W9-AYM-358

305.235 SCARDAMALIA
Scardamalia, Robert,
Millennials in America /
$100.00

MILLENNIALS
in AMERICA

MILLENNIALS
in AMERICA

2015

Robert L. Scardamalia

Lanham, MD

Published in the United States of America
by Bernan Press, a wholly owned subsidiary of
The Rowman & Littlefield Publishing Group, Inc.
4501 Forbes Boulevard, Suite 200
Lanham, Maryland 20706

Bernan Press
800-865-3457
www.bernan.com

Copyright © 2015 by Bernan Press

All rights reserved. No part of this publication may be reproduced,
stored in a retrieval system, or transmitted in any form or by any
means, electronic, mechanical, photocopying, recording, or otherwise,
without the prior permission of the publisher. Bernan Press does not claim
copyright in U.S. government information

ISBN-13: 978-1-59888-779-2
eISBN-13: 978-1-59888-780-8

∞™ The paper used in this publication meets the minimum requirements of
American National Standard for Information Sciences—Permanence of
Paper for Printed Library Materials, ANSI/NISO Z39.48-1992.
Manufactured in the United States of America.

Contents

Preface

Everyone ages. That's not a startling statement, but our national conversation on aging continues to be focused on the retirement, health, and service issues of the Baby Boom generation. The Baby Boom generation is commonly accepted to be those born between 1946 and 1964, and during those years some 76 million individuals were born. Today they are between the ages of 51 and 69. While the Boomers are swelling the ranks of the aging population, they are a declining proportion of the total U.S. population. In 2014, Boomers accounted for 22 percent of the population, but by 2040 they will account for only half that, or 11 percent. Generation "X," or the Baby Bust generation, is markedly smaller, numbering only about 55 million people compared to the 76 million births in the Baby Boom years.

So why focus on the Millennial generation? The "echo" of the Baby Boom generation is made up of 78 million births between 1982 and 2001. It is now our nation's largest generation and one that will continue to grow due to foreign immigration. Our national conversation on aging needs to shift and recognize that the Millennials will be the driving social and political force in the coming decades.

Unlike the commonly accepted period of birth for the Boomers, there is no common agreement on what birth years constitute the Millennial generation. We typically refer to the Millennials as those "coming of age" and born around the millennium but that can represent many different viewpoints. For the purposes of this portrait of the Millennials, I have defined the generation to be those born from 1982 through 2000. In the 2013 ACS used for this book, the Millennial generation is made up of those individuals between the ages of 13 (born in 2000) and 31 (born in 1982).

The Millennials are a generation who experienced the deepest recessionary period since the Great Depression while they were starting their careers. They continue to delay marriage and childbearing, are more supportive of gay rights and alternative living arrangements, have lower rates of home ownership than previous generations, and may not be able to attain as high a living standard as their parents.

It's natural to generalize about the characteristics and attitudes of any population sub-group, and outlining differences between generations is no different. However, large scale generalizations of youth, middle aged adults, seniors, low-income, high-income – you name it – completely misses the nuanced differences between our communities. The purpose of this compendium of statistics about the Millennial generation isn't a comparison with other generations but rather a comparison of characteristics across communities. Living arrangements, racial and ethnic diversity, migration patterns and many other characteristics simply aren't the same in all communities, and this volume will help to illustrate those differences.

There are a couple of important aspects of the data presented here that need explanation:

- As mentioned above, there is little agreement among demographers or in the media about what birth years constitute the Millennial generation. A search of the literature will find a number of definitions ranging from one of the earliest beginning years at 1976 to the latest year of 2004. It is unlikely that changing the definition by a year or two in either direction will have a large impact on area comparisons presented here. There is logic to maintaining a generational length of 18 to 20 years as that period when children move into adulthood, but there is also logic to lengthening that period to 25 or 28 years as delayed marriage and childbearing has extended the length of a generation. The years 1982 to 2000 were chosen to maintain a more traditional generation length yet capture the portion of the Millennials who have not quite reached the age of independence (13 to 17 years old) and also those generally completing their educations and moving into family and household formation (25 to 31 years old).

- The source of the data used here is the Census Bureau's American Community Survey. Subsequent chapters that describe many of the details of the survey will be helpful to data users in understanding some of the limitations of the ACS, but most important here is the use of the ACS microdata to define the Millennial generation. Typical Census Bureau summary data from the decennial census and the ACS is limited by predefined table structures that do not identify unique age ranges like that used to define the Millennials. The microdata provides the necessary flexibility to define specific age ranges but in that flexibility there is a limitation in terms of geography and the areas defined. This trade-off is described in much more detail in the section Defining the Millennials and readers are encouraged to pay special attention to how the geographic areas are defined.

- While the ACS is a very large survey of more than 3 million households each year, there are still significant concerns over the reliability of the estimates, especially for smaller areas. The Census Bureau continually advises users to focus on characteristic distributions rather than survey population counts, and that advice is reflected in this book. Population totals are provided to allow comparisons of area size, but the characteristics presented are percentages of the total rather than population counts. Comparisons of the percentages are less affected by relative population size and reduce misinterpretations due to sampling error.

This book is designed to include a sampling of key information about the Millennial generation but also help users understand the survey data and resources to access more detailed data available from the Census Bureau and the ACS. The 11 subject area tables in this book include data for each geographic area including all states and the District of Columbia and selected cities, counties, and metropolitan statistical areas meeting the required population threshold. This is a small sampling of the detailed data that could be presented.

The ACS survey estimates are different from the decennial census, as the Census Bureau surveys nearly 300,000 households every month as opposed to a single reference date of April 1 in the Census. The data in this book are from the 2013 ACS single year estimates, which are produced from 12 months of survey data collection. They are period estimates with sample cases spread evenly throughout the 12-month survey time period.

Finally, it is always critical to remember that all estimates are subject to sampling error. On the Census Bureau's website, every ACS number is accompanied by its margin of error. In the interests of space and simplicity, this book does not include the margins of error, but all users are encouraged to consult the Census Bureau's website and to understand some basics: small differences are very likely to represent no difference at all; do not draw conclusions from small numbers; use these numbers as a starting point to explore the wealth of information from the ACS.

Introduction

The American Community Survey (ACS) has ushered in the most substantial change in the decennial census in more than 60 years. It replaced the decennial census long form in 2010, providing more current data throughout the decade by collecting long-form-type information annually rather than only once every 10 years. The ACS provides annual estimates for states, metropolitan areas, and large cities and counties based on 12-month periods of data collection. Estimates for midsize communities (20,000 to 65,000 population) have been produced each year through 2013 based on 36-month periods of data collection, for example, 2011 to 2013. Very small communities (under 20,000 population) and statistical areas like census tracts and zip code tabulation areas require 5 years (60 months) of survey responses.

The ACS gathers demographic, social, economic, housing, and financial information about the nation's people and communities as the survey is conducted on a continuing basis by the U.S. Census Bureau in every county, American Indian and Alaska Native Area, and Hawaiian Home Land in the United States. The Puerto Rican Community Survey is conducted in every municipality in Puerto Rico. As the largest survey in the United States, it is the only source of small-area data on a wide range of important social and economic characteristics for all communities in the country. After years of planning and development, and a demonstration period, the ACS began full nationwide implementation in 2005.

Information about the ACS is available on the Census Bureau's website. The ACS main page is http://www.census.gov/programs-surveys/acs. Data from the ACS are available from American FactFinder at http://factfinder.census.gov.

A vast amount of information is collected in the ACS. In this publication, selections of these data have been assembled in various tables by subject and geographic type.

VOLUME ORGANIZATION

The data tables in this book pertain to the population age 13 to 31 and include a selection of population and housing characteristics from the ACS in 11 subject areas:

- Part A: Population Summary
- Part B: Race and Ethnicity
- Part C: Nativity and World Region of Birth
- Part D: Household Relationship
- Part E: Educational Attainment
- Part F: Field of Study
- Part G: Language Spoken at Home
- Part H: Employment and Labor Force Status
- Part I: Income and Poverty
- Part J: Mobility and Migration
- Part K: Housing Summary

The 1-year estimates from the American Community Survey provide data for all areas of 65,000 population or more. The geographic comparisons here are limited by the minimum population threshold of the microdata which is 100,000. Each subject area includes data for the United States, the 50 states and the District of Columbia, and the following:

- 622 counties, listed alphabetically within states,
- 331 cities, listed alphabetically within states, and
- 381 metropolitan areas and 34 micropolitan areas, listed alphabetically

In addition, each part is preceded by highlights, maps, and/or summary tables that show how areas diverge from the national norm, as well as the differences among areas. These research aids are invaluable for helping people understand what the census data tell us about who we are, what we do, and where we live.

In the following sections, information about the ACS and how to use the data is included, much of it excerpted from the wealth of information available on the Census Bureau's website. Especially helpful are the instructions, definitions, and guidelines on using the data in the sections on understanding and using the ACS. Readers are encouraged to explore the Census Bureau's website to expand on the information contained here and to keep up to date with this constantly changing dataset.

Robert Scardamalia is President of RLS Demographics, Inc., a firm providing data and analysis to private organizations, government agencies, and not-for-profits, especially in the areas of aging services and business development. He is an adjunct professor in the Sociology Department of the State University of New York at Albany. Prior to forming RLS Demographics, he was Chief Demographer of New York State and directed the Center for Research and Information Analysis in the New York Department of Economic Development. He also directed the New York State Data Center for more than 20 years. Mr. Scardamalia serves on the Board of the Association of Public Data Users and is a past President. He has chaired the national State Data Center Steering Committee and served on numerous Census Bureau committees. He holds a Master of Arts in Demography from Georgetown University and Bachelor of Arts in Sociology from Penn State University.

Defining the Millennials

WHAT ARE MICRODATA FILES AND WHY USE THEM?

The Census Bureau produces a large number of data profiles and detailed tables in predefined tabular formats through American FactFinder and various reports. However, these predefined products cannot meet the unique research and analysis needs of every data user. To meet those needs, the Census Bureau produces the Public Use Microdata Sample (PUMS) files which allow data users to create custom tables and characteristics not available in the standard ACS products.

The PUMS files are a set of household and person records that provide the individual characteristics as they were reported on the ACS questionnaire. They differ from the ACS summary products, which show data that have already been tabulated for specific geographic areas. For example, detailed tables on children will likely show the population tabulated for the population age 0 to 5 and 6 to 17. If a specific research task requires analysis of the population between the ages of 3 and 10, the standard products can't be used. With the PUMS files, the researcher can tabulate individuals within the specific ages of 3 and 10.

PUBLIC USE MICRODATA AREAS AND RELATION TO POLITICAL GEOGRAPHY

The increased flexibility to tabulate characteristics from the PUMS files comes with the cost of reduced geographic detail. While summary data profiles and tables from the ACS can be obtained for every community and even small statistical areas like census tracts, the PUMS geography is limited to areas of 100,000 or more population size. This is necessary to protect the confidentiality of survey respondents. Even though 1-year estimates from the ACS are produced for areas of 65,000 or more population, it is not possible to tabulate data from the PUMS for areas under 100,000 population.

This volume presents data for states and the District of Columbia because these areas are not affected by the 100,000 population threshold for the PUMS data. Also included are comparisons for counties, cities, and metropolitan areas–most of which exceed the 100,000 population threshold but some that are between 90,000 and 100,000. The inclusion of areas below the 100,000 threshold is possible because of a statistical allocation model developed that creates an equivalency table between the PUMS geographic areas and the official boundaries of county, city, and metropolitan areas. This allocation model is described on the following page.

Figure 1: Manhattan, NY PUMA 03803

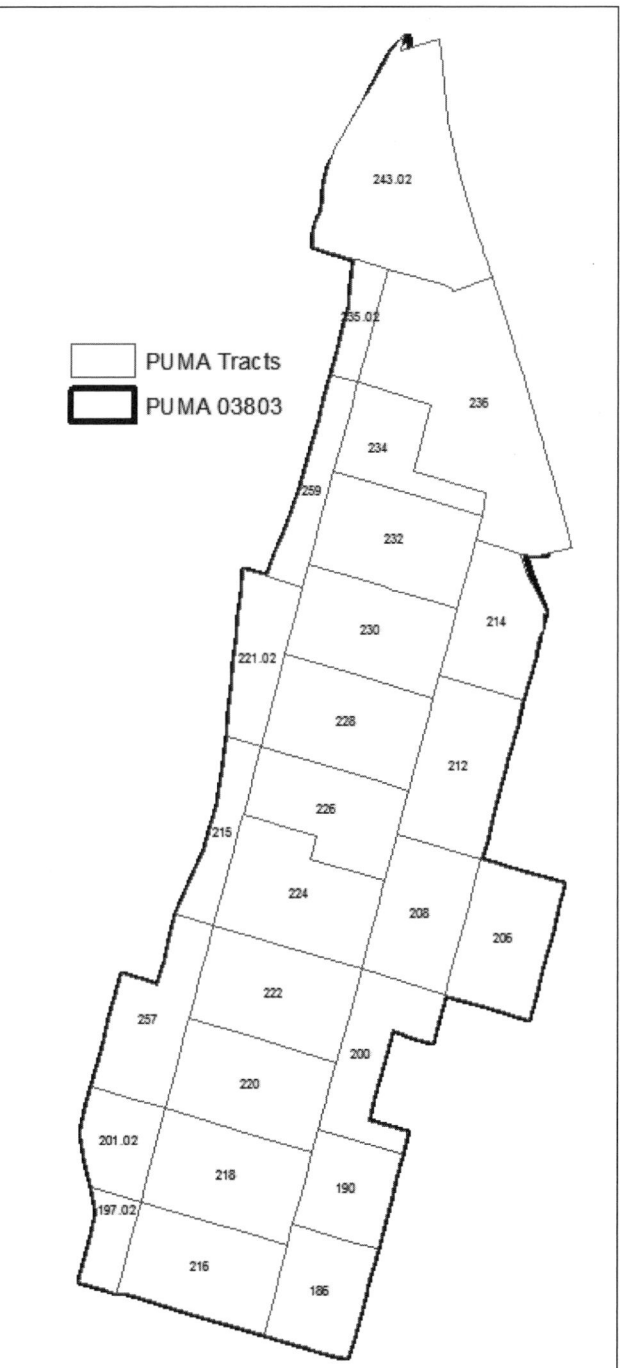

GEOGRAPHIC ALLOCATION METHOD

Understanding the allocation method first requires an understanding of the Census Bureau's PUMS geography and its relation to political and statistical geography. The following examples will help illustrate the problems and solutions.

The Census Bureau's PUMS geographic units are called Public Use Microdata Areas (PUMAs). PUMAs are constructed by the Census Bureau in cooperation with the individual states and are typically comprised of whole counties, county subdivisions and census tracts. The Census Bureau and states will aggregate the relevant statistical and political areas to make up a PUMA of at least 100,000 population. Individual counties that do not meet the 100,000 threshold are grouped with other counties until a PUMA of 100,000 or more can be identified. Counties with populations over 200,000 can theoretically have two PUMAs identified since each could potentially meet the 100,000 threshold.

In very large areas like New York City, numerous PUMAs can be created as long as each meets the required threshold. Figure 1 presents a PUMA in New York County (Manhattan - 03803) that is made up of 26 census tracts.

There are 55 PUMAs that make up the entire legal entity of New York City, which represents an illustration of exact equivalency between the PUMA definitions and the legal/political boundaries of the city. The initial PUMA delineation was done in order to ensure this exact equivalency.

Albany City, NY, is an illustration of an area that is close to the 100,000 threshold but too small to be an individual PUMA. Albany's population in the 2010 census was only 97,856. In cases such as this, the population in adjacent census tracts can be added to the PUMA to meet the 100,000 threshold. In the case of Albany, two census tracts (140.01 and 140.02) from a contiguous

Figure 2: Albany, NY PUMA 02001

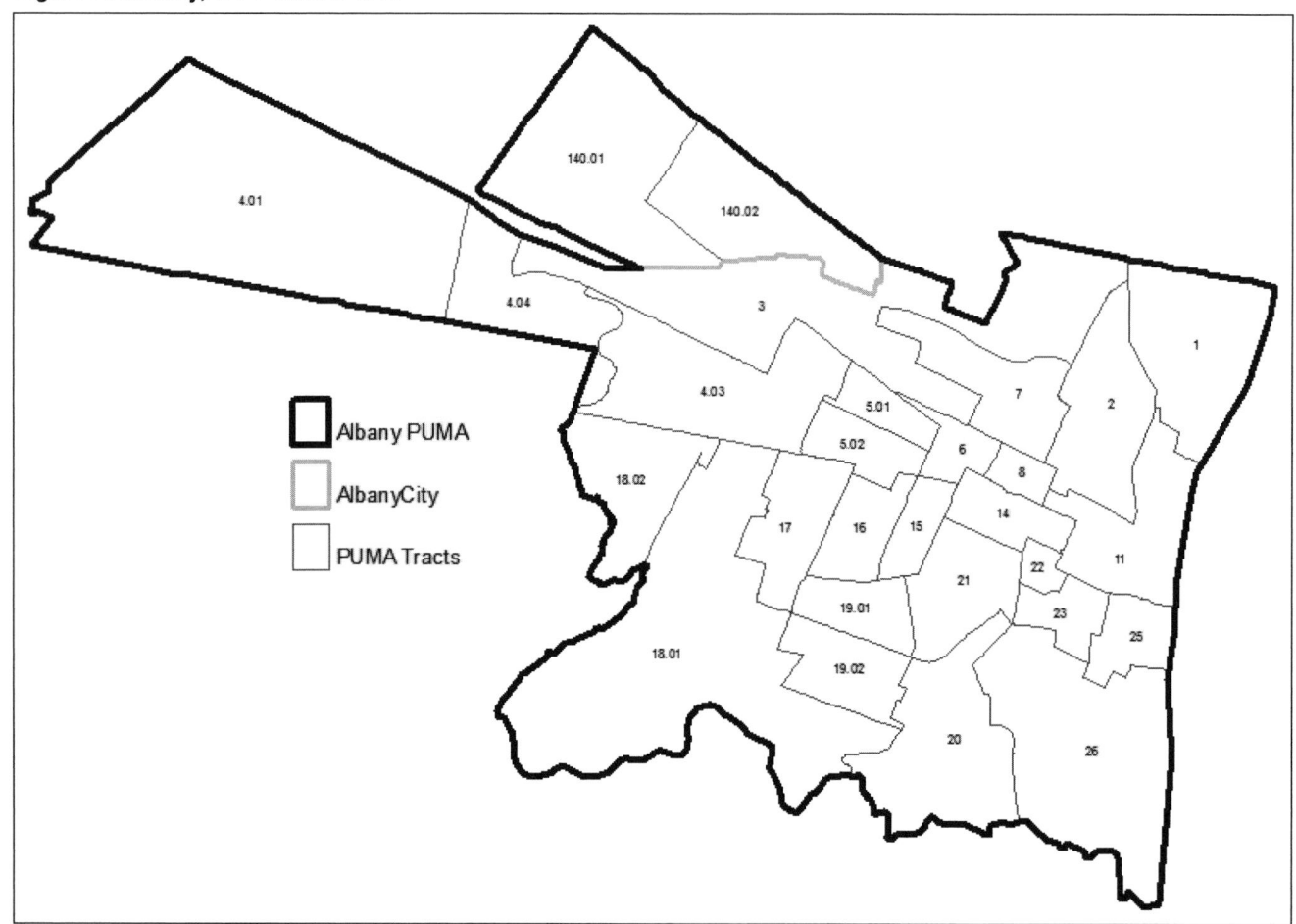

county sub-division were included in the Albany PUMA allowing it to be uniquely identified. Figure 2 illustrates this example.

Both of these cases illustrate very reasonable and workable PUMA definitions that equal or closely approximate legal/political entities. That is not the case for all PUMA definitions, and in many cases counties and cities are split by multiple PUMAs and PUMAs can be split by multiple entities. These are the cases that required the development of a statistical allocation model so that cities, counties, and metropolitan areas of over 100,000 — but not defined as individual PUMAs — could be reported. Figures 3 and 4 illustrate this situation.

Concord, CA, is a city of nearly 126,000 population as estimated for July 1, 2013. This city population in the 2010 Census was 122,000, clearly large enough to be defined as a single PUMA. Figure 3 shows that Concord is made up of portions of three separate PUMAs (black boundaries) and each PUMA includes lands outside of the city corporate limits (gray boundaries).

Atlanta, GA, is a large city of nearly 450,000 in the 2013 Census estimates and could support the definition of four PUMAs that would be exactly equivalent to the legal boundaries of Atlanta. Instead, Atlanta is made up of six PUMAs, three of which are wholly contained within the city boundaries and three which extend beyond the city borders to include land area and population outside of Atlanta, as seen in Figure 4.

In Concord, Atlanta, and hundreds of other counties, cities and metropolitan areas, the PUMA boundaries and the legal/political boundaries do not match. In all of these cases, it is necessary to allocate a portion of

Figure 3: Concord, CA

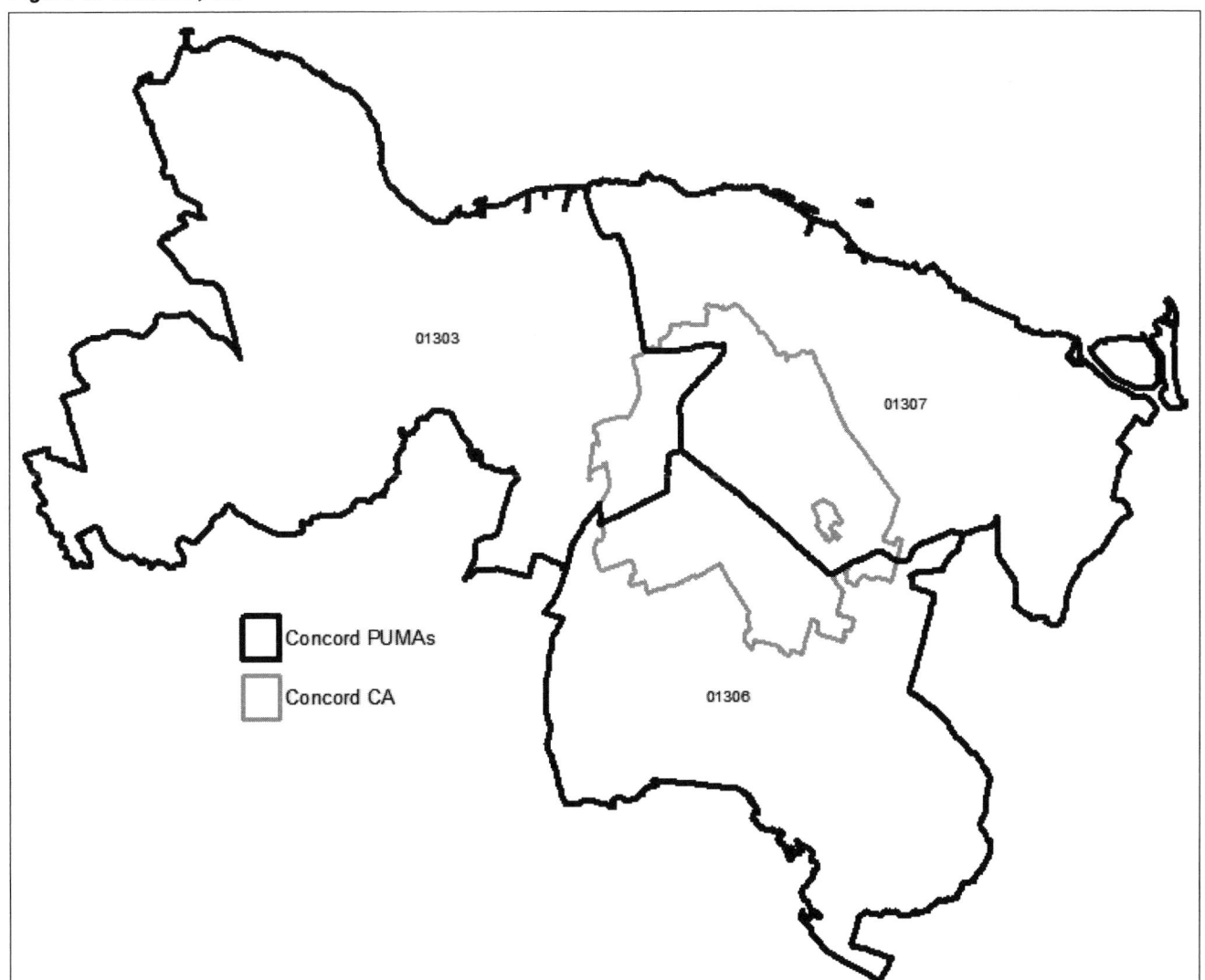

Figure 4: Atlanta, GA

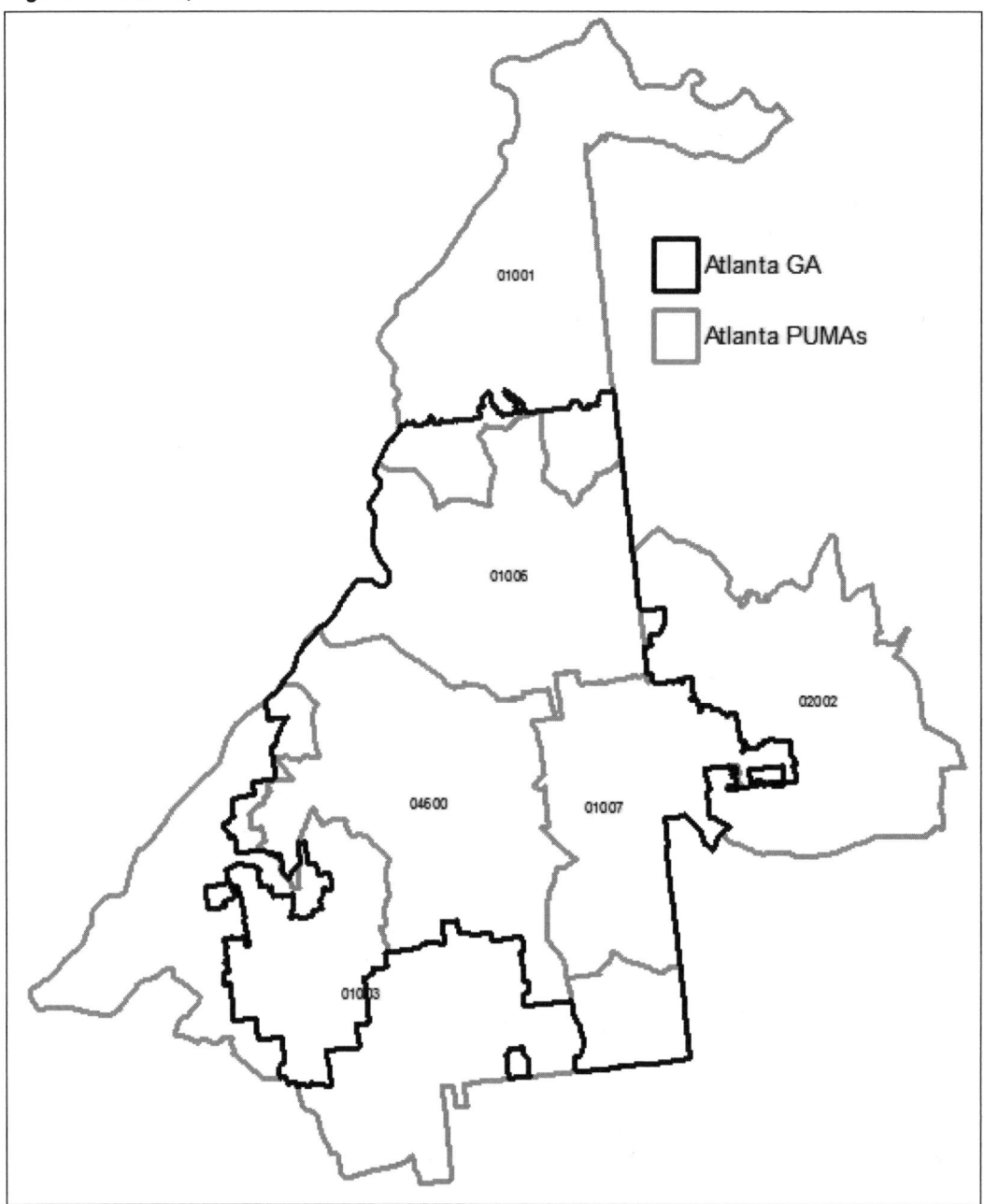

the person records in the affected PUMAs to the relevant county, city or metro area. However, due to confidentiality restrictions, there is no geographic identifier on the file that can be used to apportion records in the required fashion. An allocation method was developed that takes into account the proportional split of population between the PUMA and the legal entity and the proportion of the entity's population that is classified as the Millennial population.[1]

Based on the 2010 Census count, 46.5 percent of the population of PUMA 01306 resides within the City of Concord and 22.15 percent of the population of Concord is part of the Millennial generation, age 13 to 31. This results in a record allocation factor for PUMA 01306 of

1. The author wishes to acknowledge the assistance of Mr. Doug Hilmer, formerly with the U.S. Census Bureau, for assistance in development of the allocation method; Dr. Hui Shien Tsu with the Center for Social and Demographic Analysis at SUNY Albany; and Dr. Florio Arguillas with the Cornell Institute for Social and Economic Research at Cornell University for assistance in SAS and SPSS programming of the method.

Table 1: Illustrates the Allocation Method for Concord, CA

	PUMA	Proportion of Puma in Concord	Proportion of Concord Population that is Millennial	Total Persons Record	Proportion of Person Record to be Selected	Millennial Records to Select
Concord City, CA	01306	0.465	0.2215	1037	0.10299	107
Concord City, CA	01303	0.278	0.2215	1121	0.06157	69
Concord City, CA	01307	0.281	0.2215	1085	0.06224	68

10.299 percent. Since there are 1,037 person records in PUMA 01306, we will sample 107 records (10.299 percent times 1,037) as Millennial records residing in the City of Concord.

This method assumes an even geographic distribution of records throughout the PUMA, which is obviously not always accurate. In some cases, this method attempts to allocate more records than the number of Millennial records in the PUMA, in which case the record selection is limited to the maximum number of records available. In many other cases, like New York City, the PUMA allocation factor is 1.0, which means that all records will be selected and that the PUMA boundaries are wholly within the political/legal entity.

By applying this allocation method it is possible to approximate the characteristics of the defined Millennial population. It also allows for the reporting of estimates for some areas with populations below the PUMA threshold of 100,000. In addition to the standard cautions on the use of the American Community Survey data described in other sections, the user of these data should also understand that this allocation procedure may introduce additional error to the estimates.

Understanding the American Community Survey

Every 10 years since 1790, as required by the U.S. Constitution, Congress has authorized funds to conduct a national census of the U.S. population. From 1960 through 2000, censuses have consisted of:

- a "short form," which included basic questions about age, sex, race, Hispanic origin (since 1980), household relationship, and owner/renter status, and

- a "long form" used for a sample of approximately one of every six households that included not only the basic short-form questions but also detailed questions about socioeconomic and housing characteristics.

Beginning with the 2010 census, the American Community Survey (ACS) replaced the decennial census long form by collecting long-form-type information annually rather than only once every 10 years, providing more current data throughout the decade. The 2010 Census counted the population to support the constitutional mandate—to provide population counts needed to apportion the seats in the U.S. House of Representatives. The ACS data now provide, for the first time, a regular stream of updated information for states and local areas, revolutionizing the way we use data to understand our communities. It produces social, housing, and economic characteristics for demographic groups, even for geographic areas as small as census tracts and block groups.

SOME KEY FACTS ABOUT THE ACS

- The ACS annually provides the same kind of detailed information previously available only every 10 years from the census. The ACS is conducted under the authority of Title 13, United States Code, Sections 141 and 193.

- All answers are confidential. Any Census Bureau employee who violates that confidentiality is subject to a jail term, a fine, or both.

- The Census Bureau may use the information it collects only for statistical purposes.

- Addresses are selected at random from the Master Address File to represent similar households in the area. Approximately 290,000 addresses are selected each month, and the survey is conducted by mail, telephone, and personal visit. Response to this survey is required by Section 221 of Title 13.

- Approximately 2.9 percent of U.S. households are surveyed each year. A sample of group quarters (nursing homes, college dormitories, etc.) is included in the ACS as well.

- While the ACS sample size approximates the traditional long-form census sample, it is a smaller sample resulting in somewhat larger margins of error.

The traditional long-form census each decade provided the socio-economic portrait of the nation and communities, but that portrait was fixed in time for 10 years. Data from the ACS provides a regular update to that portrait, which is used for a variety of purposes that include: monitoring the economic well-being of America's population, children, and families; tracking trends in household living arrangements; analyzing the characteristics of the population; tracking growth in the number of grandparents responsible for their grandchildren; determining the economic status of the working-poor; or tracking social, economic, and demographic changes in the general U.S. population.

The ACS provides critical information for communities on a current basis, when they need it most. But the ACS is still a sample survey, and it is a different collection instrument and a different measure of the characteristics of the population and households than the traditional census data. It is good to be cautious in the interpretation of differences between areas and across time. Small differences may not be meaningful. On the other hand, the ACS provides annual estimates, and the frequency of updates and currency of the data far outweighs waiting 10 years for new results.

NEW OPPORTUNITIES

The main benefits of the ACS are timeliness and access to annual data for states, local areas, and small population subgroups. The ACS will deliver useful, relevant data, similar to data from previous census long forms, but updated every year rather than every 10 years. The ACS provides comparable information across and within states for program evaluation and use in funding formulas.

- ACS information is often used to determine the placement of new schools, senior residential services, hospitals, and highways.

- ACS provides information for tracking the well-being of children, families, and the elderly allowing service providers to better target populations in need.

- The data will improve the distribution of aid through federal, state, and local governments. More than $400 billion in federal program funds are distributed each year based, in whole or in part, on census and ACS data.

- The data are used by community programs, such as those for the elderly, libraries, hospitals, banks, and other organizations.

- The data are used by transportation planners to evaluate peak volumes of traffic in order to reduce congestion, plan for parking, and develop plans for carpooling and flexible work schedules.

- Corporations, small businesses, and individuals use these data to develop business plans, to set strategies for expansion or starting a business, and to determine trends in their service areas to meet current and future needs.

- Small towns and rural communities have much to gain from the ACS. Lacking the staff and resources to conduct their own research, many local communities have relied on decennial census information that became increasingly outdated throughout the decade, or used local administrative records that are not comparable with information collected in neighboring areas.

- The ACS also provides tools for those who want to conduct their own research. The ACS includes a Public Use Microdata Sample (PUMS) file each year that enables researchers to create custom universes and tabulations from individual ACS records that have been stripped of personally identifiable information. It is this file that is the basis for the data presented here.

- Because the ACS data collection occurs every month, the Census Bureau uses professional, highly trained, permanent interviewers who have improved the accuracy of ACS data compared to the decennial census long-form sample. This strategy has effectively reduced the number of refusals to complete the ACS questionnaire and allows interviewers to obtain more complete information than decennial census interviewers.

NEW CHALLENGES

The main challenges for ACS data users are understanding and using multiyear estimates and the relatively large margins of error associated with ACS data for smaller geographic areas and subgroups of the population.

- ACS data will be produced every year, but the sample size of the ACS is smaller than that of the Census 2000 long form sample. Data users need to pay more attention to the margin of error.

- Data users have access to 5-year estimates of ACS data. The sample size based on 5-year period estimates of ACS data is still smaller than the long-form sample in the decennial census, resulting in larger margins of error in the ACS 5-year estimates.

- Because the ACS will produce 1-year, 3-year, and 5-year estimates, areas of 65,000 population or more will receive three estimates of the same characteristics every year. For example, a large city will receive 1-year, 3-year, and 5-year estimates of the number of persons 65 and over in poverty. Data users will have to decide which datasets are appropriate for their needs.

- Data users will need to be aware of the implications of multiyear estimates, particularly in analyzing employment and income data that will span a full year or even a 5-year period.

- Multiyear estimates, especially the 5-year estimates, will not reflect short-term changes in the population or economy of an area. The recent recession is a good example because the 5-year ACS estimates span both the fall into recession and the resulting growth coming out.

The ACS includes several questions that are very similar to those collected in other federal surveys—especially the Current Population Survey (CPS), the American Housing Survey, and the Survey of Income and Program Participation. In some cases, there are clear guidelines about which data to use. For example, the CPS is the official source of income and poverty data. It includes detailed questions on these topics and should be used in reporting national trends in these subject areas. The Census Bureau recommends that ACS information on income and poverty be used to supplement CPS data for areas below the state level and for population subgroups (such as age, sex, race, Hispanic origin, type of household) at the state level. For an explanation of various income and poverty data sources, see the Census Bureau's guidelines at http://www.census.gov/hhes/www/poverty/about/datasources/description.html. For states, generally the Census Bureau recommends using the ACS, though the CPS is still valuable as a source for examining historical state income and poverty trends.

DATA COLLECTION VERSUS DATA REPORTING

Results from the ACS are reported each year, which is a major advantage over the traditional long-form data from the decennial census. But unlike the release of data only once every 10 years in the decennial census, the annual release of data from the ACS can be quite confusing. The ACS sample size is such that the reliability of the data is greatly affected by the length of the data collection period and the size of geographic reporting areas. In survey sampling, it is well understood that larger samples yield more reliable estimates with smaller margins of error. In order to produce reliable estimates from the ACS, it is necessary to collect the data over differing periods of time in order to provide estimates for all areas, including small areas like census tracts.

Each set of period estimates is released each year, generally between September and December, and reflects data collection ending in the previous calendar year. Thus, the collection year 2013 1-year estimates for areas of 65,000 or more were released in September of 2014. The 2011–2013 3-year estimates and the 2009–2013 5-year estimates follow as processing is completed.

THE ACS SAMPLE

The ACS is sent each month to a sample of roughly 290,000 addresses in the United States and Puerto Rico, or about 3.5 million a year, resulting in more than 2.2 million final interviews. The sample represents all housing units and group quarters in the United States and Puerto Rico. (Group quarters include places such as college dormitories, prisons, military barracks, and nursing homes.) The addresses are selected from the Census Bureau's Master Address File (MAF), which is also the basis for the decennial census.

The annual ACS sample is smaller than that of the Census 2000 long-form sample, which included about 18 million housing units. As a result, the ACS needs to combine population or housing data from multiple years to produce reliable numbers for small counties, neighborhoods, and other local areas. To provide information for communities each year, the ACS will provide 1-, 3-, and 5-year estimates.

The ACS sample is not spread evenly across all areas but includes a larger proportion of addresses in sparsely

populated rural communities and American Indian reservations and a lower proportion in densely populated areas. Over a 5-year period, the ACS will sample more than 17 million addresses and complete interviews for about 11 million. This sample is sufficient to produce estimates for small geographic areas, such as neighborhoods and sparsely-populated rural counties though the estimates will have larger margins of error than the census long-form data. In a 5-year period no address will be selected for the ACS more than once, and many addresses will never be selected for the survey. It's important to remember that the sample is address based, so while a given address will not be in sample again for at least five years, it is possible that individuals who move or have a second home could be surveyed more than once.

Geography

The ACS data are tabulated for a variety of geographic areas ranging in size from broad geographic regions (Northeast, Midwest, South, and West) to cities, towns, neighborhoods, and census block groups. Before December 2008, the ACS data were only available for geographic areas with at least 65,000 people, including regions, divisions, states, the District of Columbia, Puerto Rico, congressional districts, Public Use Microdata Areas (PUMAs)—census-constructed geographic areas, each with approximately a population of 100,000—and many large counties, metropolitan areas, cities, school districts, and American Indian areas. Starting in December 2008, 3-year estimates became available for all areas with at least 20,000 residents, and in 2010, 5-year estimates for geographic areas down to the block group level became available. One-, three-, and five-year estimates—three sets of numbers—are now available and will be refreshed every year. Less populous areas will receive only 5-year estimates. The vast majority of areas will receive only 5-year estimates.

The data tables in this book contain data from the 1-year 2013 estimates. These tables are based on the current tabulation geography for political and statistical areas, which are generally the same definitions as the 2010 Census. Changes in area boundaries can occur as a result of annexation, new incorporation or disincorporation of cities, towns, and places. For multiyear estimates, the

Data Product	Population Threshold	Year of Data Release							
		2007	2008	2009	2010	2011	2012	2013	2014
		Year(s) of Data Collection							
1-year Estimates	65,000+	2006	2007	2008	2009	2010	2011	2012	2013
3-year Estimates	20,000+		2005–2007	2006–2008	2007–2009	2008–2010	2009–2011	2010–2012	2011–2013
5-year Estimates	All Areas				2005–2009	2006–2010	2007–2011	2008–2012	2009–2013

Census Bureau reports the data based on the most current geographic boundaries incorporating any changes occurring in the multiyear period.

DATA COMPARABILITY

Since the ACS data are collected continuously, they are not always comparable with data collected from the decennial census. For example, both surveys ask about employment status during the week prior to the survey. However, data from the decennial census are typically collected between March and July with a reference date of April 1st, whereas data from the ACS are collected nearly every day and reflect employment throughout the year. Other factors that may also have an impact on the data include seasonal variation in population and minor differences in question wording and question order.

While the categories of income by source are comparable with the decennial long-form data, the monthly collection of ACS data results in a significant difference in concept. In the decennial census, income refers to the previous calendar year whereas in the ACS it refers to the previous 12-month period. Most people have a better understanding of what their calendar year income is, especially since the census is taken around tax time. With the ACS, individuals have to report income for a different period each month. A survey response in October of the year will report income from October of the previous year through September of the current year. This may require respondents to actually compute their 12-month income.

In 2006, the ACS began including samples of the population living in group quarters (e.g., jails, college dormitories, and nursing homes) for the first time. As a result, the ACS data from 2005 may not be comparable with data from later ACS surveys. This is especially true for estimates of young adults and the elderly, who are more likely than other groups to be living in group quarters facilities.

One of the most important uses of the ACS estimates is to make comparisons between estimates over time or across areas. Several key types of comparisons are of general interest to users:

- Comparisons of estimates from different geographic areas within the same time period (e.g., comparing the proportion of seniors below the poverty level in two counties).

- Comparisons of estimates for the same geographic area across time periods (e.g., comparing the proportion of people below the poverty level in a metropolitan area for 2012 and 2013).

- Comparisons of ACS estimates with the corresponding estimates from past decennial census samples (e.g., comparing the proportion of people below the poverty level in a county for 2013 and 2000).

A number of conditions must be met when comparing survey estimates.

- When comparing data for different geographic areas, always use the same period estimates. When comparing data for an area which only have 5-year estimates to an area with 1-, 3-, and 5-year estimates, it is important to compare only the 5-year estimates.

- When comparing over time for the same geographic area, again, only compare like-year period estimates. For example, it is not appropriate to compare a 1-year estimate for 2013 to a 3-year estimate for 2011–2013.

- Of primary importance is that the comparison takes into account the sampling error associated with each estimate, thus determining whether the observed differences between estimates are statistically significant. Statistical significance means that there is statistical evidence that a true difference exists within the full population, and that the observed difference is unlikely to have occurred by chance due to sampling. A method for determining statistical significance when making comparisons, as well as considerations associated with the various types of comparisons, can be found in Appendix 4 of the *ACS General Handbook*: http://www.census.gov/acs/www/Downloads/handbooks/ACSGeneralHandbook.pdf

- The statistical properties of survey samples like the ACS are dependent upon independence of samples. In the ACS multiyear period estimates, the estimates are based on the sampled households for each year. That means that when comparing estimates for the period 2010–2012 to 2011–2013, two thirds of the sample cases are the same households—those surveyed in 2011 and 2012. The only different (independent) households are those from 2010 and 2013. When comparisons over time are made, it is best to compare non-overlapping samples. That is, compare estimates for 2008–2010 to the period 2011–1013 because both periods contain independent household samples. To meet this criteria for the use of 5-year estimates, data users should wait for the 2011–2015 data to make time series comparisons.

Finally, the decennial census and the ACS have different residency rules. In the decennial census, population is tabulated by their "usual place of residence" typically where they spend six months or more of the year. This is subject to some seasonal variation due to persons with dual residences. In the ACS, there is a 2-month residency rule. That is, if the respondent has been in the sampled housing unit for 2 months or expects to be resident there for 2 months they are captured in the survey. This can have an impact on communities with highly seasonal populations and college communities.

SUBJECTS COVERED

The topics covered by the ACS focus on demographic, social, economic, and housing characteristics. These topics are virtually the same as those covered by the 2000 census long-form sample data.

Demographic Characteristics
Age, Sex, Hispanic Origin, Race, and Relationship to Householder (e.g., spouse)

Social Characteristics
Marital Status and Marital History; Fertility; Grandparents as Caregivers; Ancestry Place of Birth; Citizenship and Year of Entry; Language Spoken at Home; Educational Attainment and School Enrollment; Residence One Year Ago; Veteran Status, Period of Military Service, and VA Service-Connected Disability Rating; and Disability

Economic Characteristics
Income, Food Stamps Benefit, Labor Force Status, Industry, Occupation, Class of Worker, Place of Work and Journey to Work, Work Status Last Year, Vehicles Available, and Health Insurance Coverage

Housing Characteristics
Year Structure Built, Units in Structure, Year Moved Into Unit, Rooms, Bedrooms, Kitchen Facilities, Plumbing Facilities, House Heating Fuel, Telephone Service Available, and Farm Residence

Financial Characteristics
Tenure (Owner/Renter), Housing Value, Rent, and Selected Monthly Owner Costs

AVAILABILITY OF ACS ESTIMATES

The ACS began in 1996 and has expanded each subsequent year. From 2000 through 2004, the sample included between 740,000 and 900,000 addresses annually. In 2005, the ACS shifted from a demonstration program to the full sample size and design. It became the largest household survey in the United States, with an annual sample size of about 3 million addresses. Beginning with 2005, the

ACS single-year estimates are available for geographic areas with a population of 65,000 or more. Three-year period estimates for areas of 20,000 or more were first released for the 2005–2007 time period, while 5-year estimates for all areas were first released in 2010. The ACS will continue to accumulate samples over 3-year and 5-year intervals to produce estimates for smaller geographic areas, including census tracts and block groups, though the Census Bureau has proposed elimination of the 3-year estimates starting in 2015.

Annually, the ACS produces updated, single-year estimates of demographic, housing, social, and economic characteristics for all states, as well as for larger counties, cities, metropolitan and urban areas, and congressional districts. Geographic areas must have a minimum population of 65,000 to qualify for estimates based on a single year's sample. Every congressional district meets this threshold and therefore new single year estimates are released each year for every congressional district. Some school districts, townships, and American Indian and Alaska Native areas also meet this population threshold.

For areas with populations of at least 20,000, the Census Bureau produces estimates using data collected over a 3-year period. For rural areas and city neighborhoods (including census tracts and block groups) with fewer than 20,000 people, the Census Bureau produces estimates using data collected over a 5-year period, with plans to update these multiyear estimates every year. ACS data are released annually, about 8 months after the end of each calendar year of data collection.

For some geographic areas—including three-quarters of all counties, most school districts, and most cities, towns, and American Indian reservations—only 3-year or 5-year estimates are available because of their population size. Because some federal grant programs allocate funds directly to these areas, Congress can use the 3- and 5-year estimates to evaluate needs at the relevant geographic level, compare characteristics between areas within and among states, and analyze how various formulas distribute funds. The vast majority of areas will receive only 5-year estimates. In partnership with the states, the Census Bureau created *Public Use Microdata Areas (PUMAs)*, which are special, non-overlapping areas within a state, each with a population of about 100,000. These areas will have annual 1-year estimates.

Definitions of these geographic areas are at: http://www.census.gov/programs-surveys/acs/geography-acs.html.

Using the ACS

DIFFERENCES BETWEEN THE ACS AND THE DECENNIAL CENSUS

While the main function of the decennial census is to provide *counts* of people for the purpose of congressional apportionment and legislative redistricting, the primary purpose of the ACS is to measure the changing social and economic *characteristics* of the U.S. population. As a result, the ACS does not provide official counts of the population, though users of the data will report the estimate results as though they were counts. In nondecennial census years, the Census Bureau's Population Estimates Program continues to be the official source for annual population totals, by age, race, Hispanic origin, and sex. The ACS sample estimates are controlled to match the decennial census and the Census Bureau's annual population estimates by selected age, sex, race, and Hispanic origin categories. For more information about population estimates, visit the Census Bureau's website at http://www.census.gov/popest/estimates.html.

There are many similarities between the methods used in the past decennial census sample and the ACS, but there are also a number of differences in collection methods and concepts. Response to both the ACS and decennial census is required by law, a factor that helps improve overall response. Both the ACS and the decennial census sample data are based on information from a sample of the population. The data from the Census 2000 sample of about one-sixth of the population were collected using a "long-form" questionnaire, whose content was the model for the ACS. The sample for the ACS is somewhat smaller, approximately 1 in 7 households, resulting in larger margins of error.

While some differences exist in the specific Census 2000 question wording and that of the ACS, most questions are identical or nearly identical. Differences in the design and implementation of the two surveys are noted below with references provided to a series of evaluation studies that assess the degree to which these differences are likely to impact the estimates. The ACS produces period estimates, and these estimates do not measure characteristics for the same time frame as the decennial census estimates, which are interpreted to be a snapshot as of April 1 of the census year.

Some data items were collected by both the ACS and the Census 2000 long form with slightly different definitions or reference periods that could affect the comparability of the estimates for these items. One example is annual costs for a mobile home. Census 2000 included installment loan costs in the total annual costs but the ACS does not. In this example, the ACS could be expected to yield smaller estimates than Census 2000.

While some differences were a part of the census and survey design objectives, other differences observed between ACS and census results were not by design, but due to nonsampling error—differences related to how well the surveys were conducted. The ACS and the census experience different levels and types of coverage error, different levels and treatment of housing unit and questionnaire item nonresponse, and different instances of measurement and processing error. Both Census 2000 and the ACS had similar high levels of survey coverage and low levels of unit nonresponse. Higher levels of unit nonresponse were found in the nonresponse follow-up stage of Census 2000, while lower levels of item nonresponse were found in the ACS due to a permanent staff of trained interviewers.

Census Bureau analysts have compared sample estimates from Census 2000 with 1-year ACS estimates based on data collected in 2000 and 3-year ACS estimates based on data collected in 1999–2001 in selected counties. In general, ACS estimates were found to be quite similar to those produced from decennial census data.

Detailed information about the ACS methodology can be found at: http://www.census.gov/programs-surveys/acs/methodology.html.

RESIDENCE RULES

The fundamentally different purposes of the ACS and the census, and their timing, led to important differences in the choice of data collection methods. For example, the residence rules for a census or survey determine the sample unit's occupancy status and household membership at the time of collection. Defining the rules in a dissimilar way can affect those two very important estimates. The 2010 census residence rules, which determined where people should be counted, were based on the principle of "usual residence" on April 1, 2010, in keeping with the focus of the census on the requirements of congressional apportionment and state redistricting. To accomplish this, the decennial census attempts to restrict and determine a principal place of residence on one specific date for everyone enumerated. The ACS residence rules are based on a "current residence" concept since data are collected continuously throughout the entire year with responses provided relative to the continuously changing survey interview dates. This method is consistent with the goal of the ACS to produce estimates that reflect annual averages of the characteristics of all areas.

Residence rules determine which individuals are considered to be residents of a particular housing unit or group quarters. While many people have definite ties to a single housing unit or group quarters, some people may stay in different places for significant periods of time over the course of the year. For example, "snow birds" can maintain two residences in different states and do not live in any one location for the entire year. In the decennial census, it is their residence on April 1, or their interpretation of their "usual place of residence," that is the basis for their location. Differences in treatment of these populations in the census and ACS can lead to differences in estimates of the characteristics of some areas.

For the past several censuses, decennial census residence rules were designed to produce an accurate count of the population as of Census Day, April 1, while the ACS residence rules were designed to collect representative information to produce annual average estimates of the characteristics of all types of areas. When interviewing the population living in housing units, the decennial census uses a "usual residence" rule to enumerate people at the place where they live or stay most of the time as of April 1. The ACS uses a "current residence" rule to interview people who are currently living or staying in the sample housing unit as long as their stay at that address will exceed two months. The residence rules governing the census enumerations of people in group quarters depend on the type of group quarter and, where permitted, whether people claim a "usual residence" elsewhere. The ACS applies a straight de facto residence rule to every type of group quarter. Everyone living or staying in a group quarter on the day it is visited by an ACS interviewer is eligible to be sampled and interviewed for the survey.

Further information on residence rules can be found at: http://www2.census.gov/programs-surveys/acs/metho dology/design_and_methodology/acs_design_methodol ogy_ch06_2014.pdf

The differences in the ACS and census data, as a consequence of the different residence rules, are most likely minimal for most areas and most characteristics. However, for certain segments of the population the usual and current residence concepts could result in different residence decisions. The older population is one of those segments, as many retired and active seniors maintain dual residences. Appreciable differences may occur in areas where large proportions of the total population spend several months of the year in what would not be considered their residence under decennial census rules. In particular, data for areas that include large beach, lake, or mountain vacation areas may differ appreciably between the census and the ACS if populations live there for more than two months. In addition, college students (hence Millennials) are to be counted at the location of the college rather than their parents' home. However, during summer months, college students can meet the two-month residency rule for the ACS and be counted along with their parents rather than at the college.

REFERENCE PERIODS

Estimates produced by the ACS are not measuring exactly what decennial samples have been measuring. The ACS yearly samples, spread over 12 months, collect information that is anchored to the day on which the sampled unit was interviewed, whether it is the day that a mail questionnaire is completed or the day that an interview is conducted by telephone or personal visit. Individual questions with time references such as "last week" or "the last 12 months" all begin the reference period as of this interview date. Even the information on types and amounts of income refers to the 12 months prior to the day the question is answered. ACS interviews are conducted just about every day of the year, and all of the estimates that the survey releases are considered to be averages for a specific time period. The 1-year estimates reflect the full calendar year; 3-year and 5-year estimates reflect the full 36- or 60-month period.

Most decennial census sample estimates are anchored in this same way to the reference date of April 1. The most obvious difference between the ACS and the census is the overall time frame in which they are conducted. The census enumeration time period is less than half the time period used to collect data for each single-year ACS estimate. But a more important difference is that the distribution of census enumeration dates are highly clustered in March and April (when most census mail returns were received) with additional, smaller clusters seen in May and June (when nonresponse follow-up activities took place).

This means that the data from the decennial census, intended to reflect the characteristics of the population and housing on April 1, tend to describe the characteristics in the March through June time period (with an over-representation of March/April). The ACS data describe the characteristics nearly every day over the full calendar year. For employment and income estimates, the decennial census referred to the prior calendar year for all respondents, while the ACS asks about the 12 months preceding the interview.

Those who are interested in more information about differences in reference periods should refer to the Census Bureau's guidance on comparisons that contrasts for each question the specific reference periods used in Census 2000 with those used in the ACS: http://www.census.gov/programs-surveys/acs/guidance/comparing-acs-data.html

Some specific differences in reference periods between the ACS and the decennial census are described below. Users should consider the potential impact these different reference periods could have on distributions when comparing ACS estimates with Census 2000.

Income Data

To estimate annual income, the Census 2000 long-form sample used the calendar year prior to Census Day as the reference period, and the ACS uses the 12 months prior to the interview date as the reference period. Thus, while Census 2000 collected income information for calendar year 1999, the ACS collects income information for the 12 months preceding the interview date. The responses are a mixture of 12 reference periods ranging from, in the case of the 2013 ACS single-year estimates, the full calendar year 2012 through November 2013. The ACS income responses for each of these reference periods are individually inflation-adjusted to represent dollar values for the ACS collection year. Further inflation adjustments are made to the 3- and 5-year estimates to reflect dollar values of the final year of the estimate. It's important to note that the rotating reference period for income can result in misreporting. The calendar year reference period of the decennial census coincides with an individual's annual salary and is also collected around tax time. Respondents will have a good idea of what their annual salary is. In the ACS, the respondent has to calculate their income for the previous 12 months, a figure which can vary considerably throughout the year.

School Enrollment

The school enrollment question on the ACS asks if a person had "at any time in the last 3 months attended a school or college." A consistent 3-month reference period is used for all interviews. In contrast, Census 2000 asked if a person had "at any time since February 1 attended a school or college." Since Census 2000 data were collected from mid-March to late-August, the reference period could have been as short as about 6 weeks or as long as 7 months.

Utility Costs

The reference periods for two utility cost questions—gas and electricity—differ between Census 2000 and the ACS. The census asked for annual costs, while the ACS asks for the utility costs in the previous month.

PERIOD ESTIMATES

The ACS produces period estimates of socioeconomic and housing characteristics. It is designed to provide estimates that describe the average characteristics of an area over a specific time period. In the case of ACS single-year estimates, the period is the calendar year (e.g., the 2013 ACS covers January through December 2013). In the case of ACS multiyear estimates, the period is either 3 or 5 calendar years (e.g., the 2011–2013 ACS 3-year estimates cover January 2011 through December 2013, and the 2009–2013 ACS 5-year estimates cover January 2009 through December 2013). The ACS multiyear estimates are similar in many ways to the ACS single-year estimates, but they encompass a longer time period.

The differences in time periods between single-year and multiyear ACS estimates affect decisions about which set of estimates should be used for a particular analysis. While one may think of these estimates as representing average characteristics over a single calendar year or multiple calendar years, it must be remembered that the 1-year estimates are not calculated as an average of 12 monthly values and the multiyear estimates are not calculated as the average of either 36 or 60 monthly values, nor are the multiyear estimates calculated as the average of 3 or 5 single-year estimates. Rather, the ACS collects survey information continuously nearly every day of the year and then aggregates the results over a specific time period—1 year, 3 years, or 5 years. The data collection is spread evenly across the entire period represented so as not to over-represent any particular month or year within the period.

Because ACS estimates provide information about the characteristics of the population and housing for areas over an entire time frame, ACS single-year and multiyear estimates contrast with "point-in-time" estimates, such as those from the decennial census long-form samples or monthly employment estimates from the Current Population Survey (CPS), which are designed to measure characteristics as of a certain date or narrow time period. For example, Census 2000 was designed to measure the characteristics of the population and housing in the United States based upon data collected around April 1, 2000, and thus its data reflect a narrower time frame than ACS data. The monthly CPS collects data for an even narrower time frame, the week containing the 12th of each month.

Most areas have consistent population characteristics throughout the calendar year, and their period estimates may not look much different from estimates that would be obtained from a "point-in-time" survey design. However, some areas may experience changes in the estimated characteristics of the population, depending on when in the calendar year the measurement occurred. For these areas, the ACS period estimates (even for a single year) may noticeably differ from "point-in-time" estimates. The impact will be more noticeable in smaller areas where changes such as a factory closing can have a large impact on population characteristics, and in areas with a large natural event, such as Hurricane Katrina's impact on the New Orleans area. This logic can be extended to better interpret 3- and 5-year estimates where the periods involved are much longer. If, over the full period of time (for example, 36 months), there have been major or consistent changes in certain population or housing characteristics for an area, a period estimate for that area could differ markedly from estimates based on a "point-in-time" survey. For example, the 5-year estimates for 2009–2013 will be affected by the volatility in the economy and the housing market during those years and may mask shorter term fluctuations.

The tables in this book include 1-year estimates from 2013. Some areas will show a more rapid recovery from the recession than others and experience stronger growth between the 2000 and 2010 censuses.

The important thing to keep in mind is that ACS single-year estimates describe the population and characteristics of an area for the full year, not for any specific day or period within the year, while ACS multiyear estimates describe the population and characteristics of an area for the full 3- or 5-year period, not for any specific day, period, or year within the multiyear time period.

Single-year estimates provide more current information

Single-year estimates provide more current information about areas that have changing population and/or housing characteristics because they are based on the most current data—data from the past calendar year. In contrast, multiyear estimates provide less current information because they are based on both data from the previous year and data that are up to 5 years old. As noted earlier, for many areas with minimal change taking place, using the "less current" sample used to produce the multiyear estimates may not have a substantial influence on the estimates. However, in areas experiencing major changes over a given time period, the multiyear estimates may be quite different from the single-year estimates for any of the individual years. Single-year and multiyear estimates are not expected to be the same because they are based on data from two different time periods. This will be true even if the ACS single year is the midyear of the ACS multiyear period (e.g., 2011 single year, 2009–2013 multiyear).

Multiyear estimates are based on larger sample sizes and are therefore more reliable

The 3-year estimates are based on three times as many sample cases as the 1-year estimates. For some characteristics this increased sample is needed for the estimates to be reliable enough for use in certain applications. For other characteristics the increased sample may not be necessary.

Multiyear estimates are the only type of estimates available for geographic areas with populations of less than 65,000. Users may think that they only need to use multiyear estimates when they are working with small areas, but this isn't the case. Estimates for large geographic areas benefit from the increased sample, resulting in more precise estimates of population and housing characteristics, especially for subpopulations within those areas. In addition, users may determine that they want to use single-year estimates, despite their reduced reliability, as building blocks to produce estimates for meaningful higher levels of geography. These aggregations will similarly benefit from the increased sample sizes and gain reliability.

Currency	Reliability
1-year estimates provide information based on the most current year	Sample sizes producing estimates may be small and impact statistical reliability
3-year estimates provide information based on the last year and the 2 years before that	3-year estimates are based on 3 times as many sample cases as 1-year estimates
5-year estimates provide information based on the last year and the 4 years before that	5-year estimates are based on 5 times as many sample cases as 1-year estimates

DECIDING WHICH ACS ESTIMATE TO USE

Three primary uses of ACS estimates are:

- to understand the characteristics of the population of an area for local planning needs,
- to make comparisons across areas, and
- to assess change over time in an area.

Local planning could include making local decisions such as where to place schools or hospitals, determining the need for senior services or transportation, and carrying out other infrastructure analysis. In the past, decennial census sample data provided the most comprehensive information. However, the currency of those data suffered through the intercensal period, and the ability to assess change over time was limited. ACS estimates greatly improve the currency of data for understanding the characteristics of housing and population and enhance the ability to assess change over time. At the same time, small differences between ACS estimates can lead to misinterpretation due to larger margins of error.

Several key factors can help users decide whether to use single-year or multiyear ACS estimates for areas where both are available:

- intended use of the estimates
- required precision, or reliability, of the estimates
- currency of the estimates

All of these factors, along with an understanding of the differences between single-year and multiyear ACS estimates, should be taken into consideration when deciding which set of estimates to use.

For users interested in obtaining estimates for small geographic areas, multiyear ACS estimates are the only option. For the very smallest of these areas (less than 20,000 population), the only option is to use the 5-year ACS estimates. Users have a choice of two sets of multiyear estimates when analyzing data for small geographic areas with populations of at least 20,000. Both 3- and 5-year ACS estimates are available. Only the largest areas with populations of 65,000 and more receive all three data series.

The key trade-off to be made in deciding whether to use single-year or multiyear estimates is between currency and precision. In general, the single-year estimates are preferred, as they will be more relevant to the current conditions. However, the user must take into account the level of uncertainty present in the single-year estimates, which may be large for small subpopulation groups and rare characteristics. While single-year estimates offer more current estimates, they also have higher sampling variability. One measure, the coefficient of variation (CV), can help you determine the fitness for use of a single-year estimate in order to assess if you should opt instead to use the multiyear estimate (or if you should use a 5-year estimate rather than a 3-year estimate). The CV is calculated as the ratio of the standard error of the estimate to the estimate, times 100. A single-year estimate with a small CV is usually preferable to a multiyear estimate as it is more up to date. However, multiyear estimates are an alternative option when a single-year estimate has an unacceptably high CV. Single-year estimates for small subpopulations (e.g., Millennials age 18 to 24 by income class) will typically have larger CVs. In general, multiyear estimates are preferable to single-year estimates when looking at estimates for small subpopulations.

For the complete discussion on deciding which estimates to use and on calculating the CV, see Appendix 1 of the *ACS General Handbook*: http://www.census.gov/library/publications/2008/acs/general.html

Often users want to compare the characteristics of one area to those of another area. These comparisons can be in the form of rankings or of specific pairs of comparisons. Whenever you want to make a comparison between two different geographic areas you need to take the type of estimate into account. It is important that comparisons be made within the same estimate type. That is, 1-year estimates should only be compared with other 1-year estimates, 3-year estimates should only be compared with other 3-year estimates, and 5-year estimates should only be compared with other 5-year estimates.

You certainly can compare characteristics for areas with populations of 30,000 to areas with populations of 100,000 but you should use the data set that they have in common. In this example you could use the 3- or the 5-year estimates because they are available for areas of 30,000 and areas of 100,000. You should NOT compare the single year estimate for the area of 100,000 to the 3-year estimate for the area of 30,000. This book includes only the 3-year estimates for 2010 through 2012, so comparisons across geographic areas will be appropriate.

Users are encouraged to make comparisons between sequential single-year estimates. In American FactFinder (AFF), comparison profiles are available beginning with the 2007 single-year data. These profiles identify statistically significant differences between each year from 2007 through the most recently released year.

Caution is needed when using multiyear estimates for estimating year-to-year change in a particular characteristic. This is because roughly two-thirds of the respondents in a 3-year estimate overlap with the respondents in the next year's 3-year estimate period (the overlap is roughly four-fifths for 5-year estimates). When comparing 3-year estimates from 2010–2012 with those from 2011–2013, the differences in overlapping multiyear estimates are driven by differences in the non-overlapping years (i.e. 2011 and 2012). A more appropriate comparison of change over time would be comparing the 2008-2010 3-year estimate to the 2011–2013 3-year estimate because they include responses from total independent samples. Comparison of overlapping periods should be made with caution.

Users who are interested in comparing overlapping multiyear period estimates should refer to Appendix 4 of the *ACS General Handbook* for more information: http://www.census.gov/library/publications/2008/acs/general.html

Multiyear estimates are likely to confuse some data users, in part because of their statistical properties, and in part because this is a new product from the Census Bureau. The ACS will provide all states and communities that have at least 65,000 residents with single-year estimates of demographic, housing, social, and economic characteristics—a boon to government agencies that need to budget and plan for public services like transportation, medical care, and schools. For geographic areas with smaller populations, the ACS samples too few households to provide reliable single-year estimates. For these communities, several years of data will be pooled together to create reliable 3- or 5-year estimates.

Single-year, 3- and 5-year estimates from the ACS are all "period" estimates that represent data collected over a period of time as opposed to "point-in-time" estimates, such as the decennial census. While a single-year estimate includes information collected over a 12-month period, a 3-year estimate represents data collected over a 36-month period, and a 5-year estimate includes data collected over a 60-month period. Therefore, ACS estimates based on data collected from 2011–2013 should not be called "2012" or "2013" estimates. Nor should 2009–2013 period estimates be labeled "2011" estimates, even though that is the midpoint of the 5-year period. Multiyear estimates should be labeled to indicate clearly the full period of time (e.g., "The poverty rate for persons age 25 to 31 in 2011–2013 was X percent"). The primary advantage of using multiyear estimates is the increased statistical reliability of the data for less populated areas and small population subgroups.

Multiyear estimates should, in general, be used when single-year estimates have large CVs or when the precision of the estimates is more important than the currency of the data. Multiyear estimates should also be used when analyzing data for smaller geographies and smaller population subgroups in larger geographies. Multiyear estimates are also of value when examining change over non-overlapping time periods and for smoothing data trends over time.

Single-year estimates should, in general, be used for larger geographies and populations when currency is more important than the precision of the estimates. Single-year estimates should be used to examine year-to-year change for estimates with small CVs. Given the availability of a single-year estimate, calculating the CV provides useful information to determine if the single-year estimate should be used. For areas believed to be experiencing rapid changes in a characteristic, single-year estimates should generally be used rather than multiyear estimates as long as the CV for the single-year estimate is reasonable for the specific usage.

Local area variations may occur due to rapidly occurring changes. Multiyear estimates will tend to be insensitive to such changes when they first occur. Single-year estimates, if associated with sufficiently small CVs, can be very valuable in identifying and studying such phenomena.

Data users also need to use caution in looking at trends involving income or other measures that are adjusted for inflation, such as rental costs, home values, and energy costs. Note that inflation adjustment is based on a national-level consumer price index: it does not adjust for differences in costs of living across different geographic areas.

Appendix 5 of the *ACS General Handbook* provides information on the adjustment of single-year and multiyear ACS estimates for inflation: http://www.census.gov/library/publications/2008/acs/general.html

MARGIN OF ERROR

All data that are based on samples, such as the ACS and the census long-form samples, include a range of uncertainty. Two broad types of error can occur: sampling error and nonsampling error. Nonsampling errors can result from mistakes in how the data are reported or coded, problems in the sampling frame or survey questionnaires, or problems related to nonresponse or interviewer bias. The Census Bureau tries to minimize nonsampling errors by using trained interviewers and by carefully reviewing the survey's sampling methods, data processing techniques, and questionnaire design.

Appendix 6 of the *ACS General Handbook* includes a more detailed description of different types of errors in the ACS and other measures of ACS quality: http:// www.census.gov/library/publications/2008/acs/general. html

Sampling error occurs when data are based on a sample of a population rather than the full population. Sampling error is easier to measure than nonsampling error and can be used to assess the statistical reliability of survey data. For any given area, the larger the sample and the more months included in the data, the greater the confidence in the estimate. The Census Bureau reported the 90-percent confidence interval on all ACS estimates produced for 2005 and earlier. Beginning with the release of the 2006 ACS data, *margins of error (MOE)* are now provided for every ACS estimate. Ninety percent confidence intervals define a range expected to contain the *true* value of an estimate with a level of confidence of 90 percent. Margins of error are easily converted into these confidence ranges. By adding and subtracting the margin of error from the point estimate, we can calculate the 90-percent confidence interval for an estimate. Therefore, we can be 90 percent confident that the true number falls between the lower-bound interval and the upper-bound interval.

Detailed information about sampling error and instructions for calculating confidence intervals and margins of error are included in Appendix 3 of the *ACS General Handbook*: http://www.census.gov/library/publications/2008/acs/general.html

The margin of error around an estimate is important because it helps one draw conclusions about the data. Small differences between two estimates may not be statistically significant if the confidence intervals of those estimates overlap. However, the Census Bureau cautions data users not to rely on overlapping confidence intervals as a test for statistical significance, because this method will not always produce accurate results. Instead, the Census Bureau recommends following the detailed instructions for conducting statistical significance tests in Appendix 4 of the *ACS General Handbook*.

In some cases, data users will need to construct custom ACS estimates by combining data across multiple geographic areas or population subgroups, or it may be necessary to derive a new percentage, proportion, or ratio from published ACS data. In such cases, additional calculations are needed to produce confidence intervals and margins of error for the derived estimates. Appendix 3 of the *ACS General Handbook* provides detailed instructions on how to make these calculations. Note that these error measures do not tell us about the magnitude of nonsampling errors.

Some advanced data users will also want to construct custom ACS estimates from the Census Bureau's Public Use Microdata Samples (PUMS). There are separate instructions for conducting significance tests for PUMS estimates, available on the Census Bureau's American FactFinder (AFF) website at: http://www2. census.gov/programs-surveys/acs/tech_docs/accuracy/ ACS_Accuracy_of_Data_2013.pdf

Accessing ACS Data Online

All ACS data are available through the Census Bureau's American FactFinder (AFF) website at http://factfinder.census.gov. However, American FactFinder is the dissemination tool for all Census Bureau data sources, so it's important to make note of the source information to verify that the ACS is the source of the data presented. From the AFF home page, there are three paths to accessing the data:

- Community Facts—this will provide summary data profiles for a single geographic area. It's useful for obtaining quick demographic and economic indicators for states, cities, counties, towns, or zip codes.

- Guided Search—this "wizard" leads the user through six steps to select the characteristics and geography of interest. Guided Search is available for all Census datasets, so it is still important to verify the source of the data presented.

- Advanced Search—this path provides the most flexibility for data selection by the user but also requires a basic level of knowledge about Census datasets and characteristics. Clicking on the "Topics" button will allow the user to view and select "Datasets." For each year of available ACS data there are three datasets shown: the 1-year estimates (the most current is based on the 2013 ACS), the 3-year estimates (based on the 2011–2013 ACS), and the 5-year estimates (based on the 2009–2013 ACS). The tables in this book were produced from the 1-year estimates for 2013. It is important for all users to understand that once a data set is selected, the accessed tables will all correspond to this specific data set and period of estimate. All tables are clearly labeled, identifying the data set.

Basic help information on using the functions and features of American FactFinder can be found at http://factfinder.census.gov/help/en/index.htm#. The *American FactFinder* main page provides information about available data and guidance on using FactFinder, under the headings *Using American FactFinder* and *What We Provide*.

The various ACS data products are described below.

- **Data profiles, quick tables, and ranking tables.** The *data profiles, quick tables,* and *ranking tables* are good places to start for novice data users. *Data profiles* and *quick tables* provide separate fact sheets on the social, economic, demographic, and housing characteristics for different geographic areas, while *ranking tables* provide state-level rankings of key ACS variables.

- **Geographic comparison tables.** Those interested in geographic comparisons for areas other than states may be interested in the *geographic comparison tables*, which allow comparison of ACS data across a variety of geographic areas including metropolitan areas, cities, counties, and congressional districts.

- **Subject tables.** These are similar to *data profiles* but are specific to a more detailed characteristic or topic (e.g., employment, education, and income). *Subject tables* provide pre-tabulated numbers and percentages for a wide variety of topics, often available separately by age (for example, 60 and over and 65 and over), gender, or race/ethnicity.

- **Selected population profiles.** The most detailed race/ethnic data are available through the *selected population profiles*, which provide summary tables separately for more than 400 detailed race, ethnic, tribal, ancestry, and country of birth groups.

- **Comparison profiles.** The *comparison profiles* show data side-by-side from multiple years, indicating where there is a statistically significant difference between the two sets of estimates. Comparison profiles are only available for 1-year estimates, which limits the profiles to geographic areas of 65,000 or more population.

- **Detailed tables and summary files.** The *detailed tables* are the best source for advanced data users or those who want access to the most comprehensive ACS tables. For more advanced users, *detailed tables* are also available for download through the ACS *Summary File*: http://www.census.gov/programs-surveys/acs/technical-documentation/summary-file-documentation.html

- **Thematic maps.** The *thematic maps* provide graphic displays of the data available through the various tables. Different shades of color are used to display variations in the data across geographic areas. Data users can also highlight areas with statistically different values from a selected state, county, or metropolitan area of interest. If a mapping option is available, it will display as an option when you view a table.

- **Public Use Microdata Sample files.** Those with expertise in using SAS, SPSS, or STATA may also be interested in the *Public Use Microdata Sample (PUMS) files*, which contain a sample of individual records of people and households that responded to the survey (stripped of all identifying information). The PUMS files permit analysis of specific population groups and custom variables that are not available through the summary tables in American FactFinder. The data presented in this book was produced using the 2013 1-year micro-data files and will be explained in more detail in the chapter "Defining the Millennials." Briefly, the age definition of the millennial population used here is age 13 through 31. This age group simply isn't tabulated in the Census Bureau's summary files and requires the more detailed characteristics identified in the PUMS file. This flexibility is not provided by the pre-tabulated detailed tables provided in American Fact-Finder. Data users can also combine multiple years of PUMS data to produce data for relatively small population subgroups (e.g., female physicians over age 55). More information about the PUMS is available on the technical documentation page at: http://www.census.gov/programs-surveys/acs/technical-documentation/pums.html

For readers who are used to data from the traditional decennial census long-form, it is important to note that there are many conceptual and data collection differences in the ACS. The following is a summary of some of these differences which are described more fully in the chapter "Using the ACS."

The ACS data are complex and cover a broad range of topics and geographic areas. Because this is a relatively new survey, many people do not fully understand how to interpret and use the ACS data. The key points are summarized below.

- Use caution in comparing ACS data with data from the decennial census or other sources. Every survey uses different methods, which could affect the comparability of the numbers.

- The ACS was designed to provide estimates of the characteristics of the population, not to provide counts of the population in different geographic areas or population subgroups. However, counts of the population are often what is required by grant applications and researchers.

- Be careful in drawing conclusions about small differences between two estimates because they may not be statistically different. Statistical testing should always be considered based on the sensitivity of conclusions to differences in the data results.

- Data users need to be careful not to interpret annual fluctuations in the data as long-term trends. Again, statistical testing is necessary to determine if annual fluctuations are real or merely a result of the sample.

- Use caution in comparing data from 2006 and later surveys with data from the 2000–2005 surveys. Unlike earlier surveys, the 2006 and later ACS surveys include samples of the population living in group quarters (e.g., college dorms and nursing homes), so the data may not be comparable. This is especially important for young adults and the elderly who are more likely than other age groups to be living in group quarters facilities.

- The questionnaire series to define disability changed in 2008, making it impossible to compare disability status for periods before that date.

- Data users should not interpret or refer to 3-year or 5-year period estimates as estimates of the middle year or last year in the series. For example, a 2008–2010 estimate is not a "2009 average."

- Data users should always be consistent in comparing similar period estimates over time or between geographic areas. Compare 1-year to 1-year, 3-year to 3-year, and 5-year to 5-year estimates. Since geographic areas of different population size have different period estimates available, always make comparisons using the same period estimate. Do not compare a 1-year estimate for a large population size to a 5-year estimate for a small area or census tract.

- Data users should *not* rely on overlapping confidence intervals as a test for statistical significance because this method will not always provide an accurate result.

More ACS Resources

There is a wealth of information about the ACS on the Web with new information available on a regular basis. Each year, the ACS data release represents a new stage in the process. Consequently, many new documents are required to explain the survey, year-to-year changes, and how to use it. These resources cover many of the topics discussed in this book, but in greater detail.

The best place to start is the Census Bureau's ACS main page: http://www.census.gov/programs-surveys/acs/

BACKGROUND AND OVERVIEW INFORMATION

About the Survey provides background and general information about the importance of the ACS, how sampled households are selected, response options, privacy protections and questionnaire information.
http://www.census.gov/programs-surveys/acs/about.html

Guidance for Data Users provides detailed information that helps users understand the geographic coverage of the survey data, how and when to use the multi-year estimates, and handbooks for users of various types.
http://www.census.gov/programs-surveys/acs/guidance.html

Data & Documentation is critical for users who need to understand the details of the data that's available, research methods, and detailed documentation for the various data file products.
http://www.census.gov/programs-surveys/acs/technical-documentation.html

Methodology provides the most detailed information about the survey sample size, response rates, and data quality.
http://www.census.gov/programs-surveys/acs/methodology.html

Library is a link to volumes of research and papers describing aspects of survey methodology, research, and analytical reports categorized by year.
http://www.census.gov/programs-surveys/acs/library.html

Accuracy of the Data (2013)
Provides a basic understanding of the sample design, estimation methodology, and accuracy of the 2013 ACS data.
http://www2.census.gov/programs-surveys/acs/tech_docs/accuracy/ACS_Accuracy_of_Data_2013.pdf

ACS Sample Size and Data Quality Measures
Provides sample size information for each state for each year of the ACS. The initial sample size, the final completed response and coverage rates, as well as item allocation rates are provided. Sample sizes for all published geographic entities starting with the 2007 ACS are available in the B98 series of detailed tables on American FactFinder.
http://www.census.gov/acs/www/methodology/sample-size-and-data-quality/

ACS Multiyear Estimates and Census Comparison
Multiyear estimates were an entirely new product of Census Bureau ACS operations and their use can be confusing to data users. The ACS "Methodology" page provides content and documentation of the multiyear estimates, which are helpful to understanding the uses of multiyear estimates and making appropriate comparisons to traditional decennial census data.
http://www.census.gov/programs-surveys/acs/methodology.html

GUIDANCE ON DATA PRODUCTS AND USING THE DATA

How to Use the Data
Includes links to many documents and materials that explain the ACS data products. http://www.census.gov/programs-surveys/acs/guidance.html

Comparing ACS Data to Other Sources
Guidance on comparing the ACS data products to other years of ACS data and to Census 2000 long-form data.
http://www.census.gov/programs-surveys/acs/guidance/comparing-acs-data.html

When to Use 1-year, 3-year, or 5-year Estimates
The availability of multiple characteristic estimates for a given geographic area for different period estimates can be confusing for users of ACS data. Guidance on comparing across geographies and time periods.
http://www.census.gov/programs-surveys/acs/guidance/estimates.html

Information on Using Different Sources of Data for Income and Poverty
Highlights the sources that should be used for data on income and poverty, focusing on comparing the ACS and the Current Population Survey (CPS).
http://www.census.gov/hhes/www/poverty/about/datasources/description.html

Poverty: 2012 and 2013 American Community Survey brief on poverty.
http://www.census.gov/content/dam/Census/library/publications/2014/acs/acsbr13-01.pdf

Public Use Microdata Sample (PUMS)
Provides guidance on accessing ACS microdata.
http://www.census.gov/programs-surveys/acs/data/pums.html

ACS Data Users Group
In partnership with the U.S. Census Bureau, the Population Reference Bureau (PRB) and Sabre Systems have formed the American Community Survey (ACS) Data Users Group. The purpose of the ACS Data Users Group is to improve understanding of the value and utility of ACS data and to promote information sharing among data users about key ACS data issues and applications. Membership in the group is free and open to all interested ACS data users. You can join this online community at:
http://acsdatacommunity.leveragesoftware.com/

OTHER DATA RESOURCES

- FactFinder Help (online help, census data information, glossary, and tutorial)
  http://factfinder.census.gov/help/en/index.htm#

- Guide to the Data Products (Web page)
  http://www.census.gov/acs/www/data_documentation/product_descriptions

- *A Compass for Understanding and Using American Community Survey Data: What General Data Users Need to Know* provides a complete overview:
  http://www.census.gov/programs-surveys/acs/guidance/handbooks.html

- Other Compass handbooks are available for the business community, media, Congress and many other user groups at:
  http://www.census.gov/programs-surveys/acs/guidance/handbooks.html

- *Using the American Community Survey: Benefits and Challenges*, edited by Constance F. Citro and Graham Kalton (The National Academies Press, 2007). An excellent overview of the ACS, complete with several chapters of useful information for data users. The book is available for purchase and is also available to read online at no charge.
  http://www.nap.edu/catalog/11901/using-the-american-community-survey-benefits-and-challenges

PART A
POPULATION SUMMARY

POPULATION SUMMARY

In 1982, the population of the United States stood at 232.6 million. The Baby Boomers (age 18 to 36 at that time) represented 32.9 percent of the country's population, and their numbers pressured employment and housing opportunities. In 2013, Baby Boomers (now age 49 to 67) represented only 23.1 percent of the population and their numbers are declining. In 1982 they were also in the process of giving birth to the Millennial generation, which has now become the largest generation in the nation's history. Between the years of 1982 and 2001 more than 78 million children were born, compared to about 76 million births in the Baby Boom years.

While the aging of the Baby Boom generation captures a lot of national attention, the Millennial generation is the new economic and cultural force in the country. But it's important to note that, just as with any other demographic or economic characteristic, the portrait is not uniform. As the geographic level of analysis gets smaller, the variation across our communities grows, with some areas following national trends while others outpace or lag the nation. Analyzing population change is like telling a story of our communities. It's important to look at population change over time, the varying demographic composition of our communities, and how each compares to other areas. The text and tables in this volume are intended to provide the basic demographic portrait of the Millennial generation at the state, county, city, and metropolitan/micropolitan area levels and allow planners, researchers, and interested individuals to tell their own stories.

The tables in this book provide data for calendar year 2013 from the Census Bureau's 1-year American Community Survey (ACS). Users are encouraged to read the introductory sections describing the ACS and Public Use Microdata Sample (PUMS) and the important aspects of data collection and use that impact the interpretation of these data. In general, the book provides summaries for counties, cities, metropolitan areas, and selected micropolitan areas of approximately 100,000 population, because 100,000 is the population threshold for defining a Census Public Use Microdata Area (PUMA). However, PUMAs do not always follow the boundaries of counties and cities. The algorithm

described in the section Defining the Millennials sometimes allowed for the definition of areas smaller than 100,000 and sometimes required eliminating areas larger than 100,000.

THE MILLENNIALS

In 2013 the Millennials, now age 13 to 31, numbered 82.5 million individuals and comprised 26.1 percent of the population. Unlike the Baby Boomer generation which is aging and shrinking, the Millennial generation continues to increase due to foreign immigration, which explains why there are more Millennials in 2013 than those born during their birth years. There are slightly more males (51 percent) than females (49 percent), and this difference is also influenced by the higher number of male births and the higher proportion of foreign immigrants that are male.

In this book, the Millennial generation is categorized by age into three groups: 13 to 17 representing the pre-college ages, 18 to 24 representing those in college or early in their employment years, and 25 to 31 representing those fully into the labor force years and beginning to establish households. Unlike the Baby Boomers who were fully invested in the labor force and establishing households before their 30th birthday, the Millennials have delayed many of the traditional life cycle stages like marriage, childbearing, and family formation. Of the 82.5 million Millennials, 25.2 percent were age 13 to 17 while the 18 to 24 and 25 to 31 populations were nearly equal at 38.3 percent and 36.5 percent, respectively.

There isn't much variation in the proportion of state populations who are in the Millennial years, but a couple of states stand out. Forty-two states have between 25 and 30 percent of the population between the ages of 13 and 31. Maine has the lowest proportion at 22.9 percent, while the District of Columbia is highest at 33.4 percent. Other states with less than 25 percent include: Connecticut, Florida, New Hampshire, New Jersey, Oregon, Vermont, and West Virginia. Aside from the District of Columbia, no other state is above 30 percent, and the second highest is Alaska at 29.7 percent.

The District of Columbia also stands out with respect to the age distribution of Millennials. It has the lowest

Millennials Age 13 to 31 as a Percent of the Total Population

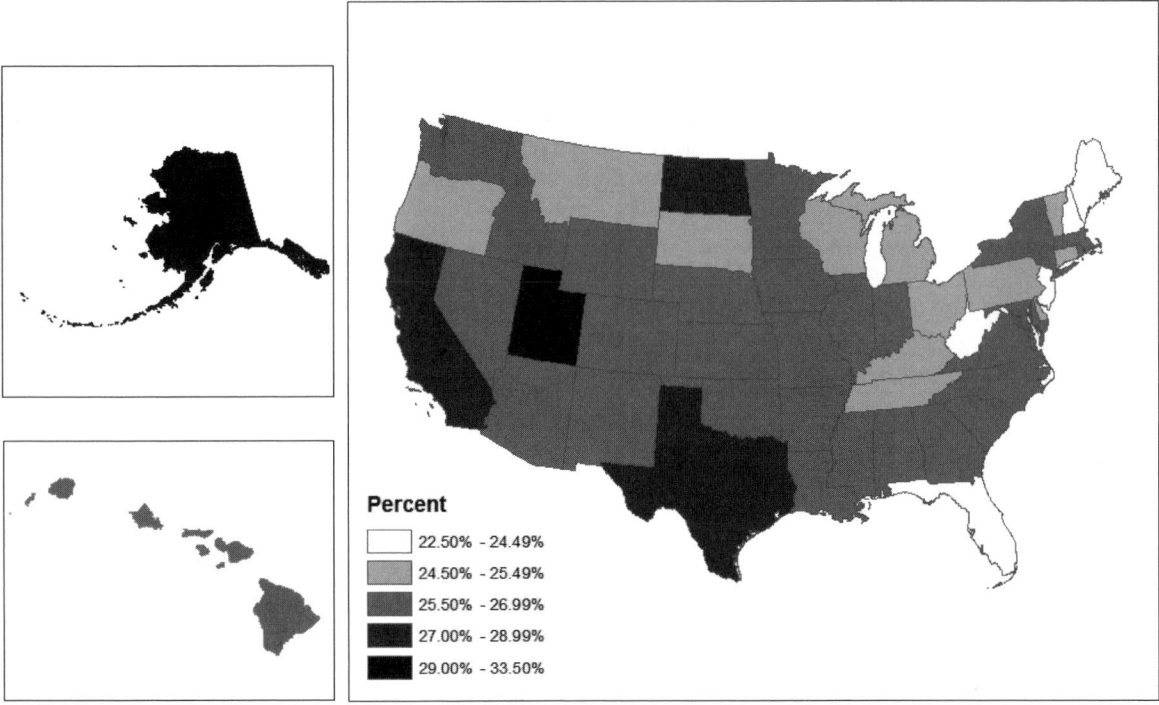

Percent

	22.50% - 24.49%
	24.50% - 25.49%
	25.50% - 26.99%
	27.00% - 28.99%
	29.00% - 33.50%

percentage age 13 to 17 (11.0 percent) and the highest percentage age 25 to 31 at 51.5 percent. North Dakota has the second lowest percentage of 13 to 17 year olds at 20.1 percent while Hawaii has the second highest percentage of 25 to 31 year olds at 40.3 percent. The 13 to 17 year olds fall in a tight range with 43 states having between 24 and 28 percent of the total Millennial population. For the 25 to 31 year olds there is a similarly tight range with 40 states falling between 34 and 39 percent.

There are 622 counties meeting the population size criteria to be included. At the county level there is much more variation in the composition of the Millennial population. Sumter County, FL has the lowest percentage of Millennials at 12.2 percent, while Brazos County, TX has the highest. In Brazos, home to the main campus of Texas A&M University at College Station, fully 48 percent of the population is between the ages of 13 and 31. Thirteen counties have a Millennial population greater than 40 percent of the total, and all are counties with large college populations such as Penn State in Centre County, PA, Virginia Tech in Montgomery County, VA, the University of Iowa in Johnson County, IA, and Purdue University in Tippecanoe County, IN. These are

good illustrations of the need to understand important community characteristics that influence their demographic compositions.

The distribution of the Millennial population by sex varies much more for counties than at the state level, with males comprising the lowest percentage in Flathead County, MT (41.6 percent) and the highest percentage in Highlands County, FL at 61.7 percent. Clark County, GA, home of the University of Georgia had the lowest percentage of 13 to 17 year olds at only 7.9 percent and Arlington County, VA had the highest percentage of 25 to 31 year olds with 64.5 percent. This is easily understood as Arlington is an easy commute to Washington, DC. Virginia is also home to the county with the lowest percentage of 25 to 31 year olds, with Montgomery County (Virginia Tech) at 16.8 percent because it has the highest percentage of 18 to 24 year olds with 67.9 percent. Forsyth County, GA has the highest percentage of 13 to 17 years old (41.0 percent), which is likely a result of its proximity to Atlanta and high proportion of married couple families with children.

Nearly one-third of the nation's Millennial population lives in the 331 cities identified here. Miami Beach,

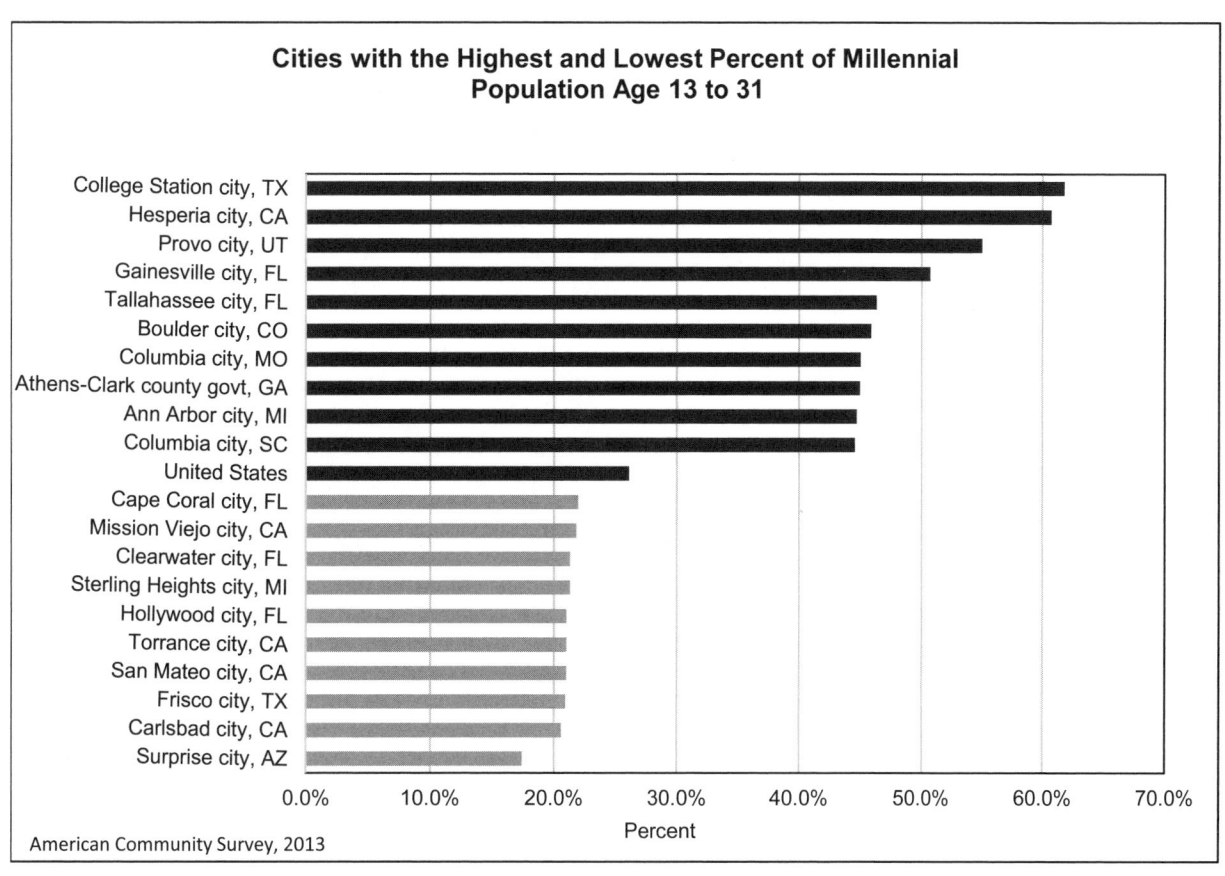

Cities with the Highest and Lowest Percent of Millennial Population Age 13 to 31

American Community Survey, 2013

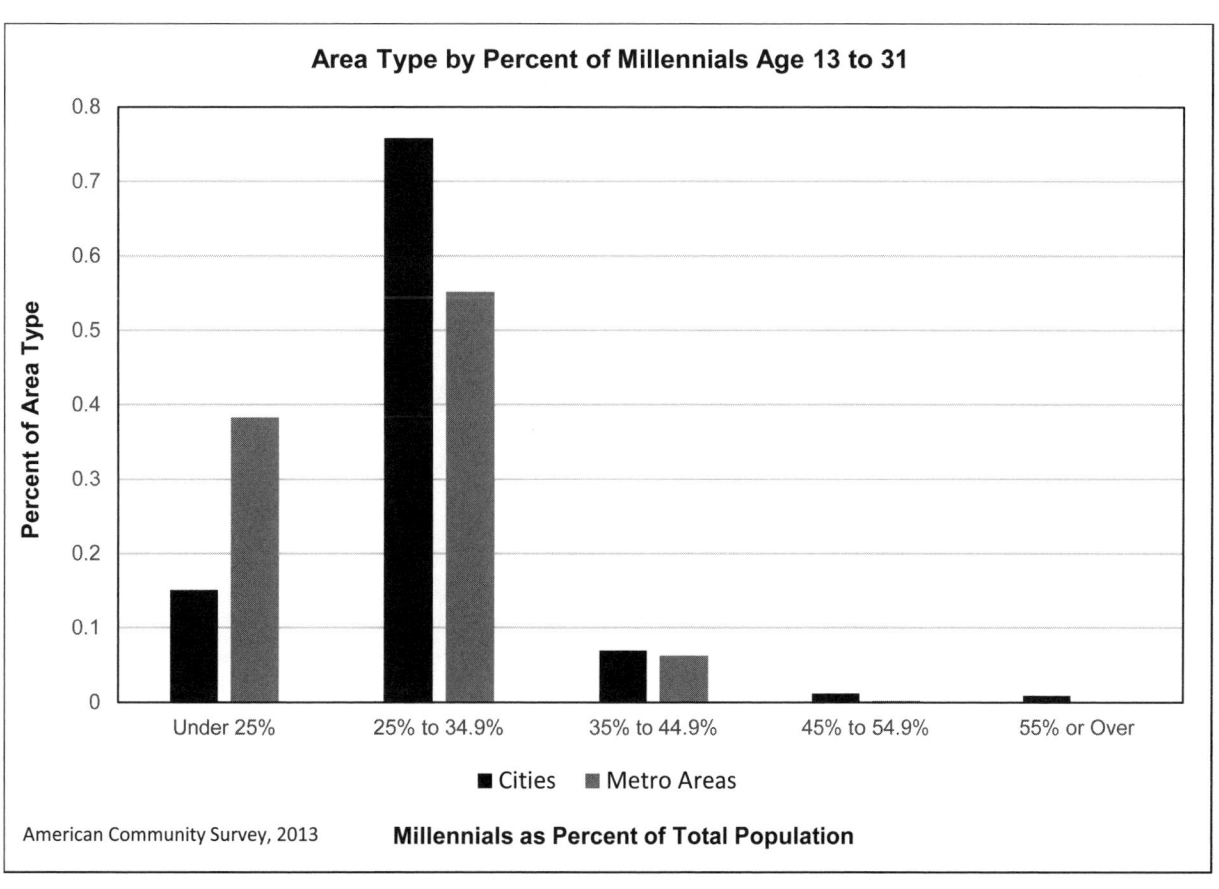

Area Type by Percent of Millennials Age 13 to 31

American Community Survey, 2013

Millennials as Percent of Total Population

FL, has the smallest number with 20,119, which is 22.1 percent of the city's population. Not surprisingly, New York City has the largest Millennial population at 2,261,947, but, as a proportion, it isn't much higher than Miami Beach at 26.9 percent. Surprise City, AZ, has the lowest percentage of population in the Millennial age category (17.4 percent) while College Station City, TX (Brazos County, TX), has the highest percentage at 61.8 percent. The Millennial population is higher than 50 percent in only five cities: College Station City, TX, Gainesville City, FL, Glendale City, CA, Hesperia City, CA, and Provo City, UT and is between 40 and 50 percent in another 11 cities. Gainesville City, FL, has the lowest percentage of Millennials age 13 to 17 at 6.3 percent, while Elk Grove City, CA, has the highest percentage at 43.1 percent. Among the 25 to 31 age group, Mission Viejo City, CA, at 21.1 percent has the lowest percentage, and Alexandria City, VA, has the highest at 67.4 percent.

Fully 86.9 percent of the nation's Millennial population lives in the 415 metropolitan/micropolitan areas identified. The New York metro area is again the largest at 5.1 million followed by Los Angeles at 3.5 million and Chicago at 2.5 million. As a percentage, however, the college dominated metro of Manhattan, KS (Kansas State University) has the largest percentage of its population in the Millennial age groups at 45.7 percent. The Villages, FL, is lowest at 10.6 percent. State College, PA (Penn State University) has the largest proportion of population in the 18 to 24 age group with more than two-thirds (67.8 percent) of the Millennials in that age category. At 28.1 percent, the Kahalui-Wailuku-Lahaina, HI, metro has the lowest percentage in the college age category.

Table A-1: States—Summary Population Characteristics

	Total 2013 ACS Population	Millennial Population Age 13 to 31	Millennials as Percent of Total	Millennial Percentage by Gender		Millennial Percentage by Age		
				Male	Female	13 to 17	18 to 24	25 to 31
United States....................	316,128,839	82,516,535	26.1%	51.0%	49.0%	25.2%	38.3%	36.5%
Alabama.............................	4,833,722	1,243,909	25.7%	50.2%	49.8%	25.5%	40.0%	34.5%
Alaska................................	735,132	218,453	29.7%	55.3%	44.7%	24.2%	38.7%	37.1%
Arizona..............................	6,626,624	1,743,604	26.3%	51.7%	48.3%	26.3%	38.0%	35.7%
Arkansas............................	2,959,373	754,902	25.5%	51.3%	48.7%	25.8%	38.0%	36.1%
California...........................	38,332,521	10,563,495	27.6%	51.6%	48.4%	24.5%	38.0%	37.5%
Colorado	5,268,367	1,404,366	26.7%	52.1%	47.9%	24.7%	36.5%	38.8%
Connecticut.......................	3,596,080	889,970	24.7%	50.8%	49.2%	26.5%	38.5%	35.0%
Delaware............................	925,749	234,000	25.3%	50.3%	49.7%	23.8%	38.7%	37.5%
District of Columbia	646,449	216,160	33.4%	46.8%	53.2%	11.0%	37.5%	51.5%
Florida...............................	19,552,860	4,703,393	24.1%	51.2%	48.8%	24.6%	38.2%	37.2%
Georgia	9,992,167	2,675,903	26.8%	50.8%	49.2%	26.2%	38.5%	35.3%
Hawaii................................	1,404,054	371,155	26.4%	53.5%	46.5%	22.9%	36.7%	40.3%
Idaho.................................	1,612,136	422,164	26.2%	51.3%	48.7%	28.4%	38.1%	33.5%
Illinois...............................	12,882,135	3,382,854	26.3%	50.6%	49.4%	25.5%	37.5%	37.1%
Indiana..............................	6,570,902	1,694,378	25.8%	50.7%	49.3%	26.3%	39.6%	34.2%
Iowa..................................	3,090,416	791,151	25.6%	51.3%	48.7%	25.4%	39.9%	34.7%
Kansas	2,893,957	763,442	26.4%	52.5%	47.5%	25.9%	39.4%	34.7%
Kentucky	4,395,295	1,113,720	25.3%	51.3%	48.7%	26.1%	38.4%	35.5%
Louisiana...........................	4,625,470	1,241,608	26.8%	50.8%	49.2%	24.2%	38.9%	36.9%
Maine................................	1,328,302	303,554	22.9%	50.7%	49.3%	27.0%	38.6%	34.3%
Maryland............................	5,928,814	1,527,405	25.8%	50.7%	49.3%	25.2%	36.9%	37.9%
Massachusetts....................	6,692,824	1,771,550	26.5%	50.0%	50.0%	23.5%	39.3%	37.3%
Michigan............................	9,895,622	2,496,925	25.2%	50.9%	49.1%	26.5%	40.1%	33.4%
Minnesota..........................	5,420,380	1,394,146	25.7%	50.7%	49.3%	25.8%	36.5%	37.8%
Mississippi.........................	2,991,207	782,547	26.2%	50.4%	49.6%	26.2%	41.2%	32.6%
Missouri.............................	6,044,171	1,551,729	25.7%	50.1%	49.9%	25.6%	38.2%	36.2%
Montana.............................	1,015,165	254,000	25.0%	51.1%	48.9%	25.5%	40.5%	33.9%
Nebraska............................	1,868,516	488,381	26.1%	51.0%	49.0%	25.0%	39.1%	35.9%
Nevada..............................	2,790,136	715,125	25.6%	51.2%	48.8%	25.5%	36.0%	38.5%
New Hampshire...................	1,323,459	320,088	24.2%	50.9%	49.1%	26.4%	39.6%	34.0%
New Jersey	8,899,339	2,179,642	24.5%	51.4%	48.6%	27.3%	36.4%	36.2%
New Mexico	2,085,287	546,092	26.2%	51.8%	48.2%	25.9%	40.0%	34.1%
New York...........................	19,651,127	5,211,620	26.5%	50.4%	49.6%	23.2%	38.2%	38.6%
North Carolina....................	9,848,060	2,517,570	25.6%	51.2%	48.8%	25.6%	39.6%	34.7%
North Dakota......................	723,393	209,265	28.9%	54.5%	45.5%	20.1%	46.4%	33.5%
Ohio..................................	11,570,808	2,922,925	25.3%	50.6%	49.4%	26.3%	38.3%	35.5%
Oklahoma...........................	3,850,568	1,014,365	26.3%	51.4%	48.6%	24.4%	39.1%	36.6%
Oregon..............................	3,930,065	981,691	25.0%	50.7%	49.3%	24.9%	37.5%	37.6%
Pennsylvania......................	12,773,801	3,194,416	25.0%	50.7%	49.3%	24.8%	39.2%	36.0%
Rhode Island......................	1,051,511	278,272	26.5%	51.0%	49.0%	22.3%	43.1%	34.6%
South Carolina	4,774,839	1,223,504	25.6%	50.4%	49.6%	25.1%	41.0%	33.9%
South Dakota	844,877	214,866	25.4%	52.3%	47.7%	25.5%	39.1%	35.4%
Tennessee	6,495,978	1,653,200	25.4%	50.7%	49.3%	25.7%	38.3%	36.0%
Texas................................	26,448,193	7,316,912	27.7%	51.4%	48.6%	26.1%	37.4%	36.6%
Utah..................................	2,900,872	868,128	29.9%	50.5%	49.5%	26.9%	38.4%	34.7%
Vermont.............................	626,630	154,073	24.6%	49.7%	50.3%	25.4%	42.1%	32.5%
Virginia..............................	8,260,405	2,153,966	26.1%	50.9%	49.1%	24.1%	38.7%	37.2%
Washington........................	6,971,406	1,808,668	25.9%	51.4%	48.6%	24.5%	36.8%	38.7%
West Virginia......................	1,854,304	436,632	23.5%	51.0%	49.0%	26.0%	40.3%	33.7%
Wisconsin	5,742,713	1,444,543	25.2%	50.9%	49.1%	25.8%	38.3%	35.9%
Wyoming	582,658	152,108	26.1%	50.5%	49.5%	25.0%	39.1%	35.9%

Table A-2: Counties—Summary Population Characteristics

	Total 2013 ACS Population	Millennial Population Age 13 to 31	Millennials as Percent of Total	Millennial Percentage by Gender		Millennial Percentage by Age		
				Male	Female	13 to 17	18 to 24	25 to 31
Alabama								
Baldwin County	182,265	43,743	24.0%	49.4%	50.6%	30.0%	37.3%	32.6%
Calhoun County	118,572	29,189	24.6%	49.7%	50.3%	22.9%	40.9%	36.1%
Etowah County	104,430	24,989	23.9%	48.9%	51.1%	30.7%	37.3%	32.1%
Houston County	101,547	25,996	25.6%	51.1%	48.9%	28.4%	33.8%	37.9%
Jefferson County	658,466	169,583	25.8%	49.3%	50.7%	25.1%	35.8%	39.1%
Lauderdale County	92,709	25,218	27.2%	50.9%	49.1%	23.1%	44.8%	32.1%
Lee County	140,247	53,402	38.1%	51.8%	48.2%	17.3%	56.2%	26.5%
Madison County	334,811	89,687	26.8%	52.1%	47.9%	25.5%	39.2%	35.2%
Marshall County	93,019	23,904	25.7%	51.8%	48.2%	31.5%	30.4%	38.2%
Mobile County	412,992	106,088	25.7%	48.8%	51.2%	24.6%	39.6%	35.8%
Montgomery County	229,363	65,733	28.7%	45.7%	54.3%	24.0%	40.8%	35.2%
Morgan County	119,490	27,865	23.3%	53.9%	46.1%	30.7%	37.6%	31.7%
Shelby County	195,085	50,021	25.6%	50.6%	49.4%	29.2%	33.9%	36.9%
Tuscaloosa County	194,656	73,097	37.6%	52.2%	47.8%	15.9%	54.5%	29.6%
Alaska								
Fairbanks North Star Borough	97,581	33,622	34.5%	53.8%	46.2%	18.4%	42.5%	39.1%
Matanuska-Susitna Borough	88,995	27,285	30.7%	57.2%	42.8%	32.2%	36.1%	31.7%
Arizona								
Cochise County	131,346	32,080	24.4%	51.9%	48.1%	25.7%	38.0%	36.2%
Coconino County	134,421	48,457	36.0%	49.0%	51.0%	16.0%	55.1%	28.9%
Maricopa County	3,817,117	1,074,489	28.1%	51.4%	48.6%	26.5%	36.0%	37.5%
Mohave County	200,186	40,348	20.2%	51.2%	48.8%	29.7%	35.0%	35.2%
Navajo County	107,449	28,502	26.5%	49.3%	50.7%	29.4%	37.0%	33.6%
Pima County	980,263	272,490	27.8%	51.1%	48.9%	23.1%	44.6%	32.3%
Pinal County	375,770	92,374	24.6%	56.2%	43.8%	30.1%	34.6%	35.3%
Yavapai County	211,033	40,349	19.1%	51.8%	48.2%	29.2%	35.6%	35.1%
Yuma County	195,751	59,396	30.3%	56.4%	43.6%	26.3%	41.0%	32.7%
Arkansas								
Benton County	221,339	61,471	27.8%	51.7%	48.3%	31.0%	32.5%	36.5%
Craighead County	96,443	27,322	28.3%	51.4%	48.6%	18.5%	40.8%	40.7%
Faulkner County	113,237	41,303	36.5%	52.9%	47.1%	22.2%	39.4%	38.4%
Garland County	96,024	20,404	21.2%	54.3%	45.7%	28.5%	41.2%	30.3%
Pulaski County	382,748	104,460	27.3%	51.7%	48.3%	24.2%	33.6%	42.2%
Saline County	107,118	27,530	25.7%	53.2%	46.8%	29.1%	29.4%	41.5%
Sebastian County	125,744	32,489	25.8%	54.4%	45.6%	27.4%	31.5%	41.1%
Washington County	203,065	68,368	33.7%	51.4%	48.6%	19.9%	45.8%	34.2%
California								
Alameda County	1,510,271	411,973	27.3%	50.7%	49.3%	22.3%	36.2%	41.4%
Butte County	220,000	65,642	29.8%	51.6%	48.4%	18.4%	51.5%	30.1%
Contra Costa County	1,049,025	260,160	24.8%	51.1%	48.9%	27.8%	36.2%	36.0%
El Dorado County	181,058	37,599	20.8%	47.7%	52.3%	30.7%	35.4%	33.9%
Fresno County	930,450	280,779	30.2%	51.7%	48.3%	25.4%	38.6%	36.0%
Humboldt County	134,623	38,357	28.5%	51.0%	49.0%	17.3%	47.2%	35.4%
Imperial County	174,528	52,602	30.1%	53.8%	46.2%	27.1%	38.6%	34.3%
Kern County	839,631	255,789	30.5%	52.1%	47.9%	26.5%	37.5%	36.0%
Kings County	152,982	45,510	29.7%	59.3%	40.7%	23.5%	38.3%	38.2%
Los Angeles County	9,818,605	2,833,691	28.9%	51.0%	49.0%	23.6%	37.7%	38.7%
Madera County	150,865	43,066	28.5%	51.1%	48.9%	27.9%	35.8%	36.3%
Marin County	252,409	49,354	19.6%	53.6%	46.4%	33.8%	35.5%	30.8%
Merced County	255,793	80,879	31.6%	52.7%	47.3%	29.4%	38.9%	31.6%
Monterey County	415,057	126,091	30.4%	52.8%	47.2%	25.8%	38.3%	35.9%
Napa County	136,484	33,246	24.4%	51.7%	48.3%	28.0%	39.6%	32.4%
Nevada County	98,764	19,138	19.4%	56.8%	43.2%	30.8%	38.6%	30.6%
Orange County	3,010,232	845,683	28.1%	51.0%	49.0%	25.7%	37.6%	36.7%
Placer County	348,432	86,972	25.0%	50.0%	50.0%	32.7%	33.7%	33.6%
Riverside County	2,189,641	639,239	29.2%	51.4%	48.6%	28.2%	38.0%	33.8%
Sacramento County	1,418,788	403,255	28.4%	50.6%	49.4%	25.9%	36.1%	38.0%
San Bernardino County	2,035,210	618,547	30.4%	51.1%	48.9%	26.8%	38.9%	34.3%
San Diego County	3,095,313	936,854	30.3%	53.0%	47.0%	21.1%	39.2%	39.7%
San Francisco County	805,235	227,668	28.3%	50.8%	49.2%	11.3%	28.3%	60.4%
San Joaquin County	685,306	195,419	28.5%	52.7%	47.3%	29.9%	38.2%	31.9%
San Luis Obispo County	269,637	80,673	29.9%	54.5%	45.5%	16.1%	54.6%	29.4%
San Mateo County	718,451	169,271	23.6%	52.0%	48.0%	25.2%	34.2%	40.5%
Santa Barbara County	423,895	138,689	32.7%	51.3%	48.7%	21.2%	49.7%	29.1%
Santa Clara County	1,781,642	475,069	26.7%	52.3%	47.7%	23.7%	34.6%	41.6%
Santa Cruz County	262,382	77,464	29.5%	53.4%	46.6%	18.9%	52.9%	28.2%
Shasta County	177,223	43,154	24.4%	52.4%	47.6%	25.5%	39.5%	35.1%
Solano County	413,344	114,250	27.6%	52.0%	48.0%	24.4%	38.0%	37.6%
Sonoma County	483,878	120,963	25.0%	52.1%	47.9%	26.4%	37.6%	36.0%
Stanislaus County	514,453	148,186	28.8%	51.2%	48.8%	28.4%	37.5%	34.1%
Sutter County	94,737	23,736	25.1%	46.9%	53.1%	19.8%	43.9%	36.3%
Tulare County	442,179	132,184	29.9%	50.3%	49.7%	27.5%	37.6%	34.9%
Ventura County	823,318	219,271	26.6%	52.0%	48.0%	26.8%	39.0%	34.1%
Yolo County	200,849	72,057	35.9%	49.3%	50.7%	17.8%	55.0%	27.2%
Colorado								
Adams County	441,603	134,668	30.5%	50.7%	49.3%	27.9%	32.8%	39.3%

Table A-2: Counties—Summary Population Characteristics—*Continued*

	Total 2013 ACS Population	Millennial Population Age 13 to 31	Millennials as Percent of Total	Millennial Percentage by Gender		Millennial Percentage by Age		
				Male	Female	13 to 17	18 to 24	25 to 31
Colorado—Cont.								
Arapahoe County	572,003	159,628	27.9%	50.3%	49.7%	28.2%	33.1%	38.7%
Boulder County	294,567	93,422	31.7%	52.2%	47.8%	22.0%	49.4%	28.6%
Denver County	600,158	198,526	33.1%	49.4%	50.6%	14.9%	31.3%	53.8%
Douglas County	285,465	68,342	23.9%	50.2%	49.8%	39.8%	31.1%	29.0%
El Paso County	622,263	185,094	29.7%	53.4%	46.6%	24.5%	38.0%	37.5%
Jefferson County	534,543	131,936	24.7%	53.6%	46.4%	27.5%	35.7%	36.8%
Larimer County	299,630	96,789	32.3%	52.7%	47.3%	20.6%	47.9%	31.5%
Mesa County	146,723	38,326	26.1%	47.5%	52.5%	21.8%	40.7%	37.4%
Pueblo County	159,063	41,292	26.0%	52.2%	47.8%	25.1%	38.2%	36.7%
Weld County	252,825	74,786	29.6%	52.2%	47.8%	23.9%	39.3%	36.8%
Connecticut								
Fairfield County	916,829	221,597	24.2%	50.5%	49.5%	29.8%	35.9%	34.3%
Hartford County	894,014	221,135	24.7%	50.8%	49.2%	27.2%	36.2%	36.6%
Litchfield County	189,927	39,336	20.7%	52.0%	48.0%	30.9%	34.7%	34.4%
Middlesex County	165,676	38,088	23.0%	53.7%	46.3%	26.5%	38.9%	34.7%
New Haven County	862,477	221,657	25.7%	49.5%	50.5%	24.8%	39.1%	36.1%
New London County	274,055	70,256	25.6%	52.5%	47.5%	22.0%	42.0%	35.9%
Tolland County	152,691	47,953	31.4%	51.7%	48.3%	20.1%	55.7%	24.2%
Windham County	118,428	29,948	25.3%	52.1%	47.9%	24.7%	39.9%	35.4%
Delaware								
Kent County	162,310	43,966	27.1%	52.2%	47.8%	24.8%	39.2%	36.0%
New Castle County	538,479	148,648	27.6%	49.7%	50.3%	23.3%	38.8%	37.9%
Sussex County	197,145	41,386	21.0%	50.4%	49.6%	24.8%	37.7%	37.5%
Florida								
Alachua County	247,336	97,705	39.5%	49.3%	50.7%	11.7%	59.2%	29.2%
Bay County	168,852	41,608	24.6%	53.2%	46.8%	23.2%	35.3%	41.5%
Brevard County	543,376	112,681	20.7%	50.3%	49.7%	26.8%	39.1%	34.1%
Broward County	1,748,066	437,509	25.0%	50.4%	49.6%	25.6%	36.0%	38.4%
Charlotte County	159,978	26,086	16.3%	50.0%	50.0%	28.5%	39.0%	32.5%
Citrus County	141,236	21,470	15.2%	53.3%	46.7%	29.1%	39.0%	31.9%
Clay County	190,865	47,604	24.9%	49.2%	50.8%	31.5%	33.5%	34.9%
Collier County	321,520	62,196	19.3%	54.1%	45.9%	27.9%	36.3%	35.8%
Duval County	864,263	241,161	27.9%	50.4%	49.6%	21.7%	36.2%	42.1%
Escambia County	297,619	86,905	29.2%	54.7%	45.3%	18.8%	45.3%	36.0%
Flagler County	95,696	20,146	21.1%	50.3%	49.7%	30.1%	41.5%	28.4%
Hernando County	172,778	33,523	19.4%	51.4%	48.6%	28.5%	34.0%	37.5%
Highlands County	98,786	17,733	18.0%	61.4%	38.6%	25.2%	39.5%	35.2%
Hillsborough County	1,229,226	347,042	28.2%	50.2%	49.8%	24.0%	36.8%	39.2%
Indian River County	138,028	25,303	18.3%	52.5%	47.5%	32.9%	34.5%	32.6%
Lake County	297,052	63,882	21.5%	51.9%	48.1%	30.3%	33.6%	36.2%
Lee County	618,754	135,429	21.9%	50.0%	50.0%	26.7%	36.5%	36.8%
Leon County	275,487	108,999	39.6%	46.9%	53.1%	13.3%	59.8%	26.9%
Manatee County	322,833	69,106	21.4%	50.1%	49.9%	28.4%	38.0%	33.6%
Marion County	331,298	67,396	20.3%	51.5%	48.5%	27.2%	36.2%	36.6%
Martin County	146,318	28,671	19.6%	56.3%	43.7%	25.7%	34.1%	40.3%
Miami-Dade County	2,496,435	676,154	27.1%	50.4%	49.6%	23.5%	36.9%	39.6%
Okaloosa County	180,822	55,617	30.8%	54.8%	45.2%	23.9%	35.3%	40.8%
Orange County	1,145,956	372,784	32.5%	49.9%	50.1%	21.4%	39.7%	39.0%
Osceola County	268,685	81,886	30.5%	50.7%	49.3%	29.1%	34.8%	36.1%
Palm Beach County	1,320,134	301,478	22.8%	52.2%	47.8%	25.2%	36.8%	38.0%
Pasco County	464,697	96,055	20.7%	52.1%	47.9%	29.4%	36.9%	33.6%
Pinellas County	916,542	194,471	21.2%	50.0%	50.0%	25.4%	35.4%	39.1%
Polk County	602,095	149,776	24.9%	51.2%	48.8%	26.0%	37.1%	36.9%
Santa Rosa County	151,372	40,422	26.7%	52.7%	47.3%	27.7%	34.7%	37.5%
Sarasota County	379,448	64,933	17.1%	53.1%	46.9%	28.6%	39.9%	31.5%
Seminole County	422,718	117,521	27.8%	51.4%	48.6%	28.3%	36.3%	35.4%
St. Johns County	190,039	47,111	24.8%	51.4%	48.6%	32.1%	38.2%	29.7%
St. Lucie County	277,789	62,007	22.3%	53.7%	46.3%	29.7%	36.7%	33.6%
Sumter County	93,420	11,428	12.2%	48.0%	52.0%	19.6%	37.2%	43.3%
Volusia County	494,593	109,532	22.1%	51.0%	49.0%	22.4%	40.0%	37.6%
Georgia								
Bartow County	100,157	28,669	28.6%	54.1%	45.9%	25.9%	42.4%	31.7%
Bibb County	155,547	41,974	27.0%	47.3%	52.7%	24.5%	39.7%	35.8%
Carroll County	110,527	32,258	29.2%	47.2%	52.8%	24.8%	44.7%	30.5%
Chatham County	265,128	83,341	31.4%	51.3%	48.7%	18.9%	40.9%	40.2%
Cherokee County	214,346	51,638	24.1%	52.6%	47.4%	31.7%	31.0%	37.3%
Clarke County	116,714	54,062	46.3%	47.2%	52.8%	7.9%	66.6%	25.5%
Clayton County	259,424	77,028	29.7%	50.6%	49.4%	27.1%	36.2%	36.7%
Cobb County	688,078	187,462	27.2%	50.2%	49.8%	27.1%	36.2%	36.7%
Columbia County	124,053	34,495	27.8%	49.7%	50.3%	31.7%	36.3%	32.0%
Coweta County	127,317	29,677	23.3%	48.9%	51.1%	27.8%	34.4%	37.9%
DeKalb County	691,893	191,237	27.6%	48.6%	51.4%	20.4%	37.0%	42.7%
Dougherty County	94,565	28,202	29.8%	49.0%	51.0%	25.1%	41.7%	33.2%
Douglas County	132,403	33,135	25.0%	52.2%	47.8%	33.7%	29.4%	36.9%
Fayette County	106,567	25,819	24.2%	48.0%	52.0%	40.7%	38.8%	20.6%
Floyd County	96,317	23,869	24.8%	47.7%	52.3%	28.2%	41.2%	30.6%
Forsyth County	175,511	42,806	24.4%	51.4%	48.6%	41.0%	30.3%	28.7%
Fulton County	920,581	276,052	30.0%	49.0%	51.0%	22.6%	36.6%	40.8%

Table A-2: Counties—Summary Population Characteristics—*Continued*

	Total 2013 ACS Population	Millennial Population Age 13 to 31	Millennials as Percent of Total	Millennial Percentage by Gender		Millennial Percentage by Age		
				Male	Female	13 to 17	18 to 24	25 to 31
Georgia—Cont.								
Gwinnett County	805,321	222,876	27.7%	51.6%	48.4%	30.5%	35.2%	34.3%
Hall County	179,684	48,065	26.7%	52.3%	47.7%	29.4%	36.5%	34.1%
Henry County	203,922	53,473	26.2%	49.2%	50.8%	34.9%	38.0%	27.2%
Houston County	139,900	41,887	29.9%	48.7%	51.3%	24.5%	37.9%	37.6%
Lowndes County	109,233	40,099	36.7%	50.0%	50.0%	18.0%	51.0%	31.0%
Muscogee County	189,885	61,172	32.2%	56.3%	43.7%	22.6%	42.1%	35.3%
Newton County	99,958	26,131	26.1%	53.7%	46.3%	31.2%	38.5%	30.3%
Paulding County	142,324	35,873	25.2%	49.0%	51.0%	33.7%	34.7%	31.6%
Richmond County	200,549	61,951	30.9%	50.5%	49.5%	21.8%	38.9%	39.3%
Whitfield County	102,599	26,807	26.1%	50.5%	49.5%	27.7%	40.7%	31.6%
Hawaii								
Hawaii County	185,079	44,614	24.1%	52.6%	47.4%	29.7%	34.2%	36.1%
Honolulu County	953,207	273,915	28.7%	53.9%	46.1%	21.3%	38.1%	40.7%
Maui County	154,834	35,448	22.9%	53.0%	47.0%	28.5%	28.8%	42.6%
Idaho								
Ada County	392,365	112,611	28.7%	50.4%	49.6%	29.3%	36.7%	34.0%
Bonneville County	104,234	27,965	26.8%	49.6%	50.4%	33.2%	31.8%	34.9%
Canyon County	188,923	51,276	27.1%	44.6%	55.4%	36.4%	32.5%	31.1%
Kootenai County	138,494	35,356	25.5%	50.2%	49.8%	27.8%	36.4%	35.8%
Illinois								
Champaign County	201,081	81,544	40.6%	52.9%	47.1%	12.9%	58.7%	28.4%
Cook County	5,194,675	1,438,037	27.7%	50.2%	49.8%	22.6%	35.3%	42.1%
DeKalb County	105,160	38,034	36.2%	49.0%	51.0%	19.1%	53.2%	27.8%
DuPage County	916,924	231,656	25.3%	52.2%	47.8%	28.8%	33.8%	37.4%
Kane County	515,269	136,039	26.4%	51.2%	48.8%	30.3%	34.8%	34.9%
Kankakee County	113,449	27,483	24.2%	49.8%	50.2%	28.2%	41.5%	30.2%
Kendall County	114,736	30,275	26.4%	51.9%	48.1%	33.1%	27.1%	39.8%
Lake County	703,462	176,831	25.1%	54.0%	46.0%	31.1%	40.0%	28.9%
LaSalle County	113,924	26,791	23.5%	50.5%	49.5%	30.9%	34.1%	35.0%
Macon County	110,768	26,140	23.6%	46.9%	53.1%	24.3%	39.1%	36.6%
Madison County	269,282	67,129	24.9%	49.9%	50.1%	22.5%	39.3%	38.2%
McHenry County	308,760	77,110	25.0%	51.1%	48.9%	34.2%	35.5%	30.3%
McLean County	169,572	57,998	34.2%	47.1%	52.9%	16.4%	53.6%	30.0%
Peoria County	186,494	49,284	26.4%	49.3%	50.7%	23.3%	37.4%	39.2%
Rock Island County	147,546	31,517	21.4%	49.8%	50.2%	24.1%	41.0%	35.0%
Sangamon County	197,465	46,845	23.7%	48.8%	51.2%	25.8%	35.7%	38.5%
St. Clair County	270,056	70,341	26.0%	47.3%	52.7%	28.2%	36.8%	35.0%
Tazewell County	135,394	31,845	23.5%	53.3%	46.7%	29.9%	33.8%	36.3%
Will County	677,560	168,570	24.9%	50.1%	49.9%	33.1%	36.0%	30.9%
Winnebago County	295,266	72,260	24.5%	49.4%	50.6%	28.8%	38.5%	32.7%
Indiana								
Allen County	355,329	93,984	26.4%	49.6%	50.4%	27.5%	36.9%	35.7%
Clark County	110,232	27,123	24.6%	50.2%	49.8%	26.2%	38.0%	35.8%
Delaware County	117,671	39,030	33.2%	47.4%	52.6%	14.3%	61.9%	23.8%
Elkhart County	197,559	49,637	25.1%	48.8%	51.2%	29.9%	35.6%	34.5%
Hamilton County	274,569	65,540	23.9%	50.3%	49.7%	33.2%	31.2%	35.7%
Hendricks County	145,448	39,350	27.1%	55.6%	44.4%	29.8%	36.5%	33.7%
Johnson County	139,654	37,878	27.1%	52.2%	47.8%	32.1%	34.4%	33.6%
Lake County	496,005	118,901	24.0%	51.7%	48.3%	29.6%	37.7%	32.7%
LaPorte County	111,467	27,693	24.8%	54.6%	45.4%	28.0%	33.0%	39.0%
Madison County	131,636	31,472	23.9%	50.4%	49.6%	30.0%	35.2%	34.8%
Marion County	903,393	259,377	28.7%	49.3%	50.7%	22.2%	35.1%	42.7%
Monroe County	137,974	59,193	42.9%	50.1%	49.9%	10.5%	67.0%	22.5%
Porter County	164,343	41,176	25.1%	49.7%	50.3%	24.3%	41.0%	34.7%
St. Joseph County	266,931	72,054	27.0%	50.0%	50.0%	27.1%	42.0%	30.9%
Tippecanoe County	172,780	70,476	40.8%	54.8%	45.2%	12.3%	62.4%	25.4%
Vanderburgh County	179,703	47,216	26.3%	46.6%	53.4%	21.4%	42.2%	36.4%
Vigo County	107,848	32,766	30.4%	51.8%	48.2%	20.6%	49.3%	30.1%
Iowa								
Black Hawk County	131,090	42,469	32.4%	46.6%	53.4%	17.1%	55.0%	28.0%
Dubuque County	93,653	24,987	26.7%	52.2%	47.8%	31.7%	39.5%	28.7%
Johnson County	130,882	56,779	43.4%	50.1%	49.9%	12.0%	54.7%	33.3%
Linn County	211,226	55,429	26.2%	48.9%	51.1%	26.7%	33.4%	39.9%
Polk County	430,640	120,544	28.0%	50.4%	49.6%	25.5%	32.8%	41.7%
Pottawattamie County	93,158	22,874	24.6%	51.8%	48.2%	29.1%	34.2%	36.7%
Scott County	165,224	42,609	25.8%	48.0%	52.0%	26.2%	35.3%	38.5%
Story County	89,542	40,969	45.8%	52.1%	47.9%	12.3%	63.1%	24.5%
Woodbury County	102,172	29,826	29.2%	55.0%	45.0%	32.2%	34.6%	33.2%
Kansas								
Douglas County..........................	110,826	44,291	40.0%	51.7%	48.3%	11.3%	55.7%	32.9%
Johnson County	544,179	134,785	24.8%	50.6%	49.4%	29.8%	32.2%	38.1%
Sedgwick County	498,365	142,587	28.6%	52.8%	47.2%	27.3%	33.8%	38.9%
Shawnee County	177,934	45,819	25.8%	51.8%	48.2%	26.2%	38.7%	35.1%
Wyandotte County......................	157,505	42,100	26.7%	51.1%	48.9%	26.8%	36.5%	36.7%
Kentucky								
Boone County	118,811	30,524	25.7%	51.8%	48.2%	29.6%	32.3%	38.0%

Table A-2: Counties—Summary Population Characteristics—*Continued*

	Total 2013 ACS Population	Millennial Population Age 13 to 31	Millennials as Percent of Total	Millennial Percentage by Gender		Millennial Percentage by Age		
				Male	Female	13 to 17	18 to 24	25 to 31
Kentucky—Cont.								
Campbell County	90,336	22,819	25.3%	48.5%	51.5%	28.8%	36.3%	34.9%
Daviess County	96,656	23,237	24.0%	50.1%	49.9%	27.6%	38.3%	34.1%
Fayette County	295,803	92,123	31.1%	49.4%	50.6%	17.3%	47.1%	35.6%
Hardin County	105,543	29,502	28.0%	47.4%	52.6%	35.6%	29.4%	35.0%
Jefferson County	741,096	192,974	26.0%	51.1%	48.9%	25.6%	35.2%	39.2%
Kenton County	159,720	42,375	26.5%	48.1%	51.9%	28.0%	33.5%	38.5%
Warren County	113,792	37,886	33.3%	49.8%	50.2%	18.0%	46.9%	35.1%
Louisiana								
Ascension Parish	107,215	29,490	27.5%	50.5%	49.5%	33.3%	33.0%	33.7%
Bossier Parish	116,979	35,157	30.1%	48.3%	51.7%	22.5%	37.0%	40.6%
Caddo Parish	254,969	68,119	26.7%	50.8%	49.2%	23.9%	37.7%	38.5%
Calcasieu Parish	192,768	52,204	27.1%	53.2%	46.8%	28.4%	39.8%	31.8%
East Baton Rouge Parish	440,171	138,439	31.5%	50.1%	49.9%	19.2%	47.6%	33.2%
Jefferson Parish	432,552	112,464	26.0%	51.5%	48.5%	21.0%	35.6%	43.3%
Lafayette Parish	221,578	65,892	29.7%	49.4%	50.6%	20.6%	39.5%	39.9%
Lafourche Parish	96,318	25,278	26.2%	48.2%	51.8%	21.4%	41.9%	36.7%
Livingston Parish	128,026	34,296	26.8%	52.8%	47.2%	27.4%	36.9%	35.7%
Orleans Parish	343,829	111,713	32.5%	47.7%	52.3%	17.7%	37.0%	45.3%
Ouachita Parish	153,720	43,511	28.3%	49.9%	50.1%	26.5%	39.6%	33.9%
Rapides Parish	131,613	35,189	26.7%	51.3%	48.7%	24.8%	37.8%	37.4%
St. Tammany Parish	233,740	56,793	24.3%	51.2%	48.8%	30.0%	33.8%	36.2%
Tangipahoa Parish	121,097	36,944	30.5%	49.0%	51.0%	23.6%	37.7%	38.7%
Terrebonne Parish	111,860	28,956	25.9%	51.6%	48.4%	25.5%	36.0%	38.6%
Maine								
Androscoggin County	107,702	26,538	24.6%	49.7%	50.3%	25.5%	36.0%	38.5%
Cumberland County	281,674	69,682	24.7%	48.8%	51.2%	21.1%	40.2%	38.6%
Kennebec County	122,151	27,602	22.6%	49.4%	50.6%	29.5%	36.9%	33.5%
Penobscot County	153,923	39,915	25.9%	50.4%	49.6%	20.8%	45.7%	33.5%
York County	197,131	42,942	21.8%	53.0%	47.0%	25.7%	36.4%	37.9%
Maryland								
Anne Arundel County	537,656	139,871	26.0%	53.5%	46.5%	25.1%	36.2%	38.7%
Baltimore County	805,029	213,682	26.5%	50.8%	49.2%	24.1%	37.1%	38.9%
Carroll County	167,134	39,345	23.5%	52.8%	47.2%	30.7%	37.1%	32.2%
Cecil County	101,108	25,431	25.2%	49.0%	51.0%	27.7%	37.1%	35.2%
Charles County	146,551	38,929	26.6%	50.0%	50.0%	29.4%	35.6%	35.0%
Frederick County	233,385	60,348	25.9%	54.3%	45.7%	29.2%	37.7%	33.0%
Harford County	244,826	61,759	25.2%	53.5%	46.5%	31.9%	33.8%	34.3%
Howard County	287,085	74,492	25.9%	52.1%	47.9%	30.9%	31.9%	37.2%
Montgomery County	971,777	237,666	24.5%	50.2%	49.8%	27.8%	32.0%	40.2%
Prince George's County	863,420	248,192	28.7%	50.2%	49.8%	23.0%	39.1%	37.9%
St. Mary's County	105,151	28,557	27.2%	52.7%	47.3%	33.9%	36.2%	29.9%
Washington County	147,430	36,422	24.7%	52.4%	47.6%	28.9%	35.6%	35.6%
Wicomico County	98,733	30,975	31.4%	46.2%	53.8%	18.6%	51.2%	30.2%
Massachusetts								
Barnstable County	215,888	40,139	18.6%	51.4%	48.6%	27.2%	36.4%	36.4%
Berkshire County	131,219	29,440	22.4%	53.1%	46.9%	24.8%	44.2%	31.0%
Bristol County	548,285	133,365	24.3%	49.0%	51.0%	26.2%	39.6%	34.2%
Essex County	743,159	189,099	25.4%	51.0%	49.0%	27.0%	37.9%	35.1%
Hampden County	463,490	130,223	28.1%	49.2%	50.8%	27.7%	42.2%	30.1%
Hampshire County	158,080	47,728	30.2%	48.4%	51.6%	18.3%	55.7%	25.9%
Middlesex County	1,503,085	417,893	27.8%	50.1%	49.9%	22.4%	35.3%	42.3%
Norfolk County	670,850	167,479	25.0%	50.1%	49.9%	30.2%	34.2%	35.7%
Plymouth County	494,919	110,941	22.4%	50.0%	50.0%	30.4%	37.0%	32.6%
Suffolk County	722,023	281,869	39.0%	49.3%	50.7%	12.7%	40.7%	46.6%
Worcester County	798,552	212,980	26.7%	51.4%	48.6%	27.0%	39.1%	33.8%
Michigan								
Allegan County	111,408	26,007	23.3%	51.7%	48.3%	32.3%	36.5%	31.1%
Bay County	107,771	26,664	24.7%	48.2%	51.8%	27.0%	36.6%	36.4%
Berrien County	156,813	34,333	21.9%	53.0%	47.0%	24.7%	39.7%	35.7%
Calhoun County	136,146	31,324	23.0%	48.7%	51.3%	31.2%	35.9%	32.9%
Eaton County	107,759	25,521	23.7%	50.5%	49.5%	28.1%	32.0%	39.9%
Genesee County	425,790	103,825	24.4%	51.6%	48.4%	28.9%	37.1%	34.0%
Ingham County	280,895	101,879	36.3%	49.5%	50.5%	15.3%	56.6%	28.1%
Jackson County	160,248	39,344	24.6%	49.7%	50.3%	26.1%	36.0%	38.0%
Kalamazoo County	250,331	81,455	32.5%	49.7%	50.3%	20.3%	50.7%	29.1%
Kent County	602,622	172,068	28.6%	50.9%	49.1%	25.5%	34.9%	39.5%
Lenawee County	99,892	24,357	24.4%	52.5%	47.5%	26.1%	38.4%	35.5%
Livingston County	180,967	43,034	23.8%	51.9%	48.1%	35.9%	35.3%	28.7%
Macomb County	840,978	202,176	24.0%	52.5%	47.5%	26.7%	36.7%	36.6%
Monroe County	152,021	35,012	23.0%	52.9%	47.1%	29.0%	37.9%	33.2%
Muskegon County	172,188	40,756	23.7%	48.6%	51.4%	32.6%	34.7%	32.7%
Oakland County	1,202,362	289,984	24.1%	50.2%	49.8%	29.1%	34.8%	36.1%
Ottawa County	263,801	78,130	29.6%	50.2%	49.8%	25.4%	46.4%	28.1%
Saginaw County	200,169	49,901	24.9%	48.8%	51.2%	26.4%	43.5%	30.1%
St. Clair County	163,040	37,367	22.9%	50.6%	49.4%	31.6%	39.0%	29.4%
Washtenaw County	344,791	119,936	34.8%	51.0%	49.0%	16.2%	53.6%	30.2%
Wayne County	1,820,584	451,782	24.8%	49.8%	50.2%	27.1%	39.0%	33.9%

Table A-2: Counties—Summary Population Characteristics—*Continued*

	Total 2013 ACS Population	Millennial Population Age 13 to 31	Millennials as Percent of Total	Millennial Percentage by Gender		Millennial Percentage by Age		
				Male	Female	13 to 17	18 to 24	25 to 31
Minnesota								
Anoka County	330,844	84,669	25.6%	51.3%	48.7%	30.4%	32.4%	37.3%
Carver County	91,042	23,348	25.6%	53.1%	46.9%	36.6%	32.1%	31.3%
Dakota County	398,552	100,432	25.2%	49.5%	50.5%	31.7%	31.5%	36.7%
Hennepin County	1,152,425	331,738	28.8%	50.3%	49.7%	20.3%	33.0%	46.7%
Olmsted County	144,248	35,580	24.7%	46.5%	53.5%	24.2%	35.2%	40.6%
Ramsey County	508,640	150,591	29.6%	49.9%	50.1%	21.4%	39.7%	38.9%
Scott County	129,928	30,250	23.3%	45.1%	54.9%	32.8%	31.5%	35.7%
St. Louis County	200,226	53,813	26.9%	51.9%	48.1%	21.1%	45.0%	33.9%
Stearns County	150,642	47,873	31.8%	54.7%	45.3%	20.1%	51.9%	28.0%
Washington County	238,136	60,484	25.4%	48.0%	52.0%	32.1%	31.7%	36.1%
Wright County	124,700	32,651	26.2%	48.1%	51.9%	33.5%	28.3%	38.2%
Mississippi								
DeSoto County	161,252	41,523	25.8%	48.0%	52.0%	33.8%	33.8%	32.4%
Harrison County	187,105	52,715	28.2%	53.3%	46.7%	22.2%	39.0%	38.8%
Hinds County	245,285	74,512	30.4%	47.6%	52.4%	22.9%	40.0%	37.1%
Jackson County	139,668	36,512	26.1%	48.5%	51.5%	24.7%	37.8%	37.4%
Madison County	95,203	26,202	27.5%	51.4%	48.6%	35.1%	34.5%	30.4%
Rankin County	141,617	35,305	24.9%	49.4%	50.6%	27.7%	32.1%	40.3%
Missouri								
Boone County	162,642	65,445	40.2%	49.0%	51.0%	13.6%	55.6%	30.7%
Cass County	99,478	24,713	24.8%	48.1%	51.9%	36.8%	33.4%	29.8%
Clay County	221,939	57,332	25.8%	48.5%	51.5%	25.9%	33.2%	40.9%
Franklin County	101,492	23,094	22.8%	47.0%	53.0%	26.9%	35.6%	37.5%
Greene County	275,174	88,273	32.1%	49.0%	51.0%	19.6%	45.4%	35.0%
Jackson County	674,158	176,380	26.2%	49.5%	50.5%	25.4%	33.7%	40.9%
Jasper County	117,404	32,081	27.3%	53.5%	46.5%	27.1%	35.7%	37.2%
Jefferson County	218,733	52,424	24.0%	51.3%	48.7%	29.6%	33.1%	37.3%
Platte County	89,322	23,767	26.6%	49.4%	50.6%	21.1%	34.7%	44.2%
St. Charles County	360,485	88,922	24.7%	48.8%	51.2%	26.4%	34.4%	39.2%
St. Louis County	998,954	244,999	24.5%	49.9%	50.1%	27.6%	36.2%	36.2%
Montana								
Flathead County	90,928	20,921	23.0%	41.6%	58.4%	32.9%	33.8%	33.4%
Gallatin County	89,513	30,983	34.6%	55.7%	44.3%	21.6%	47.3%	31.0%
Missoula County	109,299	36,652	33.5%	46.7%	53.3%	19.4%	44.8%	35.8%
Yellowstone County	147,972	38,379	25.9%	52.5%	47.5%	24.9%	39.6%	35.5%
Nebraska								
Douglas County	517,110	147,156	28.5%	49.9%	50.1%	23.8%	34.9%	41.3%
Lancaster County	285,407	95,528	33.5%	51.7%	48.3%	18.3%	48.7%	33.1%
Sarpy County	158,840	45,013	28.3%	53.4%	46.6%	29.0%	33.2%	37.8%
Nevada								
Clark County	1,951,269	527,642	27.0%	50.9%	49.1%	25.4%	35.2%	39.4%
Washoe County	421,407	113,285	26.9%	50.2%	49.8%	24.1%	38.5%	37.4%
New Hampshire								
Hillsborough County	400,721	98,359	24.5%	49.0%	51.0%	27.0%	34.7%	38.3%
Merrimack County	146,445	34,531	23.6%	53.9%	46.1%	27.1%	42.0%	30.9%
Rockingham County	295,223	64,185	21.7%	49.1%	50.9%	32.8%	36.6%	30.6%
Strafford County	123,143	36,919	30.0%	46.9%	53.1%	22.4%	49.2%	28.5%
New Jersey								
Atlantic County	274,549	67,058	24.4%	51.0%	49.0%	26.5%	39.8%	33.6%
Bergen County	905,116	207,617	22.9%	50.0%	50.0%	29.7%	35.3%	35.0%
Burlington County	448,734	108,458	24.2%	53.3%	46.7%	28.6%	37.2%	34.2%
Camden County	513,657	130,453	25.4%	51.7%	48.3%	27.5%	35.2%	37.3%
Cape May County	97,265	19,280	19.8%	53.4%	46.6%	23.3%	38.9%	37.8%
Cumberland County	156,898	41,412	26.4%	53.3%	46.7%	24.7%	32.5%	42.8%
Essex County	783,969	204,847	26.1%	50.4%	49.6%	26.3%	36.1%	37.6%
Gloucester County	288,288	70,459	24.4%	48.7%	51.3%	28.7%	37.1%	34.2%
Hudson County	634,266	196,209	30.9%	51.3%	48.7%	17.3%	31.0%	51.6%
Hunterdon County	128,349	28,211	22.0%	57.6%	42.4%	35.2%	42.8%	22.1%
Mercer County	366,513	97,275	26.5%	53.6%	46.4%	25.7%	41.7%	32.7%
Middlesex County	809,858	211,103	26.1%	51.0%	49.0%	24.7%	39.5%	35.8%
Monmouth County	630,380	146,742	23.3%	51.2%	48.8%	31.2%	36.2%	32.6%
Morris County	492,276	113,951	23.1%	51.7%	48.3%	31.9%	36.0%	32.1%
Ocean County	576,567	125,044	21.7%	52.0%	48.0%	29.5%	35.1%	35.3%
Passaic County	501,226	134,168	26.8%	51.4%	48.6%	26.5%	39.3%	34.2%
Somerset County	323,444	71,788	22.2%	51.5%	48.5%	33.9%	33.3%	32.8%
Sussex County	149,265	32,651	21.9%	50.8%	49.2%	32.5%	37.0%	30.5%
Union County	536,499	133,600	24.9%	51.9%	48.1%	27.8%	36.0%	36.3%
Warren County	108,692	24,276	22.3%	51.0%	49.0%	35.4%	38.4%	26.1%
New Mexico								
Bernalillo County	662,564	187,027	28.2%	51.3%	48.7%	23.8%	38.6%	37.6%
Doña Ana County	209,233	66,940	32.0%	52.0%	48.0%	24.3%	48.4%	27.2%
San Juan County	130,044	32,122	24.7%	49.2%	50.8%	28.4%	37.4%	34.1%
Sandoval County	131,561	32,004	24.3%	50.7%	49.3%	30.2%	34.0%	35.8%
Santa Fe County	144,170	30,956	21.5%	50.0%	50.0%	25.9%	36.4%	37.7%
New York								
Albany County	304,204	89,897	29.6%	49.4%	50.6%	19.1%	48.7%	32.2%

Table A-2: Counties—Summary Population Characteristics—*Continued*

	Total 2013 ACS Population	Millennial Population Age 13 to 31	Millennials as Percent of Total	Millennial Percentage by Gender		Millennial Percentage by Age		
				Male	Female	13 to 17	18 to 24	25 to 31
New York—Cont.								
Bronx County	1,385,108	411,710	29.7%	49.3%	50.7%	23.0%	40.3%	36.7%
Broome County	200,600	54,701	27.3%	50.5%	49.5%	20.4%	49.7%	30.0%
Chautauqua County	134,905	34,497	25.6%	55.2%	44.8%	23.7%	45.5%	30.7%
Dutchess County	297,488	78,602	26.4%	50.3%	49.7%	27.9%	44.6%	27.5%
Erie County	919,040	243,911	26.5%	51.3%	48.7%	23.3%	39.3%	37.4%
Jefferson County	116,229	35,704	30.7%	57.2%	42.8%	20.3%	41.7%	38.0%
Kings County	2,504,700	747,562	29.8%	49.4%	50.6%	20.5%	34.1%	45.4%
Monroe County	744,344	199,730	26.8%	50.7%	49.3%	22.9%	40.9%	36.2%
Nassau County	1,339,532	321,177	24.0%	51.1%	48.9%	29.1%	37.0%	33.9%
New York County	216,469	51,204	23.7%	49.9%	50.1%	26.4%	40.9%	32.6%
Niagara County	1,585,873	484,143	30.5%	46.7%	53.3%	12.0%	32.8%	55.2%
Oneida County	234,878	60,307	25.7%	50.5%	49.5%	27.4%	37.9%	34.7%
Onondaga County	467,026	128,807	27.6%	51.4%	48.6%	24.6%	40.8%	34.5%
Ontario County	107,931	25,415	23.5%	47.4%	52.6%	29.6%	38.2%	32.2%
Orange County	372,813	98,266	26.4%	53.3%	46.7%	30.2%	41.0%	28.8%
Oswego County	122,109	32,874	26.9%	52.9%	47.1%	26.4%	42.8%	30.8%
Putnam County	99,710	21,691	21.8%	51.9%	48.1%	28.9%	38.9%	32.2%
Queens County	2,230,722	607,326	27.2%	50.7%	49.3%	21.3%	35.1%	43.6%
Rensselaer County	159,429	42,068	26.4%	53.8%	46.2%	20.6%	41.8%	37.6%
Richmond County	468,730	116,248	24.8%	51.9%	48.1%	25.6%	38.6%	35.9%
Rockland County	311,687	81,322	26.1%	52.0%	48.0%	30.4%	37.6%	32.0%
Saratoga County	219,607	52,673	24.0%	50.2%	49.8%	27.6%	36.5%	35.8%
Schenectady County	154,727	38,971	25.2%	46.7%	53.3%	23.8%	37.3%	38.9%
St. Lawrence County	111,944	31,306	28.0%	53.9%	46.1%	21.1%	51.5%	27.4%
Steuben County	98,990	21,521	21.7%	52.2%	47.8%	32.9%	36.1%	31.0%
Suffolk County	1,493,350	368,366	24.7%	51.4%	48.6%	29.8%	37.3%	33.0%
Tompkins County	101,564	41,515	40.9%	53.9%	46.1%	10.6%	65.2%	24.2%
Ulster County	182,493	41,894	23.0%	48.5%	51.5%	26.7%	44.1%	29.2%
Wayne County	93,772	20,672	22.0%	49.3%	50.7%	30.1%	33.0%	36.9%
Westchester County	949,113	224,469	23.7%	51.0%	49.0%	29.0%	37.4%	33.5%
North Carolina								
Alamance County	151,131	38,845	25.7%	49.4%	50.6%	26.8%	38.4%	34.8%
Brunswick County	107,431	18,341	17.1%	49.6%	50.4%	31.1%	33.8%	35.1%
Buncombe County	238,318	56,215	23.6%	52.1%	47.9%	22.1%	33.8%	44.1%
Burke County	90,912	21,087	23.2%	48.1%	51.9%	31.8%	33.0%	35.2%
Cabarrus County	178,011	45,822	25.7%	51.5%	48.5%	31.3%	35.1%	33.6%
Catawba County	154,358	34,663	22.5%	52.0%	48.0%	28.3%	40.9%	30.8%
Cleveland County	98,078	23,149	23.6%	50.6%	49.4%	23.4%	45.3%	31.3%
Craven County	103,505	30,089	29.1%	59.1%	40.9%	17.3%	43.6%	39.1%
Cumberland County	319,431	104,204	32.6%	53.3%	46.7%	20.5%	40.9%	38.6%
Davidson County	162,878	37,301	22.9%	49.2%	50.8%	30.6%	37.2%	32.1%
Durham County	267,587	84,607	31.6%	48.8%	51.2%	17.9%	36.9%	45.2%
Forsyth County	350,670	92,178	26.3%	48.8%	51.2%	27.1%	41.1%	31.8%
Gaston County	206,086	49,851	24.2%	50.2%	49.8%	29.4%	37.2%	33.4%
Guilford County	488,406	138,056	28.3%	49.2%	50.8%	22.7%	41.8%	35.5%
Harnett County	114,678	34,876	30.4%	51.3%	48.7%	25.3%	33.7%	41.0%
Henderson County	106,740	22,375	21.0%	53.9%	46.1%	37.9%	32.1%	30.1%
Iredell County	159,437	38,933	24.4%	53.5%	46.5%	30.9%	37.8%	31.3%
Johnston County	168,878	42,338	25.1%	54.6%	45.4%	33.2%	36.5%	30.3%
Mecklenburg County	919,628	273,009	29.7%	49.7%	50.3%	22.5%	34.8%	42.6%
Moore County	88,247	18,946	21.5%	48.4%	51.6%	33.0%	28.0%	39.0%
Nash County	95,840	21,825	22.8%	44.7%	55.3%	31.0%	40.3%	28.6%
New Hanover County	202,667	59,080	29.2%	52.0%	48.0%	18.3%	47.9%	33.8%
Onslow County	177,772	80,099	45.1%	61.7%	38.3%	14.4%	51.7%	33.8%
Orange County	133,801	48,311	36.1%	47.0%	53.0%	17.8%	55.7%	26.5%
Pitt County	168,148	61,787	36.7%	49.2%	50.8%	20.7%	54.2%	25.0%
Randolph County	141,752	31,761	22.4%	52.0%	48.0%	28.2%	35.4%	36.4%
Robeson County	134,168	37,370	27.9%	50.5%	49.5%	29.6%	42.8%	27.6%
Rockingham County	93,643	19,982	21.3%	46.6%	53.4%	33.0%	26.0%	41.1%
Rowan County	138,428	32,181	23.2%	54.4%	45.6%	27.2%	40.6%	32.2%
Union County	201,292	50,048	24.9%	50.7%	49.3%	37.8%	35.6%	26.6%
Wake County	900,993	258,352	28.7%	51.0%	49.0%	27.2%	36.4%	36.4%
Wayne County	122,623	30,990	25.3%	53.4%	46.6%	24.9%	38.2%	36.8%
North Dakota								
Cass County	149,778	55,587	37.1%	51.0%	49.0%	15.3%	50.1%	34.5%
Ohio								
Allen County	106,331	26,290	24.7%	54.1%	45.9%	24.9%	41.0%	34.1%
Ashtabula County	101,497	22,736	22.4%	49.7%	50.3%	27.2%	36.3%	36.5%
Butler County	368,130	101,049	27.4%	48.6%	51.4%	23.6%	46.0%	30.4%
Clark County	138,333	32,974	23.8%	47.1%	52.9%	29.1%	37.7%	33.2%
Clermont County	197,363	49,166	24.9%	51.5%	48.5%	32.1%	31.7%	36.3%
Columbiana County	107,841	23,852	22.1%	53.6%	46.4%	28.3%	34.8%	36.9%
Cuyahoga County	1,280,122	310,929	24.3%	49.8%	50.2%	25.8%	37.2%	37.0%
Delaware County	174,214	40,420	23.2%	49.9%	50.1%	37.8%	32.2%	30.0%
Fairfield County	146,156	37,806	25.9%	52.7%	47.3%	30.8%	33.1%	36.1%
Franklin County	1,163,414	357,534	30.7%	50.4%	49.6%	20.8%	35.9%	43.3%
Geauga County	93,389	20,794	22.3%	49.1%	50.9%	34.5%	41.0%	24.5%

Table A-2: Counties—Summary Population Characteristics—*Continued*

	Total 2013 ACS Population	Millennial Population Age 13 to 31	Millennials as Percent of Total	Millennial Percentage by Gender		Millennial Percentage by Age		
				Male	Female	13 to 17	18 to 24	25 to 31
Ohio—Cont.								
Greene County	161,573	48,051	29.7%	49.0%	51.0%	22.2%	44.6%	33.2%
Hamilton County	802,374	212,839	26.5%	49.8%	50.2%	24.0%	37.6%	38.4%
Lake County	230,041	52,521	22.8%	50.3%	49.7%	27.8%	37.5%	34.7%
Licking County	166,492	41,085	24.7%	48.4%	51.6%	30.4%	36.1%	33.5%
Lorain County	301,356	71,947	23.9%	53.0%	47.0%	30.0%	37.9%	32.1%
Lucas County	441,815	117,034	26.5%	52.0%	48.0%	25.0%	40.0%	35.1%
Mahoning County	238,823	54,397	22.8%	50.3%	49.7%	27.1%	36.9%	36.0%
Medina County	172,332	39,456	22.9%	52.7%	47.3%	33.8%	33.2%	33.0%
Miami County	102,506	25,611	25.0%	52.7%	47.3%	28.6%	35.1%	36.3%
Montgomery County	535,153	134,875	25.2%	49.6%	50.4%	24.5%	39.3%	36.2%
Portage County	161,419	52,402	32.5%	48.9%	51.1%	17.3%	58.5%	24.2%
Richland County	124,475	28,039	22.5%	52.6%	47.4%	27.4%	39.1%	33.5%
Stark County	375,586	88,915	23.7%	52.0%	48.0%	27.4%	38.1%	34.5%
Summit County	541,781	132,601	24.5%	49.8%	50.2%	25.1%	37.8%	37.1%
Trumbull County	210,312	45,225	21.5%	51.4%	48.6%	31.5%	33.9%	34.6%
Tuscarawas County	92,582	21,241	22.9%	50.0%	50.0%	31.8%	34.1%	34.1%
Warren County	212,693	51,896	24.4%	54.3%	45.7%	34.8%	31.6%	33.7%
Wayne County	114,520	28,468	24.9%	50.3%	49.7%	30.3%	39.1%	30.6%
Wood County	125,488	40,741	32.5%	49.1%	50.9%	22.0%	47.6%	30.4%
Oklahoma								
Canadian County	115,541	28,837	25.0%	52.6%	47.4%	26.8%	35.7%	37.4%
Cleveland County	255,755	87,732	34.3%	52.0%	48.0%	18.1%	47.3%	34.6%
Comanche County	124,098	40,012	32.2%	58.2%	41.8%	19.7%	43.7%	36.6%
Oklahoma County	718,633	204,850	28.5%	51.0%	49.0%	21.8%	35.6%	42.6%
Tulsa County	603,403	168,279	27.9%	50.3%	49.7%	25.8%	35.4%	38.9%
Oregon								
Clackamas County	375,992	89,541	23.8%	52.9%	47.1%	30.4%	35.5%	34.1%
Deschutes County	157,733	37,987	24.1%	49.7%	50.3%	32.1%	30.3%	37.7%
Douglas County	107,667	20,735	19.3%	49.3%	50.7%	25.6%	37.1%	37.3%
Jackson County	203,206	45,840	22.6%	49.3%	50.7%	25.4%	37.8%	36.8%
Lane County	351,715	98,197	27.9%	50.0%	50.0%	20.4%	48.9%	30.7%
Linn County	116,672	30,345	26.0%	51.8%	48.2%	21.4%	51.4%	27.2%
Marion County	315,335	83,502	26.5%	53.9%	46.1%	27.3%	41.1%	31.6%
Multnomah County	735,334	204,543	27.8%	48.7%	51.3%	19.0%	33.3%	47.7%
Washington County	529,710	145,345	27.4%	49.6%	50.4%	26.7%	32.3%	41.0%
Yamhill County	99,193	24,644	24.8%	52.6%	47.4%	24.8%	39.5%	35.6%
Pennsylvania								
Adams County	101,407	24,109	23.8%	47.0%	53.0%	26.4%	46.1%	27.5%
Allegheny County	1,223,348	315,594	25.8%	50.8%	49.2%	22.1%	37.2%	40.7%
Beaver County	170,539	37,866	22.2%	49.8%	50.2%	27.3%	39.5%	33.2%
Berks County	411,442	106,444	25.9%	50.1%	49.9%	27.3%	40.2%	32.5%
Blair County	127,089	29,018	22.8%	52.2%	47.8%	22.5%	42.1%	35.4%
Bucks County	625,249	140,107	22.4%	51.0%	49.0%	30.9%	34.2%	34.9%
Butler County	183,862	44,871	24.4%	51.1%	48.9%	29.5%	38.5%	32.1%
Cambria County	143,679	32,240	22.4%	49.3%	50.7%	26.8%	40.5%	32.7%
Centre County	153,990	65,126	42.3%	52.6%	47.4%	10.7%	67.8%	21.5%
Chester County	498,886	126,204	25.3%	51.4%	48.6%	30.2%	35.8%	34.0%
Cumberland County	235,406	58,745	25.0%	48.1%	51.9%	24.8%	40.8%	34.4%
Dauphin County	268,100	63,943	23.9%	51.2%	48.8%	26.5%	33.7%	39.8%
Delaware County	558,979	147,156	26.3%	50.9%	49.1%	25.9%	40.3%	33.8%
Erie County	280,566	73,987	26.4%	51.9%	48.1%	20.9%	41.7%	37.3%
Fayette County	136,606	27,807	20.4%	51.3%	48.7%	26.6%	36.6%	36.8%
Franklin County	149,618	34,886	23.3%	50.7%	49.3%	24.8%	36.0%	39.2%
Lackawanna County	214,437	52,413	24.4%	50.5%	49.5%	22.9%	42.4%	34.6%
Lancaster County	519,445	134,345	25.9%	48.4%	51.6%	26.7%	37.9%	35.4%
Lebanon County	133,568	28,438	21.3%	50.2%	49.8%	29.3%	38.4%	32.3%
Lehigh County	349,497	86,106	24.6%	50.1%	49.9%	26.5%	37.8%	35.6%
Luzerne County	320,918	78,732	24.5%	50.2%	49.8%	25.0%	41.4%	33.6%
Lycoming County	116,111	29,371	25.3%	50.1%	49.9%	20.6%	48.2%	31.2%
Mercer County	116,638	28,430	24.4%	56.1%	43.9%	29.4%	40.3%	30.4%
Monroe County	169,842	42,860	25.2%	54.2%	45.8%	31.0%	44.4%	24.7%
Montgomery County	799,874	188,495	23.6%	50.5%	49.5%	28.1%	33.9%	38.1%
Northampton County	297,735	72,610	24.4%	52.5%	47.5%	24.7%	39.9%	35.4%
Northumberland County	94,528	20,227	21.4%	55.3%	44.7%	22.1%	38.6%	39.3%
Philadelphia County	1,526,006	477,105	31.3%	48.2%	51.8%	18.8%	39.6%	41.7%
Schuylkill County	148,289	30,617	20.6%	53.9%	46.1%	25.3%	36.5%	38.2%
Washington County	207,820	46,539	22.4%	50.8%	49.2%	27.1%	38.6%	34.3%
Westmoreland County	365,169	73,762	20.2%	52.2%	47.8%	26.9%	40.9%	32.2%
York County	434,972	102,438	23.6%	50.3%	49.7%	27.1%	38.2%	34.7%
Rhode Island								
Kent County	166,158	35,016	21.1%	51.1%	48.9%	24.5%	35.4%	40.1%
Providence County	626,667	178,704	28.5%	50.7%	49.3%	21.7%	41.5%	36.9%
Washington County	126,979	32,924	25.9%	51.2%	48.8%	21.3%	58.6%	20.0%
South Carolina								
Aiken County	160,099	40,228	25.1%	53.8%	46.2%	26.4%	37.6%	36.0%
Anderson County	187,126	45,159	24.1%	50.2%	49.8%	30.5%	34.9%	34.7%
Beaufort County	162,233	37,996	23.4%	47.3%	52.7%	22.8%	40.4%	36.9%

Table A-2: Counties—Summary Population Characteristics—*Continued*

	Total 2013 ACS Population	Millennial Population Age 13 to 31	Millennials as Percent of Total	Millennial Percentage by Gender		Millennial Percentage by Age		
				Male	Female	13 to 17	18 to 24	25 to 31
South Carolina—Cont.								
Berkeley County	177,843	54,189	30.5%	50.0%	50.0%	23.8%	37.8%	38.4%
Charleston County	350,209	105,818	30.2%	50.2%	49.8%	20.5%	39.6%	39.9%
Dorchester County	136,555	38,082	27.9%	54.5%	45.5%	28.2%	42.3%	29.6%
Florence County	136,885	34,871	25.5%	48.7%	51.3%	27.1%	40.7%	32.3%
Greenville County	451,225	124,317	27.6%	48.5%	51.5%	26.0%	37.9%	36.1%
Horry County	269,291	64,666	24.0%	52.9%	47.1%	20.6%	41.0%	38.4%
Lexington County	262,391	68,505	26.1%	49.5%	50.5%	28.9%	36.7%	34.5%
Orangeburg County	92,501	23,271	25.2%	54.1%	45.9%	30.8%	43.9%	25.3%
Pickens County	119,224	38,978	32.7%	53.2%	46.8%	22.1%	50.5%	27.4%
Richland County	384,504	131,291	34.1%	51.6%	48.4%	20.7%	48.0%	31.4%
Spartanburg County	284,307	76,183	26.8%	47.0%	53.0%	27.8%	40.5%	31.7%
Sumter County	107,456	29,711	27.6%	59.6%	40.4%	24.6%	42.9%	32.5%
York County	226,073	57,893	25.6%	47.7%	52.3%	31.0%	39.7%	29.3%
South Dakota								
Minnehaha County	169,468	50,232	29.6%	52.1%	47.9%	20.2%	37.3%	42.5%
Pennington County	100,948	25,155	24.9%	52.1%	47.9%	20.6%	44.2%	35.3%
Tennessee								
Blount County	123,010	28,615	23.3%	49.6%	50.4%	30.7%	37.9%	31.4%
Bradley County	98,963	25,327	25.6%	55.6%	44.4%	26.6%	40.5%	33.0%
Davidson County	626,681	192,958	30.8%	47.9%	52.1%	17.5%	35.8%	46.7%
Hamilton County	336,463	87,443	26.0%	50.2%	49.8%	22.2%	38.3%	39.5%
Knox County	432,226	124,022	28.7%	51.5%	48.5%	20.8%	43.8%	35.4%
Madison County	98,294	25,432	25.9%	45.6%	54.4%	28.7%	39.8%	31.5%
Montgomery County	172,331	61,480	35.7%	51.0%	49.0%	21.1%	36.8%	42.1%
Rutherford County	262,604	85,492	32.6%	50.9%	49.1%	23.6%	43.2%	33.2%
Sevier County	89,889	20,636	23.0%	53.5%	46.5%	19.6%	48.5%	31.9%
Shelby County	927,644	260,771	28.1%	49.6%	50.4%	25.8%	37.5%	36.7%
Sullivan County	156,823	33,755	21.5%	49.4%	50.6%	32.5%	35.0%	32.5%
Sumner County	160,645	41,227	25.7%	52.8%	47.2%	30.2%	34.5%	35.3%
Washington County	122,979	33,420	27.2%	49.2%	50.8%	23.7%	45.2%	31.2%
Williamson County	183,182	42,263	23.1%	49.1%	50.9%	38.2%	33.7%	28.2%
Wilson County	113,993	29,571	25.9%	53.7%	46.3%	34.3%	33.0%	32.7%
Texas								
Bell County	310,235	102,974	33.2%	50.3%	49.7%	21.3%	40.8%	38.0%
Bexar County	1,714,773	529,963	30.9%	51.8%	48.2%	25.1%	37.7%	37.1%
Bowie County	92,565	24,613	26.6%	50.6%	49.4%	20.5%	40.2%	39.3%
Brazoria County	313,166	87,769	28.0%	52.2%	47.8%	27.9%	32.7%	39.4%
Brazos County	194,851	93,443	48.0%	53.4%	46.6%	12.6%	61.4%	26.0%
Cameron County	406,220	117,741	29.0%	50.0%	50.0%	34.1%	37.5%	28.5%
Collin County	782,341	203,054	26.0%	51.3%	48.7%	32.2%	34.0%	33.8%
Comal County	108,472	27,155	25.0%	54.5%	45.5%	32.4%	35.1%	32.5%
Dallas County	2,368,139	694,588	29.3%	50.4%	49.6%	24.5%	35.2%	40.3%
Denton County	662,614	200,086	30.2%	49.1%	50.9%	26.9%	36.1%	37.0%
Ector County	137,130	45,187	33.0%	52.2%	47.8%	24.5%	37.0%	38.4%
El Paso County	800,647	246,978	30.8%	52.7%	47.3%	26.3%	40.3%	33.4%
Ellis County	149,610	41,068	27.5%	49.9%	50.1%	32.5%	35.5%	32.0%
Fort Bend County	585,375	158,317	27.0%	50.7%	49.3%	32.1%	34.4%	33.5%
Galveston County	291,309	78,839	27.1%	50.9%	49.1%	29.6%	35.8%	34.6%
Grayson County	120,877	30,811	25.5%	51.1%	48.9%	25.6%	37.4%	37.0%
Gregg County	121,730	33,454	27.5%	51.0%	49.0%	25.7%	40.3%	34.0%
Guadalupe County	131,533	35,549	27.0%	52.2%	47.8%	30.8%	36.8%	32.4%
Harris County	4,092,459	1,238,541	30.3%	51.2%	48.8%	25.0%	34.6%	40.4%
Hays County	157,107	58,556	37.3%	50.7%	49.3%	19.1%	51.8%	29.1%
Hidalgo County	774,769	240,329	31.0%	50.4%	49.6%	31.5%	37.5%	31.0%
Jefferson County	252,273	70,230	27.8%	55.5%	44.5%	24.8%	39.8%	35.5%
Johnson County	150,934	38,847	25.7%	52.1%	47.9%	28.6%	36.0%	35.5%
Kaufman County	103,350	25,319	24.5%	51.8%	48.2%	31.3%	37.6%	31.1%
Lubbock County	278,831	99,238	35.6%	52.3%	47.7%	19.8%	51.4%	28.7%
McLennan County	234,906	71,146	30.3%	49.7%	50.3%	18.7%	50.9%	30.3%
Midland County	136,872	43,594	31.9%	54.4%	45.6%	23.3%	34.7%	41.9%
Montgomery County	455,746	121,769	26.7%	48.7%	51.3%	32.2%	34.3%	33.5%
Nueces County	340,223	95,902	28.2%	50.3%	49.7%	25.6%	38.3%	36.1%
Parker County	116,927	29,995	25.7%	52.3%	47.7%	32.5%	34.5%	33.0%
Potter County	121,073	32,810	27.1%	53.4%	46.6%	24.4%	37.6%	38.0%
Randall County	120,725	34,237	28.4%	51.1%	48.9%	22.1%	37.9%	40.0%
Smith County	209,714	57,788	27.6%	49.8%	50.2%	27.0%	38.9%	34.2%
Tarrant County	1,809,034	528,418	29.2%	49.9%	50.1%	27.0%	34.6%	38.5%
Taylor County	131,506	43,355	33.0%	49.5%	50.5%	19.1%	45.6%	35.3%
Tom Green County	110,224	34,346	31.2%	54.8%	45.2%	22.3%	40.9%	36.8%
Travis County	1,024,266	344,597	33.6%	51.0%	49.0%	18.5%	34.2%	47.4%
Webb County	250,304	79,350	31.7%	50.3%	49.7%	29.5%	37.4%	33.1%
Wichita County	131,500	40,384	30.7%	58.6%	41.4%	18.5%	44.0%	37.5%
Williamson County	422,679	115,744	27.4%	51.3%	48.7%	30.7%	31.2%	38.1%
Utah								
Cache County	112,656	43,131	38.3%	48.3%	51.7%	22.9%	42.9%	34.2%
Davis County	306,479	90,315	29.5%	47.9%	52.1%	33.4%	32.8%	33.8%
Salt Lake County	1,029,655	315,374	30.6%	51.4%	48.6%	25.6%	34.1%	40.3%

Table A-2: Counties—Summary Population Characteristics—*Continued*

	Total 2013 ACS Population	Millennial Population Age 13 to 31	Millennials as Percent of Total	Millennial Percentage by Gender		Millennial Percentage by Age		
				Male	Female	13 to 17	18 to 24	25 to 31
Utah—Cont.								
Utah County	516,564	197,950	38.3%	50.4%	49.6%	23.4%	46.8%	29.8%
Washington County	138,115	36,461	26.4%	48.8%	51.2%	29.6%	41.0%	29.5%
Weber County	231,236	66,208	28.6%	50.4%	49.6%	28.6%	33.5%	37.9%
Vermont								
Chittenden County	156,545	49,483	31.6%	47.3%	52.7%	20.0%	46.9%	33.1%
Virginia								
Albemarle County	98,970	28,786	29.1%	49.7%	50.3%	24.7%	40.0%	35.3%
Arlington County	207,627	73,199	35.3%	49.3%	50.7%	10.6%	24.9%	64.5%
Chesterfield County	316,236	82,105	26.0%	49.6%	50.4%	31.9%	37.6%	30.5%
Fairfax County	1,081,726	279,011	25.8%	51.0%	49.0%	26.3%	34.4%	39.3%
Hanover County	99,863	23,207	23.2%	52.8%	47.2%	31.2%	34.3%	34.5%
Henrico County	306,935	79,944	26.0%	48.0%	52.0%	25.8%	34.2%	40.0%
Loudoun County	312,311	80,007	25.6%	50.0%	50.0%	35.6%	28.7%	35.7%
Montgomery County	94,392	44,141	46.8%	50.5%	49.5%	15.3%	67.9%	16.8%
Prince William County	402,002	113,001	28.1%	51.3%	48.7%	27.8%	33.6%	38.6%
Roanoke County	92,376	20,674	22.4%	55.2%	44.8%	27.7%	39.2%	33.1%
Spotsylvania County	122,397	32,146	26.3%	50.1%	49.9%	32.2%	37.1%	30.7%
Stafford County	128,961	38,219	29.6%	52.8%	47.2%	25.6%	43.8%	30.6%
Washington								
Benton County	175,177	46,067	26.3%	49.1%	50.9%	31.7%	33.5%	34.8%
Clark County	425,363	105,849	24.9%	49.1%	50.9%	29.0%	36.3%	34.8%
Cowlitz County	102,410	23,187	22.6%	48.5%	51.5%	30.1%	36.8%	33.1%
Grant County	89,120	25,201	28.3%	56.5%	43.5%	24.7%	46.6%	28.7%
King County	1,931,249	531,505	27.5%	51.0%	49.0%	21.3%	33.3%	45.3%
Kitsap County	251,133	65,185	26.0%	53.8%	46.2%	23.9%	39.4%	36.7%
Pierce County	795,225	221,284	27.8%	51.7%	48.3%	25.0%	36.1%	38.8%
Skagit County	116,901	27,206	23.3%	50.2%	49.8%	26.5%	40.7%	32.8%
Snohomish County	713,335	184,410	25.9%	51.7%	48.3%	26.1%	35.2%	38.7%
Spokane County	471,221	133,544	28.3%	52.2%	47.8%	24.3%	37.8%	37.9%
Thurston County	252,264	70,438	27.9%	51.9%	48.1%	24.3%	34.7%	41.0%
Whatcom County	201,140	62,149	30.9%	49.8%	50.2%	20.8%	51.0%	28.2%
Yakima County	243,231	65,994	27.1%	50.9%	49.1%	27.9%	38.2%	33.9%
West Virginia								
Berkeley County	104,169	26,793	25.7%	45.1%	54.9%	30.7%	36.9%	32.4%
Cabell County	96,319	27,010	28.0%	50.0%	50.0%	29.5%	38.4%	32.1%
Kanawha County	193,063	44,551	23.1%	52.4%	47.6%	27.4%	35.5%	37.0%
Monongalia County	96,189	41,965	43.6%	54.0%	46.0%	11.0%	55.9%	33.1%
Wisconsin								
Brown County	248,007	64,640	26.1%	52.9%	47.1%	27.3%	36.7%	36.0%
Dane County	488,073	157,015	32.2%	50.5%	49.5%	19.1%	41.3%	39.6%
Eau Claire County	98,736	33,956	34.4%	50.9%	49.1%	18.2%	50.4%	31.4%
Fond du Lac County	101,633	22,865	22.5%	55.4%	44.6%	35.2%	40.0%	24.8%
Kenosha County	166,426	42,737	25.7%	53.0%	47.0%	28.1%	38.3%	33.6%
La Crosse County	114,638	37,898	33.1%	48.4%	51.6%	20.2%	48.5%	31.2%
Marathon County	134,063	31,554	23.5%	53.2%	46.8%	29.2%	35.9%	35.0%
Milwaukee County	947,735	275,711	29.1%	48.0%	52.0%	22.4%	36.2%	41.4%
Outagamie County	176,695	44,856	25.4%	46.5%	53.5%	23.6%	37.6%	38.8%
Racine County	195,408	48,379	24.8%	54.2%	45.8%	30.9%	31.2%	38.0%
Rock County	160,331	39,734	24.8%	51.7%	48.3%	30.2%	35.9%	33.9%
Sheboygan County	115,507	25,686	22.2%	49.6%	50.4%	33.2%	31.3%	35.5%
Walworth County	102,228	27,115	26.5%	50.3%	49.7%	25.7%	41.6%	32.7%
Washington County	131,887	28,174	21.4%	50.4%	49.6%	28.3%	39.7%	32.0%
Waukesha County	389,891	85,418	21.9%	52.2%	47.8%	31.1%	36.0%	33.0%
Winnebago County	166,994	46,883	28.1%	53.3%	46.7%	20.6%	44.1%	35.3%
Wyoming								
Laramie County	91,738	25,613	27.9%	53.5%	46.5%	20.1%	48.6%	31.4%

Table A-3: Places—Summary Population Characteristics

	Total 2013 ACS Population	Millennial Population Age 13 to 31	Millennials as Percent of Total	Millennial Percentage by Gender		Millennial Percentage by Age		
				Male	Female	13 to 17	18 to 24	25 to 31
Alabama								
Birmingham city	211,933	62,699	29.6%	50.8%	49.2%	22.2%	39.6%	38.2%
Huntsville city	186,416	52,004	27.9%	49.1%	50.9%	26.5%	37.2%	36.3%
Mobile city	194,879	52,173	26.8%	49.9%	50.1%	22.4%	38.9%	38.7%
Montgomery city	201,335	58,994	29.3%	45.2%	54.8%	22.5%	39.6%	37.9%
Tuscaloosa city	95,334	39,763	41.7%	51.9%	48.1%	14.8%	60.2%	25.0%
Alaska								
Anchorage municipality	300,950	89,088	29.6%	53.4%	46.6%	21.7%	38.2%	40.0%
Arizona								
Chandler city	249,139	65,956	26.5%	52.4%	47.6%	27.7%	33.7%	38.6%
Glendale city	234,618	64,873	27.7%	52.3%	47.7%	28.2%	34.7%	37.1%
Mesa city	457,595	124,304	27.2%	50.2%	49.8%	25.3%	36.3%	38.4%
Peoria city	162,617	38,091	23.4%	52.1%	47.9%	33.4%	32.0%	34.6%
Phoenix city	1,513,350	420,298	27.8%	51.4%	48.6%	25.1%	36.9%	38.0%
Scottsdale city	226,909	49,969	22.0%	53.0%	47.0%	29.6%	32.3%	38.1%
Surprise city	123,569	21,496	17.4%	46.5%	53.5%	36.5%	28.0%	35.5%
Tempe city	168,231	74,507	44.3%	51.7%	48.3%	16.1%	48.1%	35.8%
Tucson city	526,141	164,774	31.3%	49.2%	50.8%	22.1%	46.5%	31.4%
Yuma city	91,915	27,868	30.3%	54.3%	45.7%	24.7%	39.7%	35.7%
Arkansas								
Little Rock city	197,357	52,430	26.6%	49.9%	50.1%	24.6%	30.7%	44.6%
California								
Anaheim city	345,015	95,980	27.8%	53.2%	46.8%	24.2%	38.5%	37.4%
Antioch city	107,098	31,631	29.5%	49.4%	50.6%	29.3%	38.5%	32.2%
Bakersfield city	363,630	107,664	29.6%	50.2%	49.8%	26.4%	36.6%	37.1%
Berkeley city	116,774	48,955	41.9%	47.9%	52.1%	10.5%	54.1%	35.4%
Burbank city	104,717	23,393	22.3%	46.3%	53.7%	20.4%	28.7%	50.8%
Carlsbad city	110,977	22,855	20.6%	60.1%	39.9%	26.9%	32.0%	41.1%
Carson city	92,597	25,511	27.6%	48.6%	51.4%	20.0%	42.2%	37.8%
Chula Vista city	256,765	71,383	27.8%	47.5%	52.5%	28.2%	38.5%	33.3%
Clovis city	99,758	26,910	27.0%	50.6%	49.4%	25.1%	42.8%	32.1%
Compton city	97,872	29,029	29.7%	45.6%	54.4%	28.0%	35.7%	36.3%
Concord city	125,892	31,725	25.2%	50.0%	50.0%	26.0%	34.5%	39.5%
Corona city	159,507	46,013	28.8%	55.0%	45.0%	27.0%	36.6%	36.4%
Costa Mesa city	112,184	33,705	30.0%	56.5%	43.5%	20.1%	32.1%	47.8%
Daly City city	104,747	30,077	28.7%	50.9%	49.1%	21.5%	36.8%	41.7%
Downey city	113,240	35,471	31.3%	50.1%	49.9%	21.5%	44.7%	33.7%
El Cajon city	102,207	30,019	29.4%	50.8%	49.2%	17.0%	42.7%	40.2%
El Monte city	115,685	30,902	26.7%	52.6%	47.4%	27.2%	36.5%	36.3%
Elk Grove city	161,029	42,148	26.2%	52.1%	47.9%	43.1%	32.6%	24.3%
Escondido city	148,728	44,106	29.7%	51.0%	49.0%	24.1%	37.2%	38.7%
Fairfield city	109,302	34,335	31.4%	49.4%	50.6%	22.3%	40.3%	37.4%
Fontana city	203,008	60,471	29.8%	49.8%	50.2%	31.5%	37.1%	31.4%
Fremont city	224,904	51,789	23.0%	50.2%	49.8%	25.5%	32.0%	42.5%
Fresno city	509,965	150,965	29.6%	50.9%	49.1%	23.9%	38.4%	37.7%
Fullerton city	138,979	44,549	32.1%	48.6%	51.4%	24.1%	37.1%	38.8%
Garden Grove city	175,115	46,235	26.4%	54.1%	45.9%	23.8%	39.9%	36.3%
Glendale city	196,000	47,236	24.1%	50.4%	49.6%	20.0%	31.6%	48.3%
Hayward city	151,582	42,182	27.8%	50.8%	49.2%	18.7%	37.6%	43.7%
Hesperia city	92,159	55,942	60.7%	52.7%	47.3%	27.4%	34.3%	38.3%
Inglewood city	111,544	31,386	28.1%	49.2%	50.8%	21.7%	35.4%	42.9%
Irvine city	236,724	70,736	29.9%	48.9%	51.1%	20.7%	43.2%	36.1%
Jurupa Valley city	98,036	29,796	30.4%	44.1%	55.9%	31.1%	35.1%	33.8%
Lancaster city	159,521	44,656	28.0%	49.0%	51.0%	29.6%	37.0%	33.4%
Long Beach city	469,384	132,264	28.2%	49.6%	50.4%	24.0%	37.4%	38.6%
Los Angeles city	3,884,340	1,105,809	28.5%	50.6%	49.4%	21.0%	37.5%	41.5%
Mission Viejo city	96,350	21,020	21.8%	50.1%	49.9%	36.2%	42.8%	21.1%
Modesto city	204,925	59,831	29.2%	48.4%	51.6%	27.8%	37.8%	34.4%
Moreno Valley city	201,187	65,038	32.3%	49.5%	50.5%	26.3%	34.6%	39.0%
Murrieta city	107,457	29,276	27.2%	53.4%	46.6%	37.1%	33.4%	29.5%
Norwalk city	106,588	29,652	27.8%	51.6%	48.4%	27.8%	41.8%	30.4%
Oakland city	406,228	106,839	26.3%	50.1%	49.9%	20.1%	32.6%	47.4%
Oceanside city	172,795	44,351	25.7%	61.6%	38.4%	15.0%	47.4%	37.6%
Ontario city	167,496	48,481	28.9%	48.6%	51.4%	27.6%	38.3%	34.1%
Orange city	139,983	40,584	29.0%	52.3%	47.7%	26.2%	37.7%	36.1%
Oxnard city	203,014	63,365	31.2%	55.9%	44.1%	25.8%	40.0%	34.2%
Palmdale city	157,146	45,149	28.7%	52.5%	47.5%	33.3%	37.2%	29.5%
Pasadena city	139,727	40,866	29.2%	46.2%	53.8%	15.8%	33.8%	50.4%
Pomona city	151,349	47,598	31.4%	50.7%	49.3%	20.8%	44.2%	35.0%
Rancho Cucamonga city	171,359	48,096	28.1%	56.7%	43.3%	29.5%	38.6%	31.9%
Redding city	91,124	24,640	27.0%	51.7%	48.3%	24.1%	38.7%	37.2%
Rialto city	101,889	30,933	30.4%	48.0%	52.0%	28.1%	42.0%	29.9%
Richmond city	107,580	30,165	28.0%	51.0%	49.0%	20.3%	35.7%	44.0%
Riverside city	316,613	100,148	31.6%	51.5%	48.5%	21.9%	49.4%	28.6%
Roseville city	127,039	32,207	25.4%	51.1%	48.9%	29.6%	30.2%	40.1%
Sacramento city	479,671	134,447	28.0%	50.3%	49.7%	22.8%	36.9%	40.3%
Salinas city	155,649	47,404	30.5%	48.9%	51.1%	27.2%	39.3%	33.5%

Table A-3: Places—Summary Population Characteristics—Continued

	Total 2013 ACS Population	Millennial Population Age 13 to 31	Millennials as Percent of Total	Millennial Percentage by Gender		Millennial Percentage by Age		
				Male	Female	13 to 17	18 to 24	25 to 31
California—Cont.								
San Bernardino city	213,700	67,085	31.4%	51.2%	48.8%	25.9%	43.0%	31.1%
San Buenaventura (Ventura) city	108,811	28,078	25.8%	48.4%	51.6%	21.4%	39.1%	39.5%
San Diego city	1,355,885	412,816	30.4%	52.9%	47.1%	18.9%	37.9%	43.2%
San Francisco city	837,442	216,580	25.9%	51.0%	49.0%	11.3%	28.7%	60.0%
San Jose city	998,514	250,499	25.1%	52.7%	47.3%	23.9%	34.1%	42.0%
San Mateo city	101,132	21,249	21.0%	53.9%	46.1%	25.8%	30.2%	44.1%
Santa Ana city	334,241	104,347	31.2%	49.3%	50.7%	24.3%	39.3%	36.4%
Santa Clara city	120,250	35,288	29.3%	50.0%	50.0%	12.9%	36.0%	51.1%
Santa Clarita city	179,582	46,023	25.6%	51.4%	48.6%	29.7%	35.2%	35.1%
Santa Maria city	102,205	31,713	31.0%	51.0%	49.0%	34.6%	35.0%	30.4%
Santa Monica city	92,484	21,654	23.4%	56.3%	43.7%	17.3%	23.7%	59.0%
Santa Rosa city	171,996	45,707	26.6%	55.5%	44.5%	27.9%	33.2%	38.9%
Simi Valley city	126,177	28,302	22.4%	49.1%	50.9%	31.0%	35.7%	33.3%
South Gate city	95,664	29,962	31.3%	56.9%	43.1%	25.6%	33.9%	40.5%
Stockton city	298,115	83,153	27.9%	51.4%	48.6%	26.8%	39.7%	33.5%
Sunnyvale city	147,559	35,578	24.1%	51.2%	48.8%	18.0%	27.7%	54.3%
Temecula city	106,783	31,215	29.2%	49.8%	50.2%	37.0%	39.5%	23.5%
Thousand Oaks city	128,739	30,401	23.6%	51.4%	48.6%	28.4%	41.2%	30.4%
Torrance city	147,485	31,027	21.0%	49.7%	50.3%	27.9%	39.5%	32.6%
Vacaville city	94,272	25,744	27.3%	51.5%	48.5%	26.2%	37.3%	36.5%
Vallejo city	118,855	31,222	26.3%	51.7%	48.3%	25.6%	36.4%	38.0%
Victorville city	121,080	34,079	28.1%	45.8%	54.2%	24.3%	39.4%	36.2%
Visalia city	127,758	37,794	29.6%	45.9%	54.1%	23.7%	38.2%	38.1%
Vista city	96,919	28,569	29.5%	56.1%	43.9%	15.2%	42.7%	42.1%
West Covina city	107,741	31,327	29.1%	51.3%	48.7%	24.9%	36.0%	39.1%
Westminster city	91,750	23,446	25.6%	47.9%	52.1%	28.2%	29.0%	42.8%
Colorado								
Arvada city	112,028	28,727	25.6%	50.9%	49.1%	32.7%	32.9%	34.5%
Aurora city	345,814	91,957	26.6%	48.7%	51.3%	27.1%	34.3%	38.6%
Boulder city	103,163	47,328	45.9%	51.7%	48.3%	11.3%	63.3%	25.4%
Centennial city	106,101	24,801	23.4%	53.0%	47.0%	36.1%	28.5%	35.4%
Colorado Springs city	439,858	121,448	27.6%	50.8%	49.2%	23.9%	37.6%	38.5%
Denver city	649,495	182,517	28.1%	49.2%	50.8%	15.2%	32.0%	52.8%
Fort Collins city	152,056	60,116	39.5%	54.3%	45.7%	19.3%	54.1%	26.5%
Greeley city	96,549	33,213	34.4%	54.3%	45.7%	22.4%	41.3%	36.2%
Lakewood city	147,220	35,859	24.4%	55.1%	44.9%	21.0%	38.9%	40.1%
Pueblo city	108,247	28,398	26.2%	53.4%	46.6%	26.0%	39.2%	34.8%
Thornton city	127,352	34,405	27.0%	54.1%	45.9%	35.1%	35.3%	29.6%
Westminster city	110,940	31,101	28.0%	49.5%	50.5%	27.6%	29.2%	43.2%
Connecticut								
Bridgeport city	147,216	43,377	29.5%	52.4%	47.6%	20.2%	35.3%	44.4%
Hartford city	125,035	40,826	32.7%	48.5%	51.5%	21.0%	43.9%	35.1%
New Haven city	130,654	45,402	34.7%	44.8%	55.2%	15.1%	46.9%	38.0%
Stamford city	126,455	33,807	26.7%	46.9%	53.1%	22.9%	36.0%	41.0%
Waterbury city	109,687	29,753	27.1%	53.5%	46.5%	22.4%	35.3%	42.3%
District of Columbia								
Washington city	646,449	201,595	31.2%	46.0%	54.0%	11.6%	37.4%	51.0%
Florida								
Cape Coral city	165,849	36,448	22.0%	43.7%	56.3%	29.6%	33.0%	37.3%
Clearwater city	109,705	23,401	21.3%	51.4%	48.6%	23.6%	35.4%	41.0%
Coral Springs city	126,595	32,526	25.7%	47.4%	52.6%	26.7%	43.0%	30.3%
Fort Lauderdale city	172,374	38,760	22.5%	55.0%	45.0%	22.1%	39.0%	38.9%
Gainesville city	127,493	64,700	50.7%	50.3%	49.7%	6.3%	66.5%	27.2%
Hialeah city	233,394	55,132	23.6%	47.9%	52.1%	26.4%	36.7%	36.9%
Hollywood city	146,522	30,826	21.0%	51.9%	48.1%	26.0%	36.1%	37.9%
Jacksonville city	842,588	223,251	26.5%	50.2%	49.8%	22.0%	35.9%	42.1%
Lakeland city	100,697	26,243	26.1%	53.7%	46.3%	25.7%	42.1%	32.2%
Miami Beach city	91,019	20,119	22.1%	54.6%	45.4%	25.4%	30.9%	43.7%
Miami city	417,670	99,815	23.9%	51.7%	48.3%	18.4%	34.3%	47.2%
Miami Gardens city	111,381	32,190	28.9%	49.7%	50.3%	21.5%	43.3%	35.2%
Miramar city	130,281	37,135	28.5%	47.0%	53.0%	17.5%	34.0%	48.5%
Orlando city	255,479	79,273	31.0%	53.1%	46.9%	22.4%	31.8%	45.8%
Palm Bay city	104,894	23,697	22.6%	43.7%	56.3%	26.9%	38.8%	34.3%
Pembroke Pines city	162,333	40,226	24.8%	51.7%	48.3%	26.9%	37.0%	36.1%
Pompano Beach city	104,406	25,547	24.5%	52.7%	47.3%	31.7%	28.2%	40.1%
Port St. Lucie city	170,999	38,656	22.6%	52.6%	47.4%	38.7%	34.3%	27.0%
St. Petersburg city	249,702	60,199	24.1%	50.0%	50.0%	22.7%	35.8%	41.5%
Tallahassee city	186,408	86,319	46.3%	47.3%	52.7%	12.7%	60.6%	26.7%
Tampa city	352,981	104,339	29.6%	49.2%	50.8%	19.4%	40.6%	39.9%
West Palm Beach city	102,433	29,051	28.4%	53.5%	46.5%	18.1%	36.2%	45.7%
Georgia								
Athens-Clarke County unified govt (bal)	120,212	54,062	45.0%	47.2%	52.8%	7.9%	66.6%	25.5%
Atlanta city	447,848	143,295	32.0%	51.9%	48.1%	13.3%	42.8%	43.9%
Augusta-Richmond County consolidated govt (bal)	196,711	57,457	29.2%	50.5%	49.5%	21.9%	37.5%	40.6%
Columbus city	202,824	58,130	28.7%	55.2%	44.8%	22.0%	42.6%	35.3%

Table A-3: Places—Summary Population Characteristics—*Continued*

	Total 2013 ACS Population	Millennial Population Age 13 to 31	Millennials as Percent of Total	Millennial Percentage by Gender		Millennial Percentage by Age		
				Male	Female	13 to 17	18 to 24	25 to 31
Georgia—Cont.								
Macon city	90,107	26,832	29.8%	48.7%	51.3%	23.7%	41.8%	34.4%
Roswell city	94,029	23,495	25.0%	45.5%	54.5%	28.2%	35.3%	36.5%
Sandy Springs city	99,769	25,297	25.4%	48.1%	51.9%	21.7%	19.7%	58.6%
Savannah city	142,772	45,035	31.5%	49.2%	50.8%	16.2%	44.4%	39.4%
Hawaii								
Urban Honolulu CDP	347,907	87,855	25.3%	50.9%	49.1%	21.5%	35.8%	42.7%
Idaho								
Boise City city	214,235	62,035	29.0%	52.6%	47.4%	24.7%	38.2%	37.1%
Illinois								
Aurora city	202,665	52,749	26.0%	48.6%	51.4%	27.4%	32.7%	39.9%
Chicago city	2,718,789	793,782	29.2%	49.5%	50.5%	19.6%	35.4%	45.0%
Elgin city	108,694	31,610	29.1%	51.9%	48.1%	25.2%	38.8%	36.0%
Joliet city	148,411	40,784	27.5%	45.3%	54.7%	26.8%	38.4%	34.8%
Naperville city	144,736	36,457	25.2%	47.9%	52.1%	32.9%	32.0%	35.1%
Peoria city	116,575	33,592	28.8%	50.3%	49.7%	20.4%	40.2%	39.3%
Rockford city	152,618	40,295	26.4%	46.9%	53.1%	27.8%	38.1%	34.1%
Springfield city	116,858	30,131	25.8%	44.7%	55.3%	22.1%	38.2%	39.7%
Indiana								
Evansville city	117,439	30,745	26.2%	52.1%	47.9%	21.6%	42.3%	36.1%
Fort Wayne city	251,340	67,163	26.7%	50.1%	49.9%	25.4%	37.0%	37.6%
Indianapolis city (bal)	838,425	231,827	27.7%	49.8%	50.2%	21.9%	35.4%	42.7%
South Bend city	101,975	27,619	27.1%	49.1%	50.9%	23.4%	46.6%	30.0%
Iowa								
Cedar Rapids city	128,422	34,639	27.0%	52.3%	47.7%	26.3%	32.2%	41.5%
Davenport city	102,165	26,470	25.9%	47.8%	52.2%	25.1%	36.1%	38.8%
Des Moines city	207,293	56,963	27.5%	54.2%	45.8%	18.9%	35.0%	46.2%
Kansas								
Kansas City city	148,112	39,339	26.6%	51.8%	48.2%	27.4%	36.5%	36.1%
Olathe city	131,903	32,791	24.9%	52.0%	48.0%	29.0%	36.0%	35.0%
Overland Park city	181,273	45,868	25.3%	50.5%	49.5%	32.2%	30.2%	37.6%
Topeka city	127,702	32,533	25.5%	47.9%	52.1%	24.3%	41.7%	34.0%
Wichita city	386,558	105,918	27.4%	52.1%	47.9%	27.8%	33.2%	38.9%
Kentucky								
Lexington-Fayette urban county	308,428	91,455	29.7%	49.7%	50.3%	17.4%	47.0%	35.6%
Louisville/Jefferson County metro govt (bal)	609,908	155,155	25.4%	53.1%	46.9%	25.5%	36.0%	38.4%
Louisiana								
Baton Rouge city	229,405	80,894	35.3%	49.5%	50.5%	16.3%	52.3%	31.4%
Lafayette city	124,282	41,013	33.0%	46.8%	53.2%	22.1%	39.3%	38.6%
New Orleans city	378,715	107,584	28.4%	47.9%	52.1%	17.3%	37.3%	45.4%
Shreveport city	200,191	56,474	28.2%	47.5%	52.5%	24.6%	39.6%	35.8%
Maryland								
Baltimore city	622,104	177,188	28.5%	46.8%	53.2%	16.7%	37.5%	45.9%
Massachusetts								
Boston city	644,710	233,438	36.2%	48.5%	51.5%	13.1%	39.9%	47.0%
Brockton city	94,101	25,123	26.7%	52.4%	47.6%	25.7%	27.9%	46.4%
Cambridge city	107,276	45,181	42.1%	48.0%	52.0%	8.1%	46.8%	45.2%
Lowell city	108,868	33,353	30.6%	52.1%	47.9%	21.8%	39.5%	38.7%
Lynn city	91,595	22,564	24.6%	49.4%	50.6%	24.6%	36.6%	38.8%
New Bedford city	95,079	25,019	26.3%	47.6%	52.4%	24.2%	34.8%	41.0%
Springfield city	153,694	46,473	30.2%	48.5%	51.5%	26.0%	42.9%	31.1%
Worcester city	182,538	56,561	31.0%	49.9%	50.1%	20.0%	44.4%	35.6%
Michigan								
Ann Arbor city	117,034	52,352	44.7%	54.6%	45.4%	7.7%	67.5%	24.8%
Dearborn city	95,888	27,230	28.4%	52.0%	48.0%	26.4%	41.0%	32.6%
Detroit city	688,740	188,753	27.4%	48.6%	51.4%	25.0%	43.8%	31.1%
Flint city	99,758	24,928	25.0%	48.5%	51.5%	28.2%	26.4%	45.3%
Grand Rapids city	192,285	59,157	30.8%	50.9%	49.1%	18.1%	38.8%	43.1%
Lansing city	114,113	35,463	31.1%	49.6%	50.4%	16.1%	40.1%	43.7%
Livonia city	95,212	21,256	22.3%	50.6%	49.4%	28.9%	35.5%	35.5%
Sterling Heights city	131,204	27,984	21.3%	55.8%	44.2%	29.2%	33.3%	37.5%
Warren city	134,875	33,277	24.7%	51.9%	48.1%	19.6%	40.5%	39.9%
Minnesota								
Minneapolis city	400,079	134,566	33.6%	50.9%	49.1%	12.6%	37.6%	49.8%
Rochester city	110,731	26,862	24.3%	43.9%	56.1%	23.3%	38.3%	38.5%
St. Paul city	294,873	90,558	30.7%	50.9%	49.1%	20.7%	38.9%	40.5%
Mississippi								
Jackson city	172,585	52,244	30.3%	43.7%	56.3%	21.7%	40.6%	37.7%
Missouri								
Columbia city	115,287	51,920	45.0%	48.8%	51.2%	13.7%	53.9%	32.4%
Independence city	117,246	26,867	22.9%	49.7%	50.3%	29.4%	37.4%	33.2%
Kansas City city	467,082	133,200	28.5%	50.4%	49.6%	21.3%	34.6%	44.0%
Lee's Summit city	93,669	22,267	23.8%	43.9%	56.1%	37.7%	26.0%	36.3%

Table A-3: Places—Summary Population Characteristics—*Continued*

	Total 2013 ACS Population	Millennial Population Age 13 to 31	Millennials as Percent of Total	Millennial Percentage by Gender		Millennial Percentage by Age		
				Male	Female	13 to 17	18 to 24	25 to 31
Missouri—Cont.								
Springfield city	164,133	58,414	35.6%	50.9%	49.1%	16.4%	47.9%	35.7%
St. Louis city	318,416	92,329	29.0%	47.8%	52.2%	17.2%	34.6%	48.1%
Montana								
Billings city	109,062	27,832	25.5%	51.9%	48.1%	23.1%	43.5%	33.3%
Nebraska								
Lincoln city	268,743	82,925	30.9%	51.5%	48.5%	18.9%	47.1%	34.0%
Omaha city	434,353	117,506	27.1%	49.7%	50.3%	23.4%	35.6%	41.1%
Nevada								
Henderson city	270,798	59,632	22.0%	46.8%	53.2%	25.5%	36.0%	38.4%
Las Vegas city	603,525	152,786	25.3%	52.6%	47.4%	27.3%	34.0%	38.7%
North Las Vegas city	226,872	67,469	29.7%	50.0%	50.0%	27.3%	33.7%	39.0%
Reno city	233,306	67,923	29.1%	50.0%	50.0%	21.5%	40.5%	38.1%
Sparks city	93,281	22,232	23.8%	59.3%	40.7%	22.9%	38.9%	38.1%
New Hampshire								
Manchester city	110,369	30,183	27.3%	54.4%	45.6%	18.6%	37.8%	43.6%
New Jersey								
Elizabeth city	127,552	37,355	29.3%	47.9%	52.1%	22.9%	35.2%	41.9%
Jersey City city	257,345	73,993	28.8%	49.6%	50.4%	17.4%	30.3%	52.3%
Newark city	278,436	81,864	29.4%	52.6%	47.4%	20.4%	35.5%	44.1%
Paterson city	145,952	41,976	28.8%	47.4%	52.6%	24.3%	41.9%	33.7%
New Mexico								
Albuquerque city	556,489	147,386	26.5%	51.7%	48.3%	22.9%	39.9%	37.1%
Las Cruces city	101,317	33,120	32.7%	54.9%	45.1%	19.2%	57.8%	23.0%
Rio Rancho city	91,928	22,510	24.5%	53.7%	46.3%	30.4%	35.2%	34.3%
New York								
Albany city	98,441	38,928	39.5%	50.2%	49.8%	10.1%	52.2%	37.8%
Buffalo city	258,945	79,888	30.9%	52.6%	47.4%	21.4%	40.3%	38.4%
New York city	8,405,837	2,261,947	26.9%	49.4%	50.6%	19.9%	35.3%	44.8%
Rochester city	210,345	67,543	32.1%	47.6%	52.4%	20.1%	36.4%	43.6%
Syracuse city	144,675	50,118	34.6%	46.9%	53.1%	14.4%	49.7%	35.9%
Yonkers city	199,764	48,658	24.4%	44.6%	55.4%	25.0%	37.4%	37.5%
North Carolina								
Charlotte city	792,849	218,384	27.5%	49.7%	50.3%	22.8%	34.5%	42.7%
Durham city	245,466	73,143	29.8%	49.4%	50.6%	17.0%	35.1%	47.9%
Fayetteville city	204,401	65,057	31.8%	52.4%	47.6%	20.8%	39.8%	39.4%
Greensboro city	279,651	79,997	28.6%	48.6%	51.4%	19.7%	42.6%	37.7%
High Point city	107,229	28,467	26.5%	55.4%	44.6%	23.2%	40.8%	36.0%
Raleigh city	431,897	138,360	32.0%	49.3%	50.7%	23.9%	38.1%	38.0%
Wilmington city	112,072	36,234	32.3%	49.1%	50.9%	14.6%	49.5%	35.8%
Winston-Salem city	236,457	62,381	26.4%	48.4%	51.6%	24.6%	43.8%	31.7%
North Dakota								
Fargo city	112,510	43,717	38.9%	45.8%	54.2%	11.5%	53.3%	35.2%
Ohio								
Akron city	198,095	54,485	27.5%	52.4%	47.6%	16.5%	45.5%	38.0%
Cincinnati city	297,498	91,178	30.6%	48.5%	51.5%	16.6%	43.6%	39.7%
Cleveland city	390,106	107,448	27.5%	49.1%	50.9%	22.1%	42.9%	35.1%
Columbus city	822,762	253,511	30.8%	49.3%	50.7%	22.3%	35.3%	42.4%
Dayton city	143,355	46,480	32.4%	51.3%	48.7%	19.0%	50.4%	30.6%
Toledo city	282,313	78,123	27.7%	50.5%	49.5%	20.6%	40.6%	38.9%
Oklahoma								
Broken Arrow city	105,013	26,302	25.0%	48.8%	51.2%	31.3%	31.8%	36.9%
Lawton city	97,142	33,539	34.5%	57.4%	42.6%	17.7%	45.9%	36.4%
Norman city	118,200	43,626	36.9%	50.0%	50.0%	17.4%	43.6%	39.1%
Oklahoma City city	610,617	166,433	27.3%	52.7%	47.3%	20.6%	37.3%	42.1%
Tulsa city	398,724	109,067	27.4%	52.4%	47.6%	24.6%	36.0%	39.4%
Oregon								
Beaverton city	93,525	24,936	26.7%	49.1%	50.9%	24.1%	29.7%	46.2%
Eugene city	159,161	54,972	34.5%	49.1%	50.9%	16.0%	53.3%	30.7%
Gresham city	109,410	29,749	27.2%	48.9%	51.1%	23.5%	34.7%	41.8%
Hillsboro city	97,371	25,428	26.1%	47.4%	52.6%	24.5%	31.0%	44.5%
Portland city	611,134	159,765	26.1%	48.0%	52.0%	17.4%	33.3%	49.2%
Salem city	160,618	44,757	27.9%	55.0%	45.0%	22.3%	37.9%	39.7%
Pennsylvania								
Allentown city	118,577	35,146	29.6%	50.6%	49.4%	25.5%	38.6%	35.9%
Erie city	100,676	31,041	30.8%	56.4%	43.6%	15.8%	43.0%	41.2%
Philadelphia city	1,553,165	454,880	29.3%	48.6%	51.4%	19.3%	39.5%	41.2%
Pittsburgh city	305,838	103,079	33.7%	49.6%	50.4%	14.1%	48.8%	37.2%
Rhode Island								
Providence city	177,995	64,383	36.2%	51.1%	48.9%	17.0%	47.3%	35.7%
South Carolina								
Charleston city	130,428	41,727	32.0%	46.2%	53.8%	18.1%	39.7%	42.2%

Table A-3: Places—Summary Population Characteristics—*Continued*

	Total 2013 ACS Population	Millennial Population Age 13 to 31	Millennials as Percent of Total	Millennial Percentage by Gender		Millennial Percentage by Age		
				Male	Female	13 to 17	18 to 24	25 to 31
South Carolina—Cont.								
Columbia city	133,377	59,462	44.6%	54.1%	45.9%	13.7%	55.9%	30.4%
North Charleston city	101,838	34,069	33.5%	54.6%	45.4%	19.9%	48.9%	31.2%
South Dakota								
Sioux Falls city	163,629	43,120	26.4%	52.6%	47.4%	17.8%	37.1%	45.1%
Tennessee								
Chattanooga city	173,375	47,897	27.6%	52.2%	47.8%	23.7%	37.9%	38.4%
Clarksville city	142,355	49,730	34.9%	51.8%	48.2%	19.9%	35.9%	44.2%
Knoxville city	183,261	66,524	36.3%	48.7%	51.3%	13.9%	50.6%	35.5%
Memphis city	653,450	188,820	28.9%	48.8%	51.2%	22.3%	38.9%	38.8%
Murfreesboro city	117,039	43,031	36.8%	54.6%	45.4%	14.5%	50.7%	34.8%
Nashville-Davidson metropolitan govt (bal) ..	634,465	181,961	28.7%	47.8%	52.2%	17.7%	35.3%	47.1%
Texas								
Abilene city	119,036	39,552	33.2%	49.9%	50.1%	20.0%	44.5%	35.5%
Amarillo city	196,691	54,926	27.9%	52.2%	47.8%	22.2%	38.2%	39.6%
Arlington city	379,565	112,205	29.6%	47.7%	52.3%	27.3%	33.9%	38.7%
Austin city	885,415	280,372	31.7%	50.7%	49.3%	17.9%	34.5%	47.6%
Beaumont city	117,808	34,209	29.0%	51.4%	48.6%	21.2%	45.1%	33.8%
Brownsville city	181,850	53,924	29.7%	52.8%	47.2%	32.2%	39.1%	28.7%
Carrollton city	126,695	33,385	26.4%	43.9%	56.1%	21.7%	36.8%	41.5%
College Station city	100,036	61,794	61.8%	51.1%	48.9%	12.1%	60.9%	27.0%
Corpus Christi city	316,389	86,069	27.2%	50.0%	50.0%	25.5%	38.5%	36.0%
Dallas city	1,257,676	363,191	28.9%	49.7%	50.3%	22.1%	35.6%	42.2%
Denton city	123,105	51,957	42.2%	48.9%	51.1%	17.4%	46.9%	35.8%
El Paso city	674,438	191,088	28.3%	52.2%	47.8%	26.4%	38.7%	34.8%
Fort Worth city	794,189	222,860	28.1%	50.6%	49.4%	26.1%	34.3%	39.7%
Frisco city	136,783	28,633	20.9%	51.1%	48.9%	33.8%	30.0%	36.1%
Garland city	234,694	64,933	27.7%	50.4%	49.6%	28.3%	37.2%	34.5%
Grand Prairie city	183,324	52,064	28.4%	47.9%	52.1%	30.3%	38.1%	31.7%
Houston city	2,197,374	662,760	30.2%	52.3%	47.7%	22.2%	33.9%	43.9%
Irving city	228,652	64,810	28.3%	50.1%	49.9%	22.0%	36.1%	41.9%
Killeen city	137,160	46,189	33.7%	46.7%	53.3%	21.9%	36.5%	41.6%
Laredo city	249,085	71,446	28.7%	49.7%	50.3%	29.4%	38.2%	32.5%
Lewisville city	101,154	28,237	27.9%	49.9%	50.1%	20.4%	31.0%	48.5%
Lubbock city	239,544	87,806	36.7%	52.4%	47.6%	19.5%	49.8%	30.8%
McAllen city	136,631	39,424	28.9%	47.7%	52.3%	32.8%	38.0%	29.2%
McKinney city	148,544	36,030	24.3%	57.2%	42.8%	35.1%	31.5%	33.4%
Mesquite city	143,341	40,457	28.2%	50.9%	49.1%	24.9%	39.2%	35.9%
Midland city	123,935	36,802	29.7%	55.1%	44.9%	23.4%	36.3%	40.3%
Odessa city	110,406	32,849	29.8%	51.0%	49.0%	24.4%	37.5%	38.1%
Pasadena city	152,734	44,502	29.1%	54.2%	45.8%	30.2%	40.8%	29.0%
Pearland city	102,491	24,798	24.2%	53.0%	47.0%	19.5%	35.3%	45.2%
Plano city	273,519	66,294	24.2%	47.6%	52.4%	31.0%	31.7%	37.2%
Richardson city	104,477	25,547	24.5%	47.7%	52.3%	24.9%	32.7%	42.4%
Round Rock city	109,835	30,063	27.4%	49.4%	50.6%	34.0%	31.2%	34.9%
San Angelo city	100,111	31,154	31.1%	55.5%	44.5%	23.7%	37.5%	38.7%
San Antonio city	1,409,000	410,854	29.2%	51.8%	48.2%	24.3%	38.4%	37.3%
Tyler city	100,217	28,538	28.5%	48.1%	51.9%	21.1%	38.1%	40.7%
Waco city	129,031	46,105	35.7%	50.5%	49.5%	17.8%	54.4%	27.8%
Wichita Falls city	104,900	32,437	30.9%	56.2%	43.8%	16.6%	44.4%	39.1%
Utah								
Orem city	91,650	35,056	38.2%	54.7%	45.3%	26.3%	44.0%	29.7%
Provo city	116,289	63,999	55.0%	48.6%	51.4%	9.8%	65.2%	25.0%
Salt Lake City city	191,160	62,705	32.8%	54.2%	45.8%	15.3%	42.1%	42.6%
West Jordan city	110,064	31,921	29.0%	52.1%	47.9%	37.5%	29.1%	33.4%
West Valley City city	133,597	39,676	29.7%	54.6%	45.4%	25.6%	34.9%	39.5%
Virginia								
Alexandria city	148,892	39,869	26.8%	47.5%	52.5%	11.7%	20.8%	67.4%
Chesapeake city	230,571	61,466	26.7%	52.3%	47.7%	27.0%	35.7%	37.3%
Hampton city	136,699	41,168	30.1%	46.9%	53.1%	21.3%	40.4%	38.3%
Newport News city	182,020	54,567	30.0%	48.5%	51.5%	20.1%	41.7%	38.2%
Norfolk city	246,139	92,560	37.6%	55.7%	44.3%	14.0%	48.9%	37.0%
Portsmouth city	96,205	26,744	27.8%	55.4%	44.6%	18.2%	39.5%	42.3%
Richmond city	214,114	70,765	33.1%	48.9%	51.1%	12.5%	42.7%	44.8%
Roanoke city	98,465	24,131	24.5%	47.2%	52.8%	17.1%	37.9%	45.1%
Virginia Beach city	448,479	124,962	27.9%	51.7%	48.3%	19.8%	38.0%	42.2%
Washington								
Bellevue city	133,990	32,231	24.1%	54.2%	45.8%	24.5%	24.5%	51.0%
Everett city	105,355	29,205	27.7%	54.4%	45.6%	26.1%	38.6%	35.3%
Federal Way city	92,717	26,383	28.5%	51.6%	48.4%	28.7%	32.6%	38.8%
Kent city	124,410	34,530	27.8%	49.4%	50.6%	22.0%	34.2%	43.8%
Renton city	96,987	26,083	26.9%	48.0%	52.0%	23.5%	29.8%	46.6%
Seattle city	652,429	203,636	31.2%	49.9%	50.1%	13.3%	35.0%	51.7%
Spokane city	210,722	61,518	29.2%	50.7%	49.3%	19.2%	42.1%	38.7%
Spokane Valley city	91,111	23,372	25.7%	53.4%	46.6%	28.5%	25.7%	45.9%
Tacoma city	203,451	56,132	27.6%	50.5%	49.5%	21.0%	35.7%	43.3%
Vancouver city	167,410	41,746	24.9%	52.6%	47.4%	25.9%	34.9%	39.2%
Yakima city	93,260	26,160	28.1%	51.2%	48.8%	25.4%	41.0%	33.7%

Table A-3: Places—Summary Population Characteristics—*Continued*

	Total 2013 ACS Population	Millennial Population Age 13 to 31	Millennials as Percent of Total	Millennial Percentage by Gender		Millennial Percentage by Age		
				Male	Female	13 to 17	18 to 24	25 to 31
Wisconsin								
Green Bay city...	104,773	30,520	29.1%	53.6%	46.4%	24.9%	39.2%	35.9%
Kenosha city..	99,887	27,729	27.8%	51.5%	48.5%	27.8%	41.3%	30.9%
Madison city..	243,337	94,874	39.0%	48.9%	51.1%	16.9%	43.6%	39.5%
Milwaukee city..	599,168	188,730	31.5%	47.0%	53.0%	22.1%	38.4%	39.6%

Table A-4: Metropolitan/Micropolitan Statistical Areas—Summary Population Characteristics

	Total 2013 ACS Population	Millennial Population Age 13 to 31	Millennials as Percent of Total	Millennial Percentage by Gender		Millennial Percentage by Age		
				Male	Female	13 to 17	18 to 24	25 to 31
Abilene, TX	168,144	51,282	30.5%	50.7%	49.3%	20.1%	44.9%	35.0%
Adrian, MI micro	99,188	24,684	24.9%	52.3%	47.7%	26.9%	38.0%	35.1%
Akron, OH	705,686	185,003	26.2%	49.5%	50.5%	22.9%	43.7%	33.4%
Albany-Schenectady-Troy, NY	877,905	221,152	25.2%	49.8%	50.2%	23.0%	42.6%	34.3%
Albany, GA	156,277	44,899	28.7%	51.6%	48.4%	23.2%	41.2%	35.7%
Albany, OR	118,765	30,638	25.8%	51.5%	48.5%	22.0%	51.0%	27.0%
Albertville, AL micro	94,760	22,852	24.1%	52.5%	47.5%	32.6%	29.5%	37.9%
Albuquerque, NM	901,932	232,256	25.8%	50.7%	49.3%	25.6%	37.1%	37.3%
Alexandria, LA	154,753	40,995	26.5%	52.1%	47.9%	27.1%	36.1%	36.8%
Allentown-Bethlehem-Easton, PA-NJ	827,048	200,342	24.2%	50.5%	49.5%	27.7%	37.6%	34.7%
Altoona, PA	126,314	29,018	23.0%	52.2%	47.8%	22.5%	42.1%	35.4%
Amarillo, TX	259,164	69,818	26.9%	52.8%	47.2%	23.8%	37.7%	38.5%
Ames, IA	92,406	39,514	42.8%	51.6%	48.4%	10.6%	64.1%	25.2%
Anchorage, AK	396,142	119,605	30.2%	53.5%	46.5%	24.6%	37.7%	37.7%
Ann Arbor, MI	354,240	119,936	33.9%	51.0%	49.0%	16.2%	53.6%	30.2%
Anniston-Oxford-Jacksonville, AL	116,736	29,189	25.0%	49.7%	50.3%	22.9%	40.9%	36.1%
Appleton, WI	229,962	57,198	24.9%	49.2%	50.8%	25.7%	38.1%	36.2%
Asheville, NC	437,657	97,439	22.3%	52.4%	47.6%	27.5%	34.5%	38.0%
Ashtabula, OH micro	99,811	22,736	22.8%	49.7%	50.3%	27.2%	36.3%	36.5%
Athens-Clarke County, GA	197,357	74,592	37.8%	48.2%	51.8%	14.1%	57.6%	28.3%
Atlanta-Sandy Springs-Roswell, GA	5,524,693	1,419,815	25.7%	50.1%	49.9%	27.9%	35.9%	36.2%
Atlantic City-Hammonton, NJ	275,862	67,058	24.3%	51.0%	49.0%	26.5%	39.8%	33.6%
Auburn-Opelika, AL	150,933	53,402	35.4%	51.8%	48.2%	17.3%	56.2%	26.5%
Augusta-Richmond County, GA-SC	581,551	154,121	26.5%	50.9%	49.1%	26.1%	37.7%	36.2%
Augusta-Waterville, ME micro	121,164	27,602	22.8%	49.4%	50.6%	29.5%	36.9%	33.5%
Austin-Round Rock, TX	1,883,051	549,600	29.2%	51.3%	48.7%	21.9%	35.5%	42.5%
Bakersfield, CA	864,124	253,748	29.4%	51.9%	48.1%	26.6%	37.6%	35.9%
Baltimore-Columbia-Towson, MD	2,770,738	714,534	25.8%	50.8%	49.2%	24.3%	36.5%	39.2%
Bangor, ME	153,364	39,915	26.0%	50.4%	49.6%	20.8%	45.7%	33.5%
Barnstable Town, MA	214,990	37,757	17.6%	51.0%	49.0%	28.5%	36.3%	35.2%
Baton Rouge, LA	820,159	232,828	28.4%	51.1%	48.9%	23.4%	42.8%	33.9%
Battle Creek, MI	135,012	31,074	23.0%	48.6%	51.4%	31.2%	35.7%	33.1%
Bay City, MI	106,832	25,541	23.9%	47.5%	52.5%	28.0%	36.2%	35.8%
Beaumont-Port Arthur, TX	403,622	107,793	26.7%	53.6%	46.4%	26.3%	38.1%	35.6%
Beckley, WV	124,432	27,461	22.1%	53.1%	46.9%	21.4%	41.2%	37.4%
Bellingham, WA	206,353	62,149	30.1%	49.8%	50.2%	20.8%	51.0%	28.2%
Bend-Redmond, OR	165,954	37,987	22.9%	49.7%	50.3%	32.1%	30.3%	37.7%
Billings, MT	165,730	41,323	24.9%	52.5%	47.5%	24.0%	41.6%	34.3%
Binghamton, NY	247,777	62,942	25.4%	50.5%	49.5%	22.4%	46.0%	31.6%
Birmingham-Hoover, AL	1,140,300	287,772	25.2%	49.8%	50.2%	26.6%	36.1%	37.3%
Bismarck, ND	124,817	34,202	27.4%	54.8%	45.2%	20.8%	36.9%	42.3%
Blacksburg-Christiansburg-Radford, VA	179,738	66,288	36.9%	51.5%	48.5%	13.6%	64.5%	21.9%
Bloomington, IL	192,140	63,715	33.2%	47.6%	52.4%	17.0%	52.6%	30.3%
Bloomington, IN	163,089	66,600	40.8%	49.2%	50.8%	13.4%	62.8%	23.8%
Bloomsburg-Berwick, PA	85,338	23,141	27.1%	50.0%	50.0%	23.1%	49.2%	27.7%
Boise City, ID	649,321	169,093	26.0%	50.9%	49.1%	29.5%	35.8%	34.7%
Boston-Cambridge-Newton, MA-NH	4,684,299	1,227,309	26.2%	49.9%	50.1%	23.5%	37.5%	39.0%
Boulder, CO	310,048	96,264	31.0%	52.6%	47.4%	21.3%	48.7%	29.9%
Bowling Green, KY	163,300	46,097	28.2%	51.1%	48.9%	21.4%	43.7%	34.9%
Bremerton-Silverdale, WA	253,968	65,185	25.7%	53.8%	46.2%	23.9%	39.4%	36.7%
Bridgeport-Stamford-Norwalk, CT	939,904	212,707	22.6%	50.6%	49.4%	30.2%	35.7%	34.1%
Brownsville-Harlingen, TX	417,254	117,741	28.2%	50.0%	50.0%	34.1%	37.5%	28.5%
Brunswick, GA	113,007	27,572	24.4%	53.4%	46.6%	24.9%	39.0%	36.0%
Buffalo-Cheektowaga-Niagara Falls, NY	1,134,115	286,943	25.3%	51.0%	49.0%	23.9%	39.6%	36.5%
Burlington-South Burlington, VT	215,539	59,774	27.7%	48.7%	51.3%	19.4%	46.9%	33.7%
Burlington, NC	154,378	38,845	25.2%	49.4%	50.6%	26.8%	38.4%	34.8%
California-Lexington Park, MD	109,633	28,557	26.0%	52.7%	47.3%	33.9%	36.2%	29.9%
Canton-Massillon, OH	403,707	93,351	23.1%	51.5%	48.5%	27.4%	38.1%	34.5%
Cape Coral-Fort Myers, FL	661,115	130,907	19.8%	49.6%	50.4%	26.6%	36.3%	37.1%
Cape Girardeau, MO-IL	95,463	26,340	27.6%	47.8%	52.2%	24.2%	43.0%	32.8%
Carbondale-Marion, IL	126,738	39,180	30.9%	51.6%	48.4%	23.9%	42.6%	33.5%
Carson City, NV	54,080	12,217	22.6%	53.7%	46.3%	26.8%	32.2%	41.0%
Casper, WY	80,973	21,460	26.5%	47.1%	52.9%	24.9%	36.1%	39.0%
Cedar Rapids, IA	262,421	68,286	26.0%	49.3%	50.7%	28.0%	33.6%	38.5%
Chambersburg-Waynesboro, PA	152,085	33,238	21.9%	51.3%	48.7%	24.9%	36.0%	39.1%
Champaign-Urbana, IL	234,089	90,995	38.9%	52.7%	47.3%	14.4%	56.5%	29.1%
Charleston-North Charleston, SC	712,220	192,839	27.1%	51.1%	48.9%	22.6%	38.4%	39.0%
Charleston, WV	224,727	50,342	22.4%	51.2%	48.8%	27.5%	36.6%	35.9%
Charlotte-Concord-Gastonia, NC-SC	2,335,358	579,482	24.8%	50.8%	49.2%	27.9%	36.0%	36.1%
Charlottesville, VA	225,531	60,899	27.0%	47.9%	52.1%	23.5%	45.2%	31.3%
Chattanooga, TN-GA	540,387	129,748	24.0%	51.0%	49.0%	25.9%	36.2%	37.9%
Cheyenne, WY	95,809	25,613	26.7%	53.5%	46.5%	20.1%	48.6%	31.4%
Chicago-Naperville-Elgin, IL-IN-WI	9,537,040	2,519,394	26.4%	50.8%	49.2%	25.8%	36.0%	38.2%
Chico, CA	222,090	65,642	29.6%	51.6%	48.4%	18.4%	51.5%	30.1%
Cincinnati, OH-KY-IN	2,134,109	528,404	24.8%	49.7%	50.3%	27.7%	36.5%	35.8%
Clarksburg, WV micro	89,801	18,960	21.1%	49.7%	50.3%	29.0%	34.7%	36.3%
Clarksville, TN-KY	272,452	89,743	32.9%	53.9%	46.1%	21.8%	38.0%	40.2%
Cleveland-Elyria, OH	2,064,725	488,473	23.7%	50.6%	49.4%	27.7%	36.9%	35.4%
Cleveland, TN	120,384	29,929	24.9%	53.5%	46.5%	26.2%	39.5%	34.4%

Table A-4: Metropolitan/Micropolitan Statistical Areas—Summary Population Characteristics—*Continued*

	Total 2013 ACS Population	Millennial Population Age 13 to 31	Millennials as Percent of Total	Millennial Percentage by Gender		Millennial Percentage by Age		
				Male	Female	13 to 17	18 to 24	25 to 31
Coeur d'Alene, ID	144,265	35,119	24.3%	49.3%	50.7%	27.4%	35.9%	36.7%
College Station-Bryan, TX	238,939	104,136	43.6%	53.7%	46.3%	16.0%	58.0%	26.0%
Colorado Springs, CO	678,319	189,663	28.0%	54.0%	46.0%	24.5%	37.8%	37.6%
Columbia, MO	170,773	65,445	38.3%	49.0%	51.0%	13.6%	55.6%	30.7%
Columbia, SC	793,360	224,537	28.3%	50.1%	49.9%	23.6%	43.4%	33.0%
Columbus, GA-AL	314,519	93,131	29.6%	52.9%	47.1%	22.2%	43.1%	34.7%
Columbus, IN	79,587	20,581	25.9%	55.2%	44.8%	25.5%	33.6%	40.9%
Columbus, OH	1,967,066	514,620	26.2%	50.4%	49.6%	26.0%	33.3%	40.7%
Concord, NH micro	146,849	29,353	20.0%	54.3%	45.7%	26.1%	42.1%	31.8%
Cookeville, TN micro	107,526	28,672	26.7%	51.0%	49.0%	21.0%	49.0%	30.1%
Corpus Christi, TX	444,904	123,335	27.7%	51.3%	48.7%	26.8%	38.6%	34.6%
Corvallis, OR	86,591	33,658	38.9%	52.2%	47.8%	22.0%	50.9%	27.0%
Crestview-Fort Walton Beach-Destin, FL	253,618	68,552	27.0%	54.5%	45.5%	21.6%	37.3%	41.1%
Cumberland, MD-WV	101,225	25,491	25.2%	50.1%	49.9%	26.9%	43.6%	29.5%
Dallas-Fort Worth-Arlington, TX	6,812,373	1,793,256	26.3%	50.4%	49.6%	27.2%	35.1%	37.7%
Dalton, GA	142,212	37,669	26.5%	48.1%	51.9%	27.3%	37.2%	35.5%
Danville, IL	80,329	19,265	24.0%	50.3%	49.7%	29.1%	33.7%	37.2%
Danville, VA micro	105,333	22,440	21.3%	52.4%	47.6%	27.7%	39.5%	32.8%
Daphne-Fairhope-Foley, AL	195,540	43,743	22.4%	49.4%	50.6%	30.0%	37.3%	32.6%
Davenport-Moline-Rock Island, IA-IL	383,257	92,530	24.1%	50.9%	49.1%	24.3%	40.9%	34.9%
Dayton, OH	802,489	203,642	25.4%	50.3%	49.7%	24.4%	40.0%	35.6%
Decatur, AL	153,374	35,881	23.4%	49.8%	50.2%	31.7%	36.6%	31.7%
Decatur, IL	109,278	26,140	23.9%	46.9%	53.1%	24.3%	39.1%	36.6%
Deltona-Daytona Beach-Ormond Beach, FL	600,756	128,837	21.4%	50.7%	49.3%	22.9%	40.7%	36.4%
Denver-Aurora-Lakewood, CO	2,697,476	697,150	25.8%	51.1%	48.9%	26.0%	32.8%	41.1%
Des Moines-West Des Moines, IA	599,789	151,062	25.2%	52.3%	47.7%	26.5%	31.5%	42.0%
Detroit-Warren-Dearborn, MI	4,294,983	1,027,771	23.9%	50.4%	49.6%	28.2%	37.2%	34.5%
Dothan, AL	147,691	34,752	23.5%	49.5%	50.5%	30.4%	33.0%	36.7%
Dover, DE	169,416	43,966	26.0%	52.2%	47.8%	24.8%	39.2%	36.0%
Dubuque, IA	95,697	25,299	26.4%	52.5%	47.5%	32.1%	39.4%	28.5%
Duluth, MN-WI	279,887	73,630	26.3%	53.3%	46.7%	23.0%	43.3%	33.7%
Dunn, NC micro	124,987	34,876	27.9%	51.3%	48.7%	25.3%	33.7%	41.0%
Durham-Chapel Hill, NC	534,578	150,437	28.1%	50.0%	50.0%	20.0%	41.8%	38.2%
East Stroudsburg, PA	167,148	42,860	25.6%	54.2%	45.8%	31.0%	44.4%	24.7%
Eau Claire, WI	164,570	46,385	28.2%	50.2%	49.8%	20.5%	47.4%	32.1%
El Centro, CA	176,584	52,602	29.8%	53.8%	46.2%	27.1%	38.6%	34.3%
El Paso, TX	831,935	242,820	29.2%	52.2%	47.8%	26.4%	40.0%	33.5%
Elizabethtown-Fort Knox, KY	151,740	39,917	26.3%	51.6%	48.4%	33.4%	31.1%	35.5%
Elkhart-Goshen, IN	200,563	49,637	24.7%	48.8%	51.2%	29.9%	35.6%	34.5%
Elmira, NY	88,506	21,897	24.7%	52.4%	47.6%	23.9%	36.7%	39.4%
Erie, PA	280,294	71,567	25.5%	52.3%	47.7%	21.4%	41.4%	37.2%
Eugene, OR	356,212	94,734	26.6%	50.1%	49.9%	20.4%	48.7%	30.9%
Eureka-Arcata-Fortuna, CA micro	134,493	38,357	28.5%	51.0%	49.0%	17.3%	47.2%	35.4%
Evansville, IN-KY	314,280	78,099	24.9%	48.2%	51.8%	23.9%	40.8%	35.3%
Fairbanks, AK	100,436	32,435	32.3%	53.3%	46.7%	19.0%	40.4%	40.6%
Fargo, ND-MN	223,490	79,044	35.4%	51.0%	49.0%	17.6%	49.3%	33.1%
Farmington, NM	126,503	32,645	25.8%	49.1%	50.9%	28.5%	37.7%	33.8%
Fayetteville-Springdale-Rogers, AR-MO	491,755	137,070	27.9%	51.4%	48.6%	26.2%	39.0%	34.8%
Fayetteville, NC	377,193	116,497	30.9%	52.7%	47.3%	21.0%	40.9%	38.2%
Flagstaff, AZ	136,539	48,457	35.5%	49.0%	51.0%	16.0%	55.1%	28.9%
Flint, MI	415,376	104,249	25.1%	51.7%	48.3%	28.9%	37.2%	33.9%
Florence-Muscle Shoals, AL	147,317	36,495	24.8%	51.7%	48.3%	25.8%	41.6%	32.6%
Florence, SC	206,261	49,305	23.9%	46.6%	53.4%	26.6%	40.2%	33.2%
Fond du Lac, WI	101,798	22,700	22.3%	55.9%	44.1%	35.0%	40.1%	24.9%
Fort Collins, CO	315,988	94,110	29.8%	53.2%	46.8%	20.9%	47.5%	31.6%
Fort Smith, AR-OK	279,974	71,097	25.4%	51.3%	48.7%	26.9%	35.8%	37.3%
Fort Wayne, IN	424,122	109,234	25.8%	50.7%	49.3%	27.1%	37.4%	35.4%
Fresno, CA	955,272	280,746	29.4%	51.7%	48.3%	25.4%	38.6%	36.0%
Gadsden, AL	103,931	24,989	24.0%	48.9%	51.1%	30.7%	37.3%	32.1%
Gainesville, FL	273,232	104,083	38.1%	49.7%	50.3%	12.4%	58.5%	29.1%
Gainesville, GA	187,745	48,065	25.6%	52.3%	47.7%	29.4%	36.5%	34.1%
Gettysburg, PA	101,546	23,917	23.6%	47.1%	52.9%	26.7%	46.0%	27.4%
Glens Falls, NY	128,430	27,827	21.7%	50.8%	49.2%	28.0%	37.0%	35.0%
Goldsboro, NC	124,583	30,990	24.9%	53.4%	46.6%	24.9%	38.2%	36.8%
Grand Forks, ND-MN	100,748	36,319	36.0%	52.1%	47.9%	21.3%	54.6%	24.1%
Grand Island, NE	84,168	18,823	22.4%	48.9%	51.1%	29.5%	35.9%	34.6%
Grand Junction, CO	147,554	39,345	26.7%	48.1%	51.9%	21.5%	40.4%	38.1%
Grand Rapids-Wyoming, MI	1,016,603	275,216	27.1%	50.4%	49.6%	26.2%	38.4%	35.5%
Grants Pass, OR	83,306	15,966	19.2%	52.5%	47.5%	25.1%	39.3%	35.6%
Great Falls, MT	82,384	22,162	26.9%	49.8%	50.2%	21.4%	37.4%	41.3%
Greeley, CO	269,785	75,018	27.8%	51.0%	49.0%	23.9%	39.1%	37.0%
Green Bay, WI	312,409	79,175	25.3%	51.9%	48.1%	29.3%	36.2%	34.5%
Greensboro-High Point, NC	741,065	189,386	25.6%	49.7%	50.3%	25.2%	39.0%	35.7%
Greenville-Anderson-Mauldin, SC	850,965	212,385	25.0%	49.8%	50.2%	27.2%	38.6%	34.2%
Greenville, NC	174,263	61,787	35.5%	49.2%	50.8%	20.7%	54.2%	25.0%
Greenwood, SC micro	93,996	24,086	25.6%	50.7%	49.3%	26.4%	42.9%	30.7%
Gulfport-Biloxi-Pascagoula, MS	382,516	99,555	26.0%	51.8%	48.2%	24.5%	37.0%	38.5%
Hagerstown-Martinsburg, MD-WV	258,294	63,073	24.4%	49.3%	50.7%	29.7%	36.2%	34.1%
Hammond, LA	125,412	37,246	29.7%	49.1%	50.9%	23.5%	38.1%	38.4%

Table A-4: Metropolitan/Micropolitan Statistical Areas—Summary Population Characteristics—*Continued*

	Total 2013 ACS Population	Millennial Population Age 13 to 31	Millennials as Percent of Total	Millennial Percentage by Gender		Millennial Percentage by Age		
				Male	Female	13 to 17	18 to 24	25 to 31
Hanford-Corcoran, CA	150,960	45,510	30.1%	59.3%	40.7%	23.5%	38.3%	38.2%
Harrisburg-Carlisle, PA	557,711	136,067	24.4%	49.8%	50.2%	25.2%	38.3%	36.6%
Harrisonburg, VA	129,136	45,371	35.1%	46.3%	53.7%	18.1%	56.9%	24.9%
Hartford-West Hartford-East Hartford, CT	1,215,211	305,097	25.1%	51.2%	48.8%	25.9%	39.7%	34.4%
Hattiesburg, MS	148,644	46,296	31.1%	50.5%	49.5%	19.9%	48.8%	31.3%
Hickory-Lenoir-Morganton, NC	363,572	83,615	23.0%	50.4%	49.6%	29.2%	37.5%	33.2%
Hilo, HI micro	190,821	44,614	23.4%	52.6%	47.4%	29.7%	34.2%	36.1%
Hilton Head Island-Bluffton-Beaufort, SC	198,467	48,805	24.6%	50.2%	49.8%	22.1%	41.6%	36.3%
Hinesville, GA	81,555	28,306	34.7%	50.6%	49.4%	22.0%	40.9%	37.1%
Holland, MI micro	112,531	26,007	23.1%	51.7%	48.3%	32.3%	36.5%	31.1%
Homosassa Springs, FL	139,271	21,470	15.4%	53.3%	46.7%	29.1%	39.0%	31.9%
Hot Springs, AR	97,173	20,011	20.6%	54.2%	45.8%	29.0%	40.8%	30.2%
Houma-Thibodaux, LA	209,890	57,742	27.5%	49.7%	50.3%	24.2%	37.9%	37.9%
Houston-The Woodlands-Sugar Land, TX	6,313,158	1,693,971	26.8%	50.9%	49.1%	26.8%	34.6%	38.7%
Huntington-Ashland, WV-KY-OH	364,101	89,024	24.5%	50.2%	49.8%	29.3%	36.3%	34.4%
Huntsville, AL	435,737	117,360	26.9%	51.5%	48.5%	26.0%	36.8%	37.2%
Idaho Falls, ID	137,554	37,305	27.1%	48.6%	51.4%	32.7%	36.0%	31.3%
Indianapolis-Carmel-Anderson, IN	1,953,613	498,562	25.5%	50.5%	49.5%	26.9%	34.6%	38.5%
Iowa City, IA	161,170	63,584	39.5%	50.9%	49.1%	12.5%	53.4%	34.1%
Ithaca, NY	103,617	41,515	40.1%	53.9%	46.1%	10.6%	65.2%	24.2%
Jackson, MI	160,369	39,344	24.5%	49.7%	50.3%	26.1%	36.0%	38.0%
Jackson, MS	578,361	154,147	26.7%	48.7%	51.3%	27.5%	36.3%	36.2%
Jackson, TN	130,645	34,586	26.5%	48.6%	51.4%	25.2%	41.6%	33.2%
Jacksonville, FL	1,394,624	354,593	25.4%	50.5%	49.5%	24.8%	36.3%	38.9%
Jacksonville, NC	185,220	75,082	40.5%	61.5%	38.5%	14.9%	51.9%	33.2%
Jamestown-Dunkirk-Fredonia, NY micro	133,080	34,497	25.9%	55.2%	44.8%	23.7%	45.5%	30.7%
Janesville-Beloit, WI	160,739	39,734	24.7%	51.7%	48.3%	30.2%	35.9%	33.9%
Jefferson City, MO	148,703	40,116	27.0%	51.5%	48.5%	29.7%	36.9%	33.3%
Johnson City, TN	200,591	50,488	25.2%	48.6%	51.4%	26.0%	42.4%	31.6%
Johnstown, PA	140,499	32,240	22.9%	49.3%	50.7%	26.8%	40.5%	32.7%
Jonesboro, AR	125,633	33,236	26.5%	51.1%	48.9%	22.2%	40.4%	37.3%
Joplin, MO	175,243	46,196	26.4%	49.9%	50.1%	26.6%	37.1%	36.3%
Kahului-Wailuku-Lahaina, HI	160,292	37,245	23.2%	52.5%	47.5%	28.2%	28.1%	43.7%
Kalamazoo-Portage, MI	332,180	102,518	30.9%	50.1%	49.9%	23.6%	46.9%	29.5%
Kalispell, MT micro	93,068	20,619	22.2%	42.0%	58.0%	33.2%	33.9%	32.9%
Kankakee, IL	112,120	27,483	24.5%	49.8%	50.2%	28.2%	41.5%	30.2%
Kansas City, MO-KS	2,052,048	514,311	25.1%	50.1%	49.9%	27.2%	34.6%	38.3%
Kennewick-Richland, WA	271,124	72,414	26.7%	51.4%	48.6%	30.4%	34.5%	35.1%
Killeen-Temple, TX	423,253	135,230	32.0%	51.8%	48.2%	21.9%	40.6%	37.5%
Kingsport-Bristol-Bristol, TN-VA	308,643	67,737	21.9%	50.5%	49.5%	28.2%	37.2%	34.6%
Kingston, NY	180,998	43,272	23.9%	48.1%	51.9%	26.3%	43.2%	30.5%
Knoxville, TN	852,147	211,969	24.9%	50.5%	49.5%	26.0%	39.5%	34.5%
Kokomo, IN	82,760	17,163	20.7%	49.4%	50.6%	32.1%	34.6%	33.4%
La Crosse-Onalaska, WI-MN	135,512	40,667	30.0%	48.2%	51.8%	20.2%	47.8%	32.0%
Lafayette-West Lafayette, IN	209,611	80,589	38.4%	54.7%	45.3%	14.9%	59.0%	26.2%
Lafayette, LA	479,116	134,207	28.0%	48.9%	51.1%	24.2%	40.1%	35.7%
Lake Charles, LA	202,397	53,104	26.2%	53.4%	46.6%	29.0%	39.5%	31.5%
Lake Havasu City-Kingman, AZ	203,030	40,348	19.9%	51.2%	48.8%	29.7%	35.0%	35.2%
Lakeland-Winter Haven, FL	623,009	149,776	24.0%	51.2%	48.8%	26.0%	37.1%	36.9%
Lancaster, PA	529,600	132,318	25.0%	48.3%	51.7%	26.8%	38.2%	35.0%
Lansing-East Lansing, MI	467,321	146,587	31.4%	50.0%	50.0%	19.4%	50.0%	30.6%
Laredo, TX	262,495	76,850	29.3%	50.0%	50.0%	29.9%	37.1%	33.0%
Las Cruces, NM	213,460	66,940	31.4%	52.0%	48.0%	24.3%	48.4%	27.2%
Las Vegas-Henderson-Paradise, NV	2,027,868	518,566	25.6%	50.8%	49.2%	25.5%	35.2%	39.3%
Lawrence, KS	114,322	44,291	38.7%	51.7%	48.3%	11.3%	55.7%	32.9%
Lawton, OK	131,396	41,646	31.7%	57.0%	43.0%	19.9%	44.4%	35.7%
Lebanon, PA	135,486	28,438	21.0%	50.2%	49.8%	29.3%	38.4%	32.3%
Lewiston-Auburn, ME	107,604	26,538	24.7%	49.7%	50.3%	25.5%	36.0%	38.5%
Lewiston, ID-WA	62,025	15,034	24.2%	52.6%	47.4%	20.9%	47.3%	31.8%
Lexington-Fayette, KY	489,435	138,471	28.3%	50.6%	49.4%	22.5%	42.2%	35.3%
Lima, OH	105,298	26,290	25.0%	54.1%	45.9%	24.9%	41.0%	34.1%
Lincoln, NE	316,941	100,294	31.6%	51.6%	48.4%	18.6%	48.9%	32.6%
Little Rock-North Little Rock-Conway, AR	723,743	195,299	27.0%	51.7%	48.3%	24.5%	36.2%	39.4%
Logan, UT-ID	129,956	47,715	36.7%	47.7%	52.3%	23.4%	42.7%	33.9%
Longview, TX	216,530	58,630	27.1%	51.8%	48.2%	26.5%	40.0%	33.5%
Longview, WA	101,860	23,187	22.8%	48.5%	51.5%	30.1%	36.8%	33.1%
Los Angeles-Long Beach-Anaheim, CA	13,131,431	3,542,436	27.0%	51.0%	49.0%	24.2%	37.4%	38.4%
Louisville/Jefferson County, KY-IN	1,262,928	311,466	24.7%	50.5%	49.5%	27.8%	35.2%	37.1%
Lubbock, TX	304,830	99,246	32.6%	52.1%	47.9%	20.6%	49.8%	29.6%
Lumberton, NC micro	134,841	32,622	24.2%	49.9%	50.1%	28.9%	42.8%	28.3%
Lynchburg, VA	260,792	70,265	26.9%	46.4%	53.6%	23.1%	47.1%	29.8%
Macon, GA	230,300	62,863	27.3%	47.8%	52.2%	24.4%	42.4%	33.2%
Madera, CA	152,389	43,066	28.3%	51.1%	48.9%	27.9%	35.8%	36.3%
Madison, WI	627,431	189,097	30.1%	50.9%	49.1%	20.5%	41.1%	38.4%
Manchester-Nashua, NH	403,985	94,570	23.4%	48.9%	51.1%	27.6%	34.9%	37.5%
Manhattan, KS	98,085	44,867	45.7%	58.9%	41.1%	12.3%	58.5%	29.2%
Mankato-North Mankato, MN	98,560	33,593	34.1%	49.9%	50.1%	16.9%	56.5%	26.6%
Mansfield, OH	121,773	28,039	23.0%	52.6%	47.4%	27.4%	39.1%	33.5%
McAllen-Edinburg-Mission, TX	815,996	238,715	29.3%	50.3%	49.7%	31.5%	37.4%	31.1%

Table A-4: Metropolitan/Micropolitan Statistical Areas—Summary Population Characteristics—*Continued*

	Total 2013 ACS Population	Millennial Population Age 13 to 31	Millennials as Percent of Total	Millennial Percentage by Gender		Millennial Percentage by Age		
				Male	Female	13 to 17	18 to 24	25 to 31
Medford, OR	208,545	45,840	22.0%	49.3%	50.7%	25.4%	37.8%	36.8%
Memphis, TN-MS-AR	1,343,850	367,734	27.4%	49.9%	50.1%	27.4%	37.6%	35.0%
Merced, CA	263,228	80,879	30.7%	52.7%	47.3%	29.4%	38.9%	31.6%
Meridian, MS micro	103,704	25,504	24.6%	53.1%	46.9%	22.1%	45.9%	32.0%
Miami-Fort Lauderdale-West Palm Beach, FL	5,828,191	1,390,066	23.9%	50.8%	49.2%	24.6%	36.5%	38.9%
Michigan City-La Porte, IN	111,281	27,693	24.9%	54.6%	45.4%	28.0%	33.0%	39.0%
Midland, MI	83,919	21,484	25.6%	46.9%	53.1%	25.4%	38.0%	36.6%
Midland, TX	155,723	45,864	29.5%	54.7%	45.3%	24.1%	35.0%	40.9%
Milwaukee-Waukesha-West Allis, WI	1,569,659	407,569	26.0%	49.5%	50.5%	25.0%	36.3%	38.7%
Minneapolis-St. Paul-Bloomington, MN-WI	3,459,146	874,497	25.3%	50.4%	49.6%	26.5%	33.5%	40.0%
Missoula, MT	111,807	36,652	32.8%	46.7%	53.3%	19.4%	44.8%	35.8%
Mobile, AL	414,079	106,088	25.6%	48.8%	51.2%	24.6%	39.6%	35.8%
Modesto, CA	525,491	148,186	28.2%	51.2%	48.8%	28.4%	37.5%	34.1%
Monroe, LA	178,565	50,987	28.6%	47.8%	52.2%	25.7%	39.8%	34.5%
Monroe, MI	150,376	35,012	23.3%	52.9%	47.1%	29.0%	37.9%	33.2%
Montgomery, AL	376,066	100,029	26.6%	48.4%	51.6%	24.2%	39.2%	36.6%
Morgantown, WV	136,133	49,494	36.4%	53.2%	46.8%	12.4%	56.2%	31.4%
Morristown, TN	115,197	24,459	21.2%	50.7%	49.3%	23.7%	38.3%	38.0%
Mount Vernon-Anacortes, WA	118,837	27,206	22.9%	50.2%	49.8%	26.5%	40.7%	32.8%
Muncie, IN	117,484	39,030	33.2%	47.4%	52.6%	14.3%	61.9%	23.8%
Muskegon, MI	171,008	40,756	23.8%	48.6%	51.4%	32.6%	34.7%	32.7%
Myrtle Beach-Conway-North Myrtle Beach, SC-NC	404,951	82,532	20.4%	52.1%	47.9%	23.0%	39.3%	37.7%
Napa, CA	140,326	33,246	23.7%	51.7%	48.3%	28.0%	39.6%	32.4%
Naples-Immokalee-Marco Island, FL	339,642	62,196	18.3%	54.1%	45.9%	27.9%	36.3%	35.8%
Nashville-Davidson–Murfreesboro–Franklin, TN	1,757,424	452,984	25.8%	50.3%	49.7%	24.9%	36.4%	38.7%
New Bern, NC	128,853	34,621	26.9%	61.7%	38.3%	17.9%	43.7%	38.4%
New Castle, PA micro	89,333	18,981	21.2%	49.1%	50.9%	32.2%	37.2%	30.6%
New Haven-Milford, CT	862,287	221,657	25.7%	49.5%	50.5%	24.8%	39.1%	36.1%
New Orleans-Metairie, LA	1,240,977	308,913	24.9%	49.9%	50.1%	23.4%	35.2%	41.4%
New Philadelphia-Dover, OH micro	92,672	21,241	22.9%	50.0%	50.0%	31.8%	34.1%	34.1%
New York-Newark-Jersey City, NY-NJ-PA	19,949,502	5,115,314	25.6%	50.4%	49.6%	24.4%	36.2%	39.5%
Niles-Benton Harbor, MI	155,252	34,333	22.1%	53.0%	47.0%	24.7%	39.7%	35.7%
North Port-Sarasota-Bradenton, FL	732,535	134,039	18.3%	51.5%	48.5%	28.5%	38.9%	32.6%
Norwich-New London, CT	274,150	70,256	25.6%	52.5%	47.5%	22.0%	42.0%	35.9%
Ocala, FL	337,362	66,776	19.8%	51.3%	48.7%	26.8%	36.6%	36.6%
Ocean City, NJ	95,897	19,995	20.9%	52.4%	47.6%	24.0%	39.1%	36.9%
Odessa, TX	149,378	45,187	30.3%	52.2%	47.8%	24.5%	37.0%	38.4%
Ogden-Clearfield, UT	621,853	173,619	27.9%	49.2%	50.8%	31.4%	33.5%	35.1%
Ogdensburg-Massena, NY micro	111,963	31,306	28.0%	53.9%	46.1%	21.1%	51.5%	27.4%
Oklahoma City, OK	1,319,677	350,851	26.6%	51.1%	48.9%	22.3%	38.7%	39.0%
Olympia-Tumwater, WA	262,388	68,980	26.3%	52.5%	47.5%	24.5%	34.9%	40.6%
Omaha-Council Bluffs, NE-IA	895,999	244,099	27.2%	50.0%	50.0%	25.9%	34.9%	39.2%
Orangeburg, SC micro	90,942	24,189	26.6%	52.3%	47.7%	29.6%	46.1%	24.3%
Orlando-Kissimmee-Sanford, FL	2,267,846	621,615	27.4%	50.6%	49.4%	25.2%	37.0%	37.8%
Oshkosh-Neenah, WI	169,541	46,883	27.7%	53.3%	46.7%	20.6%	44.1%	35.3%
Ottawa-Peru, IL micro	151,378	26,791	17.7%	50.5%	49.5%	30.9%	34.1%	35.0%
Owensboro, KY	117,149	27,593	23.6%	49.5%	50.5%	26.4%	37.2%	36.4%
Oxnard-Thousand Oaks-Ventura, CA	839,620	213,780	25.5%	52.0%	48.0%	27.0%	39.0%	34.0%
Palm Bay-Melbourne-Titusville, FL	550,823	112,681	20.5%	50.3%	49.7%	26.8%	39.1%	34.1%
Panama City, FL	191,522	46,495	24.3%	53.4%	46.6%	22.6%	35.5%	41.9%
Parkersburg-Vienna, WV	92,519	19,813	21.4%	46.7%	53.3%	25.6%	39.2%	35.2%
Pensacola-Ferry Pass-Brent, FL	466,913	127,327	27.3%	54.1%	45.9%	21.6%	41.9%	36.5%
Peoria, IL	382,776	96,218	25.1%	50.8%	49.2%	25.9%	36.7%	37.4%
Philadelphia-Camden-Wilmington, PA-NJ-DE-MD	6,034,678	1,580,042	26.2%	50.2%	49.8%	25.0%	37.4%	37.6%
Phoenix-Mesa-Scottsdale, AZ	4,398,762	1,160,054	26.4%	51.8%	48.2%	26.8%	35.9%	37.3%
Pine Bluff, AR	96,415	25,971	26.9%	53.7%	46.3%	25.8%	45.1%	29.1%
Pittsburgh, PA	2,360,867	559,230	23.7%	51.0%	49.0%	24.2%	38.3%	37.5%
Pittsfield, MA	129,585	30,536	23.6%	52.9%	47.1%	25.1%	43.7%	31.2%
Pocatello, ID	83,249	25,609	30.8%	49.6%	50.4%	28.7%	42.1%	29.1%
Port St. Lucie, FL	438,095	90,678	20.7%	54.5%	45.5%	28.4%	35.9%	35.7%
Portland-South Portland, ME	519,900	118,095	22.7%	49.6%	50.4%	26.8%	38.3%	35.0%
Portland-Vancouver-Hillsboro, OR-WA	2,315,089	580,285	25.1%	49.8%	50.2%	25.0%	34.4%	40.6%
Pottsville, PA micro	146,920	30,617	20.8%	53.9%	46.1%	25.3%	36.5%	38.2%
Prescott, AZ	215,133	40,349	18.8%	51.8%	48.2%	29.2%	35.6%	35.1%
Providence-Warwick, RI-MA	1,604,291	414,057	25.8%	50.4%	49.6%	23.5%	41.9%	34.5%
Provo-Orem, UT	562,338	203,200	36.1%	50.1%	49.9%	23.4%	46.9%	29.6%
Pueblo, CO	161,451	41,292	25.6%	52.2%	47.8%	25.1%	38.2%	36.7%
Punta Gorda, FL	164,736	26,086	15.8%	50.0%	50.0%	28.5%	39.0%	32.5%
Racine, WI	195,041	45,497	23.3%	54.3%	45.7%	30.4%	31.2%	38.4%
Raleigh, NC	1,214,516	320,952	26.4%	51.3%	48.7%	28.2%	36.0%	35.8%
Rapid City, SD	141,324	34,720	24.6%	55.6%	44.4%	25.7%	38.2%	36.1%
Reading, PA	413,521	103,706	25.1%	50.5%	49.5%	27.3%	40.2%	32.5%
Redding, CA	178,980	43,154	24.1%	52.4%	47.6%	25.5%	39.5%	35.1%
Reno, NV	439,047	113,990	26.0%	50.1%	49.9%	24.0%	38.6%	37.4%
Richmond, VA	1,248,513	318,467	25.5%	49.9%	50.1%	26.3%	36.4%	37.2%

Table A-4: Metropolitan/Micropolitan Statistical Areas—Summary Population Characteristics—*Continued*

	Total 2013 ACS Population	Millennial Population Age 13 to 31	Millennials as Percent of Total	Millennial Percentage by Gender		Millennial Percentage by Age		
				Male	Female	13 to 17	18 to 24	25 to 31
Riverside-San Bernardino-Ontario, CA.........	4,380,878	1,236,472	28.2%	51.2%	48.8%	27.5%	38.3%	34.2%
Roanoke, VA........................	311,607	71,344	22.9%	49.7%	50.3%	27.5%	38.3%	34.2%
Rochester, MN.......................	211,853	52,035	24.6%	48.5%	51.5%	24.2%	38.3%	37.4%
Rochester, NY.......................	1,083,278	283,108	26.1%	51.1%	48.9%	24.5%	40.5%	35.0%
Rockford, IL.........................	344,623	86,491	25.1%	48.9%	51.1%	31.2%	37.9%	30.8%
Rocky Mount, NC....................	150,667	34,744	23.1%	46.0%	54.0%	30.8%	40.8%	28.4%
Rome, GA............................	95,821	23,869	24.9%	47.7%	52.3%	28.2%	41.2%	30.6%
Roseburg, OR micro.................	106,940	20,735	19.4%	49.3%	50.7%	25.6%	37.1%	37.3%
Sacramento–Roseville–Arden-Arcade, CA.......	2,215,770	573,311	25.9%	50.2%	49.8%	26.8%	37.7%	35.5%
Saginaw, MI.........................	196,542	49,901	25.4%	48.8%	51.2%	26.4%	43.5%	30.1%
Salem, OH micro.....................	105,893	23,852	22.5%	53.6%	46.4%	28.3%	34.8%	36.9%
Salem, OR...........................	400,408	106,773	26.7%	53.6%	46.4%	26.7%	40.7%	32.6%
Salinas, CA..........................	428,826	123,388	28.8%	52.4%	47.6%	26.1%	38.3%	35.6%
Salisbury, MD-DE....................	385,438	89,343	23.2%	49.5%	50.5%	22.5%	44.1%	33.4%
Salt Lake City, UT...................	1,140,483	322,656	28.3%	51.1%	48.9%	26.4%	34.1%	39.6%
San Angelo, TX......................	116,914	34,968	29.9%	55.4%	44.6%	22.7%	40.9%	36.4%
San Antonio-New Braunfels, TX.....	2,277,516	643,590	28.3%	52.2%	47.8%	26.2%	37.7%	36.2%
San Diego-Carlsbad, CA.............	3,211,252	935,309	29.1%	53.0%	47.0%	21.1%	39.1%	39.7%
San Francisco-Oakland-Hayward, CA.............	4,516,276	1,111,639	24.6%	51.2%	48.8%	22.3%	34.2%	43.5%
San Jose-Sunnyvale-Santa Clara, CA.............	1,919,641	479,231	25.0%	52.4%	47.6%	24.2%	34.6%	41.3%
San Luis Obispo-Paso Robles-Arroyo Grande, CA........................	276,443	80,673	29.2%	54.5%	45.5%	16.1%	54.6%	29.4%
Santa Cruz-Watsonville, CA..........	269,419	75,403	28.0%	53.3%	46.7%	19.3%	52.2%	28.4%
Santa Fe, NM........................	147,423	29,956	20.3%	50.2%	49.8%	26.4%	36.8%	36.8%
Santa Maria-Santa Barbara, CA......	435,697	137,268	31.5%	51.4%	48.6%	21.3%	49.5%	29.3%
Santa Rosa, CA......................	495,025	120,963	24.4%	52.1%	47.9%	26.4%	37.6%	36.0%
Savannah, GA........................	366,047	104,999	28.7%	53.3%	46.7%	20.2%	41.8%	38.0%
Scranton–Wilkes-Barre–Hazleton, PA	562,037	135,447	24.1%	49.7%	50.3%	24.3%	41.5%	34.2%
Seattle-Tacoma-Bellevue, WA.......	3,610,105	935,702	25.9%	51.3%	48.7%	23.2%	34.4%	42.5%
Sebastian-Vero Beach, FL	141,994	27,498	19.4%	53.0%	47.0%	32.2%	35.0%	32.9%
Sebring, FL..........................	97,616	17,203	17.6%	60.7%	39.3%	25.7%	39.8%	34.5%
Sheboygan, WI.......................	114,922	25,416	22.1%	50.0%	50.0%	33.6%	31.0%	35.5%
Sherman-Denison, TX................	122,353	30,297	24.8%	50.3%	49.7%	26.0%	36.6%	37.4%
Show Low, AZ micro.................	107,322	28,335	26.4%	49.1%	50.9%	29.5%	36.9%	33.5%
Shreveport-Bossier City, LA	446,471	123,377	27.6%	51.0%	49.0%	23.1%	39.9%	37.1%
Sierra Vista-Douglas, AZ.............	129,473	32,345	25.0%	51.9%	48.1%	25.7%	38.2%	36.2%
Sioux City, IA-NE-SD................	168,491	44,165	26.2%	51.2%	48.8%	30.2%	38.1%	31.7%
Sioux Falls, SD......................	243,637	63,236	26.0%	51.2%	48.8%	21.5%	37.9%	40.6%
South Bend-Mishawaka, IN-MI	318,619	82,057	25.8%	50.6%	49.4%	29.4%	39.9%	30.7%
Spartanburg, SC......................	318,999	84,899	26.6%	47.9%	52.1%	27.7%	40.4%	31.9%
Spokane-Spokane Valley, WA........	535,189	147,190	27.5%	52.0%	48.0%	25.3%	37.0%	37.8%
Springfield, IL.......................	211,695	50,200	23.7%	48.6%	51.4%	25.7%	36.1%	38.3%
Springfield, MA......................	626,915	175,021	27.9%	48.9%	51.1%	25.0%	45.2%	29.8%
Springfield, MO......................	450,498	129,457	28.7%	49.2%	50.8%	24.0%	42.4%	33.5%
Springfield, OH......................	136,167	32,974	24.2%	47.1%	52.9%	29.1%	37.7%	33.2%
St. Cloud, MN........................	191,306	59,001	30.8%	54.1%	45.9%	20.0%	49.7%	30.3%
St. George, UT.......................	147,800	36,461	24.7%	48.8%	51.2%	29.6%	41.0%	29.5%
St. Joseph, MO-KS...................	128,989	32,200	25.0%	53.2%	46.8%	23.9%	39.8%	36.3%
St. Louis, MO-IL.....................	2,799,609	701,224	25.0%	49.1%	50.9%	25.8%	35.8%	38.4%
State College, PA....................	155,403	65,126	41.9%	52.6%	47.4%	10.7%	67.8%	21.5%
Staunton-Waynesboro, VA...........	117,077	27,051	23.1%	49.5%	50.5%	19.0%	48.3%	32.6%
Stockton-Lodi, CA....................	704,379	193,213	27.4%	52.6%	47.4%	29.9%	38.1%	31.9%
Sumter, SC..........................	108,123	30,387	28.1%	59.1%	40.9%	24.4%	43.9%	31.7%
Sunbury, PA micro...................	94,076	19,987	21.2%	55.1%	44.9%	22.0%	38.4%	39.6%
Syracuse, NY........................	661,934	170,167	25.7%	51.0%	49.0%	25.0%	42.0%	33.0%
Tallahassee, FL......................	373,961	137,443	36.8%	49.5%	50.5%	15.6%	55.1%	29.3%
Tampa-St. Petersburg-Clearwater, FL...........	2,870,569	670,366	23.4%	50.5%	49.5%	25.4%	36.3%	38.3%
Terre Haute, IN......................	168,400	46,772	27.8%	53.2%	46.8%	20.0%	44.5%	35.5%
Texarkana, TX-AR...................	149,800	38,572	25.7%	51.1%	48.9%	23.2%	36.4%	40.4%
The Villages, FL	107,056	11,362	10.6%	52.0%	48.0%	17.0%	37.0%	46.0%
Toledo, OH..........................	608,145	170,511	28.0%	49.2%	50.8%	23.8%	42.7%	33.5%
Topeka, KS..........................	234,203	54,331	23.2%	51.5%	48.5%	28.6%	35.7%	35.7%
Torrington, CT micro.................	186,924	39,336	21.0%	52.0%	48.0%	30.9%	34.7%	34.4%
Traverse City, MI micro..............	146,358	31,826	21.7%	52.5%	47.5%	29.9%	35.9%	34.2%
Trenton, NJ.........................	370,414	97,275	26.3%	53.6%	46.4%	25.7%	41.7%	32.7%
Truckee-Grass Valley, CA micro	98,200	19,138	19.5%	56.8%	43.2%	30.8%	38.6%	30.6%
Tucson, AZ..........................	996,554	272,490	27.3%	51.1%	48.9%	23.1%	44.6%	32.3%
Tullahoma-Manchester, TN micro	100,895	23,786	23.6%	51.9%	48.1%	36.0%	37.4%	26.6%
Tulsa, OK...........................	961,321	242,714	25.2%	50.6%	49.4%	27.1%	36.2%	36.7%
Tupelo, MS micro....................	139,671	35,356	25.3%	48.0%	52.0%	28.7%	39.9%	31.3%
Tuscaloosa, AL......................	234,008	77,812	33.3%	54.3%	45.7%	18.6%	51.4%	29.9%
Tyler, TX............................	216,080	57,353	26.5%	49.8%	50.2%	26.9%	38.8%	34.3%
Urban Honolulu, HI	983,429	265,827	27.0%	53.7%	46.3%	21.5%	37.6%	40.9%
Utica-Rome, NY.....................	297,766	73,705	24.8%	50.9%	49.1%	26.5%	39.7%	33.8%
Valdosta, GA........................	143,947	48,976	34.0%	52.5%	47.5%	19.7%	50.5%	29.9%
Vallejo-Fairfield, CA.................	424,788	114,250	26.9%	52.0%	48.0%	24.4%	38.0%	37.6%
Victoria, TX.........................	96,135	25,055	26.1%	53.7%	46.3%	31.7%	37.5%	30.8%
Vineland-Bridgeton, NJ..............	157,332	41,175	26.2%	53.0%	47.0%	24.9%	32.2%	42.9%
Virginia Beach-Norfolk-Newport News, VA-NC...............................	1,706,816	498,520	29.2%	51.7%	48.3%	21.2%	40.9%	37.9%

Table A-4: Metropolitan/Micropolitan Statistical Areas—Summary Population Characteristics—*Continued*

	Total 2013 ACS Population	Millennial Population Age 13 to 31	Millennials as Percent of Total	Millennial Percentage by Gender		Millennial Percentage by Age		
				Male	Female	13 to 17	18 to 24	25 to 31
Visalia-Porterville, CA..............................	454,143	132,184	29.1%	50.3%	49.7%	27.5%	37.6%	34.9%
Waco, TX..	257,083	77,186	30.0%	49.1%	50.9%	19.8%	49.3%	30.9%
Walla Walla, WA....................................	63,361	16,753	26.4%	54.6%	45.4%	20.3%	44.4%	35.3%
Warner Robins, GA	185,623	53,774	29.0%	49.0%	51.0%	26.6%	37.6%	35.8%
Washington-Arlington-Alexandria, DC-VA-MD-WV	5,950,214	1,557,927	26.2%	50.0%	50.0%	23.8%	34.7%	41.5%
Waterloo-Cedar Falls, IA........................	169,484	52,275	30.8%	46.4%	53.6%	19.3%	52.1%	28.7%
Watertown-Fort Drum, NY	119,504	36,656	30.7%	57.4%	42.6%	20.9%	41.1%	38.0%
Wausau, WI...	135,416	31,554	23.3%	53.2%	46.8%	29.2%	35.9%	35.0%
Weirton-Steubenville, WV-OH	124,718	28,248	22.6%	53.1%	46.9%	29.2%	42.5%	28.3%
Wenatchee, WA.....................................	113,438	27,971	24.7%	51.0%	49.0%	29.0%	31.2%	39.8%
Wheeling, WV-OH	145,757	32,441	22.3%	51.4%	48.6%	29.9%	40.6%	29.5%
Whitewater-Elkhorn, WI micro	102,945	27,115	26.3%	50.3%	49.7%	25.7%	41.6%	32.7%
Wichita Falls, TX	151,201	44,773	29.6%	59.5%	40.5%	20.1%	42.8%	37.1%
Wichita, KS	637,989	168,613	26.4%	51.9%	48.1%	26.8%	34.7%	38.5%
Williamsport, PA	116,754	27,887	23.9%	49.8%	50.2%	20.7%	49.6%	29.7%
Wilmington, NC......................................	268,601	70,426	26.2%	51.9%	48.1%	19.4%	46.7%	33.9%
Winchester, VA-WV	126,900	29,169	23.0%	50.3%	49.7%	31.1%	37.2%	31.7%
Winston-Salem, NC................................	650,820	156,727	24.1%	48.5%	51.5%	29.0%	38.6%	32.4%
Wooster, OH micro................................	115,071	28,468	24.7%	50.3%	49.7%	30.3%	39.1%	30.6%
Worcester, MA-CT.................................	926,710	228,311	24.6%	51.3%	48.7%	26.9%	39.3%	33.8%
Yakima, WA...	247,044	65,994	26.7%	50.9%	49.1%	27.9%	38.2%	33.9%
York-Hanover, PA..................................	438,965	97,575	22.2%	50.5%	49.5%	27.6%	38.0%	34.4%
Youngstown-Warren-Boardman, OH-PA	555,506	130,034	23.4%	52.4%	47.6%	29.4%	36.8%	33.8%
Yuba City, CA	168,690	44,330	26.3%	51.1%	48.9%	25.8%	37.6%	36.6%
Yuma, AZ	201,201	59,396	29.5%	56.4%	43.6%	26.3%	41.0%	32.7%

PART B
RACE AND ETHNICITY

PART B. RACE AND ETHNICITY

RACE AND ETHNICITY

The nation's population continues to grow more diverse, but that diversity isn't just in the large cities and metropolitan areas. Diversity is not uniform across the country, and large differences occur at smaller geographic levels.

Racial and ethnic identification in the Census is obtained in a number of different ways, including direct questions on race and Hispanic Origin. Other questions obtain data on ancestry, language spoken at home, and place of birth. The Census and American Community Survey also allow for respondents to identify with more than one racial group. The term race "Alone" means the respondent identifies with that single racial group. Those who identify with two or more racial groups are identified as "Multi-race." Hispanic Origin is obtained in a separate question, and a relatively small number of individuals identify themselves as "Some Other Race."

Some of these categories are not included in these tables because of their small sample sizes. The tables in this section present only selected major response categories–White, Non-Hispanic; Black, Non-Hispanic; Asian, Non-Hispanic; and Hispanic. The race categories, American Indian and Alaskan Native, Multi-race, and Some Other Race are excluded because of the small population size. However, the counties, cities, and metropolitan/ micropolitan areas with large populations of Native American Millennials are identified in the table below.

Unlike many other tables in this volume, some of the ACS sample population counts by race and Hispanic Origin are often too small to be reported for all geographies. This can be due to the small sample sizes noted above, but it can also be due to the geographic allocation methods described in the section Defining the Millennials. In these cases, the random sample record allocation method simply did not select any records of the Hispanic Origin group. This certainly does not mean that there are no individuals in those groups, simply that the method did not select any records. As a result, some geographic areas will have these categories indicated by "na." Part B — Race and Ethnicity presents data only for the Millennial ages of 13 to 31 and therefore may exhibit different distributions of the racial and Hispanic Origin population than that for the general population. For example, of the total U.S. Millennial population, 55.9 percent are White, Non-Hispanic, compared to 62.4 percent of the general population. The Asian, Non-Hispanic population represents 5.2 percent of Millennials much like the 5.0 percent in the general population.

White, Non-Hispanic

As noted above, 55.9 percent of the nation's Millennials are White, Non-Hispanic, but the proportion by

Percent Native American for Areas with 5 Percent or More Native American Population

Area Name	Millennials as Percent of Population		Area Name	Millennials as Percent of Population
Counties			**Counties**	
Canadian County, Oklahoma	7.3%		Pinal County, Arizona	6.7%
Cleveland County, Oklahoma	11.3%		Robeson County, North Carolina	32.3%
Coconino County, Arizona	23.1%		San Juan County, New Mexico	38.9%
Flathead County, Montana	10.9%		Sandoval County, New Mexico	16.7%
Lafourche Parish, Louisiana	5.0%		Santa Fe County, New Mexico	5.1%
Missoula County, Montana	5.5%		Tulsa County, Oklahoma	5.3%
Navajo County, Arizona	65.7%		Yellowstone County, Montana	9.6%
Places			**Places**	
Albuquerque city, New Mexico	5.4%		Rio Rancho city, New Mexico	17.8%
Billings city, Montana	6.6%			
Metropolitan Statistical Areas			**Metropolitan Statistical Areas**	
Albuquerque, NM	6.7%		Kalispell, MT micro	11.1%
Billings, MT	8.9%		Lumberton, NC micro	36.8%
Farmington, NM	39.6%		Missoula, MT	5.5%
Flagstaff, AZ	23.1%		Rapid City, SD	6.8%
Fort Smith, AR-OK	8.4%		Santa Fe, NM	5.2%
Grand Forks, ND-MN	5.6%		Show Low, AZ micro+B2	65.8%
Great Falls, MT	12.4%		Tulsa, OK	7.8%

Minority Millennials as a Percent of the Total Population

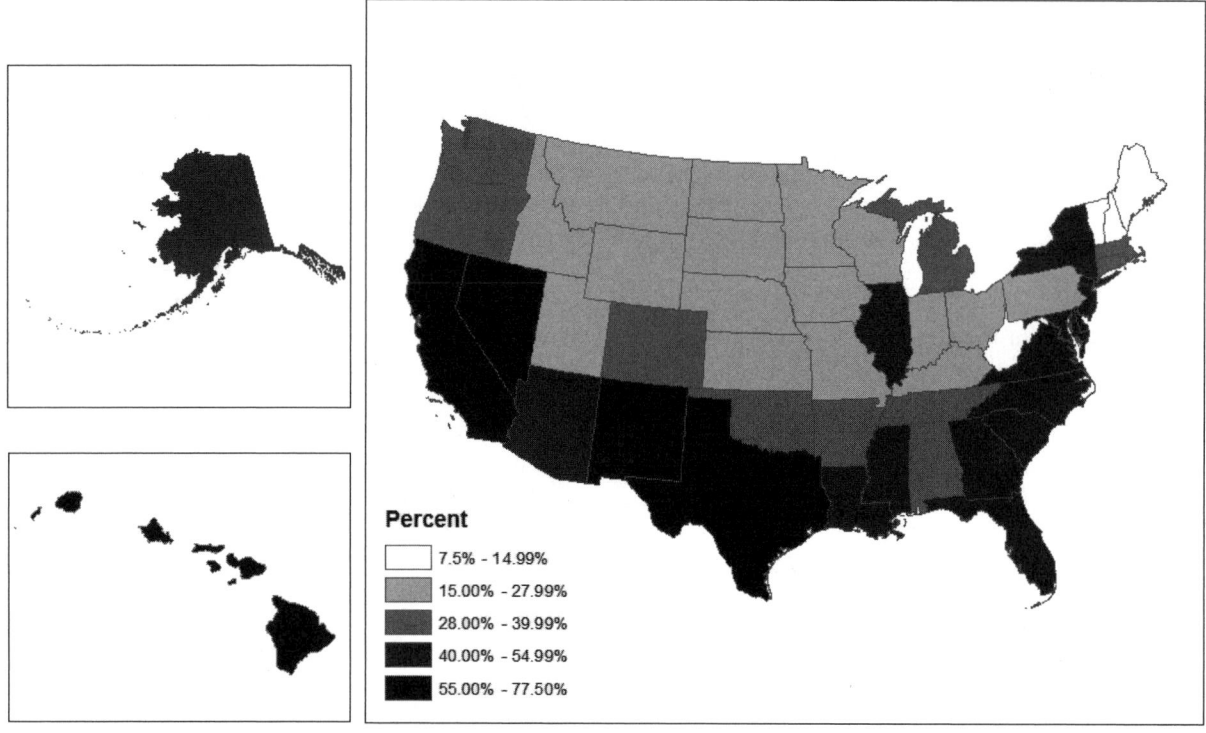

Percent
- 7.5% - 14.99%
- 15.00% - 27.99%
- 28.00% - 39.99%
- 40.00% - 54.99%
- 55.00% - 77.50%

state shows considerable variation ranging from a low of 22.6 percent in Hawaii to a high of 92.4 percent in Vermont. In 40 of the states and District of Columbia more than half of the Millennial population is White, Non-Hispanic, and in only two states (Hawaii and New Mexico) is it below 30 percent. By age, the percentage of Millennials in the 13 to 17 and 25 to 31 age groups show the greatest variation. In the 13 to 17 category, the District of Columbia is lowest at 3.5 percent and New Jersey is highest at 28.7 percent. The District of Columbia is the real outlier, as the only other state below 20 percent is Hawaii (11.9 percent). Among the 25 to 31 age group, DC has the highest percentage at 63.1 percent, with Hawaii as the second highest at 50.6 percent. Just under one-third (32.5 percent) of the Millennial population is 25 to 31 in Mississippi. In the 18 to 24 age group, all states fall between 33 and 45 percent.

There is increasing variation as the geographic area of analysis gets smaller. For counties, the percentage of their Millennial population that is White, Non-Hispanic varies from a low of 2.2 percent in Webb County, TX, to a high of 95.5 percent in Jefferson County, MO. Only

six counties are below 10 percent White, Non-Hispanic, while 31 counties are above 90 percent. By age, counties show the widest range in the 18 to 24 and 25 to 31 categories, ranging from the mid-teens to more than 70 percent.

The cities of Compton and South Gage, CA have the lowest percentage of Millennials who are White, Non-Hispanic, with values less than one percent. Thirteen cities are below 10 percent. However, 25 cities have greater than 75 percent, with Cedar Rapids, IA, the highest at 87.8 percent. At the metropolitan area level, Laredo, TX, has the lowest percentage with 2.2 percent, while Parkersburg-Vienna, WV, is highest at 96.1 percent. In 21 metros, the percentage of Millennials who are White, Non-Hispanic is greater than 90 percent.

Black, Non-Hispanic
Nationwide, 13.9 percent of Millennials are Black, Non-Hispanic. The percentage is highest in the state of Mississippi at 42.8 percent and lowest in Montana at 0.3 percent. Idaho follows closely as the second lowest percentage Black, Non-Hispanic at 0.8 percent.

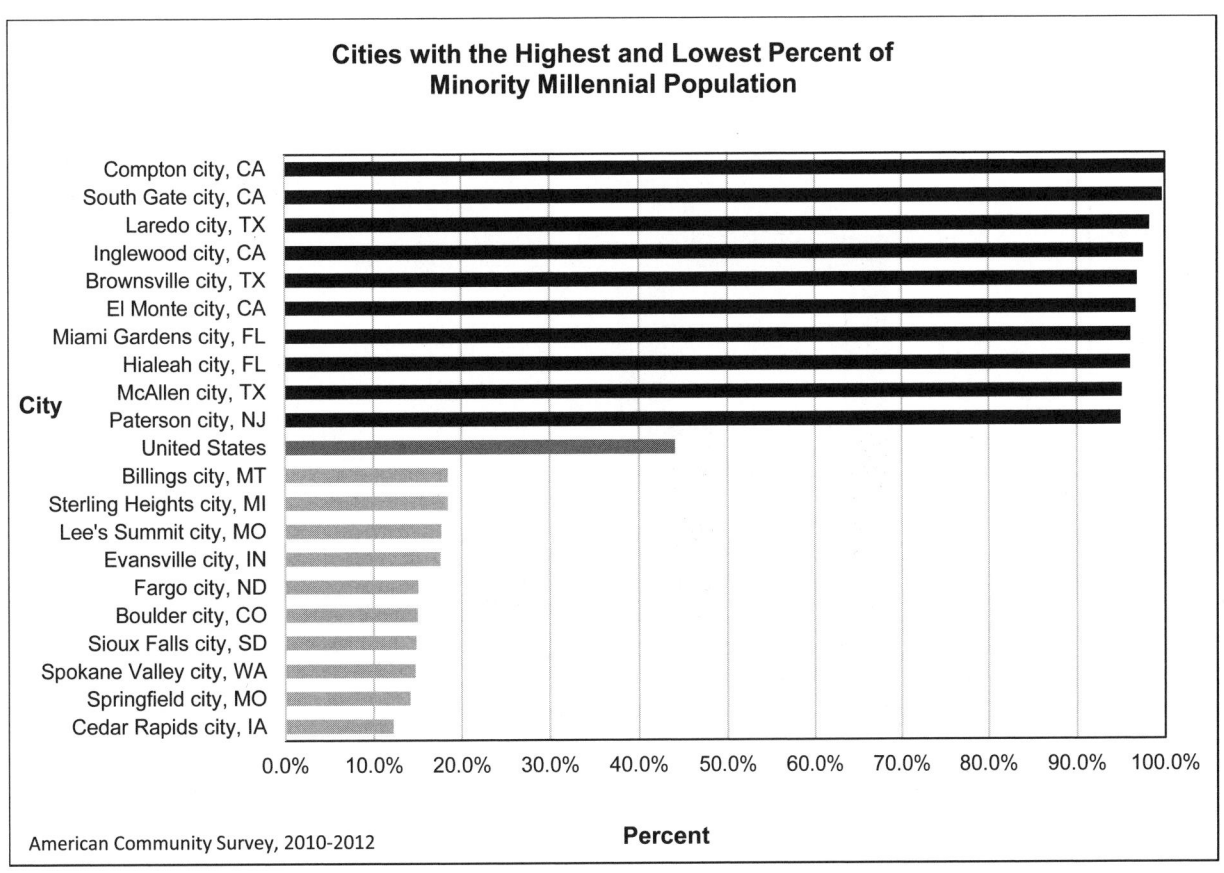

Cities with the Highest and Lowest Percent of Minority Millennial Population

American Community Survey, 2010-2012

The District of Columbia is second highest at 40.0 percent, and the third highest state is Louisiana at 36.0 percent. Thirty-four states are below the national average of 13.9 percent Black, Non-Hispanic.

Each of the Millennial age groups shows wide variation. Among the 13 to 17 population, states range from a low of 9.5 percent in North Dakota to a high of 50.0 percent in Idaho. The 18 to 24 age group varies between the low of 32.3 percent (Utah) and the high of 71.9 percent in North Dakota. While those are the extremes for the 18 to 24 population, 41 states are in a tight range from 35 to 45 percent. Maine has the lowest percentage of Millennials in the 25 to 31 age group at 11.8 percent while Hawaii is highest at 45.4 percent.

In 43 counties the percentage of Millennials who are Black, Non-Hispanic is less than 1 percent, and 214 are below 5 percent. In Hinds County, MS, three of every four (74.8 percent) Millennials is Black, Non-Hispanic, and in 15 counties the percentage is greater than 50 percent.

Similar to the county distribution, in 24 cities the Black, Non-Hispanic population have below 1 percent of the total Millennials and 158 are below 10 percent. Jackson City, MS (77.0 percent) and Detroit City, MI (77.7 percent) have the highest percentages, and 15 cities have over 50 percent. Eight metro/micro areas have too small of a Black, Non-Hispanic population to be reported, and which means that 42 metro/micros have less than one percent while 243 are less than 10 percent. Seven metropolitan/micropolitan areas have over 50 percent, with the Orangeburg, SC micro highest at 62.9 percent.

Asian, Non-Hispanic

Hawaii's Millennial population is the highest percentage at 27.1 percent, more than twice that of the second highest state (California) at 12.4 percent. West Virginia has the lowest percentage of Asian, Non-Hispanics at 0.8 percent but fully 40 states have less than 5 percent and 16 states have less than 2 percent.

There is wide variation by age among the Asian, Non-Hispanic population also. While Wyoming at 0.0 percent is likely a result of the sampling of small numbers, it is clear that the real percentage of 13 to 17 year olds is still quite low. North Dakota and Montana are Western states that are also quite low (2.6 percent and 5.4 percent, respectively), but the District of Columbia is also in that category at only 4.7 percent. Alaska has the

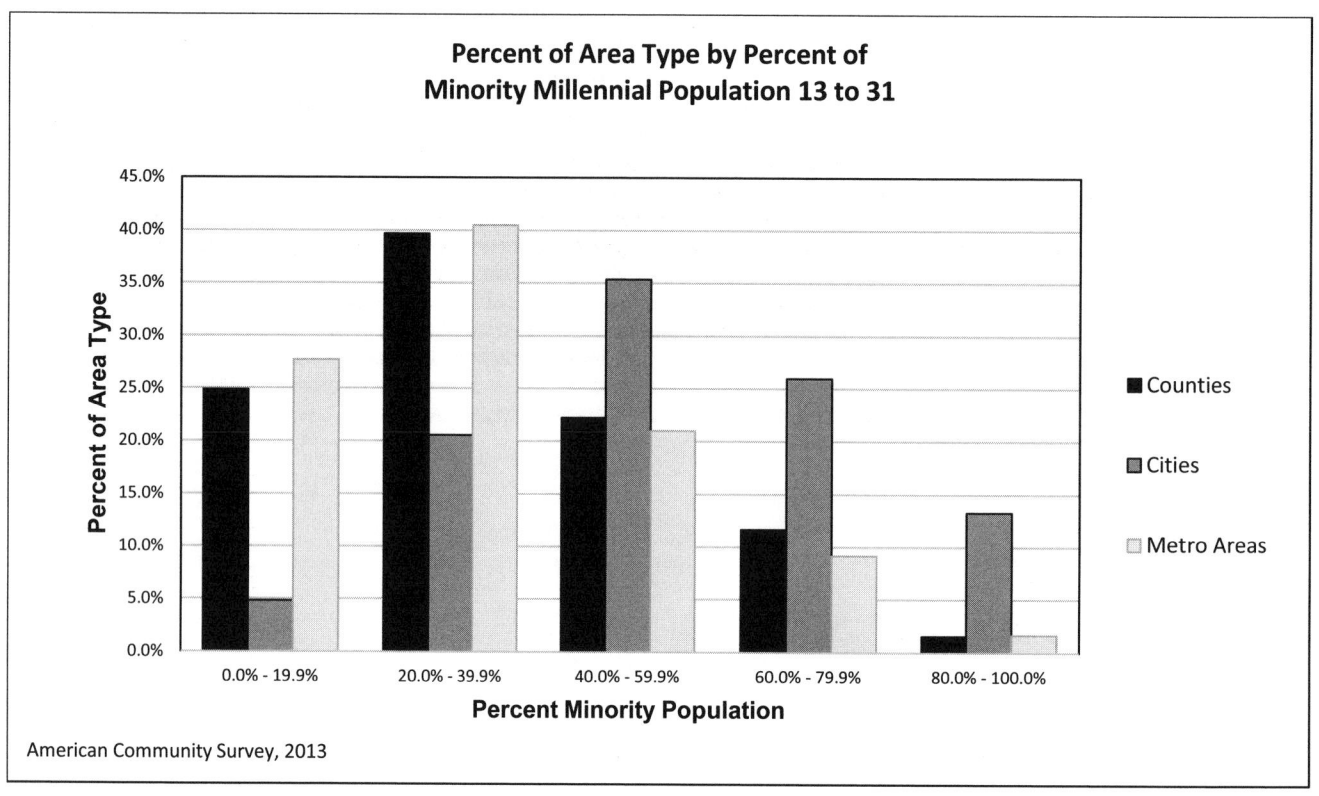

Percent of Area Type by Percent of
Minority Millennial Population 13 to 31

American Community Survey, 2013

highest percentage of 13 to 17 year olds at 28.8 percent. Montana's Millennials are concentrated in the 18 to 24 age group with the highest figure of 77.5 percent, while Wyoming has the highest percentage in the 25 to 31 age group at 61.8 percent.

The smaller Asian, Non-Hispanic population results in no data for 32 counties, and for an additional 106 counties the percentage of the Millennial population is less than 1 percent. In 500 of the 622 counties less than five percent of the Millennial population is Asian, Non-Hispanic. This minority category is highest in Santa Clara County, CA at 31.4 percent.

Among cities, the percentage of Millennials is less than one percent Asian, Non-Hispanic in 24 cities and less than 10 percent in 274 cities. Three California cities have the highest percentages: Fremont (43.6 percent), Santa Clara (44.1 percent) and Sunnyvale (45.7 percent). Metro/micros with less than one percent Asian, Non-Hispanic number 115, with all but 19 below 10 percent. The San Jose-Sunnyvale metro, known for its high-technology sector, is highest with 30.9 percent followed by the Urban Honolulu metro at 29.7 percent.

Hispanic
The Hispanic Millennials are the largest percentage of the population in New Mexico at 53.5 percent, followed

by the other Southern and Western states of California (45.9 percent), Texas (43.8 percent), Arizona (38.2 percent), and Nevada (35.3 percent). Vermont and West Virginia are tied for the lowest percentage at 1.9 percent, and 23 states are below 10 percent.

Among the 13 to 17 year olds, the District of Columbia is lowest at 10.9 percent and Vermont is highest at 39.0 percent. Vermont's Millennials have the lowest percentage in the 18 to 24 age group at 25.7 percent, while nearly two-thirds (61.3 percent) of North Dakota's Millennials are in that age group. Among the 25 to 31 year olds, Maine has the lowest percentage at 13.6 percent, while the District of Columbia is highest at 57.7 percent.

Hispanics make up less than one percent of the Millennial population in nine counties, with Fayette and Cambria counties in Pennsylvania lowest at 0.4 percent. There are 141 counties at less than five percent and 328 less than 10 percent. Webb County, TX is highest at 97.2 percent, followed closely by two other Texas counties—Hidalgo (94.5 percent) and Cameron (92.8 percent). The Millennial population is more than 50 percent Hispanic in 30 counties.

Fargo City, ND (1.0 percent) and Warren City, MI (1.9 percent) have the lowest percentage of Millennials who are Hispanic, though 75 cities are below 10 percent. Five cities are greater than 90 percent: McAllen, TX (90.4 percent), Hialeah, FL (90.6 percent), Brownsville, TX (94.5 percent), South Gate, CA (95.1 percent), and Laredo, TX (97.6 percent). The Laredo, TX metro area is also the highest metro area at 97.1 percent, with two other Texas metro areas close behind: McAllen-Edinburg-Mission (94.5 percent) and Brownsville-Harlingen (92.8 percent).

Table B-1: States—Race and Hispanic Origin by Age

	White, Non-Hispanic					Black, Non-Hispanic				
	Millennial Population		Percent by Age			Millennial Population		Percent by Age		
	Number	Percent	13 to 17	18 to 24	25 to 31	Number	Percent	13 to 17	18 to 24	25 to 31
United States	46,152,155	55.9%	24.6%	38.0%	37.4%	11,480,193	13.9%	25.4%	40.8%	33.9%
Alabama	755,707	60.8%	26.1%	38.9%	35.0%	381,881	30.7%	25.0%	41.8%	33.3%
Alaska	123,227	56.4%	22.2%	38.9%	38.9%	9,011	4.1%	32.3%	39.6%	28.1%
Arizona	802,909	46.0%	24.1%	37.3%	38.6%	82,642	4.7%	24.1%	39.9%	36.0%
Arkansas	514,778	68.2%	25.4%	38.2%	36.4%	134,477	17.8%	25.8%	39.5%	34.7%
California	3,323,444	31.5%	21.8%	37.3%	40.9%	628,033	5.9%	24.5%	41.6%	34.0%
Colorado	884,929	63.0%	22.8%	36.5%	40.7%	60,162	4.3%	26.2%	37.8%	36.0%
Connecticut	547,375	61.5%	27.3%	38.5%	34.1%	103,977	11.7%	24.8%	40.0%	35.2%
Delaware	131,871	56.4%	22.4%	39.7%	38.0%	57,477	24.6%	25.5%	39.3%	35.1%
District of Columbia	90,656	41.9%	3.5%	33.4%	63.1%	86,426	40.0%	19.7%	42.1%	38.3%
Florida	2,219,320	47.2%	23.9%	37.7%	38.4%	928,751	19.7%	24.9%	40.2%	34.9%
Georgia	1,291,153	48.3%	25.6%	38.2%	36.1%	914,382	34.2%	26.6%	39.5%	33.9%
Hawaii	84,016	22.6%	11.9%	37.5%	50.6%	12,051	3.2%	12.8%	41.8%	45.4%
Idaho	330,545	78.3%	28.4%	37.5%	34.1%	3,349	0.8%	50.0%	35.3%	14.7%
Illinois	1,922,218	56.8%	24.8%	36.4%	38.8%	525,011	15.5%	26.6%	40.5%	32.9%
Indiana	1,295,460	76.5%	25.8%	39.3%	35.0%	173,907	10.3%	28.5%	39.8%	31.8%
Iowa	654,608	82.7%	25.2%	40.0%	34.7%	35,523	4.5%	28.3%	38.1%	33.6%
Kansas	550,900	72.2%	25.2%	39.0%	35.8%	52,629	6.9%	24.7%	39.0%	36.3%
Kentucky	912,903	82.0%	26.1%	38.3%	35.6%	111,138	10.0%	24.2%	40.7%	35.1%
Louisiana	674,241	54.3%	24.4%	37.2%	38.4%	446,406	36.0%	25.0%	41.0%	34.0%
Maine	274,760	90.5%	26.9%	37.6%	35.5%	5,153	1.7%	29.0%	59.2%	11.8%
Maryland	735,656	48.2%	24.9%	36.9%	38.3%	482,744	31.6%	26.6%	38.1%	35.3%
Massachusetts	1,206,359	68.1%	23.5%	38.9%	37.7%	137,587	7.8%	24.3%	43.9%	31.7%
Michigan	1,779,678	71.3%	26.1%	39.4%	34.5%	399,875	16.0%	26.5%	42.5%	30.9%
Minnesota	1,057,243	75.8%	25.6%	36.5%	37.9%	100,663	7.2%	25.1%	36.7%	38.2%
Mississippi	403,619	51.6%	25.9%	41.6%	32.5%	334,570	42.8%	27.0%	41.4%	31.6%
Missouri	1,180,379	76.1%	25.3%	37.9%	36.8%	209,782	13.5%	26.1%	41.1%	32.8%
Montana	208,559	82.1%	24.8%	39.4%	35.8%	883	0.3%	30.1%	42.2%	27.6%
Nebraska	371,059	76.0%	24.2%	39.3%	36.5%	27,074	5.5%	25.5%	43.5%	31.0%
Nevada	304,660	42.6%	23.7%	34.3%	42.0%	63,212	8.8%	22.8%	38.5%	38.8%
New Hampshire	285,841	89.3%	26.7%	39.3%	34.0%	3,519	1.1%	36.1%	46.8%	17.1%
New Jersey	1,089,247	50.0%	28.7%	36.4%	34.9%	318,519	14.6%	27.3%	39.7%	33.0%
New Mexico	163,085	29.9%	23.5%	38.7%	37.8%	11,693	2.1%	20.1%	64.5%	15.3%
New York	2,670,007	51.2%	23.4%	37.6%	39.0%	809,266	15.5%	23.6%	39.8%	36.6%
North Carolina	1,469,250	58.4%	25.1%	39.2%	35.7%	592,416	23.5%	25.7%	41.7%	32.6%
North Dakota	174,992	83.6%	20.8%	44.3%	34.9%	6,688	3.2%	9.5%	71.9%	18.6%
Ohio	2,228,445	76.2%	26.2%	37.5%	36.3%	404,273	13.8%	26.9%	42.2%	30.9%
Oklahoma	610,607	60.2%	23.0%	38.8%	38.2%	87,769	8.7%	23.0%	45.6%	31.4%
Oregon	694,846	70.8%	23.2%	36.8%	40.0%	19,467	2.0%	21.8%	37.9%	40.3%
Pennsylvania	2,320,349	72.6%	24.4%	38.7%	36.9%	408,980	12.8%	24.7%	43.1%	32.2%
Rhode Island	186,168	66.9%	21.7%	43.0%	35.3%	17,509	6.3%	25.1%	38.9%	36.0%
South Carolina	711,275	58.1%	24.7%	39.9%	35.5%	377,499	30.9%	25.9%	43.5%	30.6%
South Dakota	170,691	79.4%	24.2%	39.5%	36.3%	4,959	2.3%	14.2%	56.2%	29.6%
Tennessee	1,145,423	69.3%	25.7%	38.2%	36.2%	336,734	20.4%	25.6%	40.7%	33.7%
Texas	2,732,589	37.3%	24.2%	36.7%	39.1%	909,918	12.4%	24.8%	39.7%	35.5%
Utah	663,228	76.4%	26.6%	38.3%	35.1%	9,488	1.1%	28.4%	32.3%	39.3%
Vermont	142,348	92.4%	24.5%	42.4%	33.1%	2,027	1.3%	20.7%	41.8%	37.5%
Virginia	1,270,802	59.0%	23.6%	38.2%	38.2%	441,988	20.5%	24.4%	41.5%	34.1%
Washington	1,165,492	64.4%	24.0%	36.5%	39.5%	73,624	4.1%	22.4%	34.8%	42.8%
West Virginia	395,821	90.7%	26.1%	39.9%	34.0%	18,337	4.2%	18.2%	49.3%	32.5%
Wisconsin	1,106,617	76.6%	25.6%	38.7%	35.7%	114,123	7.9%	25.9%	39.3%	34.8%
Wyoming	122,800	80.7%	24.5%	38.1%	37.4%	2,621	1.7%	26.9%	55.5%	17.7%

Table B-1: States—Race and Hispanic Origin by Age—*Continued*

	Asian, Non-Hispanic					Hispanic				
	Millennial Population		Percent by Age			Millennial Population		Percent by Age		
	Number	Percent	13 to 17	18 to 24	25 to 31	Number	Percent	13 to 17	18 to 24	25 to 31
United States..................	4,323,696	5.2%	21.0%	36.2%	42.9%	17,303,757	21.0%	26.6%	38.1%	35.3%
Alabama........................	16,679	1.3%	25.9%	37.4%	36.7%	63,590	5.1%	17.5%	43.4%	39.2%
Alaska..........................	10,783	4.9%	28.8%	28.3%	42.9%	19,801	9.1%	19.3%	37.8%	42.9%
Arizona.........................	51,818	3.0%	18.8%	36.5%	44.7%	666,826	38.2%	29.0%	38.5%	32.5%
Arkansas.......................	12,868	1.7%	19.5%	34.0%	46.5%	70,319	9.3%	29.1%	34.0%	36.9%
California.......................	1,307,943	12.4%	21.0%	36.3%	42.6%	4,853,246	45.9%	26.9%	38.5%	34.6%
Colorado.......................	45,094	3.2%	25.8%	33.0%	41.2%	360,412	25.7%	28.8%	36.2%	35.0%
Connecticut....................	41,193	4.6%	21.9%	30.5%	47.6%	172,020	19.3%	25.8%	38.9%	35.3%
Delaware.......................	10,644	4.5%	19.8%	32.9%	47.2%	27,925	11.9%	27.7%	34.8%	37.5%
District of Columbia	9,463	4.4%	4.7%	48.4%	46.9%	22,432	10.4%	10.9%	31.4%	57.7%
Florida..........................	128,848	2.7%	22.8%	37.6%	39.7%	1,290,518	27.4%	25.1%	37.6%	37.2%
Georgia.........................	100,258	3.7%	24.6%	39.5%	35.9%	303,115	11.3%	25.7%	35.7%	38.6%
Hawaii..........................	100,679	27.1%	25.1%	34.4%	40.5%	48,033	12.9%	23.8%	37.8%	38.4%
Idaho...........................	7,313	1.7%	17.7%	45.9%	36.4%	64,938	15.4%	27.4%	39.3%	33.3%
Illinois.........................	171,809	5.1%	19.6%	35.3%	45.1%	679,219	20.1%	27.2%	38.1%	34.7%
Indiana.........................	40,730	2.4%	11.8%	48.5%	39.6%	136,996	8.1%	28.3%	39.1%	32.7%
Iowa............................	22,010	2.8%	20.4%	33.7%	45.9%	59,034	7.5%	24.6%	41.6%	33.8%
Kansas.........................	22,973	3.0%	20.5%	43.9%	35.6%	102,902	13.5%	31.4%	39.4%	29.1%
Kentucky.......................	14,130	1.3%	20.7%	26.7%	52.6%	47,221	4.2%	23.7%	39.4%	36.9%
Louisiana......................	20,703	1.7%	19.5%	30.2%	50.2%	71,363	5.7%	15.3%	43.0%	41.6%
Maine...........................	4,528	1.5%	13.8%	52.0%	34.2%	6,951	2.3%	33.6%	52.7%	13.6%
Maryland.......................	87,002	5.7%	22.8%	34.2%	43.0%	169,608	11.1%	22.9%	34.9%	42.2%
Massachusetts................	122,467	6.9%	16.9%	38.6%	44.5%	247,617	14.0%	25.6%	38.6%	35.8%
Michigan.......................	76,609	3.1%	23.7%	36.9%	39.5%	146,988	5.9%	28.4%	41.4%	30.2%
Minnesota.....................	85,902	6.2%	18.9%	35.3%	45.7%	90,556	6.5%	26.1%	37.8%	36.1%
Mississippi....................	9,455	1.2%	23.3%	36.1%	40.6%	24,428	3.1%	16.0%	36.7%	47.3%
Missouri........................	32,542	2.1%	14.3%	34.6%	51.1%	77,105	5.0%	24.5%	37.1%	38.3%
Montana........................	2,979	1.2%	5.4%	77.5%	17.1%	13,366	5.3%	35.8%	47.0%	17.2%
Nebraska.......................	12,021	2.5%	13.0%	42.4%	44.6%	60,893	12.5%	30.0%	38.1%	31.9%
Nevada.........................	54,398	7.6%	24.6%	35.6%	39.8%	252,637	35.3%	28.1%	36.8%	35.1%
New Hampshire................	9,455	3.0%	16.4%	45.3%	38.3%	14,330	4.5%	25.6%	34.7%	39.7%
New Jersey.....................	199,750	9.2%	23.6%	30.3%	46.0%	510,469	23.4%	24.6%	37.1%	38.4%
New Mexico....................	8,952	1.6%	18.8%	34.1%	47.1%	292,414	53.5%	27.9%	40.3%	31.8%
New York.......................	437,088	8.4%	19.8%	37.2%	43.0%	1,131,952	21.7%	23.2%	38.8%	38.1%
North Carolina................	72,875	2.9%	21.5%	36.3%	42.3%	281,793	11.2%	26.4%	38.0%	35.5%
North Dakota..................	2,796	1.3%	2.6%	44.0%	53.4%	6,489	3.1%	12.7%	61.3%	26.1%
Ohio............................	63,287	2.2%	18.5%	36.2%	45.2%	126,781	4.3%	24.7%	36.8%	38.5%
Oklahoma......................	19,915	2.0%	15.5%	41.8%	42.6%	125,361	12.4%	24.4%	37.4%	38.2%
Oregon.........................	42,326	4.3%	21.1%	37.4%	41.6%	160,160	16.3%	29.6%	39.2%	31.2%
Pennsylvania..................	122,437	3.8%	20.0%	37.0%	43.1%	271,302	8.5%	27.9%	39.0%	33.1%
Rhode Island..................	10,696	3.8%	11.6%	51.2%	37.2%	50,694	18.2%	25.1%	42.4%	32.5%
South Carolina	19,522	1.6%	15.6%	46.5%	37.9%	81,267	6.6%	22.8%	37.6%	39.6%
South Dakota	3,123	1.5%	6.9%	41.5%	51.6%	7,855	3.7%	29.5%	34.2%	36.3%
Tennessee	27,810	1.7%	18.8%	24.4%	56.8%	104,000	6.3%	24.3%	36.2%	39.5%
Texas...........................	300,974	4.1%	22.2%	35.2%	42.6%	3,202,642	43.8%	28.0%	37.5%	34.5%
Utah............................	23,977	2.8%	17.9%	38.5%	43.6%	129,050	14.9%	28.4%	40.1%	31.6%
Vermont........................	3,445	2.2%	23.6%	48.4%	28.0%	2,945	1.9%	39.0%	25.7%	35.3%
Virginia........................	128,426	6.0%	22.3%	35.5%	42.2%	227,829	10.6%	23.7%	37.9%	38.5%
Washington....................	144,027	8.0%	21.9%	34.5%	43.6%	282,939	15.6%	26.5%	37.4%	36.0%
West Virginia..................	3,636	0.8%	18.2%	41.3%	40.5%	8,397	1.9%	23.3%	41.1%	35.6%
Wisconsin......................	53,458	3.7%	22.2%	36.4%	41.4%	117,220	8.1%	26.6%	34.7%	38.7%
Wyoming.......................	1,880	1.2%	0.0%	38.2%	61.8%	17,809	11.7%	26.0%	44.1%	29.8%

Table B-2: Counties—Race and Hispanic Origin by Age

	White, Non-Hispanic					Black, Non-Hispanic				
	Millennial Population		Percent by Age			Millennial Population		Percent by Age		
	Number	Percent	13 to 17	18 to 24	25 to 31	Number	Percent	13 to 17	18 to 24	25 to 31
Alabama										
Baldwin County	32,351	74.0%	29.0%	35.3%	35.7%	7,036	16.1%	24.3%	48.0%	27.8%
Calhoun County	18,859	64.6%	23.6%	39.9%	36.6%	7,480	25.6%	25.9%	51.6%	22.5%
Etowah County	18,160	72.7%	30.3%	36.5%	33.2%	4,816	19.3%	33.2%	28.7%	38.1%
Houston County	16,874	64.9%	27.1%	33.6%	39.3%	7,496	28.8%	28.3%	34.9%	36.8%
Jefferson County	76,632	45.2%	23.9%	35.0%	41.1%	77,725	45.8%	27.5%	36.6%	35.9%
Lauderdale County	19,061	75.6%	22.6%	48.3%	29.1%	4,549	18.0%	28.4%	41.3%	30.2%
Lee County	39,100	73.2%	15.2%	57.5%	27.4%	11,778	22.1%	26.3%	52.0%	21.7%
Madison County	51,489	57.4%	28.3%	35.9%	35.9%	26,125	29.1%	20.5%	46.2%	33.4%
Marshall County	19,215	80.4%	33.1%	29.7%	37.2%	503	2.1%	15.1%	42.1%	42.7%
Mobile County	57,071	53.8%	23.2%	37.6%	39.2%	41,865	39.5%	25.1%	43.4%	31.5%
Montgomery County	21,564	32.8%	28.3%	38.3%	33.4%	41,013	62.4%	21.8%	43.1%	35.1%
Morgan County	19,678	70.6%	31.0%	35.4%	33.6%	4,554	16.3%	29.1%	50.3%	20.6%
Shelby County	36,590	73.1%	31.7%	33.5%	34.9%	7,467	14.9%	28.9%	33.2%	38.0%
Tuscaloosa County	46,249	63.3%	14.0%	57.2%	28.8%	22,100	30.2%	19.0%	49.3%	31.8%
Alaska										
Fairbanks North Star Borough	22,676	67.4%	18.1%	37.8%	44.1%	1,150	3.4%	29.0%	19.3%	51.7%
Matanuska-Susitna Borough	19,051	69.8%	31.9%	30.7%	37.4%	160	0.6%	0.0%	100.0%	0.0%
Arizona										
Cochise County	11,928	37.2%	21.4%	39.1%	39.5%	651	2.0%	14.3%	41.5%	44.2%
Coconino County	25,724	53.1%	12.2%	59.2%	28.6%	515	1.1%	0.0%	61.7%	38.3%
Maricopa County	515,536	48.0%	24.8%	34.9%	40.2%	63,395	5.9%	25.3%	37.3%	37.4%
Mohave County	27,038	67.0%	29.3%	34.6%	36.0%	505	1.3%	36.0%	55.0%	8.9%
Navajo County	5,883	20.6%	32.1%	36.8%	31.1%	345	1.2%	44.6%	26.1%	29.3%
Pima County	115,844	42.5%	19.1%	45.6%	35.3%	10,517	3.9%	17.6%	50.9%	31.6%
Pinal County	40,268	43.6%	29.1%	30.1%	40.7%	5,020	5.4%	29.7%	44.9%	25.4%
Yavapai County	27,619	68.5%	30.5%	36.6%	32.8%	na	na	na	na	na
Yuma County	13,054	22.0%	18.1%	41.3%	40.6%	1,202	2.0%	8.8%	44.1%	47.1%
Arkansas										
Benton County	41,330	67.2%	29.0%	31.5%	39.5%	1,239	2.0%	3.1%	9.8%	87.1%
Craighead County	21,306	78.0%	20.8%	42.6%	36.7%	3,815	14.0%	12.8%	38.9%	48.3%
Faulkner County	33,078	80.1%	23.5%	38.6%	38.0%	3,939	9.5%	25.7%	49.1%	25.1%
Garland County	15,759	77.2%	25.0%	43.7%	31.3%	2,779	13.6%	34.8%	26.7%	38.5%
Pulaski County	47,144	45.1%	19.9%	33.0%	47.1%	42,785	41.0%	30.6%	34.2%	35.1%
Saline County	22,779	82.7%	29.8%	31.1%	39.2%	1,983	7.2%	18.4%	1.9%	79.7%
Sebastian County	22,467	69.2%	28.7%	31.2%	40.2%	1,321	4.1%	7.3%	16.7%	76.0%
Washington County	49,175	71.9%	19.2%	47.4%	33.4%	3,382	4.9%	11.2%	63.9%	24.9%
California										
Alameda County	113,122	27.5%	20.0%	33.6%	46.4%	48,113	11.7%	24.3%	43.9%	31.9%
Butte County	44,412	67.7%	16.8%	53.8%	29.4%	183	0.3%	64.5%	35.5%	0.0%
Contra Costa County	96,742	37.2%	27.8%	36.0%	36.2%	26,887	10.3%	29.8%	41.9%	28.3%
El Dorado County	25,906	68.9%	27.9%	39.0%	33.1%	293	0.8%	92.8%	0.0%	7.2%
Fresno County	66,429	23.7%	21.6%	37.0%	41.3%	14,558	5.2%	23.5%	42.2%	34.3%
Humboldt County	25,379	66.2%	15.1%	48.3%	36.7%	645	1.7%	11.8%	55.3%	32.9%
Imperial County	4,851	9.2%	24.3%	32.3%	43.4%	2,060	3.9%	16.5%	40.0%	43.5%
Kern County	73,819	28.9%	23.5%	36.4%	40.1%	14,952	5.8%	24.7%	49.1%	26.2%
Kings County	13,484	29.6%	20.4%	38.5%	41.1%	2,412	5.3%	26.0%	44.6%	29.4%
Los Angeles County	615,586	21.7%	18.9%	35.0%	46.1%	222,452	7.9%	23.7%	39.5%	36.8%
Madera County	10,255	23.8%	23.6%	34.9%	41.5%	1,498	3.5%	31.3%	29.3%	39.4%
Marin County	28,954	58.7%	40.0%	35.1%	25.0%	1,578	3.2%	13.9%	48.7%	37.4%
Merced County	18,384	22.7%	25.6%	39.1%	35.3%	2,291	2.8%	21.3%	62.5%	16.2%
Monterey County	28,062	22.3%	21.3%	39.2%	39.5%	3,052	2.4%	28.9%	53.8%	17.2%
Napa County	13,541	40.7%	27.1%	38.1%	34.8%	770	2.3%	29.9%	70.1%	0.0%
Nevada County	14,513	75.8%	27.3%	34.5%	38.3%	74	0.4%	100.0%	0.0%	0.0%
Orange County	296,392	35.0%	24.5%	37.0%	38.5%	14,794	1.7%	17.0%	40.6%	42.4%
Placer County	59,259	68.1%	30.5%	33.5%	36.0%	905	1.0%	0.0%	70.2%	29.8%
Riverside County	177,304	27.7%	26.3%	36.4%	37.3%	42,614	6.7%	29.6%	39.4%	31.0%
Sacramento County	159,456	39.5%	24.1%	34.1%	41.8%	43,589	10.8%	28.6%	41.3%	30.1%
San Bernardino County	155,115	25.1%	23.3%	38.4%	38.3%	56,171	9.1%	24.1%	41.8%	34.1%
San Diego County	376,434	40.2%	17.5%	38.9%	43.5%	48,197	5.1%	21.7%	42.6%	35.7%
San Francisco County	90,293	39.7%	5.9%	22.4%	71.7%	11,281	5.0%	20.2%	33.5%	46.3%
San Joaquin County	52,263	26.7%	26.6%	37.6%	35.8%	11,263	5.8%	26.9%	46.3%	26.8%
San Luis Obispo County	51,767	64.2%	17.6%	54.8%	27.6%	2,329	2.9%	3.6%	84.0%	12.4%
San Mateo County	55,806	33.0%	28.2%	31.8%	40.0%	4,105	2.4%	30.7%	33.9%	35.4%
Santa Barbara County	53,620	38.7%	14.7%	56.2%	29.1%	2,497	1.8%	29.0%	54.6%	16.3%
Santa Clara County	130,409	27.5%	22.1%	35.0%	42.9%	12,758	2.7%	14.4%	40.3%	45.3%
Santa Cruz County	37,949	49.0%	17.1%	55.7%	27.3%	544	0.7%	44.9%	40.6%	14.5%
Shasta County	32,227	74.7%	24.5%	36.6%	38.9%	474	1.1%	4.2%	89.2%	6.5%
Solano County	39,091	34.2%	20.4%	36.2%	43.5%	15,575	13.6%	28.9%	39.7%	31.4%
Sonoma County	65,269	54.0%	25.0%	38.0%	37.0%	2,305	1.9%	26.7%	40.4%	32.9%
Stanislaus County	55,357	37.4%	26.9%	36.2%	37.0%	3,785	2.6%	22.5%	34.1%	43.4%
Sutter County	9,430	39.7%	19.7%	44.7%	35.6%	951	4.0%	20.4%	46.3%	33.3%
Tulare County	30,561	23.1%	25.2%	35.8%	39.0%	2,583	2.0%	48.9%	37.2%	13.9%
Ventura County	83,448	38.1%	26.7%	40.2%	33.1%	2,710	1.2%	20.4%	55.9%	23.7%
Yolo County	29,054	40.3%	15.7%	53.1%	31.1%	2,385	3.3%	17.8%	72.1%	10.1%

Table B-2: Counties—Race and Hispanic Origin by Age—*Continued*

	Asian, Non-Hispanic					Hispanic				
	Millennial Population		Percent by Age			Millennial Population		Percent by Age		
	Number	Percent	13 to 17	18 to 24	25 to 31	Number	Percent	13 to 17	18 to 24	25 to 31
Alabama										
Baldwin County	539	1.2%	100.0%	0.0%	0.0%	3,758	8.6%	39.1%	40.5%	20.4%
Calhoun County	185	0.6%	0.0%	39.5%	60.5%	1,722	5.9%	14.9%	5.7%	79.4%
Etowah County	120	0.5%	100.0%	0.0%	0.0%	1,730	6.9%	15.9%	75.9%	8.2%
Houston County	166	0.6%	29.5%	0.0%	70.5%	861	3.3%	37.6%	47.6%	14.8%
Jefferson County	3,443	2.0%	20.9%	30.8%	48.3%	8,007	4.7%	19.7%	34.9%	45.4%
Lauderdale County	259	1.0%	38.2%	0.0%	61.8%	1,129	4.5%	3.5%	5.7%	90.8%
Lee County	1,189	2.2%	0.0%	47.9%	52.1%	863	1.6%	23.8%	44.1%	32.1%
Madison County	2,574	2.9%	15.0%	37.4%	47.6%	6,763	7.5%	23.8%	37.2%	39.0%
Marshall County	na	na	na	na	na	3,026	12.7%	18.5%	28.6%	53.0%
Mobile County	1,963	1.9%	33.4%	38.8%	27.9%	3,222	3.0%	20.6%	32.2%	47.2%
Montgomery County	837	1.3%	59.3%	17.2%	23.5%	1,690	2.6%	0.0%	28.2%	71.8%
Morgan County	na	na	na	na	na	2,643	9.5%	24.6%	43.0%	32.5%
Shelby County	903	1.8%	5.5%	40.6%	53.8%	3,979	8.0%	13.4%	37.5%	49.1%
Tuscaloosa County	905	1.2%	17.7%	51.8%	30.5%	2,530	3.5%	12.7%	46.3%	41.0%
Alaska										
Fairbanks North Star Borough	1,039	3.1%	15.5%	71.6%	12.9%	3,589	10.7%	0.0%	62.6%	37.4%
Matanuska-Susitna Borough	1,330	4.9%	13.6%	57.9%	28.5%	1,372	5.0%	39.9%	47.7%	12.4%
Arizona										
Cochise County	261	0.8%	0.0%	0.0%	100.0%	17,402	54.2%	27.4%	38.7%	33.9%
Coconino County	723	1.5%	0.0%	71.5%	28.5%	7,526	15.5%	15.5%	52.4%	32.2%
Maricopa County	38,786	3.6%	21.1%	33.6%	45.4%	404,023	37.6%	29.2%	37.5%	33.3%
Mohave County	234	0.6%	0.0%	13.2%	86.8%	10,144	25.1%	37.8%	30.5%	31.6%
Navajo County	39	0.1%	0.0%	100.0%	0.0%	2,797	9.8%	12.9%	37.4%	49.7%
Pima County	8,998	3.3%	9.0%	50.2%	40.9%	119,423	43.8%	27.7%	42.3%	30.0%
Pinal County	1,172	1.3%	51.9%	40.4%	7.7%	37,139	40.2%	29.5%	37.5%	33.0%
Yavapai County	649	1.6%	0.0%	0.0%	100.0%	9,608	23.8%	27.7%	34.0%	38.3%
Yuma County	606	1.0%	7.6%	54.6%	37.8%	42,979	72.4%	29.9%	40.1%	30.0%
Arkansas										
Benton County	3,041	4.9%	25.4%	20.8%	53.8%	13,660	22.2%	39.2%	40.0%	20.8%
Craighead County	352	1.3%	0.0%	100.0%	0.0%	1,439	5.3%	9.5%	7.2%	83.3%
Faulkner County	354	0.9%	0.0%	85.6%	14.4%	2,676	6.5%	14.2%	14.6%	71.2%
Garland County	263	1.3%	100.0%	0.0%	0.0%	1,250	6.1%	23.0%	63.2%	13.8%
Pulaski County	2,898	2.8%	24.3%	28.2%	47.5%	8,638	8.3%	20.6%	25.2%	54.2%
Saline County	223	0.8%	100.0%	0.0%	0.0%	1,882	6.8%	6.0%	48.0%	46.0%
Sebastian County	632	1.9%	5.2%	41.0%	53.8%	5,919	18.2%	30.8%	33.4%	35.7%
Washington County	1,702	2.5%	0.0%	10.2%	89.8%	10,525	15.4%	27.8%	41.0%	31.3%
California										
Alameda County	104,981	25.5%	21.5%	36.6%	41.9%	116,907	28.4%	23.3%	36.6%	40.1%
Butte County	4,216	6.4%	20.1%	51.9%	28.1%	13,014	19.8%	23.5%	47.3%	29.1%
Contra Costa County	34,923	13.4%	26.5%	32.8%	40.7%	85,106	32.7%	26.8%	36.8%	36.4%
El Dorado County	2,110	5.6%	44.1%	48.1%	7.8%	7,224	19.2%	29.2%	17.9%	52.8%
Fresno County	29,642	10.6%	24.7%	38.4%	36.9%	161,637	57.6%	27.0%	38.7%	34.3%
Humboldt County	1,559	4.1%	32.8%	7.1%	60.0%	5,685	14.8%	18.0%	59.0%	23.0%
Imperial County	621	1.2%	43.6%	35.1%	21.3%	44,271	84.2%	27.3%	39.4%	33.4%
Kern County	7,233	2.8%	27.9%	26.0%	46.1%	150,939	59.0%	27.5%	38.0%	34.5%
Kings County	1,547	3.4%	44.5%	18.9%	36.6%	26,531	58.3%	22.8%	39.0%	38.2%
Los Angeles County	348,001	12.3%	20.3%	36.1%	43.6%	1,559,924	55.0%	26.1%	38.9%	35.0%
Madera County	606	1.4%	0.0%	54.3%	45.7%	30,037	69.7%	29.6%	35.6%	34.8%
Marin County	3,356	6.8%	15.6%	43.8%	40.6%	13,098	26.5%	25.3%	32.1%	42.5%
Merced County	7,740	9.6%	26.0%	43.3%	30.7%	50,999	63.1%	31.2%	38.0%	30.8%
Monterey County	6,105	4.8%	18.1%	51.3%	30.7%	84,664	67.1%	27.8%	36.4%	35.8%
Napa County	2,472	7.4%	28.3%	24.5%	47.2%	15,512	46.7%	29.0%	41.0%	30.0%
Nevada County	na	na	na	na	na	3,897	20.4%	35.1%	57.2%	7.7%
Orange County	144,775	17.1%	22.0%	36.6%	41.4%	359,278	42.5%	27.9%	38.0%	34.1%
Placer County	4,807	5.5%	36.8%	30.1%	33.2%	16,882	19.4%	37.4%	31.7%	30.9%
Riverside County	33,625	5.3%	16.4%	46.1%	37.5%	361,449	56.5%	29.5%	37.8%	32.7%
Sacramento County	61,397	15.2%	25.5%	33.0%	41.5%	109,421	27.1%	26.6%	36.7%	36.6%
San Bernardino County	33,282	5.4%	21.0%	37.7%	41.3%	354,667	57.3%	29.0%	39.0%	32.0%
San Diego County	99,298	10.6%	18.1%	36.0%	45.9%	363,809	38.8%	25.0%	39.5%	35.5%
San Francisco County	66,551	29.2%	13.8%	32.8%	53.3%	44,876	19.7%	14.9%	30.4%	54.7%
San Joaquin County	29,160	14.9%	26.6%	41.3%	32.1%	93,059	47.6%	33.2%	37.0%	29.8%
San Luis Obispo County	4,540	5.6%	6.3%	69.1%	24.6%	19,635	24.3%	16.0%	46.1%	37.9%
San Mateo County	44,483	26.3%	22.8%	30.3%	46.8%	55,694	32.9%	23.6%	41.1%	35.3%
Santa Barbara County	8,549	6.2%	9.9%	68.4%	21.7%	69,787	50.3%	27.3%	41.8%	30.9%
Santa Clara County	149,355	31.4%	22.0%	29.8%	48.2%	159,373	33.5%	25.4%	37.9%	36.6%
Santa Cruz County	5,481	7.1%	6.9%	79.6%	13.5%	30,314	39.1%	20.9%	45.7%	33.4%
Shasta County	2,143	5.0%	3.1%	79.3%	17.6%	5,404	12.5%	32.1%	42.8%	25.1%
Solano County	14,861	13.0%	29.1%	31.3%	39.6%	35,113	30.7%	26.8%	38.9%	34.4%
Sonoma County	5,322	4.4%	17.5%	45.0%	37.5%	41,916	34.7%	28.3%	37.1%	34.6%
Stanislaus County	7,642	5.2%	35.4%	44.3%	20.3%	74,965	50.6%	29.9%	38.1%	32.0%
Sutter County	2,756	11.6%	12.8%	43.3%	43.9%	9,256	39.0%	22.7%	44.6%	32.6%
Tulare County	5,269	4.0%	23.3%	28.1%	48.6%	90,961	68.8%	28.3%	38.6%	33.1%
Ventura County	10,786	4.9%	25.8%	34.9%	39.3%	113,126	51.6%	27.0%	38.4%	34.6%
Yolo County	13,792	19.1%	9.0%	70.5%	20.5%	22,628	31.4%	25.5%	45.1%	29.4%

Table B-2: Counties—Race and Hispanic Origin by Age—*Continued*

	White, Non-Hispanic					Black, Non-Hispanic				
	Millennial Population		Percent by Age			Millennial Population		Percent by Age		
	Number	Percent	13 to 17	18 to 24	25 to 31	Number	Percent	13 to 17	18 to 24	25 to 31
Colorado										
Adams County	62,302	46.3%	23.7%	32.0%	44.3%	5,560	4.1%	38.0%	25.9%	36.0%
Arapahoe County	87,287	54.7%	25.1%	31.2%	43.8%	17,065	10.7%	24.7%	43.0%	32.4%
Boulder County	72,983	78.1%	20.5%	50.8%	28.7%	677	0.7%	17.7%	58.8%	23.5%
Denver County	101,270	51.0%	7.4%	26.5%	66.1%	17,798	9.0%	19.3%	41.3%	39.3%
Douglas County	54,484	79.7%	40.9%	30.5%	28.6%	364	0.5%	49.7%	0.0%	50.3%
El Paso County	120,412	65.1%	23.1%	39.7%	37.2%	11,210	6.1%	34.1%	29.1%	36.8%
Jefferson County	97,200	73.7%	26.9%	34.4%	38.8%	2,877	2.2%	38.8%	42.2%	19.0%
Larimer County	78,436	81.0%	19.7%	48.0%	32.3%	729	0.8%	0.0%	75.7%	24.3%
Mesa County	27,714	72.3%	24.6%	39.6%	35.8%	886	2.3%	62.9%	33.0%	4.2%
Pueblo County	19,084	46.2%	23.2%	36.7%	40.1%	501	1.2%	15.0%	33.1%	51.9%
Weld County	44,941	60.1%	23.2%	36.6%	40.2%	1,454	1.9%	2.3%	84.7%	13.0%
Connecticut										
Fairfield County	126,005	56.9%	32.6%	35.3%	32.2%	27,354	12.3%	25.5%	43.4%	31.2%
Hartford County	122,096	55.2%	27.6%	35.9%	36.5%	32,300	14.6%	25.8%	36.5%	37.7%
Litchfield County	33,406	84.9%	30.7%	35.5%	33.7%	857	2.2%	13.7%	35.2%	51.1%
Middlesex County	29,082	76.4%	28.1%	37.5%	34.5%	2,716	7.1%	13.6%	46.2%	40.1%
New Haven County	125,346	56.5%	24.3%	38.9%	36.8%	32,364	14.6%	27.9%	37.1%	35.1%
New London County	49,140	69.9%	24.3%	41.3%	34.3%	5,211	7.4%	8.7%	42.1%	49.3%
Tolland County	39,123	81.6%	21.1%	54.7%	24.2%	2,025	4.2%	18.4%	63.0%	18.6%
Windham County	23,177	77.4%	25.3%	40.5%	34.2%	1,150	3.8%	10.6%	78.9%	10.5%
Delaware										
Kent County	25,090	57.1%	22.6%	37.1%	40.3%	13,373	30.4%	25.4%	45.6%	29.0%
New Castle County	79,918	53.8%	21.4%	41.8%	36.8%	37,353	25.1%	26.3%	36.2%	37.5%
Sussex County	26,863	64.9%	25.1%	35.7%	39.2%	6,751	16.3%	21.5%	44.0%	34.5%
Florida										
Alachua County	57,592	58.9%	10.7%	59.7%	29.7%	16,861	17.3%	16.6%	51.8%	31.6%
Bay County	30,819	74.1%	25.5%	35.0%	39.5%	5,537	13.3%	7.2%	43.7%	49.2%
Brevard County	79,584	70.6%	27.1%	37.0%	35.9%	13,679	12.1%	29.7%	45.7%	24.6%
Broward County	136,782	31.3%	25.3%	34.3%	40.5%	145,527	33.3%	26.4%	36.9%	36.6%
Charlotte County	18,791	72.0%	28.2%	35.6%	36.1%	3,537	13.6%	23.3%	46.7%	30.0%
Citrus County	18,153	84.6%	29.7%	36.9%	33.4%	893	4.2%	10.2%	48.7%	41.1%
Clay County	34,572	72.6%	33.5%	34.0%	32.5%	5,016	10.5%	30.8%	32.0%	37.2%
Collier County	28,854	46.4%	28.6%	35.1%	36.3%	5,289	8.5%	36.5%	39.8%	23.6%
Duval County	118,568	49.2%	18.3%	35.8%	45.9%	80,476	33.4%	25.2%	36.6%	38.2%
Escambia County	53,164	61.2%	16.4%	46.0%	37.6%	19,743	22.7%	25.4%	40.7%	33.9%
Flagler County	12,919	64.1%	33.1%	33.4%	33.5%	4,011	19.9%	21.4%	64.3%	14.3%
Hernando County	23,923	71.4%	27.2%	36.4%	36.4%	2,720	8.1%	37.4%	22.5%	40.1%
Highlands County	7,451	42.0%	34.6%	27.5%	37.9%	2,487	14.0%	12.6%	52.8%	34.5%
Hillsborough County	161,419	46.5%	22.3%	35.6%	42.1%	62,354	18.0%	24.1%	39.1%	36.8%
Indian River County	15,528	61.4%	31.1%	33.3%	35.7%	3,997	15.8%	55.6%	23.4%	21.0%
Lake County	39,755	62.2%	30.0%	31.8%	38.1%	9,306	14.6%	27.4%	34.6%	38.0%
Lee County	73,963	54.6%	24.7%	37.5%	37.8%	16,449	12.1%	28.5%	34.0%	37.5%
Leon County	56,489	51.8%	12.1%	61.0%	26.9%	36,923	33.9%	14.9%	59.8%	25.4%
Manatee County	39,396	57.0%	27.8%	35.3%	36.9%	10,027	14.5%	25.4%	37.1%	37.5%
Marion County	41,203	61.1%	22.7%	36.7%	40.6%	12,741	18.9%	32.8%	39.1%	28.1%
Martin County	18,134	63.2%	27.6%	36.1%	36.3%	3,045	10.6%	22.8%	33.7%	43.5%
Miami-Dade County	99,328	14.7%	23.2%	35.7%	41.0%	134,521	19.9%	23.7%	38.6%	37.7%
Okaloosa County	39,210	70.5%	21.8%	36.4%	41.8%	6,476	11.6%	22.8%	42.7%	34.5%
Orange County	152,700	41.0%	18.9%	38.9%	42.2%	77,370	20.8%	25.4%	39.3%	35.3%
Osceola County	25,295	30.9%	25.1%	34.1%	40.8%	8,263	10.1%	34.6%	35.8%	29.6%
Palm Beach County	132,756	44.0%	25.4%	36.4%	38.3%	71,019	23.6%	24.6%	38.7%	36.7%
Pasco County	66,016	68.7%	27.6%	36.5%	35.9%	6,309	6.6%	23.9%	35.0%	41.0%
Pinellas County	128,545	66.1%	24.9%	34.6%	40.5%	25,913	13.3%	28.1%	41.0%	30.9%
Polk County	78,871	52.7%	24.8%	36.9%	38.3%	29,397	19.6%	24.4%	39.9%	35.7%
Santa Rosa County	31,931	79.0%	30.0%	34.0%	36.0%	2,593	6.4%	0.0%	53.3%	46.7%
Sarasota County	46,840	72.1%	27.4%	37.2%	35.4%	4,499	6.9%	34.2%	40.9%	24.8%
Seminole County	67,458	57.4%	26.7%	36.3%	37.0%	15,090	12.8%	33.4%	43.0%	23.6%
St. Johns County	36,737	78.0%	30.7%	37.1%	32.2%	2,771	5.9%	38.2%	42.1%	19.7%
St. Lucie County	28,715	46.3%	26.5%	37.3%	36.2%	15,952	25.7%	29.6%	35.8%	34.6%
Sumter County	7,801	68.3%	19.3%	34.3%	46.4%	2,277	19.9%	12.9%	35.2%	51.9%
Volusia County	69,071	63.1%	21.4%	38.5%	40.2%	16,831	15.4%	17.9%	53.0%	29.0%
Georgia										
Bartow County	17,450	60.9%	30.8%	34.9%	34.3%	6,943	24.2%	15.0%	53.2%	31.8%
Bibb County	15,613	37.2%	19.0%	40.6%	40.4%	23,766	56.6%	28.6%	40.5%	31.0%
Carroll County	19,967	61.9%	22.5%	47.1%	30.4%	7,753	24.0%	23.6%	37.1%	39.3%
Chatham County	35,318	42.4%	15.1%	38.5%	46.3%	36,949	44.3%	22.7%	43.8%	33.4%
Cherokee County	39,113	75.7%	31.8%	31.8%	36.4%	4,029	7.8%	34.2%	31.0%	34.8%
Clarke County	34,369	63.6%	3.0%	71.3%	25.7%	10,193	18.9%	18.7%	54.4%	26.9%
Clayton County	7,640	9.9%	22.1%	32.5%	45.5%	51,799	67.2%	26.9%	37.4%	35.6%
Cobb County	89,089	47.5%	25.3%	36.2%	38.5%	54,980	29.3%	27.6%	36.7%	35.6%
Columbia County	24,596	71.3%	32.7%	32.4%	34.9%	6,890	20.0%	31.7%	46.0%	22.3%
Coweta County	19,628	66.1%	30.2%	36.3%	33.4%	6,376	21.5%	26.3%	34.8%	38.9%
DeKalb County	46,993	24.6%	14.2%	31.9%	53.9%	105,895	55.4%	24.0%	38.7%	37.2%
Dougherty County	8,956	31.8%	23.3%	39.5%	37.2%	17,301	61.3%	25.7%	43.4%	30.9%
Douglas County	13,830	41.7%	33.7%	36.5%	29.8%	14,889	44.9%	32.0%	25.8%	42.2%
Fayette County	14,359	55.6%	40.3%	39.7%	20.0%	4,630	17.9%	32.7%	38.5%	28.7%

Table B-2: Counties—Race and Hispanic Origin by Age—*Continued*

	Asian, Non-Hispanic					Hispanic				
	Millennial Population		Percent by Age			Millennial Population		Percent by Age		
	Number	Percent	13 to 17	18 to 24	25 to 31	Number	Percent	13 to 17	18 to 24	25 to 31
Colorado										
Adams County..............................	5,086	3.8%	18.7%	33.4%	48.0%	57,071	42.4%	31.8%	34.0%	34.2%
Arapahoe County.........................	7,660	4.8%	44.9%	23.7%	31.4%	39,482	24.7%	33.7%	33.1%	33.2%
Boulder County	4,680	5.0%	23.1%	46.8%	30.1%	13,548	14.5%	25.2%	45.1%	29.7%
Denver County	8,435	4.2%	15.3%	33.9%	50.8%	65,039	32.8%	24.8%	35.7%	39.5%
Douglas County...........................	3,047	4.5%	29.4%	33.0%	37.7%	8,469	12.4%	35.2%	38.5%	26.3%
El Paso County.............................	4,764	2.6%	37.9%	28.2%	33.9%	36,698	19.8%	28.5%	33.0%	38.6%
Jefferson County..........................	3,955	3.0%	26.8%	44.7%	28.6%	24,829	18.8%	26.7%	39.6%	33.7%
Larimer County	2,076	2.1%	17.8%	61.8%	20.5%	12,387	12.8%	24.2%	43.0%	32.8%
Mesa County................................	143	0.4%	0.0%	44.8%	55.2%	8,808	23.0%	11.0%	43.4%	45.6%
Pueblo County.............................	283	0.7%	49.8%	0.0%	50.2%	20,424	49.5%	26.5%	39.5%	34.0%
Weld County................................	1,045	1.4%	20.8%	26.6%	52.6%	25,342	33.9%	27.2%	41.2%	31.6%
Connecticut										
Fairfield County	10,649	4.8%	23.5%	27.4%	49.1%	52,408	23.7%	25.8%	35.9%	38.3%
Hartford County	12,427	5.6%	20.9%	20.9%	58.2%	49,289	22.3%	29.0%	40.0%	31.1%
Litchfield County	1,577	4.0%	53.5%	14.6%	31.9%	2,670	6.8%	20.9%	32.8%	46.3%
Middlesex County	1,156	3.0%	34.4%	49.7%	15.9%	4,099	10.8%	19.8%	43.8%	36.4%
New Haven County........................	10,118	4.6%	19.0%	35.3%	45.7%	46,706	21.1%	25.1%	39.7%	35.2%
New London County......................	1,831	2.6%	24.4%	32.4%	43.3%	9,914	14.1%	20.9%	47.3%	31.8%
Tolland County	2,904	6.1%	8.8%	62.3%	28.9%	2,677	5.6%	14.9%	54.3%	30.8%
Windham County	531	1.8%	11.1%	48.0%	40.9%	4,257	14.2%	22.8%	27.6%	49.6%
Delaware										
Kent County	693	1.6%	45.7%	54.3%	0.0%	3,543	8.1%	30.5%	22.3%	47.2%
New Castle County	9,588	6.5%	18.7%	29.7%	51.6%	18,006	12.1%	26.1%	38.5%	35.5%
Sussex County.............................	363	0.9%	0.0%	77.7%	22.3%	6,376	15.4%	30.9%	31.2%	38.0%
Florida										
Alachua County...........................	7,387	7.6%	5.9%	59.2%	34.9%	11,169	11.4%	8.6%	69.8%	21.7%
Bay County..................................	1,255	3.0%	35.9%	28.6%	35.5%	2,600	6.2%	10.2%	27.8%	61.9%
Brevard County	1,678	1.5%	18.7%	63.6%	17.7%	13,612	12.1%	24.6%	41.7%	33.7%
Broward County	16,653	3.8%	23.4%	29.7%	46.9%	129,209	29.5%	25.9%	36.7%	37.4%
Charlotte County	362	1.4%	63.3%	36.7%	0.0%	2,781	10.7%	33.1%	60.5%	6.4%
Citrus County	310	1.4%	0.0%	21.3%	78.7%	2,093	9.7%	34.7%	57.0%	8.3%
Clay County	1,296	2.7%	0.0%	65.7%	34.3%	4,389	9.2%	34.3%	16.2%	49.5%
Collier County	na	na	na	na	na	26,987	43.4%	25.5%	36.9%	37.6%
Duval County...............................	10,629	4.4%	22.8%	30.7%	46.5%	24,145	10.0%	23.8%	37.2%	39.0%
Escambia County	2,681	3.1%	22.9%	42.5%	34.7%	5,508	6.3%	5.3%	53.0%	41.7%
Flagler County	474	2.4%	46.8%	53.2%	0.0%	1,925	9.6%	23.0%	54.2%	22.8%
Hernando County	528	1.6%	50.0%	10.8%	39.2%	4,581	13.7%	25.6%	32.4%	42.1%
Highlands County	83	0.5%	0.0%	100.0%	0.0%	7,413	41.8%	21.3%	45.1%	33.6%
Hillsborough County	11,656	3.4%	18.4%	36.6%	45.0%	101,019	29.1%	26.7%	37.4%	35.9%
Indian River County	257	1.0%	0.0%	52.1%	47.9%	4,416	17.5%	18.1%	45.5%	36.5%
Lake County................................	1,178	1.8%	25.0%	54.4%	20.5%	11,088	17.4%	27.7%	37.0%	35.3%
Lee County.................................	1,154	0.9%	46.7%	38.8%	14.5%	40,456	29.9%	29.4%	34.8%	35.8%
Leon County...............................	2,825	2.6%	8.4%	53.1%	38.5%	8,813	8.1%	11.0%	58.7%	30.2%
Manatee County	962	1.4%	49.1%	31.4%	19.5%	16,888	24.4%	29.7%	44.0%	26.3%
Marion County	1,217	1.8%	35.8%	13.6%	50.5%	11,278	16.7%	33.0%	34.9%	32.2%
Martin County	468	1.6%	22.0%	0.0%	78.0%	6,630	23.1%	20.8%	32.3%	46.9%
Miami-Dade County	11,190	1.7%	14.1%	35.0%	51.0%	421,422	62.3%	23.6%	36.8%	39.7%
Okaloosa County	2,136	3.8%	62.4%	25.7%	11.9%	6,202	11.2%	17.1%	27.4%	55.5%
Orange County	18,330	4.9%	18.4%	40.1%	41.5%	110,530	29.6%	21.7%	40.2%	38.2%
Osceola County	1,125	1.4%	31.6%	60.7%	7.6%	44,879	54.8%	30.0%	35.3%	34.7%
Palm Beach County	7,499	2.5%	23.6%	46.4%	30.1%	80,467	26.7%	24.6%	35.8%	39.6%
Pasco County	2,206	2.3%	37.0%	29.1%	33.9%	18,053	18.8%	33.9%	40.5%	25.6%
Pinellas County	6,766	3.5%	28.4%	28.1%	43.4%	25,262	13.0%	23.3%	36.9%	39.8%
Polk County	2,271	1.5%	25.2%	37.8%	37.0%	35,629	23.8%	28.0%	35.6%	36.4%
Santa Rosa County......................	411	1.0%	26.3%	0.0%	73.7%	2,465	6.1%	37.6%	54.4%	8.0%
Sarasota County	1,724	2.7%	39.6%	27.6%	32.9%	10,700	16.5%	26.4%	53.6%	20.0%
Seminole County	3,849	3.3%	32.6%	49.1%	18.3%	27,272	23.2%	27.9%	31.6%	40.5%
St. Johns County..........................	1,636	3.5%	75.4%	17.4%	7.2%	4,178	8.9%	26.8%	43.2%	30.0%
St. Lucie County...........................	1,515	2.4%	12.9%	55.8%	31.2%	14,605	23.6%	36.3%	33.5%	30.2%
Sumter County	na	na	na	na	na	969	8.5%	45.6%	39.8%	14.6%
Volusia County	3,297	3.0%	15.6%	40.3%	44.1%	17,235	15.7%	28.0%	36.4%	35.5%
Georgia										
Bartow County	na	na	na	na	na	4,254	14.8%	23.3%	55.7%	21.0%
Bibb County	519	1.2%	29.1%	70.9%	0.0%	1,854	4.4%	18.7%	13.5%	67.9%
Carroll County	593	1.8%	0.0%	100.0%	0.0%	2,764	8.6%	43.1%	32.1%	24.8%
Chatham County	1,929	2.3%	14.0%	58.4%	27.5%	6,902	8.3%	10.2%	33.4%	56.4%
Cherokee County	810	1.6%	21.9%	0.0%	78.1%	6,674	12.9%	31.3%	27.0%	41.7%
Clarke County..............................	3,201	5.9%	2.5%	80.5%	17.0%	5,138	9.5%	21.6%	47.1%	31.3%
Clayton County............................	4,199	5.5%	36.1%	47.4%	16.5%	11,456	14.9%	29.3%	24.9%	45.8%
Cobb County...............................	8,270	4.4%	23.3%	32.6%	44.1%	29,820	15.9%	29.7%	36.8%	33.6%
Columbia County.........................	1,335	3.9%	14.4%	52.7%	33.0%	1,559	4.5%	24.8%	43.3%	31.9%
Coweta County............................	375	1.3%	0.0%	34.1%	65.9%	2,876	9.7%	18.0%	20.0%	62.0%
DeKalb County	12,935	6.8%	12.8%	39.0%	48.1%	19,017	9.9%	18.3%	35.6%	46.2%
Dougherty County........................	250	0.9%	8.0%	71.2%	20.8%	1,354	4.8%	34.0%	36.3%	29.7%
Douglas County............................	759	2.3%	0.0%	9.6%	90.4%	2,618	7.9%	29.6%	29.9%	40.5%
Fayette County	1,689	6.5%	58.9%	0.0%	41.1%	2,845	11.0%	30.2%	64.8%	5.0%

Table B-2: Counties—Race and Hispanic Origin by Age—*Continued*

| | White, Non-Hispanic | | | | | Black, Non-Hispanic | | | | |
| | Millennial Population | | Percent by Age | | | Millennial Population | | Percent by Age | | |
	Number	Percent	13 to 17	18 to 24	25 to 31	Number	Percent	13 to 17	18 to 24	25 to 31
Georgia—Cont.										
Floyd County	17,399	72.9%	23.8%	45.9%	30.3%	2,719	11.4%	26.1%	40.7%	33.1%
Forsyth County	32,676	76.3%	42.2%	29.9%	27.9%	1,678	3.9%	25.3%	12.5%	62.2%
Fulton County	97,844	35.4%	22.5%	34.7%	42.9%	126,423	45.8%	22.3%	37.9%	39.9%
Gwinnett County	76,000	34.1%	31.1%	36.2%	32.7%	61,862	27.8%	34.1%	35.5%	30.5%
Hall County	25,756	53.6%	28.7%	35.6%	35.7%	4,662	9.7%	29.3%	46.0%	24.7%
Henry County	25,317	47.3%	34.6%	35.3%	30.1%	20,964	39.2%	37.2%	42.0%	20.8%
Houston County	22,065	52.7%	19.6%	36.5%	43.8%	13,858	33.1%	29.5%	45.7%	24.8%
Lowndes County	21,181	52.8%	15.8%	51.4%	32.8%	14,853	37.0%	17.8%	53.6%	28.6%
Muscogee County	24,265	39.7%	18.9%	42.6%	38.5%	25,684	42.0%	25.9%	39.4%	34.7%
Newton County	9,913	37.9%	24.4%	38.3%	37.3%	11,893	45.5%	35.4%	36.0%	28.6%
Paulding County	26,110	72.8%	32.5%	33.9%	33.6%	6,232	17.4%	42.2%	30.4%	27.4%
Richmond County	20,524	33.1%	14.2%	38.4%	47.4%	35,147	56.7%	26.7%	39.0%	34.3%
Whitfield County	13,851	51.7%	29.8%	38.4%	31.9%	1,142	4.3%	2.8%	64.9%	32.3%
Hawaii										
Hawaii County	8,677	19.4%	19.3%	38.6%	42.2%	na	na	na	na	na
Honolulu County	63,140	23.1%	9.4%	38.8%	51.8%	11,961	4.4%	12.9%	41.7%	45.4%
Maui County	8,273	23.3%	17.9%	26.4%	55.6%	90	0.3%	0.0%	60.0%	40.0%
Idaho										
Ada County	88,895	78.9%	28.5%	34.6%	36.8%	1,276	1.1%	59.5%	40.5%	0.0%
Bonneville County	22,490	80.4%	31.9%	33.2%	34.8%	102	0.4%	100.0%	0.0%	0.0%
Canyon County	35,254	68.8%	36.7%	29.1%	34.2%	393	0.8%	100.0%	0.0%	0.0%
Kootenai County	30,648	86.7%	29.9%	33.6%	36.5%	61	0.2%	0.0%	47.5%	52.5%
Illinois										
Champaign County	52,245	64.1%	12.6%	58.2%	29.3%	9,873	12.1%	21.5%	57.4%	21.1%
Cook County	558,822	38.9%	18.1%	31.3%	50.6%	340,687	23.7%	26.9%	40.0%	33.1%
DeKalb County	29,274	77.0%	20.2%	50.9%	29.0%	3,870	10.2%	6.7%	61.3%	32.0%
DuPage County	148,236	64.0%	28.3%	35.1%	36.6%	12,446	5.4%	31.3%	29.1%	39.6%
Kane County	67,866	49.9%	31.6%	32.7%	35.7%	8,697	6.4%	15.7%	40.4%	43.9%
Kankakee County	18,598	67.7%	26.5%	43.3%	30.2%	4,614	16.8%	32.2%	26.9%	41.0%
Kendall County	21,055	69.5%	31.3%	28.7%	40.0%	3,531	11.7%	52.4%	0.0%	47.6%
Lake County	99,816	56.4%	32.8%	39.3%	27.9%	14,167	8.0%	27.7%	45.4%	26.9%
LaSalle County	22,222	82.9%	31.8%	34.1%	34.1%	663	2.5%	11.5%	40.4%	48.1%
Macon County	18,140	69.4%	24.7%	40.4%	34.9%	4,289	16.4%	21.9%	33.4%	44.7%
Madison County	54,964	81.9%	22.2%	36.4%	41.4%	7,845	11.7%	21.5%	54.8%	23.7%
McHenry County	58,795	76.2%	34.6%	35.2%	30.2%	624	0.8%	54.5%	15.7%	29.8%
McLean County	45,787	78.9%	17.6%	56.4%	26.0%	4,786	8.3%	8.4%	43.0%	48.6%
Peoria County	32,268	65.5%	20.4%	37.1%	42.5%	9,809	19.9%	34.3%	38.7%	27.0%
Rock Island County	23,074	73.2%	22.7%	39.4%	37.9%	2,644	8.4%	24.0%	36.4%	39.6%
Sangamon County	34,790	74.3%	25.2%	35.3%	39.5%	7,901	16.9%	29.8%	35.3%	34.9%
St. Clair County	39,138	55.6%	26.0%	33.0%	41.1%	24,808	35.3%	32.1%	36.3%	31.6%
Tazewell County	28,920	90.8%	29.2%	33.3%	37.6%	343	1.1%	25.1%	24.8%	50.1%
Will County	101,594	60.3%	33.3%	34.6%	32.1%	21,636	12.8%	36.5%	41.3%	22.2%
Winnebago County	44,894	62.1%	28.5%	35.3%	36.1%	10,010	13.9%	23.6%	46.7%	29.7%
Indiana										
Allen County	67,109	71.4%	25.1%	35.6%	39.3%	11,370	12.1%	32.5%	40.7%	26.8%
Clark County	21,154	78.0%	23.3%	34.1%	42.6%	2,163	8.0%	48.2%	47.4%	4.4%
Delaware County	32,930	84.4%	13.5%	62.1%	24.4%	3,229	8.3%	27.5%	62.2%	10.3%
Elkhart County	36,130	72.8%	30.8%	34.6%	34.6%	2,346	4.7%	38.8%	22.0%	39.1%
Hamilton County	57,526	87.8%	33.1%	30.4%	36.5%	1,670	2.5%	19.8%	50.8%	29.4%
Hendricks County	31,651	80.4%	32.8%	31.3%	36.0%	3,863	9.8%	16.8%	51.1%	32.1%
Johnson County	32,191	85.0%	29.5%	34.2%	36.3%	1,758	4.6%	45.4%	48.6%	6.0%
Lake County	56,965	47.9%	26.3%	36.0%	37.7%	32,175	27.1%	32.7%	38.9%	28.4%
LaPorte County	19,895	71.8%	28.9%	35.8%	35.3%	4,683	16.9%	25.3%	34.4%	40.3%
Madison County	26,245	83.4%	27.1%	37.3%	35.7%	2,488	7.9%	28.7%	33.4%	37.8%
Marion County	139,835	53.9%	18.5%	34.9%	46.5%	73,365	28.3%	26.9%	36.0%	37.1%
Monroe County	48,446	81.8%	10.5%	67.1%	22.3%	872	1.5%	15.6%	54.1%	30.3%
Porter County	33,527	81.4%	25.1%	37.4%	37.4%	1,793	4.4%	9.0%	73.6%	17.5%
St. Joseph County	50,464	70.0%	24.4%	40.4%	35.3%	10,977	15.2%	32.1%	41.8%	26.1%
Tippecanoe County	53,583	76.0%	11.5%	61.0%	27.5%	2,622	3.7%	24.5%	51.9%	23.6%
Vanderburgh County	38,435	81.4%	20.1%	41.1%	38.8%	4,549	9.6%	36.6%	33.5%	30.0%
Vigo County	26,797	81.8%	21.5%	49.4%	29.1%	2,993	9.1%	7.0%	66.1%	26.9%
Iowa										
Black Hawk County	33,942	79.9%	17.5%	53.7%	28.8%	4,837	11.4%	25.0%	54.2%	20.8%
Dubuque County	22,407	89.7%	29.5%	39.0%	31.5%	366	1.5%	28.1%	60.9%	10.9%
Johnson County	44,171	77.8%	11.9%	54.2%	33.8%	3,570	6.3%	21.1%	31.3%	47.6%
Linn County	48,553	87.6%	25.0%	35.8%	39.2%	2,377	4.3%	53.1%	7.6%	39.3%
Polk County	92,119	76.4%	22.9%	34.3%	42.8%	9,998	8.3%	24.2%	39.2%	36.6%
Pottawattamie County	19,744	86.3%	32.6%	34.4%	32.9%	720	3.1%	10.6%	9.0%	80.4%
Scott County	31,249	73.3%	26.2%	37.9%	35.9%	4,927	11.6%	34.3%	37.5%	28.2%
Story County	33,973	82.9%	12.4%	61.6%	26.1%	747	1.8%	6.8%	93.2%	0.0%
Woodbury County	20,207	67.7%	31.2%	34.9%	33.9%	848	2.8%	26.2%	31.5%	42.3%
Kansas										
Douglas County	35,432	80.0%	11.0%	60.9%	28.0%	2,504	5.7%	32.9%	5.9%	61.2%
Johnson County	102,847	76.3%	28.7%	31.7%	39.6%	8,199	6.1%	31.9%	32.4%	35.7%
Sedgwick County	96,575	67.7%	25.6%	34.2%	40.2%	12,767	9.0%	27.0%	29.1%	43.9%
Shawnee County	32,702	71.4%	25.2%	33.9%	40.9%	3,195	7.0%	37.9%	55.0%	7.1%

Table B-2: Counties—Race and Hispanic Origin by Age—*Continued*

	Asian, Non-Hispanic					Hispanic				
	Millennial Population		Percent by Age			Millennial Population		Percent by Age		
	Number	Percent	13 to 17	18 to 24	25 to 31	Number	Percent	13 to 17	18 to 24	25 to 31
Georgia—Cont.										
Floyd County	270	1.1%	0.0%	28.5%	71.5%	2,913	12.2%	45.0%	22.5%	32.5%
Forsyth County	2,005	4.7%	47.8%	35.6%	16.6%	5,509	12.9%	36.1%	35.0%	28.9%
Fulton County	18,756	6.8%	21.8%	38.5%	39.8%	24,097	8.7%	26.2%	31.3%	42.5%
Gwinnett County	25,273	11.3%	30.8%	35.5%	33.7%	54,330	24.4%	25.4%	33.7%	41.0%
Hall County	687	1.4%	41.9%	23.0%	35.1%	16,666	34.7%	29.7%	36.5%	33.8%
Henry County	1,144	2.1%	44.1%	29.9%	26.0%	3,527	6.6%	27.0%	43.0%	30.0%
Houston County	529	1.3%	39.7%	0.0%	60.3%	5,029	12.0%	32.4%	22.9%	44.7%
Lowndes County	755	1.9%	40.9%	30.2%	28.9%	2,005	5.0%	30.8%	28.9%	40.2%
Muscogee County	883	1.4%	29.9%	40.9%	29.2%	7,069	11.6%	18.9%	48.1%	33.0%
Newton County	999	3.8%	11.8%	34.4%	53.8%	2,709	10.4%	28.8%	60.8%	10.4%
Paulding County	404	1.1%	28.7%	71.3%	0.0%	2,082	5.8%	26.1%	32.2%	41.7%
Richmond County	1,311	2.1%	14.1%	32.7%	53.2%	3,172	5.1%	22.5%	39.2%	38.3%
Whitfield County	205	0.8%	0.0%	51.7%	48.3%	11,393	42.5%	27.8%	41.8%	30.4%
Hawaii										
Hawaii County	6,836	15.3%	28.3%	36.8%	34.9%	7,467	16.7%	37.2%	28.7%	34.1%
Honolulu County	79,471	29.0%	23.6%	35.4%	41.0%	33,900	12.4%	20.4%	41.7%	37.9%
Maui County	9,591	27.1%	38.1%	23.2%	38.6%	4,396	12.4%	33.0%	21.7%	45.4%
Idaho										
Ada County	3,160	2.8%	29.4%	34.1%	36.5%	13,659	12.1%	26.7%	51.7%	21.7%
Bonneville County	491	1.8%	26.5%	13.4%	60.1%	3,938	14.1%	28.7%	31.2%	40.1%
Canyon County	728	1.4%	0.0%	84.1%	15.9%	13,451	26.2%	34.2%	38.9%	27.0%
Kootenai County	725	2.1%	19.2%	51.0%	29.8%	2,548	7.2%	14.8%	50.6%	34.5%
Illinois										
Champaign County	11,314	13.9%	3.4%	71.7%	24.9%	5,214	6.4%	13.8%	45.3%	40.8%
Cook County	95,767	6.7%	18.2%	31.8%	50.0%	408,042	28.4%	25.8%	37.4%	36.8%
DeKalb County	369	1.0%	19.0%	81.0%	0.0%	3,610	9.5%	26.1%	50.5%	23.4%
DuPage County	23,715	10.2%	27.3%	32.9%	39.8%	41,266	17.8%	29.9%	31.6%	38.5%
Kane County	5,842	4.3%	28.7%	40.7%	30.7%	51,403	37.8%	30.1%	36.0%	33.8%
Kankakee County	140	0.5%	73.6%	26.4%	0.0%	3,177	11.6%	32.0%	49.2%	18.8%
Kendall County	1,152	3.8%	19.5%	0.0%	80.5%	4,297	14.2%	31.4%	44.5%	24.0%
Lake County	9,834	5.6%	28.4%	27.9%	43.6%	46,722	26.4%	29.4%	39.8%	30.8%
LaSalle County	244	0.9%	0.0%	12.3%	87.7%	3,298	12.3%	35.1%	29.3%	35.7%
Macon County	157	0.6%	15.9%	0.0%	84.1%	1,469	5.6%	9.6%	29.0%	61.4%
Madison County	791	1.2%	65.6%	0.0%	34.4%	2,643	3.9%	21.8%	61.1%	17.1%
McHenry County	2,012	2.6%	32.8%	57.4%	9.8%	12,741	16.5%	31.5%	32.9%	35.6%
McLean County	2,838	4.9%	6.6%	21.4%	72.0%	3,092	5.3%	16.6%	69.8%	13.6%
Peoria County	2,491	5.1%	2.6%	20.6%	76.8%	2,354	4.8%	29.4%	47.1%	23.5%
Rock Island County	384	1.2%	0.0%	62.8%	37.2%	5,000	15.9%	32.9%	47.9%	19.2%
Sangamon County	912	1.9%	7.0%	43.3%	49.7%	1,847	3.9%	9.4%	40.5%	50.1%
St. Clair County	821	1.2%	24.5%	75.5%	0.0%	3,211	4.6%	28.0%	57.8%	14.1%
Tazewell County	299	0.9%	0.0%	0.0%	100.0%	1,338	4.2%	10.1%	78.0%	12.0%
Will County	5,783	3.4%	29.2%	39.5%	31.3%	36,597	21.7%	32.4%	35.8%	31.8%
Winnebago County	2,076	2.9%	23.3%	26.8%	50.0%	13,271	18.4%	28.1%	48.4%	23.5%
Indiana										
Allen County	2,197	2.3%	16.3%	49.5%	34.1%	8,238	8.8%	33.7%	36.1%	30.2%
Clark County	197	0.7%	0.0%	100.0%	0.0%	1,255	4.6%	27.9%	24.4%	47.7%
Delaware County	259	0.7%	0.0%	100.0%	0.0%	1,368	3.5%	15.9%	40.5%	43.6%
Elkhart County	612	1.2%	11.6%	32.2%	56.2%	8,672	17.5%	29.3%	41.0%	29.7%
Hamilton County	3,576	5.5%	22.6%	40.3%	37.2%	2,186	3.3%	49.6%	25.8%	24.5%
Hendricks County	406	1.0%	50.5%	16.5%	33.0%	2,226	5.7%	17.3%	76.1%	6.6%
Johnson County	735	1.9%	52.8%	0.0%	47.2%	3,194	8.4%	45.3%	36.4%	18.3%
Lake County	1,978	1.7%	18.4%	49.2%	32.4%	26,406	22.2%	32.6%	39.5%	27.9%
LaPorte County	56	0.2%	100.0%	0.0%	0.0%	2,472	8.9%	19.8%	8.7%	71.5%
Madison County	na	na	na	na	na	1,688	5.4%	60.1%	19.4%	20.6%
Marion County	7,215	2.8%	9.6%	31.0%	59.4%	29,357	11.3%	25.8%	33.8%	40.4%
Monroe County	4,967	8.4%	4.7%	61.2%	34.1%	3,391	5.7%	7.6%	84.5%	7.9%
Porter County	740	1.8%	0.0%	75.5%	24.5%	4,633	11.3%	28.6%	49.3%	22.2%
St. Joseph County	1,736	2.4%	12.7%	69.8%	17.5%	7,184	10.0%	39.8%	44.9%	15.3%
Tippecanoe County	7,615	10.8%	6.1%	73.2%	20.6%	4,259	6.0%	24.8%	54.5%	20.7%
Vanderburgh County	605	1.3%	4.6%	0.0%	95.4%	1,414	3.0%	16.1%	83.9%	0.0%
Vigo County	404	1.2%	22.8%	48.0%	29.2%	1,310	4.0%	13.8%	52.9%	33.3%
Iowa										
Black Hawk County	555	1.3%	0.0%	77.1%	22.9%	2,907	6.8%	0.0%	71.1%	28.9%
Dubuque County	61	0.2%	0.0%	0.0%	100.0%	633	2.5%	54.0%	42.0%	3.9%
Johnson County	2,921	5.1%	0.0%	37.8%	62.2%	4,776	8.4%	16.2%	74.0%	9.7%
Linn County	1,770	3.2%	21.9%	11.6%	66.4%	1,363	2.5%	23.6%	3.2%	73.1%
Polk County	5,883	4.9%	44.7%	6.6%	48.7%	8,878	7.4%	30.8%	23.9%	45.3%
Pottawattamie County	449	2.0%	0.0%	100.0%	0.0%	1,523	6.7%	9.1%	24.6%	66.3%
Scott County	1,438	3.4%	17.9%	0.0%	82.1%	3,308	7.8%	21.0%	35.1%	43.9%
Story County	3,446	8.4%	6.9%	65.7%	27.5%	2,091	5.1%	2.9%	86.1%	11.0%
Woodbury County	674	2.3%	33.8%	66.2%	0.0%	5,916	19.8%	33.0%	30.6%	36.5%
Kansas										
Douglas County	1,990	4.5%	0.0%	57.7%	42.3%	1,745	3.9%	6.6%	33.9%	59.4%
Johnson County	7,150	5.3%	37.7%	30.9%	31.4%	10,940	8.1%	33.6%	29.0%	37.4%
Sedgwick County	5,264	3.7%	24.3%	23.7%	52.0%	23,186	16.3%	35.7%	33.0%	31.3%
Shawnee County	843	1.8%	0.0%	100.0%	0.0%	5,465	11.9%	23.8%	50.3%	25.8%

Table B-2: Counties—Race and Hispanic Origin by Age—*Continued*

	White, Non-Hispanic					Black, Non-Hispanic				
	Millennial Population		Percent by Age			Millennial Population		Percent by Age		
	Number	Percent	13 to 17	18 to 24	25 to 31	Number	Percent	13 to 17	18 to 24	25 to 31
Kansas—Cont.										
Wyandotte County......................	15,700	37.3%	25.6%	31.9%	42.5%	10,246	24.3%	29.6%	38.6%	31.7%
Kentucky										
Boone County	25,734	84.3%	32.0%	33.0%	35.0%	1,097	3.6%	3.1%	45.6%	51.3%
Campbell County........................	20,737	90.9%	30.2%	38.1%	31.7%	789	3.5%	19.5%	33.7%	46.8%
Daviess County	19,708	84.8%	28.3%	37.5%	34.2%	918	4.0%	0.0%	8.9%	91.1%
Fayette County	65,669	71.3%	14.0%	50.0%	36.1%	14,587	15.8%	25.5%	43.8%	30.7%
Hardin County	22,238	75.4%	36.1%	31.8%	32.1%	4,040	13.7%	38.4%	25.7%	35.9%
Jefferson County........................	125,498	65.0%	23.4%	34.4%	42.2%	46,357	24.0%	31.3%	39.1%	29.5%
Kenton County	36,068	85.1%	26.8%	33.8%	39.4%	2,184	5.2%	1.3%	57.6%	41.1%
Warren County...........................	30,095	79.4%	17.9%	50.5%	31.5%	4,089	10.8%	15.4%	24.2%	60.4%
Louisiana										
Ascension Parish	20,423	69.3%	35.8%	32.0%	32.2%	7,271	24.7%	25.6%	32.6%	41.7%
Bossier Parish............................	20,574	58.5%	21.6%	39.3%	39.1%	10,351	29.4%	21.9%	39.4%	38.7%
Caddo Parish..............................	26,517	38.9%	22.5%	34.3%	43.3%	36,759	54.0%	25.0%	39.4%	35.5%
Calcasieu Parish.........................	36,265	69.5%	24.0%	40.5%	35.5%	12,479	23.9%	40.4%	36.4%	23.2%
East Baton Rouge Parish.............	60,732	43.9%	16.7%	49.9%	33.5%	63,342	45.8%	22.5%	46.0%	31.4%
Jefferson Parish	52,637	46.8%	22.8%	34.9%	42.2%	33,997	30.2%	20.5%	39.5%	40.0%
Lafayette Parish	42,285	64.2%	21.7%	36.8%	41.5%	18,469	28.0%	22.0%	41.1%	36.9%
Lafourche Parish	17,431	69.0%	22.9%	40.2%	36.9%	4,983	19.7%	17.4%	52.2%	30.4%
Livingston Parish	29,950	87.3%	27.9%	35.4%	36.7%	2,877	8.4%	32.8%	35.0%	32.2%
Orleans Parish............................	34,579	31.0%	10.3%	30.4%	59.3%	64,633	57.9%	22.6%	39.9%	37.5%
Ouachita Parish..........................	22,141	50.9%	25.9%	39.7%	34.5%	19,525	44.9%	25.8%	39.3%	34.9%
Rapides Parish............................	20,628	58.6%	20.9%	35.5%	43.6%	10,027	28.5%	26.9%	37.8%	35.2%
St. Tammany Parish	42,413	74.7%	31.6%	33.3%	35.1%	8,379	14.8%	27.7%	31.5%	40.8%
Tangipahoa Parish......................	21,167	57.3%	26.8%	34.5%	38.8%	11,438	31.0%	23.8%	48.7%	27.5%
Terrebonne Parish.......................	18,045	62.3%	27.8%	37.0%	35.2%	6,171	21.3%	21.1%	18.6%	60.3%
Maine										
Androscoggin County	23,319	87.9%	27.0%	35.5%	37.4%	706	2.7%	19.8%	67.7%	12.5%
Cumberland County	58,537	84.0%	20.7%	36.6%	42.7%	1,816	2.6%	38.5%	59.1%	2.4%
Kennebec County........................	25,794	93.4%	29.3%	36.3%	34.4%	531	1.9%	1.3%	98.7%	0.0%
Penobscot County.......................	36,882	92.4%	20.4%	45.9%	33.6%	670	1.7%	39.0%	38.1%	23.0%
York County	38,529	89.7%	24.8%	33.9%	41.4%	310	0.7%	0.0%	94.5%	5.5%
Maryland										
Anne Arundel County	90,483	64.7%	23.5%	36.9%	39.6%	23,745	17.0%	30.0%	29.9%	40.1%
Baltimore County	114,277	53.5%	22.6%	39.2%	38.1%	65,367	30.6%	30.2%	34.5%	35.3%
Carroll County............................	33,975	86.4%	30.4%	39.0%	30.6%	916	2.3%	47.9%	25.2%	26.9%
Cecil County	20,887	82.1%	27.5%	35.3%	37.3%	1,893	7.4%	50.2%	12.1%	37.7%
Charles County...........................	17,047	43.8%	25.4%	34.2%	40.4%	17,692	45.4%	36.6%	34.7%	28.6%
Frederick County	43,350	71.8%	27.8%	34.9%	37.2%	5,630	9.3%	32.6%	43.2%	24.1%
Harford County	45,429	73.6%	30.7%	33.9%	35.4%	9,364	15.2%	38.1%	34.9%	27.1%
Howard County	40,230	54.0%	30.8%	32.5%	36.6%	16,196	21.7%	35.0%	34.8%	30.2%
Montgomery County	96,923	40.8%	29.2%	31.4%	39.4%	46,121	19.4%	26.5%	33.9%	39.6%
Prince George's County...............	32,870	13.2%	11.2%	52.1%	36.7%	151,079	60.9%	26.5%	37.5%	36.0%
St. Mary's County........................	21,640	75.8%	33.9%	31.5%	34.6%	3,987	14.0%	35.5%	53.1%	11.4%
Washington County......................	27,140	74.5%	28.7%	34.3%	37.0%	4,781	13.1%	9.0%	46.2%	44.9%
Wicomico County........................	18,190	58.7%	17.7%	50.6%	31.8%	9,464	30.6%	22.6%	52.4%	25.0%
Massachusetts										
Barnstable County	33,999	84.7%	27.4%	36.3%	36.3%	2,447	6.1%	30.4%	25.0%	44.7%
Berkshire County........................	25,019	85.0%	26.3%	41.7%	32.0%	1,110	3.8%	8.0%	92.0%	0.0%
Bristol County	107,461	80.6%	25.3%	38.9%	35.8%	4,130	3.1%	33.6%	49.1%	17.3%
Essex County	124,796	66.0%	28.2%	36.3%	35.5%	6,223	3.3%	25.9%	42.2%	31.9%
Hampden County	73,303	56.3%	24.0%	43.7%	32.3%	12,853	9.9%	31.4%	46.8%	21.8%
Hampshire County	37,873	79.4%	19.8%	51.9%	28.3%	2,274	4.8%	6.2%	86.3%	7.5%
Middlesex County	292,327	70.0%	23.0%	34.6%	42.4%	23,203	5.6%	20.7%	42.3%	37.0%
Norfolk County...........................	123,722	73.9%	31.0%	34.4%	34.6%	14,714	8.8%	30.9%	35.8%	33.2%
Plymouth County........................	88,220	79.5%	31.4%	37.6%	31.0%	11,747	10.6%	25.9%	35.1%	39.0%
Suffolk County............................	138,871	49.3%	5.9%	40.4%	53.8%	46,714	16.6%	22.6%	43.3%	34.1%
Worcester County	157,124	73.8%	28.2%	38.2%	33.6%	11,057	5.2%	25.9%	45.1%	29.1%
Michigan										
Allegan County...........................	21,750	83.6%	30.9%	34.7%	34.4%	285	1.1%	16.1%	83.9%	0.0%
Bay County.................................	22,198	83.3%	30.5%	31.4%	38.1%	1,313	4.9%	1.1%	87.8%	11.1%
Berrien County	23,302	67.9%	26.0%	36.3%	37.7%	5,877	17.1%	18.9%	47.6%	33.5%
Calhoun County..........................	24,306	77.6%	31.0%	36.0%	32.9%	3,262	10.4%	26.4%	35.3%	38.4%
Eaton County	20,283	79.5%	27.6%	34.3%	38.1%	1,870	7.3%	8.0%	18.7%	73.3%
Genesee County..........................	69,154	66.6%	28.6%	35.8%	35.6%	26,100	25.1%	29.1%	38.7%	32.2%
Ingham County	69,381	68.1%	12.8%	58.5%	28.7%	10,805	10.6%	19.5%	53.6%	27.0%
Jackson County...........................	31,981	81.3%	26.5%	37.0%	36.5%	4,722	12.0%	22.3%	35.5%	42.2%
Kalamazoo County	59,946	73.6%	17.9%	51.7%	30.3%	10,178	12.5%	24.2%	49.3%	26.4%
Kent County	121,569	70.7%	24.0%	35.8%	40.2%	19,799	11.5%	30.8%	28.3%	41.0%
Lenawee County..........................	21,724	89.2%	25.9%	40.7%	33.4%	511	2.1%	1.6%	24.9%	73.6%
Livingston County.......................	39,674	92.2%	36.7%	34.2%	29.1%	230	0.5%	0.0%	100.0%	0.0%
Macomb County..........................	154,002	76.2%	26.2%	35.6%	38.2%	28,362	14.0%	26.2%	44.0%	29.8%
Monroe County	31,099	88.8%	28.8%	36.0%	35.2%	1,288	3.7%	37.8%	42.4%	19.8%
Muskegon County.......................	30,518	74.9%	33.1%	35.1%	31.8%	6,214	15.2%	26.5%	40.1%	33.5%
Oakland County..........................	202,876	70.0%	28.8%	33.6%	37.6%	45,370	15.6%	30.7%	39.0%	30.2%
Ottawa County............................	65,501	83.8%	25.7%	46.8%	27.5%	900	1.2%	18.6%	28.2%	53.2%

Table B-2: Counties—Race and Hispanic Origin by Age—*Continued*

| | Asian, Non-Hispanic | | | | | Hispanic | | | | |
| | Millennial Population | | Percent by Age | | | Millennial Population | | Percent by Age | | |
	Number	Percent	13 to 17	18 to 24	25 to 31	Number	Percent	13 to 17	18 to 24	25 to 31
Kansas—Cont.										
Wyandotte County......................	1,955	4.6%	14.3%	14.4%	71.3%	12,709	30.2%	30.6%	40.6%	28.8%
Kentucky										
Boone County	753	2.5%	5.6%	26.7%	67.7%	2,342	7.7%	11.7%	22.8%	65.5%
Campbell County........................	na	na	na	na	na	1,057	4.6%	15.0%	9.4%	75.6%
Daviess County	265	1.1%	67.5%	32.5%	0.0%	719	3.1%	1.0%	52.3%	46.7%
Fayette County............................	3,568	3.9%	14.0%	27.1%	58.9%	6,374	6.9%	28.5%	37.2%	34.3%
Hardin County.............................	123	0.4%	59.3%	0.0%	40.7%	1,899	6.4%	4.4%	13.4%	82.2%
Jefferson County.........................	4,137	2.1%	28.3%	17.1%	54.6%	11,196	5.8%	23.9%	41.5%	34.6%
Kenton County............................	1,042	2.5%	60.3%	0.0%	39.7%	1,174	2.8%	31.4%	30.0%	38.6%
Warren County............................	1,139	3.0%	0.0%	13.7%	86.3%	1,639	4.3%	35.6%	42.5%	21.9%
Louisiana										
Ascension Parish	74	0.3%	100.0%	0.0%	0.0%	1,522	5.2%	24.1%	53.7%	22.2%
Bossier Parish.............................	165	0.5%	0.0%	0.0%	100.0%	2,942	8.4%	12.4%	21.9%	65.8%
Caddo Parish..............................	667	1.0%	10.2%	0.0%	89.8%	2,296	3.4%	28.8%	33.2%	38.0%
Calcasieu Parish.........................	239	0.5%	0.0%	100.0%	0.0%	2,300	4.4%	26.1%	55.2%	18.7%
East Baton Rouge Parish..............	4,747	3.4%	13.6%	25.4%	61.0%	5,823	4.2%	2.0%	63.1%	34.9%
Jefferson Parish	4,241	3.8%	30.0%	17.4%	52.6%	19,732	17.5%	15.0%	35.0%	50.1%
Lafayette Parish	1,398	2.1%	7.5%	42.8%	49.6%	2,542	3.9%	8.6%	43.4%	48.0%
Lafourche Parish.........................	212	0.8%	75.5%	0.0%	24.5%	1,138	4.5%	30.5%	40.3%	29.2%
Livingston Parish	na	na	na	na	na	541	1.6%	0.0%	100.0%	0.0%
Orleans Parish............................	3,718	3.3%	12.0%	46.4%	41.6%	6,813	6.1%	10.5%	34.8%	54.6%
Ouachita Parish..........................	767	1.8%	22.6%	55.0%	22.4%	565	1.3%	38.2%	46.0%	15.8%
Rapides Parish............................	751	2.1%	75.6%	24.4%	0.0%	2,929	8.3%	28.1%	59.3%	12.6%
St. Tammany Parish	794	1.4%	24.7%	0.0%	75.3%	3,600	6.3%	14.9%	52.3%	32.7%
Tangipahoa Parish.......................	12	0.0%	100.0%	0.0%	0.0%	2,799	7.6%	5.1%	32.4%	62.4%
Terrebonne Parish.......................	na	na	na	na	na	1,895	6.5%	14.5%	43.7%	41.8%
Maine										
Androscoggin County	334	1.3%	0.0%	36.2%	63.8%	150	0.6%	27.3%	46.0%	26.7%
Cumberland County	2,928	4.2%	4.3%	66.7%	29.0%	3,936	5.6%	27.2%	68.5%	4.2%
Kennebec County........................	129	0.5%	0.0%	100.0%	0.0%	448	1.6%	57.1%	9.6%	33.3%
Penobscot County.......................	572	1.4%	35.0%	0.0%	65.0%	288	0.7%	0.0%	100.0%	0.0%
York County	396	0.9%	0.0%	78.0%	22.0%	1,270	3.0%	0.0%	100.0%	0.0%
Maryland										
Anne Arundel County	5,726	4.1%	21.8%	46.5%	31.7%	14,327	10.2%	28.9%	39.4%	31.7%
Baltimore County........................	11,157	5.2%	17.2%	37.1%	45.8%	14,056	6.6%	14.0%	24.7%	61.4%
Carroll County............................	288	0.7%	0.0%	17.7%	82.3%	2,501	6.4%	36.7%	11.1%	52.2%
Cecil County...............................	177	0.7%	0.0%	0.0%	100.0%	2,220	8.7%	16.1%	71.1%	12.8%
Charles County...........................	577	1.5%	25.6%	19.9%	54.4%	1,660	4.3%	0.0%	43.0%	57.0%
Frederick County.........................	2,647	4.4%	29.2%	54.3%	16.5%	6,766	11.2%	30.8%	44.1%	25.1%
Harford County...........................	1,625	2.6%	31.4%	17.0%	51.5%	2,762	4.5%	27.2%	35.2%	37.6%
Howard County...........................	11,149	15.0%	28.2%	30.0%	41.7%	4,267	5.7%	23.3%	15.2%	61.5%
Montgomery County	31,906	13.4%	28.3%	30.2%	41.5%	52,662	22.2%	25.4%	33.4%	41.2%
Prince George's County................	11,688	4.7%	13.4%	36.6%	50.0%	46,574	18.8%	22.2%	36.0%	41.8%
St. Mary's County........................	411	1.4%	69.1%	0.0%	30.9%	1,798	6.3%	20.1%	67.1%	12.8%
Washington County.....................	617	1.7%	42.5%	38.4%	19.1%	1,893	5.2%	43.5%	31.9%	24.6%
Wicomico County........................	704	2.3%	15.3%	70.7%	13.9%	1,981	6.4%	0.0%	46.7%	53.3%
Massachusetts										
Barnstable County......................	948	2.4%	20.9%	19.4%	59.7%	1,328	3.3%	37.6%	55.6%	6.8%
Berkshire County........................	987	3.4%	16.6%	47.1%	36.3%	1,554	5.3%	21.9%	43.4%	34.7%
Bristol County.............................	1,551	1.2%	48.5%	34.0%	17.4%	12,567	9.4%	28.9%	34.0%	37.1%
Essex County..............................	9,113	4.8%	19.5%	46.1%	34.3%	45,611	24.1%	25.0%	40.1%	34.9%
Hampden County	3,005	2.3%	32.0%	46.3%	21.7%	39,271	30.2%	32.6%	38.8%	28.7%
Hampshire County.......................	3,035	6.4%	6.0%	80.4%	13.6%	3,913	8.2%	22.2%	54.1%	23.7%
Middlesex County.......................	47,616	11.4%	17.1%	33.9%	49.0%	40,689	9.7%	23.1%	36.8%	40.1%
Norfolk County...........................	15,687	9.4%	21.4%	27.7%	50.9%	9,253	5.5%	26.1%	39.3%	34.5%
Plymouth County.........................	1,751	1.6%	16.2%	28.9%	54.9%	5,141	4.6%	25.8%	28.5%	45.7%
Suffolk County............................	26,149	9.3%	9.8%	46.6%	43.6%	58,871	20.9%	21.5%	37.5%	41.0%
Worcester County	9,876	4.6%	21.4%	32.1%	46.4%	29,920	14.0%	24.8%	41.8%	33.4%
Michigan										
Allegan County...........................	120	0.5%	100.0%	0.0%	0.0%	2,497	9.6%	32.3%	42.7%	25.0%
Bay County.................................	559	2.1%	0.0%	38.8%	61.2%	1,889	7.1%	14.6%	45.3%	40.1%
Berrien County............................	835	2.4%	28.1%	25.7%	46.1%	2,843	8.3%	18.9%	53.7%	27.4%
Calhoun County..........................	427	1.4%	45.2%	0.0%	54.8%	1,788	5.7%	42.3%	24.0%	33.7%
Eaton County..............................	241	0.9%	23.2%	76.8%	0.0%	1,979	7.8%	39.8%	25.0%	35.2%
Genesee County..........................	678	0.7%	15.8%	70.6%	13.6%	4,196	4.0%	32.2%	47.3%	20.5%
Ingham County	7,264	7.1%	11.7%	59.5%	28.8%	7,872	7.7%	19.0%	53.4%	27.6%
Jackson County...........................	40	0.1%	0.0%	100.0%	0.0%	1,623	4.1%	41.8%	17.7%	40.5%
Kalamazoo County.......................	2,115	2.6%	16.0%	21.7%	62.3%	4,716	5.8%	27.1%	53.7%	19.2%
Kent County................................	4,986	2.9%	28.9%	20.9%	50.2%	19,843	11.5%	29.1%	39.3%	31.6%
Lenawee County.........................	na	na	na	na	na	1,633	6.7%	40.2%	23.5%	36.3%
Livingston County.......................	772	1.8%	0.0%	42.4%	57.6%	1,656	3.8%	39.1%	39.1%	21.7%
Macomb County..........................	8,469	4.2%	26.7%	28.1%	45.3%	5,893	2.9%	30.2%	45.1%	24.8%
Monroe County...........................	146	0.4%	0.0%	0.0%	100.0%	1,154	3.3%	39.6%	39.2%	21.2%
Muskegon County.......................	458	1.1%	71.0%	0.0%	29.0%	1,619	4.0%	12.6%	22.4%	65.0%
Oakland County..........................	16,040	5.5%	26.0%	30.5%	43.5%	16,236	5.6%	33.1%	36.3%	30.6%
Ottawa County............................	1,778	2.3%	37.3%	23.5%	39.2%	8,030	10.3%	21.2%	48.3%	30.5%

Table B-2: Counties—Race and Hispanic Origin by Age—*Continued*

| | White, Non-Hispanic | | | | | Black, Non-Hispanic | | | | |
| | Millennial Population | | Percent by Age | | | Millennial Population | | Percent by Age | | |
	Number	Percent	13 to 17	18 to 24	25 to 31	Number	Percent	13 to 17	18 to 24	25 to 31
Michigan—Cont.										
Saginaw County	32,266	64.7%	25.5%	40.3%	34.2%	10,980	22.0%	28.7%	46.3%	25.0%
St. Clair County	32,326	86.5%	32.3%	36.6%	31.1%	1,497	4.0%	0.0%	69.7%	30.3%
Washtenaw County	82,030	68.4%	15.7%	53.8%	30.5%	15,394	12.8%	24.3%	54.4%	21.3%
Wayne County	203,950	45.1%	26.0%	35.8%	38.1%	189,620	42.0%	27.1%	42.7%	30.3%
Minnesota										
Anoka County	68,977	81.5%	29.3%	31.8%	38.9%	4,798	5.7%	34.8%	52.2%	13.0%
Carver County	21,192	90.8%	37.6%	30.0%	32.3%	224	1.0%	28.6%	0.0%	71.4%
Dakota County	74,645	74.3%	30.9%	32.9%	36.2%	9,026	9.0%	38.5%	30.7%	30.8%
Hennepin County	210,170	63.4%	20.4%	32.7%	46.9%	47,368	14.3%	21.0%	38.2%	40.8%
Olmsted County	27,750	78.0%	26.9%	32.1%	41.0%	2,217	6.2%	15.4%	56.5%	28.1%
Ramsey County	84,378	56.0%	19.6%	37.6%	42.8%	17,969	11.9%	20.0%	40.6%	39.4%
Scott County	24,839	82.1%	30.5%	33.3%	36.2%	200	0.7%	32.0%	15.0%	53.0%
St. Louis County	47,705	88.6%	20.4%	46.6%	33.0%	1,381	2.6%	5.3%	14.1%	80.6%
Stearns County	41,253	86.2%	19.9%	50.1%	30.0%	2,349	4.9%	45.6%	34.8%	19.6%
Washington County	47,082	77.8%	33.0%	32.5%	34.6%	4,456	7.4%	39.0%	19.4%	41.6%
Wright County	28,943	88.6%	32.4%	28.7%	38.9%	1,028	3.1%	64.4%	35.6%	0.0%
Mississippi										
DeSoto County	26,655	64.2%	30.8%	34.6%	34.6%	11,522	27.7%	36.9%	35.7%	27.4%
Harrison County	31,613	60.0%	22.0%	40.0%	37.9%	14,402	27.3%	27.2%	38.6%	34.3%
Hinds County	16,134	21.7%	17.6%	41.6%	40.9%	55,750	74.8%	24.8%	40.9%	34.2%
Jackson County	22,794	62.4%	26.5%	34.5%	39.0%	9,575	26.2%	24.2%	40.6%	35.2%
Madison County	11,783	45.0%	40.6%	30.6%	28.8%	13,372	51.0%	33.0%	40.1%	26.9%
Rankin County	25,158	71.3%	25.3%	32.6%	42.1%	8,925	25.3%	29.6%	35.0%	35.3%
Missouri										
Boone County	51,653	78.9%	15.0%	55.8%	29.3%	4,051	6.2%	11.6%	36.1%	52.4%
Cass County	21,390	86.6%	34.1%	35.0%	30.9%	1,131	4.6%	56.9%	25.7%	17.3%
Clay County	45,453	79.3%	27.1%	31.3%	41.6%	4,204	7.3%	34.5%	29.4%	36.1%
Franklin County	21,354	92.5%	26.1%	37.3%	36.6%	695	3.0%	46.9%	25.2%	27.9%
Greene County	77,508	87.8%	19.5%	44.8%	35.7%	3,604	4.1%	24.8%	51.3%	23.9%
Jackson County	104,449	59.2%	22.5%	32.0%	45.5%	43,608	24.7%	27.7%	38.9%	33.4%
Jasper County	26,733	83.3%	26.8%	35.9%	37.3%	914	2.8%	34.8%	27.7%	37.5%
Jefferson County	50,075	95.5%	28.6%	34.3%	37.1%	305	0.6%	84.9%	0.0%	15.1%
Platte County	18,388	77.4%	21.6%	33.1%	45.3%	2,120	8.9%	38.6%	35.9%	25.4%
St. Charles County	76,735	86.3%	27.2%	35.9%	36.9%	4,799	5.4%	9.5%	28.1%	62.4%
St. Louis County	147,545	60.2%	27.5%	34.5%	38.0%	66,969	27.3%	27.8%	41.2%	30.9%
Montana										
Flathead County	16,048	76.7%	30.5%	35.5%	34.0%	118	0.6%	0.0%	0.0%	100.0%
Gallatin County	28,404	91.7%	21.4%	45.7%	32.9%	70	0.2%	0.0%	100.0%	0.0%
Missoula County	31,371	85.6%	19.6%	43.7%	36.7%	na	na	na	na	na
Yellowstone County	29,515	76.9%	22.1%	39.3%	38.5%	392	1.0%	67.9%	0.0%	32.1%
Nebraska										
Douglas County	96,589	65.6%	22.9%	34.3%	42.8%	18,578	12.6%	30.6%	39.1%	30.3%
Lancaster County	77,248	80.9%	16.7%	48.5%	34.7%	3,791	4.0%	17.1%	66.8%	16.1%
Sarpy County	36,277	80.6%	30.0%	30.9%	39.1%	2,262	5.0%	11.0%	36.6%	52.5%
Nevada										
Clark County	193,957	36.8%	23.0%	32.4%	44.6%	58,487	11.1%	23.2%	39.4%	37.4%
Washoe County	63,586	56.1%	21.8%	38.2%	39.9%	3,120	2.8%	18.5%	17.6%	63.9%
New Hampshire										
Hillsborough County	83,019	84.4%	27.5%	34.5%	37.9%	1,214	1.2%	7.7%	87.4%	4.9%
Merrimack County	31,678	91.7%	27.1%	40.5%	32.4%	402	1.2%	62.7%	37.3%	0.0%
Rockingham County	59,208	92.2%	32.8%	36.7%	30.5%	535	0.8%	100.0%	0.0%	0.0%
Strafford County	33,889	91.8%	20.8%	49.3%	29.9%	611	1.7%	100.0%	0.0%	0.0%
New Jersey										
Atlantic County	34,112	50.9%	28.6%	40.0%	31.4%	10,320	15.4%	25.5%	41.1%	33.4%
Bergen County	110,633	53.3%	31.4%	35.7%	32.9%	10,652	5.1%	24.9%	41.8%	33.2%
Burlington County	67,547	62.3%	28.8%	36.2%	35.0%	19,711	18.2%	28.7%	42.0%	29.3%
Camden County	65,781	50.4%	25.8%	34.2%	39.9%	25,260	19.4%	32.1%	38.7%	29.2%
Cape May County	14,300	74.2%	22.0%	40.4%	37.5%	867	4.5%	48.4%	40.5%	11.1%
Cumberland County	18,829	45.5%	26.3%	37.4%	36.3%	8,777	21.2%	28.4%	29.8%	41.8%
Essex County	50,193	24.5%	29.5%	35.7%	34.8%	86,021	42.0%	25.3%	38.1%	36.7%
Gloucester County	52,358	74.3%	28.5%	38.7%	32.8%	9,092	12.9%	24.9%	42.3%	32.8%
Hudson County	53,184	27.1%	13.2%	25.2%	61.6%	22,429	11.4%	22.8%	35.6%	41.6%
Hunterdon County	22,084	78.3%	37.4%	36.0%	26.6%	2,402	8.5%	14.7%	80.4%	4.8%
Mercer County	45,570	46.8%	23.6%	44.7%	31.7%	20,495	21.1%	29.6%	41.8%	28.6%
Middlesex County	87,448	41.4%	24.7%	40.6%	34.7%	23,120	11.0%	27.0%	44.5%	28.6%
Monmouth County	102,525	69.9%	31.1%	36.6%	32.3%	12,436	8.5%	34.2%	32.7%	33.1%
Morris County	77,308	67.8%	33.7%	35.2%	31.1%	3,037	2.7%	29.5%	65.3%	5.2%
Ocean County	98,966	79.1%	30.2%	35.2%	34.5%	6,115	4.9%	29.9%	46.3%	23.7%
Passaic County	47,386	35.3%	26.1%	40.4%	33.5%	17,038	12.7%	27.1%	40.1%	32.8%
Somerset County	39,188	54.6%	34.9%	34.9%	30.2%	6,486	9.0%	33.9%	26.8%	39.3%
Sussex County	27,478	84.2%	34.0%	37.9%	28.1%	1,445	4.4%	9.5%	24.5%	66.0%
Union County	45,932	34.4%	31.6%	32.2%	36.2%	29,007	21.7%	29.7%	39.3%	31.1%
Warren County	20,094	82.8%	35.3%	36.5%	28.2%	1,108	4.6%	22.2%	55.5%	22.3%
New Mexico										
Bernalillo County	57,463	30.7%	20.1%	37.2%	42.8%	4,643	2.5%	22.0%	67.0%	11.0%

Table B-2: Counties—Race and Hispanic Origin by Age—*Continued*

	Asian, Non-Hispanic					Hispanic				
	Millennial Population		Percent by Age			Millennial Population		Percent by Age		
	Number	Percent	13 to 17	18 to 24	25 to 31	Number	Percent	13 to 17	18 to 24	25 to 31
Michigan—Cont.										
Saginaw County	620	1.2%	46.3%	15.8%	37.9%	4,269	8.6%	23.5%	56.4%	20.1%
St. Clair County	224	0.6%	100.0%	0.0%	0.0%	1,356	3.6%	6.1%	71.2%	22.7%
Washtenaw County	11,239	9.4%	9.4%	60.0%	30.5%	5,764	4.8%	8.7%	43.0%	48.2%
Wayne County	14,323	3.2%	30.7%	31.9%	37.4%	30,325	6.7%	29.5%	39.4%	31.1%
Minnesota										
Anoka County	3,405	4.0%	24.4%	30.2%	45.4%	3,883	4.6%	21.4%	35.7%	42.9%
Carver County	593	2.5%	0.0%	51.1%	48.9%	141	0.6%	51.1%	48.9%	0.0%
Dakota County	4,968	4.9%	25.3%	35.2%	39.5%	9,241	9.2%	33.7%	17.5%	48.8%
Hennepin County	29,733	9.0%	14.0%	28.3%	57.7%	30,867	9.3%	20.3%	33.0%	46.8%
Olmsted County	2,425	6.8%	6.6%	24.5%	68.9%	2,370	6.7%	10.8%	62.7%	26.5%
Ramsey County	28,875	19.2%	22.4%	41.6%	36.0%	10,959	7.3%	22.1%	50.3%	27.6%
Scott County	3,039	10.0%	55.2%	0.2%	44.6%	1,769	5.8%	31.0%	67.6%	1.5%
St. Louis County	956	1.8%	38.1%	36.9%	25.0%	500	0.9%	7.2%	13.4%	79.4%
Stearns County	623	1.3%	0.0%	100.0%	0.0%	1,926	4.0%	13.1%	76.8%	10.1%
Washington County	3,042	5.0%	7.9%	28.4%	63.7%	4,036	6.7%	35.9%	43.4%	20.8%
Wright County	788	2.4%	22.0%	0.0%	78.0%	481	1.5%	0.0%	100.0%	0.0%
Mississippi										
DeSoto County	251	0.6%	100.0%	0.0%	0.0%	2,569	6.2%	40.2%	26.9%	32.8%
Harrison County	2,762	5.2%	18.2%	30.7%	51.1%	2,742	5.2%	11.5%	46.1%	42.4%
Hinds County	854	1.1%	34.8%	26.9%	38.3%	1,353	1.8%	0.0%	0.0%	100.0%
Jackson County	1,660	4.5%	23.3%	39.8%	36.9%	2,261	6.2%	10.4%	60.2%	29.4%
Madison County	73	0.3%	0.0%	100.0%	0.0%	974	3.7%	0.0%	0.0%	100.0%
Rankin County	388	1.1%	45.1%	0.0%	54.9%	405	1.1%	34.3%	0.0%	65.7%
Missouri										
Boone County	2,572	3.9%	0.0%	57.1%	42.9%	3,161	4.8%	0.0%	78.4%	21.6%
Cass County	na	na	na	na	na	1,414	5.7%	40.8%	27.8%	31.4%
Clay County	1,042	1.8%	0.0%	41.7%	58.3%	4,640	8.1%	19.6%	39.3%	41.1%
Franklin County	na	na	na	na	na	883	3.8%	35.8%	9.2%	55.0%
Greene County	954	1.1%	0.0%	60.4%	39.6%	3,731	4.2%	18.6%	64.6%	16.8%
Jackson County	3,327	1.9%	20.6%	20.7%	58.7%	20,058	11.4%	32.5%	31.4%	36.1%
Jasper County	947	3.0%	3.4%	71.0%	25.7%	2,567	8.0%	20.8%	33.2%	46.0%
Jefferson County	587	1.1%	54.3%	31.5%	14.1%	928	1.8%	21.8%	0.0%	78.2%
Platte County	191	0.8%	0.0%	100.0%	0.0%	2,147	9.0%	3.0%	38.1%	58.9%
St. Charles County	2,811	3.2%	17.3%	14.2%	68.5%	2,687	3.0%	24.4%	19.8%	55.8%
St. Louis County	10,740	4.4%	17.2%	33.4%	49.5%	8,175	3.3%	24.3%	29.6%	46.1%
Montana										
Flathead County	33	0.2%	0.0%	0.0%	100.0%	1,687	8.1%	61.6%	4.3%	34.1%
Gallatin County	712	2.3%	13.5%	69.7%	16.9%	636	2.1%	34.3%	65.7%	0.0%
Missoula County	223	0.6%	100.0%	0.0%	0.0%	1,338	3.7%	38.9%	61.1%	0.0%
Yellowstone County	152	0.4%	0.0%	83.6%	16.4%	2,718	7.1%	49.6%	32.3%	18.1%
Nebraska										
Douglas County	5,757	3.9%	9.5%	37.2%	53.3%	19,811	13.5%	27.2%	35.4%	37.4%
Lancaster County	4,734	5.0%	15.0%	47.4%	37.6%	6,759	7.1%	28.3%	51.7%	20.0%
Sarpy County	1,001	2.2%	31.1%	23.6%	45.4%	4,517	10.0%	28.4%	44.8%	26.7%
Nevada										
Clark County	47,194	8.9%	24.6%	35.1%	40.3%	200,724	38.0%	28.1%	36.1%	35.8%
Washoe County	5,336	4.7%	32.9%	33.0%	34.0%	33,717	29.8%	28.2%	40.2%	31.6%
New Hampshire										
Hillsborough County	4,341	4.4%	21.4%	29.9%	48.7%	8,173	8.3%	25.4%	29.0%	45.6%
Merrimack County	1,406	4.1%	1.9%	89.5%	8.5%	554	1.6%	52.3%	33.2%	14.4%
Rockingham County	1,507	2.3%	32.3%	29.9%	37.8%	1,987	3.1%	16.3%	53.2%	30.5%
Strafford County	557	1.5%	13.6%	60.3%	26.0%	732	2.0%	33.3%	39.6%	27.0%
New Jersey										
Atlantic County	5,386	8.0%	25.2%	34.1%	40.7%	15,097	22.5%	24.8%	41.1%	34.1%
Bergen County	33,129	16.0%	25.9%	32.0%	42.1%	48,716	23.5%	28.6%	34.7%	36.7%
Burlington County	5,024	4.6%	26.2%	16.9%	57.0%	11,517	10.6%	25.8%	41.6%	32.6%
Camden County	8,293	6.4%	24.3%	27.8%	47.8%	26,370	20.2%	25.3%	34.7%	40.0%
Cape May County	342	1.8%	50.3%	0.0%	49.7%	3,208	16.6%	18.2%	35.3%	46.5%
Cumberland County	387	0.9%	0.0%	0.0%	100.0%	11,573	27.9%	18.6%	28.4%	53.0%
Essex County	9,632	4.7%	32.4%	30.1%	37.5%	52,413	25.6%	23.0%	34.7%	42.3%
Gloucester County	1,977	2.8%	40.2%	31.5%	28.3%	5,086	7.2%	29.1%	14.4%	56.6%
Hudson County	33,238	16.9%	9.7%	22.6%	67.7%	82,709	42.2%	21.4%	37.0%	41.7%
Hunterdon County	350	1.2%	72.3%	18.9%	8.9%	2,990	10.6%	30.4%	64.2%	5.4%
Mercer County	9,662	9.9%	22.9%	35.1%	42.1%	19,207	19.7%	26.2%	37.1%	36.7%
Middlesex County	46,586	22.1%	24.1%	35.7%	40.2%	49,136	23.3%	23.7%	40.1%	36.2%
Monmouth County	8,361	5.7%	39.6%	27.8%	32.6%	20,053	13.7%	25.6%	40.2%	34.2%
Morris County	10,284	9.0%	24.7%	28.0%	47.2%	19,027	16.7%	24.6%	36.3%	39.1%
Ocean County	2,439	2.0%	25.3%	45.1%	29.7%	15,032	12.0%	19.7%	33.5%	46.9%
Passaic County	8,153	6.1%	21.8%	32.9%	45.2%	60,075	44.8%	27.6%	38.5%	33.9%
Somerset County	10,994	15.3%	33.7%	26.1%	40.2%	13,007	18.1%	29.1%	36.2%	34.6%
Sussex County	182	0.6%	16.5%	0.0%	83.5%	3,232	9.9%	29.6%	40.6%	29.8%
Union County	4,652	3.5%	15.4%	35.7%	48.8%	46,462	34.8%	22.5%	38.0%	39.4%
Warren County	334	1.4%	52.7%	47.3%	0.0%	2,341	9.6%	38.4%	52.2%	9.4%
New Mexico										
Bernalillo County	4,934	2.6%	16.0%	38.6%	45.4%	104,585	55.9%	27.0%	37.9%	35.1%

Table B-2: Counties—Race and Hispanic Origin by Age—*Continued*

	White, Non-Hispanic					Black, Non-Hispanic				
	Millennial Population		Percent by Age			Millennial Population		Percent by Age		
	Number	Percent	13 to 17	18 to 24	25 to 31	Number	Percent	13 to 17	18 to 24	25 to 31
New Mexico—Cont.										
Doña Ana County	16,216	24.2%	17.9%	49.2%	32.9%	1,767	2.6%	29.7%	66.9%	3.4%
San Juan County	10,351	32.2%	28.8%	30.4%	40.8%	na	na	na	na	na
Sandoval County	10,906	34.1%	30.7%	34.7%	34.7%	370	1.2%	54.1%	44.9%	1.1%
Santa Fe County	7,956	25.7%	23.3%	37.1%	39.6%	106	0.3%	0.0%	100.0%	0.0%
New York										
Albany County	62,245	69.2%	18.8%	49.1%	32.2%	11,041	12.3%	21.8%	42.6%	35.6%
Bronx County	32,639	7.9%	18.6%	41.2%	40.2%	114,256	27.8%	23.3%	39.0%	37.7%
Broome County	42,966	78.5%	21.0%	47.0%	32.0%	3,537	6.5%	16.5%	57.6%	25.9%
Chautauqua County	27,721	80.4%	23.2%	43.8%	33.0%	1,700	4.9%	4.9%	74.5%	20.6%
Dutchess County	54,554	69.4%	28.2%	44.1%	27.7%	6,713	8.5%	24.9%	47.6%	27.5%
Erie County	170,360	69.8%	22.6%	38.5%	38.9%	37,843	15.5%	29.0%	43.1%	27.9%
Jefferson County	28,053	78.6%	22.7%	41.0%	36.3%	2,115	5.9%	1.2%	44.1%	54.8%
Kings County	256,807	34.4%	17.1%	28.9%	54.0%	228,640	30.6%	23.2%	37.7%	39.1%
Monroe County	129,388	64.8%	21.0%	40.8%	38.2%	34,345	17.2%	29.5%	39.2%	31.3%
Nassau County	178,827	55.7%	30.8%	37.8%	31.4%	40,537	12.6%	26.2%	38.7%	35.1%
New York County	42,160	82.3%	26.4%	38.6%	35.0%	3,864	7.5%	23.1%	54.9%	22.0%
Niagara County	223,315	46.1%	7.2%	26.9%	65.8%	59,578	12.3%	14.5%	37.1%	48.4%
Oneida County	47,314	78.5%	25.8%	36.2%	38.0%	3,918	6.5%	21.4%	39.7%	38.9%
Onondaga County	91,204	70.8%	25.2%	37.7%	37.1%	15,750	12.2%	28.1%	40.8%	31.1%
Ontario County	22,274	87.6%	30.6%	40.0%	29.4%	263	1.0%	0.0%	14.1%	85.9%
Orange County	61,755	62.8%	29.2%	39.7%	31.1%	8,307	8.5%	29.5%	49.1%	21.4%
Oswego County	29,690	90.3%	26.7%	43.0%	30.3%	628	1.9%	0.6%	31.8%	67.5%
Putnam County	16,596	76.5%	31.0%	38.3%	30.7%	749	3.5%	32.3%	12.3%	55.4%
Queens County	130,950	21.6%	17.3%	30.6%	52.1%	109,584	18.0%	24.6%	39.9%	35.5%
Rensselaer County	34,094	81.0%	21.1%	40.3%	38.6%	2,130	5.1%	13.8%	47.3%	38.8%
Richmond County	65,168	56.1%	24.6%	37.6%	37.8%	13,550	11.7%	27.4%	42.5%	30.2%
Rockland County	47,557	58.5%	34.7%	36.3%	29.0%	9,680	11.9%	29.9%	38.3%	31.8%
Saratoga County	46,405	88.1%	28.6%	36.1%	35.3%	1,581	3.0%	6.1%	48.2%	45.7%
Schenectady County	27,429	70.4%	24.1%	37.2%	38.7%	4,369	11.2%	17.9%	29.7%	52.5%
St. Lawrence County	27,615	88.2%	21.1%	51.4%	27.5%	1,550	5.0%	28.5%	46.5%	25.0%
Steuben County	20,382	94.7%	33.4%	35.1%	31.5%	376	1.7%	14.6%	54.0%	31.4%
Suffolk County	227,921	61.9%	31.2%	37.6%	31.3%	33,515	9.1%	29.4%	40.2%	30.4%
Tompkins County	28,635	69.0%	9.9%	67.0%	23.1%	1,839	4.4%	20.9%	74.3%	4.7%
Ulster County	30,235	72.2%	25.2%	41.7%	33.1%	2,858	6.8%	4.7%	66.7%	28.7%
Wayne County	17,654	85.4%	30.3%	34.4%	35.2%	918	4.4%	0.0%	13.5%	86.5%
Westchester County	104,522	46.6%	32.9%	37.8%	29.4%	35,304	15.7%	25.9%	40.1%	34.0%
North Carolina										
Alamance County	23,917	61.6%	25.1%	40.7%	34.1%	7,276	18.7%	33.0%	37.7%	29.2%
Brunswick County	14,109	76.9%	28.0%	35.2%	36.8%	2,649	14.4%	44.8%	22.3%	32.8%
Buncombe County	45,360	80.7%	20.4%	37.2%	42.5%	3,182	5.7%	17.9%	39.7%	42.4%
Burke County	17,217	81.6%	33.7%	33.7%	32.6%	946	4.5%	22.6%	46.1%	31.3%
Cabarrus County	29,687	64.8%	28.2%	34.7%	37.1%	8,390	18.3%	35.6%	41.0%	23.4%
Catawba County	24,672	71.2%	29.1%	36.9%	34.0%	3,083	8.9%	8.9%	69.9%	21.2%
Cleveland County	17,951	77.5%	24.2%	41.6%	34.2%	2,759	11.9%	9.0%	75.5%	15.5%
Craven County	18,705	62.2%	17.7%	46.9%	35.4%	7,878	26.2%	19.4%	31.1%	49.5%
Cumberland County	45,154	43.3%	15.9%	40.3%	43.8%	36,431	35.0%	25.6%	39.2%	35.3%
Davidson County	28,253	75.7%	31.9%	34.1%	34.0%	4,159	11.1%	33.3%	40.5%	26.3%
Durham County	31,080	36.7%	14.4%	31.8%	53.8%	32,775	38.7%	22.8%	42.6%	34.5%
Forsyth County	45,276	49.1%	24.1%	38.6%	37.3%	27,533	29.9%	26.8%	43.4%	29.8%
Gaston County	33,612	67.4%	28.8%	36.2%	34.9%	9,441	18.9%	29.0%	36.2%	34.8%
Guilford County	62,611	45.4%	22.6%	39.8%	37.7%	53,187	38.5%	21.9%	43.9%	34.2%
Harnett County	21,937	62.9%	24.6%	32.7%	42.7%	7,100	20.4%	27.1%	39.1%	33.9%
Henderson County	15,580	69.6%	39.1%	29.7%	31.2%	1,016	4.5%	25.0%	57.1%	17.9%
Iredell County	28,017	72.0%	32.8%	37.5%	29.7%	5,717	14.7%	28.7%	46.2%	25.1%
Johnston County	28,123	66.4%	36.0%	30.4%	33.6%	6,717	15.9%	28.4%	50.9%	20.7%
Mecklenburg County	119,831	43.9%	21.2%	32.8%	46.0%	90,624	33.2%	25.1%	39.2%	35.7%
Moore County	11,947	63.1%	33.0%	25.5%	41.5%	2,297	12.1%	22.9%	46.8%	30.3%
Nash County	7,750	35.5%	31.4%	39.2%	29.3%	12,098	55.4%	25.3%	45.0%	29.7%
New Hanover County	44,637	75.6%	15.2%	49.1%	35.8%	7,436	12.6%	28.2%	36.8%	35.0%
Onslow County	49,192	61.4%	12.2%	54.6%	33.2%	14,248	17.8%	17.2%	44.0%	38.9%
Orange County	32,352	67.0%	16.8%	58.1%	25.2%	6,366	13.2%	19.6%	42.5%	37.8%
Pitt County	35,141	56.9%	14.3%	60.7%	25.1%	20,455	33.1%	30.2%	45.4%	24.4%
Randolph County	24,471	77.0%	27.5%	36.7%	35.8%	1,873	5.9%	37.1%	30.9%	32.1%
Robeson County	7,891	21.1%	29.6%	46.3%	24.2%	11,045	29.6%	29.4%	44.4%	26.3%
Rockingham County	13,067	65.4%	33.9%	27.8%	38.3%	3,664	18.3%	35.6%	38.3%	26.0%
Rowan County	21,254	66.0%	26.2%	38.7%	35.1%	6,960	21.6%	27.3%	48.5%	24.2%
Union County	34,153	68.2%	38.9%	34.2%	26.9%	7,264	14.5%	36.6%	43.4%	20.0%
Wake County	146,429	56.7%	25.9%	35.9%	38.2%	57,020	22.1%	26.3%	38.8%	34.8%
Wayne County	16,251	52.4%	20.8%	41.6%	37.7%	9,859	31.8%	21.6%	37.4%	41.0%
North Dakota										
Cass County	48,350	87.0%	17.6%	47.7%	34.7%	2,795	5.0%	0.0%	94.7%	5.3%
Ohio										
Allen County	21,502	81.8%	24.4%	42.2%	33.4%	3,049	11.6%	31.8%	41.3%	26.9%
Ashtabula County	20,463	90.0%	30.2%	33.8%	36.0%	655	2.9%	0.0%	48.2%	51.8%
Butler County	80,603	79.8%	23.5%	45.5%	31.0%	7,249	7.2%	37.7%	34.1%	28.2%
Clark County	27,138	82.3%	29.3%	35.2%	35.4%	3,403	10.3%	26.6%	50.5%	22.9%

Table B-2: Counties—Race and Hispanic Origin by Age—*Continued*

| | Asian, Non-Hispanic | | | | | Hispanic | | | | |
| | Millennial Population | | Percent by Age | | | Millennial Population | | Percent by Age | | |
	Number	Percent	13 to 17	18 to 24	25 to 31	Number	Percent	13 to 17	18 to 24	25 to 31
New Mexico—Cont.										
Doña Ana County	428	0.6%	0.0%	0.0%	100.0%	46,724	69.8%	27.3%	47.6%	25.1%
San Juan County	54	0.2%	0.0%	100.0%	0.0%	7,550	23.5%	24.0%	42.1%	33.9%
Sandoval County	382	1.2%	0.0%	0.0%	100.0%	14,555	45.5%	30.1%	34.0%	35.8%
Santa Fe County	534	1.7%	47.4%	8.8%	43.8%	20,397	65.9%	28.3%	37.0%	34.7%
New York										
Albany County	6,178	6.9%	15.4%	53.5%	31.1%	6,815	7.6%	7.4%	56.7%	35.9%
Bronx County	14,465	3.5%	21.8%	37.9%	40.3%	242,711	59.0%	23.2%	40.8%	35.9%
Broome County	3,858	7.1%	14.0%	76.5%	9.5%	2,994	5.5%	19.5%	46.3%	34.2%
Chautauqua County	739	2.1%	33.3%	64.4%	2.3%	3,503	10.2%	31.3%	45.7%	23.0%
Dutchess County	3,056	3.9%	38.2%	44.1%	17.7%	11,403	14.5%	26.7%	43.1%	30.2%
Erie County	11,152	4.6%	17.5%	45.3%	37.1%	17,485	7.2%	23.6%	37.5%	38.9%
Jefferson County	224	0.6%	0.0%	100.0%	0.0%	3,021	8.5%	19.8%	36.9%	43.3%
Kings County	84,785	11.3%	20.8%	34.7%	44.4%	158,518	21.2%	21.3%	37.1%	41.6%
Monroe County	9,447	4.7%	16.4%	43.4%	40.2%	20,623	10.3%	30.1%	38.9%	31.0%
Nassau County	28,911	9.0%	31.1%	33.2%	35.7%	64,844	20.2%	25.7%	35.5%	38.9%
New York County	789	1.5%	26.9%	36.5%	36.6%	2,317	4.5%	34.9%	36.3%	28.9%
Niagara County	58,919	12.2%	9.5%	35.3%	55.3%	125,291	25.9%	19.7%	40.3%	40.0%
Oneida County	1,996	3.3%	47.9%	40.6%	11.5%	3,662	6.1%	32.6%	45.2%	22.2%
Onondaga County	6,142	4.8%	13.8%	51.5%	34.7%	7,353	5.7%	24.3%	54.6%	21.1%
Ontario County	343	1.3%	0.0%	40.2%	59.8%	1,893	7.4%	17.4%	23.8%	58.8%
Orange County	1,374	1.4%	24.6%	31.1%	44.3%	22,397	22.8%	32.4%	41.7%	25.9%
Oswego County	272	0.8%	32.4%	67.6%	0.0%	1,584	4.8%	26.8%	49.4%	23.8%
Putnam County	937	4.3%	25.3%	12.6%	62.1%	3,332	15.4%	16.8%	56.4%	26.8%
Queens County	143,477	23.6%	21.0%	33.9%	45.2%	191,730	31.6%	21.8%	36.1%	42.1%
Rensselaer County	1,246	3.0%	15.2%	16.3%	68.5%	2,603	6.2%	36.3%	44.6%	19.1%
Richmond County	9,183	7.9%	29.9%	43.7%	26.4%	26,172	22.5%	25.2%	37.0%	37.8%
Rockland County	4,172	5.1%	24.6%	48.5%	26.9%	18,224	22.4%	21.3%	37.9%	40.8%
Saratoga County	1,539	2.9%	7.5%	59.1%	33.5%	2,015	3.8%	28.1%	25.5%	46.4%
Schenectady County	1,577	4.0%	26.3%	34.4%	39.3%	4,341	11.1%	20.9%	48.7%	30.4%
St. Lawrence County	243	0.8%	14.0%	86.0%	0.0%	1,278	4.1%	4.9%	63.0%	32.2%
Steuben County	300	1.4%	17.7%	59.7%	22.7%	203	0.9%	0.0%	67.0%	33.0%
Suffolk County	17,512	4.8%	22.0%	39.1%	38.9%	82,761	22.5%	27.1%	35.1%	37.8%
Tompkins County	6,683	16.1%	3.5%	72.5%	24.0%	2,179	5.2%	11.3%	46.4%	42.3%
Ulster County	1,395	3.3%	26.6%	41.9%	31.5%	6,228	14.9%	39.6%	44.7%	15.7%
Wayne County	146	0.7%	3.4%	30.1%	66.4%	1,364	6.6%	45.5%	16.2%	38.3%
Westchester County	10,682	4.8%	19.0%	31.3%	49.7%	69,100	30.8%	25.1%	37.0%	38.0%
North Carolina										
Alamance County	894	2.3%	0.0%	16.4%	83.6%	6,089	15.7%	30.8%	29.3%	39.9%
Brunswick County	152	0.8%	54.6%	0.0%	45.4%	1,042	5.7%	37.2%	38.4%	24.4%
Buncombe County	320	0.6%	0.0%	100.0%	0.0%	5,253	9.3%	37.5%	5.2%	57.2%
Burke County	819	3.9%	30.2%	0.0%	69.8%	719	3.4%	0.0%	31.7%	68.3%
Cabarrus County	876	1.9%	17.9%	27.1%	55.0%	6,068	13.2%	38.4%	32.0%	29.6%
Catawba County	2,510	7.2%	27.8%	43.4%	28.8%	3,247	9.4%	30.8%	48.7%	20.6%
Cleveland County	282	1.2%	100.0%	0.0%	0.0%	1,635	7.1%	33.0%	35.4%	31.6%
Craven County	300	1.0%	0.0%	31.0%	69.0%	2,331	7.7%	7.9%	63.1%	29.0%
Cumberland County	1,828	1.8%	15.3%	48.9%	35.8%	13,699	13.1%	15.7%	46.0%	38.3%
Davidson County	786	2.1%	70.2%	29.8%	0.0%	3,360	9.0%	14.0%	50.9%	35.1%
Durham County	5,518	6.5%	4.6%	38.0%	57.4%	11,429	13.5%	14.0%	33.5%	52.6%
Forsyth County	2,200	2.4%	22.1%	50.6%	27.2%	14,475	15.7%	35.7%	41.2%	23.0%
Gaston County	833	1.7%	18.6%	52.7%	28.7%	4,285	8.6%	38.7%	36.9%	24.4%
Guilford County	7,559	5.5%	24.0%	41.2%	34.8%	11,527	8.3%	23.7%	38.3%	38.0%
Harnett County	488	1.4%	7.6%	14.8%	77.7%	3,752	10.8%	14.6%	33.4%	52.0%
Henderson County	273	1.2%	0.0%	81.7%	18.3%	3,117	13.9%	30.9%	31.6%	37.5%
Iredell County	1,243	3.2%	6.7%	40.7%	52.6%	3,042	7.8%	27.9%	22.3%	49.8%
Johnston County	184	0.4%	49.5%	50.5%	0.0%	6,872	16.2%	28.0%	47.1%	24.9%
Mecklenburg County	15,320	5.6%	11.0%	28.5%	60.6%	39,938	14.6%	23.7%	33.0%	43.3%
Moore County	260	1.4%	96.9%	0.0%	3.1%	3,340	17.6%	35.4%	24.0%	40.6%
Nash County	420	1.9%	46.2%	53.8%	0.0%	1,351	6.2%	72.8%	0.0%	27.2%
New Hanover County	1,699	2.9%	22.1%	63.0%	14.9%	2,887	4.9%	20.7%	45.7%	33.7%
Onslow County	1,860	2.3%	34.2%	27.8%	38.0%	12,571	15.7%	13.7%	55.0%	31.3%
Orange County	2,838	5.9%	28.2%	57.0%	14.8%	4,211	8.7%	18.5%	46.0%	35.5%
Pitt County	1,245	2.0%	14.1%	52.4%	33.5%	3,751	6.1%	32.3%	48.9%	18.8%
Randolph County	268	0.8%	43.7%	0.0%	56.3%	4,853	15.3%	29.2%	32.8%	38.0%
Robeson County	177	0.5%	15.8%	29.4%	54.8%	3,614	9.7%	22.7%	52.2%	25.1%
Rockingham County	na	na	na	na	na	1,871	9.4%	18.0%	5.7%	76.3%
Rowan County	376	1.2%	0.0%	22.6%	77.4%	3,344	10.4%	36.1%	39.8%	24.1%
Union County	1,102	2.2%	43.8%	49.2%	7.0%	6,681	13.3%	29.7%	32.5%	37.8%
Wake County	15,185	5.9%	29.4%	27.9%	42.7%	29,808	11.5%	29.9%	38.5%	31.6%
Wayne County	na	na	na	na	na	4,472	14.4%	42.8%	29.2%	28.0%
North Dakota										
Cass County	2,199	4.0%	0.0%	35.9%	64.1%	623	1.1%	0.0%	100.0%	0.0%
Ohio										
Allen County	na	na	na	na	na	940	3.6%	15.2%	0.0%	84.8%
Ashtabula County	na	na	na	na	na	834	3.7%	0.0%	73.3%	26.7%
Butler County	2,853	2.8%	36.0%	54.3%	9.7%	5,973	5.9%	12.4%	48.4%	39.3%
Clark County	87	0.3%	66.7%	33.3%	0.0%	1,699	5.2%	35.2%	33.1%	31.7%

Table B-2: Counties—Race and Hispanic Origin by Age—*Continued*

	White, Non-Hispanic					Black, Non-Hispanic				
	Millennial Population		Percent by Age			Millennial Population		Percent by Age		
	Number	Percent	13 to 17	18 to 24	25 to 31	Number	Percent	13 to 17	18 to 24	25 to 31
Ohio—Cont.										
Clermont County	45,209	92.0%	30.7%	32.3%	37.0%	1,035	2.1%	48.8%	31.3%	19.9%
Columbiana County	21,294	89.3%	30.6%	35.3%	34.1%	896	3.8%	6.0%	12.7%	81.3%
Cuyahoga County	167,859	54.0%	24.9%	35.0%	40.1%	102,788	33.1%	27.8%	40.8%	31.3%
Delaware County	34,703	85.9%	37.1%	32.4%	30.6%	1,122	2.8%	49.6%	36.5%	13.9%
Fairfield County	31,716	83.9%	31.1%	32.9%	36.0%	3,837	10.1%	16.8%	45.3%	37.9%
Franklin County	229,837	64.3%	18.4%	35.6%	46.0%	73,617	20.6%	27.8%	38.8%	33.3%
Geauga County	19,165	92.2%	37.4%	38.2%	24.4%	405	1.9%	0.0%	100.0%	0.0%
Greene County	37,774	78.6%	24.1%	40.4%	35.4%	5,895	12.3%	8.9%	74.7%	16.4%
Hamilton County	135,472	63.6%	22.9%	37.1%	40.0%	56,559	26.6%	27.7%	38.8%	33.5%
Lake County	43,419	82.7%	28.7%	36.4%	34.8%	2,660	5.1%	28.2%	48.5%	23.3%
Licking County	36,890	89.8%	30.4%	37.0%	32.6%	1,611	3.9%	55.8%	29.2%	15.0%
Lorain County	51,893	72.1%	28.1%	37.1%	34.7%	7,911	11.0%	34.5%	38.0%	27.5%
Lucas County	73,696	63.0%	24.3%	37.8%	37.9%	26,600	22.7%	24.4%	45.4%	30.2%
Mahoning County	37,924	69.7%	27.5%	36.9%	35.6%	9,511	17.5%	23.5%	41.1%	35.4%
Medina County	36,021	91.3%	34.2%	33.4%	32.3%	850	2.2%	34.4%	1.1%	64.6%
Miami County	22,643	88.4%	29.5%	32.4%	38.1%	467	1.8%	60.6%	39.4%	0.0%
Montgomery County	94,883	70.3%	22.7%	38.5%	38.8%	31,015	23.0%	26.7%	43.8%	29.5%
Portage County	43,845	83.7%	18.8%	56.2%	25.0%	3,115	5.9%	7.7%	67.9%	24.4%
Richland County	22,012	78.5%	28.4%	38.7%	32.9%	3,662	13.1%	21.8%	54.5%	23.7%
Stark County	76,579	86.1%	26.8%	36.9%	36.3%	4,775	5.4%	40.2%	34.3%	25.5%
Summit County	98,586	74.3%	25.1%	36.0%	38.9%	20,821	15.7%	24.6%	43.9%	31.5%
Trumbull County	38,259	84.6%	30.0%	35.8%	34.3%	4,933	10.9%	36.9%	27.3%	35.8%
Tuscarawas County	19,782	93.1%	30.8%	33.2%	36.0%	569	2.7%	100.0%	0.0%	0.0%
Warren County	45,491	87.7%	36.6%	30.5%	33.0%	3,073	5.9%	5.2%	59.6%	35.2%
Wayne County	26,675	93.7%	30.2%	40.5%	29.3%	557	2.0%	40.6%	27.1%	32.3%
Wood County	35,576	87.3%	22.5%	47.0%	30.5%	1,585	3.9%	12.9%	86.5%	0.6%
Oklahoma										
Canadian County	20,743	71.9%	27.6%	33.8%	38.6%	902	3.1%	0.0%	100.0%	0.0%
Cleveland County	60,368	68.8%	17.3%	46.5%	36.2%	4,818	5.5%	12.6%	67.9%	19.5%
Comanche County	21,762	54.4%	14.4%	42.0%	43.6%	6,995	17.5%	23.4%	51.9%	24.7%
Oklahoma County	105,754	51.6%	18.2%	35.6%	46.2%	32,332	15.8%	25.1%	35.8%	39.1%
Tulsa County	94,319	56.0%	24.5%	34.6%	40.9%	19,039	11.3%	26.9%	37.6%	35.6%
Oregon										
Clackamas County	69,773	77.9%	29.4%	35.3%	35.4%	1,183	1.3%	32.4%	55.3%	12.3%
Deschutes County	31,875	83.9%	30.5%	30.0%	39.5%	na	na	na	na	na
Douglas County	17,062	82.3%	25.8%	38.0%	36.1%	33	0.2%	33.3%	0.0%	66.7%
Jackson County	34,456	75.2%	23.2%	36.9%	39.9%	289	0.6%	44.3%	22.5%	33.2%
Lane County	76,653	78.1%	19.4%	47.4%	33.1%	1,063	1.1%	0.6%	80.3%	19.1%
Linn County	24,603	81.1%	21.2%	51.5%	27.3%	49	0.2%	100.0%	0.0%	0.0%
Marion County	48,729	58.4%	24.9%	40.2%	34.9%	937	1.1%	6.0%	26.9%	67.1%
Multnomah County	135,081	66.0%	15.7%	30.6%	53.7%	11,011	5.4%	26.6%	36.5%	36.9%
Washington County	90,479	62.3%	25.4%	31.0%	43.7%	3,489	2.4%	15.1%	33.3%	51.6%
Yamhill County	17,912	72.7%	23.4%	41.7%	34.9%	331	1.3%	42.6%	41.7%	15.7%
Pennsylvania										
Adams County	21,477	89.1%	28.2%	43.1%	28.8%	299	1.2%	0.0%	100.0%	0.0%
Allegheny County	234,852	74.4%	21.1%	36.2%	42.8%	48,052	15.2%	27.8%	42.8%	29.4%
Beaver County	32,709	86.4%	27.0%	38.1%	34.9%	2,364	6.2%	30.9%	35.9%	33.2%
Berks County	71,610	67.3%	25.9%	39.3%	34.8%	5,493	5.2%	28.7%	51.4%	19.8%
Blair County	26,359	90.8%	23.9%	41.4%	34.7%	1,205	4.2%	2.4%	47.6%	50.0%
Bucks County	115,434	82.4%	31.2%	35.5%	33.4%	7,978	5.7%	29.6%	31.2%	39.1%
Butler County	40,575	90.4%	28.3%	38.7%	33.0%	1,353	3.0%	51.9%	25.9%	22.2%
Cambria County	28,799	89.3%	27.1%	41.5%	31.4%	2,221	6.9%	15.1%	39.4%	45.5%
Centre County	51,551	79.2%	11.7%	65.4%	22.9%	3,046	4.7%	2.1%	76.7%	21.2%
Chester County	96,270	76.3%	32.1%	35.6%	32.3%	8,724	6.9%	16.0%	62.1%	21.9%
Cumberland County	49,229	83.8%	25.4%	39.7%	34.9%	3,220	5.5%	16.6%	59.6%	23.8%
Dauphin County	40,814	63.8%	26.4%	32.4%	41.2%	12,249	19.2%	22.9%	32.7%	44.4%
Delaware County	91,553	62.2%	24.6%	40.5%	34.8%	37,484	25.5%	29.5%	41.9%	28.5%
Erie County	61,650	83.3%	20.2%	42.8%	37.0%	5,713	7.7%	18.7%	42.3%	38.9%
Fayette County	25,296	91.0%	24.2%	37.2%	38.6%	1,490	5.4%	43.2%	44.7%	12.1%
Franklin County	30,284	86.8%	25.2%	37.1%	37.7%	1,006	2.9%	5.6%	37.1%	57.4%
Lackawanna County	44,092	84.1%	21.3%	43.0%	35.7%	1,502	2.9%	23.1%	44.7%	32.2%
Lancaster County	106,703	79.4%	26.0%	36.6%	37.4%	6,413	4.8%	35.0%	41.4%	23.6%
Lebanon County	23,692	83.3%	29.2%	37.8%	33.1%	627	2.2%	0.0%	83.7%	16.3%
Lehigh County	49,869	57.9%	24.8%	39.6%	35.6%	6,186	7.2%	33.3%	35.1%	31.5%
Luzerne County	61,867	78.6%	24.6%	41.1%	34.3%	4,496	5.7%	21.4%	38.9%	39.7%
Lycoming County	26,315	89.6%	21.9%	47.6%	30.5%	1,845	6.3%	12.1%	49.1%	38.8%
Mercer County	24,588	86.5%	30.4%	39.0%	30.6%	2,222	7.8%	31.9%	44.3%	23.8%
Monroe County	26,826	62.6%	29.2%	43.3%	27.4%	6,856	16.0%	32.1%	52.7%	15.2%
Montgomery County	135,865	72.1%	27.4%	34.0%	38.7%	20,498	10.9%	27.3%	36.3%	36.4%
Northampton County	53,449	73.6%	23.4%	41.2%	35.4%	4,071	5.6%	30.4%	29.7%	39.9%
Northumberland County	18,228	90.1%	24.1%	37.7%	38.2%	1,052	5.2%	8.0%	53.5%	38.5%
Philadelphia County	174,048	36.5%	10.5%	36.3%	53.2%	185,959	39.0%	23.6%	42.6%	33.8%
Schuylkill County	27,419	89.6%	27.2%	35.9%	36.9%	2,012	6.6%	0.0%	41.3%	58.7%
Washington County	42,795	92.0%	27.3%	38.1%	34.7%	1,602	3.4%	26.8%	55.1%	18.0%
Westmoreland County	66,992	90.8%	26.7%	40.3%	33.0%	3,408	4.6%	30.8%	47.7%	21.6%
York County	82,321	80.4%	26.5%	36.4%	37.1%	6,318	6.2%	21.6%	51.8%	26.6%

Table B-2: Counties—Race and Hispanic Origin by Age—*Continued*

	Asian, Non-Hispanic					Hispanic				
	Millennial Population		Percent by Age			Millennial Population		Percent by Age		
	Number	Percent	13 to 17	18 to 24	25 to 31	Number	Percent	13 to 17	18 to 24	25 to 31
Ohio—Cont.										
Clermont County	547	1.1%	0.0%	18.5%	81.5%	1,474	3.0%	62.0%	21.6%	16.4%
Columbiana County	174	0.7%	0.0%	50.6%	49.4%	1,093	4.6%	0.0%	47.2%	52.8%
Cuyahoga County	9,410	3.0%	9.0%	36.2%	54.8%	21,483	6.9%	27.9%	37.4%	34.6%
Delaware County	1,660	4.1%	29.1%	18.9%	52.0%	1,119	2.8%	50.3%	37.8%	11.9%
Fairfield County	319	0.8%	70.5%	29.5%	0.0%	823	2.2%	11.4%	0.0%	88.6%
Franklin County	16,217	4.5%	19.6%	28.1%	52.3%	19,898	5.6%	16.6%	33.5%	50.0%
Geauga County	701	3.4%	0.0%	39.8%	60.2%	175	0.8%	0.0%	100.0%	0.0%
Greene County	1,408	2.9%	29.6%	33.4%	37.0%	1,478	3.1%	11.8%	48.3%	39.9%
Hamilton County	6,134	2.9%	21.7%	31.2%	47.1%	7,234	3.4%	13.8%	33.8%	52.4%
Lake County	538	1.0%	0.0%	66.9%	33.1%	4,119	7.8%	24.7%	29.9%	45.4%
Licking County	899	2.2%	0.0%	4.9%	95.1%	523	1.3%	0.0%	37.3%	62.7%
Lorain County	616	0.9%	71.4%	28.6%	0.0%	8,568	11.9%	29.6%	44.2%	26.2%
Lucas County	2,449	2.1%	11.7%	42.4%	45.9%	10,726	9.2%	33.4%	35.3%	31.3%
Mahoning County	1,014	1.9%	42.3%	34.4%	23.3%	4,290	7.9%	23.8%	25.7%	50.5%
Medina County	484	1.2%	20.2%	0.0%	79.8%	1,398	3.5%	33.8%	36.4%	29.8%
Miami County	na	na	na	na	na	586	2.3%	59.6%	40.4%	0.0%
Montgomery County	2,756	2.0%	23.5%	36.7%	39.7%	2,884	2.1%	33.4%	41.2%	25.4%
Portage County	2,061	3.9%	2.3%	66.3%	31.4%	1,463	2.8%	20.4%	79.6%	0.0%
Richland County	na	na	na	na	na	1,075	3.8%	19.5%	10.2%	70.2%
Stark County	311	0.3%	0.0%	100.0%	0.0%	2,044	2.3%	32.2%	19.1%	48.7%
Summit County	4,143	3.1%	3.5%	44.7%	51.7%	3,266	2.5%	22.1%	54.3%	23.6%
Trumbull County	156	0.3%	0.0%	0.0%	100.0%	835	1.8%	48.3%	10.9%	40.8%
Tuscarawas County	na	na	na	na	na	639	3.0%	0.0%	81.5%	18.5%
Warren County	1,561	3.0%	60.5%	24.5%	14.9%	1,173	2.3%	11.8%	23.4%	64.8%
Wayne County	438	1.5%	0.0%	19.4%	80.6%	568	2.0%	35.6%	0.0%	64.4%
Wood County	1,077	2.6%	2.1%	40.8%	57.1%	1,885	4.6%	32.1%	30.3%	37.6%
Oklahoma										
Canadian County	1,159	4.0%	10.9%	68.7%	20.4%	2,521	8.7%	39.2%	13.2%	47.6%
Cleveland County	4,085	4.7%	14.1%	53.9%	31.9%	8,534	9.7%	23.9%	46.1%	30.0%
Comanche County	1,131	2.8%	0.0%	34.0%	66.0%	6,275	15.7%	23.8%	54.2%	22.0%
Oklahoma County	6,189	3.0%	14.3%	34.7%	51.0%	40,673	19.9%	24.9%	34.4%	40.6%
Tulsa County	4,626	2.7%	20.2%	29.7%	50.2%	23,576	14.0%	26.0%	35.7%	38.4%
Oregon										
Clackamas County	4,179	4.7%	32.8%	20.6%	46.6%	10,244	11.4%	29.9%	39.7%	30.4%
Deschutes County	885	2.3%	100.0%	0.0%	0.0%	4,023	10.6%	31.7%	27.0%	41.3%
Douglas County	323	1.6%	0.0%	100.0%	0.0%	1,648	7.9%	26.0%	26.4%	47.6%
Jackson County	406	0.9%	0.0%	0.0%	100.0%	7,971	17.4%	34.6%	36.7%	28.8%
Lane County	3,549	3.6%	12.8%	69.4%	17.8%	9,217	9.4%	26.3%	46.6%	27.2%
Linn County	2,214	7.3%	7.7%	54.4%	37.9%	2,033	6.7%	23.3%	51.0%	25.8%
Marion County	726	0.9%	0.0%	47.4%	52.6%	27,416	32.8%	32.4%	43.9%	23.8%
Multnomah County	15,550	7.6%	20.6%	38.3%	41.1%	28,119	13.7%	24.4%	36.4%	39.2%
Washington County	12,261	8.4%	20.4%	30.3%	49.3%	29,391	20.2%	30.5%	37.8%	31.7%
Yamhill County	105	0.4%	0.0%	61.0%	39.0%	4,635	18.8%	33.8%	27.0%	39.2%
Pennsylvania										
Adams County	232	1.0%	0.0%	0.0%	100.0%	1,768	7.3%	15.6%	72.1%	12.3%
Allegheny County	14,757	4.7%	11.2%	38.3%	50.6%	7,935	2.5%	18.3%	35.3%	46.4%
Beaver County	na	na	na	na	na	751	2.0%	33.2%	30.1%	36.8%
Berks County	1,540	1.4%	20.7%	48.6%	30.6%	26,254	24.7%	31.0%	39.8%	29.2%
Blair County	82	0.3%	24.4%	39.0%	36.6%	693	2.4%	0.0%	51.4%	48.6%
Bucks County	5,551	4.0%	37.8%	26.4%	35.8%	8,626	6.2%	28.0%	20.1%	51.9%
Butler County	992	2.2%	31.7%	44.9%	23.5%	1,097	2.4%	37.7%	62.3%	0.0%
Cambria County	442	1.4%	0.0%	0.0%	100.0%	136	0.4%	14.0%	86.0%	0.0%
Centre County	7,054	10.8%	7.6%	76.0%	16.4%	2,385	3.7%	15.3%	83.1%	1.7%
Chester County	5,949	4.7%	25.2%	6.3%	68.5%	13,598	10.8%	25.5%	34.2%	40.2%
Cumberland County	1,812	3.1%	0.0%	33.5%	66.5%	3,394	5.8%	41.3%	50.3%	8.4%
Dauphin County	3,125	4.9%	27.7%	32.6%	39.7%	5,577	8.7%	33.5%	41.0%	25.6%
Delaware County	8,058	5.5%	27.0%	43.7%	29.4%	6,479	4.4%	19.0%	31.4%	49.6%
Erie County	1,498	2.0%	14.7%	48.4%	36.9%	3,063	4.1%	37.0%	34.1%	29.0%
Fayette County	na	na	na	na	na	109	0.4%	0.0%	100.0%	0.0%
Franklin County	na	na	na	na	na	2,800	8.0%	25.8%	32.1%	42.1%
Lackawanna County	1,113	2.1%	42.0%	34.1%	24.0%	4,305	8.2%	35.9%	40.3%	23.8%
Lancaster County	2,547	1.9%	14.1%	51.9%	34.1%	16,818	12.5%	28.8%	43.1%	28.1%
Lebanon County	188	0.7%	0.0%	0.0%	100.0%	3,931	13.8%	36.3%	36.9%	26.8%
Lehigh County	3,663	4.3%	32.8%	10.7%	56.6%	24,439	28.4%	29.0%	37.6%	33.4%
Luzerne County	1,385	1.8%	13.6%	44.5%	41.9%	9,290	11.8%	28.4%	42.5%	29.1%
Lycoming County	na	na	na	na	na	308	1.0%	0.0%	82.5%	17.5%
Mercer County	250	0.9%	32.0%	68.0%	0.0%	620	2.2%	8.5%	70.5%	21.0%
Monroe County	1,607	3.7%	55.1%	44.9%	0.0%	6,810	15.9%	31.5%	42.0%	26.5%
Montgomery County	14,281	7.6%	25.8%	29.6%	44.6%	12,483	6.6%	27.7%	34.8%	37.5%
Northampton County	3,061	4.2%	8.9%	39.4%	51.7%	10,537	14.5%	29.4%	36.9%	33.7%
Northumberland County	68	0.3%	0.0%	0.0%	100.0%	746	3.7%	0.0%	44.2%	55.8%
Philadelphia County	37,249	7.8%	14.2%	39.4%	46.4%	69,342	14.5%	27.3%	39.4%	33.3%
Schuylkill County	63	0.2%	0.0%	0.0%	100.0%	850	2.8%	17.3%	42.4%	40.4%
Washington County	21	0.0%	0.0%	100.0%	0.0%	838	1.8%	25.9%	46.8%	27.3%
Westmoreland County	955	1.3%	20.6%	26.5%	52.9%	1,073	1.5%	0.0%	66.0%	34.0%
York County	1,505	1.5%	55.3%	21.3%	23.3%	10,083	9.8%	27.0%	47.0%	26.0%

Table B-2: Counties—Race and Hispanic Origin by Age—*Continued*

| | White, Non-Hispanic | | | | | Black, Non-Hispanic | | | | |
| | Millennial Population | | Percent by Age | | | Millennial Population | | Percent by Age | | |
	Number	Percent	13 to 17	18 to 24	25 to 31	Number	Percent	13 to 17	18 to 24	25 to 31
Rhode Island										
Kent County	29,968	85.6%	24.7%	36.3%	39.0%	617	1.8%	0.0%	4.2%	95.8%
Providence County.....................	98,573	55.2%	19.4%	41.5%	39.1%	15,486	8.7%	27.7%	37.7%	34.6%
Washington County.....................	30,025	91.2%	22.4%	55.7%	22.0%	755	2.3%	0.0%	100.0%	0.0%
South Carolina										
Aiken County........................	23,483	58.4%	24.1%	36.2%	39.6%	12,919	32.1%	33.7%	34.2%	32.2%
Anderson County....................	32,761	72.5%	29.2%	36.3%	34.5%	9,213	20.4%	30.7%	35.1%	34.2%
Beaufort County.....................	20,070	52.8%	19.5%	41.4%	39.1%	9,833	25.9%	20.0%	46.0%	34.0%
Berkeley County.....................	32,179	59.4%	24.7%	34.3%	40.9%	16,790	31.0%	22.1%	45.6%	32.3%
Charleston County...................	66,533	62.9%	18.2%	38.1%	43.8%	28,653	27.1%	25.6%	43.3%	31.1%
Dorchester County...................	21,026	55.2%	25.4%	38.4%	36.2%	13,449	35.3%	34.2%	48.3%	17.5%
Florence County.....................	16,414	47.1%	28.5%	36.1%	35.4%	16,677	47.8%	24.4%	47.1%	28.6%
Greenville County...................	80,756	65.0%	25.7%	37.8%	36.5%	25,733	20.7%	28.4%	37.7%	33.9%
Horry County........................	45,258	70.0%	20.2%	38.5%	41.3%	11,559	17.9%	25.1%	53.4%	21.5%
Lexington County....................	48,779	71.2%	30.8%	35.0%	34.3%	12,169	17.8%	26.5%	50.1%	23.5%
Orangeburg County..................	6,702	28.8%	32.1%	39.9%	28.0%	14,843	63.8%	32.7%	46.1%	21.2%
Pickens County......................	31,112	79.8%	23.0%	50.5%	26.5%	3,092	7.9%	22.3%	55.7%	22.0%
Richland County.....................	60,457	46.0%	17.9%	49.9%	32.2%	58,455	44.5%	24.0%	44.9%	31.0%
Spartanburg County..................	46,645	61.2%	25.9%	38.6%	35.5%	16,558	21.7%	26.8%	44.6%	28.6%
Sumter County.......................	11,125	37.4%	17.1%	43.0%	39.8%	16,053	54.0%	30.0%	44.3%	25.7%
York County.........................	38,559	66.6%	33.8%	37.0%	29.3%	13,431	23.2%	24.9%	45.9%	29.2%
South Dakota										
Minnehaha County...................	42,907	85.4%	19.8%	38.2%	42.1%	1,537	3.1%	0.0%	41.1%	58.9%
Pennington County...................	21,087	83.8%	18.7%	43.8%	37.6%	643	2.6%	27.4%	72.6%	0.0%
Tennessee										
Blount County.......................	24,284	84.9%	28.5%	37.5%	34.1%	1,771	6.2%	12.6%	75.3%	12.1%
Bradley County......................	21,041	83.1%	25.0%	39.7%	35.3%	3,154	12.5%	41.7%	43.1%	15.2%
Davidson County.....................	102,012	52.9%	13.1%	34.3%	52.6%	57,213	29.7%	23.9%	37.3%	38.8%
Hamilton County.....................	58,394	66.8%	22.8%	38.9%	38.3%	19,328	22.1%	26.5%	37.8%	35.7%
Knox County.........................	99,576	80.3%	20.8%	44.9%	34.4%	11,487	9.3%	16.1%	52.0%	31.9%
Madison County......................	13,563	53.3%	25.4%	43.4%	31.1%	10,291	40.5%	29.3%	38.0%	32.7%
Montgomery County..................	39,836	64.8%	18.5%	35.1%	46.4%	10,723	17.4%	28.3%	36.4%	35.4%
Rutherford County...................	62,411	73.0%	24.2%	41.9%	33.9%	13,001	15.2%	19.0%	54.5%	26.6%
Sevier County.......................	18,546	89.9%	21.1%	46.1%	32.8%	399	1.9%	14.8%	84.0%	1.3%
Shelby County.......................	82,921	31.8%	24.9%	35.2%	39.9%	149,326	57.3%	26.5%	39.9%	33.6%
Sullivan County......................	31,026	91.9%	30.4%	36.4%	33.2%	880	2.6%	13.2%	24.5%	62.3%
Sumner County......................	33,360	80.9%	31.6%	33.9%	34.5%	4,050	9.8%	37.6%	31.7%	30.7%
Washington County..................	28,584	85.5%	23.2%	45.9%	30.8%	1,743	5.2%	43.7%	25.9%	30.5%
Williamson County..................	34,929	82.6%	39.0%	33.8%	27.2%	2,626	6.2%	23.0%	55.4%	21.6%
Wilson County.......................	24,413	82.6%	34.7%	31.6%	33.8%	2,823	9.5%	38.6%	36.8%	24.6%
Texas										
Bell County..........................	45,927	44.6%	16.9%	41.1%	42.1%	22,233	21.6%	27.5%	43.8%	28.7%
Bexar County........................	132,555	25.0%	20.6%	36.8%	42.5%	35,648	6.7%	22.2%	42.7%	35.1%
Bowie County........................	15,215	61.8%	25.1%	34.3%	40.6%	5,770	23.4%	16.7%	49.9%	33.4%
Brazoria County......................	38,143	43.5%	27.7%	31.7%	40.6%	12,616	14.4%	24.1%	37.3%	38.6%
Brazos County.......................	56,109	60.0%	8.7%	67.5%	23.8%	7,615	8.1%	27.9%	49.6%	22.5%
Cameron County.....................	7,020	6.0%	45.1%	28.6%	26.3%	na	na	na	na	na
Collin County........................	116,156	57.2%	32.8%	33.1%	34.0%	19,290	9.5%	32.6%	35.7%	31.7%
Comal County.......................	15,705	57.8%	33.9%	33.9%	32.1%	900	3.3%	39.8%	0.0%	60.2%
Dallas County........................	179,890	25.9%	19.7%	32.0%	48.3%	151,095	21.8%	25.5%	37.4%	37.1%
Denton County.......................	113,908	56.9%	27.2%	35.2%	37.6%	20,453	10.2%	20.0%	41.7%	38.3%
Ector County.........................	13,455	29.8%	20.9%	38.4%	40.8%	2,013	4.5%	22.9%	26.0%	51.1%
El Paso County.......................	31,261	12.7%	15.2%	43.1%	41.7%	8,621	3.5%	15.3%	60.7%	24.0%
Ellis County.........................	23,360	56.9%	30.4%	35.1%	34.5%	3,931	9.6%	34.1%	39.4%	26.6%
Fort Bend County....................	49,101	31.0%	33.4%	30.9%	35.7%	33,314	21.0%	32.8%	40.4%	26.8%
Galveston County....................	40,081	50.8%	25.4%	35.9%	38.7%	10,568	13.4%	34.7%	33.1%	32.2%
Grayson County......................	20,978	68.1%	25.9%	40.6%	33.6%	2,601	8.4%	20.5%	52.1%	27.5%
Gregg County........................	17,599	52.6%	21.6%	39.4%	38.9%	8,049	24.1%	27.8%	45.3%	26.9%
Guadalupe County...................	16,222	45.6%	31.7%	33.2%	35.1%	3,188	9.0%	38.3%	44.6%	17.1%
Harris County........................	317,637	25.6%	23.6%	31.2%	45.2%	242,299	19.6%	23.5%	36.8%	39.7%
Hays County.........................	30,875	52.7%	15.2%	57.6%	27.1%	2,362	4.0%	20.5%	33.1%	46.4%
Hidalgo County......................	8,764	3.6%	22.3%	39.0%	38.7%	1,106	0.5%	16.6%	51.1%	32.3%
Jefferson County....................	25,264	36.0%	19.8%	36.0%	44.2%	25,011	35.6%	26.3%	46.6%	27.1%
Johnson County.....................	26,184	67.4%	30.2%	34.6%	35.2%	1,933	5.0%	0.0%	17.3%	82.7%
Kaufman County.....................	15,766	62.3%	29.8%	33.7%	36.5%	2,697	10.7%	31.0%	54.2%	14.8%
Lubbock County.....................	52,872	53.3%	14.4%	57.6%	27.9%	6,628	6.7%	16.3%	53.2%	30.6%
McLennan County....................	38,852	54.6%	16.7%	52.6%	30.7%	9,690	13.6%	19.6%	51.2%	29.2%
Midland County......................	19,277	44.2%	21.2%	33.2%	45.7%	2,109	4.8%	9.3%	26.4%	64.3%
Montgomery County..................	74,987	61.6%	30.2%	34.6%	35.2%	8,413	6.9%	36.7%	25.1%	38.1%
Nueces County.......................	25,017	26.1%	21.3%	38.7%	40.0%	3,515	3.7%	24.1%	34.8%	41.1%
Parker County.......................	23,789	79.3%	32.6%	34.5%	32.8%	485	1.6%	0.0%	40.6%	59.4%
Potter County........................	12,664	38.6%	22.6%	33.1%	44.4%	3,183	9.7%	14.4%	49.4%	36.2%
Randall County......................	22,087	64.5%	21.9%	39.6%	38.5%	1,641	4.8%	0.0%	35.0%	65.0%
Smith County........................	31,016	53.7%	25.0%	37.4%	37.6%	12,716	22.0%	27.4%	42.6%	30.0%
Tarrant County......................	228,658	43.3%	25.2%	33.4%	41.4%	86,472	16.4%	27.1%	35.5%	37.3%
Taylor County.......................	25,980	59.9%	16.0%	49.2%	34.7%	3,303	7.6%	11.2%	36.1%	52.8%

Table B-2: Counties—Race and Hispanic Origin by Age—*Continued*

	Asian, Non-Hispanic					Hispanic				
	Millennial Population		Percent by Age			Millennial Population		Percent by Age		
	Number	Percent	13 to 17	18 to 24	25 to 31	Number	Percent	13 to 17	18 to 24	25 to 31
Rhode Island										
Kent County	792	2.3%	21.8%	33.6%	44.6%	2,745	7.8%	20.3%	35.0%	44.7%
Providence County	8,996	5.0%	10.4%	50.8%	38.8%	45,548	25.5%	26.2%	41.1%	32.7%
Washington County	359	1.1%	13.1%	86.9%	0.0%	574	1.7%	15.7%	84.3%	0.0%
South Carolina										
Aiken County	na	na	na	na	na	2,430	6.0%	10.4%	56.9%	32.7%
Anderson County	141	0.3%	0.0%	0.0%	100.0%	1,987	4.4%	36.8%	16.2%	47.0%
Beaufort County	316	0.8%	0.0%	40.8%	59.2%	6,391	16.8%	25.7%	37.2%	37.1%
Berkeley County	665	1.2%	50.1%	27.2%	22.7%	3,479	6.4%	13.5%	32.7%	53.8%
Charleston County	1,293	1.2%	11.4%	39.4%	49.2%	5,968	5.6%	16.9%	35.1%	48.0%
Dorchester County	535	1.4%	49.2%	22.6%	28.2%	2,331	6.1%	18.4%	37.2%	44.4%
Florence County	195	0.6%	100.0%	0.0%	0.0%	860	2.5%	7.9%	29.0%	63.1%
Greenville County	2,547	2.0%	17.3%	40.2%	42.5%	12,062	9.7%	23.6%	37.0%	39.4%
Horry County	851	1.3%	26.2%	41.5%	32.3%	5,506	8.5%	10.9%	30.6%	58.5%
Lexington County	1,517	2.2%	0.0%	40.9%	59.1%	4,419	6.5%	23.6%	24.2%	52.2%
Orangeburg County	na	na	na	na	na	1,199	5.2%	0.0%	27.7%	72.3%
Pickens County	1,209	3.1%	0.5%	60.3%	39.2%	3,123	8.0%	19.4%	45.3%	35.3%
Richland County	3,005	2.3%	13.7%	47.8%	38.5%	6,418	4.9%	18.0%	49.0%	33.0%
Spartanburg County	3,398	4.5%	31.7%	50.7%	17.6%	6,996	9.2%	39.1%	30.2%	30.8%
Sumter County	103	0.3%	27.2%	72.8%	0.0%	1,452	4.9%	25.3%	38.1%	36.6%
York County	1,366	2.4%	8.9%	55.9%	35.2%	2,687	4.6%	25.9%	40.3%	33.8%
South Dakota										
Minnehaha County	1,151	2.3%	0.0%	26.3%	73.7%	2,338	4.7%	33.4%	26.1%	40.4%
Pennington County	316	1.3%	0.0%	66.1%	33.9%	585	2.3%	28.2%	32.1%	39.7%
Tennessee										
Blount County	na	na	na	na	na	2,129	7.4%	66.3%	16.7%	17.0%
Bradley County	9	0.0%	100.0%	0.0%	0.0%	1,051	4.1%	14.1%	44.4%	41.5%
Davidson County	6,017	3.1%	17.5%	19.1%	63.4%	20,785	10.8%	19.5%	37.7%	42.8%
Hamilton County	2,427	2.8%	10.2%	28.3%	61.5%	5,487	6.3%	10.3%	33.3%	56.4%
Knox County	3,483	2.8%	12.1%	17.9%	70.0%	6,247	5.0%	17.8%	41.1%	41.1%
Madison County	557	2.2%	33.4%	11.3%	55.3%	685	2.7%	83.9%	0.9%	15.2%
Montgomery County	1,322	2.2%	9.5%	28.4%	62.2%	6,514	10.6%	26.1%	45.9%	28.0%
Rutherford County	2,412	2.8%	18.8%	25.8%	55.4%	6,371	7.5%	27.2%	41.5%	31.3%
Sevier County	na	na	na	na	na	1,542	7.5%	4.5%	72.8%	22.6%
Shelby County	6,400	2.5%	23.7%	32.2%	44.1%	17,882	6.9%	26.4%	32.8%	40.8%
Sullivan County	262	0.8%	100.0%	0.0%	0.0%	669	2.0%	73.5%	16.6%	9.9%
Sumner County	1,258	3.1%	4.8%	24.3%	70.9%	1,877	4.6%	17.3%	44.0%	38.7%
Washington County	207	0.6%	0.0%	31.4%	68.6%	2,121	6.3%	11.8%	49.3%	38.9%
Williamson County	985	2.3%	24.5%	26.5%	49.0%	2,104	5.0%	32.4%	34.7%	32.9%
Wilson County	na	na	na	na	na	1,644	5.6%	15.3%	46.0%	38.6%
Texas										
Bell County	1,299	1.3%	12.1%	26.5%	61.4%	26,010	25.3%	22.3%	38.0%	39.6%
Bexar County	14,020	2.6%	11.4%	40.9%	47.7%	332,215	62.7%	27.1%	37.4%	35.5%
Bowie County	na	na	na	na	na	2,985	12.1%	0.0%	54.4%	45.6%
Brazoria County	4,279	4.9%	31.8%	40.6%	27.6%	31,850	36.3%	28.1%	31.3%	40.7%
Brazos County	5,868	6.3%	4.2%	62.8%	32.9%	21,288	22.8%	16.8%	53.2%	30.0%
Cameron County	668	0.6%	100.0%	0.0%	0.0%	109,220	92.8%	32.6%	38.4%	29.0%
Collin County	22,642	11.2%	29.4%	29.3%	41.3%	36,544	18.0%	30.2%	37.4%	32.4%
Comal County	na	na	na	na	na	9,309	34.3%	28.2%	41.7%	30.2%
Dallas County	38,473	5.5%	17.9%	31.1%	51.0%	307,785	44.3%	27.3%	36.5%	36.2%
Denton County	16,152	8.1%	29.4%	34.9%	35.6%	43,703	21.8%	26.4%	38.2%	35.4%
Ector County	492	1.1%	0.0%	68.7%	31.3%	28,382	62.8%	25.0%	37.5%	37.5%
El Paso County	2,395	1.0%	8.3%	1.4%	90.4%	201,073	81.4%	28.6%	39.5%	31.9%
Ellis County	681	1.7%	28.8%	42.1%	29.1%	12,591	30.7%	36.9%	36.0%	27.1%
Fort Bend County	27,253	17.2%	31.1%	34.2%	34.6%	46,335	29.3%	30.8%	34.0%	35.2%
Galveston County	2,497	3.2%	25.6%	37.2%	37.1%	23,186	29.4%	33.5%	36.1%	30.4%
Grayson County	744	2.4%	12.5%	62.6%	24.9%	5,333	17.3%	26.3%	15.6%	58.1%
Gregg County	148	0.4%	68.2%	31.8%	0.0%	7,387	22.1%	33.3%	37.4%	29.3%
Guadalupe County	794	2.2%	13.2%	16.9%	69.9%	14,627	41.1%	28.7%	39.3%	32.0%
Harris County	78,568	6.3%	21.1%	31.5%	47.3%	575,772	46.5%	26.8%	35.8%	37.3%
Hays County	581	1.0%	22.9%	61.4%	15.7%	23,648	40.4%	23.6%	45.3%	31.1%
Hidalgo County	2,999	1.2%	52.3%	27.9%	19.7%	227,206	94.5%	31.7%	37.5%	30.8%
Jefferson County	2,505	3.6%	27.4%	53.6%	19.0%	16,156	23.0%	31.0%	31.8%	37.3%
Johnson County	188	0.5%	0.0%	49.5%	50.5%	10,192	26.2%	27.9%	44.0%	28.2%
Kaufman County	154	0.6%	100.0%	0.0%	0.0%	5,969	23.6%	34.7%	41.2%	24.1%
Lubbock County	2,486	2.5%	15.6%	67.7%	16.7%	35,030	35.3%	27.7%	41.5%	30.7%
McLennan County	2,137	3.0%	11.7%	80.1%	8.2%	19,299	27.1%	21.9%	45.5%	32.6%
Midland County	196	0.4%	0.0%	50.0%	50.0%	20,759	47.6%	25.1%	38.0%	36.9%
Montgomery County	3,523	2.9%	45.6%	13.4%	41.0%	32,793	26.9%	33.9%	37.8%	28.3%
Nueces County	2,511	2.6%	20.2%	46.3%	33.6%	63,709	66.4%	27.3%	38.1%	34.6%
Parker County	51	0.2%	100.0%	0.0%	0.0%	4,825	16.1%	28.8%	38.2%	32.9%
Potter County	1,244	3.8%	33.4%	42.1%	24.4%	14,890	45.4%	26.2%	38.5%	35.3%
Randall County	854	2.5%	0.0%	60.7%	39.3%	9,239	27.0%	26.3%	32.9%	40.8%
Smith County	481	0.8%	29.3%	37.2%	33.5%	13,315	23.0%	31.2%	38.2%	30.6%
Tarrant County	23,480	4.4%	25.5%	36.0%	38.5%	169,249	32.0%	28.8%	35.6%	35.6%
Taylor County	1,193	2.8%	0.0%	57.9%	42.1%	11,379	26.2%	29.2%	41.2%	29.6%

Table B-2: Counties—Race and Hispanic Origin by Age—*Continued*

| | White, Non-Hispanic | | | | | Black, Non-Hispanic | | | | |
| | Millennial Population | | Percent by Age | | | Millennial Population | | Percent by Age | | |
	Number	Percent	13 to 17	18 to 24	25 to 31	Number	Percent	13 to 17	18 to 24	25 to 31
Texas—Cont.										
Tom Green County	16,553	48.2%	17.5%	44.4%	38.1%	1,479	4.3%	4.6%	45.7%	49.7%
Travis County	153,838	44.6%	15.7%	32.2%	52.1%	28,173	8.2%	18.0%	40.5%	41.6%
Webb County	1,722	2.2%	13.6%	19.8%	66.6%	310	0.4%	2.6%	53.2%	44.2%
Wichita County	25,615	63.4%	20.2%	42.6%	37.2%	4,620	11.4%	8.4%	49.5%	42.1%
Williamson County	63,781	55.1%	29.1%	31.2%	39.7%	6,268	5.4%	33.5%	27.8%	38.7%
Utah										
Cache County	36,030	83.5%	21.7%	45.5%	32.8%	454	1.1%	39.6%	60.4%	0.0%
Davis County	74,627	82.6%	32.6%	32.4%	35.0%	2,139	2.4%	27.0%	35.3%	37.7%
Salt Lake County	217,744	69.0%	24.7%	33.2%	42.1%	5,047	1.6%	34.3%	28.3%	37.5%
Utah County	162,937	82.3%	23.8%	47.0%	29.3%	564	0.3%	26.1%	29.6%	44.3%
Washington County	30,264	83.0%	31.8%	34.8%	33.3%	513	1.4%	0.0%	82.5%	17.5%
Weber County	47,768	72.1%	26.7%	34.7%	38.6%	638	1.0%	0.0%	0.0%	100.0%
Vermont										
Chittenden County	45,187	91.3%	19.0%	48.1%	32.9%	1,004	2.0%	0.0%	34.7%	65.3%
Virginia										
Albemarle County	21,831	75.8%	22.2%	40.8%	36.9%	2,996	10.4%	38.7%	29.7%	31.7%
Arlington County	47,221	64.5%	9.4%	20.9%	69.7%	4,744	6.5%	14.0%	46.0%	40.1%
Chesterfield County	45,389	55.3%	33.7%	34.9%	31.4%	23,498	28.6%	26.6%	45.3%	28.1%
Fairfax County	135,628	48.6%	27.0%	32.6%	40.4%	28,359	10.2%	28.4%	39.0%	32.6%
Hanover County	18,237	78.6%	31.8%	33.1%	35.2%	2,903	12.5%	18.1%	50.7%	31.2%
Henrico County	38,311	47.9%	26.6%	31.3%	42.1%	26,058	32.6%	28.2%	38.1%	33.8%
Loudoun County	47,660	59.6%	34.8%	28.0%	37.2%	5,929	7.4%	34.3%	30.2%	35.5%
Montgomery County	36,434	82.5%	16.2%	68.5%	15.3%	2,429	5.5%	20.6%	70.0%	9.3%
Prince William County	46,427	41.1%	27.1%	31.7%	41.2%	23,673	20.9%	24.0%	36.7%	39.3%
Roanoke County	17,872	86.4%	29.8%	36.9%	33.3%	2,017	9.8%	10.5%	62.4%	27.1%
Spotsylvania County	21,272	66.2%	28.4%	36.4%	35.2%	7,385	23.0%	41.1%	41.6%	17.3%
Stafford County	24,483	64.1%	22.3%	46.8%	31.0%	6,060	15.9%	28.8%	40.8%	30.3%
Washington										
Benton County	27,578	59.9%	31.4%	31.1%	37.5%	527	1.1%	44.2%	22.8%	33.0%
Clark County	81,752	77.2%	29.6%	34.4%	36.1%	2,901	2.7%	24.4%	39.3%	36.3%
Cowlitz County	17,988	77.6%	30.1%	35.7%	34.3%	na	na	na	na	na
Grant County	14,724	58.4%	21.7%	53.2%	25.1%	653	2.6%	0.0%	0.0%	100.0%
King County	301,919	56.8%	20.3%	32.4%	47.4%	34,283	6.5%	22.7%	37.9%	39.4%
Kitsap County	46,759	71.7%	24.2%	40.2%	35.6%	3,784	5.8%	7.8%	21.1%	71.1%
Pierce County	139,007	62.8%	23.8%	36.3%	39.9%	17,446	7.9%	25.7%	28.6%	45.7%
Skagit County	19,852	73.0%	24.5%	38.1%	37.4%	413	1.5%	4.6%	42.1%	53.3%
Snohomish County	126,058	68.4%	25.7%	34.9%	39.4%	3,912	2.1%	20.3%	33.8%	45.9%
Spokane County	109,611	82.1%	24.1%	37.3%	38.6%	4,033	3.0%	28.1%	30.0%	41.9%
Thurston County	48,533	68.9%	24.6%	34.0%	41.4%	2,313	3.3%	27.7%	34.4%	37.9%
Whatcom County	47,364	76.2%	20.3%	50.2%	29.5%	493	0.8%	28.0%	43.4%	28.6%
Yakima County	21,994	33.3%	27.1%	37.1%	35.8%	304	0.5%	0.0%	50.0%	50.0%
West Virginia										
Berkeley County	22,352	83.4%	31.0%	34.2%	34.8%	1,921	7.2%	32.4%	64.2%	3.4%
Cabell County	25,190	93.3%	27.8%	39.3%	32.9%	1,058	3.9%	42.9%	42.6%	14.5%
Kanawha County	37,018	83.1%	27.4%	33.8%	38.8%	2,301	5.2%	6.0%	51.0%	43.1%
Monongalia County	36,430	86.8%	12.0%	55.7%	32.3%	2,527	6.0%	0.0%	73.0%	27.0%
Wisconsin										
Brown County	50,694	78.4%	26.8%	35.9%	37.2%	1,752	2.7%	7.6%	67.4%	25.0%
Dane County	117,949	75.1%	18.0%	44.5%	37.5%	9,569	6.1%	32.0%	22.8%	45.2%
Eau Claire County	30,654	90.3%	18.3%	50.4%	31.3%	184	0.5%	0.0%	62.0%	38.0%
Fond du Lac County	20,446	89.4%	35.4%	39.1%	25.5%	100	0.4%	63.0%	37.0%	0.0%
Kenosha County	30,567	71.5%	27.8%	38.9%	33.2%	4,513	10.6%	18.8%	62.0%	19.3%
La Crosse County	31,816	84.0%	19.8%	49.6%	30.6%	318	0.8%	2.5%	25.8%	71.7%
Marathon County	26,080	82.7%	30.2%	34.2%	35.6%	294	0.9%	0.0%	41.5%	58.5%
Milwaukee County	129,052	46.8%	18.0%	34.8%	47.2%	78,114	28.3%	27.4%	39.0%	33.5%
Outagamie County	37,964	84.6%	25.0%	35.7%	39.3%	652	1.5%	0.0%	24.4%	75.6%
Racine County	30,858	63.8%	31.5%	32.7%	35.9%	7,578	15.7%	33.7%	35.0%	31.3%
Rock County	32,179	81.0%	29.6%	34.5%	35.9%	2,124	5.3%	18.5%	60.1%	21.5%
Sheboygan County	20,496	79.8%	30.4%	34.3%	35.3%	46	0.2%	0.0%	100.0%	0.0%
Walworth County	22,808	84.1%	24.3%	45.7%	30.0%	427	1.6%	75.4%	12.4%	12.2%
Washington County	25,248	89.6%	30.6%	36.5%	32.9%	349	1.2%	0.0%	79.4%	20.6%
Waukesha County	72,872	85.3%	31.5%	35.2%	33.3%	904	1.1%	26.7%	54.9%	18.5%
Winnebago County	40,468	86.3%	19.0%	46.3%	34.7%	1,851	3.9%	0.9%	55.3%	43.8%
Wyoming										
Laramie County	20,050	78.3%	20.1%	49.8%	30.1%	767	3.0%	19.3%	80.7%	0.0%

Table B-2: Counties—Race and Hispanic Origin by Age—*Continued*

	Asian, Non-Hispanic					Hispanic				
	Millennial Population		Percent by Age			Millennial Population		Percent by Age		
	Number	Percent	13 to 17	18 to 24	25 to 31	Number	Percent	13 to 17	18 to 24	25 to 31
Texas—Cont.										
Tom Green County	319	0.9%	25.1%	74.9%	0.0%	15,095	43.9%	28.2%	34.8%	37.0%
Travis County	22,519	6.5%	12.0%	36.9%	51.1%	131,424	38.1%	22.5%	34.7%	42.7%
Webb County	11	0.0%	0.0%	0.0%	100.0%	77,100	97.2%	29.8%	37.8%	32.4%
Wichita County	647	1.6%	46.4%	24.1%	29.5%	7,827	19.4%	16.6%	47.8%	35.6%
Williamson County	5,138	4.4%	27.5%	33.2%	39.3%	35,274	30.5%	31.1%	31.4%	37.5%
Utah										
Cache County	890	2.1%	31.3%	29.4%	39.2%	4,567	10.6%	29.5%	24.3%	46.2%
Davis County	2,399	2.7%	21.1%	46.6%	32.4%	8,107	9.0%	41.8%	33.2%	25.0%
Salt Lake County	12,680	4.0%	15.8%	32.1%	52.1%	62,003	19.7%	28.3%	38.8%	33.0%
Utah County	5,441	2.7%	15.8%	45.5%	38.7%	21,259	10.7%	24.3%	43.0%	32.7%
Washington County	54	0.1%	0.0%	0.0%	100.0%	4,039	11.1%	14.8%	85.2%	0.0%
Weber County	861	1.3%	34.8%	45.5%	19.6%	14,143	21.4%	30.7%	35.5%	33.9%
Vermont										
Chittenden County	1,526	3.1%	30.5%	37.4%	32.1%	702	1.4%	41.2%	13.5%	45.3%
Virginia										
Albemarle County	1,701	5.9%	10.8%	63.7%	25.6%	1,030	3.6%	46.4%	15.5%	38.1%
Arlington County	6,650	9.1%	9.9%	22.5%	67.6%	12,511	17.1%	13.7%	34.6%	51.6%
Chesterfield County	2,894	3.5%	28.5%	49.0%	22.5%	7,994	9.7%	33.7%	33.6%	32.8%
Fairfax County	47,792	17.1%	25.0%	31.7%	43.3%	52,836	18.9%	22.8%	37.4%	39.8%
Hanover County	421	1.8%	88.1%	11.9%	0.0%	976	4.2%	45.5%	24.4%	30.1%
Henrico County	7,036	8.8%	24.0%	24.0%	52.0%	6,023	7.5%	14.5%	42.6%	42.9%
Loudoun County	11,121	13.9%	34.2%	21.4%	44.5%	11,354	14.2%	36.1%	38.0%	25.9%
Montgomery County	2,179	4.9%	0.0%	59.8%	40.2%	1,948	4.4%	14.3%	79.7%	6.0%
Prince William County	8,521	7.5%	19.8%	40.1%	40.1%	29,071	25.7%	31.2%	31.6%	37.2%
Roanoke County	172	0.8%	27.9%	11.6%	60.5%	193	0.9%	0.0%	40.4%	59.6%
Spotsylvania County	781	2.4%	78.7%	19.5%	1.8%	1,656	5.2%	23.9%	37.5%	38.6%
Stafford County	1,102	2.9%	52.5%	47.5%	0.0%	4,033	10.6%	20.7%	44.0%	35.3%
Washington										
Benton County	357	0.8%	17.1%	13.2%	69.7%	15,801	34.3%	34.2%	34.1%	31.6%
Clark County	4,245	4.0%	42.9%	27.9%	29.3%	10,908	10.3%	28.6%	38.2%	33.2%
Cowlitz County	204	0.9%	31.4%	68.6%	0.0%	3,685	15.9%	22.6%	49.8%	27.5%
Grant County	488	1.9%	0.0%	100.0%	0.0%	8,005	31.8%	32.7%	39.1%	28.3%
King County	87,357	16.4%	19.6%	31.9%	48.5%	61,032	11.5%	22.6%	33.3%	44.0%
Kitsap County	1,657	2.5%	16.5%	41.9%	41.6%	6,166	9.5%	18.0%	48.2%	33.9%
Pierce County	12,895	5.8%	26.3%	39.3%	34.4%	27,825	12.6%	24.0%	38.1%	37.9%
Skagit County	1,309	4.8%	37.7%	34.1%	28.3%	3,771	13.9%	28.6%	53.2%	18.3%
Snohomish County	17,763	9.6%	25.7%	31.6%	42.7%	23,687	12.8%	26.4%	38.8%	34.8%
Spokane County	3,351	2.5%	16.8%	55.0%	28.2%	9,293	7.0%	19.0%	46.7%	34.4%
Thurston County	5,569	7.9%	32.6%	27.9%	39.5%	8,409	11.9%	24.7%	33.1%	42.1%
Whatcom County	3,211	5.2%	20.7%	60.1%	19.1%	6,542	10.5%	27.2%	45.3%	27.5%
Yakima County	578	0.9%	13.3%	68.2%	18.5%	39,337	59.6%	29.4%	38.4%	32.2%
West Virginia										
Berkeley County	226	0.8%	0.0%	100.0%	0.0%	1,228	4.6%	36.2%	10.9%	52.9%
Cabell County	29	0.1%	0.0%	100.0%	0.0%	307	1.1%	51.1%	0.0%	48.9%
Kanawha County	770	1.7%	35.6%	9.1%	55.3%	727	1.6%	2.2%	87.3%	10.5%
Monongalia County	854	2.0%	0.0%	9.3%	90.7%	1,178	2.8%	19.7%	51.6%	28.7%
Wisconsin										
Brown County	2,306	3.6%	40.8%	48.9%	10.4%	5,105	7.9%	33.7%	30.0%	36.3%
Dane County	12,748	8.1%	10.5%	42.3%	47.2%	13,088	8.3%	25.8%	30.9%	43.2%
Eau Claire County	1,555	4.6%	16.5%	40.5%	43.1%	566	1.7%	0.0%	44.7%	55.3%
Fond du Lac County	182	0.8%	0.0%	100.0%	0.0%	1,285	5.6%	43.1%	33.1%	23.8%
Kenosha County	577	1.4%	0.0%	41.6%	58.4%	5,397	12.6%	32.0%	12.5%	55.5%
La Crosse County	4,873	12.9%	25.1%	38.5%	36.4%	735	1.9%	18.4%	69.5%	12.1%
Marathon County	3,421	10.8%	29.8%	55.0%	15.3%	979	3.1%	17.8%	18.8%	63.4%
Milwaukee County	12,553	4.6%	26.6%	22.1%	51.3%	44,513	16.1%	24.0%	37.6%	38.4%
Outagamie County	1,897	4.2%	23.0%	53.1%	23.8%	2,100	4.7%	19.4%	44.6%	36.0%
Racine County	na	na	na	na	na	7,795	16.1%	23.8%	22.6%	53.5%
Rock County	229	0.6%	28.4%	71.6%	0.0%	3,071	7.7%	45.0%	27.7%	27.3%
Sheboygan County	2,112	8.2%	30.5%	32.2%	37.3%	2,178	8.5%	48.6%	10.7%	40.8%
Walworth County	251	0.9%	0.0%	0.0%	100.0%	2,841	10.5%	27.7%	27.5%	44.8%
Washington County	246	0.9%	0.0%	100.0%	0.0%	2,096	7.4%	11.9%	62.8%	25.3%
Waukesha County	4,155	4.9%	36.3%	30.7%	33.0%	4,659	5.5%	31.6%	36.4%	32.0%
Winnebago County	1,392	3.0%	0.0%	12.9%	87.1%	1,706	3.6%	42.5%	44.2%	13.3%
Wyoming										
Laramie County	614	2.4%	0.0%	0.0%	100.0%	3,461	13.5%	17.3%	53.0%	29.6%

na = not available

Table B-3: Places—Race and Hispanic Origin by Age

| | White, Non-Hispanic | | | | | Black, Non-Hispanic | | | | |
| | Millennial Population | | Percent by Age | | | Millennial Population | | Percent by Age | | |
	Number	Percent	13 to 17	18 to 24	25 to 31	Number	Percent	13 to 17	18 to 24	25 to 31
Alabama										
Birmingham city	17,730	28.3%	16.3%	36.9%	46.8%	40,349	64.4%	24.7%	41.5%	33.8%
Huntsville city	32,968	63.4%	27.4%	33.8%	38.8%	13,230	25.4%	25.9%	45.0%	29.0%
Mobile city	19,722	37.8%	21.5%	35.7%	42.8%	28,827	55.3%	23.3%	41.1%	35.6%
Montgomery city	17,786	30.1%	24.6%	36.9%	38.4%	38,052	64.5%	21.4%	41.8%	36.8%
Tuscaloosa city	21,834	54.9%	9.7%	69.0%	21.3%	15,197	38.2%	21.8%	46.6%	31.6%
Alaska										
Anchorage municipality	50,663	56.9%	19.9%	43.2%	36.9%	4,760	5.3%	29.4%	42.9%	27.7%
Arizona										
Chandler city	33,965	51.5%	25.7%	30.2%	44.1%	5,247	8.0%	29.1%	31.7%	39.2%
Glendale city	27,160	41.9%	24.4%	35.8%	39.8%	3,034	4.7%	25.2%	32.6%	42.2%
Mesa city	71,578	57.6%	21.8%	38.8%	39.5%	4,228	3.4%	23.7%	33.1%	43.2%
Peoria city	20,826	54.7%	35.4%	28.9%	35.7%	1,277	3.4%	43.5%	23.9%	32.7%
Phoenix city	161,524	38.4%	22.2%	35.0%	42.8%	30,439	7.2%	22.6%	39.8%	37.6%
Scottsdale city	35,046	70.1%	33.9%	34.5%	31.6%	1,437	2.9%	0.0%	4.9%	95.1%
Surprise city	13,733	63.9%	33.2%	26.0%	40.7%	1,124	5.2%	16.6%	40.7%	42.6%
Tempe city	41,220	55.3%	15.0%	47.5%	37.5%	3,419	4.6%	23.8%	55.3%	20.9%
Tucson city	63,486	38.5%	16.8%	48.6%	34.7%	8,238	5.0%	18.7%	48.2%	33.1%
Yuma city	6,334	22.7%	17.7%	34.5%	47.8%	817	2.9%	0.0%	42.0%	58.0%
Arkansas										
Little Rock city	19,810	37.8%	18.4%	30.5%	51.1%	24,467	46.7%	33.0%	28.3%	38.7%
California										
Anaheim city	22,613	23.6%	19.1%	39.3%	41.6%	3,925	4.1%	7.1%	43.4%	49.5%
Antioch city	8,547	27.0%	19.2%	36.0%	44.8%	6,834	21.6%	44.9%	37.6%	17.5%
Bakersfield city	31,786	29.5%	23.0%	36.6%	40.4%	7,128	6.6%	25.1%	50.2%	24.7%
Berkeley city	19,828	40.5%	12.3%	45.8%	41.8%	3,488	7.1%	18.5%	51.5%	30.0%
Burbank city	12,997	55.6%	17.7%	27.5%	54.8%	425	1.8%	0.0%	43.5%	56.5%
Carlsbad city	15,589	68.2%	28.3%	30.5%	41.2%	192	0.8%	0.0%	0.0%	100.0%
Carson city	1,290	5.1%	7.4%	38.1%	54.6%	5,264	20.6%	20.5%	37.6%	42.0%
Chula Vista city	10,784	15.1%	27.4%	30.9%	41.7%	2,839	4.0%	35.8%	34.0%	30.2%
Clovis city	12,919	48.0%	27.3%	38.9%	33.8%	1,233	4.6%	11.0%	53.2%	35.8%
Compton city	3	0.0%	0.0%	0.0%	100.0%	6,576	22.7%	20.8%	35.0%	44.2%
Concord city	13,086	41.2%	22.5%	38.8%	38.7%	2,469	7.8%	39.9%	37.7%	22.5%
Corona city	14,472	31.5%	27.6%	37.6%	34.8%	3,523	7.7%	34.3%	45.6%	20.1%
Costa Mesa city	17,006	50.5%	19.5%	30.5%	50.0%	395	1.2%	0.0%	0.0%	100.0%
Daly City city	6,589	21.9%	11.7%	58.3%	30.0%	1,082	3.6%	36.2%	12.5%	51.3%
Downey city	2,871	8.1%	22.7%	35.7%	41.6%	2,280	6.4%	10.6%	62.0%	27.4%
El Cajon city	16,065	53.5%	18.4%	36.9%	44.7%	1,203	4.0%	16.8%	37.2%	46.1%
El Monte city	1,019	3.3%	15.1%	49.7%	35.2%	16	0.1%	0.0%	100.0%	0.0%
Elk Grove city	13,025	30.9%	51.4%	31.6%	17.0%	4,949	11.7%	59.9%	27.4%	12.7%
Escondido city	16,144	36.6%	23.8%	35.8%	40.4%	275	0.6%	0.0%	49.1%	50.9%
Fairfield city	8,273	24.1%	13.3%	46.6%	40.1%	5,333	15.5%	27.0%	41.8%	31.3%
Fontana city	6,638	11.0%	19.7%	43.7%	36.6%	5,353	8.9%	30.0%	30.4%	39.6%
Fremont city	11,346	21.9%	23.1%	38.3%	38.6%	1,830	3.5%	14.1%	31.3%	54.6%
Fresno city	35,546	23.5%	16.7%	35.8%	47.4%	12,109	8.0%	26.5%	38.3%	35.2%
Fullerton city	13,834	31.1%	18.3%	43.2%	38.5%	1,048	2.4%	0.0%	22.2%	77.8%
Garden Grove city	7,206	15.6%	19.8%	48.0%	32.2%	211	0.5%	0.0%	53.6%	46.4%
Glendale city	28,770	60.9%	19.9%	29.4%	50.7%	524	1.1%	17.4%	70.0%	12.6%
Hayward city	6,287	14.9%	7.4%	42.3%	50.3%	4,899	11.6%	38.6%	36.2%	25.2%
Hesperia city	27,220	48.7%	21.4%	34.1%	44.6%	1,964	3.5%	16.9%	66.5%	16.6%
Inglewood city	774	2.5%	0.0%	15.8%	84.2%	9,000	28.7%	27.1%	31.4%	41.5%
Irvine city	28,565	40.4%	24.0%	40.9%	35.2%	1,296	1.8%	41.6%	34.8%	23.6%
Jurupa Valley city	5,218	17.5%	22.6%	25.0%	52.4%	1,110	3.7%	72.3%	10.1%	17.6%
Lancaster city	13,207	29.6%	24.2%	32.8%	42.9%	8,908	19.9%	29.5%	37.3%	33.2%
Long Beach city	26,903	20.3%	16.1%	39.2%	44.8%	18,286	13.8%	19.1%	35.7%	45.1%
Los Angeles city	271,176	24.5%	14.4%	34.5%	51.2%	89,704	8.1%	23.9%	37.1%	39.0%
Mission Viejo city	12,729	60.6%	33.4%	43.6%	23.1%	509	2.4%	32.4%	27.1%	40.5%
Modesto city	24,318	40.6%	21.6%	39.7%	38.7%	1,969	3.3%	33.2%	44.8%	22.0%
Moreno Valley city	9,250	14.2%	20.8%	33.3%	45.9%	10,856	16.7%	25.6%	34.9%	39.5%
Murrieta city	11,951	40.8%	35.9%	37.2%	26.9%	2,308	7.9%	35.9%	41.2%	22.9%
Norwalk city	1,841	6.2%	25.7%	26.3%	48.0%	1,054	3.6%	12.0%	35.9%	52.2%
Oakland city	26,467	24.8%	9.0%	24.5%	66.5%	23,079	21.6%	25.0%	43.2%	31.8%
Oceanside city	22,933	51.7%	7.9%	54.9%	37.2%	1,998	4.5%	10.6%	21.9%	67.5%
Ontario city	6,594	13.6%	21.9%	38.9%	39.3%	3,065	6.3%	13.9%	39.3%	46.8%
Orange city	16,249	40.0%	22.3%	44.1%	33.7%	70	0.2%	0.0%	100.0%	0.0%
Oxnard city	9,424	14.9%	18.2%	42.9%	38.9%	1,546	2.4%	17.3%	61.4%	21.3%
Palmdale city	9,472	21.0%	30.6%	33.4%	36.0%	6,357	14.1%	39.2%	46.1%	14.7%
Pasadena city	13,505	33.0%	16.2%	30.8%	53.1%	4,524	11.1%	10.8%	51.7%	37.5%
Pomona city	5,451	11.5%	17.1%	60.3%	22.5%	3,061	6.4%	14.3%	73.5%	12.2%
Rancho Cucamonga city	15,825	32.9%	23.8%	43.4%	32.8%	5,138	10.7%	49.9%	37.0%	13.1%
Redding city	18,832	76.4%	23.6%	37.7%	38.7%	22	0.1%	50.0%	50.0%	0.0%
Rialto city	3,963	12.8%	25.4%	20.8%	53.8%	4,346	14.0%	19.3%	60.5%	20.2%
Richmond city	3,741	12.4%	12.3%	19.1%	68.6%	4,179	13.9%	21.4%	42.4%	36.2%
Riverside city	24,008	24.0%	21.9%	47.0%	31.1%	4,858	4.9%	5.3%	65.8%	28.9%
Roseville city	20,893	64.9%	29.4%	29.1%	41.5%	258	0.8%	0.0%	67.1%	32.9%
Sacramento city	38,553	28.7%	17.9%	29.1%	53.0%	18,602	13.8%	30.7%	42.9%	26.3%

Table B-3: Places—Race and Hispanic Origin by Age—*Continued*

| | Asian, Non-Hispanic | | | | | Hispanic | | | | |
| | Millennial Population | | Percent by Age | | | Millennial Population | | Percent by Age | | |
	Number	Percent	13 to 17	18 to 24	25 to 31	Number	Percent	13 to 17	18 to 24	25 to 31
Alabama										
Birmingham city	1,303	2.1%	24.7%	34.5%	40.8%	2,975	4.7%	18.2%	34.4%	47.4%
Huntsville city	945	1.8%	14.9%	46.2%	38.8%	3,617	7.0%	19.2%	40.6%	40.2%
Mobile city	1,082	2.1%	18.2%	44.5%	37.3%	1,918	3.7%	8.0%	48.5%	43.5%
Montgomery city	837	1.4%	59.3%	17.2%	23.5%	1,690	2.9%	0.0%	28.2%	71.8%
Tuscaloosa city	624	1.6%	25.6%	65.4%	9.0%	1,070	2.7%	0.0%	60.1%	39.9%
Alaska										
Anchorage municipality	5,432	6.1%	32.1%	18.1%	49.8%	9,740	10.9%	14.7%	21.7%	63.6%
Arizona										
Chandler city	4,785	7.3%	34.1%	28.4%	37.6%	19,315	29.3%	27.2%	40.6%	32.1%
Glendale city	1,290	2.0%	18.8%	24.5%	56.7%	28,644	44.2%	34.6%	36.3%	29.2%
Mesa city	2,575	2.1%	18.5%	58.7%	22.8%	39,667	31.9%	30.9%	31.6%	37.6%
Peoria city	1,876	4.9%	30.9%	46.6%	22.5%	12,697	33.3%	32.2%	36.5%	31.3%
Phoenix city	11,633	2.8%	20.1%	14.2%	65.7%	200,939	47.8%	28.1%	39.0%	32.9%
Scottsdale city	1,995	4.0%	6.9%	15.5%	77.5%	8,560	17.1%	23.0%	34.3%	42.7%
Surprise city	730	3.4%	43.6%	30.4%	26.0%	4,753	22.1%	42.9%	35.1%	22.0%
Tempe city	6,144	8.2%	5.9%	57.2%	37.0%	17,575	23.6%	16.1%	45.0%	38.9%
Tucson city	5,814	3.5%	7.8%	55.6%	36.6%	77,185	46.8%	27.5%	43.9%	28.5%
Yuma city	152	0.5%	30.3%	69.7%	0.0%	19,989	71.7%	28.2%	40.8%	31.0%
Arkansas										
Little Rock city	1,999	3.8%	25.3%	35.9%	38.8%	3,926	7.5%	13.8%	26.8%	59.4%
California										
Anaheim city	13,231	13.8%	27.1%	31.7%	41.3%	54,139	56.4%	26.4%	38.8%	34.8%
Antioch city	2,830	8.9%	43.8%	38.4%	17.8%	11,450	36.2%	26.0%	40.1%	33.9%
Bakersfield city	3,883	3.6%	26.6%	24.7%	48.6%	61,287	56.9%	28.4%	36.2%	35.5%
Berkeley city	16,609	33.9%	5.7%	70.3%	24.0%	5,837	11.9%	12.6%	35.3%	52.1%
Burbank city	3,318	14.2%	7.6%	26.5%	65.9%	6,081	26.0%	34.0%	31.9%	34.1%
Carlsbad city	2,405	10.5%	20.6%	16.5%	63.0%	3,514	15.4%	27.5%	51.7%	20.9%
Carson city	6,314	24.8%	25.2%	40.5%	34.3%	11,105	43.5%	20.5%	42.5%	37.0%
Chula Vista city	6,834	9.6%	25.5%	43.9%	30.6%	48,009	67.3%	27.3%	39.8%	32.9%
Clovis city	2,777	10.3%	35.8%	37.5%	26.7%	8,376	31.1%	22.7%	43.2%	34.1%
Compton city	444	1.5%	22.1%	0.0%	77.9%	21,972	75.7%	30.2%	36.6%	33.2%
Concord city	2,358	7.4%	16.9%	5.9%	77.2%	10,448	32.9%	24.0%	34.9%	41.2%
Corona city	3,387	7.4%	17.6%	26.3%	56.1%	22,888	49.7%	27.0%	36.8%	36.2%
Costa Mesa city	5,634	16.7%	24.5%	22.6%	52.9%	9,740	28.9%	17.3%	41.6%	41.1%
Daly City city	11,908	39.6%	21.1%	33.5%	45.4%	9,811	32.6%	26.9%	29.1%	44.0%
Downey city	1,376	3.9%	0.0%	14.9%	85.1%	28,525	80.4%	23.2%	46.0%	30.8%
El Cajon city	545	1.8%	48.8%	29.9%	21.3%	7,734	25.8%	19.9%	33.2%	46.8%
El Monte city	6,370	20.6%	14.2%	47.1%	38.7%	23,371	75.6%	31.1%	33.0%	35.9%
Elk Grove city	10,969	26.0%	33.5%	29.3%	37.2%	9,252	22.0%	38.0%	32.5%	29.5%
Escondido city	1,285	2.9%	46.3%	34.6%	19.1%	25,211	57.2%	23.4%	37.8%	38.8%
Fairfield city	4,126	12.0%	31.6%	24.4%	44.1%	14,049	40.9%	25.0%	35.6%	39.3%
Fontana city	3,883	6.4%	31.1%	33.8%	35.1%	42,410	70.1%	34.1%	36.5%	29.4%
Fremont city	22,596	43.6%	27.3%	23.6%	49.1%	11,566	22.3%	29.5%	37.4%	33.1%
Fresno city	20,353	13.5%	21.5%	40.7%	37.9%	78,124	51.7%	27.0%	39.1%	33.9%
Fullerton city	8,217	18.4%	20.0%	42.9%	37.1%	20,160	45.3%	29.7%	32.3%	38.0%
Garden Grove city	13,651	29.5%	24.2%	35.6%	40.2%	23,658	51.2%	22.3%	41.0%	36.7%
Glendale city	7,032	14.9%	21.9%	27.2%	51.0%	8,318	17.6%	20.9%	39.2%	39.8%
Hayward city	9,597	22.8%	17.1%	35.3%	47.7%	17,966	42.6%	18.4%	37.1%	44.5%
Hesperia city	2,799	5.0%	20.5%	25.8%	53.7%	22,584	40.4%	37.3%	31.5%	31.2%
Inglewood city	398	1.3%	0.0%	24.6%	75.4%	20,889	66.6%	20.5%	38.0%	41.4%
Irvine city	26,360	37.3%	18.0%	44.0%	38.0%	11,618	16.4%	17.5%	46.6%	35.9%
Jurupa Valley city	2,052	6.9%	28.8%	39.1%	32.1%	21,212	71.2%	30.6%	38.8%	30.6%
Lancaster city	985	2.2%	14.5%	28.6%	56.9%	20,023	44.8%	34.9%	40.0%	25.1%
Long Beach city	16,450	12.4%	18.1%	32.5%	49.4%	64,231	48.6%	30.5%	38.8%	30.7%
Los Angeles city	118,969	10.8%	14.6%	42.1%	43.3%	595,701	53.9%	24.8%	38.2%	37.0%
Mission Viejo city	1,802	8.6%	43.2%	39.5%	17.3%	4,929	23.4%	41.9%	39.7%	18.4%
Modesto city	4,149	6.9%	37.7%	44.0%	18.3%	26,061	43.6%	32.2%	35.0%	32.8%
Moreno Valley city	3,021	4.6%	8.3%	29.2%	62.5%	40,791	62.7%	28.8%	35.6%	35.5%
Murrieta city	1,650	5.6%	35.6%	29.7%	34.7%	10,994	37.6%	39.9%	26.5%	33.6%
Norwalk city	2,589	8.7%	16.8%	35.7%	47.5%	23,570	79.5%	29.9%	43.7%	26.4%
Oakland city	15,913	14.9%	17.8%	38.0%	44.1%	34,043	31.9%	24.2%	30.8%	45.0%
Oceanside city	2,681	6.0%	12.4%	42.6%	45.0%	14,216	32.1%	27.3%	42.2%	30.5%
Ontario city	2,157	4.4%	17.8%	42.0%	40.2%	34,667	71.5%	30.4%	37.7%	31.9%
Orange city	3,132	7.7%	35.3%	29.0%	35.7%	20,117	49.6%	28.3%	33.1%	38.6%
Oxnard city	1,906	3.0%	23.6%	19.3%	57.1%	47,956	75.7%	27.5%	40.2%	32.4%
Palmdale city	919	2.0%	63.4%	29.2%	7.4%	26,831	59.4%	31.6%	37.2%	31.2%
Pasadena city	7,172	17.6%	9.7%	19.1%	71.2%	13,976	34.2%	18.9%	40.1%	41.0%
Pomona city	5,768	12.1%	11.6%	31.0%	57.4%	31,822	66.9%	23.5%	40.2%	36.3%
Rancho Cucamonga city	2,809	5.8%	30.2%	27.0%	42.8%	22,379	46.5%	28.0%	38.7%	33.3%
Redding city	1,279	5.2%	3.1%	82.7%	14.2%	2,803	11.4%	34.3%	29.9%	35.9%
Rialto city	na	na	na	na	na	22,551	72.9%	30.1%	42.3%	27.6%
Richmond city	5,135	17.0%	8.7%	44.4%	46.9%	15,965	52.9%	26.2%	34.8%	39.1%
Riverside city	8,386	8.4%	5.0%	78.4%	16.6%	58,525	58.4%	25.4%	44.6%	30.0%
Roseville city	2,429	7.5%	20.8%	30.9%	48.3%	7,411	23.0%	34.1%	31.4%	34.5%
Sacramento city	25,240	18.8%	20.6%	38.8%	40.6%	42,445	31.6%	24.5%	38.8%	36.7%

Table B-3: Places—Race and Hispanic Origin by Age—*Continued*

| | White, Non-Hispanic | | | | | Black, Non-Hispanic | | | | |
| | Millennial Population | | Percent by Age | | | Millennial Population | | Percent by Age | | |
	Number	Percent	13 to 17	18 to 24	25 to 31	Number	Percent	13 to 17	18 to 24	25 to 31
California—Cont.										
Salinas city	6,210	13.1%	29.7%	26.5%	43.8%	498	1.1%	64.1%	35.9%	0.0%
San Bernardino city	9,064	13.5%	15.3%	52.2%	32.5%	7,600	11.3%	16.7%	52.9%	30.4%
San Buenaventura (Ventura) city...	13,204	47.0%	14.5%	36.2%	49.3%	na	na	na	na	na
San Diego city	156,611	37.9%	13.9%	38.3%	47.8%	25,954	6.3%	19.7%	38.6%	41.7%
San Francisco city	84,604	39.1%	6.1%	23.3%	70.6%	11,020	5.1%	19.1%	34.2%	46.7%
San Jose city	61,126	24.4%	18.3%	35.3%	46.3%	6,296	2.5%	17.4%	32.4%	50.2%
San Mateo city	9,409	44.3%	27.0%	29.6%	43.4%	285	1.3%	0.0%	100.0%	0.0%
Santa Ana city	10,734	10.3%	11.0%	43.6%	45.4%	726	0.7%	25.1%	9.8%	65.2%
Santa Clara city	10,158	28.8%	7.5%	43.6%	48.9%	1,119	3.2%	4.0%	16.3%	79.7%
Santa Clarita city	19,672	42.7%	28.3%	34.7%	37.0%	2,136	4.6%	26.1%	66.5%	7.4%
Santa Maria city	5,736	18.1%	34.6%	35.7%	29.7%	164	0.5%	0.0%	100.0%	0.0%
Santa Monica city	14,486	66.9%	10.9%	21.9%	67.1%	1,205	5.6%	61.1%	17.5%	21.4%
Santa Rosa city	22,126	48.4%	24.6%	34.8%	40.6%	1,552	3.4%	32.7%	39.2%	28.1%
Simi Valley city	15,896	56.2%	27.2%	39.5%	33.3%	372	1.3%	23.4%	5.4%	71.2%
South Gate city	89	0.3%	40.4%	59.6%	0.0%	956	3.2%	36.5%	27.1%	36.4%
Stockton city	13,410	16.1%	24.4%	39.0%	36.6%	7,088	8.5%	21.9%	55.0%	23.1%
Sunnyvale city	10,211	28.7%	17.4%	31.9%	50.7%	737	2.1%	11.0%	27.4%	61.6%
Temecula city	16,043	51.4%	45.0%	32.2%	22.9%	554	1.8%	26.2%	41.5%	32.3%
Thousand Oaks city	19,475	64.1%	32.3%	41.7%	26.0%	na	na	na	na	na
Torrance city	10,540	34.0%	29.3%	48.7%	22.0%	799	2.6%	51.9%	48.1%	0.0%
Vacaville city	14,350	55.7%	27.6%	29.1%	43.4%	1,868	7.3%	33.5%	40.8%	25.7%
Vallejo city	7,498	24.0%	17.0%	33.9%	49.1%	5,670	18.2%	28.0%	39.1%	32.9%
Victorville city	6,378	18.7%	22.9%	27.9%	49.2%	6,157	18.1%	43.9%	16.3%	39.7%
Visalia city	15,049	39.8%	23.1%	33.6%	43.3%	940	2.5%	26.1%	38.6%	35.3%
Vista city	12,873	45.1%	11.1%	49.2%	39.7%	531	1.9%	71.2%	0.0%	28.8%
West Covina city	3,194	10.2%	27.5%	35.8%	36.7%	580	1.9%	0.0%	29.3%	70.7%
Westminster city	4,769	20.3%	22.5%	34.2%	43.3%	102	0.4%	0.0%	100.0%	0.0%
Colorado										
Arvada city	21,428	74.6%	32.2%	33.3%	34.5%	385	1.3%	19.5%	56.6%	23.9%
Aurora city	37,496	40.8%	24.3%	29.4%	46.3%	14,775	16.1%	23.8%	42.5%	33.7%
Boulder city	40,244	85.0%	10.6%	63.6%	25.8%	350	0.7%	0.0%	70.9%	29.1%
Centennial city	17,241	69.5%	33.4%	27.9%	38.7%	1,313	5.3%	31.0%	59.6%	9.4%
Colorado Springs city	77,307	63.7%	23.2%	38.6%	38.2%	7,376	6.1%	30.6%	31.1%	38.3%
Denver city	90,785	49.7%	7.8%	26.9%	65.3%	17,114	9.4%	16.8%	42.3%	40.9%
Fort Collins city	48,882	81.3%	17.4%	55.3%	27.3%	573	1.0%	0.0%	69.1%	30.9%
Greeley city	19,325	58.2%	23.3%	37.6%	39.1%	378	1.1%	9.0%	41.0%	50.0%
Lakewood city	26,618	74.2%	21.3%	37.3%	41.3%	328	0.9%	23.5%	47.3%	29.3%
Pueblo city	12,245	43.1%	23.0%	39.5%	37.5%	287	1.0%	26.1%	28.2%	45.6%
Thornton city	14,981	43.5%	28.6%	36.3%	35.1%	896	2.6%	81.0%	0.0%	19.0%
Westminster city	19,814	63.7%	24.1%	30.8%	45.1%	237	0.8%	4.6%	95.4%	0.0%
Connecticut										
Bridgeport city	8,589	19.8%	8.8%	35.7%	55.5%	13,149	30.3%	25.8%	41.0%	33.2%
Hartford city	7,037	17.2%	4.8%	65.9%	29.3%	13,059	32.0%	27.0%	37.8%	35.2%
New Haven city	15,463	34.1%	4.0%	52.8%	43.1%	11,525	25.4%	22.9%	39.4%	37.6%
Stamford city	16,401	48.5%	26.5%	30.7%	42.8%	5,112	15.1%	27.3%	44.4%	28.3%
Waterbury city	7,938	26.7%	9.3%	33.3%	57.4%	6,944	23.3%	31.3%	31.0%	37.7%
District of Columbia										
Washington city	80,833	40.1%	4.0%	33.7%	62.3%	84,077	41.7%	20.0%	41.8%	38.2%
Florida										
Cape Coral city	25,382	69.6%	27.2%	32.2%	40.6%	1,087	3.0%	43.9%	0.0%	56.1%
Clearwater city	14,760	63.1%	25.5%	37.0%	37.5%	2,684	11.5%	29.9%	34.0%	36.1%
Coral Springs city	16,297	50.1%	31.9%	39.1%	29.0%	6,764	20.8%	26.3%	37.7%	36.0%
Fort Lauderdale city	13,279	34.3%	17.5%	36.0%	46.5%	16,243	41.9%	27.4%	40.2%	32.4%
Gainesville city	36,583	56.5%	5.3%	68.0%	26.7%	11,263	17.4%	7.0%	57.2%	35.7%
Hialeah city	2,178	4.0%	31.4%	47.2%	21.4%	2,725	4.9%	21.5%	27.7%	50.9%
Hollywood city	13,121	42.6%	23.7%	36.5%	39.8%	5,899	19.1%	27.0%	42.4%	30.7%
Jacksonville city	108,507	48.6%	18.4%	35.4%	46.2%	77,599	34.8%	25.5%	36.4%	38.1%
Lakeland city	13,012	49.6%	25.3%	40.0%	34.8%	5,590	21.3%	27.1%	48.2%	24.7%
Miami Beach city	7,942	39.5%	17.8%	28.9%	53.4%	2,584	12.8%	41.6%	43.0%	15.5%
Miami city	11,352	11.4%	9.6%	27.4%	63.0%	19,574	19.6%	21.8%	40.6%	37.6%
Miami Gardens city	1,250	3.9%	14.6%	34.9%	50.5%	18,924	58.8%	24.4%	42.9%	32.7%
Miramar city	5,048	13.6%	17.5%	28.2%	54.3%	16,314	43.9%	14.0%	35.0%	51.1%
Orlando city	25,470	32.1%	17.1%	31.2%	51.7%	24,399	30.8%	22.2%	37.0%	40.8%
Palm Bay city	14,027	59.2%	30.1%	36.5%	33.4%	5,553	23.4%	25.3%	52.5%	22.2%
Pembroke Pines city	10,322	25.7%	29.3%	31.4%	39.3%	8,918	22.2%	14.6%	31.1%	54.3%
Pompano Beach city	4,322	16.9%	20.1%	26.3%	53.6%	14,079	55.1%	40.4%	30.9%	28.7%
Port St. Lucie city	19,058	49.3%	32.1%	36.1%	31.8%	8,675	22.4%	46.2%	30.8%	23.0%
St. Petersburg city	35,259	58.6%	18.7%	35.8%	45.5%	15,615	25.9%	30.7%	39.7%	29.6%
Tallahassee city	44,611	51.7%	11.0%	62.3%	26.7%	29,021	33.6%	14.6%	60.8%	24.6%
Tampa city	44,623	42.8%	14.2%	41.1%	44.7%	28,788	27.6%	24.3%	39.0%	36.7%
West Palm Beach city	8,264	28.4%	9.4%	37.2%	53.4%	10,258	35.3%	22.7%	46.1%	31.2%
Georgia										
Athens-Clarke County unified govt (bal)	34,369	63.6%	3.0%	71.3%	25.7%	10,193	18.9%	18.7%	54.4%	26.9%
Atlanta city	48,472	33.8%	8.4%	37.5%	54.2%	68,157	47.6%	17.3%	45.2%	37.5%

Table B-3: Places—Race and Hispanic Origin by Age—*Continued*

	Asian, Non-Hispanic					Hispanic				
	Millennial Population		Percent by Age			Millennial Population		Percent by Age		
	Number	Percent	13 to 17	18 to 24	25 to 31	Number	Percent	13 to 17	18 to 24	25 to 31
California—Cont.										
Salinas city..........................	3,069	6.5%	21.4%	44.6%	34.0%	37,346	78.8%	27.0%	40.6%	32.3%
San Bernardino city......................	2,481	3.7%	6.7%	59.2%	34.1%	45,824	68.3%	30.3%	38.1%	31.6%
San Buenaventura (Ventura) city...	911	3.2%	27.4%	58.3%	14.3%	11,456	40.8%	21.7%	43.7%	34.6%
San Diego city........................	66,138	16.0%	16.5%	36.6%	46.9%	142,003	34.4%	24.4%	38.6%	37.0%
San Francisco city.......................	63,589	29.4%	14.2%	32.9%	52.9%	42,968	19.8%	14.7%	29.7%	55.7%
San Jose city...........................	75,350	30.1%	24.2%	31.9%	43.9%	98,358	39.3%	26.4%	34.8%	38.8%
San Mateo city..........................	5,168	24.3%	26.9%	22.0%	51.2%	4,814	22.7%	23.7%	36.2%	40.1%
Santa Ana city...........................	8,015	7.7%	27.7%	33.5%	38.8%	83,479	80.0%	25.7%	39.5%	34.8%
Santa Clara city.........................	15,569	44.1%	12.3%	32.4%	55.3%	7,283	20.6%	18.5%	33.8%	47.7%
Santa Clarita city........................	4,101	8.9%	27.5%	29.8%	42.7%	17,771	38.6%	31.3%	35.7%	33.0%
Santa Maria city.........................	1,324	4.2%	17.9%	36.3%	45.8%	24,126	76.1%	35.8%	34.0%	30.2%
Santa Monica city........................	2,426	11.2%	14.1%	39.6%	46.4%	2,905	13.4%	30.0%	26.9%	43.1%
Santa Rosa city..........................	2,047	4.5%	20.6%	30.2%	49.1%	18,083	39.6%	32.5%	31.5%	36.0%
Simi Valley city..........................	1,827	6.5%	42.6%	30.9%	26.5%	8,615	30.4%	35.4%	27.4%	37.2%
South Gate city..........................	na	na	na	na	na	28,508	95.1%	25.5%	34.0%	40.5%
Stockton city............................	18,169	21.9%	20.4%	42.6%	37.0%	40,172	48.3%	31.5%	35.7%	32.8%
Sunnyvale city..........................	16,244	45.7%	12.4%	16.7%	70.9%	6,120	17.2%	27.2%	43.4%	29.4%
Temecula city...........................	2,186	7.0%	27.1%	19.0%	53.8%	8,515	27.3%	19.6%	59.1%	21.3%
Thousand Oaks city......................	2,576	8.5%	15.6%	37.0%	47.4%	7,755	25.5%	20.6%	41.0%	38.3%
Torrance city............................	9,411	30.3%	28.7%	24.1%	47.2%	7,248	23.4%	17.8%	42.9%	39.3%
Vacaville city............................	1,414	5.5%	16.0%	33.2%	50.8%	6,395	24.8%	19.9%	57.6%	22.5%
Vallejo city..............................	6,862	22.0%	31.0%	37.8%	31.2%	8,714	27.9%	29.9%	33.4%	36.8%
Victorville city..........................	965	2.8%	9.7%	73.9%	16.4%	19,964	58.6%	20.2%	49.1%	30.7%
Visalia city.............................	1,800	4.8%	43.2%	24.0%	32.8%	19,076	50.5%	23.3%	43.1%	33.5%
Vista city...............................	568	2.0%	0.0%	15.5%	84.5%	13,448	47.1%	16.2%	37.9%	45.9%
West Covina city........................	5,527	17.6%	18.3%	31.4%	50.3%	21,536	68.7%	27.1%	36.8%	36.1%
Westminster city........................	7,084	30.2%	28.7%	25.1%	46.2%	10,431	44.5%	30.5%	27.4%	42.1%
Colorado										
Arvada city.............................	477	1.7%	43.4%	44.4%	12.2%	5,720	19.9%	32.6%	29.0%	38.3%
Aurora city.............................	3,747	4.1%	32.2%	28.3%	39.5%	30,475	33.1%	31.3%	35.3%	33.4%
Boulder city............................	2,298	4.9%	8.3%	56.6%	35.1%	3,737	7.9%	16.4%	68.4%	15.2%
Centennial city.........................	1,509	6.1%	65.5%	4.8%	29.8%	3,411	13.8%	43.2%	26.9%	29.9%
Colorado Springs city...................	3,347	2.8%	45.0%	25.4%	29.6%	25,721	21.2%	25.0%	35.7%	39.3%
Denver city.............................	8,114	4.4%	15.9%	31.3%	52.8%	60,675	33.2%	25.1%	36.8%	38.1%
Fort Collins city........................	1,232	2.0%	22.2%	53.5%	24.3%	7,080	11.8%	29.4%	43.9%	26.7%
Greeley city............................	408	1.2%	7.4%	0.0%	92.6%	12,677	38.2%	22.5%	48.0%	29.5%
Lakewood city..........................	1,258	3.5%	22.5%	40.5%	37.0%	6,717	18.7%	17.9%	41.5%	40.6%
Pueblo city.............................	283	1.0%	49.8%	0.0%	50.2%	14,583	51.4%	27.6%	38.9%	33.5%
Thornton city...........................	2,086	6.1%	12.6%	54.6%	32.8%	14,591	42.4%	38.2%	35.3%	26.5%
Westminster city........................	1,174	3.8%	24.6%	5.7%	69.7%	9,016	29.0%	35.9%	27.1%	37.0%
Connecticut............................										
Bridgeport city..........................	2,404	5.5%	4.9%	36.4%	58.7%	18,103	41.7%	24.7%	30.8%	44.6%
Hartford city............................	1,858	4.6%	0.0%	24.1%	75.9%	18,352	45.0%	25.3%	41.5%	33.2%
New Haven city..........................	3,350	7.4%	11.6%	41.9%	46.5%	12,000	26.4%	23.1%	45.3%	31.7%
Stamford city...........................	1,921	5.7%	36.9%	23.9%	39.3%	9,800	29.0%	12.6%	44.1%	43.2%
Waterbury city..........................	672	2.3%	33.8%	66.2%	0.0%	13,993	47.0%	25.1%	36.7%	38.2%
District of Columbia										
Washington city.........................	8,128	4.0%	4.5%	49.4%	46.1%	21,409	10.6%	11.0%	29.3%	59.7%
Florida										
Cape Coral city..........................	299	0.8%	69.2%	0.0%	30.8%	8,889	24.4%	32.9%	41.0%	26.1%
Clearwater city..........................	394	1.7%	23.4%	0.0%	76.6%	5,059	21.6%	13.8%	33.2%	53.0%
Coral Springs city.......................	986	3.0%	23.1%	53.2%	23.6%	8,267	25.4%	15.3%	54.8%	29.9%
Fort Lauderdale city	457	1.2%	0.0%	73.1%	26.9%	8,520	22.0%	21.0%	39.7%	39.3%
Gainesville city.........................	5,092	7.9%	1.5%	63.6%	34.9%	8,630	13.3%	5.4%	74.3%	20.3%
Hialeah city............................	269	0.5%	0.0%	20.4%	79.6%	49,960	90.6%	26.6%	36.9%	36.5%
Hollywood city..........................	1,596	5.2%	25.5%	53.1%	21.4%	9,096	29.5%	29.5%	26.4%	44.1%
Jacksonville city........................	8,278	3.7%	24.5%	26.2%	49.3%	21,666	9.7%	24.3%	37.6%	38.1%
Lakeland city...........................	795	3.0%	0.0%	38.2%	61.8%	6,277	23.9%	27.4%	40.9%	31.7%
Miami Beach city........................	354	1.8%	7.9%	40.4%	51.7%	8,240	41.0%	22.2%	31.4%	46.5%
Miami city..............................	416	0.4%	13.7%	16.3%	70.0%	67,528	67.7%	19.2%	33.7%	47.1%
Miami Gardens city......................	684	2.1%	14.6%	24.7%	60.7%	10,748	33.4%	15.7%	48.1%	36.2%
Miramar city............................	933	2.5%	18.3%	20.9%	60.8%	13,523	36.4%	21.3%	34.7%	44.0%
Orlando city............................	3,582	4.5%	19.1%	40.8%	40.1%	23,690	29.9%	27.4%	25.1%	47.5%
Palm Bay city...........................	85	0.4%	0.0%	100.0%	0.0%	3,345	14.1%	21.9%	29.3%	48.8%
Pembroke Pines city	2,321	5.8%	23.7%	34.3%	42.0%	16,214	40.3%	35.4%	39.0%	25.6%
Pompano Beach city.....................	417	1.6%	0.0%	12.9%	87.1%	6,611	25.9%	21.8%	25.0%	53.2%
Port St. Lucie city.......................	1,033	2.7%	19.0%	59.4%	21.6%	9,289	24.0%	46.7%	30.1%	23.2%
St. Petersburg city	2,131	3.5%	32.3%	21.0%	46.6%	4,719	7.8%	19.4%	38.7%	41.9%
Tallahassee city.........................	2,312	2.7%	10.2%	55.7%	34.1%	6,946	8.0%	12.0%	55.6%	32.4%
Tampa city.............................	2,041	2.0%	21.5%	69.1%	9.4%	25,741	24.7%	23.1%	40.2%	36.7%
West Palm Beach city...................	63	0.2%	0.0%	100.0%	0.0%	9,386	32.3%	18.7%	24.5%	56.8%
Georgia										
Athens-Clarke County unified govt (bal)	3,201	5.9%	2.5%	80.5%	17.0%	5,138	9.5%	21.6%	47.1%	31.3%
Atlanta city.............................	10,672	7.4%	3.1%	54.8%	42.1%	11,706	8.2%	20.7%	34.9%	44.4%

Table B-3: Places—Race and Hispanic Origin by Age—*Continued*

	White, Non-Hispanic					Black, Non-Hispanic				
	Millennial Population		Percent by Age			Millennial Population		Percent by Age		
	Number	Percent	13 to 17	18 to 24	25 to 31	Number	Percent	13 to 17	18 to 24	25 to 31
Georgia—Cont.										
Augusta-Richmond County consolidated govt (bal)	18,732	32.6%	13.9%	37.7%	48.4%	32,862	57.2%	26.6%	37.5%	36.0%
Columbus city	22,581	38.8%	18.5%	43.2%	38.2%	25,097	43.2%	25.2%	39.4%	35.4%
Macon city	9,814	36.6%	22.5%	36.7%	40.7%	15,280	56.9%	24.5%	46.9%	28.5%
Roswell city	13,585	57.8%	28.2%	39.4%	32.4%	3,740	15.9%	41.2%	3.9%	54.9%
Sandy Springs city	12,583	49.7%	25.9%	19.6%	54.5%	7,968	31.5%	22.1%	18.4%	59.5%
Savannah city	18,473	41.0%	14.2%	38.8%	47.0%	21,227	47.1%	19.3%	46.8%	33.9%
Hawaii										
Urban Honolulu CDP	16,536	18.8%	3.3%	38.5%	58.2%	3,031	3.5%	19.7%	30.6%	49.7%
Idaho										
Boise City city	47,810	77.1%	21.1%	37.4%	41.5%	889	1.4%	85.4%	14.6%	0.0%
Illinois										
Aurora city	21,406	40.6%	23.2%	31.6%	45.1%	4,203	8.0%	27.9%	34.1%	37.9%
Chicago city	250,678	31.6%	9.2%	29.5%	61.3%	233,115	29.4%	25.6%	40.4%	34.0%
Elgin city	12,713	40.2%	26.9%	32.3%	40.8%	2,675	8.5%	0.6%	65.6%	33.9%
Joliet city	20,239	49.6%	27.0%	36.7%	36.3%	6,195	15.2%	27.2%	46.5%	26.3%
Naperville city	24,993	68.6%	29.7%	34.6%	35.7%	3,353	9.2%	49.3%	29.2%	21.5%
Peoria city	22,147	65.9%	17.9%	40.4%	41.7%	6,109	18.2%	29.0%	35.5%	35.6%
Rockford city	21,664	53.8%	24.7%	35.8%	39.6%	8,355	20.7%	23.9%	49.2%	26.9%
Springfield city	21,688	72.0%	22.5%	36.7%	40.8%	5,117	17.0%	21.4%	39.0%	39.5%
Indiana										
Evansville city	25,344	82.4%	21.3%	39.9%	38.8%	2,856	9.3%	25.0%	48.7%	26.3%
Fort Wayne city	45,192	67.3%	22.3%	35.8%	41.9%	9,445	14.1%	32.3%	37.7%	30.0%
Indianapolis city (bal)	125,590	54.2%	17.9%	34.8%	47.4%	63,065	27.2%	26.9%	37.0%	36.1%
South Bend city	16,604	60.1%	18.9%	47.5%	33.6%	5,717	20.7%	29.9%	43.9%	26.2%
Iowa										
Cedar Rapids city	30,406	87.8%	24.7%	34.5%	40.8%	1,339	3.9%	69.5%	13.4%	17.1%
Davenport city	19,853	75.0%	25.0%	38.3%	36.6%	2,591	9.8%	29.4%	45.3%	25.2%
Des Moines city	37,064	65.1%	11.7%	39.4%	49.0%	6,879	12.1%	26.8%	42.9%	30.3%
Kansas										
Kansas City city	14,962	38.0%	24.9%	32.6%	42.5%	8,727	22.2%	32.4%	36.3%	31.3%
Olathe city	23,530	71.8%	23.1%	38.2%	38.7%	1,554	4.7%	60.1%	7.2%	32.7%
Overland Park city	34,946	76.2%	30.7%	30.9%	38.4%	2,473	5.4%	21.1%	60.4%	18.5%
Topeka city	21,788	67.0%	22.5%	35.7%	41.8%	2,535	7.8%	36.5%	54.5%	9.0%
Wichita city	69,926	66.0%	25.1%	32.7%	42.2%	11,132	10.5%	26.6%	32.5%	40.9%
Kentucky										
Lexington-Fayette urban county	65,137	71.2%	14.1%	49.9%	36.0%	14,451	15.8%	25.7%	43.2%	31.0%
Louisville/Jefferson County metro govt (bal)	100,096	64.5%	24.5%	35.2%	40.3%	37,261	24.0%	28.7%	38.9%	32.4%
Louisiana										
Baton Rouge city	32,288	39.9%	14.8%	54.8%	30.4%	38,749	47.9%	18.1%	50.2%	31.7%
Lafayette city	26,070	63.6%	23.3%	38.5%	38.2%	11,414	27.8%	22.9%	39.5%	37.6%
New Orleans city	32,823	30.5%	9.8%	30.4%	59.8%	62,542	58.1%	22.4%	40.2%	37.3%
Shreveport city	22,867	40.5%	21.9%	37.0%	41.2%	30,524	54.0%	26.4%	40.7%	32.9%
Maryland										
Baltimore city	51,301	29.0%	9.4%	30.8%	59.8%	105,836	59.7%	21.2%	40.8%	37.9%
Massachusetts										
Boston city	114,183	48.9%	5.2%	39.4%	55.4%	43,270	18.5%	23.2%	43.0%	33.8%
Brockton city	10,280	40.9%	21.5%	23.7%	54.9%	9,506	37.8%	27.4%	32.9%	39.7%
Cambridge city	25,408	56.2%	5.0%	46.9%	48.0%	3,627	8.0%	16.7%	57.7%	25.6%
Lowell city	14,864	44.6%	16.3%	49.3%	34.4%	2,645	7.9%	22.8%	34.9%	42.4%
Lynn city	7,324	32.5%	24.9%	43.3%	31.9%	3,252	14.4%	21.8%	22.4%	55.8%
New Bedford city	15,239	60.9%	23.1%	36.7%	40.2%	460	1.8%	39.3%	42.4%	18.3%
Springfield city	12,981	27.9%	11.1%	52.6%	36.4%	10,784	23.2%	34.5%	43.0%	22.5%
Worcester city	29,940	52.9%	13.2%	49.1%	37.7%	6,270	11.1%	26.7%	37.8%	35.5%
Michigan										
Ann Arbor city	34,460	65.8%	5.4%	69.5%	25.1%	5,566	10.6%	29.6%	60.6%	9.8%
Dearborn city	22,110	81.2%	24.5%	41.6%	33.9%	2,543	9.3%	41.7%	38.0%	20.3%
Detroit city	18,483	9.8%	18.5%	37.9%	43.6%	146,612	77.7%	25.6%	45.0%	29.4%
Flint city	7,926	31.8%	21.9%	21.3%	56.8%	15,125	60.7%	30.9%	29.8%	39.3%
Grand Rapids city	35,903	60.7%	13.4%	44.0%	42.6%	11,415	19.3%	30.6%	28.8%	40.7%
Lansing city	19,638	55.4%	11.2%	38.9%	49.9%	5,462	15.4%	18.2%	40.5%	41.3%
Livonia city	15,581	73.3%	26.2%	35.5%	38.3%	3,578	16.8%	32.1%	50.4%	17.6%
Sterling Heights city	22,822	81.6%	26.4%	35.5%	38.1%	666	2.4%	26.4%	39.9%	33.6%
Warren city	21,389	64.3%	18.1%	40.0%	41.9%	7,510	22.6%	16.2%	41.4%	42.4%
Minnesota										
Minneapolis city	79,682	59.2%	8.0%	38.9%	53.0%	20,858	15.5%	18.6%	32.0%	49.4%
Rochester city	21,527	80.1%	23.7%	36.7%	39.7%	1,111	4.1%	30.8%	33.1%	36.1%
St. Paul city	41,434	45.8%	15.2%	34.1%	50.6%	13,701	15.1%	21.6%	43.6%	34.8%
Mississippi										
Jackson city	10,058	19.3%	13.4%	42.8%	43.9%	40,254	77.0%	24.5%	41.7%	33.8%

Table B-3: Places—Race and Hispanic Origin by Age—*Continued*

	Asian, Non-Hispanic					Hispanic				
	Millennial Population		Percent by Age			Millennial Population		Percent by Age		
	Number	Percent	13 to 17	18 to 24	25 to 31	Number	Percent	13 to 17	18 to 24	25 to 31
Georgia—Cont.										
Augusta-Richmond County consolidated govt (bal)	1,228	2.1%	15.1%	28.2%	56.8%	2,926	5.1%	24.4%	34.1%	41.5%
Columbus city	748	1.3%	17.2%	48.3%	34.5%	6,591	11.3%	18.8%	49.3%	31.9%
Macon city	290	1.1%	52.1%	47.9%	0.0%	1,262	4.7%	19.9%	19.8%	60.3%
Roswell city	850	3.6%	42.1%	12.5%	45.4%	3,104	13.2%	17.5%	36.4%	46.1%
Sandy Springs city	728	2.9%	0.0%	15.9%	84.1%	3,228	12.8%	15.0%	26.4%	58.6%
Savannah city	1,006	2.2%	0.0%	76.2%	23.8%	3,663	8.1%	15.4%	40.0%	44.6%
Hawaii										
Urban Honolulu CDP	35,459	40.4%	25.1%	31.4%	43.5%	8,167	9.3%	21.7%	33.4%	44.8%
Idaho										
Boise City city	1,282	2.1%	41.9%	22.5%	35.6%	7,516	12.1%	24.9%	56.3%	18.8%
Illinois										
Aurora city	2,753	5.2%	40.9%	24.2%	35.0%	23,238	44.1%	29.7%	34.1%	36.1%
Chicago city	53,063	6.7%	14.2%	35.0%	50.9%	239,813	30.2%	25.8%	36.4%	37.9%
Elgin city	1,243	3.9%	24.1%	26.6%	49.2%	14,130	44.7%	27.2%	41.1%	31.7%
Joliet city	879	2.2%	25.6%	53.4%	21.0%	12,518	30.7%	26.0%	34.1%	39.9%
Naperville city	2,498	6.9%	35.1%	19.3%	45.6%	4,353	11.9%	33.8%	26.8%	39.4%
Peoria city	1,544	4.6%	0.0%	17.5%	82.5%	1,991	5.9%	26.9%	55.7%	17.4%
Rockford city	1,043	2.6%	46.3%	12.6%	41.1%	7,955	19.7%	30.3%	40.6%	29.0%
Springfield city	592	2.0%	10.8%	55.7%	33.4%	1,441	4.8%	0.0%	49.7%	50.3%
Indiana										
Evansville city	196	0.6%	0.0%	0.0%	100.0%	1,287	4.2%	11.0%	89.0%	0.0%
Fort Wayne city	1,699	2.5%	15.0%	46.9%	38.1%	6,660	9.9%	33.7%	35.2%	31.1%
Indianapolis city (bal)	6,556	2.8%	10.6%	32.4%	57.0%	27,698	11.9%	25.7%	34.5%	39.8%
South Bend city	919	3.3%	23.9%	55.0%	21.1%	3,620	13.1%	29.3%	46.9%	23.9%
Iowa										
Cedar Rapids city	1,128	3.3%	17.2%	0.0%	82.8%	799	2.3%	0.0%	1.8%	98.2%
Davenport city	923	3.5%	18.5%	0.0%	81.5%	1,585	6.0%	28.0%	36.8%	35.1%
Des Moines city	3,705	6.5%	39.2%	4.7%	56.0%	7,019	12.3%	27.5%	18.2%	54.3%
Kansas										
Kansas City city	1,955	5.0%	14.3%	14.4%	71.3%	12,205	31.0%	31.9%	41.4%	26.8%
Olathe city	2,187	6.7%	43.7%	39.2%	17.1%	3,630	11.1%	43.4%	25.2%	31.5%
Overland Park city	3,633	7.9%	61.4%	9.0%	29.6%	2,889	6.3%	27.9%	16.4%	55.7%
Topeka city	843	2.6%	0.0%	100.0%	0.0%	4,688	14.4%	26.4%	53.8%	19.8%
Wichita city	3,425	3.2%	30.5%	20.1%	49.4%	18,267	17.2%	37.7%	35.3%	27.0%
Kentucky										
Lexington-Fayette urban county....	3,568	3.9%	14.0%	27.1%	58.9%	6,374	7.0%	28.5%	37.2%	34.3%
Louisville/Jefferson County metro govt (bal)	3,400	2.2%	29.2%	16.5%	54.3%	9,757	6.3%	20.9%	46.4%	32.7%
Louisiana										
Baton Rouge city	3,809	4.7%	10.4%	31.6%	58.0%	2,955	3.7%	2.0%	82.7%	15.3%
Lafayette city	981	2.4%	10.7%	18.6%	70.7%	1,967	4.8%	11.1%	44.4%	44.5%
New Orleans city	3,553	3.3%	8.6%	47.9%	43.5%	6,696	6.2%	10.0%	34.4%	55.6%
Shreveport city	426	0.8%	16.0%	0.0%	84.0%	1,365	2.4%	38.8%	43.9%	17.3%
Maryland										
Baltimore city	6,389	3.6%	8.0%	44.7%	47.4%	9,165	5.2%	16.2%	29.5%	54.3%
Massachusetts										
Boston city	20,777	8.9%	10.0%	45.6%	44.4%	44,672	19.1%	23.7%	37.3%	39.0%
Brockton city	698	2.8%	12.2%	5.4%	82.4%	2,118	8.4%	35.2%	14.6%	50.2%
Cambridge city	8,102	17.9%	6.5%	43.1%	50.4%	5,606	12.4%	13.8%	42.9%	43.3%
Lowell city	8,462	25.4%	19.7%	31.5%	48.8%	6,771	20.3%	31.5%	30.8%	37.7%
Lynn city	1,351	6.0%	17.2%	42.9%	39.9%	9,787	43.4%	25.1%	38.6%	36.3%
New Bedford city	140	0.6%	49.3%	0.0%	50.7%	7,618	30.4%	23.0%	27.6%	49.4%
Springfield city	589	1.3%	17.8%	45.5%	36.7%	21,579	46.4%	30.5%	37.4%	32.0%
Worcester city	4,444	7.9%	23.8%	46.8%	29.4%	14,811	26.2%	31.3%	39.5%	29.2%
Michigan										
Ann Arbor city	8,050	15.4%	2.7%	64.7%	32.5%	2,333	4.5%	0.0%	58.0%	42.0%
Dearborn city	703	2.6%	16.5%	28.6%	54.9%	608	2.2%	36.7%	17.4%	45.9%
Detroit city	3,714	2.0%	28.6%	45.1%	26.3%	15,249	8.1%	27.1%	40.3%	32.6%
Flint city	84	0.3%	0.0%	0.0%	100.0%	627	2.5%	41.6%	1.8%	56.6%
Grand Rapids city	1,507	2.5%	0.0%	19.6%	80.4%	7,614	12.9%	21.0%	40.5%	38.5%
Lansing city	1,526	4.3%	0.0%	28.8%	71.2%	4,923	13.9%	18.9%	43.3%	37.8%
Livonia city	488	2.3%	59.0%	0.0%	41.0%	1,038	4.9%	29.7%	11.8%	58.6%
Sterling Heights city	1,478	5.3%	31.1%	28.1%	40.8%	836	3.0%	63.6%	36.4%	0.0%
Warren city	3,105	9.3%	29.6%	38.5%	31.9%	622	1.9%	85.4%	14.6%	0.0%
Minnesota										
Minneapolis city	11,001	8.2%	17.7%	40.0%	42.3%	15,784	11.7%	19.3%	37.8%	42.8%
Rochester city	1,241	4.6%	13.0%	33.7%	53.3%	2,225	8.3%	11.6%	60.2%	28.2%
St. Paul city	21,344	23.6%	25.4%	42.4%	32.2%	8,650	9.6%	21.6%	48.4%	30.0%
Mississippi										
Jackson city	240	0.5%	32.1%	57.5%	10.4%	1,353	2.6%	0.0%	0.0%	100.0%

Table B-3: Places—Race and Hispanic Origin by Age—*Continued*

| | White, Non-Hispanic | | | | | Black, Non-Hispanic | | | | |
| | Millennial Population | | Percent by Age | | | Millennial Population | | Percent by Age | | |
	Number	Percent	13 to 17	18 to 24	25 to 31	Number	Percent	13 to 17	18 to 24	25 to 31
Missouri										
Columbia city	41,559	80.0%	14.6%	55.1%	30.2%	2,871	5.5%	11.7%	19.9%	68.3%
Independence city	19,052	70.9%	27.8%	37.1%	35.0%	4,288	16.0%	33.3%	54.5%	12.2%
Kansas City city	73,535	55.2%	16.7%	33.4%	49.8%	34,656	26.0%	28.2%	37.3%	34.4%
Lee's Summit city	18,327	82.3%	41.2%	22.9%	35.9%	2,142	9.6%	18.2%	38.0%	43.8%
Springfield city	50,171	85.9%	16.5%	47.2%	36.3%	2,265	3.9%	13.6%	48.4%	38.0%
St. Louis city	38,561	41.8%	8.5%	29.5%	62.0%	42,918	46.5%	24.9%	40.4%	34.7%
Montana										
Billings city	22,698	81.6%	21.6%	43.2%	35.2%	204	0.7%	38.2%	0.0%	61.8%
Nebraska										
Lincoln city	67,331	81.2%	17.3%	47.4%	35.2%	3,474	4.2%	16.6%	65.8%	17.6%
Omaha city	74,059	63.0%	21.8%	34.5%	43.7%	16,539	14.1%	29.3%	42.2%	28.6%
Nevada										
Henderson city	35,408	59.4%	25.8%	34.4%	39.8%	3,233	5.4%	2.9%	54.3%	42.8%
Las Vegas city	58,586	38.3%	24.0%	31.5%	44.5%	18,462	12.1%	26.1%	37.1%	36.8%
North Las Vegas city	19,644	29.1%	18.5%	33.6%	47.9%	10,744	15.9%	31.6%	31.9%	36.5%
Reno city	36,720	54.1%	21.7%	38.7%	39.6%	2,299	3.4%	4.9%	23.9%	71.2%
Sparks city	12,564	56.5%	17.8%	42.5%	39.6%	331	1.5%	56.8%	0.0%	43.2%
New Hampshire										
Manchester city	22,879	75.8%	17.5%	35.2%	47.3%	702	2.3%	0.0%	91.6%	8.4%
New Jersey										
Elizabeth city	3,763	10.1%	12.1%	36.6%	51.3%	5,773	15.5%	31.9%	37.3%	30.8%
Jersey City city	13,667	18.5%	11.0%	22.4%	66.6%	16,671	22.5%	23.1%	35.5%	41.5%
Newark city	7,562	9.2%	11.5%	39.1%	49.5%	40,263	49.2%	21.6%	36.2%	42.2%
Paterson city	2,105	5.0%	10.7%	47.6%	41.7%	12,776	30.4%	25.5%	40.3%	34.2%
New Mexico										
Albuquerque city	48,439	32.9%	20.0%	37.5%	42.4%	4,399	3.0%	23.2%	65.2%	11.6%
Las Cruces city	10,275	31.0%	12.6%	52.8%	34.7%	1,215	3.7%	20.4%	79.6%	0.0%
Rio Rancho city	7,938	35.3%	32.9%	34.9%	32.2%	129	0.6%	96.9%	0.0%	3.1%
New York										
Albany city	20,568	52.8%	4.5%	58.5%	36.9%	8,728	22.4%	20.1%	41.0%	38.9%
Buffalo city	33,398	41.8%	12.2%	42.2%	45.6%	28,913	36.2%	32.2%	41.6%	26.2%
New York city	675,128	29.8%	15.0%	29.9%	55.1%	506,235	22.4%	23.0%	38.2%	38.8%
Rochester city	24,589	36.4%	4.8%	30.5%	64.7%	25,964	38.4%	32.0%	36.8%	31.2%
Syracuse city	24,671	49.2%	8.8%	50.1%	41.1%	12,412	24.8%	25.5%	41.1%	33.4%
Yonkers city	15,346	31.5%	27.6%	35.4%	37.0%	7,443	15.3%	33.5%	34.2%	32.2%
North Carolina										
Charlotte city	92,311	42.3%	21.4%	31.4%	47.3%	74,705	34.2%	25.6%	40.1%	34.3%
Durham city	26,933	36.8%	11.9%	30.6%	57.5%	28,274	38.7%	23.0%	39.0%	38.0%
Fayetteville city	25,755	39.6%	14.5%	39.2%	46.3%	26,283	40.4%	24.3%	39.6%	36.0%
Greensboro city	36,112	45.1%	20.4%	41.2%	38.4%	33,671	42.1%	17.3%	46.0%	36.8%
High Point city	12,983	45.6%	21.7%	37.3%	41.0%	9,306	32.7%	21.8%	48.8%	29.4%
Raleigh city	72,117	52.1%	21.6%	38.9%	39.5%	36,153	26.1%	25.5%	37.2%	37.2%
Wilmington city	27,728	76.5%	11.4%	49.4%	39.2%	4,151	11.5%	20.4%	53.3%	26.3%
Winston-Salem city	25,571	41.0%	16.2%	42.6%	41.3%	20,715	33.2%	28.3%	46.3%	25.3%
North Dakota										
Fargo city	37,140	85.0%	13.5%	50.8%	35.6%	2,795	6.4%	0.0%	94.7%	5.3%
Ohio										
Akron city	31,148	57.2%	14.3%	44.4%	41.2%	15,804	29.0%	19.6%	43.9%	36.5%
Cincinnati city	49,865	54.7%	9.9%	46.1%	44.0%	32,254	35.4%	26.9%	39.4%	33.7%
Cleveland city	33,736	31.4%	14.7%	40.6%	44.7%	55,763	51.9%	24.8%	44.6%	30.6%
Columbus city	155,546	61.4%	20.3%	34.2%	45.5%	57,483	22.7%	29.0%	38.8%	32.2%
Dayton city	28,237	60.8%	14.7%	49.7%	35.6%	15,600	33.6%	26.4%	50.7%	22.9%
Toledo city	44,281	56.7%	17.8%	38.5%	43.7%	22,525	28.8%	21.7%	45.7%	32.6%
Oklahoma										
Broken Arrow city	15,675	59.6%	31.6%	29.0%	39.4%	1,817	6.9%	39.1%	52.8%	8.1%
Lawton city	16,476	49.1%	11.5%	44.9%	43.6%	6,848	20.4%	22.0%	52.8%	25.2%
Norman city	29,453	67.5%	15.5%	44.3%	40.2%	2,374	5.4%	12.7%	63.6%	23.7%
Oklahoma City city	83,989	50.5%	16.3%	37.3%	46.4%	23,018	13.8%	22.0%	40.7%	37.4%
Tulsa city	62,266	57.1%	23.1%	35.6%	41.2%	11,984	11.0%	26.8%	40.4%	32.8%
Oregon										
Beaverton city	14,381	57.7%	23.4%	27.0%	49.6%	906	3.6%	11.7%	74.4%	13.9%
Eugene city	41,126	74.8%	15.9%	50.7%	33.4%	1,021	1.9%	0.0%	83.6%	16.4%
Gresham city	18,411	61.9%	22.6%	36.8%	40.6%	839	2.8%	7.9%	68.5%	23.6%
Hillsboro city	16,052	63.1%	21.5%	29.9%	48.6%	223	0.9%	0.0%	0.0%	100.0%
Portland city	105,321	65.9%	13.4%	30.0%	56.6%	9,713	6.1%	28.5%	38.4%	33.0%
Salem city	28,091	62.8%	20.1%	40.5%	39.4%	624	1.4%	22.6%	9.0%	68.4%
Pennsylvania										
Allentown city	10,915	31.1%	15.2%	46.5%	38.2%	4,974	14.2%	40.1%	33.3%	26.6%
Erie city	22,068	71.1%	12.8%	46.1%	41.1%	4,458	14.4%	16.7%	39.0%	44.3%
Philadelphia city	163,480	35.9%	11.2%	36.1%	52.7%	178,019	39.1%	24.0%	42.7%	33.3%
Pittsburgh city	67,605	65.6%	10.7%	50.6%	38.7%	20,731	20.1%	29.2%	40.4%	30.4%

Table B-3: Places—Race and Hispanic Origin by Age—*Continued*

| | Asian, Non-Hispanic | | | | | Hispanic | | | | |
| | Millennial Population | | Percent by Age | | | Millennial Population | | Percent by Age | | |
	Number	Percent	13 to 17	18 to 24	25 to 31	Number	Percent	13 to 17	18 to 24	25 to 31
Missouri										
Columbia city	2,068	4.0%	0.0%	48.3%	51.7%	2,511	4.8%	0.0%	72.8%	27.2%
Independence city	208	0.8%	0.0%	0.0%	100.0%	2,662	9.9%	31.5%	20.8%	47.7%
Kansas City city	3,190	2.4%	13.9%	31.6%	54.5%	17,414	13.1%	26.4%	32.6%	41.0%
Lee's Summit city	544	2.4%	32.4%	14.7%	52.9%	1,158	5.2%	24.9%	58.8%	16.3%
Springfield city	895	1.5%	0.0%	57.8%	42.2%	2,920	5.0%	19.1%	72.7%	8.3%
St. Louis city	4,575	5.0%	16.1%	31.2%	52.7%	4,105	4.4%	18.8%	29.5%	51.7%
Montana										
Billings city	72	0.3%	0.0%	100.0%	0.0%	2,245	8.1%	59.5%	23.9%	16.6%
Nebraska										
Lincoln city	3,937	4.7%	10.9%	48.2%	40.9%	5,546	6.7%	32.0%	43.7%	24.3%
Omaha city	5,332	4.5%	10.2%	37.8%	52.0%	16,452	14.0%	28.6%	36.4%	35.0%
Nevada										
Henderson city	6,721	11.3%	20.9%	36.5%	42.6%	11,162	18.7%	28.2%	37.9%	33.8%
Las Vegas city	8,816	5.8%	39.3%	30.8%	29.9%	58,647	38.4%	30.1%	35.2%	34.6%
North Las Vegas city	3,980	5.9%	24.4%	25.3%	50.3%	28,913	42.9%	31.0%	35.6%	33.3%
Reno city	3,487	5.1%	26.6%	35.7%	37.7%	21,044	31.0%	23.2%	42.9%	33.8%
Sparks city	1,161	5.2%	40.0%	28.3%	31.7%	6,089	27.4%	28.5%	35.4%	36.1%
New Hampshire										
Manchester city	2,229	7.4%	18.3%	51.1%	30.6%	4,080	13.5%	30.0%	31.5%	38.6%
New Jersey										
Elizabeth city	605	1.6%	29.1%	21.3%	49.6%	24,620	65.9%	20.3%	35.9%	43.8%
Jersey City city	19,766	26.7%	10.4%	25.2%	64.4%	22,132	29.9%	23.1%	35.7%	41.1%
Newark city	866	1.1%	0.0%	62.4%	37.6%	29,609	36.2%	21.2%	33.6%	45.2%
Paterson city	2,873	6.8%	34.2%	52.9%	12.9%	24,132	57.5%	23.8%	40.8%	35.4%
New Mexico										
Albuquerque city	3,748	2.5%	13.0%	46.6%	40.4%	77,590	52.6%	26.2%	39.1%	34.7%
Las Cruces city	387	1.2%	0.0%	0.0%	100.0%	19,848	59.9%	23.7%	59.7%	16.6%
Rio Rancho city	382	1.7%	0.0%	0.0%	100.0%	9,794	43.5%	30.1%	37.6%	32.3%
New York										
Albany city	3,635	9.3%	4.4%	61.6%	34.0%	3,896	10.0%	6.4%	39.4%	54.2%
Buffalo city	3,880	4.9%	24.2%	47.7%	28.1%	11,573	14.5%	23.5%	33.9%	42.5%
New York city	300,706	13.3%	19.1%	34.7%	46.1%	707,144	31.3%	22.0%	38.6%	39.4%
Rochester city	1,903	2.8%	10.5%	73.8%	15.7%	12,763	18.9%	28.2%	36.1%	35.7%
Syracuse city	4,551	9.1%	7.1%	55.9%	37.0%	4,651	9.3%	28.6%	51.3%	20.2%
Yonkers city	3,064	6.3%	0.0%	49.3%	50.7%	22,308	45.8%	24.4%	37.9%	37.7%
North Carolina										
Charlotte city	12,830	5.9%	13.1%	28.3%	58.6%	32,915	15.1%	23.2%	32.1%	44.7%
Durham city	4,914	6.7%	5.1%	37.9%	57.0%	9,802	13.4%	11.6%	33.9%	54.5%
Fayetteville city	850	1.3%	32.9%	37.1%	30.0%	8,355	12.8%	20.6%	43.5%	35.9%
Greensboro city	4,520	5.7%	28.5%	31.5%	40.0%	4,984	6.2%	23.7%	38.2%	38.1%
High Point city	1,487	5.2%	19.8%	43.4%	36.8%	3,532	12.4%	30.1%	24.7%	45.2%
Raleigh city	7,488	5.4%	29.3%	31.3%	39.4%	17,668	12.8%	26.9%	37.4%	35.7%
Wilmington city	1,344	3.7%	27.9%	66.1%	6.0%	1,428	3.9%	17.2%	29.3%	53.5%
Winston-Salem city	1,272	2.0%	9.4%	56.1%	34.6%	12,518	20.1%	33.7%	39.7%	26.6%
North Dakota										
Fargo city	1,848	4.2%	0.0%	37.5%	62.5%	421	1.0%	0.0%	100.0%	0.0%
Ohio										
Akron city	2,218	4.1%	0.0%	60.5%	39.5%	1,879	3.4%	4.7%	74.9%	20.4%
Cincinnati city	2,185	2.4%	6.1%	56.1%	37.8%	3,285	3.6%	5.1%	41.0%	53.9%
Cleveland city	1,947	1.8%	5.9%	46.8%	47.3%	13,101	12.2%	28.7%	40.7%	30.5%
Columbus city	11,380	4.5%	13.1%	30.6%	56.2%	15,771	6.2%	14.4%	35.7%	49.9%
Dayton city	339	0.7%	0.0%	100.0%	0.0%	1,648	3.5%	25.1%	53.6%	21.2%
Toledo city	1,088	1.4%	26.4%	39.3%	34.3%	7,992	10.2%	32.2%	34.0%	33.8%
Oklahoma										
Broken Arrow city	1,119	4.3%	45.5%	22.8%	31.7%	3,713	14.1%	25.0%	34.0%	41.0%
Lawton city	1,131	3.4%	0.0%	34.0%	66.0%	5,673	16.9%	19.7%	58.5%	21.8%
Norman city	1,849	4.2%	31.3%	47.9%	20.8%	4,946	11.3%	26.7%	40.2%	33.1%
Oklahoma City city	6,900	4.1%	15.1%	46.4%	38.5%	35,856	21.5%	26.1%	34.0%	39.9%
Tulsa city	3,879	3.6%	18.4%	30.2%	51.4%	14,481	13.3%	26.2%	34.8%	39.0%
Oregon										
Beaverton city	2,706	10.9%	18.9%	31.8%	49.3%	5,174	20.7%	28.1%	31.8%	40.1%
Eugene city	2,731	5.0%	8.6%	70.3%	21.1%	5,802	10.6%	16.4%	53.8%	29.9%
Gresham city	1,184	4.0%	24.9%	27.0%	48.1%	7,524	25.3%	21.8%	23.8%	54.4%
Hillsboro city	2,721	10.7%	7.5%	27.1%	65.3%	5,295	20.8%	43.9%	29.2%	26.9%
Portland city	13,793	8.6%	19.9%	38.9%	41.2%	19,080	11.9%	23.9%	39.9%	36.1%
Salem city	452	1.0%	0.0%	88.5%	11.5%	11,077	24.7%	25.9%	31.6%	42.6%
Pennsylvania										
Allentown city	307	0.9%	0.0%	0.0%	100.0%	18,905	53.8%	28.1%	36.0%	36.0%
Erie city	824	2.7%	24.3%	38.0%	37.7%	2,284	7.4%	29.6%	37.3%	33.1%
Philadelphia city	35,481	7.8%	14.2%	39.3%	46.4%	67,520	14.8%	27.2%	39.3%	33.6%
Pittsburgh city	7,882	7.6%	2.4%	60.2%	37.4%	3,901	3.8%	5.9%	44.0%	50.0%

Table B-3: Places—Race and Hispanic Origin by Age—*Continued*

| | White, Non-Hispanic | | | | | Black, Non-Hispanic | | | | |
| | Millennial Population | | Percent by Age | | | Millennial Population | | Percent by Age | | |
	Number	Percent	13 to 17	18 to 24	25 to 31	Number	Percent	13 to 17	18 to 24	25 to 31
Rhode Island										
Providence city	26,217	40.7%	8.5%	54.5%	37.0%	7,154	11.1%	24.4%	51.0%	24.6%
South Carolina										
Charleston city	28,580	68.5%	14.5%	38.6%	47.0%	8,792	21.1%	29.2%	44.9%	26.0%
Columbia city	25,354	42.6%	9.6%	62.6%	27.7%	26,335	44.3%	17.9%	49.4%	32.7%
North Charleston city	16,127	47.3%	18.0%	49.2%	32.9%	12,922	37.9%	23.0%	52.1%	24.9%
South Dakota										
Sioux Falls city	36,734	85.2%	16.7%	37.4%	45.9%	1,516	3.5%	0.0%	46.4%	53.6%
Tennessee										
Chattanooga city	29,699	62.0%	20.2%	41.8%	38.0%	13,419	28.0%	34.2%	35.5%	30.3%
Clarksville city	32,465	65.3%	17.6%	34.4%	48.0%	9,058	18.2%	23.4%	38.6%	37.9%
Knoxville city	49,861	75.0%	12.2%	53.6%	34.2%	7,826	11.8%	15.1%	51.0%	33.9%
Memphis city	46,122	24.4%	18.9%	36.6%	44.5%	121,865	64.5%	23.9%	41.0%	35.0%
Murfreesboro city	31,876	74.1%	16.1%	48.9%	35.0%	7,767	18.0%	8.7%	69.0%	22.3%
Nashville-Davidson metropolitan govt (bal)	96,135	52.8%	13.1%	34.0%	52.9%	53,943	29.6%	24.2%	36.4%	39.4%
Texas										
Abilene city	23,617	59.7%	17.0%	47.4%	35.6%	3,231	8.2%	8.0%	36.9%	55.2%
Amarillo city	27,177	49.5%	20.9%	37.5%	41.6%	3,818	7.0%	7.2%	51.6%	41.2%
Arlington city	38,700	34.5%	24.6%	37.1%	38.3%	30,185	26.9%	30.6%	31.4%	38.0%
Austin city	130,679	46.6%	16.0%	32.0%	52.1%	18,887	6.7%	14.9%	44.7%	40.3%
Beaumont city	11,101	32.5%	17.7%	40.0%	42.3%	16,800	49.1%	25.4%	51.6%	23.1%
Brownsville city	1,709	3.2%	17.1%	53.2%	29.6%	na	na	na	na	na
Carrollton city	11,844	35.5%	19.4%	36.4%	44.1%	4,501	13.5%	17.3%	34.4%	48.3%
College Station city	35,327	57.2%	8.6%	65.7%	25.7%	6,311	10.2%	24.7%	53.3%	22.1%
Corpus Christi city	22,237	25.8%	21.1%	39.8%	39.1%	3,147	3.7%	26.9%	38.9%	34.2%
Dallas city	95,126	26.2%	17.7%	32.1%	50.2%	73,910	20.4%	21.3%	36.8%	41.9%
Denton city	30,341	58.4%	16.7%	47.2%	36.2%	7,181	13.8%	17.4%	56.5%	26.2%
El Paso city	24,435	12.8%	13.3%	40.2%	46.6%	6,042	3.2%	21.1%	45.9%	32.9%
Fort Worth city	92,631	41.6%	21.0%	34.6%	44.4%	32,773	14.7%	27.6%	36.5%	35.9%
Frisco city	16,967	59.3%	35.3%	24.3%	40.4%	2,432	8.5%	13.8%	55.1%	31.2%
Garland city	19,848	30.6%	22.1%	41.9%	36.0%	11,312	17.4%	25.1%	50.7%	24.2%
Grand Prairie city	12,231	23.5%	26.7%	41.3%	32.0%	12,202	23.4%	38.7%	36.6%	24.7%
Houston city	156,079	23.5%	18.9%	28.3%	52.8%	131,508	19.8%	22.7%	35.3%	42.0%
Irving city	16,899	26.1%	21.4%	33.8%	44.8%	7,516	11.6%	12.2%	39.6%	48.2%
Killeen city	16,225	35.1%	13.3%	35.0%	51.6%	12,700	27.5%	34.5%	39.0%	26.5%
Laredo city	1,246	1.7%	18.9%	21.9%	59.2%	249	0.3%	3.2%	66.3%	30.5%
Lewisville city	12,107	42.9%	13.0%	30.6%	56.4%	3,481	12.3%	12.5%	7.8%	79.7%
Lubbock city	46,132	52.5%	14.4%	55.6%	29.9%	5,292	6.0%	14.6%	50.5%	34.9%
McAllen city	1,920	4.9%	12.0%	40.4%	47.7%	13	0.0%	0.0%	0.0%	100.0%
McKinney city	20,664	57.4%	38.4%	27.6%	33.9%	4,388	12.2%	38.7%	42.8%	18.6%
Mesquite city	9,690	24.0%	19.5%	39.5%	41.0%	12,152	30.0%	20.9%	43.2%	35.9%
Midland city	16,577	45.0%	20.8%	32.3%	46.9%	1,145	3.1%	17.1%	48.6%	34.2%
Odessa city	10,460	31.8%	21.9%	33.8%	44.3%	1,559	4.7%	25.3%	16.9%	57.8%
Pasadena city	7,663	17.2%	16.7%	41.0%	42.4%	1,255	2.8%	31.7%	41.1%	27.2%
Pearland city	9,407	37.9%	24.0%	24.2%	51.8%	4,714	19.0%	18.8%	24.3%	57.0%
Plano city	33,454	50.5%	29.8%	32.4%	37.8%	6,020	9.1%	35.5%	19.4%	45.1%
Richardson city	9,501	37.2%	17.0%	34.7%	48.3%	2,419	9.5%	25.4%	30.4%	44.2%
Round Rock city	14,699	48.9%	28.0%	31.5%	40.5%	2,314	7.7%	53.8%	18.5%	27.7%
San Angelo city	14,856	47.7%	18.4%	43.0%	38.7%	1,479	4.7%	4.6%	45.7%	49.7%
San Antonio city	97,862	23.8%	19.7%	38.0%	42.2%	25,595	6.2%	23.7%	45.2%	31.1%
Tyler city	12,479	43.7%	18.3%	32.2%	49.5%	7,026	24.6%	12.7%	44.5%	42.8%
Waco city	21,695	47.1%	14.7%	60.0%	25.4%	7,758	16.8%	19.1%	54.4%	26.5%
Wichita Falls city	20,250	62.4%	17.2%	43.3%	39.4%	3,847	11.9%	4.5%	48.9%	46.6%
Utah										
Orem city	27,882	79.5%	28.0%	44.7%	27.3%	na	na	na	na	na
Provo city	48,759	76.2%	8.6%	65.7%	25.7%	417	0.7%	0.0%	40.0%	60.0%
Salt Lake City city	46,057	73.5%	14.8%	42.0%	43.3%	895	1.4%	0.0%	54.0%	46.0%
West Jordan city	23,458	73.5%	33.2%	30.8%	36.0%	685	2.1%	24.2%	0.0%	75.8%
West Valley City city	20,511	51.7%	25.7%	28.6%	45.7%	266	0.7%	0.0%	56.4%	43.6%
Virginia										
Alexandria city	18,447	46.3%	9.2%	17.7%	73.1%	9,432	23.7%	15.6%	21.4%	63.0%
Chesapeake city	33,768	54.9%	26.4%	36.2%	37.5%	19,736	32.1%	27.6%	36.4%	36.0%
Hampton city	14,133	34.3%	17.3%	38.1%	44.6%	20,601	50.0%	24.7%	43.5%	31.8%
Newport News city	23,690	43.4%	15.4%	44.9%	39.6%	21,797	39.9%	24.4%	41.0%	34.6%
Norfolk city	38,825	41.9%	9.1%	49.0%	41.9%	38,156	41.2%	18.6%	48.6%	32.9%
Portsmouth city	11,426	42.7%	12.4%	35.7%	51.9%	12,821	47.9%	23.6%	39.3%	37.0%
Richmond city	30,191	42.7%	6.4%	38.2%	55.3%	29,436	41.6%	17.9%	43.4%	38.7%
Roanoke city	16,358	67.8%	16.1%	32.6%	51.2%	3,709	15.4%	16.5%	65.2%	18.2%
Virginia Beach city	71,908	57.5%	19.1%	37.4%	43.5%	27,178	21.7%	20.7%	38.1%	41.2%
Washington										
Bellevue city	15,728	48.8%	29.6%	29.3%	41.1%	807	2.5%	9.0%	0.0%	91.0%
Everett city	16,426	56.2%	27.2%	33.0%	39.8%	834	2.9%	4.6%	71.6%	23.9%
Federal Way city	10,675	40.5%	19.5%	38.4%	42.1%	3,515	13.3%	45.3%	27.4%	27.3%
Kent city	13,846	40.1%	26.0%	30.0%	44.0%	3,719	10.8%	12.5%	40.8%	46.7%

Table B-3: Places—Race and Hispanic Origin by Age—*Continued*

	Asian, Non-Hispanic					Hispanic				
	Millennial Population		Percent by Age			Millennial Population		Percent by Age		
	Number	Percent	13 to 17	18 to 24	25 to 31	Number	Percent	13 to 17	18 to 24	25 to 31
Rhode Island										
Providence city	5,825	9.0%	3.8%	62.4%	33.8%	23,226	36.1%	27.7%	36.4%	35.9%
South Carolina										
Charleston city	858	2.1%	0.0%	43.5%	56.5%	2,516	6.0%	15.3%	41.9%	42.9%
Columbia city	2,001	3.4%	6.9%	50.3%	42.8%	3,896	6.6%	16.4%	49.7%	34.0%
North Charleston city	365	1.1%	21.1%	37.5%	41.4%	3,632	10.7%	13.4%	36.5%	50.2%
South Dakota										
Sioux Falls city	1,055	2.4%	0.0%	60.6%	39.4%	2,032	4.7%	31.8%	30.1%	38.1%
Tennessee										
Chattanooga city	1,477	3.1%	16.7%	22.7%	60.5%	2,960	6.2%	12.8%	22.2%	65.0%
Clarksville city	1,095	2.2%	11.4%	24.7%	63.8%	5,269	10.6%	25.2%	44.4%	30.4%
Knoxville city	2,742	4.1%	2.5%	19.8%	77.8%	3,759	5.7%	12.8%	58.8%	28.4%
Memphis city	4,706	2.5%	16.5%	37.5%	46.0%	12,648	6.7%	23.0%	31.4%	45.6%
Murfreesboro city	1,109	2.6%	9.5%	22.5%	68.1%	1,614	3.8%	8.7%	27.1%	64.2%
Nashville-Davidson metropolitan govt (bal)	5,575	3.1%	18.6%	16.5%	64.9%	20,040	11.0%	19.8%	37.6%	42.6%
Texas										
Abilene city	1,007	2.5%	0.0%	68.6%	31.4%	10,151	25.7%	31.2%	40.3%	28.5%
Amarillo city	1,880	3.4%	19.4%	46.6%	34.0%	20,870	38.0%	25.3%	36.1%	38.7%
Arlington city	6,022	5.4%	21.2%	38.3%	40.5%	34,133	30.4%	27.4%	32.3%	40.3%
Austin city	18,987	6.8%	13.7%	35.2%	51.1%	103,418	36.9%	21.0%	35.7%	43.3%
Beaumont city	1,401	4.1%	27.6%	38.3%	34.0%	4,674	13.7%	13.6%	32.9%	53.5%
Brownsville city	430	0.8%	100.0%	0.0%	0.0%	50,952	94.5%	31.3%	39.2%	29.4%
Carrollton city	6,379	19.1%	21.6%	38.8%	39.6%	9,227	27.6%	27.5%	37.9%	34.6%
College Station city	3,563	5.8%	0.9%	57.6%	41.5%	14,909	24.1%	15.4%	56.1%	28.4%
Corpus Christi city	2,275	2.6%	22.2%	46.7%	31.0%	57,687	67.0%	26.8%	38.1%	35.1%
Dallas city	18,032	5.0%	11.9%	33.3%	54.8%	167,586	46.1%	26.0%	37.3%	36.7%
Denton city	3,324	6.4%	14.2%	39.6%	46.2%	10,564	20.3%	19.9%	40.4%	39.8%
El Paso city	1,775	0.9%	11.2%	1.9%	87.0%	156,621	82.0%	28.9%	38.7%	32.4%
Fort Worth city	6,591	3.0%	26.4%	26.4%	47.2%	82,223	36.9%	30.8%	34.1%	35.1%
Frisco city	1,975	6.9%	44.8%	19.1%	36.1%	5,722	20.0%	30.0%	39.4%	30.7%
Garland city	5,057	7.8%	27.7%	36.9%	35.4%	24,854	38.3%	31.5%	27.7%	40.7%
Grand Prairie city	2,264	4.3%	14.1%	38.4%	47.5%	24,374	46.8%	28.4%	37.7%	33.9%
Houston city	45,427	6.9%	18.1%	28.1%	53.8%	318,263	48.0%	24.5%	36.7%	38.8%
Irving city	8,812	13.6%	11.0%	28.3%	60.7%	29,614	45.7%	27.0%	38.8%	34.2%
Killeen city	873	1.9%	18.0%	31.8%	50.2%	13,052	28.3%	22.2%	33.4%	44.4%
Laredo city	11	0.0%	0.0%	0.0%	100.0%	69,733	97.6%	29.4%	38.5%	32.1%
Lewisville city	2,580	9.1%	21.8%	28.5%	49.7%	9,154	32.4%	28.9%	44.3%	26.8%
Lubbock city	2,229	2.5%	17.4%	66.9%	15.7%	32,391	36.9%	26.6%	41.0%	32.4%
McAllen city	1,578	4.0%	35.2%	53.1%	11.7%	35,659	90.4%	34.1%	37.3%	28.7%
McKinney city	1,167	3.2%	7.4%	65.9%	26.7%	8,592	23.8%	31.5%	25.6%	43.0%
Mesquite city	1,615	4.0%	11.6%	42.8%	45.5%	16,882	41.7%	32.2%	35.8%	32.0%
Midland city	98	0.3%	0.0%	100.0%	0.0%	18,202	49.5%	24.9%	39.3%	35.8%
Odessa city	451	1.4%	0.0%	65.9%	34.1%	20,002	60.9%	24.7%	41.1%	34.2%
Pasadena city	789	1.8%	13.9%	44.4%	41.7%	34,563	77.7%	33.5%	40.8%	25.7%
Pearland city	1,952	7.9%	11.8%	74.5%	13.6%	8,635	34.8%	16.6%	44.9%	38.4%
Plano city	12,293	18.5%	35.1%	23.4%	41.5%	11,689	17.6%	23.6%	44.8%	31.6%
Richardson city	4,480	17.5%	21.1%	31.2%	47.7%	7,829	30.6%	30.3%	34.1%	35.6%
Round Rock city	1,901	6.3%	26.8%	39.5%	33.7%	9,731	32.4%	36.3%	31.4%	32.4%
San Angelo city	319	1.0%	25.1%	74.9%	0.0%	13,664	43.9%	30.4%	28.7%	40.8%
San Antonio city	11,041	2.7%	9.2%	40.1%	50.8%	266,412	64.8%	26.3%	37.8%	35.9%
Tyler city	402	1.4%	35.1%	44.5%	20.4%	8,485	29.7%	31.5%	41.0%	27.5%
Waco city	1,961	4.3%	12.7%	87.3%	0.0%	14,179	30.8%	21.6%	42.3%	36.1%
Wichita Falls city	300	0.9%	100.0%	0.0%	0.0%	6,750	20.8%	18.1%	49.2%	32.7%
Utah										
Orem city	1,614	4.6%	11.0%	22.4%	66.7%	4,570	13.0%	22.9%	41.4%	35.7%
Provo city	2,322	3.6%	11.2%	80.9%	7.8%	8,506	13.3%	15.8%	60.4%	23.8%
Salt Lake City city	2,084	3.3%	10.7%	34.7%	54.6%	11,471	18.3%	19.5%	42.4%	38.1%
West Jordan city	876	2.7%	81.7%	0.0%	18.3%	5,500	17.2%	45.8%	37.7%	16.6%
West Valley City city	727	1.8%	0.0%	40.9%	59.1%	14,309	36.1%	24.1%	45.4%	30.5%
Virginia										
Alexandria city	2,948	7.4%	6.7%	23.5%	69.8%	7,609	19.1%	13.8%	27.0%	59.2%
Chesapeake city	1,665	2.7%	21.7%	40.0%	38.3%	4,159	6.8%	18.3%	36.6%	45.1%
Hampton city	711	1.7%	32.9%	40.6%	26.4%	3,312	8.0%	8.1%	23.8%	68.1%
Newport News city	1,723	3.2%	3.8%	0.0%	96.2%	5,475	10.0%	29.3%	41.3%	29.4%
Norfolk city	3,306	3.6%	15.4%	39.4%	45.3%	7,512	8.1%	6.3%	53.0%	40.7%
Portsmouth city	135	0.5%	0.0%	100.0%	0.0%	1,101	4.1%	0.0%	61.3%	38.7%
Richmond city	2,529	3.6%	0.0%	70.6%	29.4%	5,142	7.3%	20.1%	41.8%	38.2%
Roanoke city	1,316	5.5%	18.0%	42.3%	39.7%	2,107	8.7%	13.2%	24.9%	61.8%
Virginia Beach city	6,275	5.0%	19.9%	40.0%	40.2%	13,417	10.7%	16.5%	41.7%	41.8%
Washington										
Bellevue city	10,585	32.8%	16.6%	15.2%	68.1%	3,067	9.5%	29.9%	26.7%	43.4%
Everett city	3,422	11.7%	29.6%	22.3%	48.1%	5,259	18.0%	23.2%	54.8%	22.0%
Federal Way city	2,823	10.7%	44.2%	14.7%	41.1%	6,541	24.8%	28.1%	30.5%	41.4%
Kent city	6,606	19.1%	26.2%	33.7%	40.1%	6,102	17.7%	15.8%	33.3%	50.9%

Table B-3: Places—Race and Hispanic Origin by Age—*Continued*

| | White, Non-Hispanic | | | | | Black, Non-Hispanic | | | | |
| | Millennial Population | | Percent by Age | | | Millennial Population | | Percent by Age | | |
	Number	Percent	13 to 17	18 to 24	25 to 31	Number	Percent	13 to 17	18 to 24	25 to 31
Washington—Cont.										
Renton city	12,765	48.9%	22.1%	36.9%	41.0%	1,713	6.6%	34.1%	20.8%	45.1%
Seattle city	121,967	59.9%	11.7%	30.8%	57.5%	12,525	6.2%	19.3%	42.8%	37.9%
Spokane city	49,717	80.8%	18.8%	41.6%	39.6%	2,170	3.5%	38.0%	31.2%	30.8%
Spokane Valley city	19,930	85.3%	26.4%	26.6%	47.0%	618	2.6%	21.2%	0.0%	78.8%
Tacoma city	33,974	60.5%	17.7%	37.2%	45.1%	3,830	6.8%	14.7%	30.0%	55.3%
Vancouver city	30,181	72.3%	25.9%	34.3%	39.7%	1,718	4.1%	34.7%	24.9%	40.4%
Yakima city	12,000	45.9%	28.8%	39.1%	32.1%	304	1.2%	0.0%	50.0%	50.0%
Wisconsin										
Green Bay city	21,509	70.5%	23.1%	39.0%	37.9%	1,067	3.5%	12.5%	56.6%	30.9%
Kenosha city	20,555	74.1%	28.2%	41.0%	30.8%	3,530	12.7%	17.5%	66.1%	16.4%
Madison city	68,376	72.1%	15.5%	46.9%	37.6%	6,273	6.6%	39.9%	21.4%	38.7%
Milwaukee city	64,464	34.2%	14.6%	38.6%	46.8%	73,705	39.1%	28.6%	38.5%	33.0%

Table B-3: Places—Race and Hispanic Origin by Age—*Continued*

| | Asian, Non-Hispanic | | | | | Hispanic | | | | |
| | Millennial Population | | Percent by Age | | | Millennial Population | | Percent by Age | | |
	Number	Percent	13 to 17	18 to 24	25 to 31	Number	Percent	13 to 17	18 to 24	25 to 31
Washington—Cont.										
Renton city...............................	6,624	25.4%	19.5%	24.8%	55.7%	3,510	13.5%	30.3%	13.5%	56.2%
Seattle city..............................	33,543	16.5%	11.7%	42.9%	45.4%	17,010	8.4%	13.6%	35.9%	50.5%
Spokane city	2,157	3.5%	26.1%	49.6%	24.4%	3,731	6.1%	11.5%	54.1%	34.4%
Spokane Valley city	na	na	na	na	na	1,479	6.3%	21.6%	42.1%	36.4%
Tacoma city..............................	3,512	6.3%	24.5%	43.1%	32.4%	8,296	14.8%	24.2%	37.4%	38.4%
Vancouver city	1,489	3.6%	49.3%	31.7%	19.0%	5,487	13.1%	24.5%	32.1%	43.4%
Yakima city...............................	360	1.4%	21.4%	48.9%	29.7%	12,802	48.9%	24.2%	44.0%	31.8%
Wisconsin										
Green Bay city..........................	1,919	6.3%	49.0%	38.6%	12.5%	3,067	10.0%	25.6%	25.8%	48.6%
Kenosha city	281	1.0%	0.0%	85.4%	14.6%	3,070	11.1%	42.1%	5.0%	52.9%
Madison city	8,048	8.5%	2.8%	44.5%	52.7%	10,223	10.8%	20.5%	36.2%	43.3%
Milwaukee city	7,850	4.2%	20.5%	27.9%	51.6%	34,342	18.2%	22.0%	37.4%	40.6%

na = not available

Table B-4: Metropolitan/Micropolitan Statistical Areas—Race and Hispanic Origin by Age

| | White, Non-Hispanic | | | | | Black, Non-Hispanic | | | | |
| | Millennial Population | | Percent by Age | | | Millennial Population | | Percent by Age | | |
	Number	Percent	13 to 17	18 to 24	25 to 31	Number	Percent	13 to 17	18 to 24	25 to 31
Abilene, TX	30,775	60.0%	17.9%	47.7%	34.4%	3,881	7.6%	10.7%	32.7%	56.6%
Adrian, MI micro	22,051	89.3%	26.8%	40.2%	33.0%	511	2.1%	1.6%	24.9%	73.6%
Akron, OH	142,431	77.0%	23.2%	42.2%	34.6%	23,936	12.9%	22.4%	47.1%	30.5%
Albany-Schenectady-Troy, NY	170,840	77.3%	23.8%	41.4%	34.7%	17,573	7.9%	15.9%	42.8%	41.3%
Albany, GA	16,401	36.5%	20.9%	39.7%	39.4%	25,096	55.9%	24.3%	42.5%	33.2%
Albany, OR	24,863	81.2%	21.8%	51.1%	27.1%	49	0.2%	100.0%	0.0%	0.0%
Albertville, AL micro	18,205	79.7%	34.6%	28.6%	36.8%	480	2.1%	11.0%	44.2%	44.8%
Albuquerque, NM	73,113	31.5%	22.8%	36.3%	40.9%	5,127	2.2%	23.8%	66.2%	10.0%
Alexandria, LA	24,540	59.9%	23.7%	33.8%	42.4%	11,552	28.2%	31.0%	35.6%	33.4%
Allentown-Bethlehem-Easton, PA-NJ	137,723	68.7%	26.6%	38.2%	35.2%	11,740	5.9%	30.2%	34.7%	35.1%
Altoona, PA	26,359	90.8%	23.9%	41.4%	34.7%	1,205	4.2%	2.4%	47.6%	50.0%
Amarillo, TX	36,195	51.8%	22.7%	36.8%	40.5%	4,872	7.0%	10.4%	44.0%	45.6%
Ames, IA	32,848	83.1%	10.2%	62.9%	27.0%	496	1.3%	10.3%	89.7%	0.0%
Anchorage, AK	72,846	60.9%	23.5%	39.9%	36.6%	4,720	3.9%	29.7%	42.4%	27.9%
Ann Arbor, MI	82,030	68.4%	15.7%	53.8%	30.5%	15,394	12.8%	24.3%	54.4%	21.3%
Anniston-Oxford-Jacksonville, AL	18,859	64.6%	23.6%	39.9%	36.6%	7,480	25.6%	25.9%	51.6%	22.5%
Appleton, WI	48,984	85.6%	26.5%	36.3%	37.1%	652	1.1%	0.0%	24.4%	75.6%
Asheville, NC	77,530	79.6%	26.4%	36.0%	37.6%	4,556	4.7%	18.1%	48.3%	33.6%
Ashtabula, OH micro	20,463	90.0%	30.2%	33.8%	36.0%	655	2.9%	0.0%	48.2%	51.8%
Athens-Clarke County, GA	50,026	67.1%	12.1%	59.2%	28.7%	14,641	19.6%	20.8%	51.0%	28.2%
Atlanta-Sandy Springs-Roswell, GA	612,199	43.1%	28.0%	34.8%	37.2%	510,834	36.0%	27.6%	37.4%	34.9%
Atlantic City-Hammonton, NJ	34,112	50.9%	28.6%	40.0%	31.4%	10,320	15.4%	25.5%	41.1%	33.4%
Auburn-Opelika, AL	39,100	73.2%	15.2%	57.5%	27.4%	11,778	22.1%	26.3%	52.0%	21.7%
Augusta-Richmond County, GA-SC	76,873	49.9%	25.4%	35.8%	38.8%	62,762	40.7%	28.9%	38.3%	32.7%
Augusta-Waterville, ME micro	25,794	93.4%	29.3%	36.3%	34.4%	531	1.9%	1.3%	98.7%	0.0%
Austin-Round Rock, TX	261,196	47.5%	19.8%	35.1%	45.1%	40,359	7.3%	21.0%	37.6%	41.4%
Bakersfield, CA	73,642	29.0%	23.4%	36.5%	40.2%	14,952	5.9%	24.7%	49.1%	26.2%
Baltimore-Columbia-Towson, MD	382,813	53.6%	23.8%	36.5%	39.7%	221,747	31.0%	26.7%	37.2%	36.1%
Bangor, ME	36,882	92.4%	20.4%	45.9%	33.6%	670	1.7%	39.0%	38.1%	23.0%
Barnstable Town, MA	32,566	86.3%	28.3%	35.9%	35.8%	2,203	5.8%	33.7%	24.1%	42.2%
Baton Rouge, LA	127,441	54.7%	24.4%	40.8%	34.8%	86,489	37.1%	23.3%	44.4%	32.3%
Battle Creek, MI	24,154	77.7%	30.9%	36.0%	33.1%	3,164	10.2%	27.2%	33.2%	39.6%
Bay City, MI	21,596	84.6%	31.2%	31.0%	37.9%	1,313	5.1%	1.1%	87.8%	11.1%
Beaumont-Port Arthur, TX	55,275	51.3%	24.6%	35.1%	40.4%	27,927	25.9%	25.9%	45.2%	28.9%
Beckley, WV	24,853	90.5%	22.6%	41.2%	36.2%	1,971	7.2%	6.3%	41.2%	52.4%
Bellingham, WA	47,364	76.2%	20.3%	50.2%	29.5%	493	0.8%	28.0%	43.4%	28.6%
Bend-Redmond, OR	31,875	83.9%	30.5%	30.0%	39.5%	na	na	na	na	na
Billings, MT	32,459	78.5%	21.3%	41.9%	36.8%	392	0.9%	67.9%	0.0%	32.1%
Binghamton, NY	52,098	82.8%	22.9%	43.7%	33.4%	3,244	5.2%	18.0%	60.2%	21.8%
Birmingham-Hoover, AL	164,999	57.3%	27.8%	35.1%	37.1%	96,038	33.4%	26.8%	38.0%	35.2%
Bismarck, ND	30,910	90.4%	22.3%	36.4%	41.3%	149	0.4%	0.0%	100.0%	0.0%
Blacksburg-Christiansburg-Radford, VA	55,944	84.4%	14.2%	63.7%	22.2%	3,449	5.2%	14.5%	78.9%	6.6%
Bloomington, IL	50,763	79.7%	17.9%	55.2%	27.0%	4,980	7.8%	8.1%	42.3%	49.6%
Bloomington, IN	55,861	83.9%	14.1%	62.2%	23.7%	881	1.3%	15.4%	54.6%	30.0%
Bloomsburg-Berwick, PA	20,698	89.4%	23.2%	50.0%	26.8%	1,726	7.5%	18.5%	42.2%	39.3%
Boise City, ID	127,660	75.5%	28.7%	33.9%	37.5%	1,651	1.0%	69.8%	30.2%	0.0%
Boston-Cambridge-Newton, MA-NH	827,236	67.4%	23.9%	37.1%	39.1%	99,669	8.1%	24.2%	41.1%	34.7%
Boulder, CO	74,722	77.6%	20.4%	50.3%	29.3%	604	0.6%	1.8%	71.9%	26.3%
Bowling Green, KY	37,786	82.0%	21.8%	45.7%	32.5%	4,203	9.1%	15.5%	25.8%	58.8%
Bremerton-Silverdale, WA	46,759	71.7%	24.2%	40.2%	35.6%	3,784	5.8%	7.8%	21.1%	71.1%
Bridgeport-Stamford-Norwalk, CT	124,405	58.5%	32.7%	35.2%	32.1%	24,515	11.5%	27.7%	39.2%	33.1%
Brownsville-Harlingen, TX	7,020	6.0%	45.1%	28.6%	26.3%	na	na	na	na	na
Brunswick, GA	17,697	64.2%	28.0%	39.7%	32.3%	5,851	21.2%	21.6%	25.9%	52.5%
Buffalo-Cheektowaga-Niagara Falls, NY	207,770	72.4%	23.6%	38.6%	37.8%	40,484	14.1%	28.8%	43.9%	27.3%
Burlington-South Burlington, VT	55,089	92.2%	18.3%	47.8%	33.8%	1,004	1.7%	0.0%	34.7%	65.3%
Burlington, NC	23,917	61.6%	25.1%	40.7%	34.1%	7,276	18.7%	33.0%	37.7%	29.2%
California-Lexington Park, MD	21,640	75.8%	33.9%	31.5%	34.6%	3,987	14.0%	35.5%	53.1%	11.4%
Canton-Massillon, OH	80,834	86.6%	26.5%	37.1%	36.4%	4,918	5.3%	40.2%	33.3%	26.5%
Cape Coral-Fort Myers, FL	72,705	55.5%	24.7%	37.3%	38.0%	15,338	11.7%	29.0%	32.7%	38.3%
Cape Girardeau, MO-IL	22,156	84.1%	23.8%	41.1%	35.0%	2,647	10.0%	18.0%	62.3%	19.6%
Carbondale-Marion, IL	31,666	80.8%	26.7%	42.2%	31.2%	4,224	10.8%	7.5%	44.2%	48.3%
Carson City, NV	7,011	57.4%	31.4%	30.4%	38.2%	54	0.4%	0.0%	0.0%	100.0%
Casper, WY	17,136	79.9%	23.2%	36.5%	40.3%	106	0.5%	0.0%	100.0%	0.0%
Cedar Rapids, IA	58,546	85.7%	27.2%	35.6%	37.1%	2,482	3.6%	52.6%	9.8%	37.6%
Chambersburg-Waynesboro, PA	29,281	88.1%	24.8%	37.9%	37.3%	1,006	3.0%	5.6%	37.1%	57.4%
Champaign-Urbana, IL	60,039	66.0%	14.0%	55.6%	30.3%	10,606	11.7%	22.2%	56.2%	21.6%
Charleston-North Charleston, SC	117,546	61.0%	21.3%	36.1%	42.6%	55,074	28.6%	25.6%	42.0%	32.3%
Charleston, WV	42,012	83.5%	27.4%	35.7%	36.9%	2,715	5.4%	5.0%	43.2%	51.7%
Charlotte-Concord-Gastonia, NC-SC	333,388	57.5%	28.2%	35.1%	36.7%	145,691	25.1%	28.2%	40.1%	31.7%
Charlottesville, VA	41,268	67.8%	21.0%	43.9%	35.1%	9,422	15.5%	31.6%	50.6%	17.8%
Chattanooga, TN-GA	98,213	75.7%	25.5%	37.2%	37.3%	18,537	14.3%	28.4%	33.7%	37.8%
Cheyenne, WY	20,050	78.3%	20.1%	49.8%	30.1%	767	3.0%	19.3%	80.7%	0.0%
Chicago-Naperville-Elgin, IL-IN-WI	1,224,961	48.6%	24.6%	34.1%	41.4%	443,524	17.6%	27.6%	40.2%	32.3%
Chico, CA	44,412	67.7%	16.8%	53.8%	29.4%	183	0.3%	64.5%	35.5%	0.0%
Cincinnati, OH-KY-IN	412,738	78.1%	28.0%	35.9%	36.0%	66,330	12.6%	27.1%	40.2%	32.7%
Clarksburg, WV micro	17,207	90.8%	27.6%	36.5%	35.9%	1,160	6.1%	21.9%	23.7%	54.4%
Clarksville, TN-KY	61,126	68.1%	20.7%	37.2%	42.2%	14,363	16.0%	24.3%	36.0%	39.7%
Cleveland-Elyria, OH	314,428	64.4%	27.8%	35.4%	36.8%	112,830	23.1%	28.2%	40.8%	31.0%

Table B-4: Metropolitan/Micropolitan Statistical Areas—Race and Hispanic Origin by Age—*Continued*

	Asian, Non-Hispanic					Hispanic				
	Millennial Population		Percent by Age			Millennial Population		Percent by Age		
	Number	Percent	13 to 17	18 to 24	25 to 31	Number	Percent	13 to 17	18 to 24	25 to 31
Abilene, TX...	1,193	2.3%	0.0%	57.9%	42.1%	13,686	26.7%	28.0%	43.6%	28.5%
Adrian, MI micro.....................................	na	na	na	na	na	1,633	6.6%	40.2%	23.5%	36.3%
Akron, OH...	6,204	3.4%	3.1%	51.9%	45.0%	4,729	2.6%	21.6%	62.1%	16.3%
Albany-Schenectady-Troy, NY..................	9,560	4.3%	18.3%	49.0%	32.7%	14,949	6.8%	19.0%	50.9%	30.1%
Albany, GA..	289	0.6%	6.9%	61.6%	31.5%	2,679	6.0%	28.5%	41.1%	30.4%
Albany, OR..	2,214	7.2%	7.7%	54.4%	37.9%	2,033	6.6%	23.3%	51.0%	25.8%
Albertville, AL micro................................	na	na	na	na	na	3,007	13.2%	18.6%	28.7%	52.7%
Albuquerque, NM....................................	5,500	2.4%	17.7%	34.6%	47.7%	125,858	54.2%	28.3%	36.4%	35.4%
Alexandria, LA...	751	1.8%	75.6%	24.4%	0.0%	3,275	8.0%	25.1%	59.2%	15.7%
Allentown-Bethlehem-Easton, PA-NJ	7,843	3.9%	29.9%	23.5%	46.6%	39,239	19.6%	29.9%	38.6%	31.4%
Altoona, PA...	82	0.3%	24.4%	39.0%	36.6%	693	2.4%	0.0%	51.4%	48.6%
Amarillo, TX..	2,098	3.0%	19.8%	49.7%	30.5%	25,404	36.4%	26.7%	36.8%	36.4%
Ames, IA...	3,367	8.5%	7.0%	67.2%	25.7%	2,091	5.3%	2.9%	86.1%	11.0%
Anchorage, AK..	6,762	5.7%	28.5%	25.9%	45.6%	10,864	9.1%	18.2%	25.4%	56.4%
Ann Arbor, MI..	11,239	9.4%	9.4%	60.0%	30.5%	5,764	4.8%	8.7%	43.0%	48.2%
Anniston-Oxford-Jacksonville, AL.............	185	0.6%	0.0%	39.5%	60.5%	1,722	5.9%	14.9%	5.7%	79.4%
Appleton, WI...	2,068	3.6%	21.1%	57.0%	21.9%	3,100	5.4%	31.0%	43.9%	25.1%
Asheville, NC...	593	0.6%	0.0%	91.6%	8.4%	9,329	9.6%	34.9%	17.9%	47.2%
Ashtabula, OH micro................................	na	na	na	na	na	834	3.7%	0.0%	73.3%	26.7%
Athens-Clarke County, GA.......................	3,907	5.2%	6.6%	72.2%	21.2%	4,853	6.5%	21.4%	42.1%	36.6%
Atlanta-Sandy Springs-Roswell, GA.........	76,511	5.4%	25.8%	36.8%	37.5%	180,662	12.7%	27.4%	34.2%	38.3%
Atlantic City-Hammonton, NJ...................	5,386	8.0%	25.2%	34.1%	40.7%	15,097	22.5%	24.8%	41.1%	34.1%
Auburn-Opelika, AL..................................	1,189	2.2%	0.0%	47.9%	52.1%	863	1.6%	23.8%	44.1%	32.1%
Augusta-Richmond County, GA-SC............	2,704	1.8%	13.9%	38.8%	47.3%	8,271	5.4%	16.9%	44.2%	39.0%
Augusta-Waterville, ME micro...................	129	0.5%	0.0%	100.0%	0.0%	448	1.6%	57.1%	9.6%	33.3%
Austin-Round Rock, TX............................	28,226	5.1%	15.1%	36.2%	48.7%	204,588	37.2%	24.9%	35.7%	39.4%
Bakersfield, CA.......................................	7,233	2.9%	27.9%	26.0%	46.1%	149,075	58.7%	27.7%	38.0%	34.3%
Baltimore-Columbia-Towson, MD..............	36,195	5.1%	20.4%	36.2%	43.4%	47,790	6.7%	21.8%	29.5%	48.7%
Bangor, ME...	572	1.4%	35.0%	0.0%	65.0%	288	0.7%	0.0%	100.0%	0.0%
Barnstable Town, MA...............................	504	1.3%	39.3%	36.5%	24.2%	1,044	2.8%	41.0%	50.4%	8.6%
Baton Rouge, LA......................................	4,895	2.1%	14.7%	24.6%	60.7%	8,650	3.7%	6.3%	65.3%	28.4%
Battle Creek, MI......................................	427	1.4%	45.2%	0.0%	54.8%	1,788	5.8%	42.3%	24.0%	33.7%
Bay City, MI..	273	1.1%	0.0%	79.5%	20.5%	1,654	6.5%	16.6%	37.5%	45.8%
Beaumont-Port Arthur, TX........................	3,070	2.8%	25.2%	56.0%	18.8%	19,005	17.6%	32.0%	31.9%	36.1%
Beckley, WV..	65	0.2%	0.0%	0.0%	100.0%	318	1.2%	0.0%	58.2%	41.8%
Bellingham, WA.......................................	3,211	5.2%	20.7%	60.1%	19.1%	6,542	10.5%	27.2%	45.3%	27.5%
Bend-Redmond, OR.................................	885	2.3%	100.0%	0.0%	0.0%	4,023	10.6%	31.7%	27.0%	41.3%
Billings, MT...	152	0.4%	0.0%	83.6%	16.4%	2,718	6.6%	49.6%	32.3%	18.1%
Binghamton, NY.......................................	3,200	5.1%	13.7%	74.8%	11.5%	3,068	4.9%	18.4%	44.4%	37.3%
Birmingham-Hoover, AL............................	4,725	1.6%	19.8%	33.8%	46.4%	16,112	5.6%	16.3%	35.4%	48.3%
Bismarck, ND..	73	0.2%	100.0%	0.0%	0.0%	2,006	5.9%	8.0%	35.4%	56.6%
Blacksburg-Christiansburg-Radford, VA	2,940	4.4%	9.1%	52.4%	38.5%	2,580	3.9%	10.8%	84.7%	4.5%
Bloomington, IL.......................................	2,838	4.5%	6.6%	21.4%	72.0%	3,471	5.4%	23.5%	64.3%	12.2%
Bloomington, IN.......................................	4,611	6.9%	5.1%	59.7%	35.2%	3,640	5.5%	7.1%	84.8%	8.1%
Bloomsburg-Berwick, PA..........................	29	0.1%	0.0%	100.0%	0.0%	614	2.7%	24.1%	45.8%	30.1%
Boise City, ID..	3,490	2.1%	24.4%	48.7%	27.0%	29,184	17.3%	27.8%	43.7%	28.6%
Boston-Cambridge-Newton, MA-NH...........	99,563	8.1%	16.7%	37.3%	46.0%	160,555	13.1%	24.0%	37.8%	38.2%
Boulder, CO..	4,982	5.2%	22.0%	46.8%	31.2%	14,344	14.9%	21.8%	43.8%	34.4%
Bowling Green, KY...................................	1,139	2.5%	0.0%	13.7%	86.3%	1,781	3.9%	40.0%	39.9%	20.2%
Bremerton-Silverdale, WA........................	1,657	2.5%	16.5%	41.9%	41.6%	6,166	9.5%	18.0%	48.2%	33.9%
Bridgeport-Stamford-Norwalk, CT	10,431	4.9%	24.0%	27.6%	48.3%	48,695	22.9%	25.0%	37.4%	37.6%
Brownsville-Harlingen, TX........................	668	0.6%	100.0%	0.0%	0.0%	109,220	92.8%	32.6%	38.4%	29.0%
Brunswick, GA...	162	0.6%	0.0%	22.2%	77.8%	3,277	11.9%	8.1%	66.5%	25.5%
Buffalo-Cheektowaga-Niagara Falls, NY.....	10,851	3.8%	16.8%	44.1%	39.1%	19,094	6.7%	24.2%	37.2%	38.6%
Burlington-South Burlington, VT...............	1,639	2.7%	29.8%	40.3%	29.9%	856	1.4%	51.8%	11.1%	37.1%
Burlington, NC...	894	2.3%	0.0%	16.4%	83.6%	6,089	15.7%	30.8%	29.3%	39.9%
California-Lexington Park, MD...................	411	1.4%	69.1%	0.0%	30.9%	1,798	6.3%	20.1%	67.1%	12.8%
Canton-Massillon, OH..............................	311	0.3%	0.0%	100.0%	0.0%	1,867	2.0%	36.8%	21.5%	41.7%
Cape Coral-Fort Myers, FL........................	1,062	0.8%	42.1%	42.2%	15.7%	38,395	29.3%	29.1%	34.6%	36.2%
Cape Girardeau, MO-IL.............................	82	0.3%	0.0%	51.2%	48.8%	1,083	4.1%	53.7%	27.8%	18.5%
Carbondale-Marion, IL.............................	616	1.6%	21.4%	39.9%	38.6%	1,398	3.6%	18.6%	38.8%	42.6%
Carson City, NV.......................................	101	0.8%	0.0%	100.0%	0.0%	4,026	33.0%	14.8%	35.1%	50.1%
Casper, WY...	126	0.6%	0.0%	0.0%	100.0%	3,771	17.6%	33.8%	36.8%	29.4%
Cedar Rapids, IA......................................	1,953	2.9%	24.6%	11.3%	64.2%	3,764	5.5%	17.8%	21.7%	60.5%
Chambersburg-Waynesboro, PA................	na	na	na	na	na	2,352	7.1%	30.7%	19.2%	50.1%
Champaign-Urbana, IL..............................	11,347	12.5%	3.4%	71.8%	24.8%	5,877	6.5%	18.9%	41.5%	39.6%
Charleston-North Charleston, SC..............	2,555	1.3%	15.4%	37.7%	46.9%	11,559	6.0%	20.7%	41.0%	38.4%
Charleston, WV..	770	1.5%	35.6%	9.1%	55.3%	727	1.4%	2.2%	87.3%	10.5%
Charlotte-Concord-Gastonia, NC-SC..........	19,649	3.4%	14.3%	30.3%	55.4%	66,633	11.5%	28.7%	32.6%	38.7%
Charlottesville, VA..................................	3,912	6.4%	11.3%	65.1%	23.6%	3,936	6.5%	39.5%	31.9%	28.6%
Chattanooga, TN-GA................................	2,691	2.1%	17.9%	26.3%	55.8%	6,887	5.3%	20.6%	32.2%	47.2%
Cheyenne, WY...	614	2.4%	0.0%	0.0%	100.0%	3,461	13.5%	17.3%	53.0%	29.6%
Chicago-Naperville-Elgin, IL-IN-WI............	148,328	5.9%	21.1%	33.3%	45.5%	642,875	25.5%	27.5%	37.0%	35.5%
Chico, CA..	4,216	6.4%	20.1%	51.9%	28.1%	13,014	19.8%	23.5%	47.3%	29.1%
Cincinnati, OH-KY-IN................................	12,172	2.3%	32.6%	30.5%	36.9%	20,766	3.9%	18.5%	34.0%	47.5%
Clarksburg, WV micro..............................	na	na	na	na	na	506	2.7%	81.8%	5.5%	12.6%
Clarksville, TN-KY...................................	1,606	1.8%	7.8%	32.7%	59.5%	8,130	9.1%	24.9%	47.5%	27.6%
Cleveland-Elyria, OH................................	11,522	2.4%	11.2%	35.9%	52.9%	34,645	7.1%	28.9%	37.8%	33.2%

Table B-4: Metropolitan/Micropolitan Statistical Areas—Race and Hispanic Origin by Age—*Continued*

	White, Non-Hispanic					Black, Non-Hispanic				
	Millennial Population		Percent by Age			Millennial Population		Percent by Age		
	Number	Percent	13 to 17	18 to 24	25 to 31	Number	Percent	13 to 17	18 to 24	25 to 31
Cleveland, TN	25,422	84.9%	24.9%	39.0%	36.1%	3,184	10.6%	42.2%	42.7%	15.1%
Coeur d'Alene, ID	30,659	87.3%	29.3%	33.1%	37.7%	61	0.2%	0.0%	47.5%	52.5%
College Station-Bryan, TX	61,503	59.1%	10.8%	64.7%	24.6%	9,519	9.1%	33.9%	44.2%	21.9%
Colorado Springs, CO	123,387	65.1%	23.3%	39.4%	37.3%	11,546	6.1%	33.1%	28.7%	38.2%
Columbia, MO	51,653	78.9%	15.0%	55.8%	29.3%	4,051	6.2%	11.6%	36.1%	52.4%
Columbia, SC	118,987	53.0%	24.3%	43.1%	32.6%	81,302	36.2%	24.1%	44.1%	31.8%
Columbus, GA-AL	36,441	39.1%	19.1%	43.1%	37.8%	42,059	45.2%	25.0%	41.3%	33.8%
Columbus, IN	16,437	79.9%	29.8%	33.4%	36.8%	23	0.1%	100.0%	0.0%	0.0%
Columbus, OH	370,021	71.9%	25.4%	33.0%	41.6%	81,484	15.8%	28.3%	38.1%	33.6%
Concord, NH micro	26,629	90.7%	26.3%	40.2%	33.5%	402	1.4%	62.7%	37.3%	0.0%
Cookeville, TN micro	24,768	86.4%	21.6%	48.6%	29.8%	1,743	6.1%	21.9%	71.4%	6.7%
Corpus Christi, TX	33,889	27.5%	21.8%	39.8%	38.4%	5,109	4.1%	25.9%	38.1%	36.0%
Corvallis, OR	27,319	81.2%	21.5%	51.6%	26.9%	49	0.1%	100.0%	0.0%	0.0%
Crestview-Fort Walton Beach-Destin, FL	48,554	70.8%	19.9%	38.2%	41.8%	8,477	12.4%	19.4%	47.3%	33.3%
Cumberland, MD-WV	21,617	84.8%	27.9%	40.6%	31.5%	2,210	8.7%	24.9%	55.9%	19.2%
Dallas-Fort Worth-Arlington, TX	761,901	42.5%	26.6%	33.5%	39.9%	283,531	15.8%	26.5%	36.9%	36.6%
Dalton, GA	22,925	60.9%	29.9%	35.8%	34.2%	1,185	3.1%	2.7%	62.5%	34.8%
Danville, IL	15,539	80.7%	29.0%	36.2%	34.8%	1,734	9.0%	19.4%	31.1%	49.5%
Danville, VA micro	13,933	62.1%	28.3%	37.1%	34.6%	6,959	31.0%	25.5%	43.5%	31.0%
Daphne-Fairhope-Foley, AL	32,351	74.0%	29.0%	35.3%	35.7%	7,036	16.1%	24.3%	48.0%	27.8%
Davenport-Moline-Rock Island, IA-IL	69,837	75.5%	24.1%	41.1%	34.7%	8,801	9.5%	29.2%	38.2%	32.6%
Dayton, OH	152,300	74.8%	23.8%	38.1%	38.1%	36,469	17.9%	24.7%	48.1%	27.3%
Decatur, AL	25,795	71.9%	32.0%	35.5%	32.5%	4,661	13.0%	29.5%	50.4%	20.1%
Decatur, IL	18,140	69.4%	24.7%	40.4%	34.9%	4,289	16.4%	21.9%	33.4%	44.7%
Deltona-Daytona Beach-Ormond Beach, FL	81,663	63.4%	22.7%	38.2%	39.1%	20,387	15.8%	17.3%	55.5%	27.2%
Denver-Aurora-Lakewood, CO	408,696	58.6%	24.1%	30.7%	45.2%	40,218	5.8%	26.4%	39.5%	34.1%
Des Moines-West Des Moines, IA	120,281	79.6%	25.2%	32.8%	42.0%	9,963	6.6%	23.5%	34.8%	41.7%
Detroit-Warren-Dearborn, MI	643,323	62.6%	28.1%	35.1%	36.8%	259,738	25.3%	27.7%	42.4%	30.0%
Dothan, AL	22,983	66.1%	29.7%	32.0%	38.3%	9,208	26.5%	27.1%	38.5%	34.4%
Dover, DE	25,090	57.1%	22.6%	37.1%	40.3%	13,373	30.4%	25.4%	45.6%	29.0%
Dubuque, IA	22,534	89.1%	29.9%	38.7%	31.3%	366	1.4%	28.1%	60.9%	10.9%
Duluth, MN-WI	64,485	87.6%	22.4%	44.2%	33.4%	1,649	2.2%	4.4%	15.7%	79.9%
Dunn, NC micro	21,937	62.9%	24.6%	32.7%	42.7%	7,100	20.4%	27.1%	39.1%	33.9%
Durham-Chapel Hill, NC	74,075	49.2%	18.2%	43.0%	38.8%	43,293	28.8%	23.0%	40.5%	36.5%
East Stroudsburg, PA	26,826	62.6%	29.2%	43.3%	27.4%	6,856	16.0%	32.1%	52.7%	15.2%
Eau Claire, WI	42,630	91.9%	20.2%	47.3%	32.5%	244	0.5%	0.0%	71.3%	28.7%
El Centro, CA	4,851	9.2%	24.3%	32.3%	43.4%	2,060	3.9%	16.5%	40.0%	43.5%
El Paso, TX	30,997	12.8%	15.4%	42.6%	42.0%	8,359	3.4%	15.8%	60.4%	23.8%
Elizabethtown-Fort Knox, KY	30,443	76.3%	33.9%	30.2%	36.0%	5,380	13.5%	36.8%	35.2%	28.0%
Elkhart-Goshen, IN	36,130	72.8%	30.8%	34.6%	34.6%	2,346	4.7%	38.8%	22.0%	39.1%
Elmira, NY	18,250	83.3%	22.8%	37.4%	39.8%	858	3.9%	1.6%	33.8%	64.6%
Erie, PA	59,504	83.1%	20.6%	42.5%	36.9%	5,713	8.0%	18.7%	42.3%	38.9%
Eugene, OR	73,698	77.8%	19.7%	47.0%	33.3%	1,063	1.1%	0.6%	80.3%	19.1%
Eureka-Arcata-Fortuna, CA micro	25,379	66.2%	15.1%	48.3%	36.7%	645	1.7%	11.8%	55.3%	32.9%
Evansville, IN-KY	66,094	84.6%	24.3%	40.3%	35.5%	5,547	7.1%	30.9%	32.9%	36.2%
Fairbanks, AK	22,493	69.3%	18.3%	37.3%	44.4%	1,026	3.2%	32.5%	9.6%	58.0%
Fargo, ND-MN	68,898	87.2%	19.1%	47.6%	33.3%	3,171	4.0%	3.9%	90.4%	5.7%
Farmington, NM	10,444	32.0%	28.5%	31.0%	40.5%	na	na	na	na	na
Fayetteville-Springdale-Rogers, AR-MO	97,336	71.0%	24.7%	39.5%	35.8%	4,427	3.2%	9.5%	47.1%	43.4%
Fayetteville, NC	50,632	43.5%	16.1%	39.6%	44.3%	40,759	35.0%	25.4%	40.4%	34.2%
Flagstaff, AZ	25,724	53.1%	12.2%	59.2%	28.6%	515	1.1%	0.0%	61.7%	38.3%
Flint, MI	69,485	66.7%	28.5%	35.9%	35.6%	26,100	25.0%	29.1%	38.7%	32.2%
Florence-Muscle Shoals, AL	28,048	76.9%	27.0%	41.9%	31.1%	6,081	16.7%	21.7%	46.9%	31.4%
Florence, SC	23,759	48.2%	26.7%	38.3%	34.9%	22,592	45.8%	24.8%	43.6%	31.6%
Fond du Lac, WI	20,281	89.3%	35.2%	39.2%	25.6%	100	0.4%	63.0%	37.0%	0.0%
Fort Collins, CO	76,242	81.0%	20.1%	47.7%	32.2%	573	0.6%	0.0%	69.1%	30.9%
Fort Smith, AR-OK	47,698	67.1%	27.2%	34.8%	38.0%	2,667	3.8%	8.4%	33.2%	58.4%
Fort Wayne, IN	81,252	74.4%	24.9%	36.9%	38.2%	11,517	10.5%	32.5%	41.0%	26.5%
Fresno, CA	66,396	23.6%	21.6%	37.1%	41.3%	14,558	5.2%	23.5%	42.2%	34.3%
Gadsden, AL	18,160	72.7%	30.3%	36.5%	33.2%	4,816	19.3%	33.2%	28.7%	38.1%
Gainesville, FL	61,884	59.5%	11.9%	58.7%	29.5%	18,617	17.9%	16.6%	51.6%	31.9%
Gainesville, GA	25,756	53.6%	28.7%	35.6%	35.7%	4,662	9.7%	29.3%	46.0%	24.7%
Gettysburg, PA	21,377	89.4%	28.3%	43.2%	28.5%	299	1.3%	0.0%	100.0%	0.0%
Glens Falls, NY	25,517	91.7%	28.5%	36.5%	35.0%	880	3.2%	55.1%	19.8%	25.1%
Goldsboro, NC	16,251	52.4%	20.8%	41.6%	37.7%	9,859	31.8%	21.6%	37.4%	41.0%
Grand Forks, ND-MN	29,790	82.0%	21.1%	51.6%	27.3%	613	1.7%	37.2%	45.5%	17.3%
Grand Island, NE	13,321	70.8%	26.5%	37.6%	35.9%	895	4.8%	10.4%	89.6%	0.0%
Grand Junction, CO	28,733	73.0%	24.1%	39.2%	36.7%	886	2.3%	62.9%	33.0%	4.2%
Grand Rapids-Wyoming, MI	209,492	76.1%	25.4%	39.3%	35.3%	21,108	7.7%	29.5%	27.7%	42.8%
Grants Pass, OR	13,071	81.9%	22.5%	41.5%	35.9%	na	na	na	na	na
Great Falls, MT	17,247	77.8%	21.7%	33.4%	44.8%	47	0.2%	0.0%	100.0%	0.0%
Greeley, CO	45,125	60.2%	23.1%	36.4%	40.5%	1,398	1.9%	2.4%	84.0%	13.5%
Green Bay, WI	64,698	81.7%	29.1%	35.6%	35.2%	1,364	1.7%	9.8%	51.8%	38.4%
Greensboro-High Point, NC	103,852	54.8%	26.1%	37.6%	36.3%	55,717	29.4%	23.4%	42.9%	33.7%
Greenville-Anderson-Mauldin, SC	147,059	69.2%	27.1%	39.2%	33.8%	39,608	18.6%	28.7%	38.6%	32.7%
Greenville, NC	35,141	56.9%	14.3%	60.7%	25.1%	20,455	33.1%	30.2%	45.4%	24.4%
Greenwood, SC micro	12,945	53.7%	26.0%	43.9%	30.1%	9,889	41.1%	29.5%	37.7%	32.8%
Gulfport-Biloxi-Pascagoula, MS	62,782	63.1%	26.1%	36.1%	37.8%	25,749	25.9%	25.0%	37.8%	37.3%

Table B-4: Metropolitan/Micropolitan Statistical Areas—Race and Hispanic Origin by Age—*Continued*

	Asian, Non-Hispanic					Hispanic				
	Millennial Population		Percent by Age			Millennial Population		Percent by Age		
	Number	Percent	13 to 17	18 to 24	25 to 31	Number	Percent	13 to 17	18 to 24	25 to 31
Cleveland, TN	9	0.0%	100.0%	0.0%	0.0%	1,242	4.1%	11.9%	37.6%	50.5%
Coeur d'Alene, ID	636	1.8%	21.9%	44.2%	34.0%	2,522	7.2%	14.0%	51.1%	34.9%
College Station-Bryan, TX	5,868	5.6%	4.2%	62.8%	32.9%	24,673	23.7%	22.6%	48.8%	28.5%
Colorado Springs, CO	4,827	2.5%	37.4%	29.1%	33.5%	37,412	19.7%	28.3%	33.8%	37.9%
Columbia, MO	2,572	3.9%	0.0%	57.1%	42.9%	3,161	4.8%	0.0%	78.4%	21.6%
Columbia, SC	5,869	2.6%	7.0%	45.8%	47.2%	12,795	5.7%	17.9%	38.2%	43.8%
Columbus, GA-AL	954	1.0%	27.7%	45.3%	27.0%	9,677	10.4%	17.0%	49.8%	33.1%
Columbus, IN	1,203	5.8%	0.0%	19.1%	80.9%	2,653	12.9%	7.2%	45.2%	47.6%
Columbus, OH	18,302	3.6%	23.4%	22.9%	53.6%	22,446	4.4%	18.6%	30.4%	50.9%
Concord, NH micro	1,379	4.7%	0.0%	91.3%	8.7%	452	1.5%	41.6%	40.7%	17.7%
Cookeville, TN micro	66	0.2%	100.0%	0.0%	0.0%	1,884	6.6%	6.8%	35.8%	57.4%
Corpus Christi, TX	2,574	2.1%	19.7%	45.1%	35.2%	80,508	65.3%	28.6%	38.4%	33.0%
Corvallis, OR	2,418	7.2%	7.0%	49.8%	43.2%	2,156	6.4%	21.9%	53.8%	24.3%
Crestview-Fort Walton Beach-Destin, FL	2,809	4.1%	53.2%	29.7%	17.1%	6,718	9.8%	15.9%	25.3%	58.8%
Cumberland, MD-WV	na	na	na	na	na	411	1.6%	45.7%	17.3%	37.0%
Dallas-Fort Worth-Arlington, TX	100,487	5.6%	24.4%	32.9%	42.7%	592,120	33.0%	28.3%	36.7%	34.9%
Dalton, GA	303	0.8%	0.0%	35.0%	65.0%	12,990	34.5%	25.1%	38.0%	37.0%
Danville, IL	154	0.8%	41.6%	41.6%	16.9%	1,484	7.7%	25.2%	16.4%	58.4%
Danville, VA micro	109	0.5%	0.0%	0.0%	100.0%	1,128	5.0%	32.4%	42.7%	24.8%
Daphne-Fairhope-Foley, AL	539	1.2%	100.0%	0.0%	0.0%	3,758	8.6%	39.1%	40.5%	20.4%
Davenport-Moline-Rock Island, IA-IL	1,881	2.0%	13.7%	12.8%	73.5%	9,464	10.2%	25.5%	49.8%	24.7%
Dayton, OH	4,061	2.0%	26.2%	34.0%	39.8%	4,745	2.3%	31.3%	41.8%	26.9%
Decatur, AL	na	na	na	na	na	4,332	12.1%	26.9%	36.3%	36.8%
Decatur, IL	157	0.6%	15.9%	0.0%	84.1%	1,469	5.6%	9.6%	29.0%	61.4%
Deltona-Daytona Beach-Ormond Beach, FL	3,297	2.6%	15.6%	40.3%	44.1%	19,575	15.2%	26.9%	39.5%	33.5%
Denver-Aurora-Lakewood, CO	29,122	4.2%	26.3%	31.3%	42.3%	194,404	27.9%	29.3%	35.8%	34.9%
Des Moines-West Des Moines, IA	6,438	4.3%	41.2%	7.6%	51.2%	10,152	6.7%	28.7%	25.5%	45.9%
Detroit-Warren-Dearborn, MI	39,763	3.9%	27.8%	31.0%	41.2%	54,366	5.3%	29.4%	40.6%	30.0%
Dothan, AL	166	0.5%	29.5%	0.0%	70.5%	1,234	3.6%	45.7%	35.5%	18.8%
Dover, DE	693	1.6%	45.7%	54.3%	0.0%	3,543	8.1%	30.5%	22.3%	47.2%
Dubuque, IA	61	0.2%	0.0%	0.0%	100.0%	633	2.5%	54.0%	42.0%	3.9%
Duluth, MN-WI	1,088	1.5%	33.5%	32.4%	34.1%	812	1.1%	21.1%	9.7%	69.2%
Dunn, NC micro	488	1.4%	7.6%	14.8%	77.7%	3,752	10.8%	14.6%	33.4%	52.0%
Durham-Chapel Hill, NC	7,375	4.9%	15.1%	42.2%	42.7%	19,949	13.3%	17.5%	37.6%	44.9%
East Stroudsburg, PA	1,607	3.7%	55.1%	44.9%	0.0%	6,810	15.9%	31.5%	42.0%	26.5%
Eau Claire, WI	1,732	3.7%	23.1%	38.2%	38.7%	704	1.5%	11.8%	43.8%	44.5%
El Centro, CA	621	1.2%	43.6%	35.1%	21.3%	44,271	84.2%	27.3%	39.4%	33.4%
El Paso, TX	2,159	0.9%	9.2%	1.5%	89.3%	197,559	81.4%	28.8%	39.2%	32.0%
Elizabethtown-Fort Knox, KY	169	0.4%	43.2%	27.2%	29.6%	2,319	5.8%	7.6%	25.1%	67.3%
Elkhart-Goshen, IN	612	1.2%	11.6%	32.2%	56.2%	8,672	17.5%	29.3%	41.0%	29.7%
Elmira, NY	622	2.8%	8.5%	35.4%	56.1%	947	4.3%	55.9%	32.8%	11.3%
Erie, PA	1,498	2.1%	14.7%	48.4%	36.9%	2,789	3.9%	40.6%	30.5%	28.9%
Eugene, OR	3,380	3.6%	13.4%	67.9%	18.7%	8,878	9.4%	24.1%	47.7%	28.2%
Eureka-Arcata-Fortuna, CA micro	1,559	4.1%	32.8%	7.1%	60.0%	5,685	14.8%	18.0%	59.0%	23.0%
Evansville, IN-KY	1,180	1.5%	6.5%	22.2%	71.3%	2,043	2.6%	16.2%	58.1%	25.7%
Fairbanks, AK	1,039	3.2%	15.5%	71.6%	12.9%	3,188	9.8%	0.0%	57.9%	42.1%
Fargo, ND-MN	2,737	3.5%	2.0%	38.6%	59.4%	1,811	2.3%	11.3%	59.9%	28.8%
Farmington, NM	54	0.2%	0.0%	100.0%	0.0%	7,550	23.1%	24.0%	42.1%	33.9%
Fayetteville-Springdale-Rogers, AR-MO	4,768	3.5%	16.2%	17.4%	66.4%	24,843	18.1%	35.5%	39.7%	24.8%
Fayetteville, NC	2,201	1.9%	31.2%	35.3%	33.5%	13,879	11.9%	16.9%	44.5%	38.6%
Flagstaff, AZ	723	1.5%	0.0%	71.5%	28.5%	7,526	15.5%	15.5%	52.4%	32.2%
Flint, MI	678	0.7%	15.8%	70.6%	13.6%	4,289	4.1%	33.6%	46.3%	20.1%
Florence-Muscle Shoals, AL	259	0.7%	38.2%	0.0%	61.8%	1,624	4.4%	5.5%	26.3%	68.2%
Florence, SC	195	0.4%	100.0%	0.0%	0.0%	1,251	2.5%	5.4%	33.1%	61.5%
Fond du Lac, WI	182	0.8%	0.0%	100.0%	0.0%	1,285	5.7%	43.1%	33.1%	23.8%
Fort Collins, CO	2,051	2.2%	18.0%	61.3%	20.7%	12,102	12.9%	24.1%	42.3%	33.6%
Fort Smith, AR-OK	1,073	1.5%	3.1%	41.2%	55.7%	9,387	13.2%	26.0%	39.0%	35.0%
Fort Wayne, IN	2,197	2.0%	16.3%	49.5%	34.1%	8,880	8.1%	32.2%	34.0%	33.9%
Fresno, CA	29,642	10.6%	24.7%	38.4%	36.9%	161,637	57.6%	27.0%	38.7%	34.3%
Gadsden, AL	120	0.5%	100.0%	0.0%	0.0%	1,730	6.9%	15.9%	75.9%	8.2%
Gainesville, FL	7,387	7.1%	5.9%	59.2%	34.9%	11,392	10.9%	8.4%	70.2%	21.4%
Gainesville, GA	687	1.4%	41.9%	23.0%	35.1%	16,666	34.7%	29.7%	36.5%	33.8%
Gettysburg, PA	232	1.0%	0.0%	0.0%	100.0%	1,676	7.0%	16.4%	70.6%	13.0%
Glens Falls, NY	270	1.0%	0.0%	0.0%	100.0%	1,067	3.8%	2.9%	67.9%	29.1%
Goldsboro, NC	na	na	na	na	na	4,472	14.4%	42.8%	29.2%	28.0%
Grand Forks, ND-MN	551	1.5%	9.8%	78.6%	11.6%	2,636	7.3%	26.8%	56.1%	17.0%
Grand Island, NE	na	na	na	na	na	4,166	22.1%	42.6%	16.1%	41.3%
Grand Junction, CO	143	0.4%	0.0%	44.8%	55.2%	8,808	22.4%	11.0%	43.4%	45.6%
Grand Rapids-Wyoming, MI	6,667	2.4%	33.1%	23.1%	43.8%	28,585	10.4%	27.3%	41.3%	31.4%
Grants Pass, OR	166	1.0%	4.2%	0.0%	95.8%	1,702	10.7%	51.6%	29.7%	18.7%
Great Falls, MT	na	na	na	na	na	1,408	6.4%	0.0%	80.8%	19.2%
Greeley, CO	1,178	1.6%	18.4%	23.6%	58.0%	25,205	33.6%	27.2%	41.2%	31.5%
Green Bay, WI	2,661	3.4%	35.3%	48.1%	16.6%	5,042	6.4%	37.3%	28.6%	34.1%
Greensboro-High Point, NC	7,125	3.8%	20.4%	43.8%	35.8%	17,849	9.4%	25.9%	32.6%	41.5%
Greenville-Anderson-Mauldin, SC	3,576	1.7%	12.5%	44.2%	43.3%	17,459	8.2%	24.3%	33.8%	41.8%
Greenville, NC	1,245	2.0%	14.1%	52.4%	33.5%	3,751	6.1%	32.3%	48.9%	18.8%
Greenwood, SC micro	59	0.2%	0.0%	74.6%	25.4%	1,193	5.0%	6.9%	73.0%	20.1%
Gulfport-Biloxi-Pascagoula, MS	4,422	4.4%	20.1%	34.1%	45.7%	5,184	5.2%	13.2%	51.5%	35.2%

Table B-4: Metropolitan/Micropolitan Statistical Areas—Race and Hispanic Origin by Age—*Continued*

	White, Non-Hispanic					Black, Non-Hispanic				
	Millennial Population		Percent by Age			Millennial Population		Percent by Age		
	Number	Percent	13 to 17	18 to 24	25 to 31	Number	Percent	13 to 17	18 to 24	25 to 31
Hagerstown-Martinsburg, MD-WV	49,350	78.2%	29.8%	34.4%	35.8%	6,702	10.6%	15.7%	51.3%	33.0%
Hammond, LA	21,325	57.3%	26.6%	35.0%	38.5%	11,582	31.1%	23.7%	49.1%	27.2%
Hanford-Corcoran, CA	13,484	29.6%	20.4%	38.5%	41.1%	2,412	5.3%	26.0%	44.6%	29.4%
Harrisburg-Carlisle, PA	101,316	74.5%	25.1%	37.5%	37.3%	16,346	12.0%	21.1%	40.9%	37.9%
Harrisonburg, VA	36,380	80.2%	18.0%	57.8%	24.2%	1,685	3.7%	31.7%	52.6%	15.7%
Hartford-West Hartford-East Hartford, CT	189,723	62.2%	26.3%	40.0%	33.7%	36,401	11.9%	24.2%	39.1%	36.7%
Hattiesburg, MS	28,152	60.8%	20.8%	47.3%	32.0%	15,063	32.5%	21.0%	48.5%	30.5%
Hickory-Lenoir-Morganton, NC	64,564	77.2%	29.9%	36.1%	33.9%	6,574	7.9%	13.7%	58.4%	27.9%
Hilo, HI micro	8,677	19.4%	19.3%	38.6%	42.2%	na	na	na	na	na
Hilton Head Island-Bluffton-Beaufort, SC	25,021	51.3%	19.1%	41.4%	39.5%	13,244	27.1%	21.0%	47.3%	31.7%
Hinesville, GA	14,505	51.2%	23.3%	36.3%	40.4%	8,869	31.3%	18.2%	46.8%	35.0%
Holland, MI micro	21,750	83.6%	30.9%	34.7%	34.4%	285	1.1%	16.1%	83.9%	0.0%
Homosassa Springs, FL	18,153	84.6%	29.7%	36.9%	33.4%	893	4.2%	10.2%	48.7%	41.1%
Hot Springs, AR	15,410	77.0%	25.6%	43.3%	31.1%	2,735	13.7%	35.3%	25.6%	39.1%
Houma-Thibodaux, LA	38,319	66.4%	25.8%	37.2%	37.0%	11,464	19.9%	20.3%	34.0%	45.7%
Houston-The Woodlands-Sugar Land, TX	532,927	31.5%	26.3%	32.1%	41.7%	305,468	18.0%	25.7%	37.4%	37.0%
Huntington-Ashland, WV-KY-OH	83,309	93.6%	28.3%	37.1%	34.5%	2,657	3.0%	19.9%	38.2%	41.9%
Huntsville, AL	71,840	61.2%	27.3%	33.5%	39.2%	29,352	25.0%	25.6%	41.9%	32.6%
Idaho Falls, ID	30,889	82.8%	31.6%	37.5%	30.9%	203	0.5%	100.0%	0.0%	0.0%
Indianapolis-Carmel-Anderson, IN	347,436	69.7%	26.4%	34.0%	39.6%	82,747	16.6%	26.5%	37.4%	36.1%
Iowa City, IA	50,164	78.9%	12.8%	53.1%	34.1%	3,570	5.6%	21.1%	31.3%	47.6%
Ithaca, NY	28,635	69.0%	9.9%	67.0%	23.1%	1,839	4.4%	20.9%	74.3%	4.7%
Jackson, MI	31,981	81.3%	26.5%	37.0%	36.5%	4,722	12.0%	22.3%	35.5%	42.2%
Jackson, MS	63,504	41.2%	27.9%	33.5%	38.6%	85,000	55.1%	26.6%	40.0%	33.3%
Jackson, TN	18,707	54.1%	23.2%	40.1%	36.7%	13,721	39.7%	23.0%	46.7%	30.3%
Jacksonville, FL	206,501	58.2%	23.7%	36.1%	40.3%	89,595	25.3%	26.4%	36.5%	37.1%
Jacksonville, NC	45,488	60.6%	12.5%	54.4%	33.1%	13,246	17.6%	18.5%	45.7%	35.8%
Jamestown-Dunkirk-Fredonia, NY micro	27,721	80.4%	23.2%	43.8%	33.0%	1,700	4.9%	4.9%	74.5%	20.6%
Janesville-Beloit, WI	32,179	81.0%	29.6%	34.5%	35.9%	2,124	5.3%	18.5%	60.1%	21.5%
Jefferson City, MO	32,352	80.6%	26.9%	37.1%	36.0%	4,941	12.3%	39.1%	44.2%	16.8%
Johnson City, TN	44,245	87.6%	25.6%	42.0%	32.4%	2,560	5.1%	37.3%	42.0%	20.7%
Johnstown, PA	28,799	89.3%	27.1%	41.5%	31.4%	2,221	6.9%	15.1%	39.4%	45.5%
Jonesboro, AR	23,099	69.5%	23.1%	40.7%	36.2%	7,846	23.6%	24.4%	43.7%	31.8%
Joplin, MO	37,738	81.7%	26.6%	36.3%	37.1%	985	2.1%	32.3%	32.9%	34.8%
Kahului-Wailuku-Lahaina, HI	8,505	22.8%	17.4%	25.7%	56.8%	90	0.2%	0.0%	60.0%	40.0%
Kalamazoo-Portage, MI	78,737	76.8%	21.8%	47.2%	31.0%	11,052	10.8%	24.3%	50.3%	25.4%
Kalispell, MT micro	15,902	77.1%	30.6%	35.3%	34.1%	118	0.6%	0.0%	0.0%	100.0%
Kankakee, IL	18,598	67.7%	26.5%	43.3%	30.2%	4,614	16.8%	32.2%	26.9%	41.0%
Kansas City, MO-KS	357,135	69.4%	26.7%	33.4%	39.9%	71,300	13.9%	28.6%	38.0%	33.5%
Kennewick-Richland, WA	41,324	57.1%	28.3%	33.3%	38.4%	606	0.8%	38.4%	25.4%	36.1%
Killeen-Temple, TX	64,738	47.9%	19.3%	39.7%	41.1%	25,515	18.9%	24.8%	46.4%	28.8%
Kingsport-Bristol-Bristol, TN-VA	61,618	91.0%	26.9%	37.4%	35.7%	2,912	4.3%	25.3%	47.1%	27.6%
Kingston, NY	31,037	71.7%	25.2%	40.6%	34.2%	3,434	7.9%	3.9%	61.6%	34.5%
Knoxville, TN	178,444	84.2%	25.4%	39.9%	34.8%	14,512	6.8%	18.8%	50.2%	31.0%
Kokomo, IN	13,919	81.1%	32.4%	36.0%	31.6%	726	4.2%	26.2%	55.8%	18.0%
La Crosse-Onalaska, WI-MN	34,465	84.7%	19.8%	48.5%	31.7%	318	0.8%	2.5%	25.8%	71.7%
Lafayette-West Lafayette, IN	62,809	77.9%	14.3%	57.1%	28.6%	2,564	3.2%	25.8%	49.5%	24.7%
Lafayette, LA	86,141	64.2%	24.6%	38.2%	37.2%	37,253	27.8%	26.9%	41.3%	31.8%
Lake Charles, LA	36,574	68.9%	23.8%	40.8%	35.5%	13,070	24.6%	43.1%	34.4%	22.5%
Lake Havasu City-Kingman, AZ	27,038	67.0%	29.3%	34.6%	36.0%	505	1.3%	36.0%	55.0%	8.9%
Lakeland-Winter Haven, FL	78,871	52.7%	24.8%	36.9%	38.3%	29,397	19.6%	24.4%	39.9%	35.7%
Lancaster, PA	105,511	79.7%	26.1%	36.9%	37.1%	6,004	4.5%	37.3%	42.0%	20.6%
Lansing-East Lansing, MI	105,329	71.9%	17.6%	51.0%	31.4%	13,783	9.4%	23.0%	44.5%	32.4%
Laredo, TX	1,722	2.2%	13.6%	19.8%	66.6%	310	0.4%	2.6%	53.2%	44.2%
Las Cruces, NM	16,216	24.2%	17.9%	49.2%	32.9%	1,767	2.6%	29.7%	66.9%	3.4%
Las Vegas-Henderson-Paradise, NV	192,281	37.1%	23.0%	32.4%	44.6%	56,176	10.8%	23.7%	39.9%	36.4%
Lawrence, KS	35,432	80.0%	11.0%	60.9%	28.0%	2,504	5.7%	32.9%	5.9%	61.2%
Lawton, OK	22,876	54.9%	15.4%	42.5%	42.2%	6,995	16.8%	23.4%	51.9%	24.7%
Lebanon, PA	23,692	83.3%	29.2%	37.8%	33.1%	627	2.2%	0.0%	83.7%	16.3%
Lewiston-Auburn, ME	23,319	87.9%	27.0%	35.5%	37.4%	706	2.7%	19.8%	67.7%	12.5%
Lewiston, ID-WA	11,380	75.7%	22.2%	44.8%	33.0%	192	1.3%	0.0%	100.0%	0.0%
Lexington-Fayette, KY	106,041	76.6%	21.4%	44.0%	34.6%	17,463	12.6%	22.9%	39.2%	37.9%
Lima, OH	21,502	81.8%	24.4%	42.2%	33.4%	3,049	11.6%	31.8%	41.3%	26.9%
Lincoln, NE	81,575	81.3%	17.1%	49.0%	34.0%	3,791	3.8%	17.1%	66.8%	16.1%
Little Rock-North Little Rock-Conway, AR	119,202	61.0%	23.6%	36.6%	39.8%	52,817	27.0%	28.9%	35.7%	35.4%
Logan, UT-ID	39,804	83.4%	22.0%	44.8%	33.2%	528	1.1%	48.1%	51.9%	0.0%
Longview, TX	31,866	54.4%	25.3%	36.7%	38.0%	14,271	24.3%	21.7%	50.5%	27.8%
Longview, WA	17,988	77.6%	30.1%	35.7%	34.3%	na	na	na	na	na
Los Angeles-Long Beach-Anaheim, CA	891,455	25.2%	20.9%	35.5%	43.6%	226,933	6.4%	23.3%	39.5%	37.3%
Louisville/Jefferson County, KY-IN	230,023	73.9%	27.6%	34.2%	38.2%	50,199	16.1%	29.1%	39.6%	31.3%
Lubbock, TX	51,875	52.3%	15.4%	55.3%	29.4%	6,525	6.6%	14.2%	54.8%	31.0%
Lumberton, NC micro	6,235	19.1%	23.3%	51.1%	25.6%	8,559	26.2%	29.7%	45.1%	25.2%
Lynchburg, VA	53,123	75.6%	22.6%	49.0%	28.4%	11,905	16.9%	17.5%	40.3%	42.2%
Macon, GA	27,509	43.8%	21.9%	40.7%	37.4%	31,251	49.7%	26.9%	44.2%	28.9%
Madera, CA	10,255	23.8%	23.6%	34.9%	41.5%	1,498	3.5%	31.3%	29.3%	39.4%
Madison, WI	146,908	77.7%	20.2%	43.3%	36.5%	10,370	5.5%	29.5%	23.7%	46.8%
Manchester-Nashua, NH	80,318	84.9%	28.0%	34.8%	37.2%	945	1.0%	0.0%	100.0%	0.0%
Manhattan, KS	33,449	74.6%	11.5%	59.4%	29.1%	3,891	8.7%	8.4%	55.4%	36.2%

Table B-4: Metropolitan/Micropolitan Statistical Areas—Race and Hispanic Origin by Age—*Continued*

	Asian, Non-Hispanic					Hispanic				
	Millennial Population		Percent by Age			Millennial Population		Percent by Age		
	Number	Percent	13 to 17	18 to 24	25 to 31	Number	Percent	13 to 17	18 to 24	25 to 31
Hagerstown-Martinsburg, MD-WV	843	1.3%	31.1%	54.9%	14.0%	3,121	4.9%	40.6%	23.6%	35.8%
Hammond, LA	12	0.0%	100.0%	0.0%	0.0%	2,799	7.5%	5.1%	32.4%	62.4%
Hanford-Corcoran, CA	1,547	3.4%	44.5%	18.9%	36.6%	26,531	58.3%	22.8%	39.0%	38.2%
Harrisburg-Carlisle, PA	5,472	4.0%	15.8%	34.1%	50.1%	9,577	7.0%	38.4%	43.8%	17.9%
Harrisonburg, VA	1,142	2.5%	20.1%	70.4%	9.5%	4,647	10.2%	15.4%	46.2%	38.3%
Hartford-West Hartford-East Hartford, CT	16,487	5.4%	19.7%	30.2%	50.1%	55,204	18.1%	27.6%	41.2%	31.2%
Hattiesburg, MS	462	1.0%	0.0%	56.1%	43.9%	1,691	3.7%	5.6%	79.3%	15.1%
Hickory-Lenoir-Morganton, NC	3,601	4.3%	26.2%	30.2%	43.5%	6,339	7.6%	33.7%	38.0%	28.3%
Hilo, HI micro	6,836	15.3%	28.3%	36.8%	34.9%	7,467	16.7%	37.2%	28.7%	34.1%
Hilton Head Island-Bluffton-Beaufort, SC	344	0.7%	0.0%	45.6%	54.4%	8,287	17.0%	23.2%	42.8%	34.0%
Hinesville, GA	718	2.5%	0.0%	82.2%	17.8%	2,467	8.7%	15.9%	33.8%	50.3%
Holland, MI micro	120	0.5%	100.0%	0.0%	0.0%	2,497	9.6%	32.3%	42.7%	25.0%
Homosassa Springs, FL	310	1.4%	0.0%	21.3%	78.7%	2,093	9.7%	34.7%	57.0%	8.3%
Hot Springs, AR	263	1.3%	100.0%	0.0%	0.0%	1,250	6.2%	23.0%	63.2%	13.8%
Houma-Thibodaux, LA	359	0.6%	44.6%	26.2%	29.2%	3,033	5.3%	20.5%	42.5%	37.1%
Houston-The Woodlands-Sugar Land, TX	113,075	6.7%	25.2%	31.6%	43.2%	710,648	42.0%	27.7%	35.5%	36.8%
Huntington-Ashland, WV-KY-OH	302	0.3%	8.3%	59.3%	32.5%	655	0.7%	24.0%	0.0%	76.0%
Huntsville, AL	3,245	2.8%	18.6%	36.3%	45.1%	9,303	7.9%	17.3%	45.5%	37.1%
Idaho Falls, ID	491	1.3%	26.5%	13.4%	60.1%	4,753	12.7%	28.7%	34.2%	37.1%
Indianapolis-Carmel-Anderson, IN	13,363	2.7%	15.7%	31.4%	52.9%	41,176	8.3%	29.9%	35.2%	34.9%
Iowa City, IA	3,290	5.2%	0.0%	35.7%	64.3%	4,985	7.8%	15.6%	70.9%	13.5%
Ithaca, NY	6,683	16.1%	3.5%	72.5%	24.0%	2,179	5.2%	11.3%	46.4%	42.3%
Jackson, MI	40	0.1%	0.0%	100.0%	0.0%	1,623	4.1%	41.8%	17.7%	40.5%
Jackson, MS	1,601	1.0%	47.3%	18.9%	33.7%	2,886	1.9%	22.9%	0.0%	77.1%
Jackson, TN	603	1.7%	30.8%	18.1%	51.1%	982	2.8%	74.5%	11.1%	14.4%
Jacksonville, FL	13,360	3.8%	27.2%	33.4%	39.3%	33,108	9.3%	25.2%	34.8%	40.0%
Jacksonville, NC	1,860	2.5%	34.2%	27.8%	38.0%	12,396	16.5%	13.9%	55.1%	31.0%
Jamestown-Dunkirk-Fredonia, NY micro	739	2.1%	33.3%	64.4%	2.3%	3,503	10.2%	31.3%	45.7%	23.0%
Janesville-Beloit, WI	229	0.6%	28.4%	71.6%	0.0%	3,071	7.7%	45.0%	27.7%	27.3%
Jefferson City, MO	229	0.6%	0.0%	0.0%	100.0%	1,816	4.5%	41.7%	31.4%	26.9%
Johnson City, TN	207	0.4%	0.0%	31.4%	68.6%	2,523	5.0%	19.0%	48.3%	32.7%
Johnstown, PA	442	1.4%	0.0%	0.0%	100.0%	136	0.4%	14.0%	86.0%	0.0%
Jonesboro, AR	352	1.1%	0.0%	100.0%	0.0%	1,529	4.6%	8.9%	6.8%	84.3%
Joplin, MO	983	2.1%	3.3%	68.4%	28.4%	4,244	9.2%	13.0%	48.4%	38.7%
Kahului-Wailuku-Lahaina, HI	9,814	26.3%	38.6%	22.7%	38.7%	4,425	11.9%	33.4%	21.5%	45.1%
Kalamazoo-Portage, MI	2,421	2.4%	26.6%	18.9%	54.4%	5,107	5.0%	32.7%	49.6%	17.7%
Kalispell, MT micro	33	0.2%	0.0%	0.0%	100.0%	1,531	7.4%	67.9%	4.7%	27.4%
Kankakee, IL	140	0.5%	73.6%	26.4%	0.0%	3,177	11.6%	32.0%	49.2%	18.8%
Kansas City, MO-KS	14,213	2.8%	25.8%	26.2%	48.0%	52,659	10.2%	29.1%	34.7%	36.2%
Kennewick-Richland, WA	1,009	1.4%	29.8%	16.9%	53.2%	27,339	37.8%	34.8%	34.0%	31.2%
Killeen-Temple, TX	1,437	1.1%	10.9%	27.8%	61.3%	34,289	25.4%	24.2%	37.9%	37.9%
Kingsport-Bristol-Bristol, TN-VA	299	0.4%	100.0%	0.0%	0.0%	1,368	2.0%	64.1%	13.8%	22.1%
Kingston, NY	1,395	3.2%	26.6%	41.9%	31.5%	6,228	14.4%	39.6%	44.7%	15.7%
Knoxville, TN	3,055	1.4%	15.0%	24.3%	60.7%	10,704	5.0%	32.6%	34.0%	33.5%
Kokomo, IN	386	2.2%	92.0%	0.0%	8.0%	1,911	11.1%	14.9%	26.9%	58.2%
La Crosse-Onalaska, WI-MN	4,952	12.2%	24.7%	39.5%	35.8%	750	1.8%	18.0%	70.1%	11.9%
Lafayette-West Lafayette, IN	7,303	9.1%	6.4%	74.0%	19.6%	5,298	6.6%	26.1%	55.4%	18.5%
Lafayette, LA	2,738	2.0%	8.1%	39.1%	52.7%	5,632	4.2%	14.9%	46.8%	38.2%
Lake Charles, LA	239	0.5%	0.0%	100.0%	0.0%	2,300	4.3%	26.1%	55.2%	18.7%
Lake Havasu City-Kingman, AZ	234	0.6%	0.0%	13.2%	86.8%	10,144	25.1%	37.8%	30.5%	31.6%
Lakeland-Winter Haven, FL	2,271	1.5%	25.2%	37.8%	37.0%	35,629	23.8%	28.0%	35.6%	36.4%
Lancaster, PA	2,467	1.9%	14.5%	52.2%	33.3%	16,472	12.4%	28.9%	43.2%	28.0%
Lansing-East Lansing, MI	7,974	5.4%	11.3%	62.1%	26.5%	11,169	7.6%	22.0%	48.4%	29.6%
Laredo, TX	11	0.0%	0.0%	0.0%	100.0%	74,600	97.1%	30.2%	37.6%	32.3%
Las Cruces, NM	428	0.6%	0.0%	0.0%	100.0%	46,724	69.8%	27.3%	47.6%	25.1%
Las Vegas-Henderson-Paradise, NV	46,413	9.0%	24.9%	34.2%	41.0%	196,549	37.9%	28.0%	36.3%	35.7%
Lawrence, KS	1,990	4.5%	0.0%	57.7%	42.3%	1,745	3.9%	6.6%	33.9%	59.4%
Lawton, OK	1,131	2.7%	0.0%	34.0%	66.0%	6,345	15.2%	23.9%	53.8%	22.3%
Lebanon, PA	188	0.7%	0.0%	0.0%	100.0%	3,931	13.8%	36.3%	36.9%	26.8%
Lewiston-Auburn, ME	334	1.3%	0.0%	36.2%	63.8%	150	0.6%	27.3%	46.0%	26.7%
Lewiston, ID-WA	479	3.2%	0.0%	64.5%	35.5%	1,357	9.0%	34.3%	27.6%	38.2%
Lexington-Fayette, KY	2,950	2.1%	18.4%	17.9%	63.7%	8,346	6.0%	29.6%	40.1%	30.3%
Lima, OH	na	na	na	na	na	940	3.6%	15.2%	0.0%	84.8%
Lincoln, NE	4,582	4.6%	15.5%	45.6%	38.9%	7,350	7.3%	28.6%	50.5%	20.9%
Little Rock-North Little Rock-Conway, AR	3,617	1.9%	25.7%	31.0%	43.4%	14,069	7.2%	19.2%	26.5%	54.2%
Logan, UT-ID	890	1.9%	31.3%	29.4%	39.2%	5,065	10.6%	31.5%	26.8%	41.7%
Longview, TX	211	0.4%	47.9%	52.1%	0.0%	11,915	20.3%	35.1%	36.6%	28.3%
Longview, WA	204	0.9%	31.4%	68.6%	0.0%	3,685	15.9%	22.6%	49.8%	27.5%
Los Angeles-Long Beach-Anaheim, CA	475,662	13.4%	21.0%	35.8%	43.1%	1,833,508	51.8%	26.5%	38.6%	34.9%
Louisville/Jefferson County, KY-IN	4,667	1.5%	28.4%	23.2%	48.4%	17,367	5.6%	24.1%	39.4%	36.5%
Lubbock, TX	2,483	2.5%	15.6%	68.9%	15.5%	36,320	36.6%	29.0%	40.3%	30.6%
Lumberton, NC micro	168	0.5%	16.7%	25.6%	57.7%	3,092	9.5%	26.6%	44.1%	29.4%
Lynchburg, VA	1,482	2.1%	26.8%	28.9%	44.3%	1,670	2.4%	42.9%	46.1%	11.0%
Macon, GA	1,017	1.6%	21.0%	71.7%	7.3%	2,254	3.6%	20.0%	19.7%	60.3%
Madera, CA	606	1.4%	0.0%	54.3%	45.7%	30,037	69.7%	29.6%	35.6%	34.8%
Madison, WI	13,074	6.9%	10.2%	43.7%	46.1%	14,735	7.8%	24.8%	35.4%	39.9%
Manchester-Nashua, NH	4,180	4.4%	22.2%	28.3%	49.5%	7,515	7.9%	27.6%	29.3%	43.1%
Manhattan, KS	1,609	3.6%	0.0%	78.6%	21.4%	3,793	8.5%	26.8%	59.6%	13.6%

Table B-4: Metropolitan/Micropolitan Statistical Areas—Race and Hispanic Origin by Age—*Continued*

	White, Non-Hispanic					Black, Non-Hispanic				
	Millennial Population		Percent by Age			Millennial Population		Percent by Age		
	Number	Percent	13 to 17	18 to 24	25 to 31	Number	Percent	13 to 17	18 to 24	25 to 31
Mankato-North Mankato, MN	28,301	84.2%	16.9%	56.2%	26.9%	1,151	3.4%	15.7%	32.5%	51.8%
Mansfield, OH	22,012	78.5%	28.4%	38.7%	32.9%	3,662	13.1%	21.8%	54.5%	23.7%
McAllen-Edinburg-Mission, TX	8,680	3.6%	22.5%	38.4%	39.0%	1,106	0.5%	16.6%	51.1%	32.3%
Medford, OR	34,456	75.2%	23.2%	36.9%	39.9%	289	0.6%	44.3%	22.5%	33.2%
Memphis, TN-MS-AR	147,152	40.0%	27.6%	36.5%	35.8%	185,738	50.5%	27.4%	39.6%	33.0%
Merced, CA	18,384	22.7%	25.6%	39.1%	35.3%	2,291	2.8%	21.3%	62.5%	16.2%
Meridian, MS micro	12,074	47.3%	19.2%	48.2%	32.6%	11,605	45.5%	25.8%	41.1%	33.0%
Miami-Fort Lauderdale-West Palm Beach, FL	365,932	26.3%	24.8%	35.3%	39.9%	341,196	24.5%	25.2%	38.0%	36.9%
Michigan City-La Porte, IN	19,895	71.8%	28.9%	35.8%	35.3%	4,683	16.9%	25.3%	34.4%	40.3%
Midland, MI	17,582	81.8%	28.6%	32.2%	39.2%	1,313	6.1%	1.1%	87.8%	11.1%
Midland, TX	20,555	44.8%	20.7%	34.5%	44.8%	2,208	4.8%	8.9%	26.9%	64.3%
Milwaukee-Waukesha-West Allis, WI	244,851	60.1%	24.4%	35.0%	40.6%	79,204	19.4%	27.2%	39.5%	33.4%
Minneapolis-St. Paul-Bloomington, MN-WI	632,443	72.3%	26.6%	33.5%	40.0%	76,496	8.7%	26.1%	36.4%	37.5%
Missoula, MT	31,371	85.6%	19.6%	43.7%	36.7%	na	na	na	na	na
Mobile, AL	57,071	53.8%	23.2%	37.6%	39.2%	41,865	39.5%	25.1%	43.4%	31.5%
Modesto, CA	55,357	37.4%	26.9%	36.2%	37.0%	3,785	2.6%	22.5%	34.1%	43.4%
Monroe, LA	25,566	50.1%	26.1%	37.9%	36.0%	22,842	44.8%	24.1%	41.3%	34.6%
Monroe, MI	31,099	88.8%	28.8%	36.0%	35.2%	1,288	3.7%	37.8%	42.4%	19.8%
Montgomery, AL	42,251	42.2%	26.3%	37.1%	36.6%	53,173	53.2%	22.5%	40.6%	36.8%
Morgantown, WV	43,229	87.3%	12.7%	56.5%	30.7%	2,882	5.8%	9.4%	64.0%	26.5%
Morristown, TN	22,155	90.6%	22.7%	40.4%	36.9%	127	0.5%	17.3%	78.7%	3.9%
Mount Vernon-Anacortes, WA	19,852	73.0%	24.5%	38.1%	37.4%	413	1.5%	4.6%	42.1%	53.3%
Muncie, IN	32,930	84.4%	13.5%	62.1%	24.4%	3,229	8.3%	27.5%	62.2%	10.3%
Muskegon, MI	30,518	74.9%	33.1%	35.1%	31.8%	6,214	15.2%	26.5%	40.1%	33.5%
Myrtle Beach-Conway-North Myrtle Beach, SC-NC	58,892	71.4%	22.3%	37.5%	40.3%	14,208	17.2%	28.8%	47.6%	23.6%
Napa, CA	13,541	40.7%	27.1%	38.1%	34.8%	770	2.3%	29.9%	70.1%	0.0%
Naples-Immokalee-Marco Island, FL	28,854	46.4%	28.6%	35.1%	36.3%	5,289	8.5%	36.5%	39.8%	23.6%
Nashville-Davidson–Murfreesboro–Franklin, TN	314,743	69.5%	25.3%	35.6%	39.1%	79,134	17.5%	25.0%	39.6%	35.4%
New Bern, NC	21,915	63.3%	19.7%	48.0%	32.3%	8,540	24.7%	17.9%	31.1%	51.0%
New Castle, PA micro	17,705	93.3%	30.2%	37.4%	32.4%	923	4.9%	68.7%	31.3%	0.0%
New Haven-Milford, CT	125,346	56.5%	24.3%	38.9%	36.8%	32,364	14.6%	27.9%	37.1%	35.1%
New Orleans-Metairie, LA	146,548	47.4%	24.1%	33.1%	42.8%	117,096	37.9%	24.6%	38.1%	37.3%
New Philadelphia-Dover, OH micro	19,782	93.1%	30.8%	33.2%	36.0%	569	2.7%	100.0%	0.0%	0.0%
New York-Newark-Jersey City, NY-NJ-PA	2,153,781	42.1%	25.3%	34.7%	40.1%	867,036	16.9%	24.4%	38.9%	36.7%
Niles-Benton Harbor, MI	23,302	67.9%	26.0%	36.3%	37.7%	5,877	17.1%	18.9%	47.6%	33.5%
North Port-Sarasota-Bradenton, FL	86,236	64.3%	27.6%	36.3%	36.1%	14,526	10.8%	28.2%	38.3%	33.6%
Norwich-New London, CT	49,140	69.9%	24.3%	41.3%	34.3%	5,211	7.4%	8.7%	42.1%	49.3%
Ocala, FL	41,083	61.5%	22.8%	36.8%	40.4%	12,297	18.4%	30.9%	40.5%	28.7%
Ocean City, NJ	14,509	72.6%	21.7%	41.3%	37.0%	1,284	6.4%	56.3%	36.2%	7.5%
Odessa, TX	13,455	29.8%	20.9%	38.4%	40.8%	2,013	4.5%	22.9%	26.0%	51.1%
Ogden-Clearfield, UT	136,911	78.9%	30.6%	33.6%	35.7%	2,923	1.7%	22.9%	27.7%	49.4%
Ogdensburg-Massena, NY micro	27,615	88.2%	21.1%	51.4%	27.5%	1,550	5.0%	28.5%	46.5%	25.0%
Oklahoma City, OK	207,945	59.3%	20.9%	38.2%	40.9%	39,559	11.3%	21.7%	44.6%	33.8%
Olympia-Tumwater, WA	47,715	69.2%	24.7%	34.4%	40.9%	2,313	3.4%	27.7%	34.4%	37.9%
Omaha-Council Bluffs, NE-IA	181,926	74.5%	26.5%	33.9%	39.5%	21,435	8.8%	27.6%	38.4%	34.0%
Orangeburg, SC micro	7,258	30.0%	29.6%	44.5%	25.9%	15,205	62.9%	32.0%	47.4%	20.7%
Orlando-Kissimmee-Sanford, FL	276,656	44.5%	23.5%	35.6%	40.9%	109,946	17.7%	27.7%	38.9%	33.4%
Oshkosh-Neenah, WI	40,468	86.3%	19.0%	46.3%	34.7%	1,851	3.9%	0.9%	55.3%	43.8%
Ottawa-Peru, IL micro	22,222	82.9%	31.8%	34.1%	34.1%	663	2.5%	11.5%	40.4%	48.1%
Owensboro, KY	23,304	84.5%	27.6%	36.7%	35.7%	1,540	5.6%	0.0%	14.9%	85.1%
Oxnard-Thousand Oaks-Ventura, CA	83,096	38.9%	26.8%	40.2%	33.0%	2,661	1.2%	20.8%	55.1%	24.1%
Palm Bay-Melbourne-Titusville, FL	79,584	70.6%	27.1%	37.0%	35.9%	13,679	12.1%	29.7%	45.7%	24.6%
Panama City, FL	34,440	74.1%	24.1%	35.2%	40.7%	6,281	13.5%	11.6%	41.1%	47.3%
Parkersburg-Vienna, WV	19,034	96.1%	26.0%	37.8%	36.3%	24	0.1%	100.0%	0.0%	0.0%
Pensacola-Ferry Pass-Brent, FL	85,095	66.8%	21.5%	41.5%	37.0%	22,336	17.5%	22.5%	42.1%	35.4%
Peoria, IL	74,076	77.0%	24.8%	35.9%	39.3%	10,533	10.9%	32.8%	39.0%	28.2%
Philadelphia-Camden-Wilmington, PA-NJ-DE-MD	908,598	57.5%	24.4%	36.6%	39.0%	357,335	22.6%	25.7%	41.2%	33.1%
Phoenix-Mesa-Scottsdale, AZ	554,227	47.8%	25.2%	34.6%	40.2%	68,014	5.9%	25.5%	38.1%	36.4%
Pine Bluff, AR	12,193	46.9%	25.2%	43.8%	31.0%	12,609	48.6%	26.7%	47.8%	25.5%
Pittsburgh, PA	455,514	81.5%	23.6%	37.7%	38.7%	58,436	10.4%	28.8%	43.2%	28.1%
Pittsfield, MA	26,037	85.3%	26.6%	41.0%	32.4%	1,110	3.6%	8.0%	92.0%	0.0%
Pocatello, ID	20,264	79.1%	28.9%	38.5%	32.6%	74	0.3%	100.0%	0.0%	0.0%
Port St. Lucie, FL	46,849	51.7%	26.9%	36.8%	36.3%	18,997	20.9%	28.5%	35.5%	36.0%
Portland-South Portland, ME	104,792	88.7%	26.6%	35.9%	37.5%	1,969	1.7%	34.5%	50.1%	15.4%
Portland-Vancouver-Hillsboro, OR-WA	404,805	69.8%	23.6%	33.2%	43.2%	18,330	3.2%	25.4%	38.4%	36.1%
Pottsville, PA micro	27,419	89.6%	27.2%	35.9%	36.9%	2,012	6.6%	0.0%	41.3%	58.7%
Prescott, AZ	27,619	68.5%	30.5%	36.6%	32.8%	na	na	na	na	na
Providence-Warwick, RI-MA	295,781	71.4%	23.0%	41.4%	35.6%	21,696	5.2%	26.7%	40.7%	32.6%
Provo-Orem, UT	167,191	82.3%	23.9%	47.0%	29.0%	564	0.3%	26.1%	29.6%	44.3%
Pueblo, CO	19,084	46.2%	23.2%	36.7%	40.1%	501	1.2%	15.0%	33.1%	51.9%
Punta Gorda, FL	18,791	72.0%	28.2%	35.6%	36.1%	3,537	13.6%	23.3%	46.7%	30.0%
Racine, WI	28,381	62.4%	31.2%	32.9%	35.9%	7,309	16.1%	31.3%	36.3%	32.5%
Raleigh, NC	182,712	56.9%	27.9%	34.5%	37.5%	71,869	22.4%	27.1%	39.3%	33.6%
Rapid City, SD	28,630	82.5%	22.5%	38.8%	38.7%	973	2.8%	32.4%	67.6%	0.0%
Reading, PA	70,131	67.6%	25.5%	39.6%	34.9%	5,301	5.1%	29.8%	49.7%	20.5%
Redding, CA	32,227	74.7%	24.5%	36.6%	38.9%	474	1.1%	4.2%	89.2%	6.5%
Reno, NV	64,238	56.4%	21.6%	38.7%	39.7%	3,120	2.7%	18.5%	17.6%	63.9%

Table B-4: Metropolitan/Micropolitan Statistical Areas—Race and Hispanic Origin by Age—*Continued*

	Asian, Non-Hispanic					Hispanic				
	Millennial Population		Percent by Age			Millennial Population		Percent by Age		
	Number	Percent	13 to 17	18 to 24	25 to 31	Number	Percent	13 to 17	18 to 24	25 to 31
Mankato-North Mankato, MN	1,321	3.9%	0.0%	71.7%	28.3%	1,521	4.5%	37.3%	43.4%	19.3%
Mansfield, OH	na	na	na	na	na	1,075	3.8%	19.5%	10.2%	70.2%
McAllen-Edinburg-Mission, TX	2,999	1.3%	52.3%	27.9%	19.7%	225,676	94.5%	31.7%	37.4%	30.9%
Medford, OR	406	0.9%	0.0%	0.0%	100.0%	7,971	17.4%	34.6%	36.7%	28.8%
Memphis, TN-MS-AR	6,910	1.9%	27.1%	29.8%	43.1%	22,572	6.1%	26.0%	34.0%	39.9%
Merced, CA	7,740	9.6%	26.0%	43.3%	30.7%	50,999	63.1%	31.2%	38.0%	30.8%
Meridian, MS micro	na	na	na	na	na	810	3.2%	0.0%	90.7%	9.3%
Miami-Fort Lauderdale-West Palm Beach, FL	35,002	2.5%	20.7%	34.7%	44.6%	619,599	44.6%	24.2%	36.5%	39.3%
Michigan City-La Porte, IN	56	0.2%	100.0%	0.0%	0.0%	2,472	8.9%	19.8%	8.7%	71.5%
Midland, MI	273	1.3%	0.0%	79.5%	20.5%	1,649	7.7%	16.7%	37.4%	46.0%
Midland, TX	196	0.4%	0.0%	50.0%	50.0%	21,652	47.2%	27.4%	37.2%	35.4%
Milwaukee-Waukesha-West Allis, WI	17,107	4.2%	28.3%	24.5%	47.2%	51,704	12.7%	24.2%	38.5%	37.2%
Minneapolis-St. Paul-Bloomington, MN-WI	68,651	7.9%	20.5%	32.1%	47.4%	62,291	7.1%	24.9%	34.1%	41.0%
Missoula, MT	223	0.6%	0.0%	100.0%	0.0%	1,338	3.7%	38.9%	61.1%	0.0%
Mobile, AL	1,963	1.9%	33.4%	38.8%	27.9%	3,222	3.0%	20.6%	32.2%	47.2%
Modesto, CA	7,642	5.2%	35.4%	44.3%	20.3%	74,965	50.6%	29.9%	38.1%	32.0%
Monroe, LA	767	1.5%	22.6%	55.0%	22.4%	1,160	2.3%	21.9%	56.4%	21.7%
Monroe, MI	146	0.4%	0.0%	0.0%	100.0%	1,154	3.3%	39.6%	39.2%	21.2%
Montgomery, AL	837	0.8%	59.3%	17.2%	23.5%	2,697	2.7%	10.9%	43.2%	45.9%
Morgantown, WV	996	2.0%	14.3%	7.9%	77.8%	1,367	2.8%	17.0%	58.3%	24.7%
Morristown, TN	85	0.3%	0.0%	100.0%	0.0%	1,340	5.5%	14.6%	18.4%	67.1%
Mount Vernon-Anacortes, WA	1,309	4.8%	37.7%	34.1%	28.3%	3,771	13.9%	28.6%	53.2%	18.3%
Muncie, IN	259	0.7%	0.0%	100.0%	0.0%	1,368	3.5%	15.9%	40.5%	43.6%
Muskegon, MI	458	1.1%	71.0%	0.0%	29.0%	1,619	4.0%	12.6%	22.4%	65.0%
Myrtle Beach-Conway-North Myrtle Beach, SC-NC	1,003	1.2%	30.5%	35.2%	34.3%	6,548	7.9%	15.1%	31.9%	53.0%
Napa, CA	2,472	7.4%	28.3%	24.5%	47.2%	15,512	46.7%	29.0%	41.0%	30.0%
Naples-Immokalee-Marco Island, FL	na	na	na	na	na	26,987	43.4%	25.5%	36.9%	37.6%
Nashville-Davidson–Murfreesboro–Franklin, TN	10,669	2.4%	20.3%	19.7%	60.0%	36,550	8.1%	21.3%	39.2%	39.5%
New Bern, NC	300	0.9%	0.0%	31.0%	69.0%	2,887	8.3%	6.4%	52.1%	41.6%
New Castle, PA micro	na	na	na	na	na	353	1.9%	38.5%	38.5%	22.9%
New Haven-Milford, CT	10,118	4.6%	19.0%	35.3%	45.7%	46,706	21.1%	25.1%	39.7%	35.2%
New Orleans-Metairie, LA	8,554	2.8%	23.0%	24.9%	52.2%	30,960	10.0%	14.6%	36.6%	48.8%
New Philadelphia-Dover, OH micro	na	na	na	na	na	639	3.0%	0.0%	81.5%	18.5%
New York-Newark-Jersey City, NY-NJ-PA	538,769	10.5%	21.3%	33.6%	45.1%	1,408,927	27.5%	23.5%	37.9%	38.6%
Niles-Benton Harbor, MI	835	2.4%	28.1%	25.7%	46.1%	2,843	8.3%	18.9%	53.7%	27.4%
North Port-Sarasota-Bradenton, FL	2,686	2.0%	43.0%	28.9%	28.1%	27,588	20.6%	28.4%	47.7%	23.8%
Norwich-New London, CT	1,831	2.6%	24.4%	32.4%	43.3%	9,914	14.1%	20.9%	47.3%	31.8%
Ocala, FL	1,217	1.8%	35.8%	13.6%	50.5%	11,222	16.8%	32.6%	35.1%	32.3%
Ocean City, NJ	342	1.7%	50.3%	0.0%	49.7%	3,297	16.5%	17.7%	34.3%	48.0%
Odessa, TX	492	1.1%	0.0%	68.7%	31.3%	28,382	62.8%	25.0%	37.5%	37.5%
Ogden-Clearfield, UT	3,613	2.1%	22.3%	51.5%	26.2%	24,010	13.8%	33.8%	33.9%	32.3%
Ogdensburg-Massena, NY micro	243	0.8%	14.0%	86.0%	0.0%	1,278	4.1%	4.9%	63.0%	32.2%
Oklahoma City, OK	10,365	3.0%	15.4%	45.9%	38.7%	53,490	15.2%	24.8%	35.9%	39.3%
Olympia-Tumwater, WA	5,273	7.6%	34.5%	29.5%	36.1%	8,065	11.7%	25.8%	30.3%	43.9%
Omaha-Council Bluffs, NE-IA	7,314	3.0%	11.7%	40.1%	48.2%	25,533	10.5%	24.6%	39.5%	35.9%
Orangeburg, SC micro	na	na	na	na	na	1,199	5.0%	0.0%	27.7%	72.3%
Orlando-Kissimmee-Sanford, FL	23,045	3.7%	22.6%	44.5%	32.9%	189,515	30.5%	25.6%	37.0%	37.3%
Oshkosh-Neenah, WI	1,392	3.0%	0.0%	12.9%	87.1%	1,706	3.6%	42.5%	44.2%	13.3%
Ottawa-Peru, IL micro	244	0.9%	0.0%	12.3%	87.7%	3,298	12.3%	35.1%	29.3%	35.7%
Owensboro, KY	323	1.2%	55.4%	44.6%	0.0%	799	2.9%	0.9%	47.1%	52.1%
Oxnard-Thousand Oaks-Ventura, CA	10,335	4.8%	25.1%	33.9%	41.0%	108,585	50.8%	27.3%	38.4%	34.3%
Palm Bay-Melbourne-Titusville, FL	1,678	1.5%	18.7%	63.6%	17.7%	13,612	12.1%	24.6%	41.7%	33.7%
Panama City, FL	1,255	2.7%	35.9%	28.6%	35.5%	2,765	5.9%	9.6%	28.4%	62.0%
Parkersburg-Vienna, WV	48	0.2%	100.0%	0.0%	0.0%	na	na	na	na	na
Pensacola-Ferry Pass-Brent, FL	3,092	2.4%	23.3%	36.8%	39.8%	7,973	6.3%	15.3%	53.4%	31.3%
Peoria, IL	3,006	3.1%	2.2%	17.2%	80.6%	5,110	5.3%	26.6%	56.6%	16.9%
Philadelphia-Camden-Wilmington, PA-NJ-DE-MD	96,526	6.1%	21.6%	31.9%	46.6%	178,046	11.3%	26.1%	36.6%	37.3%
Phoenix-Mesa-Scottsdale, AZ	38,777	3.3%	22.7%	33.4%	44.0%	437,985	37.8%	29.2%	37.5%	33.4%
Pine Bluff, AR	65	0.3%	0.0%	0.0%	100.0%	694	2.7%	0.0%	28.1%	71.9%
Pittsburgh, PA	17,002	3.0%	14.1%	37.6%	48.2%	11,874	2.1%	19.6%	42.1%	38.3%
Pittsfield, MA	987	3.2%	16.6%	47.1%	36.3%	1,625	5.3%	20.9%	45.8%	33.2%
Pocatello, ID	367	1.4%	0.0%	67.3%	32.7%	3,512	13.7%	30.9%	55.6%	13.5%
Port St. Lucie, FL	1,983	2.2%	15.1%	42.7%	42.3%	21,235	23.4%	31.5%	33.1%	35.4%
Portland-South Portland, ME	2,642	2.2%	4.8%	79.6%	15.6%	4,316	3.7%	28.4%	64.6%	7.1%
Portland-Vancouver-Hillsboro, OR-WA	36,352	6.3%	25.0%	31.9%	43.1%	83,654	14.4%	28.7%	36.6%	34.7%
Pottsville, PA micro	63	0.2%	0.0%	0.0%	100.0%	850	2.8%	17.3%	42.4%	40.4%
Prescott, AZ	649	1.6%	0.0%	0.0%	100.0%	9,608	23.8%	27.7%	34.0%	38.3%
Providence-Warwick, RI-MA	12,458	3.0%	16.0%	49.9%	34.1%	63,261	15.3%	25.9%	40.7%	33.4%
Provo-Orem, UT	5,441	2.7%	15.8%	45.5%	38.7%	21,429	10.5%	24.1%	43.0%	32.9%
Pueblo, CO	283	0.7%	49.8%	0.0%	50.2%	20,424	49.5%	26.5%	39.5%	34.0%
Punta Gorda, FL	362	1.4%	63.3%	36.7%	0.0%	2,781	10.7%	33.1%	60.5%	6.4%
Racine, WI	na	na	na	na	na	7,795	17.1%	23.8%	22.6%	53.5%
Raleigh, NC	15,369	4.8%	29.7%	28.1%	42.2%	39,979	12.5%	28.0%	39.8%	32.2%
Rapid City, SD	316	0.9%	0.0%	66.1%	33.9%	761	2.2%	29.6%	24.7%	45.7%
Reading, PA	1,540	1.5%	20.7%	48.6%	30.6%	25,187	24.3%	31.7%	39.5%	28.8%
Redding, CA	2,143	5.0%	3.1%	79.3%	17.6%	5,404	12.5%	32.1%	42.8%	25.1%
Reno, NV	5,149	4.5%	34.1%	30.6%	35.3%	33,812	29.7%	28.4%	40.1%	31.5%

Table B-4: Metropolitan/Micropolitan Statistical Areas—Race and Hispanic Origin by Age—*Continued*

	White, Non-Hispanic				Black, Non-Hispanic				
	Millennial Population		Percent by Age			Millennial Population		Percent by Age		
	Number	Percent	13 to 17	18 to 24	25 to 31	Number	Percent	13 to 17	18 to 24	25 to 31
Richmond, VA............................	166,355	52.2%	27.2%	33.4%	39.4%	103,934	32.6%	24.7%	40.4%	34.9%
Riverside-San Bernardino-Ontario, CA.................	328,064	26.5%	25.0%	37.3%	37.7%	97,363	7.9%	26.7%	40.4%	32.9%
Roanoke, VA.............................	55,452	77.7%	27.8%	35.7%	36.5%	7,985	11.2%	25.9%	56.2%	17.9%
Rochester, MN..........................	42,309	81.3%	25.0%	36.2%	38.8%	3,655	7.0%	25.7%	57.0%	17.3%
Rochester, NY..........................	206,471	72.9%	24.3%	40.6%	35.1%	34,132	12.1%	27.7%	37.0%	35.3%
Rockford, IL.............................	54,720	63.3%	31.1%	35.6%	33.3%	11,229	13.0%	24.8%	48.0%	27.3%
Rocky Mount, NC......................	13,406	38.6%	30.5%	40.3%	29.2%	17,628	50.7%	26.9%	42.8%	30.3%
Rome, GA...............................	17,399	72.9%	23.8%	45.9%	30.3%	2,719	11.4%	26.1%	40.7%	33.1%
Roseburg, OR micro..................	17,062	82.3%	25.8%	38.0%	36.1%	33	0.2%	33.3%	0.0%	66.7%
Sacramento–Roseville–Arden-Arcade, CA..........	264,906	46.2%	25.2%	36.0%	38.8%	46,070	8.0%	28.4%	43.1%	28.5%
Saginaw, MI............................	32,266	64.7%	25.5%	40.3%	34.2%	10,980	22.0%	28.7%	46.3%	25.0%
Salem, OH micro.......................	21,294	89.3%	30.6%	35.3%	34.1%	896	3.8%	6.0%	12.7%	81.3%
Salem, OR...............................	65,568	61.4%	24.4%	40.5%	35.0%	1,130	1.1%	17.4%	22.3%	60.3%
Salinas, CA.............................	27,842	22.6%	21.5%	38.8%	39.7%	3,052	2.5%	28.9%	53.8%	17.2%
Salisbury, MD-DE......................	54,569	61.1%	22.5%	43.8%	33.7%	20,758	23.2%	22.0%	50.1%	27.9%
Salt Lake City, UT.....................	225,101	69.8%	25.7%	33.1%	41.2%	4,714	1.5%	36.4%	27.6%	36.0%
San Angelo, TX........................	16,805	48.1%	17.2%	45.0%	37.7%	1,578	4.5%	4.3%	45.1%	50.6%
San Antonio-New Braunfels, TX....	188,794	29.3%	23.5%	36.7%	39.7%	40,841	6.3%	23.6%	42.7%	33.7%
San Diego-Carlsbad, CA.............	375,833	40.2%	17.5%	39.0%	43.5%	47,895	5.1%	21.8%	42.2%	36.0%
San Francisco-Oakland-Hayward, CA.................	383,327	34.5%	21.4%	31.4%	47.2%	90,636	8.2%	25.4%	41.4%	33.2%
San Jose-Sunnyvale-Santa Clara, CA....	131,143	27.4%	22.5%	34.6%	42.9%	12,729	2.7%	14.4%	39.2%	46.3%
San Luis Obispo-Paso Robles-Arroyo Grande, CA	51,767	64.2%	17.6%	54.8%	27.6%	2,329	2.9%	3.6%	84.0%	12.4%
Santa Cruz-Watsonville, CA..........	36,663	48.6%	17.7%	55.2%	27.2%	544	0.7%	44.9%	40.6%	14.5%
Santa Fe, NM..........................	7,826	26.1%	23.7%	36.1%	40.2%	106	0.4%	0.0%	100.0%	0.0%
Santa Maria-Santa Barbara, CA......	52,920	38.6%	14.6%	55.9%	29.5%	2,497	1.8%	29.0%	54.6%	16.3%
Santa Rosa, CA........................	65,269	54.0%	25.0%	38.0%	37.0%	2,305	1.9%	26.7%	40.4%	32.9%
Savannah, GA..........................	48,944	46.6%	16.7%	41.9%	41.4%	41,921	39.9%	24.0%	41.4%	34.6%
Scranton–Wilkes-Barre–Hazleton, PA	110,303	81.4%	23.6%	42.0%	34.4%	6,303	4.7%	19.9%	40.7%	39.4%
Seattle-Tacoma-Bellevue, WA........	566,256	60.5%	22.4%	33.9%	43.8%	55,074	5.9%	23.7%	35.1%	41.2%
Sebastian-Vero Beach, FL	17,415	63.3%	29.9%	33.7%	36.4%	4,173	15.2%	53.2%	26.7%	20.1%
Sebring, FL.............................	7,417	43.1%	34.4%	27.6%	37.9%	2,432	14.1%	12.9%	54.0%	33.1%
Sheboygan, WI.........................	20,226	79.6%	30.8%	33.9%	35.3%	46	0.2%	0.0%	100.0%	0.0%
Sherman-Denison, TX.................	20,525	67.7%	26.4%	39.3%	34.2%	2,601	8.6%	20.5%	52.1%	27.5%
Show Low, AZ micro..................	5,883	20.8%	32.1%	36.8%	31.1%	345	1.2%	44.6%	26.1%	29.3%
Shreveport-Bossier City, LA..........	57,199	46.4%	21.7%	36.8%	41.5%	55,182	44.7%	24.5%	43.3%	32.2%
Sierra Vista-Douglas, AZ.............	12,033	37.2%	21.6%	39.2%	39.2%	651	2.0%	14.3%	41.5%	44.2%
Sioux City, IA-NE-SD..................	32,314	73.2%	27.5%	40.4%	32.1%	945	2.1%	23.5%	32.5%	44.0%
Sioux Falls, SD........................	54,723	86.5%	21.3%	37.8%	40.9%	1,610	2.5%	0.0%	43.7%	56.3%
South Bend-Mishawaka, IN-MI	61,046	74.4%	27.3%	38.2%	34.5%	9,996	12.2%	30.4%	45.3%	24.3%
Spartanburg, SC.......................	52,070	61.3%	26.1%	38.7%	35.1%	19,087	22.5%	26.2%	44.5%	29.3%
Spokane-Spokane Valley, WA........	118,939	80.8%	24.9%	36.8%	38.3%	4,161	2.8%	27.3%	29.4%	43.3%
Springfield, IL.........................	37,585	74.9%	24.7%	35.7%	39.6%	7,914	15.8%	29.7%	35.5%	34.8%
Springfield, MA........................	108,812	62.2%	22.1%	45.8%	32.1%	15,080	8.6%	27.7%	52.5%	19.8%
Springfield, MO........................	114,267	88.3%	23.6%	41.5%	34.9%	4,387	3.4%	20.4%	60.0%	19.6%
Springfield, OH........................	27,138	82.3%	29.3%	35.2%	35.4%	3,403	10.3%	26.6%	50.5%	22.9%
St. Cloud, MN..........................	50,775	86.1%	20.4%	48.9%	30.7%	2,660	4.5%	40.3%	30.7%	29.0%
St. George, UT.........................	30,264	83.0%	31.8%	34.8%	33.3%	513	1.4%	0.0%	82.5%	17.5%
St. Joseph, MO-KS....................	26,777	83.2%	27.5%	37.5%	35.1%	2,215	6.9%	1.5%	62.4%	36.1%
St. Louis, MO-IL.......................	480,860	68.6%	25.3%	34.5%	40.2%	153,784	21.9%	27.0%	40.5%	32.5%
State College, PA......................	51,551	79.2%	11.7%	65.4%	22.9%	3,046	4.7%	2.1%	76.7%	21.2%
Staunton-Waynesboro, VA............	22,216	82.1%	20.7%	47.2%	32.1%	2,271	8.4%	17.4%	52.7%	29.9%
Stockton-Lodi, CA.....................	51,946	26.9%	26.7%	37.6%	35.7%	11,023	5.7%	27.5%	47.0%	25.5%
Sumter, SC.............................	11,125	36.6%	17.1%	43.0%	39.8%	16,665	54.8%	29.4%	45.8%	24.8%
Sunbury, PA micro.....................	17,988	90.0%	23.9%	37.5%	38.6%	1,052	5.3%	8.0%	53.5%	38.5%
Syracuse, NY...........................	133,715	78.6%	25.7%	40.1%	34.2%	13,590	8.0%	23.7%	44.0%	32.3%
Tallahassee, FL........................	72,285	52.6%	14.6%	56.1%	29.3%	47,314	34.4%	17.8%	53.7%	28.5%
Tampa-St. Petersburg-Clearwater, FL....	379,742	56.6%	24.4%	35.5%	40.1%	97,248	14.5%	25.5%	38.9%	35.6%
Terre Haute, IN........................	39,392	84.2%	21.1%	44.2%	34.7%	3,555	7.6%	5.9%	60.0%	34.1%
Texarkana, TX-AR......................	24,698	64.0%	26.8%	32.5%	40.6%	9,334	24.2%	19.2%	45.2%	35.6%
The Villages, FL........................	7,524	66.2%	13.1%	36.2%	50.8%	2,488	21.9%	20.3%	32.2%	47.5%
Toledo, OH.............................	121,221	71.1%	22.9%	42.0%	35.1%	28,436	16.7%	22.9%	48.3%	28.8%
Topeka, KS..............................	41,006	75.5%	29.2%	31.7%	39.1%	2,727	5.0%	37.8%	51.6%	10.6%
Torrington, CT micro..................	33,406	84.9%	30.7%	35.5%	33.7%	857	2.2%	13.7%	35.2%	51.1%
Traverse City, MI micro...............	29,500	92.7%	30.0%	35.5%	34.5%	552	1.7%	1.3%	55.8%	42.9%
Trenton, NJ.............................	45,570	46.8%	23.6%	44.7%	31.7%	20,495	21.1%	29.6%	41.8%	28.6%
Truckee-Grass Valley, CA micro	14,513	75.8%	27.3%	34.5%	38.3%	74	0.4%	100.0%	0.0%	0.0%
Tucson, AZ.............................	115,844	42.5%	19.1%	45.6%	35.3%	10,517	3.9%	17.6%	50.9%	31.6%
Tullahoma-Manchester, TN micro	19,875	83.6%	36.7%	35.7%	27.6%	1,781	7.5%	43.0%	56.0%	1.1%
Tulsa, OK...............................	141,952	58.5%	25.7%	34.8%	39.4%	22,691	9.3%	30.4%	39.5%	30.1%
Tupelo, MS micro......................	22,390	63.3%	31.1%	38.2%	30.7%	10,136	28.7%	28.2%	44.4%	27.4%
Tuscaloosa, AL.........................	47,133	60.6%	16.2%	53.9%	29.9%	25,764	33.1%	23.0%	47.4%	29.6%
Tyler, TX................................	30,863	53.8%	25.1%	37.1%	37.8%	12,513	21.8%	26.8%	42.7%	30.5%
Urban Honolulu, HI....................	60,915	22.9%	9.7%	37.7%	52.6%	11,770	4.4%	13.1%	40.8%	46.2%
Utica-Rome, NY........................	59,849	81.2%	25.4%	37.9%	36.6%	4,134	5.6%	20.3%	42.9%	36.9%
Valdosta, GA...........................	25,921	52.9%	17.1%	51.9%	30.9%	17,366	35.5%	20.1%	50.4%	29.5%
Vallejo-Fairfield, CA...................	39,091	34.2%	20.4%	36.2%	43.5%	15,575	13.6%	28.9%	39.7%	31.4%
Victoria, TX............................	9,675	38.6%	30.4%	35.6%	34.0%	2,583	10.3%	65.4%	30.9%	3.7%
Vineland-Bridgeton, NJ................	18,592	45.2%	26.6%	36.8%	36.5%	8,777	21.3%	28.4%	29.8%	41.8%
Virginia Beach-Norfolk-Newport News, VA-NC	254,087	51.0%	19.3%	40.2%	40.5%	162,957	32.7%	23.7%	41.7%	34.7%

Table B-4: Metropolitan/Micropolitan Statistical Areas—Race and Hispanic Origin by Age—*Continued*

	Asian, Non-Hispanic					Hispanic				
	Millennial Population		Percent by Age			Millennial Population		Percent by Age		
	Number	Percent	13 to 17	18 to 24	25 to 31	Number	Percent	13 to 17	18 to 24	25 to 31
Richmond, VA	12,970	4.1%	22.5%	39.8%	37.6%	23,411	7.4%	27.4%	36.8%	35.8%
Riverside-San Bernardino-Ontario, CA	65,750	5.3%	18.8%	41.8%	39.5%	702,560	56.8%	29.2%	38.3%	32.5%
Roanoke, VA	1,943	2.7%	14.7%	29.7%	55.6%	3,767	5.3%	21.0%	41.4%	37.6%
Rochester, MN	2,504	4.8%	6.4%	26.8%	66.7%	2,624	5.0%	15.3%	60.7%	23.9%
Rochester, NY	9,939	3.5%	12.4%	43.5%	44.1%	24,281	8.6%	28.6%	38.6%	32.8%
Rockford, IL	2,523	2.9%	26.0%	22.0%	51.9%	15,603	18.0%	32.6%	44.1%	23.2%
Rocky Mount, NC	420	1.2%	46.2%	53.8%	0.0%	2,428	7.0%	42.2%	34.3%	23.5%
Rome, GA	270	1.1%	0.0%	28.5%	71.5%	2,913	12.2%	45.0%	22.5%	32.5%
Roseburg, OR micro	323	1.6%	0.0%	100.0%	0.0%	1,648	7.9%	26.0%	26.4%	47.6%
Sacramento–Roseville–Arden-Arcade, CA	76,539	13.4%	24.9%	39.4%	35.7%	146,264	25.5%	28.6%	36.3%	35.1%
Saginaw, MI	620	1.2%	46.3%	15.8%	37.9%	4,269	8.6%	23.5%	56.4%	20.1%
Salem, OH micro	174	0.7%	0.0%	50.6%	49.4%	1,093	4.6%	0.0%	47.2%	52.8%
Salem, OR	831	0.8%	0.0%	49.1%	50.9%	31,965	29.9%	32.4%	41.6%	26.1%
Salinas, CA	6,105	4.9%	18.1%	51.3%	30.7%	82,181	66.6%	28.2%	36.5%	35.3%
Salisbury, MD-DE	2,392	2.7%	6.6%	35.6%	57.8%	9,708	10.9%	26.3%	32.9%	40.8%
Salt Lake City, UT	12,834	4.0%	15.7%	34.0%	50.3%	62,941	19.5%	28.5%	38.2%	33.4%
San Angelo, TX	319	0.9%	25.1%	74.9%	0.0%	15,366	43.9%	29.4%	34.2%	36.3%
San Antonio-New Braunfels, TX	14,502	2.3%	13.4%	37.3%	49.3%	380,785	59.2%	27.6%	37.6%	34.9%
San Diego-Carlsbad, CA	99,298	10.6%	18.1%	36.0%	45.9%	363,167	38.8%	25.0%	39.5%	35.5%
San Francisco-Oakland-Hayward, CA	253,268	22.8%	20.4%	34.2%	45.5%	312,941	28.2%	23.3%	36.2%	40.6%
San Jose-Sunnyvale-Santa Clara, CA	148,201	30.9%	22.0%	30.0%	47.9%	163,989	34.2%	26.3%	37.8%	35.9%
San Luis Obispo-Paso Robles-Arroyo Grande, CA	4,540	5.6%	6.3%	69.1%	24.6%	19,635	24.3%	16.0%	46.1%	37.9%
Santa Cruz-Watsonville, CA	5,106	6.8%	6.3%	79.2%	14.5%	29,914	39.7%	21.2%	44.9%	33.8%
Santa Fe, NM	534	1.8%	47.4%	8.8%	43.8%	19,527	65.2%	29.0%	38.1%	32.9%
Santa Maria-Santa Barbara, CA	8,352	6.1%	10.1%	67.7%	22.2%	69,576	50.7%	27.3%	41.9%	30.8%
Santa Rosa, CA	5,322	4.4%	17.5%	45.0%	37.5%	41,916	34.7%	28.3%	37.1%	34.6%
Savannah, GA	2,637	2.5%	10.3%	69.6%	20.1%	7,464	7.1%	12.1%	32.0%	55.9%
Scranton–Wilkes-Barre–Hazleton, PA	2,459	1.8%	18.5%	37.9%	43.7%	13,415	9.9%	31.1%	39.1%	29.8%
Seattle-Tacoma-Bellevue, WA	117,977	12.6%	21.2%	32.7%	46.1%	112,380	12.0%	23.8%	35.7%	40.5%
Sebastian-Vero Beach, FL	389	1.4%	33.9%	34.4%	31.6%	4,416	16.1%	18.1%	45.5%	36.5%
Sebring, FL	83	0.5%	0.0%	100.0%	0.0%	6,985	40.6%	22.2%	45.7%	32.1%
Sheboygan, WI	2,112	8.3%	30.5%	32.2%	37.3%	2,178	8.6%	48.6%	10.7%	40.8%
Sherman-Denison, TX	744	2.5%	12.5%	62.6%	24.9%	5,272	17.4%	26.6%	15.8%	57.6%
Show Low, AZ micro	39	0.1%	0.0%	100.0%	0.0%	2,716	9.6%	13.3%	38.5%	48.2%
Shreveport-Bossier City, LA	956	0.8%	7.1%	13.0%	79.9%	6,602	5.4%	16.7%	36.3%	47.0%
Sierra Vista-Douglas, AZ	261	0.8%	0.0%	0.0%	100.0%	17,562	54.3%	27.1%	38.9%	34.0%
Sioux City, IA-NE-SD	937	2.1%	24.3%	53.1%	22.5%	7,007	15.9%	41.0%	27.4%	31.6%
Sioux Falls, SD	1,667	2.6%	0.0%	49.1%	50.9%	2,638	4.2%	29.6%	33.7%	36.7%
South Bend-Mishawaka, IN-MI	1,851	2.3%	28.4%	55.2%	16.4%	7,054	8.6%	42.3%	42.9%	14.8%
Spartanburg, SC	3,398	4.0%	31.7%	50.7%	17.6%	7,679	9.0%	39.0%	28.9%	32.1%
Spokane-Spokane Valley, WA	3,406	2.3%	16.5%	54.1%	29.4%	11,491	7.8%	22.6%	41.4%	36.0%
Springfield, IL	912	1.8%	7.0%	43.3%	49.7%	2,226	4.4%	21.5%	37.0%	41.6%
Springfield, MA	6,085	3.5%	18.9%	61.8%	19.2%	42,678	24.4%	31.8%	39.8%	28.4%
Springfield, MO	1,356	1.0%	10.3%	61.8%	27.9%	4,888	3.8%	27.9%	55.2%	16.9%
Springfield, OH	87	0.3%	66.7%	33.3%	0.0%	1,699	5.2%	35.2%	33.1%	31.7%
St. Cloud, MN	819	1.4%	0.0%	76.1%	23.9%	2,839	4.8%	8.9%	57.5%	33.6%
St. George, UT	54	0.1%	0.0%	0.0%	100.0%	4,039	11.1%	14.8%	85.2%	0.0%
St. Joseph, MO-KS	63	0.2%	0.0%	0.0%	100.0%	1,939	6.0%	0.0%	29.8%	70.2%
St. Louis, MO-IL	21,113	3.0%	19.6%	31.3%	49.1%	24,546	3.5%	23.7%	33.3%	43.0%
State College, PA	7,054	10.8%	7.6%	76.0%	16.4%	2,385	3.7%	15.3%	83.1%	1.7%
Staunton-Waynesboro, VA	1,370	5.1%	6.9%	93.1%	0.0%	261	1.0%	0.0%	36.4%	63.6%
Stockton-Lodi, CA	28,843	14.9%	26.7%	41.4%	31.9%	91,727	47.5%	33.1%	36.9%	30.0%
Sumter, SC	103	0.3%	27.2%	72.8%	0.0%	1,516	5.0%	24.2%	40.7%	35.1%
Sunbury, PA micro	68	0.3%	0.0%	0.0%	100.0%	746	3.7%	0.0%	44.2%	55.8%
Syracuse, NY	6,013	3.5%	14.7%	50.7%	34.6%	8,345	4.9%	24.3%	56.3%	19.4%
Tallahassee, FL	3,167	2.3%	7.5%	47.4%	45.2%	10,330	7.5%	10.6%	59.7%	29.7%
Tampa-St. Petersburg-Clearwater, FL	21,114	3.1%	24.4%	32.5%	43.1%	148,488	22.2%	27.0%	37.5%	35.5%
Terre Haute, IN	404	0.9%	22.8%	48.0%	29.2%	1,917	4.1%	12.8%	44.7%	42.6%
Texarkana, TX-AR	80	0.2%	53.8%	0.0%	46.3%	3,589	9.3%	4.0%	45.2%	50.7%
The Villages, FL	na	na	na	na	na	969	8.5%	45.6%	30.8%	23.6%
Toledo, OH	3,028	1.8%	15.9%	50.1%	33.9%	13,905	8.2%	33.8%	33.6%	32.6%
Topeka, KS	872	1.6%	3.3%	96.7%	0.0%	5,753	10.6%	19.0%	48.7%	32.3%
Torrington, CT micro	1,577	4.0%	53.5%	14.6%	31.9%	2,670	6.8%	20.9%	32.8%	46.3%
Traverse City, MI micro	175	0.5%	41.1%	0.0%	58.9%	155	0.5%	87.7%	0.0%	12.3%
Trenton, NJ	9,662	9.9%	22.9%	35.1%	42.1%	19,207	19.7%	26.2%	37.1%	36.7%
Truckee-Grass Valley, CA micro	na	na	na	na	na	3,897	20.4%	35.1%	57.2%	7.7%
Tucson, AZ	8,998	3.3%	9.0%	50.2%	40.9%	119,423	43.8%	27.7%	42.3%	30.0%
Tullahoma-Manchester, TN micro	234	1.0%	63.7%	0.0%	36.3%	772	3.2%	15.9%	15.2%	68.9%
Tulsa, OK	4,927	2.0%	21.2%	32.5%	46.3%	28,250	11.6%	27.2%	35.7%	37.1%
Tupelo, MS micro	45	0.1%	0.0%	0.0%	100.0%	2,253	6.4%	2.8%	47.4%	49.8%
Tuscaloosa, AL	747	1.0%	21.4%	54.6%	24.0%	2,789	3.6%	11.5%	42.0%	46.5%
Tyler, TX	402	0.7%	35.1%	44.5%	20.4%	13,315	23.2%	31.2%	38.2%	30.6%
Urban Honolulu, HI	78,920	29.7%	23.6%	35.4%	41.0%	32,297	12.1%	20.5%	41.9%	37.5%
Utica-Rome, NY	2,019	2.7%	47.4%	41.3%	11.4%	3,908	5.3%	31.5%	46.8%	21.7%
Valdosta, GA	825	1.7%	37.5%	36.1%	26.4%	3,269	6.7%	26.2%	41.1%	32.7%
Vallejo-Fairfield, CA	14,861	13.0%	29.1%	31.3%	39.6%	35,113	30.7%	26.8%	38.9%	34.4%
Victoria, TX	928	3.7%	40.7%	22.1%	37.2%	11,783	47.0%	24.9%	41.2%	33.9%
Vineland-Bridgeton, NJ	387	0.9%	0.0%	0.0%	100.0%	11,573	28.1%	18.6%	28.4%	53.0%
Virginia Beach-Norfolk-Newport News, VA-NC	17,086	3.4%	20.0%	38.2%	41.8%	41,923	8.4%	18.7%	41.7%	39.6%

Table B-4: Metropolitan/Micropolitan Statistical Areas—Race and Hispanic Origin by Age—*Continued*

	White, Non-Hispanic					Black, Non-Hispanic				
	Millennial Population		Percent by Age			Millennial Population		Percent by Age		
	Number	Percent	13 to 17	18 to 24	25 to 31	Number	Percent	13 to 17	18 to 24	25 to 31
Visalia-Porterville, CA	30,561	23.1%	25.2%	35.8%	39.0%	2,583	2.0%	48.9%	37.2%	13.9%
Waco, TX	42,385	54.9%	18.0%	50.6%	31.5%	10,111	13.1%	21.1%	49.5%	29.4%
Walla Walla, WA	9,896	59.1%	18.5%	42.1%	39.3%	304	1.8%	0.0%	53.0%	47.0%
Warner Robins, GA	29,643	55.1%	23.5%	36.1%	40.4%	17,122	31.8%	29.3%	45.3%	25.4%
Washington-Arlington-Alexandria, DC-VA-MD-WV	693,159	44.5%	22.5%	33.0%	44.5%	403,725	25.9%	25.6%	38.0%	36.4%
Waterloo-Cedar Falls, IA	42,760	81.8%	20.2%	51.3%	28.5%	4,914	9.4%	24.6%	54.9%	20.5%
Watertown-Fort Drum, NY	28,817	78.6%	23.3%	40.5%	36.2%	2,196	6.0%	1.1%	42.4%	56.4%
Wausau, WI	26,080	82.7%	30.2%	34.2%	35.6%	294	0.9%	0.0%	41.5%	58.5%
Weirton-Steubenville, WV-OH	25,340	89.7%	29.9%	39.9%	30.2%	1,911	6.8%	17.3%	65.5%	17.2%
Wenatchee, WA	15,364	54.9%	29.3%	33.5%	37.2%	279	1.0%	0.0%	100.0%	0.0%
Wheeling, WV-OH	29,061	89.6%	30.1%	38.9%	31.0%	1,939	6.0%	21.3%	61.7%	17.0%
Whitewater-Elkhorn, WI micro	22,808	84.1%	24.3%	45.7%	30.0%	427	1.6%	75.4%	12.4%	12.2%
Wichita Falls, TX	28,665	64.0%	21.2%	41.5%	37.3%	5,054	11.3%	15.4%	45.4%	39.2%
Wichita, KS	114,655	68.0%	26.4%	34.3%	39.3%	14,491	8.6%	25.0%	31.5%	43.5%
Williamsport, PA	25,285	90.7%	21.7%	48.9%	29.4%	1,391	5.0%	16.1%	52.0%	31.8%
Wilmington, NC	51,964	73.8%	17.5%	46.5%	36.1%	9,425	13.4%	25.6%	37.5%	36.9%
Winchester, VA-WV	22,730	77.9%	31.0%	35.2%	33.8%	1,342	4.6%	19.7%	60.1%	20.3%
Winston-Salem, NC	97,451	62.2%	28.9%	36.7%	34.5%	31,732	20.2%	27.1%	42.4%	30.5%
Wooster, OH micro	26,675	93.7%	30.2%	40.5%	29.3%	557	2.0%	40.6%	27.1%	32.3%
Worcester, MA-CT	172,435	75.5%	28.4%	38.3%	33.3%	11,014	4.8%	23.7%	51.0%	25.3%
Yakima, WA	21,994	33.3%	27.1%	37.1%	35.8%	304	0.5%	0.0%	50.0%	50.0%
York-Hanover, PA	78,365	80.3%	26.8%	36.5%	36.7%	5,591	5.7%	24.5%	48.9%	26.6%
Youngstown-Warren-Boardman, OH-PA	102,161	78.6%	29.7%	37.0%	33.3%	16,666	12.8%	28.6%	37.5%	34.0%
Yuba City, CA	20,117	45.4%	25.7%	37.0%	37.3%	1,677	3.8%	23.2%	36.5%	40.3%
Yuma, AZ	13,054	22.0%	18.1%	41.3%	40.6%	1,202	2.0%	8.8%	44.1%	47.1%

Table B-4: Metropolitan/Micropolitan Statistical Areas—Race and Hispanic Origin by Age—*Continued*

	Asian, Non-Hispanic					Hispanic				
	Millennial Population		Percent by Age			Millennial Population		Percent by Age		
	Number	Percent	13 to 17	18 to 24	25 to 31	Number	Percent	13 to 17	18 to 24	25 to 31
Visalia-Porterville, CA..	5,269	4.0%	23.3%	28.1%	48.6%	90,961	68.8%	28.3%	38.6%	33.1%
Waco, TX..	2,137	2.8%	11.7%	80.1%	8.2%	21,379	27.7%	22.7%	44.6%	32.7%
Walla Walla, WA..	169	1.0%	30.2%	0.0%	69.8%	5,473	32.7%	27.8%	40.9%	31.3%
Warner Robins, GA	899	1.7%	30.4%	18.2%	51.4%	5,235	9.7%	33.2%	22.0%	44.9%
Washington-Arlington-Alexandria, DC-VA-MD-WV	138,126	8.9%	23.5%	32.5%	44.0%	260,813	16.7%	23.0%	35.2%	41.8%
Waterloo-Cedar Falls, IA....................................	628	1.2%	0.0%	79.8%	20.2%	3,727	7.1%	4.1%	55.5%	40.4%
Watertown-Fort Drum, NY	224	0.6%	0.0%	100.0%	0.0%	3,021	8.2%	19.8%	36.9%	43.3%
Wausau, WI..	3,421	10.8%	29.8%	55.0%	15.3%	979	3.1%	17.8%	18.8%	63.4%
Weirton-Steubenville, WV-OH	128	0.5%	0.0%	100.0%	0.0%	346	1.2%	16.2%	83.8%	0.0%
Wenatchee, WA..	na	na	na	na	na	10,620	38.0%	29.5%	25.8%	44.8%
Wheeling, WV-OH	128	0.4%	0.0%	100.0%	0.0%	580	1.8%	9.7%	50.0%	40.3%
Whitewater-Elkhorn, WI micro	251	0.9%	0.0%	0.0%	100.0%	2,841	10.5%	27.7%	27.5%	44.8%
Wichita Falls, TX	647	1.4%	46.4%	24.1%	29.5%	8,555	19.1%	17.0%	47.7%	35.3%
Wichita, KS..	6,731	4.0%	20.1%	33.1%	46.8%	26,901	16.0%	31.8%	35.2%	33.1%
Williamsport, PA	na	na	na	na	na	308	1.1%	0.0%	82.5%	17.5%
Wilmington, NC..	1,919	2.7%	26.0%	60.8%	13.2%	4,517	6.4%	16.4%	57.1%	26.5%
Winchester, VA-WV..	616	2.1%	14.8%	15.6%	69.6%	3,452	11.8%	41.3%	40.8%	17.9%
Winston-Salem, NC..	2,809	1.8%	37.0%	41.7%	21.3%	19,683	12.6%	32.4%	39.3%	28.3%
Wooster, OH micro..	438	1.5%	0.0%	19.4%	80.6%	568	2.0%	35.6%	0.0%	64.4%
Worcester, MA-CT..	9,482	4.2%	19.4%	31.5%	49.0%	29,802	13.1%	22.8%	41.1%	36.1%
Yakima, WA..	578	0.9%	13.3%	68.2%	18.5%	39,337	59.6%	29.4%	38.4%	32.2%
York-Hanover, PA...	1,505	1.5%	55.3%	21.3%	23.3%	9,903	10.1%	27.5%	46.0%	26.5%
Youngstown-Warren-Boardman, OH-PA	1,630	1.3%	35.3%	40.7%	24.0%	5,977	4.6%	21.4%	32.9%	45.7%
Yuba City, CA	5,664	12.8%	16.9%	38.1%	45.0%	14,490	32.7%	32.2%	40.6%	27.1%
Yuma, AZ	606	1.0%	7.6%	54.6%	37.8%	42,979	72.4%	29.9%	40.1%	30.0%

na = not available

PART C
NATIVITY AND WORLD REGION OF BIRTH

NATIVITY AND WORLD REGION OF BIRTH

The U.S. Department of Homeland Security publishes the annual *Yearbook of Immigration Statistics*, which is a compendium of data on legal permanent admissions as well as many other categories of entry for foreign nationals. Between 2008 and 2013, legal permanent admissions averaged just over 1 million per year. During that same period, the number of persons age 15 to 34 averaged nearly 450,000 or more than 40 percent of all legal permanent admissions.[1] This high percentage of foreign immigrants in the Millennial age categories implies two important trends: the Millennial generation will continue to grow as a result of foreign immigration, and it will grow more diverse than it already is.

1. U.S. Department of Homeland Security, *Yearbook of Immigration Statistics: 2008–2013*, Table 8.

Nativity in the American Community Survey is based on the answers to the question on place of birth—either in the United States or outside the United States. If born outside of the United States, respondents then indicate their foreign country of birth or U.S. territory (Puerto Rico, Guam, etc.). Persons are classified as either native or foreign born based on this and the question on citizenship. The foreign born population includes anyone who was not a U.S. citizen at birth and is shown by country or region of birth. These data are useful in understanding immigration patterns, policy, and assimilation.

More than 9.5 million Millennials, or 11.6 percent, are foreign born. By world region of birth, Latin America is the origin for 54.4 percent of the foreign born, followed by Asia (27.5 percent), Europe (10.6 percent), Africa (5.3 percent), North America (1.6 percent) and Oceania (0.6 percent). This distribution shows the clear shift in

Percent of Millennials Who are Foreign Born

Percent

- 1.00% - 3.99%
- 4.00% - 6.99%
- 7.00% - 9.99%
- 10.00% - 13.99%
- 14.00% - 19.99%

immigration from European origins to Latin America and Asia among more recent immigrants.

New Jersey (19.3 percent) and California (19.2 percent) have the highest foreign born concentrations of Millennials. Montana is lowest at only 1.4 percent. Fourteen states are less than five percent foreign born while 18 states are over 10 percent. Latin America is the foreign origin for 13.2 percent of Florida's Millennial population, and California is the second highest at 11.8 percent. In Montana the Latin origin population is only 0.3 percent. Hawaii has the highest percentage of Millennials who are of Asian origin at 9.5 percent. Less than two percent of Millennials in 17 states are of Asian origin, and European origins are highest in the District of Columbia (3.0 percent). Minnesota's percentage of African origin Millennials is highest but only 2.6 percent. Hawaii is the only state with more than a fraction of Millennials from Oceania, at 2.7 percent.

Hudson County, NJ has the highest percentage of Millennials who are of foreign birth at 39.9 percent, and 11 counties are above 25 percent. Sixty-eight counties have less and two percent foreign born. Miami-Dade County, FL has the largest percentage of Millennials who are of Latin American birth at 33.5 percent and Imperial

County, CA is the next highest with 27.1 percent. Almost two-thirds of all counties (402) have less than five percent who originate in Latin America. Millennials of Asian origin are most prevalent (17.5 percent) in Santa Clara County, CA. Walworth County, WI has 6.2 percent of European origin, and Montgomery County, MD is highest for population of African origin. North American and Oceania origins both represent small percentages, with Beaufort County, SC (2.3 percent) highest for North America and Maui County, HI highest for Oceania (3.0 percent).

In 21 cities more than 30 percent of Millennials are of foreign birth. Hialeah City, FL is highest at 53.4 percent followed by Elizabeth City, NJ (46.0 percent) and Santa Clara City, CA (42.9 percent). The majority of Hialeah's foreign born Millennials have Latin American origins with 54.0 percent from that region. In 15 cities, Latin America is the origin of more than 25 percent of Millennials. Persons of Asian origin make up 36.4 percent in Sunnyvale City, CA, and only four other cities are above 25 percent: Bellevue City, WA (28.8 percent), Fremont City, CA (26.4 percent), Glendale City, CA (35.0 percent), and Santa Clara City, CA (32.5 percent). In Alexandria City, VA, Millennials of African origin make up 10.5 percent of the total. North American origins make

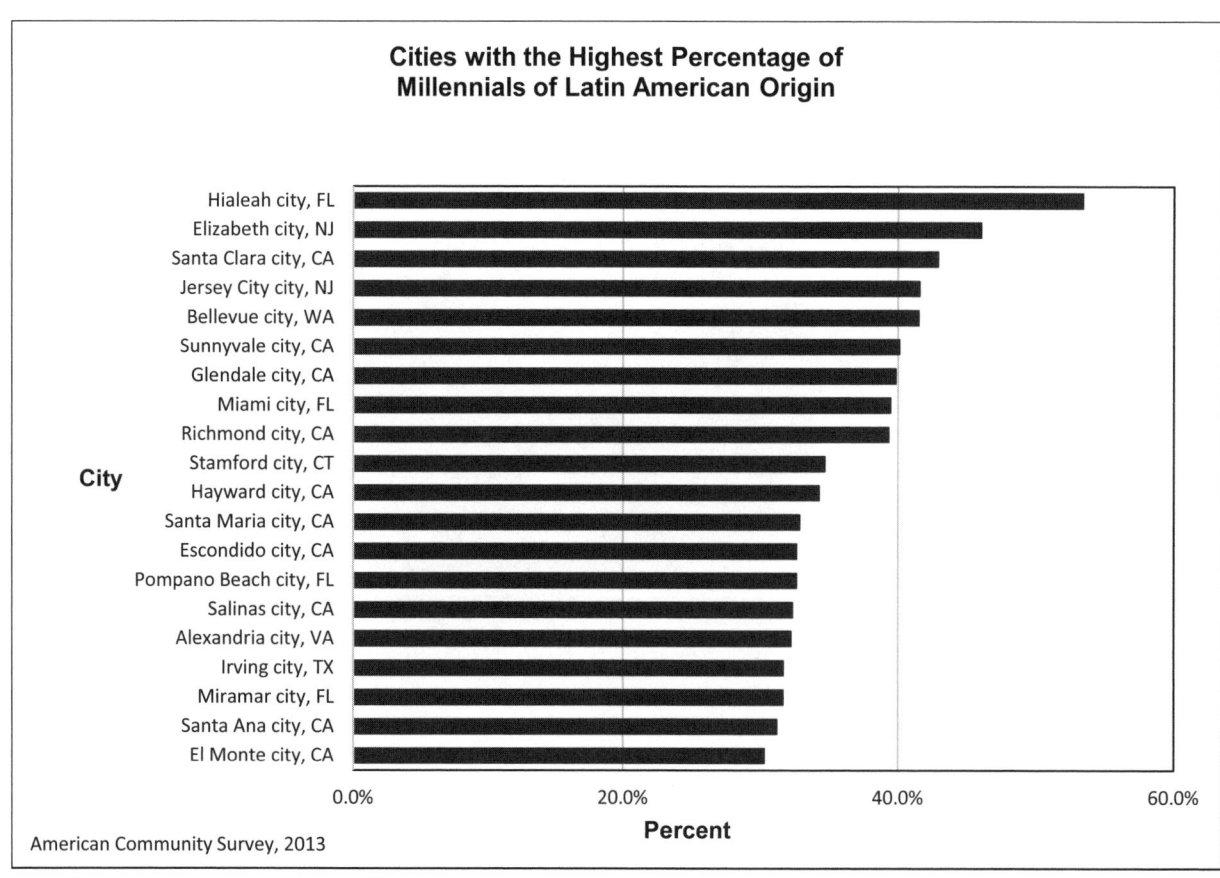

American Community Survey, 2013

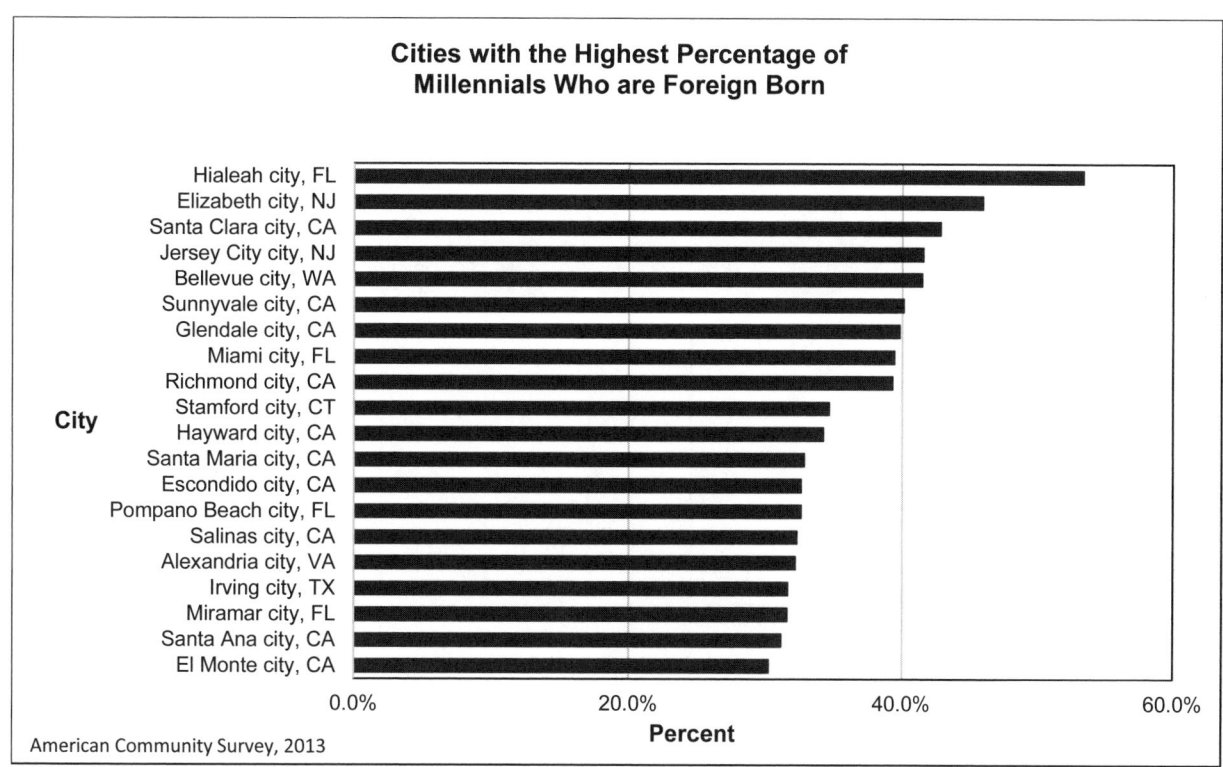

Cities with the Highest Percentage of Millennials Who are Foreign Born

American Community Survey, 2013

up 3.8 percent in Dearborn City, MI, and the Urban Honolulu CDP is highest for Oceania at 5.4 percent.

The San Jose-Sunnyvale, CA metropolitan area has the highest percentage of foreign born Millennials at 29.5 percent but is followed closely by the Miami-Fort Lauderdale, FL metro at 29.1 percent. Only 15 metro/micros are above 20 percent, while 314 are below 5 percent. In the El Centro, CA metro area Latin American Millennials make up 27.1 percent of the total. The Miami-Fort Lauderdale, FL metro is at 27.0 percent. Those of Asian origin make up 17.2 percent of the total in the San Jose-Sunnyvale, CA metro. In the Whitewater-Elkhorn, WI micropolitan area, European origins are highest at 6.2 percent, and at 4.2 percent, African origins are highest in the Rochester, MN metro area. Other North American and Oceania origins are again the lowest groups at 2.0 percent in the Hilton Head Island-Bluffton-Beaufort, SC metro and 2.8 percent in Kahululi-Wailuku-Lahaina, HI, respectively.

Table C-1: States—Nativity and World Region of Birth

	Total Millennial Population	Percent		Total Foreign Born	Percent of Foreign Born by Region of Birth					
		Native	Foreign Born		Latin America	Asia	Europe	Africa	North America	Oceania
United States	82,516,535	88.4%	11.6%	9,544,877	6.9%	3.5%	1.3%	0.7%	0.2%	0.1%
Alabama	1,243,909	95.7%	4.3%	52,925	3.0%	1.0%	0.8%	0.1%	0.1%	0.0%
Alaska	218,453	95.8%	4.2%	9,103	1.2%	2.6%	0.8%	0.2%	0.5%	0.0%
Arizona	1,743,604	88.2%	11.8%	205,463	8.4%	2.5%	1.1%	0.6%	0.2%	0.1%
Arkansas	754,902	93.6%	6.4%	48,519	4.9%	1.6%	0.5%	0.2%	0.1%	0.1%
California	10,563,495	80.8%	19.2%	2,027,943	11.8%	6.7%	1.1%	0.4%	0.2%	0.1%
Colorado	1,404,366	90.7%	9.3%	130,031	6.0%	2.2%	1.7%	0.7%	0.2%	0.1%
Connecticut	889,970	87.6%	12.4%	110,213	7.7%	3.5%	2.1%	0.4%	0.2%	0.0%
Delaware	234,000	90.2%	9.8%	23,007	4.2%	3.6%	1.1%	1.6%	0.1%	0.1%
District of Columbia	216,160	86.6%	13.4%	28,923	6.1%	3.2%	3.0%	2.4%	0.3%	0.1%
Florida	4,703,393	84.6%	15.4%	725,263	13.2%	1.8%	1.4%	0.3%	0.3%	0.0%
Georgia	2,675,903	90.4%	9.6%	258,164	5.9%	2.5%	1.3%	0.9%	0.2%	0.0%
Hawaii	371,155	87.9%	12.1%	44,786	1.0%	9.5%	1.0%	0.1%	0.2%	2.7%
Idaho	422,164	92.5%	7.5%	31,861	4.8%	2.1%	1.1%	0.4%	0.1%	0.0%
Illinois	3,382,854	88.4%	11.6%	393,658	5.9%	3.6%	2.2%	0.5%	0.1%	0.0%
Indiana	1,694,378	94.0%	6.0%	102,263	3.1%	2.2%	0.8%	0.4%	0.2%	0.0%
Iowa	791,151	92.7%	7.3%	57,695	2.8%	2.5%	1.3%	0.9%	0.4%	0.1%
Kansas	763,442	92.7%	7.3%	55,574	4.6%	2.2%	0.9%	0.4%	0.0%	0.0%
Kentucky	1,113,720	95.8%	4.2%	47,077	2.3%	1.5%	1.0%	0.3%	0.0%	0.0%
Louisiana	1,241,608	96.0%	4.0%	50,159	2.7%	1.3%	0.7%	0.1%	0.0%	0.0%
Maine	303,554	97.5%	2.5%	7,439	0.4%	1.5%	0.8%	0.6%	0.5%	0.0%
Maryland	1,527,405	86.9%	13.1%	199,477	6.3%	4.0%	1.7%	2.5%	0.1%	0.1%
Massachusetts	1,771,550	85.8%	14.2%	251,692	6.5%	4.7%	2.3%	1.3%	0.3%	0.1%
Michigan	2,496,925	94.5%	5.5%	137,739	1.3%	3.3%	1.0%	0.2%	0.5%	0.0%
Minnesota	1,394,146	90.6%	9.4%	130,906	3.0%	3.8%	0.6%	2.6%	0.1%	0.1%
Mississippi	782,547	97.9%	2.1%	16,550	1.5%	0.7%	0.4%	0.0%	0.1%	0.0%
Missouri	1,551,729	95.8%	4.2%	65,155	1.5%	1.9%	1.0%	0.3%	0.1%	0.0%
Montana	254,000	98.6%	1.4%	3,443	0.3%	0.8%	0.4%	0.0%	0.9%	0.0%
Nebraska	488,381	92.7%	7.3%	35,869	4.1%	2.5%	0.8%	0.4%	0.1%	0.0%
Nevada	715,125	84.0%	16.0%	114,575	10.7%	4.7%	1.0%	0.7%	0.2%	0.1%
New Hampshire	320,088	94.7%	5.3%	16,838	1.5%	2.7%	1.1%	0.4%	0.3%	0.0%
New Jersey	2,179,642	80.7%	19.3%	419,637	10.7%	6.1%	2.1%	1.3%	0.3%	0.0%
New Mexico	546,092	89.5%	10.5%	57,412	8.8%	1.3%	1.0%	0.2%	0.0%	0.1%
New York	5,211,620	81.8%	18.2%	949,491	10.0%	5.5%	2.4%	1.0%	0.3%	0.1%
North Carolina	2,517,570	91.1%	8.9%	222,992	5.8%	2.1%	1.3%	0.5%	0.2%	0.0%
North Dakota	209,265	95.7%	4.3%	8,938	0.5%	1.9%	0.8%	0.9%	0.7%	0.0%
Ohio	2,922,925	95.6%	4.4%	128,616	1.2%	2.1%	0.9%	0.6%	0.2%	0.0%
Oklahoma	1,014,365	92.8%	7.2%	72,553	5.2%	1.6%	0.8%	0.4%	0.0%	0.0%
Oregon	981,691	89.5%	10.5%	103,146	5.3%	3.3%	2.1%	0.4%	0.3%	0.2%
Pennsylvania	3,194,416	93.2%	6.8%	216,845	2.4%	2.9%	1.3%	0.9%	0.1%	0.0%
Rhode Island	278,272	88.3%	11.7%	32,600	6.8%	2.2%	1.8%	1.9%	0.1%	0.0%
South Carolina	1,223,504	94.8%	5.2%	63,023	3.5%	1.3%	1.0%	0.2%	0.2%	0.1%
South Dakota	214,866	96.5%	3.5%	7,508	0.9%	1.3%	0.8%	1.1%	0.0%	0.0%
Tennessee	1,653,200	93.9%	6.1%	100,571	3.6%	1.5%	0.9%	1.0%	0.1%	0.0%
Texas	7,316,912	84.8%	15.2%	1,109,707	11.6%	2.9%	1.0%	0.7%	0.2%	0.0%
Utah	868,128	91.6%	8.4%	73,052	5.1%	2.3%	1.1%	0.3%	0.5%	0.2%
Vermont	154,073	95.1%	4.9%	7,507	0.8%	2.2%	1.8%	0.3%	0.5%	0.2%
Virginia	2,153,966	89.0%	11.0%	235,968	4.7%	4.7%	2.0%	1.2%	0.1%	0.1%
Washington	1,808,668	86.0%	14.0%	253,244	5.6%	5.4%	2.8%	1.1%	0.6%	0.3%
West Virginia	436,632	98.0%	2.0%	8,840	0.9%	0.8%	0.5%	0.2%	0.1%	0.0%
Wisconsin	1,444,543	94.1%	5.9%	85,354	2.9%	2.5%	0.9%	0.2%	0.0%	0.0%
Wyoming	152,108	96.3%	3.7%	5,563	1.9%	1.2%	1.0%	0.3%	0.1%	0.0%

Table C-2: Counties—Nativity and World Region of Birth

	Total Millennial	Percent		Total Foreign Born	Percent of Foreign Born by Region of Birth					
		Native	Foreign Born		Latin America	Asia	Europe	Africa	North America	Oceania
Alabama										
Baldwin County	43,743	96.8%	3.2%	1,414	3.2%	0.0%	0.7%	0.0%	0.0%	0.0%
Calhoun County	29,189	95.0%	5.0%	1,453	1.5%	2.7%	2.4%	0.3%	0.5%	0.0%
Etowah County	24,989	95.3%	4.7%	1,178	4.7%	0.0%	0.0%	0.0%	0.0%	0.0%
Houston County	25,996	98.6%	1.4%	375	0.6%	0.7%	0.6%	0.3%	0.0%	0.0%
Jefferson County	169,583	96.0%	4.0%	6,800	3.4%	1.2%	0.5%	0.2%	0.0%	0.0%
Lauderdale County	25,218	96.0%	4.0%	1,005	3.0%	1.0%	0.9%	0.0%	0.0%	0.0%
Lee County	53,402	98.1%	1.9%	1,021	0.1%	1.8%	0.6%	0.0%	0.0%	0.0%
Madison County	89,687	91.1%	8.9%	7,953	5.7%	3.2%	1.4%	0.1%	0.2%	0.0%
Marshall County	23,904	88.3%	11.7%	2,808	10.7%	0.9%	0.0%	0.1%	0.0%	0.0%
Mobile County	106,088	97.5%	2.5%	2,639	1.4%	0.8%	0.8%	0.0%	0.0%	0.0%
Montgomery County	65,733	97.4%	2.6%	1,721	2.3%	0.2%	0.2%	0.1%	0.0%	0.0%
Morgan County	27,865	95.4%	4.6%	1,289	4.2%	0.0%	1.7%	0.0%	0.0%	0.0%
Shelby County	50,021	93.0%	7.0%	3,496	5.2%	1.8%	2.1%	0.0%	0.0%	0.0%
Tuscaloosa County	73,097	96.0%	4.0%	2,940	2.2%	0.7%	0.8%	0.4%	0.3%	0.0%
Alaska										
Fairbanks North Star Borough	33,622	95.7%	4.3%	1,429	1.0%	1.6%	1.4%	0.0%	1.3%	0.0%
Matanuska-Susitna Borough	27,285	97.7%	2.3%	626	0.6%	2.6%	0.8%	0.0%	0.0%	0.0%
Arizona										
Cochise County	32,080	90.8%	9.2%	2,950	9.0%	0.8%	0.5%	0.0%	0.0%	0.4%
Coconino County	48,457	93.9%	6.1%	2,976	4.1%	2.2%	1.3%	0.0%	0.0%	0.2%
Maricopa County	1,074,489	86.7%	13.3%	142,501	9.1%	2.9%	1.2%	0.8%	0.3%	0.1%
Mohave County	40,348	95.0%	5.0%	2,019	4.9%	0.6%	0.3%	0.0%	0.2%	0.0%
Navajo County	28,502	99.0%	1.0%	283	1.0%	0.0%	0.0%	0.0%	0.0%	0.0%
Pima County	272,490	89.0%	11.0%	30,003	7.6%	3.1%	1.2%	0.6%	0.1%	0.0%
Pinal County	92,374	93.0%	7.0%	6,447	6.2%	0.9%	0.4%	0.0%	0.1%	0.1%
Yavapai County	40,349	88.5%	11.5%	4,642	8.7%	1.6%	1.2%	0.7%	0.0%	0.0%
Yuma County	59,396	80.5%	19.5%	11,576	18.8%	1.0%	0.4%	0.0%	0.0%	0.0%
Arkansas										
Benton County	61,471	83.7%	16.3%	10,007	12.8%	3.8%	0.3%	0.3%	0.1%	0.0%
Craighead County	27,322	93.5%	6.5%	1,766	4.5%	1.2%	0.2%	0.7%	0.0%	0.0%
Faulkner County	41,303	93.0%	7.0%	2,884	3.5%	1.3%	1.8%	0.8%	0.0%	0.0%
Garland County	20,404	94.7%	5.3%	1,091	4.5%	0.8%	0.0%	0.0%	0.0%	0.0%
Pulaski County	104,460	91.7%	8.3%	8,714	6.5%	2.9%	0.0%	0.0%	0.0%	0.0%
Saline County	27,530	96.9%	3.1%	863	2.3%	0.8%	0.0%	0.0%	0.0%	0.0%
Sebastian County	32,489	92.5%	7.5%	2,422	6.0%	1.2%	0.9%	0.0%	0.2%	0.0%
Washington County	68,368	87.4%	12.6%	8,596	9.2%	1.3%	1.3%	0.6%	0.6%	0.9%
California										
Alameda County	411,973	75.3%	24.7%	101,869	9.1%	13.9%	1.6%	0.5%	0.4%	0.5%
Butte County	65,642	94.2%	5.8%	3,803	2.8%	2.6%	0.9%	0.0%	0.0%	0.0%
Contra Costa County	260,160	81.0%	19.0%	49,345	11.3%	6.6%	1.0%	0.8%	0.4%	0.1%
El Dorado County	37,599	89.8%	10.2%	3,821	6.5%	4.0%	0.1%	0.0%	0.0%	0.0%
Fresno County	280,779	84.4%	15.6%	43,888	11.1%	4.7%	0.4%	0.0%	0.2%	0.0%
Humboldt County	38,357	92.0%	8.0%	3,062	4.1%	2.2%	1.9%	0.0%	0.2%	0.0%
Imperial County	52,602	75.8%	24.2%	12,709	27.1%	0.7%	0.1%	0.0%	0.0%	0.0%
Kern County	255,789	83.2%	16.8%	43,073	14.4%	2.4%	0.6%	0.0%	0.1%	0.2%
Kings County	45,510	81.9%	18.1%	8,248	15.1%	2.7%	1.2%	0.5%	0.0%	0.0%
Los Angeles County	2,833,691	77.9%	22.1%	627,350	14.1%	7.3%	0.8%	0.4%	0.2%	0.1%
Madera County	43,066	77.9%	22.1%	9,519	20.5%	1.4%	0.0%	0.0%	0.5%	0.0%
Marin County	49,354	83.8%	16.2%	7,982	10.3%	4.7%	1.6%	0.0%	0.2%	0.0%
Merced County	80,879	81.6%	18.4%	14,852	12.6%	4.9%	0.9%	0.0%	0.0%	0.0%
Monterey County	126,091	75.7%	24.3%	30,631	21.0%	2.7%	0.7%	0.0%	0.1%	0.2%
Napa County	33,246	79.7%	20.3%	6,747	18.7%	1.2%	1.0%	0.0%	0.0%	0.0%
Nevada County	19,138	97.0%	3.0%	569	0.2%	0.0%	2.8%	0.0%	0.0%	0.0%
Orange County	845,683	80.0%	20.0%	168,787	11.7%	8.0%	0.9%	0.4%	0.1%	0.1%
Placer County	86,972	88.5%	11.5%	9,993	6.0%	3.7%	1.6%	0.5%	0.0%	0.0%
Riverside County	639,239	86.5%	13.5%	86,547	10.7%	2.7%	0.3%	0.5%	0.1%	0.1%
Sacramento County	403,255	82.5%	17.5%	70,485	6.9%	6.6%	4.0%	0.8%	0.0%	0.7%
San Bernardino County	618,547	87.7%	12.3%	75,964	9.0%	3.3%	0.2%	0.4%	0.1%	0.0%
San Diego County	936,854	81.9%	18.1%	169,658	10.7%	6.8%	1.7%	0.6%	0.2%	0.1%
San Francisco County	227,668	77.4%	22.6%	51,564	5.6%	14.0%	3.7%	0.5%	0.8%	0.3%
San Joaquin County	195,419	82.5%	17.5%	34,284	13.1%	4.8%	0.6%	0.0%	0.0%	0.1%
San Luis Obispo County	80,673	93.9%	6.1%	4,923	4.3%	1.3%	0.8%	0.3%	0.3%	0.0%
San Mateo County	169,271	74.4%	25.6%	43,297	12.1%	12.1%	1.6%	0.3%	0.1%	1.2%
Santa Barbara County	138,689	78.3%	21.7%	30,092	17.9%	3.5%	1.7%	0.3%	0.1%	0.0%
Santa Clara County	475,069	70.2%	29.8%	141,364	10.8%	17.5%	1.7%	0.8%	0.7%	0.2%
Santa Cruz County	77,464	83.1%	16.9%	13,105	12.0%	3.7%	1.4%	0.0%	0.7%	0.0%
Shasta County	43,154	91.2%	8.8%	3,783	1.8%	3.6%	2.9%	1.0%	0.0%	0.2%
Solano County	114,250	86.3%	13.7%	15,673	7.1%	5.8%	1.0%	0.1%	0.4%	0.5%
Sonoma County	120,963	87.2%	12.8%	15,527	10.5%	1.5%	0.4%	0.8%	0.0%	0.2%
Stanislaus County	148,186	83.0%	17.0%	25,136	13.9%	3.2%	0.1%	0.5%	0.0%	0.0%
Sutter County	23,736	77.7%	22.3%	5,298	15.7%	8.0%	0.7%	0.0%	0.0%	0.0%
Tulare County	132,184	81.2%	18.8%	24,908	17.1%	2.2%	0.3%	0.0%	0.1%	0.0%
Ventura County	219,271	80.9%	19.1%	41,865	15.6%	2.7%	0.9%	0.3%	0.1%	0.1%
Yolo County	72,057	82.2%	17.8%	12,800	7.3%	9.4%	2.3%	0.0%	0.0%	0.0%
Colorado										
Adams County	134,668	88.6%	11.4%	15,330	8.5%	2.0%	1.2%	0.2%	0.0%	0.0%
Arapahoe County	159,628	87.5%	12.5%	19,983	7.6%	2.9%	1.6%	1.6%	0.6%	0.0%

Table C-2: Counties—Nativity and World Region of Birth—*Continued*

		Percent			Percent of Foreign Born by Region of Birth					
	Total Millennial	Native	Foreign Born	Total Foreign Born	Latin America	Asia	Europe	Africa	North America	Oceania
Colorado—Cont.										
Boulder County	93,422	93.7%	6.3%	5,839	3.2%	2.4%	1.0%	0.1%	0.4%	0.4%
Denver County	198,526	84.0%	16.0%	31,709	10.6%	3.2%	1.4%	2.0%	0.0%	0.0%
Douglas County	68,342	95.1%	4.9%	3,353	1.8%	2.0%	2.0%	0.2%	0.7%	0.0%
El Paso County	185,094	94.1%	5.9%	10,936	3.3%	2.4%	3.6%	0.4%	0.3%	0.1%
Jefferson County	131,936	92.6%	7.4%	9,761	2.6%	1.6%	3.2%	0.5%	0.4%	0.0%
Larimer County	96,789	94.3%	5.7%	5,515	2.4%	2.6%	1.8%	0.0%	0.0%	0.0%
Mesa County	38,326	96.5%	3.5%	1,340	3.3%	0.3%	0.0%	0.0%	0.0%	0.1%
Pueblo County	41,292	93.1%	6.9%	2,862	5.8%	0.3%	1.2%	0.1%	0.0%	0.0%
Weld County	74,786	92.0%	8.0%	5,948	6.9%	1.5%	1.8%	0.4%	0.0%	0.0%
Connecticut										
Fairfield County	221,597	80.3%	19.7%	43,664	14.8%	3.8%	2.6%	0.3%	0.0%	0.0%
Hartford County	221,135	88.1%	11.9%	26,209	5.6%	4.4%	2.5%	0.5%	0.3%	0.0%
Litchfield County	39,336	95.4%	4.6%	1,820	3.2%	1.9%	1.2%	0.0%	0.2%	0.0%
Middlesex County	38,088	92.5%	7.5%	2,852	4.8%	0.7%	0.6%	0.3%	1.1%	0.0%
New Haven County	221,657	87.9%	12.1%	26,883	6.9%	3.7%	1.9%	0.7%	0.2%	0.0%
New London County	70,256	95.9%	4.1%	2,870	2.1%	2.1%	1.1%	0.0%	0.0%	0.0%
Tolland County	47,953	93.4%	6.6%	3,166	0.9%	3.3%	3.2%	0.3%	0.1%	0.0%
Windham County	29,948	90.8%	9.2%	2,749	8.4%	0.7%	0.0%	0.0%	0.1%	0.0%
Delaware										
Kent County	43,966	95.4%	4.6%	2,043	1.3%	1.5%	1.3%	1.8%	0.0%	0.0%
New Castle County	148,648	89.0%	11.0%	16,366	3.8%	5.2%	0.7%	1.9%	0.1%	0.1%
Sussex County	41,386	88.9%	11.1%	4,598	8.8%	0.2%	1.9%	0.0%	0.3%	0.0%
Florida										
Alachua County	97,705	90.0%	10.0%	9,764	4.6%	4.6%	1.4%	0.9%	0.8%	0.0%
Bay County	41,608	95.9%	4.1%	1,700	2.8%	1.2%	0.6%	0.0%	0.2%	0.0%
Brevard County	112,681	94.5%	5.5%	6,234	4.4%	0.9%	1.1%	0.0%	0.2%	0.0%
Broward County	437,509	76.2%	23.8%	104,010	20.5%	2.3%	1.5%	0.5%	0.5%	0.0%
Charlotte County	26,086	91.6%	8.4%	2,201	5.6%	1.1%	3.8%	0.0%	0.0%	0.0%
Citrus County	21,470	97.8%	2.2%	483	0.0%	1.1%	0.7%	0.0%	0.4%	0.0%
Clay County	47,604	95.0%	5.0%	2,380	2.7%	1.9%	0.9%	0.0%	0.0%	0.0%
Collier County	62,196	78.8%	21.2%	13,167	20.2%	0.0%	0.9%	0.0%	0.1%	0.0%
Duval County	241,161	92.1%	7.9%	18,983	2.6%	3.7%	2.1%	0.6%	0.2%	0.1%
Escambia County	86,905	95.1%	4.9%	4,284	2.2%	3.0%	1.7%	0.2%	0.4%	0.0%
Flagler County	20,146	94.1%	5.9%	1,189	3.2%	1.1%	1.4%	0.2%	0.0%	0.0%
Hernando County	33,523	97.3%	2.7%	917	1.8%	2.0%	1.4%	0.0%	0.0%	0.0%
Highlands County	17,733	85.1%	14.9%	2,640	16.1%	0.5%	0.0%	0.0%	0.6%	0.0%
Hillsborough County	347,042	86.8%	13.2%	45,847	10.2%	2.8%	1.7%	0.6%	0.1%	0.1%
Indian River County	25,303	91.1%	8.9%	2,244	7.2%	0.5%	0.7%	0.4%	0.0%	0.0%
Lake County	63,882	94.7%	5.3%	3,383	5.6%	0.9%	0.6%	0.0%	0.0%	0.0%
Lee County	135,429	83.6%	16.4%	22,199	14.7%	0.6%	2.0%	0.0%	0.3%	0.0%
Leon County	108,999	93.6%	6.4%	6,924	4.6%	2.2%	0.7%	0.5%	0.0%	0.0%
Manatee County	69,106	87.5%	12.5%	8,608	12.0%	0.2%	0.4%	0.0%	0.0%	0.0%
Marion County	67,396	95.3%	4.7%	3,139	3.2%	1.3%	0.6%	0.0%	0.0%	0.0%
Martin County	28,671	82.7%	17.3%	4,953	16.8%	1.3%	0.0%	0.0%	0.2%	0.0%
Miami-Dade County	676,154	65.1%	34.9%	236,058	33.5%	1.2%	1.4%	0.1%	0.3%	0.0%
Okaloosa County	55,617	93.8%	6.2%	3,424	4.6%	1.8%	2.7%	0.0%	0.1%	0.0%
Orange County	372,784	84.7%	15.3%	57,029	12.4%	2.7%	1.4%	0.2%	0.4%	0.0%
Osceola County	81,886	86.4%	13.6%	11,133	12.3%	0.4%	0.7%	1.0%	0.1%	0.0%
Palm Beach County	301,478	76.3%	23.7%	71,332	21.9%	1.7%	1.3%	0.3%	0.5%	0.0%
Pasco County	96,055	93.5%	6.5%	6,248	5.5%	0.9%	1.2%	0.2%	0.0%	0.3%
Pinellas County	194,471	91.0%	9.0%	17,533	5.0%	2.1%	2.3%	0.3%	0.3%	0.0%
Polk County	149,776	90.9%	9.1%	13,594	8.6%	1.1%	1.1%	0.1%	0.1%	0.0%
Santa Rosa County	40,422	99.0%	1.0%	417	0.2%	1.2%	2.5%	0.0%	0.0%	0.0%
Sarasota County	64,933	92.5%	7.5%	4,871	5.5%	1.6%	1.6%	0.2%	0.2%	0.0%
Seminole County	117,521	90.9%	9.1%	10,725	6.6%	2.3%	1.8%	0.7%	0.0%	0.0%
St. Johns County	47,111	98.1%	1.9%	917	2.0%	0.6%	1.3%	0.0%	1.0%	0.0%
St. Lucie County	62,007	88.0%	12.0%	7,471	10.2%	1.9%	0.1%	0.0%	0.0%	0.0%
Sumter County	11,428	96.0%	4.0%	458	4.0%	0.0%	2.2%	0.0%	0.0%	0.0%
Volusia County	109,532	94.7%	5.3%	5,845	3.2%	2.1%	1.1%	0.1%	0.1%	0.0%
Georgia										
Bartow County	28,669	94.1%	5.9%	1,698	5.7%	0.0%	0.2%	0.0%	0.0%	0.0%
Bibb County	41,974	95.0%	5.0%	2,099	4.3%	2.9%	0.2%	0.3%	0.0%	0.0%
Carroll County	32,258	94.9%	5.1%	1,635	3.5%	0.0%	0.2%	1.1%	0.3%	0.0%
Chatham County	83,341	90.6%	9.4%	7,818	5.2%	2.9%	1.8%	0.6%	0.0%	0.0%
Cherokee County	51,638	91.6%	8.4%	4,351	7.1%	0.4%	1.8%	0.0%	0.4%	0.0%
Clarke County	54,062	93.7%	6.3%	3,422	2.7%	2.9%	1.4%	0.1%	0.1%	0.1%
Clayton County	77,028	86.8%	13.2%	10,169	9.2%	3.1%	1.5%	1.0%	0.0%	0.0%
Cobb County	187,462	85.6%	14.4%	27,009	9.2%	2.7%	1.5%	2.1%	0.4%	0.1%
Columbia County	34,495	97.1%	2.9%	1,007	1.3%	1.3%	2.5%	0.0%	0.8%	0.0%
Coweta County	29,677	91.4%	8.6%	2,546	7.1%	0.9%	0.4%	0.6%	0.0%	0.0%
DeKalb County	191,237	84.0%	16.0%	30,522	6.9%	5.3%	1.2%	3.4%	0.2%	0.0%
Dougherty County	28,202	94.3%	5.7%	1,601	3.8%	2.3%	0.1%	0.4%	0.0%	0.0%
Douglas County	33,135	92.5%	7.5%	2,494	3.6%	1.8%	1.0%	2.1%	0.0%	0.0%
Fayette County	25,819	88.1%	11.9%	3,061	7.2%	5.1%	1.0%	0.0%	0.6%	0.3%
Floyd County	23,869	92.5%	7.5%	1,791	6.8%	0.6%	1.6%	0.0%	0.0%	0.0%
Forsyth County	42,806	85.9%	14.1%	6,026	8.5%	2.0%	2.9%	1.2%	0.5%	0.0%
Fulton County	276,052	88.2%	11.8%	32,506	4.6%	4.8%	1.5%	1.5%	0.4%	0.1%
Gwinnett County	222,876	76.3%	23.7%	52,931	14.0%	6.5%	2.7%	1.3%	0.1%	0.2%

Table C-2: Counties—Nativity and World Region of Birth—*Continued*

	Total Millennial	Percent		Total Foreign Born	Percent of Foreign Born by Region of Birth					
		Native	Foreign Born		Latin America	Asia	Europe	Africa	North America	Oceania
Georgia—Cont.										
Hall County	48,065	82.4%	17.6%	8,455	15.8%	1.3%	1.1%	0.0%	0.8%	0.0%
Henry County	53,473	96.8%	3.2%	1,702	0.8%	1.3%	1.7%	0.5%	0.0%	0.0%
Houston County	41,887	93.5%	6.5%	2,743	4.8%	2.0%	2.7%	0.4%	0.0%	0.0%
Lowndes County	40,099	97.9%	2.1%	823	0.4%	1.8%	1.6%	0.0%	0.2%	0.0%
Muscogee County	61,172	93.1%	6.9%	4,206	2.9%	1.4%	4.0%	0.3%	0.5%	0.0%
Newton County	26,131	93.0%	7.0%	1,829	6.0%	1.2%	0.2%	0.0%	0.3%	0.0%
Paulding County	35,873	96.7%	3.3%	1,191	2.8%	0.8%	0.0%	0.1%	0.3%	0.0%
Richmond County	61,951	97.0%	3.0%	1,830	1.1%	1.4%	2.1%	0.5%	0.0%	0.1%
Whitfield County	26,807	79.9%	20.1%	5,394	18.7%	1.0%	0.0%	0.1%	0.8%	0.0%
Hawaii										
Hawaii County	44,614	93.0%	7.0%	3,145	1.6%	5.6%	0.4%	0.0%	0.2%	1.7%
Honolulu County	273,915	88.2%	11.8%	32,372	0.7%	9.6%	1.0%	0.1%	0.2%	2.9%
Maui County	35,448	82.4%	17.6%	6,240	1.9%	12.8%	1.3%	0.0%	0.4%	3.0%
Idaho										
Ada County	112,611	93.4%	6.6%	7,439	2.6%	3.1%	2.2%	0.7%	0.0%	0.1%
Bonneville County	27,965	91.0%	9.0%	2,524	4.4%	4.6%	0.4%	0.4%	0.1%	0.0%
Canyon County	51,276	91.4%	8.6%	4,423	8.2%	1.5%	0.0%	0.0%	0.0%	0.2%
Kootenai County	35,356	97.9%	2.1%	729	0.0%	2.1%	0.3%	0.0%	0.1%	0.0%
Illinois										
Champaign County	81,544	86.3%	13.7%	11,201	2.6%	9.7%	1.2%	1.2%	0.5%	0.0%
Cook County	1,438,037	83.9%	16.1%	231,866	8.1%	4.7%	3.2%	0.8%	0.1%	0.1%
DeKalb County	38,034	96.0%	4.0%	1,537	1.0%	0.7%	1.9%	1.6%	0.0%	0.0%
DuPage County	231,656	83.7%	16.3%	37,874	6.7%	6.3%	3.7%	0.5%	0.2%	0.0%
Kane County	136,039	80.1%	19.9%	27,134	15.5%	3.3%	1.4%	0.6%	0.0%	0.0%
Kankakee County	27,483	92.6%	7.4%	2,047	6.7%	0.5%	0.2%	0.0%	0.0%	0.0%
Kendall County	30,275	97.6%	2.4%	715	0.0%	3.2%	1.5%	0.0%	0.0%	0.0%
Lake County	176,831	85.8%	14.2%	25,110	9.3%	3.3%	1.5%	0.1%	0.4%	0.0%
LaSalle County	26,791	97.0%	3.0%	799	1.9%	0.8%	0.3%	0.0%	0.0%	0.0%
Macon County	26,140	96.4%	3.6%	929	1.6%	1.2%	0.0%	0.5%	0.2%	0.0%
Madison County	67,129	98.4%	1.6%	1,079	0.7%	0.8%	0.6%	0.0%	0.0%	0.0%
McHenry County	77,110	91.2%	8.8%	6,808	5.1%	1.8%	1.9%	0.5%	0.0%	0.0%
McLean County	57,998	91.3%	8.7%	5,024	0.7%	5.7%	2.1%	0.6%	0.0%	0.0%
Peoria County	49,284	94.6%	5.4%	2,642	1.0%	4.8%	1.2%	0.0%	0.0%	0.0%
Rock Island County	31,517	91.2%	8.8%	2,780	7.0%	1.5%	0.6%	0.5%	0.8%	0.0%
Sangamon County	46,845	96.9%	3.1%	1,434	1.3%	1.5%	0.4%	0.0%	0.0%	0.0%
St. Clair County	70,341	99.0%	1.0%	674	0.3%	1.6%	0.6%	0.0%	0.0%	0.0%
Tazewell County	31,845	98.3%	1.7%	543	0.2%	0.9%	0.3%	0.5%	0.0%	0.0%
Will County	168,570	89.8%	10.2%	17,198	6.0%	1.5%	2.1%	0.8%	0.2%	0.0%
Winnebago County	72,260	91.6%	8.4%	6,038	4.5%	3.2%	0.3%	0.3%	0.2%	0.0%
Indiana										
Allen County	93,984	93.8%	6.2%	5,810	2.2%	1.9%	1.6%	0.8%	0.1%	0.0%
Clark County	27,123	96.6%	3.4%	921	2.5%	0.7%	0.2%	0.0%	0.0%	0.0%
Delaware County	39,030	96.4%	3.6%	1,404	2.0%	1.3%	0.8%	0.0%	0.0%	0.0%
Elkhart County	49,637	89.2%	10.8%	5,381	9.5%	1.1%	1.0%	0.0%	1.5%	0.0%
Hamilton County	65,540	94.6%	5.4%	3,544	1.2%	4.8%	1.4%	0.0%	0.1%	0.0%
Hendricks County	39,350	96.2%	3.8%	1,506	2.6%	0.8%	0.6%	0.3%	0.0%	0.0%
Johnson County	37,878	93.8%	6.2%	2,349	3.5%	1.8%	0.0%	0.9%	0.0%	0.0%
Lake County	118,901	94.6%	5.4%	6,406	3.4%	1.6%	0.7%	0.1%	0.0%	0.2%
LaPorte County	27,693	96.5%	3.5%	968	2.5%	0.2%	1.3%	0.0%	0.0%	0.0%
Madison County	31,472	98.4%	1.6%	509	2.7%	0.0%	0.1%	0.0%	0.0%	0.0%
Marion County	259,377	89.2%	10.8%	28,040	6.3%	2.7%	0.8%	1.4%	0.1%	0.1%
Monroe County	59,193	89.6%	10.4%	6,171	0.5%	6.9%	0.7%	1.8%	0.1%	0.4%
Porter County	41,176	95.7%	4.3%	1,754	1.7%	1.8%	0.0%	0.9%	0.0%	0.0%
St. Joseph County	72,054	94.6%	5.4%	3,890	3.3%	1.4%	0.7%	0.3%	0.1%	0.0%
Tippecanoe County	70,476	86.6%	13.4%	9,414	2.1%	10.5%	0.8%	0.4%	0.2%	0.0%
Vanderburgh County	47,216	98.1%	1.9%	880	0.4%	1.2%	1.5%	0.0%	0.0%	0.0%
Vigo County	32,766	96.4%	3.6%	1,182	1.5%	2.8%	0.0%	0.0%	0.0%	0.0%
Iowa										
Black Hawk County	42,469	92.8%	7.2%	3,073	2.5%	1.5%	3.3%	0.0%	0.0%	0.0%
Dubuque County	24,987	96.2%	3.8%	938	1.8%	0.5%	2.7%	0.0%	0.2%	0.0%
Johnson County	56,779	91.3%	8.7%	4,914	0.9%	4.6%	1.9%	2.0%	0.2%	0.0%
Linn County	55,429	93.9%	6.1%	3,379	1.1%	2.7%	0.9%	0.0%	1.7%	0.0%
Polk County	120,544	85.9%	14.1%	17,032	4.1%	3.9%	3.3%	4.4%	0.5%	0.0%
Pottawattamie County	22,874	96.1%	3.9%	889	3.6%	3.3%	0.3%	0.0%	0.5%	0.0%
Scott County	42,609	96.5%	3.5%	1,504	0.0%	1.9%	1.1%	0.9%	0.3%	0.0%
Story County	40,969	89.2%	10.8%	4,444	0.0%	9.5%	0.3%	0.3%	1.1%	0.0%
Woodbury County	29,826	89.9%	10.1%	3,020	9.9%	0.3%	0.0%	0.0%	0.0%	0.0%
Kansas										
Douglas County	44,291	95.2%	4.8%	2,142	0.4%	3.9%	1.3%	0.0%	0.0%	0.0%
Johnson County	134,785	91.8%	8.2%	11,088	3.1%	3.6%	2.0%	0.8%	0.1%	0.0%
Sedgwick County	142,587	92.2%	7.8%	11,093	3.9%	3.0%	1.5%	0.5%	0.0%	0.1%
Shawnee County	45,819	93.7%	6.3%	2,903	4.7%	1.9%	0.3%	0.0%	0.2%	0.0%
Wyandotte County	42,100	84.6%	15.4%	6,466	11.0%	4.1%	0.6%	1.1%	0.0%	0.0%
Kentucky										
Boone County	30,524	95.1%	4.9%	1,482	2.1%	2.8%	0.0%	0.0%	0.0%	0.0%
Campbell County	22,819	97.5%	2.5%	572	2.5%	0.0%	0.3%	0.0%	0.0%	0.0%

Table C-2: Counties—Nativity and World Region of Birth—Continued

	Total Millennial	Percent		Total Foreign Born	Percent of Foreign Born by Region of Birth					
		Native	Foreign Born		Latin America	Asia	Europe	Africa	North America	Oceania
Kentucky—Cont.										
Daviess County	23,237	98.4%	1.6%	364	0.4%	1.1%	0.5%	0.0%	0.0%	0.0%
Fayette County	92,123	90.7%	9.3%	8,601	3.1%	4.5%	1.4%	1.6%	0.0%	0.0%
Hardin County	29,502	95.8%	4.2%	1,226	3.0%	1.5%	2.2%	0.0%	0.0%	0.0%
Jefferson County	192,974	92.5%	7.5%	14,386	4.1%	2.6%	1.3%	0.8%	0.1%	0.0%
Kenton County	42,375	95.4%	4.6%	1,930	1.2%	2.5%	0.9%	0.2%	0.1%	0.0%
Warren County	37,886	91.1%	8.9%	3,360	3.3%	3.7%	3.4%	0.2%	0.0%	0.0%
Louisiana										
Ascension Parish	29,490	99.8%	0.2%	71	0.7%	0.0%	0.9%	0.0%	0.0%	0.0%
Bossier Parish	35,157	95.2%	4.8%	1,674	3.6%	0.8%	0.7%	0.0%	0.0%	0.0%
Caddo Parish	68,119	97.8%	2.2%	1,531	1.4%	1.0%	0.6%	0.0%	0.0%	0.0%
Calcasieu Parish	52,204	98.5%	1.5%	790	1.3%	0.6%	1.7%	0.2%	0.0%	0.0%
East Baton Rouge Parish	138,439	95.2%	4.8%	6,693	2.4%	2.8%	0.5%	0.1%	0.0%	0.0%
Jefferson Parish	112,464	85.6%	14.4%	16,235	11.4%	3.0%	0.3%	0.2%	0.0%	0.0%
Lafayette Parish	65,892	95.2%	4.8%	3,162	2.2%	2.0%	1.2%	0.2%	0.0%	0.0%
Lafourche Parish	25,278	97.3%	2.7%	671	1.3%	0.8%	0.5%	0.0%	0.0%	0.0%
Livingston Parish	34,296	100.0%	0.0%	0	0.0%	0.0%	0.2%	0.0%	0.0%	0.0%
Orleans Parish	111,713	93.9%	6.1%	6,854	3.2%	2.2%	0.8%	0.2%	0.2%	0.0%
Ouachita Parish	43,511	98.5%	1.5%	636	0.3%	1.0%	1.0%	0.0%	0.0%	0.0%
Rapides Parish	35,189	96.8%	3.2%	1,111	0.9%	2.1%	2.4%	0.0%	0.0%	0.0%
St. Tammany Parish	56,793	98.8%	1.2%	700	0.8%	1.0%	0.1%	0.0%	0.0%	0.0%
Tangipahoa Parish	36,944	95.3%	4.7%	1,747	4.7%	0.0%	0.0%	0.0%	0.0%	0.0%
Terrebonne Parish	28,956	94.5%	5.5%	1,606	5.5%	0.4%	0.0%	0.0%	0.4%	0.0%
Maine										
Androscoggin County	26,538	98.0%	2.0%	526	0.2%	0.8%	0.0%	1.0%	0.0%	0.0%
Cumberland County	69,682	94.4%	5.6%	3,885	1.4%	4.2%	0.8%	1.5%	0.3%	0.0%
Kennebec County	27,602	98.3%	1.7%	479	0.0%	1.9%	2.2%	0.0%	0.7%	0.0%
Penobscot County	39,915	97.8%	2.2%	861	0.0%	1.7%	0.1%	0.4%	0.0%	0.0%
York County	42,942	99.0%	1.0%	410	0.3%	0.4%	0.3%	0.0%	0.4%	0.0%
Maryland										
Anne Arundel County	139,871	89.4%	10.6%	14,812	5.7%	3.7%	1.7%	1.3%	0.0%	0.1%
Baltimore County	213,682	90.3%	9.7%	20,796	3.2%	4.5%	1.5%	2.0%	0.0%	0.2%
Carroll County	39,345	96.8%	3.2%	1,277	2.2%	0.4%	0.9%	0.3%	0.0%	0.0%
Cecil County	25,431	96.7%	3.3%	832	1.0%	3.1%	0.0%	0.0%	0.5%	0.0%
Charles County	38,929	97.0%	3.0%	1,163	1.8%	0.8%	1.2%	1.4%	0.0%	0.0%
Frederick County	60,348	91.6%	8.4%	5,064	4.8%	2.0%	1.2%	1.7%	0.0%	0.0%
Harford County	61,759	98.2%	1.8%	1,133	0.4%	1.3%	2.2%	0.2%	0.0%	0.0%
Howard County	74,492	84.2%	15.8%	11,770	4.4%	9.9%	1.9%	1.2%	0.0%	0.0%
Montgomery County	237,666	70.3%	29.7%	70,666	12.2%	8.3%	3.5%	7.8%	0.1%	0.0%
Prince George's County	248,192	81.6%	18.4%	45,572	12.2%	3.1%	1.2%	3.5%	0.0%	0.0%
St. Mary's County	28,557	96.2%	3.8%	1,089	2.9%	1.8%	0.2%	0.0%	0.0%	0.0%
Washington County	36,422	94.9%	5.1%	1,875	1.4%	2.2%	1.3%	0.0%	0.3%	0.2%
Wicomico County	30,975	90.2%	9.8%	3,033	6.6%	1.6%	2.3%	1.0%	0.0%	0.0%
Massachusetts										
Barnstable County	40,139	91.0%	9.0%	3,594	8.5%	1.1%	1.6%	1.6%	0.0%	0.0%
Berkshire County	29,440	93.5%	6.5%	1,923	2.2%	0.9%	0.6%	2.9%	0.0%	0.3%
Bristol County	133,365	93.7%	6.3%	8,407	3.5%	0.9%	1.9%	0.5%	0.2%	0.1%
Essex County	189,099	84.7%	15.3%	28,892	11.0%	2.6%	1.4%	0.8%	0.3%	0.0%
Hampden County	130,223	90.4%	9.6%	12,481	3.9%	2.7%	3.1%	0.8%	0.4%	0.0%
Hampshire County	47,728	92.6%	7.4%	3,528	1.5%	5.4%	0.9%	0.7%	0.3%	0.0%
Middlesex County	417,893	81.7%	18.3%	76,524	6.4%	7.9%	3.2%	1.4%	0.5%	0.1%
Norfolk County	167,479	86.4%	13.6%	22,824	3.6%	6.5%	3.5%	0.7%	0.2%	0.0%
Plymouth County	110,941	93.8%	6.2%	6,833	2.9%	0.9%	0.6%	1.6%	0.5%	0.0%
Suffolk County	281,869	77.7%	22.3%	62,862	12.8%	5.9%	2.8%	2.1%	0.4%	0.0%
Worcester County	212,980	88.0%	12.0%	25,533	4.7%	3.9%	2.0%	1.7%	0.0%	0.2%
Michigan										
Allegan County	26,007	99.5%	0.5%	124	0.2%	0.0%	0.3%	0.0%	0.4%	0.0%
Bay County	26,664	97.2%	2.8%	740	1.8%	0.7%	0.3%	0.0%	0.0%	0.0%
Berrien County	34,333	95.0%	5.0%	1,723	3.1%	1.9%	0.0%	0.0%	0.8%	0.0%
Calhoun County	31,324	97.7%	2.3%	720	0.5%	1.8%	0.0%	0.0%	0.0%	0.0%
Eaton County	25,521	97.0%	3.0%	771	1.0%	1.8%	0.2%	0.0%	0.0%	0.0%
Genesee County	103,825	98.9%	1.1%	1,095	0.3%	0.6%	0.4%	0.1%	0.0%	0.0%
Ingham County	101,879	89.1%	10.9%	11,088	1.3%	6.4%	1.0%	1.4%	1.3%	0.1%
Jackson County	39,344	99.4%	0.6%	222	0.0%	0.1%	1.6%	0.0%	0.0%	0.0%
Kalamazoo County	81,455	96.2%	3.8%	3,067	1.3%	3.3%	0.7%	0.0%	0.1%	0.0%
Kent County	172,068	91.9%	8.1%	13,939	4.6%	3.3%	0.8%	0.2%	0.7%	0.0%
Lenawee County	24,357	98.2%	1.8%	433	1.6%	0.0%	0.0%	0.0%	0.2%	0.0%
Livingston County	43,034	97.5%	2.5%	1,063	0.2%	1.3%	1.7%	0.0%	0.3%	0.2%
Macomb County	202,176	92.4%	7.6%	15,281	0.8%	5.2%	2.0%	0.0%	0.2%	0.0%
Monroe County	35,012	98.6%	1.4%	487	1.2%	0.4%	0.6%	0.0%	0.0%	0.0%
Muskegon County	40,756	98.9%	1.1%	428	0.0%	1.0%	0.5%	0.0%	0.0%	0.0%
Oakland County	289,984	89.8%	10.2%	29,653	1.2%	5.3%	2.1%	0.6%	1.5%	0.1%
Ottawa County	78,130	94.9%	5.1%	4,003	1.7%	2.2%	0.9%	0.4%	0.4%	0.0%
Saginaw County	49,901	98.8%	1.2%	619	0.2%	1.4%	0.2%	0.0%	0.4%	0.0%
St. Clair County	37,367	97.9%	2.1%	799	0.7%	0.6%	0.5%	0.0%	0.4%	0.0%
Washtenaw County	119,936	90.0%	10.0%	11,938	2.3%	6.6%	1.4%	0.3%	0.1%	0.0%
Wayne County	451,782	92.8%	7.2%	32,703	2.0%	4.8%	0.7%	0.2%	0.6%	0.0%
Minnesota										
Anoka County	84,669	94.9%	5.1%	4,304	2.2%	1.0%	1.3%	0.9%	0.0%	0.0%
Carver County	23,348	99.4%	0.6%	141	0.6%	0.0%	1.5%	0.0%	0.0%	0.0%

Table C-2: Counties—Nativity and World Region of Birth—*Continued*

	Total Millennial	Percent		Total Foreign Born	Percent of Foreign Born by Region of Birth					
		Native	Foreign Born		Latin America	Asia	Europe	Africa	North America	Oceania
Minnesota—Cont.										
Dakota County	100,432	92.3%	7.7%	7,688	3.7%	2.6%	0.4%	1.4%	0.3%	0.4%
Hennepin County	331,738	81.1%	18.9%	62,730	5.9%	7.2%	1.0%	5.5%	0.1%	0.2%
Olmsted County	35,580	88.3%	11.7%	4,180	2.8%	6.0%	0.9%	4.2%	0.0%	0.0%
Ramsey County	150,591	83.2%	16.8%	25,227	2.5%	8.5%	0.3%	6.8%	0.2%	0.0%
Scott County	30,250	94.8%	5.2%	1,574	2.3%	4.5%	0.0%	0.1%	1.2%	0.0%
St. Louis County	53,813	98.8%	1.2%	661	1.0%	0.8%	0.5%	0.0%	0.0%	0.0%
Stearns County	47,873	94.4%	5.6%	2,689	3.2%	0.6%	0.0%	2.1%	0.0%	0.0%
Washington County	60,484	96.3%	3.7%	2,226	1.0%	1.4%	0.8%	0.1%	0.0%	0.8%
Wright County	32,651	96.2%	3.8%	1,244	1.9%	1.4%	0.6%	0.0%	0.0%	0.0%
Mississippi										
DeSoto County	41,523	97.7%	2.3%	957	1.9%	0.4%	0.0%	0.0%	0.0%	0.0%
Harrison County	52,715	96.4%	3.6%	1,904	4.8%	2.4%	1.4%	0.0%	0.2%	0.0%
Hinds County	74,512	98.1%	1.9%	1,404	0.8%	0.9%	0.5%	0.2%	0.0%	0.0%
Jackson County	36,512	99.2%	0.8%	304	0.3%	0.6%	0.0%	0.0%	0.0%	0.0%
Madison County	26,202	98.9%	1.1%	297	0.9%	0.0%	0.9%	0.4%	0.0%	0.0%
Rankin County	35,305	96.4%	3.6%	1,267	0.4%	2.6%	0.2%	0.0%	1.1%	0.0%
Missouri										
Boone County	65,445	93.9%	6.1%	3,982	0.2%	3.6%	1.8%	0.6%	0.1%	0.0%
Cass County	24,713	99.8%	0.2%	57	0.0%	0.0%	0.2%	0.0%	0.0%	0.0%
Clay County	57,332	96.6%	3.4%	1,954	0.4%	1.5%	0.4%	1.3%	0.2%	0.2%
Franklin County	23,094	97.9%	2.1%	486	2.1%	0.0%	0.0%	0.0%	0.0%	0.0%
Greene County	88,273	98.3%	1.7%	1,530	0.3%	1.0%	1.0%	0.1%	0.1%	0.0%
Jackson County	176,380	92.6%	7.4%	13,056	5.4%	1.4%	0.6%	0.7%	0.0%	0.1%
Jasper County	32,081	96.3%	3.7%	1,193	0.1%	3.0%	1.1%	0.0%	0.0%	0.0%
Jefferson County	52,424	96.4%	3.6%	1,882	0.6%	0.8%	2.5%	0.0%	0.0%	0.0%
Platte County	23,767	95.5%	4.5%	1,060	3.1%	1.6%	3.4%	0.0%	0.0%	0.5%
St. Charles County	88,922	96.3%	3.7%	3,268	1.2%	2.2%	0.5%	0.0%	0.1%	0.0%
St. Louis County	244,999	93.8%	6.2%	15,133	1.2%	3.8%	1.9%	0.4%	0.2%	0.0%
Montana										
Flathead County	20,921	99.9%	0.1%	23	0.0%	0.0%	0.1%	0.0%	0.0%	0.0%
Gallatin County	30,983	96.8%	3.2%	1,001	0.4%	2.1%	0.7%	0.0%	0.3%	0.0%
Missoula County	36,652	98.7%	1.3%	482	0.7%	1.0%	0.0%	0.0%	0.1%	0.0%
Yellowstone County	38,379	99.1%	0.9%	339	0.2%	1.3%	0.4%	0.0%	0.0%	0.0%
Nebraska										
Douglas County	147,156	89.8%	10.2%	15,003	4.9%	4.3%	0.6%	0.9%	0.0%	0.0%
Lancaster County	95,528	92.8%	7.2%	6,863	1.1%	4.6%	1.2%	0.4%	0.2%	0.0%
Sarpy County	45,013	95.7%	4.3%	1,954	0.5%	2.8%	2.1%	0.0%	0.0%	0.0%
Nevada										
Clark County	527,642	82.2%	17.8%	93,804	11.7%	5.3%	1.2%	0.8%	0.3%	0.0%
Washoe County	113,285	87.6%	12.4%	14,004	8.9%	3.6%	0.5%	0.4%	0.0%	0.5%
New Hampshire										
Hillsborough County	98,359	92.1%	7.9%	7,816	2.7%	3.6%	1.4%	0.3%	0.5%	0.0%
Merrimack County	34,531	94.4%	5.6%	1,922	0.4%	3.7%	0.7%	1.1%	0.6%	0.0%
Rockingham County	64,185	93.9%	6.1%	3,918	1.8%	2.9%	0.9%	0.8%	0.3%	0.0%
Strafford County	36,919	95.1%	4.9%	1,826	1.4%	3.6%	0.9%	0.1%	0.2%	0.0%
New Jersey										
Atlantic County	67,058	86.8%	13.2%	8,826	7.3%	5.0%	1.0%	0.4%	0.0%	0.0%
Bergen County	207,617	76.2%	23.8%	49,346	8.2%	10.2%	5.1%	0.8%	0.2%	0.0%
Burlington County	108,458	93.6%	6.4%	6,912	3.0%	3.5%	0.8%	0.4%	0.3%	0.0%
Camden County	130,453	90.2%	9.8%	12,818	4.1%	3.9%	0.8%	1.3%	0.1%	0.0%
Cape May County	19,280	88.9%	11.1%	2,139	5.6%	2.2%	3.7%	0.0%	0.0%	0.0%
Cumberland County	41,412	85.3%	14.7%	6,081	10.9%	1.2%	2.9%	0.0%	0.7%	0.0%
Essex County	204,847	78.5%	21.5%	44,032	16.0%	3.6%	1.4%	2.1%	0.3%	0.0%
Gloucester County	70,459	96.4%	3.6%	2,559	1.6%	1.9%	0.9%	0.1%	0.1%	0.0%
Hudson County	196,209	60.1%	39.9%	78,302	21.1%	13.3%	2.6%	3.6%	0.4%	0.0%
Hunterdon County	28,211	97.9%	2.1%	597	1.7%	0.9%	0.8%	0.0%	0.2%	0.0%
Mercer County	97,275	77.2%	22.8%	22,184	10.1%	7.1%	4.0%	2.7%	0.7%	0.0%
Middlesex County	211,103	73.6%	26.4%	55,720	10.7%	12.8%	2.1%	1.6%	0.4%	0.0%
Monmouth County	146,742	86.5%	13.5%	19,773	8.8%	2.8%	1.7%	0.3%	0.2%	0.1%
Morris County	113,951	84.2%	15.8%	18,008	8.8%	5.8%	1.0%	1.4%	0.4%	0.4%
Ocean County	125,044	93.5%	6.5%	8,131	4.7%	2.4%	0.6%	0.1%	0.4%	0.0%
Passaic County	134,168	77.0%	23.0%	30,923	18.8%	4.8%	1.6%	0.3%	0.5%	0.0%
Somerset County	71,788	85.1%	14.9%	10,723	4.7%	5.7%	3.4%	1.0%	1.0%	0.1%
Sussex County	32,651	93.0%	7.0%	2,280	2.5%	0.5%	4.2%	1.1%	0.0%	0.0%
Union County	133,600	71.8%	28.2%	37,684	21.7%	3.3%	2.9%	2.0%	0.1%	0.0%
Warren County	24,276	96.6%	3.4%	829	2.8%	1.1%	0.0%	0.0%	0.0%	0.0%
New Mexico										
Bernalillo County	187,027	89.5%	10.5%	19,687	8.5%	1.5%	1.1%	0.2%	0.0%	0.2%
Doña Ana County	66,940	87.2%	12.8%	8,571	12.1%	0.8%	1.1%	0.0%	0.0%	0.0%
San Juan County	32,122	93.6%	6.4%	2,046	6.1%	0.4%	0.2%	0.0%	0.3%	0.0%
Sandoval County	32,004	94.5%	5.5%	1,770	4.3%	1.9%	0.1%	0.0%	0.0%	0.0%
Santa Fe County	30,956	80.2%	19.8%	6,127	16.7%	1.9%	1.4%	0.0%	0.0%	0.0%
New York										
Albany County	89,897	92.1%	7.9%	7,109	0.8%	5.2%	1.0%	0.8%	0.4%	0.0%
Bronx County	411,710	72.2%	27.8%	114,293	22.0%	2.2%	1.1%	3.8%	0.0%	0.0%
Broome County	54,701	93.9%	6.1%	3,346	0.6%	3.5%	1.7%	0.3%	0.0%	0.0%
Chautauqua County	34,497	97.2%	2.8%	977	0.1%	2.5%	0.1%	0.3%	0.1%	0.0%
Dutchess County	78,602	90.7%	9.3%	7,336	5.5%	3.1%	0.8%	0.6%	0.1%	0.0%

Table C-2: Counties—Nativity and World Region of Birth—*Continued*

	Total Millennial	Percent		Total Foreign Born	Percent of Foreign Born by Region of Birth					
		Native	Foreign Born		Latin America	Asia	Europe	Africa	North America	Oceania
New York—Cont.										
Erie County	243,911	92.5%	7.5%	18,267	1.2%	3.9%	1.3%	1.0%	0.6%	0.0%
Jefferson County	35,704	97.0%	3.0%	1,070	2.4%	0.9%	2.1%	0.0%	0.7%	0.0%
Kings County	747,562	72.4%	27.6%	206,647	14.5%	8.6%	4.4%	1.1%	0.4%	0.1%
Monroe County	199,730	92.8%	7.2%	14,329	0.9%	3.5%	2.9%	0.9%	0.3%	0.0%
Nassau County	321,177	83.2%	16.8%	53,924	11.0%	4.8%	1.4%	0.4%	0.3%	0.0%
New York County	51,204	97.0%	3.0%	1,533	0.9%	1.1%	0.9%	0.0%	0.6%	0.0%
Niagara County	484,143	78.6%	21.4%	103,583	9.1%	6.9%	4.3%	1.4%	0.9%	0.3%
Oneida County	60,307	91.7%	8.3%	4,991	2.6%	1.9%	4.6%	0.1%	0.0%	0.0%
Onondaga County	128,807	92.6%	7.4%	9,492	1.8%	3.4%	1.5%	1.0%	0.4%	0.1%
Ontario County	25,415	95.4%	4.6%	1,160	3.2%	1.3%	1.0%	0.0%	0.0%	0.0%
Orange County	98,266	91.3%	8.7%	8,523	6.6%	1.5%	1.5%	0.2%	0.2%	0.0%
Oswego County	32,874	97.4%	2.6%	845	2.1%	0.4%	0.3%	0.0%	0.0%	0.0%
Putnam County	21,691	84.3%	15.7%	3,399	7.9%	2.4%	5.7%	0.0%	0.0%	0.0%
Queens County	607,326	61.7%	38.3%	232,714	19.8%	14.9%	3.6%	1.0%	0.2%	0.1%
Rensselaer County	42,068	93.0%	7.0%	2,945	1.5%	4.4%	0.9%	0.0%	0.1%	0.0%
Richmond County	116,248	84.9%	15.1%	17,567	5.2%	4.5%	4.2%	1.9%	0.5%	0.0%
Rockland County	81,322	82.1%	17.9%	14,584	15.3%	2.6%	1.6%	0.0%	0.3%	0.0%
Saratoga County	52,673	95.9%	4.1%	2,139	1.7%	2.1%	0.7%	0.0%	0.0%	0.3%
Schenectady County	38,971	90.7%	9.3%	3,611	3.9%	4.7%	0.4%	0.2%	0.0%	0.0%
St. Lawrence County	31,306	98.1%	1.9%	608	0.8%	0.2%	0.6%	0.4%	0.0%	0.0%
Steuben County	21,521	98.2%	1.8%	385	0.2%	1.1%	0.2%	0.0%	0.5%	0.0%
Suffolk County	368,366	86.7%	13.3%	48,831	9.6%	2.9%	1.3%	0.1%	0.1%	0.0%
Tompkins County	41,515	86.8%	13.2%	5,477	0.7%	10.7%	2.5%	0.0%	0.3%	0.1%
Ulster County	41,894	95.4%	4.6%	1,907	1.7%	2.4%	0.4%	0.2%	0.1%	0.0%
Wayne County	20,672	97.7%	2.3%	471	0.3%	0.9%	1.5%	0.0%	0.0%	0.0%
Westchester County	224,469	79.5%	20.5%	46,092	14.8%	4.2%	1.9%	0.8%	0.1%	0.0%
North Carolina										
Alamance County	38,845	86.2%	13.8%	5,367	10.2%	1.9%	0.0%	1.4%	0.3%	0.0%
Brunswick County	18,341	96.3%	3.7%	672	3.4%	0.5%	1.1%	0.0%	0.0%	0.0%
Buncombe County	56,215	93.3%	6.7%	3,794	5.9%	0.6%	0.6%	0.0%	0.0%	0.0%
Burke County	21,087	96.7%	3.3%	694	2.8%	0.0%	0.5%	0.0%	0.0%	0.0%
Cabarrus County	45,822	90.5%	9.5%	4,332	6.8%	1.7%	1.8%	0.2%	0.0%	0.0%
Catawba County	34,663	89.1%	10.9%	3,790	7.0%	1.8%	2.4%	0.0%	0.0%	0.0%
Cleveland County	23,149	95.8%	4.2%	975	3.9%	0.3%	0.0%	0.0%	0.0%	0.0%
Craven County	30,089	94.0%	6.0%	1,809	4.3%	0.8%	1.1%	0.0%	0.2%	0.0%
Cumberland County	104,204	95.1%	4.9%	5,137	3.6%	1.6%	3.2%	0.0%	0.2%	0.1%
Davidson County	37,301	96.2%	3.8%	1,412	2.9%	1.4%	0.4%	0.0%	0.4%	0.0%
Durham County	84,607	83.3%	16.7%	14,144	9.2%	5.0%	1.9%	1.9%	0.7%	0.2%
Forsyth County	92,178	92.2%	7.8%	7,145	6.1%	1.6%	1.0%	0.2%	0.0%	0.0%
Gaston County	49,851	95.1%	4.9%	2,465	4.1%	0.8%	0.7%	0.2%	0.0%	0.0%
Guilford County	138,056	89.6%	10.4%	14,330	4.8%	4.7%	1.3%	1.4%	0.0%	0.0%
Harnett County	34,876	91.1%	8.9%	3,094	6.9%	1.3%	1.4%	0.1%	0.8%	0.0%
Henderson County	22,375	84.9%	15.1%	3,382	14.5%	1.0%	0.0%	0.0%	0.5%	0.0%
Iredell County	38,933	92.6%	7.4%	2,891	4.3%	1.6%	1.6%	0.0%	0.8%	0.0%
Johnston County	42,338	88.0%	12.0%	5,063	11.5%	0.4%	0.3%	0.0%	0.0%	0.0%
Mecklenburg County	273,009	84.3%	15.7%	42,998	8.6%	4.5%	1.5%	2.1%	0.1%	0.0%
Moore County	18,946	93.2%	6.8%	1,297	6.8%	0.4%	0.5%	0.0%	0.0%	0.0%
Nash County	21,825	98.1%	1.9%	409	0.5%	1.0%	2.3%	0.3%	0.0%	0.0%
New Hanover County	59,080	94.2%	5.8%	3,450	2.8%	2.6%	1.1%	0.1%	0.0%	0.0%
Onslow County	80,099	95.4%	4.6%	3,659	3.2%	1.7%	1.3%	0.3%	0.1%	0.0%
Orange County	48,311	91.2%	8.8%	4,272	3.5%	2.6%	3.7%	0.7%	0.0%	0.1%
Pitt County	61,787	97.2%	2.8%	1,738	0.7%	1.4%	1.7%	0.0%	0.0%	0.0%
Randolph County	31,761	88.6%	11.4%	3,630	11.0%	0.8%	0.0%	0.0%	0.0%	0.0%
Robeson County	37,370	92.5%	7.5%	2,811	5.5%	0.3%	1.7%	0.0%	0.0%	0.2%
Rockingham County	19,982	95.0%	5.0%	1,009	5.0%	0.0%	0.0%	0.0%	0.0%	0.0%
Rowan County	32,181	93.5%	6.5%	2,086	3.7%	1.3%	1.0%	0.0%	1.1%	0.0%
Union County	50,048	93.1%	6.9%	3,445	6.5%	1.1%	1.5%	0.0%	0.0%	0.0%
Wake County	258,352	86.5%	13.5%	34,929	6.6%	4.6%	1.8%	0.9%	0.5%	0.1%
Wayne County	30,990	93.7%	6.3%	1,938	6.0%	1.1%	0.3%	0.0%	0.0%	0.0%
North Dakota										
Cass County	55,587	91.3%	8.7%	4,814	1.5%	3.9%	0.7%	2.5%	0.2%	0.0%
Ohio										
Allen County	26,290	98.6%	1.4%	368	0.0%	0.0%	1.3%	0.1%	0.0%	0.0%
Ashtabula County	22,736	100.0%	0.0%	0	0.0%	0.0%	0.0%	0.0%	0.0%	0.0%
Butler County	101,049	93.3%	6.7%	6,811	2.3%	3.1%	1.5%	0.9%	0.0%	0.0%
Clark County	32,974	98.0%	2.0%	675	1.7%	0.2%	1.4%	0.1%	0.0%	0.0%
Clermont County	49,166	98.4%	1.6%	764	0.3%	0.8%	0.7%	0.0%	0.0%	0.2%
Columbiana County	23,852	97.7%	2.3%	551	2.1%	0.3%	0.0%	0.0%	0.0%	0.0%
Cuyahoga County	310,929	94.7%	5.3%	16,608	1.0%	2.4%	1.6%	0.5%	0.3%	0.0%
Delaware County	40,420	97.3%	2.7%	1,077	0.2%	2.2%	0.2%	0.3%	0.0%	0.0%
Fairfield County	37,806	98.5%	1.5%	564	0.0%	0.2%	1.9%	0.0%	0.0%	0.0%
Franklin County	357,534	90.1%	9.9%	35,437	3.1%	4.0%	1.0%	2.6%	0.3%	0.1%
Geauga County	20,794	97.1%	2.9%	602	0.0%	2.5%	0.4%	0.0%	0.0%	0.0%
Greene County	48,051	94.3%	5.7%	2,745	1.0%	4.8%	2.7%	0.7%	0.0%	0.0%
Hamilton County	212,839	93.6%	6.4%	13,621	2.0%	3.5%	0.7%	1.1%	0.1%	0.1%
Lake County	52,521	95.8%	4.2%	2,229	3.3%	0.5%	0.9%	0.0%	0.0%	0.0%
Licking County	41,085	98.3%	1.7%	698	0.2%	1.3%	0.7%	0.0%	0.2%	0.0%

Table C-2: Counties—Nativity and World Region of Birth—*Continued*

	Total Millennial	Percent		Total Foreign Born	Percent of Foreign Born by Region of Birth					
		Native	Foreign Born		Latin America	Asia	Europe	Africa	North America	Oceania
Ohio—Cont.										
Lorain County	71,947	97.3%	2.7%	1,969	1.3%	0.9%	0.7%	0.0%	0.0%	0.0%
Lucas County	117,034	96.8%	3.2%	3,788	0.6%	1.9%	0.3%	0.4%	0.3%	0.2%
Mahoning County	54,397	96.6%	3.4%	1,836	1.4%	1.7%	1.0%	0.2%	0.0%	0.0%
Medina County	39,456	97.9%	2.1%	835	1.4%	0.5%	0.7%	0.0%	0.0%	0.0%
Miami County	25,611	99.1%	0.9%	243	0.0%	0.0%	0.4%	0.0%	0.9%	0.0%
Montgomery County	134,875	96.0%	4.0%	5,368	0.7%	2.0%	1.5%	0.6%	0.1%	0.1%
Portage County	52,402	92.7%	7.3%	3,844	0.0%	7.0%	0.0%	0.4%	0.4%	0.0%
Richland County	28,039	99.2%	0.8%	221	0.7%	0.0%	0.1%	0.0%	0.0%	0.0%
Stark County	88,915	99.0%	1.0%	916	0.9%	0.0%	0.2%	0.0%	0.0%	0.0%
Summit County	132,601	92.6%	7.4%	9,845	1.3%	4.2%	1.9%	0.2%	0.2%	0.0%
Trumbull County	45,225	99.7%	0.3%	156	0.0%	0.3%	0.0%	0.2%	0.0%	0.0%
Tuscarawas County	21,241	97.6%	2.4%	520	2.4%	0.0%	0.0%	0.0%	0.0%	0.0%
Warren County	51,896	93.2%	6.8%	3,506	2.0%	2.5%	1.1%	0.5%	0.9%	0.0%
Wayne County	28,468	97.0%	3.0%	841	0.8%	1.6%	0.0%	0.5%	0.0%	0.0%
Wood County	40,741	94.9%	5.1%	2,093	1.7%	1.6%	1.9%	0.0%	0.0%	0.0%
Oklahoma										
Canadian County	28,837	91.7%	8.3%	2,386	5.6%	2.6%	0.0%	0.0%	0.0%	0.0%
Cleveland County	87,732	93.4%	6.6%	5,762	2.6%	4.0%	0.1%	0.7%	0.0%	0.0%
Comanche County	40,012	91.3%	8.7%	3,498	5.6%	2.4%	2.6%	1.1%	0.0%	0.0%
Oklahoma County	204,850	86.1%	13.9%	28,501	10.3%	2.4%	1.0%	1.1%	0.0%	0.0%
Tulsa County	168,279	90.0%	10.0%	16,805	7.6%	2.0%	1.3%	0.1%	0.1%	0.0%
Oregon										
Clackamas County	89,541	91.5%	8.5%	7,608	4.7%	1.8%	2.9%	0.0%	0.0%	0.1%
Deschutes County	37,987	99.1%	0.9%	334	0.7%	0.0%	0.1%	0.6%	0.0%	0.0%
Douglas County	20,735	96.1%	3.9%	814	2.2%	1.6%	0.2%	0.0%	0.0%	0.0%
Jackson County	45,840	94.2%	5.8%	2,671	5.0%	0.4%	0.3%	0.2%	0.2%	0.0%
Lane County	98,197	94.8%	5.2%	5,152	1.8%	2.9%	1.5%	0.1%	0.2%	0.7%
Linn County	30,345	90.4%	9.6%	2,903	1.7%	6.5%	0.4%	0.0%	1.6%	0.0%
Marion County	83,502	86.1%	13.9%	11,645	10.9%	1.8%	1.7%	0.1%	0.0%	0.0%
Multnomah County	204,543	82.4%	17.6%	36,078	5.8%	5.7%	5.1%	0.9%	0.3%	0.4%
Washington County	145,345	84.9%	15.1%	21,969	7.5%	6.9%	2.0%	0.8%	0.1%	0.1%
Yamhill County	24,644	93.8%	6.2%	1,517	4.8%	1.3%	0.9%	0.0%	0.0%	0.0%
Pennsylvania										
Adams County	24,109	95.8%	4.2%	1,009	2.4%	1.5%	5.9%	0.8%	0.0%	0.0%
Allegheny County	315,594	92.9%	7.1%	22,462	1.2%	3.8%	1.7%	0.9%	0.1%	0.1%
Beaver County	37,866	99.7%	0.3%	129	1.0%	0.0%	0.3%	0.0%	0.0%	0.0%
Berks County	106,444	93.4%	6.6%	7,007	5.7%	1.0%	0.5%	0.1%	0.1%	0.0%
Blair County	29,018	98.4%	1.6%	478	1.4%	0.3%	0.0%	0.2%	0.0%	0.0%
Bucks County	140,107	92.3%	7.7%	10,806	2.2%	2.7%	2.9%	1.2%	0.0%	0.2%
Butler County	44,871	98.2%	1.8%	796	0.0%	1.4%	0.2%	0.2%	0.1%	0.0%
Cambria County	32,240	99.6%	0.4%	135	0.0%	0.4%	1.2%	0.1%	0.0%	0.0%
Centre County	65,126	90.8%	9.2%	5,971	0.1%	7.4%	0.9%	1.5%	0.0%	0.0%
Chester County	126,204	89.1%	10.9%	13,783	6.9%	3.2%	1.8%	0.5%	0.1%	0.0%
Cumberland County	58,745	96.4%	3.6%	2,135	0.2%	2.2%	1.6%	0.2%	0.1%	0.0%
Dauphin County	63,943	92.7%	7.3%	4,658	1.7%	4.4%	0.8%	0.9%	0.3%	0.0%
Delaware County	147,156	89.6%	10.4%	15,316	2.5%	3.8%	0.8%	3.5%	0.1%	0.0%
Erie County	73,987	94.7%	5.3%	3,949	0.7%	2.9%	2.0%	0.6%	0.0%	0.0%
Fayette County	27,807	100.0%	0.0%	0	0.0%	0.0%	0.1%	0.0%	0.0%	0.0%
Franklin County	34,886	96.8%	3.2%	1,106	3.1%	0.2%	3.6%	0.0%	0.1%	0.0%
Lackawanna County	52,413	95.3%	4.7%	2,464	1.3%	2.9%	0.4%	0.2%	0.7%	0.0%
Lancaster County	134,345	92.5%	7.5%	10,127	2.8%	1.4%	0.7%	2.7%	0.1%	0.0%
Lebanon County	28,438	97.1%	2.9%	816	2.0%	0.7%	0.7%	0.0%	0.0%	0.0%
Lehigh County	86,106	87.3%	12.7%	10,972	6.3%	5.0%	1.6%	0.6%	0.3%	0.0%
Luzerne County	78,732	92.9%	7.1%	5,625	4.9%	1.2%	0.8%	0.5%	0.0%	0.0%
Lycoming County	29,371	99.3%	0.7%	220	0.0%	0.4%	0.0%	0.7%	0.0%	0.0%
Mercer County	28,430	99.8%	0.2%	43	0.0%	0.0%	0.1%	0.0%	0.0%	0.0%
Monroe County	42,860	95.9%	4.1%	1,777	1.3%	1.6%	0.9%	0.0%	0.5%	1.3%
Montgomery County	188,495	90.5%	9.5%	17,906	2.5%	4.7%	1.4%	1.0%	0.2%	0.0%
Northampton County	72,610	92.9%	7.1%	5,146	2.2%	3.5%	1.6%	0.2%	0.0%	0.0%
Northumberland County	20,227	99.1%	0.9%	188	0.4%	0.3%	0.4%	0.0%	0.0%	0.0%
Philadelphia County	477,105	87.7%	12.3%	58,771	3.8%	6.1%	1.9%	1.7%	0.1%	0.0%
Schuylkill County	30,617	98.4%	1.6%	503	0.6%	0.2%	0.8%	0.0%	0.0%	0.0%
Washington County	46,539	98.7%	1.3%	619	0.3%	0.0%	0.8%	0.2%	0.0%	0.0%
Westmoreland County	73,762	98.5%	1.5%	1,094	0.1%	1.0%	0.9%	0.0%	0.0%	0.0%
York County	102,438	94.9%	5.1%	5,236	3.3%	0.8%	1.1%	0.8%	0.0%	0.0%
Rhode Island										
Kent County	35,016	95.2%	4.8%	1,684	1.7%	1.9%	0.9%	1.3%	0.1%	0.1%
Providence County	178,704	84.2%	15.8%	28,227	9.4%	2.6%	2.0%	2.6%	0.1%	0.0%
Washington County	32,924	98.0%	2.0%	644	0.6%	0.6%	0.6%	0.6%	0.0%	0.0%
South Carolina										
Aiken County	40,228	98.3%	1.7%	681	1.6%	0.2%	0.4%	0.0%	0.0%	0.0%
Anderson County	45,159	97.6%	2.4%	1,097	1.3%	0.8%	0.5%	0.5%	0.0%	0.0%
Beaufort County	37,996	86.0%	14.0%	5,302	10.1%	0.9%	2.1%	0.0%	2.3%	0.0%
Berkeley County	54,189	94.4%	5.6%	3,042	4.4%	1.2%	0.6%	0.2%	0.3%	0.0%
Charleston County	105,818	94.9%	5.1%	5,365	3.1%	1.6%	1.3%	0.3%	0.0%	0.0%
Dorchester County	38,082	95.0%	5.0%	1,923	3.5%	0.7%	0.5%	0.0%	0.5%	0.0%
Florence County	34,871	95.8%	4.2%	1,454	2.6%	0.8%	0.2%	0.0%	1.3%	0.0%

Table C-2: Counties—Nativity and World Region of Birth—*Continued*

	Total Millennial	Percent		Total Foreign Born	Percent of Foreign Born by Region of Birth					
		Native	Foreign Born		Latin America	Asia	Europe	Africa	North America	Oceania
South Carolina—Cont.										
Greenville County	124,317	92.3%	7.7%	9,524	5.1%	1.5%	0.9%	0.5%	0.2%	0.2%
Horry County	64,666	91.7%	8.3%	5,350	6.1%	1.5%	1.0%	0.2%	0.3%	0.1%
Lexington County	68,505	94.6%	5.4%	3,713	3.2%	1.9%	0.4%	0.6%	0.0%	0.0%
Orangeburg County	23,271	97.7%	2.3%	537	2.3%	0.0%	0.8%	0.0%	0.0%	0.0%
Pickens County	38,978	91.8%	8.2%	3,188	4.7%	2.9%	1.8%	0.5%	0.0%	0.2%
Richland County	131,291	95.9%	4.1%	5,434	2.1%	1.9%	2.4%	0.3%	0.0%	0.1%
Spartanburg County	76,183	93.1%	6.9%	5,294	4.4%	1.7%	1.6%	0.1%	0.0%	0.0%
Sumter County	29,711	97.8%	2.2%	659	2.0%	0.5%	0.6%	0.0%	0.0%	0.2%
York County	57,893	96.5%	3.5%	2,030	1.2%	1.4%	0.9%	0.0%	0.0%	0.1%
South Dakota										
Minnehaha County	50,232	95.2%	4.8%	2,399	0.4%	1.9%	1.4%	1.7%	0.0%	0.0%
Pennington County	25,155	98.7%	1.3%	327	0.0%	1.4%	0.4%	0.5%	0.0%	0.0%
Tennessee										
Blount County	28,615	96.8%	3.2%	909	3.0%	0.0%	0.2%	0.1%	0.0%	0.0%
Bradley County	25,327	95.7%	4.3%	1,101	3.2%	0.7%	0.4%	0.0%	0.0%	0.7%
Davidson County	192,958	86.1%	13.9%	26,897	6.7%	3.6%	0.9%	3.2%	0.2%	0.0%
Hamilton County	87,443	92.8%	7.2%	6,334	4.9%	1.6%	1.8%	0.1%	0.2%	0.0%
Knox County	124,022	92.7%	7.3%	9,083	2.8%	3.0%	0.9%	1.6%	0.3%	0.0%
Madison County	25,432	95.7%	4.3%	1,088	2.3%	2.0%	0.3%	0.0%	0.0%	0.0%
Montgomery County	61,480	94.6%	5.4%	3,313	2.0%	1.4%	3.7%	3.1%	0.0%	0.0%
Rutherford County	85,492	90.4%	9.6%	8,243	5.2%	2.7%	1.5%	1.3%	0.2%	0.0%
Sevier County	20,636	93.2%	6.8%	1,411	2.9%	1.4%	2.5%	0.0%	0.0%	0.0%
Shelby County	260,771	94.0%	6.0%	15,649	3.6%	1.8%	1.2%	0.9%	0.0%	0.0%
Sullivan County	33,755	98.9%	1.1%	355	0.2%	1.8%	0.1%	0.0%	0.0%	0.0%
Sumner County	41,227	91.5%	8.5%	3,505	2.9%	1.2%	1.0%	3.5%	0.0%	0.0%
Washington County	33,420	94.9%	5.1%	1,717	2.9%	0.5%	0.1%	1.6%	0.0%	0.0%
Williamson County	42,263	95.8%	4.2%	1,789	1.7%	1.4%	1.1%	0.0%	0.2%	0.0%
Wilson County	29,571	96.2%	3.8%	1,126	4.2%	0.0%	0.0%	0.0%	0.0%	0.0%
Texas										
Bell County	102,974	96.3%	3.7%	3,822	2.8%	0.7%	4.0%	0.3%	0.0%	0.0%
Bexar County	529,963	89.0%	11.0%	58,501	8.6%	2.8%	1.2%	0.3%	0.1%	0.0%
Bowie County	24,613	94.7%	5.3%	1,312	5.0%	0.2%	0.0%	0.0%	0.0%	0.3%
Brazoria County	87,769	88.0%	12.0%	10,575	8.4%	2.6%	0.6%	0.8%	0.0%	0.0%
Brazos County	93,443	88.5%	11.5%	10,753	6.5%	4.2%	1.2%	0.3%	0.0%	0.0%
Cameron County	117,741	81.3%	18.7%	22,014	17.3%	0.2%	0.7%	0.0%	1.2%	0.0%
Collin County	203,054	86.1%	13.9%	28,217	5.2%	6.4%	2.1%	1.6%	0.3%	0.2%
Comal County	27,155	91.4%	8.6%	2,326	7.8%	3.4%	4.5%	0.0%	0.0%	0.0%
Dallas County	694,588	76.3%	23.7%	164,391	18.3%	4.0%	0.6%	1.4%	0.1%	0.0%
Denton County	200,086	86.0%	14.0%	27,971	7.5%	5.2%	1.1%	0.7%	0.2%	0.1%
Ector County	45,187	86.6%	13.4%	6,041	12.9%	0.6%	1.0%	0.3%	0.0%	0.0%
El Paso County	246,978	84.4%	15.6%	38,565	15.9%	0.8%	1.2%	0.1%	0.0%	0.2%
Ellis County	41,068	91.8%	8.2%	3,372	8.0%	1.7%	0.5%	0.6%	0.0%	0.0%
Fort Bend County	158,317	81.0%	19.0%	30,022	8.4%	7.9%	2.1%	1.6%	0.6%	0.1%
Galveston County	78,839	92.9%	7.1%	5,601	5.0%	0.9%	0.5%	0.3%	0.6%	0.0%
Grayson County	30,811	92.0%	8.0%	2,480	6.7%	1.9%	1.5%	0.3%	0.1%	0.0%
Gregg County	33,454	92.0%	8.0%	2,681	7.4%	1.1%	0.2%	0.0%	0.0%	0.0%
Guadalupe County	35,549	94.6%	5.4%	1,932	2.5%	2.7%	2.3%	0.0%	0.0%	0.7%
Harris County	1,238,541	76.1%	23.9%	296,602	18.0%	4.9%	1.1%	1.0%	0.2%	0.0%
Hays County	58,556	94.5%	5.5%	3,206	4.8%	0.6%	0.8%	0.2%	0.1%	0.0%
Hidalgo County	240,329	75.9%	24.1%	58,000	23.7%	0.9%	0.2%	0.0%	0.0%	0.0%
Jefferson County	70,230	88.2%	11.8%	8,322	10.5%	1.2%	0.3%	0.4%	0.2%	0.0%
Johnson County	38,847	93.3%	6.7%	2,616	6.7%	0.5%	0.4%	0.0%	0.0%	0.0%
Kaufman County	25,319	94.2%	5.8%	1,460	5.2%	0.8%	0.7%	0.0%	0.0%	0.0%
Lubbock County	99,238	94.7%	5.3%	5,308	3.1%	2.0%	1.0%	0.7%	0.2%	0.0%
McLennan County	71,146	90.8%	9.2%	6,575	6.0%	2.6%	0.5%	0.6%	0.2%	0.0%
Midland County	43,594	94.4%	5.6%	2,449	6.1%	0.5%	0.5%	0.0%	0.2%	0.0%
Montgomery County	121,769	88.2%	11.8%	14,400	9.3%	1.8%	1.3%	0.1%	0.2%	0.0%
Nueces County	95,902	92.0%	8.0%	7,679	6.3%	1.9%	0.6%	0.2%	0.1%	0.0%
Parker County	29,995	96.9%	3.1%	926	4.7%	0.5%	1.4%	0.0%	0.0%	0.0%
Potter County	32,810	84.1%	15.9%	5,222	11.6%	3.1%	0.0%	1.6%	0.0%	0.0%
Randall County	34,237	92.6%	7.4%	2,530	2.7%	2.3%	1.0%	2.0%	0.0%	0.0%
Smith County	57,788	89.0%	11.0%	6,377	8.2%	0.7%	0.0%	1.6%	0.7%	0.0%
Tarrant County	528,418	85.1%	14.9%	78,570	10.3%	3.2%	0.8%	1.2%	0.4%	0.0%
Taylor County	43,355	96.1%	3.9%	1,673	0.6%	2.5%	0.4%	1.0%	0.0%	0.0%
Tom Green County	34,346	97.3%	2.7%	923	2.1%	0.5%	1.8%	0.0%	0.0%	0.0%
Travis County	344,597	80.6%	19.4%	66,745	13.6%	4.9%	1.4%	0.5%	0.3%	0.2%
Webb County	79,350	84.1%	15.9%	12,597	17.0%	0.0%	0.1%	0.0%	0.0%	0.0%
Wichita County	40,384	93.9%	6.1%	2,452	3.2%	1.0%	2.1%	1.3%	0.0%	0.0%
Williamson County	115,744	89.8%	10.2%	11,820	5.8%	3.2%	1.8%	0.8%	0.0%	0.1%
Utah										
Cache County	43,131	91.6%	8.4%	3,602	5.6%	2.7%	0.4%	0.0%	0.8%	0.0%
Davis County	90,315	95.8%	4.2%	3,800	1.5%	2.0%	0.5%	0.1%	0.1%	0.5%
Salt Lake County	315,374	87.4%	12.6%	39,810	7.7%	3.2%	1.6%	0.7%	0.3%	0.0%
Utah County	197,950	91.7%	8.3%	16,403	4.8%	2.5%	1.2%	0.1%	0.9%	0.4%
Washington County	36,461	97.6%	2.4%	885	1.2%	0.3%	0.9%	0.0%	0.8%	0.0%
Weber County	66,208	94.3%	5.7%	3,777	4.2%	1.6%	0.2%	0.6%	0.5%	0.0%
Vermont										
Chittenden County	49,483	93.7%	6.3%	3,110	0.6%	2.7%	2.8%	1.0%	0.3%	0.5%

Table C-2: Counties—Nativity and World Region of Birth—*Continued*

	Total Millennial	Percent		Total Foreign Born	Percent of Foreign Born by Region of Birth					
		Native	Foreign Born		Latin America	Asia	Europe	Africa	North America	Oceania
Virginia										
Albemarle County..	28,786	93.5%	6.5%	1,882	1.1%	4.5%	2.5%	0.3%	0.0%	0.0%
Arlington County..	73,199	81.0%	19.0%	13,908	8.8%	7.7%	3.0%	2.2%	0.2%	0.1%
Chesterfield County....................................	82,105	95.3%	4.7%	3,823	2.7%	1.4%	1.4%	0.3%	0.1%	0.0%
Fairfax County..	279,011	71.6%	28.4%	79,158	10.4%	14.3%	3.1%	2.6%	0.1%	0.2%
Hanover County..	23,207	97.0%	3.0%	696	1.5%	1.2%	1.1%	0.3%	0.0%	0.0%
Henrico County..	79,944	87.1%	12.9%	10,336	4.3%	5.8%	3.0%	1.7%	0.0%	0.0%
Loudoun County..	80,007	84.4%	15.6%	12,518	4.8%	10.2%	3.6%	0.6%	0.0%	0.0%
Montgomery County....................................	44,141	94.9%	5.1%	2,264	0.0%	3.5%	3.3%	0.3%	0.0%	0.0%
Prince William County................................	113,001	75.9%	24.1%	27,262	13.1%	7.2%	3.9%	3.3%	0.3%	0.0%
Roanoke County..	20,674	98.8%	1.2%	239	0.6%	0.6%	0.0%	0.0%	0.0%	0.0%
Spotsylvania County	32,146	97.3%	2.7%	863	0.4%	2.4%	0.6%	0.0%	0.0%	0.0%
Stafford County..	38,219	91.6%	8.4%	3,207	4.3%	2.6%	1.0%	1.8%	0.0%	0.4%
Washington										
Benton County	46,067	86.8%	13.2%	6,058	10.4%	0.9%	2.2%	0.5%	0.0%	0.0%
Clark County	105,849	91.1%	8.9%	9,382	3.5%	2.6%	4.4%	0.1%	0.5%	0.0%
Cowlitz County...	23,187	93.7%	6.3%	1,456	6.0%	0.3%	0.0%	0.0%	0.0%	0.0%
Grant County..	25,201	79.9%	20.1%	5,061	14.5%	4.5%	1.7%	0.0%	0.0%	0.0%
King County..	531,505	77.4%	22.6%	119,857	5.6%	11.0%	3.4%	2.9%	1.0%	0.5%
Kitsap County...	65,185	97.8%	2.2%	1,444	1.4%	1.5%	1.2%	0.0%	0.1%	0.4%
Pierce County...	221,284	90.2%	9.8%	21,786	3.9%	3.5%	3.3%	0.7%	0.3%	0.5%
Skagit County...	27,206	89.9%	10.1%	2,737	3.7%	3.0%	4.3%	1.2%	0.9%	0.1%
Snohomish County	184,410	85.5%	14.5%	26,710	3.7%	6.8%	3.5%	0.9%	0.9%	0.1%
Spokane County..	133,544	94.1%	5.9%	7,932	0.7%	2.9%	3.5%	0.4%	0.6%	0.4%
Thurston County	70,438	92.1%	7.9%	5,581	3.5%	3.0%	0.9%	0.8%	0.8%	0.0%
Whatcom County	62,149	92.2%	7.8%	4,863	2.8%	2.5%	3.3%	0.0%	1.0%	0.1%
Yakima County...	65,994	76.4%	23.6%	15,576	23.6%	0.8%	0.0%	0.0%	0.2%	0.0%
West Virginia										
Berkeley County	26,793	95.5%	4.5%	1,197	3.2%	0.5%	0.0%	0.0%	0.7%	0.0%
Cabell County...	27,010	99.6%	0.4%	107	0.3%	0.1%	0.0%	0.0%	0.0%	0.0%
Kanawha County...	44,551	98.5%	1.5%	677	0.0%	1.5%	0.0%	0.0%	0.0%	0.0%
Monongalia County.....................................	41,965	94.6%	5.4%	2,282	0.8%	3.0%	0.4%	1.1%	0.1%	0.1%
Wisconsin										
Brown County	64,640	95.2%	4.8%	3,097	3.1%	1.3%	1.3%	0.4%	0.0%	0.0%
Dane County	157,015	88.4%	11.6%	18,156	4.7%	6.8%	0.4%	0.1%	0.1%	0.0%
Eau Claire County.......................................	33,956	96.9%	3.1%	1,045	0.3%	3.1%	0.0%	0.0%	0.0%	0.0%
Fond du Lac County....................................	22,865	96.6%	3.4%	778	2.1%	0.4%	0.7%	0.2%	0.2%	0.0%
Kenosha County..	42,737	94.7%	5.3%	2,268	2.7%	1.2%	1.4%	0.0%	0.0%	0.0%
La Crosse County.......................................	37,898	92.9%	7.1%	2,691	0.7%	6.1%	0.1%	0.2%	0.0%	0.0%
Marathon County..	31,554	90.0%	10.0%	3,166	2.6%	6.5%	2.2%	0.0%	0.0%	0.0%
Milwaukee County......................................	275,711	91.6%	8.4%	23,120	4.1%	3.3%	1.0%	0.5%	0.0%	0.0%
Outagamie County......................................	44,856	94.3%	5.7%	2,538	3.3%	1.8%	0.3%	0.0%	0.3%	0.7%
Racine County..	48,379	93.2%	6.8%	3,300	7.1%	0.0%	0.5%	0.0%	0.0%	0.0%
Rock County	39,734	95.0%	5.0%	1,981	3.9%	1.0%	0.5%	0.0%	0.0%	0.0%
Sheboygan County......................................	25,686	94.5%	5.5%	1,417	3.1%	3.3%	0.5%	0.0%	0.0%	0.0%
Walworth County..	27,115	89.5%	10.5%	2,852	7.9%	0.9%	6.2%	0.0%	0.0%	0.0%
Washington County.....................................	28,174	96.3%	3.7%	1,034	1.2%	0.9%	1.6%	0.0%	0.0%	0.0%
Waukesha County.......................................	85,418	93.8%	6.2%	5,333	1.7%	3.6%	0.8%	0.7%	0.0%	0.0%
Winnebago County......................................	46,883	97.6%	2.4%	1,128	0.5%	2.4%	0.3%	0.0%	0.0%	0.0%
Wyoming										
Laramie County..	25,613	94.3%	5.7%	1,457	2.6%	2.5%	1.2%	0.1%	0.4%	0.0%

Table C-3: Places—Nativity and World Region of Birth

	Total Millennial	Percent		Total Foreign Born	Percent of Foreign Born by Region of Birth					
		Native	Foreign Born		Latin America	Asia	Europe	Africa	North America	Oceania
Alabama										
Birmingham city	62,699	95.2%	4.8%	2,981	3.3%	1.5%	0.8%	0.1%	0.0%	0.0%
Huntsville city	52,004	93.2%	6.8%	3,525	4.2%	2.7%	1.8%	0.0%	0.0%	0.0%
Mobile city	52,173	95.2%	4.8%	2,520	2.8%	1.5%	0.8%	0.0%	0.0%	0.0%
Montgomery city	58,994	97.1%	2.9%	1,721	2.6%	0.2%	0.2%	0.1%	0.0%	0.0%
Tuscaloosa city	39,763	95.4%	4.6%	1,821	2.0%	0.5%	1.5%	0.6%	0.5%	0.0%
Alaska										
Anchorage municipality	89,088	95.1%	4.9%	4,340	1.6%	3.4%	0.5%	0.0%	0.6%	0.0%
Arizona										
Chandler city	65,956	91.6%	8.4%	5,542	5.2%	2.9%	1.7%	0.4%	0.1%	0.0%
Glendale city	64,873	83.7%	16.3%	10,592	11.6%	4.6%	2.7%	0.5%	0.1%	0.0%
Mesa city	124,304	91.4%	8.6%	10,712	7.2%	1.1%	0.4%	0.5%	0.1%	0.0%
Peoria city	38,091	93.2%	6.8%	2,606	4.1%	2.8%	1.5%	0.0%	0.0%	0.0%
Phoenix city	420,298	82.0%	18.0%	75,526	13.8%	2.6%	1.1%	1.1%	0.3%	0.0%
Scottsdale city	49,969	92.5%	7.5%	3,749	3.4%	3.5%	0.7%	1.0%	0.6%	0.4%
Surprise city	21,496	93.9%	6.1%	1,310	3.1%	2.2%	1.5%	0.0%	0.0%	0.0%
Tempe city	74,507	86.5%	13.5%	10,046	4.3%	7.4%	2.0%	0.2%	0.4%	0.0%
Tucson city	164,774	88.5%	11.5%	19,027	7.5%	3.5%	1.4%	0.6%	0.1%	0.0%
Yuma city	27,868	81.1%	18.9%	5,261	19.0%	0.4%	0.4%	0.0%	0.0%	0.0%
Arkansas										
Little Rock city	52,430	92.1%	7.9%	4,125	5.7%	4.3%	0.1%	0.0%	0.0%	0.0%
California										
Anaheim city	95,980	81.0%	19.0%	18,261	12.7%	5.7%	0.9%	0.6%	0.1%	0.0%
Antioch city	31,631	86.2%	13.8%	4,357	11.2%	4.8%	0.0%	0.0%	0.0%	0.0%
Bakersfield city	107,664	83.7%	16.3%	17,569	13.3%	2.8%	0.4%	0.0%	0.3%	0.4%
Berkeley city	48,955	73.2%	26.8%	13,125	1.0%	19.5%	4.8%	0.4%	1.0%	1.5%
Burbank city	23,393	78.4%	21.6%	5,059	6.0%	15.0%	1.0%	0.2%	0.8%	0.9%
Carlsbad city	22,855	91.2%	8.8%	2,006	1.2%	4.8%	4.2%	1.1%	0.8%	0.0%
Carson city	25,511	80.7%	19.3%	4,935	8.4%	11.2%	0.3%	0.0%	0.0%	0.0%
Chula Vista city	71,383	87.7%	12.3%	8,805	10.4%	4.1%	0.4%	0.3%	0.0%	0.1%
Clovis city	26,910	94.8%	5.2%	1,409	2.0%	3.2%	1.4%	0.2%	0.8%	0.0%
Compton city	29,029	79.4%	20.6%	5,979	20.4%	1.2%	0.0%	0.0%	0.0%	0.0%
Concord city	31,725	89.4%	10.6%	3,363	4.6%	6.4%	1.0%	0.5%	0.0%	0.0%
Corona city	46,013	86.8%	13.2%	6,088	8.2%	4.5%	0.1%	0.8%	0.2%	0.0%
Costa Mesa city	33,705	83.4%	16.6%	5,605	8.8%	7.7%	0.2%	0.0%	0.2%	0.2%
Daly City city	30,077	72.8%	27.2%	8,168	6.7%	21.2%	1.2%	0.0%	0.0%	0.0%
Downey city	35,471	85.7%	14.3%	5,069	11.0%	2.3%	0.4%	0.8%	0.0%	0.0%
El Cajon city	30,019	82.2%	17.8%	5,357	7.9%	10.6%	0.0%	0.0%	0.2%	0.0%
El Monte city	30,902	69.7%	30.3%	9,348	20.0%	11.8%	0.0%	0.0%	0.0%	0.0%
Elk Grove city	42,148	87.0%	13.0%	5,486	2.7%	8.6%	1.2%	0.2%	0.2%	0.6%
Escondido city	44,106	67.4%	32.6%	14,380	30.3%	2.5%	0.0%	0.0%	0.5%	0.0%
Fairfield city	34,335	80.8%	19.2%	6,580	11.1%	5.3%	1.6%	0.0%	0.6%	0.9%
Fontana city	60,471	82.2%	17.8%	10,759	12.7%	4.3%	0.0%	1.1%	0.0%	0.0%
Fremont city	51,789	72.5%	27.5%	14,231	1.2%	26.4%	0.3%	0.0%	0.6%	0.0%
Fresno city	150,965	87.6%	12.4%	18,705	6.9%	5.6%	0.3%	0.0%	0.3%	0.1%
Fullerton city	44,549	74.8%	25.2%	11,218	13.8%	11.2%	1.5%	0.0%	0.0%	0.0%
Garden Grove city	46,235	72.7%	27.3%	12,620	16.4%	11.2%	0.7%	0.3%	0.2%	0.0%
Glendale city	47,236	60.2%	39.8%	18,814	3.2%	35.0%	3.1%	0.5%	0.0%	0.1%
Hayward city	42,182	65.8%	34.2%	14,442	20.0%	11.2%	1.8%	1.0%	0.0%	1.4%
Hesperia city	55,942	93.5%	6.5%	3,653	4.7%	1.8%	0.2%	0.0%	0.5%	0.0%
Inglewood city	31,386	73.0%	27.0%	8,463	23.3%	1.6%	0.2%	2.8%	0.0%	0.0%
Irvine city	70,736	79.0%	21.0%	14,850	1.6%	19.2%	1.0%	0.2%	0.3%	0.4%
Jurupa Valley city	29,796	86.9%	13.1%	3,914	9.3%	3.4%	0.0%	1.1%	0.0%	0.0%
Lancaster city	44,656	92.0%	8.0%	3,552	4.8%	2.1%	0.0%	1.2%	0.0%	0.0%
Long Beach city	132,264	84.8%	15.2%	20,116	10.8%	4.1%	0.6%	0.5%	0.1%	0.1%
Los Angeles city	1,105,809	73.7%	26.3%	291,199	17.8%	7.4%	1.1%	0.4%	0.3%	0.1%
Mission Viejo city	21,020	91.7%	8.3%	1,746	3.8%	4.2%	1.0%	0.4%	0.0%	0.0%
Modesto city	59,831	86.7%	13.3%	7,952	11.0%	2.6%	0.0%	1.0%	0.0%	0.0%
Moreno Valley city	65,038	87.4%	12.6%	8,204	9.1%	3.7%	0.2%	0.6%	0.0%	0.0%
Murrieta city	29,276	91.8%	8.2%	2,406	5.0%	4.1%	0.2%	0.0%	0.0%	0.0%
Norwalk city	29,652	84.3%	15.7%	4,651	10.2%	3.9%	0.9%	0.4%	0.3%	0.0%
Oakland city	106,839	78.4%	21.6%	23,092	12.3%	7.6%	1.5%	0.5%	0.2%	0.2%
Oceanside city	44,351	90.7%	9.3%	4,146	6.4%	3.1%	0.4%	0.8%	0.5%	0.1%
Ontario city	48,481	85.6%	14.4%	6,981	12.1%	1.4%	0.7%	0.4%	0.0%	0.0%
Orange city	40,584	79.3%	20.7%	8,402	16.8%	3.9%	1.0%	0.0%	0.0%	0.0%
Oxnard city	63,365	72.4%	27.6%	17,498	25.8%	2.2%	0.2%	0.2%	0.0%	0.0%
Palmdale city	45,149	92.0%	8.0%	3,592	7.3%	0.9%	0.1%	0.0%	0.3%	0.0%
Pasadena city	40,866	79.4%	20.6%	8,399	8.7%	9.9%	0.8%	0.7%	1.5%	0.0%
Pomona city	47,598	77.2%	22.8%	10,839	16.4%	6.1%	0.2%	0.0%	0.0%	0.1%
Rancho Cucamonga city	48,096	86.3%	13.7%	6,600	4.2%	8.0%	0.3%	1.3%	0.0%	0.1%
Redding city	24,640	90.9%	9.1%	2,253	2.5%	3.5%	3.1%	0.0%	0.0%	0.0%
Rialto city	30,933	85.9%	14.1%	4,362	14.0%	0.5%	0.0%	0.8%	0.0%	0.0%
Richmond city	30,165	60.7%	39.3%	11,856	26.9%	9.8%	0.4%	2.7%	0.0%	0.0%
Riverside city	100,148	86.9%	13.1%	13,072	10.0%	3.8%	0.4%	0.1%	0.0%	0.0%
Roseville city	32,207	85.6%	14.4%	4,635	6.1%	5.8%	3.2%	0.0%	0.0%	0.0%
Sacramento city	134,447	81.0%	19.0%	25,607	10.5%	6.7%	1.5%	0.4%	0.0%	1.2%
Salinas city	47,404	67.7%	32.3%	15,315	29.1%	3.1%	0.3%	0.0%	0.0%	0.0%

Table C-3: Places—Nativity and World Region of Birth—*Continued*

	Total Millennial	Percent		Total Foreign Born	Percent of Foreign Born by Region of Birth					
		Native	Foreign Born		Latin America	Asia	Europe	Africa	North America	Oceania
California—Cont.										
San Bernardino city	67,085	85.3%	14.7%	9,882	12.9%	1.8%	0.0%	0.0%	0.2%	0.0%
San Buenaventura (Ventura) city	28,078	91.9%	8.1%	2,271	4.7%	1.9%	1.7%	0.0%	0.0%	0.0%
San Diego city	412,816	80.6%	19.4%	79,997	8.5%	9.5%	2.5%	1.0%	0.2%	0.1%
San Francisco city	216,580	77.3%	22.7%	49,144	5.6%	13.8%	3.7%	0.5%	0.8%	0.3%
San Jose city	250,499	71.5%	28.5%	71,463	12.7%	14.8%	1.1%	0.7%	0.6%	0.1%
San Mateo city	21,249	82.2%	17.8%	3,774	8.6%	7.7%	1.6%	0.0%	0.0%	1.7%
Santa Ana city	104,347	68.8%	31.2%	32,518	27.4%	3.9%	0.6%	0.0%	0.0%	0.0%
Santa Clara city	35,288	57.1%	42.9%	15,149	9.1%	32.5%	1.6%	2.0%	0.4%	0.2%
Santa Clarita city	46,023	85.5%	14.5%	6,687	9.0%	4.8%	0.6%	0.1%	0.7%	0.0%
Santa Maria city	31,713	67.2%	32.8%	10,411	31.1%	2.1%	0.0%	0.0%	0.0%	0.0%
Santa Monica city	21,654	84.9%	15.1%	3,278	3.7%	9.2%	3.3%	0.0%	0.2%	0.0%
Santa Rosa city	45,707	87.9%	12.1%	5,519	8.8%	1.7%	0.2%	1.7%	0.0%	0.2%
Simi Valley city	28,302	88.7%	11.3%	3,185	6.9%	1.8%	0.7%	1.3%	0.0%	0.7%
South Gate city	29,962	75.0%	25.0%	7,503	25.2%	0.0%	0.0%	0.0%	0.0%	0.3%
Stockton city	83,153	79.5%	20.5%	17,083	15.2%	6.2%	0.0%	0.0%	0.0%	0.1%
Sunnyvale city	35,578	59.9%	40.1%	14,273	3.2%	36.4%	1.4%	0.6%	0.5%	0.8%
Temecula city	31,215	91.4%	8.6%	2,670	1.7%	4.6%	1.0%	0.3%	1.4%	0.0%
Thousand Oaks city	30,401	83.1%	16.9%	5,137	10.4%	3.6%	3.2%	0.0%	0.0%	0.0%
Torrance city	31,027	86.8%	13.2%	4,111	2.4%	11.4%	0.3%	0.4%	0.0%	0.1%
Vacaville city	25,744	94.2%	5.8%	1,483	3.6%	2.1%	1.4%	0.0%	0.5%	0.5%
Vallejo city	31,222	83.0%	17.0%	5,317	6.5%	9.5%	0.9%	0.2%	0.3%	0.0%
Victorville city	34,079	92.6%	7.4%	2,536	7.6%	0.5%	0.0%	0.0%	0.0%	0.0%
Visalia city	37,794	91.5%	8.5%	3,194	6.9%	1.6%	0.4%	0.0%	0.0%	0.0%
Vista city	28,569	73.2%	26.8%	7,650	24.6%	1.3%	1.6%	0.3%	0.0%	0.4%
West Covina city	31,327	82.3%	17.7%	5,546	10.8%	6.8%	0.3%	0.7%	0.0%	0.0%
Westminster city	23,446	73.3%	26.7%	6,255	15.8%	11.4%	0.0%	0.0%	0.3%	0.0%
Colorado										
Arvada city	28,727	93.3%	6.7%	1,932	2.4%	0.0%	4.7%	0.0%	0.3%	0.0%
Aurora city	91,957	83.9%	16.1%	14,821	11.4%	3.0%	1.4%	2.7%	0.2%	0.0%
Boulder city	47,328	95.7%	4.3%	2,012	0.7%	2.0%	1.6%	0.1%	0.8%	0.7%
Centennial city	24,801	88.6%	11.4%	2,829	3.5%	5.2%	1.1%	0.3%	2.5%	0.0%
Colorado Springs city	121,448	93.3%	6.7%	8,111	3.9%	2.4%	4.2%	0.2%	0.0%	0.1%
Denver city	182,517	83.8%	16.2%	29,519	10.8%	3.3%	1.4%	1.9%	0.0%	0.0%
Fort Collins city	60,116	93.7%	6.3%	3,763	2.3%	3.1%	1.3%	0.0%	0.0%	0.0%
Greeley city	33,213	95.1%	4.9%	1,611	5.4%	1.6%	1.3%	0.0%	0.0%	0.0%
Lakewood city	35,859	94.4%	5.6%	2,005	2.4%	1.9%	1.2%	0.0%	0.2%	0.0%
Pueblo city	28,398	93.4%	6.6%	1,871	5.0%	0.5%	1.6%	0.0%	0.0%	0.0%
Thornton city	34,405	89.5%	10.5%	3,616	5.5%	4.0%	0.8%	0.2%	0.0%	0.0%
Westminster city	31,101	88.8%	11.2%	3,493	7.9%	1.6%	2.0%	0.0%	0.0%	0.0%
Connecticut										
Bridgeport city	43,377	72.3%	27.7%	12,010	22.4%	4.9%	0.8%	0.2%	0.0%	0.0%
Hartford city	40,826	80.1%	19.9%	8,124	16.3%	4.1%	0.4%	0.5%	0.1%	0.0%
New Haven city	45,402	84.0%	16.0%	7,263	9.0%	5.3%	1.3%	0.5%	0.5%	0.1%
Stamford city	33,807	65.3%	34.7%	11,716	29.2%	4.0%	6.6%	0.4%	0.0%	0.0%
Waterbury city	29,753	84.2%	15.8%	4,696	10.7%	2.3%	1.3%	2.8%	0.0%	0.0%
District of Columbia										
Washington city	201,595	86.4%	13.6%	27,390	6.5%	2.9%	3.0%	2.4%	0.4%	0.1%
Florida										
Cape Coral city	36,448	87.1%	12.9%	4,692	9.2%	0.2%	4.0%	0.0%	0.2%	0.0%
Clearwater city	23,401	88.5%	11.5%	2,701	8.7%	1.7%	0.6%	0.3%	1.0%	0.0%
Coral Springs city	32,526	83.1%	16.9%	5,500	14.9%	0.5%	1.2%	0.7%	1.2%	0.0%
Fort Lauderdale city	38,760	79.2%	20.8%	8,050	16.6%	2.5%	3.4%	0.2%	0.3%	0.0%
Gainesville city	64,700	88.3%	11.7%	7,602	5.9%	5.5%	1.9%	1.4%	0.5%	0.0%
Hialeah city	55,132	46.6%	53.4%	29,453	54.0%	0.3%	0.2%	0.0%	0.0%	0.0%
Hollywood city	30,826	77.7%	22.3%	6,862	15.3%	2.7%	1.8%	1.8%	0.8%	0.0%
Jacksonville city	223,251	93.1%	6.9%	15,395	2.2%	3.2%	2.1%	0.7%	0.2%	0.1%
Lakeland city	26,243	91.9%	8.1%	2,123	8.8%	1.3%	0.5%	0.0%	0.0%	0.0%
Miami Beach city	20,119	70.1%	29.9%	6,024	22.8%	0.5%	7.0%	0.0%	0.9%	0.0%
Miami city	99,815	60.6%	39.4%	39,376	36.5%	0.4%	2.6%	0.4%	0.4%	0.0%
Miami Gardens city	32,190	76.7%	23.3%	7,503	21.3%	2.3%	0.3%	0.0%	0.0%	0.7%
Miramar city	37,135	68.4%	31.6%	11,736	28.9%	1.9%	2.1%	0.0%	0.2%	0.0%
Orlando city	79,273	82.2%	17.8%	14,141	15.4%	3.0%	2.1%	0.4%	0.3%	0.0%
Palm Bay city	23,697	92.3%	7.7%	1,830	7.7%	0.4%	0.0%	0.0%	0.0%	0.0%
Pembroke Pines city	40,226	81.9%	18.1%	7,299	14.9%	2.3%	1.1%	1.4%	0.6%	0.3%
Pompano Beach city	25,547	67.4%	32.6%	8,329	29.7%	1.6%	0.4%	1.6%	0.7%	0.0%
Port St. Lucie city	38,656	92.2%	7.8%	3,000	5.7%	2.1%	0.2%	0.0%	0.0%	0.0%
St. Petersburg city	60,199	91.1%	8.9%	5,349	3.4%	1.9%	3.5%	0.2%	0.2%	0.0%
Tallahassee city	86,319	93.4%	6.6%	5,683	5.0%	2.3%	0.6%	0.3%	0.0%	0.0%
Tampa city	104,339	88.1%	11.9%	12,438	8.3%	2.6%	2.0%	1.1%	0.2%	0.2%
West Palm Beach city	29,051	74.3%	25.7%	7,480	25.9%	0.2%	1.3%	0.0%	0.0%	0.2%
Georgia										
Athens-Clarke County unified govt (bal)	54,062	93.7%	6.3%	3,422	2.7%	2.9%	1.4%	0.1%	0.1%	0.1%
Atlanta city	143,295	89.7%	10.3%	14,777	3.0%	5.3%	1.7%	1.0%	0.2%	0.1%
Augusta-Richmond County consolidated govt (bal)	57,457	97.2%	2.8%	1,584	0.8%	1.6%	2.2%	0.5%	0.0%	0.1%
Columbus city	58,130	93.3%	6.7%	3,879	2.7%	1.2%	3.7%	0.3%	0.6%	0.0%

Table C-3: Places—Nativity and World Region of Birth—*Continued*

| | Total Millennial | Percent | | Total Foreign Born | Percent of Foreign Born by Region of Birth | | | | | |
		Native	Foreign Born		Latin America	Asia	Europe	Africa	North America	Oceania
Georgia—Cont.										
Macon city	26,832	95.1%	4.9%	1,310	4.8%	2.8%	0.3%	0.2%	0.0%	0.0%
Roswell city	23,495	82.0%	18.0%	4,224	9.0%	5.3%	1.9%	2.2%	1.4%	0.3%
Sandy Springs city	25,297	80.3%	19.7%	4,994	10.4%	4.1%	1.6%	4.7%	0.0%	0.0%
Savannah city	45,035	93.2%	6.8%	3,059	3.6%	1.8%	1.5%	0.7%	0.0%	0.0%
Hawaii										
Urban Honolulu CDP	87,855	79.3%	20.7%	18,172	0.8%	16.3%	0.5%	0.1%	0.2%	5.4%
Idaho										
Boise City city	62,035	93.2%	6.8%	4,211	2.6%	2.9%	1.4%	1.2%	0.0%	0.0%
Illinois										
Aurora city	52,749	78.0%	22.0%	11,586	18.1%	3.4%	1.6%	0.1%	0.2%	0.0%
Chicago city	793,782	83.6%	16.4%	129,815	8.7%	4.8%	2.3%	1.0%	0.1%	0.0%
Elgin city	31,610	78.7%	21.3%	6,730	19.6%	1.5%	0.6%	0.5%	0.0%	0.0%
Joliet city	40,784	85.4%	14.6%	5,947	10.9%	1.7%	3.1%	0.0%	0.0%	0.0%
Naperville city	36,457	91.6%	8.4%	3,063	1.5%	3.1%	4.0%	0.2%	0.2%	0.0%
Peoria city	33,592	95.0%	5.0%	1,675	1.1%	3.8%	0.1%	0.0%	0.0%	0.0%
Rockford city	40,295	90.7%	9.3%	3,745	6.0%	3.5%	0.0%	0.2%	0.0%	0.0%
Springfield city	30,131	96.2%	3.8%	1,149	2.0%	1.6%	0.4%	0.0%	0.0%	0.0%
Indiana										
Evansville city	30,745	98.3%	1.7%	531	0.1%	1.2%	0.5%	0.0%	0.0%	0.0%
Fort Wayne city	67,163	92.4%	7.6%	5,110	2.7%	2.2%	2.0%	1.1%	0.1%	0.0%
Indianapolis city (bal)	231,827	88.5%	11.5%	26,616	6.6%	2.9%	0.9%	1.5%	0.1%	0.1%
South Bend city	27,619	94.6%	5.4%	1,503	3.2%	1.4%	0.6%	0.5%	0.0%	0.0%
Iowa										
Cedar Rapids city	34,639	94.7%	5.3%	1,851	1.1%	3.6%	0.0%	0.0%	1.2%	0.0%
Davenport city	26,470	96.9%	3.1%	809	0.0%	0.9%	1.7%	1.5%	0.0%	0.0%
Des Moines city	56,963	81.6%	18.4%	10,503	6.0%	6.8%	1.0%	7.1%	0.0%	0.0%
Kansas										
Kansas City city	39,339	84.6%	15.4%	6,074	10.8%	4.4%	0.6%	1.2%	0.0%	0.0%
Olathe city	32,791	91.3%	8.7%	2,844	4.6%	2.0%	0.5%	1.8%	0.0%	0.0%
Overland Park city	45,868	89.7%	10.3%	4,735	3.1%	5.8%	1.8%	0.0%	0.0%	0.0%
Topeka city	32,533	91.7%	8.3%	2,693	6.0%	2.6%	0.3%	0.0%	0.3%	0.0%
Wichita city	105,918	92.7%	7.3%	7,716	3.4%	2.8%	1.6%	0.7%	0.0%	0.1%
Kentucky										
Lexington-Fayette urban county	91,455	90.6%	9.4%	8,601	3.1%	4.6%	1.4%	1.6%	0.0%	0.0%
Louisville/Jefferson County metro govt (bal)	155,155	92.1%	7.9%	12,257	4.9%	2.9%	1.1%	0.5%	0.1%	0.0%
Louisiana										
Baton Rouge city	80,894	95.2%	4.8%	3,874	1.9%	3.3%	0.6%	0.2%	0.1%	0.0%
Lafayette city	41,013	95.0%	5.0%	2,070	2.5%	2.0%	1.0%	0.4%	0.0%	0.0%
New Orleans city	107,584	93.8%	6.2%	6,640	3.2%	2.2%	0.8%	0.2%	0.2%	0.0%
Shreveport city	56,474	98.9%	1.1%	599	0.4%	0.8%	0.8%	0.0%	0.0%	0.0%
Maryland										
Baltimore city	177,188	92.6%	7.4%	13,196	3.7%	2.8%	0.8%	1.0%	0.1%	0.0%
Massachusetts										
Boston city	233,438	79.3%	20.7%	48,359	11.8%	5.7%	2.7%	2.2%	0.3%	0.0%
Brockton city	25,123	83.5%	16.5%	4,133	8.0%	1.8%	1.4%	5.6%	0.3%	0.0%
Cambridge city	45,181	72.1%	27.9%	12,615	4.8%	13.1%	6.1%	2.1%	2.8%	0.5%
Lowell city	33,353	82.7%	17.3%	5,778	6.9%	9.6%	0.3%	1.6%	0.0%	0.0%
Lynn city	22,564	70.9%	29.1%	6,560	19.5%	2.6%	1.9%	5.7%	0.2%	0.0%
New Bedford city	25,019	84.5%	15.5%	3,890	10.0%	0.7%	3.8%	1.5%	0.0%	0.0%
Springfield city	46,473	90.5%	9.5%	4,412	6.8%	0.7%	0.0%	1.7%	0.8%	0.0%
Worcester city	56,561	78.0%	22.0%	12,443	7.7%	6.0%	4.4%	4.9%	0.2%	0.0%
Michigan										
Ann Arbor city	52,352	86.2%	13.8%	7,232	2.4%	9.5%	2.1%	0.4%	0.1%	0.0%
Dearborn city	27,230	76.9%	23.1%	6,302	0.0%	24.7%	0.3%	0.0%	3.8%	0.2%
Detroit city	188,753	95.2%	4.8%	9,056	3.0%	1.8%	0.5%	0.1%	0.1%	0.0%
Flint city	24,928	99.7%	0.3%	63	0.0%	0.0%	0.5%	0.3%	0.0%	0.0%
Grand Rapids city	59,157	88.9%	11.1%	6,548	6.8%	3.9%	0.8%	0.3%	0.7%	0.0%
Lansing city	35,463	91.1%	8.9%	3,166	2.1%	3.6%	0.0%	1.3%	2.1%	0.2%
Livonia city	21,256	96.4%	3.6%	757	0.7%	1.7%	1.2%	0.0%	1.2%	0.0%
Sterling Heights city	27,984	77.7%	22.3%	6,243	0.4%	17.6%	4.4%	0.4%	0.0%	0.0%
Warren city	33,277	91.1%	8.9%	2,964	1.4%	8.1%	0.8%	0.0%	0.0%	0.0%
Minnesota										
Minneapolis city	134,566	80.5%	19.5%	26,245	7.7%	7.3%	0.3%	4.8%	0.2%	0.4%
Rochester city	26,862	91.0%	9.0%	2,408	3.7%	4.6%	1.2%	2.3%	0.0%	0.0%
St. Paul city	90,558	80.0%	20.0%	18,111	3.0%	9.5%	0.5%	7.6%	0.3%	0.0%
Mississippi										
Jackson city	52,244	98.3%	1.7%	893	1.2%	0.3%	0.7%	0.4%	0.0%	0.0%
Missouri										
Columbia city	51,920	94.1%	5.9%	3,052	0.0%	3.6%	1.4%	0.7%	0.1%	0.0%
Independence city	26,867	94.7%	5.3%	1,418	4.6%	0.8%	0.6%	0.0%	0.0%	0.5%
Kansas City city	133,200	92.8%	7.2%	9,634	4.5%	1.9%	1.0%	0.8%	0.1%	0.1%
Lee's Summit city	22,267	96.3%	3.7%	825	2.2%	1.3%	0.6%	0.0%	0.0%	0.0%
Springfield city	58,414	97.6%	2.4%	1,400	0.4%	1.5%	1.1%	0.1%	0.0%	0.0%
St. Louis city	92,329	91.5%	8.5%	7,829	2.0%	4.4%	2.2%	0.6%	0.2%	0.0%

Table C-3: Places—Nativity and World Region of Birth—*Continued*

	Total Millennial	Percent		Total Foreign Born	Percent of Foreign Born by Region of Birth					
		Native	Foreign Born		Latin America	Asia	Europe	Africa	North America	Oceania
Montana										
Billings city	27,832	98.9%	1.1%	314	0.3%	1.8%	0.6%	0.0%	0.0%	0.0%
Nebraska										
Lincoln city	82,925	92.9%	7.1%	5,899	1.3%	4.4%	1.3%	0.4%	0.1%	0.0%
Omaha city	117,506	89.4%	10.6%	12,490	5.1%	4.6%	0.4%	0.9%	0.0%	0.0%
Nevada										
Henderson city	59,632	89.6%	10.4%	6,186	4.0%	5.7%	1.2%	0.0%	1.4%	0.0%
Las Vegas city	152,786	81.1%	18.9%	28,918	14.0%	4.3%	1.5%	0.2%	0.0%	0.1%
North Las Vegas city	67,469	85.9%	14.1%	9,492	12.3%	2.3%	0.7%	0.2%	0.0%	0.0%
Reno city	67,923	86.4%	13.6%	9,232	9.6%	4.4%	0.4%	0.7%	0.0%	0.8%
Sparks city	22,232	86.7%	13.3%	2,946	11.1%	2.1%	0.0%	0.0%	0.0%	0.0%
New Hampshire										
Manchester city	30,183	87.5%	12.5%	3,770	4.4%	6.0%	1.8%	0.9%	0.0%	0.0%
New Jersey										
Elizabeth city	37,355	54.0%	46.0%	17,198	41.6%	1.6%	3.1%	0.9%	0.0%	0.0%
Jersey City city	73,993	58.4%	41.6%	30,777	12.0%	20.8%	2.8%	7.0%	0.5%	0.0%
Newark city	81,864	73.8%	26.2%	21,473	21.9%	1.8%	1.4%	3.0%	0.3%	0.0%
Paterson city	41,976	73.5%	26.5%	11,109	29.5%	2.8%	0.0%	0.8%	0.0%	0.0%
New Mexico										
Albuquerque city	147,386	91.3%	8.7%	12,810	6.9%	1.2%	1.4%	0.2%	0.0%	0.3%
Las Cruces city	33,120	94.4%	5.6%	1,849	5.5%	1.2%	0.0%	0.0%	0.0%	0.1%
Rio Rancho city	22,510	92.5%	7.5%	1,690	5.8%	2.7%	0.0%	0.0%	0.0%	0.0%
New York										
Albany city	38,928	90.4%	9.6%	3,728	0.8%	5.6%	1.2%	1.7%	0.9%	0.0%
Buffalo city	79,888	90.4%	9.6%	7,651	2.5%	4.4%	0.6%	2.3%	0.3%	0.0%
New York city	2,261,947	71.4%	28.6%	647,003	15.5%	8.6%	3.6%	1.7%	0.4%	0.1%
Rochester city	67,543	95.2%	4.8%	3,229	1.0%	2.1%	1.7%	1.0%	0.3%	0.0%
Syracuse city	50,118	87.2%	12.8%	6,394	3.4%	7.3%	0.6%	2.3%	0.1%	0.2%
Yonkers city	48,658	79.0%	21.0%	10,219	14.4%	5.5%	1.4%	0.8%	0.0%	0.0%
North Carolina										
Charlotte city	218,384	84.0%	16.0%	35,015	8.7%	4.3%	1.6%	2.2%	0.1%	0.0%
Durham city	73,143	82.7%	17.3%	12,618	9.4%	5.4%	2.1%	1.8%	0.8%	0.0%
Fayetteville city	65,057	96.1%	3.9%	2,512	2.9%	1.0%	4.4%	0.0%	0.1%	0.0%
Greensboro city	79,997	90.8%	9.2%	7,323	3.7%	5.3%	1.4%	1.2%	0.0%	0.0%
High Point city	28,467	87.8%	12.2%	3,472	6.1%	3.0%	1.9%	2.7%	0.0%	0.0%
Raleigh city	138,360	84.8%	15.2%	21,058	8.3%	4.5%	1.4%	1.6%	0.2%	0.1%
Wilmington city	36,234	93.2%	6.8%	2,475	2.3%	3.8%	1.4%	0.1%	0.0%	0.0%
Winston-Salem city	62,381	91.2%	8.8%	5,516	8.1%	1.1%	0.7%	0.3%	0.0%	0.0%
North Dakota										
Fargo city	43,717	89.8%	10.2%	4,463	2.0%	4.2%	0.9%	3.2%	0.2%	0.0%
Ohio										
Akron city	54,485	89.7%	10.3%	5,630	2.2%	5.8%	2.0%	0.4%	0.1%	0.0%
Cincinnati city	91,178	93.5%	6.5%	5,967	2.8%	3.4%	0.9%	1.3%	0.0%	0.0%
Cleveland city	107,448	96.2%	3.8%	4,038	1.4%	1.1%	0.5%	0.3%	0.8%	0.0%
Columbus city	253,511	90.0%	10.0%	25,228	3.5%	4.0%	0.8%	2.7%	0.1%	0.1%
Dayton city	46,480	94.6%	5.4%	2,487	1.6%	1.5%	2.2%	0.5%	0.3%	0.0%
Toledo city	78,123	96.8%	3.2%	2,472	0.7%	1.6%	0.3%	0.6%	0.4%	0.2%
Oklahoma										
Broken Arrow city	26,302	88.0%	12.0%	3,155	8.3%	1.8%	2.7%	0.0%	0.0%	0.0%
Lawton city	33,539	89.6%	10.4%	3,498	6.7%	2.9%	2.8%	1.3%	0.0%	0.0%
Norman city	43,626	92.6%	7.4%	3,249	4.1%	3.8%	0.2%	0.6%	0.0%	0.0%
Oklahoma City city	166,433	84.3%	15.7%	26,145	11.9%	2.8%	0.7%	1.3%	0.0%	0.0%
Tulsa city	109,067	89.7%	10.3%	11,281	7.0%	2.8%	2.0%	0.1%	0.1%	0.1%
Oregon										
Beaverton city	24,936	83.7%	16.3%	4,053	9.3%	9.3%	1.0%	1.5%	0.0%	0.0%
Eugene city	54,972	93.0%	7.0%	3,872	1.8%	3.4%	1.5%	0.1%	0.1%	1.2%
Gresham city	29,749	78.4%	21.6%	6,431	11.1%	2.9%	6.4%	0.2%	0.0%	1.0%
Hillsboro city	25,428	83.0%	17.0%	4,317	9.1%	7.7%	1.5%	0.0%	0.0%	0.0%
Portland city	159,765	82.9%	17.1%	27,373	5.0%	6.4%	4.7%	1.1%	0.3%	0.4%
Salem city	44,757	86.8%	13.2%	5,900	10.4%	1.2%	2.2%	0.0%	0.0%	0.0%
Pennsylvania										
Allentown city	35,146	84.7%	15.3%	5,377	13.8%	1.3%	0.3%	0.4%	0.2%	0.0%
Erie city	31,041	90.2%	9.8%	3,051	1.6%	5.0%	3.0%	1.1%	0.1%	0.0%
Philadelphia city	454,880	87.6%	12.4%	56,241	3.8%	6.2%	2.0%	1.7%	0.1%	0.0%
Pittsburgh city	103,079	89.8%	10.2%	10,493	1.4%	6.2%	1.4%	1.7%	0.2%	0.0%
Rhode Island										
Providence city	64,383	77.1%	22.9%	14,726	13.4%	4.7%	2.8%	1.8%	0.2%	0.0%
South Carolina										
Charleston city	41,727	94.0%	6.0%	2,514	2.5%	2.2%	1.9%	0.9%	0.0%	0.0%
Columbia city	59,462	94.4%	5.6%	3,349	2.9%	2.7%	2.2%	0.3%	0.0%	0.0%
North Charleston city	34,069	89.1%	10.9%	3,720	9.7%	0.6%	0.4%	0.2%	0.0%	0.0%
South Dakota										
Sioux Falls city	43,120	95.7%	4.3%	1,847	0.2%	1.2%	1.5%	2.1%	0.0%	0.0%

Table C-3: Places—Nativity and World Region of Birth—*Continued*

	Total Millennial	Percent		Total Foreign Born	Percent of Foreign Born by Region of Birth					
		Native	Foreign Born		Latin America	Asia	Europe	Africa	North America	Oceania
Tennessee										
Chattanooga city	47,897	91.6%	8.4%	4,005	5.6%	1.7%	0.7%	0.2%	0.5%	0.0%
Clarksville city	49,730	93.9%	6.1%	3,056	2.5%	1.5%	4.3%	3.5%	0.0%	0.0%
Knoxville city	66,524	92.7%	7.3%	4,871	2.4%	4.0%	0.6%	0.0%	0.4%	0.0%
Memphis city	188,820	93.2%	6.8%	12,798	3.8%	2.0%	0.7%	1.2%	0.0%	0.0%
Murfreesboro city	43,031	92.5%	7.5%	3,211	2.2%	3.2%	2.3%	1.5%	0.0%	0.0%
Nashville-Davidson metropolitan govt (bal) ..	181,961	85.8%	14.2%	25,888	6.8%	3.6%	0.9%	3.3%	0.2%	0.0%
Texas										
Abilene city	39,552	95.2%	4.8%	1,908	1.3%	2.7%	0.4%	1.1%	0.1%	0.0%
Amarillo city	54,926	87.2%	12.8%	7,012	8.3%	3.0%	0.3%	1.5%	0.0%	0.0%
Arlington city	112,205	81.7%	18.3%	20,500	12.4%	3.8%	1.4%	1.9%	0.2%	0.0%
Austin city	280,372	81.4%	18.6%	52,141	12.5%	5.1%	1.4%	0.4%	0.2%	0.2%
Beaumont city	34,209	87.1%	12.9%	4,420	9.4%	2.4%	0.6%	0.7%	0.3%	0.0%
Brownsville city	53,924	80.0%	20.0%	10,794	18.7%	0.4%	1.0%	0.0%	1.2%	0.0%
Carrollton city	33,385	78.7%	21.3%	7,108	10.5%	9.5%	0.2%	1.9%	0.0%	0.0%
College Station city	61,794	87.8%	12.2%	7,513	7.4%	4.2%	1.2%	0.5%	0.0%	0.0%
Corpus Christi city	86,069	92.6%	7.4%	6,353	5.7%	1.9%	0.4%	0.3%	0.1%	0.0%
Dallas city	363,191	73.9%	26.1%	94,906	20.7%	3.6%	0.5%	1.7%	0.2%	0.1%
Denton city	51,957	87.9%	12.1%	6,298	5.6%	5.3%	1.0%	0.7%	0.2%	0.2%
El Paso city	191,088	84.1%	15.9%	30,334	16.1%	0.8%	1.4%	0.1%	0.2%	0.2%
Fort Worth city	222,860	86.0%	14.0%	31,236	10.9%	2.5%	0.3%	0.9%	0.2%	0.0%
Frisco city	28,633	90.1%	9.9%	2,835	5.9%	3.4%	1.9%	0.0%	0.2%	0.0%
Garland city	64,933	81.3%	18.7%	12,118	13.5%	3.9%	0.1%	2.2%	0.3%	0.5%
Grand Prairie city	52,064	79.9%	20.1%	10,470	17.1%	2.7%	1.4%	0.3%	0.0%	0.0%
Houston city	662,760	73.3%	26.7%	176,810	19.8%	5.8%	1.1%	1.3%	0.1%	0.0%
Irving city	64,810	68.4%	31.6%	20,503	19.6%	11.9%	0.8%	0.2%	0.0%	0.2%
Killeen city	46,189	96.3%	3.7%	1,695	2.1%	0.6%	4.2%	0.2%	0.0%	0.0%
Laredo city	71,446	84.2%	15.8%	11,322	16.9%	0.0%	0.1%	0.0%	0.0%	0.0%
Lewisville city	28,237	79.4%	20.6%	5,807	12.7%	5.0%	1.3%	1.0%	1.0%	0.0%
Lubbock city	87,806	94.9%	5.1%	4,453	3.1%	2.0%	0.9%	0.5%	0.0%	0.0%
McAllen city	39,424	77.4%	22.6%	8,922	20.5%	3.0%	0.9%	0.0%	0.0%	0.0%
McKinney city	36,030	91.6%	8.4%	3,028	7.2%	0.8%	0.7%	0.1%	0.0%	0.0%
Mesquite city	40,457	80.2%	19.8%	8,012	15.7%	2.7%	1.2%	2.3%	0.0%	0.0%
Midland city	36,802	94.7%	5.3%	1,933	6.0%	0.3%	0.6%	0.0%	0.3%	0.0%
Odessa city	32,849	87.3%	12.7%	4,169	12.9%	0.7%	1.0%	0.0%	0.0%	0.0%
Pasadena city	44,502	77.4%	22.6%	10,077	23.4%	1.2%	0.5%	0.4%	0.0%	0.0%
Pearland city	24,798	81.0%	19.0%	4,707	8.8%	7.3%	0.0%	2.9%	0.0%	0.0%
Plano city	66,294	81.5%	18.5%	12,235	5.1%	9.7%	2.4%	1.9%	0.2%	0.5%
Richardson city	25,547	76.1%	23.9%	6,095	9.0%	11.8%	2.3%	2.0%	0.0%	1.3%
Round Rock city	30,063	90.0%	10.0%	3,010	3.8%	3.7%	1.4%	2.5%	0.0%	0.0%
San Angelo city	31,154	97.0%	3.0%	923	2.4%	0.6%	2.0%	0.0%	0.0%	0.0%
San Antonio city	410,854	88.2%	11.8%	48,549	9.3%	2.7%	0.9%	0.4%	0.1%	0.0%
Tyler city	28,538	87.2%	12.8%	3,655	8.1%	1.1%	0.0%	2.4%	1.3%	0.0%
Waco city	46,105	88.7%	11.3%	5,215	7.1%	3.7%	0.5%	0.8%	0.3%	0.0%
Wichita Falls city	32,437	93.8%	6.2%	1,996	3.8%	1.0%	1.8%	0.9%	0.0%	0.0%
Utah										
Orem city	35,056	86.5%	13.5%	4,734	9.1%	3.6%	1.3%	0.2%	0.5%	0.3%
Provo city	63,999	89.4%	10.6%	6,809	6.5%	3.1%	1.2%	0.2%	1.5%	0.4%
Salt Lake City city	62,705	86.8%	13.2%	8,289	8.8%	3.4%	1.4%	0.6%	0.0%	0.0%
West Jordan city	31,921	93.7%	6.3%	2,012	2.2%	0.8%	2.2%	0.7%	0.7%	0.0%
West Valley City city	39,676	80.0%	20.0%	7,945	18.3%	1.1%	1.0%	0.6%	0.0%	0.0%
Virginia										
Alexandria city	39,869	67.8%	32.2%	12,836	12.7%	6.9%	1.9%	10.5%	0.1%	0.3%
Chesapeake city	61,466	94.9%	5.1%	3,140	1.8%	1.9%	2.0%	1.0%	0.0%	0.0%
Hampton city	41,168	95.3%	4.7%	1,954	2.1%	3.2%	2.5%	0.0%	0.0%	0.0%
Newport News city	54,567	93.5%	6.5%	3,569	2.8%	3.6%	1.6%	0.8%	0.1%	0.0%
Norfolk city	92,560	94.3%	5.7%	5,273	2.1%	3.0%	0.8%	1.2%	0.1%	0.0%
Portsmouth city	26,744	96.4%	3.6%	959	2.3%	0.0%	0.9%	0.9%	0.4%	0.0%
Richmond city	70,765	95.6%	4.4%	3,129	3.1%	1.3%	0.9%	0.1%	0.5%	0.1%
Roanoke city	24,131	92.1%	7.9%	1,907	5.5%	1.5%	1.4%	0.0%	0.3%	0.0%
Virginia Beach city	124,962	93.4%	6.6%	8,297	2.0%	3.4%	1.6%	1.2%	0.1%	0.0%
Washington										
Bellevue city	32,231	58.5%	41.5%	13,383	3.8%	28.8%	7.5%	2.3%	1.6%	0.8%
Everett city	29,205	81.4%	18.6%	5,429	4.4%	9.1%	4.8%	0.6%	0.7%	0.0%
Federal Way city	26,383	75.5%	24.5%	6,453	10.3%	4.4%	6.8%	3.3%	0.0%	0.6%
Kent city	34,530	69.9%	30.1%	10,397	11.8%	13.5%	2.5%	3.1%	0.0%	1.1%
Renton city	26,083	75.5%	24.5%	6,386	10.7%	12.4%	2.1%	0.0%	0.9%	0.0%
Seattle city	203,636	80.8%	19.2%	39,137	3.5%	10.7%	2.7%	2.9%	1.3%	0.2%
Spokane city	61,518	93.4%	6.6%	4,076	0.2%	2.5%	4.3%	0.3%	0.4%	0.5%
Spokane Valley city	23,372	94.0%	6.0%	1,409	1.5%	3.4%	3.1%	0.1%	1.2%	0.6%
Tacoma city	56,132	87.2%	12.8%	7,190	6.1%	3.6%	4.3%	0.8%	0.4%	0.1%
Vancouver city	41,746	89.5%	10.5%	4,401	6.0%	0.9%	3.8%	0.3%	0.6%	0.0%
Yakima city	26,160	77.4%	22.6%	5,900	23.3%	0.5%	0.0%	0.0%	0.4%	0.0%
Wisconsin										
Green Bay city	30,520	93.7%	6.3%	1,934	4.5%	2.0%	0.0%	0.8%	0.0%	0.0%
Kenosha city	27,729	96.4%	3.6%	1,003	1.3%	0.7%	1.6%	0.0%	0.0%	0.0%
Madison city	94,874	86.7%	13.3%	12,589	5.9%	7.1%	0.5%	0.1%	0.0%	0.0%
Milwaukee city	188,730	91.3%	8.7%	16,438	5.1%	2.9%	0.6%	0.7%	0.0%	0.0%

Table C-4: Metropolitan/Micropolitan Statistical Areas—Nativity and World Region of Birth

	Total Millennial	Percent		Total Foreign Born	Percent of Foreign Born by Region of Birth					
		Native	Foreign Born		Latin America	Asia	Europe	Africa	North America	Oceania
Abilene, TX	51,282	95.2%	4.8%	2,486	2.1%	2.1%	0.3%	0.8%	0.1%	0.0%
Adrian, MI micro	24,684	98.2%	1.8%	433	1.5%	0.0%	0.0%	0.0%	0.2%	0.0%
Akron, OH	185,003	92.6%	7.4%	13,689	0.9%	5.0%	1.4%	0.2%	0.3%	0.0%
Albany-Schenectady-Troy, NY	221,152	93.5%	6.5%	14,315	1.8%	3.8%	0.7%	0.2%	0.2%	0.1%
Albany, GA	44,899	94.9%	5.1%	2,303	3.9%	1.5%	0.1%	0.4%	0.0%	0.0%
Albany, OR	30,638	90.5%	9.5%	2,903	1.7%	6.4%	0.4%	0.0%	1.6%	0.0%
Albertville, AL micro	22,852	87.7%	12.3%	2,808	11.2%	0.9%	0.0%	0.1%	0.0%	0.0%
Albuquerque, NM	232,256	90.4%	9.6%	22,401	7.7%	1.5%	1.1%	0.2%	0.0%	0.2%
Alexandria, LA	40,995	97.1%	2.9%	1,177	1.0%	1.8%	2.1%	0.0%	0.0%	0.0%
Allentown-Bethlehem-Easton, PA-NJ	200,342	91.2%	8.8%	17,569	3.9%	3.7%	1.4%	0.3%	0.1%	0.0%
Altoona, PA	29,018	98.4%	1.6%	478	1.4%	0.3%	0.0%	0.2%	0.0%	0.0%
Amarillo, TX	69,818	88.7%	11.3%	7,881	7.0%	2.6%	0.5%	1.8%	0.0%	0.0%
Ames, IA	39,514	89.0%	11.0%	4,365	0.0%	9.6%	0.3%	0.3%	1.1%	0.0%
Anchorage, AK	119,605	95.8%	4.2%	4,966	1.3%	3.1%	0.5%	0.0%	0.5%	0.0%
Ann Arbor, MI	119,936	90.0%	10.0%	11,938	2.3%	6.6%	1.4%	0.3%	0.1%	0.0%
Anniston-Oxford-Jacksonville, AL	29,189	95.0%	5.0%	1,453	1.5%	2.7%	2.4%	0.3%	0.5%	0.0%
Appleton, WI	57,198	94.7%	5.3%	3,054	3.3%	1.6%	0.2%	0.0%	0.3%	0.6%
Asheville, NC	97,439	91.7%	8.3%	8,056	7.2%	0.6%	0.9%	0.0%	0.1%	0.0%
Ashtabula, OH micro	22,736	100.0%	0.0%	0	0.0%	0.0%	0.0%	0.0%	0.0%	0.0%
Athens-Clarke County, GA	74,592	94.4%	5.6%	4,187	2.8%	2.6%	1.3%	0.0%	0.2%	0.1%
Atlanta-Sandy Springs-Roswell, GA	1,419,815	87.3%	12.7%	180,646	7.1%	3.4%	1.5%	1.4%	0.2%	0.1%
Atlantic City-Hammonton, NJ	67,058	86.8%	13.2%	8,826	7.3%	5.0%	1.0%	0.4%	0.0%	0.0%
Auburn-Opelika, AL	53,402	98.1%	1.9%	1,021	0.1%	1.8%	0.6%	0.0%	0.0%	0.0%
Augusta-Richmond County, GA-SC	154,121	97.8%	2.2%	3,466	1.1%	1.0%	1.5%	0.2%	0.2%	0.0%
Augusta-Waterville, ME micro	27,602	98.3%	1.7%	479	0.0%	1.9%	2.2%	0.0%	0.7%	0.0%
Austin-Round Rock, TX	549,600	84.6%	15.4%	84,499	10.8%	3.7%	1.4%	0.5%	0.2%	0.1%
Bakersfield, CA	253,748	83.4%	16.6%	42,218	14.2%	2.4%	0.6%	0.0%	0.1%	0.2%
Baltimore-Columbia-Towson, MD	714,534	91.2%	8.8%	62,609	3.6%	3.9%	1.4%	1.2%	0.0%	0.1%
Bangor, ME	39,915	97.8%	2.2%	861	0.0%	1.7%	0.1%	0.4%	0.0%	0.0%
Barnstable Town, MA	37,757	91.5%	8.5%	3,214	6.9%	0.9%	2.0%	1.7%	0.0%	0.0%
Baton Rouge, LA	232,828	97.0%	3.0%	6,896	1.5%	1.7%	0.5%	0.1%	0.0%	0.0%
Battle Creek, MI	31,074	97.7%	2.3%	720	0.5%	1.8%	0.0%	0.0%	0.0%	0.0%
Bay City, MI	25,541	97.6%	2.4%	616	1.8%	0.2%	0.3%	0.0%	0.0%	0.0%
Beaumont-Port Arthur, TX	107,793	91.7%	8.3%	8,959	7.1%	0.8%	0.8%	0.2%	0.1%	0.0%
Beckley, WV	27,461	97.4%	2.6%	715	0.9%	0.0%	3.4%	0.0%	0.0%	0.0%
Bellingham, WA	62,149	92.2%	7.8%	4,863	2.8%	2.5%	3.3%	0.0%	1.0%	0.1%
Bend-Redmond, OR	37,987	99.1%	0.9%	334	0.7%	0.0%	0.1%	0.6%	0.0%	0.0%
Billings, MT	41,323	99.2%	0.8%	339	0.2%	1.2%	0.4%	0.0%	0.0%	0.0%
Binghamton, NY	62,942	94.7%	5.3%	3,365	0.6%	3.0%	1.6%	0.2%	0.0%	0.0%
Birmingham-Hoover, AL	287,772	95.0%	5.0%	14,365	4.0%	1.2%	0.8%	0.2%	0.0%	0.0%
Bismarck, ND	34,202	97.0%	3.0%	1,017	0.0%	2.2%	0.6%	0.2%	0.6%	0.0%
Blacksburg-Christiansburg-Radford, VA	66,288	95.2%	4.8%	3,207	0.4%	2.8%	3.1%	0.2%	0.1%	0.0%
Bloomington, IL	63,715	92.1%	7.9%	5,024	0.7%	5.2%	1.9%	0.6%	0.0%	0.0%
Bloomington, IN	66,600	90.9%	9.1%	6,060	0.6%	5.6%	0.8%	1.6%	0.1%	0.4%
Bloomsburg-Berwick, PA	23,141	99.4%	0.6%	140	0.0%	0.1%	0.4%	0.1%	0.0%	0.0%
Boise City, ID	169,093	93.0%	7.0%	11,882	4.4%	2.0%	1.5%	0.4%	0.0%	0.1%
Boston-Cambridge-Newton, MA-NH	1,227,309	84.1%	15.9%	194,913	7.5%	5.4%	2.4%	1.3%	0.4%	0.0%
Boulder, CO	96,264	92.4%	7.6%	7,272	3.6%	3.1%	1.3%	0.1%	0.4%	0.4%
Bowling Green, KY	46,097	92.6%	7.4%	3,395	2.7%	3.1%	2.8%	0.2%	0.0%	0.0%
Bremerton-Silverdale, WA	65,185	97.8%	2.2%	1,444	1.4%	1.5%	1.2%	0.0%	0.1%	0.4%
Bridgeport-Stamford-Norwalk, CT	212,707	80.5%	19.5%	41,493	14.5%	3.9%	2.7%	0.3%	0.0%	0.0%
Brownsville-Harlingen, TX	117,741	81.3%	18.7%	22,014	17.3%	0.2%	0.7%	0.0%	1.2%	0.0%
Brunswick, GA	27,572	94.7%	5.3%	1,471	4.7%	1.9%	0.6%	0.0%	0.0%	0.0%
Buffalo-Cheektowaga-Niagara Falls, NY	286,943	93.5%	6.5%	18,615	1.2%	3.2%	1.2%	0.8%	0.6%	0.0%
Burlington-South Burlington, VT	59,774	94.2%	5.8%	3,488	0.5%	2.5%	2.9%	0.8%	0.3%	0.4%
Burlington, NC	38,845	86.2%	13.8%	5,367	10.2%	1.9%	0.0%	1.4%	0.3%	0.0%
California-Lexington Park, MD	28,557	96.2%	3.8%	1,089	2.9%	1.8%	0.2%	0.0%	0.0%	0.0%
Canton-Massillon, OH	93,351	99.0%	1.0%	940	0.9%	0.1%	0.3%	0.0%	0.0%	0.0%
Cape Coral-Fort Myers, FL	130,907	84.1%	15.9%	20,819	14.2%	0.6%	2.1%	0.0%	0.3%	0.0%
Cape Girardeau, MO-IL	26,340	99.1%	0.9%	234	0.0%	0.5%	0.4%	0.0%	0.0%	0.0%
Carbondale-Marion, IL	39,180	98.1%	1.9%	745	0.6%	1.6%	0.6%	0.0%	0.0%	0.0%
Carson City, NV	12,217	85.2%	14.8%	1,814	13.5%	1.8%	0.0%	0.0%	0.0%	0.0%
Casper, WY	21,460	95.3%	4.7%	1,001	3.5%	0.6%	1.6%	0.0%	0.0%	0.0%
Cedar Rapids, IA	68,286	92.6%	7.4%	5,028	2.7%	2.5%	1.0%	0.0%	1.4%	0.0%
Chambersburg-Waynesboro, PA	33,238	96.7%	3.3%	1,106	3.3%	0.2%	3.7%	0.1%	0.1%	0.0%
Champaign-Urbana, IL	90,995	87.7%	12.3%	11,201	2.3%	8.7%	1.1%	1.1%	0.4%	0.0%
Charleston-North Charleston, SC	192,839	94.7%	5.3%	10,301	3.8%	1.5%	0.9%	0.3%	0.2%	0.0%
Charleston, WV	50,342	98.7%	1.3%	677	0.0%	1.3%	0.0%	0.0%	0.0%	0.0%
Charlotte-Concord-Gastonia, NC-SC	579,482	90.1%	9.9%	57,554	5.9%	2.5%	1.3%	0.9%	0.2%	0.0%
Charlottesville, VA	60,899	92.0%	8.0%	4,873	1.8%	4.4%	2.5%	0.1%	0.0%	0.0%
Chattanooga, TN-GA	129,748	94.6%	5.4%	6,953	3.8%	1.1%	1.4%	0.1%	0.2%	0.0%
Cheyenne, WY	25,613	94.3%	5.7%	1,457	2.6%	2.5%	1.2%	0.1%	0.4%	0.0%
Chicago-Naperville-Elgin, IL-IN-WI	2,519,394	85.8%	14.2%	358,834	7.5%	4.0%	2.7%	0.6%	0.1%	0.0%
Chico, CA	65,642	94.2%	5.8%	3,803	2.8%	2.6%	0.9%	0.0%	0.0%	0.0%
Cincinnati, OH-KY-IN	528,404	94.6%	5.4%	28,391	1.9%	2.5%	0.8%	0.7%	0.1%	0.1%
Clarksburg, WV micro	18,960	100.0%	0.0%	0	0.0%	0.0%	0.0%	0.0%	0.3%	0.0%
Clarksville, TN-KY	89,743	95.4%	4.6%	4,123	1.8%	1.1%	3.1%	2.3%	0.0%	0.0%
Cleveland-Elyria, OH	488,473	95.6%	4.4%	21,569	1.3%	1.7%	1.3%	0.3%	0.2%	0.0%
Cleveland, TN	29,929	96.0%	4.0%	1,197	3.0%	0.6%	0.3%	0.0%	0.0%	0.7%
Coeur d'Alene, ID	35,119	98.2%	1.8%	640	0.0%	1.8%	0.3%	0.0%	0.1%	0.0%

Table C-4: Metropolitan/Micropolitan Statistical Areas—Nativity and World Region of Birth—*Continued*

		Percent		Total Foreign Born	Percent of Foreign Born by Region of Birth					
	Total Millennial	Native	Foreign Born		Latin America	Asia	Europe	Africa	North America	Oceania
College Station-Bryan, TX	104,136	88.7%	11.3%	11,812	6.8%	3.8%	1.0%	0.3%	0.0%	0.0%
Colorado Springs, CO	189,663	94.1%	5.9%	11,182	3.3%	2.4%	3.6%	0.4%	0.3%	0.1%
Columbia, MO	65,445	93.9%	6.1%	3,982	0.2%	3.6%	1.8%	0.6%	0.1%	0.0%
Columbia, SC	224,537	95.3%	4.7%	10,631	2.5%	2.2%	1.7%	0.3%	0.0%	0.1%
Columbus, GA-AL	93,131	93.4%	6.6%	6,156	3.7%	0.9%	3.1%	0.4%	0.4%	0.0%
Columbus, IN	20,581	82.4%	17.6%	3,622	10.9%	5.8%	0.0%	0.0%	1.2%	0.0%
Columbus, OH	514,620	93.0%	7.0%	35,875	2.2%	3.0%	0.9%	1.8%	0.2%	0.0%
Concord, NH micro	29,353	93.5%	6.5%	1,895	0.5%	4.3%	0.8%	1.3%	0.7%	0.0%
Cookeville, TN micro	28,672	93.7%	6.3%	1,811	5.4%	0.7%	0.0%	0.0%	0.2%	0.0%
Corpus Christi, TX	123,335	93.6%	6.4%	7,913	5.3%	1.5%	0.6%	0.2%	0.1%	0.0%
Corvallis, OR	33,658	90.8%	9.2%	3,107	1.5%	6.4%	0.3%	0.0%	1.4%	0.0%
Crestview-Fort Walton Beach-Destin, FL	68,552	94.1%	5.9%	4,044	4.4%	1.7%	2.2%	0.0%	0.2%	0.0%
Cumberland, MD-WV	25,491	96.3%	3.7%	941	0.5%	0.0%	0.7%	0.3%	0.0%	2.5%
Dallas-Fort Worth-Arlington, TX	1,793,256	83.1%	16.9%	303,840	12.0%	3.8%	0.9%	1.1%	0.2%	0.0%
Dalton, GA	37,669	82.1%	17.9%	6,733	16.6%	1.0%	0.0%	0.1%	0.6%	0.0%
Danville, IL	19,265	98.6%	1.4%	272	1.1%	0.3%	0.0%	0.0%	0.0%	0.0%
Danville, VA micro	22,440	98.0%	2.0%	441	1.7%	0.5%	0.9%	0.3%	0.0%	0.0%
Daphne-Fairhope-Foley, AL	43,743	96.8%	3.2%	1,414	3.2%	0.0%	0.7%	0.0%	0.0%	0.0%
Davenport-Moline-Rock Island, IA-IL	92,530	95.3%	4.7%	4,343	2.4%	1.5%	0.8%	0.6%	0.4%	0.0%
Dayton, OH	203,642	96.0%	4.0%	8,188	0.7%	2.2%	1.7%	0.6%	0.2%	0.1%
Decatur, AL	35,881	93.2%	6.8%	2,447	6.5%	0.0%	1.3%	0.0%	0.0%	0.0%
Decatur, IL	26,140	96.4%	3.6%	929	1.6%	1.2%	0.0%	0.5%	0.2%	0.0%
Deltona-Daytona Beach-Ormond Beach, FL	128,837	94.9%	5.1%	6,560	3.0%	1.8%	1.1%	0.1%	0.1%	0.0%
Denver-Aurora-Lakewood, CO	697,150	88.7%	11.3%	78,522	6.8%	2.6%	1.7%	1.0%	0.3%	0.0%
Des Moines-West Des Moines, IA	151,062	88.5%	11.5%	17,324	3.5%	3.5%	3.2%	3.0%	0.4%	0.0%
Detroit-Warren-Dearborn, MI	1,027,771	92.4%	7.6%	78,376	1.4%	4.6%	1.4%	0.2%	0.7%	0.0%
Dothan, AL	34,752	98.9%	1.1%	398	0.5%	0.5%	0.5%	0.2%	0.0%	0.0%
Dover, DE	43,966	95.4%	4.6%	2,043	1.3%	1.5%	1.3%	1.8%	0.0%	0.0%
Dubuque, IA	25,299	96.3%	3.7%	938	1.8%	0.5%	2.7%	0.0%	0.2%	0.0%
Duluth, MN-WI	73,630	98.9%	1.1%	839	0.9%	0.6%	0.4%	0.0%	0.0%	0.0%
Dunn, NC micro	34,876	91.1%	8.9%	3,094	6.9%	1.3%	1.4%	0.1%	0.8%	0.0%
Durham-Chapel Hill, NC	150,437	86.2%	13.8%	20,810	8.4%	3.7%	2.1%	1.1%	0.4%	0.1%
East Stroudsburg, PA	42,860	95.9%	4.1%	1,777	1.3%	1.6%	0.9%	0.0%	0.5%	1.3%
Eau Claire, WI	46,385	97.4%	2.6%	1,189	0.3%	2.6%	0.0%	0.0%	0.0%	0.0%
El Centro, CA	52,602	75.8%	24.2%	12,709	27.1%	0.7%	0.1%	0.0%	0.0%	0.0%
El Paso, TX	242,820	84.4%	15.6%	37,971	15.9%	0.7%	1.2%	0.1%	0.0%	0.2%
Elizabethtown-Fort Knox, KY	39,917	96.8%	3.2%	1,272	2.2%	1.2%	2.2%	0.0%	0.0%	0.0%
Elkhart-Goshen, IN	49,637	89.2%	10.8%	5,381	9.5%	1.1%	1.0%	0.0%	1.5%	0.0%
Elmira, NY	21,897	97.2%	2.8%	617	0.0%	2.3%	0.2%	0.0%	0.4%	0.0%
Erie, PA	71,567	94.5%	5.5%	3,949	0.8%	3.0%	2.1%	0.6%	0.0%	0.0%
Eugene, OR	94,734	94.6%	5.4%	5,152	1.9%	3.0%	1.2%	0.1%	0.2%	0.7%
Eureka-Arcata-Fortuna, CA micro	38,357	92.0%	8.0%	3,062	4.1%	2.2%	1.9%	0.0%	0.2%	0.7%
Evansville, IN-KY	78,099	97.6%	2.4%	1,872	0.7%	1.5%	1.2%	0.0%	0.0%	0.0%
Fairbanks, AK	32,435	95.6%	4.4%	1,429	1.0%	1.7%	1.5%	0.0%	1.4%	0.0%
Fargo, ND-MN	79,044	92.6%	7.4%	5,817	1.7%	3.1%	0.8%	1.9%	0.1%	0.0%
Farmington, NM	32,645	93.7%	6.3%	2,046	6.0%	0.4%	0.2%	0.0%	0.3%	0.0%
Fayetteville-Springdale-Rogers, AR-MO	137,070	86.8%	13.2%	18,151	10.0%	2.4%	0.8%	0.4%	0.3%	0.5%
Fayetteville, NC	116,497	94.7%	5.3%	6,227	3.5%	1.6%	3.4%	0.0%	0.2%	0.0%
Flagstaff, AZ	48,457	93.9%	6.1%	2,976	4.1%	2.2%	1.3%	0.0%	0.0%	0.2%
Flint, MI	104,249	98.9%	1.1%	1,095	0.3%	0.6%	0.4%	0.1%	0.0%	0.0%
Florence-Muscle Shoals, AL	36,495	95.0%	5.0%	1,839	4.1%	0.7%	0.6%	0.0%	0.0%	0.3%
Florence, SC	49,305	96.3%	3.7%	1,845	2.6%	0.6%	0.3%	0.0%	0.9%	0.0%
Fond du Lac, WI	22,700	96.6%	3.4%	778	2.1%	0.4%	0.7%	0.2%	0.2%	0.0%
Fort Collins, CO	94,110	94.1%	5.9%	5,515	2.4%	2.7%	1.8%	0.0%	0.0%	0.0%
Fort Smith, AR-OK	71,097	94.5%	5.5%	3,922	4.7%	1.1%	0.6%	0.0%	0.1%	0.0%
Fort Wayne, IN	109,234	94.6%	5.4%	5,857	2.0%	1.6%	1.7%	0.7%	0.1%	0.0%
Fresno, CA	280,746	84.4%	15.6%	43,888	11.1%	4.7%	0.4%	0.0%	0.2%	0.0%
Gadsden, AL	24,989	95.3%	4.7%	1,178	4.7%	0.0%	0.0%	0.0%	0.0%	0.0%
Gainesville, FL	104,083	90.6%	9.4%	9,806	4.3%	4.3%	1.4%	0.9%	0.8%	0.0%
Gainesville, GA	48,065	82.4%	17.6%	8,455	15.8%	1.3%	1.1%	0.0%	0.8%	0.0%
Gettysburg, PA	23,917	95.8%	4.2%	1,009	2.4%	1.6%	6.0%	0.8%	0.0%	0.0%
Glens Falls, NY	27,827	97.6%	2.4%	657	0.7%	0.5%	1.2%	0.0%	0.0%	0.0%
Goldsboro, NC	30,990	93.7%	6.3%	1,938	6.0%	1.1%	0.3%	0.0%	0.0%	0.0%
Grand Forks, ND-MN	36,319	94.6%	5.4%	1,974	1.6%	0.8%	1.0%	1.1%	1.4%	0.2%
Grand Island, NE	18,823	96.6%	3.4%	634	3.4%	0.0%	0.0%	0.0%	0.0%	0.0%
Grand Junction, CO	39,345	96.6%	3.4%	1,340	3.2%	0.3%	0.0%	0.0%	0.0%	0.1%
Grand Rapids-Wyoming, MI	275,216	93.6%	6.4%	17,490	3.2%	2.7%	0.7%	0.2%	0.6%	0.0%
Grants Pass, OR	15,966	96.4%	3.6%	575	3.1%	0.5%	0.0%	0.0%	0.9%	0.0%
Great Falls, MT	22,162	99.3%	0.7%	163	0.0%	0.0%	0.5%	0.0%	1.2%	0.0%
Greeley, CO	75,018	92.0%	8.0%	5,970	6.6%	1.6%	1.9%	0.4%	0.0%	0.0%
Green Bay, WI	79,175	96.6%	3.4%	2,711	2.1%	0.9%	1.2%	0.3%	0.0%	0.0%
Greensboro-High Point, NC	189,386	90.5%	9.5%	18,020	5.6%	3.3%	1.0%	1.0%	0.0%	0.0%
Greenville-Anderson-Mauldin, SC	212,385	93.4%	6.6%	14,076	4.6%	1.5%	0.8%	0.5%	0.1%	0.2%
Greenville, NC	61,787	97.2%	2.8%	1,738	0.7%	1.4%	1.7%	0.0%	0.0%	0.0%
Greenwood, SC micro	24,086	95.6%	4.4%	1,055	3.6%	0.2%	0.5%	0.0%	0.0%	0.0%
Gulfport-Biloxi-Pascagoula, MS	99,555	97.8%	2.2%	2,208	2.6%	1.6%	0.7%	0.0%	0.1%	0.0%
Hagerstown-Martinsburg, MD-WV	63,073	95.1%	4.9%	3,072	2.2%	1.5%	0.8%	0.0%	0.5%	0.1%
Hammond, LA	37,246	95.3%	4.7%	1,747	4.7%	0.0%	0.0%	0.0%	0.0%	0.0%
Hanford-Corcoran, CA	45,510	81.9%	18.1%	8,248	15.1%	2.7%	1.2%	0.5%	0.0%	0.0%
Harrisburg-Carlisle, PA	136,067	94.7%	5.3%	7,168	0.9%	3.3%	1.0%	0.6%	0.2%	0.0%

Table C-4: Metropolitan/Micropolitan Statistical Areas—Nativity and World Region of Birth—*Continued*

	Total Millennial	Percent		Total Foreign Born	Percent of Foreign Born by Region of Birth					
		Native	Foreign Born		Latin America	Asia	Europe	Africa	North America	Oceania
Harrisonburg, VA	45,371	90.0%	10.0%	4,550	5.3%	3.7%	1.8%	0.0%	0.0%	0.1%
Hartford-West Hartford-East Hartford, CT	305,097	89.5%	10.5%	31,891	4.8%	3.8%	2.4%	0.4%	0.3%	0.0%
Hattiesburg, MS	46,296	97.5%	2.5%	1,158	0.9%	1.5%	0.1%	0.0%	0.0%	0.0%
Hickory-Lenoir-Morganton, NC	83,615	92.3%	7.7%	6,450	5.7%	1.1%	1.1%	0.0%	0.0%	0.0%
Hilo, HI micro	44,614	93.0%	7.0%	3,145	1.6%	5.6%	0.4%	0.0%	0.2%	1.7%
Hilton Head Island-Bluffton-Beaufort, SC	48,805	88.3%	11.7%	5,717	8.4%	0.7%	1.7%	0.0%	2.0%	0.0%
Hinesville, GA	28,306	98.6%	1.4%	397	1.8%	0.5%	2.1%	0.3%	0.0%	0.0%
Holland, MI micro	26,007	99.5%	0.5%	124	0.2%	0.0%	0.3%	0.0%	0.4%	0.0%
Homosassa Springs, FL	21,470	97.8%	2.2%	483	0.0%	1.1%	0.7%	0.0%	0.4%	0.0%
Hot Springs, AR	20,011	94.5%	5.5%	1,091	4.6%	0.8%	0.0%	0.0%	0.0%	0.0%
Houma-Thibodaux, LA	57,742	96.0%	4.0%	2,330	3.3%	0.7%	0.2%	0.0%	0.2%	0.0%
Houston-The Woodlands-Sugar Land, TX	1,693,971	79.2%	20.8%	352,384	15.1%	4.5%	1.2%	0.9%	0.2%	0.0%
Huntington-Ashland, WV-KY-OH	89,024	99.2%	0.8%	747	0.2%	0.8%	0.1%	0.0%	0.0%	0.0%
Huntsville, AL	117,360	92.1%	7.9%	9,281	4.9%	2.7%	1.0%	0.1%	0.3%	0.0%
Idaho Falls, ID	37,305	92.6%	7.4%	2,764	3.9%	3.4%	0.3%	0.3%	0.1%	0.0%
Indianapolis-Carmel-Anderson, IN	498,562	92.2%	7.8%	39,062	4.4%	2.4%	1.0%	0.8%	0.1%	0.0%
Iowa City, IA	63,584	91.0%	9.0%	5,726	1.1%	5.1%	1.7%	1.8%	0.1%	0.0%
Ithaca, NY	41,515	86.8%	13.2%	5,477	0.7%	10.7%	2.5%	0.0%	0.3%	0.1%
Jackson, MI	39,344	99.4%	0.6%	222	0.0%	0.1%	1.6%	0.0%	0.0%	0.0%
Jackson, MS	154,147	97.9%	2.1%	3,199	0.6%	1.0%	0.5%	0.2%	0.3%	0.0%
Jackson, TN	34,586	96.4%	3.6%	1,234	2.0%	2.3%	0.2%	0.0%	0.0%	0.0%
Jacksonville, FL	354,593	93.7%	6.3%	22,182	2.4%	2.8%	1.7%	0.4%	0.3%	0.0%
Jacksonville, NC	75,082	95.2%	4.8%	3,618	3.4%	1.8%	1.3%	0.3%	0.2%	0.0%
Jamestown-Dunkirk-Fredonia, NY micro	34,497	97.2%	2.8%	977	0.1%	2.5%	0.1%	0.3%	0.1%	0.0%
Janesville-Beloit, WI	39,734	95.0%	5.0%	1,981	3.9%	1.0%	0.5%	0.0%	0.0%	0.0%
Jefferson City, MO	40,116	97.9%	2.1%	856	1.8%	0.4%	0.0%	0.0%	0.0%	0.0%
Johnson City, TN	50,488	96.3%	3.7%	1,849	2.2%	0.3%	0.1%	1.1%	0.0%	0.0%
Johnstown, PA	32,240	99.6%	0.4%	135	0.0%	0.4%	1.2%	0.1%	0.0%	0.0%
Jonesboro, AR	33,236	94.4%	5.6%	1,856	4.0%	1.8%	0.2%	0.6%	0.0%	0.0%
Joplin, MO	46,196	96.4%	3.6%	1,678	1.1%	2.1%	1.0%	0.0%	0.0%	0.0%
Kahului-Wailuku-Lahaina, HI	37,245	82.9%	17.1%	6,371	1.8%	12.5%	1.3%	0.0%	0.3%	2.8%
Kalamazoo-Portage, MI	102,518	97.0%	3.0%	3,067	1.1%	2.9%	0.6%	0.0%	0.1%	0.0%
Kalispell, MT micro	20,619	99.9%	0.1%	23	0.0%	0.0%	0.1%	0.0%	0.0%	0.0%
Kankakee, IL	27,483	92.6%	7.4%	2,047	6.7%	0.5%	0.2%	0.0%	0.0%	0.0%
Kansas City, MO-KS	514,311	93.2%	6.8%	34,927	3.7%	2.1%	1.1%	0.8%	0.0%	0.1%
Kennewick-Richland, WA	72,414	86.5%	13.5%	9,777	11.0%	1.4%	1.9%	0.3%	0.0%	0.0%
Killeen-Temple, TX	135,230	96.0%	4.0%	5,348	3.0%	0.9%	3.3%	0.2%	0.0%	0.0%
Kingsport-Bristol-Bristol, TN-VA	67,737	99.1%	0.9%	591	0.4%	0.9%	0.2%	0.0%	0.0%	0.0%
Kingston, NY	43,272	95.2%	4.8%	2,066	2.0%	2.3%	0.4%	0.2%	0.1%	0.0%
Knoxville, TN	211,969	95.1%	4.9%	10,429	2.6%	1.6%	0.7%	0.9%	0.1%	0.0%
Kokomo, IN	17,163	92.5%	7.5%	1,292	7.3%	0.2%	0.0%	0.0%	0.0%	0.0%
La Crosse-Onalaska, WI-MN	40,667	93.1%	6.9%	2,807	0.7%	5.9%	0.0%	0.2%	0.0%	0.1%
Lafayette-West Lafayette, IN	80,589	88.1%	11.9%	9,595	2.6%	8.6%	0.7%	0.4%	0.2%	0.0%
Lafayette, LA	134,207	97.0%	3.0%	3,980	1.7%	1.0%	1.0%	0.1%	0.0%	0.0%
Lake Charles, LA	53,104	98.5%	1.5%	790	1.3%	0.5%	1.7%	0.2%	0.0%	0.0%
Lake Havasu City-Kingman, AZ	40,348	95.0%	5.0%	2,019	4.9%	0.6%	0.3%	0.0%	0.2%	0.0%
Lakeland-Winter Haven, FL	149,776	90.9%	9.1%	13,594	8.6%	1.1%	1.1%	0.1%	0.1%	0.0%
Lancaster, PA	132,318	92.4%	7.6%	10,047	2.9%	1.3%	0.7%	2.8%	0.1%	0.0%
Lansing-East Lansing, MI	146,587	91.5%	8.5%	12,530	1.1%	5.1%	0.8%	1.0%	1.0%	0.0%
Laredo, TX	76,850	84.1%	15.9%	12,218	17.0%	0.0%	0.1%	0.0%	0.0%	0.0%
Las Cruces, NM	66,940	87.2%	12.8%	8,571	12.1%	0.8%	1.1%	0.0%	0.0%	0.0%
Las Vegas-Henderson-Paradise, NV	518,566	82.2%	17.8%	92,227	11.5%	5.3%	1.2%	0.8%	0.3%	0.0%
Lawrence, KS	44,291	95.2%	4.8%	2,142	0.4%	3.9%	1.3%	0.0%	0.0%	0.0%
Lawton, OK	41,646	91.6%	8.4%	3,498	5.4%	2.3%	2.5%	1.0%	0.0%	0.0%
Lebanon, PA	28,438	97.1%	2.9%	816	2.0%	0.7%	0.7%	0.0%	0.0%	0.0%
Lewiston-Auburn, ME	26,538	98.0%	2.0%	526	0.2%	0.8%	0.0%	1.0%	0.0%	0.0%
Lewiston, ID-WA	15,034	89.7%	10.3%	1,543	3.4%	6.2%	1.2%	0.6%	0.2%	0.0%
Lexington-Fayette, KY	138,471	92.5%	7.5%	10,355	3.7%	2.4%	1.3%	1.0%	0.0%	0.0%
Lima, OH	26,290	98.6%	1.4%	368	0.0%	0.0%	1.3%	0.1%	0.0%	0.0%
Lincoln, NE	100,294	93.0%	7.0%	7,006	1.4%	4.2%	1.2%	0.3%	0.2%	0.0%
Little Rock-North Little Rock-Conway, AR	195,299	93.5%	6.5%	12,650	4.7%	2.1%	0.5%	0.2%	0.0%	0.0%
Logan, UT-ID	47,715	91.7%	8.3%	3,959	5.7%	2.7%	0.5%	0.0%	0.7%	0.0%
Longview, TX	58,630	93.5%	6.5%	3,805	5.8%	0.7%	0.5%	0.3%	0.0%	0.0%
Longview, WA	23,187	93.7%	6.3%	1,456	6.0%	0.3%	0.0%	0.0%	0.0%	0.0%
Los Angeles-Long Beach-Anaheim, CA	3,542,436	78.5%	21.5%	760,921	13.4%	7.5%	0.8%	0.4%	0.2%	0.1%
Louisville/Jefferson County, KY-IN	311,466	94.0%	6.0%	18,758	3.7%	1.8%	0.9%	0.5%	0.1%	0.0%
Lubbock, TX	99,246	94.3%	5.7%	5,618	3.4%	2.0%	1.0%	0.7%	0.0%	0.0%
Lumberton, NC micro	32,622	91.4%	8.6%	2,802	6.3%	0.3%	1.9%	0.0%	0.0%	0.2%
Lynchburg, VA	70,265	95.9%	4.1%	2,880	1.7%	2.1%	0.8%	0.6%	0.8%	0.0%
Macon, GA	62,863	96.1%	3.9%	2,431	3.0%	2.2%	0.1%	0.4%	0.0%	0.0%
Madera, CA	43,066	77.9%	22.1%	9,519	20.5%	1.4%	0.0%	0.0%	0.5%	0.0%
Madison, WI	189,097	89.8%	10.2%	19,331	4.4%	5.8%	0.4%	0.1%	0.1%	0.0%
Manchester-Nashua, NH	94,570	92.9%	7.1%	6,708	2.0%	3.6%	1.2%	0.2%	0.5%	0.0%
Manhattan, KS	44,867	98.0%	2.0%	893	0.9%	1.5%	0.2%	0.0%	0.0%	0.0%
Mankato-North Mankato, MN	33,593	91.0%	9.0%	3,015	0.0%	8.6%	0.1%	0.4%	0.2%	0.0%
Mansfield, OH	28,039	99.2%	0.8%	221	0.0%	0.0%	0.1%	0.0%	0.0%	0.0%
McAllen-Edinburg-Mission, TX	238,715	75.9%	24.1%	57,622	23.7%	0.9%	0.2%	0.0%	0.0%	0.0%
Medford, OR	45,840	94.2%	5.8%	2,671	5.0%	0.4%	0.3%	0.2%	0.2%	0.0%
Memphis, TN-MS-AR	367,734	95.2%	4.8%	17,489	3.0%	1.4%	0.9%	0.6%	0.0%	0.0%
Merced, CA	80,879	81.6%	18.4%	14,852	12.6%	4.9%	0.9%	0.0%	0.0%	0.0%

Table C-4: Metropolitan/Micropolitan Statistical Areas—Nativity and World Region of Birth—*Continued*

	Total Millennial	Percent		Total Foreign Born	Percent of Foreign Born by Region of Birth					
		Native	Foreign Born		Latin America	Asia	Europe	Africa	North America	Oceania
Meridian, MS micro	25,504	98.4%	1.6%	400	1.6%	0.0%	0.0%	0.0%	0.0%	0.0%
Miami-Fort Lauderdale-West Palm Beach, FL	1,390,066	70.9%	29.1%	404,974	27.0%	1.7%	1.4%	0.3%	0.4%	0.0%
Michigan City-La Porte, IN	27,693	96.5%	3.5%	968	2.5%	0.2%	1.3%	0.0%	0.0%	0.0%
Midland, MI	21,484	97.1%	2.9%	616	2.2%	0.3%	0.4%	0.0%	0.0%	0.0%
Midland, TX	45,864	94.3%	5.7%	2,593	6.1%	0.4%	0.5%	0.0%	0.2%	0.0%
Milwaukee-Waukesha-West Allis, WI	407,569	92.7%	7.3%	29,641	3.1%	3.1%	0.9%	0.5%	0.0%	0.0%
Minneapolis-St. Paul-Bloomington, MN-WI	874,497	88.7%	11.3%	98,404	3.5%	4.6%	0.7%	3.2%	0.1%	0.2%
Missoula, MT	36,652	98.7%	1.3%	482	0.7%	1.0%	0.0%	0.0%	0.1%	0.0%
Mobile, AL	106,088	97.5%	2.5%	2,639	1.4%	0.8%	0.8%	0.0%	0.0%	0.0%
Modesto, CA	148,186	83.0%	17.0%	25,136	13.9%	3.2%	0.1%	0.5%	0.0%	0.0%
Monroe, LA	50,987	98.2%	1.8%	915	0.6%	0.8%	1.0%	0.0%	0.0%	0.0%
Monroe, MI	35,012	98.6%	1.4%	487	1.2%	0.4%	0.6%	0.0%	0.0%	0.0%
Montgomery, AL	100,029	97.3%	2.7%	2,705	1.5%	0.5%	0.6%	0.1%	0.0%	0.4%
Morgantown, WV	49,494	95.2%	4.8%	2,385	0.7%	3.1%	1.0%	1.0%	0.1%	0.1%
Morristown, TN	24,459	95.3%	4.7%	1,153	3.9%	0.8%	0.2%	0.0%	0.0%	0.0%
Mount Vernon-Anacortes, WA	27,206	89.9%	10.1%	2,737	3.7%	3.0%	4.3%	1.2%	0.9%	0.1%
Muncie, IN	39,030	96.4%	3.6%	1,404	2.0%	1.3%	0.8%	0.0%	0.0%	0.0%
Muskegon, MI	40,756	98.9%	1.1%	428	0.0%	1.0%	0.5%	0.0%	0.0%	0.0%
Myrtle Beach-Conway-North Myrtle Beach, SC-NC	82,532	92.7%	7.3%	6,022	5.5%	1.2%	1.0%	0.1%	0.2%	0.1%
Napa, CA	33,246	79.7%	20.3%	6,747	18.7%	1.2%	1.0%	0.0%	0.0%	0.0%
Naples-Immokalee-Marco Island, FL	62,196	78.8%	21.2%	13,167	20.2%	0.0%	0.9%	0.0%	0.1%	0.0%
Nashville-Davidson–Murfreesboro–Franklin, TN	452,984	90.3%	9.7%	43,885	5.1%	2.2%	0.9%	2.0%	0.1%	0.0%
New Bern, NC	34,621	92.8%	7.2%	2,479	5.4%	0.7%	1.1%	0.0%	0.4%	0.0%
New Castle, PA micro	18,981	99.6%	0.4%	77	0.1%	0.0%	0.3%	0.0%	0.0%	0.0%
New Haven-Milford, CT	221,657	87.9%	12.1%	26,883	6.9%	3.7%	1.9%	0.7%	0.2%	0.0%
New Orleans-Metairie, LA	308,913	92.3%	7.7%	23,919	5.5%	2.0%	0.5%	0.2%	0.0%	0.0%
New Philadelphia-Dover, OH micro	21,241	97.6%	2.4%	520	2.4%	0.0%	0.0%	0.0%	0.0%	0.0%
New York-Newark-Jersey City, NY-NJ-PA	5,115,314	76.6%	23.4%	1,197,750	13.5%	6.9%	2.7%	1.3%	0.3%	0.1%
Niles-Benton Harbor, MI	34,333	95.0%	5.0%	1,723	3.1%	1.9%	0.0%	0.0%	0.8%	0.0%
North Port-Sarasota-Bradenton, FL	134,039	89.9%	10.1%	13,479	8.9%	0.9%	1.0%	0.1%	0.1%	0.0%
Norwich-New London, CT	70,256	95.9%	4.1%	2,870	2.1%	2.1%	1.1%	0.0%	0.0%	0.0%
Ocala, FL	66,776	95.3%	4.7%	3,139	3.2%	1.3%	0.6%	0.0%	0.0%	0.0%
Ocean City, NJ	19,995	89.3%	10.7%	2,139	5.4%	2.1%	3.6%	0.0%	0.0%	0.0%
Odessa, TX	45,187	86.6%	13.4%	6,041	12.9%	0.6%	1.0%	0.3%	0.0%	0.0%
Ogden-Clearfield, UT	173,619	95.3%	4.7%	8,096	2.5%	1.7%	0.3%	0.3%	0.4%	0.3%
Ogdensburg-Massena, NY micro	31,306	98.1%	1.9%	608	0.8%	0.2%	0.6%	0.4%	0.0%	0.0%
Oklahoma City, OK	350,851	89.9%	10.1%	35,329	7.2%	2.1%	0.6%	0.8%	0.0%	0.0%
Olympia-Tumwater, WA	68,980	92.3%	7.7%	5,285	3.6%	2.6%	0.9%	0.8%	0.8%	0.0%
Omaha-Council Bluffs, NE-IA	244,099	92.8%	7.2%	17,558	3.5%	3.2%	0.8%	0.5%	0.2%	0.0%
Orangeburg, SC micro	24,189	97.8%	2.2%	537	2.2%	0.0%	0.8%	0.0%	0.0%	0.0%
Orlando-Kissimmee-Sanford, FL	621,615	87.4%	12.6%	78,561	10.6%	2.0%	1.2%	0.4%	0.3%	0.0%
Oshkosh-Neenah, WI	46,883	97.6%	2.4%	1,128	0.5%	2.4%	0.3%	0.0%	0.0%	0.0%
Ottawa-Peru, IL micro	26,791	97.0%	3.0%	799	1.9%	0.8%	0.3%	0.0%	0.0%	0.0%
Owensboro, KY	27,593	98.5%	1.5%	422	0.4%	1.2%	0.4%	0.0%	0.0%	0.0%
Oxnard-Thousand Oaks-Ventura, CA	213,780	81.4%	18.6%	39,836	15.3%	2.5%	1.0%	0.3%	0.1%	0.1%
Palm Bay-Melbourne-Titusville, FL	112,681	94.5%	5.5%	6,234	4.4%	0.9%	1.1%	0.0%	0.2%	0.0%
Panama City, FL	46,495	96.0%	4.0%	1,865	2.9%	1.0%	0.5%	0.0%	0.2%	0.0%
Parkersburg-Vienna, WV	19,813	100.0%	0.0%	0	0.8%	0.0%	0.3%	0.0%	0.0%	0.0%
Pensacola-Ferry Pass-Brent, FL	127,327	96.3%	3.7%	4,701	1.6%	2.4%	1.9%	0.1%	0.2%	0.0%
Peoria, IL	96,218	96.4%	3.6%	3,448	0.6%	3.0%	0.9%	0.2%	0.0%	0.0%
Philadelphia-Camden-Wilmington, PA-NJ-DE-MD	1,580,042	89.9%	10.1%	159,224	3.6%	4.5%	1.5%	1.4%	0.1%	0.0%
Phoenix-Mesa-Scottsdale, AZ	1,160,054	87.3%	12.7%	147,623	8.9%	2.8%	1.2%	0.8%	0.3%	0.1%
Pine Bluff, AR	25,971	97.3%	2.7%	709	2.5%	0.3%	0.0%	0.0%	0.0%	0.0%
Pittsburgh, PA	559,230	95.5%	4.5%	25,134	0.8%	2.4%	1.2%	0.5%	0.1%	0.0%
Pittsfield, MA	30,536	93.7%	6.3%	1,923	2.1%	0.9%	0.6%	2.8%	0.0%	0.3%
Pocatello, ID	25,609	91.6%	8.4%	2,144	5.0%	4.3%	0.8%	0.2%	0.1%	0.0%
Port St. Lucie, FL	90,678	86.3%	13.7%	12,424	12.3%	1.7%	0.1%	0.0%	0.1%	0.0%
Portland-South Portland, ME	118,095	96.8%	3.2%	3,832	1.0%	2.2%	0.7%	0.6%	0.4%	0.0%
Portland-Vancouver-Hillsboro, OR-WA	580,285	86.9%	13.1%	76,273	5.5%	4.5%	3.6%	0.6%	0.2%	0.2%
Pottsville, PA micro	30,617	98.4%	1.6%	503	0.6%	0.2%	0.6%	0.0%	0.0%	0.0%
Prescott, AZ	40,349	88.5%	11.5%	4,642	8.7%	1.6%	1.2%	0.7%	0.0%	0.0%
Providence-Warwick, RI-MA	414,057	90.1%	9.9%	41,007	5.7%	1.7%	1.8%	1.4%	0.1%	0.1%
Provo-Orem, UT	203,200	91.9%	8.1%	16,491	4.7%	2.4%	1.2%	0.1%	0.9%	0.4%
Pueblo, CO	41,292	93.1%	6.9%	2,862	5.8%	0.3%	1.2%	0.1%	0.0%	0.0%
Punta Gorda, FL	26,086	91.6%	8.4%	2,201	5.6%	1.1%	3.8%	0.0%	0.0%	0.0%
Racine, WI	45,497	92.7%	7.3%	3,300	7.3%	0.0%	0.5%	0.0%	0.0%	0.0%
Raleigh, NC	320,952	86.8%	13.2%	42,274	7.6%	3.8%	1.5%	0.7%	0.4%	0.1%
Rapid City, SD	34,720	98.6%	1.4%	480	0.0%	1.3%	0.3%	0.8%	0.0%	0.0%
Reading, PA	103,706	93.5%	6.5%	6,723	5.6%	1.0%	0.5%	0.1%	0.1%	0.0%
Redding, CA	43,154	91.2%	8.8%	3,783	1.8%	3.6%	2.9%	1.0%	0.0%	0.2%
Reno, NV	113,990	87.8%	12.2%	13,938	8.8%	3.5%	0.5%	0.4%	0.0%	0.5%
Richmond, VA	318,467	93.9%	6.1%	19,493	2.9%	2.4%	1.5%	0.6%	0.1%	0.0%
Riverside-San Bernardino-Ontario, CA	1,236,472	87.1%	12.9%	159,307	9.9%	3.0%	0.3%	0.4%	0.1%	0.0%
Roanoke, VA	71,344	95.6%	4.4%	3,144	2.4%	1.4%	0.9%	0.0%	0.2%	0.0%
Rochester, MN	52,035	90.4%	9.6%	5,010	2.1%	4.2%	1.3%	4.2%	0.0%	0.1%
Rochester, NY	283,108	93.9%	6.1%	17,149	1.2%	2.7%	2.3%	0.7%	0.2%	0.0%

Table C-4: Metropolitan/Micropolitan Statistical Areas—Nativity and World Region of Birth—*Continued*

	Total Millennial	Percent		Total Foreign Born	Percent of Foreign Born by Region of Birth					
		Native	Foreign Born		Latin America	Asia	Europe	Africa	North America	Oceania
Rockford, IL	86,491	92.4%	7.6%	6,600	4.3%	2.7%	0.5%	0.3%	0.2%	0.0%
Rocky Mount, NC	34,744	97.0%	3.0%	1,053	2.2%	0.7%	1.5%	0.2%	0.0%	0.0%
Rome, GA	23,869	92.5%	7.5%	1,791	6.8%	0.6%	1.6%	0.0%	0.0%	0.0%
Roseburg, OR micro	20,735	96.1%	3.9%	814	2.2%	1.6%	0.2%	0.0%	0.0%	0.0%
Sacramento–Roseville–Arden-Arcade, CA	573,311	84.3%	15.7%	89,886	6.4%	6.1%	3.2%	0.6%	0.0%	0.5%
Saginaw, MI	49,901	98.8%	1.2%	619	0.2%	1.4%	0.2%	0.0%	0.4%	0.0%
Salem, OH micro	23,852	97.7%	2.3%	551	2.1%	0.3%	0.0%	0.0%	0.0%	0.0%
Salem, OR	106,773	87.7%	12.3%	13,162	9.6%	1.8%	1.5%	0.1%	0.0%	0.0%
Salinas, CA	123,388	75.8%	24.2%	29,900	20.9%	2.8%	0.7%	0.1%	0.1%	0.2%
Salisbury, MD-DE	89,343	88.9%	11.1%	9,934	6.9%	2.0%	1.9%	0.9%	0.1%	0.0%
Salt Lake City, UT	322,656	88.1%	11.9%	38,459	7.5%	2.8%	1.5%	0.6%	0.3%	0.0%
San Angelo, TX	34,968	97.4%	2.6%	923	2.1%	0.5%	1.8%	0.0%	0.0%	0.0%
San Antonio-New Braunfels, TX	643,590	90.0%	10.0%	64,412	7.9%	2.6%	1.3%	0.2%	0.1%	0.1%
San Diego-Carlsbad, CA	935,309	81.9%	18.1%	169,658	10.7%	6.8%	1.6%	0.6%	0.2%	0.1%
San Francisco-Oakland-Hayward, CA	1,111,639	77.3%	22.7%	252,061	9.4%	11.5%	1.9%	0.5%	0.4%	0.4%
San Jose-Sunnyvale-Santa Clara, CA	479,231	70.5%	29.5%	141,545	10.9%	17.2%	1.7%	0.8%	0.6%	0.2%
San Luis Obispo-Paso Robles-Arroyo Grande, CA	80,673	93.9%	6.1%	4,923	4.3%	1.3%	0.8%	0.3%	0.3%	0.0%
Santa Cruz-Watsonville, CA	75,403	82.8%	17.2%	12,970	12.3%	3.7%	1.3%	0.0%	0.7%	0.0%
Santa Fe, NM	29,956	80.4%	19.6%	5,867	16.4%	2.0%	1.4%	0.0%	0.0%	0.0%
Santa Maria-Santa Barbara, CA	137,268	78.1%	21.9%	30,006	18.0%	3.4%	1.7%	0.3%	0.1%	0.0%
Santa Rosa, CA	120,963	87.2%	12.8%	15,527	10.5%	1.5%	0.4%	0.8%	0.0%	0.2%
Savannah, GA	104,999	92.1%	7.9%	8,286	4.1%	2.4%	1.6%	0.9%	0.0%	0.0%
Scranton–Wilkes-Barre–Hazleton, PA	135,447	94.4%	5.6%	7,541	3.0%	1.8%	0.6%	0.3%	0.2%	0.0%
Seattle-Tacoma-Bellevue, WA	935,702	82.0%	18.0%	168,247	4.9%	8.4%	3.4%	1.9%	0.8%	0.4%
Sebastian-Vero Beach, FL	27,498	91.4%	8.6%	2,376	6.6%	0.9%	0.7%	0.4%	0.0%	0.0%
Sebring, FL	17,203	86.3%	13.7%	2,359	14.9%	0.5%	0.0%	0.0%	0.6%	0.0%
Sheboygan, WI	25,416	94.4%	5.6%	1,417	3.1%	3.3%	0.5%	0.0%	0.0%	0.0%
Sherman-Denison, TX	30,297	92.0%	8.0%	2,419	6.6%	1.9%	1.6%	0.3%	0.1%	0.0%
Show Low, AZ micro	28,335	99.0%	1.0%	283	1.0%	0.0%	0.0%	0.0%	0.0%	0.0%
Shreveport-Bossier City, LA	123,377	97.2%	2.8%	3,411	1.9%	1.0%	0.7%	0.0%	0.0%	0.0%
Sierra Vista-Douglas, AZ	32,345	90.7%	9.3%	3,009	8.9%	0.9%	0.7%	0.0%	0.0%	0.4%
Sioux City, IA-NE-SD	44,165	92.2%	7.8%	3,432	6.9%	0.8%	0.1%	0.1%	0.0%	0.0%
Sioux Falls, SD	63,236	95.7%	4.3%	2,723	0.4%	1.8%	1.1%	1.5%	0.0%	0.0%
South Bend-Mishawaka, IN-MI	82,057	95.8%	4.2%	3,415	2.6%	1.3%	0.6%	0.2%	0.1%	0.0%
Spartanburg, SC	84,899	93.3%	6.7%	5,686	4.3%	1.5%	1.6%	0.1%	0.0%	0.0%
Spokane-Spokane Valley, WA	147,190	93.9%	6.1%	8,910	1.2%	2.7%	3.2%	0.4%	0.5%	0.4%
Springfield, IL	50,200	97.1%	2.9%	1,434	1.2%	1.4%	0.3%	0.0%	0.0%	0.0%
Springfield, MA	175,021	90.9%	9.1%	15,863	3.2%	3.5%	2.5%	0.7%	0.4%	0.0%
Springfield, MO	129,457	98.4%	1.6%	2,029	0.3%	0.8%	0.9%	0.0%	0.1%	0.0%
Springfield, OH	32,974	98.0%	2.0%	675	1.7%	0.2%	1.4%	0.1%	0.0%	0.0%
St. Cloud, MN	59,001	95.2%	4.8%	2,842	2.9%	0.8%	0.0%	1.7%	0.0%	0.0%
St. George, UT	36,461	97.6%	2.4%	885	1.2%	0.3%	0.9%	0.0%	0.8%	0.0%
St. Joseph, MO-KS	32,200	97.4%	2.6%	851	2.0%	0.2%	0.3%	0.4%	0.0%	0.0%
St. Louis, MO-IL	701,224	95.4%	4.6%	32,125	1.2%	2.6%	1.3%	0.2%	0.1%	0.0%
State College, PA	65,126	90.8%	9.2%	5,971	0.1%	7.4%	0.9%	1.5%	0.0%	0.0%
Staunton-Waynesboro, VA	27,051	96.5%	3.5%	944	1.6%	1.9%	1.1%	0.1%	0.6%	0.0%
Stockton-Lodi, CA	193,213	82.5%	17.5%	33,723	13.0%	4.7%	0.6%	0.0%	0.0%	0.1%
Sumter, SC	30,387	97.8%	2.2%	659	2.0%	0.4%	0.6%	0.0%	0.0%	0.2%
Sunbury, PA micro	19,987	99.1%	0.9%	188	0.5%	0.3%	0.5%	0.0%	0.0%	0.0%
Syracuse, NY	170,167	94.4%	5.6%	9,511	1.5%	2.5%	1.3%	0.6%	0.3%	0.1%
Tallahassee, FL	137,443	94.0%	6.0%	8,181	4.3%	2.1%	0.6%	0.4%	0.0%	0.0%
Tampa-St. Petersburg-Clearwater, FL	670,366	89.5%	10.5%	70,301	7.6%	2.3%	1.8%	0.4%	0.1%	0.1%
Terre Haute, IN	46,772	96.4%	3.6%	1,667	2.0%	1.9%	0.1%	0.0%	0.0%	0.0%
Texarkana, TX-AR	38,572	96.0%	4.0%	1,560	3.9%	0.2%	0.0%	0.0%	0.0%	0.2%
The Villages, FL	11,362	95.2%	4.8%	546	4.8%	0.0%	2.2%	0.0%	0.0%	0.0%
Toledo, OH	170,511	96.4%	3.6%	6,089	1.1%	1.5%	0.7%	0.3%	0.2%	0.1%
Topeka, KS	54,331	94.3%	5.7%	3,112	4.3%	1.7%	0.2%	0.0%	0.2%	0.0%
Torrington, CT micro	39,336	95.4%	4.6%	1,820	3.2%	1.9%	1.2%	0.0%	0.2%	0.0%
Traverse City, MI micro	31,826	97.8%	2.2%	686	0.1%	0.5%	1.6%	0.0%	0.1%	0.0%
Trenton, NJ	97,275	77.2%	22.8%	22,184	10.1%	7.1%	4.0%	2.7%	0.7%	0.0%
Truckee-Grass Valley, CA micro	19,138	97.0%	3.0%	569	0.2%	0.0%	2.8%	0.0%	0.0%	0.0%
Tucson, AZ	272,490	89.0%	11.0%	30,003	7.6%	3.1%	1.2%	0.6%	0.1%	0.0%
Tullahoma-Manchester, TN micro	23,786	97.5%	2.5%	591	2.4%	0.6%	0.1%	0.0%	0.0%	0.0%
Tulsa, OK	242,714	92.9%	7.1%	17,347	5.5%	1.4%	1.1%	0.1%	0.1%	0.0%
Tupelo, MS micro	35,356	96.3%	3.7%	1,291	3.5%	0.1%	0.0%	0.1%	0.0%	0.0%
Tuscaloosa, AL	77,812	96.1%	3.9%	3,001	2.4%	0.4%	0.7%	0.3%	0.3%	0.0%
Tyler, TX	57,353	89.0%	11.0%	6,298	8.2%	0.5%	1.6%	0.7%	0.0%	0.0%
Urban Honolulu, HI	265,827	88.1%	11.9%	31,525	0.8%	9.6%	1.0%	0.1%	0.2%	2.8%
Utica-Rome, NY	73,705	93.0%	7.0%	5,145	2.3%	1.6%	3.9%	0.1%	0.0%	0.0%
Valdosta, GA	48,976	96.2%	3.8%	1,874	2.3%	1.6%	1.3%	0.0%	0.1%	0.0%
Vallejo-Fairfield, CA	114,250	86.3%	13.7%	15,673	7.1%	5.8%	1.0%	0.1%	0.4%	0.5%
Victoria, TX	25,055	94.1%	5.9%	1,479	4.6%	3.7%	1.5%	0.0%	0.0%	0.0%
Vineland-Bridgeton, NJ	41,175	85.2%	14.8%	6,081	11.0%	1.3%	3.0%	0.0%	0.7%	0.0%
Virginia Beach-Norfolk-Newport News, VA-NC	498,520	94.6%	5.4%	27,166	1.8%	2.7%	1.9%	0.7%	0.1%	0.1%
Visalia-Porterville, CA	132,184	81.2%	18.8%	24,908	17.1%	2.2%	0.3%	0.0%	0.1%	0.0%
Waco, TX	77,186	90.7%	9.3%	7,158	6.3%	2.4%	0.5%	0.6%	0.2%	0.0%
Walla Walla, WA	16,753	82.7%	17.3%	2,896	12.7%	4.9%	0.0%	0.5%	0.1%	0.0%
Warner Robins, GA	53,774	94.5%	5.5%	2,961	3.8%	2.0%	2.2%	0.3%	0.0%	0.0%

Table C-4: Metropolitan/Micropolitan Statistical Areas—Nativity and World Region of Birth—*Continued*

	Total Millennial	Percent		Total Foreign Born	Percent of Foreign Born by Region of Birth					
		Native	Foreign Born		Latin America	Asia	Europe	Africa	North America	Oceania
Washington-Arlington-Alexandria, DC-VA-MD-WV	1,557,927	80.0%	20.0%	311,150	9.3%	6.7%	2.5%	3.4%	0.1%	0.1%
Waterloo-Cedar Falls, IA	52,275	92.8%	7.2%	3,739	2.8%	1.4%	2.9%	0.1%	0.2%	0.0%
Watertown-Fort Drum, NY	36,656	97.1%	2.9%	1,070	2.3%	0.9%	2.0%	0.0%	0.7%	0.0%
Wausau, WI	31,554	90.0%	10.0%	3,166	2.6%	6.5%	2.2%	0.0%	0.0%	0.0%
Weirton-Steubenville, WV-OH	28,248	99.5%	0.5%	143	0.0%	0.5%	0.8%	0.0%	0.0%	0.0%
Wenatchee, WA	27,971	85.3%	14.7%	4,123	13.7%	0.0%	1.3%	0.6%	0.0%	0.0%
Wheeling, WV-OH	32,441	98.8%	1.2%	375	0.5%	0.9%	0.7%	0.0%	0.0%	0.0%
Whitewater-Elkhorn, WI micro	27,115	89.5%	10.5%	2,852	7.9%	0.9%	6.2%	0.0%	0.0%	0.0%
Wichita Falls, TX	44,773	94.0%	6.0%	2,700	3.2%	0.9%	2.1%	1.2%	0.0%	0.0%
Wichita, KS	168,613	91.9%	8.1%	13,634	4.4%	2.9%	1.4%	0.5%	0.0%	0.0%
Williamsport, PA	27,887	99.2%	0.8%	220	0.0%	0.4%	0.0%	0.7%	0.0%	0.0%
Wilmington, NC	70,426	94.1%	5.9%	4,143	3.3%	2.2%	0.9%	0.0%	0.0%	0.0%
Winchester, VA-WV	29,169	95.7%	4.3%	1,259	6.0%	1.1%	3.6%	0.0%	0.0%	0.0%
Winston-Salem, NC	156,727	94.2%	5.8%	9,138	4.9%	1.2%	0.6%	0.1%	0.1%	0.0%
Wooster, OH micro	28,468	97.0%	3.0%	841	0.8%	1.6%	0.0%	0.5%	0.0%	0.0%
Worcester, MA-CT	228,311	89.3%	10.7%	24,489	4.8%	3.3%	1.5%	1.4%	0.1%	0.2%
Yakima, WA	65,994	76.4%	23.6%	15,576	23.6%	0.8%	0.0%	0.0%	0.2%	0.0%
York-Hanover, PA	97,575	94.6%	5.4%	5,236	3.4%	0.8%	1.2%	0.8%	0.0%	0.0%
Youngstown-Warren-Boardman, OH-PA	130,034	98.3%	1.7%	2,245	0.6%	1.0%	0.4%	0.1%	0.0%	0.0%
Yuba City, CA	44,330	81.5%	18.5%	8,221	11.3%	7.4%	1.5%	0.0%	0.0%	0.0%
Yuma, AZ	59,396	80.5%	19.5%	11,576	18.8%	1.0%	0.4%	0.0%	0.0%	0.0%

PART D
HOUSEHOLD RELATIONSHIP

HOUSEHOLD RELATIONSHIP

People live in a multitude of different living arrangements, but they are all classified by the Census Bureau as living in either households or group quarters facilities. Those living in households live in either family or non-family households. A family household is comprised of two or more individuals related to the householder by blood, marriage, or adoption. Non-family households are ones where all of the individuals are unrelated or it is occupied by a single person living alone. There are no other household types. All households have a single householder, which is generally the person who owns or rents the unit.

Group quarters facilities can be either institutional or non-institutional. Examples of institutional facilities include correctional facilities, nursing homes, and other institutional health facilities. Non-institutional group quarters include college student housing, military, and other group home situations. For the Millennial population described here, those living in group quarters will be predominantly college housing, and it is often easy to identify those counties and cities with a large college or university presence.

The Millennials are notable as a generation for delayed marriage and childbearing, which dramatically alters their household composition. Whereas Baby Boomers formed family households early in life, Millennials are delaying, or not forming, family households. Today, Millennials are also faced with the unique situation of increased return to their parental home. The tables in this section focus on Millennial householders age 18 to 31 and the type of household: married couples with and without children, single male householders with and without children, single female householders with and without children, and non-family households with individuals living alone or with other non-relatives. Also included is a measure of the sons and daughters (both biological and legal) living with their parents.

More than 57 percent of Millennial householders age 18 to 24 are in non-family living situations compared to 38.4 percent of those age 25 to 31. One in four (26.3 percent) householders 18 to 24 is living alone, which is only slightly higher than those age 25 to 31 (23.7 percent).

While 31.2 percent of the 18 to 24 Millennials are living with other non-relatives, that figure drops to only 14.2 percent for those age 25 to 31. More than half (51.1 percent) of Millennials age 18 to 24 are living in their parents' households, but that figure drops to only 22.3 percent of 25 to 31 year olds.

Among family households, only 16.6 percent of the 18 to 24 year olds are in married couple families (7.7 percent are with children), compared to 38.0 percent of the 25 to 31 year olds. Though there are many more 25 to 31 year olds who are married, two out of three still do not have children. Single male and female households make up the smallest share in both age categories. Single male households make up 7.8 percent of the 18 to 24 age group and only 6.5 percent of the 25 to 31 year olds. Single females account for 18.1 percent of the 18 to 24 householders and 17.1 percent of the 25 to 31 year olds. The big difference here is single females with children, which make up 14.6 percent of 18 to 24 year old householders and 15.5 percent of the 25 to 31.

Utah has by far the highest percentage of married couple households among the 18 to 24 year olds at 44.8 percent. Hawaii is second at 32.3 percent and Idaho is close at 29.8 percent. The District of Columbia has the lowest percentage at only 1.7 percent. Nationwide, 16.6 percent of Millennial households age 18 to 24 are married couples. Marriage increases significantly for the 25 to 31 age group where 38.0 percent of Millennials are now married. Utah again has the highest percentage at 62.2 percent and the District of Columbia is still lowest at 16.2 percent.

Nevada has the highest percentage of 18 to 24 year old single male householders with no children at 9.6 percent, and three states (Alaska, Maine, and Vermont) are below one percent. Also among the 18 to 24 year olds, Mississippi has the highest percentage of single females with no children at 23.9 percent, but Alaska has the highest percentage (8.8 percent) of those with children. In Delaware, 38.5 percent of 18 to 24 year old householders are living alone but only 9.5 percent live alone in Alaska. Massachusetts has the highest percentage living with other non-relatives at 46.6 percent. More than two-thirds (68.5 percent) of New Jersey Millennials age 18 to 24 are living with their parents, and in 17 states that figure is

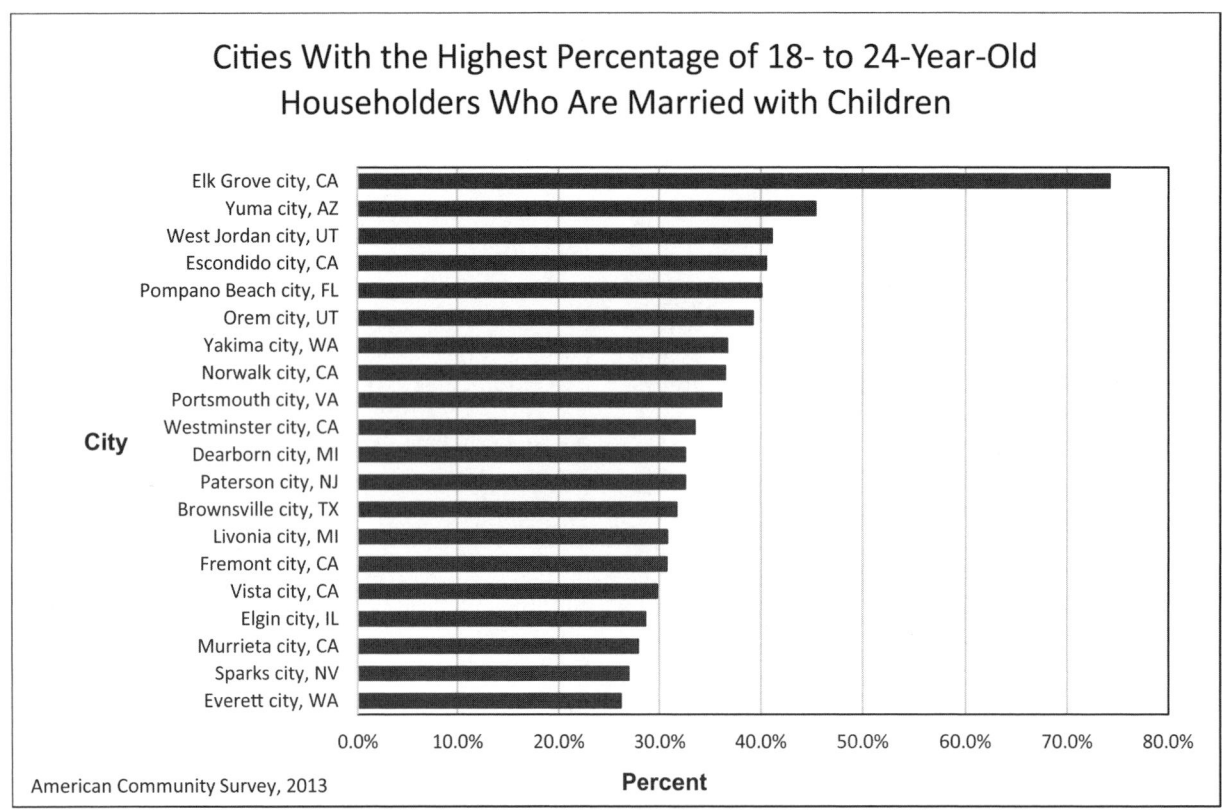

Percent Age 25 to 31 Living With Their Parents

over 50 percent. In North Dakota, only 22.2 percent are living with their parents.

The percentage of Millennial householders age 25 to 31 who are married has risen from the 18 to 24 age group mainly because the percentage of them living in non-family situations has declined. Single male and female householders, with and without children, maintain similar percentages but only 38.1 percent of 25 to 31 year olds are in non-family arrangements compared to 57.5 percent of the 18 to 24 year olds. The District of Columbia has the highest percentage of non-family households at 67.6 percent and is also highest for those living alone and living with other non-relatives. DC has the lowest share of married couples age 25 to 31. The percentage of 25 to 31 year old Millennials living with their parents drops by more than half from the 18 to 24 age group to 22.3 percent, with New Jersey still having the highest rate at 33.5 percent.

Among the 18 to 24 year old Millennial householders, Craven County, NC has the highest percentage of married couples at 82.4 percent. More than 50 percent of Millennial householders are in married couple relationships in 25 of the 622 counties. Flagler County, FL stands out as having the highest percentage of single male householders with children at 54.9 percent. Another 15.8 percent are single males with no children. Rockingham County, NC tops the list for the percentage of single females with children at 87.0 percent. Only eight counties have more than 50 percent single females households with children. The percentage of sons and daughters living with their parents ranges from a low of 5.2 percent in Johnson County, IA to a high of 87.0 percent in Sutter County, CA.

In 132 of the 622 counties more than 50 percent of Millennial householders age 25 to 31 are married. Fayette County, GA is highest at 88.0 percent, and 76.2 percent of those married couples have children. At 67.6 percent, Saline County, AR has the highest percentage of married householders with children. In Kendall County, IL, 53.1 percent of Millennial householders age 25 to 31 are single females with children while Kennebec County, ME has the highest percentage of single male householders with children at 24.8 percent. More than 70 percent (70.5 percent) of 25 to 31 year old householders in Sumter County, FL are single individuals living alone. It's one of only three counties over 50 percent. At 62.8 percent, Putnam County, NY has the highest percentage of Millennials living with their parents.

Mission Viejo City, CA is not a large city but all of its 18 to 24 year old Millennial households are married couples! Another California city, Elk Grove, has the highest percentage of married couple households with children at 74.2 percent. In 142 of the 331 cities the percentage of 18 to 24 year old householders who are married couples is less than 10 percent, but 13 cities are over 50 percent married couples. Bridgeport, CT has the highest

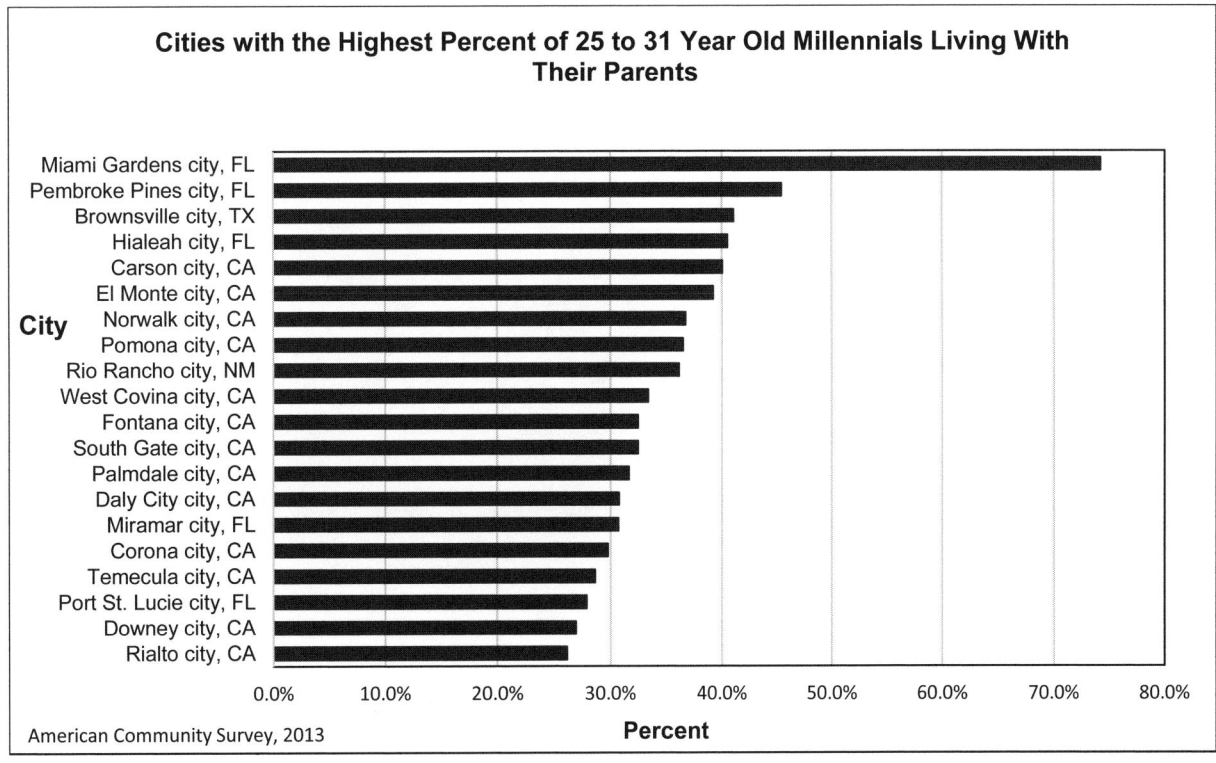

Cities with the Highest Percent of 25 to 31 Year Old Millennials Living With Their Parents

American Community Survey, 2013

percentage of single female households with children at 86.5 percent. Sandy Springs City, GA seems to be an anomaly with all of its 618 Millennial householders living alone as non-family households. In Brockton City, MA 85 percent of 18 to 24 year olds are sons or daughters living with their parents.

Among the 25 to 31 year old householders, West Jordan City, UT has the highest percentage of married couple households at 74.3 percent. Forty-two other cities are above 50 percent married couples. West Jordon City also has the highest percentage of married couples with children at 66.5 percent. Fontana City, CA has the highest percentage of single male householders with children at 27.5 percent while Paterson City, NJ is highest for single female householders with children at 51.1 percent. Even in the older ages sons and daughters are still living with their parents, with Miami Gardens City, FL having the highest percentage at 60.5 percent.

In 11 metropolitan/micropolitan areas, the percentage of 18 to 24 year old householders that are married couples is greater than 50 percent. It is highest in the Gadsden, AL metro at 82.0 percent. Gadsden is also highest with 63.3 percent being married couples with children. More than three-quarters (76.2 percent) of 18- to 24-year-old householders are single females with children in the Meridian, MS micropolitan area. The percentage of younger Millennials living alone is greatest in the Sunbury, PA micro at 76.0 percent while those living with other non-relatives is highest in the Traverse City, MI micro (80.1 percent). In 182 metro/micro areas, more than 50 percent of the 18 to 24 year old Millennials are living with their parents. It's highest in the Truckee-Grass Valley, CA micro at 83.1 percent.

Grants Pass, OR has the highest percentage of 25- to 31-year-old householders who are married couples (80.4 percent). Sixty-six metropolitan/micropolitan areas are above the 50 percent level. At 66.5 percent, the St. George, UT metro has the highest percentage of married couples with children. The Grand Island, ME metro has the highest percentage of single male householders with children (27.0 percent), while at 50.0 percent, the Greenwood, SC micro is highest for single female householders. Nearly two-thirds (66.3 percent) of 25- to 31-year-old householders are living alone in The Villages, FL metro, and the Show Low, AZ micro has the highest percentage of sons and daughters living with their parents (53.5 percent).

This page is intentionally left blank.

Table D-1: States—Household Relationship

		Married Couple Households		Male, No Spouse Present		Female, No Spouse Present		Non-Family Householders		
	Total Householders	With Children	No Children	With Children	No Children	With Children	No Children	Living Alone	Not Alone	Living With Parents
United States..........................	4,530,509	8.9%	7.7%	3.2%	4.6%	14.6%	3.5%	26.3%	31.2%	51.1%
Alabama...............................	76,876	10.6%	7.5%	2.2%	4.1%	19.8%	3.0%	28.1%	24.6%	52.1%
Alaska..................................	12,145	14.5%	15.2%	4.6%	0.9%	12.5%	8.8%	9.5%	34.0%	45.1%
Arizona................................	110,262	9.5%	7.1%	4.0%	6.7%	14.8%	4.9%	27.9%	25.1%	50.4%
Arkansas..............................	55,763	11.4%	8.3%	3.7%	2.5%	20.2%	2.6%	26.8%	24.6%	43.2%
California..............................	422,830	9.1%	7.0%	4.1%	8.0%	12.0%	5.9%	20.7%	33.1%	57.7%
Colorado..............................	98,265	8.6%	8.5%	2.0%	2.8%	10.0%	3.3%	25.8%	39.0%	43.9%
Connecticut..........................	26,507	3.9%	5.3%	2.5%	6.9%	17.5%	5.6%	30.9%	27.4%	57.4%
Delaware..............................	10,237	2.9%	7.7%	1.2%	4.7%	15.0%	4.3%	38.5%	25.7%	54.4%
District of Columbia	11,532	0.0%	1.7%	2.6%	4.3%	13.0%	0.4%	32.3%	45.6%	24.2%
Florida.................................	225,383	6.1%	7.6%	2.8%	5.8%	13.8%	5.0%	27.4%	31.5%	55.9%
Georgia................................	142,386	8.6%	9.5%	3.5%	4.4%	16.7%	3.5%	27.6%	26.2%	50.8%
Hawaii..................................	15,826	17.2%	15.1%	2.7%	2.7%	4.3%	4.4%	28.4%	25.2%	49.7%
Idaho...................................	31,836	14.2%	15.6%	3.1%	2.1%	4.8%	3.8%	20.9%	35.4%	41.0%
Illinois.................................	171,951	6.9%	6.9%	3.1%	3.7%	14.5%	2.4%	33.0%	29.4%	56.8%
Indiana................................	121,603	9.0%	7.8%	3.0%	3.3%	14.7%	2.9%	28.1%	31.2%	45.2%
Iowa....................................	71,269	3.6%	7.2%	2.4%	2.3%	10.1%	0.6%	28.3%	45.4%	34.8%
Kansas................................	68,054	13.1%	7.1%	4.0%	3.5%	14.8%	3.5%	28.1%	25.9%	37.6%
Kentucky..............................	76,956	13.5%	8.4%	2.0%	4.3%	16.0%	2.3%	24.3%	29.2%	44.9%
Louisiana.............................	83,097	6.7%	5.7%	3.2%	3.3%	20.3%	5.2%	29.5%	26.0%	48.3%
Maine..................................	13,465	3.4%	7.1%	8.2%	0.6%	5.9%	5.0%	26.6%	43.2%	47.2%
Maryland..............................	53,894	8.0%	7.1%	2.1%	6.4%	18.3%	2.8%	26.1%	29.2%	58.3%
Massachusetts......................	71,846	3.7%	3.0%	1.5%	5.6%	14.6%	4.1%	20.9%	46.6%	49.3%
Michigan..............................	159,178	5.2%	4.7%	3.5%	3.8%	16.0%	3.0%	25.9%	37.9%	49.6%
Minnesota............................	87,019	5.6%	7.5%	2.6%	2.5%	11.1%	1.6%	32.1%	37.0%	46.0%
Mississippi...........................	41,087	10.7%	9.6%	2.9%	4.0%	23.9%	3.9%	18.5%	26.5%	50.8%
Missouri...............................	110,957	9.2%	8.3%	2.8%	2.6%	16.8%	2.4%	29.2%	28.6%	45.7%
Montana...............................	18,647	6.1%	5.4%	1.9%	0.6%	22.0%	2.3%	22.2%	39.7%	38.0%
Nebraska..............................	43,497	4.3%	8.2%	4.6%	3.4%	13.3%	2.0%	31.6%	32.7%	37.1%
Nevada................................	33,768	9.8%	9.5%	3.4%	9.6%	11.5%	5.0%	25.7%	25.5%	52.7%
New Hampshire......................	15,790	6.1%	8.0%	6.3%	4.6%	14.8%	0.0%	24.6%	35.6%	50.2%
New Jersey...........................	48,322	10.6%	7.8%	3.1%	6.5%	19.9%	6.0%	21.3%	24.9%	68.5%
New Mexico..........................	34,568	14.3%	9.9%	5.2%	2.9%	18.0%	2.9%	17.5%	29.1%	49.4%
New York..............................	195,805	7.5%	5.3%	2.4%	7.2%	14.2%	4.9%	25.8%	32.7%	58.3%
North Carolina.......................	160,791	8.8%	11.1%	2.4%	3.8%	14.2%	2.1%	27.2%	30.4%	45.6%
North Dakota.........................	31,333	10.1%	9.8%	2.5%	1.7%	8.3%	2.9%	28.2%	36.5%	22.2%
Ohio....................................	192,864	8.2%	6.1%	3.2%	3.6%	18.9%	2.3%	30.2%	27.6%	47.2%
Oklahoma.............................	80,392	14.0%	9.6%	2.8%	3.5%	15.0%	2.7%	28.0%	24.3%	40.8%
Oregon................................	63,971	10.1%	7.7%	2.9%	2.1%	10.7%	3.1%	24.3%	39.0%	43.7%
Pennsylvania.........................	155,261	6.1%	3.5%	2.5%	3.8%	16.1%	2.6%	31.0%	34.3%	51.1%
Rhode Island.........................	13,433	4.6%	1.7%	3.2%	6.9%	9.7%	6.6%	27.3%	40.0%	49.5%
South Carolina.......................	76,156	5.6%	7.7%	3.1%	4.9%	20.5%	2.2%	28.8%	27.2%	46.3%
South Dakota........................	18,587	9.7%	13.2%	4.0%	2.6%	9.8%	1.5%	22.7%	36.5%	30.0%
Tennessee............................	100,771	10.5%	9.9%	4.4%	4.2%	17.5%	1.9%	26.0%	25.7%	48.9%
Texas..................................	443,553	13.0%	8.0%	3.7%	4.9%	14.7%	3.4%	26.9%	25.4%	52.5%
Utah....................................	53,405	16.7%	28.1%	2.5%	3.1%	7.8%	2.3%	11.3%	28.1%	44.5%
Vermont...............................	9,591	16.4%	0.5%	0.7%	0.5%	11.1%	3.1%	21.4%	46.3%	33.8%
Virginia................................	108,696	8.8%	10.5%	2.0%	4.5%	13.0%	3.6%	23.9%	33.7%	48.4%
Washington...........................	108,767	8.8%	7.7%	4.4%	3.7%	9.7%	4.5%	21.9%	39.2%	47.0%
West Virginia.........................	29,689	10.6%	8.0%	7.7%	2.0%	16.9%	2.3%	28.1%	24.5%	47.4%
Wisconsin.............................	107,794	6.2%	5.5%	1.7%	4.3%	14.1%	2.2%	26.2%	39.9%	44.8%
Wyoming..............................	14,834	9.0%	9.6%	0.0%	4.2%	13.2%	7.0%	32.2%	24.8%	32.6%

Table D-1: States—Household Relationship—*Continued*

		25 to 31								
		Married Couple Households		Male, No Spouse Present		Female, No Spouse Present		Non-Family Householders		
	Total Householders	With Children	No Children	With Children	No Children	With Children	No Children	Living Alone	Not Alone	Living With Parents
United States	11,833,498	25.2%	12.8%	4.0%	2.5%	15.5%	1.6%	23.7%	14.7%	22.3%
Alabama	173,083	29.1%	11.1%	3.5%	3.0%	22.4%	1.1%	23.1%	6.7%	23.1%
Alaska	29,175	26.9%	21.7%	3.1%	3.9%	13.0%	1.3%	18.6%	11.6%	21.1%
Arizona	249,521	24.3%	11.9%	5.4%	2.6%	14.8%	2.1%	24.8%	14.1%	19.3%
Arkansas	118,132	34.2%	10.7%	5.4%	1.4%	18.1%	0.9%	18.2%	11.0%	17.0%
California	1,305,113	23.9%	13.0%	4.1%	4.1%	13.0%	2.5%	21.0%	18.3%	27.3%
Colorado	232,329	27.1%	12.9%	3.1%	2.3%	11.3%	1.1%	23.8%	18.5%	15.0%
Connecticut	118,820	17.8%	13.3%	3.1%	2.6%	18.6%	1.3%	23.8%	19.5%	26.2%
Delaware	30,922	23.8%	16.2%	2.9%	1.1%	17.2%	1.6%	18.7%	18.5%	25.7%
District of Columbia	51,686	5.9%	10.3%	1.8%	2.3%	11.1%	1.0%	37.6%	30.1%	9.1%
Florida	595,359	22.4%	11.6%	4.0%	3.3%	17.1%	2.5%	24.7%	14.4%	28.7%
Georgia	370,388	24.5%	12.7%	4.9%	2.9%	18.1%	1.8%	24.2%	10.9%	20.9%
Hawaii	48,337	32.4%	12.5%	3.4%	2.3%	9.0%	2.5%	18.1%	19.9%	25.7%
Idaho	63,265	40.5%	13.7%	4.3%	0.9%	12.5%	0.4%	18.0%	9.8%	12.1%
Illinois	506,617	21.2%	14.7%	3.9%	2.9%	14.4%	1.6%	26.5%	14.8%	23.5%
Indiana	255,260	29.6%	14.5%	4.7%	1.2%	15.6%	0.5%	23.4%	10.6%	17.7%
Iowa	136,959	29.9%	13.1%	4.5%	1.2%	14.3%	0.2%	25.4%	11.4%	10.8%
Kansas	127,484	32.4%	13.8%	3.1%	1.1%	13.4%	0.9%	25.2%	10.2%	14.0%
Kentucky	166,417	31.1%	12.9%	3.1%	1.5%	18.9%	1.5%	18.6%	12.6%	18.6%
Louisiana	190,389	24.7%	9.8%	4.0%	2.9%	22.6%	1.1%	24.1%	10.8%	22.3%
Maine	48,683	19.9%	12.3%	10.8%	0.4%	15.7%	2.5%	20.9%	17.5%	17.7%
Maryland	213,830	20.4%	14.9%	3.8%	2.7%	15.8%	2.5%	25.4%	14.6%	24.8%
Massachusetts	244,639	16.7%	14.1%	2.5%	3.1%	13.6%	2.0%	24.0%	24.1%	24.4%
Michigan	346,713	24.1%	12.2%	4.7%	2.0%	17.6%	1.7%	24.4%	13.4%	22.2%
Minnesota	243,646	27.1%	13.1%	4.5%	1.9%	12.9%	0.7%	22.7%	17.0%	14.8%
Mississippi	100,007	28.9%	11.3%	4.6%	1.4%	26.6%	2.0%	16.9%	8.3%	25.6%
Missouri	264,807	27.9%	11.0%	3.3%	1.5%	17.2%	1.3%	24.3%	13.5%	15.7%
Montana	39,522	33.2%	11.0%	6.4%	1.2%	11.6%	0.8%	21.9%	14.0%	14.5%
Nebraska	86,307	29.9%	12.9%	4.4%	1.8%	13.6%	1.1%	24.2%	12.1%	11.8%
Nevada	111,081	27.3%	10.7%	4.3%	2.5%	14.3%	3.3%	25.0%	12.6%	18.8%
New Hampshire	45,344	20.4%	11.7%	6.0%	1.9%	16.7%	1.7%	19.7%	21.9%	21.1%
New Jersey	254,358	21.0%	16.0%	4.3%	3.5%	14.9%	2.2%	21.5%	16.7%	33.5%
New Mexico	68,040	28.5%	8.5%	5.8%	1.5%	19.2%	2.2%	21.8%	12.4%	25.1%
New York	695,298	19.0%	11.4%	3.3%	3.1%	14.1%	2.4%	27.8%	18.9%	28.4%
North Carolina	374,339	24.5%	14.4%	3.9%	1.6%	17.3%	1.1%	24.0%	13.1%	19.6%
North Dakota	35,017	33.3%	14.3%	2.1%	1.1%	9.6%	0.8%	19.3%	19.5%	6.5%
Ohio	458,633	24.5%	12.0%	3.4%	2.1%	17.9%	1.2%	25.1%	13.8%	18.9%
Oklahoma	170,446	32.3%	11.3%	5.3%	1.8%	16.8%	0.9%	21.7%	9.8%	13.3%
Oregon	154,288	26.5%	12.5%	5.0%	1.3%	13.3%	1.2%	22.2%	18.0%	16.6%
Pennsylvania	459,982	22.9%	13.0%	3.7%	1.8%	14.8%	1.1%	26.8%	15.8%	24.5%
Rhode Island	38,169	14.1%	12.9%	7.3%	2.8%	18.4%	2.0%	24.5%	18.1%	26.7%
South Carolina	167,127	23.1%	12.1%	3.1%	2.0%	20.6%	1.2%	25.8%	12.2%	23.5%
South Dakota	38,381	32.6%	6.9%	8.0%	0.1%	15.1%	1.3%	21.4%	14.5%	11.2%
Tennessee	258,513	26.7%	12.6%	4.7%	2.6%	16.9%	1.2%	22.7%	12.7%	18.7%
Texas	1,074,695	29.3%	12.3%	3.6%	2.4%	15.8%	1.3%	23.0%	12.2%	21.2%
Utah	115,740	45.6%	16.6%	3.4%	1.5%	7.0%	0.7%	13.8%	11.3%	17.0%
Vermont	19,170	20.6%	9.9%	3.0%	1.6%	21.3%	0.5%	22.7%	20.4%	18.2%
Virginia	318,643	24.7%	16.0%	3.2%	2.7%	14.2%	1.4%	23.5%	14.4%	19.8%
Washington	296,588	26.1%	14.2%	4.7%	1.5%	10.6%	1.5%	23.0%	18.4%	15.7%
West Virginia	58,578	29.4%	11.2%	6.7%	1.4%	18.3%	1.2%	23.9%	7.9%	22.4%
Wisconsin	237,855	24.6%	13.5%	4.4%	1.8%	15.3%	0.7%	27.3%	12.4%	16.3%
Wyoming	25,803	35.0%	15.3%	5.1%	4.4%	10.6%	0.1%	17.3%	12.3%	9.5%

Table D-2: Counties—Household Relationship

		Married Couple Households		Male, No Spouse Present		Female, No Spouse Present		Non-Family Householders		
	Total Householders	With Children	No Children	With Children	No Children	With Children	No Children	Living Alone	Not Alone	Living With Parents
Alabama										
Baldwin County	2,540	13.7%	38.8%	0.0%	0.2%	15.0%	0.0%	16.5%	15.8%	54.2%
Calhoun County	2,158	2.3%	3.4%	0.0%	16.6%	42.5%	0.0%	20.9%	14.4%	50.9%
Etowah County	822	63.3%	18.7%	0.0%	0.0%	0.0%	0.0%	18.0%	0.0%	73.3%
Houston County	1,497	13.8%	6.7%	0.0%	1.8%	21.1%	0.0%	35.2%	21.3%	61.7%
Jefferson County	10,177	7.3%	7.0%	0.4%	3.1%	22.7%	2.6%	31.1%	25.8%	50.5%
Lauderdale County	1,566	11.5%	8.7%	0.0%	14.7%	31.3%	0.0%	26.0%	7.8%	44.7%
Lee County	8,485	7.0%	3.6%	0.0%	5.3%	0.3%	6.6%	37.9%	39.3%	26.6%
Madison County	5,613	9.9%	3.0%	5.8%	0.0%	10.3%	10.6%	36.7%	23.7%	43.1%
Marshall County	1,214	42.6%	1.6%	1.3%	0.0%	38.6%	0.0%	13.8%	2.2%	57.8%
Mobile County	6,971	5.6%	2.1%	2.3%	2.4%	23.3%	1.1%	40.5%	22.7%	53.6%
Montgomery County	3,955	0.5%	0.0%	15.1%	1.2%	29.1%	1.6%	25.7%	26.8%	47.8%
Morgan County	1,735	31.0%	11.1%	0.0%	13.6%	42.5%	0.0%	1.7%	0.0%	53.0%
Shelby County	1,322	5.7%	17.3%	0.0%	0.0%	9.4%	0.0%	41.1%	26.6%	64.1%
Tuscaloosa County	6,517	13.5%	0.0%	0.6%	2.6%	8.7%	6.8%	29.2%	38.6%	36.2%
Alaska										
Fairbanks North Star Borough	2,273	0.0%	22.4%	0.0%	0.0%	21.7%	1.1%	2.5%	52.4%	33.4%
Matanuska-Susitna Borough	1,651	23.9%	6.1%	0.0%	0.0%	10.8%	43.3%	0.0%	15.9%	48.1%
Arizona										
Cochise County	3,470	15.4%	3.9%	23.5%	1.3%	7.3%	0.0%	25.4%	23.2%	38.6%
Coconino County	6,174	0.0%	7.6%	0.0%	8.2%	1.7%	0.0%	44.3%	38.3%	18.6%
Maricopa County	61,766	8.1%	7.5%	3.1%	8.1%	15.5%	4.6%	28.2%	24.9%	54.3%
Mohave County	2,575	0.0%	9.9%	16.1%	7.0%	16.1%	0.0%	34.5%	16.4%	45.7%
Navajo County	557	16.7%	0.0%	1.6%	3.8%	47.8%	0.0%	16.3%	13.8%	68.4%
Pima County	26,837	6.9%	5.6%	3.2%	5.0%	16.0%	7.0%	29.6%	26.7%	39.7%
Pinal County	2,092	52.4%	7.1%	2.4%	1.4%	10.6%	10.3%	0.0%	15.8%	59.6%
Yavapai County	1,877	29.6%	7.0%	2.8%	0.0%	14.8%	4.8%	11.7%	29.4%	53.3%
Yuma County	2,953	34.1%	11.1%	7.0%	0.0%	15.9%	7.3%	9.9%	14.6%	58.8%
Arkansas										
Benton County	2,987	26.6%	5.8%	2.9%	5.4%	22.1%	1.9%	23.8%	11.4%	49.3%
Craighead County	3,182	0.0%	0.4%	0.0%	0.5%	30.5%	11.1%	8.7%	48.6%	43.6%
Faulkner County	3,275	17.0%	13.8%	1.6%	0.3%	2.3%	0.0%	15.6%	49.3%	30.8%
Garland County	1,088	0.0%	12.0%	6.4%	0.0%	0.0%	0.0%	29.3%	52.2%	35.1%
Pulaski County	5,977	10.1%	13.0%	0.0%	0.0%	14.7%	0.0%	43.0%	19.2%	57.7%
Saline County	637	6.6%	26.4%	0.0%	8.6%	12.9%	3.3%	21.8%	20.4%	56.7%
Sebastian County	1,316	28.6%	0.0%	14.6%	0.0%	17.4%	0.0%	20.5%	18.8%	65.9%
Washington County	9,365	6.3%	3.3%	4.3%	3.0%	8.1%	4.2%	23.0%	47.8%	14.3%
California										
Alameda County	19,598	10.8%	1.4%	3.3%	6.1%	6.8%	3.6%	31.6%	36.4%	53.6%
Butte County	8,087	1.6%	10.9%	0.0%	5.5%	9.4%	0.0%	23.7%	48.8%	32.8%
Contra Costa County	9,237	4.9%	5.3%	1.4%	8.5%	16.2%	11.5%	18.3%	33.9%	62.0%
El Dorado County	1,111	17.9%	5.5%	0.0%	0.0%	23.0%	0.0%	22.5%	31.1%	74.3%
Fresno County	13,473	13.2%	5.8%	13.4%	5.4%	25.1%	5.4%	13.6%	18.1%	62.1%
Humboldt County	3,815	4.4%	1.4%	0.0%	0.0%	0.7%	15.0%	26.3%	52.1%	21.6%
Imperial County	1,125	16.9%	5.1%	0.0%	2.9%	31.6%	0.0%	23.6%	19.8%	68.8%
Kern County	12,402	13.0%	8.6%	7.3%	7.2%	19.4%	3.3%	10.4%	30.8%	59.5%
Kings County	1,235	21.7%	26.0%	0.0%	3.2%	23.1%	0.0%	0.6%	25.4%	48.4%
Los Angeles County	100,578	5.7%	5.0%	4.0%	9.7%	11.7%	7.7%	24.6%	31.5%	61.9%
Madera County	1,287	25.7%	0.0%	13.4%	0.0%	38.9%	0.0%	14.2%	7.8%	55.9%
Marin County	959	14.0%	29.2%	0.0%	0.0%	0.0%	0.0%	19.9%	36.9%	67.2%
Merced County	3,127	11.2%	12.1%	0.0%	18.3%	19.9%	6.8%	2.3%	29.4%	53.1%
Monterey County	5,039	17.5%	6.6%	2.9%	10.0%	10.7%	11.1%	15.5%	25.7%	59.2%
Napa County	1,119	11.4%	5.9%	0.0%	19.6%	18.4%	5.1%	12.1%	27.5%	55.3%
Nevada County	246	44.7%	0.0%	0.0%	4.9%	0.0%	0.0%	33.3%	17.1%	83.1%
Orange County	26,016	8.8%	6.1%	2.1%	10.6%	6.3%	8.4%	17.4%	40.2%	64.9%
Placer County	3,367	11.6%	15.7%	0.0%	7.6%	4.3%	2.2%	17.7%	40.9%	63.6%
Riverside County	18,944	14.9%	8.9%	8.2%	8.3%	17.8%	6.7%	10.4%	24.9%	65.6%
Sacramento County	20,424	11.5%	4.4%	2.9%	5.5%	15.4%	4.0%	21.7%	34.6%	53.8%
San Bernardino County	18,560	15.2%	10.1%	8.8%	11.0%	19.8%	5.8%	14.6%	14.9%	65.9%
San Diego County	42,316	10.6%	17.2%	1.6%	6.0%	6.2%	6.2%	18.5%	33.7%	50.7%
San Francisco County	10,246	2.1%	0.8%	1.1%	6.1%	1.3%	7.9%	23.1%	57.5%	27.8%
San Joaquin County	9,064	17.6%	11.7%	6.5%	6.5%	19.2%	5.0%	18.7%	14.8%	58.9%
San Luis Obispo County	7,812	3.4%	2.8%	6.4%	1.2%	11.0%	4.7%	17.4%	53.2%	23.2%
San Mateo County	4,382	18.9%	10.7%	0.0%	0.0%	1.8%	6.1%	28.3%	34.2%	66.3%
Santa Barbara County	10,140	5.7%	2.8%	3.7%	12.5%	7.8%	2.2%	9.0%	56.2%	29.2%
Santa Clara County	16,150	2.1%	5.2%	3.8%	12.6%	4.8%	6.6%	25.9%	38.9%	57.1%
Santa Cruz County	5,845	0.0%	0.0%	2.6%	10.4%	0.8%	1.6%	43.8%	40.7%	34.2%
Shasta County	2,514	5.6%	3.7%	3.5%	0.0%	13.2%	0.0%	31.2%	42.8%	33.8%
Solano County	3,615	8.1%	11.4%	2.6%	8.0%	26.4%	3.7%	20.5%	19.3%	64.4%
Sonoma County	5,775	9.6%	4.4%	0.0%	9.5%	19.4%	0.0%	15.9%	41.2%	51.0%
Stanislaus County	6,151	13.6%	2.3%	5.3%	6.1%	21.1%	6.1%	23.9%	21.7%	64.9%
Sutter County	2,197	0.0%	3.8%	13.9%	19.6%	31.8%	3.3%	22.7%	4.9%	51.5%
Tulare County	6,321	16.9%	3.0%	7.6%	11.3%	31.7%	8.2%	10.4%	10.8%	57.0%
Ventura County	4,476	14.4%	16.6%	3.7%	4.1%	6.1%	2.8%	19.3%	33.2%	64.5%
Yolo County	8,429	4.0%	6.4%	0.0%	0.7%	5.6%	4.0%	32.1%	47.2%	29.0%
Colorado										
Adams County	6,532	15.5%	7.2%	3.7%	2.9%	20.1%	2.7%	14.0%	33.8%	56.3%

Table D-2: Counties—Household Relationship—*Continued*

		25 to 31									
		Married Couple Households		Male, No Spouse Present		Female, No Spouse Present		Non-Family Householders			
	Total Householders	With Children	No Children	With Children	No Children	With Children	No Children	Living Alone	Not Alone	Living With Parents
Alabama										
Baldwin County	4,115	19.6%	16.6%	4.9%	3.3%	28.7%	5.2%	8.2%	13.5%	15.2%
Calhoun County	4,127	28.2%	3.3%	2.6%	2.7%	27.0%	0.0%	33.6%	2.6%	37.3%
Etowah County	3,277	43.7%	13.7%	0.0%	3.0%	15.8%	1.0%	18.8%	3.9%	25.3%
Houston County	4,674	44.7%	7.7%	0.0%	0.0%	20.4%	0.0%	24.5%	2.7%	18.7%
Jefferson County	26,723	25.7%	9.8%	2.1%	2.9%	25.7%	1.0%	25.0%	7.9%	20.8%
Lauderdale County	2,685	19.3%	6.2%	12.1%	5.8%	11.1%	0.0%	42.8%	2.7%	28.1%
Lee County	7,602	25.1%	14.3%	3.8%	2.2%	10.2%	2.1%	31.2%	11.2%	12.0%
Madison County	14,311	24.8%	12.0%	6.8%	4.1%	8.9%	3.3%	35.2%	4.8%	12.0%
Marshall County	2,912	27.9%	15.9%	1.1%	0.0%	44.7%	0.0%	5.9%	4.5%	12.3%
Mobile County	15,372	25.7%	9.8%	0.4%	0.0%	30.9%	0.8%	21.5%	10.9%	27.1%
Montgomery County	12,116	21.5%	2.5%	0.0%	3.0%	32.9%	0.0%	32.1%	8.1%	19.8%
Morgan County	3,553	26.9%	24.0%	0.0%	9.1%	7.8%	3.8%	28.5%	0.0%	30.6%
Shelby County	8,636	34.4%	22.6%	4.3%	0.0%	7.3%	0.3%	21.7%	9.3%	21.7%
Tuscaloosa County	8,493	30.1%	18.8%	5.9%	4.1%	15.7%	0.0%	23.9%	1.5%	21.9%
Alaska										
Fairbanks North Star Borough	5,229	19.7%	23.4%	0.0%	2.7%	6.0%	0.0%	37.7%	10.5%	24.0%
Matanuska-Susitna Borough	2,015	33.1%	8.2%	0.0%	19.3%	8.2%	0.0%	15.0%	16.3%	22.3%
Arizona										
Cochise County	5,562	33.7%	12.9%	1.2%	0.0%	19.4%	0.0%	16.3%	16.5%	9.5%
Coconino County	6,204	30.3%	15.1%	7.6%	0.0%	2.7%	0.0%	23.3%	21.0%	23.4%
Maricopa County	162,374	23.3%	12.1%	5.4%	2.4%	13.8%	2.0%	26.0%	15.0%	19.3%
Mohave County	5,255	17.5%	16.9%	5.8%	10.0%	10.0%	7.5%	18.8%	13.6%	16.8%
Navajo County	1,824	28.1%	2.6%	4.4%	0.5%	34.7%	7.6%	3.6%	18.4%	53.1%
Pima County	39,932	16.6%	11.3%	4.5%	4.9%	16.6%	2.0%	30.2%	13.9%	15.9%
Pinal County	10,564	38.3%	13.2%	10.2%	0.5%	19.1%	5.0%	8.3%	5.6%	16.3%
Yavapai County	5,237	23.5%	9.2%	9.4%	0.2%	21.9%	2.0%	19.6%	14.3%	24.4%
Yuma County	7,641	46.7%	9.0%	4.4%	1.1%	22.4%	0.0%	15.2%	1.1%	18.4%
Arkansas										
Benton County	10,143	42.7%	15.1%	3.3%	0.0%	15.1%	1.0%	11.6%	11.2%	17.1%
Craighead County	4,948	28.1%	11.2%	15.1%	6.4%	16.7%	0.0%	17.0%	5.5%	13.1%
Faulkner County	7,424	46.1%	9.6%	0.0%	0.2%	11.8%	3.1%	10.6%	18.6%	11.6%
Garland County	2,740	39.9%	10.8%	14.7%	0.0%	17.3%	0.0%	16.5%	0.9%	17.8%
Pulaski County	16,383	15.1%	10.2%	0.5%	4.9%	15.9%	2.3%	30.5%	20.7%	22.1%
Saline County	2,894	67.6%	6.0%	3.5%	0.0%	12.6%	0.0%	10.2%	0.0%	18.3%
Sebastian County	6,885	39.5%	12.4%	7.5%	3.2%	12.3%	1.2%	19.0%	4.8%	12.6%
Washington County	12,401	24.5%	17.2%	7.8%	0.0%	9.7%	0.0%	26.5%	14.2%	5.2%
California										
Alameda County	56,041	19.9%	16.4%	2.9%	3.1%	8.7%	2.7%	26.0%	20.3%	24.9%
Butte County	7,933	21.5%	16.9%	6.1%	0.8%	14.5%	2.2%	19.7%	18.3%	20.4%
Contra Costa County	29,361	28.7%	13.7%	4.4%	3.7%	15.7%	4.0%	14.7%	15.0%	29.4%
El Dorado County	2,978	47.6%	19.9%	0.0%	0.0%	6.1%	0.0%	12.8%	13.6%	24.8%
Fresno County	36,372	30.6%	11.8%	7.3%	3.0%	23.2%	1.3%	14.7%	8.0%	25.6%
Humboldt County	6,042	14.2%	11.8%	3.7%	1.0%	3.5%	0.0%	33.5%	32.3%	16.5%
Imperial County	5,587	48.7%	8.6%	3.8%	0.0%	9.5%	3.4%	14.4%	11.6%	24.6%
Kern County	32,167	37.7%	6.9%	3.6%	4.3%	24.8%	1.5%	12.5%	8.8%	20.5%
Kings County	6,465	29.2%	6.1%	17.0%	4.3%	35.0%	0.5%	5.2%	2.7%	20.5%
Los Angeles County	349,619	17.8%	11.3%	3.6%	6.1%	12.1%	3.9%	26.9%	18.3%	31.4%
Madera County	5,835	27.4%	6.2%	2.6%	8.6%	29.6%	3.6%	13.8%	8.2%	19.8%
Marin County	4,793	26.5%	12.0%	7.5%	3.5%	8.1%	0.0%	20.3%	22.1%	27.2%
Merced County	9,047	36.1%	9.2%	6.9%	0.9%	19.4%	6.1%	14.9%	6.6%	34.8%
Monterey County	12,352	32.1%	9.2%	1.4%	4.4%	15.2%	5.1%	20.4%	12.3%	31.1%
Napa County	2,563	49.9%	5.5%	3.7%	3.0%	10.3%	0.0%	16.9%	10.7%	35.0%
Nevada County	2,366	12.3%	4.9%	3.2%	0.0%	11.6%	0.0%	34.1%	33.9%	18.3%
Orange County	90,790	25.0%	16.2%	3.2%	4.7%	10.1%	2.1%	16.8%	21.9%	31.0%
Placer County	10,150	27.3%	15.8%	1.2%	4.1%	13.7%	0.8%	16.0%	21.1%	31.3%
Riverside County	62,706	34.8%	10.9%	4.9%	6.0%	14.9%	1.9%	14.4%	12.2%	35.2%
Sacramento County	59,758	23.8%	17.1%	3.2%	2.1%	15.4%	2.1%	20.6%	15.8%	20.1%
San Bernardino County	66,257	30.6%	9.1%	6.9%	3.6%	18.1%	2.8%	18.3%	10.7%	33.4%
San Diego County	136,269	24.5%	16.6%	3.4%	2.3%	9.6%	1.8%	19.6%	22.2%	19.4%
San Francisco County	58,136	3.4%	13.2%	0.0%	3.0%	3.7%	1.2%	32.4%	43.2%	10.8%
San Joaquin County	19,730	33.5%	8.2%	9.7%	2.8%	16.7%	2.1%	12.4%	14.6%	28.5%
San Luis Obispo County	8,092	21.9%	10.5%	0.8%	1.3%	22.9%	1.1%	22.4%	19.0%	23.1%
San Mateo County	19,343	19.5%	20.0%	1.9%	4.5%	5.7%	3.6%	25.2%	19.6%	29.1%
Santa Barbara County	13,355	25.1%	13.5%	10.6%	4.9%	12.0%	1.7%	17.6%	14.5%	18.3%
Santa Clara County	64,004	18.1%	18.9%	3.3%	3.6%	8.7%	2.2%	24.8%	20.2%	24.2%
Santa Cruz County	7,036	23.2%	19.5%	1.7%	1.1%	3.9%	0.0%	19.1%	31.5%	34.4%
Shasta County	6,019	41.0%	17.2%	1.8%	0.0%	15.1%	1.8%	4.1%	19.0%	16.2%
Solano County	15,558	31.9%	10.8%	6.4%	2.6%	17.2%	0.7%	16.0%	14.3%	29.1%
Sonoma County	14,688	22.5%	14.7%	2.3%	4.7%	10.0%	4.0%	16.7%	25.2%	28.1%
Stanislaus County	16,771	31.9%	6.5%	11.4%	4.5%	20.3%	1.0%	14.6%	9.8%	25.0%
Sutter County	2,534	28.1%	2.5%	7.7%	9.1%	19.5%	0.0%	17.9%	15.2%	21.1%
Tulare County	16,214	44.3%	7.1%	4.7%	4.7%	21.7%	2.0%	10.3%	5.3%	26.7%
Ventura County	20,566	36.6%	12.0%	2.4%	3.3%	18.1%	1.5%	8.1%	18.0%	30.2%
Yolo County	7,142	23.8%	16.4%	5.6%	1.6%	5.6%	0.0%	20.9%	26.1%	15.4%
Colorado										
Adams County	22,351	34.7%	11.9%	6.2%	2.9%	11.2%	1.0%	20.9%	11.1%	18.5%

Table D-2: Counties—Household Relationship—*Continued*

		18 to 24								
		Married Couple Households		Male, No Spouse Present		Female, No Spouse Present		Non-Family Householders		
	Total Householders	With Children	No Children	With Children	No Children	With Children	No Children	Living Alone	Not Alone	Living With Parents
Colorado—Cont.										
Arapahoe County	10,457	7.1%	4.6%	5.9%	0.5%	15.8%	7.6%	36.1%	22.3%	57.1%
Boulder County	11,408	0.6%	2.5%	0.0%	0.0%	2.3%	1.9%	37.3%	55.5%	29.9%
Denver County	16,302	4.1%	6.1%	2.8%	4.5%	8.8%	3.4%	32.7%	37.5%	30.7%
Douglas County	2,430	2.7%	18.5%	0.0%	24.4%	0.0%	0.0%	31.1%	23.3%	72.4%
El Paso County	11,880	17.0%	20.5%	0.0%	2.5%	9.3%	1.1%	16.7%	32.9%	41.1%
Jefferson County	10,278	5.5%	7.3%	0.0%	1.2%	12.9%	2.7%	32.1%	38.3%	49.6%
Larimer County	10,370	3.6%	6.4%	0.0%	2.8%	1.0%	4.0%	17.2%	65.0%	27.1%
Mesa County	2,290	8.1%	2.3%	0.0%	6.9%	10.8%	4.6%	26.4%	40.9%	35.1%
Pueblo County	3,933	19.2%	5.4%	10.5%	0.0%	18.8%	2.7%	21.8%	21.6%	49.4%
Weld County	5,035	5.1%	20.0%	0.0%	5.3%	10.4%	4.2%	28.7%	26.2%	46.0%
Connecticut										
Fairfield County	4,217	0.0%	1.3%	3.7%	7.2%	21.9%	9.7%	14.2%	42.1%	62.2%
Hartford County	7,854	1.0%	4.3%	6.0%	7.5%	18.1%	3.0%	37.6%	22.4%	62.3%
Litchfield County	918	47.9%	20.4%	0.0%	0.0%	13.4%	0.0%	9.3%	9.0%	76.5%
Middlesex County	1,426	2.2%	0.0%	2.9%	3.2%	20.4%	0.0%	56.9%	14.4%	61.2%
New Haven County	5,568	2.4%	4.5%	0.0%	9.5%	16.4%	13.6%	25.4%	28.2%	58.5%
New London County	3,044	10.5%	11.7%	0.0%	9.3%	17.2%	0.0%	29.6%	21.7%	44.5%
Tolland County	1,862	0.0%	0.0%	0.0%	4.1%	9.7%	3.9%	42.8%	39.5%	34.4%
Windham County	1,618	2.8%	12.6%	0.0%	0.0%	15.9%	0.0%	39.4%	29.2%	42.2%
Delaware										
Kent County	2,389	2.1%	17.9%	2.0%	11.1%	21.4%	5.0%	34.6%	5.9%	51.4%
New Castle County	7,064	3.5%	2.1%	1.1%	3.0%	13.2%	4.5%	40.4%	32.2%	53.3%
Sussex County	784	0.0%	27.2%	0.0%	0.0%	12.2%	0.0%	33.0%	27.6%	62.0%
Florida										
Alachua County	17,347	1.1%	3.8%	1.9%	2.7%	5.8%	1.0%	29.2%	54.5%	11.5%
Bay County	2,936	12.7%	20.9%	2.4%	0.0%	7.7%	0.0%	21.9%	34.3%	46.6%
Brevard County	5,074	2.9%	4.8%	4.7%	2.4%	25.6%	5.2%	27.4%	27.0%	68.1%
Broward County	13,189	10.0%	6.1%	2.4%	7.1%	19.9%	11.1%	25.2%	18.2%	67.6%
Charlotte County	1,032	26.3%	2.1%	10.0%	8.9%	10.9%	0.0%	20.8%	20.9%	60.6%
Citrus County	892	19.5%	0.0%	0.0%	0.0%	18.6%	0.0%	6.1%	55.8%	50.3%
Clay County	1,002	18.2%	31.6%	0.0%	0.0%	8.6%	0.0%	19.6%	22.1%	65.6%
Collier County	1,940	2.6%	18.9%	23.7%	4.0%	14.4%	6.9%	17.5%	12.1%	70.9%
Duval County	15,208	13.4%	8.8%	2.8%	6.4%	15.3%	5.1%	26.0%	22.1%	47.1%
Escambia County	4,153	5.9%	20.2%	5.1%	7.0%	10.9%	0.0%	19.8%	31.1%	36.4%
Flagler County	457	0.0%	11.4%	54.9%	15.8%	0.0%	0.0%	17.9%	0.0%	78.6%
Hernando County	425	0.0%	32.5%	0.0%	0.0%	24.5%	0.0%	0.0%	43.1%	74.8%
Highlands County	1,166	30.2%	0.0%	1.1%	12.3%	32.8%	0.0%	14.3%	9.2%	64.7%
Hillsborough County	23,489	2.6%	8.6%	1.2%	3.9%	10.5%	5.8%	41.2%	26.2%	49.8%
Indian River County	1,136	23.0%	0.0%	0.0%	8.0%	5.9%	0.0%	10.5%	52.6%	63.5%
Lake County	2,246	16.8%	10.0%	0.0%	0.0%	10.4%	0.0%	38.0%	24.8%	68.8%
Lee County	5,252	7.9%	6.4%	11.8%	3.0%	12.7%	4.4%	35.5%	18.3%	60.2%
Leon County	18,928	1.4%	4.2%	0.0%	8.2%	1.4%	5.3%	31.2%	48.3%	20.2%
Manatee County	2,447	13.7%	9.4%	0.0%	10.3%	14.3%	1.8%	28.1%	22.4%	62.3%
Marion County	3,020	2.2%	9.4%	0.0%	7.2%	19.3%	4.0%	13.4%	44.4%	52.5%
Martin County	982	0.0%	0.0%	0.0%	0.0%	34.8%	0.0%	0.0%	65.2%	69.1%
Miami-Dade County	18,645	5.6%	7.5%	3.7%	14.0%	12.0%	8.9%	26.4%	21.9%	67.7%
Okaloosa County	2,842	19.8%	31.4%	0.0%	0.0%	6.2%	3.6%	31.2%	8.0%	34.2%
Orange County	23,306	5.0%	3.0%	2.9%	3.0%	10.9%	4.9%	30.9%	39.3%	45.9%
Osceola County	2,878	2.5%	8.0%	4.1%	1.9%	38.0%	1.3%	13.3%	30.9%	62.0%
Palm Beach County	9,638	2.9%	7.1%	2.1%	8.2%	12.7%	7.2%	22.0%	37.7%	64.7%
Pasco County	3,754	3.9%	4.8%	7.6%	7.7%	23.3%	6.5%	14.0%	32.2%	62.5%
Pinellas County	8,938	2.4%	7.7%	4.2%	4.3%	22.3%	2.3%	32.7%	24.1%	60.2%
Polk County	5,039	9.9%	12.3%	7.0%	4.4%	19.2%	2.9%	17.4%	26.8%	58.8%
Santa Rosa County	2,463	0.0%	25.4%	0.0%	8.4%	26.2%	0.0%	7.8%	32.2%	51.0%
Sarasota County	1,999	3.9%	9.4%	0.0%	0.0%	34.4%	0.0%	33.1%	19.4%	63.6%
Seminole County	3,132	6.6%	8.7%	0.0%	2.6%	5.1%	1.1%	23.2%	52.7%	66.1%
St. Johns County	1,191	4.5%	7.0%	0.0%	21.4%	8.7%	15.7%	25.2%	17.5%	69.1%
St. Lucie County	1,883	4.8%	5.0%	0.0%	0.0%	38.8%	5.3%	27.3%	18.9%	67.6%
Sumter County	612	38.2%	0.0%	0.0%	0.0%	32.2%	0.0%	0.0%	29.6%	67.7%
Volusia County	8,133	3.5%	6.1%	1.3%	9.2%	13.5%	2.9%	29.1%	34.4%	43.9%
Georgia										
Bartow County	1,077	0.0%	0.0%	0.0%	5.5%	0.0%	0.0%	43.1%	51.4%	55.1%
Bibb County	2,472	3.7%	7.6%	3.6%	0.0%	65.1%	0.0%	8.3%	11.8%	39.9%
Carroll County	3,992	15.3%	13.5%	0.0%	0.0%	0.0%	0.0%	45.8%	25.4%	30.0%
Chatham County	5,170	2.3%	17.1%	1.8%	6.4%	16.0%	4.9%	24.6%	26.9%	39.9%
Cherokee County	1,249	5.5%	11.2%	3.3%	0.0%	16.4%	0.0%	7.8%	55.8%	56.6%
Clarke County	9,375	0.7%	3.5%	0.0%	4.8%	5.0%	0.0%	39.6%	46.3%	9.1%
Clayton County	4,037	9.5%	7.8%	5.4%	4.0%	26.7%	1.6%	30.3%	14.8%	55.9%
Cobb County	10,930	1.9%	6.3%	0.0%	5.7%	7.5%	4.9%	28.3%	45.4%	51.1%
Columbia County	343	0.0%	26.5%	0.0%	27.4%	34.7%	0.0%	11.4%	0.0%	78.1%
Coweta County	2,024	25.7%	15.0%	0.0%	6.9%	34.5%	0.0%	10.2%	7.6%	58.3%
DeKalb County	11,403	6.8%	4.7%	3.9%	3.7%	15.2%	6.3%	43.7%	15.6%	48.9%
Dougherty County	1,014	9.4%	5.6%	8.2%	4.7%	21.9%	19.2%	20.6%	10.4%	51.9%
Douglas County	785	14.6%	10.6%	0.0%	0.0%	17.5%	0.0%	57.3%	0.0%	79.0%
Fayette County	511	0.0%	55.2%	0.0%	0.0%	0.0%	44.8%	0.0%	0.0%	69.8%
Floyd County	1,748	10.8%	0.0%	4.1%	0.0%	22.0%	0.0%	43.1%	20.0%	50.0%
Forsyth County	705	34.5%	22.8%	0.0%	0.0%	0.0%	0.0%	22.3%	20.4%	82.3%

Table D-2: Counties—Household Relationship—Continued

| | | 25 to 31 | | | | | | | | |
| | | Married Couple Households | | Male, No Spouse Present | | Female, No Spouse Present | | Non-Family Householders | | |
	Total Householders	With Children	No Children	With Children	No Children	With Children	No Children	Living Alone	Not Alone	Living With Parents
Colorado—Cont.										
Arapahoe County	24,698	29.6%	12.4%	2.2%	1.9%	15.2%	2.0%	23.4%	13.3%	21.2%
Boulder County	11,036	21.4%	9.5%	2.7%	0.8%	6.0%	1.0%	25.8%	32.8%	13.9%
Denver County	48,787	13.3%	8.7%	1.6%	4.2%	7.6%	0.9%	37.4%	26.4%	10.6%
Douglas County	7,279	43.0%	30.5%	0.0%	2.9%	0.0%	0.0%	13.8%	9.8%	25.4%
El Paso County	32,259	32.4%	18.9%	3.2%	0.7%	13.0%	2.2%	16.2%	13.3%	11.8%
Jefferson County	18,010	20.8%	15.8%	3.4%	2.5%	8.0%	0.9%	28.8%	19.7%	20.9%
Larimer County	14,733	21.2%	14.7%	4.1%	0.0%	7.3%	0.9%	27.9%	23.9%	9.7%
Mesa County	7,776	43.0%	2.1%	1.3%	0.0%	29.4%	0.0%	9.1%	15.1%	11.8%
Pueblo County	5,885	48.5%	0.0%	5.4%	6.0%	20.9%	0.0%	15.7%	3.6%	19.6%
Weld County	11,866	32.9%	14.1%	2.3%	4.6%	14.5%	1.1%	21.1%	9.5%	18.4%
Connecticut										
Fairfield County	26,084	17.9%	15.1%	1.7%	2.7%	16.0%	2.7%	20.4%	23.3%	26.3%
Hartford County	32,916	18.2%	13.9%	2.9%	1.2%	18.5%	1.5%	25.7%	18.1%	26.0%
Litchfield County	5,147	22.8%	11.9%	0.0%	0.0%	13.3%	0.8%	22.9%	28.3%	26.7%
Middlesex County	5,172	19.7%	16.5%	1.6%	7.7%	1.3%	1.3%	29.1%	22.8%	26.2%
New Haven County	29,709	15.8%	13.2%	3.4%	2.2%	20.2%	0.7%	25.8%	18.7%	28.7%
New London County	11,817	21.8%	9.3%	4.0%	3.4%	28.5%	0.7%	20.2%	12.1%	21.0%
Tolland County	3,916	5.6%	13.5%	5.9%	10.9%	5.3%	0.0%	29.6%	29.3%	18.7%
Windham County	4,059	19.5%	5.1%	10.5%	1.9%	38.3%	0.0%	15.7%	8.9%	27.3%
Delaware										
Kent County	5,309	34.5%	16.4%	2.7%	2.1%	11.8%	0.0%	14.2%	18.3%	25.2%
New Castle County	20,363	18.2%	16.3%	2.7%	0.1%	18.6%	1.5%	23.2%	19.4%	26.6%
Sussex County	5,250	34.7%	15.5%	4.0%	3.9%	17.0%	3.6%	6.1%	15.1%	22.9%
Florida										
Alachua County	12,328	14.0%	11.9%	1.5%	3.5%	7.9%	0.7%	33.8%	26.8%	8.5%
Bay County	5,240	37.7%	12.3%	3.6%	1.7%	15.9%	1.9%	21.9%	5.0%	27.1%
Brevard County	14,677	25.3%	7.3%	4.9%	3.6%	20.5%	0.0%	23.8%	14.6%	29.8%
Broward County	55,183	21.6%	11.3%	3.2%	4.0%	18.4%	4.3%	24.4%	12.9%	32.3%
Charlotte County	2,228	24.3%	9.8%	9.2%	8.3%	11.8%	0.0%	14.5%	22.0%	28.4%
Citrus County	2,411	34.8%	10.5%	19.1%	0.0%	13.7%	0.0%	7.1%	14.8%	25.2%
Clay County	5,309	43.5%	10.3%	8.3%	0.0%	17.5%	1.0%	14.8%	4.6%	27.9%
Collier County	6,775	42.1%	8.3%	0.1%	2.1%	12.2%	0.0%	26.6%	8.5%	35.2%
Duval County	41,887	17.2%	12.7%	1.9%	1.7%	18.1%	2.4%	31.5%	14.6%	23.2%
Escambia County	13,848	16.9%	17.7%	0.6%	2.1%	9.5%	1.3%	30.9%	21.0%	17.8%
Flagler County	1,136	39.0%	18.8%	0.0%	7.8%	0.0%	0.0%	34.3%	0.0%	53.8%
Hernando County	3,955	27.8%	1.0%	15.5%	5.0%	32.1%	0.0%	14.7%	4.0%	39.1%
Highlands County	1,642	62.7%	0.0%	14.6%	2.1%	5.5%	0.0%	3.3%	11.7%	33.0%
Hillsborough County	54,963	22.3%	12.0%	2.4%	3.2%	16.1%	1.8%	26.5%	15.7%	23.0%
Indian River County	3,238	25.4%	6.9%	8.6%	2.3%	16.6%	0.0%	19.2%	21.0%	22.4%
Lake County	8,504	28.2%	24.6%	4.0%	7.4%	11.7%	0.0%	20.9%	3.2%	21.2%
Lee County	16,043	28.6%	11.5%	7.9%	4.1%	18.5%	2.7%	16.0%	10.8%	30.3%
Leon County	14,670	13.1%	10.9%	2.8%	0.5%	15.3%	1.9%	32.2%	23.3%	9.6%
Manatee County	8,311	24.2%	14.6%	2.9%	2.2%	18.4%	0.8%	11.7%	25.1%	22.2%
Marion County	7,765	25.9%	1.4%	0.8%	0.0%	30.2%	4.2%	32.9%	4.8%	33.0%
Martin County	3,490	25.5%	18.0%	10.1%	0.0%	11.1%	0.0%	20.9%	14.4%	35.1%
Miami-Dade County	74,151	19.1%	9.9%	3.7%	5.5%	18.7%	5.3%	26.0%	11.7%	39.7%
Okaloosa County	10,810	33.4%	12.7%	0.0%	3.6%	11.6%	4.2%	22.5%	11.9%	14.1%
Orange County	51,781	16.6%	15.6%	4.8%	3.0%	11.3%	1.9%	29.1%	17.7%	24.2%
Osceola County	7,331	34.4%	14.9%	4.9%	4.2%	27.1%	0.0%	10.8%	3.8%	40.1%
Palm Beach County	33,076	18.4%	11.3%	6.2%	4.3%	20.0%	4.3%	18.2%	17.3%	27.1%
Pasco County	9,754	28.1%	11.2%	8.2%	4.2%	14.9%	1.3%	19.9%	12.2%	30.3%
Pinellas County	28,787	17.9%	12.9%	3.5%	2.3%	15.0%	2.4%	31.7%	14.4%	25.2%
Polk County	18,203	24.6%	9.9%	7.3%	3.0%	21.6%	1.5%	17.8%	14.3%	28.6%
Santa Rosa County	6,132	31.5%	8.2%	7.8%	2.9%	21.6%	1.2%	13.7%	13.1%	15.8%
Sarasota County	6,874	30.1%	9.5%	3.4%	2.1%	7.8%	1.6%	24.7%	20.9%	28.0%
Seminole County	15,268	15.8%	12.3%	4.6%	4.0%	10.2%	2.0%	35.5%	15.6%	31.6%
St. Johns County	4,800	27.9%	19.0%	5.5%	0.0%	8.6%	0.0%	19.3%	19.8%	29.8%
St. Lucie County	6,681	30.5%	5.8%	0.0%	0.0%	29.3%	7.0%	21.8%	5.7%	35.6%
Sumter County	1,373	4.4%	18.1%	0.0%	7.1%	0.0%	0.0%	70.5%	0.0%	29.0%
Volusia County	15,364	29.9%	10.1%	5.0%	3.4%	21.3%	0.0%	13.4%	16.9%	26.5%
Georgia										
Bartow County	2,975	24.5%	5.9%	0.0%	1.6%	2.5%	0.0%	31.9%	33.5%	15.3%
Bibb County	5,328	19.0%	11.6%	1.4%	6.3%	39.2%	2.6%	16.9%	2.9%	23.4%
Carroll County	3,343	44.2%	1.9%	7.6%	0.0%	18.0%	5.3%	19.1%	3.9%	26.7%
Chatham County	13,385	20.5%	13.7%	2.5%	3.3%	15.4%	1.9%	32.6%	10.2%	19.8%
Cherokee County	6,867	37.2%	23.3%	2.2%	5.3%	6.8%	0.0%	17.1%	8.1%	26.4%
Clarke County	6,974	10.7%	14.1%	1.0%	0.0%	15.6%	0.0%	37.4%	21.2%	8.4%
Clayton County	10,841	22.3%	0.9%	5.4%	9.8%	30.1%	1.4%	23.7%	6.3%	26.4%
Cobb County	31,269	12.8%	16.7%	4.7%	4.1%	15.6%	3.2%	32.4%	10.5%	15.7%
Columbia County	2,668	54.7%	26.1%	2.8%	0.0%	2.1%	0.0%	8.0%	6.2%	41.8%
Coweta County	4,114	33.4%	9.4%	12.5%	0.0%	27.1%	0.0%	11.4%	6.1%	12.4%
DeKalb County	34,160	13.4%	9.6%	3.8%	1.4%	11.6%	4.1%	35.6%	20.5%	16.1%
Dougherty County	4,292	9.3%	11.4%	11.9%	2.2%	46.1%	3.2%	15.0%	0.8%	22.5%
Douglas County	3,652	11.7%	18.8%	0.0%	4.7%	18.0%	11.6%	24.9%	10.3%	32.8%
Fayette County	1,411	50.0%	38.1%	8.4%	0.0%	0.0%	0.0%	0.0%	3.6%	40.4%
Floyd County	2,195	33.9%	5.6%	0.0%	12.9%	17.0%	12.3%	7.8%	10.5%	21.7%
Forsyth County	3,574	36.5%	19.0%	0.0%	0.0%	15.3%	1.4%	14.3%	13.4%	33.8%

Table D-2: Counties—Household Relationship—*Continued*

		18 to 24								
		Married Couple Households		Male, No Spouse Present		Female, No Spouse Present		Non-Family Householders		
	Total Householders	With Children	No Children	With Children	No Children	With Children	No Children	Living Alone	Not Alone	Living With Parents
Georgia—Cont.										
Fulton County	16,052	1.0%	3.2%	1.9%	2.5%	12.5%	4.1%	44.8%	30.1%	39.7%
Gwinnett County	6,238	12.2%	16.0%	1.1%	1.3%	14.6%	8.9%	20.3%	25.5%	74.7%
Hall County	2,303	6.4%	16.0%	1.8%	7.6%	0.0%	10.9%	33.3%	24.1%	49.4%
Henry County	869	12.9%	9.9%	21.4%	0.0%	0.0%	0.0%	28.2%	27.6%	64.4%
Houston County	1,247	10.5%	26.8%	0.0%	0.0%	5.1%	0.0%	49.0%	8.6%	61.2%
Lowndes County	5,428	3.9%	4.9%	9.8%	5.6%	18.6%	0.0%	14.2%	43.0%	26.9%
Muscogee County	2,793	11.5%	20.1%	0.0%	0.0%	20.4%	0.0%	21.9%	26.1%	30.0%
Newton County	470	0.0%	19.1%	10.0%	58.1%	0.0%	0.0%	0.0%	12.8%	74.6%
Paulding County	435	12.6%	0.0%	0.0%	0.0%	69.4%	0.0%	0.0%	17.9%	82.9%
Richmond County	2,012	2.6%	13.9%	0.0%	5.2%	27.9%	0.0%	17.0%	33.3%	56.0%
Whitfield County	1,357	0.0%	11.9%	5.5%	24.7%	12.0%	0.0%	21.1%	24.8%	65.0%
Hawaii										
Hawaii County	1,982	0.0%	0.0%	19.1%	0.0%	1.5%	0.0%	36.5%	42.9%	59.3%
Honolulu County	12,570	19.2%	18.8%	0.4%	3.3%	3.6%	5.0%	26.1%	23.5%	46.0%
Maui County	1,057	27.5%	0.0%	0.0%	0.0%	18.5%	6.6%	30.5%	16.8%	63.9%
Idaho										
Ada County	9,293	8.7%	5.7%	4.9%	5.4%	4.3%	9.6%	14.2%	47.1%	39.1%
Bonneville County	1,091	30.5%	12.1%	0.0%	0.0%	0.0%	0.0%	0.0%	57.4%	42.7%
Canyon County	2,959	30.0%	8.7%	19.4%	0.0%	16.7%	0.0%	21.9%	3.4%	50.0%
Kootenai County	1,703	12.2%	14.5%	0.0%	0.0%	0.0%	0.0%	17.7%	55.6%	50.3%
Illinois										
Champaign County	11,859	0.9%	2.2%	0.0%	0.2%	0.7%	1.2%	48.1%	46.7%	13.4%
Cook County	60,145	5.3%	6.0%	2.1%	3.7%	13.1%	3.7%	33.6%	32.5%	59.1%
DeKalb County	4,498	0.0%	0.0%	0.0%	0.0%	17.7%	0.0%	46.7%	35.6%	33.2%
DuPage County	5,278	8.9%	4.6%	3.8%	8.1%	3.5%	3.6%	16.8%	50.5%	72.0%
Kane County	4,566	18.7%	2.0%	3.3%	24.5%	25.5%	0.0%	15.7%	10.3%	69.1%
Kankakee County	1,470	34.9%	0.0%	0.0%	0.0%	12.9%	0.0%	10.7%	41.6%	46.1%
Kendall County	303	12.9%	13.2%	0.0%	0.0%	0.0%	0.0%	73.9%	0.0%	78.9%
Lake County	6,161	9.1%	21.7%	0.0%	3.5%	9.9%	2.3%	34.8%	18.7%	65.4%
LaSalle County	1,711	5.3%	8.8%	0.0%	8.6%	46.1%	0.0%	19.3%	11.9%	58.5%
Macon County	2,131	7.4%	0.0%	0.0%	8.2%	15.6%	0.0%	11.4%	57.4%	43.6%
Madison County	5,757	11.5%	19.2%	3.2%	0.5%	13.1%	3.2%	16.8%	32.5%	44.7%
McHenry County	2,321	4.2%	7.8%	20.6%	7.5%	16.0%	0.0%	30.7%	13.1%	81.6%
McLean County	5,611	0.7%	2.4%	3.7%	1.5%	2.0%	0.0%	32.5%	57.3%	28.5%
Peoria County	4,383	0.7%	4.5%	7.2%	5.6%	15.8%	1.4%	41.7%	23.0%	42.5%
Rock Island County	1,503	18.4%	8.6%	7.8%	15.0%	46.0%	0.0%	0.0%	4.3%	47.7%
Sangamon County	3,250	0.0%	9.5%	9.2%	0.0%	4.4%	0.0%	33.7%	43.2%	51.0%
St. Clair County	4,072	1.3%	10.6%	3.3%	7.1%	42.1%	7.0%	17.6%	10.9%	63.6%
Tazewell County	2,037	24.6%	8.8%	8.5%	0.0%	15.5%	0.0%	12.3%	30.3%	58.9%
Will County	4,034	5.1%	1.5%	3.4%	9.1%	34.2%	14.1%	18.8%	13.8%	77.1%
Winnebago County	4,021	15.5%	11.9%	0.0%	0.0%	17.7%	0.0%	28.1%	26.8%	59.4%
Indiana										
Allen County	7,748	13.7%	6.1%	1.8%	2.3%	20.6%	4.5%	33.5%	17.7%	47.2%
Clark County	238	5.5%	0.0%	0.0%	0.0%	9.7%	0.0%	84.9%	0.0%	58.1%
Delaware County	5,790	1.3%	5.3%	0.0%	7.2%	2.6%	0.0%	15.5%	68.2%	22.2%
Elkhart County	4,368	30.8%	4.7%	7.2%	0.0%	14.4%	0.4%	11.2%	31.3%	52.8%
Hamilton County	3,858	6.8%	5.3%	1.4%	0.0%	0.0%	0.0%	64.4%	22.1%	69.2%
Hendricks County	1,310	1.8%	14.7%	0.0%	0.0%	30.5%	0.0%	10.2%	42.7%	63.8%
Johnson County	2,447	10.4%	0.5%	7.3%	24.4%	9.4%	19.4%	2.1%	26.5%	47.8%
Lake County	4,508	6.7%	15.1%	12.2%	1.0%	32.5%	4.7%	19.4%	8.5%	72.5%
LaPorte County	707	42.6%	0.0%	0.0%	0.0%	17.4%	0.0%	28.9%	11.2%	48.5%
Madison County	1,526	11.5%	0.0%	25.8%	0.0%	7.8%	0.0%	8.5%	46.4%	34.9%
Marion County	21,609	3.3%	6.1%	3.1%	6.8%	18.5%	4.7%	32.0%	25.5%	43.1%
Monroe County	8,953	0.0%	3.8%	0.0%	1.8%	4.7%	1.8%	41.8%	46.2%	8.1%
Porter County	2,545	11.0%	14.3%	0.0%	0.0%	14.2%	3.1%	33.6%	23.8%	53.4%
St. Joseph County	5,052	3.8%	11.3%	2.0%	4.4%	30.3%	0.7%	23.7%	23.8%	36.1%
Tippecanoe County	11,702	1.6%	7.8%	0.0%	1.3%	4.9%	1.3%	34.5%	48.6%	16.1%
Vanderburgh County	4,084	4.4%	10.4%	6.1%	0.0%	15.9%	0.0%	31.3%	31.9%	35.4%
Vigo County	2,508	26.1%	4.7%	8.9%	0.0%	14.6%	9.1%	5.1%	31.5%	21.4%
Iowa										
Black Hawk County	5,519	2.4%	3.0%	0.0%	3.5%	4.8%	0.0%	43.7%	42.6%	30.9%
Dubuque County	1,783	0.0%	17.5%	0.0%	0.0%	15.6%	0.0%	17.7%	49.1%	33.1%
Johnson County	9,123	0.0%	0.0%	0.0%	0.0%	3.9%	0.8%	28.8%	66.5%	5.2%
Linn County	3,842	0.0%	16.7%	0.0%	10.5%	23.7%	2.3%	22.5%	24.3%	41.7%
Polk County	10,417	0.0%	9.1%	1.7%	2.2%	14.0%	0.0%	21.6%	51.4%	36.8%
Pottawattamie County	1,003	6.2%	2.7%	0.0%	0.0%	26.0%	0.0%	21.3%	43.8%	60.3%
Scott County	1,792	3.2%	2.6%	0.0%	0.0%	15.8%	0.0%	51.7%	26.7%	59.7%
Story County	7,852	0.8%	1.7%	0.0%	0.0%	1.4%	1.8%	26.1%	68.3%	8.1%
Woodbury County	1,467	1.2%	0.0%	11.9%	7.0%	13.8%	2.3%	42.9%	20.9%	47.2%
Kansas										
Douglas County	5,981	0.0%	2.9%	5.0%	5.4%	0.0%	9.7%	42.3%	34.7%	13.3%
Johnson County	7,850	5.1%	10.6%	3.5%	5.6%	11.8%	0.0%	39.1%	24.2%	57.9%
Sedgwick County	10,625	14.8%	10.6%	2.8%	0.8%	19.5%	1.8%	30.8%	19.0%	53.2%
Shawnee County	3,193	4.6%	5.4%	2.5%	0.0%	20.1%	2.4%	34.3%	30.7%	42.3%
Wyandotte County	3,370	1.2%	0.0%	13.3%	8.8%	15.0%	17.8%	26.1%	17.9%	44.1%

Table D-2: Counties—Household Relationship—*Continued*

		25 to 31								
		Married Couple Households		Male, No Spouse Present		Female, No Spouse Present		Non-Family Householders		
	Total Householders	With Children	No Children	With Children	No Children	With Children	No Children	Living Alone	Not Alone	Living With Parents
Georgia—Cont.										
Fulton County	48,971	9.3%	13.7%	3.0%	2.8%	17.0%	0.6%	40.1%	13.5%	17.0%
Gwinnett County	24,344	29.1%	14.2%	7.0%	8.5%	14.9%	2.5%	16.5%	7.3%	23.7%
Hall County	5,609	31.1%	10.8%	7.4%	0.7%	16.5%	0.0%	19.0%	14.5%	19.5%
Henry County	6,390	19.3%	20.6%	3.3%	4.7%	20.7%	0.0%	23.9%	7.5%	22.2%
Houston County	8,068	16.8%	18.7%	1.1%	0.0%	21.3%	0.0%	27.6%	14.5%	13.4%
Lowndes County	6,078	23.8%	18.0%	0.6%	0.0%	22.1%	6.6%	23.0%	5.9%	14.3%
Muscogee County	8,756	34.7%	14.4%	5.1%	0.4%	19.8%	1.6%	9.8%	14.2%	16.5%
Newton County	2,048	40.0%	5.2%	0.5%	0.0%	24.9%	0.0%	19.2%	10.2%	43.2%
Paulding County	3,941	51.3%	15.0%	9.4%	2.5%	9.7%	0.0%	5.1%	7.1%	30.5%
Richmond County	9,277	10.8%	13.9%	0.9%	0.6%	25.4%	2.8%	36.5%	8.9%	33.8%
Whitfield County	2,707	61.2%	0.0%	8.6%	0.0%	21.8%	0.0%	8.4%	0.0%	32.7%
Hawaii										
Hawaii County	4,293	21.4%	18.4%	6.5%	0.0%	23.6%	0.0%	11.0%	19.2%	33.3%
Honolulu County	37,656	36.3%	12.1%	2.2%	2.5%	7.3%	2.4%	17.8%	19.3%	24.1%
Maui County	4,412	14.5%	12.8%	12.5%	0.0%	8.7%	3.9%	22.6%	25.1%	28.2%
Idaho										
Ada County	17,905	29.4%	19.9%	2.0%	1.6%	4.5%	0.7%	22.6%	19.2%	11.9%
Bonneville County	3,743	63.1%	6.5%	3.0%	0.0%	7.9%	0.0%	19.5%	0.0%	13.7%
Canyon County	7,690	51.7%	13.7%	7.6%	0.5%	5.6%	0.0%	16.6%	4.4%	12.7%
Kootenai County	5,185	56.5%	4.5%	10.7%	0.0%	15.8%	0.0%	6.6%	5.8%	9.7%
Illinois										
Champaign County	10,695	14.6%	14.1%	0.0%	0.1%	8.7%	3.1%	40.7%	18.6%	15.1%
Cook County	238,986	14.4%	13.8%	2.9%	4.0%	12.4%	2.2%	31.2%	19.0%	26.0%
DeKalb County	4,917	18.6%	1.5%	0.8%	0.0%	22.2%	0.0%	29.7%	27.2%	15.7%
DuPage County	32,667	27.6%	20.2%	2.9%	3.4%	5.9%	0.1%	28.3%	11.5%	28.6%
Kane County	15,403	28.6%	15.1%	4.9%	8.1%	12.8%	2.7%	13.8%	14.0%	25.5%
Kankakee County	2,488	10.7%	8.4%	19.1%	0.0%	38.1%	0.0%	11.8%	11.9%	21.7%
Kendall County	5,515	21.7%	0.0%	4.1%	0.0%	53.1%	0.0%	4.4%	16.7%	25.7%
Lake County	19,407	29.0%	22.6%	3.7%	1.3%	13.5%	1.6%	21.8%	6.4%	26.7%
LaSalle County	3,304	33.1%	16.1%	6.5%	4.3%	1.8%	0.0%	25.1%	13.1%	19.1%
Macon County	4,544	18.9%	5.7%	8.8%	2.1%	34.2%	0.0%	20.9%	9.4%	14.4%
Madison County	12,758	28.2%	9.2%	11.2%	0.4%	22.1%	0.9%	17.3%	10.8%	13.3%
McHenry County	9,866	25.6%	31.9%	2.9%	0.0%	11.6%	0.0%	24.0%	3.9%	27.3%
McLean County	8,907	15.7%	19.8%	1.1%	4.6%	15.0%	0.3%	32.1%	11.5%	14.8%
Peoria County	9,068	15.4%	22.1%	1.5%	0.0%	17.4%	1.3%	26.7%	15.5%	15.0%
Rock Island County	5,136	14.1%	18.1%	2.4%	0.0%	18.5%	0.0%	36.6%	10.3%	23.5%
Sangamon County	9,342	27.1%	9.9%	2.1%	0.0%	28.0%	1.6%	19.6%	11.7%	8.5%
St. Clair County	11,186	22.6%	15.1%	13.2%	0.0%	29.1%	0.8%	15.6%	3.6%	25.8%
Tazewell County	5,847	37.7%	23.7%	5.7%	0.0%	5.0%	0.0%	15.8%	12.2%	6.6%
Will County	16,683	35.5%	17.9%	4.8%	1.1%	6.7%	2.2%	19.0%	12.8%	34.6%
Winnebago County	10,561	26.3%	11.2%	5.3%	2.8%	26.6%	1.3%	18.5%	8.0%	14.1%
Indiana										
Allen County	15,997	35.2%	14.0%	2.3%	1.1%	15.5%	1.1%	18.6%	12.2%	16.8%
Clark County	3,934	50.3%	16.2%	4.0%	0.0%	9.6%	2.3%	13.7%	3.9%	20.1%
Delaware County	3,897	19.2%	11.5%	1.3%	0.0%	20.1%	0.0%	37.8%	10.1%	8.8%
Elkhart County	6,250	37.6%	14.5%	1.8%	1.3%	20.4%	0.0%	12.3%	12.1%	15.8%
Hamilton County	11,480	29.6%	24.4%	4.8%	2.8%	8.4%	0.0%	23.5%	6.4%	12.2%
Hendricks County	6,017	29.8%	26.3%	23.1%	0.0%	3.4%	0.0%	11.2%	6.1%	18.0%
Johnson County	6,404	38.9%	18.4%	0.0%	0.0%	11.7%	0.0%	17.9%	13.2%	13.0%
Lake County	16,753	25.4%	15.3%	4.4%	2.6%	23.3%	0.0%	23.6%	5.3%	29.8%
LaPorte County	4,268	22.3%	13.0%	5.1%	0.0%	32.8%	0.0%	22.5%	4.3%	12.4%
Madison County	4,344	30.2%	10.3%	6.3%	0.0%	22.3%	3.1%	13.6%	14.3%	18.7%
Marion County	50,986	16.9%	14.9%	3.0%	1.8%	20.3%	0.6%	29.4%	13.2%	16.6%
Monroe County	5,394	14.2%	7.2%	0.0%	0.0%	4.4%	0.0%	44.8%	29.4%	10.7%
Porter County	4,663	37.6%	17.0%	4.8%	0.0%	15.9%	0.0%	8.6%	16.2%	27.5%
St. Joseph County	11,626	20.1%	8.2%	2.0%	1.8%	17.9%	0.8%	35.0%	14.2%	15.4%
Tippecanoe County	9,031	24.5%	17.3%	8.1%	0.0%	6.4%	2.0%	29.3%	12.3%	5.9%
Vanderburgh County	8,452	27.8%	19.0%	0.9%	0.0%	15.8%	0.0%	26.0%	10.4%	13.2%
Vigo County	4,535	23.1%	14.2%	1.9%	5.4%	8.0%	0.0%	32.8%	14.6%	15.9%
Iowa										
Black Hawk County	6,136	33.8%	2.1%	2.5%	0.0%	22.2%	0.0%	22.4%	17.0%	12.0%
Dubuque County	3,522	12.8%	21.9%	13.1%	1.2%	13.9%	0.0%	16.1%	21.1%	10.7%
Johnson County	9,694	25.3%	20.1%	0.0%	0.0%	7.2%	1.5%	32.8%	13.1%	3.7%
Linn County	12,528	24.2%	13.2%	0.7%	1.6%	20.4%	0.0%	26.4%	13.5%	13.9%
Polk County	23,074	30.6%	9.7%	3.8%	4.2%	10.9%	0.0%	27.1%	13.8%	12.2%
Pottawattamie County	4,947	23.4%	12.5%	6.3%	0.0%	26.2%	1.5%	18.1%	12.1%	13.2%
Scott County	9,622	30.4%	9.4%	1.8%	0.0%	19.1%	0.0%	34.4%	4.9%	5.6%
Story County	5,550	24.0%	20.3%	1.8%	0.0%	8.6%	0.0%	24.5%	20.9%	5.2%
Woodbury County	5,545	30.5%	10.0%	5.7%	0.0%	27.3%	0.0%	20.7%	5.8%	6.5%
Kansas										
Douglas County	6,606	6.4%	27.7%	0.0%	1.1%	2.2%	2.5%	29.5%	30.5%	4.9%
Johnson County	25,738	25.2%	15.6%	2.2%	0.4%	9.2%	0.7%	30.9%	15.9%	14.0%
Sedgwick County	26,822	35.4%	10.0%	2.3%	0.5%	16.2%	1.2%	27.7%	6.8%	16.5%
Shawnee County	7,831	28.0%	7.4%	8.1%	0.8%	16.2%	0.3%	22.4%	16.8%	16.4%
Wyandotte County	6,782	13.4%	11.6%	1.0%	2.8%	37.2%	1.1%	24.4%	8.6%	21.7%

Table D-2: Counties—Household Relationship—*Continued*

| | | 18 to 24 | | | | | | | | |
| | | Married Couple Households | | Male, No Spouse Present | | Female, No Spouse Present | | Non-Family Householders | | |
	Total Householders	With Children	No Children	With Children	No Children	With Children	No Children	Living Alone	Not Alone	Living With Parents
Kentucky										
Boone County	702	0.0%	65.5%	0.0%	0.0%	11.4%	0.0%	0.0%	23.1%	72.1%
Campbell County	1,715	0.0%	2.6%	0.0%	0.0%	25.9%	0.0%	25.7%	45.8%	50.0%
Daviess County	1,840	15.3%	12.8%	4.5%	4.5%	29.9%	0.0%	8.6%	24.3%	56.8%
Fayette County	11,120	1.2%	5.4%	0.0%	2.3%	14.7%	6.7%	21.4%	48.3%	20.6%
Hardin County	1,012	10.1%	0.0%	2.1%	0.0%	35.0%	8.3%	18.6%	26.0%	61.9%
Jefferson County	11,990	4.9%	2.7%	0.0%	8.2%	14.4%	0.4%	42.0%	27.3%	47.2%
Kenton County	2,050	8.5%	18.4%	0.0%	0.0%	26.3%	2.1%	24.8%	19.9%	64.2%
Warren County	4,821	8.6%	7.5%	0.0%	0.0%	11.3%	1.3%	29.5%	41.8%	20.6%
Louisiana										
Ascension Parish	1,316	6.7%	0.0%	13.6%	0.0%	23.2%	0.0%	21.7%	34.9%	64.3%
Bossier Parish	1,552	5.0%	19.3%	0.0%	4.6%	11.0%	0.0%	28.0%	32.2%	53.9%
Caddo Parish	3,841	0.0%	2.8%	0.0%	9.7%	30.5%	9.2%	30.4%	17.4%	48.9%
Calcasieu Parish	3,969	17.7%	2.4%	2.7%	0.0%	18.0%	7.0%	14.0%	38.1%	50.6%
East Baton Rouge Parish	15,708	0.3%	2.8%	1.4%	0.9%	19.4%	5.9%	30.9%	38.5%	32.9%
Jefferson Parish	5,507	0.0%	2.5%	0.0%	5.5%	21.5%	5.0%	44.1%	21.4%	60.6%
Lafayette Parish	6,193	2.6%	3.8%	9.2%	4.9%	6.3%	8.8%	41.6%	22.8%	40.1%
Lafourche Parish	1,305	15.6%	0.0%	18.3%	0.0%	13.3%	0.0%	35.7%	17.1%	49.8%
Livingston Parish	2,099	1.9%	33.4%	0.0%	18.2%	14.2%	0.0%	21.2%	11.1%	51.1%
Orleans Parish	5,694	2.5%	2.9%	2.0%	4.8%	14.5%	7.3%	36.2%	29.8%	42.6%
Ouachita Parish	2,943	14.1%	5.3%	0.0%	6.1%	24.4%	0.0%	44.1%	6.0%	41.3%
Rapides Parish	2,272	34.2%	16.3%	0.0%	4.1%	19.5%	0.0%	22.5%	3.4%	44.6%
St. Tammany Parish	1,324	6.0%	10.0%	9.1%	0.0%	0.0%	9.9%	20.5%	44.5%	70.4%
Tangipahoa Parish	2,558	36.5%	0.0%	0.0%	1.9%	13.4%	0.0%	35.2%	13.0%	44.0%
Terrebonne Parish	1,836	20.4%	16.2%	0.0%	14.1%	22.2%	10.4%	5.7%	11.1%	50.7%
Maine										
Androscoggin County	1,232	0.0%	0.0%	0.0%	0.0%	14.9%	0.0%	31.2%	53.9%	43.5%
Cumberland County	3,373	0.0%	10.2%	0.9%	0.0%	0.0%	17.2%	23.5%	48.2%	48.7%
Kennebec County	1,329	0.0%	28.4%	11.4%	6.0%	0.0%	0.0%	23.3%	30.9%	43.3%
Penobscot County	2,215	6.5%	4.7%	26.1%	0.0%	2.5%	2.4%	19.1%	38.7%	34.3%
York County	1,133	0.0%	11.0%	2.6%	0.0%	8.9%	0.0%	0.0%	77.4%	66.6%
Maryland										
Anne Arundel County	3,723	14.8%	12.9%	2.3%	2.3%	4.8%	2.2%	32.5%	28.1%	56.6%
Baltimore County	8,054	6.1%	9.2%	5.4%	2.7%	25.2%	4.2%	25.7%	21.4%	55.4%
Carroll County	836	0.0%	14.7%	0.0%	0.0%	31.6%	25.5%	0.0%	28.2%	70.0%
Cecil County	789	26.4%	2.7%	0.0%	15.7%	28.9%	0.0%	0.0%	26.4%	46.6%
Charles County	1,649	26.3%	1.6%	0.0%	19.5%	29.0%	0.0%	0.0%	23.6%	65.7%
Frederick County	1,550	0.0%	9.4%	0.0%	14.5%	0.0%	0.0%	43.5%	32.5%	72.9%
Harford County	1,430	36.2%	0.0%	0.0%	6.6%	10.4%	11.8%	13.8%	21.3%	75.1%
Howard County	1,627	0.0%	11.9%	0.0%	12.7%	17.9%	0.0%	21.4%	36.1%	71.7%
Montgomery County	6,107	5.1%	3.9%	2.7%	2.9%	18.2%	3.4%	24.0%	39.8%	68.1%
Prince George's County	9,284	5.9%	6.4%	3.7%	6.5%	18.4%	1.8%	32.5%	24.8%	57.5%
St. Mary's County	908	32.0%	8.8%	0.0%	0.0%	46.6%	0.0%	0.0%	12.6%	62.5%
Washington County	1,483	4.9%	4.1%	0.0%	0.0%	10.0%	0.0%	58.0%	23.1%	52.9%
Wicomico County	2,227	10.8%	16.9%	0.0%	0.0%	27.1%	9.3%	8.8%	27.2%	40.0%
Massachusetts										
Barnstable County	1,237	0.0%	5.3%	5.2%	0.0%	0.0%	0.0%	67.7%	21.9%	73.7%
Berkshire County	1,179	13.1%	0.0%	17.9%	0.0%	35.5%	0.0%	17.6%	15.9%	44.9%
Bristol County	5,394	2.4%	5.2%	0.0%	8.6%	21.4%	5.2%	18.4%	38.7%	55.5%
Essex County	4,401	5.3%	8.5%	3.0%	10.8%	12.5%	2.0%	23.8%	34.2%	67.1%
Hampden County	5,858	13.0%	3.2%	1.5%	10.6%	15.5%	2.5%	21.0%	32.6%	55.3%
Hampshire County	2,836	0.0%	0.0%	0.0%	16.7%	6.2%	1.0%	7.6%	68.4%	22.1%
Middlesex County	16,892	3.8%	4.5%	1.6%	5.6%	10.1%	6.1%	17.3%	51.0%	42.3%
Norfolk County	3,227	0.0%	2.9%	0.0%	0.0%	21.0%	13.0%	9.9%	53.2%	67.0%
Plymouth County	1,397	0.0%	0.0%	21.5%	7.1%	20.8%	5.9%	41.9%	2.8%	74.5%
Suffolk County	18,456	0.6%	0.7%	0.0%	4.8%	11.6%	4.7%	21.3%	56.4%	26.0%
Worcester County	8,485	5.7%	3.3%	0.2%	6.2%	26.1%	0.6%	26.6%	31.3%	58.8%
Michigan										
Allegan County	1,093	12.7%	0.0%	0.0%	0.0%	2.2%	0.0%	34.0%	51.1%	77.7%
Bay County	1,780	21.3%	3.4%	1.3%	13.2%	49.7%	0.0%	10.2%	1.0%	55.2%
Berrien County	2,096	0.0%	7.2%	1.2%	1.1%	17.5%	1.4%	38.9%	32.7%	52.8%
Calhoun County	1,563	0.0%	4.9%	23.0%	0.0%	17.2%	0.0%	31.9%	23.0%	53.5%
Eaton County	1,820	1.0%	8.8%	8.6%	3.8%	2.0%	0.0%	31.0%	44.7%	40.6%
Genesee County	5,098	5.3%	0.7%	4.0%	0.0%	35.1%	0.0%	15.5%	39.4%	60.5%
Ingham County	11,173	1.5%	2.2%	0.6%	4.9%	6.3%	2.0%	28.6%	54.0%	19.6%
Jackson County	2,496	0.0%	8.2%	0.0%	0.0%	31.9%	7.6%	30.0%	22.4%	49.8%
Kalamazoo County	10,422	1.6%	2.7%	9.2%	0.0%	14.2%	2.4%	25.0%	45.0%	23.4%
Kent County	11,269	1.6%	7.3%	2.8%	4.2%	4.5%	3.4%	22.4%	53.9%	43.0%
Lenawee County	1,417	3.0%	20.7%	0.0%	5.4%	4.9%	0.0%	44.1%	21.9%	49.8%
Livingston County	1,714	3.5%	7.7%	0.0%	27.0%	7.4%	0.0%	26.0%	28.5%	72.6%
Macomb County	7,861	1.2%	4.7%	5.2%	4.9%	37.0%	6.1%	9.5%	31.4%	65.6%
Monroe County	966	0.0%	10.2%	14.1%	0.0%	6.5%	0.0%	56.5%	12.6%	75.8%
Muskegon County	2,729	4.0%	2.5%	11.2%	0.0%	29.6%	5.1%	16.8%	30.9%	47.8%
Oakland County	16,061	2.5%	3.0%	2.6%	6.0%	18.9%	4.5%	33.2%	29.3%	61.5%
Ottawa County	5,050	3.9%	5.9%	0.0%	0.8%	4.4%	0.0%	8.6%	76.4%	42.0%
Saginaw County	3,551	7.7%	0.0%	0.0%	1.9%	27.6%	0.0%	36.9%	25.9%	47.0%
St. Clair County	1,661	0.0%	5.8%	5.9%	0.0%	16.1%	22.8%	18.7%	30.8%	58.5%

Table D-2: Counties—Household Relationship—*Continued*

		25 to 31								
		Married Couple Households		Male, No Spouse Present		Female, No Spouse Present		Non-Family Householders		
	Total Householders	With Children	No Children	With Children	No Children	With Children	No Children	Living Alone	Not Alone	Living With Parents
Kentucky										
Boone County	5,844	27.1%	9.9%	8.7%	1.9%	27.2%	10.8%	10.8%	3.5%	14.2%
Campbell County	3,083	30.2%	10.6%	7.4%	0.0%	20.8%	0.0%	10.1%	21.0%	21.9%
Daviess County	2,810	34.6%	12.6%	0.0%	0.0%	17.0%	0.0%	35.8%	0.0%	24.1%
Fayette County	15,782	25.8%	17.1%	1.0%	1.0%	9.6%	1.1%	24.8%	19.6%	12.3%
Hardin County	5,207	41.0%	3.4%	2.4%	0.0%	40.3%	0.8%	7.5%	4.6%	10.9%
Jefferson County	37,224	17.2%	13.8%	1.4%	3.6%	18.1%	2.2%	26.6%	17.1%	16.7%
Kenton County	6,719	28.8%	18.5%	0.0%	0.0%	9.2%	0.5%	21.9%	21.1%	19.6%
Warren County	5,639	20.0%	6.0%	6.7%	0.0%	15.7%	1.2%	26.7%	23.7%	16.4%
Louisiana										
Ascension Parish	4,610	47.2%	18.6%	8.2%	0.0%	17.7%	0.0%	8.2%	0.0%	22.8%
Bossier Parish	6,313	12.1%	19.9%	7.6%	0.0%	25.1%	0.0%	27.9%	7.5%	15.5%
Caddo Parish	12,117	17.5%	5.3%	2.4%	0.3%	27.4%	1.1%	36.2%	9.9%	25.8%
Calcasieu Parish	7,244	25.6%	7.3%	12.4%	5.1%	15.0%	1.5%	30.6%	2.5%	17.9%
East Baton Rouge Parish	18,753	13.4%	16.0%	0.3%	5.3%	14.7%	3.1%	31.9%	15.5%	18.5%
Jefferson Parish	18,257	19.8%	9.8%	2.2%	5.7%	22.5%	1.7%	25.9%	12.3%	26.0%
Lafayette Parish	11,839	21.9%	16.3%	2.8%	0.0%	11.5%	1.0%	35.2%	11.4%	13.9%
Lafourche Parish	2,966	34.7%	4.0%	9.2%	12.2%	14.1%	0.0%	2.3%	23.6%	31.4%
Livingston Parish	5,080	46.2%	11.8%	3.2%	0.0%	11.4%	0.0%	16.9%	10.6%	19.9%
Orleans Parish	22,833	7.0%	9.5%	1.7%	2.4%	20.2%	1.1%	40.1%	18.0%	22.0%
Ouachita Parish	5,733	25.0%	14.1%	1.0%	4.2%	38.4%	1.4%	15.9%	0.0%	26.9%
Rapides Parish	5,151	41.2%	7.2%	13.9%	0.0%	18.7%	0.0%	15.6%	3.4%	23.4%
St. Tammany Parish	9,195	24.4%	10.9%	4.4%	7.1%	22.3%	0.0%	15.6%	15.4%	28.3%
Tangipahoa Parish	7,265	30.4%	5.2%	0.0%	1.7%	16.2%	4.4%	18.6%	23.6%	18.0%
Terrebonne Parish	4,413	50.2%	4.5%	4.3%	0.0%	23.1%	0.0%	12.8%	5.1%	27.1%
Maine										
Androscoggin County	6,300	16.4%	10.2%	8.4%	0.0%	25.2%	1.9%	29.2%	8.7%	8.3%
Cumberland County	13,210	9.9%	15.3%	10.9%	0.4%	11.1%	0.9%	12.6%	39.0%	11.0%
Kennebec County	5,022	9.6%	16.4%	24.8%	0.0%	20.5%	0.0%	18.9%	9.8%	21.1%
Penobscot County	6,112	15.7%	4.1%	11.1%	0.0%	12.9%	7.9%	28.0%	20.4%	22.5%
York County	8,685	30.7%	2.1%	9.5%	0.0%	17.9%	1.4%	17.9%	20.7%	12.0%
Maryland										
Anne Arundel County	20,503	36.4%	14.5%	2.3%	2.7%	16.0%	2.5%	13.7%	12.0%	19.8%
Baltimore County	31,564	23.6%	13.7%	5.2%	2.6%	10.1%	2.4%	27.5%	14.9%	23.2%
Carroll County	4,601	32.7%	12.5%	6.7%	9.8%	16.9%	3.8%	7.6%	10.0%	23.1%
Cecil County	3,639	28.7%	11.8%	2.0%	0.0%	7.9%	0.4%	36.1%	13.1%	26.8%
Charles County	5,493	21.7%	20.9%	9.6%	2.1%	16.2%	1.2%	9.6%	20.7%	25.8%
Frederick County	7,739	22.5%	26.3%	6.9%	2.1%	8.7%	1.2%	14.4%	18.0%	21.3%
Harford County	7,404	25.4%	20.2%	1.4%	4.3%	8.7%	0.0%	27.8%	12.2%	32.9%
Howard County	9,686	24.1%	27.8%	0.0%	4.8%	2.5%	5.8%	17.1%	17.9%	29.3%
Montgomery County	33,500	18.7%	18.0%	2.7%	5.0%	9.7%	3.8%	26.9%	15.1%	25.7%
Prince George's County	29,715	13.0%	8.7%	5.0%	2.7%	28.2%	2.3%	29.1%	10.9%	32.2%
St. Mary's County	2,949	41.8%	7.3%	0.0%	0.0%	11.2%	0.0%	20.4%	19.3%	26.8%
Washington County	5,065	40.2%	7.7%	0.9%	0.8%	10.9%	0.0%	12.4%	27.1%	18.1%
Wicomico County	3,991	17.7%	22.1%	7.5%	0.0%	22.4%	2.5%	19.0%	8.9%	20.9%
Massachusetts										
Barnstable County	5,614	30.2%	10.9%	1.2%	2.5%	28.4%	1.3%	11.0%	14.6%	20.1%
Berkshire County	2,964	16.6%	13.4%	9.2%	0.0%	16.2%	0.0%	19.9%	24.8%	22.5%
Bristol County	17,930	25.6%	7.2%	3.1%	3.3%	21.0%	1.3%	24.1%	14.4%	30.4%
Essex County	22,194	25.3%	12.9%	6.4%	3.8%	10.0%	2.3%	20.8%	18.5%	31.9%
Hampden County	15,497	12.0%	8.7%	4.8%	5.3%	30.7%	1.8%	18.3%	18.3%	29.1%
Hampshire County	4,754	16.7%	8.3%	4.2%	6.6%	8.0%	0.0%	29.2%	27.0%	20.2%
Middlesex County	65,828	15.4%	18.3%	0.4%	3.6%	4.4%	1.7%	27.6%	28.6%	21.5%
Norfolk County	19,725	18.2%	19.7%	0.3%	1.6%	10.4%	3.6%	21.1%	25.2%	30.5%
Plymouth County	9,560	28.4%	12.7%	2.5%	0.9%	14.0%	0.8%	28.1%	12.6%	38.9%
Suffolk County	55,055	7.0%	12.1%	2.0%	3.2%	14.2%	1.8%	28.8%	31.0%	14.4%
Worcester County	27,364	20.4%	13.9%	4.3%	2.4%	20.8%	3.0%	16.9%	18.3%	26.9%
Michigan										
Allegan County	3,446	49.1%	15.5%	0.0%	3.8%	14.9%	0.0%	14.7%	2.1%	12.2%
Bay County	4,951	44.1%	10.6%	1.4%	0.0%	17.0%	0.0%	17.7%	9.2%	15.4%
Berrien County	5,236	20.7%	10.2%	1.0%	0.0%	38.7%	0.0%	28.4%	1.1%	20.9%
Calhoun County	4,695	29.6%	3.2%	2.6%	4.2%	32.7%	3.0%	16.5%	8.3%	25.3%
Eaton County	3,825	28.8%	11.1%	7.1%	0.0%	17.9%	0.0%	16.6%	18.5%	29.5%
Genesee County	14,187	20.4%	10.6%	1.5%	0.9%	29.8%	0.0%	22.0%	15.0%	23.9%
Ingham County	15,702	27.8%	5.0%	2.7%	2.1%	13.1%	1.1%	35.4%	12.7%	11.2%
Jackson County	6,210	28.4%	11.0%	8.4%	0.0%	20.3%	0.0%	20.5%	11.4%	20.3%
Kalamazoo County	11,949	19.4%	8.4%	2.7%	0.0%	22.8%	1.7%	29.0%	16.1%	15.9%
Kent County	29,624	25.6%	14.2%	6.4%	2.4%	10.0%	2.4%	25.5%	13.4%	17.0%
Lenawee County	2,222	29.5%	12.8%	4.1%	0.0%	14.0%	0.0%	20.5%	19.1%	28.3%
Livingston County	4,611	31.9%	19.1%	0.0%	0.0%	9.0%	3.6%	20.0%	16.5%	27.4%
Macomb County	31,277	21.3%	8.8%	7.3%	2.2%	20.5%	1.9%	27.5%	10.6%	23.2%
Monroe County	3,199	36.6%	10.2%	8.3%	1.7%	14.4%	0.0%	22.2%	6.7%	39.8%
Muskegon County	5,062	19.6%	5.4%	2.2%	0.7%	39.4%	0.0%	19.9%	12.8%	19.4%
Oakland County	45,038	16.5%	17.7%	2.9%	3.0%	8.4%	2.2%	33.4%	15.8%	22.4%
Ottawa County	8,853	30.0%	24.3%	12.5%	1.4%	12.1%	0.0%	8.9%	10.9%	14.2%
Saginaw County	6,061	22.9%	8.1%	0.5%	1.9%	28.7%	0.0%	28.8%	9.1%	18.9%
St. Clair County	3,445	39.1%	14.5%	3.0%	3.0%	8.3%	1.2%	21.9%	8.9%	35.1%

Table D-2: Counties—Household Relationship—*Continued*

		18 to 24								
		Married Couple Households		Male, No Spouse Present		Female, No Spouse Present		Non-Family Householders		
	Total Householders	With Children	No Children	With Children	No Children	With Children	No Children	Living Alone	Not Alone	Living With Parents
Michigan—Cont.										
Washtenaw County	12,910	1.2%	2.4%	1.0%	0.3%	2.1%	1.1%	31.3%	60.5%	22.5%
Wayne County	22,979	9.5%	2.3%	3.4%	9.3%	25.6%	4.2%	32.1%	13.6%	62.5%
Minnesota										
Anoka County	3,220	10.1%	11.8%	3.9%	0.0%	0.0%	0.0%	50.8%	23.4%	69.0%
Carver County	398	0.0%	54.5%	0.0%	0.0%	0.0%	0.0%	45.5%	0.0%	78.2%
Dakota County	6,545	6.5%	5.1%	0.0%	2.2%	20.6%	3.6%	23.4%	38.6%	56.4%
Hennepin County	18,001	4.9%	6.3%	2.7%	1.3%	7.6%	0.8%	32.1%	44.4%	43.7%
Olmsted County	4,041	0.6%	0.0%	5.1%	0.0%	25.6%	0.8%	53.9%	14.1%	51.5%
Ramsey County	10,657	8.2%	0.9%	0.0%	1.4%	22.2%	3.1%	25.6%	38.6%	43.6%
Scott County	251	0.0%	59.4%	0.0%	29.5%	0.0%	0.0%	11.2%	0.0%	86.2%
St. Louis County	4,696	16.8%	6.4%	0.0%	0.0%	4.0%	0.0%	31.1%	41.7%	27.3%
Stearns County	4,970	0.0%	11.4%	8.0%	0.0%	4.1%	3.4%	22.4%	50.7%	20.4%
Washington County	1,639	1.3%	6.8%	0.0%	0.0%	6.2%	0.0%	40.5%	45.1%	59.3%
Wright County	657	0.0%	7.8%	0.0%	0.0%	0.0%	0.0%	0.0%	92.2%	68.1%
Mississippi										
DeSoto County	1,355	0.0%	0.0%	12.3%	7.9%	25.5%	0.0%	2.8%	51.5%	63.6%
Harrison County	3,978	0.0%	14.2%	4.2%	0.0%	28.5%	0.0%	14.0%	39.1%	43.6%
Hinds County	4,157	0.0%	8.2%	1.2%	7.4%	25.7%	7.6%	25.2%	24.8%	48.5%
Jackson County	1,562	8.0%	15.1%	0.0%	3.4%	11.6%	9.2%	23.6%	29.1%	58.8%
Madison County	572	0.0%	21.9%	0.0%	0.0%	45.8%	0.0%	0.0%	32.3%	67.6%
Rankin County	1,596	0.5%	56.7%	0.0%	0.0%	0.0%	0.0%	42.8%	0.0%	50.5%
Missouri										
Boone County	11,150	0.0%	0.7%	0.0%	2.0%	9.2%	0.0%	40.7%	47.4%	12.8%
Cass County	855	67.6%	0.0%	0.0%	0.0%	0.0%	0.0%	5.4%	27.0%	67.5%
Clay County	3,158	12.1%	7.0%	0.0%	12.0%	27.2%	0.0%	20.4%	21.3%	44.6%
Franklin County	907	33.2%	0.0%	0.0%	11.0%	17.4%	0.0%	33.1%	5.3%	61.7%
Greene County	10,750	6.3%	6.6%	5.7%	0.0%	10.5%	1.3%	26.1%	43.4%	27.0%
Jackson County	11,959	2.7%	3.2%	0.0%	1.8%	18.0%	3.8%	39.5%	31.0%	51.6%
Jasper County	2,386	18.2%	25.9%	32.1%	0.0%	0.0%	0.0%	7.0%	16.8%	41.2%
Jefferson County	2,112	21.5%	0.0%	13.2%	0.0%	45.6%	0.0%	12.5%	7.1%	58.1%
Platte County	2,114	19.4%	6.5%	0.0%	0.0%	6.0%	0.0%	65.6%	2.5%	45.2%
St. Charles County	3,861	13.7%	14.4%	2.9%	9.4%	24.0%	0.0%	22.7%	12.9%	60.6%
St. Louis County	9,443	6.0%	6.1%	0.9%	2.0%	17.8%	1.5%	36.8%	28.9%	66.9%
Montana										
Flathead County	370	6.2%	17.0%	35.1%	0.0%	13.0%	0.0%	28.6%	0.0%	63.0%
Gallatin County	3,117	2.9%	5.3%	1.3%	0.0%	9.9%	0.0%	31.8%	48.8%	19.5%
Missoula County	2,393	0.0%	0.0%	0.0%	1.7%	30.3%	1.7%	13.0%	53.3%	35.2%
Yellowstone County	3,800	9.0%	0.0%	0.1%	1.0%	46.2%	0.0%	24.1%	19.7%	42.5%
Nebraska										
Douglas County	12,008	2.7%	4.4%	2.2%	1.5%	16.1%	0.7%	36.3%	36.1%	38.6%
Lancaster County	11,291	1.9%	6.9%	9.8%	5.4%	6.7%	1.3%	21.9%	46.0%	20.4%
Sarpy County	2,760	0.0%	5.9%	0.0%	5.5%	24.9%	0.0%	27.5%	36.2%	59.8%
Nevada										
Clark County	22,814	8.6%	11.2%	3.9%	9.6%	11.5%	5.6%	27.9%	21.8%	57.1%
Washoe County	6,521	8.6%	5.5%	3.8%	6.1%	6.2%	4.8%	24.0%	41.1%	34.4%
New Hampshire										
Hillsborough County	3,570	8.7%	20.4%	0.0%	8.4%	23.8%	0.0%	17.1%	21.5%	58.2%
Merrimack County	2,156	0.0%	0.0%	38.7%	17.8%	11.2%	0.0%	2.1%	30.1%	59.2%
Rockingham County	2,120	0.0%	6.9%	0.0%	0.0%	7.7%	0.0%	60.6%	24.8%	64.3%
Strafford County	2,812	9.7%	0.0%	5.6%	0.0%	31.2%	0.0%	13.1%	40.5%	31.4%
New Jersey										
Atlantic County	1,854	26.4%	0.0%	7.0%	0.0%	26.4%	0.0%	20.3%	19.8%	61.3%
Bergen County	4,723	6.1%	3.1%	0.0%	13.4%	19.3%	9.7%	27.5%	21.0%	72.7%
Burlington County	1,483	25.1%	9.2%	0.0%	0.0%	22.7%	0.0%	17.5%	25.4%	78.9%
Camden County	4,392	5.6%	4.2%	8.0%	1.3%	24.3%	1.6%	29.9%	25.1%	69.2%
Cape May County	664	10.7%	17.8%	0.0%	0.0%	25.2%	0.0%	46.4%	0.0%	68.8%
Cumberland County	923	18.2%	0.0%	3.8%	0.0%	41.9%	8.6%	4.6%	23.0%	71.2%
Essex County	5,807	4.1%	0.0%	2.8%	7.4%	43.7%	4.0%	22.0%	16.0%	63.9%
Gloucester County	1,954	0.0%	18.4%	4.1%	10.9%	0.0%	3.4%	18.2%	45.0%	64.1%
Hudson County	4,900	6.7%	1.6%	6.0%	6.1%	8.0%	13.1%	20.1%	38.4%	61.0%
Hunterdon County	159	0.0%	56.0%	0.0%	0.0%	0.0%	0.0%	15.7%	28.3%	60.6%
Mercer County	2,419	35.1%	0.0%	4.6%	12.9%	9.5%	0.0%	0.0%	37.9%	46.1%
Middlesex County	6,040	2.6%	11.8%	1.9%	8.3%	13.3%	12.4%	22.2%	27.6%	55.6%
Monmouth County	1,964	19.5%	24.7%	0.0%	0.0%	12.8%	0.0%	28.6%	14.4%	79.1%
Morris County	805	10.8%	22.9%	0.0%	10.4%	0.0%	28.7%	0.0%	27.2%	74.7%
Ocean County	2,288	22.2%	23.9%	0.0%	1.5%	12.6%	0.0%	31.1%	8.7%	77.3%
Passaic County	2,682	17.2%	12.2%	0.0%	7.9%	26.7%	7.8%	3.6%	24.6%	75.1%
Somerset County	713	0.0%	4.5%	0.0%	0.0%	0.0%	0.0%	26.8%	68.7%	86.0%
Sussex County	194	0.0%	18.0%	0.0%	0.0%	0.0%	0.0%	32.0%	50.0%	87.0%
Union County	2,636	9.3%	12.4%	9.2%	13.8%	22.6%	5.8%	21.8%	5.2%	71.9%
Warren County	1,352	18.3%	0.0%	0.0%	0.0%	0.0%	0.0%	41.0%	40.8%	67.8%
New Mexico										
Bernalillo County	12,199	9.8%	9.1%	3.8%	6.6%	21.0%	1.7%	19.2%	28.9%	52.8%
Doña Ana County	7,395	8.9%	11.6%	0.0%	1.4%	15.7%	2.0%	10.2%	50.2%	35.8%
San Juan County	1,583	27.7%	5.6%	12.6%	0.0%	17.0%	16.4%	2.7%	18.2%	44.3%

Table D-2: Counties—Household Relationship—*Continued*

	Total Householders	Married Couple Households With Children	Married Couple Households No Children	Male, No Spouse Present With Children	Male, No Spouse Present No Children	Female, No Spouse Present With Children	Female, No Spouse Present No Children	Non-Family Householders Living Alone	Non-Family Householders Not Alone	Living With Parents
Michigan—Cont.										
Washtenaw County	18,843	10.0%	15.4%	3.9%	1.7%	14.2%	2.2%	30.5%	22.1%	14.3%
Wayne County	57,798	17.1%	11.4%	6.1%	2.5%	23.2%	3.7%	23.8%	12.2%	29.6%
Minnesota										
Anoka County	12,925	37.8%	17.2%	0.7%	1.5%	16.6%	0.0%	13.3%	12.8%	25.4%
Carver County	2,694	28.0%	17.9%	0.0%	0.0%	0.0%	0.0%	31.4%	22.8%	20.4%
Dakota County	15,229	34.7%	21.9%	5.4%	5.0%	10.7%	1.5%	11.5%	9.3%	23.3%
Hennepin County	71,397	19.8%	12.6%	3.7%	1.1%	8.2%	1.2%	28.7%	24.7%	11.2%
Olmsted County	6,429	29.7%	23.2%	0.0%	1.6%	5.9%	3.0%	27.0%	9.6%	21.8%
Ramsey County	26,760	13.0%	15.6%	1.0%	3.7%	11.9%	0.9%	38.4%	15.4%	14.5%
Scott County	3,245	39.1%	21.1%	0.0%	0.0%	3.7%	0.0%	23.5%	12.6%	33.7%
St. Louis County	10,414	21.7%	5.7%	1.1%	0.0%	27.3%	0.0%	30.5%	13.6%	13.2%
Stearns County	6,066	25.5%	14.4%	1.1%	3.7%	25.0%	0.0%	7.6%	22.7%	13.5%
Washington County	11,009	22.5%	7.0%	1.7%	1.2%	30.6%	0.0%	12.6%	24.4%	15.7%
Wright County	6,295	40.5%	2.4%	18.2%	0.0%	6.8%	0.0%	14.2%	17.9%	11.2%
Mississippi										
DeSoto County	6,765	43.4%	16.3%	10.2%	0.0%	5.5%	6.8%	12.2%	5.5%	13.2%
Harrison County	9,299	25.3%	19.7%	8.5%	0.0%	17.1%	1.0%	14.9%	13.6%	12.0%
Hinds County	11,577	13.1%	6.2%	1.6%	1.0%	32.5%	2.7%	31.9%	10.9%	25.3%
Jackson County	5,519	30.4%	12.0%	1.5%	2.4%	25.7%	1.8%	21.6%	4.5%	34.8%
Madison County	2,651	19.9%	11.1%	0.0%	0.0%	24.6%	3.4%	32.9%	8.1%	26.5%
Rankin County	5,726	56.7%	12.3%	1.3%	7.9%	5.6%	0.0%	12.9%	3.4%	16.0%
Missouri										
Boone County	11,836	9.6%	10.5%	0.0%	3.8%	18.9%	0.9%	29.6%	26.7%	7.8%
Cass County	2,899	53.4%	3.6%	0.9%	0.0%	23.6%	5.4%	7.7%	5.4%	19.1%
Clay County	11,426	23.8%	12.5%	1.1%	1.1%	10.5%	0.9%	32.5%	17.6%	19.0%
Franklin County	3,847	30.2%	1.6%	6.7%	0.0%	20.5%	13.2%	20.8%	7.1%	12.2%
Greene County	17,510	22.3%	11.6%	2.0%	1.8%	18.1%	0.7%	26.6%	16.8%	8.2%
Jackson County	35,173	23.2%	9.2%	2.0%	2.0%	17.5%	1.2%	30.4%	14.4%	14.9%
Jasper County	6,776	25.7%	13.6%	8.0%	5.1%	11.6%	1.0%	19.6%	15.5%	17.8%
Jefferson County	8,827	38.8%	13.6%	5.9%	0.0%	13.1%	0.0%	19.7%	8.9%	22.1%
Platte County	5,055	14.3%	7.0%	4.6%	0.0%	23.3%	2.1%	19.8%	28.7%	7.0%
St. Charles County	15,786	40.6%	16.4%	2.3%	0.3%	9.7%	0.5%	17.2%	13.0%	19.4%
St. Louis County	42,332	24.2%	12.6%	1.7%	0.7%	15.8%	2.0%	26.2%	16.8%	19.6%
Montana										
Flathead County	2,788	42.9%	8.8%	2.2%	1.0%	21.4%	0.0%	23.7%	0.0%	12.6%
Gallatin County	5,190	18.5%	13.5%	2.3%	0.0%	27.1%	0.0%	27.0%	11.7%	4.0%
Missoula County	5,204	32.3%	7.3%	18.1%	5.9%	3.4%	0.0%	13.4%	19.7%	14.7%
Yellowstone County	6,292	29.1%	13.7%	5.7%	0.6%	12.8%	3.9%	12.8%	21.3%	18.3%
Nebraska										
Douglas County	31,059	22.1%	11.7%	3.8%	2.2%	14.3%	1.0%	29.8%	15.0%	12.2%
Lancaster County	15,470	23.7%	16.2%	6.0%	2.9%	9.4%	3.9%	22.1%	15.8%	8.1%
Sarpy County	8,465	30.8%	10.9%	1.5%	0.0%	20.9%	0.0%	28.0%	7.8%	16.3%
Nevada										
Clark County	82,810	25.5%	11.2%	3.8%	2.9%	15.5%	3.7%	25.0%	12.5%	19.3%
Washoe County	18,318	29.1%	9.9%	4.3%	2.0%	9.0%	2.0%	30.1%	13.6%	16.1%
New Hampshire										
Hillsborough County	15,981	18.4%	9.2%	10.2%	2.7%	15.0%	0.6%	12.0%	31.9%	19.8%
Merrimack County	3,717	22.2%	3.3%	0.0%	5.6%	11.6%	0.0%	30.0%	27.4%	21.5%
Rockingham County	7,856	26.6%	14.7%	2.6%	0.7%	16.1%	1.6%	17.8%	19.9%	22.5%
Strafford County	4,396	11.1%	20.9%	13.0%	0.0%	19.0%	1.8%	24.2%	10.1%	22.7%
New Jersey										
Atlantic County	8,129	30.9%	2.6%	5.6%	3.3%	31.7%	4.7%	15.8%	5.5%	27.9%
Bergen County	22,966	26.1%	19.9%	5.0%	5.7%	9.2%	2.2%	21.5%	10.4%	39.4%
Burlington County	13,250	32.6%	13.5%	1.6%	2.1%	14.5%	0.9%	19.0%	15.9%	31.5%
Camden County	15,671	17.4%	16.2%	9.9%	0.6%	17.0%	0.6%	25.7%	12.6%	38.5%
Cape May County	1,961	40.8%	21.8%	4.2%	0.0%	10.8%	0.0%	6.9%	15.5%	34.9%
Cumberland County	6,457	33.5%	6.9%	4.4%	0.0%	25.8%	2.3%	10.3%	16.8%	25.8%
Essex County	26,340	12.6%	9.2%	5.5%	3.2%	23.3%	0.9%	29.8%	15.6%	32.9%
Gloucester County	7,884	18.8%	14.9%	1.1%	1.6%	19.3%	0.9%	13.9%	29.4%	37.6%
Hudson County	38,371	12.0%	16.6%	2.2%	6.1%	10.4%	4.2%	24.8%	23.6%	20.0%
Hunterdon County	1,008	35.7%	0.0%	3.1%	0.0%	0.0%	14.0%	10.6%	36.6%	44.7%
Mercer County	10,623	26.4%	22.5%	1.0%	1.6%	11.0%	4.3%	16.6%	16.5%	27.1%
Middlesex County	22,752	17.5%	24.9%	2.8%	4.9%	9.9%	0.8%	21.4%	17.8%	37.9%
Monmouth County	15,148	19.0%	13.3%	3.2%	2.7%	8.6%	1.1%	27.1%	25.0%	37.4%
Morris County	12,295	25.1%	13.0%	6.7%	1.9%	5.1%	6.1%	22.9%	19.1%	33.0%
Ocean County	11,639	35.7%	22.2%	6.1%	5.6%	9.4%	0.0%	18.3%	2.8%	40.3%
Passaic County	12,020	20.2%	11.4%	7.8%	0.8%	34.1%	2.7%	9.9%	13.2%	33.8%
Somerset County	5,338	22.9%	26.2%	1.9%	6.5%	7.7%	1.4%	20.0%	13.5%	41.8%
Sussex County	3,581	13.5%	14.8%	6.9%	7.6%	30.1%	0.5%	12.0%	14.6%	29.8%
Union County	14,757	23.6%	14.8%	4.4%	2.6%	16.8%	1.9%	21.3%	14.7%	37.7%
Warren County	2,512	26.0%	28.1%	1.0%	0.0%	3.9%	0.0%	23.6%	17.4%	17.8%
New Mexico										
Bernalillo County	25,852	27.5%	8.8%	4.0%	1.3%	16.8%	2.3%	27.7%	11.6%	21.1%
Doña Ana County	6,643	27.7%	10.3%	5.7%	0.0%	26.6%	1.6%	20.3%	7.9%	31.1%
San Juan County	2,856	37.7%	3.0%	5.0%	12.4%	27.1%	2.9%	7.2%	4.7%	40.9%

Table D-2: Counties—Household Relationship—*Continued*

		18 to 24								
		Married Couple Households		Male, No Spouse Present		Female, No Spouse Present		Non-Family Householders		
	Total Householders	With Children	No Children	With Children	No Children	With Children	No Children	Living Alone	Not Alone	Living With Parents
New Mexico—Cont.										
Sandoval County	416	0.0%	0.0%	8.2%	0.0%	4.3%	4.6%	4.3%	78.6%	70.7%
Santa Fe County	1,518	34.3%	4.0%	2.5%	0.0%	18.0%	0.0%	22.7%	18.6%	52.9%
New York										
Albany County	7,977	2.5%	4.2%	0.0%	1.3%	8.2%	2.1%	29.3%	52.3%	31.7%
Bronx County	13,768	11.2%	2.2%	0.7%	16.2%	21.3%	5.9%	19.7%	22.9%	66.4%
Broome County	4,200	0.0%	2.3%	0.7%	0.0%	15.9%	3.6%	40.1%	37.4%	38.3%
Chautauqua County	1,895	0.0%	2.6%	8.2%	0.0%	11.5%	5.9%	20.6%	51.1%	42.0%
Dutchess County	2,977	18.0%	5.8%	0.0%	3.2%	11.3%	3.3%	28.5%	30.0%	52.5%
Erie County	14,586	1.1%	3.9%	0.8%	9.8%	19.8%	1.2%	26.2%	37.3%	53.9%
Jefferson County	3,264	17.3%	19.1%	0.0%	2.3%	24.8%	2.0%	25.0%	9.6%	34.3%
Kings County	29,998	13.4%	7.3%	1.6%	11.9%	11.2%	9.1%	16.2%	29.3%	60.3%
Monroe County	10,886	2.2%	2.6%	2.2%	4.0%	20.4%	3.2%	29.5%	35.8%	46.8%
Nassau County	2,733	6.4%	7.3%	4.3%	9.5%	31.8%	5.3%	26.1%	9.3%	77.5%
New York County	22,533	1.2%	3.0%	0.0%	2.1%	2.7%	3.5%	35.7%	51.8%	35.3%
Niagara County	2,548	4.7%	7.3%	0.0%	0.0%	13.1%	9.7%	49.8%	15.4%	65.8%
Oneida County	2,419	4.2%	1.2%	7.4%	0.0%	1.4%	6.2%	22.4%	57.2%	48.6%
Onondaga County	7,368	7.5%	1.9%	5.3%	2.6%	18.6%	3.4%	34.5%	26.2%	45.2%
Ontario County	1,293	3.6%	16.9%	0.0%	0.0%	23.3%	0.0%	24.5%	31.8%	32.3%
Orange County	3,862	22.1%	5.6%	4.7%	3.4%	22.5%	2.0%	28.3%	11.3%	67.3%
Oswego County	1,359	8.9%	1.6%	11.4%	8.2%	6.5%	0.0%	30.3%	33.0%	45.5%
Putnam County	103	0.0%	0.0%	0.0%	0.0%	0.0%	0.0%	100.0%	0.0%	85.7%
Queens County	13,991	8.0%	4.7%	6.4%	14.1%	7.6%	10.2%	22.4%	26.6%	69.2%
Rensselaer County	2,488	8.8%	0.0%	2.4%	0.0%	29.6%	0.0%	41.8%	17.4%	53.0%
Richmond County	2,054	10.9%	7.6%	3.0%	4.9%	34.3%	2.0%	25.8%	11.5%	82.9%
Rockland County	1,167	58.4%	11.4%	0.0%	3.1%	0.0%	6.3%	8.7%	12.3%	74.6%
Saratoga County	2,763	4.5%	3.5%	0.0%	0.0%	14.6%	8.2%	16.4%	52.9%	51.6%
Schenectady County	1,297	8.7%	3.0%	0.0%	3.5%	17.5%	0.0%	30.9%	36.3%	63.5%
St. Lawrence County	1,593	16.6%	10.4%	24.4%	0.0%	13.2%	0.0%	27.4%	8.1%	33.7%
Steuben County	620	0.0%	28.2%	0.0%	4.5%	33.9%	11.6%	21.8%	0.0%	66.9%
Suffolk County	5,582	0.0%	10.1%	0.0%	18.6%	16.7%	11.0%	22.8%	20.7%	76.7%
Tompkins County	3,918	0.0%	2.2%	0.0%	0.0%	4.7%	8.1%	43.2%	41.8%	15.2%
Ulster County	2,121	0.9%	18.7%	6.7%	0.0%	24.1%	0.0%	7.8%	41.7%	41.3%
Wayne County	966	20.7%	16.3%	4.9%	0.0%	13.4%	22.0%	0.0%	22.8%	63.1%
Westchester County	5,679	0.0%	8.2%	10.0%	11.6%	16.0%	3.2%	16.0%	34.8%	66.5%
North Carolina										
Alamance County	2,799	1.0%	5.3%	10.1%	20.9%	1.6%	0.0%	37.4%	23.8%	45.1%
Brunswick County	533	31.7%	4.9%	0.0%	0.0%	58.3%	0.0%	0.0%	5.1%	63.3%
Buncombe County	2,397	1.8%	1.8%	0.0%	0.0%	19.6%	0.0%	18.7%	58.1%	44.2%
Burke County	794	10.1%	32.5%	0.0%	21.8%	15.6%	0.0%	20.0%	0.0%	58.3%
Cabarrus County	940	0.0%	7.6%	18.1%	0.0%	26.4%	0.0%	27.9%	20.1%	67.7%
Catawba County	1,281	14.3%	2.3%	0.0%	0.0%	0.0%	0.0%	12.8%	70.6%	61.2%
Cleveland County	803	0.0%	12.5%	13.1%	0.0%	5.6%	0.0%	13.4%	55.4%	64.1%
Craven County	2,933	14.9%	67.5%	0.0%	0.0%	12.2%	0.0%	5.4%	0.0%	30.7%
Cumberland County	10,002	17.0%	20.5%	4.6%	1.0%	15.2%	0.0%	25.0%	16.6%	34.7%
Davidson County	1,650	25.9%	11.4%	0.0%	25.9%	18.0%	0.0%	8.6%	10.2%	53.0%
Durham County	4,783	0.0%	5.3%	0.0%	0.0%	12.8%	0.0%	34.5%	47.4%	31.1%
Forsyth County	6,831	6.7%	3.0%	1.3%	4.5%	21.5%	3.6%	36.0%	23.3%	43.4%
Gaston County	3,582	20.7%	7.8%	0.0%	11.2%	21.0%	0.0%	8.3%	31.0%	52.5%
Guilford County	7,943	1.0%	13.4%	4.9%	5.6%	17.0%	1.8%	28.9%	27.5%	45.5%
Harnett County	1,594	14.0%	17.8%	0.0%	7.0%	9.0%	0.0%	22.8%	29.4%	48.0%
Henderson County	1,489	0.0%	32.4%	0.0%	4.9%	0.0%	15.5%	11.8%	35.5%	49.7%
Iredell County	1,166	23.8%	6.3%	0.0%	0.0%	20.1%	8.9%	28.4%	12.6%	78.8%
Johnston County	1,253	26.3%	16.8%	0.0%	19.9%	2.1%	0.0%	0.0%	35.0%	71.3%
Mecklenburg County	15,633	2.3%	4.3%	1.8%	6.2%	13.8%	5.0%	22.8%	43.8%	44.3%
Moore County	968	9.0%	0.0%	4.5%	21.3%	27.4%	0.0%	32.3%	5.5%	44.5%
Nash County	981	0.0%	0.0%	12.7%	0.0%	59.2%	0.0%	28.0%	0.0%	70.0%
New Hanover County	7,095	1.3%	3.6%	0.0%	1.6%	9.0%	0.9%	33.2%	50.5%	23.1%
Onslow County	9,855	29.0%	29.1%	4.3%	0.5%	11.4%	2.7%	18.4%	4.7%	26.0%
Orange County	4,173	1.9%	2.6%	0.0%	0.0%	0.4%	2.0%	22.0%	71.1%	14.3%
Pitt County	9,261	0.0%	2.3%	0.0%	3.0%	6.2%	0.4%	43.3%	44.9%	22.4%
Randolph County	1,795	9.1%	6.7%	0.0%	0.0%	31.0%	0.0%	17.8%	35.4%	58.2%
Robeson County	1,949	1.5%	8.6%	7.2%	14.7%	22.2%	4.5%	23.0%	18.3%	52.7%
Rockingham County	660	0.0%	13.0%	0.0%	0.0%	87.0%	0.0%	0.0%	0.0%	74.2%
Rowan County	1,451	3.6%	5.5%	0.0%	0.0%	22.6%	10.5%	48.4%	9.4%	55.3%
Union County	1,565	6.5%	9.3%	6.2%	4.2%	0.0%	0.0%	8.4%	65.5%	61.8%
Wake County	15,712	5.0%	6.8%	1.0%	0.5%	10.4%	1.3%	34.5%	40.5%	42.7%
Wayne County	2,487	15.2%	11.2%	0.0%	2.0%	18.9%	0.0%	35.9%	16.9%	47.5%
North Dakota										
Cass County	8,838	0.0%	6.3%	0.0%	4.7%	8.2%	1.2%	34.3%	45.3%	24.1%
Ohio										
Allen County	1,509	11.9%	13.2%	0.0%	0.0%	7.7%	0.0%	36.6%	30.6%	46.9%
Ashtabula County	1,002	52.9%	0.0%	0.0%	0.0%	40.9%	0.0%	6.2%	0.0%	56.8%
Butler County	6,558	5.0%	5.7%	4.3%	6.1%	18.6%	1.3%	18.5%	40.5%	38.2%
Clark County	2,728	4.5%	3.2%	11.0%	2.2%	31.8%	0.0%	27.4%	20.0%	42.8%
Clermont County	2,469	2.6%	14.1%	0.0%	0.0%	52.0%	10.2%	4.5%	16.6%	57.1%
Columbiana County	1,685	10.4%	11.9%	0.9%	0.0%	15.4%	5.5%	40.7%	15.1%	54.8%

Table D-2: Counties—Household Relationship—*Continued*

		Married Couple Households		Male, No Spouse Present		Female, No Spouse Present		Non-Family Householders		
	Total Householders	With Children	No Children	With Children	No Children	With Children	No Children	Living Alone	Not Alone	Living With Parents
New Mexico—Cont.										
Sandoval County	3,575	19.0%	8.7%	0.4%	0.7%	39.5%	2.3%	14.6%	14.7%	38.5%
Santa Fe County	4,298	22.3%	10.2%	14.4%	6.1%	19.5%	3.9%	15.4%	8.4%	24.3%
New York										
Albany County	12,923	14.8%	8.5%	3.2%	3.5%	6.3%	2.0%	43.0%	18.7%	17.8%
Bronx County	46,896	16.5%	8.5%	5.6%	5.5%	34.3%	1.8%	19.3%	8.4%	35.5%
Broome County	7,297	23.3%	10.3%	9.2%	0.0%	17.5%	0.0%	24.6%	15.2%	24.4%
Chautauqua County	4,367	36.4%	1.4%	0.5%	0.0%	17.1%	0.0%	19.3%	25.3%	17.9%
Dutchess County	7,075	16.4%	11.3%	4.0%	0.0%	12.3%	5.9%	29.4%	20.7%	38.2%
Erie County	40,545	24.1%	12.1%	3.1%	2.2%	17.5%	0.4%	23.0%	17.5%	20.2%
Jefferson County	4,977	36.7%	15.8%	15.4%	0.0%	7.1%	0.0%	16.8%	8.1%	18.3%
Kings County	121,074	20.0%	10.7%	1.9%	4.7%	10.5%	3.7%	24.7%	24.0%	25.5%
Monroe County	34,147	15.9%	11.4%	3.3%	1.2%	21.3%	1.4%	27.7%	17.7%	21.0%
Nassau County	18,766	24.7%	13.2%	5.8%	4.9%	13.6%	5.3%	18.2%	14.3%	52.8%
New York County	111,323	4.1%	9.4%	1.4%	1.0%	4.3%	2.9%	50.4%	26.4%	13.2%
Niagara County	5,265	18.1%	11.5%	5.2%	4.4%	18.5%	0.0%	25.5%	16.8%	35.7%
Oneida County	9,111	31.9%	6.6%	5.3%	4.2%	11.2%	1.3%	27.1%	12.4%	20.8%
Onondaga County	18,678	13.5%	10.8%	2.6%	3.5%	16.9%	0.7%	36.1%	15.9%	26.1%
Ontario County	3,036	42.0%	9.4%	2.9%	0.0%	25.1%	0.0%	15.1%	5.5%	19.4%
Orange County	9,810	32.5%	8.6%	2.6%	2.1%	29.9%	0.0%	18.2%	6.2%	33.8%
Oswego County	3,559	13.3%	16.6%	0.7%	3.5%	26.5%	0.0%	14.3%	25.0%	36.6%
Putnam County	1,398	28.0%	45.9%	0.0%	0.0%	13.7%	0.0%	12.4%	0.0%	62.8%
Queens County	76,669	18.7%	14.2%	4.0%	5.9%	8.7%	3.4%	23.8%	21.3%	31.8%
Rensselaer County	8,056	17.1%	13.9%	1.1%	0.9%	21.5%	0.0%	32.3%	13.2%	18.1%
Richmond County	14,053	26.0%	10.8%	5.0%	4.6%	16.7%	0.9%	21.1%	15.0%	45.9%
Rockland County	7,758	46.4%	15.5%	0.0%	0.0%	18.7%	3.1%	11.8%	4.5%	31.9%
Saratoga County	6,679	13.1%	13.9%	1.0%	2.5%	6.7%	1.8%	24.3%	36.6%	21.0%
Schenectady County	4,265	23.3%	12.0%	0.0%	0.0%	19.0%	2.3%	24.6%	18.8%	31.8%
St. Lawrence County	3,440	39.3%	2.2%	4.0%	0.0%	4.0%	0.0%	31.5%	19.0%	20.0%
Steuben County	2,995	34.1%	10.4%	4.4%	1.9%	14.3%	0.0%	21.0%	14.0%	13.2%
Suffolk County	25,661	23.4%	20.3%	2.0%	0.2%	14.8%	5.1%	19.6%	14.6%	42.9%
Tompkins County	4,746	6.6%	8.8%	0.0%	0.8%	0.9%	0.0%	60.9%	21.9%	6.6%
Ulster County	4,382	31.5%	12.3%	3.3%	0.0%	25.1%	0.0%	13.2%	14.6%	27.5%
Wayne County	2,714	41.2%	6.6%	1.7%	0.0%	23.1%	2.4%	12.5%	12.6%	15.8%
Westchester County	21,947	21.6%	13.9%	6.2%	5.1%	18.7%	4.1%	14.6%	15.8%	36.2%
North Carolina										
Alamance County	5,663	31.1%	20.4%	6.4%	4.9%	27.2%	0.1%	9.8%	0.0%	22.3%
Brunswick County	3,133	28.4%	11.9%	1.9%	2.5%	42.4%	0.0%	6.6%	6.3%	19.3%
Buncombe County	9,725	18.0%	13.3%	3.1%	0.7%	6.5%	0.0%	37.6%	20.7%	23.1%
Burke County	2,578	38.2%	8.0%	2.3%	9.2%	29.1%	0.0%	6.7%	6.6%	29.7%
Cabarrus County	6,439	25.7%	18.2%	2.6%	2.9%	13.6%	1.3%	26.2%	9.4%	25.7%
Catawba County	4,130	37.3%	8.8%	0.0%	0.0%	23.0%	4.8%	10.6%	15.5%	18.4%
Cleveland County	2,322	24.4%	29.1%	0.0%	0.0%	16.6%	0.0%	15.6%	14.3%	18.6%
Craven County	5,506	42.7%	14.5%	7.3%	0.7%	6.1%	0.0%	20.3%	8.4%	14.6%
Cumberland County	19,534	21.7%	16.8%	2.1%	0.7%	18.3%	0.5%	29.5%	10.4%	15.7%
Davidson County	4,753	21.0%	9.3%	1.3%	1.5%	28.2%	0.5%	11.9%	26.3%	23.1%
Durham County	19,150	19.8%	16.7%	5.3%	0.0%	11.6%	0.0%	31.6%	15.1%	10.5%
Forsyth County	13,622	19.8%	15.8%	2.3%	1.7%	24.0%	0.0%	27.7%	8.7%	18.3%
Gaston County	5,023	25.8%	9.4%	6.1%	0.0%	31.6%	1.3%	11.5%	14.4%	38.0%
Guilford County	25,066	18.9%	13.5%	3.9%	1.4%	14.9%	2.0%	28.4%	16.9%	14.9%
Harnett County	5,756	44.6%	17.0%	1.5%	0.5%	22.6%	0.0%	12.5%	1.5%	22.9%
Henderson County	3,255	36.5%	27.1%	0.0%	0.0%	8.6%	0.0%	19.2%	8.6%	13.5%
Iredell County	4,554	29.4%	13.1%	0.5%	0.0%	17.6%	0.0%	25.4%	14.1%	26.3%
Johnston County	5,749	32.0%	14.0%	2.7%	0.0%	10.1%	2.7%	9.4%	29.2%	14.5%
Mecklenburg County	52,735	17.2%	12.4%	5.2%	1.8%	12.9%	0.6%	34.6%	15.3%	17.9%
Moore County	3,007	8.7%	27.1%	18.6%	0.0%	15.1%	0.0%	30.5%	0.0%	29.0%
Nash County	1,844	15.6%	0.8%	9.8%	0.0%	29.9%	0.0%	33.9%	10.0%	34.2%
New Hanover County	9,769	15.4%	13.8%	9.2%	0.0%	15.9%	0.0%	24.3%	21.4%	10.5%
Onslow County	11,406	35.6%	11.8%	10.1%	1.1%	19.1%	1.0%	14.2%	7.1%	10.3%
Orange County	5,848	17.0%	28.0%	0.0%	0.0%	5.7%	0.8%	29.0%	19.4%	12.8%
Pitt County	6,783	16.3%	23.3%	0.0%	0.3%	18.0%	1.7%	31.1%	9.3%	17.8%
Randolph County	3,899	17.9%	31.9%	6.7%	0.0%	11.2%	12.9%	16.4%	3.0%	23.6%
Robeson County	4,492	25.6%	2.9%	4.9%	4.3%	36.2%	1.8%	18.6%	5.7%	27.4%
Rockingham County	3,195	50.5%	15.2%	0.0%	2.0%	15.8%	0.0%	16.4%	0.0%	33.5%
Rowan County	3,023	23.2%	12.4%	13.3%	0.0%	32.2%	2.4%	12.4%	4.0%	30.6%
Union County	4,956	25.8%	17.1%	0.4%	3.9%	26.9%	0.0%	17.1%	8.8%	26.7%
Wake County	41,773	17.5%	16.4%	2.2%	2.2%	11.1%	0.7%	27.9%	22.1%	14.8%
Wayne County	4,723	30.0%	19.7%	2.9%	1.7%	22.5%	0.0%	21.9%	1.3%	17.2%
North Dakota										
Cass County	9,607	34.8%	15.8%	1.2%	2.0%	8.9%	0.9%	21.4%	15.0%	6.8%
Ohio										
Allen County	4,158	33.6%	12.7%	3.7%	7.5%	17.4%	2.9%	22.3%	0.0%	21.6%
Ashtabula County	3,444	26.2%	2.5%	14.5%	2.6%	27.2%	0.0%	2.1%	24.9%	12.8%
Butler County	13,895	35.7%	16.1%	2.5%	5.1%	16.9%	4.4%	13.5%	5.8%	16.6%
Clark County	4,827	29.1%	14.4%	3.6%	5.3%	26.4%	0.0%	11.9%	9.4%	22.1%
Clermont County	7,763	32.8%	15.8%	0.0%	0.0%	22.8%	0.0%	19.2%	9.5%	24.3%
Columbiana County	3,830	9.2%	8.2%	4.1%	0.0%	39.2%	0.0%	21.5%	17.7%	29.1%

Table D-2: Counties—Household Relationship—*Continued*

		Married Couple Households		Male, No Spouse Present		Female, No Spouse Present		Non-Family Householders		
	Total Householders	With Children	No Children	With Children	No Children	With Children	No Children	Living Alone	Not Alone	Living With Parents
Ohio—Cont.										
Cuyahoga County	20,236	3.2%	3.9%	2.9%	1.4%	24.7%	3.6%	40.7%	19.7%	53.9%
Delaware County	1,741	10.3%	35.7%	12.3%	0.0%	0.0%	0.0%	7.4%	34.2%	60.3%
Fairfield County	1,508	27.8%	0.0%	1.3%	0.0%	1.3%	9.0%	36.1%	24.5%	48.7%
Franklin County	26,630	5.5%	3.9%	0.8%	4.3%	13.9%	2.9%	31.4%	37.4%	36.1%
Geauga County	395	30.9%	0.0%	0.0%	0.0%	0.0%	0.0%	0.0%	69.1%	76.1%
Greene County	3,856	11.8%	7.0%	5.7%	0.0%	1.1%	3.2%	27.8%	43.4%	25.5%
Hamilton County	18,204	1.7%	2.2%	1.6%	6.1%	19.0%	1.7%	38.8%	28.8%	42.0%
Lake County	743	31.1%	5.8%	0.0%	0.0%	0.0%	6.5%	10.0%	46.7%	69.8%
Licking County	1,996	17.6%	8.9%	5.9%	0.0%	32.4%	0.0%	13.8%	21.4%	53.7%
Lorain County	3,607	7.4%	9.0%	1.0%	12.0%	22.8%	0.0%	14.3%	33.5%	55.1%
Lucas County	9,530	5.3%	3.6%	4.2%	1.2%	16.6%	6.4%	34.9%	27.6%	44.7%
Mahoning County	2,912	9.3%	0.0%	0.0%	0.0%	35.4%	2.5%	18.5%	34.3%	59.4%
Medina County	1,320	9.9%	28.4%	0.0%	0.0%	15.9%	0.0%	26.0%	19.8%	72.7%
Miami County	1,219	19.4%	0.0%	0.0%	0.0%	38.6%	0.0%	18.0%	24.0%	73.3%
Montgomery County	10,660	14.7%	4.0%	3.4%	0.0%	31.6%	1.7%	30.2%	14.4%	41.0%
Portage County	4,914	0.0%	1.3%	0.0%	2.5%	13.6%	1.8%	25.9%	55.0%	36.3%
Richland County	1,984	5.6%	9.8%	0.0%	9.9%	15.8%	0.0%	19.6%	39.3%	52.5%
Stark County	4,550	10.0%	7.1%	0.0%	3.8%	25.3%	0.0%	36.8%	17.1%	59.0%
Summit County	9,224	3.2%	7.5%	4.7%	6.1%	16.4%	5.1%	20.3%	36.8%	48.4%
Trumbull County	1,869	12.7%	3.3%	10.4%	0.0%	19.7%	0.0%	37.3%	16.6%	61.1%
Tuscarawas County	754	15.8%	6.8%	0.0%	0.0%	0.0%	0.0%	64.1%	13.4%	70.7%
Warren County	1,938	15.6%	8.2%	5.7%	10.1%	12.1%	0.0%	40.6%	7.7%	65.3%
Wayne County	1,242	2.6%	37.4%	2.7%	0.0%	12.3%	0.0%	44.9%	0.0%	55.4%
Wood County	4,421	13.5%	4.6%	3.8%	1.0%	10.0%	0.0%	54.1%	13.0%	36.3%
Oklahoma										
Canadian County	976	9.3%	0.0%	0.0%	0.0%	22.5%	0.0%	56.6%	11.6%	66.6%
Cleveland County	9,808	0.7%	6.0%	0.0%	1.2%	15.3%	7.6%	29.2%	39.9%	27.6%
Comanche County	3,189	20.4%	17.1%	0.0%	0.0%	15.2%	0.0%	18.6%	28.8%	27.4%
Oklahoma County	14,925	13.2%	8.2%	1.8%	2.7%	14.0%	4.4%	36.1%	19.6%	41.2%
Tulsa County	13,465	13.4%	8.1%	3.0%	5.0%	20.2%	0.5%	31.7%	18.0%	47.4%
Oregon										
Clackamas County	4,064	6.4%	12.9%	1.7%	12.4%	11.0%	0.0%	6.1%	49.4%	59.8%
Deschutes County	1,187	44.8%	3.6%	0.0%	0.0%	3.5%	0.0%	3.2%	44.9%	52.0%
Douglas County	1,105	4.2%	3.8%	9.6%	0.0%	25.2%	0.0%	19.8%	37.5%	50.4%
Jackson County	2,787	23.9%	17.8%	0.0%	0.0%	2.8%	0.0%	24.5%	31.0%	41.7%
Lane County	11,672	5.6%	7.5%	2.5%	0.6%	12.4%	2.8%	26.5%	42.2%	31.1%
Linn County	4,206	6.1%	6.3%	0.0%	2.4%	7.9%	0.0%	18.2%	59.1%	18.4%
Marion County	6,708	17.4%	6.4%	4.6%	0.0%	11.0%	3.8%	33.2%	23.6%	51.9%
Multnomah County	12,034	0.6%	6.3%	3.1%	1.3%	4.3%	0.8%	34.3%	49.3%	37.3%
Washington County	5,564	6.4%	11.8%	3.7%	5.9%	4.0%	10.6%	15.8%	41.8%	55.7%
Yamhill County	1,632	28.5%	6.2%	0.0%	3.3%	40.0%	11.2%	0.0%	10.9%	44.0%
Pennsylvania										
Adams County	1,508	37.3%	3.3%	0.0%	0.0%	36.3%	0.0%	2.9%	20.2%	43.6%
Allegheny County	22,051	1.8%	1.6%	2.3%	1.7%	11.4%	0.8%	37.5%	42.9%	45.2%
Beaver County	1,882	3.0%	3.8%	3.7%	1.9%	48.1%	4.5%	9.6%	25.3%	60.6%
Berks County	5,126	7.5%	3.1%	7.3%	1.1%	25.6%	0.0%	30.5%	24.9%	51.4%
Blair County	1,694	7.1%	10.2%	2.5%	0.0%	26.0%	0.0%	52.5%	1.8%	51.7%
Bucks County	1,606	3.5%	13.8%	7.7%	3.1%	20.7%	6.3%	30.5%	14.3%	81.2%
Butler County	3,102	13.9%	0.0%	0.0%	7.6%	3.2%	0.0%	28.2%	47.0%	42.5%
Cambria County	1,744	7.8%	2.4%	0.0%	0.0%	17.3%	0.0%	35.7%	36.8%	46.1%
Centre County	8,430	0.3%	3.7%	0.0%	1.8%	1.9%	6.5%	26.3%	59.5%	12.2%
Chester County	5,653	3.6%	0.0%	0.4%	4.5%	5.3%	3.0%	24.8%	58.4%	46.3%
Cumberland County	3,067	5.9%	2.0%	0.0%	0.0%	32.7%	0.0%	28.7%	30.8%	39.2%
Dauphin County	4,832	4.6%	7.5%	7.3%	5.4%	15.7%	4.0%	24.7%	30.9%	56.7%
Delaware County	3,903	2.2%	3.0%	4.7%	5.9%	31.9%	0.0%	15.3%	36.9%	54.4%
Erie County	3,769	3.4%	1.2%	0.0%	11.3%	8.6%	1.2%	18.3%	56.1%	44.3%
Fayette County	1,336	7.8%	0.0%	0.0%	0.0%	51.2%	0.0%	33.1%	7.9%	71.1%
Franklin County	1,321	7.0%	2.6%	0.0%	0.0%	24.1%	0.0%	32.6%	33.7%	63.4%
Lackawanna County	1,409	5.0%	5.7%	0.0%	0.0%	19.7%	1.6%	21.3%	46.7%	49.3%
Lancaster County	7,764	5.3%	6.8%	1.4%	4.4%	19.5%	0.0%	25.6%	36.9%	50.0%
Lebanon County	1,605	29.2%	7.0%	0.0%	4.7%	0.0%	8.2%	20.8%	30.2%	44.8%
Lehigh County	3,850	2.9%	1.2%	3.8%	18.8%	31.6%	1.2%	34.8%	5.8%	57.2%
Luzerne County	3,726	0.0%	1.8%	3.1%	12.4%	11.7%	0.0%	38.0%	33.0%	45.5%
Lycoming County	2,214	8.8%	5.1%	0.0%	0.0%	27.4%	0.0%	29.9%	28.8%	44.9%
Mercer County	1,601	1.1%	12.6%	0.0%	0.0%	13.2%	20.5%	16.5%	36.0%	45.8%
Monroe County	2,243	0.0%	0.0%	17.7%	0.0%	9.7%	6.2%	21.7%	44.6%	61.8%
Montgomery County	4,420	19.1%	1.5%	3.3%	1.5%	7.4%	0.0%	42.8%	24.3%	70.8%
Northampton County	3,124	21.2%	3.2%	0.0%	3.7%	19.3%	14.9%	21.4%	16.3%	48.9%
Northumberland County	911	9.2%	4.9%	0.0%	0.0%	5.2%	0.0%	76.0%	4.7%	67.9%
Philadelphia County	23,528	4.5%	2.7%	1.4%	5.4%	10.9%	3.8%	42.1%	29.3%	46.1%
Schuylkill County	738	6.9%	0.0%	0.0%	0.0%	23.8%	0.0%	55.7%	13.6%	69.5%
Washington County	1,839	1.0%	2.1%	5.4%	0.0%	23.7%	2.3%	19.5%	45.9%	57.8%
Westmoreland County	3,896	0.0%	10.0%	0.0%	5.2%	22.7%	0.0%	44.5%	17.6%	58.5%
York County	3,339	17.3%	6.1%	5.2%	5.1%	25.4%	2.2%	17.4%	21.3%	58.9%
Rhode Island										
Kent County	1,214	1.8%	9.5%	9.2%	0.0%	0.0%	4.2%	33.2%	42.1%	68.9%

Table D-2: Counties—Household Relationship—*Continued*

		25 to 31								
		Married Couple Households		Male, No Spouse Present		Female, No Spouse Present		Non-Family Householders		
	Total Householders	With Children	No Children	With Children	No Children	With Children	No Children	Living Alone	Not Alone	Living With Parents
Ohio—Cont.										
Cuyahoga County	55,941	14.1%	8.9%	4.4%	3.5%	20.7%	1.1%	31.4%	16.0%	21.2%
Delaware County	5,758	25.6%	12.8%	7.3%	0.0%	9.4%	0.0%	41.7%	3.2%	17.7%
Fairfield County	6,625	22.3%	9.7%	6.0%	2.1%	27.9%	0.9%	20.5%	10.7%	18.8%
Franklin County	69,860	19.1%	14.5%	1.0%	1.5%	11.1%	1.2%	30.7%	20.8%	14.0%
Geauga County	1,548	63.0%	10.2%	0.0%	0.0%	0.0%	0.0%	11.8%	15.1%	36.2%
Greene County	6,640	30.2%	9.3%	0.9%	1.3%	18.8%	0.0%	20.5%	19.1%	15.8%
Hamilton County	40,671	16.8%	10.6%	2.1%	1.6%	17.1%	2.6%	33.0%	16.1%	15.6%
Lake County	7,302	21.4%	12.1%	4.8%	3.2%	13.7%	0.0%	34.9%	9.8%	21.7%
Licking County	5,478	32.8%	10.4%	1.7%	0.0%	15.0%	0.0%	33.2%	6.9%	23.3%
Lorain County	6,599	30.2%	12.9%	6.4%	1.3%	29.8%	0.0%	12.5%	7.0%	26.8%
Lucas County	20,215	16.1%	7.4%	1.5%	4.5%	27.8%	0.8%	27.2%	14.8%	20.4%
Mahoning County	9,315	25.4%	10.6%	1.1%	0.0%	21.5%	4.7%	24.7%	12.0%	21.7%
Medina County	4,667	25.9%	12.1%	0.9%	1.8%	9.4%	3.0%	19.0%	27.9%	26.9%
Miami County	4,146	28.3%	10.9%	10.4%	4.1%	10.7%	0.0%	19.8%	15.8%	19.3%
Montgomery County	21,619	22.2%	10.1%	4.5%	2.0%	20.7%	0.9%	29.9%	9.7%	17.7%
Portage County	4,776	18.0%	20.6%	4.3%	0.0%	11.4%	2.9%	25.6%	17.1%	28.1%
Richland County	3,080	40.3%	4.1%	1.5%	6.4%	22.1%	0.0%	18.3%	7.3%	17.0%
Stark County	12,511	25.4%	14.3%	0.9%	1.5%	17.6%	0.0%	28.4%	11.9%	21.3%
Summit County	22,410	21.3%	19.7%	2.1%	0.8%	19.6%	0.8%	24.1%	11.5%	23.6%
Trumbull County	7,146	24.6%	7.1%	6.0%	1.8%	25.0%	0.0%	24.4%	11.2%	25.9%
Tuscarawas County	2,723	38.8%	5.3%	0.3%	2.5%	18.4%	0.0%	19.5%	15.3%	26.7%
Warren County	6,478	31.2%	30.4%	4.0%	4.7%	6.0%	1.9%	8.0%	13.8%	11.3%
Wayne County	4,750	47.2%	11.8%	1.6%	1.0%	12.7%	0.0%	17.6%	8.0%	14.5%
Wood County	5,827	23.0%	11.4%	2.3%	2.8%	10.7%	2.6%	40.0%	7.3%	20.1%
Oklahoma										
Canadian County	4,162	52.6%	8.6%	5.0%	0.0%	13.0%	0.0%	19.7%	1.2%	29.3%
Cleveland County	15,433	26.8%	13.3%	9.5%	2.2%	12.9%	0.8%	21.4%	13.1%	8.6%
Comanche County	6,549	24.6%	9.3%	8.5%	0.0%	19.0%	0.0%	25.4%	13.2%	9.8%
Oklahoma County	40,996	24.9%	10.7%	2.5%	3.0%	12.8%	1.8%	29.0%	15.3%	10.5%
Tulsa County	31,306	26.7%	11.9%	5.1%	1.6%	21.2%	1.0%	23.5%	9.1%	15.0%
Oregon										
Clackamas County	12,232	39.6%	12.4%	2.7%	3.2%	12.9%	0.8%	16.0%	12.4%	21.1%
Deschutes County	5,478	26.1%	12.9%	11.2%	6.7%	15.4%	0.0%	14.2%	13.6%	24.8%
Douglas County	3,615	39.3%	2.8%	9.0%	0.0%	28.2%	0.0%	8.7%	12.0%	15.1%
Jackson County	8,473	34.7%	7.6%	2.6%	2.1%	24.1%	3.5%	17.3%	8.2%	14.1%
Lane County	12,797	28.9%	21.4%	3.6%	0.4%	7.5%	1.3%	25.4%	11.4%	14.2%
Linn County	3,787	20.4%	12.4%	0.0%	0.0%	9.3%	0.0%	23.1%	34.7%	19.1%
Marion County	10,752	29.7%	5.4%	12.0%	1.5%	28.5%	1.4%	15.6%	6.0%	18.1%
Multnomah County	41,942	10.8%	13.7%	4.5%	0.5%	10.0%	1.4%	28.8%	30.2%	14.3%
Washington County	23,982	23.0%	16.4%	3.4%	2.5%	8.8%	0.6%	28.1%	17.2%	19.5%
Yamhill County	3,719	44.6%	9.6%	0.2%	0.0%	5.8%	0.0%	14.0%	25.9%	8.1%
Pennsylvania										
Adams County	2,559	43.3%	6.8%	2.1%	0.0%	13.4%	12.8%	19.1%	2.5%	25.9%
Allegheny County	57,645	16.6%	12.9%	3.2%	1.4%	13.8%	0.9%	29.6%	21.5%	19.1%
Beaver County	4,263	18.0%	26.7%	3.0%	0.8%	13.7%	0.0%	26.3%	11.5%	34.6%
Berks County	13,005	31.5%	7.5%	6.8%	3.6%	11.2%	0.0%	15.0%	24.3%	24.6%
Blair County	4,153	39.8%	11.4%	2.8%	0.0%	22.9%	0.0%	18.5%	4.5%	17.0%
Bucks County	15,618	30.2%	16.1%	7.0%	5.8%	12.7%	1.5%	15.9%	10.8%	35.0%
Butler County	5,738	22.7%	25.9%	6.2%	1.1%	7.6%	0.0%	26.1%	10.4%	23.4%
Cambria County	5,039	21.8%	9.9%	2.8%	0.0%	18.0%	0.0%	35.9%	11.6%	17.9%
Centre County	6,530	19.8%	11.2%	3.0%	0.0%	5.6%	0.4%	32.6%	27.3%	18.7%
Chester County	15,283	19.8%	27.1%	0.0%	2.8%	4.1%	1.9%	23.5%	20.9%	26.0%
Cumberland County	9,132	25.7%	14.1%	8.5%	2.1%	6.4%	2.4%	25.5%	15.3%	17.9%
Dauphin County	12,860	22.4%	11.1%	0.0%	2.3%	22.9%	1.3%	32.8%	7.2%	15.9%
Delaware County	16,351	21.4%	10.9%	1.1%	2.5%	23.5%	2.1%	29.3%	9.2%	35.0%
Erie County	12,322	19.8%	11.4%	5.5%	0.0%	24.3%	2.0%	27.3%	9.8%	17.2%
Fayette County	2,819	36.1%	9.8%	1.0%	3.3%	21.4%	0.0%	13.2%	15.2%	27.3%
Franklin County	5,637	46.7%	8.5%	2.5%	0.0%	14.0%	0.0%	16.6%	11.7%	16.7%
Lackawanna County	6,156	26.0%	12.1%	4.0%	0.6%	10.6%	4.2%	26.5%	16.0%	34.3%
Lancaster County	19,592	37.9%	17.9%	2.8%	0.0%	9.7%	0.4%	21.3%	10.0%	22.3%
Lebanon County	4,154	30.4%	13.6%	7.2%	0.0%	22.3%	0.8%	11.9%	13.7%	21.3%
Lehigh County	10,112	22.8%	20.3%	2.7%	0.2%	22.4%	1.6%	15.6%	14.4%	22.5%
Luzerne County	11,285	17.0%	9.2%	6.4%	5.2%	22.3%	4.5%	20.6%	14.7%	26.4%
Lycoming County	2,737	40.3%	24.7%	2.3%	0.0%	15.7%	0.0%	9.4%	7.5%	23.3%
Mercer County	3,457	27.7%	11.0%	13.1%	1.2%	5.8%	0.0%	34.8%	6.4%	25.5%
Monroe County	3,355	23.9%	5.3%	16.0%	0.0%	18.3%	0.0%	5.7%	30.9%	36.1%
Montgomery County	26,423	21.1%	18.9%	1.0%	1.4%	4.9%	1.3%	34.3%	17.1%	32.9%
Northampton County	8,461	16.2%	26.0%	5.7%	0.0%	10.7%	0.0%	23.7%	17.8%	30.0%
Northumberland County	3,299	30.7%	12.7%	0.9%	0.0%	12.3%	0.0%	28.3%	15.1%	21.5%
Philadelphia County	86,145	12.1%	7.8%	1.9%	2.2%	16.7%	1.3%	38.4%	19.6%	22.4%
Schuylkill County	4,432	27.5%	12.8%	3.9%	1.9%	19.2%	1.2%	20.8%	13.9%	24.1%
Washington County	7,060	30.2%	10.9%	1.7%	0.6%	28.6%	1.2%	20.5%	6.2%	20.0%
Westmoreland County	10,176	35.2%	15.7%	1.0%	0.6%	12.0%	1.2%	21.5%	12.8%	23.9%
York County	14,005	32.2%	10.6%	5.0%	1.8%	17.5%	0.0%	26.2%	6.7%	24.0%
Rhode Island										
Kent County	6,482	14.9%	21.1%	16.1%	0.9%	9.0%	0.0%	22.6%	15.4%	24.2%

Table D-2: Counties—Household Relationship—*Continued*

		Married Couple Households		Male, No Spouse Present		Female, No Spouse Present		Non-Family Householders		
	Total Householders	With Children	No Children	With Children	No Children	With Children	No Children	Living Alone	Not Alone	Living With Parents
Rhode Island—Cont.										
Providence County	8,403	4.9%	0.7%	3.7%	9.6%	15.5%	5.9%	25.3%	34.3%	51.7%
Washington County	2,106	0.0%	0.0%	0.0%	0.0%	0.0%	7.7%	39.6%	52.6%	37.2%
South Carolina										
Aiken County	2,225	13.0%	24.4%	0.0%	0.0%	14.9%	2.4%	36.1%	9.2%	59.4%
Anderson County	2,858	18.3%	20.9%	0.0%	10.8%	19.6%	0.0%	21.0%	9.4%	51.6%
Beaufort County	2,176	8.0%	12.9%	0.0%	2.0%	16.8%	0.0%	39.1%	21.2%	34.8%
Berkeley County	3,356	11.5%	2.4%	1.9%	5.9%	16.6%	0.0%	32.4%	29.4%	50.4%
Charleston County	7,980	4.9%	4.1%	4.4%	6.4%	11.2%	2.5%	27.3%	39.2%	41.2%
Dorchester County	2,979	12.3%	9.7%	1.9%	0.0%	6.3%	13.4%	21.6%	34.8%	47.1%
Florence County	1,283	17.1%	0.0%	10.1%	0.0%	10.6%	0.0%	26.7%	35.6%	52.9%
Greenville County	6,514	3.1%	5.9%	4.0%	8.7%	26.2%	1.8%	31.9%	18.5%	51.4%
Horry County	3,495	8.8%	1.5%	0.0%	8.1%	22.1%	1.6%	12.2%	45.7%	47.5%
Lexington County	3,750	7.2%	11.6%	0.0%	0.0%	12.9%	3.5%	14.8%	50.0%	55.3%
Orangeburg County	1,943	12.8%	0.0%	0.0%	20.0%	31.1%	6.1%	23.7%	6.2%	41.5%
Pickens County	1,969	3.6%	2.5%	0.0%	4.9%	7.1%	7.9%	24.5%	49.6%	30.1%
Richland County	8,872	0.3%	3.0%	2.3%	2.0%	14.2%	0.0%	33.0%	45.2%	25.2%
Spartanburg County	5,356	1.3%	8.3%	7.7%	5.2%	25.3%	0.6%	41.6%	10.0%	51.5%
Sumter County	1,802	11.3%	19.2%	0.0%	14.4%	20.1%	1.4%	33.5%	0.0%	51.4%
York County	3,636	10.0%	5.6%	1.1%	5.5%	27.1%	0.0%	33.5%	17.3%	53.9%
South Dakota										
Minnehaha County	3,810	12.6%	3.8%	2.4%	0.0%	2.2%	0.0%	16.1%	63.0%	34.8%
Pennington County	2,329	0.0%	6.0%	12.6%	4.5%	3.0%	0.0%	34.7%	39.2%	29.4%
Tennessee										
Blount County	1,891	7.9%	0.0%	0.0%	11.5%	11.9%	0.0%	15.0%	53.8%	46.5%
Bradley County	1,005	11.0%	8.8%	0.0%	35.9%	40.3%	0.0%	4.0%	0.0%	45.1%
Davidson County	10,972	5.1%	7.2%	2.0%	10.9%	17.4%	3.3%	26.9%	27.4%	37.6%
Hamilton County	5,472	7.9%	6.5%	12.3%	3.6%	12.7%	0.5%	29.5%	27.0%	44.6%
Knox County	11,701	6.8%	5.7%	0.0%	1.3%	8.9%	0.5%	25.7%	50.9%	36.4%
Madison County	1,077	1.9%	16.3%	0.0%	0.0%	17.1%	0.0%	24.3%	40.3%	31.7%
Montgomery County	5,123	18.4%	20.4%	0.0%	7.7%	20.8%	5.4%	17.8%	9.5%	38.0%
Rutherford County	8,205	0.0%	12.8%	3.2%	5.5%	13.3%	1.2%	26.3%	37.7%	37.7%
Sevier County	1,414	28.1%	10.5%	0.0%	0.0%	18.7%	10.4%	23.6%	8.7%	58.9%
Shelby County	13,579	2.2%	6.3%	6.2%	2.8%	22.7%	2.9%	36.1%	20.8%	55.7%
Sullivan County	1,082	18.1%	6.3%	0.0%	0.0%	29.7%	0.0%	7.5%	38.4%	57.6%
Sumner County	1,479	35.2%	7.0%	24.4%	0.0%	9.1%	2.1%	0.0%	22.2%	65.3%
Washington County	2,698	8.5%	16.3%	0.0%	6.7%	22.6%	0.0%	22.8%	23.1%	44.2%
Williamson County	843	0.0%	15.8%	0.0%	0.0%	24.0%	0.0%	43.4%	16.8%	87.0%
Wilson County	809	11.2%	8.3%	0.0%	3.3%	54.3%	0.0%	14.1%	8.8%	60.6%
Texas										
Bell County	6,506	10.8%	23.2%	2.0%	2.5%	15.2%	1.4%	33.2%	11.7%	46.2%
Bexar County	29,081	11.2%	4.5%	6.0%	3.0%	10.2%	3.1%	34.2%	27.8%	52.9%
Bowie County	1,664	49.8%	2.8%	0.0%	0.8%	20.7%	0.0%	4.5%	21.5%	58.7%
Brazoria County	4,203	24.1%	12.1%	9.7%	9.0%	11.8%	0.0%	27.8%	5.5%	66.1%
Brazos County	16,407	1.3%	4.1%	1.4%	3.6%	0.5%	5.3%	29.7%	54.1%	14.8%
Cameron County	2,899	43.3%	4.2%	0.0%	0.0%	25.3%	0.0%	11.5%	15.8%	74.1%
Collin County	11,832	6.0%	5.9%	5.1%	4.4%	5.2%	4.1%	46.3%	23.0%	63.0%
Comal County	540	15.7%	43.3%	0.0%	0.0%	0.0%	0.0%	24.8%	16.1%	73.3%
Dallas County	41,716	12.8%	8.7%	5.9%	7.0%	20.2%	3.3%	25.2%	16.8%	53.3%
Denton County	11,897	4.5%	9.5%	0.8%	4.5%	7.1%	1.3%	25.8%	46.4%	46.3%
Ector County	3,225	25.9%	0.0%	10.3%	7.6%	28.7%	0.0%	9.6%	17.9%	47.7%
El Paso County	12,714	30.6%	9.8%	1.6%	4.6%	18.0%	4.5%	19.3%	11.6%	62.1%
Ellis County	1,975	26.0%	4.9%	0.0%	0.0%	34.7%	3.3%	0.0%	31.1%	61.3%
Fort Bend County	4,125	10.8%	0.0%	0.0%	9.4%	12.8%	0.0%	30.2%	36.9%	79.7%
Galveston County	4,779	19.5%	6.9%	0.0%	2.7%	15.6%	3.0%	35.7%	16.7%	63.9%
Grayson County	2,306	27.8%	2.4%	5.0%	0.0%	30.8%	0.0%	13.7%	20.2%	40.1%
Gregg County	3,520	10.8%	4.7%	0.0%	0.0%	36.5%	0.0%	30.0%	18.1%	40.2%
Guadalupe County	1,244	0.0%	3.6%	0.0%	4.9%	31.1%	8.7%	15.4%	36.3%	64.9%
Harris County	65,224	13.3%	7.7%	4.0%	6.5%	15.7%	6.8%	26.7%	19.2%	58.0%
Hays County	7,666	3.2%	5.3%	0.0%	0.0%	4.3%	3.3%	33.4%	50.5%	27.0%
Hidalgo County	8,746	23.8%	3.1%	0.5%	8.3%	23.3%	9.1%	13.8%	18.0%	72.3%
Jefferson County	4,699	11.6%	9.2%	6.1%	0.0%	22.0%	0.0%	49.0%	2.1%	58.2%
Johnson County	2,265	48.8%	6.4%	2.4%	5.2%	12.3%	3.3%	18.7%	2.9%	41.5%
Kaufman County	1,027	21.5%	15.0%	0.0%	0.0%	29.9%	0.0%	16.6%	17.0%	60.6%
Lubbock County	14,612	5.9%	7.1%	0.0%	5.6%	9.1%	2.5%	44.4%	25.4%	30.2%
McLennan County	7,816	3.5%	3.0%	3.2%	3.4%	18.3%	0.7%	31.9%	35.9%	37.4%
Midland County	3,405	18.2%	7.3%	0.0%	12.2%	18.6%	0.0%	14.2%	29.4%	39.8%
Montgomery County	5,535	19.1%	11.4%	6.6%	1.6%	12.2%	0.0%	35.1%	13.9%	64.0%
Nueces County	8,869	10.5%	2.5%	4.4%	10.9%	14.6%	3.9%	20.0%	33.2%	38.5%
Parker County	2,525	55.8%	7.0%	0.0%	0.0%	2.9%	1.3%	26.8%	6.2%	48.1%
Potter County	3,017	10.0%	10.3%	11.2%	0.0%	39.9%	0.0%	13.9%	14.8%	43.0%
Randall County	3,873	15.5%	9.2%	0.0%	0.0%	3.9%	2.3%	34.4%	34.6%	39.5%
Smith County	3,550	7.7%	11.7%	2.7%	0.0%	16.3%	0.0%	20.7%	41.0%	43.9%
Tarrant County	32,947	7.0%	9.6%	5.1%	8.2%	15.6%	3.9%	24.2%	26.4%	53.4%
Taylor County	6,002	7.8%	5.9%	6.2%	0.0%	9.5%	2.5%	42.8%	25.2%	28.8%
Tom Green County	2,760	13.9%	8.0%	3.9%	5.8%	12.1%	4.8%	8.6%	42.7%	24.7%
Travis County	27,624	2.2%	3.7%	1.2%	3.1%	5.6%	2.4%	30.6%	51.2%	31.8%

Table D-2: Counties—Household Relationship—*Continued*

| | | 25 to 31 | | | | | | | | |
| | Total Householders | Married Couple Households | | Male, No Spouse Present | | Female, No Spouse Present | | Non-Family Householders | | Living With Parents |
		With Children	No Children	With Children	No Children	With Children	No Children	Living Alone	Not Alone	
Rhode Island—Cont.										
Providence County....................	25,052	12.0%	10.5%	5.7%	3.7%	23.6%	2.9%	24.8%	16.7%	27.9%
Washington County....................	2,769	21.7%	21.9%	7.6%	0.0%	14.3%	0.0%	22.5%	12.0%	25.5%
South Carolina										
Aiken County...........................	4,947	39.0%	7.2%	0.0%	0.6%	10.5%	0.9%	30.9%	11.0%	32.3%
Anderson County	6,955	26.4%	17.0%	10.5%	0.0%	18.3%	0.0%	21.7%	6.1%	22.0%
Beaufort County	5,619	39.4%	4.0%	3.0%	1.4%	26.0%	0.0%	16.6%	9.5%	23.5%
Berkeley County	7,075	30.3%	10.4%	0.0%	2.6%	13.2%	1.2%	22.5%	19.8%	15.1%
Charleston County.....................	17,250	11.2%	18.9%	1.2%	1.3%	11.8%	0.8%	28.3%	26.5%	15.1%
Dorchester County	3,430	35.6%	15.6%	0.0%	5.3%	17.9%	0.0%	12.9%	12.7%	21.8%
Florence County	4,108	32.1%	18.1%	1.7%	0.0%	30.6%	0.0%	13.1%	4.4%	36.3%
Greenville County	20,249	19.0%	17.8%	3.5%	3.6%	18.1%	1.2%	27.6%	9.3%	22.9%
Horry County	8,727	24.3%	9.0%	14.0%	6.2%	14.4%	0.0%	16.5%	15.5%	16.9%
Lexington County......................	10,242	29.1%	11.9%	2.7%	0.0%	14.5%	1.5%	22.7%	17.6%	17.9%
Orangeburg County	2,655	15.6%	0.0%	0.0%	25.7%	13.4%	0.0%	32.8%	12.4%	36.1%
Pickens County	3,416	22.0%	14.0%	1.3%	0.0%	24.5%	1.4%	24.1%	12.8%	15.7%
Richland County........................	16,353	16.4%	9.7%	0.0%	0.4%	16.4%	0.6%	35.7%	20.9%	21.8%
Spartanburg County	9,433	29.2%	7.6%	4.5%	0.0%	24.0%	0.0%	22.9%	11.8%	28.4%
Sumter County	3,421	36.6%	0.8%	0.0%	0.0%	22.4%	3.8%	20.6%	15.7%	20.6%
York County	8,628	29.9%	14.9%	0.0%	2.8%	16.9%	5.4%	28.5%	1.7%	15.9%
South Dakota										
Minnehaha County	11,742	24.1%	7.5%	13.0%	0.0%	11.8%	2.7%	20.4%	20.6%	12.1%
Pennington County	4,571	49.7%	3.3%	1.2%	0.0%	24.2%	0.0%	12.7%	9.0%	11.6%
Tennessee										
Blount County	4,458	39.1%	14.0%	0.0%	4.6%	12.2%	1.7%	16.1%	12.3%	22.6%
Bradley County	3,654	14.6%	16.8%	6.8%	0.0%	19.6%	0.0%	11.5%	30.7%	13.1%
Davidson County.......................	42,266	13.9%	13.5%	0.5%	2.2%	10.4%	1.2%	35.8%	22.5%	12.1%
Hamilton County	14,112	25.0%	13.0%	2.7%	3.9%	17.0%	2.8%	26.0%	9.5%	19.9%
Knox County	21,073	22.1%	13.7%	8.0%	0.5%	8.0%	0.4%	28.7%	18.5%	15.4%
Madison County	3,261	28.1%	4.3%	14.6%	3.6%	30.1%	0.0%	16.1%	3.2%	21.8%
Montgomery County	14,010	35.9%	22.1%	6.2%	0.0%	6.7%	0.0%	19.9%	9.3%	5.6%
Rutherford County	13,392	26.8%	17.1%	5.2%	1.8%	7.8%	0.8%	18.0%	22.4%	11.3%
Sevier County	2,409	17.8%	29.2%	9.9%	3.4%	7.4%	5.7%	24.0%	2.6%	14.9%
Shelby County	41,769	18.2%	8.4%	3.4%	4.3%	26.1%	1.9%	27.9%	9.8%	23.8%
Sullivan County	4,044	31.4%	13.8%	7.0%	0.0%	11.0%	1.0%	26.4%	9.3%	27.2%
Sumner County	6,881	30.5%	11.3%	5.7%	8.2%	24.0%	1.2%	14.6%	4.6%	23.4%
Washington County....................	4,311	31.1%	18.7%	0.0%	0.0%	0.0%	2.4%	27.0%	20.8%	15.9%
Williamson County.....................	4,109	33.2%	32.5%	0.0%	0.0%	5.5%	1.3%	15.6%	11.9%	28.3%
Wilson County	3,232	52.5%	1.4%	10.3%	0.0%	18.9%	0.0%	16.9%	0.0%	27.6%
Texas										
Bell County..............................	16,777	37.0%	17.0%	1.1%	0.6%	15.3%	0.5%	25.0%	3.5%	20.7%
Bexar County............................	80,465	26.3%	11.1%	2.8%	1.7%	18.0%	2.2%	26.3%	11.6%	25.1%
Bowie County............................	3,569	26.3%	24.5%	6.9%	0.0%	23.0%	0.0%	11.7%	7.6%	21.8%
Brazoria County........................	14,174	41.1%	9.6%	7.4%	0.9%	10.4%	0.9%	20.1%	9.7%	19.2%
Brazos County..........................	10,876	22.4%	13.3%	3.3%	0.8%	14.4%	0.0%	29.6%	16.2%	11.1%
Cameron County	10,319	43.6%	11.5%	5.7%	1.1%	19.7%	0.0%	13.2%	5.2%	45.4%
Collin County	31,263	24.0%	21.5%	1.8%	0.0%	10.4%	1.4%	24.0%	17.0%	14.7%
Comal County	4,390	22.7%	10.5%	6.0%	0.0%	10.0%	0.0%	25.3%	25.5%	16.8%
Dallas County	120,908	23.5%	10.6%	5.0%	3.0%	17.8%	1.5%	26.6%	12.0%	19.0%
Denton County	31,080	23.4%	16.1%	2.4%	2.5%	11.3%	0.6%	27.4%	16.3%	18.0%
Ector County	7,064	42.4%	3.4%	6.5%	4.1%	14.3%	2.9%	16.3%	10.2%	23.1%
El Paso County.........................	28,187	37.8%	14.8%	6.4%	4.3%	14.3%	1.2%	14.5%	6.6%	29.6%
Ellis County	5,609	54.3%	6.0%	0.0%	4.0%	11.4%	0.0%	19.5%	4.8%	26.5%
Fort Bend County	17,157	27.4%	18.2%	1.2%	0.6%	19.1%	3.8%	26.4%	3.4%	37.6%
Galveston County	8,603	36.0%	8.8%	1.1%	2.9%	9.8%	1.6%	22.5%	17.3%	25.7%
Grayson County	4,127	44.7%	8.5%	4.9%	0.0%	21.1%	0.0%	14.7%	6.1%	12.5%
Gregg County...........................	4,911	45.9%	7.1%	4.6%	5.7%	15.3%	0.0%	16.4%	4.9%	20.3%
Guadalupe County.....................	5,231	34.8%	16.0%	5.4%	0.0%	19.5%	0.6%	16.7%	7.0%	28.1%
Harris County	207,424	25.4%	12.6%	3.6%	3.4%	14.0%	1.1%	27.4%	12.5%	20.9%
Hays County............................	6,426	14.5%	5.7%	7.6%	0.0%	13.7%	11.1%	15.9%	31.5%	13.7%
Hidalgo County	21,139	51.2%	3.4%	2.4%	2.2%	24.1%	1.4%	9.5%	5.7%	38.4%
Jefferson County.......................	10,871	30.0%	8.2%	0.0%	1.1%	18.6%	4.0%	30.3%	7.8%	19.6%
Johnson County........................	4,553	34.5%	17.7%	15.1%	0.0%	4.3%	0.3%	5.2%	22.8%	18.9%
Kaufman County	2,726	42.9%	6.9%	13.1%	2.2%	5.5%	1.3%	17.7%	10.6%	36.6%
Lubbock County........................	12,382	27.1%	10.2%	2.0%	4.9%	9.8%	5.9%	27.1%	13.0%	14.2%
McLennan County	10,637	19.4%	11.0%	2.7%	0.5%	27.3%	0.0%	24.5%	14.5%	15.8%
Midland County	6,282	27.9%	7.3%	1.4%	3.9%	12.3%	0.0%	29.2%	18.1%	22.9%
Montgomery County	14,424	36.3%	14.1%	0.3%	0.0%	25.6%	0.0%	15.2%	8.5%	18.2%
Nueces County	14,489	24.8%	7.7%	2.7%	1.3%	24.0%	2.0%	24.3%	13.1%	23.5%
Parker County	2,854	45.1%	4.2%	7.2%	10.5%	5.5%	0.0%	23.7%	3.7%	21.6%
Potter County	6,156	29.1%	8.5%	12.7%	2.2%	25.8%	0.0%	10.9%	10.9%	12.8%
Randall County	6,715	26.9%	8.2%	7.0%	2.2%	8.5%	0.0%	19.0%	28.2%	11.4%
Smith County	7,822	39.2%	8.4%	0.0%	1.0%	16.9%	1.2%	22.1%	11.2%	18.7%
Tarrant County	86,253	30.8%	14.4%	4.2%	2.7%	14.1%	1.9%	22.0%	9.9%	20.7%
Taylor County	5,814	37.2%	20.9%	1.1%	1.6%	11.2%	0.0%	17.9%	10.2%	11.7%
Tom Green County	5,880	43.5%	6.5%	0.0%	0.0%	4.6%	0.0%	28.2%	17.3%	5.4%
Travis County	72,399	11.3%	15.5%	1.2%	3.2%	8.9%	0.9%	28.7%	30.3%	8.9%

Table D-2: Counties—Household Relationship—*Continued*

		Married Couple Households		Male, No Spouse Present		Female, No Spouse Present		Non-Family Householders		
	Total Householders	With Children	No Children	With Children	No Children	With Children	No Children	Living Alone	Not Alone	Living With Parents
Texas—Cont.										
Webb County	2,081	12.0%	0.0%	16.4%	4.6%	35.4%	4.5%	19.3%	7.8%	71.0%
Wichita County	3,518	6.1%	17.9%	0.0%	2.7%	17.1%	0.0%	20.7%	35.5%	21.6%
Williamson County	4,760	7.9%	7.8%	1.0%	12.7%	10.7%	0.2%	32.6%	27.1%	55.5%
Utah										
Cache County	3,693	1.9%	38.5%	0.0%	0.0%	9.0%	0.0%	6.9%	43.6%	25.1%
Davis County	4,840	11.0%	43.1%	4.3%	1.5%	10.7%	7.2%	6.5%	15.8%	54.6%
Salt Lake County	16,669	13.7%	16.6%	4.6%	7.6%	11.2%	1.8%	14.4%	30.2%	50.6%
Utah County	14,823	20.9%	38.3%	1.5%	1.8%	4.8%	2.6%	2.9%	27.3%	35.3%
Washington County	1,798	51.7%	17.0%	0.0%	0.0%	0.0%	0.0%	0.0%	31.3%	42.6%
Weber County	3,833	12.1%	23.3%	0.0%	0.0%	17.7%	0.0%	6.0%	40.8%	52.5%
Vermont										
Chittenden County	3,495	16.2%	0.0%	0.0%	0.0%	5.2%	0.0%	16.7%	61.9%	26.0%
Virginia										
Albemarle County	1,980	0.0%	2.8%	0.0%	0.0%	7.3%	0.0%	4.6%	85.3%	14.6%
Arlington County	3,457	2.0%	1.0%	0.0%	15.9%	12.5%	0.0%	27.6%	41.1%	31.7%
Chesterfield County	2,600	11.7%	30.0%	0.0%	0.0%	18.8%	0.0%	19.7%	19.8%	68.4%
Fairfax County	6,379	5.0%	14.3%	0.0%	6.9%	0.8%	6.5%	31.1%	35.4%	66.7%
Hanover County	775	22.8%	0.0%	0.0%	0.0%	23.4%	0.0%	0.0%	53.8%	63.2%
Henrico County	5,202	0.0%	4.9%	0.0%	1.4%	20.5%	2.0%	22.1%	49.1%	51.2%
Loudoun County	1,112	0.0%	14.1%	11.2%	6.0%	0.0%	12.9%	47.4%	8.5%	73.5%
Montgomery County	7,857	9.7%	4.6%	0.0%	0.0%	1.2%	6.5%	17.8%	60.2%	12.1%
Prince William County	2,761	13.9%	5.4%	4.5%	12.7%	17.2%	0.0%	28.9%	17.5%	67.7%
Roanoke County	611	0.0%	35.7%	0.0%	0.0%	0.0%	0.0%	0.0%	64.3%	55.7%
Spotsylvania County	635	13.2%	2.4%	0.0%	32.9%	0.0%	0.0%	7.7%	43.8%	78.4%
Stafford County	2,338	10.8%	32.7%	0.0%	5.4%	2.3%	12.7%	10.8%	25.2%	47.1%
Washington										
Benton County	3,480	18.5%	12.7%	4.8%	7.1%	0.0%	15.2%	9.6%	32.0%	41.6%
Clark County	3,843	5.4%	11.1%	1.0%	4.1%	17.7%	9.4%	23.1%	28.3%	64.3%
Cowlitz County	1,150	0.0%	20.9%	15.3%	0.0%	21.7%	0.0%	11.5%	30.7%	62.9%
Grant County	958	9.6%	0.0%	0.0%	0.0%	18.0%	0.0%	38.7%	33.7%	38.0%
King County	33,266	2.1%	5.4%	2.6%	3.8%	4.7%	4.6%	28.1%	48.7%	42.1%
Kitsap County	3,462	25.9%	17.6%	0.0%	0.0%	11.5%	0.0%	18.1%	27.0%	46.0%
Pierce County	12,662	15.7%	10.8%	4.1%	2.9%	15.3%	1.3%	27.3%	22.6%	49.1%
Skagit County	1,688	14.6%	18.2%	0.0%	13.6%	25.9%	2.0%	22.2%	3.5%	52.6%
Snohomish County	7,524	16.6%	8.3%	5.0%	4.1%	19.2%	6.7%	13.1%	27.0%	65.8%
Spokane County	10,678	5.5%	5.4%	6.3%	3.9%	7.8%	5.4%	23.9%	41.7%	32.3%
Thurston County	4,401	8.0%	8.9%	9.8%	0.0%	3.6%	1.8%	23.5%	44.5%	52.7%
Whatcom County	5,536	0.8%	2.4%	0.0%	0.0%	3.4%	12.6%	19.7%	61.2%	31.8%
Yakima County	2,771	31.3%	10.2%	2.7%	6.9%	13.9%	5.6%	8.9%	20.4%	58.0%
West Virginia										
Berkeley County	1,183	0.0%	15.3%	20.7%	0.0%	8.6%	0.0%	44.5%	10.9%	50.7%
Cabell County	1,565	0.0%	30.9%	0.0%	0.0%	6.1%	2.5%	15.8%	44.7%	34.5%
Kanawha County	2,671	17.5%	0.0%	34.6%	0.0%	15.1%	0.0%	14.9%	18.0%	44.8%
Monongalia County	5,718	4.2%	3.7%	0.0%	0.0%	4.8%	2.0%	53.2%	32.1%	26.8%
Wisconsin										
Brown County	3,494	11.2%	4.0%	0.0%	13.5%	22.2%	0.0%	11.7%	37.3%	51.6%
Dane County	15,345	0.7%	7.2%	0.0%	2.2%	4.0%	2.2%	29.6%	54.1%	24.4%
Eau Claire County	4,273	25.3%	1.7%	0.0%	0.0%	4.0%	0.0%	17.8%	51.2%	33.2%
Fond du Lac County	2,037	7.9%	34.2%	0.0%	0.0%	0.0%	14.3%	6.6%	37.1%	47.5%
Kenosha County	2,715	0.0%	4.1%	0.0%	0.0%	10.3%	0.0%	53.6%	31.9%	50.7%
La Crosse County	5,036	5.4%	0.0%	0.0%	0.0%	14.7%	0.0%	17.1%	62.8%	19.9%
Marathon County	2,262	0.0%	2.3%	16.2%	1.2%	37.9%	0.0%	26.4%	16.0%	58.3%
Milwaukee County	20,223	2.6%	2.5%	1.7%	2.9%	22.3%	5.1%	28.6%	34.2%	42.2%
Outagamie County	2,647	0.0%	9.9%	0.0%	3.7%	0.0%	0.0%	41.3%	45.0%	58.4%
Racine County	2,295	15.6%	5.9%	14.7%	12.9%	7.3%	0.0%	26.8%	16.8%	66.1%
Rock County	3,813	0.0%	0.0%	0.0%	20.9%	42.4%	0.0%	8.4%	28.3%	48.5%
Sheboygan County	1,595	0.0%	0.0%	0.0%	13.6%	35.2%	0.0%	24.8%	26.4%	52.7%
Walworth County	2,434	3.3%	7.9%	0.0%	1.6%	0.0%	0.0%	14.5%	72.8%	35.4%
Washington County	1,796	8.8%	0.0%	0.0%	23.7%	0.0%	10.1%	40.8%	16.6%	67.6%
Waukesha County	3,991	0.0%	0.0%	0.0%	15.6%	5.3%	0.0%	45.5%	33.5%	68.5%
Winnebago County	4,984	5.4%	6.0%	0.0%	2.6%	13.1%	1.3%	13.9%	57.7%	27.4%
Wyoming										
Laramie County	3,446	5.5%	17.6%	0.0%	12.7%	15.9%	0.0%	30.6%	17.7%	31.1%

Table D-2: Counties—Household Relationship—Continued

		25 to 31								
	Total Householders	Married Couple Households		Male, No Spouse Present		Female, No Spouse Present		Non-Family Householders		Living With Parents
		With Children	No Children	With Children	No Children	With Children	No Children	Living Alone	Not Alone	
Texas—Cont.										
Webb County	8,699	42.6%	10.7%	4.8%	4.9%	24.5%	3.1%	7.2%	2.1%	29.6%
Wichita County	7,667	31.8%	4.5%	2.7%	0.6%	31.1%	1.6%	24.9%	2.7%	7.9%
Williamson County	15,826	35.7%	17.4%	4.9%	2.0%	4.6%	1.5%	21.2%	12.7%	23.0%
Utah										
Cache County	6,666	34.3%	25.7%	10.4%	0.9%	2.3%	0.0%	14.4%	11.9%	10.0%
Davis County	11,404	57.5%	20.0%	1.2%	0.0%	5.0%	0.7%	11.4%	4.3%	23.5%
Salt Lake County	46,896	34.1%	18.7%	3.6%	2.5%	7.3%	0.2%	19.0%	14.5%	20.3%
Utah County	23,587	58.7%	17.0%	2.6%	1.0%	3.8%	1.5%	6.6%	8.8%	13.1%
Washington County	5,193	66.5%	3.5%	0.6%	0.0%	12.7%	1.8%	5.7%	9.1%	4.6%
Weber County	9,382	43.4%	10.7%	3.1%	0.7%	13.5%	0.0%	17.0%	11.5%	13.8%
Vermont										
Chittenden County	6,480	10.9%	9.8%	0.0%	0.0%	21.0%	0.0%	35.5%	22.7%	18.1%
Virginia										
Albemarle County	4,748	27.3%	15.9%	0.0%	0.0%	10.2%	0.0%	28.1%	18.6%	10.6%
Arlington County	22,892	6.0%	20.8%	0.0%	6.6%	0.0%	1.1%	37.4%	28.1%	5.0%
Chesterfield County	7,922	22.8%	17.7%	0.7%	3.7%	23.0%	0.8%	14.7%	16.7%	36.5%
Fairfax County	39,979	19.7%	22.6%	2.4%	5.5%	6.7%	1.5%	20.1%	21.5%	21.0%
Hanover County	3,597	52.4%	17.9%	5.2%	0.0%	13.4%	0.4%	9.8%	0.9%	22.4%
Henrico County	13,702	22.9%	21.2%	3.5%	2.0%	24.0%	0.5%	21.1%	4.9%	16.3%
Loudoun County	11,275	31.4%	21.2%	1.0%	3.2%	4.3%	3.0%	18.3%	17.6%	23.5%
Montgomery County	2,356	31.7%	12.7%	0.0%	0.0%	15.7%	0.0%	30.3%	9.5%	8.2%
Prince William County	16,116	47.9%	9.1%	4.0%	0.0%	11.7%	4.8%	14.4%	8.2%	25.9%
Roanoke County	2,998	37.2%	7.9%	9.2%	3.8%	9.6%	0.0%	26.7%	5.6%	16.3%
Spotsylvania County	3,039	33.9%	27.6%	3.1%	2.0%	18.2%	0.0%	12.1%	3.1%	23.4%
Stafford County	4,323	24.2%	20.3%	0.0%	5.3%	15.8%	0.0%	32.5%	1.9%	33.0%
Washington										
Benton County	7,334	29.9%	7.4%	14.4%	1.6%	17.2%	7.6%	11.3%	10.6%	14.1%
Clark County	13,190	36.4%	13.4%	4.0%	1.6%	11.6%	2.4%	15.7%	14.9%	25.1%
Cowlitz County	3,186	46.9%	0.8%	16.4%	0.0%	17.6%	0.0%	5.2%	13.0%	20.1%
Grant County	3,787	47.3%	11.5%	0.0%	2.1%	1.7%	0.0%	7.7%	29.8%	8.8%
King County	107,611	13.2%	16.9%	2.5%	1.6%	6.9%	2.1%	31.5%	25.3%	12.4%
Kitsap County	11,280	34.6%	8.4%	5.6%	0.0%	14.2%	1.1%	23.9%	12.2%	16.3%
Pierce County	33,152	31.7%	14.4%	5.0%	2.0%	9.0%	1.6%	22.1%	14.2%	19.2%
Skagit County	3,904	38.1%	2.9%	9.5%	0.0%	16.2%	0.0%	20.9%	12.3%	12.9%
Snohomish County	28,926	29.5%	16.7%	3.6%	2.0%	12.5%	0.2%	19.1%	16.3%	18.0%
Spokane County	24,276	25.5%	12.2%	6.8%	0.0%	15.8%	0.7%	23.8%	15.3%	10.9%
Thurston County	10,383	34.9%	20.9%	3.3%	0.0%	14.7%	0.2%	14.4%	11.7%	22.5%
Whatcom County	7,448	31.2%	14.3%	2.9%	1.6%	10.5%	2.0%	16.6%	20.9%	10.3%
Yakima County	7,763	44.8%	8.2%	5.1%	3.9%	16.2%	0.7%	15.8%	5.4%	22.5%
West Virginia										
Berkeley County	3,560	21.0%	14.2%	10.6%	0.0%	20.6%	2.5%	22.9%	8.2%	25.2%
Cabell County	4,300	36.7%	12.9%	6.6%	4.2%	19.1%	0.0%	15.6%	4.8%	22.3%
Kanawha County	8,796	23.5%	5.8%	13.8%	0.8%	20.7%	2.8%	26.2%	6.3%	17.6%
Monongalia County	5,765	15.6%	7.5%	0.8%	1.6%	21.6%	0.0%	34.3%	18.7%	16.5%
Wisconsin										
Brown County	10,573	14.7%	20.3%	7.3%	3.1%	20.0%	0.0%	21.6%	13.0%	15.4%
Dane County	31,677	18.1%	18.0%	1.8%	1.4%	7.0%	0.7%	38.3%	14.7%	8.7%
Eau Claire County	3,027	38.0%	20.8%	0.0%	5.2%	6.5%	0.0%	21.7%	7.8%	18.3%
Fond du Lac County	2,429	32.9%	16.1%	1.4%	0.0%	5.9%	0.0%	26.2%	17.5%	18.9%
Kenosha County	6,287	30.0%	10.3%	1.2%	0.0%	19.6%	3.7%	23.5%	11.7%	24.5%
La Crosse County	5,559	30.7%	8.2%	2.9%	5.2%	8.0%	1.1%	22.3%	21.6%	8.5%
Marathon County	5,383	33.6%	10.7%	8.3%	1.5%	2.9%	3.5%	29.4%	10.2%	11.7%
Milwaukee County	56,868	14.4%	8.8%	3.4%	2.5%	23.7%	0.6%	32.4%	14.1%	17.0%
Outagamie County	8,607	29.2%	10.2%	6.3%	0.0%	21.1%	0.0%	19.1%	14.1%	10.6%
Racine County	8,048	21.2%	13.9%	7.8%	0.0%	24.0%	4.8%	25.0%	3.2%	16.2%
Rock County	5,255	29.6%	8.3%	11.1%	0.0%	8.4%	1.7%	36.6%	4.3%	26.1%
Sheboygan County	4,782	36.7%	19.9%	7.5%	0.4%	10.4%	0.0%	14.3%	10.7%	13.0%
Walworth County	3,443	42.5%	9.2%	8.5%	0.0%	19.4%	0.0%	3.0%	17.4%	16.4%
Washington County	4,393	47.3%	17.2%	3.5%	1.0%	1.2%	0.0%	26.9%	2.8%	21.3%
Waukesha County	11,738	26.9%	20.5%	0.0%	3.3%	11.0%	0.0%	24.7%	13.6%	24.6%
Winnebago County	7,242	9.4%	24.1%	5.6%	0.0%	15.0%	0.0%	34.3%	11.6%	12.6%
Wyoming										
Laramie County	3,854	31.8%	17.6%	0.0%	2.6%	6.6%	0.0%	34.0%	7.5%	8.9%

Table D-3: Places—Household Relationship

		Married Couple Households		Male, No Spouse Present		Female, No Spouse Present		Non-Family Householders		
	Total Householders	With Children	No Children	With Children	No Children	With Children	No Children	Living Alone	Not Alone	Living With Parents
Alabama										
Birmingham city	4,541	10.0%	3.8%	0.0%	3.5%	36.3%	0.0%	25.8%	20.6%	46.9%
Huntsville city	3,339	15.8%	3.0%	9.8%	0.0%	17.1%	0.0%	41.6%	12.7%	47.8%
Mobile city	4,539	5.4%	3.2%	0.0%	0.0%	25.1%	1.7%	43.8%	20.8%	44.6%
Montgomery city	3,221	0.6%	0.0%	17.1%	1.5%	29.6%	2.0%	18.3%	31.0%	45.7%
Tuscaloosa city	4,081	4.6%	0.0%	0.0%	0.0%	0.0%	3.1%	41.0%	51.4%	26.8%
Alaska										
Anchorage municipality	6,309	17.7%	17.3%	6.5%	0.0%	7.4%	4.0%	11.4%	35.7%	42.3%
Arizona										
Chandler city	2,939	2.5%	3.1%	9.7%	4.9%	11.6%	0.0%	44.0%	24.2%	67.0%
Glendale city	2,902	3.9%	2.6%	8.4%	16.8%	14.3%	0.0%	39.1%	14.9%	61.9%
Mesa city	7,981	9.8%	13.9%	2.8%	12.2%	17.4%	1.9%	20.6%	21.4%	55.5%
Peoria city	1,227	20.5%	11.7%	0.0%	13.8%	13.7%	0.0%	21.2%	19.2%	64.0%
Phoenix city	27,358	9.5%	6.1%	1.6%	9.1%	21.2%	6.9%	25.0%	20.6%	53.6%
Scottsdale city	2,581	0.0%	4.8%	15.2%	4.1%	12.8%	8.7%	13.5%	40.9%	56.7%
Surprise city	1,174	15.0%	6.7%	0.0%	0.0%	11.2%	9.5%	29.5%	28.1%	59.0%
Tempe city	8,058	1.7%	2.7%	0.0%	4.3%	2.8%	2.5%	39.5%	46.5%	22.7%
Tucson city	17,729	6.1%	7.7%	4.0%	3.4%	19.4%	8.7%	26.4%	24.3%	39.4%
Yuma city	1,403	45.4%	10.9%	2.2%	0.0%	33.6%	7.9%	0.0%	0.0%	64.8%
Arkansas										
Little Rock city	3,223	13.0%	6.7%	0.0%	0.0%	8.1%	0.0%	56.2%	16.0%	56.8%
California										
Anaheim city	2,449	14.5%	5.6%	0.0%	12.7%	17.7%	3.2%	26.2%	20.2%	69.7%
Antioch city	1,173	16.4%	0.0%	0.0%	24.9%	24.7%	0.0%	5.6%	28.4%	59.2%
Bakersfield city	5,992	11.0%	2.9%	2.3%	10.0%	19.6%	5.9%	7.3%	40.9%	57.9%
Berkeley city	6,053	0.0%	2.6%	0.0%	0.0%	0.0%	0.8%	41.8%	54.8%	12.1%
Burbank city	777	13.4%	0.0%	0.0%	0.0%	0.0%	0.0%	76.8%	9.8%	69.6%
Carlsbad city	279	22.9%	15.8%	0.0%	0.0%	25.4%	35.8%	0.0%	0.0%	73.2%
Carson city	209	0.0%	0.0%	0.0%	56.5%	0.0%	0.0%	43.5%	0.0%	81.0%
Chula Vista city	2,333	6.5%	11.3%	0.0%	1.8%	27.6%	26.6%	8.5%	17.8%	73.0%
Clovis city	1,152	5.4%	4.8%	26.1%	0.0%	30.9%	5.2%	4.2%	23.4%	69.6%
Compton city	846	16.8%	0.0%	0.0%	0.0%	17.6%	39.7%	25.9%	0.0%	69.2%
Concord city	1,311	7.3%	0.0%	0.0%	7.2%	14.6%	0.0%	27.5%	43.5%	63.7%
Corona city	558	0.0%	0.0%	0.0%	16.1%	14.3%	7.3%	62.2%	0.0%	78.0%
Costa Mesa city	1,534	3.7%	3.3%	0.0%	0.0%	8.5%	3.3%	7.4%	73.9%	54.3%
Daly City city	640	0.0%	8.0%	0.0%	0.0%	0.0%	35.8%	0.0%	56.3%	61.9%
Downey city	878	0.0%	13.9%	0.0%	0.0%	22.1%	27.3%	0.0%	36.7%	82.1%
El Cajon city	989	0.0%	22.6%	20.6%	29.0%	0.0%	4.8%	16.0%	7.0%	65.3%
El Monte city	1,152	12.8%	0.0%	0.0%	14.4%	25.4%	0.0%	33.5%	13.8%	67.7%
Elk Grove city	574	74.2%	0.0%	0.0%	0.0%	0.0%	16.6%	0.0%	9.2%	75.1%
Escondido city	1,690	40.5%	17.9%	5.0%	13.8%	5.3%	2.6%	11.8%	3.1%	59.4%
Fairfield city	632	8.7%	39.4%	14.9%	0.0%	11.4%	11.7%	0.0%	13.9%	63.6%
Fontana city	1,338	17.7%	0.0%	9.1%	27.7%	11.7%	17.9%	0.0%	16.0%	68.7%
Fremont city	1,381	30.7%	0.0%	0.0%	9.6%	24.5%	0.0%	0.0%	35.2%	68.5%
Fresno city	8,369	10.3%	4.7%	10.0%	5.9%	24.6%	5.0%	21.3%	18.2%	55.5%
Fullerton city	2,537	3.0%	0.0%	2.2%	12.2%	5.6%	17.7%	0.0%	59.4%	53.1%
Garden Grove city	1,026	25.6%	0.0%	0.0%	4.6%	27.3%	4.0%	4.8%	33.7%	66.1%
Glendale city	1,958	4.6%	0.0%	0.0%	8.7%	26.4%	7.5%	34.3%	18.5%	73.8%
Hayward city	2,133	11.7%	0.0%	7.9%	20.3%	7.4%	2.4%	11.7%	38.7%	59.1%
Hesperia city	1,548	17.8%	0.0%	11.8%	3.7%	6.7%	5.4%	29.7%	24.9%	74.9%
Inglewood city	592	0.0%	36.5%	12.3%	23.6%	17.9%	9.6%	0.0%	0.0%	68.8%
Irvine city	3,315	0.0%	0.0%	2.4%	3.4%	0.0%	6.9%	14.5%	72.9%	37.9%
Jurupa Valley city	281	0.0%	0.0%	18.9%	27.4%	53.7%	0.0%	0.0%	0.0%	72.4%
Lancaster city	1,705	3.8%	15.7%	4.6%	2.9%	26.2%	8.9%	31.0%	7.0%	70.2%
Long Beach city	4,043	10.4%	0.0%	16.6%	5.6%	2.8%	1.4%	17.6%	45.6%	61.7%
Los Angeles city	49,946	3.6%	4.0%	2.4%	7.7%	10.1%	7.7%	27.8%	36.8%	54.6%
Mission Viejo city	331	0.0%	100.0%	0.0%	0.0%	0.0%	0.0%	0.0%	0.0%	83.3%
Modesto city	2,479	6.5%	0.0%	10.6%	0.0%	36.7%	0.0%	20.7%	25.5%	62.4%
Moreno Valley city	1,547	7.4%	3.9%	0.0%	11.4%	35.0%	11.0%	3.5%	27.9%	67.8%
Murrieta city	287	27.9%	15.3%	25.8%	0.0%	0.0%	0.0%	0.0%	31.0%	68.8%
Norwalk city	488	36.5%	0.0%	0.0%	11.5%	35.2%	10.7%	0.0%	6.1%	74.3%
Oakland city	4,743	7.3%	0.0%	0.0%	6.4%	7.2%	2.7%	38.9%	37.5%	55.3%
Oceanside city	3,860	18.5%	58.2%	0.0%	0.0%	0.0%	5.1%	13.6%	4.7%	29.8%
Ontario city	1,057	10.5%	6.3%	14.4%	37.8%	0.0%	0.0%	18.0%	13.0%	74.6%
Orange city	1,101	4.4%	11.1%	18.3%	20.1%	0.0%	0.0%	4.3%	42.0%	58.2%
Oxnard city	1,082	24.4%	32.5%	3.3%	0.0%	0.0%	11.5%	9.1%	19.1%	55.2%
Palmdale city	750	22.8%	0.0%	0.0%	7.3%	17.3%	0.0%	7.1%	45.5%	79.9%
Pasadena city	2,400	3.8%	2.4%	5.4%	12.4%	5.8%	5.3%	14.4%	50.6%	35.5%
Pomona city	1,577	15.7%	0.0%	10.5%	2.2%	16.6%	2.7%	18.8%	33.7%	63.6%
Rancho Cucamonga city	1,775	0.0%	0.0%	0.0%	15.1%	6.4%	0.0%	31.5%	47.0%	68.5%
Redding city	1,910	2.3%	4.8%	4.6%	0.0%	13.4%	0.0%	30.5%	44.4%	28.1%
Rialto city	1,053	16.9%	0.0%	5.0%	21.8%	30.3%	3.6%	12.3%	10.1%	61.8%
Richmond city	1,650	0.0%	11.9%	3.3%	7.6%	17.8%	13.5%	20.7%	25.3%	58.4%
Riverside city	5,060	11.5%	4.4%	13.0%	7.1%	15.1%	0.0%	9.5%	39.5%	55.3%
Roseville city	1,365	19.9%	0.0%	0.0%	0.0%	10.5%	0.0%	13.6%	55.9%	63.3%
Sacramento city	8,001	5.0%	6.8%	0.0%	6.5%	15.9%	6.5%	34.9%	24.3%	46.4%

Table D-3: Places—Household Relationship—*Continued*

		25 to 31								
		Married Couple Households		Male, No Spouse Present		Female, No Spouse Present		Non-Family Householders		
	Total Householders	With Children	No Children	With Children	No Children	With Children	No Children	Living Alone	Not Alone	Living With Parents
Alabama										
Birmingham city	9,706	19.5%	6.3%	4.1%	5.5%	24.1%	1.3%	27.8%	11.4%	20.7%
Huntsville city	8,081	17.2%	16.6%	5.7%	1.8%	9.6%	0.7%	42.6%	5.8%	16.4%
Mobile city	8,879	14.5%	6.9%	0.6%	0.0%	36.7%	1.3%	21.8%	18.2%	27.4%
Montgomery city	11,537	21.5%	2.6%	0.0%	3.1%	34.4%	0.0%	29.9%	8.5%	20.1%
Tuscaloosa city	4,133	21.6%	10.7%	7.7%	6.8%	16.5%	0.0%	33.6%	3.1%	18.3%
Alaska										
Anchorage municipality	13,425	27.3%	30.0%	4.0%	3.2%	13.6%	2.6%	10.5%	8.8%	16.3%
Arizona										
Chandler city	9,897	25.3%	17.5%	3.3%	3.1%	6.5%	1.8%	19.5%	23.0%	23.9%
Glendale city	9,835	21.0%	12.2%	5.5%	6.0%	16.0%	2.8%	28.9%	7.5%	24.3%
Mesa city	20,436	29.3%	9.0%	2.8%	2.0%	20.3%	0.3%	28.5%	7.8%	18.6%
Peoria city	5,334	19.2%	12.8%	14.2%	2.4%	15.7%	4.3%	27.1%	4.4%	22.7%
Phoenix city	62,754	22.0%	10.2%	7.1%	2.4%	15.5%	1.3%	26.3%	15.3%	20.1%
Scottsdale city	9,741	8.4%	12.0%	0.9%	0.0%	0.0%	1.4%	53.0%	24.2%	15.3%
Surprise city	3,340	48.5%	21.7%	0.0%	0.0%	19.5%	2.5%	6.0%	1.9%	17.4%
Tempe city	12,402	8.3%	16.3%	5.5%	3.6%	6.4%	4.1%	31.0%	24.7%	9.5%
Tucson city	24,673	14.6%	8.2%	4.4%	6.1%	20.3%	0.8%	30.9%	14.6%	15.2%
Yuma city	3,939	55.0%	12.1%	3.4%	0.0%	18.5%	0.0%	10.9%	0.0%	14.0%
Arkansas										
Little Rock city	8,985	15.8%	12.3%	0.9%	5.2%	18.3%	1.3%	29.8%	16.5%	21.4%
California										
Anaheim city	10,243	26.1%	12.6%	2.8%	3.0%	20.0%	2.5%	18.6%	14.5%	34.5%
Antioch city	2,063	59.3%	2.6%	5.8%	0.0%	24.9%	0.0%	7.4%	0.0%	35.7%
Bakersfield city	15,051	31.6%	6.1%	4.2%	6.8%	27.8%	0.8%	13.6%	9.1%	22.5%
Berkeley city	5,919	9.8%	26.5%	1.5%	0.0%	1.6%	0.0%	32.0%	28.6%	12.8%
Burbank city	4,555	14.8%	12.1%	0.0%	5.5%	0.0%	0.0%	53.4%	14.3%	29.6%
Carlsbad city	3,043	12.0%	19.5%	0.0%	0.0%	2.7%	0.0%	47.2%	18.7%	32.5%
Carson city	1,090	30.6%	3.0%	10.5%	7.2%	10.3%	15.6%	17.3%	5.5%	49.6%
Chula Vista city	7,243	40.6%	15.0%	5.5%	3.8%	23.9%	2.2%	1.5%	7.4%	37.5%
Clovis city	3,599	44.3%	11.1%	7.1%	4.1%	14.1%	0.0%	8.8%	10.4%	21.4%
Compton city	2,863	39.4%	5.6%	0.0%	6.3%	34.2%	2.6%	9.0%	2.8%	39.3%
Concord city	3,754	18.4%	16.0%	5.8%	3.6%	22.7%	0.0%	28.7%	4.8%	26.9%
Corona city	4,173	34.0%	15.1%	5.3%	9.0%	9.6%	2.7%	9.3%	15.0%	43.0%
Costa Mesa city	5,738	18.2%	25.0%	0.0%	2.9%	5.8%	0.8%	11.0%	36.2%	20.0%
Daly City city	2,777	24.9%	17.7%	0.0%	7.1%	9.1%	7.6%	28.9%	4.8%	44.7%
Downey city	2,590	39.0%	5.6%	12.5%	0.0%	8.0%	0.0%	13.0%	21.9%	40.3%
El Cajon city	3,900	36.7%	3.4%	1.0%	0.0%	27.1%	2.6%	5.7%	23.5%	20.1%
El Monte city	2,992	27.8%	7.9%	7.6%	17.9%	16.3%	0.0%	15.0%	7.5%	48.1%
Elk Grove city	2,978	16.9%	25.4%	14.3%	0.0%	18.2%	3.1%	12.8%	9.3%	37.3%
Escondido city	5,427	27.0%	8.3%	7.8%	1.6%	11.8%	1.1%	7.4%	34.9%	22.2%
Fairfield city	4,786	32.3%	15.6%	3.5%	1.2%	16.8%	0.0%	18.9%	11.7%	27.0%
Fontana city	4,524	27.8%	9.1%	27.5%	8.7%	13.0%	0.0%	2.5%	11.4%	45.6%
Fremont city	5,051	20.4%	37.6%	2.2%	1.0%	9.2%	2.8%	16.8%	9.9%	39.5%
Fresno city	21,805	26.7%	13.8%	4.3%	4.1%	25.6%	0.4%	15.9%	9.3%	21.4%
Fullerton city	4,386	11.9%	16.4%	4.7%	1.5%	9.3%	2.5%	28.1%	25.5%	29.6%
Garden Grove city	4,461	28.2%	8.1%	3.4%	4.0%	20.5%	4.6%	15.3%	15.9%	30.3%
Glendale city	7,028	19.0%	9.5%	4.1%	5.7%	2.5%	13.3%	25.7%	20.2%	37.0%
Hayward city	5,554	32.4%	6.1%	5.9%	7.4%	18.0%	0.0%	19.8%	10.4%	30.9%
Hesperia city	8,589	27.9%	12.4%	2.6%	0.0%	13.5%	0.6%	22.5%	20.5%	23.2%
Inglewood city	4,462	23.4%	14.1%	6.2%	2.4%	18.4%	1.7%	23.7%	10.1%	27.3%
Irvine city	10,276	14.3%	12.6%	4.3%	6.5%	6.3%	1.3%	27.3%	27.3%	23.8%
Jurupa Valley city	2,436	37.3%	0.0%	8.7%	1.7%	9.8%	2.8%	25.9%	13.8%	35.0%
Lancaster city	4,277	42.3%	5.4%	2.2%	0.0%	13.7%	4.8%	14.0%	17.6%	25.5%
Long Beach city	20,061	16.7%	13.9%	2.4%	3.5%	13.7%	1.9%	36.9%	11.1%	25.2%
Los Angeles city	164,233	13.8%	9.8%	2.8%	5.6%	11.2%	4.0%	32.5%	20.3%	25.5%
Mission Viejo city	1,539	35.1%	14.9%	0.0%	0.0%	6.1%	0.0%	6.6%	37.2%	28.6%
Modesto city	7,228	29.1%	7.6%	16.1%	1.4%	20.2%	0.0%	13.5%	12.2%	26.6%
Moreno Valley city	6,941	22.5%	12.3%	3.9%	12.3%	26.5%	6.2%	7.2%	9.0%	38.6%
Murrieta city	4,129	35.5%	7.1%	0.0%	3.5%	11.8%	0.0%	14.3%	27.9%	19.9%
Norwalk city	2,376	29.1%	11.7%	10.2%	22.9%	3.0%	17.2%	1.8%	4.0%	47.5%
Oakland city	18,889	13.5%	12.2%	3.0%	3.1%	10.5%	1.3%	30.3%	26.1%	16.4%
Oceanside city	8,326	46.5%	12.0%	1.7%	2.1%	1.9%	0.0%	25.0%	10.8%	10.3%
Ontario city	5,088	27.7%	14.0%	9.4%	0.0%	10.9%	2.4%	27.2%	8.4%	31.6%
Orange city	3,973	27.2%	16.6%	11.5%	4.1%	10.3%	0.0%	9.5%	20.9%	33.7%
Oxnard city	5,583	40.4%	5.4%	2.3%	0.9%	33.5%	5.4%	4.0%	8.1%	30.0%
Palmdale city	3,302	21.0%	9.9%	7.5%	0.9%	30.6%	2.3%	10.7%	17.1%	45.2%
Pasadena city	8,557	8.2%	20.6%	0.0%	1.4%	2.6%	5.8%	26.3%	35.1%	18.7%
Pomona city	3,637	29.2%	8.4%	3.6%	1.5%	28.7%	6.4%	6.5%	15.5%	47.5%
Rancho Cucamonga city	4,324	26.2%	24.6%	6.3%	2.8%	6.7%	0.0%	17.4%	15.9%	36.4%
Redding city	3,388	34.0%	15.5%	0.0%	0.0%	21.2%	3.3%	4.3%	21.8%	20.1%
Rialto city	2,244	44.7%	1.7%	1.8%	3.9%	34.8%	0.0%	5.6%	7.4%	40.1%
Richmond city	5,725	33.6%	13.5%	1.6%	10.9%	19.2%	1.9%	12.0%	7.4%	21.1%
Riverside city	8,039	41.8%	10.7%	3.1%	7.1%	15.7%	0.8%	7.3%	13.5%	35.2%
Roseville city	4,380	26.3%	20.0%	0.0%	7.5%	16.6%	0.0%	19.5%	10.1%	31.6%
Sacramento city	23,760	18.9%	12.7%	2.6%	1.3%	15.1%	1.6%	28.4%	19.4%	16.5%

Table D-3: Places—Household Relationship—*Continued*

		18 to 24								
		Married Couple Households		Male, No Spouse Present		Female, No Spouse Present		Non-Family Householders		
	Total Householders	With Children	No Children	With Children	No Children	With Children	No Children	Living Alone	Not Alone	Living With Parents
California—Cont.										
Salinas city	1,707	16.6%	9.6%	5.4%	7.1%	18.1%	15.2%	15.8%	12.2%	68.9%
San Bernardino city	2,807	9.4%	0.0%	5.0%	22.4%	32.6%	14.7%	11.0%	5.0%	55.8%
San Buenaventura (Ventura) city	1,076	4.5%	27.4%	0.0%	0.0%	0.0%	0.0%	17.1%	51.0%	74.2%
San Diego city	21,401	8.7%	9.2%	1.8%	7.0%	4.3%	4.6%	20.5%	43.7%	45.1%
San Francisco city	9,551	2.3%	0.9%	1.2%	5.0%	0.9%	6.3%	24.3%	59.2%	27.7%
San Jose city	7,327	4.7%	11.5%	2.9%	9.6%	5.9%	4.6%	20.0%	40.7%	63.5%
San Mateo city	294	0.0%	60.5%	0.0%	0.0%	0.0%	0.0%	20.1%	19.4%	71.8%
Santa Ana city	2,146	20.4%	4.8%	2.8%	18.1%	13.0%	10.8%	4.2%	25.9%	66.5%
Santa Clara city	1,402	0.0%	0.0%	0.0%	0.0%	0.0%	0.0%	38.2%	61.8%	39.4%
Santa Clarita city	1,373	0.0%	0.0%	0.0%	25.5%	6.0%	0.0%	25.0%	43.5%	66.0%
Santa Maria city	1,305	7.4%	7.0%	15.7%	10.3%	39.4%	0.0%	7.9%	12.4%	51.2%
Santa Monica city	1,334	0.0%	0.0%	0.0%	0.0%	0.0%	0.0%	64.5%	35.5%	22.9%
Santa Rosa city	2,093	0.0%	0.0%	0.0%	7.3%	39.3%	0.0%	21.5%	32.0%	59.9%
Simi Valley city	568	5.8%	0.0%	0.0%	0.0%	0.0%	0.0%	50.7%	43.5%	80.1%
South Gate city	304	22.0%	0.0%	16.8%	45.7%	15.5%	0.0%	0.0%	0.0%	70.7%
Stockton city	4,924	5.6%	9.8%	10.0%	5.6%	22.2%	7.3%	28.4%	11.1%	55.6%
Sunnyvale city	1,360	0.0%	0.0%	0.0%	13.8%	0.0%	0.0%	42.3%	44.0%	50.2%
Temecula city	783	5.1%	10.5%	0.0%	9.5%	0.0%	10.2%	22.5%	42.3%	68.0%
Thousand Oaks city	825	0.0%	9.7%	0.0%	22.2%	0.0%	0.0%	9.8%	58.3%	66.3%
Torrance city	598	0.0%	0.0%	0.0%	42.0%	11.4%	0.0%	22.6%	24.1%	81.8%
Vacaville city	474	22.4%	18.6%	0.0%	0.0%	15.4%	0.0%	43.7%	0.0%	67.3%
Vallejo city	1,500	0.0%	5.1%	0.0%	8.3%	48.3%	0.0%	26.5%	11.8%	66.3%
Victorville city	708	10.7%	18.2%	0.0%	0.0%	30.1%	0.0%	41.0%	0.0%	71.7%
Visalia city	1,878	21.6%	0.0%	12.4%	11.4%	40.3%	0.0%	0.0%	14.3%	54.9%
Vista city	2,005	29.8%	21.5%	0.0%	2.7%	0.0%	0.0%	12.3%	33.7%	45.4%
West Covina city	571	0.0%	0.0%	0.0%	20.3%	63.9%	0.0%	0.0%	15.8%	71.6%
Westminster city	356	33.4%	0.0%	0.0%	48.9%	0.0%	0.0%	0.0%	17.7%	74.4%
Colorado										
Arvada city	1,787	3.9%	9.0%	0.0%	0.0%	29.5%	0.0%	14.8%	42.8%	58.0%
Aurora city	6,075	12.7%	4.4%	10.2%	0.0%	18.2%	11.4%	26.3%	16.7%	56.8%
Boulder city	8,697	0.0%	1.3%	0.0%	0.0%	0.0%	0.0%	38.9%	59.8%	10.2%
Centennial city	693	0.0%	0.0%	0.0%	0.0%	11.4%	0.0%	78.2%	10.4%	74.1%
Colorado Springs city	7,914	17.7%	20.0%	0.0%	0.0%	13.9%	0.0%	13.9%	34.5%	46.6%
Denver city	15,470	4.4%	6.4%	2.9%	4.7%	9.3%	3.6%	32.5%	36.1%	31.5%
Fort Collins city	7,672	4.0%	3.7%	0.0%	2.4%	0.0%	1.9%	22.3%	65.8%	21.0%
Greeley city	2,222	1.1%	26.2%	0.0%	4.4%	1.9%	4.1%	26.1%	36.1%	39.6%
Lakewood city	3,009	0.0%	13.5%	0.0%	0.0%	0.0%	0.0%	32.4%	54.1%	41.3%
Pueblo city	3,024	23.0%	7.0%	9.0%	0.0%	19.0%	3.5%	19.0%	19.4%	45.7%
Thornton city	1,233	3.8%	0.0%	0.0%	4.5%	35.8%	3.6%	11.8%	40.6%	55.4%
Westminster city	2,541	16.4%	7.0%	0.0%	2.2%	9.6%	2.2%	32.9%	29.6%	44.6%
Connecticut										
Bridgeport city	502	0.0%	0.0%	0.0%	13.5%	86.5%	0.0%	0.0%	0.0%	50.8%
Hartford city	3,541	0.0%	3.0%	9.3%	2.7%	26.2%	0.0%	44.8%	14.1%	38.1%
New Haven city	1,780	0.0%	3.3%	0.0%	2.6%	2.9%	18.4%	39.4%	33.5%	37.7%
Stamford city	1,166	0.0%	0.0%	0.0%	0.0%	0.0%	15.9%	22.5%	61.7%	50.7%
Waterbury city	1,021	12.8%	0.0%	0.0%	7.9%	38.9%	18.8%	17.8%	3.7%	70.4%
District of Columbia										
Washington city	10,642	0.0%	1.8%	2.9%	4.4%	14.1%	0.5%	32.6%	43.8%	25.8%
Florida										
Cape Coral city	1,174	8.8%	7.8%	34.8%	0.0%	21.0%	7.2%	11.5%	8.9%	63.7%
Clearwater city	778	4.1%	0.0%	0.0%	0.0%	30.8%	0.0%	6.7%	58.4%	50.5%
Coral Springs city	1,231	13.2%	0.0%	0.0%	5.3%	37.9%	2.6%	22.5%	18.5%	73.3%
Fort Lauderdale city	1,999	8.4%	23.9%	2.9%	4.2%	11.0%	6.1%	26.4%	17.2%	41.8%
Gainesville city	13,327	0.0%	2.9%	2.4%	3.1%	7.1%	1.3%	30.8%	52.4%	5.4%
Hialeah city	1,991	0.0%	13.9%	6.8%	15.2%	17.9%	24.0%	17.5%	4.8%	64.1%
Hollywood city	1,084	13.8%	0.0%	9.6%	20.6%	0.0%	5.9%	20.3%	29.8%	63.2%
Jacksonville city	13,617	14.6%	9.5%	3.1%	7.2%	15.3%	3.4%	27.2%	19.7%	47.4%
Lakeland city	954	11.4%	27.4%	0.0%	0.0%	25.1%	0.0%	10.8%	25.4%	70.6%
Miami Beach city	722	6.2%	40.2%	0.0%	5.1%	0.0%	0.0%	48.5%	0.0%	58.2%
Miami city	5,437	1.4%	4.5%	8.9%	12.3%	14.3%	8.5%	21.7%	28.3%	58.9%
Miami Gardens city	813	0.0%	0.0%	0.0%	6.3%	30.5%	0.0%	15.1%	48.1%	68.9%
Miramar city	969	10.8%	4.2%	0.0%	15.4%	5.4%	4.4%	43.1%	16.6%	72.5%
Orlando city	5,271	5.0%	3.7%	11.6%	6.7%	10.0%	3.3%	29.6%	30.0%	41.8%
Palm Bay city	1,211	10.7%	0.0%	4.8%	0.0%	41.1%	0.0%	22.6%	20.8%	65.8%
Pembroke Pines city	482	0.0%	0.0%	0.0%	23.7%	0.0%	13.3%	29.7%	33.4%	77.2%
Pompano Beach city	896	40.1%	0.0%	0.0%	0.0%	25.6%	25.1%	0.0%	9.3%	67.0%
Port St. Lucie city	389	23.1%	0.0%	0.0%	0.0%	34.7%	0.0%	0.0%	42.2%	75.9%
St. Petersburg city	3,837	2.9%	8.5%	5.4%	0.0%	15.2%	5.3%	43.8%	18.8%	51.8%
Tallahassee city	16,561	1.6%	3.3%	0.0%	8.9%	1.6%	6.1%	32.3%	46.2%	19.1%
Tampa city	10,868	2.5%	0.5%	0.9%	3.4%	8.5%	4.1%	56.2%	24.0%	34.1%
West Palm Beach city	1,526	0.0%	9.7%	0.0%	8.5%	21.7%	10.9%	14.2%	35.0%	45.4%
Georgia										
Athens-Clarke County unified govt (bal).	9,375	0.7%	3.5%	0.0%	4.8%	5.0%	0.0%	39.6%	46.3%	9.1%
Atlanta city	12,730	1.3%	3.4%	0.0%	2.5%	12.2%	2.8%	46.4%	31.3%	23.1%

Table D-3: Places—Household Relationship—Continued

| | | 25 to 31 | | | | | | | | |
| | | Married Couple Households | | Male, No Spouse Present | | Female, No Spouse Present | | Non-Family Householders | | |
	Total Householders	With Children	No Children	With Children	No Children	With Children	No Children	Living Alone	Not Alone	Living With Parents
California—Cont.										
Salinas city	4,144	44.4%	3.0%	0.0%	1.1%	25.4%	0.0%	18.4%	7.7%	25.4%
San Bernardino city	6,296	27.3%	7.4%	10.9%	4.2%	25.9%	2.0%	8.8%	13.5%	25.2%
San Buenaventura (Ventura) city	3,456	43.4%	14.3%	3.4%	0.0%	10.9%	0.0%	21.2%	6.8%	26.7%
San Diego city	71,191	17.4%	18.5%	2.2%	1.8%	8.6%	2.5%	23.3%	25.7%	14.2%
San Francisco city	54,300	3.5%	13.3%	0.0%	3.2%	3.7%	1.3%	33.1%	41.9%	11.4%
San Jose city	31,707	20.5%	14.8%	5.7%	4.4%	12.5%	1.7%	23.2%	17.0%	26.6%
San Mateo city	3,043	41.8%	13.9%	0.0%	0.0%	0.0%	3.2%	17.3%	23.9%	27.0%
Santa Ana city	9,286	28.3%	13.5%	3.1%	9.0%	19.6%	1.8%	14.3%	10.4%	34.2%
Santa Clara city	8,330	11.7%	27.3%	0.0%	8.0%	4.5%	2.0%	26.4%	20.0%	11.9%
Santa Clarita city	5,642	30.9%	17.4%	2.3%	9.9%	15.0%	2.1%	8.0%	14.3%	27.8%
Santa Maria city	3,008	34.6%	14.2%	0.0%	8.8%	22.3%	0.0%	7.7%	12.4%	26.1%
Santa Monica city	6,240	4.1%	14.3%	0.0%	0.0%	5.8%	3.3%	39.2%	33.2%	6.1%
Santa Rosa city	6,075	17.6%	13.3%	2.9%	3.7%	12.2%	9.6%	14.8%	25.7%	29.5%
Simi Valley city	2,436	26.5%	25.5%	0.0%	7.8%	2.1%	0.0%	10.9%	27.3%	39.2%
South Gate city	2,281	25.6%	6.1%	15.6%	0.0%	31.2%	16.0%	0.0%	5.4%	45.5%
Stockton city	10,056	24.0%	10.0%	14.3%	1.8%	18.2%	1.2%	16.1%	14.4%	31.5%
Sunnyvale city	8,427	24.3%	24.9%	0.0%	0.0%	3.1%	1.8%	23.9%	22.1%	13.1%
Temecula city	2,228	35.2%	13.0%	11.8%	0.0%	2.2%	0.0%	31.2%	6.6%	41.4%
Thousand Oaks city	2,880	30.9%	21.8%	8.7%	0.0%	10.0%	0.0%	4.3%	24.3%	24.7%
Torrance city	3,163	14.4%	18.6%	0.0%	0.0%	8.2%	0.0%	35.3%	23.4%	35.4%
Vacaville city	3,413	34.6%	7.5%	16.3%	1.6%	11.3%	2.1%	11.6%	14.9%	24.6%
Vallejo city	4,238	28.9%	6.7%	1.4%	5.5%	20.8%	0.0%	20.9%	15.8%	26.6%
Victorville city	4,641	35.3%	1.8%	0.0%	12.5%	15.0%	9.6%	18.2%	7.5%	36.7%
Visalia city	6,798	48.5%	7.6%	3.6%	0.0%	18.8%	0.0%	11.5%	9.9%	14.8%
Vista city	4,943	34.7%	23.1%	2.4%	3.1%	2.5%	0.0%	18.2%	16.0%	14.5%
West Covina city	2,410	23.7%	4.3%	11.4%	16.7%	11.4%	3.9%	4.9%	23.8%	46.6%
Westminster city	3,047	25.5%	2.2%	2.5%	0.0%	22.9%	6.8%	21.2%	18.9%	34.9%
Colorado										
Arvada city	2,948	24.3%	12.1%	3.0%	0.0%	19.8%	0.0%	11.1%	29.6%	27.2%
Aurora city	14,342	31.8%	8.7%	4.8%	1.3%	19.0%	0.0%	21.9%	12.5%	23.8%
Boulder city	5,149	8.9%	8.7%	0.0%	1.8%	1.7%	0.0%	31.9%	47.1%	8.2%
Centennial city	3,552	24.8%	25.9%	0.0%	1.8%	10.6%	9.0%	16.0%	11.9%	17.8%
Colorado Springs city	23,414	26.5%	19.8%	4.0%	0.6%	12.7%	3.1%	18.1%	15.2%	10.0%
Denver city	43,124	13.7%	9.2%	1.0%	3.5%	8.1%	1.0%	37.6%	25.9%	10.7%
Fort Collins city	7,580	14.6%	17.6%	1.8%	0.0%	7.6%	1.7%	28.2%	28.5%	6.6%
Greeley city	5,803	28.0%	17.4%	2.5%	0.0%	23.0%	2.3%	17.8%	9.1%	13.8%
Lakewood city	5,444	20.4%	12.4%	0.0%	4.7%	7.3%	1.0%	35.2%	18.9%	21.2%
Pueblo city	3,869	52.6%	0.0%	6.7%	1.1%	13.3%	0.0%	23.9%	2.5%	20.9%
Thornton city	4,531	39.2%	10.7%	14.2%	0.0%	12.3%	3.0%	17.0%	3.6%	19.5%
Westminster city	6,194	44.3%	13.9%	7.8%	1.3%	3.3%	1.9%	16.9%	10.7%	9.7%
Connecticut										
Bridgeport city	7,811	26.4%	5.3%	2.9%	0.0%	32.2%	4.4%	10.0%	18.8%	20.0%
Hartford city	6,789	2.5%	14.7%	4.9%	4.7%	44.2%	0.0%	20.6%	8.4%	24.1%
New Haven city	8,064	10.4%	7.5%	3.0%	2.3%	21.4%	0.0%	35.5%	20.0%	14.1%
Stamford city	5,536	19.7%	13.6%	0.0%	5.3%	7.9%	4.1%	19.8%	29.6%	20.6%
Waterbury city	5,107	8.7%	5.3%	5.1%	0.0%	47.7%	0.0%	20.0%	13.2%	26.4%
District of Columbia										
Washington city	47,060	6.3%	10.5%	2.0%	2.5%	11.7%	1.1%	36.6%	29.3%	9.8%
Florida										
Cape Coral city	3,499	34.9%	13.9%	7.4%	1.3%	16.9%	2.2%	14.6%	8.8%	31.8%
Clearwater city	3,064	21.5%	12.0%	14.6%	11.8%	18.5%	0.0%	9.5%	12.0%	20.2%
Coral Springs city	3,362	19.4%	7.2%	13.9%	0.0%	21.9%	8.4%	17.2%	12.1%	37.0%
Fort Lauderdale city	5,866	8.7%	14.6%	1.2%	0.0%	3.2%	3.7%	37.0%	31.5%	19.3%
Gainesville city	7,377	11.9%	11.4%	1.2%	1.2%	7.3%	0.0%	38.6%	28.3%	8.8%
Hialeah city	3,761	39.9%	8.0%	3.1%	9.4%	18.8%	4.2%	6.9%	9.7%	50.8%
Hollywood city	4,181	31.7%	8.1%	0.0%	10.9%	18.2%	5.0%	20.8%	5.4%	34.0%
Jacksonville city	38,620	17.0%	12.3%	1.9%	1.6%	18.2%	2.6%	32.8%	13.8%	23.3%
Lakeland city	2,715	18.3%	16.8%	7.2%	0.0%	16.6%	0.0%	23.2%	17.9%	31.3%
Miami Beach city	3,390	5.8%	6.4%	0.0%	2.9%	0.0%	4.9%	49.5%	30.5%	21.2%
Miami city	18,137	10.9%	8.6%	2.8%	2.0%	14.0%	8.7%	39.0%	14.1%	26.0%
Miami Gardens city	1,783	24.1%	0.0%	0.0%	0.0%	26.8%	4.0%	45.1%	0.0%	60.5%
Miramar city	5,038	22.5%	6.0%	0.0%	3.8%	32.5%	11.2%	15.7%	8.4%	43.1%
Orlando city	14,789	11.6%	18.4%	4.8%	3.1%	12.4%	3.0%	28.0%	18.6%	21.2%
Palm Bay city	2,954	42.9%	3.6%	0.0%	0.0%	29.1%	0.0%	11.4%	13.0%	25.5%
Pembroke Pines city	2,660	30.5%	27.4%	0.0%	9.9%	1.9%	5.9%	15.1%	9.1%	53.5%
Pompano Beach city	2,783	37.6%	14.9%	3.3%	0.0%	27.1%	3.1%	11.1%	3.0%	35.4%
Port St. Lucie city	3,013	37.0%	3.7%	0.0%	0.0%	35.9%	2.8%	15.2%	5.5%	40.4%
St. Petersburg city	10,265	13.4%	11.2%	1.9%	1.9%	16.3%	0.6%	40.9%	13.9%	24.4%
Tallahassee city	10,815	12.5%	11.2%	1.9%	0.7%	19.1%	2.6%	32.4%	19.6%	9.7%
Tampa city	19,197	12.5%	11.1%	0.4%	2.4%	18.9%	2.0%	35.9%	16.7%	20.6%
West Palm Beach city	4,084	15.9%	3.9%	7.8%	6.2%	21.8%	1.0%	19.8%	23.6%	27.0%
Georgia										
Athens-Clarke County unified govt (bal.)	6,974	10.7%	14.1%	1.0%	0.0%	15.6%	0.0%	37.4%	21.2%	8.4%
Atlanta city	31,272	6.2%	10.7%	0.9%	4.3%	15.4%	0.5%	46.0%	16.1%	10.3%

Table D-3: Places—Household Relationship—*Continued*

		Married Couple Households		Male, No Spouse Present		Female, No Spouse Present		Non-Family Householders		
	Total Householders	With Children	No Children	With Children	No Children	With Children	No Children	Living Alone	Not Alone	Living With Parents
Georgia—Cont.										
Augusta-Richmond County consolidated govt (bal)	1,793	3.0%	15.6%	0.0%	5.9%	28.7%	0.0%	19.1%	27.7%	55.4%
Columbus city	2,729	9.4%	20.6%	0.0%	0.0%	20.9%	0.0%	22.4%	26.7%	29.7%
Macon city	1,398	6.5%	0.0%	6.4%	0.0%	69.5%	0.0%	11.4%	6.2%	40.0%
Roswell city	281	0.0%	0.0%	0.0%	0.0%	55.5%	0.0%	0.0%	44.5%	74.9%
Sandy Springs city	618	0.0%	0.0%	0.0%	0.0%	0.0%	0.0%	100.0%	0.0%	51.5%
Savannah city	3,164	3.8%	22.6%	3.0%	9.5%	12.6%	4.9%	23.9%	19.8%	36.6%
Hawaii										
Urban Honolulu CDP	4,058	18.6%	4.5%	1.2%	3.4%	0.0%	9.7%	38.1%	24.5%	42.8%
Idaho										
Boise City city	5,980	12.1%	7.7%	0.9%	0.0%	2.4%	9.2%	17.7%	50.0%	34.7%
Illinois										
Aurora city	1,836	5.8%	7.2%	8.2%	9.0%	18.6%	7.2%	16.1%	27.9%	69.7%
Chicago city	41,039	3.8%	6.1%	2.7%	3.1%	12.0%	4.5%	33.2%	34.5%	50.5%
Elgin city	2,071	28.6%	0.0%	0.0%	6.8%	43.7%	0.0%	17.0%	3.9%	61.4%
Joliet city	1,488	13.7%	0.0%	0.0%	0.0%	29.8%	0.0%	38.4%	18.1%	71.0%
Naperville city	1,334	7.9%	9.9%	3.4%	0.0%	6.0%	25.3%	18.9%	28.6%	63.5%
Peoria city	3,594	0.0%	5.5%	4.0%	6.8%	19.3%	0.0%	39.1%	25.3%	41.8%
Rockford city	2,082	21.0%	23.0%	0.0%	0.0%	34.2%	0.0%	16.4%	5.5%	57.3%
Springfield city	2,267	0.0%	12.2%	3.4%	0.0%	1.2%	0.0%	36.7%	46.5%	52.5%
Indiana										
Evansville city	2,344	5.5%	0.0%	8.2%	0.0%	21.8%	0.0%	48.6%	15.9%	39.7%
Fort Wayne city	6,270	5.6%	7.5%	2.2%	2.9%	16.9%	5.5%	39.2%	20.2%	41.8%
Indianapolis city (bal)	19,090	3.8%	6.9%	3.4%	4.9%	16.6%	4.4%	33.5%	26.7%	43.2%
South Bend city	2,037	3.4%	2.1%	0.0%	0.0%	48.7%	1.6%	20.5%	23.7%	24.0%
Iowa										
Cedar Rapids city	2,264	0.0%	17.2%	0.0%	17.8%	0.0%	4.0%	31.8%	29.2%	39.0%
Davenport city	1,692	3.4%	0.0%	0.0%	0.0%	16.7%	0.0%	53.2%	26.7%	52.3%
Des Moines city	5,862	0.0%	16.2%	0.0%	1.8%	18.8%	0.0%	18.9%	44.4%	27.8%
Kansas										
Kansas City city	3,009	1.3%	0.0%	14.9%	9.8%	16.7%	7.9%	29.2%	20.0%	42.6%
Olathe city	2,137	10.1%	7.7%	6.1%	20.4%	0.0%	0.0%	30.4%	25.4%	58.9%
Overland Park city	2,727	6.9%	11.4%	5.4%	0.0%	10.3%	0.0%	44.6%	21.3%	62.0%
Topeka city	2,800	2.8%	0.7%	2.8%	0.0%	22.9%	0.0%	37.3%	33.5%	37.0%
Wichita city	8,091	8.8%	12.3%	1.6%	0.0%	21.6%	2.4%	32.3%	21.1%	55.7%
Kentucky										
Lexington-Fayette urban county	11,120	1.2%	5.4%	0.0%	2.3%	14.7%	6.7%	21.4%	48.3%	20.6%
Louisville/Jefferson County metro govt (bal)	9,326	5.1%	2.5%	0.0%	4.8%	17.2%	0.5%	44.4%	25.4%	46.7%
Louisiana										
Baton Rouge city	10,333	0.5%	1.1%	0.0%	0.5%	23.1%	3.0%	35.6%	36.2%	29.6%
Lafayette city	3,333	4.9%	4.2%	0.0%	9.1%	4.9%	16.4%	41.0%	19.4%	47.0%
New Orleans city	5,654	2.5%	2.9%	2.1%	4.8%	14.6%	7.4%	36.4%	29.3%	42.7%
Shreveport city	3,076	0.0%	3.5%	0.0%	1.3%	30.6%	11.4%	31.4%	21.7%	51.0%
Maryland										
Baltimore city	9,643	4.0%	2.4%	0.9%	12.0%	16.3%	0.3%	30.2%	33.8%	42.1%
Massachusetts										
Boston city	15,181	0.7%	0.5%	0.0%	4.7%	13.4%	5.5%	20.2%	55.0%	26.2%
Brockton city	82	0.0%	0.0%	0.0%	0.0%	0.0%	100.0%	0.0%	0.0%	85.0%
Cambridge city	2,558	0.0%	0.0%	0.0%	4.8%	4.9%	0.0%	40.4%	49.9%	12.4%
Lowell city	2,310	0.0%	0.0%	11.8%	1.6%	31.8%	0.0%	16.8%	38.0%	34.9%
Lynn city	359	17.8%	0.0%	36.5%	0.0%	35.4%	10.3%	0.0%	0.0%	72.1%
New Bedford city	1,260	10.5%	9.0%	0.0%	19.1%	0.0%	22.5%	10.3%	28.6%	48.5%
Springfield city	1,586	0.0%	0.0%	5.7%	18.5%	43.9%	0.0%	12.4%	19.5%	56.1%
Worcester city	2,821	9.7%	4.3%	0.0%	7.8%	15.4%	0.0%	5.1%	57.7%	40.8%
Michigan										
Ann Arbor city	7,305	0.0%	1.9%	0.0%	0.0%	0.0%	0.0%	29.6%	68.5%	10.0%
Dearborn city	917	32.5%	25.1%	0.0%	0.0%	0.0%	5.3%	26.3%	10.8%	79.9%
Detroit city	11,296	3.2%	1.9%	6.8%	10.2%	36.0%	0.5%	34.7%	6.6%	56.3%
Flint city	1,240	8.8%	0.0%	0.0%	0.0%	41.3%	0.0%	25.4%	24.5%	28.7%
Grand Rapids city	4,507	0.0%	7.8%	7.0%	0.0%	11.1%	1.6%	19.4%	53.1%	23.3%
Lansing city	4,202	3.9%	1.5%	0.0%	5.7%	13.8%	5.3%	35.0%	34.7%	31.6%
Livonia city	1,059	30.8%	0.0%	0.0%	0.0%	6.8%	0.0%	10.2%	52.2%	72.0%
Sterling Heights city	335	0.0%	0.0%	0.0%	0.0%	63.6%	0.0%	0.0%	36.4%	77.2%
Warren city	1,670	2.6%	0.0%	0.0%	0.0%	34.4%	20.0%	4.9%	38.1%	56.7%
Minnesota										
Minneapolis city	11,827	5.7%	4.9%	0.8%	0.5%	5.1%	0.4%	33.2%	49.3%	20.0%
Rochester city	2,972	0.0%	0.0%	6.9%	0.0%	34.8%	1.1%	43.5%	13.7%	54.1%
St. Paul city	6,033	14.4%	1.6%	0.0%	2.4%	18.1%	5.5%	11.0%	46.9%	40.9%
Mississippi										
Jackson city	3,095	0.0%	6.6%	1.6%	2.5%	18.0%	10.2%	31.1%	30.0%	41.3%

Table D-3: Places—Household Relationship—*Continued*

	Total Householders	25 to 31								
		Married Couple Households		Male, No Spouse Present		Female, No Spouse Present		Non-Family Householders		
		With Children	No Children	With Children	No Children	With Children	No Children	Living Alone	Not Alone	Living With Parents
Georgia—Cont.										
Augusta-Richmond County consolidated govt (bal)	8,990	8.9%	13.9%	1.0%	0.7%	25.7%	2.9%	37.7%	9.2%	34.2%
Columbus city	8,322	34.6%	13.9%	5.4%	0.4%	19.8%	1.6%	9.3%	14.9%	17.4%
Macon city	3,312	22.5%	9.3%	2.2%	2.1%	46.2%	0.0%	14.0%	3.7%	16.3%
Roswell city	3,015	8.9%	35.1%	4.1%	0.0%	10.6%	0.0%	29.2%	12.1%	25.5%
Sandy Springs city	7,340	6.6%	19.8%	0.8%	5.6%	12.1%	0.0%	40.5%	14.6%	6.6%
Savannah city	8,153	20.5%	12.1%	0.0%	1.5%	18.7%	0.6%	33.9%	12.7%	24.8%
Hawaii										
Urban Honolulu CDP	13,367	26.5%	13.2%	0.0%	4.8%	7.6%	4.6%	23.6%	19.7%	20.6%
Idaho										
Boise City city	10,762	26.9%	14.5%	0.5%	1.8%	5.4%	0.6%	22.2%	28.2%	12.2%
Illinois										
Aurora city	6,677	35.3%	7.1%	8.4%	3.5%	10.5%	0.7%	18.4%	16.0%	29.0%
Chicago city	150,328	9.6%	11.9%	2.6%	3.6%	14.3%	2.2%	33.7%	22.1%	20.9%
Elgin city	3,761	29.5%	20.3%	2.9%	11.4%	9.9%	0.0%	15.2%	10.8%	18.0%
Joliet city	3,677	40.2%	13.5%	0.0%	2.1%	9.1%	10.0%	16.0%	9.2%	34.8%
Naperville city	3,813	22.7%	22.7%	0.0%	0.0%	5.1%	1.2%	32.5%	15.9%	34.4%
Peoria city	6,967	17.9%	16.0%	1.9%	0.0%	20.2%	1.7%	25.8%	16.5%	13.4%
Rockford city	5,721	26.6%	14.6%	5.2%	1.1%	31.4%	0.0%	13.7%	7.6%	17.3%
Springfield city	6,343	29.2%	9.9%	3.1%	0.0%	29.7%	1.2%	13.9%	13.0%	7.2%
Indiana										
Evansville city	5,950	29.6%	23.9%	0.0%	0.0%	10.5%	0.0%	29.8%	6.3%	12.5%
Fort Wayne city	12,283	34.5%	15.5%	3.0%	1.4%	16.7%	0.6%	17.2%	11.2%	17.0%
Indianapolis city (bal)	46,170	17.9%	14.7%	2.9%	2.0%	20.1%	0.5%	28.3%	13.7%	14.8%
South Bend city	4,249	20.5%	4.5%	0.0%	3.5%	19.1%	0.0%	29.6%	22.8%	7.0%
Iowa										
Cedar Rapids city	7,856	25.4%	6.6%	0.0%	2.6%	19.0%	0.0%	30.4%	16.2%	14.6%
Davenport city	5,856	28.9%	15.5%	3.0%	0.0%	13.6%	0.0%	33.7%	5.4%	6.7%
Des Moines city	12,850	24.2%	12.4%	5.9%	6.3%	13.2%	0.0%	23.4%	14.6%	12.3%
Kansas										
Kansas City city	5,941	15.3%	13.2%	1.1%	0.0%	32.6%	1.2%	26.8%	9.8%	20.9%
Olathe city	4,337	42.3%	17.6%	1.7%	0.0%	7.2%	0.0%	18.2%	13.0%	17.5%
Overland Park city	9,111	16.5%	16.6%	0.0%	1.2%	12.1%	0.0%	30.9%	22.7%	13.1%
Topeka city	5,688	24.9%	4.3%	10.7%	1.1%	11.7%	0.4%	27.3%	19.6%	18.4%
Wichita city	21,244	33.3%	8.8%	2.4%	0.6%	17.1%	1.5%	30.3%	6.0%	16.4%
Kentucky										
Lexington-Fayette urban county	15,668	26.0%	17.2%	1.0%	1.0%	9.7%	1.1%	24.7%	19.3%	12.4%
Louisville/Jefferson County metro govt (bal)	29,296	16.3%	13.9%	1.7%	4.1%	16.8%	2.4%	26.6%	18.1%	17.6%
Louisiana										
Baton Rouge city	10,761	11.4%	9.5%	0.0%	8.4%	12.1%	1.3%	37.9%	19.4%	16.1%
Lafayette city	6,986	18.6%	9.6%	4.7%	0.0%	11.3%	1.7%	37.1%	17.0%	11.0%
New Orleans city	22,204	6.5%	9.4%	1.7%	2.5%	20.8%	1.1%	39.4%	18.5%	22.0%
Shreveport city	9,036	17.9%	7.0%	1.6%	0.4%	25.7%	1.4%	37.3%	8.6%	24.4%
Maryland										
Baltimore city	35,268	7.7%	10.1%	3.9%	1.3%	21.5%	2.8%	37.0%	15.6%	18.2%
Massachusetts										
Boston city	48,102	6.3%	11.6%	1.8%	3.5%	15.4%	1.9%	28.5%	30.8%	13.1%
Brockton city	2,671	39.7%	2.6%	6.0%	0.0%	17.6%	2.8%	22.1%	9.2%	38.1%
Cambridge city	8,574	3.6%	17.7%	0.0%	1.7%	0.9%	0.9%	35.5%	39.8%	3.8%
Lowell city	5,176	20.1%	17.5%	2.4%	4.1%	14.8%	6.9%	19.4%	14.9%	23.6%
Lynn city	3,568	34.3%	3.3%	13.9%	4.2%	21.4%	2.2%	17.7%	3.1%	28.8%
New Bedford city	4,840	31.3%	8.0%	0.0%	0.0%	17.1%	2.4%	27.6%	13.6%	14.9%
Springfield city	6,810	11.6%	4.1%	6.9%	0.0%	44.1%	2.7%	22.3%	8.4%	24.5%
Worcester city	8,806	25.5%	9.1%	3.2%	4.9%	21.6%	2.4%	18.2%	15.0%	13.3%
Michigan										
Ann Arbor city	7,381	10.3%	16.0%	2.9%	0.0%	4.7%	0.0%	44.3%	21.7%	8.7%
Dearborn city	3,436	50.6%	3.6%	11.5%	0.0%	15.2%	0.0%	5.5%	13.6%	28.9%
Detroit city	21,995	7.3%	4.6%	6.1%	4.9%	36.8%	6.3%	25.3%	8.6%	31.3%
Flint city	5,153	2.8%	5.7%	0.0%	0.0%	42.4%	0.0%	32.1%	17.1%	26.4%
Grand Rapids city	11,532	15.8%	12.2%	4.8%	0.0%	9.3%	3.0%	33.8%	21.2%	11.8%
Lansing city	9,292	22.8%	5.6%	5.7%	3.5%	22.4%	1.9%	36.3%	1.7%	11.3%
Livonia city	2,477	22.6%	29.7%	2.8%	0.0%	11.7%	0.0%	9.3%	23.8%	36.2%
Sterling Heights city	4,313	13.5%	15.9%	0.0%	4.1%	4.4%	8.6%	43.2%	10.3%	18.5%
Warren city	6,095	16.1%	11.0%	1.6%	4.0%	30.9%	0.8%	22.6%	13.0%	16.3%
Minnesota										
Minneapolis city	30,847	9.7%	9.9%	4.6%	1.2%	9.9%	0.8%	37.0%	26.8%	7.5%
Rochester city	5,016	32.9%	27.6%	0.0%	0.0%	6.5%	3.8%	19.1%	10.1%	20.9%
St. Paul city	17,263	14.0%	15.6%	0.7%	4.0%	13.0%	1.4%	30.2%	21.1%	9.6%
Mississippi										
Jackson city	8,223	14.1%	5.6%	1.1%	1.3%	37.1%	3.8%	24.5%	12.5%	27.9%

Table D-3: Places—Household Relationship—*Continued*

		Married Couple Households		Male, No Spouse Present		Female, No Spouse Present		Non-Family Householders		
	Total Householders	With Children	No Children	With Children	No Children	With Children	No Children	Living Alone	Not Alone	Living With Parents
Missouri										
Columbia city	7,480	0.0%	1.0%	0.0%	3.0%	7.4%	0.0%	31.8%	56.8%	11.7%
Independence city	1,741	4.3%	11.8%	0.0%	0.0%	33.3%	0.0%	15.6%	35.0%	62.9%
Kansas City city	11,117	7.8%	4.3%	0.0%	5.4%	12.4%	3.4%	45.0%	21.8%	40.7%
Lee's Summit city	601	0.0%	0.0%	0.0%	0.0%	79.4%	0.0%	20.6%	0.0%	79.4%
Springfield city	7,283	1.2%	7.7%	0.0%	0.0%	14.4%	2.0%	27.4%	47.4%	25.4%
St. Louis city	7,472	1.0%	2.2%	0.0%	4.1%	13.6%	7.3%	51.4%	20.3%	40.9%
Montana										
Billings city	3,629	8.2%	0.0%	0.0%	1.0%	48.0%	0.0%	23.3%	19.4%	35.4%
Nebraska										
Lincoln city	9,589	2.3%	8.1%	11.6%	6.3%	6.6%	1.5%	16.4%	47.2%	22.9%
Omaha city	9,937	3.1%	5.3%	1.5%	1.8%	12.3%	0.0%	36.3%	39.7%	37.6%
Nevada										
Henderson city	2,165	3.7%	4.9%	5.3%	5.8%	0.0%	0.0%	36.3%	44.0%	67.5%
Las Vegas city	5,984	8.7%	11.4%	4.1%	9.1%	19.0%	6.3%	23.0%	18.5%	60.5%
North Las Vegas city	2,857	7.4%	17.4%	0.0%	5.3%	10.1%	19.7%	29.0%	11.2%	52.4%
Reno city	4,444	3.1%	3.8%	3.6%	1.8%	8.0%	3.3%	27.9%	48.5%	31.8%
Sparks city	1,382	26.9%	13.7%	6.6%	0.0%	3.5%	12.0%	26.9%	10.3%	38.2%
New Hampshire										
Manchester city	2,169	14.4%	13.3%	0.0%	7.9%	33.7%	0.0%	15.8%	14.9%	39.9%
New Jersey										
Elizabeth city	1,170	20.9%	0.0%	20.7%	8.8%	36.6%	13.1%	0.0%	0.0%	59.8%
Jersey City city	1,994	0.0%	2.3%	0.0%	10.7%	3.3%	14.2%	29.9%	39.7%	59.2%
Newark city	2,331	4.5%	0.0%	0.0%	12.5%	51.9%	6.2%	18.2%	6.7%	56.9%
Paterson city	1,271	32.5%	0.0%	0.0%	0.0%	34.7%	10.9%	7.6%	14.2%	76.6%
New Mexico										
Albuquerque city	10,544	7.0%	10.6%	1.0%	7.6%	19.9%	1.3%	21.4%	31.2%	51.3%
Las Cruces city	5,560	8.6%	1.2%	0.0%	0.0%	14.7%	2.7%	11.9%	61.0%	22.5%
Rio Rancho city	74	0.0%	0.0%	25.7%	0.0%	24.3%	25.7%	24.3%	0.0%	74.7%
New York										
Albany city	5,151	3.8%	2.9%	0.0%	0.6%	6.8%	0.0%	34.0%	51.9%	12.6%
Buffalo city	5,800	1.9%	5.2%	1.5%	16.2%	20.3%	0.0%	20.7%	34.2%	45.0%
New York city	76,692	8.4%	5.2%	2.0%	9.9%	10.9%	7.6%	24.1%	32.1%	60.8%
Rochester city	4,598	0.0%	0.8%	5.3%	0.0%	35.9%	7.7%	20.8%	29.5%	35.9%
Syracuse city	3,443	1.6%	0.0%	2.1%	5.6%	14.4%	7.2%	33.0%	36.1%	30.2%
Yonkers city	1,583	0.0%	3.8%	0.0%	7.9%	20.9%	5.4%	31.2%	30.8%	70.1%
North Carolina										
Charlotte city	12,895	2.8%	4.9%	2.2%	5.9%	14.6%	6.1%	19.5%	44.0%	44.0%
Durham city	3,703	0.0%	5.1%	0.0%	0.0%	14.1%	0.0%	30.1%	50.7%	28.2%
Fayetteville city	6,498	7.8%	22.9%	1.6%	1.0%	20.4%	0.0%	25.5%	20.7%	39.1%
Greensboro city	4,921	0.0%	18.3%	2.2%	7.6%	11.3%	2.9%	32.0%	25.6%	40.4%
High Point city	1,411	5.5%	5.5%	20.0%	4.7%	9.9%	0.0%	21.8%	32.5%	52.3%
Raleigh city	9,575	0.8%	5.2%	1.7%	0.8%	10.3%	1.5%	37.6%	42.3%	38.4%
Wilmington city	5,238	1.8%	4.8%	0.0%	2.1%	6.2%	1.2%	31.2%	52.7%	20.1%
Winston-Salem city	5,660	8.1%	2.9%	1.6%	5.4%	21.5%	4.4%	33.7%	22.5%	37.3%
North Dakota										
Fargo city	7,385	0.0%	2.3%	0.0%	5.6%	9.9%	1.4%	38.9%	41.8%	24.9%
Ohio										
Akron city	5,629	4.3%	3.0%	6.2%	3.6%	20.3%	5.3%	13.8%	43.5%	31.6%
Cincinnati city	10,888	1.2%	0.6%	1.9%	2.9%	21.8%	2.7%	36.0%	32.9%	27.3%
Cleveland city	10,676	5.6%	3.9%	4.4%	0.0%	28.3%	4.0%	41.3%	12.5%	42.3%
Columbus city	20,106	6.9%	4.7%	1.0%	4.9%	16.4%	2.2%	30.0%	34.0%	37.7%
Dayton city	2,932	6.0%	2.1%	11.3%	0.0%	24.7%	6.1%	25.4%	24.2%	33.2%
Toledo city	7,962	5.2%	3.2%	3.2%	0.0%	15.8%	6.9%	35.6%	30.0%	36.1%
Oklahoma										
Broken Arrow city	1,436	20.9%	0.0%	0.0%	6.5%	33.4%	0.0%	21.9%	17.3%	67.4%
Lawton city	2,995	21.7%	17.1%	0.0%	0.0%	14.8%	0.0%	15.8%	30.7%	23.4%
Norman city	4,936	0.0%	6.0%	0.0%	0.0%	17.5%	0.0%	33.2%	43.3%	25.1%
Oklahoma City city	13,562	12.5%	9.8%	1.5%	1.7%	14.4%	4.9%	33.5%	21.6%	41.4%
Tulsa city	9,015	11.9%	6.3%	1.3%	6.1%	14.7%	0.0%	40.0%	19.6%	44.1%
Oregon										
Beaverton city	1,304	5.4%	8.1%	0.0%	0.0%	2.7%	3.8%	27.7%	52.3%	62.5%
Eugene city	9,232	6.3%	5.3%	2.6%	0.8%	11.6%	2.7%	22.9%	47.8%	24.5%
Gresham city	2,591	0.0%	10.7%	0.0%	2.9%	5.9%	3.6%	26.0%	50.8%	42.5%
Hillsboro city	1,294	7.3%	6.1%	0.0%	18.9%	0.0%	0.0%	24.7%	43.0%	37.7%
Portland city	9,289	0.8%	5.2%	4.0%	0.8%	4.0%	0.0%	38.3%	47.0%	35.8%
Salem city	3,286	22.9%	3.7%	0.0%	0.0%	2.5%	0.0%	53.7%	17.2%	41.9%
Pennsylvania										
Allentown city	1,764	0.0%	0.0%	8.2%	18.3%	43.5%	2.6%	27.5%	0.0%	47.3%
Erie city	2,601	0.0%	0.0%	0.0%	16.4%	5.2%	1.7%	23.6%	53.0%	29.4%
Philadelphia city	20,994	5.0%	3.0%	1.6%	4.6%	12.3%	4.2%	41.5%	27.8%	47.3%
Pittsburgh city	12,032	0.0%	0.0%	3.1%	0.5%	6.4%	0.0%	33.9%	56.1%	20.1%

Table D-3: Places—Household Relationship—*Continued*

		Married Couple Households		Male, No Spouse Present		Female, No Spouse Present		Non-Family Householders		
	Total Householders	With Children	No Children	With Children	No Children	With Children	No Children	Living Alone	Not Alone	Living With Parents
Missouri										
Columbia city	9,801	10.1%	10.3%	0.0%	4.6%	17.1%	1.1%	28.9%	27.9%	7.6%
Independence city	4,308	18.7%	13.4%	5.2%	0.0%	10.6%	0.0%	28.2%	23.9%	21.1%
Kansas City city	28,362	13.5%	10.7%	2.9%	2.1%	18.7%	1.5%	35.1%	15.5%	15.6%
Lee's Summit city	4,220	39.5%	16.8%	0.0%	0.0%	19.7%	0.0%	11.5%	12.5%	20.2%
Springfield city	11,748	19.9%	11.3%	2.0%	0.7%	14.5%	0.8%	32.6%	18.1%	5.5%
St. Louis city	21,202	10.8%	11.8%	0.6%	2.1%	18.0%	1.1%	42.1%	13.5%	12.1%
Montana										
Billings city	4,987	23.7%	16.3%	7.2%	0.0%	12.5%	4.4%	14.2%	21.8%	13.9%
Nebraska										
Lincoln city	13,866	24.0%	17.0%	6.0%	1.8%	8.9%	4.4%	20.9%	16.9%	8.6%
Omaha city	24,169	22.2%	7.9%	3.3%	1.9%	16.4%	1.3%	33.5%	13.6%	12.9%
Nevada										
Henderson city	8,659	31.0%	10.1%	0.0%	1.8%	16.9%	4.5%	16.8%	19.0%	21.0%
Las Vegas city	23,711	28.1%	14.1%	3.4%	3.8%	13.8%	3.2%	23.4%	10.0%	20.1%
North Las Vegas city	12,003	34.2%	13.5%	4.6%	3.5%	19.1%	1.3%	12.2%	11.7%	18.9%
Reno city	12,701	25.8%	9.8%	4.0%	2.9%	10.1%	2.3%	34.9%	10.2%	12.4%
Sparks city	3,009	29.2%	5.5%	8.5%	0.0%	2.9%	2.4%	29.8%	21.7%	22.0%
New Hampshire										
Manchester city	6,723	13.7%	6.8%	9.7%	5.3%	10.8%	1.4%	13.9%	38.4%	9.7%
New Jersey										
Elizabeth city	6,493	22.7%	5.0%	5.5%	2.6%	23.6%	2.4%	21.5%	16.8%	25.2%
Jersey City city	15,286	17.4%	18.6%	0.7%	6.3%	9.7%	2.9%	25.3%	19.2%	19.3%
Newark city	13,145	7.0%	1.7%	7.5%	5.7%	33.2%	1.7%	23.1%	20.1%	24.1%
Paterson city	4,009	7.7%	8.5%	5.1%	2.4%	51.1%	2.0%	12.8%	10.4%	32.9%
New Mexico										
Albuquerque city	20,522	28.2%	7.5%	3.8%	1.0%	16.4%	2.0%	31.1%	10.0%	19.0%
Las Cruces city	3,244	14.1%	6.5%	5.5%	0.0%	34.2%	0.0%	39.7%	0.0%	15.1%
Rio Rancho city	1,959	25.6%	3.5%	0.0%	1.3%	32.2%	4.2%	19.4%	13.7%	46.9%
New York										
Albany city	7,376	11.8%	8.1%	0.9%	1.0%	5.5%	3.4%	50.1%	19.1%	6.8%
Buffalo city	15,543	20.7%	7.5%	2.9%	4.2%	23.8%	0.0%	27.2%	13.6%	15.2%
New York city	352,079	15.1%	10.6%	2.9%	4.0%	11.5%	3.1%	31.3%	21.5%	26.3%
Rochester city	17,164	8.7%	7.3%	1.3%	1.0%	34.4%	2.3%	31.1%	13.7%	13.6%
Syracuse city	7,982	11.7%	11.0%	4.6%	5.9%	20.6%	1.5%	29.1%	15.6%	15.5%
Yonkers city	6,149	27.8%	8.0%	10.1%	6.9%	29.5%	1.5%	9.5%	6.8%	30.0%
North Carolina										
Charlotte city	42,607	16.2%	12.8%	3.8%	1.9%	13.0%	0.6%	35.6%	16.1%	18.2%
Durham city	17,681	20.6%	16.6%	5.7%	0.0%	11.8%	0.0%	31.4%	13.9%	10.0%
Fayetteville city	12,902	13.9%	15.7%	0.4%	1.0%	20.3%	0.7%	35.1%	12.8%	16.1%
Greensboro city	16,180	14.9%	14.2%	5.4%	1.0%	11.4%	3.2%	29.7%	20.3%	12.6%
High Point city	4,447	34.2%	15.8%	2.1%	4.4%	15.9%	6.1%	19.1%	2.4%	21.3%
Raleigh city	23,882	16.5%	12.9%	0.3%	1.2%	16.0%	0.3%	30.9%	21.9%	11.0%
Wilmington city	6,526	14.5%	11.8%	11.4%	0.0%	15.3%	0.0%	21.7%	25.2%	9.2%
Winston-Salem city	9,250	20.6%	12.9%	3.4%	1.9%	22.3%	0.0%	30.3%	8.6%	15.6%
North Dakota										
Fargo city	6,734	23.5%	19.8%	1.7%	0.0%	12.7%	1.3%	22.0%	18.9%	8.3%
Ohio										
Akron city	10,156	14.0%	22.1%	1.8%	1.8%	28.0%	1.8%	17.5%	13.0%	20.7%
Cincinnati city	20,379	9.5%	9.1%	2.2%	0.7%	21.7%	1.9%	36.7%	18.1%	13.6%
Cleveland city	18,527	10.0%	4.0%	6.5%	5.4%	36.1%	1.5%	21.2%	15.2%	20.7%
Columbus city	47,404	19.2%	14.1%	1.5%	1.8%	13.4%	0.9%	30.1%	19.1%	16.7%
Dayton city	6,781	19.4%	12.1%	6.7%	0.0%	15.6%	0.9%	39.1%	6.0%	13.8%
Toledo city	14,326	18.0%	5.3%	1.2%	2.7%	30.2%	0.0%	27.9%	14.7%	18.9%
Oklahoma										
Broken Arrow city	4,653	35.4%	10.7%	2.9%	2.5%	22.2%	0.0%	22.8%	3.5%	18.4%
Lawton city	4,692	20.0%	11.1%	9.5%	0.0%	23.4%	0.0%	18.4%	17.7%	11.5%
Norman city	9,317	31.0%	5.8%	7.0%	3.6%	10.4%	1.3%	23.9%	17.0%	7.5%
Oklahoma City city	32,071	27.7%	10.3%	3.8%	4.8%	10.9%	2.3%	26.4%	13.7%	11.8%
Tulsa city	19,867	23.1%	9.3%	5.5%	1.7%	18.1%	1.5%	29.2%	11.5%	16.6%
Oregon										
Beaverton city	5,852	13.3%	11.9%	6.8%	2.6%	2.2%	0.0%	35.2%	28.1%	9.3%
Eugene city	7,197	24.3%	21.8%	4.2%	0.7%	6.6%	1.5%	30.6%	10.3%	14.3%
Gresham city	4,162	22.4%	3.4%	17.2%	0.0%	23.0%	0.0%	24.6%	9.3%	24.0%
Hillsboro city	3,990	21.8%	14.6%	2.3%	0.0%	17.4%	0.0%	34.0%	9.9%	16.9%
Portland city	34,804	8.8%	13.9%	3.1%	0.6%	7.5%	0.7%	31.0%	34.2%	12.0%
Salem city	7,488	24.4%	5.1%	15.6%	2.1%	24.2%	2.0%	16.2%	10.3%	15.5%
Pennsylvania										
Allentown city	3,651	21.1%	6.5%	0.0%	0.0%	38.6%	4.5%	21.9%	7.3%	28.4%
Erie city	5,771	21.3%	6.2%	3.5%	0.0%	28.0%	4.2%	27.0%	9.8%	18.3%
Philadelphia city	81,343	12.3%	8.0%	2.0%	2.2%	16.4%	1.4%	38.3%	19.4%	23.2%
Pittsburgh city	17,735	11.7%	7.7%	2.2%	2.4%	12.8%	2.5%	36.3%	24.5%	13.9%

Table D-3: Places—Household Relationship—*Continued*

		18 to 24								
		Married Couple Households		Male, No Spouse Present		Female, No Spouse Present		Non-Family Householders		
	Total Householders	With Children	No Children	With Children	No Children	With Children	No Children	Living Alone	Not Alone	Living With Parents
Rhode Island										
Providence city	4,239	4.3%	0.0%	2.8%	0.0%	15.4%	7.0%	27.9%	42.7%	29.6%
South Carolina										
Charleston city	3,651	0.0%	3.5%	7.8%	3.6%	4.1%	2.9%	34.3%	43.8%	28.2%
Columbia city	5,030	0.0%	1.2%	1.7%	0.0%	23.2%	0.0%	32.9%	41.0%	13.2%
North Charleston city	3,236	13.6%	4.5%	4.6%	9.0%	22.2%	0.0%	19.3%	26.8%	51.3%
South Dakota										
Sioux Falls city	4,048	16.6%	3.6%	0.0%	5.4%	2.1%	0.0%	13.8%	58.5%	28.9%
Tennessee										
Chattanooga city	4,038	3.0%	6.4%	9.2%	4.8%	15.5%	0.7%	28.1%	32.3%	36.0%
Clarksville city	3,798	17.0%	19.2%	0.0%	10.5%	20.1%	7.3%	14.2%	11.8%	41.4%
Knoxville city	9,577	7.3%	6.4%	0.0%	0.4%	9.0%	0.7%	26.2%	50.0%	19.3%
Memphis city	11,938	2.5%	6.8%	7.1%	2.4%	25.8%	3.3%	32.3%	19.7%	50.4%
Murfreesboro city	6,381	0.0%	14.9%	0.0%	0.0%	8.9%	1.5%	32.6%	42.0%	23.1%
Nashville-Davidson metropolitan govt (bal)	10,737	5.2%	7.3%	2.0%	11.2%	17.3%	3.4%	26.5%	27.2%	37.9%
Texas										
Abilene city	5,024	9.4%	7.0%	0.8%	0.0%	8.3%	0.0%	45.9%	28.6%	28.8%
Amarillo city	5,882	12.0%	11.3%	4.4%	0.0%	23.0%	0.0%	20.0%	29.2%	40.0%
Arlington city	6,487	4.8%	11.3%	3.4%	6.1%	18.8%	3.9%	23.5%	28.2%	57.8%
Austin city	23,655	2.9%	4.2%	0.7%	2.5%	6.5%	1.9%	30.3%	51.0%	29.1%
Beaumont city	2,447	8.4%	0.0%	11.7%	0.0%	18.9%	0.0%	58.9%	2.1%	56.9%
Brownsville city	1,715	31.7%	7.1%	0.0%	0.0%	30.3%	0.0%	12.1%	18.9%	71.6%
Carrollton city	2,918	2.9%	12.6%	2.9%	12.4%	5.4%	2.1%	47.1%	14.7%	53.6%
College Station city	10,980	2.0%	2.2%	2.1%	5.4%	0.7%	7.9%	32.6%	47.0%	17.6%
Corpus Christi city	8,011	11.6%	2.8%	4.2%	11.2%	14.6%	4.3%	16.9%	34.4%	37.7%
Dallas city	26,790	11.8%	9.2%	3.2%	7.1%	20.9%	3.6%	27.4%	16.8%	49.5%
Denton city	5,023	4.7%	0.8%	0.0%	2.1%	10.6%	1.1%	19.6%	61.2%	16.9%
El Paso city	10,506	24.0%	8.2%	1.9%	5.5%	19.6%	5.2%	22.9%	12.6%	64.3%
Fort Worth city	13,133	6.3%	8.8%	3.8%	10.5%	10.4%	2.7%	25.5%	32.0%	50.2%
Frisco city	1,073	14.6%	3.0%	0.0%	0.0%	0.0%	0.0%	71.9%	10.4%	73.6%
Garland city	2,575	12.0%	8.8%	15.0%	0.0%	19.9%	0.0%	42.4%	1.9%	72.0%
Grand Prairie city	2,179	21.2%	16.8%	5.6%	12.5%	10.7%	0.0%	6.8%	26.5%	56.4%
Houston city	40,572	9.4%	8.3%	2.2%	5.7%	17.5%	7.5%	26.7%	22.8%	53.2%
Irving city	3,628	22.0%	16.2%	1.7%	8.3%	4.8%	0.0%	29.8%	17.1%	46.0%
Killeen city	2,633	12.3%	40.1%	4.8%	0.0%	19.4%	0.0%	16.1%	7.2%	59.9%
Laredo city	1,952	12.8%	0.0%	17.5%	1.8%	37.8%	4.8%	20.5%	4.9%	70.7%
Lewisville city	1,362	6.6%	5.0%	0.0%	3.3%	7.2%	2.8%	17.8%	57.3%	52.1%
Lubbock city	12,913	6.7%	6.5%	0.0%	6.3%	8.0%	2.8%	44.1%	25.6%	32.8%
McAllen city	1,960	20.2%	2.6%	0.0%	0.0%	31.2%	0.0%	22.0%	24.0%	71.6%
McKinney city	2,328	20.6%	4.8%	0.0%	15.5%	0.0%	18.8%	26.7%	13.7%	51.3%
Mesquite city	2,611	5.7%	12.4%	6.5%	3.6%	35.0%	0.0%	23.4%	13.4%	60.5%
Midland city	3,353	18.5%	5.8%	0.0%	12.4%	18.9%	0.0%	14.5%	29.9%	38.5%
Odessa city	2,146	10.6%	0.0%	12.7%	2.3%	43.1%	0.0%	20.8%	10.5%	45.1%
Pasadena city	2,445	15.6%	3.7%	4.5%	4.6%	0.0%	5.9%	37.0%	28.6%	60.6%
Pearland city	984	24.0%	0.0%	0.0%	38.6%	0.0%	0.0%	28.7%	8.7%	74.6%
Plano city	5,425	0.0%	8.9%	10.2%	3.0%	3.3%	0.0%	62.1%	12.5%	57.7%
Richardson city	1,988	5.2%	0.0%	0.0%	6.9%	18.4%	0.0%	61.3%	8.2%	54.2%
Round Rock city	1,135	0.0%	8.8%	0.0%	0.0%	29.4%	0.0%	28.4%	33.4%	53.3%
San Angelo city	2,461	15.6%	9.0%	4.4%	6.5%	8.1%	2.0%	6.4%	47.9%	20.3%
San Antonio city	25,751	11.4%	2.9%	6.3%	3.0%	9.7%	2.5%	37.2%	26.9%	51.2%
Tyler city	2,140	5.0%	10.7%	4.5%	0.0%	17.9%	0.0%	34.3%	27.6%	42.6%
Waco city	6,120	1.7%	3.3%	4.1%	4.4%	10.6%	0.0%	31.9%	43.9%	29.3%
Wichita Falls city	3,282	6.5%	17.6%	0.0%	2.9%	18.4%	0.0%	22.2%	32.5%	21.9%
Utah										
Orem city	1,761	39.2%	25.4%	0.0%	0.0%	18.4%	0.0%	0.0%	17.0%	46.6%
Provo city	8,317	15.2%	39.8%	2.6%	0.0%	1.1%	3.0%	2.2%	36.0%	13.4%
Salt Lake City city	5,447	5.9%	13.6%	0.0%	15.3%	4.5%	0.0%	17.8%	43.0%	30.5%
West Jordan city	1,348	41.1%	33.2%	4.5%	0.0%	16.5%	0.0%	0.0%	4.7%	63.2%
West Valley City city	735	8.0%	11.4%	0.0%	0.0%	0.0%	0.0%	14.1%	66.4%	55.5%
Virginia										
Alexandria city	1,605	8.2%	4.8%	5.2%	0.0%	0.0%	13.5%	20.8%	47.5%	34.3%
Chesapeake city	2,431	13.0%	3.7%	4.3%	0.0%	10.4%	2.5%	30.4%	35.8%	69.8%
Hampton city	1,961	8.6%	18.8%	3.8%	0.0%	15.9%	0.0%	42.1%	10.8%	45.0%
Newport News city	4,109	6.8%	13.3%	0.0%	1.5%	12.5%	1.5%	46.3%	18.1%	37.2%
Norfolk city	6,829	10.1%	19.3%	0.0%	0.0%	15.0%	6.1%	27.8%	21.7%	23.1%
Portsmouth city	1,706	36.1%	0.0%	0.0%	19.0%	15.9%	13.7%	15.4%	0.0%	39.9%
Richmond city	6,801	0.9%	3.0%	1.1%	5.0%	19.5%	6.9%	25.4%	38.2%	19.4%
Roanoke city	1,246	21.7%	3.8%	0.0%	0.0%	5.1%	0.0%	20.9%	48.6%	46.9%
Virginia Beach city	6,215	12.0%	21.9%	0.0%	0.5%	11.7%	6.6%	20.4%	27.0%	51.0%
Washington										
Bellevue city	979	0.0%	15.3%	0.0%	0.0%	0.0%	9.3%	18.5%	56.9%	62.8%
Everett city	1,132	26.1%	0.0%	0.0%	4.5%	11.3%	0.0%	13.7%	44.3%	61.3%
Federal Way city	1,739	0.0%	0.0%	8.6%	9.4%	16.6%	3.4%	38.4%	23.6%	48.4%
Kent city	1,491	0.0%	0.0%	3.6%	5.6%	10.9%	22.0%	20.3%	37.6%	63.5%

Table D-3: Places—Household Relationship—*Continued*

	Total Householders	25 to 31								Living With Parents
		Married Couple Households		Male, No Spouse Present		Female, No Spouse Present		Non-Family Householders		
		With Children	No Children	With Children	No Children	With Children	No Children	Living Alone	Not Alone	
Rhode Island										
Providence city	10,668	5.2%	13.9%	3.5%	0.0%	23.3%	3.4%	27.5%	23.2%	16.5%
South Carolina										
Charleston city	7,896	3.0%	16.1%	1.7%	0.0%	13.1%	0.7%	33.5%	31.9%	11.7%
Columbia city	7,610	11.4%	6.3%	0.0%	0.0%	12.2%	0.0%	46.4%	23.6%	13.1%
North Charleston city	4,434	29.7%	7.7%	0.0%	4.1%	29.9%	1.9%	24.2%	2.6%	9.4%
South Dakota										
Sioux Falls city	10,826	19.5%	6.0%	13.2%	0.0%	12.3%	2.9%	19.3%	26.7%	9.0%
Tennessee										
Chattanooga city	8,682	21.7%	8.7%	2.1%	6.3%	14.7%	0.7%	33.8%	12.0%	14.3%
Clarksville city	12,611	36.1%	23.6%	6.9%	0.0%	6.5%	0.0%	20.0%	6.8%	5.0%
Knoxville city	11,685	16.2%	11.6%	11.3%	1.0%	8.3%	0.8%	35.0%	15.8%	11.2%
Memphis city	31,689	14.3%	8.4%	4.5%	3.2%	28.0%	2.2%	27.0%	12.2%	24.3%
Murfreesboro city	6,750	14.5%	19.6%	6.6%	2.0%	3.7%	0.7%	27.9%	25.1%	11.1%
Nashville-Davidson metropolitan govt (bal)	39,575	14.2%	13.7%	0.3%	2.4%	10.8%	1.3%	35.4%	22.0%	12.3%
Texas										
Abilene city	4,986	31.3%	24.4%	0.0%	1.8%	11.4%	0.0%	19.3%	11.9%	11.7%
Amarillo city	10,646	25.9%	9.0%	11.7%	1.8%	19.9%	0.0%	13.8%	17.8%	10.4%
Arlington city	19,670	29.0%	12.0%	2.1%	5.1%	24.1%	2.9%	18.9%	5.9%	20.9%
Austin city	59,551	10.1%	14.7%	1.2%	3.2%	8.2%	0.6%	29.6%	32.4%	8.5%
Beaumont city	5,675	34.7%	7.3%	0.0%	0.0%	22.8%	5.9%	19.1%	10.2%	24.2%
Brownsville city	4,172	44.7%	11.0%	7.6%	0.0%	16.1%	0.0%	15.1%	5.6%	51.0%
Carrollton city	7,621	17.9%	15.4%	3.9%	1.3%	12.0%	0.6%	29.2%	19.7%	18.3%
College Station city	7,240	29.9%	13.3%	3.8%	1.1%	14.8%	0.0%	27.1%	10.0%	12.9%
Corpus Christi city	12,702	23.5%	7.7%	2.3%	1.5%	24.9%	2.3%	24.1%	13.7%	24.8%
Dallas city	67,148	19.4%	11.8%	5.2%	3.1%	16.6%	2.0%	26.7%	15.3%	15.9%
Denton city	8,340	11.4%	15.5%	2.7%	8.2%	16.3%	1.1%	29.0%	15.9%	12.8%
El Paso city	21,544	35.8%	11.5%	6.1%	5.5%	15.5%	1.6%	16.1%	7.8%	31.3%
Fort Worth city	36,335	35.0%	13.8%	6.4%	1.0%	12.7%	1.5%	21.0%	8.6%	21.5%
Frisco city	4,524	32.8%	20.5%	0.0%	0.0%	17.5%	2.7%	19.1%	7.4%	21.6%
Garland city	8,205	28.8%	13.3%	0.0%	5.0%	28.0%	0.0%	22.1%	2.8%	25.2%
Grand Prairie city	5,871	34.2%	9.6%	9.5%	6.4%	22.0%	1.8%	11.2%	5.2%	24.0%
Houston city	129,868	21.4%	13.3%	4.0%	3.7%	10.1%	1.4%	33.1%	13.2%	17.6%
Irving city	13,864	26.7%	12.7%	6.7%	5.4%	15.8%	0.3%	25.3%	7.0%	13.5%
Killeen city	8,976	40.7%	15.9%	0.9%	1.2%	18.9%	1.0%	20.8%	0.6%	14.9%
Laredo city	7,415	37.0%	10.0%	3.9%	5.7%	28.8%	3.6%	8.4%	2.5%	29.5%
Lewisville city	6,614	22.0%	16.9%	5.8%	0.0%	18.9%	0.5%	22.3%	13.6%	12.5%
Lubbock city	11,673	27.1%	10.8%	2.1%	5.2%	10.4%	6.3%	24.3%	13.8%	14.0%
McAllen city	4,022	31.9%	5.6%	0.0%	8.2%	14.1%	0.0%	19.6%	20.5%	37.5%
McKinney city	6,080	28.2%	17.4%	4.4%	0.0%	5.5%	0.0%	18.7%	25.9%	10.8%
Mesquite city	7,105	26.7%	3.3%	1.4%	8.0%	17.4%	6.4%	26.3%	10.4%	22.2%
Midland city	5,399	27.8%	6.5%	1.6%	4.6%	10.2%	0.0%	32.2%	17.2%	23.6%
Odessa city	5,138	44.1%	1.9%	0.0%	2.3%	21.9%	1.8%	15.2%	12.8%	21.2%
Pasadena city	4,389	26.4%	10.9%	8.7%	12.6%	24.2%	0.0%	12.5%	4.7%	27.0%
Pearland city	4,467	55.1%	8.7%	10.3%	0.0%	2.8%	0.0%	23.1%	0.0%	16.7%
Plano city	10,597	14.7%	26.1%	2.9%	0.0%	14.6%	0.5%	26.2%	15.0%	16.3%
Richardson city	4,040	21.9%	21.7%	0.0%	0.0%	17.3%	1.5%	26.5%	11.1%	19.4%
Round Rock city	4,246	39.2%	11.5%	4.5%	0.0%	2.4%	0.8%	36.1%	5.5%	11.3%
San Angelo city	5,449	45.4%	5.8%	0.0%	0.0%	2.3%	0.0%	29.4%	17.0%	5.6%
San Antonio city	62,171	24.3%	10.0%	3.3%	1.5%	19.3%	2.2%	27.4%	11.9%	27.0%
Tyler city	4,721	27.4%	10.2%	0.0%	0.0%	17.3%	1.9%	30.4%	12.8%	20.0%
Waco city	6,971	18.7%	13.9%	1.4%	0.8%	31.1%	0.0%	25.0%	9.1%	14.5%
Wichita Falls city	6,464	30.0%	4.5%	3.2%	0.7%	32.5%	0.0%	25.9%	3.2%	7.9%
Utah										
Orem city	4,298	52.1%	13.5%	10.6%	5.7%	5.3%	0.0%	7.1%	5.7%	13.1%
Provo city	6,762	47.2%	25.0%	1.4%	0.0%	1.5%	4.2%	5.7%	15.1%	8.3%
Salt Lake City city	11,980	21.1%	14.6%	3.6%	0.0%	4.8%	0.0%	32.7%	23.2%	11.1%
West Jordan city	4,702	66.5%	7.8%	1.9%	4.0%	12.5%	0.0%	1.9%	5.5%	28.4%
West Valley City city	4,465	46.3%	17.1%	4.5%	0.0%	2.4%	0.0%	19.9%	9.8%	27.3%
Virginia										
Alexandria city	11,942	11.7%	14.6%	2.5%	0.9%	11.7%	0.3%	34.5%	23.8%	6.7%
Chesapeake city	8,110	20.4%	27.4%	6.8%	0.9%	16.0%	0.0%	15.9%	12.7%	24.8%
Hampton city	7,670	16.9%	13.1%	0.0%	0.8%	28.4%	2.4%	28.8%	9.6%	18.4%
Newport News city	9,779	23.9%	10.2%	4.1%	0.4%	22.3%	1.7%	28.3%	9.0%	9.4%
Norfolk city	13,552	25.4%	11.3%	2.7%	0.4%	20.9%	1.4%	24.5%	13.5%	16.6%
Portsmouth city	4,922	25.1%	7.4%	0.0%	3.8%	20.1%	0.0%	28.2%	15.5%	18.2%
Richmond city	14,475	7.9%	10.5%	3.9%	4.0%	12.1%	2.9%	36.9%	21.7%	12.4%
Roanoke city	5,145	22.0%	11.0%	10.3%	1.3%	16.6%	0.0%	20.1%	18.7%	18.6%
Virginia Beach city	19,560	24.9%	15.9%	3.5%	3.2%	16.5%	2.1%	22.2%	11.5%	21.0%
Washington										
Bellevue city	7,824	17.5%	17.4%	0.6%	0.9%	12.3%	0.9%	23.8%	26.6%	4.5%
Everett city	4,775	21.9%	20.5%	6.2%	0.0%	21.8%	0.0%	16.4%	13.2%	15.6%
Federal Way city	4,381	22.6%	20.8%	2.7%	3.1%	13.7%	2.6%	17.7%	16.8%	22.1%
Kent city	5,305	18.8%	14.1%	1.2%	4.2%	22.0%	0.0%	18.1%	21.5%	22.2%

Table D-3: Places—Household Relationship—*Continued*

		18 to 24								
	Total Householders	Married Couple Households		Male, No Spouse Present		Female, No Spouse Present		Non-Family Householders		Living With Parents
		With Children	No Children	With Children	No Children	With Children	No Children	Living Alone	Not Alone	
Washington—Cont.										
Renton city..............................	1,364	0.0%	13.1%	0.0%	8.4%	0.0%	0.0%	36.4%	42.1%	40.9%
Seattle city..............................	16,063	0.0%	2.8%	0.0%	3.4%	0.9%	2.8%	33.3%	56.9%	24.7%
Spokane city............................	5,536	4.2%	2.7%	4.0%	2.4%	9.2%	6.8%	29.3%	41.4%	28.0%
Spokane Valley city	1,049	0.0%	0.0%	0.0%	23.2%	20.4%	0.0%	21.1%	35.4%	45.3%
Tacoma city..............................	4,102	8.4%	14.4%	1.3%	0.0%	20.5%	0.0%	28.7%	26.7%	37.5%
Vancouver city	2,000	0.0%	6.1%	0.0%	7.8%	26.4%	0.0%	20.8%	39.0%	62.9%
Yakima city..............................	1,907	36.7%	11.9%	3.9%	7.0%	7.4%	8.2%	7.4%	17.5%	50.0%
Wisconsin										
Green Bay city..........................	2,650	8.9%	0.0%	0.0%	17.8%	24.5%	0.0%	10.0%	38.8%	42.0%
Kenosha city	2,142	0.0%	0.0%	0.0%	0.0%	2.4%	0.0%	57.1%	40.5%	51.5%
Madison city	10,201	0.0%	10.8%	0.0%	2.2%	6.0%	3.4%	20.8%	56.8%	21.0%
Milwaukee city	14,544	3.7%	3.5%	2.4%	3.0%	27.1%	4.7%	29.6%	26.1%	42.8%

Table D-3: Places—Household Relationship—*Continued*

		25 to 31								
	Total Householders	Married Couple Households		Male, No Spouse Present		Female, No Spouse Present		Non-Family Householders		Living With Parents
		With Children	No Children	With Children	No Children	With Children	No Children	Living Alone	Not Alone	
Washington—Cont.										
Renton city............................	5,066	28.7%	3.7%	16.6%	3.4%	18.9%	2.3%	12.2%	14.2%	12.7%
Seattle city...........................	52,713	7.1%	15.3%	2.1%	0.6%	4.0%	2.5%	38.3%	30.1%	5.5%
Spokane city	12,635	25.2%	9.7%	8.1%	0.0%	14.5%	0.4%	24.5%	17.7%	11.7%
Spokane Valley city	4,925	9.5%	21.8%	8.6%	0.0%	23.1%	0.0%	24.3%	12.7%	7.8%
Tacoma city...........................	9,023	24.9%	15.0%	3.2%	0.6%	5.6%	2.0%	28.2%	20.5%	19.6%
Vancouver city	6,297	20.7%	9.7%	4.5%	3.4%	14.4%	2.3%	25.8%	19.3%	26.8%
Yakima city............................	2,269	32.2%	4.6%	4.1%	8.9%	17.2%	0.0%	29.1%	3.9%	28.4%
Wisconsin										
Green Bay city	5,323	11.1%	29.4%	2.6%	6.1%	19.3%	0.0%	20.5%	11.0%	15.4%
Kenosha city	3,141	50.3%	14.7%	0.0%	0.0%	5.4%	0.0%	14.3%	15.2%	34.6%
Madison city	19,846	21.6%	21.6%	1.0%	0.2%	2.8%	0.0%	33.9%	19.0%	6.7%
Milwaukee city	37,301	13.7%	6.4%	5.2%	2.0%	30.2%	0.5%	29.3%	12.7%	16.2%

Table D-4: Metropolitan/Micropolitan Statistical Areas—Household Relationship

	Total Householders	18 to 24								Living With Parents
		Married Couple Households		Male, No Spouse Present		Female, No Spouse Present		Non-Family Householders		
		With Children	No Children	With Children	No Children	With Children	No Children	Living Alone	Not Alone	
Abilene, TX	6,352	7.4%	5.6%	5.9%	4.0%	9.7%	2.4%	41.2%	23.9%	31.3%
Adrian, MI micro	1,417	3.0%	20.7%	0.0%	5.4%	4.9%	0.0%	44.1%	21.9%	49.9%
Akron, OH	14,138	2.1%	5.3%	3.0%	4.9%	15.4%	4.0%	22.2%	43.1%	43.9%
Albany-Schenectady-Troy, NY	13,614	3.7%	3.9%	0.7%	0.9%	15.1%	2.9%	28.7%	44.1%	45.7%
Albany, GA	2,060	4.6%	4.2%	26.5%	2.3%	33.5%	9.5%	14.3%	5.1%	53.4%
Albany, OR	4,206	6.1%	6.3%	0.0%	2.4%	7.9%	0.0%	18.2%	59.1%	18.4%
Albertville, AL micro	1,214	42.6%	1.6%	1.3%	0.0%	38.6%	0.0%	13.8%	2.2%	55.7%
Albuquerque, NM	13,434	11.0%	9.3%	3.7%	6.0%	19.4%	1.7%	17.8%	31.1%	53.7%
Alexandria, LA	2,420	32.1%	15.3%	0.0%	3.9%	19.5%	0.9%	21.2%	7.1%	44.8%
Allentown-Bethlehem-Easton, PA-NJ	8,518	12.0%	1.7%	1.7%	9.9%	23.1%	6.0%	27.3%	18.4%	56.8%
Altoona, PA	1,694	7.1%	10.2%	2.5%	0.0%	26.0%	0.0%	52.5%	1.8%	51.7%
Amarillo, TX	7,057	13.6%	9.4%	5.4%	0.0%	19.2%	1.3%	24.8%	26.2%	41.3%
Ames, IA	7,601	0.8%	1.7%	0.0%	0.0%	1.4%	1.9%	26.9%	67.2%	8.3%
Anchorage, AK	7,990	18.9%	14.9%	5.1%	0.0%	8.5%	12.1%	9.0%	31.5%	43.0%
Ann Arbor, MI	12,910	1.2%	2.4%	1.0%	0.3%	2.1%	1.1%	31.3%	60.5%	22.5%
Anniston-Oxford-Jacksonville, AL	2,158	2.3%	3.4%	0.0%	16.6%	42.5%	0.0%	20.9%	14.4%	50.9%
Appleton, WI	3,301	0.0%	15.8%	0.0%	3.0%	0.0%	8.8%	36.3%	36.1%	55.6%
Asheville, NC	4,904	0.9%	15.9%	1.0%	1.5%	12.2%	4.7%	16.5%	47.5%	46.5%
Ashtabula, OH micro	1,002	52.9%	0.0%	0.0%	0.0%	40.9%	0.0%	6.2%	0.0%	56.8%
Athens-Clarke County, GA	9,710	1.1%	5.5%	1.4%	3.8%	8.3%	0.0%	33.2%	46.7%	21.8%
Atlanta-Sandy Springs-Roswell, GA	64,510	8.1%	8.3%	2.3%	3.8%	13.1%	4.8%	33.9%	25.6%	57.3%
Atlantic City-Hammonton, NJ	1,854	26.4%	0.0%	7.0%	0.0%	26.4%	0.0%	20.3%	19.8%	61.3%
Auburn-Opelika, AL	8,485	7.0%	3.6%	0.0%	5.3%	0.3%	6.6%	37.9%	39.3%	26.6%
Augusta-Richmond County, GA-SC	6,050	6.5%	25.7%	0.0%	6.0%	19.2%	0.9%	29.4%	12.3%	61.8%
Augusta-Waterville, ME micro	1,329	0.0%	28.4%	11.4%	6.0%	0.0%	0.0%	23.3%	30.9%	43.3%
Austin-Round Rock, TX	39,832	3.1%	5.2%	1.0%	3.5%	5.8%	2.3%	31.2%	47.9%	38.0%
Bakersfield, CA	12,256	12.0%	8.7%	7.4%	7.3%	19.7%	3.3%	10.5%	31.1%	59.5%
Baltimore-Columbia-Towson, MD	25,876	7.0%	7.6%	2.4%	6.8%	19.5%	3.2%	26.5%	26.8%	56.6%
Bangor, ME	2,215	6.5%	4.7%	26.1%	0.0%	2.5%	2.4%	19.1%	38.7%	34.3%
Barnstable Town, MA	1,178	0.0%	5.5%	5.4%	0.0%	0.0%	0.0%	66.0%	23.0%	71.1%
Baton Rouge, LA	19,606	1.3%	6.3%	2.0%	2.7%	18.6%	4.7%	29.1%	35.2%	42.1%
Battle Creek, MI	1,563	0.0%	4.9%	23.0%	0.0%	17.2%	0.0%	31.9%	23.0%	53.2%
Bay City, MI	1,545	24.5%	3.9%	1.5%	0.0%	57.3%	0.0%	11.7%	1.1%	55.2%
Beaumont-Port Arthur, TX	6,470	15.8%	12.5%	6.7%	0.0%	20.2%	0.0%	37.9%	6.9%	59.1%
Beckley, WV	1,715	7.3%	8.8%	0.0%	12.0%	36.3%	2.7%	16.7%	16.3%	40.2%
Bellingham, WA	5,536	0.8%	2.4%	0.0%	0.0%	3.4%	12.6%	19.7%	61.2%	31.8%
Bend-Redmond, OR	1,187	44.8%	3.6%	0.0%	0.0%	3.5%	0.0%	3.2%	44.9%	52.0%
Billings, MT	4,226	8.1%	0.0%	0.0%	0.9%	41.6%	0.0%	26.0%	23.5%	39.7%
Binghamton, NY	4,437	0.7%	2.8%	0.7%	0.0%	17.2%	3.4%	37.9%	37.3%	43.5%
Birmingham-Hoover, AL	14,553	11.3%	7.6%	0.7%	2.2%	24.5%	2.3%	28.6%	23.0%	56.0%
Bismarck, ND	2,527	0.0%	0.0%	4.6%	0.0%	26.1%	13.6%	31.9%	23.8%	26.9%
Blacksburg-Christiansburg-Radford, VA.	10,109	9.2%	3.9%	3.0%	0.0%	4.0%	5.0%	17.4%	57.3%	15.7%
Bloomington, IL	6,204	0.6%	2.1%	3.3%	1.4%	3.2%	0.0%	33.9%	55.5%	28.8%
Bloomington, IN	9,790	0.2%	3.5%	0.0%	1.6%	7.6%	3.2%	38.8%	45.1%	11.6%
Bloomsburg-Berwick, PA	1,767	4.8%	2.8%	0.0%	0.0%	9.2%	0.0%	47.7%	35.5%	45.3%
Boise City, ID	11,755	17.8%	6.7%	5.3%	4.3%	6.0%	7.6%	19.4%	32.9%	46.0%
Boston-Cambridge-Newton, MA-NH	48,362	2.9%	3.0%	1.8%	4.0%	12.1%	4.6%	22.2%	49.2%	48.9%
Boulder, CO	12,192	0.5%	2.3%	0.0%	0.0%	2.1%	1.8%	35.3%	57.9%	27.4%
Bowling Green, KY	5,153	10.7%	7.6%	0.0%	0.0%	10.5%	1.2%	28.3%	41.6%	28.9%
Bremerton-Silverdale, WA	3,462	25.9%	17.6%	0.0%	0.0%	11.5%	0.0%	18.1%	27.0%	46.0%
Bridgeport-Stamford-Norwalk, CT	4,217	0.0%	1.3%	3.7%	7.2%	21.9%	9.7%	14.2%	42.1%	63.9%
Brownsville-Harlingen, TX	2,899	43.3%	4.2%	0.0%	0.0%	25.3%	0.0%	11.5%	15.8%	74.1%
Brunswick, GA	1,672	20.4%	37.3%	3.6%	0.0%	3.6%	0.0%	32.2%	2.9%	49.9%
Buffalo-Cheektowaga-Niagara Falls, NY.	16,535	1.7%	4.6%	0.5%	8.6%	17.8%	2.5%	30.1%	34.2%	56.9%
Burlington-South Burlington, VT	4,295	13.2%	0.0%	0.0%	0.0%	8.1%	0.0%	13.6%	65.1%	27.6%
Burlington, NC	2,799	1.0%	5.3%	10.1%	20.9%	1.6%	0.0%	37.4%	23.8%	45.1%
California-Lexington Park, MD	908	32.0%	8.8%	0.0%	0.0%	46.6%	0.0%	0.0%	12.6%	62.5%
Canton-Massillon, OH	4,788	9.5%	6.7%	0.0%	3.6%	24.0%	0.0%	39.9%	16.2%	59.1%
Cape Coral-Fort Myers, FL	5,098	7.8%	6.6%	12.2%	3.1%	13.1%	4.5%	34.5%	18.3%	60.7%
Cape Girardeau, MO-IL	2,411	4.4%	6.0%	0.0%	0.0%	29.1%	13.4%	19.6%	27.5%	39.2%
Carbondale-Marion, IL	3,730	4.7%	12.2%	0.0%	0.0%	11.4%	0.0%	55.4%	16.2%	42.1%
Carson City, NV	268	54.1%	0.0%	0.0%	0.0%	9.0%	36.9%	0.0%	0.0%	59.6%
Casper, WY	2,495	3.0%	11.7%	0.0%	0.0%	8.1%	4.9%	37.4%	34.9%	26.3%
Cedar Rapids, IA	4,110	0.6%	15.6%	0.0%	13.2%	22.2%	2.2%	21.0%	25.3%	44.7%
Chambersburg-Waynesboro, PA	1,303	7.1%	2.6%	0.0%	0.0%	24.4%	0.0%	31.7%	34.2%	61.7%
Champaign-Urbana, IL	12,659	0.8%	2.0%	0.0%	0.2%	1.6%	2.4%	47.4%	45.5%	15.6%
Charleston-North Charleston, SC	13,295	4.0%	6.2%	4.4%	5.5%	10.4%	5.5%	25.4%	38.6%	45.5%
Charleston, WV	2,897	17.6%	0.0%	31.9%	0.0%	13.9%	0.0%	20.0%	16.6%	50.8%
Charlotte-Concord-Gastonia, NC-SC	27,334	7.8%	6.4%	2.7%	5.8%	17.1%	3.8%	22.9%	33.5%	55.6%
Charlottesville, VA	3,799	12.8%	2.7%	0.0%	0.0%	8.8%	0.0%	13.1%	62.6%	25.5%
Chattanooga, TN-GA	7,499	13.8%	6.2%	13.1%	2.6%	11.0%	2.3%	21.9%	29.1%	45.6%
Cheyenne, WY	3,446	5.5%	17.6%	0.0%	12.7%	15.9%	0.0%	30.6%	17.7%	31.1%
Chicago-Naperville-Elgin, IL-IN-WI	97,541	6.1%	6.8%	2.9%	4.7%	14.8%	3.5%	32.1%	29.0%	63.2%
Chico, CA	8,087	1.6%	10.9%	0.0%	5.5%	9.4%	0.0%	23.7%	48.8%	32.8%
Cincinnati, OH-KY-IN	32,749	4.4%	7.3%	2.5%	5.0%	23.4%	2.1%	28.2%	27.2%	51.3%
Clarksburg, WV micro	1,276	8.5%	0.0%	4.1%	8.7%	27.4%	0.0%	13.0%	38.3%	59.3%
Clarksville, TN-KY	7,636	21.6%	17.4%	0.2%	10.1%	17.0%	3.6%	18.9%	11.0%	36.8%
Cleveland-Elyria, OH	26,000	5.4%	5.9%	1.9%	2.7%	23.2%	2.9%	35.1%	23.0%	58.2%

Table D-4: Metropolitan/Micropolitan Statistical Areas—Household Relationship

		25 to 31								
		Married Couple Households		Male, No Spouse Present		Female, No Spouse Present		Non-Family Householders		
	Total Householders	With Children	No Children	With Children	No Children	With Children	No Children	Living Alone	Not Alone	Living With Parents
Abilene, TX	6,723	38.7%	21.3%	1.0%	2.8%	9.7%	0.0%	16.5%	10.1%	11.2%
Adrian, MI	2,248	29.2%	12.6%	4.0%	0.0%	13.9%	0.0%	20.3%	20.0%	28.2%
Akron, OH	27,186	20.8%	19.9%	2.5%	0.7%	18.2%	1.2%	24.4%	12.4%	24.5%
Albany-Schenectady-Troy, NY	28,976	17.0%	11.1%	2.2%	1.1%	13.0%	0.8%	33.2%	21.6%	23.0%
Albany, GA	7,105	16.8%	9.7%	7.2%	2.2%	34.2%	1.9%	26.8%	1.2%	20.1%
Albany, OR	3,787	20.4%	12.4%	0.0%	0.0%	9.3%	0.0%	23.1%	34.7%	19.0%
Albertville, AL	2,495	27.9%	18.6%	1.2%	0.0%	40.1%	0.0%	6.9%	5.3%	12.5%
Albuquerque, NM	31,926	27.0%	8.9%	3.3%	1.1%	19.7%	2.4%	25.8%	11.7%	23.8%
Alexandria, LA	5,934	35.9%	6.3%	12.0%	0.0%	21.5%	0.0%	13.5%	10.7%	21.1%
Allentown-Bethlehem-Easton, PA-NJ	23,451	19.9%	22.5%	3.3%	0.1%	18.9%	0.7%	19.1%	15.5%	26.2%
Altoona, PA	4,153	39.8%	11.4%	2.8%	0.0%	22.9%	0.0%	18.5%	4.5%	17.0%
Amarillo, TX	13,126	28.4%	8.9%	9.8%	2.2%	16.4%	0.0%	14.8%	19.5%	11.7%
Ames, IA	5,550	24.0%	20.3%	1.8%	0.0%	8.6%	0.0%	24.5%	20.9%	5.3%
Anchorage, AK	15,800	29.4%	27.7%	3.4%	5.2%	13.2%	2.2%	10.8%	8.0%	17.8%
Ann Arbor, MI	18,843	10.0%	15.4%	3.9%	1.7%	14.2%	2.2%	30.5%	22.1%	14.3%
Anniston-Oxford-Jacksonville, AL	4,127	28.2%	3.3%	2.6%	2.7%	27.0%	0.0%	33.6%	2.6%	37.3%
Appleton, WI	10,153	30.9%	9.2%	5.6%	0.0%	18.3%	0.0%	22.4%	13.6%	13.1%
Asheville, NC	15,342	23.9%	16.2%	3.6%	0.5%	9.7%	0.0%	30.7%	15.3%	21.7%
Ashtabula, OH	3,444	26.2%	2.5%	14.5%	2.6%	27.2%	0.0%	2.1%	24.9%	12.8%
Athens-Clarke County, GA	9,101	18.4%	11.0%	0.8%	0.0%	17.5%	0.0%	30.7%	21.5%	13.9%
Atlanta-Sandy Springs-Roswell, GA	201,132	20.7%	13.3%	4.4%	4.0%	16.2%	2.3%	26.7%	12.4%	21.0%
Atlantic City-Hammonton, NJ	8,129	30.9%	2.6%	5.6%	3.3%	31.7%	4.7%	15.8%	5.5%	27.9%
Auburn-Opelika, AL	7,602	25.1%	14.3%	3.8%	2.2%	10.2%	2.1%	31.2%	11.2%	12.0%
Augusta-Richmond County, GA-SC	19,029	25.5%	14.4%	0.9%	0.5%	19.2%	1.6%	29.2%	8.8%	36.0%
Augusta-Waterville, ME	5,022	9.6%	16.4%	24.8%	0.0%	20.5%	0.0%	18.9%	9.8%	21.1%
Austin-Round Rock, TX	98,587	17.2%	15.5%	2.2%	2.5%	9.1%	1.6%	25.0%	26.9%	12.7%
Bakersfield, CA	31,847	37.1%	6.9%	3.6%	4.3%	25.0%	1.5%	12.6%	8.9%	20.6%
Baltimore-Columbia-Towson, MD	107,954	21.7%	14.2%	3.8%	2.5%	15.0%	2.7%	26.2%	13.9%	23.0%
Bangor, ME	6,112	15.7%	4.1%	11.1%	0.0%	12.9%	7.9%	28.0%	20.4%	22.5%
Barnstable Town, MA	4,533	28.9%	11.3%	1.5%	3.1%	32.0%	1.6%	13.6%	8.0%	21.8%
Baton Rouge, LA	32,075	24.7%	14.8%	1.8%	3.8%	15.3%	1.8%	24.9%	12.8%	20.0%
Battle Creek, MI	4,695	29.6%	3.2%	2.6%	4.2%	32.7%	3.0%	16.5%	8.3%	25.3%
Bay City, MI	4,748	46.0%	11.0%	0.0%	0.0%	17.8%	0.0%	18.5%	6.8%	16.4%
Beaumont-Port Arthur, TX	18,658	36.6%	10.9%	1.7%	1.3%	18.7%	2.3%	20.3%	8.1%	17.8%
Beckley, WV	3,904	32.3%	9.9%	7.4%	2.9%	25.0%	0.0%	12.7%	9.8%	13.9%
Bellingham, WA	7,448	31.2%	14.3%	2.9%	1.6%	10.5%	2.0%	16.6%	20.9%	10.3%
Bend-Redmond, OR	5,478	26.1%	12.9%	11.2%	6.7%	15.4%	0.0%	14.2%	13.6%	24.8%
Billings, MT	6,456	29.5%	13.4%	5.6%	0.6%	12.5%	3.8%	13.9%	20.8%	19.6%
Binghamton, NY	8,254	21.5%	10.8%	9.2%	0.8%	20.6%	0.0%	24.6%	12.5%	27.2%
Birmingham-Hoover, AL	42,989	31.2%	12.2%	3.0%	1.8%	21.2%	0.7%	22.3%	7.6%	20.8%
Bismarck, ND	7,762	24.3%	20.4%	4.5%	0.0%	3.8%	0.0%	10.4%	36.5%	6.6%
Blacksburg-Christiansburg-Radford, VA.	5,359	34.5%	15.0%	2.0%	0.0%	9.9%	0.0%	23.3%	15.3%	9.7%
Bloomington, IL	9,878	18.4%	18.3%	2.2%	4.1%	15.9%	0.3%	29.6%	11.1%	14.4%
Bloomington, IN	7,303	22.5%	7.3%	3.7%	0.0%	8.7%	0.0%	34.3%	23.5%	13.3%
Bloomsburg-Berwick, PA	1,702	19.4%	10.5%	8.3%	0.0%	3.0%	0.0%	25.1%	33.7%	22.8%
Boise City, ID	25,931	38.0%	15.9%	2.7%	1.3%	5.7%	0.5%	21.2%	14.8%	12.6%
Boston-Cambridge-Newton, MA-NH	176,459	15.2%	15.9%	2.2%	2.8%	10.4%	2.1%	25.3%	26.1%	23.7%
Boulder, CO	12,288	20.3%	11.2%	3.1%	1.7%	3.4%	0.9%	25.1%	34.4%	13.3%
Bowling Green, KY	6,462	24.4%	9.9%	5.8%	1.1%	13.7%	1.0%	23.3%	20.7%	16.7%
Bremerton-Silverdale, WA	11,280	34.6%	8.4%	5.6%	0.0%	14.2%	1.1%	23.9%	12.2%	16.3%
Bridgeport-Stamford-Norwalk, CT	24,596	18.9%	15.5%	1.6%	2.9%	14.8%	2.8%	19.9%	23.7%	26.8%
Brownsville-Harlingen, TX	10,319	43.6%	11.5%	5.7%	1.1%	19.7%	0.0%	13.2%	5.2%	45.4%
Brunswick, GA	3,502	48.2%	11.9%	4.3%	0.0%	11.2%	3.9%	18.0%	2.5%	20.2%
Buffalo-Cheektowaga-Niagara Falls, NY .	45,016	23.8%	12.2%	3.3%	2.5%	17.6%	0.4%	23.5%	16.7%	22.6%
Burlington-South Burlington, VT	8,316	12.3%	9.3%	2.0%	0.0%	16.4%	1.1%	35.8%	23.3%	18.7%
Burlington, NC	5,663	31.1%	20.4%	6.4%	4.9%	27.2%	0.1%	9.8%	0.0%	22.3%
California-Lexington Park, MD	2,949	41.8%	7.3%	0.0%	0.0%	11.2%	0.0%	20.4%	19.3%	26.8%
Canton-Massillon, OH	12,500	22.2%	15.1%	0.9%	1.5%	18.3%	0.7%	29.2%	12.2%	21.0%
Cape Coral-Fort Myers, FL	15,516	28.9%	11.9%	8.1%	4.2%	17.7%	2.8%	15.2%	11.2%	30.2%
Cape Girardeau, MO-IL	3,815	33.2%	7.3%	12.3%	1.5%	26.1%	0.0%	13.0%	6.6%	16.7%
Carbondale-Marion, IL	5,649	19.3%	11.0%	0.0%	1.6%	27.1%	0.6%	21.4%	19.0%	12.3%
Carson City, NV	1,854	25.1%	7.2%	2.7%	0.0%	6.7%	0.0%	12.9%	45.4%	10.3%
Casper, WY	5,010	31.1%	15.2%	15.0%	4.4%	14.3%	0.0%	6.2%	13.7%	8.0%
Cedar Rapids, IA	14,924	23.8%	17.5%	3.1%	1.3%	19.1%	0.0%	22.8%	12.2%	13.6%
Chambersburg-Waynesboro, PA	5,456	47.4%	8.8%	2.6%	0.0%	13.9%	0.0%	15.2%	12.1%	16.3%
Champaign-Urbana, IL	12,187	19.3%	13.6%	1.0%	0.1%	10.0%	2.7%	36.3%	16.9%	15.6%
Charleston-North Charleston, SC	30,599	16.4%	15.6%	0.9%	0.9%	16.3%	1.1%	28.4%	20.4%	17.4%
Charleston, WV	9,669	23.9%	5.8%	12.8%	0.8%	23.1%	2.5%	25.4%	5.8%	16.6%
Charlotte-Concord-Gastonia, NC-SC	87,265	22.9%	14.4%	3.7%	1.8%	15.8%	1.3%	28.5%	11.7%	23.0%
Charlottesville, VA	8,533	21.2%	21.0%	2.7%	0.0%	9.8%	0.0%	30.7%	14.6%	14.5%
Chattanooga, TN-GA	20,918	32.1%	11.7%	6.5%	3.0%	15.7%	1.9%	20.8%	8.3%	20.0%
Cheyenne, WY	3,854	31.8%	17.6%	0.0%	2.6%	6.6%	0.0%	34.0%	7.5%	8.9%
Chicago-Naperville-Elgin, IL-IN-WI	373,600	19.6%	15.3%	3.2%	3.4%	13.1%	1.8%	27.6%	16.1%	26.8%
Chico, CA	7,933	21.5%	16.9%	6.1%	0.8%	14.5%	2.2%	19.7%	18.3%	20.4%
Cincinnati, OH-KY-IN	84,980	25.6%	14.5%	2.7%	2.1%	16.2%	2.9%	22.3%	13.7%	17.1%
Clarksburg, WV	2,245	36.9%	11.0%	2.7%	7.3%	17.8%	2.9%	21.4%	0.0%	36.1%
Clarksville, TN-KY	18,408	35.7%	20.9%	5.7%	0.0%	5.9%	0.8%	16.3%	14.6%	7.8%
Cleveland-Elyria, OH	74,614	17.8%	9.9%	4.4%	3.2%	19.6%	1.0%	29.4%	14.7%	22.9%

Table D-4: Metropolitan/Micropolitan Statistical Areas—Household Relationship—*Continued*

		18 to 24								
		Married Couple Households		Male, No Spouse Present		Female, No Spouse Present		Non-Family Householders		
	Total Householders	With Children	No Children	With Children	No Children	With Children	No Children	Living Alone	Not Alone	Living With Parents
Cleveland, TN	1,099	18.7%	8.0%	0.0%	32.8%	36.9%	0.0%	3.6%	0.0%	42.4%
Coeur d'Alene, ID	1,703	12.2%	14.5%	0.0%	0.0%	0.0%	0.0%	17.7%	55.6%	51.4%
College Station-Bryan, TX	16,938	1.3%	4.3%	1.4%	3.5%	2.0%	5.1%	29.9%	52.4%	15.9%
Colorado Springs, CO	12,397	20.5%	19.6%	0.0%	2.4%	8.9%	1.0%	16.0%	31.5%	40.8%
Columbia, MO	11,150	0.0%	0.7%	0.0%	2.0%	9.2%	0.0%	40.7%	47.4%	12.8%
Columbia, SC	14,375	2.1%	7.3%	1.4%	1.3%	19.2%	0.9%	25.6%	42.2%	35.9%
Columbus, GA-AL	5,410	17.9%	10.4%	0.0%	10.5%	19.6%	3.2%	14.3%	24.1%	29.9%
Columbus, IN	1,275	0.9%	7.8%	0.0%	0.8%	10.7%	0.0%	46.2%	33.6%	39.5%
Columbus, OH	32,089	7.9%	8.2%	1.7%	3.5%	16.5%	2.5%	27.9%	31.8%	46.2%
Concord, NH micro	1,321	0.0%	0.0%	0.0%	29.0%	18.3%	0.0%	3.5%	49.2%	60.8%
Cookeville, TN micro	3,933	21.9%	12.5%	6.7%	6.2%	7.6%	0.8%	17.9%	26.4%	30.3%
Corpus Christi, TX	9,655	14.9%	3.8%	4.0%	10.0%	16.9%	3.6%	13.4%	33.5%	41.8%
Corvallis, OR	4,380	5.8%	8.5%	0.0%	2.3%	7.6%	0.0%	18.4%	57.4%	18.8%
Crestview-Fort Walton Beach-Destin, FL	4,748	15.6%	30.7%	0.0%	0.0%	4.7%	2.1%	24.4%	22.4%	36.3%
Cumberland, MD-WV	989	6.1%	4.3%	18.2%	0.0%	10.3%	0.0%	19.0%	42.1%	54.9%
Dallas-Fort Worth-Arlington, TX	105,654	12.3%	8.9%	4.5%	6.4%	15.8%	3.6%	26.6%	21.9%	54.5%
Dalton, GA	1,950	9.2%	8.3%	4.4%	17.2%	16.8%	3.6%	19.1%	21.5%	59.7%
Danville, IL	1,128	27.8%	0.8%	0.0%	0.0%	34.9%	13.6%	16.8%	6.0%	57.2%
Danville, VA micro	1,411	0.0%	0.0%	17.6%	0.0%	26.9%	9.1%	15.3%	31.0%	60.2%
Daphne-Fairhope-Foley, AL	2,540	13.7%	38.8%	0.0%	0.2%	15.0%	0.0%	16.5%	15.8%	54.2%
Davenport-Moline-Rock Island, IA-IL	6,945	7.3%	9.0%	1.7%	3.2%	20.2%	0.0%	29.7%	28.9%	46.4%
Dayton, OH	15,190	14.5%	4.6%	3.9%	0.0%	24.0%	2.0%	28.1%	23.0%	41.3%
Decatur, AL	1,851	29.1%	10.4%	0.0%	12.7%	39.9%	0.0%	1.6%	6.3%	59.7%
Decatur, IL	2,131	7.4%	0.0%	0.0%	8.2%	15.6%	0.0%	11.4%	57.4%	43.6%
Deltona-Daytona Beach-Ormond Beach, FL	8,933	3.2%	10.8%	4.0%	8.4%	12.3%	2.6%	27.4%	31.3%	49.8%
Denver-Aurora-Lakewood, CO	44,174	5.9%	7.0%	3.0%	3.7%	12.8%	4.1%	30.1%	33.4%	51.2%
Des Moines-West Des Moines, IA	11,678	0.4%	8.1%	5.3%	1.9%	14.2%	0.0%	26.0%	44.1%	36.9%
Detroit-Warren-Dearborn, MI	50,283	5.5%	3.2%	3.4%	7.8%	23.6%	5.1%	27.3%	24.1%	63.4%
Dothan, AL	1,815	14.1%	5.6%	0.0%	1.5%	21.8%	2.7%	35.0%	19.4%	61.4%
Dover, DE	2,389	2.1%	17.9%	2.0%	11.1%	21.4%	5.0%	34.6%	5.9%	51.4%
Dubuque, IA	1,881	0.0%	16.6%	0.0%	0.0%	14.8%	0.0%	16.8%	51.8%	32.8%
Duluth, MN-WI	5,921	15.8%	5.1%	0.0%	2.3%	9.0%	0.0%	33.6%	34.3%	29.0%
Dunn, NC micro	1,594	14.0%	17.8%	0.0%	7.0%	9.0%	0.0%	22.8%	29.4%	48.0%
Durham-Chapel Hill, NC	8,458	4.5%	4.3%	0.0%	0.8%	9.6%	1.0%	29.5%	50.3%	30.2%
East Stroudsburg, PA	2,243	0.0%	0.0%	17.7%	0.0%	9.7%	6.2%	21.7%	44.6%	61.8%
Eau Claire, WI	5,734	19.7%	6.1%	0.0%	0.0%	3.6%	0.0%	30.3%	40.2%	35.5%
El Centro, CA	1,125	16.9%	5.1%	0.0%	2.9%	31.6%	0.0%	23.6%	19.8%	68.8%
El Paso, TX	12,783	30.4%	9.8%	2.1%	4.5%	17.9%	4.5%	19.2%	11.6%	62.5%
Elizabethtown-Fort Knox, KY	2,163	27.8%	0.0%	1.0%	0.0%	16.4%	3.9%	11.4%	39.6%	53.2%
Elkhart-Goshen, IN	4,368	30.8%	4.7%	7.2%	0.0%	14.4%	0.4%	11.2%	31.3%	52.8%
Elmira, NY	1,009	0.0%	0.0%	0.0%	0.0%	27.4%	0.0%	72.6%	0.0%	55.0%
Erie, PA	3,769	3.4%	1.2%	0.0%	11.3%	8.6%	1.2%	18.3%	56.1%	44.0%
Eugene, OR	11,672	5.6%	7.5%	2.5%	0.6%	12.4%	2.8%	26.5%	42.2%	32.3%
Eureka-Arcata-Fortuna, CA micro	3,815	4.4%	1.4%	0.0%	0.0%	0.7%	15.0%	26.3%	52.1%	21.6%
Evansville, IN-KY	6,037	6.2%	8.9%	4.2%	0.0%	13.5%	0.0%	37.1%	30.2%	44.8%
Fairbanks, AK	2,218	0.0%	20.5%	0.0%	0.0%	22.3%	1.1%	2.5%	53.7%	32.4%
Fargo, ND-MN	10,766	0.0%	5.9%	0.0%	4.4%	8.5%	2.0%	38.5%	40.7%	26.7%
Farmington, NM	1,583	27.7%	5.6%	12.6%	0.0%	17.0%	16.4%	2.7%	18.2%	44.7%
Fayetteville-Springdale-Rogers, AR-MO.	11,585	10.1%	4.1%	4.2%	4.9%	12.3%	3.8%	25.5%	35.1%	31.5%
Fayetteville, NC	9,866	13.3%	20.8%	3.5%	1.0%	16.8%	0.0%	26.2%	18.4%	38.0%
Flagstaff, AZ	6,174	0.0%	7.6%	0.0%	8.2%	1.7%	0.0%	44.3%	38.3%	18.6%
Flint, MI	5,098	5.3%	0.7%	4.0%	0.0%	35.1%	0.0%	15.5%	39.4%	60.8%
Florence-Muscle Shoals, AL	2,590	6.9%	5.3%	4.3%	12.7%	18.9%	0.0%	37.5%	14.4%	43.8%
Florence, SC	1,776	12.3%	0.0%	7.3%	0.0%	12.3%	0.0%	39.2%	28.9%	51.1%
Fond du Lac, WI	2,037	7.9%	34.2%	0.0%	0.0%	0.0%	14.3%	6.6%	37.1%	47.7%
Fort Collins, CO	10,370	3.6%	6.4%	0.0%	2.8%	1.0%	4.0%	17.2%	65.0%	27.3%
Fort Smith, AR-OK	4,993	19.5%	11.5%	5.4%	1.1%	14.8%	2.1%	30.1%	15.5%	54.5%
Fort Wayne, IN	8,851	12.2%	6.3%	1.5%	2.0%	23.6%	4.6%	32.6%	17.3%	48.6%
Fresno, CA	13,473	13.2%	5.8%	13.4%	5.4%	25.1%	5.4%	13.6%	18.1%	62.1%
Gadsden, AL	822	63.3%	18.7%	0.0%	0.0%	0.0%	0.0%	18.0%	0.0%	73.3%
Gainesville, FL	17,570	1.8%	3.8%	1.8%	2.6%	6.3%	1.0%	28.8%	53.8%	13.5%
Gainesville, GA	2,303	6.4%	16.0%	1.8%	7.6%	0.0%	10.9%	33.3%	24.1%	49.4%
Gettysburg, PA	1,508	37.3%	3.3%	0.0%	0.0%	36.3%	0.0%	2.9%	20.2%	44.0%
Glens Falls, NY	1,398	2.1%	0.0%	0.0%	0.0%	52.4%	0.0%	29.8%	15.7%	66.2%
Goldsboro, NC	2,487	15.2%	11.2%	0.0%	2.0%	18.9%	0.0%	35.9%	16.9%	47.5%
Grand Forks, ND-MN	7,066	22.7%	2.6%	0.0%	2.4%	4.1%	6.0%	36.9%	25.2%	15.7%
Grand Island, NE	1,476	0.0%	12.6%	0.0%	0.0%	9.5%	11.0%	48.8%	18.0%	55.8%
Grand Junction, CO	2,290	8.1%	2.3%	0.0%	6.9%	10.8%	4.6%	26.4%	40.9%	35.8%
Grand Rapids-Wyoming, MI	17,155	2.2%	6.7%	1.5%	3.0%	6.4%	2.7%	20.9%	56.8%	43.2%
Grants Pass, OR	1,541	27.0%	1.7%	0.0%	0.0%	0.0%	32.6%	38.7%	0.0%	53.3%
Great Falls, MT	1,552	19.5%	0.0%	0.0%	0.0%	52.3%	0.0%	13.1%	15.1%	45.8%
Greeley, CO	5,234	4.9%	19.3%	0.0%	5.1%	10.0%	4.1%	29.1%	27.5%	43.8%
Green Bay, WI	4,958	4.9%	11.6%	0.0%	12.5%	15.7%	0.0%	19.5%	35.9%	51.5%
Greensboro-High Point, NC	10,508	2.3%	14.8%	3.7%	1.5%	24.4%	1.4%	26.2%	25.7%	51.4%
Greenville-Anderson-Mauldin, SC	11,512	7.3%	9.0%	2.2%	9.0%	22.3%	4.6%	26.1%	19.5%	47.4%
Greenville, NC	9,261	0.0%	2.3%	0.0%	3.0%	6.2%	0.4%	43.3%	44.9%	22.4%
Greenwood, SC micro	2,108	4.7%	0.0%	0.0%	0.0%	21.0%	0.0%	68.1%	6.2%	45.7%

Table D-4: Metropolitan/Micropolitan Statistical Areas—Household Relationship

	Total Householders	25 to 31								
		Married Couple Households		Male, No Spouse Present		Female, No Spouse Present		Non-Family Householders		
		With Children	No Children	With Children	No Children	With Children	No Children	Living Alone	Not Alone	Living With Parents
Cleveland, TN	4,582	23.2%	13.4%	7.1%	0.0%	22.7%	0.0%	9.2%	24.4%	11.8%
Coeur d'Alene, ID	5,381	54.5%	4.4%	10.4%	0.0%	20.8%	0.0%	6.0%	4.0%	9.2%
College Station-Bryan, TX	11,705	22.8%	14.4%	3.1%	0.7%	15.9%	0.0%	28.1%	15.1%	12.4%
Colorado Springs, CO	32,582	32.7%	18.5%	3.2%	0.7%	12.9%	2.2%	16.1%	13.7%	12.5%
Columbia, MO	11,836	9.6%	10.5%	0.0%	3.8%	18.9%	0.9%	29.6%	26.7%	7.8%
Columbia, SC	29,928	19.7%	10.1%	0.9%	0.2%	19.2%	0.8%	30.1%	19.0%	23.3%
Columbus, GA-AL	12,820	30.3%	11.0%	4.4%	1.4%	26.1%	2.1%	10.2%	14.5%	19.5%
Columbus, IN	4,402	41.8%	20.2%	4.5%	0.0%	2.0%	0.0%	28.9%	2.6%	19.3%
Columbus, OH	91,181	22.0%	14.3%	1.8%	1.5%	13.4%	1.2%	29.6%	16.3%	15.5%
Concord, NH	3,259	20.0%	3.8%	0.0%	6.4%	13.2%	0.0%	25.4%	31.2%	22.5%
Cookeville, TN	3,465	33.3%	8.9%	3.5%	0.0%	26.1%	0.0%	20.2%	8.0%	15.2%
Corpus Christi, TX	17,151	28.5%	6.5%	2.7%	1.6%	23.9%	2.0%	22.0%	12.7%	24.7%
Corvallis, OR	3,787	20.4%	12.4%	0.0%	0.0%	9.3%	0.0%	23.1%	34.7%	17.3%
Crestview-Fort Walton Beach-Destin, FL	12,470	36.2%	11.9%	1.2%	3.1%	11.1%	4.2%	21.5%	10.7%	18.5%
Cumberland, MD-WV	2,786	26.9%	22.5%	3.8%	0.0%	14.4%	3.2%	27.3%	1.9%	22.9%
Dallas-Fort Worth-Arlington, TX	285,436	27.9%	13.2%	4.3%	2.4%	15.1%	1.4%	23.8%	11.7%	19.7%
Dalton, GA	4,906	57.9%	2.3%	4.7%	0.0%	23.4%	0.0%	4.6%	7.1%	26.6%
Danville, IL	2,896	30.6%	4.2%	3.2%	0.0%	11.4%	0.0%	42.6%	8.0%	22.0%
Danville, VA	3,362	55.2%	5.9%	4.3%	0.0%	26.0%	0.0%	7.9%	0.6%	15.9%
Daphne-Fairhope-Foley, AL	4,115	19.6%	16.6%	4.9%	3.3%	28.7%	5.2%	8.2%	13.5%	15.2%
Davenport-Moline-Rock Island, IA-IL	16,375	26.4%	12.6%	2.1%	0.0%	16.9%	0.0%	35.3%	6.8%	12.4%
Dayton, OH	31,880	24.9%	9.9%	4.6%	2.1%	19.4%	0.6%	26.2%	12.3%	16.7%
Decatur, AL	4,636	26.6%	18.4%	0.0%	7.0%	23.3%	2.9%	21.8%	0.0%	23.8%
Decatur, IL	4,544	18.9%	5.7%	8.8%	2.1%	34.2%	0.0%	20.9%	9.4%	14.4%
Deltona-Daytona Beach-Ormond Beach, FL	16,636	30.3%	11.0%	4.6%	3.7%	20.2%	0.0%	14.7%	15.6%	29.6%
Denver-Aurora-Lakewood, CO	119,494	24.1%	12.6%	2.5%	2.9%	9.7%	1.1%	28.4%	18.7%	17.1%
Des Moines-West Des Moines, IA	29,273	27.9%	12.6%	4.3%	3.3%	9.8%	0.0%	28.7%	13.4%	12.1%
Detroit-Warren-Dearborn, MI	142,551	18.8%	13.2%	5.0%	2.5%	17.6%	2.6%	27.2%	13.1%	26.1%
Dothan, AL	5,941	42.0%	8.4%	0.0%	0.0%	23.4%	0.0%	23.0%	3.2%	19.6%
Dover, DE	5,309	34.5%	16.4%	2.7%	2.1%	11.8%	0.0%	14.2%	18.3%	25.2%
Dubuque, IA	3,553	12.7%	21.7%	13.0%	1.2%	14.6%	0.0%	16.0%	20.9%	10.6%
Duluth, MN-WI	13,660	21.2%	6.5%	4.4%	0.0%	25.4%	0.0%	25.7%	16.8%	11.8%
Dunn, NC	5,756	44.6%	17.0%	1.5%	0.5%	22.6%	0.0%	12.5%	1.5%	22.9%
Durham-Chapel Hill, NC	26,719	20.8%	17.9%	3.8%	0.0%	12.1%	0.8%	29.9%	14.7%	13.8%
East Stroudsburg, PA	3,355	23.9%	5.3%	16.0%	0.0%	18.3%	0.0%	5.7%	30.9%	36.1%
Eau Claire, WI	5,603	35.8%	13.7%	0.0%	7.0%	13.3%	0.0%	14.5%	15.6%	13.8%
El Centro, CA	5,587	48.7%	8.6%	3.8%	0.0%	9.5%	3.4%	14.4%	11.6%	24.6%
El Paso, TX	27,641	37.9%	14.7%	6.5%	4.4%	14.6%	1.2%	14.2%	6.4%	30.0%
Elizabethtown-Fort Knox, KY	6,484	44.8%	3.0%	1.9%	2.6%	34.4%	0.6%	8.8%	3.7%	14.0%
Elkhart-Goshen, IN	6,250	37.6%	14.5%	1.8%	1.3%	20.4%	0.0%	12.3%	12.1%	15.8%
Elmira, NY	4,472	19.2%	15.6%	0.3%	1.3%	28.8%	0.0%	17.9%	16.9%	10.8%
Erie, PA	11,726	20.8%	11.3%	4.5%	0.0%	24.9%	2.1%	27.1%	9.4%	17.2%
Eugene, OR	12,284	30.1%	19.2%	3.8%	0.4%	7.8%	1.4%	26.5%	10.9%	14.6%
Eureka-Arcata-Fortuna, CA	6,042	14.2%	11.8%	3.7%	1.0%	3.5%	0.0%	33.5%	32.3%	16.5%
Evansville, IN-KY	12,841	29.0%	16.4%	3.1%	0.0%	20.2%	0.0%	23.0%	8.2%	14.6%
Fairbanks, AK	5,229	19.7%	23.4%	0.0%	2.7%	6.0%	0.0%	37.7%	10.5%	24.0%
Fargo, ND-MN	12,918	34.0%	13.6%	1.4%	1.5%	11.6%	0.7%	21.3%	15.9%	9.5%
Farmington, NM	2,856	37.7%	3.0%	5.0%	12.4%	27.1%	2.9%	7.2%	4.7%	41.2%
Fayetteville-Springdale-Rogers, AR-MO.	24,012	34.7%	16.3%	5.4%	0.0%	13.0%	0.4%	18.9%	11.4%	10.7%
Fayetteville, NC	21,617	20.8%	15.2%	1.9%	0.6%	19.5%	0.4%	31.4%	10.3%	16.3%
Flagstaff, AZ	6,204	30.3%	15.1%	7.6%	0.0%	2.7%	0.0%	23.3%	21.0%	23.4%
Flint, MI	14,187	20.4%	10.6%	1.5%	0.9%	29.8%	0.0%	22.0%	15.0%	23.9%
Florence-Muscle Shoals, AL	4,873	31.1%	3.4%	15.7%	3.2%	13.6%	0.0%	23.8%	9.1%	26.9%
Florence, SC	6,822	23.3%	10.9%	1.0%	1.1%	34.7%	0.0%	25.4%	3.5%	32.9%
Fond du Lac, WI	2,429	32.9%	16.1%	1.4%	0.0%	5.9%	0.0%	26.2%	17.5%	18.9%
Fort Collins, CO	14,342	21.8%	14.1%	4.2%	0.0%	7.5%	0.9%	28.1%	23.4%	9.8%
Fort Smith, AR-OK	11,796	38.7%	9.5%	6.2%	1.9%	19.4%	0.9%	20.5%	2.8%	15.0%
Fort Wayne, IN	17,995	34.5%	14.5%	3.4%	1.3%	14.2%	1.1%	19.6%	11.4%	17.1%
Fresno, CA	36,372	30.6%	11.8%	7.3%	3.0%	23.2%	1.3%	14.7%	8.0%	25.6%
Gadsden, AL	3,277	43.7%	13.7%	0.0%	3.0%	15.8%	1.0%	18.8%	3.9%	25.3%
Gainesville, FL	13,000	16.5%	11.3%	1.4%	3.3%	8.2%	1.3%	32.7%	25.4%	9.5%
Gainesville, GA	5,609	31.1%	10.8%	7.4%	0.7%	16.5%	0.0%	19.0%	14.5%	19.5%
Gettysburg, PA	2,539	42.9%	6.8%	2.2%	0.0%	13.5%	12.9%	19.2%	2.6%	26.2%
Glens Falls, NY	3,272	22.4%	11.2%	10.5%	0.9%	24.5%	0.0%	19.7%	10.8%	31.1%
Goldsboro, NC	4,723	30.0%	19.7%	2.9%	1.7%	22.5%	0.0%	21.9%	1.3%	17.2%
Grand Forks, ND-MN	5,271	29.6%	12.0%	0.9%	0.0%	14.5%	0.0%	28.4%	14.7%	4.6%
Grand Island, NE	3,346	23.5%	14.4%	27.0%	0.0%	22.3%	0.0%	4.9%	7.8%	4.6%
Grand Junction, CO	7,873	43.7%	2.1%	1.2%	0.0%	29.1%	0.0%	9.0%	14.9%	15.0%
Grand Rapids-Wyoming, MI	41,122	27.3%	15.9%	8.3%	2.5%	10.9%	2.1%	20.5%	12.4%	17.2%
Grants Pass, OR	1,690	62.9%	17.5%	0.0%	0.0%	15.9%	0.0%	0.0%	3.7%	23.9%
Great Falls, MT	4,533	44.0%	6.7%	7.6%	0.0%	3.8%	1.9%	31.1%	4.8%	13.2%
Greeley, CO	12,120	34.6%	13.0%	2.2%	4.5%	14.3%	1.1%	20.7%	9.6%	18.6%
Green Bay, WI	11,990	16.1%	20.2%	6.7%	2.7%	18.0%	0.0%	22.4%	13.9%	15.1%
Greensboro-High Point, NC	30,497	22.5%	16.5%	4.1%	1.5%	14.0%	3.3%	24.1%	14.1%	19.5%
Greenville-Anderson-Mauldin, SC	30,792	23.0%	16.6%	5.4%	2.3%	18.1%	0.8%	24.6%	9.2%	22.2%
Greenville, NC	6,783	16.3%	23.3%	0.0%	0.3%	18.0%	1.7%	31.1%	9.3%	17.8%
Greenwood, SC	3,567	16.8%	5.9%	9.0%	1.6%	50.0%	0.0%	16.8%	0.0%	21.6%

Table D-4: Metropolitan/Micropolitan Statistical Areas—Household Relationship—*Continued*

		18 to 24								
		Married Couple Households		Male, No Spouse Present		Female, No Spouse Present		Non-Family Householders		
	Total Householders	With Children	No Children	With Children	No Children	With Children	No Children	Living Alone	Not Alone	Living With Parents
Gulfport-Biloxi-Pascagoula, MS	6,031	8.0%	14.5%	2.8%	0.9%	22.8%	2.4%	15.3%	33.3%	48.8%
Hagerstown-Martinsburg, MD-WV.........	2,666	2.7%	9.1%	9.2%	0.0%	9.4%	0.0%	52.0%	17.7%	51.9%
Hammond, LA	2,558	36.5%	0.0%	0.0%	1.9%	13.4%	0.0%	35.2%	13.0%	44.3%
Hanford-Corcoran, CA	1,235	21.7%	26.0%	0.0%	3.2%	23.1%	0.0%	0.6%	25.4%	48.4%
Harrisburg-Carlisle, PA...........................	9,230	4.6%	5.5%	5.6%	2.8%	26.1%	2.1%	22.5%	30.8%	45.2%
Harrisonburg, VA	3,379	0.0%	12.5%	0.0%	0.0%	3.9%	0.0%	9.4%	74.3%	20.0%
Hartford-West Hartford-East Hartford, CT	11,142	1.0%	3.0%	4.6%	6.4%	17.0%	2.8%	41.0%	24.3%	56.1%
Hattiesburg, MS	3,902	3.0%	4.2%	0.0%	3.7%	21.9%	2.2%	17.1%	47.9%	35.8%
Hickory-Lenoir-Morganton, NC	3,305	23.0%	12.8%	0.0%	10.1%	13.1%	0.8%	12.9%	27.4%	54.0%
Hilo, HI micro	1,982	0.0%	0.0%	19.1%	0.0%	1.5%	0.0%	36.5%	42.9%	59.3%
Hilton Head Island-Bluffton-Beaufort, SC	3,275	8.1%	14.8%	0.0%	3.2%	11.2%	0.0%	35.3%	27.3%	37.8%
Hinesville, GA	3,580	15.5%	21.2%	0.0%	2.6%	37.8%	0.0%	7.9%	14.9%	41.2%
Holland, MI micro	1,093	12.7%	0.0%	0.0%	0.0%	2.2%	0.0%	34.0%	51.1%	77.7%
Homosassa Springs, FL	892	19.5%	0.0%	0.0%	0.0%	18.6%	0.0%	6.1%	55.8%	50.3%
Hot Springs, AR	1,088	0.0%	12.0%	6.4%	0.0%	0.0%	0.0%	29.3%	52.2%	35.6%
Houma-Thibodaux, LA	3,191	18.1%	9.3%	7.5%	8.1%	18.2%	6.0%	17.9%	14.9%	48.2%
Houston-The Woodlands-Sugar Land, TX	84,698	13.7%	7.4%	4.0%	6.5%	15.7%	5.2%	27.4%	20.0%	61.3%
Huntington-Ashland, WV-KY-OH...........	6,287	7.2%	16.0%	1.5%	0.0%	7.8%	3.0%	32.3%	32.1%	44.6%
Huntsville, AL..	6,725	8.6%	5.0%	5.1%	0.0%	11.1%	6.5%	37.9%	25.9%	49.1%
Idaho Falls, ID	2,090	37.9%	21.4%	0.0%	0.0%	0.0%	0.0%	0.0%	40.7%	37.6%
Indianapolis-Carmel-Anderson, IN	34,039	6.0%	5.8%	4.3%	7.3%	16.2%	4.7%	31.2%	24.5%	49.6%
Iowa City, IA	9,864	0.0%	0.0%	0.0%	0.0%	3.6%	0.8%	31.6%	64.1%	7.7%
Ithaca, NY	3,918	0.0%	2.2%	0.0%	0.0%	4.7%	8.1%	43.2%	41.8%	15.2%
Jackson, MI	2,496	0.0%	8.2%	0.0%	0.0%	31.9%	7.6%	30.0%	22.4%	49.8%
Jackson, MS	6,399	0.1%	21.4%	2.0%	5.3%	21.4%	4.9%	27.0%	17.9%	55.4%
Jackson, TN	1,873	1.1%	9.4%	8.4%	0.0%	12.9%	0.0%	14.0%	54.1%	36.5%
Jacksonville, FL	17,765	13.8%	9.8%	2.8%	7.5%	13.4%	5.4%	26.9%	20.4%	52.6%
Jacksonville, NC......................................	9,286	30.8%	26.3%	4.5%	0.5%	10.7%	2.9%	19.5%	4.9%	27.6%
Jamestown-Dunkirk-Fredonia, NY micro	1,895	0.0%	2.6%	8.2%	0.0%	11.5%	5.9%	20.6%	51.1%	42.0%
Janesville-Beloit, WI...............................	3,813	0.0%	0.0%	0.0%	20.9%	42.4%	0.0%	8.4%	28.3%	48.5%
Jefferson City, MO..................................	1,588	21.4%	7.0%	0.0%	13.7%	16.6%	6.9%	7.2%	27.1%	46.6%
Johnson City, TN	4,647	7.9%	9.9%	11.0%	5.6%	20.3%	0.0%	32.0%	13.4%	45.3%
Johnstown, PA	1,744	7.8%	2.4%	0.0%	0.0%	17.3%	0.0%	35.7%	36.8%	46.1%
Jonesboro, AR	3,481	1.3%	3.5%	0.0%	0.5%	32.1%	10.1%	8.0%	44.5%	44.2%
Joplin, MO	4,050	17.8%	17.1%	18.9%	0.0%	1.7%	8.8%	9.8%	25.9%	35.9%
Kahului-Wailuku-Lahaina, HI..................	1,093	26.6%	0.0%	0.0%	0.0%	17.9%	6.4%	32.8%	16.3%	64.3%
Kalamazoo-Portage, MI...........................	11,424	2.1%	2.7%	8.4%	0.0%	13.7%	2.2%	27.9%	43.0%	29.2%
Kalispell, MT micro	338	6.8%	9.2%	38.5%	0.0%	14.2%	0.0%	31.4%	0.0%	63.0%
Kankakee, IL..	1,470	34.9%	0.0%	0.0%	0.0%	12.9%	0.0%	10.7%	41.6%	46.1%
Kansas City, MO-KS...............................	34,130	7.5%	7.8%	2.1%	4.0%	14.6%	3.5%	32.4%	28.0%	50.2%
Kennewick-Richland, WA........................	5,468	12.1%	10.8%	10.1%	12.0%	6.9%	9.7%	15.9%	22.6%	41.3%
Killeen-Temple, TX	8,340	15.7%	26.4%	1.8%	3.2%	13.0%	1.1%	27.4%	11.5%	44.6%
Kingsport-Bristol-Bristol, TN-VA...........	3,093	15.8%	8.6%	0.0%	5.1%	31.5%	0.0%	7.6%	31.4%	56.4%
Kingston, NY	2,121	0.9%	18.7%	6.7%	0.0%	24.1%	0.0%	7.8%	41.7%	41.9%
Knoxville, TN	15,263	11.2%	9.8%	0.4%	2.5%	14.4%	0.4%	19.3%	42.0%	44.8%
Kokomo, IN	2,074	18.8%	0.0%	2.7%	1.3%	25.8%	0.0%	38.9%	12.5%	44.8%
La Crosse-Onalaska, WI-MN	5,428	6.1%	0.0%	0.0%	0.0%	13.6%	0.0%	20.0%	60.3%	20.2%
Lafayette-West Lafayette, IN	12,524	6.7%	7.0%	0.4%	0.0%	5.7%	1.2%	30.4%	48.5%	20.8%
Lafayette, LA	9,813	5.0%	5.0%	8.7%	4.2%	16.1%	6.3%	30.0%	24.8%	54.5%
Lake Charles, LA	3,966	20.9%	2.4%	2.7%	0.0%	18.0%	7.0%	14.0%	34.9%	50.5%
Lake Havasu City-Kingman, AZ	2,575	0.0%	9.9%	16.1%	7.0%	16.1%	0.0%	34.5%	16.4%	45.7%
Lakeland-Winter Haven, FL	5,039	9.9%	12.3%	7.0%	4.4%	19.2%	2.9%	17.4%	26.8%	58.8%
Lancaster, PA	7,632	5.4%	6.9%	1.4%	4.5%	19.9%	0.0%	24.3%	37.6%	49.8%
Lansing-East Lansing, MI	13,481	1.4%	3.6%	1.6%	4.5%	5.5%	1.8%	27.9%	53.6%	24.8%
Laredo, TX	2,081	12.0%	0.0%	16.4%	4.6%	35.4%	4.5%	19.3%	7.8%	71.2%
Las Cruces, NM.......................................	7,395	8.9%	11.6%	0.0%	1.4%	15.7%	2.0%	10.2%	50.2%	35.8%
Las Vegas-Henderson-Paradise, NV.......	21,911	8.9%	11.0%	4.0%	10.0%	11.9%	5.4%	26.9%	21.8%	57.2%
Lawrence, KS	5,981	0.0%	2.9%	5.0%	5.4%	0.0%	9.7%	42.3%	34.7%	13.3%
Lawton, OK	3,510	18.5%	15.6%	0.0%	0.0%	13.8%	0.0%	26.0%	26.2%	27.2%
Lebanon, PA	1,605	29.2%	7.0%	0.0%	4.7%	0.0%	8.2%	20.8%	30.2%	44.8%
Lewiston-Auburn, ME	1,232	0.0%	0.0%	0.0%	0.0%	14.9%	0.0%	31.2%	53.9%	43.5%
Lewiston, ID-WA	827	19.3%	0.0%	0.0%	0.0%	16.1%	19.1%	9.8%	35.7%	22.9%
Lexington-Fayette, KY	12,687	1.0%	7.9%	0.7%	3.4%	17.2%	7.2%	17.9%	44.6%	32.5%
Lima, OH	1,509	11.9%	13.2%	0.0%	0.0%	7.7%	0.0%	36.6%	30.6%	46.9%
Lincoln, NE	11,721	2.3%	6.6%	9.5%	5.2%	7.1%	1.2%	23.9%	44.2%	21.4%
Little Rock-North Little Rock-Conway, AR	11,845	10.2%	12.9%	0.5%	0.6%	14.7%	0.2%	35.3%	25.7%	48.6%
Logan, UT-ID...	4,135	5.9%	37.7%	0.0%	0.0%	8.1%	0.0%	9.5%	38.9%	25.2%
Longview, TX	5,192	14.8%	7.1%	4.8%	1.2%	24.9%	0.0%	32.4%	14.8%	41.0%
Longview, WA	1,150	0.0%	20.9%	15.3%	0.0%	21.7%	0.0%	11.5%	30.7%	62.9%
Los Angeles-Long Beach-Anaheim, CA..	118,760	6.1%	5.2%	3.5%	10.1%	10.7%	8.3%	23.2%	33.0%	63.1%
Louisville/Jefferson County, KY-IN........	16,050	12.0%	4.6%	0.0%	6.1%	13.3%	0.3%	35.9%	27.7%	51.4%
Lubbock, TX	13,773	6.3%	7.5%	0.0%	5.9%	8.6%	2.6%	43.8%	25.2%	31.9%
Lumberton, NC micro	1,867	1.6%	8.9%	7.6%	15.4%	23.2%	4.7%	19.7%	19.1%	50.7%
Lynchburg, VA	4,786	6.7%	14.2%	1.8%	4.4%	12.0%	2.0%	42.9%	16.0%	41.1%
Macon, GA...	3,978	5.0%	4.7%	7.0%	0.0%	46.7%	6.1%	16.5%	14.0%	39.4%

Table D-4: Metropolitan/Micropolitan Statistical Areas—Household Relationship

	Total Householders	Married Couple Households		Male, No Spouse Present		Female, No Spouse Present		Non-Family Householders		Living With Parents
		With Children	No Children	With Children	No Children	With Children	No Children	Living Alone	Not Alone	
Gulfport-Biloxi-Pascagoula, MS	17,052	25.1%	14.6%	6.8%	0.8%	21.7%	1.1%	20.1%	9.8%	20.9%
Hagerstown-Martinsburg, MD-WV.........	8,577	31.9%	10.4%	5.0%	0.5%	15.0%	1.0%	16.8%	19.4%	21.1%
Hammond, LA...............................	7,265	30.4%	5.2%	0.0%	1.7%	16.2%	4.4%	18.6%	23.6%	18.0%
Hanford-Corcoran, CA......................	6,465	29.2%	6.1%	17.0%	4.3%	35.0%	0.5%	5.2%	2.7%	20.5%
Harrisburg-Carlisle, PA......................	24,266	23.5%	11.3%	3.3%	2.0%	14.6%	1.6%	33.3%	10.3%	16.5%
Harrisonburg, VA............................	5,292	18.3%	10.4%	12.5%	5.4%	15.5%	0.0%	27.1%	10.7%	18.4%
Hartford-West Hartford-East Hartford, CT	41,874	17.1%	14.2%	3.1%	2.9%	15.0%	1.3%	26.5%	19.8%	25.0%
Hattiesburg, MS............................	6,586	26.2%	12.4%	3.8%	0.8%	23.8%	0.8%	6.5%	25.8%	16.7%
Hickory-Lenoir-Morganton, NC	10,202	39.8%	6.9%	2.2%	2.3%	17.4%	2.0%	18.0%	11.3%	23.5%
Hilo, HI.....................................	4,293	21.4%	18.4%	6.5%	0.0%	23.6%	0.0%	11.0%	19.2%	33.3%
Hilton Head Island-Bluffton-Beaufort, SC	7,639	31.7%	9.2%	4.9%	2.5%	27.3%	0.0%	17.4%	7.0%	19.9%
Hinesville, GA..............................	4,790	35.7%	14.1%	13.1%	0.0%	9.0%	0.0%	17.6%	10.4%	11.8%
Holland, MI.................................	3,446	49.1%	15.5%	0.0%	3.8%	14.9%	0.0%	14.7%	2.1%	12.2%
Homosassa Springs, FL	2,411	34.8%	10.5%	19.1%	0.0%	13.7%	0.0%	7.1%	14.8%	25.2%
Hot Springs, AR............................	2,740	39.9%	10.8%	14.7%	0.0%	17.3%	0.0%	16.5%	0.9%	18.2%
Houma-Thibodaux, LA	8,272	39.9%	3.8%	5.6%	5.1%	24.1%	0.0%	10.3%	11.2%	29.1%
Houston-The Woodlands-Sugar Land, TX	260,045	28.4%	12.5%	3.5%	2.7%	14.8%	1.2%	25.6%	11.4%	22.1%
Huntington-Ashland, WV-KY-OH............	12,096	36.5%	9.9%	5.1%	1.5%	18.9%	1.9%	14.3%	11.8%	18.0%
Huntsville, AL..............................	19,043	26.0%	12.2%	5.7%	4.6%	10.5%	3.0%	33.7%	4.4%	14.0%
Idaho Falls, ID.............................	5,014	55.7%	7.4%	2.3%	0.0%	11.4%	0.0%	23.3%	0.0%	12.9%
Indianapolis-Carmel-Anderson, IN	87,323	23.6%	17.1%	4.8%	1.4%	15.8%	0.5%	24.2%	12.6%	16.1%
Iowa City, IA...............................	10,883	24.2%	19.1%	0.0%	0.0%	8.8%	1.3%	32.4%	14.2%	3.3%
Ithaca, NY.................................	4,746	6.6%	8.8%	0.0%	0.8%	0.9%	0.0%	60.9%	21.9%	6.6%
Jackson, MI................................	6,210	28.4%	11.0%	8.4%	0.0%	20.3%	0.0%	20.5%	11.4%	20.3%
Jackson, MS...............................	21,958	30.2%	9.3%	1.5%	3.1%	23.0%	1.9%	23.3%	7.8%	23.2%
Jackson, TN...............................	4,526	26.7%	5.3%	10.5%	2.6%	29.5%	0.0%	15.6%	9.9%	23.3%
Jacksonville, FL............................	53,413	22.3%	12.8%	3.2%	1.1%	17.9%	2.0%	27.4%	13.2%	24.8%
Jacksonville, NC...........................	9,975	33.5%	12.2%	11.6%	1.3%	18.4%	1.1%	13.8%	8.1%	11.2%
Jamestown-Dunkirk-Fredonia, NY	4,367	36.4%	1.4%	0.5%	0.0%	17.1%	0.0%	19.3%	25.3%	17.9%
Janesville-Beloit, WI.......................	5,255	29.6%	8.3%	11.1%	0.0%	8.4%	1.7%	36.6%	4.3%	26.1%
Jefferson City, MO.........................	5,738	17.1%	12.6%	0.7%	1.0%	35.3%	1.8%	14.8%	16.7%	19.3%
Johnson City, TN..........................	6,667	31.0%	18.2%	0.0%	0.9%	3.6%	1.5%	25.3%	19.5%	18.0%
Johnstown, PA.............................	5,039	21.8%	9.9%	2.8%	0.0%	18.0%	0.0%	35.9%	11.6%	17.9%
Jonesboro, AR.............................	5,465	30.7%	11.5%	13.7%	5.8%	17.9%	0.0%	15.4%	5.0%	15.3%
Joplin, MO.................................	9,227	29.5%	11.6%	6.6%	3.7%	13.0%	0.7%	21.8%	13.0%	13.8%
Kahului-Wailuku-Lahaina, HI................	4,488	14.2%	12.6%	12.3%	0.0%	8.6%	3.8%	22.2%	26.3%	30.4%
Kalamazoo-Portage, MI.....................	14,296	24.0%	11.1%	3.1%	0.0%	19.5%	1.4%	25.6%	15.2%	18.8%
Kalispell, MT...............................	2,593	46.1%	3.5%	2.4%	1.1%	21.5%	0.0%	25.5%	0.0%	12.9%
Kankakee, IL...............................	2,488	10.7%	8.4%	19.1%	0.0%	38.1%	0.0%	11.8%	11.9%	21.7%
Kansas City, MO-KS........................	92,639	25.1%	11.6%	2.3%	1.3%	16.5%	1.2%	27.9%	14.1%	16.3%
Kennewick-Richland, WA	11,101	33.2%	5.9%	12.3%	2.6%	18.1%	5.0%	10.3%	12.6%	13.2%
Killeen-Temple, TX.........................	21,041	40.8%	17.2%	0.9%	0.5%	13.4%	0.4%	23.2%	3.7%	18.1%
Kingsport-Bristol-Bristol, TN-VA	9,859	39.8%	7.7%	2.9%	2.0%	17.4%	0.4%	18.2%	11.6%	23.1%
Kingston, NY...............................	5,111	27.0%	10.6%	2.8%	0.0%	25.2%	0.0%	13.5%	21.0%	27.2%
Knoxville, TN..............................	31,407	27.0%	12.5%	5.3%	1.7%	14.9%	1.4%	22.8%	14.3%	21.4%
Kokomo, IN................................	2,446	35.9%	0.0%	17.7%	3.7%	14.6%	0.0%	14.3%	13.9%	11.1%
La Crosse-Onalaska, WI-MN	5,768	29.6%	10.4%	2.8%	5.0%	7.7%	1.0%	21.5%	22.0%	11.7%
Lafayette-West Lafayette, IN	10,008	24.3%	17.4%	9.1%	0.0%	7.8%	1.8%	27.8%	12.0%	12.1%
Lafayette, LA..............................	20,668	27.7%	14.3%	6.8%	0.8%	19.2%	0.6%	22.3%	8.2%	18.2%
Lake Charles, LA...........................	7,323	25.4%	8.3%	12.2%	5.1%	14.9%	1.5%	30.2%	2.4%	17.8%
Lake Havasu City-Kingman, AZ	5,255	17.5%	16.9%	5.8%	10.0%	10.0%	7.5%	18.8%	13.6%	16.8%
Lakeland-Winter Haven, FL	18,203	24.6%	9.9%	7.3%	3.0%	21.6%	1.5%	17.8%	14.3%	28.6%
Lancaster, PA..............................	18,985	39.1%	17.4%	2.8%	0.0%	9.0%	0.4%	20.8%	10.3%	22.7%
Lansing-East Lansing, MI	22,670	29.7%	6.1%	3.2%	1.4%	14.0%	0.8%	30.6%	14.2%	16.5%
Laredo, TX.................................	8,385	41.0%	10.6%	5.0%	5.1%	25.5%	3.2%	7.4%	2.2%	28.7%
Las Cruces, NM............................	6,643	27.7%	10.3%	5.7%	0.0%	26.6%	1.6%	20.3%	7.9%	31.1%
Las Vegas-Henderson-Paradise, NV.......	81,514	25.5%	11.3%	3.9%	2.9%	15.5%	3.7%	24.7%	12.5%	19.4%
Lawrence, KS..............................	6,606	6.4%	27.7%	0.0%	1.1%	2.2%	2.5%	29.5%	30.5%	4.9%
Lawton, OK................................	6,579	24.5%	9.3%	8.5%	0.0%	19.4%	0.0%	25.3%	13.1%	9.7%
Lebanon, PA...............................	4,154	30.4%	13.6%	7.2%	0.0%	22.3%	0.8%	11.9%	13.7%	21.3%
Lewiston-Auburn, ME	6,300	16.4%	10.2%	8.4%	0.0%	25.2%	1.9%	29.2%	8.7%	8.3%
Lewiston, ID-WA............................	1,767	48.2%	5.7%	0.0%	0.0%	12.5%	1.8%	24.4%	7.3%	19.5%
Lexington-Fayette, KY......................	22,980	27.0%	16.1%	0.6%	0.8%	16.6%	0.8%	20.2%	17.9%	14.4%
Lima, OH..................................	4,158	33.6%	12.7%	3.7%	7.5%	17.4%	2.9%	22.3%	0.0%	21.6%
Lincoln, NE................................	15,926	24.4%	15.7%	5.9%	2.8%	9.8%	3.8%	21.0%	16.5%	8.5%
Little Rock-North Little Rock-Conway, AR	29,959	30.4%	9.7%	1.8%	3.2%	14.4%	2.2%	21.7%	16.5%	18.6%
Logan, UT-ID..............................	7,899	33.4%	25.4%	10.2%	0.8%	4.9%	0.0%	13.3%	12.0%	9.3%
Longview, TX..............................	8,302	36.6%	10.1%	4.2%	3.4%	28.3%	0.0%	13.8%	3.6%	19.3%
Longview, WA..............................	3,186	46.9%	0.8%	16.4%	0.0%	17.6%	0.0%	5.2%	13.0%	20.1%
Los Angeles-Long Beach-Anaheim, CA..	424,714	19.6%	12.3%	3.5%	5.6%	11.5%	3.6%	24.8%	19.1%	31.4%
Louisville/Jefferson County, KY-IN........	51,635	23.3%	14.3%	1.9%	3.4%	17.5%	2.4%	24.0%	13.0%	19.0%
Lubbock, TX...............................	12,911	27.8%	9.8%	1.9%	4.9%	10.0%	5.7%	27.2%	12.7%	13.8%
Lumberton, NC............................	3,984	21.7%	2.5%	5.5%	4.8%	36.1%	2.0%	20.9%	6.5%	28.8%
Lynchburg, VA.............................	9,133	35.7%	13.9%	1.5%	1.7%	11.3%	1.5%	23.2%	11.0%	21.2%
Macon, GA................................	7,149	20.8%	13.5%	1.0%	6.3%	30.4%	2.5%	19.1%	6.4%	24.5%

25 to 31 (column group header)

Table D-4: Metropolitan/Micropolitan Statistical Areas—Household Relationship—*Continued*

		18 to 24								
	Total Householders	Married Couple Households		Male, No Spouse Present		Female, No Spouse Present		Non-Family Householders		Living With Parents
		With Children	No Children	With Children	No Children	With Children	No Children	Living Alone	Not Alone	
Madera, CA	1,287	25.7%	0.0%	13.4%	0.0%	38.9%	0.0%	14.2%	7.8%	55.9%
Madison, WI	17,566	0.7%	7.8%	0.2%	1.9%	4.9%	2.1%	29.7%	52.8%	28.5%
Manchester-Nashua, NH	3,125	2.4%	23.3%	0.0%	9.6%	23.4%	0.0%	19.6%	21.8%	59.0%
Manhattan, KS	7,400	31.2%	14.7%	0.0%	0.8%	1.9%	4.5%	25.3%	21.6%	12.4%
Mankato-North Mankato, MN	3,088	0.0%	5.1%	0.0%	12.9%	0.0%	0.0%	28.3%	53.7%	19.2%
Mansfield, OH	1,984	5.6%	9.8%	0.0%	9.9%	15.8%	0.0%	19.6%	39.3%	52.5%
McAllen-Edinburg-Mission, TX	8,597	24.3%	3.1%	0.5%	8.5%	23.7%	9.3%	12.3%	18.3%	72.6%
Medford, OR	2,787	23.9%	17.8%	0.0%	0.0%	2.8%	0.0%	24.5%	31.0%	41.7%
Memphis, TN-MS-AR	18,738	3.4%	6.6%	5.9%	3.2%	24.1%	2.5%	34.0%	20.2%	55.6%
Merced, CA	3,127	11.2%	12.1%	0.0%	18.3%	19.9%	6.8%	2.3%	29.4%	53.1%
Meridian, MS micro	856	3.2%	2.1%	12.5%	0.0%	76.2%	0.0%	0.0%	6.1%	56.9%
Miami-Fort Lauderdale-West Palm Beach, FL	41,036	6.2%	7.0%	2.9%	10.6%	14.5%	9.2%	25.0%	24.7%	66.9%
Michigan City-La Porte, IN	707	42.6%	0.0%	0.0%	0.0%	17.4%	0.0%	28.9%	11.2%	48.5%
Midland, MI	1,208	6.4%	2.1%	1.9%	0.0%	73.3%	0.0%	15.0%	1.4%	57.4%
Midland, TX	3,424	18.1%	7.8%	0.0%	12.1%	18.5%	0.0%	14.2%	29.2%	41.2%
Milwaukee-Waukesha-West Allis, WI	26,769	2.6%	2.0%	1.5%	6.1%	17.7%	4.6%	31.1%	34.3%	50.5%
Minneapolis-St. Paul-Bloomington, MN-WI	43,631	5.8%	6.7%	1.5%	1.6%	15.3%	1.5%	27.5%	40.1%	53.7%
Missoula, MT	2,393	0.0%	0.0%	0.0%	1.7%	30.3%	1.7%	13.0%	53.3%	35.2%
Mobile, AL	6,971	5.6%	2.1%	2.3%	2.4%	23.3%	1.1%	40.5%	22.7%	53.6%
Modesto, CA	6,151	13.6%	2.3%	5.3%	6.1%	21.1%	6.1%	23.9%	21.7%	64.9%
Monroe, LA	3,300	18.3%	4.7%	1.8%	5.5%	25.1%	0.0%	39.3%	5.4%	40.5%
Monroe, MI	966	0.0%	10.2%	14.1%	0.0%	6.5%	0.0%	56.5%	12.6%	75.8%
Montgomery, AL	4,549	0.4%	2.8%	17.0%	1.0%	27.4%	2.6%	23.9%	24.9%	57.9%
Morgantown, WV	7,064	5.9%	3.0%	0.0%	0.0%	3.9%	1.6%	55.2%	30.4%	25.9%
Morristown, TN	1,298	0.0%	0.0%	0.0%	0.0%	48.0%	0.0%	30.0%	22.0%	57.7%
Mount Vernon-Anacortes, WA	1,688	14.6%	18.2%	0.0%	13.6%	25.9%	2.0%	22.2%	3.5%	52.6%
Muncie, IN	5,790	1.3%	5.3%	0.0%	7.2%	2.6%	0.0%	15.5%	68.2%	22.2%
Muskegon, MI	2,729	4.0%	2.5%	11.2%	0.0%	29.6%	5.1%	16.8%	30.9%	47.8%
Myrtle Beach-Conway-North Myrtle Beach, SC-NC	4,028	11.8%	2.0%	0.0%	7.1%	26.9%	1.4%	10.6%	40.3%	51.0%
Napa, CA	1,119	11.4%	5.9%	0.0%	19.6%	18.4%	5.1%	12.1%	27.5%	55.3%
Naples-Immokalee-Marco Island, FL	1,940	2.6%	18.9%	23.7%	4.0%	14.4%	6.9%	17.5%	12.1%	70.9%
Nashville-Davidson–Murfreesboro–Franklin, TN	25,991	8.1%	9.5%	4.0%	6.5%	16.1%	1.9%	26.4%	27.5%	49.9%
New Bern, NC	4,012	10.9%	50.9%	5.1%	0.0%	11.6%	0.0%	15.3%	6.1%	29.7%
New Castle, PA micro	705	0.0%	3.7%	0.0%	0.0%	63.4%	0.0%	32.9%	0.0%	57.1%
New Haven-Milford, CT	5,568	2.4%	4.5%	0.0%	9.5%	16.4%	13.6%	25.4%	28.2%	58.5%
New Orleans-Metairie, LA	13,023	1.5%	4.5%	1.8%	4.4%	16.9%	7.1%	39.6%	24.2%	58.0%
New Philadelphia-Dover, OH micro	754	15.8%	6.8%	0.0%	0.0%	0.0%	0.0%	64.1%	13.4%	70.7%
New York-Newark-Jersey City, NY-NJ-PA	135,366	8.4%	6.4%	2.4%	9.5%	14.1%	7.1%	22.9%	29.2%	66.2%
Niles-Benton Harbor, MI	2,096	0.0%	7.2%	1.2%	1.1%	17.5%	1.4%	38.9%	32.7%	52.8%
North Port-Sarasota-Bradenton, FL	4,446	9.3%	9.4%	0.0%	5.7%	23.3%	1.0%	30.3%	21.0%	62.9%
Norwich-New London, CT	3,044	10.5%	11.7%	0.0%	9.3%	17.2%	0.0%	29.6%	21.7%	44.5%
Ocala, FL	3,020	2.2%	9.4%	0.0%	7.2%	19.3%	4.0%	13.4%	44.4%	52.5%
Ocean City, NJ	664	10.7%	17.8%	0.0%	0.0%	25.2%	0.0%	46.4%	0.0%	68.6%
Odessa, TX	3,225	25.9%	0.0%	10.3%	7.6%	28.7%	0.0%	9.6%	17.9%	47.7%
Ogden-Clearfield, UT	9,318	11.6%	35.8%	2.8%	0.8%	12.9%	3.7%	5.8%	26.7%	54.9%
Ogdensburg-Massena, NY micro	1,593	16.6%	10.4%	24.4%	0.0%	13.2%	0.0%	27.4%	8.1%	33.7%
Oklahoma City, OK	27,199	10.5%	7.2%	1.6%	3.3%	15.1%	4.4%	33.0%	24.8%	41.2%
Olympia-Tumwater, WA	4,345	8.1%	7.7%	9.9%	0.0%	3.6%	1.8%	23.8%	45.1%	52.6%
Omaha-Council Bluffs, NE-IA	18,826	4.6%	4.6%	1.6%	1.7%	18.8%	1.4%	31.8%	35.4%	44.5%
Orangeburg, SC micro	1,943	12.8%	0.0%	0.0%	20.0%	31.1%	6.1%	23.7%	6.2%	42.8%
Orlando-Kissimmee-Sanford, FL	30,111	6.1%	5.0%	2.6%	2.8%	14.5%	3.7%	26.0%	39.4%	56.0%
Oshkosh-Neenah, WI	4,984	5.4%	6.0%	0.0%	2.6%	13.1%	1.3%	13.9%	57.7%	27.4%
Ottawa-Peru, IL micro	1,711	5.3%	8.8%	0.0%	8.6%	46.1%	0.0%	19.3%	11.9%	58.5%
Owensboro, KY	1,995	14.1%	11.8%	4.2%	4.1%	27.6%	0.0%	15.7%	22.5%	55.2%
Oxnard-Thousand Oaks-Ventura, CA	4,476	14.4%	16.6%	3.7%	4.1%	6.1%	2.8%	19.3%	33.2%	65.1%
Palm Bay-Melbourne-Titusville, FL	5,074	2.9%	4.8%	4.7%	2.4%	25.6%	5.2%	27.4%	27.0%	68.1%
Panama City, FL	2,960	12.6%	20.8%	2.3%	0.0%	7.6%	0.0%	21.8%	34.9%	47.3%
Parkersburg-Vienna, WV	1,752	9.0%	0.0%	10.2%	0.0%	26.3%	0.0%	18.3%	36.2%	59.7%
Pensacola-Ferry Pass-Brent, FL	6,616	3.7%	22.1%	3.2%	7.5%	16.6%	0.0%	15.3%	31.5%	40.3%
Peoria, IL	7,630	7.4%	7.3%	10.1%	3.2%	13.8%	0.8%	32.2%	25.2%	48.9%
Philadelphia-Camden-Wilmington, PA-NJ-DE-MD	55,513	6.0%	3.4%	2.4%	4.4%	14.6%	3.0%	34.2%	32.1%	58.3%
Phoenix-Mesa-Scottsdale, AZ	63,457	9.2%	7.6%	3.1%	7.7%	15.5%	4.8%	27.5%	24.6%	54.8%
Pine Bluff, AR	2,439	2.6%	0.0%	14.0%	0.0%	37.7%	0.0%	39.0%	6.6%	36.8%
Pittsburgh, PA	35,430	3.1%	2.5%	1.9%	2.4%	16.0%	0.9%	34.3%	38.8%	49.7%
Pittsfield, MA	1,179	13.1%	0.0%	17.9%	0.0%	35.5%	0.0%	17.6%	15.9%	43.9%
Pocatello, ID	1,880	14.5%	26.5%	3.1%	0.0%	23.1%	0.0%	7.2%	25.5%	41.5%
Port St. Lucie, FL	2,865	3.1%	3.3%	0.0%	0.0%	37.4%	3.5%	17.9%	34.7%	68.0%
Portland-South Portland, ME	4,612	0.0%	8.9%	5.7%	0.0%	5.7%	12.6%	26.9%	40.1%	53.4%
Portland-Vancouver-Hillsboro, OR-WA	28,482	4.8%	9.9%	3.0%	4.3%	9.5%	4.4%	21.2%	42.9%	51.6%
Pottsville, PA micro	738	6.9%	0.0%	0.0%	0.0%	23.8%	0.0%	55.7%	13.6%	69.5%
Prescott, AZ	1,877	29.6%	7.0%	2.8%	0.0%	14.8%	4.8%	11.7%	29.4%	53.3%
Providence-Warwick, RI-MA	18,906	4.0%	2.7%	2.2%	7.4%	13.0%	6.2%	24.7%	39.9%	51.3%

Table D-4: Metropolitan/Micropolitan Statistical Areas—Household Relationship

		25 to 31								
		Married Couple Households		Male, No Spouse Present		Female, No Spouse Present		Non-Family Householders		
	Total Householders	With Children	No Children	With Children	No Children	With Children	No Children	Living Alone	Not Alone	Living With Parents
Madera, CA	5,835	27.4%	6.2%	2.6%	8.6%	29.6%	3.6%	13.8%	8.2%	19.8%
Madison, WI	35,834	19.5%	17.6%	2.4%	1.2%	7.1%	0.7%	37.2%	14.4%	9.8%
Manchester-Nashua, NH	15,201	18.0%	9.7%	10.7%	2.9%	15.8%	0.0%	12.7%	30.4%	20.4%
Manhattan, KS	6,164	27.5%	28.4%	1.7%	0.0%	12.7%	0.0%	24.1%	5.7%	4.9%
Mankato-North Mankato, MN	4,756	24.7%	14.6%	4.9%	3.9%	14.0%	0.0%	17.2%	20.8%	5.5%
Mansfield, OH	3,080	40.3%	4.1%	1.5%	6.4%	22.1%	0.0%	18.3%	7.3%	17.0%
McAllen-Edinburg-Mission, TX	20,945	51.7%	3.5%	2.4%	2.2%	23.4%	1.4%	9.6%	5.8%	38.3%
Medford, OR	8,473	34.7%	7.6%	2.6%	2.1%	24.1%	3.5%	17.3%	8.2%	14.1%
Memphis, TN-MS-AR	54,998	23.5%	8.7%	4.7%	3.3%	23.8%	3.0%	24.5%	8.4%	22.5%
Merced, CA	9,047	36.1%	9.2%	6.9%	0.9%	19.4%	6.1%	14.9%	6.6%	34.8%
Meridian, MS	3,238	31.2%	12.7%	0.8%	0.0%	20.0%	0.0%	29.4%	6.0%	17.6%
Miami-Fort Lauderdale-West Palm Beach, FL	159,788	19.9%	10.7%	4.1%	4.7%	18.3%	4.7%	24.1%	13.5%	34.7%
Michigan City-La Porte, IN	4,268	22.3%	13.0%	5.1%	0.0%	32.8%	0.0%	22.5%	4.3%	12.4%
Midland, MI	4,192	42.6%	10.7%	0.0%	0.0%	20.1%	0.0%	20.9%	5.6%	18.3%
Midland, TX	6,424	28.4%	7.1%	1.3%	3.9%	13.1%	0.0%	28.6%	17.7%	23.5%
Milwaukee-Waukesha-West Allis, WI	75,439	18.5%	11.5%	3.2%	2.5%	20.1%	0.5%	30.2%	13.5%	18.8%
Minneapolis-St. Paul-Bloomington, MN-WI	156,072	25.4%	13.8%	4.0%	1.7%	11.7%	0.8%	24.8%	17.8%	16.6%
Missoula, MT	5,204	32.3%	7.3%	18.1%	5.9%	3.4%	0.0%	13.4%	19.7%	14.7%
Mobile, AL	15,372	25.7%	9.8%	0.4%	0.0%	30.9%	0.8%	21.5%	10.9%	27.1%
Modesto, CA	16,771	31.9%	6.5%	11.4%	4.5%	20.3%	1.0%	14.6%	9.8%	25.0%
Monroe, LA	6,831	24.5%	11.8%	0.8%	3.5%	40.0%	1.1%	18.1%	0.0%	27.0%
Monroe, MI	3,199	36.6%	10.2%	8.3%	1.7%	14.4%	0.0%	22.2%	6.7%	39.8%
Montgomery, AL	18,978	25.5%	5.3%	0.0%	3.4%	30.5%	0.0%	26.8%	8.5%	21.5%
Morgantown, WV	6,412	18.4%	8.0%	0.7%	1.4%	19.6%	0.0%	33.5%	18.3%	18.7%
Morristown, TN	4,203	29.2%	20.9%	9.1%	3.1%	17.2%	10.1%	8.9%	1.5%	12.8%
Mount Vernon-Anacortes, WA	3,904	38.1%	2.9%	9.5%	0.0%	16.2%	0.0%	20.9%	12.3%	12.9%
Muncie, IN	3,897	19.2%	11.5%	1.3%	0.0%	20.1%	0.0%	37.8%	10.1%	8.8%
Muskegon, MI	5,062	19.6%	5.4%	2.2%	0.7%	39.4%	0.0%	19.9%	12.8%	19.4%
Myrtle Beach-Conway-North Myrtle Beach, SC-NC	11,813	25.1%	9.8%	10.9%	5.3%	21.9%	0.0%	13.9%	13.1%	17.2%
Napa, CA	2,563	49.9%	5.5%	3.7%	3.0%	10.3%	0.0%	16.9%	10.7%	35.0%
Naples-Immokalee-Marco Island, FL	6,775	42.1%	8.3%	0.1%	2.1%	12.2%	0.0%	26.6%	8.5%	35.2%
Nashville-Davidson–Murfreesboro–Franklin, TN	75,313	25.4%	14.3%	2.4%	2.5%	13.1%	1.1%	24.4%	16.7%	17.5%
New Bern, NC	5,856	42.1%	13.9%	6.9%	0.6%	7.4%	0.0%	19.1%	10.1%	16.7%
New Castle, PA	2,102	18.6%	14.3%	26.5%	5.0%	4.2%	0.0%	16.1%	15.3%	34.1%
New Haven-Milford, CT	29,709	15.8%	13.2%	3.4%	2.2%	20.2%	0.7%	25.8%	18.7%	28.7%
New Orleans-Metairie, LA	52,910	16.3%	10.2%	2.6%	3.8%	23.7%	1.1%	27.8%	14.4%	25.6%
New Philadelphia-Dover, OH	2,723	38.8%	5.3%	0.3%	2.5%	18.4%	0.0%	19.5%	15.3%	26.7%
New York-Newark-Jersey City, NY-NJ-PA	639,938	17.7%	13.1%	3.4%	3.7%	12.9%	3.0%	26.9%	19.2%	31.7%
Niles-Benton Harbor, MI	5,236	20.7%	10.2%	1.0%	0.0%	38.7%	0.0%	28.4%	1.1%	20.9%
North Port-Sarasota-Bradenton, FL	15,185	26.9%	12.3%	3.1%	2.2%	13.6%	1.1%	17.6%	23.2%	24.9%
Norwich-New London, CT	11,817	21.8%	9.3%	4.0%	3.4%	28.5%	0.7%	20.2%	12.1%	21.0%
Ocala, FL	7,660	26.3%	1.4%	0.8%	0.0%	29.9%	4.2%	32.6%	4.8%	33.2%
Ocean City, NJ	2,050	39.1%	20.8%	4.0%	0.0%	10.3%	0.0%	11.0%	14.8%	34.5%
Odessa, TX	7,064	42.4%	3.4%	6.5%	4.1%	14.3%	2.9%	16.3%	10.2%	23.1%
Ogden-Clearfield, UT	23,815	49.5%	15.0%	2.9%	0.3%	8.0%	0.3%	15.5%	8.5%	18.5%
Ogdensburg-Massena, NY	3,440	39.3%	2.2%	4.0%	0.0%	4.0%	0.0%	31.5%	19.0%	20.0%
Oklahoma City, OK	63,418	28.6%	11.2%	4.0%	2.6%	13.4%	1.5%	25.4%	13.4%	12.2%
Olympia-Tumwater, WA	10,176	33.6%	21.3%	3.3%	0.0%	15.0%	0.2%	14.7%	11.9%	21.4%
Omaha-Council Bluffs, NE-IA	48,277	25.4%	11.6%	4.0%	0.9%	16.4%	0.8%	27.2%	13.6%	12.8%
Orangeburg, SC	2,655	15.6%	0.0%	0.0%	25.7%	13.4%	0.0%	32.8%	12.4%	36.1%
Orlando-Kissimmee-Sanford, FL	81,086	19.8%	15.9%	4.7%	3.7%	12.9%	1.3%	27.4%	14.3%	27.4%
Oshkosh-Neenah, WI	7,242	9.4%	24.1%	5.6%	0.0%	15.0%	0.0%	34.3%	11.6%	12.6%
Ottawa-Peru, IL	3,304	33.1%	16.1%	6.5%	4.3%	1.8%	0.0%	25.1%	13.1%	19.1%
Owensboro, KY	4,586	29.8%	8.7%	0.0%	0.0%	25.0%	0.0%	36.5%	0.0%	20.4%
Oxnard-Thousand Oaks-Ventura, CA	20,333	35.8%	12.2%	2.4%	3.3%	18.3%	1.5%	8.2%	18.2%	29.5%
Palm Bay-Melbourne-Titusville, FL	14,677	25.3%	7.3%	4.9%	3.6%	20.5%	0.0%	23.8%	14.6%	29.8%
Panama City, FL	5,971	33.2%	10.8%	3.1%	1.5%	25.1%	1.7%	20.3%	4.4%	27.5%
Parkersburg-Vienna, WV	3,431	22.7%	3.0%	1.5%	0.0%	25.1%	4.1%	40.7%	2.9%	13.0%
Pensacola-Ferry Pass-Brent, FL	19,980	21.4%	14.8%	2.8%	2.3%	13.2%	1.2%	25.6%	18.6%	17.1%
Peoria, IL	17,511	23.9%	20.1%	3.2%	0.3%	13.4%	1.1%	23.7%	14.4%	11.8%
Philadelphia-Camden-Wilmington, PA-NJ-DE-MD	223,403	18.4%	13.4%	2.6%	2.0%	14.7%	1.3%	29.9%	17.7%	28.9%
Phoenix-Mesa-Scottsdale, AZ	172,040	24.3%	12.2%	5.7%	2.3%	14.1%	2.2%	24.8%	14.4%	19.0%
Pine Bluff, AR	3,367	41.2%	8.7%	7.4%	4.3%	17.2%	4.1%	9.7%	7.5%	15.7%
Pittsburgh, PA	89,299	21.0%	14.3%	3.3%	1.3%	14.4%	0.8%	26.7%	18.1%	21.3%
Pittsfield, MA	2,964	16.6%	13.4%	9.2%	0.0%	16.2%	0.0%	19.9%	24.8%	21.5%
Pocatello, ID	3,841	24.1%	29.5%	2.9%	0.0%	14.4%	0.0%	24.3%	4.8%	6.0%
Port St. Lucie, FL	10,171	28.8%	10.0%	3.5%	0.0%	23.0%	4.6%	21.5%	8.7%	35.4%
Portland-South Portland, ME	20,140	18.9%	16.0%	9.2%	0.3%	14.0%	2.0%	14.7%	24.9%	11.4%
Portland-Vancouver-Hillsboro, OR-WA	96,082	22.9%	13.4%	3.8%	1.6%	10.6%	1.4%	24.1%	22.2%	18.0%
Pottsville, PA	4,432	27.5%	12.8%	3.9%	1.9%	19.2%	0.0%	20.8%	13.9%	24.1%
Prescott, AZ	5,237	23.5%	9.2%	9.4%	0.2%	21.9%	2.0%	19.6%	14.3%	24.4%
Providence-Warwick, RI-MA	56,478	18.1%	11.0%	5.9%	3.0%	19.3%	1.8%	24.2%	16.8%	27.9%

Table D-4: Metropolitan/Micropolitan Statistical Areas—Household Relationship—*Continued*

		18 to 24								
		Married Couple Households		Male, No Spouse Present		Female, No Spouse Present		Non-Family Householders		
	Total Householders	With Children	No Children	With Children	No Children	With Children	No Children	Living Alone	Not Alone	Living With Parents
Provo-Orem, UT	15,524	20.1%	36.9%	1.4%	2.1%	4.6%	2.5%	6.4%	26.0%	35.1%
Pueblo, CO	3,933	19.2%	5.4%	10.5%	0.0%	18.8%	2.7%	21.8%	21.6%	49.4%
Punta Gorda, FL	1,032	26.3%	2.1%	10.0%	8.9%	10.9%	0.0%	20.8%	20.9%	60.6%
Racine, WI	2,159	16.6%	0.0%	15.6%	13.7%	7.8%	0.0%	28.4%	17.9%	65.6%
Raleigh, NC	17,677	7.0%	7.6%	0.9%	1.8%	11.4%	1.1%	31.6%	38.5%	48.0%
Rapid City, SD	2,439	0.0%	9.3%	12.0%	4.3%	2.8%	0.0%	33.2%	38.5%	32.3%
Reading, PA	5,061	7.6%	3.2%	7.4%	1.1%	25.9%	0.0%	29.6%	25.2%	51.3%
Redding, CA	2,514	5.6%	3.7%	3.5%	0.0%	13.2%	0.0%	31.2%	42.8%	33.8%
Reno, NV	6,666	10.6%	5.3%	3.8%	5.9%	6.1%	4.7%	23.5%	40.2%	34.3%
Richmond, VA	16,353	4.3%	7.8%	1.8%	1.3%	21.3%	3.5%	23.3%	36.6%	50.9%
Riverside-San Bernardino-Ontario, CA	36,545	14.6%	9.1%	8.7%	9.9%	18.8%	6.3%	12.7%	19.9%	65.8%
Roanoke, VA	4,829	10.4%	16.9%	3.1%	0.0%	9.1%	0.0%	27.7%	32.9%	46.5%
Rochester, MN	6,686	4.7%	0.9%	3.1%	0.0%	21.5%	0.5%	58.2%	11.1%	43.1%
Rochester, NY	14,422	3.6%	7.3%	2.4%	3.7%	17.5%	3.9%	28.5%	33.1%	47.8%
Rockford, IL	4,174	14.9%	11.5%	0.0%	0.0%	17.1%	0.0%	28.7%	27.8%	61.8%
Rocky Mount, NC	2,034	0.0%	33.0%	6.1%	0.0%	32.9%	0.0%	27.9%	0.0%	66.0%
Rome, GA	1,748	10.8%	0.0%	4.1%	0.0%	22.0%	0.0%	43.1%	20.0%	50.0%
Roseburg, OR micro	1,105	4.2%	3.8%	9.6%	0.0%	25.2%	0.0%	19.8%	37.5%	50.4%
Sacramento–Roseville–Arden-Arcade, CA	30,593	9.8%	5.1%	1.9%	4.7%	13.1%	3.1%	23.0%	39.2%	53.2%
Saginaw, MI	3,551	7.7%	0.0%	0.0%	1.9%	27.6%	0.0%	36.9%	25.9%	47.0%
Salem, OH micro	1,685	10.4%	11.9%	0.9%	0.0%	15.4%	5.5%	40.7%	15.1%	54.8%
Salem, OR	8,279	19.7%	6.4%	3.7%	0.7%	16.8%	5.3%	26.9%	20.5%	50.6%
Salinas, CA	4,985	17.7%	6.7%	2.9%	10.2%	9.8%	11.2%	15.6%	26.0%	58.5%
Salisbury, MD-DE	3,978	6.1%	14.8%	0.0%	0.0%	19.9%	5.2%	18.3%	35.8%	49.8%
Salt Lake City, UT	16,645	14.2%	17.0%	4.9%	6.6%	11.2%	2.6%	14.0%	29.6%	52.5%
San Angelo, TX	2,760	13.9%	8.0%	3.9%	5.8%	12.1%	4.8%	8.6%	42.7%	25.8%
San Antonio-New Braunfels, TX	32,161	10.3%	5.2%	5.8%	3.4%	12.6%	3.2%	33.5%	26.0%	55.2%
San Diego-Carlsbad, CA	42,316	10.6%	17.2%	1.6%	6.0%	6.2%	6.2%	18.5%	33.7%	50.8%
San Francisco-Oakland-Hayward, CA	43,869	8.6%	3.6%	2.0%	5.9%	6.3%	6.5%	26.5%	40.5%	53.8%
San Jose-Sunnyvale-Santa Clara, CA	15,999	2.1%	5.7%	4.2%	11.1%	4.8%	6.7%	26.1%	39.3%	57.3%
San Luis Obispo-Paso Robles-Arroyo Grande, CA	7,812	3.4%	2.8%	6.4%	1.2%	11.0%	4.7%	17.4%	53.2%	23.2%
Santa Cruz-Watsonville, CA	5,715	0.0%	0.0%	2.7%	10.7%	0.8%	1.7%	44.8%	39.4%	34.7%
Santa Fe, NM	1,518	34.3%	4.0%	2.5%	0.0%	18.0%	0.0%	22.7%	18.6%	53.1%
Santa Maria-Santa Barbara, CA	10,140	5.7%	2.8%	3.7%	12.5%	7.8%	2.2%	9.0%	56.2%	29.3%
Santa Rosa, CA	5,775	9.6%	4.4%	0.0%	9.5%	19.4%	0.0%	15.9%	41.2%	51.0%
Savannah, GA	7,958	5.9%	17.4%	2.0%	5.3%	15.2%	4.6%	18.3%	31.3%	36.7%
Scranton–Wilkes-Barre–Hazleton, PA	5,715	1.2%	2.0%	2.0%	9.1%	15.3%	0.4%	29.7%	40.2%	47.3%
Seattle-Tacoma-Bellevue, WA	53,276	7.4%	7.1%	3.3%	3.7%	9.3%	4.1%	25.5%	39.6%	48.7%
Sebastian-Vero Beach, FL	1,244	21.0%	0.0%	0.0%	7.3%	5.4%	8.7%	9.6%	48.1%	63.9%
Sebring, FL	1,153	30.5%	0.0%	0.0%	12.5%	33.2%	0.0%	14.5%	9.3%	65.0%
Sheboygan, WI	1,595	0.0%	0.0%	0.0%	13.6%	35.2%	0.0%	24.8%	26.4%	51.6%
Sherman-Denison, TX	2,306	27.8%	2.4%	5.0%	0.0%	30.8%	0.0%	13.7%	20.2%	41.1%
Show Low, AZ micro	557	16.7%	0.0%	1.6%	3.8%	47.8%	0.0%	16.3%	13.8%	68.7%
Shreveport-Bossier City, LA	9,383	1.7%	7.3%	0.0%	4.7%	26.0%	9.4%	27.9%	23.0%	44.1%
Sierra Vista-Douglas, AZ	3,470	15.4%	3.9%	23.5%	1.3%	7.3%	0.0%	25.4%	23.2%	38.8%
Sioux City, IA-NE-SD	3,068	0.6%	1.4%	5.7%	6.0%	10.8%	1.1%	23.9%	50.6%	45.1%
Sioux Falls, SD	4,953	16.2%	5.4%	1.8%	4.9%	1.7%	0.0%	15.6%	54.4%	34.4%
South Bend-Mishawaka, IN-MI	5,476	4.9%	10.4%	1.9%	2.1%	27.2%	0.6%	30.9%	22.0%	43.0%
Spartanburg, SC	5,439	1.2%	8.2%	9.1%	5.1%	24.9%	0.6%	40.9%	9.9%	53.7%
Spokane-Spokane Valley, WA	11,056	5.4%	5.4%	6.6%	3.7%	8.3%	6.0%	23.4%	41.3%	34.4%
Springfield, IL	3,825	0.0%	8.1%	7.8%	0.0%	6.0%	0.0%	35.5%	42.7%	49.6%
Springfield, MA	7,977	9.5%	2.4%	1.1%	10.7%	14.4%	2.2%	17.6%	42.0%	46.4%
Springfield, MO	13,701	6.3%	16.1%	4.5%	2.2%	13.9%	1.1%	21.3%	34.8%	34.4%
Springfield, OH	2,728	4.5%	3.2%	11.0%	2.2%	31.8%	0.0%	27.4%	20.0%	42.8%
St. Cloud, MN	5,448	0.0%	10.8%	7.3%	0.0%	3.7%	3.1%	20.4%	54.6%	29.0%
St. George, UT	1,798	51.7%	17.0%	0.0%	0.0%	0.0%	0.0%	0.0%	31.3%	42.6%
St. Joseph, MO-KS	2,085	9.5%	7.0%	0.0%	0.0%	47.1%	0.0%	6.9%	29.5%	44.7%
St. Louis, MO-IL	36,657	7.7%	8.1%	2.2%	3.6%	21.9%	3.1%	32.5%	20.9%	58.0%
State College, PA	8,430	0.3%	3.7%	0.0%	1.8%	1.9%	6.5%	26.3%	59.5%	12.2%
Staunton-Waynesboro, VA	1,380	5.4%	4.9%	0.0%	6.4%	27.1%	0.0%	45.1%	11.0%	42.1%
Stockton-Lodi, CA	8,828	16.9%	12.0%	5.6%	6.7%	19.3%	5.1%	19.2%	15.2%	59.3%
Sumter, SC	1,802	11.3%	19.2%	0.0%	14.4%	20.1%	1.4%	33.5%	0.0%	51.1%
Sunbury, PA micro	911	9.2%	4.9%	0.0%	0.0%	5.2%	0.0%	76.0%	4.7%	67.4%
Syracuse, NY	8,715	7.1%	1.8%	5.5%	2.1%	15.0%	2.8%	35.3%	30.3%	45.7%
Tallahassee, FL	19,917	1.4%	4.0%	0.0%	7.7%	2.3%	7.5%	30.7%	46.4%	24.2%
Tampa-St. Petersburg-Clearwater, FL	36,518	2.7%	8.1%	2.5%	4.4%	14.9%	5.0%	35.9%	26.6%	55.8%
Terre Haute, IN	3,513	21.3%	15.2%	6.4%	4.6%	11.0%	6.5%	3.6%	31.3%	28.5%
Texarkana, TX-AR	2,232	37.8%	2.1%	3.2%	4.0%	15.4%	0.0%	19.1%	18.5%	60.3%
The Villages, FL	612	38.2%	0.0%	0.0%	0.0%	32.2%	0.0%	0.0%	29.6%	67.4%
Toledo, OH	15,797	7.4%	4.4%	3.0%	3.0%	14.6%	3.9%	37.9%	25.7%	40.8%
Topeka, KS	3,453	6.8%	7.5%	2.3%	0.0%	22.7%	2.3%	31.7%	26.8%	44.7%
Torrington, CT micro	918	47.9%	20.4%	0.0%	0.0%	13.4%	0.0%	9.3%	9.0%	76.5%
Traverse City, MI micro	743	2.3%	1.7%	0.0%	0.0%	11.8%	0.0%	4.0%	80.1%	63.4%
Trenton, NJ	2,419	35.1%	0.0%	4.6%	12.9%	9.5%	0.0%	0.0%	37.9%	46.1%
Truckee-Grass Valley, CA micro	246	44.7%	0.0%	0.0%	4.9%	0.0%	0.0%	33.3%	17.1%	83.1%
Tucson, AZ	26,837	6.9%	5.6%	3.2%	5.0%	16.0%	7.0%	29.6%	26.7%	39.7%
Tullahoma-Manchester, TN micro	1,651	0.0%	0.0%	0.0%	0.0%	31.6%	4.7%	38.3%	25.4%	44.5%

Table D-4: Metropolitan/Micropolitan Statistical Areas—Household Relationship

		Married Couple Households		Male, No Spouse Present		Female, No Spouse Present		Non-Family Householders		
	Total Householders	With Children	No Children	With Children	No Children	With Children	No Children	Living Alone	Not Alone	Living With Parents
Provo-Orem, UT	23,980	57.8%	16.9%	2.5%	1.0%	3.8%	1.5%	6.8%	9.6%	12.9%
Pueblo, CO	5,885	48.5%	0.0%	5.4%	6.0%	20.9%	0.0%	15.7%	3.6%	19.6%
Punta Gorda, FL	2,228	24.3%	9.8%	9.2%	8.3%	11.8%	0.0%	14.5%	22.0%	28.4%
Racine, WI	7,575	18.3%	12.8%	8.3%	0.0%	25.5%	5.1%	26.6%	3.4%	17.0%
Raleigh, NC	50,776	19.8%	15.2%	3.3%	2.0%	12.7%	0.9%	24.7%	21.5%	15.3%
Rapid City, SD	6,786	51.1%	5.9%	0.8%	0.0%	18.4%	0.0%	10.6%	13.2%	10.1%
Reading, PA	12,354	29.7%	7.9%	7.2%	3.8%	10.9%	0.0%	15.3%	25.1%	24.9%
Redding, CA	6,019	41.0%	17.2%	1.8%	0.0%	15.1%	1.8%	4.1%	19.0%	16.2%
Reno, NV	18,413	29.0%	10.3%	4.3%	2.0%	8.9%	2.0%	30.0%	13.6%	16.1%
Richmond, VA	46,569	21.4%	15.9%	3.2%	2.6%	21.4%	0.8%	23.3%	11.4%	21.8%
Riverside-San Bernardino-Ontario, CA	126,617	32.5%	10.0%	6.0%	4.7%	16.3%	2.4%	16.5%	11.6%	34.5%
Roanoke, VA	10,440	26.1%	14.5%	7.7%	1.7%	10.1%	0.0%	24.7%	15.2%	17.5%
Rochester, MN	8,096	31.9%	22.3%	2.7%	1.2%	5.9%	2.4%	22.9%	10.8%	25.3%
Rochester, NY	43,522	21.1%	11.2%	3.5%	1.6%	20.5%	1.3%	24.9%	15.8%	20.7%
Rockford, IL	11,921	28.9%	12.1%	4.7%	2.4%	26.1%	1.2%	17.5%	7.1%	14.9%
Rocky Mount, NC	3,354	24.0%	7.7%	10.3%	8.3%	22.3%	0.0%	21.9%	5.5%	32.5%
Rome, GA	2,195	33.9%	5.6%	0.0%	12.9%	17.0%	12.3%	7.8%	10.5%	21.7%
Roseburg, OR	3,615	39.3%	2.8%	9.0%	0.0%	28.2%	0.0%	8.7%	12.0%	15.1%
Sacramento–Roseville–Arden-Arcade, CA	77,259	25.3%	17.6%	2.9%	2.3%	13.9%	1.7%	19.3%	17.0%	21.4%
Saginaw, MI	6,061	22.9%	8.1%	0.5%	1.9%	28.7%	0.0%	28.8%	9.1%	18.9%
Salem, OH	3,830	9.2%	8.2%	4.1%	0.0%	39.2%	0.0%	21.5%	17.7%	29.1%
Salem, OR	14,272	32.8%	6.6%	9.1%	1.1%	23.0%	1.0%	15.2%	11.2%	15.4%
Salinas, CA	11,849	33.5%	9.6%	1.4%	3.1%	14.3%	5.3%	20.9%	11.9%	31.3%
Salisbury, MD-DE	10,295	28.3%	17.9%	4.9%	2.0%	20.9%	2.8%	12.0%	11.2%	24.1%
Salt Lake City, UT	47,932	35.7%	17.9%	4.1%	2.3%	7.3%	0.2%	17.8%	14.7%	20.9%
San Angelo, TX	5,880	43.5%	6.5%	0.0%	0.0%	4.6%	0.0%	28.2%	17.3%	5.3%
San Antonio-New Braunfels, TX	93,972	27.4%	11.3%	3.0%	2.3%	17.8%	2.1%	24.1%	11.9%	25.6%
San Diego-Carlsbad, CA	135,913	24.5%	16.7%	3.4%	2.3%	9.6%	1.8%	19.5%	22.3%	19.4%
San Francisco-Oakland-Hayward, CA	166,675	16.0%	15.2%	2.2%	3.4%	7.8%	2.4%	25.8%	27.2%	22.4%
San Jose-Sunnyvale-Santa Clara, CA	63,913	17.9%	19.0%	3.6%	3.6%	9.0%	2.2%	24.3%	20.3%	23.9%
San Luis Obispo-Paso Robles-Arroyo Grande, CA	8,092	21.9%	10.5%	0.8%	1.3%	22.9%	1.1%	22.4%	19.0%	23.1%
Santa Cruz-Watsonville, CA	7,001	23.3%	19.6%	1.7%	0.6%	3.9%	0.0%	19.2%	31.6%	34.4%
Santa Fe, NM	3,893	23.0%	11.2%	9.3%	6.7%	19.3%	4.3%	17.0%	9.2%	24.7%
Santa Maria-Santa Barbara, CA	13,355	25.1%	13.5%	10.6%	4.9%	12.0%	1.7%	17.6%	14.5%	18.4%
Santa Rosa, CA	14,688	22.5%	14.7%	2.3%	4.7%	10.0%	4.0%	16.7%	25.2%	28.1%
Savannah, GA	16,225	20.4%	19.1%	4.4%	4.1%	13.3%	1.5%	28.5%	8.7%	18.0%
Scranton–Wilkes-Barre–Hazleton, PA	17,641	21.2%	11.0%	5.1%	3.5%	17.1%	4.4%	20.4%	17.2%	28.9%
Seattle-Tacoma-Bellevue, WA	169,487	19.6%	16.4%	3.1%	1.7%	8.3%	1.7%	27.6%	21.6%	14.9%
Sebastian-Vero Beach, FL	3,521	23.4%	8.6%	7.9%	2.1%	21.0%	0.0%	17.7%	19.3%	24.0%
Sebring, FL	1,611	63.9%	0.0%	14.9%	2.1%	5.6%	0.0%	1.5%	11.9%	34.8%
Sheboygan, WI	4,725	37.1%	18.9%	7.6%	0.4%	10.6%	0.0%	14.5%	10.9%	13.1%
Sherman-Denison, TX	4,127	44.7%	8.5%	4.9%	0.0%	21.1%	0.0%	14.7%	6.1%	12.1%
Show Low, AZ	1,824	28.1%	2.6%	4.4%	0.5%	34.7%	7.6%	3.6%	18.4%	53.5%
Shreveport-Bossier City, LA	21,254	17.9%	9.0%	6.0%	0.7%	24.1%	0.6%	33.1%	8.6%	21.7%
Sierra Vista-Douglas, AZ	5,641	33.2%	12.7%	1.2%	0.0%	20.5%	0.0%	16.1%	16.3%	9.5%
Sioux City, IA-NE-SD	7,649	30.3%	15.9%	4.4%	0.0%	23.7%	0.0%	21.5%	4.2%	7.5%
Sioux Falls, SD	13,950	24.7%	8.6%	10.9%	0.0%	11.8%	2.3%	18.4%	23.3%	11.3%
South Bend-Mishawaka, IN-MI	12,543	24.8%	10.0%	2.8%	1.7%	15.7%	0.7%	31.9%	12.4%	17.6%
Spartanburg, SC	10,596	30.4%	8.4%	4.5%	0.0%	21.7%	0.0%	24.5%	10.5%	28.2%
Spokane-Spokane Valley, WA	26,594	28.6%	12.2%	6.2%	0.3%	15.0%	0.6%	22.7%	14.3%	11.0%
Springfield, IL	10,060	29.1%	9.3%	2.0%	0.0%	28.4%	1.5%	18.9%	10.9%	8.7%
Springfield, MA	20,550	15.8%	8.5%	4.2%	4.3%	25.0%	1.7%	20.6%	19.8%	27.1%
Springfield, MO	23,668	30.9%	12.9%	2.8%	1.3%	16.2%	1.0%	21.2%	13.7%	12.7%
Springfield, OH	4,827	29.1%	14.4%	3.6%	5.3%	26.4%	0.0%	11.9%	9.4%	22.1%
St. Cloud, MN	8,350	25.8%	12.0%	5.8%	2.7%	27.4%	0.0%	7.9%	18.4%	13.3%
St. George, UT	5,193	66.5%	3.5%	0.6%	0.0%	12.7%	1.8%	5.7%	9.1%	4.6%
St. Joseph, MO-KS	4,024	23.9%	8.4%	0.0%	4.6%	32.2%	0.0%	23.7%	7.2%	17.8%
St. Louis, MO-IL	125,647	26.2%	12.2%	4.3%	0.7%	17.3%	1.5%	24.9%	13.0%	17.8%
State College, PA	6,530	19.8%	11.2%	3.0%	0.0%	5.6%	0.4%	32.6%	27.3%	18.7%
Staunton-Waynesboro, VA	3,914	29.4%	21.6%	3.2%	2.2%	15.4%	0.0%	20.7%	7.5%	26.0%
Stockton-Lodi, CA	19,413	34.1%	8.3%	9.5%	2.2%	16.2%	2.1%	12.6%	14.9%	28.5%
Sumter, SC	3,421	36.6%	0.8%	0.0%	0.0%	22.4%	3.8%	20.6%	15.7%	20.6%
Sunbury, PA	3,267	30.1%	12.8%	0.9%	0.0%	12.4%	0.0%	28.6%	15.2%	21.6%
Syracuse, NY	22,540	16.3%	11.2%	2.4%	2.5%	16.8%	0.6%	32.4%	17.8%	28.7%
Tallahassee, FL	17,396	14.9%	10.1%	2.4%	1.1%	17.6%	1.8%	30.2%	21.9%	14.1%
Tampa-St. Petersburg-Clearwater, FL	97,317	21.9%	11.7%	3.8%	3.1%	16.3%	1.9%	26.8%	14.5%	25.3%
Terre Haute, IN	6,550	26.0%	19.6%	4.4%	3.7%	6.4%	0.0%	29.7%	10.1%	20.3%
Texarkana, TX-AR	5,816	37.5%	20.4%	4.2%	0.9%	19.9%	0.0%	8.0%	9.0%	20.3%
The Villages, FL	1,461	10.1%	17.0%	0.0%	6.6%	0.0%	0.0%	66.3%	0.0%	29.8%
Toledo, OH	25,889	20.6%	9.0%	1.2%	2.9%	26.1%	0.8%	27.7%	11.8%	22.6%
Topeka, KS	9,412	34.2%	7.6%	6.9%	0.7%	13.6%	0.2%	20.1%	16.7%	16.3%
Torrington, CT	5,147	22.8%	11.9%	0.0%	0.0%	13.3%	0.8%	22.9%	28.3%	26.7%
Traverse City, MI	4,596	21.9%	9.5%	0.5%	0.0%	24.0%	0.0%	32.3%	11.7%	20.0%
Trenton, NJ	10,623	26.4%	22.5%	1.0%	1.6%	11.0%	4.3%	16.6%	16.5%	27.1%
Truckee-Grass Valley, CA	2,366	12.3%	4.9%	3.2%	0.0%	11.6%	0.0%	34.1%	33.9%	18.3%
Tucson, AZ	39,932	16.6%	11.3%	4.5%	4.9%	16.6%	2.0%	30.2%	13.9%	15.9%
Tullahoma-Manchester, TN	2,496	28.4%	32.3%	0.0%	0.0%	22.8%	0.0%	9.0%	7.6%	11.5%

Table D-4: Metropolitan/Micropolitan Statistical Areas—Household Relationship—*Continued*

		18 to 24								
		Married Couple Households		Male, No Spouse Present		Female, No Spouse Present		Non-Family Householders		
	Total Householders	With Children	No Children	With Children	No Children	With Children	No Children	Living Alone	Not Alone	Living With Parents
Tulsa, OK	18,846	9.6%	9.6%	3.6%	5.0%	19.2%	0.7%	31.4%	21.0%	46.0%
Tupelo, MS micro	1,028	10.0%	12.2%	0.0%	0.0%	42.2%	0.0%	17.4%	18.2%	72.8%
Tuscaloosa, AL	5,911	14.9%	0.0%	0.0%	0.0%	9.6%	7.4%	29.1%	38.9%	38.1%
Tyler, TX	3,468	7.9%	11.9%	2.8%	0.0%	16.6%	0.0%	21.2%	39.6%	44.4%
Urban Honolulu, HI	12,228	18.4%	18.9%	0.4%	3.4%	3.7%	5.2%	26.9%	23.0%	46.3%
Utica-Rome, NY	3,228	1.5%	0.9%	5.5%	2.0%	3.0%	4.7%	25.2%	57.2%	52.2%
Valdosta, GA	6,227	6.0%	10.9%	8.5%	4.9%	17.2%	0.0%	12.9%	39.6%	30.4%
Vallejo-Fairfield, CA	3,615	8.1%	11.4%	2.6%	8.0%	26.4%	3.7%	20.5%	19.3%	64.4%
Victoria, TX	1,169	6.8%	0.0%	2.7%	8.0%	62.9%	0.0%	11.6%	8.0%	62.6%
Vineland-Bridgeton, NJ	923	18.2%	0.0%	3.8%	0.0%	41.9%	8.6%	4.6%	23.0%	70.8%
Virginia Beach-Norfolk-Newport News, VA-NC	26,929	10.1%	15.6%	0.7%	4.9%	14.4%	4.8%	25.9%	23.6%	46.8%
Visalia-Porterville, CA	6,321	16.9%	3.0%	7.6%	11.3%	31.7%	8.2%	10.4%	10.8%	57.0%
Waco, TX	8,159	3.7%	2.9%	3.1%	3.3%	19.9%	0.7%	32.1%	34.4%	38.4%
Walla Walla, WA	1,068	10.7%	7.7%	0.0%	23.2%	0.0%	0.0%	14.1%	44.3%	28.7%
Warner Robins, GA	2,325	14.9%	16.9%	0.0%	0.0%	4.3%	10.5%	37.3%	16.2%	55.3%
Washington-Arlington-Alexandria, DC-VA-MD-WV	53,302	5.9%	7.0%	2.5%	7.4%	13.7%	3.1%	27.3%	33.2%	57.0%
Waterloo-Cedar Falls, IA	6,471	2.0%	2.6%	0.0%	3.0%	7.8%	1.5%	39.9%	43.2%	32.0%
Watertown-Fort Drum, NY	3,264	17.3%	19.1%	0.0%	2.3%	24.8%	2.0%	25.0%	9.6%	34.6%
Wausau, WI	2,262	0.0%	2.3%	16.2%	1.2%	37.9%	0.0%	26.4%	16.0%	58.3%
Weirton-Steubenville, WV-OH	2,377	19.1%	0.0%	4.2%	6.2%	31.1%	0.0%	15.2%	24.2%	39.1%
Wenatchee, WA	725	0.0%	8.1%	0.0%	0.0%	17.4%	8.7%	61.5%	4.3%	81.3%
Wheeling, WV-OH	2,412	18.8%	0.0%	4.1%	6.1%	30.2%	0.0%	15.0%	25.8%	40.5%
Whitewater-Elkhorn, WI micro	2,434	3.3%	7.9%	0.0%	1.6%	0.0%	0.0%	14.5%	72.8%	35.4%
Wichita Falls, TX	3,680	10.2%	17.1%	0.0%	2.6%	16.4%	0.0%	19.8%	33.9%	24.8%
Wichita, KS	12,418	12.8%	10.5%	2.4%	2.4%	21.6%	1.5%	27.6%	21.1%	51.5%
Williamsport, PA	2,214	8.8%	5.1%	0.0%	0.0%	27.4%	0.0%	29.9%	28.8%	44.0%
Wilmington, NC	7,815	1.2%	9.4%	2.4%	1.4%	8.2%	0.8%	30.8%	45.8%	28.7%
Winchester, VA-WV	1,135	0.0%	4.0%	15.9%	0.0%	36.2%	7.7%	16.9%	19.4%	52.2%
Winston-Salem, NC	9,013	10.3%	6.1%	2.1%	10.1%	20.0%	2.8%	28.8%	19.7%	50.9%
Wooster, OH micro	1,242	2.6%	37.4%	2.7%	0.0%	12.3%	0.0%	44.9%	0.0%	55.4%
Worcester, MA-CT	9,016	5.9%	5.3%	0.2%	5.1%	23.5%	0.6%	32.1%	27.3%	58.7%
Yakima, WA	2,771	31.3%	10.2%	2.7%	6.9%	13.9%	5.6%	8.9%	20.4%	58.0%
York-Hanover, PA	3,177	18.2%	6.5%	5.4%	5.4%	26.7%	2.3%	16.9%	18.6%	60.1%
Youngstown-Warren-Boardman, OH-PA	6,753	7.8%	3.9%	6.2%	0.0%	21.7%	6.0%	26.5%	27.9%	56.5%
Yuba City, CA	3,193	7.4%	6.0%	9.6%	22.0%	24.8%	5.2%	17.6%	7.4%	49.0%
Yuma, AZ	2,953	34.1%	11.1%	7.0%	0.0%	15.9%	7.3%	9.9%	14.6%	58.8%

Table D-4: Metropolitan/Micropolitan Statistical Areas—Household Relationship—*Continued*

		25 to 31								
		Married Couple Households		Male, No Spouse Present		Female, No Spouse Present		Non-Family Householders		
	Total Householders	With Children	No Children	With Children	No Children	With Children	No Children	Living Alone	Not Alone	Living With Parents
Tulsa, OK	41,854	33.7%	10.8%	4.5%	2.3%	19.6%	0.5%	20.8%	7.8%	16.0%
Tupelo, MS	5,436	36.7%	8.2%	6.7%	1.3%	24.2%	0.7%	17.9%	4.3%	13.9%
Tuscaloosa, AL	8,913	33.2%	18.6%	4.8%	3.9%	15.1%	0.0%	22.8%	1.4%	24.4%
Tyler, TX	7,822	39.2%	8.4%	0.0%	1.0%	16.9%	1.2%	22.1%	11.2%	18.8%
Urban Honolulu, HI	36,557	35.7%	12.0%	2.2%	2.6%	7.5%	2.5%	18.1%	19.3%	24.6%
Utica-Rome, NY	10,693	33.2%	7.5%	5.1%	3.6%	13.7%	1.1%	22.5%	13.4%	22.0%
Valdosta, GA	7,056	24.3%	16.4%	0.5%	0.0%	21.1%	7.6%	25.0%	5.1%	14.1%
Vallejo-Fairfield, CA	15,558	31.9%	10.8%	6.4%	2.6%	17.2%	0.7%	16.0%	14.3%	29.1%
Victoria, TX	3,590	33.1%	10.3%	1.3%	5.5%	20.1%	0.0%	17.9%	11.8%	19.1%
Vineland-Bridgeton, NJ	6,457	33.5%	6.9%	4.4%	0.0%	25.8%	2.3%	10.3%	16.8%	25.8%
Virginia Beach-Norfolk-Newport News, VA-NC	75,639	21.5%	13.8%	2.7%	1.5%	21.7%	1.5%	24.2%	13.0%	19.5%
Visalia-Porterville, CA	16,214	44.3%	7.1%	4.7%	4.7%	21.7%	2.0%	10.3%	5.3%	26.7%
Waco, TX	11,420	22.0%	10.2%	2.7%	0.5%	27.2%	0.0%	23.9%	13.5%	17.3%
Walla Walla, WA	2,519	61.4%	9.2%	7.3%	4.6%	12.2%	0.0%	5.2%	0.0%	15.4%
Warner Robins, GA	9,316	17.3%	23.1%	0.9%	1.2%	19.4%	0.0%	23.9%	14.2%	13.7%
Washington-Arlington-Alexandria, DC-VA-MD-WV	251,124	17.7%	15.8%	2.8%	3.5%	11.7%	1.9%	27.0%	19.6%	20.5%
Waterloo-Cedar Falls, IA	7,612	31.1%	6.6%	2.0%	0.0%	21.0%	0.0%	25.6%	13.7%	11.3%
Watertown-Fort Drum, NY	5,112	36.2%	15.4%	15.0%	0.0%	6.9%	0.0%	18.6%	7.9%	18.1%
Wausau, WI	5,383	33.6%	10.7%	8.3%	1.5%	2.9%	3.5%	29.4%	10.2%	11.7%
Weirton-Steubenville, WV-OH	3,297	29.9%	5.9%	7.2%	0.0%	14.6%	0.0%	27.8%	14.6%	15.2%
Wenatchee, WA	5,727	22.7%	9.6%	15.8%	3.8%	19.4%	0.0%	10.8%	17.8%	16.1%
Wheeling, WV-OH	4,033	25.5%	4.8%	5.9%	0.0%	11.9%	0.0%	35.8%	16.1%	16.6%
Whitewater-Elkhorn, WI	3,443	42.5%	9.2%	8.5%	0.0%	19.4%	0.0%	3.0%	17.4%	16.4%
Wichita Falls, TX	8,101	33.7%	4.7%	2.5%	0.5%	30.5%	1.6%	23.6%	2.9%	8.3%
Wichita, KS	30,890	36.1%	9.3%	2.3%	0.4%	15.7%	1.1%	27.7%	7.4%	16.3%
Williamsport, PA	2,406	37.2%	28.1%	2.6%	0.0%	12.8%	0.0%	10.7%	8.6%	25.2%
Wilmington, NC	11,213	19.5%	12.9%	8.0%	0.0%	13.9%	0.0%	25.8%	20.0%	13.0%
Winchester, VA-WV	3,660	23.7%	27.5%	0.0%	0.0%	14.4%	2.4%	18.8%	13.3%	15.9%
Winston-Salem, NC	21,021	27.7%	14.1%	1.8%	2.1%	21.8%	0.6%	20.9%	11.0%	23.2%
Wooster, OH	4,750	47.2%	11.8%	1.6%	1.0%	12.7%	0.0%	17.6%	8.0%	14.5%
Worcester, MA-CT	28,912	21.4%	13.2%	5.1%	1.6%	22.4%	2.4%	17.3%	16.6%	27.3%
Yakima, WA	7,763	44.8%	8.2%	5.1%	3.9%	16.2%	0.7%	15.8%	5.4%	22.5%
York-Hanover, PA	13,310	32.4%	10.4%	5.3%	1.9%	18.4%	0.0%	24.5%	7.1%	23.9%
Youngstown-Warren-Boardman, OH-PA	20,304	24.7%	8.6%	4.7%	0.8%	19.5%	2.2%	28.5%	11.0%	23.0%
Yuba City, CA	5,195	36.5%	4.5%	8.4%	4.4%	11.5%	0.0%	20.9%	13.6%	22.9%
Yuma, AZ	7,641	46.7%	9.0%	4.4%	1.1%	22.4%	0.0%	15.2%	1.1%	18.4%

PART E

EDUCATIONAL ATTAINMENT

EDUCATIONAL ATTAINMENT

Unlike the Baby Boom generation, completion of a bachelor's degree is more universally expected of the Millennials. Today's economy is more knowledge based, and Millennials find that in many fields even a bachelor's degree isn't sufficient for advancement. Millennials are also facing a very different economic climate having weathered the Great Recession and a slow recovery of the labor market. Yet, as the largest generation in the United States, they will be an important driver of the economy in the future. As noted by the President's Council of Economic Advisors, "this is the first generation to have had access to the Internet during their formative years."[1]

The Millennial age categories defined here span the ages where they are entering or completing their education (18 to 24) or are at the beginning of their careers (25 to 31). As expected, these two age groups vary in levels of educational accomplishment, though the 18 to 24 year olds likely aren't finished with formal schooling. In comparison to older Americans, less than one in four (22.2 percent) of those age 65 and over have a bachelor's degree or higher, but among the 25 to 31 age group, 32.4 percent have already attained that level of education.

The Millennial generation is also highly diverse, and many Millennials are immigrants having entered this country on student visas. In 1983 there were 339,000 foreign students being educated in the U.S., but by 2013 that number swelled to 886,000[2]. This is a generation facing a very different economic climate, labor force competition, and continued advancement of educational attainment for women.

Education

Nationally, 29.7 percent of Millennials age 18 to 24 have only a high school education, and that percentage falls to 24.1 percent for the 25 to 31 year olds. For the population age 65 and over, 33.9 percent have only a high school

1. Council of Economic Advisors, Executive Office of the President, "15 Economic Facts About Millennials," October 2014.
2. Institute of International Education, Open Doors Data, International Students, http://www.iie.org/Research-and-Publications/Open-Doors/Data/International-Students

or equivalent education. Younger Millennials continue their education as 40.8 percent have had some college experience and five percent have attained an associate's degree. Nearly 10 percent have gone on and hold a bachelor's degree or higher. Among the 25 to 31 year olds, fewer have some college (23.8 percent), but 32.4 percent have completed a bachelor's or advanced degree.

By state, West Virginia has the highest percentage of 18 to 24 year olds with only a high school education (38.9 percent), while North Dakota is lowest at 22.0 percent. In 26 states more than 30 percent of the younger Millennials stopped their educations after high school. In Florida, 9.2 percent have an associate's degree, but only 1.8 percent in the District of Columbia. DC also has the highest percentage in this age group with a bachelor's or advanced degree (25.2 percent), while Alaska has the lowest percentage at 3.7 percent. Alaska also has the highest percentage of 25 to 31 year olds who have only a high school education (34.3 percent). The District of Columbia is lowest at 12.6 percent. Associates degrees are held by 20.1 percent of North Dakota's older Millennials. The District of Columbia has the highest percentage with bachelor's degrees (35.4 percent) and advanced degrees (35.0 percent). In total, 70.5 percent of DC's older Millennials have a bachelor's degree or higher. Mississippi has the lowest percentage with a bachelor's degree (14.5 percent), and Nevada is lowest for advanced degrees at 3.5 percent. Virtually all 13- to 17-year-old Millennials are still enrolled in school (97.5 percent). Alaska is lowest at 94.9 percent.

Blair County, PA has the highest percentage of 18 to 24 year olds who have only a high school education (56.6 percent), but in 64 additional counties, high school is the highest level of accomplishment for 40 percent of this younger group. Story County, IA has the lowest percentage at 6.2 percent. In Arlington County, VA almost half (47.5 percent) of the 18 to 24 year olds have attained a bachelor's degree or higher. In 379 counties, less than 10 percent have completed that level of education. Among the older age group, Fayette County, PA has the highest percentage who have only completed high school (47.0 percent). Many in this age group have at least experienced college, with some attaining an associate's degree. In 355 counties, more than one-third have an associate's degree or some college experience.

Percent Age 25 to 31 Holding an Advanced Degree

Percent

☐ 3.50% - 5.99%
▨ 6.00% - 7.99%
▨ 8.00% - 12.99%
▨ 13.00% - 16.99%
■ 17.00% - 35.99%

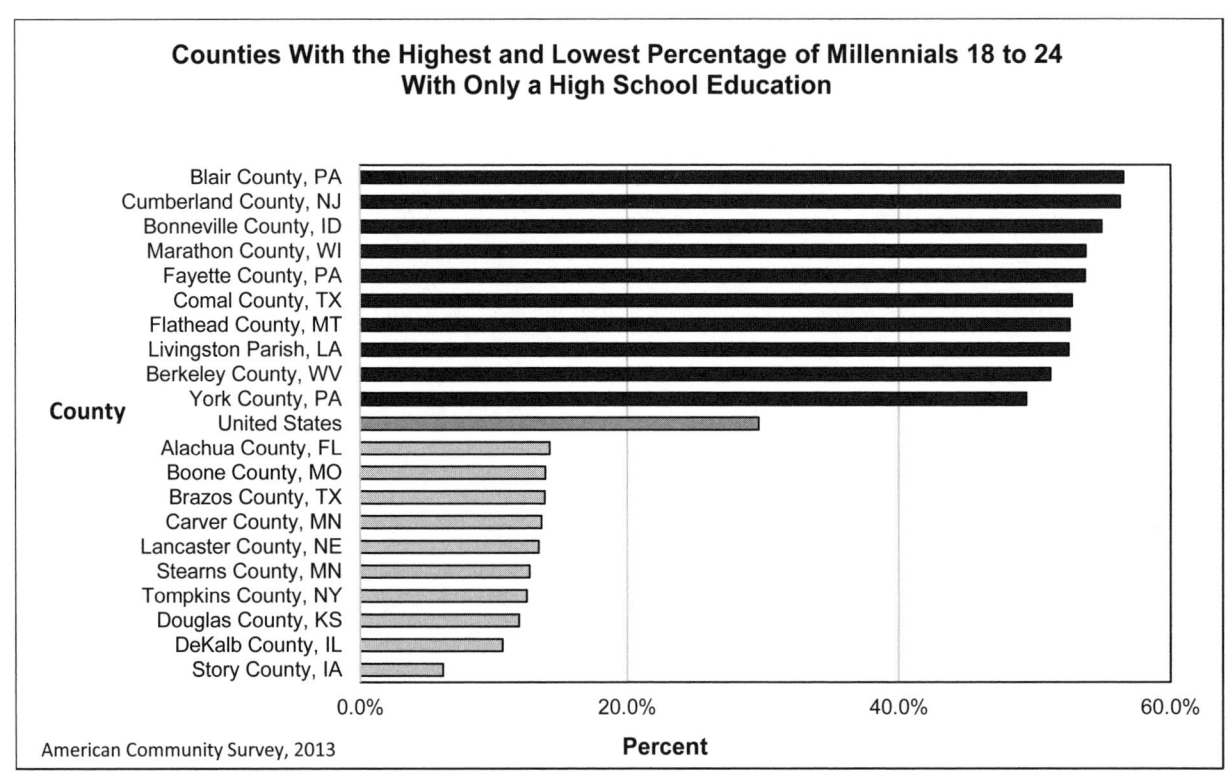

Counties With the Highest and Lowest Percentage of Millennials 18 to 24 With Only a High School Education

American Community Survey, 2013

A bachelor's degree is held by 53.8 percent in New York County, NY (Manhattan), where an additional 21 percent hold an advanced degree. Citrus County, FL has the lowest percentage holding a bachelor's degree at 3.2 percent. Most 13 to 17 year olds are enrolled in school, but

in Geauga County, OH only 83.0 percent are enrolled. In only eight counties is the percentage less than 90 percent.

Ann Arbor City, MI has the lowest percentage of 18 to 24 year olds with only a high school education,

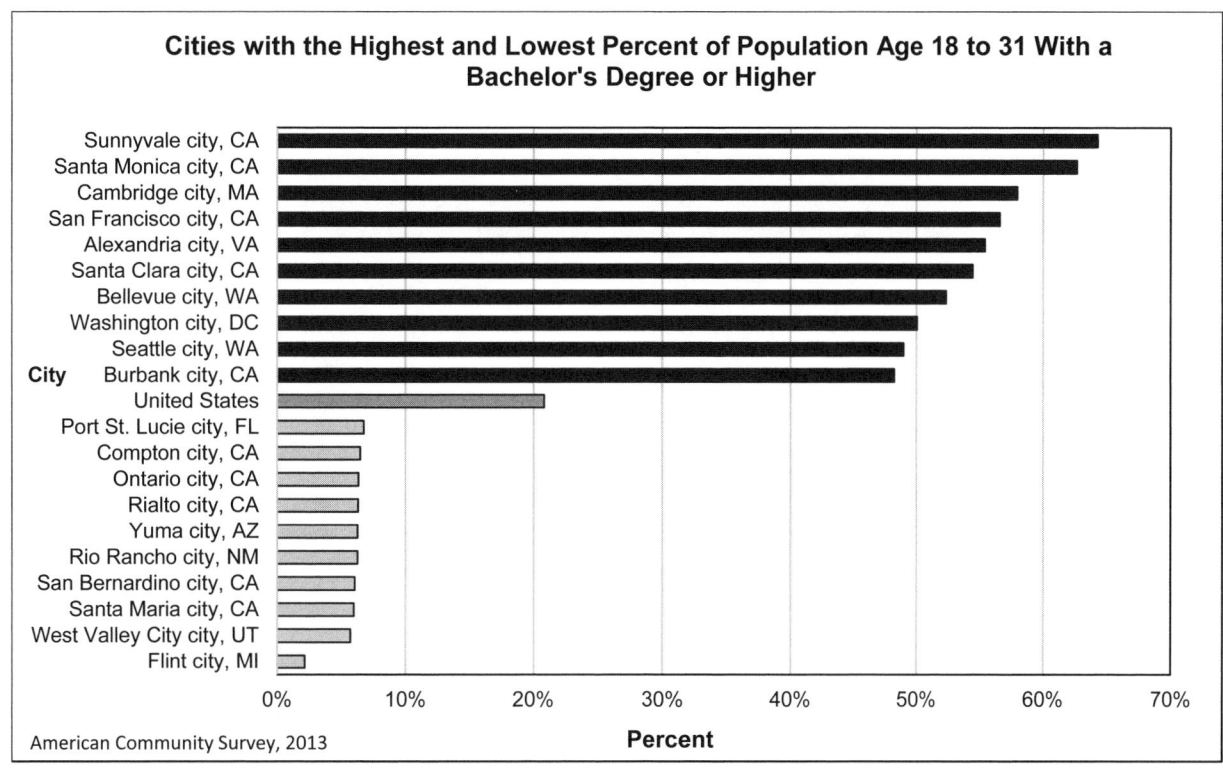

Cities with the Highest and Lowest Percent of Population Age 18 to 31 With a Bachelor's Degree or Higher

American Community Survey, 2013

while Victorville City, CA is highest at 50.9 percent. More than 70 percent (71.6 percent) in Berkeley City, CA have already experienced some college time, and in Clearwater City, FL 16.6 percent have attained an associate's degree. Bachelor's degrees are held by 34.9 percent of younger Millennials in Sunnyvale City, CA, where 10.9 percent also hold advanced degrees. Among the older Millennial age group, 46.1 percent in Paterson City, NJ still have only completed high school. Cambridge City, MA has the lowest percentage at 3.9 percent. In 56 cities more than one-third hold a bachelor's degree, and Boulder City, CO is highest at 59.8 percent. Cambridge City, MA has the highest percentage holding an advanced degree (40.6 percent). In 94 cities, less than five percent of the 25 to 31 year olds hold an advanced degree. Anchorage Municipality, AK has the lowest percentage of the 13 to 17 population enrolled in school (88.8 percent), but 170 cities are above 98 percent.

The Columbus, IN metropolitan area has the highest percentage of 18 to 24 year olds with only a high school education (57.1 percent), while the Ames, IA metro is lowest at 5.8 percent. In 224 metros more than 40 percent of younger Millennials have experienced some college. The Ithaca, NY metro is highest at 71.8 percent. The Lawrence, KS metro has the highest percentage with a bachelor's degree or higher (24.7 percent). Among the older Millennials, the Danville, IL metro has the highest percentage (58.8 percent) with only a high school education. The Goldsboro, NC metro is lowest at 9.9 percent. The Bismarck, ND metro has the highest percentage with an associate's degree at 31.3 percent, but an associate's degree is held by less than 10 percent in 251 metros. The Ithaca, NY metro (home to Cornell University and Ithaca College) has the highest percentage with a bachelor's or advanced degree (61.3 percent). It's also highest for just a bachelor's degree, but State College, PA (Penn State University) is highest for advanced degrees (25.8 percent). At the metro/micro level the percentage of 13 to 17 year olds enrolled in school is below 90 percent in only four areas: the Dalton, GA metro and the Lumberton, NC, Ogdensburg-Massena, NY, and Wooster, OH micropolitan areas.

Table E-1: States—Educational Attainment

	13 to 17		18 to 24					25 to 31					
				Percent					Percent				
	Total Population	Percent Enrolled in School	Total Population	High School	Some College	Associates Degree	Bachelors Degree	Total Population	High School	Some College	Associates Degree	Bachelors Degree	Advanced Degree
United States	20,794,322	97.5%	31,635,759	29.7%	40.8%	5.0%	9.8%	30,086,454	24.1%	23.8%	8.6%	23.5%	8.9%
Alabama	317,143	96.7%	497,511	30.4%	39.3%	3.9%	8.3%	429,255	28.5%	25.2%	8.8%	17.3%	6.9%
Alaska	52,922	94.9%	84,545	36.1%	41.5%	1.8%	3.7%	80,986	29.4%	32.1%	5.2%	21.3%	6.2%
Arizona	458,064	96.4%	662,724	31.2%	38.2%	5.0%	7.5%	622,816	24.8%	26.8%	8.8%	18.5%	7.0%
Arkansas	194,868	96.2%	287,155	34.9%	40.3%	3.6%	6.9%	272,879	34.3%	24.2%	7.7%	16.0%	5.8%
California	2,588,851	98.2%	4,016,509	28.6%	43.0%	4.8%	9.4%	3,958,135	21.9%	24.6%	7.6%	23.7%	8.2%
Colorado	347,310	97.6%	512,098	25.1%	43.4%	4.8%	11.1%	544,958	20.2%	25.0%	8.9%	28.7%	7.3%
Connecticut	235,916	98.1%	342,884	27.3%	42.3%	3.8%	13.3%	311,170	24.0%	19.8%	7.4%	26.7%	13.6%
Delaware	55,750	96.8%	90,525	33.8%	33.8%	3.9%	13.2%	87,725	25.8%	18.1%	8.8%	23.3%	11.8%
District of Columbia	23,781	96.3%	80,974	22.9%	38.9%	1.8%	25.2%	111,405	12.6%	10.1%	2.7%	35.4%	35.0%
Florida	1,157,139	97.1%	1,796,924	30.7%	35.6%	9.2%	7.7%	1,749,330	27.6%	23.0%	11.3%	20.0%	6.5%
Georgia	701,865	97.2%	1,029,573	30.0%	40.1%	3.7%	8.2%	944,465	25.7%	25.0%	7.4%	20.0%	8.1%
Hawaii	85,036	96.8%	136,384	33.7%	42.9%	6.0%	9.2%	149,735	26.3%	27.9%	11.7%	23.4%	4.9%
Idaho	120,090	96.9%	160,655	37.2%	34.8%	5.5%	8.2%	141,419	28.5%	26.5%	10.0%	19.0%	4.8%
Illinois	861,332	97.7%	1,267,572	27.4%	41.2%	5.7%	12.2%	1,253,950	21.8%	22.6%	7.5%	27.8%	11.3%
Indiana	444,803	96.4%	670,827	31.7%	39.1%	3.4%	8.7%	578,748	26.8%	26.0%	8.7%	19.8%	6.7%
Iowa	200,763	97.5%	315,687	26.1%	43.5%	7.9%	11.3%	274,701	24.4%	24.5%	13.5%	22.5%	7.3%
Kansas	197,499	98.4%	301,166	25.1%	44.1%	7.6%	10.4%	264,777	20.4%	25.9%	11.0%	25.1%	8.2%
Kentucky	290,213	97.5%	427,893	32.8%	41.2%	3.3%	7.5%	395,614	27.0%	26.0%	9.6%	17.9%	7.7%
Louisiana	300,317	96.4%	482,665	30.6%	39.2%	2.5%	6.9%	458,626	27.3%	25.7%	5.8%	19.1%	5.7%
Maine	82,081	97.7%	117,248	29.3%	49.1%	4.0%	8.2%	104,225	29.7%	25.7%	12.7%	20.8%	6.4%
Maryland	384,899	97.6%	564,004	28.5%	42.3%	4.9%	12.7%	578,502	23.3%	21.5%	7.4%	25.9%	12.7%
Massachusetts	415,765	97.9%	695,854	27.8%	42.1%	3.2%	15.9%	659,931	20.3%	17.3%	7.2%	31.8%	17.0%
Michigan	661,571	97.3%	1,000,327	28.0%	44.5%	4.8%	9.2%	835,027	23.0%	27.8%	9.9%	22.1%	8.0%
Minnesota	359,295	98.0%	508,343	24.6%	44.6%	6.3%	10.9%	526,508	20.1%	21.4%	12.2%	30.2%	8.7%
Mississippi	204,811	96.1%	322,350	28.6%	42.4%	4.2%	5.4%	255,386	29.3%	25.8%	10.3%	14.5%	5.3%
Missouri	397,250	97.5%	593,075	31.4%	40.7%	4.7%	10.9%	561,404	24.8%	23.6%	9.2%	23.9%	9.4%
Montana	64,848	95.8%	102,961	29.0%	44.1%	3.0%	6.0%	86,191	25.7%	25.0%	11.0%	22.8%	8.6%
Nebraska	122,024	98.5%	190,963	24.4%	49.0%	6.9%	9.5%	175,394	18.6%	25.4%	12.3%	25.0%	10.1%
Nevada	182,501	96.8%	257,114	34.3%	35.1%	4.9%	5.4%	275,510	28.7%	27.6%	8.6%	17.4%	3.5%
New Hampshire	84,658	98.2%	126,757	30.4%	43.5%	4.1%	12.8%	108,673	25.9%	24.5%	8.5%	25.6%	8.6%
New Jersey	595,382	97.8%	794,360	29.4%	39.4%	4.9%	14.1%	789,900	23.7%	19.2%	7.1%	29.1%	11.9%
New Mexico	141,557	97.4%	218,255	28.7%	43.6%	4.8%	5.3%	186,280	25.2%	27.1%	9.6%	15.1%	7.4%
New York	1,208,404	97.5%	1,992,311	25.4%	40.6%	6.1%	14.5%	2,010,905	20.8%	17.5%	8.6%	28.7%	13.2%
North Carolina	645,484	96.9%	998,003	28.9%	41.3%	4.3%	9.4%	874,083	22.0%	26.2%	8.8%	22.3%	8.2%
North Dakota	42,043	97.4%	97,140	22.0%	44.5%	9.0%	12.4%	70,082	18.2%	25.3%	20.1%	23.0%	9.2%
Ohio	767,800	97.6%	1,118,384	30.9%	41.7%	4.1%	9.3%	1,036,741	25.3%	24.7%	9.2%	22.1%	9.2%
Oklahoma	247,021	96.7%	396,186	32.1%	37.9%	5.4%	7.4%	371,158	28.4%	26.1%	8.2%	19.9%	4.7%
Oregon	244,438	97.3%	368,263	30.5%	43.8%	4.5%	6.9%	368,990	23.2%	28.3%	9.5%	22.5%	7.5%
Pennsylvania	793,189	97.0%	1,251,852	32.2%	39.6%	4.7%	11.4%	1,149,375	26.5%	18.4%	9.2%	25.8%	11.6%
Rhode Island	62,151	96.0%	119,895	27.5%	44.8%	4.3%	12.8%	96,226	20.4%	24.3%	6.9%	29.3%	9.7%
South Carolina	306,746	97.2%	502,074	29.7%	41.6%	4.1%	8.0%	414,684	23.3%	26.7%	8.5%	20.2%	7.5%
South Dakota	54,808	97.3%	84,051	31.1%	39.8%	6.9%	8.7%	76,007	24.0%	22.5%	14.8%	24.3%	6.7%
Tennessee	424,842	97.9%	632,614	35.5%	39.2%	3.7%	8.5%	595,744	29.5%	23.6%	7.1%	21.3%	7.9%
Texas	1,909,547	97.4%	2,733,033	31.6%	39.5%	4.0%	7.9%	2,674,332	25.2%	26.3%	6.8%	21.3%	6.8%
Utah	233,633	97.8%	333,429	28.9%	44.8%	7.9%	5.8%	301,066	22.2%	28.2%	10.5%	24.9%	6.5%
Vermont	39,154	98.0%	64,873	29.1%	48.2%	3.1%	10.8%	50,046	27.7%	24.1%	8.5%	25.3%	6.4%
Virginia	518,191	97.8%	833,573	31.4%	40.5%	4.6%	12.1%	802,202	22.6%	24.1%	7.2%	26.0%	12.7%
Washington	442,740	97.8%	665,504	30.1%	37.7%	6.8%	10.4%	700,424	22.7%	25.7%	8.9%	24.7%	8.1%
West Virginia	113,555	98.0%	176,100	38.9%	36.6%	4.5%	5.7%	146,977	32.2%	24.0%	9.1%	15.1%	10.3%
Wisconsin	372,227	97.6%	553,079	31.3%	41.5%	5.1%	9.1%	519,237	24.6%	23.1%	12.1%	25.2%	7.2%
Wyoming	38,045	97.7%	59,513	29.9%	43.7%	7.3%	7.9%	54,550	22.4%	28.0%	9.4%	25.3%	8.0%

Table E-2: Counties—Educational Attainment

| | 13 to 17 | | 18 to 24 | | | | | 25 to 31 | | | | | |
| | | | | Percent | | | | | Percent | | | | |
	Total Population	Percent Enrolled in School	Total Population	High School	Some College	Associates Degree	Bachelors Degree	Total Population	High School	Some College	Associates Degree	Bachelors Degree	Advanced Degree
Alabama													
Baldwin County	13,134	97.8%	16,338	38.6%	20.0%	7.2%	12.3%	14,271	25.4%	27.3%	9.0%	26.4%	2.7%
Calhoun County	6,696	98.8%	11,943	28.0%	47.1%	1.5%	7.9%	10,550	41.0%	23.9%	3.6%	14.3%	4.1%
Etowah County	7,662	100.0%	9,315	33.2%	43.9%	7.5%	0.0%	8,012	35.7%	32.9%	7.5%	7.3%	2.5%
Houston County	7,382	99.4%	8,774	46.1%	29.3%	6.7%	4.0%	9,840	36.1%	26.3%	10.8%	17.2%	1.8%
Jefferson County	42,598	96.3%	60,692	26.6%	43.0%	1.7%	12.2%	66,293	24.3%	20.1%	7.8%	24.0%	10.8%
Lauderdale County	5,814	92.5%	11,302	23.7%	46.8%	2.5%	7.4%	8,102	39.4%	35.4%	7.9%	8.3%	3.1%
Lee County	9,237	97.8%	30,018	20.4%	49.4%	6.0%	15.6%	14,147	23.1%	17.4%	10.2%	21.3%	20.2%
Madison County	22,909	96.5%	35,171	28.6%	43.6%	3.6%	11.8%	31,607	16.3%	24.8%	12.8%	26.1%	9.6%
Marshall County	7,521	98.4%	7,257	40.7%	31.0%	4.5%	7.9%	9,126	22.8%	13.3%	23.0%	18.7%	1.4%
Mobile County	26,092	91.6%	42,048	30.6%	34.7%	2.1%	10.9%	37,948	24.1%	30.1%	9.5%	16.5%	5.2%
Montgomery County	15,773	97.5%	26,815	30.7%	34.0%	0.5%	12.3%	23,145	21.0%	30.0%	8.1%	17.1%	7.5%
Morgan County	8,545	95.7%	10,480	39.9%	24.3%	1.9%	4.9%	8,840	32.0%	20.5%	14.0%	19.1%	1.4%
Shelby County	14,600	99.8%	16,952	25.0%	42.2%	4.2%	15.7%	18,469	25.9%	21.5%	7.3%	28.2%	11.6%
Tuscaloosa County	11,590	97.0%	39,838	25.7%	54.4%	2.8%	5.9%	21,669	25.1%	28.3%	8.0%	21.1%	11.7%
Alaska													
Fairbanks North Star Borough	6,177	99.2%	14,290	30.8%	43.0%	2.4%	0.4%	13,155	25.0%	21.8%	3.4%	40.5%	7.0%
Matanuska-Susitna Borough	8,792	100.0%	9,851	21.6%	50.4%	0.9%	0.3%	8,642	34.2%	22.9%	4.0%	17.1%	0.9%
Arizona													
Cochise County	8,258	93.0%	12,200	36.3%	42.2%	4.6%	3.8%	11,622	15.0%	40.8%	5.6%	18.1%	7.1%
Coconino County	7,738	96.5%	26,701	22.9%	53.6%	7.6%	9.8%	14,018	19.5%	19.7%	12.3%	23.5%	10.3%
Maricopa County	284,537	96.6%	386,757	31.6%	36.4%	5.3%	8.7%	403,195	23.8%	24.8%	9.1%	20.8%	7.8%
Mohave County	12,002	93.3%	14,136	37.7%	29.2%	0.9%	4.9%	14,210	34.5%	30.4%	7.9%	10.7%	2.8%
Navajo County	8,371	97.1%	10,545	32.7%	36.2%	3.3%	1.8%	9,586	30.6%	30.0%	5.5%	11.5%	1.8%
Pima County	62,937	97.8%	121,550	31.0%	41.4%	3.7%	8.2%	88,003	23.3%	29.6%	8.3%	17.8%	7.9%
Pinal County	27,764	92.5%	32,006	34.7%	29.2%	2.9%	2.0%	32,604	31.8%	31.4%	10.3%	8.4%	3.0%
Yavapai County	11,799	94.4%	14,382	26.5%	38.0%	10.1%	5.2%	14,168	27.2%	40.5%	5.4%	7.4%	5.3%
Yuma County	15,620	100.0%	24,334	24.3%	48.9%	7.1%	1.9%	19,442	31.5%	24.3%	11.2%	11.4%	1.3%
Arkansas													
Benton County	19,059	98.1%	19,984	45.7%	29.3%	4.7%	6.4%	22,428	26.4%	20.4%	5.0%	24.1%	10.9%
Craighead County	5,049	98.0%	11,153	33.2%	42.7%	5.2%	6.9%	11,120	27.8%	31.6%	9.2%	16.4%	4.4%
Faulkner County	9,156	99.3%	16,274	33.0%	43.9%	5.7%	7.7%	15,873	26.5%	22.8%	18.8%	16.4%	7.0%
Garland County	5,813	96.2%	8,413	38.1%	41.3%	3.8%	5.6%	6,178	41.8%	37.5%	3.8%	5.0%	3.2%
Pulaski County	25,229	94.3%	35,099	31.3%	44.2%	1.8%	10.4%	44,132	27.6%	24.7%	5.7%	18.8%	9.1%
Saline County	8,012	89.4%	8,095	35.4%	48.3%	4.0%	3.5%	11,423	34.2%	34.5%	3.2%	23.1%	0.7%
Sebastian County	8,906	97.4%	10,237	44.9%	35.1%	0.9%	1.1%	13,346	33.7%	27.4%	7.8%	15.9%	2.0%
Washington County	13,619	96.2%	31,341	25.7%	48.2%	2.9%	13.0%	23,408	19.3%	24.3%	5.8%	23.6%	12.7%
California													
Alameda County	91,937	98.9%	149,330	22.7%	47.7%	2.9%	14.9%	170,706	17.4%	21.4%	5.5%	32.1%	13.4%
Butte County	12,100	97.3%	33,787	30.9%	43.1%	7.0%	7.8%	19,755	19.3%	38.2%	9.3%	17.3%	5.5%
Contra Costa County	72,371	98.8%	94,235	30.1%	40.1%	5.4%	11.2%	93,554	23.0%	23.8%	6.1%	25.8%	6.6%
El Dorado County	11,561	100.0%	13,295	37.5%	39.1%	4.0%	5.4%	12,743	21.6%	37.4%	7.6%	19.1%	2.8%
Fresno County	71,245	98.3%	108,464	27.3%	43.4%	5.7%	4.5%	101,070	23.7%	30.8%	10.0%	14.7%	4.0%
Humboldt County	6,652	98.8%	18,113	21.0%	60.4%	5.4%	6.7%	13,592	29.6%	33.9%	3.6%	24.8%	3.1%
Imperial County	14,236	99.9%	20,303	25.0%	39.2%	3.2%	5.5%	18,063	29.2%	37.1%	7.1%	8.3%	1.1%
Kern County	67,823	97.8%	95,971	35.2%	39.0%	6.3%	3.4%	91,995	30.6%	28.9%	7.2%	8.6%	3.6%
Kings County	10,697	100.0%	17,431	41.8%	30.5%	1.0%	3.2%	17,382	25.3%	29.1%	10.5%	7.7%	1.2%
Los Angeles County	669,035	98.3%	1,067,750	26.9%	43.5%	4.0%	10.0%	1,096,906	21.9%	23.0%	6.7%	26.0%	7.8%
Madera County	12,013	98.0%	15,435	24.9%	36.8%	4.6%	3.3%	15,618	24.8%	25.8%	6.3%	5.6%	1.3%
Marin County	16,661	96.7%	17,512	16.3%	52.4%	1.5%	14.4%	15,181	19.1%	18.6%	8.1%	24.9%	6.5%
Merced County	23,797	98.6%	31,498	27.7%	58.6%	2.3%	1.4%	25,584	32.7%	28.9%	5.5%	12.1%	2.7%
Monterey County	32,539	98.8%	48,230	27.9%	43.1%	4.1%	6.2%	45,322	29.0%	27.0%	5.9%	13.6%	4.0%
Napa County	9,311	100.0%	13,156	28.1%	47.0%	3.4%	1.7%	10,779	22.3%	29.7%	10.6%	20.7%	0.5%
Nevada County	5,901	100.0%	7,382	20.6%	49.0%	3.4%	6.0%	5,855	23.1%	25.5%	26.5%	20.2%	1.2%
Orange County	217,538	97.8%	317,913	23.1%	47.3%	6.1%	11.2%	310,232	17.5%	23.9%	8.3%	29.2%	7.8%
Placer County	28,449	97.4%	29,285	32.6%	44.9%	4.9%	4.7%	29,238	21.6%	29.7%	11.0%	24.6%	6.1%
Riverside County	180,238	98.1%	243,003	37.6%	35.2%	5.1%	4.5%	215,998	29.6%	28.0%	7.8%	14.0%	5.1%
Sacramento County	104,329	97.7%	145,677	32.6%	39.8%	5.9%	8.5%	153,249	22.7%	29.4%	7.3%	21.9%	6.5%
San Bernardino County	165,643	98.5%	240,638	34.0%	40.3%	4.7%	6.5%	212,266	27.2%	29.2%	9.1%	14.0%	5.4%
San Diego County	197,801	98.0%	366,780	32.1%	38.2%	5.7%	10.5%	372,273	20.7%	23.1%	9.2%	26.0%	10.5%
San Francisco County	25,622	96.1%	64,495	19.3%	43.0%	3.4%	28.4%	137,551	6.5%	12.1%	4.6%	49.1%	21.3%
San Joaquin County	58,390	98.8%	74,649	36.3%	34.1%	6.0%	5.5%	62,376	25.3%	28.4%	12.4%	11.8%	1.7%
San Luis Obispo County	12,954	98.3%	44,013	18.8%	65.5%	4.0%	7.6%	23,706	21.6%	38.7%	6.3%	21.6%	4.4%
San Mateo County	42,716	98.6%	57,975	20.8%	49.1%	4.3%	16.4%	68,580	14.6%	20.0%	8.7%	35.7%	13.1%
Santa Barbara County	29,415	99.7%	68,915	16.6%	57.1%	4.1%	10.9%	40,359	19.9%	18.3%	8.7%	17.1%	6.9%
Santa Clara County	112,666	98.7%	164,573	25.2%	40.5%	4.4%	17.5%	197,830	14.0%	18.6%	5.5%	31.0%	20.5%
Santa Cruz County	14,645	98.2%	40,992	20.1%	60.3%	2.5%	9.1%	21,827	16.3%	32.7%	11.5%	22.5%	6.4%
Shasta County	10,988	97.6%	17,040	28.4%	48.4%	7.6%	4.9%	15,126	25.9%	37.3%	8.6%	11.7%	3.7%
Solano County	27,829	97.0%	43,457	38.3%	38.4%	3.0%	6.1%	42,964	19.8%	36.2%	12.3%	16.3%	4.0%
Sonoma County	31,888	99.8%	45,516	28.2%	49.3%	4.0%	5.2%	43,559	23.7%	24.6%	10.6%	22.0%	4.0%
Stanislaus County	42,105	97.0%	55,502	33.0%	46.5%	4.9%	3.7%	50,579	33.4%	29.1%	7.4%	11.5%	2.9%
Sutter County	4,709	99.5%	10,422	31.0%	41.8%	6.9%	6.8%	8,605	35.7%	22.8%	13.2%	10.1%	1.3%
Tulare County	36,363	97.9%	49,699	30.8%	46.3%	6.5%	2.7%	46,122	36.9%	20.4%	6.9%	6.9%	5.3%
Ventura County	58,861	98.4%	85,580	23.4%	46.4%	8.6%	9.0%	74,830	21.5%	28.0%	8.3%	19.2%	6.2%
Yolo County	12,811	94.1%	39,633	23.8%	51.3%	5.8%	12.9%	19,613	11.3%	27.5%	11.0%	26.2%	15.2%

Table E-2: Counties—Educational Attainment—*Continued*

| | 13 to 17 | | 18 to 24 | | | | | 25 to 31 | | | | | |
| | | | | Percent | | | | | Percent | | | | |
	Total Population	Percent Enrolled in School	Total Population	High School	Some College	Associates Degree	Bachelors Degree	Total Population	High School	Some College	Associates Degree	Bachelors Degree	Advanced Degree
Colorado													
Adams County	37,555	96.5%	44,213	28.0%	39.4%	5.6%	4.6%	52,900	21.3%	25.3%	9.8%	20.8%	4.4%
Arapahoe County	44,980	97.7%	52,812	30.6%	33.3%	4.9%	11.0%	61,836	19.7%	29.8%	8.5%	26.8%	6.9%
Boulder County	20,549	98.2%	46,153	20.1%	57.2%	3.1%	13.2%	26,720	14.4%	14.6%	6.6%	42.7%	15.3%
Denver County	29,542	93.5%	62,202	21.3%	39.2%	3.5%	20.1%	106,782	14.0%	18.3%	3.8%	41.1%	10.0%
Douglas County	27,216	99.4%	21,277	27.3%	32.6%	4.6%	15.4%	19,849	20.2%	18.0%	8.3%	41.2%	10.1%
El Paso County	45,330	98.8%	70,362	27.3%	45.0%	5.2%	8.8%	69,402	16.9%	32.8%	16.6%	21.7%	4.8%
Jefferson County	36,223	98.5%	47,146	24.3%	41.2%	7.9%	11.6%	48,567	18.7%	26.2%	9.1%	29.7%	10.6%
Larimer County	19,902	99.4%	46,410	19.6%	56.5%	4.1%	12.1%	30,477	19.3%	23.8%	12.8%	30.9%	10.0%
Mesa County	8,373	99.5%	15,610	27.9%	53.4%	4.6%	4.1%	14,343	40.6%	34.1%	3.8%	12.7%	1.1%
Pueblo County	10,360	98.1%	15,775	21.8%	42.5%	6.7%	9.8%	15,157	26.7%	37.5%	9.7%	9.9%	2.0%
Weld County	17,897	95.2%	29,369	27.9%	44.8%	3.5%	9.5%	27,520	27.2%	25.8%	10.9%	18.0%	4.4%
Connecticut													
Fairfield County	66,065	98.1%	79,561	23.2%	40.5%	2.4%	17.5%	75,971	18.5%	19.5%	6.4%	29.2%	14.2%
Hartford County	60,054	98.6%	80,061	23.2%	41.3%	5.2%	14.8%	81,020	23.2%	18.4%	8.2%	29.6%	12.9%
Litchfield County	12,168	92.5%	13,642	33.6%	39.2%	2.0%	13.5%	13,526	26.2%	25.1%	5.4%	30.3%	11.4%
Middlesex County	10,078	99.0%	14,810	32.2%	40.4%	3.9%	12.7%	13,200	15.1%	19.7%	11.1%	33.3%	16.7%
New Haven County	55,017	97.7%	86,612	32.4%	38.5%	3.5%	12.0%	80,028	26.6%	17.3%	7.1%	25.6%	16.5%
New London County	15,491	99.4%	29,528	36.6%	42.9%	3.0%	10.3%	25,237	33.6%	29.3%	4.3%	16.1%	5.5%
Tolland County	9,638	99.8%	26,722	21.6%	58.5%	6.9%	8.4%	11,593	26.3%	12.7%	9.5%	21.8%	21.4%
Windham County	7,405	100.0%	11,948	20.9%	56.4%	3.3%	4.6%	10,595	30.6%	28.5%	14.4%	13.2%	2.3%
Delaware													
Kent County	10,917	97.8%	17,233	27.2%	45.4%	4.5%	11.9%	15,816	24.2%	20.0%	11.8%	21.0%	9.0%
New Castle County	34,584	97.8%	57,691	32.7%	33.2%	4.2%	15.1%	56,373	23.4%	18.1%	6.0%	27.2%	14.4%
Sussex County	10,249	92.2%	15,601	45.1%	23.3%	2.1%	7.4%	15,536	35.9%	15.9%	15.8%	11.3%	5.4%
Florida													
Alachua County	11,393	98.2%	57,810	14.2%	57.8%	9.8%	14.2%	28,502	14.8%	14.6%	9.0%	35.6%	22.3%
Bay County	9,643	98.1%	14,680	29.5%	35.9%	11.1%	4.7%	17,285	38.6%	22.2%	8.3%	11.4%	2.0%
Brevard County	30,170	94.1%	44,051	31.3%	32.1%	12.0%	9.6%	38,460	24.5%	20.8%	21.4%	19.2%	7.8%
Broward County	112,099	97.5%	157,400	29.5%	33.7%	10.7%	9.4%	168,010	23.3%	25.6%	10.5%	20.3%	9.1%
Charlotte County	7,440	100.0%	10,166	44.3%	17.1%	4.3%	3.3%	8,480	44.2%	18.2%	11.1%	5.4%	3.8%
Citrus County	6,239	92.4%	8,383	43.5%	20.1%	7.7%	0.8%	6,848	44.6%	26.6%	11.1%	3.2%	1.4%
Clay County	15,005	98.4%	15,970	27.0%	36.3%	5.3%	11.1%	16,629	19.1%	40.4%	14.3%	15.6%	0.0%
Collier County	17,383	95.2%	22,554	38.9%	29.6%	8.9%	5.8%	22,259	31.2%	16.6%	15.4%	18.3%	4.0%
Duval County	52,351	96.9%	87,274	33.0%	31.9%	7.2%	8.4%	101,536	25.9%	23.2%	13.5%	24.5%	4.7%
Escambia County	16,302	97.6%	39,340	29.3%	43.3%	8.3%	3.5%	31,263	19.5%	25.8%	16.9%	25.5%	4.7%
Flagler County	6,063	97.1%	8,355	41.4%	44.2%	4.4%	0.7%	5,728	41.0%	27.9%	10.5%	9.8%	0.0%
Hernando County	9,567	90.4%	11,400	40.0%	35.7%	8.6%	1.5%	12,556	41.2%	29.8%	13.6%	6.7%	1.2%
Highlands County	4,471	94.1%	7,013	44.3%	18.3%	11.1%	0.0%	6,249	43.9%	29.8%	4.2%	3.2%	2.6%
Hillsborough County	83,199	96.6%	127,839	26.9%	36.5%	9.0%	11.4%	136,004	23.7%	21.7%	10.0%	23.9%	8.4%
Indian River County	8,321	100.0%	8,737	38.8%	17.6%	16.4%	0.0%	8,245	24.7%	25.1%	13.9%	9.5%	10.3%
Lake County	19,345	93.0%	21,438	32.7%	29.0%	5.9%	6.9%	23,099	32.3%	22.5%	9.6%	16.1%	1.2%
Lee County	36,197	97.9%	49,443	39.1%	30.6%	8.9%	5.2%	49,789	35.5%	19.8%	7.6%	18.6%	3.5%
Leon County	14,519	100.0%	65,187	19.2%	48.2%	12.4%	12.8%	29,293	11.4%	19.0%	13.1%	32.0%	17.8%
Manatee County	19,630	93.8%	26,263	39.9%	20.8%	6.8%	8.5%	23,213	27.1%	20.7%	5.0%	18.1%	12.0%
Marion County	18,327	98.9%	24,424	35.2%	23.8%	9.7%	5.7%	24,645	42.6%	27.1%	4.2%	8.8%	3.4%
Martin County	7,357	99.4%	9,764	27.6%	42.2%	10.5%	2.3%	11,550	42.8%	14.9%	6.1%	11.7%	7.0%
Miami-Dade County	158,899	96.7%	249,341	28.4%	37.3%	10.7%	7.8%	267,914	28.0%	21.8%	11.6%	21.2%	7.5%
Okaloosa County	13,303	96.8%	19,619	39.4%	31.4%	8.6%	8.7%	22,695	28.1%	31.6%	11.9%	18.5%	5.5%
Orange County	79,736	97.9%	147,814	23.5%	43.6%	11.6%	10.0%	145,234	24.8%	20.6%	11.0%	25.8%	7.3%
Osceola County	23,796	99.8%	28,518	33.7%	30.6%	6.3%	7.1%	29,572	28.2%	33.4%	11.3%	10.9%	1.8%
Palm Beach County	75,950	99.0%	111,040	33.2%	35.7%	6.8%	6.3%	114,488	25.2%	22.4%	9.8%	19.3%	6.8%
Pasco County	28,277	98.1%	35,466	35.4%	35.3%	9.2%	4.7%	32,312	31.9%	20.9%	15.7%	17.1%	4.7%
Pinellas County	49,492	96.5%	68,856	32.2%	33.2%	9.7%	7.9%	76,123	27.2%	24.9%	13.6%	19.7%	5.9%
Polk County	38,905	96.7%	55,573	36.0%	30.3%	5.2%	2.8%	55,298	37.6%	20.6%	11.7%	13.0%	3.3%
Santa Rosa County	11,213	100.0%	14,039	44.1%	21.4%	11.6%	5.4%	15,170	27.7%	31.5%	13.3%	16.6%	1.9%
Sarasota County	18,595	99.0%	25,916	35.8%	37.8%	5.7%	4.6%	20,422	32.3%	30.7%	11.7%	15.9%	5.6%
Seminole County	33,283	96.7%	42,621	28.9%	33.5%	13.9%	11.1%	41,617	19.4%	23.2%	11.8%	32.3%	7.1%
St. Johns County	15,143	97.2%	17,994	37.8%	30.9%	4.3%	11.1%	13,974	24.8%	33.3%	5.6%	23.4%	6.0%
St. Lucie County	18,393	99.1%	22,765	36.3%	39.2%	2.6%	2.3%	20,849	30.7%	27.5%	11.2%	8.7%	5.1%
Sumter County	2,238	100.0%	4,246	32.5%	43.1%	5.0%	0.0%	4,944	23.5%	32.5%	8.9%	13.3%	0.0%
Volusia County	24,502	94.8%	43,828	33.4%	40.0%	10.5%	4.6%	41,202	31.7%	23.8%	14.9%	13.3%	4.2%
Georgia													
Bartow County	7,422	97.4%	12,166	23.1%	18.9%	2.8%	8.0%	9,081	30.3%	24.1%	10.9%	5.9%	0.6%
Bibb County	10,274	99.6%	16,655	31.1%	43.5%	1.1%	8.6%	15,045	35.2%	14.0%	9.3%	14.5%	5.4%
Carroll County	8,001	96.9%	14,416	34.0%	51.9%	2.6%	4.5%	9,841	37.8%	28.3%	3.0%	5.0%	4.3%
Chatham County	15,743	99.7%	34,089	29.9%	43.6%	3.2%	7.3%	33,509	17.8%	30.2%	4.5%	24.0%	9.6%
Cherokee County	16,364	95.1%	16,011	26.2%	46.8%	0.0%	9.6%	19,263	26.4%	25.2%	7.8%	27.5%	5.7%
Clarke County	4,249	97.7%	36,028	22.0%	47.8%	3.8%	19.5%	13,785	15.4%	26.9%	2.6%	29.7%	16.9%
Clayton County	20,872	96.5%	27,881	37.2%	32.2%	2.7%	5.0%	28,275	36.4%	20.5%	7.8%	9.5%	3.0%
Cobb County	50,742	98.4%	67,950	24.8%	42.4%	2.3%	14.4%	68,770	16.1%	24.7%	8.2%	30.0%	10.8%
Columbia County	10,922	98.3%	12,527	31.0%	40.8%	5.2%	4.8%	11,046	11.6%	44.2%	16.8%	12.0%	11.9%
Coweta County	8,243	100.0%	10,199	35.4%	39.5%	0.2%	9.8%	11,235	23.9%	18.1%	6.1%	30.1%	5.0%
DeKalb County	38,998	95.7%	70,674	27.2%	42.8%	3.3%	8.9%	81,565	20.9%	19.3%	5.5%	30.6%	14.8%
Dougherty County	7,070	93.9%	11,759	29.9%	37.7%	2.9%	3.1%	9,373	18.8%	43.3%	5.3%	13.1%	5.1%
Douglas County	11,167	99.1%	9,740	30.4%	37.8%	3.8%	2.5%	12,228	18.0%	37.9%	5.6%	21.8%	9.7%
Fayette County	10,505	100.0%	10,008	26.3%	33.2%	1.2%	18.3%	5,306	22.6%	25.9%	13.5%	18.6%	16.4%

Table E-2: Counties—Educational Attainment—*Continued*

| | 13 to 17 | | 18 to 24 | | | | | 25 to 31 | | | | | |
	Total Population	Percent Enrolled in School	Total Population	High School	Some College	Associates Degree	Bachelors Degree	Total Population	High School	Some College	Associates Degree	Bachelors Degree	Advanced Degree
Georgia—Cont.													
Floyd County	6,730	94.9%	9,834	30.4%	31.7%	1.5%	7.2%	7,305	20.6%	27.4%	5.7%	19.1%	5.0%
Forsyth County	17,561	98.7%	12,959	33.1%	25.7%	11.5%	13.4%	12,286	26.0%	28.7%	5.5%	27.8%	8.1%
Fulton County	62,359	97.7%	101,164	23.6%	45.3%	3.4%	14.5%	112,529	16.5%	22.1%	6.7%	31.5%	15.7%
Gwinnett County	68,051	96.4%	78,434	28.8%	37.7%	5.4%	9.4%	76,391	21.1%	22.9%	8.5%	21.5%	6.3%
Hall County	14,136	99.2%	17,558	30.3%	37.1%	3.5%	3.4%	16,371	32.9%	24.1%	6.8%	13.3%	3.1%
Henry County	18,645	99.6%	20,309	35.8%	33.0%	4.4%	6.6%	14,519	23.2%	26.5%	12.3%	24.2%	6.4%
Houston County	10,265	98.4%	15,867	38.8%	38.1%	2.9%	5.1%	15,755	47.0%	22.7%	13.2%	12.9%	1.7%
Lowndes County	7,219	99.8%	20,465	22.2%	56.6%	4.4%	5.5%	12,415	17.5%	20.1%	12.6%	28.1%	12.6%
Muscogee County	13,840	99.2%	25,723	26.3%	46.9%	2.1%	11.2%	21,609	22.5%	36.4%	8.8%	15.7%	5.2%
Newton County	8,144	97.5%	10,070	28.8%	37.8%	2.5%	0.0%	7,917	32.0%	19.2%	13.3%	11.5%	8.2%
Paulding County	12,087	100.0%	12,434	37.2%	46.5%	1.2%	3.1%	11,352	32.9%	33.0%	4.3%	12.2%	5.5%
Richmond County	13,528	95.1%	24,088	40.9%	32.0%	1.8%	8.3%	24,335	25.0%	24.6%	8.0%	19.7%	9.2%
Whitfield County	7,413	88.1%	10,922	28.4%	40.1%	4.9%	9.7%	8,472	12.2%	36.4%	11.4%	5.1%	0.8%
Hawaii													
Hawaii County	13,272	97.2%	15,240	33.2%	43.0%	3.6%	10.7%	16,102	40.5%	23.1%	10.0%	21.4%	2.5%
Honolulu County	58,210	97.4%	104,322	32.8%	44.1%	6.1%	9.2%	111,383	22.4%	29.3%	11.5%	25.5%	5.2%
Maui County	10,112	94.0%	10,226	43.0%	30.3%	7.6%	6.4%	15,110	32.4%	23.7%	13.7%	16.3%	4.1%
Idaho													
Ada County	32,998	97.6%	41,286	33.8%	38.5%	7.2%	8.9%	38,327	24.4%	28.8%	10.8%	24.7%	7.0%
Bonneville County	9,290	89.4%	8,902	55.0%	16.9%	3.4%	11.5%	9,773	23.3%	28.5%	6.4%	17.7%	8.0%
Canyon County	18,650	97.9%	16,673	45.7%	25.9%	2.6%	6.1%	15,953	26.6%	32.1%	16.6%	11.0%	1.5%
Kootenai County	9,826	98.6%	12,876	34.9%	30.5%	4.5%	12.4%	12,654	33.9%	25.1%	8.2%	18.2%	6.8%
Illinois													
Champaign County	10,534	99.9%	47,858	14.5%	61.1%	3.9%	14.9%	23,152	22.6%	19.6%	6.8%	32.1%	13.6%
Cook County	324,964	97.3%	508,028	26.7%	39.5%	5.0%	15.1%	605,045	19.1%	19.4%	6.0%	33.0%	14.2%
DeKalb County	7,258	99.0%	20,217	10.7%	60.5%	11.2%	12.5%	10,559	12.4%	27.0%	7.0%	35.1%	15.6%
DuPage County	66,690	98.7%	78,288	21.9%	45.1%	4.3%	20.1%	86,678	16.7%	25.0%	5.7%	33.1%	13.7%
Kane County	41,236	97.6%	47,275	28.5%	39.2%	5.3%	8.4%	47,528	26.1%	19.4%	9.0%	16.2%	6.5%
Kankakee County	7,763	94.9%	11,416	28.0%	53.6%	5.1%	4.8%	8,304	30.8%	45.6%	7.8%	9.2%	4.6%
Kendall County	10,017	94.4%	8,195	21.0%	31.6%	2.0%	14.0%	12,063	19.2%	40.5%	12.9%	17.4%	5.1%
Lake County	54,910	97.9%	70,753	32.9%	38.6%	3.2%	12.8%	51,168	18.8%	28.6%	6.5%	24.5%	9.1%
LaSalle County	8,288	97.2%	9,127	39.8%	32.0%	6.3%	6.8%	9,376	42.3%	18.6%	7.8%	16.1%	6.5%
Macon County	6,354	100.0%	10,229	37.0%	41.0%	7.5%	3.7%	9,557	24.3%	36.7%	2.8%	13.3%	6.7%
Madison County	15,120	96.3%	26,372	31.6%	44.1%	6.2%	6.4%	25,637	28.5%	21.9%	10.5%	27.8%	9.4%
McHenry County	26,378	98.5%	27,383	27.9%	39.2%	10.2%	9.0%	23,349	28.0%	22.0%	7.3%	30.0%	4.9%
McLean County	9,536	97.1%	31,067	14.8%	57.3%	11.2%	12.0%	17,395	16.7%	16.2%	11.8%	37.8%	13.8%
Peoria County	11,507	94.0%	18,445	24.3%	40.5%	6.9%	16.0%	19,332	19.7%	15.1%	13.8%	32.1%	11.9%
Rock Island County	7,586	98.8%	12,911	32.6%	38.7%	6.9%	10.0%	11,020	21.0%	32.0%	10.0%	17.3%	7.5%
Sangamon County	12,075	99.1%	16,718	20.4%	45.3%	3.8%	15.0%	18,052	17.7%	32.0%	6.9%	27.3%	13.0%
St. Clair County	19,828	97.0%	25,896	29.8%	40.0%	7.8%	6.5%	24,617	24.5%	27.0%	14.5%	18.4%	6.6%
Tazewell County	9,526	99.0%	10,753	47.4%	27.4%	5.5%	5.2%	11,566	31.3%	34.2%	6.2%	21.9%	4.0%
Will County	55,873	98.9%	60,678	31.9%	37.9%	5.4%	10.8%	52,019	23.2%	27.0%	5.2%	24.5%	9.4%
Winnebago County	20,782	98.7%	27,837	39.8%	29.5%	8.9%	6.5%	23,641	27.4%	23.3%	10.8%	21.7%	4.4%
Indiana													
Allen County	25,831	96.7%	34,640	34.3%	36.6%	5.0%	5.7%	33,513	18.5%	31.2%	12.6%	22.1%	3.4%
Clark County	7,109	98.5%	10,298	39.8%	42.9%	2.6%	2.0%	9,716	41.4%	24.5%	8.3%	14.5%	1.0%
Delaware County	5,589	100.0%	24,150	17.2%	62.2%	1.6%	9.8%	9,291	34.8%	28.2%	10.1%	11.8%	4.4%
Elkhart County	14,822	94.8%	17,694	39.9%	30.5%	1.4%	3.2%	17,121	38.6%	20.1%	6.6%	14.1%	3.4%
Hamilton County	21,744	96.3%	20,418	30.1%	29.6%	4.0%	24.6%	23,378	11.4%	23.6%	5.6%	36.8%	19.2%
Hendricks County	11,742	93.6%	14,344	31.0%	46.4%	0.7%	4.6%	13,264	11.1%	27.6%	11.2%	30.6%	5.8%
Johnson County	12,141	100.0%	13,025	37.2%	35.9%	3.7%	9.4%	12,712	26.3%	32.7%	6.3%	13.7%	5.1%
Lake County	35,237	96.8%	44,830	32.5%	32.5%	4.1%	7.9%	38,834	30.6%	32.0%	6.5%	18.8%	3.1%
LaPorte County	7,767	100.0%	9,137	41.6%	26.7%	4.2%	2.4%	10,789	33.3%	30.7%	10.5%	8.3%	2.5%
Madison County	9,450	98.8%	11,067	36.4%	37.7%	2.9%	5.8%	10,955	30.5%	28.8%	7.3%	17.3%	3.0%
Marion County	57,618	94.9%	91,053	28.2%	35.7%	2.7%	12.6%	110,706	20.8%	28.2%	5.9%	24.2%	8.5%
Monroe County	6,199	98.6%	39,652	20.6%	61.3%	1.2%	14.7%	13,342	17.4%	20.5%	0.6%	39.2%	18.3%
Porter County	10,002	95.6%	16,877	33.8%	35.6%	2.6%	11.2%	14,297	21.4%	24.6%	11.9%	23.1%	4.6%
St. Joseph County	19,494	96.9%	30,290	35.1%	44.2%	0.7%	7.8%	22,270	25.0%	30.0%	8.7%	18.2%	9.3%
Tippecanoe County	8,636	97.5%	43,959	25.3%	59.0%	1.2%	10.2%	17,881	22.0%	22.7%	10.3%	22.1%	18.7%
Vanderburgh County	10,109	99.0%	19,927	26.1%	54.4%	2.8%	5.7%	17,180	25.6%	35.4%	7.5%	17.3%	7.3%
Vigo County	6,745	99.4%	16,164	27.6%	54.3%	1.9%	4.9%	9,857	19.9%	25.9%	11.0%	11.9%	13.2%
Iowa													
Black Hawk County	7,244	99.9%	23,342	26.9%	48.4%	5.7%	6.5%	11,883	20.5%	27.8%	15.4%	17.1%	11.7%
Dubuque County	7,929	99.1%	9,876	16.9%	49.9%	16.1%	5.7%	7,182	21.0%	33.8%	14.7%	19.1%	4.3%
Johnson County	6,795	100.0%	31,053	17.0%	57.2%	2.7%	18.4%	18,931	16.1%	22.4%	8.1%	28.6%	19.2%
Linn County	14,796	93.9%	18,517	36.2%	41.1%	8.7%	7.3%	22,116	16.7%	25.9%	21.6%	20.8%	8.8%
Polk County	30,744	96.4%	39,587	32.9%	29.7%	8.6%	20.0%	50,213	24.0%	22.1%	10.7%	28.7%	4.0%
Pottawattamie County	6,660	99.1%	7,814	26.0%	35.3%	5.1%	4.2%	8,400	31.0%	26.3%	13.0%	17.8%	4.9%
Scott County	11,143	95.8%	15,048	36.1%	27.5%	7.1%	11.0%	16,418	14.6%	24.6%	9.1%	30.0%	14.3%
Story County	5,049	97.1%	25,869	6.2%	67.9%	9.3%	14.1%	10,051	17.4%	18.2%	4.5%	35.3%	23.8%
Woodbury County	9,614	98.0%	10,317	35.5%	37.2%	9.1%	2.4%	9,895	22.5%	23.5%	16.3%	19.1%	0.5%
Kansas													
Douglas County	5,015	100.0%	24,686	11.9%	57.3%	3.9%	24.7%	14,590	11.1%	25.2%	7.1%	35.1%	21.4%
Johnson County	40,126	99.8%	43,369	23.1%	41.6%	7.8%	15.6%	51,290	10.6%	19.9%	12.0%	40.3%	11.9%
Sedgwick County	38,903	97.3%	48,246	24.7%	46.5%	7.2%	8.9%	55,438	20.4%	31.6%	8.7%	23.4%	6.0%

Table E-2: Counties—Educational Attainment—*Continued*

	13 to 17		18 to 24					25 to 31					
				Percent					Percent				
	Total Population	Percent Enrolled in School	Total Population	High School	Some College	Associates Degree	Bachelors Degree	Total Population	High School	Some College	Associates Degree	Bachelors Degree	Advanced Degree
Kansas—Cont.													
Shawnee County	11,984	98.6%	17,750	30.1%	40.2%	4.2%	5.7%	16,085	26.1%	25.5%	5.1%	27.7%	7.0%
Wyandotte County	11,278	96.7%	15,375	40.7%	29.8%	6.4%	6.9%	15,447	31.0%	12.2%	10.6%	12.0%	6.6%
Kentucky													
Boone County	9,046	96.9%	9,870	28.2%	32.1%	4.8%	18.3%	11,608	26.8%	31.2%	14.4%	22.3%	3.0%
Campbell County	6,568	99.7%	8,276	35.7%	35.6%	0.0%	20.1%	7,975	23.6%	30.6%	7.5%	19.0%	2.5%
Daviess County	6,414	95.7%	8,905	33.4%	35.3%	16.6%	5.9%	7,918	17.1%	36.9%	14.9%	9.0%	9.4%
Fayette County	15,950	97.0%	43,417	24.2%	50.5%	2.8%	13.0%	32,756	15.0%	20.1%	13.4%	23.8%	13.2%
Hardin County	10,516	98.7%	8,668	44.2%	34.3%	4.0%	4.1%	10,318	38.2%	25.3%	5.0%	21.1%	3.3%
Jefferson County	49,409	99.3%	67,944	27.0%	41.1%	4.5%	10.7%	75,621	21.2%	23.6%	9.1%	24.9%	13.4%
Kenton County	11,875	99.1%	14,183	35.8%	38.3%	1.3%	9.3%	16,317	24.7%	26.9%	8.7%	25.3%	8.0%
Warren County	6,811	100.0%	17,778	24.9%	52.9%	3.7%	6.9%	13,297	32.2%	20.9%	9.6%	13.3%	20.4%
Louisiana													
Ascension Parish	9,816	100.0%	9,729	26.6%	54.3%	3.5%	3.8%	9,945	42.5%	11.1%	11.0%	26.0%	3.5%
Bossier Parish	7,900	100.0%	12,994	27.8%	37.4%	5.9%	9.5%	14,263	18.5%	26.1%	9.8%	21.7%	2.3%
Caddo Parish	16,260	95.7%	25,659	35.9%	28.2%	1.2%	5.8%	26,200	32.1%	26.0%	6.2%	17.6%	4.1%
Calcasieu Parish	14,824	98.1%	20,801	38.7%	38.0%	2.7%	3.6%	16,579	40.5%	25.7%	8.8%	12.3%	3.8%
East Baton Rouge Parish	26,536	98.1%	65,930	24.5%	47.9%	2.7%	8.5%	45,973	23.4%	23.8%	4.9%	31.1%	10.1%
Jefferson Parish	23,648	99.2%	40,088	26.8%	35.9%	2.4%	7.7%	48,728	24.0%	24.4%	8.3%	16.6%	7.2%
Lafayette Parish	13,605	95.0%	26,004	19.1%	53.7%	0.3%	11.9%	26,283	16.1%	33.7%	3.5%	31.5%	5.5%
Lafourche Parish	5,421	100.0%	10,583	44.2%	34.2%	4.2%	4.8%	9,274	39.3%	22.9%	2.4%	13.1%	0.9%
Livingston Parish	9,382	99.0%	12,671	52.6%	20.2%	4.5%	0.5%	12,243	28.0%	30.2%	6.4%	19.4%	0.0%
Orleans Parish	19,732	93.4%	41,346	23.8%	46.3%	1.4%	11.1%	50,635	16.3%	23.7%	4.1%	28.5%	15.6%
Ouachita Parish	11,534	93.8%	17,225	29.0%	42.9%	1.8%	9.2%	14,752	24.7%	37.7%	3.9%	9.2%	7.6%
Rapides Parish	8,741	96.4%	13,288	41.2%	33.8%	2.0%	8.7%	13,160	28.6%	29.0%	8.5%	13.7%	2.2%
St. Tammany Parish	17,036	98.4%	19,189	28.1%	31.4%	0.4%	15.3%	20,568	18.8%	27.9%	2.8%	31.9%	3.1%
Tangipahoa Parish	8,725	93.9%	13,931	35.5%	41.9%	1.2%	4.3%	14,288	27.1%	28.5%	2.2%	11.9%	0.0%
Terrebonne Parish	7,372	94.1%	10,410	38.3%	32.1%	1.9%	4.5%	11,174	34.1%	30.1%	3.6%	15.2%	0.0%
Maine													
Androscoggin County	6,766	100.0%	9,557	20.3%	69.0%	2.6%	0.0%	10,215	31.1%	26.4%	18.7%	15.2%	2.1%
Cumberland County	14,723	99.0%	28,028	24.3%	51.2%	2.3%	15.4%	26,931	22.8%	28.5%	14.0%	26.2%	7.1%
Kennebec County	8,147	94.1%	10,198	34.6%	44.3%	10.2%	7.8%	9,257	26.9%	33.8%	9.9%	20.3%	8.2%
Penobscot County	8,286	100.0%	18,248	32.0%	45.1%	7.1%	3.2%	13,381	28.6%	22.4%	10.9%	19.3%	7.0%
York County	11,016	99.3%	15,638	30.6%	43.3%	0.0%	14.6%	16,288	32.7%	32.6%	15.1%	11.2%	7.1%
Maryland													
Anne Arundel County	35,080	98.5%	50,657	21.0%	53.6%	4.6%	11.6%	54,134	22.8%	26.3%	7.7%	25.1%	11.0%
Baltimore County	51,418	98.6%	79,202	27.7%	46.0%	6.2%	11.2%	83,062	25.7%	22.3%	10.8%	24.5%	9.8%
Carroll County	12,078	98.4%	14,608	34.3%	38.8%	8.2%	12.9%	12,659	30.0%	22.8%	13.6%	14.4%	8.0%
Cecil County	7,042	92.3%	9,432	32.8%	29.8%	16.4%	5.2%	8,957	13.6%	23.3%	16.1%	23.1%	12.4%
Charles County	11,442	96.3%	13,872	36.6%	38.2%	4.9%	10.2%	13,615	26.3%	20.0%	15.2%	27.0%	2.9%
Frederick County	17,642	98.2%	22,769	30.0%	47.5%	5.2%	12.0%	19,937	22.8%	15.3%	7.5%	37.5%	13.0%
Harford County	19,721	93.5%	20,860	39.9%	34.4%	6.8%	11.0%	21,178	19.6%	30.1%	8.1%	23.2%	10.8%
Howard County	22,986	100.0%	23,779	25.5%	32.5%	4.9%	27.2%	27,727	10.6%	17.5%	6.4%	40.4%	20.3%
Montgomery County	66,053	98.1%	76,058	21.1%	39.8%	4.7%	20.2%	95,555	16.3%	19.0%	7.0%	29.5%	20.4%
Prince George's County	57,013	98.3%	97,121	29.4%	44.5%	3.4%	9.6%	94,058	25.3%	22.7%	5.3%	23.8%	9.0%
St. Mary's County	9,687	97.0%	10,336	34.2%	34.9%	5.1%	6.0%	8,534	24.2%	32.5%	11.9%	24.1%	1.7%
Washington County	10,513	98.9%	12,958	38.8%	35.2%	4.8%	9.7%	12,951	32.1%	23.8%	9.4%	18.3%	2.6%
Wicomico County	5,775	95.7%	15,847	39.9%	41.5%	2.8%	5.8%	9,353	31.3%	22.3%	4.6%	18.6%	10.6%
Massachusetts													
Barnstable County	10,912	98.4%	14,628	34.4%	34.1%	1.7%	13.0%	14,599	41.7%	14.9%	7.3%	21.6%	9.5%
Berkshire County	7,314	98.0%	13,013	29.3%	47.7%	1.8%	6.8%	9,113	24.1%	16.0%	11.7%	23.9%	9.3%
Bristol County	34,944	98.5%	52,838	38.1%	34.3%	3.9%	13.8%	45,583	28.3%	23.7%	10.6%	18.4%	7.6%
Essex County	51,071	96.6%	71,656	27.6%	37.9%	3.8%	12.8%	66,372	20.6%	21.1%	9.6%	29.0%	12.2%
Hampden County	36,061	96.9%	54,906	27.7%	43.4%	3.7%	8.9%	39,256	30.1%	21.6%	9.3%	16.5%	7.3%
Hampshire County	8,751	99.3%	26,597	16.9%	69.1%	2.3%	6.8%	12,380	30.4%	22.7%	8.9%	25.3%	9.3%
Middlesex County	93,680	97.7%	147,617	28.6%	37.5%	1.6%	22.4%	176,596	16.5%	11.7%	7.1%	36.6%	23.7%
Norfolk County	50,495	98.2%	57,195	17.9%	43.1%	4.1%	22.4%	59,789	17.0%	15.7%	6.3%	37.6%	21.0%
Plymouth County	33,740	96.5%	41,066	31.8%	37.2%	6.8%	11.7%	36,135	23.4%	26.5%	6.2%	26.0%	10.8%
Suffolk County	35,835	99.3%	114,663	22.7%	50.2%	2.3%	16.8%	131,371	15.1%	14.8%	4.8%	39.1%	22.0%
Worcester County	57,599	98.2%	83,318	38.1%	33.0%	3.4%	15.6%	72,063	24.9%	18.9%	6.9%	32.1%	10.5%
Michigan													
Allegan County	8,408	98.8%	9,499	34.1%	39.9%	2.9%	3.2%	8,100	34.1%	25.4%	17.3%	12.4%	0.0%
Bay County	7,193	96.7%	9,763	48.3%	26.5%	10.3%	3.9%	9,708	33.0%	18.3%	9.5%	23.0%	13.8%
Berrien County	8,469	93.4%	13,614	31.9%	41.6%	8.7%	6.8%	12,250	35.0%	15.5%	16.2%	17.6%	7.9%
Calhoun County	9,780	99.4%	11,245	35.4%	38.3%	2.9%	3.4%	10,299	36.3%	25.6%	10.2%	13.6%	2.4%
Eaton County	7,164	99.0%	8,168	20.8%	52.2%	4.3%	12.5%	10,189	25.2%	23.0%	12.4%	25.7%	5.9%
Genesee County	30,043	96.8%	38,494	28.4%	40.5%	3.4%	6.4%	35,288	24.8%	37.9%	9.3%	13.1%	3.0%
Ingham County	15,618	92.8%	57,613	18.4%	62.3%	1.7%	12.5%	28,648	8.9%	32.2%	9.6%	29.8%	14.9%
Jackson County	10,254	96.6%	14,147	27.8%	44.2%	0.6%	7.4%	14,943	33.8%	33.9%	8.3%	10.2%	4.7%
Kalamazoo County	16,510	97.6%	41,267	19.1%	60.1%	4.2%	8.7%	23,678	15.1%	33.4%	10.0%	29.5%	7.8%
Kent County	43,955	98.4%	60,117	24.8%	39.1%	6.8%	15.7%	67,996	17.4%	23.6%	10.5%	29.1%	9.1%
Lenawee County	6,357	96.5%	9,357	40.4%	42.3%	4.2%	1.1%	8,643	23.9%	39.5%	9.4%	14.9%	4.3%
Livingston County	15,463	99.6%	15,203	30.0%	36.5%	4.3%	13.3%	12,368	22.8%	32.5%	12.0%	26.1%	3.7%
Macomb County	53,989	98.7%	74,161	30.4%	40.9%	9.1%	7.6%	74,026	23.6%	32.4%	10.8%	18.7%	5.8%
Monroe County	10,149	97.1%	13,255	40.6%	37.9%	4.8%	7.5%	11,608	26.4%	26.4%	17.1%	23.9%	2.3%
Muskegon County	13,279	99.2%	14,142	43.3%	24.2%	4.7%	5.7%	13,335	36.4%	25.2%	5.3%	12.5%	1.3%

Table E-2: Counties—Educational Attainment—*Continued*

| | 13 to 17 | | 18 to 24 | | | | | 25 to 31 | | | | | |
| | | | | Percent | | | | | Percent | | | | |
	Total Population	Percent Enrolled in School	Total Population	High School	Some College	Associates Degree	Bachelors Degree	Total Population	High School	Some College	Associates Degree	Bachelors Degree	Advanced Degree
Michigan—Cont.													
Oakland County	84,263	97.3%	101,005	23.3%	42.7%	3.9%	15.5%	104,716	14.5%	24.4%	7.5%	34.1%	14.3%
Ottawa County	19,883	98.4%	36,260	25.2%	53.2%	5.7%	8.6%	21,987	19.8%	26.7%	7.6%	32.8%	7.9%
Saginaw County	13,195	100.0%	21,690	30.7%	47.8%	5.7%	5.6%	15,016	19.0%	25.9%	15.5%	22.3%	6.1%
St. Clair County	11,815	98.7%	14,562	38.7%	32.0%	5.3%	7.4%	10,990	29.6%	23.9%	10.1%	21.6%	3.8%
Washtenaw County	19,383	97.0%	64,295	15.6%	53.5%	2.7%	23.2%	36,258	10.6%	23.5%	6.5%	32.9%	22.4%
Wayne County	122,329	96.5%	176,187	29.3%	41.9%	4.2%	6.5%	153,266	24.4%	28.8%	8.7%	16.7%	7.0%
Minnesota													
Anoka County	25,704	97.9%	27,416	35.0%	39.0%	3.7%	8.6%	31,549	20.9%	27.8%	13.1%	24.3%	2.6%
Carver County	8,553	100.0%	7,496	13.6%	56.8%	5.0%	14.8%	7,299	29.5%	13.6%	5.7%	46.8%	4.4%
Dakota County	31,886	98.4%	31,660	29.6%	43.2%	4.3%	9.9%	36,886	14.7%	23.4%	12.8%	33.3%	8.1%
Hennepin County	67,480	99.0%	109,313	18.6%	45.0%	6.3%	17.0%	154,945	14.3%	17.4%	7.8%	39.3%	13.7%
Olmsted County	8,626	98.4%	12,514	14.4%	43.5%	12.7%	19.5%	14,440	19.5%	21.2%	11.1%	23.2%	22.1%
Ramsey County	32,242	98.7%	59,746	24.3%	43.6%	3.3%	11.4%	58,603	15.1%	16.3%	8.6%	39.7%	10.6%
Scott County	9,913	100.0%	9,533	43.1%	25.0%	4.2%	8.3%	10,804	23.5%	21.0%	9.3%	31.6%	13.1%
St. Louis County	11,337	98.6%	24,221	14.8%	54.4%	5.1%	14.9%	18,255	20.2%	27.4%	17.5%	23.5%	3.9%
Stearns County	9,625	98.4%	24,867	12.7%	68.9%	7.6%	3.3%	13,381	28.0%	19.9%	22.4%	27.0%	1.9%
Washington County	19,434	99.9%	19,201	31.7%	41.5%	3.2%	6.1%	21,849	27.6%	17.8%	16.4%	30.4%	4.4%
Wright County	10,933	100.0%	9,249	22.1%	36.4%	14.4%	11.8%	12,469	25.7%	29.0%	18.1%	12.3%	2.3%
Mississippi													
DeSoto County	14,018	92.8%	14,031	24.5%	47.2%	2.0%	9.6%	13,474	23.2%	32.5%	8.7%	23.1%	2.0%
Harrison County	11,692	95.0%	20,561	33.2%	43.8%	1.7%	4.3%	20,462	31.5%	29.6%	9.1%	12.8%	4.3%
Hinds County	17,049	96.8%	29,826	27.7%	43.5%	2.3%	9.3%	27,637	26.1%	25.3%	5.7%	16.9%	13.5%
Jackson County	9,032	98.1%	13,816	27.8%	44.2%	5.8%	2.1%	13,664	28.4%	28.0%	14.8%	14.5%	4.0%
Madison County	9,197	97.2%	9,042	32.3%	31.5%	4.1%	12.1%	7,963	15.0%	26.5%	15.1%	13.6%	11.6%
Rankin County	9,764	91.5%	11,321	46.4%	28.0%	4.9%	6.1%	14,220	31.7%	28.2%	11.3%	18.4%	4.0%
Missouri													
Boone County	8,915	99.1%	36,413	13.9%	62.0%	3.1%	15.6%	20,117	21.6%	21.5%	7.9%	29.7%	15.3%
Cass County	9,097	98.2%	8,261	22.4%	35.1%	3.9%	18.2%	7,355	17.4%	34.7%	10.7%	21.1%	4.1%
Clay County	14,860	99.4%	19,027	37.9%	29.2%	1.5%	13.9%	23,445	22.7%	26.9%	12.0%	27.1%	7.5%
Franklin County	6,220	100.0%	8,224	28.4%	42.5%	15.2%	5.1%	8,650	45.7%	8.5%	6.4%	24.9%	0.0%
Greene County	17,287	98.5%	40,080	24.2%	50.9%	3.5%	12.7%	30,906	18.4%	22.8%	7.9%	25.2%	12.1%
Jackson County	44,774	97.3%	59,386	36.1%	33.0%	4.2%	13.3%	72,220	21.3%	27.5%	7.4%	24.2%	9.6%
Jasper County	8,694	98.0%	11,453	27.6%	47.2%	1.7%	19.0%	11,934	30.2%	35.1%	6.6%	17.8%	4.0%
Jefferson County	15,502	98.5%	17,351	39.1%	34.7%	10.5%	4.6%	19,571	27.5%	22.6%	14.0%	19.7%	7.1%
Platte County	5,017	100.0%	8,248	33.7%	45.6%	0.8%	11.9%	10,502	21.4%	30.4%	8.5%	19.9%	17.9%
St. Charles County	23,492	97.9%	30,614	28.7%	44.6%	7.5%	14.9%	34,816	15.6%	22.7%	14.2%	36.6%	8.9%
St. Louis County	67,609	97.5%	88,692	28.1%	40.6%	5.7%	13.5%	88,698	16.2%	22.3%	9.5%	32.3%	14.0%
Montana													
Flathead County	6,875	94.5%	7,067	52.6%	21.6%	2.9%	4.4%	6,979	28.1%	18.3%	21.2%	21.3%	3.1%
Gallatin County	6,700	93.7%	14,670	18.2%	66.7%	1.1%	8.7%	9,613	17.7%	37.3%	4.6%	31.6%	8.1%
Missoula County	7,120	97.8%	16,419	26.1%	38.2%	2.7%	7.8%	13,113	28.1%	19.9%	5.6%	30.6%	9.8%
Yellowstone County	9,552	97.0%	15,195	33.2%	39.1%	2.3%	5.9%	13,632	26.7%	31.2%	8.5%	19.1%	8.4%
Nebraska													
Douglas County	35,085	98.8%	51,301	26.0%	50.0%	2.5%	12.7%	60,770	14.2%	24.0%	9.0%	31.6%	12.0%
Lancaster County	17,456	98.4%	46,475	13.4%	62.1%	6.1%	11.6%	31,597	18.8%	25.9%	12.8%	25.7%	11.4%
Sarpy County	13,038	99.2%	14,951	25.0%	44.2%	10.3%	10.8%	17,024	25.3%	28.6%	16.1%	24.5%	4.8%
Nevada													
Clark County	134,264	96.3%	185,550	36.1%	34.8%	4.3%	5.0%	207,828	29.1%	28.2%	9.2%	16.6%	2.9%
Washoe County	27,255	99.0%	43,605	27.0%	41.0%	7.5%	7.2%	42,425	24.4%	27.6%	5.9%	24.7%	4.6%
New Hampshire													
Hillsborough County	26,570	97.5%	34,112	33.2%	34.9%	4.3%	16.6%	37,677	28.5%	24.1%	7.3%	25.1%	8.0%
Merrimack County	9,362	99.4%	14,498	29.6%	37.1%	8.9%	11.0%	10,671	26.7%	16.4%	10.0%	27.6%	7.9%
Rockingham County	21,028	99.9%	23,488	29.6%	40.7%	5.0%	15.2%	19,669	20.4%	23.1%	9.6%	30.7%	11.6%
Strafford County	8,257	98.8%	18,156	25.9%	55.6%	3.0%	7.8%	10,506	21.3%	29.6%	11.1%	20.1%	10.4%
New Jersey													
Atlantic County	17,790	97.4%	26,718	35.8%	36.4%	4.3%	9.3%	22,550	29.7%	19.7%	3.2%	24.8%	6.0%
Bergen County	61,727	97.2%	73,274	24.0%	40.9%	5.4%	19.9%	72,616	20.8%	16.2%	6.2%	38.0%	13.2%
Burlington County	31,051	98.2%	40,355	35.6%	36.6%	5.8%	12.6%	37,052	24.6%	23.5%	11.2%	30.2%	7.9%
Camden County	35,887	97.6%	45,958	31.1%	39.6%	4.2%	9.6%	48,608	25.1%	24.1%	8.9%	23.7%	8.9%
Cape May County	4,486	100.0%	7,503	31.7%	29.4%	2.7%	20.4%	7,291	32.0%	13.6%	4.9%	33.4%	2.9%
Cumberland County	10,242	96.9%	13,442	56.3%	20.1%	5.3%	5.4%	17,728	37.5%	27.5%	3.4%	12.3%	2.9%
Essex County	53,893	98.3%	73,948	30.3%	41.8%	3.4%	11.3%	77,006	28.1%	20.8%	7.9%	23.3%	7.3%
Gloucester County	20,226	98.5%	26,112	32.3%	41.5%	4.8%	11.9%	24,121	29.9%	23.7%	6.2%	25.7%	7.0%
Hudson County	34,014	97.6%	60,876	23.2%	39.4%	2.8%	20.8%	101,319	18.6%	14.4%	5.4%	33.1%	19.8%
Hunterdon County	9,918	95.3%	12,070	28.3%	36.1%	3.9%	9.8%	6,223	20.9%	30.3%	5.2%	34.4%	7.5%
Mercer County	24,958	98.5%	40,520	27.1%	46.4%	1.3%	13.0%	31,797	24.9%	13.4%	5.1%	24.3%	18.6%
Middlesex County	52,221	96.6%	83,384	24.6%	47.3%	4.1%	14.3%	75,498	17.4%	20.5%	7.7%	29.4%	17.0%
Monmouth County	45,724	99.3%	53,159	30.1%	37.6%	5.3%	16.2%	47,859	22.3%	15.9%	7.5%	34.2%	12.1%
Morris County	36,391	97.9%	40,984	29.1%	38.0%	5.7%	18.1%	36,576	14.7%	10.4%	7.2%	44.2%	17.5%
Ocean County	36,944	99.0%	43,910	26.8%	41.1%	9.2%	10.7%	44,190	27.7%	26.9%	8.0%	22.2%	6.7%
Passaic County	35,597	95.7%	52,748	31.4%	38.1%	6.1%	10.2%	45,823	35.2%	16.5%	5.0%	23.0%	6.4%
Somerset County	24,310	98.4%	23,900	26.8%	32.1%	3.8%	20.0%	23,578	14.8%	19.5%	7.1%	37.9%	17.4%
Sussex County	10,599	99.4%	12,094	35.8%	31.4%	8.9%	12.7%	9,958	17.8%	20.0%	12.9%	38.4%	6.8%
Union County	37,116	97.7%	48,047	30.8%	35.8%	5.2%	15.0%	48,437	23.4%	22.9%	8.0%	23.8%	10.7%
Warren County	8,596	98.0%	9,333	36.2%	32.0%	13.7%	9.1%	6,347	22.6%	26.4%	5.1%	33.0%	9.9%

Table E-2: Counties—Educational Attainment—*Continued*

| | 13 to 17 | | 18 to 24 | | | | | 25 to 31 | | | | | |
| | | | | Percent | | | | | Percent | | | | |
	Total Population	Percent Enrolled in School	Total Population	High School	Some College	Associates Degree	Bachelors Degree	Total Population	High School	Some College	Associates Degree	Bachelors Degree	Advanced Degree
New Mexico													
Bernalillo County	44,531	97.2%	72,174	27.8%	41.1%	5.6%	6.7%	70,322	25.2%	24.5%	6.8%	18.1%	11.7%
Doña Ana County	16,277	99.3%	32,427	27.1%	62.4%	2.9%	4.4%	18,236	20.1%	32.2%	12.2%	14.1%	6.2%
San Juan County	9,133	98.9%	12,029	25.5%	40.4%	10.5%	2.5%	10,960	29.3%	41.9%	7.3%	5.8%	0.9%
Sandoval County	9,675	97.4%	10,885	25.0%	34.5%	7.1%	2.3%	11,444	22.7%	36.8%	5.4%	13.3%	5.7%
Santa Fe County	8,016	97.3%	11,267	28.2%	45.9%	2.5%	5.2%	11,673	33.9%	25.4%	8.8%	14.1%	9.3%
New York													
Albany County	17,152	98.7%	43,769	25.9%	43.7%	10.6%	14.4%	28,976	15.9%	16.8%	12.1%	29.0%	23.0%
Bronx County	94,578	97.9%	165,974	24.8%	40.5%	4.8%	6.8%	151,158	25.3%	23.1%	8.2%	15.8%	5.7%
Broome County	11,152	98.0%	27,164	29.0%	40.3%	10.7%	11.2%	16,385	30.3%	24.4%	9.3%	19.1%	5.4%
Chautauqua County	8,192	90.6%	15,702	23.6%	48.6%	5.2%	7.8%	10,603	30.7%	18.6%	12.9%	11.6%	9.7%
Dutchess County	21,898	98.4%	35,052	28.8%	44.8%	6.6%	10.8%	21,652	30.9%	21.8%	13.9%	16.0%	10.5%
Erie County	56,943	98.8%	95,801	25.7%	42.8%	5.2%	17.0%	91,167	17.8%	18.6%	13.4%	24.6%	16.4%
Jefferson County	7,232	99.3%	14,889	43.3%	36.6%	4.8%	2.9%	13,583	35.3%	33.2%	7.5%	11.6%	4.7%
Kings County	153,421	97.0%	254,944	27.9%	34.5%	5.3%	16.5%	339,197	21.9%	15.6%	6.5%	31.8%	11.9%
Monroe County	45,735	97.7%	81,663	23.4%	45.4%	7.8%	11.2%	72,332	20.5%	21.5%	8.5%	27.3%	13.4%
Nassau County	93,396	98.5%	118,749	27.4%	40.9%	5.6%	17.2%	109,032	17.3%	16.5%	8.5%	29.9%	17.2%
New York County	58,237	97.3%	158,748	14.7%	40.1%	2.1%	31.4%	267,158	8.5%	6.1%	3.4%	53.8%	21.0%
Niagara County	13,527	95.0%	20,964	32.4%	33.8%	10.2%	10.2%	16,713	26.0%	26.5%	10.0%	24.2%	12.2%
Oneida County	16,545	95.9%	22,861	24.6%	42.7%	6.4%	8.0%	20,901	29.4%	24.7%	15.0%	9.7%	13.9%
Onondaga County	31,745	99.2%	52,600	23.6%	46.3%	4.0%	14.3%	44,462	20.7%	19.8%	10.8%	28.1%	12.7%
Ontario County	7,525	93.2%	9,713	24.3%	46.6%	7.9%	6.6%	8,177	21.4%	20.1%	13.3%	18.4%	17.5%
Orange County	29,651	98.5%	40,299	33.9%	34.3%	7.6%	9.8%	28,316	25.6%	27.2%	10.0%	21.0%	6.4%
Oswego County	8,684	99.7%	14,062	23.1%	48.1%	11.4%	7.4%	10,128	36.4%	22.7%	12.5%	13.3%	5.8%
Putnam County	6,266	100.0%	8,442	20.7%	42.9%	0.0%	22.7%	6,983	33.4%	27.1%	6.7%	16.7%	12.1%
Queens County	129,542	97.4%	212,998	23.5%	39.6%	6.1%	15.5%	264,786	22.3%	17.6%	9.7%	27.2%	12.2%
Rensselaer County	8,677	98.4%	17,570	27.6%	44.3%	7.8%	12.6%	15,821	21.7%	20.9%	17.5%	25.9%	11.5%
Richmond County	29,713	95.4%	44,851	22.5%	44.3%	5.7%	15.6%	41,684	20.7%	22.3%	8.7%	24.1%	13.8%
Rockland County	24,743	98.0%	30,572	32.2%	26.6%	6.5%	19.2%	26,007	23.8%	17.6%	5.9%	22.7%	9.3%
Saratoga County	14,558	98.9%	19,250	23.6%	41.0%	5.6%	13.1%	18,865	22.1%	15.7%	15.2%	22.3%	20.2%
Schenectady County	9,275	95.4%	14,529	29.7%	37.4%	11.9%	7.1%	15,167	32.9%	20.7%	8.2%	19.7%	10.7%
St. Lawrence County	6,608	84.5%	16,127	20.4%	52.6%	3.7%	5.3%	8,571	30.3%	26.8%	6.5%	17.4%	4.6%
Steuben County	7,076	98.4%	7,766	25.3%	36.6%	9.8%	12.1%	6,679	29.0%	19.7%	21.4%	13.4%	12.6%
Suffolk County	109,596	97.7%	137,312	25.1%	40.5%	7.9%	16.1%	121,458	22.4%	20.2%	10.8%	23.5%	12.5%
Tompkins County	4,388	100.0%	27,064	12.5%	71.8%	0.7%	14.1%	10,063	11.5%	11.3%	11.6%	41.6%	19.7%
Ulster County	11,176	97.7%	18,478	27.3%	43.5%	9.0%	8.8%	12,240	23.7%	25.5%	11.3%	19.2%	8.5%
Wayne County	6,223	96.1%	6,813	30.7%	31.2%	16.9%	7.9%	7,636	22.3%	21.0%	20.4%	16.4%	3.4%
Westchester County	65,177	97.9%	84,010	26.1%	41.1%	5.9%	15.9%	75,282	14.1%	19.0%	5.8%	30.9%	17.6%
North Carolina													
Alamance County	10,421	99.3%	14,914	22.6%	32.4%	3.0%	17.1%	13,510	30.6%	18.0%	8.6%	19.9%	8.6%
Brunswick County	5,706	98.2%	6,204	22.5%	38.6%	4.9%	12.3%	6,431	14.6%	45.4%	10.8%	9.1%	0.0%
Buncombe County	12,414	99.3%	19,015	25.9%	38.2%	8.6%	11.5%	24,786	28.9%	19.2%	4.7%	26.1%	13.0%
Burke County	6,705	97.2%	6,960	41.1%	35.7%	9.5%	0.0%	7,422	21.7%	25.5%	6.6%	19.6%	5.6%
Cabarrus County	14,356	95.6%	16,063	39.7%	30.7%	7.0%	4.8%	15,403	18.4%	33.2%	8.9%	20.3%	9.0%
Catawba County	9,820	97.2%	14,162	33.8%	37.3%	4.6%	7.0%	10,681	23.3%	19.6%	14.6%	15.6%	3.8%
Cleveland County	5,418	99.8%	10,491	28.7%	27.6%	7.3%	8.6%	7,240	19.2%	24.1%	11.7%	12.9%	0.5%
Craven County	5,204	97.3%	13,109	44.2%	44.2%	2.7%	2.4%	11,776	21.0%	40.0%	12.6%	5.4%	7.0%
Cumberland County	21,359	98.2%	42,645	30.6%	47.4%	3.9%	7.2%	40,200	19.5%	41.8%	8.5%	16.9%	4.7%
Davidson County	11,421	100.0%	13,893	39.0%	31.6%	4.0%	3.0%	11,987	23.5%	34.4%	9.1%	12.6%	8.0%
Durham County	15,132	98.5%	31,255	19.5%	47.9%	0.9%	18.5%	38,220	11.1%	16.1%	5.6%	37.0%	19.8%
Forsyth County	24,965	96.7%	37,917	34.7%	39.2%	2.5%	11.1%	29,296	22.3%	25.0%	6.6%	24.3%	11.1%
Gaston County	14,672	96.3%	18,530	32.6%	41.2%	5.7%	2.3%	16,649	24.8%	33.5%	6.7%	23.3%	1.8%
Guilford County	31,332	96.1%	57,650	27.8%	49.4%	3.3%	8.3%	49,074	21.8%	28.7%	5.7%	24.1%	9.3%
Harnett County	8,830	98.8%	11,742	26.3%	45.6%	5.7%	4.0%	14,304	22.5%	25.1%	10.3%	23.2%	4.7%
Henderson County	8,472	99.0%	7,177	24.6%	28.0%	6.8%	12.1%	6,726	37.0%	15.8%	2.9%	23.1%	13.0%
Iredell County	12,029	93.7%	14,727	25.7%	31.8%	13.4%	6.2%	12,177	31.8%	22.9%	11.5%	14.3%	4.5%
Johnston County	14,056	96.1%	15,471	41.5%	19.0%	0.0%	4.0%	12,811	29.8%	19.2%	18.6%	14.4%	5.2%
Mecklenburg County	61,481	98.6%	95,115	26.6%	39.9%	2.2%	17.2%	116,413	14.2%	21.7%	7.1%	33.5%	10.8%
Moore County	6,255	96.8%	5,301	34.2%	37.3%	13.2%	6.8%	7,390	28.1%	19.4%	8.3%	16.5%	11.8%
Nash County	6,770	96.2%	8,804	28.5%	34.2%	7.8%	7.7%	6,251	21.7%	42.7%	6.1%	6.9%	6.2%
New Hanover County	10,798	94.5%	28,308	21.2%	55.0%	1.5%	11.5%	19,974	20.9%	22.9%	15.9%	25.9%	6.3%
Onslow County	11,543	96.4%	41,443	40.9%	36.2%	5.1%	3.3%	27,113	28.3%	42.6%	10.0%	7.7%	1.5%
Orange County	8,604	99.8%	26,907	22.0%	51.1%	3.8%	14.0%	12,800	4.7%	29.5%	3.3%	30.9%	25.8%
Pitt County	12,815	97.1%	33,517	19.9%	51.6%	5.5%	14.9%	15,455	19.4%	29.0%	8.5%	22.6%	14.9%
Randolph County	8,957	90.7%	11,229	30.2%	37.6%	3.9%	4.5%	11,575	33.3%	18.1%	9.9%	17.4%	3.4%
Robeson County	11,057	90.7%	15,994	32.2%	32.0%	7.7%	1.7%	10,319	34.6%	26.3%	9.4%	5.8%	1.7%
Rockingham County	6,587	95.0%	5,190	36.1%	35.7%	6.3%	6.6%	8,205	40.1%	29.3%	4.5%	5.8%	3.0%
Rowan County	8,759	96.0%	13,058	25.4%	42.4%	3.6%	8.6%	10,364	34.7%	20.6%	12.0%	14.9%	2.7%
Union County	18,915	97.3%	17,838	27.1%	34.2%	6.3%	12.3%	13,295	36.0%	28.4%	11.5%	17.3%	3.1%
Wake County	70,257	97.9%	93,995	20.8%	46.7%	2.4%	17.8%	94,100	14.7%	18.7%	5.8%	38.5%	14.3%
Wayne County	7,730	98.0%	11,846	32.0%	50.1%	4.0%	3.8%	11,414	9.9%	37.6%	20.2%	18.0%	3.3%
North Dakota													
Cass County	8,511	100.0%	27,874	15.1%	48.9%	8.5%	21.7%	19,202	16.9%	26.1%	16.4%	27.4%	11.7%
Ohio													
Allen County	6,547	97.8%	10,770	33.6%	21.6%	5.4%	11.1%	8,973	22.3%	37.1%	15.3%	11.7%	3.6%

Table E-2: Counties—Educational Attainment—*Continued*

| | 13 to 17 | | 18 to 24 | | | | | 25 to 31 | | | | | |
| | | | | Percent | | | | | Percent | | | | |
	Total Population	Percent Enrolled in School	Total Population	High School	Some College	Associates Degree	Bachelors Degree	Total Population	High School	Some College	Associates Degree	Bachelors Degree	Advanced Degree
Ohio—Cont.													
Ashtabula County	6,190	96.8%	8,246	37.7%	31.6%	3.1%	0.4%	8,300	26.4%	41.2%	8.2%	10.4%	1.7%
Butler County	23,887	96.6%	46,473	37.4%	45.0%	3.4%	8.7%	30,689	30.7%	22.4%	5.3%	25.4%	7.6%
Clark County	9,593	97.5%	12,435	30.5%	48.8%	2.2%	2.4%	10,946	30.0%	28.2%	8.3%	20.4%	3.4%
Clermont County	15,776	99.8%	15,562	44.9%	26.6%	3.6%	12.6%	17,828	29.1%	26.3%	11.8%	18.5%	7.7%
Columbiana County	6,746	97.1%	8,311	34.4%	38.8%	6.7%	3.1%	8,795	32.4%	24.2%	8.0%	13.5%	5.2%
Cuyahoga County	80,244	97.3%	115,543	27.6%	38.3%	3.2%	12.5%	115,142	19.0%	25.2%	7.2%	25.6%	12.2%
Delaware County	15,291	100.0%	13,023	31.9%	41.4%	6.1%	17.2%	12,106	17.6%	19.0%	6.2%	37.3%	16.6%
Fairfield County	11,627	99.0%	12,513	46.4%	33.9%	1.8%	8.1%	13,666	30.9%	25.7%	12.4%	18.1%	5.0%
Franklin County	74,512	98.5%	128,229	24.6%	43.7%	3.2%	14.7%	154,793	20.6%	21.4%	6.6%	29.0%	14.3%
Geauga County	7,164	83.0%	8,535	27.9%	38.5%	0.7%	8.6%	5,095	25.0%	24.4%	3.6%	28.1%	14.8%
Greene County	10,650	98.5%	21,436	19.5%	64.6%	1.0%	8.2%	15,965	22.1%	18.9%	9.2%	35.1%	8.7%
Hamilton County	51,107	99.3%	79,971	32.2%	40.6%	2.8%	13.4%	81,761	18.5%	18.5%	8.6%	30.0%	11.2%
Lake County	14,613	94.3%	19,679	26.2%	45.6%	7.0%	7.2%	18,229	22.3%	23.4%	8.1%	28.6%	9.7%
Licking County	12,504	98.7%	14,831	30.4%	43.8%	4.7%	8.5%	13,750	25.9%	23.7%	17.8%	18.3%	7.8%
Lorain County	21,562	97.4%	27,287	24.2%	49.2%	3.8%	5.0%	23,098	26.2%	28.7%	10.2%	16.0%	6.6%
Lucas County	29,236	99.2%	46,770	29.0%	43.5%	3.4%	8.3%	41,028	23.3%	29.0%	11.9%	16.0%	10.5%
Mahoning County	14,721	98.8%	20,067	29.0%	44.6%	4.4%	8.0%	19,609	21.1%	25.4%	7.2%	28.3%	6.8%
Medina County	13,348	96.9%	13,092	33.1%	40.3%	5.8%	9.1%	13,016	21.5%	17.6%	16.1%	29.5%	8.6%
Miami County	7,318	99.6%	9,000	35.3%	36.2%	5.4%	7.7%	9,293	27.0%	35.3%	13.8%	9.1%	2.2%
Montgomery County	33,093	99.7%	52,950	24.7%	49.4%	3.2%	7.4%	48,832	17.6%	35.0%	11.0%	20.4%	8.7%
Portage County	9,086	97.1%	30,634	28.5%	57.6%	0.8%	9.6%	12,682	22.7%	28.8%	10.6%	23.7%	8.6%
Richland County	7,676	98.8%	10,958	36.4%	24.8%	4.0%	2.9%	9,405	40.1%	23.0%	7.4%	16.5%	2.5%
Stark County	24,335	98.3%	33,908	30.9%	45.5%	3.9%	8.4%	30,672	25.7%	36.2%	6.7%	17.1%	4.9%
Summit County	33,307	98.3%	50,125	32.5%	38.3%	7.1%	9.7%	49,169	25.4%	18.0%	12.5%	26.1%	11.6%
Trumbull County	14,264	96.8%	15,334	40.8%	28.7%	4.0%	4.8%	15,627	43.8%	17.0%	4.9%	15.6%	4.9%
Tuscarawas County	6,749	100.0%	7,243	45.7%	29.3%	6.5%	7.7%	7,249	31.1%	27.2%	10.9%	16.5%	6.0%
Warren County	18,040	100.0%	16,382	37.9%	34.0%	1.9%	9.9%	17,474	22.3%	11.2%	13.5%	34.3%	14.3%
Wayne County	8,612	88.1%	11,137	31.5%	36.5%	2.4%	3.7%	8,719	30.4%	20.0%	9.2%	11.1%	8.6%
Wood County	8,979	100.0%	19,374	34.1%	43.4%	5.7%	6.9%	12,388	22.5%	19.9%	8.3%	29.8%	15.5%
Oklahoma													
Canadian County	7,741	100.0%	10,297	31.4%	45.6%	8.8%	1.2%	10,799	25.7%	43.6%	11.8%	10.2%	2.9%
Cleveland County	15,890	97.5%	41,466	36.4%	46.7%	1.2%	8.4%	30,376	20.9%	26.3%	6.1%	30.0%	7.3%
Comanche County	7,888	93.8%	17,467	45.6%	30.2%	5.5%	7.1%	14,657	27.8%	42.8%	1.6%	16.6%	1.2%
Oklahoma County	44,685	97.4%	72,868	23.5%	38.6%	4.9%	12.9%	87,297	20.8%	23.6%	9.1%	23.2%	6.1%
Tulsa County	43,334	97.3%	59,491	32.0%	35.3%	4.1%	9.9%	65,454	25.5%	26.3%	8.7%	20.4%	6.3%
Oregon													
Clackamas County	27,212	99.3%	31,816	29.0%	43.5%	5.8%	9.6%	30,513	22.7%	30.8%	12.4%	18.1%	5.9%
Deschutes County	12,180	95.6%	11,498	40.1%	38.5%	3.1%	6.4%	14,309	26.1%	25.0%	8.2%	26.2%	6.9%
Douglas County	5,316	99.1%	7,684	15.6%	45.0%	14.2%	4.6%	7,735	30.0%	32.5%	11.0%	9.9%	4.3%
Jackson County	11,641	97.5%	17,320	45.8%	34.4%	5.2%	4.2%	16,879	20.0%	41.8%	6.2%	13.2%	4.0%
Lane County	19,984	98.1%	48,062	26.0%	56.3%	3.6%	5.2%	30,151	22.7%	42.2%	6.3%	18.0%	7.1%
Linn County	6,504	98.4%	15,594	29.7%	58.2%	3.2%	4.7%	8,247	21.0%	20.2%	11.6%	38.3%	7.2%
Marion County	22,772	96.0%	34,348	41.8%	39.5%	4.4%	3.0%	26,382	32.0%	27.6%	10.0%	12.0%	7.5%
Multnomah County	38,870	96.7%	68,115	25.8%	44.2%	3.8%	11.8%	97,558	16.4%	23.4%	10.1%	31.7%	10.5%
Washington County	38,757	98.9%	47,001	32.3%	38.2%	5.3%	10.6%	59,587	22.2%	24.8%	7.4%	29.4%	7.9%
Yamhill County	6,122	100.0%	9,740	23.7%	47.2%	1.8%	2.6%	8,782	31.9%	28.2%	3.3%	23.3%	8.9%
Pennsylvania													
Adams County	6,375	97.7%	11,103	38.7%	37.8%	1.6%	7.9%	6,631	38.1%	15.7%	9.2%	27.7%	2.4%
Allegheny County	69,744	97.4%	117,461	25.9%	40.4%	6.0%	19.0%	128,389	15.4%	18.2%	11.7%	34.6%	16.3%
Beaver County	10,331	97.6%	14,952	29.2%	39.0%	5.5%	11.2%	12,583	30.6%	17.4%	12.0%	27.0%	8.1%
Berks County	29,106	95.4%	42,753	33.3%	43.7%	5.0%	3.3%	34,585	30.4%	23.5%	8.6%	19.9%	7.7%
Blair County	6,521	99.2%	12,217	56.6%	27.2%	1.3%	5.5%	10,280	43.9%	11.6%	12.5%	16.7%	2.8%
Bucks County	43,272	97.5%	47,975	29.5%	36.3%	6.0%	17.4%	48,860	27.6%	18.9%	9.8%	28.4%	11.0%
Butler County	13,224	99.1%	17,255	26.1%	39.9%	8.2%	17.4%	14,392	19.4%	19.2%	8.4%	36.4%	10.7%
Cambria County	8,630	99.7%	13,064	31.0%	37.0%	3.9%	10.2%	10,546	30.2%	23.6%	10.4%	20.5%	3.9%
Centre County	6,996	96.8%	44,131	22.3%	60.3%	4.5%	9.3%	13,999	35.9%	7.8%	9.9%	17.0%	25.8%
Chester County	38,126	95.4%	45,204	32.7%	38.0%	2.5%	15.6%	42,874	19.5%	20.2%	6.8%	29.9%	15.7%
Cumberland County	14,570	97.4%	23,970	25.3%	52.2%	3.7%	8.2%	20,205	28.6%	18.3%	10.0%	28.6%	6.8%
Dauphin County	16,950	95.6%	21,555	36.0%	25.0%	8.2%	11.6%	25,438	28.8%	17.0%	10.9%	24.4%	10.7%
Delaware County	38,175	97.4%	59,250	27.9%	45.6%	4.3%	10.1%	49,731	21.2%	18.6%	8.5%	28.7%	12.0%
Erie County	15,496	97.1%	30,889	31.6%	45.2%	2.3%	11.5%	27,602	32.9%	14.3%	8.8%	22.3%	12.8%
Fayette County	7,384	97.0%	10,191	53.7%	17.3%	5.1%	7.1%	10,232	47.0%	11.4%	11.4%	21.1%	1.0%
Franklin County	8,647	98.1%	12,550	43.5%	37.3%	5.4%	4.9%	13,689	32.4%	23.3%	5.4%	18.4%	10.1%
Lackawanna County	12,024	99.2%	22,248	26.1%	46.2%	3.4%	10.6%	18,141	28.1%	18.9%	8.4%	20.1%	14.7%
Lancaster County	35,871	95.1%	50,977	39.9%	32.8%	3.1%	8.7%	47,497	29.6%	13.8%	9.4%	25.6%	4.2%
Lebanon County	8,334	94.7%	10,926	26.1%	36.0%	7.3%	14.7%	9,178	25.9%	26.8%	11.0%	17.8%	5.9%
Lehigh County	22,847	95.9%	32,576	29.1%	44.6%	9.4%	7.8%	30,683	20.5%	20.0%	11.0%	27.7%	11.2%
Luzerne County	19,687	98.5%	32,579	30.3%	48.1%	2.5%	7.6%	26,466	30.7%	22.4%	12.2%	19.1%	8.1%
Lycoming County	6,042	98.2%	14,169	35.4%	36.5%	8.8%	9.4%	9,160	41.9%	9.1%	9.6%	24.5%	6.9%
Mercer County	8,346	98.4%	11,450	40.5%	19.0%	4.1%	14.6%	8,634	42.7%	13.7%	8.9%	16.7%	7.8%
Monroe County	13,266	99.4%	19,021	40.2%	40.3%	9.6%	6.8%	10,573	32.9%	12.3%	14.9%	26.4%	4.0%
Montgomery County	52,880	97.7%	63,883	29.4%	37.0%	5.0%	17.6%	71,732	16.2%	18.0%	5.7%	38.4%	17.6%
Northampton County	17,941	100.0%	28,977	34.8%	39.5%	4.0%	11.7%	25,692	24.0%	19.5%	5.7%	29.9%	11.7%
Northumberland County	4,473	91.7%	7,804	32.0%	23.7%	7.9%	6.5%	7,950	31.4%	11.9%	11.9%	14.6%	16.9%
Philadelphia County	89,645	96.1%	188,718	31.4%	40.5%	3.4%	11.9%	198,742	26.1%	17.1%	4.3%	27.0%	15.3%
Schuylkill County	7,752	98.0%	11,168	39.3%	28.0%	7.2%	9.4%	11,697	32.1%	21.9%	12.8%	15.5%	5.1%
Washington County	12,596	97.7%	17,971	31.2%	42.2%	9.8%	6.1%	15,972	28.6%	17.5%	16.1%	20.3%	8.4%

Table E-2: Counties—Educational Attainment—*Continued*

| | 13 to 17 | | 18 to 24 | | | | | 25 to 31 | | | | | |
| | | | | Percent | | | | | Percent | | | | |
	Total Population	Percent Enrolled in School	Total Population	High School	Some College	Associates Degree	Bachelors Degree	Total Population	High School	Some College	Associates Degree	Bachelors Degree	Advanced Degree
Pennsylvania—*Cont.*													
Westmoreland County	19,863	99.4%	30,175	26.1%	49.2%	3.4%	12.0%	23,724	26.1%	23.2%	12.8%	16.8%	15.3%
York County	27,741	98.9%	39,152	49.5%	28.4%	3.1%	7.7%	35,545	32.2%	22.4%	13.6%	18.5%	3.8%
Rhode Island													
Kent County	8,562	98.8%	12,404	24.4%	44.7%	1.6%	21.0%	14,050	22.0%	25.3%	6.5%	31.1%	10.0%
Providence County	38,699	94.8%	74,088	27.3%	43.7%	5.1%	11.0%	65,917	20.5%	26.7%	6.6%	26.0%	8.4%
Washington County	7,020	97.3%	19,306	25.5%	53.2%	3.9%	11.8%	6,598	12.7%	15.5%	9.1%	40.1%	18.2%
South Carolina													
Aiken County	10,610	93.5%	15,125	34.1%	32.4%	4.7%	9.8%	14,493	29.9%	32.8%	4.8%	10.4%	7.3%
Anderson County	13,756	99.0%	15,743	28.2%	32.9%	11.6%	5.1%	15,660	15.3%	31.7%	8.3%	18.9%	9.3%
Beaufort County	8,656	98.6%	15,335	36.1%	29.1%	0.7%	7.5%	14,005	17.1%	41.3%	5.3%	15.6%	5.1%
Berkeley County	12,922	98.7%	20,467	32.3%	34.0%	4.3%	14.9%	20,800	14.7%	24.1%	16.5%	24.4%	6.7%
Charleston County	21,693	98.7%	41,902	24.5%	45.6%	6.4%	13.5%	42,223	14.0%	20.3%	11.6%	35.0%	10.5%
Dorchester County	10,726	99.1%	16,093	38.6%	35.8%	6.4%	7.0%	11,263	20.4%	28.7%	11.8%	11.5%	8.6%
Florence County	9,435	97.8%	14,181	15.1%	43.3%	3.6%	5.9%	11,255	24.0%	27.2%	5.6%	27.6%	4.1%
Greenville County	32,336	96.7%	47,093	28.1%	44.1%	3.7%	9.6%	44,888	19.3%	22.6%	6.0%	20.8%	12.2%
Horry County	13,308	93.6%	26,544	25.5%	46.4%	2.8%	9.4%	24,814	26.1%	29.8%	10.7%	16.1%	3.6%
Lexington County	19,792	97.5%	25,109	30.5%	43.6%	3.4%	12.8%	23,604	27.6%	24.2%	7.7%	20.5%	8.8%
Orangeburg County	7,159	94.2%	10,222	28.7%	30.9%	9.0%	5.4%	5,890	30.5%	12.4%	11.3%	16.5%	5.2%
Pickens County	8,610	96.9%	19,673	16.0%	57.9%	2.4%	7.8%	10,695	29.0%	18.1%	10.3%	16.8%	8.3%
Richland County	27,131	96.5%	62,983	26.8%	50.8%	3.2%	9.9%	41,177	15.7%	30.0%	6.7%	25.4%	8.4%
Spartanburg County	21,150	96.9%	30,878	38.9%	35.7%	5.1%	4.7%	24,155	27.0%	29.0%	9.7%	15.8%	5.9%
Sumter County	7,316	97.9%	12,753	40.0%	25.4%	5.2%	8.5%	9,642	31.6%	29.7%	8.4%	7.1%	6.4%
York County	17,957	99.0%	22,992	26.7%	48.3%	1.9%	6.4%	16,944	19.9%	25.5%	13.9%	22.6%	9.1%
South Dakota													
Minnehaha County	10,156	96.1%	18,746	20.5%	45.9%	10.8%	11.8%	21,330	22.2%	19.1%	15.7%	29.9%	7.4%
Pennington County	5,173	100.0%	11,112	32.6%	45.3%	6.2%	9.3%	8,870	26.1%	24.7%	13.3%	24.6%	8.2%
Tennessee													
Blount County	8,783	86.9%	10,855	36.1%	39.7%	3.4%	9.5%	8,977	46.7%	19.7%	9.7%	16.6%	1.2%
Bradley County	6,726	96.7%	10,249	44.2%	37.5%	1.5%	0.0%	8,352	34.1%	29.7%	8.3%	14.5%	4.1%
Davidson County	33,719	99.2%	69,097	26.7%	43.8%	3.8%	15.3%	90,142	16.4%	17.5%	6.2%	37.5%	12.2%
Hamilton County	19,372	98.3%	33,512	26.4%	44.8%	3.5%	8.8%	34,559	23.2%	26.2%	10.4%	17.4%	9.1%
Knox County	25,759	98.3%	54,317	30.6%	47.2%	5.1%	10.4%	43,946	25.0%	19.2%	7.6%	29.7%	14.6%
Madison County	7,298	96.9%	10,133	26.5%	52.2%	1.0%	5.7%	8,001	42.5%	24.9%	3.2%	17.3%	5.5%
Montgomery County	12,997	96.7%	22,598	33.8%	44.2%	3.8%	10.1%	25,885	23.6%	36.5%	10.9%	21.1%	5.9%
Rutherford County	20,158	99.2%	36,951	32.9%	43.8%	3.2%	10.4%	28,383	23.0%	28.7%	6.2%	27.0%	7.9%
Sevier County	4,044	100.0%	10,006	31.7%	44.0%	4.3%	12.3%	6,586	25.9%	23.0%	6.6%	16.6%	11.4%
Shelby County	67,246	98.0%	97,843	31.9%	38.6%	2.4%	10.0%	95,682	23.4%	26.3%	7.3%	19.3%	7.5%
Sullivan County	10,967	97.3%	11,805	41.1%	28.0%	7.5%	4.2%	10,983	35.4%	29.8%	5.8%	15.5%	9.3%
Sumner County	12,450	99.1%	14,205	39.7%	25.9%	9.6%	6.3%	14,572	32.0%	21.4%	7.0%	26.1%	9.1%
Washington County	7,909	98.8%	15,096	27.5%	50.8%	3.8%	13.4%	10,415	13.2%	27.3%	4.2%	30.7%	17.5%
Williamson County	16,127	98.8%	14,237	30.1%	30.9%	9.3%	8.4%	11,899	18.3%	29.7%	3.5%	35.5%	12.9%
Wilson County	10,149	98.5%	9,764	46.1%	16.9%	1.6%	13.5%	9,658	31.3%	20.2%	6.0%	28.2%	4.2%
Texas													
Bell County	21,906	97.0%	41,977	42.0%	38.0%	3.3%	6.5%	39,091	31.4%	37.6%	12.3%	10.0%	6.2%
Bexar County	133,146	98.2%	199,950	32.1%	39.1%	4.1%	9.3%	196,867	26.0%	28.1%	7.2%	21.2%	7.2%
Bowie County	5,049	97.5%	9,884	45.4%	34.0%	4.6%	2.2%	9,680	32.0%	33.9%	3.7%	11.4%	7.3%
Brazoria County	24,523	99.0%	28,706	26.0%	48.1%	5.0%	9.3%	34,540	27.7%	28.6%	5.4%	20.9%	7.1%
Brazos County	11,792	98.5%	57,384	13.8%	64.0%	4.0%	13.2%	24,267	14.9%	22.4%	9.6%	26.7%	14.6%
Cameron County	40,096	96.4%	44,095	33.3%	38.9%	6.1%	3.2%	33,550	23.3%	30.0%	6.2%	15.0%	1.8%
Collin County	65,384	97.7%	69,090	30.4%	39.4%	3.1%	13.7%	68,580	13.4%	21.9%	8.8%	36.1%	15.3%
Comal County	8,810	100.0%	9,523	52.8%	17.9%	4.0%	11.1%	8,822	32.9%	20.9%	2.4%	26.2%	5.6%
Dallas County	170,331	97.6%	244,435	29.8%	35.9%	4.4%	9.0%	279,822	22.5%	22.3%	6.1%	22.0%	8.6%
Denton County	53,763	98.4%	72,238	23.4%	50.9%	5.5%	8.4%	74,085	18.7%	26.2%	6.9%	32.0%	9.5%
Ector County	11,080	99.3%	16,738	39.4%	25.1%	4.0%	6.2%	17,369	32.1%	31.0%	3.8%	12.7%	4.3%
El Paso County	64,922	96.3%	99,494	31.7%	44.7%	5.2%	4.8%	82,562	21.8%	38.5%	6.4%	17.6%	5.2%
Ellis County	13,358	95.5%	14,570	34.0%	35.4%	6.7%	4.3%	13,140	33.0%	19.8%	11.3%	19.6%	7.8%
Fort Bend County	50,862	98.4%	54,417	25.4%	42.4%	4.6%	10.2%	53,038	23.2%	24.3%	7.9%	27.4%	10.2%
Galveston County	23,372	98.2%	28,221	32.4%	36.9%	6.9%	12.7%	27,246	28.7%	25.0%	7.8%	23.2%	9.9%
Grayson County	7,874	99.2%	11,527	33.3%	39.5%	3.4%	7.0%	11,410	28.6%	27.7%	9.9%	11.6%	3.6%
Gregg County	8,605	100.0%	13,487	26.3%	40.6%	4.0%	7.9%	11,362	38.8%	27.2%	9.4%	9.9%	2.6%
Guadalupe County	10,943	98.3%	13,089	41.3%	34.2%	1.1%	6.3%	11,517	25.8%	30.1%	4.2%	22.2%	4.7%
Harris County	309,621	97.0%	428,939	31.5%	36.5%	3.1%	9.2%	499,981	24.4%	23.7%	6.1%	22.5%	8.4%
Hays County	11,213	99.5%	30,303	26.2%	48.4%	4.6%	12.7%	17,040	26.1%	39.4%	5.5%	24.6%	2.6%
Hidalgo County	75,624	97.3%	90,122	27.4%	40.5%	2.9%	6.0%	74,583	26.2%	28.3%	5.7%	12.6%	2.1%
Jefferson County	17,384	93.6%	27,930	33.4%	40.7%	4.0%	3.0%	24,916	33.3%	29.9%	6.3%	17.4%	2.8%
Johnson County	11,098	95.9%	13,976	34.7%	34.9%	2.9%	4.6%	13,773	26.8%	27.1%	11.1%	13.8%	7.2%
Kaufman County	7,925	100.0%	9,526	34.4%	35.2%	8.5%	4.5%	7,868	31.7%	29.4%	6.8%	14.9%	1.7%
Lubbock County	19,693	95.4%	51,030	25.0%	48.8%	4.2%	11.2%	28,515	25.4%	28.3%	10.2%	20.4%	7.2%
McLennan County	13,339	95.8%	36,248	24.8%	49.2%	4.3%	11.6%	21,559	20.2%	32.8%	13.9%	13.1%	6.3%
Midland County	10,168	100.0%	15,147	34.5%	32.4%	1.7%	11.6%	18,279	25.4%	24.4%	1.4%	22.1%	9.0%
Montgomery County	39,235	97.9%	41,800	40.3%	39.4%	3.9%	3.3%	40,734	26.5%	26.0%	5.3%	22.4%	5.5%
Nueces County	24,532	96.8%	36,773	31.4%	39.6%	5.7%	11.2%	34,597	31.5%	30.4%	9.0%	15.1%	2.3%
Parker County	9,752	96.2%	10,340	45.7%	25.3%	12.6%	1.8%	9,903	37.5%	23.4%	3.3%	19.1%	4.2%

Table E-2: Counties—Educational Attainment—*Continued*

| | 13 to 17 | | 18 to 24 | | | | | 25 to 31 | | | | | |
	Total Population	Percent Enrolled in School	Total Population	High School	Some College	Associates Degree	Bachelors Degree	Total Population	High School	Some College	Associates Degree	Bachelors Degree	Advanced Degree
Texas—Cont.													
Potter County	8,010	97.8%	12,335	37.4%	31.6%	7.2%	3.8%	12,465	20.3%	26.5%	10.9%	9.8%	1.6%
Randall County	7,557	97.4%	12,985	29.0%	47.4%	3.0%	11.8%	13,695	21.6%	32.2%	6.3%	20.7%	8.5%
Smith County	15,574	92.6%	22,466	29.4%	36.3%	11.8%	6.2%	19,748	24.9%	29.7%	8.2%	25.2%	2.7%
Tarrant County	142,599	98.5%	182,581	30.1%	38.9%	4.6%	8.8%	203,238	24.2%	25.0%	7.2%	23.8%	5.9%
Taylor County	8,285	98.0%	19,774	30.9%	47.6%	5.0%	5.0%	15,296	20.3%	35.7%	8.3%	20.2%	7.8%
Tom Green County	7,665	99.6%	14,049	33.7%	52.2%	1.6%	6.8%	12,632	31.4%	13.6%	16.0%	21.2%	0.8%
Travis County	63,713	97.0%	117,682	23.8%	49.5%	2.4%	12.0%	163,202	14.7%	22.2%	4.6%	37.7%	10.9%
Webb County	23,409	99.5%	29,655	35.3%	43.1%	2.3%	2.3%	26,286	27.5%	26.5%	11.2%	13.4%	4.1%
Wichita County	7,490	97.8%	17,764	37.1%	43.0%	6.3%	7.7%	15,130	38.0%	26.7%	9.0%	14.7%	3.9%
Williamson County	35,527	97.8%	36,128	33.1%	42.2%	2.7%	7.4%	44,089	22.9%	30.4%	6.2%	24.3%	7.2%
Utah													
Cache County	9,876	99.8%	18,490	20.4%	49.4%	14.0%	10.7%	14,765	16.9%	31.9%	7.5%	32.2%	5.7%
Davis County	30,135	94.0%	29,660	39.5%	34.3%	6.3%	6.9%	30,520	23.5%	31.5%	10.4%	27.0%	5.7%
Salt Lake County	80,671	98.8%	107,464	30.7%	41.4%	7.3%	6.9%	127,239	22.7%	25.9%	8.7%	25.1%	9.6%
Utah County	46,338	98.5%	92,638	21.9%	54.4%	7.9%	6.0%	58,974	13.5%	31.0%	11.2%	32.9%	5.4%
Washington County	10,787	96.9%	14,931	23.9%	39.1%	8.8%	2.4%	10,743	19.3%	38.2%	13.8%	17.8%	3.9%
Weber County	18,953	98.9%	22,158	32.8%	43.3%	8.4%	1.6%	25,097	28.7%	24.9%	11.7%	18.0%	0.6%
Vermont													
Chittenden County	9,908	97.6%	23,207	15.6%	59.8%	2.6%	15.1%	16,368	16.0%	22.0%	8.6%	37.5%	6.9%
Virginia													
Albemarle County	7,120	100.0%	11,502	28.1%	49.1%	6.1%	13.5%	10,164	28.5%	13.4%	4.9%	25.8%	25.0%
Arlington County	7,751	93.2%	18,217	26.3%	17.2%	2.5%	47.5%	47,231	5.8%	7.9%	3.5%	49.4%	31.2%
Chesterfield County	26,193	97.2%	30,892	40.0%	36.1%	5.1%	12.7%	25,020	21.8%	29.8%	7.0%	19.9%	15.4%
Fairfax County	73,325	98.1%	95,982	24.3%	36.5%	5.0%	21.0%	109,704	11.3%	17.4%	4.2%	36.9%	22.3%
Hanover County	7,237	97.6%	7,969	38.4%	30.6%	2.6%	18.1%	8,001	21.1%	21.2%	17.8%	27.2%	9.7%
Henrico County	20,646	99.2%	27,360	31.3%	30.6%	6.0%	15.9%	31,938	21.7%	27.9%	5.2%	24.9%	12.6%
Loudoun County	28,480	99.0%	22,990	34.4%	34.9%	3.2%	13.6%	28,537	15.4%	16.2%	4.6%	42.7%	20.9%
Montgomery County	6,734	97.8%	29,989	15.4%	65.2%	3.6%	11.4%	7,418	16.5%	25.4%	6.2%	24.7%	27.2%
Prince William County	31,371	98.8%	37,966	29.4%	34.2%	6.9%	12.4%	43,664	19.8%	32.6%	7.7%	25.5%	7.1%
Roanoke County	5,731	95.1%	8,101	25.4%	28.6%	8.8%	11.2%	6,842	28.9%	33.7%	3.0%	18.3%	6.0%
Spotsylvania County	10,344	95.8%	11,918	40.5%	33.4%	5.2%	4.6%	9,884	39.4%	19.7%	13.0%	17.4%	3.5%
Stafford County	9,772	100.0%	16,747	32.5%	37.1%	0.4%	21.2%	11,700	31.5%	35.7%	7.3%	18.6%	4.5%
Washington													
Benton County	14,605	98.3%	15,433	34.2%	39.7%	7.9%	3.5%	16,029	22.7%	24.2%	14.2%	16.6%	4.7%
Clark County	30,646	97.6%	38,418	34.7%	31.2%	10.9%	7.5%	36,785	30.5%	30.4%	12.9%	11.8%	4.6%
Cowlitz County	6,983	100.0%	8,540	36.0%	34.8%	2.4%	1.6%	7,664	39.3%	41.6%	2.0%	7.2%	1.2%
Grant County	6,236	97.7%	11,733	29.1%	33.8%	8.7%	3.1%	7,232	29.4%	27.0%	5.9%	19.2%	0.6%
King County	113,272	98.2%	177,207	23.3%	36.5%	7.0%	20.7%	241,026	14.0%	19.8%	6.9%	38.0%	14.1%
Kitsap County	15,581	96.5%	25,705	37.0%	42.9%	4.6%	7.1%	23,899	21.7%	42.2%	7.3%	20.6%	2.6%
Pierce County	55,338	98.3%	79,988	31.9%	40.8%	4.8%	8.4%	85,958	26.9%	28.2%	11.0%	16.6%	6.2%
Skagit County	7,220	96.0%	11,075	45.5%	27.8%	3.8%	0.8%	8,911	26.4%	43.6%	9.6%	6.3%	1.8%
Snohomish County	48,188	97.1%	64,845	28.9%	38.7%	7.7%	8.5%	71,377	20.7%	27.0%	13.1%	23.6%	5.3%
Spokane County	32,408	99.2%	50,514	27.6%	47.5%	6.1%	10.2%	50,622	32.1%	27.0%	9.2%	19.7%	5.4%
Thurston County	17,119	97.0%	24,463	29.8%	39.3%	7.8%	10.4%	28,856	22.4%	29.9%	9.5%	21.4%	8.8%
Whatcom County	12,958	100.0%	31,693	25.1%	43.7%	14.2%	6.4%	17,498	15.9%	32.6%	8.3%	31.2%	3.3%
Yakima County	18,411	94.7%	25,232	35.4%	26.1%	4.3%	3.8%	22,351	32.3%	25.8%	6.1%	14.9%	1.9%
West Virginia													
Berkeley County	8,235	98.1%	9,880	51.2%	21.2%	6.7%	6.9%	8,678	24.9%	32.5%	6.7%	18.6%	9.2%
Cabell County	7,962	98.9%	10,375	25.0%	52.1%	3.5%	2.9%	8,673	20.1%	37.3%	6.1%	17.4%	12.3%
Kanawha County	12,228	99.8%	15,818	30.5%	35.2%	2.5%	8.5%	16,505	28.2%	26.7%	10.3%	11.6%	13.8%
Monongalia County	4,599	100.0%	23,460	27.4%	57.3%	2.0%	10.4%	13,906	23.0%	19.2%	2.2%	16.7%	27.3%
Wisconsin													
Brown County	17,666	96.1%	23,708	30.8%	41.1%	3.9%	10.5%	23,266	26.9%	17.6%	16.0%	28.7%	3.1%
Dane County	30,018	98.4%	64,801	20.1%	48.5%	4.7%	18.9%	62,196	12.5%	15.7%	9.4%	40.8%	17.4%
Eau Claire County	6,195	99.0%	17,113	32.0%	42.6%	3.6%	7.7%	10,648	16.8%	31.4%	17.9%	24.2%	4.5%
Fond du Lac County	8,056	100.0%	9,137	34.4%	35.3%	8.2%	4.9%	5,672	40.0%	19.0%	16.4%	17.4%	4.2%
Kenosha County	12,019	100.0%	16,352	30.8%	38.2%	6.5%	9.6%	14,366	30.7%	27.6%	10.7%	19.4%	3.7%
La Crosse County	7,672	99.2%	18,390	26.0%	55.7%	4.3%	6.6%	11,836	11.0%	34.0%	23.6%	26.5%	3.5%
Marathon County	9,211	99.2%	11,313	53.8%	27.0%	5.2%	0.3%	11,030	27.9%	16.7%	18.3%	22.5%	4.5%
Milwaukee County	61,747	98.2%	99,896	28.6%	42.6%	4.2%	8.1%	114,068	21.9%	22.1%	9.2%	28.6%	8.5%
Outagamie County	10,595	100.0%	16,864	41.0%	38.2%	3.4%	7.4%	17,397	29.8%	31.6%	10.9%	23.9%	2.6%
Racine County	14,948	99.7%	15,071	29.4%	45.3%	1.1%	7.3%	18,360	23.1%	30.4%	7.6%	13.6%	3.9%
Rock County	12,012	92.4%	14,267	38.5%	41.1%	8.2%	3.7%	13,455	43.9%	18.2%	9.1%	13.4%	7.0%
Sheboygan County	8,528	98.8%	8,049	32.3%	37.7%	0.7%	9.2%	9,109	20.5%	26.6%	15.0%	19.5%	8.4%
Walworth County	6,980	94.9%	11,281	27.9%	50.9%	6.2%	8.0%	8,854	29.3%	25.5%	10.3%	18.8%	6.3%
Washington County	7,985	98.0%	11,187	38.6%	30.7%	9.0%	10.3%	9,002	34.8%	9.5%	8.3%	38.9%	6.7%
Waukesha County	26,526	96.3%	30,739	35.5%	36.3%	5.1%	12.0%	28,153	14.9%	25.3%	13.4%	34.4%	9.3%
Winnebago County	9,642	95.0%	20,693	31.7%	48.0%	4.2%	7.6%	16,548	25.5%	18.9%	12.5%	29.2%	5.6%
Wyoming													
Laramie County	5,137	100.0%	12,437	26.1%	47.9%	6.3%	6.6%	8,039	18.8%	22.4%	13.4%	20.4%	20.6%

Table E-3: Places—Educational Attainment

	13 to 17		18 to 24					25 to 31					
				Percent					Percent				
	Total Population	Percent Enrolled in School	Total Population	High School	Some College	Associates Degree	Bachelors Degree	Total Population	High School	Some College	Associates Degree	Bachelors Degree	Advanced Degree
Alabama													
Birmingham city	13,899	95.1%	24,818	29.3%	39.7%	0.0%	10.7%	23,982	27.7%	16.2%	2.8%	23.1%	11.6%
Huntsville city	13,760	98.0%	19,366	35.1%	33.2%	3.3%	13.5%	18,878	15.0%	23.0%	18.3%	25.7%	7.8%
Mobile city	11,666	89.3%	20,293	27.8%	35.5%	2.1%	15.0%	20,214	22.3%	31.8%	7.9%	17.6%	7.0%
Montgomery city	13,270	97.0%	23,367	27.9%	36.0%	0.5%	12.4%	22,357	21.4%	30.8%	8.4%	16.7%	6.9%
Tuscaloosa city	5,873	98.9%	23,953	15.0%	65.7%	2.5%	6.4%	9,937	30.3%	16.3%	12.8%	21.3%	13.2%
Alaska													
Anchorage municipality	19,361	88.8%	34,074	39.0%	40.2%	2.4%	7.1%	35,653	20.1%	39.4%	6.7%	23.5%	9.0%
Arizona													
Chandler city	18,302	94.3%	22,227	29.1%	41.7%	7.2%	6.6%	25,427	17.1%	28.5%	9.0%	22.6%	11.9%
Glendale city	18,310	96.4%	22,520	39.7%	27.2%	3.9%	10.2%	24,043	21.6%	27.9%	6.8%	15.1%	6.5%
Mesa city	31,497	93.1%	45,070	30.7%	38.9%	4.2%	8.9%	47,737	24.6%	28.1%	8.9%	16.9%	7.6%
Peoria city	12,708	98.7%	12,190	35.7%	30.6%	4.9%	7.2%	13,193	26.8%	27.8%	10.8%	22.2%	4.8%
Phoenix city	105,482	98.3%	154,915	32.6%	31.3%	5.4%	7.3%	159,901	24.9%	23.5%	9.7%	17.3%	6.8%
Scottsdale city	14,768	97.2%	16,139	25.1%	40.1%	0.8%	18.0%	19,062	11.8%	17.9%	12.2%	39.8%	16.4%
Surprise city	7,841	100.0%	6,025	40.4%	35.9%	12.6%	4.9%	7,630	28.0%	34.5%	8.8%	22.6%	3.7%
Tempe city	11,967	94.2%	35,874	25.9%	52.6%	3.4%	13.4%	26,666	16.3%	14.7%	10.2%	37.2%	9.9%
Tucson city	36,362	96.6%	76,603	30.8%	41.1%	3.7%	7.5%	51,809	24.4%	30.2%	7.0%	14.2%	8.8%
Yuma city	6,871	100.0%	11,052	26.5%	41.2%	10.0%	1.4%	9,945	36.0%	25.1%	12.4%	11.3%	0.4%
Arkansas													
Little Rock city	12,920	91.4%	16,118	24.7%	43.2%	1.6%	15.2%	23,392	22.2%	27.6%	3.4%	21.1%	9.0%
California													
Anaheim city	23,186	99.8%	36,943	30.1%	43.6%	4.4%	6.6%	35,851	16.7%	26.9%	6.5%	25.2%	7.2%
Antioch city	9,261	98.7%	12,180	37.0%	36.6%	6.7%	3.7%	10,190	30.0%	28.2%	6.3%	16.8%	0.0%
Bakersfield city	28,392	98.2%	39,371	31.7%	42.5%	7.9%	5.5%	39,901	28.2%	29.1%	7.6%	11.8%	6.5%
Berkeley city	5,136	98.3%	26,469	9.7%	71.6%	0.7%	16.1%	17,350	4.7%	16.4%	5.2%	43.8%	24.7%
Burbank city	4,783	100.0%	6,721	20.4%	35.2%	4.7%	28.2%	11,889	14.2%	23.1%	3.2%	50.5%	9.1%
Carlsbad city	6,142	100.0%	7,319	31.6%	49.7%	3.8%	9.8%	9,394	10.8%	20.6%	7.9%	36.0%	21.0%
Carson city	5,110	97.7%	10,757	29.3%	50.7%	1.6%	11.3%	9,644	26.1%	32.4%	13.6%	17.5%	3.2%
Chula Vista city	20,122	98.5%	27,506	29.1%	37.6%	9.1%	6.4%	23,755	22.4%	26.8%	11.5%	18.5%	6.0%
Clovis city	6,764	100.0%	11,520	19.5%	48.8%	6.4%	11.1%	8,626	17.1%	27.4%	7.8%	31.9%	9.7%
Compton city	8,128	97.3%	10,355	24.7%	40.5%	1.4%	3.4%	10,546	27.8%	27.8%	3.0%	6.0%	3.6%
Concord city	8,257	97.8%	10,951	30.7%	31.7%	6.4%	22.0%	12,517	18.8%	20.2%	5.7%	31.5%	11.6%
Corona city	12,434	99.5%	16,818	45.2%	30.6%	6.5%	6.5%	16,761	24.6%	28.3%	4.0%	15.2%	8.6%
Costa Mesa city	6,774	91.3%	10,818	29.6%	41.4%	11.4%	8.6%	16,113	20.9%	21.3%	3.0%	41.3%	4.3%
Daly City city	6,466	98.2%	11,075	19.3%	58.0%	6.3%	13.6%	12,536	14.6%	15.3%	12.0%	40.3%	3.7%
Downey city	7,627	99.5%	15,873	30.8%	45.3%	5.0%	4.1%	11,971	33.8%	27.0%	2.9%	18.7%	5.1%
El Cajon city	5,117	96.0%	12,830	25.3%	38.6%	5.9%	7.8%	12,072	34.7%	25.3%	10.4%	14.2%	2.8%
El Monte city	8,408	98.0%	11,284	25.2%	47.7%	2.0%	6.8%	11,210	35.7%	21.8%	8.5%	9.2%	0.0%
Elk Grove city	18,155	97.5%	13,742	32.3%	41.0%	3.0%	9.6%	10,251	24.7%	20.4%	6.3%	34.4%	8.0%
Escondido city	10,612	93.3%	16,403	35.1%	27.9%	4.7%	5.5%	17,091	20.4%	20.7%	11.8%	12.0%	2.7%
Fairfield city	7,655	93.6%	13,826	43.8%	35.5%	0.6%	6.3%	12,854	18.6%	43.0%	12.3%	13.6%	2.2%
Fontana city	19,050	99.7%	22,450	37.5%	42.7%	1.4%	7.2%	18,971	24.0%	35.4%	9.6%	11.8%	4.1%
Fremont city	13,227	98.6%	16,568	21.8%	39.7%	2.9%	25.3%	21,994	18.0%	22.6%	5.9%	31.3%	16.8%
Fresno city	36,152	98.1%	57,906	27.3%	45.6%	4.8%	4.4%	56,907	21.6%	33.7%	10.7%	14.4%	4.2%
Fullerton city	10,742	98.1%	16,518	18.5%	57.3%	5.2%	10.6%	17,289	14.8%	36.4%	4.9%	26.0%	5.5%
Garden Grove city	11,020	94.2%	18,446	24.9%	41.1%	8.5%	8.4%	16,769	23.2%	19.6%	6.2%	21.1%	2.5%
Glendale city	9,459	98.5%	14,944	19.1%	50.6%	6.6%	16.0%	22,833	11.7%	22.5%	11.0%	38.9%	11.5%
Hayward city	7,885	99.1%	15,875	28.3%	45.5%	4.6%	8.3%	18,422	18.4%	30.0%	6.0%	21.4%	7.5%
Hesperia city	15,319	98.2%	19,216	27.5%	46.3%	9.7%	4.4%	21,407	24.4%	25.1%	10.7%	18.9%	10.9%
Inglewood city	6,819	100.0%	11,099	39.5%	31.5%	0.0%	6.2%	13,468	22.2%	34.7%	6.0%	16.6%	1.4%
Irvine city	14,623	98.7%	30,544	15.6%	57.0%	3.2%	20.0%	25,569	8.5%	22.9%	10.7%	46.8%	6.5%
Jurupa Valley city	9,260	97.7%	10,455	29.3%	38.9%	2.5%	8.6%	10,081	17.3%	36.4%	10.1%	15.5%	5.5%
Lancaster city	13,212	100.0%	16,534	35.8%	33.8%	4.5%	2.7%	14,910	41.3%	29.0%	4.9%	13.8%	1.5%
Long Beach city	31,717	99.0%	49,447	27.1%	49.9%	3.8%	6.8%	51,100	19.1%	32.0%	6.4%	22.1%	10.4%
Los Angeles city	232,150	98.5%	414,272	24.4%	43.0%	4.1%	11.8%	459,387	20.0%	21.1%	5.6%	28.4%	8.8%
Mission Viejo city	7,600	98.5%	8,995	20.3%	52.4%	3.8%	13.3%	4,425	25.0%	19.8%	21.2%	27.1%	4.7%
Modesto city	16,645	96.6%	22,619	33.5%	48.8%	5.4%	3.4%	20,567	29.5%	28.2%	8.4%	14.1%	3.7%
Moreno Valley city	17,136	98.2%	22,518	37.7%	33.1%	5.6%	2.2%	25,384	37.7%	27.8%	9.3%	10.5%	3.3%
Murrieta city	10,866	100.0%	9,771	21.6%	40.2%	9.9%	5.9%	8,639	16.8%	42.3%	7.0%	23.0%	4.8%
Norwalk city	8,233	98.1%	12,390	35.9%	38.8%	6.7%	5.5%	9,029	23.2%	22.2%	15.8%	9.5%	6.8%
Oakland city	21,442	98.6%	34,793	23.6%	42.9%	2.7%	16.6%	50,604	15.3%	22.6%	3.8%	29.6%	16.1%
Oceanside city	6,636	100.0%	21,035	49.9%	37.4%	5.7%	2.8%	16,680	24.9%	22.9%	16.4%	18.3%	7.9%
Ontario city	13,368	99.6%	18,592	20.5%	56.8%	4.9%	2.7%	16,521	29.8%	39.9%	6.7%	6.8%	3.6%
Orange city	10,644	96.1%	15,291	21.8%	52.6%	6.7%	9.8%	14,649	24.4%	22.6%	4.7%	16.9%	8.7%
Oxnard city	16,353	94.9%	25,335	26.1%	44.0%	4.1%	7.0%	21,677	29.2%	28.2%	4.0%	13.6%	1.4%
Palmdale city	15,050	100.0%	16,777	33.3%	29.6%	2.1%	5.8%	13,322	23.9%	38.3%	8.1%	10.9%	2.7%
Pasadena city	6,467	96.9%	13,797	20.2%	35.8%	8.8%	19.7%	20,602	9.1%	18.5%	4.6%	41.4%	17.7%
Pomona city	9,893	99.3%	21,042	25.8%	48.0%	1.6%	7.9%	16,663	23.3%	24.1%	6.3%	17.9%	3.1%
Rancho Cucamonga city	14,183	98.1%	18,570	25.8%	45.3%	6.5%	9.6%	15,343	25.6%	17.4%	12.9%	22.8%	18.1%
Redding city	5,931	97.8%	9,543	29.8%	48.5%	7.0%	3.1%	9,166	33.8%	28.7%	4.4%	11.5%	6.1%
Rialto city	8,699	100.0%	12,998	33.9%	41.0%	4.9%	1.5%	9,236	24.4%	28.9%	14.1%	10.1%	3.0%
Richmond city	6,121	100.0%	10,767	32.1%	41.5%	5.1%	6.1%	13,277	14.1%	17.4%	0.2%	24.1%	10.8%
Riverside city	21,974	97.6%	49,495	29.5%	48.1%	2.7%	6.7%	28,679	22.0%	30.5%	8.8%	18.2%	5.6%
Roseville city	9,540	100.0%	9,740	31.2%	47.7%	2.8%	4.5%	12,927	23.1%	26.7%	11.0%	27.9%	4.7%

Table E-3: Places—Educational Attainment—*Continued*

| | 13 to 17 | | 18 to 24 | | | | | 25 to 31 | | | | | |
| | | | | Percent | | | | | Percent | | | | |
	Total Population	Percent Enrolled in School	Total Population	High School	Some College	Associates Degree	Bachelors Degree	Total Population	High School	Some College	Associates Degree	Bachelors Degree	Advanced Degree
California—Cont.													
Sacramento city	30,668	98.1%	49,576	31.3%	38.8%	5.3%	10.7%	54,203	18.6%	28.5%	6.3%	24.2%	8.9%
Salinas city	12,910	98.6%	18,628	32.9%	40.2%	4.1%	1.9%	15,866	33.2%	21.2%	4.6%	9.6%	3.6%
San Bernardino city	17,350	95.9%	28,852	37.4%	35.8%	3.0%	4.8%	20,883	25.6%	22.0%	9.9%	6.4%	1.3%
San Buenaventura (Ventura) city...	6,004	100.0%	10,980	25.3%	46.4%	11.4%	13.6%	11,094	13.3%	33.0%	17.6%	17.5%	11.4%
San Diego city	78,041	98.8%	156,541	28.2%	41.2%	4.7%	14.1%	178,234	15.9%	22.7%	8.6%	33.2%	13.9%
San Francisco city	24,561	96.0%	62,062	19.1%	43.0%	3.5%	28.9%	129,957	6.7%	12.4%	4.6%	49.5%	20.4%
San Jose city	59,825	98.1%	85,425	25.3%	41.0%	5.2%	14.6%	105,249	17.4%	22.8%	7.7%	26.7%	12.8%
San Mateo city	5,472	99.0%	6,413	21.5%	38.1%	1.7%	17.9%	9,364	15.5%	20.0%	6.0%	32.2%	23.4%
Santa Ana city	25,400	99.6%	40,982	29.0%	41.2%	2.7%	7.0%	37,965	25.9%	24.5%	4.2%	14.9%	3.4%
Santa Clara city	4,554	98.7%	12,714	28.8%	41.6%	1.1%	21.1%	18,020	6.9%	12.8%	0.6%	40.2%	37.9%
Santa Clarita city	13,653	98.4%	16,200	25.4%	46.1%	4.0%	10.0%	16,170	20.7%	31.3%	6.9%	26.7%	3.7%
Santa Maria city	10,972	99.5%	11,107	24.9%	30.6%	5.6%	3.0%	9,634	26.3%	21.6%	9.4%	7.6%	1.8%
Santa Monica city	3,737	100.0%	5,131	23.3%	36.2%	6.5%	32.2%	12,786	5.0%	15.9%	0.6%	46.8%	28.1%
Santa Rosa city	12,740	100.0%	15,177	36.3%	44.6%	1.7%	2.0%	17,790	28.6%	23.5%	11.3%	22.5%	6.0%
Simi Valley city	8,782	99.1%	10,104	21.5%	41.7%	15.9%	13.4%	9,416	19.4%	23.8%	7.6%	31.1%	8.0%
South Gate city	7,663	97.7%	10,170	36.3%	36.6%	1.3%	2.2%	12,129	25.5%	30.2%	4.5%	10.7%	1.5%
Stockton city	22,258	98.4%	33,029	31.0%	36.6%	5.6%	7.9%	27,866	24.7%	29.8%	11.0%	12.1%	0.8%
Sunnyvale city	6,404	98.2%	9,863	11.6%	41.0%	1.4%	34.9%	19,311	6.6%	12.4%	1.0%	46.4%	32.9%
Temecula city	11,539	95.4%	12,331	40.3%	30.2%	3.2%	7.5%	7,345	19.5%	30.1%	18.1%	24.2%	2.8%
Thousand Oaks city	8,631	100.0%	12,516	23.4%	45.0%	12.5%	13.5%	9,254	12.6%	29.1%	6.4%	28.0%	16.3%
Torrance city	8,662	100.0%	12,260	20.7%	48.3%	10.9%	9.7%	10,105	9.3%	25.0%	9.1%	42.5%	11.8%
Vacaville city	6,745	95.7%	9,594	32.6%	44.4%	0.9%	4.5%	9,405	14.3%	40.8%	13.0%	15.8%	4.6%
Vallejo city	7,997	100.0%	11,369	30.5%	43.0%	4.4%	8.9%	11,856	23.8%	28.0%	11.8%	18.4%	4.2%
Victorville city	8,289	100.0%	13,437	50.9%	28.0%	2.5%	4.3%	12,353	28.6%	28.4%	6.0%	7.2%	6.5%
Visalia city	8,950	94.4%	14,451	36.2%	22.4%	15.4%	2.4%	14,393	35.4%	16.5%	14.2%	9.9%	13.6%
Vista city	4,332	100.0%	12,213	30.6%	27.7%	14.6%	5.4%	12,024	33.0%	15.1%	13.2%	6.5%	5.8%
West Covina city	7,801	100.0%	11,275	35.7%	47.3%	0.8%	7.4%	12,251	28.0%	21.9%	10.1%	22.8%	3.7%
Westminster city	6,620	92.1%	6,793	22.5%	33.3%	13.7%	15.0%	10,033	18.5%	23.7%	19.5%	18.7%	4.5%
Colorado													
Arvada city	9,383	99.3%	9,441	23.6%	43.2%	12.3%	10.9%	9,903	17.2%	38.6%	3.0%	27.6%	7.8%
Aurora city	24,916	94.5%	31,521	31.5%	32.7%	6.1%	8.6%	35,520	19.3%	32.1%	11.6%	20.1%	3.9%
Boulder city	5,359	95.6%	29,961	11.8%	69.0%	3.8%	12.2%	12,008	9.2%	5.9%	1.8%	59.8%	22.5%
Centennial city	8,965	100.0%	7,068	25.4%	45.2%	2.7%	10.9%	8,768	10.1%	32.9%	7.9%	31.8%	10.5%
Colorado Springs city	29,007	98.5%	45,636	27.8%	39.6%	6.5%	9.4%	46,805	16.2%	29.4%	15.1%	24.1%	6.0%
Denver city	27,684	93.1%	58,403	21.9%	39.3%	3.6%	19.2%	96,430	13.7%	18.2%	3.8%	41.5%	9.4%
Fort Collins city	11,622	99.0%	32,540	17.2%	60.6%	4.2%	11.9%	15,954	14.2%	22.4%	14.5%	34.7%	11.6%
Greeley city	7,448	96.1%	13,727	24.4%	46.3%	2.1%	10.3%	12,038	27.1%	31.0%	10.0%	17.0%	4.2%
Lakewood city	7,538	96.7%	13,949	22.9%	42.5%	7.6%	13.6%	14,372	27.1%	16.8%	16.3%	24.6%	9.1%
Pueblo city	7,372	97.3%	11,131	22.6%	49.8%	4.7%	7.8%	9,895	30.0%	33.3%	12.2%	7.4%	3.0%
Thornton city	12,083	97.5%	12,131	25.7%	40.8%	11.9%	2.8%	10,191	28.4%	12.6%	17.0%	10.7%	3.7%
Westminster city	8,578	98.2%	9,091	28.1%	47.7%	4.2%	8.2%	13,432	12.0%	33.2%	10.1%	19.6%	8.2%
Connecticut													
Bridgeport city	8,781	95.2%	15,330	22.7%	46.7%	2.3%	7.7%	19,266	24.5%	21.6%	2.1%	19.4%	10.8%
Hartford city	8,558	97.3%	17,926	26.3%	41.7%	1.4%	3.8%	14,342	24.5%	24.1%	4.0%	16.3%	10.9%
New Haven city	6,843	95.3%	21,287	32.6%	45.0%	1.5%	6.9%	17,272	26.5%	14.4%	4.3%	18.3%	28.3%
Stamford city	7,752	98.1%	12,181	19.5%	34.2%	0.0%	24.0%	13,874	22.1%	17.2%	7.7%	26.2%	14.3%
Waterbury city	6,658	100.0%	10,499	30.6%	34.2%	4.1%	3.3%	12,596	39.7%	20.2%	4.7%	15.3%	7.1%
District of Columbia													
Washington city	23,448	96.2%	75,399	23.4%	38.2%	1.9%	24.5%	102,748	13.2%	10.6%	2.9%	34.4%	34.4%
Florida													
Cape Coral city	10,806	100.0%	12,044	33.8%	38.1%	7.3%	1.0%	13,598	42.2%	23.2%	2.0%	24.2%	3.0%
Clearwater city	5,523	92.5%	8,279	37.2%	21.7%	16.2%	8.7%	9,599	29.6%	23.5%	11.9%	21.3%	2.9%
Coral Springs city	8,687	100.0%	13,970	41.9%	30.2%	7.7%	10.0%	9,869	19.6%	31.0%	9.3%	25.9%	6.7%
Fort Lauderdale city	8,570	96.3%	15,103	22.2%	35.3%	12.0%	5.5%	15,087	21.1%	19.8%	10.1%	19.1%	16.3%
Gainesville city	4,051	100.0%	43,021	12.7%	61.2%	10.6%	13.0%	17,628	10.3%	17.8%	8.0%	36.8%	22.3%
Hialeah city	14,554	96.2%	20,256	28.2%	36.9%	10.7%	6.2%	20,322	36.6%	25.3%	14.4%	12.5%	2.5%
Hollywood city	8,007	94.8%	11,122	18.8%	37.3%	13.7%	6.7%	11,697	23.7%	23.3%	11.1%	24.4%	6.7%
Jacksonville city	49,164	96.9%	80,071	34.3%	30.6%	6.6%	8.7%	94,016	26.3%	23.3%	12.9%	24.7%	4.7%
Lakeland city	6,754	98.6%	11,043	47.9%	28.3%	2.0%	1.2%	8,446	34.0%	20.5%	13.7%	19.7%	0.3%
Miami Beach city	5,105	97.7%	6,216	19.8%	29.8%	13.2%	13.9%	8,798	25.1%	10.4%	9.5%	34.8%	17.9%
Miami city	18,402	93.8%	34,280	34.3%	26.1%	8.3%	11.8%	47,133	28.7%	18.6%	7.9%	23.3%	9.8%
Miami Gardens city	6,910	96.1%	13,952	38.3%	41.9%	5.3%	3.7%	11,328	36.1%	24.5%	12.8%	10.2%	2.3%
Miramar city	6,517	100.0%	12,626	22.8%	36.5%	16.6%	12.3%	17,992	14.6%	33.8%	14.8%	18.7%	11.1%
Orlando city	17,769	97.2%	25,196	32.0%	37.7%	6.4%	8.9%	36,308	35.3%	18.6%	10.6%	17.1%	10.6%
Palm Bay city	6,369	97.7%	9,200	15.2%	38.6%	4.8%	8.9%	8,128	20.4%	27.7%	23.4%	16.6%	4.4%
Pembroke Pines city	10,823	100.0%	14,893	28.1%	39.3%	13.6%	8.4%	14,510	13.3%	27.4%	11.9%	22.7%	17.7%
Pompano Beach city	8,091	96.0%	7,215	26.3%	32.1%	5.5%	14.5%	10,241	28.9%	18.0%	4.5%	12.0%	5.8%
Port St. Lucie city	14,965	99.4%	13,266	38.3%	41.8%	1.5%	3.3%	10,425	34.2%	29.8%	10.3%	5.6%	5.5%
St. Petersburg city	13,662	98.8%	21,540	34.5%	36.2%	6.7%	9.7%	24,997	30.9%	18.7%	14.7%	22.2%	7.3%
Tallahassee city	10,982	100.0%	52,303	19.3%	47.0%	13.3%	12.6%	23,034	11.8%	18.5%	13.1%	34.3%	15.6%
Tampa city	20,286	93.4%	42,412	26.0%	33.0%	6.2%	15.8%	41,641	21.4%	18.6%	9.6%	29.3%	9.2%
West Palm Beach city	5,269	98.6%	10,514	43.4%	28.9%	3.7%	5.2%	13,268	29.0%	13.6%	6.0%	21.3%	4.2%

Table E-3: Places—Educational Attainment—*Continued*

	13 to 17		18 to 24					25 to 31					
				Percent					Percent				
	Total Population	Percent Enrolled in School	Total Population	High School	Some College	Associates Degree	Bachelors Degree	Total Population	High School	Some College	Associates Degree	Bachelors Degree	Advanced Degree
Georgia													
Athens-Clarke County unified govt (bal)	4,249	97.7%	36,028	22.0%	47.8%	3.8%	19.5%	13,785	15.4%	26.9%	2.6%	29.7%	16.9%
Atlanta city	19,055	97.9%	61,305	17.8%	51.8%	2.8%	16.8%	62,935	14.8%	18.2%	5.9%	35.7%	20.1%
Augusta-Richmond County consolidated govt (bal)	12,556	94.7%	21,555	40.5%	34.1%	2.0%	8.1%	23,346	25.0%	24.2%	7.8%	20.3%	8.8%
Columbus city	12,803	99.1%	24,790	25.8%	46.3%	2.2%	11.6%	20,537	21.3%	36.6%	9.3%	15.9%	5.4%
Macon city	6,372	100.0%	11,218	33.8%	44.1%	0.0%	6.8%	9,242	37.7%	14.5%	8.1%	12.6%	4.8%
Roswell city	6,632	99.4%	8,294	23.3%	40.5%	0.0%	20.8%	8,569	13.8%	18.9%	11.5%	36.4%	9.4%
Sandy Springs city	5,499	100.0%	4,983	19.2%	33.7%	3.0%	24.8%	14,815	20.7%	17.6%	4.3%	36.5%	14.6%
Savannah city	7,282	99.3%	20,003	32.4%	46.2%	1.9%	5.7%	17,750	20.0%	28.4%	5.2%	19.3%	12.2%
Hawaii													
Urban Honolulu CDP	18,889	97.3%	31,461	27.8%	46.6%	8.6%	10.8%	37,505	21.7%	24.4%	8.0%	29.9%	8.4%
Idaho													
Boise City city	15,322	95.9%	23,692	29.7%	42.0%	7.2%	10.1%	23,021	26.8%	27.8%	9.8%	23.4%	7.5%
Illinois													
Aurora city	14,448	95.2%	17,229	20.6%	35.7%	5.0%	12.0%	21,072	15.2%	23.1%	3.6%	19.7%	9.0%
Chicago city	155,567	96.5%	281,004	26.9%	39.3%	4.3%	14.1%	357,011	18.0%	18.3%	5.0%	33.3%	16.1%
Elgin city	7,963	96.5%	12,274	34.8%	43.0%	4.0%	6.1%	11,373	36.1%	11.3%	11.7%	17.3%	8.1%
Joliet city	10,942	98.6%	15,649	33.9%	41.0%	3.1%	9.6%	14,193	30.4%	19.0%	3.9%	21.0%	8.7%
Naperville city	12,006	97.4%	11,662	18.6%	51.8%	2.1%	20.9%	12,789	12.3%	24.9%	7.0%	41.6%	9.2%
Peoria city	6,867	89.9%	13,512	23.7%	43.2%	6.1%	15.8%	13,213	23.0%	15.0%	8.5%	33.0%	11.8%
Rockford city	11,191	98.8%	15,357	42.0%	28.7%	10.4%	3.7%	13,747	19.1%	27.7%	9.7%	19.3%	6.4%
Springfield city	6,652	99.7%	11,506	19.9%	44.5%	4.4%	14.6%	11,973	18.8%	32.8%	6.0%	26.2%	12.9%
Indiana													
Evansville city	6,633	98.4%	13,002	30.1%	47.4%	0.3%	7.2%	11,110	33.1%	32.6%	9.6%	13.7%	5.2%
Fort Wayne city	17,031	98.2%	24,853	35.8%	35.0%	4.8%	7.3%	25,279	17.3%	32.9%	11.0%	23.2%	2.3%
Indianapolis city (bal)	50,763	94.7%	82,156	28.4%	34.8%	3.0%	12.6%	98,908	20.8%	27.3%	6.3%	24.6%	8.5%
South Bend city	6,461	94.8%	12,876	38.3%	48.2%	0.0%	6.0%	8,282	29.6%	31.9%	3.1%	16.4%	11.8%
Iowa													
Cedar Rapids city	9,113	98.9%	11,166	32.0%	43.3%	6.9%	9.2%	14,360	12.8%	25.1%	23.4%	23.4%	9.5%
Davenport city	6,652	100.0%	9,550	34.5%	27.3%	9.3%	11.4%	10,268	20.5%	18.3%	3.2%	33.9%	14.7%
Des Moines city	10,741	99.1%	19,910	33.2%	32.1%	7.9%	17.7%	26,312	30.0%	22.5%	12.1%	20.6%	5.1%
Kansas													
Kansas City city	10,777	97.9%	14,343	40.0%	31.2%	6.9%	7.4%	14,219	29.2%	13.2%	11.5%	13.0%	7.2%
Olathe city	9,513	100.0%	11,796	25.4%	41.8%	12.0%	12.1%	11,482	11.8%	22.0%	16.7%	36.8%	5.7%
Overland Park city	14,789	100.0%	13,831	19.4%	42.9%	2.7%	13.7%	17,248	10.5%	12.2%	11.0%	48.3%	13.2%
Topeka city	7,891	98.0%	13,574	27.6%	41.8%	4.8%	5.8%	11,068	26.0%	26.7%	5.5%	26.4%	4.7%
Wichita city	29,488	96.9%	35,181	24.1%	43.9%	8.6%	8.9%	41,249	21.0%	31.6%	8.6%	22.6%	6.0%
Kentucky													
Lexington-Fayette urban county	15,950	97.0%	42,981	24.3%	50.4%	2.8%	13.1%	32,524	15.1%	20.3%	13.5%	23.3%	13.1%
Louisville/Jefferson County metro govt (bal)	39,634	99.5%	55,865	25.9%	40.3%	4.5%	10.6%	59,656	22.5%	22.8%	9.1%	25.5%	11.6%
Louisiana													
Baton Rouge city	13,155	97.3%	42,340	24.3%	49.1%	2.4%	8.1%	25,399	27.7%	22.7%	4.4%	31.1%	8.0%
Lafayette city	9,071	97.7%	16,123	19.6%	54.3%	0.6%	9.9%	15,819	17.1%	30.1%	4.4%	33.1%	7.9%
New Orleans city	18,610	93.7%	40,095	24.0%	45.6%	1.5%	11.0%	48,879	16.1%	23.9%	4.2%	28.5%	14.9%
Shreveport city	13,881	94.9%	22,368	35.1%	27.2%	0.9%	6.3%	20,225	29.8%	24.9%	7.0%	18.8%	2.5%
Maryland													
Baltimore city	29,538	96.8%	66,366	26.5%	38.6%	3.2%	15.8%	81,284	26.0%	18.2%	3.0%	24.5%	17.5%
Massachusetts													
Boston city	30,568	99.4%	93,252	22.6%	48.9%	2.7%	17.9%	109,618	14.1%	14.9%	5.2%	41.2%	22.0%
Brockton city	6,446	88.9%	7,019	25.4%	41.7%	3.9%	8.1%	11,658	33.8%	26.1%	6.0%	18.0%	9.3%
Cambridge city	3,640	97.8%	21,135	26.1%	42.8%	2.0%	27.0%	20,406	3.9%	2.2%	1.3%	49.5%	40.6%
Lowell city	7,272	93.3%	13,159	40.4%	38.2%	1.6%	12.2%	12,922	26.7%	17.8%	7.6%	27.5%	13.2%
Lynn city	5,551	99.3%	8,255	25.5%	40.6%	0.0%	3.9%	8,758	28.5%	25.3%	9.3%	11.9%	5.8%
New Bedford city	6,054	96.6%	8,700	41.8%	29.7%	0.9%	13.9%	10,265	33.9%	15.9%	14.4%	13.2%	6.1%
Springfield city	12,077	92.1%	19,946	29.7%	40.8%	3.3%	2.6%	14,450	29.7%	23.5%	8.5%	13.7%	6.1%
Worcester city	11,319	99.2%	25,113	38.0%	40.3%	3.6%	14.5%	20,129	25.8%	19.8%	7.6%	25.2%	13.0%
Michigan													
Ann Arbor city	4,021	100.0%	35,322	7.9%	59.8%	0.2%	28.8%	13,009	6.0%	14.3%	7.1%	36.2%	32.4%
Dearborn city	7,181	96.8%	11,174	21.0%	55.4%	8.3%	8.6%	8,875	14.6%	30.6%	13.5%	13.3%	19.6%
Detroit city	47,250	96.3%	82,750	33.3%	36.8%	1.7%	3.3%	58,753	27.5%	31.5%	6.1%	11.2%	4.1%
Flint city	7,032	91.2%	6,592	37.5%	36.2%	3.0%	2.2%	11,304	32.0%	42.5%	4.6%	2.1%	0.0%
Grand Rapids city	10,731	96.7%	22,957	23.0%	45.1%	4.3%	19.5%	25,469	16.1%	20.3%	11.4%	31.0%	7.6%
Lansing city	5,727	90.6%	14,224	18.4%	44.9%	0.5%	19.1%	15,512	9.9%	41.3%	7.9%	23.3%	12.3%
Livonia city	6,151	98.6%	7,551	27.9%	32.7%	11.1%	11.0%	7,554	28.7%	14.9%	10.1%	22.9%	16.1%
Sterling Heights city	8,168	99.3%	9,328	23.6%	44.0%	4.0%	11.3%	10,488	26.4%	25.4%	5.5%	20.1%	17.9%
Warren city	6,537	100.0%	13,462	21.7%	36.2%	11.9%	6.4%	13,278	31.6%	25.4%	8.2%	18.6%	6.0%
Minnesota													
Minneapolis city	16,951	97.7%	50,657	18.0%	47.3%	6.1%	19.8%	66,958	13.5%	17.6%	6.8%	40.9%	13.3%
Rochester city	6,253	97.9%	10,278	15.7%	41.6%	14.4%	21.4%	10,331	18.5%	17.2%	11.6%	27.4%	21.5%
St. Paul city	18,717	97.7%	35,185	23.6%	43.5%	4.4%	9.3%	36,656	16.9%	16.3%	4.4%	41.6%	9.8%

Table E-3: Places—Educational Attainment—*Continued*

	13 to 17		18 to 24					25 to 31					
				Percent					Percent				
	Total Population	Percent Enrolled in School	Total Population	High School	Some College	Associates Degree	Bachelors Degree	Total Population	High School	Some College	Associates Degree	Bachelors Degree	Advanced Degree
Mississippi													
Jackson city	11,334	96.7%	21,229	22.9%	48.4%	2.5%	9.3%	19,681	22.9%	25.4%	5.3%	18.8%	11.6%
Missouri													
Columbia city	7,104	98.9%	28,006	14.2%	67.9%	1.8%	12.8%	16,810	23.4%	23.0%	6.0%	27.3%	16.3%
Independence city	7,908	100.0%	10,039	30.3%	43.4%	8.5%	3.8%	8,920	21.3%	34.4%	8.5%	15.0%	7.2%
Kansas City city	28,430	96.0%	46,153	36.4%	30.2%	1.8%	16.8%	58,617	22.6%	27.0%	6.7%	26.0%	10.1%
Lee's Summit city	8,398	100.0%	5,779	32.8%	36.8%	4.3%	10.9%	8,090	9.0%	28.3%	6.8%	30.9%	13.5%
Springfield city	9,578	97.2%	27,960	20.7%	52.5%	3.2%	13.3%	20,876	17.3%	28.5%	6.6%	27.6%	13.5%
St. Louis city	15,920	97.6%	31,990	28.6%	34.2%	2.2%	19.0%	44,419	15.0%	16.5%	6.4%	30.5%	20.0%
Montana													
Billings city	6,438	97.5%	12,115	30.5%	41.2%	2.3%	6.6%	9,279	25.9%	30.0%	8.5%	17.5%	10.6%
Nebraska													
Lincoln city	15,690	98.2%	39,030	13.2%	60.3%	6.5%	12.0%	28,205	19.3%	26.1%	11.5%	26.5%	11.2%
Omaha city	27,454	99.4%	41,799	24.7%	51.8%	2.3%	11.8%	48,253	14.8%	22.2%	9.1%	31.6%	12.5%
Nevada													
Henderson city	15,235	95.9%	21,476	39.7%	32.6%	5.7%	9.7%	22,921	16.6%	38.4%	9.0%	19.5%	4.5%
Las Vegas city	41,666	98.2%	51,928	35.8%	33.6%	4.6%	4.7%	59,192	29.3%	26.7%	7.8%	16.1%	3.3%
North Las Vegas city	18,438	96.7%	22,742	32.9%	32.7%	5.7%	6.1%	26,289	28.7%	24.2%	14.9%	12.1%	2.0%
Reno city	14,578	98.6%	27,486	25.7%	41.4%	8.0%	8.5%	25,859	21.8%	21.5%	7.2%	29.9%	5.9%
Sparks city	5,092	98.7%	8,659	26.9%	43.5%	8.5%	1.0%	8,481	28.6%	33.8%	2.5%	14.0%	0.0%
New Hampshire													
Manchester city	5,627	92.9%	11,409	37.8%	32.1%	3.4%	10.4%	13,147	23.9%	22.2%	5.8%	25.5%	5.9%
New Jersey													
Elizabeth city	8,550	97.1%	13,165	39.6%	39.3%	2.8%	4.8%	15,640	34.8%	23.4%	6.9%	9.9%	6.8%
Jersey City city	12,868	96.6%	22,404	19.0%	42.2%	1.7%	26.4%	38,721	19.8%	14.0%	4.3%	30.9%	25.5%
Newark city	16,673	96.3%	29,094	29.4%	43.9%	6.0%	8.4%	36,097	34.3%	24.0%	4.7%	15.2%	2.8%
Paterson city	10,214	92.7%	17,606	29.7%	38.7%	7.4%	3.6%	14,156	46.1%	19.0%	4.0%	9.1%	3.2%
New Mexico													
Albuquerque city	33,796	97.6%	58,842	28.3%	41.5%	4.0%	7.5%	54,748	26.1%	27.1%	7.0%	18.3%	11.7%
Las Cruces city	6,347	99.9%	19,157	18.6%	66.5%	4.8%	6.9%	7,616	14.1%	34.8%	10.5%	21.7%	11.3%
Rio Rancho city	6,850	98.5%	7,932	22.8%	31.0%	9.4%	0.0%	7,728	25.6%	41.7%	6.9%	4.9%	7.8%
New York													
Albany city	3,915	100.0%	20,309	21.7%	44.6%	13.8%	18.3%	14,704	16.9%	15.2%	9.9%	28.5%	24.5%
Buffalo city	17,057	98.9%	32,188	29.3%	40.0%	2.4%	13.4%	30,643	17.2%	20.2%	10.7%	22.9%	15.4%
New York city	449,663	97.2%	798,163	23.4%	38.4%	5.0%	17.0%	1014,121	19.1%	15.2%	7.0%	33.2%	13.5%
Rochester city	13,571	95.4%	24,555	25.8%	33.4%	6.1%	8.6%	29,417	19.0%	22.2%	9.8%	21.2%	11.6%
Syracuse city	7,218	98.4%	24,887	16.9%	57.9%	1.7%	9.9%	18,013	25.5%	17.5%	9.5%	24.0%	11.7%
Yonkers city	12,187	98.1%	18,205	21.1%	45.0%	4.6%	15.9%	18,266	18.0%	19.7%	6.0%	23.5%	12.4%
North Carolina													
Charlotte city	49,767	98.2%	75,363	26.9%	38.6%	1.9%	17.6%	93,254	14.1%	20.2%	6.8%	34.4%	10.9%
Durham city	12,441	99.2%	25,653	16.8%	48.2%	1.1%	19.1%	35,049	10.1%	16.4%	5.1%	35.9%	21.6%
Fayetteville city	13,528	99.0%	25,924	29.2%	47.8%	3.6%	9.0%	25,605	19.4%	41.1%	9.2%	13.7%	5.2%
Greensboro city	15,724	93.7%	34,083	25.8%	49.0%	4.6%	10.0%	30,190	18.9%	29.4%	4.6%	28.4%	10.4%
High Point city	6,602	99.2%	11,627	28.7%	46.9%	1.8%	6.0%	10,238	30.0%	24.3%	8.1%	15.6%	4.7%
Raleigh city	33,064	96.9%	52,777	22.0%	46.1%	2.5%	19.5%	52,519	14.3%	15.2%	4.6%	39.3%	15.8%
Wilmington city	5,293	93.0%	17,952	24.2%	57.2%	1.7%	9.0%	12,989	15.5%	28.1%	17.5%	21.4%	7.7%
Winston-Salem city	15,317	97.8%	27,308	31.1%	41.0%	1.8%	12.9%	19,756	23.4%	19.4%	8.1%	23.6%	11.0%
North Dakota													
Fargo city	5,023	100.0%	23,311	15.2%	46.7%	8.8%	23.8%	15,383	15.3%	32.6%	14.6%	23.9%	11.7%
Ohio													
Akron city	8,990	98.8%	24,800	24.6%	45.2%	7.7%	8.4%	20,695	31.0%	16.8%	13.9%	20.9%	8.0%
Cincinnati city	15,160	99.8%	39,783	29.7%	42.8%	1.8%	12.2%	36,235	21.1%	13.7%	5.6%	31.2%	11.4%
Cleveland city	23,722	95.5%	46,059	33.1%	32.5%	1.5%	10.2%	37,667	23.3%	26.6%	4.9%	15.4%	7.2%
Columbus city	56,527	98.4%	89,448	24.7%	41.4%	3.4%	14.1%	107,536	22.4%	20.0%	7.8%	28.6%	12.0%
Dayton city	8,849	100.0%	23,431	21.4%	46.2%	3.9%	6.3%	14,200	16.9%	33.3%	10.2%	16.3%	8.8%
Toledo city	16,083	99.4%	31,680	28.8%	45.6%	2.8%	4.7%	30,360	26.8%	32.5%	10.7%	12.0%	6.5%
Oklahoma													
Broken Arrow city	8,235	100.0%	8,364	31.5%	36.1%	9.2%	5.6%	9,703	29.3%	31.3%	4.8%	24.5%	4.0%
Lawton city	5,921	93.0%	15,406	47.2%	32.1%	2.3%	7.8%	12,212	29.0%	38.2%	1.7%	18.4%	1.5%
Norman city	7,582	100.0%	19,002	35.5%	46.8%	0.2%	10.8%	17,042	17.9%	22.1%	8.3%	34.3%	8.0%
Oklahoma City city	34,238	97.3%	62,132	24.3%	41.6%	6.4%	11.3%	70,063	19.7%	26.8%	8.6%	21.1%	5.2%
Tulsa city	26,852	97.3%	39,294	31.1%	36.2%	4.8%	10.4%	42,921	24.4%	26.5%	7.0%	21.2%	7.9%
Oregon													
Beaverton city	6,011	100.0%	7,397	34.3%	24.3%	6.5%	19.4%	11,528	29.3%	20.8%	7.4%	32.1%	8.9%
Eugene city	8,787	95.6%	29,300	20.6%	63.9%	4.3%	5.7%	16,885	21.8%	43.3%	4.6%	17.9%	8.2%
Gresham city	6,992	99.0%	10,336	31.7%	40.3%	6.1%	4.9%	12,421	29.8%	30.0%	12.0%	9.5%	1.6%
Hillsboro city	6,241	100.0%	7,870	20.0%	43.3%	7.8%	11.4%	11,317	20.2%	20.5%	3.9%	32.1%	8.7%
Portland city	27,860	97.6%	53,240	24.3%	46.0%	3.5%	13.1%	78,665	13.8%	22.2%	9.8%	35.1%	12.5%
Salem city	9,997	94.0%	16,978	35.7%	44.4%	4.0%	3.9%	17,782	29.5%	28.8%	6.7%	14.0%	7.8%

Table E-3: Places—Educational Attainment—*Continued*

| | 13 to 17 | | 18 to 24 | | | | | 25 to 31 | | | | | |
| | | | | Percent | | | | | Percent | | | | |
	Total Population	Percent Enrolled in School	Total Population	High School	Some College	Associates Degree	Bachelors Degree	Total Population	High School	Some College	Associates Degree	Bachelors Degree	Advanced Degree
Pennsylvania													
Allentown city	8,964	91.4%	13,580	33.5%	39.4%	10.1%	1.5%	12,602	29.4%	26.2%	9.1%	13.2%	4.1%
Erie city	4,892	91.4%	13,353	32.3%	38.4%	1.2%	15.9%	12,796	44.9%	11.2%	5.3%	19.5%	8.2%
Philadelphia city	87,644	96.2%	179,729	32.1%	40.2%	3.6%	11.2%	187,507	26.8%	17.4%	4.3%	26.4%	14.7%
Pittsburgh city	14,531	97.0%	50,254	18.3%	49.6%	3.3%	23.0%	38,294	16.1%	16.2%	11.1%	31.2%	22.5%
Rhode Island													
Providence city	10,962	91.2%	30,447	20.2%	49.5%	3.8%	14.4%	22,974	15.4%	28.8%	5.1%	24.5%	15.0%
South Carolina													
Charleston city	7,539	100.0%	16,578	22.0%	52.5%	3.5%	15.3%	17,610	10.1%	17.5%	9.0%	38.9%	17.0%
Columbia city	8,176	92.8%	33,216	25.3%	56.3%	1.6%	8.5%	18,070	14.2%	28.1%	7.3%	26.6%	9.1%
North Charleston city	6,796	96.2%	16,645	37.4%	37.1%	5.2%	3.8%	10,628	10.3%	21.0%	19.3%	25.9%	3.0%
South Dakota													
Sioux Falls city	7,691	100.0%	15,987	24.3%	50.8%	8.2%	10.3%	19,442	22.9%	19.2%	15.0%	30.6%	7.2%
Tennessee													
Chattanooga city	11,328	98.9%	18,173	26.3%	41.8%	3.8%	11.6%	18,396	18.4%	27.3%	8.2%	19.3%	10.2%
Clarksville city	9,909	96.3%	17,831	34.8%	40.5%	4.8%	11.7%	21,990	21.6%	36.0%	11.9%	22.8%	6.1%
Knoxville city	9,223	95.3%	33,690	30.5%	49.7%	2.9%	11.3%	23,611	23.5%	19.2%	7.0%	28.7%	15.8%
Memphis city	42,111	97.0%	73,486	33.9%	36.1%	2.6%	10.4%	73,223	23.9%	27.1%	6.8%	16.4%	7.2%
Murfreesboro city	6,260	97.4%	21,810	27.7%	47.9%	4.5%	13.2%	14,961	20.8%	33.6%	6.6%	21.2%	7.9%
Nashville-Davidson metropolitan govt (bal)	32,158	99.2%	64,157	26.8%	44.1%	3.7%	14.9%	85,646	16.7%	17.3%	6.4%	37.3%	11.8%
Texas													
Abilene city	7,916	97.9%	17,581	29.1%	50.3%	4.0%	5.5%	14,055	17.9%	37.0%	8.9%	18.7%	6.7%
Amarillo city	12,209	97.5%	20,974	31.3%	39.9%	5.6%	6.9%	21,743	22.8%	28.8%	8.4%	12.9%	4.9%
Arlington city	30,675	99.5%	38,088	25.6%	45.3%	7.3%	5.7%	43,442	25.0%	24.8%	9.7%	23.9%	2.9%
Austin city	50,107	96.0%	96,859	23.9%	49.2%	2.1%	13.0%	133,406	13.0%	22.9%	3.9%	40.0%	10.8%
Beaumont city	7,244	93.4%	15,412	38.2%	44.2%	1.7%	3.8%	11,553	22.6%	37.7%	7.4%	20.0%	3.3%
Brownsville city	17,348	95.7%	21,080	32.4%	41.7%	6.7%	4.6%	15,496	24.3%	37.4%	6.0%	9.6%	3.2%
Carrollton city	7,244	99.1%	12,278	26.5%	43.8%	5.9%	17.8%	13,863	13.1%	28.8%	7.9%	30.7%	13.1%
College Station city	7,447	97.6%	37,647	14.8%	61.2%	5.0%	14.1%	16,700	12.4%	19.1%	13.0%	30.5%	15.7%
Corpus Christi city	21,957	98.2%	33,162	32.1%	38.8%	6.0%	12.3%	30,950	32.0%	29.4%	9.4%	15.4%	2.5%
Dallas city	80,397	97.6%	129,394	29.3%	33.1%	4.1%	10.5%	153,400	24.4%	18.6%	5.5%	23.0%	8.8%
Denton city	9,021	96.0%	24,350	18.8%	58.6%	4.7%	7.3%	18,586	20.0%	28.6%	8.9%	23.4%	10.6%
El Paso city	50,508	95.6%	74,001	28.7%	45.7%	5.8%	5.8%	66,579	22.8%	39.2%	6.0%	16.0%	6.1%
Fort Worth city	58,152	98.5%	76,339	29.7%	39.9%	3.7%	9.5%	88,369	23.5%	24.5%	7.4%	21.5%	6.4%
Frisco city	9,692	97.2%	8,604	38.3%	35.9%	6.5%	11.4%	10,337	12.8%	27.9%	6.6%	30.6%	15.8%
Garland city	18,363	99.7%	24,159	23.9%	50.1%	4.0%	8.6%	22,411	25.7%	28.5%	9.2%	11.0%	7.1%
Grand Prairie city	15,751	98.2%	19,830	35.0%	41.4%	6.6%	1.2%	16,483	36.2%	21.4%	3.9%	13.2%	3.1%
Houston city	147,061	97.1%	224,553	29.0%	34.9%	2.6%	12.2%	291,146	23.6%	19.5%	5.6%	25.2%	10.9%
Irving city	14,236	94.6%	23,396	31.2%	40.6%	3.0%	7.9%	27,178	16.5%	22.9%	8.8%	22.6%	11.3%
Killeen city	10,138	100.0%	16,852	37.2%	36.3%	4.3%	7.0%	19,199	27.1%	46.1%	10.3%	11.7%	2.8%
Laredo city	20,972	99.5%	27,273	36.5%	41.0%	2.3%	2.5%	23,201	30.5%	25.7%	10.3%	10.5%	4.6%
Lewisville city	5,761	100.0%	8,767	28.4%	38.4%	4.9%	8.8%	13,709	19.4%	20.0%	6.4%	36.6%	8.4%
Lubbock city	17,086	94.7%	43,705	26.7%	46.4%	3.9%	11.3%	27,015	26.4%	28.3%	10.3%	19.6%	6.4%
McAllen city	12,943	96.4%	14,982	21.2%	48.3%	2.1%	6.2%	11,499	21.0%	20.9%	7.2%	29.7%	4.4%
McKinney city	12,649	98.0%	11,353	33.7%	35.2%	4.0%	10.0%	12,028	24.0%	20.4%	8.7%	33.1%	7.3%
Mesquite city	10,082	98.3%	15,853	28.1%	44.5%	4.1%	7.8%	14,522	16.1%	38.9%	6.6%	13.6%	3.0%
Midland city	8,615	100.0%	13,360	32.5%	32.4%	0.4%	12.2%	14,827	22.8%	24.8%	1.7%	23.5%	8.0%
Odessa city	8,009	99.1%	12,319	33.1%	26.8%	5.4%	7.4%	12,521	26.5%	32.3%	5.3%	12.7%	4.1%
Pasadena city	13,451	92.5%	18,164	35.3%	25.8%	4.0%	8.6%	12,887	28.5%	24.3%	5.9%	11.4%	0.7%
Pearland city	4,841	98.0%	8,755	11.5%	62.2%	4.6%	12.9%	11,202	13.4%	28.2%	5.4%	37.7%	13.6%
Plano city	20,584	94.8%	21,028	23.3%	41.0%	2.0%	21.6%	24,682	10.8%	21.3%	7.4%	41.6%	16.6%
Richardson city	6,349	100.0%	8,366	12.9%	41.3%	3.8%	16.4%	10,832	27.0%	21.2%	3.0%	22.2%	19.0%
Round Rock city	10,216	98.9%	9,366	32.4%	38.9%	2.0%	10.8%	10,481	28.3%	29.5%	4.3%	16.4%	8.5%
San Angelo city	7,399	99.6%	11,694	34.2%	50.1%	2.0%	7.4%	12,061	32.3%	13.1%	16.1%	20.0%	0.8%
San Antonio city	99,976	98.3%	157,599	32.0%	38.8%	3.9%	9.8%	153,279	25.5%	28.1%	7.5%	20.3%	7.0%
Tyler city	6,031	95.3%	10,887	29.1%	41.3%	5.0%	7.6%	11,620	21.4%	34.2%	8.3%	26.1%	2.4%
Waco city	8,203	96.1%	25,064	18.7%	52.7%	2.8%	13.0%	12,838	23.0%	32.5%	8.9%	10.1%	7.8%
Wichita Falls city	5,381	96.9%	14,389	38.1%	42.0%	6.5%	7.8%	12,667	37.4%	25.3%	9.7%	15.0%	3.5%
Utah													
Orem city	9,224	99.5%	15,432	31.6%	45.6%	10.8%	2.4%	10,400	9.3%	44.1%	10.2%	27.9%	3.7%
Provo city	6,291	98.4%	41,722	12.2%	67.0%	7.9%	8.0%	15,986	9.6%	24.6%	11.2%	44.9%	5.2%
Salt Lake City city	9,576	100.0%	26,404	26.8%	45.5%	9.8%	10.1%	26,725	19.6%	24.6%	5.4%	30.5%	13.6%
West Jordan city	11,957	97.4%	9,300	39.4%	31.9%	8.8%	2.6%	10,664	22.5%	28.4%	19.9%	18.9%	5.1%
West Valley City city	10,153	99.4%	13,843	45.4%	30.2%	2.5%	1.3%	15,680	45.0%	22.8%	12.2%	8.5%	1.1%
Virginia													
Alexandria city	4,681	95.5%	8,303	12.7%	41.4%	6.4%	27.2%	26,885	10.8%	15.4%	2.9%	41.0%	23.2%
Chesapeake city	16,601	98.8%	21,964	41.9%	32.7%	4.0%	8.7%	22,901	25.6%	31.0%	9.4%	20.4%	6.0%
Hampton city	8,750	100.0%	16,646	25.8%	56.9%	3.6%	3.5%	15,772	18.8%	45.9%	10.2%	9.8%	2.5%
Newport News city	10,976	99.8%	22,747	27.8%	43.2%	5.7%	13.9%	20,844	26.1%	34.6%	7.3%	14.7%	8.9%
Norfolk city	13,003	97.9%	45,302	40.1%	43.4%	3.0%	5.1%	34,255	25.0%	30.6%	11.3%	18.6%	5.8%
Portsmouth city	4,858	97.6%	10,561	43.1%	33.7%	3.1%	12.3%	11,325	24.6%	27.6%	13.3%	20.9%	4.5%
Richmond city	8,840	94.1%	30,207	31.7%	42.2%	2.5%	11.3%	31,718	20.2%	24.1%	3.8%	25.3%	15.0%
Roanoke city	4,118	97.1%	9,135	32.2%	42.5%	2.1%	7.6%	10,878	32.2%	14.5%	11.1%	21.5%	8.7%
Virginia Beach city	24,779	97.8%	47,498	32.4%	44.0%	3.7%	8.7%	52,685	22.6%	34.3%	12.4%	21.7%	6.6%

Table E-3: Places—Educational Attainment—*Continued*

	13 to 17		18 to 24					25 to 31					
				Percent					Percent				
	Total Population	Percent Enrolled in School	Total Population	High School	Some College	Associates Degree	Bachelors Degree	Total Population	High School	Some College	Associates Degree	Bachelors Degree	Advanced Degree
Washington													
Bellevue city	7,907	100.0%	7,892	24.3%	35.0%	5.3%	16.5%	16,432	7.8%	14.1%	7.1%	43.4%	26.3%
Everett city	7,608	97.6%	11,276	32.2%	48.4%	3.5%	5.5%	10,321	29.8%	29.8%	11.3%	22.3%	0.9%
Federal Way city	7,561	100.0%	8,597	41.2%	36.4%	10.5%	4.9%	10,225	29.4%	36.3%	8.8%	12.0%	0.5%
Kent city	7,583	98.4%	11,821	16.8%	38.1%	13.0%	8.6%	15,126	22.4%	22.8%	9.9%	16.8%	7.8%
Renton city	6,135	97.3%	7,783	33.8%	28.1%	13.8%	16.1%	12,165	18.3%	25.8%	3.6%	20.2%	11.5%
Seattle city	27,121	96.6%	71,283	18.3%	39.5%	5.1%	28.5%	105,232	8.9%	18.0%	4.4%	45.2%	17.7%
Spokane city	11,781	98.9%	25,919	20.5%	53.0%	4.7%	11.5%	23,818	32.8%	27.3%	8.2%	16.8%	6.4%
Spokane Valley city	6,650	98.0%	5,998	33.4%	42.9%	5.0%	7.6%	10,724	35.2%	24.2%	8.0%	21.6%	4.5%
Tacoma city	11,780	98.3%	20,040	21.9%	42.4%	2.4%	10.8%	24,312	19.8%	27.3%	11.9%	18.0%	4.4%
Vancouver city	10,825	96.6%	14,568	37.0%	32.6%	8.9%	9.7%	16,353	29.2%	30.1%	16.0%	9.6%	3.3%
Yakima city	6,635	90.2%	10,717	27.5%	26.9%	2.8%	5.7%	8,808	40.1%	30.5%	3.3%	8.8%	0.5%
Wisconsin													
Green Bay city	7,600	93.3%	11,960	25.1%	46.7%	3.3%	10.7%	10,960	35.0%	13.6%	11.6%	20.1%	5.2%
Kenosha city	7,710	100.0%	11,446	26.6%	37.3%	9.2%	12.2%	8,573	29.6%	32.4%	11.4%	16.8%	6.2%
Madison city	16,034	99.2%	41,339	16.7%	51.7%	5.9%	18.8%	37,501	11.3%	16.0%	5.1%	40.7%	20.0%
Milwaukee city	41,626	98.0%	72,453	29.0%	41.0%	4.3%	5.3%	74,651	25.2%	24.4%	9.2%	22.6%	6.6%

Table E-4: Metropolitan/Micropolitan Statistical Areas—Educational Attainment

| | 13 to 17 | | 18 to 24 | | | | | 25 to 31 | | | | | |
| | | | | Percent | | | | | Percent | | | | |
	Total Population	Percent Enrolled in School	Total Population	High School	Some College	Associates Degree	Bachelors Degree	Total Population	High School	Some College	Associates Degree	Bachelors Degree	Advanced Degree
Abilene, TX	10,295	98.0%	23,017	30.4%	47.9%	4.3%	4.3%	17,970	21.6%	34.5%	7.4%	18.0%	6.8%
Adrian, MI micro	6,644	96.7%	9,371	40.3%	42.2%	4.2%	1.2%	8,669	23.8%	39.4%	9.7%	14.8%	4.3%
Akron, OH	42,393	98.0%	80,759	31.0%	45.7%	4.7%	9.7%	61,851	24.9%	20.2%	12.1%	25.6%	11.0%
Albany-Schenectady-Troy, NY	50,969	98.0%	94,295	25.8%	42.2%	9.2%	12.7%	75,888	23.2%	17.7%	14.3%	23.4%	16.5%
Albany, GA	10,397	93.3%	18,490	32.9%	31.3%	2.6%	2.1%	16,012	26.9%	39.3%	5.0%	10.0%	4.8%
Albany, OR	6,733	98.4%	15,636	29.8%	58.2%	3.2%	4.6%	8,269	21.1%	20.2%	11.5%	38.2%	7.3%
Albertville, AL micro	7,439	98.4%	6,743	43.8%	30.4%	4.8%	4.9%	8,670	22.9%	13.3%	20.7%	19.7%	1.5%
Albuquerque, NM	59,465	97.2%	86,268	27.5%	39.7%	5.8%	6.4%	86,523	25.5%	25.6%	6.6%	17.2%	10.2%
Alexandria, LA	11,127	97.2%	14,798	39.5%	35.6%	2.0%	7.8%	15,070	25.9%	31.9%	7.6%	12.4%	2.0%
Allentown-Bethlehem-Easton, PA-NJ	55,437	98.0%	75,340	31.9%	40.5%	7.4%	10.0%	69,565	24.4%	20.7%	7.9%	27.4%	11.3%
Altoona, PA	6,521	99.2%	12,217	56.6%	27.2%	1.3%	5.5%	10,280	43.9%	11.6%	12.5%	16.7%	2.8%
Amarillo, TX	16,606	97.8%	26,298	33.6%	39.0%	5.5%	7.6%	26,914	21.6%	29.6%	8.5%	15.4%	5.1%
Ames, IA	4,194	96.6%	25,348	5.8%	67.8%	9.5%	14.4%	9,972	17.5%	18.4%	4.5%	34.8%	24.0%
Anchorage, AK	29,436	92.0%	45,083	35.9%	42.5%	2.0%	5.4%	45,086	23.8%	36.6%	6.1%	21.7%	6.5%
Ann Arbor, MI	19,383	97.0%	64,295	15.6%	53.5%	2.7%	23.2%	36,258	10.6%	23.5%	6.5%	32.9%	22.4%
Anniston-Oxford-Jacksonville, AL	6,696	98.8%	11,943	28.0%	47.1%	1.5%	7.9%	10,550	41.0%	23.9%	3.6%	14.3%	4.1%
Appleton, WI	14,719	100.0%	21,776	38.3%	38.8%	3.7%	7.8%	20,703	33.0%	28.3%	11.5%	22.8%	3.0%
Asheville, NC	26,814	98.4%	33,633	26.6%	36.0%	7.2%	10.8%	36,992	29.5%	20.0%	5.3%	24.6%	12.6%
Ashtabula, OH micro	6,190	96.8%	8,246	37.7%	31.6%	3.1%	0.4%	8,300	26.4%	41.2%	8.2%	10.4%	1.7%
Athens-Clarke County, GA	10,529	97.1%	42,955	25.2%	46.6%	4.0%	16.0%	21,108	22.8%	27.5%	3.5%	22.9%	13.3%
Atlanta-Sandy Springs-Roswell, GA	395,662	97.4%	510,259	29.4%	39.3%	3.6%	9.6%	513,894	22.4%	23.7%	7.6%	24.0%	9.6%
Atlantic City-Hammonton, NJ	17,790	97.4%	26,718	35.8%	36.4%	4.3%	9.3%	22,550	29.7%	19.7%	3.2%	24.8%	6.0%
Auburn-Opelika, AL	9,237	97.8%	30,018	20.4%	49.4%	6.0%	15.6%	14,147	23.1%	17.4%	10.2%	21.3%	20.2%
Augusta-Richmond County, GA-SC	40,233	96.2%	58,079	34.6%	37.3%	3.5%	8.0%	55,809	25.3%	29.6%	8.9%	15.4%	8.2%
Augusta-Waterville, ME micro	8,147	94.1%	10,198	34.6%	44.3%	10.2%	7.8%	9,257	26.9%	33.8%	9.9%	20.3%	8.2%
Austin-Round Rock, TX	120,571	97.6%	195,346	28.1%	46.2%	2.8%	10.5%	233,683	18.2%	25.4%	5.3%	32.4%	9.2%
Bakersfield, CA	67,483	97.8%	95,288	35.3%	38.9%	6.3%	3.4%	90,977	30.5%	29.1%	7.2%	8.7%	3.7%
Baltimore-Columbia-Towson, MD	173,961	97.8%	260,777	27.6%	42.9%	5.3%	13.6%	279,796	23.7%	22.2%	7.4%	25.5%	12.6%
Bangor, ME	8,286	100.0%	18,248	32.0%	45.1%	7.1%	3.2%	13,381	28.6%	22.4%	10.9%	19.3%	7.0%
Barnstable Town, MA	10,775	98.4%	13,695	31.9%	33.8%	1.8%	12.9%	13,287	37.7%	19.9%	8.5%	22.5%	6.8%
Baton Rouge, LA	54,371	97.4%	99,623	28.7%	42.8%	2.8%	6.3%	78,834	27.5%	22.3%	7.0%	26.0%	6.7%
Battle Creek, MI	9,689	99.4%	11,086	35.9%	37.4%	2.9%	3.4%	10,299	36.3%	25.6%	10.2%	13.6%	2.4%
Bay City, MI	7,155	96.6%	9,251	49.5%	23.9%	10.9%	4.1%	9,135	33.7%	18.6%	8.7%	21.8%	14.7%
Beaumont-Port Arthur, TX	28,297	95.0%	41,111	38.1%	37.4%	3.3%	2.6%	38,385	35.0%	28.7%	5.1%	18.4%	3.5%
Beckley, WV	5,876	100.0%	11,317	46.5%	31.1%	5.9%	3.2%	10,268	33.2%	24.3%	8.8%	18.0%	7.9%
Bellingham, WA	12,958	100.0%	31,693	25.1%	43.7%	14.2%	6.4%	17,498	15.9%	32.6%	8.3%	31.2%	3.3%
Bend-Redmond, OR	12,180	95.6%	11,498	40.1%	38.5%	3.1%	6.4%	14,309	26.1%	25.0%	8.2%	26.2%	6.9%
Billings, MT	9,934	97.1%	17,198	32.5%	41.5%	1.9%	6.0%	14,191	27.1%	31.5%	8.2%	19.0%	8.3%
Binghamton, NY	14,084	98.5%	28,948	31.2%	39.4%	10.8%	9.7%	19,910	31.2%	22.8%	10.8%	20.2%	4.7%
Birmingham-Hoover, AL	76,510	96.7%	103,964	29.9%	39.4%	2.3%	10.6%	107,298	26.0%	21.9%	8.5%	21.6%	9.1%
Bismarck, ND	7,121	94.2%	12,626	20.9%	29.5%	21.1%	8.1%	14,455	10.5%	28.3%	31.3%	17.5%	10.8%
Blacksburg-Christiansburg-Radford, VA	9,013	98.4%	42,782	17.0%	63.6%	4.4%	11.1%	14,493	26.6%	21.5%	5.4%	22.8%	20.7%
Bloomington, IL	10,855	97.5%	33,533	16.4%	55.2%	10.9%	12.0%	19,327	20.6%	16.2%	12.2%	34.8%	12.7%
Bloomington, IN	8,946	99.0%	41,831	21.7%	58.9%	1.2%	14.8%	15,823	19.2%	21.0%	5.4%	32.6%	14.0%
Bloomsburg-Berwick, PA	5,342	93.5%	11,393	21.8%	51.0%	4.7%	8.9%	6,406	41.1%	12.7%	15.7%	16.3%	8.6%
Boise City, ID	49,831	98.1%	60,531	37.6%	32.7%	6.3%	8.4%	58,731	26.0%	29.0%	12.1%	21.3%	4.5%
Boston-Cambridge-Newton, MA-NH	287,948	98.1%	460,199	26.2%	41.6%	3.2%	17.7%	479,162	17.5%	16.6%	6.9%	34.8%	19.3%
Boulder, CO	20,523	98.2%	46,928	20.5%	57.6%	3.3%	12.8%	28,813	13.9%	15.5%	5.7%	41.7%	15.3%
Bowling Green, KY	9,845	98.0%	20,162	28.8%	48.1%	3.6%	7.2%	16,090	33.9%	21.5%	7.9%	11.9%	16.8%
Bremerton-Silverdale, WA	15,581	96.5%	25,705	37.0%	42.9%	4.6%	7.1%	23,899	21.7%	42.2%	7.3%	20.6%	2.6%
Bridgeport-Stamford-Norwalk, CT	64,222	98.0%	75,893	23.8%	39.6%	2.6%	18.1%	72,592	18.0%	19.2%	6.4%	29.9%	14.6%
Brownsville-Harlingen, TX	40,096	96.4%	44,095	33.3%	38.9%	6.1%	3.2%	33,550	23.3%	30.0%	6.2%	15.0%	1.8%
Brunswick, GA	6,878	97.8%	10,762	52.5%	26.4%	3.8%	1.8%	9,932	33.4%	26.1%	9.2%	14.8%	3.2%
Buffalo-Cheektowaga-Niagara Falls, NY	68,577	98.0%	113,628	27.2%	40.4%	6.2%	16.0%	104,738	19.4%	20.2%	12.9%	23.8%	15.6%
Burlington-South Burlington, VT	11,601	97.4%	28,043	16.9%	59.9%	2.3%	14.0%	20,130	19.4%	20.9%	8.2%	36.4%	7.7%
Burlington, NC	10,421	99.3%	14,914	22.6%	32.4%	3.0%	17.1%	13,510	30.6%	18.0%	8.6%	19.9%	8.6%
California-Lexington Park, MD	9,687	97.0%	10,336	34.2%	34.9%	5.1%	6.0%	8,534	24.2%	32.5%	11.9%	24.1%	1.7%
Canton-Massillon, OH	25,547	98.4%	35,605	31.0%	45.7%	4.2%	7.9%	32,199	25.4%	36.0%	7.1%	17.0%	5.6%
Cape Coral-Fort Myers, FL	34,853	97.8%	47,505	38.5%	30.7%	8.9%	5.4%	48,549	36.0%	20.0%	7.2%	18.8%	3.4%
Cape Girardeau, MO-IL	6,381	100.0%	11,316	31.4%	47.2%	1.6%	6.0%	8,643	27.2%	29.9%	11.2%	21.0%	7.1%
Carbondale-Marion, IL	9,377	100.0%	16,679	25.8%	49.9%	6.3%	4.6%	13,124	20.9%	44.2%	7.7%	9.9%	9.9%
Carson City, NV	3,278	97.3%	3,934	29.9%	43.6%	11.5%	0.0%	5,005	24.1%	23.8%	16.5%	4.9%	12.8%
Casper, WY	5,346	100.0%	7,750	29.6%	39.4%	5.9%	9.9%	8,364	27.7%	34.4%	11.6%	15.7%	3.0%
Cedar Rapids, IA	19,102	94.8%	22,914	33.6%	42.0%	8.1%	6.0%	26,270	17.1%	28.1%	19.9%	21.3%	7.8%
Chambersburg-Waynesboro, PA	8,275	98.0%	11,960	43.6%	38.1%	5.6%	5.0%	13,003	32.8%	20.9%	5.3%	19.4%	10.6%
Champaign-Urbana, IL	13,077	99.4%	51,413	16.6%	58.5%	3.9%	14.5%	26,505	27.4%	18.7%	7.4%	28.7%	12.1%
Charleston-North Charleston, SC	43,634	98.7%	74,064	29.1%	41.1%	5.3%	11.1%	75,141	17.1%	25.8%	10.1%	28.4%	8.5%
Charleston, WV	13,854	98.2%	18,423	34.0%	32.0%	3.5%	8.3%	18,065	28.1%	27.8%	10.5%	11.8%	13.0%
Charlotte-Concord-Gastonia, NC-SC	161,725	97.3%	208,491	28.8%	39.0%	4.3%	10.6%	209,266	21.5%	24.1%	8.5%	26.0%	8.0%
Charlottesville, VA	14,286	96.7%	27,546	29.9%	45.3%	4.1%	10.0%	19,067	25.4%	13.3%	3.6%	28.7%	22.9%
Chattanooga, TN-GA	33,567	97.8%	46,961	30.1%	40.9%	5.5%	6.1%	49,220	27.3%	25.7%	9.5%	17.0%	7.1%
Cheyenne, WY	5,137	100.0%	12,437	26.1%	47.9%	6.3%	6.6%	8,039	18.8%	22.4%	13.4%	20.4%	20.6%
Chicago-Naperville-Elgin, IL-IN-WI	650,051	97.7%	907,719	27.5%	39.5%	5.0%	13.9%	961,624	20.4%	22.0%	6.4%	29.9%	12.1%
Chico, CA	12,100	97.3%	33,787	30.9%	43.1%	7.0%	7.8%	19,755	19.3%	38.2%	9.3%	17.3%	5.5%
Cincinnati, OH-KY-IN	146,384	98.5%	193,039	36.2%	37.1%	3.0%	11.9%	188,981	24.4%	21.9%	8.7%	26.2%	9.3%
Clarksburg, WV micro	5,506	100.0%	6,577	38.6%	43.8%	6.4%	1.7%	6,877	39.9%	12.8%	7.5%	13.3%	17.3%
Clarksville, TN-KY	19,577	96.6%	34,064	35.4%	39.6%	3.6%	8.7%	36,102	26.1%	34.2%	10.5%	17.4%	4.8%

Table E-4: Metropolitan/Micropolitan Statistical Areas—Educational Attainment—*Continued*

| | 13 to 17 | | 18 to 24 | | | | | 25 to 31 | | | | | |
| | Total Population | Percent Enrolled in School | Total Population | Percent | | | | Total Population | Percent | | | | |
				High School	Some College	Associates Degree	Bachelors Degree		High School	Some College	Associates Degree	Bachelors Degree	Advanced Degree
Cleveland-Elyria, OH	135,379	96.4%	180,390	27.1%	40.7%	3.9%	10.2%	172,704	20.8%	24.7%	8.3%	25.0%	11.0%
Cleveland, TN	7,830	96.8%	11,815	43.5%	36.5%	1.3%	0.9%	10,284	35.6%	29.2%	7.9%	12.7%	3.4%
Coeur d'Alene, ID	9,617	98.6%	12,617	35.0%	30.3%	4.6%	12.7%	12,885	33.0%	23.5%	11.3%	17.8%	6.6%
College Station-Bryan, TX	16,637	96.8%	60,432	14.8%	63.0%	3.9%	12.5%	27,067	16.2%	23.1%	9.9%	25.8%	13.4%
Colorado Springs, CO	46,539	98.9%	71,720	26.7%	45.5%	5.1%	8.7%	71,404	17.1%	33.1%	16.4%	21.3%	4.7%
Columbia, MO	8,915	99.1%	36,413	13.9%	62.0%	3.1%	15.6%	20,117	21.6%	21.5%	7.9%	29.7%	15.3%
Columbia, SC	52,961	97.3%	97,384	28.9%	46.7%	3.7%	10.5%	74,192	20.6%	28.2%	7.6%	23.3%	7.8%
Columbus, GA-AL	20,674	98.9%	40,180	26.6%	45.3%	4.1%	7.7%	32,277	27.5%	33.0%	9.2%	13.6%	4.3%
Columbus, IN	5,242	99.0%	6,922	57.1%	22.5%	2.9%	12.7%	8,417	39.3%	7.8%	9.5%	20.5%	5.6%
Columbus, OH	133,803	98.9%	171,487	30.8%	38.6%	4.4%	12.0%	209,330	23.8%	22.7%	8.1%	25.1%	11.5%
Concord, NH micro	7,647	99.3%	12,366	25.9%	40.5%	10.4%	11.8%	9,340	28.4%	14.0%	10.1%	25.5%	9.0%
Cookeville, TN micro	6,015	100.0%	14,041	39.0%	46.9%	0.6%	4.7%	8,616	43.5%	25.6%	0.5%	12.3%	6.4%
Corpus Christi, TX	33,021	95.8%	47,608	36.7%	35.3%	4.5%	8.6%	42,706	33.3%	31.2%	8.3%	12.6%	2.2%
Corvallis, OR	7,419	98.6%	17,148	30.0%	56.3%	3.8%	4.9%	9,091	19.2%	20.9%	14.5%	37.0%	6.6%
Crestview-Fort Walton Beach-Destin, FL	14,790	97.1%	25,602	34.5%	33.8%	9.7%	8.4%	28,160	29.8%	31.0%	11.4%	16.3%	4.8%
Cumberland, MD-WV	6,863	94.8%	11,119	34.2%	46.4%	5.2%	4.3%	7,509	39.6%	26.2%	5.4%	17.8%	7.0%
Dallas-Fort Worth-Arlington, TX	488,661	97.9%	628,923	30.3%	38.3%	4.6%	8.8%	675,672	22.8%	24.0%	6.8%	24.4%	8.0%
Dalton, GA	10,281	90.0%	14,006	33.7%	37.1%	3.8%	8.9%	13,382	22.2%	32.5%	8.7%	3.2%	0.5%
Danville, IL	5,607	95.3%	6,498	39.9%	30.8%	2.6%	3.5%	7,160	58.8%	13.1%	7.4%	7.0%	0.9%
Danville, VA micro	6,207	95.3%	8,865	37.5%	45.9%	3.8%	5.0%	7,368	31.3%	35.7%	9.8%	10.1%	6.9%
Daphne-Fairhope-Foley, AL	13,134	97.8%	16,338	38.6%	20.0%	7.2%	12.3%	14,271	25.4%	27.3%	9.0%	26.4%	2.7%
Davenport-Moline-Rock Island, IA-IL	22,450	96.0%	37,821	34.5%	35.0%	7.1%	10.1%	32,259	21.3%	26.2%	9.5%	23.3%	10.8%
Dayton, OH	49,753	99.4%	81,355	24.7%	51.4%	2.9%	7.7%	72,534	19.9%	31.8%	11.1%	21.7%	8.0%
Decatur, AL	11,377	96.8%	13,146	38.5%	26.6%	4.9%	5.3%	11,358	26.8%	20.6%	11.9%	18.3%	1.1%
Decatur, IL	6,354	100.0%	10,229	37.0%	41.0%	7.5%	3.7%	9,557	24.3%	36.7%	2.8%	13.3%	6.7%
Deltona-Daytona Beach-Ormond Beach, FL	29,506	95.1%	52,478	34.6%	40.8%	9.5%	4.0%	46,853	32.7%	24.3%	14.8%	12.5%	3.7%
Denver-Aurora-Lakewood, CO	181,495	97.2%	228,854	25.6%	37.8%	5.2%	12.9%	286,801	17.6%	23.7%	7.2%	32.4%	8.6%
Des Moines-West Des Moines, IA	40,085	96.8%	47,538	30.5%	33.1%	7.9%	17.8%	63,439	23.9%	21.9%	12.1%	28.3%	5.1%
Detroit-Warren-Dearborn, MI	290,039	97.4%	382,812	28.0%	41.5%	5.1%	9.5%	354,920	21.8%	28.3%	9.1%	22.5%	8.6%
Dothan, AL	10,557	99.0%	11,453	42.8%	30.9%	5.6%	4.7%	12,742	33.3%	27.0%	10.1%	16.7%	2.3%
Dover, DE	10,917	97.8%	17,233	27.2%	45.4%	4.5%	11.9%	15,816	24.2%	20.0%	11.8%	21.0%	9.0%
Dubuque, IA	8,112	99.1%	9,974	17.7%	49.4%	16.0%	5.6%	7,213	20.9%	34.1%	14.6%	19.0%	4.3%
Duluth, MN-WI	16,919	97.4%	31,911	18.2%	49.7%	6.5%	14.0%	24,800	21.8%	26.0%	16.3%	22.1%	4.0%
Dunn, NC micro	8,830	98.8%	11,742	26.3%	45.6%	5.7%	4.0%	14,304	22.5%	25.1%	10.3%	23.2%	4.7%
Durham-Chapel Hill, NC	30,036	98.5%	62,916	22.1%	47.5%	3.6%	15.2%	57,485	12.0%	23.0%	6.2%	29.5%	19.3%
East Stroudsburg, PA	13,266	99.4%	19,021	40.2%	40.3%	9.6%	6.8%	10,573	32.9%	12.3%	14.9%	26.4%	4.0%
Eau Claire, WI	9,486	98.2%	21,989	37.5%	39.8%	3.4%	7.7%	14,910	18.2%	33.5%	15.9%	23.0%	3.7%
El Centro, CA	14,236	99.9%	20,303	25.0%	39.2%	3.2%	5.5%	18,063	29.2%	37.1%	7.1%	8.3%	1.1%
El Paso, TX	64,210	96.1%	97,204	31.5%	45.3%	5.4%	5.0%	81,406	22.2%	38.6%	6.4%	17.0%	5.3%
Elizabethtown-Fort Knox, KY	13,326	97.0%	12,405	42.6%	36.2%	3.3%	4.0%	14,186	35.6%	25.5%	5.9%	18.1%	4.1%
Elkhart-Goshen, IN	14,822	94.8%	17,694	39.9%	30.5%	1.4%	3.2%	17,121	38.6%	20.1%	6.6%	14.1%	3.4%
Elmira, NY	5,234	100.0%	8,030	28.6%	36.7%	15.8%	10.3%	8,633	31.2%	18.4%	17.1%	16.2%	9.6%
Erie, PA	15,298	97.1%	29,620	32.5%	45.8%	2.4%	10.8%	26,649	33.4%	13.8%	8.6%	22.8%	12.4%
Eugene, OR	19,356	98.0%	46,109	26.6%	55.1%	3.7%	5.4%	29,269	22.7%	42.8%	6.4%	16.9%	7.3%
Eureka-Arcata-Fortuna, CA micro	6,652	98.8%	18,113	21.0%	60.4%	5.4%	6.7%	13,592	29.6%	33.9%	3.6%	24.8%	3.1%
Evansville, IN-KY	18,675	99.1%	31,837	30.8%	46.6%	3.8%	5.6%	27,587	26.6%	32.7%	12.4%	14.9%	5.4%
Fairbanks, AK	6,177	99.2%	13,103	33.1%	42.3%	2.6%	0.4%	13,155	25.0%	21.8%	3.4%	40.5%	7.0%
Fargo, ND-MN	13,889	99.3%	39,007	20.6%	48.0%	7.6%	17.1%	26,148	18.1%	22.9%	17.8%	28.2%	10.1%
Farmington, NM	9,310	98.9%	12,308	25.7%	40.3%	10.3%	2.4%	11,027	29.1%	42.2%	7.3%	5.7%	0.9%
Fayetteville-Springdale-Rogers, AR-MO	35,894	97.0%	53,424	34.0%	40.7%	3.4%	10.1%	47,752	24.8%	22.2%	5.3%	22.5%	10.9%
Fayetteville, NC	24,421	98.2%	47,605	30.7%	44.2%	4.5%	7.3%	44,471	20.8%	39.5%	8.8%	16.6%	5.6%
Flagstaff, AZ	7,738	96.5%	26,701	22.9%	53.6%	7.6%	9.8%	14,018	19.5%	19.7%	12.3%	23.5%	10.3%
Flint, MI	30,158	96.8%	38,737	28.3%	40.7%	3.4%	6.4%	35,354	24.7%	38.0%	9.3%	13.0%	3.0%
Florence-Muscle Shoals, AL	9,406	92.7%	15,187	22.0%	47.1%	1.9%	7.3%	11,902	35.4%	35.9%	6.2%	9.9%	3.3%
Florence, SC	13,118	98.1%	19,834	16.7%	45.5%	3.8%	5.2%	16,353	28.6%	25.0%	7.9%	23.5%	4.2%
Fond du Lac, WI	7,948	100.0%	9,105	34.5%	35.1%	8.2%	4.9%	5,647	40.2%	19.1%	16.5%	17.5%	3.8%
Fort Collins, CO	19,699	99.4%	44,712	19.8%	55.7%	4.0%	12.6%	29,699	19.8%	24.5%	11.9%	31.2%	9.3%
Fort Smith, AR-OK	19,126	97.0%	25,420	37.4%	30.0%	6.5%	5.5%	26,551	35.1%	25.1%	8.9%	12.4%	3.1%
Fort Wayne, IN	29,642	95.6%	40,876	33.9%	35.9%	4.5%	5.6%	38,716	20.4%	30.3%	11.9%	22.0%	3.1%
Fresno, CA	71,245	98.3%	108,464	27.3%	43.4%	5.7%	4.5%	101,037	23.7%	30.8%	10.0%	14.7%	4.0%
Gadsden, AL	7,662	100.0%	9,315	33.2%	43.9%	7.5%	0.0%	8,012	35.7%	32.9%	7.5%	7.3%	2.5%
Gainesville, FL	12,923	98.4%	60,876	15.0%	56.5%	9.4%	13.6%	30,284	15.8%	14.9%	8.7%	33.6%	21.9%
Gainesville, GA	14,136	99.2%	17,558	30.3%	37.1%	3.5%	3.4%	16,371	32.9%	24.1%	6.8%	13.3%	3.1%
Gettysburg, PA	6,375	97.7%	10,996	39.1%	37.1%	1.6%	8.0%	6,546	37.6%	15.9%	9.3%	27.8%	2.4%
Glens Falls, NY	7,781	99.5%	10,305	39.6%	38.4%	3.0%	6.1%	9,741	38.3%	12.7%	17.4%	14.1%	8.3%
Goldsboro, NC	7,730	98.0%	11,846	32.0%	50.1%	4.0%	3.8%	11,414	9.9%	37.6%	20.2%	18.0%	3.3%
Grand Forks, ND-MN	7,718	98.8%	19,839	20.2%	65.7%	1.1%	4.4%	8,762	17.6%	17.2%	18.6%	29.2%	11.7%
Grand Island, NE	5,560	100.0%	6,752	31.4%	39.7%	0.0%	17.9%	6,511	11.0%	25.9%	12.7%	12.6%	10.4%
Grand Junction, CO	8,466	99.5%	15,894	27.6%	53.7%	4.5%	4.1%	14,985	42.5%	33.3%	3.6%	12.1%	1.1%
Grand Rapids-Wyoming, MI	71,978	98.2%	105,657	24.5%	45.5%	6.2%	11.1%	97,581	20.7%	24.3%	10.0%	28.1%	8.4%
Grants Pass, OR	4,012	92.6%	6,276	39.7%	24.2%	6.8%	7.3%	5,678	41.5%	32.0%	7.4%	4.9%	0.0%
Great Falls, MT	4,735	95.9%	8,278	25.0%	36.8%	1.4%	5.4%	9,149	20.4%	18.2%	14.6%	19.4%	12.3%
Greeley, CO	17,892	95.2%	29,349	26.8%	45.9%	3.3%	10.3%	27,777	28.4%	25.0%	10.7%	18.6%	4.8%
Green Bay, WI	23,180	96.5%	28,652	29.9%	41.9%	7.3%	10.8%	27,343	27.6%	17.6%	16.6%	26.5%	3.0%
Greensboro-High Point, NC	47,780	95.0%	73,916	29.6%	46.0%	4.1%	7.0%	67,690	25.4%	26.5%	6.7%	20.6%	7.4%
Greenville-Anderson-Mauldin, SC	57,700	96.9%	81,975	26.1%	44.2%	4.9%	7.5%	72,710	20.5%	24.8%	6.3%	19.2%	11.3%
Greenville, NC	12,815	97.1%	33,517	19.9%	51.6%	5.5%	14.9%	15,455	19.4%	29.0%	8.5%	22.6%	14.9%

Table E-4: Metropolitan/Micropolitan Statistical Areas—Educational Attainment—*Continued*

	13 to 17		18 to 24					25 to 31					
				Percent					Percent				
	Total Population	Percent Enrolled in School	Total Population	High School	Some College	Associates Degree	Bachelors Degree	Total Population	High School	Some College	Associates Degree	Bachelors Degree	Advanced Degree
Greenwood, SC micro	6,366	93.1%	10,326	32.7%	40.9%	1.4%	8.9%	7,394	35.7%	20.4%	11.8%	14.1%	8.4%
Gulfport-Biloxi-Pascagoula, MS	24,417	96.0%	36,851	31.8%	42.5%	3.9%	3.2%	38,287	31.8%	29.5%	10.8%	12.4%	3.9%
Hagerstown-Martinsburg, MD-WV	18,748	98.6%	22,838	44.2%	29.2%	5.6%	8.5%	21,487	29.4%	27.2%	8.4%	18.1%	5.3%
Hammond, LA	8,755	94.0%	14,203	34.8%	43.0%	1.1%	4.2%	14,288	27.1%	28.5%	2.2%	11.9%	0.0%
Hanford-Corcoran, CA	10,697	100.0%	17,431	41.8%	30.5%	1.0%	3.2%	17,382	25.3%	29.1%	10.5%	7.7%	1.2%
Harrisburg-Carlisle, PA	34,226	96.4%	52,087	30.9%	40.3%	5.1%	8.8%	49,754	29.3%	17.7%	10.0%	26.5%	9.0%
Harrisonburg, VA	8,231	99.3%	25,833	22.8%	59.9%	2.4%	7.4%	11,307	34.2%	23.0%	4.5%	23.5%	6.8%
Hartford-West Hartford-East Hartford, CT	78,990	98.8%	121,030	24.1%	44.7%	5.4%	13.2%	105,077	22.7%	17.8%	8.8%	29.4%	14.0%
Hattiesburg, MS	9,195	98.3%	22,591	23.5%	48.6%	4.7%	5.4%	14,510	29.2%	28.9%	3.4%	21.8%	4.5%
Hickory-Lenoir-Morganton, NC	24,437	97.3%	31,386	35.1%	36.0%	4.9%	3.3%	27,792	27.7%	23.4%	10.7%	13.8%	2.9%
Hilo, HI micro	13,272	97.2%	15,240	33.2%	43.0%	3.6%	10.7%	16,102	40.5%	23.1%	10.0%	21.4%	2.5%
Hilton Head Island-Bluffton-Beaufort, SC	10,794	98.9%	20,318	35.9%	29.9%	1.8%	7.2%	17,693	17.0%	42.2%	4.8%	17.0%	4.5%
Hinesville, GA	6,218	100.0%	11,580	33.1%	46.1%	6.2%	2.8%	10,508	30.9%	31.6%	7.6%	12.6%	4.7%
Holland, MI micro	8,408	98.8%	9,499	34.1%	39.9%	2.9%	3.2%	8,100	34.1%	25.4%	17.3%	12.4%	0.0%
Homosassa Springs, FL	6,239	92.4%	8,383	43.5%	20.1%	7.7%	0.8%	6,848	44.6%	26.6%	11.1%	3.2%	1.4%
Hot Springs, AR	5,813	96.2%	8,161	39.3%	41.2%	3.9%	4.1%	6,037	40.5%	38.4%	3.9%	5.1%	3.3%
Houma-Thibodaux, LA	13,955	96.9%	21,875	41.3%	33.6%	2.9%	5.0%	21,912	35.9%	28.2%	2.9%	13.3%	0.6%
Houston-The Woodlands-Sugar Land, TX	453,816	97.5%	585,394	32.1%	37.1%	3.5%	8.6%	654,761	25.0%	24.2%	6.5%	22.3%	8.0%
Huntington-Ashland, WV-KY-OH	26,073	96.6%	32,303	30.2%	48.5%	3.4%	3.0%	30,648	24.7%	28.4%	10.9%	14.3%	11.5%
Huntsville, AL	30,524	96.3%	43,181	27.4%	38.7%	4.8%	12.2%	43,655	19.3%	24.6%	11.9%	25.2%	7.4%
Idaho Falls, ID	12,212	91.9%	13,418	42.8%	28.7%	4.5%	11.0%	11,675	21.7%	31.7%	6.4%	17.6%	6.7%
Indianapolis-Carmel-Anderson, IN	133,996	95.9%	172,522	30.5%	35.9%	3.5%	11.5%	192,044	20.2%	27.0%	6.6%	24.8%	9.4%
Iowa City, IA	7,948	100.0%	33,957	17.2%	54.7%	4.0%	17.5%	21,679	16.8%	23.1%	8.3%	28.3%	17.6%
Ithaca, NY	4,388	100.0%	27,064	12.5%	71.8%	0.7%	14.1%	10,063	11.5%	11.3%	11.6%	41.6%	19.7%
Jackson, MI	10,254	96.6%	14,147	27.8%	44.2%	0.6%	7.4%	14,943	33.8%	33.9%	8.3%	10.2%	4.7%
Jackson, MS	42,346	95.3%	55,933	31.8%	39.5%	2.8%	9.1%	55,868	25.4%	24.8%	9.5%	19.1%	9.3%
Jackson, TN	8,709	97.4%	14,392	26.5%	55.7%	0.7%	4.3%	11,485	46.7%	24.5%	2.4%	12.7%	5.7%
Jacksonville, FL	87,849	97.4%	128,721	34.5%	32.0%	6.3%	8.6%	138,023	26.0%	26.7%	12.4%	22.2%	4.0%
Jacksonville, NC	11,202	96.2%	38,939	40.0%	35.7%	5.4%	3.5%	24,941	29.5%	40.3%	10.8%	6.9%	1.6%
Jamestown-Dunkirk-Fredonia, NY micro	8,192	90.6%	15,702	23.6%	48.6%	5.2%	7.8%	10,603	30.7%	18.6%	12.9%	11.6%	9.7%
Janesville-Beloit, WI	12,012	92.4%	14,267	38.5%	41.1%	8.2%	3.7%	13,455	43.9%	18.2%	9.1%	13.4%	7.0%
Jefferson City, MO	11,932	99.8%	14,811	28.6%	44.1%	6.7%	2.3%	13,373	43.6%	18.0%	19.4%	13.4%	0.5%
Johnson City, TN	13,143	97.5%	21,384	27.4%	51.4%	3.7%	10.9%	15,961	26.1%	22.1%	5.3%	26.3%	13.3%
Johnstown, PA	8,630	99.7%	13,064	31.0%	37.0%	3.9%	10.2%	10,546	30.2%	23.6%	10.4%	20.5%	3.9%
Jonesboro, AR	7,390	97.1%	13,440	33.7%	43.2%	4.6%	5.7%	12,406	30.7%	28.7%	9.1%	15.4%	3.9%
Joplin, MO	12,281	98.6%	17,153	33.9%	39.7%	3.8%	13.7%	16,762	28.8%	33.4%	6.1%	16.8%	5.2%
Kahului-Wailuku-Lahaina, HI	10,520	91.9%	10,449	42.4%	31.2%	7.5%	6.3%	16,276	32.5%	23.2%	16.3%	15.2%	3.8%
Kalamazoo-Portage, MI	24,233	96.5%	48,062	23.9%	55.5%	3.6%	7.7%	30,223	18.8%	31.4%	10.0%	25.9%	7.0%
Kalispell, MT micro	6,850	94.5%	6,985	52.1%	21.8%	2.9%	4.4%	6,784	28.9%	16.6%	21.8%	21.9%	3.2%
Kankakee, IL	7,763	94.9%	11,416	28.0%	53.6%	5.1%	4.8%	8,304	30.8%	45.6%	7.8%	9.2%	4.6%
Kansas City, MO-KS	139,847	98.3%	177,722	32.2%	37.4%	5.2%	12.3%	196,742	20.0%	24.9%	10.0%	26.5%	9.7%
Kennewick-Richland, WA	22,018	97.9%	24,991	42.2%	37.2%	5.7%	4.7%	25,405	25.4%	24.1%	12.3%	14.6%	4.7%
Killeen-Temple, TX	29,682	97.1%	54,892	42.7%	35.8%	4.5%	5.8%	50,656	30.9%	36.5%	10.4%	12.1%	5.7%
Kingsport-Bristol-Bristol, TN-VA	19,106	97.9%	25,175	39.6%	36.0%	5.8%	6.0%	23,456	35.0%	26.4%	6.0%	17.2%	8.9%
Kingston, NY	11,368	97.7%	18,701	27.0%	43.1%	10.0%	8.7%	13,203	22.8%	26.4%	10.5%	15.8%	7.9%
Knoxville, TN	55,117	97.0%	83,818	34.4%	41.3%	5.4%	8.7%	73,034	31.9%	20.5%	7.4%	22.7%	9.5%
Kokomo, IN	5,501	100.0%	5,932	36.0%	27.7%	4.2%	3.7%	5,730	26.9%	20.9%	18.6%	16.1%	1.2%
La Crosse-Onalaska, WI-MN	8,223	98.5%	19,433	27.2%	54.5%	4.0%	6.5%	13,011	15.7%	32.2%	22.3%	24.5%	4.1%
Lafayette-West Lafayette, IN	11,974	98.2%	47,508	28.5%	56.2%	1.5%	8.2%	21,107	25.6%	23.2%	8.5%	21.8%	15.8%
Lafayette, LA	32,527	95.2%	53,794	26.2%	45.0%	1.7%	6.6%	47,886	23.8%	26.9%	5.3%	23.7%	5.0%
Lake Charles, LA	15,397	98.2%	20,994	37.5%	38.7%	3.3%	3.6%	16,713	40.0%	26.2%	8.6%	12.6%	3.8%
Lake Havasu City-Kingman, AZ	12,002	93.3%	14,136	37.7%	29.2%	0.9%	4.9%	14,210	34.5%	30.4%	7.9%	10.7%	2.8%
Lakeland-Winter Haven, FL	38,905	96.7%	55,573	36.0%	30.3%	5.2%	2.8%	55,298	37.6%	20.6%	11.7%	13.0%	3.3%
Lancaster, PA	35,519	95.0%	50,538	39.6%	33.0%	3.1%	8.8%	46,261	29.6%	13.5%	9.2%	26.1%	3.8%
Lansing-East Lansing, MI	28,397	95.8%	73,289	19.5%	59.4%	2.3%	12.7%	44,901	12.7%	32.2%	10.7%	28.1%	11.2%
Laredo, TX	22,946	99.5%	28,519	35.9%	41.6%	2.4%	2.4%	25,385	28.5%	26.4%	9.9%	13.5%	4.2%
Las Cruces, NM	16,277	99.3%	32,427	27.1%	62.4%	2.9%	4.4%	18,236	20.1%	32.2%	12.2%	14.1%	6.2%
Las Vegas-Henderson-Paradise, NV	132,184	96.4%	182,345	36.4%	34.6%	4.0%	5.1%	204,037	28.9%	28.2%	9.1%	16.8%	3.0%
Lawrence, KS	5,015	100.0%	24,686	11.9%	57.3%	3.9%	24.7%	14,590	11.1%	25.2%	7.1%	35.1%	21.4%
Lawton, OK	8,293	93.5%	18,502	45.2%	32.0%	4.0%	6.7%	14,851	27.7%	43.7%	1.6%	16.0%	1.2%
Lebanon, PA	8,334	94.7%	10,926	26.1%	36.0%	7.3%	14.7%	9,178	25.9%	26.8%	11.0%	17.8%	5.9%
Lewiston-Auburn, ME	6,766	100.0%	9,557	20.3%	69.0%	2.6%	0.0%	10,215	31.1%	26.4%	18.7%	15.2%	2.1%
Lewiston, ID-WA	3,148	98.6%	7,110	38.6%	42.2%	2.2%	7.2%	4,776	24.2%	29.2%	2.3%	31.1%	4.3%
Lexington-Fayette, KY	31,170	98.2%	58,404	29.2%	44.6%	3.0%	9.9%	48,897	19.5%	25.4%	13.4%	21.9%	9.6%
Lima, OH	6,547	97.8%	10,770	33.6%	21.6%	5.4%	11.1%	8,973	22.3%	37.1%	15.3%	11.7%	3.6%
Lincoln, NE	18,631	98.2%	49,014	14.2%	61.6%	5.6%	11.7%	32,649	19.3%	25.8%	12.5%	25.0%	11.0%
Little Rock-North Little Rock-Conway, AR	47,818	94.0%	70,624	33.0%	44.1%	3.3%	8.6%	76,857	28.8%	25.1%	8.8%	18.7%	7.5%
Logan, UT-ID	11,167	99.8%	20,371	23.2%	47.6%	13.6%	10.4%	16,177	18.2%	32.3%	6.8%	31.3%	5.8%
Longview, TX	15,519	97.8%	23,450	30.3%	41.8%	4.0%	5.1%	19,661	37.1%	28.8%	7.6%	11.7%	2.8%
Longview, WA	6,983	100.0%	8,540	36.0%	34.8%	2.4%	1.6%	7,664	39.3%	41.6%	2.0%	7.2%	1.2%
Los Angeles-Long Beach-Anaheim, CA	857,172	98.2%	1,326,162	25.9%	44.4%	4.5%	10.4%	1,359,102	21.0%	23.3%	7.0%	26.7%	7.8%
Louisville/Jefferson County, KY-IN	86,468	98.4%	109,505	32.4%	37.9%	4.0%	8.2%	115,493	27.0%	22.7%	9.0%	22.2%	10.4%
Lubbock, TX	20,461	95.5%	49,404	26.7%	47.0%	4.1%	10.8%	29,381	25.2%	29.1%	10.1%	19.7%	6.3%
Lumberton, NC micro	9,433	89.1%	13,959	35.8%	33.6%	5.3%	1.9%	9,230	32.7%	29.2%	9.9%	5.8%	1.9%
Lynchburg, VA	16,213	96.1%	33,122	32.9%	45.5%	5.1%	9.1%	20,930	27.6%	29.5%	9.5%	20.0%	5.0%
Macon, GA	15,319	95.4%	26,659	30.4%	42.3%	1.6%	7.9%	20,885	42.3%	13.9%	8.5%	13.0%	6.1%
Madera, CA	12,013	98.0%	15,435	24.9%	36.8%	4.6%	3.3%	15,618	24.8%	25.8%	6.3%	5.6%	1.3%

Table E-4: Metropolitan/Micropolitan Statistical Areas—Educational Attainment—*Continued*

| | 13 to 17 | | 18 to 24 | | | | | 25 to 31 | | | | | |
| | Total Population | Percent Enrolled in School | Total Population | Percent | | | | Total Population | Percent | | | | |
				High School	Some College	Associates Degree	Bachelors Degree		High School	Some College	Associates Degree	Bachelors Degree	Advanced Degree
Madison, WI	38,821	97.5%	77,713	21.8%	47.1%	5.3%	16.4%	72,563	16.5%	16.2%	10.6%	37.0%	15.5%
Manchester-Nashua, NH	26,068	97.5%	32,994	33.3%	34.6%	4.5%	16.8%	35,508	29.4%	24.3%	7.7%	23.5%	8.4%
Manhattan, KS	5,522	100.0%	26,254	19.7%	66.5%	2.5%	5.5%	13,091	18.4%	33.3%	12.0%	23.0%	9.5%
Mankato-North Mankato, MN	5,686	99.5%	18,983	17.4%	70.8%	4.5%	3.5%	8,924	28.5%	18.6%	9.2%	35.2%	8.6%
Mansfield, OH	7,676	98.8%	10,958	36.4%	24.8%	4.0%	2.9%	9,405	40.1%	23.0%	7.4%	16.5%	2.5%
McAllen-Edinburg-Mission, TX	75,231	97.3%	89,264	27.2%	40.9%	2.9%	5.9%	74,220	25.9%	28.5%	5.8%	12.6%	2.2%
Medford, OR	11,641	97.5%	17,320	45.8%	34.4%	5.2%	4.2%	16,879	20.0%	41.8%	6.2%	13.2%	4.0%
Memphis, TN-MS-AR	100,716	97.1%	138,386	33.2%	38.4%	2.4%	8.8%	128,632	26.6%	26.1%	7.7%	18.3%	6.1%
Merced, CA	23,797	98.6%	31,498	27.7%	58.6%	2.3%	1.4%	25,584	32.7%	28.9%	5.5%	12.1%	2.7%
Meridian, MS micro	5,641	98.4%	11,710	44.6%	27.8%	3.3%	2.4%	8,153	22.2%	22.5%	22.2%	14.9%	8.5%
Miami-Fort Lauderdale-West Palm Beach, FL	341,643	97.5%	507,492	29.7%	35.8%	9.9%	8.1%	540,931	26.0%	22.9%	10.9%	20.8%	7.9%
Michigan City-La Porte, IN	7,767	100.0%	9,137	41.6%	26.7%	4.2%	2.4%	10,789	33.3%	30.7%	10.5%	8.3%	2.5%
Midland, MI	5,454	95.6%	8,172	52.0%	24.9%	5.3%	4.7%	7,858	32.9%	16.4%	10.1%	20.7%	17.0%
Midland, TX	11,045	100.0%	16,050	33.6%	31.7%	3.8%	10.9%	18,769	24.9%	25.7%	1.4%	21.5%	8.8%
Milwaukee-Waukesha-West Allis, WI	101,921	97.8%	147,919	30.6%	40.2%	4.5%	9.5%	157,729	21.6%	22.2%	9.7%	30.4%	8.4%
Minneapolis-St. Paul-Bloomington, MN-WI	231,875	98.9%	293,062	26.9%	41.7%	5.4%	11.7%	349,560	18.6%	20.2%	10.6%	33.3%	9.3%
Missoula, MT	7,120	97.8%	16,419	26.1%	38.2%	2.7%	7.8%	13,113	28.1%	19.9%	5.6%	30.6%	9.8%
Mobile, AL	26,092	91.6%	42,048	30.6%	34.7%	2.1%	10.9%	37,948	24.1%	30.1%	9.5%	16.5%	5.2%
Modesto, CA	42,105	97.0%	55,502	33.0%	46.5%	4.9%	3.7%	50,579	33.4%	29.1%	7.4%	11.5%	2.9%
Monroe, LA	13,105	94.5%	20,311	28.5%	43.2%	1.5%	7.8%	17,571	29.9%	33.7%	3.3%	8.3%	7.5%
Monroe, MI	10,149	97.1%	13,255	37.9%	37.9%	4.8%	7.5%	11,608	26.4%	26.4%	17.1%	23.9%	2.3%
Montgomery, AL	24,219	97.4%	39,232	30.3%	34.4%	3.3%	11.1%	36,578	26.4%	30.1%	7.6%	14.0%	7.3%
Morgantown, WV	6,143	100.0%	27,833	28.0%	56.6%	1.7%	9.5%	15,518	25.8%	19.0%	2.1%	17.3%	25.6%
Morristown, TN	5,792	99.4%	9,379	39.6%	40.2%	4.6%	7.7%	9,288	34.7%	24.3%	8.5%	12.8%	8.2%
Mount Vernon-Anacortes, WA	7,220	96.0%	11,075	45.5%	27.8%	3.8%	0.8%	8,911	26.4%	43.6%	9.6%	6.3%	1.8%
Muncie, IN	5,589	100.0%	24,150	17.2%	62.2%	1.6%	9.8%	9,291	34.8%	28.2%	10.1%	11.8%	4.4%
Muskegon, MI	13,279	99.2%	14,142	43.3%	24.2%	4.7%	5.7%	13,335	36.4%	25.2%	5.3%	12.5%	1.3%
Myrtle Beach-Conway-North Myrtle Beach, SC-NC	19,014	95.0%	32,427	25.1%	44.4%	3.3%	10.0%	31,091	23.4%	33.2%	10.8%	14.7%	2.9%
Napa, CA	9,311	100.0%	13,156	28.1%	47.0%	3.4%	1.7%	10,779	22.3%	29.7%	10.6%	20.7%	0.5%
Naples-Immokalee-Marco Island, FL	17,383	95.2%	22,554	38.9%	29.6%	8.9%	5.8%	22,259	31.2%	16.6%	15.4%	18.3%	4.0%
Nashville-Davidson–Murfreesboro–Franklin, TN	112,956	98.4%	164,808	32.8%	37.8%	4.8%	11.2%	175,220	24.2%	21.5%	5.9%	30.3%	9.3%
New Bern, NC	6,204	97.8%	15,130	40.1%	42.3%	3.7%	2.8%	13,287	23.6%	36.3%	11.1%	4.9%	6.4%
New Castle, PA micro	6,112	98.3%	7,055	37.1%	24.7%	14.3%	7.6%	5,814	38.5%	10.5%	20.5%	15.4%	2.9%
New Haven-Milford, CT	55,017	97.7%	86,612	32.4%	38.5%	3.5%	12.0%	80,028	26.6%	17.3%	7.1%	25.6%	16.5%
New Orleans-Metairie, LA	72,223	97.0%	108,886	27.8%	37.6%	1.6%	9.2%	127,804	21.5%	25.5%	6.0%	22.6%	8.4%
New Philadelphia-Dover, OH micro	6,749	100.0%	7,243	45.7%	29.3%	6.5%	7.7%	7,249	31.1%	27.2%	10.9%	15.6%	6.0%
New York-Newark-Jersey City, NY-NJ-PA	1,246,080	97.6%	1,851,065	25.7%	39.2%	5.4%	16.2%	2,018,169	20.2%	16.9%	7.3%	31.3%	13.5%
Niles-Benton Harbor, MI	8,469	93.4%	13,614	31.9%	41.6%	8.7%	6.8%	12,250	35.0%	15.5%	16.2%	17.6%	7.9%
North Port-Sarasota-Bradenton, FL	38,225	96.3%	52,179	37.8%	29.2%	6.3%	6.6%	43,635	29.5%	25.4%	8.2%	17.1%	9.0%
Norwich-New London, CT	15,491	99.4%	29,528	36.6%	42.9%	3.0%	10.3%	25,237	33.6%	29.3%	4.3%	16.1%	5.5%
Ocala, FL	17,883	98.9%	24,424	35.2%	23.8%	9.7%	5.7%	24,469	42.7%	27.3%	4.3%	8.9%	3.2%
Ocean City, NJ	4,789	100.0%	7,826	30.4%	28.6%	2.6%	21.8%	7,380	31.6%	14.7%	4.9%	33.0%	2.9%
Odessa, TX	11,080	99.3%	16,738	39.4%	25.1%	4.0%	6.2%	17,369	32.1%	31.0%	3.8%	12.7%	4.3%
Ogden-Clearfield, UT	54,531	96.2%	58,172	35.0%	38.7%	7.5%	4.4%	60,916	27.5%	28.5%	10.5%	22.6%	3.2%
Ogdensburg-Massena, NY micro	6,608	84.5%	16,127	20.4%	52.6%	3.7%	5.3%	8,571	30.3%	26.8%	6.5%	17.4%	4.6%
Oklahoma City, OK	78,325	97.5%	135,749	28.5%	41.2%	4.6%	9.4%	136,777	23.2%	25.1%	8.7%	22.9%	6.0%
Olympia-Tumwater, WA	16,923	97.0%	24,063	30.3%	38.7%	7.9%	10.1%	27,994	22.7%	30.8%	9.8%	21.9%	8.0%
Omaha-Council Bluffs, NE-IA	63,199	98.1%	85,177	27.0%	44.2%	4.9%	10.6%	95,723	20.0%	24.4%	10.5%	27.9%	9.8%
Orangeburg, SC micro	7,159	94.2%	11,140	28.2%	34.0%	8.3%	5.6%	5,890	30.5%	12.4%	11.3%	16.5%	5.2%
Orlando-Kissimmee-Sanford, FL	156,899	97.3%	230,036	27.7%	36.9%	10.5%	9.7%	234,680	25.3%	23.0%	10.8%	23.9%	5.8%
Oshkosh-Neenah, WI	9,642	95.0%	20,693	31.7%	48.0%	4.2%	7.6%	16,548	25.5%	18.9%	12.5%	29.2%	5.6%
Ottawa-Peru, IL micro	8,288	97.2%	9,127	39.8%	32.0%	6.3%	6.8%	9,376	42.3%	18.6%	7.8%	16.1%	6.5%
Owensboro, KY	7,282	96.2%	10,277	30.5%	37.0%	14.7%	5.1%	10,034	14.5%	43.1%	14.4%	9.2%	7.6%
Oxnard-Thousand Oaks-Ventura, CA	57,805	98.4%	83,390	23.6%	46.1%	8.8%	9.3%	72,585	21.2%	28.2%	8.5%	19.5%	6.1%
Palm Bay-Melbourne-Titusville, FL	30,170	94.1%	44,051	31.3%	32.1%	12.0%	9.6%	38,460	24.5%	20.8%	21.4%	19.2%	7.8%
Panama City, FL	10,522	98.2%	16,496	30.9%	33.4%	11.0%	4.2%	19,477	38.0%	25.7%	7.6%	10.3%	1.7%
Parkersburg-Vienna, WV	5,079	95.2%	7,766	36.9%	30.1%	7.3%	5.1%	6,968	29.3%	30.2%	13.1%	20.6%	3.2%
Pensacola-Ferry Pass-Brent, FL	27,515	98.6%	53,379	33.2%	37.5%	9.2%	4.0%	46,433	22.2%	27.7%	15.7%	22.6%	3.8%
Peoria, IL	24,935	96.5%	35,324	33.0%	37.7%	5.7%	10.1%	35,959	27.6%	21.1%	10.8%	27.5%	8.1%
Philadelphia-Camden-Wilmington, PA-NJ-DE-MD	395,794	96.9%	590,688	31.3%	38.7%	4.5%	13.1%	593,560	24.0%	19.1%	6.7%	28.5%	13.4%
Phoenix-Mesa-Scottsdale, AZ	310,618	96.2%	416,357	31.9%	35.8%	5.1%	8.2%	433,079	24.3%	25.4%	9.2%	19.8%	7.5%
Pine Bluff, AR	6,699	95.3%	11,714	42.4%	39.7%	3.2%	3.7%	7,558	44.9%	21.9%	9.4%	5.5%	5.5%
Pittsburgh, PA	135,474	97.9%	214,247	28.2%	41.1%	6.0%	15.1%	209,509	20.5%	18.7%	11.8%	30.3%	13.7%
Pittsfield, MA	7,662	98.1%	13,341	28.7%	48.8%	1.8%	6.6%	9,533	23.1%	15.3%	11.2%	25.3%	8.8%
Pocatello, ID	7,359	96.1%	10,790	38.0%	40.2%	4.6%	6.7%	7,460	42.5%	22.8%	9.4%	14.6%	7.6%
Port St. Lucie, FL	25,750	99.2%	32,529	33.7%	40.1%	5.0%	2.3%	32,399	35.0%	23.0%	9.4%	9.8%	5.8%
Portland-South Portland, ME	31,599	98.7%	45,220	28.6%	49.0%	1.9%	13.6%	41,276	25.7%	28.7%	12.8%	22.7%	8.3%
Portland-Vancouver-Hillsboro, OR-WA	145,334	98.0%	199,536	29.6%	40.1%	5.8%	9.7%	235,415	21.8%	25.9%	10.5%	25.4%	8.1%
Pottsville, PA micro	7,752	98.0%	11,168	39.3%	28.0%	7.2%	9.4%	11,697	32.1%	12.0%	12.8%	15.5%	5.1%
Prescott, AZ	11,799	94.4%	14,382	26.5%	38.0%	10.1%	5.2%	14,168	27.2%	40.5%	5.4%	7.4%	5.3%
Providence-Warwick, RI-MA	97,420	96.9%	173,628	30.8%	41.5%	4.2%	13.2%	143,009	22.8%	24.2%	8.0%	25.7%	9.0%
Provo-Orem, UT	47,624	98.6%	95,374	21.7%	54.8%	8.1%	5.8%	60,202	14.1%	31.3%	11.0%	32.1%	5.3%
Pueblo, CO	10,360	98.1%	15,775	21.8%	42.5%	6.7%	9.8%	15,157	26.7%	37.5%	9.7%	9.9%	2.0%
Punta Gorda, FL	7,440	100.0%	10,166	44.3%	17.1%	4.3%	3.3%	8,480	44.2%	18.2%	11.1%	5.4%	3.8%

Table E-4: Metropolitan/Micropolitan Statistical Areas—Educational Attainment—*Continued*

| | 13 to 17 | | 18 to 24 | | | | | 25 to 31 | | | | | |
| | Total Population | Percent Enrolled in School | Total Population | Percent | | | | Total Population | Percent | | | | |
				High School	Some College	Associates Degree	Bachelors Degree		High School	Some College	Associates Degree	Bachelors Degree	Advanced Degree
Racine, WI	13,831	99.7%	14,201	29.7%	46.6%	1.1%	4.6%	17,465	22.5%	32.0%	8.0%	13.1%	2.1%
Raleigh, NC	90,582	97.8%	115,499	24.8%	41.7%	2.3%	15.0%	114,871	17.7%	18.3%	7.2%	34.1%	12.6%
Rapid City, SD	8,917	100.0%	13,254	34.2%	42.6%	8.5%	8.0%	12,549	23.8%	26.4%	19.4%	20.4%	7.3%
Reading, PA	28,314	95.2%	41,660	33.0%	44.2%	5.0%	3.0%	33,732	29.7%	24.1%	8.3%	19.8%	7.9%
Redding, CA	10,988	97.6%	17,040	28.4%	48.4%	7.6%	4.9%	15,126	25.9%	37.3%	8.6%	11.7%	3.7%
Reno, NV	27,350	99.0%	43,965	26.8%	40.9%	7.8%	7.1%	42,675	24.6%	27.8%	5.9%	24.5%	4.6%
Richmond, VA	83,841	97.7%	116,039	34.1%	36.9%	4.3%	11.7%	118,587	25.7%	25.4%	6.5%	22.0%	11.9%
Riverside-San Bernardino-Ontario, CA	339,960	98.3%	474,163	35.8%	37.9%	4.9%	5.5%	422,349	28.3%	28.7%	8.4%	14.1%	5.2%
Roanoke, VA	19,632	95.3%	27,320	37.3%	35.1%	7.5%	6.3%	24,392	27.3%	22.6%	8.8%	22.2%	6.6%
Rochester, MN	12,613	98.2%	19,938	16.8%	49.9%	9.3%	13.7%	19,484	22.5%	22.8%	10.7%	24.6%	17.2%
Rochester, NY	69,422	96.8%	114,616	25.4%	44.6%	8.0%	9.9%	99,070	20.4%	22.0%	10.2%	23.7%	12.2%
Rockford, IL	27,011	99.0%	32,814	38.0%	31.6%	7.6%	6.2%	26,666	26.0%	25.2%	11.6%	20.7%	4.8%
Rocky Mount, NC	10,711	96.1%	14,182	31.1%	33.9%	8.0%	5.9%	9,851	26.2%	37.1%	6.7%	9.7%	5.0%
Rome, GA	6,730	94.9%	9,834	30.4%	31.7%	1.5%	7.2%	7,305	20.6%	27.4%	5.7%	19.1%	5.0%
Roseburg, OR micro	5,316	99.1%	7,684	15.6%	45.0%	14.2%	4.6%	7,735	30.0%	32.5%	11.0%	9.9%	4.3%
Sacramento–Roseville–Arden-Arcade, CA	153,429	97.7%	216,145	31.3%	42.4%	5.7%	8.4%	203,737	21.5%	29.6%	8.2%	22.7%	6.8%
Saginaw, MI	13,195	100.0%	21,690	30.7%	47.8%	5.7%	5.6%	15,016	19.0%	25.9%	15.5%	22.3%	6.1%
Salem, OH micro	6,746	97.1%	8,311	34.4%	38.8%	6.7%	3.1%	8,795	32.4%	24.2%	8.0%	13.5%	5.2%
Salem, OR	28,501	96.8%	43,413	38.1%	40.6%	3.9%	3.0%	34,859	31.4%	28.0%	8.4%	14.9%	7.9%
Salinas, CA	32,192	98.8%	47,254	27.1%	43.6%	4.2%	6.3%	43,942	29.6%	27.5%	5.3%	13.5%	4.1%
Salisbury, MD-DE	20,077	94.2%	39,407	38.6%	38.3%	2.2%	7.0%	29,859	33.8%	19.2%	11.2%	14.4%	6.6%
Salt Lake City, UT	85,071	98.8%	109,954	30.6%	40.7%	7.6%	6.5%	127,631	24.2%	26.5%	8.8%	23.8%	8.9%
San Angelo, TX	7,936	99.6%	14,311	33.1%	51.6%	1.6%	6.7%	12,721	31.4%	14.0%	15.9%	21.1%	0.8%
San Antonio-New Braunfels, TX	168,358	98.1%	242,475	34.0%	36.3%	3.8%	8.8%	232,757	27.0%	28.4%	6.8%	20.5%	6.4%
San Diego-Carlsbad, CA	197,480	98.0%	366,084	32.0%	38.3%	5.7%	10.6%	371,745	20.8%	23.1%	9.2%	26.0%	10.4%
San Francisco-Oakland-Hayward, CA	248,359	98.4%	380,272	23.3%	45.4%	3.8%	16.6%	483,008	15.1%	18.8%	5.9%	36.1%	14.1%
San Jose-Sunnyvale-Santa Clara, CA	115,758	98.7%	165,780	25.3%	40.3%	4.5%	17.4%	197,693	13.9%	18.8%	5.7%	30.7%	20.6%
San Luis Obispo-Paso Robles-Arroyo Grande, CA	12,954	98.3%	44,013	18.8%	65.5%	4.0%	7.6%	23,706	21.6%	38.7%	6.3%	21.6%	4.4%
Santa Cruz-Watsonville, CA	14,588	98.2%	39,381	20.9%	58.7%	2.6%	9.5%	21,434	15.9%	33.2%	11.7%	22.4%	6.0%
Santa Fe, NM	7,907	97.2%	11,027	28.8%	46.0%	2.5%	4.2%	11,022	35.6%	25.0%	7.0%	14.3%	9.8%
Santa Maria-Santa Barbara, CA	29,172	99.7%	67,925	16.7%	57.0%	4.2%	10.9%	40,171	20.0%	18.4%	8.7%	17.1%	6.6%
Santa Rosa, CA	31,888	99.8%	45,516	28.2%	49.3%	4.0%	5.2%	43,559	23.7%	24.6%	10.6%	22.0%	4.0%
Savannah, GA	21,245	99.8%	43,891	29.1%	46.2%	3.8%	6.4%	39,863	19.0%	30.1%	3.8%	23.6%	8.7%
Scranton–Wilkes-Barre–Hazleton, PA	32,972	99.0%	56,196	28.7%	46.8%	2.7%	9.1%	46,279	31.1%	20.8%	10.7%	19.3%	10.0%
Seattle-Tacoma-Bellevue, WA	216,743	98.0%	321,593	26.5%	38.1%	6.6%	15.2%	397,366	18.0%	22.9%	9.0%	30.7%	10.8%
Sebastian-Vero Beach, FL	8,844	100.0%	9,614	37.1%	16.0%	19.3%	0.0%	9,040	24.6%	26.4%	14.3%	9.5%	9.4%
Sebring, FL	4,417	94.5%	6,849	43.9%	17.8%	11.4%	0.0%	5,937	42.1%	30.8%	4.4%	3.4%	2.2%
Sheboygan, WI	8,528	98.8%	7,877	30.8%	38.6%	0.7%	9.4%	9,011	20.3%	26.9%	15.1%	19.1%	8.5%
Sherman-Denison, TX	7,874	99.2%	11,094	33.4%	41.0%	3.6%	7.2%	11,329	28.8%	27.4%	9.9%	11.5%	3.7%
Show Low, AZ micro	8,371	97.1%	10,459	32.8%	36.1%	3.3%	1.8%	9,505	30.0%	30.3%	5.5%	11.6%	1.8%
Shreveport-Bossier City, LA	28,463	97.0%	49,166	31.0%	34.5%	4.2%	7.4%	45,748	28.5%	25.9%	7.0%	18.6%	4.3%
Sierra Vista-Douglas, AZ	8,304	93.1%	12,340	35.9%	42.8%	4.6%	3.7%	11,701	14.9%	40.5%	5.5%	18.0%	7.0%
Sioux City, IA-NE-SD	13,318	98.5%	16,841	31.4%	43.4%	7.9%	3.6%	14,006	21.8%	22.0%	17.0%	19.7%	5.8%
Sioux Falls, SD	13,580	97.1%	23,954	23.0%	44.0%	9.9%	13.2%	25,702	22.3%	18.3%	15.5%	30.0%	8.7%
South Bend-Mishawaka, IN-MI	24,107	95.9%	32,769	38.9%	41.0%	0.5%	6.7%	25,181	25.2%	29.8%	7.9%	18.3%	8.8%
Spartanburg, SC	23,490	97.2%	34,337	36.2%	35.6%	5.9%	4.5%	27,072	25.9%	28.0%	9.9%	15.9%	6.0%
Spokane-Spokane Valley, WA	37,179	99.3%	54,440	28.6%	46.6%	5.8%	9.7%	55,571	31.8%	27.9%	9.1%	19.0%	5.1%
Springfield, IL	12,890	99.2%	18,107	21.8%	43.8%	3.7%	15.2%	19,203	19.9%	31.1%	7.3%	26.4%	12.3%
Springfield, MA	43,682	97.3%	79,118	23.1%	52.4%	3.3%	8.3%	52,221	30.4%	21.3%	9.2%	18.9%	8.0%
Springfield, MO	31,094	96.1%	54,954	28.3%	45.4%	4.6%	11.3%	43,409	19.9%	24.5%	8.5%	22.9%	10.2%
Springfield, OH	9,593	97.5%	12,435	30.5%	48.8%	2.2%	2.4%	10,946	30.0%	28.2%	8.3%	20.4%	3.4%
St. Cloud, MN	11,797	98.3%	29,346	17.7%	62.5%	7.0%	3.2%	17,858	25.9%	21.5%	19.7%	27.0%	1.4%
St. George, UT	10,787	96.9%	14,931	23.9%	39.1%	8.8%	2.4%	10,743	19.3%	38.2%	13.8%	17.8%	3.9%
St. Joseph, MO-KS	7,692	95.6%	12,829	37.1%	33.4%	4.1%	4.5%	11,679	38.5%	21.8%	5.8%	18.2%	7.6%
St. Louis, MO-IL	181,026	97.3%	250,869	30.1%	40.0%	6.2%	11.5%	269,329	20.2%	21.6%	10.4%	28.6%	11.8%
State College, PA	6,996	96.8%	44,131	22.3%	60.3%	4.5%	9.3%	13,999	35.9%	7.8%	9.9%	17.0%	25.8%
Staunton-Waynesboro, VA	5,147	92.8%	13,074	49.1%	31.2%	2.1%	11.4%	8,830	48.0%	10.9%	8.4%	18.0%	3.5%
Stockton-Lodi, CA	57,808	98.9%	73,709	36.3%	34.4%	6.0%	5.5%	61,696	25.5%	28.2%	12.3%	11.7%	1.7%
Sumter, SC	7,412	97.9%	13,333	39.7%	25.4%	5.0%	8.1%	9,642	31.6%	29.7%	8.4%	7.1%	6.4%
Sunbury, PA micro	4,390	91.5%	7,679	30.9%	24.0%	8.1%	6.7%	7,918	31.2%	12.0%	11.9%	14.7%	17.0%
Syracuse, NY	42,521	99.4%	71,514	25.2%	47.3%	6.1%	11.6%	56,132	23.9%	22.0%	10.8%	25.7%	10.3%
Tallahassee, FL	21,444	99.9%	75,689	21.9%	46.3%	11.1%	11.4%	40,310	18.7%	19.7%	11.0%	26.6%	13.2%
Tampa-St. Petersburg-Clearwater, FL	170,417	96.4%	243,210	30.3%	35.3%	9.2%	9.0%	256,739	26.6%	23.0%	12.0%	21.0%	6.8%
Terre Haute, IN	9,373	99.4%	20,793	27.5%	46.9%	3.2%	6.8%	16,606	29.3%	25.3%	7.5%	12.1%	8.6%
Texarkana, TX-AR	8,947	98.6%	14,037	45.0%	33.2%	6.3%	2.4%	15,588	40.0%	26.7%	3.5%	12.1%	4.7%
The Villages, FL	1,930	100.0%	4,200	32.9%	41.5%	5.1%	0.0%	5,232	22.2%	30.7%	8.4%	15.0%	0.0%
Toledo, OH	40,545	99.1%	72,817	27.8%	45.8%	3.8%	9.0%	57,149	24.4%	27.4%	11.0%	19.1%	8.9%
Topeka, KS	15,563	97.1%	19,391	29.3%	40.8%	4.7%	5.3%	19,377	28.1%	25.2%	5.9%	24.7%	8.0%
Torrington, CT micro	12,168	92.5%	13,642	33.6%	39.2%	2.0%	13.5%	13,526	26.2%	25.1%	5.4%	30.3%	11.4%
Traverse City, MI micro	9,525	99.4%	11,425	42.8%	39.5%	1.7%	4.1%	10,876	33.9%	12.6%	15.2%	19.5%	7.8%
Trenton, NJ	24,958	98.5%	40,520	27.1%	46.4%	1.3%	13.0%	31,797	24.9%	13.4%	5.1%	24.3%	18.6%
Truckee-Grass Valley, CA micro	5,901	100.0%	7,382	20.6%	49.0%	3.4%	6.0%	5,855	23.1%	25.5%	26.5%	20.2%	1.2%
Tucson, AZ	62,937	97.8%	121,550	31.0%	41.4%	3.7%	8.2%	88,003	23.3%	29.6%	8.3%	17.8%	7.9%
Tullahoma-Manchester, TN micro	8,553	99.0%	8,902	43.0%	38.0%	3.9%	4.0%	6,331	35.7%	23.3%	6.6%	11.9%	3.7%
Tulsa, OK	65,890	97.7%	87,792	33.9%	36.2%	5.1%	7.8%	89,032	29.3%	27.3%	9.6%	17.3%	5.2%
Tupelo, MS micro	10,149	99.4%	14,124	29.1%	41.4%	8.0%	3.2%	11,083	25.8%	22.0%	13.0%	9.7%	4.5%

Table E-4: Metropolitan/Micropolitan Statistical Areas—Educational Attainment—*Continued*

| | 13 to 17 | | 18 to 24 | | | | | 25 to 31 | | | | | |
| | Total Population | Percent Enrolled in School | Total Population | Percent | | | | Total Population | Percent | | | | |
				High School	Some College	Associates Degree	Bachelors Degree		High School	Some College	Associates Degree	Bachelors Degree	Advanced Degree
Tuscaloosa, AL	14,476	96.7%	40,034	27.6%	51.9%	3.2%	5.6%	23,302	26.5%	29.6%	7.7%	20.8%	9.9%
Tyler, TX	15,454	92.6%	22,230	29.2%	36.1%	11.9%	6.3%	19,669	25.0%	29.8%	8.2%	24.9%	2.7%
Urban Honolulu, HI	57,221	97.5%	99,988	32.3%	44.9%	6.2%	9.6%	108,618	21.6%	29.5%	11.7%	26.0%	5.3%
Utica-Rome, NY	19,567	96.3%	29,255	25.1%	42.4%	6.8%	7.8%	24,883	28.4%	26.6%	15.0%	9.4%	11.9%
Valdosta, GA	9,624	96.2%	24,729	29.1%	49.9%	3.6%	5.0%	14,623	21.1%	19.1%	12.7%	24.6%	11.8%
Vallejo-Fairfield, CA	27,829	97.0%	43,457	38.3%	38.4%	3.0%	6.1%	42,964	19.8%	36.2%	12.3%	16.3%	4.0%
Victoria, TX	7,946	99.3%	9,386	44.4%	18.9%	3.8%	2.0%	7,723	40.0%	28.9%	7.3%	9.7%	3.6%
Vineland-Bridgeton, NJ	10,242	96.9%	13,253	57.1%	20.4%	4.0%	5.5%	17,680	37.4%	27.6%	3.4%	12.3%	2.9%
Virginia Beach-Norfolk-Newport News, VA-NC	105,756	98.4%	203,677	33.5%	42.7%	4.4%	8.4%	189,087	23.9%	32.3%	10.1%	19.7%	6.6%
Visalia-Porterville, CA	36,363	97.9%	49,699	35.5%	30.8%	6.5%	2.7%	46,122	36.9%	20.4%	6.9%	6.9%	5.3%
Waco, TX	15,318	96.4%	38,050	24.9%	49.0%	4.6%	11.1%	23,818	22.4%	31.9%	13.0%	13.2%	5.7%
Walla Walla, WA	3,406	100.0%	7,436	31.3%	61.2%	2.5%	2.0%	5,911	20.5%	36.3%	15.0%	9.5%	2.6%
Warner Robins, GA	14,319	94.3%	20,230	35.0%	38.4%	3.6%	6.5%	19,225	46.1%	22.3%	12.5%	13.2%	2.0%
Washington-Arlington-Alexandria, DC-VA-MD-WV	371,020	98.0%	540,511	27.3%	38.3%	4.1%	17.8%	646,396	17.0%	18.3%	5.4%	32.5%	19.7%
Waterloo-Cedar Falls, IA	10,071	99.9%	27,213	24.7%	51.6%	6.1%	6.5%	14,991	22.1%	24.4%	15.9%	17.0%	10.7%
Watertown-Fort Drum, NY	7,667	99.3%	15,064	42.8%	37.2%	4.8%	2.9%	13,925	34.8%	33.2%	7.9%	11.8%	4.6%
Wausau, WI	9,211	99.2%	11,313	53.8%	27.0%	5.2%	0.3%	11,030	27.9%	16.7%	18.3%	22.5%	4.5%
Weirton-Steubenville, WV-OH	8,246	99.3%	12,018	31.1%	42.7%	10.1%	3.2%	7,984	48.7%	20.9%	13.1%	11.0%	4.7%
Wenatchee, WA	8,121	98.3%	8,718	41.6%	19.9%	8.0%	5.1%	11,132	42.7%	25.4%	5.9%	7.0%	1.9%
Wheeling, WV-OH	9,707	99.4%	13,164	31.3%	40.5%	10.9%	4.8%	9,570	47.5%	19.5%	14.1%	12.3%	3.9%
Whitewater-Elkhorn, WI micro	6,980	94.9%	11,281	27.9%	50.9%	6.2%	8.0%	8,854	29.3%	25.5%	10.3%	18.8%	6.3%
Wichita Falls, TX	9,009	98.2%	19,163	35.9%	42.9%	6.1%	7.6%	16,601	39.1%	26.4%	8.2%	14.2%	3.7%
Wichita, KS	45,238	97.7%	58,427	24.3%	45.7%	7.0%	9.5%	64,948	20.9%	30.8%	9.1%	23.4%	5.7%
Williamsport, PA	5,763	98.1%	13,832	34.8%	36.4%	9.0%	9.6%	8,292	40.2%	9.5%	10.6%	25.0%	7.7%
Wilmington, NC	13,683	95.6%	32,892	21.5%	50.4%	2.3%	12.2%	23,851	19.6%	23.4%	17.9%	25.0%	6.0%
Winchester, VA-WV	9,063	99.2%	10,846	50.8%	29.2%	0.5%	6.7%	9,260	18.7%	31.8%	6.8%	19.8%	13.0%
Winston-Salem, NC	45,514	97.1%	60,502	36.2%	34.5%	4.1%	8.5%	50,711	27.7%	26.2%	7.7%	18.4%	8.1%
Wooster, OH micro	8,612	88.1%	11,137	31.5%	36.5%	2.4%	3.7%	8,719	30.4%	20.0%	9.2%	11.1%	8.6%
Worcester, MA-CT	61,447	98.3%	89,748	35.8%	36.1%	3.2%	14.1%	77,116	25.5%	20.4%	8.2%	29.7%	9.7%
Yakima, WA	18,411	94.7%	25,232	35.4%	26.1%	4.3%	3.8%	22,351	32.3%	25.8%	6.1%	14.9%	1.9%
York-Hanover, PA	26,969	98.9%	37,083	49.9%	28.6%	2.8%	8.2%	33,523	33.3%	20.7%	13.7%	18.3%	3.8%
Youngstown-Warren-Boardman, OH-PA	38,178	98.1%	47,862	35.9%	33.4%	3.5%	8.8%	43,994	31.8%	21.9%	8.0%	22.5%	5.7%
Yuba City, CA	11,439	98.1%	16,677	32.4%	40.0%	5.9%	6.6%	16,214	27.8%	29.8%	11.3%	14.7%	0.9%
Yuma, AZ	15,620	100.0%	24,334	24.3%	48.9%	7.1%	1.9%	19,442	31.5%	24.3%	11.2%	11.4%	1.3%

PART F
FIELD OF STUDY

FIELD OF STUDY

The Millennial generation and the technological world they are growing into is far different from the decades when the Baby Boomers were this age. The President's Council of Economic Advisors notes that they are "the first generation to have had access to the Internet during their formative years."[1] Yet that technological advantage may not be required in the industry sectors where employment is increasing most rapidly. One of their challenges will be obtaining an education in the appropriate fields for future employment and growth. The American Community Survey questions respondents on their bachelor's degree field of study. The data are used primarily by the National Science Foundation to study the characteristics of the population in science and engineering fields, but they are more generally applicable to understanding the educational focus of the Millennials. The question is asked only of persons with a bachelor's degree or higher. Tables presented here follow the Census Bureau's category scheme for field of degree classification.

Nationwide, Millennials age 18 to 31 with a bachelor's degree or higher favor Business as their primary field of study. At 19.1 percent, Business is chosen at a rate more than twice that of the Social Sciences (8.5 percent). While Business stands out for almost one in five degree holders, other disciplines are pretty evenly distributed, as seen in Table 1.

Business is the field of choice for more than 20 percent of Millennials in 17 states. Nevada is highest at 24.9 percent, but New Hampshire is a close second at 24.7 percent. Vermont has the lowest percentage of Business degree holders at 10.4 percent. The Millennials are thought of as the "tech" generation, but 34.3 percent in the District of Columbia hold degrees in the Social Sciences. California is a distant second at 11.7 percent, and North Dakota has the lowest percentage at 2.7 percent. Engineering is most prevalent in Delaware (11.0 percent), and fields related to Science and Engineering are most important in North Dakota (15.5 percent). Degrees in Computers and Mathematics are held by 8.6 percent of Millennials in Washington state, which is possibly due to the location of

Table 1: Percent of Population 18 to 31 With a Bachelor's Degree or Higher by Field of Study

Field of Study	Percent
Business	19.1%
Social Science	8.5%
Science and Engineering Related	8.3%
Education	7.8%
Biological Sciences	7.6%
Engineering	7.0%
Psychology	5.9%
Communications	5.8%
Visual and Performing Arts	5.6%
Liberal Arts	4.6%
Literature	4.0%
Computers and Mathematical	3.6%
Physical Sciences	2.7%

Microsoft's corporate headquarters. Washington is one of only five states that are above 5.0 percent–Arkansas, Maryland, New Jersey and Virginia are the others. In the Biological Sciences, Idaho is highest at 15.1 percent followed by Maine at 14.8 percent. Eleven states have more than 10 percent in the Biological Sciences. The Education fields also have large percentages with 18 states having more than 10 percent degree holders. Wyoming is the highest at 18.0 percent while the District of Columbia is lowest at 2.0 percent.

Science and Engineering Related, Business, the Social Sciences, and Education are the field of degree categories with the highest percentages at the county level. Bradley County, TN (60.7 percent) has the highest percentage in the Science and Engineering Related category. In Business, Canadian County, OK is at the top with 56.7 percent of Millennials holding business degrees. Social Science degrees are held by 58.7 percent in Saline County, AR, and in Education, Marshall County, AL is highest at 59.7 percent. Terrebonne Parish, LA (39.6 percent) has the highest percentage of Engineering degree holders while Linn County, OR is highest in the Biological Sciences. In 316 counties, one out of every five degree holder Millennials holds a degree in Business.

---

1. The Council of Economic Advisors, "15 Economic Facts About Millennials," Executive Office of the President, October 2014.

Percent of Age 18 to 31 With Business Field of Degree

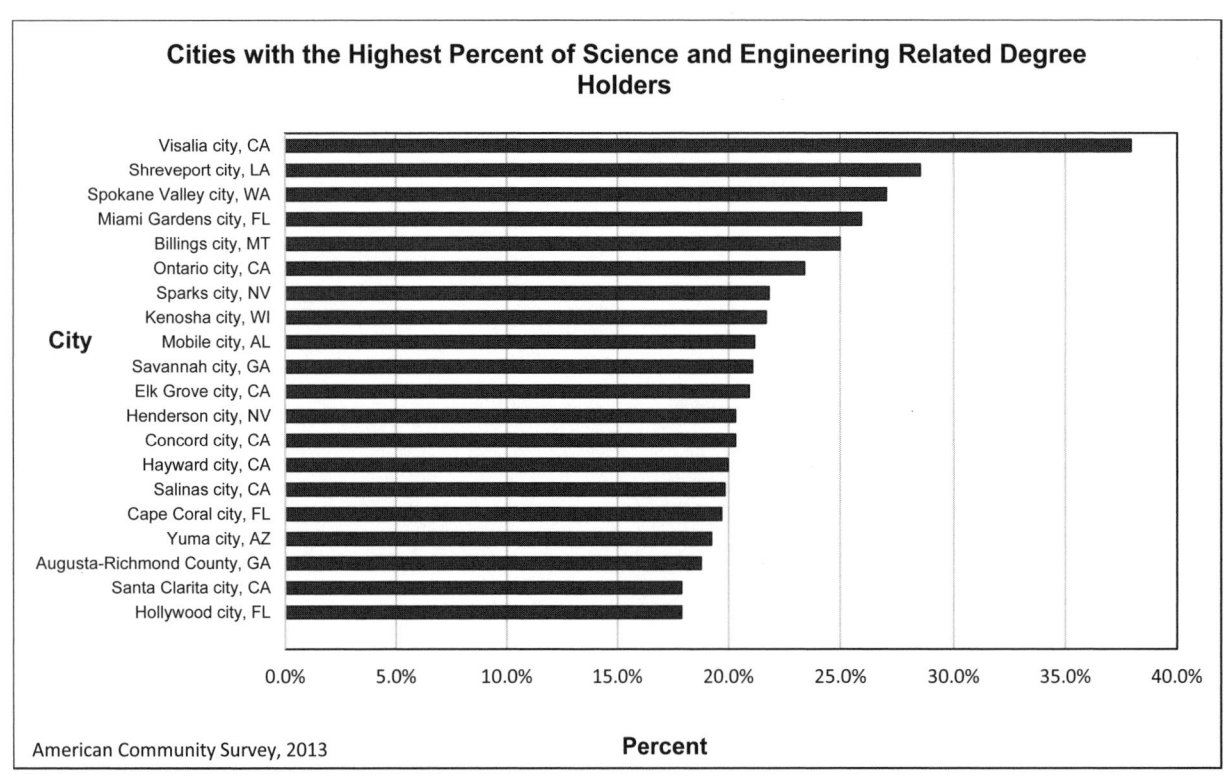

Among cities, Psychology ranks highest in Palm Bay City, FL at 50.4 percent, which is unusually high since the next highest city is Compton, CA at 37.5 percent. Engineering degree holders are highest in Sunnyvale City, CA (39.3 percent), and Science and Engineering Related fields are top in another California city—Visalia at 37.9 percent. Pompano Beach City, FL has a concentration of degree holders in Computers and Mathematics with 33.6 percent. Business is important in 128 cities where the percentage of degree holders exceeds 20 percent. Fort Lauderdale City, FL tops the list at 47.4 percent. Flint City, MI is highest in three fields of degree: Liberal Arts (37.1 percent), Education (30.9 percent), and the Visual and Performing Arts (31.9 percent).

The Albertville, AL metropolitan area has the largest percentage of its Millennials in the Education field at 57.4 percent. It's one of 26 metro/micro areas with more than 25 percent of its degree holders in Education. In Science and Engineering Related fields, Cleveland, TN ranks highest at 54.6 percent, with Dalton, GA following at 42.4 percent. Business degree holders are most prevalent in Wenatchee, WA, where more than half (52.6 percent) of Millennials are business minded. The Biological Sciences are strong in Grants Pass, OR (49.0 percent), while Racine, WI has the highest percentage (35.6 percent) of Communications degree holders.

Table F-1: States—Educational Field of Study

	Total Millennial Population	Percent of the Population 18 to 31 by Field of Study												
		Engineering	Computers and Math	Science and Engineering Related	Business	Physical Science	Social Science	Communications	Biological Sciences	Literature	Liberal Arts	Psychology	Education	Visual and Performing Arts
United States	12,861,801	7.0%	3.6%	8.3%	19.1%	2.7%	8.5%	5.8%	7.6%	4.0%	4.6%	5.9%	7.8%	5.6%
Alabama	145,197	7.1%	2.5%	10.8%	19.7%	2.8%	6.5%	3.9%	8.6%	4.2%	3.6%	4.9%	12.0%	3.3%
Alaska	25,471	8.0%	1.4%	9.3%	16.1%	6.2%	9.3%	0.9%	6.7%	8.9%	4.6%	8.9%	5.9%	1.1%
Arizona	208,435	8.0%	4.4%	8.9%	17.1%	2.0%	8.4%	5.1%	7.4%	2.9%	4.0%	6.7%	10.6%	4.4%
Arkansas	79,060	4.7%	5.4%	10.0%	17.1%	3.8%	5.3%	4.6%	9.4%	4.1%	6.1%	4.6%	11.1%	3.6%
California	1,639,023	8.4%	4.2%	6.6%	17.1%	2.6%	11.7%	6.3%	7.7%	4.5%	5.6%	6.6%	3.2%	7.0%
Colorado	253,289	6.8%	2.9%	6.2%	19.8%	1.8%	8.5%	5.8%	8.4%	4.4%	5.5%	6.3%	4.8%	6.5%
Connecticut	171,074	7.4%	3.3%	7.0%	18.1%	2.2%	8.6%	5.6%	8.0%	3.7%	4.4%	6.5%	7.5%	6.5%
Delaware	42,699	11.0%	4.4%	7.3%	18.3%	3.5%	6.6%	2.6%	7.4%	3.9%	6.7%	6.3%	7.9%	5.3%
District of Columbia	98,921	5.4%	2.3%	2.5%	10.9%	1.9%	34.3%	7.9%	3.7%	6.3%	9.8%	3.3%	2.0%	3.3%
Florida	604,023	6.1%	3.3%	8.6%	23.1%	2.3%	7.5%	5.9%	6.9%	3.0%	3.7%	6.7%	8.5%	4.4%
Georgia	349,404	5.5%	4.3%	8.8%	20.6%	2.7%	7.7%	6.1%	7.1%	3.2%	4.1%	5.6%	9.4%	5.0%
Hawaii	54,914	5.4%	1.4%	12.7%	22.0%	4.0%	8.4%	6.5%	9.8%	3.2%	2.7%	6.4%	8.9%	3.7%
Idaho	46,811	7.5%	1.6%	8.2%	13.1%	1.4%	7.3%	6.8%	15.1%	3.7%	4.1%	5.8%	13.0%	2.1%
Illinois	644,401	6.9%	3.7%	8.7%	20.6%	3.0%	8.2%	5.9%	6.7%	3.3%	4.2%	6.2%	8.5%	6.2%
Indiana	211,765	7.1%	4.3%	12.6%	15.9%	3.3%	5.4%	5.0%	8.6%	3.4%	5.6%	4.4%	11.1%	4.0%
Iowa	117,457	9.9%	2.7%	7.8%	20.2%	1.3%	5.7%	6.0%	10.0%	3.8%	3.6%	4.8%	9.7%	3.7%
Kansas	119,588	6.4%	2.6%	10.7%	19.2%	2.4%	5.3%	4.9%	9.9%	3.9%	5.1%	5.5%	11.5%	4.5%
Kentucky	133,575	6.2%	2.0%	9.6%	19.6%	2.8%	7.2%	5.6%	5.7%	2.5%	5.5%	5.7%	11.5%	3.8%
Louisiana	147,074	7.2%	2.5%	12.0%	17.3%	3.3%	6.8%	5.3%	8.1%	3.5%	7.9%	4.9%	7.5%	4.8%
Maine	37,880	8.3%	0.9%	6.6%	13.6%	0.9%	7.3%	4.1%	14.8%	2.9%	4.8%	4.9%	9.5%	8.7%
Maryland	294,483	7.1%	5.4%	8.2%	16.6%	3.1%	9.1%	5.1%	7.1%	5.3%	4.3%	7.4%	5.9%	4.7%
Massachusetts	433,045	8.5%	3.8%	7.5%	18.7%	3.2%	9.7%	4.6%	7.7%	4.5%	4.5%	7.0%	4.7%	6.6%
Michigan	343,509	9.2%	2.6%	10.2%	19.2%	2.7%	6.2%	6.3%	7.3%	4.4%	4.4%	5.9%	8.6%	3.5%
Minnesota	260,252	5.9%	3.0%	9.3%	19.7%	2.0%	10.1%	5.8%	9.1%	3.5%	3.0%	4.7%	8.7%	5.5%
Mississippi	68,243	3.8%	1.2%	14.7%	21.8%	4.0%	3.1%	2.9%	8.7%	2.0%	4.2%	3.2%	16.1%	3.7%
Missouri	251,660	4.3%	2.5%	10.3%	20.4%	3.0%	4.9%	6.6%	9.3%	3.2%	5.2%	4.1%	12.1%	5.0%
Montana	33,220	6.4%	1.8%	10.8%	13.1%	1.3%	8.3%	2.7%	14.6%	2.4%	8.5%	5.0%	13.5%	2.7%
Nebraska	79,825	5.0%	1.9%	10.6%	21.7%	1.7%	4.2%	4.6%	12.8%	3.4%	2.1%	4.8%	13.3%	4.4%
Nevada	71,449	4.2%	3.8%	9.6%	24.9%	3.2%	4.5%	4.1%	7.7%	2.5%	2.8%	7.0%	8.1%	3.7%
New Hampshire	53,429	7.8%	2.9%	10.3%	24.7%	1.1%	6.2%	4.3%	4.7%	5.8%	5.0%	6.6%	6.0%	6.9%
New Jersey	436,053	7.7%	5.1%	8.2%	22.3%	2.8%	7.2%	6.2%	5.6%	3.4%	4.2%	5.9%	8.5%	4.8%
New Mexico	53,379	9.8%	3.0%	12.0%	11.0%	6.2%	5.7%	4.1%	7.6%	5.5%	3.1%	5.7%	9.7%	6.9%
New York	1,132,000	5.2%	3.0%	6.6%	20.3%	2.5%	10.4%	6.7%	5.5%	4.6%	4.9%	6.3%	6.8%	9.5%
North Carolina	360,386	6.0%	3.1%	8.2%	16.8%	3.1%	7.5%	5.3%	9.2%	3.9%	4.3%	7.1%	8.8%	5.2%
North Dakota	34,592	3.9%	0.8%	15.5%	23.9%	2.1%	2.7%	5.6%	7.1%	3.5%	0.8%	4.1%	12.8%	1.8%
Ohio	428,906	7.4%	3.0%	10.5%	19.4%	2.5%	6.3%	6.4%	7.8%	4.6%	3.9%	5.8%	9.5%	4.2%
Oklahoma	120,412	5.5%	1.7%	8.8%	20.1%	3.4%	6.1%	5.7%	10.1%	3.7%	4.3%	6.3%	8.7%	5.3%
Oregon	136,117	7.3%	3.5%	6.5%	13.9%	3.3%	10.9%	5.5%	11.5%	4.9%	5.7%	6.5%	4.1%	7.1%
Pennsylvania	572,029	6.2%	2.9%	9.0%	20.3%	3.2%	6.3%	6.1%	7.0%	3.5%	3.9%	6.1%	11.0%	5.4%
Rhode Island	52,936	5.9%	2.3%	8.3%	15.3%	5.2%	6.1%	5.4%	6.9%	5.0%	4.0%	7.2%	7.2%	7.9%
South Carolina	155,032	4.3%	2.1%	10.1%	19.8%	3.6%	7.5%	4.7%	8.0%	3.3%	5.5%	5.4%	10.6%	5.2%
South Dakota	30,902	3.1%	2.9%	8.6%	21.2%	1.8%	10.4%	4.3%	11.4%	3.5%	0.9%	4.1%	15.1%	4.1%
Tennessee	227,798	4.5%	3.0%	9.9%	20.0%	2.6%	6.9%	6.6%	8.3%	3.5%	4.6%	6.2%	10.3%	4.6%
Texas	966,066	8.6%	3.2%	7.9%	22.0%	2.8%	6.4%	5.4%	7.6%	3.3%	4.2%	4.5%	8.4%	4.1%
Utah	113,648	6.4%	4.1%	9.6%	16.4%	1.9%	7.0%	5.9%	6.0%	5.9%	3.2%	5.6%	9.3%	4.1%
Vermont	22,900	5.4%	2.4%	4.6%	10.4%	0.9%	11.0%	5.1%	10.3%	8.1%	5.5%	3.8%	5.6%	10.1%
Virginia	411,394	7.0%	5.1%	7.1%	17.1%	3.2%	11.0%	5.5%	7.4%	4.4%	5.8%	6.6%	5.8%	4.8%
Washington	298,868	8.6%	8.6%	7.2%	15.2%	2.4%	10.7%	5.8%	7.9%	5.0%	4.8%	5.1%	4.4%	5.3%
West Virginia	47,331	7.9%	4.6%	11.0%	15.3%	2.2%	3.3%	5.5%	11.1%	2.9%	3.4%	4.8%	13.9%	3.4%
Wisconsin	218,971	6.7%	3.8%	9.1%	15.6%	3.1%	8.3%	7.1%	8.5%	3.7%	3.4%	5.1%	9.0%	6.5%
Wyoming	22,905	6.1%	2.5%	10.2%	12.9%	3.1%	3.2%	3.0%	12.8%	5.5%	8.1%	2.6%	18.0%	1.7%

Table F-2: Counties—Educational Field of Study

	Total Millennial Population	Percent of the Population 18 to 31 by Field of Study												
		Engineering	Computers and Math	Science and Engineering Related	Business	Physical Science	Social Science	Communications	Biological Sciences	Literature	Liberal Arts	Psychology	Education	Visual and Performing Arts
Alabama														
Baldwin County	5,211	0.0%	17.0%	11.9%	17.0%	4.8%	7.9%	5.0%	6.1%	7.1%	6.7%	2.2%	11.4%	2.9%
Calhoun County	2,566	3.5%	5.8%	10.8%	19.9%	0.0%	4.5%	8.7%	16.3%	3.7%	0.0%	12.9%	13.8%	0.0%
Etowah County	542	0.0%	0.0%	4.6%	0.0%	0.0%	0.0%	15.1%	0.0%	0.0%	0.0%	34.7%	34.9%	10.7%
Houston County	1,947	5.9%	4.1%	11.4%	27.7%	3.5%	0.9%	2.8%	7.4%	1.0%	4.0%	5.0%	24.3%	2.0%
Jefferson County	28,181	4.5%	1.5%	11.9%	24.7%	2.6%	4.5%	4.5%	16.0%	3.5%	4.9%	6.1%	9.7%	5.7%
Lauderdale County	1,758	0.0%	0.0%	0.0%	37.3%	4.5%	0.0%	7.8%	0.0%	28.0%	0.0%	0.0%	3.4%	19.0%
Lee County	9,378	14.4%	4.8%	14.4%	19.3%	4.0%	1.0%	5.3%	13.1%	2.0%	4.9%	1.6%	11.7%	3.5%
Madison County	14,839	16.3%	1.5%	6.3%	20.8%	9.3%	5.3%	1.2%	9.6%	5.0%	5.1%	4.8%	13.0%	2.0%
Marshall County	2,082	12.4%	0.0%	0.9%	23.3%	0.0%	0.0%	1.3%	0.5%	0.0%	1.1%	0.4%	59.7%	0.4%
Mobile County	12,358	9.7%	1.1%	25.0%	25.9%	3.5%	6.8%	2.5%	3.5%	4.3%	6.2%	7.8%	3.7%	0.0%
Montgomery County	7,679	1.7%	4.5%	18.4%	18.2%	0.7%	16.0%	2.4%	7.4%	1.0%	1.2%	6.0%	19.7%	2.8%
Morgan County	1,971	16.4%	3.8%	0.8%	5.5%	0.0%	12.3%	10.0%	0.0%	0.0%	2.9%	0.0%	42.8%	5.5%
Shelby County	8,564	6.7%	2.9%	14.2%	20.9%	0.0%	11.8%	6.5%	11.0%	3.4%	1.8%	9.6%	2.9%	8.3%
Tuscaloosa County	8,775	3.9%	0.8%	10.9%	19.4%	1.9%	8.0%	3.2%	6.8%	14.7%	5.4%	4.3%	17.8%	2.9%
Alaska														
Fairbanks North Star Borough	5,074	14.2%	0.0%	9.7%	2.0%	10.9%	18.1%	0.0%	5.4%	18.6%	5.7%	2.5%	12.6%	0.3%
Matanuska-Susitna Borough	1,200	0.0%	23.3%	0.0%	45.6%	0.0%	0.0%	0.0%	7.1%	3.9%	0.0%	4.6%	11.6%	4.0%
Arizona														
Cochise County	3,121	2.4%	2.3%	10.4%	7.9%	0.0%	8.3%	4.0%	21.7%	10.9%	4.2%	4.6%	23.3%	0.0%
Coconino County	6,241	17.2%	0.0%	15.3%	5.8%	2.8%	14.2%	4.9%	10.9%	0.0%	3.0%	7.9%	5.5%	12.4%
Maricopa County	134,425	8.7%	5.7%	9.5%	21.3%	1.6%	8.2%	6.1%	7.9%	2.7%	3.5%	8.4%	12.0%	4.5%
Mohave County	2,176	0.0%	0.0%	11.7%	25.6%	0.0%	2.8%	3.5%	12.4%	0.0%	9.7%	15.3%	14.3%	4.7%
Navajo County	1,463	0.0%	0.0%	11.8%	7.2%	0.0%	10.7%	0.0%	3.0%	0.8%	29.6%	8.2%	17.8%	10.8%
Pima County	29,740	10.7%	2.4%	9.2%	13.7%	5.6%	14.8%	3.0%	8.9%	5.6%	7.3%	3.8%	8.5%	6.5%
Pinal County	3,860	4.5%	10.2%	5.9%	26.0%	2.0%	8.8%	6.8%	7.3%	2.7%	0.0%	7.3%	16.9%	1.6%
Yavapai County	1,934	18.4%	14.9%	21.7%	7.8%	0.0%	10.7%	0.0%	0.0%	0.0%	18.5%	0.0%	8.0%	0.0%
Yuma County	2,620	3.5%	0.0%	21.8%	11.1%	2.9%	4.5%	23.2%	2.5%	1.6%	7.2%	3.7%	12.5%	5.6%
Arkansas														
Benton County	8,265	12.2%	15.1%	5.3%	32.5%	0.8%	1.7%	2.8%	4.4%	0.7%	0.7%	5.2%	12.0%	6.6%
Craighead County	2,539	0.0%	10.4%	11.5%	9.7%	3.7%	3.9%	21.9%	3.7%	0.0%	8.5%	2.4%	24.4%	0.0%
Faulkner County	4,951	0.0%	7.8%	23.9%	12.2%	2.1%	5.2%	6.0%	16.8%	5.7%	13.2%	0.0%	5.4%	1.8%
Garland County	646	0.0%	0.0%	0.0%	53.6%	2.9%	0.0%	0.0%	36.2%	0.0%	0.0%	0.0%	7.3%	0.0%
Pulaski County	13,618	2.2%	5.5%	14.6%	15.3%	5.9%	3.0%	4.3%	12.8%	6.2%	8.8%	4.8%	10.2%	6.4%
Saline County	2,883	0.0%	6.4%	9.3%	16.2%	0.0%	58.7%	6.8%	0.0%	0.0%	0.0%	2.6%	0.0%	0.0%
Sebastian County	2,393	17.6%	5.2%	4.4%	15.7%	1.8%	1.9%	4.2%	0.0%	0.0%	0.0%	0.0%	35.6%	13.7%
Washington County	11,570	6.0%	2.1%	8.6%	22.5%	1.5%	7.9%	8.5%	13.0%	4.5%	6.4%	7.3%	10.4%	1.3%
California														
Alameda County	93,299	12.3%	7.2%	8.4%	16.7%	3.8%	14.3%	5.5%	7.9%	6.2%	4.7%	5.3%	0.9%	6.6%
Butte County	5,980	4.4%	3.1%	7.6%	23.3%	1.2%	6.4%	0.3%	8.3%	6.5%	13.0%	8.7%	11.7%	5.6%
Contra Costa County	36,158	8.6%	4.0%	9.1%	16.7%	2.9%	12.2%	11.1%	9.0%	2.8%	8.0%	5.7%	3.6%	6.4%
El Dorado County	3,452	15.6%	3.6%	13.2%	16.4%	0.0%	5.1%	12.9%	4.8%	5.6%	17.5%	0.0%	3.9%	1.5%
Fresno County	19,647	3.0%	2.4%	8.2%	14.5%	5.0%	10.4%	7.5%	13.4%	2.7%	12.6%	6.4%	9.8%	4.2%
Humboldt County	4,962	0.0%	3.0%	1.4%	13.8%	0.0%	13.6%	0.3%	9.2%	3.8%	23.8%	11.5%	5.7%	13.9%
Imperial County	1,827	9.5%	9.9%	8.9%	7.2%	0.0%	15.7%	5.0%	0.0%	0.0%	21.7%	12.6%	9.5%	0.0%
Kern County	12,512	7.4%	1.9%	15.6%	23.9%	0.6%	10.9%	6.8%	3.3%	3.5%	12.1%	5.2%	8.4%	0.5%
Kings County	1,680	0.0%	4.4%	10.0%	20.2%	0.8%	38.6%	5.0%	2.4%	0.0%	14.9%	3.8%	0.0%	0.0%
Los Angeles County	443,557	6.4%	2.9%	7.0%	17.5%	2.7%	13.2%	9.1%	7.0%	5.7%	6.1%	6.9%	3.4%	12.0%
Madera County	1,298	6.4%	0.0%	15.5%	17.5%	0.0%	7.9%	0.0%	0.0%	15.9%	31.7%	0.0%	5.2%	0.0%
Marin County	6,395	0.0%	6.3%	10.0%	5.0%	4.3%	16.9%	15.5%	7.8%	10.6%	11.3%	8.1%	0.0%	4.3%
Merced County	3,591	1.4%	3.3%	10.1%	27.3%	2.9%	6.2%	8.0%	10.6%	1.6%	13.5%	12.6%	2.5%	0.0%
Monterey County	10,041	4.2%	4.1%	15.6%	16.0%	0.9%	10.3%	4.9%	6.7%	8.3%	6.9%	6.1%	4.8%	11.2%
Napa County	2,275	8.0%	0.0%	11.3%	23.6%	1.8%	9.9%	10.3%	8.4%	3.8%	2.5%	7.8%	10.6%	2.0%
Nevada County	1,612	0.0%	0.0%	0.0%	36.2%	16.9%	22.3%	0.0%	9.6%	0.0%	2.1%	0.0%	5.8%	7.2%
Orange County	137,165	8.9%	3.0%	5.0%	23.8%	2.5%	12.9%	8.2%	10.4%	5.6%	6.4%	5.6%	3.1%	4.6%
Placer County	8,448	4.1%	0.4%	5.7%	21.3%	1.4%	14.9%	8.9%	9.5%	2.4%	7.8%	11.2%	1.8%	10.8%
Riverside County	46,129	4.3%	2.2%	8.2%	24.8%	1.5%	12.6%	3.4%	10.1%	5.4%	5.3%	10.3%	7.0%	5.0%
Sacramento County	50,438	10.9%	3.3%	6.8%	21.8%	2.2%	17.5%	5.4%	8.8%	4.4%	3.4%	7.1%	3.8%	4.6%
San Bernardino County	50,306	4.8%	3.2%	14.4%	19.3%	1.3%	9.9%	3.1%	12.2%	4.7%	5.9%	10.6%	4.1%	6.3%
San Diego County	155,656	11.6%	4.3%	6.6%	18.6%	3.3%	12.0%	5.7%	7.9%	3.9%	7.6%	8.0%	4.1%	6.3%
San Francisco County	107,929	10.4%	5.9%	5.0%	21.3%	3.7%	15.2%	6.4%	7.5%	4.5%	3.8%	7.6%	1.5%	7.2%
San Joaquin County	11,606	3.9%	3.0%	5.7%	21.6%	0.0%	10.6%	7.6%	21.0%	2.6%	2.7%	14.7%	3.6%	3.1%
San Luis Obispo County	8,602	10.6%	3.6%	11.7%	11.2%	0.0%	11.3%	4.9%	10.8%	8.0%	14.8%	2.6%	1.5%	9.0%
San Mateo County	40,157	8.7%	9.7%	6.8%	22.7%	2.1%	9.5%	7.8%	6.8%	2.6%	6.2%	6.2%	3.4%	7.4%
Santa Barbara County	15,270	9.5%	4.0%	4.4%	10.9%	7.1%	17.0%	6.4%	5.3%	6.5%	4.8%	12.0%	2.9%	9.0%
Santa Clara County	123,144	22.3%	14.3%	5.6%	17.2%	3.1%	10.4%	4.0%	6.1%	2.8%	2.6%	6.0%	2.4%	3.3%
Santa Cruz County	9,618	2.5%	3.1%	4.4%	10.1%	6.0%	13.8%	10.3%	19.5%	4.2%	4.7%	7.8%	0.4%	13.3%
Shasta County	2,593	8.4%	0.0%	2.4%	13.7%	3.1%	8.5%	8.6%	5.3%	9.1%	4.8%	17.8%	8.2%	9.9%
Solano County	9,490	6.3%	1.9%	11.3%	11.7%	1.9%	20.8%	6.1%	17.2%	4.1%	4.2%	5.1%	1.6%	7.6%
Sonoma County	12,310	1.5%	0.5%	14.0%	21.3%	1.6%	15.7%	4.0%	14.4%	6.6%	4.0%	6.4%	4.5%	5.5%
Stanislaus County	8,050	0.0%	0.7%	6.2%	14.4%	2.0%	12.7%	6.8%	13.9%	10.0%	15.1%	11.5%	4.1%	2.7%
Sutter County	1,656	0.0%	0.0%	7.3%	23.1%	0.0%	15.8%	7.2%	1.8%	4.2%	22.2%	2.7%	0.0%	15.7%
Tulare County	5,892	5.8%	0.3%	25.9%	9.4%	0.0%	6.1%	5.5%	4.1%	1.6%	15.4%	6.5%	16.1%	3.3%
Ventura County	24,596	10.1%	1.5%	5.7%	17.5%	3.3%	11.1%	6.1%	7.2%	5.1%	6.6%	12.5%	5.8%	7.6%
Yolo County	12,314	7.7%	1.5%	4.1%	4.3%	7.5%	8.9%	1.6%	29.3%	4.7%	13.5%	6.8%	2.0%	8.1%

Table F-2: Counties—Educational Field of Study—*Continued*

	Total Millennial Population	Percent of the Population 18 to 31 by Field of Study												
		Engineering	Computers and Math	Science and Engineering Related	Business	Physical Science	Social Science	Communications	Biological Sciences	Literature	Liberal Arts	Psychology	Education	Visual and Performing Arts
Colorado														
Adams County	12,165	5.5%	5.5%	8.0%	27.5%	0.5%	4.8%	6.5%	14.5%	2.2%	6.1%	8.6%	6.3%	3.9%
Arapahoe County	22,966	9.9%	5.6%	7.7%	21.3%	1.0%	11.1%	8.5%	10.5%	3.6%	4.0%	5.0%	7.3%	4.5%
Boulder County	18,836	16.1%	1.8%	3.2%	15.9%	4.6%	8.5%	3.6%	7.4%	3.6%	7.0%	11.2%	4.5%	12.6%
Denver County	59,586	5.7%	1.3%	7.4%	30.3%	1.1%	10.6%	9.4%	6.2%	6.2%	5.7%	4.7%	3.8%	7.6%
Douglas County	11,284	4.6%	4.7%	6.4%	32.3%	2.0%	7.0%	3.3%	5.5%	4.0%	5.9%	11.2%	8.2%	4.8%
El Paso County	21,484	7.5%	7.1%	8.1%	16.0%	1.8%	14.2%	5.5%	4.1%	5.9%	6.0%	13.5%	3.8%	6.4%
Jefferson County	22,162	13.6%	2.9%	7.9%	13.3%	3.9%	11.0%	6.5%	8.5%	6.3%	4.7%	6.2%	5.9%	9.2%
Larimer County	16,241	5.8%	1.2%	7.1%	14.2%	1.9%	12.5%	4.6%	20.2%	4.0%	7.5%	9.7%	6.8%	4.4%
Mesa County	2,625	0.0%	0.0%	15.6%	20.4%	0.0%	0.0%	0.0%	25.0%	0.0%	0.0%	10.2%	21.6%	7.2%
Pueblo County	3,028	12.4%	3.8%	3.0%	42.9%	0.0%	8.0%	3.9%	2.0%	4.3%	14.2%	3.5%	0.0%	1.9%
Weld County	7,866	3.6%	4.7%	9.2%	18.4%	0.8%	4.8%	6.9%	12.3%	2.4%	9.4%	13.4%	10.9%	3.2%
Connecticut														
Fairfield County	43,655	4.8%	2.9%	5.2%	25.1%	2.7%	10.5%	9.4%	6.5%	5.1%	4.6%	5.8%	8.9%	8.6%
Hartford County	39,912	13.5%	4.8%	9.8%	22.8%	0.5%	7.5%	6.3%	8.1%	3.0%	3.5%	6.3%	7.7%	6.3%
Litchfield County	6,266	15.4%	2.9%	4.9%	21.7%	0.7%	5.5%	6.7%	5.4%	3.4%	8.7%	12.2%	7.5%	5.2%
Middlesex County	7,717	15.0%	4.6%	5.8%	8.9%	5.5%	14.8%	5.8%	5.7%	5.8%	9.3%	13.0%	3.8%	2.0%
New Haven County	38,232	4.2%	3.3%	10.2%	17.0%	2.3%	10.1%	4.7%	11.6%	4.5%	5.1%	9.5%	9.5%	8.1%
New London County	7,893	14.4%	4.7%	8.4%	14.1%	4.3%	12.1%	2.3%	12.5%	3.1%	7.6%	2.8%	8.4%	5.5%
Tolland County	6,318	3.8%	3.0%	3.8%	16.2%	10.1%	3.5%	1.3%	21.1%	4.2%	5.9%	5.1%	9.7%	12.4%
Windham County	1,991	8.2%	2.8%	10.4%	14.7%	0.0%	30.8%	4.7%	0.0%	7.2%	0.0%	7.8%	8.9%	4.4%
Delaware														
Kent County	6,017	2.2%	2.4%	10.9%	20.7%	7.7%	6.0%	0.0%	10.0%	0.5%	5.7%	14.2%	9.0%	10.9%
New Castle County	29,828	14.7%	5.8%	7.2%	20.5%	3.4%	6.8%	3.2%	8.1%	4.9%	8.1%	4.8%	7.5%	4.9%
Sussex County	3,091	6.3%	0.0%	10.7%	15.2%	0.0%	13.1%	5.8%	5.0%	5.6%	2.4%	13.1%	18.6%	4.2%
Florida														
Alachua County	21,796	11.2%	1.3%	8.7%	10.0%	7.9%	8.0%	5.6%	24.2%	3.8%	5.4%	4.1%	3.7%	6.2%
Bay County	2,856	0.0%	4.9%	13.7%	17.5%	13.7%	3.3%	4.8%	2.8%	13.3%	10.9%	3.3%	2.9%	9.1%
Brevard County	13,127	16.6%	9.4%	9.2%	22.8%	3.0%	3.4%	3.1%	4.8%	3.0%	1.4%	15.0%	6.8%	1.5%
Broward County	57,311	5.6%	5.5%	9.6%	29.2%	2.1%	8.1%	7.2%	10.1%	3.0%	1.5%	7.4%	8.1%	2.6%
Charlotte County	1,067	0.0%	0.0%	17.5%	19.1%	0.0%	15.3%	3.8%	0.0%	9.7%	15.7%	0.0%	10.5%	8.4%
Citrus County	262	38.9%	0.0%	0.0%	0.0%	0.0%	0.0%	0.0%	24.0%	0.0%	0.0%	0.0%	37.0%	0.0%
Clay County	4,227	0.0%	0.0%	10.7%	11.4%	0.0%	0.0%	0.0%	0.0%	0.0%	5.6%	31.0%	41.3%	0.0%
Collier County	5,272	0.6%	0.0%	7.8%	42.8%	0.0%	8.2%	2.9%	3.8%	3.3%	5.3%	7.7%	15.4%	2.4%
Duval County	33,312	8.6%	4.1%	12.9%	24.7%	1.0%	7.9%	8.2%	6.7%	4.4%	6.7%	5.4%	8.6%	0.8%
Escambia County	9,597	11.0%	2.6%	8.6%	22.9%	3.6%	5.2%	9.3%	7.9%	4.3%	6.4%	4.3%	5.7%	8.3%
Flagler County	576	0.0%	0.0%	33.5%	0.0%	0.0%	0.0%	0.0%	0.0%	0.0%	0.0%	33.9%	32.6%	0.0%
Hernando County	950	4.3%	0.0%	11.2%	29.8%	0.0%	23.9%	9.5%	2.7%	0.0%	0.0%	0.0%	16.6%	2.0%
Highlands County	310	0.0%	0.0%	34.5%	0.0%	0.0%	0.0%	0.0%	0.0%	32.3%	0.0%	0.0%	33.2%	0.0%
Hillsborough County	53,599	8.1%	3.2%	9.0%	28.0%	1.5%	8.8%	8.0%	7.6%	3.2%	4.1%	5.4%	8.0%	5.1%
Indian River County	1,502	20.8%	0.0%	9.6%	17.2%	0.0%	23.5%	0.0%	22.4%	0.0%	0.0%	0.0%	6.5%	0.0%
Lake County	4,842	3.9%	0.7%	5.3%	18.3%	5.8%	3.0%	14.3%	7.8%	2.5%	9.7%	1.1%	18.2%	9.5%
Lee County	11,944	0.2%	1.6%	14.3%	28.6%	10.1%	3.6%	8.8%	3.9%	5.8%	6.2%	6.3%	6.6%	4.0%
Leon County	20,705	4.8%	2.8%	13.8%	17.5%	2.5%	9.3%	5.0%	6.9%	4.5%	4.0%	12.9%	10.1%	6.0%
Manatee County	8,333	4.1%	5.1%	6.5%	16.9%	1.5%	10.5%	3.2%	21.5%	6.9%	0.4%	5.1%	11.4%	7.0%
Marion County	4,276	8.2%	0.0%	14.2%	13.0%	0.0%	0.0%	6.0%	17.3%	0.0%	2.0%	18.3%	18.0%	3.1%
Martin County	2,296	4.3%	0.0%	14.2%	22.5%	0.0%	6.6%	3.4%	6.0%	18.7%	8.0%	0.0%	16.5%	0.0%
Miami-Dade County	86,794	6.8%	2.8%	9.2%	27.6%	2.8%	9.2%	6.7%	6.5%	3.9%	3.7%	7.4%	7.4%	6.2%
Okaloosa County	6,711	6.6%	9.4%	6.8%	17.3%	0.7%	7.6%	10.9%	12.0%	2.6%	7.6%	9.0%	5.1%	4.3%
Orange County	56,199	8.6%	6.4%	8.7%	28.7%	1.7%	6.9%	7.2%	3.6%	1.9%	2.9%	9.1%	9.0%	5.4%
Osceola County	5,371	2.9%	0.0%	4.6%	24.4%	1.2%	3.8%	7.9%	6.3%	10.6%	8.0%	10.6%	11.2%	8.3%
Palm Beach County	34,043	4.9%	3.2%	8.2%	27.7%	2.8%	7.8%	6.2%	7.7%	3.3%	3.4%	8.5%	8.0%	8.3%
Pasco County	8,451	3.1%	2.7%	11.3%	20.3%	3.1%	13.6%	5.1%	4.8%	5.1%	6.1%	8.6%	16.2%	0.0%
Pinellas County	22,460	3.7%	3.2%	8.7%	31.2%	3.0%	9.1%	6.6%	5.7%	2.8%	1.6%	8.5%	10.2%	5.6%
Polk County	10,148	2.2%	3.5%	6.6%	18.6%	2.8%	11.5%	6.3%	7.5%	2.2%	9.5%	11.7%	13.6%	3.9%
Santa Rosa County	2,979	6.5%	0.0%	3.8%	35.1%	2.7%	12.4%	0.0%	21.6%	3.0%	6.9%	0.0%	8.1%	0.0%
Sarasota County	5,154	3.6%	2.3%	3.1%	27.0%	1.2%	7.3%	3.8%	5.4%	1.0%	3.2%	7.3%	19.2%	15.6%
Seminole County	18,333	9.7%	3.8%	10.0%	25.5%	0.6%	12.9%	4.2%	4.6%	1.2%	4.5%	4.8%	13.6%	4.5%
St. Johns County	5,263	6.1%	5.0%	6.3%	45.3%	1.1%	7.2%	10.3%	4.9%	0.0%	4.1%	4.6%	2.8%	2.2%
St. Lucie County	2,105	0.0%	13.1%	26.3%	3.7%	0.0%	0.0%	9.9%	4.1%	5.2%	8.9%	0.0%	28.7%	0.0%
Sumter County	494	0.0%	0.0%	24.1%	0.0%	0.0%	28.9%	0.0%	0.0%	0.0%	33.2%	0.0%	13.8%	0.0%
Volusia County	7,975	11.4%	3.3%	8.2%	15.1%	6.9%	9.0%	4.5%	7.5%	0.8%	7.2%	1.7%	14.8%	9.6%
Georgia														
Bartow County	1,075	10.2%	0.0%	0.0%	0.0%	3.6%	21.9%	3.9%	0.0%	0.0%	0.0%	39.0%	21.4%	0.0%
Bibb County	4,022	1.6%	6.7%	7.8%	19.5%	0.0%	16.6%	2.9%	18.0%	1.5%	5.5%	0.0%	6.7%	13.2%
Carroll County	1,192	0.0%	7.3%	14.8%	23.6%	0.0%	0.0%	0.0%	4.4%	6.5%	4.8%	0.0%	31.2%	7.5%
Chatham County	12,193	4.1%	8.7%	22.3%	12.9%	1.2%	16.2%	3.0%	3.3%	2.5%	7.7%	2.8%	7.1%	8.2%
Cherokee County	7,049	3.5%	19.2%	6.9%	11.8%	0.0%	5.4%	3.6%	6.8%	0.0%	21.9%	1.2%	12.5%	7.3%
Clarke County	12,801	5.5%	0.0%	4.6%	14.7%	5.7%	19.6%	7.2%	13.1%	8.2%	3.6%	5.3%	7.7%	4.8%
Clayton County	4,073	0.0%	3.0%	26.4%	12.2%	1.8%	5.4%	5.9%	15.2%	5.9%	8.8%	10.2%	2.4%	2.7%
Cobb County	35,076	11.7%	3.9%	8.7%	24.3%	2.3%	8.3%	8.5%	6.6%	3.9%	2.9%	7.7%	7.4%	3.8%
Columbia County	2,578	1.9%	3.6%	42.6%	20.1%	0.0%	0.0%	3.4%	13.5%	0.0%	1.0%	5.9%	8.1%	0.0%
Coweta County	4,591	4.3%	0.0%	9.9%	44.4%	0.0%	2.6%	4.8%	7.8%	1.9%	5.0%	9.9%	6.9%	2.6%
DeKalb County	39,136	5.0%	6.8%	7.7%	31.2%	1.6%	6.4%	6.0%	10.7%	4.1%	1.7%	7.5%	5.0%	6.1%
Dougherty County	1,778	0.0%	0.0%	35.9%	31.4%	0.0%	0.0%	0.0%	8.3%	1.0%	9.3%	5.1%	0.0%	8.9%
Douglas County	3,695	0.0%	0.0%	0.0%	13.1%	5.8%	5.7%	16.5%	17.8%	0.0%	0.0%	0.0%	35.9%	5.2%

Table F-2: Counties—Educational Field of Study—*Continued*

	Total Millennial Population	Engineering	Computers and Math	Science and Engineering Related	Business	Physical Science	Social Science	Communications	Biological Sciences	Literature	Liberal Arts	Psychology	Education	Visual and Performing Arts
Georgia—Cont.														
Fayette County	3,682	2.9%	0.0%	4.0%	13.9%	11.6%	0.0%	0.5%	21.1%	3.8%	20.2%	5.0%	7.7%	9.4%
Floyd County	2,275	10.2%	5.5%	16.2%	12.9%	16.9%	6.9%	0.0%	11.4%	0.0%	0.6%	3.5%	12.9%	3.1%
Forsyth County	4,951	6.4%	12.8%	2.0%	16.7%	3.3%	6.4%	7.3%	5.2%	11.8%	8.4%	4.3%	10.6%	4.8%
Fulton County	63,458	8.2%	4.3%	6.3%	26.5%	3.9%	8.7%	11.3%	4.8%	5.1%	3.3%	6.7%	4.5%	6.6%
Gwinnett County	24,719	6.9%	3.9%	8.5%	26.0%	2.5%	5.6%	8.4%	7.3%	1.8%	4.3%	5.2%	13.1%	6.5%
Hall County	3,228	1.5%	3.4%	14.5%	13.6%	15.6%	3.9%	0.0%	6.8%	2.5%	0.0%	0.0%	29.8%	8.4%
Henry County	5,796	3.9%	0.0%	16.1%	15.9%	2.0%	8.5%	10.4%	6.0%	2.0%	0.7%	7.5%	22.2%	4.8%
Houston County	2,898	7.8%	3.1%	0.0%	31.3%	0.0%	0.0%	4.9%	14.9%	1.1%	11.2%	14.3%	11.4%	0.0%
Lowndes County	5,112	6.3%	0.0%	11.6%	19.0%	8.0%	2.8%	5.7%	5.3%	6.1%	2.0%	11.2%	18.8%	3.2%
Muscogee County	5,958	7.5%	2.5%	7.2%	24.0%	0.0%	12.9%	7.0%	8.0%	5.4%	4.4%	13.3%	5.9%	1.8%
Newton County	1,558	0.0%	3.0%	12.7%	3.2%	0.0%	28.9%	0.0%	0.0%	0.0%	6.5%	8.7%	13.0%	24.0%
Paulding County	2,399	0.0%	3.0%	2.1%	32.4%	6.4%	10.8%	9.3%	9.3%	4.8%	0.0%	4.4%	17.5%	0.0%
Richmond County	7,414	4.6%	0.0%	21.8%	17.6%	0.0%	23.8%	6.9%	7.7%	3.4%	2.1%	8.8%	1.3%	1.9%
Whitfield County	1,564	0.0%	0.0%	47.4%	2.6%	0.0%	0.0%	0.0%	19.6%	0.0%	3.3%	4.5%	21.2%	1.5%
Hawaii														
Hawaii County	5,336	0.0%	0.0%	17.4%	19.6%	1.1%	26.5%	12.6%	9.8%	0.0%	0.0%	5.1%	5.2%	2.8%
Honolulu County	41,350	6.5%	1.6%	12.7%	25.2%	2.9%	7.2%	6.6%	9.2%	4.1%	3.4%	7.5%	10.1%	3.1%
Maui County	3,626	7.8%	0.0%	17.8%	16.5%	25.2%	2.2%	3.3%	6.2%	1.9%	1.8%	2.0%	4.7%	10.6%
Idaho														
Ada County	14,744	9.9%	2.1%	13.2%	12.1%	2.4%	4.0%	8.7%	19.5%	3.8%	3.3%	8.0%	10.6%	2.4%
Bonneville County	2,934	7.7%	11.9%	7.9%	15.8%	3.0%	4.0%	1.9%	2.7%	2.1%	1.9%	5.7%	33.2%	2.2%
Canyon County	3,007	7.0%	0.0%	8.4%	15.8%	0.0%	0.0%	15.5%	30.4%	0.0%	8.1%	7.0%	6.9%	1.0%
Kootenai County	4,508	12.6%	0.0%	0.0%	21.1%	0.0%	9.9%	1.2%	10.4%	0.0%	7.0%	8.5%	27.2%	2.3%
Illinois														
Champaign County	15,852	13.3%	6.0%	4.1%	12.6%	12.7%	1.9%	7.7%	15.6%	3.0%	8.7%	2.6%	7.7%	4.1%
Cook County	339,166	6.9%	4.2%	7.2%	23.6%	2.6%	10.7%	7.0%	6.2%	4.5%	5.0%	7.0%	7.4%	7.8%
DeKalb County	7,576	1.7%	7.9%	17.3%	15.1%	2.2%	9.1%	11.2%	3.7%	2.2%	3.8%	4.3%	11.5%	10.0%
DuPage County	51,215	11.0%	5.3%	11.4%	20.4%	2.1%	7.6%	6.2%	6.3%	2.3%	3.7%	8.5%	11.6%	3.5%
Kane County	13,249	4.0%	5.3%	11.7%	27.1%	5.2%	2.6%	2.6%	9.1%	2.3%	4.3%	2.1%	16.4%	7.2%
Kankakee County	1,112	13.1%	0.0%	0.0%	27.0%	0.0%	4.9%	8.5%	2.2%	14.9%	0.0%	11.8%	11.9%	5.6%
Kendall County	3,532	3.5%	0.0%	10.4%	23.3%	15.8%	0.0%	7.6%	0.7%	8.4%	3.7%	0.0%	24.5%	2.2%
Lake County	23,702	9.2%	2.2%	13.4%	22.4%	5.4%	10.6%	6.0%	5.4%	3.4%	3.3%	5.9%	7.9%	4.9%
LaSalle County	2,635	1.3%	0.0%	26.2%	23.3%	0.0%	1.1%	13.3%	6.9%	4.9%	2.4%	12.1%	7.3%	1.2%
Macon County	1,823	16.8%	0.0%	3.0%	39.9%	0.0%	10.5%	2.4%	10.2%	0.0%	7.6%	0.0%	3.4%	6.1%
Madison County	9,940	3.9%	3.1%	10.4%	23.8%	2.2%	7.8%	8.3%	10.1%	1.1%	2.7%	6.2%	13.0%	7.3%
McHenry County	10,467	8.0%	4.6%	10.7%	23.2%	0.9%	13.8%	1.6%	4.8%	4.4%	4.4%	2.9%	14.4%	6.2%
McLean County	11,218	12.0%	8.8%	10.8%	17.4%	6.6%	5.1%	4.1%	9.8%	0.0%	0.0%	11.3%	11.0%	3.1%
Peoria County	10,451	17.5%	2.8%	15.9%	17.8%	1.0%	2.9%	2.9%	7.4%	2.6%	2.9%	9.6%	8.8%	8.0%
Rock Island County	3,142	10.8%	6.2%	3.9%	34.7%	0.0%	0.0%	0.0%	2.4%	2.2%	3.3%	7.5%	13.8%	15.2%
Sangamon County	8,829	5.3%	2.0%	14.8%	16.5%	3.0%	14.4%	8.8%	10.4%	3.4%	8.9%	6.7%	4.9%	1.1%
St. Clair County	6,812	7.0%	1.2%	14.7%	19.4%	9.1%	0.0%	21.4%	7.1%	1.1%	1.9%	1.8%	12.5%	2.9%
Tazewell County	3,401	8.8%	1.3%	12.7%	26.9%	3.2%	3.9%	5.0%	0.8%	2.1%	10.5%	0.0%	19.0%	5.7%
Will County	21,653	6.2%	5.5%	15.4%	21.7%	2.2%	7.4%	3.0%	8.5%	1.5%	0.7%	7.1%	14.9%	5.9%
Winnebago County	7,702	9.8%	1.8%	12.9%	9.8%	6.3%	8.4%	6.1%	7.0%	2.5%	6.4%	8.7%	13.9%	6.3%
Indiana														
Allen County	9,147	3.8%	3.4%	12.7%	27.1%	2.5%	7.9%	4.4%	7.4%	1.1%	5.8%	3.9%	10.7%	9.3%
Clark County	1,599	7.9%	0.0%	32.2%	15.8%	4.4%	0.0%	9.1%	0.0%	0.0%	12.9%	17.8%	0.0%	0.0%
Delaware County	3,195	1.9%	9.4%	11.9%	20.8%	4.6%	0.0%	0.0%	8.3%	0.0%	21.8%	12.4%	6.5%	2.5%
Elkhart County	3,257	5.9%	0.0%	16.1%	13.0%	0.0%	1.3%	0.0%	5.7%	0.0%	23.6%	3.5%	22.4%	8.5%
Hamilton County	16,822	7.4%	6.5%	16.1%	21.6%	2.5%	2.7%	4.3%	9.5%	2.8%	8.1%	4.6%	11.3%	2.4%
Hendricks County	4,741	6.3%	1.9%	11.7%	22.5%	3.4%	3.8%	12.8%	4.6%	0.0%	9.0%	1.9%	16.5%	5.6%
Johnson County	3,604	6.0%	1.9%	12.2%	41.3%	0.0%	0.0%	4.4%	4.1%	2.2%	6.0%	0.0%	17.8%	4.1%
Lake County	11,324	3.8%	7.2%	6.2%	23.0%	2.9%	9.5%	7.7%	9.5%	1.1%	5.7%	8.0%	11.0%	4.5%
LaPorte County	1,322	2.2%	7.6%	37.9%	28.1%	0.0%	3.6%	3.3%	3.3%	0.0%	0.8%	12.2%	0.9%	0.0%
Madison County	2,590	0.0%	0.0%	22.3%	16.9%	7.6%	0.0%	11.9%	19.6%	3.4%	5.1%	0.0%	3.3%	9.8%
Marion County	43,577	5.3%	6.0%	11.6%	18.2%	3.8%	5.7%	8.3%	12.3%	4.5%	5.1%	6.4%	10.1%	2.7%
Monroe County	12,601	2.8%	7.4%	4.0%	4.8%	4.5%	17.4%	0.9%	9.7%	10.5%	7.3%	5.6%	7.2%	17.8%
Porter County	5,361	7.9%	12.7%	11.9%	10.6%	0.2%	4.9%	2.1%	16.0%	4.8%	5.5%	2.7%	20.7%	0.0%
St. Joseph County	7,325	10.2%	1.1%	11.0%	13.5%	7.6%	5.2%	1.6%	5.9%	9.7%	7.3%	3.9%	18.4%	4.4%
Tippecanoe County	11,101	11.7%	5.9%	21.4%	9.9%	17.1%	1.6%	6.9%	10.7%	7.1%	1.3%	1.1%	3.4%	1.9%
Vanderburgh County	4,783	12.1%	5.6%	12.2%	21.1%	0.0%	3.9%	5.8%	9.0%	1.0%	0.0%	3.1%	23.8%	2.4%
Vigo County	2,580	12.1%	8.7%	40.5%	1.3%	0.0%	4.9%	10.9%	8.4%	1.4%	0.0%	5.2%	6.7%	0.0%
Iowa														
Black Hawk County	4,084	3.9%	0.0%	16.3%	8.5%	0.0%	9.3%	6.5%	2.7%	9.2%	2.4%	15.9%	20.7%	4.6%
Dubuque County	2,162	0.0%	18.5%	5.1%	33.3%	0.0%	0.0%	13.7%	3.5%	6.2%	0.0%	8.1%	6.1%	5.5%
Johnson County	12,543	1.4%	6.3%	5.8%	14.9%	0.7%	4.4%	10.7%	23.4%	8.7%	7.4%	7.2%	6.9%	2.2%
Linn County	7,405	26.3%	5.1%	5.8%	27.4%	0.0%	8.0%	6.9%	5.2%	9.3%	1.8%	1.7%	2.6%	0.0%
Polk County	22,263	7.5%	1.2%	5.1%	37.4%	0.0%	9.7%	10.0%	5.6%	4.2%	3.6%	3.5%	10.6%	1.6%
Pottawattamie County	1,630	6.0%	0.0%	0.0%	47.2%	0.0%	4.2%	9.8%	5.5%	4.0%	5.0%	7.3%	7.2%	3.9%
Scott County	8,577	16.0%	5.7%	10.4%	15.3%	9.0%	11.6%	2.3%	10.9%	2.6%	0.0%	3.0%	4.6%	8.5%
Story County	8,044	34.3%	0.0%	3.8%	16.1%	0.0%	2.6%	2.0%	18.4%	2.9%	2.4%	5.9%	8.5%	3.0%
Woodbury County	1,933	3.7%	0.0%	2.7%	24.3%	0.0%	0.0%	0.0%	15.4%	0.0%	21.9%	0.0%	19.0%	12.9%
Kansas														
Douglas County	14,177	10.3%	4.6%	16.5%	6.7%	2.0%	7.7%	10.4%	6.4%	9.0%	4.5%	5.3%	3.8%	12.7%
Johnson County	30,820	8.2%	4.9%	9.4%	26.7%	1.4%	4.9%	7.0%	11.6%	3.7%	6.9%	4.2%	7.6%	3.6%

Percent of the Population 18 to 31 by Field of Study

Table F-2: Counties—Educational Field of Study—*Continued*

	Total Millennial Population	Percent of the Population 18 to 31 by Field of Study												
		Engineering	Computers and Math	Science and Engineering Related	Business	Physical Science	Social Science	Communications	Biological Sciences	Literature	Liberal Arts	Psychology	Education	Visual and Performing Arts
Kansas—Cont.														
Sedgwick County	19,234	12.1%	0.0%	14.8%	22.4%	4.4%	1.4%	2.6%	5.8%	5.2%	5.6%	4.3%	17.7%	3.7%
Shawnee County	5,886	4.3%	3.0%	9.4%	21.7%	0.0%	5.9%	4.3%	12.3%	5.6%	0.0%	8.5%	20.7%	4.2%
Wyandotte County	3,319	19.2%	0.0%	1.7%	20.2%	5.9%	1.6%	0.0%	24.9%	2.3%	3.8%	9.5%	11.0%	0.0%
Kentucky														
Boone County	4,587	6.9%	0.0%	22.0%	23.5%	0.0%	6.2%	5.7%	2.4%	0.0%	5.0%	2.7%	18.3%	7.2%
Campbell County	3,128	4.9%	3.8%	21.3%	18.3%	0.0%	0.0%	9.7%	8.5%	0.0%	11.3%	8.3%	5.1%	8.8%
Daviess County	1,868	22.4%	4.1%	8.0%	26.5%	0.0%	0.0%	16.8%	0.0%	4.4%	0.0%	0.0%	17.8%	0.0%
Fayette County	15,451	11.8%	2.0%	13.3%	16.7%	6.3%	12.2%	1.4%	4.9%	5.8%	2.2%	12.5%	5.8%	5.0%
Hardin County	2,325	0.3%	0.0%	0.0%	52.2%	0.0%	10.0%	0.0%	0.0%	0.0%	0.0%	7.2%	26.5%	3.8%
Jefferson County	32,389	8.9%	1.5%	10.1%	25.7%	3.2%	7.4%	10.1%	6.3%	3.0%	5.0%	7.1%	7.9%	3.8%
Kenton County	6,327	5.9%	0.0%	7.8%	28.0%	0.3%	10.7%	12.5%	8.5%	0.0%	3.6%	4.4%	8.1%	10.3%
Warren County	5,461	2.3%	2.4%	16.2%	20.5%	3.6%	8.6%	9.0%	2.8%	8.1%	8.6%	2.6%	7.5%	7.6%
Louisiana														
Ascension Parish	2,814	17.2%	0.0%	19.4%	8.0%	0.0%	0.0%	15.5%	0.0%	4.9%	11.9%	7.1%	6.4%	9.7%
Bossier Parish	4,482	8.2%	3.5%	21.5%	19.8%	0.0%	2.7%	9.4%	6.6%	13.9%	1.9%	3.7%	8.8%	0.0%
Caddo Parish	6,678	7.0%	0.0%	22.3%	27.2%	5.1%	1.3%	0.0%	18.2%	1.9%	7.5%	4.3%	5.1%	0.0%
Calcasieu Parish	2,889	7.7%	0.0%	29.5%	5.6%	0.0%	7.6%	2.4%	14.8%	0.0%	8.1%	5.0%	14.2%	5.0%
East Baton Rouge Parish	23,228	12.4%	0.9%	13.1%	16.7%	5.0%	12.9%	4.8%	14.1%	2.7%	5.8%	2.8%	5.6%	3.1%
Jefferson Parish	12,986	7.9%	1.6%	12.7%	18.3%	8.1%	0.8%	8.8%	8.7%	6.1%	4.2%	6.6%	9.5%	6.9%
Lafayette Parish	12,052	14.9%	11.5%	5.2%	13.2%	5.2%	1.4%	6.0%	3.5%	2.1%	15.8%	7.5%	3.2%	10.7%
Lafourche Parish	1,812	0.0%	2.9%	50.4%	13.1%	0.0%	0.0%	11.2%	0.0%	4.5%	9.5%	6.7%	1.7%	0.0%
Livingston Parish	2,160	6.2%	11.7%	28.8%	0.7%	0.0%	0.0%	1.4%	0.0%	5.0%	19.7%	0.0%	26.6%	0.0%
Orleans Parish	24,914	4.2%	0.8%	10.5%	18.9%	3.6%	16.9%	7.7%	9.6%	5.1%	6.5%	5.6%	2.3%	8.3%
Ouachita Parish	3,744	0.0%	3.6%	20.5%	35.9%	0.7%	2.2%	4.1%	5.1%	2.6%	7.3%	4.4%	13.5%	0.0%
Rapides Parish	3,148	0.0%	1.3%	0.0%	33.9%	3.7%	13.9%	7.0%	2.5%	5.0%	11.1%	10.4%	11.2%	0.0%
St. Tammany Parish	9,287	8.8%	1.8%	4.0%	23.6%	5.1%	6.4%	7.8%	9.3%	1.4%	11.0%	0.0%	7.1%	13.6%
Tangipahoa Parish	2,226	0.0%	0.0%	0.0%	11.0%	0.0%	0.0%	7.1%	5.8%	14.4%	8.0%	31.2%	17.2%	5.3%
Terrebonne Parish	2,021	39.6%	0.0%	24.4%	11.1%	0.0%	0.0%	0.0%	0.0%	6.9%	9.4%	4.5%	4.2%	0.0%
Maine														
Androscoggin County	1,074	0.0%	0.0%	0.0%	21.5%	0.0%	29.8%	0.0%	12.1%	5.8%	0.0%	0.0%	30.8%	0.0%
Cumberland County	12,729	1.6%	0.0%	5.3%	13.8%	0.9%	11.4%	6.0%	23.3%	4.7%	4.8%	8.9%	5.5%	14.0%
Kennebec County	2,533	3.5%	0.0%	0.0%	3.0%	4.4%	0.0%	3.8%	20.2%	2.4%	15.1%	1.4%	31.2%	15.1%
Penobscot County	3,747	16.7%	0.0%	20.1%	22.5%	0.8%	9.8%	9.2%	2.3%	2.8%	6.9%	0.0%	8.9%	0.0%
York County	5,111	12.3%	0.0%	6.1%	11.2%	0.0%	0.5%	7.0%	38.5%	0.0%	0.0%	10.0%	12.5%	1.9%
Maryland														
Anne Arundel County	22,089	9.5%	8.1%	6.0%	27.1%	2.7%	8.1%	4.2%	5.0%	7.0%	6.2%	3.8%	4.7%	7.8%
Baltimore County	33,447	6.3%	8.6%	11.8%	19.0%	4.3%	5.0%	5.9%	3.7%	11.0%	4.0%	7.5%	7.8%	5.4%
Carroll County	3,822	5.7%	4.5%	13.5%	16.4%	3.0%	4.9%	13.9%	7.3%	2.1%	4.9%	1.9%	6.4%	15.5%
Cecil County	3,647	8.4%	11.4%	1.9%	14.9%	17.2%	0.0%	3.2%	5.6%	2.1%	18.3%	10.7%	3.3%	2.9%
Charles County	4,533	5.2%	0.0%	11.2%	19.6%	0.0%	2.2%	10.3%	1.5%	5.2%	7.1%	9.8%	28.0%	0.0%
Frederick County	11,235	1.7%	12.2%	7.5%	16.8%	3.1%	5.7%	7.4%	11.0%	8.6%	9.1%	5.6%	4.9%	6.5%
Harford County	8,219	13.4%	3.4%	10.3%	16.3%	4.9%	5.4%	3.2%	18.2%	1.6%	5.4%	4.8%	10.9%	2.1%
Howard County	20,705	8.2%	7.1%	8.5%	20.6%	2.8%	8.3%	4.7%	7.7%	4.5%	2.8%	16.0%	5.4%	3.5%
Montgomery County	56,703	10.1%	5.9%	10.0%	14.6%	2.9%	13.6%	5.9%	7.7%	5.3%	5.8%	8.4%	6.0%	3.9%
Prince George's County	35,616	7.3%	4.4%	5.4%	21.2%	4.3%	14.9%	6.6%	6.0%	6.9%	2.4%	7.9%	5.1%	7.6%
St. Mary's County	2,375	16.2%	12.8%	5.7%	9.7%	0.0%	24.8%	0.0%	14.9%	0.0%	2.6%	2.4%	10.9%	0.0%
Washington County	3,502	7.1%	1.8%	14.4%	32.6%	1.9%	12.4%	5.7%	6.8%	1.1%	0.0%	3.9%	12.3%	0.0%
Wicomico County	3,375	0.0%	2.2%	28.5%	17.4%	11.6%	5.3%	5.7%	0.0%	4.7%	0.0%	3.9%	9.8%	11.1%
Massachusetts														
Barnstable County	6,263	8.4%	2.8%	10.9%	15.6%	6.0%	4.1%	3.3%	10.8%	11.9%	9.0%	10.5%	1.6%	5.1%
Berkshire County	3,403	12.7%	6.3%	1.0%	4.2%	3.8%	3.5%	1.1%	6.1%	19.1%	16.9%	6.7%	12.0%	6.4%
Bristol County	17,097	6.6%	3.0%	9.8%	27.7%	2.3%	5.1%	3.5%	2.9%	2.6%	6.9%	11.7%	10.8%	7.2%
Essex County	32,405	8.2%	5.7%	9.1%	22.5%	1.6%	4.6%	3.5%	6.5%	6.3%	4.2%	6.2%	6.9%	14.6%
Hampden County	12,869	2.4%	7.2%	8.0%	30.4%	3.6%	5.6%	6.6%	2.2%	4.0%	3.1%	11.5%	7.5%	7.9%
Hampshire County	5,424	6.3%	0.0%	4.5%	23.6%	1.5%	10.1%	3.7%	9.3%	5.5%	8.8%	10.1%	0.0%	16.6%
Middlesex County	128,209	13.1%	4.9%	7.5%	18.3%	4.8%	11.9%	4.7%	8.2%	5.1%	4.9%	5.9%	5.2%	5.4%
Norfolk County	42,587	6.4%	3.8%	10.2%	25.0%	3.3%	8.1%	6.0%	6.1%	2.9%	7.1%	7.4%	7.0%	6.8%
Plymouth County	16,373	7.7%	3.2%	8.6%	20.2%	2.1%	12.2%	6.6%	2.8%	3.8%	4.6%	12.9%	5.9%	9.4%
Suffolk County	93,241	9.5%	2.6%	7.7%	22.7%	1.7%	13.8%	5.4%	11.3%	4.9%	4.5%	6.9%	2.4%	6.7%
Worcester County	38,459	8.3%	3.6%	12.0%	15.8%	5.8%	6.7%	6.0%	8.8%	4.4%	4.3%	9.8%	7.5%	6.8%
Michigan														
Allegan County	1,303	1.5%	2.7%	9.3%	9.4%	0.0%	23.0%	2.8%	2.8%	5.4%	28.2%	4.8%	10.1%	0.0%
Bay County	3,627	26.0%	0.0%	13.7%	16.0%	0.7%	13.4%	0.0%	9.9%	0.0%	0.0%	0.0%	8.4%	11.9%
Berrien County	4,051	4.2%	0.0%	10.1%	7.8%	2.8%	6.8%	6.9%	9.5%	2.8%	27.5%	5.8%	15.9%	0.0%
Calhoun County	1,855	3.8%	0.0%	8.4%	10.8%	0.0%	13.5%	0.0%	0.0%	28.5%	0.0%	0.0%	24.0%	11.1%
Eaton County	3,647	3.2%	6.7%	11.4%	18.7%	3.7%	20.8%	0.9%	8.1%	4.3%	3.4%	6.8%	6.3%	5.7%
Genesee County	6,935	6.6%	1.4%	7.1%	20.0%	0.0%	2.8%	8.4%	8.1%	11.3%	5.0%	7.7%	19.9%	1.8%
Ingham County	16,755	8.5%	1.2%	9.8%	20.9%	3.1%	11.7%	4.1%	16.4%	5.1%	4.5%	8.2%	6.2%	0.3%
Jackson County	2,788	6.5%	0.0%	21.3%	26.7%	3.7%	3.3%	0.0%	2.8%	1.3%	0.0%	20.3%	7.4%	6.7%
Kalamazoo County	11,170	11.5%	1.8%	10.6%	26.8%	3.0%	7.6%	12.4%	3.3%	7.9%	0.2%	4.5%	6.0%	4.2%
Kent County	31,441	8.4%	3.2%	19.6%	18.9%	2.8%	3.4%	9.0%	4.7%	4.5%	6.5%	5.6%	11.1%	2.4%
Lenawee County	1,603	4.0%	0.0%	0.0%	4.3%	0.0%	0.0%	7.3%	12.6%	18.4%	12.4%	2.1%	39.0%	0.0%
Livingston County	5,118	11.1%	4.1%	7.8%	31.0%	2.0%	6.4%	8.0%	5.0%	7.1%	0.0%	3.0%	9.7%	4.9%
Macomb County	21,366	8.6%	3.4%	10.7%	24.0%	1.5%	2.0%	6.1%	7.5%	4.0%	9.2%	7.0%	13.3%	2.8%
Monroe County	3,283	2.9%	0.0%	6.6%	53.8%	0.0%	2.0%	6.6%	3.4%	0.0%	0.0%	0.0%	20.5%	4.2%

Table F-2: Counties—Educational Field of Study—*Continued*

	Total Millennial Population	Percent of the Population 18 to 31 by Field of Study												
		Engineering	Computers and Math	Science and Engineering Related	Business	Physical Science	Social Science	Communications	Biological Sciences	Literature	Liberal Arts	Psychology	Education	Visual and Performing Arts
Michigan—Cont.														
Muskegon County	2,566	9.0%	3.4%	28.8%	24.6%	0.0%	0.0%	2.0%	1.2%	5.6%	0.0%	1.2%	22.6%	1.6%
Oakland County	62,218	11.1%	3.4%	10.6%	24.6%	3.2%	7.6%	8.5%	5.7%	4.6%	3.8%	5.6%	7.1%	4.2%
Ottawa County	10,675	7.0%	7.9%	14.5%	22.5%	0.0%	3.5%	3.9%	12.0%	1.7%	7.9%	8.8%	3.4%	6.8%
Saginaw County	4,241	23.9%	4.4%	5.7%	22.0%	2.9%	5.4%	12.5%	1.1%	0.0%	0.0%	4.7%	11.3%	6.1%
St. Clair County	2,683	6.9%	2.9%	19.2%	17.8%	1.9%	0.0%	6.1%	3.4%	0.0%	8.9%	13.5%	19.3%	0.0%
Washtenaw County	33,032	16.6%	4.0%	8.3%	13.8%	3.5%	11.5%	4.5%	11.2%	7.8%	4.7%	6.7%	3.5%	4.1%
Wayne County	43,598	11.4%	1.5%	8.0%	21.3%	5.5%	7.8%	8.7%	10.3%	3.2%	2.7%	7.2%	8.4%	4.1%
Minnesota														
Anoka County	9,860	8.6%	3.4%	2.8%	25.3%	1.7%	9.6%	5.1%	8.7%	4.0%	2.2%	2.5%	18.1%	8.0%
Carver County	4,577	0.0%	0.0%	16.2%	21.1%	0.0%	4.2%	8.5%	13.6%	0.0%	0.0%	9.7%	22.7%	4.0%
Dakota County	16,702	4.0%	2.8%	8.5%	28.7%	0.0%	9.3%	3.2%	5.6%	4.3%	6.0%	5.9%	12.8%	8.9%
Hennepin County	91,950	8.5%	3.8%	7.3%	23.8%	1.9%	13.1%	9.2%	8.2%	4.5%	3.5%	5.9%	4.7%	5.8%
Olmsted County	8,015	11.5%	6.4%	16.0%	18.4%	5.4%	10.4%	1.7%	15.8%	0.8%	2.9%	0.0%	8.2%	2.2%
Ramsey County	33,025	6.0%	3.7%	10.8%	14.8%	3.2%	10.3%	5.7%	9.6%	5.7%	4.5%	5.6%	7.7%	12.5%
Scott County	5,609	2.0%	0.0%	18.9%	31.5%	0.0%	5.6%	0.9%	34.4%	0.0%	0.0%	2.6%	4.1%	0.0%
St. Louis County	7,862	4.8%	4.0%	10.7%	16.7%	6.5%	13.0%	9.5%	10.9%	1.9%	2.1%	5.7%	12.6%	1.5%
Stearns County	3,838	2.8%	4.9%	10.4%	12.6%	4.2%	4.0%	3.4%	7.0%	0.0%	0.0%	8.8%	32.0%	10.1%
Washington County	7,189	6.4%	0.0%	18.6%	25.4%	2.0%	15.8%	3.0%	8.6%	0.3%	0.0%	5.4%	12.3%	2.1%
Wright County	2,820	4.4%	0.0%	11.2%	10.2%	0.0%	0.0%	4.3%	25.0%	1.8%	8.6%	3.3%	28.5%	2.7%
Mississippi														
DeSoto County	4,174	1.3%	0.0%	12.6%	32.7%	5.7%	1.0%	1.7%	5.4%	0.0%	16.5%	2.0%	21.1%	0.0%
Harrison County	3,957	1.9%	0.0%	14.8%	19.0%	8.3%	4.5%	6.5%	6.6%	3.6%	14.1%	4.2%	15.9%	0.7%
Hinds County	9,616	6.2%	0.5%	8.1%	19.9%	0.4%	6.9%	4.9%	14.6%	5.5%	3.0%	6.8%	14.1%	9.0%
Jackson County	2,728	4.7%	6.5%	2.2%	30.3%	10.0%	3.5%	0.0%	0.9%	2.5%	12.4%	0.0%	14.6%	12.4%
Madison County	2,913	0.0%	0.0%	33.1%	19.2%	0.0%	19.9%	3.3%	13.0%	0.0%	0.0%	0.0%	6.9%	4.6%
Rankin County	3,630	5.0%	0.0%	36.8%	27.6%	0.0%	0.0%	3.1%	2.6%	7.3%	7.6%	1.5%	6.3%	2.1%
Missouri														
Boone County	12,838	6.4%	7.0%	10.9%	10.2%	2.5%	6.4%	11.9%	21.0%	2.7%	5.9%	4.0%	9.4%	1.7%
Cass County	3,107	11.4%	2.4%	11.2%	28.6%	0.0%	0.0%	3.0%	7.1%	0.0%	0.0%	0.0%	34.0%	2.3%
Clay County	8,960	9.0%	6.5%	8.8%	19.2%	1.2%	1.9%	4.8%	20.8%	0.0%	3.9%	7.2%	15.3%	1.4%
Franklin County	2,301	0.0%	0.0%	47.2%	17.8%	0.0%	0.0%	0.0%	0.0%	0.0%	6.0%	0.0%	23.9%	5.1%
Greene County	14,950	0.0%	0.9%	9.7%	21.5%	5.7%	8.0%	6.8%	5.9%	7.6%	5.2%	5.0%	14.4%	9.3%
Jackson County	30,377	4.9%	2.0%	10.1%	20.6%	2.4%	4.2%	8.8%	7.2%	6.2%	7.0%	6.0%	10.2%	10.4%
Jasper County	3,522	5.5%	0.0%	6.3%	38.2%	0.0%	0.7%	0.0%	11.2%	0.0%	9.7%	0.0%	22.9%	5.5%
Jefferson County	5,629	1.8%	3.1%	17.1%	24.6%	0.0%	3.9%	15.5%	7.7%	0.0%	1.7%	6.0%	17.3%	1.3%
Platte County	4,241	11.5%	10.8%	3.2%	25.8%	9.3%	0.0%	1.7%	6.6%	0.0%	11.2%	2.9%	9.7%	7.3%
St. Charles County	18,642	5.0%	4.4%	14.2%	33.5%	0.4%	7.3%	5.6%	3.0%	0.7%	6.4%	3.1%	11.0%	5.4%
St. Louis County	48,969	4.1%	2.1%	13.4%	27.0%	2.5%	6.0%	7.1%	10.4%	3.2%	5.0%	2.2%	10.8%	6.1%
Montana														
Flathead County	1,739	0.0%	4.7%	27.3%	15.8%	10.4%	4.1%	12.1%	0.0%	3.2%	10.6%	0.0%	11.8%	0.0%
Gallatin County	5,082	13.9%	4.3%	3.1%	22.2%	0.0%	8.0%	0.5%	20.9%	6.8%	6.0%	0.8%	3.3%	10.3%
Missoula County	6,439	5.9%	0.0%	1.2%	2.3%	0.0%	17.7%	8.9%	22.4%	4.8%	13.3%	12.1%	11.4%	0.0%
Yellowstone County	3,168	6.7%	0.0%	29.8%	14.6%	0.0%	1.2%	0.0%	3.7%	0.0%	15.9%	15.8%	6.8%	5.5%
Nebraska														
Douglas County	29,903	4.4%	2.9%	11.1%	25.3%	1.6%	6.0%	6.1%	9.9%	6.6%	2.0%	6.6%	12.4%	5.1%
Lancaster County	15,095	8.8%	1.4%	8.9%	25.0%	3.5%	8.0%	7.9%	11.4%	2.9%	1.8%	3.6%	8.1%	8.8%
Sarpy County	6,054	9.1%	4.1%	19.2%	22.9%	0.0%	3.3%	0.0%	16.2%	2.0%	6.9%	1.7%	13.3%	1.3%
Nevada														
Clark County	42,858	2.9%	3.8%	10.7%	31.9%	3.3%	5.2%	5.1%	8.7%	3.5%	2.6%	10.5%	7.2%	4.5%
Washoe County	13,690	4.5%	3.0%	12.3%	27.8%	6.1%	6.3%	1.9%	10.9%	1.7%	3.6%	1.8%	14.6%	5.4%
New Hampshire														
Hillsborough County	16,712	9.7%	3.9%	5.6%	39.5%	0.6%	5.4%	3.3%	4.3%	1.8%	4.8%	6.5%	4.4%	10.2%
Merrimack County	4,858	7.7%	0.0%	20.2%	12.8%	0.0%	15.1%	1.5%	3.9%	12.3%	12.0%	2.0%	4.5%	8.0%
Rockingham County	11,138	11.1%	6.1%	8.8%	28.9%	0.6%	1.4%	6.0%	3.2%	8.1%	5.5%	10.0%	5.2%	5.1%
Strafford County	4,076	6.5%	0.0%	4.9%	18.0%	5.5%	5.2%	14.8%	13.1%	4.4%	0.0%	11.2%	11.8%	4.8%
New Jersey														
Atlantic County	7,548	7.6%	3.1%	15.1%	28.1%	3.6%	8.3%	10.2%	3.6%	1.3%	3.5%	6.3%	6.7%	2.6%
Bergen County	48,068	9.0%	5.6%	6.6%	29.1%	2.6%	9.4%	6.7%	3.4%	3.2%	3.2%	6.8%	9.9%	4.6%
Burlington County	17,936	4.2%	2.6%	9.2%	21.7%	3.7%	9.6%	8.0%	8.8%	2.3%	5.4%	2.6%	10.7%	11.2%
Camden County	18,854	3.8%	4.0%	14.1%	22.3%	2.5%	3.5%	7.3%	10.4%	6.1%	6.3%	6.0%	7.9%	5.8%
Cape May County	3,759	3.0%	5.2%	13.0%	21.1%	0.0%	0.0%	8.0%	14.9%	0.0%	7.5%	10.6%	10.7%	6.1%
Cumberland County	2,709	17.3%	1.1%	3.3%	4.9%	0.0%	0.0%	2.4%	12.6%	4.2%	4.2%	9.5%	17.0%	23.4%
Essex County	29,470	7.8%	3.8%	9.1%	21.4%	3.4%	13.6%	7.1%	6.9%	1.4%	2.8%	10.3%	8.5%	3.8%
Gloucester County	9,869	8.2%	1.6%	8.9%	14.1%	3.0%	2.8%	10.4%	8.7%	5.3%	7.0%	9.6%	18.4%	2.0%
Hudson County	62,659	11.4%	10.2%	10.5%	27.3%	2.0%	6.5%	4.4%	3.1%	4.7%	3.3%	6.0%	4.6%	6.0%
Hunterdon County	2,846	1.8%	0.0%	2.7%	28.0%	1.1%	17.9%	1.9%	5.4%	10.8%	9.2%	14.8%	1.4%	5.0%
Mercer County	17,796	8.4%	5.1%	4.6%	24.5%	4.5%	9.2%	3.8%	2.5%	3.5%	6.8%	4.8%	10.8%	11.6%
Middlesex County	42,965	10.8%	7.7%	10.1%	21.0%	6.5%	7.6%	6.2%	7.8%	4.0%	2.0%	4.0%	8.0%	4.2%
Monmouth County	27,326	8.7%	5.3%	7.2%	24.7%	0.4%	7.0%	11.6%	8.3%	4.0%	3.9%	6.0%	9.3%	3.6%
Morris County	27,481	10.8%	2.1%	6.3%	29.9%	1.3%	9.7%	7.1%	7.1%	2.7%	4.8%	6.1%	7.8%	4.2%
Ocean County	15,556	3.5%	3.2%	7.5%	20.2%	1.1%	10.0%	10.3%	6.1%	4.0%	15.3%	5.3%	12.4%	1.1%
Passaic County	17,601	7.8%	1.7%	11.4%	26.8%	6.0%	3.1%	4.7%	4.0%	3.8%	5.3%	7.7%	13.3%	4.4%
Somerset County	16,815	7.6%	10.7%	6.9%	18.2%	2.5%	8.1%	5.7%	9.7%	3.4%	3.9%	6.1%	12.0%	5.2%
Sussex County	4,706	4.4%	0.0%	11.8%	21.8%	11.4%	4.4%	1.0%	4.1%	2.9%	5.4%	13.4%	18.5%	0.7%
Union County	22,369	7.1%	6.1%	10.0%	23.9%	2.9%	6.5%	7.2%	7.9%	4.8%	4.6%	5.6%	8.4%	5.1%

Table F-2: Counties—Educational Field of Study—*Continued*

	Total Millennial Population	Percent of the Population 18 to 31 by Field of Study												
		Engineering	Computers and Math	Science and Engineering Related	Business	Physical Science	Social Science	Communications	Biological Sciences	Literature	Liberal Arts	Psychology	Education	Visual and Performing Arts
New Jersey—Cont.														
Warren County	3,296	3.7%	0.0%	13.7%	25.2%	0.0%	7.5%	0.5%	2.0%	3.2%	9.8%	15.4%	18.5%	0.6%
New Mexico														
Bernalillo County	23,029	9.6%	5.9%	12.8%	14.6%	2.7%	9.9%	4.4%	7.2%	4.9%	3.5%	5.9%	9.2%	9.5%
Doña Ana County	4,004	9.8%	0.0%	13.7%	6.3%	2.4%	9.5%	2.9%	11.8%	6.5%	0.0%	16.6%	14.6%	5.9%
San Juan County	962	7.7%	0.0%	0.0%	5.8%	0.0%	0.0%	20.3%	0.0%	0.0%	7.8%	17.6%	38.5%	2.4%
Sandoval County	2,221	0.5%	0.0%	23.3%	7.2%	7.2%	2.1%	11.1%	0.9%	0.0%	0.0%	23.0%	2.1%	22.6%
Santa Fe County	3,113	0.3%	1.8%	12.1%	9.0%	3.3%	2.5%	11.3%	8.3%	11.4%	18.5%	2.9%	4.9%	13.7%
New York														
Albany County	20,226	6.8%	1.0%	12.7%	18.9%	5.4%	8.2%	6.3%	9.0%	3.3%	10.6%	8.1%	6.6%	3.2%
Bronx County	38,795	5.3%	7.0%	15.0%	23.1%	3.1%	9.5%	3.6%	5.0%	3.7%	5.8%	7.8%	7.1%	3.8%
Broome County	6,608	17.8%	5.7%	5.2%	31.3%	3.0%	8.6%	6.3%	0.0%	4.4%	2.2%	9.2%	5.3%	1.1%
Chautauqua County	2,855	6.1%	6.5%	9.0%	6.1%	1.5%	14.1%	3.7%	14.4%	14.2%	3.4%	4.7%	14.2%	2.2%
Dutchess County	8,671	6.4%	1.1%	15.8%	15.4%	2.0%	10.3%	3.6%	5.2%	3.4%	10.8%	5.9%	14.2%	5.8%
Erie County	48,809	7.3%	3.3%	7.1%	17.2%	3.8%	9.5%	7.2%	8.3%	6.7%	6.0%	7.1%	12.3%	4.1%
Jefferson County	2,323	1.6%	2.3%	10.4%	32.3%	1.1%	15.1%	0.0%	7.7%	0.0%	0.7%	5.8%	22.2%	0.9%
Kings County	179,537	2.9%	2.6%	7.7%	20.8%	1.7%	12.2%	8.1%	3.3%	6.0%	5.8%	5.9%	4.0%	18.8%
Monroe County	36,138	8.7%	5.3%	9.7%	18.2%	4.0%	4.6%	7.9%	7.4%	4.4%	4.5%	4.7%	12.4%	8.2%
Nassau County	65,464	2.5%	4.5%	8.5%	23.2%	2.7%	7.9%	8.8%	6.7%	4.7%	7.0%	7.7%	9.4%	6.5%
New York County	235,508	5.6%	2.1%	2.7%	25.7%	2.5%	16.9%	9.6%	5.2%	5.6%	3.9%	5.9%	2.5%	11.8%
Niagara County	7,827	5.6%	8.1%	6.3%	17.2%	6.4%	5.3%	7.7%	6.3%	1.2%	4.2%	7.4%	15.5%	9.0%
Oneida County	5,496	1.1%	4.3%	9.0%	8.6%	6.6%	10.5%	3.5%	8.2%	11.3%	4.2%	10.3%	19.2%	3.2%
Onondaga County	22,891	6.6%	1.2%	7.0%	20.2%	2.6%	8.9%	6.2%	13.2%	4.2%	6.6%	5.4%	9.9%	8.1%
Ontario County	3,021	10.6%	10.1%	0.0%	5.5%	12.0%	10.8%	1.1%	0.0%	2.2%	12.4%	10.2%	21.5%	3.5%
Orange County	10,234	7.6%	1.3%	11.2%	15.1%	2.0%	6.0%	8.5%	6.6%	1.4%	12.3%	8.2%	9.4%	10.5%
Oswego County	2,905	3.9%	0.8%	6.7%	15.5%	1.1%	4.0%	7.5%	23.6%	0.0%	1.4%	21.8%	6.8%	6.9%
Putnam County	3,659	7.0%	0.0%	12.7%	27.7%	10.0%	8.1%	6.4%	2.2%	0.0%	0.0%	3.1%	18.6%	4.2%
Queens County	127,003	6.4%	3.9%	6.7%	23.0%	2.9%	11.1%	5.8%	5.9%	4.6%	4.3%	7.8%	6.7%	10.9%
Rensselaer County	7,030	15.3%	3.3%	10.0%	23.1%	5.7%	1.5%	4.7%	10.6%	3.8%	7.4%	4.4%	8.1%	2.1%
Richmond County	22,004	1.9%	5.6%	9.8%	31.8%	2.5%	10.1%	5.8%	3.3%	1.6%	4.6%	7.9%	9.0%	6.0%
Rockland County	12,801	4.2%	0.8%	9.4%	36.7%	1.2%	7.2%	10.1%	5.1%	0.0%	4.5%	3.4%	9.6%	7.6%
Saratoga County	9,736	9.0%	3.0%	9.5%	19.3%	1.1%	4.1%	8.0%	9.8%	2.8%	7.1%	3.5%	12.6%	10.2%
Schenectady County	4,589	7.9%	3.5%	1.3%	25.4%	3.2%	6.2%	4.8%	11.9%	3.9%	3.7%	15.6%	8.4%	4.2%
St. Lawrence County	2,371	9.7%	1.4%	8.1%	4.0%	0.0%	1.6%	11.7%	30.6%	1.7%	0.5%	6.1%	10.0%	14.5%
Steuben County	2,427	2.8%	3.7%	5.6%	9.1%	0.0%	7.3%	12.8%	6.3%	1.9%	1.2%	19.6%	19.7%	10.0%
Suffolk County	59,309	5.7%	3.2%	7.3%	17.4%	2.4%	7.2%	5.7%	5.8%	5.5%	5.2%	8.9%	15.7%	10.0%
Tompkins County	8,451	20.3%	4.6%	5.7%	6.6%	8.5%	11.0%	6.6%	10.9%	10.5%	5.0%	0.0%	2.4%	8.0%
Ulster County	4,712	2.7%	0.0%	15.4%	18.4%	0.0%	4.8%	5.3%	2.0%	2.0%	3.9%	0.0%	22.8%	22.8%
Wayne County	1,941	10.5%	5.8%	12.4%	27.3%	0.0%	5.9%	0.0%	5.2%	7.4%	9.4%	10.7%	5.5%	0.0%
Westchester County	45,245	6.7%	4.6%	9.4%	23.5%	2.3%	12.1%	5.7%	5.4%	4.4%	7.3%	7.0%	5.8%	5.6%
North Carolina														
Alamance County	5,635	2.6%	8.0%	12.5%	8.1%	0.0%	7.2%	23.4%	13.8%	0.7%	5.2%	2.1%	4.3%	12.0%
Brunswick County	1,325	0.0%	0.0%	6.3%	11.4%	0.0%	20.8%	0.0%	1.8%	11.3%	0.0%	11.4%	5.6%	31.4%
Buncombe County	10,283	5.9%	0.0%	5.1%	7.1%	0.0%	9.6%	10.0%	22.9%	7.1%	8.5%	5.6%	7.8%	10.5%
Burke County	1,550	0.0%	0.0%	7.3%	28.0%	0.0%	0.0%	4.8%	9.9%	0.0%	10.1%	23.9%	15.9%	0.0%
Cabarrus County	4,824	5.2%	5.0%	9.7%	19.4%	0.0%	4.9%	6.7%	8.6%	6.1%	12.2%	0.0%	15.9%	6.2%
Catawba County	2,770	1.9%	3.7%	42.9%	3.6%	0.0%	5.5%	0.0%	3.5%	0.4%	0.0%	6.1%	24.9%	7.6%
Cleveland County	1,692	12.8%	0.0%	8.1%	12.5%	8.3%	16.4%	2.7%	0.0%	2.5%	4.6%	0.0%	32.1%	0.0%
Craven County	1,777	0.0%	0.0%	4.7%	17.0%	0.0%	0.0%	14.4%	2.1%	0.0%	0.0%	36.7%	21.5%	3.5%
Cumberland County	9,482	5.8%	1.1%	9.5%	22.7%	13.2%	7.8%	3.9%	3.3%	1.6%	9.2%	4.5%	10.8%	6.5%
Davidson County	2,420	6.3%	1.1%	0.0%	16.8%	0.0%	9.0%	9.6%	6.3%	4.1%	6.4%	27.4%	3.4%	9.5%
Durham County	24,000	7.7%	4.4%	4.6%	7.7%	7.1%	16.1%	5.3%	18.3%	3.5%	6.3%	11.1%	3.3%	4.7%
Forsyth County	13,222	3.6%	1.3%	13.7%	13.6%	4.1%	4.8%	2.0%	17.9%	6.5%	8.1%	7.0%	9.2%	8.2%
Gaston County	4,235	4.8%	5.0%	9.9%	22.7%	6.6%	7.1%	7.2%	2.1%	8.6%	4.3%	5.1%	14.9%	1.8%
Guilford County	18,362	5.4%	3.3%	6.2%	22.8%	1.1%	5.3%	5.6%	7.5%	5.8%	3.6%	13.2%	13.7%	6.4%
Harnett County	4,213	13.0%	2.2%	14.8%	7.5%	5.9%	3.6%	0.8%	11.0%	2.5%	5.9%	19.6%	13.2%	0.0%
Henderson County	3,147	0.0%	0.0%	2.6%	19.6%	0.0%	18.9%	7.1%	17.3%	2.9%	5.6%	19.1%	6.8%	0.0%
Iredell County	2,665	3.4%	4.5%	7.0%	20.0%	0.0%	0.0%	4.6%	9.7%	0.0%	3.2%	4.9%	38.8%	3.8%
Johnston County	3,035	0.0%	16.1%	12.9%	10.8%	18.3%	6.5%	0.0%	0.0%	0.0%	0.0%	13.0%	13.1%	9.3%
Mecklenburg County	61,037	7.2%	2.3%	7.0%	31.4%	2.3%	9.7%	7.1%	4.6%	3.2%	3.0%	9.5%	6.1%	6.5%
Moore County	2,105	21.1%	0.0%	29.4%	1.3%	0.0%	11.7%	0.0%	14.0%	0.0%	10.6%	6.5%	5.3%	0.0%
Nash County	1,313	0.0%	0.0%	3.1%	26.2%	0.0%	0.0%	23.5%	0.0%	0.0%	0.0%	29.3%	17.9%	0.0%
New Hanover County	8,355	5.0%	0.0%	11.0%	21.4%	4.2%	10.5%	4.2%	3.7%	8.9%	3.4%	6.5%	10.8%	10.5%
Onslow County	2,985	1.8%	0.0%	26.3%	4.7%	0.0%	0.8%	0.0%	18.0%	1.2%	14.1%	3.6%	25.3%	4.3%
Orange County	10,229	4.4%	0.8%	4.6%	7.1%	8.7%	16.4%	5.0%	19.0%	10.2%	8.6%	5.8%	0.7%	8.8%
Pitt County	8,575	7.1%	3.2%	23.3%	8.0%	2.9%	4.8%	1.6%	20.5%	1.3%	0.0%	10.6%	16.7%	0.0%
Randolph County	2,745	4.4%	9.9%	0.0%	20.5%	20.2%	0.0%	4.0%	4.8%	0.0%	6.7%	7.7%	14.9%	6.8%
Robeson County	980	0.0%	8.0%	9.8%	3.0%	0.0%	12.9%	10.0%	20.1%	0.0%	0.0%	6.0%	25.4%	4.9%
Rockingham County	1,064	0.0%	2.5%	0.0%	15.4%	15.9%	6.5%	0.0%	0.0%	20.5%	28.2%	0.0%	11.0%	0.0%
Rowan County	2,538	0.0%	7.7%	0.0%	25.8%	0.0%	1.4%	3.3%	23.2%	0.0%	4.4%	8.6%	22.7%	2.9%
Union County	3,828	10.5%	4.6%	8.5%	20.2%	0.2%	1.8%	4.6%	4.8%	7.4%	3.2%	4.9%	22.9%	6.4%
Wake County	59,093	12.4%	7.5%	7.1%	20.1%	3.2%	8.1%	7.2%	9.8%	4.8%	2.8%	3.9%	7.1%	6.1%
Wayne County	2,315	5.4%	8.0%	7.7%	33.0%	6.5%	5.6%	0.0%	30.6%	0.0%	0.0%	0.0%	3.2%	0.0%
North Dakota														
Cass County	12,524	8.6%	0.0%	18.9%	18.7%	0.9%	4.9%	8.5%	7.5%	7.7%	0.0%	5.7%	18.4%	0.2%

Table F-2: Counties—Educational Field of Study—*Continued*

	Total Millennial Population	Engineering	Computers and Math	Science and Engineering Related	Business	Physical Science	Social Science	Communications	Biological Sciences	Literature	Liberal Arts	Psychology	Education	Visual and Performing Arts
Ohio														
Allen County	2,236	7.9%	0.0%	22.5%	9.5%	0.0%	3.0%	5.9%	0.0%	2.1%	9.3%	15.8%	24.1%	0.0%
Ashtabula County	717	0.0%	0.0%	8.5%	26.6%	0.0%	0.0%	0.0%	12.4%	0.0%	0.0%	19.8%	28.3%	4.3%
Butler County	12,973	10.0%	6.0%	5.9%	13.9%	4.1%	8.9%	6.3%	9.9%	9.3%	5.1%	4.2%	13.1%	3.5%
Clark County	2,910	3.0%	3.1%	8.6%	28.5%	1.6%	5.4%	6.2%	10.3%	1.5%	7.1%	7.2%	17.6%	0.0%
Clermont County	5,268	3.2%	7.6%	13.9%	14.7%	0.0%	12.2%	8.7%	6.8%	5.0%	8.1%	9.1%	10.3%	0.4%
Columbiana County	1,905	2.8%	7.7%	12.0%	0.0%	12.6%	0.0%	11.7%	0.0%	33.1%	13.2%	0.0%	6.9%	0.0%
Cuyahoga County	53,317	8.7%	4.5%	11.9%	23.8%	1.8%	9.1%	9.1%	8.1%	5.1%	3.0%	3.6%	4.9%	6.3%
Delaware County	8,427	1.5%	1.0%	12.5%	22.8%	2.4%	0.0%	5.2%	16.2%	3.5%	3.5%	11.5%	12.3%	7.6%
Fairfield County	3,778	0.0%	0.8%	14.6%	16.7%	0.0%	3.3%	5.6%	9.3%	2.9%	0.0%	20.3%	10.1%	16.5%
Franklin County	78,060	6.1%	2.6%	10.1%	19.3%	4.1%	8.5%	8.7%	9.8%	5.0%	4.9%	8.3%	6.9%	5.7%
Geauga County	2,495	12.7%	0.8%	27.8%	12.5%	0.0%	0.0%	8.3%	12.3%	0.0%	14.5%	5.0%	2.2%	3.8%
Greene County	7,943	14.9%	5.0%	14.7%	19.8%	3.3%	14.6%	0.0%	4.4%	2.7%	3.3%	2.6%	12.7%	2.1%
Hamilton County	40,993	10.4%	3.9%	11.2%	19.3%	1.9%	6.6%	6.8%	9.0%	4.3%	5.4%	5.9%	8.3%	7.0%
Lake County	7,569	17.1%	3.5%	12.4%	29.8%	1.3%	4.0%	10.0%	5.3%	1.1%	3.5%	2.6%	5.0%	4.5%
Licking County	4,613	9.9%	5.0%	6.9%	34.3%	0.9%	7.8%	2.8%	1.3%	0.2%	0.0%	8.1%	21.0%	1.8%
Lorain County	5,981	9.5%	0.7%	8.2%	16.6%	6.0%	7.9%	5.8%	4.5%	2.8%	4.6%	14.1%	14.8%	4.6%
Lucas County	13,408	7.3%	4.4%	12.0%	26.0%	0.5%	5.6%	5.4%	15.2%	3.4%	7.7%	4.0%	3.5%	5.1%
Mahoning County	8,050	3.6%	1.2%	21.8%	31.3%	1.0%	2.0%	10.7%	5.5%	6.9%	0.0%	6.6%	7.2%	2.0%
Medina County	5,119	5.6%	2.6%	14.1%	28.6%	0.0%	6.7%	1.0%	1.9%	1.1%	3.8%	7.9%	20.5%	6.3%
Miami County	1,663	3.2%	0.0%	9.8%	33.4%	0.0%	12.6%	0.0%	14.9%	0.0%	12.6%	0.0%	2.1%	11.4%
Montgomery County	17,039	18.2%	2.7%	10.1%	18.3%	1.2%	3.4%	7.4%	5.6%	9.0%	3.8%	2.7%	14.2%	3.3%
Portage County	6,781	3.2%	5.4%	11.4%	8.9%	3.2%	6.1%	13.1%	22.4%	14.6%	4.0%	0.2%	7.4%	0.0%
Richland County	2,100	0.0%	0.0%	4.3%	35.1%	0.0%	14.6%	0.0%	0.0%	17.8%	0.0%	11.8%	16.4%	0.0%
Stark County	8,760	5.1%	5.3%	17.2%	26.9%	1.7%	3.8%	5.0%	4.0%	7.8%	4.2%	5.6%	12.9%	0.6%
Summit County	21,379	13.2%	3.6%	7.1%	27.9%	3.4%	9.4%	5.1%	4.3%	5.6%	2.0%	3.5%	12.4%	2.7%
Trumbull County	3,416	1.9%	0.0%	20.7%	17.4%	15.5%	6.6%	11.7%	3.5%	0.0%	4.5%	5.9%	10.1%	2.0%
Tuscarawas County	2,062	2.8%	0.0%	8.5%	27.5%	2.3%	0.0%	2.9%	3.0%	6.2%	2.1%	13.6%	25.8%	5.5%
Warren County	9,159	10.1%	7.2%	9.6%	19.6%	6.7%	0.0%	4.7%	12.0%	2.8%	4.8%	8.2%	11.5%	2.7%
Wayne County	2,032	14.3%	6.9%	1.4%	7.3%	0.0%	8.5%	5.3%	16.9%	5.7%	9.3%	6.9%	12.1%	5.4%
Wood County	6,538	5.4%	1.5%	17.7%	20.0%	0.0%	6.8%	3.2%	8.7%	9.4%	6.5%	6.2%	11.9%	2.7%
Oklahoma														
Canadian County	1,223	0.0%	17.4%	0.0%	56.9%	0.0%	4.0%	0.0%	0.0%	0.0%	0.0%	0.0%	21.7%	0.0%
Cleveland County	14,141	8.2%	0.7%	7.0%	9.6%	4.1%	13.7%	7.0%	8.9%	4.6%	8.6%	11.0%	4.9%	11.7%
Comanche County	3,457	32.3%	0.0%	17.8%	4.0%	0.0%	12.3%	0.0%	6.7%	2.5%	5.6%	14.6%	4.1%	0.0%
Oklahoma County	32,172	5.0%	0.9%	6.9%	23.6%	3.7%	8.2%	7.6%	11.8%	7.6%	4.5%	7.4%	6.1%	6.7%
Tulsa County	21,169	2.7%	0.6%	11.0%	26.6%	3.2%	4.0%	8.4%	7.9%	2.6%	6.1%	8.1%	12.2%	6.6%
Oregon														
Clackamas County	9,750	5.9%	6.0%	5.7%	20.4%	3.1%	10.0%	9.2%	8.4%	2.1%	7.2%	1.5%	8.3%	12.2%
Deschutes County	3,834	3.0%	0.0%	17.9%	26.0%	0.0%	21.1%	3.8%	4.2%	5.7%	3.4%	5.8%	0.0%	9.2%
Douglas County	1,380	0.0%	0.0%	10.5%	19.9%	0.0%	0.0%	0.0%	25.7%	0.0%	0.0%	8.9%	35.0%	0.0%
Jackson County	3,395	3.7%	8.2%	2.2%	9.8%	14.4%	13.3%	6.3%	13.2%	9.3%	5.5%	12.3%	1.8%	0.0%
Lane County	9,138	1.8%	0.6%	1.3%	14.1%	1.4%	24.4%	7.0%	13.6%	4.1%	7.0%	11.7%	5.4%	7.5%
Linn County	3,874	5.3%	2.7%	3.0%	12.0%	6.5%	5.6%	0.0%	39.2%	5.7%	4.4%	4.9%	4.7%	6.0%
Marion County	5,524	13.2%	3.8%	2.9%	6.8%	11.8%	9.6%	5.4%	18.5%	0.3%	8.1%	12.5%	5.3%	1.9%
Multnomah County	44,133	8.3%	2.6%	7.2%	13.0%	1.8%	14.8%	5.3%	12.9%	6.5%	6.9%	6.3%	2.9%	11.4%
Washington County	25,789	10.8%	7.8%	9.9%	18.6%	4.2%	7.9%	6.6%	6.1%	5.3%	5.1%	7.9%	3.3%	6.5%
Yamhill County	2,746	2.8%	1.8%	4.4%	36.6%	0.0%	1.5%	5.5%	14.1%	6.6%	8.1%	5.4%	8.7%	4.6%
Pennsylvania														
Adams County	2,517	6.2%	2.0%	13.6%	9.8%	5.0%	3.3%	0.0%	10.1%	3.6%	8.6%	3.3%	30.4%	4.1%
Allegheny County	79,987	8.7%	3.5%	8.3%	25.6%	4.2%	6.0%	8.0%	5.6%	5.0%	4.9%	6.3%	8.1%	5.8%
Beaver County	5,290	10.8%	1.7%	8.1%	31.6%	0.0%	1.6%	3.9%	5.8%	0.7%	10.2%	10.0%	11.9%	3.7%
Berks County	10,158	6.9%	3.7%	11.7%	29.2%	1.9%	7.9%	7.3%	3.1%	3.8%	0.2%	4.5%	16.4%	3.3%
Blair County	2,584	1.7%	4.6%	41.4%	10.1%	0.0%	0.0%	7.9%	6.3%	9.9%	0.0%	4.6%	12.6%	0.9%
Bucks County	25,734	7.6%	4.3%	10.0%	22.7%	4.2%	3.4%	5.9%	10.0%	5.2%	3.5%	8.1%	8.1%	7.0%
Butler County	8,983	10.8%	5.4%	6.9%	34.3%	1.7%	12.9%	1.0%	1.6%	0.8%	7.9%	2.3%	13.2%	1.2%
Cambria County	3,797	0.0%	2.1%	24.4%	15.1%	1.9%	10.3%	7.4%	3.6%	3.7%	15.3%	5.3%	9.9%	0.9%
Centre County	8,944	22.5%	2.2%	2.6%	16.9%	11.6%	6.1%	2.5%	7.6%	4.7%	5.4%	13.5%	3.5%	0.8%
Chester County	24,082	5.9%	5.5%	5.1%	26.0%	2.3%	4.4%	10.3%	8.3%	4.2%	2.5%	5.6%	14.7%	5.0%
Cumberland County	8,233	11.9%	6.8%	11.4%	21.0%	1.0%	8.2%	8.2%	4.1%	2.0%	7.7%	6.7%	6.5%	4.4%
Dauphin County	10,556	8.1%	1.0%	13.6%	13.6%	3.3%	11.8%	7.3%	10.1%	2.0%	1.0%	2.3%	23.5%	2.6%
Delaware County	24,436	6.0%	4.1%	13.9%	24.1%	1.5%	5.9%	8.2%	3.8%	5.0%	7.7%	5.3%	13.3%	1.3%
Erie County	11,718	3.0%	3.3%	12.8%	21.3%	0.0%	2.8%	4.9%	14.7%	4.3%	1.2%	11.1%	16.5%	3.9%
Fayette County	2,315	0.0%	0.0%	30.3%	24.0%	0.0%	0.0%	8.8%	1.1%	2.0%	2.2%	9.4%	20.1%	2.1%
Franklin County	4,429	8.8%	3.2%	20.4%	9.9%	4.0%	14.4%	0.0%	0.9%	0.2%	6.5%	2.3%	24.8%	4.5%
Lackawanna County	7,774	0.0%	3.5%	7.4%	22.9%	3.2%	10.3%	1.7%	15.6%	4.6%	6.2%	1.3%	14.0%	9.4%
Lancaster County	16,753	9.5%	1.2%	16.8%	25.6%	3.5%	1.1%	3.4%	2.7%	5.3%	5.8%	2.2%	17.6%	5.4%
Lebanon County	3,388	0.0%	0.0%	3.2%	9.7%	0.0%	0.0%	8.9%	10.2%	12.3%	6.6%	22.3%	21.4%	5.5%
Lehigh County	12,897	8.1%	3.1%	7.0%	21.3%	1.7%	1.5%	10.4%	4.1%	2.7%	7.9%	7.4%	16.5%	8.3%
Luzerne County	8,017	2.7%	1.9%	15.2%	15.2%	0.6%	7.0%	12.0%	6.6%	0.0%	2.2%	7.8%	18.9%	10.0%
Lycoming County	3,193	0.0%	1.0%	17.6%	10.0%	2.7%	5.7%	0.0%	11.9%	3.4%	8.7%	5.2%	28.6%	5.3%
Mercer County	3,749	1.3%	0.0%	14.0%	16.1%	1.9%	3.0%	1.4%	13.3%	0.0%	6.3%	3.1%	27.0%	12.6%
Monroe County	3,991	0.0%	0.0%	23.2%	17.9%	0.0%	0.0%	3.6%	2.9%	13.4%	0.0%	7.2%	22.1%	9.6%
Montgomery County	48,659	6.9%	2.6%	7.6%	26.0%	3.6%	8.6%	5.6%	8.3%	3.2%	3.6%	6.2%	13.2%	4.6%
Northampton County	13,073	15.2%	2.2%	2.7%	15.6%	4.6%	4.6%	4.6%	4.5%	7.2%	0.8%	8.1%	23.1%	6.9%
Northumberland County	2,744	3.6%	10.6%	19.0%	12.5%	18.7%	3.0%	7.9%	4.7%	0.0%	8.1%	3.5%	8.3%	0.0%
Philadelphia County	98,556	5.5%	3.6%	7.4%	19.7%	4.7%	11.8%	7.5%	12.0%	3.3%	3.5%	7.1%	4.2%	9.7%
Schuylkill County	2,700	0.0%	0.0%	16.1%	22.7%	0.9%	1.1%	11.5%	1.1%	1.7%	0.9%	4.3%	37.6%	2.0%

Table F-2: Counties—Educational Field of Study—*Continued*

	Total Millennial Population	Percent of the Population 18 to 31 by Field of Study												
		Engineering	Computers and Math	Science and Engineering Related	Business	Physical Science	Social Science	Communications	Biological Sciences	Literature	Liberal Arts	Psychology	Education	Visual and Performing Arts
Pennsylvania—Cont.														
Washington County	5,260	9.4%	0.0%	9.4%	40.0%	0.4%	7.1%	4.1%	4.0%	9.2%	1.9%	2.1%	10.0%	2.4%
Westmoreland County	10,197	12.9%	2.6%	13.4%	20.3%	1.3%	7.6%	2.9%	10.5%	0.0%	0.0%	13.7%	8.5%	6.4%
York County	8,775	1.9%	2.9%	14.5%	17.0%	4.5%	2.3%	8.3%	7.5%	0.0%	5.0%	15.2%	14.2%	6.8%
Rhode Island														
Kent County	7,303	5.4%	9.3%	7.7%	15.4%	0.7%	3.9%	6.3%	8.3%	6.5%	3.0%	16.3%	5.7%	11.8%
Providence County	27,264	5.4%	2.1%	9.1%	19.3%	8.1%	6.0%	5.5%	7.3%	4.3%	6.5%	7.6%	9.3%	9.7%
Washington County	5,170	16.5%	0.0%	13.1%	10.7%	7.7%	17.2%	6.6%	10.3%	1.6%	0.8%	4.4%	6.4%	4.6%
South Carolina														
Aiken County	3,362	9.3%	2.1%	31.7%	10.5%	4.7%	6.5%	0.0%	5.6%	6.3%	3.2%	8.3%	9.7%	2.2%
Anderson County	4,343	0.0%	2.3%	23.6%	5.5%	0.0%	5.8%	10.2%	5.6%	5.8%	0.0%	16.4%	13.1%	11.7%
Beaufort County	3,733	0.0%	5.9%	3.3%	41.8%	0.0%	6.8%	5.7%	1.2%	0.0%	5.2%	0.0%	10.6%	19.6%
Berkeley County	9,125	9.9%	1.8%	6.0%	15.5%	1.7%	11.8%	1.8%	29.9%	3.7%	4.5%	5.8%	4.5%	2.9%
Charleston County	23,097	7.8%	3.2%	5.8%	16.5%	3.2%	8.3%	6.0%	20.2%	4.7%	5.6%	10.6%	4.9%	3.3%
Dorchester County	2,696	14.7%	3.2%	11.9%	13.1%	2.2%	6.6%	10.3%	4.6%	0.0%	10.1%	5.0%	8.5%	9.8%
Florence County	4,407	7.6%	1.6%	18.3%	34.6%	2.8%	4.8%	0.0%	6.9%	0.9%	12.2%	1.5%	7.9%	1.0%
Greenville County	18,091	7.7%	1.7%	10.6%	28.3%	3.5%	6.2%	5.6%	4.1%	7.1%	5.9%	2.2%	8.2%	8.8%
Horry County	6,905	0.0%	0.0%	3.4%	35.0%	1.3%	12.2%	6.0%	4.0%	5.5%	5.4%	11.4%	11.4%	4.2%
Lexington County	8,567	6.6%	2.1%	11.7%	17.1%	2.3%	13.0%	6.9%	6.9%	1.1%	8.4%	2.3%	17.5%	4.2%
Orangeburg County	1,665	0.0%	0.0%	6.2%	47.1%	0.4%	24.0%	0.0%	0.0%	0.0%	0.0%	4.4%	13.1%	4.9%
Pickens County	4,135	10.1%	2.5%	4.1%	11.2%	9.9%	6.9%	0.0%	19.3%	0.0%	8.5%	1.4%	13.8%	12.3%
Richland County	17,567	2.1%	3.2%	8.0%	22.3%	2.5%	8.8%	8.4%	10.6%	4.6%	6.2%	8.9%	9.5%	4.9%
Spartanburg County	6,400	5.5%	1.9%	3.9%	19.6%	2.3%	2.3%	9.1%	7.8%	2.9%	2.7%	8.7%	28.0%	5.4%
Sumter County	1,580	0.0%	0.0%	18.6%	27.5%	0.0%	0.0%	0.0%	4.0%	0.0%	7.2%	0.0%	42.7%	0.0%
York County	6,557	6.0%	0.0%	16.4%	34.7%	0.0%	8.2%	0.9%	5.3%	0.0%	7.6%	0.9%	14.1%	5.9%
South Dakota														
Minnehaha County	9,934	1.0%	8.3%	6.5%	20.1%	4.9%	4.2%	12.1%	12.3%	3.7%	0.0%	5.5%	17.3%	4.2%
Pennington County	3,795	2.7%	0.0%	10.1%	25.7%	0.0%	11.6%	3.1%	2.6%	3.7%	1.6%	0.6%	24.5%	13.8%
Tennessee														
Blount County	2,410	10.8%	0.0%	3.4%	32.5%	0.0%	22.2%	7.2%	7.0%	6.0%	0.0%	0.0%	10.8%	0.0%
Bradley County	1,421	4.9%	0.0%	60.7%	0.0%	0.0%	0.0%	0.0%	7.0%	0.0%	0.0%	10.7%	16.7%	0.0%
Davidson County	51,737	4.9%	4.0%	8.1%	20.9%	4.2%	5.2%	11.0%	8.2%	4.2%	5.1%	8.9%	4.8%	10.5%
Hamilton County	11,135	5.1%	3.4%	13.9%	23.0%	3.3%	4.4%	9.7%	9.1%	3.2%	9.2%	4.1%	8.7%	3.0%
Knox County	22,512	9.5%	3.3%	7.7%	26.6%	3.2%	9.2%	5.4%	8.1%	6.6%	7.8%	2.6%	7.0%	3.1%
Madison County	2,297	1.6%	5.8%	22.1%	26.1%	2.0%	11.7%	3.0%	1.5%	0.0%	2.0%	1.7%	22.6%	0.0%
Montgomery County	8,677	2.6%	0.0%	5.3%	30.6%	0.1%	5.3%	8.6%	0.0%	3.2%	7.4%	7.8%	20.9%	8.2%
Rutherford County	11,844	6.6%	4.4%	10.3%	25.2%	7.4%	10.2%	2.8%	7.1%	5.4%	1.2%	7.7%	8.9%	2.8%
Sevier County	2,737	13.2%	5.4%	17.2%	16.5%	0.0%	33.9%	2.3%	0.0%	0.0%	0.0%	4.9%	0.0%	6.5%
Shelby County	31,756	4.7%	4.0%	6.3%	17.4%	3.2%	10.2%	9.3%	11.9%	5.4%	4.4%	7.1%	11.9%	4.2%
Sullivan County	2,902	4.7%	0.0%	37.8%	14.1%	0.0%	6.4%	8.3%	2.2%	0.3%	4.0%	5.0%	17.2%	0.0%
Sumner County	5,758	3.6%	3.7%	22.6%	25.2%	0.0%	4.8%	9.3%	3.2%	2.2%	3.9%	1.9%	13.0%	6.8%
Washington County	6,474	3.1%	1.6%	10.5%	24.9%	1.3%	14.9%	0.0%	23.2%	0.6%	5.1%	6.4%	8.3%	0.0%
Williamson County	6,366	1.4%	6.7%	13.4%	29.9%	0.0%	5.1%	5.2%	12.0%	1.6%	4.3%	7.9%	8.6%	3.9%
Wilson County	3,899	2.6%	6.4%	17.3%	20.9%	0.0%	1.4%	13.2%	18.9%	0.0%	0.0%	4.9%	14.3%	0.0%
Texas														
Bell County	7,251	5.8%	0.0%	13.2%	20.4%	2.4%	16.2%	7.0%	11.5%	6.2%	7.8%	2.1%	5.8%	1.6%
Bexar County	65,635	8.9%	6.0%	7.3%	23.9%	2.1%	7.9%	6.5%	10.0%	4.2%	4.7%	7.7%	7.2%	3.5%
Bowie County	1,719	7.2%	0.0%	4.1%	28.2%	0.0%	11.9%	0.0%	0.0%	0.0%	0.0%	7.1%	34.3%	7.3%
Brazoria County	10,183	13.4%	1.6%	2.4%	27.3%	3.0%	8.9%	11.1%	2.6%	1.7%	1.1%	5.3%	20.6%	1.1%
Brazos County	15,724	13.0%	0.7%	8.0%	13.3%	5.1%	11.2%	2.3%	29.7%	3.6%	3.2%	6.7%	2.8%	0.3%
Cameron County	6,157	2.6%	0.8%	5.3%	21.9%	2.6%	0.7%	4.2%	19.4%	3.4%	2.4%	0.8%	34.4%	1.3%
Collin County	40,059	15.6%	9.3%	7.0%	26.8%	1.6%	5.1%	4.2%	6.9%	3.7%	2.4%	5.3%	8.4%	3.7%
Comal County	3,348	29.1%	0.0%	13.4%	10.4%	7.7%	2.2%	1.7%	12.2%	0.0%	0.0%	2.6%	4.8%	15.9%
Dallas County	97,662	6.7%	4.3%	10.2%	28.4%	2.1%	6.4%	9.5%	8.6%	3.5%	4.3%	4.3%	6.2%	5.5%
Denton County	33,135	5.2%	2.6%	8.7%	31.2%	0.9%	3.8%	5.5%	7.6%	4.5%	7.9%	3.4%	11.3%	7.3%
Ector County	3,210	2.6%	4.7%	18.6%	22.1%	5.1%	0.0%	3.7%	8.3%	31.0%	0.0%	0.0%	2.0%	1.8%
El Paso County	21,632	6.7%	1.6%	11.1%	26.3%	2.0%	4.0%	1.4%	13.6%	3.6%	7.1%	6.1%	13.1%	3.6%
Ellis County	3,456	0.0%	0.0%	2.6%	23.1%	0.0%	2.6%	18.1%	15.2%	3.2%	11.9%	1.8%	10.7%	10.9%
Fort Bend County	22,592	11.4%	0.9%	15.1%	27.9%	2.8%	8.1%	4.6%	8.8%	1.8%	2.2%	5.3%	7.8%	3.4%
Galveston County	11,211	7.3%	0.0%	7.9%	15.1%	2.5%	11.8%	1.2%	18.9%	2.2%	11.8%	6.6%	12.0%	2.7%
Grayson County	2,001	5.3%	17.4%	35.3%	12.4%	0.2%	0.0%	0.7%	2.9%	0.0%	7.8%	3.2%	14.7%	0.0%
Gregg County	2,266	18.2%	0.0%	9.6%	2.6%	12.9%	17.1%	5.5%	2.3%	8.7%	0.0%	2.2%	0.0%	20.7%
Guadalupe County	3,654	3.5%	0.0%	7.1%	23.5%	5.2%	15.3%	3.5%	9.3%	5.3%	5.0%	15.4%	4.6%	2.3%
Harris County	171,803	13.7%	4.3%	8.9%	25.4%	4.9%	7.5%	5.8%	7.1%	3.2%	3.6%	4.0%	7.3%	4.3%
Hays County	6,812	6.9%	2.0%	16.2%	27.8%	0.0%	6.4%	13.0%	2.0%	0.3%	1.6%	12.6%	7.1%	4.1%
Hidalgo County	14,343	3.7%	3.7%	10.2%	20.0%	3.2%	7.5%	1.9%	6.6%	2.9%	2.0%	12.2%	25.0%	1.0%
Jefferson County	5,163	21.3%	3.2%	7.9%	19.9%	0.0%	2.6%	10.3%	3.2%	8.4%	5.6%	1.4%	12.9%	3.3%
Johnson County	3,317	16.7%	0.0%	6.2%	49.3%	0.0%	2.5%	4.7%	0.3%	0.0%	3.0%	0.0%	14.4%	2.9%
Kaufman County	1,455	0.0%	0.0%	16.5%	45.0%	0.0%	0.0%	4.1%	0.0%	10.7%	0.0%	14.4%	9.3%	0.0%
Lubbock County	11,567	6.8%	0.0%	10.3%	25.3%	6.5%	8.7%	2.6%	13.0%	3.8%	4.5%	4.9%	11.3%	2.2%
McLennan County	7,131	4.9%	0.4%	1.2%	22.4%	1.1%	9.2%	3.4%	8.6%	4.7%	9.3%	8.6%	14.5%	11.7%
Midland County	6,086	9.2%	0.0%	1.6%	25.3%	3.5%	11.5%	11.7%	5.8%	9.3%	13.4%	0.0%	8.7%	0.0%
Montgomery County	12,213	7.5%	3.5%	8.7%	36.9%	0.5%	1.7%	2.0%	0.1%	3.9%	8.1%	5.4%	21.7%	0.0%
Nueces County	9,005	17.2%	2.5%	9.1%	21.5%	9.5%	3.5%	3.7%	8.5%	0.0%	6.1%	10.3%	7.2%	0.9%
Parker County	2,462	9.0%	11.4%	5.1%	31.2%	0.0%	12.6%	0.0%	7.5%	0.0%	7.2%	6.7%	9.3%	0.0%

Table F-2: Counties—Educational Field of Study—Continued

	Total Millennial Population	Percent of the Population 18 to 31 by Field of Study												
		Engineering	Computers and Math	Science and Engineering Related	Business	Physical Science	Social Science	Communications	Biological Sciences	Literature	Liberal Arts	Psychology	Education	Visual and Performing Arts
Texas—Cont.														
Potter County	1,640	6.2%	0.0%	0.0%	28.6%	0.0%	0.0%	9.0%	13.6%	3.1%	6.2%	15.3%	0.0%	18.0%
Randall County	4,824	7.3%	1.7%	12.9%	19.1%	4.2%	2.1%	9.2%	10.9%	5.5%	6.7%	0.0%	11.6%	8.8%
Smith County	5,728	1.4%	0.0%	9.5%	36.0%	0.0%	4.7%	12.6%	6.1%	3.2%	4.9%	5.9%	11.1%	4.6%
Tarrant County	65,677	7.3%	2.6%	10.1%	30.4%	2.1%	6.2%	6.0%	10.9%	2.5%	5.5%	4.6%	8.4%	3.4%
Taylor County	4,466	4.4%	6.2%	15.2%	27.9%	0.0%	5.0%	2.9%	0.7%	0.0%	9.8%	11.9%	8.4%	7.6%
Tom Green County	2,928	5.0%	9.1%	7.3%	17.6%	0.0%	4.8%	18.4%	10.9%	1.9%	0.0%	6.5%	18.5%	0.0%
Travis County	85,925	11.0%	3.9%	4.7%	20.0%	3.8%	13.1%	8.9%	5.0%	5.8%	5.2%	4.1%	5.0%	9.4%
Webb County	4,736	6.7%	0.0%	14.5%	32.5%	1.6%	5.8%	0.0%	8.0%	1.7%	2.2%	8.3%	18.6%	0.0%
Wichita County	3,487	3.1%	4.1%	2.0%	30.3%	0.0%	10.4%	8.9%	3.5%	0.0%	6.0%	0.0%	23.7%	7.8%
Williamson County	14,238	13.3%	4.3%	10.0%	15.5%	2.8%	5.0%	5.9%	8.5%	5.7%	3.8%	6.6%	15.2%	3.4%
Utah														
Cache County	5,375	6.7%	1.0%	3.3%	17.8%	2.3%	8.8%	7.9%	10.3%	2.6%	7.6%	2.9%	25.4%	3.4%
Davis County	10,725	11.2%	3.8%	15.9%	21.0%	1.8%	13.9%	10.4%	3.8%	3.1%	1.6%	2.7%	4.7%	6.0%
Salt Lake County	45,244	7.8%	3.7%	10.4%	21.3%	2.8%	7.3%	6.1%	7.2%	8.6%	4.2%	7.8%	7.2%	5.6%
Utah County	23,184	6.2%	6.8%	9.8%	16.0%	1.3%	6.9%	7.6%	6.8%	8.6%	3.1%	7.1%	15.2%	4.6%
Washington County	2,489	6.0%	0.0%	21.7%	12.9%	0.0%	4.9%	4.7%	13.3%	0.0%	7.1%	21.5%	5.5%	2.4%
Weber County	4,681	10.1%	12.9%	16.0%	19.7%	0.0%	9.0%	5.6%	6.7%	0.7%	1.7%	0.0%	13.2%	4.3%
Vermont														
Chittenden County	8,963	4.1%	6.1%	3.9%	15.8%	0.9%	15.0%	4.1%	12.3%	13.0%	5.0%	5.3%	1.3%	13.3%
Virginia														
Albemarle County	6,175	6.7%	4.0%	10.3%	4.0%	2.5%	8.1%	1.7%	24.2%	17.7%	11.6%	5.1%	2.4%	1.5%
Arlington County	44,349	8.2%	1.4%	3.2%	24.4%	2.9%	19.4%	9.2%	5.7%	5.9%	4.9%	7.4%	4.1%	3.2%
Chesterfield County	11,982	3.6%	7.0%	8.0%	19.9%	1.8%	10.5%	6.8%	4.9%	8.5%	6.8%	2.5%	13.3%	6.4%
Fairfax County	78,098	11.6%	8.6%	6.3%	19.9%	2.5%	14.1%	4.9%	7.5%	3.6%	6.1%	5.6%	3.6%	5.6%
Hanover County	3,797	5.0%	0.0%	8.0%	22.7%	18.9%	15.7%	2.0%	5.2%	2.3%	0.6%	6.6%	7.3%	5.9%
Henrico County	15,336	7.1%	5.4%	9.5%	20.9%	3.9%	16.1%	2.6%	7.9%	3.4%	6.7%	7.6%	7.6%	1.5%
Loudoun County	18,515	10.4%	9.3%	6.3%	24.2%	3.7%	8.5%	5.3%	9.5%	1.6%	5.4%	3.5%	4.8%	7.7%
Montgomery County	6,366	2.6%	9.8%	11.3%	7.1%	1.5%	9.0%	0.0%	10.6%	11.0%	7.2%	17.0%	12.9%	0.0%
Prince William County	17,647	7.2%	7.1%	13.6%	19.1%	0.9%	9.0%	8.1%	4.2%	0.9%	5.8%	7.5%	11.9%	4.8%
Roanoke County	2,238	4.6%	3.9%	11.0%	16.0%	1.2%	8.8%	3.5%	5.3%	0.0%	11.1%	24.5%	10.1%	0.0%
Spotsylvania County	2,112	0.0%	6.3%	0.0%	29.7%	6.0%	9.6%	0.0%	0.0%	0.0%	7.6%	11.8%	9.3%	19.8%
Stafford County	4,603	10.2%	6.6%	5.5%	10.8%	0.0%	8.8%	8.6%	9.1%	3.6%	13.1%	12.6%	3.9%	7.3%
Washington														
Benton County	3,441	1.9%	0.0%	3.2%	38.5%	3.0%	7.9%	8.1%	13.4%	5.3%	4.0%	2.9%	10.2%	1.6%
Clark County	7,464	7.0%	16.2%	5.3%	15.5%	4.2%	8.1%	1.8%	4.6%	9.6%	13.8%	4.8%	3.5%	5.6%
Cowlitz County	782	0.0%	0.0%	35.3%	5.1%	0.0%	0.0%	0.0%	17.4%	0.0%	14.3%	11.9%	0.0%	16.0%
Grant County	1,790	6.8%	26.8%	5.1%	5.2%	0.0%	0.0%	13.4%	0.0%	2.3%	1.8%	11.6%	6.6%	20.4%
King County	150,321	11.4%	13.3%	5.9%	13.8%	2.5%	13.4%	6.3%	8.2%	5.3%	5.2%	6.0%	2.6%	6.3%
Kitsap County	6,879	28.3%	9.2%	6.7%	16.5%	3.3%	4.1%	0.0%	2.9%	2.3%	9.6%	3.4%	9.2%	4.4%
Pierce County	24,460	3.9%	4.6%	13.2%	18.0%	2.2%	11.8%	5.9%	7.5%	5.8%	3.3%	9.1%	9.3%	5.2%
Skagit County	732	5.3%	11.6%	9.3%	10.2%	0.0%	7.4%	0.0%	2.6%	0.0%	5.2%	24.2%	2.7%	21.4%
Snohomish County	22,693	12.2%	6.0%	11.0%	22.0%	1.4%	10.4%	4.9%	11.1%	4.9%	3.6%	3.0%	4.3%	5.3%
Spokane County	16,249	3.8%	0.0%	20.0%	25.8%	1.8%	9.7%	10.1%	4.5%	4.2%	2.1%	5.8%	6.1%	6.1%
Thurston County	9,184	1.6%	3.9%	4.1%	21.2%	4.2%	17.4%	10.8%	9.0%	8.5%	9.0%	2.0%	8.1%	0.3%
Whatcom County	7,804	3.2%	1.9%	2.6%	14.6%	13.2%	10.5%	7.4%	5.6%	12.6%	12.0%	0.0%	7.9%	8.5%
Yakima County	4,000	3.6%	0.0%	13.2%	22.8%	0.0%	4.0%	2.1%	18.7%	4.7%	9.4%	2.7%	18.9%	0.0%
West Virginia														
Berkeley County	2,815	3.5%	2.5%	8.9%	12.0%	0.0%	3.1%	3.0%	7.9%	0.0%	6.1%	10.8%	29.0%	13.2%
Cabell County	2,722	9.6%	4.8%	12.3%	9.1%	6.0%	0.0%	0.0%	31.1%	0.0%	16.7%	1.8%	8.6%	0.0%
Kanawha County	4,973	15.7%	11.1%	14.2%	20.4%	0.0%	6.3%	9.1%	2.2%	6.8%	2.0%	0.0%	12.3%	0.0%
Monongalia County	8,082	18.8%	1.3%	10.2%	11.5%	5.9%	3.8%	10.8%	8.9%	9.7%	0.7%	4.6%	10.2%	3.5%
Wisconsin														
Brown County	8,668	8.0%	5.5%	8.4%	16.1%	0.9%	2.9%	10.7%	10.4%	1.1%	4.0%	21.5%	5.6%	5.0%
Dane County	43,729	10.2%	6.6%	8.0%	10.2%	6.7%	11.2%	8.9%	11.7%	5.9%	2.7%	4.0%	5.1%	8.8%
Eau Claire County	4,019	0.8%	15.7%	8.1%	40.0%	3.8%	2.7%	1.0%	13.3%	3.2%	1.2%	2.6%	2.7%	4.9%
Fond du Lac County	1,306	11.3%	0.0%	5.5%	47.5%	11.1%	0.0%	0.0%	1.8%	0.0%	13.5%	0.0%	0.0%	9.3%
Kenosha County	4,204	0.0%	0.0%	17.3%	31.4%	0.0%	16.4%	3.4%	1.5%	6.2%	12.9%	1.7%	0.0%	9.2%
La Crosse County	4,580	16.1%	3.3%	14.7%	11.3%	6.0%	10.3%	4.4%	6.9%	6.2%	0.0%	0.0%	20.9%	0.0%
Marathon County	2,634	3.1%	0.0%	36.9%	23.2%	0.0%	12.0%	7.9%	7.2%	1.6%	0.0%	8.0%	0.0%	0.0%
Milwaukee County	45,198	7.4%	3.7%	8.4%	18.6%	4.9%	11.3%	8.9%	5.9%	3.3%	4.1%	4.7%	7.7%	11.2%
Outagamie County	4,814	12.4%	0.0%	10.9%	29.9%	0.0%	8.6%	4.2%	4.0%	5.4%	0.0%	15.2%	7.6%	1.8%
Racine County	3,994	3.8%	0.0%	9.2%	13.4%	0.0%	0.0%	38.3%	8.3%	2.0%	12.2%	0.0%	7.5%	5.2%
Rock County	3,162	0.0%	0.0%	27.1%	9.1%	0.8%	6.3%	3.3%	5.6%	0.0%	12.8%	0.0%	21.1%	13.9%
Sheboygan County	3,283	5.8%	16.3%	0.0%	30.1%	3.6%	1.2%	7.1%	13.3%	10.0%	0.0%	0.0%	9.8%	2.9%
Walworth County	3,017	1.4%	0.0%	11.2%	25.4%	0.0%	4.7%	10.9%	13.4%	5.5%	0.0%	1.7%	15.2%	10.6%
Washington County	4,752	6.9%	8.4%	0.0%	21.0%	0.0%	6.9%	10.4%	9.0%	6.4%	3.8%	4.2%	14.6%	8.3%
Waukesha County	14,560	11.8%	1.0%	12.2%	24.6%	0.2%	16.1%	6.0%	5.3%	0.8%	3.1%	9.2%	7.4%	2.3%
Winnebago County	7,170	13.5%	11.3%	4.5%	19.4%	0.0%	5.3%	4.1%	3.4%	10.4%	0.0%	10.5%	4.0%	13.7%
Wyoming														
Laramie County	2,970	7.1%	7.2%	14.7%	15.4%	0.0%	4.6%	0.0%	26.4%	11.3%	0.0%	3.3%	9.9%	0.0%

Table F-3: Places—Educational Field of Study

	Total Millennial Population	Percent of the Population 18 to 31 by Field of Study												
		Engineering	Computers and Math	Science and Engineering Related	Business	Physical Science	Social Science	Communications	Biological Sciences	Literature	Liberal Arts	Psychology	Education	Visual and Performing Arts
Alabama														
Birmingham city	10,984	0.5%	4.7%	8.9%	23.6%	4.9%	4.2%	6.3%	12.2%	2.1%	5.6%	4.5%	5.6%	5.6%
Huntsville city	8,942	13.9%	0.7%	4.1%	17.3%	10.2%	6.5%	2.0%	11.3%	5.1%	1.7%	7.9%	14.7%	3.3%
Mobile city	7,995	13.7%	0.8%	21.2%	22.7%	3.9%	2.2%	3.9%	5.4%	5.4%	4.5%	10.1%	1.8%	0.0%
Montgomery city	8,167	1.6%	0.5%	17.3%	15.3%	0.7%	15.0%	2.3%	6.7%	0.9%	1.1%	4.9%	17.5%	2.7%
Tuscaloosa city	4,955	1.6%	2.0%	2.7%	17.8%	3.5%	14.1%	4.4%	11.6%	11.4%	6.6%	2.5%	14.0%	0.0%
Alaska														
Anchorage municipality	14,015	6.9%	1.2%	10.7%	18.1%	6.6%	8.2%	0.7%	8.1%	8.2%	4.6%	11.6%	4.4%	0.8%
Arizona														
Chandler city	10,264	4.5%	10.3%	14.8%	23.4%	2.4%	0.7%	7.5%	4.5%	4.3%	4.5%	9.0%	5.7%	1.2%
Glendale city	7,496	2.6%	4.0%	10.5%	15.3%	1.4%	4.4%	14.9%	11.6%	0.5%	0.0%	9.5%	10.2%	0.0%
Mesa city	15,693	9.9%	5.0%	8.8%	19.3%	1.1%	10.8%	0.8%	4.0%	3.0%	2.4%	7.2%	20.1%	3.4%
Peoria city	4,437	12.1%	6.2%	1.7%	22.5%	0.0%	5.7%	0.0%	12.4%	0.0%	2.5%	16.9%	10.0%	2.9%
Phoenix city	49,950	8.3%	6.0%	8.8%	17.6%	1.7%	8.6%	5.4%	8.9%	2.5%	3.0%	6.7%	9.0%	4.4%
Scottsdale city	13,637	5.1%	4.1%	7.1%	21.0%	5.1%	6.1%	10.0%	7.8%	3.6%	2.8%	9.3%	3.9%	5.7%
Surprise city	2,304	3.3%	0.0%	9.5%	38.0%	0.0%	14.5%	3.7%	2.0%	0.0%	0.0%	7.4%	13.2%	0.0%
Tempe city	17,368	14.4%	5.5%	7.0%	21.6%	1.2%	8.3%	5.4%	5.3%	3.5%	4.6%	5.2%	6.3%	4.9%
Tucson city	17,628	9.5%	2.6%	6.8%	12.3%	3.9%	12.5%	1.3%	11.4%	7.3%	8.4%	3.2%	5.6%	6.5%
Yuma city	1,316	4.9%	0.0%	19.2%	11.8%	0.0%	9.0%	20.1%	0.0%	0.0%	0.0%	0.0%	22.3%	5.8%
Arkansas														
Little Rock city	9,500	2.0%	4.9%	10.6%	16.8%	5.3%	3.1%	4.0%	12.5%	3.6%	9.9%	1.9%	7.6%	4.9%
California														
Anaheim city	14,059	8.6%	4.9%	5.0%	25.7%	5.4%	10.3%	4.2%	5.8%	4.1%	5.6%	4.2%	3.6%	3.1%
Antioch city	2,170	9.9%	0.0%	3.8%	21.8%	0.0%	3.4%	4.3%	3.4%	0.0%	4.7%	0.0%	0.0%	17.3%
Bakersfield city	9,461	7.2%	4.1%	12.4%	21.2%	0.7%	9.6%	7.8%	3.8%	2.0%	9.0%	5.7%	5.0%	0.7%
Berkeley city	16,147	7.7%	9.3%	3.0%	12.9%	10.0%	18.5%	1.9%	13.9%	6.6%	2.9%	5.8%	0.0%	3.0%
Burbank city	8,975	1.3%	1.4%	4.0%	12.7%	2.8%	11.1%	8.4%	4.4%	6.3%	11.1%	6.9%	3.8%	21.5%
Carlsbad city	6,070	3.3%	8.6%	0.0%	39.9%	1.9%	2.9%	10.8%	11.7%	5.8%	4.2%	1.6%	2.4%	1.0%
Carson city	3,209	4.3%	3.2%	9.4%	16.2%	7.5%	7.3%	18.2%	4.7%	1.7%	9.2%	2.0%	11.4%	0.0%
Chula Vista city	7,571	3.1%	1.2%	6.2%	27.0%	0.0%	13.6%	2.5%	4.4%	5.3%	13.6%	3.5%	1.8%	8.3%
Clovis city	4,864	1.0%	1.3%	2.2%	15.0%	2.7%	9.1%	2.4%	10.9%	2.2%	8.4%	6.5%	13.0%	4.9%
Compton city	1,355	0.0%	0.0%	0.0%	5.1%	5.9%	10.9%	0.0%	0.0%	0.0%	3.5%	37.5%	17.0%	0.0%
Concord city	7,804	7.0%	7.0%	20.3%	6.8%	3.4%	9.0%	11.3%	8.7%	1.8%	7.5%	6.2%	0.0%	3.4%
Corona city	5,095	4.3%	0.0%	11.8%	11.3%	1.5%	4.9%	8.0%	8.0%	2.6%	11.2%	7.8%	5.4%	7.5%
Costa Mesa city	8,270	2.9%	1.3%	2.7%	27.2%	1.1%	15.6%	8.1%	14.3%	3.4%	9.3%	5.4%	1.2%	0.0%
Daly City city	7,030	6.4%	6.1%	10.9%	14.4%	4.7%	6.9%	3.0%	3.4%	3.0%	11.6%	10.5%	2.6%	7.0%
Downey city	3,501	0.0%	2.6%	7.3%	18.9%	0.0%	14.9%	8.5%	8.3%	8.9%	2.1%	6.9%	2.4%	0.0%
El Cajon city	3,051	5.9%	0.0%	8.4%	13.8%	0.0%	0.0%	2.4%	7.3%	9.8%	13.8%	0.0%	8.5%	0.0%
El Monte city	1,800	3.2%	7.3%	4.4%	23.2%	0.0%	21.1%	6.4%	13.6%	0.0%	6.8%	10.2%	3.7%	0.0%
Elk Grove city	5,658	1.5%	6.9%	20.9%	33.0%	0.0%	3.6%	0.8%	13.4%	3.7%	4.3%	1.3%	1.9%	1.5%
Escondido city	3,406	5.3%	7.2%	6.6%	12.9%	0.0%	7.0%	3.4%	11.7%	4.2%	19.4%	1.4%	10.3%	1.6%
Fairfield city	2,908	2.5%	0.0%	2.3%	9.8%	6.2%	22.8%	1.9%	5.2%	3.7%	3.8%	8.9%	2.8%	12.2%
Fontana city	4,632	12.1%	13.8%	11.7%	10.3%	0.0%	6.5%	8.5%	2.4%	5.6%	4.9%	1.3%	5.9%	0.0%
Fremont city	14,778	22.6%	14.2%	15.6%	14.3%	2.8%	6.3%	2.4%	2.0%	3.8%	7.8%	3.6%	1.3%	2.5%
Fresno city	13,119	3.5%	3.0%	9.8%	11.7%	2.7%	9.2%	7.9%	8.7%	2.6%	10.6%	4.0%	4.6%	2.5%
Fullerton city	7,188	15.0%	9.8%	6.3%	14.5%	2.9%	6.8%	12.1%	5.2%	2.4%	6.8%	3.3%	1.6%	5.6%
Garden Grove city	5,527	6.8%	1.1%	3.0%	32.7%	8.6%	14.4%	5.4%	7.8%	6.5%	0.0%	6.7%	4.3%	2.7%
Glendale city	13,901	5.4%	4.9%	6.2%	10.8%	5.6%	11.2%	8.5%	4.4%	1.4%	4.5%	9.7%	0.0%	21.9%
Hayward city	6,637	5.1%	9.2%	20.0%	10.4%	1.4%	8.1%	6.4%	2.7%	3.7%	7.8%	3.7%	0.0%	10.1%
Hesperia city	7,243	7.0%	6.7%	9.8%	19.2%	0.9%	0.8%	4.8%	12.3%	7.9%	4.4%	10.1%	0.0%	8.4%
Inglewood city	3,109	3.7%	2.8%	8.5%	9.5%	8.0%	31.2%	9.1%	0.0%	4.1%	0.0%	0.0%	0.0%	5.3%
Irvine city	19,772	13.0%	2.8%	3.0%	24.6%	0.0%	21.3%	3.5%	10.2%	5.8%	4.4%	4.4%	0.4%	4.5%
Jurupa Valley city	3,016	8.1%	5.8%	3.5%	37.4%	0.0%	4.5%	0.0%	3.7%	2.8%	0.0%	18.7%	5.7%	4.1%
Lancaster city	2,728	12.4%	4.3%	0.0%	18.0%	0.0%	15.0%	0.0%	2.1%	15.2%	20.1%	6.0%	0.0%	1.9%
Long Beach city	19,947	4.9%	2.2%	5.2%	18.0%	4.4%	13.3%	3.7%	5.0%	9.6%	4.9%	9.7%	5.4%	4.9%
Los Angeles city	219,489	4.9%	3.6%	6.3%	14.9%	2.2%	13.8%	10.3%	6.2%	5.5%	4.7%	5.7%	2.9%	14.2%
Mission Viejo city	2,602	5.8%	4.0%	3.7%	17.7%	0.0%	0.0%	2.5%	21.0%	4.4%	0.0%	10.3%	5.6%	8.6%
Modesto city	4,408	0.0%	4.0%	5.7%	10.3%	3.6%	12.5%	4.8%	20.3%	4.4%	9.2%	11.8%	2.3%	4.9%
Moreno Valley city	4,023	2.0%	0.0%	11.1%	20.2%	4.1%	12.7%	3.5%	17.4%	4.4%	1.8%	11.8%	0.0%	7.8%
Murrieta city	2,977	9.2%	0.0%	1.6%	27.8%	0.0%	6.0%	4.6%	16.3%	18.0%	2.4%	3.3%	10.8%	0.0%
Norwalk city	2,146	8.5%	0.0%	2.5%	17.9%	2.3%	8.5%	0.0%	18.8%	5.3%	11.6%	6.2%	11.2%	3.4%
Oakland city	28,880	7.2%	6.1%	6.2%	9.2%	1.0%	15.8%	8.1%	8.5%	8.9%	3.0%	7.2%	1.7%	11.4%
Oceanside city	4,956	3.8%	0.0%	6.8%	35.4%	0.0%	0.0%	1.9%	11.0%	6.1%	11.1%	12.6%	6.5%	0.0%
Ontario city	2,226	0.0%	3.5%	23.4%	11.2%	2.1%	0.0%	0.0%	13.6%	2.2%	15.5%	5.0%	9.5%	4.0%
Orange city	5,248	5.7%	1.2%	3.2%	32.9%	0.0%	6.1%	9.0%	1.3%	3.8%	7.5%	2.5%	6.2%	7.0%
Oxnard city	5,038	4.9%	0.0%	1.7%	28.0%	3.8%	13.7%	4.3%	9.1%	2.2%	0.7%	10.0%	12.8%	2.8%
Palmdale city	2,781	3.9%	2.7%	16.2%	7.3%	18.9%	8.5%	5.9%	2.8%	0.0%	8.4%	3.8%	0.0%	2.2%
Pasadena city	14,880	9.6%	2.2%	7.7%	15.4%	6.6%	8.4%	3.1%	12.5%	5.5%	4.3%	4.1%	1.1%	11.4%
Pomona city	5,164	2.0%	1.3%	15.6%	12.8%	0.0%	12.4%	3.1%	7.5%	2.9%	0.0%	28.9%	1.5%	7.3%
Rancho Cucamonga city	8,060	0.9%	6.8%	8.6%	28.6%	0.0%	12.9%	3.7%	6.6%	9.2%	9.0%	6.4%	0.0%	0.9%
Redding city	1,917	0.0%	0.0%	3.3%	0.7%	4.2%	4.2%	11.6%	7.2%	12.4%	3.8%	24.1%	7.9%	4.3%
Rialto city	1,401	0.0%	16.7%	0.0%	7.2%	0.0%	18.7%	0.0%	0.0%	16.4%	11.1%	16.9%	0.0%	4.7%
Richmond city	5,292	10.1%	7.7%	3.9%	14.6%	2.8%	3.8%	7.5%	14.7%	1.4%	3.3%	7.7%	6.6%	7.3%
Riverside city	10,161	2.2%	8.9%	7.8%	15.0%	2.3%	12.1%	1.0%	12.0%	5.4%	5.4%	5.8%	3.7%	8.1%
Roseville city	4,649	3.3%	5.8%	1.7%	19.8%	0.0%	6.6%	12.5%	3.3%	2.6%	5.7%	10.0%	0.0%	11.4%
Sacramento city	23,234	7.5%	2.5%	5.7%	18.3%	2.8%	22.1%	5.0%	5.6%	4.2%	3.7%	6.4%	3.6%	6.1%

Table F-3: Places—Educational Field of Study—*Continued*

	Total Millennial Population	Engineering	Computers and Math	Science and Engineering Related	Business	Physical Science	Social Science	Communications	Biological Sciences	Literature	Liberal Arts	Psychology	Education	Visual and Performing Arts
California—Cont.														
Salinas city	2,455	7.7%	0.0%	19.8%	10.4%	2.3%	2.4%	3.4%	5.3%	2.3%	7.7%	13.8%	13.9%	11.0%
San Bernardino city	3,003	0.0%	0.0%	12.7%	31.6%	2.8%	3.7%	0.0%	6.3%	5.1%	0.0%	13.0%	7.8%	5.3%
San Buenaventura (Ventura) city	4,696	15.2%	8.7%	1.8%	3.4%	1.1%	9.9%	6.0%	10.4%	3.9%	4.0%	12.8%	8.7%	3.4%
San Diego city	105,950	12.2%	6.0%	6.6%	14.8%	3.0%	11.1%	5.0%	7.7%	2.8%	6.4%	6.6%	3.2%	6.3%
San Francisco city	108,719	10.1%	6.4%	5.0%	20.0%	3.7%	14.3%	5.8%	7.2%	4.2%	3.3%	7.2%	1.0%	6.8%
San Jose city	54,029	16.9%	8.8%	6.8%	17.3%	3.3%	10.0%	5.2%	4.2%	3.1%	2.7%	7.7%	3.2%	3.9%
San Mateo city	6,351	16.3%	8.1%	6.9%	20.0%	2.6%	3.0%	12.0%	6.5%	2.4%	6.5%	3.7%	2.0%	3.0%
Santa Ana city	9,813	2.2%	4.8%	3.3%	18.9%	2.5%	10.1%	3.1%	5.7%	6.6%	9.1%	14.0%	4.1%	6.0%
Santa Clara city	16,754	21.9%	14.0%	6.8%	23.6%	2.0%	7.5%	1.7%	6.5%	0.9%	6.1%	4.9%	1.0%	2.0%
Santa Clarita city	6,531	6.2%	3.9%	17.9%	8.3%	0.0%	10.7%	0.7%	11.3%	0.8%	14.3%	3.7%	2.9%	14.1%
Santa Maria city	1,237	8.2%	4.4%	13.8%	12.0%	5.7%	0.0%	5.7%	0.0%	0.0%	0.0%	10.6%	20.5%	0.0%
Santa Monica city	11,224	10.3%	4.1%	2.7%	9.3%	0.0%	22.4%	17.9%	4.5%	4.0%	1.6%	7.5%	2.4%	6.3%
Santa Rosa city	5,390	0.0%	0.0%	12.9%	20.3%	3.7%	12.4%	1.1%	13.1%	10.7%	4.0%	6.5%	5.0%	4.3%
Simi Valley city	5,039	8.8%	0.0%	6.9%	19.9%	0.0%	7.2%	6.3%	4.2%	6.1%	3.4%	17.4%	3.9%	7.8%
South Gate city	1,710	10.5%	3.3%	2.9%	10.3%	0.0%	28.1%	4.5%	3.9%	0.0%	12.7%	4.9%	3.4%	2.7%
Stockton city	6,217	3.8%	0.0%	4.2%	26.6%	0.0%	5.5%	4.5%	26.2%	2.3%	0.4%	12.6%	1.8%	5.7%
Sunnyvale city	18,738	39.3%	19.1%	4.9%	9.1%	1.7%	2.4%	1.7%	7.9%	2.2%	0.0%	4.7%	4.6%	2.0%
Temecula city	2,903	2.7%	0.0%	7.7%	32.4%	0.0%	3.3%	4.8%	8.4%	2.9%	6.6%	12.6%	0.0%	5.4%
Thousand Oaks city	5,788	13.7%	2.7%	3.5%	20.2%	7.4%	2.1%	10.0%	4.7%	6.9%	10.5%	6.4%	4.4%	3.0%
Torrance city	6,679	18.3%	2.2%	11.5%	13.3%	3.7%	13.1%	4.0%	7.4%	6.1%	2.1%	3.4%	1.2%	9.4%
Vacaville city	2,359	5.8%	3.0%	11.8%	7.7%	0.0%	20.1%	5.6%	16.0%	0.0%	2.5%	3.4%	0.0%	8.6%
Vallejo city	3,692	6.1%	2.9%	8.9%	8.6%	0.0%	12.6%	10.7%	13.6%	7.7%	3.2%	3.9%	1.9%	2.7%
Victorville city	2,274	0.0%	2.3%	0.0%	25.6%	0.0%	19.8%	0.0%	0.0%	0.0%	0.0%	7.0%	25.0%	0.0%
Visalia city	3,722	0.0%	0.0%	37.9%	3.8%	0.0%	7.8%	8.7%	5.2%	0.0%	12.5%	4.5%	12.3%	0.0%
Vista city	2,134	6.8%	1.4%	4.7%	12.4%	0.0%	0.0%	9.3%	10.8%	13.2%	0.0%	20.8%	20.6%	0.0%
West Covina city	4,088	9.8%	0.0%	17.4%	10.2%	1.9%	14.6%	3.2%	9.0%	6.4%	3.6%	12.9%	0.0%	4.3%
Westminster city	3,349	5.6%	4.6%	12.2%	29.3%	0.0%	2.2%	6.3%	14.2%	11.4%	2.1%	0.0%	1.9%	3.6%
Colorado														
Arvada city	4,532	10.5%	3.1%	1.6%	5.9%	0.0%	19.4%	13.9%	3.5%	15.4%	6.2%	7.5%	8.8%	0.0%
Aurora city	11,222	8.7%	9.3%	8.3%	18.1%	1.0%	6.5%	7.6%	7.3%	2.7%	3.8%	4.3%	6.9%	2.9%
Boulder city	13,541	19.8%	6.0%	1.9%	11.4%	3.4%	8.7%	3.6%	7.5%	1.7%	4.2%	10.1%	0.8%	11.5%
Centennial city	4,481	13.4%	3.8%	2.2%	26.8%	1.3%	14.2%	7.0%	4.8%	4.5%	1.0%	8.6%	2.3%	2.7%
Colorado Springs city	18,390	6.0%	12.9%	7.4%	12.4%	2.2%	14.1%	5.4%	3.8%	6.1%	5.3%	14.4%	0.7%	5.1%
Denver city	60,360	4.9%	1.8%	5.8%	28.0%	1.1%	9.0%	8.2%	5.6%	5.9%	4.6%	4.1%	3.1%	6.8%
Fort Collins city	11,242	7.9%	2.5%	7.6%	12.1%	2.2%	11.1%	6.1%	18.8%	2.4%	9.1%	7.8%	4.7%	2.6%
Greeley city	3,978	3.5%	0.0%	9.8%	11.3%	0.0%	7.5%	2.0%	10.9%	3.1%	18.6%	12.1%	7.6%	1.7%
Lakewood city	6,732	11.7%	1.7%	7.6%	11.5%	3.4%	4.0%	3.8%	9.4%	7.3%	9.6%	5.0%	2.3%	11.5%
Pueblo city	1,892	0.0%	6.1%	4.8%	35.1%	0.0%	2.4%	0.0%	3.2%	6.9%	22.7%	5.7%	0.0%	3.1%
Thornton city	1,812	12.6%	23.7%	0.0%	15.4%	0.0%	9.1%	0.0%	0.0%	0.0%	0.0%	0.0%	18.7%	2.8%
Westminster city	4,480	4.3%	4.8%	4.9%	31.1%	2.2%	3.1%	5.6%	9.1%	0.0%	3.7%	9.2%	0.0%	1.5%
Connecticut														
Bridgeport city	6,998	8.5%	7.6%	2.0%	27.1%	0.5%	7.0%	9.4%	7.8%	7.2%	1.6%	1.7%	3.2%	10.2%
Hartford city	4,571	16.3%	5.0%	0.0%	15.7%	0.0%	14.4%	1.7%	6.0%	2.8%	2.8%	11.4%	3.6%	8.5%
New Haven city	9,515	1.4%	5.6%	2.0%	8.3%	1.8%	12.5%	1.1%	19.1%	9.2%	12.3%	8.0%	1.2%	7.1%
Stamford city	8,541	3.0%	2.9%	6.2%	21.6%	3.5%	14.2%	6.8%	3.1%	8.0%	9.0%	2.6%	7.6%	11.5%
Waterbury city	3,176	0.0%	1.7%	1.4%	33.5%	2.4%	2.4%	0.0%	5.0%	0.0%	7.3%	9.0%	22.2%	4.9%
District of Columbia														
Washington city	89,158	5.0%	2.9%	2.6%	11.7%	2.0%	33.3%	8.5%	3.9%	6.5%	9.3%	3.4%	2.3%	3.3%
Florida														
Cape Coral city	3,810	0.0%	0.0%	19.7%	45.9%	6.0%	0.0%	10.5%	0.0%	1.0%	5.5%	1.6%	3.1%	0.8%
Clearwater city	3,040	0.0%	0.0%	7.1%	21.3%	5.0%	4.1%	18.6%	6.8%	2.3%	6.7%	1.1%	5.2%	17.7%
Coral Springs city	4,617	4.5%	0.0%	6.4%	25.6%	0.0%	6.2%	11.3%	8.4%	2.3%	0.0%	13.1%	12.3%	1.2%
Fort Lauderdale city	6,155	5.1%	0.7%	1.8%	47.4%	0.0%	2.0%	9.6%	8.9%	6.2%	0.9%	3.2%	4.3%	3.3%
Gainesville city	16,018	12.1%	2.7%	6.5%	11.4%	9.2%	6.2%	2.3%	23.0%	2.8%	1.8%	2.9%	1.1%	3.6%
Hialeah city	4,288	4.4%	3.4%	2.0%	18.9%	0.0%	16.1%	3.3%	13.4%	5.5%	0.0%	12.2%	13.3%	0.0%
Hollywood city	4,384	7.4%	5.9%	17.9%	21.3%	0.0%	5.5%	1.8%	6.5%	3.0%	1.8%	7.6%	11.0%	1.3%
Jacksonville city	34,541	8.3%	3.4%	11.4%	22.5%	1.0%	7.6%	6.9%	5.5%	4.0%	5.7%	5.2%	7.5%	0.2%
Lakeland city	1,818	9.1%	0.0%	11.2%	14.7%	0.0%	9.6%	10.5%	1.2%	10.3%	12.2%	5.0%	4.7%	8.2%
Miami Beach city	5,502	3.0%	5.0%	9.9%	27.4%	0.0%	4.0%	4.5%	11.7%	11.5%	1.7%	4.0%	3.8%	6.4%
Miami city	19,656	5.4%	1.0%	5.6%	31.3%	3.0%	9.0%	9.4%	8.3%	3.2%	3.8%	5.1%	1.4%	5.5%
Miami Gardens city	1,929	8.1%	6.3%	25.9%	20.5%	0.0%	0.0%	0.0%	4.5%	0.0%	0.0%	4.6%	5.1%	0.0%
Miramar city	6,916	3.3%	5.2%	5.4%	13.8%	0.0%	12.9%	7.1%	11.0%	1.0%	3.7%	6.2%	4.9%	0.7%
Orlando city	12,284	8.6%	4.9%	8.1%	24.8%	0.4%	5.5%	6.1%	4.0%	3.2%	3.1%	9.5%	6.2%	4.0%
Palm Bay city	2,528	2.9%	1.5%	7.7%	10.3%	0.0%	0.0%	4.8%	0.0%	9.8%	0.0%	50.4%	0.0%	0.0%
Pembroke Pines city	7,115	4.6%	1.2%	6.1%	19.7%	1.2%	18.3%	3.1%	7.1%	2.9%	0.0%	5.0%	7.6%	1.5%
Pompano Beach city	2,860	0.0%	33.6%	0.0%	17.7%	0.0%	16.0%	9.0%	13.7%	0.0%	0.0%	0.0%	9.9%	0.0%
Port St. Lucie city	1,599	0.0%	0.0%	0.0%	4.9%	0.0%	0.0%	6.8%	0.0%	6.9%	11.8%	0.0%	20.4%	0.0%
St. Petersburg city	9,463	1.5%	3.2%	8.1%	31.7%	0.0%	13.0%	3.9%	6.0%	2.3%	1.1%	7.7%	6.2%	3.9%
Tallahassee city	18,092	4.4%	3.0%	14.2%	15.4%	2.9%	9.9%	4.4%	6.0%	3.3%	3.4%	11.7%	7.3%	6.1%
Tampa city	22,743	3.4%	2.2%	8.2%	32.2%	1.3%	7.9%	11.0%	7.6%	4.4%	1.9%	4.4%	4.1%	6.5%
West Palm Beach city	3,920	6.4%	0.9%	14.5%	15.2%	1.1%	7.5%	9.8%	1.3%	1.0%	0.0%	17.6%	6.8%	3.2%
Georgia														
Athens-Clarke County unified govt (bal)	13,460	5.2%	1.3%	4.4%	14.0%	5.4%	18.7%	6.9%	12.5%	7.8%	3.4%	5.0%	7.4%	4.5%

Table F-3: Places—Educational Field of Study—*Continued*

	Total Millennial Population	Percent of the Population 18 to 31 by Field of Study												
		Engineering	Computers and Math	Science and Engineering Related	Business	Physical Science	Social Science	Communications	Biological Sciences	Literature	Liberal Arts	Psychology	Education	Visual and Performing Arts
Georgia—Cont.														
Atlanta city	45,435	6.3%	5.4%	4.9%	26.7%	3.5%	8.7%	7.8%	5.5%	5.4%	3.5%	6.9%	3.2%	6.9%
Augusta-Richmond County consolidated govt (bal)	8,544	4.0%	1.6%	18.8%	11.7%	0.0%	20.7%	6.0%	6.7%	3.0%	1.8%	6.8%	1.2%	1.6%
Columbus city	7,245	6.1%	2.7%	5.9%	18.1%	0.0%	10.6%	5.8%	6.6%	4.4%	3.6%	10.9%	4.9%	1.5%
Macon city	2,375	2.7%	11.3%	7.5%	17.4%	0.0%	8.9%	4.9%	15.6%	2.5%	2.4%	0.0%	0.0%	18.0%
Roswell city	5,657	18.7%	1.7%	4.8%	19.5%	7.2%	6.6%	8.1%	0.0%	0.0%	6.5%	7.6%	7.1%	5.5%
Sandy Springs city	8,804	3.4%	7.7%	8.0%	29.2%	5.4%	6.0%	6.6%	1.0%	10.1%	3.3%	2.6%	1.6%	6.8%
Savannah city	6,741	3.8%	6.3%	21.1%	11.1%	1.2%	7.4%	1.1%	5.0%	2.7%	10.9%	1.6%	9.6%	5.8%
Hawaii														
Urban Honolulu CDP	17,755	8.2%	1.4%	10.4%	30.1%	1.8%	4.3%	5.1%	9.4%	6.5%	2.7%	6.9%	8.6%	1.2%
Idaho														
Boise City city	9,485	9.7%	0.6%	14.7%	12.9%	3.8%	4.1%	6.7%	12.0%	2.9%	4.4%	10.1%	9.8%	2.7%
Illinois														
Aurora city	8,105	5.6%	4.8%	10.2%	16.5%	7.4%	2.5%	7.2%	1.9%	2.9%	2.7%	10.7%	11.4%	7.9%
Chicago city	215,935	5.6%	4.5%	6.7%	21.7%	2.5%	10.9%	7.0%	6.0%	4.8%	4.9%	6.2%	5.4%	8.7%
Elgin city	3,646	8.0%	12.5%	5.1%	26.6%	0.0%	8.9%	0.0%	8.7%	8.3%	0.0%	0.0%	9.5%	0.0%
Joliet city	5,720	1.6%	2.1%	7.7%	20.9%	14.1%	0.0%	6.7%	6.4%	0.0%	5.0%	8.0%	16.5%	5.7%
Naperville city	8,933	6.3%	5.8%	13.9%	18.3%	1.2%	3.8%	5.3%	7.2%	0.7%	0.0%	13.9%	10.7%	4.0%
Peoria city	8,043	16.9%	4.5%	14.2%	21.5%	0.5%	0.0%	3.8%	2.0%	3.3%	3.8%	7.9%	8.3%	7.0%
Rockford city	4,106	7.2%	3.4%	12.9%	9.9%	11.8%	1.3%	6.6%	8.4%	0.0%	1.9%	2.0%	15.6%	11.8%
Springfield city	6,357	1.3%	2.0%	12.3%	10.4%	4.1%	17.0%	5.8%	12.4%	1.6%	10.5%	3.7%	6.2%	0.3%
Indiana														
Evansville city	3,041	10.4%	8.4%	12.9%	25.0%	0.0%	2.1%	6.0%	4.1%	1.6%	0.0%	4.8%	16.9%	3.7%
Fort Wayne city	8,284	2.5%	4.8%	11.1%	20.2%	1.9%	8.7%	4.0%	5.9%	1.2%	5.0%	3.2%	8.5%	10.1%
Indianapolis city (bal)	43,076	4.2%	6.4%	8.8%	16.8%	3.7%	5.7%	6.8%	12.1%	4.4%	5.2%	6.3%	8.7%	2.5%
South Bend city	3,110	18.2%	9.4%	3.7%	8.6%	13.9%	2.0%	0.0%	4.8%	10.2%	14.5%	8.2%	2.8%	3.1%
Iowa														
Cedar Rapids city	5,753	24.9%	8.3%	7.5%	21.3%	0.0%	10.3%	3.0%	6.2%	4.0%	2.3%	2.2%	3.4%	0.0%
Davenport city	6,082	17.3%	6.3%	13.9%	6.5%	11.5%	10.0%	3.3%	14.1%	3.7%	0.0%	4.3%	3.9%	5.2%
Des Moines city	10,307	6.2%	1.7%	3.1%	32.3%	0.0%	8.6%	11.6%	8.0%	1.4%	6.4%	4.8%	8.7%	0.8%
Kansas														
Kansas City city	3,939	16.2%	2.6%	1.4%	17.0%	5.0%	1.4%	0.0%	21.0%	1.9%	3.2%	8.0%	9.3%	0.0%
Olathe city	6,307	7.9%	11.7%	10.8%	21.3%	1.2%	9.3%	5.4%	5.2%	1.3%	2.6%	2.5%	10.8%	1.4%
Overland Park city	12,505	5.5%	2.2%	9.7%	31.7%	0.0%	7.8%	7.6%	8.1%	2.5%	4.6%	6.3%	2.5%	4.2%
Topeka city	4,228	4.4%	0.0%	10.3%	16.5%	0.0%	6.0%	6.0%	8.7%	7.8%	0.0%	11.9%	13.7%	2.9%
Wichita city	14,912	9.5%	0.0%	14.5%	20.7%	5.7%	1.8%	2.3%	7.5%	4.0%	4.9%	3.5%	16.3%	4.0%
Kentucky														
Lexington-Fayette urban county	17,489	10.4%	2.1%	11.8%	14.4%	5.3%	10.1%	1.3%	4.4%	5.1%	1.9%	11.0%	5.2%	4.4%
Louisville/Jefferson County metro govt (bal)	28,050	9.0%	3.1%	8.2%	23.3%	2.6%	6.5%	8.9%	5.7%	1.9%	3.6%	6.9%	7.9%	3.6%
Louisiana														
Baton Rouge city	13,364	14.9%	3.0%	8.0%	14.6%	3.3%	15.9%	7.6%	10.1%	2.4%	7.2%	3.3%	3.8%	4.1%
Lafayette city	8,073	16.8%	7.5%	6.2%	4.8%	6.3%	2.0%	3.1%	2.6%	1.9%	20.8%	11.1%	3.4%	7.8%
New Orleans city	25,636	4.1%	1.7%	9.7%	17.7%	3.5%	15.4%	6.6%	9.3%	5.0%	6.3%	5.2%	2.3%	7.5%
Shreveport city	5,725	6.2%	0.0%	28.5%	22.9%	3.1%	1.5%	0.0%	17.0%	2.2%	6.4%	5.0%	2.1%	0.0%
Maryland														
Baltimore city	44,703	7.7%	4.7%	8.4%	16.3%	3.4%	10.5%	4.7%	12.2%	3.2%	5.3%	9.3%	3.8%	4.9%
Massachusetts														
Boston city	85,917	8.4%	4.2%	7.6%	22.2%	1.6%	12.9%	4.9%	10.4%	4.7%	4.8%	6.5%	2.1%	5.1%
Brockton city	3,752	2.7%	7.8%	12.8%	21.5%	9.2%	5.9%	2.4%	2.0%	0.0%	5.2%	14.6%	0.0%	7.0%
Cambridge city	24,086	20.3%	5.9%	5.3%	12.9%	8.7%	12.6%	1.0%	10.7%	5.7%	3.3%	6.8%	2.5%	3.1%
Lowell city	6,848	16.9%	6.7%	5.6%	10.1%	1.6%	5.2%	3.1%	4.7%	4.9%	5.8%	5.6%	8.1%	14.1%
Lynn city	1,873	13.1%	2.2%	4.0%	13.9%	6.9%	10.5%	3.7%	3.2%	0.0%	8.4%	7.7%	2.3%	24.0%
New Bedford city	3,191	4.2%	4.0%	4.5%	7.9%	1.1%	8.4%	2.6%	0.0%	4.7%	10.3%	13.0%	11.3%	21.0%
Springfield city	3,371	4.9%	0.0%	5.3%	18.9%	6.4%	4.3%	10.1%	2.6%	2.2%	3.0%	25.1%	0.0%	11.7%
Worcester city	11,329	12.3%	8.0%	5.6%	14.1%	9.0%	8.4%	1.7%	14.5%	6.8%	1.5%	8.6%	1.8%	1.0%
Michigan														
Ann Arbor city	19,109	20.9%	7.2%	7.5%	9.6%	3.1%	14.2%	0.8%	12.9%	8.8%	3.0%	4.7%	0.9%	2.7%
Dearborn city	3,880	7.1%	7.2%	9.6%	9.1%	1.6%	16.6%	11.1%	18.0%	0.0%	0.0%	7.5%	10.4%	0.0%
Detroit city	11,709	5.9%	0.5%	5.9%	20.3%	5.1%	9.0%	7.2%	11.3%	6.9%	0.5%	6.7%	2.4%	7.7%
Flint city	385	0.0%	0.0%	0.0%	0.0%	0.0%	0.0%	0.0%	0.0%	0.0%	37.1%	0.0%	30.9%	31.9%
Grand Rapids city	14,306	3.0%	3.2%	12.6%	11.8%	5.0%	3.7%	13.7%	7.1%	4.3%	10.0%	7.4%	10.1%	1.7%
Lansing city	8,241	5.0%	6.1%	3.7%	19.3%	3.4%	5.6%	2.4%	13.7%	5.4%	6.9%	9.0%	3.6%	0.0%
Livonia city	3,778	6.0%	0.0%	5.2%	9.3%	0.0%	6.8%	15.5%	17.8%	2.5%	0.0%	9.0%	11.7%	6.6%
Sterling Heights city	5,044	16.1%	2.7%	1.7%	17.4%	0.0%	0.0%	4.6%	10.3%	2.9%	12.5%	8.0%	18.0%	2.7%
Warren city	4,125	1.8%	14.3%	3.8%	47.7%	0.0%	0.0%	0.0%	8.0%	8.6%	0.0%	8.1%	0.0%	0.0%
Minnesota														
Minneapolis city	46,356	6.5%	4.9%	6.1%	18.1%	2.0%	13.7%	8.8%	9.7%	4.2%	2.8%	6.5%	1.9%	7.3%
Rochester city	7,248	12.7%	4.8%	17.7%	11.4%	6.0%	10.0%	1.9%	13.9%	0.9%	2.6%	0.0%	7.1%	1.2%
St. Paul city	22,134	4.4%	2.5%	11.1%	13.1%	4.0%	11.1%	6.3%	5.6%	4.0%	5.5%	4.2%	7.3%	11.2%

Table F-3: Places—Educational Field of Study—*Continued*

	Total Millennial Population	Percent of the Population 18 to 31 by Field of Study												
		Engineering	Computers and Math	Science and Engineering Related	Business	Physical Science	Social Science	Communications	Biological Sciences	Literature	Liberal Arts	Psychology	Education	Visual and Performing Arts
Mississippi														
Jackson city	7,949	5.7%	0.6%	4.5%	17.3%	0.4%	8.3%	3.6%	12.4%	5.8%	1.5%	7.6%	9.1%	6.7%
Missouri														
Columbia city	10,914	4.1%	10.0%	6.6%	9.7%	2.7%	2.8%	10.9%	21.3%	0.6%	7.0%	4.7%	8.6%	2.0%
Independence city	2,357	0.0%	5.9%	2.5%	16.5%	0.0%	3.0%	0.0%	0.0%	0.0%	2.8%	25.9%	24.1%	10.9%
Kansas City city	28,909	5.9%	4.1%	8.5%	19.2%	3.6%	2.7%	8.2%	9.2%	3.5%	4.6%	5.9%	8.3%	6.8%
Lee's Summit city	4,219	12.6%	0.0%	16.0%	16.7%	0.0%	3.1%	11.4%	1.5%	13.8%	4.7%	2.1%	12.7%	2.4%
Springfield city	12,309	0.0%	1.9%	7.6%	22.8%	3.6%	5.6%	5.7%	5.5%	8.7%	3.8%	4.0%	11.0%	9.2%
St. Louis city	28,507	3.6%	1.5%	5.5%	19.5%	5.7%	7.6%	5.7%	12.4%	5.9%	7.5%	7.1%	7.3%	4.6%
Montana														
Billings city	3,402	0.0%	0.0%	25.0%	11.0%	0.0%	0.0%	0.0%	3.0%	0.0%	11.5%	12.3%	0.7%	5.1%
Nebraska														
Lincoln city	15,326	7.8%	2.7%	7.7%	21.6%	3.3%	5.6%	7.8%	10.6%	2.9%	1.7%	3.5%	6.6%	8.6%
Omaha city	26,189	3.8%	3.9%	10.9%	22.9%	1.5%	6.1%	5.1%	8.0%	6.5%	2.2%	6.9%	10.6%	4.3%
Nevada														
Henderson city	7,571	2.1%	4.2%	20.3%	35.5%	0.0%	1.7%	7.6%	12.2%	0.0%	0.0%	1.6%	1.2%	1.1%
Las Vegas city	13,891	4.6%	4.4%	3.9%	21.0%	1.1%	5.0%	2.9%	7.7%	4.0%	3.1%	15.4%	11.0%	7.2%
North Las Vegas city	5,095	2.1%	1.8%	8.2%	30.6%	8.8%	0.6%	6.1%	3.8%	0.0%	3.8%	5.6%	4.7%	0.0%
Reno city	11,606	4.0%	5.0%	8.5%	20.6%	6.2%	4.9%	1.8%	9.8%	2.1%	2.2%	2.1%	16.5%	2.5%
Sparks city	1,270	9.0%	4.0%	21.8%	37.6%	9.6%	12.2%	0.0%	0.0%	0.0%	0.0%	0.0%	5.7%	0.0%
New Hampshire														
Manchester city	5,321	8.6%	4.5%	7.7%	33.4%	0.9%	6.3%	1.1%	4.2%	1.8%	4.9%	9.5%	0.0%	10.6%
New Jersey														
Elizabeth city	3,253	10.2%	16.5%	9.8%	24.5%	0.0%	0.0%	0.0%	8.2%	0.0%	3.4%	0.0%	7.8%	10.2%
Jersey City city	27,758	13.1%	12.3%	9.0%	22.9%	1.2%	6.4%	2.4%	1.6%	6.0%	2.1%	5.1%	3.1%	9.1%
Newark city	8,938	8.5%	3.5%	11.1%	19.0%	0.9%	16.9%	6.9%	6.6%	0.0%	0.0%	8.2%	4.8%	3.4%
Paterson city	2,375	7.5%	0.0%	16.0%	18.5%	20.9%	0.0%	2.5%	0.0%	0.0%	9.6%	0.0%	3.0%	0.0%
New Mexico														
Albuquerque city	20,811	10.1%	5.2%	13.1%	11.1%	3.0%	10.4%	4.8%	4.8%	4.3%	3.5%	4.7%	9.9%	9.2%
Las Cruces city	3,827	10.3%	0.0%	4.3%	6.6%	2.6%	2.4%	1.8%	8.4%	6.8%	0.0%	16.5%	5.4%	6.1%
Rio Rancho city	980	1.0%	0.0%	6.6%	0.0%	16.4%	0.0%	0.0%	1.9%	0.0%	0.0%	25.4%	4.7%	24.2%
New York														
Albany city	11,499	3.4%	2.5%	10.7%	18.3%	5.0%	11.0%	5.9%	8.1%	4.1%	12.5%	7.3%	3.0%	5.6%
Buffalo city	16,029	5.3%	4.6%	5.4%	10.0%	2.7%	8.5%	4.3%	9.3%	6.4%	8.9%	12.6%	11.0%	6.1%
New York city	608,982	4.4%	4.2%	6.0%	22.4%	2.3%	12.9%	7.1%	4.4%	4.9%	4.4%	6.2%	4.2%	11.8%
Rochester city	11,734	8.5%	0.3%	6.0%	11.8%	4.0%	7.7%	5.9%	10.4%	6.0%	5.0%	6.4%	14.3%	5.3%
Syracuse city	8,868	6.2%	3.5%	3.9%	20.3%	2.1%	9.1%	4.2%	15.9%	4.6%	9.2%	2.5%	3.2%	6.3%
Yonkers city	9,458	7.1%	10.3%	14.7%	17.5%	0.0%	5.9%	4.1%	6.5%	2.5%	4.2%	6.1%	6.0%	4.1%
North Carolina														
Charlotte city	55,530	5.1%	3.0%	5.8%	28.8%	1.4%	8.9%	6.8%	3.9%	2.8%	3.3%	9.3%	5.1%	5.6%
Durham city	25,014	7.4%	5.6%	4.4%	6.4%	6.5%	13.9%	4.7%	14.3%	2.8%	5.6%	10.4%	3.2%	4.0%
Fayetteville city	7,175	4.5%	5.4%	7.5%	14.8%	14.1%	9.8%	5.2%	3.3%	2.1%	3.3%	3.3%	10.7%	3.2%
Greensboro city	15,108	5.6%	2.5%	5.5%	17.2%	1.3%	2.2%	6.1%	6.1%	6.1%	1.4%	13.8%	11.7%	5.7%
High Point city	2,773	0.0%	2.1%	4.7%	33.3%	0.0%	4.3%	1.8%	3.1%	0.0%	13.7%	5.1%	8.6%	11.8%
Raleigh city	39,236	8.8%	8.0%	3.9%	16.2%	3.7%	8.3%	4.4%	9.1%	5.6%	3.0%	2.4%	7.9%	6.9%
Wilmington city	5,387	7.7%	0.0%	6.5%	22.2%	6.6%	1.5%	0.8%	4.4%	9.8%	1.6%	7.6%	12.0%	7.9%
Winston-Salem city	10,370	3.8%	1.8%	13.7%	10.4%	4.1%	4.6%	0.4%	15.7%	6.8%	7.6%	7.1%	7.3%	8.8%
North Dakota														
Fargo city	11,023	7.6%	0.0%	17.1%	15.8%	1.0%	5.5%	6.7%	6.4%	8.8%	0.0%	6.2%	17.1%	0.3%
Ohio														
Akron city	8,056	11.6%	7.9%	10.2%	14.8%	4.6%	15.7%	6.2%	3.1%	6.5%	2.9%	1.0%	11.3%	2.0%
Cincinnati city	20,271	7.1%	4.3%	6.3%	18.7%	1.5%	9.2%	9.6%	9.0%	6.3%	3.3%	5.4%	6.4%	6.9%
Cleveland city	13,209	6.3%	2.9%	11.2%	30.2%	1.6%	7.4%	8.8%	8.6%	7.0%	1.4%	3.6%	2.9%	3.9%
Columbus city	56,192	4.7%	3.8%	10.2%	19.4%	2.9%	7.4%	7.6%	9.9%	4.9%	3.2%	7.8%	5.5%	4.2%
Dayton city	5,037	12.7%	0.0%	13.3%	15.4%	1.5%	3.3%	8.8%	0.0%	9.8%	3.5%	0.0%	21.8%	3.8%
Toledo city	7,100	8.8%	3.3%	5.4%	18.8%	1.0%	5.2%	4.9%	15.3%	3.6%	4.5%	1.8%	5.7%	6.8%
Oklahoma														
Broken Arrow city	3,225	0.0%	9.4%	15.7%	22.3%	2.9%	6.2%	11.5%	3.1%	0.0%	4.2%	8.0%	6.1%	6.4%
Lawton city	3,624	30.8%	2.9%	17.0%	3.8%	0.0%	11.7%	0.0%	6.4%	2.4%	5.3%	10.2%	1.7%	0.0%
Norman city	9,260	6.5%	0.8%	2.9%	9.1%	6.3%	14.5%	10.7%	2.2%	4.6%	5.1%	15.0%	0.0%	16.6%
Oklahoma City city	25,418	4.4%	2.5%	5.4%	19.3%	2.0%	9.5%	8.3%	8.8%	4.5%	3.3%	7.0%	5.9%	10.1%
Tulsa city	16,600	1.7%	1.4%	9.6%	22.5%	4.0%	5.1%	8.9%	7.8%	2.2%	5.8%	5.8%	9.2%	5.2%
Oregon														
Beaverton city	6,153	12.4%	1.9%	13.4%	21.9%	7.1%	12.0%	0.0%	0.7%	2.4%	5.5%	14.3%	2.8%	4.3%
Eugene city	6,090	2.7%	3.9%	0.0%	11.1%	0.0%	11.9%	7.7%	13.5%	5.3%	8.6%	14.2%	3.3%	9.1%
Gresham city	1,885	3.7%	2.3%	15.9%	9.0%	4.8%	3.7%	4.2%	6.2%	5.7%	13.6%	5.5%	3.9%	13.3%
Hillsboro city	5,512	15.8%	21.4%	3.9%	15.6%	8.7%	1.3%	0.6%	2.7%	3.7%	1.6%	5.7%	3.1%	12.1%
Portland city	44,419	7.4%	3.6%	6.2%	11.9%	1.2%	14.0%	4.7%	11.8%	5.5%	6.7%	6.3%	2.7%	9.0%
Salem city	4,547	5.8%	20.2%	2.6%	10.8%	13.3%	9.4%	2.4%	21.0%	0.0%	6.3%	8.2%	0.0%	0.0%
Pennsylvania														
Allentown city	2,386	3.1%	3.8%	2.3%	15.3%	5.4%	1.3%	6.1%	0.0%	4.2%	4.4%	12.2%	0.0%	18.6%

Table F-3: Places—Educational Field of Study—*Continued*

	Total Millennial Population	Percent of the Population 18 to 31 by Field of Study												
		Engineering	Computers and Math	Science and Engineering Related	Business	Physical Science	Social Science	Communications	Biological Sciences	Literature	Liberal Arts	Psychology	Education	Visual and Performing Arts
Pennsylvania—Cont.														
Erie city	5,673	0.0%	6.8%	17.3%	12.6%	0.0%	3.0%	6.0%	9.5%	7.0%	2.5%	7.2%	8.7%	5.7%
Philadelphia city	97,199	4.8%	3.2%	6.8%	18.7%	4.8%	10.7%	6.4%	11.3%	2.9%	3.5%	7.1%	3.2%	9.1%
Pittsburgh city	32,117	10.9%	7.8%	7.1%	14.4%	4.5%	6.5%	6.9%	7.3%	7.4%	3.6%	6.3%	4.5%	6.5%
Rhode Island														
Providence city	13,489	6.4%	6.9%	4.6%	9.9%	14.4%	4.4%	2.4%	7.7%	4.0%	6.1%	7.9%	4.5%	9.3%
South Carolina														
Charleston city	12,365	4.3%	5.7%	7.1%	14.5%	3.5%	5.7%	7.9%	17.3%	3.4%	6.4%	12.2%	4.6%	1.9%
Columbia city	9,279	3.3%	4.4%	7.6%	25.2%	0.8%	11.3%	8.2%	7.7%	4.3%	6.4%	6.7%	0.3%	6.1%
North Charleston city	3,692	24.8%	2.0%	7.2%	13.3%	1.6%	8.7%	1.9%	12.2%	0.0%	5.6%	6.8%	11.3%	0.0%
South Dakota														
Sioux Falls city	8,973	2.5%	4.4%	7.0%	19.0%	0.0%	6.5%	11.5%	12.3%	3.6%	0.0%	6.1%	18.9%	4.6%
Tennessee														
Chattanooga city	7,527	5.5%	3.2%	12.1%	20.6%	3.7%	3.6%	7.6%	7.4%	3.9%	10.7%	4.7%	6.8%	3.8%
Clarksville city	8,443	2.7%	0.0%	4.2%	29.2%	0.0%	5.5%	6.2%	0.0%	3.3%	6.7%	5.3%	21.5%	8.4%
Knoxville city	14,322	9.1%	2.6%	6.6%	20.5%	1.0%	9.3%	5.7%	6.7%	8.5%	7.3%	1.3%	7.3%	4.9%
Memphis city	24,879	3.8%	4.3%	5.9%	13.6%	1.2%	7.4%	6.9%	11.1%	5.8%	4.3%	8.6%	11.8%	4.5%
Murfreesboro city	7,236	7.3%	0.0%	7.8%	27.2%	11.4%	5.0%	3.6%	6.9%	5.6%	0.0%	8.4%	5.2%	3.0%
Nashville-Davidson metropolitan govt (bal)	51,621	4.3%	4.1%	7.7%	20.6%	4.2%	4.9%	10.4%	6.8%	3.7%	5.0%	7.5%	4.4%	9.8%
Texas														
Abilene city	4,531	3.0%	6.2%	10.9%	25.8%	0.0%	4.9%	2.9%	0.7%	0.0%	9.7%	3.6%	7.3%	7.5%
Amarillo city	5,303	5.5%	3.9%	6.7%	19.7%	0.5%	1.9%	6.5%	12.3%	6.0%	6.8%	4.7%	1.6%	10.9%
Arlington city	13,787	6.2%	3.7%	10.9%	28.4%	2.9%	3.3%	3.7%	9.3%	0.6%	4.0%	3.7%	11.2%	3.3%
Austin city	80,303	10.3%	4.5%	5.5%	16.9%	3.4%	13.2%	8.9%	4.3%	5.6%	4.8%	3.5%	5.2%	8.4%
Beaumont city	3,290	12.3%	4.6%	12.3%	16.9%	0.0%	4.0%	3.4%	0.0%	6.3%	4.9%	2.2%	10.2%	5.2%
Brownsville city	2,947	2.5%	3.5%	2.6%	17.1%	0.0%	1.5%	8.8%	18.6%	4.4%	5.1%	0.0%	29.7%	0.0%
Carrollton city	8,258	15.1%	8.2%	2.2%	37.4%	0.8%	2.5%	9.6%	3.6%	2.9%	1.5%	0.9%	2.1%	4.8%
College Station city	13,013	12.1%	1.6%	8.0%	9.1%	5.8%	10.5%	2.8%	26.0%	4.3%	2.5%	5.9%	2.4%	0.4%
Corpus Christi city	9,622	16.1%	3.2%	6.5%	18.0%	8.9%	3.3%	3.5%	7.9%	0.0%	5.7%	9.6%	6.7%	0.9%
Dallas city	62,347	7.1%	3.8%	9.7%	26.2%	2.6%	7.1%	7.9%	6.9%	2.9%	4.5%	3.2%	3.9%	7.0%
Denton city	8,107	1.7%	4.2%	14.9%	21.3%	2.0%	1.5%	4.3%	10.4%	2.3%	7.4%	3.7%	7.4%	13.7%
El Paso city	19,029	5.2%	1.3%	7.6%	24.9%	2.3%	3.6%	1.6%	14.4%	1.3%	8.0%	6.3%	12.8%	3.2%
Fort Worth city	31,888	5.8%	2.2%	10.5%	24.5%	1.3%	5.3%	7.0%	11.4%	1.2%	2.9%	6.0%	7.3%	2.7%
Frisco city	5,785	9.1%	3.5%	13.0%	15.3%	2.0%	9.1%	8.2%	0.8%	3.2%	1.5%	7.6%	15.8%	0.0%
Garland city	6,152	9.1%	0.8%	1.9%	27.6%	0.0%	2.2%	13.4%	11.2%	9.3%	0.0%	8.7%	3.9%	0.0%
Grand Prairie city	2,923	4.1%	4.2%	5.5%	19.7%	5.7%	16.0%	3.8%	4.4%	6.2%	0.0%	9.8%	0.0%	10.2%
Houston city	132,358	11.9%	5.7%	9.0%	21.0%	5.3%	9.4%	4.2%	7.9%	1.4%	3.0%	3.4%	6.0%	3.9%
Irving city	11,068	11.3%	16.7%	4.7%	24.8%	1.5%	6.9%	7.0%	8.7%	4.0%	1.1%	3.4%	4.0%	2.6%
Killeen city	3,949	7.4%	1.8%	11.9%	11.4%	0.0%	20.6%	0.0%	0.0%	11.4%	10.1%	0.0%	3.2%	3.0%
Laredo city	4,185	7.6%	1.6%	16.4%	21.8%	1.8%	6.6%	0.0%	7.1%	1.9%	2.5%	9.4%	16.4%	0.0%
Lewisville city	6,927	1.3%	3.1%	1.6%	28.9%	1.0%	2.8%	3.7%	10.6%	1.7%	9.2%	2.6%	14.5%	9.0%
Lubbock city	11,956	5.9%	2.2%	9.4%	23.6%	5.0%	4.9%	1.8%	10.9%	3.7%	3.8%	3.9%	9.6%	1.6%
McAllen city	4,855	5.0%	1.7%	11.9%	18.1%	2.5%	3.2%	1.8%	7.6%	4.0%	4.7%	13.2%	15.8%	2.9%
McKinney city	5,997	7.7%	0.5%	4.9%	29.9%	1.9%	2.3%	3.6%	1.9%	4.8%	0.0%	4.0%	20.8%	0.0%
Mesquite city	3,645	1.7%	14.8%	3.9%	23.8%	1.8%	0.9%	0.0%	2.3%	15.5%	0.0%	4.7%	8.6%	1.0%
Midland city	6,303	8.9%	0.0%	0.0%	18.2%	3.4%	11.1%	7.6%	3.5%	7.8%	12.3%	0.0%	8.4%	0.0%
Odessa city	3,004	2.8%	5.0%	17.6%	18.9%	0.0%	0.0%	1.8%	5.1%	33.1%	0.0%	0.0%	2.2%	2.0%
Pasadena city	3,123	7.6%	5.0%	10.1%	16.5%	6.4%	0.0%	12.4%	2.8%	0.0%	5.3%	3.2%	15.0%	0.0%
Pearland city	6,880	8.5%	0.0%	5.9%	21.2%	4.4%	14.1%	15.0%	0.0%	2.5%	0.0%	5.5%	21.2%	1.1%
Plano city	18,900	17.4%	8.4%	7.5%	27.1%	1.6%	6.1%	3.0%	7.9%	4.4%	2.3%	1.9%	2.9%	4.2%
Richardson city	5,835	21.6%	12.3%	7.8%	19.0%	0.0%	4.3%	3.9%	9.3%	1.0%	1.8%	1.7%	0.0%	13.3%
Round Rock city	3,616	11.7%	2.1%	15.9%	5.4%	8.5%	3.5%	6.4%	10.1%	1.4%	0.0%	0.0%	15.9%	7.4%
San Angelo city	3,382	1.7%	7.8%	2.9%	15.2%	0.0%	4.2%	15.9%	9.5%	1.7%	0.0%	5.6%	13.5%	0.0%
San Antonio city	57,297	7.3%	8.0%	6.4%	21.4%	1.6%	7.5%	5.0%	8.9%	4.1%	4.1%	6.5%	6.8%	2.7%
Tyler city	4,135	0.0%	1.5%	8.9%	38.1%	0.0%	4.4%	2.0%	8.5%	4.4%	2.2%	8.2%	4.6%	3.1%
Waco city	5,556	5.1%	0.4%	1.5%	23.2%	1.3%	5.2%	4.4%	7.8%	6.0%	9.2%	7.8%	3.8%	4.9%
Wichita Falls city	3,480	1.6%	2.1%	0.0%	30.4%	0.0%	10.4%	9.0%	0.0%	0.0%	6.0%	0.0%	23.8%	2.9%
Utah														
Orem city	3,647	3.8%	8.4%	1.8%	27.7%	0.0%	0.0%	11.1%	5.1%	1.0%	1.9%	3.4%	8.3%	10.2%
Provo city	11,330	6.6%	5.6%	9.3%	7.9%	2.6%	11.5%	4.8%	7.4%	9.4%	2.9%	3.9%	11.5%	1.3%
Salt Lake City city	14,460	7.8%	2.1%	8.1%	13.7%	3.7%	9.4%	8.4%	10.5%	9.5%	3.4%	4.5%	5.2%	4.8%
West Jordan city	2,802	2.3%	3.1%	5.9%	41.3%	0.0%	0.0%	6.7%	0.0%	9.6%	0.0%	9.1%	5.2%	0.0%
West Valley City city	1,685	27.6%	0.0%	0.0%	10.1%	0.0%	3.9%	8.9%	5.8%	24.8%	0.0%	0.0%	4.7%	3.9%
Virginia														
Alexandria city	19,521	10.5%	6.2%	9.5%	22.6%	1.5%	16.4%	2.7%	2.9%	4.5%	5.3%	5.1%	2.3%	5.2%
Chesapeake city	7,962	5.9%	3.5%	8.3%	12.6%	10.5%	6.3%	3.6%	11.9%	0.5%	1.5%	14.1%	7.7%	4.0%
Hampton city	2,521	5.7%	0.0%	16.2%	19.3%	6.0%	0.0%	7.8%	0.0%	3.1%	0.0%	10.7%	0.0%	9.2%
Newport News city	8,090	3.1%	7.1%	14.0%	18.4%	2.3%	4.4%	6.3%	5.7%	2.9%	7.5%	8.3%	6.1%	1.5%
Norfolk city	10,695	14.0%	4.2%	7.3%	18.1%	5.3%	8.9%	2.8%	13.4%	5.1%	4.4%	2.9%	5.8%	1.9%
Portsmouth city	4,172	3.8%	4.4%	8.5%	6.9%	3.7%	1.8%	9.6%	30.2%	9.5%	0.0%	7.3%	1.2%	6.5%
Richmond city	16,175	4.6%	3.9%	5.3%	8.4%	2.9%	15.9%	9.6%	6.1%	8.7%	3.4%	14.1%	3.7%	6.8%
Roanoke city	3,979	2.9%	2.2%	8.0%	14.6%	10.2%	8.5%	0.0%	16.2%	7.5%	5.0%	3.3%	8.5%	11.3%
Virginia Beach city	19,035	3.8%	4.8%	5.5%	14.9%	0.6%	10.3%	10.9%	7.3%	3.9%	3.8%	8.6%	4.2%	9.5%

Table F-3: Places—Educational Field of Study—*Continued*

	Total Millennial Population	Percent of the Population 18 to 31 by Field of Study												
		Engineering	Computers and Math	Science and Engineering Related	Business	Physical Science	Social Science	Communications	Biological Sciences	Literature	Liberal Arts	Psychology	Education	Visual and Performing Arts
Washington														
Bellevue city	12,755	26.4%	23.2%	14.9%	7.6%	3.4%	3.0%	5.8%	2.9%	0.0%	4.7%	3.0%	0.0%	3.2%
Everett city	3,008	28.6%	5.8%	4.9%	7.6%	5.7%	16.1%	2.9%	1.8%	4.8%	4.9%	3.7%	0.0%	4.5%
Federal Way city	1,699	13.6%	0.0%	3.3%	40.0%	0.0%	0.0%	7.9%	11.9%	0.0%	0.0%	0.0%	0.0%	20.3%
Kent city	4,727	6.1%	22.9%	4.0%	20.6%	0.0%	23.5%	2.1%	6.9%	1.0%	0.0%	3.0%	7.3%	2.6%
Renton city	5,110	15.6%	12.2%	4.8%	22.7%	1.3%	4.0%	6.1%	5.2%	5.0%	2.4%	3.8%	8.8%	1.5%
Seattle city	86,418	8.1%	9.1%	5.5%	10.3%	3.0%	15.0%	7.3%	8.6%	5.4%	5.2%	6.2%	2.3%	7.2%
Spokane city	8,493	2.0%	1.5%	14.2%	20.6%	3.5%	12.6%	10.9%	3.5%	5.7%	2.9%	7.3%	6.9%	3.8%
Spokane Valley city	3,253	4.2%	0.0%	27.0%	14.8%	0.0%	7.7%	13.5%	8.4%	0.0%	0.0%	0.0%	6.0%	11.4%
Tacoma city	7,596	5.1%	2.9%	6.5%	11.7%	2.6%	17.8%	8.5%	5.9%	14.2%	1.6%	8.2%	6.9%	2.5%
Vancouver city	3,520	5.8%	22.2%	4.7%	11.3%	0.0%	7.2%	0.0%	3.4%	0.0%	12.7%	7.2%	1.7%	7.5%
Yakima city	1,433	0.0%	0.0%	8.6%	39.0%	0.0%	0.0%	5.9%	16.6%	7.3%	0.0%	7.5%	15.1%	0.0%
Wisconsin														
Green Bay city	4,056	14.3%	3.7%	6.2%	18.2%	0.0%	5.3%	5.9%	14.9%	0.0%	5.1%	8.3%	7.1%	0.0%
Kenosha city	3,361	0.0%	0.0%	21.7%	24.9%	0.0%	12.8%	0.0%	0.0%	0.0%	16.1%	2.1%	0.0%	11.5%
Madison city	30,505	11.8%	7.0%	6.7%	9.6%	5.0%	8.8%	8.2%	12.2%	4.4%	2.1%	4.5%	4.2%	9.4%
Milwaukee city	25,637	5.8%	3.5%	7.3%	17.5%	2.7%	13.3%	10.8%	5.5%	2.8%	2.1%	4.7%	6.6%	9.2%

Table F-4: Metropolitan/Micropolitan Statistical Areas—Educational Field of Study

	Total Millennial Population	Percent of the Population 18 to 31 by Field of Study												
		Engineering	Computers and Math	Science and Engineering Related	Business	Physical Science	Social Science	Communications	Biological Sciences	Literature	Liberal Arts	Psychology	Education	Visual and Performing Arts
Abilene, TX	5,449	3.6%	5.1%	12.5%	23.9%	0.0%	4.1%	2.4%	2.1%	0.0%	8.0%	9.7%	7.1%	6.8%
Adrian, MI micro	1,772	3.6%	0.0%	0.0%	3.9%	0.0%	0.0%	6.6%	11.4%	16.6%	11.2%	1.9%	36.1%	0.0%
Akron, OH	30,464	10.0%	3.7%	7.5%	21.6%	3.1%	7.9%	6.5%	8.0%	7.2%	2.3%	2.5%	10.3%	1.9%
Albany-Schenectady-Troy, NY	42,268	7.9%	2.4%	10.3%	17.7%	3.0%	4.7%	5.2%	9.0%	3.5%	6.7%	7.2%	8.3%	4.5%
Albany, GA	2,767	0.0%	0.0%	24.5%	22.8%	0.0%	9.2%	0.0%	6.4%	0.6%	10.3%	4.6%	5.3%	5.7%
Albany, OR	4,485	4.6%	2.3%	2.6%	10.3%	5.6%	4.8%	0.0%	33.9%	4.9%	3.8%	4.2%	4.0%	5.2%
Albertville, AL micro	2,167	11.9%	0.0%	0.0%	22.4%	0.0%	0.0%	1.2%	0.5%	0.0%	1.0%	0.4%	57.4%	0.4%
Albuquerque, NM	29,255	9.4%	4.6%	12.5%	13.0%	2.7%	8.0%	4.3%	6.1%	4.0%	2.8%	5.3%	8.3%	9.2%
Alexandria, LA	3,329	0.0%	1.3%	0.0%	34.3%	3.5%	13.2%	6.6%	2.3%	5.1%	10.5%	9.8%	10.6%	0.0%
Allentown-Bethlehem-Easton, PA-NJ	34,504	9.1%	1.6%	5.2%	17.3%	2.4%	2.7%	6.4%	3.8%	4.7%	4.5%	8.4%	18.7%	5.8%
Altoona, PA	2,685	1.6%	4.4%	39.9%	9.0%	0.0%	0.0%	7.6%	6.1%	9.5%	0.0%	4.4%	12.1%	0.9%
Amarillo, TX	7,496	6.1%	1.1%	8.3%	18.5%	2.7%	1.4%	7.9%	10.0%	4.2%	6.1%	3.3%	7.4%	10.2%
Ames, IA	9,518	28.2%	0.0%	3.2%	13.6%	0.0%	2.2%	1.7%	15.5%	2.5%	2.0%	5.0%	7.2%	2.6%
Anchorage, AK	15,159	6.6%	1.8%	11.1%	18.2%	6.1%	7.6%	0.6%	8.0%	6.3%	2.7%	12.0%	5.0%	1.1%
Ann Arbor, MI	34,954	15.7%	3.8%	7.8%	13.0%	3.3%	10.9%	4.2%	10.5%	7.4%	4.4%	6.3%	3.3%	3.9%
Anniston-Oxford-Jacksonville, AL	2,890	3.1%	5.1%	9.6%	17.7%	0.0%	4.0%	7.7%	14.5%	3.3%	0.0%	11.5%	12.3%	0.4%
Appleton, WI	7,024	10.6%	0.0%	7.8%	28.0%	2.1%	5.9%	2.9%	3.1%	3.7%	2.5%	10.4%	5.2%	3.0%
Asheville, NC	17,376	3.5%	0.1%	3.9%	9.4%	0.1%	9.7%	8.7%	18.2%	6.4%	6.5%	7.6%	8.2%	6.7%
Ashtabula, OH micro	1,042	0.0%	0.0%	5.9%	18.3%	0.0%	0.0%	0.0%	8.5%	0.0%	0.0%	13.6%	19.5%	3.0%
Athens-Clarke County, GA	14,511	4.8%	1.4%	5.1%	13.5%	5.0%	17.6%	6.8%	12.4%	7.2%	4.2%	2.4%	8.6%	3.9%
Atlanta-Sandy Springs-Roswell, GA	221,833	6.3%	4.8%	7.0%	22.6%	2.8%	6.9%	7.3%	7.0%	3.5%	3.9%	6.0%	7.8%	5.2%
Atlantic City-Hammonton, NJ	9,424	6.1%	2.5%	12.1%	22.5%	2.9%	6.7%	8.1%	2.8%	1.0%	2.8%	5.1%	5.4%	2.1%
Auburn-Opelika, AL	10,574	12.8%	4.3%	12.8%	17.1%	3.5%	0.4%	4.7%	11.6%	1.8%	4.4%	1.4%	10.4%	3.1%
Augusta-Richmond County, GA-SC	17,788	3.9%	4.1%	21.8%	11.3%	0.9%	11.4%	3.6%	6.2%	3.2%	2.6%	6.9%	4.8%	1.2%
Augusta-Waterville, ME micro	3,424	2.6%	0.0%	0.0%	2.2%	3.2%	0.0%	2.8%	14.9%	1.8%	11.2%	1.0%	23.1%	11.2%
Austin-Round Rock, TX	117,703	10.0%	3.5%	5.6%	18.1%	3.1%	10.3%	7.9%	5.1%	4.9%	4.4%	4.5%	6.0%	7.2%
Bakersfield, CA	14,529	6.4%	1.6%	13.4%	20.6%	0.5%	9.4%	5.9%	2.9%	3.1%	10.4%	4.5%	7.2%	0.5%
Baltimore-Columbia-Towson, MD	142,339	7.1%	5.6%	8.0%	17.8%	3.2%	7.2%	4.8%	7.6%	5.6%	4.3%	7.5%	5.7%	5.0%
Bangor, ME	4,091	15.3%	0.0%	18.4%	20.6%	0.8%	9.0%	8.4%	2.1%	2.6%	6.3%	0.0%	8.2%	0.0%
Barnstable Town, MA	5,660	9.3%	1.2%	9.5%	17.3%	6.6%	5.2%	3.6%	13.0%	9.2%	8.2%	6.5%	1.8%	5.7%
Baton Rouge, LA	32,050	10.9%	1.6%	13.3%	15.2%	3.6%	9.7%	5.4%	10.7%	2.9%	6.8%	2.8%	7.3%	3.1%
Battle Creek, MI	2,031	3.5%	0.0%	7.6%	9.8%	0.0%	12.3%	0.0%	0.0%	26.0%	0.0%	0.0%	21.9%	10.1%
Bay City, MI	3,708	25.5%	0.0%	13.4%	13.3%	0.7%	13.1%	0.0%	9.7%	0.0%	0.0%	0.0%	3.9%	11.6%
Beaumont-Port Arthur, TX	9,459	14.6%	1.7%	10.9%	18.7%	0.0%	1.4%	6.4%	1.8%	4.6%	3.1%	0.8%	15.1%	3.6%
Beckley, WV	3,030	0.0%	2.8%	9.8%	19.8%	0.0%	7.3%	0.0%	13.2%	3.5%	8.8%	19.6%	6.0%	0.0%
Bellingham, WA	8,080	3.1%	1.9%	2.5%	14.1%	12.7%	10.2%	7.1%	5.4%	12.2%	11.6%	0.0%	7.6%	8.2%
Bend-Redmond, OR	5,471	2.1%	0.0%	12.5%	18.2%	0.0%	14.8%	2.7%	2.9%	4.0%	2.4%	4.1%	0.0%	6.4%
Billings, MT	4,893	4.3%	0.0%	19.3%	12.0%	0.0%	3.3%	0.0%	2.4%	0.0%	10.3%	10.3%	4.4%	3.6%
Binghamton, NY	7,757	17.3%	4.9%	5.5%	25.2%	2.6%	7.3%	6.7%	0.4%	3.7%	1.9%	8.7%	8.5%	1.6%
Birmingham-Hoover, AL	43,950	5.5%	1.7%	10.8%	21.6%	2.0%	6.3%	4.0%	12.6%	3.0%	3.9%	5.3%	7.7%	5.5%
Bismarck, ND	5,114	0.0%	1.7%	11.9%	34.4%	6.9%	0.0%	8.8%	5.0%	0.0%	0.2%	0.0%	9.7%	0.3%
Blacksburg-Christiansburg-Radford, VA	11,057	5.5%	8.0%	8.0%	9.6%	2.6%	5.2%	2.7%	10.8%	7.2%	6.2%	10.9%	10.4%	0.0%
Bloomington, IL	13,218	10.2%	7.5%	9.5%	15.7%	5.7%	4.4%	3.7%	8.6%	0.0%	1.3%	9.6%	9.5%	2.6%
Bloomington, IN	13,583	2.6%	6.9%	3.7%	5.1%	4.2%	16.1%	2.0%	8.5%	8.2%	5.6%	5.2%	5.4%	16.8%
Bloomsburg-Berwick, PA	2,614	5.7%	0.0%	7.2%	11.2%	8.6%	5.4%	7.5%	4.8%	0.0%	1.8%	10.4%	4.2%	0.0%
Boise City, ID	20,275	7.7%	0.9%	10.0%	11.7%	1.8%	3.8%	11.7%	19.7%	3.0%	3.9%	8.2%	8.9%	1.9%
Boston-Cambridge-Newton, MA-NH	340,751	9.1%	4.0%	7.3%	19.6%	2.7%	10.1%	5.0%	7.7%	4.6%	4.6%	6.3%	4.4%	6.4%
Boulder, CO	22,427	13.3%	2.6%	2.8%	14.3%	4.4%	8.0%	3.4%	6.9%	2.0%	5.2%	10.4%	3.3%	11.8%
Bowling Green, KY	6,074	2.1%	2.2%	15.3%	18.4%	3.3%	7.8%	8.1%	4.0%	7.9%	7.8%	2.4%	7.7%	6.8%
Bremerton-Silverdale, WA	7,379	26.4%	8.6%	6.3%	15.4%	3.1%	3.8%	0.0%	2.7%	2.1%	9.0%	3.2%	8.6%	4.1%
Bridgeport-Stamford-Norwalk, CT	46,005	4.5%	2.7%	4.6%	23.1%	2.6%	10.0%	8.9%	6.0%	4.8%	4.4%	5.5%	8.5%	7.8%
Brownsville-Harlingen, TX	7,071	2.3%	0.7%	4.6%	19.1%	2.3%	0.6%	3.7%	16.9%	3.0%	2.1%	0.7%	30.0%	1.1%
Brunswick, GA	1,976	0.0%	0.0%	6.1%	27.2%	0.0%	7.3%	8.2%	0.8%	2.3%	10.0%	5.9%	5.3%	11.1%
Buffalo-Cheektowaga-Niagara Falls, NY	59,418	6.3%	3.8%	6.5%	15.5%	3.7%	8.3%	6.9%	7.3%	5.1%	5.4%	6.5%	11.5%	4.6%
Burlington-South Burlington, VT	12,818	5.6%	4.2%	3.8%	11.7%	0.6%	11.1%	5.3%	9.8%	9.1%	5.1%	3.7%	2.1%	9.8%
Burlington, NC	6,401	2.2%	7.1%	11.0%	7.1%	0.0%	6.3%	20.6%	12.2%	0.6%	4.6%	1.9%	3.8%	10.6%
California-Lexington Park, MD	2,820	13.7%	10.8%	4.8%	8.2%	0.0%	20.9%	0.0%	12.6%	0.0%	2.2%	2.0%	9.2%	0.0%
Canton-Massillon, OH	10,053	4.5%	4.6%	15.0%	23.9%	1.5%	2.5%	5.4%	3.5%	6.8%	3.9%	4.9%	14.9%	0.5%
Cape Coral-Fort Myers, FL	13,317	0.2%	1.2%	12.2%	25.7%	8.8%	3.2%	7.9%	3.5%	5.0%	5.6%	5.3%	5.9%	3.1%
Cape Girardeau, MO-IL	3,105	7.3%	0.0%	31.2%	16.6%	5.2%	0.0%	3.1%	11.5%	1.5%	2.3%	8.1%	10.5%	1.3%
Carbondale-Marion, IL	3,362	2.5%	1.8%	9.0%	12.4%	1.2%	1.3%	7.2%	19.7%	4.1%	0.0%	6.5%	9.4%	9.9%
Carson City, NV	885	0.0%	0.0%	0.0%	0.0%	0.0%	0.0%	0.0%	0.0%	0.0%	36.8%	27.7%	35.5%	0.0%
Casper, WY	2,330	5.7%	0.0%	8.4%	38.2%	0.0%	5.4%	0.0%	0.0%	0.0%	7.6%	0.0%	17.8%	8.8%
Cedar Rapids, IA	9,024	21.6%	4.2%	4.8%	22.6%	0.0%	6.5%	5.9%	6.4%	8.9%	1.4%	3.9%	3.0%	0.0%
Chambersburg-Waynesboro, PA	4,500	8.6%	3.1%	20.1%	9.7%	3.6%	14.2%	0.0%	0.9%	0.2%	6.4%	2.3%	24.4%	4.4%
Champaign-Urbana, IL	18,233	11.5%	5.2%	3.9%	11.8%	11.1%	1.7%	6.9%	13.9%	2.6%	8.5%	2.2%	6.9%	3.6%
Charleston-North Charleston, SC	35,995	5.8%	2.3%	8.7%	15.3%	5.2%	8.1%	4.9%	13.5%	4.2%	5.8%	9.0%	5.1%	4.9%
Charleston, WV	6,007	13.0%	9.2%	11.7%	19.9%	1.3%	5.2%	7.5%	1.8%	5.6%	1.6%	1.1%	10.2%	0.0%
Charlotte-Concord-Gastonia, NC-SC	93,418	5.9%	2.5%	6.8%	27.0%	1.2%	7.1%	5.6%	5.1%	3.0%	3.7%	6.6%	9.2%	5.1%
Charlottesville, VA	12,612	7.8%	2.0%	9.2%	6.1%	4.2%	7.7%	3.3%	18.5%	12.3%	12.8%	5.0%	2.1%	3.5%
Chattanooga, TN-GA	14,740	5.2%	2.7%	10.9%	20.2%	3.4%	3.8%	6.4%	6.2%	2.5%	8.1%	3.7%	13.2%	3.5%
Cheyenne, WY	4,118	5.1%	5.2%	10.6%	11.1%	0.0%	3.3%	0.0%	19.1%	8.2%	0.0%	2.4%	7.1%	0.0%
Chicago-Naperville-Elgin, IL-IN-WI	529,636	6.6%	4.1%	8.2%	21.3%	2.6%	9.2%	6.0%	5.9%	3.7%	4.2%	6.3%	8.3%	6.4%
Chico, CA	7,132	3.7%	2.6%	6.4%	19.6%	1.0%	5.4%	0.2%	7.0%	5.4%	10.9%	7.3%	9.8%	4.7%
Cincinnati, OH-KY-IN	90,146	8.1%	3.8%	10.2%	16.7%	2.0%	5.9%	6.5%	8.3%	3.9%	4.8%	5.3%	10.2%	5.3%
Clarksburg, WV micro	2,214	5.0%	8.8%	19.2%	20.2%	0.0%	0.0%	0.0%	22.4%	0.0%	0.0%	1.8%	14.5%	0.0%

Table F-4: Metropolitan/Micropolitan Statistical Areas—Educational Field of Study—*Continued*

	Total Millennial Population	Engineering	Computers and Math	Science and Engineering Related	Business	Physical Science	Social Science	Communications	Biological Sciences	Literature	Liberal Arts	Psychology	Education	Visual and Performing Arts
					Percent of the Population 18 to 31 by Field of Study									
Clarksville, TN-KY	10,995	2.0%	0.0%	4.1%	31.0%	0.1%	7.2%	6.8%	0.4%	2.5%	8.9%	4.7%	17.8%	7.1%
Cleveland-Elyria, OH	80,523	9.5%	3.4%	11.3%	21.4%	1.7%	7.2%	7.4%	6.0%	3.7%	3.2%	4.3%	6.2%	5.3%
Cleveland, TN	1,758	4.0%	0.0%	54.6%	0.0%	0.0%	0.0%	6.0%	5.6%	0.0%	0.0%	8.6%	13.5%	0.0%
Coeur d'Alene, ID	4,752	11.9%	0.0%	0.0%	20.0%	0.0%	9.4%	1.1%	9.8%	0.0%	6.6%	8.0%	25.8%	2.2%
College Station-Bryan, TX	18,194	11.2%	1.3%	7.7%	11.8%	4.4%	9.7%	2.0%	26.0%	3.1%	2.7%	5.8%	3.7%	0.3%
Colorado Springs, CO	24,751	6.5%	6.4%	7.5%	13.9%	1.6%	12.1%	4.8%	3.5%	5.1%	5.3%	11.7%	3.3%	5.6%
Columbia, MO	14,754	5.5%	6.1%	9.5%	8.9%	2.2%	5.6%	10.3%	18.3%	2.4%	5.2%	3.5%	8.1%	1.5%
Columbia, SC	33,328	2.8%	2.2%	9.1%	16.6%	2.9%	9.3%	6.4%	8.4%	2.7%	5.6%	5.3%	10.2%	4.6%
Columbus, GA-AL	8,869	5.0%	1.7%	6.7%	20.6%	0.0%	10.4%	8.9%	5.7%	3.6%	4.0%	8.9%	6.5%	1.2%
Columbus, IN	3,070	30.1%	0.0%	5.0%	5.3%	9.8%	1.9%	1.9%	19.4%	0.0%	1.0%	0.0%	14.9%	5.0%
Columbus, OH	97,168	5.3%	2.6%	10.0%	19.1%	2.4%	6.4%	7.2%	8.8%	3.8%	4.0%	8.5%	7.6%	5.2%
Concord, NH micro	4,678	1.5%	0.0%	21.0%	13.3%	0.0%	15.7%	1.5%	4.1%	8.0%	12.5%	1.4%	4.6%	8.3%
Cookeville, TN micro	2,275	4.0%	0.0%	4.9%	10.1%	0.0%	3.6%	0.0%	13.6%	4.6%	5.7%	4.8%	19.6%	4.4%
Corpus Christi, TX	10,379	14.9%	2.2%	7.8%	18.5%	8.3%	3.1%	3.2%	8.2%	0.0%	6.1%	9.4%	6.5%	0.8%
Corvallis, OR	4,797	4.3%	2.1%	2.4%	11.1%	8.1%	4.5%	0.0%	31.7%	6.9%	3.5%	4.0%	3.8%	4.9%
Crestview-Fort Walton Beach-Destin, FL	8,116	5.5%	7.8%	9.0%	15.7%	5.4%	7.5%	9.0%	9.9%	2.5%	6.3%	7.4%	5.0%	3.6%
Cumberland, MD-WV	2,342	0.0%	3.2%	10.7%	24.4%	0.0%	18.1%	12.0%	3.0%	5.0%	3.7%	0.0%	12.9%	3.0%
Dallas-Fort Worth-Arlington, TX	274,252	7.3%	4.0%	8.5%	25.5%	1.5%	5.1%	6.2%	7.8%	2.9%	4.3%	4.1%	7.5%	4.4%
Dalton, GA	1,747	0.0%	0.0%	42.4%	2.3%	0.0%	0.0%	0.0%	17.5%	2.7%	2.9%	4.0%	26.8%	1.3%
Danville, IL	793	0.0%	0.0%	11.1%	4.5%	0.0%	1.1%	13.1%	9.0%	0.0%	1.0%	17.4%	31.7%	0.0%
Danville, VA micro	1,699	7.1%	0.0%	28.8%	10.1%	5.6%	5.7%	10.2%	17.2%	0.0%	5.7%	0.0%	2.5%	0.0%
Daphne-Fairhope-Foley, AL	6,171	0.0%	14.3%	10.1%	14.4%	4.0%	6.7%	4.2%	5.1%	6.0%	5.7%	1.8%	9.6%	2.5%
Davenport-Moline-Rock Island, IA-IL	14,818	12.5%	5.0%	7.0%	16.7%	5.2%	7.6%	1.6%	11.7%	2.0%	1.0%	4.2%	7.8%	7.9%
Dayton, OH	27,820	14.9%	3.1%	9.5%	18.9%	1.7%	6.4%	4.5%	5.6%	6.3%	3.9%	2.4%	12.5%	3.3%
Decatur, AL	2,895	11.2%	2.6%	6.6%	6.9%	0.0%	8.4%	6.8%	0.0%	2.7%	2.0%	0.0%	35.5%	3.7%
Decatur, IL	2,289	13.4%	0.0%	2.4%	31.8%	0.0%	8.4%	1.9%	8.1%	0.0%	6.1%	0.0%	2.7%	4.9%
Deltona-Daytona Beach-Ormond Beach, FL	9,638	9.4%	2.8%	7.4%	12.5%	5.7%	7.4%	3.7%	6.2%	0.6%	5.9%	3.4%	14.2%	8.0%
Denver-Aurora-Lakewood, CO	147,212	7.1%	2.8%	6.5%	21.9%	1.5%	8.1%	7.0%	7.3%	4.9%	4.6%	5.2%	4.4%	6.3%
Des Moines-West Des Moines, IA	29,665	6.5%	2.5%	6.0%	30.2%	0.0%	7.4%	8.7%	6.2%	3.2%	4.5%	3.6%	9.9%	2.4%
Detroit-Warren-Dearborn, MI	146,891	9.9%	2.6%	9.2%	21.1%	3.1%	5.8%	7.3%	6.6%	4.0%	3.8%	6.1%	8.2%	3.5%
Dothan, AL	2,963	5.4%	2.7%	10.4%	23.3%	2.3%	0.6%	1.8%	8.5%	0.6%	2.6%	5.5%	19.0%	1.9%
Dover, DE	6,786	1.9%	2.1%	9.6%	18.3%	6.8%	5.3%	0.0%	8.9%	0.4%	5.0%	12.6%	7.9%	9.6%
Dubuque, IA	2,242	0.0%	17.8%	4.9%	32.2%	0.0%	0.0%	13.2%	3.4%	6.0%	0.0%	7.8%	5.8%	5.3%
Duluth, MN-WI	10,938	3.9%	3.2%	13.3%	13.6%	4.9%	9.4%	7.6%	9.5%	1.4%	1.5%	6.0%	13.8%	1.1%
Dunn, NC micro	4,463	12.3%	2.1%	14.0%	7.1%	5.5%	3.4%	0.8%	10.4%	2.4%	5.6%	18.5%	12.5%	0.0%
Durham-Chapel Hill, NC	37,648	6.7%	3.0%	4.0%	6.8%	7.5%	13.0%	5.4%	15.9%	4.5%	6.7%	7.9%	2.6%	5.1%
East Stroudsburg, PA	4,492	0.0%	0.0%	20.6%	15.9%	0.0%	0.0%	3.2%	2.6%	11.9%	0.0%	6.4%	19.6%	8.5%
Eau Claire, WI	5,673	0.6%	11.1%	6.6%	30.9%	2.7%	1.9%	2.0%	16.0%	2.3%	0.9%	1.9%	10.8%	3.5%
El Centro, CA	2,807	6.2%	6.4%	5.8%	4.7%	0.0%	10.2%	3.2%	0.0%	0.0%	14.1%	8.2%	6.2%	0.0%
El Paso, TX	22,990	6.3%	1.5%	10.4%	23.9%	1.9%	3.4%	1.3%	12.6%	3.0%	6.6%	5.5%	12.3%	3.4%
Elizabethtown-Fort Knox, KY	3,648	0.2%	0.0%	6.2%	33.3%	0.0%	8.4%	0.0%	0.0%	0.0%	0.0%	7.8%	24.9%	2.4%
Elkhart-Goshen, IN	3,557	5.4%	0.0%	14.8%	11.9%	0.0%	1.2%	0.0%	5.3%	0.0%	21.6%	3.2%	20.5%	7.8%
Elmira, NY	3,058	8.2%	2.1%	1.4%	20.1%	0.0%	1.3%	11.9%	6.5%	0.0%	5.4%	14.6%	22.6%	0.0%
Erie, PA	12,569	2.8%	3.1%	12.0%	18.5%	0.0%	2.6%	3.8%	13.7%	2.5%	1.1%	10.4%	14.1%	3.6%
Eugene, OR	9,564	1.7%	0.6%	1.2%	12.0%	1.3%	21.1%	6.7%	13.0%	3.9%	6.7%	10.6%	4.3%	7.2%
Eureka-Arcata-Fortuna, CA micro	5,007	0.0%	2.9%	1.3%	13.7%	0.0%	13.5%	0.3%	9.1%	3.8%	23.6%	11.4%	5.7%	13.8%
Evansville, IN-KY	7,372	10.8%	3.6%	8.8%	29.1%	1.0%	1.5%	7.2%	6.3%	0.7%	1.1%	2.0%	16.4%	1.5%
Fairbanks, AK	6,302	11.5%	0.0%	7.8%	1.7%	8.7%	14.5%	0.0%	4.4%	14.9%	4.6%	2.0%	10.1%	0.3%
Fargo, ND-MN	16,671	8.5%	0.1%	16.2%	15.1%	0.7%	3.8%	6.5%	9.3%	5.8%	1.0%	7.0%	15.3%	0.5%
Farmington, NM	1,030	7.2%	0.0%	0.0%	5.4%	0.0%	0.0%	18.9%	0.0%	0.0%	7.3%	16.4%	35.9%	2.2%
Fayetteville-Springdale-Rogers, AR-MO	21,370	7.0%	7.0%	7.3%	24.7%	1.1%	3.2%	5.7%	8.7%	2.8%	3.5%	5.1%	12.0%	3.2%
Fayetteville, NC	13,367	4.8%	0.8%	10.4%	20.0%	9.4%	5.5%	2.8%	2.3%	1.1%	6.5%	3.8%	9.7%	5.8%
Flagstaff, AZ	7,365	14.6%	0.0%	13.0%	4.9%	2.4%	12.1%	4.2%	9.2%	0.0%	2.6%	6.7%	4.6%	10.5%
Flint, MI	8,135	5.6%	1.2%	6.0%	17.0%	0.0%	2.3%	7.2%	6.9%	9.6%	4.3%	6.5%	17.0%	1.5%
Florence-Muscle Shoals, AL	2,687	0.0%	0.0%	0.0%	29.7%	2.9%	12.4%	5.1%	0.0%	18.3%	4.5%	0.0%	4.3%	12.4%
Florence, SC	5,561	6.0%	1.2%	14.5%	32.1%	2.2%	8.1%	0.0%	5.4%	0.7%	9.7%	3.6%	13.8%	2.0%
Fond du Lac, WI	1,647	8.9%	0.0%	4.4%	36.2%	8.8%	0.0%	0.0%	1.4%	0.0%	10.7%	0.0%	0.0%	7.4%
Fort Collins, CO	17,665	5.3%	1.1%	6.5%	12.8%	1.8%	11.1%	3.9%	18.2%	3.7%	6.4%	8.9%	5.8%	4.0%
Fort Smith, AR-OK	5,512	11.4%	6.5%	6.4%	12.7%	5.2%	0.8%	1.8%	8.6%	0.0%	0.5%	12.1%	17.2%	10.0%
Fort Wayne, IN	11,991	4.6%	2.6%	9.7%	22.2%	1.9%	11.3%	3.9%	5.6%	0.8%	4.4%	3.1%	10.8%	7.1%
Fresno, CA	23,824	2.4%	2.0%	6.7%	12.0%	4.1%	8.6%	6.2%	11.1%	2.2%	10.4%	5.3%	8.1%	3.4%
Gadsden, AL	786	0.0%	0.0%	3.2%	0.0%	0.0%	0.0%	10.4%	0.0%	0.0%	0.0%	23.9%	24.0%	7.4%
Gainesville, FL	25,094	9.7%	1.1%	8.7%	9.1%	6.8%	7.0%	4.8%	21.0%	3.3%	4.7%	3.5%	3.2%	5.4%
Gainesville, GA	3,283	1.5%	3.4%	14.3%	13.4%	15.4%	3.8%	0.0%	6.7%	2.5%	0.0%	0.0%	29.3%	8.3%
Gettysburg, PA	2,859	5.5%	1.8%	12.0%	8.6%	4.4%	2.9%	0.0%	8.2%	3.1%	7.6%	2.9%	26.7%	3.6%
Glens Falls, NY	2,812	15.8%	2.2%	10.4%	10.1%	7.4%	7.7%	0.0%	10.7%	0.0%	2.0%	9.5%	17.6%	2.2%
Goldsboro, NC	2,879	4.3%	6.5%	6.2%	26.5%	5.2%	4.5%	0.0%	24.6%	0.0%	0.0%	0.0%	2.6%	0.0%
Grand Forks, ND-MN	4,465	6.0%	0.0%	26.5%	1.4%	0.4%	0.0%	1.8%	10.2%	3.0%	1.4%	18.0%	3.7%	1.1%
Grand Island, NE	2,705	2.4%	0.0%	5.1%	27.8%	0.0%	0.0%	10.4%	6.6%	0.0%	0.0%	7.7%	30.7%	0.0%
Grand Junction, CO	2,625	0.0%	0.0%	15.6%	20.4%	0.0%	0.0%	0.0%	25.0%	0.0%	0.0%	10.2%	21.6%	7.2%
Grand Rapids-Wyoming, MI	47,308	7.2%	3.4%	14.8%	17.1%	1.8%	3.6%	6.7%	6.3%	4.0%	6.1%	5.5%	8.6%	3.5%
Grants Pass, OR	736	0.0%	0.0%	11.0%	21.5%	0.0%	0.0%	0.0%	49.0%	0.0%	18.5%	0.0%	0.0%	0.0%
Great Falls, MT	3,344	4.4%	0.0%	8.1%	14.7%	0.0%	14.4%	0.0%	6.6%	0.0%	13.3%	0.0%	21.5%	5.9%
Greeley, CO	9,507	3.0%	3.9%	9.2%	16.5%	0.7%	5.4%	6.9%	9.4%	2.0%	7.8%	11.1%	10.7%	2.6%
Green Bay, WI	11,154	5.6%	4.2%	8.3%	13.7%	0.9%	2.2%	8.3%	8.6%	2.4%	3.1%	16.7%	5.4%	4.2%

Table F-4: Metropolitan/Micropolitan Statistical Areas—Educational Field of Study—*Continued*

	Total Millennial Population	Engineering	Computers and Math	Science and Engineering Related	Business	Physical Science	Social Science	Communications	Biological Sciences	Literature	Liberal Arts	Psychology	Education	Visual and Performing Arts
						Percent of the Population 18 to 31 by Field of Study								
Greensboro-High Point, NC	24,152	4.0%	3.4%	4.6%	20.7%	3.8%	3.1%	3.8%	6.0%	5.2%	4.8%	11.3%	11.6%	5.7%
Greenville-Anderson-Mauldin, SC	28,367	6.5%	1.8%	10.8%	19.3%	3.0%	5.8%	5.2%	6.0%	5.4%	4.9%	4.3%	9.5%	9.4%
Greenville, NC	10,775	5.6%	2.5%	18.6%	6.4%	2.3%	3.8%	1.3%	16.3%	1.0%	0.0%	8.4%	13.3%	0.0%
Greenwood, SC micro	2,582	3.8%	4.2%	25.9%	5.0%	7.4%	5.5%	0.0%	1.5%	0.0%	7.8%	0.0%	21.8%	0.0%
Gulfport-Biloxi-Pascagoula, MS	7,413	2.7%	2.4%	10.4%	20.2%	7.5%	3.0%	3.5%	3.8%	2.8%	12.8%	2.3%	16.7%	4.9%
Hagerstown-Martinsburg, MD-WV	6,971	5.0%	1.9%	10.9%	21.2%	0.9%	7.5%	4.1%	5.2%	0.5%	2.5%	6.3%	17.9%	5.3%
Hammond, LA	2,296	0.0%	0.0%	0.0%	10.7%	0.0%	0.0%	6.9%	5.6%	13.9%	7.8%	30.2%	16.7%	5.1%
Hanford-Corcoran, CA	2,114	0.0%	3.5%	7.9%	16.0%	0.6%	30.7%	4.0%	1.9%	0.0%	11.8%	3.0%	0.0%	0.0%
Harrisburg-Carlisle, PA	22,235	8.2%	3.9%	11.1%	16.2%	1.9%	8.7%	6.6%	6.5%	2.2%	4.0%	4.5%	14.0%	2.9%
Harrisonburg, VA	5,353	1.6%	4.1%	10.4%	28.7%	0.0%	1.5%	10.7%	7.8%	9.1%	3.1%	5.3%	0.9%
Hartford-West Hartford-East Hartford, CT	61,586	11.0%	4.0%	7.5%	17.6%	2.0%	7.1%	4.9%	7.5%	3.1%	4.0%	6.2%	6.5%	5.6%
Hattiesburg, MS	5,034	5.9%	2.7%	16.7%	18.6%	18.2%	2.6%	0.0%	8.2%	1.3%	3.2%	0.7%	16.2%	3.5%
Hickory-Lenoir-Morganton, NC	5,691	0.9%	1.8%	30.9%	10.1%	0.0%	2.7%	1.3%	4.4%	0.2%	4.4%	9.5%	16.5%	5.6%
Hilo, HI micro	5,483	0.0%	0.0%	16.9%	19.1%	1.1%	25.8%	12.3%	9.5%	0.0%	0.0%	5.0%	5.0%	2.7%
Hilton Head Island-Bluffton-Beaufort, SC	5,270	0.0%	4.2%	7.6%	34.4%	0.0%	9.2%	4.0%	4.8%	0.0%	3.7%	0.0%	9.3%	14.3%
Hinesville, GA	2,137	0.0%	20.1%	2.9%	6.5%	0.0%	16.9%	0.0%	0.0%	6.0%	14.0%	5.8%	3.6%	10.6%
Holland, MI micro	1,303	1.5%	2.7%	9.3%	9.4%	0.0%	23.0%	2.8%	2.8%	5.4%	28.2%	4.8%	10.1%	0.0%
Homosassa Springs, FL	381	26.8%	0.0%	0.0%	0.0%	0.0%	0.0%	0.0%	16.5%	0.0%	0.0%	0.0%	25.5%	0.0%
Hot Springs, AR	843	0.0%	0.0%	0.0%	35.8%	2.3%	0.0%	0.0%	27.8%	0.0%	0.0%	0.0%	5.6%	0.0%
Houma-Thibodaux, LA	4,143	20.6%	1.3%	35.1%	11.2%	0.0%	0.0%	4.9%	0.0%	6.9%	8.7%	5.1%	2.8%	0.0%
Houston-The Woodlands-Sugar Land, TX	249,310	11.4%	3.2%	8.1%	22.6%	3.7%	6.8%	4.5%	6.4%	2.6%	3.5%	3.8%	8.1%	3.4%
Huntington-Ashland, WV-KY-OH	8,883	6.7%	2.9%	11.1%	10.1%	5.2%	4.0%	1.8%	13.9%	2.2%	9.2%	1.8%	19.9%	4.3%
Huntsville, AL	19,500	17.7%	0.6%	4.6%	20.3%	7.1%	6.4%	0.9%	10.6%	4.6%	3.9%	3.6%	15.2%	1.5%
Idaho Falls, ID	4,312	5.2%	8.1%	6.1%	14.7%	2.0%	2.7%	1.3%	10.6%	1.4%	1.3%	3.9%	25.5%	1.5%
Indianapolis-Carmel-Anderson, IN	85,579	4.8%	5.0%	14.3%	18.1%	3.0%	4.5%	6.3%	9.6%	3.6%	5.5%	4.4%	9.6%	2.6%
Iowa City, IA	15,899	1.1%	5.0%	7.3%	12.4%	1.3%	3.5%	8.4%	19.1%	6.8%	5.8%	5.7%	7.3%	1.8%
Ithaca, NY	9,982	17.2%	3.9%	4.8%	5.6%	7.2%	9.3%	5.6%	9.2%	8.9%	4.2%	0.0%	2.0%	6.8%
Jackson, MI	3,270	5.5%	0.0%	18.2%	22.8%	3.1%	2.8%	0.0%	2.4%	1.1%	0.0%	17.3%	6.3%	5.7%
Jackson, MS	20,919	4.0%	1.0%	16.8%	21.9%	1.5%	4.1%	4.0%	9.5%	3.8%	2.7%	3.6%	11.8%	5.0%
Jackson, TN	2,728	1.3%	4.9%	23.4%	22.0%	1.7%	9.8%	2.5%	1.2%	0.0%	1.7%	2.4%	23.8%	0.0%
Jacksonville, FL	47,338	7.1%	3.1%	10.9%	23.6%	0.8%	6.4%	6.6%	5.3%	3.1%	5.5%	7.1%	10.1%	0.6%
Jacksonville, NC	3,498	1.5%	0.0%	22.5%	4.0%	0.0%	0.7%	0.0%	15.4%	1.0%	12.0%	1.3%	15.5%	3.6%
Jamestown-Dunkirk-Fredonia, NY micro	3,492	5.0%	5.4%	7.4%	5.0%	1.2%	11.5%	3.0%	11.8%	11.6%	2.8%	3.8%	11.6%	1.8%
Janesville-Beloit, WI	3,275	0.0%	0.0%	26.2%	8.8%	0.7%	6.1%	3.2%	5.4%	0.0%	12.4%	0.0%	20.3%	13.4%
Jefferson City, MO	2,209	2.7%	9.9%	2.3%	25.8%	6.6%	0.7%	14.7%	6.2%	0.0%	5.6%	5.6%	6.2%	0.0%
Johnson City, TN	8,656	2.3%	1.2%	8.9%	22.4%	2.3%	11.2%	0.0%	18.2%	2.5%	5.9%	7.6%	10.2%	0.0%
Johnstown, PA	3,912	0.0%	2.0%	23.7%	14.7%	1.9%	10.0%	7.2%	3.5%	3.6%	14.8%	5.1%	9.6%	0.9%
Jonesboro, AR	3,167	0.0%	8.3%	9.2%	7.8%	2.9%	3.1%	17.6%	5.8%	0.0%	6.8%	1.9%	19.5%	0.0%
Joplin, MO	6,036	3.2%	0.0%	8.8%	23.0%	0.0%	0.9%	6.8%	6.5%	0.2%	6.8%	0.0%	17.6%	3.8%
Kahului-Wailuku-Lahaina, HI	3,747	7.6%	0.0%	17.2%	16.0%	24.4%	2.1%	3.1%	6.0%	1.8%	1.8%	1.9%	4.6%	10.3%
Kalamazoo-Portage, MI	13,630	10.4%	2.0%	12.3%	22.6%	3.3%	5.6%	10.2%	2.7%	7.1%	0.4%	3.7%	6.9%	3.5%
Kalispell, MT micro	2,009	0.0%	4.1%	23.6%	13.6%	9.0%	3.6%	10.5%	0.0%	2.8%	9.2%	0.0%	10.3%	0.0%
Kankakee, IL	1,696	8.6%	0.0%	0.0%	17.7%	0.0%	3.2%	5.6%	1.5%	9.8%	0.0%	7.7%	7.8%	3.7%
Kansas City, MO-KS	93,156	6.9%	3.2%	8.7%	21.2%	2.4%	3.3%	6.3%	10.3%	3.3%	5.7%	4.6%	10.4%	4.8%
Kennewick-Richland, WA	6,081	5.9%	0.7%	5.1%	24.1%	3.7%	4.5%	10.4%	9.2%	3.0%	2.2%	3.6%	9.6%	4.6%
Killeen-Temple, TX	12,238	4.1%	0.0%	8.5%	13.2%	4.3%	18.0%	6.8%	8.8%	3.8%	5.0%	3.7%	4.9%	3.2%
Kingsport-Bristol-Bristol, TN-VA	7,625	3.5%	2.9%	24.1%	12.9%	1.5%	6.6%	5.4%	8.9%	2.4%	5.2%	1.9%	14.2%	0.8%
Kingston, NY	4,748	2.7%	0.0%	15.2%	18.3%	0.0%	4.7%	5.2%	1.9%	2.0%	3.9%	0.0%	17.2%	22.6%
Knoxville, TN	30,784	6.8%	2.7%	9.3%	20.8%	2.2%	8.5%	4.5%	9.4%	5.0%	6.3%	2.5%	7.7%	2.8%
Kokomo, IN	1,206	0.0%	6.3%	0.0%	11.9%	0.0%	8.6%	2.2%	0.0%	1.5%	21.6%	28.8%	11.4%	7.6%
La Crosse-Onalaska, WI-MN	4,985	14.8%	3.0%	13.5%	11.7%	5.5%	10.2%	4.0%	6.6%	5.7%	0.0%	0.0%	19.5%	1.7%
Lafayette-West Lafayette, IN	11,848	11.0%	3.6%	22.4%	9.4%	11.4%	2.1%	6.5%	9.6%	6.6%	1.2%	1.0%	4.2%	2.3%
Lafayette, LA	17,288	11.8%	9.9%	4.3%	12.0%	3.9%	1.8%	4.2%	3.8%	1.4%	14.7%	7.3%	8.5%	8.2%
Lake Charles, LA	3,495	6.4%	0.0%	24.4%	4.6%	0.0%	6.3%	2.0%	12.2%	0.0%	6.7%	4.1%	13.8%	4.1%
Lake Havasu City-Kingman, AZ	2,599	0.0%	0.0%	9.8%	21.5%	0.0%	2.3%	3.0%	10.4%	0.0%	8.1%	12.8%	12.0%	4.0%
Lakeland-Winter Haven, FL	10,637	2.1%	3.4%	6.3%	17.7%	2.7%	11.0%	6.0%	7.2%	2.1%	9.0%	11.2%	13.0%	3.7%
Lancaster, PA	18,252	8.7%	1.1%	15.4%	23.5%	3.2%	1.0%	3.2%	2.4%	4.9%	5.4%	2.0%	16.1%	4.7%
Lansing-East Lansing, MI	26,916	6.1%	2.3%	8.3%	17.6%	2.4%	11.4%	2.7%	11.7%	5.0%	3.4%	6.5%	5.4%	0.9%
Laredo, TX	5,188	6.1%	0.0%	13.3%	29.6%	1.5%	5.3%	0.0%	5.7%	1.5%	2.0%	7.6%	17.0%	0.0%
Las Cruces, NM	5,109	7.7%	0.0%	10.7%	5.0%	1.9%	7.4%	2.3%	9.3%	5.1%	0.0%	13.0%	11.5%	4.6%
Las Vegas-Henderson-Paradise, NV	49,658	2.4%	3.3%	9.3%	27.4%	2.8%	4.5%	4.4%	7.5%	3.0%	2.2%	9.1%	6.2%	3.9%
Lawrence, KS	14,328	10.2%	4.5%	16.3%	6.7%	2.0%	7.7%	10.3%	6.4%	8.9%	4.5%	5.3%	3.8%	12.5%
Lawton, OK	3,796	29.5%	0.0%	16.2%	3.6%	0.0%	11.2%	0.0%	6.1%	2.3%	5.1%	13.3%	2.5%	0.0%
Lebanon, PA	3,775	0.0%	0.0%	2.9%	8.7%	0.0%	0.0%	7.9%	9.2%	11.0%	6.0%	20.0%	19.2%	4.9%
Lewiston-Auburn, ME	1,764	0.0%	0.0%	0.0%	13.1%	0.0%	18.1%	0.0%	7.4%	3.5%	0.0%	0.0%	18.8%	0.0%
Lewiston, ID-WA	2,203	3.2%	0.0%	9.5%	8.5%	0.0%	9.8%	11.8%	14.6%	12.8%	7.4%	6.8%	5.1%	2.9%
Lexington-Fayette, KY	21,198	6.7%	1.5%	9.6%	17.8%	3.8%	10.7%	3.1%	5.4%	4.2%	2.5%	6.3%	6.9%	4.4%
Lima, OH	2,563	6.9%	0.0%	19.6%	8.3%	0.0%	2.6%	5.1%	0.0%	1.8%	8.2%	13.8%	21.0%	0.0%
Lincoln, NE	17,481	7.6%	1.2%	7.7%	21.3%	3.0%	6.9%	6.8%	9.8%	2.5%	1.5%	3.1%	9.1%	7.6%
Little Rock-North Little Rock-Conway, AR	26,188	1.5%	5.1%	15.5%	14.1%	3.5%	9.0%	4.3%	9.9%	5.0%	7.1%	2.8%	6.6%	4.8%
Logan, UT-ID	8,121	4.4%	0.7%	4.5%	13.8%	1.5%	5.8%	6.5%	6.8%	1.7%	5.0%	1.9%	17.1%	3.2%
Longview, TX	4,047	10.2%	0.0%	18.2%	6.2%	15.4%	9.6%	3.1%	2.0%	4.9%	0.0%	1.2%	6.4%	13.1%
Longview, WA	782	0.0%	0.0%	35.3%	5.1%	0.0%	0.0%	0.0%	17.4%	0.0%	14.3%	11.9%	0.0%	16.0%

Table F-4: Metropolitan/Micropolitan Statistical Areas—Educational Field of Study—*Continued*

	Total Millennial Population	Engineering	Computers and Math	Science and Engineering Related	Business	Physical Science	Social Science	Communications	Biological Sciences	Literature	Liberal Arts	Psychology	Education	Visual and Performing Arts
Los Angeles-Long Beach-Anaheim, CA.	607,608	6.4%	2.7%	6.0%	17.4%	2.4%	12.2%	8.3%	7.2%	5.3%	5.7%	6.1%	3.2%	9.4%
Louisville/Jefferson County, KY-IN........	46,595	7.0%	2.3%	10.5%	23.3%	3.0%	5.8%	8.5%	5.6%	2.1%	5.2%	6.6%	5.8%	3.8%
Lubbock, TX..................................	12,947	6.1%	0.0%	8.6%	22.2%	5.3%	7.1%	1.7%	11.0%	3.4%	4.0%	4.2%	10.1%	1.5%
Lumberton, NC micro	980	0.0%	8.0%	9.8%	3.0%	0.0%	6.9%	10.0%	20.1%	0.0%	0.0%	6.0%	25.4%	4.9%
Lynchburg, VA................................	8,264	2.8%	2.2%	5.5%	13.5%	2.3%	2.4%	4.5%	3.7%	7.4%	15.2%	8.4%	11.6%	5.9%
Macon, GA...................................	6,103	4.5%	4.4%	15.9%	18.4%	0.0%	11.0%	1.9%	11.9%	1.0%	3.6%	0.9%	9.7%	8.7%
Madera, CA	1,580	5.3%	0.0%	12.7%	14.4%	0.0%	6.5%	0.0%	0.0%	13.0%	26.0%	0.0%	4.2%	0.0%
Madison, WI.................................	50,860	9.0%	5.9%	8.0%	9.1%	5.9%	10.0%	7.8%	10.9%	5.2%	2.3%	3.6%	4.9%	7.7%
Manchester-Nashua, NH	16,895	9.5%	3.9%	5.5%	35.3%	0.4%	5.4%	3.3%	3.7%	1.8%	4.3%	5.7%	4.4%	8.4%
Manhattan, KS	5,695	3.5%	0.0%	13.9%	11.6%	0.0%	26.9%	1.3%	21.1%	4.7%	3.6%	0.6%	0.9%	0.0%
Mankato-North Mankato, MN...............	4,580	2.7%	0.0%	10.0%	20.5%	0.0%	30.5%	1.0%	2.2%	7.6%	1.1%	0.6%	18.5%	4.2%
Mansfield, OH	2,100	0.0%	0.0%	4.3%	35.1%	0.0%	14.6%	0.0%	0.0%	17.8%	0.0%	11.8%	16.4%	0.0%
McAllen-Edinburg-Mission, TX	16,204	3.3%	3.3%	9.0%	17.7%	2.9%	5.7%	1.7%	5.8%	2.6%	1.7%	10.8%	22.2%	0.9%
Medford, OR	3,641	3.4%	7.6%	2.0%	9.1%	13.4%	12.4%	5.9%	12.3%	8.7%	5.2%	11.5%	1.7%	0.0%
Memphis, TN-MS-AR........................	43,619	4.3%	3.5%	6.9%	17.5%	2.9%	7.7%	7.2%	8.9%	4.2%	5.3%	6.0%	12.7%	2.8%
Merced, CA	4,226	1.2%	2.8%	8.6%	23.2%	2.5%	5.3%	6.8%	9.0%	1.3%	11.5%	10.7%	2.2%	0.0%
Meridian, MS micro	2,183	3.1%	0.0%	21.8%	11.1%	3.4%	0.0%	0.0%	27.9%	0.0%	2.2%	10.4%	2.9%	2.4%
Miami-Fort Lauderdale-West Palm Beach, FL..................................	196,094	5.4%	3.4%	8.3%	25.4%	2.3%	7.7%	6.1%	7.1%	3.2%	2.7%	6.9%	6.9%	4.9%
Michigan City-La Porte, IN..................	1,375	2.1%	7.3%	36.4%	27.1%	0.0%	3.5%	3.1%	3.2%	0.0%	0.8%	11.7%	0.9%	0.0%
Midland, MI.................................	3,346	26.0%	0.0%	14.9%	14.8%	0.8%	14.5%	0.0%	10.7%	0.0%	0.0%	0.0%	4.3%	4.3%
Midland, TX.................................	7,447	7.5%	0.0%	1.3%	20.7%	2.9%	9.4%	9.5%	4.7%	7.6%	10.9%	0.0%	7.1%	0.0%
Milwaukee-Waukesha-West Allis, WI ...	75,340	7.2%	2.9%	8.3%	18.3%	3.0%	11.4%	7.6%	5.1%	2.5%	3.8%	4.9%	7.9%	7.7%
Minneapolis-St. Paul-Bloomington, MN-WI...................................	183,090	6.2%	2.7%	8.2%	20.7%	1.5%	10.4%	5.7%	8.5%	3.6%	3.3%	5.3%	7.9%	6.5%
Missoula, MT	6,578	5.8%	0.0%	1.2%	2.2%	0.0%	17.3%	8.7%	22.0%	4.7%	13.0%	11.9%	11.2%	0.0%
Mobile, AL..................................	12,843	9.3%	1.1%	24.0%	24.9%	3.3%	6.5%	2.5%	3.4%	4.2%	6.0%	7.5%	3.6%	0.0%
Modesto, CA	9,289	0.0%	0.6%	5.3%	12.5%	1.7%	11.0%	5.9%	12.0%	8.7%	13.1%	9.9%	3.6%	2.3%
Monroe, LA.................................	4,364	0.0%	3.1%	19.9%	32.0%	0.6%	1.9%	3.6%	4.4%	2.2%	6.3%	3.8%	11.5%	0.0%
Monroe, MI.................................	4,035	2.4%	0.0%	5.4%	43.8%	0.0%	1.6%	5.4%	2.7%	0.0%	0.0%	0.0%	16.7%	3.4%
Montgomery, AL............................	12,135	2.9%	4.9%	12.9%	17.0%	0.5%	12.4%	3.8%	4.9%	4.0%	0.8%	5.2%	14.3%	4.3%
Morgantown, WV............................	9,292	16.4%	1.1%	8.9%	10.0%	5.1%	4.3%	10.5%	10.6%	8.9%	1.6%	4.8%	9.7%	3.0%
Morristown, TN.............................	2,674	2.4%	0.0%	24.0%	25.2%	0.0%	17.7%	2.4%	0.0%	3.3%	3.6%	1.5%	11.2%	8.8%
Mount Vernon-Anacortes, WA	803	4.9%	10.6%	8.5%	9.3%	0.0%	6.7%	0.0%	2.4%	0.0%	4.7%	22.0%	2.5%	19.6%
Muncie, IN.................................	3,874	1.5%	7.7%	9.8%	17.1%	3.8%	0.0%	0.0%	6.8%	0.0%	18.0%	10.2%	5.3%	2.1%
Muskegon, MI...............................	2,644	8.8%	3.3%	28.0%	23.9%	0.0%	0.0%	2.0%	1.2%	5.4%	0.0%	1.1%	21.9%	1.5%
Myrtle Beach-Conway-North Myrtle Beach, SC-NC.............................	8,729	0.0%	0.0%	3.7%	29.4%	1.0%	12.8%	4.8%	3.5%	6.1%	4.2%	10.7%	9.9%	8.1%
Napa, CA...................................	2,512	7.2%	0.0%	10.2%	21.3%	1.6%	9.0%	9.4%	7.6%	3.4%	2.3%	7.1%	9.6%	1.8%
Naples-Immokalee-Marco Island, FL.....	6,267	0.5%	0.0%	6.5%	36.0%	0.0%	6.9%	2.4%	3.2%	2.8%	4.4%	6.4%	12.9%	2.0%
Nashville-Davidson—Murfreesboro–Franklin, TN...............................	87,885	4.1%	4.1%	10.2%	21.9%	3.6%	5.1%	7.8%	7.2%	3.3%	4.1%	6.9%	7.3%	6.8%
New Bern, NC...............................	1,924	0.0%	0.0%	4.4%	15.7%	0.0%	0.0%	13.3%	2.0%	0.7%	5.2%	33.9%	19.9%	5.0%
New Castle, PA micro........................	1,604	7.5%	0.0%	19.6%	11.0%	1.1%	2.2%	0.0%	0.0%	0.0%	10.5%	1.8%	33.4%	0.0%
New Haven-Milford, CT......................	44,122	3.6%	2.9%	8.8%	14.7%	2.0%	8.8%	4.1%	10.0%	3.9%	4.4%	8.3%	8.2%	7.0%
New Orleans-Metairie, LA	49,599	5.9%	1.2%	9.0%	19.0%	4.9%	8.6%	6.8%	8.6%	4.1%	6.0%	4.4%	5.0%	7.9%
New Philadelphia-Dover, OH micro	2,190	2.6%	0.0%	8.0%	25.9%	2.2%	0.0%	2.7%	2.8%	5.8%	2.0%	12.8%	24.2%	5.2%
New York-Newark-Jersey City, NY-NJ-PA.................................	1,203,462	5.6%	3.7%	6.8%	21.9%	2.4%	10.4%	6.8%	4.9%	4.3%	4.5%	6.2%	6.3%	8.8%
Niles-Benton Harbor, MI....................	4,051	4.2%	0.0%	10.1%	7.8%	2.8%	6.8%	6.9%	9.5%	2.8%	27.5%	5.8%	15.9%	0.0%
North Port-Sarasota-Bradenton, FL.......	14,808	3.5%	3.7%	4.7%	18.9%	1.3%	8.4%	3.1%	14.0%	4.2%	1.3%	5.4%	13.1%	9.3%
Norwich-New London, CT...................	8,483	13.4%	4.4%	7.8%	13.1%	4.0%	11.2%	2.1%	11.6%	2.9%	7.1%	2.6%	7.8%	5.1%
Ocala, FL...................................	4,355	8.1%	0.0%	13.9%	12.8%	0.0%	0.0%	5.9%	16.9%	0.0%	2.0%	17.9%	17.6%	3.1%
Ocean City, NJ..............................	4,353	2.5%	4.5%	11.2%	18.2%	0.0%	0.0%	11.0%	12.8%	0.0%	6.5%	9.1%	9.2%	5.2%
Odessa, TX..................................	3,971	2.1%	3.8%	15.1%	17.8%	4.1%	0.0%	3.0%	6.7%	25.1%	0.0%	0.0%	1.6%	1.5%
Ogden-Clearfield, UT........................	18,294	9.6%	5.6%	14.2%	19.5%	1.2%	10.4%	8.6%	3.2%	2.1%	1.8%	1.6%	6.4%	4.6%
Ogdensburg-Massena, NY micro	2,737	8.4%	1.2%	7.1%	3.5%	0.0%	1.4%	10.2%	26.5%	1.5%	0.5%	5.3%	8.7%	12.6%
Oklahoma City, OK	52,295	4.4%	1.2%	5.9%	19.3%	3.4%	8.5%	6.9%	10.5%	5.3%	4.1%	8.0%	5.8%	8.2%
Olympia-Tumwater, WA.....................	10,786	1.4%	3.3%	3.5%	18.0%	3.6%	14.8%	8.7%	7.7%	7.3%	7.6%	1.7%	6.9%	0.3%
Omaha-Council Bluffs, NE-IA...............	45,201	3.9%	2.0%	10.6%	24.1%	1.5%	4.9%	4.5%	10.2%	4.5%	2.8%	6.0%	10.7%	4.5%
Orangeburg, SC micro	1,906	0.0%	0.0%	5.4%	41.1%	0.3%	21.0%	0.0%	0.0%	0.0%	0.0%	3.8%	11.4%	4.2%
Orlando-Kissimmee-Sanford, FL...........	91,920	7.1%	4.2%	7.8%	24.6%	0.9%	7.0%	6.4%	3.8%	2.1%	3.3%	6.9%	9.8%	5.0%
Oshkosh-Neenah, WI	7,318	13.2%	11.1%	4.4%	19.0%	0.0%	5.2%	4.0%	3.3%	10.2%	0.0%	10.3%	3.9%	13.4%
Ottawa-Peru, IL micro.......................	2,743	1.2%	0.0%	25.2%	22.4%	0.0%	1.0%	12.8%	6.6%	4.7%	2.3%	11.7%	7.0%	1.1%
Owensboro, KY	2,202	19.0%	3.5%	6.8%	32.0%	0.0%	0.0%	14.3%	0.0%	3.7%	0.0%	0.0%	15.6%	0.0%
Oxnard-Thousand Oaks-Ventura, CA.....	26,322	9.4%	1.4%	5.3%	16.4%	3.1%	9.0%	5.7%	6.7%	4.8%	6.1%	11.4%	5.3%	7.1%
Palm Bay-Melbourne-Titusville, FL........	14,627	14.9%	8.4%	8.3%	20.4%	2.7%	3.0%	2.7%	4.3%	2.7%	1.3%	13.5%	6.1%	1.3%
Panama City, FL.............................	3,027	0.0%	4.6%	12.9%	16.5%	12.9%	3.1%	4.5%	3.6%	12.5%	10.3%	3.1%	2.7%	8.6%
Parkersburg-Vienna, WV....................	2,055	4.7%	6.8%	1.8%	31.3%	2.9%	0.0%	0.0%	8.8%	0.0%	0.0%	15.2%	15.3%	0.0%
Pensacola-Ferry Pass-Brent, FL............	14,374	8.7%	1.8%	6.5%	22.6%	2.9%	6.0%	6.2%	9.7%	3.5%	5.7%	2.9%	5.5%	5.5%
Peoria, IL...................................	16,378	13.1%	2.1%	14.1%	18.7%	1.3%	3.3%	3.5%	5.2%	2.1%	4.0%	6.5%	11.4%	7.1%
Philadelphia-Camden-Wilmington, PA-NJ-DE-MD.............................	326,125	6.3%	3.6%	7.8%	20.3%	3.5%	7.3%	6.5%	8.8%	3.7%	4.5%	5.9%	8.3%	6.2%
Phoenix-Mesa-Scottsdale, AZ	152,273	7.7%	5.0%	8.6%	19.4%	1.4%	7.3%	5.5%	7.1%	2.4%	3.1%	7.6%	11.0%	4.0%
Pine Bluff, AR...............................	1,269	0.0%	20.4%	25.1%	13.0%	0.0%	0.0%	0.0%	3.5%	0.0%	9.9%	4.2%	21.0%	0.0%
Pittsburgh, PA..............................	124,607	8.3%	3.0%	8.5%	24.1%	2.9%	5.9%	6.0%	5.0%	3.5%	4.3%	6.1%	8.3%	4.6%
Pittsfield, MA...............................	4,136	10.4%	5.2%	0.8%	3.5%	3.2%	8.6%	0.9%	5.0%	15.7%	13.9%	5.5%	9.9%	5.3%
Pocatello, ID................................	2,387	0.0%	0.0%	10.7%	25.0%	0.0%	14.5%	4.2%	13.3%	4.1%	10.7%	2.9%	1.0%	6.2%

Table F-4: Metropolitan/Micropolitan Statistical Areas—Educational Field of Study—*Continued*

	Total Millennial Population	Engineering	Computers and Math	Science and Engineering Related	Business	Physical Science	Social Science	Communications	Biological Sciences	Literature	Liberal Arts	Psychology	Education	Visual and Performing Arts
Port St. Lucie, FL	5,788	1.7%	4.8%	15.2%	10.3%	0.0%	2.6%	4.9%	3.9%	9.3%	6.4%	0.0%	17.0%	0.0%
Portland-South Portland, ME	18,948	5.9%	0.8%	6.9%	15.6%	0.0%	8.0%	5.9%	17.5%	3.2%	4.1%	7.5%	7.1%	12.4%
Portland-Vancouver-Hillsboro, OR-WA	98,305	7.6%	5.1%	6.9%	14.9%	2.5%	10.1%	5.1%	9.2%	5.5%	6.5%	5.5%	3.4%	8.5%
Pottsville, PA micro	3,471	0.0%	0.0%	12.6%	17.7%	0.7%	0.9%	9.0%	0.9%	1.4%	0.7%	3.3%	29.2%	1.5%
Prescott, AZ	2,544	14.0%	11.4%	16.5%	5.9%	0.0%	8.1%	0.0%	0.0%	0.0%	14.1%	0.0%	6.1%	0.0%
Providence-Warwick, RI-MA	72,439	5.9%	2.4%	8.3%	17.3%	4.4%	5.8%	4.9%	5.7%	4.3%	4.6%	8.2%	7.8%	7.6%
Provo-Orem, UT	28,063	5.1%	5.7%	8.1%	13.2%	1.1%	5.7%	6.3%	5.6%	7.1%	2.6%	5.9%	12.3%	3.8%
Pueblo, CO	3,347	11.2%	3.4%	2.7%	38.8%	0.0%	7.3%	3.5%	1.8%	3.9%	12.8%	3.2%	0.0%	1.7%
Punta Gorda, FL	1,116	0.0%	0.0%	16.8%	18.3%	0.0%	14.6%	3.7%	0.0%	9.2%	15.0%	0.0%	10.0%	8.1%
Racine, WI	3,301	0.0%	0.0%	11.2%	16.3%	0.0%	0.0%	35.6%	10.0%	2.4%	11.7%	0.0%	2.9%	0.0%
Raleigh, NC	70,958	10.6%	6.9%	6.7%	17.3%	3.4%	7.2%	6.2%	8.4%	4.0%	2.5%	3.9%	6.5%	5.8%
Rapid City, SD	4,532	6.3%	0.0%	8.5%	27.1%	0.0%	9.7%	2.6%	3.6%	3.1%	1.9%	0.5%	20.5%	11.5%
Reading, PA	10,600	6.7%	3.6%	9.3%	27.0%	1.8%	7.5%	7.0%	3.0%	3.2%	0.2%	4.3%	15.7%	3.2%
Redding, CA	3,173	6.9%	0.0%	2.0%	11.2%	2.6%	7.0%	7.0%	4.3%	7.5%	3.9%	14.6%	6.7%	8.1%
Reno, NV	15,547	4.0%	2.6%	10.9%	24.5%	5.4%	5.5%	1.7%	9.6%	1.5%	3.2%	1.6%	12.9%	4.7%
Richmond, VA	53,784	4.5%	3.7%	7.4%	15.7%	4.0%	12.9%	4.7%	5.9%	5.9%	5.3%	7.6%	8.0%	5.4%
Riverside-San Bernardino-Ontario, CA	107,348	4.0%	2.2%	10.3%	19.6%	1.3%	9.6%	2.9%	10.0%	4.5%	5.0%	9.3%	4.9%	5.1%
Roanoke, VA	8,743	3.5%	1.5%	6.5%	16.1%	4.9%	7.1%	0.9%	8.9%	5.5%	6.0%	16.4%	5.9%	5.1%
Rochester, MN	10,884	8.5%	4.7%	12.1%	17.7%	5.6%	8.6%	2.2%	12.8%	0.9%	2.7%	0.1%	7.1%	3.9%
Rochester, NY	46,921	8.6%	5.0%	8.7%	16.9%	4.2%	4.8%	6.1%	6.9%	3.6%	5.1%	4.5%	11.8%	6.3%
Rockford, IL	8,820	8.5%	1.6%	13.4%	10.3%	5.5%	7.3%	5.4%	6.1%	2.2%	6.9%	7.6%	14.4%	7.4%
Rocky Mount, NC	2,287	0.0%	0.0%	1.8%	18.5%	5.2%	0.0%	15.5%	0.0%	0.0%	0.0%	23.7%	22.7%	0.0%
Rome, GA	2,471	9.3%	5.0%	14.9%	11.9%	15.5%	6.4%	0.0%	10.5%	0.0%	0.6%	3.2%	11.9%	2.9%
Roseburg, OR micro	1,458	0.0%	0.0%	9.9%	18.9%	0.0%	0.0%	0.0%	24.3%	0.0%	0.0%	8.4%	33.1%	0.0%
Sacramento–Roseville–Arden-Arcade, CA	78,436	9.3%	2.4%	5.5%	17.4%	2.6%	13.5%	5.1%	10.8%	3.8%	5.2%	5.8%	3.0%	5.1%
Saginaw, MI	5,465	18.5%	3.4%	4.4%	17.1%	2.3%	4.2%	9.7%	0.9%	0.0%	0.0%	3.7%	8.8%	4.7%
Salem, OH micro	1,905	2.8%	7.7%	12.0%	0.0%	12.6%	0.0%	11.7%	0.0%	33.1%	13.2%	0.0%	6.9%	0.0%
Salem, OR	9,265	8.7%	2.8%	3.0%	14.9%	7.0%	6.1%	4.8%	15.2%	2.2%	7.2%	9.0%	5.7%	2.5%
Salinas, CA	10,725	3.9%	3.8%	14.6%	14.9%	0.9%	9.7%	4.1%	6.3%	7.8%	6.5%	5.7%	4.5%	10.5%
Salisbury, MD-DE	9,053	2.1%	2.0%	14.3%	16.7%	4.3%	6.4%	5.4%	2.4%	3.7%	0.8%	5.9%	12.0%	7.7%
Salt Lake City, UT	48,841	6.2%	3.3%	9.7%	19.9%	2.1%	6.5%	5.4%	4.8%	7.8%	3.1%	6.9%	6.3%	5.1%
San Angelo, TX	3,735	3.9%	7.1%	5.7%	13.8%	0.0%	3.8%	14.4%	8.6%	1.5%	0.0%	5.1%	14.5%	0.0%
San Antonio-New Braunfels, TX	83,991	8.6%	4.5%	7.4%	20.5%	2.0%	6.7%	5.3%	8.6%	3.6%	3.8%	6.6%	6.7%	3.4%
San Diego-Carlsbad, CA	173,979	10.4%	3.9%	5.9%	16.6%	3.0%	10.8%	5.0%	7.1%	3.4%	6.8%	7.1%	3.6%	5.6%
San Francisco-Oakland-Hayward, CA	305,098	9.5%	6.2%	6.5%	17.7%	3.2%	12.7%	6.6%	7.2%	4.4%	4.8%	6.0%	1.7%	6.3%
San Jose-Sunnyvale-Santa Clara, CA	130,168	20.8%	13.6%	5.4%	16.3%	3.0%	9.7%	3.6%	5.7%	2.6%	2.5%	5.7%	2.3%	3.1%
San Luis Obispo-Paso Robles-Arroyo Grande, CA	9,508	9.5%	3.2%	10.6%	10.1%	0.0%	10.2%	4.5%	9.8%	7.2%	13.4%	2.4%	1.3%	8.2%
Santa Cruz-Watsonville, CA	9,820	2.5%	3.0%	4.3%	9.9%	5.9%	12.7%	10.1%	19.1%	3.0%	4.6%	7.7%	0.4%	13.0%
Santa Fe, NM	3,116	0.3%	1.8%	9.7%	9.0%	3.3%	2.5%	11.3%	8.3%	11.4%	14.3%	2.9%	4.9%	13.6%
Santa Maria-Santa Barbara, CA	16,896	8.6%	3.6%	4.0%	9.9%	6.4%	14.1%	5.8%	4.8%	5.9%	4.4%	10.1%	2.6%	8.2%
Santa Rosa, CA	13,694	1.3%	0.5%	12.6%	19.2%	1.5%	14.1%	3.6%	13.0%	5.9%	3.6%	5.7%	4.0%	5.0%
Savannah, GA	15,694	3.1%	5.9%	17.1%	12.7%	2.0%	14.2%	2.7%	5.1%	2.0%	5.6%	1.5%	10.1%	6.8%
Scranton–Wilkes-Barre–Hazleton, PA	18,646	1.3%	2.5%	9.7%	17.3%	1.4%	7.6%	7.1%	7.6%	1.7%	3.5%	4.0%	13.9%	8.2%
Seattle-Tacoma-Bellevue, WA	214,200	9.7%	10.5%	6.8%	13.8%	2.1%	11.8%	5.6%	7.8%	4.9%	4.4%	5.5%	3.3%	5.5%
Sebastian-Vero Beach, FL	1,714	18.3%	0.0%	8.4%	15.1%	0.0%	20.6%	0.0%	19.8%	0.0%	0.0%	0.0%	5.7%	4.6%
Sebring, FL	332	0.0%	0.0%	22.9%	0.0%	0.0%	0.0%	0.0%	0.0%	30.1%	0.0%	0.0%	31.0%	0.0%
Sheboygan, WI	3,226	5.9%	16.6%	0.0%	30.7%	3.6%	1.2%	7.3%	13.5%	10.1%	0.0%	0.0%	8.2%	3.0%
Sherman-Denison, TX	2,519	4.2%	13.0%	28.0%	9.8%	0.2%	0.0%	0.6%	2.3%	0.0%	6.2%	2.5%	11.7%	0.0%
Show Low, AZ micro	1,463	0.0%	0.0%	11.8%	7.2%	0.0%	10.7%	0.0%	3.0%	0.8%	29.6%	8.2%	17.8%	10.8%
Shreveport-Bossier City, LA	14,104	5.9%	1.1%	18.8%	19.9%	2.4%	3.3%	3.0%	12.5%	5.4%	7.4%	3.6%	5.9%	0.0%
Sierra Vista-Douglas, AZ	3,392	2.2%	2.1%	9.6%	7.3%	0.0%	7.7%	3.7%	19.9%	10.1%	3.8%	4.2%	21.4%	0.0%
Sioux City, IA-NE-SD	4,179	9.3%	5.0%	4.1%	16.5%	7.4%	0.7%	2.6%	13.4%	1.1%	10.1%	0.0%	15.7%	7.3%
Sioux Falls, SD	13,106	1.7%	6.3%	8.3%	18.7%	4.2%	4.7%	9.2%	13.4%	2.9%	0.0%	5.6%	16.7%	3.5%
South Bend-Mishawaka, IN-MI	9,043	9.1%	1.6%	13.8%	8.9%	7.5%	4.2%	1.3%	4.8%	6.9%	5.9%	3.2%	17.1%	2.8%
Spartanburg, SC	7,471	4.7%	1.6%	4.6%	19.1%	2.0%	1.9%	7.8%	6.7%	3.9%	3.0%	7.4%	25.1%	4.6%
Spokane-Spokane Valley, WA	18,713	3.3%	0.0%	18.2%	23.7%	1.7%	8.4%	9.4%	4.0%	3.6%	1.8%	5.3%	6.3%	5.3%
Springfield, IL	10,176	4.6%	1.7%	13.3%	15.1%	2.7%	12.6%	7.7%	9.5%	3.0%	9.4%	5.8%	4.2%	0.9%
Springfield, MA	20,612	4.6%	4.5%	6.8%	25.2%	2.7%	6.7%	5.1%	4.9%	2.9%	3.7%	9.5%	4.7%	9.4%
Springfield, MO	20,591	1.6%	0.7%	7.5%	20.3%	4.2%	6.2%	5.2%	4.2%	7.0%	4.1%	4.0%	14.7%	8.9%
Springfield, OH	2,910	3.0%	3.1%	8.6%	28.5%	1.6%	5.4%	6.2%	10.3%	1.5%	7.1%	7.2%	17.6%	0.0%
St. Cloud, MN	6,015	1.8%	3.1%	8.2%	17.9%	2.7%	2.5%	2.2%	4.5%	0.0%	1.0%	8.9%	20.8%	6.4%
St. George, UT	2,681	5.6%	0.0%	20.1%	12.0%	0.0%	4.6%	4.4%	12.3%	0.0%	6.6%	20.0%	5.1%	2.2%
St. Joseph, MO-KS	3,586	0.6%	0.0%	20.1%	19.3%	0.3%	15.2%	0.0%	9.8%	3.2%	4.7%	5.7%	17.0%	1.2%
St. Louis, MO-IL	137,666	3.9%	2.1%	11.2%	23.3%	2.9%	5.5%	6.9%	9.4%	2.7%	4.9%	3.6%	10.2%	4.8%
State College, PA	10,087	19.9%	2.0%	2.3%	15.0%	10.3%	5.4%	2.2%	6.7%	4.2%	4.8%	12.0%	3.1%	0.7%
Staunton-Waynesboro, VA	3,391	14.5%	0.0%	7.9%	16.4%	23.1%	4.4%	0.0%	6.0%	0.0%	9.2%	8.6%	6.7%	1.4%
Stockton-Lodi, CA	12,338	3.7%	2.9%	5.4%	20.3%	0.0%	9.1%	7.1%	19.8%	2.4%	2.5%	13.9%	3.3%	2.9%
Sumter, SC	2,377	0.0%	0.0%	12.4%	18.3%	0.0%	0.0%	0.0%	2.7%	0.0%	4.8%	0.0%	28.4%	0.0%
Sunbury, PA micro	3,018	3.2%	9.7%	17.3%	11.4%	17.0%	2.8%	7.2%	4.3%	0.0%	7.4%	3.2%	7.5%	0.0%
Syracuse, NY	28,488	6.7%	1.2%	6.1%	18.0%	2.5%	8.7%	6.0%	10.7%	3.4%	4.7%	7.5%	8.4%	6.9%
Tallahassee, FL	24,708	4.1%	2.3%	11.6%	17.2%	2.1%	8.4%	4.4%	6.1%	3.9%	3.5%	10.9%	10.3%	5.2%
Tampa-St. Petersburg-Clearwater, FL	93,196	5.9%	2.9%	8.4%	25.8%	1.9%	8.7%	6.8%	6.2%	3.0%	3.3%	6.0%	8.7%	4.3%
Terre Haute, IN	4,849	15.8%	4.6%	23.8%	2.8%	0.0%	5.5%	5.8%	4.5%	0.7%	2.2%	2.8%	7.0%	0.9%
Texarkana, TX-AR	2,970	4.1%	0.0%	3.6%	17.4%	0.0%	6.9%	0.0%	0.0%	0.0%	1.4%	11.6%	27.1%	4.2%
The Villages, FL	786	0.0%	0.0%	15.1%	0.0%	0.0%	18.2%	0.0%	0.0%	0.0%	37.0%	0.0%	8.7%	0.0%

Table F-4: Metropolitan/Micropolitan Statistical Areas—Educational Field of Study—*Continued*

	Total Millennial Population	Percent of the Population 18 to 31 by Field of Study												
		Engineering	Computers and Math	Science and Engineering Related	Business	Physical Science	Social Science	Communications	Biological Sciences	Literature	Liberal Arts	Psychology	Education	Visual and Performing Arts
Toledo, OH	22,493	4.5%	3.1%	11.7%	21.7%	1.0%	6.1%	3.7%	11.4%	4.3%	5.1%	4.4%	11.0%	4.1%
Topeka, KS	7,367	3.5%	4.8%	5.0%	21.1%	1.1%	4.7%	3.4%	14.7%	4.5%	0.0%	6.8%	20.3%	3.3%
Torrington, CT micro	7,480	12.9%	2.4%	4.1%	18.2%	0.6%	4.6%	5.6%	4.6%	2.8%	7.3%	10.2%	6.3%	4.3%
Traverse City, MI micro	3,430	0.0%	0.0%	8.4%	19.8%	0.0%	13.7%	8.7%	6.2%	4.4%	9.8%	7.6%	11.6%	2.9%
Trenton, NJ	18,915	7.9%	4.8%	4.4%	23.1%	4.2%	8.6%	3.6%	2.4%	3.3%	6.4%	4.5%	10.1%	10.9%
Truckee-Grass Valley, CA micro	1,694	0.0%	0.0%	0.0%	34.5%	16.1%	21.2%	0.0%	9.1%	0.0%	2.0%	0.0%	5.5%	6.8%
Tucson, AZ	32,546	9.8%	2.2%	8.4%	12.5%	5.1%	13.6%	2.7%	8.1%	5.1%	6.6%	3.5%	7.8%	5.9%
Tullahoma-Manchester, TN micro	1,348	5.0%	0.0%	13.6%	7.8%	0.0%	1.6%	6.5%	13.2%	5.9%	10.2%	4.4%	11.3%	11.3%
Tulsa, OK	26,831	2.9%	1.7%	11.0%	24.5%	3.1%	3.9%	7.5%	7.5%	1.8%	4.8%	7.0%	11.3%	3.8%
Tupelo, MS micro	2,032	0.0%	0.0%	21.0%	37.8%	0.0%	2.9%	1.0%	2.9%	0.0%	0.0%	2.6%	31.8%	0.0%
Tuscaloosa, AL	9,404	3.6%	0.7%	10.2%	19.5%	1.8%	7.4%	3.0%	6.4%	11.3%	5.0%	4.0%	18.0%	2.7%
Tyler, TX	6,813	0.0%	0.0%	8.0%	30.3%	0.0%	3.9%	10.6%	5.1%	2.7%	4.1%	5.0%	9.3%	3.9%
Urban Honolulu, HI	43,660	6.1%	1.5%	12.0%	23.9%	2.8%	6.8%	6.2%	8.6%	3.8%	3.2%	7.1%	9.5%	3.0%
Utica-Rome, NY	7,608	0.8%	3.1%	7.5%	6.5%	5.5%	10.7%	3.8%	6.0%	8.9%	5.4%	6.0%	15.9%	2.3%
Valdosta, GA	6,550	4.9%	0.0%	10.8%	15.8%	6.3%	2.2%	4.4%	4.2%	5.4%	3.3%	8.7%	15.3%	2.5%
Vallejo-Fairfield, CA	11,355	5.3%	1.6%	9.4%	9.8%	1.6%	17.4%	5.1%	14.4%	3.4%	3.5%	4.3%	1.3%	6.4%
Victoria, TX	1,215	12.3%	14.5%	4.6%	0.0%	0.0%	0.0%	0.0%	14.2%	0.0%	21.2%	0.0%	22.0%	0.0%
Vineland-Bridgeton, NJ	3,425	13.7%	0.9%	2.6%	3.9%	0.0%	0.0%	1.9%	10.0%	3.3%	3.4%	7.5%	13.4%	18.5%
Virginia Beach-Norfolk-Newport News, VA-NC	66,908	5.3%	4.4%	7.8%	15.0%	4.1%	7.9%	6.7%	9.2%	3.8%	4.4%	8.2%	5.8%	5.0%
Visalia-Porterville, CA	7,005	4.9%	0.3%	21.8%	7.9%	0.0%	5.1%	4.6%	3.4%	1.3%	12.9%	5.4%	13.5%	2.8%
Waco, TX	8,719	4.0%	0.3%	1.1%	18.6%	2.1%	7.6%	2.8%	7.1%	3.8%	7.6%	7.1%	12.4%	9.6%
Walla Walla, WA	864	8.2%	0.0%	3.9%	11.5%	12.0%	0.0%	0.0%	4.7%	0.0%	0.0%	0.0%	26.4%	0.0%
Warner Robins, GA	4,248	8.9%	2.1%	6.3%	24.6%	0.0%	4.1%	3.3%	10.2%	0.8%	7.7%	9.7%	14.5%	0.0%
Washington-Arlington-Alexandria, DC-VA-MD-WV	433,381	7.6%	4.8%	5.6%	16.4%	2.4%	17.6%	6.1%	5.5%	4.6%	6.2%	5.5%	4.5%	4.5%
Waterloo-Cedar Falls, IA	5,919	2.7%	0.0%	14.6%	9.4%	0.0%	6.8%	4.5%	2.6%	7.2%	2.5%	10.9%	16.7%	3.2%
Watertown-Fort Drum, NY	2,714	3.5%	2.0%	8.9%	27.6%	0.9%	12.9%	0.0%	6.6%	0.0%	0.6%	5.0%	19.0%	0.8%
Wausau, WI	3,012	2.7%	0.0%	32.3%	20.3%	0.0%	10.5%	6.9%	6.3%	1.4%	0.0%	7.0%	0.0%	0.0%
Weirton-Steubenville, WV-OH	1,637	0.0%	0.0%	8.1%	18.2%	0.0%	5.7%	0.0%	5.9%	0.0%	3.9%	0.0%	35.4%	0.0%
Wenatchee, WA	1,433	4.0%	0.0%	0.0%	52.6%	0.0%	0.0%	19.7%	18.7%	0.9%	0.0%	2.9%	0.6%	0.0%
Wheeling, WV-OH	2,188	0.0%	0.0%	31.3%	13.6%	0.0%	4.3%	0.0%	4.4%	0.0%	2.9%	0.0%	26.5%	0.0%
Whitewater-Elkhorn, WI micro	3,121	1.3%	0.0%	10.8%	24.6%	0.0%	4.6%	10.5%	12.9%	5.4%	0.0%	1.6%	14.7%	10.2%
Wichita Falls, TX	4,420	2.5%	3.2%	1.6%	25.8%	0.0%	8.2%	7.1%	4.0%	0.0%	4.8%	0.0%	21.0%	6.2%
Wichita, KS	24,454	9.5%	0.0%	12.3%	22.4%	6.6%	1.1%	2.0%	5.8%	4.5%	4.6%	3.7%	15.8%	3.7%
Williamsport, PA	4,036	0.0%	0.8%	13.9%	7.9%	2.1%	4.5%	0.0%	9.4%	2.7%	6.9%	4.1%	18.3%	4.2%
Wilmington, NC	11,389	3.6%	0.0%	12.4%	20.2%	3.1%	7.7%	3.1%	5.2%	7.4%	2.9%	4.8%	8.9%	7.7%
Winchester, VA-WV	3,763	7.5%	8.0%	10.1%	18.4%	7.9%	12.5%	8.0%	0.6%	0.0%	2.4%	0.3%	10.3%	8.0%
Winston-Salem, NC	18,583	4.0%	1.2%	9.7%	14.0%	3.8%	4.9%	2.5%	12.4%	6.2%	6.9%	8.5%	9.0%	6.7%
Wooster, OH micro	2,131	13.7%	6.6%	1.4%	7.0%	0.0%	8.1%	5.1%	16.1%	5.4%	8.9%	6.6%	11.5%	5.1%
Worcester, MA-CT	43,054	7.1%	3.3%	10.6%	13.1%	5.0%	6.9%	5.6%	6.4%	4.0%	3.9%	8.6%	7.1%	6.3%
Yakima, WA	4,712	3.1%	0.0%	11.2%	19.3%	0.0%	3.4%	1.8%	15.9%	3.9%	8.0%	2.3%	16.0%	
York-Hanover, PA	10,468	1.6%	2.4%	12.2%	14.3%	0.5%	1.9%	6.9%	6.3%	0.0%	3.2%	12.2%	11.9%	5.7%
Youngstown-Warren-Boardman, OH-PA	16,600	2.4%	0.6%	17.8%	22.7%	4.1%	3.0%	7.9%	6.4%	3.3%	2.4%	5.3%	13.2%	4.3%
Yuba City, CA	3,618	2.6%	6.5%	6.0%	26.8%	0.0%	11.3%	8.0%	1.9%	1.9%	13.7%	6.7%	0.0%	11.9%
Yuma, AZ	2,944	3.2%	0.0%	19.4%	9.9%	2.5%	4.0%	20.7%	2.2%	1.4%	6.4%	3.3%	11.1%	5.0%

PART G

LANGUAGE SPOKEN AT HOME

LANGUAGE SPOKEN AT HOME

The nation's racial and ethnic diversity grows even in the smallest of communities and is also seen in the growth of Spanish and Asian languages spoken at home. Today, immigration from many different origin countries, especially Latin America and Asia, has added to the mix of languages spoken. These differences are shown in the data on education and language spoken. Some estimates indicate that as many as 800 different languages are spoken in New York City.[1]

_____

1. "Say What?" *The Economist*, September 10, 2011, http://www.economist.com/node/21528592, accessed 7/7/2015.

American Community Survey data on language is gathered through a question on whether each person speaks a language other than English at home and a write-in response of what that language is. The respondent is then asked a question on how well they speak English—Very Well, Well, Not Well, or Not At All. The data presented in the following tables report on the percentage of population by major categories of Language Spoken at Home and how well the population speaks English.

There is an interesting difference between today's Millennial generation and the population 65 and over. Nationwide, more than 85 percent of the population over age 65 speaks English at home, while only 77 percent of Millennials speak only English. And while Spanish

Percent of Millennials Who Speak Spanish at Home

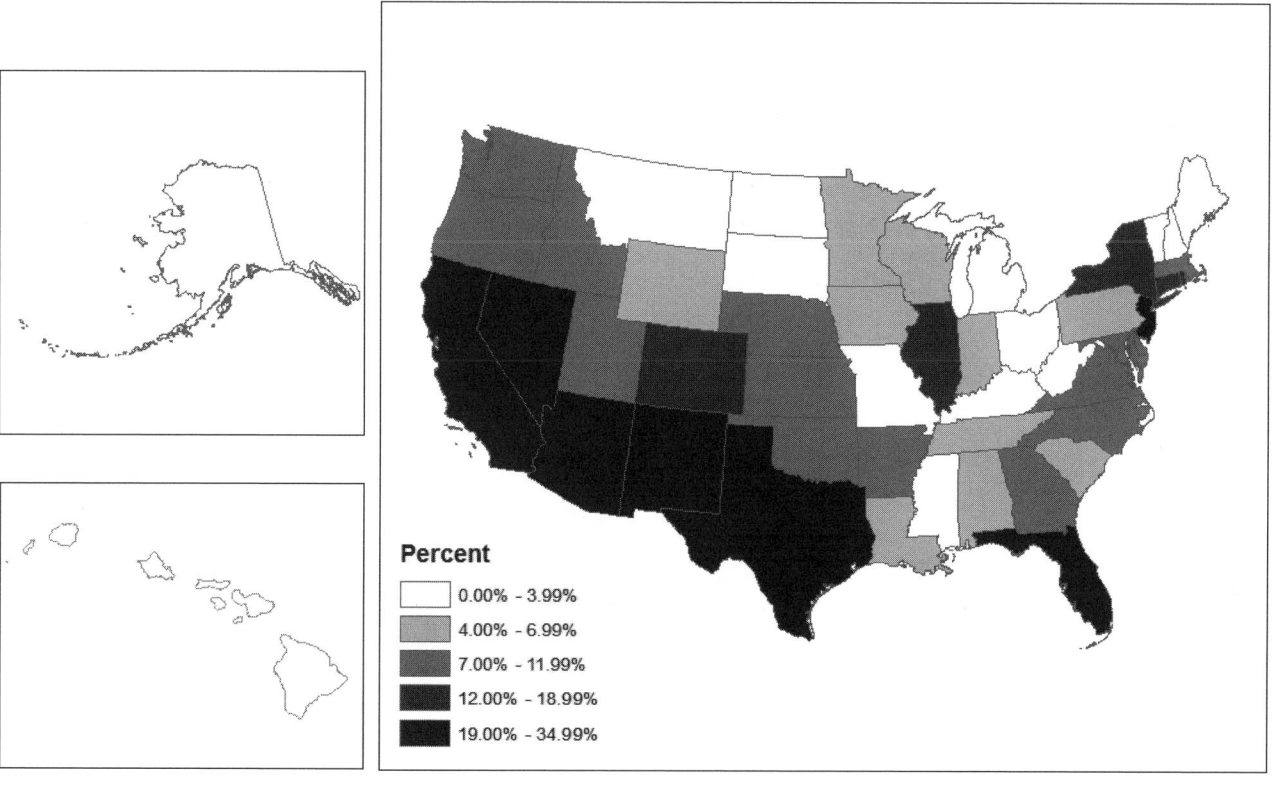

Percent

- 0.00% - 3.99%
- 4.00% - 6.99%
- 7.00% - 11.99%
- 12.00% - 18.99%
- 19.00% - 34.99%

is spoken by only 6.7 percent of the older population, 15.7 percent of Millennials speak Spanish at home. Indo-European and Asian languages are spoken by 3.3 percent and 3.1 percent of Millennials, respectively. By state, West Virginia (96.2 percent) has the highest percentage of the younger generation speaking only English, while California is lowest with a little over half the population (53.5 percent) speaking English. California also has the highest percentage of those speaking Spanish at home at 34.0 percent. More than 90 percent of the Millennial population speaks only English in 18 states, and in five additional states Spanish is spoken by more than 20 percent of the younger population—Arizona (24.4 percent), Florida (23.0 percent), Nevada (26.5 percent), New Mexico (28.8 percent), and Texas (31.9 percent). Asian languages are spoken at home by 14.5 percent of Hawaii's Millennials and by 7.7 percent in California. Massachusetts and New York have the highest percentage who speak Indo-European languages at 8.1 percent and 8.0 percent, respectively.

While many languages can be spoken in the home, the ability to speak English is an important measure of assimilation. The question on ability to speak English is only asked of those who speak a language other than English at home. Montana has the highest percentage of Millennials who speak another language and speak English "Very Well" (88.0 percent), while Hawaii is lowest at 58.4 percent. In Louisiana 21.7 percent speak another language at home and speak English "Not Well" or "Not At All."

Virtually everyone (99.5 percent) in Cambria County, PA speaks only English at home, and 243 counties are above the 90 percent mark. Webb County, TX has the lowest percentage at 11.3 percent where it's also the highest for Spanish speaking population with 88.7 percent speaking Spanish at home. Rockland County, NY has the highest percentage of those speaking Indo-European languages (20.9 percent) while San Francisco County, CA tops the list for Asian languages at 19.6 percent.

Of Millennials who speak another language at home, more than 90 percent indicate that they speak English "Very Well" in 50 counties. The lowest percentage who speak English "Very Well" is in Madison County, TN (15.7 percent). Columbiana County, OH has the highest percentage of those who speak English "Not Well" or "Not At All" at 76.2 percent.

In Shreveport City, LA, 98.1 percent of Millennials speak only English at home, but in 48 cities less than 50 percent of the generation speaks English at home. It's lowest in Hialeah City, FL where 88.3 percent speak Spanish at home. Hialeah isn't the highest though—Laredo City, TX is tops at 89.0 percent. Spanish is spoken at home by more than 25 percent in 96 cities. At 36.2 percent, Glendale City, CA has the highest percentage who speak Indo-European languages and Urban Honolunu CDP, HI has the most speaking Asian languages (28.9 percent). Of those who speak a language other than English, 99.2 percent speak English "Very Well" in Springfield City, IL. Wilmington City, NC has the highest

Table 1: Counties with the Highest Percentage of Another Language Spoken At Home

Asian Language		Spanish Language	
County	Percent	County	Percent
San Francisco County, CA	19.6%	Webb County, TX	88.7%
Santa Clara County, CA	18.9%	Hidalgo County, TX	86.3%
Honolulu County, HI	16.1%	Cameron County, TX	77.0%
San Mateo County, CA	15.5%	Imperial County, CA	74.3%
Ramsey County, MN	15.0%	El Paso County, TX	67.8%
Alameda County, CA	14.7%	Miami-Dade County, FL	59.7%
Maui County, HI	12.8%	Yuma County, AZ	56.8%
Yolo County, CA	12.3%	Doña Ana County, NM	53.6%
Queens County, NY	11.7%	Madera County, CA	53.3%
Orange County, CA	11.2%	Tulare County, CA	53.1%

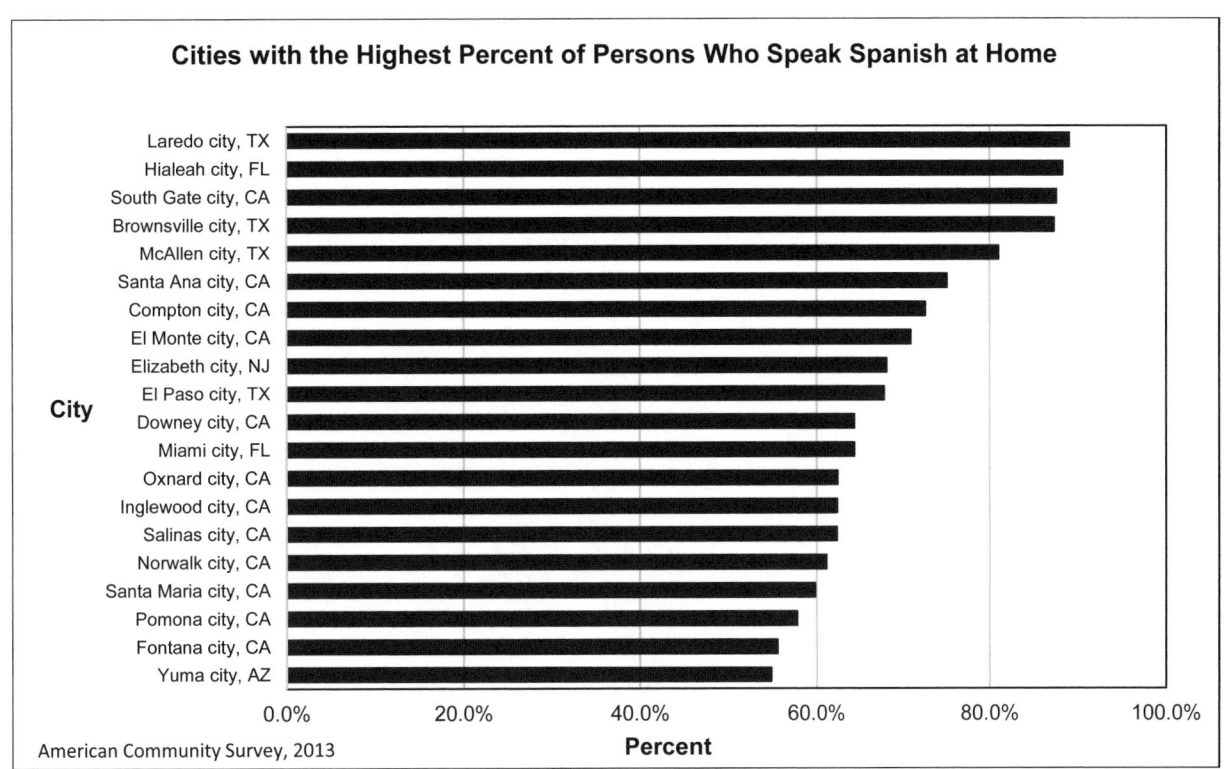

Cities with the Highest Percent of Persons Who Speak Spanish at Home

American Community Survey, 2013

percentage who speak English "Not Well" or "Not At All" at 54.3 percent.

In 185 metropolitan/micropolitan areas English is spoken at home by more than 90 percent of Millennials over age 18. The Johnstown, PA metro is highest at 99.5 percent, but 19 other metro/micros are above 97 percent. Spanish is the primary language in the Laredo, TX metro with 88.4 percent, but in 22 metro/micros less than one percent speak Spanish at home.

Indo-European languages are spoken by 12.8 percent in the Wooster, OH micro and in the San Jose-Sunnyvale, CA metro, 18.6 percent speak Asian languages at home. Among those who speak a language other than English, 83.3 percent in the Cookeville, TN micropolitan area speak English "Not Well" or "Not At All." Seven metro/micros are over 50 percent. The Roseburg, OR micro has the highest percentage (65.0 percent) who speak English "Very Well" even though they don't speak English at home.

Table G-1: States—Language Spoken and English Ability

	Millennial Population 13 to 31	Percent by Language Spoken at Home					Percent Who Speak Only English	Percent by Ability to Speak English		
		English Only	Spanish	Other Indo-European Language	Asian and Pacific Island Language	Other Language		Speak English "Very Well"	Speak English "Well"	Speak English "Not Well" or "Not at All"
United States	82,516,535	76.8%	15.7%	3.3%	3.1%	1.1%	76.8%	17.0%	3.4%	2.8%
Alabama	1,243,909	93.8%	4.4%	0.7%	0.8%	0.3%	93.8%	3.7%	1.2%	1.3%
Alaska	218,453	86.1%	2.8%	2.3%	3.4%	5.4%	86.1%	12.0%	1.7%	0.2%
Arizona	1,743,604	69.6%	24.4%	1.5%	1.8%	2.6%	69.6%	24.3%	3.0%	3.1%
Arkansas	754,902	90.5%	7.3%	1.0%	0.7%	0.4%	90.5%	6.0%	1.8%	1.6%
California	10,563,495	53.5%	34.0%	3.6%	7.7%	1.1%	53.5%	35.1%	6.2%	5.2%
Colorado	1,404,366	80.7%	14.1%	2.2%	2.0%	1.0%	80.7%	14.6%	2.8%	1.9%
Connecticut	889,970	76.2%	14.8%	5.6%	2.5%	0.9%	76.2%	16.9%	4.3%	2.7%
Delaware	234,000	84.1%	9.1%	3.2%	2.3%	1.3%	84.1%	11.2%	2.5%	2.2%
District of Columbia	216,160	81.8%	8.7%	4.3%	2.8%	2.5%	81.8%	13.2%	3.6%	1.4%
Florida	4,703,393	70.0%	23.0%	4.9%	1.5%	0.6%	70.0%	22.4%	3.9%	3.6%
Georgia	2,675,903	84.0%	10.5%	2.3%	2.3%	0.9%	84.0%	11.2%	2.4%	2.5%
Hawaii	371,155	78.0%	2.7%	1.3%	14.5%	3.5%	78.0%	12.8%	7.7%	1.5%
Idaho	422,164	86.7%	10.2%	1.8%	0.8%	0.6%	86.7%	9.3%	1.9%	2.1%
Illinois	3,382,854	75.6%	15.8%	4.7%	2.7%	1.2%	75.6%	18.6%	3.5%	2.3%
Indiana	1,694,378	89.5%	5.9%	2.7%	1.4%	0.5%	89.5%	7.0%	2.0%	1.5%
Iowa	791,151	89.7%	5.3%	2.3%	1.8%	0.9%	89.7%	6.6%	2.4%	1.3%
Kansas	763,442	87.0%	9.0%	1.3%	2.1%	0.6%	87.0%	9.6%	1.9%	1.5%
Kentucky	1,113,720	93.1%	3.8%	1.7%	0.8%	0.6%	93.1%	4.6%	1.2%	1.1%
Louisiana	1,241,608	92.3%	4.4%	1.8%	1.1%	0.4%	92.3%	4.9%	1.1%	1.7%
Maine	303,554	95.0%	1.0%	2.5%	1.1%	0.5%	95.0%	4.1%	0.9%	0.0%
Maryland	1,527,405	82.4%	8.7%	3.9%	3.1%	1.9%	82.4%	12.3%	2.7%	2.6%
Massachusetts	1,771,550	75.1%	11.0%	8.1%	4.1%	1.6%	75.1%	18.4%	4.1%	2.3%
Michigan	2,496,925	90.4%	3.5%	2.2%	1.6%	2.2%	90.4%	7.3%	1.3%	1.0%
Minnesota	1,394,146	86.0%	5.4%	1.6%	4.4%	2.5%	86.0%	9.8%	2.8%	1.4%
Mississippi	782,547	95.7%	2.6%	0.6%	0.8%	0.3%	95.7%	2.9%	0.7%	0.8%
Missouri	1,551,729	92.8%	3.4%	2.0%	1.3%	0.5%	92.8%	5.1%	1.6%	0.4%
Montana	254,000	95.4%	1.0%	2.2%	0.5%	0.9%	95.4%	4.1%	0.3%	0.2%
Nebraska	488,381	87.4%	9.0%	1.3%	1.6%	0.8%	87.4%	8.4%	2.0%	2.1%
Nevada	715,125	66.1%	26.5%	2.1%	4.3%	1.0%	66.1%	26.5%	4.6%	2.9%
New Hampshire	320,088	92.2%	3.1%	2.8%	1.5%	0.4%	92.2%	5.6%	1.2%	1.0%
New Jersey	2,179,642	67.9%	19.0%	7.4%	3.9%	1.7%	67.9%	24.0%	4.3%	3.9%
New Mexico	546,092	64.2%	28.8%	1.2%	1.2%	4.6%	64.2%	29.0%	3.3%	3.6%
New York	5,211,620	68.4%	17.5%	8.0%	4.5%	1.6%	68.4%	22.0%	5.3%	4.3%
North Carolina	2,517,570	86.2%	9.7%	1.6%	1.8%	0.7%	86.2%	9.0%	2.1%	2.7%
North Dakota	209,265	93.1%	2.2%	2.0%	1.3%	1.4%	93.1%	5.2%	1.2%	0.5%
Ohio	2,922,925	91.8%	3.0%	2.7%	1.3%	1.1%	91.8%	5.5%	1.7%	0.9%
Oklahoma	1,014,365	87.7%	9.3%	0.8%	1.5%	0.7%	87.7%	8.2%	2.1%	2.0%
Oregon	981,691	80.6%	12.0%	3.3%	2.9%	1.2%	80.6%	15.1%	2.1%	2.2%
Pennsylvania	3,194,416	87.2%	5.9%	3.6%	2.2%	1.0%	87.2%	8.9%	2.5%	1.4%
Rhode Island	278,272	74.9%	16.3%	5.4%	2.7%	0.7%	74.9%	20.5%	2.1%	2.5%
South Carolina	1,223,504	91.7%	5.9%	1.1%	0.9%	0.4%	91.7%	5.7%	1.2%	1.3%
South Dakota	214,866	91.9%	3.4%	2.0%	0.8%	1.8%	91.9%	5.1%	1.6%	1.4%
Tennessee	1,653,200	91.5%	5.4%	1.2%	1.1%	0.8%	91.5%	5.7%	1.3%	1.5%
Texas	7,316,912	63.1%	31.9%	1.9%	2.3%	0.7%	63.1%	26.8%	5.5%	4.6%
Utah	868,128	84.8%	10.0%	2.0%	2.2%	0.9%	84.8%	11.9%	1.7%	1.6%
Vermont	154,073	94.7%	0.8%	2.9%	1.2%	0.4%	94.7%	3.8%	0.9%	0.6%
Virginia	2,153,966	83.4%	8.2%	3.4%	3.3%	1.8%	83.4%	12.5%	2.4%	1.7%
Washington	1,808,668	77.7%	11.2%	4.5%	5.1%	1.5%	77.7%	16.4%	3.5%	2.4%
West Virginia	436,632	96.2%	2.2%	1.0%	0.3%	0.3%	96.2%	2.4%	0.9%	0.6%
Wisconsin	1,444,543	88.4%	6.8%	1.8%	2.8%	0.3%	88.4%	7.8%	2.1%	1.7%
Wyoming	152,108	92.0%	4.9%	0.8%	1.0%	1.4%	92.0%	6.4%	1.0%	0.6%

Table G-2: Counties—Language Spoken and English Ability

	Millennial Population 13 to 31	Percent by Language Spoken at Home					Percent Who Speak Only English	Percent by Ability to Speak English		
		English Only	Spanish	Other Indo-European Language	Asian and Pacific Island Language	Other Language		Speak English "Very Well"	Speak English "Well"	Speak English "Not Well" or "Not at All"
Alabama										
Baldwin County	43,743	92.5%	6.0%	0.3%	1.2%	0.0%	92.5%	6.1%	0.2%	1.2%
Calhoun County	29,189	94.8%	3.0%	0.3%	1.9%	0.0%	94.8%	3.2%	0.6%	1.3%
Etowah County	24,989	98.0%	1.4%	0.5%	0.0%	0.2%	98.0%	0.4%	0.4%	1.3%
Houston County	25,996	97.4%	2.2%	0.1%	0.3%	0.0%	97.4%	2.0%	0.2%	0.4%
Jefferson County	169,583	92.9%	4.7%	1.2%	0.6%	0.5%	92.9%	3.6%	2.0%	1.5%
Lauderdale County	25,218	95.0%	3.5%	1.4%	0.0%	0.0%	95.0%	2.0%	0.0%	3.0%
Lee County	53,402	96.8%	0.9%	0.0%	2.0%	0.3%	96.8%	2.4%	0.5%	0.3%
Madison County	89,687	89.5%	7.2%	1.3%	1.7%	0.4%	89.5%	5.4%	2.6%	2.6%
Marshall County	23,904	85.5%	13.8%	0.6%	0.0%	0.2%	85.5%	3.2%	2.5%	8.9%
Mobile County	106,088	95.6%	1.6%	1.0%	1.5%	0.3%	95.6%	3.4%	0.7%	0.3%
Montgomery County	65,733	96.0%	3.2%	0.3%	0.3%	0.2%	96.0%	1.2%	0.9%	1.9%
Morgan County	27,865	90.3%	9.5%	0.2%	0.0%	0.0%	90.3%	5.9%	0.3%	3.5%
Shelby County	50,021	90.1%	7.2%	1.6%	1.2%	0.0%	90.1%	7.0%	1.8%	1.2%
Tuscaloosa County	73,097	96.0%	2.7%	0.7%	0.5%	0.0%	96.0%	2.0%	1.2%	0.8%
Alaska										
Fairbanks North Star Borough	33,622	94.0%	3.1%	0.5%	2.0%	0.3%	94.0%	5.5%	0.3%	0.2%
Matanuska-Susitna Borough	27,285	88.2%	2.3%	3.0%	4.0%	2.4%	88.2%	10.6%	1.2%	0.0%
Arizona										
Cochise County	32,080	58.7%	39.3%	1.2%	0.8%	0.0%	58.7%	35.3%	2.4%	3.5%
Coconino County	48,457	81.9%	6.5%	1.7%	1.0%	8.8%	81.9%	15.9%	1.8%	0.3%
Maricopa County	1,074,489	69.7%	25.0%	1.9%	2.0%	1.4%	69.7%	23.8%	3.2%	3.3%
Mohave County	40,348	86.0%	13.0%	0.0%	0.5%	0.6%	86.0%	11.1%	1.8%	1.2%
Navajo County	28,502	59.3%	2.5%	0.6%	0.0%	37.6%	59.3%	33.9%	3.3%	3.5%
Pima County	272,490	67.3%	26.5%	1.4%	3.0%	1.8%	67.3%	27.3%	3.2%	2.2%
Pinal County	92,374	79.4%	18.7%	0.4%	0.5%	1.1%	79.4%	16.0%	0.7%	3.9%
Yavapai County	40,349	84.8%	13.9%	0.3%	0.3%	0.7%	84.8%	10.3%	1.8%	3.1%
Yuma County	59,396	42.2%	56.8%	0.3%	0.3%	0.4%	42.2%	45.1%	5.9%	6.8%
Arkansas										
Benton County	61,471	83.0%	15.1%	1.2%	0.4%	0.3%	83.0%	11.0%	3.4%	2.6%
Craighead County	27,322	91.5%	6.5%	0.1%	0.5%	1.4%	91.5%	4.6%	3.3%	0.6%
Faulkner County	41,303	91.0%	5.4%	2.2%	0.6%	0.8%	91.0%	5.9%	0.9%	2.2%
Garland County	20,404	93.2%	5.6%	0.4%	0.8%	0.0%	93.2%	5.2%	0.8%	0.8%
Pulaski County	104,460	91.3%	6.8%	0.9%	0.9%	0.1%	91.3%	3.2%	2.7%	2.7%
Saline County	27,530	94.6%	4.2%	1.1%	0.0%	0.0%	94.6%	4.2%	0.0%	1.1%
Sebastian County	32,489	82.2%	16.1%	0.0%	1.7%	0.0%	82.2%	15.2%	1.7%	0.9%
Washington County	68,368	83.5%	12.1%	2.3%	1.0%	1.2%	83.5%	7.9%	5.4%	3.3%
California										
Alameda County	411,973	57.0%	20.3%	6.4%	14.7%	1.6%	57.0%	30.8%	7.0%	5.2%
Butte County	65,642	84.6%	9.4%	1.0%	5.1%	0.0%	84.6%	9.9%	4.7%	0.8%
Contra Costa County	260,160	64.4%	23.1%	4.0%	7.2%	1.2%	64.4%	24.3%	6.0%	5.3%
El Dorado County	37,599	81.5%	11.5%	0.9%	5.1%	1.0%	81.5%	13.3%	3.4%	1.9%
Fresno County	280,779	54.8%	34.6%	3.5%	6.9%	0.2%	54.8%	32.3%	6.6%	6.3%
Humboldt County	38,357	79.9%	11.1%	5.0%	2.7%	1.4%	79.9%	12.5%	2.6%	5.0%
Imperial County	52,602	24.5%	74.3%	0.0%	1.0%	0.2%	24.5%	51.7%	16.6%	7.3%
Kern County	255,789	51.3%	44.3%	1.6%	1.3%	1.4%	51.3%	36.5%	6.2%	6.0%
Kings County	45,510	52.8%	41.5%	2.8%	1.6%	1.2%	52.8%	28.7%	12.6%	5.9%
Los Angeles County	2,833,691	41.6%	44.8%	4.1%	8.4%	1.0%	41.6%	45.2%	7.1%	6.0%
Madera County	43,066	44.2%	53.3%	2.5%	0.1%	0.0%	44.2%	37.4%	2.7%	15.7%
Marin County	49,354	72.9%	20.3%	2.4%	4.1%	0.3%	72.9%	18.4%	4.4%	4.4%
Merced County	80,879	41.8%	46.2%	5.6%	6.0%	0.6%	41.8%	43.0%	9.9%	5.4%
Monterey County	126,091	45.0%	50.1%	1.3%	3.2%	0.4%	45.0%	34.8%	7.1%	13.1%
Napa County	33,246	63.3%	34.0%	0.4%	2.3%	0.0%	63.3%	26.7%	7.8%	2.2%
Nevada County	19,138	88.6%	7.7%	3.1%	0.6%	0.0%	88.6%	10.5%	0.0%	0.8%
Orange County	845,683	52.2%	32.5%	2.8%	11.2%	1.2%	52.2%	36.8%	6.0%	4.9%
Placer County	86,972	81.6%	10.5%	3.8%	2.4%	1.6%	81.6%	14.4%	2.6%	1.3%
Riverside County	639,239	56.1%	38.7%	1.4%	2.8%	1.0%	56.1%	36.2%	4.0%	3.7%
Sacramento County	403,255	64.5%	16.1%	8.8%	10.0%	0.6%	64.5%	25.9%	5.7%	4.0%
San Bernardino County	618,547	58.2%	35.9%	1.1%	3.6%	1.2%	58.2%	34.6%	4.5%	2.7%
San Diego County	936,854	60.6%	28.7%	3.1%	5.5%	2.1%	60.6%	28.8%	6.8%	3.9%
San Francisco County	227,668	61.2%	12.7%	4.9%	19.6%	1.6%	61.2%	28.2%	7.1%	3.5%
San Joaquin County	195,419	54.7%	31.6%	4.2%	9.2%	0.3%	54.7%	33.7%	6.5%	5.1%
San Luis Obispo County	80,673	79.8%	15.9%	1.3%	2.9%	0.1%	79.8%	15.8%	1.9%	2.5%
San Mateo County	169,271	54.1%	24.4%	4.7%	15.5%	1.3%	54.1%	32.7%	6.1%	7.2%
Santa Barbara County	138,689	53.1%	38.2%	2.6%	4.2%	1.9%	53.1%	31.3%	6.4%	9.2%
Santa Clara County	475,069	48.4%	23.4%	7.8%	18.9%	1.4%	48.4%	38.0%	7.3%	6.2%
Santa Cruz County	77,464	57.1%	34.8%	1.7%	5.9%	0.5%	57.1%	32.6%	6.8%	3.4%
Shasta County	43,154	86.8%	6.5%	1.9%	4.7%	0.2%	86.8%	7.6%	2.2%	3.4%
Solano County	114,250	71.2%	21.3%	1.5%	5.9%	0.2%	71.2%	22.4%	3.2%	3.2%
Sonoma County	120,963	68.8%	26.3%	2.4%	1.8%	0.7%	68.8%	24.2%	4.1%	3.0%
Stanislaus County	148,186	56.7%	37.1%	3.0%	1.1%	2.0%	56.7%	33.2%	4.0%	6.1%
Sutter County	23,736	63.1%	24.2%	8.6%	3.3%	0.8%	63.1%	29.2%	4.7%	3.1%
Tulare County	132,184	42.2%	53.1%	1.1%	2.5%	1.1%	42.2%	38.4%	10.8%	8.6%
Ventura County	219,271	55.5%	39.3%	2.2%	2.5%	0.5%	55.5%	32.0%	3.6%	8.8%
Yolo County	72,057	59.9%	21.6%	5.7%	12.3%	0.4%	59.9%	28.4%	8.7%	3.0%

Table G-2: Counties—Language Spoken and English Ability—*Continued*

	Millennial Population 13 to 31	Percent by Language Spoken at Home					Percent Who Speak Only English	Percent by Ability to Speak English		
		English Only	Spanish	Other Indo-European Language	Asian and Pacific Island Language	Other Language		Speak English "Very Well"	Speak English "Well"	Speak English "Not Well" or "Not at All"
Colorado										
Adams County	134,668	72.3%	21.9%	2.5%	2.8%	0.5%	72.3%	19.7%	4.7%	3.3%
Arapahoe County	159,628	74.3%	17.6%	2.8%	3.1%	2.2%	74.3%	19.3%	4.8%	1.6%
Boulder County	93,422	86.2%	8.7%	2.6%	2.3%	0.2%	86.2%	11.8%	1.7%	0.3%
Denver County	198,526	71.9%	21.4%	2.3%	2.5%	2.0%	71.9%	22.0%	2.6%	3.5%
Douglas County	68,342	89.3%	6.2%	1.8%	2.7%	0.1%	89.3%	8.8%	1.3%	0.6%
El Paso County	185,094	88.0%	7.8%	2.1%	1.5%	0.6%	88.0%	9.2%	1.8%	1.0%
Jefferson County	131,936	82.5%	9.0%	4.9%	2.5%	1.0%	82.5%	14.4%	2.3%	0.7%
Larimer County	96,789	89.2%	6.6%	1.8%	1.5%	1.0%	89.2%	8.6%	1.2%	1.1%
Mesa County	38,326	92.9%	6.4%	0.2%	0.4%	0.0%	92.9%	5.8%	0.8%	0.5%
Pueblo County	41,292	84.4%	14.1%	0.9%	0.7%	0.0%	84.4%	10.2%	2.6%	2.8%
Weld County	74,786	76.7%	20.7%	1.1%	0.5%	1.1%	76.7%	18.1%	3.3%	1.9%
Connecticut										
Fairfield County	221,597	68.5%	19.5%	7.9%	3.2%	0.9%	68.5%	20.3%	6.6%	4.6%
Hartford County	221,135	72.0%	17.5%	6.8%	2.9%	0.8%	72.0%	21.1%	4.6%	2.3%
Litchfield County	39,336	90.7%	3.9%	2.4%	1.7%	1.3%	90.7%	7.0%	2.3%	0.1%
Middlesex County	38,088	88.0%	5.9%	5.0%	0.8%	0.3%	88.0%	6.6%	4.6%	0.8%
New Haven County	221,657	75.7%	16.0%	5.0%	2.1%	1.2%	75.7%	18.5%	3.5%	2.3%
New London County	70,256	88.5%	7.9%	1.9%	1.3%	0.3%	88.5%	8.3%	1.7%	1.5%
Tolland County	47,953	88.6%	2.7%	3.8%	3.2%	1.7%	88.6%	8.5%	2.1%	0.8%
Windham County	29,948	84.7%	11.7%	1.9%	1.8%	0.0%	84.7%	7.3%	2.3%	5.8%
Delaware										
Kent County	43,966	90.9%	3.8%	3.5%	0.4%	1.4%	90.9%	8.0%	1.2%	0.0%
New Castle County	148,648	82.3%	9.4%	3.2%	3.6%	1.6%	82.3%	13.0%	3.3%	1.5%
Sussex County	41,386	83.7%	13.5%	2.8%	0.0%	0.0%	83.7%	8.5%	0.8%	7.0%
Florida										
Alachua County	97,705	82.3%	8.0%	3.3%	5.3%	1.1%	82.3%	13.7%	3.3%	0.7%
Bay County	41,608	91.5%	4.3%	1.4%	2.7%	0.0%	91.5%	6.4%	0.4%	1.6%
Brevard County	112,681	89.2%	7.0%	2.3%	1.1%	0.3%	89.2%	8.2%	1.9%	0.7%
Broward County	437,509	62.0%	24.7%	10.5%	1.6%	1.2%	62.0%	30.2%	4.2%	3.7%
Charlotte County	26,086	91.7%	6.2%	1.6%	0.5%	0.0%	91.7%	8.3%	0.0%	0.0%
Citrus County	21,470	96.2%	1.1%	2.8%	0.0%	0.0%	96.2%	2.7%	0.4%	0.7%
Clay County	47,604	89.9%	7.0%	1.3%	1.8%	0.0%	89.9%	9.1%	0.2%	0.7%
Collier County	62,196	56.6%	38.4%	5.0%	0.0%	0.0%	56.6%	32.7%	4.2%	6.4%
Duval County	241,161	86.0%	7.1%	3.3%	2.8%	0.8%	86.0%	10.0%	2.1%	1.9%
Escambia County	86,905	92.6%	2.4%	1.8%	2.4%	0.8%	92.6%	5.8%	1.5%	0.1%
Flagler County	20,146	93.7%	1.7%	4.6%	0.0%	0.0%	93.7%	4.0%	0.8%	1.4%
Hernando County	33,523	89.3%	7.7%	2.2%	0.6%	0.3%	89.3%	8.0%	1.3%	1.4%
Highlands County	17,733	60.8%	37.3%	1.2%	0.5%	0.3%	60.8%	23.6%	9.5%	6.2%
Hillsborough County	347,042	71.6%	22.3%	3.1%	1.9%	1.2%	71.6%	22.0%	3.0%	3.4%
Indian River County	25,303	83.5%	14.3%	1.2%	0.5%	0.5%	83.5%	11.3%	4.8%	0.4%
Lake County	63,882	86.0%	11.7%	1.5%	0.8%	0.0%	86.0%	12.3%	0.8%	0.9%
Lee County	135,429	68.4%	25.8%	5.3%	0.3%	0.2%	68.4%	21.7%	4.1%	5.8%
Leon County	108,999	88.3%	5.7%	3.6%	2.0%	0.4%	88.3%	10.3%	1.0%	0.4%
Manatee County	69,106	80.0%	18.0%	1.1%	0.7%	0.2%	80.0%	9.6%	5.5%	4.9%
Marion County	67,396	84.9%	13.9%	0.1%	1.1%	0.0%	84.9%	12.1%	0.4%	2.6%
Martin County	28,671	76.3%	21.3%	0.7%	1.7%	0.0%	76.3%	8.3%	9.6%	5.7%
Miami-Dade County	676,154	31.1%	59.7%	7.9%	0.7%	0.5%	31.1%	52.1%	9.2%	7.6%
Okaloosa County	55,617	88.6%	8.0%	1.2%	2.2%	0.0%	88.6%	9.1%	1.2%	1.0%
Orange County	372,784	67.1%	24.2%	5.8%	2.3%	0.7%	67.1%	25.4%	3.7%	3.8%
Osceola County	81,886	47.3%	48.7%	1.7%	0.2%	2.0%	47.3%	42.9%	4.6%	5.2%
Palm Beach County	301,478	64.0%	22.3%	11.8%	1.2%	0.6%	64.0%	23.3%	6.6%	6.1%
Pasco County	96,055	83.5%	11.0%	3.7%	1.6%	0.2%	83.5%	14.1%	1.0%	1.4%
Pinellas County	194,471	85.5%	9.2%	2.9%	2.0%	0.4%	85.5%	9.5%	2.3%	2.7%
Polk County	149,776	77.8%	18.2%	2.8%	0.7%	0.5%	77.8%	15.9%	2.1%	4.2%
Santa Rosa County	40,422	96.2%	2.1%	0.2%	1.2%	0.3%	96.2%	2.9%	0.7%	0.1%
Sarasota County	64,933	85.0%	11.3%	0.9%	2.0%	0.8%	85.0%	11.9%	2.7%	0.4%
Seminole County	117,521	81.5%	14.1%	2.4%	1.9%	0.1%	81.5%	14.1%	3.6%	0.9%
St. Johns County	47,111	91.3%	6.3%	1.9%	0.3%	0.1%	91.3%	8.3%	0.3%	0.2%
St. Lucie County	62,007	77.5%	15.6%	4.9%	1.8%	0.1%	77.5%	15.7%	2.6%	4.2%
Sumter County	11,428	92.8%	6.3%	0.8%	0.0%	0.0%	92.8%	7.2%	0.0%	0.0%
Volusia County	109,532	85.4%	10.9%	1.8%	1.2%	0.7%	85.4%	11.6%	2.1%	1.0%
Georgia										
Bartow County	28,669	85.8%	14.2%	0.0%	0.0%	0.0%	85.8%	12.8%	0.0%	1.4%
Bibb County	41,974	94.1%	4.3%	0.4%	0.9%	0.3%	94.1%	4.2%	0.7%	1.0%
Carroll County	32,258	87.4%	9.0%	0.2%	1.8%	1.6%	87.4%	9.8%	1.0%	1.8%
Chatham County	83,341	86.6%	7.7%	3.3%	2.4%	0.0%	86.6%	9.1%	1.9%	2.5%
Cherokee County	51,638	85.6%	12.6%	0.3%	1.6%	0.0%	85.6%	8.6%	4.9%	0.9%
Clarke County	54,062	85.3%	8.7%	3.5%	2.5%	0.1%	85.3%	10.1%	3.1%	1.6%
Clayton County	77,028	76.7%	15.9%	1.7%	3.8%	1.8%	76.7%	15.7%	4.1%	3.5%
Cobb County	187,462	76.8%	15.1%	3.3%	3.0%	1.9%	76.8%	16.9%	2.7%	3.6%
Columbia County	34,495	94.6%	0.9%	1.2%	3.3%	0.0%	94.6%	5.3%	0.1%	0.0%
Coweta County	29,677	89.8%	8.1%	1.8%	0.0%	0.2%	89.8%	3.5%	3.0%	3.6%
DeKalb County	191,237	79.1%	9.6%	4.5%	3.0%	3.7%	79.1%	12.5%	3.9%	4.5%
Dougherty County	28,202	89.8%	8.7%	1.3%	0.2%	0.0%	89.8%	7.0%	1.4%	1.9%
Douglas County	33,135	83.1%	11.3%	2.3%	2.4%	0.9%	83.1%	13.4%	3.3%	0.2%
Fayette County	25,819	80.5%	13.6%	0.7%	5.1%	0.0%	80.5%	17.3%	1.4%	0.8%

Table G-2: Counties—Language Spoken and English Ability—*Continued*

	Millennial Population 13 to 31	Percent by Language Spoken at Home					Percent Who Speak Only English	Percent by Ability to Speak English		
		English Only	Spanish	Other Indo-European Language	Asian and Pacific Island Language	Other Language		Speak English "Very Well"	Speak English "Well"	Speak English "Not Well" or "Not at All"
Georgia—Cont.										
Floyd County	23,869	85.3%	13.4%	0.5%	0.6%	0.3%	85.3%	10.5%	1.5%	2.6%
Forsyth County	42,806	82.0%	11.9%	3.4%	2.8%	0.0%	82.0%	12.6%	2.8%	2.7%
Fulton County	276,052	81.8%	8.6%	4.5%	3.6%	1.4%	81.8%	13.6%	3.1%	1.5%
Gwinnett County	222,876	62.5%	23.0%	5.0%	7.7%	1.8%	62.5%	26.9%	5.3%	5.4%
Hall County	48,065	67.0%	30.7%	1.4%	0.5%	0.5%	67.0%	23.5%	1.7%	7.9%
Henry County	53,473	86.2%	7.3%	4.8%	1.8%	0.0%	86.2%	11.6%	0.9%	1.3%
Houston County	41,887	91.5%	6.9%	1.0%	0.2%	0.3%	91.5%	5.4%	1.8%	1.3%
Lowndes County	40,099	92.0%	5.4%	2.3%	0.3%	0.0%	92.0%	5.7%	1.4%	0.9%
Muscogee County	61,172	86.7%	9.2%	2.8%	0.6%	0.6%	86.7%	8.2%	2.8%	2.2%
Newton County	26,131	86.8%	10.5%	1.1%	1.6%	0.0%	86.8%	6.0%	6.5%	0.7%
Paulding County	35,873	94.9%	2.0%	2.3%	0.7%	0.1%	94.9%	5.1%	0.0%	0.0%
Richmond County	61,951	92.8%	4.1%	0.7%	1.7%	0.7%	92.8%	5.5%	1.1%	0.6%
Whitfield County	26,807	63.5%	34.5%	1.6%	0.4%	0.0%	63.5%	25.7%	4.6%	6.1%
Hawaii										
Hawaii County	44,614	86.5%	0.3%	0.0%	7.4%	5.7%	86.5%	10.1%	3.2%	0.2%
Honolulu County	273,915	76.4%	3.4%	1.4%	16.1%	2.7%	76.4%	13.6%	8.4%	1.7%
Maui County	35,448	78.3%	1.1%	1.6%	12.8%	6.2%	78.3%	12.0%	8.0%	1.7%
Idaho										
Ada County	112,611	89.2%	5.8%	2.9%	1.2%	0.9%	89.2%	7.1%	2.2%	1.5%
Bonneville County	27,965	89.1%	8.1%	1.6%	0.9%	0.4%	89.1%	7.4%	1.6%	1.8%
Canyon County	51,276	80.8%	17.2%	1.4%	0.2%	0.3%	80.8%	13.6%	3.3%	2.3%
Kootenai County	35,356	97.1%	1.3%	1.4%	0.3%	0.0%	97.1%	2.6%	0.3%	0.0%
Illinois										
Champaign County	81,544	79.4%	5.1%	4.0%	9.9%	1.6%	79.4%	13.0%	5.7%	2.0%
Cook County	1,438,037	64.9%	22.9%	6.6%	3.7%	1.9%	64.9%	26.8%	5.3%	3.1%
DeKalb County	38,034	87.6%	8.3%	2.1%	2.0%	0.0%	87.6%	9.7%	1.3%	1.4%
DuPage County	231,656	72.8%	13.1%	10.5%	3.1%	0.6%	72.8%	20.4%	3.9%	3.0%
Kane County	136,039	62.1%	31.9%	2.0%	2.8%	1.2%	62.1%	27.3%	5.6%	5.0%
Kankakee County	27,483	89.5%	8.2%	1.7%	0.1%	0.4%	89.5%	9.5%	0.6%	0.4%
Kendall County	30,275	87.6%	9.3%	0.1%	3.1%	0.0%	87.6%	8.4%	1.5%	2.5%
Lake County	176,831	68.3%	22.7%	5.2%	3.2%	0.7%	68.3%	26.6%	2.8%	2.3%
LaSalle County	26,791	90.6%	6.2%	0.3%	2.9%	0.0%	90.6%	8.5%	0.6%	0.3%
Macon County	26,140	94.5%	3.2%	1.4%	0.3%	0.6%	94.5%	5.2%	0.3%	0.0%
Madison County	67,129	97.2%	1.5%	0.5%	0.5%	0.2%	97.2%	2.3%	0.5%	0.0%
McHenry County	77,110	82.4%	12.3%	4.3%	1.0%	0.0%	82.4%	13.1%	1.7%	2.8%
McLean County	57,998	89.0%	3.0%	3.5%	2.9%	1.6%	89.0%	8.1%	2.8%	0.6%
Peoria County	49,284	89.9%	4.1%	2.2%	3.8%	0.0%	89.9%	7.5%	2.1%	0.6%
Rock Island County	31,517	83.8%	13.4%	2.4%	0.0%	0.4%	83.8%	12.4%	1.5%	2.2%
Sangamon County	46,845	95.5%	1.7%	1.9%	0.5%	0.4%	95.5%	4.2%	0.0%	0.2%
St. Clair County	70,341	94.7%	4.5%	0.0%	0.5%	0.3%	94.7%	4.4%	0.5%	0.4%
Tazewell County	31,845	93.5%	5.0%	0.3%	0.6%	0.5%	93.5%	5.9%	0.4%	0.2%
Will County	168,570	77.2%	15.6%	4.7%	0.9%	1.5%	77.2%	18.2%	2.4%	2.1%
Winnebago County	72,260	84.7%	11.0%	1.6%	2.1%	0.6%	84.7%	11.5%	2.5%	1.3%
Indiana										
Allen County	93,984	89.9%	5.0%	2.5%	1.6%	0.9%	89.9%	5.9%	2.0%	2.1%
Clark County	27,123	96.1%	2.9%	0.2%	0.7%	0.0%	96.1%	3.5%	0.3%	0.0%
Delaware County	39,030	94.1%	1.3%	2.9%	0.4%	1.3%	94.1%	5.2%	0.4%	0.4%
Elkhart County	49,637	77.8%	14.4%	6.9%	0.9%	0.0%	77.8%	17.6%	1.4%	3.3%
Hamilton County	65,540	93.3%	1.9%	3.6%	1.1%	0.0%	93.3%	5.2%	1.4%	0.1%
Hendricks County	39,350	93.9%	5.4%	0.7%	0.0%	0.0%	93.9%	4.3%	1.5%	0.3%
Johnson County	37,878	92.1%	3.3%	2.2%	1.2%	1.2%	92.1%	6.1%	1.4%	0.5%
Lake County	118,901	84.5%	12.0%	1.8%	1.0%	0.7%	84.5%	12.1%	2.2%	1.2%
LaPorte County	27,693	94.0%	4.6%	0.7%	0.7%	0.0%	94.0%	3.0%	0.7%	2.2%
Madison County	31,472	95.6%	4.1%	0.2%	0.0%	0.0%	95.6%	1.9%	2.5%	0.0%
Marion County	259,377	84.5%	10.6%	2.6%	1.1%	1.2%	84.5%	9.3%	2.7%	3.6%
Monroe County	59,193	83.3%	5.1%	4.3%	7.0%	0.3%	83.3%	12.2%	4.2%	0.4%
Porter County	41,176	92.5%	4.5%	1.7%	1.2%	0.1%	92.5%	6.3%	0.6%	0.6%
St. Joseph County	72,054	91.0%	5.5%	1.5%	1.7%	0.2%	91.0%	7.4%	1.3%	0.3%
Tippecanoe County	70,476	82.3%	4.2%	3.6%	8.6%	1.3%	82.3%	10.6%	5.8%	1.3%
Vanderburgh County	47,216	95.4%	0.2%	4.2%	0.0%	0.2%	95.4%	3.7%	0.9%	0.0%
Vigo County	32,766	92.6%	3.6%	0.6%	0.6%	2.6%	92.6%	4.1%	1.5%	1.7%
Iowa										
Black Hawk County	42,469	91.3%	4.6%	3.2%	0.4%	0.5%	91.3%	6.1%	1.9%	0.7%
Dubuque County	24,987	94.4%	1.8%	3.8%	0.0%	0.0%	94.4%	4.5%	0.2%	0.8%
Johnson County	56,779	87.8%	4.4%	4.3%	2.7%	0.8%	87.8%	8.6%	3.2%	0.4%
Linn County	55,429	94.1%	1.6%	2.1%	2.0%	0.2%	94.1%	5.7%	0.2%	0.0%
Polk County	120,544	83.6%	6.3%	3.3%	2.8%	4.0%	83.6%	8.5%	5.4%	2.4%
Pottawattamie County	22,874	95.2%	4.0%	0.8%	0.0%	0.0%	95.2%	3.8%	1.0%	0.0%
Scott County	42,609	94.7%	2.0%	2.0%	0.4%	0.9%	94.7%	3.8%	1.1%	0.3%
Story County	40,969	86.7%	4.1%	0.6%	8.6%	0.0%	86.7%	8.6%	4.5%	0.3%
Woodbury County	29,826	83.4%	14.3%	0.0%	2.3%	0.0%	83.4%	7.7%	7.1%	1.8%
Kansas										
Douglas County	44,291	91.7%	0.8%	0.4%	6.3%	0.9%	91.7%	4.0%	3.1%	1.2%
Johnson County	134,785	87.1%	5.6%	3.4%	2.6%	1.4%	87.1%	10.2%	1.5%	1.2%
Sedgwick County	142,587	85.6%	10.7%	0.8%	2.9%	0.1%	85.6%	11.4%	1.7%	1.3%
Shawnee County	45,819	90.0%	7.5%	1.0%	1.2%	0.3%	90.0%	8.0%	1.3%	0.7%

Table G-2: Counties—Language Spoken and English Ability—*Continued*

	Millennial Population 13 to 31	Percent by Language Spoken at Home					Percent Who Speak Only English	Percent by Ability to Speak English		
		English Only	Spanish	Other Indo-European Language	Asian and Pacific Island Language	Other Language		Speak English "Very Well"	Speak English "Well"	Speak English "Not Well" or "Not at All"
Kansas —Cont.										
Wyandotte County	42,100	70.3%	23.9%	1.5%	3.6%	0.6%	70.3%	20.8%	4.6%	4.3%
Kentucky										
Boone County	30,524	90.3%	6.8%	0.0%	2.9%	0.0%	90.3%	7.6%	0.0%	2.1%
Campbell County	22,819	95.4%	4.6%	0.0%	0.0%	0.0%	95.4%	1.5%	2.9%	0.2%
Daviess County	23,237	97.2%	1.2%	0.2%	0.6%	0.8%	97.2%	2.0%	0.0%	0.8%
Fayette County	92,123	85.3%	8.0%	2.5%	2.6%	1.7%	85.3%	9.6%	2.3%	2.8%
Hardin County	29,502	92.5%	5.8%	1.7%	0.0%	0.0%	92.5%	5.1%	1.6%	0.8%
Jefferson County	192,974	89.8%	5.1%	2.2%	1.3%	1.7%	89.8%	7.3%	1.6%	1.4%
Kenton County	42,375	93.6%	3.9%	1.9%	0.6%	0.0%	93.6%	3.8%	2.6%	0.0%
Warren County	37,886	89.0%	3.6%	5.2%	1.1%	1.0%	89.0%	6.9%	1.5%	2.5%
Louisiana										
Ascension Parish	29,490	94.9%	4.6%	0.4%	0.0%	0.0%	94.9%	5.1%	0.0%	0.0%
Bossier Parish	35,157	93.9%	4.7%	0.9%	0.5%	0.0%	93.9%	3.1%	0.8%	2.2%
Caddo Parish	68,119	96.8%	2.4%	0.5%	0.4%	0.0%	96.8%	1.9%	1.0%	0.4%
Calcasieu Parish	52,204	95.9%	2.4%	1.1%	0.6%	0.0%	95.9%	3.5%	0.5%	0.1%
East Baton Rouge Parish	138,439	90.7%	4.1%	2.2%	2.4%	0.6%	90.7%	6.3%	1.8%	1.2%
Jefferson Parish	112,464	75.9%	15.1%	4.0%	2.8%	2.2%	75.9%	13.4%	3.3%	7.4%
Lafayette Parish	65,892	91.4%	3.1%	5.0%	0.4%	0.1%	91.4%	6.9%	0.8%	0.9%
Lafourche Parish	25,278	93.8%	1.9%	4.0%	0.0%	0.3%	93.8%	5.0%	0.5%	0.7%
Livingston Parish	34,296	97.4%	1.4%	0.3%	0.9%	0.0%	97.4%	2.6%	0.0%	0.0%
Orleans Parish	111,713	90.6%	4.7%	1.4%	2.6%	0.6%	90.6%	5.4%	1.8%	2.1%
Ouachita Parish	43,511	97.7%	1.4%	0.6%	0.3%	0.0%	97.7%	1.4%	0.4%	0.5%
Rapides Parish	35,189	92.6%	4.8%	0.4%	2.1%	0.0%	92.6%	3.7%	2.5%	1.2%
St. Tammany Parish	56,793	95.8%	2.0%	1.3%	0.9%	0.0%	95.8%	3.3%	0.6%	0.3%
Tangipahoa Parish	36,944	91.2%	7.8%	1.0%	0.0%	0.0%	91.2%	4.1%	2.8%	1.9%
Terrebonne Parish	28,956	94.5%	3.8%	0.2%	0.0%	1.6%	94.5%	3.5%	0.0%	2.1%
Maine										
Androscoggin County	26,538	92.7%	1.3%	5.0%	0.5%	0.5%	92.7%	7.3%	0.0%	0.0%
Cumberland County	69,682	89.1%	2.6%	3.4%	3.4%	1.5%	89.1%	8.2%	2.7%	0.0%
Kennebec County	27,602	97.5%	0.5%	1.3%	0.7%	0.0%	97.5%	2.5%	0.0%	0.0%
Penobscot County	39,915	98.4%	0.1%	0.3%	0.9%	0.3%	98.4%	1.5%	0.0%	0.1%
York County	42,942	97.2%	0.8%	1.6%	0.4%	0.0%	97.2%	2.6%	0.2%	0.0%
Maryland										
Anne Arundel County	139,871	85.3%	9.3%	2.4%	2.5%	0.5%	85.3%	10.5%	2.6%	1.6%
Baltimore County	213,682	86.9%	4.2%	4.5%	2.2%	2.3%	86.9%	9.0%	2.8%	1.2%
Carroll County	39,345	93.0%	5.5%	0.9%	0.3%	0.4%	93.0%	4.6%	0.2%	2.3%
Cecil County	25,431	95.6%	1.6%	1.6%	0.7%	0.4%	95.6%	4.4%	0.0%	0.0%
Charles County	38,929	94.4%	2.4%	0.9%	0.2%	2.2%	94.4%	4.8%	0.3%	0.5%
Frederick County	60,348	86.5%	9.0%	1.9%	1.9%	0.6%	86.5%	11.9%	1.5%	0.0%
Harford County	61,759	96.3%	1.7%	1.3%	0.6%	0.2%	96.3%	2.9%	0.6%	0.2%
Howard County	74,492	78.3%	4.9%	5.9%	9.2%	1.7%	78.3%	16.8%	2.2%	2.7%
Montgomery County	237,666	58.9%	18.4%	9.5%	8.1%	5.1%	58.9%	30.7%	5.1%	5.3%
Prince George's County	248,192	78.3%	14.4%	3.0%	2.5%	1.8%	78.3%	13.4%	3.8%	4.5%
St. Mary's County	28,557	93.0%	4.6%	2.3%	0.1%	0.0%	93.0%	3.4%	1.1%	2.5%
Washington County	36,422	90.0%	5.8%	1.3%	2.6%	0.3%	90.0%	8.4%	0.8%	0.8%
Wicomico County	30,975	89.9%	5.1%	2.7%	1.5%	0.7%	89.9%	3.6%	3.5%	3.0%
Massachusetts										
Barnstable County	40,139	89.2%	0.9%	9.4%	0.5%	0.0%	89.2%	7.9%	2.8%	0.2%
Berkshire County	29,440	90.8%	4.5%	2.1%	1.1%	1.4%	90.8%	7.3%	0.7%	1.2%
Bristol County	133,365	84.3%	6.4%	8.6%	0.4%	0.4%	84.3%	11.0%	2.7%	2.0%
Essex County	189,099	71.2%	20.4%	4.9%	2.6%	0.9%	71.2%	21.4%	3.2%	4.2%
Hampden County	130,223	69.7%	21.9%	5.6%	1.2%	1.6%	69.7%	22.4%	5.2%	2.7%
Hampshire County	47,728	90.1%	3.4%	1.8%	4.3%	0.4%	90.1%	7.0%	2.5%	0.4%
Middlesex County	417,893	73.3%	7.5%	10.7%	6.5%	2.1%	73.3%	19.8%	4.6%	2.3%
Norfolk County	167,479	77.5%	4.4%	9.5%	7.0%	1.5%	77.5%	18.2%	3.2%	1.1%
Plymouth County	110,941	86.2%	3.2%	8.7%	1.1%	0.8%	86.2%	10.3%	2.7%	0.8%
Suffolk County	281,869	64.6%	17.4%	10.8%	5.1%	2.1%	64.6%	26.2%	5.3%	3.9%
Worcester County	212,980	76.7%	11.7%	6.1%	3.0%	2.5%	76.7%	16.8%	4.9%	1.6%
Michigan										
Allegan County	26,007	96.9%	3.1%	0.0%	0.0%	0.0%	96.9%	2.7%	0.3%	0.1%
Bay County	26,664	91.1%	1.4%	0.9%	1.8%	4.7%	91.1%	6.7%	0.6%	1.6%
Berrien County	34,333	91.9%	5.6%	1.4%	1.2%	0.0%	91.9%	5.7%	1.3%	1.1%
Calhoun County	31,324	95.5%	2.0%	1.0%	1.4%	0.0%	95.5%	2.9%	0.6%	1.0%
Eaton County	25,521	96.0%	2.2%	0.0%	0.9%	0.9%	96.0%	1.2%	1.6%	1.2%
Genesee County	103,825	97.3%	1.2%	0.8%	0.2%	0.4%	97.3%	2.6%	0.1%	0.0%
Ingham County	101,879	87.6%	2.3%	2.9%	5.0%	2.1%	87.6%	7.2%	4.3%	0.9%
Jackson County	39,344	99.2%	0.4%	0.0%	0.2%	0.2%	99.2%	0.7%	0.1%	0.0%
Kalamazoo County	81,455	91.0%	5.9%	1.7%	1.2%	0.2%	91.0%	7.7%	0.8%	0.5%
Kent County	172,068	88.3%	8.0%	1.7%	1.5%	0.5%	88.3%	7.5%	2.1%	2.1%
Lenawee County	24,357	96.7%	2.2%	1.1%	0.0%	0.0%	96.7%	2.7%	0.3%	0.4%
Livingston County	43,034	97.0%	1.7%	1.0%	0.0%	0.3%	97.0%	2.4%	0.2%	0.5%
Macomb County	202,176	86.8%	2.0%	4.1%	2.1%	5.0%	86.8%	9.7%	1.7%	1.8%
Monroe County	35,012	96.3%	1.8%	1.7%	0.0%	0.3%	96.3%	3.4%	0.2%	0.1%
Muskegon County	40,756	97.1%	1.5%	1.1%	0.1%	0.2%	97.1%	2.6%	0.2%	0.1%
Oakland County	289,984	86.6%	2.9%	4.3%	2.9%	3.2%	86.6%	10.8%	1.9%	0.6%
Ottawa County	78,130	93.0%	4.2%	0.6%	1.5%	0.7%	93.0%	5.2%	0.3%	1.5%

Table G-2: Counties—Language Spoken and English Ability—Continued

	Millennial Population 13 to 31	Percent by Language Spoken at Home					Percent Who Speak Only English	Percent by Ability to Speak English		
		English Only	Spanish	Other Indo-European Language	Asian and Pacific Island Language	Other Language		Speak English "Very Well"	Speak English "Well"	Speak English "Not Well" or "Not at All"
Michigan—Cont.										
Saginaw County	49,901	96.8%	1.4%	0.6%	0.6%	0.6%	96.8%	1.8%	0.7%	0.8%
St. Clair County	37,367	94.6%	4.5%	0.9%	0.0%	0.0%	94.6%	4.5%	0.4%	0.5%
Washtenaw County	119,936	85.4%	3.6%	2.4%	6.5%	2.1%	85.4%	10.7%	2.6%	1.3%
Wayne County	451,782	85.0%	5.2%	2.6%	1.4%	5.9%	85.0%	11.9%	1.5%	1.6%
Minnesota										
Anoka County	84,669	89.6%	4.2%	1.4%	3.3%	1.5%	89.6%	6.4%	2.7%	1.3%
Carver County	23,348	95.5%	2.0%	2.0%	0.5%	0.0%	95.5%	2.7%	1.6%	0.2%
Dakota County	100,432	84.8%	8.2%	0.5%	4.1%	2.3%	84.8%	12.7%	1.8%	0.7%
Hennepin County	331,738	78.2%	7.7%	3.5%	6.0%	4.5%	78.2%	14.6%	4.7%	2.4%
Olmsted County	35,580	86.6%	5.6%	2.1%	2.5%	3.2%	86.6%	11.6%	1.8%	0.0%
Ramsey County	150,591	73.4%	5.3%	1.4%	15.0%	4.9%	73.4%	17.6%	6.1%	3.0%
Scott County	30,250	85.3%	8.2%	0.3%	5.9%	0.2%	85.3%	13.3%	1.0%	0.4%
St. Louis County	53,813	94.1%	2.5%	1.7%	1.2%	0.5%	94.1%	4.7%	0.7%	0.5%
Stearns County	47,873	92.9%	3.0%	0.2%	1.5%	2.4%	92.9%	3.5%	1.6%	2.1%
Washington County	60,484	88.3%	6.0%	0.9%	4.3%	0.6%	88.3%	9.7%	1.5%	0.6%
Wright County	32,651	98.3%	0.0%	1.7%	0.0%	0.0%	98.3%	1.6%	0.1%	0.0%
Mississippi										
DeSoto County	41,523	94.7%	5.1%	0.0%	0.2%	0.0%	94.7%	4.8%	0.5%	0.0%
Harrison County	52,715	90.0%	5.6%	0.2%	4.2%	0.0%	90.0%	7.8%	0.5%	1.7%
Hinds County	74,512	96.9%	1.2%	1.0%	0.6%	0.2%	96.9%	2.1%	0.2%	0.8%
Jackson County	36,512	92.0%	3.1%	0.3%	4.5%	0.0%	92.0%	5.7%	1.7%	0.6%
Madison County	26,202	97.9%	1.8%	0.3%	0.0%	0.0%	97.9%	0.3%	0.4%	1.4%
Rankin County	35,305	96.1%	1.0%	0.2%	1.1%	1.5%	96.1%	1.1%	1.5%	1.3%
Missouri										
Boone County	65,445	92.1%	1.9%	2.4%	3.1%	0.6%	92.1%	5.2%	2.6%	0.0%
Cass County	24,713	98.7%	0.0%	1.3%	0.0%	0.0%	98.7%	1.3%	0.0%	0.0%
Clay County	57,332	93.7%	4.3%	0.5%	0.4%	1.0%	93.7%	4.6%	1.2%	0.4%
Franklin County	23,094	96.0%	4.0%	0.0%	0.0%	0.0%	96.0%	4.0%	0.0%	0.0%
Greene County	88,273	95.3%	2.2%	1.2%	1.0%	0.2%	95.3%	3.0%	1.6%	0.2%
Jackson County	176,380	88.3%	8.6%	1.0%	1.2%	0.8%	88.3%	6.6%	2.8%	2.3%
Jasper County	32,081	93.2%	2.9%	3.0%	0.5%	0.4%	93.2%	6.6%	0.0%	0.2%
Jefferson County	52,424	95.8%	1.6%	1.9%	0.7%	0.0%	95.8%	3.8%	0.4%	0.0%
Platte County	23,767	94.1%	4.8%	0.6%	0.6%	0.0%	94.1%	3.3%	2.6%	0.0%
St. Charles County	88,922	92.4%	3.3%	1.9%	2.4%	0.0%	92.4%	6.2%	1.2%	0.2%
St. Louis County	244,999	91.9%	1.9%	2.6%	2.5%	1.1%	91.9%	6.3%	1.8%	0.0%
Montana										
Flathead County	20,921	98.9%	0.8%	0.1%	0.2%	0.0%	98.9%	0.3%	0.0%	0.8%
Gallatin County	30,983	94.8%	1.5%	1.8%	1.3%	0.6%	94.8%	5.1%	0.0%	0.0%
Missoula County	36,652	97.4%	0.8%	1.6%	0.0%	0.2%	97.4%	1.8%	0.5%	0.2%
Yellowstone County	38,379	95.1%	0.9%	1.5%	0.3%	2.3%	95.1%	4.8%	0.2%	0.0%
Nebraska										
Douglas County	147,156	85.6%	9.9%	1.6%	1.8%	1.1%	85.6%	8.4%	3.6%	2.4%
Lancaster County	95,528	89.0%	3.8%	1.8%	4.4%	1.0%	89.0%	8.0%	1.0%	2.0%
Sarpy County	45,013	91.3%	3.5%	2.5%	0.8%	2.0%	91.3%	5.2%	1.8%	1.7%
Nevada										
Clark County	527,642	62.5%	29.1%	2.2%	4.9%	1.2%	62.5%	29.2%	5.1%	3.2%
Washoe County	113,285	73.6%	20.7%	1.7%	3.4%	0.7%	73.6%	20.8%	3.4%	2.2%
New Hampshire										
Hillsborough County	98,359	86.2%	6.4%	3.9%	2.7%	0.8%	86.2%	9.0%	2.7%	2.1%
Merrimack County	34,531	93.8%	0.9%	5.0%	0.0%	0.3%	93.8%	4.2%	0.9%	1.1%
Rockingham County	64,185	93.7%	1.7%	2.7%	1.2%	0.7%	93.7%	4.3%	1.0%	0.9%
Strafford County	36,919	93.8%	1.7%	2.1%	1.5%	0.9%	93.8%	5.5%	0.2%	0.4%
New Jersey										
Atlantic County	67,058	72.0%	17.1%	7.1%	3.1%	0.7%	72.0%	22.0%	3.1%	2.9%
Bergen County	207,617	56.4%	19.5%	11.1%	10.4%	2.6%	56.4%	36.6%	4.4%	2.6%
Burlington County	108,458	86.9%	6.6%	4.6%	1.2%	0.8%	86.9%	11.1%	1.4%	0.6%
Camden County	130,453	78.9%	13.3%	3.1%	4.1%	0.6%	78.9%	15.1%	3.1%	2.9%
Cape May County	19,280	74.6%	16.5%	7.6%	1.3%	0.0%	74.6%	16.7%	5.7%	3.0%
Cumberland County	41,412	70.9%	24.7%	3.6%	0.8%	0.0%	70.9%	18.8%	4.1%	6.2%
Essex County	204,847	67.2%	20.7%	8.3%	2.1%	1.8%	67.2%	23.2%	5.0%	4.6%
Gloucester County	70,459	92.2%	3.7%	2.2%	1.3%	0.6%	92.2%	6.4%	1.0%	0.4%
Hudson County	196,209	41.2%	37.6%	10.6%	7.1%	3.5%	41.2%	42.2%	9.1%	7.6%
Hunterdon County	28,211	92.1%	5.2%	1.7%	0.7%	0.2%	92.1%	6.4%	0.6%	0.9%
Mercer County	97,275	66.2%	17.8%	8.8%	6.0%	1.1%	66.2%	23.5%	6.3%	3.9%
Middlesex County	211,103	61.6%	17.8%	12.2%	6.5%	1.9%	61.6%	28.8%	4.9%	4.6%
Monmouth County	146,742	82.9%	8.9%	5.4%	2.0%	0.8%	82.9%	10.6%	3.0%	3.5%
Morris County	113,951	75.2%	13.5%	6.3%	3.6%	1.4%	75.2%	20.8%	3.0%	0.9%
Ocean County	125,044	86.5%	8.0%	2.6%	1.0%	1.8%	86.5%	8.5%	2.6%	2.4%
Passaic County	134,168	49.4%	36.8%	7.4%	2.7%	3.7%	49.4%	38.2%	5.5%	6.9%
Somerset County	71,788	74.4%	12.6%	7.6%	4.2%	1.1%	74.4%	20.8%	3.8%	1.0%
Sussex County	32,651	89.9%	5.1%	3.2%	0.0%	1.8%	89.9%	7.9%	0.3%	1.9%
Union County	133,600	52.0%	35.6%	9.2%	1.2%	2.1%	52.0%	35.4%	4.9%	7.8%
Warren County	24,276	91.9%	6.0%	1.3%	0.8%	0.0%	91.9%	6.0%	2.1%	0.0%
New Mexico										
Bernalillo County	187,027	71.7%	24.2%	1.0%	1.6%	1.5%	71.7%	22.6%	3.2%	2.6%

Table G-2: Counties—Language Spoken and English Ability—*Continued*

	Millennial Population 13 to 31	Percent by Language Spoken at Home					Percent Who Speak Only English	Percent by Ability to Speak English		
		English Only	Spanish	Other Indo-European Language	Asian and Pacific Island Language	Other Language		Speak English "Very Well"	Speak English "Well"	Speak English "Not Well" or "Not at All"
New Mexico—Cont.										
Doña Ana County	66,940	43.9%	53.6%	1.1%	0.6%	0.8%	43.9%	46.6%	5.6%	4.0%
San Juan County	32,122	72.0%	13.6%	0.3%	0.2%	13.9%	72.0%	24.4%	0.3%	3.3%
Sandoval County	32,004	72.5%	14.7%	0.1%	0.0%	12.6%	72.5%	25.2%	1.6%	0.6%
Santa Fe County	30,956	60.5%	34.6%	1.7%	1.9%	1.4%	60.5%	28.2%	5.8%	5.5%
New York										
Albany County	89,897	87.8%	5.0%	2.3%	3.3%	1.6%	87.8%	9.3%	2.3%	0.7%
Bronx County	411,710	41.2%	49.7%	4.6%	1.0%	3.4%	41.2%	41.5%	8.3%	9.0%
Broome County	54,701	88.3%	2.6%	3.0%	5.2%	0.9%	88.3%	8.3%	1.8%	1.5%
Chautauqua County	34,497	88.4%	5.8%	4.3%	1.4%	0.1%	88.4%	7.6%	1.1%	2.9%
Dutchess County	78,602	83.7%	10.7%	3.6%	1.9%	0.1%	83.7%	12.3%	1.4%	2.5%
Erie County	243,911	88.3%	4.2%	3.0%	3.0%	1.5%	88.3%	8.8%	1.9%	1.1%
Jefferson County	35,704	92.3%	3.5%	2.9%	0.2%	1.0%	92.3%	6.7%	0.1%	0.8%
Kings County	747,562	55.3%	17.5%	16.7%	7.2%	3.3%	55.3%	29.3%	8.7%	6.7%
Monroe County	199,730	86.2%	6.0%	4.1%	2.6%	1.0%	86.2%	10.8%	2.2%	0.8%
Nassau County	321,177	71.1%	16.9%	7.9%	3.3%	0.9%	71.1%	19.2%	4.7%	5.1%
New York County	484,143	60.9%	22.7%	7.1%	7.2%	2.1%	60.9%	30.6%	5.2%	3.3%
Niagara County	51,204	97.3%	1.1%	0.7%	0.8%	0.1%	97.3%	1.7%	1.0%	0.0%
Oneida County	60,307	86.3%	4.4%	6.7%	1.9%	0.7%	86.3%	8.7%	3.1%	1.9%
Onondaga County	128,807	89.1%	3.5%	3.6%	2.7%	1.1%	89.1%	7.4%	2.8%	0.7%
Ontario County	25,415	85.1%	7.9%	6.3%	0.7%	0.0%	85.1%	11.9%	2.2%	0.8%
Orange County	98,266	74.3%	15.8%	8.0%	0.9%	0.9%	74.3%	17.6%	3.6%	4.5%
Oswego County	32,874	90.6%	5.0%	3.9%	0.6%	0.0%	90.6%	6.8%	1.6%	1.0%
Putnam County	21,691	75.0%	8.2%	13.0%	3.8%	0.0%	75.0%	19.6%	1.8%	3.6%
Queens County	607,326	45.0%	27.0%	14.6%	11.7%	1.8%	45.0%	35.4%	10.8%	8.8%
Rensselaer County	42,068	92.8%	2.9%	1.7%	2.4%	0.3%	92.8%	5.0%	1.6%	0.6%
Richmond County	116,248	71.0%	12.4%	9.6%	4.6%	2.4%	71.0%	25.0%	3.1%	0.8%
Rockland County	81,322	58.4%	18.1%	20.9%	1.2%	1.4%	58.4%	26.4%	7.9%	7.3%
Saratoga County	52,673	91.0%	4.4%	1.4%	2.8%	0.3%	91.0%	7.4%	0.5%	1.2%
Schenectady County	38,971	89.0%	4.6%	4.8%	0.8%	0.8%	89.0%	7.5%	3.6%	0.0%
St. Lawrence County	31,306	87.1%	2.7%	9.6%	0.3%	0.2%	87.1%	11.8%	1.0%	0.0%
Steuben County	21,521	94.6%	0.9%	4.3%	0.1%	0.1%	94.6%	4.1%	1.3%	0.0%
Suffolk County	368,366	75.8%	17.2%	5.0%	1.8%	0.2%	75.8%	15.2%	5.0%	4.0%
Tompkins County	41,515	86.4%	0.7%	2.7%	9.5%	0.7%	86.4%	9.6%	2.6%	1.3%
Ulster County	41,894	86.4%	7.2%	3.6%	2.6%	0.2%	86.4%	9.6%	2.4%	1.6%
Wayne County	20,672	94.2%	3.0%	2.0%	0.6%	0.2%	94.2%	4.3%	0.6%	1.0%
Westchester County	224,469	62.0%	26.6%	6.5%	2.9%	2.0%	62.0%	29.3%	4.6%	4.1%
North Carolina										
Alamance County	38,845	81.1%	14.8%	1.9%	1.7%	0.4%	81.1%	9.9%	6.2%	2.8%
Brunswick County	18,341	93.1%	5.8%	0.7%	0.5%	0.0%	93.1%	3.7%	1.0%	2.2%
Buncombe County	56,215	89.2%	8.5%	1.7%	0.4%	0.1%	89.2%	5.3%	1.5%	4.1%
Burke County	21,087	93.4%	3.9%	0.0%	2.7%	0.0%	93.4%	5.0%	0.8%	0.9%
Cabarrus County	45,822	87.0%	9.5%	1.9%	1.5%	0.1%	87.0%	10.8%	0.6%	1.5%
Catawba County	34,663	83.3%	8.1%	1.3%	7.2%	0.0%	83.3%	11.0%	1.2%	4.5%
Cleveland County	23,149	89.2%	10.3%	0.0%	0.5%	0.0%	89.2%	7.9%	0.2%	2.7%
Craven County	30,089	90.0%	8.5%	0.0%	1.5%	0.0%	90.0%	2.0%	4.6%	3.4%
Cumberland County	104,204	86.8%	9.4%	1.7%	1.6%	0.4%	86.8%	9.4%	2.4%	1.3%
Davidson County	37,301	90.3%	9.0%	0.0%	0.6%	0.0%	90.3%	7.6%	0.6%	1.4%
Durham County	84,607	79.7%	12.3%	2.1%	4.0%	1.8%	79.7%	12.5%	2.1%	5.7%
Forsyth County	92,178	82.9%	13.9%	1.2%	1.7%	0.3%	82.9%	12.8%	1.8%	2.4%
Gaston County	49,851	88.3%	9.7%	0.7%	1.2%	0.1%	88.3%	9.7%	1.6%	0.5%
Guilford County	138,056	85.0%	7.1%	2.3%	4.1%	1.6%	85.0%	9.2%	3.9%	1.9%
Harnett County	34,876	89.1%	9.3%	0.2%	0.8%	0.6%	89.1%	3.9%	2.8%	4.2%
Henderson County	22,375	85.8%	12.3%	0.1%	0.9%	0.9%	85.8%	6.3%	1.0%	6.9%
Iredell County	38,933	88.0%	7.5%	2.2%	2.3%	0.0%	88.0%	7.8%	2.9%	1.4%
Johnston County	42,338	82.6%	16.0%	0.9%	0.4%	0.0%	82.6%	10.8%	3.2%	3.5%
Mecklenburg County	273,009	78.6%	13.5%	3.1%	3.3%	1.5%	78.6%	13.6%	3.2%	4.7%
Moore County	18,946	84.1%	15.1%	0.8%	0.0%	0.0%	84.1%	6.3%	6.8%	2.8%
Nash County	21,825	93.4%	4.4%	0.0%	1.9%	0.3%	93.4%	6.5%	0.1%	0.0%
New Hanover County	59,080	92.3%	4.6%	0.6%	1.2%	1.2%	92.3%	3.8%	0.5%	3.4%
Onslow County	80,099	87.9%	8.8%	2.1%	0.9%	0.4%	87.9%	9.9%	0.8%	1.5%
Orange County	48,311	85.6%	7.8%	3.8%	1.5%	1.3%	85.6%	12.2%	1.5%	0.7%
Pitt County	61,787	91.2%	6.3%	1.2%	1.2%	0.0%	91.2%	7.1%	0.8%	0.9%
Randolph County	31,761	87.1%	12.1%	0.8%	0.0%	0.0%	87.1%	8.6%	2.6%	1.8%
Robeson County	37,370	89.7%	8.6%	1.4%	0.3%	0.0%	89.7%	6.5%	0.5%	3.3%
Rockingham County	19,982	92.6%	7.4%	0.0%	0.0%	0.0%	92.6%	4.6%	0.8%	2.0%
Rowan County	32,181	86.9%	9.7%	1.4%	1.2%	0.8%	86.9%	8.7%	2.3%	2.2%
Union County	50,048	87.8%	9.3%	1.3%	1.5%	0.1%	87.8%	8.2%	1.9%	2.1%
Wake County	258,352	82.0%	9.7%	3.3%	3.2%	1.8%	82.0%	12.7%	2.4%	2.9%
Wayne County	30,990	86.2%	13.1%	0.5%	0.0%	0.2%	86.2%	10.7%	0.6%	2.5%
North Dakota										
Cass County	55,587	87.2%	1.6%	4.7%	3.7%	2.8%	87.2%	9.4%	3.1%	0.2%
Ohio										
Allen County	26,290	97.0%	0.2%	2.7%	0.0%	0.1%	97.0%	2.7%	0.4%	0.0%
Ashtabula County	22,736	95.3%	3.6%	1.1%	0.0%	0.0%	95.3%	4.3%	0.0%	0.4%
Butler County	101,049	91.0%	4.1%	1.9%	1.7%	1.3%	91.0%	5.3%	2.6%	1.1%
Clark County	32,974	93.5%	4.8%	0.6%	0.6%	0.4%	93.5%	4.0%	1.4%	1.1%

Table G-2: Counties—Language Spoken and English Ability—*Continued*

	Millennial Population 13 to 31	Percent by Language Spoken at Home					Percent Who Speak Only English	Percent by Ability to Speak English		
		English Only	Spanish	Other Indo-European Language	Asian and Pacific Island Language	Other Language		Speak English "Very Well"	Speak English "Well"	Speak English "Not Well" or "Not at All"
Ohio—Cont.										
Clermont County	49,166	95.7%	2.3%	1.4%	0.4%	0.2%	95.7%	3.6%	0.7%	0.0%
Columbiana County	23,852	97.1%	2.4%	0.6%	0.0%	0.0%	97.1%	0.6%	0.1%	2.2%
Cuyahoga County	310,929	89.5%	4.1%	3.1%	1.7%	1.7%	89.5%	7.8%	1.9%	0.9%
Delaware County	40,420	91.6%	2.7%	2.4%	1.5%	1.7%	91.6%	6.9%	1.4%	0.0%
Fairfield County	37,806	99.2%	0.4%	0.3%	0.2%	0.0%	99.2%	0.8%	0.0%	0.0%
Franklin County	357,534	86.7%	4.6%	2.8%	3.0%	2.9%	86.7%	8.6%	2.5%	2.3%
Geauga County	20,794	81.9%	1.2%	15.5%	1.3%	0.0%	81.9%	10.8%	6.6%	0.6%
Greene County	48,051	90.0%	1.4%	3.5%	2.8%	2.3%	90.0%	8.8%	0.9%	0.3%
Hamilton County	212,839	90.7%	3.8%	2.9%	1.6%	1.0%	90.7%	6.0%	2.0%	1.3%
Lake County	52,521	91.3%	5.7%	2.4%	0.3%	0.2%	91.3%	4.6%	2.2%	1.8%
Licking County	41,085	95.8%	2.1%	0.2%	2.0%	0.0%	95.8%	3.7%	0.5%	0.0%
Lorain County	71,947	91.5%	5.7%	1.6%	0.3%	0.8%	91.5%	5.0%	0.8%	2.6%
Lucas County	117,034	92.2%	3.6%	1.4%	1.3%	1.5%	92.2%	5.5%	2.0%	0.3%
Mahoning County	54,397	90.4%	4.9%	3.6%	0.8%	0.3%	90.4%	6.3%	2.5%	0.7%
Medina County	39,456	92.1%	3.9%	3.7%	0.3%	0.0%	92.1%	5.6%	1.1%	1.3%
Miami County	25,611	99.5%	0.5%	0.0%	0.0%	0.0%	99.5%	0.5%	0.0%	0.0%
Montgomery County	134,875	94.3%	1.4%	1.9%	1.9%	0.4%	94.3%	3.6%	1.5%	0.6%
Portage County	52,402	90.0%	0.7%	2.1%	3.5%	3.7%	90.0%	4.5%	4.1%	1.5%
Richland County	28,039	94.1%	3.4%	2.6%	0.0%	0.0%	94.1%	5.1%	0.4%	0.4%
Stark County	88,915	96.0%	2.9%	0.5%	0.6%	0.1%	96.0%	3.2%	0.2%	0.6%
Summit County	132,601	92.3%	2.4%	2.8%	1.1%	1.5%	92.3%	3.6%	3.1%	1.0%
Trumbull County	45,225	94.2%	1.6%	3.5%	0.3%	0.4%	94.2%	4.3%	1.5%	0.0%
Tuscarawas County	21,241	95.2%	1.1%	3.7%	0.0%	0.0%	95.2%	3.8%	1.0%	0.0%
Warren County	51,896	91.2%	2.6%	2.0%	2.5%	1.6%	91.2%	6.3%	1.1%	1.4%
Wayne County	28,468	83.0%	2.7%	12.8%	1.5%	0.0%	83.0%	10.3%	6.4%	0.3%
Wood County	40,741	90.8%	3.8%	4.0%	1.4%	0.0%	90.8%	7.6%	1.1%	0.5%
Oklahoma										
Canadian County	28,837	90.1%	6.0%	0.0%	2.6%	1.2%	90.1%	6.6%	2.7%	0.5%
Cleveland County	87,732	90.0%	4.5%	0.4%	3.8%	1.3%	90.0%	6.8%	1.9%	1.3%
Comanche County	40,012	87.8%	9.7%	0.6%	1.4%	0.5%	87.8%	5.6%	2.7%	3.9%
Oklahoma County	204,850	77.8%	17.5%	1.7%	1.9%	1.1%	77.8%	13.7%	4.6%	4.0%
Tulsa County	168,279	85.1%	11.1%	1.3%	2.3%	0.2%	85.1%	9.3%	2.5%	3.2%
Oregon										
Clackamas County	89,541	83.0%	10.3%	3.4%	3.2%	0.2%	83.0%	12.7%	2.1%	2.2%
Deschutes County	37,987	92.0%	3.4%	0.7%	3.9%	0.0%	92.0%	6.8%	1.1%	0.0%
Douglas County	20,735	95.9%	3.9%	0.2%	0.0%	0.0%	95.9%	1.2%	2.6%	0.3%
Jackson County	45,840	87.6%	11.3%	0.6%	0.4%	0.2%	87.6%	10.6%	0.5%	1.3%
Lane County	98,197	86.5%	7.7%	1.6%	3.1%	1.0%	86.5%	11.2%	1.4%	0.9%
Linn County	30,345	87.9%	4.6%	3.4%	3.0%	1.2%	87.9%	9.8%	2.3%	0.0%
Marion County	83,502	68.7%	25.8%	3.8%	0.7%	1.1%	68.7%	24.8%	3.4%	3.1%
Multnomah County	204,543	76.0%	9.9%	7.0%	5.3%	1.8%	76.0%	17.5%	3.2%	3.3%
Washington County	145,345	72.0%	16.0%	4.0%	5.1%	3.0%	72.0%	22.4%	2.9%	2.8%
Yamhill County	24,644	88.3%	9.4%	0.7%	0.1%	1.5%	88.3%	11.7%	0.0%	0.0%
Pennsylvania										
Adams County	24,109	92.0%	6.5%	0.2%	1.3%	0.0%	92.0%	4.0%	4.0%	0.0%
Allegheny County	315,594	90.8%	1.5%	3.5%	2.9%	1.3%	90.8%	6.1%	2.9%	0.2%
Beaver County	37,866	97.5%	1.7%	0.7%	0.1%	0.0%	97.5%	2.0%	0.5%	0.0%
Berks County	106,444	77.4%	19.8%	1.6%	1.1%	0.1%	77.4%	15.7%	4.1%	2.8%
Blair County	29,018	95.7%	2.0%	1.5%	0.0%	0.8%	95.7%	2.9%	0.8%	0.6%
Bucks County	140,107	86.4%	4.5%	5.8%	2.3%	0.9%	86.4%	9.1%	3.2%	1.3%
Butler County	44,871	98.6%	0.2%	0.3%	0.7%	0.2%	98.6%	1.2%	0.2%	0.0%
Cambria County	32,240	99.5%	0.5%	0.0%	0.0%	0.0%	99.5%	0.5%	0.0%	0.0%
Centre County	65,126	87.1%	1.3%	3.0%	6.8%	1.8%	87.1%	8.9%	2.8%	1.2%
Chester County	126,204	86.4%	8.3%	3.2%	1.5%	0.7%	86.4%	7.2%	2.0%	4.5%
Cumberland County	58,745	92.4%	1.9%	3.7%	1.6%	0.4%	92.4%	7.0%	0.5%	0.1%
Dauphin County	63,943	88.5%	4.3%	3.9%	2.4%	0.9%	88.5%	6.0%	3.2%	2.3%
Delaware County	147,156	86.8%	4.4%	5.0%	2.5%	1.4%	86.8%	10.1%	1.6%	1.5%
Erie County	73,987	92.4%	2.4%	3.0%	0.6%	1.7%	92.4%	5.4%	1.5%	0.8%
Fayette County	27,807	97.9%	0.7%	1.0%	0.4%	0.0%	97.9%	1.3%	0.0%	0.7%
Franklin County	34,886	91.0%	7.0%	0.9%	1.0%	0.0%	91.0%	5.2%	0.5%	3.2%
Lackawanna County	52,413	87.9%	6.6%	4.1%	0.2%	1.2%	87.9%	6.7%	3.8%	1.6%
Lancaster County	134,345	78.0%	8.6%	10.4%	1.0%	2.0%	78.0%	15.6%	4.3%	2.1%
Lebanon County	28,438	90.3%	6.7%	2.3%	0.7%	0.0%	90.3%	3.1%	4.4%	2.2%
Lehigh County	86,106	70.2%	21.8%	2.7%	1.9%	3.4%	70.2%	19.2%	8.4%	2.2%
Luzerne County	78,732	86.1%	10.9%	1.5%	1.4%	0.2%	86.1%	9.3%	1.1%	3.5%
Lycoming County	29,371	95.6%	1.2%	3.0%	0.1%	0.0%	95.6%	3.6%	0.7%	0.0%
Mercer County	28,430	93.0%	2.0%	5.0%	0.0%	0.0%	93.0%	4.4%	2.5%	0.1%
Monroe County	42,860	87.0%	4.4%	7.2%	0.5%	0.8%	87.0%	11.5%	1.5%	0.0%
Montgomery County	188,495	87.0%	3.7%	4.0%	3.7%	1.6%	87.0%	10.3%	2.1%	0.7%
Northampton County	72,610	85.5%	8.3%	3.6%	1.8%	0.8%	85.5%	11.4%	1.9%	1.1%
Northumberland County	20,227	90.6%	2.8%	6.3%	0.3%	0.0%	90.6%	7.0%	1.8%	0.6%
Philadelphia County	477,105	78.3%	10.2%	4.3%	5.6%	1.6%	78.3%	15.6%	3.8%	2.3%
Schuylkill County	30,617	95.7%	2.4%	1.1%	0.8%	0.0%	95.7%	2.9%	1.4%	0.0%
Washington County	46,539	97.3%	1.6%	0.9%	0.0%	0.2%	97.3%	2.2%	0.0%	0.5%
Westmoreland County	73,762	95.6%	1.0%	2.2%	1.3%	0.0%	95.6%	3.9%	0.4%	0.1%
York County	102,438	89.6%	7.7%	1.2%	0.3%	1.1%	89.6%	4.7%	2.0%	3.7%

Table G-2: Counties—Language Spoken and English Ability—*Continued*

	Millennial Population 13 to 31	Percent by Language Spoken at Home					Percent Who Speak Only English	Percent by Ability to Speak English		
		English Only	Spanish	Other Indo-European Language	Asian and Pacific Island Language	Other Language		Speak English "Very Well"	Speak English "Well"	Speak English "Not Well" or "Not at All"
Rhode Island										
Kent County	35,016	94.1%	2.2%	2.1%	1.1%	0.4%	94.1%	4.9%	0.7%	0.2%
Providence County	178,704	64.6%	23.9%	7.0%	3.8%	0.8%	64.6%	29.3%	2.9%	3.2%
Washington County	32,924	95.5%	1.8%	2.2%	0.0%	0.6%	95.5%	4.2%	0.2%	0.1%
South Carolina										
Aiken County	40,228	95.8%	3.5%	0.7%	0.0%	0.0%	95.8%	2.8%	0.7%	0.7%
Anderson County	45,159	95.9%	2.2%	1.1%	0.3%	0.5%	95.9%	3.3%	0.7%	0.2%
Beaufort County	37,996	83.1%	13.8%	2.3%	0.8%	0.0%	83.1%	11.5%	2.6%	2.8%
Berkeley County	54,189	90.4%	7.1%	1.2%	1.2%	0.2%	90.4%	6.0%	1.7%	1.8%
Charleston County	105,818	91.7%	6.2%	0.8%	0.7%	0.6%	91.7%	5.0%	1.6%	1.7%
Dorchester County	38,082	93.5%	5.2%	0.6%	0.7%	0.0%	93.5%	2.8%	0.7%	3.0%
Florence County	34,871	95.7%	2.2%	1.0%	0.3%	0.8%	95.7%	3.4%	0.9%	0.0%
Greenville County	124,317	86.8%	10.0%	0.4%	1.8%	1.0%	86.8%	9.0%	1.6%	2.6%
Horry County	64,666	92.0%	6.6%	1.0%	0.4%	0.1%	92.0%	4.4%	1.8%	1.8%
Lexington County	68,505	92.0%	4.8%	1.6%	1.5%	0.1%	92.0%	5.6%	1.1%	1.3%
Orangeburg County	23,271	92.3%	6.0%	0.0%	1.6%	0.1%	92.3%	5.1%	1.2%	1.4%
Pickens County	38,978	91.4%	5.2%	0.8%	2.7%	0.0%	91.4%	3.3%	2.7%	2.6%
Richland County	131,291	93.4%	4.3%	1.3%	0.8%	0.2%	93.4%	4.4%	1.0%	1.1%
Spartanburg County	76,183	86.4%	8.1%	2.9%	2.1%	0.6%	86.4%	9.9%	2.8%	0.9%
Sumter County	29,711	90.8%	7.7%	1.5%	0.0%	0.0%	90.8%	7.0%	0.4%	1.9%
York County	57,893	91.8%	3.8%	3.2%	1.1%	0.1%	91.8%	6.8%	1.3%	0.1%
South Dakota										
Minnehaha County	50,232	87.9%	5.2%	3.3%	2.0%	1.6%	87.9%	8.4%	2.2%	1.5%
Pennington County	25,155	96.4%	1.3%	0.7%	1.0%	0.6%	96.4%	2.1%	0.5%	1.0%
Tennessee										
Blount County	28,615	96.9%	3.0%	0.0%	0.0%	0.1%	96.9%	1.0%	1.4%	0.6%
Bradley County	25,327	92.7%	5.5%	1.8%	0.0%	0.0%	92.7%	3.0%	2.8%	1.5%
Davidson County	192,958	82.2%	10.2%	2.5%	1.8%	3.3%	82.2%	12.0%	2.7%	3.2%
Hamilton County	87,443	91.4%	5.7%	1.6%	1.1%	0.1%	91.4%	4.8%	1.0%	2.7%
Knox County	124,022	90.6%	3.7%	2.3%	2.7%	0.8%	90.6%	6.0%	2.3%	1.1%
Madison County	25,432	95.8%	2.2%	0.2%	1.8%	0.0%	95.8%	4.1%	0.1%	0.0%
Montgomery County	61,480	87.4%	7.6%	1.3%	1.8%	1.9%	87.4%	10.6%	1.5%	0.4%
Rutherford County	85,492	87.6%	7.8%	1.0%	2.3%	1.4%	87.6%	9.6%	1.0%	1.9%
Sevier County	20,636	90.5%	5.1%	4.3%	0.0%	0.0%	90.5%	6.8%	1.0%	1.7%
Shelby County	260,771	90.4%	6.1%	0.9%	1.3%	1.3%	90.4%	6.0%	1.6%	2.0%
Sullivan County	33,755	95.8%	2.9%	1.4%	0.0%	0.0%	95.8%	3.8%	0.2%	0.2%
Sumner County	41,227	88.5%	4.8%	3.9%	2.1%	0.8%	88.5%	9.5%	1.1%	1.0%
Washington County	33,420	95.2%	3.8%	0.8%	0.2%	0.0%	95.2%	2.7%	0.9%	1.3%
Williamson County	42,263	95.0%	1.6%	1.8%	0.6%	1.0%	95.0%	4.2%	0.8%	0.0%
Wilson County	29,571	98.6%	1.4%	0.0%	0.0%	0.0%	98.6%	1.0%	0.4%	0.0%
Texas										
Bell County	102,974	85.2%	13.1%	1.1%	0.4%	0.3%	85.2%	10.6%	3.3%	1.0%
Bexar County	529,963	64.6%	31.6%	1.3%	1.5%	1.0%	64.6%	28.1%	4.3%	3.0%
Bowie County	24,613	95.5%	4.2%	0.0%	0.0%	0.3%	95.5%	3.2%	0.0%	1.3%
Brazoria County	87,769	69.4%	24.5%	1.1%	3.2%	1.8%	69.4%	24.2%	5.0%	1.4%
Brazos County	93,443	77.7%	14.9%	3.4%	3.6%	0.5%	77.7%	16.5%	4.2%	1.6%
Cameron County	117,741	22.3%	77.0%	0.5%	0.2%	0.0%	22.3%	62.7%	9.6%	5.4%
Collin County	203,054	77.6%	10.8%	5.6%	5.1%	0.9%	77.6%	17.7%	2.6%	2.1%
Comal County	27,155	79.7%	19.8%	0.5%	0.0%	0.0%	79.7%	14.6%	2.0%	3.7%
Dallas County	694,588	53.7%	39.5%	2.2%	3.1%	1.5%	53.7%	29.2%	9.5%	7.6%
Denton County	200,086	76.0%	16.1%	3.5%	3.9%	0.6%	76.0%	18.3%	3.2%	2.5%
Ector County	45,187	48.9%	49.0%	1.3%	0.4%	0.3%	48.9%	39.7%	5.8%	5.6%
El Paso County	246,978	30.9%	67.8%	0.2%	0.8%	0.2%	30.9%	48.9%	14.8%	5.4%
Ellis County	41,068	78.1%	18.7%	1.4%	0.8%	1.0%	78.1%	14.4%	5.8%	1.7%
Fort Bend County	158,317	65.1%	20.5%	6.8%	6.3%	1.4%	65.1%	28.4%	3.3%	3.2%
Galveston County	78,839	79.5%	16.9%	2.6%	1.0%	0.1%	79.5%	16.7%	1.8%	2.1%
Grayson County	30,811	83.3%	13.5%	1.3%	1.9%	0.0%	83.3%	12.5%	0.4%	3.8%
Gregg County	33,454	79.9%	19.4%	0.0%	0.1%	0.5%	79.9%	15.1%	1.7%	3.3%
Guadalupe County	35,549	80.0%	16.8%	0.9%	2.3%	0.0%	80.0%	17.5%	0.8%	1.8%
Harris County	1,238,541	54.0%	38.4%	2.7%	3.9%	1.1%	54.0%	31.0%	7.6%	7.4%
Hays County	58,556	80.6%	17.0%	1.1%	0.3%	1.0%	80.6%	13.3%	4.6%	1.5%
Hidalgo County	240,329	12.9%	86.3%	0.0%	0.8%	0.0%	12.9%	70.3%	5.8%	10.9%
Jefferson County	70,230	72.7%	22.5%	1.9%	2.2%	0.6%	72.7%	19.7%	4.7%	2.8%
Johnson County	38,847	80.8%	17.8%	0.9%	0.5%	0.0%	80.8%	13.7%	0.7%	4.7%
Kaufman County	25,319	79.3%	20.1%	0.0%	0.6%	0.0%	79.3%	15.6%	3.1%	2.0%
Lubbock County	99,238	76.8%	19.1%	1.9%	1.5%	0.6%	76.8%	19.7%	2.0%	1.5%
McLennan County	71,146	78.3%	17.1%	1.4%	3.1%	0.0%	78.3%	13.2%	6.8%	1.8%
Midland County	43,594	75.8%	23.6%	0.0%	0.4%	0.1%	75.8%	19.0%	2.7%	2.5%
Montgomery County	121,769	78.0%	20.2%	1.4%	0.5%	0.0%	78.0%	15.6%	2.8%	3.6%
Nueces County	95,902	68.8%	28.4%	1.5%	1.1%	0.3%	68.8%	27.1%	2.3%	1.8%
Parker County	29,995	91.3%	8.7%	0.0%	0.0%	0.0%	91.3%	4.7%	1.1%	2.9%
Potter County	32,810	65.2%	29.5%	0.0%	2.8%	2.5%	65.2%	22.9%	5.6%	6.4%
Randall County	34,237	82.5%	12.6%	1.3%	1.1%	2.5%	82.5%	11.3%	4.2%	2.0%
Smith County	57,788	75.6%	20.9%	1.9%	0.0%	1.6%	75.6%	17.8%	4.0%	2.6%
Tarrant County	528,418	69.8%	23.6%	2.8%	2.6%	1.2%	69.8%	21.7%	4.1%	4.4%
Taylor County	43,355	82.9%	12.1%	2.7%	1.1%	1.3%	82.9%	15.1%	0.6%	1.5%

Table G-2: Counties—Language Spoken and English Ability—*Continued*

	Millennial Population 13 to 31	Percent by Language Spoken at Home					Percent Who Speak Only English	Percent by Ability to Speak English		
		English Only	Spanish	Other Indo-European Language	Asian and Pacific Island Language	Other Language		Speak English "Very Well"	Speak English "Well"	Speak English "Not Well" or "Not at All"
Texas—Cont.										
Tom Green County	34,346	77.3%	22.0%	0.7%	0.0%	0.0%	77.3%	20.9%	1.4%	0.4%
Travis County	344,597	67.7%	24.6%	2.6%	4.3%	0.9%	67.7%	22.4%	3.9%	6.0%
Webb County	79,350	11.3%	88.7%	0.0%	0.0%	0.0%	11.3%	67.4%	13.1%	8.2%
Wichita County	40,384	87.3%	10.2%	1.2%	0.9%	0.4%	87.3%	8.9%	3.3%	0.5%
Williamson County	115,744	76.9%	16.9%	2.7%	2.5%	0.9%	76.9%	18.6%	2.2%	2.4%
Utah										
Cache County	43,131	83.9%	10.7%	3.0%	2.3%	0.1%	83.9%	11.1%	1.1%	3.9%
Davis County	90,315	92.9%	3.2%	1.2%	2.3%	0.3%	92.9%	5.9%	1.1%	0.1%
Salt Lake County	315,374	77.6%	15.2%	2.5%	3.5%	1.3%	77.6%	18.1%	2.3%	2.1%
Utah County	197,950	86.3%	8.5%	2.9%	1.9%	0.4%	86.3%	10.5%	1.6%	1.6%
Washington County	36,461	94.6%	5.0%	0.4%	0.0%	0.0%	94.6%	4.8%	0.0%	0.5%
Weber County	66,208	89.5%	9.3%	0.3%	0.9%	0.0%	89.5%	8.2%	1.4%	1.0%
Vermont										
Chittenden County	49,483	93.9%	0.3%	3.2%	1.5%	1.0%	93.9%	3.5%	1.2%	1.3%
Virginia										
Albemarle County	28,786	92.6%	2.3%	1.3%	3.0%	0.7%	92.6%	5.1%	1.0%	1.3%
Arlington County	73,199	71.7%	16.1%	5.4%	4.3%	2.5%	71.7%	25.8%	1.9%	0.7%
Chesterfield County	82,105	87.9%	8.2%	2.0%	1.8%	0.1%	87.9%	9.6%	1.8%	0.7%
Fairfax County	279,011	60.9%	14.7%	8.9%	10.3%	5.2%	60.9%	30.4%	5.7%	3.0%
Hanover County	23,207	95.2%	2.9%	1.1%	0.4%	0.4%	95.2%	3.9%	0.7%	0.2%
Henrico County	79,944	80.5%	6.5%	3.9%	6.7%	2.3%	80.5%	13.7%	3.1%	2.6%
Loudoun County	80,007	72.9%	12.1%	8.9%	5.1%	1.0%	72.9%	23.5%	3.1%	0.5%
Montgomery County	44,141	93.5%	1.4%	1.5%	2.4%	1.2%	93.5%	3.5%	2.0%	1.0%
Prince William County	113,001	66.0%	21.5%	5.5%	2.4%	4.6%	66.0%	27.0%	2.4%	4.6%
Roanoke County	20,674	95.6%	2.6%	0.4%	1.0%	0.5%	95.6%	3.1%	0.9%	0.4%
Spotsylvania County	32,146	93.4%	4.2%	0.4%	2.0%	0.0%	93.4%	3.8%	1.6%	1.3%
Stafford County	38,219	88.4%	5.8%	1.9%	1.8%	2.1%	88.4%	8.8%	1.6%	1.2%
Washington										
Benton County	46,067	69.0%	27.4%	3.4%	0.2%	0.0%	69.0%	21.9%	5.8%	3.3%
Clark County	105,849	83.3%	6.2%	8.4%	1.4%	0.7%	83.3%	13.6%	1.7%	1.4%
Cowlitz County	23,187	86.7%	11.7%	0.6%	1.0%	0.0%	86.7%	7.3%	2.1%	3.8%
Grant County	25,201	73.1%	24.2%	2.3%	0.4%	0.0%	73.1%	18.0%	3.7%	5.2%
King County	531,505	70.6%	8.9%	6.8%	10.5%	3.3%	70.6%	21.5%	5.2%	2.8%
Kitsap County	65,185	95.2%	2.8%	0.8%	1.1%	0.0%	95.2%	3.9%	0.9%	0.0%
Pierce County	221,284	83.7%	7.4%	3.3%	4.9%	0.7%	83.7%	12.0%	3.0%	1.3%
Skagit County	27,206	83.6%	9.4%	4.2%	2.3%	0.5%	83.6%	11.9%	3.9%	0.6%
Snohomish County	184,410	78.8%	7.7%	6.9%	5.8%	0.7%	78.8%	17.0%	2.5%	1.7%
Spokane County	133,544	90.7%	2.4%	3.3%	1.9%	1.7%	90.7%	5.4%	3.0%	0.9%
Thurston County	70,438	83.1%	7.7%	2.3%	6.1%	0.8%	83.1%	12.7%	1.9%	2.4%
Whatcom County	62,149	86.8%	7.0%	5.7%	0.4%	0.1%	86.8%	10.5%	1.9%	0.7%
Yakima County	65,994	47.3%	51.0%	0.5%	0.6%	0.7%	47.3%	42.1%	4.8%	5.9%
West Virginia										
Berkeley County	26,793	94.6%	4.0%	0.9%	0.5%	0.0%	94.6%	3.3%	2.0%	0.0%
Cabell County	27,010	98.1%	0.5%	1.4%	0.0%	0.0%	98.1%	1.8%	0.0%	0.1%
Kanawha County	44,551	97.8%	0.7%	1.1%	0.3%	0.2%	97.8%	1.0%	1.2%	0.0%
Monongalia County	41,965	93.2%	2.2%	2.9%	0.2%	1.5%	93.2%	4.9%	1.5%	0.4%
Wisconsin										
Brown County	64,640	86.4%	8.4%	1.7%	3.1%	0.4%	86.4%	10.1%	2.5%	0.9%
Dane County	157,015	84.8%	7.5%	1.0%	6.6%	0.1%	84.8%	10.0%	2.7%	2.6%
Eau Claire County	33,956	93.8%	1.5%	2.4%	2.3%	0.0%	93.8%	4.8%	0.9%	0.5%
Fond du Lac County	22,865	91.8%	5.5%	1.4%	1.2%	0.2%	91.8%	5.3%	0.4%	2.6%
Kenosha County	42,737	87.8%	10.0%	0.8%	1.4%	0.0%	87.8%	7.8%	1.6%	2.8%
La Crosse County	37,898	85.9%	4.3%	0.6%	9.1%	0.2%	85.9%	4.8%	6.7%	2.6%
Marathon County	31,554	88.0%	3.9%	0.3%	7.9%	0.0%	88.0%	6.3%	4.3%	1.4%
Milwaukee County	275,711	82.4%	11.4%	2.1%	3.2%	0.9%	82.4%	11.9%	2.8%	2.9%
Outagamie County	44,856	89.4%	5.8%	1.0%	3.6%	0.2%	89.4%	8.8%	1.5%	0.4%
Racine County	48,379	89.6%	9.5%	0.7%	0.1%	0.0%	89.6%	6.2%	1.5%	2.7%
Rock County	39,734	92.2%	6.9%	0.2%	0.7%	0.0%	92.2%	6.0%	1.3%	0.6%
Sheboygan County	25,686	81.9%	9.0%	1.1%	8.0%	0.0%	81.9%	12.2%	2.2%	3.6%
Walworth County	27,115	80.3%	12.3%	7.4%	0.0%	0.0%	80.3%	7.8%	7.2%	4.6%
Washington County	28,174	89.3%	6.1%	4.6%	0.0%	0.0%	89.3%	9.7%	0.8%	0.2%
Waukesha County	85,418	89.8%	5.8%	2.3%	2.2%	0.0%	89.8%	8.0%	1.6%	0.7%
Winnebago County	46,883	93.9%	3.2%	0.9%	2.0%	0.0%	93.9%	4.6%	1.1%	0.3%
Wyoming										
Laramie County	25,613	91.9%	5.0%	0.4%	2.5%	0.1%	91.9%	5.4%	1.5%	1.1%

Table G-3: Places—Language Spoken and English Ability

	Millennial Population 13 to 31	Percent by Language Spoken at Home					Percent Who Speak Only English	Percent by Ability to Speak English		
		English Only	Spanish	Other Indo-European Language	Asian and Pacific Island Language	Other Language		Speak English "Very Well"	Speak English "Well"	Speak English "Not Well" or "Not at All"
Alabama										
Birmingham city	62,699	93.2%	4.3%	1.6%	0.7%	0.2%	93.2%	2.2%	3.3%	1.3%
Huntsville city	52,004	91.5%	6.0%	0.8%	1.2%	0.4%	91.5%	3.7%	2.8%	1.9%
Mobile city	52,173	94.1%	2.7%	1.1%	1.4%	0.7%	94.1%	4.1%	1.2%	0.5%
Montgomery city	58,994	95.8%	3.4%	0.4%	0.3%	0.2%	95.8%	1.1%	1.0%	2.1%
Tuscaloosa city	39,763	96.0%	1.9%	1.1%	1.0%	0.0%	96.0%	2.3%	0.9%	0.9%
Alaska										
Anchorage municipality	89,088	88.0%	2.9%	2.7%	4.2%	2.2%	88.0%	9.3%	2.3%	0.4%
Arizona										
Chandler city	65,956	76.1%	19.4%	1.0%	3.0%	0.6%	76.1%	19.6%	2.2%	2.0%
Glendale city	64,873	67.6%	26.7%	1.6%	1.0%	3.1%	67.6%	26.7%	1.8%	3.9%
Mesa city	124,304	76.7%	20.8%	0.7%	1.1%	0.8%	76.7%	18.1%	2.2%	3.1%
Peoria city	38,091	75.2%	18.8%	1.7%	3.4%	0.9%	75.2%	20.7%	3.8%	0.3%
Phoenix city	420,298	61.0%	34.0%	2.0%	1.7%	1.2%	61.0%	29.8%	4.3%	4.8%
Scottsdale city	49,969	84.5%	9.5%	3.1%	1.9%	1.1%	84.5%	12.8%	2.2%	0.5%
Surprise city	21,496	84.4%	11.5%	1.1%	3.1%	0.0%	84.4%	13.4%	0.7%	1.5%
Tempe city	74,507	71.9%	16.1%	3.3%	5.6%	3.1%	71.9%	20.6%	5.2%	2.3%
Tucson city	164,774	65.9%	28.1%	1.3%	3.2%	1.5%	65.9%	28.4%	3.4%	2.3%
Yuma city	27,868	45.0%	54.8%	0.0%	0.0%	0.2%	45.0%	43.0%	3.3%	8.8%
Arkansas										
Little Rock city	52,430	91.6%	5.5%	1.4%	1.5%	0.0%	91.6%	4.9%	1.8%	1.7%
California										
Anaheim city	95,980	41.4%	45.5%	1.7%	9.9%	1.5%	41.4%	47.6%	6.9%	4.1%
Antioch city	31,631	64.6%	26.1%	5.3%	2.6%	1.4%	64.6%	29.9%	1.6%	3.9%
Bakersfield city	107,664	55.5%	39.6%	2.2%	0.6%	2.1%	55.5%	34.8%	4.3%	5.5%
Berkeley city	48,955	66.3%	6.9%	7.9%	17.0%	1.9%	66.3%	24.8%	7.2%	1.7%
Burbank city	23,393	54.3%	20.9%	14.7%	8.3%	1.8%	54.3%	39.8%	3.8%	2.1%
Carlsbad city	22,855	79.7%	10.2%	5.4%	4.7%	0.0%	79.7%	17.3%	3.0%	0.0%
Carson city	25,511	48.5%	35.5%	1.1%	12.4%	2.5%	48.5%	42.7%	5.3%	3.5%
Chula Vista city	71,383	44.1%	51.1%	1.5%	2.9%	0.3%	44.1%	50.2%	4.4%	1.2%
Clovis city	26,910	79.4%	9.2%	5.6%	5.6%	0.2%	79.4%	17.0%	3.3%	0.2%
Compton city	29,029	26.3%	72.5%	0.0%	1.2%	0.0%	26.3%	60.5%	6.8%	6.4%
Concord city	31,725	74.2%	18.0%	2.5%	5.3%	0.0%	74.2%	19.5%	4.6%	1.6%
Corona city	46,013	60.7%	30.6%	2.8%	4.2%	1.7%	60.7%	34.2%	4.4%	0.7%
Costa Mesa city	33,705	66.9%	19.5%	1.6%	9.9%	2.0%	66.9%	26.1%	1.5%	5.4%
Daly City city	30,077	52.6%	18.7%	3.7%	23.4%	1.6%	52.6%	34.4%	5.1%	7.9%
Downey city	35,471	31.4%	64.4%	0.3%	3.1%	0.8%	31.4%	63.1%	2.9%	2.6%
El Cajon city	30,019	71.4%	15.0%	3.5%	1.2%	8.8%	71.4%	18.3%	5.7%	4.6%
El Monte city	30,902	11.4%	70.8%	0.0%	17.7%	0.0%	11.4%	48.0%	27.2%	13.4%
Elk Grove city	42,148	68.5%	7.6%	8.7%	14.9%	0.3%	68.5%	23.9%	5.0%	2.6%
Escondido city	44,106	46.8%	50.6%	0.6%	2.0%	0.0%	46.8%	30.3%	11.4%	11.5%
Fairfield city	34,335	65.1%	27.2%	2.8%	4.7%	0.2%	65.1%	26.8%	4.5%	3.6%
Fontana city	60,471	37.2%	55.5%	0.8%	5.0%	1.5%	37.2%	49.2%	9.6%	4.0%
Fremont city	51,789	47.7%	9.5%	16.5%	25.0%	1.3%	47.7%	44.8%	6.3%	1.2%
Fresno city	150,965	61.7%	25.2%	3.3%	9.5%	0.2%	61.7%	27.5%	6.2%	4.6%
Fullerton city	44,549	51.4%	31.3%	3.0%	13.9%	0.4%	51.4%	32.6%	9.9%	6.1%
Garden Grove city	46,235	29.0%	43.8%	0.9%	25.9%	0.3%	29.0%	56.7%	6.1%	8.1%
Glendale city	47,236	35.9%	16.8%	36.2%	9.4%	1.8%	35.9%	49.2%	10.7%	4.2%
Hayward city	42,182	48.7%	31.4%	5.3%	13.0%	1.5%	48.7%	33.6%	7.5%	10.2%
Hesperia city	55,942	72.7%	23.6%	0.1%	3.4%	0.1%	72.7%	22.2%	2.5%	2.6%
Inglewood city	31,386	31.6%	62.4%	1.8%	0.9%	3.3%	31.6%	52.4%	10.6%	5.5%
Irvine city	70,736	64.0%	5.3%	7.0%	20.4%	3.3%	64.0%	27.0%	6.6%	2.3%
Jurupa Valley city	29,796	44.6%	49.1%	0.3%	4.6%	1.4%	44.6%	44.7%	8.2%	2.6%
Lancaster city	44,656	84.2%	13.0%	0.4%	2.0%	0.4%	84.2%	12.6%	1.5%	1.8%
Long Beach city	132,264	50.7%	39.5%	1.7%	8.0%	0.1%	50.7%	41.4%	4.6%	3.3%
Los Angeles city	1,105,809	38.9%	47.4%	5.6%	6.8%	1.3%	38.9%	45.8%	7.9%	7.4%
Mission Viejo city	21,020	78.2%	14.5%	4.3%	2.5%	0.4%	78.2%	17.7%	3.2%	0.8%
Modesto city	59,831	65.5%	29.0%	1.5%	2.3%	1.7%	65.5%	26.7%	2.9%	4.9%
Moreno Valley city	65,038	47.2%	47.3%	1.4%	2.7%	1.4%	47.2%	46.9%	2.1%	3.8%
Murrieta city	29,276	78.9%	17.0%	0.6%	3.4%	0.0%	78.9%	17.9%	0.5%	2.7%
Norwalk city	29,652	32.9%	61.2%	0.4%	4.9%	0.7%	32.9%	55.4%	7.4%	4.3%
Oakland city	106,839	59.2%	25.6%	2.9%	10.5%	1.8%	59.2%	26.9%	6.0%	7.9%
Oceanside city	44,351	79.5%	15.7%	1.7%	2.3%	0.8%	79.5%	12.6%	5.5%	2.4%
Ontario city	48,481	46.1%	49.8%	0.9%	2.6%	0.7%	46.1%	45.1%	4.6%	4.3%
Orange city	40,584	58.2%	36.8%	2.2%	2.6%	0.2%	58.2%	27.8%	5.7%	8.3%
Oxnard city	63,365	33.9%	62.4%	1.3%	2.1%	0.3%	33.9%	44.3%	3.8%	18.1%
Palmdale city	45,149	65.7%	33.2%	0.4%	0.5%	0.2%	65.7%	29.5%	3.1%	1.7%
Pasadena city	40,866	52.6%	29.8%	5.3%	11.2%	1.1%	52.6%	39.5%	3.5%	4.4%
Pomona city	47,598	33.7%	57.8%	0.5%	7.5%	0.5%	33.7%	53.1%	5.6%	7.7%
Rancho Cucamonga city	48,096	71.0%	17.5%	2.9%	4.2%	4.4%	71.0%	23.5%	3.1%	2.4%
Redding city	24,640	85.2%	7.3%	2.5%	5.0%	0.0%	85.2%	8.2%	3.4%	3.2%
Rialto city	30,933	44.5%	51.2%	3.6%	0.0%	0.8%	44.5%	48.6%	5.7%	1.2%
Richmond city	30,165	35.2%	47.3%	2.5%	11.5%	3.5%	35.2%	34.7%	12.1%	18.1%
Riverside city	100,148	58.9%	33.5%	1.2%	5.4%	0.9%	58.9%	34.9%	3.4%	2.7%
Roseville city	32,207	82.4%	8.8%	4.1%	2.6%	2.1%	82.4%	14.5%	2.7%	0.4%
Sacramento city	134,447	60.2%	20.7%	5.6%	13.0%	0.5%	60.2%	27.1%	6.2%	6.5%

Table G-3: Places—Language Spoken and English Ability—*Continued*

	Millennial Population 13 to 31	Percent by Language Spoken at Home					Percent Who Speak Only English	Percent by Ability to Speak English		
		English Only	Spanish	Other Indo-European Language	Asian and Pacific Island Language	Other Language		Speak English "Very Well"	Speak English "Well"	Speak English "Not Well" or "Not at All"
California—Cont.										
Salinas city	47,404	34.3%	62.4%	0.1%	3.1%	0.0%	34.3%	37.3%	8.1%	20.3%
San Bernardino city	67,085	46.5%	49.5%	0.7%	3.1%	0.2%	46.5%	43.0%	5.3%	5.2%
San Buenaventura (Ventura) city	28,078	65.5%	26.2%	5.2%	3.0%	0.0%	65.5%	28.6%	4.3%	1.6%
San Diego city	412,816	59.4%	25.3%	4.0%	9.1%	2.3%	59.4%	31.7%	6.3%	2.6%
San Francisco city	216,580	60.9%	12.6%	5.0%	19.8%	1.7%	60.9%	28.3%	7.2%	3.6%
San Jose city	250,499	45.8%	27.8%	5.9%	18.9%	1.6%	45.8%	38.8%	7.5%	7.9%
San Mateo city	21,249	62.0%	17.4%	5.3%	15.2%	0.0%	62.0%	29.1%	5.2%	3.7%
Santa Ana city	104,347	17.5%	75.1%	0.7%	6.3%	0.3%	17.5%	63.6%	8.3%	10.5%
Santa Clara city	35,288	48.2%	13.2%	10.6%	26.2%	1.8%	48.2%	35.1%	10.6%	6.1%
Santa Clarita city	46,023	69.5%	23.4%	0.6%	5.3%	1.2%	69.5%	22.3%	4.7%	3.5%
Santa Maria city	31,713	33.3%	59.8%	0.6%	3.3%	3.0%	33.3%	42.6%	5.4%	18.7%
Santa Monica city	21,654	81.0%	6.9%	4.9%	7.2%	0.0%	81.0%	15.8%	1.9%	1.2%
Santa Rosa city	45,707	66.3%	28.1%	2.4%	1.6%	1.7%	66.3%	26.7%	3.8%	3.2%
Simi Valley city	28,302	79.5%	14.9%	2.0%	2.7%	0.9%	79.5%	16.0%	1.1%	3.4%
South Gate city	29,962	12.4%	87.6%	0.0%	0.0%	0.0%	12.4%	72.1%	5.5%	10.0%
Stockton city	83,153	49.4%	33.7%	1.6%	15.0%	0.3%	49.4%	35.6%	8.5%	6.5%
Sunnyvale city	35,578	49.3%	8.5%	13.7%	26.5%	2.0%	49.3%	37.6%	12.0%	1.1%
Temecula city	31,215	81.6%	9.9%	3.9%	4.3%	0.3%	81.6%	13.7%	3.5%	1.2%
Thousand Oaks city	30,401	73.2%	18.8%	4.2%	2.8%	1.0%	73.2%	22.3%	3.4%	1.1%
Torrance city	31,027	68.0%	8.3%	1.4%	19.6%	2.6%	68.0%	22.1%	7.8%	2.1%
Vacaville city	25,744	82.5%	14.0%	0.8%	2.4%	0.3%	82.5%	12.1%	2.4%	2.9%
Vallejo city	31,222	66.4%	21.1%	0.9%	11.3%	0.2%	66.4%	26.3%	3.4%	3.9%
Victorville city	34,079	68.1%	29.6%	0.3%	1.8%	0.2%	68.1%	27.3%	2.1%	2.5%
Visalia city	37,794	64.2%	29.0%	0.7%	3.0%	3.0%	64.2%	27.3%	7.0%	1.5%
Vista city	28,569	58.4%	38.6%	2.3%	0.7%	0.0%	58.4%	9.9%	13.7%	18.0%
West Covina city	31,327	42.0%	45.1%	0.7%	11.6%	0.7%	42.0%	48.0%	5.4%	4.7%
Westminster city	23,446	39.5%	32.2%	0.0%	27.4%	0.9%	39.5%	41.8%	10.3%	8.4%
Colorado										
Arvada city	28,727	84.9%	8.3%	5.0%	1.8%	0.0%	84.9%	13.5%	0.3%	1.3%
Aurora city	91,957	67.7%	25.4%	2.1%	2.0%	2.8%	67.7%	22.1%	7.6%	2.6%
Boulder city	47,328	90.1%	3.2%	3.9%	2.6%	0.2%	90.1%	8.3%	1.2%	0.4%
Centennial city	24,801	83.1%	7.6%	4.3%	5.1%	0.0%	83.1%	12.0%	4.2%	0.8%
Colorado Springs city	121,448	87.5%	8.0%	2.5%	1.3%	0.6%	87.5%	8.9%	2.4%	1.1%
Denver city	182,517	70.9%	22.2%	2.2%	2.6%	2.0%	70.9%	23.0%	2.6%	3.5%
Fort Collins city	60,116	88.5%	6.7%	2.2%	1.2%	1.4%	88.5%	9.2%	1.3%	1.0%
Greeley city	33,213	77.5%	19.6%	0.9%	0.6%	1.3%	77.5%	17.0%	2.7%	2.7%
Lakewood city	35,859	83.4%	8.6%	3.5%	3.7%	0.8%	83.4%	11.9%	3.6%	1.1%
Pueblo city	28,398	84.2%	14.6%	0.2%	1.0%	0.0%	84.2%	9.8%	1.9%	4.0%
Thornton city	34,405	76.8%	16.5%	1.9%	4.8%	0.0%	76.8%	17.4%	3.1%	2.7%
Westminster city	31,101	77.3%	15.0%	4.3%	3.3%	0.0%	77.3%	17.7%	2.1%	2.9%
Connecticut										
Bridgeport city	43,377	53.1%	32.3%	7.6%	5.4%	1.6%	53.1%	29.3%	11.7%	6.0%
Hartford city	40,826	58.3%	34.2%	5.4%	1.6%	0.4%	58.3%	28.8%	7.9%	5.0%
New Haven city	45,240	66.5%	24.1%	4.1%	4.0%	1.4%	66.5%	28.6%	3.6%	1.4%
Stamford city	33,807	56.0%	26.8%	13.2%	3.1%	0.9%	56.0%	23.4%	9.0%	11.6%
Waterbury city	29,753	58.9%	35.2%	3.2%	0.0%	2.8%	58.9%	28.7%	8.4%	4.0%
District of Columbia										
Washington city	201,595	81.5%	8.9%	4.5%	2.5%	2.6%	81.5%	13.3%	3.6%	1.5%
Florida										
Cape Coral city	36,448	73.2%	20.7%	5.9%	0.0%	0.2%	73.2%	19.6%	5.0%	2.2%
Clearwater city	23,401	78.7%	18.2%	1.8%	1.3%	0.0%	78.7%	11.7%	4.5%	5.1%
Coral Springs city	32,526	72.7%	17.4%	8.2%	0.5%	1.1%	72.7%	23.1%	1.5%	2.6%
Fort Lauderdale city	38,760	65.8%	17.1%	14.8%	0.0%	2.3%	65.8%	24.3%	5.3%	4.6%
Gainesville city	64,700	82.8%	8.0%	3.0%	4.5%	1.6%	82.8%	12.4%	4.5%	0.2%
Hialeah city	55,132	10.8%	88.3%	0.6%	0.3%	0.0%	10.8%	60.4%	12.1%	16.7%
Hollywood city	30,826	59.5%	28.6%	6.7%	1.3%	3.8%	59.5%	33.1%	3.7%	3.8%
Jacksonville city	223,251	87.1%	6.6%	3.4%	2.0%	0.8%	87.1%	9.4%	2.0%	1.5%
Lakeland city	26,243	76.0%	20.9%	1.7%	1.0%	0.4%	76.0%	17.5%	1.0%	5.5%
Miami Beach city	20,119	44.6%	44.8%	9.9%	0.2%	0.5%	44.6%	36.1%	12.3%	6.9%
Miami city	99,815	27.6%	64.4%	7.5%	0.1%	0.4%	27.6%	51.6%	8.9%	11.9%
Miami Gardens city	32,190	58.9%	21.1%	17.0%	1.8%	1.3%	58.9%	35.4%	3.2%	2.5%
Miramar city	37,135	50.6%	33.6%	14.5%	0.5%	0.8%	50.6%	38.9%	6.8%	3.7%
Orlando city	79,273	66.7%	24.2%	6.0%	2.6%	0.5%	66.7%	23.3%	6.9%	3.1%
Palm Bay city	23,697	86.6%	9.0%	2.6%	0.4%	1.3%	86.6%	11.6%	1.8%	0.0%
Pembroke Pines city	40,226	55.1%	32.9%	10.0%	0.4%	1.5%	55.1%	39.2%	4.1%	1.6%
Pompano Beach city	25,547	59.2%	24.1%	16.4%	0.0%	0.2%	59.2%	26.9%	2.3%	11.6%
Port St. Lucie city	38,656	81.3%	14.3%	2.4%	1.9%	0.2%	81.3%	15.0%	0.6%	3.1%
St. Petersburg city	60,199	88.0%	6.0%	3.2%	1.7%	1.1%	88.0%	8.3%	2.5%	1.2%
Tallahassee city	86,319	87.8%	5.8%	4.0%	2.0%	0.3%	87.8%	11.1%	0.9%	0.1%
Tampa city	104,339	75.6%	18.2%	3.0%	1.5%	1.7%	75.6%	19.5%	2.3%	2.6%
West Palm Beach city	29,051	66.4%	26.1%	7.1%	0.0%	0.4%	66.4%	16.0%	5.7%	11.9%
Georgia										
Athens-Clarke County unified govt (bal).	54,062	85.3%	8.7%	3.5%	2.5%	0.1%	85.3%	10.1%	3.1%	1.6%
Atlanta city	143,295	83.9%	6.9%	4.1%	4.2%	1.0%	83.9%	11.9%	2.6%	1.6%
Augusta-Richmond County consolidated govt (bal)	57,457	92.8%	4.0%	0.7%	1.7%	0.7%	92.8%	5.3%	1.2%	0.7%

Table G-3: Places—Language Spoken and English Ability—*Continued*

	Millennial Population 13 to 31	Percent by Language Spoken at Home					Percent Who Speak Only English	Percent by Ability to Speak English		
		English Only	Spanish	Other Indo-European Language	Asian and Pacific Island Language	Other Language		Speak English "Very Well"	Speak English "Well"	Speak English "Not Well" or "Not at All"
Georgia—Cont.										
Columbus city	58,130	87.0%	8.9%	2.7%	0.7%	0.7%	87.0%	8.0%	2.8%	2.2%
Macon city	26,832	93.6%	5.1%	0.6%	0.5%	0.2%	93.6%	4.9%	0.8%	0.7%
Roswell city	23,495	77.7%	11.5%	5.4%	2.3%	3.0%	77.7%	13.9%	4.3%	4.0%
Sandy Springs city	25,297	70.1%	13.3%	11.4%	1.6%	3.6%	70.1%	21.9%	2.8%	5.2%
Savannah city	45,035	88.8%	6.4%	2.0%	2.8%	0.0%	88.8%	9.1%	1.1%	1.0%
Hawaii										
Urban Honolulu CDP	87,855	64.1%	1.5%	1.6%	28.9%	3.8%	64.1%	15.3%	17.0%	3.5%
Idaho										
Boise City city	62,035	88.9%	6.0%	2.9%	0.9%	1.4%	88.9%	7.1%	2.9%	1.2%
Illinois										
Aurora city	52,749	56.5%	37.3%	3.3%	1.1%	1.8%	56.5%	32.7%	5.7%	5.0%
Chicago city	793,782	65.0%	24.9%	4.8%	3.9%	1.4%	65.0%	26.3%	5.3%	3.4%
Elgin city	31,610	57.8%	36.7%	2.9%	1.9%	0.7%	57.8%	29.7%	7.7%	4.8%
Joliet city	40,784	69.6%	23.9%	4.5%	1.6%	0.4%	69.6%	26.0%	1.4%	2.9%
Naperville city	36,457	83.0%	5.1%	8.2%	1.3%	2.3%	83.0%	14.1%	1.4%	1.4%
Peoria city	33,592	89.9%	5.1%	0.7%	4.3%	0.0%	89.9%	8.4%	1.1%	0.6%
Rockford city	40,295	84.0%	13.3%	0.3%	1.6%	0.7%	84.0%	13.2%	1.8%	1.0%
Springfield city	30,131	95.3%	2.1%	1.3%	0.7%	0.6%	95.3%	4.7%	0.0%	0.0%
Indiana										
Evansville city	30,745	97.5%	0.1%	2.1%	0.0%	0.3%	97.5%	1.9%	0.7%	0.0%
Fort Wayne city	67,163	89.1%	6.0%	2.0%	1.8%	1.1%	89.1%	6.0%	2.4%	2.6%
Indianapolis city (bal)	231,827	83.5%	11.3%	2.7%	1.1%	1.3%	83.5%	9.8%	2.8%	3.9%
South Bend city	27,619	87.5%	8.5%	2.3%	1.7%	0.0%	87.5%	11.0%	1.4%	0.0%
Iowa										
Cedar Rapids city	34,639	94.1%	1.6%	1.2%	2.7%	0.4%	94.1%	5.5%	0.4%	0.0%
Davenport city	26,470	95.5%	1.4%	0.9%	0.6%	1.5%	95.5%	2.1%	1.8%	0.6%
Des Moines city	56,963	78.5%	8.6%	1.0%	4.1%	7.8%	78.5%	11.9%	5.2%	4.4%
Kansas										
Kansas City city	39,339	69.5%	24.3%	1.6%	3.9%	0.7%	69.5%	22.0%	3.9%	4.6%
Olathe city	32,791	86.7%	8.8%	1.5%	1.9%	1.1%	86.7%	12.0%	0.2%	1.1%
Overland Park city	45,868	83.5%	5.2%	5.5%	4.5%	1.3%	83.5%	11.7%	3.3%	1.5%
Topeka city	32,533	88.1%	8.5%	1.2%	1.7%	0.4%	88.1%	9.1%	1.8%	1.0%
Wichita city	105,918	85.1%	11.5%	0.8%	2.4%	0.1%	85.1%	11.9%	1.4%	1.6%
Kentucky										
Lexington-Fayette urban county	91,455	85.2%	8.0%	2.5%	2.7%	1.7%	85.2%	9.6%	2.3%	2.8%
Louisville/Jefferson County metro govt (bal)	155,155	89.6%	5.6%	2.0%	1.3%	1.5%	89.6%	7.7%	1.2%	1.5%
Louisiana										
Baton Rouge city	80,894	89.8%	3.7%	3.1%	3.5%	0.0%	89.8%	7.6%	1.9%	0.7%
Lafayette city	41,013	88.7%	4.4%	6.3%	0.4%	0.2%	88.7%	9.5%	1.3%	0.5%
New Orleans city	107,584	90.4%	4.7%	1.5%	2.7%	0.6%	90.4%	5.5%	1.9%	2.2%
Shreveport city	56,474	98.1%	1.4%	0.6%	0.0%	0.0%	98.1%	1.7%	0.3%	0.0%
Maryland										
Baltimore city	177,188	90.6%	4.3%	2.4%	1.2%	1.4%	90.6%	6.1%	1.5%	1.8%
Massachusetts										
Boston city	233,438	67.0%	15.7%	10.2%	4.9%	2.2%	67.0%	25.3%	4.6%	3.2%
Brockton city	25,123	64.2%	6.7%	26.0%	2.2%	0.8%	64.2%	25.1%	9.5%	1.2%
Cambridge city	45,181	65.0%	9.1%	10.4%	11.9%	3.6%	65.0%	31.3%	3.6%	0.1%
Lowell city	33,353	52.0%	18.7%	9.1%	17.4%	2.8%	52.0%	30.9%	12.7%	4.4%
Lynn city	22,564	48.6%	35.7%	8.8%	2.7%	4.2%	48.6%	32.0%	8.9%	10.6%
New Bedford city	25,019	64.0%	22.1%	13.2%	0.6%	0.2%	64.0%	21.0%	7.6%	7.5%
Springfield city	46,473	60.8%	35.3%	3.0%	0.4%	0.4%	60.8%	30.1%	5.3%	3.8%
Worcester city	56,561	56.9%	22.4%	8.2%	5.7%	6.8%	56.9%	27.7%	12.4%	3.0%
Michigan										
Ann Arbor city	52,352	80.5%	2.5%	3.5%	11.6%	2.0%	80.5%	15.3%	3.7%	0.6%
Dearborn city	27,230	47.6%	0.7%	2.8%	0.7%	48.2%	47.6%	43.0%	5.2%	4.2%
Detroit city	188,753	89.0%	6.9%	2.2%	0.4%	1.5%	89.0%	7.9%	1.4%	1.7%
Flint city	24,928	98.0%	0.4%	1.0%	0.0%	0.7%	98.0%	1.7%	0.4%	0.0%
Grand Rapids city	59,157	88.6%	9.7%	0.3%	1.4%	0.0%	88.6%	5.1%	3.4%	2.9%
Lansing city	35,463	88.2%	3.7%	3.4%	1.7%	3.0%	88.2%	8.7%	3.1%	0.0%
Livonia city	21,256	91.5%	2.3%	2.4%	1.3%	2.4%	91.5%	6.4%	1.1%	0.9%
Sterling Heights city	27,984	59.2%	3.0%	10.9%	3.5%	23.3%	59.2%	33.8%	2.9%	4.1%
Warren city	33,277	87.5%	0.2%	4.2%	2.8%	5.3%	87.5%	7.8%	1.2%	3.6%
Minnesota										
Minneapolis city	134,566	79.4%	9.1%	2.7%	5.2%	3.6%	79.4%	12.0%	4.9%	3.7%
Rochester city	26,862	89.8%	5.9%	1.9%	1.5%	1.0%	89.8%	9.7%	0.5%	0.0%
St. Paul city	90,558	65.9%	6.8%	1.1%	21.0%	5.2%	65.9%	22.7%	7.3%	4.2%
Mississippi										
Jackson city	52,244	97.2%	1.7%	1.1%	0.0%	0.0%	97.2%	1.4%	0.3%	1.2%
Missouri										
Columbia city	51,920	92.4%	1.6%	2.1%	3.2%	0.7%	92.4%	4.8%	2.8%	0.0%

Table G-3: Places—Language Spoken and English Ability—*Continued*

| | Millennial Population 13 to 31 | Percent by Language Spoken at Home | | | | | Percent Who Speak Only English | Percent by Ability to Speak English | | |
		English Only	Spanish	Other Indo-European Language	Asian and Pacific Island Language	Other Language		Speak English "Very Well"	Speak English "Well"	Speak English "Not Well" or "Not at All"
Missouri—Cont.										
Independence city	26,867	92.0%	6.9%	0.0%	1.1%	0.0%	92.0%	3.6%	2.2%	2.2%
Kansas City city	133,200	87.5%	9.5%	1.0%	1.0%	1.0%	87.5%	8.5%	2.1%	1.9%
Lee's Summit city	22,267	93.8%	2.1%	2.1%	2.1%	0.0%	93.8%	1.8%	3.7%	0.6%
Springfield city	58,414	95.2%	2.4%	0.7%	1.5%	0.1%	95.2%	3.2%	1.4%	0.2%
St. Louis city	92,329	88.7%	3.5%	3.6%	2.9%	1.3%	88.7%	9.2%	1.7%	0.3%
Montana										
Billings city	27,832	96.7%	1.2%	1.9%	0.3%	0.0%	96.7%	3.1%	0.2%	0.0%
Nebraska										
Lincoln city	82,925	89.3%	3.8%	1.5%	4.3%	1.0%	89.3%	7.8%	0.5%	2.4%
Omaha city	117,506	84.9%	10.1%	1.6%	2.1%	1.3%	84.9%	8.3%	3.9%	2.9%
Nevada										
Henderson city	59,632	84.6%	8.0%	1.9%	5.3%	0.2%	84.6%	12.0%	2.2%	1.2%
Las Vegas city	152,786	61.7%	31.4%	2.8%	3.2%	0.9%	61.7%	29.8%	4.4%	4.1%
North Las Vegas city	67,469	61.2%	35.8%	0.5%	2.1%	0.5%	61.2%	32.0%	3.4%	3.3%
Reno city	67,923	70.7%	22.2%	2.3%	3.7%	1.0%	70.7%	22.2%	4.2%	2.9%
Sparks city	22,232	77.7%	18.8%	0.0%	3.3%	0.2%	77.7%	18.3%	2.5%	1.5%
New Hampshire										
Manchester city	30,183	78.9%	9.3%	5.0%	5.3%	1.5%	78.9%	10.9%	5.0%	5.1%
New Jersey										
Elizabeth city	37,355	20.3%	68.1%	11.4%	0.0%	0.3%	20.3%	51.7%	11.7%	16.3%
Jersey City city	73,993	45.2%	23.0%	14.0%	12.4%	5.4%	45.2%	38.6%	12.0%	4.1%
Newark city	81,864	56.2%	32.2%	8.7%	0.5%	2.4%	56.2%	30.7%	4.7%	8.5%
Paterson city	41,976	40.8%	49.6%	5.8%	0.3%	3.4%	40.8%	42.3%	7.6%	9.2%
New Mexico										
Albuquerque city	147,386	74.5%	21.5%	1.0%	1.6%	1.3%	74.5%	20.6%	2.5%	2.3%
Las Cruces city	33,120	55.8%	41.7%	0.3%	1.3%	0.9%	55.8%	36.0%	4.3%	3.9%
Rio Rancho city	22,510	71.7%	14.7%	0.0%	0.0%	13.6%	71.7%	26.2%	1.9%	0.2%
New York										
Albany city	38,928	89.7%	3.7%	0.8%	2.5%	3.3%	89.7%	7.5%	1.8%	1.0%
Buffalo city	79,888	83.7%	8.9%	2.4%	3.2%	1.8%	83.7%	10.9%	2.7%	2.7%
New York city	2,261,947	52.1%	26.2%	11.8%	7.3%	2.6%	52.1%	33.0%	8.3%	6.6%
Rochester city	67,543	81.8%	12.7%	2.3%	1.9%	1.3%	81.8%	13.6%	3.8%	0.8%
Syracuse city	50,118	81.9%	6.1%	4.6%	4.9%	2.5%	81.9%	11.0%	6.4%	0.7%
Yonkers city	48,658	47.0%	39.9%	5.9%	4.5%	2.7%	47.0%	42.9%	4.9%	5.2%
North Carolina										
Charlotte city	218,384	77.8%	14.0%	3.0%	3.7%	1.5%	77.8%	14.0%	3.3%	4.9%
Durham city	73,143	79.8%	12.5%	2.0%	4.0%	1.8%	79.8%	12.0%	2.2%	6.1%
Fayetteville city	65,057	88.3%	8.7%	1.4%	1.1%	0.5%	88.3%	8.3%	2.4%	1.0%
Greensboro city	79,997	87.2%	5.3%	1.5%	4.1%	1.8%	87.2%	6.7%	4.2%	1.8%
High Point city	28,467	76.5%	12.8%	3.4%	4.9%	2.4%	76.5%	17.2%	3.2%	3.1%
Raleigh city	138,360	80.1%	11.4%	3.6%	2.8%	2.1%	80.1%	13.6%	2.8%	3.6%
Wilmington city	36,234	93.2%	2.7%	1.0%	1.2%	2.0%	93.2%	2.3%	0.8%	3.7%
Winston-Salem city	62,381	79.5%	17.6%	1.2%	1.3%	0.4%	79.5%	15.2%	1.8%	3.4%
North Dakota										
Fargo city	43,717	84.6%	2.0%	6.0%	3.9%	3.5%	84.6%	11.2%	4.0%	0.3%
Ohio										
Akron city	54,485	89.5%	3.3%	3.7%	1.4%	2.0%	89.5%	3.8%	4.9%	1.9%
Cincinnati city	91,178	91.0%	4.3%	1.6%	2.0%	1.1%	91.0%	5.7%	2.1%	1.1%
Cleveland city	107,448	88.6%	8.1%	1.0%	1.5%	0.7%	88.6%	8.4%	2.2%	0.9%
Columbus city	253,511	86.0%	5.4%	2.7%	2.5%	3.5%	86.0%	8.4%	2.9%	2.8%
Dayton city	46,480	92.3%	2.8%	2.9%	1.9%	0.0%	92.3%	4.4%	2.2%	1.0%
Toledo city	78,123	92.6%	3.5%	1.0%	1.1%	1.8%	92.6%	5.0%	2.1%	0.3%
Oklahoma										
Broken Arrow city	26,302	82.9%	11.6%	2.3%	2.9%	0.2%	82.9%	10.8%	1.8%	4.5%
Lawton city	33,539	86.2%	10.7%	0.7%	1.7%	0.6%	86.2%	5.9%	3.3%	4.6%
Norman city	43,626	90.5%	5.1%	0.0%	3.6%	0.7%	90.5%	6.9%	1.3%	1.3%
Oklahoma City city	166,433	76.0%	18.5%	1.7%	2.8%	1.0%	76.0%	14.1%	5.7%	4.2%
Tulsa city	109,067	84.8%	10.2%	1.8%	3.0%	0.3%	84.8%	9.3%	2.5%	3.5%
Oregon										
Beaverton city	24,936	68.2%	17.7%	6.2%	6.0%	1.9%	68.2%	22.0%	6.4%	3.5%
Eugene city	54,972	83.9%	8.8%	2.2%	4.3%	0.8%	83.9%	13.4%	1.3%	1.4%
Gresham city	29,749	67.4%	18.9%	8.9%	3.3%	1.5%	67.4%	19.8%	4.3%	8.5%
Hillsboro city	25,428	76.7%	16.6%	2.1%	4.3%	0.3%	76.7%	18.6%	1.5%	3.3%
Portland city	159,765	77.1%	8.6%	6.6%	5.8%	1.9%	77.1%	17.3%	3.1%	2.4%
Salem city	44,757	76.7%	19.1%	1.7%	0.9%	1.6%	76.7%	16.6%	2.9%	3.9%
Pennsylvania										
Allentown city	35,146	53.9%	43.7%	0.2%	0.3%	1.9%	53.9%	28.5%	12.2%	5.4%
Erie city	31,041	86.7%	4.4%	4.4%	0.8%	3.7%	86.7%	8.4%	3.6%	1.3%
Philadelphia city	454,880	77.8%	10.5%	4.4%	5.7%	1.6%	77.8%	15.9%	3.9%	2.4%
Pittsburgh city	103,079	85.7%	2.7%	3.0%	6.1%	2.6%	85.7%	9.6%	4.4%	0.3%
Rhode Island										
Providence city	64,383	53.2%	35.5%	4.0%	6.8%	0.6%	53.2%	39.0%	4.2%	3.7%

Table G-3: Places—Language Spoken and English Ability—*Continued*

	Millennial Population 13 to 31	Percent by Language Spoken at Home					Percent Who Speak Only English	Percent by Ability to Speak English		
		English Only	Spanish	Other Indo-European Language	Asian and Pacific Island Language	Other Language		Speak English "Very Well"	Speak English "Well"	Speak English "Not Well" or "Not at All"
South Carolina										
Charleston city	41,727	92.1%	6.1%	0.6%	0.2%	1.0%	92.1%	4.9%	1.3%	1.7%
Columbia city	59,462	92.0%	5.2%	1.6%	1.1%	0.1%	92.0%	4.2%	1.9%	2.0%
North Charleston city	34,069	85.0%	11.8%	1.3%	1.4%	0.5%	85.0%	9.7%	3.2%	2.1%
South Dakota										
Sioux Falls city	43,120	87.6%	5.3%	3.1%	1.9%	2.1%	87.6%	7.7%	2.4%	2.3%
Tennessee										
Chattanooga city	47,897	91.1%	6.0%	1.9%	0.8%	0.2%	91.1%	4.7%	1.0%	3.1%
Clarksville city	49,730	87.0%	7.1%	1.6%	2.0%	2.3%	87.0%	10.6%	1.9%	0.6%
Knoxville city	66,524	90.5%	3.7%	1.3%	3.7%	0.9%	90.5%	5.7%	2.4%	1.4%
Memphis city	188,820	89.9%	7.1%	0.7%	1.5%	0.8%	89.9%	5.8%	2.0%	2.3%
Murfreesboro city	43,031	91.9%	4.1%	1.4%	1.8%	0.8%	91.9%	6.2%	0.2%	1.7%
Nashville-Davidson metropolitan govt (bal)	181,961	81.9%	10.4%	2.6%	1.6%	3.4%	81.9%	12.1%	2.9%	3.1%
Texas										
Abilene city	39,552	82.5%	12.5%	2.4%	1.2%	1.4%	82.5%	14.5%	0.8%	2.2%
Amarillo city	54,926	72.8%	22.4%	0.4%	2.1%	2.3%	72.8%	17.5%	4.7%	5.0%
Arlington city	112,205	68.1%	24.0%	2.1%	3.5%	2.4%	68.1%	21.2%	4.8%	5.9%
Austin city	280,372	67.7%	23.9%	3.0%	4.4%	0.9%	67.7%	23.0%	3.2%	6.0%
Beaumont city	34,209	75.1%	20.2%	2.1%	1.7%	0.8%	75.1%	18.9%	2.9%	3.1%
Brownsville city	53,924	11.8%	87.3%	0.4%	0.4%	0.0%	11.8%	70.6%	11.7%	5.9%
Carrollton city	33,385	58.7%	20.9%	6.6%	10.3%	3.5%	58.7%	34.4%	3.5%	3.4%
College Station city	61,794	75.6%	17.2%	3.2%	3.4%	0.6%	75.6%	18.2%	5.0%	1.2%
Corpus Christi city	86,069	69.0%	28.4%	1.3%	1.0%	0.3%	69.0%	26.9%	2.3%	1.7%
Dallas city	363,191	51.7%	41.9%	2.2%	2.6%	1.7%	51.7%	28.7%	10.5%	9.0%
Denton city	51,957	78.8%	14.2%	2.5%	4.1%	0.5%	78.8%	14.9%	3.6%	2.8%
El Paso city	191,088	31.0%	67.8%	0.3%	0.8%	0.2%	31.0%	48.8%	15.0%	5.2%
Fort Worth city	222,860	68.0%	27.3%	2.0%	1.6%	1.1%	68.0%	23.9%	4.6%	3.6%
Frisco city	28,633	80.6%	12.1%	3.6%	3.7%	0.0%	80.6%	16.9%	2.3%	0.1%
Garland city	64,933	58.6%	32.9%	1.4%	5.4%	1.6%	58.6%	32.1%	5.6%	3.7%
Grand Prairie city	52,064	55.0%	40.8%	0.7%	3.2%	0.3%	55.0%	25.0%	12.8%	7.1%
Houston city	662,760	50.2%	41.4%	2.9%	4.1%	1.4%	50.2%	33.5%	7.7%	8.6%
Irving city	64,810	42.7%	42.0%	6.9%	6.8%	1.6%	42.7%	39.8%	9.1%	8.4%
Killeen city	46,189	83.0%	15.1%	1.1%	0.6%	0.2%	83.0%	13.4%	2.5%	1.1%
Laredo city	71,446	11.0%	89.0%	0.0%	0.0%	0.0%	11.0%	67.0%	13.4%	8.6%
Lewisville city	28,237	62.4%	28.7%	2.5%	6.0%	0.4%	62.4%	28.2%	4.7%	4.7%
Lubbock city	87,806	75.9%	20.2%	1.8%	1.6%	0.6%	75.9%	20.2%	2.2%	1.7%
McAllen city	39,424	16.5%	81.1%	0.0%	2.5%	0.0%	16.5%	67.4%	8.0%	8.1%
McKinney city	36,030	83.6%	14.1%	1.4%	0.9%	0.0%	83.6%	10.0%	3.2%	3.1%
Mesquite city	40,457	60.7%	34.8%	1.6%	2.7%	0.3%	60.7%	26.3%	7.2%	5.8%
Midland city	36,802	75.7%	24.0%	0.0%	0.3%	0.0%	75.7%	18.8%	2.5%	3.0%
Odessa city	32,849	53.7%	44.9%	0.9%	0.5%	0.0%	53.7%	36.2%	6.3%	3.8%
Pasadena city	44,502	53.9%	44.1%	1.1%	0.5%	0.4%	53.9%	29.2%	6.5%	10.4%
Pearland city	24,798	63.9%	24.6%	3.3%	4.2%	4.0%	63.9%	31.0%	5.2%	0.0%
Plano city	66,294	68.1%	11.3%	9.5%	9.1%	2.0%	68.1%	26.9%	3.2%	1.8%
Richardson city	25,547	59.9%	22.3%	8.2%	8.1%	1.5%	59.9%	31.3%	5.3%	3.5%
Round Rock city	30,063	73.2%	18.9%	1.2%	4.3%	2.4%	73.2%	21.8%	2.5%	2.5%
San Angelo city	31,154	76.3%	22.9%	0.7%	0.0%	0.0%	76.3%	21.7%	1.5%	0.5%
San Antonio city	410,854	63.0%	33.2%	1.2%	1.5%	1.1%	63.0%	29.5%	4.3%	3.2%
Tyler city	28,538	72.1%	22.7%	2.7%	0.0%	2.4%	72.1%	20.0%	4.5%	3.4%
Waco city	46,105	76.6%	17.5%	1.6%	4.3%	0.0%	76.6%	12.1%	9.0%	2.3%
Wichita Falls city	32,437	86.9%	11.4%	1.1%	0.6%	0.1%	86.9%	9.2%	3.4%	0.6%
Utah										
Orem city	35,056	82.8%	10.8%	4.1%	2.3%	0.0%	82.8%	8.8%	3.2%	5.1%
Provo city	63,999	81.3%	11.3%	3.7%	2.9%	0.7%	81.3%	16.2%	2.0%	0.4%
Salt Lake City city	62,705	78.6%	14.8%	2.4%	3.3%	0.8%	78.6%	18.2%	1.5%	1.6%
West Jordan city	31,921	83.0%	10.7%	3.7%	2.0%	0.7%	83.0%	15.2%	1.0%	0.7%
West Valley City city	39,676	64.3%	29.7%	0.8%	3.2%	2.0%	64.3%	30.5%	1.9%	3.3%
Virginia										
Alexandria city	39,869	69.0%	13.9%	6.1%	4.8%	6.2%	69.0%	15.7%	6.5%	8.8%
Chesapeake city	61,466	89.7%	6.0%	1.6%	1.8%	1.0%	89.7%	7.6%	1.4%	1.3%
Hampton city	41,168	89.5%	6.5%	0.9%	0.4%	2.7%	89.5%	7.5%	1.2%	1.8%
Newport News city	54,567	89.9%	5.4%	3.1%	1.4%	0.3%	89.9%	7.1%	1.6%	1.4%
Norfolk city	92,560	88.7%	5.9%	1.9%	3.0%	0.5%	88.7%	9.3%	1.4%	0.7%
Portsmouth city	26,744	94.6%	3.7%	0.9%	0.7%	0.0%	94.6%	4.4%	0.9%	0.0%
Richmond city	70,765	91.2%	5.6%	0.6%	2.2%	0.3%	91.2%	6.0%	0.6%	2.2%
Roanoke city	24,131	88.4%	7.0%	1.5%	1.2%	1.9%	88.4%	4.7%	4.5%	2.4%
Virginia Beach city	124,962	86.5%	6.1%	2.7%	3.0%	1.7%	86.5%	10.1%	2.5%	0.9%
Washington										
Bellevue city	32,231	54.1%	7.6%	15.3%	21.7%	1.4%	54.1%	33.1%	10.1%	2.7%
Everett city	29,205	72.0%	9.3%	11.0%	7.2%	0.5%	72.0%	23.6%	3.8%	0.6%
Federal Way city	26,383	66.5%	16.1%	7.2%	6.5%	3.7%	66.5%	25.8%	5.6%	2.1%
Kent city	34,530	61.1%	15.8%	11.1%	8.2%	3.8%	61.1%	31.2%	2.5%	5.2%
Renton city	26,083	64.2%	12.1%	6.2%	17.3%	0.3%	64.2%	25.3%	7.9%	2.6%
Seattle city	203,636	74.3%	6.3%	4.4%	11.8%	3.2%	74.3%	18.9%	5.1%	1.7%
Spokane city	61,518	92.1%	1.4%	2.6%	2.5%	1.3%	92.1%	5.2%	1.9%	0.8%

Table G-3: Places—Language Spoken and English Ability—*Continued*

	Millennial Population 13 to 31	Percent by Language Spoken at Home					Percent Who Speak Only English	Percent by Ability to Speak English		
		English Only	Spanish	Other Indo-European Language	Asian and Pacific Island Language	Other Language		Speak English "Very Well"	Speak English "Well"	Speak English "Not Well" or "Not at All"
Washington—Cont.										
Spokane Valley city	23,372	85.7%	3.4%	6.0%	1.3%	3.6%	85.7%	8.3%	4.9%	1.1%
Tacoma city	56,132	79.5%	9.4%	4.5%	5.7%	0.9%	79.5%	13.8%	4.9%	1.9%
Vancouver city	41,746	81.4%	9.4%	8.4%	0.6%	0.1%	81.4%	14.7%	1.7%	2.2%
Yakima city...	26,160	55.7%	43.1%	0.4%	0.7%	0.0%	55.7%	33.7%	6.2%	4.4%
Wisconsin										
Green Bay city	30,520	82.8%	9.2%	1.4%	5.7%	0.8%	82.8%	13.7%	2.1%	1.5%
Kenosha city	27,729	87.2%	11.0%	0.7%	1.0%	0.0%	87.2%	10.0%	1.9%	0.8%
Madison city	94,874	81.5%	10.0%	1.3%	7.0%	0.2%	81.5%	12.2%	2.6%	3.7%
Milwaukee city	188,730	80.2%	13.8%	1.4%	3.7%	0.9%	80.2%	12.9%	3.4%	3.5%

Table G-4: Metropolitan/Micropolitan Statistical Areas—Language Spoken and English Ability

	Millennial Population 13 to 31	Percent by Language Spoken at Home					Percent Who Speak Only English	Percent by Ability to Speak English		
		English Only	Spanish	Other Indo-European Language	Asian and Pacific Island Language	Other Language		Speak English "Very Well"	Speak English "Well"	Speak English "Not Well" or "Not at All"
Abilene, TX..............................	51,282	82.6%	13.2%	2.3%	0.9%	1.1%	82.6%	14.4%	0.8%	2.2%
Adrian, MI micro....................	24,684	96.7%	2.2%	1.1%	0.0%	0.0%	96.7%	2.6%	0.3%	0.4%
Akron, OH..............................	185,003	91.6%	1.9%	2.6%	1.8%	2.1%	91.6%	3.9%	3.4%	1.1%
Albany-Schenectady-Troy, NY	221,152	89.9%	4.3%	2.7%	2.4%	0.6%	89.9%	7.7%	1.8%	0.6%
Albany, GA..............................	44,899	90.7%	8.1%	0.8%	0.2%	0.2%	90.7%	5.8%	0.9%	2.7%
Albany, OR..............................	30,638	87.9%	4.5%	3.4%	3.0%	1.2%	87.9%	9.7%	2.3%	0.0%
Albertville, AL micro................	22,852	84.9%	14.3%	0.6%	0.0%	0.2%	84.9%	3.2%	2.6%	9.3%
Albuquerque, NM....................	232,256	71.8%	22.3%	1.1%	1.3%	3.4%	71.8%	22.8%	3.2%	2.2%
Alexandria, LA........................	40,995	93.3%	4.5%	0.4%	1.8%	0.0%	93.3%	3.4%	2.3%	1.0%
Allentown-Bethlehem-Easton, PA-NJ	200,342	80.0%	13.7%	2.8%	1.7%	1.8%	80.0%	14.0%	4.5%	1.5%
Altoona, PA..............................	29,018	95.7%	2.0%	1.5%	0.0%	0.8%	95.7%	2.9%	0.8%	0.6%
Amarillo, TX..............................	69,818	73.9%	21.2%	0.6%	1.9%	2.4%	73.9%	17.3%	4.7%	4.1%
Ames, IA..............................	39,514	86.4%	4.2%	0.6%	8.8%	0.0%	86.4%	8.9%	4.4%	0.3%
Anchorage, AK........................	119,605	88.1%	2.5%	2.9%	4.1%	2.4%	88.1%	9.6%	2.0%	0.3%
Ann Arbor, MI........................	119,936	85.4%	3.6%	2.4%	6.5%	2.1%	85.4%	10.7%	2.6%	1.3%
Anniston-Oxford-Jacksonville, AL..........	29,189	94.8%	3.0%	0.3%	1.9%	0.0%	94.8%	3.2%	0.6%	1.3%
Appleton, WI..........................	57,198	89.4%	6.2%	1.1%	3.1%	0.2%	89.4%	8.0%	1.3%	1.3%
Asheville, NC..........................	97,439	89.3%	8.5%	1.5%	0.5%	0.3%	89.3%	5.0%	1.7%	3.9%
Ashtabula, OH micro................	22,736	95.3%	3.6%	1.1%	0.0%	0.0%	95.3%	4.3%	0.0%	0.4%
Athens-Clarke County, GA............	74,592	88.1%	6.5%	3.1%	2.2%	0.1%	88.1%	8.1%	2.4%	1.3%
Atlanta-Sandy Springs-Roswell, GA......	1,419,815	79.7%	12.3%	3.2%	3.3%	1.4%	79.7%	14.3%	3.2%	2.8%
Atlantic City-Hammonton, NJ............	67,058	72.0%	17.1%	7.1%	3.1%	0.7%	72.0%	22.0%	3.1%	2.9%
Auburn-Opelika, AL................	53,402	96.8%	0.9%	0.0%	2.0%	0.3%	96.8%	2.4%	0.5%	0.3%
Augusta-Richmond County, GA-SC........	154,121	94.5%	2.9%	0.8%	1.4%	0.3%	94.5%	4.3%	0.7%	0.4%
Augusta-Waterville, ME micro..............	27,602	97.5%	0.5%	1.3%	0.7%	0.0%	97.5%	2.5%	0.0%	0.0%
Austin-Round Rock, TX..............	549,600	70.9%	22.6%	2.5%	3.2%	0.9%	70.9%	20.8%	3.8%	4.5%
Bakersfield, CA........................	253,748	51.6%	44.0%	1.6%	1.3%	1.4%	51.6%	36.4%	6.1%	5.9%
Baltimore-Columbia-Towson, MD.........	714,534	88.0%	5.1%	3.1%	2.5%	1.3%	88.0%	8.4%	2.0%	1.6%
Bangor, ME..............................	39,915	98.4%	0.1%	0.3%	0.9%	0.3%	98.4%	1.5%	0.0%	0.1%
Barnstable Town, MA	37,757	89.9%	0.6%	8.8%	0.8%	0.0%	89.9%	7.6%	2.6%	0.0%
Baton Rouge, LA......................	232,828	93.1%	3.3%	1.6%	1.6%	0.4%	93.1%	5.1%	1.1%	0.7%
Battle Creek, MI......................	31,074	95.5%	2.1%	1.0%	1.4%	0.0%	95.5%	2.9%	0.6%	1.0%
Bay City, MI..........................	25,541	91.9%	1.5%	0.5%	1.2%	4.9%	91.9%	6.4%	0.6%	1.2%
Beaumont-Port Arthur, TX............	107,793	81.2%	15.5%	1.3%	1.7%	0.4%	81.2%	13.6%	3.3%	1.9%
Beckley, WV..........................	27,461	94.6%	3.5%	1.8%	0.0%	0.0%	94.6%	4.3%	0.6%	0.5%
Bellingham, WA......................	62,149	86.8%	7.0%	5.7%	0.4%	0.1%	86.8%	10.5%	1.9%	0.7%
Bend-Redmond, OR..................	37,987	92.0%	3.4%	0.7%	3.9%	0.0%	92.0%	6.8%	1.1%	0.0%
Billings, MT..........................	41,323	95.4%	0.8%	1.4%	0.2%	2.1%	95.4%	4.4%	0.2%	0.0%
Binghamton, NY......................	62,942	90.6%	2.4%	2.5%	3.9%	0.6%	90.6%	6.5%	1.6%	1.3%
Birmingham-Hoover, AL..............	287,772	92.6%	5.3%	1.2%	0.6%	0.4%	92.6%	4.2%	2.0%	1.2%
Bismarck, ND	34,202	94.4%	2.7%	1.8%	0.0%	1.0%	94.4%	5.6%	0.0%	0.0%
Blacksburg-Christiansburg-Radford, VA.....	66,288	93.5%	1.4%	1.7%	2.6%	0.8%	93.5%	4.5%	1.3%	0.6%
Bloomington, IL......................	63,715	89.5%	3.2%	3.2%	2.6%	1.5%	89.5%	7.7%	2.5%	0.2%
Bloomington, IN......................	66,600	85.1%	5.0%	3.9%	5.7%	0.3%	85.1%	11.2%	3.4%	0.3%
Bloomsburg-Berwick, PA............	23,141	96.0%	1.6%	1.8%	0.0%	0.5%	96.0%	3.1%	0.3%	0.6%
Boise City, ID..........................	169,093	86.8%	9.6%	2.2%	0.7%	0.7%	86.8%	9.3%	2.3%	1.7%
Boston-Cambridge-Newton, MA-NH	1,227,309	74.4%	10.6%	8.6%	4.8%	1.6%	74.4%	19.2%	3.8%	2.6%
Boulder, CO..........................	96,264	85.2%	9.6%	2.9%	2.2%	0.1%	85.2%	12.5%	1.7%	0.6%
Bowling Green, KY..................	46,097	89.4%	3.0%	5.1%	1.6%	0.9%	89.4%	6.5%	1.7%	2.3%
Bremerton-Silverdale, WA............	65,185	95.2%	2.8%	0.8%	1.1%	0.0%	95.2%	3.9%	0.9%	0.0%
Bridgeport-Stamford-Norwalk, CT	212,707	69.3%	19.0%	7.7%	3.2%	0.9%	69.3%	19.9%	6.4%	4.5%
Brownsville-Harlingen, TX................	117,741	22.3%	77.0%	0.5%	0.2%	0.0%	22.3%	62.7%	9.6%	5.4%
Brunswick, GA........................	27,572	87.5%	11.2%	0.8%	0.6%	0.0%	87.5%	8.9%	1.9%	1.8%
Buffalo-Cheektowaga-Niagara Falls, NY .	286,943	90.1%	3.6%	2.5%	2.4%	1.3%	90.1%	7.3%	1.7%	0.9%
Burlington-South Burlington, VT........	59,774	94.6%	0.2%	3.0%	1.3%	0.8%	94.6%	3.0%	1.3%	1.1%
Burlington, NC........................	38,845	81.1%	14.8%	1.9%	1.7%	0.4%	81.1%	9.9%	6.2%	2.8%
California-Lexington Park, MD	28,557	93.0%	4.6%	2.3%	0.1%	0.0%	93.0%	3.4%	1.1%	2.5%
Canton-Massillon, OH................	93,351	96.0%	2.5%	0.7%	0.7%	0.1%	96.0%	3.1%	0.2%	0.6%
Cape Coral-Fort Myers, FL............	130,907	68.7%	25.4%	5.4%	0.4%	0.2%	68.7%	21.7%	4.1%	5.5%
Cape Girardeau, MO-IL	26,340	98.9%	0.0%	0.6%	0.5%	0.0%	98.9%	0.9%	0.2%	0.0%
Carbondale-Marion, IL................	39,180	94.1%	3.0%	1.4%	0.6%	0.8%	94.1%	4.7%	0.5%	0.7%
Carson City, NV......................	12,217	72.8%	25.7%	0.0%	1.5%	0.0%	72.8%	18.3%	5.7%	3.2%
Casper, WY..........................	21,460	91.2%	8.2%	0.0%	0.6%	0.0%	91.2%	5.5%	0.8%	2.4%
Cedar Rapids, IA......................	68,286	92.1%	3.7%	2.3%	1.7%	0.3%	92.1%	6.8%	0.2%	0.9%
Chambersburg-Waynesboro, PA............	33,238	91.3%	6.6%	1.0%	1.1%	0.0%	91.3%	4.7%	0.6%	3.4%
Champaign-Urbana, IL................	90,995	81.0%	4.9%	3.7%	8.9%	1.5%	81.0%	11.9%	5.1%	1.9%
Charleston-North Charleston, SC	192,839	91.4%	6.2%	1.2%	0.6%	0.6%	91.4%	5.7%	1.3%	1.7%
Charleston, WV......................	50,342	98.1%	0.6%	1.0%	0.2%	0.1%	98.1%	0.9%	1.0%	0.0%
Charlotte-Concord-Gastonia, NC-SC	579,482	84.7%	10.2%	2.2%	2.1%	0.8%	84.7%	10.6%	2.2%	2.6%
Charlottesville, VA....................	60,899	91.1%	3.2%	2.8%	2.5%	0.3%	91.1%	5.7%	1.6%	1.6%
Chattanooga, TN-GA	129,748	92.7%	4.7%	1.7%	0.8%	0.1%	92.7%	4.4%	1.0%	1.9%
Cheyenne, WY........................	25,613	91.9%	5.0%	0.4%	2.5%	0.1%	91.9%	5.4%	1.5%	1.1%
Chicago-Naperville-Elgin, IL-IN-WI	2,519,394	69.7%	20.1%	5.8%	3.0%	1.4%	69.7%	23.2%	4.2%	2.9%
Chico, CA..............................	65,642	84.6%	9.4%	1.0%	5.1%	0.0%	84.6%	9.9%	4.7%	0.8%
Cincinnati, OH-KY-IN................	528,404	92.0%	3.8%	2.0%	1.3%	0.8%	92.0%	5.1%	1.9%	1.0%
Clarksburg, WV micro................	18,960	96.9%	2.1%	1.0%	0.0%	0.0%	96.9%	1.9%	0.5%	0.8%
Clarksville, TN-KY	89,743	89.0%	5.8%	2.2%	1.4%	1.7%	89.0%	9.0%	1.7%	0.4%

Table G-4: Metropolitan/Micropolitan Statistical Areas—Language Spoken and English Ability—*Continued*

	Millennial Population 13 to 31	Percent by Language Spoken at Home					Percent Who Speak Only English	Percent by Ability to Speak English		
		English Only	Spanish	Other Indo-European Language	Asian and Pacific Island Language	Other Language		Speak English "Very Well"	Speak English "Well"	Speak English "Not Well" or "Not at All"
Cleveland-Elyria, OH	488,473	89.8%	4.3%	3.5%	1.2%	1.2%	89.8%	7.1%	1.8%	1.3%
Cleveland, TN	29,929	92.4%	6.1%	1.5%	0.0%	0.0%	92.4%	3.7%	2.6%	1.3%
Coeur d'Alene, ID	35,119	97.1%	1.5%	1.4%	0.0%	0.0%	97.1%	2.9%	0.0%	0.0%
College Station-Bryan, TX	104,136	77.5%	15.9%	3.0%	3.2%	0.4%	77.5%	17.1%	3.8%	1.5%
Colorado Springs, CO	189,663	88.2%	7.6%	2.1%	1.5%	0.5%	88.2%	9.1%	1.8%	0.9%
Columbia, MO	65,445	92.1%	1.9%	2.4%	3.1%	0.6%	92.1%	5.2%	2.6%	0.0%
Columbia, SC	224,537	92.5%	4.8%	1.3%	1.3%	0.1%	92.5%	5.4%	1.0%	1.1%
Columbus, GA-AL	93,131	88.0%	8.9%	2.3%	0.4%	0.4%	88.0%	8.1%	1.9%	2.0%
Columbus, IN	20,581	78.8%	15.3%	1.7%	4.1%	0.0%	78.8%	9.5%	5.2%	6.5%
Columbus, OH	514,620	89.6%	3.8%	2.2%	2.2%	2.1%	89.6%	7.0%	1.7%	1.6%
Concord, NH micro	29,353	93.0%	1.0%	5.6%	0.0%	0.4%	93.0%	4.7%	1.0%	1.3%
Cookeville, TN micro	28,672	94.3%	5.7%	0.0%	0.0%	0.0%	94.3%	1.0%	0.0%	4.8%
Corpus Christi, TX	123,335	69.3%	28.3%	1.4%	0.8%	0.2%	69.3%	26.5%	2.5%	1.7%
Corvallis, OR	33,658	88.8%	4.1%	3.1%	2.9%	1.1%	88.8%	9.1%	2.1%	0.0%
Crestview-Fort Walton Beach-Destin, FL	68,552	88.7%	7.4%	1.1%	2.8%	0.0%	88.7%	9.1%	1.2%	1.0%
Cumberland, MD-WV	25,491	96.7%	1.9%	0.8%	0.0%	0.7%	96.7%	2.6%	0.8%	0.0%
Dallas-Fort Worth-Arlington, TX	1,793,256	66.7%	26.5%	2.7%	3.0%	1.1%	66.7%	22.7%	5.7%	4.9%
Dalton, GA	37,669	70.0%	28.2%	1.3%	0.5%	0.0%	70.0%	18.8%	4.9%	6.3%
Danville, IL	19,265	94.2%	4.3%	1.3%	0.1%	0.0%	94.2%	5.5%	0.0%	0.3%
Danville, VA micro	22,440	94.5%	4.7%	0.5%	0.0%	0.3%	94.5%	2.7%	0.5%	2.3%
Daphne-Fairhope-Foley, AL	43,743	92.5%	6.0%	0.3%	1.2%	0.0%	92.5%	6.1%	0.2%	1.2%
Davenport-Moline-Rock Island, IA-IL	92,530	90.7%	6.7%	1.9%	0.2%	0.6%	90.7%	7.2%	1.2%	1.0%
Dayton, OH	203,642	93.9%	1.3%	2.1%	1.9%	0.8%	93.9%	4.5%	1.2%	0.4%
Decatur, AL	35,881	88.0%	11.8%	0.2%	0.0%	0.0%	88.0%	8.1%	0.8%	3.1%
Decatur, IL	26,140	94.5%	3.2%	1.4%	0.3%	0.6%	94.5%	5.2%	0.3%	0.0%
Deltona-Daytona Beach-Ormond Beach, FL	128,837	86.2%	10.0%	2.2%	1.1%	0.6%	86.2%	10.9%	1.9%	1.0%
Denver-Aurora-Lakewood, CO	697,150	76.9%	16.3%	2.7%	2.8%	1.2%	76.9%	17.5%	3.4%	2.1%
Des Moines-West Des Moines, IA	151,062	86.3%	5.6%	3.0%	2.4%	2.7%	86.3%	7.4%	4.1%	2.2%
Detroit-Warren-Dearborn, MI	1,027,771	87.1%	3.6%	3.3%	1.8%	4.3%	87.1%	10.1%	1.6%	1.3%
Dothan, AL	34,752	97.3%	2.3%	0.2%	0.2%	0.0%	97.3%	1.9%	0.2%	0.7%
Dover, DE	43,966	90.9%	3.8%	3.5%	0.4%	1.4%	90.9%	8.0%	1.2%	0.0%
Dubuque, IA	25,299	94.5%	1.8%	3.7%	0.0%	0.0%	94.5%	4.5%	0.2%	0.8%
Duluth, MN-WI	73,630	94.8%	2.1%	1.6%	1.0%	0.5%	94.8%	4.3%	0.5%	0.4%
Dunn, NC micro	34,876	89.1%	9.3%	0.2%	0.8%	0.6%	89.1%	3.9%	2.8%	4.2%
Durham-Chapel Hill, NC	150,437	81.7%	12.2%	2.3%	2.4%	1.3%	81.7%	12.1%	2.0%	4.2%
East Stroudsburg, PA	42,860	87.0%	4.4%	7.2%	0.5%	0.8%	87.0%	11.5%	1.5%	0.0%
Eau Claire, WI	46,385	93.8%	1.4%	2.7%	2.1%	0.0%	93.8%	4.8%	1.0%	0.4%
El Centro, CA	52,602	24.5%	74.3%	0.0%	1.0%	0.2%	24.5%	51.7%	16.6%	7.3%
El Paso, TX	242,820	30.9%	68.0%	0.3%	0.7%	0.2%	30.9%	49.2%	14.6%	5.3%
Elizabethtown-Fort Knox, KY	39,917	92.2%	5.9%	1.9%	0.0%	0.0%	92.2%	5.5%	1.7%	0.6%
Elkhart-Goshen, IN	49,637	77.8%	14.4%	6.9%	0.9%	0.0%	77.8%	17.6%	1.4%	3.3%
Elmira, NY	21,897	97.1%	0.8%	1.2%	0.8%	0.1%	97.1%	2.7%	0.1%	0.0%
Erie, PA	71,567	92.4%	2.2%	3.1%	0.6%	1.8%	92.4%	5.3%	1.5%	0.8%
Eugene, OR	94,734	86.4%	7.7%	1.7%	3.1%	1.1%	86.4%	11.2%	1.5%	0.9%
Eureka-Arcata-Fortuna, CA micro	38,357	79.9%	11.1%	5.0%	2.7%	1.4%	79.9%	12.5%	2.6%	5.0%
Evansville, IN-KY	78,099	95.3%	1.0%	3.2%	0.4%	0.2%	95.3%	3.5%	1.1%	0.0%
Fairbanks, AK	32,435	93.8%	3.2%	0.5%	2.1%	0.3%	93.8%	5.7%	0.7%	0.2%
Fargo, ND-MN	79,044	88.7%	2.3%	3.6%	2.9%	2.5%	88.7%	8.1%	2.7%	0.6%
Farmington, NM	32,645	72.2%	13.4%	0.3%	0.2%	13.9%	72.2%	24.2%	0.3%	3.2%
Fayetteville-Springdale-Rogers, AR-MO	137,070	83.6%	13.1%	1.8%	0.7%	0.7%	83.6%	9.5%	4.2%	2.7%
Fayetteville, NC	116,497	88.1%	8.7%	1.3%	1.6%	0.4%	88.1%	8.3%	2.1%	1.5%
Flagstaff, AZ	48,457	81.9%	6.5%	1.7%	1.0%	8.8%	81.9%	15.9%	1.8%	0.3%
Flint, MI	104,249	97.2%	1.3%	0.8%	0.2%	0.4%	97.2%	2.7%	0.1%	0.0%
Florence-Muscle Shoals, AL	36,495	94.1%	4.7%	1.0%	0.0%	0.3%	94.1%	2.9%	0.0%	3.0%
Florence, SC	49,305	96.6%	1.9%	0.7%	0.2%	0.6%	96.6%	2.8%	0.6%	0.0%
Fond du Lac, WI	22,700	91.7%	5.5%	1.4%	1.2%	0.2%	91.7%	5.3%	0.4%	2.6%
Fort Collins, CO	94,110	89.0%	6.7%	1.8%	1.5%	1.0%	89.0%	8.7%	1.2%	1.1%
Fort Smith, AR-OK	71,097	88.0%	10.1%	0.5%	0.9%	0.6%	88.0%	9.9%	1.3%	0.8%
Fort Wayne, IN	109,234	90.2%	4.9%	2.7%	1.4%	0.8%	90.2%	6.2%	1.8%	1.8%
Fresno, CA	280,746	54.8%	34.6%	3.5%	6.9%	0.2%	54.8%	32.3%	6.6%	6.3%
Gadsden, AL	24,989	98.0%	1.4%	0.5%	0.0%	0.2%	98.0%	0.4%	0.0%	1.3%
Gainesville, FL	104,083	83.4%	7.6%	3.1%	5.0%	1.0%	83.4%	12.9%	3.1%	0.6%
Gainesville, GA	48,065	67.0%	30.7%	1.4%	0.5%	0.5%	67.0%	23.5%	1.7%	7.9%
Gettysburg, PA	23,917	92.3%	6.2%	0.2%	1.3%	0.0%	92.3%	3.6%	4.1%	0.0%
Glens Falls, NY	27,827	94.3%	3.1%	2.1%	0.5%	0.0%	94.3%	4.0%	1.0%	0.8%
Goldsboro, NC	30,990	86.2%	13.1%	0.5%	0.0%	0.2%	86.2%	10.7%	0.6%	2.5%
Grand Forks, ND-MN	36,319	91.6%	5.6%	1.9%	0.7%	0.2%	91.6%	5.1%	2.4%	0.9%
Grand Island, NE	18,823	90.8%	7.6%	1.6%	0.0%	0.0%	90.8%	6.7%	0.5%	2.0%
Grand Junction, CO	39,345	93.1%	6.3%	0.2%	0.4%	0.0%	93.1%	5.7%	0.8%	0.5%
Grand Rapids-Wyoming, MI	275,216	90.4%	6.2%	1.4%	1.5%	0.5%	90.4%	6.2%	1.4%	1.9%
Grants Pass, OR	15,966	96.4%	2.6%	0.5%	0.5%	0.0%	96.4%	3.6%	0.0%	0.0%
Great Falls, MT	22,162	92.7%	1.1%	5.0%	0.0%	1.1%	92.7%	6.8%	0.5%	0.0%
Greeley, CO	75,018	76.6%	20.4%	1.2%	0.6%	1.1%	76.6%	17.9%	3.5%	1.9%
Green Bay, WI	79,175	88.6%	6.8%	1.4%	2.8%	0.3%	88.6%	8.4%	2.6%	0.5%
Greensboro-High Point, NC	189,386	86.5%	8.0%	1.8%	2.6%	1.2%	86.5%	8.4%	3.3%	1.8%
Greenville-Anderson-Mauldin, SC	212,385	89.5%	7.6%	0.6%	1.5%	0.7%	89.5%	6.6%	1.6%	2.3%

Table G-4: Metropolitan/Micropolitan Statistical Areas—Language Spoken and English Ability—*Continued*

	Millennial Population 13 to 31	Percent by Language Spoken at Home					Percent Who Speak Only English	Percent by Ability to Speak English		
		English Only	Spanish	Other Indo-European Language	Asian and Pacific Island Language	Other Language		Speak English "Very Well"	Speak English "Well"	Speak English "Not Well" or "Not at All"
Greenville, NC	61,787	91.2%	6.3%	1.2%	1.2%	0.0%	91.2%	7.1%	0.8%	0.9%
Greenwood, SC micro	24,086	95.1%	4.4%	0.4%	0.2%	0.0%	95.1%	2.1%	1.1%	1.8%
Gulfport-Biloxi-Pascagoula, MS	99,555	91.6%	4.3%	0.2%	3.9%	0.0%	91.6%	6.4%	0.9%	1.1%
Hagerstown-Martinsburg, MD-WV	63,073	91.9%	5.0%	1.1%	1.7%	0.2%	91.9%	6.3%	1.3%	0.4%
Hammond, LA	37,246	91.2%	7.8%	1.0%	0.0%	0.0%	91.2%	4.1%	2.8%	1.9%
Hanford-Corcoran, CA	45,510	52.8%	41.5%	2.8%	1.6%	1.2%	52.8%	28.7%	12.6%	5.9%
Harrisburg-Carlisle, PA	136,067	90.8%	2.9%	3.8%	2.0%	0.6%	90.8%	6.4%	1.7%	1.1%
Harrisonburg, VA	45,371	85.9%	8.3%	2.7%	2.3%	0.8%	85.9%	8.2%	4.4%	1.5%
Hartford-West Hartford-East Hartford, CT	305,097	76.6%	13.7%	6.1%	2.7%	0.9%	76.6%	17.4%	4.1%	1.9%
Hattiesburg, MS	46,296	96.6%	2.1%	0.4%	0.4%	0.5%	96.6%	2.4%	0.6%	0.3%
Hickory-Lenoir-Morganton, NC	83,615	88.6%	6.9%	0.6%	4.0%	0.0%	88.6%	7.5%	1.7%	2.2%
Hilo, HI micro	44,614	86.5%	0.3%	0.0%	7.4%	5.7%	86.5%	10.1%	3.2%	0.2%
Hilton Head Island-Bluffton-Beaufort, SC	48,805	83.7%	13.7%	1.8%	0.7%	0.1%	83.7%	11.6%	2.1%	2.6%
Hinesville, GA	28,306	92.6%	5.7%	1.0%	0.5%	0.4%	92.6%	5.6%	1.8%	0.0%
Holland, MI micro	26,007	96.9%	3.1%	0.0%	0.0%	0.0%	96.9%	2.7%	0.3%	0.1%
Homosassa Springs, FL	21,470	96.2%	1.1%	2.8%	0.0%	0.0%	96.2%	2.7%	0.4%	0.7%
Hot Springs, AR	20,011	93.1%	5.7%	0.4%	0.8%	0.0%	93.1%	5.3%	0.8%	0.8%
Houma-Thibodaux, LA	57,742	94.2%	3.0%	1.9%	0.0%	0.9%	94.2%	4.3%	0.2%	1.3%
Houston-The Woodlands-Sugar Land, TX	1,693,971	59.2%	33.4%	2.8%	3.6%	1.0%	59.2%	28.2%	6.5%	6.1%
Huntington-Ashland, WV-KY-OH	89,024	98.1%	0.7%	0.6%	0.3%	0.3%	98.1%	1.4%	0.4%	0.2%
Huntsville, AL	117,360	89.5%	7.1%	1.1%	1.7%	0.6%	89.5%	4.8%	3.2%	2.5%
Idaho Falls, ID	37,305	88.8%	8.5%	1.8%	0.7%	0.3%	88.8%	8.1%	1.8%	1.4%
Indianapolis-Carmel-Anderson, IN	498,562	89.0%	7.1%	2.4%	0.8%	0.7%	89.0%	6.7%	2.1%	2.2%
Iowa City, IA	63,584	87.0%	4.5%	5.2%	2.5%	0.7%	87.0%	8.6%	3.0%	1.4%
Ithaca, NY	41,515	86.4%	0.7%	2.7%	9.5%	0.7%	86.4%	9.6%	2.6%	1.3%
Jackson, MI	39,344	99.2%	0.4%	0.0%	0.2%	0.2%	99.2%	0.7%	0.1%	0.0%
Jackson, MS	154,147	96.9%	1.3%	0.8%	0.6%	0.5%	96.9%	1.7%	0.5%	0.9%
Jackson, TN	34,586	95.5%	2.0%	0.1%	2.4%	0.0%	95.5%	3.9%	0.5%	0.1%
Jacksonville, FL	354,593	88.1%	6.5%	2.7%	2.1%	0.5%	88.1%	9.1%	1.4%	1.4%
Jacksonville, NC	75,082	87.8%	9.3%	1.7%	0.9%	0.3%	87.8%	9.8%	0.9%	1.5%
Jamestown-Dunkirk-Fredonia, NY micro	34,497	88.4%	5.8%	4.3%	1.4%	0.1%	88.4%	7.6%	1.1%	2.9%
Janesville-Beloit, WI	39,734	92.2%	6.9%	0.2%	0.7%	0.0%	92.2%	6.0%	1.3%	0.6%
Jefferson City, MO	40,116	93.2%	4.3%	1.8%	0.6%	0.1%	93.2%	5.9%	0.9%	0.0%
Johnson City, TN	50,488	96.5%	2.8%	0.5%	0.1%	0.0%	96.5%	2.0%	0.7%	0.9%
Johnstown, PA	32,240	99.5%	0.5%	0.0%	0.0%	0.0%	99.5%	0.5%	0.0%	0.0%
Jonesboro, AR	33,236	91.8%	5.8%	0.0%	0.4%	1.9%	91.8%	4.2%	2.7%	1.3%
Joplin, MO	46,196	91.8%	5.2%	2.3%	0.5%	0.3%	91.8%	7.3%	0.3%	0.7%
Kahului-Wailuku-Lahaina, HI	37,245	78.8%	1.2%	1.5%	12.5%	6.0%	78.8%	12.0%	7.6%	1.6%
Kalamazoo-Portage, MI	102,518	92.0%	5.2%	1.6%	0.9%	0.3%	92.0%	6.8%	0.7%	0.5%
Kalispell, MT micro	20,619	98.9%	0.9%	0.1%	0.2%	0.0%	98.9%	0.3%	0.0%	0.9%
Kankakee, IL	27,483	89.5%	8.2%	1.7%	0.1%	0.4%	89.5%	9.5%	0.6%	0.4%
Kansas City, MO-KS	514,311	88.9%	6.9%	1.7%	1.6%	0.9%	88.9%	7.6%	2.0%	1.5%
Kennewick-Richland, WA	72,414	65.7%	30.8%	2.4%	1.1%	0.0%	65.7%	24.2%	5.4%	4.8%
Killeen-Temple, TX	135,230	85.6%	12.4%	1.3%	0.5%	0.2%	85.6%	10.3%	2.8%	1.3%
Kingsport-Bristol-Bristol, TN-VA	67,737	97.3%	1.8%	0.8%	0.0%	0.0%	97.3%	2.4%	0.1%	0.1%
Kingston, NY	43,272	86.5%	7.4%	3.5%	2.5%	0.2%	86.5%	9.6%	2.4%	1.5%
Knoxville, TN	211,969	93.6%	3.2%	1.5%	1.2%	0.5%	93.6%	4.2%	1.4%	0.8%
Kokomo, IN	17,163	89.3%	9.2%	0.4%	1.2%	0.0%	89.3%	5.2%	4.2%	1.4%
La Crosse-Onalaska, WI-MN	40,667	86.3%	4.2%	0.7%	8.6%	0.2%	86.3%	4.7%	6.4%	2.6%
Lafayette-West Lafayette, IN	80,589	83.5%	4.7%	3.7%	7.2%	1.0%	83.5%	10.4%	5.0%	1.1%
Lafayette, LA	134,207	90.8%	3.1%	4.9%	1.1%	0.1%	90.8%	7.6%	0.9%	0.7%
Lake Charles, LA	53,104	96.0%	2.3%	1.1%	0.6%	0.0%	96.0%	3.4%	0.5%	0.1%
Lake Havasu City-Kingman, AZ	40,348	86.0%	13.0%	0.0%	0.5%	0.6%	86.0%	11.1%	1.8%	1.2%
Lakeland-Winter Haven, FL	149,776	77.8%	18.2%	2.8%	0.7%	0.5%	77.8%	15.9%	2.1%	4.2%
Lancaster, PA	132,318	78.0%	8.5%	10.5%	1.0%	2.0%	78.0%	15.7%	4.2%	2.1%
Lansing-East Lansing, MI	146,587	89.6%	2.7%	2.3%	3.8%	1.6%	89.6%	6.0%	3.5%	0.8%
Laredo, TX	76,850	11.6%	88.4%	0.0%	0.0%	0.0%	11.6%	66.8%	13.3%	8.4%
Las Cruces, NM	66,940	43.9%	53.6%	1.1%	0.6%	0.8%	43.9%	46.6%	5.6%	4.0%
Las Vegas-Henderson-Paradise, NV	518,566	62.6%	28.9%	2.2%	5.0%	1.2%	62.6%	29.1%	5.1%	3.1%
Lawrence, KS	44,291	91.7%	0.8%	0.4%	6.3%	0.9%	91.7%	4.0%	3.1%	1.2%
Lawton, OK	41,646	88.2%	9.3%	0.6%	1.4%	0.5%	88.2%	5.4%	2.6%	3.7%
Lebanon, PA	28,438	90.3%	6.7%	2.3%	0.7%	0.0%	90.3%	3.1%	4.4%	2.2%
Lewiston-Auburn, ME	26,538	92.7%	1.3%	5.0%	0.5%	0.5%	92.7%	7.3%	0.0%	0.0%
Lewiston, ID-WA	15,034	82.3%	9.3%	2.2%	2.1%	4.1%	82.3%	9.1%	4.2%	4.3%
Lexington-Fayette, KY	138,471	89.1%	6.5%	2.2%	1.4%	0.8%	89.1%	7.1%	1.8%	2.0%
Lima, OH	26,290	97.0%	0.2%	2.7%	0.0%	0.1%	97.0%	2.7%	0.4%	0.0%
Lincoln, NE	100,294	89.3%	4.0%	1.7%	4.0%	1.0%	89.3%	7.8%	0.9%	2.0%
Little Rock-North Little Rock-Conway, AR	195,299	92.2%	5.9%	1.1%	0.6%	0.2%	92.2%	4.0%	1.6%	2.1%
Logan, UT-ID	47,715	83.6%	11.3%	2.9%	2.1%	0.1%	83.6%	11.2%	1.4%	3.8%
Longview, TX	58,630	81.6%	17.7%	0.0%	0.2%	0.5%	81.6%	15.1%	1.1%	2.1%
Longview, WA	23,187	86.7%	11.7%	0.6%	1.0%	0.0%	86.7%	7.3%	2.1%	3.8%
Los Angeles-Long Beach-Anaheim, CA	3,542,436	44.6%	41.4%	3.8%	9.1%	1.0%	44.6%	42.9%	6.8%	5.7%
Louisville/Jefferson County, KY-IN	311,466	91.6%	4.7%	1.8%	0.9%	1.1%	91.6%	5.9%	1.3%	1.2%
Lubbock, TX	99,246	75.9%	20.1%	1.9%	1.5%	0.6%	75.9%	20.2%	2.1%	1.9%
Lumberton, NC micro	32,622	88.9%	9.1%	1.6%	0.3%	0.0%	88.9%	6.7%	0.6%	3.8%

Table G-4: Metropolitan/Micropolitan Statistical Areas—Language Spoken and English Ability—*Continued*

	Millennial Population 13 to 31	Percent by Language Spoken at Home					Percent Who Speak Only English	Percent by Ability to Speak English		
		English Only	Spanish	Other Indo-European Language	Asian and Pacific Island Language	Other Language		Speak English "Very Well"	Speak English "Well"	Speak English "Not Well" or "Not at All"
Lynchburg, VA	70,265	94.2%	2.4%	1.3%	1.4%	0.7%	94.2%	4.1%	1.5%	0.3%
Macon, GA	62,863	94.3%	3.3%	0.6%	1.1%	0.7%	94.3%	4.2%	0.7%	0.8%
Madera, CA	43,066	44.2%	53.3%	2.5%	0.1%	0.0%	44.2%	37.4%	2.7%	15.7%
Madison, WI	189,097	85.3%	7.5%	1.4%	5.6%	0.1%	85.3%	9.8%	2.8%	2.1%
Manchester-Nashua, NH	94,570	86.9%	6.0%	3.8%	2.6%	0.7%	86.9%	8.9%	2.6%	1.7%
Manhattan, KS	44,867	95.7%	2.6%	0.3%	1.4%	0.0%	95.7%	2.7%	1.4%	0.3%
Mankato-North Mankato, MN	33,593	88.7%	3.3%	0.3%	2.1%	5.6%	88.7%	9.0%	2.4%	0.0%
Mansfield, OH	28,039	94.1%	3.4%	2.6%	0.0%	0.0%	94.1%	5.1%	0.4%	0.4%
McAllen-Edinburg-Mission, TX	238,715	12.9%	86.3%	0.0%	0.8%	0.0%	12.9%	70.3%	5.9%	11.0%
Medford, OR	45,840	87.6%	11.3%	0.6%	0.4%	0.2%	87.6%	10.6%	0.5%	1.3%
Memphis, TN-MS-AR	367,734	92.0%	5.4%	0.7%	1.0%	0.9%	92.0%	5.2%	1.3%	1.4%
Merced, CA	80,879	41.8%	46.2%	5.6%	6.0%	0.6%	41.8%	43.0%	9.9%	5.4%
Meridian, MS micro	25,504	96.2%	1.4%	0.7%	0.0%	1.7%	96.2%	3.5%	0.3%	0.0%
Miami-Fort Lauderdale-West Palm Beach, FL	1,390,066	47.7%	40.9%	9.5%	1.1%	0.8%	47.7%	39.1%	7.1%	6.1%
Michigan City-La Porte, IN	27,693	94.0%	4.6%	0.7%	0.7%	0.0%	94.0%	3.0%	0.7%	2.2%
Midland, MI	21,484	93.5%	1.4%	0.6%	1.5%	3.1%	93.5%	4.8%	0.7%	1.0%
Midland, TX	45,864	76.2%	23.2%	0.0%	0.4%	0.1%	76.2%	18.8%	2.6%	2.4%
Milwaukee-Waukesha-West Allis, WI	407,569	85.2%	9.4%	2.1%	2.6%	0.6%	85.2%	10.4%	2.3%	2.1%
Minneapolis-St. Paul-Bloomington, MN-WI	874,497	83.7%	6.1%	1.8%	5.7%	2.7%	83.7%	11.6%	3.2%	1.5%
Missoula, MT	36,652	97.4%	0.8%	1.6%	0.0%	0.2%	97.4%	1.8%	0.5%	0.2%
Mobile, AL	106,088	95.6%	1.6%	1.0%	1.5%	0.3%	95.6%	3.4%	0.7%	0.3%
Modesto, CA	148,186	56.7%	37.1%	3.0%	1.1%	2.0%	56.7%	33.2%	4.0%	6.1%
Monroe, LA	50,987	96.9%	2.3%	0.5%	0.3%	0.0%	96.9%	1.9%	0.4%	0.8%
Monroe, MI	35,012	96.3%	1.8%	1.7%	0.0%	0.3%	96.3%	3.4%	0.2%	0.1%
Montgomery, AL	100,029	96.0%	2.8%	0.3%	0.3%	0.5%	96.0%	2.0%	0.7%	1.3%
Morgantown, WV	49,494	93.8%	2.0%	2.5%	0.4%	1.2%	93.8%	4.6%	1.3%	0.3%
Morristown, TN	24,459	94.0%	5.2%	0.4%	0.3%	0.0%	94.0%	2.1%	2.2%	1.7%
Mount Vernon-Anacortes, WA	27,206	83.6%	9.4%	4.2%	2.3%	0.5%	83.6%	11.9%	3.9%	0.6%
Muncie, IN	39,030	94.1%	1.3%	2.9%	0.4%	1.3%	94.1%	5.2%	0.4%	0.4%
Muskegon, MI	40,756	97.1%	1.5%	1.1%	0.1%	0.2%	97.1%	2.6%	0.2%	0.1%
Myrtle Beach-Conway-North Myrtle Beach, SC-NC	82,532	92.2%	6.4%	0.9%	0.4%	0.1%	92.2%	4.3%	1.6%	1.9%
Napa, CA	33,246	63.3%	34.0%	0.4%	2.3%	0.0%	63.3%	26.7%	7.8%	2.2%
Naples-Immokalee-Marco Island, FL	62,196	56.6%	38.4%	5.0%	0.0%	0.0%	56.6%	32.7%	4.2%	6.4%
Nashville-Davidson–Murfreesboro–Franklin, TN	452,984	87.7%	7.5%	1.8%	1.4%	1.7%	87.7%	8.5%	1.8%	2.1%
New Bern, NC	34,621	89.6%	9.0%	0.1%	1.3%	0.0%	89.6%	1.9%	5.1%	3.5%
New Castle, PA micro	18,981	99.2%	0.4%	0.1%	0.3%	0.0%	99.2%	0.4%	0.0%	0.4%
New Haven-Milford, CT	221,657	75.7%	16.0%	5.0%	2.1%	1.2%	75.7%	18.5%	3.5%	2.3%
New Orleans-Metairie, LA	308,913	86.9%	7.8%	2.3%	2.1%	1.0%	86.9%	7.5%	2.0%	3.6%
New Philadelphia-Dover, OH micro	21,241	95.2%	1.1%	3.7%	0.0%	0.0%	95.2%	3.8%	1.0%	0.0%
New York-Newark-Jersey City, NY-NJ-PA	5,115,314	60.3%	22.8%	9.6%	5.2%	2.1%	60.3%	28.0%	6.2%	5.4%
Niles-Benton Harbor, MI	34,333	91.9%	5.6%	1.4%	1.2%	0.0%	91.9%	5.7%	1.3%	1.1%
North Port-Sarasota-Bradenton, FL	134,039	82.4%	14.7%	1.0%	1.3%	0.5%	82.4%	10.7%	4.1%	2.7%
Norwich-New London, CT	70,256	88.5%	7.9%	1.9%	1.3%	0.3%	88.5%	8.3%	1.7%	1.5%
Ocala, FL	66,776	84.7%	14.1%	0.1%	1.1%	0.0%	84.7%	12.2%	0.4%	2.6%
Ocean City, NJ	19,995	75.6%	15.9%	7.3%	1.3%	0.0%	75.6%	16.1%	5.5%	2.8%
Odessa, TX	45,187	48.9%	49.0%	1.3%	0.4%	0.3%	48.9%	39.7%	5.8%	5.6%
Ogden-Clearfield, UT	173,619	91.8%	5.6%	0.8%	1.6%	0.2%	91.8%	6.7%	1.1%	0.5%
Ogdensburg-Massena, NY micro	31,306	87.1%	2.7%	9.6%	0.3%	0.2%	87.1%	11.8%	1.0%	0.0%
Oklahoma City, OK	350,851	83.8%	12.2%	1.1%	2.1%	0.8%	83.8%	10.4%	3.2%	2.6%
Olympia-Tumwater, WA	68,980	83.4%	7.7%	2.4%	5.8%	0.8%	83.4%	12.3%	1.9%	2.4%
Omaha-Council Bluffs, NE-IA	244,099	89.3%	7.0%	1.3%	1.4%	1.0%	89.3%	6.4%	2.4%	2.0%
Orangeburg, SC micro	24,189	92.6%	5.7%	0.0%	1.6%	0.1%	92.6%	4.9%	1.1%	1.4%
Orlando-Kissimmee-Sanford, FL	621,615	69.2%	24.4%	4.1%	1.7%	0.6%	69.2%	24.1%	3.5%	3.2%
Oshkosh-Neenah, WI	46,883	93.9%	3.2%	0.9%	2.0%	0.0%	93.9%	4.6%	1.1%	0.3%
Ottawa-Peru, IL micro	26,791	90.6%	6.2%	0.3%	2.9%	0.0%	90.6%	8.5%	0.6%	0.3%
Owensboro, KY	27,593	97.4%	1.0%	0.2%	0.5%	0.9%	97.4%	1.7%	0.0%	0.9%
Oxnard-Thousand Oaks-Ventura, CA	213,780	56.5%	38.3%	2.2%	2.5%	0.5%	56.5%	31.4%	3.5%	8.6%
Palm Bay-Melbourne-Titusville, FL	112,681	89.2%	7.0%	2.3%	1.1%	0.3%	89.2%	8.2%	1.9%	0.7%
Panama City, FL	46,495	91.4%	4.0%	2.1%	2.4%	0.1%	91.4%	6.7%	0.4%	1.6%
Parkersburg-Vienna, WV	19,813	97.0%	2.5%	0.3%	0.2%	0.0%	97.0%	2.3%	0.2%	0.5%
Pensacola-Ferry Pass-Brent, FL	127,327	93.8%	2.3%	1.3%	2.0%	0.6%	93.8%	4.9%	1.2%	0.1%
Peoria, IL	96,218	91.6%	4.8%	1.3%	2.2%	0.2%	91.6%	6.3%	1.7%	0.3%
Philadelphia-Camden-Wilmington, PA-NJ-DE-MD	1,580,042	83.4%	7.9%	4.0%	3.5%	1.2%	83.4%	12.0%	2.7%	1.9%
Phoenix-Mesa-Scottsdale, AZ	1,160,054	70.5%	24.4%	1.8%	1.9%	1.4%	70.5%	23.2%	3.0%	3.3%
Pine Bluff, AR	25,971	96.2%	3.6%	0.0%	0.0%	0.3%	96.2%	1.9%	0.7%	1.2%
Pittsburgh, PA	559,230	93.4%	1.3%	2.6%	1.9%	0.8%	93.4%	4.6%	1.8%	0.2%
Pittsfield, MA	30,536	91.0%	4.4%	2.2%	1.1%	1.3%	91.0%	7.2%	0.7%	1.1%
Pocatello, ID	25,609	86.2%	9.8%	1.4%	0.3%	2.3%	86.2%	7.1%	3.5%	3.2%
Port St. Lucie, FL	90,678	77.1%	17.4%	3.6%	1.8%	0.1%	77.1%	13.3%	4.8%	4.7%
Portland-South Portland, ME	118,095	92.8%	1.9%	2.7%	2.0%	0.6%	92.8%	5.6%	1.6%	0.0%
Portland-Vancouver-Hillsboro, OR-WA	580,285	78.3%	10.7%	5.6%	3.9%	1.6%	78.3%	16.8%	2.4%	2.5%
Pottsville, PA micro	30,617	95.7%	2.4%	1.1%	0.8%	0.0%	95.7%	2.9%	1.4%	0.0%

Table G-4: Metropolitan/Micropolitan Statistical Areas—Language Spoken and English Ability—*Continued*

	Millennial Population 13 to 31	Percent by Language Spoken at Home					Percent Who Speak Only English	Percent by Ability to Speak English		
		English Only	Spanish	Other Indo-European Language	Asian and Pacific Island Language	Other Language		Speak English "Very Well"	Speak English "Well"	Speak English "Not Well" or "Not at All"
Prescott, AZ	40,349	84.8%	13.9%	0.3%	0.3%	0.7%	84.8%	10.3%	1.8%	3.1%
Providence-Warwick, RI-MA	414,057	78.1%	13.0%	6.4%	1.9%	0.6%	78.1%	17.4%	2.3%	2.3%
Provo-Orem, UT	203,200	86.6%	8.4%	2.8%	1.8%	0.4%	86.6%	10.3%	1.6%	1.5%
Pueblo, CO	41,292	84.4%	14.1%	0.9%	0.7%	0.0%	84.4%	10.2%	2.6%	2.8%
Punta Gorda, FL	26,086	91.7%	6.2%	1.6%	0.5%	0.0%	91.7%	8.3%	0.0%	0.0%
Racine, WI	45,497	89.5%	9.9%	0.5%	0.1%	0.0%	89.5%	6.0%	1.6%	2.9%
Raleigh, NC	320,952	82.3%	10.8%	2.8%	2.6%	1.5%	82.3%	12.1%	2.4%	3.2%
Rapid City, SD	34,720	96.5%	1.1%	0.5%	0.7%	1.1%	96.5%	2.0%	0.8%	0.7%
Reading, PA	103,706	77.8%	19.4%	1.7%	1.1%	0.1%	77.8%	15.6%	3.7%	2.9%
Redding, CA	43,154	86.8%	6.5%	1.9%	4.7%	0.2%	86.8%	7.6%	2.2%	3.4%
Reno, NV	113,990	73.8%	20.6%	1.6%	3.3%	0.6%	73.8%	20.8%	3.2%	2.2%
Richmond, VA	318,467	88.4%	5.9%	1.9%	2.7%	1.0%	88.4%	8.4%	1.7%	1.5%
Riverside-San Bernardino-Ontario, CA	1,236,472	57.2%	37.2%	1.2%	3.2%	1.1%	57.2%	35.3%	4.3%	3.2%
Roanoke, VA	71,344	92.7%	4.0%	1.7%	0.9%	0.6%	92.7%	4.1%	2.1%	1.0%
Rochester, MN	52,035	88.6%	5.1%	2.2%	1.9%	2.2%	88.6%	9.5%	1.7%	0.1%
Rochester, NY	283,108	87.7%	5.7%	4.0%	1.9%	0.7%	87.7%	9.3%	1.9%	1.1%
Rockford, IL	86,491	85.5%	10.3%	1.5%	2.1%	0.5%	85.5%	11.2%	2.2%	1.1%
Rocky Mount, NC	34,744	94.3%	4.3%	0.0%	1.2%	0.2%	94.3%	4.3%	0.8%	0.6%
Rome, GA	23,869	85.3%	13.4%	0.5%	0.6%	0.3%	85.3%	10.5%	1.5%	2.6%
Roseburg, OR micro	20,735	95.9%	3.9%	0.2%	0.0%	0.0%	95.9%	1.2%	2.6%	0.3%
Sacramento–Roseville–Arden-Arcade, CA	573,311	68.1%	15.2%	7.3%	8.7%	0.7%	68.1%	23.5%	5.0%	3.4%
Saginaw, MI	49,901	96.8%	1.4%	0.6%	0.6%	0.6%	96.8%	1.8%	0.7%	0.8%
Salem, OH micro	23,852	97.1%	2.4%	0.6%	0.0%	0.0%	97.1%	0.6%	0.1%	2.2%
Salem, OR	106,773	72.8%	22.3%	3.1%	0.6%	1.1%	72.8%	22.1%	2.7%	2.5%
Salinas, CA	123,388	45.2%	49.8%	1.3%	3.3%	0.4%	45.2%	34.7%	7.2%	13.0%
Salisbury, MD-DE	89,343	85.4%	9.4%	2.8%	1.9%	0.6%	85.4%	7.4%	2.4%	4.8%
Salt Lake City, UT	322,656	78.5%	14.6%	2.3%	3.2%	1.3%	78.5%	17.2%	2.2%	2.1%
San Angelo, TX	34,968	77.7%	21.6%	0.7%	0.0%	0.0%	77.7%	20.6%	1.3%	0.4%
San Antonio-New Braunfels, TX	643,590	66.8%	30.0%	1.1%	1.3%	0.8%	66.8%	26.4%	3.9%	2.8%
San Diego-Carlsbad, CA	935,309	60.5%	28.7%	3.1%	5.5%	2.1%	60.5%	28.8%	6.8%	3.9%
San Francisco-Oakland-Hayward, CA	1,111,639	59.9%	19.9%	5.1%	13.6%	1.4%	59.9%	28.4%	6.5%	5.1%
San Jose-Sunnyvale-Santa Clara, CA	479,231	48.5%	23.9%	7.6%	18.6%	1.4%	48.5%	38.1%	7.3%	6.2%
San Luis Obispo-Paso Robles-Arroyo Grande, CA	80,673	79.8%	15.9%	1.3%	2.9%	0.1%	79.8%	15.8%	1.9%	2.5%
Santa Cruz-Watsonville, CA	75,403	57.2%	35.2%	1.6%	5.6%	0.4%	57.2%	32.3%	7.0%	3.5%
Santa Fe, NM	29,956	60.4%	34.5%	1.7%	2.0%	1.4%	60.4%	28.2%	5.7%	5.7%
Santa Maria-Santa Barbara, CA	137,268	52.9%	38.5%	2.6%	4.1%	2.0%	52.9%	31.4%	6.4%	9.3%
Santa Rosa, CA	120,963	68.8%	26.3%	2.4%	1.8%	0.7%	68.8%	24.2%	4.1%	3.0%
Savannah, GA	104,999	88.8%	6.4%	2.9%	1.9%	0.0%	88.8%	7.6%	1.7%	2.0%
Scranton–Wilkes-Barre–Hazleton, PA	135,447	87.6%	8.5%	2.1%	1.1%	0.6%	87.6%	8.1%	2.1%	2.2%
Seattle-Tacoma-Bellevue, WA	935,702	75.2%	8.3%	6.0%	8.3%	2.2%	75.2%	18.4%	4.1%	2.2%
Sebastian-Vero Beach, FL	27,498	84.4%	13.2%	1.1%	0.9%	0.5%	84.4%	10.4%	4.9%	0.4%
Sebring, FL	17,203	62.0%	35.9%	1.2%	0.5%	0.3%	62.0%	21.8%	9.8%	6.4%
Sheboygan, WI	25,416	82.0%	9.0%	0.8%	8.1%	0.0%	82.0%	12.1%	2.3%	3.7%
Sherman-Denison, TX	30,297	83.2%	13.5%	1.3%	1.9%	0.0%	83.2%	12.5%	0.4%	3.9%
Show Low, AZ micro	28,335	59.4%	2.5%	0.6%	0.0%	37.5%	59.4%	33.8%	3.3%	3.5%
Shreveport-Bossier City, LA	123,377	96.0%	3.2%	0.5%	0.3%	0.0%	96.0%	2.3%	0.8%	1.0%
Sierra Vista-Douglas, AZ	32,345	58.4%	39.4%	1.3%	0.8%	0.0%	58.4%	35.5%	2.6%	3.5%
Sioux City, IA-NE-SD	44,165	86.7%	11.0%	0.2%	2.1%	0.0%	86.7%	7.1%	4.9%	1.4%
Sioux Falls, SD	63,236	88.5%	4.7%	3.1%	2.3%	1.4%	88.5%	7.9%	1.7%	1.9%
South Bend-Mishawaka, IN-MI	82,057	92.3%	4.8%	1.5%	1.3%	0.2%	92.3%	6.6%	1.1%	0.1%
Spartanburg, SC	84,899	87.1%	7.9%	2.6%	1.9%	0.5%	87.1%	9.6%	2.6%	0.8%
Spokane-Spokane Valley, WA	147,190	90.2%	3.4%	3.0%	1.7%	1.6%	90.2%	6.1%	2.7%	1.0%
Springfield, IL	50,200	95.5%	1.9%	1.8%	0.4%	0.3%	95.5%	4.3%	0.0%	0.2%
Springfield, MA	175,021	74.7%	17.2%	4.6%	2.1%	1.4%	74.7%	18.6%	4.5%	2.2%
Springfield, MO	129,457	94.1%	1.8%	3.3%	0.7%	0.2%	94.1%	3.1%	2.7%	0.2%
Springfield, OH	32,974	93.5%	4.8%	0.6%	0.6%	0.4%	93.5%	4.0%	1.4%	1.1%
St. Cloud, MN	59,001	92.5%	3.7%	0.6%	1.3%	1.9%	92.5%	4.5%	1.3%	1.7%
St. George, UT	36,461	94.6%	5.0%	0.4%	0.0%	0.0%	94.6%	4.8%	0.0%	0.5%
St. Joseph, MO-KS	32,200	95.9%	3.6%	0.0%	0.0%	0.4%	95.9%	3.9%	0.1%	0.0%
St. Louis, MO-IL	701,224	92.9%	2.7%	2.0%	1.8%	0.6%	92.9%	5.7%	1.2%	0.2%
State College, PA	65,126	87.1%	1.3%	3.0%	6.8%	1.8%	87.1%	8.9%	2.8%	1.2%
Staunton-Waynesboro, VA	27,051	92.4%	0.7%	4.6%	2.2%	0.1%	92.4%	6.4%	0.7%	0.5%
Stockton-Lodi, CA	193,213	54.9%	31.3%	4.2%	9.2%	0.3%	54.9%	33.5%	6.5%	5.1%
Sumter, SC	30,387	90.7%	7.8%	1.5%	0.0%	0.0%	90.7%	7.0%	0.3%	1.9%
Sunbury, PA micro	19,987	90.7%	2.8%	6.2%	0.3%	0.0%	90.7%	6.9%	1.8%	0.7%
Syracuse, NY	170,167	90.3%	3.4%	3.4%	2.0%	0.9%	90.3%	6.6%	2.3%	0.7%
Tallahassee, FL	137,443	88.8%	5.7%	3.4%	1.8%	0.4%	88.8%	9.4%	0.9%	0.9%
Tampa-St. Petersburg-Clearwater, FL	670,366	78.3%	16.1%	3.1%	1.8%	0.8%	78.3%	16.5%	2.4%	2.8%
Terre Haute, IN	46,772	93.2%	3.5%	1.0%	0.4%	1.9%	93.2%	4.3%	1.2%	1.3%
Texarkana, TX-AR	38,572	95.5%	4.1%	0.0%	0.2%	0.2%	95.5%	2.3%	0.8%	1.5%
The Villages, FL	11,362	92.0%	7.1%	0.8%	0.0%	0.0%	92.0%	7.2%	0.8%	0.0%
Toledo, OH	170,511	92.6%	3.4%	1.8%	1.0%	1.2%	92.6%	5.6%	1.5%	0.3%
Topeka, KS	54,331	90.8%	6.8%	0.8%	1.3%	0.3%	90.8%	7.1%	1.5%	0.6%
Torrington, CT micro	39,336	90.7%	3.9%	2.4%	1.7%	1.3%	90.7%	7.0%	2.3%	0.1%
Traverse City, MI micro	31,826	92.9%	3.4%	3.0%	0.2%	0.5%	92.9%	6.1%	0.8%	0.2%
Trenton, NJ	97,275	66.2%	17.8%	8.8%	6.0%	1.1%	66.2%	23.5%	6.3%	3.9%

Table G-4: Metropolitan/Micropolitan Statistical Areas—Language Spoken and English Ability—*Continued*

	Millennial Population 13 to 31	Percent by Language Spoken at Home					Percent Who Speak Only English	Percent by Ability to Speak English		
		English Only	Spanish	Other Indo-European Language	Asian and Pacific Island Language	Other Language		Speak English "Very Well"	Speak English "Well"	Speak English "Not Well" or "Not at All"
Truckee-Grass Valley, CA micro	19,138	88.6%	7.7%	3.1%	0.6%	0.0%	88.6%	10.5%	0.0%	0.8%
Tucson, AZ..	272,490	67.3%	26.5%	1.4%	3.0%	1.8%	67.3%	27.3%	3.2%	2.2%
Tullahoma-Manchester, TN micro	23,786	93.4%	5.4%	0.0%	1.2%	0.0%	93.4%	4.0%	0.9%	1.7%
Tulsa, OK..	242,714	88.6%	8.5%	1.0%	1.6%	0.3%	88.6%	7.6%	1.8%	2.0%
Tupelo, MS micro..................................	35,356	93.7%	5.4%	0.9%	0.0%	0.0%	93.7%	1.6%	2.7%	2.1%
Tuscaloosa, AL	77,812	95.8%	3.1%	0.6%	0.5%	0.0%	95.8%	2.4%	1.1%	0.7%
Tyler, TX	57,353	75.7%	20.9%	1.7%	0.0%	1.6%	75.7%	17.7%	4.0%	2.6%
Urban Honolulu, HI	265,827	76.3%	3.5%	1.5%	16.2%	2.5%	76.3%	13.5%	8.6%	1.6%
Utica-Rome, NY	73,705	88.4%	3.7%	5.7%	1.7%	0.5%	88.4%	7.5%	2.6%	1.5%
Valdosta, GA	48,976	90.9%	6.8%	1.9%	0.4%	0.0%	90.9%	6.1%	2.0%	1.1%
Vallejo-Fairfield, CA	114,250	71.2%	21.3%	1.5%	5.9%	0.2%	71.2%	22.4%	3.2%	3.2%
Victoria, TX	25,055	84.6%	14.0%	0.0%	1.4%	0.0%	84.6%	11.9%	1.8%	1.7%
Vineland-Bridgeton, NJ	41,175	70.7%	24.8%	3.6%	0.8%	0.0%	70.7%	18.9%	4.1%	6.2%
Virginia Beach-Norfolk-Newport News, VA-NC..	498,520	89.7%	5.4%	2.0%	2.0%	1.0%	89.7%	7.5%	1.8%	1.0%
Visalia-Porterville, CA..........................	132,184	42.2%	53.1%	1.1%	2.5%	1.1%	42.2%	38.4%	10.8%	8.6%
Waco, TX...	77,186	77.6%	18.0%	1.4%	2.9%	0.0%	77.6%	13.7%	6.8%	1.9%
Walla Walla, WA	16,753	68.7%	26.7%	1.0%	0.6%	3.0%	68.7%	16.4%	6.0%	8.9%
Warner Robins, GA	53,774	92.0%	5.6%	1.1%	0.7%	0.7%	92.0%	5.0%	1.8%	1.1%
Washington-Arlington-Alexandria, DC-VA-MD-WV	1,557,927	72.8%	13.5%	5.6%	4.9%	3.2%	72.8%	20.4%	3.8%	3.1%
Waterloo-Cedar Falls, IA......................	52,275	91.1%	4.9%	3.0%	0.5%	0.4%	91.1%	5.6%	1.6%	1.7%
Watertown-Fort Drum, NY	36,656	92.3%	3.7%	2.9%	0.2%	0.9%	92.3%	6.7%	0.1%	0.8%
Wausau, WI..	31,554	88.0%	3.9%	0.3%	7.9%	0.0%	88.0%	6.3%	4.3%	1.4%
Weirton-Steubenville, WV-OH	28,248	97.2%	1.3%	1.3%	0.2%	0.1%	97.2%	2.4%	0.1%	0.3%
Wenatchee, WA....................................	27,971	62.8%	34.5%	2.0%	0.0%	0.6%	62.8%	29.5%	2.9%	4.8%
Wheeling, WV-OH	32,441	96.8%	1.7%	1.1%	0.2%	0.2%	96.8%	2.3%	0.1%	0.8%
Whitewater-Elkhorn, WI micro	27,115	80.3%	12.3%	7.4%	0.0%	0.0%	80.3%	7.8%	7.2%	4.6%
Wichita Falls, TX	44,773	87.1%	10.6%	1.1%	0.8%	0.4%	87.1%	9.1%	3.0%	0.8%
Wichita, KS	168,613	85.0%	10.8%	1.0%	3.1%	0.1%	85.0%	11.6%	1.8%	1.5%
Williamsport, PA	27,887	96.5%	0.7%	2.7%	0.1%	0.0%	96.5%	3.0%	0.5%	0.0%
Wilmington, NC....................................	70,426	91.6%	6.0%	0.5%	1.0%	1.0%	91.6%	4.7%	0.8%	3.0%
Winchester, VA-WV..............................	29,169	85.7%	12.2%	0.0%	2.1%	0.0%	85.7%	10.0%	3.9%	0.4%
Winston-Salem, NC...............................	156,727	86.7%	11.5%	0.5%	1.1%	0.1%	86.7%	10.2%	1.4%	1.8%
Wooster, OH micro...............................	28,468	83.0%	2.7%	12.8%	1.5%	0.0%	83.0%	10.3%	6.4%	0.3%
Worcester, MA-CT................................	228,311	79.1%	10.8%	5.3%	2.8%	2.0%	79.1%	14.5%	4.3%	2.1%
Yakima, WA...	65,994	47.3%	51.0%	0.5%	0.6%	0.7%	47.3%	42.1%	4.8%	5.9%
York-Hanover, PA	97,575	89.3%	7.9%	1.3%	0.4%	1.2%	89.3%	4.8%	2.1%	3.8%
Youngstown-Warren-Boardman, OH-PA ...	130,034	92.6%	3.3%	3.4%	0.4%	0.3%	92.6%	5.1%	2.0%	0.3%
Yuba City, CA	44,330	63.9%	21.4%	11.0%	2.9%	0.8%	63.9%	29.0%	4.5%	2.6%
Yuma, AZ	59,396	42.2%	56.8%	0.3%	0.3%	0.4%	42.2%	45.1%	5.9%	6.8%

PART H
EMPLOYMENT AND LABOR FORCE STATUS

EMPLOYMENT AND LABOR FORCE STATUS

Understanding the employment situation of the Millennials is complicated by changes in the economy, its impact on labor force participation, and the fact that many Millennials are still pursuing formal education. Younger Millennials who are still in school are not generally captured as part of the labor force by official U.S. Bureau of Labor Statistics (BLS) standards because they are not "looking for work." However, their response to employment questions in the American Community Survey may well have them classified as labor force participants if they are working while in school.

Official BLS employment data for 2013 show an unemployment rate for younger Millennials age 18 to 24 of 14.4 percent, yet in 2008 during the depth of the recession the unemployment rate for that age group was only 11.6 percent. This apparent anomaly illustrates the importance of looking at the size of the labor force in addition to the number of unemployed. While the population base increased between 2008 and 2013, the size of the labor force declined slightly indicating that labor force participation declined during this period. Employment status is a dynamic process with individuals moving in and out of the labor force as education and life cycle changes take place.

About two-thirds (66.4 percent) of younger Millennials are engaged in the civilian labor force meaning they are not in the military and are either employed or unemployed and actively looking for work. A bit more than half (55.4 percent) of all persons age 18 to 24 are employed, 11.0 percent are unemployed, and 1.2 percent

Percent Age 25 to 31 Who Are Employed

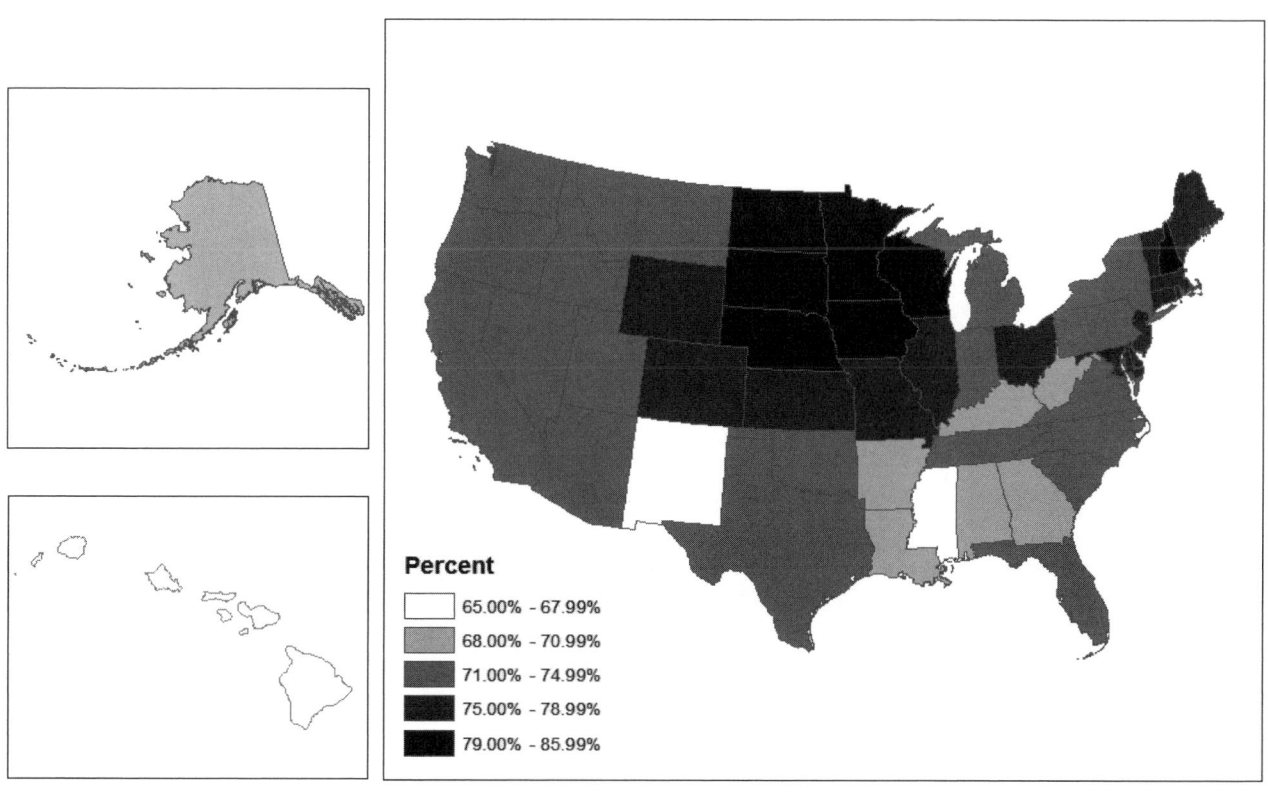

Percent
65.00% - 67.99%
68.00% - 70.99%
71.00% - 74.99%
75.00% - 78.99%
79.00% - 85.99%

are in the armed forces. The remaining young Millennials are classified as not in the labor force. While 11.0 percent of the population is unemployed, the overall unemployment rate for those age 18 to 24 is 16.5 percent because the unemployment rate is based on the civilian labor force not the total population.

The highest unemployment rate is in the District of Columbia at 24.9 percent while the lowest is in North Dakota (3.9 percent). Nebraska has the highest percentage of young Millennials participating in the labor force at 76.6 percent. The District of Columbia is lowest at 55.8 percent. South Dakota has the highest percentage of employed (70.6 percent), and only two states are below 50 percent: the District of Columbia (41.9 percent) and Georgia (49.0 percent). Among the older age group, the highest rate of unemployment is in Mississippi at 14.1 percent, and North Dakota is lowest at 2.3 percent. Labor force participation is high at 81.1 percent nationwide, and it's above 80 percent in 35 states. It's highest in the District of Columbia (88.0 percent) and lowest in Hawaii at 68.7 percent. However, Hawaii also has the highest percentage of older Millennials in the armed forces (11.3 percent). At 85.8 percent, North Dakota has the highest percentage of 25- to 31-year-olds who are employed.

Participation in the civilian labor force among Millennials age 18 to 24 is highest (91.5 percent) in Livingston Parish, LA and lowest in St. Lawrence County, NY at 39.5 percent. Cass County, ND has the highest

percentage who are employed (83.1 percent), and in 99 counties more than two-thirds of the younger age group is employed. Local unemployment can be very high with 322 counties having unemployment rates greater than 15 percent. Sutter County, CA has the highest rate at 42.2 percent, and 63 other counties are above 25 percent. Unemployment declines for the older Millennial age group where the highest rate is 28.3 percent in Rowan County, NC. Still, unemployment is less than 10 percent in 399 counties. Labor force participation ranges from a low of 50.2 percent in Onslow County, NC to 96.1 percent in Dubuque County, IA where 95.5 percent of persons 25 to 31 are employed. A number of counties have a high percentage of armed forces population such as Cumberland County, NC at 27.6 percent. Twenty-one counties are above 10 percent.

In West Jordan City, UT 88.2 percent of Millennials age 18 to 24 are participating in the labor force, and in 58 cities the rate is above 75 percent. The lowest rate (38.8 percent) is in Lawton City, OK. Fargo City, ND has the highest percentage of those employed (84.8 percent), but less than one-third (29.5 percent) are employed in Columbus City, GA. The armed forces presence is highest in Oceanside City, CA due to the nearby Camp Pendleton Marine Corps base. The city with the highest rate of unemployment is Inglewood, CA at 42.2 percent. Fifty-one cities have unemployment rates above 25 percent, while 59 cities are below 10 percent.

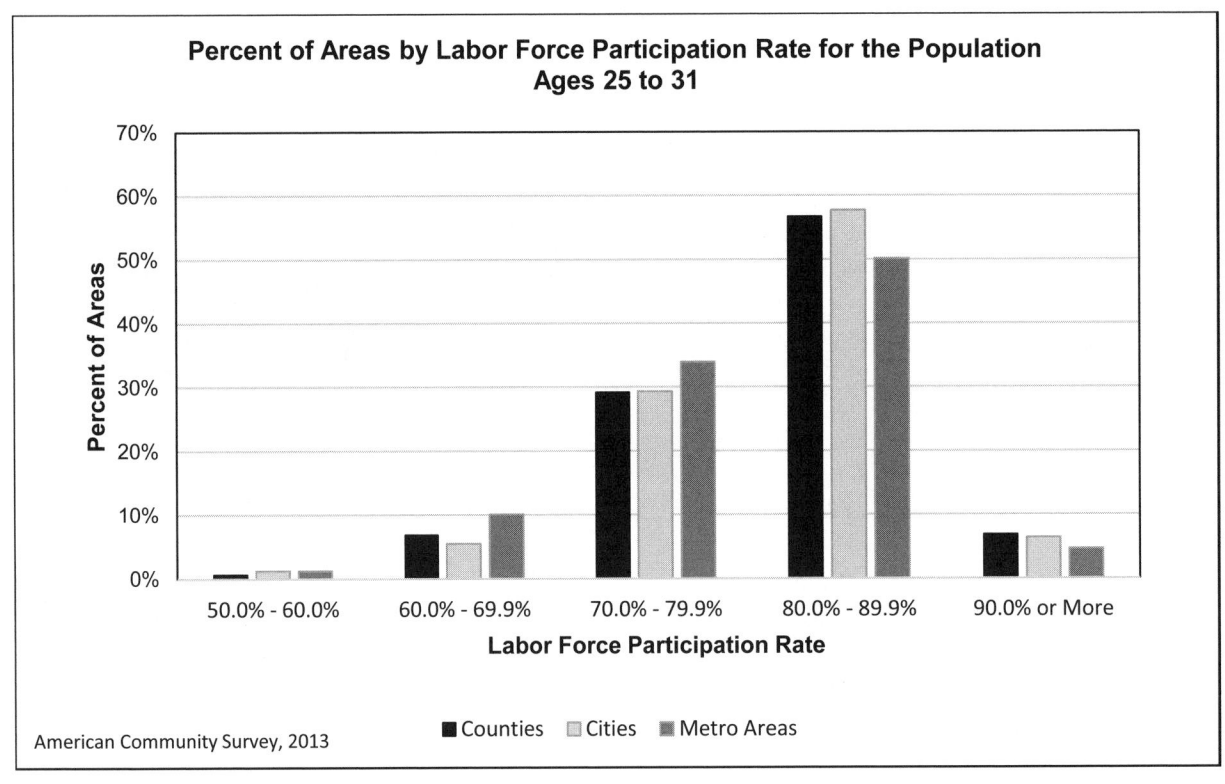

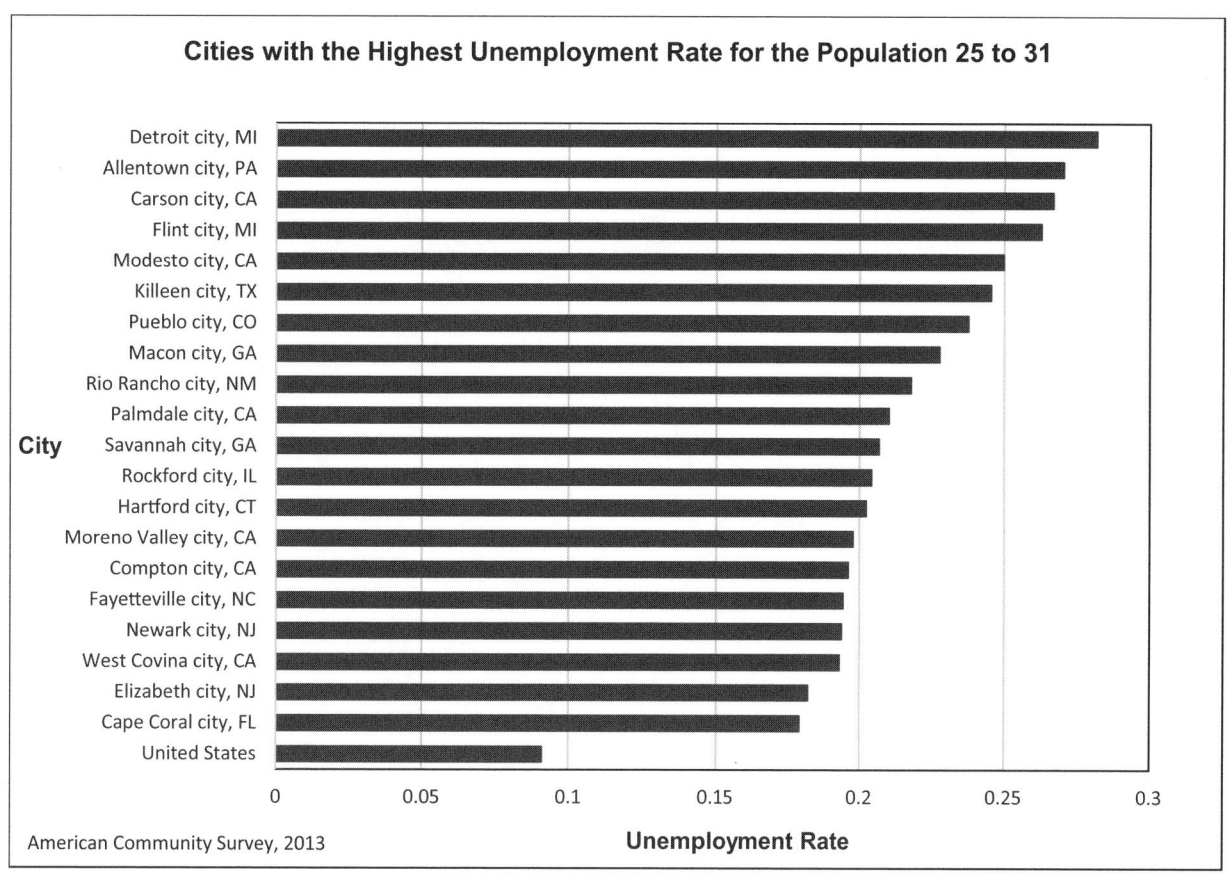

Cities with the Highest Unemployment Rate for the Population 25 to 31

American Community Survey, 2013

Almost all 25 to 31 year olds are participating in the labor force in Independence City, MO (95.4 percent), but just over one-half (54.6 percent) are participating in Fayetteville City, NC. However, Fayetteville does have the largest armed forces percentage at 23.0 percent due to nearby Ft. Bragg, a U.S. Army base. In San Mateo City, CA 92.6 percent of older Millennials are employed, and the percent employed is greater than 75 percent in 145 cities. Unemployment among this age group is below five percent in 56 cities, but it's also greater than 20 percent in 13 cities, with Detroit City, MI having the highest rate at 28.2 percent.

The Grand Island, NE metropolitan area has the highest percent of young Millennials participating in the labor force at 89.9 percent while the Odgensburg-Massena, NY micropolitan area is lowest at 39.5 percent. Labor force participation is above 75 percent in 74 metro areas

but less than 50 percent in 12. The highest percentage of employed 18 to 24 year olds is in the Kokomo, IN metro area at 79.5 percent and the lowest is in the Show Low, AZ micro (28.6 percent). The Jacksonville, NC metro has the highest percentage (42.3 percent) of young Millennials in the armed forces and is home to the U.S. Marine Corps base Camp Lejeune. Unemployment, at 39.0 percent, is highest in the Cleveland, TN metro area.

Among Millennials age 25 to 31, labor force participation ranges from a low of 52.7 percent in the Jacksonville, NC metro to a high of 95.7 percent in the Dubuque, IA metro. Jacksonville is understandably low because of the large armed forces population. Dubuque also has the highest percentage of older Millennials who are employed. The unemployment rate for older Millennials is highest in the Sebring, FL metro area at 23.8 percent and above 20 percent in 14 other metropolitan areas.

Table H-1: States—Labor Force Status

	18 to 24					25 to 31				
	In the Labor Force	Percent			Labor Force Participation Rate	In the Labor Force	Percent			Labor Force Participation Rate
		Employed	Unemployed	In Armed Forces			Employed	Unemployed	In Armed Forces	
United States	21,371,633	55.4%	11.0%	1.2%	67.6%	24,692,915	73.8%	7.4%	0.9%	82.1%
Alabama	323,618	50.4%	13.8%	0.8%	65.0%	337,955	69.9%	8.2%	0.6%	78.7%
Alaska	63,021	56.7%	11.0%	6.9%	74.5%	70,119	69.4%	8.9%	8.3%	86.6%
Arizona	440,256	54.7%	10.8%	0.9%	66.4%	490,078	71.2%	6.8%	0.6%	78.7%
Arkansas	189,489	54.6%	11.1%	0.3%	66.0%	212,922	70.2%	7.4%	0.4%	78.0%
California	2,578,905	50.7%	12.1%	1.4%	64.2%	3,200,738	71.6%	8.3%	1.0%	80.9%
Colorado	372,870	59.6%	10.7%	2.5%	72.8%	459,279	77.3%	5.4%	1.6%	84.3%
Connecticut	239,654	56.7%	11.8%	1.4%	69.9%	264,210	75.9%	8.7%	0.4%	84.9%
Delaware	58,686	51.2%	13.0%	0.6%	64.8%	73,172	75.0%	7.4%	1.0%	83.4%
District of Columbia	46,874	41.9%	13.9%	2.1%	57.9%	98,144	80.0%	8.0%	0.1%	88.1%
Florida	1,175,885	52.7%	11.7%	1.1%	65.4%	1,413,749	71.1%	9.0%	0.8%	80.8%
Georgia	661,364	49.0%	13.6%	1.6%	64.2%	767,197	70.9%	8.8%	1.5%	81.2%
Hawaii	96,782	52.7%	6.5%	11.8%	71.0%	119,731	65.1%	3.5%	11.3%	80.0%
Idaho	114,163	59.6%	10.8%	0.7%	71.1%	115,608	73.5%	7.8%	0.4%	81.7%
Illinois	885,184	57.1%	12.2%	0.6%	69.8%	1,057,814	76.3%	7.9%	0.2%	84.4%
Indiana	450,841	57.7%	9.5%	0.0%	67.2%	469,911	73.6%	7.4%	0.2%	81.2%
Iowa	232,550	67.2%	6.4%	0.1%	73.7%	235,649	81.1%	4.6%	0.1%	85.8%
Kansas	218,233	63.0%	7.6%	1.9%	72.5%	226,726	78.1%	5.5%	2.0%	85.6%
Kentucky	302,026	58.7%	10.7%	1.2%	70.6%	309,557	69.4%	8.1%	0.7%	78.2%
Louisiana	307,070	50.9%	11.4%	1.4%	63.6%	359,586	70.7%	7.1%	0.7%	78.4%
Maine	86,508	65.5%	8.2%	0.1%	73.8%	86,876	76.3%	6.8%	0.2%	83.4%
Maryland	390,255	57.5%	10.1%	1.6%	69.2%	492,323	77.3%	6.5%	1.3%	85.1%
Massachusetts	472,282	58.0%	9.8%	0.1%	67.9%	565,798	78.8%	6.8%	0.2%	85.7%
Michigan	716,216	58.5%	13.1%	0.0%	71.6%	684,148	73.0%	8.7%	0.2%	81.9%
Minnesota	387,493	68.5%	7.7%	0.0%	76.2%	458,140	82.0%	4.9%	0.1%	87.0%
Mississippi	195,537	46.0%	13.5%	1.2%	60.7%	202,027	67.4%	11.0%	0.7%	79.1%
Missouri	431,347	61.1%	9.7%	2.0%	72.7%	465,702	76.4%	6.1%	0.5%	83.0%
Montana	75,736	62.6%	9.3%	1.7%	73.6%	70,903	74.2%	6.9%	1.2%	82.3%
Nebraska	147,257	69.2%	7.4%	0.5%	77.1%	150,956	82.3%	2.7%	1.1%	86.1%
Nevada	186,633	57.4%	14.5%	0.7%	72.6%	227,209	71.9%	9.5%	1.0%	82.5%
New Hampshire	89,227	62.1%	8.1%	0.2%	70.4%	93,311	79.4%	6.3%	0.1%	85.9%
New Jersey	515,627	54.2%	10.4%	0.3%	64.9%	666,270	75.3%	8.8%	0.3%	84.3%
New Mexico	145,059	52.0%	13.2%	1.2%	66.5%	141,652	66.9%	8.0%	1.1%	76.0%
New York	1,218,329	50.3%	10.3%	0.5%	61.2%	1,657,769	74.2%	7.9%	0.3%	82.4%
North Carolina	676,808	52.1%	12.1%	3.6%	67.8%	721,276	71.1%	8.1%	3.3%	82.5%
North Dakota	73,901	69.0%	2.8%	4.3%	76.1%	63,063	85.8%	2.1%	2.1%	90.0%
Ohio	805,728	61.4%	10.5%	0.1%	72.0%	858,101	75.8%	6.6%	0.4%	82.8%
Oklahoma	269,173	56.9%	9.2%	1.9%	67.9%	297,874	73.7%	5.5%	1.1%	80.3%
Oregon	254,440	56.4%	12.7%	0.0%	69.1%	298,745	71.9%	8.8%	0.3%	81.0%
Pennsylvania	829,093	55.0%	11.1%	0.1%	66.2%	956,783	74.8%	8.3%	0.1%	83.2%
Rhode Island	84,289	58.7%	11.2%	0.4%	70.3%	82,344	76.8%	8.2%	0.6%	85.6%
South Carolina	338,936	52.2%	13.0%	2.3%	67.5%	338,699	71.6%	8.4%	1.7%	81.7%
South Dakota	64,591	70.6%	5.9%	0.4%	76.8%	66,235	80.0%	5.0%	2.2%	87.1%
Tennessee	438,529	56.5%	12.4%	0.4%	69.3%	485,652	72.5%	7.9%	1.1%	81.5%
Texas	1,828,422	55.8%	9.7%	1.4%	66.9%	2,159,735	74.1%	5.7%	0.9%	80.8%
Utah	255,186	68.5%	7.8%	0.1%	76.5%	233,497	72.9%	4.3%	0.4%	77.6%
Vermont	40,372	56.8%	5.5%	0.0%	62.2%	40,989	77.2%	4.7%	0.0%	81.9%
Virginia	569,489	54.1%	10.0%	4.2%	68.3%	666,296	74.3%	5.8%	3.0%	83.1%
Washington	457,971	55.7%	10.6%	2.5%	68.8%	572,954	72.8%	6.3%	2.7%	81.8%
West Virginia	107,993	50.6%	10.6%	0.1%	61.3%	114,478	70.0%	7.8%	0.1%	77.9%
Wisconsin	417,828	66.5%	9.0%	0.0%	75.5%	445,067	79.8%	5.8%	0.1%	85.7%
Wyoming	43,907	62.4%	9.7%	1.7%	73.8%	45,898	78.0%	4.1%	2.0%	84.1%

Table H-2: Counties—Labor Force Status

	18 to 24					25 to 31				
	In the Labor Force	Percent				In the Labor Force	Percent			
		Employed	Unemployed	In Armed Forces	Labor Force Participation Rate		Employed	Unemployed	In Armed Forces	Labor Force Participation Rate
Alabama										
Baldwin County	12,198	67.8%	6.8%	0.0%	74.7%	10,608	70.4%	4.0%	0.0%	74.3%
Calhoun County	7,946	51.3%	13.2%	2.0%	66.5%	8,612	67.1%	14.5%	0.0%	81.6%
Etowah County	5,484	45.5%	13.4%	0.0%	58.9%	5,764	68.3%	3.6%	0.0%	71.9%
Houston County	6,236	45.5%	21.2%	4.4%	71.1%	8,274	67.2%	11.0%	5.9%	84.1%
Jefferson County	41,191	51.3%	16.6%	0.0%	67.9%	54,878	76.0%	6.8%	0.0%	82.8%
Lauderdale County	6,447	43.8%	13.2%	0.0%	57.0%	6,697	71.6%	11.1%	0.0%	82.7%
Lee County	16,504	46.4%	5.7%	2.9%	55.0%	12,274	74.6%	7.6%	4.6%	86.8%
Madison County	24,782	58.8%	11.1%	0.6%	70.5%	26,762	78.7%	6.0%	0.0%	84.7%
Marshall County	5,754	59.9%	19.4%	0.0%	79.3%	7,952	82.5%	4.6%	0.1%	87.1%
Mobile County	28,629	51.2%	16.9%	0.0%	68.1%	29,811	68.3%	9.7%	0.6%	78.6%
Montgomery County	16,612	46.9%	9.8%	5.2%	62.0%	17,216	68.7%	4.9%	0.7%	74.4%
Morgan County	7,620	55.0%	17.7%	0.0%	72.7%	6,902	68.5%	9.6%	0.0%	78.1%
Shelby County	11,161	58.4%	7.5%	0.0%	65.8%	16,218	81.6%	6.2%	0.0%	87.8%
Tuscaloosa County	22,304	45.6%	10.4%	0.0%	56.0%	17,922	75.4%	7.3%	0.0%	82.7%
Alaska										
Fairbanks North Star Borough	11,014	51.4%	14.5%	11.2%	77.1%	12,470	64.9%	14.5%	15.4%	94.8%
Matanuska-Susitna Borough	8,015	64.9%	16.4%	0.0%	81.4%	7,146	65.6%	15.6%	1.5%	82.7%
Arizona										
Cochise County	7,898	50.4%	2.4%	11.9%	64.7%	8,609	60.5%	4.1%	9.5%	74.1%
Coconino County	15,812	47.1%	12.1%	0.0%	59.2%	11,639	77.2%	5.9%	0.0%	83.0%
Maricopa County	261,156	58.0%	9.4%	0.1%	67.5%	326,619	74.7%	6.1%	0.2%	81.0%
Mohave County	9,638	51.0%	17.2%	0.0%	68.2%	11,229	70.9%	8.1%	0.0%	79.0%
Navajo County	4,738	28.4%	16.5%	0.0%	44.9%	5,780	47.2%	13.1%	0.0%	60.3%
Pima County	82,074	53.6%	12.4%	1.5%	67.5%	70,130	69.8%	8.9%	1.0%	79.7%
Pinal County	21,042	53.9%	11.8%	0.0%	65.7%	19,752	56.6%	4.0%	0.0%	60.6%
Yavapai County	10,831	58.1%	17.2%	0.0%	75.3%	10,539	69.4%	3.8%	1.2%	74.4%
Yuma County	15,589	45.7%	10.4%	8.0%	64.1%	14,771	63.6%	9.2%	3.2%	76.0%
Arkansas										
Benton County	14,380	66.1%	5.8%	0.0%	72.0%	16,996	72.7%	2.9%	0.3%	75.8%
Craighead County	7,132	46.6%	17.4%	0.0%	63.9%	8,642	71.2%	6.5%	0.0%	77.7%
Faulkner County	10,587	56.6%	6.5%	1.9%	65.1%	13,117	74.6%	6.6%	1.4%	82.6%
Garland County	6,352	56.7%	18.8%	0.0%	75.5%	4,490	66.2%	6.5%	0.0%	72.7%
Pulaski County	24,927	62.9%	6.9%	1.2%	71.0%	37,692	76.5%	7.7%	1.2%	85.4%
Saline County	6,511	74.9%	5.5%	0.0%	80.4%	10,526	87.3%	4.9%	0.0%	92.1%
Sebastian County	6,883	58.9%	8.4%	0.0%	67.2%	10,645	65.9%	13.9%	0.0%	79.8%
Washington County	19,439	58.2%	3.9%	0.0%	62.0%	19,848	77.1%	7.7%	0.0%	84.8%
California										
Alameda County	91,092	50.4%	10.3%	0.3%	61.0%	140,988	73.6%	8.4%	0.5%	82.6%
Butte County	20,171	50.2%	9.5%	0.0%	59.7%	14,764	68.7%	6.1%	0.0%	74.7%
Contra Costa County	64,839	57.0%	11.8%	0.0%	68.8%	75,459	71.2%	8.9%	0.5%	80.7%
El Dorado County	10,079	51.8%	24.0%	0.0%	75.8%	9,023	62.6%	8.2%	0.0%	70.8%
Fresno County	65,962	49.9%	10.9%	0.0%	60.8%	78,564	66.6%	10.9%	0.3%	77.7%
Humboldt County	11,734	46.9%	17.5%	0.3%	64.8%	10,194	68.0%	7.0%	0.0%	75.0%
Imperial County	13,724	48.8%	17.9%	0.9%	67.6%	12,690	59.9%	8.8%	1.5%	70.3%
Kern County	58,582	47.6%	13.1%	0.4%	61.0%	64,263	61.0%	8.0%	0.9%	69.9%
Kings County	11,337	45.4%	10.2%	9.5%	65.0%	11,799	59.9%	4.6%	3.3%	67.9%
Los Angeles County	657,530	48.6%	12.9%	0.1%	61.6%	898,581	73.3%	8.5%	0.1%	81.9%
Madera County	8,571	46.4%	9.1%	0.0%	55.5%	10,492	55.6%	11.6%	0.0%	67.2%
Marin County	10,614	48.4%	12.2%	0.0%	60.6%	12,063	73.6%	5.9%	0.0%	79.5%
Merced County	20,801	41.5%	24.6%	0.0%	66.0%	18,720	61.5%	11.7%	0.0%	73.2%
Monterey County	26,906	44.5%	7.5%	3.8%	55.8%	34,198	64.8%	7.5%	3.1%	75.5%
Napa County	9,918	72.7%	2.7%	0.0%	75.4%	9,966	83.4%	9.0%	0.0%	92.5%
Nevada County	4,518	56.6%	4.6%	0.0%	61.2%	5,025	82.5%	3.4%	0.0%	85.8%
Orange County	206,341	56.0%	8.7%	0.2%	64.9%	257,017	77.5%	5.1%	0.3%	82.8%
Placer County	18,905	56.7%	7.9%	0.0%	64.6%	24,983	77.1%	7.0%	1.4%	85.4%
Riverside County	159,694	48.3%	17.2%	0.2%	65.7%	172,605	67.7%	11.6%	0.6%	79.9%
Sacramento County	98,071	50.0%	17.3%	0.1%	67.3%	123,944	71.2%	9.6%	0.1%	80.9%
San Bernardino County	153,945	48.1%	13.7%	2.1%	64.0%	160,334	64.6%	9.5%	1.4%	75.5%
San Diego County	249,565	47.8%	10.1%	10.2%	68.0%	305,217	69.4%	7.0%	5.5%	82.0%
San Francisco County	41,593	52.8%	11.7%	0.0%	64.5%	124,697	84.5%	5.6%	0.6%	90.7%
San Joaquin County	51,823	54.9%	14.6%	0.0%	69.4%	49,492	69.6%	9.6%	0.2%	79.3%
San Luis Obispo County	24,719	48.6%	2.8%	4.7%	56.2%	18,852	74.1%	5.4%	0.0%	79.5%
San Mateo County	41,762	61.7%	10.3%	0.0%	72.0%	59,353	79.3%	6.9%	0.3%	86.5%
Santa Barbara County	46,712	59.1%	7.9%	0.8%	67.8%	33,464	74.8%	7.3%	0.8%	82.9%
Santa Clara County	109,658	56.6%	10.1%	0.0%	66.6%	167,110	76.0%	8.3%	0.2%	84.5%
Santa Cruz County	25,454	54.2%	7.8%	0.0%	62.1%	18,450	79.8%	4.7%	0.0%	84.5%
Shasta County	9,259	40.8%	13.5%	0.0%	54.3%	10,705	66.1%	4.7%	0.0%	70.8%
Solano County	30,261	52.1%	13.3%	4.2%	69.6%	35,069	69.9%	6.7%	5.1%	81.6%
Sonoma County	30,447	57.0%	9.7%	0.2%	66.9%	35,803	73.0%	7.8%	1.5%	82.2%
Stanislaus County	40,789	57.4%	16.1%	0.0%	73.5%	38,083	61.1%	14.2%	0.0%	75.3%
Sutter County	6,773	36.5%	26.7%	1.8%	65.0%	7,064	61.5%	19.1%	1.5%	82.1%
Tulare County	30,966	48.1%	14.3%	0.0%	62.3%	35,253	64.3%	11.6%	0.6%	76.4%
Ventura County	60,983	60.8%	8.8%	1.6%	71.3%	63,219	74.3%	7.9%	2.2%	84.5%
Yolo County	20,094	43.4%	7.3%	0.0%	50.7%	15,993	69.1%	12.0%	0.5%	81.5%

Table H-2: Counties—Labor Force Status—*Continued*

	18 to 24					25 to 31				
	In the Labor Force	Percent				In the Labor Force	Percent			
		Employed	Unemployed	In Armed Forces	Labor Force Participation Rate		Employed	Unemployed	In Armed Forces	Labor Force Participation Rate
Colorado										
Adams County	34,581	65.7%	12.1%	0.4%	78.2%	44,508	79.0%	5.2%	0.0%	84.1%
Arapahoe County	38,689	59.0%	13.7%	0.6%	73.3%	55,278	82.2%	7.0%	0.2%	89.4%
Boulder County	30,680	59.7%	6.8%	0.0%	66.5%	23,683	84.2%	3.9%	0.5%	88.6%
Denver County	47,143	67.1%	8.1%	0.6%	75.8%	90,536	79.5%	5.0%	0.3%	84.8%
Douglas County	15,225	63.0%	8.6%	0.0%	71.6%	17,008	82.7%	3.0%	0.0%	85.7%
El Paso County	54,671	49.7%	13.6%	14.4%	77.7%	57,298	67.5%	4.9%	10.2%	82.6%
Jefferson County	34,187	62.7%	9.9%	0.0%	72.5%	41,193	77.5%	7.3%	0.0%	84.8%
Larimer County	31,886	60.0%	8.7%	0.0%	68.7%	27,040	84.1%	4.3%	0.4%	88.7%
Mesa County	10,335	55.0%	11.2%	0.0%	66.2%	11,617	71.6%	9.4%	0.0%	81.0%
Pueblo County	9,981	52.1%	10.3%	0.9%	63.3%	11,563	64.3%	12.0%	0.0%	76.3%
Weld County	21,881	57.6%	16.6%	0.4%	74.5%	21,988	71.6%	8.0%	0.2%	79.9%
Connecticut										
Fairfield County	57,238	57.2%	14.7%	0.0%	71.9%	66,639	79.2%	8.6%	0.0%	87.7%
Hartford County	55,849	55.5%	14.3%	0.0%	69.8%	69,335	75.9%	9.3%	0.3%	85.6%
Litchfield County	10,011	57.8%	15.6%	0.0%	73.4%	12,783	90.0%	4.5%	0.0%	94.5%
Middlesex County	10,634	65.2%	6.6%	0.0%	71.8%	11,573	80.7%	6.2%	0.8%	87.7%
New Haven County	55,007	53.7%	9.7%	0.1%	63.5%	64,673	73.5%	7.2%	0.1%	80.8%
New London County	23,219	54.9%	8.2%	15.6%	78.6%	21,357	69.6%	12.2%	2.8%	84.6%
Tolland County	18,500	63.6%	5.6%	0.0%	69.2%	9,077	69.7%	8.6%	0.0%	78.3%
Windham County	9,196	60.5%	16.5%	0.0%	77.0%	8,773	67.1%	15.7%	0.0%	82.8%
Delaware										
Kent County	11,469	48.7%	15.2%	2.6%	66.6%	13,318	74.0%	5.9%	4.3%	84.2%
New Castle County	36,461	51.4%	11.6%	0.2%	63.2%	46,595	74.7%	7.9%	0.1%	82.7%
Sussex County	10,756	53.1%	15.8%	0.0%	68.9%	13,259	77.1%	7.2%	1.0%	85.3%
Florida										
Alachua County	31,691	47.3%	7.5%	0.0%	54.8%	21,817	70.6%	5.9%	0.0%	76.5%
Bay County	10,683	63.2%	7.3%	2.2%	72.8%	11,092	53.2%	8.0%	2.9%	64.2%
Brevard County	32,330	56.9%	15.3%	1.3%	73.4%	32,463	74.7%	8.9%	0.7%	84.4%
Broward County	102,361	50.9%	14.0%	0.2%	65.0%	138,942	73.1%	9.4%	0.2%	82.7%
Charlotte County	7,327	59.5%	12.6%	0.0%	72.1%	5,703	57.1%	10.2%	0.0%	67.3%
Citrus County	7,109	57.6%	27.2%	0.0%	84.8%	4,636	51.8%	15.9%	0.0%	67.7%
Clay County	11,051	59.4%	9.8%	0.0%	69.2%	14,338	72.2%	6.4%	7.6%	86.2%
Collier County	17,069	66.1%	9.5%	0.0%	75.7%	18,545	75.3%	8.0%	0.0%	83.3%
Duval County	60,344	50.7%	12.3%	6.1%	69.1%	86,519	72.7%	10.6%	1.8%	85.2%
Escambia County	28,706	48.8%	6.3%	17.9%	73.0%	25,941	69.1%	7.8%	6.1%	83.0%
Flagler County	5,377	58.9%	5.4%	0.0%	64.4%	3,659	61.3%	2.5%	0.0%	63.9%
Hernando County	7,212	48.9%	14.4%	0.0%	63.3%	9,142	60.3%	12.5%	0.0%	72.8%
Highlands County	5,031	47.3%	24.4%	0.0%	71.7%	4,914	58.0%	20.6%	0.0%	78.6%
Hillsborough County	85,431	55.8%	10.2%	0.8%	66.8%	112,639	73.9%	8.1%	0.8%	82.8%
Indian River County	5,460	49.1%	13.4%	0.0%	62.5%	6,840	68.9%	14.1%	0.0%	83.0%
Lake County	14,475	54.9%	12.6%	0.0%	67.5%	19,473	78.3%	6.0%	0.0%	84.3%
Lee County	34,540	58.3%	11.6%	0.0%	69.9%	40,617	70.1%	11.5%	0.0%	81.6%
Leon County	42,473	50.2%	15.0%	0.0%	65.2%	24,598	76.2%	7.2%	0.6%	84.0%
Manatee County	16,285	51.1%	10.0%	0.8%	62.0%	18,570	69.3%	10.7%	0.0%	80.0%
Marion County	14,220	43.4%	14.8%	0.0%	58.2%	17,764	62.9%	9.2%	0.0%	72.1%
Martin County	7,006	54.4%	17.4%	0.0%	71.8%	10,305	84.0%	5.3%	0.0%	89.2%
Miami-Dade County	148,389	47.9%	11.5%	0.1%	59.5%	214,655	70.4%	9.5%	0.2%	80.1%
Okaloosa County	15,216	59.0%	3.7%	14.9%	77.6%	18,360	61.6%	6.2%	13.1%	80.9%
Orange County	93,324	53.4%	9.8%	0.0%	63.1%	123,337	73.4%	11.1%	0.4%	84.9%
Osceola County	18,916	55.6%	10.7%	0.0%	66.3%	20,997	66.9%	4.1%	0.0%	71.0%
Palm Beach County	79,684	58.1%	13.5%	0.1%	71.8%	99,204	77.6%	9.0%	0.1%	86.7%
Pasco County	23,039	56.7%	8.2%	0.1%	65.0%	24,992	69.6%	7.5%	0.3%	77.3%
Pinellas County	48,666	59.0%	11.0%	0.7%	70.7%	62,686	72.6%	9.2%	0.6%	82.3%
Polk County	35,163	51.2%	12.1%	0.0%	63.3%	41,878	67.3%	8.5%	0.0%	75.7%
Santa Rosa County	9,739	58.9%	6.6%	3.8%	69.4%	11,266	58.9%	9.2%	6.2%	74.3%
Sarasota County	16,462	49.2%	14.3%	0.0%	63.5%	18,074	84.9%	3.6%	0.0%	88.5%
Seminole County	31,824	59.0%	15.7%	0.0%	74.7%	36,887	79.7%	8.9%	0.0%	88.6%
St. Johns County	10,213	50.3%	6.5%	0.0%	56.8%	11,500	72.6%	9.7%	0.0%	82.3%
St. Lucie County	14,444	53.1%	10.3%	0.0%	63.4%	16,742	71.0%	9.3%	0.0%	80.3%
Sumter County	3,297	63.7%	13.9%	0.0%	77.6%	4,229	68.8%	16.8%	0.0%	85.5%
Volusia County	26,300	52.4%	7.7%	0.0%	60.0%	29,860	66.6%	5.9%	0.0%	72.5%
Georgia										
Bartow County	7,431	54.4%	6.7%	0.0%	61.1%	7,756	72.0%	13.4%	0.0%	85.4%
Bibb County	9,799	41.3%	17.5%	0.0%	58.8%	12,705	67.7%	16.7%	0.0%	84.4%
Carroll County	8,414	48.1%	10.2%	0.0%	58.4%	7,142	63.1%	9.5%	0.0%	72.6%
Chatham County	22,364	46.8%	16.0%	2.8%	65.6%	26,442	64.8%	11.1%	3.1%	78.9%
Cherokee County	10,488	58.4%	7.1%	0.0%	65.5%	16,902	79.8%	7.9%	0.0%	87.7%
Clarke County	19,684	43.9%	10.7%	0.1%	54.6%	12,448	78.4%	11.1%	0.8%	90.3%
Clayton County	17,860	42.1%	20.6%	1.3%	64.1%	22,225	61.1%	17.5%	0.0%	78.6%
Cobb County	49,370	60.7%	11.9%	0.1%	72.7%	59,308	78.9%	7.3%	0.0%	86.2%
Columbia County	8,890	51.2%	19.2%	0.6%	71.0%	9,184	74.8%	2.7%	5.6%	83.1%
Coweta County	7,584	66.5%	7.9%	0.0%	74.4%	8,979	68.2%	9.5%	2.2%	79.9%
DeKalb County	47,756	48.1%	19.5%	0.0%	67.6%	71,663	79.6%	8.3%	0.0%	87.9%
Dougherty County	6,139	31.1%	21.1%	0.0%	52.2%	8,038	67.1%	16.8%	1.8%	85.8%
Douglas County	5,699	41.3%	17.2%	0.0%	58.5%	11,443	87.3%	6.3%	0.0%	93.6%

Table H-2: Counties—Labor Force Status—Continued

| | 18 to 24 | | | | | 25 to 31 | | | | |
| | In the Labor Force | Percent | | | | In the Labor Force | Percent | | | |
		Employed	Unemployed	In Armed Forces	Labor Force Participation Rate		Employed	Unemployed	In Armed Forces	Labor Force Participation Rate
Georgia—Cont.										
Fayette County	6,591	55.8%	10.1%	0.0%	65.9%	4,346	66.5%	15.4%	0.0%	81.9%
Floyd County	5,871	50.3%	9.4%	0.0%	59.7%	5,578	66.0%	10.4%	0.0%	76.4%
Forsyth County	8,254	52.7%	11.0%	0.0%	63.7%	10,966	80.5%	8.8%	0.0%	89.3%
Fulton County	62,917	50.8%	11.4%	0.0%	62.2%	96,979	77.1%	8.9%	0.1%	86.2%
Gwinnett County	51,231	54.8%	10.5%	0.0%	65.3%	61,713	74.1%	6.2%	0.5%	80.8%
Hall County	13,362	61.9%	14.0%	0.3%	76.1%	14,697	78.6%	11.2%	0.0%	89.8%
Henry County	13,048	56.2%	8.0%	0.0%	64.2%	12,004	77.2%	4.2%	1.3%	82.7%
Houston County	9,340	40.4%	15.4%	3.0%	58.9%	12,840	70.7%	8.7%	2.1%	81.5%
Lowndes County	14,819	55.0%	13.1%	4.3%	72.4%	10,981	73.8%	7.8%	6.9%	88.4%
Muscogee County	18,157	30.2%	14.6%	25.8%	70.6%	16,477	50.0%	8.5%	17.8%	76.3%
Newton County	8,181	52.9%	28.3%	0.0%	81.2%	5,783	68.1%	5.0%	0.0%	73.0%
Paulding County	7,192	51.6%	6.2%	0.0%	57.8%	9,065	76.3%	3.5%	0.0%	79.9%
Richmond County	16,095	42.8%	14.6%	9.4%	66.8%	18,927	62.6%	10.3%	4.9%	77.8%
Whitfield County	9,338	71.9%	11.8%	1.8%	85.5%	6,734	65.6%	13.9%	0.0%	79.5%
Hawaii										
Hawaii County	8,640	45.4%	11.3%	0.0%	56.7%	11,344	63.3%	4.7%	2.4%	70.5%
Honolulu County	74,840	50.5%	5.9%	15.4%	71.7%	89,660	62.5%	3.2%	14.7%	80.5%
Maui County	7,585	71.0%	3.1%	0.0%	74.2%	12,673	79.7%	4.1%	0.0%	83.9%
Idaho										
Ada County	30,467	63.8%	9.9%	0.1%	73.8%	32,696	77.5%	7.4%	0.4%	85.3%
Bonneville County	5,716	63.6%	0.7%	0.0%	64.2%	8,088	78.9%	3.8%	0.0%	82.8%
Canyon County	10,607	57.7%	5.9%	0.0%	63.6%	13,488	78.6%	5.9%	0.0%	84.5%
Kootenai County	9,528	58.6%	14.3%	1.1%	74.0%	9,289	59.7%	13.7%	0.0%	73.4%
Illinois										
Champaign County	25,128	44.2%	8.3%	0.0%	52.5%	19,577	79.8%	4.8%	0.0%	84.6%
Cook County	339,080	53.0%	13.7%	0.0%	66.7%	512,693	76.8%	7.9%	0.0%	84.7%
DeKalb County	15,102	59.7%	15.0%	0.0%	74.7%	8,933	81.8%	2.8%	0.0%	84.6%
DuPage County	58,091	63.7%	10.5%	0.0%	74.2%	75,318	80.5%	6.3%	0.1%	86.9%
Kane County	37,131	68.9%	9.6%	0.0%	78.5%	40,395	79.3%	5.7%	0.0%	85.0%
Kankakee County	7,120	53.6%	8.7%	0.0%	62.4%	7,586	77.6%	13.8%	0.0%	91.4%
Kendall County	5,600	64.8%	3.5%	0.0%	68.3%	10,001	66.3%	16.6%	0.0%	82.9%
Lake County	53,126	57.4%	7.4%	10.3%	75.1%	45,555	76.3%	10.7%	2.0%	89.0%
LaSalle County	7,629	56.5%	27.1%	0.0%	83.6%	8,545	82.0%	9.2%	0.0%	91.1%
Macon County	7,943	64.9%	12.7%	0.0%	77.7%	7,901	71.1%	11.0%	0.6%	82.7%
Madison County	20,473	62.2%	15.4%	0.0%	77.6%	21,675	76.0%	8.3%	0.2%	84.5%
McHenry County	21,917	69.7%	10.3%	0.0%	80.0%	20,431	76.6%	10.9%	0.0%	87.5%
McLean County	23,609	68.8%	7.2%	0.0%	76.0%	16,056	89.3%	3.0%	0.0%	92.3%
Peoria County	13,477	62.3%	10.7%	0.0%	73.1%	16,262	73.0%	10.7%	0.4%	84.1%
Rock Island County	9,854	72.0%	4.4%	0.0%	76.3%	8,843	75.8%	4.4%	0.0%	80.2%
Sangamon County	12,008	65.0%	6.4%	0.4%	71.8%	15,156	79.9%	4.1%	0.0%	84.0%
St. Clair County	16,859	53.4%	10.6%	1.1%	65.1%	20,386	72.1%	9.2%	1.5%	82.8%
Tazewell County	7,628	47.0%	24.0%	0.0%	70.9%	9,281	77.9%	2.3%	0.0%	80.2%
Will County	44,451	61.6%	11.7%	0.0%	73.3%	44,247	77.3%	7.8%	0.0%	85.1%
Winnebago County	20,896	59.0%	16.1%	0.0%	75.1%	19,392	69.9%	12.2%	0.0%	82.0%
Indiana										
Allen County	24,848	59.3%	12.5%	0.0%	71.7%	27,592	73.6%	8.7%	0.0%	82.3%
Clark County	6,596	60.8%	3.2%	0.0%	64.1%	8,081	74.9%	8.3%	0.0%	83.2%
Delaware County	16,349	55.9%	11.8%	0.0%	67.7%	7,654	66.0%	16.1%	0.3%	82.4%
Elkhart County	13,238	72.1%	2.7%	0.0%	74.8%	13,059	71.0%	5.3%	0.0%	76.3%
Hamilton County	15,481	66.3%	9.5%	0.0%	75.8%	19,948	78.9%	5.5%	1.0%	85.3%
Hendricks County	9,262	54.4%	10.2%	0.0%	64.6%	11,321	82.5%	2.9%	0.0%	85.4%
Johnson County	9,598	69.8%	3.9%	0.0%	73.7%	10,234	67.8%	12.8%	0.0%	80.5%
Lake County	27,359	51.4%	9.7%	0.0%	61.0%	32,178	72.9%	9.9%	0.0%	82.9%
LaPorte County	6,971	65.5%	10.8%	0.0%	76.3%	7,030	60.9%	4.2%	0.0%	65.2%
Madison County	7,663	59.8%	9.5%	0.0%	69.2%	8,122	71.4%	2.7%	0.0%	74.1%
Marion County	65,568	58.1%	13.7%	0.2%	72.0%	93,471	75.0%	9.3%	0.0%	84.4%
Monroe County	20,985	47.4%	5.5%	0.0%	52.9%	10,884	76.3%	5.2%	0.0%	81.6%
Porter County	11,404	56.4%	11.2%	0.0%	67.6%	11,538	70.0%	10.7%	0.0%	80.7%
St. Joseph County	18,943	52.9%	9.7%	0.0%	62.5%	19,584	78.0%	9.3%	0.6%	87.9%
Tippecanoe County	21,864	46.1%	3.6%	0.0%	49.7%	14,409	78.8%	1.8%	0.0%	80.6%
Vanderburgh County	12,731	55.3%	8.6%	0.0%	63.9%	13,272	72.8%	4.5%	0.0%	77.3%
Vigo County	10,364	58.7%	5.4%	0.0%	64.1%	6,433	54.6%	9.8%	0.9%	65.3%
Iowa										
Black Hawk County	17,262	69.9%	4.0%	0.0%	74.0%	10,769	76.8%	13.8%	0.0%	90.6%
Dubuque County	7,416	68.6%	6.5%	0.0%	75.1%	6,904	95.5%	0.7%	0.0%	96.1%
Johnson County	18,825	57.5%	3.1%	0.0%	60.6%	15,194	79.4%	0.9%	0.0%	80.3%
Linn County	15,039	70.8%	10.4%	0.0%	81.2%	20,245	81.9%	8.7%	1.0%	91.5%
Polk County	31,055	70.2%	8.2%	0.1%	78.4%	42,407	78.5%	5.9%	0.0%	84.5%
Pottawattamie County	5,425	65.9%	3.5%	0.0%	69.4%	7,303	85.2%	1.7%	0.0%	86.9%
Scott County	9,945	58.8%	7.2%	0.0%	66.1%	13,418	80.2%	1.5%	0.0%	81.7%
Story County	15,860	58.6%	2.7%	0.0%	61.3%	8,393	75.5%	8.0%	0.0%	83.5%
Woodbury County	8,044	73.0%	5.0%	0.0%	78.0%	9,171	86.9%	5.8%	0.0%	92.7%
Kansas										
Douglas County	17,262	64.3%	5.6%	0.0%	69.9%	13,010	80.8%	8.4%	0.0%	89.2%
Johnson County	31,891	63.7%	9.8%	0.0%	73.5%	45,591	86.1%	2.6%	0.2%	88.9%

Table H-2: Counties—Labor Force Status—*Continued*

| | 18 to 24 | | | | | 25 to 31 | | | | |
| | In the Labor Force | Percent | | | | In the Labor Force | Percent | | | |
		Employed	Unemployed	In Armed Forces	Labor Force Participation Rate		Employed	Unemployed	In Armed Forces	Labor Force Participation Rate
Kansas—Cont.										
Sedgwick County	37,669	67.4%	10.1%	0.7%	78.1%	47,142	73.5%	7.6%	4.0%	85.0%
Shawnee County	13,277	60.6%	14.2%	0.0%	74.8%	14,168	82.6%	5.5%	0.0%	88.1%
Wyandotte County	11,641	65.1%	10.6%	0.0%	75.7%	12,321	71.1%	8.7%	0.0%	79.8%
Kentucky										
Boone County	7,943	76.5%	4.0%	0.0%	80.5%	10,761	79.3%	13.4%	0.0%	92.7%
Campbell County	6,059	60.8%	12.4%	0.0%	73.2%	6,236	73.6%	4.6%	0.0%	78.2%
Daviess County	6,872	67.0%	10.2%	0.0%	77.2%	6,372	71.0%	9.5%	0.0%	80.5%
Fayette County	30,810	60.5%	10.5%	0.0%	71.0%	28,085	78.0%	7.4%	0.4%	85.7%
Hardin County	7,031	58.9%	14.4%	7.8%	81.1%	8,570	70.5%	3.7%	8.9%	83.1%
Jefferson County	50,385	62.9%	10.7%	0.6%	74.2%	64,574	78.5%	6.9%	0.0%	85.4%
Kenton County	11,601	67.6%	14.2%	0.0%	81.8%	14,189	78.3%	7.7%	1.0%	87.0%
Warren County	12,554	67.2%	3.0%	0.5%	70.6%	11,497	79.7%	6.8%	0.0%	86.5%
Louisiana										
Ascension Parish	7,317	69.0%	6.2%	0.0%	75.2%	8,454	81.6%	3.4%	0.0%	85.0%
Bossier Parish	8,691	42.6%	7.9%	16.4%	66.9%	11,704	71.5%	7.4%	3.1%	82.1%
Caddo Parish	14,497	49.0%	7.2%	0.2%	56.5%	20,910	73.4%	6.4%	0.0%	79.8%
Calcasieu Parish	13,588	45.2%	20.1%	0.0%	65.3%	13,319	73.5%	6.6%	0.2%	80.3%
East Baton Rouge Parish	42,452	55.1%	9.3%	0.0%	64.4%	38,992	76.7%	8.1%	0.0%	84.8%
Jefferson Parish	25,443	49.8%	12.4%	1.3%	63.5%	38,919	75.9%	3.3%	0.7%	79.9%
Lafayette Parish	18,581	65.1%	6.4%	0.0%	71.5%	23,688	85.1%	5.0%	0.0%	90.1%
Lafourche Parish	6,202	54.0%	4.6%	0.0%	58.6%	8,183	84.1%	4.1%	0.0%	88.2%
Livingston Parish	11,588	68.2%	23.2%	0.0%	91.5%	9,745	70.9%	8.7%	0.0%	79.6%
Orleans Parish	21,701	40.9%	11.3%	0.3%	52.5%	39,708	70.6%	7.4%	0.4%	78.4%
Ouachita Parish	8,499	39.4%	10.0%	0.0%	49.3%	10,080	62.6%	5.7%	0.0%	68.3%
Rapides Parish	7,833	29.8%	10.6%	18.5%	58.9%	10,402	66.7%	5.3%	7.0%	79.0%
St. Tammany Parish	13,991	58.3%	14.6%	0.0%	72.9%	17,563	76.6%	7.6%	1.2%	85.4%
Tangipahoa Parish	10,397	53.1%	21.5%	0.0%	74.6%	11,297	61.6%	16.6%	0.9%	79.1%
Terrebonne Parish	7,315	60.3%	9.1%	0.9%	70.3%	8,503	72.0%	3.0%	1.1%	76.1%
Maine										
Androscoggin County	7,221	73.4%	2.1%	0.0%	75.6%	8,640	81.0%	3.6%	0.0%	84.6%
Cumberland County	21,233	68.8%	6.9%	0.1%	75.8%	23,250	74.1%	11.8%	0.4%	86.3%
Kennebec County	7,568	71.8%	2.4%	0.0%	74.2%	8,804	91.1%	2.7%	1.3%	95.1%
Penobscot County	12,620	56.6%	12.6%	0.0%	69.2%	9,762	65.0%	8.0%	0.0%	73.0%
York County	11,600	66.9%	7.0%	0.2%	74.2%	14,543	75.8%	13.4%	0.1%	89.3%
Maryland										
Anne Arundel County	41,807	57.6%	10.9%	14.0%	82.5%	44,592	74.0%	4.2%	4.2%	82.4%
Baltimore County	52,042	56.6%	9.1%	0.0%	65.7%	72,190	80.9%	5.9%	0.1%	86.9%
Carroll County	11,748	75.2%	5.2%	0.0%	80.4%	10,921	85.3%	1.0%	0.0%	86.3%
Cecil County	7,928	66.9%	16.6%	0.5%	84.1%	7,917	78.6%	9.8%	0.0%	88.4%
Charles County	10,466	62.0%	10.5%	2.9%	75.4%	11,427	75.0%	7.5%	1.5%	83.9%
Frederick County	18,312	69.2%	10.3%	0.9%	80.4%	17,767	81.9%	5.9%	1.3%	89.1%
Harford County	16,171	67.9%	9.1%	0.6%	77.5%	17,694	79.1%	3.7%	0.7%	83.5%
Howard County	14,700	57.0%	4.8%	0.0%	61.8%	24,874	83.1%	4.9%	1.8%	89.7%
Montgomery County	53,878	60.8%	9.5%	0.5%	70.8%	84,955	81.7%	6.5%	0.6%	88.9%
Prince George's County	63,864	54.7%	10.7%	0.3%	65.8%	82,333	77.6%	8.5%	1.4%	87.5%
St. Mary's County	7,389	59.9%	9.0%	2.6%	71.5%	7,161	61.7%	7.9%	14.3%	83.9%
Washington County	8,960	60.0%	9.1%	0.0%	69.1%	9,471	66.5%	6.7%	0.0%	73.1%
Wicomico County	10,710	56.6%	11.0%	0.0%	67.6%	7,883	77.3%	7.0%	0.0%	84.3%
Massachusetts										
Barnstable County	12,192	75.4%	7.9%	0.0%	83.3%	13,050	82.6%	5.5%	1.3%	89.4%
Berkshire County	8,850	51.7%	16.3%	0.0%	68.0%	7,719	80.7%	4.0%	0.0%	84.7%
Bristol County	39,144	60.5%	13.6%	0.0%	74.1%	37,042	70.3%	10.8%	0.2%	81.3%
Essex County	48,311	58.0%	9.4%	0.0%	67.4%	57,278	77.8%	8.1%	0.4%	86.3%
Hampden County	35,661	53.0%	11.9%	0.0%	64.9%	32,909	71.2%	12.6%	0.0%	83.8%
Hampshire County	17,911	54.4%	12.9%	0.0%	67.3%	10,301	73.1%	10.2%	0.0%	83.2%
Middlesex County	97,883	58.7%	7.5%	0.1%	66.3%	151,185	80.6%	4.6%	0.4%	85.6%
Norfolk County	37,294	56.3%	8.9%	0.0%	65.2%	52,053	81.7%	5.3%	0.0%	87.1%
Plymouth County	32,435	64.4%	14.6%	0.0%	79.0%	32,421	83.6%	5.6%	0.5%	89.7%
Suffolk County	74,433	54.6%	10.1%	0.2%	64.9%	115,654	81.4%	6.5%	0.1%	88.0%
Worcester County	58,934	61.0%	9.3%	0.5%	70.7%	60,201	78.6%	5.0%	0.0%	83.5%
Michigan										
Allegan County	7,116	68.1%	6.8%	0.0%	74.9%	6,721	78.1%	4.9%	0.0%	83.0%
Bay County	7,640	63.5%	14.7%	0.0%	78.3%	7,298	67.5%	7.7%	0.0%	75.2%
Berrien County	9,380	57.2%	11.6%	0.0%	68.9%	10,054	72.7%	9.4%	0.0%	82.1%
Calhoun County	8,115	58.2%	14.0%	0.0%	72.2%	8,495	79.8%	2.7%	0.0%	82.5%
Eaton County	5,588	61.9%	6.5%	0.0%	68.4%	8,539	80.0%	3.8%	0.0%	83.8%
Genesee County	26,180	50.1%	17.9%	0.0%	68.0%	27,732	64.4%	14.2%	0.0%	78.6%
Ingham County	38,139	57.1%	9.1%	0.0%	66.2%	25,375	80.4%	8.2%	0.0%	88.6%
Jackson County	9,723	59.8%	8.9%	0.0%	68.7%	10,781	59.6%	12.6%	0.0%	72.1%
Kalamazoo County	30,371	57.6%	16.0%	0.0%	73.6%	20,364	80.1%	5.6%	0.3%	86.0%
Kent County	49,486	70.1%	12.2%	0.0%	82.3%	59,515	79.9%	7.6%	0.0%	87.5%
Lenawee County	6,468	59.8%	9.4%	0.0%	69.1%	7,150	80.7%	2.0%	0.0%	82.7%
Livingston County	11,022	62.0%	10.5%	0.0%	72.5%	11,033	87.1%	2.1%	0.0%	89.2%
Macomb County	57,128	66.1%	10.9%	0.0%	77.0%	62,041	76.9%	6.7%	0.2%	83.8%
Monroe County	11,466	71.6%	14.9%	0.0%	86.5%	10,508	77.3%	13.2%	0.0%	90.5%

Table H-2: Counties—Labor Force Status—*Continued*

	18 to 24					25 to 31				
	In the Labor Force	Percent				In the Labor Force	Percent			
		Employed	Unemployed	In Armed Forces	Labor Force Participation Rate		Employed	Unemployed	In Armed Forces	Labor Force Participation Rate
Michigan—Cont.										
Muskegon County	11,254	52.2%	27.4%	0.0%	79.6%	10,546	64.0%	14.2%	0.8%	79.1%
Oakland County	78,263	66.1%	11.2%	0.1%	77.5%	89,914	79.6%	6.1%	0.2%	85.9%
Ottawa County	26,847	66.6%	7.1%	0.4%	74.0%	17,308	66.7%	12.1%	0.0%	78.7%
Saginaw County	16,607	65.6%	11.0%	0.0%	76.6%	11,646	71.8%	5.2%	0.5%	77.6%
St. Clair County	10,792	53.8%	20.3%	0.0%	74.1%	8,525	72.0%	5.5%	0.0%	77.6%
Washtenaw County	37,268	50.1%	7.8%	0.0%	58.0%	30,023	78.8%	4.0%	0.0%	82.8%
Wayne County	119,837	49.4%	18.5%	0.1%	68.0%	118,275	64.7%	12.5%	0.0%	77.2%
Minnesota										
Anoka County	22,759	74.1%	8.9%	0.0%	83.0%	26,311	78.8%	4.6%	0.0%	83.4%
Carver County	6,231	76.7%	6.5%	0.0%	83.1%	6,710	85.9%	6.0%	0.0%	91.9%
Dakota County	24,225	62.5%	14.0%	0.0%	76.5%	33,428	85.5%	5.1%	0.0%	90.6%
Hennepin County	81,109	65.3%	8.9%	0.0%	74.2%	137,919	83.6%	5.3%	0.2%	89.0%
Olmsted County	9,959	74.1%	5.4%	0.0%	79.6%	12,509	82.4%	4.2%	0.0%	86.6%
Ramsey County	44,658	65.6%	9.2%	0.0%	74.7%	49,834	78.6%	6.4%	0.0%	85.0%
Scott County	7,866	68.9%	13.6%	0.0%	82.5%	10,212	91.9%	2.6%	0.0%	94.5%
St. Louis County	16,034	63.0%	2.8%	0.4%	66.2%	14,040	73.6%	3.3%	0.0%	76.9%
Stearns County	20,951	76.9%	7.3%	0.0%	84.3%	12,662	93.1%	1.6%	0.0%	94.6%
Washington County	15,198	74.9%	4.3%	0.0%	79.2%	19,253	83.9%	4.2%	0.0%	88.1%
Wright County	7,278	78.7%	0.0%	0.0%	78.7%	10,597	81.8%	3.2%	0.0%	85.0%
Mississippi										
DeSoto County	10,927	60.8%	17.1%	0.0%	77.9%	11,521	79.3%	6.2%	0.0%	85.5%
Harrison County	16,111	56.3%	8.5%	13.5%	78.4%	17,792	74.6%	7.0%	5.4%	87.0%
Hinds County	20,498	52.6%	16.1%	0.0%	68.7%	23,540	72.7%	10.6%	1.8%	85.2%
Jackson County	8,852	49.6%	13.1%	1.4%	64.1%	11,341	74.9%	8.1%	0.0%	83.0%
Madison County	5,784	47.6%	16.3%	0.0%	64.0%	6,082	63.2%	6.9%	6.4%	76.4%
Rankin County	6,491	48.0%	9.3%	0.0%	57.3%	11,447	70.4%	10.1%	0.0%	80.5%
Missouri										
Boone County	23,374	61.7%	2.5%	0.0%	64.2%	18,223	86.5%	4.1%	0.0%	90.6%
Cass County	6,789	71.5%	10.7%	0.0%	82.2%	6,436	72.1%	13.6%	1.9%	87.5%
Clay County	14,928	73.1%	5.4%	0.0%	78.5%	19,630	81.3%	2.0%	0.5%	83.7%
Franklin County	6,572	70.9%	9.0%	0.0%	79.9%	6,598	74.0%	2.3%	0.0%	76.3%
Greene County	28,621	63.1%	8.3%	0.0%	71.4%	25,582	77.7%	5.1%	0.0%	82.8%
Jackson County	45,816	67.8%	9.4%	0.0%	77.1%	62,517	81.2%	5.3%	0.1%	86.6%
Jasper County	9,233	67.3%	13.3%	0.0%	80.6%	9,545	75.9%	4.0%	0.0%	80.0%
Jefferson County	13,897	59.3%	20.8%	0.0%	80.1%	16,913	82.3%	3.7%	0.4%	86.4%
Platte County	6,979	78.9%	5.7%	0.0%	84.6%	10,092	86.5%	9.6%	0.0%	96.1%
St. Charles County	23,404	70.5%	6.0%	0.0%	76.4%	30,645	82.3%	5.8%	0.0%	88.0%
St. Louis County	65,902	61.3%	13.0%	0.0%	74.3%	75,433	78.7%	6.3%	0.0%	85.0%
Montana										
Flathead County	5,409	66.2%	10.4%	0.0%	76.5%	5,181	71.9%	2.3%	0.0%	74.2%
Gallatin County	10,926	72.0%	2.5%	0.0%	74.5%	8,983	88.7%	4.8%	0.0%	93.4%
Missoula County	11,422	54.2%	15.4%	0.0%	69.6%	10,729	64.2%	17.6%	0.0%	81.8%
Yellowstone County	12,509	70.3%	12.1%	0.0%	82.3%	11,121	77.3%	4.3%	0.0%	81.6%
Nebraska										
Douglas County	40,442	73.7%	5.1%	0.0%	78.8%	52,788	84.3%	2.5%	0.0%	86.9%
Lancaster County	34,562	66.5%	7.9%	0.0%	74.4%	27,643	83.2%	3.9%	0.3%	87.5%
Sarpy County	12,448	74.9%	3.6%	4.8%	83.3%	14,043	71.9%	4.3%	6.3%	82.5%
Nevada										
Clark County	135,267	56.7%	15.4%	0.8%	72.9%	172,381	72.2%	9.6%	1.1%	82.9%
Washoe County	30,862	61.2%	9.2%	0.3%	70.8%	35,630	75.0%	8.8%	0.2%	84.0%
New Hampshire										
Hillsborough County	25,142	63.0%	10.7%	0.0%	73.7%	33,480	81.2%	7.3%	0.3%	88.9%
Merrimack County	9,284	59.0%	5.1%	0.0%	64.0%	8,957	81.0%	3.0%	0.0%	83.9%
Rockingham County	16,121	60.0%	7.3%	1.3%	68.6%	16,531	77.2%	6.8%	0.0%	84.0%
Strafford County	12,678	61.4%	8.4%	0.0%	69.8%	8,913	79.7%	5.1%	0.0%	84.8%
New Jersey										
Atlantic County	18,577	57.0%	12.6%	0.0%	69.5%	18,543	67.9%	13.1%	1.1%	82.2%
Bergen County	44,668	54.0%	6.6%	0.3%	61.0%	60,113	76.7%	6.0%	0.1%	82.8%
Burlington County	30,120	59.1%	10.5%	5.0%	74.6%	30,610	74.3%	5.6%	2.7%	82.6%
Camden County	31,985	56.1%	13.5%	0.0%	69.6%	40,873	75.9%	7.8%	0.4%	84.1%
Cape May County	5,168	64.2%	4.7%	0.0%	68.9%	5,899	73.4%	6.2%	1.3%	80.9%
Cumberland County	11,035	62.8%	18.8%	0.5%	82.1%	11,343	49.5%	14.5%	0.0%	64.0%
Essex County	45,925	43.4%	18.7%	0.0%	62.1%	64,836	71.7%	12.5%	0.0%	84.2%
Gloucester County	19,172	60.4%	13.0%	0.0%	73.4%	20,366	73.6%	10.8%	0.0%	84.4%
Hudson County	37,189	51.0%	10.1%	0.0%	61.1%	86,544	78.8%	6.6%	0.0%	85.4%
Hunterdon County	7,000	49.9%	8.1%	0.0%	58.0%	4,849	66.0%	11.9%	0.0%	77.9%
Mercer County	24,667	49.2%	11.6%	0.0%	60.9%	26,036	71.0%	10.9%	0.0%	81.9%
Middlesex County	45,487	45.6%	9.0%	0.0%	54.6%	64,808	77.0%	8.9%	0.0%	85.8%
Monmouth County	33,952	55.6%	8.3%	0.0%	63.9%	42,445	80.3%	8.4%	0.0%	88.7%
Morris County	25,738	54.1%	8.7%	0.0%	62.8%	32,299	82.5%	5.8%	0.0%	88.3%
Ocean County	31,073	59.5%	11.0%	0.3%	70.8%	37,435	76.3%	7.6%	0.8%	84.7%
Passaic County	32,342	58.0%	3.3%	0.0%	61.3%	37,074	70.3%	10.6%	0.0%	80.9%
Somerset County	16,772	62.1%	8.0%	0.0%	70.2%	20,602	82.2%	5.2%	0.0%	87.4%
Sussex County	9,393	67.0%	10.7%	0.0%	77.7%	8,560	73.2%	12.8%	0.0%	86.0%
Union County	34,413	60.2%	11.2%	0.2%	71.6%	42,434	76.5%	11.1%	0.0%	87.6%

Table H-2: Counties—Labor Force Status—*Continued*

	18 to 24					25 to 31				
	In the Labor Force	Percent				In the Labor Force	Percent			
		Employed	Unemployed	In Armed Forces	Labor Force Participation Rate		Employed	Unemployed	In Armed Forces	Labor Force Participation Rate
New Jersey—Cont.										
Warren County	6,418	62.3%	6.5%	0.0%	68.8%	5,794	85.0%	6.2%	0.0%	91.3%
New Mexico										
Bernalillo County	49,657	56.9%	11.4%	0.6%	68.8%	54,525	68.6%	8.2%	0.7%	77.5%
Doña Ana County	24,200	55.8%	17.0%	1.9%	74.6%	14,788	73.5%	6.2%	1.4%	81.1%
San Juan County	7,870	50.4%	15.0%	0.0%	65.4%	7,577	60.9%	7.9%	0.3%	69.1%
Sandoval County	6,924	51.2%	12.4%	0.0%	63.6%	8,789	64.3%	12.5%	0.0%	76.8%
Santa Fe County	6,872	48.7%	11.7%	0.6%	61.0%	9,156	75.3%	3.1%	0.0%	78.4%
New York										
Albany County	27,050	54.4%	7.4%	0.0%	61.8%	25,518	80.2%	7.6%	0.3%	88.1%
Bronx County	91,951	39.4%	15.7%	0.3%	55.4%	115,981	63.6%	12.7%	0.3%	76.7%
Broome County	16,196	50.4%	9.2%	0.0%	59.6%	12,930	67.7%	11.2%	0.0%	78.9%
Chautauqua County	9,253	46.8%	12.2%	0.0%	58.9%	8,899	73.7%	10.2%	0.0%	83.9%
Dutchess County	24,270	59.5%	9.7%	0.0%	69.2%	17,951	70.3%	11.8%	0.8%	82.9%
Erie County	63,066	59.4%	6.3%	0.1%	65.8%	77,073	77.2%	7.1%	0.3%	84.5%
Jefferson County	11,081	42.4%	6.0%	26.1%	74.4%	11,169	47.9%	13.6%	20.8%	82.2%
Kings County	138,711	42.5%	11.8%	0.1%	54.4%	274,753	72.9%	7.9%	0.2%	81.0%
Monroe County	56,015	55.0%	13.5%	0.1%	68.6%	59,796	75.4%	6.9%	0.4%	82.7%
Nassau County	79,360	57.5%	9.3%	0.0%	66.8%	91,025	76.2%	7.3%	0.0%	83.5%
New York County	15,409	59.0%	14.2%	0.3%	73.5%	13,636	72.3%	9.3%	0.0%	81.6%
Niagara County	84,821	45.3%	8.1%	0.0%	53.4%	234,156	82.3%	5.4%	0.0%	87.6%
Oneida County	15,612	59.0%	9.3%	0.0%	68.3%	17,193	75.0%	6.7%	0.6%	82.3%
Onondaga County	32,900	55.0%	7.6%	0.0%	62.5%	38,503	77.7%	8.8%	0.1%	86.6%
Ontario County	7,593	72.3%	5.9%	0.0%	78.2%	7,049	74.4%	11.8%	0.0%	86.2%
Orange County	30,867	55.0%	12.5%	9.1%	76.6%	22,403	68.1%	10.3%	0.7%	79.1%
Oswego County	9,425	54.8%	12.2%	0.0%	67.0%	8,225	62.0%	18.2%	1.0%	81.2%
Putnam County	6,156	71.6%	1.3%	0.0%	72.9%	6,304	85.9%	4.4%	0.0%	90.3%
Queens County	121,927	46.0%	11.2%	0.0%	57.2%	215,556	73.5%	7.8%	0.1%	81.4%
Rensselaer County	11,095	57.6%	5.6%	0.0%	63.1%	13,531	79.2%	6.4%	0.0%	85.5%
Richmond County	23,957	42.8%	10.6%	0.0%	53.4%	31,264	68.7%	6.3%	0.0%	75.0%
Rockland County	20,079	54.9%	10.8%	0.0%	65.7%	21,687	75.6%	7.8%	0.0%	83.4%
Saratoga County	13,249	53.4%	10.5%	4.9%	68.8%	17,748	85.5%	7.7%	0.9%	94.1%
Schenectady County	10,867	58.5%	16.3%	0.0%	74.8%	13,737	78.3%	12.2%	0.0%	90.6%
St. Lawrence County	6,416	32.5%	7.1%	0.2%	39.8%	6,805	66.5%	10.9%	2.0%	79.4%
Steuben County	4,794	49.3%	12.4%	0.0%	61.7%	5,006	69.0%	6.0%	0.0%	75.0%
Suffolk County	92,890	57.9%	9.7%	0.0%	67.6%	100,865	76.9%	6.1%	0.0%	83.0%
Tompkins County	12,412	42.8%	3.1%	0.0%	45.9%	7,303	71.9%	0.7%	0.0%	72.6%
Ulster County	11,012	49.2%	10.4%	0.0%	59.6%	9,976	70.2%	11.3%	0.0%	81.5%
Wayne County	5,542	79.1%	2.2%	0.0%	81.3%	5,750	70.9%	4.4%	0.0%	75.3%
Westchester County	54,231	51.7%	12.8%	0.0%	64.6%	65,751	79.2%	8.1%	0.0%	87.3%
North Carolina										
Alamance County	9,352	57.2%	5.5%	0.0%	62.7%	10,990	72.6%	8.7%	0.0%	81.3%
Brunswick County	4,184	59.0%	8.4%	0.0%	67.4%	4,989	65.9%	11.7%	0.0%	77.6%
Buncombe County	15,296	69.9%	10.5%	0.0%	80.4%	21,477	81.8%	4.8%	0.0%	86.6%
Burke County	4,625	45.5%	21.0%	0.0%	66.5%	5,776	69.5%	8.3%	0.0%	77.8%
Cabarrus County	12,438	54.1%	23.4%	0.0%	77.4%	13,170	78.5%	7.0%	0.0%	85.5%
Catawba County	8,821	57.5%	4.8%	0.0%	62.3%	8,920	75.3%	8.2%	0.0%	83.5%
Cleveland County	7,513	54.0%	17.7%	0.0%	71.6%	5,669	68.2%	10.1%	0.0%	78.3%
Craven County	11,396	46.4%	7.3%	33.2%	86.9%	9,402	58.6%	4.6%	16.7%	79.8%
Cumberland County	31,119	35.5%	12.7%	24.7%	73.0%	31,333	41.7%	8.7%	27.6%	77.9%
Davidson County	9,914	49.9%	21.5%	0.0%	71.4%	9,093	63.4%	12.5%	0.0%	75.9%
Durham County	17,357	48.9%	6.6%	0.0%	55.5%	31,793	77.6%	5.1%	0.5%	83.2%
Forsyth County	24,889	57.4%	8.3%	0.0%	65.6%	23,355	74.4%	5.3%	0.0%	79.7%
Gaston County	13,595	58.8%	14.5%	0.0%	73.4%	14,950	79.2%	10.6%	0.0%	89.8%
Guilford County	32,089	44.1%	11.6%	0.0%	55.7%	41,824	75.2%	8.9%	1.1%	85.2%
Harnett County	6,886	47.4%	8.8%	2.4%	58.6%	11,159	49.2%	13.9%	14.9%	78.0%
Henderson County	5,866	68.1%	13.6%	0.0%	81.7%	5,687	77.8%	6.8%	0.0%	84.6%
Iredell County	10,667	59.1%	13.3%	0.0%	72.4%	9,753	68.1%	12.0%	0.0%	80.1%
Johnston County	10,688	53.0%	16.1%	0.0%	69.1%	10,026	73.2%	5.1%	0.0%	78.3%
Mecklenburg County	70,803	61.3%	12.9%	0.2%	74.4%	102,359	79.5%	8.2%	0.2%	87.9%
Moore County	3,523	53.2%	13.3%	0.0%	66.5%	5,978	74.1%	4.7%	2.1%	80.9%
Nash County	6,165	55.5%	14.5%	0.0%	70.0%	5,129	67.5%	14.5%	0.0%	82.1%
New Hanover County	20,977	60.3%	13.4%	0.4%	74.1%	17,761	82.7%	5.1%	1.1%	88.9%
Onslow County	35,067	30.9%	9.9%	43.8%	84.6%	21,008	43.5%	6.7%	27.2%	77.5%
Orange County	15,091	51.3%	4.8%	0.0%	56.1%	10,945	76.6%	8.9%	0.0%	85.5%
Pitt County	21,283	54.9%	8.6%	0.0%	63.5%	13,515	80.6%	6.0%	0.9%	87.4%
Randolph County	7,393	59.6%	6.2%	0.0%	65.8%	9,658	75.3%	8.1%	0.0%	83.4%
Robeson County	8,106	33.4%	17.3%	0.0%	50.7%	7,643	64.5%	9.5%	0.0%	74.1%
Rockingham County	3,360	46.4%	18.3%	0.0%	64.7%	6,201	68.2%	7.4%	0.0%	75.6%
Rowan County	9,124	50.1%	19.8%	0.0%	69.9%	8,604	59.5%	23.5%	0.0%	83.0%
Union County	13,609	66.6%	9.7%	0.0%	76.3%	11,016	80.9%	1.9%	0.0%	82.9%
Wake County	60,967	55.1%	9.8%	0.0%	64.9%	82,201	80.3%	6.3%	0.8%	87.4%
Wayne County	9,874	60.6%	13.6%	9.2%	83.4%	10,019	65.5%	8.8%	13.5%	87.8%
North Dakota										
Cass County	23,937	83.1%	2.1%	0.6%	85.9%	17,922	88.1%	5.1%	0.2%	93.3%

Table H-2: Counties—Labor Force Status—*Continued*

	18 to 24					25 to 31				
	In the Labor Force	Percent				In the Labor Force	Percent			
		Employed	Unemployed	In Armed Forces	Labor Force Participation Rate		Employed	Unemployed	In Armed Forces	Labor Force Participation Rate
Ohio										
Allen County	8,907	66.1%	16.6%	0.0%	82.7%	7,793	79.2%	7.6%	0.0%	86.8%
Ashtabula County	5,119	52.1%	10.0%	0.0%	62.1%	6,455	69.2%	6.2%	2.3%	77.8%
Butler County	31,608	59.5%	8.5%	0.0%	68.0%	22,683	69.9%	4.1%	0.0%	73.9%
Clark County	8,985	65.2%	7.1%	0.0%	72.3%	9,703	80.0%	8.7%	0.0%	88.6%
Clermont County	12,119	72.6%	5.3%	0.0%	77.9%	14,369	75.7%	4.9%	0.0%	80.6%
Columbiana County	6,316	54.0%	22.0%	0.0%	76.0%	5,546	57.6%	5.5%	0.0%	63.1%
Cuyahoga County	85,103	59.7%	13.9%	0.0%	73.7%	97,348	77.0%	7.5%	0.1%	84.5%
Delaware County	9,496	70.9%	2.0%	0.0%	72.9%	10,772	85.2%	3.8%	0.0%	89.0%
Fairfield County	9,435	68.0%	7.4%	0.0%	75.4%	12,439	84.2%	6.8%	0.0%	91.0%
Franklin County	86,505	59.0%	8.4%	0.1%	67.5%	135,098	82.4%	4.2%	0.6%	87.3%
Geauga County	6,710	68.3%	10.3%	0.0%	78.6%	4,529	88.4%	0.5%	0.0%	88.9%
Greene County	14,227	54.5%	8.5%	3.4%	66.4%	12,873	69.1%	4.3%	7.2%	80.6%
Hamilton County	58,639	64.5%	8.8%	0.0%	73.3%	70,111	78.9%	6.9%	0.0%	85.8%
Lake County	15,666	66.4%	12.9%	0.3%	79.6%	16,814	87.6%	4.6%	0.0%	92.2%
Licking County	11,631	65.7%	12.7%	0.0%	78.4%	12,619	79.7%	12.1%	0.0%	91.8%
Lorain County	20,495	64.6%	10.5%	0.0%	75.1%	18,699	73.4%	7.6%	0.0%	81.0%
Lucas County	36,121	61.6%	15.6%	0.0%	77.2%	33,557	70.8%	10.9%	0.0%	81.8%
Mahoning County	15,248	59.4%	16.0%	0.6%	76.0%	15,335	73.1%	2.4%	2.8%	78.2%
Medina County	10,935	79.8%	3.7%	0.0%	83.5%	11,171	85.4%	0.4%	0.0%	85.8%
Miami County	6,353	63.8%	6.8%	0.0%	70.6%	7,567	70.9%	10.5%	0.0%	81.4%
Montgomery County	36,558	55.3%	13.6%	0.1%	69.0%	40,863	76.5%	6.0%	1.2%	83.7%
Portage County	22,811	66.5%	8.0%	0.0%	74.5%	10,440	79.8%	2.5%	0.0%	82.3%
Richland County	7,484	55.8%	12.5%	0.0%	68.3%	6,004	58.6%	5.3%	0.0%	63.8%
Stark County	25,058	63.4%	10.5%	0.0%	73.9%	25,181	71.7%	10.4%	0.0%	82.1%
Summit County	37,137	64.3%	9.8%	0.0%	74.1%	42,846	78.1%	8.8%	0.3%	87.1%
Trumbull County	10,831	63.6%	7.0%	0.0%	70.6%	12,116	73.4%	4.1%	0.0%	77.5%
Tuscarawas County	4,760	60.6%	5.1%	0.0%	65.7%	5,854	74.5%	6.2%	0.0%	80.8%
Warren County	12,662	57.9%	19.4%	0.0%	77.3%	14,036	78.1%	2.2%	0.0%	80.3%
Wayne County	8,484	75.3%	0.8%	0.0%	76.2%	6,690	76.1%	0.6%	0.0%	76.7%
Wood County	14,646	65.9%	9.7%	0.0%	75.6%	11,212	82.4%	8.1%	0.0%	90.5%
Oklahoma										
Canadian County	7,429	57.1%	15.0%	0.0%	72.1%	9,763	90.1%	0.3%	0.0%	90.4%
Cleveland County	28,164	58.1%	9.8%	0.0%	67.9%	24,285	79.3%	0.6%	0.0%	79.9%
Comanche County	12,402	40.7%	2.5%	27.7%	71.0%	11,657	53.0%	12.2%	14.4%	79.5%
Oklahoma County	52,613	62.3%	7.7%	2.2%	72.2%	73,055	78.8%	3.8%	1.1%	83.7%
Tulsa County	42,748	60.8%	11.1%	0.0%	71.9%	54,192	75.5%	7.3%	0.0%	82.8%
Oregon										
Clackamas County	23,528	60.5%	13.4%	0.0%	74.0%	25,387	71.5%	11.7%	0.0%	83.2%
Deschutes County	8,472	67.8%	5.9%	0.0%	73.7%	11,348	73.8%	5.5%	0.0%	79.3%
Douglas County	4,611	42.6%	17.4%	0.0%	60.0%	5,692	64.1%	9.5%	0.0%	73.6%
Jackson County	13,305	69.7%	7.1%	0.0%	76.8%	13,453	72.9%	6.8%	0.0%	79.7%
Lane County	31,111	54.6%	10.1%	0.0%	64.7%	23,731	68.2%	9.9%	0.6%	78.7%
Linn County	9,141	47.2%	11.4%	0.0%	58.6%	5,510	61.1%	5.7%	0.0%	66.8%
Marion County	24,479	61.0%	10.3%	0.0%	71.3%	20,081	67.4%	8.7%	0.0%	76.1%
Multnomah County	47,309	55.3%	14.1%	0.1%	69.5%	81,545	73.6%	9.6%	0.3%	83.6%
Washington County	35,474	61.0%	14.4%	0.0%	75.5%	50,346	79.0%	5.5%	0.0%	84.5%
Yamhill County	6,442	42.5%	23.7%	0.0%	66.1%	7,359	71.5%	12.3%	0.0%	83.8%
Pennsylvania										
Adams County	8,526	62.4%	14.4%	0.0%	76.8%	5,172	74.9%	3.1%	0.0%	78.0%
Allegheny County	76,834	54.9%	10.5%	0.0%	65.4%	113,217	80.2%	7.8%	0.1%	88.2%
Beaver County	12,103	68.9%	12.1%	0.0%	80.9%	10,980	76.2%	11.1%	0.0%	87.3%
Berks County	27,720	53.7%	11.1%	0.0%	64.8%	30,987	82.7%	6.9%	0.0%	89.6%
Blair County	8,214	62.0%	5.3%	0.0%	67.2%	7,950	69.7%	7.7%	0.0%	77.3%
Bucks County	38,138	68.0%	11.5%	0.0%	79.5%	42,276	76.6%	9.5%	0.4%	86.5%
Butler County	13,668	73.0%	6.2%	0.0%	79.2%	12,533	82.1%	5.0%	0.0%	87.1%
Cambria County	8,740	55.7%	11.2%	0.0%	66.9%	8,267	64.7%	13.0%	0.7%	78.4%
Centre County	21,004	38.5%	9.1%	0.0%	47.6%	10,600	70.4%	5.3%	0.0%	75.7%
Chester County	33,680	64.7%	9.5%	0.3%	74.5%	37,772	82.6%	5.5%	0.0%	88.1%
Cumberland County	17,175	61.5%	10.1%	0.0%	71.7%	16,435	69.6%	10.8%	0.9%	81.3%
Dauphin County	15,466	58.4%	13.3%	0.0%	71.8%	23,118	81.7%	7.2%	2.0%	90.9%
Delaware County	33,563	46.8%	9.9%	0.0%	56.6%	42,179	72.5%	12.3%	0.0%	84.8%
Erie County	19,435	55.4%	7.5%	0.0%	62.9%	23,026	74.1%	9.4%	0.0%	83.4%
Fayette County	6,900	57.3%	10.5%	0.0%	67.7%	6,491	59.8%	3.7%	0.0%	63.4%
Franklin County	9,078	61.5%	10.8%	0.0%	72.3%	11,735	76.0%	9.8%	0.0%	85.7%
Lackawanna County	15,863	63.2%	8.1%	0.0%	71.3%	14,662	72.8%	8.0%	0.0%	80.8%
Lancaster County	37,934	64.3%	10.1%	0.0%	74.4%	40,892	81.1%	5.0%	0.0%	86.1%
Lebanon County	8,216	56.2%	19.0%	0.0%	75.2%	7,446	75.7%	5.4%	0.0%	81.1%
Lehigh County	21,280	56.1%	9.2%	0.0%	65.3%	25,867	71.0%	13.3%	0.0%	84.3%
Luzerne County	21,446	58.6%	7.2%	0.0%	65.8%	21,706	69.5%	12.6%	0.0%	82.0%
Lycoming County	8,499	49.2%	10.8%	0.0%	60.0%	7,111	60.7%	16.9%	0.0%	77.6%
Mercer County	7,368	52.7%	10.7%	1.0%	64.3%	7,038	79.1%	2.4%	0.0%	81.5%
Monroe County	13,851	57.8%	14.1%	0.9%	72.8%	9,134	75.9%	10.5%	0.0%	86.4%
Montgomery County	44,469	58.1%	11.1%	0.4%	69.6%	62,755	81.4%	6.1%	0.0%	87.5%
Northampton County	17,531	49.4%	11.1%	0.0%	60.5%	22,841	80.4%	7.9%	0.5%	88.9%
Northumberland County	5,812	59.7%	14.7%	0.0%	74.5%	5,970	63.8%	11.3%	0.0%	75.1%
Philadelphia County	108,210	42.6%	14.8%	0.0%	57.3%	158,514	69.1%	10.7%	0.0%	79.8%

Table H-2: Counties—Labor Force Status—*Continued*

	18 to 24					25 to 31				
	In the Labor Force	Percent				In the Labor Force	Percent			
		Employed	Unemployed	In Armed Forces	Labor Force Participation Rate		Employed	Unemployed	In Armed Forces	Labor Force Participation Rate
Pennsylvania—Cont.										
Schuylkill County	7,314	47.3%	18.2%	0.0%	65.5%	9,309	70.1%	9.4%	0.0%	79.6%
Washington County	12,966	57.0%	15.2%	0.0%	72.1%	11,986	69.2%	5.9%	0.0%	75.0%
Westmoreland County	23,301	65.3%	11.9%	0.0%	77.2%	18,970	71.6%	8.4%	0.0%	80.0%
York County	28,401	65.1%	7.5%	0.0%	72.5%	29,501	77.8%	5.2%	0.0%	83.0%
Rhode Island										
Kent County	10,659	69.2%	16.8%	0.0%	85.9%	12,111	82.8%	2.1%	1.3%	86.2%
Providence County	49,820	55.4%	11.8%	0.1%	67.2%	55,688	75.7%	8.8%	0.1%	84.5%
Washington County	12,686	60.4%	5.3%	0.0%	65.7%	6,069	76.0%	14.2%	1.8%	92.0%
South Carolina										
Aiken County	12,190	69.4%	11.2%	0.0%	80.6%	11,420	73.7%	4.6%	0.5%	78.8%
Anderson County	9,299	48.1%	11.0%	0.0%	59.1%	13,886	79.1%	9.5%	0.0%	88.7%
Beaufort County	12,809	68.0%	6.4%	9.1%	83.5%	10,479	59.8%	6.6%	8.5%	74.8%
Berkeley County	14,384	55.0%	12.6%	2.7%	70.3%	17,310	73.2%	8.3%	1.7%	83.2%
Charleston County	27,029	49.4%	13.5%	1.6%	64.5%	36,863	77.3%	8.3%	1.7%	87.3%
Dorchester County	11,999	57.6%	15.5%	1.4%	74.6%	8,397	67.6%	3.9%	3.1%	74.6%
Florence County	9,155	48.0%	16.6%	0.0%	64.6%	8,585	58.9%	17.3%	0.0%	76.3%
Greenville County	32,506	57.1%	11.7%	0.3%	69.0%	35,113	73.2%	5.0%	0.0%	78.2%
Horry County	20,012	63.1%	12.3%	0.0%	75.4%	22,032	80.7%	8.1%	0.0%	88.8%
Lexington County	18,354	60.0%	13.1%	0.0%	73.1%	20,000	75.2%	9.5%	0.0%	84.7%
Orangeburg County	6,884	41.5%	25.9%	0.0%	67.3%	4,526	70.0%	6.9%	0.0%	76.8%
Pickens County	9,682	42.4%	6.8%	0.0%	49.2%	8,841	71.9%	10.8%	0.0%	82.7%
Richland County	43,371	44.4%	14.2%	10.2%	68.9%	32,727	66.3%	10.0%	3.1%	79.5%
Spartanburg County	21,914	60.1%	10.9%	0.0%	71.0%	18,998	68.1%	10.5%	0.0%	78.7%
Sumter County	9,185	46.6%	22.7%	2.7%	72.0%	7,854	55.7%	12.8%	12.9%	81.5%
York County	15,638	55.1%	12.9%	0.0%	68.0%	15,589	84.3%	7.7%	0.0%	92.0%
South Dakota										
Minnehaha County	14,258	72.2%	3.8%	0.0%	76.1%	19,219	84.3%	5.8%	0.0%	90.1%
Pennington County	9,603	80.5%	5.2%	0.7%	86.4%	8,183	73.3%	8.8%	10.1%	92.3%
Tennessee										
Blount County	7,999	65.6%	8.1%	0.0%	73.7%	8,118	66.2%	24.2%	0.0%	90.4%
Bradley County	7,634	46.6%	27.9%	0.0%	74.5%	7,401	83.8%	4.8%	0.0%	88.6%
Davidson County	47,139	59.2%	9.0%	0.1%	68.2%	77,578	80.5%	5.6%	0.0%	86.1%
Hamilton County	23,834	58.9%	12.2%	0.0%	71.1%	27,859	72.3%	8.3%	0.0%	80.6%
Knox County	35,366	57.3%	7.8%	0.0%	65.1%	37,975	77.2%	9.1%	0.1%	86.4%
Madison County	6,551	49.9%	14.7%	0.0%	64.7%	5,997	65.0%	10.0%	0.0%	75.0%
Montgomery County	18,379	63.4%	7.7%	10.3%	81.3%	20,153	52.1%	5.2%	20.6%	77.9%
Rutherford County	25,900	62.3%	7.8%	0.0%	70.1%	24,539	84.3%	2.1%	0.0%	86.5%
Sevier County	7,196	64.2%	7.7%	0.0%	71.9%	5,113	70.6%	7.1%	0.0%	77.6%
Shelby County	65,240	49.4%	16.9%	0.3%	66.7%	79,798	72.1%	10.6%	0.6%	83.4%
Sullivan County	7,924	57.1%	10.0%	0.0%	67.1%	8,866	72.1%	8.6%	0.0%	80.7%
Sumner County	10,302	63.7%	8.9%	0.0%	72.5%	12,627	78.9%	7.3%	0.5%	86.7%
Washington County	12,045	76.8%	3.0%	0.0%	79.8%	8,704	80.2%	3.4%	0.0%	83.6%
Williamson County	9,674	62.9%	5.0%	0.0%	67.9%	10,772	88.8%	1.7%	0.0%	90.5%
Wilson County	6,746	58.9%	10.2%	0.0%	69.1%	8,494	79.4%	8.5%	0.0%	87.9%
Texas										
Bell County	29,953	44.9%	10.2%	16.3%	71.4%	31,766	56.4%	10.1%	14.8%	81.3%
Bexar County	139,219	57.6%	8.9%	3.1%	69.6%	166,188	77.1%	6.3%	1.1%	84.4%
Bowie County	6,974	48.7%	21.9%	0.0%	70.6%	7,407	70.3%	6.1%	0.1%	76.5%
Brazoria County	22,541	66.9%	11.2%	0.3%	78.5%	28,989	81.4%	2.5%	0.0%	83.9%
Brazos County	32,117	50.3%	5.7%	0.0%	56.0%	20,239	77.3%	6.1%	0.0%	83.4%
Cameron County	22,975	37.3%	14.8%	0.0%	52.1%	25,636	65.7%	10.7%	0.0%	76.4%
Collin County	50,434	66.9%	5.5%	0.6%	73.0%	58,723	81.0%	4.6%	0.0%	85.6%
Comal County	6,616	66.1%	3.4%	0.0%	69.5%	7,935	85.5%	4.5%	0.0%	89.9%
Dallas County	165,570	57.3%	10.3%	0.2%	67.7%	236,858	79.5%	5.2%	0.0%	84.6%
Denton County	51,638	62.3%	9.2%	0.0%	71.5%	64,042	79.4%	7.1%	0.0%	86.4%
Ector County	13,094	68.0%	10.2%	0.0%	78.2%	14,451	78.6%	4.6%	0.0%	83.2%
El Paso County	65,500	47.9%	9.4%	8.5%	65.8%	64,884	64.1%	7.0%	7.5%	78.6%
Ellis County	9,889	52.9%	15.0%	0.0%	67.9%	10,891	78.9%	4.0%	0.0%	82.9%
Fort Bend County	33,368	51.4%	9.9%	0.0%	61.3%	43,344	76.8%	5.0%	0.0%	81.7%
Galveston County	18,756	56.6%	8.9%	0.9%	66.5%	20,969	66.4%	10.3%	0.3%	77.0%
Grayson County	7,546	57.2%	8.3%	0.0%	65.5%	8,956	71.8%	6.7%	0.0%	78.5%
Gregg County	10,362	66.6%	10.3%	0.0%	76.8%	8,266	68.9%	3.9%	0.0%	72.8%
Guadalupe County	8,901	59.7%	8.3%	0.0%	68.0%	9,007	72.1%	3.4%	2.7%	78.2%
Harris County	291,941	57.6%	10.4%	0.0%	68.1%	413,662	77.0%	5.7%	0.1%	82.7%
Hays County	19,004	51.5%	11.3%	0.0%	62.7%	14,237	80.2%	3.4%	0.0%	83.6%
Hidalgo County	53,133	47.3%	11.7%	0.0%	59.0%	52,860	64.7%	6.2%	0.0%	70.9%
Jefferson County	15,812	48.4%	8.2%	0.0%	56.6%	17,983	68.4%	3.3%	0.5%	72.2%
Johnson County	8,692	49.7%	12.5%	0.0%	62.2%	9,341	56.5%	11.3%	0.0%	67.8%
Kaufman County	6,980	63.3%	10.0%	0.0%	73.3%	6,008	76.4%	0.0%	0.0%	76.4%
Lubbock County	31,482	53.3%	8.4%	0.0%	61.7%	23,156	76.0%	4.8%	0.4%	81.2%
McLennan County	21,980	56.1%	4.5%	0.0%	60.6%	17,510	75.5%	5.4%	0.3%	81.2%
Midland County	11,647	69.1%	7.8%	0.0%	76.9%	15,339	82.5%	1.4%	0.0%	83.9%
Montgomery County	27,160	55.6%	9.4%	0.0%	65.0%	33,268	75.7%	6.0%	0.0%	81.7%
Nueces County	27,130	63.4%	6.4%	4.0%	73.8%	28,942	76.7%	6.3%	0.7%	83.7%

Table H-2: Counties—Labor Force Status—Continued

	18 to 24					25 to 31				
	In the Labor Force	Percent				In the Labor Force	Percent			
		Employed	Unemployed	In Armed Forces	Labor Force Participation Rate		Employed	Unemployed	In Armed Forces	Labor Force Participation Rate
Texas—Cont.										
Parker County	6,691	56.4%	8.3%	0.0%	64.7%	6,019	53.6%	7.2%	0.0%	60.8%
Potter County	9,628	71.6%	6.5%	0.0%	78.1%	9,023	68.5%	3.4%	0.4%	72.4%
Randall County	9,605	66.1%	7.4%	0.4%	74.0%	11,642	81.1%	3.9%	0.0%	85.0%
Smith County	14,319	48.2%	15.6%	0.0%	63.7%	16,447	75.9%	7.4%	0.0%	83.3%
Tarrant County	133,916	62.5%	10.5%	0.3%	73.3%	171,343	78.6%	5.5%	0.2%	84.3%
Taylor County	14,339	60.2%	9.2%	3.2%	72.5%	12,240	63.0%	6.6%	10.4%	80.0%
Tom Green County	10,713	52.8%	4.9%	18.6%	76.3%	10,259	69.2%	4.4%	7.6%	81.2%
Travis County	79,679	57.5%	10.2%	0.0%	67.7%	145,882	85.0%	4.4%	0.0%	89.4%
Webb County	16,367	46.7%	8.5%	0.0%	55.2%	16,816	60.2%	3.8%	0.0%	64.0%
Wichita County	14,748	51.3%	10.7%	21.0%	83.0%	10,471	58.4%	3.3%	7.6%	69.2%
Williamson County	26,519	64.7%	8.7%	0.0%	73.4%	37,413	77.5%	6.2%	1.2%	84.9%
Utah										
Cache County	14,320	69.3%	8.2%	0.0%	77.4%	11,875	79.6%	0.9%	0.0%	80.4%
Davis County	23,784	72.5%	6.2%	1.4%	80.2%	22,573	68.6%	3.4%	1.9%	74.0%
Salt Lake County	83,242	68.5%	8.9%	0.0%	77.5%	104,762	78.0%	4.2%	0.1%	82.3%
Utah County	69,014	68.7%	5.8%	0.0%	74.5%	42,262	66.5%	5.0%	0.2%	71.7%
Washington County	11,225	63.6%	11.6%	0.0%	75.2%	8,579	79.4%	0.0%	0.5%	79.9%
Weber County	18,155	70.4%	11.5%	0.0%	81.9%	18,908	72.9%	1.9%	0.6%	75.3%
Vermont										
Chittenden County	14,474	58.7%	3.7%	0.0%	62.4%	14,522	81.7%	7.0%	0.0%	88.7%
Virginia										
Albemarle County	4,994	37.2%	6.2%	0.0%	43.4%	8,208	77.2%	3.6%	0.0%	80.8%
Arlington County	14,860	65.6%	11.1%	4.9%	81.6%	41,396	84.5%	1.9%	1.3%	87.6%
Chesterfield County	24,110	64.7%	13.4%	0.0%	78.0%	22,098	78.1%	10.2%	0.0%	88.3%
Fairfax County	65,206	58.3%	8.6%	1.0%	67.9%	95,958	82.8%	3.6%	1.0%	87.5%
Hanover County	7,041	68.7%	19.6%	0.0%	88.4%	7,045	86.7%	1.3%	0.0%	88.1%
Henrico County	19,674	57.0%	14.4%	0.5%	71.9%	27,304	78.4%	7.1%	0.0%	85.5%
Loudoun County	18,040	65.5%	12.9%	0.0%	78.5%	24,710	83.4%	2.3%	0.8%	86.6%
Montgomery County	13,609	41.6%	3.0%	0.8%	45.4%	4,965	66.7%	0.2%	0.0%	66.9%
Prince William County	28,921	62.1%	11.1%	3.0%	76.2%	38,581	80.6%	5.5%	2.2%	88.4%
Roanoke County	5,619	65.9%	3.5%	0.0%	69.4%	5,045	65.4%	8.0%	0.3%	73.7%
Spotsylvania County	8,472	60.5%	10.5%	0.1%	71.1%	7,479	65.7%	9.1%	0.9%	75.7%
Stafford County	11,656	55.8%	5.8%	8.0%	69.6%	9,003	62.9%	7.1%	6.9%	76.9%
Washington										
Benton County	11,310	60.1%	11.9%	1.3%	73.3%	13,542	78.4%	5.6%	0.5%	84.5%
Clark County	28,432	56.5%	17.4%	0.1%	74.0%	27,368	67.2%	7.2%	0.0%	74.4%
Cowlitz County	6,657	64.9%	12.3%	0.8%	78.0%	5,431	61.4%	4.5%	5.0%	70.9%
Grant County	6,699	46.3%	10.8%	0.0%	57.1%	5,132	65.1%	5.8%	0.0%	71.0%
King County	121,267	59.3%	8.9%	0.2%	68.4%	205,590	79.6%	4.9%	0.8%	85.3%
Kitsap County	19,217	46.8%	8.2%	19.7%	74.8%	20,607	69.1%	5.1%	12.0%	86.2%
Pierce County	58,179	53.5%	11.8%	7.5%	72.7%	70,504	65.9%	7.7%	8.5%	82.0%
Skagit County	8,395	59.4%	7.2%	9.2%	75.8%	6,903	51.1%	13.4%	13.0%	77.5%
Snohomish County	45,282	59.1%	9.4%	1.3%	69.8%	59,557	75.4%	6.8%	1.2%	83.4%
Spokane County	32,720	54.4%	9.1%	1.3%	64.8%	39,575	70.3%	6.7%	1.2%	78.2%
Thurston County	17,854	52.5%	16.7%	3.8%	73.0%	21,513	58.2%	8.2%	8.1%	74.6%
Whatcom County	21,789	60.6%	8.2%	0.0%	68.8%	14,766	77.3%	4.7%	2.4%	84.4%
Yakima County	16,606	48.5%	17.1%	0.3%	65.8%	18,184	73.8%	7.6%	0.0%	81.4%
West Virginia										
Berkeley County	7,023	45.6%	23.5%	2.0%	71.1%	6,315	66.4%	6.3%	0.0%	72.8%
Cabell County	5,681	52.5%	2.3%	0.0%	54.8%	6,926	75.4%	4.4%	0.0%	79.9%
Kanawha County	10,589	54.0%	12.9%	0.0%	66.9%	14,454	79.1%	8.5%	0.0%	87.6%
Monongalia County	14,154	53.8%	6.6%	0.0%	60.3%	10,177	64.2%	9.0%	0.0%	73.2%
Wisconsin										
Brown County	18,880	72.3%	7.3%	0.0%	79.6%	21,096	81.7%	9.0%	0.0%	90.7%
Dane County	47,259	69.1%	3.9%	0.0%	72.9%	56,624	87.3%	3.8%	0.0%	91.0%
Eau Claire County	13,399	70.3%	8.0%	0.0%	78.3%	8,823	79.6%	3.2%	0.0%	82.9%
Fond du Lac County	7,119	69.9%	8.0%	0.0%	77.9%	4,764	73.3%	10.6%	0.0%	84.0%
Kenosha County	12,471	55.3%	21.0%	0.0%	76.3%	12,487	76.9%	8.8%	1.2%	86.9%
La Crosse County	13,526	72.0%	1.6%	0.0%	73.6%	10,894	85.7%	6.3%	0.0%	92.0%
Marathon County	7,702	52.9%	15.2%	0.0%	68.1%	9,646	83.2%	4.2%	0.0%	87.5%
Milwaukee County	67,072	55.6%	11.5%	0.0%	67.1%	95,525	75.2%	8.5%	0.0%	83.7%
Outagamie County	12,909	69.9%	6.7%	0.0%	76.5%	16,004	90.2%	0.8%	1.1%	92.0%
Racine County	10,956	58.5%	14.1%	0.0%	72.7%	14,995	70.7%	11.0%	0.0%	81.7%
Rock County	10,507	54.5%	19.2%	0.0%	73.6%	9,553	68.2%	2.8%	0.0%	71.0%
Sheboygan County	6,543	78.7%	2.6%	0.0%	81.3%	7,840	79.5%	6.5%	0.0%	86.1%
Walworth County	8,300	60.4%	13.2%	0.0%	73.6%	6,704	70.0%	5.7%	0.0%	75.7%
Washington County	9,007	72.9%	7.7%	0.0%	80.5%	8,191	89.3%	1.7%	0.0%	91.0%
Waukesha County	24,687	74.8%	5.5%	0.0%	80.3%	25,164	87.0%	2.3%	0.0%	89.4%
Winnebago County	16,225	76.4%	2.0%	0.0%	78.4%	13,353	79.5%	1.2%	0.0%	80.7%
Wyoming										
Laramie County	7,450	46.1%	10.6%	3.2%	59.9%	6,819	74.9%	0.0%	9.9%	84.8%

Table H-3: Places—Labor Force Status

	18 to 24					25 to 31				
	In the Labor Force	Percent				In the Labor Force	Percent			
		Employed	Unemployed	In Armed Forces	Labor Force Participation Rate		Employed	Unemployed	In Armed Forces	Labor Force Participation Rate
Alabama										
Birmingham city	24,818	46.1%	22.5%	0.0%	68.6%	23,982	72.2%	9.5%	0.0%	81.7%
Huntsville city	19,366	57.3%	11.6%	0.0%	68.9%	18,878	74.0%	7.3%	0.0%	81.2%
Mobile city	20,293	56.5%	11.2%	0.0%	67.6%	20,214	72.2%	11.7%	0.3%	84.1%
Montgomery city	23,367	45.8%	7.2%	5.9%	58.9%	22,357	69.0%	4.7%	0.8%	74.4%
Tuscaloosa city	23,953	37.4%	9.8%	0.0%	47.2%	9,937	77.4%	2.0%	0.0%	79.5%
Alaska										
Anchorage municipality	34,074	61.0%	5.9%	8.6%	75.5%	35,653	73.2%	5.5%	10.3%	89.0%
Arizona										
Chandler city	22,227	70.0%	5.9%	0.0%	75.9%	25,427	77.2%	4.8%	0.0%	82.0%
Glendale city	22,520	56.7%	9.0%	0.5%	66.2%	24,043	67.6%	7.2%	0.6%	75.5%
Mesa city	45,070	58.1%	7.8%	0.0%	65.9%	47,737	76.2%	6.6%	0.1%	82.9%
Peoria city	12,190	62.0%	8.5%	0.0%	70.5%	13,193	73.1%	8.0%	0.0%	81.2%
Phoenix city	154,915	53.9%	12.4%	0.0%	66.3%	159,901	72.4%	7.0%	0.1%	79.6%
Scottsdale city	16,139	71.5%	8.9%	0.0%	80.3%	19,062	89.3%	1.5%	0.0%	90.8%
Surprise city	6,025	67.3%	6.2%	0.0%	73.4%	7,630	80.7%	2.5%	0.0%	83.2%
Tempe city	35,874	58.2%	5.5%	0.0%	63.7%	26,666	83.8%	5.6%	0.1%	89.5%
Tucson city	76,603	53.8%	12.3%	1.7%	67.7%	51,809	69.9%	9.7%	0.9%	80.4%
Yuma city	11,052	44.7%	4.1%	8.7%	57.5%	9,945	60.7%	7.6%	4.5%	72.9%
Arkansas										
Little Rock city	16,118	58.1%	7.6%	0.0%	65.7%	23,392	72.1%	10.5%	0.4%	83.0%
California										
Anaheim city	36,943	53.3%	13.1%	0.0%	66.3%	35,851	77.5%	5.2%	0.0%	82.7%
Antioch city	12,180	48.2%	13.2%	0.0%	61.4%	10,190	66.1%	10.5%	0.0%	76.6%
Bakersfield city	39,371	47.9%	10.9%	0.0%	58.9%	39,901	67.3%	7.8%	0.0%	75.1%
Berkeley city	26,469	36.6%	9.5%	0.0%	46.1%	17,350	70.6%	5.2%	0.6%	76.4%
Burbank city	6,721	46.5%	9.9%	1.1%	57.4%	11,889	82.8%	6.6%	0.0%	89.5%
Carlsbad city	7,319	65.9%	7.3%	0.0%	73.2%	9,394	67.0%	5.7%	1.2%	74.0%
Carson city	10,757	52.8%	13.1%	0.0%	65.8%	9,644	66.9%	24.3%	1.0%	92.2%
Chula Vista city	27,506	43.7%	12.5%	6.2%	62.4%	23,755	63.5%	11.8%	6.0%	81.3%
Clovis city	11,520	66.4%	9.2%	0.0%	75.6%	8,626	78.4%	6.9%	0.9%	86.2%
Compton city	10,355	43.3%	22.8%	0.0%	66.0%	10,546	54.7%	13.4%	0.0%	68.0%
Concord city	10,951	58.4%	15.1%	0.0%	73.5%	12,517	72.5%	8.6%	0.8%	81.9%
Corona city	16,818	49.4%	9.7%	0.0%	59.1%	16,761	68.6%	10.6%	0.0%	79.2%
Costa Mesa city	10,818	60.0%	8.6%	0.0%	68.7%	16,113	81.1%	4.1%	0.0%	85.2%
Daly City city	11,075	71.3%	6.2%	0.0%	77.5%	12,536	78.6%	8.0%	0.0%	86.6%
Downey city	15,873	53.6%	7.0%	0.0%	60.7%	11,971	77.2%	4.1%	0.0%	81.3%
El Cajon city	12,830	46.4%	25.4%	0.0%	71.8%	12,072	73.5%	9.4%	1.3%	84.1%
El Monte city	11,284	34.9%	20.9%	0.0%	55.8%	11,210	67.0%	13.9%	0.0%	80.9%
Elk Grove city	13,742	41.7%	20.0%	0.0%	61.7%	10,251	69.3%	8.4%	0.0%	77.7%
Escondido city	16,403	60.5%	13.1%	0.0%	73.7%	17,091	70.9%	6.4%	0.0%	77.3%
Fairfield city	13,826	44.3%	16.4%	8.3%	69.0%	12,854	70.1%	3.4%	9.7%	83.3%
Fontana city	22,450	55.3%	22.7%	0.0%	77.9%	18,971	75.1%	11.5%	0.0%	86.6%
Fremont city	16,568	52.4%	4.9%	0.0%	57.3%	21,994	64.7%	8.9%	0.0%	73.6%
Fresno city	57,906	45.9%	11.5%	0.0%	57.4%	56,907	65.1%	9.8%	0.4%	75.3%
Fullerton city	16,518	52.7%	13.1%	0.0%	65.8%	17,289	83.7%	4.4%	0.0%	88.1%
Garden Grove city	18,446	47.0%	17.3%	1.1%	65.4%	16,769	77.7%	6.1%	0.0%	83.8%
Glendale city	14,944	52.8%	11.7%	0.0%	64.5%	22,833	78.8%	7.5%	0.0%	86.3%
Hayward city	15,875	56.1%	10.3%	0.6%	67.0%	18,422	76.8%	10.5%	0.0%	87.3%
Hesperia city	19,216	50.9%	15.8%	0.5%	67.2%	21,407	74.1%	4.5%	0.0%	78.7%
Inglewood city	11,099	46.0%	33.5%	0.0%	79.5%	13,468	72.1%	15.7%	0.0%	87.8%
Irvine city	30,544	49.5%	2.9%	0.0%	52.4%	25,569	69.6%	4.1%	0.0%	73.7%
Jurupa Valley city	10,455	47.3%	28.6%	0.0%	75.9%	10,081	81.6%	3.8%	0.0%	85.3%
Lancaster city	16,534	44.3%	5.4%	0.0%	49.7%	14,910	59.2%	7.4%	0.0%	66.7%
Long Beach city	49,447	49.3%	16.4%	0.0%	65.7%	51,100	71.6%	9.0%	0.4%	81.0%
Los Angeles city	414,272	48.0%	12.4%	0.2%	60.5%	459,387	75.7%	7.3%	0.0%	83.0%
Mission Viejo city	8,995	57.0%	13.6%	2.7%	73.4%	4,425	72.9%	0.0%	0.0%	72.9%
Modesto city	22,619	51.4%	15.5%	0.0%	66.9%	20,567	59.1%	19.7%	0.0%	78.8%
Moreno Valley city	22,518	51.5%	14.8%	0.4%	66.7%	25,384	66.8%	16.5%	0.0%	83.2%
Murrieta city	9,771	58.8%	13.0%	0.0%	71.8%	8,639	71.8%	9.8%	2.4%	84.0%
Norwalk city	12,390	51.7%	8.5%	0.0%	60.1%	9,029	72.0%	2.8%	0.0%	74.7%
Oakland city	34,793	53.0%	17.1%	0.0%	70.1%	50,604	74.7%	8.4%	0.7%	83.7%
Oceanside city	21,035	36.3%	7.2%	40.1%	83.5%	16,680	52.3%	4.2%	19.7%	76.2%
Ontario city	18,592	59.2%	10.9%	0.0%	70.1%	16,521	68.7%	10.9%	0.0%	79.6%
Orange city	15,291	49.7%	3.9%	0.0%	53.6%	14,649	80.1%	2.3%	0.0%	82.5%
Oxnard city	25,335	65.9%	7.4%	3.8%	77.0%	21,677	75.3%	7.7%	2.7%	85.6%
Palmdale city	16,777	38.2%	16.9%	0.0%	55.1%	13,322	64.0%	17.0%	0.0%	81.0%
Pasadena city	13,797	49.5%	19.4%	0.0%	68.9%	20,602	80.8%	6.3%	0.0%	87.1%
Pomona city	21,042	47.1%	12.2%	0.2%	59.5%	16,663	67.1%	7.5%	1.5%	76.0%
Rancho Cucamonga city	18,570	48.6%	18.8%	0.0%	67.4%	15,343	71.8%	11.7%	0.0%	83.5%
Redding city	9,543	45.3%	11.9%	0.0%	57.2%	9,166	66.9%	3.7%	0.0%	70.6%
Rialto city	12,998	55.3%	13.2%	0.0%	68.6%	9,236	70.5%	5.6%	0.0%	76.1%
Richmond city	10,767	59.7%	10.3%	0.0%	70.1%	13,277	73.3%	8.7%	0.0%	82.0%
Riverside city	49,495	47.9%	18.6%	0.0%	66.5%	28,679	65.5%	10.1%	0.0%	75.6%
Roseville city	9,740	54.5%	5.7%	0.0%	60.2%	12,927	77.1%	7.5%	0.4%	85.1%

Table H-3: Places—Labor Force Status—*Continued*

	18 to 24					25 to 31				
	In the Labor Force	Percent				In the Labor Force	Percent			
		Employed	Unemployed	In Armed Forces	Labor Force Participation Rate		Employed	Unemployed	In Armed Forces	Labor Force Participation Rate
California—Cont.										
Sacramento city	49,576	47.3%	19.1%	0.0%	66.4%	54,203	73.4%	9.9%	0.1%	83.4%
Salinas city	18,628	42.4%	8.5%	0.0%	50.9%	15,866	64.7%	7.5%	0.0%	72.2%
San Bernardino city	28,852	45.5%	15.3%	0.0%	60.8%	20,883	52.9%	11.2%	0.0%	64.1%
San Buenaventura (Ventura) city	10,980	51.0%	8.7%	0.0%	59.7%	11,094	70.4%	7.8%	0.5%	78.7%
San Diego city	156,541	47.9%	8.7%	8.8%	65.4%	178,234	71.7%	7.2%	6.3%	85.2%
San Francisco city	62,062	53.4%	11.5%	0.0%	64.9%	129,957	84.1%	5.7%	0.6%	90.4%
San Jose city	85,425	56.1%	9.9%	0.0%	66.0%	105,249	76.5%	8.8%	0.2%	85.5%
San Mateo city	6,413	58.3%	18.7%	0.0%	76.9%	9,364	92.6%	2.1%	0.7%	95.4%
Santa Ana city	40,982	60.7%	9.5%	0.0%	70.2%	37,965	77.5%	4.9%	0.0%	82.4%
Santa Clara city	12,714	53.1%	6.9%	0.0%	60.0%	18,020	77.2%	6.8%	0.0%	83.9%
Santa Clarita city	16,200	56.2%	13.4%	0.0%	69.5%	16,170	75.3%	5.9%	0.0%	81.2%
Santa Maria city	11,107	64.0%	4.7%	0.9%	69.6%	9,634	79.5%	1.7%	0.0%	81.3%
Santa Monica city	5,131	66.9%	9.2%	0.0%	76.1%	12,786	87.4%	3.6%	0.0%	91.0%
Santa Rosa city	15,177	64.1%	14.5%	0.1%	78.7%	17,790	74.4%	8.2%	2.1%	84.6%
Simi Valley city	10,104	59.7%	3.8%	0.6%	64.0%	9,416	71.7%	10.2%	0.0%	81.9%
South Gate city	10,170	41.3%	8.4%	0.0%	49.8%	12,129	68.8%	12.3%	0.0%	81.1%
Stockton city	33,029	51.6%	11.3%	0.0%	62.9%	27,866	66.8%	12.7%	0.4%	79.9%
Sunnyvale city	9,863	75.9%	1.9%	0.0%	77.8%	19,311	73.5%	5.8%	0.6%	79.9%
Temecula city	12,331	44.1%	16.1%	1.1%	61.3%	7,345	62.5%	11.2%	3.6%	77.2%
Thousand Oaks city	12,516	65.0%	8.7%	0.0%	73.7%	9,254	85.4%	3.0%	0.0%	88.4%
Torrance city	12,260	48.5%	20.6%	0.0%	69.1%	10,105	86.4%	7.2%	0.0%	93.6%
Vacaville city	9,594	65.7%	5.2%	0.0%	70.9%	9,405	67.3%	3.3%	6.1%	76.7%
Vallejo city	11,369	55.6%	15.2%	0.0%	70.7%	11,856	69.2%	12.6%	0.0%	81.8%
Victorville city	13,437	36.7%	11.5%	0.0%	48.2%	12,353	58.4%	10.9%	0.0%	69.3%
Visalia city	14,451	45.5%	23.4%	0.0%	68.9%	14,393	66.3%	8.8%	1.8%	76.8%
Vista city	12,213	52.9%	2.5%	6.0%	61.5%	12,024	70.7%	0.6%	1.3%	72.6%
West Covina city	11,275	48.9%	21.6%	1.6%	72.1%	12,251	64.1%	15.3%	0.0%	79.4%
Westminster city	6,793	55.1%	15.2%	0.0%	70.4%	10,033	63.1%	10.5%	0.6%	74.2%
Colorado										
Arvada city	9,441	69.8%	5.2%	0.0%	75.0%	9,903	79.9%	5.5%	0.0%	85.4%
Aurora city	31,521	57.2%	12.0%	1.0%	70.3%	35,520	77.8%	8.3%	0.4%	86.4%
Boulder city	29,961	53.8%	6.2%	0.0%	60.0%	12,008	89.5%	2.7%	1.1%	93.2%
Centennial city	7,068	50.4%	7.8%	0.0%	58.2%	8,768	89.0%	1.5%	0.8%	91.2%
Colorado Springs city	45,636	56.4%	14.4%	4.8%	75.5%	46,805	72.8%	3.5%	6.7%	83.1%
Denver city	58,403	67.0%	8.4%	0.7%	76.1%	96,430	78.9%	5.2%	0.3%	84.4%
Fort Collins city	32,540	62.5%	6.5%	0.0%	68.9%	15,954	80.8%	5.3%	0.7%	86.8%
Greeley city	13,727	53.2%	19.9%	0.0%	73.2%	12,038	66.6%	13.9%	0.5%	81.1%
Lakewood city	13,949	61.8%	10.6%	0.0%	72.3%	14,372	73.9%	10.4%	0.0%	84.3%
Pueblo city	11,131	48.8%	11.6%	0.7%	61.1%	9,895	58.3%	18.2%	0.0%	76.5%
Thornton city	12,131	65.0%	12.0%	0.0%	77.1%	10,191	68.3%	7.5%	0.0%	75.8%
Westminster city	9,091	66.9%	13.4%	0.0%	80.3%	13,432	78.3%	6.4%	0.0%	84.7%
Connecticut										
Bridgeport city	15,330	51.2%	17.1%	0.0%	68.3%	19,266	78.8%	8.0%	0.0%	86.8%
Hartford city	17,926	38.6%	19.8%	0.0%	58.4%	14,342	69.2%	17.6%	0.0%	86.8%
New Haven city	21,287	45.5%	6.8%	0.4%	52.8%	17,272	57.9%	9.1%	0.0%	67.0%
Stamford city	12,181	68.3%	12.2%	0.0%	80.4%	13,874	83.8%	6.8%	0.0%	90.5%
Waterbury city	10,499	57.7%	16.4%	0.0%	74.1%	12,596	69.6%	6.6%	0.0%	76.2%
District of Columbia										
Washington city	75,399	41.8%	13.9%	2.1%	57.7%	102,748	79.3%	8.4%	0.1%	87.8%
Florida										
Cape Coral city	12,044	55.3%	15.6%	0.0%	70.9%	13,598	70.4%	15.4%	0.0%	85.7%
Clearwater city	8,279	68.3%	6.4%	0.0%	74.7%	9,599	68.8%	7.5%	0.0%	76.2%
Coral Springs city	13,970	59.5%	14.3%	0.6%	74.4%	9,869	72.6%	14.1%	0.0%	86.8%
Fort Lauderdale city	15,103	50.7%	12.0%	0.0%	62.7%	15,087	80.0%	7.0%	0.0%	87.0%
Gainesville city	43,021	45.3%	8.1%	0.0%	53.4%	17,628	67.9%	4.6%	0.0%	72.5%
Hialeah city	20,256	50.5%	11.7%	0.0%	62.2%	20,322	62.7%	2.5%	0.0%	65.2%
Hollywood city	11,122	64.2%	7.7%	0.0%	71.9%	11,697	78.6%	9.9%	1.2%	89.7%
Jacksonville city	80,071	51.6%	13.0%	5.2%	69.9%	94,016	72.4%	11.2%	1.7%	85.3%
Lakeland city	11,043	47.0%	17.0%	0.0%	63.9%	8,446	64.1%	11.7%	0.0%	75.8%
Miami Beach city	6,216	50.2%	16.5%	0.0%	66.7%	8,798	83.4%	7.3%	1.1%	91.8%
Miami city	34,280	59.1%	10.6%	0.1%	69.8%	47,133	67.6%	11.9%	0.0%	79.5%
Miami Gardens city	13,952	53.7%	9.8%	0.0%	63.5%	11,328	66.0%	12.8%	0.0%	78.9%
Miramar city	12,626	49.3%	17.6%	0.0%	66.9%	17,992	74.1%	11.4%	0.0%	85.5%
Orlando city	25,196	61.1%	17.0%	0.0%	78.1%	36,308	80.3%	9.2%	0.2%	89.8%
Palm Bay city	9,200	59.8%	15.5%	0.0%	75.3%	8,128	62.9%	7.8%	0.0%	70.8%
Pembroke Pines city	14,893	55.2%	9.3%	0.0%	64.4%	14,510	74.4%	10.5%	1.0%	85.8%
Pompano Beach city	7,215	50.4%	11.7%	0.0%	62.0%	10,241	72.4%	11.4%	1.1%	84.9%
Port St. Lucie city	13,266	58.0%	13.2%	0.0%	71.2%	10,425	77.8%	7.3%	0.0%	85.2%
St. Petersburg city	21,540	60.2%	12.4%	1.6%	74.2%	24,997	70.5%	6.1%	1.0%	77.6%
Tallahassee city	52,303	47.8%	16.6%	0.0%	64.4%	23,034	74.8%	8.3%	0.7%	83.8%
Tampa city	42,412	47.7%	13.8%	0.6%	62.0%	41,641	72.6%	10.9%	0.9%	84.4%
West Palm Beach city	10,514	45.5%	18.3%	0.0%	63.8%	13,268	75.0%	7.0%	0.0%	82.0%
Georgia										
Athens-Clarke County unified govt (bal)	36,028	43.9%	10.7%	0.1%	54.6%	13,785	78.4%	11.1%	0.8%	90.3%

Table H-3: Places—Labor Force Status—*Continued*

	18 to 24					25 to 31				
	In the Labor Force	Percent				In the Labor Force	Percent			
		Employed	Unemployed	In Armed Forces	Labor Force Participation Rate		Employed	Unemployed	In Armed Forces	Labor Force Participation Rate
Georgia—Cont.										
Atlanta city	61,305	47.6%	11.9%	0.0%	59.5%	62,935	79.6%	7.1%	0.1%	86.7%
Augusta-Richmond County consolidated govt (bal)	21,555	42.0%	14.9%	9.3%	66.2%	23,346	63.4%	10.4%	4.2%	78.1%
Columbus city	24,790	29.5%	15.1%	26.1%	70.7%	20,537	51.8%	8.9%	17.0%	77.7%
Macon city	11,218	42.4%	20.4%	0.0%	62.8%	9,242	63.6%	18.8%	0.0%	82.3%
Roswell city	8,294	60.2%	3.5%	0.0%	63.7%	8,569	86.8%	3.6%	0.0%	90.5%
Sandy Springs city	4,983	75.0%	5.4%	0.0%	80.4%	14,815	80.5%	9.1%	0.7%	90.3%
Savannah city	20,003	46.1%	14.2%	4.0%	64.3%	17,750	61.1%	15.9%	3.0%	80.1%
Hawaii										
Urban Honolulu CDP	31,461	54.6%	4.3%	7.8%	66.6%	37,505	65.3%	4.6%	8.6%	78.5%
Idaho										
Boise City city	23,692	65.2%	9.8%	0.0%	75.0%	23,021	76.0%	8.9%	0.6%	85.6%
Illinois										
Aurora city	17,229	63.4%	7.3%	0.0%	70.7%	21,072	73.6%	10.3%	0.0%	83.9%
Chicago city	281,204	47.9%	16.7%	0.0%	64.6%	357,011	76.1%	8.4%	0.0%	84.5%
Elgin city	12,274	67.7%	12.2%	1.6%	81.6%	11,373	90.0%	0.8%	0.0%	90.8%
Joliet city	15,649	63.8%	11.0%	0.0%	74.8%	14,193	66.7%	9.3%	0.0%	76.1%
Naperville city	11,662	68.0%	5.9%	0.0%	73.8%	12,789	78.6%	10.3%	0.0%	88.9%
Peoria city	13,512	65.6%	8.0%	0.0%	73.6%	13,213	75.6%	10.6%	0.6%	86.8%
Rockford city	15,357	63.5%	14.1%	0.0%	77.6%	13,747	64.1%	16.4%	0.0%	80.6%
Springfield city	11,506	63.5%	5.8%	0.6%	69.9%	11,973	77.9%	3.4%	0.0%	81.3%
Indiana										
Evansville city	13,002	52.0%	9.3%	0.0%	61.3%	11,110	73.5%	2.1%	0.0%	75.6%
Fort Wayne city	24,853	60.2%	12.7%	0.0%	72.9%	25,279	74.0%	9.3%	0.0%	83.4%
Indianapolis city (bal)	82,156	58.2%	12.6%	0.0%	70.8%	98,908	77.0%	7.8%	0.1%	84.9%
South Bend city	12,876	51.2%	8.2%	0.0%	59.5%	8,282	76.2%	12.6%	0.0%	88.8%
Iowa										
Cedar Rapids city	11,166	71.6%	9.2%	0.0%	80.8%	14,360	86.7%	3.9%	0.0%	90.6%
Davenport city	9,550	64.5%	7.5%	0.0%	72.0%	10,268	85.6%	0.0%	0.0%	85.6%
Des Moines city	19,910	73.0%	7.6%	0.3%	80.8%	26,312	80.2%	9.1%	0.0%	89.4%
Kansas										
Kansas City city	14,343	65.5%	11.3%	0.0%	76.8%	14,219	72.7%	8.1%	0.0%	80.8%
Olathe city	11,796	78.8%	5.4%	0.0%	84.2%	11,482	73.9%	1.6%	0.0%	75.5%
Overland Park city	13,831	55.4%	11.7%	0.0%	67.1%	17,248	90.6%	2.2%	0.0%	92.8%
Topeka city	13,574	60.6%	12.2%	0.0%	72.7%	11,068	78.9%	7.4%	0.0%	86.3%
Wichita city	35,181	64.9%	12.1%	0.6%	77.6%	41,249	71.9%	7.7%	4.4%	84.0%
Kentucky										
Lexington-Fayette urban county	42,981	60.7%	10.6%	0.0%	71.3%	32,524	78.0%	7.4%	0.4%	85.8%
Louisville/Jefferson County metro govt (bal)	55,865	61.8%	10.7%	0.7%	73.2%	59,656	78.2%	7.6%	0.0%	85.8%
Louisiana										
Baton Rouge city	42,340	54.9%	9.6%	0.0%	64.5%	25,399	76.1%	8.0%	0.0%	84.0%
Lafayette city	16,123	60.6%	9.7%	0.0%	70.3%	15,819	86.6%	3.1%	0.0%	89.8%
New Orleans city	40,095	41.0%	10.6%	0.3%	51.9%	48,879	70.6%	7.3%	0.4%	78.2%
Shreveport city	22,368	50.0%	6.7%	1.2%	57.9%	20,225	70.0%	8.0%	0.0%	78.0%
Maryland										
Baltimore city	66,366	47.4%	14.7%	0.0%	62.1%	81,284	69.9%	8.0%	0.5%	78.3%
Massachusetts										
Boston city	93,252	55.7%	10.6%	0.3%	66.5%	109,618	81.3%	6.5%	0.1%	87.9%
Brockton city	7,019	58.9%	24.2%	0.0%	83.1%	11,658	78.9%	7.0%	0.5%	86.5%
Cambridge city	21,135	57.7%	2.8%	0.0%	60.5%	20,406	69.7%	3.1%	0.0%	72.8%
Lowell city	13,159	68.1%	6.1%	0.0%	74.2%	12,922	71.3%	14.5%	0.0%	85.7%
Lynn city	8,255	55.5%	8.5%	0.0%	64.0%	8,758	77.7%	11.6%	0.0%	89.3%
New Bedford city	8,700	60.3%	15.9%	0.0%	76.2%	10,265	66.5%	12.6%	0.0%	79.2%
Springfield city	19,946	52.2%	9.9%	0.0%	62.1%	14,450	66.2%	9.5%	0.0%	75.7%
Worcester city	25,113	55.1%	7.9%	0.9%	63.9%	20,129	77.7%	4.5%	0.0%	82.2%
Michigan										
Ann Arbor city	35,322	41.8%	7.6%	0.0%	49.4%	13,009	76.0%	3.8%	0.0%	79.8%
Dearborn city	11,174	63.3%	4.0%	0.0%	67.3%	8,875	60.1%	8.1%	0.0%	68.2%
Detroit city	82,750	36.8%	24.9%	0.0%	61.6%	58,753	50.3%	19.7%	0.0%	70.0%
Flint city	6,592	45.3%	28.0%	0.0%	73.3%	11,304	54.8%	19.5%	0.0%	74.3%
Grand Rapids city	22,957	71.2%	13.3%	0.0%	84.6%	25,469	77.1%	9.0%	0.0%	86.1%
Lansing city	14,224	61.5%	13.7%	0.0%	75.2%	15,512	79.3%	7.8%	0.0%	87.1%
Livonia city	7,551	67.4%	8.4%	1.5%	77.4%	7,554	82.1%	8.8%	0.0%	90.8%
Sterling Heights city	9,328	62.7%	13.2%	0.0%	75.9%	10,488	70.9%	9.4%	0.0%	80.3%
Warren city	13,462	60.8%	9.1%	0.0%	69.9%	13,278	76.4%	8.8%	0.0%	85.2%
Minnesota										
Minneapolis city	50,657	62.8%	10.5%	0.0%	73.3%	66,958	83.6%	6.0%	0.0%	89.6%
Rochester city	10,278	76.4%	2.3%	0.0%	78.7%	10,331	84.3%	3.0%	0.0%	87.3%
St. Paul city	35,185	68.2%	7.9%	0.0%	76.1%	36,656	84.5%	6.5%	0.0%	91.0%
Mississippi										
Jackson city	21,229	53.7%	12.8%	0.0%	66.6%	19,681	69.9%	12.6%	2.6%	85.0%

Table H-3: Places—Labor Force Status—*Continued*

	18 to 24					25 to 31				
	In the Labor Force	Percent				In the Labor Force	Percent			
		Employed	Unemployed	In Armed Forces	Labor Force Participation Rate		Employed	Unemployed	In Armed Forces	Labor Force Participation Rate
Missouri										
Columbia city	28,006	64.3%	3.1%	0.0%	67.4%	16,810	87.1%	4.6%	0.0%	91.8%
Independence city	10,039	68.1%	8.3%	0.0%	76.4%	8,920	89.7%	5.7%	0.0%	95.4%
Kansas City city	46,153	71.6%	7.0%	0.0%	78.6%	58,617	81.2%	5.4%	0.2%	86.8%
Lee's Summit city	5,779	57.2%	11.9%	0.0%	69.1%	8,090	79.8%	3.7%	0.0%	83.5%
Springfield city	27,960	60.8%	7.8%	0.0%	68.6%	20,876	80.6%	5.0%	0.0%	85.6%
St. Louis city	31,990	52.4%	13.2%	0.0%	65.6%	44,419	76.0%	4.8%	0.0%	80.8%
Montana										
Billings city	12,115	69.5%	13.9%	0.0%	83.4%	9,279	83.2%	0.0%	0.0%	83.2%
Nebraska										
Lincoln city	39,030	67.8%	7.0%	0.0%	74.8%	28,205	82.3%	4.1%	0.0%	86.4%
Omaha city	41,799	72.9%	6.3%	0.0%	79.2%	48,253	82.9%	2.7%	0.0%	85.6%
Nevada										
Henderson city	21,476	58.8%	15.8%	0.0%	74.6%	22,921	68.6%	13.2%	1.5%	83.4%
Las Vegas city	51,928	52.9%	18.5%	0.1%	71.5%	59,192	71.7%	8.2%	0.9%	80.8%
North Las Vegas city	22,742	54.0%	18.0%	1.7%	73.7%	26,289	70.7%	10.4%	3.1%	84.2%
Reno city	27,486	58.5%	7.8%	0.5%	66.8%	25,859	75.8%	11.7%	0.2%	87.6%
Sparks city	8,659	60.8%	17.8%	0.0%	78.6%	8,481	73.2%	8.3%	0.0%	81.4%
New Hampshire										
Manchester city	11,409	55.2%	13.6%	0.0%	68.8%	13,147	73.4%	9.6%	0.8%	83.8%
New Jersey										
Elizabeth city	13,165	65.0%	7.4%	0.0%	72.3%	15,640	69.7%	15.5%	0.0%	85.2%
Jersey City city	22,404	47.4%	7.5%	0.0%	54.8%	38,721	76.7%	5.9%	0.0%	82.7%
Newark city	29,094	34.8%	20.4%	0.0%	55.2%	36,097	64.4%	15.5%	0.0%	79.9%
Paterson city	17,606	48.4%	3.4%	0.0%	51.8%	14,156	64.4%	6.7%	0.0%	71.2%
New Mexico										
Albuquerque city	58,842	56.4%	11.4%	0.7%	68.5%	54,748	73.6%	7.2%	0.9%	81.6%
Las Cruces city	19,157	54.3%	14.6%	0.9%	69.7%	7,616	74.5%	10.1%	0.0%	84.6%
Rio Rancho city	7,932	49.6%	6.4%	0.0%	56.0%	7,728	60.5%	16.8%	0.0%	77.3%
New York										
Albany city	20,309	46.7%	6.6%	0.0%	53.4%	14,704	76.8%	5.8%	0.5%	83.1%
Buffalo city	32,188	52.4%	5.3%	0.0%	57.7%	30,643	72.7%	8.4%	0.0%	81.1%
New York city	798,163	43.1%	11.8%	0.0%	55.0%	1,014,121	73.8%	7.9%	0.2%	81.9%
Rochester city	24,555	52.2%	19.4%	0.0%	71.6%	29,417	70.7%	7.2%	0.3%	78.3%
Syracuse city	24,887	46.3%	7.6%	0.0%	53.9%	18,013	73.1%	8.3%	0.0%	81.5%
Yonkers city	18,205	47.7%	15.0%	0.0%	62.7%	18,266	69.7%	9.8%	0.0%	79.6%
North Carolina										
Charlotte city	75,363	61.2%	13.4%	0.2%	74.8%	93,254	78.5%	8.4%	0.2%	87.2%
Durham city	25,653	45.3%	7.9%	0.0%	53.1%	35,049	77.9%	4.6%	0.6%	83.1%
Fayetteville city	25,924	38.3%	15.8%	17.2%	71.2%	25,605	44.0%	10.6%	23.0%	77.6%
Greensboro city	34,083	42.5%	11.0%	0.0%	53.6%	30,190	76.0%	9.2%	1.8%	87.0%
High Point city	11,627	40.8%	10.1%	0.0%	50.9%	10,238	70.2%	8.0%	0.0%	78.3%
Raleigh city	52,777	50.2%	12.2%	0.0%	62.4%	52,519	81.0%	6.3%	0.1%	87.5%
Wilmington city	17,952	59.4%	12.9%	0.6%	72.9%	12,989	86.7%	3.3%	0.7%	90.6%
Winston-Salem city	27,308	54.6%	9.1%	0.0%	63.7%	19,756	73.1%	5.1%	0.0%	78.2%
North Dakota										
Fargo city	23,311	84.8%	2.5%	0.0%	87.3%	15,383	87.4%	6.4%	0.2%	94.0%
Ohio										
Akron city	24,800	63.3%	8.6%	0.0%	71.9%	20,695	74.8%	8.9%	0.3%	84.0%
Cincinnati city	39,783	57.7%	8.3%	0.0%	66.0%	36,235	75.5%	11.0%	0.0%	86.6%
Cleveland city	46,059	52.6%	19.2%	0.0%	71.8%	37,667	66.4%	11.6%	0.0%	78.0%
Columbus city	89,448	58.6%	8.0%	0.0%	66.6%	107,536	81.6%	4.7%	0.8%	87.1%
Dayton city	23,431	44.0%	14.7%	0.3%	59.0%	14,200	63.2%	9.5%	2.1%	74.8%
Toledo city	31,680	58.0%	18.6%	0.0%	76.6%	30,360	68.5%	12.2%	0.0%	80.7%
Oklahoma										
Broken Arrow city	8,364	62.5%	16.5%	0.0%	79.0%	9,703	79.2%	3.2%	0.0%	82.3%
Lawton city	15,406	36.1%	2.6%	30.4%	69.1%	12,212	56.0%	6.8%	15.9%	78.7%
Norman city	19,002	60.7%	11.0%	0.0%	71.6%	17,042	82.5%	0.6%	0.0%	83.1%
Oklahoma City city	62,132	61.1%	8.5%	2.3%	71.9%	70,063	81.8%	3.5%	0.7%	86.0%
Tulsa city	39,294	61.9%	11.0%	0.0%	72.9%	42,921	77.5%	5.5%	0.0%	83.0%
Oregon										
Beaverton city	7,397	48.0%	21.4%	0.0%	69.5%	11,528	84.9%	1.4%	0.0%	86.4%
Eugene city	29,300	54.7%	8.7%	0.0%	63.3%	16,885	61.4%	12.7%	0.6%	74.7%
Gresham city	10,336	58.1%	18.7%	0.0%	76.8%	12,421	71.4%	15.2%	0.8%	87.4%
Hillsboro city	7,870	78.2%	1.4%	0.0%	79.5%	11,317	70.7%	13.8%	0.0%	84.6%
Portland city	53,240	52.9%	14.0%	0.1%	67.0%	78,665	73.3%	10.2%	0.3%	83.8%
Salem city	16,978	49.6%	17.1%	0.0%	66.7%	17,782	65.8%	10.7%	0.0%	76.5%
Pennsylvania										
Allentown city	13,580	50.2%	13.7%	0.0%	64.0%	12,602	59.4%	22.0%	0.0%	81.4%
Erie city	13,353	53.8%	8.3%	0.0%	62.1%	12,796	67.7%	13.2%	0.0%	80.9%
Philadelphia city	179,729	42.8%	14.4%	0.0%	57.2%	187,507	69.0%	10.6%	0.0%	79.6%
Pittsburgh city	50,254	47.3%	8.8%	0.0%	56.1%	38,294	78.4%	8.2%	0.5%	87.1%

Table H-3: Places—Labor Force Status—*Continued*

	18 to 24					25 to 31				
	In the Labor Force	Percent			Labor Force Participation Rate	In the Labor Force	Percent			Labor Force Participation Rate
		Employed	Unemployed	In Armed Forces			Employed	Unemployed	In Armed Forces	
Rhode Island										
Providence city	30,447	46.3%	10.9%	0.0%	57.2%	22,974	73.9%	10.5%	0.2%	84.6%
South Carolina										
Charleston city	16,578	39.1%	18.9%	0.7%	58.7%	17,610	75.2%	7.0%	1.6%	83.8%
Columbia city	33,216	43.1%	12.3%	12.0%	67.4%	18,070	64.4%	12.2%	4.6%	81.1%
North Charleston city	16,645	52.9%	10.9%	6.1%	69.9%	10,628	76.4%	5.9%	3.9%	86.3%
South Dakota										
Sioux Falls city.....................	15,987	74.9%	4.4%	0.0%	79.3%	19,442	86.5%	6.1%	0.0%	92.6%
Tennessee										
Chattanooga city	18,173	57.0%	14.3%	0.0%	71.4%	18,396	74.5%	6.9%	0.0%	81.4%
Clarksville city	17,831	64.1%	9.4%	8.1%	81.6%	21,990	51.6%	6.1%	21.5%	79.2%
Knoxville city........................	33,690	54.7%	6.3%	0.0%	61.0%	23,611	73.9%	10.9%	0.2%	85.0%
Memphis city	73,486	47.9%	18.4%	0.0%	66.3%	73,223	68.3%	12.5%	0.5%	81.3%
Murfreesboro city	21,810	62.4%	10.6%	0.0%	73.0%	14,961	84.3%	2.1%	0.0%	86.4%
Nashville-Davidson metropolitan govt (bal)	64,157	60.0%	8.4%	0.1%	68.5%	85,646	80.7%	5.7%	0.0%	86.5%
Texas										
Abilene city	17,581	59.1%	9.2%	3.6%	71.9%	14,055	60.8%	7.2%	10.4%	78.5%
Amarillo city	20,974	71.8%	6.9%	0.0%	78.7%	21,743	72.3%	4.4%	0.3%	77.0%
Arlington city	38,088	66.1%	9.3%	0.5%	75.9%	43,442	74.8%	7.7%	0.0%	82.5%
Austin city	96,859	60.1%	8.2%	0.0%	68.3%	133,406	85.3%	4.4%	0.0%	89.7%
Beaumont city	15,412	48.8%	4.0%	0.0%	52.7%	11,553	81.9%	0.8%	0.0%	82.7%
Brownsville city....................	21,080	39.3%	17.9%	0.0%	57.1%	15,496	66.0%	13.2%	0.0%	79.1%
Carrollton city	12,278	70.1%	4.7%	0.0%	74.8%	13,863	82.0%	6.9%	0.0%	88.9%
College Station city	37,647	51.7%	6.1%	0.0%	57.8%	16,700	77.2%	3.6%	0.0%	80.8%
Corpus Christi city	33,162	63.3%	6.3%	4.4%	74.0%	30,950	76.4%	6.9%	0.8%	84.0%
Dallas city	129,394	57.4%	10.9%	0.1%	68.3%	153,400	77.0%	5.9%	0.0%	82.9%
Denton city...........................	24,350	56.1%	7.3%	0.0%	63.4%	18,586	79.8%	3.7%	0.0%	83.4%
El Paso city	74,001	52.4%	9.2%	4.6%	66.2%	66,579	63.8%	7.6%	7.3%	78.7%
Fort Worth city	76,339	62.9%	10.8%	0.4%	74.1%	88,369	75.3%	5.9%	0.4%	81.6%
Frisco city	8,604	70.3%	7.6%	0.0%	77.8%	10,337	71.8%	7.7%	0.0%	79.5%
Garland city..........................	24,159	55.4%	13.9%	0.0%	69.3%	22,411	73.0%	8.8%	0.0%	81.8%
Grand Prairie city	19,830	59.1%	6.2%	0.0%	65.3%	16,483	77.2%	8.3%	0.0%	85.6%
Houston city	224,553	57.4%	10.3%	0.1%	67.7%	291,146	77.3%	5.4%	0.1%	82.8%
Irving city	23,396	63.0%	7.2%	0.0%	70.2%	27,178	83.3%	2.5%	0.0%	85.9%
Killeen city...........................	16,852	40.5%	8.5%	12.4%	61.5%	19,199	50.2%	16.3%	17.2%	83.7%
Laredo city............................	27,273	47.0%	8.4%	0.0%	55.4%	23,201	57.9%	3.8%	0.0%	61.7%
Lewisville city......................	8,767	82.4%	2.3%	0.0%	84.6%	13,709	82.5%	6.9%	0.0%	89.4%
Lubbock city.........................	43,705	52.7%	8.9%	0.0%	61.5%	27,015	75.6%	4.6%	0.4%	80.7%
McAllen city	14,982	49.3%	9.2%	0.0%	58.4%	11,499	71.6%	7.6%	0.0%	79.2%
McKinney city	11,353	59.9%	4.7%	0.0%	64.7%	12,028	85.1%	2.4%	0.0%	87.5%
Mesquite city	15,853	60.9%	6.3%	0.0%	67.3%	14,522	74.3%	8.6%	0.0%	82.9%
Midland city	13,360	69.1%	8.8%	0.0%	78.0%	14,827	83.3%	1.7%	0.0%	85.0%
Odessa city	12,319	62.5%	11.6%	0.0%	74.1%	12,521	76.8%	4.2%	0.0%	81.0%
Pasadena city	18,164	59.0%	12.4%	0.0%	71.4%	12,887	69.4%	12.8%	0.0%	82.2%
Pearland city	8,755	64.1%	7.7%	0.0%	71.8%	11,202	81.1%	2.3%	0.3%	83.8%
Plano city	21,028	61.7%	5.1%	0.0%	66.8%	24,682	82.2%	4.4%	0.0%	86.6%
Richardson city	8,366	54.6%	16.1%	0.0%	70.8%	10,832	77.8%	6.6%	0.0%	84.4%
Round Rock city....................	9,366	51.1%	9.1%	0.0%	60.1%	10,481	77.3%	9.1%	0.9%	87.4%
San Angelo city	11,694	52.4%	3.7%	19.8%	75.9%	12,061	69.9%	4.6%	6.4%	81.0%
San Antonio city...................	157,599	56.7%	8.2%	3.0%	67.9%	153,279	77.1%	7.1%	1.0%	85.2%
Tyler city	10,887	52.7%	8.6%	0.0%	61.3%	11,620	73.2%	7.7%	0.0%	80.9%
Waco city	25,064	49.9%	5.9%	0.0%	55.8%	12,838	70.8%	7.1%	0.0%	77.9%
Wichita Falls city	14,389	55.8%	10.2%	18.9%	84.9%	12,667	55.5%	3.9%	5.7%	65.1%
Utah										
Orem city	15,432	77.3%	8.3%	0.0%	85.6%	10,400	69.7%	8.3%	1.3%	79.3%
Provo city	41,722	63.7%	5.5%	0.0%	69.3%	15,986	63.6%	4.2%	0.0%	67.8%
Salt Lake City city................	26,404	65.1%	9.0%	0.0%	74.1%	26,725	80.6%	3.1%	0.0%	83.6%
West Jordan city	9,300	72.1%	16.0%	0.0%	88.2%	10,664	65.4%	10.6%	0.5%	76.6%
West Valley City city............	13,843	62.8%	19.7%	0.0%	82.5%	15,680	75.7%	6.4%	0.0%	82.1%
Virginia										
Alexandria city.....................	8,303	63.6%	11.4%	1.0%	76.0%	26,885	86.7%	2.9%	2.2%	91.7%
Chesapeake city	21,964	46.7%	19.2%	3.0%	68.9%	22,901	68.0%	5.8%	5.3%	79.0%
Hampton city........................	16,646	49.3%	8.5%	11.7%	69.5%	15,772	53.2%	10.0%	11.1%	74.3%
Newport News city...............	22,747	52.1%	5.6%	13.3%	71.1%	20,844	70.8%	5.5%	10.8%	87.1%
Norfolk city	45,302	35.9%	8.8%	28.2%	72.8%	34,255	60.2%	7.2%	15.2%	82.6%
Portsmouth city	10,561	48.2%	7.4%	21.3%	77.0%	11,325	68.6%	7.3%	10.3%	86.2%
Richmond city.......................	30,207	45.7%	19.0%	0.1%	64.8%	31,718	76.4%	5.9%	0.0%	82.3%
Roanoke city	9,135	57.1%	9.6%	3.6%	70.3%	10,878	70.0%	7.2%	0.9%	78.2%
Virginia Beach city	47,498	57.8%	6.4%	15.0%	79.1%	52,685	73.8%	5.5%	8.8%	88.1%
Washington										
Bellevue city	7,892	42.3%	5.9%	0.0%	48.3%	16,432	74.6%	6.5%	0.0%	81.0%
Everett city	11,276	47.9%	10.5%	5.5%	63.9%	10,321	74.0%	6.6%	1.6%	82.1%
Federal Way city	8,597	64.6%	11.6%	0.0%	76.2%	10,225	75.0%	8.8%	4.3%	88.1%

Table H-3: Places—Labor Force Status—*Continued*

	18 to 24					25 to 31				
	In the Labor Force	Percent				In the Labor Force	Percent			
		Employed	Unemployed	In Armed Forces	Labor Force Participation Rate		Employed	Unemployed	In Armed Forces	Labor Force Participation Rate
Washington—Cont.										
Kent city	11,821	53.3%	5.9%	0.0%	59.2%	15,126	67.2%	9.4%	0.0%	76.5%
Renton city	7,783	53.4%	4.1%	0.0%	57.5%	12,165	76.5%	6.1%	0.0%	82.6%
Seattle city	71,283	58.2%	9.8%	0.5%	68.5%	105,232	85.7%	3.4%	0.8%	89.8%
Spokane city	25,919	52.9%	6.9%	1.1%	60.9%	23,818	72.3%	7.5%	0.1%	79.8%
Spokane Valley city	5,998	48.4%	16.9%	1.2%	66.5%	10,724	75.3%	9.8%	0.0%	85.1%
Tacoma city	20,040	58.8%	12.5%	2.5%	73.8%	24,312	67.2%	10.3%	4.0%	81.4%
Vancouver city	14,568	58.2%	16.6%	0.0%	74.8%	16,353	70.4%	7.6%	0.0%	78.0%
Yakima city	10,717	49.9%	9.2%	0.7%	59.8%	8,808	75.8%	3.8%	0.0%	79.7%
Wisconsin										
Green Bay city	11,960	76.6%	4.8%	0.0%	81.4%	10,960	81.0%	10.0%	0.0%	91.0%
Kenosha city	11,446	57.3%	22.7%	0.0%	80.1%	8,573	72.7%	9.3%	2.0%	84.0%
Madison city	41,339	69.1%	3.7%	0.0%	72.8%	37,501	87.3%	3.5%	0.0%	90.9%
Milwaukee city	72,453	51.8%	12.6%	0.0%	64.4%	74,651	70.9%	9.0%	0.0%	79.9%

Table H-4: Metropolitan/Micropolitan Statistical Areas—Labor Force Status

	18 to 24					25 to 31				
	In the Labor Force	Percent				In the Labor Force	Percent			
		Employed	Unemployed	In Armed Forces	Labor Force Participation Rate		Employed	Unemployed	In Armed Forces	Labor Force Participation Rate
Abilene, TX	16,209	59.5%	8.2%	2.7%	70.4%	13,524	60.3%	6.1%	8.9%	75.3%
Adrian, MI micro	6,482	59.7%	9.5%	0.0%	69.2%	7,176	80.8%	2.0%	0.0%	82.8%
Akron, OH	59,948	65.1%	9.1%	0.0%	74.2%	53,286	78.4%	7.5%	0.2%	86.2%
Albany-Schenectady-Troy, NY	62,032	55.8%	9.0%	1.0%	65.8%	67,560	79.7%	9.0%	0.3%	89.0%
Albany, GA	10,395	34.9%	21.3%	0.0%	56.2%	12,303	60.8%	14.7%	1.4%	76.8%
Albany, OR	9,183	47.4%	11.4%	0.0%	58.7%	5,532	61.2%	5.7%	0.0%	66.9%
Albertville, AL micro	5,240	60.8%	16.9%	0.0%	77.7%	7,496	81.6%	4.8%	0.1%	86.5%
Albuquerque, NM	57,981	54.9%	11.8%	0.5%	67.2%	66,314	66.9%	9.2%	0.6%	76.6%
Alexandria, LA	8,837	33.3%	9.8%	16.6%	59.7%	11,348	60.9%	8.4%	6.1%	75.3%
Allentown-Bethlehem-Easton, PA-NJ	48,818	55.2%	9.6%	0.0%	64.8%	60,926	78.0%	9.4%	0.2%	87.6%
Altoona, PA	8,214	62.0%	5.3%	0.0%	67.2%	7,950	69.7%	7.7%	0.0%	77.3%
Amarillo, TX	19,645	67.8%	6.7%	0.2%	74.7%	21,143	74.8%	3.6%	0.2%	78.6%
Ames, IA	15,609	58.8%	2.7%	0.0%	61.6%	8,314	75.4%	8.0%	0.0%	83.4%
Anchorage, AK	34,456	61.8%	8.1%	6.5%	76.4%	38,801	71.0%	7.4%	7.7%	86.1%
Ann Arbor, MI	37,268	50.1%	7.8%	0.0%	58.0%	30,023	78.8%	4.0%	0.0%	82.8%
Anniston-Oxford-Jacksonville, AL	7,946	51.3%	13.2%	2.0%	66.5%	8,612	67.1%	14.5%	0.0%	81.6%
Appleton, WI	16,880	71.2%	6.4%	0.0%	77.5%	18,553	86.8%	1.9%	0.9%	89.6%
Asheville, NC	25,761	67.0%	9.6%	0.0%	76.6%	31,567	80.4%	4.9%	0.0%	85.3%
Ashtabula, OH micro	5,119	52.1%	10.0%	0.0%	62.1%	6,455	69.2%	6.2%	2.3%	77.8%
Athens-Clarke County, GA	24,051	46.4%	9.5%	0.1%	56.0%	17,926	76.2%	8.5%	0.2%	84.9%
Atlanta-Sandy Springs-Roswell, GA	334,330	52.5%	12.8%	0.1%	65.5%	430,131	75.3%	8.2%	0.2%	83.7%
Atlantic City-Hammonton, NJ	18,577	57.0%	12.6%	0.0%	69.5%	18,543	67.9%	13.1%	1.1%	82.2%
Auburn-Opelika, AL	16,504	46.4%	5.7%	2.9%	55.0%	12,274	74.6%	7.6%	4.6%	86.8%
Augusta-Richmond County, GA-SC	39,821	50.0%	15.0%	3.6%	68.6%	43,555	68.3%	6.7%	3.0%	78.0%
Augusta-Waterville, ME micro	7,568	71.8%	2.4%	0.0%	74.2%	8,804	91.1%	2.7%	1.3%	95.1%
Austin-Round Rock, TX	131,822	57.6%	9.9%	0.0%	67.5%	204,664	82.8%	4.5%	0.2%	87.6%
Bakersfield, CA	58,421	47.7%	13.1%	0.4%	61.3%	63,575	61.0%	8.0%	0.9%	69.9%
Baltimore-Columbia-Towson, MD	181,737	56.7%	10.2%	2.8%	69.7%	233,289	76.5%	5.8%	1.1%	83.4%
Bangor, ME	12,620	56.6%	12.6%	0.0%	69.2%	9,762	65.0%	8.0%	0.0%	73.0%
Barnstable Town, MA	11,210	73.0%	8.8%	0.0%	81.9%	12,083	84.3%	5.2%	1.4%	90.9%
Baton Rouge, LA	67,123	56.5%	10.8%	0.1%	67.4%	64,648	74.0%	8.0%	0.0%	82.0%
Battle Creek, MI	8,090	59.0%	13.9%	0.0%	73.0%	8,495	79.8%	2.7%	0.0%	82.5%
Bay City, MI	7,128	62.5%	14.5%	0.0%	77.1%	6,919	67.5%	8.2%	0.0%	75.7%
Beaumont-Port Arthur, TX	24,558	50.3%	9.4%	0.0%	59.7%	28,932	70.1%	4.4%	1.0%	75.4%
Beckley, WV	6,730	47.7%	11.8%	0.0%	59.5%	8,377	74.0%	7.6%	0.0%	81.6%
Bellingham, WA	21,789	60.6%	8.2%	0.0%	68.8%	14,766	77.3%	4.7%	2.4%	84.4%
Bend-Redmond, OR	8,472	67.8%	5.9%	0.0%	73.7%	11,348	73.8%	5.5%	0.0%	79.3%
Billings, MT	14,036	69.3%	12.3%	0.0%	81.6%	11,505	77.0%	4.1%	0.0%	81.1%
Binghamton, NY	18,059	52.8%	9.6%	0.0%	62.4%	15,498	66.6%	11.2%	0.0%	77.8%
Birmingham-Hoover, AL	71,521	55.1%	13.7%	0.0%	68.8%	86,778	73.3%	7.5%	0.0%	80.9%
Bismarck, ND	9,801	76.1%	1.5%	0.0%	77.6%	13,563	93.8%	0.0%	0.0%	93.8%
Blacksburg-Christiansburg-Radford, VA	20,439	44.1%	3.1%	0.6%	47.8%	10,045	65.6%	3.7%	0.0%	69.3%
Bloomington, IL	25,522	67.4%	8.7%	0.0%	76.1%	17,830	89.4%	2.9%	0.0%	92.3%
Bloomington, IN	23,029	49.1%	5.9%	0.0%	55.1%	12,917	74.6%	7.1%	0.0%	81.6%
Bloomsburg-Berwick, PA	6,376	52.1%	3.9%	0.0%	56.0%	5,144	71.3%	9.0%	0.0%	80.3%
Boise City, ID	44,486	61.8%	11.7%	0.0%	73.5%	50,762	79.6%	6.6%	0.3%	86.4%
Boston-Cambridge-Newton, MA-NH	310,618	58.3%	9.1%	0.2%	67.5%	415,944	80.7%	5.9%	0.2%	86.8%
Boulder, CO	30,760	58.7%	6.8%	0.0%	65.5%	25,811	85.5%	3.6%	0.4%	89.6%
Bowling Green, KY	14,142	66.8%	2.9%	0.4%	70.1%	13,620	76.7%	8.0%	0.0%	84.6%
Bremerton-Silverdale, WA	19,217	46.8%	8.2%	19.7%	74.8%	20,607	69.1%	5.1%	12.0%	86.2%
Bridgeport-Stamford-Norwalk, CT	54,608	57.1%	14.8%	0.0%	72.0%	63,732	79.5%	8.2%	0.0%	87.8%
Brownsville-Harlingen, TX	22,975	37.3%	14.8%	0.0%	52.1%	25,636	65.7%	10.7%	0.0%	76.4%
Brunswick, GA	7,745	48.3%	18.9%	4.8%	72.0%	7,087	52.5%	11.4%	7.5%	71.4%
Buffalo-Cheektowaga-Niagara Falls, NY	76,689	59.5%	7.8%	0.2%	67.5%	88,559	76.8%	7.5%	0.2%	84.6%
Burlington-South Burlington, VT	17,799	60.1%	3.4%	0.0%	63.5%	18,054	83.5%	6.2%	0.0%	89.7%
Burlington, NC	9,352	57.2%	5.5%	0.0%	62.7%	10,990	72.6%	8.7%	0.0%	81.3%
California-Lexington Park, MD	7,389	59.9%	9.0%	2.6%	71.5%	7,161	61.7%	7.9%	14.3%	83.9%
Canton-Massillon, OH	26,337	62.6%	11.3%	0.0%	74.0%	26,511	71.1%	11.2%	0.0%	82.3%
Cape Coral-Fort Myers, FL	32,832	57.5%	11.6%	0.0%	69.1%	39,489	69.8%	11.6%	0.0%	81.3%
Cape Girardeau, MO-IL	8,468	65.9%	8.9%	0.0%	74.8%	7,197	74.7%	8.6%	0.0%	83.3%
Carbondale-Marion, IL	8,780	41.9%	10.8%	0.0%	52.6%	9,290	68.2%	2.5%	0.0%	70.8%
Carson City, NV	2,865	58.7%	14.2%	0.0%	72.8%	4,190	80.0%	3.7%	0.0%	83.7%
Casper, WY	5,570	57.2%	14.7%	0.0%	71.9%	6,779	74.2%	6.8%	0.0%	81.0%
Cedar Rapids, IA	18,690	72.6%	8.9%	0.0%	81.6%	24,043	83.4%	7.3%	0.8%	91.5%
Chambersburg-Waynesboro, PA	8,729	61.6%	11.3%	0.0%	73.0%	11,391	78.6%	9.0%	0.0%	87.6%
Champaign-Urbana, IL	27,989	45.1%	9.3%	0.0%	54.4%	22,111	78.6%	4.9%	0.0%	83.4%
Charleston-North Charleston, SC	50,898	51.6%	14.0%	3.1%	68.7%	64,814	76.9%	7.0%	2.4%	86.3%
Charleston, WV	12,324	55.5%	11.4%	0.0%	66.9%	15,380	76.8%	8.3%	0.0%	85.1%
Charlotte-Concord-Gastonia, NC-SC	153,098	59.5%	13.8%	0.1%	73.4%	179,106	76.9%	8.6%	0.1%	85.6%
Charlottesville, VA	12,140	35.5%	7.7%	0.9%	44.1%	15,649	80.0%	2.1%	0.0%	82.1%
Chattanooga, TN-GA	33,372	59.7%	11.3%	0.0%	71.1%	39,531	71.3%	9.0%	0.0%	80.3%
Cheyenne, WY	7,450	46.1%	10.6%	3.2%	59.9%	6,819	74.9%	0.0%	9.9%	84.8%
Chicago-Naperville-Elgin, IL-IN-WI	632,469	56.6%	12.3%	0.8%	69.7%	818,424	76.9%	8.0%	0.2%	85.1%
Chico, CA	20,171	50.2%	9.5%	0.0%	59.7%	14,764	68.7%	6.1%	0.0%	74.7%

Table H-4: Metropolitan/Micropolitan Statistical Areas—Labor Force Status—*Continued*

	18 to 24					25 to 31				
	In the Labor Force	Percent				In the Labor Force	Percent			
		Employed	Unemployed	In Armed Forces	Labor Force Participation Rate		Employed	Unemployed	In Armed Forces	Labor Force Participation Rate
Cincinnati, OH-KY-IN	142,737	64.5%	9.4%	0.0%	73.9%	156,747	76.7%	6.2%	0.1%	82.9%
Clarksburg, WV micro	4,715	67.3%	4.4%	0.0%	71.7%	5,822	74.1%	10.6%	0.0%	84.7%
Clarksville, TN-KY	26,262	53.7%	8.1%	15.2%	77.1%	27,032	50.8%	5.6%	18.5%	74.9%
Cleveland-Elyria, OH	135,438	62.6%	12.4%	0.0%	75.1%	146,925	78.7%	6.3%	0.1%	85.1%
Cleveland, TN	9,116	47.0%	30.1%	0.0%	77.2%	8,804	81.7%	3.9%	0.0%	85.6%
Coeur d'Alene, ID	9,375	59.2%	14.0%	1.1%	74.3%	9,221	59.2%	12.4%	0.0%	71.6%
College Station-Bryan, TX	33,965	49.6%	6.6%	0.0%	56.2%	22,401	77.0%	5.8%	0.0%	82.8%
Colorado Springs, CO	55,719	48.7%	13.4%	15.6%	77.7%	58,293	66.2%	4.9%	10.6%	81.6%
Columbia, MO	23,374	61.7%	2.5%	0.0%	64.2%	18,223	86.5%	4.1%	0.0%	90.6%
Columbia, SC	68,404	50.3%	13.3%	6.6%	70.2%	60,735	69.5%	9.5%	2.9%	81.9%
Columbus, GA-AL	26,946	33.1%	14.2%	19.8%	67.1%	24,828	52.7%	11.0%	13.2%	76.9%
Columbus, IN	5,398	65.4%	11.0%	1.6%	78.0%	6,713	76.8%	3.0%	0.0%	79.8%
Columbus, OH	120,803	61.9%	8.5%	0.0%	70.4%	179,852	79.8%	5.7%	0.4%	85.9%
Concord, NH micro	7,775	59.0%	3.9%	0.0%	62.9%	7,792	80.0%	3.4%	0.0%	83.4%
Cookeville, TN micro	8,471	49.8%	10.5%	0.0%	60.3%	6,071	66.2%	3.1%	1.3%	70.5%
Corpus Christi, TX	33,403	62.1%	5.0%	3.1%	70.2%	34,335	72.8%	6.5%	1.2%	80.4%
Corvallis, OR	10,058	48.3%	10.4%	0.0%	58.7%	6,037	61.2%	5.2%	0.0%	66.4%
Crestview-Fort Walton Beach-Destin, FL	20,005	61.8%	4.9%	11.5%	78.1%	21,993	59.7%	7.1%	11.3%	78.1%
Cumberland, MD-WV	7,074	53.9%	9.8%	0.0%	63.6%	5,052	60.0%	7.3%	0.0%	67.3%
Dallas-Fort Worth-Arlington, TX	443,446	60.2%	10.0%	0.2%	70.5%	566,888	78.3%	5.5%	0.1%	83.9%
Dalton, GA	10,967	64.6%	12.3%	1.4%	78.3%	10,764	69.6%	10.8%	0.0%	80.4%
Danville, IL	4,624	50.0%	21.1%	0.0%	71.2%	5,716	61.7%	18.1%	0.0%	79.8%
Danville, VA micro	6,754	55.7%	20.5%	0.0%	76.2%	5,557	68.7%	6.7%	0.0%	75.4%
Daphne-Fairhope-Foley, AL	12,198	67.8%	6.8%	0.0%	74.7%	10,608	70.4%	4.0%	0.0%	74.3%
Davenport-Moline-Rock Island, IA-IL	26,409	62.9%	7.0%	0.0%	69.8%	25,865	74.3%	5.8%	0.0%	80.2%
Dayton, OH	55,425	55.6%	11.6%	1.0%	68.1%	59,944	74.2%	6.2%	2.2%	82.6%
Decatur, AL	9,346	52.8%	18.3%	0.0%	71.1%	8,613	63.7%	12.1%	0.0%	75.8%
Decatur, IL	7,943	64.9%	12.7%	0.0%	77.7%	7,901	71.1%	11.0%	0.6%	82.7%
Deltona-Daytona Beach-Ormond Beach, FL	32,232	54.2%	7.3%	0.0%	61.4%	33,522	65.9%	5.6%	0.0%	71.5%
Denver-Aurora-Lakewood, CO	170,938	63.6%	10.7%	0.4%	74.7%	247,124	80.5%	5.4%	0.2%	86.2%
Des Moines-West Des Moines, IA	37,578	70.1%	8.8%	0.1%	79.0%	53,808	79.7%	5.0%	0.1%	84.8%
Detroit-Warren-Dearborn, MI	278,348	57.9%	14.7%	0.1%	72.7%	290,523	72.8%	8.9%	0.1%	81.9%
Dothan, AL	7,964	46.1%	18.0%	5.4%	69.5%	10,595	68.7%	9.5%	5.0%	83.2%
Dover, DE	11,469	48.7%	15.2%	2.6%	66.6%	13,318	74.0%	5.9%	4.3%	84.2%
Dubuque, IA	7,514	68.9%	6.4%	0.0%	75.3%	6,904	95.1%	0.7%	0.0%	95.7%
Duluth, MN-WI	22,242	66.2%	3.2%	0.3%	69.7%	19,440	75.2%	3.2%	0.0%	78.4%
Dunn, NC micro	6,886	47.4%	8.8%	2.4%	58.6%	11,159	49.2%	13.9%	14.9%	78.0%
Durham-Chapel Hill, NC	38,479	53.3%	7.7%	0.1%	61.2%	47,610	76.3%	6.1%	0.4%	82.8%
East Stroudsburg, PA	13,851	57.8%	14.1%	0.9%	72.8%	9,134	75.9%	10.5%	0.0%	86.4%
Eau Claire, WI	17,749	68.7%	12.0%	0.0%	80.7%	12,575	81.2%	3.2%	0.0%	84.3%
El Centro, CA	13,724	48.8%	17.9%	0.9%	67.6%	12,690	59.9%	8.8%	1.5%	70.3%
El Paso, TX	63,960	48.6%	9.5%	7.7%	65.8%	63,629	64.2%	7.1%	6.9%	78.2%
Elizabethtown-Fort Knox, KY	10,421	65.9%	11.5%	6.7%	84.0%	11,106	67.1%	4.0%	7.1%	78.3%
Elkhart-Goshen, IN	13,238	72.1%	2.7%	0.0%	74.8%	13,059	71.0%	5.3%	0.0%	76.3%
Elmira, NY	5,003	53.3%	9.0%	0.0%	62.3%	6,640	68.8%	8.1%	0.0%	76.9%
Erie, PA	18,709	55.5%	7.6%	0.1%	63.2%	22,155	73.8%	9.3%	0.0%	83.1%
Eugene, OR	30,582	55.8%	10.5%	0.0%	66.3%	22,849	67.3%	10.2%	0.6%	78.1%
Eureka-Arcata-Fortuna, CA micro	11,734	46.9%	17.5%	0.3%	64.8%	10,194	68.0%	7.0%	0.0%	75.0%
Evansville, IN-KY	21,665	58.0%	10.0%	0.0%	68.0%	20,448	70.8%	3.3%	0.0%	74.1%
Fairbanks, AK	10,480	55.6%	12.2%	12.2%	80.0%	12,470	64.9%	14.5%	15.4%	94.8%
Fargo, ND-MN	30,844	76.5%	2.1%	0.5%	79.1%	23,533	84.5%	5.4%	0.1%	90.0%
Farmington, NM	7,984	50.2%	14.6%	0.0%	64.9%	7,644	61.1%	7.9%	0.3%	69.3%
Fayetteville-Springdale-Rogers, AR-MO	35,195	60.2%	5.6%	0.0%	65.9%	38,401	75.0%	5.3%	0.1%	80.4%
Fayetteville, NC	34,354	36.8%	14.5%	20.9%	72.2%	34,601	44.9%	9.6%	23.3%	77.8%
Flagstaff, AZ	15,812	47.1%	12.1%	0.0%	59.2%	11,639	77.2%	5.9%	0.0%	83.0%
Flint, MI	26,423	50.4%	17.8%	0.0%	68.2%	27,798	64.4%	14.2%	0.0%	78.6%
Florence-Muscle Shoals, AL	8,642	45.5%	11.4%	0.0%	56.9%	9,408	69.9%	9.2%	0.0%	79.0%
Florence, SC	13,586	50.5%	18.0%	0.0%	68.5%	12,156	59.5%	14.9%	0.0%	74.3%
Fond du Lac, WI	7,087	69.8%	8.0%	0.0%	77.8%	4,739	73.2%	10.7%	0.0%	83.9%
Fort Collins, CO	30,670	59.5%	9.1%	0.0%	68.6%	26,396	84.1%	4.4%	0.4%	88.9%
Fort Smith, AR-OK	17,113	56.3%	11.0%	0.0%	67.3%	20,212	63.5%	12.0%	0.5%	76.1%
Fort Wayne, IN	29,645	60.5%	12.1%	0.0%	72.5%	32,020	74.3%	8.4%	0.0%	82.7%
Fresno, CA	65,962	49.9%	10.9%	0.0%	60.8%	78,531	66.5%	10.9%	0.3%	77.7%
Gadsden, AL	5,484	45.5%	13.4%	0.0%	58.9%	5,764	68.3%	3.6%	0.0%	71.9%
Gainesville, FL	33,441	46.9%	8.0%	0.0%	54.9%	23,019	70.3%	5.7%	0.0%	76.0%
Gainesville, GA	13,362	61.9%	14.0%	0.3%	76.1%	14,697	78.6%	11.2%	0.0%	89.8%
Gettysburg, PA	8,419	62.1%	14.4%	0.0%	76.6%	5,087	74.5%	3.2%	0.0%	77.7%
Glens Falls, NY	7,605	64.8%	9.0%	0.0%	73.8%	7,753	68.1%	11.5%	0.0%	79.6%
Goldsboro, NC	9,874	60.6%	13.6%	9.2%	83.4%	10,019	65.5%	8.8%	13.5%	87.8%
Grand Forks, ND-MN	14,273	62.4%	6.8%	2.7%	71.9%	7,899	82.2%	5.3%	2.7%	90.2%
Grand Island, NE	6,073	67.2%	22.8%	0.0%	89.9%	5,433	79.6%	3.9%	0.0%	83.4%
Grand Junction, CO	10,566	55.5%	11.0%	0.0%	66.5%	12,259	72.8%	9.0%	0.0%	81.8%
Grand Rapids-Wyoming, MI	81,344	66.2%	10.6%	0.1%	77.0%	82,623	76.3%	8.4%	0.0%	84.7%
Grants Pass, OR	4,243	47.1%	20.5%	0.0%	67.6%	4,838	72.4%	9.6%	3.2%	85.2%

Table H-4: Metropolitan/Micropolitan Statistical Areas—Labor Force Status—*Continued*

	18 to 24					25 to 31				
	In the Labor Force	Percent				In the Labor Force	Percent			
		Employed	Unemployed	In Armed Forces	Labor Force Participation Rate		Employed	Unemployed	In Armed Forces	Labor Force Participation Rate
Great Falls, MT..............................	5,844	59.2%	5.9%	5.5%	70.6%	7,223	73.3%	1.5%	4.2%	78.9%
Greeley, CO..................................	21,563	57.4%	16.1%	0.0%	73.5%	21,899	70.4%	8.2%	0.2%	78.8%
Green Bay, WI..............................	23,227	74.7%	6.4%	0.0%	81.1%	24,557	81.4%	8.4%	0.0%	89.8%
Greensboro-High Point, NC..............	43,490	47.3%	11.5%	0.0%	58.8%	57,259	75.4%	8.4%	0.8%	84.6%
Greenville-Anderson-Mauldin, SC	50,106	50.9%	10.1%	0.1%	61.1%	58,774	74.1%	6.7%	0.0%	80.8%
Greenville, NC......................	21,283	54.9%	8.6%	0.0%	63.5%	13,515	80.6%	6.0%	0.9%	87.4%
Greenwood, SC micro......................	6,881	45.9%	20.8%	0.0%	66.6%	6,781	71.4%	20.3%	0.0%	91.7%
Gulfport-Biloxi-Pascagoula, MS.......	26,929	54.3%	11.0%	7.8%	73.1%	32,649	73.3%	9.1%	2.9%	85.3%
Hagerstown-Martinsburg, MD-WV...	15,983	53.8%	15.3%	0.9%	70.0%	15,644	66.2%	6.6%	0.0%	72.8%
Hammond, LA................................	10,555	53.2%	21.1%	0.0%	74.3%	11,297	61.6%	16.6%	0.9%	79.1%
Hanford-Corcoran, CA.....................	11,337	45.4%	10.2%	9.5%	65.0%	11,799	59.9%	4.6%	3.3%	67.9%
Harrisburg-Carlisle, PA...................	37,041	58.6%	12.5%	0.0%	71.1%	43,058	77.1%	8.1%	1.4%	86.5%
Harrisonburg, VA	15,309	51.8%	7.5%	0.0%	59.3%	9,943	79.3%	8.6%	0.0%	87.9%
Hartford-West Hartford-East Hartford, CT...............................	84,565	58.4%	11.5%	0.0%	69.9%	89,335	76.2%	8.5%	0.4%	85.0%
Hattiesburg, MS............................	14,942	57.4%	8.7%	0.0%	66.1%	12,733	70.9%	16.3%	0.6%	87.8%
Hickory-Lenoir-Morganton, NC.......	20,178	52.9%	11.4%	0.0%	64.3%	22,629	70.8%	10.7%	0.0%	81.4%
Hilo, HI micro...............................	8,640	45.4%	11.3%	0.0%	56.7%	11,344	63.3%	4.7%	2.4%	70.5%
Hilton Head Island-Bluffton-Beaufort, SC..............................	16,416	65.8%	5.1%	9.9%	80.8%	13,936	64.9%	5.2%	8.6%	78.8%
Hinesville, GA..............................	7,987	37.1%	15.4%	16.5%	69.0%	8,347	51.0%	7.1%	21.3%	79.4%
Holland, MI micro	7,116	68.1%	6.8%	0.0%	74.9%	6,721	78.1%	4.9%	0.0%	83.0%
Homosassa Springs, FL	7,109	57.6%	27.2%	0.0%	84.8%	4,636	51.8%	15.9%	0.0%	67.7%
Hot Springs, AR............................	6,114	56.7%	18.2%	0.0%	74.9%	4,349	65.4%	6.7%	0.0%	72.0%
Houma-Thibodaux, LA	14,204	57.0%	7.5%	0.4%	64.9%	17,832	77.3%	3.5%	0.6%	81.4%
Houston-The Woodlands-Sugar Land, TX...................................	395,572	57.1%	10.4%	0.1%	67.6%	535,829	76.2%	5.6%	0.1%	81.8%
Huntington-Ashland, WV-KY-OH......	21,001	55.8%	9.2%	0.0%	65.0%	22,736	68.4%	5.8%	0.0%	74.2%
Huntsville, AL...............................	30,366	57.7%	11.5%	1.2%	70.3%	37,151	78.6%	6.5%	0.0%	85.1%
Idaho Falls, ID.............................	8,454	60.0%	3.0%	0.0%	63.0%	9,868	80.3%	4.2%	0.0%	84.5%
Indianapolis-Carmel-Anderson, IN....	122,803	59.5%	11.6%	0.1%	71.2%	159,741	75.4%	7.6%	0.1%	83.2%
Iowa City, IA...............................	20,651	56.9%	3.9%	0.0%	60.8%	17,108	78.2%	0.8%	0.0%	78.9%
Ithaca, NY	12,412	42.8%	3.1%	0.0%	45.9%	7,303	71.9%	0.7%	0.0%	72.6%
Jackson, MI	9,723	59.8%	8.9%	0.0%	68.7%	10,781	59.6%	12.6%	0.0%	72.1%
Jackson, MS..................................	35,203	48.8%	14.2%	0.0%	62.9%	45,789	71.3%	9.7%	0.9%	82.0%
Jackson, TN..................................	10,424	52.9%	19.5%	0.0%	72.4%	8,852	67.9%	9.1%	0.0%	77.1%
Jacksonville, FL............................	85,383	51.3%	11.1%	3.9%	66.3%	116,768	72.6%	9.8%	2.2%	84.6%
Jacksonville, NC............................	32,657	31.0%	10.6%	42.3%	83.9%	19,536	45.2%	7.5%	25.6%	78.3%
Jamestown-Dunkirk-Fredonia, NY micro..	9,253	46.8%	12.2%	0.0%	58.9%	8,899	73.7%	10.2%	0.0%	83.9%
Janesville-Beloit, WI......................	10,507	54.5%	19.2%	0.0%	73.6%	9,553	68.2%	2.8%	0.0%	71.0%
Jefferson City, MO.........................	7,713	46.3%	5.7%	0.0%	52.1%	9,155	62.8%	5.7%	0.0%	68.5%
Johnson City, TN...........................	16,511	71.1%	6.1%	0.0%	77.2%	12,630	72.2%	6.9%	0.0%	79.1%
Johnstown, PA..............................	8,740	55.7%	11.2%	0.0%	66.9%	8,267	64.7%	13.0%	0.7%	78.4%
Jonesboro, AR...............................	8,765	46.0%	19.2%	0.0%	65.2%	9,428	67.9%	8.1%	0.0%	76.0%
Joplin, MO...................................	14,349	72.5%	10.8%	0.4%	83.7%	13,125	73.6%	4.7%	0.0%	78.3%
Kahului-Wailuku-Lahaina, HI...........	7,640	70.1%	3.1%	0.0%	73.1%	13,839	80.7%	3.8%	0.5%	85.0%
Kalamazoo-Portage, MI...................	34,566	56.1%	15.8%	0.0%	71.9%	26,275	80.2%	6.5%	0.3%	86.9%
Kalispell, MT micro	5,327	65.8%	10.5%	0.0%	76.3%	4,986	71.1%	2.4%	0.0%	73.5%
Kankakee, IL................................	7,120	53.6%	8.7%	0.0%	62.4%	7,586	77.6%	13.8%	0.0%	91.4%
Kansas City, MO-KS.......................	134,312	65.4%	8.8%	1.4%	75.6%	169,147	80.5%	5.2%	0.3%	86.0%
Kennewick-Richland, WA.................	17,722	56.5%	13.6%	0.8%	70.9%	21,001	76.7%	5.6%	0.3%	82.7%
Killeen-Temple, TX........................	39,709	43.6%	10.6%	18.2%	72.3%	39,148	52.8%	8.5%	16.0%	77.3%
Kingsport-Bristol-Bristol, TN-VA......	17,225	53.4%	15.0%	0.0%	68.4%	16,947	65.2%	7.1%	0.0%	72.3%
Kingston, NY................................	11,012	48.6%	10.3%	0.0%	58.9%	10,593	66.5%	13.8%	0.0%	80.2%
Knoxville, TN................................	56,401	56.3%	11.0%	0.0%	67.3%	59,271	70.8%	10.4%	0.0%	81.2%
Kokomo, IN..................................	5,268	79.5%	9.3%	0.0%	88.8%	4,793	82.5%	1.1%	0.0%	83.6%
La Crosse-Onalaska, WI-MN	14,315	72.2%	1.5%	0.0%	73.7%	12,026	86.1%	6.4%	0.0%	92.4%
Lafayette-West Lafayette, IN	25,263	48.6%	4.6%	0.0%	53.2%	17,491	78.8%	3.8%	0.3%	82.9%
Lafayette, LA................................	38,135	61.3%	9.5%	0.0%	70.9%	39,789	77.8%	5.2%	0.1%	83.1%
Lake Charles, LA...........................	13,554	44.6%	19.9%	0.0%	64.6%	13,484	73.9%	6.5%	0.2%	80.7%
Lake Havasu City-Kingman, AZ	9,638	51.0%	17.2%	0.0%	68.2%	11,229	70.9%	8.1%	0.0%	79.0%
Lakeland-Winter Haven, FL	35,163	51.2%	12.1%	0.0%	63.3%	41,878	67.3%	8.5%	0.0%	75.7%
Lancaster, PA...............................	37,661	64.3%	10.2%	0.0%	74.5%	39,724	80.7%	5.1%	0.0%	85.9%
Lansing-East Lansing, MI	48,185	57.3%	8.4%	0.0%	65.7%	39,128	79.2%	8.0%	0.0%	87.1%
Laredo, TX...................................	15,719	46.7%	8.4%	0.0%	55.1%	16,070	59.4%	3.9%	0.0%	63.3%
Las Cruces, NM.............................	24,200	55.8%	17.0%	1.9%	74.6%	14,788	73.5%	6.2%	1.4%	81.1%
Las Vegas-Henderson-Paradise, NV	133,004	56.6%	15.6%	0.7%	72.9%	169,313	72.3%	9.6%	1.1%	83.0%
Lawrence, KS................................	17,262	64.3%	5.6%	0.0%	69.9%	13,010	80.8%	8.4%	0.0%	89.2%
Lawton, OK..................................	12,506	38.7%	2.7%	26.2%	67.6%	11,898	52.9%	13.0%	14.2%	80.1%
Lebanon, PA.................................	8,216	56.2%	19.0%	0.0%	75.2%	7,446	75.7%	5.4%	0.0%	81.1%
Lewiston-Auburn, ME	7,221	73.4%	2.1%	0.0%	75.6%	8,640	81.0%	3.6%	0.0%	84.6%
Lewiston, ID-WA...........................	3,924	46.3%	8.9%	0.0%	55.2%	3,665	73.7%	3.0%	0.0%	76.7%
Lexington-Fayette, KY	40,292	58.4%	10.6%	0.0%	69.0%	41,246	76.7%	7.4%	0.3%	84.4%
Lima, OH....................................	8,907	66.1%	16.6%	0.0%	82.7%	7,793	79.2%	7.6%	0.0%	86.8%
Lincoln, NE.................................	36,480	66.6%	7.8%	0.0%	74.4%	27,920	81.2%	4.0%	0.3%	85.5%

Table H-4: Metropolitan/Micropolitan Statistical Areas—Labor Force Status—*Continued*

	18 to 24					25 to 31				
	In the Labor Force	Percent				In the Labor Force	Percent			
		Employed	Unemployed	In Armed Forces	Labor Force Participation Rate		Employed	Unemployed	In Armed Forces	Labor Force Participation Rate
Little Rock-North Little Rock-Conway, AR	49,473	61.5%	7.5%	1.1%	70.1%	65,578	77.3%	6.7%	1.3%	85.3%
Logan, UT-ID	15,925	70.2%	8.0%	0.0%	78.2%	12,973	79.2%	1.0%	0.0%	80.2%
Longview, TX	17,921	66.4%	10.0%	0.0%	76.4%	14,878	70.2%	5.5%	0.0%	75.7%
Longview, WA	6,657	64.9%	12.3%	0.8%	78.0%	5,431	61.4%	4.5%	5.0%	70.9%
Los Angeles-Long Beach-Anaheim, CA	828,101	50.5%	11.8%	0.1%	62.4%	1,118,443	74.5%	7.7%	0.1%	82.3%
Louisville/Jefferson County, KY-IN	80,066	61.4%	11.3%	0.4%	73.1%	97,444	77.0%	7.4%	0.0%	84.4%
Lubbock, TX	29,997	52.5%	8.2%	0.0%	60.7%	23,678	75.5%	4.7%	0.4%	80.6%
Lumberton, NC micro	7,044	34.7%	15.7%	0.0%	50.5%	6,680	61.7%	10.7%	0.0%	72.4%
Lynchburg, VA	20,428	52.7%	8.9%	0.0%	61.7%	16,955	76.2%	4.3%	0.5%	81.0%
Macon, GA	16,198	45.6%	15.2%	0.0%	60.8%	17,979	72.1%	14.0%	0.0%	86.1%
Madera, CA	8,571	46.4%	9.1%	0.0%	55.5%	10,492	55.6%	11.6%	0.0%	67.2%
Madison, WI	57,449	69.3%	4.6%	0.0%	73.9%	65,252	86.1%	3.6%	0.2%	89.9%
Manchester-Nashua, NH	24,081	61.9%	11.1%	0.0%	73.0%	31,908	81.8%	7.8%	0.3%	89.9%
Manhattan, KS	15,055	39.4%	3.0%	14.9%	57.3%	10,672	63.6%	3.6%	14.3%	81.5%
Mankato-North Mankato, MN	12,850	65.7%	2.0%	0.0%	67.7%	8,200	88.8%	3.1%	0.0%	91.9%
Mansfield, OH	7,484	55.8%	12.5%	0.0%	68.3%	6,004	58.6%	5.3%	0.0%	63.8%
McAllen-Edinburg-Mission, TX	52,822	47.5%	11.7%	0.0%	59.2%	52,497	64.5%	6.2%	0.0%	70.7%
Medford, OR	13,305	69.7%	7.1%	0.0%	76.8%	13,453	72.9%	6.8%	0.0%	79.7%
Memphis, TN-MS-AR	90,496	49.1%	16.1%	0.2%	65.4%	106,438	72.1%	10.2%	0.5%	82.7%
Merced, CA	20,801	41.5%	24.6%	0.0%	66.0%	18,720	61.5%	11.7%	0.0%	73.2%
Meridian, MS micro	6,963	41.0%	14.7%	3.8%	59.5%	6,584	73.8%	7.0%	0.0%	80.8%
Miami-Fort Lauderdale-West Palm Beach, FL	323,784	51.0%	12.7%	0.1%	63.8%	446,180	73.1%	9.2%	0.2%	82.5%
Michigan City-La Porte, IN	6,971	65.5%	10.8%	0.0%	76.3%	7,030	60.9%	4.2%	0.0%	65.2%
Midland, MI	6,297	63.4%	13.6%	0.0%	77.1%	5,929	68.3%	7.1%	0.0%	75.5%
Midland, TX	12,288	69.2%	7.3%	0.0%	76.6%	15,624	81.9%	1.3%	0.0%	83.2%
Milwaukee-Waukesha-West Allis, WI	105,828	61.7%	9.9%	0.0%	71.5%	135,112	78.7%	6.9%	0.0%	85.7%
Minneapolis-St. Paul-Bloomington, MN-WI	228,267	68.6%	9.3%	0.0%	77.9%	306,875	83.0%	4.7%	0.1%	87.8%
Missoula, MT	11,422	54.2%	15.4%	0.0%	69.6%	10,729	64.2%	17.6%	0.0%	81.8%
Mobile, AL	28,629	51.2%	16.9%	0.0%	68.1%	29,811	68.3%	9.7%	0.6%	78.6%
Modesto, CA	40,789	57.4%	16.1%	0.0%	73.5%	38,083	61.1%	14.2%	0.0%	75.3%
Monroe, LA	10,179	40.2%	10.0%	0.0%	50.1%	12,214	61.9%	7.6%	0.0%	69.5%
Monroe, MI	11,466	71.6%	14.9%	0.0%	86.5%	10,508	77.3%	13.2%	0.0%	90.5%
Montgomery, AL	23,537	47.5%	9.0%	3.5%	60.0%	26,849	68.5%	4.4%	0.5%	73.4%
Morgantown, WV	16,513	53.8%	5.5%	0.0%	59.3%	11,550	66.3%	8.1%	0.0%	74.4%
Morristown, TN	7,290	64.8%	12.9%	0.0%	77.7%	7,197	72.2%	5.2%	0.0%	77.5%
Mount Vernon-Anacortes, WA	8,395	59.4%	7.2%	9.2%	75.8%	6,903	51.1%	13.4%	13.0%	77.5%
Muncie, IN	16,349	55.9%	11.8%	0.0%	67.7%	7,654	66.0%	16.1%	0.3%	82.4%
Muskegon, MI	11,254	52.2%	27.4%	0.0%	79.6%	10,546	64.0%	14.2%	0.8%	79.1%
Myrtle Beach-Conway-North Myrtle Beach, SC-NC	24,001	62.3%	11.7%	0.0%	74.0%	26,867	77.9%	8.5%	0.0%	86.4%
Napa, CA	9,918	72.7%	2.7%	0.0%	75.4%	9,966	83.4%	9.0%	0.0%	92.5%
Naples-Immokalee-Marco Island, FL	17,069	66.1%	9.5%	0.0%	75.7%	18,545	75.3%	8.0%	0.0%	83.3%
Nashville-Davidson—Murfreesboro—Franklin, TN	115,118	61.3%	8.5%	0.0%	69.8%	150,013	80.4%	5.1%	0.1%	85.6%
New Bern, NC	13,064	47.0%	10.2%	29.2%	86.3%	10,782	59.4%	7.0%	14.8%	81.1%
New Castle, PA micro	4,719	59.5%	7.4%	0.0%	66.9%	5,276	83.8%	7.0%	0.0%	90.7%
New Haven-Milford, CT	55,007	53.7%	9.7%	0.1%	63.5%	64,673	73.5%	7.2%	0.1%	80.8%
New Orleans-Metairie, LA	66,522	47.5%	12.7%	0.8%	61.1%	102,112	73.2%	6.0%	0.7%	79.9%
New Philadelphia-Dover, OH micro	4,760	60.6%	5.1%	0.0%	65.7%	5,854	74.5%	6.2%	0.0%	80.8%
New York-Newark-Jersey City, NY-NJ-PA	1,122,509	49.6%	10.8%	0.3%	60.6%	1,680,546	75.1%	8.0%	0.1%	83.3%
Niles-Benton Harbor, MI	9,380	57.2%	11.6%	0.0%	68.9%	10,054	72.7%	9.4%	0.0%	82.1%
North Port-Sarasota-Bradenton, FL	32,747	50.2%	12.1%	0.4%	62.8%	36,644	76.6%	7.4%	0.0%	84.0%
Norwich-New London, CT	23,219	54.9%	8.2%	15.6%	78.6%	21,357	69.6%	12.2%	2.8%	84.6%
Ocala, FL	14,220	43.4%	14.8%	0.0%	58.2%	17,708	63.1%	9.2%	0.0%	72.4%
Ocean City, NJ	5,377	64.2%	4.5%	0.0%	68.7%	5,899	72.5%	6.1%	1.3%	79.9%
Odessa, TX	13,094	68.0%	10.2%	0.0%	78.2%	14,451	78.6%	4.6%	0.0%	83.2%
Ogden-Clearfield, UT	45,528	68.6%	8.9%	0.8%	78.3%	45,877	71.0%	3.1%	1.2%	75.3%
Ogdensburg-Massena, NY micro	6,416	32.5%	7.1%	0.2%	39.8%	6,805	66.5%	10.9%	2.0%	79.4%
Oklahoma City, OK	94,978	59.7%	8.9%	1.3%	70.0%	113,437	79.3%	2.9%	0.7%	82.9%
Olympia-Tumwater, WA	17,685	52.7%	17.0%	3.8%	73.5%	20,743	58.2%	7.7%	8.2%	74.1%
Omaha-Council Bluffs, NE-IA	67,569	72.7%	5.5%	1.1%	79.3%	82,488	81.8%	2.8%	1.5%	86.2%
Orangeburg, SC micro	6,884	38.1%	23.7%	0.0%	61.8%	4,526	70.0%	6.9%	0.0%	76.8%
Orlando-Kissimmee-Sanford, FL	156,007	56.1%	11.7%	0.0%	67.8%	196,292	73.8%	9.7%	0.1%	83.6%
Oshkosh-Neenah, WI	16,225	76.4%	2.0%	0.0%	78.4%	13,353	79.5%	1.2%	0.0%	80.7%
Ottawa-Peru, IL micro	7,629	56.5%	27.1%	0.0%	83.6%	8,545	82.0%	9.2%	0.0%	91.1%
Owensboro, KY	7,664	64.6%	10.0%	0.0%	74.6%	7,928	71.2%	7.8%	0.0%	79.0%
Oxnard-Thousand Oaks-Ventura, CA	59,105	60.2%	9.0%	1.7%	70.9%	61,426	74.7%	7.8%	2.1%	84.6%
Palm Bay-Melbourne-Titusville, FL	32,330	56.9%	15.3%	1.3%	73.4%	32,463	74.7%	8.9%	0.7%	84.4%
Panama City, FL	11,582	59.4%	8.9%	2.0%	70.2%	12,647	53.5%	8.9%	2.6%	64.9%
Parkersburg-Vienna, WV	5,471	62.5%	7.9%	0.0%	70.4%	5,400	75.2%	2.3%	0.0%	77.5%
Pensacola-Ferry Pass-Brent, FL	38,445	51.5%	6.4%	14.2%	72.0%	37,207	65.7%	8.3%	6.1%	80.1%

Table H-4: Metropolitan/Micropolitan Statistical Areas—Labor Force Status—*Continued*

	18 to 24					25 to 31				
	In the Labor Force	Percent				In the Labor Force	Percent			
		Employed	Unemployed	In Armed Forces	Labor Force Participation Rate		Employed	Unemployed	In Armed Forces	Labor Force Participation Rate
Peoria, IL	25,428	57.5%	14.5%	0.0%	72.0%	30,166	76.9%	6.8%	0.2%	83.9%
Philadelphia-Camden-Wilmington, PA-NJ-DE-MD	388,721	52.9%	12.5%	0.4%	65.8%	494,271	74.1%	8.9%	0.2%	83.3%
Phoenix-Mesa-Scottsdale, AZ	280,666	57.7%	9.6%	0.1%	67.4%	344,309	73.5%	5.8%	0.2%	79.5%
Pine Bluff, AR	6,997	45.2%	14.6%	0.0%	59.7%	5,730	68.5%	7.3%	0.0%	75.8%
Pittsburgh, PA	150,138	59.1%	11.0%	0.0%	70.1%	177,961	77.4%	7.4%	0.1%	84.9%
Pittsfield, MA	9,031	51.8%	15.9%	0.0%	67.7%	8,139	79.6%	5.8%	0.0%	85.4%
Pocatello, ID	7,885	62.8%	10.3%	0.0%	73.1%	6,013	78.5%	1.1%	1.1%	80.6%
Port St. Lucie, FL	21,450	53.5%	12.5%	0.0%	65.9%	27,047	75.6%	7.8%	0.0%	83.5%
Portland-South Portland, ME	34,277	68.5%	7.1%	0.2%	75.8%	35,590	77.6%	8.3%	0.3%	86.2%
Portland-Vancouver-Hillsboro, OR-WA	144,510	57.3%	15.1%	0.1%	72.4%	193,713	73.5%	8.7%	0.1%	82.3%
Pottsville, PA micro	7,314	47.3%	18.2%	0.0%	65.5%	9,309	70.1%	9.4%	0.0%	79.6%
Prescott, AZ	10,831	58.1%	17.2%	0.0%	75.3%	10,539	69.4%	3.8%	1.2%	74.4%
Providence-Warwick, RI-MA	124,114	59.2%	12.1%	0.3%	71.5%	120,291	74.6%	9.0%	0.5%	84.1%
Provo-Orem, UT	71,353	69.1%	5.7%	0.0%	74.8%	43,299	66.8%	4.9%	0.2%	71.9%
Pueblo, CO	9,981	52.1%	10.3%	0.9%	63.3%	11,563	64.3%	12.0%	0.0%	76.3%
Punta Gorda, FL	7,327	59.5%	12.6%	0.0%	72.1%	5,703	57.1%	10.2%	0.0%	67.3%
Racine, WI	10,389	58.1%	15.0%	0.0%	73.2%	14,100	69.1%	11.6%	0.0%	80.7%
Raleigh, NC	75,608	54.6%	10.9%	0.0%	65.5%	98,391	78.3%	6.8%	0.6%	85.7%
Rapid City, SD	11,216	77.9%	5.5%	1.2%	84.6%	11,324	71.7%	7.8%	10.7%	90.2%
Reading, PA	27,122	54.5%	10.6%	0.0%	65.1%	30,249	83.7%	6.0%	0.0%	89.7%
Redding, CA	9,259	40.8%	13.5%	0.0%	54.3%	10,705	66.1%	4.7%	0.0%	70.8%
Reno, NV	30,956	60.9%	9.2%	0.3%	70.4%	35,797	74.9%	8.7%	0.2%	83.9%
Richmond, VA	84,245	57.0%	15.1%	0.5%	72.6%	96,574	73.2%	7.8%	0.4%	81.4%
Riverside-San Bernardino-Ontario, CA	308,255	48.4%	15.5%	1.1%	65.0%	327,740	66.0%	10.6%	1.0%	77.6%
Roanoke, VA	20,161	64.0%	5.6%	4.2%	73.8%	19,144	68.7%	9.3%	0.5%	78.5%
Rochester, MN	15,712	67.5%	11.3%	0.0%	78.8%	17,104	83.5%	4.3%	0.0%	87.8%
Rochester, NY	79,202	58.4%	10.6%	0.1%	69.1%	81,125	74.7%	6.9%	0.3%	81.9%
Rockford, IL	24,985	60.0%	16.1%	0.0%	76.1%	22,119	71.2%	11.8%	0.0%	82.9%
Rocky Mount, NC	11,155	60.6%	18.1%	0.0%	78.7%	8,059	64.1%	17.7%	0.0%	81.8%
Rome, GA	5,871	50.3%	9.4%	0.0%	59.7%	5,578	66.0%	10.4%	0.0%	76.4%
Roseburg, OR micro	4,611	42.6%	17.4%	0.0%	60.0%	5,692	64.1%	9.5%	0.0%	73.6%
Sacramento–Roseville–Arden-Arcade, CA	140,145	49.9%	14.9%	0.0%	64.8%	164,600	71.9%	8.6%	0.3%	80.8%
Saginaw, MI	16,607	65.6%	11.0%	0.0%	76.6%	11,646	71.8%	5.2%	0.5%	77.6%
Salem, OH micro	6,316	54.0%	22.0%	0.0%	76.0%	5,546	57.6%	5.5%	0.0%	63.1%
Salem, OR	30,617	57.7%	12.8%	0.0%	70.5%	27,331	68.8%	9.7%	0.0%	78.4%
Salinas, CA	26,326	44.6%	7.3%	3.8%	55.7%	32,998	64.3%	7.6%	3.2%	75.1%
Salisbury, MD-DE	25,468	53.3%	11.4%	0.0%	64.6%	25,393	77.1%	7.4%	0.5%	85.0%
Salt Lake City, UT	84,860	67.7%	9.4%	0.0%	77.2%	105,694	77.9%	4.7%	0.1%	82.8%
San Angelo, TX	10,713	51.8%	4.8%	18.2%	74.9%	10,285	68.9%	4.4%	7.6%	80.9%
San Antonio-New Braunfels, TX	167,121	58.2%	8.2%	2.5%	68.9%	191,677	75.2%	6.1%	1.1%	82.4%
San Diego-Carlsbad, CA	249,053	47.8%	10.1%	10.1%	68.0%	304,689	69.4%	7.0%	5.5%	82.0%
San Francisco-Oakland-Hayward, CA	247,318	53.9%	11.0%	0.1%	65.0%	410,121	77.0%	7.4%	0.5%	84.9%
San Jose-Sunnyvale-Santa Clara, CA	110,126	56.4%	9.9%	0.1%	66.4%	166,412	75.7%	8.3%	0.2%	84.2%
San Luis Obispo-Paso Robles-Arroyo Grande, CA	24,719	48.6%	2.8%	4.7%	56.2%	18,852	74.1%	5.4%	0.0%	79.5%
Santa Cruz-Watsonville, CA	24,328	53.6%	8.2%	0.0%	61.8%	18,057	79.5%	4.8%	0.0%	84.2%
Santa Fe, NM	6,632	47.6%	11.9%	0.6%	60.1%	8,620	74.9%	3.3%	0.0%	78.2%
Santa Maria-Santa Barbara, CA	46,109	59.1%	8.0%	0.8%	67.9%	33,333	74.8%	7.4%	0.8%	83.0%
Santa Rosa, CA	30,447	57.0%	9.7%	0.2%	66.9%	35,803	73.0%	7.8%	1.5%	82.2%
Savannah, GA	28,122	46.1%	13.6%	4.4%	64.1%	31,660	64.3%	11.1%	4.0%	79.4%
Scranton–Wilkes-Barre–Hazleton, PA	37,660	59.1%	7.9%	0.0%	67.0%	37,548	70.6%	10.5%	0.0%	81.1%
Seattle-Tacoma-Bellevue, WA	224,552	57.9%	9.7%	2.2%	69.8%	334,656	75.8%	5.8%	2.5%	84.2%
Sebastian-Vero Beach, FL	6,161	47.6%	16.5%	0.0%	64.1%	7,257	67.4%	12.9%	0.0%	80.3%
Sebring, FL	4,935	47.1%	25.0%	0.0%	72.1%	4,705	60.4%	18.9%	0.0%	79.2%
Sheboygan, WI	6,371	78.2%	2.7%	0.0%	80.9%	7,783	79.8%	6.6%	0.0%	86.4%
Sherman-Denison, TX	7,113	55.5%	8.6%	0.0%	64.1%	8,875	71.6%	6.8%	0.0%	78.3%
Show Low, AZ micro	4,738	28.6%	16.7%	0.0%	45.3%	5,699	46.8%	13.2%	0.0%	60.0%
Shreveport-Bossier City, LA	29,478	45.9%	8.9%	5.2%	60.0%	36,888	72.8%	6.9%	1.0%	80.6%
Sierra Vista-Douglas, AZ	7,898	49.8%	2.4%	11.8%	64.0%	8,609	60.1%	4.1%	9.4%	73.6%
Sioux City, IA-NE-SD	13,496	76.0%	4.1%	0.0%	80.1%	12,649	85.5%	4.8%	0.0%	90.3%
Sioux Falls, SD	18,071	71.1%	4.4%	0.0%	75.4%	23,126	85.1%	4.8%	0.0%	90.0%
South Bend-Mishawaka, IN-MI	19,990	50.8%	10.2%	0.0%	61.0%	22,718	81.6%	8.6%	0.0%	90.2%
Spartanburg, SC	24,285	60.1%	10.6%	0.0%	70.7%	20,982	67.6%	9.9%	0.0%	77.5%
Spokane-Spokane Valley, WA	35,559	54.9%	9.3%	1.2%	65.3%	43,074	69.5%	7.0%	1.1%	77.5%
Springfield, IL	13,340	64.3%	9.0%	0.4%	73.7%	16,271	80.8%	3.9%	0.0%	84.7%
Springfield, MA	51,690	54.2%	11.2%	0.0%	65.3%	43,324	71.5%	11.5%	0.0%	83.0%
Springfield, MO	38,714	64.0%	6.4%	0.0%	70.4%	35,354	76.5%	5.0%	0.0%	81.4%
Springfield, OH	8,985	65.2%	7.1%	0.0%	72.3%	9,703	80.0%	8.7%	0.0%	88.6%
St. Cloud, MN	24,849	78.4%	6.3%	0.0%	84.7%	16,601	91.8%	1.2%	0.0%	93.0%
St. George, UT	11,225	63.6%	11.6%	0.0%	75.2%	8,579	79.4%	0.0%	0.5%	79.9%
St. Joseph, MO-KS	8,752	55.9%	12.3%	0.0%	68.2%	8,612	68.0%	5.7%	0.0%	73.7%

Table H-4: Metropolitan/Micropolitan Statistical Areas—Labor Force Status—*Continued*

	18 to 24					25 to 31				
	In the Labor Force	Percent				In the Labor Force	Percent			
		Employed	Unemployed	In Armed Forces	Labor Force Participation Rate		Employed	Unemployed	In Armed Forces	Labor Force Participation Rate
St. Louis, MO-IL............................	184,041	60.6%	12.7%	0.1%	73.4%	224,562	77.1%	6.1%	0.2%	83.4%
State College, PA............................	21,004	38.5%	9.1%	0.0%	47.6%	10,600	70.4%	5.3%	0.0%	75.7%
Staunton-Waynesboro, VA..............	8,145	56.5%	5.8%	0.0%	62.3%	7,039	76.3%	3.4%	0.0%	79.7%
Stockton-Lodi, CA...........................	51,312	54.9%	14.7%	0.0%	69.6%	48,812	69.4%	9.6%	0.2%	79.1%
Sumter, SC....................................	9,688	46.0%	24.0%	2.6%	72.7%	7,854	55.7%	12.8%	12.9%	81.5%
Sunbury, PA micro..........................	5,812	60.7%	15.0%	0.0%	75.7%	5,938	63.7%	11.3%	0.0%	75.0%
Syracuse, NY.................................	45,339	55.1%	8.3%	0.0%	63.4%	47,898	74.1%	10.9%	0.3%	85.3%
Tallahassee, FL..............................	48,537	48.4%	15.7%	0.0%	64.1%	30,882	69.0%	7.2%	0.4%	76.6%
Tampa-St. Petersburg-Clearwater, FL...	164,140	56.5%	10.3%	0.6%	67.5%	209,203	72.3%	8.6%	0.6%	81.5%
Terre Haute, IN..............................	13,325	58.6%	5.5%	0.0%	64.1%	10,658	56.8%	6.9%	0.5%	64.2%
Texarkana, TX-AR..........................	9,339	47.1%	19.4%	0.0%	66.5%	11,643	70.6%	4.0%	0.1%	74.7%
The Villages, FL.............................	3,339	65.4%	14.1%	0.0%	79.5%	4,517	70.5%	15.8%	0.0%	86.3%
Toledo, OH....................................	53,124	59.9%	13.1%	0.0%	73.0%	48,454	74.0%	10.8%	0.0%	84.8%
Topeka, KS....................................	13,876	60.4%	11.2%	0.0%	71.6%	16,645	79.1%	6.8%	0.0%	85.9%
Torrington, CT micro......................	10,011	57.8%	15.6%	0.0%	73.4%	12,783	90.0%	4.5%	0.0%	94.5%
Traverse City, MI micro..................	9,080	59.0%	20.5%	0.0%	79.5%	9,020	78.0%	3.4%	1.5%	82.9%
Trenton, NJ...................................	24,667	49.2%	11.6%	0.0%	60.9%	26,036	71.0%	10.9%	0.0%	81.9%
Truckee-Grass Valley, CA micro	4,518	56.6%	4.6%	0.0%	61.2%	5,025	82.5%	3.4%	0.0%	85.8%
Tucson, AZ....................................	82,074	53.6%	12.4%	1.5%	67.5%	70,130	69.8%	8.9%	1.0%	79.7%
Tullahoma-Manchester, TN micro	5,530	48.6%	13.5%	0.0%	62.1%	5,613	69.7%	18.7%	0.3%	88.7%
Tulsa, OK......................................	61,613	60.5%	9.7%	0.0%	70.2%	72,841	74.8%	6.8%	0.2%	81.8%
Tupelo, MS micro...........................	9,385	49.9%	16.6%	0.0%	66.4%	8,476	70.0%	6.4%	0.0%	76.5%
Tuscaloosa, AL..............................	22,840	47.7%	9.3%	0.0%	57.1%	19,164	75.3%	6.9%	0.0%	82.2%
Tyler, TX......................................	14,166	48.0%	15.7%	0.0%	63.7%	16,447	76.2%	7.4%	0.0%	83.6%
Urban Honolulu, HI........................	72,245	51.3%	5.6%	15.4%	72.3%	88,035	63.2%	3.3%	14.6%	81.1%
Utica-Rome, NY.............................	20,140	59.7%	9.1%	0.0%	68.8%	20,426	73.4%	8.2%	0.5%	82.1%
Valdosta, GA.................................	17,730	52.0%	16.2%	3.5%	71.7%	12,074	69.3%	7.4%	5.9%	82.6%
Vallejo-Fairfield, CA.......................	30,261	52.1%	13.3%	4.2%	69.6%	35,069	69.9%	6.7%	5.1%	81.6%
Victoria, TX..................................	6,459	66.2%	2.6%	0.0%	68.8%	6,105	76.3%	2.7%	0.0%	79.0%
Vineland-Bridgeton, NJ...................	10,846	62.3%	19.0%	0.6%	81.8%	11,343	49.6%	14.5%	0.0%	64.2%
Virginia Beach-Norfolk-Newport News, VA-NC................................	149,014	49.2%	10.9%	13.1%	73.2%	156,721	66.9%	6.6%	9.3%	82.9%
Visalia-Porterville, CA....................	30,966	48.1%	14.3%	0.0%	62.3%	35,253	64.3%	11.6%	0.6%	76.4%
Waco, TX......................................	23,493	57.0%	4.8%	0.0%	61.7%	19,338	73.3%	7.6%	0.3%	81.2%
Walla Walla, WA............................	4,075	43.7%	11.1%	0.0%	54.8%	4,107	61.1%	8.4%	0.0%	69.5%
Warner Robins, GA.........................	11,861	42.1%	13.6%	2.9%	58.6%	15,902	71.8%	8.6%	2.3%	82.7%
Washington-Arlington-Alexandria, DC-VA-MD-WV	372,130	56.9%	10.4%	1.5%	68.8%	565,159	80.3%	6.0%	1.2%	87.4%
Waterloo-Cedar Falls, IA.................	20,462	70.2%	5.0%	0.0%	75.2%	13,613	79.5%	11.3%	0.0%	90.8%
Watertown-Fort Drum, NY	11,223	41.9%	6.4%	26.2%	74.5%	11,385	47.7%	13.2%	20.8%	81.8%
Wausau, WI...................................	7,702	52.9%	15.2%	0.0%	68.1%	9,646	83.2%	4.2%	0.0%	87.5%
Weirton-Steubenville, WV-OH	7,320	51.6%	9.3%	0.0%	60.9%	5,962	70.8%	3.8%	0.0%	74.7%
Wenatchee, WA..............................	6,834	66.2%	12.2%	0.0%	78.4%	9,573	82.8%	3.2%	0.0%	86.0%
Wheeling, WV-OH...........................	7,911	50.7%	9.4%	0.0%	60.1%	7,377	73.9%	3.2%	0.0%	77.1%
Whitewater-Elkhorn, WI micro	8,300	60.4%	13.2%	0.0%	73.6%	6,704	70.0%	5.7%	0.0%	75.7%
Wichita Falls, TX	15,622	51.4%	10.7%	19.5%	81.5%	11,711	60.4%	3.3%	6.9%	70.5%
Wichita, KS...................................	44,600	66.7%	9.1%	0.5%	76.3%	55,609	74.8%	7.5%	3.4%	85.6%
Williamsport, PA............................	8,399	49.7%	11.1%	0.0%	60.7%	6,739	62.7%	18.5%	0.0%	81.3%
Wilmington, NC..............................	24,492	57.8%	16.3%	0.4%	74.5%	21,003	82.8%	4.3%	0.9%	88.1%
Winchester, VA-WV........................	7,982	65.1%	8.5%	0.0%	73.6%	6,573	64.6%	6.4%	0.0%	71.0%
Winston-Salem, NC.........................	41,029	56.7%	11.1%	0.0%	67.8%	39,930	70.3%	8.4%	0.0%	78.7%
Wooster, OH micro.........................	8,484	75.3%	0.8%	0.0%	76.2%	6,690	76.1%	0.6%	0.0%	76.7%
Worcester, MA-CT..........................	64,784	61.4%	10.4%	0.4%	72.2%	64,884	77.3%	6.8%	0.0%	84.1%
Yakima, WA...................................	16,606	48.5%	17.1%	0.3%	65.8%	18,184	73.8%	7.6%	0.0%	81.4%
York-Hanover, PA...........................	27,433	66.7%	7.2%	0.0%	74.0%	28,243	78.7%	5.5%	0.0%	84.2%
Youngstown-Warren-Boardman, OH-PA..	34,621	59.9%	12.0%	0.5%	72.3%	35,309	75.0%	4.1%	1.2%	80.3%
Yuba City, CA................................	10,734	38.9%	22.2%	3.3%	64.4%	12,311	56.7%	15.3%	4.0%	75.9%
Yuma, AZ......................................	15,589	45.7%	10.4%	8.0%	64.1%	14,771	63.6%	9.2%	3.2%	76.0%

PART I
INCOME AND POVERTY

INCOME AND POVERTY

Income reported in the American Community Survey pertains only to the population age 15 and older. While some Millennials who are 15 to 17 will have income, they are not included in the following tables because of their small numbers and low income. The Census definition of income includes all sources of cash income: wages and salary, social security, retirement, interest, dividends and rent, for example. However, sources such as social security and retirement income are largely not applicable to a younger population. The Census money income definition also does not include measures of assets.

INCOME

The Census Bureau reports that median household income for householders under age 25 increased from $24,476 in 2012 to $25,391 in 2013, but this masks the fact that median income in 2013 is just slightly above the $24,903 figure from 2009. This is another indication of the difficult economic climate faced by Millennials as they continue their formal educations and move into the work force. The tables presented here reflect individual incomes rather than household income, which is an important difference. The median income of young Millennials age 18 to 24 was only $5,605 in 2013, and for those age 25 to 31 it was only $18,225. If these incomes

Percent Age 25 to 31 With Income Over $100,000

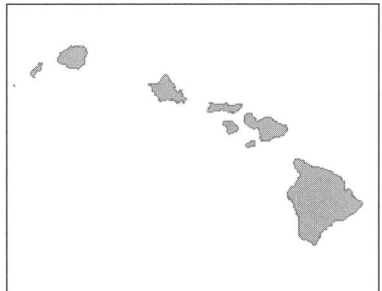

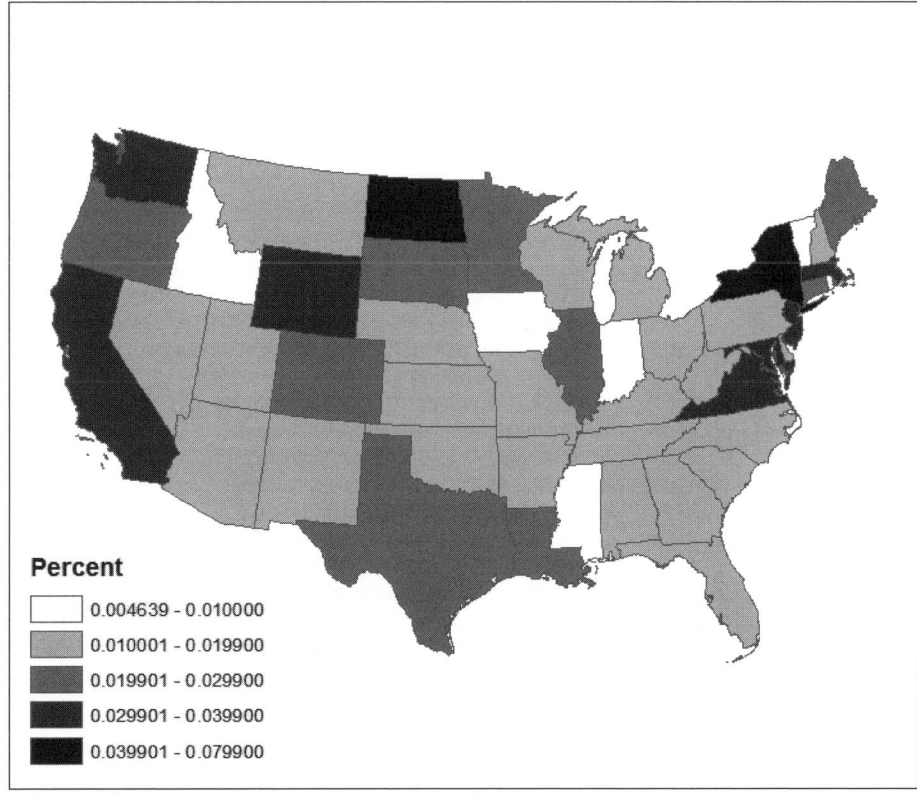

Percent

	0.004639 - 0.010000
	0.010001 - 0.019900
	0.019901 - 0.029900
	0.029901 - 0.039900
	0.039901 - 0.079900

are also just returning to their pre-recession levels, then it's an indicator that Millennials are continuing to struggle with a difficult economy.

Not surprisingly, most young Millennials age 18 to 24 have low incomes. Nationwide, 64.2 percent have less than $10,000 in income from all sources and less than 2 percent have incomes over $50,000. Almost one out of five (18.7 percent) have between $10,000 and $19,999 in annual income. Mississippi has the highest percentage of low income Millennials at 72.7 percent, and the District of Columbia is close behind with 70 percent. By this measure, Alaska is doing the best with the lowest percentage at 44.3 percent. At the higher income levels, Wyoming has the highest percentage (5.8 percent) with incomes over $50,000. Only 19 states have more than two percent of this youngest age group making over $50,000. Incomes rise with age, and only one-third (33.2 percent) of the older Millennial age group has income below $10,000. New Jersey has the highest percentage at 37.1 percent, while North Carolina is lowest at 15.9 percent. Some older Millennials are doing quite well, with incomes over $150,000. Delaware has the highest percentage at 2.6 percent, but it's one of only three states above one percent with Alabama (1.1 percent) and New Mexico (1.4 percent).

Dougherty County, GA has the highest percentage of younger Millennials in the under $10,000 category at 87.5 percent, and 201 counties have more than two-thirds of the 18 to 24 year olds in the lowest income category. Onslow County, NC has the lowest percentage at 34.6 percent. Arlington County, VA has the highest percentage of young, high income Millennials where 14.6 percent have incomes above $50,000, but in 443 counties less than two percent of this group is in the high income category. Among the older Millennial age category, those making under $10,000 range from a low of 6.7 percent in Litchfield County, CT to a high of 54.2 percent in Navajo County, AZ. In 47 counties, more than 10 percent of those age 25 to 31 make more than $75,000, and in New York County, NY (Manhattan) 29.4 percent have over $75,000. In Berkshire County, MA 6.4 percent make over $150,000.

More than 80 percent of those age 18 to 24 in West Palm Beach City, FL have incomes below $10,000, and in 115 cities more than two-thirds of the younger population is in the low income category. Oceanside City, CA has the lowest percentage (37.4 percent) of low income persons. In Ann Arbor City, MI, 11.9 percent of young Millennials make more than $50,000, and it is one of only seven cities above 10 percent. In Miami Beach City, FL only 9.2 percent of older Millennials are in the lowest income category. Almost three-quarters (72.7 percent) in Brownsville City, TX make under $20,000. In the high income categories, 16 cities have greater than 15 percent of the 25 to 31 year old population making more than $75,000. The highest is Sunnyvale city, CA, at 38.1 percent. In San Francisco city, CA, 5.1 percent make more than $150,000.

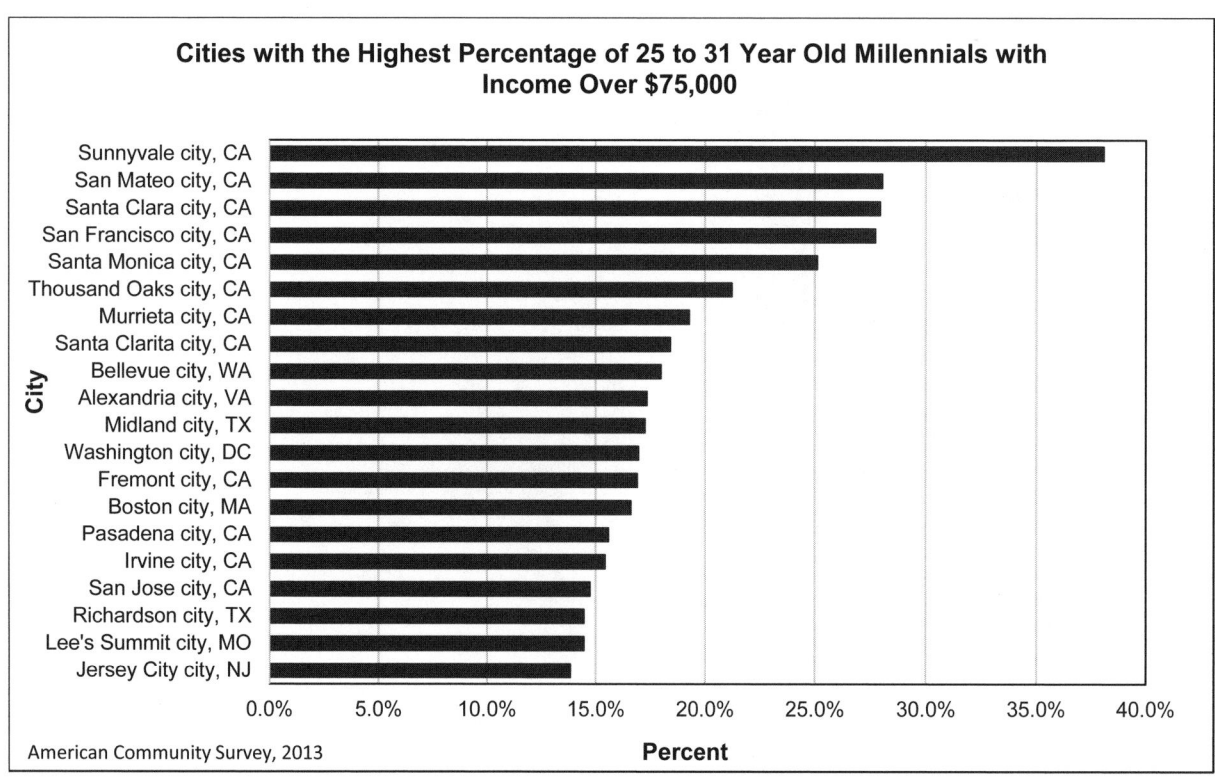

Cities with the Highest Percentage of 25 to 31 Year Old Millennials with Income Over $75,000

American Community Survey, 2013

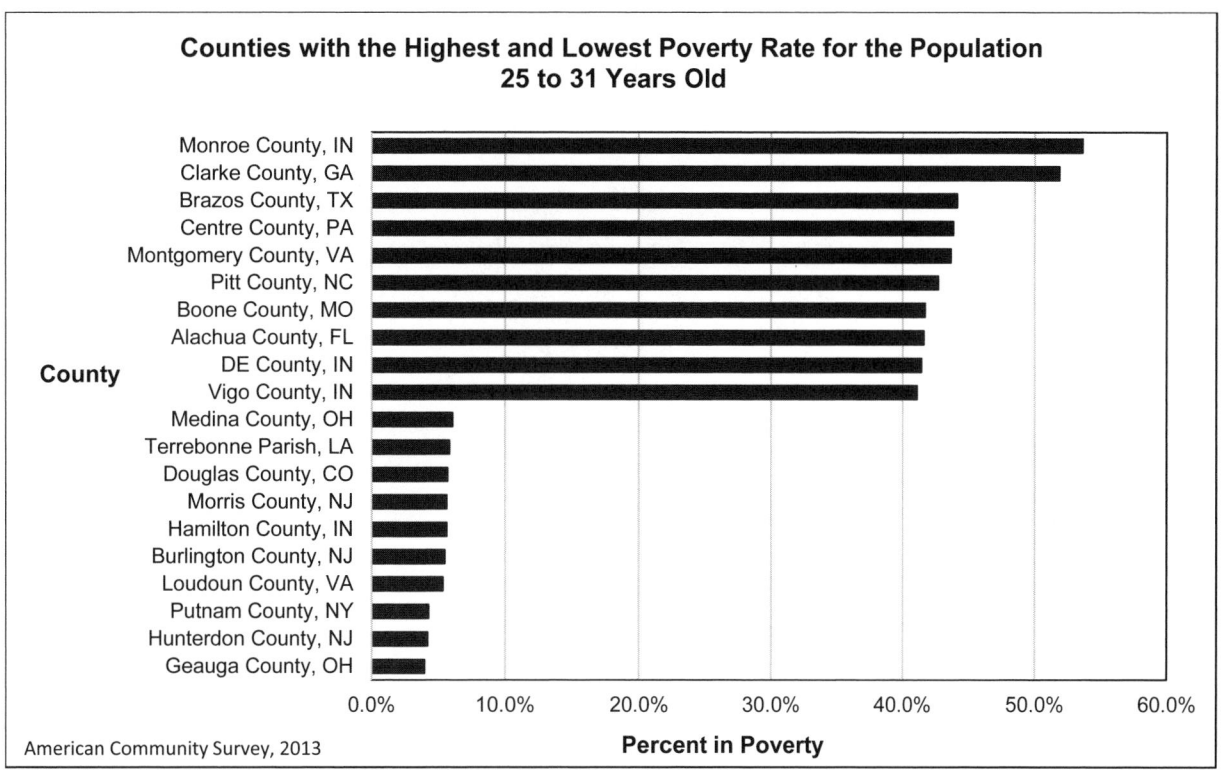

Counties with the Highest and Lowest Poverty Rate for the Population 25 to 31 Years Old

American Community Survey, 2013

In 26 metropolitan/micropolitan areas more than 75 percent of Millennials in the younger age group make less than $10,000. The Albany, GA metro is the highest at 85.9 percent, while the Fairbanks, AK metro is lowest with 33.1 percent. Only 6.7 percent of older Millennials make less than $10,000 in the Torrington, CT micro, but more than half (54.6 percent) are low income earners in the Show Low, AZ micropolitan area. It's one of only three areas above 50 percent; also included are the Panama City, FL and the Rocky Mount, NC metropolitan areas. High income earners are most prevalent in the San Jose-Sunnyvale, CA metro area where more than one in five (20.7 percent) make more than $75,000. Fifteen metro/micros have more than 15 percent of the older Millennials in the high income category.

POVERTY

Poverty status is determined by comparing total family or unrelated individual income to the established national poverty thresholds which vary by size and type of household and number of children. When a family or single person household is determined to be in poverty, every member of the family is so defined. College students living in group quarters (dormitories or other college housing) are not part of the poverty population universe so the poverty data presented here is only for the 25- to 31-year-old Millennials to minimize the effect of college populations.

The national poverty rate for all persons from the 2013 ACS is 15.8 percent, but for the older Millennials, 20.4 percent have incomes below the poverty level. Mississippi has the highest poverty rate at 30.3 percent while Alaska is lowest at 11.0 percent. Of the 622 counties, 295 have poverty rates above the national average for Millennials. Geauga County, GA has the lowest rate of poverty at 4.0 percent. Poverty was highest in Monroe County, IN at 53.6 percent. However, Monroe County is the home of Indiana University, and while college students living in dormitories are excluded from the poverty definition, college students living in non-university, private housing off-campus are included. For this reason, most large college counties and cities will have very high poverty rates.

The University of Georgia accounts for the high poverty rate (51.9 percent) in the Athens-Clark County, GA unified government. Sixteen cities have poverty rates above 40 percent, but 30 cities have poverty rates below 10 percent. Mission Viejo City, CA is lowest at 3.6 percent. The impact of college populations is less important at the metropolitan level, but Bloomington City, IN (Indiana University) still has the highest poverty rate at 47.7 percent. More than 30 percent of Millennials are in poverty in 61 metro/micro areas. The Torrington, CT micro is lowest at 6.2 percent.

Table I-1: States—Income Class by Age

| | Personal Income, Percent by Income Class, Ages 18 to 24 | | | | | | |
	Total Millennials	Under $10,000	$10,000 to $19,999	$20,000 to $29,999	$30,000 to $49,999	$50,000 to $74,999	$75,000 to $99,999	$100,000 or More
United States	31,635,759	64.2%	18.7%	9.4%	5.9%	1.4%	0.2%	0.2%
Alabama	497,511	68.7%	17.1%	8.3%	4.6%	0.9%	0.3%	0.1%
Alaska	84,545	44.3%	22.6%	16.5%	11.9%	4.6%	0.1%	0.0%
Arizona	662,724	63.0%	20.4%	10.1%	5.6%	0.8%	0.1%	0.1%
Arkansas	287,155	64.1%	18.7%	10.1%	5.8%	1.2%	0.2%	0.0%
California	4,016,509	65.7%	18.3%	9.0%	5.2%	1.3%	0.3%	0.2%
Colorado	512,098	58.5%	21.1%	11.4%	7.0%	1.5%	0.2%	0.3%
Connecticut	342,884	63.7%	19.1%	10.0%	4.8%	1.8%	0.3%	0.3%
Delaware	90,525	64.4%	18.4%	10.1%	4.4%	1.7%	0.9%	0.0%
District of Columbia	80,974	70.0%	11.3%	4.9%	9.4%	4.0%	0.4%	0.0%
Florida	1,796,924	65.0%	20.4%	9.3%	4.3%	0.7%	0.2%	0.0%
Georgia	1,029,573	68.4%	17.4%	7.9%	5.2%	0.8%	0.2%	0.1%
Hawaii	136,384	54.4%	17.3%	13.7%	9.0%	4.2%	1.4%	0.0%
Idaho	160,655	63.5%	20.4%	10.9%	4.4%	0.6%	0.2%	0.0%
Illinois	1,267,572	66.1%	17.2%	9.0%	5.7%	1.6%	0.2%	0.1%
Indiana	670,827	64.1%	19.8%	9.4%	5.3%	1.3%	0.0%	0.1%
Iowa	315,687	58.2%	20.2%	11.4%	8.1%	1.9%	0.1%	0.1%
Kansas	301,166	58.0%	22.5%	10.4%	7.2%	1.8%	0.0%	0.1%
Kentucky	427,893	62.6%	20.5%	10.2%	5.4%	1.1%	0.0%	0.2%
Louisiana	482,665	67.1%	16.8%	7.3%	6.1%	1.7%	0.8%	0.2%
Maine	117,248	63.9%	20.4%	8.4%	5.0%	1.6%	0.0%	0.8%
Maryland	564,004	60.7%	17.6%	9.6%	9.4%	2.3%	0.2%	0.1%
Massachusetts	695,854	65.8%	15.8%	8.8%	7.1%	2.3%	0.2%	0.1%
Michigan	1,000,327	64.7%	19.3%	8.5%	5.8%	1.5%	0.1%	0.0%
Minnesota	508,343	59.4%	20.2%	11.6%	6.7%	1.9%	0.2%	0.0%
Mississippi	322,350	72.7%	13.3%	8.4%	5.0%	0.5%	0.1%	0.0%
Missouri	593,075	61.7%	21.9%	9.3%	5.9%	1.1%	0.1%	0.1%
Montana	102,961	62.5%	21.0%	8.0%	7.1%	0.5%	0.4%	0.4%
Nebraska	190,963	60.7%	19.6%	11.4%	7.3%	0.9%	0.0%	0.1%
Nevada	257,114	60.3%	20.1%	10.7%	7.2%	1.1%	0.4%	0.1%
New Hampshire	126,757	64.4%	17.9%	8.8%	6.4%	2.0%	0.1%	0.3%
New Jersey	794,360	66.7%	17.1%	7.9%	5.9%	2.0%	0.2%	0.2%
New Mexico	218,255	66.9%	19.1%	6.7%	6.1%	0.9%	0.3%	0.0%
New York	1,992,311	67.5%	15.9%	7.7%	6.4%	1.9%	0.3%	0.3%
North Carolina	998,003	65.3%	17.8%	10.3%	5.5%	0.8%	0.1%	0.2%
North Dakota	97,140	47.8%	25.5%	11.7%	10.0%	3.2%	1.4%	0.4%
Ohio	1,118,384	63.3%	20.3%	9.6%	5.6%	1.0%	0.1%	0.1%
Oklahoma	396,186	58.2%	20.4%	11.6%	7.2%	2.1%	0.2%	0.2%
Oregon	368,263	62.3%	21.8%	9.5%	5.3%	0.9%	0.1%	0.1%
Pennsylvania	1,251,852	67.0%	16.4%	8.8%	6.1%	1.5%	0.1%	0.1%
Rhode Island	119,895	65.1%	20.2%	8.0%	5.6%	0.7%	0.3%	0.1%
South Carolina	502,074	66.0%	19.0%	9.0%	5.4%	0.5%	0.1%	0.0%
South Dakota	84,051	51.9%	25.3%	15.7%	5.3%	1.1%	0.1%	0.5%
Tennessee	632,614	65.3%	19.3%	9.0%	5.2%	1.0%	0.0%	0.1%
Texas	2,733,033	62.4%	19.7%	10.1%	5.9%	1.5%	0.3%	0.2%
Utah	333,429	59.1%	20.9%	12.3%	6.4%	0.9%	0.2%	0.2%
Vermont	64,873	63.7%	18.1%	12.3%	4.6%	0.8%	0.6%	0.0%
Virginia	833,573	62.6%	17.6%	10.7%	7.1%	1.6%	0.2%	0.2%
Washington	665,504	60.5%	18.2%	11.3%	7.2%	1.8%	0.6%	0.5%
West Virginia	176,100	70.3%	15.9%	6.7%	5.1%	1.3%	0.5%	0.2%
Wisconsin	553,079	60.6%	21.0%	10.7%	5.9%	1.6%	0.1%	0.1%
Wyoming	59,513	48.4%	24.7%	11.8%	9.2%	4.0%	1.3%	0.5%

Table I-1: States—Income Class by Age—*Continued*

| | Personal Income, Percent by Income Class, Ages 25 to 31 | | | | | | | | |
	Total Millennials	Under $10,000	$10,000 to $19,999	$20,000 to $29,999	$30,000 to $49,999	$50,000 to $74,999	$75,000 to $99,999	$100,000 to $149,999	$150,000 or More	Poverty Rate
United States	30,086,454	33.2%	18.4%	15.5%	20.6%	8.6%	2.3%	1.0%	0.3%	20.4%
Alabama	429,255	22.1%	12.7%	18.6%	24.0%	13.0%	6.3%	2.2%	1.1%	23.9%
Alaska	80,986	31.2%	14.7%	17.1%	22.2%	10.4%	2.8%	1.2%	0.4%	11.0%
Arizona	622,816	31.8%	20.9%	16.7%	20.8%	6.4%	2.2%	0.7%	0.5%	23.8%
Arkansas	272,879	29.5%	17.7%	15.2%	19.0%	10.8%	4.2%	2.8%	0.8%	25.0%
California	3,958,135	23.2%	15.0%	15.9%	27.3%	13.0%	3.2%	1.7%	0.7%	20.4%
Colorado	544,958	23.8%	14.8%	14.3%	25.1%	14.6%	4.6%	2.1%	0.6%	18.4%
Connecticut	311,170	27.1%	14.1%	16.2%	27.1%	11.5%	2.6%	1.3%	0.1%	14.2%
Delaware	87,725	20.8%	7.6%	8.9%	20.3%	24.5%	10.8%	4.5%	2.6%	16.9%
District of Columbia	111,405	30.8%	18.2%	18.3%	21.9%	7.5%	2.0%	0.9%	0.3%	23.8%
Florida	1,749,330	30.9%	18.2%	16.8%	20.8%	9.0%	2.6%	1.3%	0.5%	21.3%
Georgia	944,465	27.7%	12.4%	14.4%	26.3%	14.2%	3.4%	1.5%	0.1%	23.4%
Hawaii	149,735	31.9%	21.0%	18.3%	21.1%	6.0%	1.4%	0.2%	0.3%	14.0%
Idaho	141,419	25.5%	15.3%	15.8%	22.2%	13.6%	4.7%	1.9%	1.0%	23.1%
Illinois	1,253,950	29.6%	18.2%	16.5%	23.4%	9.3%	2.3%	0.5%	0.3%	18.3%
Indiana	578,748	21.3%	16.3%	18.3%	29.0%	12.0%	2.0%	0.6%	0.4%	21.6%
Iowa	274,701	23.1%	15.2%	18.3%	29.5%	10.6%	2.1%	1.0%	0.3%	20.1%
Kansas	264,777	31.6%	17.9%	17.4%	21.7%	8.2%	1.9%	1.1%	0.2%	19.2%
Kentucky	395,614	31.6%	17.0%	13.2%	23.0%	10.2%	2.7%	1.6%	0.7%	23.3%
Louisiana	458,626	24.4%	18.4%	19.9%	22.8%	10.5%	1.7%	1.8%	0.5%	24.5%
Maine	104,225	23.0%	12.3%	13.9%	25.3%	16.9%	5.5%	2.2%	0.8%	17.2%
Maryland	578,502	20.9%	13.4%	14.2%	25.1%	16.8%	5.8%	3.0%	0.9%	12.2%
Massachusetts	659,931	30.0%	18.8%	16.3%	21.3%	9.8%	2.5%	1.0%	0.4%	16.7%
Michigan	835,027	21.9%	13.3%	16.0%	28.0%	14.9%	3.7%	1.6%	0.7%	23.4%
Minnesota	526,508	36.6%	19.1%	15.7%	19.9%	6.3%	1.4%	0.7%	0.3%	16.9%
Mississippi	255,386	27.6%	17.2%	17.3%	23.9%	10.0%	2.3%	1.3%	0.4%	30.3%
Missouri	561,404	28.6%	16.3%	18.0%	24.8%	9.9%	1.3%	0.6%	0.6%	22.1%
Montana	86,191	19.3%	17.7%	20.7%	26.9%	11.7%	2.4%	1.0%	0.4%	25.8%
Nebraska	175,394	26.7%	17.6%	17.6%	23.1%	10.7%	2.7%	1.2%	0.3%	18.5%
Nevada	275,510	22.1%	13.7%	14.7%	32.9%	11.9%	3.1%	1.2%	0.3%	20.0%
New Hampshire	108,673	26.0%	15.3%	14.1%	20.6%	15.6%	4.8%	2.8%	0.8%	13.5%
New Jersey	789,900	37.1%	17.8%	15.7%	18.6%	7.4%	2.3%	1.0%	0.1%	13.8%
New Mexico	186,280	27.1%	14.8%	14.5%	20.4%	13.2%	5.3%	3.2%	1.4%	29.3%
New York	2,010,905	29.4%	17.7%	17.5%	23.3%	8.7%	2.0%	1.0%	0.4%	19.7%
North Carolina	874,083	15.9%	11.7%	13.5%	34.2%	14.4%	5.8%	3.5%	1.0%	23.6%
North Dakota	70,082	27.1%	17.1%	17.5%	22.6%	11.4%	2.6%	1.2%	0.5%	18.2%
Ohio	1,036,741	30.0%	16.8%	17.2%	23.6%	8.1%	2.3%	1.6%	0.3%	20.8%
Oklahoma	371,158	30.5%	17.8%	17.4%	20.5%	9.0%	2.8%	1.4%	0.6%	21.3%
Oregon	368,990	25.9%	15.2%	15.3%	25.6%	12.7%	3.4%	1.4%	0.5%	24.0%
Pennsylvania	1,149,375	23.6%	17.3%	15.0%	26.2%	13.0%	4.0%	0.7%	0.2%	19.2%
Rhode Island	96,226	32.1%	17.2%	17.1%	22.9%	7.6%	1.9%	0.9%	0.2%	18.6%
South Carolina	414,684	21.7%	12.4%	22.1%	32.4%	7.7%	1.7%	1.2%	0.8%	24.0%
South Dakota	76,007	30.3%	18.6%	16.5%	23.7%	7.8%	1.8%	0.9%	0.5%	18.3%
Tennessee	595,744	28.1%	16.8%	16.4%	22.0%	10.8%	3.4%	1.8%	0.7%	23.2%
Texas	2,674,332	30.1%	16.1%	15.7%	23.6%	10.7%	2.2%	1.2%	0.4%	21.1%
Utah	301,066	24.1%	16.7%	17.8%	32.6%	6.6%	1.7%	0.2%	0.3%	17.6%
Vermont	50,046	23.9%	13.6%	16.5%	24.0%	14.2%	4.8%	2.3%	0.7%	19.6%
Virginia	802,202	25.1%	16.2%	16.1%	24.2%	12.0%	3.4%	2.5%	0.6%	15.8%
Washington	700,424	34.0%	16.5%	17.7%	17.0%	10.3%	3.0%	1.1%	0.4%	19.2%
West Virginia	146,977	22.0%	18.1%	19.1%	24.8%	12.3%	2.3%	1.0%	0.4%	24.8%
Wisconsin	519,237	21.2%	14.5%	15.1%	26.6%	11.0%	8.3%	2.7%	0.5%	19.2%
Wyoming	54,550	27.8%	16.5%	16.2%	22.5%	11.2%	3.4%	1.8%	0.6%	16.0%

Table I-2: Counties—Income Class by Age

| | Personal Income, Percent by Income Class, Ages 18 to 24 | | | | | | |
	Total Millennials	Under $10,000	$10,000 to $19,999	$20,000 to $29,999	$30,000 to $49,999	$50,000 to $74,999	$75,000 to $99,999	$100,000 or More
Alabama								
Baldwin County	16,338	66.9%	18.1%	12.2%	2.9%	0.0%	0.0%	0.0%
Calhoun County	11,943	70.1%	18.2%	7.3%	2.8%	1.4%	0.0%	0.0%
Etowah County	9,315	81.2%	13.5%	3.2%	2.1%	0.0%	0.0%	0.0%
Houston County	8,774	65.8%	20.1%	9.9%	3.3%	1.0%	0.0%	0.0%
Jefferson County	60,692	73.3%	13.8%	6.3%	4.6%	1.6%	0.4%	0.1%
Lauderdale County	11,302	74.9%	16.8%	4.4%	3.1%	0.8%	0.0%	0.0%
Lee County	30,018	66.1%	18.0%	7.4%	6.4%	2.1%	0.0%	0.0%
Madison County	35,171	63.4%	22.8%	8.7%	3.4%	1.6%	0.0%	0.0%
Marshall County	7,257	64.0%	27.9%	5.2%	2.6%	0.3%	0.0%	0.0%
Mobile County	42,048	69.5%	16.5%	5.5%	7.2%	0.4%	0.9%	0.0%
Montgomery County	26,815	63.7%	15.2%	13.1%	7.2%	0.5%	0.0%	0.1%
Morgan County	10,480	61.3%	25.9%	10.1%	2.7%	0.0%	0.0%	0.0%
Shelby County	16,952	73.4%	12.5%	9.1%	1.4%	1.5%	0.0%	2.1%
Tuscaloosa County	39,838	74.6%	10.5%	7.0%	7.8%	0.0%	0.0%	0.1%
Alaska								
Fairbanks North Star Borough	14,290	34.9%	33.3%	21.0%	5.0%	5.6%	0.3%	0.0%
Matanuska-Susitna Borough	9,851	47.2%	16.7%	17.3%	18.7%	0.0%	0.0%	0.0%
Arizona								
Cochise County	12,200	49.5%	29.2%	19.1%	0.6%	1.6%	0.0%	0.0%
Coconino County	26,701	66.2%	21.5%	7.1%	3.5%	1.7%	0.0%	0.0%
Maricopa County	386,757	61.3%	20.8%	10.6%	6.3%	0.9%	0.1%	0.0%
Mohave County	14,136	73.1%	16.7%	5.4%	3.8%	0.9%	0.0%	0.0%
Navajo County	10,545	76.3%	15.0%	3.6%	4.2%	0.8%	0.0%	0.0%
Pima County	121,550	64.0%	21.5%	8.7%	5.2%	0.5%	0.0%	0.1%
Pinal County	32,006	62.8%	19.4%	14.3%	2.2%	0.1%	1.2%	0.0%
Yavapai County	14,382	68.0%	16.3%	5.3%	9.0%	0.5%	0.0%	0.9%
Yuma County	24,334	64.9%	18.0%	10.6%	6.6%	0.0%	0.0%	0.0%
Arkansas								
Benton County	19,984	55.5%	18.1%	15.6%	8.8%	2.0%	0.0%	0.0%
Craighead County	11,153	55.4%	32.0%	5.0%	7.6%	0.0%	0.0%	0.0%
Faulkner County	16,274	63.1%	15.1%	9.4%	9.2%	1.4%	1.6%	0.2%
Garland County	8,413	63.2%	20.1%	12.8%	0.0%	3.8%	0.0%	0.0%
Pulaski County	35,099	56.2%	19.3%	14.3%	8.6%	1.6%	0.0%	0.0%
Saline County	8,095	41.2%	28.3%	28.2%	1.7%	0.7%	0.0%	0.0%
Sebastian County	10,237	65.0%	19.4%	10.1%	5.4%	0.0%	0.0%	0.0%
Washington County	31,341	61.7%	23.7%	11.8%	2.4%	0.4%	0.0%	0.0%
California								
Alameda County	149,330	62.3%	18.3%	9.2%	6.8%	2.3%	0.6%	0.4%
Butte County	33,787	64.0%	18.7%	10.2%	5.7%	0.6%	0.0%	0.8%
Contra Costa County	94,235	61.9%	20.4%	7.8%	8.2%	1.3%	0.4%	0.0%
El Dorado County	13,295	74.7%	10.2%	9.5%	5.7%	0.0%	0.0%	0.0%
Fresno County	108,464	71.5%	18.7%	6.3%	3.0%	0.4%	0.0%	0.1%
Humboldt County	18,113	66.2%	19.4%	9.7%	2.8%	1.9%	0.0%	0.0%
Imperial County	20,303	74.1%	14.2%	8.4%	1.3%	2.0%	0.0%	0.0%
Kern County	95,971	64.9%	18.9%	9.1%	5.4%	1.3%	0.4%	0.1%
Kings County	17,431	63.1%	18.5%	10.1%	8.2%	0.1%	0.0%	0.0%
Los Angeles County	1,067,750	67.7%	18.2%	7.9%	4.6%	1.1%	0.3%	0.1%
Madera County	15,435	74.1%	20.7%	3.7%	0.6%	0.2%	0.0%	0.7%
Marin County	17,512	71.7%	18.1%	5.4%	2.8%	2.0%	0.0%	0.0%
Merced County	31,498	65.5%	19.4%	6.1%	8.8%	0.3%	0.0%	0.0%
Monterey County	48,230	65.0%	23.7%	7.4%	3.3%	0.0%	0.0%	0.6%
Napa County	13,156	66.7%	15.5%	12.0%	4.0%	1.4%	0.0%	0.3%
Nevada County	7,382	77.5%	17.4%	4.9%	0.3%	0.0%	0.0%	0.0%
Orange County	317,913	65.7%	17.8%	9.3%	5.3%	1.7%	0.2%	0.0%
Placer County	29,285	62.5%	21.8%	6.7%	6.0%	2.8%	0.0%	0.3%
Riverside County	243,003	68.9%	18.6%	7.8%	4.0%	0.6%	0.1%	0.1%
Sacramento County	145,677	67.2%	20.3%	6.3%	4.9%	0.9%	0.4%	0.0%
San Bernardino County	240,638	67.3%	17.4%	10.0%	4.0%	1.2%	0.1%	0.0%
San Diego County	366,780	58.2%	18.4%	14.1%	6.8%	2.0%	0.4%	0.0%
San Francisco County	64,495	60.8%	13.2%	7.5%	7.9%	6.1%	1.5%	2.9%
San Joaquin County	74,649	66.8%	17.7%	9.8%	4.9%	0.8%	0.0%	0.0%
San Luis Obispo County	44,013	70.8%	12.0%	9.1%	5.6%	0.8%	1.6%	0.0%
San Mateo County	57,975	60.7%	18.0%	13.8%	5.1%	1.0%	1.0%	0.5%
Santa Barbara County	68,915	68.2%	15.5%	7.6%	7.0%	1.2%	0.5%	0.0%
Santa Clara County	164,573	63.4%	16.4%	7.7%	7.1%	3.9%	0.6%	0.8%
Santa Cruz County	40,992	67.3%	14.1%	13.5%	5.0%	0.0%	0.0%	0.1%
Shasta County	17,040	65.9%	19.6%	8.1%	6.1%	0.0%	0.0%	0.2%
Solano County	43,457	64.3%	19.4%	9.6%	5.6%	0.7%	0.4%	0.0%
Sonoma County	45,516	63.2%	19.5%	10.9%	4.5%	1.3%	0.0%	0.5%
Stanislaus County	55,502	59.3%	26.4%	8.3%	4.1%	1.9%	0.0%	0.0%
Sutter County	10,422	70.5%	15.7%	10.8%	2.5%	0.4%	0.0%	0.0%
Tulare County	49,699	70.9%	16.2%	9.6%	3.0%	0.0%	0.3%	0.0%
Ventura County	85,580	58.1%	23.0%	10.7%	7.0%	0.6%	0.4%	0.2%
Yolo County	39,633	69.6%	12.7%	11.9%	5.8%	0.0%	0.0%	0.0%
Colorado								
Adams County	44,213	58.6%	18.8%	13.3%	7.6%	1.3%	0.2%	0.2%

Table I-2: Counties—Income Class by Age—*Continued*

					Personal Income, Percent by Income Class, Ages 25 to 31					
	Total Millennials	Under $10,000	$10,000 to $19,999	$20,000 to $29,999	$30,000 to $49,999	$50,000 to $74,999	$75,000 to $99,999	$100,000 to $149,999	$150,000 or More	Poverty Rate
Alabama										
Baldwin County	14,271	27.4%	19.4%	23.8%	18.3%	8.0%	2.0%	1.1%	0.0%	21.9%
Calhoun County	10,550	28.8%	22.6%	21.2%	14.1%	12.6%	0.0%	0.7%	0.0%	31.6%
Etowah County	8,012	33.4%	18.8%	13.3%	29.0%	5.0%	0.4%	0.0%	0.0%	21.0%
Houston County	9,840	28.3%	14.5%	13.3%	29.1%	7.7%	5.2%	2.0%	0.0%	20.8%
Jefferson County	66,293	32.1%	16.6%	14.8%	19.8%	11.6%	3.8%	1.1%	0.4%	25.2%
Lauderdale County	8,102	33.3%	25.0%	16.8%	20.4%	4.4%	0.0%	0.0%	0.0%	28.6%
Lee County	14,147	22.7%	20.7%	15.4%	26.3%	4.4%	4.4%	6.1%	0.0%	28.4%
Madison County	31,607	20.5%	22.2%	16.2%	25.0%	11.0%	3.8%	1.2%	0.0%	22.2%
Marshall County	9,126	12.5%	42.3%	11.0%	27.5%	5.8%	1.0%	0.0%	0.0%	18.1%
Mobile County	37,948	36.5%	16.1%	12.7%	21.5%	10.5%	1.5%	1.1%	0.1%	21.1%
Montgomery County	23,145	35.7%	18.5%	16.8%	23.2%	3.5%	0.3%	0.5%	1.4%	29.8%
Morgan County	8,840	33.8%	16.8%	27.3%	11.2%	10.9%	0.0%	0.0%	0.0%	20.6%
Shelby County	18,469	23.1%	8.7%	11.2%	32.4%	18.2%	3.3%	0.9%	2.0%	11.6%
Tuscaloosa County	21,669	27.9%	16.2%	19.8%	22.9%	7.7%	3.4%	2.0%	0.0%	23.7%
Alaska										
Fairbanks North Star Borough	13,155	11.6%	10.2%	20.6%	31.7%	19.7%	4.3%	0.9%	1.0%	8.0%
Matanuska-Susitna Borough	8,642	25.4%	14.1%	9.1%	18.4%	18.8%	10.8%	3.3%	0.0%	12.2%
Arizona										
Cochise County	11,622	34.1%	21.0%	11.5%	20.4%	7.1%	3.5%	2.4%	0.0%	20.2%
Coconino County	14,018	27.7%	12.4%	17.8%	23.9%	14.2%	3.6%	0.2%	0.0%	30.4%
Maricopa County	403,195	28.8%	13.5%	17.9%	23.6%	11.6%	2.8%	1.3%	0.5%	21.9%
Mohave County	14,210	34.5%	14.9%	14.3%	23.8%	10.4%	2.2%	0.0%	0.0%	26.6%
Navajo County	9,586	54.2%	11.8%	10.3%	19.6%	2.5%	1.6%	0.0%	0.0%	39.6%
Pima County	88,003	32.6%	18.2%	17.8%	18.6%	7.8%	3.4%	1.4%	0.3%	29.0%
Pinal County	32,604	41.1%	12.8%	15.0%	17.9%	8.8%	2.9%	1.2%	0.4%	22.0%
Yavapai County	14,168	36.3%	24.5%	10.7%	23.8%	4.4%	0.0%	0.0%	0.2%	26.9%
Yuma County	19,442	29.9%	21.4%	19.0%	18.7%	7.4%	2.7%	0.6%	0.3%	16.6%
Arkansas										
Benton County	22,428	28.9%	13.0%	15.5%	20.9%	11.1%	8.6%	1.6%	0.5%	12.1%
Craighead County	11,120	30.2%	29.8%	19.4%	12.7%	7.9%	0.0%	0.0%	0.0%	27.9%
Faulkner County	15,873	21.3%	14.1%	24.1%	28.7%	9.1%	1.7%	0.0%	1.0%	17.6%
Garland County	6,178	32.5%	25.1%	19.2%	21.1%	2.1%	0.0%	0.0%	0.0%	29.8%
Pulaski County	44,132	30.2%	25.5%	16.3%	19.9%	6.9%	0.9%	0.3%	0.0%	20.3%
Saline County	11,423	25.6%	13.3%	24.6%	27.5%	7.7%	0.7%	0.0%	0.6%	9.6%
Sebastian County	13,346	41.7%	17.1%	16.6%	18.3%	1.7%	3.2%	1.5%	0.0%	28.5%
Washington County	23,408	22.6%	21.5%	19.9%	23.3%	6.2%	4.3%	0.6%	1.6%	30.0%
California										
Alameda County	170,706	26.6%	13.6%	11.4%	23.4%	13.9%	4.9%	4.9%	1.3%	17.4%
Butte County	19,755	34.8%	20.8%	11.8%	16.5%	11.2%	1.4%	0.7%	2.7%	34.5%
Contra Costa County	93,554	28.5%	17.2%	15.2%	17.5%	12.5%	4.6%	3.7%	0.7%	15.1%
El Dorado County	12,743	39.0%	18.7%	13.7%	14.6%	8.8%	1.7%	3.2%	0.1%	17.1%
Fresno County	101,070	38.8%	17.9%	15.1%	16.1%	8.2%	2.8%	0.9%	0.2%	31.7%
Humboldt County	13,592	30.4%	32.7%	13.7%	13.8%	9.0%	0.0%	0.0%	0.3%	30.6%
Imperial County	18,063	41.8%	12.1%	15.3%	18.6%	11.3%	0.2%	0.7%	0.0%	23.9%
Kern County	91,995	37.7%	21.4%	15.7%	15.0%	6.1%	2.3%	1.2%	0.6%	23.2%
Kings County	17,382	39.2%	16.3%	20.7%	18.2%	4.9%	0.0%	0.5%	0.1%	21.5%
Los Angeles County	1,096,906	29.4%	19.3%	15.9%	18.5%	10.6%	3.6%	2.0%	0.7%	21.3%
Madera County	15,618	43.5%	25.9%	13.1%	8.6%	8.8%	0.0%	0.0%	0.0%	28.2%
Marin County	15,181	31.2%	19.4%	14.8%	22.9%	6.5%	3.9%	1.4%	0.0%	16.6%
Merced County	25,584	37.3%	20.2%	14.0%	19.6%	7.4%	0.2%	0.9%	0.4%	28.7%
Monterey County	45,322	32.7%	23.0%	16.5%	16.9%	8.0%	1.6%	1.3%	0.0%	19.7%
Napa County	10,779	16.4%	15.2%	33.5%	19.9%	10.7%	1.5%	2.8%	0.0%	10.3%
Nevada County	5,855	27.2%	15.8%	7.6%	28.5%	20.4%	0.5%	0.0%	0.0%	20.2%
Orange County	310,232	25.8%	18.1%	15.7%	19.5%	13.2%	4.9%	2.1%	0.7%	16.0%
Placer County	29,238	31.3%	10.9%	20.7%	18.6%	14.1%	3.3%	0.7%	0.2%	11.0%
Riverside County	215,998	33.2%	19.2%	15.7%	16.7%	9.1%	2.6%	3.3%	0.3%	20.1%
Sacramento County	153,249	30.0%	15.6%	14.3%	24.8%	8.8%	4.5%	1.8%	0.3%	21.7%
San Bernardino County	212,266	35.5%	18.6%	14.8%	20.2%	7.0%	2.9%	1.0%	0.0%	21.6%
San Diego County	372,273	26.4%	15.3%	16.9%	21.3%	12.4%	4.7%	2.4%	0.5%	18.5%
San Francisco County	137,551	16.5%	10.4%	8.9%	18.9%	16.9%	12.7%	10.5%	5.1%	17.3%
San Joaquin County	62,376	30.7%	20.3%	16.3%	20.9%	7.9%	2.5%	1.2%	0.0%	23.8%
San Luis Obispo County	23,706	27.2%	23.9%	16.1%	23.4%	7.4%	1.0%	0.6%	0.4%	29.9%
San Mateo County	68,580	21.8%	10.4%	19.9%	17.8%	15.1%	8.6%	5.3%	1.1%	10.1%
Santa Barbara County	40,359	23.2%	21.6%	20.4%	19.6%	9.5%	2.9%	2.6%	0.0%	27.4%
Santa Clara County	197,830	26.4%	12.0%	10.6%	16.5%	13.9%	8.8%	9.1%	2.8%	13.6%
Santa Cruz County	21,827	17.6%	29.2%	13.8%	27.0%	6.9%	2.0%	3.0%	0.5%	24.0%
Shasta County	15,126	40.3%	27.8%	9.6%	14.8%	6.1%	0.5%	0.8%	0.0%	30.6%
Solano County	42,964	29.1%	15.3%	15.9%	19.3%	13.0%	4.0%	2.8%	0.7%	16.1%
Sonoma County	43,559	23.6%	18.3%	16.5%	23.9%	11.6%	3.4%	1.5%	1.2%	14.4%
Stanislaus County	50,579	37.9%	21.7%	14.5%	14.1%	7.0%	3.5%	1.2%	0.0%	25.2%
Sutter County	8,605	26.6%	15.8%	28.5%	21.9%	5.1%	2.2%	0.0%	0.0%	20.7%
Tulare County	46,122	42.9%	20.7%	15.5%	10.4%	5.9%	2.7%	1.4%	0.4%	33.6%
Ventura County	74,830	26.7%	22.4%	15.0%	17.2%	10.7%	4.1%	3.2%	0.5%	16.1%
Yolo County	19,613	30.3%	17.1%	20.2%	21.2%	9.3%	1.4%	0.5%	0.0%	29.9%
Colorado										
Adams County	52,900	23.4%	14.6%	16.8%	28.6%	10.7%	4.1%	1.3%	0.5%	13.1%

Table I-2: Counties—Income Class by Age—*Continued*

	Total Millennials	Under $10,000	$10,000 to $19,999	$20,000 to $29,999	$30,000 to $49,999	$50,000 to $74,999	$75,000 to $99,999	$100,000 or More
				Personal Income, Percent by Income Class, Ages 18 to 24				
Colorado—Cont.								
Arapahoe County	52,812	62.2%	16.6%	10.8%	10.0%	0.1%	0.2%	0.1%
Boulder County	46,153	63.7%	18.0%	10.6%	5.7%	0.7%	1.0%	0.3%
Denver County	62,202	50.1%	23.0%	12.3%	12.2%	2.1%	0.1%	0.2%
Douglas County	21,277	57.9%	22.0%	8.7%	8.6%	2.7%	0.0%	0.0%
El Paso County	70,362	53.9%	23.3%	13.6%	6.9%	1.3%	0.1%	0.8%
Jefferson County	47,146	52.7%	23.8%	11.9%	9.3%	0.1%	1.1%	1.1%
Larimer County	46,410	62.0%	22.3%	12.3%	1.6%	1.6%	0.1%	0.0%
Mesa County	15,610	62.0%	16.6%	10.7%	5.6%	4.9%	0.0%	0.2%
Pueblo County	15,775	69.5%	23.8%	4.0%	2.8%	0.0%	0.0%	0.0%
Weld County	29,369	65.6%	21.3%	6.5%	6.5%	0.1%	0.0%	0.0%
Connecticut								
Fairfield County	79,561	62.4%	18.2%	12.0%	4.7%	2.0%	0.2%	0.5%
Hartford County	80,061	66.7%	17.1%	9.0%	4.9%	2.3%	0.0%	0.1%
Litchfield County	13,642	48.3%	29.5%	10.6%	8.0%	1.7%	0.5%	1.4%
Middlesex County	14,810	59.2%	20.6%	11.2%	6.1%	1.4%	1.5%	0.0%
New Haven County	86,612	66.6%	18.7%	9.7%	3.7%	1.0%	0.2%	0.2%
New London County	29,528	51.6%	29.9%	11.5%	2.9%	2.2%	1.1%	0.8%
Tolland County	26,722	69.2%	12.8%	4.8%	10.1%	3.1%	0.0%	0.0%
Windham County	11,948	73.3%	15.9%	10.2%	0.6%	0.0%	0.0%	0.0%
Delaware								
Kent County	17,233	64.3%	19.2%	8.4%	5.8%	2.3%	0.0%	0.0%
New Castle County	57,691	68.0%	16.7%	8.9%	3.9%	1.5%	1.0%	0.0%
Sussex County	15,601	51.6%	23.8%	16.5%	4.9%	1.8%	1.4%	0.0%
Florida								
Alachua County	57,810	68.6%	20.3%	6.9%	2.9%	0.8%	0.4%	0.0%
Bay County	14,680	48.9%	25.5%	16.7%	7.8%	1.1%	0.0%	0.0%
Brevard County	44,051	61.4%	23.9%	9.1%	3.6%	0.8%	1.2%	0.0%
Broward County	157,400	68.8%	18.7%	7.8%	3.6%	0.7%	0.2%	0.1%
Charlotte County	10,166	57.8%	24.0%	9.4%	8.1%	0.2%	0.0%	0.4%
Citrus County	8,383	72.6%	18.2%	4.7%	2.8%	0.0%	1.7%	0.0%
Clay County	15,970	63.6%	22.5%	10.1%	3.7%	0.0%	0.0%	0.0%
Collier County	22,554	50.6%	25.0%	17.8%	6.4%	0.2%	0.0%	0.0%
Duval County	87,274	58.7%	22.7%	9.9%	7.4%	1.0%	0.3%	0.1%
Escambia County	39,340	57.5%	26.6%	12.0%	2.1%	1.1%	0.8%	0.0%
Flagler County	8,355	65.2%	25.1%	9.0%	0.7%	0.0%	0.0%	0.0%
Hernando County	11,400	71.4%	17.1%	6.6%	4.8%	0.0%	0.0%	0.0%
Highlands County	7,013	69.2%	14.5%	14.2%	2.1%	0.0%	0.0%	0.0%
Hillsborough County	127,839	60.8%	21.0%	10.9%	6.3%	0.9%	0.1%	0.0%
Indian River County	8,737	74.4%	17.8%	3.5%	2.9%	1.3%	0.0%	0.0%
Lake County	21,438	60.6%	24.2%	8.3%	5.8%	1.0%	0.0%	0.0%
Lee County	49,443	60.0%	22.1%	11.7%	4.3%	1.8%	0.1%	0.0%
Leon County	65,187	73.6%	14.5%	7.0%	4.6%	0.2%	0.0%	0.0%
Manatee County	26,263	59.5%	25.0%	9.5%	4.3%	1.1%	0.0%	0.6%
Marion County	24,424	64.8%	25.0%	6.9%	3.2%	0.0%	0.0%	0.0%
Martin County	9,764	78.4%	17.7%	3.1%	0.9%	0.0%	0.0%	0.0%
Miami-Dade County	249,341	68.2%	18.6%	8.5%	3.8%	0.7%	0.0%	0.0%
Okaloosa County	19,619	50.5%	19.5%	21.3%	7.9%	0.8%	0.0%	0.0%
Orange County	147,814	65.2%	20.7%	8.6%	4.4%	0.9%	0.2%	0.0%
Osceola County	28,518	69.3%	15.7%	9.1%	5.6%	0.2%	0.0%	0.0%
Palm Beach County	111,040	66.3%	17.9%	10.8%	4.2%	0.6%	0.2%	0.1%
Pasco County	35,466	67.1%	24.0%	5.5%	2.9%	0.3%	0.0%	0.3%
Pinellas County	68,856	62.8%	21.7%	11.0%	4.0%	0.3%	0.1%	0.0%
Polk County	55,573	62.6%	19.7%	12.3%	3.8%	0.7%	1.0%	0.0%
Santa Rosa County	14,039	62.6%	25.7%	7.7%	1.6%	2.3%	0.0%	0.0%
Sarasota County	25,916	64.7%	22.1%	8.5%	3.9%	0.8%	0.0%	0.1%
Seminole County	42,621	65.2%	20.1%	10.7%	3.8%	0.0%	0.0%	0.2%
St. Johns County	17,994	75.8%	16.6%	4.2%	3.5%	0.0%	0.0%	0.0%
St. Lucie County	22,765	68.2%	21.2%	7.3%	3.3%	0.0%	0.0%	0.0%
Sumter County	4,246	50.0%	30.4%	17.3%	2.3%	0.0%	0.0%	0.0%
Volusia County	43,828	64.7%	20.9%	10.2%	3.9%	0.0%	0.4%	0.0%
Georgia								
Bartow County	12,166	69.5%	21.8%	5.1%	3.2%	0.0%	0.4%	0.0%
Bibb County	16,655	78.5%	11.4%	3.8%	6.3%	0.0%	0.0%	0.0%
Carroll County	14,416	67.2%	20.6%	2.9%	7.9%	0.0%	0.0%	1.4%
Chatham County	34,089	66.9%	19.9%	7.2%	4.7%	1.2%	0.0%	0.1%
Cherokee County	16,011	55.0%	17.6%	11.7%	15.5%	0.2%	0.0%	0.0%
Clarke County	36,028	76.2%	13.2%	5.6%	2.5%	2.6%	0.0%	0.0%
Clayton County	27,881	66.2%	20.3%	7.8%	4.9%	0.7%	0.0%	0.0%
Cobb County	67,950	63.6%	18.9%	10.4%	6.1%	1.1%	0.0%	0.0%
Columbia County	12,527	70.7%	21.8%	5.4%	2.0%	0.0%	0.0%	0.0%
Coweta County	10,199	54.7%	23.6%	13.5%	5.2%	0.0%	3.0%	0.0%
DeKalb County	70,674	67.4%	18.3%	7.3%	4.9%	1.4%	0.4%	0.3%
Dougherty County	11,759	87.5%	8.4%	3.2%	0.3%	0.5%	0.0%	0.0%
Douglas County	9,740	75.5%	16.9%	4.1%	2.8%	0.7%	0.0%	0.0%
Fayette County	10,008	68.1%	8.7%	7.7%	10.7%	1.8%	0.0%	3.0%
Floyd County	9,834	75.1%	14.6%	6.5%	3.7%	0.0%	0.0%	0.0%
Forsyth County	12,959	66.9%	10.2%	7.6%	14.9%	0.4%	0.0%	0.0%
Fulton County	101,164	70.4%	15.7%	6.8%	5.4%	1.2%	0.4%	0.1%

Table I-2: Counties—Income Class by Age—*Continued*

| | Personal Income, Percent by Income Class, Ages 25 to 31 | | | | | | | | | |
	Total Millennials	Under $10,000	$10,000 to $19,999	$20,000 to $29,999	$30,000 to $49,999	$50,000 to $74,999	$75,000 to $99,999	$100,000 to $149,999	$150,000 or More	Poverty Rate
Colorado—Cont.										
Arapahoe County	61,836	19.2%	15.6%	20.0%	27.1%	13.3%	2.7%	1.5%	0.7%	15.2%
Boulder County	26,720	16.8%	13.6%	13.9%	28.3%	16.9%	7.2%	1.0%	2.3%	23.4%
Denver County	106,782	21.9%	12.7%	14.8%	27.5%	15.9%	3.6%	2.8%	0.7%	21.7%
Douglas County	19,849	19.6%	12.9%	11.5%	31.2%	13.3%	8.2%	2.9%	0.4%	5.7%
El Paso County	69,402	23.8%	14.6%	16.2%	27.3%	13.9%	3.0%	1.3%	0.0%	15.9%
Jefferson County	48,567	19.6%	19.5%	15.4%	26.3%	14.0%	3.9%	0.9%	0.4%	13.4%
Larimer County	30,477	18.8%	18.1%	18.2%	24.7%	13.3%	3.4%	0.7%	2.9%	27.8%
Mesa County	14,343	36.4%	11.5%	14.6%	15.3%	16.0%	0.9%	4.4%	1.0%	23.6%
Pueblo County	15,157	41.3%	16.8%	17.1%	19.0%	3.6%	0.8%	1.4%	0.0%	29.4%
Weld County	27,520	26.6%	13.5%	10.6%	27.3%	17.5%	3.0%	1.0%	0.6%	19.5%
Connecticut										
Fairfield County	75,971	22.7%	16.2%	13.8%	19.3%	17.7%	5.8%	2.8%	1.8%	12.3%
Hartford County	81,020	26.1%	12.0%	11.7%	26.7%	14.3%	5.6%	3.4%	0.3%	14.8%
Litchfield County	13,526	6.7%	20.8%	15.7%	30.2%	13.5%	9.7%	3.3%	0.0%	6.2%
Middlesex County	13,200	15.9%	16.6%	19.5%	26.0%	15.7%	5.1%	0.6%	0.7%	9.5%
New Haven County	80,028	25.7%	13.6%	13.8%	27.9%	14.8%	2.9%	1.0%	0.3%	17.4%
New London County	25,237	29.1%	17.3%	15.1%	24.6%	9.8%	3.0%	1.2%	0.0%	16.0%
Tolland County	11,593	20.1%	12.5%	17.1%	34.2%	15.2%	0.9%	0.0%	0.0%	9.8%
Windham County	10,595	25.3%	23.0%	27.2%	17.6%	4.1%	2.2%	0.7%	0.0%	19.9%
Delaware										
Kent County	15,816	21.1%	19.1%	15.6%	28.7%	13.6%	1.9%	0.0%	0.0%	13.1%
New Castle County	56,373	28.3%	12.1%	14.1%	27.9%	12.6%	3.0%	1.9%	0.1%	17.7%
Sussex County	15,536	28.8%	16.3%	24.7%	22.7%	5.2%	2.1%	0.1%	0.1%	18.0%
Florida										
Alachua County	28,502	30.9%	17.6%	20.9%	20.5%	7.6%	2.0%	0.5%	0.0%	41.7%
Bay County	17,285	51.5%	13.3%	17.5%	10.9%	3.8%	2.2%	0.4%	0.3%	23.6%
Brevard County	38,460	27.7%	26.0%	19.1%	18.1%	6.8%	1.5%	0.6%	0.1%	19.8%
Broward County	168,010	29.8%	15.5%	18.1%	23.1%	9.1%	2.5%	1.4%	0.5%	18.1%
Charlotte County	8,480	36.6%	19.7%	17.0%	19.7%	3.5%	2.6%	1.0%	0.0%	15.9%
Citrus County	6,848	49.8%	20.0%	5.3%	22.8%	0.6%	1.5%	0.0%	0.0%	33.8%
Clay County	16,629	36.9%	9.4%	20.2%	26.5%	7.1%	0.0%	0.0%	0.0%	9.1%
Collier County	22,259	31.4%	19.3%	15.9%	20.2%	6.7%	4.4%	0.3%	1.7%	14.1%
Duval County	101,536	26.8%	15.6%	17.6%	27.8%	9.1%	2.3%	0.8%	0.0%	20.8%
Escambia County	31,263	27.1%	15.0%	24.2%	27.1%	5.5%	0.8%	0.3%	0.0%	18.2%
Flagler County	5,728	39.8%	21.4%	25.5%	10.9%	0.0%	0.0%	2.3%	0.0%	18.1%
Hernando County	12,556	43.1%	15.5%	19.2%	11.8%	10.4%	0.0%	0.0%	0.0%	15.9%
Highlands County	6,249	48.5%	11.7%	18.6%	16.6%	3.1%	1.6%	0.0%	0.0%	29.8%
Hillsborough County	136,004	27.4%	18.6%	19.0%	20.2%	10.8%	2.5%	1.2%	0.3%	20.7%
Indian River County	8,245	29.5%	21.9%	22.0%	16.6%	6.2%	0.0%	1.1%	2.7%	24.3%
Lake County	23,099	28.2%	16.0%	22.3%	25.2%	3.8%	4.0%	0.5%	0.0%	13.9%
Lee County	49,789	32.5%	20.5%	19.9%	18.7%	6.5%	1.8%	0.1%	0.1%	23.1%
Leon County	29,293	28.7%	16.6%	16.1%	29.6%	6.7%	2.4%	0.0%	0.0%	40.8%
Manatee County	23,213	34.3%	14.5%	14.0%	27.4%	5.9%	2.4%	1.4%	0.1%	23.2%
Marion County	24,645	38.4%	24.5%	16.1%	12.9%	5.9%	1.3%	0.4%	0.4%	26.0%
Martin County	11,550	23.0%	27.8%	19.3%	19.8%	8.8%	1.3%	0.0%	0.0%	19.4%
Miami-Dade County	267,914	29.5%	19.3%	19.3%	20.6%	8.2%	1.8%	1.1%	0.3%	20.7%
Okaloosa County	22,695	28.3%	15.7%	13.5%	21.8%	14.4%	4.6%	0.8%	0.9%	21.4%
Orange County	145,234	27.9%	17.2%	19.2%	23.5%	8.3%	2.8%	1.0%	0.2%	23.5%
Osceola County	29,572	41.1%	18.6%	23.1%	12.2%	4.1%	0.8%	0.0%	0.0%	20.3%
Palm Beach County	114,488	26.7%	23.7%	15.9%	23.6%	5.5%	3.0%	1.2%	0.5%	19.6%
Pasco County	32,312	31.4%	18.7%	18.2%	23.0%	6.4%	1.7%	0.4%	0.1%	15.1%
Pinellas County	76,123	26.6%	16.4%	18.5%	27.3%	7.7%	2.2%	0.9%	0.4%	19.7%
Polk County	55,298	37.0%	20.1%	14.9%	20.3%	7.0%	0.2%	0.1%	0.4%	22.3%
Santa Rosa County	15,170	31.6%	13.4%	22.8%	19.8%	9.6%	1.7%	1.2%	0.0%	17.8%
Sarasota County	20,422	22.3%	21.3%	20.1%	26.3%	7.0%	0.4%	2.5%	0.2%	14.6%
Seminole County	41,617	22.9%	17.0%	20.5%	29.0%	7.6%	1.8%	1.3%	0.0%	16.8%
St. Johns County	13,974	28.3%	19.6%	18.9%	26.4%	5.1%	0.4%	0.8%	0.4%	16.1%
St. Lucie County	20,849	35.5%	20.3%	16.9%	20.9%	4.9%	1.2%	0.3%	0.0%	24.1%
Sumter County	4,944	38.3%	8.7%	36.5%	12.9%	1.2%	0.0%	2.4%	0.0%	14.7%
Volusia County	41,202	36.8%	20.5%	16.8%	16.7%	5.9%	0.6%	2.0%	0.7%	24.8%
Georgia										
Bartow County	9,081	32.3%	40.2%	8.8%	16.3%	1.1%	0.0%	1.2%	0.0%	30.4%
Bibb County	15,045	44.8%	17.8%	12.2%	19.4%	5.4%	0.4%	0.0%	0.0%	37.6%
Carroll County	9,841	37.4%	10.5%	25.2%	24.3%	1.8%	0.9%	0.0%	0.0%	18.8%
Chatham County	33,509	29.3%	21.3%	12.0%	20.7%	11.0%	2.9%	0.0%	2.7%	24.5%
Cherokee County	19,263	24.6%	14.5%	12.7%	33.0%	9.5%	5.3%	0.4%	0.0%	13.3%
Clarke County	13,785	27.3%	27.4%	21.8%	16.8%	6.3%	0.0%	0.0%	0.5%	51.9%
Clayton County	28,275	44.4%	21.2%	17.6%	12.4%	2.3%	1.6%	0.0%	0.5%	31.6%
Cobb County	68,770	22.3%	20.8%	14.5%	24.5%	12.0%	4.0%	2.0%	0.0%	20.0%
Columbia County	11,046	18.8%	10.4%	14.9%	36.1%	15.9%	2.5%	1.5%	0.0%	8.5%
Coweta County	11,235	34.8%	17.3%	7.7%	15.3%	16.1%	5.7%	3.1%	0.0%	19.7%
DeKalb County	81,565	26.9%	16.2%	13.2%	21.0%	14.1%	5.0%	2.6%	0.9%	22.7%
Dougherty County	9,373	42.1%	18.4%	16.8%	10.9%	9.2%	2.5%	0.0%	0.0%	35.4%
Douglas County	12,228	14.6%	28.6%	5.7%	33.4%	14.9%	1.0%	1.9%	0.0%	23.1%
Fayette County	5,306	42.1%	12.7%	14.2%	17.2%	7.5%	2.2%	4.1%	0.0%	15.1%
Floyd County	7,305	35.0%	21.5%	16.2%	13.6%	10.5%	3.1%	0.0%	0.0%	25.6%
Forsyth County	12,286	23.4%	15.0%	21.8%	19.2%	13.1%	4.5%	1.8%	1.2%	9.5%
Fulton County	112,529	24.0%	13.5%	16.4%	22.9%	13.3%	5.8%	3.6%	0.4%	19.7%

Table I-2: Counties—Income Class by Age—*Continued*

	Total Millennials	Personal Income, Percent by Income Class, Ages 18 to 24						
		Under $10,000	$10,000 to $19,999	$20,000 to $29,999	$30,000 to $49,999	$50,000 to $74,999	$75,000 to $99,999	$100,000 or More
Georgia—Cont.								
Gwinnett County	78,434	66.9%	22.2%	6.0%	4.5%	0.4%	0.0%	0.0%
Hall County	17,558	59.9%	22.8%	10.8%	4.9%	1.2%	0.0%	0.3%
Henry County	20,309	67.0%	16.8%	10.3%	5.3%	0.6%	0.0%	0.0%
Houston County	15,867	68.6%	17.2%	5.7%	6.7%	1.9%	0.0%	0.0%
Lowndes County	20,465	65.1%	19.6%	11.7%	2.9%	0.7%	0.0%	0.0%
Muscogee County	25,723	51.6%	19.8%	19.0%	8.8%	0.7%	0.1%	0.0%
Newton County	10,070	78.1%	10.8%	8.2%	2.9%	0.0%	0.0%	0.0%
Paulding County	12,434	70.7%	24.7%	3.7%	0.9%	0.0%	0.0%	0.0%
Richmond County	24,088	65.8%	20.2%	8.5%	4.8%	0.6%	0.0%	0.0%
Whitfield County	10,922	48.3%	28.5%	12.3%	10.9%	0.0%	0.0%	0.0%
Hawaii								
Hawaii County	15,240	76.2%	11.9%	6.2%	5.0%	0.5%	0.0%	0.0%
Honolulu County	104,322	52.4%	16.8%	14.6%	10.2%	4.3%	1.8%	0.0%
Maui County	10,226	49.5%	16.7%	14.5%	8.0%	11.3%	0.0%	0.0%
Idaho								
Ada County	41,286	66.6%	19.5%	11.2%	2.4%	0.1%	0.3%	0.0%
Bonneville County	8,902	59.8%	27.1%	12.2%	0.9%	0.0%	0.0%	0.0%
Canyon County	16,673	65.2%	20.2%	13.3%	1.3%	0.0%	0.0%	0.0%
Kootenai County	12,876	55.3%	28.2%	8.0%	8.4%	0.0%	0.0%	0.0%
Illinois								
Champaign County	47,858	77.4%	11.0%	7.5%	3.6%	0.4%	0.0%	0.0%
Cook County	508,028	68.1%	15.8%	8.8%	4.8%	2.1%	0.2%	0.1%
DeKalb County	20,217	72.0%	14.4%	7.1%	6.3%	0.2%	0.0%	0.0%
DuPage County	78,288	64.6%	18.4%	7.8%	7.0%	2.1%	0.2%	0.0%
Kane County	47,275	60.9%	17.0%	12.2%	7.4%	1.9%	0.2%	0.4%
Kankakee County	11,416	73.8%	12.9%	4.8%	5.2%	3.4%	0.0%	0.0%
Kendall County	8,195	61.5%	19.3%	6.5%	11.8%	0.9%	0.0%	0.0%
Lake County	70,753	55.6%	21.0%	10.7%	8.1%	2.9%	1.7%	0.0%
LaSalle County	9,127	55.1%	28.5%	10.0%	6.4%	0.0%	0.0%	0.0%
Macon County	10,229	66.1%	19.5%	7.9%	5.1%	1.4%	0.0%	0.0%
Madison County	26,372	63.7%	17.6%	8.8%	6.2%	3.7%	0.0%	0.0%
McHenry County	27,383	57.9%	23.8%	9.5%	7.2%	1.5%	0.0%	0.0%
McLean County	31,067	67.5%	13.8%	9.4%	9.2%	0.1%	0.0%	0.0%
Peoria County	18,445	62.6%	16.5%	10.3%	10.5%	0.0%	0.0%	0.0%
Rock Island County	12,911	63.5%	25.9%	4.3%	5.2%	1.1%	0.0%	0.0%
Sangamon County	16,718	62.4%	21.8%	10.7%	4.2%	0.8%	0.0%	0.0%
St. Clair County	25,896	70.2%	18.2%	8.2%	2.9%	0.5%	0.0%	0.0%
Tazewell County	10,753	64.0%	16.9%	9.4%	8.3%	1.4%	0.0%	0.0%
Will County	60,678	64.0%	20.5%	10.4%	4.0%	0.9%	0.2%	0.0%
Winnebago County	27,837	62.6%	19.9%	12.2%	4.9%	0.5%	0.0%	0.0%
Indiana								
Allen County	34,640	59.7%	22.2%	11.1%	6.5%	0.0%	0.2%	0.3%
Clark County	10,298	58.0%	33.7%	5.5%	2.8%	0.0%	0.0%	0.0%
Delaware County	24,150	73.3%	17.9%	6.0%	2.5%	0.3%	0.0%	0.0%
Elkhart County	17,694	48.6%	31.3%	5.1%	13.5%	1.4%	0.0%	0.0%
Hamilton County	20,418	59.3%	12.7%	14.1%	8.9%	5.0%	0.0%	0.0%
Hendricks County	14,344	57.3%	29.2%	11.8%	1.7%	0.0%	0.0%	0.0%
Johnson County	13,025	51.2%	27.0%	7.0%	13.5%	0.0%	0.0%	1.3%
Lake County	44,830	68.2%	20.0%	7.5%	2.9%	1.3%	0.0%	0.0%
LaPorte County	9,137	49.9%	34.3%	11.0%	4.8%	0.0%	0.0%	0.0%
Madison County	11,067	56.9%	33.4%	8.8%	0.6%	0.4%	0.0%	0.0%
Marion County	91,053	60.3%	20.4%	11.7%	6.0%	1.6%	0.0%	0.0%
Monroe County	39,652	85.9%	10.7%	1.8%	1.2%	0.4%	0.0%	0.0%
Porter County	16,877	61.7%	12.6%	11.0%	11.3%	1.8%	0.0%	1.6%
St. Joseph County	30,290	68.4%	17.7%	10.1%	3.2%	0.7%	0.0%	0.0%
Tippecanoe County	43,959	72.5%	13.0%	10.8%	2.8%	0.9%	0.0%	0.0%
Vanderburgh County	19,927	73.7%	13.9%	5.1%	6.6%	0.6%	0.0%	0.0%
Vigo County	16,164	70.0%	20.3%	7.1%	2.2%	0.0%	0.4%	0.0%
Iowa								
Black Hawk County	23,342	63.6%	17.6%	15.9%	2.0%	0.9%	0.0%	0.0%
Dubuque County	9,876	55.9%	22.9%	13.2%	7.7%	0.4%	0.0%	0.0%
Johnson County	31,053	64.5%	15.2%	10.7%	8.9%	0.7%	0.0%	0.0%
Linn County	18,517	59.9%	21.8%	9.0%	8.0%	1.3%	0.0%	0.0%
Polk County	39,587	44.5%	28.5%	13.4%	10.9%	2.2%	0.4%	0.0%
Pottawattamie County	7,814	54.9%	24.1%	8.9%	4.0%	8.0%	0.0%	0.0%
Scott County	15,048	62.3%	24.9%	6.5%	3.5%	2.3%	0.0%	0.5%
Story County	25,869	67.2%	16.4%	6.0%	9.1%	1.3%	0.0%	0.0%
Woodbury County	10,317	61.5%	23.5%	10.3%	4.8%	0.0%	0.0%	0.0%
Kansas								
Douglas County	24,686	65.3%	16.4%	6.4%	7.1%	3.4%	0.0%	1.4%
Johnson County	43,369	56.4%	23.0%	7.2%	10.2%	3.2%	0.0%	0.0%
Sedgwick County	48,246	57.1%	21.8%	11.6%	7.5%	2.1%	0.0%	0.0%
Shawnee County	17,750	59.1%	24.0%	11.5%	4.5%	0.9%	0.0%	0.0%
Wyandotte County	15,375	49.9%	23.0%	15.6%	11.5%	0.0%	0.0%	0.0%
Kentucky								
Boone County	9,870	56.4%	18.2%	19.6%	5.7%	0.0%	0.0%	0.0%

Table I-2: Counties—Income Class by Age—*Continued*

	Total Millennials	Under $10,000	$10,000 to $19,999	$20,000 to $29,999	$30,000 to $49,999	$50,000 to $74,999	$75,000 to $99,999	$100,000 to $149,999	$150,000 or More	Poverty Rate
Georgia—Cont.										
Gwinnett County	76,391	29.4%	19.1%	23.4%	18.8%	6.4%	2.7%	0.4%	0.0%	13.8%
Hall County	16,371	27.4%	16.2%	26.2%	13.2%	14.4%	0.3%	2.0%	0.3%	24.6%
Henry County	14,519	24.6%	15.3%	16.5%	27.8%	14.5%	1.2%	0.0%	0.0%	16.6%
Houston County	15,755	31.0%	11.3%	22.6%	31.7%	2.5%	0.9%	0.0%	0.0%	18.7%
Lowndes County	12,415	31.1%	19.2%	16.9%	24.3%	5.3%	2.5%	0.7%	0.0%	33.8%
Muscogee County	21,609	37.3%	17.1%	17.4%	16.7%	8.6%	2.0%	0.8%	0.2%	24.3%
Newton County	7,917	40.0%	17.4%	13.7%	23.8%	5.1%	0.0%	0.0%	0.0%	24.6%
Paulding County	11,352	38.2%	16.1%	21.4%	12.9%	8.2%	0.8%	1.3%	1.1%	17.4%
Richmond County	24,335	33.8%	25.5%	13.1%	16.6%	8.8%	1.2%	0.8%	0.3%	33.6%
Whitfield County	8,472	34.6%	24.0%	11.8%	28.4%	0.0%	1.2%	0.0%	0.0%	20.9%
Hawaii										
Hawaii County	16,102	41.2%	10.2%	20.8%	17.6%	7.5%	2.7%	0.0%	0.0%	25.9%
Honolulu County	111,383	26.1%	13.2%	13.6%	26.0%	15.4%	3.6%	2.0%	0.2%	12.6%
Maui County	15,110	24.2%	8.1%	16.2%	38.3%	12.5%	0.6%	0.0%	0.0%	11.9%
Idaho										
Ada County	38,327	29.0%	21.8%	17.5%	22.8%	5.9%	2.1%	0.2%	0.7%	26.6%
Bonneville County	9,773	26.8%	30.3%	10.5%	25.0%	7.4%	0.0%	0.0%	0.0%	13.0%
Canyon County	15,953	32.3%	24.9%	15.3%	19.5%	2.9%	3.2%	0.0%	1.8%	23.8%
Kootenai County	12,654	35.3%	19.3%	9.0%	25.1%	9.2%	0.9%	1.2%	0.0%	14.8%
Illinois										
Champaign County	23,152	24.4%	16.3%	24.2%	23.1%	10.6%	0.6%	0.8%	0.0%	36.5%
Cook County	605,045	25.3%	14.2%	13.6%	22.3%	14.9%	5.7%	2.6%	1.3%	20.2%
DeKalb County	10,559	25.8%	21.1%	12.0%	26.3%	8.3%	3.7%	2.9%	0.0%	31.5%
DuPage County	86,678	22.9%	13.4%	13.1%	24.8%	14.6%	8.0%	2.4%	0.9%	7.7%
Kane County	47,528	25.2%	16.3%	18.0%	23.4%	13.0%	2.3%	0.4%	1.4%	10.5%
Kankakee County	8,304	31.3%	9.3%	28.3%	20.8%	4.3%	6.0%	0.0%	0.0%	27.0%
Kendall County	12,063	34.5%	6.0%	18.6%	24.1%	8.0%	4.9%	3.8%	0.0%	19.0%
Lake County	51,168	21.2%	17.5%	23.0%	17.3%	13.6%	4.7%	1.8%	0.9%	11.2%
LaSalle County	9,376	19.4%	28.7%	15.7%	20.3%	15.3%	0.6%	0.0%	0.0%	16.1%
Macon County	9,557	17.3%	32.0%	16.3%	21.0%	10.9%	1.8%	0.7%	0.0%	25.6%
Madison County	25,637	22.4%	14.2%	19.1%	21.3%	18.0%	3.5%	0.7%	0.8%	17.8%
McHenry County	23,349	21.7%	12.5%	19.3%	25.5%	16.0%	5.1%	0.0%	0.0%	7.7%
McLean County	17,395	19.6%	13.7%	13.4%	27.6%	22.7%	3.0%	0.0%	0.0%	28.1%
Peoria County	19,332	25.9%	10.2%	10.6%	28.2%	11.6%	9.1%	1.9%	2.4%	19.4%
Rock Island County	11,020	27.4%	14.1%	15.7%	24.6%	15.2%	3.0%	0.0%	0.0%	15.2%
Sangamon County	18,052	27.9%	15.5%	14.1%	24.8%	12.0%	2.9%	1.7%	1.1%	22.2%
St. Clair County	24,617	24.4%	18.3%	18.6%	21.6%	13.8%	2.5%	0.7%	0.0%	23.3%
Tazewell County	11,566	22.0%	17.2%	15.9%	25.4%	14.6%	4.1%	0.9%	0.0%	12.4%
Will County	52,019	25.0%	16.3%	18.6%	22.5%	11.3%	2.8%	2.1%	1.3%	9.0%
Winnebago County	23,641	32.6%	16.0%	24.9%	19.7%	6.3%	0.5%	0.0%	0.0%	21.0%
Indiana										
Allen County	33,513	31.5%	17.9%	14.6%	25.7%	8.5%	1.7%	0.0%	0.0%	22.2%
Clark County	9,716	23.2%	21.6%	23.1%	25.5%	6.7%	0.0%	0.0%	0.0%	17.2%
Delaware County	9,291	31.5%	24.4%	22.4%	15.1%	4.1%	2.4%	0.0%	0.0%	41.5%
Elkhart County	17,121	34.8%	19.2%	17.2%	17.2%	6.9%	4.8%	0.0%	0.0%	21.1%
Hamilton County	23,378	15.8%	13.7%	14.7%	27.9%	19.3%	5.4%	3.3%	0.0%	5.6%
Hendricks County	13,264	16.8%	18.2%	15.7%	30.8%	13.4%	3.3%	1.9%	0.0%	9.3%
Johnson County	12,712	30.1%	15.0%	16.1%	31.5%	6.2%	1.0%	0.0%	0.0%	13.1%
Lake County	38,834	26.2%	18.1%	17.6%	23.4%	9.3%	5.1%	0.3%	0.0%	19.2%
LaPorte County	10,789	47.4%	13.1%	14.5%	14.1%	11.0%	0.0%	0.0%	0.0%	22.2%
Madison County	10,955	35.2%	16.4%	15.8%	22.4%	9.6%	0.0%	0.6%	0.0%	25.9%
Marion County	110,706	29.8%	20.3%	14.9%	23.1%	9.0%	1.2%	0.8%	0.8%	25.3%
Monroe County	13,342	33.3%	25.5%	16.7%	17.8%	5.2%	1.6%	0.0%	0.0%	53.6%
Porter County	14,297	34.3%	15.4%	10.6%	27.3%	7.5%	3.6%	1.2%	0.0%	19.4%
St. Joseph County	22,270	25.2%	22.6%	16.2%	23.1%	8.3%	3.9%	0.4%	0.2%	24.4%
Tippecanoe County	17,881	28.4%	16.7%	19.0%	27.8%	7.4%	0.6%	0.0%	0.0%	33.7%
Vanderburgh County	17,180	28.0%	15.6%	21.2%	24.5%	6.5%	3.9%	0.0%	0.3%	24.6%
Vigo County	9,857	41.9%	15.2%	19.4%	17.0%	4.4%	0.9%	1.2%	0.0%	41.1%
Iowa										
Black Hawk County	11,883	32.8%	10.3%	13.1%	31.3%	9.7%	1.9%	0.9%	0.0%	29.8%
Dubuque County	7,182	7.5%	19.1%	30.4%	33.2%	9.8%	0.0%	0.0%	0.0%	18.6%
Johnson County	18,931	22.4%	10.5%	14.6%	29.6%	21.8%	0.3%	0.0%	0.8%	30.0%
Linn County	22,116	14.9%	20.3%	15.5%	23.6%	22.9%	2.8%	0.0%	0.0%	10.7%
Polk County	50,213	23.7%	12.6%	17.7%	29.3%	14.8%	0.7%	0.7%	0.4%	19.9%
Pottawattamie County	8,400	18.7%	8.4%	32.8%	28.9%	10.3%	0.8%	0.0%	0.0%	16.9%
Scott County	16,418	26.1%	13.6%	18.6%	27.0%	10.6%	4.0%	0.0%	0.0%	21.3%
Story County	10,051	16.3%	20.5%	14.8%	30.4%	13.3%	4.7%	0.0%	0.0%	40.6%
Woodbury County	9,895	19.4%	18.4%	22.2%	31.6%	8.5%	0.0%	0.0%	0.0%	19.7%
Kansas										
Douglas County	14,590	23.3%	17.3%	8.2%	30.3%	20.8%	0.0%	0.0%	0.0%	22.7%
Johnson County	51,290	14.8%	12.5%	17.7%	35.9%	11.4%	4.5%	2.1%	1.1%	7.7%
Sedgwick County	55,438	28.7%	17.8%	16.6%	24.9%	10.1%	0.8%	0.9%	0.1%	18.3%
Shawnee County	16,085	17.5%	8.7%	20.9%	38.0%	12.9%	0.7%	1.3%	0.0%	20.3%
Wyandotte County	15,447	30.4%	22.9%	16.3%	19.1%	6.6%	4.4%	0.2%	0.0%	25.2%
Kentucky										
Boone County	11,608	25.1%	12.0%	26.6%	16.6%	11.9%	4.6%	2.5%	0.7%	10.7%

Table I-2: Counties—Income Class by Age—*Continued*

	Personal Income, Percent by Income Class, Ages 18 to 24						
	Total Millennials	Under $10,000	$10,000 to $19,999	$20,000 to $29,999	$30,000 to $49,999	$50,000 to $74,999	$75,000 to $99,999	$100,000 or More
Kentucky—Cont.								
Campbell County	8,276	55.4%	28.8%	3.8%	3.4%	8.5%	0.0%	0.0%
Daviess County	8,905	46.8%	26.8%	8.3%	15.5%	2.6%	0.0%	0.0%
Fayette County	43,417	65.3%	25.0%	7.1%	2.6%	0.0%	0.0%	0.0%
Hardin County	8,668	53.3%	25.9%	18.7%	1.3%	0.8%	0.0%	0.0%
Jefferson County	67,944	62.0%	19.7%	10.3%	6.4%	1.4%	0.2%	0.0%
Kenton County	14,183	61.9%	15.0%	13.0%	6.5%	0.0%	0.0%	3.5%
Warren County	17,778	70.2%	16.6%	8.9%	4.3%	0.0%	0.0%	0.1%
Louisiana								
Ascension Parish	9,729	59.8%	26.6%	7.4%	1.8%	0.9%	0.6%	2.9%
Bossier Parish	12,994	57.9%	17.6%	18.7%	4.8%	1.0%	0.0%	0.0%
Caddo Parish	25,659	68.1%	19.8%	7.1%	4.5%	0.5%	0.0%	0.0%
Calcasieu Parish	20,801	66.5%	17.1%	7.3%	4.4%	2.3%	2.4%	0.0%
East Baton Rouge Parish	65,930	70.2%	16.7%	3.2%	6.6%	2.2%	1.1%	0.0%
Jefferson Parish	40,088	63.3%	20.4%	6.8%	6.5%	1.4%	1.4%	0.1%
Lafayette Parish	26,004	56.1%	23.2%	9.6%	9.0%	0.8%	1.2%	0.0%
Lafourche Parish	10,583	68.9%	11.8%	13.5%	5.0%	0.0%	0.0%	0.8%
Livingston Parish	12,671	57.1%	18.8%	8.0%	8.9%	4.0%	3.2%	0.0%
Orleans Parish	41,346	74.7%	14.5%	5.2%	4.3%	1.1%	0.0%	0.2%
Ouachita Parish	17,225	69.5%	14.0%	6.5%	10.0%	0.0%	0.0%	0.0%
Rapides Parish	13,288	71.3%	9.9%	10.7%	7.9%	0.2%	0.0%	0.0%
St. Tammany Parish	19,189	64.2%	18.9%	8.0%	4.3%	1.9%	0.0%	2.7%
Tangipahoa Parish	13,931	64.6%	12.0%	11.4%	5.9%	3.5%	2.6%	0.0%
Terrebonne Parish	10,410	52.8%	11.6%	14.0%	21.6%	0.0%	0.0%	0.0%
Maine								
Androscoggin County	9,557	66.5%	21.3%	10.6%	0.0%	1.6%	0.0%	0.0%
Cumberland County	28,028	64.0%	22.9%	9.8%	2.5%	0.8%	0.0%	0.0%
Kennebec County	10,198	50.8%	17.6%	17.7%	4.9%	7.6%	0.0%	1.5%
Penobscot County	18,248	64.7%	22.7%	3.5%	8.4%	0.8%	0.0%	0.0%
York County	15,638	64.2%	25.5%	4.0%	2.3%	0.0%	0.0%	4.0%
Maryland								
Anne Arundel County	50,657	50.2%	23.0%	12.6%	10.3%	3.1%	0.8%	0.0%
Baltimore County	79,202	62.0%	19.0%	9.2%	7.9%	1.7%	0.2%	0.0%
Carroll County	14,608	46.3%	28.2%	13.2%	9.7%	0.3%	0.9%	1.5%
Cecil County	9,432	42.4%	15.6%	15.4%	26.6%	0.0%	0.0%	0.0%
Charles County	13,872	54.7%	26.9%	8.7%	7.5%	2.2%	0.0%	0.0%
Frederick County	22,769	58.4%	17.6%	13.7%	8.9%	1.2%	0.0%	0.2%
Harford County	20,860	53.5%	24.1%	14.0%	6.2%	2.1%	0.0%	0.0%
Howard County	23,779	64.7%	13.8%	8.8%	10.9%	1.3%	0.0%	0.5%
Montgomery County	76,058	62.3%	17.3%	7.1%	9.7%	3.4%	0.1%	0.2%
Prince George's County	97,121	60.8%	14.9%	10.3%	9.9%	4.1%	0.0%	0.0%
St. Mary's County	10,336	57.3%	19.5%	6.5%	15.6%	1.1%	0.0%	0.0%
Washington County	12,958	55.8%	18.3%	13.4%	8.7%	3.8%	0.0%	0.0%
Wicomico County	15,847	69.2%	17.6%	8.3%	4.2%	0.7%	0.0%	0.0%
Massachusetts								
Barnstable County	14,628	47.6%	26.0%	13.2%	5.8%	7.5%	0.0%	0.0%
Berkshire County	13,013	77.7%	15.3%	4.4%	1.4%	1.1%	0.1%	0.0%
Bristol County	52,838	59.4%	18.7%	10.8%	7.4%	3.7%	0.0%	0.0%
Essex County	71,656	65.0%	19.4%	7.4%	7.4%	0.7%	0.0%	0.0%
Hampden County	54,906	64.3%	16.6%	9.7%	5.9%	2.1%	0.7%	0.6%
Hampshire County	26,597	79.0%	10.7%	5.1%	3.5%	1.6%	0.0%	0.0%
Middlesex County	147,617	62.5%	15.4%	9.0%	9.4%	3.2%	0.5%	0.0%
Norfolk County	57,195	69.3%	14.9%	8.6%	4.8%	2.0%	0.2%	0.2%
Plymouth County	41,066	61.7%	20.6%	9.6%	7.3%	0.8%	0.0%	0.0%
Suffolk County	114,663	68.6%	12.5%	8.1%	7.7%	2.7%	0.2%	0.1%
Worcester County	83,318	64.9%	17.0%	10.1%	6.3%	1.4%	0.1%	0.2%
Michigan								
Allegan County	9,499	55.4%	26.0%	7.4%	11.2%	0.0%	0.0%	0.0%
Bay County	9,763	57.7%	25.4%	12.8%	4.1%	0.0%	0.0%	0.0%
Berrien County	13,614	73.3%	17.7%	1.3%	5.1%	2.7%	0.0%	0.0%
Calhoun County	11,245	53.1%	30.4%	9.3%	7.2%	0.0%	0.0%	0.0%
Eaton County	8,168	57.9%	30.9%	6.8%	3.1%	1.3%	0.0%	0.0%
Genesee County	38,494	71.4%	19.4%	6.2%	2.3%	0.7%	0.0%	0.0%
Ingham County	57,613	76.2%	12.3%	4.0%	5.9%	1.4%	0.3%	0.0%
Jackson County	14,147	64.4%	23.2%	4.3%	8.2%	0.0%	0.0%	0.0%
Kalamazoo County	41,267	61.2%	23.6%	9.3%	5.2%	0.6%	0.0%	0.0%
Kent County	60,117	56.3%	22.4%	10.3%	9.4%	1.5%	0.0%	0.0%
Lenawee County	9,357	64.3%	14.8%	14.8%	4.6%	0.2%	1.2%	0.0%
Livingston County	15,203	58.9%	24.4%	11.4%	3.0%	2.2%	0.0%	0.0%
Macomb County	74,161	60.7%	21.7%	10.0%	6.0%	1.2%	0.3%	0.0%
Monroe County	13,255	49.0%	34.5%	11.0%	3.3%	2.2%	0.0%	0.0%
Muskegon County	14,142	62.4%	21.2%	8.0%	6.1%	2.2%	0.0%	0.0%
Oakland County	101,005	62.2%	19.2%	8.0%	8.2%	2.3%	0.1%	0.0%
Ottawa County	36,260	64.1%	19.2%	9.9%	5.9%	0.9%	0.0%	0.0%
Saginaw County	21,690	64.2%	25.9%	5.1%	4.6%	0.3%	0.0%	0.0%
St. Clair County	14,562	62.6%	17.8%	10.1%	5.8%	3.8%	0.0%	0.0%
Washtenaw County	64,295	53.3%	15.9%	13.1%	10.6%	7.1%	0.0%	0.0%
Wayne County	176,187	70.3%	16.0%	8.2%	4.0%	1.2%	0.1%	0.1%

Table I-2: Counties—Income Class by Age—*Continued*

	Personal Income, Percent by Income Class, Ages 25 to 31									Poverty Rate
	Total Millennials	Under $10,000	$10,000 to $19,999	$20,000 to $29,999	$30,000 to $49,999	$50,000 to $74,999	$75,000 to $99,999	$100,000 to $149,999	$150,000 or More	
Kentucky—Cont.										
Campbell County	7,975	33.7%	21.4%	4.0%	27.8%	11.7%	0.4%	0.9%	0.0%	22.0%
Daviess County	7,918	31.0%	24.3%	16.4%	19.7%	5.8%	2.7%	0.0%	0.0%	14.7%
Fayette County	32,756	23.7%	21.1%	22.2%	21.7%	6.6%	2.6%	1.8%	0.2%	31.3%
Hardin County	10,318	22.1%	23.5%	25.5%	23.3%	4.4%	0.5%	0.6%	0.0%	20.9%
Jefferson County	75,621	22.0%	15.9%	22.8%	24.2%	10.2%	3.1%	1.7%	0.1%	20.7%
Kenton County	16,317	20.3%	15.0%	24.2%	21.9%	12.1%	5.5%	0.9%	0.0%	12.3%
Warren County	13,297	27.6%	15.2%	15.8%	18.8%	22.6%	0.0%	0.0%	0.0%	29.2%
Louisiana										
Ascension Parish	9,945	18.4%	9.1%	6.1%	32.3%	23.4%	8.6%	2.1%	0.0%	15.4%
Bossier Parish	14,263	34.9%	18.9%	7.6%	26.1%	9.7%	2.8%	0.0%	0.0%	25.1%
Caddo Parish	26,200	30.2%	17.9%	17.6%	22.0%	9.0%	1.3%	1.6%	0.5%	31.2%
Calcasieu Parish	16,579	28.6%	17.2%	15.8%	20.8%	11.1%	3.2%	2.7%	0.7%	20.5%
East Baton Rouge Parish	45,973	26.8%	16.6%	14.0%	24.6%	13.4%	2.3%	2.0%	0.3%	30.5%
Jefferson Parish	48,728	28.9%	19.3%	17.2%	23.8%	8.1%	1.3%	0.9%	0.5%	23.3%
Lafayette Parish	26,283	14.1%	18.8%	13.1%	26.1%	16.2%	4.4%	3.8%	3.5%	16.1%
Lafourche Parish	9,274	22.3%	16.3%	13.1%	22.5%	17.8%	4.7%	2.7%	0.5%	21.8%
Livingston Parish	12,243	27.8%	11.9%	4.7%	35.8%	10.7%	6.2%	1.3%	1.5%	20.6%
Orleans Parish	50,635	31.1%	17.9%	12.8%	23.0%	8.1%	3.8%	2.3%	0.9%	30.3%
Ouachita Parish	14,752	49.8%	17.0%	10.5%	16.1%	3.3%	2.9%	0.4%	0.0%	30.4%
Rapides Parish	13,160	31.4%	11.0%	21.8%	26.9%	5.7%	1.1%	2.2%	0.0%	23.7%
St. Tammany Parish	20,568	23.9%	19.2%	15.3%	23.3%	13.7%	1.9%	2.3%	0.3%	13.2%
Tangipahoa Parish	14,288	32.9%	22.6%	14.4%	17.0%	9.6%	1.3%	0.0%	2.2%	26.6%
Terrebonne Parish	11,174	29.4%	13.2%	7.3%	37.2%	8.0%	1.7%	1.4%	1.8%	5.9%
Maine										
Androscoggin County	10,215	14.8%	14.5%	44.4%	18.2%	6.6%	1.6%	0.0%	0.0%	14.7%
Cumberland County	26,931	21.4%	16.0%	15.6%	30.9%	12.6%	2.0%	1.2%	0.4%	16.6%
Kennebec County	9,257	14.6%	20.1%	34.2%	18.2%	12.9%	0.0%	0.0%	0.0%	11.6%
Penobscot County	13,381	36.4%	14.2%	19.2%	18.1%	11.7%	0.4%	0.0%	0.0%	22.4%
York County	16,288	19.3%	14.6%	14.7%	32.0%	12.2%	1.0%	4.9%	1.3%	14.0%
Maryland										
Anne Arundel County	54,134	22.6%	9.6%	11.9%	22.8%	21.4%	6.8%	3.3%	1.6%	7.6%
Baltimore County	83,062	18.5%	11.6%	12.7%	33.4%	17.6%	3.5%	1.5%	1.1%	13.4%
Carroll County	12,659	17.9%	11.5%	15.8%	39.7%	12.5%	0.6%	2.2%	0.0%	7.4%
Cecil County	8,957	24.0%	10.0%	15.8%	22.5%	16.5%	10.6%	0.6%	0.0%	8.7%
Charles County	13,615	27.7%	6.8%	17.2%	23.3%	18.7%	4.3%	1.5%	0.5%	8.6%
Frederick County	19,937	17.8%	10.5%	13.0%	24.1%	23.1%	6.8%	2.6%	2.3%	6.9%
Harford County	21,178	24.5%	10.7%	14.4%	19.4%	23.8%	5.9%	1.3%	0.0%	7.2%
Howard County	27,727	17.5%	13.4%	8.5%	18.8%	23.7%	13.1%	3.9%	1.0%	7.0%
Montgomery County	95,555	19.3%	10.7%	14.3%	22.3%	22.2%	6.7%	3.7%	0.9%	8.2%
Prince George's County	94,058	22.9%	15.0%	18.6%	26.4%	10.9%	4.5%	1.5%	0.2%	12.4%
St. Mary's County	8,534	29.4%	9.6%	8.8%	23.6%	15.3%	7.7%	5.7%	0.0%	6.9%
Washington County	12,951	29.1%	19.7%	14.5%	22.4%	11.4%	2.7%	0.0%	0.2%	14.8%
Wicomico County	9,353	21.8%	22.3%	11.9%	35.3%	6.2%	0.0%	2.5%	0.0%	21.6%
Massachusetts										
Barnstable County	14,599	15.8%	6.5%	24.8%	35.9%	11.2%	5.0%	0.0%	0.7%	11.1%
Berkshire County	9,113	16.5%	23.6%	17.7%	25.2%	6.6%	4.0%	0.0%	6.4%	14.6%
Bristol County	45,583	28.8%	16.7%	14.6%	26.4%	9.1%	2.8%	1.6%	0.0%	18.0%
Essex County	66,372	21.6%	17.6%	14.9%	22.7%	15.5%	3.9%	3.6%	0.1%	14.4%
Hampden County	39,256	25.0%	20.2%	14.2%	26.9%	9.0%	3.4%	0.8%	0.5%	22.2%
Hampshire County	12,380	22.6%	11.9%	15.4%	30.2%	15.3%	1.6%	2.8%	0.2%	23.8%
Middlesex County	176,596	19.0%	10.9%	12.4%	25.4%	20.5%	7.4%	3.7%	0.7%	12.3%
Norfolk County	59,789	20.0%	8.8%	13.0%	23.7%	24.5%	5.9%	3.6%	0.6%	10.4%
Plymouth County	36,135	20.6%	13.0%	19.5%	24.2%	15.7%	5.1%	1.8%	0.0%	11.3%
Suffolk County	131,371	16.9%	12.8%	13.1%	22.9%	18.7%	8.1%	5.6%	2.0%	24.3%
Worcester County	72,063	22.6%	13.8%	16.5%	25.2%	16.1%	3.9%	1.2%	0.6%	18.6%
Michigan										
Allegan County	8,100	29.1%	11.0%	25.7%	24.8%	6.4%	0.8%	2.2%	0.0%	16.1%
Bay County	9,708	36.4%	12.8%	9.7%	28.7%	11.6%	0.8%	0.0%	0.0%	16.3%
Berrien County	12,250	35.5%	18.3%	18.5%	21.0%	4.4%	2.0%	0.2%	0.0%	24.6%
Calhoun County	10,299	19.4%	26.6%	19.0%	26.8%	6.6%	1.6%	0.0%	0.0%	16.9%
Eaton County	10,189	24.1%	31.9%	11.5%	17.9%	14.0%	0.6%	0.0%	0.0%	24.7%
Genesee County	35,288	36.5%	25.1%	12.6%	17.4%	7.3%	0.4%	0.8%	0.0%	26.6%
Ingham County	28,648	28.3%	11.2%	19.5%	24.1%	14.7%	1.2%	0.0%	0.9%	33.8%
Jackson County	14,943	41.8%	13.1%	15.7%	19.0%	7.4%	3.0%	0.0%	0.0%	24.0%
Kalamazoo County	23,678	20.4%	33.3%	16.4%	20.2%	7.4%	1.0%	1.3%	0.1%	26.0%
Kent County	67,996	26.5%	18.3%	17.4%	24.5%	9.9%	2.2%	1.0%	0.2%	21.2%
Lenawee County	8,643	34.2%	23.5%	20.0%	13.4%	5.2%	3.7%	0.1%	0.0%	24.1%
Livingston County	12,368	20.0%	11.7%	13.3%	33.2%	18.6%	2.4%	0.0%	0.8%	6.4%
Macomb County	74,026	26.5%	21.1%	14.6%	24.3%	9.7%	2.8%	0.2%	0.8%	16.7%
Monroe County	11,608	18.1%	23.6%	22.2%	23.3%	9.4%	2.6%	0.4%	0.4%	15.3%
Muskegon County	13,335	40.7%	15.6%	18.7%	19.5%	3.6%	1.9%	0.0%	0.0%	25.3%
Oakland County	104,716	23.4%	13.1%	16.1%	21.8%	16.2%	6.7%	2.1%	0.6%	13.1%
Ottawa County	21,987	23.3%	16.9%	20.4%	24.8%	10.2%	3.7%	0.5%	0.2%	19.1%
Saginaw County	15,016	37.6%	23.3%	15.9%	13.6%	7.7%	0.0%	1.9%	0.0%	22.9%
St. Clair County	10,990	35.3%	18.4%	21.3%	13.6%	7.2%	1.5%	2.7%	0.0%	26.4%
Washtenaw County	36,258	22.2%	18.1%	19.4%	21.6%	12.5%	3.0%	3.1%	0.2%	32.4%
Wayne County	153,266	37.3%	18.4%	13.8%	17.9%	8.6%	2.3%	1.1%	0.6%	30.9%

Table I-2: Counties—Income Class by Age—*Continued*

	Personal Income, Percent by Income Class, Ages 18 to 24							
	Total Millennials	Under $10,000	$10,000 to $19,999	$20,000 to $29,999	$30,000 to $49,999	$50,000 to $74,999	$75,000 to $99,999	$100,000 or More
Minnesota								
Anoka County	27,416	62.9%	16.9%	14.6%	5.6%	0.0%	0.0%	0.0%
Carver County	7,496	53.2%	35.8%	7.3%	1.1%	2.6%	0.0%	0.0%
Dakota County	31,660	47.3%	28.2%	15.4%	5.0%	4.2%	0.0%	0.0%
Hennepin County	109,313	57.8%	21.2%	8.7%	9.2%	3.2%	0.0%	0.0%
Olmsted County	12,514	55.4%	15.0%	20.8%	8.2%	0.6%	0.0%	0.0%
Ramsey County	59,746	61.0%	19.4%	14.6%	4.6%	0.4%	0.0%	0.0%
Scott County	9,533	58.9%	23.5%	13.5%	1.6%	2.2%	0.0%	0.3%
St. Louis County	24,221	66.1%	19.8%	5.3%	8.2%	0.3%	0.2%	0.0%
Stearns County	24,867	60.5%	14.7%	13.7%	9.8%	1.4%	0.0%	0.0%
Washington County	19,201	62.0%	14.0%	13.0%	10.7%	0.3%	0.0%	0.0%
Wright County	9,249	38.9%	19.5%	28.9%	9.3%	3.4%	0.0%	0.0%
Mississippi								
DeSoto County	14,031	54.9%	23.6%	11.4%	8.4%	1.7%	0.0%	0.0%
Harrison County	20,561	54.2%	16.0%	23.8%	6.1%	0.0%	0.0%	0.0%
Hinds County	29,826	72.8%	10.5%	9.9%	6.4%	0.3%	0.0%	0.0%
Jackson County	13,816	64.5%	17.4%	8.5%	9.5%	0.2%	0.0%	0.0%
Madison County	9,042	74.5%	14.6%	5.4%	5.2%	0.3%	0.0%	0.0%
Rankin County	11,321	57.0%	25.5%	6.4%	8.3%	2.9%	0.0%	0.0%
Missouri								
Boone County	36,413	75.5%	17.8%	4.0%	1.9%	0.0%	0.8%	0.0%
Cass County	8,261	54.4%	20.9%	9.3%	15.0%	0.3%	0.0%	0.0%
Clay County	19,027	49.5%	34.2%	8.2%	7.3%	0.8%	0.0%	0.0%
Franklin County	8,224	48.8%	35.7%	11.5%	4.0%	0.0%	0.0%	0.0%
Greene County	40,080	60.1%	24.8%	6.6%	7.9%	0.6%	0.0%	0.0%
Jackson County	59,386	57.9%	21.3%	10.9%	7.1%	2.2%	0.6%	0.0%
Jasper County	11,453	51.7%	19.0%	6.5%	20.2%	2.6%	0.0%	0.0%
Jefferson County	17,351	69.1%	17.3%	5.7%	6.3%	1.6%	0.0%	0.0%
Platte County	8,248	46.3%	20.9%	20.4%	11.0%	1.3%	0.0%	0.0%
St. Charles County	30,614	52.8%	27.2%	13.2%	5.4%	1.3%	0.0%	0.0%
St. Louis County	88,692	62.8%	19.9%	10.2%	5.5%	1.5%	0.0%	0.2%
Montana								
Flathead County	7,067	68.3%	17.6%	13.7%	0.0%	0.5%	0.0%	0.0%
Gallatin County	14,670	70.7%	14.7%	4.8%	9.4%	0.0%	0.0%	0.3%
Missoula County	16,419	68.3%	16.2%	2.5%	9.4%	1.8%	0.0%	1.8%
Yellowstone County	15,195	60.5%	22.9%	9.0%	5.4%	0.0%	1.9%	0.5%
Nebraska								
Douglas County	51,301	57.0%	20.6%	14.3%	7.3%	0.8%	0.0%	0.2%
Lancaster County	46,475	67.1%	17.8%	8.6%	6.2%	0.3%	0.0%	0.0%
Sarpy County	14,951	55.6%	22.3%	14.8%	6.6%	0.7%	0.0%	0.0%
Nevada								
Clark County	185,550	60.3%	19.4%	11.1%	8.2%	0.8%	0.0%	0.1%
Washoe County	43,605	57.5%	25.4%	11.0%	4.3%	0.4%	1.4%	0.0%
New Hampshire								
Hillsborough County	34,112	61.2%	18.4%	7.4%	7.6%	4.8%	0.4%	0.3%
Merrimack County	14,498	66.6%	19.2%	9.8%	3.1%	0.5%	0.0%	0.7%
Rockingham County	23,488	67.8%	17.0%	6.2%	6.4%	2.2%	0.0%	0.4%
Strafford County	18,156	70.4%	10.4%	12.0%	5.7%	0.9%	0.0%	0.5%
New Jersey								
Atlantic County	26,718	66.7%	18.9%	8.7%	4.3%	1.2%	0.2%	0.0%
Bergen County	73,274	67.8%	15.8%	7.3%	5.7%	2.8%	0.1%	0.4%
Burlington County	40,355	65.7%	16.6%	9.5%	7.3%	0.9%	0.0%	0.0%
Camden County	45,958	66.4%	20.4%	8.9%	3.9%	0.3%	0.0%	0.1%
Cape May County	7,503	51.8%	35.1%	3.9%	8.2%	1.0%	0.0%	0.0%
Cumberland County	13,442	55.6%	23.0%	9.4%	9.9%	2.1%	0.0%	0.0%
Essex County	73,948	74.0%	15.8%	5.2%	4.4%	0.5%	0.0%	0.1%
Gloucester County	26,112	63.7%	14.9%	10.8%	7.8%	2.8%	0.0%	0.0%
Hudson County	60,876	62.4%	17.3%	7.9%	6.7%	4.1%	1.1%	0.6%
Hunterdon County	12,070	62.4%	17.2%	11.8%	7.5%	0.6%	0.5%	0.0%
Mercer County	40,520	70.8%	15.8%	7.2%	4.1%	2.0%	0.0%	0.0%
Middlesex County	83,384	71.8%	11.8%	7.5%	5.7%	3.2%	0.0%	0.0%
Monmouth County	53,159	66.7%	17.9%	7.2%	4.6%	2.2%	0.9%	0.5%
Morris County	40,984	71.7%	13.0%	7.0%	6.5%	1.5%	0.3%	0.0%
Ocean County	43,910	65.7%	21.9%	6.9%	4.0%	1.4%	0.1%	0.0%
Passaic County	52,748	63.2%	18.1%	9.9%	6.4%	2.0%	0.1%	0.3%
Somerset County	23,900	59.4%	16.2%	9.6%	11.0%	3.7%	0.1%	0.0%
Sussex County	12,094	55.8%	25.6%	10.8%	6.9%	0.8%	0.0%	0.0%
Union County	48,047	64.4%	18.3%	8.8%	5.9%	1.9%	0.4%	0.3%
Warren County	9,333	57.0%	26.4%	7.9%	6.9%	1.1%	0.0%	0.7%
New Mexico								
Bernalillo County	72,174	62.0%	22.8%	7.5%	6.0%	1.4%	0.2%	0.0%
Doña Ana County	32,427	64.3%	22.9%	7.0%	5.3%	0.6%	0.0%	0.0%
San Juan County	12,029	76.5%	15.7%	5.4%	1.4%	0.0%	1.0%	0.0%
Sandoval County	10,885	68.1%	12.0%	8.3%	11.6%	0.0%	0.0%	0.0%
Santa Fe County	11,267	65.8%	23.8%	7.6%	2.2%	0.5%	0.0%	0.0%
New York								
Albany County	43,769	72.6%	11.6%	4.8%	8.5%	2.5%	0.0%	0.0%

Table I-2: Counties—Income Class by Age—*Continued*

	Personal Income, Percent by Income Class, Ages 25 to 31									Poverty Rate
	Total Millennials	Under $10,000	$10,000 to $19,999	$20,000 to $29,999	$30,000 to $49,999	$50,000 to $74,999	$75,000 to $99,999	$100,000 to $149,999	$150,000 or More	
Minnesota										
Anoka County	31,549	18.6%	8.9%	24.3%	30.6%	11.5%	2.7%	2.9%	0.4%	10.5%
Carver County	7,299	10.0%	15.0%	13.1%	30.7%	25.0%	1.5%	2.6%	2.0%	6.2%
Dakota County	36,886	18.9%	22.2%	11.3%	24.9%	15.6%	6.5%	0.3%	0.3%	13.6%
Hennepin County	154,945	20.8%	11.5%	15.4%	26.0%	18.3%	4.6%	2.5%	0.9%	15.8%
Olmsted County	14,440	22.5%	7.3%	16.0%	29.7%	20.3%	3.0%	1.3%	0.0%	11.6%
Ramsey County	58,603	28.5%	8.6%	14.3%	28.1%	17.3%	1.7%	1.5%	0.0%	22.4%
Scott County	10,804	20.2%	5.9%	17.4%	26.2%	17.4%	11.0%	1.4%	0.6%	6.4%
St. Louis County	18,255	29.9%	19.1%	14.6%	21.6%	7.1%	7.0%	0.3%	0.4%	31.1%
Stearns County	13,381	10.3%	25.2%	13.1%	34.4%	13.8%	0.8%	0.9%	1.5%	29.7%
Washington County	21,849	20.2%	18.1%	12.9%	27.9%	17.6%	1.4%	2.0%	0.0%	11.2%
Wright County	12,469	22.9%	18.5%	24.1%	16.2%	13.2%	5.0%	0.0%	0.2%	8.7%
Mississippi										
DeSoto County	13,474	24.2%	13.4%	9.1%	38.4%	8.4%	6.1%	0.0%	0.4%	16.0%
Harrison County	20,462	23.1%	18.2%	26.1%	20.9%	10.4%	1.3%	0.0%	0.0%	25.0%
Hinds County	27,637	33.3%	25.6%	12.6%	19.1%	6.0%	2.5%	1.0%	0.0%	34.9%
Jackson County	13,664	30.1%	19.4%	13.4%	28.4%	6.3%	0.0%	2.5%	0.0%	14.0%
Madison County	7,963	34.4%	17.6%	10.3%	17.5%	17.9%	2.0%	0.3%	0.0%	23.7%
Rankin County	14,220	24.8%	13.4%	18.0%	29.7%	10.1%	0.9%	3.0%	0.2%	18.8%
Missouri										
Boone County	20,117	33.6%	21.1%	18.0%	21.8%	2.5%	1.7%	1.4%	0.0%	41.7%
Cass County	7,355	20.8%	19.3%	18.0%	25.5%	10.1%	6.3%	0.0%	0.0%	13.0%
Clay County	23,445	26.3%	9.8%	13.6%	29.6%	15.4%	3.6%	1.7%	0.0%	10.1%
Franklin County	8,650	30.7%	17.4%	18.1%	13.0%	18.2%	2.7%	0.0%	0.0%	15.0%
Greene County	30,906	31.9%	17.1%	19.4%	21.1%	6.8%	1.7%	0.7%	1.3%	27.4%
Jackson County	72,220	21.8%	16.3%	21.1%	25.2%	10.9%	3.3%	0.9%	0.6%	22.6%
Jasper County	11,934	26.0%	23.5%	12.6%	30.5%	6.9%	0.5%	0.0%	0.0%	19.7%
Jefferson County	19,571	20.9%	17.2%	20.9%	25.0%	13.2%	1.1%	1.6%	0.0%	19.3%
Platte County	10,502	8.4%	18.0%	18.9%	27.9%	22.2%	2.8%	0.8%	1.1%	14.8%
St. Charles County	34,816	19.0%	14.2%	14.3%	28.4%	16.6%	5.0%	2.1%	0.4%	10.8%
St. Louis County	88,698	26.3%	13.8%	18.7%	23.5%	11.9%	3.0%	2.3%	0.5%	15.2%
Montana										
Flathead County	6,979	33.6%	7.5%	13.3%	34.9%	6.6%	2.9%	1.2%	0.0%	20.6%
Gallatin County	9,613	8.4%	19.1%	14.6%	33.2%	19.2%	4.0%	0.2%	1.4%	30.9%
Missoula County	13,113	34.9%	14.3%	16.5%	22.2%	11.0%	1.1%	0.0%	0.0%	33.9%
Yellowstone County	13,632	33.3%	13.8%	16.2%	21.9%	11.8%	0.0%	0.6%	2.5%	21.4%
Nebraska										
Douglas County	60,770	20.0%	17.3%	18.2%	25.1%	15.0%	3.2%	1.2%	0.0%	19.0%
Lancaster County	31,597	21.6%	15.0%	24.9%	25.1%	11.1%	1.3%	0.6%	0.3%	27.4%
Sarpy County	17,024	22.9%	16.7%	21.8%	20.8%	14.2%	1.7%	0.6%	1.3%	12.3%
Nevada										
Clark County	207,828	26.3%	17.7%	18.2%	23.6%	9.9%	2.4%	1.3%	0.4%	19.8%
Washoe County	42,425	26.4%	16.0%	15.0%	24.2%	14.0%	3.2%	1.2%	0.1%	21.0%
New Hampshire										
Hillsborough County	37,677	20.2%	13.8%	12.7%	36.2%	9.5%	5.4%	1.3%	0.8%	13.9%
Merrimack County	10,671	23.0%	14.8%	21.7%	28.4%	10.9%	0.6%	0.0%	0.6%	13.6%
Rockingham County	19,669	21.9%	9.7%	13.4%	34.3%	14.6%	5.3%	0.7%	0.0%	9.5%
Strafford County	10,506	21.4%	16.3%	19.2%	24.0%	10.8%	4.3%	4.0%	0.0%	12.5%
New Jersey										
Atlantic County	22,550	32.5%	19.7%	12.5%	19.5%	11.4%	2.2%	1.5%	0.7%	23.0%
Bergen County	72,616	22.7%	11.5%	12.3%	21.3%	17.7%	8.2%	4.8%	1.6%	8.3%
Burlington County	37,052	25.2%	12.0%	12.3%	25.1%	17.8%	4.1%	2.7%	0.7%	5.5%
Camden County	48,608	27.9%	18.0%	16.8%	20.6%	13.8%	1.0%	0.8%	1.0%	17.3%
Cape May County	7,291	41.4%	10.5%	19.1%	12.7%	15.0%	0.0%	1.2%	0.0%	14.4%
Cumberland County	17,728	47.1%	14.3%	10.6%	15.6%	9.5%	1.5%	1.3%	0.0%	19.1%
Essex County	77,006	31.3%	18.8%	16.8%	18.7%	9.7%	1.8%	2.3%	0.7%	20.4%
Gloucester County	24,121	25.1%	22.3%	15.2%	17.7%	16.7%	2.8%	0.0%	0.2%	14.1%
Hudson County	101,319	22.9%	13.6%	13.0%	17.6%	17.5%	8.8%	4.6%	2.1%	18.9%
Hunterdon County	6,223	36.1%	8.6%	8.5%	19.8%	20.9%	1.3%	0.0%	5.3%	4.2%
Mercer County	31,797	29.5%	16.5%	13.0%	20.4%	14.7%	4.3%	1.5%	0.0%	16.0%
Middlesex County	75,498	25.0%	11.0%	13.6%	21.6%	16.3%	8.1%	4.2%	0.2%	12.6%
Monmouth County	47,859	19.2%	15.7%	14.3%	24.8%	18.9%	2.9%	4.0%	0.3%	11.2%
Morris County	36,576	18.2%	11.2%	10.7%	21.0%	27.1%	8.3%	2.7%	0.8%	5.7%
Ocean County	44,190	27.8%	17.7%	15.8%	23.7%	10.6%	1.5%	2.2%	0.6%	11.3%
Passaic County	45,823	29.9%	18.6%	13.8%	21.8%	9.5%	3.4%	2.6%	0.4%	20.8%
Somerset County	23,394	20.2%	19.9%	10.6%	18.0%	21.1%	6.3%	3.4%	0.6%	8.4%
Sussex County	9,958	22.8%	17.4%	16.5%	22.0%	13.1%	6.3%	1.9%	0.0%	8.1%
Union County	48,437	26.0%	14.2%	18.6%	21.9%	15.4%	2.2%	1.2%	0.4%	14.0%
Warren County	6,347	13.3%	19.0%	9.2%	16.1%	32.6%	7.7%	1.6%	0.6%	10.3%
New Mexico										
Bernalillo County	70,322	33.3%	18.2%	17.5%	19.3%	8.0%	2.7%	0.6%	0.3%	26.2%
Doña Ana County	18,236	35.3%	25.2%	16.4%	18.6%	2.8%	1.8%	0.0%	0.0%	38.0%
San Juan County	10,960	46.3%	12.7%	19.0%	13.2%	6.5%	2.3%	0.0%	0.0%	31.9%
Sandoval County	11,444	44.3%	18.8%	7.1%	22.5%	4.5%	0.1%	2.8%	0.0%	23.1%
Santa Fe County	11,673	29.0%	26.1%	16.8%	16.6%	10.2%	0.0%	1.2%	0.0%	31.1%
New York										
Albany County	28,976	19.9%	20.1%	12.4%	27.9%	12.0%	4.0%	3.1%	0.6%	22.1%

Table I-2: Counties—Income Class by Age—Continued

	Total Millennials	Personal Income, Percent by Income Class, Ages 18 to 24						
		Under $10,000	$10,000 to $19,999	$20,000 to $29,999	$30,000 to $49,999	$50,000 to $74,999	$75,000 to $99,999	$100,000 or More
New York—Cont.								
Bronx County	165,974	74.5%	14.6%	5.7%	3.9%	1.4%	0.0%	0.0%
Broome County	27,164	75.4%	12.5%	5.8%	5.6%	0.7%	0.0%	0.0%
Chautauqua County	15,702	70.0%	17.4%	10.4%	1.3%	0.9%	0.0%	0.0%
Dutchess County	35,052	73.1%	15.2%	8.0%	2.6%	1.0%	0.2%	0.0%
Erie County	95,801	61.4%	20.1%	10.1%	6.0%	2.0%	0.3%	0.1%
Jefferson County	14,889	39.3%	24.0%	22.9%	12.9%	0.8%	0.0%	0.0%
Kings County	254,944	69.0%	13.2%	7.3%	7.9%	1.9%	0.3%	0.3%
Monroe County	81,663	68.0%	17.2%	11.1%	3.0%	0.7%	0.0%	0.0%
Nassau County	118,749	66.5%	17.0%	6.6%	8.0%	1.6%	0.0%	0.3%
New York County	158,748	66.3%	11.4%	4.4%	9.3%	5.4%	1.6%	1.5%
Niagara County	20,964	58.3%	27.1%	9.5%	3.0%	2.1%	0.0%	0.0%
Oneida County	22,861	64.5%	21.1%	7.6%	5.5%	1.3%	0.0%	0.0%
Onondaga County	52,600	66.8%	14.5%	9.8%	6.5%	1.3%	0.0%	1.1%
Ontario County	9,713	67.1%	12.3%	8.9%	10.6%	0.5%	0.0%	0.5%
Orange County	40,299	56.0%	24.8%	12.7%	4.7%	1.7%	0.0%	0.0%
Oswego County	14,062	65.8%	17.6%	9.1%	6.3%	1.2%	0.0%	0.0%
Putnam County	8,442	54.3%	21.4%	17.8%	6.3%	0.1%	0.0%	0.0%
Queens County	212,998	69.7%	15.0%	7.5%	5.7%	1.7%	0.4%	0.1%
Rensselaer County	17,570	67.6%	15.7%	10.0%	5.8%	0.9%	0.0%	0.0%
Richmond County	44,851	73.1%	13.2%	5.3%	5.0%	3.0%	0.4%	0.0%
Rockland County	30,572	62.6%	16.2%	9.6%	9.3%	2.3%	0.0%	0.0%
Saratoga County	19,250	66.2%	14.8%	12.2%	5.7%	0.5%	0.6%	0.0%
Schenectady County	14,529	62.4%	23.0%	5.5%	7.3%	1.8%	0.0%	0.0%
St. Lawrence County	16,127	80.3%	13.1%	5.7%	0.5%	0.5%	0.0%	0.0%
Steuben County	7,766	65.2%	25.0%	6.7%	2.8%	0.4%	0.0%	0.0%
Suffolk County	137,312	64.0%	16.0%	8.8%	8.4%	2.2%	0.3%	0.3%
Tompkins County	27,064	71.3%	17.4%	6.4%	3.8%	1.0%	0.0%	0.0%
Ulster County	18,478	65.3%	18.6%	8.2%	6.6%	1.3%	0.0%	0.0%
Wayne County	6,813	44.4%	27.9%	17.3%	8.4%	2.0%	0.0%	0.0%
Westchester County	84,010	67.1%	15.3%	6.0%	8.0%	2.2%	0.5%	0.8%
North Carolina								
Alamance County	14,914	66.7%	27.3%	4.8%	1.2%	0.0%	0.0%	0.0%
Brunswick County	6,204	60.5%	25.7%	11.3%	1.7%	0.8%	0.0%	0.0%
Buncombe County	19,015	66.8%	22.2%	8.2%	1.9%	0.9%	0.0%	0.0%
Burke County	6,960	64.2%	30.2%	2.1%	3.4%	0.0%	0.0%	0.0%
Cabarrus County	16,063	76.1%	13.5%	8.2%	1.9%	0.3%	0.0%	0.0%
Catawba County	14,162	60.2%	24.3%	11.8%	3.7%	0.0%	0.0%	0.0%
Cleveland County	10,491	68.7%	14.3%	12.1%	4.9%	0.0%	0.0%	0.0%
Craven County	13,109	47.1%	18.1%	21.5%	13.3%	0.0%	0.0%	0.0%
Cumberland County	42,645	53.0%	17.8%	20.4%	6.9%	1.5%	0.0%	0.3%
Davidson County	13,893	66.3%	22.4%	7.1%	4.2%	0.0%	0.0%	0.0%
Durham County	31,255	70.2%	14.0%	9.2%	5.1%	0.2%	0.0%	1.5%
Forsyth County	37,917	73.3%	14.5%	7.4%	4.1%	0.7%	0.0%	0.0%
Gaston County	18,530	66.0%	16.8%	9.5%	7.4%	0.3%	0.0%	0.0%
Guilford County	57,650	72.5%	16.4%	7.2%	3.1%	0.9%	0.0%	0.0%
Harnett County	11,742	72.7%	12.8%	7.4%	6.1%	0.8%	0.2%	0.0%
Henderson County	7,177	56.9%	27.0%	14.3%	1.8%	0.0%	0.0%	0.0%
Iredell County	14,727	70.1%	20.9%	4.0%	3.8%	1.3%	0.0%	0.0%
Johnston County	15,471	61.6%	33.9%	3.8%	0.6%	0.0%	0.0%	0.0%
Mecklenburg County	95,115	61.0%	17.7%	12.1%	6.3%	1.6%	0.1%	1.1%
Moore County	5,301	61.4%	23.9%	8.2%	5.7%	0.9%	0.0%	0.0%
Nash County	8,804	78.1%	13.9%	6.6%	1.4%	0.0%	0.0%	0.0%
New Hanover County	28,308	58.9%	23.5%	9.5%	5.5%	2.6%	0.0%	0.0%
Onslow County	41,443	34.6%	20.2%	28.5%	14.5%	1.9%	0.0%	0.3%
Orange County	26,907	81.2%	10.7%	4.7%	3.2%	0.2%	0.0%	0.0%
Pitt County	33,517	64.1%	26.3%	4.4%	5.2%	0.0%	0.0%	0.0%
Randolph County	11,229	49.0%	19.0%	24.6%	7.3%	0.0%	0.0%	0.0%
Robeson County	15,994	77.4%	10.7%	7.1%	4.5%	0.3%	0.0%	0.0%
Rockingham County	5,190	75.2%	16.5%	4.7%	1.7%	0.0%	0.0%	1.9%
Rowan County	13,058	64.9%	17.3%	7.1%	6.9%	3.8%	0.0%	0.0%
Union County	17,838	59.7%	18.7%	7.0%	14.3%	0.0%	0.2%	0.0%
Wake County	93,995	64.1%	17.4%	10.1%	7.2%	1.1%	0.0%	0.0%
Wayne County	11,846	70.4%	8.1%	10.4%	8.0%	1.7%	1.4%	0.0%
North Dakota								
Cass County	27,874	44.1%	32.3%	12.2%	10.4%	0.2%	0.7%	0.0%
Ohio								
Allen County	10,770	62.2%	13.0%	17.2%	7.5%	0.0%	0.0%	0.0%
Ashtabula County	8,246	67.0%	15.5%	8.0%	9.5%	0.0%	0.0%	0.0%
Butler County	46,473	68.4%	17.4%	6.7%	6.6%	0.8%	0.1%	0.0%
Clark County	12,435	60.9%	28.8%	6.4%	3.9%	0.0%	0.0%	0.0%
Clermont County	15,562	43.7%	28.5%	18.2%	6.4%	2.4%	0.7%	0.0%
Columbiana County	8,311	59.3%	26.5%	10.2%	2.3%	1.7%	0.0%	0.0%
Cuyahoga County	115,543	62.2%	23.1%	9.0%	4.6%	1.1%	0.0%	0.0%
Delaware County	13,023	53.8%	23.8%	16.4%	5.2%	0.8%	0.0%	0.0%
Fairfield County	12,513	62.8%	23.5%	10.9%	2.0%	0.7%	0.0%	0.0%
Franklin County	128,229	62.9%	18.9%	8.6%	8.5%	1.1%	0.0%	0.0%
Geauga County	8,535	62.6%	24.4%	10.2%	0.3%	2.6%	0.0%	0.0%
Greene County	21,436	69.7%	18.3%	9.7%	1.7%	0.7%	0.0%	0.0%

Table I-2: Counties—Income Class by Age—*Continued*

| | Personal Income, Percent by Income Class, Ages 25 to 31 | | | | | | | | | |
	Total Millennials	Under $10,000	$10,000 to $19,999	$20,000 to $29,999	$30,000 to $49,999	$50,000 to $74,999	$75,000 to $99,999	$100,000 to $149,999	$150,000 or More	Poverty Rate
New York—Cont.										
Bronx County	151,158	41.1%	17.0%	15.1%	16.8%	6.9%	1.9%	1.0%	0.2%	32.6%
Broome County	16,385	29.0%	19.9%	20.6%	17.5%	11.4%	1.1%	0.5%	0.0%	27.8%
Chautauqua County	10,603	27.2%	23.8%	22.6%	22.9%	2.4%	0.3%	0.8%	0.0%	24.5%
Dutchess County	21,652	29.2%	15.0%	21.3%	15.4%	14.5%	2.6%	2.0%	0.0%	12.7%
Erie County	91,167	20.9%	18.8%	15.9%	26.6%	13.2%	3.3%	0.5%	0.6%	20.7%
Jefferson County	13,583	26.6%	15.6%	26.8%	17.7%	7.3%	2.7%	2.2%	1.0%	19.3%
Kings County	339,197	30.2%	12.9%	14.2%	19.1%	14.2%	4.9%	2.8%	1.8%	24.2%
Monroe County	72,332	25.2%	16.8%	19.3%	22.7%	12.0%	2.7%	0.8%	0.5%	22.0%
Nassau County	109,032	25.1%	14.2%	15.0%	20.0%	16.6%	6.2%	2.3%	0.7%	7.9%
New York County	267,158	18.4%	10.4%	7.2%	17.7%	16.9%	11.5%	11.9%	6.0%	22.0%
Niagara County	16,713	34.5%	15.6%	12.3%	19.2%	17.9%	0.2%	0.3%	0.0%	21.1%
Oneida County	20,901	23.7%	15.4%	21.1%	32.4%	3.5%	2.9%	0.6%	0.5%	20.1%
Onondaga County	44,462	27.1%	15.4%	19.7%	21.8%	10.7%	4.0%	1.2%	0.2%	22.6%
Ontario County	8,177	23.0%	22.1%	21.4%	15.7%	10.8%	3.8%	3.1%	0.0%	12.8%
Orange County	28,316	30.2%	15.4%	13.4%	22.0%	9.2%	6.6%	3.0%	0.2%	16.6%
Oswego County	10,128	33.8%	30.5%	19.6%	7.3%	5.7%	2.7%	0.4%	0.0%	25.3%
Putnam County	6,983	28.5%	11.9%	29.2%	13.8%	8.3%	4.6%	3.7%	0.0%	4.3%
Queens County	264,786	27.7%	15.2%	14.3%	21.0%	13.2%	5.3%	2.3%	1.0%	18.5%
Rensselaer County	15,821	15.2%	13.0%	26.4%	23.4%	12.7%	8.7%	0.7%	0.0%	21.7%
Richmond County	41,684	32.4%	12.3%	11.7%	19.4%	17.1%	4.6%	2.3%	0.3%	19.6%
Rockland County	26,007	26.1%	21.7%	14.7%	17.3%	13.6%	4.6%	2.0%	0.0%	19.1%
Saratoga County	18,865	10.6%	10.0%	19.7%	33.7%	17.3%	5.4%	1.8%	1.4%	12.9%
Schenectady County	15,167	18.1%	21.5%	21.8%	27.5%	7.8%	1.3%	2.0%	0.0%	11.3%
St. Lawrence County	8,571	42.2%	17.8%	13.6%	16.9%	8.7%	0.0%	0.8%	0.0%	32.3%
Steuben County	6,679	31.8%	20.0%	9.0%	14.7%	19.1%	3.4%	1.8%	0.2%	23.7%
Suffolk County	121,458	24.1%	16.0%	14.9%	21.3%	14.5%	7.5%	1.2%	0.5%	7.5%
Tompkins County	10,063	19.9%	20.5%	22.1%	17.7%	16.2%	2.8%	0.8%	0.0%	32.6%
Ulster County	12,240	27.7%	16.1%	24.9%	19.5%	5.5%	5.2%	0.0%	1.2%	22.5%
Wayne County	7,636	25.0%	15.6%	15.5%	27.7%	6.6%	8.3%	0.6%	0.7%	12.6%
Westchester County	75,282	24.2%	11.7%	13.8%	24.5%	15.0%	7.0%	2.8%	0.9%	12.1%
North Carolina										
Alamance County	13,510	36.5%	18.9%	19.9%	10.3%	12.5%	1.9%	0.0%	0.0%	29.2%
Brunswick County	6,431	43.2%	8.0%	18.1%	19.4%	8.1%	0.0%	0.0%	3.2%	24.6%
Buncombe County	24,786	23.7%	31.4%	15.8%	17.9%	7.1%	2.0%	2.0%	0.0%	22.4%
Burke County	7,422	35.7%	14.1%	29.5%	15.4%	0.8%	4.4%	0.0%	0.0%	29.4%
Cabarrus County	15,403	19.3%	28.9%	12.4%	26.5%	9.0%	1.2%	2.7%	0.0%	18.6%
Catawba County	10,681	30.2%	13.8%	21.1%	29.4%	2.3%	2.2%	0.9%	0.0%	18.5%
Cleveland County	7,240	40.9%	19.6%	16.8%	14.4%	8.3%	0.0%	0.0%	0.0%	22.9%
Craven County	11,776	33.6%	17.2%	15.1%	24.8%	4.7%	1.0%	3.7%	0.0%	13.4%
Cumberland County	40,200	32.9%	12.0%	15.9%	24.8%	12.9%	1.1%	0.3%	0.0%	18.3%
Davidson County	11,987	36.0%	13.5%	23.2%	18.8%	6.9%	0.9%	0.0%	0.8%	27.1%
Durham County	38,220	23.8%	20.8%	17.8%	22.1%	12.9%	1.4%	0.8%	0.5%	24.6%
Forsyth County	29,296	34.6%	14.8%	16.6%	22.9%	8.1%	2.2%	0.0%	0.8%	30.0%
Gaston County	16,649	30.2%	22.6%	16.9%	24.6%	5.0%	0.3%	0.0%	0.3%	27.2%
Guilford County	49,074	23.8%	27.5%	19.2%	19.9%	6.8%	2.0%	0.4%	0.4%	26.0%
Harnett County	14,304	39.3%	17.0%	9.3%	13.6%	16.5%	3.2%	1.0%	0.0%	21.5%
Henderson County	6,726	17.3%	32.9%	17.9%	26.0%	3.0%	0.0%	1.7%	1.2%	12.7%
Iredell County	12,177	34.9%	18.4%	16.8%	22.0%	6.3%	0.9%	0.7%	0.0%	16.7%
Johnston County	12,811	31.1%	11.4%	13.8%	34.4%	9.3%	0.0%	0.0%	0.0%	23.0%
Mecklenburg County	116,413	22.6%	14.9%	19.7%	24.5%	11.4%	4.2%	1.8%	0.8%	19.7%
Moore County	7,390	31.6%	11.1%	7.5%	33.8%	12.0%	3.3%	0.7%	0.0%	18.8%
Nash County	6,251	53.4%	13.6%	10.0%	21.2%	0.0%	1.9%	0.0%	0.0%	26.3%
New Hanover County	19,974	20.4%	18.8%	18.1%	30.8%	7.7%	2.8%	1.5%	0.0%	31.3%
Onslow County	27,113	29.8%	21.3%	14.9%	25.5%	7.9%	0.3%	0.0%	0.3%	18.2%
Orange County	12,800	17.8%	18.5%	19.6%	28.7%	12.0%	0.8%	2.1%	0.5%	33.2%
Pitt County	15,455	23.0%	15.3%	13.1%	28.4%	12.0%	5.6%	1.9%	0.8%	42.7%
Randolph County	11,575	23.4%	21.1%	19.1%	29.1%	6.4%	0.0%	1.0%	0.0%	25.6%
Robeson County	10,319	43.3%	24.0%	13.6%	13.5%	4.2%	0.4%	1.1%	0.0%	38.8%
Rockingham County	8,205	27.0%	22.3%	20.5%	26.8%	3.4%	0.0%	0.0%	0.0%	22.8%
Rowan County	10,364	47.8%	15.8%	11.4%	23.1%	1.9%	0.0%	0.0%	0.0%	20.7%
Union County	13,295	23.1%	15.3%	17.7%	33.2%	5.6%	1.4%	3.6%	0.0%	9.6%
Wake County	94,100	21.8%	15.6%	14.7%	28.9%	13.5%	3.5%	1.5%	0.4%	16.1%
Wayne County	11,414	25.9%	13.5%	23.7%	22.2%	12.1%	2.5%	0.0%	0.0%	18.2%
North Dakota										
Cass County	19,202	16.6%	11.4%	15.3%	40.2%	12.4%	1.6%	2.5%	0.0%	21.1%
Ohio										
Allen County	8,973	28.2%	26.0%	16.5%	19.8%	8.3%	0.5%	0.7%	0.0%	19.0%
Ashtabula County	8,300	27.9%	17.3%	18.2%	21.3%	14.4%	0.9%	0.0%	0.0%	19.8%
Butler County	30,689	30.8%	11.3%	18.6%	24.2%	9.3%	2.6%	2.7%	0.4%	20.2%
Clark County	10,946	29.9%	18.4%	23.2%	22.9%	4.8%	0.8%	0.0%	0.0%	28.8%
Clermont County	17,828	20.3%	19.3%	20.4%	24.4%	10.1%	5.2%	0.3%	0.0%	10.3%
Columbiana County	8,795	44.3%	13.1%	18.1%	14.2%	10.4%	0.0%	0.0%	0.0%	22.7%
Cuyahoga County	115,142	27.6%	15.8%	18.4%	22.2%	12.4%	2.3%	0.8%	0.5%	23.2%
Delaware County	12,106	14.0%	16.9%	13.6%	33.3%	17.2%	3.9%	0.4%	0.6%	6.4%
Fairfield County	13,666	22.4%	17.1%	16.1%	27.6%	13.8%	2.3%	0.7%	0.0%	15.7%
Franklin County	154,793	20.0%	16.5%	18.4%	26.6%	13.2%	2.5%	1.9%	1.0%	21.5%
Geauga County	5,095	12.0%	28.8%	16.8%	25.8%	8.4%	8.2%	0.0%	0.0%	4.0%
Greene County	15,965	25.5%	11.6%	18.2%	21.2%	13.1%	6.1%	3.9%	0.4%	22.0%

Table I-2: Counties—Income Class by Age—*Continued*

	Total Millennials	Under $10,000	$10,000 to $19,999	$20,000 to $29,999	$30,000 to $49,999	$50,000 to $74,999	$75,000 to $99,999	$100,000 or More
Ohio—Cont.								
Hamilton County	79,971	57.7%	22.4%	11.3%	6.6%	1.2%	0.3%	0.4%
Lake County	19,679	65.0%	24.4%	7.9%	1.4%	0.7%	0.5%	0.0%
Licking County	14,831	65.0%	18.0%	11.7%	5.2%	0.1%	0.0%	0.0%
Lorain County	27,287	67.4%	18.6%	7.6%	5.3%	1.1%	0.0%	0.0%
Lucas County	46,770	62.4%	23.8%	9.5%	4.2%	0.1%	0.0%	0.0%
Mahoning County	20,067	68.9%	21.9%	6.8%	1.8%	0.5%	0.0%	0.0%
Medina County	13,092	56.7%	20.3%	14.6%	8.5%	0.0%	0.0%	0.0%
Miami County	9,000	44.3%	23.3%	9.6%	19.9%	2.9%	0.0%	0.0%
Montgomery County	52,950	67.4%	20.0%	8.3%	3.4%	0.8%	0.0%	0.0%
Portage County	30,634	63.8%	19.8%	12.1%	3.5%	0.5%	0.0%	0.2%
Richland County	10,958	76.6%	11.3%	9.0%	1.5%	1.6%	0.0%	0.0%
Stark County	33,908	59.1%	22.1%	11.7%	3.7%	2.7%	0.0%	0.6%
Summit County	50,125	63.0%	17.6%	9.5%	8.1%	1.4%	0.0%	0.4%
Trumbull County	15,334	62.1%	23.6%	12.7%	1.6%	0.0%	0.0%	0.0%
Tuscarawas County	7,243	66.2%	13.4%	9.7%	7.0%	1.0%	2.6%	0.0%
Warren County	16,382	66.7%	25.9%	4.1%	2.9%	0.3%	0.0%	0.0%
Wayne County	11,137	56.7%	20.8%	16.8%	5.8%	0.0%	0.0%	0.0%
Wood County	19,374	74.4%	8.5%	11.5%	5.6%	0.1%	0.0%	0.0%
Oklahoma								
Canadian County	10,297	61.1%	5.9%	14.3%	15.2%	3.5%	0.0%	0.0%
Cleveland County	41,466	56.5%	24.9%	11.1%	6.7%	0.4%	0.0%	0.5%
Comanche County	17,467	47.3%	27.6%	7.1%	15.4%	2.5%	0.0%	0.0%
Oklahoma County	72,868	55.1%	17.7%	15.8%	7.9%	2.5%	0.6%	0.4%
Tulsa County	59,491	55.8%	22.8%	12.9%	7.2%	0.9%	0.1%	0.2%
Oregon								
Clackamas County	31,816	56.2%	24.3%	11.7%	5.9%	0.9%	0.7%	0.3%
Deschutes County	11,498	53.9%	26.6%	13.9%	5.1%	0.6%	0.0%	0.0%
Douglas County	7,684	65.1%	19.1%	10.1%	4.1%	1.7%	0.0%	0.0%
Jackson County	17,320	50.5%	29.9%	11.1%	6.8%	1.7%	0.0%	0.0%
Lane County	48,062	74.8%	16.0%	5.4%	3.2%	0.4%	0.0%	0.3%
Linn County	15,594	68.2%	23.1%	5.1%	3.6%	0.0%	0.0%	0.0%
Marion County	34,348	56.9%	24.1%	10.8%	6.6%	1.6%	0.0%	0.0%
Multnomah County	68,115	61.4%	22.0%	8.9%	6.2%	1.4%	0.1%	0.0%
Washington County	47,001	57.6%	25.8%	8.9%	5.8%	1.6%	0.1%	0.2%
Yamhill County	9,740	57.7%	25.7%	16.1%	0.5%	0.0%	0.0%	0.0%
Pennsylvania								
Adams County	11,103	68.5%	15.5%	13.3%	2.2%	0.5%	0.0%	0.0%
Allegheny County	117,461	62.8%	17.7%	10.0%	7.4%	1.9%	0.0%	0.2%
Beaver County	14,952	59.7%	27.7%	6.5%	2.6%	3.1%	0.3%	0.0%
Berks County	42,753	67.0%	15.8%	10.9%	6.3%	0.0%	0.0%	0.8%
Blair County	12,217	69.7%	8.9%	11.7%	6.0%	3.7%	0.0%	0.0%
Bucks County	47,975	66.9%	14.5%	7.7%	10.4%	0.5%	0.0%	0.0%
Butler County	17,255	64.8%	17.3%	8.8%	7.2%	1.4%	0.0%	0.5%
Cambria County	13,064	66.7%	14.4%	7.0%	6.1%	5.1%	0.8%	0.0%
Centre County	44,131	74.3%	13.5%	6.4%	4.4%	1.3%	0.0%	0.0%
Chester County	45,204	56.5%	19.0%	11.0%	12.1%	1.4%	0.0%	0.0%
Cumberland County	23,970	65.5%	19.2%	10.1%	4.2%	1.0%	0.0%	0.0%
Dauphin County	21,555	61.2%	17.8%	13.7%	6.2%	1.0%	0.0%	0.0%
Delaware County	59,250	77.3%	11.0%	5.5%	4.6%	1.4%	0.0%	0.1%
Erie County	30,889	71.3%	17.5%	8.4%	2.1%	0.0%	0.0%	0.6%
Fayette County	10,191	71.0%	14.5%	8.9%	5.1%	0.5%	0.0%	0.0%
Franklin County	12,550	65.2%	18.4%	10.9%	4.8%	0.0%	0.0%	0.7%
Lackawanna County	22,248	68.0%	20.4%	4.3%	5.4%	0.7%	0.0%	1.3%
Lancaster County	50,977	59.3%	23.6%	10.2%	5.2%	1.4%	0.0%	0.3%
Lebanon County	10,926	60.0%	16.3%	13.5%	8.5%	1.6%	0.0%	0.0%
Lehigh County	32,576	65.1%	17.8%	9.3%	5.6%	2.3%	0.0%	0.0%
Luzerne County	32,579	62.0%	21.1%	9.1%	5.7%	1.8%	0.3%	0.0%
Lycoming County	14,169	70.8%	16.4%	3.9%	7.6%	1.4%	0.1%	0.0%
Mercer County	11,450	71.0%	17.1%	6.7%	3.3%	0.0%	1.9%	0.0%
Monroe County	19,021	70.7%	12.6%	12.3%	4.0%	0.4%	0.0%	0.0%
Montgomery County	63,883	65.0%	16.6%	7.9%	8.1%	2.4%	0.1%	0.0%
Northampton County	28,977	73.8%	8.4%	10.7%	3.8%	1.8%	1.6%	0.0%
Northumberland County	7,804	59.5%	14.8%	15.7%	4.1%	6.0%	0.0%	0.0%
Philadelphia County	188,718	73.6%	12.1%	6.6%	5.9%	1.6%	0.0%	0.0%
Schuylkill County	11,168	68.6%	21.5%	6.1%	3.8%	0.0%	0.0%	0.0%
Washington County	17,971	62.0%	19.4%	12.0%	3.8%	1.7%	0.7%	0.3%
Westmoreland County	30,175	60.8%	20.1%	11.9%	4.0%	2.1%	1.1%	0.0%
York County	39,152	57.4%	26.3%	9.3%	6.0%	0.7%	0.3%	0.0%
Rhode Island								
Kent County	12,404	60.9%	17.0%	16.5%	4.4%	1.2%	0.0%	0.0%
Providence County	74,088	66.0%	19.9%	8.8%	4.6%	0.3%	0.4%	0.1%
Washington County	19,306	71.3%	19.9%	3.9%	5.0%	0.0%	0.0%	0.0%
South Carolina								
Aiken County	15,125	70.7%	14.3%	6.1%	7.3%	1.6%	0.0%	0.0%
Anderson County	15,743	67.6%	14.8%	10.8%	6.8%	0.0%	0.0%	0.0%
Beaufort County	15,335	52.3%	26.9%	5.6%	15.2%	0.0%	0.0%	0.0%
Berkeley County	20,467	57.0%	28.2%	6.0%	7.8%	1.0%	0.0%	0.0%

The header spanning the data columns reads: Personal Income, Percent by Income Class, Ages 18 to 24

Table I-2: Counties—Income Class by Age—*Continued*

	Total Millennials	Under $10,000	$10,000 to $19,999	$20,000 to $29,999	$30,000 to $49,999	$50,000 to $74,999	$75,000 to $99,999	$100,000 to $149,999	$150,000 or More	Poverty Rate
Ohio—Cont.										
Hamilton County	81,761	25.8%	13.8%	18.6%	25.2%	11.6%	2.9%	1.7%	0.4%	23.2%
Lake County	18,229	16.5%	12.8%	15.3%	34.0%	16.1%	4.5%	0.7%	0.7%	12.5%
Licking County	13,750	16.3%	20.0%	26.3%	16.6%	17.2%	0.7%	2.9%	0.0%	10.9%
Lorain County	23,098	36.8%	17.1%	14.5%	18.7%	8.0%	2.8%	2.2%	0.0%	19.5%
Lucas County	41,028	33.1%	20.0%	11.8%	21.6%	11.3%	0.6%	1.3%	0.2%	24.4%
Mahoning County	19,609	29.1%	16.8%	19.5%	14.7%	14.1%	2.9%	0.7%	2.2%	20.5%
Medina County	13,016	18.0%	17.8%	19.5%	20.5%	21.3%	2.3%	0.6%	0.0%	6.1%
Miami County	9,293	34.1%	15.3%	16.5%	22.5%	11.6%	0.0%	0.0%	0.0%	11.7%
Montgomery County	48,832	27.5%	19.5%	19.2%	17.9%	13.3%	1.3%	0.5%	0.8%	25.3%
Portage County	12,682	27.7%	14.7%	20.1%	24.1%	11.1%	2.3%	0.0%	0.0%	32.3%
Richland County	9,405	38.1%	27.4%	14.3%	13.9%	6.3%	0.0%	0.0%	0.0%	19.0%
Stark County	30,672	30.6%	19.7%	19.6%	20.7%	5.4%	0.2%	2.3%	1.5%	18.7%
Summit County	49,169	24.2%	15.3%	19.7%	21.6%	11.6%	6.3%	0.8%	0.4%	20.1%
Trumbull County	15,627	35.6%	24.3%	17.8%	12.1%	8.6%	1.6%	0.0%	0.0%	29.8%
Tuscarawas County	7,249	35.7%	17.0%	13.6%	25.1%	8.6%	0.0%	0.0%	0.0%	18.6%
Warren County	17,474	20.5%	14.0%	13.0%	20.9%	17.5%	5.7%	4.6%	3.8%	9.3%
Wayne County	8,719	32.1%	21.5%	9.6%	28.5%	4.2%	4.0%	0.0%	0.0%	16.6%
Wood County	12,388	22.0%	17.3%	17.0%	22.4%	18.3%	0.7%	2.3%	0.0%	22.2%
Oklahoma										
Canadian County	10,799	16.1%	11.2%	20.0%	38.8%	7.7%	1.9%	3.5%	0.8%	6.4%
Cleveland County	30,376	31.1%	14.1%	17.5%	20.9%	12.8%	2.9%	0.7%	0.0%	24.1%
Comanche County	14,657	36.6%	17.7%	24.5%	18.0%	1.8%	0.5%	0.9%	0.0%	27.0%
Oklahoma County	87,297	25.8%	15.7%	19.9%	23.9%	8.2%	3.1%	2.9%	0.5%	20.1%
Tulsa County	65,454	27.5%	18.0%	21.1%	21.3%	7.5%	3.2%	1.2%	0.2%	19.7%
Oregon										
Clackamas County	30,513	28.3%	18.9%	16.2%	26.6%	5.1%	2.0%	1.4%	1.5%	15.1%
Deschutes County	14,309	28.8%	15.3%	23.2%	19.9%	8.3%	2.3%	2.3%	0.0%	14.4%
Douglas County	7,735	36.8%	26.1%	7.9%	17.9%	7.5%	1.3%	2.5%	0.0%	24.8%
Jackson County	16,879	29.0%	10.2%	17.0%	28.6%	13.5%	1.7%	0.0%	0.0%	18.1%
Lane County	30,151	34.4%	17.2%	17.0%	24.5%	3.4%	0.2%	2.4%	1.0%	36.4%
Linn County	8,247	41.3%	20.9%	15.0%	14.8%	6.1%	1.9%	0.0%	0.0%	40.8%
Marion County	26,382	36.3%	16.0%	18.0%	17.3%	8.0%	4.2%	0.3%	0.0%	24.8%
Multnomah County	97,558	27.4%	19.2%	18.3%	17.6%	11.1%	3.6%	2.1%	0.8%	27.1%
Washington County	59,587	25.2%	14.0%	18.6%	21.8%	13.1%	5.1%	1.6%	0.6%	14.0%
Yamhill County	8,782	30.5%	14.8%	17.6%	22.9%	13.1%	0.0%	1.0%	0.0%	28.8%
Pennsylvania										
Adams County	6,631	32.4%	16.4%	14.3%	21.4%	10.4%	4.2%	1.0%	0.0%	12.6%
Allegheny County	128,389	20.1%	15.7%	16.3%	27.5%	14.4%	3.1%	1.9%	1.0%	20.6%
Beaver County	12,583	24.2%	18.2%	18.5%	27.8%	9.3%	1.7%	0.3%	0.0%	16.3%
Berks County	34,585	18.4%	15.3%	14.9%	35.6%	12.3%	2.0%	1.0%	0.5%	17.7%
Blair County	10,280	21.2%	27.0%	17.9%	20.5%	7.5%	5.7%	0.0%	0.3%	20.4%
Bucks County	48,860	25.4%	14.2%	12.6%	25.5%	16.1%	3.2%	1.8%	1.2%	8.1%
Butler County	14,392	16.5%	17.4%	9.4%	23.5%	17.0%	12.0%	4.3%	0.0%	13.6%
Cambria County	10,546	33.4%	21.1%	17.5%	21.8%	5.2%	0.9%	0.0%	0.0%	22.3%
Centre County	13,999	29.1%	19.1%	20.7%	19.2%	7.3%	2.7%	0.2%	1.7%	43.9%
Chester County	42,874	17.8%	11.0%	14.3%	33.3%	17.4%	3.1%	2.8%	0.2%	9.5%
Cumberland County	20,205	25.2%	18.0%	17.9%	22.9%	9.6%	6.0%	0.0%	0.4%	16.4%
Dauphin County	25,438	25.2%	12.9%	12.2%	29.5%	17.3%	1.6%	1.1%	0.3%	19.3%
Delaware County	49,731	30.5%	13.9%	14.0%	25.4%	11.0%	3.2%	1.8%	0.3%	14.3%
Erie County	27,602	23.4%	17.4%	20.4%	28.4%	7.0%	3.1%	0.3%	0.0%	24.4%
Fayette County	10,232	40.0%	17.0%	13.0%	19.0%	2.5%	3.3%	4.8%	0.4%	24.3%
Franklin County	13,689	25.4%	13.0%	15.8%	23.8%	17.5%	1.7%	2.8%	0.0%	12.4%
Lackawanna County	18,141	23.6%	22.4%	17.7%	21.3%	11.7%	2.1%	1.1%	0.2%	13.5%
Lancaster County	47,497	22.5%	12.5%	15.2%	29.4%	14.4%	2.6%	1.5%	1.9%	15.7%
Lebanon County	9,178	31.1%	11.0%	12.0%	32.3%	12.3%	1.1%	0.3%	0.0%	17.7%
Lehigh County	30,683	28.9%	17.2%	14.1%	23.0%	13.0%	1.7%	1.7%	0.5%	21.7%
Luzerne County	26,466	31.0%	19.1%	17.8%	22.1%	7.8%	1.9%	0.5%	0.0%	22.6%
Lycoming County	9,160	35.8%	12.2%	14.5%	25.6%	9.2%	2.4%	0.0%	0.3%	15.1%
Mercer County	8,634	26.7%	21.4%	22.6%	19.6%	7.9%	1.9%	0.0%	0.0%	18.5%
Monroe County	10,573	24.9%	14.1%	11.7%	40.9%	5.7%	2.8%	0.0%	0.0%	20.7%
Montgomery County	71,732	17.7%	11.2%	16.5%	25.7%	19.0%	7.1%	2.2%	0.6%	7.0%
Northampton County	25,692	26.5%	15.3%	15.3%	23.9%	11.8%	4.7%	0.3%	2.2%	17.4%
Northumberland County	7,950	34.1%	14.8%	20.2%	8.8%	13.6%	3.9%	3.5%	1.2%	20.6%
Philadelphia County	198,742	31.8%	13.3%	13.4%	22.7%	13.3%	3.9%	1.4%	0.2%	31.5%
Schuylkill County	11,697	29.7%	20.2%	13.7%	28.3%	6.7%	0.2%	1.2%	0.0%	18.6%
Washington County	15,972	27.1%	16.1%	15.9%	25.3%	11.4%	2.8%	1.4%	0.0%	17.0%
Westmoreland County	23,724	23.5%	19.8%	16.0%	20.2%	16.2%	2.6%	1.3%	0.4%	14.8%
York County	35,545	21.1%	14.4%	17.3%	32.7%	9.9%	2.1%	2.4%	0.0%	15.2%
Rhode Island										
Kent County	14,050	15.3%	13.9%	21.4%	26.6%	20.6%	2.3%	0.0%	0.0%	9.9%
Providence County	65,917	26.4%	19.1%	14.1%	26.0%	9.0%	4.4%	0.8%	0.2%	22.4%
Washington County	6,598	19.7%	20.5%	8.2%	26.9%	21.3%	2.9%	0.5%	0.0%	17.2%
South Carolina										
Aiken County	14,493	35.0%	21.2%	22.2%	13.7%	5.7%	1.3%	0.9%	0.0%	20.0%
Anderson County	15,660	25.6%	16.8%	25.3%	22.7%	8.9%	0.7%	0.0%	0.0%	22.5%
Beaufort County	14,005	36.0%	17.2%	16.8%	20.8%	9.3%	0.0%	0.0%	0.0%	19.5%
Berkeley County	20,800	23.9%	19.8%	15.6%	21.0%	10.9%	7.9%	0.8%	0.0%	21.3%

Table I-2: Counties—Income Class by Age—*Continued*

	Personal Income, Percent by Income Class, Ages 18 to 24							
	Total Millennials	Under $10,000	$10,000 to $19,999	$20,000 to $29,999	$30,000 to $49,999	$50,000 to $74,999	$75,000 to $99,999	$100,000 or More
South Carolina—Cont.								
Charleston County	41,902	64.9%	19.2%	8.2%	6.7%	0.9%	0.0%	0.0%
Dorchester County	16,093	62.5%	19.0%	10.8%	5.0%	2.7%	0.0%	0.0%
Florence County	14,181	71.6%	16.9%	6.0%	3.5%	2.0%	0.0%	0.0%
Greenville County	47,093	68.0%	18.3%	9.7%	3.8%	0.2%	0.0%	0.0%
Horry County	26,544	55.0%	33.2%	8.6%	2.0%	1.3%	0.0%	0.0%
Lexington County	25,109	62.0%	13.5%	14.7%	8.8%	0.5%	0.4%	0.0%
Orangeburg County	10,222	75.1%	8.7%	9.9%	6.3%	0.0%	0.0%	0.0%
Pickens County	19,673	76.8%	14.1%	6.7%	2.3%	0.0%	0.0%	0.0%
Richland County	62,983	62.1%	22.9%	10.3%	4.8%	0.0%	0.0%	0.0%
Spartanburg County	30,878	61.1%	22.7%	9.6%	6.2%	0.3%	0.0%	0.0%
Sumter County	12,753	62.5%	20.3%	10.2%	6.9%	0.0%	0.0%	0.0%
York County	22,992	71.4%	11.4%	9.2%	7.5%	0.4%	0.0%	0.0%
South Dakota								
Minnehaha County	18,746	47.9%	24.9%	19.0%	6.1%	0.2%	0.0%	1.9%
Pennington County	11,112	48.2%	24.1%	21.1%	6.6%	0.0%	0.0%	0.0%
Tennessee								
Blount County	10,855	57.8%	34.8%	2.8%	3.4%	1.2%	0.0%	0.0%
Bradley County	10,249	71.9%	14.2%	12.4%	1.5%	0.0%	0.0%	0.0%
Davidson County	69,097	60.3%	20.8%	9.0%	5.9%	3.5%	0.3%	0.2%
Hamilton County	33,512	68.0%	19.0%	9.4%	2.7%	0.9%	0.0%	0.0%
Knox County	54,317	68.2%	15.3%	12.0%	4.3%	0.2%	0.0%	0.0%
Madison County	10,133	78.5%	9.7%	8.3%	2.9%	0.6%	0.0%	0.0%
Montgomery County	22,598	52.1%	16.7%	12.5%	16.7%	2.1%	0.0%	0.0%
Rutherford County	36,951	54.9%	28.7%	10.9%	3.9%	1.2%	0.0%	0.5%
Sevier County	10,006	60.9%	22.7%	11.9%	4.5%	0.0%	0.0%	0.0%
Shelby County	97,843	69.0%	16.6%	7.4%	6.3%	0.7%	0.0%	0.1%
Sullivan County	11,805	65.4%	25.8%	4.0%	4.8%	0.0%	0.0%	0.0%
Sumner County	14,205	60.5%	14.5%	14.8%	8.8%	1.3%	0.0%	0.0%
Washington County	15,096	69.6%	22.1%	7.0%	0.5%	0.7%	0.0%	0.1%
Williamson County	14,237	77.1%	16.8%	3.0%	1.6%	1.4%	0.0%	0.0%
Wilson County	9,764	60.3%	26.5%	7.7%	5.4%	0.0%	0.0%	0.0%
Texas								
Bell County	41,977	55.3%	19.0%	17.2%	7.7%	0.3%	0.5%	0.0%
Bexar County	199,950	64.2%	19.7%	9.6%	4.8%	1.4%	0.2%	0.2%
Bowie County	9,884	67.6%	23.4%	8.1%	0.5%	0.4%	0.0%	0.0%
Brazoria County	28,706	54.1%	25.2%	13.6%	4.4%	2.0%	0.7%	0.0%
Brazos County	57,384	70.5%	16.9%	6.8%	5.0%	0.7%	0.0%	0.0%
Cameron County	44,095	76.2%	14.1%	5.8%	3.7%	0.0%	0.1%	0.0%
Collin County	69,090	57.5%	20.0%	10.7%	7.4%	4.0%	0.4%	0.0%
Comal County	9,523	58.3%	27.1%	4.6%	10.0%	0.0%	0.0%	0.0%
Dallas County	244,435	59.6%	20.0%	11.1%	6.9%	2.1%	0.2%	0.1%
Denton County	72,238	61.6%	21.5%	9.3%	6.4%	0.8%	0.2%	0.2%
Ector County	16,738	52.5%	17.4%	13.7%	7.4%	3.1%	4.8%	1.2%
El Paso County	99,494	65.1%	18.4%	12.3%	3.9%	0.4%	0.0%	0.0%
Ellis County	14,570	68.1%	15.5%	13.5%	2.3%	0.7%	0.0%	0.0%
Fort Bend County	54,417	72.3%	11.6%	9.9%	5.1%	0.8%	0.4%	0.0%
Galveston County	28,221	61.3%	20.2%	7.7%	7.2%	2.5%	1.0%	0.0%
Grayson County	11,527	62.7%	15.9%	11.4%	7.8%	1.9%	0.3%	0.0%
Gregg County	13,487	55.6%	33.8%	5.7%	3.2%	1.6%	0.0%	0.0%
Guadalupe County	13,089	67.5%	17.8%	6.6%	4.4%	0.8%	1.7%	1.1%
Harris County	428,939	60.0%	19.9%	11.8%	6.1%	1.6%	0.3%	0.2%
Hays County	30,303	65.2%	20.5%	10.7%	3.0%	0.6%	0.0%	0.0%
Hidalgo County	90,122	74.9%	14.5%	6.3%	3.4%	0.8%	0.0%	0.0%
Jefferson County	27,930	71.6%	12.4%	8.6%	4.0%	3.1%	0.3%	0.0%
Johnson County	13,976	59.3%	19.9%	11.5%	6.2%	3.0%	0.0%	0.0%
Kaufman County	9,526	68.8%	18.9%	7.7%	1.5%	3.1%	0.0%	0.0%
Lubbock County	51,030	64.6%	19.2%	9.6%	6.1%	0.5%	0.0%	0.0%
McLennan County	36,248	65.4%	21.1%	6.9%	5.2%	1.2%	0.2%	0.0%
Midland County	15,147	41.2%	24.5%	9.2%	14.0%	6.6%	2.7%	1.9%
Montgomery County	41,800	65.4%	17.6%	8.5%	5.9%	2.3%	0.0%	0.3%
Nueces County	36,773	52.7%	22.9%	7.8%	11.7%	3.6%	0.0%	1.3%
Parker County	10,340	54.5%	26.3%	13.1%	1.7%	4.4%	0.0%	0.0%
Potter County	12,335	50.2%	34.6%	8.9%	6.3%	0.0%	0.0%	0.0%
Randall County	12,985	57.8%	18.4%	11.9%	9.9%	0.0%	0.0%	1.9%
Smith County	22,466	70.6%	10.6%	14.4%	2.8%	1.0%	0.3%	0.4%
Tarrant County	182,581	57.6%	24.0%	10.2%	6.4%	1.2%	0.1%	0.4%
Taylor County	19,774	56.8%	21.3%	11.6%	8.6%	1.7%	0.0%	0.0%
Tom Green County	14,049	42.5%	33.1%	9.2%	9.9%	1.6%	3.4%	0.5%
Travis County	117,682	60.2%	20.6%	10.9%	6.1%	1.7%	0.2%	0.2%
Webb County	29,655	68.6%	21.6%	5.4%	4.1%	0.3%	0.0%	0.0%
Wichita County	17,764	55.9%	25.7%	8.1%	9.1%	0.0%	0.0%	1.3%
Williamson County	36,128	59.3%	23.0%	10.9%	5.7%	0.7%	0.1%	0.3%
Utah								
Cache County	18,490	55.9%	23.7%	14.3%	6.0%	0.0%	0.0%	0.0%
Davis County	29,660	56.8%	21.5%	11.7%	9.7%	0.2%	0.0%	0.0%
Salt Lake County	107,464	54.8%	21.5%	15.0%	7.2%	0.8%	0.5%	0.2%
Utah County	92,638	65.8%	19.0%	10.3%	3.9%	0.7%	0.0%	0.3%

Table I-2: Counties—Income Class by Age—*Continued*

	Personal Income, Percent by Income Class, Ages 25 to 31									
	Total Millennials	Under $10,000	$10,000 to $19,999	$20,000 to $29,999	$30,000 to $49,999	$50,000 to $74,999	$75,000 to $99,999	$100,000 to $149,999	$150,000 or More	Poverty Rate
South Carolina—Cont.										
Charleston County	42,223	20.3%	18.7%	15.7%	24.5%	13.8%	4.9%	1.7%	0.4%	22.6%
Dorchester County	11,263	28.2%	20.5%	20.9%	15.6%	10.2%	3.8%	0.8%	0.0%	23.8%
Florence County	11,255	41.4%	14.8%	12.2%	23.9%	7.8%	0.0%	0.0%	0.0%	31.8%
Greenville County	44,888	35.5%	12.6%	17.2%	21.5%	7.2%	3.3%	2.4%	0.3%	21.6%
Horry County	24,814	30.0%	22.9%	20.0%	22.6%	2.6%	1.7%	0.4%	0.0%	28.7%
Lexington County	23,604	27.3%	18.2%	20.8%	24.5%	7.2%	0.7%	0.6%	0.6%	16.9%
Orangeburg County	5,890	37.6%	10.6%	26.3%	17.2%	8.2%	0.0%	0.0%	0.0%	29.2%
Pickens County	10,695	41.2%	18.7%	20.6%	15.9%	2.8%	0.8%	0.0%	0.0%	25.8%
Richland County	41,177	34.2%	16.8%	11.6%	27.9%	7.3%	2.0%	0.0%	0.2%	28.1%
Spartanburg County	24,155	31.2%	22.0%	17.2%	19.8%	8.4%	0.2%	0.4%	0.9%	24.2%
Sumter County	9,642	40.3%	13.4%	15.3%	25.0%	5.4%	0.6%	0.0%	0.0%	32.1%
York County	16,944	23.7%	15.1%	22.7%	22.6%	8.9%	4.4%	2.6%	0.0%	19.1%
South Dakota										
Minnehaha County	21,330	15.9%	8.7%	24.0%	37.5%	10.6%	0.9%	2.4%	0.0%	11.8%
Pennington County	8,870	17.1%	14.4%	31.9%	22.0%	9.4%	4.2%	0.0%	0.9%	23.3%
Tennessee										
Blount County	8,977	28.1%	30.3%	14.8%	21.9%	2.9%	0.0%	0.0%	1.9%	25.5%
Bradley County	8,352	20.0%	10.0%	31.4%	28.4%	5.3%	0.0%	4.9%	0.0%	20.4%
Davidson County	90,142	21.5%	19.6%	18.1%	27.5%	9.1%	2.7%	1.1%	0.3%	20.3%
Hamilton County	34,559	32.1%	22.2%	17.1%	21.1%	4.9%	0.7%	1.4%	0.5%	22.6%
Knox County	43,946	24.3%	18.3%	20.6%	23.9%	7.8%	3.0%	2.1%	0.0%	25.5%
Madison County	8,001	42.8%	12.4%	13.7%	22.2%	8.9%	0.0%	0.0%	0.0%	30.5%
Montgomery County	25,885	27.3%	12.8%	13.6%	29.2%	13.2%	2.3%	1.5%	0.0%	19.0%
Rutherford County	28,383	20.6%	15.1%	17.6%	21.5%	20.1%	4.1%	0.6%	0.4%	18.3%
Sevier County	6,586	40.4%	9.9%	15.3%	31.1%	3.3%	0.0%	0.0%	0.0%	20.2%
Shelby County	95,682	32.7%	17.3%	14.0%	26.0%	7.5%	1.1%	0.9%	0.4%	27.0%
Sullivan County	10,983	32.5%	22.8%	18.8%	17.3%	1.9%	4.3%	0.6%	1.8%	21.0%
Sumner County	14,572	26.1%	20.4%	12.6%	23.8%	9.9%	3.6%	1.5%	2.2%	15.4%
Washington County	10,415	30.8%	16.6%	23.8%	18.9%	6.6%	2.3%	0.0%	1.0%	27.6%
Williamson County	11,899	13.8%	15.5%	14.5%	28.2%	20.1%	5.8%	0.7%	1.4%	7.6%
Wilson County	9,658	11.5%	19.6%	14.6%	37.0%	14.4%	2.2%	0.7%	0.0%	16.2%
Texas										
Bell County	39,091	31.7%	13.8%	13.1%	29.8%	8.4%	1.4%	0.5%	1.2%	14.5%
Bexar County	196,867	27.6%	17.5%	20.5%	20.9%	9.2%	2.5%	1.5%	0.2%	20.5%
Bowie County	9,680	37.8%	12.7%	27.2%	11.2%	4.2%	1.8%	2.0%	3.1%	28.3%
Brazoria County	34,540	25.3%	11.5%	17.0%	17.2%	18.4%	6.6%	3.2%	0.8%	11.6%
Brazos County	24,267	27.4%	20.1%	18.3%	19.7%	10.3%	3.5%	0.0%	0.8%	44.1%
Cameron County	33,550	41.2%	25.8%	9.9%	17.0%	4.6%	0.8%	0.7%	0.0%	33.1%
Collin County	68,580	19.7%	11.6%	13.0%	26.5%	19.5%	6.7%	2.4%	0.5%	11.1%
Comal County	8,822	16.0%	20.3%	13.4%	30.3%	16.0%	0.0%	1.1%	2.8%	15.3%
Dallas County	279,822	22.9%	20.0%	17.3%	23.4%	10.4%	3.2%	1.9%	0.8%	21.4%
Denton County	74,085	21.3%	12.1%	15.0%	30.8%	14.0%	4.4%	2.3%	0.2%	13.8%
Ector County	17,369	23.5%	14.5%	18.8%	16.7%	12.1%	5.4%	4.2%	4.7%	16.5%
El Paso County	82,562	33.8%	24.5%	14.4%	18.9%	5.1%	2.4%	0.6%	0.3%	25.8%
Ellis County	13,140	25.5%	19.8%	15.1%	25.3%	12.2%	0.7%	1.5%	0.0%	20.8%
Fort Bend County	53,038	25.9%	15.9%	17.5%	17.0%	11.4%	4.4%	6.8%	1.0%	11.9%
Galveston County	27,246	36.7%	10.8%	14.3%	19.6%	11.6%	3.7%	3.2%	0.0%	16.6%
Grayson County	11,410	33.3%	11.9%	18.7%	23.5%	9.0%	3.2%	0.5%	0.0%	21.9%
Gregg County	11,362	30.1%	24.1%	16.5%	19.5%	6.0%	3.7%	0.1%	0.0%	23.2%
Guadalupe County	11,517	22.1%	25.1%	14.0%	22.0%	13.2%	2.4%	0.7%	0.5%	11.8%
Harris County	499,981	26.2%	15.7%	16.3%	22.8%	11.5%	4.4%	1.9%	1.2%	20.3%
Hays County	17,040	28.5%	19.9%	16.1%	24.1%	9.0%	1.7%	0.0%	0.8%	28.6%
Hidalgo County	74,583	44.9%	19.1%	12.1%	15.3%	6.4%	1.2%	0.7%	0.3%	37.6%
Jefferson County	24,916	30.1%	18.6%	17.1%	16.0%	10.1%	1.9%	3.7%	2.5%	25.1%
Johnson County	13,773	41.0%	15.2%	8.2%	19.0%	8.4%	5.8%	1.6%	0.8%	16.8%
Kaufman County	7,868	28.3%	6.8%	19.6%	27.5%	13.0%	1.4%	1.6%	1.7%	11.1%
Lubbock County	28,515	27.1%	18.1%	17.2%	24.8%	8.5%	2.6%	0.3%	1.4%	24.6%
McLennan County	21,559	32.4%	20.9%	14.4%	25.9%	4.8%	0.5%	1.0%	0.0%	31.1%
Midland County	18,279	19.8%	11.4%	12.7%	20.2%	20.7%	8.2%	5.8%	1.3%	9.9%
Montgomery County	40,734	20.9%	18.8%	15.9%	25.1%	15.6%	3.2%	0.5%	0.1%	12.9%
Nueces County	34,597	26.2%	14.9%	19.8%	20.2%	12.1%	3.1%	3.4%	0.2%	18.9%
Parker County	9,903	45.1%	13.2%	13.3%	11.6%	12.7%	1.9%	0.0%	2.3%	14.1%
Potter County	12,465	34.4%	25.4%	18.2%	15.5%	5.5%	0.4%	0.7%	0.0%	28.8%
Randall County	13,695	27.4%	9.3%	14.7%	28.1%	10.4%	2.2%	7.5%	0.5%	23.5%
Smith County	19,748	25.0%	17.1%	22.1%	27.4%	6.1%	2.0%	0.0%	0.2%	21.5%
Tarrant County	203,238	22.3%	16.5%	17.4%	24.2%	14.9%	2.5%	1.7%	0.5%	18.9%
Taylor County	15,296	28.0%	9.3%	26.8%	20.9%	12.8%	2.2%	0.0%	0.0%	21.6%
Tom Green County	12,632	17.7%	21.9%	11.7%	34.8%	10.2%	1.4%	1.7%	0.6%	12.8%
Travis County	163,202	18.0%	18.0%	18.7%	25.2%	11.8%	5.6%	1.7%	1.1%	23.0%
Webb County	26,286	41.3%	19.0%	14.3%	11.2%	8.8%	4.2%	1.3%	0.0%	30.5%
Wichita County	15,130	33.6%	15.1%	17.1%	18.7%	15.0%	0.0%	0.5%	0.0%	25.7%
Williamson County	44,089	26.3%	14.3%	19.2%	23.8%	10.4%	3.3%	1.9%	0.8%	11.5%
Utah										
Cache County	14,765	26.2%	19.5%	13.1%	25.3%	13.9%	1.8%	0.1%	0.0%	17.8%
Davis County	30,520	37.0%	13.6%	15.9%	17.0%	14.5%	1.5%	0.4%	0.0%	13.1%
Salt Lake County	127,239	24.4%	16.0%	17.4%	27.2%	11.6%	1.8%	1.2%	0.5%	15.4%
Utah County	58,974	37.0%	17.1%	11.2%	20.6%	8.9%	3.2%	1.7%	0.4%	22.5%

Table I-2: Counties—Income Class by Age—*Continued*

		Personal Income, Percent by Income Class, Ages 18 to 24						
	Total Millennials	Under $10,000	$10,000 to $19,999	$20,000 to $29,999	$30,000 to $49,999	$50,000 to $74,999	$75,000 to $99,999	$100,000 or More
Utah—Cont.								
Washington County	14,931	62.6%	16.9%	14.1%	4.8%	0.0%	0.0%	1.6%
Weber County	22,158	53.8%	22.2%	15.7%	7.2%	1.1%	0.0%	0.0%
Vermont								
Chittenden County	23,207	59.5%	21.1%	12.8%	3.4%	1.6%	1.6%	0.0%
Virginia								
Albemarle County	11,502	80.5%	7.5%	4.4%	4.6%	3.0%	0.0%	0.0%
Arlington County	18,217	42.6%	14.2%	13.7%	14.9%	11.6%	3.0%	0.0%
Chesterfield County	30,892	58.4%	26.3%	7.3%	5.9%	1.5%	0.0%	0.6%
Fairfax County	95,982	63.1%	15.2%	8.8%	8.3%	3.6%	0.3%	0.7%
Hanover County	7,969	52.7%	14.0%	15.8%	17.5%	0.0%	0.0%	0.0%
Henrico County	27,360	58.7%	19.0%	13.9%	6.7%	1.4%	0.3%	0.0%
Loudoun County	22,990	63.1%	16.4%	10.1%	9.8%	0.3%	0.2%	0.0%
Montgomery County	29,989	79.4%	11.4%	4.9%	3.5%	0.0%	0.5%	0.2%
Prince William County	37,966	50.9%	23.4%	10.8%	11.6%	2.0%	0.6%	0.6%
Roanoke County	8,101	66.2%	23.1%	6.4%	3.3%	0.8%	0.0%	0.0%
Spotsylvania County	11,918	60.4%	22.4%	11.9%	3.3%	2.0%	0.0%	0.0%
Stafford County	16,747	52.4%	9.4%	17.9%	18.2%	2.0%	0.0%	0.0%
Washington								
Benton County	15,433	47.6%	22.1%	22.9%	6.5%	0.9%	0.0%	0.0%
Clark County	38,418	65.1%	17.6%	12.6%	2.7%	1.6%	0.2%	0.1%
Cowlitz County	8,540	61.6%	19.0%	15.4%	3.4%	0.6%	0.0%	0.0%
Grant County	11,733	59.5%	26.8%	7.4%	3.6%	0.7%	2.0%	0.0%
King County	177,207	59.5%	17.0%	10.1%	7.6%	2.6%	1.8%	1.4%
Kitsap County	25,705	53.3%	19.0%	19.5%	6.9%	1.3%	0.0%	0.0%
Pierce County	79,988	55.8%	19.0%	15.5%	7.4%	2.1%	0.0%	0.1%
Skagit County	11,075	61.6%	11.7%	12.6%	13.4%	0.8%	0.0%	0.0%
Snohomish County	64,845	59.7%	14.9%	11.4%	11.6%	2.0%	0.4%	0.0%
Spokane County	50,514	66.3%	17.8%	8.2%	5.8%	1.6%	0.0%	0.3%
Thurston County	24,463	61.6%	14.4%	11.1%	10.1%	1.6%	0.6%	0.6%
Whatcom County	31,693	59.7%	23.3%	12.0%	4.0%	0.6%	0.0%	0.4%
Yakima County	25,232	65.7%	20.1%	7.8%	6.3%	0.0%	0.0%	0.0%
West Virginia								
Berkeley County	9,880	79.2%	11.5%	3.6%	5.6%	0.0%	0.0%	0.0%
Cabell County	10,375	68.6%	11.1%	11.9%	3.9%	1.6%	2.8%	0.0%
Kanawha County	15,818	61.4%	25.8%	8.0%	3.3%	0.9%	0.6%	0.0%
Monongalia County	23,460	73.0%	13.0%	5.3%	7.4%	1.3%	0.0%	0.0%
Wisconsin								
Brown County	23,708	52.0%	30.8%	8.1%	8.1%	0.9%	0.0%	0.0%
Dane County	64,801	62.8%	18.4%	8.6%	5.2%	4.6%	0.0%	0.4%
Eau Claire County	17,113	60.5%	19.1%	13.1%	4.5%	2.8%	0.0%	0.0%
Fond du Lac County	9,137	60.8%	13.8%	15.5%	9.4%	0.4%	0.0%	0.0%
Kenosha County	16,352	67.8%	14.4%	15.6%	2.2%	0.0%	0.0%	0.0%
La Crosse County	18,390	58.1%	24.6%	10.4%	6.0%	0.9%	0.0%	0.0%
Marathon County	11,313	60.0%	23.1%	6.3%	10.6%	0.0%	0.0%	0.0%
Milwaukee County	99,896	65.5%	20.9%	8.8%	2.8%	2.0%	0.1%	0.0%
Outagamie County	16,864	68.8%	13.3%	11.2%	5.3%	1.3%	0.0%	0.0%
Racine County	15,071	63.5%	21.2%	8.1%	6.5%	0.7%	0.0%	0.0%
Rock County	14,267	57.7%	18.3%	20.2%	3.7%	0.0%	0.0%	0.0%
Sheboygan County	8,049	54.3%	7.4%	13.9%	24.3%	0.0%	0.0%	0.0%
Walworth County	11,281	76.7%	14.0%	8.2%	1.2%	0.0%	0.0%	0.0%
Washington County	11,187	73.0%	12.6%	8.1%	4.0%	2.3%	0.0%	0.0%
Waukesha County	30,739	56.0%	20.7%	14.0%	8.5%	0.8%	0.0%	0.0%
Winnebago County	20,693	55.5%	26.5%	9.2%	8.9%	0.0%	0.0%	0.0%
Wyoming								
Laramie County	12,437	60.4%	17.3%	12.6%	8.7%	0.0%	0.0%	1.0%

Table I-2: Counties—Income Class by Age—*Continued*

| | Personal Income, Percent by Income Class, Ages 25 to 31 | | | | | | | | | |
	Total Millennials	Under $10,000	$10,000 to $19,999	$20,000 to $29,999	$30,000 to $49,999	$50,000 to $74,999	$75,000 to $99,999	$100,000 to $149,999	$150,000 or More	Poverty Rate
Utah—Cont.										
Washington County	10,743	24.6%	10.6%	25.6%	22.8%	10.9%	4.5%	1.0%	0.0%	26.2%
Weber County	25,097	27.8%	18.0%	17.4%	25.2%	9.1%	0.6%	0.0%	1.9%	15.7%
Vermont										
Chittenden County	16,368	17.8%	14.0%	19.2%	35.3%	10.4%	2.6%	0.0%	0.7%	16.7%
Virginia										
Albemarle County	10,164	21.2%	19.2%	9.7%	28.5%	11.2%	5.5%	2.9%	1.7%	25.7%
Arlington County	47,231	12.9%	8.1%	8.2%	18.4%	28.6%	15.3%	6.3%	2.1%	13.7%
Chesterfield County	25,020	24.8%	17.5%	18.7%	26.5%	8.9%	1.8%	1.9%	0.0%	10.7%
Fairfax County	109,704	17.7%	9.4%	12.0%	20.7%	23.0%	10.1%	5.7%	1.4%	6.3%
Hanover County	8,001	13.4%	15.8%	13.3%	33.7%	20.7%	0.9%	0.8%	1.3%	7.7%
Henrico County	31,938	27.9%	9.5%	19.3%	25.3%	12.6%	3.5%	1.5%	0.5%	14.9%
Loudoun County	28,537	16.6%	9.0%	12.2%	21.9%	21.1%	9.1%	7.4%	2.6%	5.4%
Montgomery County	7,418	31.6%	10.1%	19.5%	26.4%	10.2%	0.0%	2.2%	0.0%	43.7%
Prince William County	43,664	19.4%	13.9%	19.0%	24.7%	14.3%	5.8%	2.7%	0.2%	6.8%
Roanoke County	6,842	32.8%	13.8%	15.9%	28.9%	7.2%	1.3%	0.0%	0.0%	19.6%
Spotsylvania County	9,884	35.7%	9.0%	10.3%	27.4%	11.1%	3.7%	1.8%	1.0%	15.1%
Stafford County	11,700	37.8%	15.3%	4.9%	23.6%	14.3%	2.9%	1.2%	0.0%	8.5%
Washington										
Benton County	16,029	26.3%	20.8%	14.4%	24.9%	10.8%	1.4%	0.7%	0.7%	19.5%
Clark County	36,785	31.5%	20.8%	18.7%	17.7%	7.8%	1.9%	1.4%	0.1%	15.9%
Cowlitz County	7,664	37.7%	20.6%	16.6%	12.9%	12.1%	0.0%	0.0%	0.0%	24.1%
Grant County	7,232	38.7%	10.4%	5.6%	28.8%	14.7%	1.8%	0.0%	0.0%	29.4%
King County	241,026	19.6%	14.8%	14.7%	24.6%	14.8%	4.5%	5.5%	1.5%	16.1%
Kitsap County	23,899	26.5%	15.8%	11.9%	25.5%	17.2%	2.0%	1.0%	0.0%	15.1%
Pierce County	85,958	24.5%	14.1%	20.5%	24.9%	12.3%	2.3%	0.9%	0.5%	18.1%
Skagit County	8,911	41.8%	16.8%	6.2%	28.6%	2.2%	4.4%	0.0%	0.0%	20.3%
Snohomish County	71,377	22.9%	12.9%	15.6%	27.1%	16.1%	4.1%	1.2%	0.0%	14.7%
Spokane County	50,622	28.1%	17.8%	17.3%	26.8%	6.5%	3.3%	0.0%	0.3%	24.9%
Thurston County	28,856	31.8%	18.7%	10.3%	21.6%	10.3%	4.9%	1.7%	0.7%	21.2%
Whatcom County	17,498	26.8%	18.8%	23.0%	19.1%	4.9%	4.4%	3.0%	0.0%	23.6%
Yakima County	22,351	24.3%	20.8%	20.4%	23.5%	9.1%	1.3%	0.6%	0.0%	20.5%
West Virginia										
Berkeley County	8,678	20.8%	22.8%	25.4%	16.9%	10.3%	2.9%	0.8%	0.0%	20.9%
Cabell County	8,673	30.8%	12.5%	25.1%	18.7%	10.4%	2.5%	0.0%	0.0%	30.2%
Kanawha County	16,505	20.7%	12.5%	25.1%	19.3%	18.2%	1.2%	2.3%	0.9%	21.6%
Monongalia County	13,906	39.9%	12.4%	19.9%	11.7%	8.7%	5.0%	2.0%	0.5%	32.6%
Wisconsin										
Brown County	23,266	16.5%	17.3%	28.0%	27.9%	7.6%	1.1%	0.6%	1.0%	14.7%
Dane County	62,196	15.7%	16.9%	16.3%	29.0%	13.5%	5.0%	2.9%	0.8%	23.9%
Eau Claire County	10,648	24.1%	13.4%	11.5%	24.5%	22.3%	0.4%	0.0%	3.8%	16.6%
Fond du Lac County	5,672	24.6%	14.3%	20.5%	28.3%	12.3%	0.0%	0.0%	0.0%	11.4%
Kenosha County	14,366	25.9%	13.3%	35.6%	12.1%	10.6%	1.1%	1.4%	0.0%	19.0%
La Crosse County	11,836	31.2%	12.7%	12.4%	27.9%	11.4%	3.4%	0.0%	0.9%	25.3%
Marathon County	11,030	21.5%	14.8%	27.8%	22.8%	7.2%	2.8%	1.9%	1.2%	20.0%
Milwaukee County	114,068	24.0%	20.4%	16.5%	23.7%	12.9%	2.0%	0.4%	0.1%	27.7%
Outagamie County	17,397	15.8%	15.3%	18.0%	30.4%	17.6%	2.8%	0.0%	0.0%	12.4%
Racine County	18,360	20.4%	28.3%	16.9%	24.5%	7.0%	3.0%	0.0%	0.0%	19.0%
Rock County	13,455	29.4%	16.7%	21.3%	22.5%	9.2%	0.4%	0.5%	0.0%	20.6%
Sheboygan County	9,109	19.0%	26.4%	18.6%	29.4%	5.1%	1.5%	0.0%	0.0%	13.6%
Walworth County	8,854	30.4%	21.3%	18.8%	16.8%	11.9%	0.9%	0.0%	0.0%	29.7%
Washington County	9,002	14.1%	11.4%	34.8%	18.9%	17.3%	2.1%	1.5%	0.0%	12.1%
Waukesha County	28,153	20.9%	14.7%	20.9%	18.2%	16.3%	5.7%	3.3%	0.0%	6.2%
Winnebago County	16,548	20.5%	17.8%	16.5%	25.0%	16.9%	2.4%	0.0%	0.9%	21.2%
Wyoming										
Laramie County	8,039	16.4%	8.7%	22.9%	31.9%	16.0%	3.1%	0.0%	1.1%	19.1%

Table I-3: Places—Income Class by Age

	Total Millennials	Personal Income, Percent by Income Class, Ages 18 to 24						
		Under $10,000	$10,000 to $19,999	$20,000 to $29,999	$30,000 to $49,999	$50,000 to $74,999	$75,000 to $99,999	$100,000 or More
Alabama								
Birmingham city	17,581	78.4%	13.4%	2.7%	4.1%	1.5%	0.0%	0.0%
Huntsville city	24,800	64.1%	23.0%	8.7%	3.1%	1.2%	0.0%	0.0%
Mobile city	20,309	63.2%	18.9%	8.3%	8.9%	0.3%	0.4%	0.0%
Montgomery city	58,842	66.4%	15.5%	13.1%	4.3%	0.6%	0.0%	0.1%
Tuscaloosa city	8,303	79.0%	7.8%	4.4%	8.7%	0.0%	0.0%	0.0%
Alaska								
Anchorage municipality	13,580	40.7%	18.1%	18.2%	15.4%	7.5%	0.1%	0.0%
Arizona								
Chandler city	20,974	52.8%	24.7%	16.8%	3.4%	1.9%	0.4%	0.0%
Glendale city	36,943	63.0%	14.7%	13.5%	8.8%	0.0%	0.0%	0.0%
Mesa city	34,074	60.4%	22.4%	11.0%	5.3%	0.6%	0.2%	0.0%
Peoria city	35,322	52.9%	29.2%	13.1%	4.7%	0.0%	0.0%	0.0%
Phoenix city	12,180	62.7%	19.7%	9.9%	7.0%	0.5%	0.1%	0.1%
Scottsdale city	38,088	57.6%	21.6%	8.3%	9.7%	2.9%	0.0%	0.0%
Surprise city	9,441	50.9%	21.6%	21.3%	3.1%	3.2%	0.0%	0.0%
Tempe city	36,028	66.4%	18.7%	9.7%	4.8%	0.5%	0.0%	0.0%
Tucson city	61,305	63.1%	21.2%	9.4%	5.9%	0.3%	0.0%	0.1%
Yuma city	21,555	64.8%	20.2%	7.9%	7.1%	0.0%	0.0%	0.0%
Arkansas								
Little Rock city	31,521	58.3%	15.6%	14.1%	11.0%	0.9%	0.0%	0.0%
California								
Anaheim city	17,229	63.3%	21.5%	10.1%	3.4%	1.6%	0.0%	0.2%
Antioch city	96,859	65.3%	14.4%	10.1%	8.6%	1.6%	0.0%	0.0%
Bakersfield city	39,371	62.5%	19.9%	9.4%	5.8%	1.2%	1.0%	0.2%
Berkeley city	66,366	64.8%	10.3%	11.8%	8.7%	3.7%	0.7%	0.1%
Burbank city	42,340	66.3%	21.7%	9.9%	2.2%	0.0%	0.0%	0.0%
Carlsbad city	15,412	66.5%	17.0%	9.2%	7.3%	0.0%	0.0%	0.0%
Carson city	7,397	74.6%	16.8%	2.4%	5.7%	0.5%	0.0%	0.0%
Chula Vista city	7,892	68.2%	16.9%	9.7%	3.2%	2.0%	0.0%	0.0%
Clovis city	26,469	58.6%	26.5%	11.2%	3.3%	0.4%	0.0%	0.0%
Compton city	12,115	68.9%	25.3%	5.8%	0.0%	0.0%	0.0%	0.0%
Concord city	24,818	53.4%	32.0%	10.2%	1.6%	2.8%	0.0%	0.0%
Corona city	23,692	70.7%	18.8%	5.9%	3.4%	1.1%	0.0%	0.0%
Costa Mesa city	93,252	57.3%	15.6%	16.0%	8.7%	2.4%	0.0%	0.0%
Daly City city	29,961	58.9%	18.5%	7.9%	12.6%	0.6%	0.0%	1.5%
Downey city	15,330	59.3%	14.3%	19.4%	6.8%	0.3%	0.0%	0.0%
El Cajon city	7,019	67.8%	24.9%	6.5%	0.8%	0.0%	0.0%	0.0%
El Monte city	8,364	72.8%	16.4%	7.1%	3.4%	0.0%	0.0%	0.2%
Elk Grove city	21,080	75.5%	15.2%	0.6%	6.5%	0.3%	1.6%	0.3%
Escondido city	32,188	57.3%	24.5%	15.6%	2.3%	0.3%	0.0%	0.0%
Fairfield city	6,721	69.3%	16.4%	8.0%	5.7%	0.7%	0.0%	0.0%
Fontana city	21,135	63.8%	16.7%	13.4%	4.1%	1.2%	0.8%	0.0%
Fremont city	12,044	63.9%	14.9%	10.8%	7.7%	0.9%	1.8%	0.0%
Fresno city	7,319	76.0%	16.3%	5.8%	1.9%	0.0%	0.0%	0.1%
Fullerton city	12,278	71.3%	18.6%	3.7%	3.9%	2.0%	0.0%	0.4%
Garden Grove city	10,757	64.2%	23.6%	6.5%	5.7%	0.0%	0.0%	0.0%
Glendale city	11,166	68.2%	15.3%	8.7%	3.8%	4.0%	0.0%	0.0%
Hayward city	7,068	53.6%	23.8%	11.8%	5.6%	4.3%	0.0%	0.9%
Hesperia city	22,227	63.6%	22.2%	8.3%	5.8%	0.0%	0.0%	0.0%
Inglewood city	16,578	70.8%	17.5%	8.1%	3.6%	0.0%	0.0%	0.0%
Irvine city	75,363	74.1%	9.1%	9.1%	5.6%	2.1%	0.0%	0.0%
Jurupa Valley city	18,173	76.3%	14.8%	6.0%	1.9%	1.1%	0.0%	0.0%
Lancaster city	21,964	63.4%	19.9%	10.6%	5.4%	0.7%	0.0%	0.0%
Long Beach city	281,204	69.2%	15.3%	7.8%	6.1%	0.8%	0.8%	0.0%
Los Angeles city	27,506	68.2%	18.1%	7.2%	4.7%	1.1%	0.6%	0.2%
Mission Viejo city	39,783	66.8%	18.0%	6.4%	3.0%	5.7%	0.0%	0.0%
Modesto city	17,831	54.6%	32.6%	7.3%	3.2%	2.4%	0.0%	0.0%
Moreno Valley city	8,279	59.5%	24.2%	7.3%	6.5%	2.5%	0.0%	0.0%
Murrieta city	46,059	79.8%	13.0%	3.3%	3.8%	0.0%	0.0%	0.0%
Norwalk city	11,520	74.1%	17.4%	5.1%	3.1%	0.2%	0.0%	0.0%
Oakland city	37,647	59.8%	21.9%	8.5%	8.3%	0.9%	0.1%	0.6%
Oceanside city	45,636	37.4%	20.5%	24.6%	14.9%	0.5%	2.1%	0.0%
Ontario city	28,006	63.4%	23.5%	8.1%	4.3%	0.7%	0.0%	0.0%
Orange city	33,216	71.3%	14.7%	5.2%	8.5%	0.4%	0.0%	0.0%
Oxnard city	24,790	52.5%	28.4%	11.2%	7.7%	0.2%	0.0%	0.0%
Palmdale city	89,448	71.9%	15.1%	11.9%	1.1%	0.0%	0.0%	0.0%
Pasadena city	10,355	65.9%	20.8%	5.4%	5.1%	0.7%	0.4%	1.7%
Pomona city	10,951	65.2%	19.7%	9.2%	2.9%	2.5%	0.5%	0.0%
Rancho Cucamonga city	13,970	64.6%	15.4%	12.1%	3.7%	4.2%	0.0%	0.0%
Redding city	16,818	58.8%	22.8%	10.4%	7.5%	0.0%	0.0%	0.4%
Rialto city	33,162	54.7%	21.0%	13.7%	8.5%	2.1%	0.0%	0.0%
Richmond city	10,818	66.0%	17.6%	10.9%	4.5%	0.0%	1.0%	0.0%
Riverside city	129,394	68.7%	19.3%	6.8%	4.6%	0.6%	0.0%	0.0%
Roseville city	11,075	64.5%	23.6%	1.2%	7.2%	3.6%	0.0%	0.0%
Sacramento city	9,550	69.3%	18.4%	7.3%	3.8%	1.1%	0.1%	0.0%
Salinas city	23,431	69.4%	22.0%	7.7%	0.9%	0.0%	0.0%	0.0%

Table I-3: Places—Income Class by Age—*Continued*

| | Personal Income, Percent by Income Class, Ages 25 to 31 | | | | | | | | | |
	Total Millennials	Under $10,000	$10,000 to $19,999	$20,000 to $29,999	$30,000 to $49,999	$50,000 to $74,999	$75,000 to $99,999	$100,000 to $149,999	$150,000 or More	Poverty Rate
Alabama										
Birmingham city	14,055	42.2%	18.6%	9.3%	18.7%	7.3%	2.6%	1.0%	0.3%	21.6%
Huntsville city	20,695	24.6%	23.3%	17.3%	19.1%	12.6%	2.4%	0.8%	0.0%	30.3%
Mobile city	14,704	35.3%	16.7%	17.6%	20.0%	5.8%	2.5%	2.0%	0.3%	33.5%
Montgomery city	54,748	36.2%	18.7%	16.8%	22.4%	3.6%	0.2%	0.5%	1.5%	25.2%
Tuscaloosa city	26,885	27.7%	10.2%	23.5%	26.3%	6.7%	2.4%	3.2%	0.0%	11.1%
Alaska										
Anchorage municipality	12,602	17.3%	12.3%	21.6%	28.2%	9.6%	8.1%	2.8%	0.0%	38.3%
Arizona										
Chandler city	21,743	23.7%	11.7%	14.0%	27.1%	13.6%	5.0%	4.4%	0.6%	27.1%
Glendale city	35,851	39.6%	13.6%	17.5%	19.7%	8.1%	0.9%	0.0%	0.6%	15.8%
Mesa city	35,653	26.1%	18.1%	21.8%	23.9%	6.6%	2.7%	0.5%	0.2%	7.4%
Peoria city	13,009	28.4%	11.6%	14.6%	21.7%	15.9%	2.4%	4.2%	1.1%	48.1%
Phoenix city	10,190	31.6%	13.7%	17.8%	22.3%	11.0%	2.0%	1.2%	0.5%	11.2%
Scottsdale city	43,442	17.3%	3.8%	15.1%	33.8%	21.4%	3.3%	3.8%	1.4%	20.4%
Surprise city	9,903	19.6%	5.9%	17.9%	21.5%	34.1%	1.0%	0.0%	0.0%	14.1%
Tempe city	13,785	20.8%	14.1%	20.1%	22.2%	16.0%	6.1%	0.7%	0.0%	51.9%
Tucson city	62,935	33.9%	19.1%	18.3%	18.1%	6.1%	2.6%	1.6%	0.4%	27.0%
Yuma city	23,346	33.0%	20.6%	16.7%	19.2%	5.6%	3.1%	1.2%	0.7%	34.3%
Arkansas										
Little Rock city	35,520	34.9%	25.8%	18.6%	16.8%	3.4%	0.5%	0.1%	0.0%	20.1%
California										
Anaheim city	21,072	28.4%	18.6%	17.2%	19.3%	9.8%	5.6%	1.1%	0.0%	15.6%
Antioch city	133,406	32.9%	21.9%	13.9%	21.6%	7.6%	2.2%	0.0%	0.0%	22.7%
Bakersfield city	39,901	34.4%	18.9%	19.1%	15.7%	7.4%	3.2%	0.9%	0.6%	23.2%
Berkeley city	81,284	23.9%	10.1%	8.0%	26.8%	18.5%	4.1%	4.6%	4.0%	24.6%
Burbank city	25,399	15.9%	13.4%	17.7%	31.4%	10.4%	3.7%	7.1%	0.3%	35.5%
Carlsbad city	11,553	26.2%	9.9%	13.3%	22.1%	15.4%	3.8%	6.4%	2.9%	23.1%
Carson city	11,528	36.2%	14.1%	12.0%	16.1%	11.5%	7.8%	0.0%	2.2%	13.5%
Chula Vista city	16,432	35.1%	15.3%	22.3%	13.8%	7.1%	2.7%	3.6%	0.0%	15.0%
Clovis city	17,350	19.3%	14.0%	16.5%	33.7%	7.7%	6.0%	1.3%	1.3%	34.4%
Compton city	9,279	36.1%	20.0%	23.5%	17.3%	2.4%	0.7%	0.0%	0.0%	23.9%
Concord city	23,982	20.4%	12.9%	15.6%	17.3%	21.1%	5.7%	6.4%	0.6%	37.5%
Corona city	23,021	26.7%	23.9%	14.6%	20.9%	8.4%	2.2%	2.8%	0.5%	30.7%
Costa Mesa city	109,618	21.7%	12.0%	13.2%	25.5%	15.2%	5.7%	4.5%	2.2%	24.9%
Daly City city	12,008	22.2%	15.5%	24.9%	19.5%	8.8%	7.4%	1.6%	0.0%	37.4%
Downey city	19,266	25.9%	15.2%	24.8%	25.6%	8.1%	0.0%	0.4%	0.0%	20.8%
El Cajon city	11,658	34.1%	22.6%	18.3%	17.6%	6.5%	1.0%	0.0%	0.0%	19.9%
El Monte city	9,703	32.5%	25.1%	22.3%	14.6%	3.0%	1.2%	1.3%	0.0%	15.1%
Elk Grove city	15,496	29.9%	12.6%	12.6%	30.4%	5.7%	8.1%	0.6%	0.0%	37.1%
Escondido city	30,643	30.9%	14.3%	27.1%	16.4%	6.3%	4.5%	0.6%	0.0%	33.6%
Fairfield city	11,889	25.7%	12.8%	22.1%	20.4%	14.9%	0.5%	3.6%	0.0%	16.9%
Fontana city	20,406	24.1%	28.0%	19.0%	21.6%	4.1%	1.9%	1.4%	0.0%	19.0%
Fremont city	13,598	34.8%	4.5%	8.8%	17.6%	17.4%	6.0%	9.0%	1.9%	21.4%
Fresno city	9,394	42.7%	16.3%	13.1%	14.7%	8.9%	3.0%	1.1%	0.1%	13.4%
Fullerton city	13,863	16.6%	25.9%	21.1%	21.9%	11.5%	2.5%	0.0%	0.4%	9.5%
Garden Grove city	9,644	27.9%	28.5%	12.2%	19.5%	10.6%	0.9%	0.4%	0.0%	10.1%
Glendale city	14,360	25.1%	20.1%	18.1%	15.2%	15.8%	4.2%	0.9%	0.5%	9.0%
Hayward city	8,768	23.2%	17.5%	15.9%	26.6%	7.2%	4.2%	5.4%	0.0%	6.7%
Hesperia city	25,427	33.7%	12.0%	10.7%	24.7%	11.7%	5.4%	1.7%	0.0%	15.5%
Inglewood city	17,610	29.0%	26.4%	12.2%	18.6%	8.8%	4.3%	0.8%	0.0%	26.3%
Irvine city	93,254	27.7%	9.5%	12.6%	15.3%	19.6%	11.1%	3.8%	0.5%	19.9%
Jurupa Valley city	18,396	21.8%	15.5%	11.9%	23.4%	17.8%	2.9%	6.7%	0.0%	29.7%
Lancaster city	22,901	43.8%	12.5%	7.2%	27.2%	7.5%	1.3%	0.4%	0.0%	12.9%
Long Beach city	357,011	28.8%	17.0%	16.0%	17.5%	14.7%	3.9%	1.5%	0.6%	24.9%
Los Angeles city	23,755	28.4%	20.4%	15.6%	18.1%	10.9%	3.5%	2.1%	1.1%	20.8%
Mission Viejo city	36,235	28.9%	20.7%	4.0%	20.7%	25.7%	0.0%	0.0%	0.0%	37.9%
Modesto city	21,990	37.1%	22.9%	15.7%	11.6%	9.3%	3.1%	0.4%	0.0%	18.6%
Moreno Valley city	9,599	34.5%	19.9%	14.8%	21.3%	5.7%	3.0%	0.9%	0.0%	22.2%
Murrieta city	37,667	28.4%	11.6%	11.8%	21.5%	7.4%	12.6%	6.6%	0.0%	40.4%
Norwalk city	8,626	24.9%	21.4%	22.6%	15.1%	6.8%	7.5%	1.7%	0.0%	9.8%
Oakland city	16,700	28.3%	16.9%	14.7%	20.7%	10.7%	3.1%	4.1%	1.6%	42.6%
Oceanside city	46,805	30.4%	18.1%	15.0%	19.5%	8.7%	6.4%	1.8%	0.0%	17.2%
Ontario city	16,810	31.7%	16.2%	22.3%	18.5%	6.9%	3.6%	0.8%	0.0%	41.5%
Orange city	18,070	22.2%	19.3%	21.2%	17.8%	12.2%	2.3%	4.0%	1.1%	39.3%
Oxnard city	20,537	27.3%	30.4%	18.1%	14.0%	7.8%	1.1%	1.1%	0.0%	23.1%
Palmdale city	107,536	37.4%	17.0%	18.2%	17.2%	7.5%	0.9%	1.7%	0.0%	21.9%
Pasadena city	10,546	20.5%	13.8%	12.4%	22.3%	15.5%	8.4%	6.5%	0.7%	24.2%
Pomona city	12,517	34.5%	20.2%	17.2%	15.8%	8.1%	2.6%	1.4%	0.2%	13.4%
Rancho Cucamonga city	9,869	31.3%	11.7%	10.2%	26.0%	13.8%	4.4%	2.5%	0.0%	11.4%
Redding city	16,761	45.4%	23.6%	9.0%	10.9%	8.9%	0.9%	1.3%	0.0%	15.9%
Rialto city	30,950	33.2%	12.7%	16.8%	26.4%	5.7%	4.3%	1.0%	0.0%	17.9%
Richmond city	16,113	25.4%	22.0%	15.9%	18.8%	13.9%	2.5%	0.9%	0.6%	14.1%
Riverside city	153,400	39.6%	18.5%	14.5%	15.1%	7.2%	2.0%	2.8%	0.2%	23.5%
Roseville city	12,536	33.2%	12.4%	19.6%	16.4%	13.1%	3.0%	1.7%	0.5%	11.2%
Sacramento city	10,268	27.3%	16.9%	13.3%	26.7%	9.1%	3.1%	3.3%	0.3%	20.3%
Salinas city	14,200	32.4%	30.9%	14.0%	16.1%	4.4%	2.2%	0.0%	0.0%	40.0%

Table I-3: Places—Income Class by Age—*Continued*

	Personal Income, Percent by Income Class, Ages 18 to 24							
	Total Millennials	Under $10,000	$10,000 to $19,999	$20,000 to $29,999	$30,000 to $49,999	$50,000 to $74,999	$75,000 to $99,999	$100,000 or More
California—Cont.								
San Bernardino city	11,174	71.9%	17.7%	8.5%	1.9%	0.0%	0.0%	0.0%
San Buenaventura (Ventura) city	24,350	59.8%	20.4%	9.9%	7.6%	0.0%	2.3%	0.0%
San Diego city	58,403	60.2%	17.8%	12.2%	6.7%	2.7%	0.5%	0.0%
San Francisco city	19,910	60.4%	13.3%	7.8%	7.9%	6.3%	1.6%	2.8%
San Jose city	82,750	62.4%	17.2%	8.8%	7.3%	3.7%	0.1%	0.4%
San Mateo city	15,873	65.7%	20.4%	7.4%	2.9%	2.3%	1.3%	0.0%
Santa Ana city	25,653	58.2%	22.5%	13.8%	4.4%	0.2%	0.8%	0.0%
Santa Clara city	12,830	65.3%	14.9%	2.4%	6.9%	8.8%	0.5%	1.1%
Santa Clarita city	11,284	67.6%	20.3%	6.4%	3.2%	1.9%	0.6%	0.0%
Santa Maria city	74,001	63.1%	17.6%	12.1%	4.4%	2.7%	0.0%	0.0%
Santa Monica city	12,274	48.9%	11.1%	12.4%	17.4%	2.6%	7.6%	0.0%
Santa Rosa city	13,165	57.0%	26.1%	13.0%	3.2%	0.0%	0.0%	0.7%
Simi Valley city	13,742	62.7%	15.6%	15.5%	4.8%	1.3%	0.0%	0.0%
South Gate city	13,353	65.9%	23.0%	7.0%	3.3%	0.0%	0.8%	0.0%
Stockton city	16,403	69.3%	16.6%	8.5%	5.2%	0.5%	0.0%	0.0%
Sunnyvale city	29,300	51.7%	11.6%	11.2%	14.8%	6.8%	3.1%	0.7%
Temecula city	13,002	77.3%	15.6%	4.2%	2.3%	0.0%	0.0%	0.6%
Thousand Oaks city	11,276	58.5%	20.4%	13.5%	5.6%	1.3%	0.6%	0.0%
Torrance city	13,826	64.4%	16.6%	13.2%	4.2%	0.7%	1.0%	0.0%
Vacaville city	23,311	53.9%	30.1%	10.2%	2.5%	1.7%	1.7%	0.0%
Vallejo city	25,924	69.1%	15.6%	11.7%	2.8%	0.6%	0.2%	0.0%
Victorville city	8,597	75.3%	8.2%	15.0%	1.5%	0.0%	0.0%	0.0%
Visalia city	6,592	69.9%	12.8%	10.5%	5.8%	0.0%	1.0%	0.0%
Vista city	22,450	49.0%	22.4%	19.0%	6.1%	0.0%	3.6%	0.0%
West Covina city	32,540	66.1%	10.5%	18.8%	4.6%	0.0%	0.0%	0.0%
Westminster city	15,103	72.0%	14.4%	4.6%	8.2%	0.8%	0.0%	0.0%
Colorado								
Arvada city	24,853	44.8%	30.0%	12.6%	11.6%	0.0%	0.9%	0.0%
Aurora city	76,339	64.1%	15.0%	13.3%	7.0%	0.5%	0.0%	0.2%
Boulder city	16,568	67.4%	15.9%	9.4%	5.0%	0.3%	1.5%	0.5%
Centennial city	57,906	62.0%	18.2%	14.0%	5.8%	0.0%	0.0%	0.0%
Colorado Springs city	8,604	57.7%	23.1%	10.2%	6.2%	1.9%	0.2%	0.7%
Denver city	16,518	50.1%	22.3%	12.7%	12.4%	2.2%	0.1%	0.2%
Fort Collins city	43,021	60.8%	21.3%	14.3%	2.0%	1.7%	0.0%	0.0%
Greeley city	18,446	67.6%	19.0%	6.6%	6.6%	0.2%	0.0%	0.0%
Lakewood city	24,159	57.2%	19.5%	15.0%	6.9%	0.0%	0.0%	1.3%
Pueblo city	22,520	69.7%	24.1%	4.4%	1.8%	0.0%	0.0%	0.0%
Thornton city	14,944	51.7%	29.2%	10.1%	8.2%	0.0%	0.7%	0.0%
Westminster city	19,830	50.0%	21.3%	17.5%	9.8%	0.4%	0.0%	1.1%
Connecticut								
Bridgeport city	22,957	68.3%	17.1%	10.7%	2.3%	1.6%	0.0%	0.0%
Hartford city	13,727	73.5%	16.3%	7.5%	1.1%	1.5%	0.0%	0.0%
New Haven city	11,960	69.5%	18.0%	8.6%	3.1%	0.2%	0.2%	0.4%
Stamford city	34,083	52.9%	20.4%	15.3%	7.4%	2.9%	1.1%	0.0%
Waterbury city	10,336	62.2%	24.5%	7.2%	4.9%	0.4%	0.0%	0.8%
District of Columbia								
Washington city	16,646	70.1%	10.9%	5.0%	9.5%	3.9%	0.5%	0.0%
Florida								
Cape Coral city	17,926	61.0%	26.6%	10.4%	1.7%	0.3%	0.0%	0.0%
Clearwater city	15,875	49.5%	31.7%	13.0%	5.0%	0.0%	0.8%	0.0%
Coral Springs city	21,476	59.3%	21.3%	13.7%	5.4%	0.2%	0.0%	0.0%
Fort Lauderdale city	19,216	70.7%	19.9%	3.7%	4.2%	1.5%	0.0%	0.0%
Gainesville city	20,256	71.2%	19.8%	5.8%	2.6%	0.6%	0.0%	0.0%
Hialeah city	11,627	63.0%	19.3%	10.7%	7.0%	0.0%	0.0%	0.0%
Hollywood city	7,870	65.1%	15.0%	8.6%	8.9%	2.0%	0.0%	0.4%
Jacksonville city	11,122	58.8%	22.3%	9.6%	7.9%	1.0%	0.4%	0.1%
Lakeland city	224,553	60.7%	23.1%	15.9%	0.3%	0.0%	0.0%	0.0%
Miami Beach city	19,366	53.7%	31.0%	10.8%	4.5%	0.0%	0.0%	0.0%
Miami city	10,039	59.7%	25.1%	9.2%	3.0%	2.8%	0.0%	0.3%
Miami Gardens city	82,156	72.9%	12.8%	11.6%	2.7%	0.0%	0.0%	0.0%
Miramar city	11,099	65.1%	17.7%	9.0%	5.9%	0.2%	2.1%	0.0%
Orlando city	30,544	59.1%	18.8%	13.7%	7.6%	0.2%	0.7%	0.0%
Palm Bay city	23,396	76.4%	19.0%	3.3%	1.3%	0.0%	0.0%	0.0%
Pembroke Pines city	21,229	74.0%	11.6%	8.3%	3.9%	0.2%	1.8%	0.3%
Pompano Beach city	80,071	71.9%	15.5%	9.2%	2.3%	1.1%	0.0%	0.0%
Port St. Lucie city	22,404	68.8%	25.1%	3.6%	2.6%	0.0%	0.0%	0.0%
St. Petersburg city	15,649	63.8%	24.0%	5.4%	6.1%	0.7%	0.0%	0.0%
Tallahassee city	10,455	76.0%	11.8%	7.1%	4.8%	0.3%	0.0%	0.0%
Tampa city	14,343	64.8%	16.4%	9.9%	7.0%	1.6%	0.3%	0.0%
West Palm Beach city	46,153	80.4%	10.9%	5.9%	2.2%	0.6%	0.0%	0.0%
Georgia								
Athens-Clarke County unified govt (bal)	11,446	76.2%	13.2%	5.6%	2.5%	2.6%	0.0%	0.0%
Atlanta city	11,821	69.7%	14.9%	6.4%	7.3%	0.9%	0.7%	0.0%
Augusta-Richmond County consolidated govt (bal)	16,852	67.3%	19.2%	9.5%	3.3%	0.7%	0.0%	0.0%

Table I-3: Places—Income Class by Age—*Continued*

	Personal Income, Percent by Income Class, Ages 25 to 31								
	Total Millennials	Under $10,000	$10,000 to $19,999	$20,000 to $29,999	$30,000 to $49,999	$50,000 to $74,999	$75,000 to $99,999	$100,000 to $149,999	$150,000 or More	Poverty Rate
California—Cont.										
San Bernardino city	8,875	45.4%	22.3%	16.6%	7.6%	3.9%	4.1%	0.0%	0.0%	26.7%
San Buenaventura (Ventura) city	18,586	24.9%	17.3%	13.4%	17.5%	17.2%	7.0%	2.2%	0.5%	27.7%
San Diego city	96,430	23.4%	13.4%	13.9%	23.8%	15.9%	6.3%	2.5%	0.8%	21.5%
San Francisco city	26,312	17.0%	10.4%	8.9%	18.5%	17.4%	11.9%	10.7%	5.1%	24.4%
San Jose city	58,753	26.8%	13.2%	11.8%	19.1%	14.3%	7.2%	5.7%	1.9%	46.3%
San Mateo city	11,971	9.6%	7.6%	24.7%	10.6%	19.4%	20.4%	6.9%	0.8%	9.6%
Santa Ana city	35,049	28.0%	28.0%	19.2%	17.3%	5.6%	0.9%	0.8%	0.2%	24.2%
Santa Clara city	12,072	24.0%	7.8%	9.6%	12.8%	17.9%	11.3%	14.8%	1.9%	25.4%
Santa Clarita city	11,210	20.9%	16.0%	19.5%	15.1%	10.1%	10.0%	7.7%	0.7%	28.0%
Santa Maria city	66,579	23.7%	18.8%	22.5%	23.7%	11.2%	0.0%	0.0%	0.0%	26.3%
Santa Monica city	11,373	12.1%	7.5%	11.6%	24.8%	18.9%	7.3%	17.2%	0.6%	8.9%
Santa Rosa city	15,640	24.8%	23.9%	12.3%	25.3%	7.7%	2.3%	0.8%	2.9%	18.9%
Simi Valley city	10,251	27.6%	14.4%	12.7%	24.1%	13.4%	3.0%	4.7%	0.0%	16.5%
South Gate city	12,796	37.4%	20.1%	17.8%	11.7%	10.5%	2.5%	0.0%	0.0%	34.7%
Stockton city	17,091	30.7%	22.6%	14.7%	22.0%	7.3%	1.7%	1.1%	0.0%	19.2%
Sunnyvale city	16,885	25.8%	6.9%	3.6%	13.3%	12.2%	13.7%	20.1%	4.3%	42.2%
Temecula city	11,110	25.2%	15.9%	6.3%	32.7%	12.9%	0.0%	5.8%	1.0%	25.1%
Thousand Oaks city	10,321	26.3%	14.4%	16.2%	15.0%	6.9%	7.2%	10.3%	3.7%	17.8%
Torrance city	12,854	20.4%	23.7%	18.4%	22.3%	13.4%	1.7%	0.0%	0.0%	14.5%
Vacaville city	15,383	35.4%	12.4%	7.9%	24.0%	10.7%	5.5%	3.1%	0.9%	22.0%
Vallejo city	25,605	32.5%	18.8%	14.8%	15.0%	9.5%	8.0%	0.5%	0.9%	21.2%
Victorville city	10,225	47.5%	22.7%	8.4%	12.8%	7.0%	1.6%	0.0%	0.0%	27.6%
Visalia city	11,304	38.2%	20.4%	14.1%	14.0%	5.3%	5.7%	2.3%	0.0%	45.8%
Vista city	18,971	31.7%	14.2%	28.3%	15.0%	7.8%	1.7%	1.4%	0.0%	16.8%
West Covina city	15,954	35.8%	24.4%	11.2%	19.4%	8.8%	0.0%	0.4%	0.0%	32.0%
Westminster city	15,087	44.5%	20.5%	12.3%	11.9%	4.4%	5.6%	0.8%	0.0%	28.3%
Colorado										
Arvada city	25,279	11.8%	30.7%	16.0%	27.2%	12.4%	1.8%	0.0%	0.0%	25.8%
Aurora city	88,369	22.2%	17.9%	21.2%	24.3%	11.4%	2.2%	0.3%	0.4%	21.0%
Boulder city	21,994	13.8%	10.3%	14.6%	31.1%	16.7%	7.2%	2.0%	4.4%	10.2%
Centennial city	56,907	15.4%	8.5%	18.7%	33.8%	21.1%	2.6%	0.0%	0.0%	36.3%
Colorado Springs city	10,337	23.8%	17.1%	15.6%	24.8%	15.2%	2.2%	1.2%	0.0%	6.7%
Denver city	17,289	22.3%	12.6%	14.2%	27.7%	15.9%	3.7%	3.0%	0.5%	22.1%
Fort Collins city	17,628	19.4%	11.1%	16.8%	27.5%	16.7%	4.1%	1.3%	3.1%	50.9%
Greeley city	16,769	29.2%	14.2%	9.1%	30.2%	13.0%	2.5%	1.2%	0.6%	18.3%
Lakewood city	22,411	25.3%	19.5%	14.6%	27.9%	8.7%	1.5%	1.7%	0.8%	21.3%
Pueblo city	24,043	43.0%	17.9%	14.2%	19.1%	3.7%	0.0%	2.2%	0.0%	27.8%
Thornton city	22,833	27.9%	20.0%	14.8%	24.2%	8.4%	4.1%	0.5%	0.0%	19.9%
Westminster city	16,483	19.9%	18.5%	13.7%	26.6%	13.8%	6.0%	1.2%	0.4%	22.0%
Connecticut										
Bridgeport city	25,469	28.4%	16.8%	23.3%	13.7%	12.2%	3.1%	0.8%	1.7%	32.1%
Hartford city	12,038	32.5%	15.1%	12.1%	23.8%	14.3%	0.9%	1.4%	0.0%	23.3%
New Haven city	10,960	35.6%	12.3%	14.7%	18.5%	14.4%	2.4%	1.4%	0.7%	19.1%
Stamford city	30,190	17.4%	19.2%	12.8%	22.6%	15.6%	7.8%	3.4%	1.1%	23.7%
Waterbury city	12,421	32.3%	15.7%	21.9%	20.6%	8.7%	0.4%	0.4%	0.0%	30.5%
District of Columbia										
Washington city	15,772	21.7%	7.9%	8.9%	20.5%	24.0%	10.0%	4.6%	2.4%	20.8%
Florida										
Cape Coral city	14,342	33.8%	20.5%	19.3%	20.5%	4.1%	1.8%	0.0%	0.0%	35.5%
Clearwater city	18,422	25.3%	15.3%	22.5%	24.2%	9.7%	1.5%	1.5%	0.0%	13.6%
Coral Springs city	22,921	25.2%	17.5%	13.6%	26.5%	10.0%	3.9%	3.4%	0.0%	15.9%
Fort Lauderdale city	21,407	27.3%	14.5%	14.9%	28.5%	7.8%	4.6%	1.6%	0.9%	19.7%
Gainesville city	20,322	36.7%	16.9%	19.2%	19.9%	5.8%	1.3%	0.3%	0.0%	30.1%
Hialeah city	10,238	43.9%	11.9%	27.3%	12.2%	3.6%	1.0%	0.0%	0.0%	30.9%
Hollywood city	11,317	29.8%	20.8%	15.2%	22.3%	6.5%	4.1%	0.3%	0.9%	13.1%
Jacksonville city	11,697	26.9%	15.7%	17.2%	27.8%	9.3%	2.3%	0.8%	0.0%	17.6%
Lakeland city	291,146	44.4%	13.8%	9.5%	24.2%	8.2%	0.0%	0.0%	0.0%	22.1%
Miami Beach city	18,878	9.2%	30.6%	16.6%	22.8%	18.4%	0.5%	1.1%	0.8%	24.5%
Miami city	8,920	32.4%	21.7%	13.5%	16.3%	9.6%	3.3%	2.6%	0.5%	22.8%
Miami Gardens city	98,908	30.8%	20.7%	29.7%	15.1%	2.7%	0.0%	1.1%	0.0%	26.0%
Miramar city	13,468	31.9%	14.7%	25.8%	17.2%	7.7%	2.3%	0.4%	0.0%	28.6%
Orlando city	25,569	23.1%	18.6%	18.7%	24.7%	9.2%	4.6%	0.8%	0.2%	23.8%
Palm Bay city	27,178	44.2%	18.2%	25.8%	7.9%	2.7%	1.1%	0.0%	0.0%	16.8%
Pembroke Pines city	19,681	25.6%	18.6%	23.8%	16.8%	11.0%	2.6%	1.6%	0.0%	40.6%
Pompano Beach city	94,016	34.4%	14.4%	33.4%	14.6%	2.1%	0.0%	0.0%	1.1%	21.3%
Port St. Lucie city	38,721	39.3%	21.3%	6.9%	22.9%	7.8%	1.0%	0.7%	0.0%	20.7%
St. Petersburg city	14,193	28.7%	14.1%	16.2%	28.5%	8.8%	2.0%	1.3%	0.5%	16.2%
Tallahassee city	10,081	28.4%	17.3%	16.7%	29.3%	5.9%	2.2%	0.0%	0.0%	13.4%
Tampa city	14,219	26.8%	19.5%	16.9%	19.1%	12.6%	3.0%	1.7%	0.3%	25.3%
West Palm Beach city	58,617	25.2%	36.5%	19.8%	8.7%	4.6%	4.9%	0.0%	0.3%	21.2%
Georgia										
Athens-Clarke County unified govt (bal)	8,573	27.3%	27.4%	21.8%	16.8%	6.3%	0.0%	0.0%	0.5%	18.9%
Atlanta city	15,126	22.5%	12.3%	15.9%	21.2%	17.5%	5.9%	4.0%	0.7%	20.9%
Augusta-Richmond County consolidated govt (bal)	19,199	34.7%	25.3%	13.3%	16.2%	8.2%	1.2%	0.8%	0.3%	11.3%

Table I-3: Places—Income Class by Age—*Continued*

	Personal Income, Percent by Income Class, Ages 18 to 24							
	Total Millennials	Under $10,000	$10,000 to $19,999	$20,000 to $29,999	$30,000 to $49,999	$50,000 to $74,999	$75,000 to $99,999	$100,000 or More
Georgia—Cont.								
Columbus city	33,690	51.0%	20.6%	19.7%	7.9%	0.7%	0.1%	0.0%
Macon city	16,123	75.8%	11.6%	4.3%	8.4%	0.0%	0.0%	0.0%
Roswell city	11,043	70.2%	17.1%	9.9%	0.0%	2.7%	0.0%	0.0%
Sandy Springs city	13,949	44.8%	29.7%	11.3%	5.1%	7.6%	1.5%	0.0%
Savannah city	16,534	66.7%	20.9%	7.1%	3.6%	1.6%	0.0%	0.0%
Hawaii								
Urban Honolulu CDP	14,224	60.3%	18.3%	12.9%	6.8%	1.4%	0.3%	0.0%
Idaho								
Boise City city	27,273	66.7%	18.0%	11.0%	3.8%	0.0%	0.5%	0.0%
Illinois								
Aurora city	19,157	57.4%	18.7%	11.8%	9.2%	2.3%	0.6%	0.0%
Chicago city	51,928	70.7%	14.2%	7.7%	4.6%	2.3%	0.2%	0.3%
Elgin city	15,406	58.0%	15.5%	19.3%	4.3%	2.8%	0.0%	0.0%
Joliet city	5,779	61.5%	26.8%	8.0%	2.9%	0.0%	0.7%	0.0%
Naperville city	8,767	60.7%	18.7%	8.2%	9.0%	3.3%	0.0%	0.0%
Peoria city	42,981	60.4%	17.4%	13.8%	8.4%	0.0%	0.0%	0.0%
Rockford city	39,030	61.5%	16.9%	13.1%	7.6%	0.9%	0.0%	0.0%
Springfield city	16,118	67.4%	18.5%	10.1%	4.0%	0.0%	0.0%	0.0%
Indiana								
Evansville city	7,551	76.1%	14.7%	4.0%	4.3%	0.9%	0.0%	0.0%
Fort Wayne city	49,447	57.5%	25.4%	11.9%	4.7%	0.0%	0.3%	0.2%
Indianapolis city (bal)	414,272	61.1%	20.4%	11.0%	5.7%	1.8%	0.0%	0.0%
South Bend city	55,865	74.4%	16.4%	8.4%	0.7%	0.0%	0.0%	0.0%
Iowa								
Cedar Rapids city	13,159	59.7%	20.4%	6.1%	11.6%	2.1%	0.0%	0.0%
Davenport city	43,705	56.1%	32.2%	9.2%	1.7%	0.0%	0.0%	0.8%
Des Moines city	8,255	40.3%	29.3%	12.8%	15.7%	1.8%	0.0%	0.0%
Kansas								
Kansas City city	11,218	50.7%	22.8%	14.2%	12.4%	0.0%	0.0%	0.0%
Olathe city	41,339	48.9%	37.6%	3.0%	2.6%	7.9%	0.0%	0.0%
Overland Park city	11,409	64.7%	11.6%	8.9%	13.5%	1.3%	0.0%	0.0%
Topeka city	14,982	60.9%	24.8%	10.5%	2.7%	1.1%	0.0%	0.0%
Wichita city	11,353	60.3%	22.0%	11.0%	5.1%	1.5%	0.0%	0.0%
Kentucky								
Lexington-Fayette urban county	73,486	65.2%	25.0%	7.2%	2.6%	0.0%	0.0%	0.0%
Louisville/Jefferson County metro govt (bal)	45,070	61.2%	20.3%	9.7%	7.2%	1.6%	0.0%	0.0%
Louisiana								
Baton Rouge city	15,853	73.6%	14.6%	2.5%	4.7%	3.5%	1.2%	0.0%
Lafayette city	6,216	59.3%	20.2%	9.4%	7.9%	1.4%	1.9%	0.0%
New Orleans city	34,280	74.8%	14.9%	5.4%	3.9%	0.9%	0.0%	0.1%
Shreveport city	13,952	68.3%	18.0%	7.9%	5.2%	0.5%	0.0%	0.0%
Maryland								
Baltimore city	13,360	69.4%	12.6%	6.7%	9.5%	1.6%	0.1%	0.0%
Massachusetts								
Boston city	72,453	68.7%	12.3%	8.2%	7.3%	3.1%	0.3%	0.2%
Brockton city	50,657	67.8%	20.7%	9.0%	2.5%	0.0%	0.0%	0.0%
Cambridge city	12,626	69.9%	11.1%	9.1%	5.7%	3.5%	0.7%	0.0%
Lowell city	8,995	57.1%	19.7%	10.8%	9.1%	3.3%	0.0%	0.0%
Lynn city	20,293	60.8%	25.4%	7.2%	6.6%	0.0%	0.0%	0.0%
New Bedford city	22,619	53.7%	26.8%	13.5%	2.4%	3.6%	0.0%	0.0%
Springfield city	23,367	65.3%	19.7%	11.3%	3.0%	0.8%	0.0%	0.0%
Worcester city	22,518	69.3%	15.9%	10.6%	3.2%	0.4%	0.0%	0.5%
Michigan								
Ann Arbor city	21,810	51.6%	9.1%	14.0%	13.5%	11.9%	0.0%	0.0%
Dearborn city	9,771	79.2%	10.1%	4.3%	5.6%	0.9%	0.0%	0.0%
Detroit city	11,662	78.2%	14.2%	5.7%	1.5%	0.2%	0.0%	0.1%
Flint city	64,157	75.7%	23.0%	1.4%	0.0%	0.0%	0.0%	0.0%
Grand Rapids city	8,700	59.4%	19.3%	8.6%	9.8%	2.9%	0.0%	0.0%
Lansing city	21,287	73.7%	12.9%	3.7%	9.2%	0.5%	0.0%	0.0%
Livonia city	40,095	46.4%	19.7%	14.1%	11.1%	4.5%	2.8%	1.4%
Sterling Heights city	798,163	67.7%	16.6%	5.0%	9.0%	1.8%	0.0%	0.0%
Warren city	29,094	67.6%	16.8%	11.5%	3.6%	0.5%	0.0%	0.0%
Minnesota								
Minneapolis city	22,747	60.2%	19.8%	8.2%	9.0%	2.9%	0.0%	0.0%
Rochester city	45,302	55.9%	16.6%	16.7%	10.0%	0.7%	0.0%	0.0%
St. Paul city	19,002	60.5%	21.8%	15.2%	2.5%	0.0%	0.0%	0.0%
Mississippi								
Jackson city	16,645	75.8%	9.1%	9.7%	5.2%	0.2%	0.0%	0.0%
Missouri								
Columbia city	22,742	75.5%	18.6%	5.2%	0.8%	0.0%	0.0%	0.0%
Independence city	12,390	58.3%	18.3%	12.0%	9.3%	2.2%	0.0%	0.0%

Table I-3: Places—Income Class by Age—*Continued*

	Personal Income, Percent by Income Class, Ages 25 to 31									
	Total Millennials	Under $10,000	$10,000 to $19,999	$20,000 to $29,999	$30,000 to $49,999	$50,000 to $74,999	$75,000 to $99,999	$100,000 to $149,999	$150,000 or More	Poverty Rate
Georgia—Cont.										
Columbus city	23,611	36.0%	17.8%	17.8%	17.1%	8.9%	1.5%	0.8%	0.2%	33.9%
Macon city	15,819	46.3%	15.8%	14.1%	17.9%	5.3%	0.6%	0.0%	0.0%	16.6%
Roswell city	8,446	16.3%	22.5%	32.1%	17.6%	4.9%	6.0%	0.5%	0.0%	19.2%
Sandy Springs city	14,372	14.4%	16.9%	18.5%	24.4%	13.3%	10.1%	1.3%	1.0%	16.9%
Savannah city	14,910	31.9%	21.1%	13.7%	24.6%	7.2%	1.2%	0.1%	0.2%	18.0%
Hawaii										
Urban Honolulu CDP	15,512	30.9%	10.8%	9.5%	27.1%	15.6%	3.9%	1.9%	0.3%	33.6%
Idaho										
Boise City city	23,201	28.6%	24.8%	17.1%	22.5%	5.5%	1.5%	0.0%	0.0%	32.5%
Illinois										
Aurora city	7,616	30.3%	16.5%	18.8%	18.1%	9.8%	4.5%	1.7%	0.3%	40.2%
Chicago city	59,192	26.3%	14.0%	13.4%	20.3%	15.8%	5.8%	2.8%	1.5%	20.3%
Elgin city	12,212	20.1%	17.3%	14.5%	30.5%	10.4%	3.9%	1.2%	2.1%	29.2%
Joliet city	8,090	32.0%	16.5%	19.0%	21.5%	5.5%	3.9%	1.6%	0.0%	8.7%
Naperville city	13,709	23.4%	14.0%	16.4%	20.7%	16.9%	3.0%	5.0%	0.5%	10.6%
Peoria city	32,524	22.0%	11.3%	9.3%	28.6%	15.1%	9.5%	2.8%	1.5%	31.0%
Rockford city	28,205	39.7%	14.7%	17.9%	21.0%	5.9%	0.9%	0.0%	0.0%	26.1%
Springfield city	23,392	30.1%	18.0%	14.7%	24.4%	7.7%	2.5%	0.9%	1.6%	21.9%
Indiana										
Evansville city	7,554	24.4%	15.5%	18.0%	26.8%	8.6%	6.1%	0.0%	0.5%	9.7%
Fort Wayne city	51,100	32.1%	21.4%	14.9%	22.5%	8.4%	0.6%	0.0%	0.0%	23.6%
Indianapolis city (bal)	459,387	28.8%	20.4%	16.1%	23.3%	9.0%	1.1%	0.8%	0.5%	25.2%
South Bend city	59,656	28.0%	16.3%	24.5%	18.3%	10.6%	1.3%	1.1%	0.0%	21.5%
Iowa										
Cedar Rapids city	12,922	12.6%	14.8%	18.9%	22.9%	28.2%	2.7%	0.0%	0.0%	25.1%
Davenport city	27,015	23.8%	11.3%	16.5%	30.2%	11.8%	6.4%	0.0%	0.0%	24.5%
Des Moines city	8,758	20.1%	18.2%	19.8%	25.6%	15.1%	0.4%	0.4%	0.2%	19.0%
Kansas										
Kansas City city	9,242	28.9%	24.4%	15.0%	19.4%	7.2%	4.8%	0.3%	0.0%	40.5%
Olathe city	37,501	17.7%	24.6%	19.0%	25.7%	5.9%	6.0%	0.0%	0.9%	27.8%
Overland Park city	13,147	15.4%	8.6%	15.1%	40.1%	9.9%	7.3%	3.0%	0.6%	19.6%
Topeka city	11,499	17.2%	8.6%	21.9%	43.2%	8.1%	1.0%	0.0%	0.0%	31.4%
Wichita city	12,028	27.7%	19.1%	17.5%	24.6%	9.5%	0.7%	0.7%	0.2%	9.8%
Kentucky										
Lexington-Fayette urban county	73,223	23.8%	20.9%	22.3%	21.6%	6.7%	2.6%	1.8%	0.2%	31.6%
Louisville/Jefferson County metro govt (bal)	47,737	22.2%	16.2%	22.2%	25.0%	10.3%	3.0%	1.0%	0.0%	20.3%
Louisiana										
Baton Rouge city	14,522	30.4%	18.7%	13.0%	23.8%	8.6%	2.8%	2.1%	0.6%	20.0%
Lafayette city	8,798	12.2%	19.3%	15.9%	26.7%	16.4%	5.1%	2.2%	2.2%	13.8%
New Orleans city	47,133	30.9%	18.2%	13.1%	22.5%	8.1%	3.9%	2.4%	0.9%	27.0%
Shreveport city	11,328	35.0%	19.0%	15.1%	17.5%	9.8%	1.6%	1.5%	0.6%	19.1%
Maryland										
Baltimore city	14,827	30.2%	11.9%	12.3%	24.1%	14.0%	4.9%	1.6%	1.0%	10.9%
Massachusetts										
Boston city	74,651	16.3%	12.7%	12.4%	22.8%	19.1%	8.2%	6.2%	2.2%	33.8%
Brockton city	66,958	27.6%	6.6%	19.3%	23.4%	19.5%	3.5%	0.0%	0.0%	27.6%
Cambridge city	17,992	19.7%	6.7%	11.7%	29.4%	21.6%	5.9%	3.8%	1.3%	13.4%
Lowell city	4,425	28.3%	17.1%	17.0%	17.9%	16.7%	2.9%	0.0%	0.0%	3.6%
Lynn city	20,214	29.6%	19.8%	19.7%	18.0%	9.4%	3.0%	0.5%	0.0%	31.9%
New Bedford city	20,567	31.9%	16.3%	12.6%	28.3%	8.6%	0.0%	2.2%	0.0%	23.4%
Springfield city	22,357	28.0%	27.5%	15.7%	21.4%	4.9%	1.9%	0.0%	0.6%	31.9%
Worcester city	25,384	28.4%	13.3%	17.9%	23.0%	11.8%	3.0%	2.4%	0.3%	20.8%
Michigan										
Ann Arbor city	14,961	23.1%	18.3%	18.2%	20.4%	13.2%	4.5%	2.2%	0.0%	23.8%
Dearborn city	8,639	39.6%	17.0%	11.3%	23.8%	4.0%	0.0%	0.0%	4.3%	12.3%
Detroit city	12,789	52.3%	18.9%	11.0%	10.9%	4.3%	1.9%	0.0%	0.7%	5.5%
Flint city	85,646	36.5%	27.9%	16.1%	16.5%	3.0%	0.0%	0.0%	0.0%	20.2%
Grand Rapids city	10,265	26.9%	23.4%	18.8%	20.2%	6.9%	2.5%	1.2%	0.0%	30.9%
Lansing city	17,272	26.0%	13.0%	21.4%	23.5%	14.4%	1.7%	0.0%	0.0%	28.0%
Livonia city	48,879	13.8%	18.3%	21.2%	25.6%	18.8%	2.3%	0.0%	0.0%	30.2%
Sterling Heights city	1,014,121	35.9%	12.9%	10.5%	22.8%	11.5%	6.3%	0.0%	0.0%	23.5%
Warren city	36,097	29.0%	22.9%	19.6%	25.0%	3.6%	0.0%	0.0%	0.0%	29.2%
Minnesota										
Minneapolis city	20,844	22.3%	13.9%	15.7%	23.6%	15.8%	3.8%	3.7%	1.1%	21.0%
Rochester city	34,255	20.8%	7.0%	18.6%	27.9%	19.7%	4.2%	1.8%	0.0%	26.9%
St. Paul city	17,042	21.5%	10.0%	16.9%	31.5%	16.0%	2.0%	2.0%	0.0%	24.1%
Mississippi										
Jackson city	10,628	35.0%	28.9%	13.1%	14.9%	5.7%	2.5%	0.0%	0.0%	22.6%
Missouri										
Columbia city	26,289	34.6%	17.8%	20.6%	21.9%	2.4%	2.0%	0.8%	0.0%	17.5%
Independence city	9,029	21.7%	14.4%	21.8%	31.7%	7.5%	2.8%	0.0%	0.0%	11.7%

Table I-3: Places—Income Class by Age—*Continued*

	Personal Income, Percent by Income Class, Ages 18 to 24							
	Total Millennials	Under $10,000	$10,000 to $19,999	$20,000 to $29,999	$30,000 to $49,999	$50,000 to $74,999	$75,000 to $99,999	$100,000 or More
Missouri—Cont.								
Kansas City city	34,793	50.4%	30.2%	9.6%	7.3%	2.6%	0.0%	0.0%
Lee's Summit city	21,035	66.9%	21.7%	7.0%	4.4%	0.0%	0.0%	0.0%
Springfield city	12,319	61.6%	25.7%	3.2%	8.7%	0.8%	0.0%	0.0%
St. Louis city	62,132	62.4%	20.5%	8.3%	6.5%	2.3%	0.0%	0.0%
Montana								
Billings city	11,796	59.2%	24.3%	10.2%	3.9%	0.0%	2.3%	0.0%
Nebraska								
Lincoln city	41,799	65.2%	19.6%	8.6%	6.2%	0.4%	0.0%	0.0%
Omaha city	18,592	57.0%	22.1%	13.8%	6.1%	0.8%	0.0%	0.2%
Nevada								
Henderson city	15,291	59.0%	20.0%	9.7%	10.8%	0.5%	0.0%	0.0%
Las Vegas city	15,432	63.7%	17.3%	12.7%	5.8%	0.5%	0.0%	0.0%
North Las Vegas city	25,196	63.6%	14.1%	10.2%	11.2%	0.7%	0.0%	0.2%
Reno city	13,831	63.8%	18.2%	14.0%	3.5%	0.4%	0.0%	0.0%
Sparks city	25,335	47.4%	31.6%	7.1%	6.8%	0.0%	7.1%	0.0%
New Hampshire								
Manchester city	9,200	59.5%	12.7%	10.1%	13.3%	3.2%	1.2%	0.0%
New Jersey								
Elizabeth city	16,777	51.3%	34.2%	9.3%	3.5%	1.8%	0.0%	0.0%
Jersey City city	13,797	66.4%	15.2%	5.5%	6.3%	4.8%	0.6%	1.2%
Newark city	18,164	78.7%	14.0%	4.6%	1.8%	0.7%	0.0%	0.2%
Paterson city	17,606	64.9%	11.9%	18.4%	2.6%	2.1%	0.0%	0.0%
New Mexico								
Albuquerque city	8,755	60.9%	22.5%	8.1%	6.6%	1.5%	0.3%	0.0%
Las Cruces city	14,893	61.7%	27.8%	4.0%	6.0%	0.4%	0.0%	0.0%
Rio Rancho city	12,190	78.5%	10.2%	3.7%	7.6%	0.0%	0.0%	0.0%
New York								
Albany city	13,512	77.0%	6.0%	5.7%	9.9%	1.4%	0.0%	0.0%
Buffalo city	179,729	66.2%	19.2%	6.9%	6.0%	1.6%	0.0%	0.0%
New York city	154,915	70.2%	13.6%	6.3%	6.5%	2.5%	0.5%	0.4%
Rochester city	50,254	63.5%	17.5%	12.4%	5.9%	0.8%	0.0%	0.0%
Syracuse city	21,028	70.6%	14.8%	5.0%	6.5%	0.8%	0.0%	2.3%
Yonkers city	21,042	70.1%	13.9%	4.3%	7.0%	3.5%	1.2%	0.0%
North Carolina								
Charlotte city	7,215	62.0%	17.7%	10.7%	6.0%	2.0%	0.1%	1.4%
Durham city	13,266	72.9%	12.1%	9.4%	3.7%	0.2%	0.0%	1.8%
Fayetteville city	53,240	60.0%	16.5%	16.4%	4.9%	2.2%	0.0%	0.0%
Greensboro city	10,561	70.5%	15.7%	8.1%	4.2%	1.5%	0.0%	0.0%
High Point city	30,447	77.9%	15.4%	4.2%	2.5%	0.0%	0.0%	0.0%
Raleigh city	41,722	65.8%	18.9%	7.5%	7.3%	0.3%	0.0%	0.1%
Wilmington city	11,131	59.6%	25.2%	9.9%	2.7%	2.5%	0.0%	0.0%
Winston-Salem city	52,777	72.6%	16.2%	6.0%	4.2%	1.0%	0.0%	0.0%
North Dakota								
Fargo city	18,570	41.8%	34.1%	12.9%	11.0%	0.3%	0.0%	0.0%
Ohio								
Akron city	9,543	62.4%	22.3%	10.8%	2.4%	1.5%	0.0%	0.6%
Cincinnati city	27,486	60.9%	20.4%	8.6%	7.4%	1.9%	0.5%	0.2%
Cleveland city	7,783	67.7%	19.8%	7.3%	4.8%	0.4%	0.0%	0.0%
Columbus city	12,998	61.3%	19.6%	8.5%	9.5%	1.2%	0.0%	0.0%
Dayton city	8,366	76.7%	14.6%	6.5%	2.1%	0.0%	0.0%	0.0%
Toledo city	10,767	62.6%	25.0%	8.2%	4.1%	0.2%	0.0%	0.0%
Oklahoma								
Broken Arrow city	30,207	62.6%	18.1%	10.9%	7.4%	0.0%	1.0%	0.0%
Lawton city	7,932	48.4%	29.1%	8.1%	11.5%	2.9%	0.0%	0.0%
Norman city	49,495	61.4%	18.0%	13.4%	6.2%	0.8%	0.0%	0.1%
Oklahoma City city	9,135	56.6%	15.3%	15.8%	9.9%	1.8%	0.3%	0.3%
Tulsa city	10,278	56.7%	21.9%	11.8%	8.2%	0.9%	0.2%	0.3%
Oregon								
Beaverton city	24,555	68.4%	19.1%	10.5%	2.1%	0.0%	0.0%	0.0%
Eugene city	15,357	75.9%	15.8%	4.9%	2.6%	0.3%	0.0%	0.6%
Gresham city	9,740	64.5%	25.3%	7.7%	2.5%	0.0%	0.0%	0.0%
Hillsboro city	8,294	43.0%	34.3%	9.0%	10.4%	2.8%	0.5%	0.0%
Portland city	9,366	61.7%	21.1%	9.1%	6.5%	1.4%	0.2%	0.0%
Salem city	49,576	57.8%	24.7%	12.7%	2.1%	2.8%	0.0%	0.0%
Pennsylvania								
Allentown city	16,978	63.9%	21.5%	8.1%	4.9%	1.5%	0.0%	0.0%
Erie city	18,628	69.3%	14.4%	12.9%	1.8%	0.0%	0.0%	1.4%
Philadelphia city	26,404	73.9%	12.3%	6.5%	6.0%	1.2%	0.1%	0.0%
Pittsburgh city	11,694	74.0%	13.3%	5.2%	5.6%	1.8%	0.0%	0.0%
Rhode Island								
Providence city	157,599	77.8%	12.4%	6.3%	2.2%	0.4%	0.9%	0.0%

Table I-3: Places—Income Class by Age—*Continued*

	Personal Income, Percent by Income Class, Ages 25 to 31									
	Total Millennials	Under $10,000	$10,000 to $19,999	$20,000 to $29,999	$30,000 to $49,999	$50,000 to $74,999	$75,000 to $99,999	$100,000 to $149,999	$150,000 or More	Poverty Rate
Missouri—Cont.										
Kansas City city	50,604	20.2%	17.2%	19.6%	27.0%	12.7%	2.3%	0.8%	0.1%	23.0%
Lee's Summit city	16,680	22.5%	8.1%	19.8%	19.2%	16.0%	10.1%	0.0%	4.3%	10.2%
Springfield city	12,521	27.3%	17.9%	22.4%	21.1%	8.8%	1.4%	1.1%	0.0%	20.4%
St. Louis city	70,063	28.4%	14.9%	12.8%	27.7%	11.4%	1.9%	1.5%	1.4%	21.5%
Montana										
Billings city	11,482	30.3%	17.1%	20.1%	23.4%	9.2%	0.0%	0.0%	0.0%	8.5%
Nebraska										
Lincoln city	48,253	21.7%	14.5%	25.5%	25.6%	10.9%	0.7%	0.7%	0.4%	20.0%
Omaha city	16,521	22.0%	17.4%	17.4%	25.4%	13.2%	3.0%	1.5%	0.0%	20.3%
Nevada										
Henderson city	14,649	24.2%	15.3%	19.8%	26.2%	10.6%	1.6%	2.3%	0.0%	13.0%
Las Vegas city	10,400	29.6%	16.2%	17.2%	23.2%	9.8%	2.5%	1.1%	0.4%	21.8%
North Las Vegas city	36,308	23.2%	19.3%	16.5%	28.1%	9.4%	2.2%	1.3%	0.0%	24.6%
Reno city	17,248	24.8%	18.2%	17.5%	20.8%	12.2%	4.4%	1.9%	0.2%	9.2%
Sparks city	21,677	26.9%	7.3%	18.3%	27.4%	17.5%	1.5%	1.1%	0.0%	22.7%
New Hampshire										
Manchester city	8,128	20.2%	15.0%	14.4%	35.5%	12.1%	2.7%	0.0%	0.0%	36.0%
New Jersey										
Elizabeth city	13,322	35.2%	12.4%	19.1%	21.5%	10.5%	0.8%	0.5%	0.0%	22.9%
Jersey City city	20,602	26.1%	12.8%	13.4%	17.2%	16.7%	6.1%	5.5%	2.2%	20.3%
Newark city	12,887	40.8%	21.7%	17.2%	12.4%	7.0%	0.4%	0.0%	0.5%	24.4%
Paterson city	14,156	37.3%	28.8%	12.4%	15.9%	3.7%	1.9%	0.0%	0.0%	36.4%
New Mexico										
Albuquerque city	11,202	31.1%	18.1%	18.3%	19.3%	9.1%	2.9%	0.8%	0.4%	5.1%
Las Cruces city	14,510	26.8%	22.4%	22.3%	20.7%	3.6%	4.3%	0.0%	0.0%	8.1%
Rio Rancho city	13,193	47.9%	20.8%	2.9%	19.2%	4.9%	0.1%	4.1%	0.0%	12.2%
New York										
Albany city	13,213	24.6%	17.8%	12.0%	24.3%	13.7%	3.2%	3.1%	1.3%	18.9%
Buffalo city	187,507	23.1%	24.5%	12.0%	24.7%	12.2%	2.2%	0.8%	0.6%	31.5%
New York city	159,901	28.2%	13.4%	12.6%	19.0%	13.5%	6.2%	4.8%	2.3%	26.6%
Rochester city	38,294	28.9%	21.3%	22.9%	16.1%	7.6%	1.5%	1.6%	0.0%	36.3%
Syracuse city	24,682	33.8%	15.7%	22.5%	16.7%	7.7%	3.1%	0.5%	0.0%	13.0%
Yonkers city	16,663	31.2%	17.5%	13.8%	19.7%	7.2%	7.0%	3.6%	0.0%	22.8%
North Carolina										
Charlotte city	10,241	23.2%	14.5%	19.6%	24.9%	10.9%	4.0%	2.0%	1.0%	30.9%
Durham city	10,425	23.9%	20.0%	18.1%	21.2%	13.9%	1.5%	0.8%	0.5%	20.4%
Fayetteville city	78,665	35.5%	11.2%	16.1%	20.0%	14.8%	1.7%	0.5%	0.0%	27.9%
Greensboro city	11,325	21.2%	28.2%	19.5%	21.3%	7.4%	2.1%	0.4%	0.0%	25.4%
High Point city	22,974	33.1%	23.3%	22.0%	13.3%	6.1%	1.0%	1.2%	0.0%	35.9%
Raleigh city	15,986	19.6%	17.4%	17.8%	28.4%	11.6%	3.4%	1.4%	0.4%	41.0%
Wilmington city	9,895	18.2%	20.8%	18.8%	28.3%	10.1%	2.4%	1.4%	0.0%	29.7%
Winston-Salem city	52,519	34.7%	16.6%	18.0%	21.5%	7.3%	1.4%	0.0%	0.7%	20.0%
North Dakota										
Fargo city	15,343	18.4%	12.4%	17.8%	34.9%	11.4%	2.0%	3.1%	0.0%	8.0%
Ohio										
Akron city	9,166	27.3%	16.5%	19.7%	23.0%	6.6%	6.9%	0.0%	0.0%	32.0%
Cincinnati city	25,859	27.8%	18.5%	13.7%	26.0%	8.5%	2.7%	2.5%	0.2%	24.5%
Cleveland city	12,165	38.1%	19.3%	15.4%	16.6%	8.0%	1.2%	0.8%	0.6%	20.6%
Columbus city	9,236	20.7%	15.4%	18.5%	28.4%	12.5%	2.4%	1.2%	1.1%	19.8%
Dayton city	10,832	37.5%	20.1%	20.7%	9.9%	10.7%	1.2%	0.0%	0.0%	24.1%
Toledo city	13,277	37.1%	19.6%	12.5%	20.1%	9.7%	0.4%	0.3%	0.3%	24.1%
Oklahoma										
Broken Arrow city	31,718	21.3%	22.7%	18.2%	17.4%	8.2%	7.0%	5.3%	0.0%	33.0%
Lawton city	7,728	35.5%	15.8%	27.9%	17.2%	1.9%	0.6%	1.1%	0.0%	22.2%
Norman city	28,679	35.7%	10.2%	18.2%	24.6%	9.8%	1.4%	0.0%	0.0%	26.5%
Oklahoma City city	10,878	24.8%	12.1%	22.6%	27.8%	8.3%	3.0%	1.2%	0.3%	26.0%
Tulsa city	10,331	26.0%	20.0%	20.3%	21.4%	7.6%	3.7%	1.0%	0.0%	12.3%
Oregon										
Beaverton city	29,417	19.0%	9.3%	20.9%	28.8%	14.0%	7.5%	0.5%	0.0%	37.1%
Eugene city	13,747	40.3%	19.7%	13.0%	20.1%	4.2%	0.0%	0.9%	1.8%	26.4%
Gresham city	12,927	34.9%	27.0%	14.8%	11.3%	8.7%	1.0%	2.3%	0.0%	12.0%
Hillsboro city	8,569	26.7%	13.4%	11.8%	28.5%	12.9%	3.5%	3.2%	0.0%	11.9%
Portland city	10,481	26.5%	18.6%	19.0%	18.0%	10.5%	4.4%	1.9%	1.0%	12.1%
Salem city	54,203	38.7%	16.9%	15.5%	13.1%	10.9%	4.9%	0.0%	0.0%	25.9%
Pennsylvania										
Allentown city	17,782	38.7%	22.5%	9.7%	22.7%	5.8%	0.6%	0.0%	0.0%	28.6%
Erie city	15,866	30.6%	18.8%	22.4%	25.5%	1.5%	1.2%	0.0%	0.0%	21.9%
Philadelphia city	26,725	32.3%	13.3%	13.8%	22.3%	12.8%	4.0%	1.4%	0.2%	22.8%
Pittsburgh city	12,061	21.9%	17.1%	19.8%	19.7%	14.6%	2.5%	2.4%	2.0%	12.8%
Rhode Island										
Providence city	153,279	24.0%	22.9%	17.9%	28.1%	3.0%	3.1%	0.5%	0.5%	21.7%

Table I-3: Places—Income Class by Age—*Continued*

	Total Millennials	Under $10,000	$10,000 to $19,999	$20,000 to $29,999	$30,000 to $49,999	$50,000 to $74,999	$75,000 to $99,999	$100,000 or More
				Personal Income, Percent by Income Class, Ages 18 to 24				
South Carolina								
Charleston city	28,852	71.5%	13.6%	9.0%	4.8%	1.1%	0.0%	0.0%
Columbia city	10,980	57.6%	26.5%	12.0%	3.8%	0.0%	0.0%	0.0%
North Charleston city	156,541	60.2%	23.7%	8.9%	5.6%	1.7%	0.0%	0.0%
South Dakota								
Sioux Falls city	62,062	41.5%	26.3%	23.6%	6.5%	0.0%	0.0%	2.2%
Tennessee								
Chattanooga city	85,425	65.9%	18.9%	10.3%	3.8%	1.0%	0.0%	0.0%
Clarksville city	6,413	55.8%	16.0%	12.2%	13.7%	2.3%	0.0%	0.0%
Knoxville city	4,983	67.8%	15.0%	11.4%	5.4%	0.3%	0.0%	0.0%
Memphis city	40,982	69.0%	16.7%	7.3%	6.7%	0.3%	0.0%	0.1%
Murfreesboro city	12,714	49.8%	33.0%	11.3%	4.3%	1.7%	0.0%	0.0%
Nashville-Davidson metropolitan govt (bal)	16,200	60.3%	20.0%	9.4%	6.3%	3.5%	0.4%	0.2%
Texas								
Abilene city	11,107	58.4%	19.3%	12.7%	9.7%	0.0%	0.0%	0.0%
Amarillo city	5,131	52.3%	29.2%	9.7%	7.5%	0.0%	0.0%	1.2%
Arlington city	15,177	55.5%	27.3%	9.0%	5.8%	0.7%	0.2%	1.4%
Austin city	20,003	58.0%	21.4%	11.6%	6.8%	1.7%	0.3%	0.2%
Beaumont city	16,139	73.7%	12.3%	8.9%	2.7%	2.4%	0.0%	0.0%
Brownsville city	71,283	76.3%	13.6%	4.2%	5.6%	0.0%	0.2%	0.0%
Carrollton city	22,368	50.1%	19.8%	11.9%	14.8%	2.8%	0.7%	0.0%
College Station city	10,104	71.8%	17.7%	5.2%	4.3%	1.0%	0.0%	0.0%
Corpus Christi city	15,987	50.5%	23.7%	8.4%	12.5%	3.4%	0.0%	1.4%
Dallas city	12,876	57.7%	20.1%	11.2%	7.8%	3.0%	0.1%	0.0%
Denton city	10,170	65.6%	26.0%	3.5%	4.0%	0.8%	0.1%	0.0%
El Paso city	8,659	67.8%	17.6%	9.7%	4.4%	0.5%	0.1%	0.0%
Fort Worth city	25,919	55.3%	23.3%	12.1%	6.7%	2.0%	0.2%	0.3%
Frisco city	5,998	53.3%	23.9%	15.7%	6.3%	0.9%	0.0%	0.0%
Garland city	11,506	60.9%	27.7%	5.7%	4.8%	1.0%	0.0%	0.0%
Grand Prairie city	19,946	64.3%	18.2%	11.4%	5.1%	0.0%	0.9%	0.0%
Houston city	27,960	59.9%	18.6%	12.5%	6.5%	1.8%	0.4%	0.2%
Irving city	31,990	58.7%	14.3%	17.9%	7.7%	0.4%	0.4%	0.6%
Killeen city	35,185	64.7%	14.7%	12.6%	5.9%	0.8%	1.3%	0.0%
Laredo city	21,540	69.3%	22.1%	4.8%	3.7%	0.2%	0.0%	0.0%
Lewisville city	12,181	40.4%	27.9%	18.2%	11.2%	1.9%	0.0%	0.4%
Lubbock city	9,328	65.7%	18.2%	9.8%	6.3%	0.1%	0.0%	0.0%
McAllen city	33,029	79.3%	15.2%	2.7%	2.8%	0.0%	0.0%	0.0%
McKinney city	9,863	52.6%	17.2%	10.1%	18.7%	0.3%	1.2%	0.0%
Mesquite city	6,025	60.5%	17.7%	14.5%	5.0%	2.2%	0.0%	0.0%
Midland city	24,887	42.0%	21.8%	9.7%	14.9%	6.3%	3.1%	2.1%
Odessa city	20,040	57.5%	17.3%	9.2%	7.1%	3.5%	5.4%	0.0%
Pasadena city	52,303	58.2%	23.9%	10.9%	6.5%	0.5%	0.0%	0.0%
Pearland city	42,412	59.0%	33.9%	7.0%	0.0%	0.0%	0.0%	0.0%
Plano city	12,331	56.1%	14.3%	8.2%	9.6%	11.0%	0.8%	0.0%
Richardson city	35,874	65.1%	19.2%	7.3%	5.6%	2.7%	0.0%	0.0%
Round Rock city	12,131	70.1%	17.8%	9.6%	2.6%	0.0%	0.0%	0.0%
San Angelo city	12,516	44.7%	30.2%	9.3%	9.9%	1.9%	4.0%	0.0%
San Antonio city	31,680	64.9%	19.1%	9.5%	5.0%	1.3%	0.2%	0.1%
Tyler city	13,574	67.8%	13.3%	14.8%	2.8%	0.0%	0.5%	0.8%
Waco city	12,260	68.7%	21.8%	5.1%	2.6%	1.4%	0.3%	0.0%
Wichita Falls city	76,603	56.3%	26.8%	7.4%	8.8%	0.0%	0.0%	0.6%
Utah								
Orem city	39,294	57.0%	19.5%	16.8%	6.7%	0.0%	0.0%	0.0%
Provo city	23,953	69.4%	20.6%	7.7%	1.1%	0.5%	0.0%	0.7%
Salt Lake City city	10,887	58.1%	16.8%	20.0%	3.4%	1.0%	0.6%	0.0%
West Jordan city	31,461	47.2%	23.8%	17.0%	9.9%	0.7%	1.4%	0.0%
West Valley City city	9,594	54.2%	25.5%	17.3%	3.0%	0.0%	0.0%	0.0%
Virginia								
Alexandria city	11,369	46.3%	19.6%	13.8%	16.7%	3.0%	0.5%	0.0%
Chesapeake city	14,568	67.2%	16.5%	7.3%	5.6%	2.7%	0.4%	0.3%
Hampton city	13,437	46.2%	26.1%	15.6%	10.7%	1.4%	0.0%	0.0%
Newport News city	47,498	48.8%	18.6%	23.2%	8.0%	1.3%	0.0%	0.0%
Norfolk city	14,451	53.6%	20.8%	17.5%	6.4%	1.6%	0.2%	0.0%
Portsmouth city	12,213	49.9%	25.6%	17.2%	5.2%	1.3%	0.7%	0.0%
Richmond city	25,064	72.0%	13.7%	4.7%	7.2%	2.1%	0.4%	0.0%
Roanoke city	13,462	64.8%	27.2%	6.6%	1.4%	0.0%	0.0%	0.0%
Virginia Beach city	75,399	51.2%	29.5%	13.5%	5.0%	0.6%	0.1%	0.0%
Washington								
Bellevue city	10,499	67.6%	19.5%	3.6%	3.4%	3.4%	1.2%	1.3%
Everett city	11,275	62.6%	11.3%	11.3%	13.9%	0.9%	0.0%	0.0%
Federal Way city	9,300	57.3%	19.2%	10.6%	6.5%	6.4%	0.0%	0.0%
Kent city	10,514	65.3%	18.5%	8.5%	6.2%	1.5%	0.0%	0.0%
Renton city	13,843	67.0%	9.0%	9.9%	9.8%	4.2%	0.0%	0.0%
Seattle city	6,793	57.6%	16.8%	9.6%	8.5%	2.8%	2.3%	2.4%
Spokane city	9,091	63.9%	19.8%	8.2%	6.6%	1.0%	0.0%	0.5%
Spokane Valley city	35,181	65.1%	18.2%	7.1%	5.8%	3.8%	0.0%	0.0%

Table I-3: Places—Income Class by Age—*Continued*

	Personal Income, Percent by Income Class, Ages 25 to 31									
	Total Millennials	Under $10,000	$10,000 to $19,999	$20,000 to $29,999	$30,000 to $49,999	$50,000 to $74,999	$75,000 to $99,999	$100,000 to $149,999	$150,000 or More	Poverty Rate
South Carolina										
Charleston city	20,883	28.2%	13.3%	11.6%	24.9%	18.3%	1.4%	2.4%	0.0%	39.8%
Columbia city	11,094	36.0%	22.1%	11.0%	23.0%	6.4%	1.1%	0.0%	0.4%	15.1%
North Charleston city	178,234	24.6%	18.2%	16.6%	22.0%	11.1%	6.8%	0.7%	0.0%	20.5%
South Dakota										
Sioux Falls city	129,957	13.2%	8.4%	21.4%	42.7%	10.2%	0.8%	2.5%	0.9%	17.0%
Tennessee										
Chattanooga city	105,249	28.5%	25.3%	19.0%	19.7%	4.2%	0.7%	1.6%	1.0%	15.1%
Clarksville city	9,364	25.8%	14.6%	12.9%	28.9%	13.7%	2.3%	1.8%	0.0%	5.3%
Knoxville city	14,815	26.9%	18.9%	22.0%	22.4%	6.3%	1.6%	1.9%	0.0%	4.7%
Memphis city	37,965	37.5%	17.1%	13.1%	23.7%	6.4%	1.1%	0.0%	0.0%	23.1%
Murfreesboro city	18,020	22.6%	18.4%	15.3%	17.6%	18.8%	5.7%	1.0%	0.5%	9.3%
Nashville-Davidson metropolitan govt (bal)	16,170	21.2%	20.0%	18.6%	27.4%	9.1%	2.3%	1.2%	0.1%	12.7%
Texas										
Abilene city	9,634	29.9%	9.1%	25.1%	20.9%	12.6%	2.4%	0.0%	0.0%	19.5%
Amarillo city	12,786	31.2%	18.7%	15.1%	20.5%	8.7%	1.6%	4.0%	0.3%	12.7%
Arlington city	17,790	23.2%	22.0%	16.7%	24.7%	10.8%	0.6%	0.9%	1.0%	15.3%
Austin city	17,750	18.1%	18.4%	19.0%	24.7%	11.1%	5.6%	1.9%	1.2%	26.0%
Beaumont city	19,062	23.0%	17.4%	26.3%	16.7%	10.0%	2.1%	2.9%	1.6%	9.3%
Brownsville city	105,232	43.2%	29.5%	8.4%	14.9%	2.2%	0.2%	1.5%	0.0%	18.7%
Carrollton city	20,225	17.1%	10.5%	17.3%	32.7%	18.1%	2.6%	1.5%	0.0%	32.6%
College Station city	9,416	29.4%	19.7%	19.1%	18.3%	8.2%	4.2%	0.0%	1.1%	6.8%
Corpus Christi city	19,442	26.8%	14.0%	20.5%	20.6%	10.5%	3.4%	3.9%	0.3%	11.2%
Dallas city	8,282	24.4%	20.0%	17.5%	20.5%	11.0%	3.0%	2.4%	1.3%	31.2%
Denton city	12,129	25.0%	13.7%	19.6%	28.9%	8.2%	3.6%	0.6%	0.4%	16.6%
El Paso city	8,481	34.0%	24.6%	14.9%	18.4%	5.2%	2.1%	0.6%	0.3%	20.3%
Fort Worth city	23,818	24.8%	16.8%	15.7%	19.6%	17.0%	2.7%	3.1%	0.3%	26.7%
Frisco city	10,724	22.9%	11.9%	12.1%	19.9%	22.3%	7.0%	3.9%	0.0%	13.8%
Garland city	11,973	28.7%	16.6%	21.8%	22.1%	7.8%	2.8%	0.2%	0.0%	25.5%
Grand Prairie city	14,450	26.9%	25.1%	19.4%	18.3%	8.6%	1.2%	0.4%	0.0%	32.9%
Houston city	20,876	24.8%	15.3%	16.2%	22.9%	11.5%	5.5%	2.1%	1.7%	29.5%
Irving city	44,419	19.1%	18.3%	11.9%	33.9%	9.0%	6.5%	1.0%	0.3%	25.8%
Killeen city	36,656	36.6%	10.7%	13.5%	23.8%	11.2%	1.5%	0.4%	2.4%	27.2%
Laredo city	24,997	44.8%	18.5%	13.3%	10.1%	8.7%	3.2%	1.4%	0.0%	22.0%
Lewisville city	13,874	16.5%	7.3%	20.8%	34.7%	12.5%	6.5%	1.7%	0.0%	16.7%
Lubbock city	10,488	27.4%	17.2%	18.0%	24.3%	8.7%	2.8%	0.3%	1.4%	10.1%
McAllen city	27,866	35.3%	15.5%	11.1%	25.8%	9.6%	0.4%	0.4%	1.9%	28.9%
McKinney city	19,311	15.3%	4.9%	19.7%	27.4%	22.9%	6.8%	2.3%	0.7%	7.9%
Mesquite city	7,630	25.8%	20.3%	16.0%	25.9%	9.2%	2.0%	0.0%	0.8%	8.0%
Midland city	18,013	20.7%	9.0%	7.3%	23.4%	22.3%	9.8%	6.3%	1.2%	40.9%
Odessa city	24,312	28.7%	13.2%	21.3%	10.2%	13.4%	6.7%	4.2%	2.3%	25.4%
Pasadena city	23,034	33.8%	23.7%	15.0%	14.4%	10.8%	1.5%	0.7%	0.0%	41.7%
Pearland city	41,641	21.8%	10.3%	22.8%	12.5%	26.5%	3.9%	2.2%	0.0%	27.2%
Plano city	7,345	17.1%	16.3%	10.0%	32.2%	15.5%	5.6%	2.8%	0.4%	12.5%
Richardson city	26,666	24.8%	18.5%	7.6%	18.4%	16.2%	6.4%	7.5%	0.5%	27.8%
Round Rock city	10,191	23.7%	17.5%	27.6%	19.6%	8.1%	2.9%	0.3%	0.3%	14.3%
San Angelo city	9,254	18.5%	21.2%	11.8%	34.9%	10.3%	1.5%	1.8%	0.0%	15.7%
San Antonio city	30,360	27.7%	18.0%	21.2%	21.6%	7.6%	2.3%	1.6%	0.1%	30.4%
Tyler city	11,068	27.1%	13.8%	24.9%	23.6%	9.5%	1.0%	0.0%	0.0%	24.7%
Waco city	10,105	37.6%	23.2%	11.1%	24.6%	1.9%	0.9%	0.8%	0.0%	7.0%
Wichita Falls city	51,809	38.5%	14.4%	14.6%	18.3%	13.6%	0.0%	0.6%	0.0%	30.8%
Utah										
Orem city	42,921	34.0%	14.0%	18.0%	22.6%	9.9%	0.8%	0.7%	0.0%	18.1%
Provo city	9,937	40.2%	21.1%	9.7%	18.6%	7.1%	3.4%	0.0%	0.0%	31.8%
Salt Lake City city	11,620	22.3%	19.6%	20.0%	23.2%	11.3%	1.7%	1.5%	0.3%	23.7%
West Jordan city	37,505	24.9%	14.5%	20.3%	28.3%	3.7%	3.7%	2.7%	1.9%	18.3%
West Valley City city	9,405	25.4%	23.0%	16.0%	27.7%	7.9%	0.0%	0.0%	0.0%	9.4%
Virginia										
Alexandria city	11,856	15.5%	5.3%	18.2%	22.3%	21.3%	13.7%	2.3%	1.3%	22.2%
Chesapeake city	16,353	30.2%	12.9%	14.6%	25.9%	10.8%	3.2%	1.9%	0.5%	17.9%
Hampton city	12,353	35.7%	7.4%	16.7%	31.6%	7.3%	1.3%	0.0%	0.0%	29.9%
Newport News city	52,685	23.3%	15.9%	15.3%	33.5%	8.4%	3.3%	0.3%	0.0%	9.9%
Norfolk city	14,393	25.5%	14.7%	20.8%	22.5%	13.9%	1.0%	1.4%	0.2%	27.8%
Portsmouth city	12,024	22.9%	10.5%	25.7%	34.7%	4.5%	0.7%	1.0%	0.0%	12.6%
Richmond city	12,838	24.7%	16.7%	21.2%	23.1%	8.0%	3.7%	0.8%	1.6%	40.4%
Roanoke city	13,278	25.1%	27.3%	16.2%	18.0%	10.0%	3.5%	0.0%	0.0%	29.1%
Virginia Beach city	102,748	15.5%	18.4%	21.1%	24.6%	16.1%	2.1%	1.6%	0.6%	24.0%
Washington										
Bellevue city	12,596	21.6%	14.5%	12.3%	14.9%	18.8%	7.6%	8.6%	1.8%	27.9%
Everett city	12,251	25.6%	7.4%	10.0%	34.9%	13.0%	6.0%	3.2%	0.0%	13.7%
Federal Way city	10,664	28.5%	15.8%	24.8%	18.1%	9.2%	3.6%	0.0%	0.0%	7.2%
Kent city	13,268	31.6%	16.7%	20.3%	19.5%	7.0%	2.1%	1.1%	1.7%	38.2%
Renton city	15,680	25.8%	22.6%	16.7%	22.9%	6.8%	0.6%	4.2%	0.5%	18.4%
Seattle city	10,033	14.4%	14.6%	15.2%	28.6%	15.9%	4.8%	4.7%	1.8%	19.2%
Spokane city	13,432	29.1%	17.7%	18.5%	25.4%	5.7%	3.0%	0.0%	0.6%	8.2%
Spokane Valley city	41,249	17.5%	22.1%	22.0%	33.2%	4.0%	1.2%	0.0%	0.0%	19.7%

Table I-3: Places—Income Class by Age—*Continued*

		Personal Income, Percent by Income Class, Ages 18 to 24						
	Total Millennials	Under $10,000	$10,000 to $19,999	$20,000 to $29,999	$30,000 to $49,999	$50,000 to $74,999	$75,000 to $99,999	$100,000 or More
Washington—Cont.								
Tacoma city....................................	14,389	57.7%	17.2%	14.0%	7.2%	3.7%	0.0%	0.2%
Vancouver city	17,952	63.4%	18.4%	12.1%	3.7%	2.1%	0.0%	0.4%
Yakima city....................................	27,308	65.0%	19.7%	10.6%	4.6%	0.0%	0.0%	0.0%
Wisconsin								
Green Bay city................................	25,113	50.9%	37.0%	8.2%	3.8%	0.0%	0.0%	0.0%
Kenosha city	10,717	67.6%	13.6%	15.7%	3.1%	0.0%	0.0%	0.0%
Madison city	18,205	60.5%	21.7%	8.3%	3.9%	5.6%	0.0%	0.0%
Milwaukee city	11,052	70.5%	17.8%	8.3%	1.9%	1.5%	0.1%	0.0%

Table I-3: Places—Income Class by Age—*Continued*

| | Personal Income, Percent by Income Class, Ages 25 to 31 | | | | | | | | | |
	Total Millennials	Under $10,000	$10,000 to $19,999	$20,000 to $29,999	$30,000 to $49,999	$50,000 to $74,999	$75,000 to $99,999	$100,000 to $149,999	$150,000 or More	Poverty Rate
Washington—Cont.										
Tacoma city................................	12,667	29.7%	18.5%	13.5%	21.9%	11.2%	4.0%	0.4%	0.7%	27.8%
Vancouver city	12,989	29.2%	20.3%	19.3%	22.4%	4.7%	2.0%	1.8%	0.3%	33.3%
Yakima city..................................	19,756	24.8%	19.9%	16.4%	25.9%	9.6%	2.9%	0.5%	0.0%	37.2%
Wisconsin										
Green Bay city.............................	20,129	18.6%	18.8%	27.6%	27.0%	6.7%	0.0%	1.3%	0.0%	35.1%
Kenosha city	8,808	30.1%	7.1%	33.6%	15.3%	13.1%	0.8%	0.0%	0.0%	20.0%
Madison city	18,266	18.3%	18.4%	14.6%	27.2%	13.5%	3.7%	3.7%	0.5%	24.6%
Milwaukee city	9,945	27.7%	22.9%	17.2%	19.5%	11.0%	1.4%	0.4%	0.0%	17.7%

Table I-4: Metropolitan/Micropolitan Statistical Areas—Income Class by Age

	Total Millennials	\multicolumn{7}{c}{Personal Income, Percent by Income, Ages 18 to 24}
		Under $10,000	$10,000 to $19,999	$20,000 to $29,999	$30,000 to $49,999	$50,000 to $74,999	$75,000 to $99,999	$100,000 or More
Abilene, TX	23,017	56.0%	22.1%	10.0%	10.1%	1.8%	0.0%	0.1%
Adrian, MI micro	9,371	64.4%	14.8%	14.8%	4.6%	0.2%	1.2%	0.0%
Akron, OH	80,759	63.3%	18.4%	10.5%	6.4%	1.1%	0.0%	0.3%
Albany-Schenectady-Troy, NY	94,295	69.7%	14.9%	7.4%	6.2%	1.7%	0.1%	0.0%
Albany, GA	18,490	85.9%	8.7%	4.8%	0.4%	0.3%	0.0%	0.0%
Albany, OR	15,636	68.0%	23.3%	5.0%	3.6%	0.0%	0.0%	0.0%
Albertville, AL micro	6,743	61.2%	30.0%	5.6%	2.8%	0.3%	0.0%	0.0%
Albuquerque, NM	86,268	64.2%	20.5%	7.8%	6.2%	1.1%	0.2%	0.0%
Alexandria, LA	14,798	70.2%	12.6%	9.6%	7.5%	0.2%	0.0%	0.0%
Allentown-Bethlehem-Easton, PA-NJ	75,340	67.0%	15.6%	10.1%	4.8%	1.8%	0.7%	0.1%
Altoona, PA	12,217	69.7%	8.9%	11.7%	6.0%	3.7%	0.0%	0.0%
Amarillo, TX	26,298	54.9%	25.4%	10.6%	8.1%	0.2%	0.0%	1.0%
Ames, IA	25,348	66.5%	16.7%	6.2%	9.3%	1.3%	0.0%	0.0%
Anchorage, AK	45,083	41.8%	19.1%	17.5%	15.7%	5.7%	0.1%	0.0%
Ann Arbor, MI	64,295	53.3%	15.9%	13.1%	10.6%	7.1%	0.0%	0.0%
Anniston-Oxford-Jacksonville, AL	11,943	70.1%	18.2%	7.3%	2.8%	1.4%	0.0%	0.0%
Appleton, WI	21,776	66.6%	13.1%	13.7%	5.4%	1.2%	0.0%	0.0%
Asheville, NC	33,633	65.1%	23.3%	9.1%	2.1%	0.5%	0.0%	0.0%
Ashtabula, OH micro	8,246	67.0%	15.5%	8.0%	9.5%	0.0%	0.0%	0.0%
Athens-Clarke County, GA	42,955	73.6%	14.8%	6.2%	3.1%	2.2%	0.0%	0.0%
Atlanta-Sandy Springs-Roswell, GA	510,259	66.8%	18.5%	7.6%	5.8%	0.8%	0.3%	0.2%
Atlantic City-Hammonton, NJ	26,718	66.7%	18.9%	8.7%	4.3%	1.2%	0.2%	0.0%
Auburn-Opelika, AL	30,018	66.1%	18.0%	7.4%	6.4%	2.1%	0.0%	0.0%
Augusta-Richmond County, GA-SC	58,079	70.3%	17.9%	7.4%	3.7%	0.7%	0.0%	0.0%
Augusta-Waterville, ME micro	10,198	50.8%	17.6%	17.7%	4.9%	7.6%	0.0%	1.5%
Austin-Round Rock, TX	195,346	61.3%	20.7%	10.6%	5.7%	1.3%	0.2%	0.2%
Bakersfield, CA	95,288	64.7%	19.1%	9.0%	5.5%	1.3%	0.4%	0.1%
Baltimore-Columbia-Towson, MD	260,777	60.3%	18.7%	9.8%	9.0%	1.7%	0.3%	0.1%
Bangor, ME	18,248	64.7%	22.7%	3.5%	8.4%	0.8%	0.0%	0.0%
Barnstable Town, MA	13,695	52.6%	23.4%	9.7%	6.8%	7.5%	0.0%	0.0%
Baton Rouge, LA	99,623	67.7%	17.7%	4.5%	6.2%	2.2%	1.3%	0.3%
Battle Creek, MI	11,086	52.5%	30.8%	9.4%	7.3%	0.0%	0.0%	0.0%
Bay City, MI	9,251	57.9%	24.3%	13.5%	4.3%	0.0%	0.0%	0.0%
Beaumont-Port Arthur, TX	41,111	69.1%	15.8%	8.4%	4.3%	2.3%	0.2%	0.0%
Beckley, WV	11,317	72.7%	18.5%	4.3%	2.0%	1.6%	0.0%	0.9%
Bellingham, WA	31,693	59.7%	23.3%	12.0%	4.0%	0.6%	0.0%	0.4%
Bend-Redmond, OR	11,498	53.9%	26.6%	13.9%	5.1%	0.6%	0.0%	0.0%
Billings, MT	17,198	60.8%	22.6%	8.8%	5.8%	0.0%	1.6%	0.4%
Binghamton, NY	28,948	72.5%	13.2%	7.2%	6.5%	0.6%	0.0%	0.0%
Birmingham-Hoover, AL	103,964	68.8%	16.8%	8.8%	3.6%	1.3%	0.4%	0.4%
Bismarck, ND	12,626	41.9%	29.3%	10.0%	13.2%	5.6%	0.0%	0.0%
Blacksburg-Christiansburg-Radford, VA	42,782	77.5%	12.8%	5.1%	4.1%	0.0%	0.4%	0.2%
Bloomington, IL	33,533	68.1%	13.3%	9.8%	8.7%	0.1%	0.0%	0.0%
Bloomington, IN	41,831	82.3%	12.0%	2.7%	2.6%	0.5%	0.0%	0.0%
Bloomsburg-Berwick, PA	11,393	70.0%	11.9%	6.3%	6.7%	5.1%	0.0%	0.0%
Boise City, ID	60,531	66.1%	19.0%	13.1%	1.6%	0.1%	0.2%	0.0%
Boston-Cambridge-Newton, MA-NH	460,199	65.8%	15.1%	8.6%	7.8%	2.3%	0.2%	0.1%
Boulder, CO	46,928	64.1%	17.5%	10.3%	6.3%	0.6%	1.0%	0.3%
Bowling Green, KY	20,162	69.2%	16.4%	8.7%	5.5%	0.0%	0.0%	0.1%
Bremerton-Silverdale, WA	25,705	53.3%	19.0%	19.5%	6.9%	1.3%	0.0%	0.0%
Bridgeport-Stamford-Norwalk, CT	75,893	62.9%	17.5%	12.4%	4.4%	2.1%	0.2%	0.6%
Brownsville-Harlingen, TX	44,095	76.2%	14.1%	5.8%	3.7%	0.0%	0.1%	0.0%
Brunswick, GA	10,762	57.1%	18.4%	17.2%	6.0%	1.2%	0.0%	0.0%
Buffalo-Cheektowaga-Niagara Falls, NY	113,628	60.5%	21.7%	9.9%	5.6%	1.9%	0.2%	0.1%
Burlington-South Burlington, VT	28,043	61.8%	20.5%	12.2%	2.8%	1.3%	1.3%	0.0%
Burlington, NC	14,914	66.7%	27.3%	4.8%	1.2%	0.0%	0.0%	0.0%
California-Lexington Park, MD	10,336	57.3%	19.5%	6.5%	15.6%	1.1%	0.0%	0.0%
Canton-Massillon, OH	35,605	58.8%	22.2%	11.4%	3.5%	3.5%	0.0%	0.6%
Cape Coral-Fort Myers, FL	47,505	60.2%	22.0%	12.0%	4.2%	1.5%	0.1%	0.0%
Cape Girardeau, MO-IL	11,316	62.7%	20.3%	15.0%	0.4%	1.5%	0.0%	0.0%
Carbondale-Marion, IL	16,679	79.9%	11.6%	4.6%	2.8%	1.2%	0.0%	0.0%
Carson City, NV	3,934	61.7%	20.9%	5.9%	7.9%	3.7%	0.0%	0.0%
Casper, WY	7,750	47.6%	31.6%	3.0%	7.4%	6.8%	0.9%	2.6%
Cedar Rapids, IA	22,914	60.9%	20.5%	8.6%	8.8%	1.0%	0.0%	0.2%
Chambersburg-Waynesboro, PA	11,960	64.7%	18.2%	11.4%	5.0%	0.0%	0.0%	0.8%
Champaign-Urbana, IL	51,413	76.5%	11.3%	8.1%	3.7%	0.4%	0.0%	0.0%
Charleston-North Charleston, SC	74,064	63.8%	18.6%	9.5%	6.3%	1.3%	0.4%	0.0%
Charleston, WV	18,423	63.4%	22.8%	7.6%	3.9%	1.8%	0.5%	0.0%
Charlotte-Concord-Gastonia, NC-SC	208,491	66.0%	16.4%	9.2%	6.9%	0.9%	0.1%	0.5%
Charlottesville, VA	27,546	81.9%	6.5%	4.5%	5.2%	1.3%	0.6%	0.0%
Chattanooga, TN-GA	46,961	67.9%	19.1%	9.8%	2.6%	0.7%	0.0%	0.0%
Cheyenne, WY	12,437	60.4%	17.3%	12.6%	8.7%	0.0%	0.0%	1.0%
Chicago-Naperville-Elgin, IL-IN-WI	907,719	65.8%	17.2%	9.2%	5.5%	1.9%	0.3%	0.1%
Chico, CA	33,787	64.0%	18.7%	10.2%	5.7%	0.6%	0.0%	0.8%
Cincinnati, OH-KY-IN	193,039	59.9%	21.5%	10.5%	6.2%	1.3%	0.2%	0.4%
Clarksburg, WV micro	6,577	48.4%	36.8%	9.1%	5.8%	0.0%	0.0%	0.0%
Clarksville, TN-KY	34,064	50.8%	18.4%	15.6%	12.6%	2.7%	0.0%	0.0%
Cleveland-Elyria, OH	180,390	62.8%	22.2%	9.4%	4.5%	1.0%	0.1%	0.0%
Cleveland, TN	11,815	72.6%	13.7%	10.7%	3.0%	0.0%	0.0%	0.0%

Table I-4: Metropolitan/Micropolitan Statistical Areas—Income Class by Age—*Continued*

	Total Millennials	Personal Income, Ages 25 to 31								Poverty Rate
		Under $10,000	$10,000 to $19,999	$20,000 to $29,999	$30,000 to $49,999	$50,000 to $74,999	$75,000 to $99,999	$100,000 to $149,999	$150,000 or More	
Abilene, TX	17,970	30.7%	11.2%	23.8%	20.3%	12.0%	1.9%	0.0%	0.0%	21.0%
Adrian, MI micro	8,669	34.1%	23.4%	20.2%	13.4%	5.2%	3.7%	0.1%	0.0%	23.8%
Akron, OH	61,851	24.9%	15.2%	19.8%	22.1%	11.5%	5.5%	0.6%	0.3%	23.3%
Albany-Schenectady-Troy, NY	75,888	16.0%	17.3%	19.8%	28.1%	12.0%	4.6%	1.7%	0.5%	18.0%
Albany, GA	16,012	42.0%	18.4%	17.5%	13.2%	6.2%	1.4%	1.2%	0.0%	34.1%
Albany, OR	8,269	41.2%	20.8%	15.1%	14.7%	6.2%	1.9%	0.0%	0.0%	40.7%
Albertville, AL micro	8,670	13.1%	43.8%	8.1%	27.9%	6.1%	1.0%	0.0%	0.0%	18.3%
Albuquerque, NM	86,523	35.6%	18.0%	15.6%	19.8%	7.3%	2.3%	1.1%	0.3%	26.4%
Alexandria, LA	15,070	34.9%	14.3%	19.0%	24.1%	4.9%	0.9%	1.9%	0.0%	25.9%
Allentown-Bethlehem-Easton, PA-NJ	69,565	25.0%	16.3%	15.9%	23.0%	14.2%	3.5%	1.0%	1.1%	18.2%
Altoona, PA	10,280	21.2%	27.0%	17.9%	20.5%	7.5%	5.7%	0.0%	0.3%	20.4%
Amarillo, TX	26,914	30.9%	16.7%	16.2%	22.5%	7.9%	1.5%	4.1%	0.2%	25.9%
Ames, IA	9,972	16.5%	19.9%	14.9%	30.6%	13.4%	4.7%	0.0%	0.0%	39.7%
Anchorage, AK	45,086	20.4%	11.9%	18.9%	25.8%	11.6%	8.5%	2.9%	0.0%	8.5%
Ann Arbor, MI	36,258	22.2%	18.1%	19.4%	21.6%	12.5%	3.0%	3.1%	0.2%	32.4%
Anniston-Oxford-Jacksonville, AL	10,550	28.8%	22.6%	21.2%	14.1%	12.6%	0.0%	0.7%	0.0%	31.6%
Appleton, WI	20,703	18.0%	14.9%	17.7%	28.8%	18.2%	2.4%	0.0%	0.0%	11.7%
Asheville, NC	36,992	23.6%	30.7%	16.0%	20.3%	5.7%	1.5%	2.0%	0.2%	21.6%
Ashtabula, OH micro	8,300	27.9%	17.3%	18.2%	21.3%	14.4%	0.9%	0.0%	0.0%	19.8%
Athens-Clarke County, GA	21,108	27.8%	26.0%	20.9%	17.6%	6.5%	0.4%	0.4%	0.3%	40.8%
Atlanta-Sandy Springs-Roswell, GA	513,894	27.9%	17.6%	16.9%	21.5%	10.3%	3.7%	1.7%	0.5%	19.1%
Atlantic City-Hammonton, NJ	22,550	32.5%	19.7%	12.5%	19.5%	11.4%	2.2%	1.5%	0.7%	23.0%
Auburn-Opelika, AL	14,147	22.7%	20.7%	15.4%	26.3%	4.4%	4.4%	6.1%	0.0%	28.4%
Augusta-Richmond County, GA-SC	55,809	33.3%	20.8%	15.6%	19.1%	8.6%	1.5%	0.9%	0.1%	22.9%
Augusta-Waterville, ME micro	9,257	14.6%	20.1%	34.2%	18.2%	12.9%	0.0%	0.0%	0.0%	11.6%
Austin-Round Rock, TX	233,683	20.9%	17.4%	18.2%	24.7%	11.5%	4.8%	1.5%	1.0%	20.7%
Bakersfield, CA	90,977	37.8%	21.3%	15.5%	15.1%	6.1%	2.3%	1.3%	0.7%	23.2%
Baltimore-Columbia-Towson, MD	279,796	23.3%	11.6%	12.4%	26.2%	17.7%	5.7%	2.1%	1.0%	13.7%
Bangor, ME	13,381	36.4%	14.2%	19.2%	18.1%	11.7%	0.4%	0.0%	0.0%	22.4%
Barnstable Town, MA	13,287	13.0%	9.0%	23.7%	36.3%	11.7%	5.5%	0.0%	0.7%	10.4%
Baton Rouge, LA	78,834	28.0%	14.7%	11.4%	26.4%	13.3%	4.1%	1.6%	0.4%	25.8%
Battle Creek, MI	10,299	19.4%	26.6%	19.0%	26.8%	6.6%	1.6%	0.0%	0.0%	17.1%
Bay City, MI	9,135	34.7%	13.6%	10.3%	29.4%	11.1%	0.9%	0.0%	0.0%	16.1%
Beaumont-Port Arthur, TX	38,385	26.8%	19.6%	17.3%	17.8%	10.5%	3.5%	2.6%	1.8%	19.7%
Beckley, WV	10,268	37.7%	21.7%	12.0%	19.8%	3.6%	5.0%	0.0%	0.0%	38.3%
Bellingham, WA	17,498	26.8%	18.8%	23.0%	19.1%	4.9%	4.4%	3.0%	0.0%	23.6%
Bend-Redmond, OR	14,309	28.8%	15.3%	23.2%	19.9%	8.3%	2.3%	2.3%	0.0%	14.4%
Billings, MT	14,191	32.5%	15.3%	16.3%	21.0%	12.0%	0.0%	0.5%	2.4%	23.6%
Binghamton, NY	19,910	32.1%	18.1%	18.4%	17.6%	11.1%	1.7%	0.4%	0.5%	27.3%
Birmingham-Hoover, AL	107,298	33.0%	15.0%	13.5%	21.5%	12.1%	3.1%	1.2%	0.6%	21.8%
Bismarck, ND	14,455	8.1%	8.5%	15.8%	37.1%	23.0%	6.3%	1.2%	0.0%	8.9%
Blacksburg-Christiansburg-Radford, VA	14,493	32.8%	8.7%	17.4%	28.9%	10.0%	1.0%	1.1%	0.0%	38.8%
Bloomington, IL	19,327	19.4%	15.3%	14.1%	26.3%	22.3%	2.7%	0.0%	0.0%	27.9%
Bloomington, IN	15,823	34.9%	21.9%	19.3%	17.2%	5.4%	1.3%	0.0%	0.0%	47.7%
Bloomsburg-Berwick, PA	6,406	27.8%	12.1%	16.7%	21.7%	18.9%	2.9%	0.0%	0.0%	18.2%
Boise City, ID	58,731	27.7%	22.6%	19.9%	22.1%	5.6%	1.6%	0.1%	0.5%	24.8%
Boston-Cambridge-Newton, MA-NH	479,162	19.1%	12.6%	13.7%	24.6%	18.7%	6.8%	3.6%	0.9%	14.6%
Boulder, CO	28,813	16.1%	13.6%	16.9%	28.0%	15.7%	6.8%	0.9%	1.8%	25.0%
Bowling Green, KY	16,090	28.4%	15.9%	16.4%	20.3%	19.0%	0.0%	0.0%	0.0%	27.2%
Bremerton-Silverdale, WA	23,899	26.5%	15.8%	11.9%	25.6%	17.2%	2.0%	1.0%	0.0%	15.1%
Bridgeport-Stamford-Norwalk, CT	72,592	22.2%	16.4%	13.2%	19.2%	18.2%	6.0%	2.9%	1.8%	12.2%
Brownsville-Harlingen, TX	33,550	41.2%	25.8%	9.9%	17.0%	4.6%	0.8%	0.7%	0.0%	33.1%
Brunswick, GA	9,932	37.6%	12.4%	17.7%	27.6%	4.5%	0.0%	0.0%	0.2%	20.3%
Buffalo-Cheektowaga-Niagara Falls, NY	104,738	22.7%	18.3%	15.7%	25.2%	14.2%	2.9%	0.5%	0.5%	20.5%
Burlington-South Burlington, VT	20,130	16.5%	14.5%	20.4%	35.4%	9.4%	3.3%	0.0%	0.6%	17.1%
Burlington, NC	13,510	36.5%	18.9%	19.9%	10.3%	12.5%	1.9%	0.0%	0.0%	29.2%
California-Lexington Park, MD	8,534	29.4%	9.6%	8.8%	23.6%	15.3%	7.7%	5.7%	0.0%	6.9%
Canton-Massillon, OH	32,199	31.0%	17.6%	18.8%	22.4%	6.2%	0.2%	2.2%	1.5%	18.2%
Cape Coral-Fort Myers, FL	48,549	32.3%	20.1%	20.4%	18.7%	6.5%	1.9%	0.1%	0.1%	22.7%
Cape Girardeau, MO-IL	8,643	27.9%	19.8%	13.0%	23.9%	10.9%	0.7%	3.8%	0.0%	22.0%
Carbondale-Marion, IL	13,124	42.6%	14.6%	19.5%	16.9%	5.6%	0.8%	0.0%	0.0%	31.3%
Carson City, NV	5,005	26.6%	18.3%	23.7%	19.6%	6.5%	5.4%	0.0%	0.0%	16.4%
Casper, WY	8,364	22.4%	21.1%	14.6%	19.9%	4.8%	17.1%	0.0%	0.0%	18.0%
Cedar Rapids, IA	26,270	14.4%	21.7%	15.9%	23.0%	21.8%	2.4%	0.8%	0.0%	11.9%
Chambersburg-Waynesboro, PA	13,003	22.9%	13.5%	16.3%	24.2%	18.4%	1.8%	2.9%	0.0%	12.3%
Champaign-Urbana, IL	26,505	25.3%	17.9%	22.8%	22.0%	10.8%	0.6%	0.7%	0.0%	34.8%
Charleston-North Charleston, SC	75,141	22.6%	18.5%	14.4%	25.9%	12.9%	3.8%	1.7%	0.2%	20.3%
Charleston, WV	18,065	22.9%	12.4%	24.0%	19.7%	16.6%	1.5%	2.1%	0.8%	21.2%
Charlotte-Concord-Gastonia, NC-SC	209,266	27.2%	16.3%	17.8%	24.6%	9.1%	2.7%	1.8%	0.5%	19.2%
Charlottesville, VA	19,067	20.1%	17.1%	13.2%	30.6%	11.9%	3.3%	2.3%	1.4%	26.2%
Chattanooga, TN-GA	49,220	30.6%	19.8%	18.9%	22.5%	5.1%	1.5%	1.0%	0.6%	23.2%
Cheyenne, WY	8,039	16.4%	8.7%	22.9%	31.9%	3.1%	0.0%	0.0%	1.1%	19.1%
Chicago-Naperville-Elgin, IL-IN-WI	961,624	25.1%	14.7%	15.2%	22.5%	13.9%	5.3%	2.2%	1.1%	16.8%
Chico, CA	19,755	34.8%	20.8%	11.8%	16.5%	11.2%	1.4%	0.7%	2.7%	34.5%
Cincinnati, OH-KY-IN	188,981	25.6%	14.2%	18.7%	24.5%	11.1%	3.4%	1.9%	0.6%	17.0%
Clarksburg, WV micro	6,877	29.0%	6.9%	16.8%	18.1%	27.6%	1.6%	0.0%	0.0%	11.0%
Clarksville, TN-KY	36,102	30.6%	12.2%	13.5%	25.3%	14.7%	2.4%	1.3%	0.0%	19.5%
Cleveland-Elyria, OH	172,704	26.2%	16.0%	17.8%	23.0%	12.6%	3.2%	0.9%	0.4%	19.1%
Cleveland, TN	10,284	21.4%	14.1%	27.7%	27.4%	5.3%	0.0%	4.0%	0.0%	23.9%

Table I-4: Metropolitan/Micropolitan Statistical Areas—Income Class by Age—*Continued*

	Total Millennials	Under $10,000	$10,000 to $19,999	$20,000 to $29,999	$30,000 to $49,999	$50,000 to $74,999	$75,000 to $99,999	$100,000 or More
Coeur d'Alene, ID	12,617	55.1%	28.1%	8.2%	8.6%	0.0%	0.0%	0.0%
College Station-Bryan, TX	60,432	70.5%	16.7%	6.6%	5.5%	0.7%	0.0%	0.0%
Colorado Springs, CO	71,720	53.6%	23.5%	13.6%	7.1%	1.3%	0.1%	0.8%
Columbia, MO	36,413	75.5%	17.8%	4.0%	1.9%	0.0%	0.8%	0.0%
Columbia, SC	97,384	62.0%	20.5%	11.4%	5.9%	0.1%	0.1%	0.0%
Columbus, GA-AL	40,180	56.4%	18.5%	17.1%	7.2%	0.4%	0.3%	0.0%
Columbus, IN	6,922	44.3%	28.3%	13.9%	7.4%	6.1%	0.0%	0.0%
Columbus, OH	171,487	60.0%	20.4%	10.8%	7.8%	0.9%	0.0%	0.0%
Concord, NH micro	12,366	70.1%	22.6%	4.6%	2.8%	0.0%	0.0%	0.0%
Cookeville, TN micro	14,041	71.5%	15.6%	9.3%	3.1%	0.5%	0.0%	0.0%
Corpus Christi, TX	47,608	53.8%	21.4%	8.1%	11.7%	4.0%	0.0%	1.0%
Corvallis, OR	17,148	66.4%	25.1%	5.2%	3.3%	0.0%	0.0%	0.0%
Crestview-Fort Walton Beach-Destin, FL	25,602	48.3%	21.7%	21.6%	7.2%	1.1%	0.0%	0.0%
Cumberland, MD-WV	11,119	77.6%	13.2%	4.6%	4.2%	0.4%	0.0%	0.0%
Dallas-Fort Worth-Arlington, TX	628,923	59.3%	21.6%	10.6%	6.4%	1.8%	0.2%	0.2%
Dalton, GA	14,006	51.9%	24.7%	12.2%	9.9%	0.0%	1.4%	0.0%
Danville, IL	6,498	48.3%	27.6%	18.7%	3.2%	1.7%	0.0%	0.4%
Danville, VA micro	8,865	71.6%	15.5%	8.2%	3.9%	0.8%	0.0%	0.0%
Daphne-Fairhope-Foley, AL	16,338	66.9%	18.1%	12.2%	2.9%	0.0%	0.0%	0.0%
Davenport-Moline-Rock Island, IA-IL	37,821	63.5%	21.8%	8.3%	4.6%	1.6%	0.0%	0.2%
Dayton, OH	81,355	65.5%	19.8%	8.8%	4.9%	1.0%	0.0%	0.0%
Decatur, AL	13,146	62.9%	25.1%	8.9%	3.1%	0.0%	0.0%	0.0%
Decatur, IL	10,229	66.1%	19.5%	7.9%	5.1%	1.4%	0.0%	0.0%
Deltona-Daytona Beach-Ormond Beach, FL	52,478	64.9%	20.9%	9.7%	4.1%	0.0%	0.3%	0.0%
Denver-Aurora-Lakewood, CO	228,854	56.0%	21.0%	11.9%	9.0%	1.4%	0.3%	0.3%
Des Moines-West Des Moines, IA	47,538	45.5%	27.6%	13.6%	10.9%	2.1%	0.4%	0.0%
Detroit-Warren-Dearborn, MI	382,812	65.4%	18.6%	8.6%	5.6%	1.7%	0.1%	0.1%
Dothan, AL	11,453	67.6%	18.1%	10.5%	3.1%	0.8%	0.0%	0.0%
Dover, DE	17,233	64.3%	19.2%	8.4%	5.8%	2.3%	0.0%	0.0%
Dubuque, IA	9,974	55.4%	23.6%	13.0%	7.6%	0.4%	0.0%	0.0%
Duluth, MN-WI	31,911	61.7%	22.7%	6.0%	8.8%	0.5%	0.2%	0.0%
Dunn, NC micro	11,742	72.7%	12.8%	7.4%	6.1%	0.8%	0.2%	0.0%
Durham-Chapel Hill, NC	62,916	73.5%	12.9%	7.9%	4.7%	0.3%	0.0%	0.7%
East Stroudsburg, PA	19,021	70.7%	12.6%	12.3%	4.0%	0.4%	0.0%	0.0%
Eau Claire, WI	21,989	59.9%	18.3%	14.4%	5.2%	2.2%	0.0%	0.0%
El Centro, CA	20,303	74.1%	14.2%	8.4%	1.3%	2.0%	0.0%	0.0%
El Paso, TX	97,204	65.4%	18.7%	11.8%	3.7%	0.4%	0.0%	0.0%
Elizabethtown-Fort Knox, KY	12,405	48.5%	32.4%	16.0%	1.3%	1.8%	0.0%	0.0%
Elkhart-Goshen, IN	17,694	48.6%	31.3%	5.1%	13.5%	1.4%	0.0%	0.0%
Elmira, NY	8,030	60.5%	23.4%	5.5%	10.6%	0.0%	0.0%	0.0%
Erie, PA	29,620	71.1%	17.2%	8.8%	2.2%	0.0%	0.0%	0.7%
Eugene, OR	46,109	74.9%	16.4%	5.6%	2.4%	0.4%	0.0%	0.4%
Eureka-Arcata-Fortuna, CA micro	18,113	66.2%	19.4%	9.7%	2.8%	1.9%	0.0%	0.0%
Evansville, IN-KY	31,837	64.8%	21.1%	6.1%	7.7%	0.4%	0.0%	0.0%
Fairbanks, AK	13,103	33.1%	32.6%	22.9%	5.0%	6.1%	0.3%	0.0%
Fargo, ND-MN	39,007	51.1%	26.7%	12.2%	8.1%	1.3%	0.5%	0.0%
Farmington, NM	12,308	76.3%	15.3%	6.0%	1.3%	0.0%	1.0%	0.0%
Fayetteville-Springdale-Rogers, AR-MO	53,424	60.0%	21.1%	13.1%	4.8%	1.0%	0.0%	0.0%
Fayetteville, NC	47,605	56.6%	18.1%	17.4%	6.3%	1.6%	0.0%	0.0%
Flagstaff, AZ	26,701	66.2%	21.5%	7.1%	3.5%	1.7%	0.0%	0.0%
Flint, MI	38,737	71.0%	19.9%	6.2%	2.3%	0.7%	0.0%	0.0%
Florence-Muscle Shoals, AL	15,187	73.9%	19.9%	3.3%	2.3%	0.6%	0.0%	0.0%
Florence, SC	19,834	69.5%	19.2%	6.5%	3.4%	1.4%	0.0%	0.0%
Fond du Lac, WI	9,105	60.7%	13.9%	15.6%	9.4%	0.4%	0.0%	0.0%
Fort Collins, CO	44,712	63.0%	21.2%	12.4%	1.7%	1.6%	0.1%	0.0%
Fort Smith, AR-OK	25,420	63.5%	24.5%	6.9%	4.7%	0.4%	0.0%	0.0%
Fort Wayne, IN	40,876	59.4%	23.1%	10.8%	6.2%	0.0%	0.2%	0.2%
Fresno, CA	108,464	71.5%	18.7%	6.3%	3.0%	0.4%	0.0%	0.1%
Gadsden, AL	9,315	81.2%	13.5%	3.2%	2.1%	0.0%	0.0%	0.0%
Gainesville, FL	60,876	68.7%	20.7%	6.6%	2.9%	0.8%	0.4%	0.0%
Gainesville, GA	17,558	59.9%	22.8%	10.8%	4.9%	1.2%	0.0%	0.3%
Gettysburg, PA	10,996	68.2%	15.6%	13.5%	2.2%	0.5%	0.0%	0.0%
Glens Falls, NY	10,305	61.4%	24.4%	8.9%	4.5%	0.8%	0.0%	0.0%
Goldsboro, NC	11,846	70.4%	8.1%	10.4%	8.0%	1.7%	1.4%	0.0%
Grand Forks, ND-MN	19,839	62.6%	25.0%	7.1%	1.7%	3.0%	0.6%	0.0%
Grand Island, NE	6,752	57.2%	23.9%	6.7%	12.1%	0.0%	0.0%	0.2%
Grand Junction, CO	15,894	61.4%	16.6%	11.5%	5.5%	4.8%	0.0%	0.0%
Grand Rapids-Wyoming, MI	105,657	60.6%	21.5%	9.3%	7.6%	1.1%	0.0%	0.0%
Grants Pass, OR	6,276	67.4%	9.8%	10.7%	12.0%	0.0%	0.0%	0.0%
Great Falls, MT	8,278	50.1%	25.7%	14.8%	7.6%	1.2%	0.7%	0.0%
Greeley, CO	29,349	65.7%	21.6%	6.5%	6.2%	0.1%	0.0%	0.0%
Green Bay, WI	28,652	49.4%	27.1%	12.5%	10.0%	1.0%	0.0%	0.0%
Greensboro-High Point, NC	73,916	69.3%	16.4%	9.5%	3.9%	0.7%	0.0%	0.1%
Greenville-Anderson-Mauldin, SC	81,975	69.8%	17.2%	8.7%	4.1%	0.1%	0.0%	0.0%
Greenville, NC	33,517	64.1%	26.3%	4.4%	5.2%	0.0%	0.0%	0.0%
Greenwood, SC micro	10,326	73.7%	23.0%	0.8%	1.7%	0.7%	0.0%	0.0%
Gulfport-Biloxi-Pascagoula, MS	36,851	58.6%	16.4%	17.6%	7.5%	0.1%	0.0%	0.0%
Hagerstown-Martinsburg, MD-WV	22,838	66.0%	15.4%	9.2%	7.3%	2.1%	0.0%	0.0%

Table I-4: Metropolitan/Micropolitan Statistical Areas—Income Class by Age—*Continued*

| | Personal Income, Ages 25 to 31 | | | | | | | | | |
	Total Millennials	Under $10,000	$10,000 to $19,999	$20,000 to $29,999	$30,000 to $49,999	$50,000 to $74,999	$75,000 to $99,999	$100,000 to $149,999	$150,000 or More	Poverty Rate
Coeur d'Alene, ID	12,885	35.6%	19.8%	9.4%	24.0%	9.0%	0.8%	1.2%	0.0%	15.3%
College Station-Bryan, TX	27,067	27.5%	20.6%	17.0%	20.7%	10.2%	3.3%	0.0%	0.7%	42.2%
Colorado Springs, CO	71,404	24.8%	14.4%	15.9%	27.4%	13.5%	2.8%	1.2%	0.0%	15.6%
Columbia, MO	20,117	33.6%	21.1%	18.0%	21.8%	2.5%	1.7%	1.4%	0.0%	41.7%
Columbia, SC	74,192	31.4%	17.2%	15.5%	26.6%	7.2%	1.6%	0.3%	0.3%	23.7%
Columbus, GA-AL	32,277	35.5%	21.4%	17.7%	15.9%	7.1%	1.6%	0.5%	0.2%	26.4%
Columbus, IN	8,417	24.2%	22.2%	13.9%	22.5%	16.1%	1.1%	0.0%	0.0%	14.0%
Columbus, OH	209,330	22.1%	16.6%	18.0%	25.5%	13.2%	2.3%	1.5%	0.7%	17.3%
Concord, NH micro	9,340	23.6%	14.1%	23.7%	28.8%	8.4%	0.7%	0.0%	0.7%	15.6%
Cookeville, TN micro	8,616	47.9%	17.1%	15.0%	11.6%	7.2%	0.0%	1.2%	0.0%	42.1%
Corpus Christi, TX	42,706	27.9%	13.9%	19.7%	20.2%	11.7%	3.4%	2.9%	0.2%	18.1%
Corvallis, OR	9,091	40.8%	19.2%	13.7%	15.0%	5.6%	5.7%	0.0%	0.0%	41.1%
Crestview-Fort Walton Beach-Destin, FL	28,160	32.3%	15.8%	12.9%	20.5%	12.9%	4.2%	0.7%	0.7%	20.5%
Cumberland, MD-WV	7,509	41.3%	16.6%	13.8%	19.6%	4.7%	1.8%	2.1%	0.0%	18.2%
Dallas-Fort Worth-Arlington, TX	675,672	23.3%	16.8%	16.5%	24.5%	13.1%	3.4%	1.8%	0.6%	18.0%
Dalton, GA	13,382	34.0%	20.9%	14.2%	25.3%	3.0%	0.7%	1.7%	0.0%	20.7%
Danville, IL	7,160	26.7%	21.9%	10.6%	18.2%	21.7%	0.0%	0.9%	0.0%	16.7%
Danville, VA micro	7,368	32.2%	16.4%	12.9%	27.7%	9.0%	1.7%	0.0%	0.0%	27.7%
Daphne-Fairhope-Foley, AL	14,271	27.4%	19.4%	23.8%	18.3%	8.0%	2.0%	1.1%	0.0%	21.9%
Davenport-Moline-Rock Island, IA-IL	32,259	29.3%	14.4%	16.0%	24.9%	11.7%	3.6%	0.0%	0.0%	21.1%
Dayton, OH	72,534	27.7%	17.3%	18.8%	19.6%	12.6%	2.2%	1.2%	0.6%	22.8%
Decatur, AL	11,358	34.8%	16.7%	28.2%	11.8%	8.5%	0.0%	0.0%	0.0%	21.5%
Decatur, IL	9,557	17.3%	32.0%	16.3%	21.0%	10.9%	1.8%	0.7%	0.0%	25.6%
Deltona-Daytona Beach-Ormond Beach, FL	46,853	37.3%	20.7%	17.8%	16.0%	5.2%	0.8%	1.7%	0.6%	23.5%
Denver-Aurora-Lakewood, CO	286,801	20.6%	15.4%	15.9%	28.1%	13.8%	3.7%	1.9%	0.6%	15.1%
Des Moines-West Des Moines, IA	63,439	22.0%	13.3%	17.7%	32.0%	12.6%	1.6%	0.6%	0.3%	17.8%
Detroit-Warren-Dearborn, MI	354,920	30.2%	17.3%	14.9%	20.6%	11.5%	3.7%	1.3%	0.6%	21.6%
Dothan, AL	12,742	27.8%	14.7%	16.4%	28.0%	6.9%	4.5%	1.6%	0.0%	21.4%
Dover, DE	15,816	21.1%	19.1%	15.6%	28.7%	13.6%	1.9%	0.0%	0.0%	13.1%
Dubuque, IA	7,213	7.9%	19.0%	30.3%	33.0%	9.7%	0.0%	0.0%	0.0%	18.5%
Duluth, MN-WI	24,800	27.9%	20.0%	15.1%	20.0%	11.0%	5.3%	0.4%	0.4%	29.0%
Dunn, NC micro	14,304	39.3%	17.0%	9.3%	13.6%	16.5%	3.2%	0.8%	0.2%	21.5%
Durham-Chapel Hill, NC	57,485	23.8%	20.3%	18.4%	22.3%	12.4%	1.1%	1.4%	0.3%	25.1%
East Stroudsburg, PA	10,573	24.9%	14.1%	11.7%	40.9%	5.7%	2.8%	0.0%	0.0%	20.7%
Eau Claire, WI	14,910	23.8%	14.3%	14.4%	26.8%	16.7%	0.3%	0.0%	3.8%	18.2%
El Centro, CA	18,063	41.8%	12.1%	15.3%	18.6%	11.3%	0.2%	0.7%	0.0%	23.9%
El Paso, TX	81,406	34.2%	24.4%	14.7%	18.4%	5.0%	2.4%	0.6%	0.3%	25.9%
Elizabethtown-Fort Knox, KY	14,186	27.4%	19.6%	21.5%	26.5%	4.2%	0.3%	0.4%	0.0%	21.8%
Elkhart-Goshen, IN	17,121	34.8%	19.2%	17.2%	17.2%	6.9%	4.8%	0.0%	0.0%	21.1%
Elmira, NY	8,633	32.9%	13.2%	9.0%	21.9%	18.3%	2.8%	2.0%	0.0%	19.5%
Erie, PA	26,649	22.9%	16.8%	20.8%	29.4%	6.5%	3.3%	0.3%	0.0%	23.4%
Eugene, OR	29,269	35.1%	17.6%	15.8%	24.3%	3.5%	0.2%	2.4%	1.0%	36.1%
Eureka-Arcata-Fortuna, CA micro	13,592	30.4%	32.7%	13.7%	13.8%	9.0%	0.0%	0.0%	0.3%	30.6%
Evansville, IN-KY	27,587	30.2%	15.7%	18.6%	23.3%	7.8%	4.2%	0.0%	0.2%	21.2%
Fairbanks, AK	13,155	11.6%	10.2%	20.6%	31.7%	19.7%	4.3%	0.9%	1.0%	6.7%
Fargo, ND-MN	26,148	19.5%	11.5%	14.7%	37.6%	13.5%	1.5%	1.8%	0.0%	20.5%
Farmington, NM	11,027	46.6%	12.6%	18.9%	13.2%	6.5%	2.3%	0.0%	0.0%	32.4%
Fayetteville-Springdale-Rogers, AR-MO	47,752	25.5%	18.4%	16.8%	21.9%	8.4%	6.9%	1.0%	1.0%	20.8%
Fayetteville, NC	44,471	34.5%	12.5%	16.2%	22.4%	12.6%	1.4%	0.2%	0.2%	20.8%
Flagstaff, AZ	14,018	27.7%	12.4%	17.8%	23.9%	14.2%	3.6%	0.2%	0.0%	30.4%
Flint, MI	35,354	36.4%	25.0%	12.5%	17.3%	7.5%	0.4%	0.8%	0.0%	26.6%
Florence-Muscle Shoals, AL	11,902	36.8%	18.0%	19.8%	20.6%	4.8%	0.0%	0.0%	0.0%	28.7%
Florence, SC	16,353	41.5%	17.9%	8.6%	22.9%	9.1%	0.0%	0.0%	0.0%	31.9%
Fond du Lac, WI	5,647	24.7%	14.4%	20.6%	28.0%	12.4%	0.0%	0.0%	0.0%	11.4%
Fort Collins, CO	29,699	18.8%	18.1%	18.4%	23.8%	13.7%	3.4%	0.7%	3.0%	27.8%
Fort Smith, AR-OK	26,551	38.2%	20.7%	13.1%	17.7%	6.6%	2.0%	1.5%	0.2%	28.6%
Fort Wayne, IN	38,716	30.5%	17.4%	16.1%	24.4%	9.8%	1.8%	0.0%	0.0%	21.2%
Fresno, CA	101,037	38.8%	17.9%	15.1%	16.1%	8.2%	2.8%	0.9%	0.2%	31.7%
Gadsden, AL	8,012	33.4%	18.8%	13.3%	29.0%	5.0%	0.4%	0.0%	0.0%	21.0%
Gainesville, FL	30,284	30.8%	17.6%	21.5%	20.3%	7.2%	2.2%	0.4%	0.0%	40.4%
Gainesville, GA	16,371	27.4%	16.2%	26.2%	13.2%	14.4%	0.3%	2.0%	0.3%	24.6%
Gettysburg, PA	6,546	31.8%	16.6%	14.5%	21.3%	10.5%	4.3%	1.0%	0.0%	12.7%
Glens Falls, NY	9,741	30.3%	12.1%	24.6%	16.2%	15.2%	1.6%	0.0%	0.0%	15.6%
Goldsboro, NC	11,414	25.9%	13.5%	23.7%	22.2%	12.1%	2.5%	0.0%	0.0%	18.2%
Grand Forks, ND-MN	8,762	17.3%	13.3%	7.9%	39.3%	14.8%	6.2%	0.2%	1.0%	22.9%
Grand Island, NE	6,511	20.3%	35.8%	11.1%	23.0%	5.4%	2.3%	2.1%	0.0%	23.8%
Grand Junction, CO	14,985	35.7%	11.0%	14.0%	15.3%	18.1%	0.8%	4.2%	1.0%	23.0%
Grand Rapids-Wyoming, MI	97,581	25.3%	18.4%	17.8%	25.5%	9.6%	2.4%	0.8%	0.2%	20.5%
Grants Pass, OR	5,678	28.3%	34.2%	13.0%	19.9%	2.4%	2.0%	0.0%	0.2%	21.9%
Great Falls, MT	9,149	22.2%	17.9%	20.3%	34.8%	3.6%	0.9%	0.0%	0.3%	22.5%
Greeley, CO	27,777	26.8%	15.0%	10.5%	26.7%	16.5%	2.9%	0.9%	0.5%	20.2%
Green Bay, WI	27,343	18.3%	16.3%	27.2%	27.9%	7.6%	1.4%	0.5%	0.8%	12.5%
Greensboro-High Point, NC	67,690	23.6%	26.5%	19.8%	21.6%	6.3%	1.3%	0.7%	0.3%	25.2%
Greenville-Anderson-Mauldin, SC	72,710	35.1%	14.7%	19.5%	20.0%	7.1%	2.4%	0.9%	0.3%	22.1%
Greenville, NC	15,455	23.0%	15.3%	13.1%	28.4%	12.0%	5.6%	1.9%	0.8%	42.7%
Greenwood, SC micro	7,394	35.1%	22.6%	10.1%	28.4%	3.4%	0.3%	0.0%	0.0%	39.4%
Gulfport-Biloxi-Pascagoula, MS	38,287	28.0%	18.6%	19.1%	23.2%	9.7%	0.5%	0.9%	0.0%	22.2%
Hagerstown-Martinsburg, MD-WV	21,487	26.0%	20.8%	19.0%	20.3%	10.6%	2.8%	0.3%	0.1%	17.5%

Table I-4: Metropolitan/Micropolitan Statistical Areas—Income Class by Age—*Continued*

	Total Millennials	Under $10,000	$10,000 to $19,999	$20,000 to $29,999	$30,000 to $49,999	$50,000 to $74,999	$75,000 to $99,999	$100,000 or More
			Personal Income, Percent by Income, Ages 18 to 24					
Hammond, LA	14,203	65.3%	11.8%	11.1%	5.8%	3.5%	2.6%	0.0%
Hanford-Corcoran, CA	17,431	63.1%	18.5%	10.1%	8.2%	0.1%	0.0%	0.0%
Harrisburg-Carlisle, PA	52,087	64.8%	17.6%	11.5%	5.1%	0.9%	0.0%	0.0%
Harrisonburg, VA	25,833	76.7%	11.1%	9.3%	2.2%	0.6%	0.0%	0.0%
Hartford-West Hartford-East Hartford, CT	121,030	66.3%	16.5%	8.3%	6.2%	2.4%	0.2%	0.1%
Hattiesburg, MS	22,591	79.0%	14.9%	3.9%	2.1%	0.0%	0.0%	0.0%
Hickory-Lenoir-Morganton, NC	31,386	64.0%	23.3%	8.9%	3.6%	0.0%	0.0%	0.2%
Hilo, HI micro	15,240	76.2%	11.9%	6.2%	5.0%	0.5%	0.0%	0.0%
Hilton Head Island-Bluffton-Beaufort, SC.	20,318	53.6%	26.4%	8.2%	11.8%	0.0%	0.0%	0.0%
Hinesville, GA	11,580	59.6%	18.1%	10.3%	11.6%	0.4%	0.0%	0.0%
Holland, MI micro	9,499	55.4%	26.0%	7.4%	11.2%	0.0%	0.0%	0.0%
Homosassa Springs, FL	8,383	72.6%	18.2%	4.7%	2.8%	0.0%	1.7%	0.0%
Hot Springs, AR	8,161	63.3%	19.6%	13.2%	0.0%	3.9%	0.0%	0.0%
Houma-Thibodaux, LA	21,875	60.3%	11.7%	13.2%	12.7%	0.2%	1.5%	0.4%
Houston-The Woodlands-Sugar Land, TX	585,394	61.3%	19.4%	11.3%	6.0%	1.5%	0.4%	0.2%
Huntington-Ashland, WV-KY-OH	32,303	67.5%	14.5%	10.4%	4.6%	2.0%	1.1%	0.0%
Huntsville, AL	43,181	62.0%	22.8%	8.9%	3.4%	2.5%	0.5%	0.0%
Idaho Falls, ID	13,418	63.2%	24.5%	9.1%	3.1%	0.0%	0.0%	0.0%
Indianapolis-Carmel-Anderson, IN	172,522	59.8%	20.6%	12.4%	5.6%	1.5%	0.0%	0.1%
Iowa City, IA	33,957	64.2%	15.2%	10.5%	9.4%	0.7%	0.0%	0.0%
Ithaca, NY	27,064	71.3%	17.4%	6.4%	3.8%	1.0%	0.0%	0.0%
Jackson, MI	14,147	64.4%	23.2%	4.3%	8.2%	0.0%	0.0%	0.0%
Jackson, MS	55,933	71.8%	13.4%	7.7%	6.2%	0.8%	0.1%	0.0%
Jackson, TN	14,392	74.4%	13.9%	7.7%	3.0%	0.9%	0.0%	0.0%
Jacksonville, FL	128,721	62.4%	22.2%	8.6%	5.9%	0.7%	0.2%	0.0%
Jacksonville, NC	38,939	36.6%	19.1%	27.6%	14.4%	2.0%	0.0%	0.3%
Jamestown-Dunkirk-Fredonia, NY micro.	15,702	70.0%	17.4%	10.4%	1.3%	0.9%	0.0%	0.0%
Janesville-Beloit, WI	14,267	57.7%	18.3%	20.2%	3.7%	0.0%	0.0%	0.0%
Jefferson City, MO	14,811	67.1%	16.4%	11.8%	4.0%	0.6%	0.0%	0.0%
Johnson City, TN	21,384	67.4%	19.4%	8.5%	4.2%	0.5%	0.0%	0.1%
Johnstown, PA	13,064	66.7%	14.4%	7.0%	6.1%	5.1%	0.8%	0.0%
Jonesboro, AR	13,440	61.1%	26.6%	4.5%	7.8%	0.0%	0.0%	0.0%
Joplin, MO	17,153	54.0%	18.7%	10.2%	15.0%	2.1%	0.0%	0.0%
Kahului-Wailuku-Lahaina, HI	10,449	50.1%	16.7%	14.3%	7.9%	11.0%	0.0%	0.0%
Kalamazoo-Portage, MI	48,062	62.7%	22.0%	9.6%	5.1%	0.5%	0.0%	0.0%
Kalispell, MT micro	6,985	69.1%	16.6%	13.9%	0.0%	0.5%	0.0%	0.0%
Kankakee, IL	11,416	73.8%	12.9%	4.8%	5.2%	3.4%	0.0%	0.0%
Kansas City, MO-KS	177,722	55.9%	23.1%	10.5%	8.7%	1.6%	0.2%	0.0%
Kennewick-Richland, WA	24,991	54.0%	22.5%	17.2%	5.1%	1.3%	0.0%	0.0%
Killeen-Temple, TX	54,892	53.5%	19.5%	18.2%	8.1%	0.4%	0.4%	0.0%
Kingsport-Bristol-Bristol, TN-VA	25,175	68.0%	21.9%	5.0%	4.8%	0.3%	0.0%	0.0%
Kingston, NY	18,701	65.7%	18.4%	8.1%	6.5%	1.3%	0.0%	0.0%
Knoxville, TN	83,818	66.5%	18.7%	10.1%	4.3%	0.5%	0.0%	0.0%
Kokomo, IN	5,932	51.3%	30.4%	8.4%	4.6%	5.3%	0.0%	0.0%
La Crosse-Onalaska, WI-MN	19,433	58.2%	23.9%	10.6%	6.5%	0.8%	0.0%	0.0%
Lafayette-West Lafayette, IN	47,508	70.5%	13.8%	12.1%	2.7%	0.8%	0.0%	0.0%
Lafayette, LA	53,794	60.5%	19.5%	8.8%	8.9%	1.4%	0.6%	0.2%
Lake Charles, LA	20,994	66.8%	17.0%	7.3%	4.4%	2.3%	2.4%	0.0%
Lake Havasu City-Kingman, AZ	14,136	73.1%	16.7%	5.4%	3.8%	0.9%	0.0%	0.0%
Lakeland-Winter Haven, FL	55,573	62.6%	19.7%	12.3%	3.8%	0.7%	1.0%	0.0%
Lancaster, PA	50,538	59.2%	23.5%	10.3%	5.3%	1.4%	0.0%	0.3%
Lansing-East Lansing, MI	73,289	73.7%	14.9%	4.4%	5.5%	1.4%	0.2%	0.0%
Laredo, TX	28,519	69.2%	21.6%	5.3%	3.5%	0.3%	0.0%	0.0%
Las Cruces, NM	32,427	64.3%	22.9%	7.0%	5.3%	0.6%	0.0%	0.0%
Las Vegas-Henderson-Paradise, NV	182,345	60.2%	19.6%	11.2%	8.1%	0.8%	0.0%	0.1%
Lawrence, KS	24,686	65.3%	16.4%	6.4%	7.1%	3.4%	0.0%	1.4%
Lawton, OK	18,502	49.9%	26.1%	6.7%	14.9%	2.4%	0.0%	0.0%
Lebanon, PA	10,926	60.0%	16.3%	13.5%	8.5%	1.6%	0.0%	0.0%
Lewiston-Auburn, ME	9,557	66.5%	21.3%	10.6%	0.0%	1.6%	0.0%	0.0%
Lewiston, ID-WA	7,110	69.0%	17.2%	13.0%	0.4%	0.3%	0.0%	0.0%
Lexington-Fayette, KY	58,404	64.7%	23.7%	7.7%	3.6%	0.0%	0.0%	0.2%
Lima, OH	10,770	62.2%	13.0%	17.2%	7.5%	0.0%	0.0%	0.0%
Lincoln, NE	49,014	66.7%	17.8%	8.8%	6.3%	0.3%	0.0%	0.0%
Little Rock-North Little Rock-Conway, AR	70,624	57.7%	20.2%	13.0%	7.2%	1.2%	0.6%	0.0%
Logan, UT-ID	20,371	54.8%	24.4%	13.6%	7.2%	0.0%	0.0%	0.0%
Longview, TX	23,450	64.0%	27.2%	4.3%	3.0%	1.3%	0.2%	0.0%
Longview, WA	8,540	61.6%	19.0%	15.4%	3.4%	0.6%	0.0%	0.0%
Los Angeles-Long Beach-Anaheim, CA	1,326,162	67.2%	18.1%	8.3%	4.8%	1.2%	0.3%	0.1%
Louisville/Jefferson County, KY-IN	109,505	59.8%	21.8%	11.0%	5.7%	1.5%	0.1%	0.1%
Lubbock, TX	49,404	65.3%	18.9%	9.0%	6.2%	0.6%	0.0%	0.0%
Lumberton, NC micro	13,959	74.7%	12.2%	8.1%	4.6%	0.4%	0.0%	0.0%
Lynchburg, VA	33,122	73.1%	15.5%	7.2%	3.8%	0.4%	0.0%	0.0%
Macon, GA	26,659	78.0%	13.5%	3.7%	4.6%	0.0%	0.0%	0.2%
Madera, CA	15,435	74.1%	20.7%	3.7%	0.6%	0.2%	0.0%	0.7%
Madison, WI	77,713	61.6%	20.2%	8.7%	5.2%	4.0%	0.0%	0.3%
Manchester-Nashua, NH	32,994	61.7%	18.6%	6.7%	7.6%	4.7%	0.4%	0.3%

Table I-4: Metropolitan/Micropolitan Statistical Areas—Income Class by Age—*Continued*

	Personal Income, Ages 25 to 31								Poverty Rate
	Total Millennials	Under $10,000	$10,000 to $19,999	$20,000 to $29,999	$30,000 to $49,999	$50,000 to $74,999	$75,000 to $99,999	$100,000 to $149,999	$150,000 or More	
Hammond, LA	14,288	32.9%	22.6%	14.4%	17.0%	9.6%	1.3%	0.0%	2.2%	26.6%
Hanford-Corcoran, CA	17,382	39.2%	16.3%	20.7%	18.2%	4.9%	0.0%	0.5%	0.1%	21.5%
Harrisburg-Carlisle, PA	49,754	24.7%	14.3%	14.4%	28.5%	14.0%	3.3%	0.6%	0.3%	18.7%
Harrisonburg, VA	11,307	14.0%	32.5%	12.5%	31.8%	6.0%	3.1%	0.1%	0.0%	33.5%
Hartford-West Hartford-East Hartford, CT	105,077	23.6%	12.6%	13.4%	27.6%	14.7%	5.0%	2.7%	0.3%	13.3%
Hattiesburg, MS	14,510	38.1%	10.6%	24.2%	17.3%	7.2%	1.1%	1.0%	0.4%	38.6%
Hickory-Lenoir-Morganton, NC	27,792	36.6%	12.4%	22.9%	23.5%	1.8%	2.3%	0.4%	0.0%	21.6%
Hilo, HI micro	16,102	41.2%	10.2%	20.8%	17.6%	7.5%	2.7%	0.0%	0.0%	25.9%
Hilton Head Island-Bluffton-Beaufort, SC.	17,693	32.4%	16.2%	17.1%	24.4%	9.9%	0.0%	0.0%	0.0%	21.5%
Hinesville, GA	10,508	28.3%	18.2%	10.9%	35.0%	4.9%	2.9%	0.0%	0.0%	24.5%
Holland, MI micro	8,100	29.1%	11.0%	25.7%	24.8%	6.4%	0.8%	2.2%	0.0%	16.1%
Homosassa Springs, FL	6,848	49.8%	20.0%	5.3%	22.8%	0.6%	1.5%	0.0%	0.0%	33.8%
Hot Springs, AR	6,037	33.3%	25.7%	19.6%	19.3%	2.1%	0.0%	0.0%	0.0%	30.4%
Houma-Thibodaux, LA	21,912	25.9%	15.3%	9.5%	28.5%	14.2%	3.1%	2.4%	1.1%	13.7%
Houston-The Woodlands-Sugar Land, TX	654,761	26.7%	15.3%	16.4%	21.8%	12.1%	4.4%	2.3%	0.9%	18.4%
Huntington-Ashland, WV-KY-OH	30,648	36.8%	17.8%	15.5%	18.2%	5.0%	4.1%	1.1%	1.5%	25.1%
Huntsville, AL	43,655	23.7%	21.6%	16.9%	22.3%	10.1%	4.2%	1.0%	0.2%	21.0%
Idaho Falls, ID	11,675	28.9%	26.5%	14.9%	23.6%	6.2%	0.0%	0.0%	0.0%	18.1%
Indianapolis-Carmel-Anderson, IN	192,044	27.0%	18.5%	15.0%	24.8%	11.3%	2.0%	1.0%	0.5%	18.7%
Iowa City, IA	21,679	23.8%	11.4%	14.9%	28.7%	20.2%	0.3%	0.0%	0.7%	28.8%
Ithaca, NY	10,063	19.9%	20.5%	22.1%	17.7%	16.2%	2.8%	0.8%	0.0%	32.6%
Jackson, MI	14,943	41.8%	13.1%	15.7%	19.0%	7.4%	3.0%	0.0%	0.0%	24.0%
Jackson, MS	55,868	31.8%	20.2%	13.2%	22.1%	9.5%	1.9%	1.3%	0.0%	28.0%
Jackson, TN	11,485	37.7%	17.5%	16.8%	21.1%	6.4%	0.0%	0.5%	0.0%	28.1%
Jacksonville, FL	138,023	28.7%	15.2%	18.6%	26.4%	8.6%	1.7%	0.7%	0.1%	18.7%
Jacksonville, NC	24,941	29.6%	21.0%	15.4%	24.7%	8.6%	0.4%	0.0%	0.3%	18.2%
Jamestown-Dunkirk-Fredonia, NY micro.	10,603	27.2%	23.8%	22.6%	22.9%	2.4%	0.3%	0.8%	0.0%	24.5%
Janesville-Beloit, WI	13,455	29.4%	16.7%	21.3%	22.5%	9.2%	0.4%	0.5%	0.0%	20.6%
Jefferson City, MO	13,373	34.3%	17.5%	11.6%	27.2%	6.1%	2.8%	0.2%	0.3%	21.9%
Johnson City, TN	15,961	37.1%	17.8%	20.5%	17.4%	5.0%	1.5%	0.0%	0.7%	26.5%
Johnstown, PA	10,546	33.4%	21.1%	17.5%	21.8%	5.2%	0.9%	0.0%	0.0%	22.3%
Jonesboro, AR	12,406	33.2%	30.1%	17.0%	12.2%	7.1%	0.0%	0.0%	0.3%	33.6%
Joplin, MO	16,762	26.7%	21.5%	13.1%	30.2%	8.1%	0.4%	0.1%	0.0%	21.0%
Kahului-Wailuku-Lahaina, HI	16,276	26.0%	8.2%	15.6%	36.5%	13.1%	0.6%	0.0%	0.0%	11.4%
Kalamazoo-Portage, MI	30,223	20.4%	30.5%	19.0%	20.0%	8.3%	0.8%	1.0%	0.1%	24.8%
Kalispell, MT micro	6,784	34.6%	7.1%	13.7%	33.6%	6.8%	3.0%	1.2%	0.0%	20.8%
Kankakee, IL	8,304	31.3%	9.3%	28.3%	20.8%	4.3%	6.0%	0.0%	0.0%	27.0%
Kansas City, MO-KS	196,742	21.5%	15.6%	18.3%	27.8%	11.2%	3.8%	1.2%	0.5%	16.8%
Kennewick-Richland, WA	25,405	29.1%	21.6%	12.9%	21.4%	10.3%	4.0%	0.4%	0.4%	22.8%
Killeen-Temple, TX	50,656	34.8%	12.5%	13.4%	27.3%	8.8%	2.0%	0.4%	0.9%	14.6%
Kingsport-Bristol-Bristol, TN-VA	23,456	37.3%	16.7%	17.3%	18.3%	3.3%	5.3%	1.0%	0.8%	22.4%
Kingston, NY	13,203	31.1%	17.9%	21.1%	18.1%	5.9%	4.8%	0.0%	1.1%	23.3%
Knoxville, TN	73,034	30.8%	20.1%	18.8%	20.6%	5.2%	2.1%	1.6%	0.8%	25.4%
Kokomo, IN	5,730	23.2%	11.0%	25.6%	20.7%	17.4%	0.0%	0.0%	2.1%	20.0%
La Crosse-Onalaska, WI-MN	13,011	29.8%	14.9%	11.5%	28.1%	11.1%	3.1%	0.7%	0.8%	24.9%
Lafayette-West Lafayette, IN	21,107	30.3%	15.8%	19.4%	26.1%	7.8%	0.7%	0.0%	0.0%	30.9%
Lafayette, LA	47,886	23.7%	18.0%	10.1%	26.0%	13.0%	4.8%	2.5%	1.9%	17.9%
Lake Charles, LA	16,713	28.2%	17.0%	16.2%	21.0%	11.0%	3.2%	2.7%	0.7%	20.8%
Lake Havasu City-Kingman, AZ	14,210	34.5%	14.9%	14.3%	23.8%	10.4%	2.2%	0.0%	0.0%	26.6%
Lakeland-Winter Haven, FL	55,298	37.0%	20.1%	14.9%	20.3%	7.0%	0.2%	0.1%	0.4%	22.3%
Lancaster, PA	46,261	23.0%	12.5%	15.0%	28.9%	14.6%	2.7%	1.5%	1.9%	15.7%
Lansing-East Lansing, MI	44,901	26.6%	18.4%	16.9%	22.7%	13.6%	1.1%	0.0%	0.6%	30.3%
Laredo, TX	25,385	42.5%	17.9%	14.8%	11.0%	8.6%	3.8%	1.3%	0.0%	30.9%
Las Cruces, NM	18,236	35.3%	25.2%	16.4%	18.6%	2.8%	1.8%	0.0%	0.0%	38.0%
Las Vegas-Henderson-Paradise, NV	204,037	26.2%	17.6%	18.3%	23.7%	10.0%	2.5%	1.4%	0.4%	19.9%
Lawrence, KS	14,590	23.3%	17.3%	8.2%	30.3%	20.8%	0.0%	0.0%	0.0%	22.7%
Lawton, OK	14,851	37.3%	17.4%	24.2%	17.6%	2.0%	0.5%	0.9%	0.0%	26.2%
Lebanon, PA	9,178	31.1%	11.0%	12.0%	32.3%	12.3%	1.1%	0.3%	0.0%	17.7%
Lewiston-Auburn, ME	10,215	14.8%	14.5%	44.4%	18.2%	6.6%	1.6%	0.0%	0.0%	14.7%
Lewiston, ID-WA	4,776	36.4%	15.8%	22.8%	11.0%	10.8%	0.0%	1.5%	1.7%	21.3%
Lexington-Fayette, KY	48,897	26.0%	16.9%	21.1%	23.2%	9.4%	2.1%	1.2%	0.2%	25.4%
Lima, OH	8,973	28.2%	26.0%	16.5%	19.8%	8.3%	0.5%	0.7%	0.0%	19.0%
Lincoln, NE	32,649	22.7%	15.4%	24.2%	24.8%	10.8%	1.3%	0.6%	0.3%	27.0%
Little Rock-North Little Rock-Conway, AR	76,857	27.0%	21.5%	19.1%	22.8%	7.7%	1.1%	0.4%	0.4%	19.7%
Logan, UT-ID	16,177	25.7%	20.4%	12.0%	26.4%	12.7%	2.8%	0.1%	0.0%	18.6%
Longview, TX	19,661	31.7%	21.6%	17.7%	19.5%	4.9%	3.0%	0.4%	1.2%	25.8%
Longview, WA	7,664	37.7%	20.6%	16.6%	12.9%	12.1%	0.0%	0.0%	0.0%	24.1%
Los Angeles-Long Beach-Anaheim, CA	1,359,102	28.5%	18.9%	15.9%	18.8%	11.3%	3.9%	2.0%	0.7%	19.7%
Louisville/Jefferson County, KY-IN	115,493	24.2%	15.8%	22.5%	24.6%	9.2%	2.3%	1.2%	0.1%	17.6%
Lubbock, TX	29,381	27.6%	17.2%	17.5%	25.0%	8.0%	2.8%	0.3%	1.6%	23.7%
Lumberton, NC micro	9,230	43.3%	26.8%	10.5%	13.1%	4.7%	0.4%	1.2%	0.0%	38.4%
Lynchburg, VA	20,930	30.9%	15.3%	19.7%	25.6%	7.9%	0.0%	0.0%	0.6%	19.7%
Macon, GA	20,885	37.0%	19.4%	13.1%	19.9%	9.1%	0.4%	1.1%	0.0%	35.8%
Madera, CA	15,618	43.5%	25.9%	13.1%	8.6%	8.8%	0.0%	0.0%	0.0%	28.2%
Madison, WI	72,563	16.6%	17.5%	16.4%	28.8%	12.8%	4.7%	2.6%	0.7%	23.0%
Manchester-Nashua, NH	35,508	20.0%	14.3%	12.7%	35.0%	10.1%	5.7%	1.4%	0.8%	14.2%

Table I-4: Metropolitan/Micropolitan Statistical Areas—Income Class by Age—*Continued*

	Personal Income, Percent by Income, Ages 18 to 24							
	Total Millennials	Under $10,000	$10,000 to $19,999	$20,000 to $29,999	$30,000 to $49,999	$50,000 to $74,999	$75,000 to $99,999	$100,000 or More
Manhattan, KS	26,254	59.7%	23.8%	14.0%	1.5%	1.0%	0.0%	0.0%
Mankato-North Mankato, MN	18,983	75.0%	16.8%	3.9%	4.3%	0.0%	0.0%	0.0%
Mansfield, OH	10,958	76.6%	11.3%	9.0%	1.5%	1.6%	0.0%	0.0%
McAllen-Edinburg-Mission, TX	89,264	74.7%	14.7%	6.4%	3.4%	0.8%	0.0%	0.0%
Medford, OR	17,320	50.5%	29.9%	11.1%	6.8%	1.7%	0.0%	0.0%
Memphis, TN-MS-AR	138,386	68.8%	16.1%	8.0%	5.9%	1.0%	0.0%	0.2%
Merced, CA	31,498	65.5%	19.4%	6.1%	8.8%	0.3%	0.0%	0.0%
Meridian, MS micro	11,710	73.2%	13.3%	5.7%	6.7%	0.9%	0.2%	0.0%
Miami-Fort Lauderdale-West Palm Beach, FL	507,492	68.0%	18.4%	8.9%	3.9%	0.7%	0.1%	0.1%
Michigan City-La Porte, IN	9,137	49.9%	34.3%	11.0%	4.8%	0.0%	0.0%	0.0%
Midland, MI	8,172	58.3%	27.1%	13.4%	1.2%	0.0%	0.0%	0.0%
Midland, TX	16,050	43.6%	23.9%	8.7%	13.2%	6.3%	2.6%	1.8%
Milwaukee-Waukesha-West Allis, WI	147,919	63.2%	21.2%	9.7%	4.0%	1.8%	0.0%	0.0%
Minneapolis-St. Paul-Bloomington, MN-WI	293,062	56.0%	22.6%	12.0%	6.8%	2.2%	0.4%	0.0%
Missoula, MT	16,419	68.3%	16.2%	2.5%	9.4%	1.8%	0.0%	1.8%
Mobile, AL	42,048	69.5%	16.5%	5.5%	7.2%	0.4%	0.9%	0.0%
Modesto, CA	55,502	59.3%	26.4%	8.3%	4.1%	1.9%	0.0%	0.0%
Monroe, LA	20,311	69.0%	16.2%	5.5%	9.2%	0.0%	0.0%	0.0%
Monroe, MI	13,255	49.0%	34.5%	11.0%	3.3%	2.2%	0.0%	0.0%
Montgomery, AL	39,232	66.6%	14.2%	12.0%	6.5%	0.5%	0.0%	0.1%
Morgantown, WV	27,833	74.6%	13.3%	4.8%	6.2%	1.1%	0.0%	0.0%
Morristown, TN	9,379	60.9%	27.7%	7.0%	4.4%	0.0%	0.0%	0.0%
Mount Vernon-Anacortes, WA	11,075	61.6%	11.7%	12.6%	13.4%	0.8%	0.0%	0.0%
Muncie, IN	24,150	73.3%	17.9%	6.0%	2.5%	0.3%	0.0%	0.0%
Muskegon, MI	14,142	62.4%	21.2%	8.0%	6.1%	2.2%	0.0%	0.0%
Myrtle Beach-Conway-North Myrtle Beach, SC-NC	32,427	55.6%	32.1%	9.2%	1.9%	1.2%	0.0%	0.0%
Napa, CA	13,156	66.7%	15.5%	12.0%	4.0%	1.4%	0.0%	0.3%
Naples-Immokalee-Marco Island, FL	22,554	50.6%	25.0%	17.8%	6.4%	0.2%	0.0%	0.0%
Nashville-Davidson–Murfreesboro–Franklin, TN	164,808	60.7%	22.3%	9.0%	5.7%	2.1%	0.1%	0.2%
New Bern, NC	15,130	49.4%	16.9%	19.1%	14.6%	0.0%	0.0%	0.0%
New Castle, PA micro	7,055	59.9%	19.1%	13.4%	7.7%	0.0%	0.0%	0.0%
New Haven-Milford, CT	86,612	66.6%	18.7%	9.7%	3.7%	1.0%	0.2%	0.2%
New Orleans-Metairie, LA	108,886	68.6%	16.8%	7.0%	5.0%	1.4%	0.7%	0.6%
New Philadelphia-Dover, OH micro	7,243	66.2%	13.4%	9.7%	7.0%	1.0%	2.6%	0.0%
New York-Newark-Jersey City, NY-NJ-PA	1,851,065	67.9%	15.3%	7.2%	6.6%	2.3%	0.4%	0.3%
Niles-Benton Harbor, MI	13,614	73.3%	17.7%	1.3%	5.1%	2.7%	0.0%	0.0%
North Port-Sarasota-Bradenton, FL	52,179	62.1%	23.6%	9.0%	4.1%	0.9%	0.0%	0.3%
Norwich-New London, CT	29,528	51.6%	29.9%	11.5%	2.9%	2.2%	1.1%	0.8%
Ocala, FL	24,424	64.8%	25.0%	6.9%	3.2%	0.0%	0.0%	0.0%
Ocean City, NJ	7,826	53.8%	33.7%	3.7%	7.9%	0.9%	0.0%	0.0%
Odessa, TX	16,738	52.5%	17.4%	13.7%	7.4%	3.1%	4.8%	1.2%
Ogden-Clearfield, UT	58,172	57.5%	21.5%	12.0%	8.4%	0.5%	0.0%	0.0%
Ogdensburg-Massena, NY micro	16,127	80.3%	13.1%	5.7%	0.5%	0.5%	0.0%	0.0%
Oklahoma City, OK	135,749	57.9%	17.6%	13.8%	7.9%	2.3%	0.3%	0.2%
Olympia-Tumwater, WA	24,063	61.2%	14.6%	11.3%	10.0%	1.6%	0.6%	0.6%
Omaha-Council Bluffs, NE-IA	85,177	55.1%	20.8%	14.4%	8.0%	1.6%	0.0%	0.1%
Orangeburg, SC micro	11,140	77.1%	8.0%	9.1%	5.8%	0.0%	0.0%	0.0%
Orlando-Kissimmee-Sanford, FL	230,036	64.1%	21.1%	9.2%	4.7%	0.7%	0.1%	0.0%
Oshkosh-Neenah, WI	20,693	55.5%	26.5%	9.2%	8.9%	0.0%	0.0%	0.0%
Ottawa-Peru, IL micro	9,127	55.1%	28.5%	10.0%	6.4%	0.0%	0.0%	0.0%
Owensboro, KY	10,277	50.1%	24.0%	9.1%	14.6%	2.2%	0.0%	0.0%
Oxnard-Thousand Oaks-Ventura, CA	83,390	58.1%	23.2%	10.6%	6.9%	0.6%	0.4%	0.2%
Palm Bay-Melbourne-Titusville, FL	44,051	61.4%	23.9%	9.1%	3.6%	0.8%	1.2%	0.0%
Panama City, FL	16,496	52.1%	23.8%	16.1%	6.9%	1.0%	0.0%	0.0%
Parkersburg-Vienna, WV	7,766	67.5%	12.1%	6.7%	13.6%	0.0%	0.0%	0.0%
Pensacola-Ferry Pass-Brent, FL	53,379	58.9%	26.4%	10.8%	2.0%	1.4%	0.6%	0.0%
Peoria, IL	35,324	62.5%	17.7%	9.4%	9.9%	0.5%	0.0%	0.0%
Philadelphia-Camden-Wilmington, PA-NJ-DE-MD	590,688	68.5%	14.9%	7.9%	7.1%	1.5%	0.1%	0.0%
Phoenix-Mesa-Scottsdale, AZ	416,357	61.4%	20.7%	11.0%	5.9%	0.8%	0.2%	0.0%
Pine Bluff, AR	11,714	76.2%	13.9%	4.7%	3.8%	0.0%	1.4%	0.0%
Pittsburgh, PA	214,247	63.0%	18.6%	9.9%	6.2%	1.9%	0.2%	0.2%
Pittsfield, MA	13,341	78.1%	15.0%	4.3%	1.5%	1.0%	0.1%	0.0%
Pocatello, ID	10,790	57.4%	27.4%	10.7%	4.5%	0.0%	0.0%	0.0%
Port St. Lucie, FL	32,529	71.2%	20.1%	6.0%	2.6%	0.0%	0.0%	0.0%
Portland-South Portland, ME	45,220	63.1%	21.3%	9.4%	4.3%	0.5%	0.0%	1.4%
Portland-Vancouver-Hillsboro, OR-WA	199,536	59.7%	22.7%	10.7%	5.2%	1.3%	0.2%	0.2%
Pottsville, PA micro	11,168	68.6%	21.5%	6.1%	3.8%	0.0%	0.0%	0.0%
Prescott, AZ	14,382	68.0%	16.3%	5.3%	9.0%	0.5%	0.0%	0.9%
Providence-Warwick, RI-MA	173,628	63.4%	19.7%	8.8%	6.1%	1.7%	0.2%	0.2%
Provo-Orem, UT	95,374	65.5%	19.7%	10.0%	3.8%	0.7%	0.0%	0.3%
Pueblo, CO	15,775	69.5%	23.8%	4.0%	2.8%	0.0%	0.0%	0.0%
Punta Gorda, FL	10,166	57.8%	24.0%	9.4%	8.1%	0.2%	0.0%	0.4%
Racine, WI	14,201	64.4%	22.5%	6.9%	5.4%	0.7%	0.0%	0.0%
Raleigh, NC	115,499	63.7%	20.1%	9.3%	6.0%	0.9%	0.0%	0.0%
Rapid City, SD	13,254	51.0%	22.9%	18.2%	7.3%	0.0%	0.6%	0.0%

Table I-4: Metropolitan/Micropolitan Statistical Areas—Income Class by Age—*Continued*

	Personal Income, Ages 25 to 31								Poverty Rate
	Total Millennials	Under $10,000	$10,000 to $19,999	$20,000 to $29,999	$30,000 to $49,999	$50,000 to $74,999	$75,000 to $99,999	$100,000 to $149,999	$150,000 or More	
Manhattan, KS	13,091	23.9%	19.3%	11.8%	31.6%	12.3%	1.0%	0.0%	0.0%	36.5%
Mankato-North Mankato, MN	8,924	16.8%	11.7%	24.7%	35.4%	4.7%	5.8%	0.9%	0.0%	44.9%
Mansfield, OH	9,405	38.1%	27.4%	14.3%	13.9%	6.3%	0.0%	0.0%	0.0%	19.0%
McAllen-Edinburg-Mission, TX	74,220	45.1%	19.2%	11.9%	15.1%	6.5%	1.2%	0.7%	0.3%	37.5%
Medford, OR	16,879	29.0%	10.2%	17.0%	28.6%	13.5%	1.7%	0.0%	0.0%	18.1%
Memphis, TN-MS-AR	128,632	32.3%	17.8%	14.3%	25.9%	7.2%	1.6%	0.7%	0.3%	25.6%
Merced, CA	25,584	37.3%	20.2%	14.0%	19.6%	7.4%	0.2%	0.9%	0.4%	28.7%
Meridian, MS micro	8,153	25.5%	28.4%	11.1%	28.1%	1.3%	1.4%	3.4%	0.8%	31.8%
Miami-Fort Lauderdale-West Palm Beach, FL	540,931	28.7%	19.1%	18.3%	22.1%	7.9%	2.3%	1.2%	0.4%	19.6%
Michigan City-La Porte, IN	10,789	47.4%	13.1%	14.5%	14.1%	11.0%	0.0%	0.0%	0.0%	22.2%
Midland, MI	7,858	31.2%	10.7%	12.0%	33.0%	12.0%	1.0%	0.0%	0.0%	15.9%
Midland, TX	18,769	20.0%	11.1%	14.0%	19.8%	20.3%	7.9%	5.7%	1.3%	10.2%
Milwaukee-Waukesha-West Allis, WI	157,729	22.1%	18.7%	18.4%	22.8%	14.4%	2.6%	1.0%	0.1%	20.7%
Minneapolis-St. Paul-Bloomington, MN-WI	349,560	20.8%	12.5%	16.8%	27.3%	16.4%	3.8%	1.8%	0.6%	13.5%
Missoula, MT	13,113	34.9%	14.3%	16.5%	22.2%	11.0%	1.1%	0.0%	0.0%	33.9%
Mobile, AL	37,948	36.5%	16.1%	12.7%	21.5%	10.5%	1.5%	1.1%	0.1%	21.1%
Modesto, CA	50,579	37.9%	21.7%	14.5%	14.1%	7.0%	3.5%	1.2%	0.0%	25.2%
Monroe, LA	17,571	49.1%	17.2%	11.2%	14.3%	4.6%	2.4%	1.2%	0.0%	30.5%
Monroe, MI	11,608	18.1%	23.6%	22.2%	23.3%	9.4%	2.6%	0.4%	0.4%	15.3%
Montgomery, AL	36,578	36.3%	18.6%	13.3%	23.8%	6.2%	0.6%	0.3%	0.9%	26.6%
Morgantown, WV	15,518	38.8%	14.1%	18.6%	13.5%	7.8%	4.4%	2.4%	0.4%	33.0%
Morristown, TN	9,288	34.4%	20.3%	15.2%	22.8%	5.9%	0.0%	0.0%	1.4%	24.6%
Mount Vernon-Anacortes, WA	8,911	41.8%	16.8%	6.2%	28.6%	2.2%	4.4%	0.0%	0.0%	20.3%
Muncie, IN	9,291	31.5%	24.4%	22.4%	15.1%	4.1%	2.4%	0.0%	0.0%	41.5%
Muskegon, MI	13,335	40.7%	15.6%	18.7%	19.5%	3.6%	1.9%	0.0%	0.0%	25.3%
Myrtle Beach-Conway-North Myrtle Beach, SC-NC	31,091	32.5%	19.9%	19.5%	22.0%	3.8%	1.3%	0.3%	0.7%	27.4%
Napa, CA	10,779	16.4%	15.2%	33.5%	19.9%	10.7%	1.5%	2.8%	0.0%	10.3%
Naples-Immokalee-Marco Island, FL	22,259	31.4%	19.3%	15.9%	20.2%	6.7%	4.4%	0.3%	1.7%	14.1%
Nashville-Davidson–Murfreesboro–Franklin, TN	175,220	22.5%	18.8%	16.7%	26.8%	11.2%	2.7%	0.9%	0.4%	17.6%
New Bern, NC	13,287	33.7%	16.5%	14.8%	25.7%	5.1%	0.9%	3.2%	0.0%	15.5%
New Castle, PA micro	5,814	26.9%	12.1%	16.7%	20.4%	21.6%	1.9%	0.4%	0.0%	12.9%
New Haven-Milford, CT	80,028	25.7%	13.6%	13.8%	27.9%	14.8%	2.9%	1.0%	0.3%	17.4%
New Orleans-Metairie, LA	127,804	29.1%	18.2%	15.7%	22.7%	9.6%	2.4%	1.7%	0.5%	22.8%
New Philadelphia-Dover, OH micro	7,249	35.7%	17.0%	13.6%	25.1%	8.6%	0.0%	0.0%	0.0%	18.6%
New York-Newark-Jersey City, NY-NJ-PA	2,018,169	26.7%	14.1%	13.4%	19.9%	14.5%	6.0%	3.8%	1.6%	17.3%
Niles-Benton Harbor, MI	12,250	35.5%	18.3%	18.5%	21.0%	4.4%	2.0%	0.2%	0.0%	24.6%
North Port-Sarasota-Bradenton, FL	43,635	28.6%	17.7%	16.8%	26.9%	6.4%	1.5%	1.9%	0.2%	19.0%
Norwich-New London, CT	25,237	29.1%	17.3%	15.1%	24.6%	9.8%	3.0%	1.2%	0.0%	16.0%
Ocala, FL	24,469	38.2%	24.7%	16.0%	13.0%	5.9%	1.4%	0.4%	0.4%	25.5%
Ocean City, NJ	7,380	42.1%	10.4%	18.9%	12.6%	14.8%	0.0%	1.2%	0.0%	15.1%
Odessa, TX	17,369	23.5%	14.5%	18.8%	16.7%	12.1%	5.4%	4.2%	4.7%	16.5%
Ogden-Clearfield, UT	60,916	32.6%	15.2%	16.2%	21.2%	11.6%	2.0%	0.4%	0.8%	14.6%
Ogdensburg-Massena, NY micro	8,571	42.2%	17.8%	13.6%	16.9%	8.7%	0.0%	0.8%	0.0%	32.3%
Oklahoma City, OK	136,777	27.2%	15.7%	18.3%	24.6%	8.6%	2.7%	2.5%	0.4%	19.4%
Olympia-Tumwater, WA	27,994	32.4%	18.5%	9.9%	22.3%	10.6%	4.9%	0.7%	0.7%	21.5%
Omaha-Council Bluffs, NE-IA	95,723	19.8%	16.9%	20.2%	25.9%	13.5%	2.5%	1.0%	0.2%	17.3%
Orangeburg, SC micro	5,890	37.6%	10.6%	26.3%	17.2%	8.2%	0.0%	0.0%	0.0%	29.5%
Orlando-Kissimmee-Sanford, FL	234,680	28.9%	17.4%	20.1%	23.1%	6.9%	2.5%	1.0%	0.1%	20.6%
Oshkosh-Neenah, WI	16,548	20.5%	17.8%	16.5%	25.0%	16.9%	2.4%	0.0%	0.9%	21.2%
Ottawa-Peru, IL micro	9,376	19.4%	28.7%	15.7%	20.3%	15.3%	0.6%	0.0%	0.0%	16.1%
Owensboro, KY	10,034	32.7%	25.5%	15.4%	18.1%	6.1%	2.1%	0.0%	0.0%	18.8%
Oxnard-Thousand Oaks-Ventura, CA	72,585	26.2%	22.4%	14.9%	17.3%	11.1%	4.2%	3.3%	0.5%	16.0%
Palm Bay-Melbourne-Titusville, FL	38,460	27.7%	26.0%	19.1%	18.1%	6.8%	1.5%	0.6%	0.1%	19.8%
Panama City, FL	19,477	50.5%	17.3%	16.5%	9.7%	3.4%	2.0%	0.4%	0.3%	26.1%
Parkersburg-Vienna, WV	6,968	29.5%	21.0%	9.1%	22.5%	7.1%	7.9%	2.9%	0.0%	23.7%
Pensacola-Ferry Pass-Brent, FL	46,433	28.5%	14.5%	23.7%	24.7%	6.9%	1.1%	0.6%	0.0%	18.1%
Peoria, IL	35,959	23.0%	14.7%	13.2%	26.8%	12.6%	6.5%	1.9%	1.3%	16.4%
Philadelphia-Camden-Wilmington, PA-NJ-DE-MD	593,560	27.1%	13.5%	14.3%	24.6%	14.7%	3.8%	1.7%	0.4%	17.6%
Phoenix-Mesa-Scottsdale, AZ	433,079	29.6%	13.4%	17.7%	23.3%	11.4%	2.7%	1.3%	0.5%	21.8%
Pine Bluff, AR	7,558	36.1%	24.8%	7.3%	20.3%	6.5%	0.0%	2.8%	2.2%	42.3%
Pittsburgh, PA	209,509	22.0%	16.6%	15.7%	26.0%	13.6%	3.5%	2.0%	0.7%	18.8%
Pittsfield, MA	9,533	17.8%	22.5%	16.9%	26.5%	6.3%	3.8%	0.0%	6.1%	14.9%
Pocatello, ID	7,460	18.2%	29.2%	23.6%	23.5%	2.0%	2.9%	0.5%	0.0%	21.3%
Port St. Lucie, FL	32,399	31.0%	23.0%	17.7%	20.5%	6.3%	1.2%	0.0%	0.0%	22.6%
Portland-South Portland, ME	41,276	21.3%	15.2%	15.0%	28.5%	13.8%	1.7%	3.8%	0.8%	13.4%
Portland-Vancouver-Hillsboro, OR-WA	235,415	27.9%	18.0%	17.9%	20.2%	10.5%	3.3%	1.6%	0.7%	19.7%
Pottsville, PA micro	11,697	29.7%	20.2%	13.7%	28.3%	6.7%	0.2%	1.2%	0.0%	18.6%
Prescott, AZ	14,168	36.3%	24.5%	10.7%	23.8%	4.4%	0.0%	0.0%	0.2%	26.9%
Providence-Warwick, RI-MA	143,009	25.5%	16.8%	15.0%	26.3%	11.7%	3.6%	1.0%	0.2%	18.4%
Provo-Orem, UT	60,202	36.5%	17.3%	12.0%	20.2%	8.8%	3.1%	1.8%	0.4%	22.2%
Pueblo, CO	15,157	41.3%	16.8%	17.1%	19.0%	3.6%	0.8%	1.4%	0.0%	29.4%
Punta Gorda, FL	8,480	36.6%	19.7%	17.0%	19.7%	3.5%	2.6%	1.0%	0.0%	15.9%
Racine, WI	17,465	21.4%	29.3%	15.9%	23.7%	6.5%	3.1%	0.0%	0.0%	20.2%
Raleigh, NC	114,871	23.6%	15.9%	15.4%	28.4%	12.2%	2.8%	1.2%	0.5%	17.6%
Rapid City, SD	12,549	17.0%	21.9%	24.0%	24.9%	8.1%	3.5%	0.0%	0.7%	21.5%

Table I-4: Metropolitan/Micropolitan Statistical Areas—Income Class by Age—*Continued*

	Total Millennials	Under $10,000	$10,000 to $19,999	$20,000 to $29,999	$30,000 to $49,999	$50,000 to $74,999	$75,000 to $99,999	$100,000 or More
Reading, PA	41,660	67.0%	15.4%	11.2%	6.4%	0.0%	0.0%	0.0%
Redding, CA	17,040	65.9%	19.6%	8.1%	6.1%	0.0%	0.0%	0.2%
Reno, NV	43,965	57.5%	25.5%	10.9%	4.3%	0.4%	1.4%	0.0%
Richmond, VA	116,039	62.2%	18.2%	10.4%	7.4%	1.5%	0.2%	0.1%
Riverside-San Bernardino-Ontario, CA	474,163	68.0%	18.0%	8.9%	4.0%	0.9%	0.1%	0.1%
Roanoke, VA	27,320	60.4%	23.0%	14.4%	2.0%	0.2%	0.0%	0.0%
Rochester, MN	19,938	57.3%	17.8%	15.7%	8.9%	0.4%	0.0%	0.0%
Rochester, NY	114,616	66.6%	17.5%	10.6%	4.6%	0.7%	0.0%	0.1%
Rockford, IL	32,814	62.1%	21.8%	11.1%	4.6%	0.4%	0.0%	0.0%
Rocky Mount, NC	14,182	71.7%	11.9%	14.9%	1.5%	0.0%	0.0%	0.0%
Rome, GA	9,834	75.1%	14.6%	6.5%	3.7%	0.0%	0.0%	0.0%
Roseburg, OR micro	7,684	65.1%	19.1%	10.1%	4.1%	1.7%	0.0%	0.0%
Sacramento–Roseville–Arden-Arcade, CA	216,145	67.7%	18.9%	7.0%	5.1%	0.9%	0.2%	0.1%
Saginaw, MI	21,690	64.2%	25.9%	5.1%	4.6%	0.3%	0.0%	0.0%
Salem, OH micro	8,311	59.3%	26.5%	10.2%	2.3%	1.7%	0.0%	0.0%
Salem, OR	43,413	56.4%	24.9%	12.2%	5.3%	1.2%	0.0%	0.0%
Salinas, CA	47,254	65.2%	23.4%	7.5%	3.3%	0.0%	0.0%	0.6%
Salisbury, MD-DE	39,407	62.9%	19.6%	11.0%	4.7%	1.0%	0.8%	0.0%
Salt Lake City, UT	109,954	55.4%	21.3%	14.7%	7.2%	0.7%	0.5%	0.2%
San Angelo, TX	14,311	43.5%	32.5%	9.0%	9.7%	1.5%	3.3%	0.4%
San Antonio-New Braunfels, TX	242,475	63.9%	19.9%	9.4%	5.0%	1.3%	0.3%	0.2%
San Diego-Carlsbad, CA	366,084	58.2%	18.4%	14.1%	6.8%	2.0%	0.4%	0.0%
San Francisco-Oakland-Hayward, CA	380,272	62.3%	17.9%	9.0%	6.9%	2.4%	0.8%	0.7%
San Jose-Sunnyvale-Santa Clara, CA	165,780	63.3%	16.9%	7.5%	7.1%	3.9%	0.6%	0.8%
San Luis Obispo-Paso Robles-Arroyo Grande, CA	44,013	70.8%	12.0%	9.1%	5.6%	0.8%	1.6%	0.0%
Santa Cruz-Watsonville, CA	39,381	66.0%	14.7%	14.0%	5.2%	0.0%	0.0%	0.1%
Santa Fe, NM	11,027	66.0%	23.4%	7.8%	2.2%	0.5%	0.0%	0.0%
Santa Maria-Santa Barbara, CA	67,925	68.0%	15.5%	7.7%	7.1%	1.2%	0.5%	0.0%
Santa Rosa, CA	45,516	63.2%	19.5%	10.9%	4.5%	1.3%	0.0%	0.5%
Savannah, GA	43,891	67.8%	17.3%	7.7%	5.9%	1.2%	0.0%	0.1%
Scranton–Wilkes-Barre–Hazleton, PA	56,196	66.9%	18.9%	6.8%	5.4%	1.3%	0.1%	0.5%
Seattle-Tacoma-Bellevue, WA	321,593	58.7%	17.1%	11.7%	8.4%	2.4%	1.1%	0.8%
Sebastian-Vero Beach, FL	9,614	76.8%	16.2%	3.2%	2.6%	1.2%	0.0%	0.0%
Sebring, FL	6,849	69.7%	13.9%	14.5%	1.9%	0.0%	0.0%	0.0%
Sheboygan, WI	7,877	53.3%	7.6%	14.2%	24.8%	0.0%	0.0%	0.0%
Sherman-Denison, TX	11,094	64.5%	16.6%	9.2%	8.1%	1.3%	0.3%	0.0%
Show Low, AZ micro	10,459	76.1%	15.1%	3.6%	4.3%	0.9%	0.0%	0.0%
Shreveport-Bossier City, LA	49,166	67.6%	16.6%	10.0%	4.3%	1.6%	0.0%	0.0%
Sierra Vista-Douglas, AZ	12,340	49.6%	29.4%	18.8%	0.6%	1.6%	0.0%	0.0%
Sioux City, IA-NE-SD	16,841	68.7%	17.3%	8.9%	5.0%	0.1%	0.0%	0.0%
Sioux Falls, SD	23,954	48.0%	26.1%	18.6%	5.3%	0.5%	0.0%	1.4%
South Bend-Mishawaka, IN-MI	32,769	69.2%	17.2%	9.6%	3.8%	0.2%	0.0%	0.0%
Spartanburg, SC	34,337	63.3%	21.1%	8.8%	6.5%	0.3%	0.0%	0.0%
Spokane-Spokane Valley, WA	54,440	65.8%	18.3%	8.5%	5.6%	1.5%	0.0%	0.3%
Springfield, IL	18,107	63.6%	20.9%	10.9%	3.9%	0.8%	0.0%	0.0%
Springfield, MA	79,118	69.1%	14.7%	8.2%	5.1%	2.0%	0.5%	0.4%
Springfield, MO	54,954	62.4%	23.1%	7.4%	6.6%	0.4%	0.0%	0.0%
Springfield, OH	12,435	60.9%	28.8%	6.4%	3.9%	0.0%	0.0%	0.0%
St. Cloud, MN	29,346	56.5%	18.8%	13.6%	9.9%	1.2%	0.0%	0.0%
St. George, UT	14,931	62.6%	16.9%	14.1%	4.8%	0.0%	0.0%	1.6%
St. Joseph, MO-KS	12,829	64.9%	24.1%	8.7%	2.0%	0.3%	0.0%	0.0%
St. Louis, MO-IL	250,869	62.2%	21.0%	9.8%	5.2%	1.6%	0.0%	0.1%
State College, PA	44,131	74.3%	13.5%	6.4%	4.4%	1.3%	0.0%	0.0%
Staunton-Waynesboro, VA	13,074	69.6%	20.4%	3.0%	7.0%	0.0%	0.0%	0.0%
Stockton-Lodi, CA	73,709	67.1%	17.7%	9.9%	4.6%	0.8%	0.0%	0.0%
Sumter, SC	13,333	62.7%	19.5%	9.8%	8.1%	0.0%	0.0%	0.0%
Sunbury, PA micro	7,679	60.4%	15.0%	14.3%	4.2%	6.1%	0.0%	0.0%
Syracuse, NY	71,514	66.9%	15.0%	9.9%	6.3%	1.2%	0.0%	0.8%
Tallahassee, FL	75,689	73.5%	14.8%	7.3%	4.3%	0.2%	0.0%	0.0%
Tampa-St. Petersburg-Clearwater, FL	243,210	62.8%	21.4%	10.0%	5.1%	0.6%	0.1%	0.1%
Terre Haute, IN	20,793	68.1%	21.1%	6.7%	3.6%	0.1%	0.3%	0.1%
Texarkana, TX-AR	14,037	69.3%	22.3%	7.0%	0.3%	1.0%	0.0%	0.0%
The Villages, FL	4,200	49.4%	30.7%	17.5%	2.4%	0.0%	0.0%	0.0%
Toledo, OH	72,817	66.7%	19.4%	9.2%	4.6%	0.1%	0.0%	0.0%
Topeka, KS	19,391	57.7%	25.1%	11.8%	4.5%	0.8%	0.0%	0.0%
Torrington, CT micro	13,642	48.3%	29.5%	10.6%	8.0%	1.7%	0.5%	1.4%
Traverse City, MI micro	11,425	68.4%	19.8%	7.6%	3.7%	0.5%	0.0%	0.0%
Trenton, NJ	40,520	70.8%	15.8%	7.2%	4.1%	2.0%	0.0%	0.0%
Truckee-Grass Valley, CA micro	7,382	77.5%	17.4%	4.9%	0.3%	0.0%	0.0%	0.0%
Tucson, AZ	121,550	64.0%	21.5%	8.7%	5.2%	0.5%	0.0%	0.1%
Tullahoma-Manchester, TN micro	8,902	69.3%	12.7%	15.5%	2.4%	0.0%	0.0%	0.0%
Tulsa, OK	87,792	56.5%	21.9%	12.5%	6.9%	1.8%	0.1%	0.3%
Tupelo, MS micro	14,124	74.3%	16.1%	9.2%	0.4%	0.0%	0.0%	0.0%
Tuscaloosa, AL	40,034	73.2%	13.1%	6.7%	7.0%	0.0%	0.0%	0.0%
Tyler, TX	22,230	71.0%	10.7%	14.2%	2.8%	0.6%	0.3%	0.4%
Urban Honolulu, HI	99,988	51.9%	16.9%	14.6%	10.3%	4.4%	1.9%	0.0%
Utica-Rome, NY	29,255	65.1%	18.4%	10.0%	5.0%	1.5%	0.0%	0.0%

Table I-4: Metropolitan/Micropolitan Statistical Areas—Income Class by Age—*Continued*

	Total Millennials	Under $10,000	$10,000 to $19,999	$20,000 to $29,999	$30,000 to $49,999	$50,000 to $74,999	$75,000 to $99,999	$100,000 to $149,999	$150,000 or More	Poverty Rate
					Personal Income, Ages 25 to 31					
Reading, PA	33,732	17.5%	15.5%	14.8%	36.1%	12.4%	2.1%	1.1%	0.6%	17.2%
Redding, CA	15,126	40.3%	27.8%	9.6%	14.8%	6.1%	0.5%	0.8%	0.0%	30.6%
Reno, NV	42,675	26.4%	15.9%	15.2%	24.1%	13.9%	3.2%	1.2%	0.1%	21.2%
Richmond, VA	118,587	29.1%	14.5%	17.8%	24.6%	10.2%	2.2%	1.1%	0.5%	17.5%
Riverside-San Bernardino-Ontario, CA	422,349	34.6%	18.8%	15.1%	18.3%	8.0%	2.8%	2.2%	0.1%	20.7%
Roanoke, VA	24,392	29.1%	23.8%	13.7%	24.6%	6.7%	1.6%	0.0%	0.4%	20.3%
Rochester, MN	19,484	22.8%	9.8%	14.3%	32.0%	17.3%	2.4%	1.4%	0.1%	14.7%
Rochester, NY	99,070	25.9%	16.6%	19.0%	22.6%	11.5%	3.1%	0.9%	0.4%	19.2%
Rockford, IL	26,666	32.0%	16.7%	22.9%	19.6%	7.3%	1.1%	0.4%	0.0%	19.9%
Rocky Mount, NC	9,851	51.5%	12.3%	9.0%	22.2%	3.9%	1.2%	0.0%	0.0%	25.2%
Rome, GA	7,305	35.0%	21.5%	16.2%	13.6%	10.5%	3.1%	0.0%	0.0%	25.6%
Roseburg, OR micro	7,735	36.8%	26.1%	7.9%	17.9%	7.5%	1.3%	2.5%	0.0%	24.8%
Sacramento–Roseville–Arden-Arcade, CA	203,737	30.3%	15.2%	15.9%	23.1%	9.9%	3.7%	1.6%	0.3%	20.2%
Saginaw, MI	15,016	37.6%	23.3%	15.9%	13.6%	7.7%	0.0%	1.9%	0.0%	22.9%
Salem, OH micro	8,795	44.3%	13.1%	18.1%	14.2%	10.4%	0.0%	0.0%	0.0%	22.7%
Salem, OR	34,859	34.6%	15.8%	17.9%	18.6%	9.4%	3.2%	0.5%	0.0%	25.2%
Salinas, CA	43,942	32.9%	22.6%	16.5%	16.9%	8.2%	1.6%	1.3%	0.0%	19.6%
Salisbury, MD-DE	29,859	29.0%	18.4%	19.7%	25.4%	5.5%	1.1%	0.8%	0.0%	20.0%
Salt Lake City, UT	127,631	24.4%	16.0%	17.0%	27.4%	11.3%	2.1%	1.3%	0.5%	15.0%
San Angelo, TX	12,721	18.1%	21.7%	11.6%	34.8%	10.1%	1.4%	1.7%	0.6%	12.6%
San Antonio-New Braunfels, TX	232,757	28.9%	17.6%	18.8%	21.1%	9.3%	2.3%	1.6%	0.3%	19.7%
San Diego-Carlsbad, CA	371,745	26.4%	15.3%	17.0%	21.3%	12.3%	4.7%	2.4%	0.5%	18.5%
San Francisco-Oakland-Hayward, CA	483,008	23.6%	13.1%	12.7%	20.2%	14.5%	7.5%	6.2%	2.2%	15.6%
San Jose-Sunnyvale-Santa Clara, CA	197,693	26.6%	12.0%	10.7%	16.4%	13.8%	8.8%	9.1%	2.8%	13.7%
San Luis Obispo-Paso Robles-Arroyo Grande, CA	23,706	27.2%	23.9%	16.1%	23.4%	7.4%	1.0%	0.6%	0.4%	29.9%
Santa Cruz-Watsonville, CA	21,434	17.9%	28.7%	13.9%	26.8%	7.1%	2.0%	3.1%	0.5%	23.3%
Santa Fe, NM	11,022	29.7%	26.3%	17.6%	15.3%	9.9%	0.0%	1.3%	0.0%	30.8%
Santa Maria-Santa Barbara, CA	40,171	23.2%	21.7%	20.5%	19.7%	9.6%	2.6%	2.7%	0.0%	27.3%
Santa Rosa, CA	43,559	23.6%	18.3%	16.5%	23.9%	11.6%	3.4%	1.5%	1.2%	14.4%
Savannah, GA	39,863	29.7%	20.6%	13.8%	21.0%	10.5%	2.1%	0.0%	2.3%	25.7%
Scranton–Wilkes-Barre–Hazleton, PA	46,279	29.4%	19.3%	17.2%	22.2%	9.5%	1.6%	0.7%	0.2%	19.7%
Seattle-Tacoma-Bellevue, WA	397,366	21.3%	14.3%	16.1%	25.0%	14.5%	4.0%	3.7%	1.0%	16.3%
Sebastian-Vero Beach, FL	9,040	32.1%	20.8%	21.1%	16.8%	5.7%	0.0%	1.0%	2.5%	23.1%
Sebring, FL	5,937	46.5%	12.3%	18.8%	17.4%	3.2%	1.7%	0.0%	0.0%	30.4%
Sheboygan, WI	9,011	19.2%	26.7%	18.4%	29.1%	5.2%	1.5%	0.0%	0.0%	13.7%
Sherman-Denison, TX	11,329	33.5%	11.8%	18.8%	23.1%	9.0%	3.2%	0.5%	0.0%	22.3%
Show Low, AZ micro	9,505	54.6%	11.9%	10.4%	18.9%	2.6%	1.6%	0.0%	0.0%	39.6%
Shreveport-Bossier City, LA	45,748	31.7%	17.1%	14.3%	24.5%	9.4%	1.9%	0.9%	0.3%	31.1%
Sierra Vista-Douglas, AZ	11,701	34.6%	20.9%	11.4%	20.2%	7.0%	3.5%	2.4%	0.0%	20.3%
Sioux City, IA-NE-SD	14,006	19.1%	15.5%	22.0%	30.8%	10.2%	1.3%	0.8%	0.2%	20.5%
Sioux Falls, SD	25,702	15.2%	8.5%	22.0%	40.8%	10.0%	0.9%	2.0%	0.7%	10.9%
South Bend-Mishawaka, IN-MI	25,181	22.3%	21.6%	20.8%	22.2%	9.5%	3.0%	0.4%	0.2%	22.3%
Spartanburg, SC	27,072	32.8%	20.4%	17.1%	19.0%	7.7%	0.3%	1.5%	1.2%	23.8%
Spokane-Spokane Valley, WA	55,571	28.9%	17.4%	18.4%	25.6%	6.2%	3.2%	0.0%	0.2%	24.7%
Springfield, IL	19,203	26.6%	16.2%	15.0%	24.0%	12.8%	2.8%	1.6%	1.0%	22.6%
Springfield, MA	52,221	25.2%	18.2%	14.1%	27.9%	10.3%	3.3%	0.7%	0.4%	21.9%
Springfield, MO	43,409	31.6%	17.1%	18.0%	23.4%	6.1%	1.5%	1.4%	0.9%	25.4%
Springfield, OH	10,946	29.9%	18.4%	23.2%	22.9%	4.8%	0.8%	0.0%	0.0%	28.8%
St. Cloud, MN	17,858	12.1%	20.8%	13.5%	40.0%	11.3%	0.6%	0.6%	1.1%	25.3%
St. George, UT	10,743	24.6%	10.6%	25.6%	22.8%	10.9%	4.5%	1.0%	0.0%	26.2%
St. Joseph, MO-KS	11,679	35.8%	18.6%	19.5%	18.8%	4.7%	1.9%	0.4%	0.2%	18.5%
St. Louis, MO-IL	269,329	25.1%	15.2%	17.1%	24.1%	13.6%	2.8%	1.6%	0.5%	17.8%
State College, PA	13,999	29.1%	19.1%	20.7%	19.2%	7.3%	2.7%	0.2%	1.7%	43.9%
Staunton-Waynesboro, VA	8,830	16.6%	24.7%	19.0%	33.2%	6.5%	0.0%	0.0%	0.0%	22.6%
Stockton-Lodi, CA	61,696	30.7%	20.5%	15.9%	21.1%	7.9%	2.6%	1.2%	0.0%	23.6%
Sumter, SC	9,642	40.3%	13.4%	15.3%	25.0%	5.4%	0.6%	0.0%	0.0%	31.4%
Sunbury, PA micro	7,918	34.2%	14.8%	20.2%	8.8%	13.7%	3.5%	3.5%	1.2%	20.8%
Syracuse, NY	56,132	27.8%	18.9%	19.4%	19.0%	10.0%	3.7%	1.1%	0.1%	21.5%
Tallahassee, FL	40,310	35.2%	16.8%	15.4%	25.8%	5.1%	1.7%	0.0%	0.0%	38.4%
Tampa-St. Petersburg-Clearwater, FL	256,739	28.5%	17.8%	18.8%	22.2%	9.3%	2.2%	1.0%	0.3%	19.4%
Terre Haute, IN	16,606	45.4%	14.9%	15.0%	19.0%	4.3%	0.8%	0.7%	0.0%	34.3%
Texarkana, TX-AR	15,588	39.9%	14.7%	19.2%	17.6%	3.4%	1.8%	1.4%	1.9%	25.1%
The Villages, FL	5,232	36.2%	12.0%	36.2%	12.2%	1.1%	0.0%	2.3%	0.0%	16.3%
Toledo, OH	57,149	30.9%	20.6%	13.9%	19.9%	12.7%	0.7%	1.0%	0.3%	24.4%
Topeka, KS	19,377	20.1%	9.0%	17.3%	37.0%	14.2%	1.3%	1.1%	0.0%	17.8%
Torrington, CT micro	13,526	6.7%	20.8%	15.7%	30.2%	13.5%	9.7%	3.3%	0.0%	6.2%
Traverse City, MI micro	10,876	23.6%	27.3%	17.9%	24.3%	3.5%	3.3%	0.0%	0.2%	21.3%
Trenton, NJ	31,797	29.5%	16.5%	13.0%	20.4%	14.7%	4.3%	1.5%	0.0%	16.0%
Truckee-Grass Valley, CA micro	5,855	27.2%	15.8%	7.6%	28.5%	20.4%	0.5%	0.0%	0.0%	20.2%
Tucson, AZ	88,003	32.6%	18.2%	17.8%	18.6%	7.8%	3.4%	1.4%	0.3%	29.0%
Tullahoma-Manchester, TN micro	6,331	29.1%	28.2%	9.7%	26.8%	4.1%	0.0%	0.0%	2.2%	26.6%
Tulsa, OK	89,032	29.4%	17.5%	19.1%	21.5%	8.2%	2.9%	1.3%	0.1%	18.6%
Tupelo, MS micro	11,083	33.9%	18.0%	17.3%	21.4%	6.2%	1.5%	0.0%	1.8%	25.5%
Tuscaloosa, AL	23,302	27.3%	17.2%	19.0%	22.4%	9.0%	3.2%	1.9%	0.0%	23.3%
Tyler, TX	19,669	24.7%	17.2%	22.2%	27.5%	6.2%	2.0%	0.0%	0.2%	21.6%
Urban Honolulu, HI	108,618	25.9%	12.9%	13.4%	26.3%	15.7%	3.6%	2.0%	0.2%	12.5%
Utica-Rome, NY	24,883	24.7%	15.7%	20.8%	30.4%	4.9%	2.4%	0.5%	0.5%	19.9%

Table I-4: Metropolitan/Micropolitan Statistical Areas—Income Class by Age—*Continued*

	Total Millennials	Under $10,000	$10,000 to $19,999	$20,000 to $29,999	$30,000 to $49,999	$50,000 to $74,999	$75,000 to $99,999	$100,000 or More
				Personal Income, Percent by Income, Ages 18 to 24				
Valdosta, GA	24,729	66.7%	19.2%	10.1%	3.4%	0.6%	0.0%	0.0%
Vallejo-Fairfield, CA.................................	43,457	64.3%	19.4%	9.6%	5.6%	0.7%	0.4%	0.0%
Victoria, TX.................................	9,386	51.8%	25.8%	10.2%	10.6%	0.5%	1.1%	0.0%
Vineland-Bridgeton, NJ	13,253	56.4%	21.9%	9.6%	10.0%	2.2%	0.0%	0.0%
Virginia Beach-Norfolk-Newport News, VA-NC	203,677	55.9%	22.0%	14.6%	6.2%	1.1%	0.1%	0.0%
Visalia-Porterville, CA...........................	49,699	70.9%	16.2%	9.6%	3.0%	0.0%	0.3%	0.0%
Waco, TX.................................	38,050	64.4%	22.3%	6.7%	5.0%	1.4%	0.2%	0.0%
Walla Walla, WA.................................	7,436	59.8%	12.9%	14.8%	12.5%	0.0%	0.0%	0.0%
Warner Robins, GA	20,230	69.5%	18.1%	5.2%	5.8%	1.5%	0.0%	0.0%
Washington-Arlington-Alexandria, DC-VA-MD-WV	540,511	61.0%	15.9%	9.3%	10.1%	3.3%	0.3%	0.2%
Waterloo-Cedar Falls, IA.......................	27,213	61.5%	20.6%	14.9%	2.2%	0.8%	0.0%	0.0%
Watertown-Fort Drum, NY	15,064	39.6%	23.8%	23.0%	12.8%	0.8%	0.0%	0.0%
Wausau, WI.................................	11,313	60.0%	23.1%	6.3%	10.6%	0.0%	0.0%	0.0%
Weirton-Steubenville, WV-OH	12,018	70.9%	15.5%	3.8%	4.7%	4.5%	0.6%	0.0%
Wenatchee, WA.................................	8,718	48.7%	32.5%	11.0%	5.3%	2.5%	0.0%	0.0%
Wheeling, WV-OH	13,164	74.1%	13.5%	3.4%	4.3%	4.1%	0.6%	0.0%
Whitewater-Elkhorn, WI micro	11,281	76.7%	14.0%	8.2%	1.2%	0.0%	0.0%	0.0%
Wichita Falls, TX	19,163	56.4%	26.0%	7.5%	8.8%	0.0%	0.0%	1.2%
Wichita, KS	58,427	56.1%	24.0%	10.4%	6.7%	2.8%	0.0%	0.0%
Williamsport, PA	13,832	70.2%	16.8%	3.9%	7.7%	1.4%	0.1%	0.0%
Wilmington, NC.................................	32,892	62.1%	21.5%	9.4%	4.8%	2.2%	0.0%	0.0%
Winchester, VA-WV.................................	10,846	64.4%	14.4%	15.5%	5.7%	0.0%	0.0%	0.0%
Winston-Salem, NC.................................	60,502	68.0%	18.3%	8.3%	4.8%	0.4%	0.0%	0.2%
Wooster, OH micro.................................	11,137	56.7%	20.8%	16.8%	5.8%	0.0%	0.0%	0.0%
Worcester, MA-CT.................................	89,748	65.7%	16.6%	10.3%	5.9%	1.3%	0.1%	0.1%
Yakima, WA.................................	25,232	65.7%	20.1%	7.8%	6.3%	0.0%	0.0%	0.0%
York-Hanover, PA.................................	37,083	57.6%	26.1%	9.7%	5.6%	0.8%	0.3%	0.0%
Youngstown-Warren-Boardman, OH-PA...	47,862	67.4%	21.4%	7.9%	2.6%	0.2%	0.4%	0.0%
Yuba City, CA	16,677	64.3%	22.2%	11.2%	1.6%	0.3%	0.0%	0.5%
Yuma, AZ	24,334	64.9%	18.0%	10.6%	6.6%	0.0%	0.0%	0.0%

Table I-4: Metropolitan/Micropolitan Statistical Areas—Income Class by Age—*Continued*

| | Personal Income, Ages 25 to 31 | | | | | | | | | |
	Total Millennials	Under $10,000	$10,000 to $19,999	$20,000 to $29,999	$30,000 to $49,999	$50,000 to $74,999	$75,000 to $99,999	$100,000 to $149,999	$150,000 or More	Poverty Rate
Valdosta, GA	14,623	35.3%	16.9%	14.3%	25.5%	5.2%	2.1%	0.6%	0.0%	35.2%
Vallejo-Fairfield, CA	42,964	29.1%	15.3%	15.9%	19.3%	13.0%	4.0%	2.8%	0.7%	16.1%
Victoria, TX	7,723	28.7%	12.4%	13.0%	12.2%	16.8%	12.8%	4.0%	0.0%	16.6%
Vineland-Bridgeton, NJ	17,680	47.2%	14.1%	10.7%	15.7%	9.5%	1.5%	1.3%	0.0%	19.2%
Virginia Beach-Norfolk-Newport News, VA-NC	189,087	24.5%	14.8%	19.4%	25.9%	11.8%	2.2%	1.2%	0.3%	16.9%
Visalia-Porterville, CA	46,122	42.9%	20.7%	15.5%	10.4%	5.9%	2.7%	1.4%	0.4%	33.6%
Waco, TX	23,818	34.5%	21.0%	13.4%	24.3%	5.3%	0.5%	1.1%	0.0%	30.3%
Walla Walla, WA	5,911	42.9%	26.6%	14.1%	10.2%	5.1%	0.0%	1.2%	0.0%	34.6%
Warner Robins, GA	19,225	28.9%	13.6%	21.5%	31.3%	2.9%	0.8%	1.2%	0.0%	19.7%
Washington-Arlington-Alexandria, DC-VA-MD-WV	646,396	19.9%	10.4%	13.7%	22.4%	20.2%	8.2%	3.8%	1.3%	10.8%
Waterloo-Cedar Falls, IA	14,991	33.5%	9.7%	14.3%	30.1%	9.3%	2.3%	0.7%	0.0%	28.6%
Watertown-Fort Drum, NY	13,925	26.9%	15.3%	26.2%	17.8%	8.0%	2.6%	2.2%	1.0%	19.0%
Wausau, WI	11,030	21.5%	14.8%	27.8%	22.8%	7.2%	2.8%	1.9%	1.2%	20.0%
Weirton-Steubenville, WV-OH	7,984	31.8%	20.8%	13.1%	21.8%	7.4%	2.0%	1.7%	1.5%	23.3%
Wenatchee, WA	11,132	24.3%	23.0%	15.3%	24.8%	8.8%	1.4%	2.5%	0.0%	15.8%
Wheeling, WV-OH	9,570	29.8%	27.9%	14.7%	16.2%	6.2%	3.5%	0.6%	1.2%	21.7%
Whitewater-Elkhorn, WI micro	8,854	30.4%	21.3%	18.8%	16.8%	11.9%	0.9%	0.0%	0.0%	29.7%
Wichita Falls, TX	16,601	33.1%	14.3%	16.1%	20.1%	15.9%	0.0%	0.5%	0.0%	24.9%
Wichita, KS	64,948	27.9%	18.0%	17.1%	25.3%	9.4%	1.2%	0.9%	0.1%	18.4%
Williamsport, PA	8,292	35.5%	13.0%	11.5%	27.9%	9.1%	2.7%	0.0%	0.3%	14.8%
Wilmington, NC	23,851	19.6%	16.4%	21.6%	30.1%	8.8%	2.8%	0.8%	0.0%	29.4%
Winchester, VA-WV	9,260	30.6%	12.5%	12.1%	28.3%	15.0%	1.4%	0.1%	0.0%	10.5%
Winston-Salem, NC	50,711	34.6%	15.3%	20.5%	21.5%	5.9%	1.7%	0.0%	0.6%	26.5%
Wooster, OH micro	8,719	32.1%	21.5%	9.6%	28.5%	4.2%	4.0%	0.0%	0.0%	16.6%
Worcester, MA-CT	77,116	22.3%	15.0%	17.5%	24.7%	15.1%	4.0%	1.2%	0.3%	17.2%
Yakima, WA	22,351	24.3%	20.8%	20.4%	23.5%	9.1%	1.3%	0.6%	0.0%	20.5%
York-Hanover, PA	33,523	21.1%	13.9%	17.2%	32.8%	10.5%	2.0%	2.6%	0.0%	14.9%
Youngstown-Warren-Boardman, OH-PA	43,994	30.0%	21.0%	19.1%	14.8%	10.7%	2.2%	1.1%	1.0%	23.6%
Yuba City, CA	16,214	33.8%	15.2%	23.6%	22.7%	3.5%	1.1%	0.0%	0.0%	20.9%
Yuma, AZ	19,442	29.9%	21.4%	19.0%	18.7%	7.4%	2.7%	0.6%	0.3%	16.6%

PART J
MOBILITY AND MIGRATION

MOBILITY AND MIGRATION

While the mobility of younger Millennials may still be tied to their parents, the mobility of those in the 18 to 24 age group will often be related to college attendance, and the older Millennials may be following their first job or career move. People in their late 20s and early 30s typically have high rates of migration as this stage in the lifecycle is one of transition: finding jobs, finding partners, starting families, and finding a location to settle in. Today, metropolitan areas have become primary destinations. Millennials aren't so different from other generations in that sense, except that they are often staying in school longer and delaying marriage and career decisions. A recent Census Bureau report on young adult migration provides a useful portrait of

the characteristics of Millennial migrants at the national level.[1]

The American Community Survey data comes from response to the question on residence one year ago. This is used to determine the extent of mobility and migration. From these data it is possible to identify specific migration flows such as retirees from northern states to southern states or even economic moves between specific Public Use Microdata Areas. The tables presented here are summarized to identify persons living in the same house as one year ago (non-migrants), those who have moved but were residing in the same state one year

1. U.S. Census Bureau, "Young Adult Migration: 2007–2009 to 2010–2012," Report Number: ACS-31, March 2015.

Percent Age 25 to 31 Living in the Same House One Year Ago

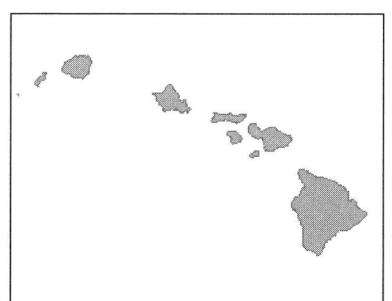

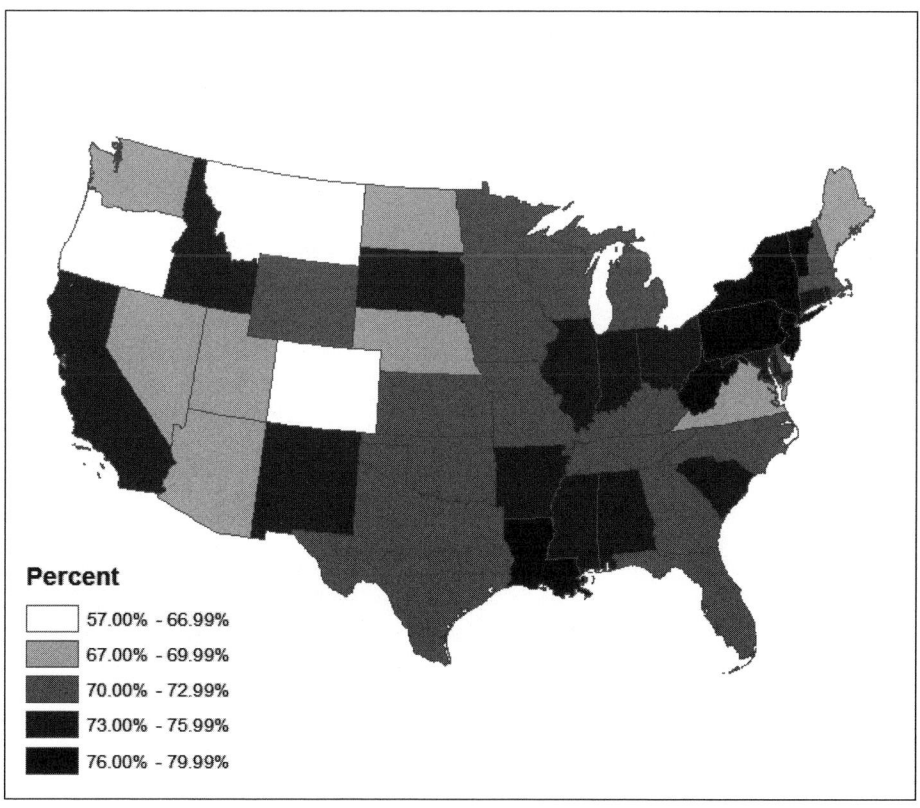

Percent

- 57.00% - 66.99%
- 67.00% - 69.99%
- 70.00% - 72.99%
- 73.00% - 75.99%
- 76.00% - 79.99%

ago, those who lived in a different state but within the same Census region, one year ago, those who lived in a different region, and those who lived outside of the United States one year ago (primarily foreign immigrants). It's important to remember that for someone who has moved, these data don't always represent migration. Someone who moves but stays in the same state would only be considered a migrant if their move was to or from a different county.

Not surprisingly, 88.2 percent of young Millennials age 13 to 17 live in the same house as they did one year ago, but they're more mobile in Nevada where only 81.0 percent stayed in the same house. They're most stable in Vermont where 94.2 percent didn't move. While nearly three of every four older Millennials are still in the same house, they are much more mobile. The percentage of stable 18 to 24 and 25 to 31 year olds is 70.0 percent and 73.1 percent, respectively. When they do move, most stay within the same state – 23.6 percent of the 18 to 24 age group and 21.3 percent for the 25 to 31 year olds. In the younger age category only 11.9 percent of New Jersey residents stayed in the same state while 13.0 percent of the 25 to 31 year olds in the District of Columbia where in the same state. Among the 18 to 24 age group, 14.2 percent of the District of Columbia residents lived in a different region one year ago. DC also has the highest percentage who

lived outside the U.S. at 3.2 percent for the 18 to 24 year olds compared to 3.0 percent for those 25 to 31.

Sussex County, DE (98.7 percent) has the highest percentage of 13 to 17 year olds who remain in the same house year to year. Cape May County, NJ and Lycoming County, PA are also above 98 percent. Henderson County, NC is the most mobile with only 63.7 percent staying in the same house. Among the 18 to 24 age group, Johnson County, IA has the lowest percentage who stay home at only 30.8 percent, compared to Putnam County, NY, where 95.5 percent are stable. In Moore County, NC only 1.8 percent live in a different house but in the same state, while La Crosse County, WI has the highest percentage at 64.4 percent. Living in a different state from one year ago is most common in Comanche County, OK, where 34.6 percent moved, but in 357 counties less than five percent of the 18 to 24 year olds lived in a different state. Ector County, TX has the highest percentage of those living abroad in the previous year at 8.9 percent. Among the older age group, 99.0 percent of residents in Saline County, AR stayed in the same house as a year ago. The most mobile were in Missoula County, MT, where only 43.6 percent stayed at home. In Sumter County, FL 49.8 percent moved but stayed within Florida. With Saline County, AR having the highest percentage of stable residents, they also have the lowest percent moving, and the 1.0 percent who changed

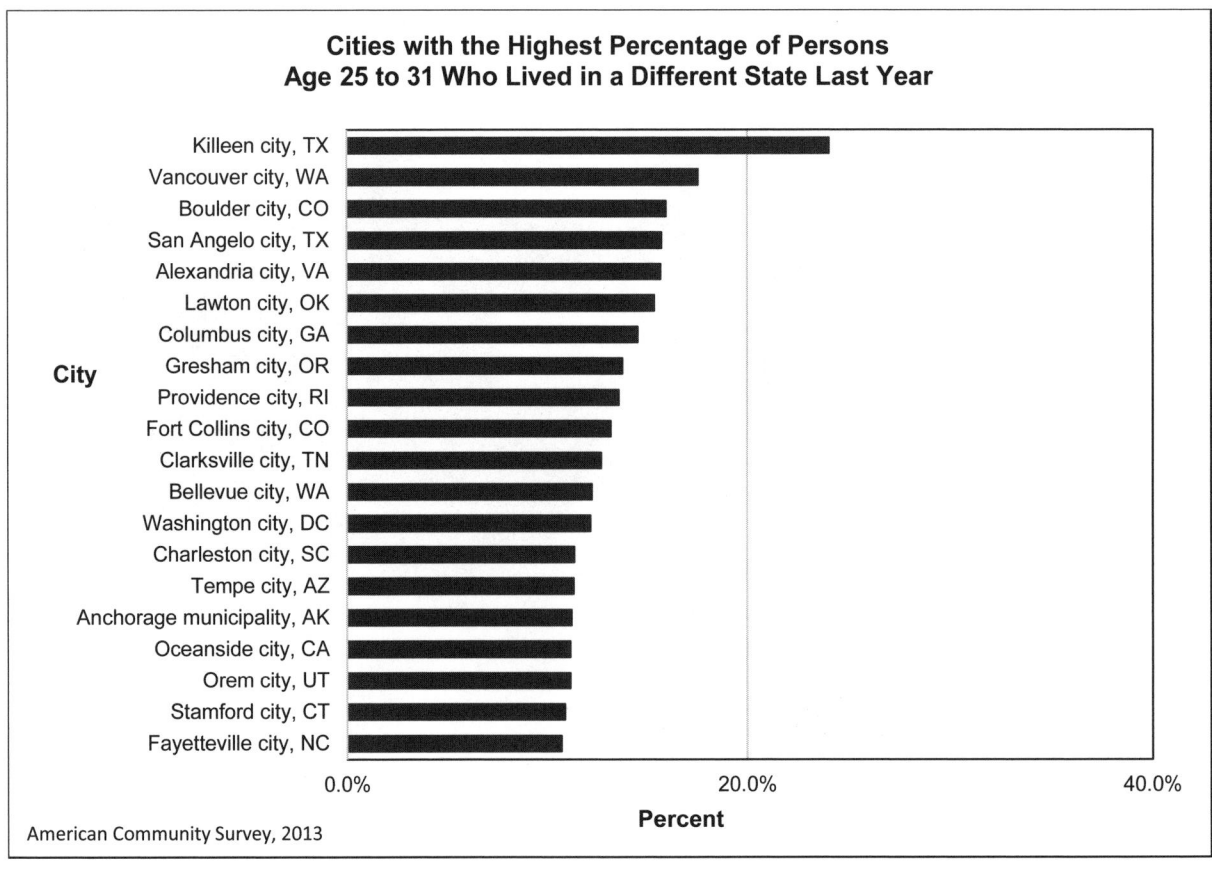

Cities with the Highest Percentage of Persons Age 25 to 31 Who Lived in a Different State Last Year

American Community Survey, 2013

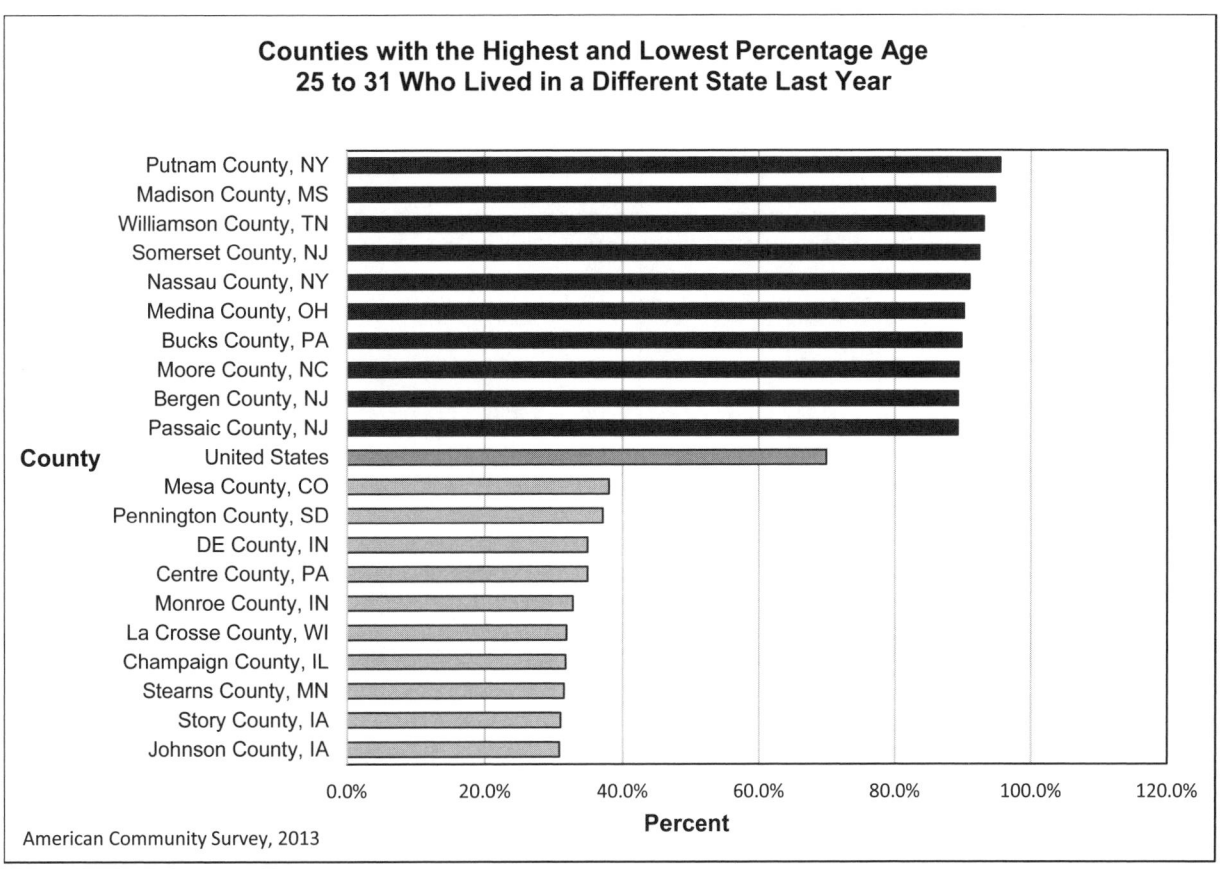

Counties with the Highest and Lowest Percentage Age 25 to 31 Who Lived in a Different State Last Year

American Community Survey, 2013

houses all stayed within Arkansas. Beaufort County, SC has the highest percentage who changed states at 17.9 percent, and in 391 counties the percentage was below five percent. Story County, IA has the highest percentage moving from outside the U.S. at 6.6 percent.

In Santa Monica City, CA, the ACS reports that all 13 to 17 year olds live in the same house as one year ago. It's reported as the highest, but 84 other cities are above 90 percent. Roanoke City, VA has the lowest percentage (62.6 percent) of young Millennials who live in the same house. Among the 18 to 24 year olds, El Monte City, CA is the most stable, with 95.5 percent not moving. In Boulder City, CO only 28.1 percent did not move, but 52.5 moved and stayed within Colorado. In Lawton City, OK 35.8 percent previously lived in a different state, though 19.6 percent were still within the same Census region. The city with the highest percentage (10.0. percent) who lived abroad in the previous year was Odessa City, TX. El Monte City, CA has the highest percentage of 25 to 31 year olds who live in the same house as a year ago. Akron City, OH (90.5 percent) is the only other city above 90 percent. In Killeen City, TX, 24.1 percent of the older Millennials lived in a different state last year. Only five other cities were above 15 percent: Alexandria City, VA (15.7 percent), Boulder City, CO (16.0 percent),

Lawton City, OK (15.4 percent), San Angelo City, TX (15.7 percent) and Vancouver City, WA (17.5 percent). Foreign locations were the origin for 12.0 percent of Millennials age 25 to 31 in Temecula City, CA.

More than 70 percent of the youngest Millennials live in the same house as a year ago in every metropolitan/micropolitan area except for the Clarksville, TN-KY metro at 69.4 percent. In 144 of the 415 metro areas more than 90 percent have not moved. The Ames, IA metro has the lowest percentage of 18 to 24 year olds who live in the same house at 31.6 percent, while the Ocean City, NJ metro is highest (89.1 percent). The Lawton, OK metro area has the highest percentage who lived in a different state last year at 31.5 percent. Only three other metros are above 20 percent: Cheyenne, WY (23.0 percent), Columbus, GA-AL (21.6 percent), and Watertown-Fort Drum, NY (23.7 percent). In the Odessa, TX metropolitan area, 8.9 percent of the 24 to 31 year olds lived abroad last year. Seventy metros had less than two percent from abroad. Among the older Millennials, the Farmington, NM metro had the highest percentage (93.7) who stayed in the same house as last year, and in 146 metros more than 75 percent did not move. In the Hilton Head Island-Bluffton-Beaufort, SC metro, 18.6 percent of the older Millennials lived abroad.

Table J-1: States—Mobility Status by Age

| | 13 to 17 | | 18 to 24 | | | | | | 25 to 31 | | | | | |
| | | | | | Percent Living in a Different House | | | | | | Percent Living in a Different House | | | |
	Total Population	Percent Living in Same House	Total Population	Percent Living in Same House	Same State	Different State, Same Region	Different Region	Outside US	Total Population	Percent Living in Same House	Same State	Different State, Same Region	Different Region	Outside US
United States	20,794,322	88.2%	31,635,759	70.0%	23.6%	2.7%	2.6%	1.1%	30,086,454	73.1%	21.3%	2.0%	2.4%	1.2%
Alabama	317,143	85.2%	497,511	71.1%	22.4%	4.2%	1.6%	0.6%	429,255	74.6%	21.2%	2.6%	1.0%	0.7%
Alaska	52,922	88.2%	84,545	62.6%	26.8%	3.8%	4.8%	2.0%	80,986	57.5%	32.1%	3.8%	5.3%	1.2%
Arizona	458,064	84.1%	662,724	66.4%	26.6%	3.3%	2.6%	1.2%	622,816	68.3%	24.4%	2.7%	3.3%	1.3%
Arkansas	194,868	88.4%	287,155	69.1%	26.7%	2.4%	1.3%	0.6%	272,879	75.8%	19.7%	2.3%	1.5%	0.6%
California	2,588,851	88.4%	4,016,509	74.2%	21.6%	1.0%	1.7%	1.5%	3,958,135	75.2%	20.8%	0.8%	1.8%	1.3%
Colorado	347,310	86.7%	512,098	57.7%	31.6%	3.1%	6.3%	1.4%	544,958	64.6%	26.4%	2.1%	5.6%	1.3%
Connecticut	235,916	91.6%	342,884	78.4%	15.0%	3.6%	1.9%	1.1%	311,170	74.3%	19.1%	2.9%	2.2%	1.5%
Delaware	55,750	89.2%	90,525	69.4%	19.9%	2.9%	7.0%	0.9%	87,725	71.3%	21.1%	3.4%	4.1%	0.1%
District of Columbia	23,781	85.8%	80,974	54.1%	20.1%	8.5%	14.2%	3.2%	111,405	71.5%	13.3%	7.8%	4.4%	3.0%
Florida	1,157,139	85.5%	1,796,924	72.7%	21.7%	1.8%	2.7%	1.1%	1,749,330	72.4%	22.3%	1.6%	2.3%	1.3%
Georgia	701,865	85.0%	1,029,573	68.6%	25.2%	2.8%	2.3%	1.0%	944,465	72.9%	21.5%	2.7%	1.9%	1.0%
Hawaii	85,036	90.2%	136,384	72.3%	15.1%	5.2%	5.3%	2.1%	149,735	69.1%	16.9%	4.0%	7.8%	2.2%
Idaho	120,090	85.8%	160,655	54.4%	31.1%	8.8%	3.5%	2.2%	141,419	73.2%	19.7%	5.0%	0.9%	1.1%
Illinois	861,332	90.2%	1,267,572	72.6%	21.9%	2.0%	2.5%	1.0%	1,253,950	74.7%	20.0%	1.5%	2.6%	1.1%
Indiana	444,803	88.0%	670,827	66.2%	28.3%	2.6%	2.0%	0.9%	578,748	73.2%	22.1%	1.7%	2.5%	0.5%
Iowa	200,763	89.5%	315,687	59.7%	33.0%	4.3%	2.1%	0.9%	274,701	70.5%	23.4%	2.7%	2.2%	1.1%
Kansas	197,499	85.9%	301,166	63.9%	27.5%	3.2%	4.1%	1.4%	264,777	72.8%	19.9%	2.6%	3.9%	0.8%
Kentucky	290,213	85.4%	427,893	67.1%	27.1%	1.8%	3.5%	0.5%	395,614	72.3%	22.3%	1.7%	2.7%	1.1%
Louisiana	300,317	88.8%	482,665	74.3%	19.5%	3.5%	1.6%	1.1%	458,626	76.4%	19.2%	2.4%	1.4%	0.5%
Maine	82,081	88.8%	117,248	68.2%	24.0%	4.5%	2.5%	0.8%	104,225	68.8%	26.4%	2.0%	2.7%	0.2%
Maryland	384,899	90.0%	564,004	76.8%	16.7%	2.5%	2.9%	1.1%	578,502	73.3%	18.8%	3.6%	2.7%	1.6%
Massachusetts	415,765	91.4%	695,854	71.4%	20.4%	4.0%	2.7%	1.5%	659,931	71.8%	21.9%	2.2%	2.5%	1.6%
Michigan	661,571	86.4%	1,000,327	65.3%	29.9%	1.5%	2.4%	0.9%	835,027	72.9%	23.1%	1.0%	1.8%	1.1%
Minnesota	359,295	89.8%	508,343	64.2%	29.2%	4.1%	1.6%	0.9%	526,508	72.5%	21.4%	2.3%	2.0%	1.8%
Mississippi	204,811	86.0%	322,350	72.7%	21.5%	4.1%	1.5%	0.2%	255,386	73.9%	21.4%	2.9%	1.4%	0.4%
Missouri	397,250	87.3%	593,075	65.2%	27.3%	3.4%	3.7%	0.4%	561,404	70.1%	24.5%	2.1%	2.7%	0.6%
Montana	64,848	82.3%	102,961	59.8%	27.5%	7.3%	3.7%	1.6%	86,191	65.0%	25.9%	2.3%	6.5%	0.2%
Nebraska	122,024	89.1%	190,963	59.5%	32.4%	3.6%	3.7%	0.8%	175,394	68.8%	26.2%	1.2%	3.3%	0.5%
Nevada	182,501	81.0%	257,114	67.8%	24.0%	5.6%	2.0%	0.5%	275,510	68.9%	23.8%	4.2%	2.3%	0.7%
New Hampshire	84,658	91.4%	126,757	68.9%	18.6%	9.2%	1.6%	1.7%	108,673	70.7%	19.8%	5.3%	3.3%	0.9%
New Jersey	595,382	92.8%	794,360	84.2%	11.9%	1.5%	1.3%	1.1%	789,900	79.2%	14.9%	2.6%	2.0%	1.3%
New Mexico	141,557	87.8%	218,255	71.5%	20.6%	1.8%	3.9%	2.2%	186,280	74.3%	18.9%	2.0%	3.4%	1.4%
New York	1,208,404	92.2%	1,992,311	78.3%	16.2%	1.4%	2.5%	1.6%	2,010,905	79.6%	16.0%	1.1%	2.0%	1.3%
North Carolina	645,484	88.1%	998,003	67.9%	24.3%	3.3%	3.4%	1.0%	874,083	71.7%	21.5%	3.0%	2.6%	1.2%
North Dakota	42,043	91.5%	97,140	51.7%	28.7%	13.1%	4.7%	1.8%	70,082	70.0%	20.7%	7.0%	2.1%	0.2%
Ohio	767,800	88.2%	1,118,384	65.8%	29.3%	1.4%	2.4%	1.1%	1,036,741	73.0%	22.7%	1.0%	2.4%	0.9%
Oklahoma	247,021	86.7%	396,186	66.3%	26.0%	4.4%	2.6%	0.6%	371,158	71.2%	23.0%	2.4%	2.6%	0.9%
Oregon	244,438	86.0%	368,263	59.2%	32.3%	5.9%	1.7%	0.9%	368,990	66.5%	24.7%	5.1%	2.6%	1.1%
Pennsylvania	793,189	90.9%	1,251,852	72.4%	21.8%	2.4%	2.4%	1.1%	1,149,375	76.5%	18.8%	1.3%	2.4%	1.0%
Rhode Island	62,151	92.6%	119,895	74.3%	13.8%	7.3%	2.3%	2.3%	96,226	75.2%	17.1%	2.5%	3.6%	1.5%
South Carolina	306,746	88.4%	502,074	67.1%	24.2%	4.4%	3.8%	0.4%	414,684	73.5%	19.9%	3.1%	2.8%	0.8%
South Dakota	54,808	89.0%	84,051	54.4%	33.7%	9.5%	1.9%	0.5%	76,007	75.0%	20.6%	2.6%	1.8%	0.1%
Tennessee	424,842	86.1%	632,614	71.2%	22.4%	3.6%	2.4%	0.5%	595,744	72.7%	20.8%	3.5%	2.1%	0.8%
Texas	1,909,547	87.0%	2,733,033	69.1%	25.8%	1.6%	2.3%	1.1%	2,674,332	70.5%	24.1%	1.5%	2.4%	1.5%
Utah	233,633	87.0%	333,429	60.4%	27.6%	5.7%	4.0%	2.2%	301,066	69.2%	25.0%	3.2%	1.7%	0.8%
Vermont	39,154	94.2%	64,873	63.5%	21.7%	8.8%	3.3%	2.6%	50,046	76.4%	18.9%	3.5%	0.6%	0.7%
Virginia	518,191	87.6%	833,573	69.3%	22.1%	3.8%	3.7%	1.2%	802,202	69.7%	22.1%	3.6%	3.2%	1.4%
Washington	442,740	87.6%	665,504	64.5%	27.9%	3.5%	2.6%	1.5%	700,424	68.9%	23.3%	2.9%	3.6%	1.3%
West Virginia	113,555	89.9%	176,100	72.5%	18.7%	3.0%	5.3%	0.5%	146,977	77.1%	17.8%	2.3%	2.5%	0.3%
Wisconsin	372,227	90.4%	553,079	63.1%	30.6%	4.2%	1.5%	0.6%	519,237	72.7%	23.6%	1.4%	1.5%	0.7%
Wyoming	38,045	85.2%	59,513	57.0%	30.0%	6.3%	5.9%	0.8%	54,550	70.0%	18.5%	5.5%	5.3%	0.7%

Table J-2: Counties—Mobility Status by Age

	13 to 17		18 to 24						25 to 31					
					Percent Living in a Different House						Percent Living in a Different House			
	Total Population	Percent Living in Same House	Total Population	Percent Living in Same House	Same State	Different State, Same Region	Different Region	Outside US	Total Population	Percent Living in Same House	Same State	Different State, Same Region	Different Region	Outside US
Alabama														
Baldwin County	13,134	88.0%	16,338	71.4%	8.5%	12.2%	0.1%	7.8%	14,271	51.8%	39.0%	9.3%	0.0%	0.0%
Calhoun County	6,696	78.2%	11,943	55.6%	36.9%	5.6%	1.8%	0.1%	10,550	75.5%	17.3%	1.5%	0.0%	5.7%
Etowah County	7,662	80.1%	9,315	86.2%	13.4%	0.5%	0.0%	0.0%	8,012	70.7%	24.9%	2.8%	1.6%	0.0%
Houston County	7,382	85.6%	8,774	71.7%	17.3%	4.0%	7.0%	0.0%	9,840	74.6%	15.8%	9.6%	0.0%	0.0%
Jefferson County	42,598	83.9%	60,692	68.6%	25.2%	3.7%	2.4%	0.0%	66,293	71.8%	23.3%	3.1%	1.1%	0.7%
Lauderdale County	5,814	84.5%	11,302	73.8%	15.3%	6.2%	4.7%	0.0%	8,102	75.1%	23.6%	1.3%	0.0%	0.0%
Lee County	9,237	90.1%	30,018	48.3%	37.8%	13.1%	0.8%	0.0%	14,147	65.2%	20.1%	5.2%	5.9%	3.6%
Madison County	22,909	83.6%	35,171	67.3%	26.0%	1.7%	4.3%	0.6%	31,607	73.0%	24.5%	1.4%	0.9%	0.2%
Marshall County	7,521	88.1%	7,257	77.6%	20.6%	1.8%	0.0%	0.0%	9,126	74.6%	25.0%	0.5%	0.0%	0.0%
Mobile County	26,092	90.2%	42,048	72.2%	26.0%	1.5%	0.2%	0.2%	37,948	77.7%	18.9%	0.9%	1.1%	1.4%
Montgomery County	15,773	67.9%	26,815	55.7%	37.4%	5.0%	1.6%	0.2%	23,145	68.9%	26.6%	1.7%	2.1%	0.7%
Morgan County	8,545	78.9%	10,480	77.0%	20.9%	0.0%	2.1%	0.0%	8,840	78.2%	20.3%	1.5%	0.0%	0.0%
Shelby County	14,600	88.4%	16,952	76.2%	17.8%	0.5%	3.8%	1.7%	18,469	73.6%	22.5%	2.1%	1.6%	0.3%
Tuscaloosa County	11,590	78.1%	39,838	58.8%	25.6%	11.1%	3.2%	1.4%	21,669	71.6%	21.7%	5.0%	1.3%	0.4%
Alaska														
Fairbanks North Star Borough..	6,177	88.5%	14,290	50.4%	28.4%	3.9%	11.5%	5.8%	13,155	45.4%	47.8%	0.8%	6.0%	0.0%
Matanuska-Susitna Borough.....	8,792	82.5%	9,851	62.3%	35.6%	2.1%	0.0%	0.0%	8,642	56.4%	26.7%	8.4%	3.9%	4.6%
Arizona														
Cochise County	8,258	92.1%	12,200	58.8%	29.0%	2.0%	7.7%	2.5%	11,622	53.3%	26.2%	4.9%	10.6%	5.0%
Coconino County	7,738	79.3%	26,701	48.9%	36.8%	12.7%	1.3%	0.3%	14,018	67.6%	24.8%	1.3%	6.3%	0.0%
Maricopa County	284,531	84.7%	386,757	69.3%	24.9%	2.5%	2.2%	1.1%	403,195	68.7%	24.6%	2.3%	3.3%	1.1%
Mohave County	12,002	72.5%	14,136	59.1%	31.0%	4.9%	4.9%	0.0%	14,210	63.7%	27.5%	4.9%	3.5%	0.4%
Navajo County	8,371	91.7%	10,545	86.4%	10.9%	0.4%	1.7%	0.6%	9,586	83.3%	14.6%	0.0%	0.0%	2.2%
Pima County	62,937	85.6%	121,550	55.3%	35.8%	2.9%	4.2%	1.8%	88,003	65.3%	26.0%	3.4%	3.3%	2.0%
Pinal County	27,764	79.0%	32,006	75.6%	19.4%	2.5%	0.9%	1.7%	32,604	70.8%	20.3%	4.8%	1.9%	2.1%
Yavapai County	11,799	70.3%	14,382	61.2%	24.1%	11.9%	2.3%	0.5%	14,168	70.8%	22.7%	4.5%	1.3%	0.7%
Yuma County	15,620	88.6%	24,334	76.1%	15.2%	3.8%	2.7%	2.2%	19,442	74.2%	18.8%	2.4%	3.0%	1.6%
Arkansas														
Benton County	19,059	91.3%	19,984	74.4%	18.8%	2.0%	3.3%	1.6%	22,428	73.6%	18.0%	1.9%	3.4%	3.2%
Craighead County	5,049	73.0%	11,153	69.1%	29.2%	0.7%	0.0%	0.9%	11,120	79.1%	16.4%	3.0%	0.4%	1.2%
Faulkner County	9,156	81.0%	16,274	68.6%	23.3%	2.8%	2.5%	2.7%	15,873	71.4%	27.1%	0.1%	1.4%	0.0%
Garland County	5,813	87.2%	8,413	68.1%	25.7%	6.1%	0.0%	0.0%	6,178	80.7%	18.2%	1.1%	0.0%	0.0%
Pulaski County	25,229	92.3%	35,099	72.4%	25.2%	1.4%	0.9%	0.0%	44,132	71.3%	26.0%	1.3%	1.0%	0.4%
Saline County	8,012	95.4%	8,095	77.3%	21.5%	0.3%	0.9%	0.0%	11,423	99.0%	1.0%	0.0%	0.0%	0.0%
Sebastian County	8,906	91.1%	10,237	76.8%	19.0%	2.2%	0.4%	1.7%	13,346	76.2%	16.9%	5.4%	1.5%	0.0%
Washington County	13,619	87.6%	31,341	43.2%	43.9%	7.6%	5.2%	0.0%	23,408	75.7%	20.1%	2.3%	1.9%	0.0%
California														
Alameda County	91,937	89.6%	149,330	71.7%	21.8%	0.7%	2.6%	3.2%	170,706	72.8%	21.4%	1.0%	2.1%	2.8%
Butte County	12,100	82.6%	33,787	53.0%	43.6%	0.1%	1.3%	2.1%	19,755	76.1%	22.0%	0.0%	1.9%	0.0%
Contra Costa County	72,371	87.9%	94,235	74.0%	22.0%	1.3%	1.1%	1.6%	93,554	75.7%	22.2%	0.4%	1.1%	0.6%
El Dorado County	11,561	79.8%	13,295	79.3%	18.2%	1.0%	0.0%	1.6%	12,743	57.2%	40.0%	2.3%	0.5%	0.0%
Fresno County	71,245	87.1%	108,464	78.2%	20.8%	0.4%	0.4%	0.2%	101,070	76.3%	22.5%	0.3%	0.5%	0.5%
Humboldt County	6,652	74.5%	18,113	57.3%	41.7%	0.6%	0.3%	0.0%	13,592	72.5%	23.7%	2.9%	0.9%	0.0%
Imperial County	14,236	87.9%	20,303	82.4%	15.6%	0.1%	0.0%	1.9%	18,063	81.9%	14.9%	1.4%	0.4%	1.4%
Kern County	67,823	87.2%	95,971	75.2%	21.3%	0.7%	1.3%	1.5%	91,995	69.7%	27.3%	0.2%	1.9%	0.9%
Kings County	10,697	83.2%	17,431	73.4%	21.5%	1.4%	2.4%	1.3%	17,382	72.9%	26.2%	0.0%	0.7%	0.3%
Los Angeles County	669,035	90.2%	1,067,750	78.5%	17.4%	0.8%	1.8%	1.5%	1,096,906	78.1%	18.2%	0.6%	1.9%	1.2%
Madera County	12,013	95.3%	15,435	80.3%	19.1%	0.0%	0.0%	0.6%	15,618	85.8%	12.7%	0.0%	0.0%	1.5%
Marin County	16,661	86.8%	17,512	66.4%	29.4%	2.3%	0.7%	1.2%	15,181	67.8%	24.1%	2.1%	1.8%	4.2%
Merced County	23,797	88.0%	31,498	75.5%	23.4%	0.6%	0.5%	0.0%	25,584	76.4%	22.0%	1.6%	0.0%	0.0%
Monterey County	32,539	92.1%	48,230	76.6%	18.0%	1.4%	2.9%	1.1%	45,322	83.2%	12.3%	0.9%	2.1%	1.6%
Napa County	9,311	88.9%	13,156	69.6%	14.8%	9.9%	2.5%	3.2%	10,779	83.3%	16.1%	0.0%	0.6%	0.0%
Nevada County	5,901	86.7%	7,382	71.2%	26.0%	2.7%	0.0%	0.0%	5,855	80.8%	19.2%	0.0%	0.0%	0.0%
Orange County	217,538	87.6%	317,913	77.6%	19.3%	0.9%	1.4%	0.8%	310,232	74.9%	22.1%	0.8%	1.3%	1.0%
Placer County	28,449	93.0%	29,285	76.5%	19.4%	1.9%	1.4%	0.8%	29,238	75.6%	22.9%	0.7%	0.4%	0.4%
Riverside County	180,238	88.2%	243,003	79.9%	18.5%	0.6%	0.5%	0.5%	215,998	76.4%	21.0%	0.6%	0.7%	1.3%
Sacramento County	104,329	84.2%	145,677	69.8%	27.9%	0.8%	0.6%	0.9%	153,249	66.0%	32.3%	0.4%	0.8%	0.5%
San Bernardino County	165,643	85.3%	240,638	78.1%	18.4%	1.2%	1.0%	1.3%	212,266	76.8%	19.5%	1.3%	1.6%	0.9%
San Diego County	197,801	89.1%	366,780	71.5%	21.1%	1.1%	4.2%	2.1%	372,273	73.3%	20.4%	1.2%	3.2%	1.9%
San Francisco County	25,622	93.8%	64,495	58.1%	31.4%	1.9%	4.2%	4.5%	137,551	69.7%	20.6%	1.5%	5.4%	2.8%
San Joaquin County	58,394	84.4%	74,649	69.0%	29.8%	0.6%	0.5%	0.2%	62,376	75.0%	24.7%	0.1%	0.1%	0.0%
San Luis Obispo County	12,954	90.1%	44,013	44.0%	54.3%	0.0%	1.5%	0.2%	23,706	75.0%	21.1%	2.2%	0.7%	1.1%
San Mateo County	42,716	87.3%	57,975	80.7%	15.1%	1.0%	1.5%	1.7%	68,580	79.4%	16.0%	0.7%	1.8%	2.1%
Santa Barbara County	29,415	87.8%	68,915	47.1%	45.2%	1.9%	1.7%	4.0%	40,359	68.7%	25.6%	3.1%	0.5%	2.2%
Santa Clara County	112,666	90.3%	164,573	70.2%	23.5%	1.2%	2.0%	3.1%	197,830	72.8%	20.6%	0.6%	3.2%	2.8%
Santa Cruz County	14,645	96.6%	40,992	63.9%	31.0%	2.2%	0.9%	2.0%	21,827	84.2%	15.2%	0.0%	0.3%	0.3%
Shasta County	10,988	92.3%	17,040	64.1%	25.5%	5.5%	3.2%	1.8%	15,126	67.3%	26.7%	2.2%	1.2%	2.5%
Solano County	27,829	85.7%	43,457	77.2%	19.0%	1.0%	1.4%	1.5%	42,964	74.2%	21.4%	0.0%	3.5%	0.9%
Sonoma County	31,888	90.2%	45,516	72.2%	26.1%	0.1%	0.8%	0.8%	43,559	73.2%	23.7%	0.7%	1.9%	0.5%
Stanislaus County	42,105	87.3%	55,502	75.5%	23.2%	0.7%	0.1%	0.4%	50,579	75.3%	23.6%	0.6%	0.0%	0.5%
Sutter County	4,709	86.3%	10,422	69.9%	27.9%	0.9%	0.7%	0.7%	8,605	51.1%	41.9%	1.6%	3.3%	2.2%
Tulare County	36,363	88.4%	49,699	76.7%	21.3%	0.2%	1.8%	0.0%	46,122	79.8%	16.6%	2.3%	1.3%	0.0%
Ventura County	58,861	87.5%	85,580	82.3%	13.5%	1.7%	1.8%	0.7%	74,830	81.9%	13.6%	0.9%	1.8%	1.7%

Table J-2: Counties—Mobility Status by Age—*Continued*

| | 13 to 17 | | 18 to 24 | | | | | | 25 to 31 | | | | | |
| | | | | | Percent Living in a Different House | | | | | | Percent Living in a Different House | | | |
	Total Population	Percent Living in Same House	Total Population	Percent Living in Same House	Same State	Different State, Same Region	Different Region	Outside US	Total Population	Percent Living in Same House	Same State	Different State, Same Region	Different Region	Outside US
California—Cont.														
Yolo County	12,811	81.9%	39,633	47.9%	44.2%	1.1%	1.6%	5.3%	19,613	66.6%	31.0%	0.0%	0.7%	1.8%
Colorado														
Adams County	37,555	90.8%	44,213	66.9%	23.9%	4.8%	3.1%	1.3%	52,900	71.4%	23.0%	1.9%	3.4%	0.3%
Arapahoe County	44,980	81.9%	52,812	68.5%	24.1%	3.5%	3.2%	0.8%	61,836	66.3%	25.3%	2.1%	5.5%	0.9%
Boulder County	20,549	88.9%	46,153	41.9%	41.8%	5.6%	9.7%	1.0%	26,720	53.1%	34.8%	3.6%	7.5%	1.0%
Denver County	29,542	89.7%	62,202	54.5%	34.0%	3.2%	7.1%	1.3%	106,782	65.1%	25.8%	2.5%	6.2%	0.4%
Douglas County	27,216	90.7%	21,277	70.6%	25.3%	0.3%	1.2%	2.6%	19,849	62.5%	26.8%	4.6%	4.5%	1.6%
El Paso County	45,330	87.2%	70,362	56.3%	27.1%	2.4%	11.1%	3.2%	69,402	61.0%	25.4%	1.0%	8.4%	4.2%
Jefferson County	36,223	92.9%	47,146	69.5%	23.2%	2.4%	3.8%	1.1%	48,567	67.2%	25.0%	2.8%	4.8%	0.3%
Larimer County	19,902	85.6%	46,410	44.1%	46.1%	2.5%	5.5%	1.7%	30,477	62.5%	26.1%	2.5%	6.7%	2.2%
Mesa County	8,373	82.3%	15,610	38.0%	53.5%	3.4%	5.1%	0.0%	14,343	67.2%	27.7%	0.0%	4.7%	0.4%
Pueblo County	10,360	83.9%	15,775	58.8%	34.6%	0.2%	5.1%	1.3%	15,157	57.2%	34.2%	0.0%	7.0%	1.6%
Weld County	17,897	80.5%	29,369	52.1%	36.8%	3.2%	7.6%	0.2%	27,520	65.0%	29.6%	3.3%	1.8%	0.3%
Connecticut														
Fairfield County	66,065	91.4%	79,561	82.4%	10.8%	3.7%	1.0%	2.2%	75,971	72.6%	17.0%	5.2%	2.5%	2.6%
Hartford County	60,054	89.8%	80,061	77.3%	16.1%	3.3%	2.4%	1.0%	81,020	77.5%	18.9%	1.8%	1.1%	0.8%
Litchfield County	12,168	97.2%	13,642	87.9%	10.6%	0.3%	0.6%	0.6%	13,526	72.0%	24.6%	0.0%	2.7%	0.7%
Middlesex County	10,078	96.9%	14,810	74.0%	15.3%	6.8%	2.8%	1.1%	13,200	61.8%	22.9%	5.2%	6.6%	3.5%
New Haven County	55,017	91.5%	86,612	81.9%	13.2%	2.4%	1.9%	0.6%	80,028	75.6%	18.2%	3.2%	1.4%	1.7%
New London County	15,491	95.3%	29,528	73.8%	12.7%	8.4%	4.4%	0.7%	25,237	75.0%	18.9%	0.7%	5.4%	0.0%
Tolland County	9,638	95.1%	26,722	66.9%	29.0%	2.7%	0.7%	0.6%	11,593	72.4%	22.3%	1.9%	3.5%	0.0%
Windham County	7,405	79.5%	11,948	66.7%	29.4%	3.9%	0.0%	0.0%	10,595	70.9%	28.1%	0.9%	0.0%	0.2%
Delaware														
Kent County	10,917	91.2%	17,233	72.5%	14.4%	8.1%	4.5%	0.5%	15,816	76.6%	21.4%	1.6%	0.4%	0.0%
New Castle County	34,584	85.7%	57,691	67.5%	21.2%	1.0%	9.2%	1.1%	56,373	67.2%	22.8%	4.0%	5.8%	0.2%
Sussex County	10,249	98.7%	15,601	73.0%	21.2%	3.9%	1.5%	0.4%	15,536	81.0%	14.5%	2.7%	1.7%	0.0%
Florida														
Alachua County	11,393	87.0%	57,810	54.2%	40.4%	2.4%	0.7%	2.3%	28,502	60.0%	31.9%	4.5%	1.0%	2.6%
Bay County	9,643	86.0%	14,680	68.0%	21.4%	4.8%	4.7%	1.1%	17,285	74.3%	22.1%	1.8%	1.8%	0.0%
Brevard County	30,170	89.6%	44,051	76.7%	16.7%	1.4%	2.8%	2.4%	38,460	82.5%	14.1%	1.3%	0.9%	1.2%
Broward County	112,099	86.0%	157,400	78.9%	17.2%	1.2%	1.3%	1.4%	168,010	69.9%	25.7%	1.4%	1.7%	1.3%
Charlotte County	7,440	79.1%	10,166	72.4%	24.4%	0.0%	3.2%	0.0%	8,480	81.7%	14.4%	1.4%	2.5%	0.0%
Citrus County	6,239	74.3%	8,383	66.0%	29.7%	0.0%	4.3%	0.0%	6,848	86.9%	7.4%	3.2%	2.4%	0.0%
Clay County	15,005	91.5%	15,970	75.0%	24.1%	0.9%	0.1%	0.0%	16,629	77.7%	19.6%	1.6%	1.1%	0.0%
Collier County	17,383	77.5%	22,554	64.4%	27.4%	0.6%	7.3%	0.2%	22,259	70.2%	22.9%	1.9%	3.9%	1.0%
Duval County	52,351	83.1%	87,274	67.5%	23.8%	6.4%	1.9%	0.3%	101,536	63.6%	30.9%	2.1%	2.9%	0.5%
Escambia County	16,302	84.8%	39,340	64.3%	14.8%	6.4%	12.8%	1.7%	31,263	72.1%	17.2%	5.7%	3.4%	1.6%
Flagler County	6,063	87.1%	8,355	83.9%	12.5%	2.8%	0.9%	0.0%	5,728	81.7%	15.4%	2.2%	0.6%	0.0%
Hernando County	9,567	79.4%	11,400	70.1%	26.3%	0.0%	3.6%	0.0%	12,556	61.4%	35.6%	0.4%	2.4%	0.2%
Highlands County	4,471	91.7%	7,013	85.4%	12.7%	0.0%	0.0%	1.8%	6,249	71.8%	18.4%	9.0%	0.8%	0.0%
Hillsborough County	83,199	82.3%	127,839	67.5%	25.4%	1.7%	4.2%	1.2%	136,004	67.0%	25.9%	2.3%	2.6%	2.2%
Indian River County	8,321	96.0%	8,737	79.3%	16.1%	0.0%	4.6%	0.0%	8,245	60.4%	33.1%	1.6%	3.5%	1.3%
Lake County	19,345	89.1%	21,438	77.0%	20.7%	0.4%	1.7%	0.2%	23,099	76.3%	21.2%	1.5%	1.0%	0.1%
Lee County	36,197	81.5%	49,443	69.3%	25.9%	0.4%	3.7%	0.7%	49,789	66.2%	26.0%	1.8%	4.4%	1.7%
Leon County	14,519	77.7%	65,187	48.8%	47.8%	1.4%	1.6%	0.4%	29,293	60.7%	32.4%	3.3%	2.9%	0.6%
Manatee County	19,630	84.8%	26,263	73.4%	19.6%	3.9%	2.3%	0.8%	23,213	65.0%	29.9%	1.6%	2.4%	1.1%
Marion County	18,327	85.1%	24,424	71.2%	27.5%	0.3%	1.0%	0.0%	24,645	60.5%	37.7%	0.8%	0.8%	0.2%
Martin County	7,357	84.7%	9,764	76.7%	22.2%	0.0%	1.1%	0.0%	11,550	75.3%	23.7%	0.0%	1.0%	0.0%
Miami-Dade County	158,899	89.3%	249,341	83.6%	11.3%	0.9%	2.2%	2.1%	267,914	79.4%	15.9%	0.9%	2.1%	1.6%
Okaloosa County	13,303	88.0%	19,619	70.7%	16.2%	6.9%	5.2%	1.0%	22,695	68.1%	19.1%	3.4%	7.0%	2.4%
Orange County	79,736	79.6%	147,814	67.3%	26.4%	2.2%	2.7%	1.5%	145,234	72.5%	22.1%	0.8%	1.9%	2.6%
Osceola County	23,796	88.1%	28,518	86.8%	9.5%	1.0%	1.8%	0.9%	29,572	86.0%	12.0%	0.1%	0.7%	1.1%
Palm Beach County	75,950	84.6%	111,040	77.3%	17.6%	0.9%	2.9%	1.3%	114,488	74.2%	19.8%	1.1%	3.8%	1.1%
Pasco County	28,277	91.1%	35,466	82.9%	14.0%	0.2%	2.3%	0.6%	32,312	84.5%	13.6%	1.2%	0.7%	0.0%
Pinellas County	49,492	86.1%	68,856	68.3%	25.7%	1.3%	3.9%	0.7%	76,123	72.0%	22.8%	1.5%	2.7%	0.9%
Polk County	38,905	85.4%	55,573	76.3%	18.4%	1.1%	3.0%	1.2%	55,298	76.0%	20.7%	1.5%	1.8%	0.0%
Santa Rosa County	11,213	76.8%	14,039	62.8%	31.1%	2.5%	3.5%	0.0%	15,170	61.1%	24.1%	10.1%	4.8%	0.0%
Sarasota County	18,595	87.0%	25,916	68.4%	29.8%	0.8%	0.8%	0.2%	20,422	62.8%	31.2%	0.3%	2.9%	2.8%
Seminole County	33,283	90.8%	42,621	79.8%	17.7%	1.4%	0.7%	0.3%	41,617	74.7%	18.9%	1.5%	2.9%	2.0%
St. Johns County	15,143	90.3%	17,994	79.4%	12.4%	3.6%	4.6%	0.0%	13,974	59.5%	32.7%	2.8%	3.9%	1.1%
St. Lucie County	18,393	88.2%	22,765	77.8%	19.4%	0.3%	2.4%	0.0%	20,849	72.5%	22.2%	2.1%	1.8%	1.5%
Sumter County	2,238	96.4%	4,246	61.8%	38.2%	0.0%	0.0%	0.0%	4,944	50.2%	49.8%	0.0%	0.0%	0.0%
Volusia County	24,502	90.4%	43,828	72.0%	20.1%	3.2%	4.1%	0.7%	41,202	80.9%	15.7%	0.8%	2.6%	0.0%
Georgia														
Bartow County	7,422	74.6%	12,166	67.4%	30.7%	0.4%	1.6%	0.0%	9,081	83.3%	12.7%	0.0%	4.0%	0.0%
Bibb County	10,274	75.3%	16,655	68.7%	23.9%	4.8%	2.1%	0.4%	15,045	79.6%	18.1%	0.7%	0.0%	1.5%
Carroll County	8,001	79.2%	14,416	61.6%	38.4%	0.0%	0.0%	0.0%	9,841	79.8%	15.7%	2.8%	1.2%	0.5%
Chatham County	15,743	83.6%	34,089	60.5%	28.4%	6.8%	2.6%	1.7%	33,509	73.1%	15.9%	4.2%	4.0%	2.8%
Cherokee County	16,364	92.9%	16,011	82.1%	16.4%	0.7%	0.8%	0.0%	19,263	73.3%	22.0%	2.9%	0.8%	1.1%
Clarke County	4,249	84.4%	36,028	51.9%	43.4%	3.3%	0.8%	0.6%	13,785	68.3%	21.8%	2.4%	3.5%	4.0%
Clayton County	20,872	79.4%	27,881	59.3%	34.6%	3.3%	2.7%	0.0%	28,275	70.7%	23.8%	3.0%	1.5%	1.0%
Cobb County	50,742	82.4%	67,950	54.5%	36.7%	4.0%	2.4%	2.4%	68,770	62.5%	33.1%	1.2%	2.7%	0.5%
Columbia County	10,922	96.4%	12,527	88.8%	7.1%	4.0%	0.0%	0.0%	11,046	77.7%	11.2%	10.4%	0.7%	0.0%
Coweta County	8,243	95.3%	10,199	76.0%	18.8%	0.0%	3.5%	1.7%	11,235	82.8%	15.4%	0.0%	1.5%	0.3%

Table J-2: Counties—Mobility Status by Age—*Continued*

| | 13 to 17 | | 18 to 24 | | | | | | 25 to 31 | | | | | |
| | | | | | Percent Living in a Different House | | | | | | Percent Living in a Different House | | | |
	Total Population	Percent Living in Same House	Total Population	Percent Living in Same House	Same State	Different State, Same Region	Different Region	Outside US	Total Population	Percent Living in Same House	Same State	Different State, Same Region	Different Region	Outside US
Georgia—Cont.														
DeKalb County	38,998	77.3%	70,674	63.9%	27.3%	2.7%	3.2%	3.0%	81,565	67.1%	26.5%	2.7%	2.3%	1.4%
Dougherty County	7,070	93.4%	11,759	66.2%	32.5%	0.0%	0.9%	0.4%	9,373	79.6%	17.7%	1.6%	1.0%	0.0%
Douglas County	11,167	90.7%	9,740	69.7%	18.9%	0.9%	10.4%	0.0%	12,228	78.1%	19.8%	0.0%	2.1%	0.0%
Fayette County	10,505	90.4%	10,008	80.3%	15.1%	4.5%	0.0%	0.0%	5,306	60.4%	25.5%	7.3%	6.7%	0.0%
Floyd County	6,730	72.4%	9,834	71.9%	24.7%	3.4%	0.0%	0.0%	7,305	76.9%	18.8%	3.1%	1.2%	0.0%
Forsyth County	17,561	90.6%	12,959	83.3%	15.0%	0.5%	1.2%	0.0%	12,286	80.4%	13.7%	0.9%	5.0%	0.0%
Fulton County	62,359	85.5%	101,164	63.3%	28.7%	2.3%	3.8%	2.0%	112,529	72.3%	21.3%	3.2%	2.3%	0.9%
Gwinnett County	68,051	86.8%	78,434	82.7%	14.4%	0.8%	1.1%	0.9%	76,391	73.7%	23.1%	1.8%	1.2%	0.4%
Hall County	14,136	88.1%	17,558	64.3%	27.0%	1.8%	4.0%	2.9%	16,371	72.4%	23.0%	0.5%	2.0%	2.1%
Henry County	18,645	80.1%	20,309	83.4%	12.0%	1.5%	3.0%	0.0%	14,519	71.0%	26.7%	2.3%	0.0%	0.0%
Houston County	10,265	73.9%	15,867	80.0%	18.1%	1.9%	0.0%	0.0%	15,755	71.9%	26.4%	1.2%	0.2%	0.3%
Lowndes County	7,219	92.2%	20,465	52.7%	41.3%	3.9%	1.3%	0.8%	12,415	68.3%	21.1%	3.0%	3.3%	4.2%
Muscogee County	13,840	79.4%	25,723	40.0%	28.9%	10.9%	17.9%	2.2%	21,609	57.5%	23.8%	8.1%	6.6%	4.0%
Newton County	8,144	82.4%	10,070	77.6%	13.7%	6.6%	0.0%	2.1%	7,917	85.9%	6.9%	0.0%	5.7%	1.6%
Paulding County	12,087	80.6%	12,434	68.2%	27.5%	0.0%	4.3%	0.0%	11,352	78.5%	21.5%	0.0%	0.0%	0.0%
Richmond County	13,528	89.5%	24,088	66.9%	23.3%	5.2%	4.3%	0.3%	24,335	73.7%	19.1%	3.4%	2.7%	1.1%
Whitfield County	7,413	88.1%	10,922	80.5%	14.6%	1.9%	3.1%	0.0%	8,472	74.3%	16.9%	6.2%	0.0%	2.7%
Hawaii														
Hawaii County	13,272	93.9%	15,240	87.7%	10.2%	0.1%	1.5%	0.5%	16,102	85.6%	12.1%	1.3%	1.0%	0.0%
Honolulu County	58,210	89.6%	104,322	69.3%	15.7%	5.9%	6.6%	2.5%	111,383	67.2%	16.5%	4.6%	9.1%	2.6%
Maui County	10,112	88.5%	10,226	71.1%	20.1%	6.9%	1.1%	0.7%	15,110	64.5%	21.3%	3.3%	8.5%	2.4%
Idaho														
Ada County	32,998	86.5%	41,286	53.4%	36.0%	7.2%	2.3%	1.1%	38,327	66.7%	25.0%	6.8%	0.3%	1.2%
Bonneville County	9,290	87.8%	8,902	63.4%	35.3%	1.3%	0.0%	0.0%	9,773	68.1%	23.2%	5.1%	2.0%	1.6%
Canyon County	18,650	80.9%	16,673	68.1%	25.2%	5.6%	0.0%	1.1%	15,953	75.2%	22.6%	0.2%	0.0%	0.0%
Kootenai County	9,826	93.2%	12,876	65.9%	22.0%	5.9%	1.9%	4.4%	12,654	90.1%	7.7%	0.8%	1.4%	0.0%
Illinois														
Champaign County	10,534	85.9%	47,858	31.7%	60.9%	2.0%	2.6%	2.9%	23,152	65.7%	23.1%	0.5%	7.8%	2.8%
Cook County	324,964	90.1%	508,028	76.2%	16.5%	2.9%	2.8%	1.6%	605,045	74.5%	19.9%	1.6%	2.6%	1.4%
DeKalb County	7,258	89.0%	20,217	42.7%	55.4%	1.7%	0.3%	0.0%	10,559	69.9%	27.6%	0.5%	1.9%	0.0%
DuPage County	66,690	90.9%	78,288	79.1%	17.1%	1.3%	1.3%	1.2%	86,678	73.8%	21.1%	0.4%	2.5%	2.2%
Kane County	41,236	92.2%	47,275	80.3%	16.5%	0.2%	1.0%	2.0%	47,528	81.9%	15.1%	0.9%	1.8%	0.4%
Kankakee County	7,763	90.7%	11,416	79.6%	17.9%	1.5%	0.7%	0.3%	8,304	76.8%	22.8%	0.5%	0.0%	0.0%
Kendall County	10,017	85.3%	8,195	77.7%	17.6%	2.9%	0.9%	1.0%	12,063	71.4%	11.1%	13.8%	3.7%	0.0%
Lake County	54,910	92.6%	70,753	72.8%	13.6%	3.2%	10.2%	0.2%	51,168	73.7%	18.8%	1.4%	5.0%	1.0%
LaSalle County	8,288	88.3%	9,127	71.6%	27.7%	0.7%	0.0%	0.0%	9,376	80.7%	19.1%	0.2%	0.0%	0.0%
Macon County	6,354	92.0%	10,229	66.5%	32.2%	0.0%	1.3%	0.0%	9,557	62.0%	32.0%	2.8%	3.2%	0.0%
Madison County	15,120	90.8%	26,372	62.9%	34.9%	1.1%	0.9%	0.2%	25,637	79.6%	18.9%	1.6%	0.0%	0.0%
McHenry County	26,378	89.6%	27,383	71.9%	21.6%	1.9%	3.0%	1.5%	23,349	76.3%	19.1%	0.3%	4.3%	0.0%
McLean County	9,536	93.5%	31,067	45.5%	52.1%	0.0%	1.9%	0.5%	17,395	70.1%	23.4%	0.5%	1.4%	4.7%
Peoria County	11,507	93.3%	18,445	67.6%	28.2%	3.0%	1.1%	0.0%	19,332	73.0%	16.7%	4.9%	4.9%	0.5%
Rock Island County	7,586	94.7%	12,911	64.3%	29.7%	4.7%	0.4%	0.9%	11,020	83.9%	13.5%	1.3%	1.4%	0.0%
Sangamon County	12,075	85.3%	16,718	72.0%	22.8%	1.4%	3.6%	0.2%	18,052	73.3%	16.8%	0.5%	8.1%	1.4%
St. Clair County	19,828	92.1%	25,896	84.6%	11.9%	0.7%	2.8%	0.0%	24,617	80.2%	13.9%	1.5%	3.1%	1.3%
Tazewell County	9,526	90.3%	10,753	73.4%	26.6%	0.0%	0.0%	0.0%	11,566	84.2%	13.6%	1.5%	0.8%	0.0%
Will County	55,873	89.7%	60,678	86.2%	12.8%	0.3%	0.5%	0.2%	52,019	81.1%	17.3%	0.3%	1.1%	0.2%
Winnebago County	20,782	85.3%	27,837	77.5%	21.3%	1.0%	0.2%	0.0%	23,641	65.3%	27.8%	2.6%	3.8%	0.5%
Indiana														
Allen County	25,831	89.0%	34,640	65.8%	29.4%	3.5%	1.4%	0.0%	33,513	71.3%	26.4%	1.7%	0.6%	0.0%
Clark County	7,109	91.3%	10,298	83.0%	14.3%	0.0%	2.7%	0.0%	9,716	82.6%	12.1%	2.4%	3.0%	0.0%
Delaware County	5,589	78.3%	24,150	34.9%	61.6%	3.0%	0.5%	0.0%	9,291	56.9%	41.7%	0.6%	0.8%	0.0%
Elkhart County	14,822	95.5%	17,694	77.6%	20.1%	0.1%	1.2%	1.0%	17,121	77.9%	18.9%	1.2%	2.0%	0.0%
Hamilton County	21,744	94.4%	20,418	79.7%	15.6%	1.5%	1.6%	1.6%	23,378	73.7%	14.8%	6.0%	4.1%	1.4%
Hendricks County	11,742	88.7%	14,344	70.5%	28.7%	0.7%	0.0%	0.0%	13,264	57.6%	35.4%	1.1%	5.9%	0.0%
Johnson County	12,141	95.1%	13,025	75.6%	21.5%	0.0%	1.8%	1.1%	12,712	77.9%	22.1%	0.0%	0.0%	0.0%
Lake County	35,237	82.9%	44,830	76.9%	18.2%	2.3%	0.9%	1.8%	38,834	76.8%	18.9%	3.8%	0.2%	0.2%
LaPorte County	7,767	84.3%	9,137	67.4%	31.8%	0.8%	0.0%	0.0%	10,789	72.9%	24.5%	0.1%	2.5%	0.0%
Madison County	9,450	83.7%	11,067	70.7%	26.2%	1.8%	1.0%	0.3%	10,955	74.8%	23.8%	0.0%	1.4%	0.0%
Marion County	57,618	86.8%	91,053	70.3%	24.6%	2.0%	2.2%	1.0%	110,706	71.2%	23.0%	1.6%	3.8%	0.5%
Monroe County	6,199	94.5%	39,652	32.7%	56.9%	3.8%	3.4%	3.1%	13,342	53.9%	42.1%	0.0%	1.6%	2.4%
Porter County	10,002	76.1%	16,877	65.6%	23.1%	9.9%	1.1%	0.3%	14,297	75.1%	23.9%	1.0%	0.0%	0.0%
St. Joseph County	19,494	79.1%	30,290	65.3%	21.7%	6.5%	5.5%	0.9%	22,270	66.8%	22.5%	4.1%	5.7%	0.9%
Tippecanoe County	8,636	87.2%	43,959	45.6%	41.7%	4.7%	5.4%	2.5%	17,881	65.0%	28.2%	4.2%	1.1%	1.4%
Vanderburgh County	10,109	86.1%	19,927	71.8%	24.5%	3.1%	0.1%	0.5%	17,180	77.0%	19.9%	0.0%	3.1%	0.0%
Vigo County	6,745	75.9%	16,164	60.9%	32.1%	3.3%	2.9%	0.8%	9,857	70.8%	20.1%	3.2%	5.9%	0.0%
Iowa														
Black Hawk County	7,244	95.1%	23,342	75.5%	23.6%	0.0%	0.0%	0.9%	11,883	77.6%	18.3%	2.4%	1.7%	0.0%
Dubuque County	7,929	92.7%	9,876	69.3%	23.7%	7.0%	0.0%	0.0%	7,182	76.0%	23.5%	0.0%	0.0%	0.5%
Johnson County	6,795	85.0%	31,053	30.8%	58.5%	6.6%	2.7%	1.5%	18,931	78.3%	17.6%	1.5%	0.0%	2.6%
Linn County	14,796	93.3%	18,517	74.2%	25.8%	0.0%	0.0%	0.0%	22,116	77.0%	17.7%	4.1%	0.7%	0.6%
Polk County	30,744	87.9%	39,587	54.6%	36.2%	4.5%	4.0%	0.8%	50,213	66.6%	23.9%	3.0%	4.2%	2.3%
Pottawattamie County	6,660	94.1%	7,814	72.8%	22.1%	3.0%	2.1%	0.0%	8,400	80.1%	18.6%	0.0%	1.3%	0.0%
Scott County	11,143	84.3%	15,048	77.6%	16.7%	3.7%	2.1%	0.0%	16,418	74.1%	17.8%	3.9%	2.0%	2.2%

Table J-2: Counties—Mobility Status by Age—*Continued*

	13 to 17		18 to 24						25 to 31					
					Percent Living in a Different House						Percent Living in a Different House			
	Total Population	Percent Living in Same House	Total Population	Percent Living in Same House	Same State	Different State, Same Region	Different Region	Outside US	Total Population	Percent Living in Same House	Same State	Different State, Same Region	Different Region	Outside US
Iowa—Cont.														
Story County	5,049	90.2%	25,869	31.0%	56.8%	7.5%	1.9%	2.9%	10,051	55.6%	26.2%	8.3%	3.3%	6.6%
Woodbury County	9,614	90.4%	10,317	67.8%	22.4%	5.6%	3.4%	0.7%	9,895	66.3%	26.0%	6.2%	1.5%	0.0%
Kansas														
Douglas County	5,015	86.3%	24,686	47.3%	35.7%	5.5%	6.3%	5.2%	14,590	70.4%	19.0%	4.4%	3.8%	2.3%
Johnson County	40,126	82.8%	43,369	66.6%	24.7%	6.2%	2.1%	0.3%	51,290	64.0%	24.3%	7.9%	3.0%	0.8%
Sedgwick County	38,903	86.9%	48,246	70.6%	24.5%	0.5%	2.6%	1.9%	55,438	75.7%	19.0%	0.4%	4.6%	0.3%
Shawnee County	11,984	79.3%	17,750	72.6%	23.0%	1.9%	2.1%	0.4%	16,085	79.6%	13.7%	4.4%	1.4%	1.0%
Wyandotte County	11,278	77.8%	15,375	75.7%	16.5%	5.0%	2.8%	0.0%	15,447	78.0%	18.7%	0.9%	2.0%	0.4%
Kentucky														
Boone County	9,046	92.4%	9,870	69.1%	21.6%	0.6%	8.8%	0.0%	11,608	69.7%	15.7%	6.0%	8.6%	0.0%
Campbell County	6,568	76.3%	8,276	65.9%	26.7%	0.0%	7.4%	0.0%	7,975	74.7%	13.1%	0.9%	11.2%	0.0%
Daviess County	6,414	90.1%	8,905	73.1%	26.9%	0.0%	0.0%	0.0%	7,918	76.5%	22.3%	1.3%	0.0%	0.0%
Fayette County	15,950	75.9%	43,417	41.6%	49.0%	2.2%	6.8%	0.4%	32,756	63.3%	28.2%	3.4%	1.8%	3.3%
Hardin County	10,516	67.2%	8,668	74.7%	22.0%	0.2%	1.2%	1.9%	10,318	60.4%	28.5%	2.7%	4.5%	3.8%
Jefferson County	49,409	86.8%	67,944	71.4%	21.7%	2.1%	3.6%	1.2%	75,621	70.2%	25.2%	2.2%	1.0%	1.5%
Kenton County	11,875	90.6%	14,183	84.3%	12.7%	0.0%	3.1%	0.0%	16,317	66.0%	18.4%	0.0%	14.7%	0.9%
Warren County	6,811	83.3%	17,778	41.5%	52.1%	2.5%	3.0%	1.0%	13,297	61.1%	32.5%	1.3%	1.8%	3.4%
Louisiana														
Ascension Parish	9,816	90.4%	9,729	89.0%	11.0%	0.0%	0.0%	0.0%	9,945	92.9%	7.1%	0.0%	0.0%	0.0%
Bossier Parish	7,900	91.1%	12,994	66.9%	13.6%	16.3%	3.2%	0.0%	14,263	74.9%	15.7%	4.3%	4.6%	0.5%
Caddo Parish	16,260	83.0%	25,659	83.9%	14.3%	0.9%	0.3%	0.6%	26,200	78.6%	18.2%	1.9%	0.5%	0.9%
Calcasieu Parish	14,824	81.2%	20,801	68.2%	29.6%	2.0%	0.2%	0.0%	16,579	70.1%	24.8%	3.4%	1.7%	0.0%
East Baton Rouge Parish	26,536	86.3%	65,930	70.4%	22.4%	4.6%	2.5%	0.1%	45,973	74.9%	21.1%	1.2%	1.5%	1.3%
Jefferson Parish	23,648	89.3%	40,088	82.2%	15.5%	0.3%	1.0%	1.0%	48,728	70.4%	24.2%	3.9%	1.4%	0.1%
Lafayette Parish	13,605	93.1%	26,004	71.5%	18.3%	3.1%	3.0%	4.1%	26,283	71.6%	23.9%	1.9%	1.4%	1.2%
Lafourche Parish	5,421	97.5%	10,583	76.8%	19.3%	0.0%	0.0%	3.9%	9,274	79.4%	18.4%	2.2%	0.0%	0.0%
Livingston Parish	9,382	97.9%	12,671	68.6%	23.4%	5.2%	2.8%	0.0%	12,243	81.5%	12.4%	2.3%	2.5%	1.3%
Orleans Parish	19,732	87.3%	41,346	68.3%	21.4%	4.8%	4.2%	1.2%	50,635	72.0%	20.5%	4.0%	3.0%	0.4%
Ouachita Parish	11,534	90.5%	17,225	76.8%	21.8%	1.4%	0.0%	0.0%	14,752	80.5%	19.4%	0.1%	0.0%	0.0%
Rapides Parish	8,741	76.5%	13,288	63.3%	15.9%	14.4%	6.0%	0.5%	13,160	81.8%	10.2%	5.4%	2.5%	0.2%
St. Tammany Parish	17,036	89.9%	19,189	84.8%	9.0%	4.8%	1.1%	0.3%	20,568	78.4%	18.7%	2.9%	0.0%	0.0%
Tangipahoa Parish	8,725	83.2%	13,931	72.3%	21.4%	1.1%	5.2%	0.0%	14,288	72.5%	23.3%	4.2%	0.0%	0.0%
Terrebonne Parish	7,372	88.2%	10,410	71.7%	26.5%	1.8%	0.0%	0.0%	11,174	82.8%	11.4%	3.5%	2.3%	0.0%
Maine														
Androscoggin County	6,766	91.4%	9,557	78.4%	15.8%	1.4%	4.4%	0.0%	10,215	68.2%	30.5%	0.0%	1.3%	0.0%
Cumberland County	14,723	88.3%	28,028	61.8%	29.4%	6.4%	1.9%	0.4%	26,931	55.7%	38.3%	2.9%	3.1%	0.0%
Kennebec County	8,147	75.1%	10,198	77.4%	12.1%	0.5%	7.9%	2.1%	9,257	86.0%	11.1%	0.0%	2.9%	0.0%
Penobscot County	8,286	94.5%	18,248	69.2%	26.1%	3.2%	1.2%	0.4%	13,381	69.7%	23.6%	2.1%	4.6%	0.0%
York County	11,016	95.5%	15,638	79.5%	9.0%	8.4%	2.4%	0.7%	16,288	72.1%	26.7%	0.7%	0.6%	0.0%
Maryland														
Anne Arundel County	35,080	92.9%	50,657	76.4%	12.6%	4.0%	6.2%	0.8%	54,134	72.5%	18.0%	5.0%	3.4%	1.1%
Baltimore County	51,418	91.9%	79,202	76.3%	20.6%	1.5%	1.0%	0.6%	83,062	76.2%	19.2%	0.8%	3.1%	0.7%
Carroll County	12,078	95.0%	14,608	82.6%	11.5%	1.6%	2.1%	2.3%	12,659	75.5%	23.0%	0.8%	0.8%	0.0%
Cecil County	7,042	93.5%	9,432	77.0%	21.4%	0.0%	0.2%	1.5%	8,957	75.6%	13.0%	5.1%	6.3%	0.0%
Charles County	11,442	96.4%	13,872	81.5%	10.6%	6.4%	1.5%	0.0%	13,615	80.2%	13.1%	5.8%	0.9%	0.0%
Frederick County	17,642	94.6%	22,769	84.5%	9.5%	1.1%	4.5%	0.3%	19,937	76.6%	15.6%	5.0%	1.8%	1.0%
Harford County	19,721	92.3%	20,860	87.6%	11.7%	0.4%	0.2%	0.0%	21,178	81.8%	15.8%	0.4%	2.0%	0.0%
Howard County	22,986	93.7%	23,779	87.6%	8.0%	1.5%	2.3%	0.6%	27,727	76.8%	16.7%	0.9%	5.4%	0.1%
Montgomery County	66,053	89.0%	76,058	75.3%	16.8%	2.5%	2.1%	3.2%	95,555	68.6%	18.0%	5.5%	3.2%	4.7%
Prince George's County	57,013	87.1%	97,121	74.7%	16.4%	3.8%	3.3%	1.9%	94,058	72.2%	18.2%	6.9%	1.2%	1.5%
St. Mary's County	9,687	97.1%	10,336	87.2%	9.2%	1.9%	1.1%	0.5%	8,534	79.3%	11.5%	6.9%	1.7%	0.5%
Washington County	10,513	92.2%	12,958	78.9%	16.8%	0.3%	3.5%	0.5%	12,951	70.2%	24.5%	1.1%	3.5%	0.7%
Wicomico County	5,775	84.7%	15,847	66.2%	22.0%	8.1%	3.8%	0.0%	9,353	71.4%	26.6%	0.0%	2.0%	0.0%
Massachusetts														
Barnstable County	10,912	91.6%	14,628	78.1%	14.2%	0.1%	7.6%	0.0%	14,599	74.0%	21.5%	1.6%	3.0%	0.0%
Berkshire County	7,314	94.5%	13,013	73.6%	17.0%	3.6%	3.7%	2.0%	9,113	63.5%	33.2%	1.4%	1.9%	0.0%
Bristol County	34,944	93.1%	52,838	81.0%	16.3%	1.6%	0.8%	0.4%	45,583	73.9%	21.4%	3.3%	1.5%	0.0%
Essex County	51,071	91.8%	71,656	80.5%	15.2%	2.9%	0.6%	0.8%	66,372	73.8%	20.4%	1.8%	2.5%	1.5%
Hampden County	36,061	87.8%	54,906	76.3%	18.9%	3.0%	1.3%	0.5%	39,256	76.1%	20.6%	1.1%	1.3%	1.0%
Hampshire County	8,751	90.2%	26,597	58.1%	32.6%	4.8%	2.3%	2.3%	12,380	61.6%	29.7%	2.7%	4.0%	2.0%
Middlesex County	93,680	93.1%	147,617	68.3%	22.3%	4.2%	3.4%	1.8%	176,596	69.4%	21.8%	2.4%	3.5%	2.9%
Norfolk County	50,495	91.6%	57,195	78.0%	12.4%	4.2%	2.9%	2.5%	59,789	74.8%	21.0%	1.7%	1.7%	0.8%
Plymouth County	33,740	94.7%	41,066	83.1%	14.7%	1.0%	0.6%	0.6%	36,135	76.1%	21.1%	1.3%	1.1%	0.4%
Suffolk County	35,835	84.2%	114,663	60.4%	24.0%	6.9%	5.3%	3.4%	131,371	70.1%	22.5%	2.6%	2.7%	2.1%
Worcester County	57,599	91.6%	83,318	74.6%	20.5%	2.9%	1.3%	0.6%	72,063	75.2%	20.7%	1.7%	1.6%	0.7%
Michigan														
Allegan County	8,408	85.7%	9,499	81.5%	18.0%	0.5%	0.0%	0.0%	8,100	82.2%	17.8%	0.0%	0.0%	0.0%
Bay County	7,193	90.5%	9,763	73.5%	23.5%	1.6%	0.5%	1.0%	9,708	74.5%	17.3%	0.0%	8.2%	0.0%
Berrien County	8,469	91.4%	13,614	65.0%	28.4%	3.3%	2.7%	0.6%	12,250	63.5%	28.8%	1.8%	2.6%	3.3%
Calhoun County	9,780	77.1%	11,245	74.3%	20.3%	2.9%	1.5%	1.0%	10,299	63.1%	35.5%	0.0%	1.4%	0.0%
Eaton County	7,164	96.0%	8,168	53.7%	38.7%	3.1%	1.8%	2.7%	10,189	62.0%	35.2%	1.4%	0.0%	1.3%
Genesee County	30,043	87.1%	38,494	73.2%	25.1%	0.0%	1.6%	0.0%	35,288	67.3%	28.3%	1.6%	2.5%	0.2%
Ingham County	15,618	85.7%	57,613	41.4%	51.5%	2.4%	2.6%	2.2%	28,648	70.1%	25.9%	0.2%	1.5%	2.3%

Table J-2: Counties—Mobility Status by Age—*Continued*

	13 to 17		18 to 24						25 to 31					
					Percent Living in a Different House						Percent Living in a Different House			
	Total Population	Percent Living in Same House	Total Population	Percent Living in Same House	Same State	Different State, Same Region	Different Region	Outside US	Total Population	Percent Living in Same House	Same State	Different State, Same Region	Different Region	Outside US
Michigan—Cont.														
Jackson County	10,254	90.9%	14,147	53.8%	42.6%	0.5%	3.1%	0.0%	14,943	70.1%	27.1%	0.0%	1.9%	0.9%
Kalamazoo County	16,510	90.2%	41,267	45.4%	49.0%	2.3%	2.1%	1.2%	23,678	75.5%	19.9%	1.5%	2.8%	0.4%
Kent County	43,955	83.3%	60,117	55.0%	37.3%	2.1%	5.4%	0.3%	67,996	72.0%	24.7%	1.4%	1.3%	0.6%
Lenawee County	6,357	80.3%	9,357	72.1%	22.3%	1.9%	3.7%	0.0%	8,643	72.5%	22.2%	3.0%	2.3%	0.0%
Livingston County	15,463	79.2%	15,203	82.7%	15.1%	0.7%	0.3%	1.2%	12,368	78.5%	20.0%	1.5%	0.0%	0.0%
Macomb County	53,989	84.6%	74,161	78.2%	19.6%	0.5%	0.3%	1.4%	74,026	74.8%	22.9%	0.4%	0.7%	1.1%
Monroe County	10,149	95.4%	13,255	82.0%	13.9%	0.5%	3.6%	0.0%	11,608	89.8%	8.8%	0.5%	0.0%	0.9%
Muskegon County	13,279	91.1%	14,142	59.1%	39.9%	0.0%	1.0%	0.0%	13,335	79.2%	18.0%	0.0%	2.3%	0.5%
Oakland County	84,263	87.0%	101,005	72.8%	23.8%	1.1%	1.5%	0.6%	104,716	70.7%	23.5%	0.7%	3.3%	1.8%
Ottawa County	19,883	87.9%	36,260	53.8%	42.9%	1.9%	1.4%	0.0%	21,987	67.0%	31.2%	1.2%	0.0%	0.6%
Saginaw County	13,195	92.5%	21,690	65.9%	33.0%	0.0%	0.7%	0.5%	15,016	74.3%	22.8%	0.0%	2.5%	0.4%
St. Clair County	11,815	79.8%	14,562	65.4%	27.4%	0.7%	6.6%	0.0%	10,990	80.5%	18.4%	0.0%	1.1%	0.0%
Washtenaw County	19,383	90.5%	64,295	41.3%	45.9%	3.2%	6.6%	3.0%	36,258	60.1%	29.4%	3.1%	4.0%	3.4%
Wayne County	122,329	83.7%	176,187	77.0%	20.3%	0.4%	1.9%	0.5%	153,266	76.3%	19.7%	0.7%	1.7%	1.6%
Minnesota														
Anoka County	25,704	87.4%	27,416	72.7%	23.2%	3.3%	0.8%	0.0%	31,549	81.4%	12.5%	1.5%	3.0%	1.6%
Carver County	8,553	91.2%	7,496	81.4%	16.1%	1.0%	0.0%	1.5%	7,299	71.9%	24.2%	0.0%	4.0%	0.0%
Dakota County	31,886	81.6%	31,660	69.0%	23.5%	5.5%	1.0%	1.0%	36,886	70.1%	23.9%	2.2%	2.1%	1.7%
Hennepin County	67,480	91.7%	109,313	61.9%	29.0%	3.9%	3.5%	1.6%	154,945	68.0%	23.0%	3.4%	2.6%	3.0%
Olmsted County	8,626	95.0%	12,514	68.9%	26.0%	5.2%	0.0%	0.0%	14,440	80.8%	13.7%	2.2%	1.1%	2.3%
Ramsey County	32,242	90.9%	59,746	66.7%	25.5%	5.0%	1.1%	1.7%	58,603	64.0%	27.6%	2.1%	2.6%	3.7%
Scott County	9,913	90.2%	9,533	66.8%	33.2%	0.0%	0.0%	0.0%	10,804	89.9%	6.1%	4.0%	0.0%	0.0%
St. Louis County	11,337	90.1%	24,221	58.9%	36.3%	2.3%	1.8%	0.8%	18,255	77.1%	19.0%	1.4%	1.1%	1.4%
Stearns County	9,625	96.8%	24,867	31.5%	62.6%	4.5%	1.1%	0.3%	13,381	77.8%	21.6%	0.0%	0.6%	0.0%
Washington County	19,434	86.9%	19,201	83.4%	13.0%	0.6%	1.0%	2.0%	21,849	70.8%	26.9%	2.1%	0.0%	0.2%
Wright County	10,933	90.2%	9,249	68.7%	25.4%	0.0%	3.5%	2.3%	12,469	80.9%	17.7%	1.1%	0.3%	0.0%
Mississippi														
DeSoto County	14,018	76.3%	14,031	82.3%	13.3%	3.7%	0.0%	0.7%	13,474	78.3%	14.6%	5.7%	0.5%	0.9%
Harrison County	11,692	75.4%	20,561	56.6%	21.7%	10.7%	10.5%	0.5%	20,462	61.2%	22.0%	8.7%	6.0%	2.0%
Hinds County	17,049	84.1%	29,826	74.9%	21.7%	2.2%	0.8%	0.4%	27,637	76.3%	18.6%	2.1%	2.7%	0.2%
Jackson County	9,032	91.6%	13,816	75.8%	21.4%	1.7%	1.2%	0.0%	13,664	70.2%	29.5%	0.3%	0.0%	0.0%
Madison County	9,197	88.9%	9,042	94.7%	5.3%	0.0%	0.0%	0.0%	7,963	80.2%	17.9%	1.9%	0.0%	0.0%
Rankin County	9,764	78.1%	11,321	87.8%	9.8%	2.4%	0.0%	0.0%	14,220	67.6%	28.9%	0.5%	1.8%	1.2%
Missouri														
Boone County	8,915	88.7%	36,413	48.4%	37.5%	8.3%	4.9%	0.8%	20,117	57.8%	33.9%	5.0%	2.1%	1.3%
Cass County	9,097	79.1%	8,261	71.7%	27.5%	0.0%	0.8%	0.0%	7,355	67.0%	31.7%	1.3%	0.0%	0.0%
Clay County	14,860	77.9%	19,027	67.4%	29.2%	2.0%	1.4%	0.0%	23,445	66.8%	26.5%	0.5%	6.2%	0.0%
Franklin County	6,220	84.9%	8,224	78.4%	21.6%	0.0%	0.0%	0.0%	8,650	79.6%	20.4%	0.0%	0.0%	0.0%
Greene County	17,287	88.3%	40,080	62.5%	32.6%	0.8%	4.1%	0.0%	30,906	75.2%	22.3%	0.7%	1.8%	0.0%
Jackson County	44,774	89.7%	59,386	68.2%	25.1%	4.7%	1.2%	0.9%	72,220	71.7%	23.1%	4.0%	0.7%	0.4%
Jasper County	8,694	86.3%	11,453	65.5%	25.4%	2.0%	6.4%	0.7%	11,934	70.7%	25.2%	2.4%	1.7%	0.0%
Jefferson County	15,502	89.2%	17,351	71.6%	27.3%	0.5%	0.6%	0.0%	19,571	77.4%	21.2%	0.0%	1.5%	0.0%
Platte County	5,017	91.1%	8,248	66.3%	13.1%	17.8%	2.8%	0.0%	10,502	57.9%	30.7%	4.7%	6.6%	0.0%
St. Charles County	23,492	92.9%	30,614	79.0%	20.1%	0.5%	0.3%	0.1%	34,816	69.2%	28.1%	1.3%	1.4%	0.0%
St. Louis County	67,609	89.0%	88,692	72.9%	22.4%	2.5%	2.0%	0.2%	88,698	69.1%	23.8%	3.1%	3.2%	0.8%
Montana														
Flathead County	6,875	74.1%	7,067	75.8%	8.9%	14.0%	1.2%	0.0%	6,979	69.2%	21.1%	3.9%	5.8%	0.0%
Gallatin County	6,700	78.0%	14,670	56.0%	26.9%	8.0%	6.4%	2.7%	9,613	63.6%	28.1%	2.2%	4.8%	1.2%
Missoula County	7,120	78.6%	16,419	51.3%	39.9%	5.2%	2.1%	1.6%	13,113	43.6%	44.6%	2.4%	9.5%	0.0%
Yellowstone County	9,552	73.6%	15,195	58.4%	27.3%	7.6%	3.9%	2.7%	13,632	63.7%	25.0%	2.5%	8.9%	0.0%
Nebraska														
Douglas County	35,085	88.5%	51,301	60.9%	29.8%	4.7%	3.6%	1.0%	60,770	70.8%	23.6%	1.2%	2.8%	1.5%
Lancaster County	17,456	93.1%	46,475	49.8%	42.5%	2.4%	3.1%	2.2%	31,597	63.8%	30.7%	1.0%	4.4%	0.0%
Sarpy County	13,038	92.0%	14,951	70.4%	15.5%	9.9%	3.7%	0.5%	17,024	59.1%	33.0%	3.7%	4.1%	0.0%
Nevada														
Clark County	134,264	79.8%	185,550	70.9%	22.3%	4.2%	2.1%	0.5%	207,828	69.8%	23.0%	4.3%	2.2%	0.7%
Washoe County	27,255	82.7%	43,605	53.5%	31.4%	12.8%	1.4%	1.0%	42,425	69.9%	23.6%	3.4%	1.5%	1.6%
New Hampshire														
Hillsborough County	26,570	92.5%	34,112	75.6%	15.0%	5.5%	2.7%	1.2%	37,677	68.2%	23.5%	5.2%	1.6%	1.6%
Merrimack County	9,362	96.0%	14,498	84.6%	11.6%	3.1%	0.0%	0.8%	10,671	62.2%	32.2%	3.1%	2.4%	0.0%
Rockingham County	21,028	95.6%	23,488	74.3%	10.3%	11.8%	1.5%	2.1%	19,669	78.3%	13.2%	6.0%	0.9%	1.5%
Strafford County	8,257	90.8%	18,156	48.7%	29.7%	17.1%	0.9%	3.5%	10,506	75.1%	15.5%	3.4%	3.0%	3.0%
New Jersey														
Atlantic County	17,790	90.4%	26,718	82.1%	13.8%	2.7%	1.2%	0.2%	22,550	77.8%	16.5%	3.0%	2.3%	0.4%
Bergen County	61,727	93.6%	73,274	89.3%	5.1%	2.1%	1.5%	2.0%	72,616	83.5%	11.8%	1.4%	2.0%	1.2%
Burlington County	31,051	91.1%	40,355	88.1%	6.8%	2.7%	2.5%	0.0%	37,052	77.4%	16.1%	1.9%	2.1%	2.6%
Camden County	35,887	89.3%	45,958	82.6%	14.5%	1.9%	0.9%	0.1%	48,608	78.4%	14.7%	2.2%	4.0%	0.7%
Cape May County	4,486	98.1%	7,503	88.6%	6.2%	4.4%	0.7%	0.0%	7,291	72.6%	18.3%	3.5%	5.6%	0.0%
Cumberland County	10,242	95.7%	13,442	85.2%	12.5%	1.5%	0.7%	0.0%	17,728	76.9%	17.7%	3.9%	1.5%	0.0%
Essex County	53,893	88.8%	73,948	84.0%	11.6%	1.5%	2.0%	0.9%	77,006	79.8%	15.5%	2.3%	1.8%	0.5%
Gloucester County	20,226	96.8%	26,112	70.2%	27.6%	1.3%	0.5%	0.3%	24,121	88.5%	10.0%	0.8%	0.0%	0.7%
Hudson County	34,014	91.7%	60,876	83.1%	11.9%	1.5%	0.7%	2.8%	101,319	73.5%	15.7%	5.5%	1.9%	3.5%
Hunterdon County	9,918	91.3%	12,070	80.9%	19.0%	0.2%	0.0%	0.0%	6,223	78.6%	17.4%	4.0%	0.0%	0.0%

Table J-2: Counties—Mobility Status by Age—*Continued*

| | 13 to 17 | | 18 to 24 | | | | | | 25 to 31 | | | | | |
| | | | | | Percent Living in a Different House | | | | | | Percent Living in a Different House | | | |
	Total Population	Percent Living in Same House	Total Population	Percent Living in Same House	Same State	Different State, Same Region	Different Region	Outside US	Total Population	Percent Living in Same House	Same State	Different State, Same Region	Different Region	Outside US
New Jersey—Cont.														
Mercer County	24,958	93.4%	40,520	73.9%	19.0%	1.7%	3.4%	1.9%	31,797	72.5%	20.0%	1.8%	3.4%	2.2%
Middlesex County	52,221	92.9%	83,384	80.5%	16.7%	1.3%	0.6%	0.9%	75,498	78.2%	14.1%	3.8%	1.7%	2.2%
Monmouth County	45,724	94.9%	53,159	87.9%	9.0%	1.3%	1.0%	0.9%	47,859	80.2%	14.5%	1.3%	3.4%	0.5%
Morris County	36,391	97.9%	40,984	86.0%	9.2%	1.4%	1.7%	1.7%	36,576	77.9%	16.7%	2.5%	2.8%	0.2%
Ocean County	36,944	92.4%	43,910	81.9%	12.6%	2.0%	2.4%	1.0%	44,190	82.4%	14.5%	0.7%	2.1%	0.2%
Passaic County	35,597	94.0%	52,748	89.3%	8.8%	0.0%	1.2%	0.7%	45,823	83.3%	12.0%	2.5%	0.6%	1.6%
Somerset County	24,310	93.4%	23,900	92.5%	6.1%	0.8%	0.0%	0.6%	23,578	86.4%	10.0%	1.0%	0.7%	1.9%
Sussex County	10,599	94.1%	12,094	87.2%	10.8%	2.0%	0.0%	0.0%	9,958	71.0%	23.6%	4.3%	0.6%	0.6%
Union County	37,116	91.4%	48,047	84.3%	11.3%	0.6%	1.3%	2.5%	48,437	82.5%	15.1%	1.3%	1.0%	0.0%
Warren County	8,596	89.1%	9,333	89.0%	10.4%	0.0%	0.5%	0.0%	6,347	79.5%	18.2%	1.4%	0.9%	0.0%
New Mexico														
Bernalillo County	44,531	88.9%	72,174	70.1%	23.1%	2.3%	2.2%	2.3%	70,322	70.1%	23.6%	1.4%	3.1%	1.7%
Doña Ana County	16,277	76.3%	32,427	69.1%	23.1%	0.6%	5.3%	1.9%	18,236	79.7%	15.4%	0.0%	3.1%	1.8%
San Juan County	9,133	92.3%	12,029	67.2%	28.3%	0.0%	0.0%	4.6%	10,960	93.7%	2.5%	1.7%	0.0%	2.1%
Sandoval County	9,675	91.7%	10,885	75.7%	13.6%	2.1%	8.6%	0.0%	11,444	71.4%	16.2%	5.0%	7.4%	0.0%
Santa Fe County	8,016	86.8%	11,267	76.7%	14.3%	2.7%	6.0%	0.4%	11,673	69.9%	21.4%	3.2%	3.0%	2.6%
New York														
Albany County	17,152	89.5%	43,769	69.2%	26.0%	2.0%	2.3%	0.5%	28,976	61.4%	31.9%	2.0%	3.7%	1.0%
Bronx County	94,578	90.5%	165,974	83.8%	13.0%	0.7%	0.7%	1.8%	151,158	83.4%	13.2%	0.5%	0.8%	2.1%
Broome County	11,152	90.1%	27,164	63.3%	31.8%	0.2%	1.3%	3.4%	16,385	69.8%	25.8%	1.8%	1.4%	1.2%
Chautauqua County	8,192	93.5%	15,702	62.3%	36.1%	1.3%	0.2%	0.2%	10,603	68.5%	24.0%	3.9%	3.6%	0.0%
Dutchess County	21,898	92.2%	35,052	76.7%	17.1%	2.7%	2.9%	0.7%	21,652	80.4%	17.6%	0.5%	0.8%	0.6%
Erie County	56,943	91.4%	95,801	74.6%	21.9%	0.6%	1.4%	1.5%	91,167	72.2%	23.9%	0.1%	1.6%	2.2%
Jefferson County	7,232	84.9%	14,889	49.0%	20.8%	5.8%	18.0%	6.3%	13,583	64.0%	22.3%	0.0%	11.2%	2.5%
Kings County	153,421	93.8%	254,944	86.5%	9.0%	0.8%	2.0%	1.7%	339,197	82.2%	13.1%	1.2%	2.3%	1.3%
Monroe County	45,735	88.5%	81,663	64.8%	26.8%	2.7%	5.0%	0.7%	72,332	74.4%	21.5%	1.1%	1.5%	1.5%
Nassau County	93,396	95.4%	118,749	91.1%	5.8%	0.4%	1.8%	1.0%	109,032	87.6%	9.8%	0.4%	1.5%	0.6%
New York County	58,237	89.5%	158,748	66.9%	18.1%	2.8%	7.8%	4.5%	267,158	75.7%	16.9%	2.2%	3.5%	1.7%
Niagara County	13,527	93.3%	20,964	82.9%	16.3%	0.0%	0.4%	0.4%	16,713	85.6%	12.1%	0.0%	2.3%	0.0%
Oneida County	16,545	87.0%	22,861	61.6%	34.8%	1.0%	2.1%	0.5%	20,901	71.2%	25.1%	0.0%	2.8%	1.0%
Onondaga County	31,745	92.2%	52,600	58.6%	32.0%	3.3%	4.3%	1.9%	44,462	74.5%	21.7%	0.9%	2.2%	0.6%
Ontario County	7,525	88.7%	9,713	68.8%	29.7%	0.0%	1.5%	0.0%	8,177	70.2%	24.2%	0.0%	5.6%	0.0%
Orange County	29,651	96.8%	40,299	87.0%	9.9%	1.0%	2.1%	0.0%	28,316	85.1%	12.3%	0.1%	1.3%	1.2%
Oswego County	8,684	90.9%	14,062	63.4%	34.9%	0.4%	0.5%	0.9%	10,128	75.3%	22.0%	0.0%	2.7%	0.0%
Putnam County	6,266	95.8%	8,442	95.5%	2.8%	0.0%	0.0%	1.7%	6,983	84.5%	11.9%	0.0%	3.6%	0.0%
Queens County	129,542	91.6%	212,998	86.2%	9.8%	0.6%	1.5%	2.0%	264,786	83.9%	11.7%	1.3%	1.3%	1.9%
Rensselaer County	8,677	89.5%	17,570	70.9%	24.6%	2.3%	1.8%	0.4%	15,821	62.7%	30.8%	0.7%	4.7%	1.1%
Richmond County	29,713	94.5%	44,851	88.9%	8.5%	0.7%	0.5%	1.4%	41,684	90.6%	7.7%	0.8%	0.6%	0.4%
Rockland County	24,743	96.8%	30,572	88.7%	8.2%	1.8%	0.5%	0.8%	26,007	83.8%	13.6%	1.2%	0.7%	0.6%
Saratoga County	14,558	92.9%	19,250	72.2%	19.0%	2.4%	6.5%	0.0%	18,865	70.1%	23.2%	4.2%	2.5%	0.0%
Schenectady County	9,275	95.2%	14,529	80.1%	16.3%	2.1%	0.8%	0.8%	15,167	80.6%	16.3%	1.4%	1.7%	0.0%
St. Lawrence County	6,608	78.1%	16,127	68.0%	28.2%	1.8%	1.5%	0.6%	8,571	79.1%	18.7%	0.0%	1.5%	0.6%
Steuben County	7,076	97.0%	7,766	76.8%	22.2%	1.0%	0.0%	0.0%	6,679	79.2%	20.1%	0.4%	0.3%	0.0%
Suffolk County	109,596	96.3%	137,312	88.0%	9.3%	0.4%	1.3%	1.0%	121,458	87.5%	10.4%	0.3%	1.3%	0.5%
Tompkins County	4,388	85.2%	27,064	54.6%	21.8%	8.9%	9.1%	5.5%	10,063	69.2%	21.9%	1.4%	5.0%	2.6%
Ulster County	11,176	92.3%	18,478	60.6%	37.2%	2.1%	0.0%	0.0%	12,240	76.9%	19.7%	1.3%	0.9%	1.2%
Wayne County	6,223	93.3%	6,813	73.0%	23.1%	0.0%	3.9%	0.0%	7,636	59.9%	34.4%	0.4%	5.4%	0.0%
Westchester County	65,177	88.6%	84,010	82.5%	12.8%	2.1%	1.1%	1.5%	75,282	80.6%	15.6%	0.6%	1.4%	1.7%
North Carolina														
Alamance County	10,421	93.3%	14,914	72.4%	15.1%	3.6%	8.9%	0.0%	13,510	71.5%	23.9%	4.3%	0.2%	0.1%
Brunswick County	5,706	73.0%	6,204	74.6%	22.3%	0.0%	3.1%	0.0%	6,431	70.7%	28.2%	1.1%	0.0%	0.0%
Buncombe County	12,414	86.5%	19,015	60.7%	25.8%	7.0%	5.4%	1.1%	24,786	73.7%	18.9%	3.7%	2.8%	0.9%
Burke County	6,705	92.3%	6,960	84.4%	10.2%	3.4%	0.0%	2.0%	7,422	77.7%	19.3%	3.0%	0.0%	0.0%
Cabarrus County	14,356	86.4%	16,063	80.9%	16.2%	2.3%	0.6%	0.0%	15,403	83.9%	11.1%	2.0%	1.7%	1.3%
Catawba County	9,820	87.6%	14,162	73.4%	21.9%	2.7%	2.0%	0.0%	10,681	72.9%	23.4%	0.5%	3.2%	0.0%
Cleveland County	5,418	95.9%	10,491	73.3%	21.1%	2.6%	0.0%	3.0%	7,240	84.8%	10.6%	4.6%	0.0%	0.0%
Craven County	5,204	79.8%	13,109	67.5%	16.1%	8.0%	5.0%	3.3%	11,776	60.2%	32.0%	0.4%	7.4%	0.0%
Cumberland County	21,359	83.6%	42,645	60.9%	23.5%	4.7%	10.1%	0.8%	40,200	67.5%	17.5%	5.8%	4.9%	4.3%
Davidson County	11,421	78.9%	13,893	77.7%	19.6%	1.0%	1.7%	0.0%	11,987	79.0%	18.9%	1.5%	0.7%	0.0%
Durham County	15,132	80.3%	31,255	53.8%	30.8%	4.1%	7.7%	3.6%	38,220	61.3%	25.1%	4.0%	6.7%	2.8%
Forsyth County	24,965	86.9%	37,917	66.3%	22.1%	7.1%	3.9%	0.7%	29,296	72.3%	21.1%	3.3%	2.7%	0.6%
Gaston County	14,672	89.4%	18,530	73.1%	25.3%	0.3%	1.3%	0.0%	16,649	77.7%	20.0%	1.1%	1.2%	0.0%
Guilford County	31,332	90.9%	57,650	72.4%	21.5%	2.6%	2.8%	0.7%	49,074	79.7%	14.8%	1.5%	3.1%	0.9%
Harnett County	8,830	77.7%	11,742	77.0%	15.6%	5.6%	1.7%	0.0%	14,304	72.1%	22.2%	4.2%	0.5%	1.0%
Henderson County	8,472	63.7%	7,177	77.4%	7.8%	4.0%	10.8%	0.0%	6,726	81.5%	14.6%	1.2%	0.7%	2.0%
Iredell County	12,029	87.9%	14,727	79.0%	18.2%	0.7%	2.1%	0.0%	12,177	74.8%	18.3%	1.7%	1.4%	3.8%
Johnston County	14,056	93.7%	15,471	88.6%	10.1%	1.3%	0.0%	0.0%	12,811	66.5%	33.5%	0.0%	0.0%	0.0%
Mecklenburg County	61,481	90.4%	95,115	61.2%	27.4%	4.1%	6.5%	0.9%	116,413	69.1%	22.6%	4.6%	2.5%	1.2%
Moore County	6,255	97.3%	5,301	89.4%	1.8%	5.7%	0.0%	3.1%	7,390	85.1%	5.6%	2.1%	2.6%	4.7%
Nash County	6,770	90.6%	8,804	82.0%	11.3%	3.8%	3.0%	0.0%	6,251	87.5%	12.5%	0.0%	0.0%	0.0%
New Hanover County	10,798	85.9%	28,308	45.1%	43.2%	5.1%	4.0%	2.5%	19,974	57.7%	36.6%	3.1%	2.1%	0.4%
Onslow County	11,543	82.0%	41,443	60.1%	25.9%	6.5%	5.1%	2.3%	27,113	62.0%	17.7%	8.0%	8.7%	3.6%
Orange County	8,604	88.7%	26,907	48.4%	44.0%	1.2%	4.1%	2.3%	12,800	57.8%	30.4%	3.5%	6.5%	1.7%
Pitt County	12,815	78.5%	33,517	45.1%	49.4%	3.1%	2.3%	0.0%	15,455	73.5%	22.1%	0.0%	2.8%	1.6%

Table J-2: Counties—Mobility Status by Age—*Continued*

| | 13 to 17 | | 18 to 24 | | | | | | 25 to 31 | | | | | |
| | | | | | Percent Living in a Different House | | | | | | Percent Living in a Different House | | | |
	Total Population	Percent Living in Same House	Total Population	Percent Living in Same House	Same State	Different State, Same Region	Different Region	Outside US	Total Population	Percent Living in Same House	Same State	Different State, Same Region	Different Region	Outside US
North Carolina—Cont.														
Randolph County	8,957	95.8%	11,229	84.5%	15.5%	0.0%	0.0%	0.0%	11,575	81.9%	17.1%	1.0%	0.0%	0.0%
Robeson County	11,057	83.7%	15,994	74.8%	24.7%	0.0%	0.5%	0.0%	10,319	83.1%	16.9%	0.0%	0.0%	0.0%
Rockingham County	6,587	86.6%	5,190	79.7%	16.0%	1.8%	2.6%	0.0%	8,205	85.9%	14.1%	0.0%	0.0%	0.0%
Rowan County	8,759	93.9%	13,058	85.1%	12.3%	0.9%	1.7%	0.0%	10,364	68.7%	26.2%	2.5%	2.6%	0.0%
Union County	18,915	89.7%	17,838	74.4%	18.4%	4.6%	2.6%	0.0%	13,295	73.5%	22.5%	3.1%	0.8%	0.0%
Wake County	70,257	88.2%	93,995	65.8%	27.5%	2.0%	3.3%	1.5%	94,100	61.5%	30.3%	3.4%	3.2%	1.6%
Wayne County	7,730	91.9%	11,846	72.3%	20.8%	3.8%	1.8%	1.3%	11,414	63.6%	30.4%	4.6%	1.5%	0.0%
North Dakota														
Cass County	8,511	94.8%	27,874	53.0%	27.2%	17.6%	1.9%	0.2%	19,202	73.6%	19.3%	6.2%	0.0%	0.9%
Ohio														
Allen County	6,547	78.6%	10,770	59.7%	33.9%	0.9%	5.5%	0.0%	8,973	58.3%	39.9%	0.0%	1.5%	0.4%
Ashtabula County	6,190	94.4%	8,246	87.4%	12.6%	0.0%	0.0%	0.0%	8,300	83.3%	16.7%	0.0%	0.0%	0.0%
Butler County	23,887	91.5%	46,473	68.5%	24.4%	2.6%	4.0%	0.4%	30,689	67.1%	26.4%	0.9%	4.8%	0.9%
Clark County	9,593	90.6%	12,435	71.5%	27.4%	1.1%	0.0%	0.0%	10,946	66.6%	25.2%	0.0%	4.8%	3.4%
Clermont County	15,776	92.8%	15,562	73.8%	23.4%	0.7%	2.0%	0.0%	17,828	73.0%	24.8%	1.1%	1.1%	0.0%
Columbiana County	6,746	85.4%	8,311	68.0%	28.3%	0.0%	3.7%	0.0%	8,795	67.0%	30.2%	0.0%	2.9%	0.0%
Cuyahoga County	80,244	86.9%	115,543	70.5%	25.4%	1.5%	2.1%	0.6%	115,142	69.3%	26.1%	1.2%	2.7%	0.8%
Delaware County	15,291	94.9%	13,023	68.6%	29.0%	1.0%	1.0%	0.5%	12,106	77.1%	18.9%	1.6%	0.9%	1.4%
Fairfield County	11,627	90.6%	12,513	67.1%	32.9%	0.0%	0.0%	0.0%	13,666	67.6%	31.2%	0.0%	1.2%	0.0%
Franklin County	74,512	84.2%	128,229	57.4%	37.5%	1.6%	2.4%	1.1%	154,793	70.8%	23.0%	1.8%	2.6%	1.8%
Geauga County	7,164	91.8%	8,535	83.3%	12.1%	0.7%	3.9%	0.0%	5,095	82.8%	16.1%	1.1%	0.0%	0.0%
Greene County	10,650	83.4%	21,436	41.9%	44.2%	4.5%	6.1%	3.3%	15,965	70.5%	21.9%	1.1%	4.0%	2.5%
Hamilton County	51,107	85.1%	79,971	62.1%	30.8%	2.5%	3.8%	0.9%	81,761	69.4%	24.1%	0.7%	4.1%	1.7%
Lake County	14,613	97.7%	19,679	86.8%	12.0%	0.3%	0.5%	0.3%	18,229	85.1%	14.8%	0.1%	0.0%	0.0%
Licking County	12,504	92.9%	14,831	65.2%	27.6%	2.2%	3.9%	1.1%	13,750	79.0%	17.7%	0.0%	3.3%	0.0%
Lorain County	21,562	87.8%	27,287	66.7%	25.3%	1.1%	5.7%	1.2%	23,098	78.3%	20.8%	0.0%	0.4%	0.5%
Lucas County	29,236	83.8%	46,770	61.9%	33.1%	2.1%	1.4%	1.5%	41,028	75.4%	21.5%	1.3%	0.4%	1.4%
Mahoning County	14,721	90.6%	20,067	68.1%	27.5%	0.2%	1.2%	2.9%	19,609	70.2%	25.2%	0.0%	4.6%	0.0%
Medina County	13,348	89.9%	13,092	90.2%	8.4%	0.8%	0.6%	0.0%	13,016	75.1%	24.1%	0.8%	0.0%	0.0%
Miami County	7,318	90.1%	9,000	70.5%	29.5%	0.0%	0.0%	0.0%	9,293	80.6%	19.4%	0.0%	0.0%	0.0%
Montgomery County	33,093	83.8%	52,950	55.1%	40.4%	2.0%	1.9%	0.6%	48,832	66.0%	30.7%	1.3%	1.0%	1.0%
Portage County	9,086	92.6%	30,634	53.3%	37.2%	0.9%	2.1%	6.4%	12,682	63.4%	17.0%	1.9%	15.2%	2.4%
Richland County	7,676	81.5%	10,958	71.4%	28.6%	0.0%	0.0%	0.0%	9,405	64.9%	30.2%	1.4%	1.5%	2.1%
Stark County	24,335	91.4%	33,908	73.6%	22.8%	0.7%	2.9%	0.0%	30,672	73.8%	23.1%	0.3%	2.2%	0.5%
Summit County	33,307	93.4%	50,125	75.3%	19.7%	1.1%	2.3%	1.5%	49,169	84.3%	12.3%	0.8%	1.7%	1.0%
Trumbull County	14,264	87.0%	15,334	77.0%	22.0%	0.0%	1.0%	0.0%	15,627	76.6%	18.8%	1.1%	3.5%	0.0%
Tuscarawas County	6,749	93.5%	7,243	84.4%	13.3%	0.7%	1.6%	0.0%	7,249	66.8%	19.6%	0.0%	13.6%	0.0%
Warren County	18,040	92.2%	16,382	71.0%	22.4%	2.4%	1.0%	3.1%	17,474	69.1%	25.8%	4.5%	0.0%	0.7%
Wayne County	8,612	93.0%	11,137	63.4%	29.9%	0.4%	5.6%	0.8%	8,719	70.9%	24.9%	1.9%	2.3%	0.0%
Wood County	8,979	90.7%	19,374	61.7%	34.1%	2.6%	0.8%	0.7%	12,388	74.3%	23.7%	0.3%	1.6%	0.0%
Oklahoma														
Canadian County	7,741	80.7%	10,297	73.7%	18.7%	7.0%	0.6%	0.0%	10,799	61.9%	31.8%	2.0%	2.8%	1.5%
Cleveland County	15,890	88.6%	41,466	52.6%	37.1%	5.9%	3.1%	1.3%	30,376	69.7%	23.1%	1.7%	3.5%	2.0%
Comanche County	7,888	75.7%	17,467	46.5%	18.4%	17.4%	17.2%	0.5%	14,657	59.8%	22.0%	10.0%	3.0%	5.2%
Oklahoma County	44,685	84.5%	72,868	60.3%	30.9%	4.5%	3.3%	1.0%	87,297	65.6%	26.9%	2.8%	2.9%	1.8%
Tulsa County	43,334	83.7%	59,491	67.9%	24.2%	3.5%	3.1%	1.2%	65,454	67.2%	29.0%	1.3%	2.6%	0.0%
Oregon														
Clackamas County	27,212	92.3%	31,816	67.2%	28.2%	3.7%	0.5%	0.4%	30,513	61.5%	32.2%	4.9%	0.9%	0.5%
Deschutes County	12,180	84.6%	11,498	58.0%	41.2%	0.0%	0.7%	0.0%	14,309	79.9%	17.3%	0.7%	2.2%	0.0%
Douglas County	5,316	88.9%	7,684	68.4%	21.9%	9.7%	0.0%	0.0%	7,735	80.2%	17.8%	0.0%	1.9%	0.0%
Jackson County	11,641	87.5%	17,320	62.7%	23.1%	7.3%	5.1%	1.8%	16,879	76.8%	16.3%	5.6%	0.7%	0.6%
Lane County	19,984	84.1%	48,062	41.5%	47.8%	9.1%	1.1%	0.5%	30,151	68.9%	24.9%	2.7%	1.7%	1.8%
Linn County	6,504	85.5%	15,594	46.6%	49.1%	1.9%	2.4%	0.0%	8,247	60.0%	20.9%	7.2%	5.5%	6.3%
Marion County	22,772	86.9%	34,348	73.9%	21.8%	3.2%	0.3%	0.8%	26,382	69.9%	23.8%	3.8%	2.3%	0.3%
Multnomah County	38,870	86.4%	68,115	53.6%	33.0%	9.0%	2.1%	2.4%	97,558	61.4%	27.6%	5.9%	4.0%	1.2%
Washington County	38,757	84.1%	47,001	61.8%	30.4%	5.3%	2.3%	0.2%	59,587	65.6%	26.3%	4.8%	2.4%	0.9%
Yamhill County	6,122	88.4%	9,740	68.3%	19.3%	6.2%	4.4%	1.8%	8,782	50.3%	39.0%	8.2%	2.5%	0.0%
Pennsylvania														
Adams County	6,375	87.4%	11,103	73.6%	18.3%	4.2%	3.9%	0.1%	6,631	66.1%	24.8%	0.0%	7.9%	1.2%
Allegheny County	69,744	91.5%	117,461	64.5%	28.3%	1.8%	3.3%	2.0%	128,389	71.8%	23.3%	0.9%	2.8%	1.1%
Beaver County	10,331	85.3%	14,952	71.8%	19.9%	0.0%	8.2%	0.0%	12,583	81.4%	18.0%	0.0%	0.7%	0.0%
Berks County	29,106	91.7%	42,753	75.2%	21.4%	1.3%	0.6%	1.5%	34,585	79.4%	18.6%	0.6%	0.6%	0.8%
Blair County	6,521	96.7%	12,217	71.9%	23.6%	2.4%	2.1%	0.0%	10,280	71.5%	28.1%	0.0%	0.4%	0.0%
Bucks County	43,272	93.7%	47,975	89.8%	7.3%	0.3%	0.7%	1.7%	48,860	83.4%	12.6%	1.2%	1.1%	1.8%
Butler County	13,224	90.0%	17,255	59.3%	36.9%	0.3%	2.5%	0.9%	14,392	72.4%	27.1%	0.0%	0.5%	0.0%
Cambria County	8,630	84.6%	13,064	71.8%	24.4%	1.5%	1.2%	1.1%	10,546	77.3%	19.5%	0.0%	3.2%	0.0%
Centre County	6,996	93.6%	44,131	34.9%	48.0%	8.5%	4.5%	4.2%	13,999	59.2%	30.4%	6.7%	3.2%	0.6%
Chester County	38,126	95.6%	45,204	73.9%	19.2%	2.8%	3.7%	0.4%	42,874	81.7%	12.4%	0.8%	2.8%	2.2%
Cumberland County	14,570	91.4%	23,970	65.9%	29.7%	1.5%	1.9%	1.0%	20,205	80.6%	17.2%	0.0%	1.3%	0.9%
Dauphin County	16,950	84.9%	21,555	76.8%	17.3%	1.0%	0.5%	4.4%	25,438	73.3%	22.3%	0.0%	3.3%	1.1%
Delaware County	38,175	91.6%	59,250	81.8%	13.7%	3.0%	1.0%	0.5%	49,731	81.5%	15.0%	0.7%	2.0%	0.9%
Erie County	15,496	94.3%	30,889	56.9%	36.3%	3.1%	3.1%	0.6%	27,602	74.9%	20.9%	2.6%	1.7%	0.0%
Fayette County	7,384	92.0%	10,191	86.2%	9.5%	1.0%	2.0%	1.3%	10,232	78.2%	20.8%	0.0%	1.0%	0.0%

Table J-2: Counties—Mobility Status by Age—*Continued*

| | 13 to 17 | | 18 to 24 | | | | | | 25 to 31 | | | | | |
| | | | | | Percent Living in a Different House | | | | | | Percent Living in a Different House | | | |
	Total Population	Percent Living in Same House	Total Population	Percent Living in Same House	Same State	Different State, Same Region	Different Region	Outside US	Total Population	Percent Living in Same House	Same State	Different State, Same Region	Different Region	Outside US
Pennsylvania—Cont.														
Franklin County	8,647	94.0%	12,550	78.9%	16.3%	0.4%	4.4%	0.0%	13,689	86.1%	9.2%	0.0%	4.7%	0.0%
Lackawanna County	12,024	91.2%	22,248	82.5%	8.1%	5.9%	3.2%	0.4%	18,141	77.3%	16.7%	1.8%	2.3%	1.9%
Lancaster County	35,871	90.9%	50,977	79.4%	16.6%	1.1%	1.9%	0.9%	47,497	80.5%	15.2%	0.5%	3.3%	0.5%
Lebanon County	8,334	86.1%	10,926	75.0%	18.5%	0.0%	3.4%	3.1%	9,178	86.3%	11.9%	1.8%	0.0%	0.0%
Lehigh County	22,847	86.5%	32,576	76.4%	17.2%	4.0%	0.7%	1.7%	30,683	72.2%	18.4%	2.7%	3.0%	3.7%
Luzerne County	19,687	92.3%	32,579	71.4%	23.2%	3.6%	0.5%	1.3%	26,466	74.2%	21.5%	3.6%	0.8%	0.0%
Lycoming County	6,042	98.2%	14,169	67.4%	31.8%	0.3%	0.5%	0.0%	9,160	81.5%	14.1%	0.0%	4.4%	0.0%
Mercer County	8,346	81.9%	11,450	70.8%	18.7%	0.2%	10.3%	0.0%	8,634	83.4%	12.5%	3.3%	0.8%	0.0%
Monroe County	13,266	93.9%	19,021	72.6%	22.8%	3.4%	1.2%	0.0%	10,573	89.8%	3.1%	0.0%	4.5%	2.6%
Montgomery County	52,880	94.0%	63,883	81.5%	14.3%	1.6%	1.6%	1.0%	71,732	79.3%	15.7%	1.0%	2.5%	1.4%
Northampton County	17,941	93.8%	28,977	69.8%	23.3%	4.9%	1.6%	0.4%	25,692	71.1%	20.9%	5.0%	3.0%	0.0%
Northumberland County	4,473	95.6%	7,804	81.9%	18.1%	0.0%	0.0%	0.0%	7,950	79.8%	19.1%	0.0%	0.2%	0.9%
Philadelphia County	89,645	86.9%	188,718	74.0%	17.9%	4.4%	2.7%	1.0%	198,742	74.6%	19.0%	2.3%	2.8%	1.3%
Schuylkill County	7,752	91.1%	11,168	85.9%	12.9%	0.0%	1.2%	0.0%	11,697	72.1%	24.9%	1.8%	1.2%	0.0%
Washington County	12,596	89.8%	17,971	71.6%	24.8%	0.0%	3.2%	0.4%	15,972	70.9%	25.4%	1.6%	2.2%	0.0%
Westmoreland County	19,863	87.7%	30,175	72.8%	22.8%	0.4%	3.9%	0.0%	23,724	73.2%	24.7%	0.0%	2.2%	0.0%
York County	27,741	93.3%	39,152	71.9%	24.9%	0.4%	2.2%	0.6%	35,545	71.9%	21.8%	0.0%	4.4%	1.9%
Rhode Island														
Kent County	8,562	88.7%	12,404	86.8%	12.7%	0.5%	0.0%	0.0%	14,050	74.8%	24.5%	0.0%	0.7%	0.0%
Providence County	38,699	95.4%	74,088	75.7%	11.2%	7.0%	2.3%	3.8%	65,917	76.7%	15.0%	3.3%	3.7%	1.4%
Washington County	7,020	89.6%	19,306	69.7%	21.0%	9.3%	0.0%	0.0%	6,598	81.2%	10.4%	1.5%	6.9%	0.0%
South Carolina														
Aiken County	10,610	83.3%	15,125	83.2%	10.4%	2.9%	1.7%	1.8%	14,493	82.4%	14.4%	1.6%	1.7%	0.0%
Anderson County	13,756	90.6%	15,743	80.2%	15.4%	2.8%	1.6%	0.0%	15,660	76.6%	20.3%	3.1%	0.0%	0.0%
Beaufort County	8,656	91.6%	15,335	71.0%	11.9%	11.7%	5.5%	0.0%	14,005	66.9%	14.5%	12.4%	5.5%	0.7%
Berkeley County	12,922	97.5%	20,467	60.9%	28.0%	5.8%	4.9%	0.4%	20,800	65.6%	26.3%	5.6%	2.3%	0.2%
Charleston County	21,693	92.1%	41,902	56.4%	31.4%	5.2%	6.5%	0.5%	42,223	67.6%	21.8%	6.6%	3.5%	0.5%
Dorchester County	10,726	95.7%	16,093	70.9%	23.7%	1.6%	3.8%	0.0%	11,263	67.1%	30.0%	1.8%	1.2%	0.0%
Florence County	9,435	86.2%	14,181	84.0%	13.6%	2.5%	0.0%	0.0%	11,255	83.4%	12.4%	3.5%	0.6%	0.0%
Greenville County	32,336	89.5%	47,093	75.5%	18.2%	2.9%	2.5%	0.8%	44,888	74.6%	20.7%	1.9%	1.8%	1.0%
Horry County	13,308	84.9%	26,544	67.5%	26.4%	2.7%	3.5%	0.0%	24,814	71.4%	20.8%	3.8%	3.9%	0.0%
Lexington County	19,792	84.8%	25,109	69.8%	23.1%	4.3%	2.2%	0.6%	23,604	76.9%	19.1%	1.1%	2.1%	0.7%
Orangeburg County	7,159	88.4%	10,222	81.7%	18.0%	0.2%	0.0%	0.2%	5,890	83.9%	16.1%	0.0%	0.0%	0.0%
Pickens County	8,610	91.3%	19,673	44.7%	47.0%	6.4%	2.1%	0.2%	10,695	72.7%	25.1%	1.2%	0.0%	0.9%
Richland County	27,131	87.2%	62,983	41.8%	34.8%	9.8%	13.0%	0.7%	41,177	67.8%	20.3%	3.0%	7.4%	1.6%
Spartanburg County	21,150	84.7%	30,878	71.5%	24.0%	3.0%	1.5%	0.0%	24,155	74.3%	20.0%	0.5%	1.9%	3.3%
Sumter County	7,316	86.6%	12,753	66.2%	26.3%	6.4%	1.1%	0.0%	9,642	81.5%	8.2%	7.9%	2.5%	0.0%
York County	17,957	84.9%	22,992	75.2%	20.0%	3.7%	1.0%	0.1%	16,944	74.6%	19.9%	3.5%	2.0%	0.0%
South Dakota														
Minnehaha County	10,156	81.6%	18,746	63.5%	23.7%	10.6%	1.7%	0.4%	21,330	82.3%	15.9%	1.8%	0.0%	0.0%
Pennington County	5,173	84.6%	11,112	37.1%	54.3%	7.6%	1.0%	0.0%	8,870	64.7%	27.2%	6.4%	1.6%	0.0%
Tennessee														
Blount County	8,783	80.0%	10,855	75.6%	23.6%	0.2%	0.0%	0.7%	8,977	80.8%	17.7%	1.1%	0.4%	0.0%
Bradley County	6,726	75.4%	10,249	64.3%	25.4%	5.7%	2.8%	1.8%	8,352	73.6%	24.5%	0.0%	1.8%	0.0%
Davidson County	33,719	76.4%	69,097	63.2%	21.3%	6.7%	7.7%	1.1%	90,142	68.3%	21.2%	5.1%	3.4%	1.9%
Hamilton County	19,372	85.4%	33,512	71.5%	20.4%	4.9%	2.3%	0.8%	34,559	69.6%	19.0%	8.4%	0.7%	2.3%
Knox County	25,759	88.3%	54,317	68.1%	27.7%	2.2%	1.8%	0.2%	43,946	77.2%	18.9%	2.1%	1.4%	0.4%
Madison County	7,298	89.1%	10,133	71.9%	22.2%	2.2%	3.7%	0.0%	8,001	67.8%	26.9%	4.4%	0.8%	0.0%
Montgomery County	12,997	71.4%	22,598	60.8%	22.7%	11.0%	4.3%	1.2%	25,885	65.1%	20.6%	7.5%	3.9%	2.8%
Rutherford County	20,158	90.9%	36,951	56.7%	32.8%	6.4%	3.8%	0.3%	28,383	64.8%	31.9%	2.0%	1.2%	0.0%
Sevier County	4,044	79.9%	10,006	68.3%	21.9%	9.7%	0.0%	0.0%	6,586	75.7%	17.0%	7.3%	0.0%	0.0%
Shelby County	67,246	84.8%	97,843	75.6%	19.8%	2.9%	1.1%	0.6%	95,682	72.6%	21.9%	3.6%	1.5%	0.3%
Sullivan County	10,967	91.3%	11,805	80.4%	15.8%	0.8%	2.7%	0.2%	10,983	75.0%	14.7%	8.0%	2.4%	0.0%
Sumner County	12,450	89.7%	14,205	72.8%	22.7%	4.5%	0.0%	0.0%	14,572	71.4%	23.0%	4.7%	0.9%	0.0%
Washington County	7,909	93.4%	15,096	70.8%	25.3%	3.5%	0.5%	0.0%	10,415	70.8%	25.1%	2.8%	1.3%	0.0%
Williamson County	16,127	87.9%	14,237	93.1%	3.8%	1.7%	1.3%	0.0%	11,899	65.1%	23.2%	3.0%	4.8%	3.9%
Wilson County	10,149	82.8%	9,764	81.7%	17.7%	0.6%	0.0%	0.0%	9,658	80.5%	16.4%	0.0%	2.0%	1.2%
Texas														
Bell County	21,906	86.8%	41,977	68.4%	20.3%	4.6%	4.2%	2.5%	39,091	66.3%	15.5%	3.9%	11.9%	2.4%
Bexar County	133,146	87.1%	199,950	66.7%	25.5%	2.0%	3.7%	2.1%	196,867	71.5%	24.0%	1.5%	1.8%	1.2%
Bowie County	5,049	75.5%	9,884	74.0%	22.8%	1.6%	1.6%	0.0%	9,680	79.9%	11.1%	8.5%	0.5%	0.0%
Brazoria County	24,523	94.8%	28,706	79.7%	15.5%	1.2%	3.5%	0.0%	34,540	80.8%	17.0%	0.3%	0.4%	1.4%
Brazos County	11,792	90.4%	57,384	44.2%	51.6%	0.8%	1.9%	1.4%	24,267	62.6%	33.6%	1.3%	1.0%	1.6%
Cameron County	40,096	87.2%	44,095	84.4%	12.9%	0.6%	0.6%	1.6%	33,550	82.1%	16.4%	0.0%	1.0%	0.4%
Collin County	65,384	89.3%	69,090	74.0%	21.5%	1.4%	1.8%	1.3%	68,580	65.8%	27.0%	0.5%	5.1%	1.6%
Comal County	8,810	96.2%	9,523	75.7%	24.3%	0.0%	0.0%	0.0%	8,822	58.0%	34.0%	0.0%	4.0%	4.0%
Dallas County	170,331	86.1%	244,435	70.7%	25.3%	1.0%	2.3%	0.6%	279,822	70.5%	24.6%	0.9%	2.3%	1.8%
Denton County	53,763	85.5%	72,238	60.6%	35.1%	1.3%	1.8%	1.2%	74,085	68.7%	26.6%	1.4%	1.5%	1.8%
Ector County	11,080	78.6%	16,738	56.7%	27.7%	0.0%	6.7%	8.9%	17,369	68.3%	25.8%	0.4%	0.7%	4.9%
El Paso County	64,922	91.6%	99,494	78.8%	12.9%	2.6%	3.5%	2.2%	82,562	75.2%	17.2%	1.1%	4.2%	2.3%
Ellis County	13,358	83.0%	14,570	67.7%	29.2%	1.9%	0.7%	0.6%	13,140	73.5%	26.5%	0.0%	0.0%	0.0%
Fort Bend County	50,862	92.0%	54,417	83.3%	12.2%	0.0%	3.7%	0.9%	53,038	75.7%	18.5%	3.2%	0.3%	2.3%

Table J-2: Counties—Mobility Status by Age—*Continued*

| | 13 to 17 | | 18 to 24 | | | | | | 25 to 31 | | | | | |
| | | | | | Percent Living in a Different House | | | | | | Percent Living in a Different House | | | |
	Total Population	Percent Living in Same House	Total Population	Percent Living in Same House	Same State	Different State, Same Region	Different Region	Outside US	Total Population	Percent Living in Same House	Same State	Different State, Same Region	Different Region	Outside US
Texas—Cont.														
Galveston County	23,372	86.1%	28,221	61.8%	32.5%	1.5%	4.2%	0.0%	27,246	59.5%	36.0%	1.8%	1.2%	1.5%
Grayson County	7,874	86.6%	11,527	69.5%	23.7%	3.3%	0.0%	3.6%	11,410	77.2%	20.7%	1.4%	0.7%	0.0%
Gregg County	8,605	89.1%	13,487	62.4%	29.4%	6.7%	1.5%	0.0%	11,362	59.8%	37.4%	1.9%	1.0%	0.0%
Guadalupe County..................	10,943	90.3%	13,089	85.6%	12.8%	0.6%	0.0%	1.0%	11,517	78.6%	16.8%	3.0%	1.6%	0.0%
Harris County.........................	309,621	86.5%	428,939	73.5%	22.4%	1.6%	1.4%	1.1%	499,981	69.4%	24.3%	1.7%	2.6%	1.9%
Hays County............................	11,213	87.2%	30,303	60.4%	38.4%	0.7%	0.0%	0.4%	17,040	49.1%	44.7%	2.4%	3.8%	0.0%
Hidalgo County	75,624	91.2%	90,122	87.6%	11.4%	0.4%	0.3%	0.3%	74,583	83.5%	13.2%	0.5%	1.8%	1.0%
Jefferson County.....................	17,384	94.3%	27,930	83.3%	15.0%	0.5%	0.4%	0.9%	24,916	72.6%	22.9%	0.7%	3.4%	0.4%
Johnson County	11,098	89.9%	13,976	58.4%	41.3%	0.0%	0.0%	0.3%	13,773	61.9%	37.7%	0.0%	0.3%	0.0%
Kaufman County	7,925	91.5%	9,526	88.1%	10.5%	0.0%	1.3%	0.0%	7,868	80.9%	15.7%	0.0%	0.5%	2.9%
Lubbock County......................	19,693	85.5%	51,030	49.8%	47.1%	0.2%	2.1%	0.7%	28,515	63.1%	32.9%	1.0%	2.6%	0.4%
McLennan County	13,339	89.2%	36,248	58.3%	36.3%	1.4%	3.5%	0.5%	21,559	59.3%	35.1%	2.2%	2.5%	0.8%
Midland County.......................	10,168	75.2%	15,147	57.8%	36.1%	0.0%	5.3%	0.8%	18,279	72.0%	22.1%	0.4%	5.4%	0.0%
Montgomery County	39,235	88.8%	41,800	69.0%	23.3%	0.8%	4.1%	2.8%	40,734	66.9%	26.5%	1.9%	1.5%	3.2%
Nueces County	24,532	77.3%	36,773	57.0%	31.6%	6.7%	3.6%	1.1%	34,597	73.0%	24.9%	0.7%	1.2%	0.2%
Parker County	9,752	89.0%	10,340	73.0%	24.9%	0.0%	2.1%	0.0%	9,903	70.5%	27.3%	0.0%	2.2%	0.0%
Potter County	8,010	74.9%	12,335	54.6%	40.5%	4.1%	0.8%	0.0%	12,465	66.9%	26.9%	2.6%	2.0%	1.7%
Randall County.......................	7,557	80.7%	12,985	59.8%	31.8%	4.9%	2.7%	0.7%	13,695	64.8%	27.2%	2.7%	5.2%	0.0%
Smith County	15,574	81.2%	22,466	65.5%	29.0%	2.1%	3.4%	0.0%	19,748	73.1%	20.5%	0.0%	5.1%	1.4%
Tarrant County	142,599	85.5%	182,581	67.2%	27.9%	1.9%	2.5%	0.4%	203,238	70.7%	26.2%	1.4%	1.0%	0.7%
Taylor County	8,285	78.3%	19,774	56.2%	38.4%	2.1%	3.3%	0.0%	15,296	57.2%	35.5%	6.0%	1.0%	0.3%
Tom Green County	7,665	81.8%	14,049	45.9%	34.3%	3.6%	14.8%	1.4%	12,632	64.8%	17.3%	10.3%	5.3%	2.4%
Travis County	63,713	85.5%	117,682	53.3%	39.7%	1.3%	3.2%	2.4%	163,202	62.1%	29.3%	1.2%	5.2%	2.2%
Webb County	23,409	90.7%	29,655	86.2%	12.4%	0.2%	0.5%	0.7%	26,286	85.6%	10.0%	1.6%	0.2%	2.6%
Wichita County	7,490	87.9%	17,764	57.2%	18.9%	7.8%	12.2%	3.9%	15,130	69.0%	21.8%	3.2%	6.0%	0.0%
Williamson County..................	35,527	85.9%	36,128	64.7%	28.5%	4.3%	2.3%	0.1%	44,089	64.4%	28.4%	2.4%	4.2%	0.6%
Utah														
Cache County	9,876	85.3%	18,490	52.4%	34.3%	8.9%	0.9%	3.5%	14,765	70.4%	25.6%	1.8%	1.3%	0.9%
Davis County...........................	30,135	94.6%	29,660	72.8%	19.7%	2.7%	3.9%	0.9%	30,520	74.7%	20.8%	1.9%	1.5%	1.2%
Salt Lake County	80,671	86.1%	107,464	69.5%	20.8%	3.1%	4.7%	2.0%	127,239	67.0%	27.6%	2.4%	1.8%	1.2%
Utah County	46,338	86.2%	92,638	47.0%	34.9%	8.5%	6.4%	3.3%	58,974	68.1%	25.0%	3.8%	2.6%	0.5%
Washington County.................	10,787	72.7%	14,931	49.6%	31.5%	17.2%	1.5%	0.2%	10,743	73.0%	22.5%	3.0%	1.5%	0.0%
Weber County	18,953	88.8%	22,158	60.5%	34.7%	2.6%	0.0%	2.2%	25,097	65.7%	30.2%	3.1%	0.9%	0.0%
Vermont														
Chittenden County...................	9,908	96.1%	23,207	53.7%	27.6%	11.7%	2.5%	4.6%	16,368	76.8%	18.8%	2.6%	0.8%	1.0%
Virginia														
Albemarle County....................	7,120	84.3%	11,502	58.1%	35.9%	1.3%	3.6%	1.2%	10,164	66.1%	26.4%	1.8%	2.9%	2.8%
Arlington County	7,751	96.3%	18,217	57.6%	21.9%	8.7%	9.0%	2.8%	47,231	66.5%	15.2%	9.7%	6.2%	2.5%
Chesterfield County.................	26,193	91.0%	30,892	84.2%	13.0%	1.0%	1.4%	0.4%	25,020	77.8%	19.7%	1.1%	0.6%	0.8%
Fairfax County	73,325	89.8%	95,982	77.8%	13.2%	4.6%	2.0%	2.4%	109,704	67.4%	22.7%	4.7%	3.3%	1.9%
Hanover County	7,237	88.5%	7,969	81.7%	17.2%	1.0%	0.0%	0.0%	8,001	66.2%	26.9%	6.9%	0.0%	0.0%
Henrico County	20,646	88.4%	27,360	66.5%	28.0%	1.7%	2.8%	1.0%	31,938	65.0%	28.0%	1.4%	2.4%	3.3%
Loudoun County......................	28,480	88.9%	22,990	81.7%	14.3%	1.4%	1.2%	1.4%	28,537	71.9%	22.4%	2.8%	2.9%	0.0%
Montgomery County	6,734	90.8%	29,989	43.3%	46.2%	4.8%	5.2%	0.6%	7,418	79.1%	14.7%	4.9%	0.0%	1.3%
Prince William County..............	31,371	87.7%	37,966	77.2%	13.7%	4.6%	2.4%	2.0%	43,664	67.7%	24.0%	3.8%	2.3%	2.2%
Roanoke County......................	5,731	94.0%	8,101	78.1%	20.5%	0.9%	0.6%	0.0%	6,842	72.4%	25.4%	1.8%	0.4%	0.0%
Spotsylvania County	10,344	82.3%	11,918	88.5%	8.3%	2.9%	0.2%	0.0%	9,884	72.7%	24.1%	0.8%	0.0%	2.4%
Stafford County.......................	9,772	93.1%	16,747	66.4%	18.6%	7.2%	7.0%	0.8%	11,700	68.2%	20.7%	5.2%	3.4%	2.5%
Washington														
Benton County	14,605	85.3%	15,433	70.2%	25.3%	3.9%	0.2%	0.4%	16,029	71.9%	21.7%	3.3%	2.6%	0.5%
Clark County	30,646	88.7%	38,418	72.0%	19.6%	6.7%	1.7%	0.0%	36,785	67.0%	18.8%	7.5%	4.6%	2.1%
Cowlitz County	6,983	90.4%	8,540	62.2%	36.0%	1.8%	0.0%	0.0%	7,664	64.9%	28.6%	6.1%	0.3%	0.0%
Grant County	6,236	88.9%	11,733	60.7%	38.3%	0.6%	0.2%	0.2%	7,232	70.9%	18.0%	0.0%	11.0%	0.0%
King County	113,272	87.3%	177,207	61.6%	28.4%	3.9%	3.8%	2.3%	241,026	64.0%	26.8%	2.8%	4.3%	2.1%
Kitsap County..........................	15,581	83.4%	25,705	57.4%	30.3%	4.0%	8.1%	0.3%	23,899	70.1%	18.4%	4.8%	6.3%	0.4%
Pierce County	55,338	88.5%	79,988	65.6%	22.8%	4.4%	3.8%	3.4%	85,958	69.4%	21.6%	2.4%	5.0%	1.6%
Skagit County..........................	7,220	76.9%	11,075	74.7%	25.3%	0.0%	0.0%	0.0%	8,911	75.2%	20.8%	0.7%	3.3%	0.0%
Snohomish County	48,188	89.9%	64,845	73.4%	20.0%	3.0%	2.7%	0.9%	71,377	68.6%	26.3%	2.8%	2.3%	0.0%
Spokane County......................	32,408	90.1%	50,514	60.0%	30.9%	4.3%	3.7%	1.1%	50,622	74.3%	20.6%	2.0%	2.9%	0.2%
Thurston County	17,119	81.3%	24,463	67.5%	27.7%	2.7%	1.0%	1.2%	28,856	71.5%	17.6%	3.3%	4.2%	3.3%
Whatcom County	12,958	98.0%	31,693	69.9%	27.0%	2.5%	0.3%	0.3%	17,498	78.5%	17.0%	2.8%	1.0%	0.8%
Yakima County	18,411	89.9%	25,232	69.9%	28.7%	1.4%	0.0%	0.0%	22,351	73.6%	26.4%	0.0%	0.0%	0.0%
West Virginia														
Berkeley County......................	8,235	87.4%	9,880	68.7%	23.0%	4.4%	3.8%	0.0%	8,678	78.8%	7.7%	7.0%	6.5%	0.0%
Cabell County..........................	7,962	86.8%	10,375	64.3%	30.8%	1.1%	3.8%	0.0%	8,673	67.0%	28.9%	0.5%	1.9%	1.6%
Kanawha County	12,228	89.9%	15,818	77.3%	16.2%	1.0%	5.5%	0.0%	16,505	75.7%	20.2%	2.1%	1.9%	0.0%
Monongalia County..................	4,599	83.2%	23,460	63.9%	18.4%	5.7%	11.3%	0.6%	13,906	72.9%	20.5%	3.1%	2.8%	0.7%
Wisconsin														
Brown County	17,666	88.4%	23,708	67.2%	27.0%	3.8%	1.4%	0.5%	23,266	68.8%	29.3%	0.0%	1.6%	0.3%
Dane County	30,018	86.8%	64,801	48.7%	37.1%	7.0%	5.0%	2.2%	62,196	65.2%	28.1%	2.2%	2.5%	1.9%
Eau Claire County....................	6,195	93.6%	17,113	50.5%	40.9%	6.7%	1.7%	0.2%	10,648	67.0%	33.0%	0.0%	0.0%	0.0%
Fond du Lac County	8,056	94.1%	9,137	58.4%	37.8%	2.8%	0.0%	1.0%	5,672	71.6%	23.4%	5.0%	0.0%	0.0%

Table J-2: Counties—Mobility Status by Age—*Continued*

	13 to 17		18 to 24						25 to 31					
					Percent Living in a Different House						Percent Living in a Different House			
	Total Population	Percent Living in Same House	Total Population	Percent Living in Same House	Same State	Different State, Same Region	Different Region	Outside US	Total Population	Percent Living in Same House	Same State	Different State, Same Region	Different Region	Outside US
Wisconsin—Cont.														
Kenosha County.....................	12,019	93.0%	16,352	61.7%	26.4%	9.3%	1.6%	1.0%	14,366	77.5%	19.2%	1.8%	1.5%	0.0%
La Crosse County...................	7,672	96.5%	18,390	31.8%	64.4%	3.6%	0.0%	0.1%	11,836	57.7%	31.2%	3.0%	6.5%	1.5%
Marathon County	9,211	92.8%	11,313	65.6%	33.3%	0.3%	0.0%	0.8%	11,030	72.7%	27.0%	0.0%	0.2%	0.0%
Milwaukee County..................	61,747	87.4%	99,896	63.5%	31.7%	2.6%	1.6%	0.5%	114,068	71.5%	24.6%	1.3%	1.6%	0.9%
Outagamie County..................	10,595	90.4%	16,864	72.8%	26.1%	0.7%	0.0%	0.4%	17,397	63.2%	34.2%	0.6%	2.0%	0.0%
Racine County........................	14,948	95.3%	15,071	84.2%	15.8%	0.0%	0.0%	0.0%	18,360	83.3%	14.1%	1.4%	1.2%	0.0%
Rock County	12,012	92.2%	14,267	79.6%	13.2%	4.5%	1.3%	1.4%	13,455	81.2%	16.3%	0.0%	0.0%	2.5%
Sheboygan County.................	8,528	93.1%	8,049	78.0%	16.8%	5.3%	0.0%	0.0%	9,109	79.1%	18.8%	0.0%	2.1%	0.0%
Walworth County	6,980	88.0%	11,281	39.6%	57.4%	0.3%	2.8%	0.0%	8,854	71.8%	22.5%	0.8%	0.0%	4.9%
Washington County................	7,985	92.2%	11,187	71.4%	25.2%	3.4%	0.0%	0.0%	9,002	87.1%	12.5%	0.4%	0.0%	0.0%
Waukesha County	26,526	90.7%	30,739	79.3%	18.3%	0.9%	1.6%	0.0%	28,153	75.9%	17.3%	4.0%	2.1%	0.7%
Winnebago County..................	9,642	87.7%	20,693	68.5%	29.7%	1.1%	0.7%	0.0%	16,548	64.7%	31.4%	0.0%	3.9%	0.0%
Wyoming														
Laramie County......................	5,137	80.5%	12,437	46.5%	29.7%	12.0%	11.0%	0.8%	8,039	60.8%	22.9%	9.9%	6.0%	0.3%

Table J-3: Places—Mobility Status by Age

| | 13 to 17 | | 18 to 24 | | | | | | 25 to 31 | | | | | |
| | | | | | Percent Living in a Different House | | | | | | Percent Living in a Different House | | | |
	Total Population	Percent Living in Same House	Total Population	Percent Living in Same House	Same State	Different State, Same Region	Different Region	Outside US	Total Population	Percent Living in Same House	Same State	Different State, Same Region	Different Region	Outside US
Alabama														
Birmingham city	13,899	83.1%	24,818	62.8%	31.6%	2.6%	3.1%	0.0%	23,982	74.4%	22.7%	0.9%	0.1%	1.8%
Huntsville city	13,760	84.5%	19,366	69.6%	25.9%	2.1%	1.7%	0.7%	18,878	75.1%	23.4%	0.1%	1.5%	0.0%
Mobile city	11,666	91.9%	20,293	67.3%	29.3%	3.0%	0.3%	0.0%	20,214	70.8%	23.8%	1.7%	1.0%	2.7%
Montgomery city	13,270	71.3%	23,367	53.8%	38.7%	5.8%	1.5%	0.3%	22,357	68.6%	26.7%	1.8%	2.1%	0.8%
Tuscaloosa city	5,873	63.3%	23,953	46.3%	32.5%	15.5%	4.9%	0.8%	9,937	64.8%	27.7%	5.0%	1.6%	0.9%
Alaska														
Anchorage municipality	19,361	87.2%	34,074	63.8%	25.1%	5.2%	3.7%	2.1%	35,653	57.1%	30.2%	4.7%	6.6%	1.4%
Arizona														
Chandler city	18,302	87.7%	22,227	74.8%	18.1%	1.5%	5.1%	0.6%	25,427	63.4%	28.0%	2.7%	5.6%	0.3%
Glendale city	18,310	86.9%	22,520	71.7%	22.3%	1.9%	1.2%	2.8%	24,043	73.8%	19.4%	3.2%	1.3%	2.3%
Mesa city	31,497	80.3%	45,070	66.6%	28.7%	2.3%	1.1%	1.3%	47,737	70.4%	23.6%	2.4%	2.0%	1.6%
Peoria city	12,708	94.3%	12,190	87.5%	10.3%	2.1%	0.0%	0.1%	13,193	72.0%	23.4%	2.7%	1.4%	0.5%
Phoenix city	105,482	84.3%	154,915	70.4%	25.4%	2.2%	1.4%	0.5%	159,901	68.6%	25.1%	2.0%	3.3%	1.0%
Scottsdale city	14,768	79.1%	16,139	61.4%	26.2%	2.7%	8.8%	0.8%	19,062	57.4%	31.3%	1.5%	5.2%	4.6%
Surprise city	7,841	85.8%	6,025	66.7%	33.3%	0.0%	0.0%	0.0%	7,630	72.8%	21.5%	0.0%	5.7%	0.0%
Tempe city	11,967	81.5%	35,874	47.0%	42.5%	5.3%	3.0%	2.2%	26,666	56.2%	31.2%	3.1%	8.3%	1.2%
Tucson city	36,362	80.7%	76,603	55.3%	34.9%	3.2%	4.6%	1.9%	51,809	63.3%	30.2%	1.9%	3.5%	1.1%
Yuma city	6,871	97.1%	11,052	77.3%	12.9%	5.1%	3.8%	1.0%	9,945	73.9%	17.6%	3.9%	3.2%	1.4%
Arkansas														
Little Rock city	12,920	97.0%	16,118	84.7%	12.2%	3.0%	0.0%	0.0%	23,392	75.9%	20.5%	1.3%	1.7%	0.5%
California														
Anaheim city	23,186	83.7%	36,943	80.6%	15.9%	1.0%	2.1%	0.4%	35,851	73.8%	23.5%	0.8%	1.1%	0.7%
Antioch city	9,261	79.1%	12,180	68.7%	30.7%	0.0%	0.0%	0.7%	10,190	83.9%	16.1%	0.0%	0.0%	0.0%
Bakersfield city	28,392	85.2%	39,371	71.6%	23.6%	0.8%	1.3%	2.7%	39,901	73.7%	23.2%	0.0%	2.1%	1.0%
Berkeley city	5,136	79.1%	26,469	41.2%	46.1%	1.8%	3.7%	7.2%	17,350	58.1%	25.3%	1.3%	6.9%	8.4%
Burbank city	4,783	92.7%	6,721	68.4%	13.3%	0.0%	18.3%	0.1%	11,889	79.7%	13.9%	1.7%	4.7%	0.0%
Carlsbad city	6,142	95.1%	7,319	92.4%	4.9%	2.8%	0.0%	0.0%	9,394	79.0%	17.2%	0.0%	3.1%	0.7%
Carson city	5,110	75.5%	10,757	81.3%	14.8%	1.8%	0.4%	1.7%	9,644	83.2%	13.6%	0.0%	2.0%	1.2%
Chula Vista city	20,122	90.3%	27,506	83.7%	12.9%	0.6%	0.2%	2.6%	23,755	82.1%	10.9%	1.0%	5.2%	0.8%
Clovis city	6,764	85.2%	11,520	84.6%	14.4%	0.4%	0.6%	0.0%	8,626	74.4%	21.8%	0.0%	3.9%	0.0%
Compton city	8,128	94.4%	10,355	90.7%	6.6%	0.0%	1.3%	1.3%	10,546	88.4%	9.4%	2.2%	0.0%	0.0%
Concord city	8,257	90.7%	10,951	71.6%	25.2%	1.0%	2.1%	0.0%	12,517	65.1%	33.8%	0.0%	0.5%	0.5%
Corona city	12,434	93.6%	16,818	91.6%	8.4%	0.0%	0.0%	0.0%	16,761	80.0%	17.8%	0.5%	1.7%	0.0%
Costa Mesa city	6,774	83.5%	10,818	70.5%	24.4%	1.7%	3.3%	0.0%	16,113	65.8%	28.4%	3.0%	0.0%	2.8%
Daly City city	6,466	73.9%	11,075	79.5%	18.9%	0.0%	1.6%	0.0%	12,536	88.1%	9.7%	0.8%	0.8%	0.7%
Downey city	7,627	89.4%	15,873	91.6%	7.6%	0.0%	0.0%	0.8%	11,971	84.6%	14.5%	0.0%	0.0%	0.9%
El Cajon city	5,117	92.2%	12,830	74.0%	19.8%	0.0%	3.1%	3.1%	12,072	64.6%	28.3%	0.0%	3.8%	3.3%
El Monte city	8,408	96.2%	11,284	95.5%	4.5%	0.0%	0.0%	0.0%	11,210	94.6%	4.2%	0.0%	0.0%	1.1%
Elk Grove city	18,155	82.5%	13,742	77.7%	21.2%	1.1%	0.0%	0.0%	10,251	76.4%	23.6%	0.0%	0.0%	0.0%
Escondido city	10,612	77.9%	16,403	70.4%	28.5%	0.7%	0.5%	0.0%	17,091	83.6%	15.8%	0.6%	0.0%	0.0%
Fairfield city	7,655	73.5%	13,826	80.8%	17.1%	0.5%	1.7%	0.0%	12,854	65.6%	25.3%	0.0%	7.3%	1.8%
Fontana city	19,050	85.5%	22,450	82.9%	16.7%	0.0%	0.0%	0.4%	18,971	89.1%	9.0%	1.9%	0.0%	0.0%
Fremont city	13,227	97.1%	16,568	86.0%	12.8%	0.0%	0.0%	1.2%	21,994	73.0%	22.7%	0.5%	0.8%	2.9%
Fresno city	36,152	85.0%	57,906	72.7%	26.1%	0.2%	0.5%	0.5%	56,907	72.6%	26.1%	0.6%	0.1%	0.5%
Fullerton city	10,742	80.8%	16,518	68.6%	25.0%	0.8%	1.1%	4.5%	17,289	73.0%	23.4%	0.0%	3.6%	0.0%
Garden Grove city	11,020	90.8%	18,446	83.0%	16.0%	0.3%	0.3%	0.4%	16,769	85.3%	13.2%	0.0%	0.0%	1.5%
Glendale city	9,459	90.1%	14,944	81.6%	11.6%	0.0%	2.0%	4.7%	22,833	76.4%	16.7%	0.0%	5.9%	1.0%
Hayward city	7,885	93.3%	15,875	77.6%	18.1%	0.0%	1.0%	3.3%	18,422	80.0%	17.8%	0.0%	0.9%	1.3%
Hesperia city	15,319	80.1%	19,216	74.9%	24.2%	0.0%	0.5%	0.4%	21,407	80.9%	18.1%	0.4%	0.3%	0.4%
Inglewood city	6,819	85.9%	11,099	82.5%	17.5%	0.0%	0.0%	0.0%	13,468	83.7%	15.6%	0.0%	0.7%	0.0%
Irvine city	14,623	85.9%	30,544	64.5%	30.3%	1.3%	2.3%	1.6%	25,569	66.0%	27.3%	1.9%	1.8%	3.1%
Jurupa Valley city	9,260	90.1%	10,455	84.7%	8.1%	0.0%	0.0%	7.2%	10,081	71.0%	27.2%	0.6%	0.0%	1.2%
Lancaster city	13,212	89.0%	16,534	90.0%	10.0%	0.0%	0.0%	0.0%	14,910	81.6%	15.9%	1.3%	0.5%	0.6%
Long Beach city	31,717	91.2%	49,447	80.5%	17.7%	0.7%	0.0%	1.1%	51,100	76.7%	22.1%	0.1%	1.1%	0.0%
Los Angeles city	232,150	89.8%	414,272	72.9%	21.2%	1.0%	2.8%	2.0%	459,387	75.7%	19.6%	0.8%	2.4%	1.4%
Mission Viejo city	7,600	96.1%	8,995	81.1%	15.9%	0.0%	3.0%	0.0%	4,425	67.3%	30.6%	0.0%	0.0%	2.1%
Modesto city	16,645	85.1%	22,619	69.2%	30.6%	0.2%	0.0%	0.0%	20,567	66.7%	31.9%	0.8%	0.0%	0.7%
Moreno Valley city	17,136	85.2%	22,518	80.7%	19.0%	0.3%	0.0%	0.0%	25,384	81.6%	16.0%	0.3%	0.6%	1.5%
Murrieta city	10,866	87.2%	9,771	84.1%	15.9%	0.0%	0.0%	0.0%	8,639	69.0%	28.3%	0.0%	1.0%	1.6%
Norwalk city	8,233	94.8%	12,390	92.5%	5.4%	0.0%	1.0%	1.1%	9,029	88.7%	11.3%	0.0%	0.0%	0.0%
Oakland city	21,442	88.5%	34,793	74.1%	18.8%	0.7%	2.7%	3.7%	50,604	69.5%	24.2%	2.3%	2.2%	1.7%
Oceanside city	6,636	97.6%	21,035	59.8%	18.6%	1.9%	14.6%	5.0%	16,680	73.5%	13.2%	5.2%	6.0%	2.1%
Ontario city	13,368	89.9%	18,592	86.2%	13.8%	0.0%	0.0%	0.0%	16,521	82.3%	15.9%	0.0%	0.0%	1.8%
Orange city	10,644	85.7%	15,291	74.0%	18.7%	5.0%	1.2%	1.1%	14,649	83.1%	16.9%	0.0%	0.0%	0.0%
Oxnard city	16,353	85.6%	25,335	82.0%	9.4%	5.1%	1.9%	1.7%	21,677	85.6%	11.3%	1.6%	1.0%	0.5%
Palmdale city	15,050	87.6%	16,777	89.5%	8.2%	0.0%	1.8%	0.5%	13,322	76.1%	22.7%	1.2%	0.0%	0.0%
Pasadena city	6,467	90.9%	13,797	68.1%	22.0%	1.8%	5.3%	2.7%	20,602	64.6%	31.1%	0.1%	2.7%	1.5%
Pomona city	9,893	84.5%	21,042	75.4%	21.9%	0.5%	0.5%	1.6%	16,663	84.5%	14.0%	0.0%	0.9%	0.6%
Rancho Cucamonga city	14,183	88.3%	18,570	72.8%	21.7%	0.0%	1.8%	3.6%	15,343	73.2%	26.2%	0.0%	0.5%	0.0%
Redding city	5,931	91.5%	9,543	57.1%	36.3%	2.6%	2.3%	1.8%	9,166	73.6%	18.5%	3.6%	2.0%	2.2%
Rialto city	8,699	86.4%	12,998	75.2%	20.8%	2.9%	0.0%	1.1%	9,236	80.1%	19.4%	0.0%	0.0%	0.5%
Richmond city	6,121	87.2%	10,767	73.7%	17.3%	2.6%	1.2%	5.2%	13,277	83.0%	14.7%	0.0%	1.0%	1.3%

Table J-3: Places—Mobility Status by Age—*Continued*

| | 13 to 17 | | 18 to 24 | | | | | | 25 to 31 | | | | | |
| | | | | | Percent Living in a Different House | | | | | | Percent Living in a Different House | | | |
	Total Population	Percent Living in Same House	Total Population	Percent Living in Same House	Same State	Different State, Same Region	Different Region	Outside US	Total Population	Percent Living in Same House	Same State	Different State, Same Region	Different Region	Outside US
California—Cont.														
Riverside city	21,974	89.2%	49,495	75.8%	23.1%	0.4%	0.2%	0.5%	28,679	76.4%	21.9%	0.0%	0.8%	0.9%
Roseville city	9,540	92.8%	9,740	71.0%	25.4%	1.8%	1.9%	0.0%	12,927	74.4%	23.8%	1.5%	0.3%	0.0%
Sacramento city	30,668	82.1%	49,576	66.1%	30.9%	0.7%	0.5%	1.7%	54,203	62.2%	34.5%	0.7%	1.7%	0.8%
Salinas city	12,910	93.1%	18,628	87.8%	10.9%	0.0%	0.3%	1.0%	15,866	87.2%	10.8%	1.0%	1.0%	0.0%
San Bernardino city	17,350	79.8%	28,852	78.9%	16.0%	2.2%	1.3%	1.6%	20,883	69.9%	24.5%	3.2%	2.4%	0.0%
San Buenaventura (Ventura) city	6,004	86.9%	10,980	81.2%	17.9%	0.0%	0.0%	0.8%	11,094	76.1%	19.9%	0.0%	1.8%	2.2%
San Diego city	78,041	88.0%	156,541	68.1%	23.1%	1.5%	4.8%	2.5%	178,234	70.1%	22.2%	1.3%	3.8%	2.7%
San Francisco city	24,561	93.8%	62,062	57.7%	31.6%	1.8%	4.3%	4.5%	129,957	69.7%	20.9%	1.6%	5.0%	2.8%
San Jose city	59,825	91.7%	85,425	74.9%	22.0%	0.8%	0.7%	1.6%	105,249	76.3%	19.9%	0.7%	1.5%	1.7%
San Mateo city	5,472	87.7%	6,413	75.2%	18.9%	3.8%	0.0%	2.0%	9,364	59.4%	36.3%	0.0%	3.7%	0.6%
Santa Ana city	25,400	93.1%	40,982	86.1%	12.1%	0.7%	0.2%	1.0%	37,965	82.4%	15.9%	0.0%	0.1%	1.6%
Santa Clara city	4,554	89.1%	12,714	51.2%	34.0%	0.5%	4.1%	10.2%	18,020	60.3%	26.2%	0.0%	6.9%	6.7%
Santa Clarita city	13,653	87.4%	16,200	70.6%	24.4%	0.0%	3.6%	1.4%	16,170	69.6%	27.7%	0.3%	1.8%	0.6%
Santa Maria city	10,972	88.0%	11,107	74.1%	17.7%	0.0%	0.0%	8.2%	9,634	69.5%	21.5%	6.1%	0.0%	3.0%
Santa Monica city	3,737	100.0%	5,131	50.1%	40.0%	0.0%	7.0%	2.9%	12,786	63.1%	29.9%	0.0%	6.5%	0.5%
Santa Rosa city	12,740	85.9%	15,177	76.9%	22.3%	0.0%	0.8%	0.0%	17,790	72.1%	23.0%	0.6%	4.3%	0.0%
Simi Valley city	8,782	96.2%	10,104	89.6%	8.3%	1.6%	0.5%	0.0%	9,416	81.8%	13.8%	2.7%	1.6%	0.0%
South Gate city	7,663	96.8%	10,170	89.3%	10.7%	0.0%	0.0%	0.0%	12,129	88.8%	10.4%	0.8%	0.0%	0.0%
Stockton city	22,258	82.8%	33,029	67.0%	31.9%	0.5%	0.5%	0.1%	27,866	74.2%	25.8%	0.0%	0.0%	0.0%
Sunnyvale city	6,404	98.5%	9,863	64.7%	29.7%	2.1%	1.2%	2.3%	19,311	65.2%	20.8%	0.5%	5.9%	7.7%
Temecula city	11,539	82.5%	12,331	79.6%	12.7%	4.8%	2.9%	0.0%	7,345	61.2%	23.6%	3.3%	0.0%	12.0%
Thousand Oaks city	8,631	87.8%	12,516	77.9%	21.3%	0.0%	0.5%	0.3%	9,254	67.3%	20.6%	0.0%	7.1%	5.0%
Torrance city	8,662	83.1%	12,260	76.7%	18.4%	2.3%	0.9%	1.7%	10,105	65.0%	22.7%	2.5%	1.3%	8.5%
Vacaville city	6,745	85.1%	9,594	77.9%	20.5%	0.0%	1.6%	0.0%	9,405	84.4%	13.9%	0.0%	1.0%	0.8%
Vallejo city	7,997	97.6%	11,369	74.9%	20.3%	1.9%	0.0%	2.9%	11,856	75.1%	21.4%	0.0%	3.5%	0.0%
Victorville city	8,289	91.8%	13,437	87.1%	10.3%	1.6%	0.9%	0.0%	12,353	73.3%	22.5%	1.8%	1.5%	0.8%
Visalia city	8,950	85.0%	14,451	74.2%	20.1%	0.0%	5.7%	0.0%	14,393	76.6%	21.9%	0.2%	1.3%	0.0%
Vista city	4,332	86.1%	12,213	84.2%	12.3%	1.1%	2.3%	0.0%	12,024	82.4%	14.6%	0.0%	3.0%	0.0%
West Covina city	7,801	88.1%	11,275	86.0%	13.5%	0.0%	0.5%	0.0%	12,251	84.9%	11.2%	0.0%	2.3%	1.6%
Westminster city	6,620	90.1%	6,793	84.3%	15.0%	0.8%	0.0%	0.0%	10,033	75.0%	17.8%	3.0%	2.7%	1.4%
Colorado														
Arvada city	9,383	91.5%	9,441	60.8%	36.5%	0.9%	0.0%	1.8%	9,903	66.2%	27.0%	2.4%	4.3%	0.0%
Aurora city	24,916	77.5%	31,521	68.7%	24.7%	1.6%	3.5%	1.4%	35,520	66.8%	28.2%	1.4%	3.0%	0.6%
Boulder city	5,359	87.6%	29,961	28.1%	52.5%	6.0%	11.8%	1.6%	12,008	49.3%	32.4%	2.4%	13.6%	2.3%
Centennial city	8,965	91.4%	7,068	80.2%	15.2%	3.6%	0.9%	0.0%	8,768	57.5%	32.3%	1.8%	6.3%	2.2%
Colorado Springs city	29,007	86.5%	45,636	55.7%	31.8%	2.7%	7.9%	1.9%	46,805	61.5%	27.8%	1.1%	7.0%	2.6%
Denver city	27,684	89.6%	58,403	55.4%	33.2%	3.3%	7.1%	1.1%	96,430	64.5%	26.2%	2.4%	6.5%	0.5%
Fort Collins city	11,622	89.3%	32,540	40.4%	47.1%	3.3%	7.0%	2.1%	15,954	57.1%	26.7%	4.1%	9.1%	3.0%
Greeley city	7,448	72.7%	13,727	47.2%	45.1%	1.5%	5.7%	0.5%	12,038	63.5%	30.1%	3.1%	2.6%	0.6%
Lakewood city	7,538	92.5%	13,949	67.2%	23.7%	2.9%	3.8%	2.4%	14,372	68.6%	23.5%	1.8%	5.3%	0.8%
Pueblo city	7,372	85.7%	11,131	59.5%	33.0%	0.3%	6.4%	0.7%	9,895	60.8%	27.2%	0.0%	9.5%	2.4%
Thornton city	12,083	85.5%	12,131	60.5%	29.1%	2.8%	4.6%	3.0%	10,191	81.6%	12.9%	0.2%	5.2%	0.0%
Westminster city	8,578	96.6%	9,091	66.8%	22.3%	7.4%	3.5%	0.0%	13,432	64.9%	26.8%	4.3%	4.0%	0.0%
Connecticut														
Bridgeport city	8,781	81.5%	15,330	74.8%	15.4%	2.9%	0.7%	6.1%	19,266	76.5%	11.9%	4.5%	1.2%	5.8%
Hartford city	8,558	80.4%	17,926	55.9%	29.1%	8.0%	5.2%	1.8%	14,342	77.6%	20.3%	0.0%	0.6%	1.5%
New Haven city	6,843	83.4%	21,287	78.4%	16.1%	2.0%	1.9%	1.6%	17,272	75.9%	14.5%	4.4%	1.6%	3.5%
Stamford city	7,752	97.6%	12,181	84.3%	8.1%	4.8%	1.2%	1.6%	13,874	65.1%	20.3%	7.1%	3.9%	3.7%
Waterbury city	6,658	86.8%	10,499	80.8%	8.9%	4.7%	5.6%	0.0%	12,596	63.2%	28.3%	5.1%	3.3%	0.0%
District of Columbia														
Washington city	23,448	86.0%	75,399	56.0%	18.8%	8.2%	13.7%	3.4%	102,748	71.6%	13.5%	7.9%	4.3%	2.7%
Florida														
Cape Coral city	10,806	87.9%	12,044	84.6%	13.4%	0.0%	0.7%	1.3%	13,598	66.2%	23.4%	2.1%	6.2%	2.1%
Clearwater city	5,523	94.0%	8,279	49.7%	33.9%	0.0%	16.3%	0.0%	9,599	63.7%	24.0%	2.2%	6.8%	3.2%
Coral Springs city	8,687	79.9%	13,970	76.7%	19.2%	0.5%	1.7%	1.8%	9,869	72.5%	20.8%	0.0%	5.7%	1.0%
Fort Lauderdale city	8,570	80.0%	15,103	61.2%	33.3%	1.2%	3.2%	1.1%	15,087	63.6%	32.0%	0.0%	4.4%	0.0%
Gainesville city	4,051	74.8%	43,021	49.6%	45.0%	1.9%	0.7%	2.8%	17,628	57.7%	35.8%	2.8%	1.2%	2.5%
Hialeah city	14,554	91.5%	20,256	89.7%	7.4%	0.0%	0.6%	2.3%	20,322	87.0%	7.2%	0.9%	0.0%	4.9%
Hollywood city	8,007	81.1%	11,122	88.0%	10.6%	0.0%	1.5%	0.0%	11,697	65.7%	30.9%	2.9%	0.0%	0.5%
Jacksonville city	49,164	82.5%	80,071	69.0%	23.4%	5.4%	1.9%	0.3%	94,016	63.9%	30.9%	2.1%	3.0%	0.2%
Lakeland city	6,754	82.6%	11,043	83.4%	11.0%	2.1%	1.7%	1.8%	8,446	82.9%	9.8%	6.1%	1.1%	0.0%
Miami Beach city	5,105	88.1%	6,216	67.5%	20.2%	4.2%	3.2%	4.8%	8,798	54.2%	31.7%	3.6%	5.4%	5.2%
Miami city	18,402	89.7%	34,280	78.0%	14.9%	0.7%	4.2%	2.2%	47,133	71.9%	21.4%	0.5%	4.5%	1.6%
Miami Gardens city	6,910	92.4%	13,952	80.6%	16.4%	0.0%	3.0%	0.0%	11,328	89.4%	8.6%	0.9%	1.1%	0.0%
Miramar city	6,517	87.3%	12,626	83.1%	16.9%	0.0%	0.0%	0.0%	17,992	70.4%	27.4%	0.4%	0.0%	1.8%
Orlando city	17,769	64.8%	25,196	69.1%	25.7%	1.7%	1.7%	1.8%	36,308	64.7%	29.9%	1.6%	0.9%	2.9%
Palm Bay city	6,369	93.9%	9,200	88.7%	10.0%	0.0%	1.3%	0.0%	8,128	80.2%	17.4%	2.4%	0.0%	0.0%
Pembroke Pines city	10,823	85.6%	14,893	94.4%	4.8%	0.0%	0.8%	0.0%	14,510	79.5%	19.2%	1.4%	0.0%	0.0%
Pompano Beach city	8,091	80.5%	7,215	75.8%	23.0%	0.0%	0.0%	1.2%	10,241	68.5%	16.2%	1.4%	9.1%	4.8%
Port St. Lucie city	14,965	85.9%	13,266	77.8%	19.1%	0.0%	3.2%	0.0%	10,425	67.8%	26.4%	0.7%	3.5%	1.5%
St. Petersburg city	13,662	82.3%	21,540	71.8%	22.9%	3.0%	2.3%	0.0%	24,997	70.2%	25.0%	1.8%	2.4%	0.5%
Tallahassee city	10,982	80.4%	52,303	49.6%	46.5%	1.6%	1.8%	0.5%	23,034	60.9%	32.6%	2.7%	3.2%	0.6%

Table J-3: Places—Mobility Status by Age—*Continued*

	13 to 17		18 to 24						25 to 31					
					Percent Living in a Different House						Percent Living in a Different House			
	Total Population	Percent Living in Same House	Total Population	Percent Living in Same House	Same State	Different State, Same Region	Different Region	Outside US	Total Population	Percent Living in Same House	Same State	Different State, Same Region	Different Region	Outside US
Florida—Cont.														
Tampa city	20,286	81.9%	42,412	60.4%	30.3%	1.1%	6.5%	1.8%	41,641	73.0%	22.1%	2.1%	1.5%	1.3%
West Palm Beach city	5,269	81.6%	10,514	63.1%	27.6%	1.2%	6.9%	1.2%	13,268	75.8%	15.9%	3.1%	3.7%	1.5%
Georgia														
Athens-Clarke County unified govt (bal)	4,249	84.4%	36,028	51.9%	43.4%	3.3%	0.8%	0.6%	13,785	68.3%	21.8%	2.4%	3.5%	4.0%
Atlanta city	19,055	83.2%	61,305	59.0%	31.2%	1.8%	5.1%	2.9%	62,935	70.4%	23.0%	2.1%	3.4%	1.0%
Augusta-Richmond County consolidated govt (bal)	12,556	89.2%	21,555	65.2%	25.0%	5.4%	4.4%	0.0%	23,346	73.7%	19.3%	3.2%	2.5%	1.1%
Columbus city	12,803	78.0%	24,790	39.9%	28.8%	11.3%	17.7%	2.3%	20,537	56.7%	24.5%	7.6%	7.0%	4.2%
Macon city	6,372	66.1%	11,218	74.5%	18.7%	4.6%	1.7%	0.5%	9,242	84.5%	12.4%	0.6%	0.0%	2.5%
Roswell city	6,632	79.7%	8,294	77.1%	20.3%	0.0%	0.0%	2.7%	8,569	69.4%	25.8%	1.7%	0.5%	2.5%
Sandy Springs city	5,499	89.7%	4,983	75.6%	15.4%	9.0%	0.0%	0.0%	14,815	76.0%	19.2%	0.0%	4.5%	0.4%
Savannah city	7,282	89.2%	20,003	56.5%	28.2%	9.3%	3.6%	2.4%	17,750	70.1%	17.8%	1.7%	6.0%	4.4%
Hawaii														
Urban Honolulu CDP	18,889	89.6%	31,461	72.9%	16.7%	5.4%	3.1%	1.9%	37,505	74.3%	14.4%	4.0%	4.1%	3.3%
Idaho														
Boise City city	15,322	86.3%	23,692	46.4%	39.2%	10.3%	2.9%	1.2%	23,021	67.8%	22.5%	7.9%	0.5%	1.4%
Illinois														
Aurora city	14,448	86.9%	17,229	70.8%	23.3%	0.6%	0.7%	4.7%	21,072	77.0%	18.9%	1.5%	1.0%	1.5%
Chicago city	155,567	86.8%	281,204	72.9%	18.5%	3.0%	3.4%	2.2%	357,011	72.2%	21.2%	2.0%	3.1%	1.4%
Elgin city	7,963	91.8%	12,274	86.5%	12.9%	0.6%	0.0%	0.0%	11,373	88.7%	9.9%	1.0%	0.0%	0.4%
Joliet city	10,942	80.3%	15,649	78.6%	21.4%	0.0%	0.0%	0.0%	14,193	76.1%	20.6%	0.0%	3.3%	0.0%
Naperville city	12,006	92.2%	11,662	76.8%	17.9%	1.5%	2.6%	1.1%	12,789	71.3%	23.3%	0.0%	3.5%	1.9%
Peoria city	6,867	96.2%	13,512	69.0%	27.4%	3.5%	0.2%	0.0%	13,213	75.6%	16.2%	6.5%	1.7%	0.0%
Rockford city	11,191	80.5%	15,357	72.3%	26.9%	0.4%	0.4%	0.0%	13,747	64.3%	29.0%	2.0%	3.8%	0.8%
Springfield city	6,652	83.9%	11,506	73.2%	21.3%	0.8%	4.4%	0.4%	11,973	75.3%	14.0%	0.7%	9.0%	1.0%
Indiana														
Evansville city	6,633	85.4%	13,002	76.0%	20.5%	2.5%	0.2%	0.7%	11,110	82.6%	15.6%	0.0%	1.8%	0.0%
Fort Wayne city	17,031	87.0%	24,853	62.3%	31.8%	4.0%	1.9%	0.0%	25,279	66.6%	30.7%	2.3%	0.4%	0.0%
Indianapolis city (bal)	50,763	85.9%	82,156	71.4%	23.6%	1.7%	2.1%	1.1%	98,908	70.9%	23.5%	1.6%	3.6%	0.5%
South Bend city	6,461	67.3%	12,876	63.3%	20.3%	8.7%	6.6%	1.1%	8,282	64.9%	23.7%	5.6%	3.7%	2.1%
Iowa														
Cedar Rapids city	9,113	97.9%	11,166	73.1%	26.9%	0.0%	0.0%	0.0%	14,360	71.0%	20.8%	6.3%	1.0%	0.9%
Davenport city	6,652	93.6%	9,550	75.9%	17.8%	4.7%	1.6%	0.0%	10,268	76.9%	16.9%	6.2%	0.0%	0.0%
Des Moines city	10,741	81.2%	19,910	52.5%	39.6%	3.7%	2.6%	1.6%	26,312	67.8%	20.6%	4.9%	5.4%	1.3%
Kansas														
Kansas City city	10,777	76.8%	14,343	76.4%	15.2%	5.3%	3.0%	0.0%	14,219	79.3%	18.5%	1.0%	0.8%	0.4%
Olathe city	9,513	85.1%	11,796	68.1%	24.2%	3.9%	3.8%	0.0%	11,482	69.6%	24.6%	1.9%	3.8%	0.0%
Overland Park city	14,789	85.7%	13,831	63.8%	24.8%	8.1%	3.2%	0.0%	17,248	61.7%	27.7%	5.2%	3.7%	1.7%
Topeka city	7,891	74.6%	13,574	70.6%	25.9%	1.5%	1.9%	0.1%	11,068	79.3%	13.4%	6.3%	0.9%	0.0%
Wichita city	29,488	85.6%	35,181	73.2%	22.0%	0.7%	2.8%	1.4%	41,249	74.3%	18.8%	0.6%	6.0%	0.3%
Kentucky														
Lexington-Fayette urban county	15,950	75.9%	42,981	41.6%	49.0%	2.2%	6.7%	0.4%	32,524	63.4%	28.1%	3.4%	1.9%	3.3%
Louisville/Jefferson County metro govt (bal)	39,634	86.1%	55,865	71.1%	22.2%	2.2%	3.0%	1.4%	59,656	71.1%	25.5%	1.3%	0.3%	1.7%
Louisiana														
Baton Rouge city	13,155	91.2%	42,340	70.4%	23.5%	4.6%	1.4%	0.1%	25,399	69.1%	25.4%	1.8%	1.3%	2.4%
Lafayette city	9,071	92.3%	16,123	72.6%	16.8%	2.5%	4.1%	4.0%	15,819	72.0%	24.7%	1.8%	1.6%	0.0%
New Orleans city	18,610	87.3%	40,095	68.6%	21.0%	4.8%	4.4%	1.3%	48,879	72.2%	20.1%	4.1%	3.1%	0.5%
Shreveport city	13,881	80.3%	22,368	84.0%	13.3%	2.0%	0.0%	0.7%	20,225	79.7%	17.2%	1.3%	0.6%	1.1%
Maryland														
Baltimore city	29,538	79.8%	66,366	67.3%	25.1%	2.2%	4.8%	0.6%	81,284	68.2%	24.5%	2.3%	3.1%	1.9%
Massachusetts														
Boston city	30,568	84.4%	93,252	60.1%	24.7%	6.1%	5.9%	3.2%	109,618	68.9%	23.1%	2.6%	3.0%	2.4%
Brockton city	6,446	91.7%	7,019	88.9%	9.7%	0.0%	0.0%	1.4%	11,658	79.2%	19.2%	1.6%	0.0%	0.0%
Cambridge city	3,640	83.5%	21,135	61.5%	21.7%	6.7%	7.9%	2.2%	20,406	56.9%	25.4%	1.7%	7.2%	8.9%
Lowell city	7,272	82.7%	13,159	58.4%	37.7%	0.8%	2.2%	1.0%	12,922	72.2%	18.4%	7.7%	0.0%	1.8%
Lynn city	5,551	82.6%	8,255	86.4%	13.6%	0.0%	0.0%	0.0%	8,758	73.6%	24.5%	0.0%	0.0%	1.9%
New Bedford city	6,054	95.2%	8,700	81.2%	15.0%	3.1%	0.0%	0.6%	10,265	70.8%	24.8%	4.0%	0.5%	0.0%
Springfield city	12,077	80.1%	19,946	74.7%	19.9%	2.8%	1.7%	0.8%	14,450	79.7%	18.1%	0.5%	0.0%	1.8%
Worcester city	11,319	83.4%	25,113	63.2%	28.0%	5.5%	2.4%	1.0%	20,129	75.1%	19.5%	2.2%	0.8%	2.5%
Michigan														
Ann Arbor city	4,021	91.9%	35,322	29.9%	52.4%	5.0%	10.5%	2.2%	13,009	53.4%	29.4%	3.8%	5.9%	7.5%
Dearborn city	7,181	88.6%	11,174	89.6%	10.4%	0.0%	0.0%	0.0%	8,875	71.6%	20.3%	5.4%	2.8%	0.0%
Detroit city	47,250	83.9%	82,750	77.0%	21.4%	0.1%	1.1%	0.4%	58,753	77.7%	19.9%	0.4%	1.6%	0.5%
Flint city	7,032	81.4%	6,592	61.0%	39.0%	0.0%	0.0%	0.0%	11,304	68.0%	30.1%	0.0%	2.0%	0.0%
Grand Rapids city	10,731	76.5%	22,957	50.2%	39.9%	1.9%	7.3%	0.6%	25,469	67.4%	29.1%	1.1%	2.4%	0.0%
Lansing city	5,727	85.7%	14,224	52.1%	45.4%	2.4%	0.0%	0.0%	15,512	69.5%	27.9%	0.0%	2.1%	0.5%

Table J-3: Places—Mobility Status by Age—*Continued*

| | 13 to 17 | | 18 to 24 | | | | | | 25 to 31 | | | | | |
| | | | | | Percent Living in a Different House | | | | | | Percent Living in a Different House | | | |
	Total Population	Percent Living in Same House	Total Population	Percent Living in Same House	Same State	Different State, Same Region	Different Region	Outside US	Total Population	Percent Living in Same House	Same State	Different State, Same Region	Different Region	Outside US
Michigan—Cont.														
Livonia city	6,151	93.3%	7,551	78.5%	18.2%	1.0%	2.3%	0.0%	7,554	63.8%	32.0%	0.0%	0.9%	3.2%
Sterling Heights city	8,168	88.0%	9,328	79.7%	20.3%	0.0%	0.0%	0.0%	10,488	84.5%	12.9%	0.0%	0.0%	2.6%
Warren city	6,537	79.7%	13,462	82.8%	13.4%	0.5%	0.0%	3.3%	13,278	66.7%	30.6%	0.0%	0.0%	2.7%
Minnesota														
Minneapolis city	16,951	79.4%	50,657	44.5%	42.9%	6.8%	3.8%	1.9%	66,958	64.1%	25.9%	4.6%	3.3%	2.1%
Rochester city	6,253	93.3%	10,278	73.7%	20.1%	6.3%	0.0%	0.0%	10,331	78.5%	15.4%	1.4%	1.5%	3.2%
St. Paul city	18,717	88.3%	35,185	69.0%	21.9%	4.7%	1.5%	3.0%	36,656	59.9%	31.7%	3.3%	2.2%	2.8%
Mississippi														
Jackson city	11,334	79.4%	21,229	69.4%	27.0%	1.9%	1.1%	0.6%	19,681	78.2%	16.7%	1.6%	3.4%	0.1%
Missouri														
Columbia city	7,104	92.7%	28,006	49.3%	36.1%	8.9%	5.0%	0.7%	16,810	60.1%	30.0%	6.0%	2.3%	1.5%
Independence city	7,908	86.4%	10,039	82.6%	15.2%	1.2%	0.9%	0.0%	8,920	84.1%	15.9%	0.0%	0.0%	0.0%
Kansas City city	28,430	83.6%	46,153	60.9%	29.9%	7.0%	1.6%	0.7%	58,617	64.7%	27.5%	4.8%	2.8%	0.2%
Lee's Summit city	8,398	97.0%	5,779	71.2%	26.3%	1.8%	0.8%	0.0%	8,090	84.0%	16.0%	0.0%	0.0%	0.0%
Springfield city	9,578	89.2%	27,960	62.3%	34.5%	0.3%	2.9%	0.0%	20,876	75.2%	21.1%	1.1%	2.6%	0.0%
St. Louis city	15,920	88.6%	31,990	62.9%	29.6%	4.0%	2.9%	0.6%	44,419	67.2%	24.9%	2.5%	3.4%	1.9%
Montana														
Billings city	6,438	63.1%	12,115	51.0%	31.9%	9.6%	4.1%	3.4%	9,279	60.6%	29.0%	1.4%	9.1%	0.0%
Nebraska														
Lincoln city	15,690	92.3%	39,030	52.9%	39.9%	2.7%	3.0%	1.4%	28,205	65.0%	29.3%	1.1%	4.5%	0.0%
Omaha city	27,454	89.2%	41,799	63.2%	28.5%	4.6%	3.1%	0.6%	48,253	72.4%	22.5%	1.3%	2.5%	1.4%
Nevada														
Henderson city	15,235	80.4%	21,476	71.9%	18.5%	8.3%	0.8%	0.5%	22,921	75.5%	20.5%	2.9%	1.0%	0.0%
Las Vegas city	41,666	79.8%	51,928	68.1%	26.1%	3.9%	1.1%	0.8%	59,192	64.4%	29.1%	3.8%	2.0%	0.7%
North Las Vegas city	18,438	77.3%	22,742	65.9%	24.4%	5.4%	4.3%	0.0%	26,289	60.0%	32.1%	3.4%	2.2%	2.3%
Reno city	14,578	75.6%	27,486	48.2%	35.5%	14.0%	1.2%	1.1%	25,859	68.0%	24.3%	3.6%	1.9%	2.2%
Sparks city	5,092	87.3%	8,659	66.7%	20.8%	9.9%	2.7%	0.0%	8,481	74.9%	17.8%	4.5%	1.6%	1.2%
New Hampshire														
Manchester city	5,627	76.4%	11,409	63.6%	24.8%	5.8%	3.3%	2.6%	13,147	54.3%	35.1%	5.7%	1.3%	3.7%
New Jersey														
Elizabeth city	8,550	85.2%	13,165	81.6%	14.3%	0.0%	2.2%	1.8%	15,640	81.3%	18.1%	0.0%	0.6%	0.0%
Jersey City city	12,868	91.4%	22,404	86.1%	5.9%	1.6%	0.4%	5.9%	38,721	71.1%	15.0%	6.4%	2.5%	5.1%
Newark city	16,673	82.4%	29,094	81.7%	12.5%	2.0%	3.0%	0.9%	36,097	79.5%	16.0%	1.0%	2.5%	1.0%
Paterson city	10,214	90.9%	17,606	94.0%	4.0%	0.0%	0.0%	2.0%	14,156	85.1%	10.8%	1.9%	0.0%	2.3%
New Mexico														
Albuquerque city	33,796	87.6%	58,842	68.8%	24.1%	2.6%	2.6%	1.9%	54,748	71.6%	21.7%	1.7%	3.5%	1.5%
Las Cruces city	6,347	83.6%	19,157	65.6%	26.2%	0.8%	4.2%	3.2%	7,616	83.1%	14.9%	0.0%	2.0%	0.0%
Rio Rancho city	6,850	91.4%	7,932	78.7%	16.2%	1.3%	3.8%	0.0%	7,728	71.3%	21.4%	3.7%	3.6%	0.0%
New York														
Albany city	3,915	74.5%	20,309	72.4%	24.7%	2.0%	0.1%	0.7%	14,704	58.5%	36.2%	1.6%	3.7%	0.0%
Buffalo city	17,057	85.7%	32,188	73.8%	22.6%	0.3%	0.7%	2.7%	30,643	68.6%	26.8%	0.0%	2.2%	2.3%
New York city	449,663	92.0%	798,163	82.7%	11.4%	1.1%	2.5%	2.2%	1,014,121	81.7%	13.5%	1.3%	2.1%	1.6%
Rochester city	13,571	83.0%	24,555	59.9%	31.2%	3.0%	5.3%	0.6%	29,417	71.6%	22.8%	2.2%	2.2%	1.2%
Syracuse city	7,218	87.4%	24,887	42.6%	42.6%	6.3%	5.2%	3.3%	18,013	68.9%	26.3%	1.1%	2.2%	1.5%
Yonkers city	12,187	90.1%	18,205	77.2%	18.3%	3.0%	0.3%	1.3%	18,266	79.2%	18.4%	0.0%	0.6%	1.8%
North Carolina														
Charlotte city	49,767	89.6%	75,363	60.7%	27.7%	4.6%	6.1%	0.9%	93,254	68.2%	23.2%	5.4%	2.3%	1.0%
Durham city	12,441	76.4%	25,653	53.2%	29.8%	4.3%	8.3%	4.4%	35,049	61.8%	24.5%	4.0%	6.6%	3.1%
Fayetteville city	13,528	86.0%	25,924	61.9%	24.9%	4.4%	8.3%	0.6%	25,605	69.2%	17.8%	5.3%	5.4%	2.3%
Greensboro city	15,724	91.6%	34,083	70.4%	23.6%	3.0%	2.5%	0.5%	30,190	80.2%	12.8%	2.1%	3.4%	1.5%
High Point city	6,602	94.3%	11,627	83.1%	12.4%	1.6%	1.7%	1.2%	10,238	83.1%	14.3%	1.1%	1.5%	0.0%
Raleigh city	33,064	85.0%	52,777	59.4%	33.1%	2.2%	3.4%	1.9%	52,519	61.0%	33.5%	0.7%	2.8%	2.1%
Wilmington city	5,293	89.0%	17,952	42.9%	43.2%	5.9%	4.6%	3.4%	12,989	59.9%	35.7%	2.5%	1.3%	0.6%
Winston-Salem city	15,317	82.1%	27,308	65.5%	21.2%	7.3%	5.4%	0.6%	19,756	72.3%	22.0%	2.4%	2.4%	0.9%
North Dakota														
Fargo city	5,023	96.6%	23,311	54.8%	27.7%	16.0%	1.5%	0.0%	15,383	74.2%	18.7%	6.1%	0.0%	1.1%
Ohio														
Akron city	8,990	88.3%	24,800	63.0%	30.6%	1.8%	2.1%	2.4%	20,695	90.5%	8.2%	0.1%	0.0%	1.1%
Cincinnati city	15,160	77.9%	39,783	52.4%	39.0%	2.8%	4.4%	1.4%	36,235	68.7%	23.5%	1.1%	5.5%	1.2%
Cleveland city	23,722	80.4%	46,059	58.1%	35.7%	2.8%	2.7%	0.7%	37,667	64.8%	31.5%	1.0%	2.3%	0.4%
Columbus city	56,527	84.3%	89,448	61.0%	33.6%	1.9%	2.7%	0.8%	107,536	71.6%	22.2%	1.8%	2.4%	2.0%
Dayton city	8,849	76.4%	23,431	45.1%	47.5%	2.8%	3.9%	0.7%	14,200	59.3%	39.3%	0.8%	0.6%	0.0%
Toledo city	16,083	81.3%	31,680	56.9%	39.0%	2.2%	0.9%	1.1%	30,360	74.8%	21.7%	1.7%	0.5%	1.3%
Oklahoma														
Broken Arrow city	8,235	78.7%	8,364	79.3%	18.5%	2.2%	0.0%	0.0%	9,703	72.6%	23.7%	1.8%	2.0%	0.0%
Lawton city	5,921	73.6%	15,406	45.5%	18.2%	19.6%	16.1%	0.6%	12,212	61.7%	16.7%	11.8%	3.6%	6.2%
Norman city	7,582	89.5%	19,002	61.4%	29.4%	5.7%	2.6%	0.9%	17,042	74.3%	18.3%	1.6%	5.2%	0.6%
Oklahoma City city	34,238	88.2%	62,132	61.3%	29.4%	4.6%	4.0%	0.7%	70,063	66.8%	24.9%	3.0%	3.2%	2.1%
Tulsa city	26,852	85.6%	39,294	66.3%	25.0%	3.1%	4.0%	1.6%	42,921	68.5%	27.3%	1.4%	2.8%	0.0%

Table J-3: Places—Mobility Status by Age—Continued

| | 13 to 17 | | 18 to 24 | | | | | | 25 to 31 | | | | | |
| | | | | | Percent Living in a Different House | | | | | | Percent Living in a Different House | | | |
	Total Population	Percent Living in Same House	Total Population	Percent Living in Same House	Same State	Different State, Same Region	Different Region	Outside US	Total Population	Percent Living in Same House	Same State	Different State, Same Region	Different Region	Outside US
Oregon														
Beaverton city	6,011	85.1%	7,397	57.3%	21.9%	19.5%	1.3%	0.0%	11,528	65.9%	25.7%	6.0%	2.4%	0.0%
Eugene city	8,787	81.3%	29,300	39.7%	46.3%	12.1%	1.9%	0.0%	16,885	71.9%	24.0%	1.4%	0.9%	1.7%
Gresham city	6,992	89.6%	10,336	63.2%	30.4%	4.3%	2.1%	0.0%	12,421	70.4%	15.8%	7.8%	6.0%	0.0%
Hillsboro city	6,241	81.1%	7,870	57.6%	40.3%	1.3%	0.8%	0.0%	11,317	56.1%	34.7%	1.7%	5.5%	2.0%
Portland city	27,860	85.1%	53,240	52.9%	32.6%	9.6%	2.1%	2.8%	78,665	59.8%	28.8%	5.7%	4.3%	1.5%
Salem city	9,997	87.9%	16,978	69.9%	23.2%	3.5%	1.6%	1.8%	17,782	62.3%	32.3%	2.6%	2.8%	0.0%
Pennsylvania														
Allentown city	8,964	67.0%	13,580	64.5%	25.3%	7.0%	0.4%	2.8%	12,602	72.3%	16.1%	4.2%	4.7%	2.8%
Erie city	4,892	97.8%	13,353	48.6%	42.4%	3.6%	4.7%	0.6%	12,796	81.5%	15.4%	0.8%	2.3%	0.0%
Philadelphia city	87,644	86.6%	179,729	74.2%	17.6%	4.5%	2.6%	1.0%	187,507	74.1%	19.5%	2.4%	2.7%	1.4%
Pittsburgh city	14,531	85.3%	50,254	48.4%	39.1%	3.4%	4.8%	4.3%	38,294	68.5%	23.4%	1.4%	4.1%	2.7%
Rhode Island														
Providence city	10,962	92.6%	30,447	64.8%	11.3%	12.3%	3.9%	7.7%	22,974	64.6%	19.4%	5.4%	8.2%	2.3%
South Carolina														
Charleston city	7,539	84.9%	16,578	52.0%	33.3%	3.5%	10.0%	1.2%	17,610	66.3%	21.6%	8.4%	2.9%	0.7%
Columbia city	8,176	78.3%	33,216	29.3%	40.0%	11.5%	18.2%	1.0%	18,070	64.4%	24.7%	4.0%	3.8%	3.1%
North Charleston city	6,796	94.4%	16,645	62.6%	27.5%	2.7%	6.8%	0.3%	10,628	62.2%	31.2%	3.6%	3.0%	0.0%
South Dakota														
Sioux Falls city	7,691	77.0%	15,987	60.3%	27.2%	9.6%	2.1%	0.9%	19,442	81.3%	17.4%	1.3%	0.0%	0.0%
Tennessee														
Chattanooga city	11,328	80.5%	18,173	67.0%	25.1%	5.2%	1.2%	1.6%	18,396	69.3%	19.6%	8.1%	0.3%	2.7%
Clarksville city	9,909	69.9%	17,831	62.2%	22.5%	9.6%	4.2%	1.5%	21,990	62.9%	21.5%	8.4%	4.3%	2.8%
Knoxville city	9,223	81.1%	33,690	63.3%	33.0%	1.3%	2.1%	0.4%	23,611	77.7%	18.2%	2.0%	1.5%	0.7%
Memphis city	42,111	82.6%	73,486	73.1%	22.0%	2.7%	1.3%	0.8%	73,223	71.6%	23.3%	3.4%	1.3%	0.4%
Murfreesboro city	6,260	91.8%	21,810	45.9%	41.0%	8.9%	4.2%	0.0%	14,961	62.8%	36.1%	0.5%	0.5%	0.0%
Nashville-Davidson metropolitan govt (bal)	32,158	76.2%	64,157	63.1%	21.1%	6.7%	8.0%	1.1%	85,646	68.4%	21.2%	5.0%	3.5%	1.9%
Texas														
Abilene city	7,916	80.4%	17,581	55.2%	38.7%	2.3%	3.7%	0.0%	14,055	58.9%	33.2%	6.6%	1.0%	0.3%
Amarillo city	12,209	77.0%	20,974	57.6%	36.1%	4.8%	1.1%	0.4%	21,743	66.5%	26.0%	2.2%	4.4%	1.0%
Arlington city	30,675	83.4%	38,088	66.5%	28.7%	1.7%	3.0%	0.1%	43,442	72.4%	24.2%	2.0%	1.1%	0.2%
Austin city	50,107	83.7%	96,859	52.4%	39.4%	1.9%	3.6%	2.8%	133,406	60.3%	31.7%	1.3%	4.2%	2.4%
Beaumont city	7,244	93.5%	15,412	84.8%	15.2%	0.0%	0.0%	0.0%	11,553	80.1%	15.4%	1.3%	2.2%	1.0%
Brownsville city	17,348	89.7%	21,080	83.3%	14.7%	0.4%	1.3%	0.3%	15,496	78.3%	19.5%	0.0%	1.3%	0.9%
Carrollton city	7,244	76.4%	12,278	63.3%	34.3%	0.0%	2.4%	0.1%	13,863	55.5%	39.4%	1.5%	3.6%	0.0%
College Station city	7,447	90.9%	37,647	46.9%	48.2%	0.3%	2.7%	1.9%	16,700	65.5%	30.7%	0.0%	1.4%	2.4%
Corpus Christi city	21,957	77.5%	33,162	56.4%	31.0%	7.4%	4.0%	1.2%	30,950	74.4%	23.6%	0.8%	1.0%	0.3%
Dallas city	80,397	86.6%	129,394	68.5%	28.0%	0.6%	2.2%	0.5%	153,400	70.7%	24.6%	0.9%	2.1%	1.5%
Denton city	9,021	82.9%	24,350	46.6%	50.7%	0.0%	1.3%	1.4%	18,586	71.1%	26.2%	0.0%	2.1%	0.6%
El Paso city	50,508	92.4%	74,001	81.0%	12.8%	1.7%	3.0%	1.5%	66,579	74.1%	18.1%	1.2%	4.8%	1.8%
Fort Worth city	58,152	84.5%	76,339	67.0%	28.1%	2.1%	2.2%	0.6%	88,369	74.7%	22.2%	1.6%	0.6%	0.9%
Frisco city	9,692	84.8%	8,604	63.7%	25.8%	4.2%	6.2%	0.0%	10,337	70.6%	19.5%	1.0%	8.9%	0.0%
Garland city	18,363	84.4%	24,159	76.7%	17.1%	2.9%	2.6%	0.7%	22,411	75.5%	22.4%	0.8%	0.3%	1.1%
Grand Prairie city	15,751	91.2%	19,830	79.0%	14.9%	1.9%	3.3%	1.0%	16,483	77.4%	19.1%	1.6%	0.6%	1.4%
Houston city	147,061	86.5%	224,553	70.8%	23.7%	1.5%	2.3%	1.7%	291,146	65.9%	26.6%	1.9%	2.9%	2.8%
Irving city	14,236	84.7%	23,396	65.9%	27.3%	1.6%	3.8%	1.5%	27,178	60.4%	27.6%	0.5%	6.9%	4.6%
Killeen city	10,138	85.6%	16,852	67.2%	19.0%	7.1%	4.9%	1.9%	19,199	58.8%	12.8%	4.8%	19.2%	4.4%
Laredo city	20,972	89.7%	27,273	86.2%	12.3%	0.3%	0.5%	0.7%	23,201	86.3%	10.9%	0.0%	0.2%	2.6%
Lewisville city	5,761	80.0%	8,767	71.7%	25.3%	1.2%	1.1%	0.7%	13,709	68.4%	25.1%	4.4%	1.9%	0.3%
Lubbock city	17,086	83.8%	43,705	53.3%	43.8%	0.0%	2.2%	0.6%	27,015	64.0%	32.2%	0.7%	2.7%	0.3%
McAllen city	12,943	86.1%	14,982	79.4%	18.6%	0.0%	0.6%	1.3%	11,499	73.8%	24.0%	0.0%	0.0%	2.1%
McKinney city	12,649	82.5%	11,353	69.9%	26.0%	2.6%	1.5%	0.0%	12,028	73.2%	22.9%	0.0%	4.0%	0.0%
Mesquite city	10,082	82.7%	15,853	68.6%	28.5%	0.0%	2.8%	0.0%	14,522	80.2%	17.5%	0.0%	0.0%	2.3%
Midland city	8,615	79.1%	13,360	55.7%	37.4%	0.0%	6.0%	0.9%	14,827	68.2%	24.6%	0.5%	6.7%	0.0%
Odessa city	8,009	79.4%	12,319	57.4%	25.4%	0.0%	7.2%	10.0%	12,521	64.1%	28.7%	0.5%	0.0%	6.8%
Pasadena city	13,451	82.6%	18,164	68.0%	29.4%	2.4%	0.0%	0.2%	12,887	71.1%	28.0%	0.0%	0.9%	0.0%
Pearland city	4,841	97.7%	8,755	85.3%	3.5%	0.0%	11.1%	0.0%	11,202	84.5%	13.1%	0.0%	0.5%	1.9%
Plano city	20,584	94.0%	21,028	72.9%	22.1%	1.4%	1.0%	2.5%	24,682	61.1%	29.9%	0.6%	4.7%	3.7%
Richardson city	6,349	85.5%	8,366	57.6%	36.8%	0.0%	5.1%	0.5%	10,832	61.9%	34.5%	0.8%	1.1%	1.7%
Round Rock city	10,216	83.6%	9,366	65.8%	30.9%	1.1%	2.2%	0.0%	10,481	61.1%	30.1%	1.6%	4.6%	2.5%
San Angelo city	7,399	82.4%	11,694	41.6%	37.1%	4.4%	15.2%	1.7%	12,061	65.3%	16.4%	10.7%	5.0%	2.5%
San Antonio city	99,976	87.3%	157,599	65.5%	26.6%	2.2%	3.4%	2.3%	153,279	71.7%	23.7%	1.5%	1.9%	1.2%
Tyler city	6,031	82.4%	10,887	70.3%	19.5%	3.6%	6.6%	0.0%	11,620	73.2%	20.4%	0.0%	4.1%	2.2%
Waco city	8,203	84.1%	25,064	56.9%	36.0%	2.0%	4.4%	0.7%	12,838	57.6%	36.2%	1.6%	3.3%	1.4%
Wichita Falls city	5,381	88.4%	14,389	57.0%	20.3%	7.1%	11.1%	4.5%	12,667	71.1%	20.8%	3.8%	4.3%	0.0%
Utah														
Orem city	9,224	85.3%	15,432	60.8%	24.6%	9.3%	5.2%	0.1%	10,400	63.0%	24.6%	4.9%	6.2%	1.2%
Provo city	6,291	78.2%	41,722	32.5%	40.6%	12.0%	8.6%	6.4%	15,986	56.4%	34.8%	4.7%	3.0%	1.0%
Salt Lake City city	9,576	74.2%	26,404	51.2%	32.3%	5.0%	9.4%	2.1%	26,725	57.6%	33.2%	3.8%	3.9%	1.5%
West Jordan city	11,957	88.7%	9,300	80.4%	15.6%	1.8%	0.0%	2.2%	10,664	80.0%	19.4%	0.0%	0.6%	0.0%
West Valley City city	10,153	76.9%	13,843	72.8%	18.4%	2.9%	5.6%	0.0%	15,680	68.6%	24.5%	3.8%	2.8%	0.3%

Table J-3: Places—Mobility Status by Age—*Continued*

	13 to 17		18 to 24						25 to 31					
					Percent Living in a Different House						Percent Living in a Different House			
	Total Population	Percent Living in Same House	Total Population	Percent Living in Same House	Same State	Different State, Same Region	Different Region	Outside US	Total Population	Percent Living in Same House	Same State	Different State, Same Region	Different Region	Outside US
Virginia														
Alexandria city	4,681	85.6%	8,303	62.6%	14.5%	7.5%	9.4%	5.9%	26,885	53.7%	24.2%	11.0%	4.7%	6.4%
Chesapeake city	16,601	94.2%	21,964	84.8%	13.4%	1.0%	0.8%	0.0%	22,901	71.9%	18.7%	5.1%	4.0%	0.3%
Hampton city	8,750	77.3%	16,646	68.8%	22.9%	2.7%	5.1%	0.4%	15,772	67.3%	25.3%	2.6%	3.0%	1.8%
Newport News city	10,976	90.8%	22,747	49.0%	38.9%	5.2%	6.9%	0.0%	20,844	62.9%	28.4%	2.7%	4.5%	1.5%
Norfolk city	13,003	76.4%	45,302	56.8%	27.1%	6.8%	7.6%	1.6%	34,255	66.6%	22.9%	2.7%	7.4%	0.3%
Portsmouth city	4,858	77.2%	10,561	57.6%	22.1%	8.0%	9.8%	2.5%	11,325	76.2%	19.2%	0.6%	2.8%	1.2%
Richmond city	8,840	79.9%	30,207	56.1%	38.0%	2.1%	3.6%	0.1%	31,718	67.4%	29.5%	2.2%	1.0%	0.0%
Roanoke city	4,118	62.6%	9,135	62.3%	31.7%	1.4%	4.6%	0.0%	10,878	66.9%	28.0%	1.4%	3.1%	0.6%
Virginia Beach city	24,779	85.7%	47,498	66.8%	19.7%	3.9%	8.1%	1.5%	52,685	67.0%	24.4%	2.7%	5.1%	0.8%
Washington														
Bellevue city	7,907	94.0%	7,892	78.9%	17.4%	0.4%	1.4%	2.1%	16,432	52.0%	24.3%	3.7%	8.6%	11.4%
Everett city	7,608	89.9%	11,276	70.2%	28.5%	0.5%	0.8%	0.0%	10,321	67.9%	30.5%	1.6%	0.0%	0.0%
Federal Way city	7,561	95.1%	8,597	60.6%	37.1%	2.4%	0.0%	0.0%	10,225	77.5%	15.7%	3.6%	2.7%	0.5%
Kent city	7,583	89.6%	11,821	76.3%	18.9%	1.8%	1.3%	1.7%	15,126	81.9%	14.5%	0.4%	1.4%	1.8%
Renton city	6,135	79.2%	7,783	50.8%	35.0%	14.2%	0.0%	0.0%	12,165	66.5%	24.6%	5.8%	3.1%	0.0%
Seattle city	27,121	86.1%	71,283	51.8%	32.5%	6.6%	6.9%	2.3%	105,232	63.3%	27.7%	2.9%	4.8%	1.4%
Spokane city	11,781	91.9%	25,919	55.7%	32.7%	5.3%	5.1%	1.3%	23,818	70.5%	24.8%	1.3%	3.4%	0.0%
Spokane Valley city	6,650	93.4%	5,998	89.6%	5.6%	4.8%	0.0%	0.0%	10,724	83.1%	10.2%	4.1%	2.6%	0.0%
Tacoma city	11,780	88.1%	20,040	57.3%	26.7%	6.3%	5.4%	4.2%	24,312	69.1%	20.0%	3.8%	5.9%	1.3%
Vancouver city	10,825	86.8%	14,568	73.0%	16.9%	8.1%	2.0%	0.0%	16,353	60.7%	21.8%	11.1%	6.4%	0.0%
Yakima city	6,635	80.9%	10,717	61.6%	37.8%	0.6%	0.0%	0.0%	8,808	65.1%	34.9%	0.0%	0.0%	0.0%
Wisconsin														
Green Bay city	7,600	81.8%	11,960	64.9%	30.0%	2.4%	1.9%	0.8%	10,960	66.0%	33.4%	0.0%	0.0%	0.6%
Kenosha city	7,710	91.5%	11,446	56.7%	32.1%	7.5%	2.3%	1.4%	8,573	79.5%	17.4%	3.1%	0.0%	0.0%
Madison city	16,034	92.3%	41,339	47.8%	39.4%	6.7%	4.0%	2.1%	37,501	68.1%	27.1%	1.8%	1.6%	1.4%
Milwaukee city	41,626	84.5%	72,453	61.7%	33.2%	2.8%	1.8%	0.5%	74,651	68.5%	26.8%	1.9%	1.5%	1.3%

Table J-4: Metropolitan/Micropolitan Statistical Areas—Mobility Status by Age

	13 to 17		18 to 24						25 to 31					
					Percent Living in a Different House						Percent Living in a Different House			
	Total Population	Percent Living in Same House	Total Population	Percent Living in Same House	Same State	Different State, Same Region	Different Region	Outside US	Total Population	Percent Living in Same House	Same State	Different State, Same Region	Different Region	Outside US
Abilene, TX	10,295	81.5%	23,017	57.4%	37.2%	1.8%	3.2%	0.5%	17,970	61.1%	32.7%	5.2%	0.8%	0.2%
Adrian, MI micro	6,644	81.1%	9,371	72.2%	22.2%	1.9%	3.7%	0.0%	8,669	72.5%	22.2%	3.0%	2.3%	0.0%
Akron, OH	42,393	93.2%	80,759	67.0%	26.4%	1.0%	2.2%	3.4%	61,851	80.0%	13.3%	1.0%	4.5%	1.3%
Albany-Schenectady-Troy, NY	50,969	91.7%	94,295	70.4%	24.1%	2.1%	2.9%	0.5%	75,888	68.3%	25.7%	2.2%	3.2%	0.6%
Albany, GA	10,397	90.9%	18,490	72.4%	26.8%	0.0%	0.6%	0.2%	16,012	82.1%	15.3%	2.1%	0.6%	0.0%
Albany, OR	6,733	86.0%	15,636	46.6%	49.1%	1.9%	2.4%	0.0%	8,269	60.0%	21.0%	7.2%	5.5%	6.3%
Albertville, AL micro	7,439	88.5%	6,743	75.9%	22.1%	2.0%	0.0%	0.0%	8,670	76.9%	22.6%	0.5%	0.0%	0.0%
Albuquerque, NM	59,465	90.1%	86,268	70.3%	22.2%	2.4%	2.9%	2.1%	86,523	71.5%	21.5%	2.0%	3.5%	1.4%
Alexandria, LA	11,127	77.7%	14,798	65.0%	16.3%	12.9%	5.3%	0.4%	15,070	82.9%	9.5%	4.9%	2.6%	0.2%
Allentown-Bethlehem-Easton, PA-NJ	55,437	90.1%	75,340	76.5%	18.0%	3.8%	0.9%	0.8%	69,565	73.0%	19.4%	3.1%	2.9%	1.7%
Altoona, PA	6,521	96.7%	12,217	71.9%	23.6%	2.4%	2.1%	0.0%	10,280	71.5%	28.1%	0.0%	0.4%	0.0%
Amarillo, TX	16,606	79.1%	26,298	58.0%	35.5%	4.3%	1.9%	0.3%	26,914	66.7%	26.4%	2.6%	3.6%	0.8%
Ames, IA	4,194	88.2%	25,348	31.6%	55.9%	7.6%	1.9%	2.9%	9,972	56.1%	25.6%	8.3%	3.3%	6.7%
Anchorage, AK	29,436	86.4%	45,083	63.0%	28.6%	4.4%	2.4%	1.6%	45,086	57.0%	30.3%	5.7%	5.4%	1.6%
Ann Arbor, MI	19,383	90.5%	64,295	41.3%	45.9%	3.2%	6.6%	3.0%	36,258	60.1%	29.4%	3.1%	4.0%	3.4%
Anniston-Oxford-Jacksonville, AL	6,696	78.2%	11,943	55.6%	36.9%	5.6%	1.8%	0.1%	10,550	75.5%	17.3%	1.5%	0.0%	5.7%
Appleton, WI	14,719	91.7%	21,776	69.3%	28.3%	1.7%	0.0%	0.7%	20,703	63.6%	32.8%	1.8%	1.7%	0.0%
Asheville, NC	26,814	79.9%	33,633	64.6%	21.9%	5.0%	6.6%	1.9%	36,992	76.3%	17.4%	3.0%	2.3%	1.0%
Ashtabula, OH micro	6,190	94.4%	8,246	87.4%	12.6%	0.0%	0.0%	0.0%	8,300	83.3%	16.7%	0.0%	0.0%	0.0%
Athens-Clarke County, GA	10,529	91.6%	42,955	60.2%	36.2%	2.2%	0.8%	0.7%	21,108	73.7%	19.6%	1.8%	2.4%	2.4%
Atlanta-Sandy Springs-Roswell, GA	395,662	85.1%	510,259	70.1%	24.1%	2.1%	2.5%	1.3%	513,894	71.9%	23.4%	2.1%	1.9%	0.7%
Atlantic City-Hammonton, NJ	17,790	90.4%	26,718	82.1%	13.8%	2.7%	1.2%	0.2%	22,550	77.8%	16.5%	3.0%	2.3%	0.4%
Auburn-Opelika, AL	9,237	90.1%	30,018	48.3%	37.8%	13.1%	0.8%	0.0%	14,147	65.2%	20.1%	5.2%	5.9%	3.6%
Augusta-Richmond County, GA-SC	40,233	88.7%	58,079	77.8%	14.6%	4.2%	2.9%	0.5%	55,809	77.2%	15.9%	4.8%	1.6%	0.5%
Augusta-Waterville, ME micro	8,147	75.1%	10,198	77.4%	12.1%	0.5%	7.9%	2.1%	9,257	86.0%	11.1%	0.0%	2.9%	0.0%
Austin-Round Rock, TX	120,571	85.9%	195,346	57.9%	36.4%	1.7%	2.5%	1.5%	233,683	62.5%	29.6%	1.4%	4.8%	1.6%
Bakersfield, CA	67,483	87.2%	95,288	75.0%	21.5%	0.7%	1.3%	1.6%	90,977	69.6%	27.3%	0.2%	1.9%	0.9%
Baltimore-Columbia-Towson, MD	173,961	90.6%	260,777	76.6%	17.6%	2.0%	3.0%	0.7%	279,796	74.1%	20.0%	2.0%	3.1%	0.8%
Bangor, ME	8,286	94.5%	18,248	69.2%	26.1%	3.2%	1.2%	0.4%	13,381	69.7%	23.6%	2.1%	4.6%	0.0%
Barnstable Town, MA	10,775	90.7%	13,695	80.4%	12.4%	0.4%	6.9%	0.0%	13,287	76.4%	19.4%	0.5%	3.3%	0.5%
Baton Rouge, LA	54,371	88.3%	99,623	73.0%	20.6%	4.3%	2.0%	0.1%	78,834	78.6%	17.3%	1.2%	1.5%	1.4%
Battle Creek, MI	9,689	76.9%	11,086	73.9%	20.6%	3.0%	1.5%	1.0%	10,299	63.1%	35.5%	0.0%	1.4%	0.0%
Bay City, MI	7,155	90.4%	9,251	74.6%	22.2%	1.7%	0.5%	1.0%	9,135	75.1%	16.2%	0.0%	8.7%	0.0%
Beaumont-Port Arthur, TX	28,297	90.8%	41,111	81.1%	17.1%	0.6%	0.7%	0.6%	38,385	73.4%	22.9%	0.5%	2.2%	1.0%
Beckley, WV	5,876	94.5%	11,317	72.8%	15.5%	4.5%	5.3%	1.9%	10,268	83.5%	12.9%	2.3%	1.3%	0.0%
Bellingham, WA	12,958	98.0%	31,693	69.9%	27.0%	2.5%	0.3%	0.3%	17,498	78.5%	17.0%	2.8%	1.0%	0.8%
Bend-Redmond, OR	12,180	84.6%	11,498	58.0%	41.2%	0.0%	0.7%	0.0%	14,309	79.9%	17.3%	0.7%	2.2%	0.0%
Billings, MT	9,934	74.6%	17,198	59.1%	27.0%	7.1%	4.5%	2.4%	14,191	64.1%	24.0%	2.4%	9.5%	0.0%
Binghamton, NY	14,084	91.7%	28,948	67.6%	27.6%	0.2%	1.4%	3.2%	19,910	70.7%	24.5%	2.1%	1.6%	1.0%
Birmingham-Hoover, AL	76,510	85.1%	103,964	72.4%	22.3%	2.9%	2.0%	0.3%	107,298	74.7%	21.9%	1.8%	1.0%	0.6%
Bismarck, ND	7,121	95.6%	12,626	69.2%	22.3%	4.0%	4.5%	0.0%	14,455	71.1%	21.9%	7.0%	0.0%	0.0%
Blacksburg-Christiansburg-Radford, VA	9,013	88.8%	42,782	47.3%	43.2%	4.1%	5.0%	0.4%	14,493	80.2%	14.2%	2.5%	2.5%	0.7%
Bloomington, IL	10,855	93.2%	33,533	46.4%	51.1%	0.2%	1.8%	0.5%	19,327	69.8%	23.7%	0.7%	1.7%	4.2%
Bloomington, IN	8,946	92.2%	41,831	35.1%	55.1%	3.6%	3.2%	2.9%	15,823	58.2%	39.0%	0.6%	0.0%	2.3%
Bloomsburg-Berwick, PA	5,342	98.5%	11,393	75.4%	22.3%	2.2%	0.0%	0.0%	6,406	86.1%	12.6%	0.0%	1.3%	0.0%
Boise City, ID	49,831	85.9%	60,531	59.7%	31.8%	6.2%	1.5%	0.8%	58,731	71.1%	21.3%	5.9%	0.6%	1.2%
Boston-Cambridge-Newton, MA-NH	287,948	91.9%	460,199	70.4%	19.4%	5.0%	3.0%	2.1%	479,162	71.8%	21.2%	2.5%	2.7%	1.8%
Boulder, CO	20,523	87.8%	46,928	40.3%	42.5%	6.1%	9.9%	1.2%	28,813	52.5%	35.3%	3.3%	7.5%	1.4%
Bowling Green, KY	9,845	88.6%	20,162	47.8%	45.8%	2.9%	2.6%	0.9%	16,090	65.2%	29.5%	1.1%	1.5%	2.8%
Bremerton-Silverdale, WA	15,581	83.4%	25,705	57.4%	30.3%	4.0%	8.1%	0.3%	23,899	70.1%	18.4%	4.8%	6.3%	0.4%
Bridgeport-Stamford-Norwalk, CT	64,222	91.2%	75,893	83.1%	10.2%	3.7%	1.0%	1.9%	72,592	72.0%	17.6%	5.2%	2.7%	2.6%
Brownsville-Harlingen, TX	40,096	87.2%	44,095	84.4%	12.9%	0.6%	0.6%	1.6%	33,550	82.1%	16.4%	0.0%	1.0%	0.4%
Brunswick, GA	6,878	72.0%	10,762	49.8%	40.7%	4.2%	4.8%	0.6%	9,932	66.2%	24.0%	3.1%	1.7%	5.0%
Buffalo-Cheektowaga-Niagara Falls, NY	68,577	92.2%	113,628	76.4%	20.8%	0.5%	1.2%	1.1%	104,738	74.9%	21.3%	0.1%	1.8%	1.9%
Burlington-South Burlington, VT	11,601	95.6%	28,043	55.1%	27.5%	10.9%	2.2%	4.3%	20,130	76.3%	20.1%	2.2%	0.6%	0.8%
Burlington, NC	10,421	93.3%	14,914	72.4%	15.1%	3.6%	8.9%	0.0%	13,510	71.5%	23.9%	4.3%	0.2%	0.1%
California-Lexington Park, MD	9,687	97.1%	10,336	87.2%	9.2%	1.9%	1.1%	0.5%	8,534	79.3%	11.5%	6.9%	1.7%	0.5%
Canton-Massillon, OH	25,547	91.8%	35,605	74.0%	23.0%	0.7%	2.4%	0.0%	32,199	72.1%	23.7%	0.3%	3.4%	0.5%
Cape Coral-Fort Myers, FL	34,853	81.5%	47,505	68.4%	26.7%	0.4%	3.8%	0.7%	48,549	65.7%	26.3%	1.9%	4.5%	1.7%
Cape Girardeau, MO-IL	6,381	95.5%	11,316	70.9%	18.8%	7.0%	2.9%	0.4%	8,643	80.4%	18.9%	0.0%	0.6%	0.0%
Carbondale-Marion, IL	9,377	88.7%	16,679	68.8%	27.2%	1.0%	2.9%	0.0%	13,124	73.4%	22.7%	1.7%	0.9%	1.3%
Carson City, NV	3,278	86.2%	3,934	71.0%	26.8%	2.2%	0.0%	0.0%	5,005	66.5%	28.7%	4.8%	0.0%	0.0%
Casper, WY	5,346	94.8%	7,750	50.5%	42.5%	0.0%	5.3%	1.7%	8,364	63.1%	30.3%	4.6%	0.5%	1.5%
Cedar Rapids, IA	19,102	93.6%	22,914	76.3%	22.5%	1.0%	0.2%	0.0%	26,270	70.8%	24.1%	3.4%	0.7%	0.9%
Chambersburg-Waynesboro, PA	8,275	93.7%	11,960	79.4%	15.6%	0.3%	4.6%	0.0%	13,003	85.6%	9.5%	0.0%	4.9%	0.0%

Table J-4: Metropolitan/Micropolitan Statistical Areas—Mobility Status by Age—*Continued*

	13 to 17		18 to 24						25 to 31					
					Percent Living in a Different House						Percent Living in a Different House			
	Total Population	Percent Living in Same House	Total Population	Percent Living in Same House	Same State	Different State, Same Region	Different Region	Outside US	Total Population	Percent Living in Same House	Same State	Different State, Same Region	Different Region	Outside US
Champaign-Urbana, IL	13,077	85.1%	51,413	34.3%	58.7%	2.0%	2.4%	2.7%	26,505	66.1%	23.7%	0.6%	7.1%	2.5%
Charleston-North Charleston, SC	43,634	91.3%	74,064	62.1%	27.8%	4.2%	5.5%	0.3%	75,141	67.5%	24.1%	4.5%	3.3%	0.5%
Charleston, WV	13,854	89.5%	18,423	77.2%	16.3%	0.9%	5.7%	0.0%	18,065	77.8%	18.5%	1.9%	1.8%	0.0%
Charlotte-Concord-Gastonia, NC-SC	161,725	90.0%	208,491	72.1%	21.2%	3.0%	3.3%	0.4%	209,266	73.5%	20.0%	3.4%	2.2%	1.0%
Charlottesville, VA	14,286	84.3%	27,546	66.5%	26.8%	1.3%	2.7%	2.6%	19,067	66.5%	25.0%	2.8%	4.1%	1.5%
Chattanooga, TN-GA	33,567	86.5%	46,961	71.3%	20.7%	5.6%	1.8%	0.6%	49,220	75.7%	15.4%	6.7%	0.5%	1.6%
Cheyenne, WY	5,137	80.5%	12,437	46.5%	29.7%	12.0%	11.0%	0.8%	8,039	60.8%	22.9%	9.9%	6.0%	0.3%
Chicago-Naperville-Elgin, IL-IN-WI	650,051	89.9%	907,719	75.8%	17.5%	2.6%	2.8%	1.3%	961,624	75.3%	19.4%	1.6%	2.4%	1.2%
Chico, CA	12,100	82.6%	33,787	53.0%	43.6%	0.1%	1.3%	2.1%	19,755	76.1%	22.0%	0.0%	1.9%	0.0%
Cincinnati, OH-KY-IN	146,384	88.8%	193,039	69.0%	24.6%	1.8%	3.9%	0.6%	188,981	70.1%	22.6%	1.4%	5.0%	1.0%
Clarksburg, WV micro	5,506	79.8%	6,577	80.4%	17.5%	0.4%	1.8%	0.0%	6,877	88.6%	11.4%	0.0%	0.0%	0.0%
Clarksville, TN-KY	19,577	69.4%	34,064	62.9%	20.9%	9.1%	5.9%	1.2%	36,102	69.0%	17.7%	6.8%	4.5%	2.0%
Cleveland-Elyria, OH	135,379	88.8%	180,390	73.8%	22.0%	1.1%	2.5%	0.6%	172,704	73.2%	23.5%	0.9%	1.8%	0.6%
Cleveland, TN	7,830	78.1%	11,815	63.8%	25.8%	6.2%	2.5%	1.8%	10,284	69.8%	25.4%	0.0%	4.8%	0.0%
Coeur d'Alene, ID	9,617	93.1%	12,617	67.3%	21.1%	6.0%	1.9%	3.7%	12,885	90.0%	7.8%	0.8%	1.4%	0.0%
College Station-Bryan, TX	16,637	90.2%	60,432	45.7%	50.3%	0.8%	1.8%	1.4%	27,067	64.1%	32.5%	1.1%	0.9%	1.5%
Colorado Springs, CO	46,539	86.4%	71,720	56.5%	26.2%	2.3%	11.8%	3.2%	71,404	60.9%	24.9%	0.9%	8.9%	4.3%
Columbia, MO	8,915	88.7%	36,413	48.4%	37.5%	8.3%	4.9%	0.8%	20,117	57.8%	33.9%	5.0%	2.1%	1.3%
Columbia, SC	52,961	85.0%	97,384	51.4%	30.8%	7.7%	9.1%	1.0%	74,192	71.9%	19.9%	2.0%	5.1%	1.1%
Columbus, GA-AL	20,674	80.0%	40,180	51.8%	24.9%	9.0%	12.6%	1.7%	32,277	59.9%	23.2%	9.0%	5.0%	2.9%
Columbus, IN	5,242	95.8%	6,922	78.5%	14.4%	2.9%	4.2%	0.0%	8,417	75.6%	17.1%	0.0%	0.7%	6.7%
Columbus, OH	133,803	87.6%	171,487	64.7%	31.3%	1.3%	2.1%	0.6%	209,330	72.0%	22.7%	1.5%	2.3%	1.4%
Concord, NH micro	7,647	95.2%	12,366	83.4%	12.1%	3.6%	0.0%	0.9%	9,340	60.1%	33.6%	3.5%	2.8%	0.0%
Cookeville, TN micro	6,015	99.4%	14,041	71.7%	25.6%	2.2%	0.5%	0.0%	8,616	85.6%	11.6%	0.0%	1.0%	1.8%
Corpus Christi, TX	33,021	78.0%	47,608	61.2%	29.9%	5.2%	2.8%	1.0%	42,706	72.5%	25.6%	0.6%	1.0%	0.3%
Corvallis, OR	7,419	85.0%	17,148	43.8%	52.3%	1.7%	2.2%	0.0%	9,091	56.1%	24.3%	6.6%	5.0%	8.0%
Crestview-Fort Walton Beach-Destin, FL	14,790	87.3%	25,602	66.4%	19.4%	7.1%	5.9%	1.3%	28,160	71.2%	18.9%	2.5%	5.8%	1.6%
Cumberland, MD-WV	6,863	88.2%	11,119	85.6%	11.1%	1.5%	1.7%	0.1%	7,509	84.6%	9.6%	4.2%	1.7%	0.0%
Dallas-Fort Worth-Arlington, TX	488,661	86.4%	628,923	69.4%	26.4%	1.3%	2.1%	0.8%	675,672	70.4%	25.4%	1.1%	1.9%	1.3%
Dalton, GA	10,281	88.5%	14,006	79.7%	16.0%	1.9%	2.4%	0.0%	13,382	74.6%	19.6%	4.1%	0.0%	1.7%
Danville, IL	5,607	91.1%	6,498	74.7%	19.7%	0.9%	4.8%	0.0%	7,160	75.1%	23.5%	0.0%	1.4%	0.0%
Danville, VA micro	6,207	91.0%	8,865	77.6%	17.6%	2.0%	2.1%	0.8%	7,368	73.3%	21.8%	3.3%	1.5%	0.0%
Daphne-Fairhope-Foley, AL	13,134	88.0%	16,338	71.4%	8.5%	12.2%	0.1%	7.8%	14,271	51.8%	39.0%	9.3%	0.0%	0.0%
Davenport-Moline-Rock Island, IA-IL	22,450	89.2%	37,821	70.8%	23.9%	3.9%	1.0%	0.5%	32,259	77.4%	17.6%	2.4%	1.5%	1.1%
Dayton, OH	49,753	84.2%	81,355	53.9%	39.5%	2.5%	2.8%	1.2%	72,534	68.8%	27.5%	1.0%	1.5%	1.2%
Decatur, AL	11,377	81.5%	13,146	75.9%	21.9%	0.0%	2.3%	0.0%	11,358	74.9%	24.0%	1.2%	0.0%	0.0%
Decatur, IL	6,354	92.0%	10,229	66.5%	32.2%	0.0%	1.3%	0.0%	9,557	62.0%	32.0%	2.8%	3.2%	0.0%
Deltona-Daytona Beach-Ormond Beach, FL	29,506	90.1%	52,478	73.5%	19.0%	3.3%	3.6%	0.6%	46,853	81.2%	15.5%	1.0%	2.3%	0.0%
Denver-Aurora-Lakewood, CO	181,495	88.6%	228,854	64.8%	27.1%	2.8%	4.2%	1.1%	286,801	66.4%	25.5%	2.3%	5.1%	0.6%
Des Moines-West Des Moines, IA	40,085	88.3%	47,538	54.8%	36.7%	4.3%	3.4%	0.8%	63,439	64.4%	27.9%	2.4%	3.5%	1.8%
Detroit-Warren-Dearborn, MI	290,039	84.6%	382,812	75.8%	21.3%	0.6%	1.6%	0.7%	354,920	74.3%	21.7%	0.7%	1.9%	1.5%
Dothan, AL	10,557	85.4%	11,453	75.0%	15.1%	4.1%	5.8%	0.0%	12,742	74.9%	16.6%	8.1%	0.4%	0.0%
Dover, DE	10,917	91.2%	17,233	72.5%	14.4%	8.1%	4.5%	0.5%	15,816	76.6%	21.4%	1.6%	0.4%	0.0%
Dubuque, IA	8,112	92.8%	9,974	68.6%	24.5%	6.9%	0.0%	0.0%	7,213	76.1%	23.4%	0.0%	0.0%	0.5%
Duluth, MN-WI	16,919	90.8%	31,911	62.1%	33.1%	2.8%	1.4%	0.6%	24,800	70.9%	24.8%	1.8%	1.4%	1.0%
Dunn, NC micro	8,830	77.7%	11,742	77.0%	15.6%	5.6%	1.7%	0.0%	14,304	72.1%	22.2%	4.2%	0.5%	1.0%
Durham-Chapel Hill, NC	30,036	86.1%	62,916	55.1%	33.4%	3.7%	5.4%	2.4%	57,485	64.3%	24.4%	3.7%	5.6%	2.0%
East Stroudsburg, PA	13,266	93.9%	19,021	72.6%	22.8%	3.4%	1.2%	0.0%	10,573	89.8%	3.1%	0.0%	4.5%	2.6%
Eau Claire, WI	9,486	85.7%	21,989	49.2%	42.9%	5.2%	2.6%	0.1%	14,910	70.7%	27.1%	1.7%	0.2%	0.2%
El Centro, CA	14,236	87.9%	20,303	82.4%	15.6%	0.1%	0.0%	1.9%	18,063	81.9%	14.9%	1.4%	0.4%	1.4%
El Paso, TX	64,210	91.5%	97,204	79.1%	13.0%	2.3%	3.6%	2.0%	81,406	75.3%	17.2%	1.1%	4.2%	2.1%
Elizabethtown-Fort Knox, KY	13,326	71.6%	12,405	67.4%	26.2%	3.5%	1.2%	1.7%	14,186	61.3%	29.8%	2.1%	3.3%	3.5%
Elkhart-Goshen, IN	14,822	95.5%	17,694	77.6%	20.1%	0.1%	1.2%	1.0%	17,121	77.9%	18.9%	1.2%	2.0%	0.0%
Elmira, NY	5,234	92.5%	8,030	68.5%	28.6%	2.8%	0.2%	0.0%	8,633	63.2%	35.5%	0.5%	0.0%	0.8%
Erie, PA	15,298	94.2%	29,620	56.8%	36.4%	2.9%	3.3%	0.6%	26,649	75.3%	20.3%	2.7%	1.7%	0.0%
Eugene, OR	19,356	83.6%	46,109	42.7%	46.5%	9.1%	1.2%	0.5%	29,269	70.4%	23.6%	2.8%	1.4%	1.9%
Eureka-Arcata-Fortuna, CA micro	6,652	74.5%	18,113	57.3%	41.7%	0.6%	0.3%	0.0%	13,592	72.5%	23.7%	2.9%	0.9%	0.0%
Evansville, IN-KY	18,675	90.7%	31,837	74.2%	21.5%	2.9%	1.1%	0.3%	27,587	79.7%	17.4%	0.0%	2.6%	0.4%
Fairbanks, AK	6,177	88.5%	13,103	54.5%	26.4%	3.3%	12.6%	3.3%	13,155	45.4%	47.8%	0.8%	6.0%	0.0%
Fargo, ND-MN	13,889	95.0%	39,007	56.7%	26.6%	14.2%	2.0%	0.4%	26,148	76.9%	16.0%	5.8%	0.0%	1.3%
Farmington, NM	9,310	92.1%	12,308	67.9%	27.6%	0.0%	0.0%	4.5%	11,027	93.7%	2.5%	1.7%	0.0%	2.1%
Fayetteville-Springdale-Rogers, AR-MO	35,894	90.1%	53,424	59.1%	31.1%	5.1%	4.1%	0.6%	47,752	75.4%	18.4%	2.0%	2.7%	1.5%
Fayetteville, NC	24,421	86.6%	47,605	63.1%	23.0%	4.1%	9.0%	0.9%	44,471	67.0%	19.6%	5.1%	4.6%	3.7%
Flagstaff, AZ	7,738	79.3%	26,701	48.9%	36.8%	12.7%	1.3%	0.3%	14,018	67.6%	24.8%	1.3%	6.3%	0.0%
Flint, MI	30,158	87.2%	38,737	73.4%	25.0%	0.0%	1.6%	0.0%	35,354	67.2%	28.5%	1.6%	2.5%	0.2%
Florence-Muscle Shoals, AL	9,406	83.9%	15,187	71.3%	19.6%	4.6%	4.4%	0.0%	11,902	76.4%	19.6%	4.0%	0.0%	0.0%
Florence, SC	13,118	83.7%	19,834	78.6%	19.6%	1.8%	0.0%	0.0%	16,353	80.0%	16.9%	2.4%	0.7%	0.0%

Table J-4: Metropolitan/Micropolitan Statistical Areas—Mobility Status by Age—*Continued*

| | 13 to 17 | | 18 to 24 | | | | | | 25 to 31 | | | | | |
| | | | | | Percent Living in a Different House | | | | | | Percent Living in a Different House | | | |
	Total Population	Percent Living in Same House	Total Population	Percent Living in Same House	Same State	Different State, Same Region	Different Region	Outside US	Total Population	Percent Living in Same House	Same State	Different State, Same Region	Different Region	Outside US
Fond du Lac, WI	7,948	94.0%	9,105	58.3%	37.9%	2.8%	0.0%	1.0%	5,647	71.5%	23.5%	5.0%	0.0%	0.0%
Fort Collins, CO	19,699	85.4%	44,712	45.0%	45.2%	2.6%	5.5%	1.8%	29,699	62.2%	26.8%	2.4%	6.6%	2.0%
Fort Smith, AR-OK	19,126	90.0%	25,420	77.0%	19.7%	2.2%	0.5%	0.7%	26,551	75.9%	17.5%	4.6%	2.0%	0.0%
Fort Wayne, IN	29,642	89.9%	40,876	66.6%	28.4%	3.5%	1.6%	0.0%	38,716	72.6%	25.0%	1.5%	0.9%	0.0%
Fresno, CA	71,245	87.1%	108,464	78.2%	20.8%	0.4%	0.4%	0.2%	101,037	76.3%	22.5%	0.3%	0.5%	0.5%
Gadsden, AL	7,662	80.1%	9,315	86.2%	13.4%	0.5%	0.0%	0.0%	8,012	70.7%	24.9%	2.8%	1.6%	0.0%
Gainesville, FL	12,923	88.5%	60,876	54.9%	39.9%	2.3%	0.7%	2.2%	30,284	60.5%	31.5%	4.3%	1.3%	2.4%
Gainesville, GA	14,136	88.1%	17,558	64.3%	27.0%	1.8%	4.0%	2.9%	16,371	72.4%	23.0%	0.5%	2.0%	2.1%
Gettysburg, PA	6,375	87.4%	10,996	74.3%	17.5%	4.2%	4.0%	0.1%	6,546	65.9%	24.8%	0.0%	8.0%	1.3%
Glens Falls, NY	7,781	90.4%	10,305	73.6%	18.3%	3.5%	3.3%	1.3%	9,741	68.6%	28.5%	0.0%	2.9%	0.0%
Goldsboro, NC	7,730	91.9%	11,846	72.3%	20.8%	3.8%	1.8%	1.3%	11,414	63.6%	30.4%	4.6%	1.5%	0.0%
Grand Forks, ND-MN	7,718	96.1%	19,839	47.2%	38.8%	10.7%	0.4%	2.9%	8,762	86.3%	6.9%	3.4%	1.6%	1.8%
Grand Island, NE	5,560	88.6%	6,752	63.9%	36.1%	0.0%	0.0%	0.0%	6,511	79.1%	20.9%	0.0%	0.0%	0.0%
Grand Junction, CO	8,466	82.5%	15,894	37.9%	53.6%	3.5%	5.0%	0.0%	14,985	68.0%	27.2%	0.0%	4.5%	0.3%
Grand Rapids-Wyoming, MI	71,978	83.7%	105,657	56.0%	38.2%	1.8%	3.8%	0.3%	97,581	70.1%	27.1%	1.2%	1.0%	0.6%
Grants Pass, OR	4,012	76.9%	6,276	55.8%	38.7%	0.0%	5.5%	0.0%	5,678	68.2%	19.8%	7.1%	4.9%	0.0%
Great Falls, MT	4,735	84.4%	8,278	62.1%	32.6%	3.5%	0.9%	0.9%	9,149	66.4%	23.1%	1.4%	8.5%	0.6%
Greeley, CO	17,892	79.0%	29,349	51.7%	37.4%	3.1%	7.5%	0.2%	27,777	62.9%	31.7%	3.3%	1.8%	0.3%
Green Bay, WI	23,180	89.9%	28,652	72.3%	23.5%	2.5%	1.2%	0.5%	27,343	70.9%	27.8%	0.0%	1.4%	0.0%
Greensboro-High Point, NC	47,780	91.5%	73,916	75.7%	19.4%	2.0%	2.3%	0.7%	67,690	80.4%	15.2%	1.7%	2.0%	0.7%
Greenville-Anderson-Mauldin, SC	57,700	90.0%	81,975	71.7%	22.8%	2.9%	2.1%	0.5%	72,710	75.4%	20.8%	1.9%	1.1%	0.8%
Greenville, NC	12,815	78.5%	33,517	45.1%	49.4%	3.1%	2.3%	0.0%	15,455	73.5%	22.1%	0.0%	2.8%	1.6%
Greenwood, SC micro	6,366	82.4%	10,326	73.3%	21.5%	1.8%	3.4%	0.0%	7,394	64.2%	33.3%	0.5%	2.0%	0.0%
Gulfport-Biloxi-Pascagoula, MS	24,417	83.8%	36,851	63.8%	23.6%	6.3%	6.0%	0.3%	38,287	66.4%	22.9%	6.1%	3.6%	1.1%
Hagerstown-Martinsburg, MD-WV	18,748	90.1%	22,838	74.5%	19.5%	2.1%	3.6%	0.3%	21,487	73.5%	17.8%	3.5%	4.7%	0.4%
Hammond, LA	8,755	83.2%	14,203	72.8%	21.0%	1.1%	5.1%	0.0%	14,288	72.5%	23.3%	4.2%	0.0%	0.0%
Hanford-Corcoran, CA	10,697	83.2%	17,431	73.4%	21.5%	1.4%	2.4%	1.3%	17,382	72.9%	26.2%	0.0%	0.7%	0.3%
Harrisburg-Carlisle, PA	34,226	87.1%	52,087	69.2%	24.5%	1.1%	2.8%	2.5%	49,754	76.0%	20.9%	0.0%	2.2%	1.0%
Harrisonburg, VA	8,231	88.7%	25,833	47.0%	42.2%	4.0%	6.1%	0.8%	11,307	62.1%	31.6%	1.2%	2.9%	2.2%
Hartford-West Hartford-East Hartford, CT	78,990	91.4%	121,030	74.6%	18.9%	3.6%	2.0%	0.9%	105,077	74.8%	19.9%	2.2%	2.1%	1.0%
Hattiesburg, MS	9,195	84.2%	22,591	54.1%	41.1%	3.5%	1.2%	0.0%	14,510	64.8%	31.1%	3.7%	0.0%	0.4%
Hickory-Lenoir-Morganton, NC	24,437	88.2%	31,386	78.3%	16.3%	4.0%	0.9%	0.4%	27,792	73.9%	20.5%	2.4%	3.3%	0.0%
Hilo, HI micro	13,272	93.9%	15,240	87.7%	10.2%	0.1%	1.5%	0.5%	16,102	85.6%	12.1%	1.3%	1.0%	0.0%
Hilton Head Island-Bluffton-Beaufort, SC	10,794	83.6%	20,318	68.9%	14.1%	11.3%	5.7%	0.0%	17,693	62.8%	17.6%	13.0%	5.6%	1.0%
Hinesville, GA	6,218	84.5%	11,580	56.7%	29.7%	11.5%	1.1%	1.0%	10,508	64.2%	20.1%	7.6%	2.7%	5.5%
Holland, MI micro	8,408	85.7%	9,499	81.5%	18.0%	0.5%	0.0%	0.0%	8,100	82.2%	17.8%	0.0%	0.0%	0.0%
Homosassa Springs, FL	6,239	74.3%	8,383	66.0%	29.7%	0.0%	4.3%	0.0%	6,848	86.9%	7.4%	3.2%	2.4%	0.0%
Hot Springs, AR	5,813	87.2%	8,161	67.1%	26.5%	6.3%	0.0%	0.0%	6,037	80.2%	18.6%	1.2%	0.0%	0.0%
Houma-Thibodaux, LA	13,955	92.8%	21,875	73.6%	23.7%	0.8%	0.0%	1.9%	21,912	79.5%	16.6%	2.7%	1.2%	0.0%
Houston-The Woodlands-Sugar Land, TX	453,816	88.0%	585,394	73.9%	21.6%	1.4%	2.1%	1.0%	654,761	70.0%	24.0%	1.9%	2.1%	1.9%
Huntington-Ashland, WV-KY-OH	26,073	83.7%	32,303	72.5%	24.8%	0.3%	2.4%	0.0%	30,648	74.1%	22.1%	0.8%	2.5%	0.5%
Huntsville, AL	30,524	84.4%	43,181	71.1%	23.1%	1.8%	3.5%	0.5%	43,655	75.8%	21.6%	1.8%	0.6%	0.1%
Idaho Falls, ID	12,212	80.9%	13,418	53.2%	33.6%	10.8%	2.4%	0.0%	11,675	67.0%	21.7%	8.2%	1.7%	1.3%
Indianapolis-Carmel-Anderson, IN	133,996	88.7%	172,522	71.2%	24.5%	1.7%	1.6%	1.0%	192,044	71.8%	22.3%	1.9%	3.4%	0.5%
Iowa City, IA	7,948	87.2%	33,957	33.2%	56.8%	6.0%	2.5%	1.5%	21,679	79.2%	16.6%	1.3%	0.6%	2.3%
Ithaca, NY	4,388	85.2%	27,064	54.6%	21.8%	8.9%	9.1%	5.5%	10,063	69.2%	21.9%	1.4%	5.0%	2.6%
Jackson, MI	10,254	90.9%	14,147	53.8%	42.6%	0.5%	3.1%	0.0%	14,943	70.1%	27.1%	0.0%	1.9%	0.9%
Jackson, MS	42,346	85.1%	55,933	81.7%	15.4%	2.3%	0.4%	0.3%	55,868	73.2%	22.1%	2.4%	1.8%	0.4%
Jackson, TN	8,709	88.1%	14,392	74.8%	20.6%	1.5%	3.1%	0.0%	11,485	69.5%	26.6%	3.3%	0.6%	0.0%
Jacksonville, FL	87,849	86.5%	128,721	71.4%	21.7%	4.8%	2.0%	0.2%	138,023	65.5%	29.3%	2.0%	2.7%	0.4%
Jacksonville, NC	11,202	81.5%	38,939	61.2%	25.4%	6.3%	5.4%	1.7%	24,941	63.6%	17.6%	6.2%	8.7%	3.9%
Jamestown-Dunkirk-Fredonia, NY micro	8,192	93.5%	15,702	62.3%	36.1%	1.3%	0.2%	0.2%	10,603	68.5%	24.0%	3.9%	3.6%	0.0%
Janesville-Beloit, WI	12,012	92.2%	14,267	79.6%	13.2%	4.5%	1.3%	1.4%	13,455	81.2%	16.3%	0.0%	0.0%	2.5%
Jefferson City, MO	11,932	87.9%	14,811	78.5%	20.8%	0.5%	0.2%	0.0%	13,373	67.7%	27.7%	4.4%	0.0%	0.3%
Johnson City, TN	13,143	93.2%	21,384	70.0%	27.2%	2.5%	0.3%	0.0%	15,961	68.2%	29.1%	1.8%	0.8%	0.0%
Johnstown, PA	8,630	84.6%	13,064	71.8%	24.4%	1.5%	1.2%	1.1%	10,546	77.3%	19.5%	0.0%	3.2%	0.0%
Jonesboro, AR	7,390	72.5%	13,440	70.8%	26.3%	2.2%	0.0%	0.8%	12,406	79.2%	16.8%	2.7%	0.4%	1.0%
Joplin, MO	12,281	89.6%	17,153	63.4%	26.3%	4.4%	5.4%	0.5%	16,762	72.3%	24.5%	1.7%	1.4%	0.0%
Kahului-Wailuku-Lahaina, HI	10,520	89.0%	10,449	71.8%	19.7%	6.8%	1.1%	0.7%	16,276	63.4%	23.4%	3.1%	7.8%	2.2%
Kalamazoo-Portage, MI	24,233	89.7%	48,062	50.6%	44.2%	3.2%	1.8%	1.0%	30,223	74.9%	21.4%	1.3%	2.2%	0.3%
Kalispell, MT micro	6,850	74.4%	6,985	76.2%	9.0%	14.2%	0.5%	0.0%	6,784	68.3%	21.7%	4.1%	5.9%	0.0%
Kankakee, IL	7,763	90.7%	11,416	79.6%	17.9%	1.5%	0.7%	0.3%	8,304	76.8%	22.8%	0.5%	0.0%	0.0%
Kansas City, MO-KS	139,847	83.4%	177,722	66.7%	25.4%	5.5%	2.1%	0.4%	196,742	70.1%	22.9%	4.2%	2.3%	0.5%
Kennewick-Richland, WA	22,018	85.9%	24,991	63.5%	33.1%	2.7%	0.1%	0.6%	25,405	72.8%	22.5%	2.7%	1.7%	0.3%
Killeen-Temple, TX	29,682	84.6%	54,892	66.7%	22.2%	4.5%	3.9%	2.7%	50,656	66.3%	17.4%	3.5%	9.7%	3.1%
Kingsport-Bristol-Bristol, TN-VA	19,106	87.4%	25,175	75.7%	17.7%	2.0%	2.1%	2.6%	23,456	76.0%	17.0%	3.8%	3.2%	0.0%
Kingston, NY	11,368	92.4%	18,701	59.9%	38.0%	2.1%	0.0%	0.0%	13,203	73.7%	23.1%	1.2%	0.9%	1.1%
Knoxville, TN	55,117	87.9%	83,818	71.8%	24.9%	1.8%	1.3%	0.2%	73,034	78.0%	18.8%	1.6%	1.4%	0.2%

Table J-4: Metropolitan/Micropolitan Statistical Areas—Mobility Status by Age—*Continued*

	13 to 17		18 to 24						25 to 31					
					Percent Living in a Different House						Percent Living in a Different House			
	Total Population	Percent Living in Same House	Total Population	Percent Living in Same House	Same State	Different State, Same Region	Different Region	Outside US	Total Population	Percent Living in Same House	Same State	Different State, Same Region	Different Region	Outside US
Kokomo, IN	5,501	94.8%	5,932	57.3%	40.8%	1.5%	0.4%	0.0%	5,730	77.0%	23.0%	0.0%	0.0%	0.0%
La Crosse-Onalaska, WI-MN	8,223	96.4%	19,433	33.2%	62.1%	4.0%	0.6%	0.1%	13,011	60.6%	29.3%	2.7%	5.9%	1.4%
Lafayette-West Lafayette, IN	11,974	86.0%	47,508	49.1%	39.2%	4.2%	5.3%	2.2%	21,107	65.2%	27.8%	3.7%	2.1%	1.2%
Lafayette, LA	32,527	91.5%	53,794	75.4%	17.9%	2.4%	1.4%	2.9%	47,886	72.3%	25.2%	1.0%	0.8%	0.7%
Lake Charles, LA	15,397	81.9%	20,994	68.0%	29.8%	2.0%	0.2%	0.0%	16,713	70.1%	24.9%	3.4%	1.7%	0.0%
Lake Havasu City-Kingman, AZ	12,002	72.5%	14,136	59.1%	31.0%	4.9%	4.9%	0.0%	14,210	63.7%	27.5%	4.9%	3.5%	0.4%
Lakeland-Winter Haven, FL	38,905	85.4%	55,573	76.3%	18.4%	1.1%	3.0%	1.2%	55,298	76.0%	20.7%	1.5%	1.8%	0.0%
Lancaster, PA	35,519	90.9%	50,538	79.5%	16.5%	1.1%	1.9%	0.9%	46,261	80.6%	15.0%	0.5%	3.4%	0.6%
Lansing-East Lansing, MI	28,397	89.9%	73,289	45.0%	48.4%	2.2%	2.4%	2.0%	44,901	68.7%	28.1%	0.4%	1.0%	1.8%
Laredo, TX	22,946	90.6%	28,519	86.3%	12.2%	0.3%	0.5%	0.7%	25,385	85.6%	10.2%	1.6%	0.2%	2.4%
Las Cruces, NM	16,277	76.3%	32,427	69.1%	23.1%	0.6%	5.3%	1.9%	18,236	79.7%	15.4%	0.0%	3.1%	1.8%
Las Vegas-Henderson-Paradise, NV	132,184	79.9%	182,345	70.7%	22.4%	4.2%	2.2%	0.5%	204,037	70.0%	22.8%	4.4%	2.1%	0.7%
Lawrence, KS	5,015	86.3%	24,686	47.3%	35.7%	5.5%	6.3%	5.2%	14,590	70.4%	19.0%	4.4%	3.8%	2.3%
Lawton, OK	8,293	76.9%	18,502	50.6%	17.4%	16.4%	15.1%	0.5%	14,851	60.3%	21.7%	9.9%	3.0%	5.1%
Lebanon, PA	8,334	86.1%	10,926	75.0%	18.5%	0.0%	3.4%	3.1%	9,178	86.3%	11.9%	1.8%	0.0%	0.0%
Lewiston-Auburn, ME	6,766	91.4%	9,557	78.4%	15.8%	1.4%	4.4%	0.0%	10,215	68.2%	30.5%	0.0%	1.3%	0.0%
Lewiston, ID-WA	3,148	90.7%	7,110	49.0%	31.9%	11.0%	0.0%	8.1%	4,776	82.5%	11.3%	5.7%	0.4%	0.0%
Lexington-Fayette, KY	31,170	83.9%	58,404	50.4%	42.8%	2.2%	4.2%	0.4%	48,897	67.9%	24.9%	3.1%	2.3%	1.9%
Lima, OH	6,547	78.6%	10,770	59.7%	33.9%	0.9%	5.5%	0.0%	8,973	58.3%	39.9%	0.0%	1.5%	0.4%
Lincoln, NE	18,631	92.6%	49,014	50.3%	41.8%	2.6%	3.6%	1.8%	32,649	63.4%	31.1%	1.0%	4.5%	0.0%
Little Rock-North Little Rock-Conway, AR	47,818	89.9%	70,624	71.4%	24.9%	1.7%	1.3%	0.7%	76,857	76.3%	21.3%	0.9%	1.3%	0.2%
Logan, UT-ID	11,167	85.8%	20,371	53.5%	33.2%	8.9%	1.0%	3.4%	16,177	70.4%	25.3%	2.3%	1.2%	0.8%
Longview, TX	15,519	86.0%	23,450	71.2%	23.7%	3.9%	0.9%	0.3%	19,661	67.7%	29.7%	2.0%	0.6%	0.0%
Longview, WA	6,983	90.4%	8,540	62.2%	36.0%	1.8%	0.0%	0.0%	7,664	64.9%	28.6%	6.1%	0.3%	0.0%
Los Angeles-Long Beach-Anaheim, CA	857,172	89.5%	1,326,162	78.5%	17.6%	0.8%	1.7%	1.3%	1,359,102	77.2%	19.2%	0.7%	1.7%	1.1%
Louisville/Jefferson County, KY-IN	86,468	88.4%	109,505	75.5%	18.7%	1.7%	3.3%	0.9%	115,493	73.7%	21.8%	1.7%	1.3%	1.5%
Lubbock, TX	20,461	85.5%	49,404	51.6%	45.2%	0.2%	2.3%	0.7%	29,381	62.8%	32.4%	1.0%	2.8%	1.1%
Lumberton, NC micro	9,433	83.8%	13,959	72.8%	26.6%	0.0%	0.6%	0.0%	9,230	82.1%	17.9%	0.0%	0.0%	0.0%
Lynchburg, VA	16,213	81.3%	33,122	65.9%	20.9%	5.8%	6.4%	1.0%	20,930	77.0%	16.9%	3.8%	2.0%	0.4%
Macon, GA	15,319	77.9%	26,659	66.1%	28.3%	3.3%	2.0%	0.3%	20,885	79.5%	17.4%	0.9%	1.1%	1.1%
Madera, CA	12,013	95.3%	15,435	80.3%	19.1%	0.0%	0.0%	0.6%	15,618	85.8%	12.7%	0.0%	0.0%	1.5%
Madison, WI	38,821	86.7%	77,713	51.6%	35.1%	7.3%	4.1%	1.9%	72,563	67.4%	26.7%	2.0%	2.2%	1.7%
Manchester-Nashua, NH	26,068	92.7%	32,994	76.3%	14.0%	5.7%	2.8%	1.2%	35,508	69.0%	22.8%	5.1%	1.4%	1.7%
Manhattan, KS	5,522	96.1%	26,254	59.4%	21.8%	1.9%	13.8%	3.2%	13,091	75.2%	9.0%	1.0%	11.3%	3.5%
Mankato-North Mankato, MN	5,686	90.6%	18,983	44.2%	50.3%	4.5%	0.2%	0.8%	8,924	68.7%	21.9%	3.0%	6.3%	0.0%
Mansfield, OH	7,676	81.5%	10,958	71.4%	28.6%	0.0%	0.0%	0.0%	9,405	64.9%	30.2%	1.4%	1.5%	2.1%
McAllen-Edinburg-Mission, TX	75,231	91.1%	89,264	87.8%	11.4%	0.5%	0.1%	0.3%	74,220	83.5%	13.3%	0.5%	1.8%	1.1%
Medford, OR	11,641	87.5%	17,320	62.7%	23.1%	7.3%	5.1%	1.8%	16,879	76.8%	16.3%	5.6%	0.7%	0.6%
Memphis, TN-MS-AR	100,716	85.5%	138,386	76.0%	19.5%	3.1%	0.9%	0.5%	128,632	74.3%	20.2%	3.4%	1.6%	0.5%
Merced, CA	23,797	88.0%	31,498	75.5%	23.4%	0.6%	0.5%	0.0%	25,584	76.4%	22.0%	1.6%	0.0%	0.0%
Meridian, MS micro	5,641	86.8%	11,710	71.5%	19.4%	6.5%	2.6%	0.0%	8,153	79.7%	18.7%	0.5%	1.1%	0.0%
Miami-Fort Lauderdale-West Palm Beach, FL	341,643	87.3%	507,492	80.6%	14.5%	1.0%	2.1%	1.7%	540,931	75.3%	19.8%	1.2%	2.4%	1.4%
Michigan City-La Porte, IN	7,767	84.3%	9,137	67.4%	31.8%	0.8%	0.0%	0.0%	10,789	72.9%	24.5%	0.1%	2.5%	0.0%
Midland, MI	5,454	87.6%	8,172	74.1%	24.2%	0.0%	0.5%	1.2%	7,858	72.1%	17.8%	0.0%	10.1%	0.0%
Midland, TX	11,045	76.8%	16,050	59.5%	34.8%	0.0%	5.0%	0.7%	18,769	72.4%	21.9%	0.4%	5.3%	0.0%
Milwaukee-Waukesha-West Allis, WI	101,921	89.3%	147,919	67.9%	27.6%	2.5%	1.4%	0.6%	157,729	73.7%	22.3%	1.6%	1.6%	0.8%
Minneapolis-St. Paul-Bloomington, MN-WI	231,875	88.6%	293,062	68.6%	23.8%	4.7%	1.6%	1.3%	349,560	71.8%	21.9%	2.1%	2.0%	2.2%
Missoula, MT	7,120	78.6%	16,419	51.3%	39.9%	5.2%	2.1%	1.6%	13,113	43.6%	44.6%	2.4%	9.5%	0.0%
Mobile, AL	26,092	90.2%	42,048	72.2%	26.0%	1.5%	0.2%	0.2%	37,948	77.7%	18.9%	0.9%	1.1%	1.4%
Modesto, CA	42,105	87.3%	55,502	75.5%	23.2%	0.7%	0.1%	0.4%	50,579	75.3%	23.6%	0.6%	0.0%	0.5%
Monroe, LA	13,105	91.6%	20,311	77.5%	21.3%	1.2%	0.0%	0.0%	17,571	83.2%	16.7%	0.1%	0.0%	0.0%
Monroe, MI	10,149	95.4%	13,255	82.0%	13.9%	0.5%	3.6%	0.0%	11,608	89.8%	8.8%	0.5%	0.0%	0.9%
Montgomery, AL	24,219	73.6%	39,232	62.2%	32.0%	3.4%	1.1%	1.2%	36,578	74.0%	21.9%	2.3%	1.3%	0.5%
Morgantown, WV	6,143	83.8%	27,833	63.4%	17.9%	7.1%	10.7%	0.9%	15,518	70.7%	19.1%	3.8%	5.7%	0.7%
Morristown, TN	5,792	80.1%	9,379	73.0%	22.6%	4.4%	0.0%	0.0%	9,288	71.8%	22.6%	5.6%	0.0%	0.0%
Mount Vernon-Anacortes, WA	7,220	76.9%	11,075	74.7%	25.3%	0.0%	0.0%	0.0%	8,911	75.2%	20.8%	0.7%	3.3%	0.0%
Muncie, IN	5,589	78.3%	24,150	34.9%	61.6%	3.0%	0.5%	0.0%	9,291	56.9%	41.7%	0.6%	0.8%	0.0%
Muskegon, MI	13,279	91.1%	14,142	59.1%	39.9%	0.0%	1.0%	0.0%	13,335	79.2%	18.0%	0.0%	2.3%	0.5%
Myrtle Beach-Conway-North Myrtle Beach, SC-NC	19,014	81.3%	32,427	68.9%	25.9%	2.2%	3.1%	0.0%	31,091	71.3%	22.3%	3.3%	3.1%	0.0%
Napa, CA	9,311	88.9%	13,156	69.6%	14.8%	9.9%	2.5%	3.2%	10,779	83.3%	16.1%	0.0%	0.6%	0.0%
Naples-Immokalee-Marco Island, FL	17,383	77.5%	22,554	64.4%	27.4%	0.6%	7.3%	0.2%	22,259	70.2%	22.9%	1.9%	3.9%	1.0%
Nashville-Davidson–Murfreesboro–Franklin, TN	112,956	84.5%	164,808	68.7%	20.7%	5.3%	4.7%	0.6%	175,220	69.7%	22.8%	3.6%	2.7%	1.3%
New Bern, NC	6,204	82.4%	15,130	68.4%	17.4%	6.9%	4.4%	2.9%	13,287	63.9%	28.9%	0.4%	6.6%	0.2%
New Castle, PA micro	6,112	89.4%	7,055	73.5%	21.7%	0.0%	4.9%	0.0%	5,814	87.5%	10.5%	0.0%	1.9%	0.0%
New Haven-Milford, CT	55,017	91.5%	86,612	81.9%	13.2%	2.4%	1.9%	0.6%	80,028	75.6%	18.2%	3.2%	1.4%	1.7%
New Orleans-Metairie, LA	72,223	89.3%	108,886	78.2%	16.1%	2.7%	1.8%	1.2%	127,804	73.6%	21.0%	3.5%	1.7%	0.2%
New Philadelphia-Dover, OH micro	6,749	93.5%	7,243	84.4%	13.3%	0.7%	1.6%	0.0%	7,249	66.8%	19.6%	0.0%	13.6%	0.0%

Table J-4: Metropolitan/Micropolitan Statistical Areas—Mobility Status by Age—*Continued*

| | 13 to 17 | | 18 to 24 | | | | | | 25 to 31 | | | | | |
| | | | | | Percent Living in a Different House | | | | | | Percent Living in a Different House | | | |
	Total Population	Percent Living in Same House	Total Population	Percent Living in Same House	Same State	Different State, Same Region	Different Region	Outside US	Total Population	Percent Living in Same House	Same State	Different State, Same Region	Different Region	Outside US
New York-Newark-Jersey City, NY-NJ-PA	1,246,080	93.0%	1,851,065	84.4%	10.8%	1.1%	1.9%	1.7%	2,018,169	81.7%	13.5%	1.5%	1.9%	1.4%
Niles-Benton Harbor, MI	8,469	91.4%	13,614	65.0%	28.4%	3.3%	2.7%	0.6%	12,250	63.5%	28.8%	1.8%	2.6%	3.3%
North Port-Sarasota-Bradenton, FL	38,225	85.9%	52,179	70.9%	24.7%	2.4%	1.5%	0.5%	43,635	63.9%	30.5%	1.0%	2.6%	1.9%
Norwich-New London, CT	15,491	95.3%	29,528	73.8%	12.7%	8.4%	4.4%	0.7%	25,237	75.0%	18.9%	0.7%	5.4%	0.0%
Ocala, FL	17,883	84.8%	24,424	71.2%	27.5%	0.3%	1.0%	0.0%	24,469	60.8%	37.7%	0.6%	0.8%	0.2%
Ocean City, NJ	4,789	98.2%	7,826	89.1%	6.0%	4.2%	0.7%	0.0%	7,380	71.7%	19.3%	3.5%	5.5%	0.0%
Odessa, TX	11,080	78.6%	16,738	56.7%	27.7%	0.0%	6.7%	8.9%	17,369	68.3%	25.8%	0.4%	0.7%	4.9%
Ogden-Clearfield, UT	54,531	92.0%	58,172	67.9%	25.8%	2.6%	2.3%	1.4%	60,916	70.3%	24.6%	3.4%	1.1%	0.6%
Ogdensburg-Massena, NY micro	6,608	78.1%	16,127	68.0%	28.2%	1.8%	1.5%	0.6%	8,571	79.1%	18.7%	0.0%	1.5%	0.6%
Oklahoma City, OK	78,325	85.4%	135,749	60.9%	30.9%	4.7%	2.7%	0.7%	136,777	68.1%	25.1%	2.5%	2.9%	1.4%
Olympia-Tumwater, WA	16,923	81.1%	24,063	67.2%	28.1%	2.5%	1.0%	1.2%	27,994	70.7%	18.2%	3.4%	4.4%	3.4%
Omaha-Council Bluffs, NE-IA	63,199	89.9%	85,177	62.9%	27.4%	5.9%	3.1%	0.7%	95,723	69.6%	25.5%	1.4%	2.6%	0.8%
Orangeburg, SC micro	7,159	88.4%	11,140	82.9%	16.8%	0.2%	0.0%	0.2%	5,890	83.9%	16.1%	0.0%	0.0%	0.0%
Orlando-Kissimmee-Sanford, FL	156,899	84.5%	230,036	73.7%	21.4%	1.8%	2.0%	1.1%	234,680	75.2%	20.3%	0.8%	1.8%	1.8%
Oshkosh-Neenah, WI	9,642	87.7%	20,693	68.5%	29.7%	1.1%	0.7%	0.0%	16,548	64.7%	31.4%	0.0%	3.9%	0.0%
Ottawa-Peru, IL micro	8,288	88.3%	9,127	71.6%	27.7%	0.7%	0.0%	0.0%	9,376	80.7%	19.1%	0.2%	0.0%	0.0%
Owensboro, KY	7,282	89.5%	10,277	71.5%	27.4%	0.1%	0.0%	0.9%	10,034	76.7%	22.3%	1.0%	0.0%	0.0%
Oxnard-Thousand Oaks-Ventura, CA	57,805	87.8%	83,390	82.8%	12.9%	1.7%	1.9%	0.7%	72,585	81.4%	14.0%	1.0%	1.9%	1.8%
Palm Bay-Melbourne-Titusville, FL	30,170	89.6%	44,051	76.7%	16.7%	1.4%	2.8%	2.4%	38,460	82.5%	14.1%	1.3%	0.9%	1.2%
Panama City, FL	10,522	84.3%	16,496	64.5%	26.1%	4.2%	4.1%	1.0%	19,477	74.6%	21.6%	1.7%	1.6%	0.5%
Parkersburg-Vienna, WV	5,079	96.4%	7,766	88.9%	7.4%	1.3%	2.4%	0.0%	6,968	69.9%	25.3%	1.4%	3.3%	0.0%
Pensacola-Ferry Pass-Brent, FL	27,515	81.5%	53,379	63.9%	19.1%	5.4%	10.4%	1.3%	46,433	68.5%	19.5%	7.2%	3.8%	1.1%
Peoria, IL	24,935	91.7%	35,324	72.0%	25.6%	1.6%	0.8%	0.0%	35,959	78.6%	15.0%	3.2%	2.9%	0.3%
Philadelphia-Camden-Wilmington, PA-NJ-DE-MD	395,794	91.1%	590,688	77.9%	16.0%	2.6%	2.6%	0.8%	593,560	77.3%	16.6%	1.9%	2.8%	1.3%
Phoenix-Mesa-Scottsdale, AZ	310,618	84.3%	416,357	69.8%	24.5%	2.5%	2.1%	1.1%	433,079	69.0%	24.2%	2.5%	3.2%	1.1%
Pine Bluff, AR	6,699	94.0%	11,714	77.9%	21.3%	0.0%	0.8%	0.0%	7,558	87.7%	12.1%	0.2%	0.0%	0.0%
Pittsburgh, PA	135,474	90.3%	214,247	67.3%	26.6%	1.2%	3.6%	1.3%	209,509	72.9%	23.4%	0.7%	2.4%	0.7%
Pittsfield, MA	7,662	94.7%	13,341	73.0%	17.8%	3.6%	3.6%	1.9%	9,533	65.1%	31.7%	1.3%	1.8%	0.0%
Pocatello, ID	7,359	81.3%	10,790	59.2%	28.2%	5.4%	4.3%	2.8%	7,460	76.6%	18.7%	1.4%	0.0%	3.4%
Port St. Lucie, FL	25,750	87.2%	32,529	77.5%	20.3%	0.2%	2.0%	0.0%	32,399	73.5%	22.7%	1.3%	1.5%	0.9%
Portland-South Portland, ME	31,599	89.6%	45,220	66.3%	25.1%	5.9%	2.0%	0.7%	41,276	63.9%	30.4%	3.1%	2.7%	0.0%
Portland-Vancouver-Hillsboro, OR-WA	145,334	87.1%	199,536	62.7%	28.1%	6.4%	1.9%	1.0%	235,415	60.0%	26.6%	6.1%	3.2%	1.1%
Pottsville, PA micro	7,752	91.1%	11,168	85.9%	12.9%	0.0%	1.2%	0.0%	11,697	72.1%	24.9%	1.8%	1.2%	0.0%
Prescott, AZ	11,799	70.3%	14,382	61.2%	24.1%	11.9%	2.3%	0.5%	14,168	70.8%	22.7%	4.5%	1.3%	0.7%
Providence-Warwick, RI-MA	97,420	92.7%	173,628	76.3%	14.7%	5.4%	1.8%	1.7%	143,009	74.7%	18.5%	2.8%	3.0%	1.0%
Provo-Orem, UT	47,624	86.7%	95,374	46.6%	35.7%	8.2%	6.2%	3.2%	60,202	68.4%	24.9%	3.7%	2.6%	0.5%
Pueblo, CO	10,360	83.9%	15,775	58.8%	34.6%	0.2%	5.1%	1.3%	15,157	57.2%	34.2%	0.0%	7.0%	1.6%
Punta Gorda, FL	7,440	79.1%	10,166	72.4%	24.4%	0.0%	3.2%	0.0%	8,480	81.7%	14.4%	1.4%	2.5%	0.0%
Racine, WI	13,831	95.1%	14,201	84.8%	15.2%	0.0%	0.0%	0.0%	17,465	83.7%	14.8%	1.5%	0.0%	0.0%
Raleigh, NC	90,582	88.8%	115,499	69.8%	24.5%	1.8%	2.7%	1.2%	114,871	63.1%	30.1%	2.8%	2.6%	1.5%
Rapid City, SD	8,917	86.6%	13,254	37.5%	53.1%	8.1%	1.3%	0.0%	12,549	66.1%	24.9%	4.5%	4.5%	0.0%
Reading, PA	28,314	91.4%	41,660	74.8%	21.8%	1.2%	0.7%	1.5%	33,732	79.9%	18.4%	0.7%	0.3%	0.8%
Redding, CA	10,988	92.3%	17,040	64.1%	25.5%	5.5%	3.2%	1.8%	15,126	67.3%	26.7%	2.2%	1.2%	2.5%
Reno, NV	27,350	82.7%	43,965	53.3%	31.7%	12.7%	1.4%	1.0%	42,675	69.8%	23.5%	3.7%	1.5%	1.6%
Richmond, VA	83,841	87.1%	116,039	72.5%	23.8%	1.3%	2.1%	0.4%	118,587	69.7%	25.2%	2.3%	1.5%	1.3%
Riverside-San Bernardino-Ontario, CA	339,960	86.7%	474,163	79.0%	18.4%	0.9%	0.8%	0.9%	422,349	76.5%	20.3%	0.9%	1.2%	1.1%
Roanoke, VA	19,632	85.4%	27,320	70.3%	25.2%	1.6%	2.7%	0.3%	24,392	68.8%	28.4%	1.1%	1.4%	0.3%
Rochester, MN	12,613	95.4%	19,938	60.0%	34.5%	4.8%	0.6%	0.0%	19,484	82.8%	13.1%	1.6%	0.8%	1.7%
Rochester, NY	69,422	89.4%	114,616	65.9%	27.6%	1.8%	3.9%	0.8%	99,070	73.0%	22.6%	0.8%	2.5%	1.1%
Rockford, IL	27,011	87.4%	32,814	79.6%	19.3%	0.9%	0.2%	0.0%	26,666	67.2%	26.6%	2.3%	3.4%	0.4%
Rocky Mount, NC	10,711	88.5%	14,182	83.2%	9.4%	5.3%	2.0%	0.0%	9,851	84.7%	13.3%	1.9%	0.1%	0.0%
Rome, GA	6,730	72.4%	9,834	71.9%	24.7%	3.4%	0.0%	0.0%	7,305	76.9%	18.8%	3.1%	1.2%	0.0%
Roseburg, OR micro	5,316	88.9%	7,684	68.4%	21.9%	9.7%	0.0%	0.0%	7,735	80.2%	17.8%	0.0%	1.9%	0.0%
Sacramento–Roseville–Arden-Arcade, CA	153,429	85.5%	216,145	68.0%	28.5%	0.9%	0.9%	1.7%	203,737	66.7%	31.5%	0.5%	0.8%	0.6%
Saginaw, MI	13,195	92.5%	21,690	65.9%	33.0%	0.0%	0.7%	0.5%	15,016	74.3%	22.8%	0.0%	2.5%	0.4%
Salem, OH micro	6,746	85.4%	8,311	68.0%	28.3%	0.0%	3.7%	0.0%	8,795	67.0%	30.2%	0.0%	2.9%	0.0%
Salem, OR	28,501	87.1%	43,413	73.0%	21.1%	3.9%	0.9%	1.0%	34,859	65.2%	27.3%	5.0%	2.4%	0.2%
Salinas, CA	32,192	92.1%	47,254	76.2%	18.2%	1.4%	3.0%	1.2%	43,942	83.5%	12.2%	0.7%	2.0%	1.6%
Salisbury, MD-DE	20,077	89.1%	39,407	68.9%	22.8%	5.3%	2.5%	0.6%	29,859	79.4%	17.2%	1.9%	1.5%	0.0%
Salt Lake City, UT	85,071	86.2%	109,954	70.7%	20.3%	2.8%	4.4%	1.8%	127,631	67.9%	26.7%	3.1%	1.7%	0.6%
San Angelo, TX	7,936	82.4%	14,311	46.9%	33.6%	3.6%	14.5%	1.4%	12,721	65.0%	17.1%	10.2%	5.3%	2.4%
San Antonio-New Braunfels, TX	168,358	87.9%	242,475	68.6%	24.7%	1.7%	3.3%	1.7%	232,757	71.3%	24.1%	1.5%	2.0%	1.1%
San Diego-Carlsbad, CA	197,480	89.0%	366,084	71.5%	21.1%	1.1%	4.1%	2.1%	371,745	73.3%	20.4%	1.2%	3.2%	1.9%
San Francisco-Oakland-Hayward, CA	248,359	89.0%	380,272	71.2%	22.7%	1.2%	2.2%	2.7%	483,008	73.3%	20.5%	1.1%	2.8%	2.3%
San Jose-Sunnyvale-Santa Clara, CA	115,758	90.5%	165,780	70.5%	23.2%	1.2%	2.1%	3.1%	197,693	73.1%	20.3%	0.6%	3.2%	2.8%
San Luis Obispo-Paso Robles-Arroyo Grande, CA	12,954	90.1%	44,013	44.0%	54.3%	0.0%	1.5%	0.2%	23,706	75.0%	21.1%	2.2%	0.7%	1.1%

Table J-4: Metropolitan/Micropolitan Statistical Areas—Mobility Status by Age—*Continued*

	13 to 17		18 to 24						25 to 31					
					Percent Living in a Different House						Percent Living in a Different House			
	Total Population	Percent Living in Same House	Total Population	Percent Living in Same House	Same State	Different State, Same Region	Different Region	Outside US	Total Population	Percent Living in Same House	Same State	Different State, Same Region	Different Region	Outside US
Santa Cruz-Watsonville, CA......	14,588	96.6%	39,381	63.8%	31.0%	2.3%	0.9%	2.0%	21,434	84.2%	15.2%	0.0%	0.3%	0.3%
Santa Fe, NM..........	7,907	86.7%	11,027	77.4%	14.5%	2.7%	4.9%	0.4%	11,022	69.0%	21.7%	3.3%	3.2%	2.7%
Santa Maria-Santa Barbara, CA	29,172	87.7%	67,925	47.6%	44.6%	2.0%	1.7%	4.1%	40,171	68.5%	25.7%	3.1%	0.5%	2.2%
Santa Rosa, CA	31,888	90.2%	45,516	72.2%	26.1%	0.1%	0.8%	0.8%	43,559	73.2%	23.7%	0.7%	1.9%	0.5%
Savannah, GA..........	21,245	84.5%	43,891	60.3%	28.3%	7.6%	2.2%	1.6%	39,863	71.2%	18.6%	4.3%	3.5%	2.5%
Scranton–Wilkes-Barre–Hazleton, PA..........	32,972	92.5%	56,196	76.9%	16.6%	4.2%	1.4%	0.9%	46,279	76.1%	18.8%	2.7%	1.5%	0.9%
Seattle-Tacoma-Bellevue, WA...	216,743	88.2%	321,593	65.0%	25.3%	3.8%	3.6%	2.3%	397,366	65.9%	25.7%	2.7%	4.1%	1.6%
Sebastian-Vero Beach, FL	8,844	94.3%	9,614	79.4%	16.4%	0.0%	4.2%	0.0%	9,040	59.2%	34.9%	1.5%	3.2%	1.2%
Sebring, FL..........	4,417	91.6%	6,849	86.1%	12.1%	0.0%	0.0%	1.9%	5,937	70.9%	18.8%	9.4%	0.9%	0.0%
Sheboygan, WI..........	8,528	93.1%	7,877	77.5%	17.1%	5.4%	0.0%	0.0%	9,011	78.9%	19.0%	0.0%	2.1%	0.0%
Sherman-Denison, TX............	7,874	86.6%	11,094	68.3%	24.6%	3.4%	0.0%	3.8%	11,329	77.0%	20.8%	1.4%	0.7%	0.0%
Show Low, AZ micro.....	8,371	91.7%	10,459	86.3%	11.0%	0.4%	1.7%	0.6%	9,505	84.0%	13.8%	0.0%	0.0%	2.2%
Shreveport-Bossier City, LA	28,463	85.3%	49,166	77.4%	15.0%	6.2%	1.0%	0.4%	45,748	77.3%	17.3%	2.7%	2.1%	0.7%
Sierra Vista-Douglas, AZ.........	8,304	92.1%	12,340	59.3%	28.7%	2.0%	7.6%	2.5%	11,701	52.9%	26.7%	4.8%	10.5%	5.0%
Sioux City, IA-NE-SD..............	13,318	92.5%	16,841	66.1%	25.0%	5.2%	2.9%	0.8%	14,006	67.5%	25.3%	5.6%	1.6%	0.0%
Sioux Falls, SD	13,580	84.9%	23,954	61.5%	23.8%	11.9%	2.1%	0.6%	25,702	82.1%	16.0%	1.5%	0.4%	0.0%
South Bend-Mishawaka, IN-MI	24,107	81.2%	32,769	69.1%	19.9%	5.9%	4.5%	0.5%	25,181	67.0%	24.1%	3.5%	4.6%	0.8%
Spartanburg, SC.....................	23,490	85.3%	34,337	72.2%	23.8%	2.7%	1.4%	0.0%	27,072	75.9%	19.1%	0.4%	1.7%	3.0%
Spokane-Spokane Valley, WA...	37,179	90.6%	54,440	61.6%	29.5%	4.4%	3.5%	1.0%	55,571	73.9%	21.0%	2.2%	2.7%	0.2%
Springfield, IL	12,890	86.2%	18,107	69.6%	25.2%	1.6%	3.3%	0.2%	19,203	72.8%	17.7%	0.7%	7.6%	1.3%
Springfield, MA	43,682	88.0%	79,118	70.5%	22.8%	3.8%	1.9%	1.0%	52,221	72.7%	22.7%	1.6%	1.8%	1.2%
Springfield, MO	31,094	85.8%	54,954	63.9%	31.4%	1.0%	3.7%	0.0%	43,409	76.0%	20.8%	0.8%	2.4%	0.0%
Springfield, OH	9,593	90.6%	12,435	71.5%	27.4%	1.1%	0.0%	0.0%	10,946	66.6%	25.2%	0.0%	4.8%	3.4%
St. Cloud, MN..........	11,797	94.8%	29,346	39.3%	54.1%	5.4%	1.0%	0.2%	17,858	76.6%	21.8%	0.0%	0.5%	1.1%
St. George, UT	10,787	72.7%	14,931	49.6%	31.5%	17.2%	1.5%	0.2%	10,743	73.0%	22.5%	3.0%	1.5%	0.0%
St. Joseph, MO-KS..........	7,692	89.5%	12,829	69.1%	26.6%	2.5%	1.8%	0.0%	11,679	59.1%	29.5%	3.0%	8.3%	0.0%
St. Louis, MO-IL..........	181,026	89.7%	250,869	72.4%	23.9%	1.7%	1.7%	0.2%	269,329	72.4%	22.5%	2.0%	2.5%	0.7%
State College, PA.....................	6,996	93.6%	44,131	34.9%	48.0%	8.5%	4.5%	4.2%	13,999	59.2%	30.4%	6.7%	3.2%	0.6%
Staunton-Waynesboro, VA.......	5,147	85.1%	13,074	61.1%	27.3%	6.7%	4.0%	0.9%	8,830	75.3%	23.1%	0.0%	1.6%	0.0%
Stockton-Lodi, CA...................	57,808	84.4%	73,709	69.4%	29.3%	0.6%	0.5%	0.2%	61,696	75.0%	24.7%	0.1%	0.1%	0.0%
Sumter, SC..........	7,412	86.8%	13,333	67.7%	25.1%	6.1%	1.1%	0.0%	9,642	81.5%	8.2%	7.9%	2.5%	0.0%
Sunbury, PA micro	4,390	95.5%	7,679	81.6%	18.4%	0.0%	0.0%	0.0%	7,918	79.7%	19.2%	0.0%	0.2%	0.9%
Syracuse, NY	42,521	93.0%	71,514	62.1%	31.1%	2.4%	3.1%	1.3%	56,132	75.7%	20.8%	0.8%	2.2%	0.5%
Tallahassee, FL	21,444	80.8%	75,689	51.2%	45.7%	1.3%	1.3%	0.4%	40,310	65.9%	28.7%	2.6%	2.1%	0.8%
Tampa-St. Petersburg-Clearwater, FL	170,417	84.7%	243,210	70.1%	23.9%	1.3%	3.8%	0.9%	256,739	70.4%	23.9%	1.9%	2.3%	1.4%
Terre Haute, IN	9,373	79.1%	20,793	64.7%	28.9%	2.6%	2.3%	1.6%	16,606	74.4%	18.2%	1.9%	5.5%	0.0%
Texarkana, TX-AR...................	8,947	82.9%	14,037	72.8%	23.2%	2.5%	1.5%	0.0%	15,588	80.9%	9.8%	8.6%	0.7%	0.0%
The Villages, FL.....................	1,930	95.8%	4,200	60.4%	39.6%	0.0%	0.0%	0.0%	5,232	50.5%	49.5%	0.0%	0.0%	0.0%
Toledo, OH..........	40,545	84.5%	72,817	60.1%	34.9%	2.6%	1.1%	1.3%	57,149	75.5%	21.7%	1.3%	0.9%	0.7%
Topeka, KS	15,563	80.3%	19,391	72.8%	21.1%	2.2%	3.5%	0.4%	19,377	78.2%	13.0%	5.1%	2.9%	0.8%
Torrington, CT micro............	12,168	97.2%	13,642	87.9%	10.6%	0.3%	0.6%	0.6%	13,526	72.0%	24.6%	0.0%	2.7%	0.7%
Traverse City, MI micro	9,525	83.9%	11,425	55.9%	35.8%	3.0%	3.8%	1.6%	10,876	77.9%	14.8%	6.0%	1.3%	0.0%
Trenton, NJ	24,958	93.4%	40,520	73.9%	19.0%	1.7%	3.4%	1.9%	31,797	72.5%	20.0%	1.8%	3.4%	2.2%
Truckee-Grass Valley, CA micro	5,901	86.7%	7,382	71.2%	26.0%	2.7%	0.0%	0.0%	5,855	80.8%	19.2%	0.0%	0.0%	0.0%
Tucson, AZ	62,937	85.6%	121,550	55.3%	35.8%	2.9%	4.2%	1.8%	88,003	65.3%	26.0%	3.4%	3.3%	2.0%
Tullahoma-Manchester, TN micro	8,553	92.6%	8,902	54.7%	37.5%	5.1%	2.7%	0.0%	6,331	69.1%	23.4%	1.3%	6.1%	0.0%
Tulsa, OK..........	65,890	85.7%	87,792	71.2%	22.5%	2.9%	2.3%	1.0%	89,032	71.7%	24.2%	1.4%	2.7%	0.0%
Tupelo, MS micro.....................	10,149	87.8%	14,124	80.3%	18.8%	0.7%	0.3%	0.0%	11,083	64.8%	33.7%	0.4%	0.0%	1.0%
Tuscaloosa, AL..........	14,476	81.7%	40,034	61.0%	23.3%	11.4%	2.9%	1.4%	23,302	71.1%	23.3%	4.0%	1.2%	0.4%
Tyler, TX..........	15,454	81.8%	22,230	65.9%	28.6%	2.1%	3.4%	0.0%	19,669	73.3%	20.6%	0.0%	4.7%	1.4%
Urban Honolulu, HI	57,221	89.6%	99,988	69.3%	15.9%	6.1%	6.3%	2.5%	108,618	67.3%	16.4%	4.7%	9.0%	2.7%
Utica-Rome, NY	19,567	85.0%	29,255	64.3%	31.9%	0.8%	2.4%	0.6%	24,883	70.4%	25.9%	0.2%	2.2%	1.4%
Valdosta, GA	9,624	87.6%	24,729	55.5%	39.5%	3.2%	1.1%	0.7%	14,623	70.4%	20.7%	2.6%	2.8%	3.5%
Vallejo-Fairfield, CA................	27,829	85.7%	43,457	77.2%	19.0%	1.0%	1.4%	1.5%	42,964	74.2%	21.4%	0.0%	3.5%	0.9%
Victoria, TX	7,946	87.2%	9,386	76.3%	19.3%	2.5%	2.0%	0.0%	7,723	71.1%	27.0%	2.0%	0.0%	0.0%
Vineland-Bridgeton, NJ............	10,242	95.7%	13,253	86.5%	11.3%	1.6%	0.7%	0.0%	17,680	76.8%	17.8%	3.9%	1.5%	0.0%
Virginia Beach-Norfolk-Newport News, VA-NC	105,756	86.3%	203,677	67.5%	21.5%	4.2%	5.6%	1.2%	189,087	68.3%	22.7%	3.1%	4.9%	1.1%
Visalia-Porterville, CA.............	36,363	88.4%	49,699	76.7%	21.3%	0.2%	1.8%	0.0%	46,122	79.8%	16.6%	2.3%	1.3%	0.0%
Waco, TX..........	15,318	88.0%	38,050	59.3%	35.5%	1.3%	3.5%	0.4%	23,818	61.1%	33.3%	2.0%	2.9%	0.7%
Walla Walla, WA.....................	3,406	91.6%	7,436	50.2%	34.7%	5.9%	0.4%	8.8%	5,911	74.9%	21.3%	2.4%	0.0%	1.4%
Warner Robins, GA	14,319	76.9%	20,230	78.3%	19.2%	2.2%	0.2%	0.0%	19,225	72.8%	24.3%	1.0%	1.3%	0.6%
Washington-Arlington-Alexandria, DC-VA-MD-WV	371,020	89.4%	540,511	72.8%	15.9%	4.6%	4.6%	2.1%	646,396	69.6%	18.6%	6.1%	3.1%	2.5%
Waterloo-Cedar Falls, IA.........	10,071	93.5%	27,213	74.6%	23.8%	0.3%	0.5%	0.8%	14,991	74.5%	22.2%	1.9%	1.3%	0.0%
Watertown-Fort Drum, NY	7,667	85.2%	15,064	49.5%	20.6%	5.8%	17.8%	6.2%	13,925	64.5%	22.2%	0.0%	10.9%	2.5%
Wausau, WI..........	9,211	92.8%	11,313	65.6%	33.3%	0.3%	0.0%	0.8%	11,030	72.7%	27.0%	0.0%	0.2%	0.0%
Weirton-Steubenville, WV-OH ..	8,246	88.7%	12,018	70.1%	21.0%	0.6%	6.8%	1.4%	7,984	80.7%	15.4%	0.0%	3.8%	0.2%
Wenatchee, WA..........	8,121	92.0%	8,718	88.8%	10.0%	0.0%	1.2%	0.0%	11,132	87.6%	12.1%	0.0%	0.2%	0.0%
Wheeling, WV-OH	9,707	87.3%	13,164	72.3%	19.3%	0.0%	7.1%	1.3%	9,570	79.8%	13.8%	0.0%	3.8%	2.6%
Whitewater-Elkhorn, WI micro.	6,980	88.0%	11,281	39.6%	57.4%	0.3%	2.8%	0.0%	8,854	71.8%	22.5%	0.8%	0.0%	4.9%
Wichita Falls, TX	9,009	89.4%	19,163	59.2%	18.7%	7.2%	11.3%	3.6%	16,601	70.4%	21.2%	2.9%	5.4%	0.0%
Wichita, KS..........	45,238	86.9%	58,427	69.5%	25.9%	0.6%	2.3%	1.8%	64,948	75.1%	19.2%	0.4%	4.5%	0.8%
Williamsport, PA	5,763	98.1%	13,832	67.2%	32.0%	0.3%	0.5%	0.0%	8,292	82.8%	14.5%	0.0%	2.8%	0.0%
Wilmington, NC.....................	13,683	89.2%	32,892	48.4%	41.2%	4.5%	3.8%	2.1%	23,851	59.9%	35.4%	2.6%	1.8%	0.3%

Table J-4: Metropolitan/Micropolitan Statistical Areas—Mobility Status by Age—*Continued*

	13 to 17		18 to 24						25 to 31					
					Percent Living in a Different House						Percent Living in a Different House			
	Total Population	Percent Living in Same House	Total Population	Percent Living in Same House	Same State	Different State, Same Region	Different Region	Outside US	Total Population	Percent Living in Same House	Same State	Different State, Same Region	Different Region	Outside US
Winchester, VA-WV	9,063	90.1%	10,846	58.7%	33.1%	7.1%	1.1%	0.0%	9,260	70.7%	24.1%	3.0%	2.1%	0.0%
Winston-Salem, NC	45,514	86.4%	60,502	70.0%	22.4%	4.4%	3.0%	0.3%	50,711	78.1%	17.8%	2.3%	1.4%	0.4%
Wooster, OH micro	8,612	93.0%	11,137	63.4%	29.9%	0.4%	5.6%	0.8%	8,719	70.9%	24.9%	1.9%	2.3%	0.0%
Worcester, MA-CT	61,447	90.6%	89,748	74.5%	21.0%	2.8%	1.2%	0.6%	77,116	74.6%	22.0%	1.3%	1.5%	0.7%
Yakima, WA	18,411	89.9%	25,232	69.9%	28.7%	1.4%	0.0%	0.0%	22,351	73.6%	26.4%	0.0%	0.0%	0.0%
York-Hanover, PA	26,969	93.1%	37,083	71.8%	24.9%	0.4%	2.2%	0.7%	33,523	71.9%	21.5%	0.0%	4.7%	2.0%
Youngstown-Warren-Boardman, OH-PA	38,178	88.0%	47,862	71.5%	23.9%	0.1%	3.3%	1.2%	43,994	73.9%	21.5%	1.1%	3.4%	0.0%
Yuba City, CA	11,439	88.5%	16,677	67.2%	28.2%	1.2%	2.6%	0.9%	16,214	59.0%	34.8%	1.4%	3.2%	1.6%
Yuma, AZ	15,620	88.6%	24,334	76.1%	15.2%	3.8%	2.7%	2.2%	19,442	74.2%	18.8%	2.4%	3.0%	1.6%

PART K
HOUSING SUMMARY

HOUSING SUMMARY

As the Baby Boom entered its household formation years in the late 1960s and 1970s, housing development grew to accommodate the growing adult population and their children. As the Millennials enter their household formation years, times have changed. The structure of living arrangements has shifted to more single person households or non-relatives living together. Millennials have delayed marriage and childbearing, and many more are living with other non-relative friends and have pushed home ownership until later in life. One thing that is almost universal, regardless of housing arrangements, is their access to the Internet and use of technology.

The tables presented here are for Millennial householders rather than all persons. The householder is the person who owns or rents the housing unit and other individuals in the household are defined in reference to the householder. This also means that Millennials who live in group quarters (primarily college housing) are excluded because they are not part of the household population and are not householders. While most of the tables in this book relate to the 82.5 million Millennials age 13 to 31, this section describes the housing characteristics for the 16.4 million householders age 18 to 31.

HOUSING STATUS

Nationwide, 72.6 percent of Millennial householders are age 25 to 31 compared to only 27.6 percent in the 18 to 24 age group. Among householders in North Dakota, almost half (47.2 percent) are 18 to 24 year olds, leaving

Percent Age 25 to 31 Who Are Home Owner Households

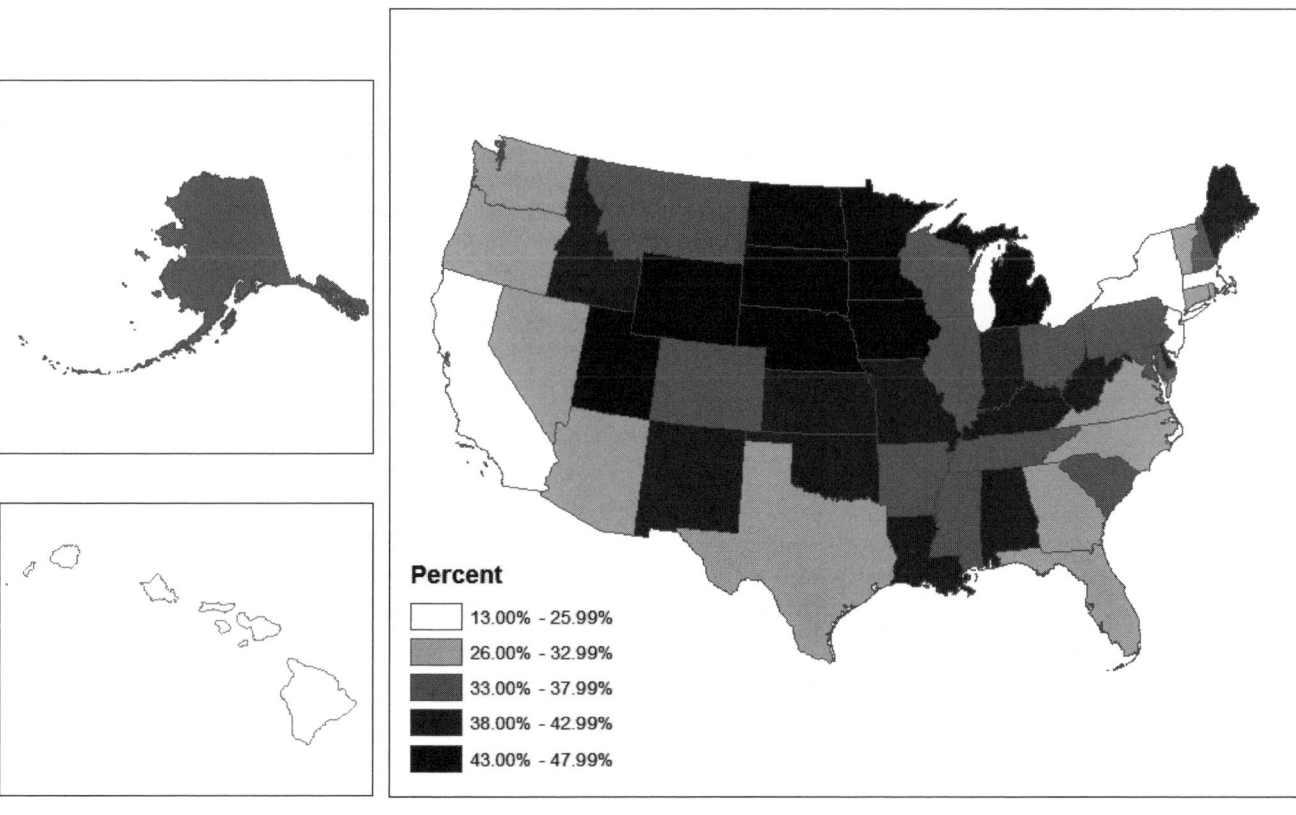

Percent
13.00% - 25.99%
26.00% - 32.99%
33.00% - 37.99%
38.00% - 42.99%
43.00% - 47.99%

only 52.8 percent of older Millennials. In New Jersey only 15.9 percent of the householders are 18 to 24 year olds, making it the highest percentage for the 25 to 31 age group at 83.8 percent.

Tenure describes whether a housing unit is owned or rented. As expected, Millennials in the older age group are more frequently owners compared to the younger ages. Among the 18 to 24 year olds, 87.3 percent are renters compared to 67.1 percent of the older age group. The District of Columbia has the highest percentage of renters (95.1 percent) among 18 to 24 year old Millennials, while West Virginia is lowest at 74.5 percent. That means West Virginia also has the highest percentage of home owners at 25.5 percent. For the older age group, almost half (47.9 percent) are home owners in North Dakota. The District of Columbia is lowest at only 14.0 percent. While home ownership is still a struggle, 22.6 percent of the nation's Millennials hold mortgage debt. The percentage ranges from a low of 9.5 percent in Hawaii to 35.2 percent in Utah.

Cumberland County, PA has the lowest percentage of young Millennial householders at 5.3 percent, while Montgomery County, VA is highest with 76.3 percent and therefore the lowest percentage in the older age group. In most counties there is a much higher percentage of

older Millennials as householders, but in 24 counties the reverse is true—there are more younger householders. The gap is largest in Montgomery County, VA followed by Monroe County, IN. In 267 of the 622 counties more than 90 percent of householders age 18 to 24 are renters. In 28 counties the data shows that all (100 percent) young householders are renters while three counties (Forsyth County, GA, Newton County, GA and Scott County, MN) are above 80 percent owners. Among older Millennials, Jefferson County, MO has the highest percentage of homeowners at 86.6 percent while Nash County, NC is lowest with 1.6 percent ownership.

Virtually all householders (97.6 percent) are age 25 to 31 in Brockton City, MA, and in eight other cities the percentage is above 90 percent. Gainesville City, FL (home to the University of Florida) has the lowest share of older householders at 35.7 percent. Renters are by far most common among the younger Millennials, as 214 of 331 cities have renter rates above 90 percent. The ACS data shows that all householders (100 percent) are renters in 38 cities. Among the older age group, owners are more prevalent than renters in only 14 cities. Rochester City, MN has the largest difference between owners and renters with 72.9 percent owning their homes. Livonia City, MI is a close second at 72.7 percent. Livonia also has the highest percentage of Millennials who hold mortgage

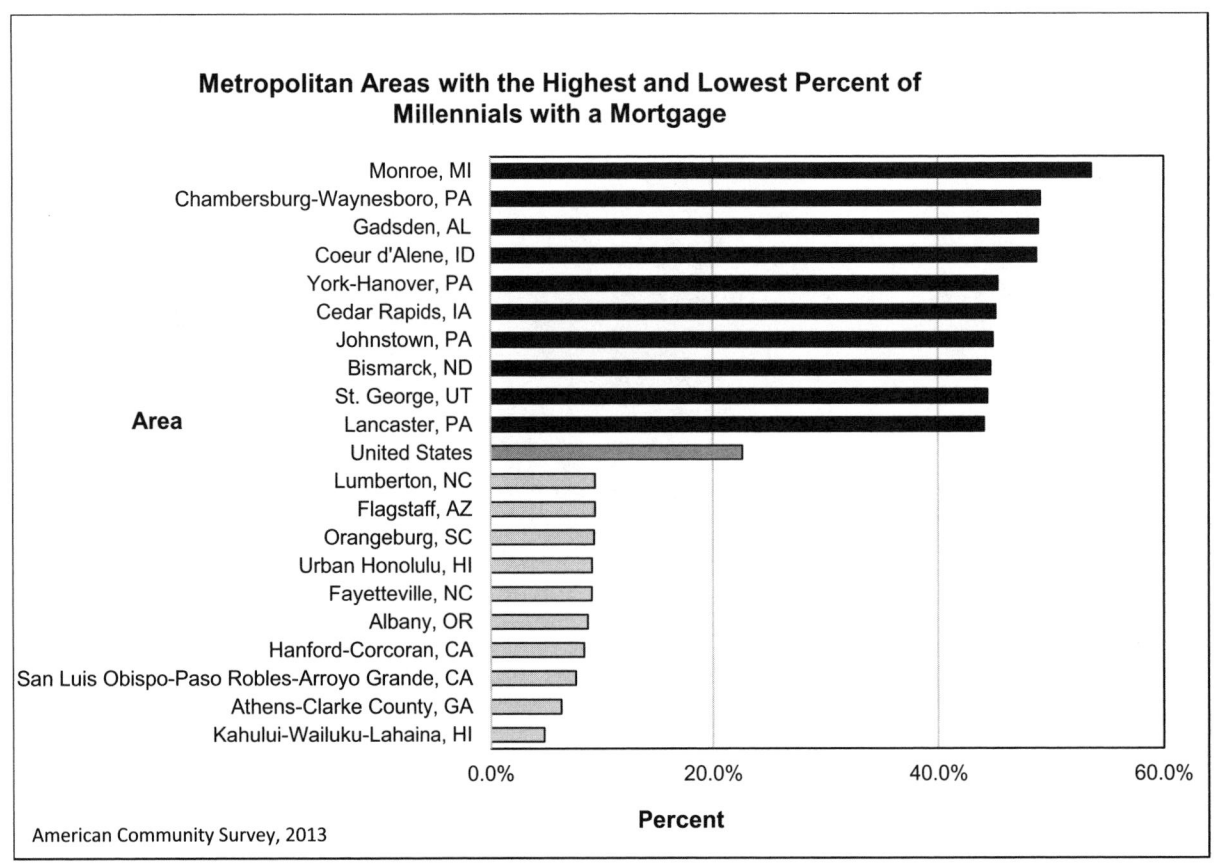

American Community Survey, 2013

debt at 70.0 percent. In 54 cities mortgages are held by less than 10 percent.

The 25- to 31-year-old Millennial householders are 90.6 percent of all householders in the Truckee-Grass Valley, CA micropolitan area. In 34 metro/micros they are more than 80 percent of the total. As with the other area types, the younger Millennials are mostly renters with renters being more than 80 percent of the total in 166 metro/micro areas. However, in the Tupelo, MS micropolitan area, 63.6 percent are home owners. Among the older ages, owners are more than 50 percent of the total in 43 metro/micros, and the highest level of ownership is in the Monroe, MI metro area. Monroe also has the highest percentage of Millennials with mortgage debt at 53.6 percent. The lowest level of ownership is in the Kahalui-Wailuku-Lahaina, HI metro at 7.8 percent.

INTERNET ACCESS

The President's Council of Economic Advisors notes that the Millennials are the first generation to have grown up with access to the Internet. That technology is important to them is illustrated by the fact that 84.6 percent of Millennial householders age 25 to 31 have Internet access. Younger Millennials are only slightly behind at 80.8 percent. Among the older age group, residents of Mississippi have the lowest level of access at 73.9 percent compared to Massachusetts with 92.9 percent. Internet and phone access is carried with 38.8 percent who have a mobile communications plan. Wyoming has the lowest level of access to a mobile plan at 30.5 percent, while Hawaii is highest with 51.3 percent. Among older Millennials, in 178 counties 90 percent or more of those age 25 to 31 have Internet access, but in Robeson County, NC only 37.4 percent have access at home. Mobile communications plans are held by 69.0 percent in Anchorage Municipality, AK.

The Internet is accessible to more than 90 percent of younger Millennials in 105 cities and 113 cities for older Millennials. Mobile communications plans are held by 83.9 percent in Mission Viejo City, CA but only 8.3 percent in Flint City, MI. The Midland, MI metropolitan area has the lowest level of Internet access among the younger Millennials at only 20.4 percent, while in 100 metro/micros access is greater than 90 percent. Among older Millennials, the Lumberton, NC micro has the lowest access at 41.6 percent, and only 79 metro/micros are above 90 percent. At the metropolitan/micropolitan area level, mobile communications plans are held be 68.4 percent in the Whitewater-Elkhorn, WI micro but only 4.2 percent in the Danville, IL metro area.

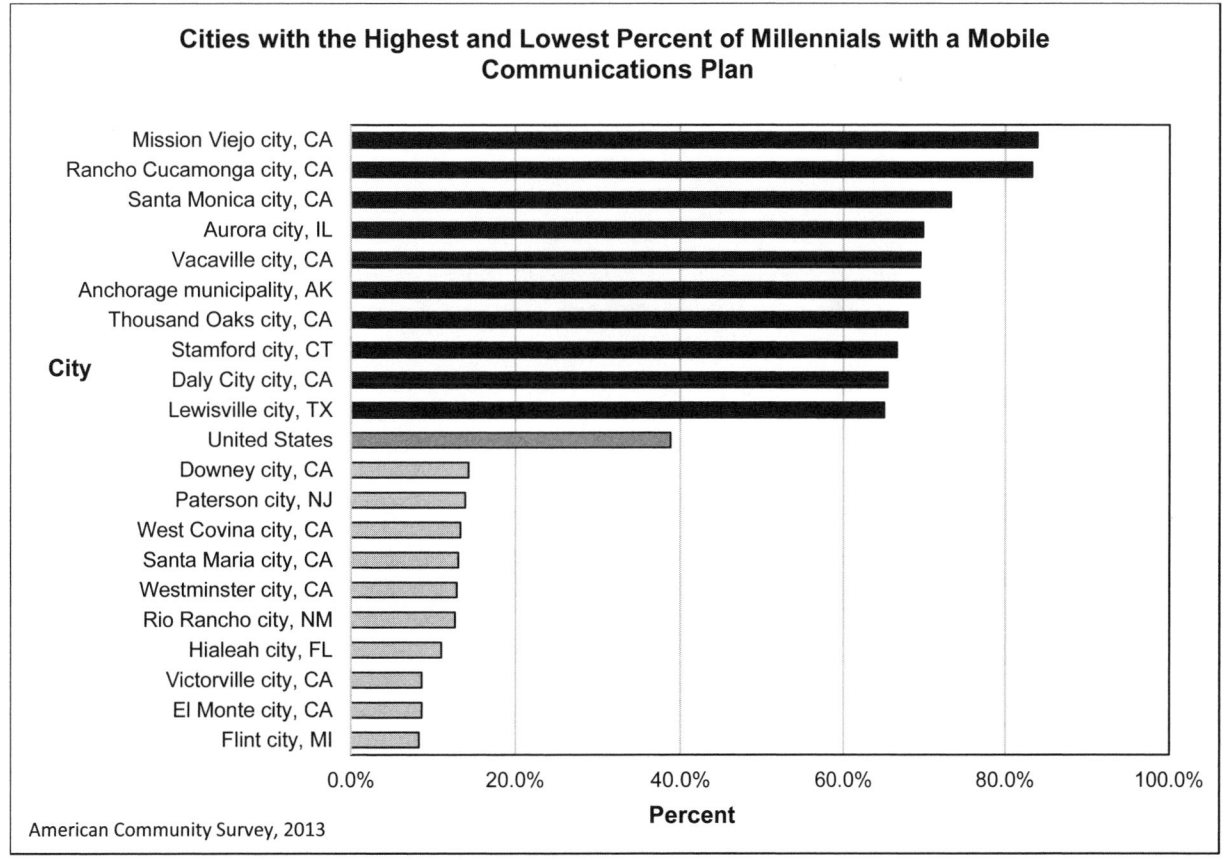

American Community Survey, 2013

Table K-1: States—Summary Housing Characteristics

	Millennial Householders	Age of Householders		18 to 24 Years Old		25 to 31 Years Old			Percent with Internet Access		Percent with Mobile Access Plan
		18 to 24	25 to 31	Owners	Renters	Owners	Renters	With Mortgage	18 to 24	25 to 31	
United States	16,387,392	27.6%	72.2%	12.7%	87.3%	32.9%	67.1%	22.6%	80.8%	84.6%	38.8%
Alabama	250,003	30.8%	69.2%	14.8%	85.2%	40.0%	60.0%	25.3%	75.0%	75.3%	37.8%
Alaska	41,320	29.4%	70.6%	9.2%	90.8%	33.5%	66.5%	21.2%	72.0%	81.7%	49.0%
Arizona	360,645	30.6%	69.2%	14.3%	85.7%	32.0%	68.0%	21.5%	80.1%	81.8%	35.7%
Arkansas	173,969	32.1%	67.9%	16.5%	83.5%	34.6%	65.4%	23.7%	71.4%	77.7%	31.7%
California	1,730,647	24.4%	75.4%	8.5%	91.5%	23.1%	76.9%	16.6%	83.6%	85.6%	41.5%
Colorado	330,961	29.7%	70.2%	11.5%	88.5%	36.7%	63.3%	26.0%	88.2%	89.1%	43.2%
Connecticut	145,454	18.2%	81.7%	14.4%	85.6%	29.2%	70.8%	23.0%	81.6%	87.6%	37.6%
Delaware	41,691	24.6%	74.2%	23.3%	76.7%	40.6%	59.4%	28.0%	83.4%	88.4%	36.4%
District of Columbia	63,291	18.2%	81.7%	4.9%	95.1%	14.0%	86.0%	10.6%	89.8%	88.6%	50.0%
Florida	822,171	27.4%	72.4%	11.5%	88.5%	27.7%	72.3%	18.2%	80.2%	82.7%	32.5%
Georgia	513,244	27.7%	72.2%	11.4%	88.6%	32.5%	67.5%	21.5%	78.7%	81.2%	36.7%
Hawaii	64,289	24.6%	75.2%	4.2%	95.8%	14.4%	85.6%	9.5%	87.2%	89.7%	51.3%
Idaho	95,101	33.5%	66.5%	12.8%	87.2%	42.8%	57.2%	29.4%	81.6%	87.2%	37.4%
Illinois	679,556	25.3%	74.6%	11.3%	88.7%	35.7%	64.3%	24.9%	81.3%	86.1%	42.5%
Indiana	377,181	32.2%	67.7%	16.8%	83.2%	42.6%	57.4%	29.4%	77.7%	83.2%	34.3%
Iowa	208,256	34.2%	65.8%	18.1%	81.9%	47.1%	52.9%	32.4%	79.5%	86.6%	40.5%
Kansas	195,674	34.8%	65.2%	11.6%	88.4%	40.3%	59.7%	25.3%	83.5%	86.4%	37.2%
Kentucky	243,620	31.6%	68.3%	15.4%	84.6%	40.3%	59.7%	26.4%	79.4%	82.3%	37.5%
Louisiana	273,824	30.3%	69.5%	17.7%	82.3%	39.3%	60.7%	25.0%	69.4%	79.0%	33.7%
Maine	62,148	21.7%	78.3%	14.4%	85.6%	38.1%	61.9%	27.5%	81.8%	84.7%	36.9%
Maryland	268,323	20.1%	79.7%	16.2%	83.8%	34.0%	66.0%	26.6%	86.9%	89.0%	40.4%
Massachusetts	317,059	22.7%	77.2%	6.2%	93.8%	25.2%	74.8%	19.0%	87.7%	92.9%	42.9%
Michigan	506,316	31.4%	68.5%	17.5%	82.5%	45.1%	54.9%	27.1%	79.4%	85.2%	38.1%
Minnesota	330,863	26.3%	73.6%	14.3%	85.7%	47.2%	52.8%	33.7%	89.1%	88.4%	42.3%
Mississippi	141,392	29.1%	70.7%	20.4%	79.6%	36.6%	63.4%	21.5%	70.0%	73.9%	32.4%
Missouri	375,896	29.5%	70.4%	14.6%	85.4%	40.8%	59.2%	28.3%	79.7%	84.3%	37.0%
Montana	58,427	31.9%	67.6%	8.2%	91.8%	35.9%	64.1%	22.0%	80.4%	87.5%	34.9%
Nebraska	130,109	33.4%	66.3%	11.6%	88.4%	43.6%	56.4%	27.9%	84.4%	83.6%	34.3%
Nevada	144,917	23.3%	76.7%	18.3%	81.7%	27.9%	72.1%	21.2%	86.0%	83.4%	37.6%
New Hampshire	61,191	25.8%	74.1%	9.5%	90.5%	34.9%	65.1%	22.8%	92.9%	88.1%	35.1%
New Jersey	303,609	15.9%	83.8%	9.8%	90.2%	25.1%	74.9%	19.9%	81.3%	88.3%	36.8%
New Mexico	103,153	33.5%	66.0%	15.5%	84.5%	38.8%	61.2%	24.0%	75.9%	80.8%	38.4%
New York	892,932	21.9%	77.9%	8.7%	91.3%	21.5%	78.5%	15.0%	81.4%	87.4%	35.8%
North Carolina	536,376	30.0%	69.8%	11.4%	88.6%	32.6%	67.4%	21.4%	80.8%	81.8%	41.2%
North Dakota	66,350	47.2%	52.8%	14.1%	85.9%	47.9%	52.1%	26.6%	89.8%	90.4%	42.5%
Ohio	652,626	29.6%	70.3%	12.8%	87.2%	37.5%	62.5%	25.6%	80.1%	84.1%	38.1%
Oklahoma	251,534	32.0%	67.8%	16.8%	83.2%	40.2%	59.8%	25.7%	72.7%	80.4%	41.5%
Oregon	218,434	29.3%	70.6%	7.0%	93.0%	26.7%	73.3%	18.2%	87.1%	89.8%	42.7%
Pennsylvania	615,672	25.2%	74.7%	13.6%	86.4%	37.5%	62.5%	26.7%	83.6%	85.6%	38.3%
Rhode Island	51,602	26.0%	74.0%	9.3%	90.7%	26.8%	73.2%	19.8%	82.3%	86.2%	38.2%
South Carolina	243,574	31.3%	68.6%	12.7%	87.3%	36.0%	64.0%	22.2%	72.1%	78.8%	36.0%
South Dakota	56,991	32.6%	67.3%	18.1%	81.9%	47.3%	52.7%	28.4%	90.8%	89.1%	42.5%
Tennessee	359,651	28.0%	71.9%	14.2%	85.8%	35.5%	64.5%	24.8%	73.4%	78.9%	35.8%
Texas	1,520,732	29.2%	70.7%	11.7%	88.3%	30.9%	69.1%	20.1%	77.7%	81.8%	39.1%
Utah	169,284	31.5%	68.4%	22.2%	77.8%	46.4%	53.6%	35.2%	88.7%	89.2%	39.4%
Vermont	28,761	33.3%	66.7%	16.1%	83.9%	31.4%	68.6%	20.2%	82.5%	84.9%	37.3%
Virginia	428,226	25.4%	74.4%	10.5%	89.5%	32.4%	67.6%	24.0%	85.3%	88.4%	40.8%
Washington	405,541	26.8%	73.1%	11.7%	88.3%	28.1%	71.9%	20.9%	86.5%	87.4%	46.0%
West Virginia	88,285	33.6%	66.4%	25.5%	74.5%	40.4%	59.6%	25.4%	80.4%	81.8%	39.8%
Wisconsin	345,884	31.2%	68.8%	12.7%	87.3%	36.8%	63.2%	26.8%	83.2%	85.2%	39.9%
Wyoming	40,637	36.5%	63.5%	16.4%	83.6%	45.2%	54.8%	26.9%	86.9%	87.7%	30.1%

Table K-2: Counties—Summary Housing Characteristics

	Millennial Householders	Age of Householders		18 to 24 Years Old		25 to 31 Years Old			Percent with Internet Access		Percent with Mobile Access Plan
		18 to 24	25 to 31	Owners	Renters	Owners	Renters	With Mortgage	18 to 24	25 to 31	
Alabama											
Baldwin County	6,655	38.2%	61.8%	19.6%	80.4%	51.5%	48.5%	28.9%	48.3%	76.3%	19.5%
Calhoun County	6,285	34.3%	65.7%	10.8%	89.2%	41.8%	58.2%	18.7%	98.7%	73.9%	42.5%
Etowah County	4,099	20.1%	79.9%	33.2%	66.8%	58.5%	41.5%	48.9%	75.3%	83.1%	14.7%
Houston County	6,171	24.3%	75.7%	9.9%	90.1%	26.8%	73.2%	22.1%	70.9%	86.1%	21.5%
Jefferson County	36,900	27.6%	72.4%	6.4%	93.6%	33.6%	66.4%	21.4%	79.4%	76.3%	31.3%
Lauderdale County	4,251	36.8%	63.2%	9.7%	90.3%	34.1%	65.9%	22.0%	69.2%	69.3%	34.8%
Lee County	16,087	52.7%	47.3%	20.9%	79.1%	18.4%	81.6%	14.1%	92.8%	72.5%	44.3%
Madison County	19,924	28.2%	71.8%	14.4%	85.6%	37.1%	62.9%	27.8%	71.2%	84.6%	44.9%
Marshall County	4,126	29.4%	70.6%	28.2%	71.8%	43.1%	56.9%	35.1%	55.0%	67.0%	14.6%
Mobile County	22,343	31.2%	68.8%	11.2%	88.8%	32.6%	67.4%	22.6%	62.1%	70.5%	29.7%
Montgomery County	16,071	24.6%	75.4%	3.5%	96.5%	25.3%	74.7%	17.8%	87.9%	71.7%	53.6%
Morgan County	5,288	32.8%	67.2%	15.3%	84.7%	71.2%	28.8%	32.4%	71.3%	67.6%	36.9%
Shelby County	9,958	13.3%	86.7%	21.1%	78.9%	54.8%	45.2%	45.8%	88.9%	89.1%	56.6%
Tuscaloosa County	15,010	43.4%	56.6%	23.7%	76.3%	41.8%	58.2%	23.6%	93.6%	92.3%	57.9%
Alaska											
Fairbanks North Star Borough	7,502	30.3%	69.7%	1.4%	98.6%	19.3%	80.7%	13.9%	44.3%	59.0%	13.7%
Matanuska-Susitna Borough	3,666	45.0%	55.0%	26.4%	73.6%	35.3%	64.7%	27.6%	60.6%	78.5%	33.6%
Arizona											
Cochise County	9,083	38.2%	61.2%	11.7%	88.3%	20.6%	79.4%	12.0%	93.5%	90.8%	28.3%
Coconino County	12,378	49.9%	50.1%	5.2%	94.8%	25.3%	74.7%	9.5%	94.0%	89.0%	37.8%
Maricopa County	224,470	27.5%	72.3%	15.2%	84.8%	31.8%	68.2%	22.6%	74.8%	80.4%	34.3%
Mohave County	8,096	31.8%	64.9%	25.7%	74.3%	27.1%	72.9%	24.4%	82.5%	75.4%	28.3%
Navajo County	2,381	23.4%	76.6%	13.1%	86.9%	47.0%	53.0%	16.9%	60.9%	64.5%	33.3%
Pima County	66,847	40.1%	59.7%	9.6%	90.4%	27.7%	72.3%	15.7%	89.5%	86.7%	43.4%
Pinal County	12,656	16.5%	83.5%	34.2%	65.8%	54.3%	45.7%	46.9%	68.4%	86.4%	28.9%
Yavapai County	7,251	25.9%	72.2%	6.6%	93.4%	21.3%	78.7%	12.8%	77.7%	88.7%	32.9%
Yuma County	10,594	27.9%	72.1%	32.1%	67.9%	43.9%	56.1%	31.4%	63.5%	85.4%	35.2%
Arkansas											
Benton County	13,130	22.7%	77.3%	19.2%	80.8%	35.4%	64.6%	27.8%	91.0%	88.9%	24.3%
Craighead County	8,130	39.1%	60.9%	15.7%	84.3%	28.2%	71.8%	17.0%	92.5%	77.3%	38.1%
Faulkner County	10,699	30.6%	69.4%	20.8%	79.2%	55.6%	44.4%	40.2%	76.7%	87.1%	50.8%
Garland County	3,828	28.4%	71.6%	0.0%	100.0%	28.1%	71.9%	17.1%	100.0%	88.5%	51.4%
Pulaski County	22,360	26.7%	73.3%	4.3%	95.7%	18.2%	81.8%	13.3%	82.0%	76.0%	32.9%
Saline County	3,531	18.0%	82.0%	53.5%	46.5%	55.6%	44.4%	47.4%	49.9%	89.8%	49.8%
Sebastian County	8,201	16.0%	84.0%	50.5%	49.5%	33.5%	66.5%	32.4%	88.5%	67.9%	22.4%
Washington County	21,766	43.0%	57.0%	4.5%	95.5%	28.9%	71.1%	17.1%	89.3%	91.5%	21.6%
California											
Alameda County	75,639	25.9%	74.1%	3.9%	96.1%	21.7%	78.3%	15.6%	82.6%	92.8%	50.5%
Butte County	16,020	50.5%	49.5%	4.7%	95.3%	35.2%	64.8%	17.7%	94.8%	89.0%	40.3%
Contra Costa County	38,740	23.8%	75.8%	8.6%	91.4%	28.9%	71.1%	20.0%	90.5%	92.3%	49.6%
El Dorado County	4,089	27.2%	72.8%	5.5%	94.5%	42.4%	57.6%	28.4%	42.5%	88.5%	35.6%
Fresno County	49,982	27.0%	72.8%	7.5%	92.5%	33.5%	66.5%	23.0%	75.5%	81.8%	44.3%
Humboldt County	9,938	38.4%	60.8%	0.0%	100.0%	22.3%	77.7%	12.2%	96.9%	83.1%	24.8%
Imperial County	6,712	16.8%	83.2%	29.0%	71.0%	44.6%	55.4%	36.1%	63.7%	88.6%	19.8%
Kern County	44,569	27.8%	72.2%	6.6%	93.4%	32.1%	67.9%	21.1%	70.5%	73.7%	32.6%
Kings County	7,700	16.0%	84.0%	5.4%	94.6%	11.5%	88.5%	8.5%	91.7%	81.1%	58.7%
Los Angeles County	450,828	22.3%	77.6%	7.7%	92.3%	16.1%	83.9%	11.8%	80.7%	83.5%	37.1%
Madera County	7,122	18.1%	81.9%	2.0%	98.0%	42.6%	57.4%	34.0%	80.0%	66.6%	17.9%
Marin County	5,752	16.7%	83.3%	0.0%	100.0%	19.1%	80.9%	10.8%	100.0%	82.3%	46.4%
Merced County	12,174	25.7%	74.3%	12.6%	87.4%	35.8%	64.2%	24.7%	86.7%	85.4%	54.5%
Monterey County	17,429	28.9%	70.9%	6.9%	93.1%	23.5%	76.5%	16.3%	75.1%	82.6%	39.6%
Napa County	3,682	30.4%	69.6%	5.1%	94.9%	65.8%	34.2%	43.7%	74.0%	92.6%	54.4%
Nevada County	2,612	9.4%	90.6%	22.0%	78.0%	22.4%	77.6%	16.5%	72.4%	70.5%	30.4%
Orange County	116,861	22.3%	77.7%	9.3%	90.7%	22.7%	77.3%	15.7%	91.2%	90.6%	43.4%
Placer County	13,517	24.9%	75.1%	10.6%	89.4%	41.1%	58.9%	30.9%	83.4%	87.1%	55.0%
Riverside County	81,650	23.2%	76.8%	13.5%	86.5%	44.7%	55.3%	33.7%	80.1%	84.4%	38.0%
Sacramento County	80,519	25.4%	74.2%	7.5%	92.5%	27.5%	72.5%	20.3%	84.1%	86.5%	40.3%
San Bernardino County	85,070	21.8%	77.9%	15.7%	84.3%	29.8%	70.2%	22.5%	73.8%	77.1%	33.2%
San Diego County	179,013	23.6%	76.1%	7.7%	92.3%	19.0%	81.0%	13.9%	93.5%	89.1%	45.5%
San Francisco County	68,423	15.0%	85.0%	5.9%	94.1%	7.6%	92.4%	5.2%	99.1%	94.9%	57.0%
San Joaquin County	28,826	31.4%	68.4%	9.3%	90.7%	34.5%	65.5%	21.3%	65.7%	79.7%	32.9%
San Luis Obispo County	15,904	49.1%	50.9%	4.1%	95.9%	13.2%	86.8%	7.7%	91.4%	90.6%	32.6%
San Mateo County	23,799	18.4%	81.3%	5.2%	94.8%	22.3%	77.7%	15.1%	95.3%	92.2%	51.0%
Santa Barbara County	23,552	43.1%	56.7%	4.2%	95.8%	16.9%	83.1%	9.7%	84.5%	73.9%	45.0%
Santa Clara County	80,290	20.1%	79.7%	6.3%	93.7%	19.4%	80.6%	14.0%	92.8%	92.9%	42.1%
Santa Cruz County	12,881	45.4%	54.6%	15.5%	84.5%	18.4%	81.6%	10.6%	100.0%	85.0%	49.6%
Shasta County	8,533	29.5%	70.5%	17.2%	82.8%	23.7%	76.3%	19.1%	81.8%	75.2%	27.8%
Solano County	19,173	18.9%	81.1%	12.5%	87.5%	30.7%	69.3%	25.9%	98.0%	87.8%	55.1%
Sonoma County	20,463	28.2%	71.8%	4.2%	95.8%	17.8%	82.2%	10.6%	83.3%	91.8%	43.0%
Stanislaus County	22,922	26.8%	73.2%	18.8%	81.2%	31.3%	68.7%	26.4%	66.4%	80.2%	53.9%
Sutter County	4,756	46.2%	53.3%	6.1%	93.9%	45.6%	54.4%	26.3%	69.5%	91.7%	50.1%
Tulare County	22,574	28.0%	71.8%	17.1%	82.9%	39.6%	60.4%	31.0%	62.7%	69.5%	40.9%
Ventura County	25,042	17.9%	82.1%	16.0%	84.0%	28.5%	71.5%	21.1%	74.5%	80.7%	48.5%
Yolo County	15,617	54.0%	45.7%	3.9%	96.1%	11.6%	88.4%	5.0%	94.6%	90.0%	38.4%
Colorado											
Adams County	28,883	22.6%	77.4%	10.7%	89.3%	45.4%	54.6%	33.6%	90.2%	85.6%	38.9%
Arapahoe County	35,155	29.7%	70.3%	4.8%	95.2%	35.4%	64.6%	24.2%	87.6%	90.9%	33.4%

Table K-2: Counties—Summary Housing Characteristics—*Continued*

	Millennial Householders	Age of Householders		18 to 24 Years Old		25 to 31 Years Old			Percent with Internet Access		Percent with Mobile Access Plan
		18 to 24	25 to 31	Owners	Renters	Owners	Renters	With Mortgage	18 to 24	25 to 31	
Colorado—Cont.											
Boulder County	22,444	50.8%	49.2%	10.4%	89.6%	35.3%	64.7%	18.6%	94.6%	93.6%	47.4%
Denver County	65,456	24.9%	74.5%	7.2%	92.8%	25.2%	74.8%	19.2%	84.8%	86.8%	38.0%
Douglas County	9,709	25.0%	75.0%	26.7%	73.3%	58.0%	42.0%	50.2%	96.7%	89.8%	57.9%
El Paso County	44,139	26.9%	73.1%	9.5%	90.5%	38.3%	61.7%	28.4%	91.7%	92.0%	52.2%
Jefferson County	28,288	36.3%	63.7%	18.4%	81.6%	42.5%	57.5%	30.1%	84.9%	93.0%	47.8%
Larimer County	25,103	41.3%	58.7%	5.7%	94.3%	35.9%	64.1%	19.9%	95.3%	93.6%	38.8%
Mesa County	10,066	22.7%	77.3%	25.1%	74.9%	40.7%	59.3%	35.0%	96.6%	86.5%	60.5%
Pueblo County	9,818	40.1%	59.9%	11.2%	88.8%	35.2%	64.8%	18.8%	88.5%	98.7%	48.5%
Weld County	16,901	29.8%	70.2%	7.7%	92.3%	45.0%	55.0%	27.5%	83.3%	80.9%	38.2%
Connecticut											
Fairfield County	30,321	13.9%	86.0%	13.9%	86.1%	26.2%	73.8%	22.8%	86.9%	93.6%	48.4%
Hartford County	40,820	19.2%	80.6%	11.1%	88.9%	31.0%	69.0%	24.0%	81.0%	91.0%	41.5%
Litchfield County	6,065	15.1%	84.9%	8.4%	91.6%	44.8%	55.2%	34.4%	83.6%	88.7%	25.1%
Middlesex County	6,598	21.6%	78.4%	6.5%	93.5%	43.6%	56.4%	29.5%	93.3%	81.8%	35.4%
New Haven County	35,307	15.8%	84.1%	17.8%	82.2%	28.4%	71.6%	22.3%	72.6%	80.7%	29.1%
New London County	14,861	20.5%	79.5%	9.3%	90.7%	23.6%	76.4%	18.6%	86.1%	85.6%	36.3%
Tolland County	5,805	32.1%	67.5%	31.7%	68.3%	27.9%	72.1%	22.7%	76.9%	96.4%	31.3%
Windham County	5,677	28.5%	71.5%	19.9%	80.1%	17.8%	82.2%	13.8%	88.0%	74.6%	31.4%
Delaware											
Kent County	7,698	31.0%	69.0%	26.2%	73.8%	46.2%	53.8%	21.3%	79.4%	91.3%	37.2%
New Castle County	27,959	25.3%	72.8%	22.7%	77.3%	35.9%	64.1%	27.3%	85.8%	88.7%	35.6%
Sussex County	6,034	13.0%	87.0%	19.8%	80.2%	53.0%	47.0%	39.7%	73.5%	84.5%	39.1%
Florida											
Alachua County	29,675	58.5%	41.5%	10.2%	89.8%	22.8%	77.2%	10.2%	92.2%	88.8%	43.3%
Bay County	8,176	35.9%	64.1%	4.8%	95.2%	30.3%	69.7%	10.6%	81.7%	77.9%	49.9%
Brevard County	19,751	25.7%	74.3%	18.4%	81.6%	34.8%	65.2%	25.8%	89.7%	94.8%	39.2%
Broward County	68,407	19.3%	80.7%	16.0%	84.0%	23.0%	77.0%	16.4%	82.9%	87.2%	37.3%
Charlotte County	3,260	31.7%	68.3%	15.9%	84.1%	53.4%	46.6%	23.7%	81.4%	78.9%	29.0%
Citrus County	3,303	27.0%	73.0%	6.8%	93.2%	45.6%	54.4%	33.3%	52.7%	83.6%	21.5%
Clay County	6,396	15.7%	83.0%	33.3%	66.7%	32.4%	67.6%	30.3%	100.0%	92.9%	44.0%
Collier County	8,715	22.3%	77.7%	16.4%	83.6%	26.2%	73.8%	16.5%	86.2%	80.6%	55.3%
Duval County	57,127	26.6%	73.3%	13.0%	87.0%	27.4%	72.6%	20.5%	76.0%	85.4%	42.0%
Escambia County	18,094	23.0%	76.5%	2.0%	98.0%	21.0%	79.0%	15.1%	78.6%	84.3%	24.5%
Flagler County	1,593	28.7%	71.3%	70.7%	29.3%	50.9%	49.1%	49.2%	82.1%	76.1%	31.2%
Hernando County	4,380	9.7%	90.3%	26.1%	73.9%	23.0%	77.0%	21.9%	56.9%	84.6%	27.7%
Highlands County	2,808	41.5%	58.5%	42.6%	57.4%	52.7%	47.3%	21.2%	40.2%	49.6%	7.7%
Hillsborough County	78,660	29.9%	69.9%	7.9%	92.1%	26.5%	73.5%	16.4%	79.4%	82.2%	23.9%
Indian River County	4,374	26.0%	74.0%	8.0%	92.0%	34.4%	65.6%	22.5%	73.9%	85.0%	27.0%
Lake County	10,750	20.9%	79.1%	4.9%	95.1%	42.1%	57.9%	31.4%	81.7%	86.3%	23.6%
Lee County	21,324	24.6%	75.2%	16.5%	83.5%	27.0%	73.0%	18.2%	78.4%	81.7%	33.4%
Leon County	33,667	56.2%	43.6%	3.7%	96.3%	19.0%	81.0%	8.5%	93.0%	90.8%	38.6%
Manatee County	10,758	22.7%	77.3%	9.4%	90.6%	29.8%	70.2%	24.4%	66.1%	82.4%	38.0%
Marion County	10,785	28.0%	72.0%	6.6%	93.4%	30.4%	69.6%	15.6%	65.3%	60.2%	13.7%
Martin County	4,472	22.0%	78.0%	0.0%	100.0%	35.2%	64.8%	23.3%	100.0%	81.5%	41.1%
Miami-Dade County	92,965	20.1%	79.8%	14.2%	85.8%	21.2%	78.8%	14.2%	73.2%	79.1%	25.7%
Okaloosa County	13,652	20.8%	79.2%	2.5%	97.5%	34.6%	65.4%	25.5%	81.9%	91.3%	31.9%
Orange County	75,130	31.0%	68.9%	7.7%	92.3%	21.5%	78.5%	13.3%	85.3%	88.7%	31.1%
Osceola County	10,209	28.2%	71.8%	17.7%	82.3%	29.3%	70.7%	23.0%	67.9%	58.5%	18.9%
Palm Beach County	42,894	22.5%	77.1%	10.0%	90.0%	31.6%	68.4%	20.3%	80.7%	80.1%	28.9%
Pasco County	13,508	27.8%	72.2%	26.6%	73.4%	39.2%	60.8%	20.6%	93.1%	86.9%	36.8%
Pinellas County	37,849	23.6%	76.1%	6.3%	93.7%	25.2%	74.8%	16.1%	77.5%	84.7%	29.7%
Polk County	23,242	21.7%	78.3%	18.2%	81.8%	37.2%	62.8%	28.5%	63.0%	78.7%	31.0%
Santa Rosa County	8,595	28.7%	71.3%	0.0%	100.0%	35.8%	64.2%	22.3%	93.4%	88.7%	52.7%
Sarasota County	8,873	22.5%	77.5%	15.1%	84.9%	31.8%	68.2%	21.1%	72.6%	86.2%	45.1%
Seminole County	18,443	17.0%	82.8%	5.1%	94.9%	39.4%	60.6%	27.0%	79.2%	92.6%	49.2%
St. Johns County	6,002	19.8%	80.0%	19.6%	80.4%	33.1%	66.9%	25.3%	64.2%	85.5%	33.6%
St. Lucie County	8,564	22.0%	78.0%	10.0%	90.0%	21.8%	78.2%	18.7%	46.8%	65.1%	23.2%
Sumter County	1,985	30.8%	69.2%	0.0%	100.0%	23.4%	76.6%	11.3%	100.0%	71.5%	4.9%
Volusia County	23,535	34.6%	65.3%	25.3%	74.7%	32.5%	67.5%	25.1%	76.4%	68.9%	29.3%
Georgia											
Bartow County	4,052	26.6%	73.4%	0.0%	100.0%	39.3%	60.7%	19.9%	100.0%	89.6%	45.0%
Bibb County	7,819	31.6%	68.1%	9.3%	90.7%	24.1%	75.9%	14.3%	43.5%	66.0%	26.8%
Carroll County	7,335	54.4%	45.6%	5.9%	94.1%	37.2%	62.8%	17.7%	98.1%	85.3%	62.5%
Chatham County	18,555	27.9%	72.1%	6.8%	93.2%	26.1%	73.9%	15.6%	73.4%	82.8%	38.2%
Cherokee County	8,116	15.4%	84.6%	3.0%	97.0%	52.9%	47.1%	42.6%	89.7%	89.6%	52.7%
Clarke County	16,349	57.3%	42.7%	6.8%	93.2%	6.6%	93.4%	3.9%	82.8%	80.8%	42.5%
Clayton County	14,956	27.0%	72.5%	11.4%	88.6%	16.7%	83.3%	10.0%	67.1%	55.2%	29.0%
Cobb County	42,199	25.9%	74.1%	8.1%	91.9%	27.8%	72.2%	20.9%	87.2%	83.2%	37.8%
Columbia County	3,011	11.4%	88.6%	30.0%	70.0%	74.6%	25.4%	63.9%	100.0%	94.2%	42.7%
Coweta County	6,138	33.0%	67.0%	24.5%	75.5%	60.0%	40.0%	43.6%	88.7%	88.8%	39.2%
DeKalb County	45,563	25.0%	75.0%	5.5%	94.5%	18.0%	82.0%	13.6%	86.4%	89.5%	49.4%
Dougherty County	5,306	19.1%	80.9%	14.3%	85.7%	15.2%	84.8%	11.9%	61.5%	82.0%	22.1%
Douglas County	4,437	17.7%	82.3%	21.0%	79.0%	29.4%	70.6%	15.6%	85.4%	87.9%	30.8%
Fayette County	1,922	26.6%	73.4%	0.0%	100.0%	50.5%	49.5%	19.6%	100.0%	94.4%	53.2%
Floyd County	3,943	44.3%	55.7%	29.6%	70.4%	23.8%	76.2%	18.3%	97.0%	92.1%	56.8%
Forsyth County	4,279	16.5%	83.5%	87.1%	12.9%	65.0%	35.0%	62.8%	94.2%	86.6%	41.2%
Fulton County	65,186	24.6%	75.1%	5.9%	94.1%	23.4%	76.6%	16.5%	81.2%	88.4%	42.0%
Gwinnett County	30,614	20.4%	79.5%	12.8%	87.2%	33.7%	66.3%	23.8%	89.9%	83.1%	33.1%
Hall County	7,912	29.1%	70.9%	31.0%	69.0%	28.9%	71.1%	26.2%	74.2%	76.8%	30.7%

Table K-2: Counties—Summary Housing Characteristics—*Continued*

	Millennial Householders	Age of Householders		18 to 24 Years Old		25 to 31 Years Old			Percent with Internet Access		Percent with Mobile Access Plan
		18 to 24	25 to 31	Owners	Renters	Owners	Renters	With Mortgage	18 to 24	25 to 31	
Georgia—Cont.											
Henry County	7,259	12.0%	88.0%	18.8%	81.2%	48.2%	51.8%	39.6%	91.1%	94.0%	48.4%
Houston County	9,315	13.4%	86.6%	6.4%	93.6%	38.6%	61.4%	19.5%	65.0%	75.7%	20.3%
Lowndes County	11,506	47.2%	52.8%	2.7%	97.3%	40.0%	60.0%	21.1%	74.2%	81.0%	25.0%
Muscogee County	11,549	24.2%	75.8%	14.1%	85.9%	20.3%	79.7%	16.7%	89.1%	84.0%	45.9%
Newton County	2,518	18.7%	81.3%	90.0%	10.0%	67.0%	33.0%	55.2%	47.7%	77.7%	46.1%
Paulding County	4,376	9.9%	90.1%	0.0%	100.0%	68.1%	31.9%	53.7%	30.6%	98.7%	59.9%
Richmond County	11,289	17.8%	82.2%	10.1%	89.9%	23.8%	76.2%	18.9%	83.4%	80.4%	32.8%
Whitfield County	4,064	33.4%	66.6%	16.4%	83.6%	36.2%	63.8%	22.5%	39.9%	88.7%	20.3%
Hawaii											
Hawaii County	6,275	31.6%	68.4%	0.0%	100.0%	34.8%	65.2%	16.8%	70.2%	65.4%	31.2%
Honolulu County	50,280	25.0%	74.9%	3.7%	96.3%	12.9%	87.1%	9.0%	90.1%	92.8%	55.1%
Maui County	5,541	19.1%	79.6%	15.6%	84.4%	7.9%	92.1%	5.0%	90.2%	86.2%	48.7%
Idaho											
Ada County	27,198	34.2%	65.8%	9.2%	90.8%	42.5%	57.5%	29.5%	78.2%	92.5%	38.9%
Bonneville County	4,834	22.6%	77.4%	27.7%	72.3%	39.9%	60.1%	31.0%	67.0%	80.7%	48.9%
Canyon County	10,649	27.8%	72.2%	21.9%	78.1%	57.0%	43.0%	42.8%	85.9%	92.9%	47.4%
Kootenai County	6,888	24.7%	75.3%	0.0%	100.0%	62.4%	37.6%	45.8%	64.6%	82.2%	26.4%
Illinois											
Champaign County	22,554	52.6%	47.4%	4.9%	95.1%	33.8%	66.2%	15.4%	97.4%	90.9%	36.3%
Cook County	299,597	20.1%	79.8%	6.3%	93.7%	24.4%	75.6%	16.5%	85.6%	87.6%	43.7%
DeKalb County	9,415	47.8%	52.2%	5.9%	94.1%	27.6%	72.4%	16.8%	85.0%	98.0%	57.6%
DuPage County	37,945	13.9%	86.1%	12.6%	87.4%	39.1%	60.9%	31.3%	94.2%	87.7%	52.0%
Kane County	19,969	22.9%	77.1%	23.3%	76.7%	40.5%	59.5%	31.8%	87.0%	87.3%	59.1%
Kankakee County	3,958	37.1%	62.9%	34.9%	65.1%	45.0%	55.0%	19.9%	99.2%	84.7%	24.0%
Kendall County	5,818	5.2%	94.8%	17.2%	82.8%	34.7%	65.3%	31.5%	91.7%	100.0%	66.7%
Lake County	25,568	24.1%	75.9%	5.1%	94.9%	37.1%	62.9%	26.6%	88.7%	84.5%	41.3%
LaSalle County	5,015	34.1%	65.9%	27.1%	72.9%	58.2%	41.8%	35.5%	49.2%	88.0%	26.9%
Macon County	6,699	31.8%	67.8%	15.0%	85.0%	35.8%	64.2%	27.5%	75.6%	77.3%	43.9%
Madison County	18,572	31.0%	68.7%	11.4%	88.6%	44.4%	55.6%	31.3%	82.4%	89.3%	45.5%
McHenry County	12,187	19.0%	81.0%	33.0%	67.0%	60.3%	39.7%	50.5%	77.9%	90.3%	62.4%
McLean County	14,518	38.6%	61.4%	5.6%	94.4%	37.6%	62.4%	23.3%	84.9%	87.0%	31.0%
Peoria County	13,451	32.6%	67.4%	1.6%	98.4%	41.4%	58.6%	27.7%	62.6%	83.7%	40.0%
Rock Island County	6,639	22.6%	77.4%	18.0%	82.0%	41.2%	58.8%	33.4%	72.3%	93.0%	52.3%
Sangamon County	12,592	25.8%	74.2%	5.8%	94.2%	40.5%	59.5%	26.9%	79.7%	93.9%	42.6%
St. Clair County	15,258	26.7%	73.3%	15.1%	84.9%	44.0%	56.0%	32.6%	61.1%	66.9%	38.8%
Tazewell County	7,884	25.8%	74.2%	34.0%	66.0%	59.9%	40.1%	45.5%	38.5%	90.8%	51.1%
Will County	20,810	19.4%	80.2%	32.7%	67.3%	60.6%	39.4%	49.5%	82.2%	79.8%	28.0%
Winnebago County	14,582	27.6%	72.4%	5.5%	94.5%	40.0%	60.0%	27.1%	75.2%	83.8%	44.0%
Indiana											
Allen County	23,745	32.6%	67.4%	23.2%	76.8%	49.2%	50.8%	36.8%	74.5%	88.3%	39.8%
Clark County	4,172	5.7%	94.3%	17.6%	82.4%	32.2%	67.8%	25.2%	100.0%	78.8%	22.5%
Delaware County	9,687	59.8%	40.2%	7.0%	93.0%	30.4%	69.6%	10.4%	92.2%	94.0%	52.9%
Elkhart County	10,618	41.1%	58.9%	33.0%	67.0%	55.1%	44.9%	43.0%	73.6%	78.7%	43.5%
Hamilton County	15,338	25.2%	74.8%	37.9%	62.1%	57.0%	43.0%	50.6%	92.5%	96.9%	44.8%
Hendricks County	7,327	17.9%	82.1%	3.2%	96.8%	70.3%	29.7%	57.4%	60.2%	99.8%	44.7%
Johnson County	8,851	27.6%	72.4%	18.3%	81.7%	47.7%	52.3%	35.3%	97.8%	86.9%	21.6%
Lake County	21,261	21.2%	78.8%	8.9%	91.1%	34.5%	65.5%	25.0%	77.9%	82.4%	41.8%
LaPorte County	4,975	14.2%	85.8%	26.7%	73.3%	36.5%	63.5%	25.3%	87.3%	62.6%	15.0%
Madison County	5,870	26.0%	74.0%	14.7%	85.3%	36.9%	63.1%	26.6%	74.8%	76.4%	48.7%
Marion County	72,744	29.7%	70.1%	12.2%	87.8%	25.2%	74.8%	19.0%	71.5%	81.9%	29.1%
Monroe County	14,424	62.1%	37.4%	4.7%	95.3%	21.6%	78.4%	8.0%	98.2%	92.8%	25.5%
Porter County	7,208	35.3%	64.7%	19.3%	80.7%	61.2%	38.8%	36.3%	72.4%	79.5%	51.0%
St. Joseph County	16,678	30.3%	69.7%	9.8%	90.2%	34.7%	65.3%	23.5%	73.5%	86.6%	33.8%
Tippecanoe County	20,733	56.4%	43.6%	6.5%	93.5%	20.9%	79.1%	9.0%	91.9%	100.0%	32.0%
Vanderburgh County	12,536	32.6%	67.4%	8.4%	91.6%	36.4%	63.6%	19.5%	81.0%	90.1%	36.5%
Vigo County	7,043	35.6%	64.4%	25.0%	75.0%	30.7%	69.3%	18.2%	80.3%	62.5%	16.9%
Iowa											
Black Hawk County	11,655	47.4%	52.6%	14.6%	85.4%	45.7%	54.3%	26.0%	92.1%	81.0%	51.7%
Dubuque County	5,305	33.6%	66.4%	18.0%	82.0%	60.7%	39.3%	40.4%	86.2%	88.3%	42.4%
Johnson County	18,817	48.5%	51.5%	2.7%	97.3%	30.3%	69.7%	14.2%	100.0%	87.7%	44.7%
Linn County	16,370	23.5%	76.5%	9.3%	90.7%	57.0%	43.0%	44.0%	76.8%	94.5%	32.0%
Polk County	33,491	31.1%	68.9%	14.1%	85.9%	44.0%	56.0%	31.3%	75.0%	87.6%	53.1%
Pottawattamie County	5,950	16.9%	83.1%	14.0%	86.0%	30.3%	69.7%	27.5%	64.9%	91.6%	36.3%
Scott County	11,414	15.7%	84.3%	19.9%	80.1%	41.2%	58.8%	34.0%	85.4%	67.8%	31.8%
Story County	13,402	58.6%	41.4%	5.3%	94.7%	28.7%	71.3%	10.2%	92.7%	97.2%	35.0%
Woodbury County	7,012	20.9%	79.1%	17.9%	82.1%	45.6%	54.4%	32.0%	70.3%	88.0%	27.9%
Kansas											
Douglas County	12,587	47.5%	52.5%	2.7%	97.3%	22.3%	77.7%	13.0%	94.2%	88.0%	47.1%
Johnson County	33,588	23.4%	76.6%	12.5%	87.5%	37.0%	63.0%	28.4%	92.2%	92.4%	58.2%
Sedgwick County	37,542	28.3%	71.4%	8.8%	91.2%	38.4%	61.6%	26.0%	78.2%	87.7%	29.9%
Shawnee County	11,065	28.9%	70.8%	4.0%	96.0%	41.8%	58.2%	27.7%	82.3%	90.4%	38.6%
Wyandotte County	10,152	33.2%	66.8%	5.8%	94.2%	24.9%	75.1%	15.4%	78.4%	74.9%	35.1%
Kentucky											
Boone County	6,546	10.7%	89.3%	11.4%	88.6%	62.0%	38.0%	39.1%	88.6%	91.4%	30.4%
Campbell County	4,798	35.7%	64.3%	0.0%	100.0%	32.3%	67.7%	18.6%	96.9%	85.3%	36.7%
Daviess County	4,650	39.6%	60.4%	27.4%	72.6%	35.6%	64.4%	30.1%	92.0%	95.5%	65.2%
Fayette County	26,902	41.3%	58.7%	1.2%	98.8%	21.7%	78.3%	11.9%	88.1%	86.8%	45.0%

Table K-2: Counties—Summary Housing Characteristics—*Continued*

	Millennial Householders	Age of Householders		18 to 24 Years Old		25 to 31 Years Old			Percent with Internet Access		Percent with Mobile Access Plan
		18 to 24	25 to 31	Owners	Renters	Owners	Renters	With Mortgage	18 to 24	25 to 31	
Kentucky—Cont.											
Hardin County	6,219	16.3%	83.7%	25.8%	74.2%	36.4%	63.6%	30.7%	78.8%	74.1%	40.9%
Jefferson County	49,214	24.4%	75.6%	4.8%	95.2%	33.4%	66.6%	23.5%	83.4%	86.1%	42.3%
Kenton County	8,769	23.4%	76.6%	26.2%	73.8%	40.3%	59.7%	36.8%	87.3%	86.6%	56.0%
Warren County	10,460	46.1%	53.9%	20.1%	79.9%	31.3%	68.7%	24.2%	86.7%	95.8%	41.7%
Louisiana											
Ascension Parish	5,926	22.2%	77.8%	45.5%	54.5%	85.0%	15.0%	61.7%	87.2%	100.0%	41.4%
Bossier Parish	7,865	19.7%	80.3%	7.5%	92.5%	43.0%	57.0%	30.6%	74.7%	68.7%	40.1%
Caddo Parish	15,958	24.1%	75.9%	37.5%	62.5%	24.5%	75.5%	19.6%	73.1%	83.9%	41.0%
Calcasieu Parish	11,213	35.4%	64.6%	46.3%	53.7%	41.0%	59.0%	27.1%	47.8%	94.7%	30.7%
East Baton Rouge Parish	34,511	45.5%	54.3%	4.2%	95.8%	26.3%	73.7%	14.1%	71.9%	84.1%	37.5%
Jefferson Parish	23,805	23.1%	76.7%	10.3%	89.7%	26.2%	73.8%	18.6%	73.0%	79.2%	34.8%
Lafayette Parish	18,032	34.3%	65.7%	21.7%	78.3%	48.3%	51.7%	32.3%	94.8%	95.7%	21.7%
Lafourche Parish	4,271	30.6%	69.4%	20.5%	79.5%	64.7%	35.3%	29.7%	75.2%	85.7%	40.9%
Livingston Parish	7,179	29.2%	70.8%	45.0%	55.0%	73.5%	26.5%	61.9%	66.4%	62.3%	17.6%
Orleans Parish	28,645	19.9%	79.7%	3.6%	96.4%	19.1%	80.9%	13.5%	77.7%	73.0%	26.0%
Ouachita Parish	8,805	33.4%	65.1%	17.3%	82.7%	22.6%	77.4%	18.9%	68.3%	73.1%	50.6%
Rapides Parish	7,423	30.6%	69.4%	5.4%	94.6%	41.1%	58.9%	19.3%	70.4%	88.8%	49.1%
St. Tammany Parish	10,519	12.6%	87.4%	18.1%	81.9%	49.7%	50.3%	42.7%	96.8%	86.5%	56.1%
Tangipahoa Parish	9,823	26.0%	74.0%	15.0%	85.0%	34.5%	65.5%	17.3%	53.2%	71.2%	25.3%
Terrebonne Parish	6,249	29.4%	70.6%	36.4%	63.6%	55.0%	45.0%	32.5%	74.8%	84.1%	50.0%
Maine											
Androscoggin County	7,532	16.4%	83.6%	36.7%	63.3%	13.8%	86.2%	15.9%	85.4%	81.9%	45.8%
Cumberland County	16,583	20.3%	79.7%	3.9%	96.1%	30.9%	69.1%	21.6%	91.4%	90.3%	41.7%
Kennebec County	6,351	20.9%	79.1%	19.9%	80.1%	42.8%	57.2%	36.4%	88.1%	82.2%	35.7%
Penobscot County	8,327	26.6%	73.4%	25.1%	74.9%	22.0%	78.0%	15.3%	76.6%	79.1%	48.1%
York County	9,818	11.5%	88.5%	0.0%	100.0%	51.3%	48.7%	34.7%	65.6%	84.5%	28.5%
Maryland											
Anne Arundel County	24,226	15.4%	84.6%	30.3%	69.7%	36.9%	63.1%	30.8%	95.2%	91.3%	39.8%
Baltimore County	39,618	20.3%	79.7%	11.8%	88.2%	34.9%	65.1%	24.7%	83.5%	92.0%	46.4%
Carroll County	5,437	15.4%	84.6%	40.2%	59.8%	53.8%	46.2%	46.1%	100.0%	92.6%	38.6%
Cecil County	4,428	17.8%	82.2%	19.9%	80.1%	42.3%	57.7%	35.5%	89.1%	80.2%	19.0%
Charles County	7,142	23.1%	76.9%	32.5%	67.5%	59.7%	40.3%	48.5%	100.0%	94.8%	22.6%
Frederick County	9,479	16.4%	81.6%	53.2%	46.8%	48.8%	51.2%	47.9%	89.0%	97.4%	48.2%
Harford County	8,834	16.2%	83.8%	20.7%	79.3%	70.0%	30.0%	54.5%	92.4%	95.6%	36.0%
Howard County	11,313	14.4%	85.6%	32.0%	68.0%	47.1%	52.9%	41.6%	100.0%	98.0%	66.8%
Montgomery County	39,607	15.4%	84.6%	16.0%	84.0%	29.0%	71.0%	23.9%	95.2%	96.2%	42.5%
Prince George's County	38,999	23.8%	76.2%	7.4%	92.6%	25.3%	74.7%	18.2%	78.6%	80.0%	34.9%
St. Mary's County	3,857	23.5%	76.5%	12.6%	87.4%	45.3%	54.7%	32.8%	82.8%	96.8%	38.1%
Washington County	6,548	22.6%	77.4%	18.1%	81.9%	23.3%	76.7%	19.9%	90.3%	91.9%	50.3%
Wicomico County	6,218	35.8%	64.2%	12.6%	87.4%	39.6%	60.4%	26.4%	94.3%	85.6%	36.9%
Massachusetts											
Barnstable County	6,851	18.1%	81.9%	19.7%	80.3%	38.9%	61.1%	34.5%	100.0%	88.2%	37.5%
Berkshire County	4,143	28.5%	71.5%	17.6%	82.4%	31.4%	68.6%	24.7%	82.1%	89.7%	50.3%
Bristol County	23,562	22.9%	76.1%	4.4%	95.6%	34.0%	66.0%	26.5%	74.5%	88.1%	37.4%
Essex County	26,804	16.4%	82.8%	4.2%	95.8%	29.4%	70.6%	24.0%	80.8%	93.4%	59.6%
Hampden County	21,355	27.4%	72.6%	6.5%	93.5%	26.6%	73.4%	19.1%	81.8%	88.1%	41.9%
Hampshire County	7,631	37.2%	62.3%	23.9%	76.1%	29.4%	70.6%	23.9%	77.4%	96.3%	17.8%
Middlesex County	82,772	20.4%	79.5%	5.2%	94.8%	22.3%	77.7%	16.5%	92.0%	94.8%	48.1%
Norfolk County	22,952	14.1%	85.9%	14.3%	85.7%	28.0%	72.0%	23.4%	97.4%	97.0%	49.6%
Plymouth County	10,957	12.7%	87.3%	29.7%	70.3%	44.2%	55.8%	38.2%	100.0%	94.8%	40.7%
Suffolk County	73,511	25.1%	74.9%	2.8%	97.2%	14.7%	85.3%	9.7%	92.6%	93.6%	42.6%
Worcester County	35,883	23.6%	76.3%	5.8%	94.2%	29.7%	70.3%	22.4%	72.1%	90.5%	27.2%
Michigan											
Allegan County	4,539	24.1%	75.9%	46.8%	53.2%	65.8%	34.2%	37.9%	46.8%	73.8%	23.6%
Bay County	6,731	26.4%	73.6%	7.4%	92.6%	65.8%	34.2%	33.6%	46.0%	89.8%	30.2%
Berrien County	7,430	28.2%	70.5%	5.3%	94.7%	48.1%	51.9%	24.4%	68.1%	82.2%	55.0%
Calhoun County	6,258	25.0%	75.0%	12.3%	87.7%	33.4%	66.6%	25.5%	71.6%	81.0%	34.8%
Eaton County	5,645	32.2%	67.8%	17.1%	82.9%	35.6%	64.4%	26.4%	100.0%	91.0%	44.1%
Genesee County	19,391	26.3%	73.2%	17.7%	82.3%	43.1%	56.9%	21.7%	55.7%	69.3%	27.0%
Ingham County	26,875	41.6%	58.4%	13.0%	87.0%	37.2%	62.8%	22.0%	86.7%	94.8%	49.5%
Jackson County	8,706	28.7%	71.3%	20.7%	79.3%	41.5%	58.5%	34.5%	78.4%	81.3%	42.6%
Kalamazoo County	22,371	46.6%	53.4%	10.3%	89.7%	36.3%	63.7%	18.5%	92.8%	89.2%	60.6%
Kent County	40,893	27.6%	72.4%	10.2%	89.8%	46.4%	53.6%	31.2%	93.2%	84.8%	42.6%
Lenawee County	3,639	38.9%	61.1%	49.4%	50.6%	35.2%	64.8%	25.3%	50.0%	89.2%	25.2%
Livingston County	6,325	27.1%	72.9%	29.6%	70.4%	56.3%	43.7%	43.0%	78.2%	84.3%	52.1%
Macomb County	39,138	20.1%	79.9%	19.2%	80.8%	44.8%	55.2%	26.0%	75.9%	88.3%	33.8%
Monroe County	4,165	23.2%	76.8%	30.5%	69.5%	70.8%	29.2%	53.6%	31.8%	92.3%	39.4%
Muskegon County	7,791	35.0%	65.0%	33.5%	66.5%	36.5%	63.5%	31.9%	74.3%	83.6%	27.7%
Oakland County	61,165	26.3%	73.6%	14.0%	86.0%	45.3%	54.7%	26.6%	83.5%	91.2%	42.2%
Ottawa County	13,903	36.3%	63.7%	25.8%	74.2%	56.1%	43.9%	38.3%	97.9%	92.7%	42.8%
Saginaw County	9,612	36.9%	63.1%	23.2%	76.8%	53.2%	46.8%	29.1%	80.3%	75.1%	32.4%
St. Clair County	5,106	32.5%	67.5%	23.2%	76.8%	64.4%	35.6%	47.6%	84.5%	93.2%	64.4%
Washtenaw County	31,753	40.7%	59.3%	2.9%	97.1%	28.2%	71.8%	11.8%	91.3%	92.0%	51.5%
Wayne County	80,864	28.4%	71.5%	23.6%	76.4%	37.4%	62.6%	20.9%	72.2%	83.4%	27.1%
Minnesota											
Anoka County	16,145	19.9%	80.1%	9.2%	90.8%	62.5%	37.5%	48.7%	87.5%	79.6%	44.9%
Carver County	3,092	12.9%	87.1%	60.6%	39.4%	62.5%	37.5%	57.3%	100.0%	100.0%	58.2%
Dakota County	21,774	30.1%	69.9%	13.6%	86.4%	56.5%	43.5%	42.3%	100.0%	95.2%	48.5%

Table K-2: Counties—Summary Housing Characteristics—*Continued*

	Millennial Householders	Age of Householders		18 to 24 Years Old		25 to 31 Years Old			Percent with Internet Access		Percent with Mobile Access Plan
		18 to 24	25 to 31	Owners	Renters	Owners	Renters	With Mortgage	18 to 24	25 to 31	
Minnesota—Cont.											
Hennepin County	89,398	20.1%	79.9%	8.1%	91.9%	30.8%	69.2%	22.2%	88.7%	89.2%	46.3%
Olmsted County	10,470	38.6%	61.4%	28.0%	72.0%	68.4%	31.6%	42.6%	88.9%	91.0%	58.6%
Ramsey County	37,417	28.5%	71.5%	6.6%	93.4%	33.3%	66.7%	21.1%	86.0%	95.8%	45.8%
Scott County	3,496	7.2%	92.8%	100.0%	0.0%	57.1%	42.9%	56.9%	100.0%	91.5%	42.2%
St. Louis County	15,110	31.1%	68.9%	14.5%	85.5%	34.0%	66.0%	25.4%	97.3%	89.4%	23.4%
Stearns County	11,036	45.0%	55.0%	21.6%	78.4%	64.8%	35.2%	40.5%	88.8%	94.5%	22.4%
Washington County	12,648	13.0%	87.0%	5.2%	94.8%	58.1%	41.9%	47.4%	88.4%	80.1%	30.4%
Wright County	6,952	9.5%	90.5%	7.8%	92.2%	59.4%	40.6%	51.3%	100.0%	81.1%	44.1%
Mississippi											
DeSoto County	8,233	16.5%	82.2%	10.6%	89.4%	53.7%	46.3%	32.4%	58.6%	73.4%	30.0%
Harrison County	13,277	30.0%	70.0%	0.9%	99.1%	34.3%	65.7%	13.3%	96.4%	83.4%	47.1%
Hinds County	15,734	26.4%	73.6%	8.9%	91.1%	20.6%	79.4%	12.6%	66.9%	77.1%	32.9%
Jackson County	7,081	22.1%	77.9%	20.4%	79.6%	35.0%	65.0%	19.4%	82.9%	75.8%	17.4%
Madison County	3,223	17.7%	82.3%	21.9%	78.1%	50.4%	49.6%	23.5%	79.9%	78.0%	46.8%
Rankin County	7,322	21.8%	78.2%	12.2%	87.8%	50.2%	49.8%	34.2%	100.0%	85.9%	62.2%
Missouri											
Boone County	22,986	48.5%	51.5%	2.9%	97.1%	26.4%	73.6%	13.6%	93.6%	82.5%	34.7%
Cass County	3,754	22.8%	77.2%	53.5%	46.5%	62.1%	37.9%	54.7%	51.3%	83.0%	57.1%
Clay County	14,584	21.7%	78.3%	0.0%	100.0%	30.3%	69.7%	20.2%	70.7%	90.9%	44.6%
Franklin County	4,754	19.1%	80.9%	7.5%	92.5%	60.3%	39.7%	48.5%	84.8%	85.0%	17.7%
Greene County	28,260	38.0%	62.0%	4.5%	95.5%	39.0%	61.0%	24.6%	82.3%	83.0%	29.8%
Jackson County	47,132	25.4%	74.6%	6.7%	93.3%	32.9%	67.1%	22.5%	81.4%	83.7%	40.7%
Jasper County	9,162	26.0%	74.0%	27.2%	72.8%	39.4%	60.6%	33.6%	84.2%	81.8%	21.0%
Jefferson County	10,939	19.3%	80.7%	38.9%	61.1%	86.6%	13.4%	70.0%	48.6%	91.4%	33.7%
Platte County	7,169	29.5%	70.5%	3.5%	96.5%	30.5%	69.5%	19.4%	97.2%	96.5%	60.1%
St. Charles County	19,647	19.7%	80.3%	31.3%	68.7%	51.3%	48.7%	44.8%	90.3%	90.1%	43.4%
St. Louis County	51,775	18.2%	81.8%	14.3%	85.7%	35.8%	64.2%	29.2%	81.6%	88.0%	42.2%
Montana											
Flathead County	3,158	11.7%	88.3%	24.1%	75.9%	44.0%	56.0%	33.2%	80.5%	79.1%	30.6%
Gallatin County	8,565	36.4%	60.6%	3.6%	96.4%	30.8%	69.2%	15.9%	79.1%	96.0%	43.6%
Missoula County	7,597	31.5%	68.5%	0.0%	100.0%	29.7%	70.3%	18.9%	50.9%	92.3%	36.2%
Yellowstone County	10,092	37.7%	62.3%	5.4%	94.6%	39.2%	60.8%	23.2%	73.9%	87.1%	32.8%
Nebraska											
Douglas County	43,067	27.9%	72.1%	8.3%	91.7%	38.7%	61.3%	26.1%	89.4%	81.5%	37.4%
Lancaster County	26,939	41.9%	57.4%	5.3%	94.7%	43.4%	56.6%	22.9%	93.9%	88.6%	27.6%
Sarpy County	11,225	24.6%	75.4%	14.6%	85.4%	41.6%	58.4%	32.7%	75.1%	91.2%	40.7%
Nevada											
Clark County	105,663	21.6%	78.4%	18.5%	81.5%	27.1%	72.9%	21.7%	86.3%	82.5%	36.0%
Washoe County	24,868	26.2%	73.7%	8.3%	91.7%	29.7%	70.3%	18.8%	84.4%	86.4%	47.1%
New Hampshire											
Hillsborough County	19,551	18.3%	81.7%	5.9%	94.1%	24.8%	75.2%	19.5%	82.5%	88.3%	43.6%
Merrimack County	5,930	36.4%	62.7%	48.5%	51.5%	30.8%	69.2%	22.4%	94.0%	91.6%	30.0%
Rockingham County	9,976	21.3%	78.7%	0.0%	100.0%	40.9%	59.1%	28.6%	100.0%	91.5%	31.9%
Strafford County	7,208	39.0%	61.0%	2.7%	97.3%	34.6%	65.4%	16.0%	97.4%	87.6%	24.5%
New Jersey											
Atlantic County	9,983	18.6%	81.4%	27.7%	72.3%	36.7%	63.3%	27.0%	39.0%	79.6%	28.5%
Bergen County	28,123	16.8%	81.7%	19.2%	80.8%	27.6%	72.4%	22.3%	94.2%	87.5%	31.5%
Burlington County	14,733	10.1%	89.9%	9.2%	90.8%	42.4%	57.6%	32.5%	73.8%	90.4%	42.0%
Camden County	20,063	21.9%	78.1%	5.3%	94.7%	39.7%	60.3%	27.8%	84.5%	84.2%	42.8%
Cape May County	2,625	25.3%	74.7%	17.3%	82.7%	46.1%	53.9%	34.5%	74.8%	85.3%	48.7%
Cumberland County	7,380	12.5%	87.5%	21.2%	78.8%	35.1%	64.9%	31.7%	81.3%	70.3%	30.0%
Essex County	32,273	18.0%	81.6%	0.6%	99.4%	10.5%	89.5%	7.4%	80.3%	87.6%	33.4%
Gloucester County	9,975	19.6%	79.0%	14.5%	85.5%	33.0%	67.0%	25.8%	79.7%	86.9%	61.9%
Hudson County	43,271	11.3%	88.7%	3.6%	96.4%	12.2%	87.8%	9.2%	93.4%	91.9%	33.5%
Hunterdon County	1,199	13.3%	84.1%	61.6%	38.4%	28.6%	71.4%	28.4%	71.7%	97.3%	45.9%
Mercer County	13,042	18.5%	81.5%	1.7%	98.3%	20.5%	79.5%	14.8%	85.3%	91.3%	50.5%
Middlesex County	28,792	21.0%	79.0%	12.5%	87.5%	19.8%	80.2%	15.2%	82.3%	92.4%	40.5%
Monmouth County	17,112	11.5%	88.5%	18.4%	81.6%	26.8%	73.2%	21.6%	85.2%	95.1%	35.8%
Morris County	13,162	6.1%	93.4%	16.0%	84.0%	32.8%	67.2%	30.4%	100.0%	96.0%	37.1%
Ocean County	13,927	16.4%	83.6%	14.5%	85.5%	42.4%	57.6%	36.8%	59.0%	87.2%	32.9%
Passaic County	14,794	18.1%	81.2%	5.7%	94.3%	14.0%	86.0%	11.2%	86.9%	73.0%	38.2%
Somerset County	6,051	11.8%	88.2%	29.9%	70.1%	44.6%	55.4%	42.5%	100.0%	95.8%	28.3%
Sussex County	3,821	5.1%	93.7%	50.0%	50.0%	27.9%	72.1%	26.0%	50.0%	74.3%	27.7%
Union County	17,393	15.2%	84.8%	0.0%	100.0%	19.4%	80.6%	15.5%	74.2%	88.6%	33.5%
Warren County	3,864	35.0%	65.0%	0.0%	100.0%	40.7%	59.3%	26.5%	81.7%	100.0%	26.8%
New Mexico											
Bernalillo County	38,524	31.7%	67.1%	10.8%	89.2%	36.2%	63.8%	24.2%	81.3%	86.4%	36.9%
Doña Ana County	14,038	52.7%	47.3%	15.7%	84.3%	30.8%	69.2%	15.4%	87.2%	85.4%	52.7%
San Juan County	4,439	35.7%	64.3%	29.8%	70.2%	50.5%	49.5%	28.9%	48.2%	82.9%	36.4%
Sandoval County	3,991	10.4%	89.6%	8.9%	91.1%	24.1%	75.9%	15.8%	82.9%	79.7%	35.4%
Santa Fe County	5,816	26.1%	73.9%	26.7%	73.3%	33.1%	66.9%	27.3%	66.4%	82.9%	32.1%
New York											
Albany County	20,900	38.2%	61.8%	7.0%	93.0%	24.9%	75.1%	17.4%	90.3%	93.9%	37.4%
Bronx County	60,881	22.6%	77.0%	2.3%	97.7%	3.9%	96.1%	2.9%	84.1%	83.9%	28.4%
Broome County	11,530	36.4%	63.3%	0.0%	100.0%	34.1%	65.9%	15.4%	68.1%	84.7%	34.0%
Chautauqua County	6,262	30.3%	69.7%	3.6%	96.4%	42.1%	57.9%	24.3%	68.9%	79.4%	22.6%
Dutchess County	10,052	29.6%	70.4%	19.5%	80.5%	31.8%	68.2%	20.2%	94.8%	91.2%	39.0%
Erie County	55,131	26.5%	73.5%	8.1%	91.9%	32.7%	67.3%	22.3%	75.7%	89.3%	34.8%

Table K-2: Counties—Summary Housing Characteristics—*Continued*

	Millennial Householders	Age of Householders		18 to 24 Years Old		25 to 31 Years Old			Percent with Internet Access		Percent with Mobile Access Plan
		18 to 24	25 to 31	Owners	Renters	Owners	Renters	With Mortgage	18 to 24	25 to 31	
New York —Cont.											
Jefferson County	8,241	39.6%	60.4%	17.9%	82.1%	19.2%	80.8%	15.6%	87.7%	95.9%	49.0%
Kings County	151,377	19.8%	80.0%	6.3%	93.7%	8.8%	91.2%	5.8%	79.4%	84.9%	36.1%
Monroe County	45,033	24.2%	75.8%	4.6%	95.4%	32.1%	67.9%	21.7%	81.5%	85.1%	40.8%
Nassau County	21,499	12.7%	87.3%	26.4%	73.6%	37.7%	62.3%	31.8%	96.4%	90.5%	36.4%
New York County	134,036	16.8%	83.1%	2.6%	97.4%	5.7%	94.3%	2.7%	95.0%	94.9%	46.5%
Niagara County	7,813	32.6%	67.4%	18.7%	81.3%	42.5%	57.5%	28.6%	71.0%	69.8%	34.4%
Oneida County	11,607	20.8%	78.5%	12.8%	87.2%	35.4%	64.6%	21.6%	87.1%	82.1%	21.4%
Onondaga County	26,078	28.3%	71.6%	10.6%	89.4%	40.5%	59.5%	28.7%	74.6%	88.8%	35.2%
Ontario County	4,329	29.9%	70.1%	17.7%	82.3%	61.6%	38.4%	42.3%	66.6%	66.6%	30.2%
Orange County	13,672	28.2%	71.8%	7.8%	92.2%	45.4%	54.6%	26.5%	78.6%	82.3%	48.5%
Oswego County	4,918	27.6%	72.4%	16.3%	83.7%	37.3%	62.7%	23.2%	79.6%	87.8%	24.9%
Putnam County	1,501	6.9%	93.1%	0.0%	100.0%	21.7%	78.3%	20.2%	0.0%	80.1%	38.6%
Queens County	91,204	15.3%	84.1%	12.5%	87.5%	16.8%	83.2%	12.8%	83.2%	88.3%	27.6%
Rensselaer County	10,595	23.5%	76.0%	3.7%	96.3%	24.6%	75.4%	14.8%	93.3%	97.7%	52.2%
Richmond County	16,107	12.8%	87.2%	29.5%	70.5%	30.4%	69.6%	23.9%	71.8%	77.7%	27.7%
Rockland County	8,925	13.1%	86.9%	14.7%	85.3%	21.2%	78.8%	16.9%	34.8%	68.9%	20.3%
Saratoga County	9,718	28.4%	68.7%	10.2%	89.8%	37.9%	62.1%	25.2%	72.7%	92.3%	50.0%
Schenectady County	5,562	23.3%	76.7%	11.7%	88.3%	32.4%	67.6%	20.0%	81.0%	65.2%	28.0%
St. Lawrence County	5,033	31.7%	68.3%	13.4%	86.6%	39.7%	60.3%	26.2%	44.0%	68.4%	24.3%
Steuben County	3,615	17.2%	82.8%	31.6%	68.4%	50.2%	49.8%	40.7%	63.5%	76.6%	38.5%
Suffolk County	31,322	17.8%	81.9%	13.9%	86.1%	45.9%	54.1%	36.5%	84.2%	93.2%	25.9%
Tompkins County	8,664	45.2%	54.8%	0.0%	100.0%	20.1%	79.9%	11.0%	98.6%	96.9%	32.1%
Ulster County	6,503	32.6%	67.4%	4.3%	95.7%	42.0%	58.0%	23.1%	100.0%	72.8%	26.0%
Wayne County	3,680	26.3%	73.8%	19.4%	80.6%	72.1%	27.9%	58.3%	53.3%	93.0%	26.4%
Westchester County	27,626	20.6%	79.4%	10.1%	89.9%	13.8%	86.2%	10.1%	84.4%	91.7%	44.2%
North Carolina											
Alamance County	8,462	33.1%	66.9%	27.5%	72.5%	35.1%	64.9%	18.7%	86.8%	75.6%	36.2%
Brunswick County	3,666	14.5%	85.5%	9.9%	90.1%	29.4%	70.6%	22.4%	27.2%	82.2%	44.5%
Buncombe County	12,122	19.8%	80.2%	13.6%	86.4%	40.8%	59.2%	24.2%	86.8%	84.5%	53.4%
Burke County	3,372	23.5%	76.5%	36.0%	64.0%	41.7%	58.3%	35.8%	89.8%	78.3%	33.9%
Cabarrus County	7,379	12.7%	87.3%	4.4%	95.6%	41.1%	58.9%	32.3%	70.4%	92.2%	38.0%
Catawba County	5,458	23.5%	75.7%	11.7%	88.3%	33.4%	66.6%	28.2%	74.8%	81.5%	30.7%
Cleveland County	3,125	25.7%	74.3%	13.1%	86.9%	63.1%	36.9%	32.5%	39.2%	100.0%	13.8%
Craven County	8,439	34.8%	65.2%	9.0%	91.0%	19.1%	80.9%	12.8%	81.8%	94.6%	60.5%
Cumberland County	29,536	33.9%	66.1%	6.6%	93.4%	13.5%	86.5%	9.9%	83.6%	80.1%	44.3%
Davidson County	6,403	25.8%	74.2%	29.3%	70.7%	40.5%	59.5%	24.8%	76.6%	79.8%	27.4%
Durham County	23,933	20.0%	80.0%	2.0%	98.0%	21.8%	78.2%	17.5%	98.1%	88.1%	57.0%
Forsyth County	20,675	33.0%	65.9%	6.4%	93.6%	34.9%	65.1%	23.0%	83.9%	82.8%	26.0%
Gaston County	8,605	41.6%	58.4%	4.6%	95.4%	46.6%	53.4%	26.4%	76.3%	81.0%	46.8%
Guilford County	33,027	24.1%	75.9%	8.0%	92.0%	24.7%	75.3%	18.1%	75.3%	84.1%	33.7%
Harnett County	7,369	21.6%	78.1%	26.9%	73.1%	51.5%	48.5%	36.7%	82.0%	81.4%	42.4%
Henderson County	4,744	31.4%	68.6%	19.5%	80.5%	56.8%	43.2%	19.7%	70.7%	62.1%	36.0%
Iredell County	5,770	20.2%	78.9%	37.0%	63.0%	27.2%	72.8%	24.0%	87.0%	73.2%	25.5%
Johnston County	7,002	17.9%	82.1%	29.6%	70.4%	54.6%	45.4%	45.7%	88.1%	82.3%	47.9%
Mecklenburg County	68,412	22.9%	77.1%	6.6%	93.4%	26.5%	73.5%	19.1%	80.5%	85.2%	39.7%
Moore County	3,975	24.4%	75.6%	21.0%	79.0%	10.3%	89.7%	10.7%	68.1%	40.4%	26.7%
Nash County	3,100	31.6%	59.5%	0.0%	100.0%	1.6%	98.4%	0.5%	72.9%	68.8%	25.9%
New Hanover County	16,950	41.9%	57.6%	5.5%	94.5%	27.7%	72.3%	15.2%	86.7%	85.8%	36.5%
Onslow County	21,261	46.4%	53.6%	20.1%	79.9%	33.6%	66.4%	24.4%	88.8%	82.5%	52.6%
Orange County	10,021	41.6%	58.4%	5.7%	94.3%	18.2%	81.8%	9.6%	95.2%	97.8%	63.0%
Pitt County	16,044	57.7%	42.3%	7.7%	92.3%	31.8%	68.2%	12.1%	91.9%	94.3%	30.2%
Randolph County	5,694	31.5%	68.5%	43.6%	56.4%	39.0%	61.0%	20.0%	78.4%	60.6%	37.2%
Robeson County	6,441	30.3%	69.7%	8.8%	91.2%	22.8%	77.2%	9.0%	49.6%	37.4%	14.1%
Rockingham County	3,855	17.1%	82.9%	13.0%	87.0%	59.2%	40.8%	33.1%	100.0%	61.5%	45.0%
Rowan County	4,474	32.4%	67.6%	15.7%	84.3%	47.2%	52.8%	32.1%	92.7%	76.6%	28.3%
Union County	6,521	24.0%	76.0%	14.7%	85.3%	42.6%	57.4%	34.4%	78.3%	86.5%	44.0%
Wake County	57,485	27.3%	72.7%	3.5%	96.5%	35.6%	64.4%	25.2%	88.2%	89.4%	51.9%
Wayne County	7,210	34.5%	65.5%	2.3%	97.7%	39.0%	61.0%	24.4%	87.1%	87.7%	55.4%
North Dakota											
Cass County	18,445	47.9%	52.1%	2.6%	97.4%	39.0%	61.0%	17.1%	91.4%	79.7%	34.0%
Ohio											
Allen County	5,667	26.6%	73.4%	21.3%	78.7%	33.2%	66.8%	28.0%	67.2%	65.9%	14.8%
Ashtabula County	4,446	22.5%	77.5%	52.9%	47.1%	37.0%	63.0%	26.5%	47.1%	87.3%	11.2%
Butler County	20,453	32.1%	67.9%	6.4%	93.6%	46.8%	53.2%	26.3%	86.5%	93.5%	36.0%
Clark County	7,555	36.1%	63.9%	18.5%	81.5%	41.2%	58.8%	28.0%	66.3%	86.8%	39.3%
Clermont County	10,232	24.1%	75.9%	2.9%	97.1%	39.6%	60.4%	29.0%	74.8%	90.0%	47.4%
Columbiana County	5,515	30.6%	69.4%	11.0%	89.0%	41.0%	59.0%	23.1%	50.2%	71.6%	40.2%
Cuyahoga County	76,387	26.5%	73.2%	6.6%	93.4%	27.6%	72.4%	18.4%	80.5%	87.0%	39.0%
Delaware County	7,499	23.2%	76.8%	47.0%	53.0%	39.8%	60.2%	39.4%	87.7%	84.4%	34.6%
Fairfield County	8,133	18.5%	81.5%	9.7%	90.3%	40.4%	59.6%	29.4%	93.8%	90.3%	64.0%
Franklin County	96,520	27.6%	72.4%	3.8%	96.2%	29.3%	70.7%	19.3%	81.2%	89.2%	43.0%
Geauga County	1,943	20.3%	79.7%	41.8%	58.2%	70.7%	29.3%	53.2%	56.7%	100.0%	28.3%
Greene County	10,496	36.7%	63.3%	7.0%	93.0%	33.1%	66.9%	19.6%	91.1%	76.9%	45.0%
Hamilton County	58,958	30.9%	69.0%	6.6%	93.4%	31.0%	69.0%	21.5%	79.8%	82.7%	35.6%
Lake County	8,362	8.9%	87.3%	31.1%	68.9%	40.1%	59.9%	36.7%	90.0%	92.7%	27.3%
Licking County	7,512	26.6%	72.9%	1.5%	98.5%	50.5%	49.5%	33.5%	96.4%	89.6%	58.2%
Lorain County	10,206	35.3%	64.7%	24.5%	75.5%	38.8%	61.2%	29.2%	83.6%	80.8%	46.4%
Lucas County	29,745	32.0%	68.0%	12.8%	87.2%	27.8%	72.2%	19.0%	76.7%	79.6%	33.9%

Table K-2: Counties—Summary Housing Characteristics—*Continued*

	Millennial Householders	Age of Householders		18 to 24 Years Old		25 to 31 Years Old			Percent with Internet Access		Percent with Mobile Access Plan
		18 to 24	25 to 31	Owners	Renters	Owners	Renters	With Mortgage	18 to 24	25 to 31	
Ohio—Cont.											
Mahoning County...............	12,227	23.8%	76.2%	17.1%	82.9%	45.1%	54.9%	32.2%	81.6%	83.4%	28.3%
Medina County...............	5,987	22.0%	78.0%	35.8%	64.2%	59.6%	40.4%	52.6%	89.2%	84.4%	54.8%
Miami County...............	5,365	22.7%	77.3%	30.4%	69.6%	44.4%	55.6%	38.4%	100.0%	86.3%	53.6%
Montgomery County............	32,321	33.0%	66.9%	12.1%	87.9%	36.2%	63.8%	24.4%	76.4%	90.6%	45.7%
Portage County...............	9,690	50.7%	49.3%	8.5%	91.5%	23.9%	76.1%	14.2%	86.3%	93.3%	21.3%
Richland County...............	5,200	38.2%	59.2%	29.6%	70.4%	43.3%	56.7%	24.1%	88.1%	92.0%	32.3%
Stark County...............	17,117	26.6%	73.1%	14.3%	85.7%	42.5%	57.5%	27.2%	85.1%	88.7%	59.5%
Summit County...............	31,851	29.0%	70.4%	8.9%	91.1%	43.5%	56.5%	29.8%	89.6%	83.7%	39.8%
Trumbull County...............	9,015	20.7%	79.3%	21.4%	78.6%	36.0%	64.0%	22.4%	50.1%	63.3%	15.8%
Tuscarawas County............	3,477	21.7%	78.3%	37.3%	62.7%	19.4%	80.6%	22.0%	68.3%	87.4%	44.4%
Warren County...............	8,416	23.0%	77.0%	21.3%	78.7%	60.6%	39.4%	41.3%	80.6%	86.8%	37.6%
Wayne County...............	5,992	20.7%	79.3%	10.9%	89.1%	37.1%	62.9%	25.8%	51.4%	75.1%	42.8%
Wood County...............	10,248	43.1%	56.9%	15.3%	84.7%	35.7%	64.3%	20.5%	81.4%	95.6%	18.5%
Oklahoma											
Canadian County...............	5,138	19.0%	81.0%	20.9%	79.1%	71.0%	29.0%	42.7%	66.1%	98.0%	40.0%
Cleveland County...............	25,511	38.4%	60.5%	14.2%	85.8%	43.3%	56.7%	27.8%	83.2%	91.8%	53.3%
Comanche County............	9,738	32.7%	67.3%	1.1%	98.9%	22.3%	77.7%	12.6%	55.0%	79.1%	41.2%
Oklahoma County...............	55,921	26.7%	73.3%	14.4%	85.6%	28.6%	71.4%	21.6%	82.5%	85.2%	43.2%
Tulsa County...............	44,922	30.0%	69.7%	9.1%	90.9%	31.6%	68.4%	21.6%	68.8%	82.2%	38.7%
Oregon											
Clackamas County...............	16,296	24.9%	75.1%	22.0%	78.0%	25.3%	74.7%	20.9%	91.2%	91.6%	44.1%
Deschutes County...............	6,665	17.8%	82.2%	3.2%	96.8%	25.5%	74.5%	16.8%	91.1%	78.2%	47.1%
Douglas County...............	4,720	23.4%	76.6%	0.0%	100.0%	40.1%	59.9%	20.6%	50.2%	69.7%	22.0%
Jackson County...............	11,435	24.4%	74.1%	28.3%	71.7%	25.0%	75.0%	17.5%	72.0%	85.2%	20.2%
Lane County...............	24,469	47.7%	52.3%	7.9%	92.1%	32.8%	67.2%	18.5%	90.3%	93.2%	43.9%
Linn County...............	7,993	52.6%	47.4%	3.2%	96.8%	23.7%	76.3%	8.8%	94.1%	91.0%	33.4%
Marion County...............	17,460	38.4%	61.6%	1.5%	98.5%	21.1%	78.9%	13.4%	92.8%	84.2%	34.5%
Multnomah County...............	53,976	22.3%	77.7%	3.1%	96.9%	24.0%	76.0%	17.3%	90.3%	92.9%	56.0%
Washington County............	29,546	18.8%	81.2%	5.1%	94.9%	22.5%	77.5%	17.6%	90.8%	94.6%	51.1%
Yamhill County...............	5,351	30.5%	69.5%	0.0%	100.0%	24.1%	75.9%	16.7%	100.0%	96.8%	25.7%
Pennsylvania											
Adams County...............	4,067	37.1%	62.9%	19.4%	80.6%	39.0%	61.0%	20.9%	62.9%	84.3%	34.7%
Allegheny County...............	79,769	27.6%	72.3%	7.1%	92.9%	32.5%	67.5%	21.8%	84.3%	90.7%	43.5%
Beaver County...............	6,256	30.1%	68.1%	8.2%	91.8%	57.2%	42.8%	42.0%	89.7%	84.4%	46.7%
Berks County...............	18,198	28.2%	71.5%	13.0%	87.0%	48.5%	51.5%	31.7%	73.4%	92.2%	41.8%
Blair County...............	5,847	29.0%	71.0%	25.1%	74.9%	32.7%	67.3%	22.4%	94.0%	83.2%	47.5%
Bucks County...............	17,224	9.3%	90.7%	19.1%	80.9%	31.5%	68.5%	28.1%	94.1%	94.9%	35.7%
Butler County...............	8,840	35.1%	64.9%	38.7%	61.3%	61.4%	38.6%	47.6%	95.8%	89.1%	48.2%
Cambria County...............	6,783	25.7%	74.3%	44.2%	55.8%	49.6%	50.4%	44.9%	87.0%	82.5%	42.8%
Centre County...............	14,960	56.4%	43.6%	4.0%	96.0%	29.1%	70.9%	11.7%	95.8%	94.5%	28.4%
Chester County...............	20,936	27.0%	73.0%	11.4%	88.6%	37.8%	62.2%	28.8%	90.0%	84.9%	32.2%
Cumberland County............	12,199	25.1%	74.9%	7.2%	92.8%	32.3%	67.7%	20.2%	92.6%	92.1%	51.1%
Dauphin County...............	17,692	27.3%	72.7%	14.3%	85.7%	34.4%	65.6%	25.1%	98.5%	84.5%	44.9%
Delaware County...............	20,254	19.3%	80.7%	13.7%	86.3%	40.6%	59.4%	32.8%	83.5%	90.9%	38.2%
Erie County...............	16,091	23.4%	76.6%	19.4%	80.6%	48.3%	51.7%	36.5%	95.0%	88.3%	45.0%
Fayette County...............	4,179	32.0%	67.5%	7.5%	92.5%	52.8%	47.2%	24.5%	23.8%	80.2%	22.6%
Franklin County...............	6,958	19.0%	81.0%	26.5%	73.5%	58.7%	41.3%	49.2%	91.6%	83.2%	32.0%
Lackawanna County............	7,565	18.6%	81.4%	4.7%	95.3%	32.1%	67.9%	23.5%	78.9%	82.9%	43.7%
Lancaster County...............	27,356	28.4%	71.6%	18.6%	81.4%	58.6%	41.4%	43.6%	67.3%	80.0%	29.6%
Lebanon County...............	5,759	27.9%	72.1%	10.5%	89.5%	40.8%	59.2%	21.6%	68.7%	71.7%	34.7%
Lehigh County...............	13,962	27.6%	72.4%	20.6%	79.4%	34.4%	65.6%	24.0%	78.5%	87.4%	36.4%
Luzerne County...............	15,011	24.8%	75.2%	10.6%	89.4%	29.8%	70.2%	18.9%	85.3%	83.1%	18.6%
Lycoming County...............	4,951	44.7%	55.3%	24.2%	75.8%	48.8%	51.2%	23.3%	81.6%	78.0%	26.6%
Mercer County...............	5,058	31.7%	68.3%	5.5%	94.5%	35.3%	64.7%	21.6%	80.5%	69.0%	29.6%
Monroe County...............	5,598	40.1%	59.9%	11.5%	88.5%	60.5%	39.5%	28.8%	90.3%	67.7%	45.1%
Montgomery County............	30,926	14.3%	85.4%	18.6%	81.4%	38.6%	61.4%	33.1%	92.6%	90.3%	46.3%
Northampton County............	11,585	27.0%	73.0%	3.2%	96.8%	41.0%	59.0%	25.9%	87.8%	89.2%	37.1%
Northumberland County..........	4,210	21.6%	78.4%	26.7%	73.3%	45.6%	54.4%	34.9%	95.3%	72.1%	22.6%
Philadelphia County...............	109,719	21.4%	78.5%	8.9%	91.1%	20.3%	79.7%	14.1%	82.2%	84.0%	37.6%
Schuylkill County...............	5,170	14.3%	85.7%	34.0%	66.0%	47.0%	53.0%	37.0%	35.0%	79.4%	21.7%
Washington County............	8,899	20.7%	79.3%	11.9%	88.1%	45.4%	54.6%	25.4%	70.1%	77.4%	49.9%
Westmoreland County............	14,072	27.7%	72.3%	11.0%	89.0%	46.2%	53.8%	30.3%	66.6%	78.9%	35.5%
York County...............	17,344	19.3%	80.7%	16.4%	83.6%	55.9%	44.1%	45.7%	69.0%	78.6%	39.0%
Rhode Island											
Kent County...............	7,696	15.8%	84.2%	22.7%	77.3%	45.1%	54.9%	40.4%	100.0%	96.6%	54.3%
Providence County............	33,455	25.1%	74.9%	8.5%	91.5%	20.3%	79.7%	14.7%	78.1%	82.4%	35.0%
Washington County............	4,875	43.2%	56.8%	7.7%	92.3%	23.5%	76.5%	13.3%	96.9%	89.7%	38.3%
South Carolina											
Aiken County...............	7,172	31.0%	69.0%	47.6%	52.4%	34.6%	65.4%	29.6%	66.2%	89.9%	51.1%
Anderson County............	9,906	28.9%	70.2%	37.5%	62.5%	44.2%	55.8%	32.3%	72.3%	75.6%	34.1%
Beaufort County...............	7,795	27.9%	72.1%	18.9%	81.1%	52.8%	47.2%	36.7%	82.3%	90.0%	19.2%
Berkeley County...............	10,431	32.2%	67.8%	4.2%	95.8%	33.6%	66.4%	20.4%	77.0%	79.9%	34.1%
Charleston County...............	25,230	31.6%	68.4%	3.6%	96.4%	32.4%	67.6%	20.1%	87.7%	82.1%	41.7%
Dorchester County...............	6,409	46.5%	53.5%	1.9%	98.1%	29.5%	70.5%	15.4%	53.8%	87.8%	44.3%
Florence County...............	5,391	23.8%	76.2%	10.6%	89.4%	43.8%	56.2%	23.4%	69.8%	86.3%	26.5%
Greenville County...............	26,782	24.3%	75.6%	10.9%	89.1%	31.5%	68.5%	20.3%	72.9%	75.3%	34.4%
Horry County...............	12,222	28.6%	71.4%	12.0%	88.0%	36.2%	63.8%	18.8%	83.0%	86.4%	55.9%
Lexington County...............	13,992	26.8%	73.2%	18.9%	81.1%	48.9%	51.1%	31.4%	82.6%	81.0%	44.6%

Table K-2: Counties—Summary Housing Characteristics—*Continued*

	Millennial Householders	Age of Householders		18 to 24 Years Old		25 to 31 Years Old			Percent with Internet Access		Percent with Mobile Access Plan
		18 to 24	25 to 31	Owners	Renters	Owners	Renters	With Mortgage	18 to 24	25 to 31	
South Carolina—Cont.											
Orangeburg County	4,598	42.3%	57.7%	17.3%	82.7%	25.7%	74.3%	9.4%	50.8%	65.3%	28.2%
Pickens County	5,385	36.6%	63.4%	4.2%	95.8%	42.1%	57.9%	18.5%	96.6%	72.4%	42.8%
Richland County	25,225	35.2%	64.8%	7.0%	93.0%	28.0%	72.0%	15.7%	77.4%	79.3%	40.3%
Spartanburg County	14,789	36.2%	63.8%	8.6%	91.4%	44.1%	55.9%	27.2%	74.0%	79.6%	47.7%
Sumter County	5,380	33.5%	63.6%	30.0%	70.0%	33.6%	66.4%	23.2%	74.7%	94.3%	28.5%
York County	12,264	29.6%	70.4%	10.0%	90.0%	49.2%	50.8%	32.8%	83.5%	77.8%	20.4%
South Dakota											
Minnehaha County	15,552	24.5%	75.5%	17.6%	82.4%	43.1%	56.9%	27.6%	93.8%	94.5%	37.0%
Pennington County	6,900	33.8%	66.2%	16.3%	83.7%	53.8%	46.2%	26.4%	92.0%	90.5%	44.0%
Tennessee											
Blount County	6,349	29.8%	70.2%	8.7%	91.3%	51.6%	48.4%	36.5%	61.5%	77.7%	29.8%
Bradley County	4,659	21.6%	78.4%	18.2%	81.8%	34.7%	65.3%	27.5%	43.2%	77.4%	41.9%
Davidson County	53,291	20.6%	79.3%	12.1%	87.9%	25.7%	74.3%	19.2%	74.1%	84.1%	36.3%
Hamilton County	19,584	27.9%	72.1%	11.4%	88.6%	30.1%	69.9%	21.6%	46.3%	81.4%	29.7%
Knox County	32,774	35.7%	64.3%	2.8%	97.2%	36.6%	63.4%	20.6%	80.4%	87.5%	40.4%
Madison County	4,338	24.8%	75.2%	11.4%	88.6%	27.6%	72.4%	21.2%	68.7%	76.9%	17.1%
Montgomery County	19,133	26.8%	73.2%	26.3%	73.7%	33.4%	66.6%	26.9%	87.3%	88.4%	41.9%
Rutherford County	21,597	38.0%	62.0%	6.7%	93.3%	44.1%	55.9%	27.1%	86.4%	75.7%	23.0%
Sevier County	3,823	37.0%	63.0%	0.0%	100.0%	43.3%	56.7%	25.2%	60.0%	80.0%	41.5%
Shelby County	55,348	24.5%	75.5%	8.3%	91.7%	23.2%	76.8%	16.7%	80.1%	71.3%	29.5%
Sullivan County	5,187	20.9%	78.0%	23.0%	77.0%	61.8%	38.2%	45.2%	73.2%	85.5%	29.4%
Sumner County	8,360	17.7%	82.3%	32.4%	67.6%	47.3%	52.7%	37.9%	86.3%	84.0%	56.1%
Washington County	7,009	38.5%	61.5%	6.7%	93.3%	37.5%	62.5%	25.6%	98.4%	89.6%	55.3%
Williamson County	5,025	16.8%	81.8%	24.1%	75.9%	52.2%	47.8%	41.4%	100.0%	97.5%	68.7%
Wilson County	4,041	20.0%	80.0%	11.2%	88.8%	60.4%	39.6%	38.6%	64.0%	80.6%	37.4%
Texas											
Bell County	23,283	27.9%	72.1%	5.5%	94.5%	28.6%	71.4%	17.9%	77.5%	93.0%	30.9%
Bexar County	109,672	26.5%	73.4%	6.1%	93.9%	27.0%	73.0%	18.1%	79.6%	83.5%	38.4%
Bowie County	5,249	31.7%	68.0%	0.8%	99.2%	34.7%	65.3%	15.2%	26.6%	72.3%	15.8%
Brazoria County	18,377	22.9%	77.1%	32.7%	67.3%	56.0%	44.0%	42.2%	73.0%	79.6%	42.1%
Brazos County	27,283	60.1%	39.9%	5.3%	94.7%	23.1%	76.9%	10.7%	93.4%	85.2%	45.0%
Cameron County	13,218	21.9%	78.1%	15.7%	84.3%	37.6%	62.4%	19.7%	69.9%	60.5%	33.6%
Collin County	43,095	27.5%	72.5%	10.3%	89.7%	30.3%	69.7%	22.6%	81.2%	93.3%	31.0%
Comal County	4,930	11.0%	89.0%	43.3%	56.7%	38.2%	61.8%	32.8%	87.4%	83.8%	47.9%
Dallas County	162,886	25.6%	74.2%	7.6%	92.4%	19.4%	80.6%	13.2%	71.6%	78.0%	37.8%
Denton County	43,177	27.6%	72.0%	8.0%	92.0%	28.7%	71.3%	19.3%	84.8%	87.4%	42.3%
Ector County	10,289	31.3%	68.7%	30.0%	70.0%	44.4%	55.6%	25.5%	92.4%	88.3%	59.5%
El Paso County	40,974	31.0%	68.8%	8.4%	91.6%	32.9%	67.1%	18.3%	70.7%	78.2%	37.4%
Ellis County	7,584	26.0%	74.0%	10.7%	89.3%	34.1%	65.9%	24.3%	74.9%	76.1%	36.6%
Fort Bend County	21,282	19.4%	80.6%	7.0%	93.0%	52.7%	47.3%	36.7%	48.6%	85.1%	47.9%
Galveston County	13,382	35.7%	64.3%	16.2%	83.8%	30.2%	69.8%	19.6%	85.0%	88.4%	43.2%
Grayson County	6,433	35.8%	64.2%	25.9%	74.1%	55.8%	44.2%	37.4%	80.1%	81.9%	43.1%
Gregg County	8,431	41.8%	58.2%	0.0%	100.0%	38.0%	62.0%	20.6%	73.8%	79.2%	53.1%
Guadalupe County	6,475	19.2%	80.8%	5.5%	94.5%	47.0%	53.0%	33.4%	38.7%	98.7%	39.5%
Harris County	272,978	23.9%	76.0%	10.9%	89.1%	23.8%	76.2%	17.6%	76.0%	82.7%	42.5%
Hays County	14,092	54.4%	45.6%	3.1%	96.9%	37.5%	62.5%	14.2%	86.0%	79.3%	40.4%
Hidalgo County	29,987	29.2%	70.5%	18.5%	81.5%	36.7%	63.3%	18.5%	62.7%	67.0%	32.0%
Jefferson County	15,570	30.2%	69.8%	17.0%	83.0%	43.2%	56.8%	23.9%	54.3%	72.5%	22.8%
Johnson County	7,057	32.1%	64.5%	11.2%	88.8%	44.3%	55.7%	31.6%	88.6%	69.1%	31.9%
Kaufman County	3,753	27.4%	72.6%	40.2%	59.8%	66.5%	33.5%	46.3%	97.5%	62.1%	32.9%
Lubbock County	26,994	54.1%	45.9%	7.1%	92.9%	33.0%	67.0%	14.3%	88.4%	87.8%	30.9%
McLennan County	18,519	42.2%	57.4%	5.3%	94.7%	21.2%	78.8%	12.1%	82.1%	79.2%	20.8%
Midland County	9,687	35.2%	64.8%	15.5%	84.5%	48.7%	51.3%	27.6%	89.3%	93.7%	38.5%
Montgomery County	19,959	27.7%	72.3%	15.3%	84.7%	55.0%	45.0%	38.2%	85.3%	81.7%	41.5%
Nueces County	23,422	37.9%	61.9%	14.0%	86.0%	26.9%	73.1%	15.9%	88.0%	87.6%	47.8%
Parker County	5,379	46.9%	53.1%	32.1%	67.9%	28.9%	71.1%	14.0%	74.0%	68.5%	36.3%
Potter County	9,173	32.9%	67.1%	10.8%	89.2%	24.9%	75.1%	18.1%	67.6%	51.1%	17.3%
Randall County	10,588	36.6%	63.4%	5.1%	94.9%	37.0%	63.0%	24.1%	89.6%	83.3%	28.0%
Smith County	11,595	30.6%	67.5%	21.6%	78.4%	44.6%	55.4%	29.4%	90.5%	90.4%	61.9%
Tarrant County	119,355	27.6%	72.3%	12.2%	87.8%	34.3%	65.7%	24.4%	79.9%	83.4%	36.5%
Taylor County	11,816	50.8%	49.2%	12.5%	87.5%	39.0%	61.0%	18.6%	37.9%	78.3%	35.8%
Tom Green County	8,640	31.9%	68.1%	14.9%	85.1%	48.6%	51.4%	34.9%	73.2%	85.4%	34.1%
Travis County	100,285	27.5%	72.2%	3.0%	97.0%	17.6%	82.4%	12.1%	92.2%	88.3%	49.7%
Webb County	10,780	19.3%	80.7%	14.0%	86.0%	42.0%	58.0%	32.5%	63.9%	62.7%	21.0%
Wichita County	11,185	31.5%	68.5%	9.9%	90.1%	40.8%	59.2%	25.4%	100.0%	78.3%	34.6%
Williamson County	20,618	23.1%	76.8%	10.4%	89.6%	39.1%	60.9%	29.7%	88.7%	85.2%	46.6%
Utah											
Cache County	10,359	35.7%	64.3%	6.0%	94.0%	41.8%	58.2%	22.8%	90.8%	78.3%	31.7%
Davis County	16,244	29.8%	70.2%	30.6%	69.4%	55.7%	44.3%	44.7%	94.8%	94.2%	37.8%
Salt Lake County	63,647	26.2%	73.7%	21.2%	78.8%	41.4%	58.6%	32.9%	90.6%	91.7%	39.4%
Utah County	38,467	38.5%	61.3%	18.4%	81.6%	44.6%	55.4%	30.0%	91.9%	89.1%	47.4%
Washington County	6,991	25.7%	74.3%	33.9%	66.1%	48.0%	52.0%	44.4%	66.1%	99.1%	38.3%
Weber County	13,215	29.0%	71.0%	27.0%	73.0%	51.3%	48.7%	41.3%	86.4%	71.1%	26.8%
Vermont											
Chittenden County	9,975	35.0%	65.0%	8.9%	91.1%	27.4%	72.6%	13.6%	78.6%	83.7%	44.9%

Table K-2: Counties—Summary Housing Characteristics—*Continued*

	Millennial Householders	Age of Householders		18 to 24 Years Old		25 to 31 Years Old			Percent with Internet Access		Percent with Mobile Access Plan
		18 to 24	25 to 31	Owners	Renters	Owners	Renters	With Mortgage	18 to 24	25 to 31	
Virginia											
Albemarle County	6,728	29.4%	70.6%	2.7%	97.3%	38.8%	61.2%	27.4%	97.9%	79.3%	35.8%
Arlington County	26,349	13.1%	86.9%	3.7%	96.3%	12.1%	87.9%	10.0%	87.3%	96.5%	46.4%
Chesterfield County	10,522	24.7%	75.3%	10.7%	89.3%	39.4%	60.6%	29.0%	61.8%	92.6%	32.7%
Fairfax County	46,549	13.7%	85.9%	11.5%	88.5%	28.8%	71.2%	23.8%	90.1%	93.8%	51.8%
Hanover County	4,372	17.7%	82.3%	22.8%	77.2%	60.4%	39.6%	51.1%	100.0%	92.6%	56.3%
Henrico County	18,904	27.5%	72.5%	12.7%	87.3%	29.7%	70.3%	24.8%	88.1%	77.0%	32.7%
Loudoun County	12,387	9.0%	91.0%	17.7%	82.3%	53.1%	46.9%	45.9%	100.0%	95.8%	55.7%
Montgomery County	10,291	76.3%	22.9%	11.2%	88.8%	20.6%	79.4%	11.1%	97.6%	79.9%	29.6%
Prince William County	18,951	14.6%	85.0%	7.6%	92.4%	42.3%	57.7%	36.0%	100.0%	93.5%	46.6%
Roanoke County	3,609	16.9%	83.1%	0.0%	100.0%	45.1%	54.9%	30.6%	73.0%	76.4%	25.6%
Spotsylvania County	3,674	17.3%	82.7%	36.5%	63.5%	59.9%	40.1%	48.0%	100.0%	90.3%	55.1%
Stafford County	6,661	35.1%	64.9%	6.7%	93.3%	22.4%	77.6%	16.9%	89.0%	89.2%	61.4%
Washington											
Benton County	10,814	32.2%	67.8%	1.8%	98.2%	40.7%	59.3%	27.6%	68.4%	70.9%	37.5%
Clark County	17,033	22.6%	77.4%	7.2%	92.8%	26.7%	73.3%	21.3%	92.7%	88.7%	56.9%
Cowlitz County	4,336	26.5%	73.5%	2.3%	97.7%	33.7%	66.3%	24.2%	90.1%	81.4%	65.3%
Grant County	4,745	20.2%	79.8%	9.6%	90.4%	28.0%	72.0%	19.1%	91.4%	85.4%	48.0%
King County	140,877	23.6%	76.4%	13.5%	86.5%	19.4%	80.6%	15.4%	92.4%	93.0%	51.9%
Kitsap County	14,742	23.5%	76.5%	22.1%	77.9%	27.6%	72.4%	22.9%	100.0%	88.7%	59.4%
Pierce County	45,814	27.6%	72.4%	7.4%	92.6%	30.1%	69.9%	21.2%	82.5%	89.6%	42.7%
Skagit County	5,592	30.2%	69.8%	7.2%	92.8%	27.5%	72.5%	20.9%	99.2%	86.9%	39.3%
Snohomish County	36,450	20.6%	79.4%	20.8%	79.2%	41.5%	58.5%	34.6%	96.2%	86.1%	53.3%
Spokane County	34,954	30.5%	69.5%	8.3%	91.7%	32.8%	67.2%	22.5%	85.6%	86.6%	45.3%
Thurston County	14,784	29.8%	70.2%	19.9%	80.1%	33.8%	66.2%	27.3%	72.1%	84.7%	41.1%
Whatcom County	12,984	42.6%	57.4%	1.2%	98.8%	29.7%	70.3%	14.1%	92.7%	86.6%	31.6%
Yakima County	10,592	26.2%	73.3%	29.4%	70.6%	34.8%	65.2%	26.1%	74.4%	64.9%	33.7%
West Virginia											
Berkeley County	4,743	24.9%	75.1%	27.4%	72.6%	35.7%	64.3%	25.0%	70.2%	80.4%	44.9%
Cabell County	5,865	26.7%	73.3%	26.1%	73.9%	29.2%	70.8%	24.8%	97.3%	88.7%	49.1%
Kanawha County	11,467	23.3%	76.7%	25.4%	74.6%	43.7%	56.3%	31.4%	83.3%	88.4%	50.6%
Monongalia County	11,483	49.8%	50.2%	18.7%	81.3%	36.1%	63.9%	21.4%	100.0%	87.5%	32.8%
Wisconsin											
Brown County	14,087	24.8%	75.1%	8.6%	91.4%	39.2%	60.8%	29.3%	81.1%	94.4%	45.3%
Dane County	47,022	32.6%	67.4%	4.4%	95.6%	29.6%	70.4%	19.9%	89.9%	93.9%	41.7%
Eau Claire County	7,300	58.5%	41.5%	3.7%	96.3%	50.2%	49.8%	22.1%	95.0%	93.6%	42.4%
Fond du Lac County	4,466	45.6%	54.4%	50.0%	50.0%	43.8%	56.2%	43.4%	78.7%	91.3%	42.5%
Kenosha County	9,002	30.2%	69.8%	5.0%	95.0%	27.3%	72.7%	17.2%	71.2%	83.5%	28.5%
La Crosse County	10,595	47.5%	52.5%	0.0%	100.0%	47.1%	52.9%	21.0%	95.8%	89.9%	37.6%
Marathon County	7,645	29.6%	70.4%	7.6%	92.4%	49.2%	50.8%	33.2%	93.4%	76.0%	50.4%
Milwaukee County	77,168	26.2%	73.7%	2.7%	97.3%	22.5%	77.5%	14.7%	72.0%	81.3%	43.6%
Outagamie County	11,254	23.5%	76.5%	7.1%	92.9%	43.0%	57.0%	31.6%	77.8%	81.3%	27.9%
Racine County	10,343	22.2%	77.8%	51.1%	48.9%	32.3%	67.7%	36.5%	100.0%	74.2%	33.0%
Rock County	9,068	42.0%	58.0%	31.1%	68.9%	43.3%	56.7%	34.1%	97.2%	80.0%	28.6%
Sheboygan County	6,377	25.0%	75.0%	40.3%	59.7%	37.8%	62.2%	34.0%	89.2%	81.6%	36.5%
Walworth County	5,877	41.4%	58.6%	7.4%	92.6%	40.9%	59.1%	25.3%	96.1%	100.0%	68.4%
Washington County	6,189	29.0%	71.0%	8.8%	91.2%	55.5%	44.5%	40.4%	76.3%	92.5%	22.2%
Waukesha County	15,729	25.4%	74.6%	14.2%	85.8%	48.8%	51.2%	39.1%	83.5%	93.8%	48.9%
Winnebago County	12,226	40.8%	59.2%	5.1%	94.9%	32.2%	67.8%	19.8%	88.5%	79.8%	27.8%
Wyoming											
Laramie County	7,300	47.2%	52.8%	8.4%	91.6%	36.0%	64.0%	15.3%	96.5%	88.9%	23.7%

Table K-3: Places—Summary Housing Characteristics

	Millennial Householders	Age of Householders		18 to 24 Years Old		25 to 31 Years Old			Percent with Internet Access		Percent with Mobile Access Plan
		18 to 24	25 to 31	Owners	Renters	Owners	Renters	With Mortgage	18 to 24	25 to 31	
Alabama											
Birmingham city	14,247	31.9%	68.1%	6.7%	93.3%	26.9%	73.1%	20.0%	73.2%	65.5%	25.0%
Huntsville city	11,420	29.2%	70.8%	21.7%	78.3%	31.6%	68.4%	26.4%	58.7%	82.7%	33.6%
Mobile city	13,418	33.8%	66.2%	5.0%	95.0%	23.7%	76.3%	15.4%	57.0%	66.7%	24.9%
Montgomery city	14,758	21.8%	78.2%	4.3%	95.7%	25.3%	74.7%	18.5%	86.6%	71.6%	52.1%
Tuscaloosa city	8,214	49.7%	50.3%	20.0%	80.0%	23.5%	76.5%	13.0%	95.3%	94.3%	57.9%
Alaska											
Anchorage municipality	19,734	32.0%	68.0%	5.6%	94.4%	40.4%	59.6%	25.3%	86.9%	85.6%	69.4%
Arizona											
Chandler city	12,836	22.9%	77.1%	3.4%	96.6%	40.6%	59.4%	30.3%	77.1%	90.0%	43.8%
Glendale city	12,737	22.8%	77.2%	13.1%	86.9%	27.8%	72.2%	20.3%	59.0%	62.6%	22.8%
Mesa city	28,417	28.1%	71.9%	14.1%	85.9%	29.7%	70.3%	20.6%	78.9%	70.4%	27.5%
Peoria city	6,561	18.7%	81.3%	25.7%	74.3%	51.8%	48.2%	40.5%	83.5%	90.8%	24.1%
Phoenix city	90,291	30.3%	69.5%	16.3%	83.7%	26.3%	73.7%	18.3%	64.7%	77.6%	34.6%
Scottsdale city	12,322	20.9%	79.1%	4.6%	95.4%	33.3%	66.7%	25.9%	88.7%	96.4%	44.7%
Surprise city	4,578	25.6%	73.0%	19.2%	80.8%	53.4%	46.6%	42.8%	100.0%	97.4%	30.4%
Tempe city	20,547	39.2%	60.4%	8.6%	91.4%	19.1%	80.9%	11.5%	96.6%	89.2%	42.9%
Tucson city	42,402	41.8%	58.2%	9.5%	90.5%	21.9%	78.1%	13.4%	89.5%	85.6%	48.9%
Yuma city	5,342	26.3%	73.7%	33.6%	66.4%	46.6%	53.4%	34.6%	64.2%	88.0%	36.2%
Arkansas											
Little Rock city	12,208	26.4%	73.6%	4.0%	96.0%	14.0%	86.0%	9.1%	87.0%	83.9%	30.9%
California											
Anaheim city	12,692	19.3%	80.7%	9.3%	90.7%	24.3%	75.7%	17.2%	94.4%	83.1%	45.6%
Antioch city	3,236	36.2%	63.8%	21.1%	78.9%	28.7%	71.3%	19.8%	86.1%	100.0%	48.0%
Bakersfield city	21,043	28.5%	71.5%	7.8%	92.2%	31.2%	68.8%	21.8%	77.6%	79.3%	39.0%
Berkeley city	11,972	50.6%	49.4%	0.0%	100.0%	15.2%	84.8%	7.5%	97.6%	97.0%	57.8%
Burbank city	5,332	14.6%	85.4%	0.0%	100.0%	10.2%	89.8%	8.7%	86.6%	100.0%	54.2%
Carlsbad city	3,322	8.4%	91.6%	35.8%	64.2%	32.5%	67.5%	30.0%	100.0%	86.5%	51.8%
Carson city	1,299	16.1%	83.9%	27.8%	72.2%	60.9%	39.1%	43.6%	56.5%	82.4%	34.9%
Chula Vista city	9,576	24.4%	75.6%	0.0%	100.0%	28.6%	71.4%	20.5%	91.3%	84.2%	40.3%
Clovis city	4,751	24.2%	75.8%	5.2%	94.8%	42.2%	57.8%	31.9%	100.0%	98.7%	45.2%
Compton city	3,709	22.8%	77.2%	29.8%	70.2%	22.7%	77.3%	21.7%	65.6%	62.9%	14.5%
Concord city	5,065	25.9%	74.1%	3.7%	96.3%	35.6%	64.4%	18.5%	100.0%	93.5%	44.8%
Corona city	4,731	11.8%	88.2%	59.1%	40.9%	48.5%	51.5%	45.9%	100.0%	95.0%	27.8%
Costa Mesa city	7,272	21.1%	78.9%	3.8%	96.2%	8.0%	92.0%	5.7%	88.9%	85.2%	31.3%
Daly City city	3,417	18.7%	81.3%	35.8%	64.2%	24.5%	75.5%	18.3%	100.0%	100.0%	65.4%
Downey city	3,507	25.0%	73.9%	0.0%	100.0%	0.0%	100.0%	0.0%	77.9%	57.7%	14.3%
El Cajon city	4,889	20.2%	79.8%	6.7%	93.3%	17.8%	82.2%	14.3%	100.0%	88.9%	63.0%
El Monte city	4,144	27.8%	72.2%	10.3%	89.7%	18.1%	81.9%	8.3%	59.7%	55.6%	8.6%
Elk Grove city	3,552	16.2%	83.8%	17.1%	82.9%	52.2%	47.8%	38.4%	61.1%	83.4%	47.4%
Escondido city	7,117	23.7%	76.3%	6.4%	93.6%	34.6%	65.4%	26.1%	68.7%	89.5%	23.5%
Fairfield city	5,418	11.7%	88.3%	14.9%	85.1%	23.3%	76.7%	22.3%	100.0%	93.4%	58.2%
Fontana city	5,862	22.8%	77.2%	20.7%	79.3%	46.8%	53.2%	34.9%	90.9%	84.5%	64.2%
Fremont city	6,432	21.5%	78.5%	5.2%	94.8%	30.1%	69.9%	22.6%	44.8%	100.0%	62.2%
Fresno city	30,270	27.6%	72.0%	7.3%	92.7%	28.6%	71.4%	20.0%	79.6%	80.6%	46.1%
Fullerton city	6,923	36.6%	63.4%	7.3%	92.7%	12.7%	87.3%	8.0%	97.0%	94.1%	55.4%
Garden Grove city	5,487	18.7%	81.3%	4.0%	96.0%	21.4%	78.6%	14.2%	80.1%	82.7%	23.0%
Glendale city	8,986	21.8%	78.2%	4.6%	95.4%	11.4%	88.6%	8.6%	91.4%	94.5%	26.8%
Hayward city	7,687	27.7%	72.3%	2.6%	97.4%	15.8%	84.2%	10.7%	78.5%	84.4%	55.7%
Hesperia city	10,137	15.3%	84.7%	15.2%	84.8%	28.4%	71.6%	16.8%	76.0%	74.9%	17.1%
Inglewood city	5,054	11.7%	88.3%	0.0%	100.0%	24.3%	75.7%	18.8%	39.9%	90.7%	41.6%
Irvine city	13,591	24.4%	75.6%	19.6%	80.4%	15.9%	84.1%	11.2%	98.3%	95.4%	50.4%
Jurupa Valley city	2,717	10.3%	89.7%	18.9%	81.1%	68.9%	31.1%	51.3%	100.0%	100.0%	57.7%
Lancaster city	5,982	28.5%	71.5%	23.2%	76.8%	42.7%	57.3%	26.2%	53.4%	69.9%	29.7%
Long Beach city	24,104	16.8%	83.2%	1.5%	98.5%	16.6%	83.4%	11.9%	90.1%	86.1%	54.4%
Los Angeles city	214,343	23.3%	76.6%	4.5%	95.5%	11.5%	88.5%	7.9%	82.3%	83.7%	37.5%
Mission Viejo city	1,870	17.7%	82.3%	74.0%	26.0%	36.5%	63.5%	43.2%	100.0%	100.0%	83.9%
Modesto city	9,707	25.5%	74.5%	5.3%	94.7%	30.6%	69.4%	21.2%	58.6%	70.5%	50.8%
Moreno Valley city	8,488	18.2%	81.8%	7.4%	92.6%	47.2%	52.8%	38.1%	90.4%	67.2%	20.5%
Murrieta city	4,416	6.5%	93.5%	41.1%	58.9%	38.2%	61.8%	38.4%	100.0%	70.0%	17.5%
Norwalk city	2,864	17.0%	83.0%	52.0%	48.0%	39.4%	60.6%	41.6%	28.3%	63.0%	19.8%
Oakland city	23,632	20.1%	79.9%	3.5%	96.5%	14.3%	85.7%	10.0%	68.3%	92.6%	53.3%
Oceanside city	12,186	31.7%	68.3%	0.0%	100.0%	14.0%	86.0%	8.1%	100.0%	95.9%	60.5%
Ontario city	6,145	17.2%	82.8%	23.0%	77.0%	24.2%	75.8%	15.9%	62.0%	82.3%	23.7%
Orange city	5,074	21.7%	78.3%	5.1%	94.9%	31.7%	68.3%	21.7%	100.0%	84.2%	58.9%
Oxnard city	6,665	16.2%	83.8%	29.5%	70.5%	20.1%	79.9%	14.2%	72.3%	70.4%	27.8%
Palmdale city	4,052	18.5%	81.5%	11.2%	88.8%	44.5%	55.5%	34.6%	74.4%	57.8%	15.2%
Pasadena city	10,994	21.8%	77.8%	7.9%	92.1%	17.1%	82.9%	13.3%	72.3%	91.1%	30.1%
Pomona city	5,214	30.2%	69.8%	7.4%	92.6%	26.3%	73.7%	18.6%	92.9%	75.5%	54.6%
Rancho Cucamonga city	6,099	29.1%	70.9%	2.8%	97.2%	18.1%	81.9%	11.1%	93.6%	95.7%	83.3%
Redding city	5,298	36.1%	63.9%	8.9%	91.1%	19.9%	80.1%	14.3%	80.4%	69.5%	29.9%
Rialto city	3,350	31.4%	67.0%	23.8%	76.2%	38.0%	62.0%	27.0%	87.7%	91.7%	26.0%
Richmond city	7,517	22.0%	76.2%	3.8%	96.2%	16.7%	83.3%	11.4%	84.8%	86.7%	47.8%
Riverside city	13,099	38.6%	61.4%	2.9%	97.1%	25.9%	74.1%	15.8%	79.9%	86.9%	60.0%
Roseville city	5,745	23.8%	76.2%	0.0%	100.0%	33.7%	66.3%	24.3%	80.3%	90.2%	46.8%
Sacramento city	31,803	25.2%	74.7%	5.0%	95.0%	23.5%	76.5%	17.0%	86.8%	83.3%	33.7%
Salinas city	5,851	29.2%	70.8%	13.1%	86.9%	28.8%	71.2%	19.0%	64.3%	88.3%	30.0%
San Bernardino city	9,261	30.3%	68.0%	12.0%	88.0%	21.2%	78.8%	17.3%	64.5%	81.5%	18.8%

Table K-3: Places—Summary Housing Characteristics—*Continued*

	Millennial Householders	Age of Householders		18 to 24 Years Old		25 to 31 Years Old			Percent with Internet Access		Percent with Mobile Access Plan
		18 to 24	25 to 31	Owners	Renters	Owners	Renters	With Mortgage	18 to 24	25 to 31	
California—Cont.											
San Buenaventura (Ventura) city.....	4,532	23.7%	76.3%	0.0%	100.0%	25.6%	74.4%	19.5%	86.9%	97.0%	54.1%
San Diego city..............................	92,786	23.1%	76.7%	5.5%	94.5%	16.6%	83.4%	11.6%	97.5%	92.3%	47.0%
San Francisco city........................	63,892	14.9%	85.0%	6.4%	93.6%	8.1%	91.9%	5.5%	99.1%	94.7%	55.9%
San Jose city...............................	39,127	18.7%	81.0%	9.9%	90.1%	22.8%	77.2%	17.8%	92.0%	89.6%	42.6%
San Mateo city	3,337	8.8%	91.2%	0.0%	100.0%	7.5%	92.5%	4.5%	100.0%	84.9%	55.1%
Santa Ana city	11,432	18.8%	81.2%	6.6%	93.4%	16.9%	83.1%	11.2%	84.4%	78.5%	33.9%
Santa Clara city	9,732	14.4%	85.6%	4.1%	95.9%	19.9%	80.1%	16.9%	66.1%	96.1%	54.9%
Santa Clarita city	7,015	19.6%	80.4%	3.4%	96.6%	41.9%	58.1%	27.0%	88.3%	91.2%	34.9%
Santa Maria city	4,313	30.3%	69.7%	0.0%	100.0%	24.2%	75.8%	16.9%	53.2%	44.3%	13.1%
Santa Monica city	7,574	17.6%	82.4%	0.0%	100.0%	7.8%	92.2%	4.9%	100.0%	98.3%	73.4%
Santa Rosa city	8,168	25.6%	74.4%	0.0%	100.0%	15.7%	84.3%	6.5%	100.0%	95.4%	52.7%
Simi Valley city	3,004	18.9%	81.1%	38.7%	61.3%	30.7%	69.3%	27.5%	100.0%	74.5%	58.4%
South Gate city	2,585	11.8%	88.2%	15.5%	84.5%	23.4%	76.6%	20.6%	83.2%	73.6%	43.0%
Stockton city	15,012	32.8%	67.0%	6.3%	93.7%	28.4%	71.6%	17.0%	67.6%	77.4%	31.7%
Sunnyvale city.............................	9,787	13.9%	86.1%	4.9%	95.1%	11.7%	88.3%	6.5%	100.0%	98.3%	40.5%
Temecula city	3,011	26.0%	74.0%	21.1%	78.9%	35.1%	64.9%	28.9%	41.9%	100.0%	26.9%
Thousand Oaks city.......................	3,705	22.3%	77.7%	0.0%	100.0%	29.0%	71.0%	19.2%	100.0%	92.7%	67.9%
Torrance city................................	3,761	15.9%	84.1%	0.0%	100.0%	8.5%	91.5%	7.2%	100.0%	84.6%	52.1%
Vacaville city	3,887	12.2%	87.8%	0.0%	100.0%	49.8%	50.2%	42.1%	84.6%	100.0%	69.5%
Vallejo city	5,738	26.1%	73.9%	14.2%	85.8%	30.3%	69.7%	22.7%	100.0%	83.4%	46.0%
Victorville city	5,349	13.2%	86.8%	29.0%	71.0%	40.2%	59.8%	32.8%	69.9%	49.7%	8.6%
Visalia city	8,676	21.6%	78.4%	9.2%	90.8%	41.4%	58.6%	32.7%	87.6%	84.1%	41.0%
Vista city	6,948	28.9%	71.1%	4.4%	95.6%	17.2%	82.8%	11.8%	83.4%	71.8%	23.5%
West Covina city	2,981	19.2%	80.8%	0.0%	100.0%	20.7%	79.3%	14.9%	100.0%	92.5%	13.4%
Westminster city	3,403	10.5%	89.5%	0.0%	100.0%	18.8%	81.2%	12.9%	51.1%	82.4%	12.9%
Colorado											
Arvada city	4,735	37.7%	62.3%	9.3%	90.7%	44.2%	55.8%	27.3%	92.1%	88.4%	28.6%
Aurora city	20,417	29.8%	70.2%	8.2%	91.8%	34.0%	66.0%	25.0%	87.3%	88.4%	28.0%
Boulder city	13,846	62.8%	37.2%	8.7%	91.3%	20.6%	79.4%	10.9%	97.7%	100.0%	56.5%
Centennial city.............................	4,245	16.3%	83.7%	0.0%	100.0%	28.5%	71.5%	22.8%	100.0%	98.2%	42.1%
Colorado Springs city....................	31,328	25.3%	74.7%	5.1%	94.9%	36.6%	63.4%	27.6%	93.0%	91.6%	53.6%
Denver city	58,961	26.2%	73.1%	6.3%	93.7%	25.5%	74.5%	18.8%	83.9%	86.1%	37.7%
Fort Collins city	15,252	50.3%	49.7%	7.7%	92.3%	49.1%	50.9%	24.5%	99.3%	97.9%	45.6%
Greeley city	8,025	27.7%	72.3%	6.6%	93.4%	40.7%	59.3%	29.5%	80.5%	71.3%	37.5%
Lakewood city	8,453	35.6%	64.4%	19.2%	80.8%	45.2%	54.8%	32.3%	100.0%	91.1%	49.9%
Pueblo city	6,893	43.9%	56.1%	14.6%	85.4%	35.2%	64.8%	16.4%	87.0%	98.9%	49.5%
Thornton city................................	5,764	21.4%	78.6%	17.4%	82.6%	60.0%	40.0%	42.9%	100.0%	92.6%	42.1%
Westminster city	8,735	29.1%	70.9%	0.0%	100.0%	27.8%	72.2%	18.7%	95.1%	93.1%	42.4%
Connecticut											
Bridgeport city	8,313	6.0%	94.0%	0.0%	100.0%	15.1%	84.9%	14.2%	72.9%	90.8%	30.9%
Hartford city	10,330	34.3%	65.7%	1.5%	98.5%	12.1%	87.9%	7.7%	65.6%	73.0%	32.3%
New Haven city	9,844	18.1%	81.9%	4.9%	95.1%	6.3%	93.7%	2.2%	58.9%	73.0%	20.0%
Stamford city...............................	6,722	17.3%	82.4%	0.0%	100.0%	15.2%	84.8%	12.5%	93.5%	86.2%	66.6%
Waterbury city..............................	6,128	16.7%	83.3%	26.9%	73.1%	39.8%	60.2%	33.0%	86.2%	74.6%	25.3%
District of Columbia											
Washington city	57,775	18.4%	81.5%	4.8%	95.2%	13.8%	86.2%	10.3%	88.9%	87.7%	50.3%
Florida											
Cape Coral city	4,673	25.1%	74.9%	14.9%	85.1%	35.3%	64.7%	22.3%	83.1%	93.5%	42.1%
Clearwater city	3,842	20.2%	79.8%	0.0%	100.0%	26.6%	73.4%	15.0%	60.7%	78.6%	30.8%
Coral Springs city.........................	4,593	26.8%	73.2%	7.6%	92.4%	29.2%	70.8%	13.7%	97.7%	90.5%	58.1%
Fort Lauderdale city	7,865	25.4%	74.6%	0.0%	100.0%	15.3%	84.7%	9.8%	55.9%	83.2%	26.1%
Gainesville city	20,704	64.4%	35.6%	5.5%	94.5%	16.2%	83.8%	6.6%	93.6%	90.2%	44.6%
Hialeah city	5,792	34.4%	64.9%	9.5%	90.5%	17.5%	82.5%	12.3%	58.8%	59.9%	11.0%
Hollywood city	5,265	20.6%	79.4%	50.7%	49.3%	27.3%	72.7%	27.7%	94.1%	93.1%	47.2%
Jacksonville city...........................	52,269	26.1%	73.9%	14.6%	85.4%	27.0%	73.0%	21.0%	75.8%	85.1%	40.3%
Lakeland city	3,669	26.0%	74.0%	28.5%	71.5%	26.7%	73.3%	22.8%	47.6%	67.4%	24.0%
Miami Beach city	4,112	17.6%	82.4%	6.1%	93.9%	10.5%	89.5%	7.3%	74.8%	94.2%	43.1%
Miami city	23,608	23.0%	76.8%	10.8%	89.2%	13.7%	86.3%	7.3%	76.2%	77.7%	31.8%
Miami Gardens city	2,596	31.3%	68.7%	22.6%	77.4%	30.5%	69.5%	19.1%	86.2%	60.2%	20.6%
Miramar city.................................	6,007	16.1%	83.9%	20.7%	79.3%	32.9%	67.1%	26.3%	81.4%	93.0%	18.4%
Orlando city.................................	20,103	26.2%	73.6%	6.8%	93.2%	13.8%	86.2%	9.8%	71.0%	88.3%	30.1%
Palm Bay city	4,165	29.1%	70.9%	16.2%	83.8%	43.8%	56.2%	34.0%	82.8%	95.9%	40.9%
Pembroke Pines city	3,142	15.3%	84.7%	36.9%	63.1%	36.8%	63.2%	30.1%	86.7%	97.4%	41.2%
Pompano Beach city	3,679	24.4%	75.6%	6.9%	93.1%	12.5%	87.5%	9.4%	78.0%	87.4%	40.6%
Port St. Lucie city	3,402	11.4%	88.6%	36.5%	63.5%	39.0%	61.0%	38.7%	100.0%	80.6%	25.6%
St. Petersburg city	14,102	27.2%	72.8%	3.9%	96.1%	23.4%	76.6%	12.8%	74.0%	84.1%	33.6%
Tallahassee city	27,445	60.3%	39.4%	4.0%	96.0%	14.8%	85.2%	6.5%	92.0%	91.3%	38.7%
Tampa city...................................	30,083	36.1%	63.8%	4.1%	95.9%	22.9%	77.1%	13.3%	84.5%	80.2%	20.6%
West Palm Beach city....................	5,610	27.2%	72.8%	13.0%	87.0%	23.5%	76.5%	7.4%	64.5%	57.7%	19.7%
Georgia											
Athens-Clarke County unified govt (bal)	16,349	57.3%	42.7%	6.8%	93.2%	6.6%	93.4%	3.9%	82.8%	80.8%	42.5%
Atlanta city..................................	44,081	28.9%	70.9%	6.5%	93.5%	18.4%	81.6%	12.8%	83.7%	87.9%	46.2%
Augusta-Richmond County consolidated govt (bal)	10,783	16.6%	83.4%	1.8%	98.2%	23.0%	77.0%	17.3%	81.4%	80.3%	32.1%
Columbus city...............................	11,051	24.7%	75.3%	14.5%	85.5%	21.4%	78.6%	17.5%	88.8%	84.3%	47.4%
Macon city	4,729	29.6%	70.0%	16.5%	83.5%	28.6%	71.4%	17.7%	25.2%	63.6%	34.3%

Table K-3: Places—Summary Housing Characteristics—*Continued*

	Millennial Householders	Age of Householders		18 to 24 Years Old		25 to 31 Years Old			Percent with Internet Access		Percent with Mobile Access Plan
		18 to 24	25 to 31	Owners	Renters	Owners	Renters	With Mortgage	18 to 24	25 to 31	
Georgia—Cont.											
Roswell city	3,296	8.5%	91.5%	0.0%	100.0%	24.7%	75.3%	22.6%	100.0%	92.1%	32.9%
Sandy Springs city	7,958	7.8%	92.2%	7.9%	92.1%	13.3%	86.7%	9.2%	100.0%	91.5%	35.4%
Savannah city	11,317	28.0%	72.0%	7.1%	92.9%	23.9%	76.1%	16.1%	71.7%	82.0%	37.6%
Hawaii											
Urban Honolulu CDP	17,479	23.2%	76.5%	5.3%	94.7%	7.1%	92.9%	4.7%	89.4%	86.4%	42.3%
Idaho											
Boise City city	16,742	35.7%	64.3%	10.3%	89.7%	37.8%	62.2%	26.3%	72.0%	91.9%	35.9%
Illinois											
Aurora city	8,513	21.6%	78.4%	9.3%	90.7%	34.3%	65.7%	26.9%	91.8%	91.2%	69.8%
Chicago city	191,787	21.4%	78.4%	5.1%	94.9%	18.8%	81.2%	12.6%	88.2%	86.6%	45.2%
Elgin city	5,832	35.5%	64.5%	11.3%	88.7%	59.1%	40.9%	31.1%	73.5%	87.6%	52.6%
Joliet city	5,165	28.8%	71.2%	6.0%	94.0%	46.4%	53.6%	25.7%	89.2%	84.9%	23.8%
Naperville city	5,147	25.9%	74.1%	18.7%	81.3%	48.2%	51.8%	33.6%	92.1%	98.4%	49.1%
Peoria city	10,561	34.0%	66.0%	2.0%	98.0%	32.7%	67.3%	21.4%	65.2%	82.5%	39.9%
Rockford city	7,803	26.7%	73.3%	4.7%	95.3%	33.1%	66.9%	23.9%	57.6%	76.5%	33.1%
Springfield city	8,610	26.3%	73.7%	2.8%	97.2%	39.7%	60.3%	24.1%	81.4%	92.6%	36.5%
Indiana											
Evansville city	8,294	28.3%	71.7%	5.6%	94.4%	40.9%	59.1%	21.2%	69.4%	86.7%	41.9%
Fort Wayne city	18,553	33.8%	66.2%	18.3%	81.7%	45.7%	54.3%	33.1%	73.3%	87.9%	40.1%
Indianapolis city (bal)	65,409	29.2%	70.6%	12.7%	87.3%	23.8%	76.2%	17.9%	70.9%	82.6%	29.6%
South Bend city	6,286	32.4%	67.6%	14.7%	85.3%	39.0%	61.0%	28.3%	76.7%	87.5%	24.8%
Iowa											
Cedar Rapids city	10,120	22.4%	77.6%	8.1%	91.9%	55.5%	44.5%	42.0%	92.0%	93.5%	30.9%
Davenport city	7,548	22.4%	77.6%	19.4%	80.6%	44.0%	56.0%	35.3%	84.6%	71.4%	30.7%
Des Moines city	18,712	31.3%	68.7%	13.0%	87.0%	46.1%	53.9%	31.4%	69.5%	86.8%	49.4%
Kansas											
Kansas City city	8,950	33.6%	66.4%	6.5%	93.5%	28.5%	71.5%	17.5%	75.8%	80.0%	39.8%
Olathe city	6,474	33.0%	67.0%	20.7%	79.3%	49.5%	50.5%	37.4%	97.8%	93.9%	55.4%
Overland Park city	11,838	23.0%	77.0%	13.0%	87.0%	31.6%	68.4%	23.1%	84.0%	89.2%	59.1%
Topeka city	8,529	32.8%	66.7%	3.8%	96.2%	36.7%	63.3%	24.2%	82.3%	88.4%	29.1%
Wichita city	29,430	27.5%	72.2%	9.8%	90.2%	35.1%	64.9%	23.6%	71.8%	88.7%	31.4%
Kentucky											
Lexington-Fayette urban county	26,788	41.5%	58.5%	1.2%	98.8%	21.8%	78.2%	11.9%	88.1%	86.7%	44.7%
Louisville/Jefferson County metro govt (bal)	38,622	24.1%	75.9%	3.2%	96.8%	32.6%	67.4%	23.6%	82.5%	86.1%	40.5%
Louisiana											
Baton Rouge city	21,094	49.0%	51.0%	1.9%	98.1%	20.1%	79.9%	9.4%	72.9%	87.7%	37.4%
Lafayette city	10,319	32.3%	67.7%	12.5%	87.5%	44.2%	55.8%	28.8%	95.8%	97.9%	22.9%
New Orleans city	27,976	20.2%	79.4%	3.6%	96.4%	19.0%	81.0%	13.8%	77.5%	73.0%	26.3%
Shreveport city	12,112	25.4%	74.6%	37.2%	62.8%	27.5%	72.5%	22.2%	83.6%	81.6%	36.2%
Maryland											
Baltimore city	45,320	21.3%	77.8%	5.7%	94.3%	18.0%	82.0%	13.0%	80.7%	80.0%	36.5%
Massachusetts											
Boston city	63,283	24.0%	76.0%	2.6%	97.4%	14.6%	85.4%	10.0%	92.2%	93.6%	41.1%
Brockton city	2,753	3.0%	97.0%	100.0%	0.0%	29.5%	70.5%	31.6%	100.0%	95.6%	33.9%
Cambridge city	11,132	23.0%	77.0%	7.8%	92.2%	10.9%	89.1%	5.4%	100.0%	92.8%	54.1%
Lowell city	7,486	30.9%	69.1%	0.0%	100.0%	11.2%	88.8%	7.3%	81.1%	87.3%	29.1%
Lynn city	4,136	8.7%	86.3%	0.0%	100.0%	20.7%	79.3%	16.2%	100.0%	83.5%	63.6%
New Bedford city	6,100	20.7%	79.3%	5.7%	94.3%	23.1%	76.9%	19.5%	67.2%	86.7%	45.6%
Springfield city	8,396	18.9%	81.1%	6.0%	94.0%	21.1%	78.9%	17.2%	69.7%	85.5%	41.4%
Worcester city	11,627	24.3%	75.7%	2.1%	97.9%	24.4%	75.6%	17.2%	86.1%	89.1%	27.3%
Michigan											
Ann Arbor city	14,686	49.7%	50.3%	0.0%	100.0%	25.3%	74.7%	7.1%	95.2%	100.0%	45.4%
Dearborn city	4,353	21.1%	78.9%	20.2%	79.8%	30.2%	69.8%	21.6%	92.9%	87.5%	26.5%
Detroit city	33,331	33.9%	66.0%	15.0%	85.0%	27.7%	72.3%	7.2%	64.7%	74.4%	19.0%
Flint city	6,393	19.4%	80.6%	14.2%	85.8%	51.0%	49.0%	13.8%	35.0%	53.0%	8.3%
Grand Rapids city	16,039	28.1%	71.9%	9.2%	90.8%	33.9%	66.1%	22.8%	93.1%	89.5%	42.5%
Lansing city	13,494	31.1%	68.9%	10.6%	89.4%	37.7%	62.3%	23.7%	82.2%	93.7%	42.0%
Livonia city	3,536	29.9%	70.1%	75.1%	24.9%	72.7%	27.3%	70.0%	73.5%	100.0%	55.8%
Sterling Heights city	4,648	7.2%	92.8%	0.0%	100.0%	46.4%	53.6%	40.8%	100.0%	100.0%	28.1%
Warren city	7,765	21.5%	78.5%	24.9%	75.1%	44.2%	55.8%	14.0%	62.6%	79.7%	51.2%
Minnesota											
Minneapolis city	42,674	27.7%	72.3%	7.0%	93.0%	17.8%	82.2%	11.5%	86.3%	87.2%	41.2%
Rochester city	7,988	37.2%	62.8%	38.1%	61.9%	72.9%	27.1%	54.0%	85.8%	98.5%	61.3%
St. Paul city	23,296	25.9%	74.1%	8.4%	91.6%	29.0%	71.0%	20.6%	83.1%	96.7%	38.5%
Mississippi											
Jackson city	11,318	27.3%	72.7%	11.9%	88.1%	17.9%	82.1%	10.1%	68.1%	79.4%	30.2%
Missouri											
Columbia city	17,281	43.3%	56.7%	4.3%	95.7%	24.8%	75.2%	14.1%	95.5%	82.5%	32.5%
Independence city	6,049	28.8%	71.2%	0.0%	100.0%	22.4%	77.6%	12.4%	90.8%	80.9%	47.9%
Kansas City city	39,479	28.2%	71.8%	7.9%	92.1%	23.8%	76.2%	15.3%	84.4%	81.4%	37.3%
Lee's Summit city	4,821	12.5%	87.5%	0.0%	100.0%	68.1%	31.9%	57.0%	52.4%	91.9%	51.2%
Springfield city	19,031	38.3%	61.7%	1.1%	98.9%	37.7%	62.3%	22.7%	88.5%	82.7%	28.8%

Table K-3: Places—Summary Housing Characteristics—*Continued*

	Millennial Householders	Age of Householders		18 to 24 Years Old		25 to 31 Years Old			Percent with Internet Access		Percent with Mobile Access Plan
		18 to 24	25 to 31	Owners	Renters	Owners	Renters	With Mortgage	18 to 24	25 to 31	
Missouri—Cont.											
St. Louis city	28,674	26.1%	73.9%	16.7%	83.3%	26.8%	73.2%	18.1%	86.1%	82.3%	40.2%
Montana											
Billings city	8,616	42.1%	57.9%	4.0%	96.0%	38.4%	61.6%	23.2%	73.2%	87.6%	30.0%
Nebraska											
Lincoln city	23,633	40.6%	58.7%	6.3%	93.7%	44.0%	56.0%	24.3%	94.2%	90.9%	26.6%
Omaha city	34,106	29.1%	70.9%	6.8%	93.2%	36.9%	63.1%	23.9%	90.8%	79.8%	37.2%
Nevada											
Henderson city	10,824	20.0%	80.0%	24.2%	75.8%	42.7%	57.3%	34.8%	97.8%	91.5%	36.0%
Las Vegas city	29,734	20.1%	79.7%	16.7%	83.3%	23.3%	76.7%	18.4%	81.7%	77.9%	41.6%
North Las Vegas city	14,860	19.2%	80.8%	16.5%	83.5%	35.6%	64.4%	28.8%	83.9%	93.5%	42.6%
Reno city	17,174	25.9%	74.0%	8.5%	91.5%	21.7%	78.3%	13.3%	83.4%	83.5%	47.1%
Sparks city	4,391	31.5%	68.5%	11.9%	88.1%	46.6%	53.4%	25.9%	79.6%	88.7%	37.4%
New Hampshire											
Manchester city	8,892	24.4%	75.6%	4.1%	95.9%	26.1%	73.9%	18.9%	76.8%	83.2%	40.5%
New Jersey											
Elizabeth city	7,663	15.3%	84.7%	0.0%	100.0%	7.5%	92.5%	6.4%	75.1%	83.8%	15.6%
Jersey City city	17,280	11.5%	88.5%	7.3%	92.7%	13.3%	86.7%	9.5%	90.5%	91.4%	33.0%
Newark city	15,602	14.9%	84.3%	1.6%	98.4%	4.6%	95.4%	2.7%	77.3%	80.7%	36.4%
Paterson city	5,280	24.1%	75.9%	0.0%	100.0%	2.5%	97.5%	1.2%	72.3%	49.5%	13.9%
New Mexico											
Albuquerque city	31,539	33.4%	65.1%	9.3%	90.7%	32.4%	67.6%	20.9%	79.3%	87.2%	34.7%
Las Cruces city	8,804	63.2%	36.8%	14.3%	85.7%	14.6%	85.4%	7.0%	87.2%	96.6%	60.7%
Rio Rancho city	2,033	3.6%	96.4%	50.0%	50.0%	35.5%	64.5%	27.3%	24.3%	78.6%	12.6%
New York											
Albany city	12,527	41.1%	58.9%	3.6%	96.4%	18.0%	82.0%	12.0%	96.3%	93.5%	34.1%
Buffalo city	21,343	27.2%	72.8%	1.1%	98.9%	15.2%	84.8%	7.1%	82.3%	83.3%	30.7%
New York city	429,884	17.8%	81.9%	6.7%	93.3%	9.8%	90.2%	6.7%	84.3%	88.2%	36.2%
Rochester city	21,762	21.1%	78.9%	1.3%	98.7%	20.9%	79.1%	12.3%	66.4%	77.0%	37.6%
Syracuse city	11,425	30.1%	69.9%	2.0%	98.0%	19.9%	80.1%	12.8%	79.1%	90.4%	37.2%
Yonkers city	7,732	20.5%	79.5%	8.1%	91.9%	16.9%	83.1%	12.3%	72.7%	89.9%	26.9%
North Carolina											
Charlotte city	55,546	23.2%	76.7%	7.4%	92.6%	25.7%	74.3%	18.0%	81.1%	84.2%	39.6%
Durham city	21,384	17.3%	82.7%	2.6%	97.4%	20.8%	79.2%	17.2%	97.5%	87.2%	58.2%
Fayetteville city	19,400	33.5%	66.5%	3.1%	96.9%	14.3%	85.7%	9.2%	83.7%	78.5%	48.8%
Greensboro city	21,101	23.3%	76.7%	13.0%	87.0%	22.3%	77.7%	16.7%	87.6%	84.1%	32.9%
High Point city	5,876	24.0%	75.7%	0.0%	100.0%	37.5%	62.5%	26.2%	40.3%	90.6%	32.8%
Raleigh city	33,457	28.6%	71.4%	3.6%	96.4%	36.5%	63.5%	25.4%	87.1%	89.7%	53.1%
Wilmington city	11,850	44.2%	55.1%	6.0%	94.0%	24.2%	75.8%	14.0%	84.8%	85.6%	40.8%
Winston-Salem city	15,132	37.4%	61.1%	7.0%	93.0%	34.4%	65.6%	21.1%	84.5%	86.6%	25.5%
North Dakota											
Fargo city	14,119	52.3%	47.7%	3.1%	96.9%	41.5%	58.5%	17.2%	92.5%	82.2%	36.1%
Ohio											
Akron city	15,785	35.7%	64.3%	6.2%	93.8%	38.1%	61.9%	22.8%	84.3%	72.3%	39.5%
Cincinnati city	31,304	34.8%	65.1%	7.2%	92.8%	19.7%	80.3%	14.2%	76.8%	78.1%	31.0%
Cleveland city	29,369	36.4%	63.1%	1.6%	98.4%	15.7%	84.3%	7.6%	78.0%	80.6%	42.1%
Columbus city	67,540	29.8%	70.2%	2.2%	97.8%	27.3%	72.7%	17.6%	78.6%	87.4%	41.9%
Dayton city	9,713	30.2%	69.8%	7.3%	92.7%	20.0%	80.0%	12.3%	79.4%	83.6%	47.2%
Toledo city	22,288	35.7%	64.3%	13.6%	86.4%	24.2%	75.8%	16.5%	80.4%	76.1%	33.9%
Oklahoma											
Broken Arrow city	6,089	23.6%	76.4%	20.9%	79.1%	44.4%	55.6%	38.9%	85.7%	86.4%	31.4%
Lawton city	7,687	39.0%	61.0%	0.0%	100.0%	20.9%	79.1%	9.3%	52.1%	92.4%	43.0%
Norman city	14,253	34.6%	65.4%	19.8%	80.2%	49.9%	50.1%	34.7%	81.2%	96.4%	60.3%
Oklahoma City city	45,633	29.7%	70.3%	12.0%	88.0%	34.6%	65.4%	22.9%	79.7%	86.4%	43.6%
Tulsa city	28,919	31.2%	68.7%	10.5%	89.5%	25.7%	74.3%	17.8%	73.3%	79.4%	37.8%
Oregon											
Beaverton city	7,156	18.2%	81.8%	9.3%	90.7%	24.8%	75.2%	18.5%	97.3%	98.5%	53.1%
Eugene city	16,429	56.2%	43.8%	3.2%	96.8%	27.2%	72.8%	11.0%	90.0%	93.7%	36.9%
Gresham city	6,753	38.4%	61.6%	3.6%	96.4%	21.6%	78.4%	14.7%	87.5%	95.2%	62.0%
Hillsboro city	5,284	24.5%	75.5%	3.6%	96.4%	18.8%	81.2%	12.4%	86.6%	74.6%	54.8%
Portland city	44,093	21.1%	78.9%	2.5%	97.5%	22.4%	77.6%	16.2%	88.9%	92.4%	55.5%
Salem city	10,774	30.5%	69.5%	1.4%	98.6%	20.4%	79.6%	14.6%	97.0%	85.1%	25.5%
Pennsylvania											
Allentown city	5,415	32.6%	67.4%	6.3%	93.7%	20.2%	79.8%	14.0%	80.9%	87.5%	29.6%
Erie city	8,372	31.1%	68.9%	23.2%	76.8%	34.5%	65.5%	27.6%	95.7%	86.9%	40.8%
Philadelphia city	102,383	20.5%	79.4%	7.4%	92.6%	21.1%	78.9%	14.9%	81.3%	83.3%	37.8%
Pittsburgh city	29,840	40.3%	59.4%	3.9%	96.1%	20.2%	79.8%	10.0%	95.9%	89.1%	37.5%
Rhode Island											
Providence city	14,907	28.4%	71.6%	3.9%	96.1%	8.6%	91.4%	5.7%	80.4%	78.2%	35.1%
South Carolina											
Charleston city	11,547	31.6%	68.4%	3.2%	96.8%	22.4%	77.6%	14.9%	93.7%	88.4%	47.1%
Columbia city	12,640	39.8%	60.2%	5.0%	95.0%	20.5%	79.5%	11.3%	75.2%	83.1%	47.0%
North Charleston city	7,670	42.2%	57.8%	11.0%	89.0%	34.1%	65.9%	20.7%	79.5%	60.2%	32.8%

Table K-3: Places—Summary Housing Characteristics—*Continued*

	Millennial Householders	Age of Householders		18 to 24 Years Old		25 to 31 Years Old			Percent with Internet Access		Percent with Mobile Access Plan
		18 to 24	25 to 31	Owners	Renters	Owners	Renters	With Mortgage	18 to 24	25 to 31	
South Dakota											
Sioux Falls city	14,874	27.2%	72.8%	22.0%	78.0%	42.2%	57.8%	30.6%	93.1%	94.1%	37.8%
Tennessee											
Chattanooga city	12,720	31.7%	68.3%	7.5%	92.5%	25.0%	75.0%	17.5%	43.2%	79.3%	28.1%
Clarksville city	16,409	23.1%	76.9%	23.6%	76.4%	34.0%	66.0%	28.1%	82.8%	87.1%	40.7%
Knoxville city	21,262	45.0%	55.0%	2.4%	97.6%	26.1%	73.9%	12.1%	84.0%	88.5%	39.5%
Memphis city	43,627	27.4%	72.6%	8.8%	91.2%	17.7%	82.3%	12.6%	79.3%	69.9%	27.9%
Murfreesboro city	13,131	48.6%	51.4%	5.0%	95.0%	42.7%	57.3%	20.2%	82.5%	67.3%	18.0%
Nashville-Davidson metropolitan govt (bal)	50,365	21.3%	78.6%	11.9%	88.1%	26.2%	73.8%	19.4%	73.7%	83.3%	35.4%
Texas											
Abilene city	10,010	50.2%	49.8%	6.5%	93.5%	34.4%	65.6%	14.8%	40.1%	85.8%	38.3%
Amarillo city	16,528	35.6%	64.4%	8.1%	91.9%	28.9%	71.1%	20.3%	83.4%	64.6%	22.0%
Arlington city	26,157	24.8%	75.2%	13.1%	86.9%	31.9%	68.1%	24.3%	80.6%	81.0%	29.0%
Austin city	83,468	28.3%	71.3%	2.5%	97.5%	14.9%	85.1%	10.0%	91.7%	89.2%	47.6%
Beaumont city	8,122	30.1%	69.9%	11.8%	88.2%	37.6%	62.4%	22.0%	63.9%	57.0%	19.3%
Brownsville city	5,887	29.1%	70.9%	7.8%	92.2%	22.7%	77.3%	9.1%	72.3%	56.7%	37.9%
Carrollton city	10,539	27.7%	72.3%	3.4%	96.6%	14.2%	85.8%	9.1%	73.1%	91.2%	35.7%
College Station city	18,220	60.3%	39.7%	7.8%	92.2%	23.1%	76.9%	11.4%	92.6%	86.0%	43.6%
Corpus Christi city	20,777	38.6%	61.1%	15.6%	84.4%	25.7%	74.3%	15.3%	91.5%	86.4%	48.9%
Dallas city	94,160	28.5%	71.3%	7.6%	92.4%	17.5%	82.5%	11.5%	69.1%	76.2%	36.3%
Denton city	13,563	37.0%	61.5%	5.9%	94.1%	23.0%	77.0%	11.8%	83.9%	79.4%	31.8%
El Paso city	32,123	32.7%	67.1%	6.7%	93.3%	25.8%	74.2%	12.6%	73.1%	77.8%	35.4%
Fort Worth city	49,623	26.5%	73.2%	6.7%	93.3%	37.2%	62.8%	25.0%	75.2%	83.5%	34.8%
Frisco city	5,597	19.2%	80.8%	4.8%	95.2%	34.3%	65.7%	22.3%	38.4%	90.8%	40.2%
Garland city	10,780	23.9%	76.1%	9.7%	90.3%	16.6%	83.4%	14.2%	95.8%	91.8%	49.8%
Grand Prairie city	8,050	27.1%	72.9%	12.7%	87.3%	31.3%	68.7%	21.0%	87.7%	71.2%	24.7%
Houston city	170,770	23.8%	76.0%	7.9%	92.1%	18.7%	81.3%	13.7%	76.1%	83.5%	44.5%
Irving city	17,532	20.7%	79.1%	0.0%	100.0%	10.0%	90.0%	5.9%	64.4%	82.1%	36.6%
Killeen city	11,609	22.7%	77.3%	3.4%	96.6%	22.5%	77.5%	14.3%	91.4%	94.8%	28.3%
Laredo city	9,367	20.8%	79.2%	11.8%	88.2%	37.1%	62.9%	27.1%	61.5%	56.8%	17.3%
Lewisville city	7,976	17.1%	82.9%	6.7%	93.3%	18.0%	82.0%	15.4%	100.0%	93.6%	65.0%
Lubbock city	24,586	52.5%	47.5%	8.0%	92.0%	33.4%	66.6%	14.9%	88.2%	87.7%	30.1%
McAllen city	6,006	32.6%	67.0%	4.6%	95.4%	29.2%	70.8%	10.5%	92.5%	80.3%	46.2%
McKinney city	8,408	27.7%	72.3%	11.9%	88.1%	35.0%	65.0%	27.4%	76.3%	86.8%	27.9%
Mesquite city	9,716	26.9%	73.1%	11.1%	88.9%	28.5%	71.5%	19.0%	79.1%	74.1%	30.5%
Midland city	8,752	38.3%	61.7%	15.7%	84.3%	47.2%	52.8%	26.6%	89.1%	92.7%	39.6%
Odessa city	7,284	29.5%	70.5%	34.8%	65.2%	47.4%	52.6%	24.1%	91.4%	89.9%	57.7%
Pasadena city	6,834	35.8%	64.2%	19.6%	80.4%	15.1%	84.9%	14.8%	77.1%	82.5%	48.1%
Pearland city	5,451	18.1%	81.9%	11.9%	88.1%	56.5%	43.5%	46.9%	88.1%	94.3%	45.6%
Plano city	16,022	33.9%	66.1%	15.0%	85.0%	27.9%	72.1%	21.6%	87.3%	95.0%	18.2%
Richardson city	6,028	33.0%	67.0%	0.0%	100.0%	18.5%	81.5%	12.4%	72.3%	89.1%	20.0%
Round Rock city	5,413	21.0%	78.4%	0.0%	100.0%	28.8%	71.2%	22.7%	100.0%	75.9%	45.7%
San Angelo city	7,910	31.1%	68.9%	16.7%	83.3%	49.4%	50.6%	36.0%	73.1%	86.9%	34.2%
San Antonio city	88,048	29.2%	70.6%	5.7%	94.3%	23.8%	76.2%	15.2%	78.3%	82.9%	36.2%
Tyler city	7,084	30.2%	66.6%	20.4%	79.6%	33.7%	66.3%	21.7%	95.2%	93.3%	63.7%
Waco city	13,091	46.7%	53.3%	4.3%	95.7%	19.7%	80.3%	9.5%	88.2%	70.5%	20.1%
Wichita Falls city	9,746	33.7%	66.3%	10.6%	89.4%	37.4%	62.6%	21.9%	100.0%	76.6%	36.7%
Utah											
Orem city	6,059	29.1%	70.9%	25.7%	74.3%	27.7%	72.3%	21.2%	81.6%	83.6%	48.9%
Provo city	15,136	54.9%	44.7%	9.9%	90.1%	24.3%	75.7%	12.4%	92.8%	94.1%	41.1%
Salt Lake City city	17,427	31.3%	68.7%	8.5%	91.5%	24.1%	75.9%	17.2%	93.6%	90.9%	43.1%
West Jordan city	6,050	22.3%	77.7%	64.7%	35.3%	60.0%	40.0%	55.5%	100.0%	100.0%	34.3%
West Valley City city	5,200	14.1%	85.9%	28.0%	72.0%	45.9%	54.1%	40.5%	85.9%	100.0%	34.5%
Virginia											
Alexandria city	13,547	11.8%	88.2%	2.7%	97.3%	19.9%	80.1%	17.3%	78.3%	88.7%	43.8%
Chesapeake city	10,541	23.1%	76.9%	10.1%	89.9%	38.9%	61.1%	29.4%	60.5%	90.2%	32.7%
Hampton city	9,631	20.4%	79.6%	7.5%	92.5%	25.6%	74.4%	20.8%	88.0%	85.3%	53.8%
Newport News city	13,955	29.4%	70.1%	2.2%	97.8%	21.8%	78.2%	14.5%	93.2%	81.4%	41.5%
Norfolk city	20,381	33.5%	66.5%	7.0%	93.0%	19.7%	80.3%	14.5%	91.2%	85.5%	44.8%
Portsmouth city	6,628	25.7%	74.3%	19.0%	81.0%	19.7%	80.3%	15.0%	100.0%	96.8%	53.9%
Richmond city	21,420	31.8%	67.6%	2.7%	97.3%	11.8%	88.2%	8.3%	87.2%	88.0%	44.6%
Roanoke city	6,391	19.5%	80.5%	17.6%	82.4%	24.5%	75.5%	19.7%	75.3%	93.2%	37.9%
Virginia Beach city	25,775	24.1%	75.9%	11.3%	88.7%	25.9%	74.1%	21.6%	94.3%	96.4%	23.9%
Washington											
Bellevue city	8,803	11.1%	88.9%	27.6%	72.4%	7.7%	92.3%	7.5%	100.0%	100.0%	62.5%
Everett city	5,907	19.2%	80.8%	8.0%	92.0%	44.2%	55.8%	32.6%	74.6%	74.3%	39.5%
Federal Way city	6,120	28.4%	71.6%	30.6%	69.4%	24.9%	75.1%	17.8%	85.2%	86.7%	37.0%
Kent city	6,796	21.9%	78.1%	9.8%	90.2%	19.7%	80.3%	17.5%	81.6%	75.5%	28.7%
Renton city	6,430	21.2%	78.8%	0.0%	100.0%	21.3%	78.7%	16.8%	82.0%	94.1%	55.6%
Seattle city	68,776	23.4%	76.6%	6.7%	93.3%	15.4%	84.6%	11.6%	94.3%	92.3%	50.7%
Spokane city	18,171	30.5%	69.5%	5.7%	94.3%	30.4%	69.6%	18.4%	91.2%	86.0%	41.8%
Spokane Valley city	5,974	17.6%	82.4%	4.3%	95.7%	25.6%	74.4%	20.6%	67.5%	91.1%	61.3%
Tacoma city	13,125	31.3%	68.7%	8.3%	91.7%	29.4%	70.6%	21.5%	82.6%	84.4%	50.8%
Vancouver city	8,297	24.1%	75.9%	1.9%	98.2%	17.2%	82.8%	13.2%	92.7%	86.9%	53.1%
Yakima city	4,176	45.7%	54.3%	27.1%	72.9%	31.6%	68.4%	22.1%	87.2%	87.8%	44.3%

Table K-3: Places—Summary Housing Characteristics—*Continued*

	Millennial Householders	Age of Householders		18 to 24 Years Old		25 to 31 Years Old			Percent with Internet Access		Percent with Mobile Access Plan
		18 to 24	25 to 31	Owners	Renters	Owners	Renters	With Mortgage	18 to 24	25 to 31	
Wisconsin											
Green Bay city..............................	7,993	33.2%	66.6%	5.8%	94.2%	40.6%	59.4%	26.4%	84.6%	96.0%	45.7%
Kenosha city	5,283	40.5%	59.5%	1.1%	98.9%	11.4%	88.6%	6.0%	81.8%	97.5%	35.0%
Madison city	30,047	34.0%	66.0%	5.0%	95.0%	24.5%	75.5%	16.6%	91.6%	95.3%	40.7%
Milwaukee city	51,922	28.0%	71.8%	2.7%	97.3%	21.8%	78.2%	14.6%	70.1%	77.2%	39.7%

Table K-4: Metropolitan/Micropolitan Statistical Areas—Summary Housing Characteristics

	Millennial Householders	Age of Householders		18 to 24 Years Old		25 to 31 Years Old			Percent with Internet Access		Percent with Mobile Access Plan
		18 to 24	25 to 31	Owners	Renters	Owners	Renters	With Mortgage	18 to 24	25 to 31	
Abilene, TX	13,075	48.6%	51.4%	11.8%	88.2%	39.6%	60.4%	18.9%	36.7%	80.1%	36.1%
Adrian, MI micro	3,665	38.7%	61.3%	49.4%	50.6%	35.9%	64.1%	25.1%	50.0%	88.1%	25.0%
Akron, OH	41,541	34.0%	65.4%	8.8%	91.2%	40.1%	59.9%	26.1%	88.4%	85.4%	35.4%
Albany-Schenectady-Troy, NY	42,917	31.7%	67.5%	8.3%	91.7%	30.2%	69.8%	13.1%	85.2%	90.1%	22.1%
Albany, GA	9,339	22.1%	76.1%	7.0%	93.0%	24.8%	75.2%	8.8%	49.6%	73.3%	33.4%
Albany, OR	7,993	52.6%	47.4%	3.2%	96.8%	23.7%	76.3%	19.2%	94.1%	91.0%	42.4%
Albertville, AL micro	3,709	32.7%	67.3%	28.2%	71.8%	45.7%	54.3%	38.4%	55.0%	61.5%	16.3%
Albuquerque, NM	45,833	29.3%	69.7%	10.9%	89.1%	37.7%	62.3%	24.3%	79.9%	82.2%	34.8%
Alexandria, LA	8,354	29.0%	71.0%	6.0%	94.0%	37.4%	62.6%	18.6%	67.4%	85.0%	43.6%
Allentown-Bethlehem-Easton, PA-NJ	31,969	26.6%	73.4%	14.2%	85.8%	37.5%	62.5%	26.3%	81.7%	90.4%	37.5%
Altoona, PA	5,847	29.0%	71.0%	25.1%	74.9%	32.7%	67.3%	22.4%	94.0%	83.2%	47.5%
Amarillo, TX	20,183	35.0%	65.0%	8.1%	91.9%	30.7%	69.3%	20.9%	79.6%	68.5%	22.9%
Ames, IA	13,151	57.8%	42.2%	5.5%	94.5%	28.7%	71.3%	10.4%	92.5%	97.2%	35.7%
Anchorage, AK	23,790	33.6%	66.4%	9.9%	90.1%	39.2%	60.8%	26.5%	81.1%	84.3%	63.1%
Ann Arbor, MI	31,753	40.7%	59.3%	2.9%	97.1%	28.2%	71.8%	11.8%	91.3%	92.0%	51.5%
Anniston-Oxford-Jacksonville, AL	6,285	34.3%	65.7%	10.8%	89.2%	41.8%	58.2%	18.7%	98.7%	73.9%	42.5%
Appleton, WI	13,454	24.5%	75.5%	17.7%	82.3%	41.8%	58.2%	32.4%	82.2%	83.3%	33.7%
Asheville, NC	20,324	24.1%	75.5%	19.4%	80.6%	44.8%	55.2%	24.8%	79.7%	77.8%	46.0%
Ashtabula, OH micro	4,446	22.5%	77.5%	52.9%	47.1%	37.0%	63.0%	26.5%	47.1%	87.3%	11.2%
Athens-Clarke County, GA	18,811	51.6%	48.4%	6.9%	93.1%	13.8%	86.2%	6.4%	85.4%	79.5%	39.6%
Atlanta-Sandy Springs-Roswell, GA	265,915	24.3%	75.6%	11.4%	88.6%	31.5%	68.5%	22.9%	83.2%	84.9%	41.5%
Atlantic City-Hammonton, NJ	9,983	18.6%	81.4%	27.7%	72.3%	36.7%	63.3%	27.0%	39.0%	79.6%	28.5%
Auburn-Opelika, AL	16,087	52.7%	47.3%	20.9%	79.1%	18.4%	81.6%	14.1%	92.8%	72.5%	44.3%
Augusta-Richmond County, GA-SC	25,083	24.1%	75.9%	24.6%	75.4%	37.7%	62.3%	26.0%	80.1%	84.3%	41.0%
Augusta-Waterville, ME micro	6,351	20.9%	79.1%	19.9%	80.1%	42.8%	57.2%	36.4%	88.1%	82.2%	35.7%
Austin-Round Rock, TX	138,713	28.7%	71.1%	4.2%	95.8%	24.1%	75.9%	15.6%	89.7%	87.0%	48.1%
Bakersfield, CA	44,103	27.8%	72.2%	5.9%	94.1%	32.4%	67.6%	21.1%	71.3%	74.4%	32.9%
Baltimore-Columbia-Towson, MD	134,239	19.3%	80.4%	15.5%	84.5%	34.4%	65.6%	26.5%	87.0%	88.6%	42.9%
Bangor, ME	8,327	26.6%	73.4%	25.1%	74.9%	22.0%	78.0%	15.3%	76.6%	79.1%	48.1%
Barnstable Town, MA	5,711	20.6%	79.4%	20.7%	79.3%	42.1%	57.9%	36.6%	100.0%	97.8%	45.6%
Baton Rouge, LA	51,731	37.9%	62.0%	12.1%	87.9%	44.7%	55.3%	28.2%	72.6%	82.0%	34.3%
Battle Creek, MI	6,258	25.0%	75.0%	12.3%	87.7%	33.4%	66.6%	25.5%	71.6%	81.0%	34.8%
Bay City, MI	6,293	24.6%	75.4%	8.5%	91.5%	64.4%	35.6%	33.8%	37.7%	91.7%	27.1%
Beaumont-Port Arthur, TX	25,128	25.7%	74.3%	21.2%	78.8%	48.4%	51.6%	26.8%	63.4%	79.1%	35.5%
Beckley, WV	5,619	30.5%	69.5%	16.0%	84.0%	45.9%	54.1%	12.1%	54.4%	76.7%	54.9%
Bellingham, WA	12,984	42.6%	57.4%	1.2%	98.8%	29.7%	70.3%	14.1%	92.7%	86.6%	31.6%
Bend-Redmond, OR	6,665	17.8%	82.2%	3.2%	96.8%	25.5%	74.5%	16.8%	91.1%	78.2%	47.1%
Billings, MT	10,682	39.6%	60.4%	4.9%	95.1%	38.2%	61.8%	22.0%	72.2%	86.4%	32.2%
Binghamton, NY	12,724	34.9%	64.9%	2.5%	97.5%	35.9%	64.1%	16.7%	67.3%	83.1%	32.8%
Birmingham-Hoover, AL	57,542	25.3%	74.7%	10.1%	89.9%	40.5%	59.5%	28.1%	69.4%	79.1%	34.9%
Bismarck, ND	10,289	24.6%	75.4%	6.9%	93.1%	65.8%	34.2%	44.7%	91.5%	98.6%	41.9%
Blacksburg-Christiansburg-Radford, VA	15,546	65.0%	34.5%	9.6%	90.4%	43.9%	56.1%	17.9%	96.0%	86.4%	31.8%
Bloomington, IL	16,082	38.6%	61.4%	5.4%	94.6%	39.8%	60.2%	24.4%	85.1%	88.3%	31.5%
Bloomington, IN	17,170	57.0%	42.5%	9.2%	90.8%	32.0%	68.0%	14.2%	95.3%	85.8%	24.8%
Bloomsburg-Berwick, PA	3,469	50.9%	49.1%	7.6%	92.4%	39.5%	60.5%	21.4%	100.0%	83.8%	17.9%
Boise City, ID	37,686	31.2%	68.8%	12.7%	87.3%	48.3%	51.7%	33.7%	78.5%	91.0%	40.3%
Boston-Cambridge-Newton, MA-NH	225,030	21.5%	78.4%	4.7%	95.3%	24.2%	75.8%	17.7%	93.2%	94.3%	45.8%
Boulder, CO	24,480	49.8%	50.2%	9.8%	90.2%	31.2%	68.8%	16.4%	94.9%	94.7%	45.3%
Bowling Green, KY	11,615	44.4%	55.6%	22.0%	78.0%	34.9%	65.1%	27.1%	87.6%	95.1%	42.6%
Bremerton-Silverdale, WA	14,742	23.5%	76.5%	22.1%	77.9%	27.6%	72.4%	22.9%	100.0%	88.7%	59.4%
Bridgeport-Stamford-Norwalk, CT	28,833	14.6%	85.3%	13.9%	86.1%	27.8%	72.2%	24.0%	86.9%	93.3%	49.8%
Brownsville-Harlingen, TX	13,218	21.9%	78.1%	15.7%	84.3%	37.6%	62.4%	19.7%	69.9%	60.5%	33.6%
Brunswick, GA	5,174	32.3%	67.7%	30.1%	69.9%	26.6%	73.4%	25.1%	87.2%	66.1%	28.2%
Buffalo-Cheektowaga-Niagara Falls, NY	61,551	26.9%	73.1%	10.0%	90.0%	34.4%	65.6%	23.6%	75.9%	86.9%	35.1%
Burlington-South Burlington, VT	12,611	34.1%	65.9%	7.2%	92.8%	27.3%	72.7%	18.7%	79.0%	86.2%	36.2%
Burlington, NC	8,462	33.1%	66.9%	27.5%	72.5%	35.1%	64.9%	13.3%	86.8%	75.6%	44.0%
California-Lexington Park, MD	3,857	23.5%	76.5%	12.6%	87.4%	45.3%	54.7%	32.8%	82.8%	96.8%	38.1%
Canton-Massillon, OH	17,344	27.6%	72.1%	13.8%	86.2%	45.6%	54.4%	28.5%	85.7%	88.2%	56.7%
Cape Coral-Fort Myers, FL	20,643	24.7%	75.2%	17.0%	83.0%	27.6%	72.4%	18.6%	80.1%	81.9%	34.1%
Cape Girardeau, MO-IL	6,226	38.7%	61.3%	18.7%	81.3%	57.4%	42.6%	37.7%	94.4%	74.4%	37.7%
Carbondale-Marion, IL	9,379	39.8%	60.2%	7.4%	92.6%	36.6%	63.4%	21.1%	58.9%	69.1%	25.5%
Carson City, NV	2,122	12.6%	87.4%	36.9%	63.1%	23.3%	76.7%	25.0%	45.9%	77.1%	32.0%
Casper, WY	7,505	33.2%	66.8%	10.9%	89.1%	44.3%	55.7%	25.8%	70.2%	85.9%	25.2%
Cedar Rapids, IA	19,034	21.6%	78.4%	12.7%	87.3%	57.4%	42.6%	45.2%	78.3%	91.8%	33.3%
Chambersburg-Waynesboro, PA	6,759	19.3%	80.7%	26.9%	73.1%	57.8%	42.2%	49.1%	92.9%	82.6%	33.0%
Champaign-Urbana, IL	24,846	50.9%	49.1%	4.8%	95.2%	35.6%	64.4%	16.6%	95.6%	92.0%	35.5%
Charleston-North Charleston, SC	43,894	30.3%	69.7%	7.2%	92.8%	29.9%	70.1%	30.8%	79.4%	78.6%	49.3%
Charleston, WV	12,566	23.1%	76.9%	24.9%	75.1%	42.9%	57.1%	19.1%	84.6%	85.1%	40.8%
Charlotte-Concord-Gastonia, NC-SC	114,693	23.8%	76.1%	11.6%	88.4%	34.8%	65.2%	25.7%	81.1%	83.2%	37.1%
Charlottesville, VA	12,332	30.8%	69.2%	4.2%	95.8%	39.6%	60.4%	26.6%	88.7%	82.5%	33.4%
Chattanooga, TN-GA	28,417	26.4%	73.6%	10.5%	89.5%	38.6%	61.4%	26.5%	55.1%	82.6%	32.3%
Cheyenne, WY	7,300	47.2%	52.8%	8.4%	91.6%	36.0%	64.0%	15.3%	96.5%	88.9%	23.7%
Chicago-Naperville-Elgin, IL-IN-WI	471,700	20.7%	79.2%	9.6%	90.4%	31.2%	68.8%	22.4%	84.8%	87.1%	45.0%
Chico, CA	16,020	50.5%	49.5%	4.7%	95.3%	35.2%	64.8%	17.7%	94.8%	89.0%	40.3%
Cincinnati, OH-KY-IN	117,812	27.8%	72.1%	9.9%	90.1%	41.1%	58.9%	27.8%	79.3%	86.4%	38.5%
Clarksburg, WV micro	3,539	36.1%	63.4%	36.2%	63.8%	57.1%	42.9%	37.0%	91.1%	90.4%	53.5%
Clarksville, TN-KY	26,044	29.3%	70.7%	20.5%	79.5%	34.0%	66.0%	25.0%	80.1%	87.1%	37.0%

Table K-4: Metropolitan/Micropolitan Statistical Areas—Summary Housing Characteristics—*Continued*

	Millennial Householders	Age of Householders		18 to 24 Years Old		25 to 31 Years Old			Percent with Internet Access		Percent with Mobile Access Plan
		18 to 24	25 to 31	Owners	Renters	Owners	Renters	With Mortgage	18 to 24	25 to 31	
Cleveland-Elyria, OH	101,141	25.7%	73.8%	12.4%	87.6%	33.1%	66.9%	26.0%	81.0%	87.3%	46.0%
Cleveland, TN	5,681	19.3%	80.7%	16.7%	83.3%	32.0%	68.0%	24.0%	48.0%	75.3%	40.2%
Coeur d'Alene, ID	7,084	24.0%	76.0%	0.0%	100.0%	65.7%	34.3%	48.8%	64.6%	80.7%	24.4%
College Station-Bryan, TX	28,643	59.1%	40.9%	5.8%	94.2%	25.0%	75.0%	10.2%	92.1%	84.3%	44.9%
Colorado Springs, CO	44,979	27.6%	72.4%	10.1%	89.9%	38.5%	61.5%	28.5%	92.0%	92.0%	51.4%
Columbia, MO	22,986	48.5%	51.5%	2.9%	97.1%	26.4%	73.6%	13.6%	93.6%	82.5%	34.7%
Columbia, SC	44,303	32.4%	67.6%	11.6%	88.4%	36.1%	63.9%	22.3%	76.0%	80.3%	38.7%
Columbus, GA-AL	18,230	29.7%	70.3%	12.0%	88.0%	23.5%	76.5%	16.5%	72.4%	80.6%	41.6%
Columbus, IN	5,677	22.5%	77.5%	20.2%	79.8%	43.5%	56.5%	30.6%	68.9%	88.5%	19.7%
Columbus, OH	123,338	26.0%	73.9%	9.7%	90.3%	34.2%	65.8%	24.4%	84.1%	87.4%	43.9%
Concord, NH micro	4,637	28.5%	70.3%	16.0%	84.0%	28.2%	71.8%	23.8%	90.2%	90.4%	31.0%
Cookeville, TN micro	7,398	53.2%	46.8%	14.1%	85.9%	37.2%	62.8%	21.7%	72.9%	53.4%	20.7%
Corpus Christi, TX	26,870	35.9%	63.8%	13.8%	86.2%	25.2%	74.8%	15.4%	90.6%	86.2%	45.9%
Corvallis, OR	8,167	53.6%	46.4%	5.5%	94.5%	23.7%	76.3%	9.9%	94.3%	91.0%	32.7%
Crestview-Fort Walton Beach-Destin, FL	17,218	27.6%	72.4%	3.1%	96.9%	34.9%	65.1%	21.1%	82.9%	90.7%	38.4%
Cumberland, MD-WV	3,775	26.2%	73.8%	9.3%	90.7%	58.2%	41.8%	36.1%	95.3%	76.9%	33.5%
Dallas-Fort Worth-Arlington, TX	391,746	27.0%	72.9%	11.0%	89.0%	28.3%	71.7%	20.1%	75.8%	81.8%	36.3%
Dalton, GA	6,856	28.4%	71.6%	15.0%	85.0%	33.3%	66.7%	22.3%	46.6%	81.8%	31.8%
Danville, IL	4,024	28.0%	72.0%	27.4%	72.6%	29.6%	70.4%	26.8%	37.2%	58.6%	4.2%
Danville, VA micro	4,773	29.6%	70.4%	9.1%	90.9%	36.8%	63.2%	28.6%	90.9%	68.4%	15.8%
Daphne-Fairhope-Foley, AL	6,655	38.2%	61.8%	19.6%	80.4%	51.5%	48.5%	28.9%	48.3%	76.3%	19.5%
Davenport-Moline-Rock Island, IA-IL	23,320	29.8%	70.2%	17.2%	82.8%	42.6%	57.4%	31.0%	74.8%	78.3%	35.1%
Dayton, OH	47,112	32.2%	67.7%	12.7%	87.3%	37.2%	62.8%	25.5%	81.5%	87.0%	46.7%
Decatur, AL	6,487	28.5%	71.5%	14.4%	85.6%	57.8%	42.2%	26.4%	66.8%	59.3%	35.4%
Decatur, IL	6,699	31.8%	67.8%	15.0%	85.0%	35.8%	64.2%	27.5%	75.6%	77.3%	43.9%
Deltona-Daytona Beach-Ormond Beach, FL	25,607	34.9%	65.0%	25.9%	74.1%	34.3%	65.7%	26.4%	77.6%	69.8%	28.9%
Denver-Aurora-Lakewood, CO	164,035	26.9%	72.8%	12.3%	87.7%	37.2%	62.8%	28.0%	86.8%	88.2%	40.8%
Des Moines-West Des Moines, IA	40,951	28.5%	71.5%	12.9%	87.1%	47.9%	52.1%	33.9%	70.4%	91.1%	52.0%
Detroit-Warren-Dearborn, MI	192,987	26.1%	73.9%	19.7%	80.3%	42.9%	57.1%	25.3%	76.3%	87.2%	35.6%
Dothan, AL	7,756	23.4%	76.6%	8.2%	91.8%	28.3%	71.7%	22.2%	71.1%	83.5%	22.4%
Dover, DE	7,698	31.0%	69.0%	26.2%	73.8%	46.2%	53.8%	21.3%	79.4%	91.3%	37.2%
Dubuque, IA	5,434	34.6%	65.4%	17.1%	82.9%	60.2%	39.8%	39.4%	86.9%	87.5%	43.2%
Duluth, MN-WI	19,581	30.2%	69.8%	15.5%	84.5%	32.4%	67.6%	24.9%	93.2%	89.7%	26.8%
Dunn, NC micro	7,369	21.6%	78.1%	26.9%	73.1%	51.5%	48.5%	36.7%	82.0%	81.4%	42.4%
Durham-Chapel Hill, NC	35,177	24.0%	76.0%	5.2%	94.8%	21.9%	78.1%	16.5%	92.9%	89.3%	58.7%
East Stroudsburg, PA	5,598	40.1%	59.9%	11.5%	88.5%	60.5%	39.5%	28.8%	90.3%	67.7%	45.1%
Eau Claire, WI	11,337	50.6%	49.4%	8.9%	91.1%	45.7%	54.3%	25.8%	89.3%	92.1%	33.0%
El Centro, CA	6,712	16.8%	83.2%	29.0%	71.0%	44.6%	55.4%	36.1%	63.7%	88.6%	19.8%
El Paso, TX	40,497	31.6%	68.3%	8.3%	91.7%	32.5%	67.5%	18.0%	70.8%	77.9%	37.2%
Elizabethtown-Fort Knox, KY	8,647	25.0%	75.0%	14.7%	85.3%	44.6%	55.4%	33.3%	82.8%	73.9%	32.7%
Elkhart-Goshen, IN	10,618	41.1%	58.9%	33.0%	67.0%	55.1%	44.9%	43.0%	73.6%	78.7%	43.5%
Elmira, NY	5,481	18.4%	81.6%	2.9%	97.1%	50.3%	49.7%	35.9%	79.0%	86.0%	28.8%
Erie, PA	15,495	24.3%	75.7%	19.4%	80.6%	48.7%	51.3%	36.3%	95.0%	87.7%	45.1%
Eugene, OR	23,956	48.7%	51.3%	7.9%	92.1%	32.2%	67.8%	17.9%	90.3%	92.9%	43.7%
Eureka-Arcata-Fortuna, CA micro	9,938	38.4%	60.8%	0.0%	100.0%	22.3%	77.7%	12.2%	96.9%	83.1%	24.8%
Evansville, IN-KY	18,878	32.0%	68.0%	14.2%	85.8%	44.1%	55.9%	29.0%	82.5%	88.5%	34.1%
Fairbanks, AK	7,447	29.8%	70.2%	1.4%	98.6%	19.3%	80.7%	14.0%	43.0%	59.0%	13.8%
Fargo, ND-MN	23,684	45.5%	54.5%	4.0%	96.0%	45.5%	54.5%	21.4%	85.1%	84.0%	31.3%
Farmington, NM	4,439	35.7%	64.3%	29.8%	70.2%	50.5%	49.5%	28.9%	48.2%	82.9%	36.4%
Fayetteville-Springdale-Rogers, AR-MO	35,597	32.5%	67.5%	9.9%	90.1%	33.7%	66.3%	9.2%	89.4%	89.8%	46.0%
Fayetteville, NC	31,502	31.3%	68.6%	4.3%	95.7%	15.4%	84.6%	22.8%	81.1%	81.5%	23.0%
Flagstaff, AZ	12,378	49.9%	50.1%	5.2%	94.8%	25.3%	74.7%	9.5%	94.0%	89.0%	37.8%
Flint, MI	19,391	26.3%	73.2%	17.7%	82.3%	43.1%	56.9%	21.7%	55.7%	69.3%	27.0%
Florence-Muscle Shoals, AL	7,463	34.7%	65.3%	9.7%	90.3%	31.8%	68.2%	20.9%	77.1%	66.8%	27.2%
Florence, SC	8,598	20.7%	79.3%	12.3%	87.7%	34.9%	65.1%	21.6%	59.9%	87.3%	42.0%
Fond du Lac, WI	4,466	45.6%	54.4%	50.0%	50.0%	43.8%	56.2%	43.4%	78.7%	91.3%	42.5%
Fort Collins, CO	24,712	42.0%	58.0%	5.7%	94.3%	35.2%	64.8%	19.9%	95.3%	93.4%	39.1%
Fort Smith, AR-OK	16,822	29.7%	70.1%	26.7%	73.3%	34.4%	65.6%	26.3%	60.1%	66.1%	22.6%
Fort Wayne, IN	26,846	33.0%	67.0%	24.6%	75.4%	50.6%	49.4%	38.0%	71.9%	88.8%	38.9%
Fresno, CA	49,982	27.0%	72.8%	7.5%	92.5%	33.5%	66.5%	23.0%	75.5%	81.8%	44.3%
Gadsden, AL	4,099	20.1%	79.9%	33.2%	66.8%	58.5%	41.5%	48.9%	75.3%	83.1%	14.7%
Gainesville, FL	30,570	57.5%	42.5%	10.0%	90.0%	23.9%	76.1%	10.6%	92.1%	88.1%	43.2%
Gainesville, GA	7,912	29.1%	70.9%	31.0%	69.0%	28.9%	71.1%	26.2%	74.2%	76.8%	30.7%
Gettysburg, PA	4,047	37.3%	62.7%	19.4%	80.6%	38.6%	61.4%	20.6%	62.9%	84.1%	34.9%
Glens Falls, NY	4,670	29.9%	70.1%	2.1%	97.9%	36.1%	63.9%	17.5%	76.9%	79.6%	35.9%
Goldsboro, NC	7,210	34.5%	65.5%	2.3%	97.7%	39.0%	61.0%	24.4%	87.1%	87.7%	55.4%
Grand Forks, ND-MN	12,337	57.3%	42.7%	6.6%	93.4%	58.8%	41.2%	23.3%	89.5%	98.3%	40.5%
Grand Island, NE	4,822	30.6%	69.4%	10.0%	90.0%	33.1%	66.9%	24.6%	86.5%	74.0%	29.8%
Grand Junction, CO	10,163	22.5%	77.5%	25.1%	74.9%	41.4%	58.6%	35.7%	96.6%	86.7%	59.9%
Grand Rapids-Wyoming, MI	58,277	29.4%	70.6%	16.2%	83.8%	49.7%	50.3%	33.8%	92.5%	86.6%	41.3%
Grants Pass, OR	3,231	47.7%	52.3%	23.4%	76.6%	32.4%	67.6%	22.0%	73.0%	91.2%	6.9%
Great Falls, MT	6,085	25.5%	74.5%	8.4%	91.6%	41.4%	58.6%	24.5%	90.7%	87.2%	32.1%
Greeley, CO	17,354	30.2%	69.8%	9.3%	90.7%	45.1%	54.9%	28.0%	83.9%	80.2%	38.1%
Green Bay, WI	16,968	29.2%	70.7%	24.1%	75.9%	40.9%	59.1%	33.4%	84.0%	94.3%	42.4%
Greensboro-High Point, NC	41,122	25.6%	74.2%	14.3%	85.7%	31.5%	68.5%	20.5%	76.2%	78.1%	35.0%
Greenville-Anderson-Mauldin, SC	42,416	27.1%	72.6%	15.9%	84.1%	37.1%	62.9%	12.1%	76.4%	75.5%	30.2%

Table K-4: Metropolitan/Micropolitan Statistical Areas—Summary Housing Characteristics—*Continued*

	Millennial Householders	Age of Householders		18 to 24 Years Old		25 to 31 Years Old			Percent with Internet Access		Percent with Mobile Access Plan
		18 to 24	25 to 31	Owners	Renters	Owners	Renters	With Mortgage	18 to 24	25 to 31	
Greenville, NC	16,044	57.7%	42.3%	7.7%	92.3%	31.8%	68.2%	23.8%	91.9%	94.3%	35.2%
Greenwood, SC micro	5,675	37.1%	62.9%	0.0%	100.0%	33.2%	66.8%	20.1%	78.2%	92.9%	50.2%
Gulfport-Biloxi-Pascagoula, MS	23,268	25.9%	73.3%	9.2%	90.8%	33.2%	66.8%	15.9%	93.2%	78.5%	35.6%
Hagerstown-Martinsburg, MD-WV	11,243	23.7%	76.3%	22.2%	77.8%	28.6%	71.4%	22.1%	81.4%	87.1%	48.2%
Hammond, LA	9,823	26.0%	74.0%	15.0%	85.0%	34.5%	65.5%	17.3%	53.2%	71.2%	25.3%
Hanford-Corcoran, CA	7,700	16.0%	84.0%	5.4%	94.6%	11.5%	88.5%	8.5%	91.7%	81.1%	58.7%
Harrisburg-Carlisle, PA	33,496	27.6%	72.4%	12.2%	87.8%	35.3%	64.7%	24.2%	94.8%	86.2%	48.9%
Harrisonburg, VA	8,671	39.0%	61.0%	7.6%	92.4%	41.5%	58.5%	23.7%	94.0%	91.5%	47.9%
Hartford-West Hartford-East Hartford, CT	53,093	21.0%	78.9%	14.0%	86.0%	32.3%	67.7%	24.6%	81.9%	90.5%	39.7%
Hattiesburg, MS	10,488	37.2%	62.8%	12.1%	87.9%	32.5%	67.5%	18.4%	98.2%	81.3%	34.4%
Hickory-Lenoir-Morganton, NC	13,554	24.4%	75.3%	18.5%	81.5%	35.6%	64.4%	28.2%	67.9%	77.1%	31.7%
Hilo, HI micro	6,275	31.6%	68.4%	0.0%	100.0%	34.8%	65.2%	16.8%	70.2%	65.4%	31.2%
Hilton Head Island-Bluffton-Beaufort, SC	10,914	30.0%	70.0%	27.9%	72.1%	41.4%	58.6%	32.6%	72.9%	79.4%	16.9%
Hinesville, GA	8,370	42.8%	57.2%	5.8%	94.2%	26.3%	73.7%	13.6%	76.5%	82.7%	23.1%
Holland, MI micro	4,539	24.1%	75.9%	46.8%	53.2%	65.8%	34.2%	37.9%	46.8%	73.8%	23.6%
Homosassa Springs, FL	3,303	27.0%	73.0%	6.8%	93.2%	45.6%	54.4%	33.3%	52.7%	83.6%	21.5%
Hot Springs, AR	3,828	28.4%	71.6%	0.0%	100.0%	28.1%	71.9%	17.1%	100.0%	88.5%	51.4%
Houma-Thibodaux, LA	11,463	27.8%	72.2%	30.9%	69.1%	59.2%	40.8%	34.1%	75.4%	85.0%	42.5%
Houston-The Woodlands-Sugar Land, TX	345,073	24.5%	75.4%	12.5%	87.5%	30.5%	69.5%	21.9%	75.7%	82.3%	42.5%
Huntington-Ashland, WV-KY-OH	18,383	34.2%	65.8%	15.3%	84.7%	32.3%	67.7%	19.7%	72.2%	85.7%	30.7%
Huntsville, AL	25,768	26.1%	73.9%	14.6%	85.4%	47.0%	53.0%	33.5%	73.6%	87.3%	50.0%
Idaho Falls, ID	7,104	29.4%	70.6%	22.0%	78.0%	34.8%	65.2%	26.2%	80.6%	68.2%	37.5%
Indianapolis-Carmel-Anderson, IN	121,511	28.0%	71.9%	17.4%	82.6%	38.6%	61.4%	29.7%	76.8%	85.7%	33.1%
Iowa City, IA	20,747	47.5%	52.5%	6.7%	93.3%	33.3%	66.7%	16.9%	94.8%	87.6%	43.1%
Ithaca, NY	8,664	45.2%	54.8%	0.0%	100.0%	20.1%	79.9%	11.0%	98.6%	96.9%	32.1%
Jackson, MI	8,706	28.7%	71.3%	20.7%	79.3%	41.5%	58.5%	34.5%	78.4%	81.3%	42.6%
Jackson, MS	28,357	22.6%	77.4%	12.0%	88.0%	37.0%	63.0%	23.4%	75.8%	78.4%	41.8%
Jackson, TN	6,399	29.3%	70.7%	23.2%	76.8%	24.1%	75.9%	22.2%	72.1%	66.9%	19.6%
Jacksonville, FL	71,306	24.9%	74.9%	15.0%	85.0%	29.4%	70.6%	22.8%	75.4%	85.4%	39.5%
Jacksonville, NC	19,261	48.2%	51.8%	17.9%	82.1%	34.3%	65.7%	23.1%	89.3%	79.4%	52.9%
Jamestown-Dunkirk-Fredonia, NY micro	6,262	30.3%	69.7%	3.6%	96.4%	42.1%	57.9%	24.3%	68.9%	79.4%	22.6%
Janesville-Beloit, WI	9,068	42.0%	58.0%	31.1%	68.9%	43.3%	56.7%	34.1%	97.2%	80.0%	28.6%
Jefferson City, MO	7,326	21.7%	78.3%	41.4%	58.6%	42.7%	57.3%	35.6%	67.3%	69.2%	25.0%
Johnson City, TN	11,348	40.9%	58.8%	13.9%	86.1%	36.5%	63.5%	22.6%	84.6%	86.6%	46.2%
Johnstown, PA	6,783	25.7%	74.3%	44.2%	55.8%	49.6%	50.4%	44.9%	87.0%	82.5%	42.8%
Jonesboro, AR	8,946	38.9%	61.1%	15.6%	84.4%	26.9%	73.1%	16.8%	93.2%	74.8%	39.0%
Joplin, MO	13,277	30.5%	69.5%	22.0%	78.0%	42.4%	57.6%	31.5%	69.1%	75.7%	18.9%
Kahului-Wailuku-Lahaina, HI	5,653	19.3%	79.4%	18.4%	81.6%	7.8%	92.2%	4.9%	90.5%	86.5%	49.1%
Kalamazoo-Portage, MI	25,720	44.4%	55.6%	10.2%	89.8%	43.3%	56.7%	22.6%	90.4%	88.7%	58.3%
Kalispell, MT micro	2,931	11.5%	88.5%	16.9%	83.1%	41.3%	58.7%	35.8%	78.7%	77.5%	27.6%
Kankakee, IL	3,958	37.1%	62.9%	34.9%	65.1%	45.0%	55.0%	19.9%	99.2%	84.7%	24.0%
Kansas City, MO-KS	126,769	26.9%	73.1%	10.9%	89.1%	34.9%	65.1%	25.0%	85.0%	86.4%	46.3%
Kennewick-Richland, WA	16,569	33.0%	67.0%	10.6%	89.4%	41.8%	58.2%	28.8%	59.4%	74.8%	32.1%
Killeen-Temple, TX	29,381	28.4%	71.6%	8.7%	91.3%	26.3%	73.7%	17.5%	77.4%	92.4%	34.7%
Kingsport-Bristol-Bristol, TN-VA	13,013	23.8%	75.8%	27.2%	72.8%	49.7%	50.3%	32.2%	57.8%	86.5%	23.1%
Kingston, NY	7,232	29.3%	70.7%	4.3%	95.7%	36.0%	64.0%	20.8%	100.0%	73.0%	23.4%
Knoxville, TN	46,740	32.7%	67.2%	7.8%	92.2%	41.5%	58.5%	26.3%	74.5%	84.2%	41.1%
Kokomo, IN	4,520	45.9%	54.1%	17.8%	82.2%	52.1%	47.9%	27.1%	77.5%	93.3%	47.0%
La Crosse-Onalaska, WI-MN	11,196	48.5%	51.5%	0.0%	100.0%	49.0%	51.0%	21.7%	95.0%	90.2%	37.9%
Lafayette-West Lafayette, IN	22,532	55.6%	44.4%	8.6%	91.4%	23.9%	76.1%	30.5%	91.4%	96.2%	23.1%
Lafayette, LA	30,481	32.2%	67.8%	19.8%	80.2%	50.0%	50.0%	11.8%	82.3%	89.7%	29.4%
Lake Charles, LA	11,289	35.1%	64.9%	46.3%	53.7%	41.6%	58.4%	27.6%	51.0%	94.8%	31.5%
Lake Havasu City-Kingman, AZ	8,096	31.8%	64.9%	25.7%	74.3%	27.1%	72.9%	24.4%	82.5%	75.4%	28.3%
Lakeland-Winter Haven, FL	23,242	21.7%	78.3%	18.2%	81.8%	37.2%	62.8%	28.5%	63.0%	78.7%	31.0%
Lancaster, PA	26,617	28.7%	71.3%	18.9%	81.1%	59.4%	40.6%	44.1%	68.5%	79.4%	28.9%
Lansing-East Lansing, MI	36,151	37.3%	62.7%	13.8%	86.2%	40.7%	59.3%	24.9%	88.9%	93.1%	45.8%
Laredo, TX	10,466	19.9%	80.1%	14.0%	86.0%	40.5%	59.5%	31.0%	63.9%	61.8%	19.9%
Las Cruces, NM	14,038	52.7%	47.3%	15.7%	84.3%	30.8%	69.2%	15.4%	87.2%	85.4%	52.7%
Las Vegas-Henderson-Paradise, NV	103,464	21.2%	78.8%	18.8%	81.2%	27.3%	72.7%	21.9%	85.8%	82.3%	35.7%
Lawrence, KS	12,587	47.5%	52.5%	2.7%	97.3%	22.3%	77.7%	13.0%	94.2%	88.0%	47.1%
Lawton, OK	10,089	34.8%	65.2%	2.4%	97.6%	22.2%	77.8%	12.2%	50.0%	78.8%	39.8%
Lebanon, PA	5,759	27.9%	72.1%	10.5%	89.5%	40.8%	59.2%	21.6%	68.7%	71.7%	34.7%
Lewiston-Auburn, ME	7,532	16.4%	83.6%	36.7%	63.3%	13.8%	86.2%	37.0%	85.4%	81.9%	11.7%
Lewiston, ID-WA	2,594	31.9%	68.1%	41.6%	58.4%	46.4%	53.6%	15.9%	46.3%	59.6%	45.8%
Lexington-Fayette, KY	35,667	35.6%	64.4%	5.1%	94.9%	31.4%	68.6%	17.9%	87.3%	82.0%	40.5%
Lima, OH	5,667	26.6%	73.4%	21.3%	78.7%	33.2%	66.8%	28.0%	67.2%	65.9%	14.8%
Lincoln, NE	27,825	42.1%	57.2%	6.8%	93.2%	43.6%	56.4%	23.5%	94.1%	88.5%	27.7%
Little Rock-North Little Rock-Conway, AR	41,804	28.3%	71.7%	13.0%	87.0%	33.8%	66.2%	25.3%	76.9%	80.7%	39.5%
Logan, UT-ID	12,034	34.4%	65.6%	7.6%	92.4%	41.2%	58.8%	23.4%	88.5%	81.7%	33.7%
Longview, TX	13,494	38.5%	61.5%	15.9%	84.1%	42.8%	57.2%	25.1%	74.2%	71.0%	37.5%
Longview, WA	4,336	26.5%	73.5%	2.3%	97.7%	33.7%	66.3%	24.2%	90.1%	81.4%	65.3%
Los Angeles-Long Beach-Anaheim, CA	544,160	21.8%	78.0%	8.4%	91.6%	17.5%	82.5%	12.7%	82.9%	85.1%	38.3%
Louisville/Jefferson County, KY-IN	67,777	23.7%	76.2%	11.8%	88.2%	38.2%	61.8%	27.8%	76.9%	85.1%	40.0%
Lubbock, TX	26,684	51.6%	48.4%	7.5%	92.5%	32.6%	67.4%	14.8%	87.7%	87.8%	29.9%
Lumberton, NC micro	5,851	31.9%	68.1%	9.2%	90.8%	24.2%	75.8%	9.5%	47.4%	41.6%	13.7%

Table K-4: Metropolitan/Micropolitan Statistical Areas—Summary Housing Characteristics—*Continued*

	Millennial Householders	Age of Householders		18 to 24 Years Old		25 to 31 Years Old			Percent with Internet Access		Percent with Mobile Access Plan
		18 to 24	25 to 31	Owners	Renters	Owners	Renters	With Mortgage	18 to 24	25 to 31	
Lynchburg, VA	13,919	34.4%	65.6%	14.5%	85.5%	58.4%	41.6%	40.5%	76.2%	85.9%	30.8%
Macon, GA	11,146	35.7%	64.1%	6.1%	93.9%	30.1%	69.9%	14.7%	64.5%	70.4%	31.7%
Madera, CA	7,122	18.1%	81.9%	2.0%	98.0%	42.6%	57.4%	34.0%	80.0%	66.6%	17.9%
Madison, WI	53,400	32.9%	67.1%	6.7%	93.3%	31.6%	68.4%	21.5%	90.5%	91.0%	40.8%
Manchester-Nashua, NH	18,326	17.1%	82.9%	6.7%	93.3%	26.1%	73.9%	20.8%	83.9%	88.3%	42.8%
Manhattan, KS	13,564	54.6%	45.4%	3.4%	96.6%	48.4%	51.6%	17.3%	100.0%	94.0%	43.6%
Mankato-North Mankato, MN	7,844	39.4%	60.6%	5.1%	94.9%	57.2%	42.8%	24.7%	97.5%	89.4%	51.2%
Mansfield, OH	5,200	38.2%	59.2%	29.6%	70.4%	43.3%	56.7%	24.1%	88.1%	92.0%	32.3%
McAllen-Edinburg-Mission, TX	29,644	29.0%	70.7%	18.9%	81.1%	37.1%	62.9%	18.7%	62.0%	66.7%	31.7%
Medford, OR	11,435	24.4%	74.1%	28.3%	71.7%	25.0%	75.0%	17.5%	72.0%	85.2%	20.2%
Memphis, TN-MS-AR	73,849	25.4%	74.5%	9.2%	90.8%	28.8%	71.2%	19.2%	72.5%	70.4%	28.6%
Merced, CA	12,174	25.7%	74.3%	12.6%	87.4%	35.8%	64.2%	24.7%	86.7%	85.4%	54.5%
Meridian, MS micro	4,094	20.9%	79.1%	17.8%	82.2%	54.1%	45.9%	19.6%	52.0%	61.3%	17.0%
Miami-Fort Lauderdale-West Palm Beach, FL	201,208	20.4%	79.4%	13.9%	86.1%	24.0%	76.0%	16.2%	78.2%	82.2%	30.3%
Michigan City-La Porte, IN	4,975	14.2%	85.8%	26.7%	73.3%	36.5%	63.5%	25.3%	87.3%	62.6%	15.0%
Midland, MI	5,400	22.4%	77.6%	8.0%	92.0%	63.5%	36.5%	31.5%	20.4%	92.7%	29.5%
Midland, TX	9,848	34.8%	65.2%	16.0%	84.0%	48.8%	51.2%	28.1%	89.3%	93.9%	38.8%
Milwaukee-Waukesha-West Allis, WI	102,285	26.2%	73.8%	5.0%	95.0%	29.5%	70.5%	20.7%	74.8%	84.5%	44.1%
Minneapolis-St. Paul-Bloomington, MN-WI	199,703	21.8%	78.2%	13.1%	86.9%	44.0%	56.0%	33.7%	90.7%	89.4%	45.9%
Missoula, MT	7,597	31.5%	68.5%	0.0%	100.0%	29.7%	70.3%	18.9%	50.9%	92.3%	36.2%
Mobile, AL	22,343	31.2%	68.8%	11.2%	88.8%	32.6%	67.4%	22.6%	62.1%	70.5%	29.7%
Modesto, CA	22,922	26.8%	73.2%	18.8%	81.2%	31.3%	68.7%	26.4%	66.4%	80.2%	53.9%
Monroe, LA	10,260	32.2%	66.6%	17.2%	82.8%	22.5%	77.5%	19.2%	64.2%	71.1%	48.1%
Monroe, MI	4,165	23.2%	76.8%	30.5%	69.5%	70.8%	29.2%	53.6%	31.8%	92.3%	39.4%
Montgomery, AL	23,527	19.3%	80.7%	7.1%	92.9%	42.9%	57.1%	28.4%	88.9%	75.4%	52.4%
Morgantown, WV	13,476	52.4%	47.6%	16.2%	83.8%	35.2%	64.8%	20.1%	98.9%	87.2%	31.7%
Morristown, TN	5,501	23.6%	76.4%	0.0%	100.0%	48.9%	51.1%	32.9%	26.0%	75.4%	37.8%
Mount Vernon-Anacortes, WA	5,592	30.2%	69.8%	7.2%	92.8%	27.5%	72.5%	20.9%	99.2%	86.9%	39.3%
Muncie, IN	9,687	59.8%	40.2%	7.0%	93.0%	30.4%	69.6%	10.4%	92.2%	94.0%	52.9%
Muskegon, MI	7,791	35.0%	65.0%	33.5%	66.5%	36.5%	63.5%	31.9%	74.3%	83.6%	27.7%
Myrtle Beach-Conway-North Myrtle Beach, SC-NC	15,841	25.4%	74.6%	11.8%	88.2%	34.2%	65.8%	19.4%	75.6%	85.7%	53.4%
Napa, CA	3,682	30.4%	69.6%	5.1%	94.9%	65.8%	34.2%	43.7%	74.0%	92.6%	54.4%
Naples-Immokalee-Marco Island, FL	8,715	22.3%	77.7%	16.4%	83.6%	26.2%	73.8%	16.5%	86.2%	80.6%	55.3%
Nashville-Davidson–Murfreesboro–Franklin, TN	101,430	25.6%	74.3%	16.0%	84.0%	38.4%	61.6%	28.0%	80.0%	82.7%	37.5%
New Bern, NC	9,868	40.7%	59.3%	17.9%	82.1%	20.1%	79.9%	12.1%	70.3%	92.8%	56.1%
New Castle, PA micro	2,807	25.1%	74.9%	3.7%	96.3%	44.1%	55.9%	26.4%	100.0%	71.9%	22.7%
New Haven-Milford, CT	35,307	15.8%	84.1%	17.8%	82.2%	28.4%	71.6%	22.3%	72.6%	80.7%	29.1%
New Orleans-Metairie, LA	66,092	19.7%	80.1%	13.6%	86.4%	29.3%	70.7%	22.5%	77.8%	76.1%	33.4%
New Philadelphia-Dover, OH micro	3,477	21.7%	78.3%	37.3%	62.7%	19.4%	80.6%	22.0%	68.3%	87.4%	44.4%
New York-Newark-Jersey City, NY-NJ-PA	777,288	17.4%	82.3%	8.5%	91.5%	16.4%	83.6%	12.3%	84.3%	88.7%	35.7%
Niles-Benton Harbor, MI	7,430	28.2%	70.5%	5.3%	94.7%	48.1%	51.9%	24.4%	68.1%	82.2%	55.0%
North Port-Sarasota-Bradenton, FL	19,631	22.6%	77.4%	11.9%	88.1%	30.7%	69.3%	22.9%	69.1%	84.1%	41.2%
Norwich-New London, CT	14,861	20.5%	79.5%	9.3%	90.7%	23.6%	76.4%	18.6%	86.1%	85.6%	36.3%
Ocala, FL	10,680	28.3%	71.7%	6.6%	93.4%	30.2%	69.8%	15.3%	65.3%	59.6%	13.8%
Ocean City, NJ	2,714	24.5%	75.5%	17.3%	82.7%	44.1%	55.9%	33.3%	74.8%	86.0%	47.1%
Odessa, TX	10,289	31.3%	68.7%	30.0%	70.0%	44.4%	55.6%	25.5%	92.4%	88.3%	59.5%
Ogden-Clearfield, UT	33,133	28.1%	71.9%	27.9%	72.1%	53.8%	46.2%	43.1%	91.7%	85.2%	31.8%
Ogdensburg-Massena, NY micro	5,033	31.7%	68.3%	13.4%	86.6%	39.7%	60.3%	26.2%	44.0%	68.4%	24.3%
Oklahoma City, OK	90,904	29.9%	69.8%	15.4%	84.6%	37.6%	62.4%	26.0%	80.7%	86.7%	45.8%
Olympia-Tumwater, WA	14,521	29.9%	70.1%	20.1%	79.9%	34.5%	65.5%	27.8%	71.7%	84.4%	41.9%
Omaha-Council Bluffs, NE-IA	67,103	28.1%	71.9%	9.6%	90.4%	40.2%	59.8%	28.2%	83.6%	85.2%	37.0%
Orangeburg, SC micro	4,598	42.3%	57.7%	17.3%	82.7%	25.7%	74.3%	9.4%	50.8%	65.3%	28.2%
Orlando-Kissimmee-Sanford, FL	111,283	27.1%	72.9%	8.4%	91.6%	27.7%	72.3%	18.3%	82.7%	86.0%	33.1%
Oshkosh-Neenah, WI	12,226	40.8%	59.2%	5.1%	94.9%	32.2%	67.8%	19.8%	88.5%	79.8%	27.8%
Ottawa-Peru, IL micro	5,015	34.1%	65.9%	27.1%	72.9%	58.2%	41.8%	35.5%	49.2%	88.0%	26.9%
Owensboro, KY	6,581	30.3%	69.7%	33.0%	67.0%	34.0%	66.0%	32.1%	92.6%	88.0%	56.3%
Oxnard-Thousand Oaks-Ventura, CA	24,809	18.0%	82.0%	16.0%	84.0%	28.8%	71.2%	21.3%	74.5%	81.6%	49.0%
Palm Bay-Melbourne-Titusville, FL	19,751	25.7%	74.3%	18.4%	81.6%	34.8%	65.2%	25.8%	89.7%	94.8%	39.2%
Panama City, FL	8,931	33.1%	66.9%	4.7%	95.3%	27.7%	72.3%	10.5%	81.9%	76.3%	51.0%
Parkersburg-Vienna, WV	5,183	33.8%	66.2%	49.8%	50.2%	41.4%	58.6%	29.0%	63.9%	77.7%	50.2%
Pensacola-Ferry Pass-Brent, FL	26,689	24.8%	74.9%	1.2%	98.8%	25.6%	74.4%	17.5%	84.1%	85.7%	33.6%
Peoria, IL	25,141	30.3%	69.7%	15.5%	84.5%	50.2%	49.8%	35.8%	59.5%	84.7%	42.7%
Philadelphia-Camden-Wilmington, PA-NJ-DE-MD	279,714	19.8%	79.9%	12.5%	87.5%	30.9%	69.1%	23.7%	84.1%	86.9%	38.9%
Phoenix-Mesa-Scottsdale, AZ	235,827	26.9%	73.0%	15.8%	84.2%	33.2%	66.8%	23.8%	74.6%	80.8%	33.9%
Pine Bluff, AR	5,806	42.0%	58.0%	6.9%	93.1%	32.2%	67.8%	21.6%	43.7%	63.6%	27.2%
Pittsburgh, PA	124,937	28.4%	71.5%	10.9%	89.1%	38.8%	61.2%	26.1%	80.7%	87.6%	42.9%
Pittsfield, MA	4,143	28.5%	71.5%	17.6%	82.4%	31.4%	68.6%	24.7%	82.1%	89.7%	50.3%
Pocatello, ID	5,721	32.9%	67.1%	20.4%	79.6%	45.7%	54.3%	30.2%	82.4%	84.7%	29.1%
Port St. Lucie, FL	13,036	22.0%	78.0%	6.6%	93.4%	26.4%	73.6%	20.3%	65.1%	70.7%	29.3%
Portland-South Portland, ME	24,752	18.6%	81.4%	5.2%	94.8%	40.2%	59.8%	28.4%	91.5%	89.3%	37.3%
Portland-Vancouver-Hillsboro, OR-WA	124,564	22.9%	77.1%	6.8%	93.2%	24.4%	75.6%	18.7%	91.7%	92.7%	51.7%

Table K-4: Metropolitan/Micropolitan Statistical Areas—Summary Housing Characteristics—*Continued*

	Millennial Householders	Age of Householders		18 to 24 Years Old		25 to 31 Years Old			Percent with Internet Access		Percent with Mobile Access Plan
		18 to 24	25 to 31	Owners	Renters	Owners	Renters	With Mortgage	18 to 24	25 to 31	
Pottsville, PA micro.......................	5,170	14.3%	85.7%	34.0%	66.0%	47.0%	53.0%	37.0%	35.0%	79.4%	21.7%
Prescott, AZ	7,251	25.9%	72.2%	6.6%	93.4%	21.3%	78.7%	12.8%	77.7%	88.7%	32.9%
Providence-Warwick, RI-MA..........	75,622	25.0%	74.7%	7.8%	92.2%	29.2%	70.8%	22.0%	80.1%	86.9%	38.1%
Provo-Orem, UT............................	39,561	39.2%	60.6%	17.9%	82.1%	44.0%	56.0%	29.4%	88.2%	89.3%	46.2%
Pueblo, CO..................................	9,818	40.1%	59.9%	11.2%	88.8%	35.2%	64.8%	18.8%	88.5%	98.7%	48.5%
Punta Gorda, FL............................	3,260	31.7%	68.3%	15.9%	84.1%	53.4%	46.6%	23.7%	81.4%	78.9%	29.0%
Racine, WI...................................	9,734	22.2%	77.8%	54.3%	45.7%	28.1%	71.9%	33.9%	100.0%	72.6%	32.1%
Raleigh, NC..................................	68,453	25.8%	74.2%	7.4%	92.6%	36.5%	63.5%	26.6%	86.6%	86.6%	50.0%
Rapid City, SD..............................	9,225	26.4%	73.6%	19.1%	80.9%	59.8%	40.2%	38.0%	92.3%	93.6%	52.8%
Reading, PA..................................	17,482	28.9%	70.7%	13.1%	86.9%	48.6%	51.4%	32.7%	73.0%	91.8%	41.8%
Redding, CA.................................	8,533	29.5%	70.5%	17.2%	82.8%	23.7%	76.3%	19.1%	81.8%	75.2%	27.8%
Reno, NV.....................................	25,108	26.5%	73.3%	8.1%	91.9%	29.6%	70.4%	18.7%	82.5%	86.5%	46.6%
Richmond, VA...............................	63,066	25.9%	73.8%	9.2%	90.8%	28.6%	71.4%	22.5%	84.4%	85.5%	39.3%
Riverside-San Bernardino-Ontario, CA	163,415	22.4%	77.5%	15.0%	85.0%	36.7%	63.3%	27.8%	76.9%	80.3%	35.2%
Roanoke, VA.................................	15,269	31.6%	68.4%	4.7%	95.3%	33.2%	66.8%	18.6%	79.0%	87.7%	34.8%
Rochester, MN..............................	14,782	45.2%	54.8%	16.9%	83.1%	70.0%	30.0%	38.1%	87.7%	91.3%	56.1%
Rochester, NY...............................	57,944	24.9%	75.1%	9.0%	91.0%	39.6%	60.4%	27.9%	79.5%	82.5%	37.8%
Rockford, IL	16,095	25.9%	74.1%	5.3%	94.7%	42.1%	57.9%	29.5%	76.1%	85.6%	43.6%
Rocky Mount, NC..........................	5,830	34.9%	57.5%	3.0%	97.0%	32.4%	67.6%	16.0%	79.6%	71.7%	32.0%
Rome, GA.....................................	3,943	44.3%	55.7%	29.6%	70.4%	23.8%	76.2%	18.3%	97.0%	92.1%	56.8%
Roseburg, OR micro	4,720	23.4%	76.6%	0.0%	100.0%	40.1%	59.9%	20.6%	50.2%	69.7%	22.0%
Sacramento–Roseville–Arden-Arcade, CA	108,235	28.3%	71.4%	7.2%	92.8%	28.7%	71.3%	20.5%	84.3%	87.7%	42.1%
Saginaw, MI.................................	9,612	36.9%	63.1%	23.2%	76.8%	53.2%	46.8%	29.1%	80.3%	75.1%	32.4%
Salem, OH micro...........................	5,515	30.6%	69.4%	11.0%	89.0%	41.0%	59.0%	23.1%	50.2%	71.6%	40.2%
Salem, OR....................................	22,551	36.7%	63.3%	1.2%	98.8%	22.1%	77.9%	14.4%	94.2%	87.3%	32.6%
Salinas, CA..................................	16,872	29.5%	70.2%	5.9%	94.1%	24.5%	75.5%	16.8%	75.9%	82.9%	39.1%
Salisbury, MD-DE..........................	14,273	27.9%	72.1%	17.7%	82.3%	43.7%	56.3%	29.9%	84.4%	81.8%	35.5%
Salt Lake City, UT	64,659	25.7%	74.1%	20.7%	79.3%	43.6%	56.4%	34.5%	90.5%	92.0%	38.6%
San Angelo, TX.............................	8,640	31.9%	68.1%	14.9%	85.1%	48.6%	51.4%	34.9%	73.2%	85.4%	34.1%
San Antonio-New Braunfels, TX......	126,280	25.5%	74.4%	7.3%	92.7%	29.3%	70.7%	19.7%	76.1%	83.5%	38.5%
San Diego-Carlsbad, CA.................	178,657	23.7%	76.1%	7.7%	92.3%	19.1%	80.9%	13.9%	93.5%	89.1%	45.4%
San Francisco-Oakland-Hayward, CA	210,801	20.8%	79.1%	5.5%	94.5%	18.1%	81.9%	12.9%	89.5%	93.0%	52.3%
San Jose-Sunnyvale-Santa Clara, CA	80,048	20.0%	79.8%	6.4%	93.6%	19.5%	80.5%	14.1%	92.3%	92.9%	41.6%
San Luis Obispo-Paso Robles-Arroyo Grande, CA	15,904	49.1%	50.9%	4.1%	95.9%	13.2%	86.8%	7.7%	91.4%	90.6%	32.6%
Santa Cruz-Watsonville, CA.............	12,716	44.9%	55.1%	15.8%	84.2%	18.5%	81.5%	10.8%	100.0%	84.9%	49.2%
Santa Fe, NM................................	5,411	28.1%	71.9%	26.7%	73.3%	36.5%	63.5%	29.3%	66.4%	83.3%	33.4%
Santa Maria-Santa Barbara, CA.......	23,552	43.1%	56.7%	4.2%	95.8%	16.9%	83.1%	9.7%	84.5%	73.9%	45.0%
Santa Rosa, CA.............................	20,463	28.2%	71.8%	4.2%	95.8%	17.8%	82.2%	10.6%	83.3%	91.8%	43.0%
Savannah, GA................................	24,183	32.9%	67.1%	6.3%	93.7%	28.2%	71.8%	16.4%	77.9%	81.9%	34.3%
Scranton–Wilkes-Barre–Hazleton, PA	23,356	24.5%	75.5%	9.0%	91.0%	29.6%	70.4%	19.1%	85.2%	83.8%	26.0%
Seattle-Tacoma-Bellevue, WA.........	222,763	23.9%	76.1%	13.1%	86.9%	25.3%	74.7%	19.8%	90.5%	91.1%	50.3%
Sebastian-Vero Beach, FL	4,765	26.1%	73.9%	16.0%	84.0%	31.7%	68.3%	23.0%	76.2%	84.6%	26.4%
Sebring, FL..................................	2,764	41.7%	58.3%	43.1%	56.9%	53.8%	46.2%	21.5%	39.5%	48.7%	7.8%
Sheboygan, WI..............................	6,320	25.2%	74.8%	40.3%	59.7%	37.0%	63.0%	33.4%	89.2%	81.4%	35.9%
Sherman-Denison, TX.....................	6,433	35.8%	64.2%	25.9%	74.1%	55.8%	44.2%	37.4%	80.1%	81.9%	43.1%
Show Low, AZ micro.......................	2,381	23.4%	76.6%	13.1%	86.9%	47.0%	53.0%	16.9%	60.9%	64.5%	33.3%
Shreveport-Bossier City, LA............	30,637	30.6%	69.4%	18.4%	81.6%	34.5%	65.5%	22.4%	67.1%	76.7%	37.7%
Sierra Vista-Douglas, AZ.................	9,162	37.9%	61.6%	11.7%	88.3%	20.4%	79.6%	11.9%	93.5%	89.6%	28.1%
Sioux City, IA-NE-SD.....................	10,745	28.6%	71.2%	11.0%	89.0%	44.5%	55.5%	27.2%	77.2%	88.4%	26.3%
Sioux Falls, SD.............................	18,903	26.2%	73.8%	21.9%	78.1%	45.3%	54.7%	31.0%	93.7%	93.9%	42.1%
South Bend-Mishawaka, IN-MI	18,019	30.4%	69.6%	8.5%	91.5%	40.6%	59.4%	26.6%	72.8%	85.8%	36.2%
Spartanburg, SC............................	16,035	33.9%	66.1%	10.0%	90.0%	44.3%	55.7%	28.7%	74.4%	78.7%	46.8%
Spokane-Spokane Valley, WA..........	37,650	29.4%	70.6%	8.5%	91.5%	33.5%	66.5%	23.5%	85.1%	86.5%	45.1%
Springfield, IL	13,885	27.5%	72.5%	4.9%	95.1%	42.1%	57.9%	27.3%	81.2%	94.3%	41.9%
Springfield, MA.............................	28,568	27.9%	71.9%	11.1%	88.9%	28.7%	71.3%	22.3%	81.7%	89.2%	35.9%
Springfield, MO.............................	37,369	36.7%	63.3%	9.8%	90.2%	48.6%	51.4%	30.3%	79.2%	84.9%	29.8%
Springfield, OH.............................	7,555	36.1%	63.9%	18.5%	81.5%	41.2%	58.8%	28.0%	66.3%	86.8%	39.3%
St. Cloud, MN...............................	13,798	39.5%	60.5%	20.1%	79.9%	63.0%	37.0%	39.2%	89.8%	92.3%	24.8%
St. George, UT	6,991	25.7%	74.3%	33.9%	66.1%	48.0%	52.0%	44.4%	66.1%	99.1%	38.3%
St. Joseph, MO-KS........................	6,109	34.1%	65.9%	28.0%	72.0%	21.1%	78.9%	16.5%	50.3%	92.5%	44.0%
St. Louis, MO-IL............................	162,361	22.6%	77.4%	18.9%	81.1%	43.4%	56.6%	33.4%	79.5%	85.2%	40.6%
State College, PA..........................	14,960	56.4%	43.6%	4.0%	96.0%	29.1%	70.9%	11.7%	95.8%	94.5%	28.4%
Staunton-Waynesboro, VA..............	5,294	26.1%	73.9%	5.4%	94.6%	55.5%	44.5%	37.8%	93.6%	80.6%	30.7%
Stockton-Lodi, CA.........................	28,273	31.2%	68.7%	9.5%	90.5%	33.8%	66.2%	21.2%	66.3%	80.1%	32.9%
Sumter, SC..................................	5,380	33.5%	63.6%	30.0%	70.0%	33.6%	66.4%	23.2%	74.7%	94.3%	28.5%
Sunbury, PA micro.........................	4,178	21.8%	78.2%	26.7%	73.3%	45.1%	54.9%	34.4%	95.3%	72.8%	22.8%
Syracuse, NY................................	31,287	27.9%	72.0%	11.7%	88.3%	41.1%	58.9%	28.7%	74.1%	88.3%	34.0%
Tallahassee, FL.............................	37,382	53.3%	46.5%	5.1%	94.9%	21.1%	78.9%	9.8%	91.5%	86.9%	38.3%
Tampa-St. Petersburg-Clearwater, FL	134,167	27.2%	72.5%	9.7%	90.3%	27.2%	72.8%	17.0%	80.0%	83.5%	26.9%
Terre Haute, IN.............................	10,063	34.9%	65.1%	23.7%	76.3%	30.2%	69.8%	17.4%	63.4%	66.5%	22.9%
Texarkana, TX-AR..........................	8,064	27.7%	72.1%	0.6%	99.4%	35.7%	64.3%	18.3%	31.6%	82.2%	27.6%
The Villages, FL.............................	2,073	29.5%	70.5%	0.0%	100.0%	22.0%	78.0%	10.8%	100.0%	73.2%	8.9%
Toledo, OH..................................	41,686	37.9%	62.1%	10.8%	89.2%	31.9%	68.1%	19.5%	81.1%	81.7%	31.7%

Table K-4: Metropolitan/Micropolitan Statistical Areas—Summary Housing Characteristics—*Continued*

	Millennial Householders	Age of Householders		18 to 24 Years Old		25 to 31 Years Old			Percent with Internet Access		Percent with Mobile Access Plan
		18 to 24	25 to 31	Owners	Renters	Owners	Renters	With Mortgage	18 to 24	25 to 31	
Topeka, KS	12,906	26.8%	72.9%	5.1%	94.9%	49.3%	50.7%	32.3%	85.4%	88.5%	37.8%
Torrington, CT micro	6,065	15.1%	84.9%	8.4%	91.6%	44.8%	55.2%	34.4%	83.6%	88.7%	25.1%
Traverse City, MI micro	5,339	13.9%	86.1%	11.0%	89.0%	60.5%	39.5%	35.2%	56.0%	76.8%	30.6%
Trenton, NJ	13,042	18.5%	81.5%	1.7%	98.3%	20.5%	79.5%	14.8%	85.3%	91.3%	50.5%
Truckee-Grass Valley, CA micro	2,612	9.4%	90.6%	22.0%	78.0%	22.4%	77.6%	16.5%	72.4%	70.5%	30.4%
Tucson, AZ	66,847	40.1%	59.7%	9.6%	90.4%	27.7%	72.3%	15.7%	89.5%	86.7%	43.4%
Tullahoma-Manchester, TN micro ...	4,147	39.8%	60.2%	11.6%	88.4%	29.5%	70.5%	16.4%	74.1%	86.3%	21.2%
Tulsa, OK	60,973	30.9%	68.6%	13.9%	86.1%	38.3%	61.7%	25.2%	70.6%	81.1%	42.1%
Tupelo, MS micro	6,464	15.9%	84.1%	63.6%	36.4%	46.5%	53.5%	37.7%	35.0%	79.2%	44.4%
Tuscaloosa, AL	14,824	39.9%	60.1%	23.2%	76.8%	41.3%	58.7%	24.7%	92.7%	90.5%	56.3%
Tyler, TX	11,513	30.1%	67.9%	22.1%	77.9%	44.6%	55.4%	29.6%	90.3%	90.4%	62.3%
Urban Honolulu, HI	48,839	25.0%	74.9%	3.6%	96.4%	13.0%	87.0%	9.2%	89.9%	92.9%	55.7%
Utica-Rome, NY	13,998	23.1%	76.4%	9.6%	90.4%	35.1%	64.9%	21.5%	82.8%	81.7%	24.3%
Valdosta, GA	13,283	46.9%	53.1%	10.0%	90.0%	41.3%	58.7%	23.5%	77.5%	76.0%	24.1%
Vallejo-Fairfield, CA	19,173	18.9%	81.1%	12.5%	87.5%	30.7%	69.3%	25.9%	98.0%	87.8%	55.1%
Victoria, TX	4,759	24.6%	75.4%	52.4%	47.6%	29.1%	70.9%	28.4%	100.0%	84.4%	38.6%
Vineland-Bridgeton, NJ	7,380	12.5%	87.5%	21.2%	78.8%	35.1%	64.9%	31.7%	81.3%	70.3%	30.0%
Virginia Beach-Norfolk-Newport News, VA-NC	102,757	26.2%	73.6%	8.8%	91.2%	26.2%	73.8%	19.2%	86.1%	87.7%	39.5%
Visalia-Porterville, CA....................	22,574	28.0%	71.8%	17.1%	82.9%	39.6%	60.4%	31.0%	62.7%	69.5%	40.9%
Waco, TX.................................	19,645	41.5%	58.1%	7.8%	92.2%	22.4%	77.6%	13.1%	82.8%	78.6%	20.3%
Walla Walla, WA.........................	3,587	29.8%	70.2%	27.3%	72.7%	62.7%	37.3%	40.4%	77.2%	78.0%	46.5%
Warner Robins, GA	11,641	20.0%	80.0%	3.4%	96.6%	40.6%	59.4%	19.3%	76.6%	75.2%	23.6%
Washington-Arlington-Alexandria, DC-VA-MD-WV	304,954	17.5%	82.3%	10.8%	89.2%	27.8%	72.2%	22.5%	88.1%	91.0%	46.0%
Waterloo-Cedar Falls, IA.................	14,083	45.9%	54.1%	16.5%	83.5%	44.4%	55.6%	27.5%	92.3%	81.0%	52.5%
Watertown-Fort Drum, NY	8,376	39.0%	61.0%	17.9%	82.1%	19.1%	80.9%	15.5%	87.7%	96.0%	49.6%
Wausau, WI.............................	7,645	29.6%	70.4%	7.6%	92.4%	49.2%	50.8%	33.2%	93.4%	76.0%	50.4%
Weirton-Steubenville, WV-OH.........	5,674	41.9%	58.1%	18.6%	81.4%	32.1%	67.9%	23.2%	44.0%	86.0%	20.4%
Wenatchee, WA..........................	6,516	11.1%	87.9%	0.0%	100.0%	20.4%	79.6%	12.9%	30.3%	60.3%	19.0%
Wheeling, WV-OH	6,445	37.4%	62.6%	18.3%	81.7%	30.4%	69.6%	23.1%	44.9%	75.6%	19.3%
Whitewater-Elkhorn, WI micro	5,877	41.4%	58.6%	7.4%	92.6%	40.9%	59.1%	25.3%	96.1%	100.0%	68.4%
Wichita Falls, TX	11,781	31.2%	68.8%	11.6%	88.4%	42.6%	57.4%	26.8%	100.0%	79.1%	36.8%
Wichita, KS	43,403	28.6%	71.2%	8.4%	91.6%	38.0%	62.0%	25.6%	78.0%	87.4%	29.6%
Williamsport, PA	4,620	47.9%	52.1%	24.2%	75.8%	46.3%	53.7%	24.4%	81.6%	80.8%	24.7%
Wilmington, NC..........................	19,114	40.9%	58.7%	5.0%	95.0%	29.6%	70.4%	16.7%	85.5%	87.6%	39.9%
Winchester, VA-WV	4,795	23.7%	76.3%	12.6%	87.4%	42.1%	57.9%	26.1%	51.6%	93.7%	37.3%
Winston-Salem, NC......................	30,306	29.7%	69.4%	12.5%	87.5%	43.7%	56.3%	26.9%	83.7%	80.8%	28.6%
Wooster, OH micro.......................	5,992	20.7%	79.3%	10.9%	89.1%	37.1%	62.9%	25.8%	51.4%	75.1%	42.8%
Worcester, MA-CT........................	37,962	23.8%	76.2%	8.3%	91.7%	29.5%	70.5%	22.6%	74.8%	88.4%	27.8%
Yakima, WA..............................	10,592	26.2%	73.3%	29.4%	70.6%	34.8%	65.2%	26.1%	74.4%	64.9%	33.7%
York-Hanover, PA........................	16,487	19.3%	80.7%	17.3%	82.7%	55.5%	44.5%	45.3%	67.5%	77.9%	36.7%
Youngstown-Warren-Boardman, OH-PA....................................	27,057	25.0%	75.0%	12.4%	87.6%	40.9%	59.1%	27.5%	70.3%	77.1%	24.6%
Yuba City, CA	8,413	38.0%	61.7%	12.7%	87.3%	33.6%	66.4%	22.7%	77.9%	81.8%	41.3%
Yuma, AZ	10,594	27.9%	72.1%	32.1%	67.9%	43.9%	56.1%	31.4%	63.5%	85.4%	35.2%

APPENDIXES

Metropolitan and Micropolitan Areas and Components (as defined February 2013)

Metropolitan and Micropolitan Area Code	State/County FIPS code	Title and Geographic Components
10180		Abilene, TX Metro area
	48059	Callahan County, TX
	48253	Jones County, TX
	48441	Taylor County, TX
10300		Adrian, MI Micro area
	26091	Lenawee County, MI
10420		Akron, OH Metro area
	39133	Portage County, OH
	39153	Summit County, OH
10500		Albany, GA Metro area
	13007	Baker County, GA
	13095	Dougherty County, GA
	13177	Lee County, GA
	13273	Terrell County, GA
	13321	Worth County, GA
10580		Albany-Schenectady-Troy, NY Metro area
	36001	Albany County, NY
	36083	Rensselaer County, NY
	36091	Saratoga County, NY
	36093	Schenectady County, NY
	36095	Schoharie County, NY
10700		Albertville, AL Micro area
	01095	Marshall County, AL
10740		Albuquerque, NM Metro area
	35001	Bernalillo County, NM
	35043	Sandoval County, NM
	35057	Torrance County, NM
	35061	Valencia County, NM
10780		Alexandria, LA Metro area
	22043	Grant Parish, LA
	22079	Rapides Parish, LA
10900		Allentown-Bethlehem-Easton, PA-NJ Metro area
	34041	Warren County, NJ
	42025	Carbon County, PA
	42077	Lehigh County, PA
	42095	Northampton County, PA
11020		Altoona, PA Metro area
	42013	Blair County, PA
11100		Amarillo, TX Metro area
	48011	Armstrong County, TX
	48065	Carson County, TX
	48359	Oldham County, TX
	48375	Potter County, TX
	48381	Randall County, TX
11180		Ames, IA Metro area
	19169	Story County, IA
11260		Anchorage, AK Metro area
	02020	Anchorage Municipality, AK
	02170	Matanuska-Susitna Borough, AK
11460		Ann Arbor, MI Metro area
	26161	Washtenaw County, MI
11500		Anniston-Oxford-Jacksonville, AL Metro area
	01015	Calhoun County, AL
11540		Appleton, WI Metro area
	55015	Calumet County, WI
	55087	Outagamie County, WI
11700		Asheville, NC Metro area
	37021	Buncombe County, NC
	37087	Haywood County, NC
	37089	Henderson County, NC
	37115	Madison County, NC
11780		Astabula, OH Micro area
	39007	Astabula County, OH
12020		Athens-Clarke County, GA Metro area
	13059	Clarke County, GA
	13195	Madison County, GA
	13219	Oconee County, GA
	13221	Oglethorpe County, GA
12060		Atlanta-Sandy Springs-Roswell, GA Metro area
	13013	Barrow County, GA
	13015	Bartow County, GA
	13035	Butts County, GA
	13045	Carroll County, GA
	13057	Cherokee County, GA
	13063	Clayton County, GA
	13067	Cobb County, GA
	13077	Coweta County, GA
	13085	Dawson County, GA
	13089	DeKalb County, GA
	13097	Douglas County, GA
	13113	Fayette County, GA
	13117	Forsyth County, GA
	13121	Fulton County, GA
	13135	Gwinnett County, GA
	13143	Haralson County, GA
	13149	Heard County, GA
	13151	Henry County, GA
	13159	Jasper County, GA
	13171	Lamar County, GA
	13199	Meriwether County, GA
	13211	Morgan County, GA
	13217	Newton County, GA
	13223	Paulding County, GA
	13227	Pickens County, GA
	13231	Pike County, GA
	13247	Rockdale County, GA
	13255	Spalding County, GA
	13297	Walton County, GA
12100		Atlantic City-Hammonton, NJ Metro area
	34001	Atlantic County, NJ
12220		Auburn-Opelika, AL Metro area
	01081	Lee County, AL
12260		Augusta-Richmond County, GA-SC Metro area
	13033	Burke County, GA
	13073	Columbia County, GA
	13181	Lincoln County, GA
	13189	McDuffie County, GA
	13245	Richmond County, GA
	45003	Aiken County, SC
	45037	Edgefield County, SC
12300		Augusta-Waterville, ME Micro area
	23011	Kennebec County, ME
12420		Austin-Round Rock, TX Metro area
	48021	Bastrop County, TX
	48055	Caldwell County, TX
	48209	Hays County, TX
	48453	Travis County, TX
	48491	Williamson County, TX
12540		Bakersfield, CA Metro area
	06029	Kern County, CA
12580		Baltimore-Columbia-Towson, MD Metro area
	24003	Anne Arundel County, MD
	24005	Baltimore County, MD
	24013	Carroll County, MD
	24025	Harford County, MD
	24027	Howard County, MD
	24035	Queen Anne's County, MD
	24510	Baltimore city, MD
12620		Bangor, ME Metro area
	23019	Penobscot County, ME
12700		Barnstable Town, MA Metro area
	25001	Barnstable County, MA
12940		Baton Rouge, LA Metro area
	22005	Ascension Parish, LA
	22033	East Baton Rouge Parish, LA
	22037	East Feliciana Parish, LA
	22047	Iberville Parish, LA
	22063	Livingston Parish, LA
	22077	Pointe Coupee Parish, LA
	22091	St. Helena Parish, LA
	22121	West Baton Rouge Parish, LA
	22125	West Feliciana Parish, LA
12980		Battle Creek, MI Metro area
	26025	Calhoun County, MI
13020		Bay City, MI Metro area
	26017	Bay County, MI
13140		Beaumont-Port Arthur, TX Metro area
	48199	Hardin County, TX
	48245	Jefferson County, TX
	48351	Newton County, TX
	48361	Orange County, TX
13220		Beckley, WV Metro area
	54019	Fayette County, WV
	54081	Raleigh County, WV
13380		Bellingham, WA Metro area
	53073	Whatcom County, WA
13460		Bend-Redmond, OR Metro area

381

Metropolitan and Micropolitan Areas and Components (as defined February 2013)		
Metropolitan and Micropolitan Area Code	State/County FIPS code	Title and Geographic Components
	41017	Deschutes County, OR
13740		Billings, MT Metro area
	30009	Carbon County, MT
	30037	Golden Valley County, MT
	30111	Yellowstone County, MT
13780		Binghamton, NY Metro area
	36007	Broome County, NY
	36107	Tioga County, NY
13820		Birmingham-Hoover, AL Metro area
	01007	Bibb County, AL
	01009	Blount County, AL
	01021	Chilton County, AL
	01073	Jefferson County, AL
	01115	St. Clair County, AL
	01117	Shelby County, AL
	01127	Walker County, AL
13900		Bismarck, ND Metro area
	38015	Burleigh County, ND
	38059	Morton County, ND
	38065	Oliver County, ND
	38085	Sioux County, ND
13980		Blacksburg-Christiansburg-Radford, VA Metro area
	51063	Floyd County, VA
	51071	Giles County, VA
	51121	Montgomery County, VA
	51155	Pulaski County, VA
	51750	Radford city, VA
14010		Bloomington, IL Metro area
	17039	De Witt County, IL
	17113	McLean County, IL
14020		Bloomington, IN Metro area
	18105	Monroe County, IN
	18119	Owen County, IN
14100		Bloomsburg-Berwick, PA Metro area
	42037	Columbia County, PA
	42093	Montour County, PA
14260		Boise City, ID Metro area
	16001	Ada County, ID
	16015	Boise County, ID
	16027	Canyon County, ID
	16045	Gem County, ID
	16073	Owyhee County, ID
14460		Boston-Cambridge Newton, MA-NH Metro area
14460		Boston, MA Metro Div 14454
	25021	Norfolk County, MA
	25023	Plymouth County, MA
	25025	Suffolk County, MA
14460		Cambridge-Newton-Framingham, MA Metro Div 15764
	25009	Essex County, MA
	25017	Middlesex County, MA
14460		Rockingham County-Strafford County-NH Metro Div 40484
	33015	Rockingham County, NH
	33017	Strafford County, NH
14500		Boulder, CO Metro area
	08013	Boulder County, CO
14540		Bowling Green, KY Metro area
	21003	Allen County, KY
	21031	Butler County, KY
	21061	Edmonson County, KY
	21227	Warren County, KY
14740		Bremerton-Silverdale, WA Metro area
	53035	Kitsap County, WA
14860		Bridgeport-Stamford-Norwalk, CT Metro area
	09001	Fairfield County, CT
15180		Brownsville-Harlingen, TX Metro area
	48061	Cameron County, TX
15260		Brunswick, GA Metro area
	13025	Brantley County, GA
	13127	Glynn County, GA
	13191	McIntosh County, GA
15380		Buffalo-Cheektowaga-Niagara Falls, NY Metro area
	36029	Erie County, NY
	36063	Niagara County, NY
15500		Burlington, NC Metro area
	37001	Alamance County, NC
15540		Burlington-South Burlington, VT Metro area
	50007	Chittenden County, VT
	50011	Franklin County, VT
	50013	Grand Isle County, VT
15680		California-Lexington Park, MD Metro area
	24037	St. Mary's County, MD
15940		Canton-Massillon, OH Metro area
	39019	Carroll County, OH
	39151	Stark County, OH
15980		Cape Coral-Fort Myers, FL Metro area
	12071	Lee County, FL

Metropolitan and Micropolitan Areas and Components (as defined February 2013)		
Metropolitan and Micropolitan Area Code	State/County FIPS code	Title and Geographic Components
16020		Cape Girardeau, MO-IL Metro area
	17003	Alexander County, IL
	29017	Bollinger County, MO
	29031	Cape Girardeau County, MO
16060		Carbondale-Marion, IL Metro area
	17077	Jackson County, IL
	17199	Williamson County, IL
16180		Carson City, NV Metro area
	32510	Carson City, NV
16220		Casper, WY Metro area
	56025	Natrona County, WY
16300		Cedar Rapids, IA Metro area
	19011	Benton County, IA
	19105	Jones County, IA
	19113	Linn County, IA
16540		Chambersburg-Waynesboro, PA Metro area
	42055	Franklin County, PA
16580		Champaign-Urbana, IL Metro area
	17019	Champaign County, IL
	17053	Ford County, IL
	17147	Piatt County, IL
16620		Charleston, WV Metro area
	54005	Boone County, WV
	54015	Clay County, WV
	54039	Kanawha County, WV
16700		Charleston-North Charleston, SC Metro area
	45015	Berkeley County, SC
	45019	Charleston County, SC
	45035	Dorchester County, SC
16740		Charlotte-Concord-Gastonia, NC-SC Metro area
	37025	Cabarrus County, NC
	37071	Gaston County, NC
	37097	Iredell County, NC
	37109	Lincoln County, NC
	37119	Mecklenburg County, NC
	37159	Rowan County, NC
	37179	Union County, NC
	45023	Chester County, SC
	45057	Lancaster County, SC
	45091	York County, SC
16820		Charlottesville, VA Metro area
	51003	Albemarle County, VA
	51029	Buckingham County, VA
	51065	Fluvanna County, VA
	51079	Greene County, VA
	51125	Nelson County, VA
	51540	Charlottesville city, VA
16860		Chattanooga, TN-GA Metro area
	13047	Catoosa County, GA
	13083	Dade County, GA
	13295	Walker County, GA
	47065	Hamilton County, TN
	47115	Marion County, TN
	47153	Sequatchie County, TN
16940		Cheyenne, WY Metro area
	56021	Laramie County, WY
16980		Chicago-Naperville-Elgin, IL-IN-WI Metro area
16980		Chicago-Naperville-Arlington Heights, IL Metro Div 16974
	17031	Cook County, IL
	17043	DuPage County, IL
	17063	Grundy County, IL
	17093	Kendall County, IL
	17111	McHenry County, IL
	17197	Will County, IL
16980		Gary, IN Metro Div 23844
	18073	Jasper County, IN
	18089	Lake County, IN
	18111	Newton County, IN
	18127	Porter County, IN
16980		Lake County-Kenosha County, IL-WI Metro Div 29404
	17097	Lake County, IL
	55059	Kenosha County, WI
17020		Chico, CA Metro area
	06007	Butte County, CA
17140		Cincinnati, OH-KY-IN Metro area
	18029	Dearborn County, IN
	18115	Ohio County, IN
	18161	Union County, IN
	21015	Boone County, KY
	21023	Bracken County, KY
	21037	Campbell County, KY
	21077	Gallatin County, KY
	21081	Grant County, KY
	21117	Kenton County, KY
	21191	Pendleton County, KY
	39015	Brown County, OH

Metropolitan and Micropolitan Area Code	State/County FIPS code	Title and Geographic Components
		Metropolitan and Micropolitan Areas and Components (as defined February 2013)
	39017	Butler County, OH
	39025	Clermont County, OH
	39061	Hamilton County, OH
	39165	Warren County, OH
17220		Clarksburg, WV Micro area
	54017	Doddridge County, WV
	54033	Harrison County, WV
	54091	Taylor County, WV
17300		Clarksville, TN-KY Metro area
	21047	Christian County, KY
	21221	Trigg County, KY
	47125	Montgomery County, TN
17420		Cleveland, TN Metro area
	47011	Bradley County, TN
	47139	Polk County, TN
17460		Cleveland-Elyria, OH Metro area
	39035	Cuyahoga County, OH
	39055	Geauga County, OH
	39085	Lake County, OH
	39093	Lorain County, OH
	39103	Medina County, OH
17660		Coeur d'Alene, ID Metro area
	16055	Kootenai County, ID
17780		College Station-Bryan, TX Metro area
	48041	Brazos County, TX
	48051	Burleson County, TX
	48395	Robertson County, TX
17820		Colorado Springs, CO Metro area
	08041	El Paso County, CO
	08119	Teller County, CO
17860		Columbia, MO Metro area
	29019	Boone County, MO
17900		Columbia, SC Metro area
	45017	Calhoun County, SC
	45039	Fairfield County, SC
	45055	Kershaw County, SC
	45063	Lexington County, SC
	45079	Richland County, SC
	45081	Saluda County, SC
17980		Columbus, GA-AL Metro area
	01113	Russell County, AL
	13053	Chattahoochee County, GA
	13145	Harris County, GA
	13197	Marion County, GA
	13215	Muscogee County, GA
18020		Columbus, IN Metro area
	18005	Bartholomew County, IN
18140		Columbus, OH Metro area
	39041	Delaware County, OH
	39045	Fairfield County, OH
	39049	Franklin County, OH
	39073	Hocking County, OH
	39089	Licking County, OH
	39097	Madison County, OH
	39117	Morrow County, OH
	39127	Perry County, OH
	39129	Pickaway County, OH
	39159	Union County, OH
18180		Concord, NH Micro area
	33013	Merrimack County, NH
18260		Cookeville, TN Micro area
	47087	Jackson County, TN
	47133	Overton County, TN
	47141	Putnam County, TN
18580		Corpus Christi, TX Metro area
	48007	Aransas County, TX
	48355	Nueces County, TX
	48409	San Patricio County, TX
18700		Corvallis, OR Metro area
	41003	Benton County, OR
18880		Crestview-Fort Walton Beach-Destin, FL Metro area
	12091	Okaloosa County, FL
	12131	Walton County, FL
19060		Cumberland, MD-WV Metro area
	24001	Allegany County, MD
	54057	Mineral County, WV
19100		Dallas-Fort Worth-Arlington, TX Metro area
19100		Dallas-Plano-Irving, TX Metro Div 19124
	48085	Collin County, TX
	48113	Dallas County, TX
	48121	Denton County, TX
	48139	Ellis County, TX
	48231	Hunt County, TX
	48257	Kaufman County, TX
	48397	Rockwall County, TX
19100		Fort Worth-Arlington, TX Metro Div 23104
	48221	Hood County, TX

Metropolitan and Micropolitan Area Code	State/County FIPS code	Title and Geographic Components
		Metropolitan and Micropolitan Areas and Components (as defined February 2013)
	48251	Johnson County, TX
	48367	Parker County, TX
	48425	Somervell County, TX
	48439	Tarrant County, TX
	48497	Wise County, TX
19140		Dalton, GA Metro area
	13213	Murray County, GA
	13313	Whitfield County, GA
19180		Danville, IL Metro area
	17183	Vermilion County, IL
19260		Danville, VA Micro area
	51143	Pittsylvania County, VA
	51590	Danville city, VA
19300		Daphne-Fairhope-Foley, AL Metro area
	01003	Baldwin County, AL
19340		Davenport-Moline-Rock Island, IA-IL Metro area
	17073	Henry County, IL
	17131	Mercer County, IL
	17161	Rock Island County, IL
	19163	Scott County, IA
19380		Dayton, OH Metro area
	39057	Greene County, OH
	39109	Miami County, OH
	39113	Montgomery County, OH
19460		Decatur, AL Metro area
	01079	Lawrence County, AL
	01103	Morgan County, AL
19500		Decatur, IL Metro area
	17115	Macon County, IL
19660		Deltona-Daytona Beach-Ormond Beach, FL Metro area
	12035	Flagler County, FL
	12127	Volusia County, FL
19740		Denver-Aurora-Lakewood, CO Metro area
	08001	Adams County, CO
	08005	Arapahoe County, CO
	08014	Broomfield County, CO
	08019	Clear Creek County, CO
	08031	Denver County, CO
	08035	Douglas County, CO
	08039	Elbert County, CO
	08047	Gilpin County, CO
	08059	Jefferson County, CO
	08093	Park County, CO
19780		Des Moines-West Des Moines, IA Metro area
	19049	Dallas County, IA
	19077	Guthrie County, IA
	19121	Madison County, IA
	19153	Polk County, IA
	19181	Warren County, IA
19820		Detroit-Warren-Dearborn, MI Metro area
19820		Detroit-Dearborn-Livonia, MI Metro Div 19804
	26163	Wayne County, MI
19820		Warren-Troy-Farmington Hills, MI Metro Div 47664
	26087	Lapeer County, MI
	26093	Livingston County, MI
	26099	Macomb County, MI
	26125	Oakland County, MI
	26147	St. Clair County, MI
20020		Dothan, AL Metro area
	01061	Geneva County, AL
	01067	Henry County, AL
	01069	Houston County, AL
20100		Dover, DE Metro area
	10001	Kent County, Delaware
20220		Dubuque, IA Metro area
	19061	Dubuque County, IA
20260		Duluth, MN-WI Metro area
	27017	Carlton County, MN
	27137	St. Louis County, MN
	55031	Douglas County, WI
20380		Dunn, NC Micro area
	37085	Harnett County, NC
20500		Durham-Chapel Hill, NC Metro area
	37037	Chatham County, NC
	37063	Durham County, NC
	37135	Orange County, NC
	37145	Person County, NC
20700		East Stroudsburg, PA Metro area
	42089	Monroe County, PA
20740		Eau Claire, WI Metro area
	55017	Chippewa County, WI
	55035	Eau Claire County, WI
20940		El Centro, CA Metro area
	06025	Imperial County, CA
21340		El Paso, TX Metro area
	48141	El Paso County, TX
	48229	Hudspeth County, TX

Metropolitan and Micropolitan Area Code	State/County FIPS code	Title and Geographic Components
21060		Elizabethtown-Fort Knox, KY Metro area
	21093	Hardin County, KY
	21123	Larue County, KY
	21163	Meade County, KY
21140		Elkhart-Goshen, IN Metro area
	18039	Elkhart County, IN
21300		Elmira, NY Metro area
	36015	Chemung County, NY
21500		Erie, PA Metro area
	42049	Erie County, PA
21660		Eugene, OR Metro area
	41039	Lane County, OR
21700		Eureka-Arcata-Fortuna, CA Micro area
	06023	Humboldt County, CA
21780		Evansville, IN-KY Metro area
	18129	Posey County, IN
	18163	Vanderburgh County, IN
	18173	Warrick County, IN
	21101	Henderson County, KY
21820		Fairbanks, AK Metro area
	02090	Fairbanks North Star Borough, AK
22020		Fargo, ND-MN Metro area
	27027	Clay County, MN
	38017	Cass County, ND
22140		Farmington, NM Metro area
	35045	San Juan County, NM
22180		Fayetteville, NC Metro area
	37051	Cumberland County, NC
	37093	Hoke County, NC
22220		Fayetteville-Springdale-Rogers, AR-MO Metro area
	05007	Benton County, AR
	05087	Madison County, AR
	05143	Washington County, AR
	29119	McDonald County, MO
22380		Flagstaff, AZ Metro area
	04005	Coconino County, AZ
22420		Flint, MI Metro area
	26049	Genesee County, MI
22500		Florence, SC Metro area
	45031	Darlington County, SC
	45041	Florence County, SC
22520		Florence-Muscle Shoals, AL Metro area
	01033	Colbert County, AL
	01077	Lauderdale County, AL
22540		Fond du Lac, WI Metro area
	55039	Fond du Lac County, WI
22660		Fort Collins, CO Metro area
	08069	Larimer County, CO
22900		Fort Smith, AR-OK Metro area
	05033	Crawford County, AR
	05131	Sebastian County, AR
	40079	Le Flore County, OK
	40135	Sequoyah County, OK
23060		Fort Wayne, IN Metro area
	18003	Allen County, IN
	18179	Wells County, IN
	18183	Whitley County, IN
23420		Fresno, CA Metro area
	06019	Fresno County, CA
23460		Gadsden, AL Metro area
	01055	Etowah County, AL
23540		Gainesville, FL Metro area
	12001	Alachua County, FL
	12041	Gilchrist County, FL
23580		Gainesville, GA Metro area
	13139	Hall County, GA
		Gettysburg, PA Metro area
	42001	Adams County, PA
24020		Glens Falls, NY Metro area
	36113	Warren County, NY
	36115	Washington County, NY
24140		Goldsboro, NC Metro area
	37191	Wayne County, NC
24220		Grand Forks, ND-MN Metro area
	27119	Polk County, MN
	38035	Grand Forks County, ND
24260		Grand Island, NE Metro area
	31079	Hall County, NE
	31081	Hamilton County, NE
	31093	Howard County, NE
	31121	Merrick County, NE
24300		Grand Junction, CO Metro area
	08077	Mesa County, CO
24340		Grand Rapids-Wyoming, MI Metro area
	26015	Barry County, MI
	26081	Kent County, MI

Metropolitan and Micropolitan Area Code	State/County FIPS code	Title and Geographic Components
	26117	Montcalm County, MI
	26139	Ottawa County, MI
24420		Grants Pass, OR Metro area
	41033	Josephine County, OR
24500		Great Falls, MT Metro area
	30013	Cascade County, MT
24540		Greeley, CO Metro area
	08123	Weld County, CO
24580		Green Bay, WI Metro area
	55009	Brown County, WI
	55061	Kewaunee County, WI
	55083	Oconto County, WI
24660		Greensboro-High Point, NC Metro area
	37081	Guilford County, NC
	37151	Randolph County, NC
	37157	Rockingham County, NC
24780		Greenville, NC Metro area
	37147	Pitt County, NC
24860		Greenville-Anderson-Mauldin, SC Metro area
	45007	Anderson County, SC
	45045	Greenville County, SC
	45059	Laurens County, SC
	45077	Pickens County, SC
29940		Greenwood, SC Micro area
	45001	Abeville County, SC
	45045	Greenwood County, SC
25060		Gulfport-Biloxi-Pascagoula, MS Metro area
	28045	Hancock County, MS
	28047	Harrison County, MS
	28059	Jackson County, MS
25180		Hagerstown-Martinsburg, MD-WV Metro area
	24043	Washington County, MD
	54003	Berkeley County, WV
25220		Hammond, LA Metro area
	22105	Tangipahoa Parish, LA
25260		Hanford-Corcoran, CA Metro area
	06031	Kings County, CA
25420		Harrisburg-Carlisle, PA Metro area
	42041	Cumberland County, PA
	42043	Dauphin County, PA
	42099	Perry County, PA
25500		Harrisonburg, VA Metro area
	51165	Rockingham County, VA
	51660	Harrisonburg city, VA
25540		Hartford-West Hartford-East Hartford, CT Metro area
	09003	Hartford County, CT
	09007	Middlesex County, CT
	09013	Tolland County, CT
25620		Hattiesburg, MS Metro area
	28035	Forrest County, MS
	28073	Lamar County, MS
	28111	Perry County, MS
25860		Hickory-Lenoir-Morganton, NC Metro area
	37003	Alexander County, NC
	37023	Burke County, NC
	37027	Caldwell County, NC
	37035	Catawba County, NC
25900		Hilo, HI Micro area
	15001	Hawaii County, HI
25940		Hilton Head Island-Bluffton-Beaufort, SC Metro area
	45013	Beaufort County, SC
	45053	Jasper County, SC
25980		Hinesville, GA Metro area
	13179	Liberty County, GA
	13183	Long County, GA
26090		Holland, MI Micro area
	26005	Allegan County, MI
26140		Homosassa Springs, FL Metro area
	12017	Citrus County, FL
26300		Hot Springs, AR Metro area
	05051	Garland County, AR
26380		Houma-Thibodaux, LA Metro area
	22057	Lafourche Parish, LA
	22109	Terrebonne Parish, LA
26420		Houston-The Woodlands-Sugar Land, TX Metro area
	48015	Austin County, TX
	48039	Brazoria County, TX
	48071	Chambers County, TX
	48157	Fort Bend County, TX
	48167	Galveston County, TX
	48201	Harris County, TX
	48291	Liberty County, TX
	48339	Montgomery County, TX
	48473	Waller County, TX
26580		Huntington-Ashland, WV-KY-OH Metro area
	21019	Boyd County, KY

Metropolitan and Micropolitan Area Code	State/County FIPS code	Title and Geographic Components
	21089	Greenup County, KY
	39087	Lawrence County, OH
	54011	Cabell County, WV
	54043	Lincoln County, WV
	54079	Putnam County, WV
	54099	Wayne County, WV
26620		Huntsville, AL Metro area
	01083	Limestone County, AL
	01089	Madison County, AL
26820		Idaho Falls, ID Metro area
	16019	Bonneville County, ID
	16023	Butte County, ID
	16051	Jefferson County, ID
26900		Indianapolis-Carmel-Anderson, IN Metro area
	18011	Boone County, IN
	18013	Brown County, IN
	18057	Hamilton County, IN
	18059	Hancock County, IN
	18063	Hendricks County, IN
	18081	Johnson County, IN
	18095	Madison County, IN
	18097	Marion County, IN
	18109	Morgan County, IN
	18133	Putnam County, IN
	18145	Shelby County, IN
26980		Iowa City, IA Metro area
	19103	Johnson County, IA
	19183	Washington County, IA
27060		Ithaca, NY Metro area
	36109	Tompkins County, NY
27100		Jackson, MI Metro area
	26075	Jackson County, MI
27140		Jackson, MS Metro area
	28029	Copiah County, MS
	28049	Hinds County, MS
	28089	Madison County, MS
	28121	Rankin County, MS
	28127	Simpson County, MS
	28163	Yazoo County, MS
27180		Jackson, TN Metro area
	47023	Chester County, TN
	47033	Crockett County, TN
	47113	Madison County, TN
27260		Jacksonville, FL Metro area
	12003	Baker County, FL
	12019	Clay County, FL
	12031	Duval County, FL
	12089	Nassau County, FL
	12109	St. Johns County, FL
27340		Jacksonville, NC Metro area
	37133	Onslow County, NC
27460		Jamestown-Dunkirk-Fredonia, NY Micro area
	36013	Chautauqua County, NY
27500		Janesville-Beloit, WI Metro area
	55105	Rock County, WI
27620		Jefferson City, MO Metro area
	29027	Callaway County, MO
	29051	Cole County, MO
	29135	Moniteau County, MO
	29151	Osage County, MO
27740		Johnson City, TN Metro area
	47019	Carter County, TN
	47171	Unicoi County, TN
	47179	Washington County, TN
27780		Johnstown, PA Metro area
	42021	Cambria County, PA
27860		Jonesboro, AR Metro area
	05031	Craighead County, AR
	05111	Poinsett County, AR
27900		Joplin, MO Metro area
	29097	Jasper County, MO
	29145	Newton County, MO
27980		Kahului-Wailuku-Lahaina, HI Metro area
	15005	Kalawao County, HI
	15009	Maui County, HI
28020		Kalamazoo-Portage, MI Metro area
	26077	Kalamazoo County, MI
	26159	Van Buren County, MI
28060		Kalispell, MT Micro area
	30029	Flathead County, MT
28100		Kankakee, IL Metro area
	17091	Kankakee County, IL
28140		Kansas City, MO-KS Metro area
	20091	Johnson County, KS
	20103	Leavenworth County, KS
	20107	Linn County, KS
	20121	Miami County, KS
	20209	Wyandotte County, KS
	29013	Bates County, MO
	29025	Caldwell County, MO
	29037	Cass County, MO
	29047	Clay County, MO
	29049	Clinton County, MO
	29095	Jackson County, MO
	29107	Lafayette County, MO
	29165	Platte County, MO
	29177	Ray County, MO
28420		Kennewick-Richland, WA Metro area
	53005	Benton County, WA
	53021	Franklin County, WA
28660		Killeen-Temple, TX Metro area
	48027	Bell County, TX
	48099	Coryell County, TX
	48281	Lampasas County, TX
28700		Kingsport-Bristol-Bristol, TN-VA Metro area
	47073	Hawkins County, TN
	47163	Sullivan County, TN
	51169	Scott County, VA
	51191	Washington County, VA
	51520	Bristol city, VA
28740		Kingston, NY Metro area
	36111	Ulster County, NY
28940		Knoxville, TN Metro area
	47001	Anderson County, TN
	47009	Blount County, TN
	47013	Campbell County, TN
	47057	Grainger County, TN
	47093	Knox County, TN
	47105	Loudon County, TN
	47129	Morgan County, TN
	47145	Roane County, TN
	47173	Union County, TN
29020		Kokomo, IN Metro area
	18067	Howard County, IN
29100		La Crosse-Onalaska, WI-MN Metro area
	27055	Houston County, MN
	55063	La Crosse County, WI
29180		Lafayette, LA Metro area
	22001	Acadia Parish, LA
	22045	Iberia Parish, LA
	22055	Lafayette Parish, LA
	22099	St. Martin Parish, LA
	22113	Vermilion Parish, LA
29200		Lafayette-West Lafayette, IN Metro area
	18007	Benton County, IN
	18015	Carroll County, IN
	18157	Tippecanoe County, IN
29340		Lake Charles, LA Metro area
	22019	Calcasieu Parish, LA
	22023	Cameron Parish, LA
29420		Lake Havasu City-Kingman, AZ Metro area
	04015	Mohave County, AZ
29460		Lakeland-Winter Haven, FL Metro area
	12105	Polk County, FL
29540		Lancaster, PA Metro area
	42071	Lancaster County, PA
29620		Lansing-East Lansing, MI Metro area
	26037	Clinton County, MI
	26045	Eaton County, MI
	26065	Ingham County, MI
29700		Laredo, TX Metro area
	48479	Webb County, TX
29740		Las Cruces, NM Metro area
	35013	Doña Ana County, NM
29820		Las Vegas-Henderson-Paradise, NV Metro area
	32003	Clark County, NV
29940		Lawrence, KS Metro area
	20045	Douglas County, KS
30020		Lawton, OK Metro area
	40031	Comanche County, OK
	40033	Cotton County, OK
30060		Lebanon, MO Micro area
	29105	Laclede County, MO
30340		Lewiston-Auburn, ME Metro area
	23001	Androscoggin County, ME
30300		Lewiston, ID-WA Metro area
	16069	Nez Perce County, ID
	53003	Asotin County, WA
30460		Lexington-Fayette, KY Metro area
	21017	Bourbon County, KY
	21049	Clark County, KY
	21067	Fayette County, KY

Metropolitan and Micropolitan Areas and Components (as defined February 2013)

Metropolitan and Micropolitan Areas and Components (as defined February 2013)

Metropolitan and Micropolitan Area Code	State/County FIPS code	Title and Geographic Components
	21113	Jessamine County, KY
	21209	Scott County, KY
	21239	Woodford County, KY
30620		Lima, OH Metro area
	39003	Allen County, OH
30660		Lincoln, IL Micro area
	17107	Logan County, IL
30780		Little Rock-North Little Rock-Conway, AR Metro area
	05045	Faulkner County, AR
	05053	Grant County, AR
	05085	Lonoke County, AR
	05105	Perry County, AR
	05119	Pulaski County, AR
	05125	Saline County, AR
30860		Logan, UT-ID Metro area
	16041	Franklin County, ID
	49005	Cache County, UT
30980		Longview, TX Metro area
	48183	Gregg County, TX
	48401	Rusk County, TX
	48459	Upshur County, TX
31020		Longview, WA Metro area
	53015	Cowlitz County, WA
31080		Los Angeles-Long Beach-Anaheim, CA Metro area
31080		Anaheim-Santa Ana-Irvine, CA Metro Div 11244
	06059	Orange County, CA
31080		Los Angeles-Long Beach-Glendale, CA Metro Div 31084
	06037	Los Angeles County, CA
31140		Louisville/Jefferson County, KY-IN Metro area
	18019	Clark County, IN
	18043	Floyd County, IN
	18061	Harrison County, IN
	18143	Scott County, IN
	18175	Washington County, IN
	21029	Bullitt County, KY
	21103	Henry County, KY
	21111	Jefferson County, KY
	21185	Oldham County, KY
	21211	Shelby County, KY
	21215	Spencer County, KY
	21223	Trimble County, KY
31180		Lubbock, TX Metro area
	48107	Crosby County, TX
	48303	Lubbock County, TX
	48305	Lynn County, TX
31300		Lumberton, NC Micro area
	37155	Robeson County, NC
31340		Lynchburg, VA Metro area
	51009	Amherst County, VA
	51011	Appomattox County, VA
	51019	Bedford County, VA
	51031	Campbell County, VA
	51515	Bedford city, VA
	51680	Lynchburg city, VA
31420		Macon, GA Metro area
	13021	Bibb County, GA
	13079	Crawford County, GA
	13169	Jones County, GA
	13207	Monroe County, GA
	13289	Twiggs County, GA
31460		Madera, CA Metro area
	06039	Madera County, CA
31540		Madison, WI Metro area
	55021	Columbia County, WI
	55025	Dane County, WI
	55045	Green County, WI
	55049	Iowa County, WI
31700		Manchester-Nashua, NH Metro area
	33011	Hillsborough County, NH
31740		Manhattan, KS Metro area
	20149	Pottawatomie County, KS
	20161	Riley County, KS
31860		Mankato-North Mankato, MN Metro area
	27013	Blue Earth County, MN
	27103	Nicollet County, MN
31900		Mansfield, OH Metro area
	39139	Richland County, OH
32580		McAllen-Edinburg-Mission, TX Metro area
	48215	Hidalgo County, TX
32780		Medford, OR Metro area
	41029	Jackson County, OR
32820		Memphis, TN-MS-AR Metro area
	05035	Crittenden County, AR
	28009	Benton County, MS
	28033	DeSoto County, MS
	28093	Marshall County, MS
	28137	Tate County, MS

Metropolitan and Micropolitan Areas and Components (as defined February 2013)

Metropolitan and Micropolitan Area Code	State/County FIPS code	Title and Geographic Components
	28143	Tunica County, MS
	47047	Fayette County, TN
	47157	Shelby County, TN
	47167	Tipton County, TN
32900		Merced, CA Metro area
	06047	Merced County, CA
32940		Meridian, MS Micro area
	28023	Clarke County, MS
	28069	Kemper County, MS
	28075	Lauderdale County, MS
33100		Miami-Fort Lauderdale-West Palm Beach, FL Metro area
33100		Fort Lauderdale-Pompano Beach-Deerfield Beach, FL Metro Div 22744
	12011	Broward County, FL
33100		Miami-Miami Beach-Kendall, FL Metro Div 33124
	12086	Miami-Dade County, FL
33100		West Palm Beach-Boca Raton-Delray Beach, FL Metro Div 48424
	12099	Palm Beach County, FL
33140		Michigan City-La Porte, IN Metro area
	18091	LaPorte County, IN
33220		Midland, MI Metro area
	26111	Midland County, MI
33260		Midland, TX Metro area
	48317	Martin County, TX
	48329	Midland County, TX
33340		Milwaukee-Waukesha-West Allis, WI Metro area
	55079	Milwaukee County, WI
	55089	Ozaukee County, WI
	55131	Washington County, WI
	55133	Waukesha County, WI
33460		Minneapolis-St. Paul-Bloomington, MN Metro area
	27003	Anoka County, MN
	27019	Carver County, MN
	27025	Chisago County, MN
	27037	Dakota County, MN
	27053	Hennepin County, MN
	27059	Isanti County, MN
	27079	Le Sueur County, MN
	27095	Mille Lacs County, MN
	27123	Ramsey County, MN
	27139	Scott County, MN
	27141	Sherburne County, MN
	27143	Sibley County, MN
	27163	Washington County, MN
	27171	Wright County, MN
	55093	Pierce County, WI
	55109	St. Croix County, WI
33540		Missoula, MT Metro area
	30063	Missoula County, MT
33660		Mobile, AL Metro area
	01097	Mobile County, AL
33700		Modesto, CA Metro area
	06099	Stanislaus County, CA
33740		Monroe, LA Metro area
	22073	Ouachita Parish, LA
	22111	Union Parish, LA
33780		Monroe, MI Metro area
	26115	Monroe County, MI
33860		Montgomery, AL Metro area
	01001	Autauga County, AL
	01051	Elmore County, AL
	01085	Lowndes County, AL
	01101	Montgomery County, AL
34060		Morgantown, WV Metro area
	54061	Monongalia County, WV
	54077	Preston County, WV
34100		Morristown, TN Metro area
	47063	Hamblen County, TN
	47089	Jefferson County, TN
34540		Mount Vernon, OH Micro area
	39083	Knox County, OH
34620		Muncie, IN Metro area
	18035	Delaware County, IN
34740		Muskegon, MI Metro area
	26121	Muskegon County, MI
34820		Myrtle Beach-Conway-North Myrtle Beach, NC-SC Metro area
	37019	Brunswick County, NC
	45051	Horry County, SC
34900		Napa, CA Metro area
	06055	Napa County, CA
34940		Naples-Immokalee-Marco Island, FL Metro area
	12021	Collier County, FL
34980		Nashville-Davidson–Murfreesboro–Franklin, TN Metro area
	47015	Cannon County, TN
	47021	Cheatham County, TN
	47037	Davidson County, TN

Metropolitan and Micropolitan Area Code	State/County FIPS code	Title and Geographic Components
	47043	Dickson County, TN
	47081	Hickman County, TN
	47111	Macon County, TN
	47119	Maury County, TN
	47147	Robertson County, TN
	47149	Rutherford County, TN
	47159	Smith County, TN
	47165	Sumner County, TN
	47169	Trousdale County, TN
	47187	Williamson County, TN
	47189	Wilson County, TN
35100		New Bern, NC Metro area
	37049	Craven County, NC
	37103	Jones County, NC
	37137	Pamlico County, NC
35260		New Castle, PA Micro area
	42073	Lawrence County, PA
35300		New Haven-Milford, CT Metro area
	09009	New Haven County, CT
35380		New Orleans-Metairie, LA Metro area
	22051	Jefferson Parish, LA
	22071	Orleans Parish, LA
	22075	Plaquemines Parish, LA
	22087	St. Bernard Parish, LA
	22089	St. Charles Parish, LA
	22093	St. James Parish, LA
	22095	St. John the Baptist Parish, LA
	22103	St. Tammany Parish, LA
35420		New Philadelphia-Dover, OH Micro area
	39157	Tuscarawas County, OH
35620		New York-Newark-Jersey City, NY-NJ-PA Metro area
35620		Dutchess County-Putnam County, NY Metro Div 20524
	36027	Dutchess County, NY
	36079	Putnam County, NY
35620		Nassau County-Suffolk County, NY Metro Div 35004
	36059	Nassau County, NY
	36103	Suffolk County, NY
35620		Newark, NJ-PA Metro Div 35084
	34013	Essex County, NJ
	34019	Hunterdon County, NJ
	34027	Morris County, NJ
	34035	Somerset County, NJ
	34037	Sussex County, NJ
	34039	Union County, NJ
	42103	Pike County, PA
35620		New York-Jersey City-White Plains, NY-NJ Metro Div 35614
	34003	Bergen County, NJ
	34017	Hudson County, NJ
	34023	Middlesex County, NJ
	34025	Monmouth County, NJ
	34029	Ocean County, NJ
	34031	Passaic County, NJ
	36005	Bronx County, NY
	36047	Kings County, NY
	36061	New York County, NY
	36071	Orange County, NY
	36081	Queens County, NY
	36085	Richmond County, NY
	36087	Rockland County, NY
	36119	Westchester County, NY
35660		Niles-Benton Harbor, MI Metro area
	26021	Berrien County, MI
35840		North Port-Sarasota-Bradenton, FL Metro area
	12081	Manatee County, FL
	12115	Sarasota County, FL
35980		Norwich-New London, CT Metro area
	09011	New London County, CT
36100		Ocala, FL Metro area
	12083	Marion County, FL
36140		Ocean City, NJ Metro area
	34009	Cape May County, NJ
36220		Odessa, TX Metro area
	48135	Ector County, TX
36260		Ogden-Clearfield, UT Metro area
	49003	Box Elder County, UT
	49011	Davis County, UT
	49029	Morgan County, UT
	49057	Weber County, UT
36300		Ogdensburg-Massena, NY Micro area
	36089	St. Lawrence County, NY
36420		Oklahoma City, OK Metro area
	40017	Canadian County, OK
	40027	Cleveland County, OK
	40051	Grady County, OK
	40081	Lincoln County, OK
	40083	Logan County, OK
	40087	McClain County, OK

Metropolitan and Micropolitan Area Code	State/County FIPS code	Title and Geographic Components
	40109	Oklahoma County, OK
36500		Olympia-Tumwater, WA Metro area
	53067	Thurston County, WA
36540		Omaha-Council Bluffs, NE-IA Metro area
	19085	Harrison County, IA
	19129	Mills County, IA
	19155	Pottawattamie County, IA
	31025	Cass County, NE
	31055	Douglas County, NE
	31153	Sarpy County, NE
	31155	Saunders County, NE
	31177	Washington County, NE
36700		Orangeburg, SC Micro area
	45075	Orangeburg County, SC
36740		Orlando-Kissimmee-Sanford, FL Metro
	12069	Lake County, FL
	12095	Orange County, FL
	12097	Osceola County, FL
	12117	Seminole County, FL
36780		Oshkosh-Neenah, WI Metro area
	55139	Winnebago County, WI
36860		Ottaw-Peru, IL Micro area
	17011	Bureau County, IL
	17099	LaSalle County, IL
	17155	Putnam County, IL
36980		Owensboro, KY Metro area
	21059	Daviess County, KY
	21091	Hancock County, KY
	21149	McLean County, KY
37100		Oxnard-Thousand Oaks-Ventura, CA Metro area
	06111	Ventura County, CA
37340		Palm Bay-Melbourne-Titusville, FL Metro area
	12009	Brevard County, FL
37460		Panama City, FL Metro area
	12005	Bay County, FL
	12045	Gulf County, FL
37620		Parkersburg-Vienna, WV Metro area
	54105	Wirt County, WV
	54107	Wood County, WV
37860		Pensacola-Ferry Pass-Brent, FL Metro area
	12033	Escambia County, FL
	12113	Santa Rosa County, FL
37900		Peoria, IL Metro area
	17123	Marshall County, IL
	17143	Peoria County, IL
	17175	Stark County, IL
	17179	Tazewell County, IL
	17203	Woodford County, IL
37980		Philadelphia-Camden-Wilmington, PA-NJ-DE-MD Metro area
37980		Camden, NJ Metro Div 15804
	34005	Burlington County, NJ
	34007	Camden County, NJ
	34015	Gloucester County, NJ
37980		Montgomery County-Bucks County-Chester County, PA Metro Div 33874
	42017	Bucks County, PA
	42029	Chester County, PA
	42091	Montgomery County, PA
37980		Philadelphia, PA Metro Div 37964
	42045	Delaware County, PA
	42101	Philadelphia County, PA
37980		Wilmington, DE-MD-NJ Metro Div 48864
	10003	New Castle County, Delaware
	24015	Cecil County, MD
	34033	Salem County, NJ
38060		Phoenix-Mesa-Scottsdale, AZ Metro area
	04013	Maricopa County, AZ
	04021	Pinal County, AZ
38220		Pine Bluff, AR Metro area
	05025	Cleveland County, AR
	05069	Jefferson County, AR
	05079	Lincoln County, AR
38300		Pittsburgh, PA Metro area
	42003	Allegheny County, PA
	42005	Armstrong County, PA
	42007	Beaver County, PA
	42019	Butler County, PA
	42051	Fayette County, PA
	42125	Washington County, PA
	42129	Westmoreland County, PA
38340		Pittsfield, MA Metro area
	25003	Berkshire County, MA
38540		Pocatello, ID Metro area
	16005	Bannock County, ID
38860		Portland-South Portland, ME Metro area
	23005	Cumberland County, ME
	23023	Sagadahoc County, ME

Metropolitan and Micropolitan Areas and Components (as defined February 2013)

Metropolitan and Micropolitan Area Code	State/County FIPS code	Title and Geographic Components
	23031	York County, ME
38900		Portland-Vancouver-Hillsboro, OR-WA Metro area
	41005	Clackamas County, OR
	41009	Columbia County, OR
	41051	Multnomah County, OR
	41067	Washington County, OR
	41071	Yamhill County, OR
	53011	Clark County, WA
	53059	Skamania County, WA
38940		Port St. Lucie, FL Metro area
	12085	Martin County, FL
	12111	St. Lucie County, FL
39060		Pottsville, PA Micro area
	42107	Schuylkill County, PA
39140		Prescott, AZ Metro area
	04025	Yavapai County, AZ
39300		Providence-Warwick, RI-MA Metro area
	25005	Bristol County, MA
	44001	Bristol County, RI
	44003	Kent County, RI
	44005	Newport County, RI
	44007	Providence County, RI
	44009	Washington County, RI
39340		Provo-Orem, UT Metro area
	49023	Juab County, UT
	49049	Utah County, UT
39380		Pueblo, CO Metro area
	08101	Pueblo County, CO
39460		Punta Gorda, FL Metro area
	12015	Charlotte County, FL
39540		Racine, WI Metro area
	55101	Racine County, WI
39580		Raleigh, NC Metro area
	37069	Franklin County, NC
	37101	Johnston County, NC
	37183	Wake County, NC
39660		Rapid City, SD Metro area
	46033	Custer County, SD
	46093	Meade County, SD
	46103	Pennington County, SD
39740		Reading, PA Metro area
	42011	Berks County, PA
39820		Redding, CA Metro area
	06089	Shasta County, CA
39900		Reno, NV Metro area
	32029	Storey County, NV
	32031	Washoe County, NV
40060		Richmond, VA Metro area
	51007	Amelia County, VA
	51033	Caroline County, VA
	51036	Charles City County, VA
	51041	Chesterfield County, VA
	51053	Dinwiddie County, VA
	51075	Goochland County, VA
	51085	Hanover County, VA
	51087	Henrico County, VA
	51101	King William County, VA
	51127	New Kent County, VA
	51145	Powhatan County, VA
	51149	Prince George County, VA
	51183	Sussex County, VA
	51570	Colonial Heights city, VA
	51670	Hopewell city, VA
	51730	Petersburg city, VA
	51760	Richmond city, VA
40140		Riverside-San Bernardino-Ontario, CA
	06065	Riverside County, CA
	06071	San Bernardino County, CA
40220		Roanoke, VA Metro area
	51023	Botetourt County, VA
	51045	Craig County, VA
	51067	Franklin County, VA
	51161	Roanoke County, VA
	51770	Roanoke city, VA
	51775	Salem city, VA
40340		Rochester, MN Metro area
	27039	Dodge County, MN
	27045	Fillmore County, MN
	27109	Olmsted County, MN
	27157	Wabasha County, MN
40380		Rochester, NY Metro area
	36051	Livingston County, NY
	36055	Monroe County, NY
	36069	Ontario County, NY
	36073	Orleans County, NY
	36117	Wayne County, NY

Metropolitan and Micropolitan Areas and Components (as defined February 2013)

Metropolitan and Micropolitan Area Code	State/County FIPS code	Title and Geographic Components
	36123	Yates County, NY
40420		Rockford, IL Metro area
	17007	Boone County, IL
	17201	Winnebago County, IL
40580		Rocky Mount, NC Metro area
	37065	Edgecombe County, NC
	37127	Nash County, NC
40660		Rome, GA Metro area
	13115	Floyd County, GA
40700		Roseburg, OR Micro area
	41019	Douglas County, OR
40900		Sacramento–Roseville–Arden-Arcade, CA Metro area
	06017	El Dorado County, CA
	06061	Placer County, CA
	06067	Sacramento County, CA
	06113	Yolo County, CA
40980		Saginaw, MI Metro area
	26145	Saginaw County, MI
41400		Salem, OH Micro area
	39029	Columbiana County, OH
41420		Salem, OR Metro area
	41047	Marion County, OR
	41053	Polk County, OR
41500		Salinas, CA Metro area
	06053	Monterey County, CA
41540		Salisbury, MD-DE Metro area
	10005	Sussex County, DE
	24039	Somerset County, MD
	24045	Wicomico County, MD
	24047	Worcester County, MD
41620		Salt Lake City, UT Metro area
	49035	Salt Lake County, UT
	49045	Tooele County, UT
41660		San Angelo, TX Metro area
	48235	Irion County, TX
	48451	Tom Green County, TX
41700		San Antonio-New Braunfels, TX Metro
	48013	Atascosa County, TX
	48019	Bandera County, TX
	48029	Bexar County, TX
	48091	Comal County, TX
	48187	Guadalupe County, TX
	48259	Kendall County, TX
	48325	Medina County, TX
	48493	Wilson County, TX
41740		San Diego-Carlsbad, CA Metro area
	06073	San Diego County, CA
41860		San Francisco-Oakland-Hayward, CA Metro area
41860		Oakland-Hayward-Berkeley, CA Metro Div 36084
	06001	Alameda County, CA
	06013	Contra Costa County, CA
		San Francisco-Redwood City-South San Francisco, CA
41860		Metro Div 41884
	06075	San Francisco County, CA
	06081	San Mateo County, CA
41860		San Rafael, CA Metropolitan Div 42034
	06041	Marin County, CA
41940		San Jose-Sunnyvale-Santa Clara, CA Metro area
	06069	San Benito County, CA
	06085	Santa Clara County, CA
42020		San Luis Obispo-Paso Robles-Arroyo Grande, CA Metro area
	06079	San Luis Obispo County, CA
42100		Santa Cruz-Watsonville, CA Metro area
	06087	Santa Cruz County, CA
42140		Santa Fe, NM Metro area
	35049	Santa Fe County, NM
42200		Santa Maria-Santa Barbara, CA Metro
	06083	Santa Barbara County, CA
42220		Santa Rosa, CA Metro area
	06097	Sonoma County, CA
42340		Savannah, GA Metro area
	13029	Bryan County, GA
	13051	Chatham County, GA
	13103	Effingham County, GA
42540		Scranton–Wilkes-Barre–Hazleton, PA Metro area
	42069	Lackawanna County, PA
	42079	Luzerne County, PA
	42131	Wyoming County, PA
42660		Seattle-Tacoma-Bellevue, WA Metro area
42660		Seattle-Bellevue-Everett, WA Metro Div 42644
	53033	King County, WA
	53061	Snohomish County, WA
42660		Tacoma-Lakewood, WA Metro Div 45104
	53053	Pierce County, WA
42680		Sebastian-Vero Beach, FL Metro area
	12061	Indian River County, FL

Metropolitan and Micropolitan Area Code	State/County FIPS code	Title and Geographic Components
		Metropolitan and Micropolitan Areas and Components (as defined February 2013)
42700		Sebring, FL Metro area
	12055	Highlands County, FL
43100		Sheboygan, WI Metro area
	55117	Sheboygan County, WI
43300		Sherman-Denison, TX Metro area
	48181	Grayson County, TX
43320		Show Low, AZ Micro area
	04017	Navajo County, AZ
43340		Shreveport-Bossier City, LA Metro area
	22015	Bossier Parish, LA
	22017	Caddo Parish, LA
	22031	De Soto Parish, LA
	22119	Webster Parish, LA
43420		Sierra Vista-Douglas, AZ Metro area
	04003	Cochise County, AZ
43580		Sioux City, IA-NE-SD Metro area
	19149	Plymouth County, IA
	19193	Woodbury County, IA
	31043	Dakota County, NE
	31051	Dixon County, NE
	46127	Union County, SD
43620		Sioux Falls, SD Metro area
	46083	Lincoln County, SD
	46087	McCook County, SD
	46099	Minnehaha County, SD
	46125	Turner County, SD
43780		South Bend-Mishawaka, IN-MI Metro area
	18141	St. Joseph County, IN
	26027	Cass County, MI
43900		Spartanburg, SC Metro area
	45083	Spartanburg County, SC
	45087	Union County, SC
44060		Spokane-Spokane Valley, WA Metro area
	53051	Pend Oreille County, WA
	53063	Spokane County, WA
	53065	Stevens County, WA
44100		Springfield, IL Metro area
	17129	Menard County, IL
	17167	Sangamon County, IL
44140		Springfield, MA Metro area
	25013	Hampden County, MA
	25015	Hampshire County, MA
44180		Springfield, MO Metro area
	29043	Christian County, MO
	29059	Dallas County, MO
	29077	Greene County, MO
	29167	Polk County, MO
	29225	Webster County, MO
44220		Springfield, OH Metro area
	39023	Clark County, OH
41060		St. Cloud, MN Metro area
	27009	Benton County, MN
	27145	Stearns County, MN
41100		St. George, UT Metro area
	49053	Washington County, UT
41140		St. Joseph, MO-KS Metro area
	20043	Doniphan County, KS
	29003	Andrew County, MO
	29021	Buchanan County, MO
	29063	DeKalb County, MO
41180		St. Louis, MO-IL Metro area
	17005	Bond County, IL
	17013	Calhoun County, IL
	17027	Clinton County, IL
	17083	Jersey County, IL
	17117	Macoupin County, IL
	17119	Madison County, IL
	17133	Monroe County, IL
	17163	St. Clair County, IL
	29071	Franklin County, MO
	29099	Jefferson County, MO
	29113	Lincoln County, MO
	29183	St. Charles County, MO
	29189	St. Louis County, MO
	29219	Warren County, MO
	29510	St. Louis city, MO
44300		State College, PA Metro area
	42027	Centre County, PA
44420		Staunton-Waynesboro, VA Metro area
	51015	Augusta County, VA
	51790	Staunton, VA
	51820	Waynesboro City, VA
44700		Stockton-Lodi, CA Metro area
	06077	San Joaquin County, CA
44940		Sumter, SC Metro area
	45085	Sumter County, SC

Metropolitan and Micropolitan Area Code	State/County FIPS code	Title and Geographic Components
		Metropolitan and Micropolitan Areas and Components (as defined February 2013)
44980		Sunbury, PA Micro area
	42097	Northumberland County, PA
45060		Syracuse, NY Metro area
	36053	Madison County, NY
	36067	Onondaga County, NY
	36075	Oswego County, NY
45220		Tallahassee, FL Metro area
	12039	Gadsden County, FL
	12065	Jefferson County, FL
	12073	Leon County, FL
	12129	Wakulla County, FL
45300		Tampa-St. Petersburg-Clearwater, FL Metro area
	12053	Hernando County, FL
	12057	Hillsborough County, FL
	12101	Pasco County, FL
	12103	Pinellas County, FL
45460		Terre Haute, IN Metro area
	18021	Clay County, IN
	18153	Sullivan County, IN
	18165	Vermillion County, IN
	18167	Vigo County, IN
45500		Texarkana, TX-AR Metro area
	05081	Little River County, AR
	05091	Miller County, AR
	48037	Bowie County, TX
45540		The Villages, FL Metro area
	12119	Sumter County, FL
45780		Toledo, OH Metro area
	39051	Fulton County, OH
	39095	Lucas County, OH
	39173	Wood County, OH
45820		Topeka, KS Metro area
	20085	Jackson County, KS
	20087	Jefferson County, KS
	20139	Osage County, KS
	20177	Shawnee County, KS
	20197	Wabaunsee County, KS
45860		Torrington, CT Micro area
	09005	Litchfield County, CT
45900		Traverse City, MI Micro area
	26019	Benzie County, MI
	26055	Grand Traverse County, MI
	26079	Kalkaska County, MI
	26089	Leelanau County, MI
45940		Trenton, NJ Metro area
	34021	Mercer County, NJ
46020		Truckee-Grass Valley, CA Micro area
	06057	Nevada County, CA
46060		Tucson, AZ Metro area
	04019	Pima County, AZ
		Tullahoma-Manchester, TN Micro area
	47031	Coffee County, TN
	47051	Franklin County, TN
	47127	Moore County, TN
46140		Tulsa, OK Metro area
	40037	Creek County, OK
	40111	Okmulgee County, OK
	40113	Osage County, OK
	40117	Pawnee County, OK
	40131	Rogers County, OK
	40143	Tulsa County, OK
	40145	Wagoner County, OK
46180		Tupelo, MS Micro area
	28057	Itawamba County, MS
	28081	Lee County, MS
	28115	Pontotoc County, MS
46220		Tuscaloosa, AL Metro area
	01065	Hale County, AL
	01107	Pickens County, AL
	01125	Tuscaloosa County, AL
46340		Tyler, TX Metro area
	48423	Smith County, TX
46520		Urban Honolulu, HI Metro area
	15003	Honolulu County, HI
46540		Utica-Rome, NY Metro area
	36043	Herkimer County, NY
	36065	Oneida County, NY
46660		Valdosta, GA Metro area
	13027	Brooks County, GA
	13101	Echols County, GA
	13173	Lanier County, GA
	13185	Lowndes County, GA
46700		Vallejo-Fairfield, CA Metro area
	06095	Solano County, CA
47020		Victoria, TX Metro area
	48175	Goliad County, TX

Metropolitan and Micropolitan Area Code	State/County FIPS code	Title and Geographic Components
	48469	Victoria County, TX
47220		Vineland-Bridgeton, NJ Metro area
	34011	Cumberland County, NJ
47260		Virginia Beach-Norfolk-Newport News, VA-NC Metro area
	37053	Currituck County, NC
	37073	Gates County, NC
	51073	Gloucester County, VA
	51093	Isle of Wight County, VA
	51095	James City County, VA
	51115	Mathews County, VA
	51199	York County, VA
	51550	Chesapeake city, VA
	51650	Hampton city, VA
	51700	Newport News city, VA
	51710	Norfolk city, VA
	51735	Poquoson city, VA
	51740	Portsmouth city, VA
	51800	Suffolk city, VA
	51810	Virginia Beach city, VA
	51830	Williamsburg city, VA
47300		Visalia-Porterville, CA Metro area
	06107	Tulare County, CA
47380		Waco, TX Metro area
	48145	Falls County, TX
	48309	McLennan County, TX
47460		Walla Walla, WA Metro area
	53013	Columbia County, WA
	53071	Walla Walla County, WA
47580		Warner Robins, GA Metro area
	13153	Houston County, GA
	13225	Peach County, GA
	13235	Pulaski County, GA
47900		Washington-Arlington-Alexandria, DC-VA-MD-WV Metro area
47900		Silver Spring-Frederick-Rockville, MD Metro Div 43524
	24021	Frederick County, MD
	24031	Montgomery County, MD
47900		Washington-Arlington-Alexandria, DC-VA-MD-WV Metro Div 47894
	11001	District of Columbia, DC
	24009	Calvert County, MD
	24017	Charles County, MD
	24033	Prince George's County, MD
	51013	Arlington County, VA
	51043	Clarke County, VA
	51047	Culpeper County, VA
	51059	Fairfax County, VA
	51061	Fauquier County, VA
	51107	Loudoun County, VA
	51153	Prince William County, VA
	51157	Rappahannock County, VA
	51177	Spotsylvania County, VA
	51179	Stafford County, VA
	51187	Warren County, VA
	51510	Alexandria city, VA
	51600	Fairfax city, VA
	51610	Falls Church city, VA
	51630	Fredericksburg city, VA
	51683	Manassas city, VA
	51685	Manassas Park city, VA
	54037	Jefferson County, WV
47940		Waterloo-Cedar Falls, IA Metro area
	19013	Black Hawk County, IA

Metropolitan and Micropolitan Area Code	State/County FIPS code	Title and Geographic Components
	19017	Bremer County, IA
	19075	Grundy County, IA
48060		Watertown-Fort Drum, NY Metro area
	36045	Jefferson County, NY
48140		Wausau, WI Metro area
	55073	Marathon County, WI
48260		Weirton-Steubenville, WV-OH Metro area
	39081	Jefferson County, OH
	54009	Brooke County, WV
	54029	Hancock County, WV
48300		Wenatchee, WA Metro area
	53007	Chelan County, WA
	53017	Douglas County, WA
48540		Wheeling, WV-OH Metro area
	39013	Belmont County, OH
	54051	Marshall County, WV
	54069	Ohio County, WV
48580		Whitewater-Elkhorn, WI Micro area
	55127	Walworth County, WI
48620		Wichita, KS Metro area
	20015	Butler County, KS
	20079	Harvey County, KS
	20095	Kingman County, KS
	20173	Sedgwick County, KS
	20191	Sumner County, KS
48660		Wichita Falls, TX Metro area
	48009	Archer County, TX
	48077	Clay County, TX
	48485	Wichita County, TX
48700		Williamsport, PA Metro area
	42081	Lycoming County, PA
48900		Wilmington, NC Metro area
	37129	New Hanover County, NC
	37141	Pender County, NC
49020		Winchester, VA-WV Metro area
	51069	Frederick County, VA
	51840	Winchester city, VA
	54027	Hampshire County, WV
49180		Winston-Salem, NC Metro area
	37057	Davidson County, NC
	37059	Davie County, NC
	37067	Forsyth County, NC
	37169	Stokes County, NC
	37197	Yadkin County, NC
49300		Wooster, OH Micro area
	39169	Wayne County, OH
49340		Worcester, MA-CT Metro area
	09015	Windham County, CT
	25027	Worcester County, MA
49420		Yakima, WA Metro area
	53077	Yakima County, WA
49620		York-Hanover, PA Metro area
	42133	York County, PA
49660		Youngstown-Warren-Boardman, OH-PA Metro area
	39099	Mahoning County, OH
	39155	Trumbull County, OH
	42085	Mercer County, PA
49700		Yuba City, CA Metro area
	06101	Sutter County, CA
	06115	Yuba County, CA
49740		Yuma, AZ Metro area
	04027	Yuma County, AZ

APPENDIX B. CITIES BY COUNTY

The following table is arranged alphabetically by state. Under each state heading are listed all cities identifiable based on the PUMA allocation procedure, along with their component counties. The population in each city and component reflects the 2010 Census population, which in some cases is less than the 100,000 PUMA threshold.

State code	County Code	Place Code	Geographic Area Name	2010 census population
01			**ALABAMA**	4,779,736
01		07000	Birmingham city	212,237
01	073		Jefferson County	210,609
01	117		Shelby County	1,628
01		37000	Huntsville city	180,105
01	083		Limestone County	1,521
01	089		Madison County	178,584
01		50000	Mobile city	195,111
01	097		Mobile County	195,111
01		51000	Montgomery city	205,764
01	101		Montgomery County	205,764
01		77256	Tuscaloosa city	90,468
01	125		Tuscaloosa County	90,468
02			**ALASKA**	710,231
02		03000	Anchorage municipality	291,826
02	020		Anchorage Municipality	291,826
04			**ARIZONA**	6,392,017
04		12000	Chandler city	236,123
04	013		Maricopa County	236,123
04		27820	Glendale city	226,721
04	013		Maricopa County	226,721
04		46000	Mesa city	439,041
04	013		Maricopa County	439,041
04		54050	Peoria city	154,065
04	013		Maricopa County	154,058
04	025		Yavapai County	7
04		55000	Phoenix city	1,445,632
04	013		Maricopa County	1,445,632
04		65000	Scottsdale city	217,385
04	013		Maricopa County	217,385
04		71510	Surprise city	117,517
04	013		Maricopa County	117,517
04		73000	Tempe city	161,719
04	013		Maricopa County	161,719
04		77000	Tucson city	520,116
04	019		Pima County	520,116
04		85540	Yuma city	93,064
04	027		Yuma County	93,064
05			**ARKANSAS**	2,915,918
05		41000	Little Rock city	193,524
05	119		Pulaski County	193,524
06			**CALIFORNIA**	37,253,956
06		02000	Anaheim city	336,265
06	059		Orange County	336,265
06		02252	Antioch city	102,372
06	013		Contra Costa County	102,372
06		03526	Bakersfield city	347,483
06	029		Kern County	347,483
06		06000	Berkeley city	112,580
06	001		Alameda County	112,580
06		08954	Burbank city	103,340
06	037		Los Angeles County	103,340

State code	County Code	Place Code	Geographic Area Name	2010 census population
06		11194	Carlsbad city	105,328
06	073		San Diego County	105,328
06		11530	Carson city	91,714
06	037		Los Angeles County	91,714
06		13392	Chula Vista city	243,916
06	073		San Diego County	243,916
06		14218	Clovis city	95,631
06	019		Fresno County	95,631
06		15044	Compton city	96,455
06	037		Los Angeles County	96,455
06		16000	Concord city	122,067
06	013		Contra Costa County	122,067
06		16350	Corona city	152,374
06	065		Riverside County	152,374
06		16532	Costa Mesa city	109,960
06	059		Orange County	109,960
06		17918	Daly City city	101,123
06	081		San Mateo County	101,123
06		19766	Downey city	111,772
06	037		Los Angeles County	111,772
06		21712	El Cajon city	99,478
06	073		San Diego County	99,478
06		22230	El Monte city	113,475
06	037		Los Angeles County	113,475
06	067	22020	Elk Grove city	153,015
06			Sacramento County	153,015
06		22804	Escondido city	143,911
06	073		San Diego County	143,911
06		23182	Fairfield city	105,321
06	095		Solano County	105,321
06		24680	Fontana city	196,069
06	071		San Bernardino County	196,069
06		26000	Fremont city	214,089
06	001		Alameda County	214,089
06		27000	Fresno city	494,665
06	019		Fresno County	494,665
06		28000	Fullerton city	135,161
06	059		Orange County	135,161
06		29000	Garden Grove city	170,883
06	059		Orange County	170,883
06		30000	Glendale city	191,719
06	037		Los Angeles County	191,719
06		33000	Hayward city	144,186
06	001		Alameda County	144,186
06		33434	Hesperia city	90,173
06	071		San Bernardino County	90,173
06		36546	Inglewood city	109,673
06	037		Los Angeles County	109,673
06		36770	Irvine city	212,375
06	059		Orange County	212,375
06		37692	Jurupa Valley city	95,004
06	065		Riverside County	95,004
06		40130	Lancaster city	156,633
06	037		Los Angeles County	156,633

State code	County Code	Place Code	Geographic Area Name	2010 census population
06		43000	Long Beach city	462,257
06	037		Los Angeles County	462,257
06		44000	Los Angeles city	3,792,621
06	037		Los Angeles County	3,792,621
06		48256	Mission Viejo city	93,305
06	059		Orange County	93,305
06		48354	Modesto city	201,165
06	099		Stanislaus County	201,165
06		49270	Moreno Valley city	193,365
06	065		Riverside County	193,365
06		50076	Murrieta city	103,466
06	065		Riverside County	103,466
06		52526	Norwalk city	105,549
06	037		Los Angeles County	105,549
06		53000	Oakland city	390,724
06	001		Alameda County	390,724
06		53322	Oceanside city	167,086
06	073		San Diego County	167,086
06		53896	Ontario city	163,924
06	071		San Bernardino County	163,924
06		53980	Orange city	136,416
06	059		Orange County	136,416
06		54652	Oxnard city	197,899
06	111		Ventura County	197,899
06		55156	Palmdale city	152,750
06	037		Los Angeles County	152,750
06		56000	Pasadena city	137,122
06	037		Los Angeles County	137,122
06		58072	Pomona city	149,058
06	037		Los Angeles County	149,058
06		59451	Rancho Cucamonga city	165,269
06	071		San Bernardino County	165,269
06		59920	Redding city	89,861
06	089		Shasta County	89,861
06		60466	Rialto city	99,171
06	071		San Bernardino County	99,171
06		60620	Richmond city	103,701
06	013		Contra Costa County	103,701
06		62000	Riverside city	303,871
06	065		Riverside County	303,871
06		62938	Roseville city	118,788
06	061		Placer County	118,788
06		64000	Sacramento city	466,488
06	067		Sacramento County	466,488
06		64224	Salinas city	150,441
06	053		Monterey County	150,441
06		65000	San Bernardino city	209,924
06	071		San Bernardino County	209,924
06		65042	San Buenaventura (Ventura) city	106,433
06	111		Ventura County	106,433
06		66000	San Diego city	1,307,402
06	073		San Diego County	1,307,402
06		67000	San Francisco city	805,235
06	075		San Francisco County	805,235
06		68000	San Jose city	945,942
06	085		Santa Clara County	945,942
06		68252	San Mateo city	97,207
06	081		San Mateo County	97,207
06		69000	Santa Ana city	324,528
06	059		Orange County	324,528

State code	County Code	Place Code	Geographic Area Name	2010 census population
06		69084	Santa Clara city	116,468
06	085		Santa Clara County	116,468
06		69088	Santa Clarita city	176,320
06	037		Los Angeles County	176,320
06		69196	Santa Maria city	99,553
06	083		Santa Barbara County	99,553
06		70000	Santa Monica city	89,736
06	037		Los Angeles County	89,736
06		70098	Santa Rosa city	167,815
06	097		Sonoma County	167,815
06		72016	Simi Valley city	124,237
06	111		Ventura County	124,237
06		73080	South Gate city	94,396
06	037		Los Angeles County	94,396
06		75000	Stockton city	291,707
06	077		San Joaquin County	291,707
06		77000	Sunnyvale city	140,081
06	085		Santa Clara County	140,081
06		78120	Temecula city	100,097
06	065		Riverside County	100,097
06		78582	Thousand Oaks city	126,683
06	111		Ventura County	126,683
06		80000	Torrance city	145,438
06	037		Los Angeles County	145,438
06		81554	Vacaville city	92,428
06	095		Solano County	92,428
06		81666	Vallejo city	115,942
06	095		Solano County	115,942
06		82590	Victorville city	115,903
06	071		San Bernardino County	115,903
06		82954	Visalia city	124,442
06	107		Tulare County	124,442
06		82996	Vista city	93,834
06	073		San Diego County	93,834
06		84200	West Covina city	106,098
06	037		Los Angeles County	106,098
06		84550	Westminster city	89,701
06	059		Orange County	89,701
08			**COLORADO**	5,029,196
08		03455	Arvada city	106,433
08	001		Adams County	2,849
08	059		Jefferson County	103,584
08		04000	Aurora city	325,078
08	001		Adams County	39,871
08	005		Arapahoe County	285,090
08	035		Douglas County	117
08		07850	Boulder city	97,385
08	013		Boulder County	97,385
08		12815	Centennial city	100,377
08	005		Arapahoe County	100,377
08		16000	Colorado Springs city	416,427
08	041		El Paso County	416,427
08		20000	Denver city	600,158
08	031		Denver County	600,158
08		27425	Fort Collins city	143,986
08	069		Larimer County	143,986
08		32155	Greeley city	92,889
08	123		Weld County	92,889
08		43000	Lakewood city	142,980
08	059		Jefferson County	142,980

State code	County Code	Place Code	Geographic Area Name	2010 census population
08		62000	Pueblo city	106,595
08	101		Pueblo County	106,595
08		77290	Thornton city	118,772
08	001		Adams County	118,772
08	123		Weld County	0
08		83835	Westminster city	106,114
08	001		Adams County	63,696
08	059		Jefferson County	42,418
09			**CONNECTICUT**	3,574,097
09		08000	Bridgeport city	144,229
09	001		Fairfield County	144,229
09		37000	Hartford city	124,775
09	003		Hartford County	124,775
09		52000	New Haven city	129,779
09	009		New Haven County	129,779
09		73000	Stamford city	122,643
09	001		Fairfield County	122,643
09		80000	Waterbury city	110,366
09	009		New Haven County	110,366
11			**DISTRICT OF COLUMBIA**	601,723
11		50000	Washington city	601,723
11	001		District of Columbia	601,723
12			**FLORIDA**	18,801,310
12		10275	Cape Coral city	154,305
12	071		Lee County	154,305
12		12875	Clearwater city	107,685
12	103		Pinellas County	107,685
12		14400	Coral Springs city	121,096
12	011		Broward County	121,096
12		24000	Fort Lauderdale city	165,521
12	011		Broward County	165,521
12		25175	Gainesville city	124,354
12	001		Alachua County	124,354
12		30000	Hialeah city	224,669
12	086		Miami-Dade County	224,669
12		32000	Hollywood city	140,768
12	011		Broward County	140,768
12		35000	Jacksonville city	821,784
12	031		Duval County	821,784
12		38250	Lakeland city	97,422
12	105		Polk County	97,422
12		45000	Miami city	399,457
12	086		Miami-Dade County	399,457
12		45025	Miami Beach city	87,779
12	086		Miami-Dade County	87,779
12		45060	Miami Gardens city	107,167
12	086		Miami-Dade County	107,167
12		45975	Miramar city	122,041
12	011		Broward County	122,041
12		53000	Orlando city	238,300
12	095		Orange County	238,300
12		54000	Palm Bay city	103,190
12	009		Brevard County	103,190
12		55775	Pembroke Pines city	154,750
12	011		Broward County	154,750
12		58050	Pompano Beach city	99,845
12	011		Broward County	99,845
12		58715	Port St. Lucie city	164,603
12	111		St. Lucie County	164,603
12		63000	St. Petersburg city	244,769
12	103		Pinellas County	244,769

State code	County Code	Place Code	Geographic Area Name	2010 census population
12		70600	Tallahassee city	181,376
12	073		Leon County	181,376
12		71000	Tampa city	335,709
12	057		Hillsborough County	335,709
12		76600	West Palm Beach city	99,919
12	099		Palm Beach County	99,919
13			**GEORGIA**	9,687,653
13		04000	Atlanta city	420,003
13	089		DeKalb County	28,292
13	121		Fulton County	391,711
13		19000	Columbus city	189,885
13	215		Muscogee County	189,885
13		49000	Macon city	91,351
13	021		Bibb County	90,885
13	169		Jones County	466
13		67284	Roswell city	88,346
13	121		Fulton County	88,346
13		68516	Sandy Springs city	93,853
13	121		Fulton County	93,853
13		69000	Savannah city	136,286
13	051		Chatham County	136,286
15			**HAWAII**	1,360,301
15		71550	Urban Honolulu CDP	337,256
15	003		Honolulu County	337,256
16			**IDAHO**	1,567,582
16		08830	Boise City city	205,671
16	001		Ada County	205,671
17			**ILLINOIS**	12,830,632
17		03012	Aurora city	197,899
17	043		DuPage County	49,433
17	089		Kane County	130,976
17	093		Kendall County	6,019
17	197		Will County	11,471
17		14000	Chicago city	2,695,598
17	031		Cook County	2,695,598
17	043		DuPage County	0
17		23074	Elgin city	108,188
17	031		Cook County	24,032
17	089		Kane County	84,156
17		38570	Joliet city	147,433
17	093		Kendall County	9,749
17	197		Will County	137,684
17		51622	Naperville city	141,853
17	043		DuPage County	94,533
17	197		Will County	47,320
17		59000	Peoria city	115,007
17	143		Peoria County	115,007
17		65000	Rockford city	152,871
17	201		Winnebago County	152,871
17		72000	Springfield city	116,250
17	167		Sangamon County	116,250
18			**INDIANA**	6,483,802
18		22000	Evansville city	117,429
18	163		Vanderburgh County	117,429
18		25000	Fort Wayne city	253,691
18	003		Allen County	253,691
18		71000	South Bend city	101,168
18	141		St. Joseph County	101,168
19			**IOWA**	3,046,355
19		12000	Cedar Rapids city	126,326
19	113		Linn County	126,326

State code	County Code	Place Code	Geographic Area Name	2010 census population
19		19000	Davenport city	99,685
19	163		Scott County	99,685
19		21000	Des Moines city	203,433
19	153		Polk County	203,419
19	181		Warren County	14
20			**KANSAS**	2,853,118
20		36000	Kansas City city	145,786
20	209		Wyandotte County	145,786
20		52575	Olathe city	125,872
20	091		Johnson County	125,872
20		53775	Overland Park city	173,372
20	091		Johnson County	173,372
20		71000	Topeka city	127,473
20	177		Shawnee County	127,473
20		79000	Wichita city	382,368
20	173		Sedgwick County	382,368
21			**KENTUCKY**	4,339,367
21		46027	Lexington-Fayette urban county	295,803
21	067		Fayette County	295,803
22			**LOUISIANA**	4,533,372
22		05000	Baton Rouge city	229,493
22	033		East Baton Rouge Parish	229,493
22		40735	Lafayette city	120,623
22	055		Lafayette Parish	120,623
22		55000	New Orleans city	343,829
22	071		Orleans Parish	343,829
22		70000	Shreveport city	199,311
22	015		Bossier Parish	2,702
22	017		Caddo Parish	196,609
24			**MARYLAND**	5,773,552
24		04000	Baltimore city	620,961
24	510		Baltimore city	620,961
25			**MASSACHUSETTS**	6,547,629
25		07000	Boston city	617,594
25	025		Suffolk County	617,594
25		09000	Brockton city	93,810
25	023		Plymouth County	93,810
25		11000	Cambridge city	105,162
25	017		Middlesex County	105,162
25		37000	Lowell city	106,519
25	017		Middlesex County	106,519
25		37490	Lynn city	90,329
25	009		Essex County	90,329
25		45000	New Bedford city	95,072
25	005		Bristol County	95,072
25		67000	Springfield city	153,060
25	013		Hampden County	153,060
25		82000	Worcester city	181,045
25	027		Worcester County	181,045
26			**MICHIGAN**	9,883,640
26		03000	Ann Arbor city	113,934
26	161		Washtenaw County	113,934
26		21000	Dearborn city	98,153
26	163		Wayne County	98,153
26		22000	Detroit city	713,777
26	163		Wayne County	713,777
26		29000	Flint city	102,434
26	049		Genesee County	102,434
26		34000	Grand Rapids city	188,040
26	081		Kent County	188,040
26		46000	Lansing city	114,297
26	045		Eaton County	4,734
26	065		Ingham County	109,563
26		49000	Livonia city	96,942
26	163		Wayne County	96,942
26		76460	Sterling Heights city	129,699
26	099		Macomb County	129,699
26		84000	Warren city	134,056
26	099		Macomb County	134,056
27			**MINNESOTA**	5,303,925
27		43000	Minneapolis city	382,578
27	053		Hennepin County	382,578
27		54880	Rochester city	106,769
27	109		Olmsted County	106,769
27		58000	St. Paul city	285,068
27	123		Ramsey County	285,068
28			**MISSISSIPPI**	2,967,297
28		36000	Jackson city	173,514
28	049		Hinds County	172,891
28	089		Madison County	622
28	121		Rankin County	1
29			**MISSOURI**	5,988,927
29		15670	Columbia city	108,500
29	019		Boone County	108,500
29		35000	Independence city	116,830
29	047		Clay County	0
29	095		Jackson County	116,830
29		38000	Kansas City city	459,787
29	037		Cass County	197
29	047		Clay County	113,415
29	095		Jackson County	302,499
29	165		Platte County	43,676
29		41348	Lee's Summit city	91,364
29	037		Cass County	1,917
29	095		Jackson County	89,447
29		65000	St. Louis city	319,294
29	510		St. Louis city	319,294
29		70000	Springfield city	159,498
29	043		Christian County	2
29	077		Greene County	159,496
30			**MONTANA**	989,415
30		06550	Billings city	104,170
30	111		Yellowstone County	104,170
31			**NEBRASKA**	1,826,341
31		28000	Lincoln city	258,379
31	109		Lancaster County	258,379
31		37000	Omaha city	408,958
31	055		Douglas County	408,958
32			**NEVADA**	2,700,551
32		31900	Henderson city	257,729
32	003		Clark County	257,729
32		40000	Las Vegas city	583,756
32	003		Clark County	583,756
32		51800	North Las Vegas city	216,961
32	003		Clark County	216,961
32		60600	Reno city	225,221
32	031		Washoe County	225,221
32		68400	Sparks city	90,264
32	031		Washoe County	90,264

State code	County Code	Place Code	Geographic Area Name	2010 census population
33			**NEW HAMPSHIRE**	1,316,470
33		45140	Manchester city	109,565
33	011		Hillsborough County	109,565
34			**NEW JERSEY**	8,791,894
34		21000	Elizabeth city	124,969
34	039		Union County	124,969
34		36000	Jersey City city	247,597
34	017		Hudson County	247,597
34		51000	Newark city	277,140
34	013		Essex County	277,140
34		57000	Paterson city	146,199
34	031		Passaic County	146,199
35			**NEW MEXICO**	2,059,179
35		02000	Albuquerque city	545,852
35	001		Bernalillo County	545,852
35		39380	Las Cruces city	97,618
35	013		Doña Ana County	97,618
35		63460	Rio Rancho city	87,521
35	001		Bernalillo County	130
35	043		Sandoval County	87,391
36			**NEW YORK**	19,378,102
36		01000	Albany city	97,856
36	001		Albany County	97,856
36		11000	Buffalo city	261,310
36	029		Erie County	261,310
36		51000	New York city	8,175,133
36	005		Bronx County	1,385,108
36	047		Kings County	2,504,700
36	061		New York County	1,585,873
36	081		Queens County	2,230,722
36	085		Richmond County	468,730
36		63000	Rochester city	210,565
36	055		Monroe County	210,565
36		73000	Syracuse city	145,170
36	067		Onondaga County	145,170
36		84000	Yonkers	195,976
36	119		Westchester County	195,976
37			**NORTH CAROLINA**	9,535,483
37		12000	Charlotte city	731,424
37	119		Mecklenburg County	731,424
37		19000	Durham city	228,330
37	063		Durham County	228,300
37	135		Orange County	30
37	183		Wake County	0
37		22920	Fayetteville city	200,564
37	051		Cumberland County	200,564
37		28000	Greensboro city	269,666
37	081		Guilford County	269,666
37		31400	High Point city	104,371
37	057		Davidson County	5,310
37	067		Forsyth County	8
37	081		Guilford County	99,042
37	151		Randolph County	11
37		55000	Raleigh city	403,892
37	063		Durham County	1,067
37	183		Wake County	402,825
37		74440	Wilmington city	106,476
37	129		New Hanover County	106,476
37		75000	Winston-Salem city	229,617
37	067		Forsyth County	229,617

State code	County Code	Place Code	Geographic Area Name	2010 census population
38			**NORTH DAKOTA**	672,591
38		25700	Fargo city	105,549
38	017		Cass County	105,549
39			**OHIO**	11,536,504
39		01000	Akron city	199,110
39	153		Summit County	199,110
39		15000	Cincinnati city	296,943
39	061		Hamilton County	296,943
39		16000	Cleveland city	396,815
39	035		Cuyahoga County	396,815
39		18000	Columbus city	787,033
39	041		Delaware County	7,245
39	045		Fairfield County	9,666
39	049		Franklin County	770,122
39		21000	Dayton city	141,527
39	113		Montgomery County	141,527
39		77000	Toledo city	287,208
39	095		Lucas County	287,208
40			**OKLAHOMA**	3,751,351
40		09050	Broken Arrow city	98,850
40	143		Tulsa County	80,634
40	145		Wagoner County	18,216
40		41850	Lawton city	96,867
40	031		Comanche County	96,867
40		52500	Norman city	110,925
40	027		Cleveland County	110,925
40		55000	Oklahoma City city	579,999
40	017		Canadian County	44,541
40	027		Cleveland County	63,723
40	109		Oklahoma County	471,671
40	125		Pottawatomie County	64
40		75000	Tulsa city	391,906
40	113		Osage County	6,136
40	131		Rogers County	0
40	143		Tulsa County	385,613
40	145		Wagoner County	157
41			**OREGON**	3,831,074
41		05350	Beaverton city	89,803
41	067		Washington County	89,803
41		23850	Eugene city	156,185
41	039		Lane County	156,185
41		31250	Gresham city	105,594
41	051		Multnomah County	105,594
41		34100	Hillsboro city	91,611
41	067		Washington County	91,611
41		59000	Portland city	583,776
41	005		Clackamas County	744
41	051		Multnomah County	581,485
41	067		Washington County	1,547
41		64900	Salem city	154,637
41	047		Marion County	130,398
41	053		Polk County	24,239
42			**PENNSYLVANIA**	12,702,379
42		02000	Allentown city	118,032
42	077		Lehigh County	118,032
42		24000	Erie city	101,786
42	049		Erie County	101,786
42		60000	Philadelphia city	1,526,006
42	101		Philadelphia County	1,526,006
42		61000	Pittsburgh city	305,704
42	003		Allegheny County	305,704

State code	County Code	Place Code	Geographic Area Name	2010 census population
44			**RHODE ISLAND**	1,052,567
44		59000	Providence city	178,042
44	007		Providence County	178,042
45			**SOUTH CAROLINA**	4,625,364
45		13330	Charleston city	120,083
45	015		Berkeley County	8,095
45	019		Charleston County	111,988
45		16000	Columbia city	129,272
45	063		Lexington County	559
45	079		Richland County	128,713
45		50875	North Charleston city	97,471
45	015		Berkeley County	0
45	019		Charleston County	78,393
45	035		Dorchester County	19,078
46			**SOUTH DAKOTA**	814,180
46		59020	Sioux Falls city	153,888
46	083		Lincoln County	21,095
46	099		Minnehaha County	132,793
47			**TENNESSEE**	6,346,105
47		14000	Chattanooga city	167,674
47	065		Hamilton County	167,674
47		15160	Clarksville city	132,929
47	125		Montgomery County	132,929
47		40000	Knoxville city	178,874
47	093		Knox County	178,874
47		48000	Memphis city	646,889
47	157		Shelby County	646,889
47		51560	Murfreesboro city	108,755
47	149		Rutherford County	108,755
48			**TEXAS**	25,145,561
48		01000	Abilene city	117,063
48	253		Jones County	5,145
48	441		Taylor County	111,918
48		03000	Amarillo city	190,695
48	375		Potter County	105,486
48	381		Randall County	85,209
48		04000	Arlington city	365,438
48	439		Tarrant County	365,438
48		05000	Austin city	790,390
48	209		Hays County	2
48	453		Travis County	754,691
48	491		Williamson County	35,697
48		07000	Beaumont city	118,296
48	245		Jefferson County	118,296
48		10768	Brownsville city	175,023
48	061		Cameron County	175,023
48		13024	Carrollton city	119,097
48	085		Collin County	2
48	113		Dallas County	49,352
48	121		Denton County	69,743
48		15976	College Station city	93,857
48	041		Brazos County	93,857
48		17000	Corpus Christi city	305,215
48	007		Aransas County	0
48	273		Kleberg County	0
48	355		Nueces County	305,215
48	409		San Patricio County	0
48		19000	Dallas city	1,197,816
48	085		Collin County	46,885
48	113		Dallas County	1,124,296
48	121		Denton County	26,579
48	257		Kaufman County	0
48	397		Rockwall County	56
48		19972	Denton city	113,383
48	121		Denton County	113,383

State code	County Code	Place Code	Geographic Area Name	2010 census population
48		24000	El Paso city	649,121
48	141		El Paso County	649,121
48		27000	Fort Worth city	741,206
48	121		Denton County	7,813
48	367		Parker County	7
48	439		Tarrant County	733,386
48	497		Wise County	0
48		27684	Frisco city	116,989
48	085		Collin County	72,489
48	121		Denton County	44,500
48		29000	Garland city	226,876
48	085		Collin County	266
48	113		Dallas County	226,608
48	397		Rockwall County	2
48		30464	Grand Prairie city	175,396
48	113		Dallas County	123,487
48	139		Ellis County	45
48	439		Tarrant County	51,864
48		35000	Houston city	2,099,451
48	157		Fort Bend County	38,124
48	201		Harris County	2,057,280
48	339		Montgomery County	4,047
48		37000	Irving city	216,290
48	113		Dallas County	216,290
48		39148	Killeen city	127,921
48	027		Bell County	127,921
48		41464	Laredo city	236,091
48	479		Webb County	236,091
48		42508	Lewisville city	95,290
48	113		Dallas County	841
48	121		Denton County	94,449
48		45000	Lubbock city	229,573
48	303		Lubbock County	229,573
48		45384	McAllen city	129,877
48	215		Hidalgo County	129,877
48		45744	McKinney city	131,117
48	085		Collin County	131,117
48		47892	Mesquite city	139,824
48	113		Dallas County	139,824
48		48072	Midland city	111,147
48	317		Martin County	0
48	329		Midland County	111,147
48		53388	Odessa city	99,940
48	135		Ector County	98,270
48	329		Midland County	1,670
48		56000	Pasadena city	149,043
48	201		Harris County	149,043
48		56348	Pearland city	91,252
48	039		Brazoria County	86,706
48	157		Fort Bend County	721
48	201		Harris County	3,825
48		58016	Plano city	259,841
48	085		Collin County	254,525
48	121		Denton County	5,316
48		61796	Richardson city	99,223
48	085		Collin County	28,569
48	113		Dallas County	70,654
48		63500	Round Rock city	99,887
48	453		Travis County	1,362
48	491		Williamson County	98,525
48		64472	San Angelo city	93,200
48	451		Tom Green County	93,200
48		65000	San Antonio city	1,327,407
48	029		Bexar County	1,327,381
48	091		Comal County	0
48	325		Medina County	26

State code	County Code	Place Code	Geographic Area Name	2010 census population
48		74144	Tyler city	96,900
48	423		Smith County	96,900
48		76000	Waco city	124,805
48	309		McLennan County	124,805
48		79000	Wichita Falls city	104,553
48	485		Wichita County	104,553
49			**UTAH**	2,763,885
49		57300	Orem city	88,328
49	049		Utah County	88,328
49		62470	Provo city	112,488
49	049		Utah County	112,488
49		67000	Salt Lake City city	186,440
49	035		Salt Lake County	186,440
49		82950	West Jordan city	103,712
49	035		Salt Lake County	103,712
49		83470	West Valley City city	129,480
49	035		Salt Lake County	129,480
51			**VIRGINIA**	8,001,024
51		01000	Alexandria city	139,966
51	510		Alexandria city	139,966
51		16000	Chesapeake city	222,209
51	550		Chesapeake city	222,209
51		35000	Hampton city	137,436
51	650		Hampton city	137,436
51		56000	Newport News city	180,719
51	700		Newport News city	180,719
51		57000	Norfolk city	242,803
51	710		Norfolk city	242,803
51		64000	Portsmouth city	95,535
51	740		Portsmouth city	95,535
51		67000	Richmond city	204,214
51	760		Richmond city	204,214
51		68000	Roanoke city	97,032
51	770		Roanoke city	97,032
51		82000	Virginia Beach city	437,994
51	810		Virginia Beach city	437,994
53			**WASHINGTON**	6,724,540
53		05210	Bellevue city	122,363
53	033		King County	122,363
53		22640	Everett city	103,019
53	061		Snohomish County	103,019
53		35415	Kent city	92,411
53	033		King County	92,411
53		57745	Renton city	90,927
53	033		King County	90,927
53		63000	Seattle city	608,660
53	033		King County	608,660
53		67000	Spokane city	208,916
53	063		Spokane County	208,916
53		67167	Spokane Valley city	89,755
53	063		Spokane County	89,755
53		70000	Tacoma city	198,397
53	053		Pierce County	198,397
53		74060	Vancouver city	161,791
53	011		Clark County	161,791
53		80010	Yakima city	91,067
53	077		Yakima County	91,067
55			**WISCONSIN**	5,686,986
55		31000	Green Bay city	104,057
55	009		Brown County	104,057
55		39225	Kenosha city	99,218
55	059		Kenosha County	99,218
55		48000	Madison city	233,209
55	025		Dane County	233,209
55		53000	Milwaukee city	594,833
55	079		Milwaukee County	594,833
55	131		Washington County	0
55	133		Waukesha County	0

The following consolidated cities are included here. They are listed here with their 2010 census populations, followed by the separate entities that make up the consolidated city. Data from the American Community Survey include only the "balance," the major city of each consolidated city.

State code	County Code	Place Code	Geographic Area Name	2010 census population
13			**GEORGIA**	9,687,653
13		03436	Athens-Clark county	116,714
13		03440	Athens-Clark county (balance)	115,452
13		09068	Bogart town	140
13		83728	Winterville city	1,122
13		04200	Augusta-Richmond county	200,549
13		04204	Augusta-Richmond county (balance)	195,844
13		09040	Blythe city	694
13		38040	Hephzibah city	4,011
18			**INDIANA**	6,483,802
18		36000	Indianapolis city	829,718
18		04204	Beech Grove city	0
18		13492	Clermont town	1,356
18		16156	Crows Nest town	73
18		16336	Cumberland town	2,597
18		34420	Homecroft town	722
18		36003	Indianapolis city (balance)	820,445
18		42426	Lawrence city	42
18		48456	Meridian Hills town	1,616
18		54612	North Crows Nest town	45
18		65556	Rocky Ripple town	606
18		72232	Spring Hill town	98
18		80234	Warren Park town	1,480
18		84374	Williams Creek town	407
18		85742	Wynnedale town	231
21			**KENTUCKY**	4,339,367
21		46003	Louisville/Jefferson County	741,096
21		01504	Anchorage city	2,348
21		02656	Audubon Park city	1,473
21		03376	Bancroft city	494
21		03556	Barbourmeade city	1,218
21		05068	Beechwood Village city	1,324
21		05392	Bellemeade city	865
21		05464	Bellewood city	321
21		07858	Blue Ridge Manor city	767
21		09532	Briarwood city	435
21		09847	Broeck Pointe city	272
21		10162	Brownsboro Farm city	648
21		10198	Brownsboro Village city	319
21		12066	Cambridge city	175
21		16395	Coldstream city	1,100
21		18270	Creekside city	305
21		18766	Crossgate city	225
21		22204	Douglass Hills city	5,484
21		22474	Druid Hills city	308
21		27262	Fincastle city	817
21		28342	Forest Hills city	444
21		31348	Glenview city	531
21		31402	Glenview Hills city	319
21		31420	Glenview Manor city	191
21		31870	Goose Creek city	294
21		32523	Graymoor-Devondale city	2,870
21		32986	Green Spring city	715
21		36102	Heritage Creek city	1,076
21		36374	Hickory Hill city	114
21		36865	Hills and Dales city	142
21		37576	Hollow Creek city	783
21		37630	Hollyvilla city	537
21		38170	Houston Acres city	507
21		38814	Hurstbourne city	4,216
21		38818	Hurstbourne Acres city	1,811
21		39304	Indian Hills city	2,868
21		40222	Jeffersontown city	26,595
21		42598	Kingsley city	381
21		43900	Langdon Place city	936

State code	County Code	Place Code	Geographic Area Name	2010 census population
21		46540	Lincolnshire city	148
21		48006	Louisville/Jefferson County (balance)	597,337
21		48558	Lyndon city	11,002
21		48648	Lynnview city	914
21		49800	Manor Creek city	140
21		50412	Maryhill Estates city	179
21		51193	Meadowbrook Farm city	136
21		51258	Meadow Vale city	736
21		51294	Meadowview Estates city	363
21		51978	Middletown city	7,218
21		52842	Mockingbird Valley city	167
21		53328	Moorland city	431
21		54660	Murray Hill city	582
21		56550	Norbourne Estates city	441
21		56730	Northfield city	1,020
21		56928	Norwood city	370
21		57658	Old Brownsboro Place city	353
21		59322	Parkway Village city	650
21		61554	Plantation city	832
21		62370	Poplar Hills city	362
21		63264	Prospect city	4,636
21		65208	Richlawn city	405
21		65766	Riverwood city	446
21		66486	Rolling Fields city	646
21		66504	Rolling Hills city	959
21		67944	St. Matthews city	17,472
21		67998	St. Regis Park city	1,454
21		69384	Seneca Gardens city	696
21		70284	Shively city	15,264

State code	County Code	Place Code	Geographic Area Name	2010 census population
21		72138	South Park View city	7
21		72770	Spring Mill city	287
21		72790	Spring Valley city	654
21		74064	Strathmoor Manor city	337
21		74082	Strathmoor Village city	648
21		75190	Sycamore city	160
21		75963	Ten Broeck city	103
21		76380	Thornhill city	178
21		80913	Watterson Park city	976
21		81372	Wellington city	565
21		81624	West Buechel city	1,230
21		82164	Westwood city	634
21		83208	Wildwood city	261
21		83784	Windy Hills city	2,385
21		84486	Woodland Hills city	696
21		84576	Woodlawn Park city	942
21		84891	Worthington Hills city	1,446
47			**TENNESSEE**	6,346,105
47		52004	Nashville-Davidson	626,681
47	04620		Belle Meade city	2,912
47	05140		Berry Hill city	537
47	27020		Forest Hills city	4,812
47	29920		Goodlettsville city	10,319
47	40720		Lakewood city	2,302
47	52006		Nashville-Davidson (balance)	601,222
47	54780		Oak Hill city	4,529
47	63140		Ridgetop city	48

INDEX

INDEX